DAY BY DAY: THE EIGHTIES

Volume II
1986–Index

Ellen Meltzer
and
Marc Aronson

Facts On File®

AN INFOBASE HOLDINGS COMPANY

Day By Day: The Eighties

Facts On File, Inc.
460 Park Avenue South
New York, NY 10016

Library of Congress Cataloging-in-Publication Data

Meltzer, Ellen.
  Day by day, the eighties / by Ellen Meltzer, Marc Aronson.
    p. cm.
  Includes index.
  Contents: v. 1. 1980–1989
  ISBN 0-8160-1592-9 (alk. paper)
  1. History, Modern—1945– —Chronology. I. Aronson, Marc.
II. Title. III. Title: Day by day.
D848.M45   1995
909.82'02'02—dc20   94-26632

Facts On File books are available at special discounts when purchased in bulk quantities for businesses, associations, institutions or sales promotions. Please contact our Special Sales Department in New York at 212/683-2244 or 800/322-8755.

Jacket design by Catherine Hyman
Photographs: AP/Wide World

Printed in the United States of America

KP LOG 10 9 8 7 6 5 4 3 2 1

This book is printed on acid-free paper.

CONTENTS

Editor's Preface IV

Introduction V

Yearly summary of events 2

Monthly and daily chronology of events

1980 6

1981 138

1982 258

1983 386

1984 570

1985 736

1986 900

1987 1074

1988 1226

1989 1406

Index 1541

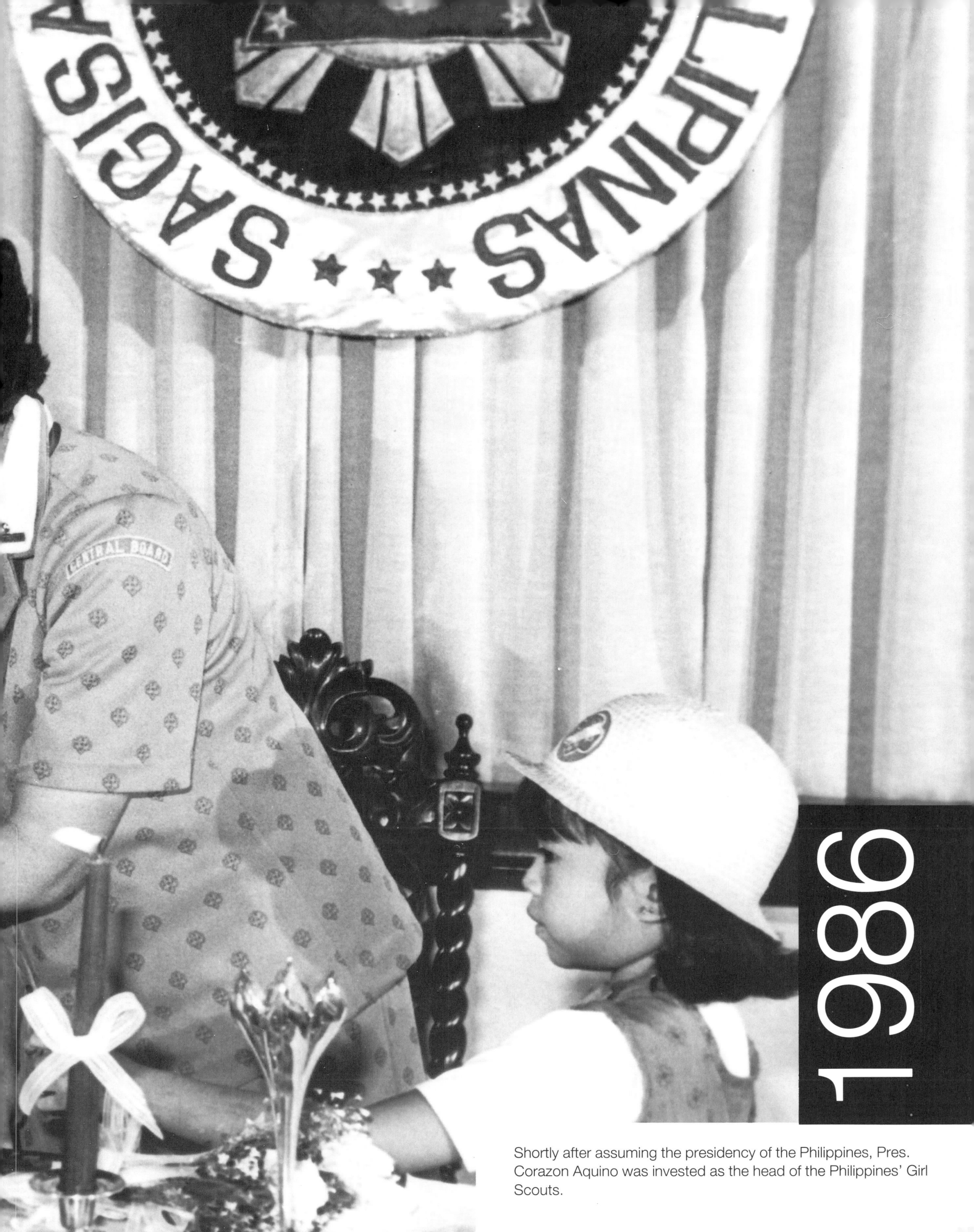

1986

Shortly after assuming the presidency of the Philippines, Pres. Corazon Aquino was invested as the head of the Philippines' Girl Scouts.

	World Affairs	Europe	Africa & the Middle East	The Americas	Asia & the Pacific
Jan.	A two-week decline in crude oil prices, caused by an oversupply of petroleum on world markets, brings prices to their lowest levels in six years.	Soviet leader Mikhail S. Gorbachev proposes a total ban on nuclear weapons by the year 2000 and announces a three-month extension of the Soviet moratorium on nuclear testing.	African National Congress Pres. Oliver Tambo says the ANC will step up its military campaign to overthrow South Africa's white-ruled apartheid system of government.	The foreign ministers of Costa Rica, El Salvador, Honduras, Nicaragua and Guatemala formally back renewed peace talks sponsored by the Contadora Group.	A U.S. delegation visits Vietnam and talks with government officials in Hanoi. The focus of the discussions is on U.S. servicemen missing in action and Americans still in Vietnam.
Feb.	Over 700 artists, scientists, business executives and public officials from 80 nations attend the Soviet Union's international forum on peace.	Premier Olof Palme of Sweden is shot and killed as he and his wife, Lisbeth, walk away from a movie theater in central Stockholm.	Iranian forces capture Fao, a disused Iraqi oil port near Kuwait, in a thrust that alarms Iraq's Arab supporters in the Persian Gulf.	President-for-life Jean-Claude Duvalier flees Haiti aboard a U.S. Air Force jet, ending the Duvalier family's 28-year dictatorship.	After leading military allies pledge their support to Corazon Aquino, Philippines President Ferdinand E. Marcos flees to the United States.
March	In an unprecedented coordinated action, the central banks of West Germany, France, Japan and the United States move to reduce key interest rates.	Spanish voters vote to retain their country's four-year-old membership in the North Atlantic Treaty Org. The vote is a victory for the socialist government of P.M. Felipe Gonzalez.	A U.S. Navy task force in the Mediterranean Sea off Libya conducts "freedom of navigation" exercises in the Gulf of Sidra, which Libya claims as territorial waters.	The UN Human Rights Commission passes a resolution urging Chile to halt human rights abuses. The resolution is similar to one drafted by the United States.	Philippine Pres. Corazon Aquino abolishes the National Assembly, abrogates the 1973 constitution and claims all legislative powers for herself pending approval of a new charter.
April	The central banks of France, the United States, Japan and several smaller nations reduce by half a percentage point the interest rate they charge to member financial institutions.	A serious accident at the Chernobyl nuclear plant in the Soviet Ukraine about 60 miles north of Kiev spews clouds of radiation that eventually spread across Europe.	South Africa's Pres. Pieter W. Botha announces that the pass laws that severely control the movements of blacks will be rescinded.	Efforts to revive peace negotiations sponsored by the Contadora Group founder over Nicaragua's insistence that the United States cease supporting anti-Sandinista Contras.	Benazir Bhutto, leader of the opposition Pakistan People's Party, returns to Pakistan from exile in London and is greeted by thousands of supporters.
May	At their 12th annual summit, leaders of the seven major industrial democracies agree to denounce terrorism and single out Libya as a key target in the fight against terrorism.	Moscow claims the situation at the Chernobyl nuclear power plant is under control; nine people are confirmed dead, with 299 hospitalized for "radiation sickness of varying degrees."	South Africa provokes international outrage when its forces raid African National Congress guerrilla strongholds in and around the capitals of Zimbabwe, Botswana and Zambia.	Liberal Party candidate Virgilio Barco Vargas wins a landslide victory in presidential elections in Colombia.	China and Taiwan hold their first direct talks since the communists took power in China in 1949. The talks are on the return of a Taiwanese plane hijacked to China by its pilot.
June	The World Court rules that the United States has violated international law and Nicaraguan sovereignty in its support of the Contras fighting to overthrow the Sandinista government.	Despite questions about his activities in the German Army in World War II, former UN Sec. Gen. Kurt Waldheim is elected president of Austria in a run-off election.	The South African government declares a state of emergency, giving virtually unlimited powers to the security forces and imposing severe restrictions on the media.	Nicaraguan Contras free eight West Germans held prisoner since May 17. The incident caused tensions between West Germany and the United States, which backs the Contra rebels.	In the Philippines, a 48-member constitutional commission begins work on drafting a new charter. Pres. Corazon Aquino currently rules under an interim "freedom constitution."
July	UN Sec. Gen. Javier Perez de Cuellar mediates a settlement between France and New Zealand over France's role in the sinking of the Greenpeace ship *Rainbow Warrior*.	Soviet Foreign Min. Eduard A. Shevardnadze visits Britain as part of an apparent Soviet diplomatic initiative to improve relations with Western Europe.	After meeting with an European Community-sponsored peace mission, South Africa's Pres. Pieter W. Botha says his government will not allow "direct interference in our internal affairs."	In Chile, at least six people are shot to death, and a Chilean-born U.S. resident set on fire dies later of his burns, during a two-day general strike to demand a return to democracy.	A bid by backers of former Pres. Ferdinand E. Marcos to set up a rebel government under Arturo Tolentino, Marcos's running mate in the Philippines' February elections, fails.
Aug.	Org. of Petroleum Exporting Countries ministers agree to cut their combined oil production by more than 3 million barrels per day for two months in a move that quickly boosts oil prices by as much as 50%.	Nicholas S. Daniloff, Moscow correspondent for *U.S. News & World Report*, is detained by Soviet authorities under suspicion of espionage.	At a National Party congress, South Africa's Pres. Pieter W. Botha and other officials prepare the party faithful for more international sanctions.	The Bolivian government imposes a state of siege in an effort to curb unrest among workers protesting the austerity policies of Pres. Victor Paz Estenssoro.	Pakistan's current president, Gen. Muhammad Zia ul-Haq, orders the arrest of Benazir Bhutto and virtually all the leading opposition leaders.
Sept.	The eighth summit meeting of the 101-member Nonaligned Movement is dominated by the issue of sanctions against South Africa and wide-ranging criticism of U.S. foreign policy.	In Paris, France, eight people are killed and some 170 injured in a series of five explosions over 10 days. The bombing campaign is attributed to a Lebanese-based group.	Egypt's Pres. Hosni Mubarak and Israel's P.M. Shimon Peres meet in Alexandria, Egypt, in the first summit meeting between the two nations in five years.	Chile's Pres. Augusto Pinochet Ugarte survives an assassination attempt and hours later widens government control from a state of emergency to a state of siege.	Twenty-one of nearly 400 passengers are killed when four Arab terrorists posing as ground crew seize a Pan American Airways jet in Karachi, Pakistan, for 16 hours.
Oct.	A pre-summit meeting between Pres. Reagan and Soviet leader Mikhail S. Gorbachev in Reykjavik, Iceland, collapses over the Strategic Defense Initiative program.	Britain breaks diplomatic ties with Syria after Nezar Hindawi is convicted of plotting to use his girlfriend to smuggle a bomb aboard an Israeli jet flying from London to Tel Aviv.	Mozambique's Pres. Samora M. Machel is killed when a plane carrying him home from a meeting in Zambia crashes just inside the border of South Africa.	Despite claims of an ex-Marine who parachuted to safety, the United States denies any link to a Contra supply plane shot down over southern Nicaragua October 5.	Amid charges of voter fraud, Bangladesh's Pres. Hossein Mohammed Ershad wins an overwhelming majority in a presidential election boycotted by all major opposition parties.
Nov.	Leaders of the member nations of the Council for Mutual Economic Assistance (Comecon) gather in Moscow for Comecon's first formal summit since June 1984.	A chemical spill at a chemical warehouse near Basel, Switzerland, pollutes the Rhine River in the worst nonnuclear environmental disaster in Europe in a decade.	The release of an American held hostage in Lebanon for 17 months is reportedly linked to a secret deal involving the U.S. transfer of military spare parts to Iran via Israel.	Britain rejects an Argentine offer to end formal hostilities if Britain drops its 150-mile "military protection zone" around the Falkland/Malvinas Islands.	Amid rumors of a coup planned by members of the military loyal to Defense Min. Juan Ponce Enrile, Philippines Pres. Corazon Aquino dismisses her entire cabinet.
Dec.	The United States and Iran resume negotiations for the release of about $500 mil. in Iranian funds frozen in U.S. banks since 1981.	In separate meetings, North Atlantic Treaty Org. ministers endorse proposals to negotiate separate accords for the reduction of conventional forces and U.S. and Soviet strategic weapons in Europe.	An Iraqi Airways passenger jet crashes during an emergency landing in northwest Saudi Arabia after hijackers exploded two grenades in the cabin; 67 of 107 passengers died.	Honduran aircraft attack Nicaraguan troops on their common border after Sandinista soldiers penetrate Honduran territory in an operation against Contras based in that country.	Fighting between ethnic Pathans and Muhajirs in Karachi leaves at least 150 people dead and hundreds of buildings in ruins in the worst domestic violence in Pakistan's history.

A	B	C	D	E
Includes developments that affect more than one world region, international organizations and important meetings of major world leaders.	Includes all domestic and regional developments in Europe, including the Soviet Union, Turkey, Cyprus and Malta.	Includes all domestic and regional developments in Africa and the Middle East, including Iraq and Iran and excluding Cyprus, Turkey and Afghanistan.	Includes all domestic and regional developments in Latin America, the Caribbean and Canada.	Includes all domestic and regional developments in Asia and Pacific nations, extending from Afghanistan through all the Pacific Islands, except Hawaii.

U.S. Politics & Social Issues	U.S. Foreign Policy & Defense	U.S. Economy & Environment	Science, Technology & Nature	Culture, Leisure & Life Style	
The Supreme Court overturns a 23-year-old murder conviction because the defendant was indicted by a grand jury from which members of his own race had been unconstitutionally excluded.	Pres. Reagan announces economic sanctions against Libya and the freezing of all Libyan assets in the United States, and orders the 1,000 to 1,500 Americans in Libya to leave immediately.	The Office of Management and Budget orders federal agencies to prepare $11.7 bil. in spending cuts in the first round of automatic cuts mandated by the Gramm-Rudman law.	The space shuttle *Challenger* explodes shortly after launch, killing all seven crew members—including teacher Christa McAuliffe—and plunging the nation into mourning.	L. Ron Hubbard, 74, author whose *Dianetics: The Modern Science of Mental Health* is the bible for the Church of Scientology, dies of a stroke near San Luis Obispo, Calif.	Jan.
A Peekskill, N.Y., woman dies after taking a potassium cyanide-contaminated capsule of Tylenol. Johnson & Johnson later ends production of nonprescription capsule medicines.	The Senate votes to ratify the UN treaty outlawing genocide, formally known as the International Convention on the Prevention and Punishment of the Crime of Genocide.	Pres. Reagan submits a $994 bil. FY1987 federal budget that proposes reducing the deficit through cuts in domestic programs and privatization of government agencies.	The chairman of the presidential commission investigating the loss of the *Challenger* charges that National Aeronautics and Space Admin. officials mishandled safety issues prior to the fateful launch.	Robert Penn Warren, poet, critic and novelist, is named the first official poet laureate of the United States.	Feb.
Abortion rights demonstrators gather in Washington, D.C., for what is thought to be the largest rally ever staged by the National Org. for Women.	The Senate approves Pres. Reagan's request to send $100 mil. in aid to Nicaraguan Contras after a Sandinista incursion into Honduras is reported.	The government's consumer price index fell at a compounded annual rate of 4.6%, the largest decline in the index since November 1953.	An unmanned Soviet spacecraft penetrates the atmosphere of Halley's comet to come within 5,600 miles of its icy core in what a U.S. observer calls "a watershed day for world science."	Georgia O'Keeffe, 98, painter who for seven decades was a leading figure in American art, dies in Santa Fe, New Mexico.	March
The House votes by a wide margin to ease firearms restrictions in a move that will result in the first significant changes in the landmark 1968 Gun Control Act.	U.S. warplanes bomb "terrorist-related targets" in Tripoli and Benghazi, Libya, in an effort to pressure Col. Muammer el-Qaddafi to stop his support for anti-American terrorism.	The Republican-controlled Senate overwhelmingly rejects Pres. Reagan's proposals to eliminate a wide array of domestic programs.	Astronauts tell the presidential commission investigating the *Challenger* explosion of their concern over safety in the space shuttle program.	Simone De Beauvoir, 78, French leftist intellectual whose 1949 book *The Second Sex* is considered the literary cornerstone of the contemporary feminist movement, dies in Paris.	April
A federal jury in Tucson, Ariz., convicts eight Christian activists of smuggling or harboring illegal immigrants from El Salvador and Guatemala in the United States.	Pres. Reagan affirms a tentative decision to stay within the limits of the 1979 SALT II agreement by dismantling two Poseidon ballistic submarines.	In a triumphant scene, members of the Senate Finance Committee celebrate their unanimous approval of a sweeping plan to overhaul and simplify the nation's tax code.	A team of medical specialists reveal that 35 people are suffering from serious radiation poisoning as a result of the Chernobyl nuclear plant accident.	Expo 86, the 1986 World's Fair, opens in Vancouver, British Columbia. More than 50 nations and 40 corporations are represented at the fair, which will run through October 31.	May
Pres. Reagan announces Chief Justice Warren E. Burger's retirement and names Associate Justice William H. Rehnquist to succeed him and Antonin Scalia to succeed Rehnquist.	The House approves Pres. Reagan's request for $100 mil. in aid for the Nicaraguan Contras in its first grant of overt military aid to the Contras.	After more than 100 hours of debate spanning 16 days, the Senate approves a bill that would represent the most radical overhaul of the nation's tax code in decades.	The presidential shuttle commission report on the *Challenger* disaster says the National Aeronautics and Space Admin. could have avoided the tragedy, which was caused by a faulty seal in a booster rocket.	Benny (Benjamin David) Goodman, 77, bandleader and clarinetist known for some five decades as "The King of Swing," dies of cardiac arrest in New York City.	June
In a firm rebuff to the Reagan administration, the Supreme Court upholds affirmative action and the use of numerical goals as a remedy for past job discrimination.	Pres. Reagan urges the white minority government of South Africa to end its apartheid system of government but says new economic sanctions would be a "historic act of folly."	The Supreme Court rules that the Gramm-Rudman-Hollings budget-balancing law's mechanism for automatic spending cuts is unconstitutional because it violates the separation of powers.	Soviet cosmonauts Col. Leonid D. Kizim and Vladimir A. Solovyov return safely to Earth after a 125-day mission in space.	New York City hosts a four-day international centennial celebration of the newly restored Statue of Liberty.	July
Roy Marcus Cohn, 59, controversial trial attorney famous for his role as chief counsel to McCarthy during his communist subversion in the 1950s, dies in New York of AIDS-related symptoms.	The Senate votes, 84-14, to impose economic sanctions on South Africa to pressure it to dismantle its apartheid system of racial segregation.	House and Senate conferees approve a sweeping measure that will represent by far the most extensive restructuring of the federal tax system since World War II.	An eruption of poisonous gas from a volcanic lake in the central African nation of Cameroon kills more than 1,700 people.	Henry Moore, 88, leading 20th-century sculptor and one of Britain's most acclaimed artists, dies in Much Hadham, England.	Aug.
The Committee for the Study of the American Electorate reports that voter turnout in the 1986 primary elections was the lowest in more than 20 years.	The Senate votes to override Pres. Reagan's veto of legislation imposing strict economic sanctions against South Africa, and the bill becomes law.	The House and Senate overwhelmingly approve sweeping legislation for the most radical overhaul of the nation's tax code in at least 40 years.	Federal health officials announce that testing has found significant success for the drug AZT (azidothymidine) as a palliative for some cases of AIDS.	Lorin Maazel is appointed to a four-year term as music director of the Pittsburgh Symphony, which has been without a music director since Andre Previn's departure in 1984.	Sept.
U.S. Dist. Judge Harry E. Claiborne is automatically removed from office when the Senate votes to convict him on three of the four articles of impeachment.	V.P. George Bush and Bush aide Donald Gregg are linked to a private supply operation to provide arms to Nicaraguan Contras after a U.S. supply plane is shot down by Sandinista troops.	Pres. Reagan signs into law the most sweeping overhaul of the nation's tax code in 40 years. The Congress passed the bill in September.	Surgeon Gen. C. Everett Koop issues a report calling for education of school children "at the lowest grade possible" about sex and the fatal disease AIDS.	Wole Soyinka, Nigerian playwright, poet, novelist and essayist, becomes the first African and the first black of any nationality to win the Nobel Prize for literature.	Oct.
The Democratic Party makes a net gain of eight seats to regain control of the Senate with a 55-45 majority; Democrats solidify their majority in the House with a net gain of five seats.	Pres. Reagan says the United States secretly sent "defensive weapons and spare parts" to Iran, but denies that the shipments were in exchange for the release of hostages in Lebanon.	The Securities and Exchange Comm. announces that arbitrager Ivan F. Boesky has agreed to pay $100 mil. in fines for insider trading.	The director of the World Health Org. announces a top-priority drive against AIDS, a disease that is expected to affect 500,000 to 3.5 million people worldwide by 1990.	Exacerbating tensions between the Vatican and U.S. Catholics, the National Conference of Catholic Bishops approves a controversial pastoral letter on "economic justice."	Nov.
At the request of Pres. Reagan, a special panel of three federal judges selects Lawrence E. Walsh as the independent counsel in the Iran-Contra arms scandal.	Reagan administration officials testify before Congress on U.S. arms sales to Iran and on the diversion of funds from the sales to the Nicaraguan Contra rebels.	The nation's state insurance regulators approve non-binding model guidelines barring insurance applicants from being asked whether they are homosexual.	The experimental aircraft *Voyager* touches down at the end of the first round-the-world flight made without stopping or refueling.	Desi Arnaz, 69, Cuban-born entertainer who with his wife, Lucille Ball, starred in and produced the "I Love Lucy" TV comedy series, dies of lung cancer in Del Mar, Calif.	Dec.

F	G	H	I	J
Includes elections, federal-state relations, civil rights and liberties, crime, the judiciary, education, health care, poverty, urban affairs and population.	*Includes formation and debate of U.S. foreign and defense policies, veterans' affairs and defense spending. (Relations with specific foreign countries are usually found under the region concerned.)*	*Includes business, labor, agriculture, taxation, transportation, consumer affairs, monetary and fiscal policy, natural resources, and pollution.*	*Includes worldwide scientific, medical and technological developments, natural phenomena, U.S. weather, natural disasters, and accidents.*	*Includes the arts, religion, scholarship, communications media, sports, entertainments, fashions, fads and social life.*

	World Affairs	Europe	Africa & the Middle East	The Americas	Asia & the Pacific
Jan. 1	Pres. Reagan and Soviet Gen. Sec. Mikhail S. Gorbachev express their desire for peace in separate five-minute messages broadcast on television in each other's nation.	In the Netherlands, the government introduces a program cutting the 40-hour work week by two hours for public employees.... Spain and Portugal automatically become official members of the European Community (EC). Their formal entry is set forth in a treaty ratified by their own and the parliaments of the 10 other members of the EC.		The Caribbean island of Aruba secedes from the Netherlands Antilles to become a self-governing member of the Kingdom of the Netherlands. P.M. Henny Eman of the People's Party and his six cabinet ministers are sworn in by the island's first governor, Felipe Tromp.... Continuing a three-month campaign against the opposition media, the Nicaraguan government closes down the official Roman Catholic radio station.	Farmers in South Australia lost between A$20 mil. and A$40 mil. in the current grain harvest because of poor weather, the United Farmers and Stockowners report. Losses in New South Wales and Victoria reportedly also ranged in the tens of millions of dollars.
Jan. 2		A publication known as "Britain 1986" and described as an official handbook is released by the government. It indicates, among other findings, that 98% of British households have a television set, while refrigerators, found in 94% of households, are the next most commonplace home appliance.			
Jan. 3				Mexican Pres. Miguel de la Madrid Hurtado meets with Pres. Reagan in Mexicali. Trade and Mexico's foreign debt are at the top of the agenda.	
Jan. 4			U.S. officials report that Syria withdrew recently deployed mobile antiaircraft missiles from Lebanon in a move that appears to ease regional tensions.		Australians consumed more alcohol than any other English-speaking people, according to a survey published in the *Medical Journal of Australia*. The survey says the nation ranks 12th in the world in per capita alcohol consumption.
Jan. 5					

A	B	C	D	E
Includes developments that affect more than one world region, international organizations and important meetings of major world leaders.	Includes all domestic and regional developments in Europe, including the Soviet Union, Turkey, Cyprus and Malta.	Includes all domestic and regional developments in Africa and the Middle East, including Iraq and Iran and excluding Cyprus, Turkey and Afghanistan.	Includes all domestic and regional developments in Latin America, the Caribbean and Canada.	Includes all domestic and regional developments in Asia and Pacific nations, extending from Afghanistan through all the Pacific Islands, except Hawaii.

U.S. Politics & Social Issues	U.S. Foreign Policy & Defense	U.S. Economy & Environment	Science, Technology & Nature	Culture, Leisure & Life Style	
Rioting prisoners seize 16 guards as hostages at West Virginia's penitentiary in Moundsville. They return to their cells shortly before Gov. Arch A. Moore Jr. (R) meets with a group of prisoners to discuss inmate grievances.				College bowl results: Orange: Oklahoma 25, Penn State 10; Sugar: Tennessee 35, Miami 7; Rose: Univ. of California, Los Angeles 45, Iowa 28; Cotton: Texas A&M 36, Auburn 16. . . . Lord (Edward Christian) David (Gascoyne) Cecil, 83, eminent British literary historian and biographer, dies. Best known for his biography of Lord Melbourne, Queen Victoria's first prime minister, he was Goldsmith's Professor of English literature at Oxford from 1948 to 1969 and appeared on such British television programs as the British Broadcasting Corp.'s "Brains Trust."	Jan. 1
Barbara Aronstein Black becomes the first woman to head an Ivy League law school when she is appointed dean of Columbia Univ. Law School, effective February 4.	Pres. Reagan accuses the Soviet Union and Cuba of sponsoring terrorism and narcotics trafficking in Latin America. His statements are in a written response to questions submitted by Noticias de Mexico, a Mexican news agency. . . . A federal grand jury in Alexandria, Va., delivers a new espionage indictment against Larry Wu-Tai Chin, a naturalized American citizen who worked for the Central Intelligence Agency (CIA) from 1952 until his retirement in 1981. Chin was arrested on espionage charges in November 1985. The second indictment alleges that among other things he supplied a Chinese agent with classified information from the CIA about the West's assessment of China's "strategic, military, economic, scientific and technical capabilities and intentions."	The Treasury Dept. announces that the San Francisco-based Bank of America has been fined a record $4.75 mil. for failing to report some 17,000 large cash transactions between 1980 and 1985.	The first woman to receive an artificial heart emerges from a coma at Abbott Northwestern Hospital in Minneapolis. The patient, Mary Lund, remains on a respirator, but doctors say she has a better than 50% chance of survival.	The National Society of Film Critics names Akira Kurosawa's *Ran* best film of 1985. Jack Nicholson is voted best actor and John Huston is voted best director for *Prizzi's Honor*. Vanessa Redgrave is named best actress for *Wetherby*. . . . Oklahoma is named the nation's best college football team in polls conducted by the Associated Press and United Press International. . . . Bill Veeck, 71, former owner of three major league baseball teams—the Cleveland Indians, the St. Louis Browns, and the Chicago White Sox (twice)—and known as the "Barnum of Baseball" for his creative and occasionally outrageous promotional activities, dies of a heart attack in Chicago.	Jan. 2
The Rev. Jerry Falwell announces that he is forming a new political group to rally support for conservative causes on a wide spectrum of domestic and foreign issues.					Jan. 3
Sen. Gary Hart (D, Colo.) announces that he will not run for reelection in 1986 and strongly hints at a run for the presidency in 1988.				In National Football League playoff games, the Miami Dolphins beat the Cleveland Browns, 24-21, and the Los Angeles Rams beat the Dallas Cowboys, 20-0. . . . Christopher (William Bradshaw) Isherwood, 81, noted British-born author, dies of cancer in Santa Monica, Calif. Since the 1940s he lived in California and for some years supported himself as a screenwriter, best known for his stories written in the 1930s about prewar Berlin that became the basis for the play and film *I Am a Camera* and the stage and screen musical *Cabaret*. He was one of the first international figures to publicly admit he was a homosexual and in the 1970s became a leading spokesman for gay rights.	Jan. 4
		A gas leak at a Kerr-McGee Corp. uranium-processing plant in Gore, Okla., kills one employee and causes the brief hospitalization of 26 workers and four local residents.		In National Football League playoff games, the Chicago Bears beat the New York Giants, 21-0, and the New England Patriots beat the Los Angeles Raiders, 27-20.	Jan. 5

F	G	H	I	J
Includes elections, federal-state relations, civil rights and liberties, crime, the judiciary, education, health care, poverty, urban affairs and population.	Includes formation and debate of U.S. foreign and defense policies, veterans' affairs and defense spending. (Relations with specific foreign countries are usually found under the region concerned.)	Includes business, labor, agriculture, taxation, transportation, consumer affairs, monetary and fiscal policy, natural resources, and pollution.	Includes worldwide scientific, medical and technological developments, natural phenomena, U.S. weather, natural disasters, and accidents.	Includes the arts, religion, scholarship, communications media, sports, entertainments, fashions, fads and social life.

	World Affairs	Europe	Africa & the Middle East	The Americas	Asia & the Pacific
Jan. 6		Yugoslavia's state president designates Branko Mikulic as the next premier. Mikulic, 57, a Croat from the province of Bosnia-Herzegovina, will replace Premier Milka Planinc, who is near the end of a four-year term.	Impala Platinum Holdings Ltd., the second-largest platinum producer in the world, fires 20,000 workers at three mines in the South African tribal homeland of Bophuthatswana after they refuse to call off a five-day-old strike. Platinum future prices reportedly soar at the news.	In Liberia, Gen. Samuel K. Doe is sworn in as Liberia's elected president, returning the country to civilian rule. Doe has ruled Liberia since seizing power in a bloody 1980 coup. He was declared the winner of a nationwide election—widely regarded as having been rigged—in October 1985, and crushed an attempted coup shortly afterward.	
Jan. 7			Kurdish rebels fighting for regional autonomy in northern Iraq have begun to pose a serious challenge to the Iraqi Army's control of the area, the *Financial Times* of London reports. Improved relations with their anti-Baghdad allies, Iran, Syria, and Libya, have been accompanied by new supplies of heavy weapons.		Soviet Jewish dissident Anatoly B. Shcharansky is reported to have been sentenced again to forced labor. Shcharansky, 38, was sentenced in 1978 to three years in prison and 10 years in a labor camp for alleged spying for the United States.... The highest ranking U.S. delegation to visit Vietnam since the end of the Vietnam War in 1975 holds talks with government officials in Hanoi. The two sides agree to try to resolve the question of U.S. servicemen missing in action and to investigate reports that living Americans remain in Vietnam.
Jan. 8		The West German industrial concern formally known as the Flick Group says it has paid 5 mil. Deutsche Marks (about $2 mil.) to Jews it used as slave labor during World War II.		The Canadian and U.S. special envoys on acid rain issue a joint report calling for a $5 bil. program on pollution control.... In an effort to quell increasing antigovernment protests, Haiti's Pres. Jean-Claude Duvalier declares that security forces have been instructed to "rigorously put down all illegal action." He also orders all schools and universities to close indefinitely.	
Jan. 9	Finance ministers and central bankers from the Group of Five nations (the United States, Japan, West Germany, France, Britain) adjourn a two-day meeting after agreeing "that any movement in interest rates ought to be down rather than up," according to one participant in the talks quoted in the *Financial Times* newspaper. There is, however, no plan for a concerted effort to cut rates.	Michael Heseltine, the British secretary of state for defense, resigns suddenly by stalking out of a cabinet meeting with P.M. Margaret Thatcher over a rescue battle for the ailing Westland PLC, Britain's sole helicopter manufacturer. Prior to his resignation Heseltine had sought support for a European-backed rescue of Westland.... In East Germany, the Communist Party had an overall gain of 121,000 members from 1980 to 1985, according to *Neues Deutschland*, the party's main newspaper. The paper asserts that the party's membership stood at 2,194,585 at the end of 1985, out of a total East German population of 17 million.	In Lusaka, Zambia, Oliver Tambo, president of the African National Congress (ANC), pledges that the ANC will step up its military campaign to overthrow South Africa's white-ruled government and its apartheid system of racial segregation, and that the struggle will inevitably lead to increased civilian casualties.	The *Washington Post* reports that at least three people have died and scores have been injured in 11 days of protests against alleged fraud in municipal elections in Mexico.	In Indonesia, a former secretary general of the Assoc. of Southeast Asian Nations is reported sentenced to 10 years in prison for subversion.

A	B	C	D	E
Includes developments that affect more than one world region, international organizations and important meetings of major world leaders.	Includes all domestic and regional developments in Europe, including the Soviet Union, Turkey, Cyprus and Malta.	Includes all domestic and regional developments in Africa and the Middle East, including Iraq and Iran and excluding Cyprus, Turkey and Afghanistan.	Includes all domestic and regional developments in Latin America, the Caribbean and Canada.	Includes all domestic and regional developments in Asia and Pacific nations, extending from Afghanistan through all the Pacific Islands, except Hawaii.

U.S. Politics & Social Issues	U.S. Foreign Policy & Defense	U.S. Economy & Environment	Science, Technology & Nature	Culture, Leisure & Life Style	
		Paul N. Carlin is dismissed as postmaster general and replaced by Albert V. Casey, 65, retired chairman and chief executive officer of AMR Corp., parent company of American Airlines.			**Jan. 6**
Sen. Lloyd Bentsen (D, Tex.) says he will hold hearings on the political influence wielded by foreign investors in the United States, particularly with respect to contributions by political action committees run by foreign-owned U.S. companies.	Pres. Reagan announces the imposition of economic sanctions against Libya and orders the 1,000 to 1,500 Americans remaining in Libya to leave immediately.	Agriculture Sec. John R. Block announces his resignation, effective mid-February. . . . The Labor Dept.'s Occupational Safety and Health Admin. (OSHA) announces a revised policy of workplace safety inspections. OSHA will continue its current policy of keying the inspection effort on high-hazard manufacturing companies, but it will expand the scope of the program to include spot checks of companies in industries with injury rates below the national average.		Spend a Buck wins the Eclipse Award as the top three-year-old American race horse of 1985. The colt was winner of the Kentucky Derby.	**Jan. 7**
		Stock prices tumble, with the nation's most widely followed indicator, the Dow Jones Industrial Average of 30 blue-chip stocks falling, a record 39.10 points to close at 1526.61. . . . The nation's unemployment rate fell to a seasonally adjusted level of 6.8% of the work force in December 1985, the Labor Dept. reports. . . . Finding that Kodak's instant camera and film violates patents held by Polaroid Corp., the U.S. Court of Appeals in Washington D.C. and Supreme Court Justice Lewis F. Powell refuse to lift an injunction prohibiting Kodak from selling its instant system.		Pierre Fournier, 79, cellist whose elegant and subdued manner of playing typified French musical style, dies in Geneva, Switz. His repertoire ranged from the unaccompanied sonatas of Bach to music written for him by 20th-century composers. . . . In his first year of eligibility, Willie McCovey is elected to baseball's Hall of Fame. McCovey's 521 lifetime home runs ranked him ninth on the all-time list and first among National League left-handers. . . . U.S.-Soviet cultural exchanges begin with a premiere performance in Moscow by an American theater group. Pres. Reagan and Soviet leader Mikhail S. Gorbachev signed the cultural agreement at the close of the 1985 Geneva summit.	**Jan. 8**
		Barry Bingham Sr. puts up for sale his family's Kentucky media empire, including the Courier-Journal and Louisville Times Co. In a statement he cited the "divergent interests" of family members, together with problems that include tax complications and rising costs.	Researchers in Virginia and Australia report the first practical use of any drug in halting the spread of the common cold virus. The two studies, which appear in the *New England Journal of Medicine*, report that the drug interferon alpha 2 is useful in preventing the spread of cold virus infections in family members. . . . A U.S. study prepared by the Federal Centers for Disease Control and the San Francisco Dept. of Public Health says the first 10,000 acquired immune deficiency syndrome (AIDS) cases in the United States will result in costs to the economy of some $6.3 bil. Critics question the high figure and warn that the fight against AIDS would be best served through unexaggerated data. . . . Women who exercise regularly throughout their lives establish a style of life that significantly lowers their risk of developing cancer of the breast or reproductive organs later in life, according to a Harvard Univ. study.	Lucia (Mrs. Thomas Ewing Jr.) Chase, 88, leading figure in American dance, dies in News York City. She helped found the American Ballet Theater (ABT) in 1940 and officially codirected the company for most of its existence; she not only gave the company considerable financial support but also danced character roles with it well into her 70s.	**Jan. 9**

F	G	H	I	J
Includes elections, federal-state relations, civil rights and liberties, crime, the judiciary, education, health care, poverty, urban affairs and population.	Includes formation and debate of U.S. foreign and defense policies, veterans' affairs and defense spending. (Relations with specific foreign countries are usually found under the region concerned.)	Includes business, labor, agriculture, taxation, transportation, consumer affairs, monetary and fiscal policy, natural resources, and pollution.	Includes worldwide scientific, medical and technological developments, natural phenomena, U.S. weather, natural disasters, and accidents.	Includes the arts, religion, scholarship, communications media, sports, entertainments, fashions, fads and social life.

	World Affairs	Europe	Africa & the Middle East	The Americas	Asia & the Pacific
Jan. 10		Dutch unemployment fell to a two-year low of 15.4% in December 1985. In addition, unemployment for the year fell for the first time in a decade.	Six U.S. congressmen conclude a visit to South Africa undertaken in order to see whether limited sanctions imposed in 1985 were having any effect and to ''express our solidarity with the [black] majority.'' The delegation was led by Rep. William H. Gray III (D, Pa.), one of the leading black members of Congress.		British and Australian officials conclude two days of meetings in Canberra, Australia, to discuss for the first time the Royal Comm. report on British nuclear testing in Australia during the 1950s and 1960s. The commission, chaired by Justice James McClelland, recommends that Britain finance the cleanup of the South Australia testing sites.
Jan. 11		In Poland, the government announces the arrest of Bogdan Borusewicz, a major figure in the underground leadership of Solidarity, the outlawed labor movement.		Some 17,000 Bolivian coca growers end a five-day siege of a camp of 245 narcotics police of the U.S.-financed ''Leopards'' unit. The angry farmers were protesting a government program to reduce coca production.	
Jan. 12			An Iranian Navy ship stops an American merchant vessel in international waters outside the Persian Gulf and sends sailors aboard to search for Iraq-bound war material. None is found, and the freighter is allowed to go on its way.	Japan's Premier Yasuhiro Nakasone visits Canada, with trade issues dominating his discussions with Canadian officials.	Tamil guerrillas say they are calling off a seven-month-old truce with Sri Lanka's security forces in the island's ongoing ethnic conflict. The guerrillas are members of Sri Lanka's largely Hindu Tamil minority who have been fighting against its predominantly Buddhist Sinhalese majority for a separate Tamil state.
Jan. 13		West Germany's visible trade surplus jumped in 1985 to a record 72.3 bil. Deutsche Marks, compared with 50.1 bil. Deutsche Marks in 1984, the federal statistical offices announce.		Mexico's central bank announces that inflation in 1985 was 63.7%, up from 59.2% in 1984.... In Argentina, leftist demonstrators stage violent protests against visiting U.S. banker David Rockefeller. The visit is also opposed by political leaders who associate Rockefeller with former repressive military regimes that borrowed millions of dollars from U.S. banks in the 1970s.	
Jan. 14				The foreign ministers of Costa Rica, El Salvador, Honduras, Nicaragua, and Guatemala meeting in Guatemala City formally endorse a document calling for the resumption of talks between the United States and Nicaragua and back renewal of Contadora Group-sponsored peace talks suspended in December 1985.	

A	B	C	D	E
Includes developments that affect more than one world region, international organizations and important meetings of major world leaders.	Includes all domestic and regional developments in Europe, including the Soviet Union, Turkey, Cyprus and Malta.	Includes all domestic and regional developments in Africa and the Middle East, including Iraq and Iran and excluding Cyprus, Turkey and Afghanistan.	Includes all domestic and regional developments in Latin America, the Caribbean and Canada.	Includes all domestic and regional developments in Asia and Pacific nations, extending from Afghanistan through all the Pacific Islands, except Hawaii.

U.S. Politics & Social Issues	U.S. Foreign Policy & Defense	U.S. Economy & Environment	Science, Technology & Nature	Culture, Leisure & Life Style	
James Terry Roach is executed by electrocution at South Carolina's state penitentiary in Columbia. He is the first person in 22 years to be executed for a juvenile offense without waiving his right to appeal. Roach, 25, had pleaded guilty to the 1977 killing of two teenagers. Roach's lawyers had sought clemency not only on account of his age but also on the grounds that he was mentally retarded and suffered from the brain disease Huntington's chorea.		The government's producer price index (PPI) rose a seasonally adjusted 0.4% in December 1985, the Labor Dept. reports. That gain brought the total increase in the PPI to 1.8% for 1985.		Joseph Kraft, 61, Washington-based journalist whose columns on public affairs were carried by more than 200 newspapers in the United States and abroad, dies in Washington, D.C., of apparent heart failure. . . . Jaroslav Seifert, 84, Czechoslovak poet, dies of heart disease in Prague. Winner of the Nobel Prize for literature in 1984, he was unable to go to Stockholm to receive the prize personally because of a chronic heart ailment.	Jan. 10
				It is reported that North American hardback and paperback rights to *Whirlwind*, the latest novel by James Clavell, were sold at auction for $5 mil. to William Morrow & Co. and Avon Books. Clavell is the author of *Shogun*, the best-selling novel that became a successful television mini-series in 1980.	Jan. 11
			A new mapping of part of the universe reveals patterns suggesting that galaxies, far from being randomly distributed, tend to cluster at the intersections of expanding "bubbles" of empty space. The theory, proposed by Margaret Geller of the Harvard-Smithsonian Center for Astrophysics and explored at recent meetings of the American Astronomical Society, has been picking up support among astronomers. Geller is preparing new three-dimensional sky charts of distant regions of space. . . . A weather satellite is launched successfully from Vandenberg Air Force Base, Calif., by a 25 year-old Atlas-E rocket. . . . A report by 150 scientists from 11 countries warns that human industry is changing the Earth's atmosphere in ways whose long-term consequences are still unknown, the *New York Times* reports. The report was sponsored by international and U.S. organizations and coordinated by National Aeronautics and Space Admin.	Bob Kaufman, 60, one of the original San Francisco Beat poets, dies of emphysema in San Francisco. With Allen Ginsberg and two other poets, he founded *Beatitude* magazine in 1959. His books include *Solitudes Crowded with Loneliness* and *Golden Sardine*. . . . The New England Patriots win the National Football League's American Conf. championship and advance to the Super Bowl in a 31-14 victory over the Miami Dolphins. The Chicago Bears also advance to the Super Bowl, beating the Los Angeles Rams 24-0 in the National Football League's National Conf. championship.	Jan. 12
	Ecuador's Pres. Leon Febres Cordero makes a state visit to the United States to meet with Pres. Reagan and to sign new loan agreements with international lending agencies.	Outgoing Agriculture Sec. John Block announces severe cuts in price-support loan levels for corn and wheat during the 1986 growing season. The cuts are made under authority of a sweeping new agricultural bill passed in late 1985.		It is reported that Peter F. Fleischmann will be stepping down at the end of the month as chairman of the New Yorker Magazine Inc., publisher of the weekly magazine founded by his father in 1925. The magazine was acquired by publishing magnate Samuel I. Newhouse Jr. in 1984.	Jan. 13
The Supreme Court rules unanimously that a suspect's right to remain silent under the 1966 Miranda warnings cannot be used against him later by the prosecution as proof of the suspect's sanity at the time of arrest. . . . The Supreme Court overturns the 23-year-old murder conviction of a defendant because he was indicted by a grand jury from which members of his own race were excluded unconstitutionally. . . . A report by a private panel says that in 1984 the federal food stamp program served just 55% of those eligible, down from 65% in 1980.		Outstanding consumer installment credit grew a seasonally adjusted $4.88 bil. in November 1985, or at an annual rate of 11%, the Federal Reserve Board reports. The November gain was the smallest since August 1983. . . . The Federal Communications Comm. bars zoning and other rules that single out backyard satellite dishes from other antennas.		Donna Reed (born Donna Belle Mullenger), 64, actress who portrayed the ideal suburban American wife and mother on television's "The Donna Reed Show" in the 1950s and 1960s, dies in Beverly Hills, Calif., of pancreatic cancer. She starred in the 1946 Frank Capra film *It's a Wonderful Life* and won the Academy Award for best supporting actress in *From Here to Eternity* (1953). She returned to television briefly in 1984 as Miss Ellie on "Dallas," replacing Barbara Bel Geddes, who reclaimed the role in 1985. . . . The National Collegiate Athletic Assoc. votes to institute eligibility requirements for student athletes based on standardized test results and to implement drug testing at championship events.	Jan. 14
F	G	H	I	J	
Includes elections, federal-state relations, civil rights and liberties, crime, the judiciary, education, health care, poverty, urban affairs and population.	Includes formation and debate of U.S. foreign and defense policies, veterans' affairs and defense spending. (Relations with specific foreign countries are usually found under the region concerned.)	Includes business, labor, agriculture, taxation, transportation, consumer affairs, monetary and fiscal policy, natural resources, and pollution.	Includes worldwide scientific, medical and technological developments, natural phenomena, U.S. weather, natural disasters, and accidents.	Includes the arts, religion, scholarship, communications media, sports, entertainments, fashions, fads and social life.	

	World Affairs	Europe	Africa & the Middle East	The Americas	Asia & the Pacific
Jan. 15		Soviet leader Mikhail S. Gorbachev proposes a worldwide ban on nuclear weapons by the year 2000. His proposal is read by an announcer on Soviet television's evening news and published by Tass, the official news agency.	A revised draft proposal of Algeria's national charter is approved by an overwhelming majority (more than 98%) of the nation's voters. . . . Heavy fighting between rival Lebanese Christian militias broke out Jan. 13 in east Beirut. On this day forces loyal to Pres. Amin Gemayel defeat those of Elie Hobeika, commander of the Lebanese Forces militia. Hobeika's defeat appears to doom the Syrian-brokered peace accord signed by Christian and Moslem militia leaders in December 1985.	Dow Chemical Canada Inc. pleads guilty to four counts of violating the Ontario Water Resources Act. The charges concern an accidental discharge of dry-cleaning solvent into the St. Clair River in August 1985.	
Jan. 16		The fourth round of the U.S.-Soviet disarmament talks opens in Geneva. The U.S. negotiators hope to make gains on the issue of verification and medium-range missiles in Europe. The Moscow contingent is optimistic regarding the proposal by Gen. Sec. Mikhail Gorbachev to eliminate nuclear weapons in stages by the year 2000.			
Jan. 17			The leaders of Mali and Burkina Faso (formerly Upper Volta) meet in Yamoussoukro, Ivory Coast, for the first time since their two countries fought a five-day border war at the end of 1985.		Japan's world trade surplus reached a record $46.14 bil. in 1985, according to preliminary figures released by the finance ministry.
Jan. 18					
Jan. 19				Colombia's Pres. Belisario Betancur nationalizes four subsidiaries of Grand Colombian Financial Group that have been in difficulties since 1983.	In India, P.M. Rajiv Gandhi drops three senior ministers from his cabinet and appoints them to top posts in his ruling Congress (I) Party. . . . At the end of a four-day mission to Japan designed to improve Sino-Soviet relations, Soviet Foreign Min. Eduard A. Shevardnadze reports that there is no "coincidence of views" regarding the Soviet occupation, since August 1945, of four of the Kurile Islands northeast of the Japanese island of Hokkaido.

A	B	C	D	E
Includes developments that affect more than one world region, international organizations and important meetings of major world leaders.	Includes all domestic and regional developments in Europe, including the Soviet Union, Turkey, Cyprus and Malta.	Includes all domestic and regional developments in Africa and the Middle East, including Iraq and Iran and excluding Cyprus, Turkey and Afghanistan.	Includes all domestic and regional developments in Latin America, the Caribbean and Canada.	Includes all domestic and regional developments in Asia and Pacific nations, extending from Afghanistan through all the Pacific Islands, except Hawaii.

U.S. Politics & Social Issues	U.S. Foreign Policy & Defense	U.S. Economy & Environment	Science, Technology & Nature	Culture, Leisure & Life Style	
A panel convened by the National Institutes of Health says the use of snuff and chewing tobacco is "health endangering." The panel links smokeless tobacco to "increased risk of oral cancer" as well as to recession of the gums and to the gum disease leukopenia. . . . Saying that a record number of approved drugs offered improvement in treatment, the Federal Food and Drug Admin. says it approved 30 new drugs for marketing in 1985; 16 in the last weeks of December.		The Office of Management and Budget orders federal agencies to prepare to make $11.7 bil. in spending cuts in 1986. They represent the first round of automatic spending cuts mandated by the 1985 Gramm-Rudman balanced-budget law.		Herbert W. Armstrong, 93, founder of the Worldwide Church of God, an 80,000-member fundamentalist Christian sect that incorporated certain elements of Judaism, dies in Pasadena, Calif. of heart disease. Over the years the church built up an extremely prosperous base. In the late 1970s, charges by Armstrong's son that Herbert Armstrong siphoned off millions of dollars of church funds for his personal enrichment led to a much-publicized investigation by the California attorney general.	Jan. 15
All charges of assault and attempted murder lodged against Bernhard H. Goetz, the "subway vigilante," are dismissed by a New York State Supreme Court justice in a decision leaves open the possibility of another grand jury hearing on the case. In December 1984, Goetz created a national sensation by shooting four youths whom he believed to be threatening him. . . . The Family Policy Panel issues a report that says the "work and family lives" of most Americans are "increasingly coming into conflict," and warns of an economic cost to the nation. According to the panel's report, the labor force includes 50% of women with children aged under three, as well as 70% of women whose youngest children are six to 13 years old.		The United Steelworkers of America says it plans to negotiate contracts with major steel makers on a company-by-company basis rather than on an industry-wide basis as it has for the past 30 years.			Jan. 16
		New housing starts rose 17.5% in December 1985 to a seasonally adjusted annual rate of 1.84 million units, the Commerce Dept. reports. . . . Apple Computer Inc. reaches a settlement with Steven Jobs, the company's 30-year-old cofounder and former chairman, barring him from marketing his new computer until July 1987.		Some 800 writers conclude a five-day gathering in New York City of the 48th annual congress of PEN, the international organization of poets, playwrights, editors, essayists, and novelists. An opening address by U.S. Sec. of State George P.Shultz is greeted with a letter of protest signed by 65 PEN members.	Jan. 17
The White House announces that laboratory tests show that three colonic growths and a facial patch removed from Pres. Reagan yesterday are benign.			The space shuttle *Columbia* successfully completes a much-delayed scientific mission. The launch from Cape Canaveral, Fla., originally scheduled for Dec. 18, 1985, was postponed seven times. The landing was postponed twice, and the site shifted finally from Florida to California's Edwards Air Force Base.		Jan. 18
Douglas J. Brown, 87, Princeton Univ. economist, dies in Princeton, N.J. Brown, who worked for Pres. Franklin D. Roosevelt's Committee on Economic Security in 1934, was one of the architects of the U.S. Social Security system.				James L. Hicks, 70, pioneering black journalist, dies in New York City, after a stroke. Hicks was the first black American accredited to cover the UN, the first black member of the State Dept. Correspondents Assoc., and the first black sent to cover the Korean War. As editor of the *Amsterdam News* he helped turn the New York City weekly into one of the most influential U.S. newspapers aimed at blacks.	Jan. 19

F	G	H	I	J
Includes elections, federal-state relations, civil rights and liberties, crime, the judiciary, education, health care, poverty, urban affairs and population.	Includes formation and debate of U.S. foreign and defense policies, veterans' affairs and defense spending. (Relations with specific foreign countries are usually found under the region concerned.)	Includes business, labor, agriculture, taxation, transportation, consumer affairs, monetary and fiscal policy, natural resources, and pollution.	Includes worldwide scientific, medical and technological developments, natural phenomena, U.S. weather, natural disasters, and accidents.	Includes the arts, religion, scholarship, communications media, sports, entertainments, fashions, fads and social life.

	World Affairs	Europe	Africa & the Middle East	The Americas	Asia & the Pacific
Jan. 20		Britain and France approve the construction of a rail tunnel beneath the English Channel that will link the two countries by 1993. . . . Galvan Enrique Tierno, 67, Spanish socialist intellectual, dies of cancer in Madrid. From 1979, he was mayor of Madrid and one of Spain's best-loved political figures of the post-Franco period; his administration is credited with having transformed the Spanish capital into one of the most vibrant and livable cities of Europe. Earlier, as a professor of political science, he had been a leading opponent of Francisco Franco's regime.		Premier Robert Bourassa wins a seat in the Quebec National Assembly in a by-election. . . . The prime minister of Lesotho, Chief Leabua Jonathan, is overthrown in a military coup following three weeks of tension resulting from an economic blockade imposed by South Africa.	North Korea says it is suspending political and economic talks with South Korea in protest of joint U.S.-South Korean military maneuvers.
Jan. 21		In Poland, the government announces that Lech Walesa, the founder of Solidarity, will be tried on charges of slandering state elections officials. No trial date is set.		In Canada, the national inflation rate in 1985 is the lowest in 14 years, according to Statistics Canada. The 1985 inflation rate was 4% compared with 4.4% in 1984. The newest figure is the lowest inflation rate since the 2.9% in 1971. . . . El Salvador's Pres. Jose Napoleon Duarte devalues the nation's currency and announces new austerity measures as part of an effort to revive the economy.	
Jan. 22				A 1,800-mile trek through Central America by an estimated 300 peace activists ends in Mexico City with a rally in support of the group's initiatives. Participants in the international march for peace in Central America hail from more than 40 countries. They began their journey in Panama Dec. 10, 1985, with the goal of drawing world attention to U.S. involvement in the region and to human rights issues.	In India, three Sikhs convicted of the October 1984 assassination of P.M. Indira Gandhi are sentenced to be hanged.
Jan. 23	A two-week decline in crude oil prices on the world markets has brought prices to their lowest levels in six years. The precipitous decline, caused by an oversupply of petroleum on world markets, is influencing aspects of the world economy ranging from the value of the British pound to the foreign debt problems of Mexico.	In Northern Ireland, 14 of the 15 unionist members of Parliament from Ulster are reelected in by-elections. The unionists all had resigned in late 1985 to protest the recent Anglo-Irish accord that gave the Republic of Ireland a consultative role for the first time in governing Ulster.	In South Yemen, rebel forces gain the upper hand in a virtual civil war against supporters of Pres. Ali Nasser Mohammed al-Hasani.		The Australian dollar reaches a five-month high, rising to 71.55 cents. Dealers attribute the increase to growing confidence in the Australian economy resulting in part from the reserve bank's tight monetary policy, which pushed interest rates up to record levels, according to the newspaper the *Australian*.

A	B	C	D	E
Includes developments that affect more than one world region, international organizations and important meetings of major world leaders.	*Includes all domestic and regional developments in Europe, including the Soviet Union, Turkey, Cyprus and Malta.*	*Includes all domestic and regional developments in Africa and the Middle East, including Iraq and Iran and excluding Cyprus, Turkey and Afghanistan.*	*Includes all domestic and regional developments in Latin America, the Caribbean and Canada.*	*Includes all domestic and regional developments in Asia and Pacific nations, extending from Afghanistan through all the Pacific Islands, except Hawaii.*

U.S. Politics & Social Issues	U.S. Foreign Policy & Defense	U.S. Economy & Environment	Science, Technology & Nature	Culture, Leisure & Life Style	
The United States observes the first federal holiday in honor of slain civil rights leader Martin Luther King Jr. His widow, Coretta Scott King, marches with some 6,000 people through heavy crowds in King's home city of Atlanta.		The General Accounting Office sends Pres. Reagan the first detailed list of mandatory federal spending cuts required by the 1985 Gramm-Rudman balanced-budget law.		The American Library Assoc. announces the recipient of the John Newberry Medal for best children's book of 1985, Patricia MacLachlan for *Sarah, Plain and Tall*, and the Randolph Caldecott Medal for best illustrations in an American picture book for children, Chris Van Allsburg for *The Polar Express*.	Jan. 20
Five reputed underworld figures are convicted in Kansas City, Mo., on eight counts linked to the skimming of the profits of Las Vegas gambling casinos. The casinos are said to have been bought with money from the Teamsters union. ... A report issued by the U.S. Conf. of Mayors at the group's annual meeting in Washington, D.C., says that serious hunger continues in their cities and that economic recovery has failed to house those left homeless by the recession of 1982.					Jan. 21
A chart in the *Washington Post* chronicling the growth of the White House staff at assorted intervals from 1937 through 1985 shows the greatest number of White House staff to have been 593 employees under Pres. Reagan in December 1985. ... At their meeting in Washington, D.C., members of the U.S. Conf. of Mayors, are critical of the Gramm-Rudman balanced-budget law, which seeks to curb federal deficits by mandating automatic cutbacks in federal spending, cutbacks that mayors of both parties say could devastate city programs.	An unarmed U.S. cruise missile crashes in northwestern Canada during a test flight. The mishap prompts authorities to indefinitely postpone a second cruise test set for the following day. ... The heads of the Selective Service System and the Education Dept. announce that male applicants for federal college aid are being checked for compliance with mandatory draft registration. Under a 1982 law, male college students are barred from receiving federal aid if they do not register for the draft upon turning 18 years of age.	The gross national product, adjusted for inflation, grew 2.3% in 1985, the Commerce Dept. reports, as against a dynamic 6.6% expansion in 1984 and a 3.4% gain in 1983. ... The government's consumer price index (CPI) rose a seasonally adjusted 0.4% in December 1985, according to the Labor Dept. CPI for all of 1985 rose only 3.8%. ... The Supreme Court rules unanimously that the Federal Reserve Board overextended its authority in attempting to control limited-service banks.		The American Broadcasting Co. (ABC) television network announces that it will proceed with the production of a controversial miniseries. The 12-hour "Amerika" depicts life in the United States after a Soviet takeover. ABC announced a production delay Jan. 8, a few days after the planned miniseries was denounced by Moscow. ... *Variety*'s top-grossing films for the week are: *The Color Purple, Iron Eagle, Out of Africa, The Jewel of the Nile* and *Rocky IV*.	Jan. 22
The Federal Election Comm. issues a ruling that will limit the use of special political action committees (PACs) to finance the activities of unannounced presidential candidates. The election commission rules that expenditures by the PACs for travel, entertainment, and other activities related to "testing the waters" for a candidacy must be counted against the $5,000 limit. ... The National Urban League says that during 1985 the United States came closer to becoming "permanently divided between the haves and the have-nots." The warning comes in the league's 11th annual assessment of the "State of Black America."	The Reagan administration orders two aircraft carrier battle groups in the Mediterranean to commence flight operations near Libya. The maneuvers are described by one U.S. official as "part of the war of nerves" between the administration and Libya's Col. Muammar el-Qaddafi, following U.S. accusations of Libyan involvement in the December 1985 terrorist attacks on Rome and Vienna airports.	Americans' total personal income rose only 1.6% in 1985 after adjusting for inflation, the Commerce Dept. reports. ... The Environmental Protection Agency proposes a 10-year phaseout of all uses of asbestos. The agency proposes an immediate ban on use of the cancer-causing substance in clothing, roofing felt, flooring felt, vinyl floor tile, cement pipe and fittings.		Willard Van Dyke, 79, photographer and documentary film maker dies of a heart attack in Jackson, Tenn. A founding member of the San Francisco-based f.64 group with Ansel Adams and others, from 1965 to 1974 he was director of the film department at New York City's Museum of Modern Art. ... Joseph Beuys, 64, West German sculptor, teacher, and conceptual artist, dies of heart failure in Dusseldorf. One of the most controversial and influential artists in post-World War II Europe, he was unafraid to draw upon images of Germany's Nazi past for his highly politicized work. In the 1970s he helped found West Germany's environmentalist Green Party. ... The Rock and Roll Hall of Fame Foundation names its first 12 inductees: living performers Chuck Berry, James Brown, Ray Charles, Fats Domino, the Everly Brothers, Jerry Lee Lewis, and Little Richard; the late Sam Cooke, Buddy Holly, and Elvis Presley; and Sun Records founder Sam Phillips and disc jockey Alan Freed are also inducted.	Jan. 23

F	G	H	I	J
Includes elections, federal-state relations, civil rights and liberties, crime, the judiciary, education, health care, poverty, urban affairs and population.	Includes formation and debate of U.S. foreign and defense policies, veterans' affairs and defense spending. (Relations with specific foreign countries are usually found under the region concerned.)	Includes business, labor, agriculture, taxation, transportation, consumer affairs, monetary and fiscal policy, natural resources, and pollution.	Includes worldwide scientific, medical and technological developments, natural phenomena, U.S. weather, natural disasters, and accidents.	Includes the arts, religion, scholarship, communications media, sports, entertainments, fashions, fads and social life.

	World Affairs	Europe	Africa & the Middle East	The Americas	Asia & the Pacific
Jan. 24		Britain's Trade and Industry Sec. Leon Brittan, resigns amid growing criticism of his role in the controversial rescue of Britain's only helicopter maker, Westland PLC. Brittan is the second cabinet minister to resign in the controversy, following the Jan. 9 resignation of Defense Sec. Michael Heseltine.		Argentina's main labor organization calls a general strike to protest against the government's economic program. The strike is the fourth against the government of Pres. Raul Alfonsin since it took office in 1983; it is virtually halting commercial and government activity.	
Jan. 25			After a fierce 12-day civil war that toppled South Yemen's Pres. Ali Nasser Mohammed al-Hasani, the Marxist faction that emerged victorious consolidates its power and names former Premier Haydar Bakr al-Attas to be interim president. Attas is flown in from Moscow, where he has been waiting out the fighting.		
Jan. 26		In Portugal, Diogo Freitas do Amaral, the conservative former Christian Democratic leader, wins the first round of voting in presidential elections. A run-off election between Freitas do Amaral and the second-place winner, Socialist Party leader and former Premier Mario Soares, is scheduled for February 16.	The Ugandan rebel group known as the National Resistance Army abandons a peace treaty signed with government forces in December 1985, seizes control of the capital city of Kampala in fierce fighting, and ousts the country's ruling military council.		Tensions flare in the troubled northern India state of Punjab when Sikh extremists seize control of Sikhdom's holy Golden Temple in Amritsar and oust the five official high priests of Sikhism. The Golden Temple, the Sikhs' holiest shrine, was the site whose occupation by extremists in 1984 prompted an Indian Army assault, resulting in hundreds of deaths and months of unrest.
Jan. 27				Jose Azcona Hoyo, 59, is inaugurated as president of Honduras in a ceremony that marks the first time in more than 50 years that one elected civilian president has handed over power to another in Honduras.	
Jan. 28		The European Community issues a declaration condemning international terrorism. The 12 member nations agree to ban arms sales to countries that are ''clearly implicated in supporting terrorism.''			

A	B	C	D	E
Includes developments that affect more than one world region, international organizations and important meetings of major world leaders.	Includes all domestic and regional developments in Europe, including the Soviet Union, Turkey, Cyprus and Malta.	Includes all domestic and regional developments in Africa and the Middle East, including Iraq and Iran and excluding Cyprus, Turkey and Afghanistan.	Includes all domestic and regional developments in Latin America, the Caribbean and Canada.	Includes all domestic and regional developments in Asia and Pacific nations, extending from Afghanistan through all the Pacific Islands, except Hawaii.

U.S. Politics & Social Issues	U.S. Foreign Policy & Defense	U.S. Economy & Environment	Science, Technology & Nature	Culture, Leisure & Life Style	
			The U.S. spacecraft Voyager 2 makes its closest approach to the planet Uranus, passing within 50,679 miles of the planet's cloud tops.	Gordon MacRae, 64, baritone singer and actor, dies in Lincoln, Nebr., after a long bout with cancer. Best known for his role as the singing cowboy in the 1955 film version of Rodgers and Hammerstein's landmark musical *Oklahoma!*, he also starred in the 1956 film version of their musical *Carousel*. He was a highly successful recording artist for more than a decade beginning in 1948. . . . L. Ron Hubbard, 74, science fiction writer whose best-selling, nonfiction *Dianetics: The Modern Science of Mental Health* (1950), became the bible for the Church of Scientology, a "new religion" he founded with his third wife in 1954, dies of a stroke at his ranch near San Luis Obispo, Calif. Hubbard was the target of investigations by both the Federal Bureau of Investigation and the Internal Revenue Service.	**Jan. 24**
The Senate Finance Committee holds a two-day closed meeting with top Treasury Dept. officials, signaling the formal start of work on a Senate tax bill. In December 1985, the House passed a tax overhaul bill modeled on the proposals submitted to Congress by Pres. Reagan in May 1985.				Albert B. Grossman, 59, one of the most influential personal managers in the history of American popular music, dies of a heart attack while aboard a plane flying from the United States to England. With George Wein he organized the first Newport Folk Festival in 1959, and he played a key role in the careers of such artists as Odetta, Joan Baez, the folk trio Peter, Paul and Mary, Bob Dylan, Richie Havens, Gordon Lightfoot, and Janis Joplin. . . . Up-and-coming heavyweight Mike Tyson knocks out Mike Jameson to record his 17th consecutive knockout.	**Jan. 25**
	Women were part of the flight crews airlifting troops and supplies during the U.S. invasion of Grenada in 1983, according to the *Los Angeles Times*.			The Chicago Bears beat the New England Patriots, 46-10, in Super Bowl XX. Richard Dent, primarily a defensive end for the Bears is named the game's most valuable player. The broadcast of the game receives a Nielsen television rating of 48.3.	**Jan. 26**
		The first-year pay increases negotiated in major collective-bargaining contracts in 1985 averaged 2.3%, the smallest increase since the Labor Dept. began keeping the statistics 18 years ago, the department reports. . . . The Supreme Court refuses to hear Exxon Corp.'s appeal of a $2 bil. judgment against it for overpricing oil from a Texas field from 1975 through 1980. . . . Pepsi-Cola was the nation's largest-selling soft drink in 1985, according to figures from *Beverage Digest*. Pepsi, made by PepsiCo Inc., captured an 18.6% share of the U.S. market.		Lilli (born Lilli Marie Peiser) Palmer, 71, German-born actress and author, dies in Los Angeles. In 1943 she married Rex Harrison, with whom she appeared on Broadway and on television until their divorce in 1957. Palmer appeared in more than 50 films including Alfred Hitchcock's *The Secret Agent* (1936), *The Four Poster* (1952) and her last, *The Boys From Brazil* (1978). She published several novels and an autobiography, *Change Lobsters— And Dance* which became an international best-seller.	**Jan. 27**
Pres. Reagan continues to enjoy strong personal popularity with the American people, according to a CBS News/*New York Times* poll published today, with 65% approving of his handling of the job.			The U.S. space shuttle *Challenger* explodes 73 seconds after lifting off from Cape Canaveral, Florida. All seven crew, including schoolteacher Christa McAuliffe, are killed as millions watch the fiery explosion on television.	Scottish poet Douglas Dunn is named the winner of the Whitbread Book of the Year Award, Britain's biggest literary prize, for his collection of poems, *Elegies*. . . . Five players are voted into the Pro Football Hall of Fame: Paul Hornung, Fran Tarkenton, Ken Houston, Willie Lanier, and Doak Walker.	**Jan. 28**

F	G	H	I	J
Includes elections, federal-state relations, civil rights and liberties, crime, the judiciary, education, health care, poverty, urban affairs and population.	*Includes formation and debate of U.S. foreign and defense policies, veterans' affairs and defense spending. (Relations with specific foreign countries are usually found under the region concerned.)*	*Includes business, labor, agriculture, taxation, transportation, consumer affairs, monetary and fiscal policy, natural resources, and pollution.*	*Includes worldwide scientific, medical and technological developments, natural phenomena, U.S. weather, natural disasters, and accidents.*	*Includes the arts, religion, scholarship, communications media, sports, entertainments, fashions, fads and social life.*

	World Affairs	Europe	Africa & the Middle East	The Americas	Asia & the Pacific
Jan. 29	In Moscow, officials of Argentina and the Soviet Union sign a five-year trade agreement; a previous five-year accord expired in December 1985.		In Uganda, the National Resistance Army leader Yoweri Museveni names himself as Uganda's president and promises to usher in a new era of peace for the war-racked East African nation. Museveni's forces seized control of the capital of Kampala, January 26.		The Bank of Japan announces that it is cutting the official discount rate to 4.5% from 5%, effective Jan. 30. The reduction in the discount rate, which is the fee the central bank charges on loans to commercial banks, is expected to lead to a reduction in other domestic interest rates.
Jan. 30		Prince Felipe of Spain is sworn in as the heir apparent to the Spanish throne. The swearing-in ceremony coincided with the prince's 18th birthday.			Foreign investment in China increased sharply in 1985, to $4.6 bil. However, the foreign trade ministry concedes that the increased investment has not brought the advanced technology that is desired, and few ventures are in key sectors such as transportation, communications, and energy.
Jan. 31	Philip Caryl Jessup, 89, U.S. authority on international law who for many years taught at Columbia Univ., dies in Newtown, Pa.; he had been suffering from Parkinson's disease. As a member of the U.S. delegation to the UN, he played a key role in the diplomatic effort to end the 1948 to 1949 Berlin blockade, and he was a member of the International Court of Justice at The Hague from 1960 to 1969.	In Britain, the jobless rate, on a seasonally adjusted basis, reached record levels in December 1985 and January 1986. A report by the Org. for Economic Cooperation and Development warns that Britain's unemployment problem seems more persistent and deep-rooted than during the great economic depression of the 1930s.	South Africa's Pres. Pieter W. Botha promises to end the nation's system of racial pass laws and offers to give blacks an advisory role in government for the first time. Botha also suggests that jailed black nationalist leader Nelson Mandela might be freed in exchange for the release of two Soviet dissidents and a South African soldier captured by Angola. . . . Ministers from the member states of the Southern African Development Coordination Conf. meet in Harare, Zimbabwe, to review the nations' economic performance over the previous five years. The conference was set up in 1980 to help the region's black-ruled states reduce their economic dependence on white-ruled South Africa.	Haiti's Pres. Jean Claude Duvalier declares a state of siege as unprecedented protests against his government continue. . . . Cuba and a British company sign a five-year trade deal that amounts to a government-to-government trading program aimed at increasing bilateral trade by $491 mil., it is reported. The deal is described as the first between a British private-sector company and a Cuban state trade organization.	
Feb. 1	Alva Myrdal, 84, Swedish diplomat who was a cowinner of the 1982 Nobel Peace Prize for her efforts to promote world disarmament, dies in Stockholm. She is survived by her husband, Gunnar Myrdal, a 1974 Nobel laureate in economics.			As a result of unrest in Haiti, the neighboring Dominican Republic is reported to have closed its border with Haiti and reinforced its military strength.	
Feb. 2				Oscar Arias Sanchez, leader of the ruling National Liberation Party, emerges as the winner of presidential elections held in Costa Rica. . . . Peru unilaterally declares that it will roll over for a further three months debt payments due to foreign creditor banks. The debts concerned amount to more than $2.2 bil.	

A	B	C	D	E
Includes developments that affect more than one world region, international organizations and important meetings of major world leaders.	Includes all domestic and regional developments in Europe, including the Soviet Union, Turkey, Cyprus and Malta.	Includes all domestic and regional developments in Africa and the Middle East, including Iraq and Iran and excluding Cyprus, Turkey and Afghanistan.	Includes all domestic and regional developments in Latin America, the Caribbean and Canada.	Includes all domestic and regional developments in Asia and Pacific nations, extending from Afghanistan through all the Pacific Islands, except Hawaii.

U.S. Politics & Social Issues	U.S. Foreign Policy & Defense	U.S. Economy & Environment	Science, Technology & Nature	Culture, Leisure & Life Style	
		Productivity among the nation's nonfarm businesses fell at a seasonally adjusted annual rate of 1.8% during the fourth quarter of 1985, according to the Labor Dept. . . . Pres. Reagan announces that he is nominating fellow Californian and long-time associate Richard E. Lyng to be secretary of agriculture. Lyng will succeed John R. Block, who is to resign February 14.	Rounding out the data from the fly-by of the planet Uranus by the spacecraft Voyager 2, National Aeronautics and Space Admin. scientists report that the craft discovered an 11th ring around the planet, a diffuse sheet of material orbiting inside the planet's other rings.	*Billboard*'s best-selling albums for the week are: *The Broadway Album*, Barbra Streisand; *Promise*, Sade; *Miami Vice* (television soundtrack); and *Scarecrow*, John Cougar Mellencamp.	Jan. 29
Irina Astakova McClellan, a Soviet citizen, is reunited with her American husband in Baltimore. In November 1985, Moscow notified the State Dept. that 10 Soviets would be permitted to reunite with American relatives. Eight in that group, including McClellan, had either husbands or wives in the United States.		The U.S. deficit on merchandise trade increased in December 1985 to a seasonally adjusted level of $17.37 bil., the Commerce Dept. reports. The U.S. deficit on merchandise trade totaled a record $148.49 bil. in 1985, $25 bil. more than in 1984. . . . The government's index of leading economic indicators rose 0.9% in December 1985, the Commerce Dept. reports. . . . Imported steel captured a 25.2% share of the U.S. market in 1985, according to data released by the American Iron and Steel Institute.	A panel of 10 leading scientists proposes the first uniform public-safety guidelines for the nascent genetic engineering industry. The recommendations are contained in a report to the Environmental Protection Agency, one of four federal agencies attempting to coordinate government policy.		Jan. 30
Pres. and Mrs. Reagan attend a memorial service at Johnson Space Center in Houston for the astronauts lost in the January 28 *Challenger* explosion. At least 90 members of Congress and an estimated 10,000 people attend the outdoor memorial ceremony.	In the face of overwhelming congressional opposition, the Reagan administration indefinitely postpones plans to sell $1.9 bil. in advanced U.S. arms to Jordan.	The Dow Jones sets a record high closing this day, 1570.99. . . . Prices received by farmers for their raw agricultural goods fell 3.1% in January from December 1985 levels, the Agriculture Dept. reports. . . . Sales of both new and existing homes in 1985 hit their highest levels since 1979, according to data released by the National Assoc. of Realtors. The average price of a new home was a record $108,600 in December.		*Publishers Weekly*'s hardback fiction best-sellers for the week are: *The Mammoth Hunters*, Jean M. Auel; *Lake Wobegon Days*, Garrison Keillor; *Texas*, James Michener, *Secrets*, Danielle Steel; and *Contact*, Carl Sagan.	Jan. 31
The Conservative Political Action Conf., an umbrella group of conservative political organizations, concludes its four-day annual meeting in Washington, D.C. V.P. George Bush led the field of prospective Republican presidential candidates in a survey of member organizations.				Craig Phillips a self-described professional horse player, amasses $1,906,491.90 in one day by picking winners in all nine races at Santa Anita Park in Arcadia, Calif. . . . Pope John Paul II begins a ten-day tour of India with restraint and references to "religious pluralism" and a call for "the spirit of tolerance."	Feb. 1
		A three-judge federal district panel in Washington, D.C., rules unanimously that a key provision of the so-called Gramm-Rudman balanced budget law is unconstitutional. If upheld on appeal, the ruling will invalidate the first round of FY1986 spending cuts already ordered.		A team of three drivers led by Al Holbert, with teammates Derek Bell and Al Unser, wins the Sunbank Daytona 24 Hours endurance race in Daytona Beach, Fla. . . . The National Football Conf. defeats the American Football Conf., 28-24, in the Pro-Bowl all-star game. Phil Simms of the New York Giants is named most valuable player.	Feb. 2

F	G	H	I	J
Includes elections, federal-state relations, civil rights and liberties, crime, the judiciary, education, health care, poverty, urban affairs and population.	*Includes formation and debate of U.S. foreign and defense policies, veterans' affairs and defense spending. (Relations with specific foreign countries are usually found under the region concerned.)*	*Includes business, labor, agriculture, taxation, transportation, consumer affairs, monetary and fiscal policy, natural resources, and pollution.*	*Includes worldwide scientific, medical and technological developments, natural phenomena, U.S. weather, natural disasters, and accidents.*	*Includes the arts, religion, scholarship, communications media, sports, entertainments, fashions, fads and social life.*

	World Affairs	Europe	Africa & the Middle East	The Americas	Asia & the Pacific
Feb. 3			A senior British official meets with executive members of the African National Congress (ANC) in Lusaka, Zambia. It is the first formal contact between Britain and the ANC, the main South African rebel group. Previously, Britain refused to meet with the ANC because of its dedication to overthrowing the white minority government by force.		
Feb. 4			Israeli warplanes intercept a Libyan civilian jet flying from Tripoli to Damascus and force it to land at an airfield in northern Israel. Israel had erroneously suspected that the plane was carrying Palestinian terrorist leaders. The plane was allowed to proceed to Syria following a five-hour search.		In South Korea, 19 defendants charged with occupying the U.S. Information Service building in 1985 have their prison sentences reduced by an appeals court.
Feb. 5		Three well-known Paris commercial sites were bombed over the last three days, wounding 21 people, at least six seriously. Several factors have lead the police to suggest that the explosions might be linked to Middle Eastern terrorism.			
Feb. 6					

A	B	C	D	E
Includes developments that affect more than one world region, international organizations and important meetings of major world leaders.	Includes all domestic and regional developments in Europe, including the Soviet Union, Turkey, Cyprus and Malta.	Includes all domestic and regional developments in Africa and the Middle East, including Iraq and Iran and excluding Cyprus, Turkey and Afghanistan.	Includes all domestic and regional developments in Latin America, the Caribbean and Canada.	Includes all domestic and regional developments in Asia and Pacific nations, extending from Afghanistan through all the Pacific Islands, except Hawaii.

U.S. Politics & Social Issues	U.S. Foreign Policy & Defense	U.S. Economy & Environment	Science, Technology & Nature	Culture, Leisure & Life Style	
Charles Abraham Halleck, 85, Indiana Republican who was elected to 16 consecutive full terms in the House of Representatives, dies of pneumonia in Lafayette, Ind. He first won a special election in 1935 to fill the remainder of the term of an incumbent who had died. A two-time majority leader, he was a conservative party loyalist generally allied with the conservative Southern Democrats. He parted company with them on the issue of civil rights. His regularly scheduled broadcasts with Sen. Everett Dirksen (R, Ill.) attacking Democratic administration policies, came to be known as "the Ev and Charlie Show."		Reports by three private national organizations conclude that state and local governments could lose as much as $10 bil. in federal-state programs in FY1987 if the Gramm-Rudman automatic budget-cutting process goes into effect.	Pres. Reagan appoints an independent commission to investigate the January 28 explosion of the space shuttle *Challenger*, in which all seven crew members lost their lives.		Feb. 3
Pres. Reagan delivers his fifth State of the Union address to a joint session of Congress and a nationwide television audience. In the unusually short speech, Reagan repeatedly put issues in the context of traditional family values. . . . In a televised response to the president's message, Democratic leaders counter Reagan's optimistic picture of America with an acknowledgment of severe existing problems that they say arise from the administration's "failed fiscal policies" and massive trade deficits.		Citicorp expanded its lead in 1985 as the nation's largest bank holding company as measured by assets. By the end of 1985, the New York City bank's assets grew by 15.3%, to $173.6 bil., according to the *New York Times*. . . . A Waynesboro, Ga., farmer kills himself to stop the auction of 711 acres of his 1,300-acre farm. Before killing himself, the farmer turns his life insurance policies over to his wife. The Federal Land Bank and the Credit Assoc. had begun foreclosure proceedings against 293 of Georgia's 50,000 farms. Farms in Burke Co., where Hill lived, are said to have been auctioned off in every month of 1985.			Feb. 4
	Defense Sec. Caspar W. Weinberger presents his fifth annual report on the state of the U.S. military at a hearing of the Senate Armed Services Committee.	Pres. Reagan submits to Congress a $994 bil. federal budget for FY1987. The budget proposes a substantial increase in defense spending while meeting the $144 bil. deficit requirement of the 1985 Gramm-Rudman balanced budget law. The administration proposes reducing the deficit through cutbacks and the elimination of a wide variety of domestic programs, sales of existing federal operations and assets to private business, and increases in charges for federal services.		The Alfred I. duPont-Columbia Univ. Awards for excellence in broadcast journalism are presented. The top duPont Award goes to American Broadcasting Co.'s news program "NightLine," for a series of reports on South Africa aired in March 1985.	Feb. 5
Two members of the neo-Nazi group Order (also called the Bruder Schweigen) are sentenced by U.S. District Judge Walter T. McGovern in Seattle for crimes including racketeering and murder.		Pres. Reagan issues his annual economic report for 1986. The report highlights the economic accomplishments of his administration and calls for further government deregulation, particularly in the nation's banking and agricultural sectors. . . . The Treasury Dept. sells $24 bil. worth of notes and bonds at its regular quarterly refinancing auction. Interest yields resulting from the auction are the lowest in seven to eight years.	Individuals who live with victims of acquired immune deficiency syndrome but are not sexual partners do not become infected with disease even after months of close personal contact, according to the largest and most thorough study to date, published by the *New England Journal of Medicine*.		Feb. 6

F	G	H	I	J
Includes elections, federal-state relations, civil rights and liberties, crime, the judiciary, education, health care, poverty, urban affairs and population.	*Includes formation and debate of U.S. foreign and defense policies, veterans' affairs and defense spending. (Relations with specific foreign countries are usually found under the region concerned.)*	*Includes business, labor, agriculture, taxation, transportation, consumer affairs, monetary and fiscal policy, natural resources, and pollution.*	*Includes worldwide scientific, medical and technological developments, natural phenomena, U.S. weather, natural disasters, and accidents.*	*Includes the arts, religion, scholarship, communications media, sports, entertainments, fashions, fads and social life.*

	World Affairs	Europe	Africa & the Middle East	The Americas	Asia & the Pacific
Feb. 7				President-for-Life Jean Claude Duvalier flees Haiti, ending a 28-year dictatorship by the Duvalier family. Upon leaving for France aboard a U.S. Air Force jet, he hands over power to a military-civilian council. . . . The Communist Party of Cuba concludes its third congress, in Havana. Pres. Fidel Castro announces extensive changes in the Politburo as part of a program of bringing women, blacks, and youth into the party leadership.	Filipinos vote in presidential elections amid allegations of fraud, bribery, and intimidation. The two major candidates, Pres. Ferdinand E. Marcos, 68, and Corazon Aquino, 53, charge each other with planning to cheat, and both say they might challenge the results if they lost. . . . In Australia, Lindy Chamberlain, the woman imprisoned for life after being convicted in the 1980 murder of her nine-month-old daughter, Azaria, is freed unconditionally. Her release follows the February 2 discovery of a baby jacket at Ayers Rock, the Northern Territory landmark near the site of the infant's disappearance.
Feb. 8					
Feb. 9					
Feb. 10		The largest trial of Mafia suspects in history opens in a specially built courtroom in Palermo, Sicily. Some 474 defendants, about 115 of them still at large, face charges ranging from assassination to auto theft.	Libyan-backed Chadian rebels launch an attack on government forces in central Chad, in the first major outbreak of fighting since a joint troop withdrawal agreement was signed by France and Libya in 1984.	Haiti's interim National Council of Government names a new cabinet and pledges to hand over power to a democratically elected government at an unspecified time. Meanwhile, tensions arise between France and the United States as those nations seek to find a refuge for deposed Haitian Pres. Jean-Claude Duvalier.	

A	B	C	D	E
Includes developments that affect more than one world region, international organizations and important meetings of major world leaders.	Includes all domestic and regional developments in Europe, including the Soviet Union, Turkey, Cyprus and Malta.	Includes all domestic and regional developments in Africa and the Middle East, including Iraq and Iran and excluding Cyprus, Turkey and Afghanistan.	Includes all domestic and regional developments in Latin America, the Caribbean and Canada.	Includes all domestic and regional developments in Asia and Pacific nations, extending from Afghanistan through all the Pacific Islands, except Hawaii.

U.S. Politics & Social Issues	U.S. Foreign Policy & Defense	U.S. Economy & Environment	Science, Technology & Nature	Culture, Leisure & Life Style	
	Larry Wu-Tai Chin is convicted by a federal jury in Alexandria, Va., of charges of spying for China for more than 30 years. Chin, a retired Central Intelligence Agency analyst, was arrested in November 1985.... Acting for the Defense Dept., the U.S. Navy lifts the suspension of General Dynamics Corp. from receiving new federal contracts. The ban was imposed in December 1985 after the company and four current or former executives were indicted for conspiring to defraud the government on a weapons contract.	The nation's unemployment rate fell to a seasonally adjusted level of 6.6% of the work force in January, the Labor Dept. reports.	Scientists have found the so-called monocyte/macrophages, a type of body cell found in the brain and lung, are attacked by the acquired immune deficiency syndrome virus.	The film *Hannah and Her Sisters* opens in New York. The comedy-drama, set in New York City, portrays three sisters whose lives interconnect in a variety of ways. The film wins three Academy Awards: best supporting actor, Michael Caine; best supporting actress, Dianne Wiest; and best original screenplay, Woody Allen. Allen also starred in and directed the film.	**Feb. 7**
	Jonas Savimbi, leader of the Org. for the Total Independence of Angola (UNITA), a rebel group fighting to overthrow the Soviet- and Cuban- backed government of Angola, concludes a visit to the United States. The guerrilla chief received a red-carpet welcome from the Reagan administration and wide media exposure, and apparently leaves with promises of U.S. aid for the UNITA struggle.	A bitter strike by 1,400 meat packers at Geo. A. Hormel & Co.'s hog-packing plant in Austin, Minn., drags on into its 25th week. The strikers are members of Local P-9 of the United Food and Commercial Workers.		Debi Thomas becomes the first black skater to win a senior U.S. singles figure skating championship, when she wins the U.S. women's title. Brian Boitano defends his men's title. The ice dancing title goes to Renee Roca and Donald Adair.... Abram Nicholas Pritzker, 90, billionaire Chicago entrepreneur, dies in Chicago. He founded the vast privately held group that included the Hyatt hotel chain, Braniff Airlines, and *McCall's* magazine. A leading philanthropist, his gifts ranged from a $16 mil. donation to the Univ. of Chicago for its Pritzker School of Medicine to the endowment of the annual Pritzker Architecture Prize, awarded for creative accomplishments in architecture.	**Feb. 8**
The House Select Committee on Children, Youth and Families makes public a study on the problem of teenage pregnancy, a report entitled "Teen Pregnancy: What Is Being Done? A State by State Study." Rep. George Miller (D, Calif.), chairman of the House committee, attacks policy makers for the "incredible failure to dedicate the resources necessary to reduce the incidence of teenage pregnancy."			William Henry Menard, 65, marine geologist long associated with the Scripps Institute of Oceanography in La Jolla, Calif., dies of cancer in La Jolla. His discoveries on the Pacific Ocean floor were crucial to the development of the theory of plate tectonics, which conjectures that continents and ocean basins are in constant motion relative to one another. From 1978 to 1981 he headed the Dept. of the Interior's U.S. Geological Survey.... A Phoenix, Ariz., woman, Bernadette Chayrez, becomes the first person known to have received a second artificial heart.	In the National Basketball Assoc. All-Star Game in Dallas, the Eastern Conf. defeats the Western Conf., 139-132. The East is lead by Detroit Piston point guard Isaiah Thomas, who is named most valuable player.	**Feb. 9**
	One of three Japanese-Americans convicted in 1942 for resisting federal internment has his conviction vacated in Seattle. The case dates from World War II, when the military rounded up West Coast Japanese-Americans as potential traitors. The defendant, Gordon Hirabayashi, was convicted of refusing to register with military authorities for relocation. A 1943 Supreme Court ruling upheld the conviction, and Hirabayashi served two years in prison.				**Feb. 10**

F	G	H	I	J
Includes elections, federal-state relations, civil rights and liberties, crime, the judiciary, education, health care, poverty, urban affairs and population.	Includes formation and debate of U.S. foreign and defense policies, veterans' affairs and defense spending. (Relations with specific foreign countries are usually found under the region concerned.)	Includes business, labor, agriculture, taxation, transportation, consumer affairs, monetary and fiscal policy, natural resources, and pollution.	Includes worldwide scientific, medical and technological developments, natural phenomena, U.S. weather, natural disasters, and accidents.	Includes the arts, religion, scholarship, communications media, sports, entertainments, fashions, fads and social life.

	World Affairs	Europe	Africa & the Middle East	The Americas	Asia & the Pacific
Feb. 11		In Poland, the government drops criminal slander charges against Lech Walesa, founder of the Solidarity labor movement. The move comes on the opening day of his trial in a provincial court in Gdansk.	Iranian forces capture Fao (Faw), a disused Iraqi oil port near Kuwait. The Iranian thrust appears to be one of the most daring of the five-and-a-half-year-old war, and its initial success alarms Iraq's Arab supporters in the Persian Gulf.	The value of the Canadian dollar rises to 71.56 cents after falling to a historic low against the U.S. dollar one week earlier. The latest valuation is approximately where the Canadian dollar was at the start of 1986, before its steady decline.	
Feb. 12	Shareholders in Westland PLC, Britain's ailing and only helicopter maker, approve a rescue package proposed by United Technologies Corp. of the United States and Fiat S.p.A. of Italy. The competition between this and a rival group generated a wide-ranging political controversy that prompted the resignation of two Conservative cabinet ministers in Britain.				
Feb. 13			Members of Britain's elite and secretive Special Air Services regiment are scheduled to take part in an extended training exercise with Botswanan troops in a remote northern part of the country, the *Guardian* (newspaper) reports.		After a delayed start in the official vote count, a tally by the Philippine National Assembly shows that, with almost half the votes counted, Pres. Ferdinand Marcos is leading his principal rival Corazon Aquino in the presidential election held February 7. . . . Japan announces that it will extend for a sixth year curbs on automobile exports to the United States. However, Japan raises the ceiling on exports to the United States by 24.3%, to 2.3 million units.
Feb. 14		In Czechoslovakia, economic performance in 1985 was mixed, according to a Czechoslovakian government data report. Modest growth in national income and industrial production are listed among the successes in 1985.			The Roman Catholic Bishops' Conf. of the Philippines issues a statement declaring that the February 7 presidential election polls "were unparalleled in the fraudulence of their conduct."
Feb. 15		Andrija Artukovic, 86, an official in the former, Nazi-controlled puppet state of Croatia (now part of Yugoslavia), is extradited from the United States, where he had lived for 38 years. Artukovic is formally charged by a Yugoslav court with ordering the murder of 231,000 Serbs, Jews, and Gypsies during World War II. . . . A letter written by Andrei D. Sakharov and smuggled out of the Soviet Union describes his physical and mental abuse by Soviet authorities in 1984. Relatives of Sakharov living in the United States vouch for the authenticity of the letter.			

A	B	C	D	E
Includes developments that affect more than one world region, international organizations and important meetings of major world leaders.	*Includes all domestic and regional developments in Europe, including the Soviet Union, Turkey, Cyprus and Malta.*	*Includes all domestic and regional developments in Africa and the Middle East, including Iraq and Iran and excluding Cyprus, Turkey and Afghanistan.*	*Includes all domestic and regional developments in Latin America, the Caribbean and Canada.*	*Includes all domestic and regional developments in Asia and Pacific nations, extending from Afghanistan through all the Pacific Islands, except Hawaii.*

U.S. Politics & Social Issues	U.S. Foreign Policy & Defense	U.S. Economy & Environment	Science, Technology & Nature	Culture, Leisure & Life Style	
The Equal Employment Opportunity Comm. (EEOC) unofficially abandons the use of hiring goals and timetables to correct job discrimination, the *Washington Post* reports. EEOC chairman Clarence Thomas is cited in the *Post* article as saying that the group has not used goals and timetables since early 1985.	Soviet dissident Anatoly B. Shcharansky is freed in an East-West exchange that involves a total of nine persons either accused or convicted of espionage. Shcharansky, 38, was convicted in the Soviet Union in 1978 of spying for the West.	Outstanding consumer installment credit grew a seasonally adjusted $5.14 bil. in December 1985, or at annual rate of 11.5%, the Federal Reserve Board reports. . . . Eastman Kodak Co. says it will seek to reduce its worldwide work force by 10%, or 12,900 employees, by the end of 1986. The huge Rochester, N.Y.-based photographic concern says it will cut its staff and seek to reduce other expenses by 5% in order to improve profitability. . . . Pres. Reagan defends the budget he has proposed for FY1987 and, as in the past, says he will veto any tax increase that Congress passes. His remarks come in a nationally televised news conference.		Frank Herbert, 65, science fiction writer best known for his 1965 epic novel *Dune*, an international best-seller, dies in Madison, Wis., of a pulmonary blood clot while undergoing treatment for cancer.	Feb. 11
		Bert Lance, Pres. Jimmy Carter's former budget director, agrees to a court order permanently barring him from becoming an official of any federally insured bank without prior consent of the government. He also agrees to pay a $50,000 fine as part of a settlement of a lawsuit brought against him by the comptroller of the currency.		Chrysler Corp. Chairman Lee Iacocca is fired as chairman of the Statue of Liberty-Ellis Island Centennial Comm. after refusing Interior Sec. Donald P. Hodel's request that he resign. Hodel says the ouster is necessary to avoid any appearance of a conflict of interest between Iacocca's chairmanship of the commission and of the private Statue of Liberty-Ellis Island Foundation.	Feb. 12
More than a year after being barred from attending Western Middle School in Russiaville, Ind., because he had contracted acquired immune deficiency syndrome, 14-year-old Ryan White wins a county medical ruling that he poses no health threat to his fellow classmates and should be allowed to return to the classroom.	The State Dept. issues its annual report on human rights. The 1,454-page document, mandated by Congress, assesses the situation in 164 countries in 1985.				Feb. 13
		The government's producer price index fell a seasonally adjusted 0.7% in January, the Labor Dept. reports. . . . Industrial production in January rose a seasonally adjusted 0.3%, the Federal Reserve Board reports. . . . Dr. Kenneth W. Kizer, California's director of health services, attributes almost 1,000 outbreaks of illness due to watermelon grown with the pesticide aldicarb during 1985 and calls the incident "the largest foodborne pesticide outbreak in North American history."			Feb. 14
Benjamin L. Hooks, executive director of the National Assoc. for the Advancement of Colored People (NAACP), answers critics who say the NAACP has declined since the start of his stewardship in 1977. His remarks come in a "State of the Association" address delivered to the annual meeting of the NAACP board of directors.	The Soviet Union secretly attempted to acquire four California banks in the 1970s in an effort to gain access to U.S. high-technology secrets, according to the *New York Times*.		The presidential panel investigating the explosion of the space shuttle *Challenger* asserts that the decision to launch the craft on Jan. 28 "may have been flawed."		Feb. 15

F	G	H	I	J
Includes elections, federal-state relations, civil rights and liberties, crime, the judiciary, education, health care, poverty, urban affairs and population.	Includes formation and debate of U.S. foreign and defense policies, veterans' affairs and defense spending. (Relations with specific foreign countries are usually found under the region concerned.)	Includes business, labor, agriculture, taxation, transportation, consumer affairs, monetary and fiscal policy, natural resources, and pollution.	Includes worldwide scientific, medical and technological developments, natural phenomena, U.S. weather, natural disasters, and accidents.	Includes the arts, religion, scholarship, communications media, sports, entertainments, fashions, fads and social life.

	World Affairs	Europe	Africa & the Middle East	The Americas	Asia & the Pacific
Feb. 16		Mario Soares, the former socialist premier of Portugal, is elected president in what is described as a stunning political recovery. Soares had polled only 25% in the first round of voting, compared with 46% drawn by his chief rival, rightist Diogo Freitas do Amaral.... Canada's Transportation Min. Donald Mazankowski orders a crackdown on railroad safety violations in the wake of 10 accidents since the start of 1986.			The Philippine National Assembly proclaims Pres. Ferdinand E. Marcos the winner of the presidential elections held February 7. His main rival, Corazon Aquino, responds by announcing a program of nonviolent resistance to bring down Marcos.
Feb. 17				Fifty-eight people are believed dead in the collision of two passenger trains in Chile. Injured passengers and crew number 510, of whom 154 are said to be hurt severely.	Queen Elizabeth II of England concludes a tour of Nepal, New Zealand, and Australia with her husband, Prince Philip. The trip combined official functions of a political and social nature.
Feb. 18				In Canada, the Ontario Court of Appeals rules, 3-2, that the province's funding of Roman Catholic high schools does not violate the Charter of Rights and Freedoms.	
Feb. 19	After a 37-year stalemate, the Senate votes 83-11 to ratify the International Convention on the Prevention and Punishment of the Crime of Genocide, which defines as an international crime any act "committed with intent to destroy, in whole or part, a national, ethnical, racial or religious group."	The leaders and representatives of 41 French-speaking nations conclude a two-day summit. The gathering, held in the Versailles Palace outside Paris, is the first of its kind. Over 100 million people worldwide speak French as a primary or secondary language.	King Hussein of Jordan declares that he is ending a year-long joint effort with the Palestine Liberation Org. (PLO) to revitalize the Arab-Israeli peace process. He accuses PLO leader Yasir Arafat of breaking his word after Jordan won major diplomatic concessions from the United States.		

A	B	C	D	E
Includes developments that affect more than one world region, international organizations and important meetings of major world leaders.	Includes all domestic and regional developments in Europe, including the Soviet Union, Turkey, Cyprus and Malta.	Includes all domestic and regional developments in Africa and the Middle East, including Iraq and Iran and excluding Cyprus, Turkey and Afghanistan.	Includes all domestic and regional developments in Latin America, the Caribbean and Canada.	Includes all domestic and regional developments in Asia and Pacific nations, extending from Afghanistan through all the Pacific Islands, except Hawaii.

U.S. Politics & Social Issues	U.S. Foreign Policy & Defense	U.S. Economy & Environment	Science, Technology & Nature	Culture, Leisure & Life Style	
				Geoff Bodine wins the National Assoc. for Stock Car Racing Daytona 500.	Feb. 16
Johnson and Johnson announces that it will end production of all its nonprescription capsule medications. The action comes after a Peekskill, N.Y., woman died February 8 after taking a capsule of the pain-killer Tylenol that was mysteriously contaminated with potassium cyanide.... Prince Charles, heir to the British throne, arrives in Dallas for a five-day visit to help celebrate the 150th anniversary of the establishment of the Texas Republic. He was invited as a gesture of gratitude to Britain, which had recognized Texas as a republic after it gained independence from Mexico in 1836.				Jiddu Krishnamurti, 90, Indian philosopher, teacher, and author, dies of pancreatic cancer at the Krishnamurti Foundation in Ojai, Calif. Despite his insistence that he was neither a guru nor an authority figure, many regarded him as a spiritual leader. He lectured widely on the importance of achieving maximum self-awareness, and set up nonprofit foundations and schools in California, England, and India. Unlike many Eastern gurus with a Western following, he was rarely accused of exploiting the trust of his supporters.... Charles "Red" Ruffing, 81, baseball Hall of Famer considered the best-hitting pitcher of his era, dies in Mayfield, Ohio. Retiring in 1947 after 22 seasons, 15 with the New York Yankees, he had a regular-season record of 273 wins and 225 losses. His .269 career batting average included four consecutive seasons with 20 or more wins and eight seasons when he hit above .300.... National Book Critics Circle award winners are: for fiction, Anne Tyler for *The Accidental Tourist*; general nonfiction, J. Anthony Lukas for *Common Ground: A Turbulent Decade in the Lives of Three American families*; biography, Leon Edel for *Henry James: A Life*; poetry, Louise Gluck for *Triumph of Achilles*; and criticism, William Gass's *Habitations of the Word*.	Feb. 17
The *Washington Post* reports that the Democratic National Committee (DNC) raised only $7 mil. in 1985, less than one-third its 1984 total and the lowest since 1981. The drop in contributions reverses three years of steady gains in the DNC fund raising. The decline is attributed to Pres. Reagan's 1984 landslide victory and to competition from a rival Democratic group, the Democratic Leadership Council.		The Farm Credit System reports a net loss of $2.69 bil. for 1985. Officials of the system, a federation of institutions that holds almost one-third of the nation's farm debt, had predicted the huge losses in late 1985.			Feb. 18
James Oliver Eastland, 81, Mississippi Democrat who served in the U.S. Senate for more than 36 years, dies in Greenwood, Miss. At his retirement in 1979, he had been chairman of the Senate Judiciary Committee for 22 years and president pro tem of the Senate for six. Although best known as a stubborn segregationist and militant anticommunist, he was nevertheless respected and even liked by Senate liberals.		New housing starts rose 15.7% in January to a seasonally adjusted annual rate of 2.088 million units, the Commerce Dept. reports.	The presidential panel investigating the explosion of the space shuttle *Challenger* reports that Morton Thiokol Inc., builder of the main parts of the shuttle's solid-fuel booster rockets, recommended strongly against the launch "due to weather conditions" the day before the explosion but reversed its decision later that day.	*Billboard's* best-selling albums for the week are: *Promise*, Sade; *Welcome to the Real World*, Mr. Mister; *The Broadway Album*, Barbra Streisand; *Whitney Houston*, Whitney Houston; *Heart*, Heart.... *Variety's* top-grossing films for the week are: *Down and Out in Beverly Hills*; *The Color Purple*; *The Delta Force*; *Wildcats*; and *F/X*.	Feb. 19

F	G	H	I	J
Includes elections, federal-state relations, civil rights and liberties, crime, the judiciary, education, health care, poverty, urban affairs and population.	*Includes formation and debate of U.S. foreign and defense policies, veterans' affairs and defense spending. (Relations with specific foreign countries are usually found under the region concerned.)*	*Includes business, labor, agriculture, taxation, transportation, consumer affairs, monetary and fiscal policy, natural resources, and pollution.*	*Includes worldwide scientific, medical and technological developments, natural phenomena, U.S. weather, natural disasters, and accidents.*	*Includes the arts, religion, scholarship, communications media, sports, entertainments, fashions, fads and social life.*

	World Affairs	Europe	Africa & the Middle East	The Americas	Asia & the Pacific
Feb. 20		At the Mutual and Balanced Force reduction talks in Vienna, the Warsaw Pact proposes a draft agreement to balance its conventional forces with those of North Atlantic Treaty Org. Under the plan, the Soviet Union would withdraw a total of 11,500 troops from East Germany, Poland, and Czechoslovakia. The United States would match that by pulling a total of 6,500 soldiers out of West Germany, Belgium, the Netherlands, and Luxembourg. The remaining Soviet and U.S. troop levels would be frozen for three years.... The man described as the acknowledged leader of the entire Mafia crime syndicate in Sicily is arrested in a farmhouse outside Palermo, Sicily, in a huge police sweep. A senior judge in Palermo describes the arrest of the man, Michele Greco, as "the single most important Mafia arrest in the post-war period."		Pres. Reagan visits Grenada to attend a summit of Caribbean leaders. He also commemorates the American servicemen slain in the 1983 U.S.-backed invasion of Grenada that followed the slaying of P.M. Maurice Bishop by hard-line Marxists.	
Feb. 21					
Feb. 22			The *New York Times* reports that the rupture between Jordan and the Palestine Liberation Org. (PLO) has improved the chances of reconciliation between Arafat's faction of the PLO and the anti-Arafat factions based in Syria. A dialogue, backed by the Soviet Union, is said to be under way to heal the PLO's rifts.		Two leading military allies of Philippine Pres. Ferdinand E. Marcos call on him to resign. Juan Ponce Enrile, defense minister since 1970, and Lt. Gen. Fidel Ramos, recently named to become Marcos's armed forces chief of staff, pledge their support to Corazon Aquino. Both men maintain that Marcos rigged the February 7 presidential election in which he was proclaimed the victor over Corazon Aquino.
Feb. 23			Crisis talks among senior members of the Israeli cabinet fail to resolve a growing split in the national unity coalition over proposed changes in economic policy. With runaway inflation apparently under control, P.M. Shimon Peres and his Labor Party are now calling for renewed growth in the economy, while the Likud bloc continues to advocate fiscal restraint.		

A	B	C	D	E
Includes developments that affect more than one world region, international organizations and important meetings of major world leaders.	Includes all domestic and regional developments in Europe, including the Soviet Union, Turkey, Cyprus and Malta.	Includes all domestic and regional developments in Africa and the Middle East, including Iraq and Iran and excluding Cyprus, Turkey and Afghanistan.	Includes all domestic and regional developments in Latin America, the Caribbean and Canada.	Includes all domestic and regional developments in Asia and Pacific nations, extending from Afghanistan through all the Pacific Islands, except Hawaii.

U.S. Politics & Social Issues	U.S. Foreign Policy & Defense	U.S. Economy & Environment	Science, Technology & Nature	Culture, Leisure & Life Style	
A "startling" surge of illegal entries into the United States by aliens from Mexico is reported by Alan Nelson, commissioner of the Immigration and Naturalization Service. Nelson said that apprehension of illegal aliens from Mexico is up nearly 40% over the previous year, when a record total of 1.2 million illegal aliens were seized at the border.... A survey by the Education Dept. finds graduation rates and standardized test scores to be on the rise among the nation's public school students.		Petroleum prices continue their precipitous decline in late January through mid-February. Prices for West Texas Intermediate, a benchmark U.S. crude, fell below $15 per barrel in New York Mercantile Exchange futures contract trading. ... Federal Reserve Board Chairman Paul Volcker gives his regular semiannual testimony before Congress. Volcker's congressional testimony spanned topics ranging from the falling dollar to the massive debt burden taken on in recent years by corporations.	A week of heavy rain, snow, floods, and avalanches in the Western United States and Canada's British Columbia, blamed for the death of 17 people and for forcing more than 33,000 from their homes, finally ends. The storms began February 14 when waves of water-heavy air from the Pacific Ocean struck northern California.		Feb. 20
An Indiana county judge bars Ryan White from returning to school until a hearing is held to determine whether a 1949 Indiana law dealing with communicable diseases applies to acquired immune deficiency syndrome. The county medical office had ruled in White's favor on February 13.... The State Dept.'s Bureau of International Narcotics Matters releases to Congress its annual report on the world production of illegal drugs. The paper says some countries have made gains in combating narcotics production, but assails Mexico's performance as the "principal disappointment" of 1985.... A class-action suit seeking damages on behalf of all Japanese-Americans interned during World War II is reinstated by a panel of the U.S. Court of Appeals in Washington, D.C. The ruling is expected to allow damage suits by any of the 120,000 Japanese-Americans whom the government had interned.		Americans' total personal income fell 0.1%, or $3 bil., in January to a seasonally adjusted annual rate of $3.383 trillion, according to the Commerce Dept. Consumer spending fell an adjusted 0.4%.	Helen Hooven Santmyer, 90, author of "...And Ladies of the Club," the mammoth novel about life in a small Midwestern town that turned her into a celebrity at age 88, dies of emphysema in Xenia, Ohio. The book shot to the top of U.S. best-seller lists in 1984 after being published commercially; Ohio State Univ. Press had brought out a limited edition in 1982. She labored on the book for more than 50 years while working as an English professor, college dean, and librarian.		Feb. 21
Members of Congress in 1984 and 1985 spent at least $9.28 mil. on overseas travel, according to Congress Watch, a watchdog group. The 1984 total of $4.96 mil. is up 36% over that of 1982, the previous year studied, Congress Watch says.					Feb. 22
					Feb. 23

	World Affairs	Europe	Africa & the Middle East	The Americas	Asia & the Pacific
Feb. 24			The popularity of Nigeria's president, Maj. Gen. Ibrahim Babangida, has continued to grow despite his institution of tough austerity measures to bolster the country's ailing economy, according to reports over the past five weeks. Meanwhile, the military government's efforts to reschedule its foreign debt have taken on added urgency because of plummeting oil prices on the world market.		After cracking down on political opponents campaigning for constitutional reform in February, South Korea's Pres. Chun Doo Hwan invites opposition leaders to meet with him to discuss the issue.
Feb. 25		The 27th Congress of the Communist Party of the Soviet Union opens in Moscow. The gathering, held once every five years, is attended by an estimated 5,000 Soviet delegates and thousands of visitors from 113 countries. Soviet leader Mikhail S. Gorbachev gives the keynote address; although he touches on many issues, the heart of the speech calls for sweeping economic reforms.			Pres. Ferdinand E. Marcos flees the Philippines hours after his inauguration in a private ceremony at Manila's Malacanang Palace. In a separate inaugural, Corazon Aquino is sworn in as president by Supreme Court Justice Claudio Teehankee. Sixty-two National Assembly members earlier voided the assembly's proclamation of Marcos as winner of the recent elections.
Feb. 26				After three years of negotiations, Venezuela signs a $21.2 bil. debt refinancing agreement with its international bank creditors.... Haiti's government vows to prosecute those accused of abuses during the regime of ousted Pres. Jean Claude Duvalier and says it has arrested two former police officials alleged to have committed human rights violations. The government accedes to public demands when riots erupt after it is revealed that the chief of the secret police under Duvalier, Col. Albert Pierre, was permitted to leave the country late February 23. His exit also causes a rift in the ruling National Council of Government.... In El Salvador, two former members of the national guard are sentenced to 30 years in prison for the 1981 slayings of the head of the Salvadoran land reform agency and two U.S. labor advisers.	Ending a 20-year tenure as president of the Philippines, Ferdinand E. Marcos arrives in the United States.
Feb. 27		Danish voters approve proposed reforms to the European Community founding charter, the Treaty of Rome, in a referendum. The vote means that Denmark will now sign the reform package. The other two countries that had declined to do so, Greece and Italy, are also expected to sign.			

A	B	C	D	E
Includes developments that affect more than one world region, international organizations and important meetings of major world leaders.	Includes all domestic and regional developments in Europe, including the Soviet Union, Turkey, Cyprus and Malta.	Includes all domestic and regional developments in Africa and the Middle East, including Iraq and Iran and excluding Cyprus, Turkey and Afghanistan.	Includes all domestic and regional developments in Latin America, the Caribbean and Canada.	Includes all domestic and regional developments in Asia and Pacific nations, extending from Afghanistan through all the Pacific Islands, except Hawaii.

U.S. Politics & Social Issues	U.S. Foreign Policy & Defense	U.S. Economy & Environment	Science, Technology & Nature	Culture, Leisure & Life Style	
The Supreme Court strikes down as unconstitutional an Indianapolis ordinance that defined and penalized pornography as discrimination against women. The court affirms, without issuing an opinion, lower federal court rulings that the statute violated the First Amendment right of free speech.... The National Governors Assoc. begins its three-day winter conference in Washington, D.C. The centerpiece of the session is a meeting between the governors and Pres. Reagan over cuts in aid to state governments called for in the Reagan budget and threatened under the Gramm-Rudman balanced-budget law.... The Los Angeles Unified School District board votes to start a phase-in of year-round classes during the 1987-88 school year. Ninety-three of the district's 618 schools already stay open all year to fight over-crowding.	Pres. Reagan proposes an elimination of U.S. nuclear missiles over a three-year period. The plan is presented by the U.S. arms-control negotiators in Geneva.			Marathoner Joan Benoit Samuelson is named the winner of the Sullivan Award, presented annually to the top U.S. amateur athlete. Samuelson is the seventh woman to win the award in its 56-year history.	Feb. 24
	As expected, Pres. Reagan asks Congress to authorize $100 mil. in military and non-lethal aid to the Nicaraguan Contras fighting to overthrow the Sandinista government.	The government's consumer price index rose a seasonally adjusted 0.3% in January, or at a compounded annual rate of 4.1% after rounding, according to the Labor Dept.... Advanced Genetic Sciences, a pioneering genetic engineering firm, and the Environmental Protection Agency are both embarrassed by the revelation that the company tested genetically altered bacteria outdoors without explicit authorization from the agency.		At the 28th annual Grammy awards, Lionel Richie and Michael Jackson's "We Are the World" wins awards for best song, record of the year, and pop group performance. Best male pop vocalist is Phil Collins, *No Jacket Required*; female pop vocalist, Whitney Houston, *Saving All My Love for You*; rock female vocalist, Tina Turner, *One of the Living*; rock male vocalist, Don Henley, *The Boys of Summer*. Best new artist award goes to Nigerian-born British pop star Sade.	Feb. 25
	The U.S. administration releases $25.5 mil. in economic and military aid to Haiti that was withheld in January because of human rights abuses under Jean-Claude Duvalier. In announcing that the aid for FY1986 would be released, the State Dept. cites moves toward democracy by Haiti's new interim government and improvements in human rights.	A new analysis by the Congressional Budget Office indicates that Pres. Reagan's budget proposals will fall short of the deficit targets mandated by the Gramm-Rudman balanced-budget law.... Major strike activity is at a record low, according to the Labor Dept. Fewer major labor strikes and lockouts took place in 1985 than at anytime since the department began compiling such data in 1947.		Robert Penn Warren, for many years a major figure in American literature as poet, critic, and novelist, is designated the first official poet laureate of the United States.... Dr. James I. McCord, a 66-year-old Presbyterian theologian, is named the 1986 recipient of the Templeton Prize for Progress in Religion.	Feb. 26
The Senate votes to allow live television and radio coverage of its proceedings on a trial basis from June 1 to July 15. After a two-week period, the Senate will vote on whether to make the coverage permanent.... Pres. Reagan signs the Comprehensive Smokeless Tobacco Education Act of 1986, legislation that requires warning labels on packages of smokeless tobacco.		A report by the accounting firm of Arthur Andersen & Co. says the way the federal budget is written "obscures the costs of current programs" by failing to give an accurate picture of the government's long-term obligations.... As part of an investigation into charges of bribery and connections with organized crime, a federal grand jury issues a subpoena to the Recording Industry Assoc. of America for papers pertaining to record company dealings with independent record promoters.... The Dow Jones Industrial Average closes at a record high 1713.99.	The chairman of the presidential commission investigating the explosion of the space shuttle *Challenger* charges that space agency officials abandoned "good judgment and common sense" in handling safety problems prior to the fateful launch.		Feb. 27

F	G	H	I	J
Includes elections, federal-state relations, civil rights and liberties, crime, the judiciary, education, health care, poverty, urban affairs and population.	*Includes formation and debate of U.S. foreign and defense policies, veterans' affairs and defense spending. (Relations with specific foreign countries are usually found under the region concerned.)*	*Includes business, labor, agriculture, taxation, transportation, consumer affairs, monetary and fiscal policy, natural resources, and pollution.*	*Includes worldwide scientific, medical and technological developments, natural phenomena, U.S. weather, natural disasters, and accidents.*	*Includes the arts, religion, scholarship, communications media, sports, entertainments, fashions, fads and social life.*

	World Affairs	Europe	Africa & the Middle East	The Americas	Asia & the Pacific
Feb. 28		Premier Olof Palme of Sweden is shot and killed as he and his wife Lisbeth walk away from a movie theater in central Stockholm. . . . Pres. Francois Mitterrand of France and Chancellor Helmut Kohl of West Germany end a two-day summit meeting by signing an agreement to strengthen military cooperation between their two countries. In the accord, France agrees, in the event of a conflict with Warsaw Pact forces, to consult West Germany before using nuclear weapons located on West German soil. . . . In the Netherlands, the lower house of parliament approves a U.S.-Dutch agreement calling for the deployment of 48 nuclear cruise missiles in the Netherlands by the end of 1988.		Brazil's Pres. Jose Sarney introduces sweeping economic changes to fight inflation, including a price freeze, changes in the wage structure, and the introduction of a new currency, the cruzado.	
March 1					In the Philippine's, the government of Pres. Corazon Aquino moves to recover millions of dollars worth of assets from former Pres. Ferdinand E. Marcos and his family; the assets were allegedly gained with illegally amassed wealth.
March 2			Zafir al-Masri, the recently appointed Arab mayor of the occupied West Bank city of Nablus, is shot to death while walking to work. The lone killer escapes, and two radical Palestinian splinter groups claim responsibility for the assassination. . . . John Demjanjuk is formally charged in a Jerusalem court with crimes against humanity. Demjanjuk, a retired Ohio auto worker accused of murdering thousands of Jews at the Nazi death camp, Treblinka, in World War II, was deported from the United States to Israel February 27.		Queen Elizabeth II of England signs a proclamation activating an Australian act abolishing remaining constitutional links between Australia and the United Kingdom. The signing takes place at a ceremony attended by Australian P.M. Bob Hawke at Government House in Canberra.
March 3		In Northern Ireland, Protestant unionists stage a one-day general strike to protest the Anglo-Irish accord giving Dublin a consultative role in governing Northern Ireland. There are reports of widespread violence and intimidation, despite promises by the Ulster unionist leaders that participation would be voluntary and paramilitary groups would not be involved. . . . Five teachers' unions in England and Wales reach an agreement with employers on an accord ending their 13-month-old labor dispute. However, the National Union of Teachers, the largest teacher's union, does not endorse the deal.			In Australia, the federal cabinet votes to abandon plans to enact national legislation to protect the land rights of Aborigines. Critics immediately accuse the cabinet of breaching the platform of the ruling Australian Labor Party and revoking the party's commitment to meaningful land rights laws.
March 4		The *New York Times* reports that Kurt Waldheim, a candidate for election as president of Austria, and UN secretary-general from 1972 to 1982, belonged to Nazi organizations in Austria during World War II and served under a notorious war criminal.	In South Africa, the white city council of East London in eastern Cape Province votes in favor of allowing racially integrated residential areas. The move is reported today, one week after the vote was secretly taken.	Canada's Justice Min. John Crosbie introduces in the House of Commons a report proposing measures to bring federal laws into compliance with the equality provisions of the Charter of Rights and Freedoms.	

A	B	C	D	E
Includes developments that affect more than one world region, international organizations and important meetings of major world leaders.	Includes all domestic and regional developments in Europe, including the Soviet Union, Turkey, Cyprus and Malta.	Includes all domestic and regional developments in Africa and the Middle East, including Iraq and Iran and excluding Cyprus, Turkey and Afghanistan.	Includes all domestic and regional developments in Latin America, the Caribbean and Canada.	Includes all domestic and regional developments in Asia and Pacific nations, extending from Afghanistan through all the Pacific Islands, except Hawaii.

U.S. Politics & Social Issues	U.S. Foreign Policy & Defense	U.S. Economy & Environment	Science, Technology & Nature	Culture, Leisure & Life Style	
		The U.S. deficit on merchandise trade increased in January to $16.46 bil., the Commerce Dept. reports.		Publishers Weekly's hardback fiction best-sellers for the week are: The Mammoth Hunters, Jean M. Auel; Lie Down With Lions, Ken Follett; Lake Wobegon Days, Garrison Keillor; Cyclops, Clive Cussler; and Angels of September, Andrew M. Greeley.... Baseball Commissioner Peter Ueberroth announces the suspension of 11 major league players for their past involvement with illegal drugs. The commissioner offers the 11 players an alternative to the suspensions that includes fines, drug testing for the duration of their careers, and community service work.... Max Frisch, author of the novel I'm Not Stiller and the play Andora, is named the winner of the $25,000 Neustadt International Prize for literature.	Feb. 28
		Spending in hundreds of federal programs is cut by 4.3% as the first round of automatic spending cuts required by the 1985 Gramm-Rudman balanced-budget law takes effect.	Pres. Reagan selects James C. Fletcher to head National Aeronautics and Space Admin. (NASA), for the second time. Fletcher, 66, lead NASA from 1971 to 1977, a period during which the space shuttle project was undertaken.	The Associated Press and United Press International announce their All-American basketball teams. Four players are named to both teams: Len Bias, Maryland; Kenny Walker, Kentucky; Walter Berry, St. John's; and Johnny Dawkins, Duke. Steve Alford, Indiana, is named by the Associated Press, and Scott Skiles, Michigan State, is chosen by United Press International.	March 1
		Business failures rose 9.6% in 1985 from a year earlier, to 57,067, according to data from Dun & Bradstreet Corp. The business information company says that failures of service concerns, which rose 30% to 16,626, were largely responsible for the increase.			March 2
The President's Comm. on Organized Crime issues a report on the federal government's effort against illegal narcotics. Drug trafficking, the paper says, is "the most serious problem presented by organized crime in this country."			Veteran astronauts say that they were unaware that the National Aeronautics and Space Admin. was facing serious problems with solid-fuel rocket booster seals for some time prior to the Jan. 28 explosion of the shuttle Challenger, which killed the seven astronauts aboard.		March 3
Education Sec. William J. Bennett presents Pres. Reagan with "What Works: Research about Learning and Teaching," an Education Dept. book that lists 41 findings about how elementary and secondary students can be taught effectively. ... The Los Angeles Police Comm. releases a 1,453-page summary of the Los Angeles Police Dept.'s investigation into the 1968 assassination of presidential candidate Robert F. Kennedy. The summary says assassin Sirhan Bishara Sirhan acted alone and not as part of a conspiracy.		The government's index of leading economic indicators fell 0.6% in January, the Commerce Dept. reports.... The nation's unemployment rate fell to a seasonally adjusted level of 7.1% of the work force in March, the Labor Dept. reports.... The United Steel Workers of America approves new three-year contracts with four of the largest can makers. The settlement ends a strike that began February 17.	Albert Lester Lehninger, 69, leading biochemist at Johns Hopkins Univ., dies of a respiratory ailment in Baltimore. Credited with developing the field of bioenergetics, which deals with how nutrients are converted into biochemically usable forms, he was the author of Biochemistry, perhaps the most influential of all general textbooks on the subject.		March 4

F	G	H	I	J
Includes elections, federal-state relations, civil rights and liberties, crime, the judiciary, education, health care, poverty, urban affairs and population.	Includes formation and debate of U.S. foreign and defense policies, veterans' affairs and defense spending. (Relations with specific foreign countries are usually found under the region concerned.)	Includes business, labor, agriculture, taxation, transportation, consumer affairs, monetary and fiscal policy, natural resources, and pollution.	Includes worldwide scientific, medical and technological developments, natural phenomena, U.S. weather, natural disasters, and accidents.	Includes the arts, religion, scholarship, communications media, sports, entertainments, fashions, fads and social life.

	World Affairs	Europe	Africa & the Middle East	The Americas	Asia & the Pacific
March 5			One of four French hostages being held by Shiite Moslem extremists in Lebanon is reported executed.		Overruling objections by military leaders, Pres. Corazon Aquino of the Philippines frees two leading communists, fulfilling a campaign pledge to free all political prisoners.
March 6		The 27th Congress of the Communist Party of the Soviet Union concludes with the announcement of a new makeup of the Central Committee and its two powerful organs, the policy-making Politburo and the Secretariat.			
March 7	Within a two-day period the central banks of West Germany, France, Japan, and the United States move to reduce key interest rates. The coordinated action by four of the Group of Five nations (Britain is the fifth) is hailed by one U.S. central banker as "unprecedented." . . . The United States orders the Soviet Union to reduce the staff members of the Soviet, Ukrainian, and Byelorussian missions to the UN. Under the order, issued by the White House, the three missions are to trim their UN personnel from a total of 275 to 170 by Apr. 1, 1988.	Britain posts its sixth consecutive balance of payment surplus in 1985, according to Central Statistical Office data.	South Africa lifts the state of emergency that it had imposed on riot-torn black areas in July 1985 and frees the last 329 of the nearly 8,000 people who were detained without charges under the decree. Pres. Pieter W. Botha signs a proclamation officially ending the emergency in the magisterial districts where it was in force.		The government of P.M. Rajiv Gandhi imposes central rule on the Moslem-dominated northern border state of Jammu and Kashmir. A Congress (I) official says Gandhi acted because of a breakdown of law and order in the state.
March 8	UN officials disclose that they are studying the legality of the March 7 order by the United States that the Soviet Union reduce the number of staff attached to the Soviet, Ukrainian, and Byelorussian missions to the UN.		Four more French citizens are abducted by Shiite Moslem extremists in Beirut.		
March 9		Mario Soares is formally installed as Portugal's first civilian president in 60 years at a swearing-in ceremony in parliament.		Colombia's opposition Liberal Party claims victory in congressional elections over Pres. Belisario Betancur's Conservative Party.	

A	B	C	D	E
Includes developments that affect more than one world region, international organizations and important meetings of major world leaders.	Includes all domestic and regional developments in Europe, including the Soviet Union, Turkey, Cyprus and Malta.	Includes all domestic and regional developments in Africa and the Middle East, including Iraq and Iran and excluding Cyprus, Turkey and Afghanistan.	Includes all domestic and regional developments in Latin America, the Caribbean and Canada.	Includes all domestic and regional developments in Asia and Pacific nations, extending from Afghanistan through all the Pacific Islands, except Hawaii.

U.S. Politics & Social Issues	U.S. Foreign Policy & Defense	U.S. Economy & Environment	Science, Technology & Nature	Culture, Leisure & Life Style	
Six alleged members of New York City's Gambino crime group are convicted of involvement in an auto theft ring. A federal jury delivered the verdict in New York. Paul Castellano, the group's reputed boss was a defendant until his shooting death in December 1985. . . . The Supreme Court rules that police officers are liable to pay damages for an unreasonable arrest even if they have obtained a court warrant for the arrest.			Scientists report a new genetic engineering technique that will facilitate the custom design of food crops. The breakthrough is reported in the British scientific journal *Nature* by Virginia Walbot and colleagues at Stanford Univ.	*Salvador*, a film about an American journalist caught up in the turmoil in El Salvador in the early 1980s, is released in New York. Directed by Oliver Stone and written by Stone and Richard Boyle, the film stars James Woods, James Belushi and Elpedia Carrillo.	March 5
A commission appointed by Philadelphia's Mayor W. Wilson Goode (D) reports that he was "grossly negligent" in his failure to halt a fatal police showdown with armed members of the radical group MOVE in May 1985. But the panel says the direct blame for the resulting deaths lay with the city's fire commissioner and former police commissioner. To break a stalemate with the group, the police dropped a bomb on a row house, and the resulting fire killed 11 people and destroyed 61 homes. . . . The President's Comm. on Organized Crime issues a report calling for a more aggressive law enforcement assault upon the "enduring problem" of organized crime's influence among labor unions. The paper says four major unions are deeply under the mob's sway. The Teamsters are singled out as the "most controlled union."		The nation's air traffic control system is severely over-taxed and poses a threat to proper maintenance of safety standards, a General Accounting Office reports warns.	An unmanned Soviet spacecraft penetrates the atmosphere of Halley's comet and comes within 5,600 miles of its icy core. An American witnessing the event at the Institute for Space Research in Moscow calls it "a watershed day for world science." . . . A continuing study of nearly 17,000 Harvard Univ. alumni, reported in the *New England Journal of Medicine*, indicates that moderate physical exercise in adult life can significantly increase life expectancy. . . . Australian scientists have reportedly developed a contraceptive bullet designed to reduce kangaroo populations through birth control rather than culling.	Georgia O'Keeffe, 98, painter who for seven decades was a leading figure in American art, dies in Santa Fe, N.Mex. Her work was noted for its stunning use of color, its subtle eroticism and the transcendental quality with which she invested objects ranging from skyscrapers to flowers to animal skulls. She was the wife of photographer Alfred Stieglitz.	March 6
Jacob Koppel Javits, 81, U.S. senator from New York from 1957 to 1981 and a leader of the liberal wing of the Republican Party, dies of a heart attack in Palm Beach, Fla. His legislative achievements include the 1973 War Powers Act, creation of the National Endowment for the Humanities, and the 1974 Pension Reform Act. . . . The Food and Drug Admin. announces that all nonprescription aspirin products and medicine containing aspirin has to bear a label warning of Reye's syndrome, which produces swelling of the brain and enlargement of the liver. The federal requirement is simply intended to provide consistency, since most aspirin makers started using such labels in 1985. . . . In New York City, a federal jury convicts six self-described revolutionaries on 33 counts stemming from 10 bombings and an unsuccessful bombing attempt against military and corporate sites in the New York area. A mistrial is declared on 39 other counts.		The Republican-controlled Senate Budget Committee decisively rejects Pres. Reagan's proposed FY1987 budget, by a vote of 16 to 6. The vote, although expected, points up sharp differences between the president and Congress, including congressional Republicans, over federal spending and revenue priorities. . . . The House approves a deficit reduction package for FY1986 that would, if enacted, reduce the deficit by $6.8 bil. in FY1986 and by $18.1 bil. over three years. A last-ditch effort to reach a compromise deficit reduction package for FY1986 failed at the end of the 1985 legislative session. . . . The nation's unemployment rate rose to a seasonally adjusted level of 7.2% of the work force in February, the Labor Dept. reports.		*My Beautiful Laundrette* is released in New York. The English film comedy set in London revolves around a coin laundry operated by two young men, a Pakistani immigrant and his cockney lover. Directed by Stephen Frears, screenplay by Hanif Kureishi, with Daniel Day Lewis. . . . *A Room With A View*, based on the 1908 novel by E. M. Forster, is released in New York. Screenwriter Ruth Prawer Jhabvala will win the Academy Award for her adaptation; the film is directed by James Ivory, produced by Ismail Merchant, and stars Helena Bonham Carter, Maggie Smith, Denholm Elliott and Daniel Day Lewis.	March 7
In a generally harmonious session, the Democratic National Committee approves minor changes in the party's presidential nominating rules for 1988. It is the first time in 16 years that the party has avoided a major mid-term rules overhaul.					March 8
Demonstrators rally in Washington, D.C., for an abortion rights march sponsored by the National Org. for Women. It is thought to be the largest demonstration in the history of its organizer.					March 9

F	G	H	I	J
Includes elections, federal-state relations, civil rights and liberties, crime, the judiciary, education, health care, poverty, urban affairs and population.	Includes formation and debate of U.S. foreign and defense policies, veterans' affairs and defense spending. (Relations with specific foreign countries are usually found under the region concerned.)	Includes business, labor, agriculture, taxation, transportation, consumer affairs, monetary and fiscal policy, natural resources, and pollution.	Includes worldwide scientific, medical and technological developments, natural phenomena, U.S. weather, natural disasters, and accidents.	Includes the arts, religion, scholarship, communications media, sports, entertainments, fashions, fads and social life.

	World Affairs	Europe	Africa & the Middle East	The Americas	Asia & the Pacific
March 10					
March 11				In Canada, Deputy P.M. Erik Nielsen presents to the House of Commons a massive report that criticizes federal spending and the federal bureaucracy. The study's basic finding is that spending on many programs is wasteful and unproductive. Overall, it urges that the nation rely less on Ottawa and more on private enterprise.	China becomes the 47th member of the Asian Development Bank (ADB). Under a 1985 arrangement with Beijing, the ADB, on admitting China, changed the name of the Taiwan delegation to "Taipei, China" from "Republic of China." Taiwan protests the name change.
March 12		Spanish voters vote to retain their country's four-year-old membership in the North Atlantic Treaty Org. The vote is a victory for the socialist government of P.M. Felipe Gonzalez.... Traders on the London Metal Exchange settle outstanding contracts for exchanges of tin at a price fixed earlier by the London Metal Exchange. The contracts had remained unsettled since October 1985, when the International Tin Council announced that it could not meet obligations it had undertaken to support the price of tin.... In Sweden, Ingvar Carlson, acting premier since the assassination of Premier Olof Palme, is elected in the Riksdag (parliament) as the new Swedish premier.	Iran continues to report new battlefield successes in its war with Iraq, and warns Persian Gulf Arab states that unless they stop supporting Baghdad in the conflict they will face an Iranian "military option."		
March 13		Soviet leader Mikhail S. Gorbachev announces that the Soviet Union will indefinitely continue its moratorium on nuclear testing if the United States will refrain from further testing. Moscow's moratorium, which began in August 1985, is scheduled to expire March 31.		In Colombia, Alvaro Fayad, the leader and founding member of the leftist April 19 (M-19) guerrilla group, is killed in a police raid on an apartment in Bogota.	The repatriation to the Phillipines of ill-gotten assets of Pres. Ferdinand E. Marcos, his family, and allies— estimated at as much as $10 bil.— is held up in the United States when a federal district court in Hawaii issues a temporary restraining order barring the U.S. Customs Service from turning over some 1,500 documents the Marcos party brought to the United States in late February.

A	B	C	D	E
Includes developments that affect more than one world region, international organizations and important meetings of major world leaders.	Includes all domestic and regional developments in Europe, including the Soviet Union, Turkey, Cyprus and Malta.	Includes all domestic and regional developments in Africa and the Middle East, including Iraq and Iran and excluding Cyprus, Turkey and Afghanistan.	Includes all domestic and regional developments in Latin America, the Caribbean and Canada.	Includes all domestic and regional developments in Asia and Pacific nations, extending from Afghanistan through all the Pacific Islands, except Hawaii.

U.S. Politics & Social Issues	U.S. Foreign Policy & Defense	U.S. Economy & Environment	Science, Technology & Nature	Culture, Leisure & Life Style	
The president of the National League of Cities, Mayor Henry Cisneros (D) of San Antonio, Tex. says proposed federal cuts in aid to cities will amount to a "disastrous dismantling of federal-local partnerships" that will require imposition of "regressive" taxes on city residents. . . . In a 6-3 decision, the Supreme Court finds no legal fault with deceit by police to keep a lawyer from a criminal suspect during interrogation. Nor do the police have to inform the suspect of the attorney's effort to reach him, the court rules. . . . Texas becomes the second state to test the basic academic skills of its public school teachers and administrators some 210,000 of whom take an examination in reading and writing competency as part of a package of education reforms pushed into law by Gov. Mark White.		The Supreme Court bars imposition of a New Jersey state tax on chemical manufacturers for total cleanup of toxic waste sites already covered by the federal Superfund law.	Researchers working with the National Institutes of Health have had such success with a new clot-dissolving drug, TPA or tissue-type plasminogen activator, that they are urging expedited approval by the Food and Drug Admin.	Undisputed middleweight champion "Marvelous" Marvin Hagler retains his title with an 11th-round knockout of John (The Beast) Mugabi. . . . Ray (born Reginald Truscott-Jones) Milland, 78, suave Welsh-born actor, dies in Los Angeles of cancer. His performance as an alcoholic writer in the 1945 film *The Lost Weekend* won him an Academy Award for best actor. His 56-year career in Britain and the United States included numerous television roles and parts in almost 150 films, including *Lady in the Dark* and *Dial M for Murder*.	March 10
The Georgia Board of Pardons and Paroles awards a posthumous pardon to Leo M. Frank, a Jewish factory manager lynched in 1915 in Cobb County, two years after he was convicted of murdering one of his employees, 13-year-old Mary Phagan. . . . The *Washington Post* reports that under a 1985 policy, the Justice Dept. has asked all prospective assistant U.S. attorneys and department lawyers if they are homosexual and are keeping it secret, ostensibly to see if they are susceptible to blackmail.	Citing concerns about the recent intensification of the Iran-Iraq war, the Reagan administration, notifies Congress that it plans to sell $354 mil. in advanced missiles to Saudi Arabia. Congressional supporters of Israel oppose the deal although Israeli reaction is mild.				March 11
The Dept. of Health and Human Services releases lists of hospitals with abnormal death and discharge rates. It says the move was forced under the Freedom of Information Act.	The Reagan administration has stepped up its campaign over the last several weeks to win aid for the Nicaraguan Contras fighting to overthrow the Sandinista government. But the administration provokes a storm in Congress by charging that those who do not back Pres. Reagan on the issue are supporting communism.	Farmers begin receiving notices from the Farmers Home Admin. that they will have to restructure or renegotiate their loans from the agency or face foreclosure. The notices are being mailed to some 65,000 farmers in an attempt by the government to collect payments on some $5.8 bil. in delinquent loans.			March 12
	Pres. Reagan nominates former Republican congressman Barber B. Conable Jr. to head the World Bank. He would replace outgoing A.W. (Tom) Clausen.	The House decisively rejects Pres. Reagan's FY1987 budget by a vote of 312-12. The action comes a week after the Republican-controlled Senate budget committee did the same. . . . Outstanding consumer installment credit grew a seasonally adjusted $6.88 bil. in January, or at an annual rate of 15.2%, the Federal Reserve Board reports.		Susan Butcher crosses the finish line in Nome, Alaska, to win the 1,158-mile Iditarod dog-sled race in the record time of 11 days, 15 hours, and 6 minutes. Butcher, who has twice finished second in the annual event, is the second woman to win the Iditarod.	March 13

F	G	H	I	J
Includes elections, federal-state relations, civil rights and liberties, crime, the judiciary, education, health care, poverty, urban affairs and population.	*Includes formation and debate of U.S. foreign and defense policies, veterans' affairs and defense spending. (Relations with specific foreign countries are usually found under the region concerned.)*	*Includes business, labor, agriculture, taxation, transportation, consumer affairs, monetary and fiscal policy, natural resources, and pollution.*	*Includes worldwide scientific, medical and technological developments, natural phenomena, U.S. weather, natural disasters, and accidents.*	*Includes the arts, religion, scholarship, communications media, sports, entertainments, fashions, fads and social life.*

	World Affairs	Europe	Africa & the Middle East	The Americas	Asia & the Pacific
March 14	The United Nations Human Rights Comm. passes a resolution urging Chile to halt human rights abuses. The resolution is similar to a draft version submitted the previous week by the United States marking the first time that nation has taken the lead in criticizing the military government of Pres. Augusto Pinochet Ugarte on the human rights question.		UN Sec. Gen. Javier Perez de Cuellar issues a report by a team of experts charging that Iraq used chemical weapons "on many occasions" against Iran. It is the third UN probe of chemical warfare in the Iran-Iraq war, but the first report that specifically names Iraq as having used poison gas.	In Ecuador, army troops quell a revolt by the former armed forces chief of staff, Gen. Frank Vargas Pazos, when they storm a base held by the mutineer and arrest him.	
March 15		Allied rightist parties win a narrow victory against the ruling Socialist Party in elections for the French National Assembly. The rightist victory means that a premier and president from opposing political camps will govern together for the first time since the Fifth Republic was established in 1958.			
March 16		The Swiss vote by a 3-1 margin against joining the UN. Although both houses of parliament had approved a proposal to join the UN, the proposal required the majority support of both the voters and the cantons in a national referendum.	Some 125 airmen of the Canadian Forces 408 Squadron join the multinational observers based at the abandoned Israeli air base at El-Gharra in the Sinai Desert. The multinational force was established in 1981 to monitor the 1979 Camp David accords.	Paraguay witnesses its first antigovernment demonstrations and strikes in 32 years as antigovernment opponents and dissidents within the ruling Colorado Party begin defying the Gen. Alfredo Stroessner's dictatorial rule.	
March 17		Sir John Bagot Glubb, 88, British Army officer who built Jordan's Arab Legion into one of the most effective fighting forces in the Middle East, dies in Sussex, England. In 1939 he took formal command of the legion, and he served as a close confidant of Jordan's King Abdullah until the king's assassination in Jerusalem in 1951. In 1956 a growing, militant Arab nationalism led to his being dismissed by Abdullah's successor, King Hussein. Expelled from Jordan, he returned to England and wrote many books about the Arab world.		Brazil summons the U.S. charge d'affaires to demand a clarification of Pres. Reagan's assertions in a March 16 speech that the Sandinista government of Nicaragua is aiding Brazilian radicals.	

A	B	C	D	E
Includes developments that affect more than one world region, international organizations and important meetings of major world leaders.	Includes all domestic and regional developments in Europe, including the Soviet Union, Turkey, Cyprus and Malta.	Includes all domestic and regional developments in Africa and the Middle East, including Iraq and Iran and excluding Cyprus, Turkey and Afghanistan.	Includes all domestic and regional developments in Latin America, the Caribbean and Canada.	Includes all domestic and regional developments in Asia and Pacific nations, extending from Afghanistan through all the Pacific Islands, except Hawaii.

U.S. Politics & Social Issues	U.S. Foreign Policy & Defense	U.S. Economy & Environment	Science, Technology & Nature	Culture, Leisure & Life Style	
	A report on acid rain concludes that there is a definite link in Eastern North America between environmental damage and industrial sulfur emissions. The report, issued by the U.S. National Academy of Sciences, connects the burning of coal, gasoline and other fossil fuels to acidifying of the countryside, killing lakes and fish and quite possibly trees. . . . Pres. Reagan reveals that he has offered Soviet Gen. Sec. Mikhail Gorbachev "a new, very specific and far-reaching proposal concerning nuclear-testing limitations." The president says he has invited Soviet scientists to visit the nuclear site in Nevada and witness an underground test in April.	The government's producer price index fell a seasonally adjusted 1.6% in February, the Labor Dept. reports. The decline is the largest in the index since it was first used in 1947. . . . Industrial production in February fell a seasonally adjusted 0.6%, the Federal Reserve Board reports. The February output performance follows a revised 0.1% rise in January and a 0.8% gain in December 1985.			**March 14**
		LTV Corp. and the United Steelworkers of America (USWA) settle upon a 40-month labor contract that will reduce wages but extend profit sharing to workers. . . . The House passes a FY1987 budget that rejects Pres. Reagan's request for massive new growth in military spending. The vote is largely along party lines, 245-179, with 17 Republicans voting in favor and 19 Democrats opposed. . . . Industrial production in April rose a seasonally adjusted 0.2%, the Federal Reserve Board reports.	Two Soviet cosmonauts board the new Soviet space station *Mir*, after a successful docking of the Soyuz T-15 spacecraft. The Soyuz was launched March 13.		**March 15**
White House officials agree to finance the renovation of a dilapidated shelter for the homeless in Washington, D.C. The deal appears to end two years of wrangling over the shelter's fate. Mitch Snyder, director of the Community for Creative Non-Violence and head of the shelter, had been pressing the federal government for the funds.	In a bluntly worded speech to the nation, Pres. Reagan depicts Nicaragua as a "cancer" posing a direct threat to the security of the United States. He urges Congress to put partisanship aside in dealing with the issue.			The British Academy Awards are presented. Woody Allen's *Purple Rose of Cairo* is named best film; William Hurt, best actor for *Kiss of the Spider Woman*; and Dame Peggy Ashcroft, best actress for *A Passage to India*.	**March 16**
		A study undertaken for the Joint Economic Committee of Congress finds that budget cuts have hurt federal agencies that compile economic statistics. The study warns that the 4.3% across-the-board budget cuts mandated by the Gramm-Rudman balanced budget law for the current year would "have serious consequences" for the quality of some statistics. . . . The value of mergers and acquisitions undertaken in 1985 totaled a record $179.6 bil. up 47% from the previous record of $122.2 bil. in 1984, according to data compiled by W.T. Grimm & Co. . . . The United Auto Workers (UAW) suspends an organizing drive at Honda Motor Co.'s plant at Marysville, Ohio. The UAW has not yet attained a union representation election at a Japanese-owned auto plant in the United States, although several plants have agreed to union representation without a vote.			**March 17**

F	G	H	I	J
Includes elections, federal-state relations, civil rights and liberties, crime, the judiciary, education, health care, poverty, urban affairs and population.	*Includes formation and debate of U.S. foreign and defense policies, veterans' affairs and defense spending. (Relations with specific foreign countries are usually found under the region concerned.)*	*Includes business, labor, agriculture, taxation, transportation, consumer affairs, monetary and fiscal policy, natural resources, and pollution.*	*Includes worldwide scientific, medical and technological developments, natural phenomena, U.S. weather, natural disasters, and accidents.*	*Includes the arts, religion, scholarship, communications media, sports, entertainments, fashions, fads and social life.*

	World Affairs	Europe	Africa & the Middle East	The Americas	Asia & the Pacific
March 18		The Kremlin protests an incursion by two U.S. Navy ships into Soviet territorial waters. The protest is contained in a note delivered to the U.S. Embassy in Moscow. U.S. officials confirm that the guided missile cruiser USS *Yorktown* and the destroyer USS *Caron* entered the Black Sea from the Turkish straits and sailed within six nautical miles of the southern Crimea coast March 10.			Japan's central bank intervenes in foreign exchange markets to brake the rapid rise of the yen and lift the U.S. dollar, according to the *Wall Street Journal*.
March 19			Evidence surfaces in Israel raising doubts about whether John Demjanjuk, recently extradited from the United States to stand trial for war crimes, is in fact the notorious Treblinka death camp guard known only as "Ivan the Terrible."	Canadian P.M. Brian Mulroney concludes a two-day visit to Washington, D.C., during which he and Pres. Reagan discuss various issues, including free trade and defense; but acid rain is the central issue at the summit. . . . Panamanian workers stage a general nine-day strike to protest reforms in the nation's 1972 labor code. The proposed reforms satisfy conditions for a loan from the World Bank, and were approved by the congress March 16.	
March 20		Jacques Chirac, leader of the neo-Gaullist Rassemblement pour la Republic and current mayor of Paris, assumes the office of premier of France and names a 37-member government. The occasion marks a shift of the political balance in France back to the rightists, who had governed steadily for 23 years before the socialists were swept to power in 1981.			Some 2,300 pages of documents released by the United States indicate that former Philippine Pres. Ferdinand E. Marcos, his wife, Imelda, and their associates accumulated wealth totaling millions of dollars over a 20-year period and had concealed it in a network of bank accounts, dummy corporations, and real estate transactions worldwide. . . . The Australian domestic economy grew by 4.9% during the 1985 calendar year, according to figures released by the Australian Bureau of Statistics.
March 21		In Bulgaria, Georgi Atanasov is promoted to Politburo full membership and named premier, capping a series of high-level changes begun in January.			

A	B	C	D	E
Includes developments that affect more than one world region, international organizations and important meetings of major world leaders.	Includes all domestic and regional developments in Europe, including the Soviet Union, Turkey, Cyprus and Malta.	Includes all domestic and regional developments in Africa and the Middle East, including Iraq and Iran and excluding Cyprus, Turkey and Afghanistan.	Includes all domestic and regional developments in Latin America, the Caribbean and Canada.	Includes all domestic and regional developments in Asia and Pacific nations, extending from Afghanistan through all the Pacific Islands, except Hawaii.

U.S. Politics & Social Issues	U.S. Foreign Policy & Defense	U.S. Economy & Environment	Science, Technology & Nature	Culture, Leisure & Life Style	
Adlai E. Stevenson III easily wins the Democratic nomination for governor in the Illinois primary, only to be stunned by the discovery that two of his running mates are followers of ultra-right-wing political organizer Lyndon H. LaRouche Jr. . . . Hotly disputed city council elections in seven newly created Chicago wards leave both Mayor Harold Washington (D) and his chief political opponent, Alderman Edward R. Vrdolyak (D), claiming victory. The predominantly black and Hispanic wards were created in response to an order by a federal judge, who held that the city's 1981 redistricting had unfairly discriminated against minority voters.		The U.S. balance of payments on current account shows a record deficit of $36.56 bil. in the fourth quarter of 1985, the Commerce Dept. reports. The deficit is larger than a revised $29.30 bil. gap in the third quarter of 1985 and brings the payments deficit for all of 1985 to $117.66 bil., up 9.6% from 1984's record of $107.36 bil. . . . New housing starts fell 3.5% in February to a seasonally adjusted annual rate of 1.985 million units, the Commerce Dept. reports.		Ending months of speculation, Buckingham Palace announces the engagement of Prince Andrew, 26, to Sarah Ferguson, 26. Prince Andrew, Queen Elizabeth's second son, is currently fourth in line to the British throne. . . . Bernard Malamud, 71, novelist and short story writer regarded as one of the most distinctive Jewish voices in post-war American literature, dies in New York City. His first novel, *The Natural* (1952), is an allegory about the rise and fall of a baseball player. His later novels include *The Assistant* (1957), *The Fixer* (1966), *The Tenants* (1971), and the short story collections *The Magic Barrel* (1958) and *Idiots First* (1963).	March 18
Variety's top-grossing films for the week are: *Gung Ho!, Pretty in Pink, Hannah and Her Sisters, Down and Out in Beverly Hills* and *The Color Purple*.		In a blow to Pres. Reagan, the Senate Budget Committee approves a bipartisan FY1987 budget plan that will slash $25 bil. from the president's military spending request, raise taxes and other revenues by $18.7 bil., and scale back many of Reagan's requested cutbacks in domestic programs. . . . Trading activity in tax-free municipal bonds grinds to a virtual halt when it is discovered that the tax overhaul bill the Senate is working on would subject municipal bond income to federal taxation. . . . After-tax profits of U.S. corporations rose a seasonally adjusted 6% in the fourth quarter of 1985, the Commerce Dept. reports; but profits for the year were off 2.2%, to $140.9 bil.		*The House of Blue Leaves*, a revival of John Guare's black comedy first produced in 1970, opens at New York City's Lincoln Center. The play, which takes place on the day of Pope Paul VI's 1965 visit to New York City, is directed by Jerry Zaks and stars Swoosie Kurtz, John Mahoney, Stockard Channing, and Julie Haggerty. The production later moves to Broadway, and Zaks goes on to win the Tony Award for best director.	March 19
The New York city council passes a bill that amends the city's code to forbid discrimination on the basis of sexual orientation. The measure, a so-called gay rights bill, passes by 21 to 14 votes, a surprisingly wide margin. . . . The President's Council on Physical Fitness and Sports issues a report on the physical condition of young Americans in 1985. The survey, which covered 18,857 public school students age six to 17, finds a "low level of performance" in many key areas. For example, 45% of the boys aged six to 14 and 55% of the girls could not sustain a chin-up for more than 10 seconds.	The House of Representatives rejects Pres. Reagan's appeal for $70 mil. in military aid and $30 mil. in humanitarian aid for Contras in Nicaragua fighting the Sandinista government.	The House, defying its Democratic leadership, approves a Senate bill setting $18.4 bil. in deficit reductions over the three fiscal years beginning with the current year, FY1986. . . . Americans' total personal income rose 0.6% or $19 bil. in February, to a seasonally adjusted annual rate of $3.406 trillion, according to the Commerce Dept. Consumer spending gained an adjusted 0.3%	Replacing saturated fats in the diet with olive oil could reduce blood cholesterol levels as effectively as adopting a low-fat diet, according to a study published in the *New England Journal of Medicine*.	The Genie awards are presented by the Academy of Canadian Cinema and Television. *My American Cousin* wins awards for best picture, best actor, John Wildman, and best actress, Margaret Langrick.	March 20
Smith-Kline Beckman Corp. recalls three of its nonprescription capsule products after the discovery of traces of rat poison in about half a dozen capsules. . . . Anthony "Fat Tony" Salerno, described as boss of "the Genovese organized crime family of La Cosa Nostra," and 14 others are indicted in New York City on 29 counts ranging from murder conspiracy to labor racketeering.			National Aeronautics and Space Admin. officials concede that failure of a joint on a solid-fuel booster rocket is the probable cause of the explosion that destroyed the shuttle *Challenger* on Jan. 28 and killed its crew of seven. . . . The chances that a person infected with the acquired immune deficiency syndrome virus will develop the disease are greater than previously estimated, according to a new study made by the National Cancer Institute and published in *Science*.	Lyudmila Rudenko, 81, first women's world chess champion, dies in Leningrad. A native of the Ukraine, she won the first world chess competition for women in 1950 and held the title for three years. In 1977, she became the first woman to be ranked an international grandmaster by the World Chess Federation. . . . Debi Thomas of the United States becomes the first black woman to win the women's world figure skating championship, in Geneva, Switzerland. Brian Boitano of the United States wins the men's world figure skating championship. Natalya Bestiamanova and Andrei Bukin of the Soviet Union win the ice dancing world championship.	March 21

F	G	H	I	J
Includes elections, federal-state relations, civil rights and liberties, crime, the judiciary, education, health care, poverty, urban affairs and population.	*Includes formation and debate of U.S. foreign and defense policies, veterans' affairs and defense spending. (Relations with specific foreign countries are usually found under the region concerned.)*	*Includes business, labor, agriculture, taxation, transportation, consumer affairs, monetary and fiscal policy, natural resources, and pollution.*	*Includes worldwide scientific, medical and technological developments, natural phenomena, U.S. weather, natural disasters, and accidents.*	*Includes the arts, religion, scholarship, communications media, sports, entertainments, fashions, fads and social life.*

	World Affairs	Europe	Africa & the Middle East	The Americas	Asia & the Pacific
March 22					Bangladesh's military Pres. Hossein Mohammed Ershad announces that parliamentary elections will be postponed until May 7.
March 23			A huge U.S. Navy task force gathers in the Mediterranean Sea off Libya and begins conducting "freedom of navigation" exercises in the Gulf of Sidra, which Libya claims as its territorial waters.		The New Korea Democratic Party (NKDP) begins staging a series of rallies in major Korean cities to gain 10 million signatures on a petition asking for constitutional reform to allow for direct presidential elections in 1987.
March 24	Members of Org. of Petroleum Exporting Countries (OPEC) adjourn a nine-day meeting in Geneva without taking any action to reverse recent steep declines in world prices. A proposal for cutting crude oil output was discussed, but agreement could not be reached on apportioning the cuts among OPEC's 13 member nations. The failure of the meeting causes further declines in world oil prices.				The Indian government rejects a proposed $350 mil. settlement by the U.S.-based Union Carbide Corp. of claims arising from the 1984 fatal gas leak at its subsidiary in Bhopal, India. The tentative settlement had been agreed upon by Union Carbide and U.S. lawyers representing Indian victims of the disaster, in which about 2,000 people died and 20,000 others were injured.
March 25				Canada's Federal Supply Services Min. Stewart McInnes, announces that a bronze-plated, nickel $1 coin will be in circulation in 1987 and will eventually supplant the paper dollar. . . . Thousands of Argentine workers stage a 10-hour general strike to protest the government's economic policies. It is the third such strike against the anti-inflation Austral Plan imposed by the government in June 1985 and the fifth strike against the government of Pres. Raul Alfonsin since it took power in December 1983.	Philippine Pres. Corazon Aquino abolishes the National Assembly, abrogates the 1973 constitution and claims all legislative powers for herself. She announces an interim "freedom constitution" under which she will hold power until a new charter is written and submitted to a referendum, and legislative elections are held. . . . In an unprecedented move, Switzerland says it is freezing "until further notice" all Swiss banks deposits belonging to former Philippine Pres. Ferdinand E. Marcos, his family and allies. . . . China's preeminent leader, Deng Xiaoping, 81, makes his first public appearance in three months and hints that he is considering retirement.

A	B	C	D	E
Includes developments that affect more than one world region, international organizations and important meetings of major world leaders.	Includes all domestic and regional developments in Europe, including the Soviet Union, Turkey, Cyprus and Malta.	Includes all domestic and regional developments in Africa and the Middle East, including Iraq and Iran and excluding Cyprus, Turkey and Afghanistan.	Includes all domestic and regional developments in Latin America, the Caribbean and Canada.	Includes all domestic and regional developments in Asia and Pacific nations, extending from Afghanistan through all the Pacific Islands, except Hawaii.

U.S. Politics & Social Issues	U.S. Foreign Policy & Defense	U.S. Economy & Environment	Science, Technology & Nature	Culture, Leisure & Life Style	
The General Accounting Office concludes that the Defense Dept. violated its own rules during the 1984 election campaign by giving mailing lists to the reelection committee of Pres. Reagan.	The United States conducts its first underground nuclear test of 1986. The test is criticized by both the Soviet Union and many members of Congress. . . . A poll sponsored by the Union of Concerned Scientists, an anti-Strategic Defense Initiative (SDI) organization, purports to show that many U.S. physicists involved in SDI research have doubts about the program. The physicists favor basic SDI research by a margin of 77% to 21%. However, the poll finds that 54% of the scientists believe that SDI represents "a step in the wrong direction for America's national security policy."	The General Accounting Office (GAO) reports considerable laxity in federal monitoring of toxic waste storage and disposal sites to prevent closing of the sites without proper environmental safeguards. The GAO says that 67 of 176 such sites closed in 1984 were not inspected by the Environmental Protection Agency for potential threats to health and safety.		*Billboard*'s best-selling albums for the week are: *Whitney Houston*, Whitney Houston; *Promise*, Sade; *Heart*, Heart; *Scarecrow*, John Cougar Mellencamp; and *Welcome to the Real World*, Mr. Mister.	March 22
Surgeon Gen. C. Everett Koop distributes summaries of a report on smokeless tobacco scheduled for release April 1. He compares the paper to the government's landmark 1964 report on the risks of smoking.				Nelson Piquet wins auto racing's Brazilian Grand Prix. . . . Trevor Berbick wins the World Boxing Council heavyweight title in a unanimous 12-round decision over Pinklon Thomas. . . . Zola Budd, a native of South Africa running for Britain, wins the women's world cross-country championship in Colombier, Switz., John Ngugi of Kenya wins the men's division. . . . Marc Girardelli of Luxembourg wins the men's overall World Cup skiing title, Roswitha Steiner of Austria wins the women's slalom title, and Vreni Schneider of Switzerland wins the giant slalom.	March 23
			The Environmental Protection Agency suspends a California biotechnology company's permit to conduct an outdoor test of a genetically engineered bacterium. The company, Advanced Genetic Sciences, admits making unauthorized preliminary outdoor tests during the previous year.	The 58th annual Oscar awards are presented. *Out of Africa* wins seven awards, including best picture and best director, Sydney Pollack. William Hurt wins best actor for *Kiss of the Spider Woman*; Geraldine Page, best actress for *The Trip to Bountiful*; Don Ameche, best supporting actor for *Cocoon*; Anjelica Houston, best supporting actress for *Prizzi's Honor*. Best foreign-language film is *The Official Story* (Argentina). *The Color Purple*, nominated for 11 awards, fails to win any.	March 24
	A constitutional amendment to require a balanced federal budget after 1991 falls one vote short of passage in the Republican-controlled Senate, despite a last-minute plea for its passage from Pres. Reagan. . . . The government's consumer price index fell a seasonally adjusted 0.4% in February, or at a compounded annual rate of 4.6%, according to the Labor Dept. The decline is the largest since November 1953.				March 25

F	G	H	I	J
Includes elections, federal-state relations, civil rights and liberties, crime, the judiciary, education, health care, poverty, urban affairs and population.	Includes formation and debate of U.S. foreign and defense policies, veterans' affairs and defense spending. (Relations with specific foreign countries are usually found under the region concerned.)	Includes business, labor, agriculture, taxation, transportation, consumer affairs, monetary and fiscal policy, natural resources, and pollution.	Includes worldwide scientific, medical and technological developments, natural phenomena, U.S. weather, natural disasters, and accidents.	Includes the arts, religion, scholarship, communications media, sports, entertainments, fashions, fads and social life.

	World Affairs	Europe	Africa & the Middle East	The Americas	Asia & the Pacific
March 26					
March 27			The U.S. fleet leaves the Gulf of Sidra after two days of trading hostile fire with Libyan forces. Libya fired antiaircraft missiles at American carrier-based planes, and the United States responded with attacks on a number of installations on the Libyan mainland. Both Pres. Reagan and Libyan leader Col. Muammar el-Qaddafi proclaim victory in the brief conflict.		
March 28		Czechoslovakia holds its 17th Communist Party congress in Prague. The congress, which takes place once every five years, opens amid reports that the conservative Czechoslovakian party leadership is resisting the promptings of Soviet leader Mikhail S. Gorbachev to adopt wholesale economic reforms and oust obstructionist officials.			
March 29		Soviet leader Mikhail S. Gorbachev calls for Pres. Reagan to join him "in the nearest future" to discuss a ban on nuclear weapons tests.... Three Bulgarians and three Turks charged with complicity in the 1981 assassination attempt on Pope John Paul II are acquitted in an Italian court for lack of proof. Under Italian law, the ruling implies that the evidence in the case is too ambiguous to allow a clear-cut verdict of guilt or innocence.		After almost three weeks of tough negotiations, Nicaraguan Contra leaders formally announce a unity agreement and say they have resolved an internal dispute on leadership that threatened to split apart their organization, the United Nicaraguan Opposition.	

A	B	C	D	E
Includes developments that affect more than one world region, international organizations and important meetings of major world leaders.	Includes all domestic and regional developments in Europe, including the Soviet Union, Turkey, Cyprus and Malta.	Includes all domestic and regional developments in Africa and the Middle East, including Iraq and Iran and excluding Cyprus, Turkey and Afghanistan.	Includes all domestic and regional developments in Latin America, the Caribbean and Canada.	Includes all domestic and regional developments in Asia and Pacific nations, extending from Afghanistan through all the Pacific Islands, except Hawaii.

U.S. Politics & Social Issues	U.S. Foreign Policy & Defense	U.S. Economy & Environment	Science, Technology & Nature	Culture, Leisure & Life Style	
The Supreme Court decides unanimously that the presence of armed, uniformed guards near defendants during their trial does not deny them the right to a fair trial.	The Justice Dept. files a civil suit against General Dynamics Corp. in the U.S. District Court in Los Angeles. The suit seeks unspecified damages from the company for alleged fraud on a contract to produce a prototype of the army DIVAD (division air defense) antiaircraft gun.	The Senate votes by voice to authorize $11.5 bil. in water projects and substantial increases in cost sharing by localities and beneficiaries of the works. The bill is sent to conference with the House, which approved a $20 bil. version of the legislation in 1985. ... The Supreme Court rules against the Zenith Electronics Corp. in its antitrust lawsuit against Japanese television manufacturers. The litigation, dating back to 1974, contends that the Japanese companies sought to undercut American producers by conspiring to charge artificially high prices in Japan and artificially low prices in the United States.			March 26
	The Senate narrowly approves Pres. Reagan's request to spend $100 mil. in aid to Nicaraguan Contras fighting to overthrow the Sandinista government. Reagan received a boost for his request when details surfaced March 24-25 of a Sandinista incursion into Honduras. Nicaragua denies an invasion took place, and opponents of the aid request accuse Reagan of exaggerating the threat to Honduras in order to win the aid.	The U.S. deficit on merchandise trade decreased in February to $12.49 bil., the Commerce Dept. reports.... The Dow Jones Industrial Averaged closes at a record high of 1821.72.	A Canadian scientist discovers that the speed of sound has been incorrectly given for more than 40 years. George S.K. Wong of the National Research Council of Canada establishes that the true figure of 741.1 miles per hour is about a half-mile per hour slower than the accepted figure. Wong says he traced the erroneous figure to a 1942 calculation error that had worked its way through the scientific literature unchallenged.... A volcano erupts on Alaska's unpopulated Augustine Island. The 4,025-foot mountain, dormant since 1976, is located in southern Alaska's Cook Inlet, about 175 miles southwest of Anchorage.		March 27
The Justice Dept. releases documents intended to show that the Labor Dept.'s denial of federal contracts to businesses that did not meet the department's goals for the hiring and promotion of women and minorities were improperly enforced so as to promote discrimination.... A new, inexpensive, and highly potent form of heroin, "black tar," is spreading rapidly among U.S. drug users, according to a report issued by the Drug Enforcement Agency.... A serious decline in U.S. college-level programs in science, mathematics, and engineering poses a "grave and long-term threat" to the nation, according to a report issued by the National Science Board, the policy-making body of the National Science Foundation.		The government's index of leading economic indicators rose 0.7% in February, the Commerce Dept. reports.... Some 1.55 million cattle will be slaughtered as part of the federal effort to reduce dairy output, Agriculture Sec. Richard Lyng announces. The total exceeds the Agriculture Dept.'s earlier estimate of 900,000 head.		*Publisher Weekly*'s hardback fiction best-sellers for the week are: *The Bourne Supremacy*, Robert Ludlum; *Lie Down with Lions*, Ken Follett; *Lake Wobegon Days*, Garrison Keillor; *The Mammoth Hunters*, Jean M. Auel; and *The Handmaid's Tale*, Margaret Atwood.	March 28
	According to 75% of the Americans surveyed in a *Newsweek* poll, the United States was justified in attacking Libyan ships and a missile site in the Gulf of Sidra March 24 and 25. However, respondents were evenly divided over whether the U.S. naval maneuvers in the gulf were a deliberate attempt to provoke an attack by Libya.			Cambridge wins the 132nd University Boat Race on the River Thames in London, ending an Oxford winning streak that dates to 1975.... Michigan State wins the National Collegiate Athletic Assoc. Division I hockey championship with a 6-5 victory over Harvard.	March 29

F	G	H	I	J
Includes elections, federal-state relations, civil rights and liberties, crime, the judiciary, education, health care, poverty, urban affairs and population.	*Includes formation and debate of U.S. foreign and defense policies, veterans' affairs and defense spending. (Relations with specific foreign countries are usually found under the region concerned.)*	*Includes business, labor, agriculture, taxation, transportation, consumer affairs, monetary and fiscal policy, natural resources, and pollution.*	*Includes worldwide scientific, medical and technological developments, natural phenomena, U.S. weather, natural disasters, and accidents.*	*Includes the arts, religion, scholarship, communications media, sports, entertainments, fashions, fads and social life.*

	World Affairs	Europe	Africa & the Middle East	The Americas	Asia & the Pacific
March 30			A conference of black teachers, students, and parents meets in Durban, South Africa, and urges blacks not to resume a national boycott of segregated schools. Instead, the National Education Crisis Committee calls for a change in strategy that will emphasize general strikes and rent and consumer boycotts.		
March 31		In Northern Ireland, rioting erupts on Easter Monday after unionists defy a British government ban on a planned march through Portadown, southwest of Belfast in County Armagh. As many as 77 people, including 38 police officers, are reported injured in the clashes.		A Mexicana Airlines jet crashes against a mountainside about 100 miles northwest of Mexico City, killing the eight crew members and 158 passengers aboard.	
April 1					Japanese police dramatically step up security in Tokyo after radicals unleash a series of rocket attacks and vow to disrupt an upcoming economic conference of industrialized nations.
April 2		A bomb explodes aboard a Trans World Airlines jet flying from Rome to Athens. The blast tears a hole in the plane's fuselage, through which the bodies of four passengers, all of them Americans, fall to their death. The jet manages to land in Athens without further injuries to the passengers. A previously unknown terrorist group says the bombing is in response to the U.S. clashes with Libya in the Gulf of Sidra the week before.	Desmond Tutu, the black Anglican bishop of Johannesburg, calls on Western countries to apply "punitive sanctions" against the South African government to force it to end its apartheid system of racial segregation. . . . In South Africa, it is announced that the government has stopped enforcing a long-standing banning order on black activist Winnie Mandela, wife of imprisoned African National Congress leader Nelson Mandela. . . . The International Monetary Fund (IMF) declares Sudan ineligible to receive new loans. The East African nation is overdue in repaying $250 mil. in IMF loans, the largest arrearage of any nation in the fund.		

A	B	C	D	E
Includes developments that affect more than one world region, international organizations and important meetings of major world leaders.	Includes all domestic and regional developments in Europe, including the Soviet Union, Turkey, Cyprus and Malta.	Includes all domestic and regional developments in Africa and the Middle East, including Iraq and Iran and excluding Cyprus, Turkey and Afghanistan.	Includes all domestic and regional developments in Latin America, the Caribbean and Canada.	Includes all domestic and regional developments in Asia and Pacific nations, extending from Afghanistan through all the Pacific Islands, except Hawaii.

U.S. Politics & Social Issues	U.S. Foreign Policy & Defense	U.S. Economy & Environment	Science, Technology & Nature	Culture, Leisure & Life Style	
	In response to yesterday's proposal by Soviet leader Mikhail S. Gorbachev, Pres. Reagan dismisses the notion that a summit meeting should be held to discuss only the test-ban issue. . . . A study conducted by the aides of three U.S. senators concludes that "Congress should maintain a certain degree of skepticism over claims of tremendous advances in the Strategic Defense Initiative research."			The Lady Longhorns of the Univ. of Texas beat the Univ. of Southern California, 97-81, in the women's National Collegiate Athletic Assoc. basketball championship. Texas's Clarissa Davis is named most valuable player. . . . James Cagney, 86, Irish-American actor who rose from the streets of New York City to become one of the great stars of Hollywood's Golden Age, dies at his farm in Stanfordville, N.Y. Starting out as a song and dance man on Broadway, in 1931 became an overnight sensation with the release of the film *The Public Enemy*, his first gangster role. In 1942 he won an Oscar for best actor for his portrayal of songwriter George M. Cohan in *Yankee Doodle Dandy*. His more than 60 films include *Angels with Dirty Faces* (1938), *White Heat* (1949), *Mister Roberts* (1955), and *Ragtime* (1981). . . . John Anthony Ciardi, 69, poet, critic, and essayist, dies in Edison, N.J., after a heart attack. The author of some 40 books, including an internationally acclaimed translation of Dante's *Inferno* (1954), he was poetry editor of the *Saturday Review* magazine from 1956 to 1972.	March 30
The Dept. of Housing and Urban Development orders an end to federal housing aid to illegal aliens. A department spokesman says the rule applies to 4.2 million units of federally assisted housing with more than 10 million tenants, but no estimate of the number of illegal aliens in the housing is available.		Prices received by farmers for their raw agricultural goods fell 0.8% in March, the Agriculture Dept. reports.	The second of two earthquakes in as many days jolts the San Francisco Bay area and measures 5.3-5.6 on the open-ended Richter scale of ground motion. The March 29 quake measured 4.0 on the Richter scale. The two quakes are said to be unrelated.	The Louisville Cardinals beat Duke, 72-69, in the men's National Collegiate Athletic Assoc. Division I basketball championship. Louisville's Pervis Ellison is named most valuable player.	March 31
The President's Comm. on Organized Crime details racketeering's cost to the United States in the third and last of an ambitious series of reports. But nine of the panel's 18 members charge that commission missteps made its record "a saga of missed opportunities." . . . The Supreme Court rules that police cannot interrogate a defendant at his arraignment without his lawyer present if the defendant has requested a lawyer.		The Labor Dept. announces it is seeking a $1.4 mil. fine against Union Carbide Corp. for 221 alleged health and safety violations at its Institute, W. Va. plant. . . . Stopgap funding for the Superfund hazardous waste cleanup program is signed by Pres. Reagan; Congress approves the funding March 21. . . . A General Accounting Office study concludes that federal agencies generally succeeded in cutting their budget outlays in accordance with the 1985 Gramm-Rudman balanced-budget law.		Erik Bruhn, 57, Danish-born ballet star who came to be regarded as one of the greatest classical dancers of the 20th century, dies of lung cancer in Toronto. From 1953 to 1972 he was a principal dancer and a choreogrpher with the American Ballet Theater. From 1967 to 1972 he directed the Royal Swedish Ballet, and since 1983 he had been the artistic director of the National Ballet of Canada.	April 1
	Pres. Reagan calls for a reorganization of the Pentagon along the lines of the recommendations of his Blue Ribbon Comm. on Defense Management.				April 2

F	G	H	I	J
Includes elections, federal-state relations, civil rights and liberties, crime, the judiciary, education, health care, poverty, urban affairs and population.	Includes formation and debate of U.S. foreign and defense policies, veterans' affairs and defense spending. (Relations with specific foreign countries are usually found under the region concerned.)	Includes business, labor, agriculture, taxation, transportation, consumer affairs, monetary and fiscal policy, natural resources, and pollution.	Includes worldwide scientific, medical and technological developments, natural phenomena, U.S. weather, natural disasters, and accidents.	Includes the arts, religion, scholarship, communications media, sports, entertainments, fashions, fads and social life.

	World Affairs	Europe	Africa & the Middle East	The Americas	Asia & the Pacific
April 3			The emir of Kuwait, Sheik Jabir al-Ahmad Al Sabah, dissolves the country's parliament, imposes censorship and suspends parts of the constitution. Citing pressure from the Iran-Iraq war, Jabir tells the nation that it faces a "foreign conspiracy" as well as an "acute economic crisis."		
April 4				In El Salvador, in an unprecedented move, two senior army officers have been detained in connection with a kidnapping ring with ties to the political right. They are among some 20 military men and civilians being detained; leading ultra-right businessmen, politicians, and other military officers are also under investigation. A probe into the ring has been under way since February, and the first announcements of arrests were made April 1.	
April 5		A bomb explodes in a West Berlin discotheque killing two people, including an American serviceman. The United States says that Libyan leader Col. Muammar el-Qaddafi might have ordered the blast.			
April 6		The European Monetary System (EMS) of eight European currencies is realigned for the ninth time in its seven-year history. The French franc is devalued as part of the broad EMS readjustment, which was initiated by the new rightist government in France and is expected to "pave the way for a fall in interest rates."			
April 7		In Greece, some 500,000 businessmen and workers stage a 24-hour strike to protest a two-year freeze in salaries and wages outlined in the government's austerity program announced in October 1985.		Efforts to revive peace negotiations sponsored by the Contadora Group founder over Nicaragua's insistence that the United States cease supporting anti-Sandinista Contras before Nicaragua will sign a Central American peace accord.	

A	B	C	D	E
Includes developments that affect more than one world region, international organizations and important meetings of major world leaders.	Includes all domestic and regional developments in Europe, including the Soviet Union, Turkey, Cyprus and Malta.	Includes all domestic and regional developments in Africa and the Middle East, including Iraq and Iran and excluding Cyprus, Turkey and Afghanistan.	Includes all domestic and regional developments in Latin America, the Caribbean and Canada.	Includes all domestic and regional developments in Asia and Pacific nations, extending from Afghanistan through all the Pacific Islands, except Hawaii.

U.S. Politics & Social Issues	U.S. Foreign Policy & Defense	U.S. Economy & Environment	Science, Technology & Nature	Culture, Leisure & Life Style	
	Twenty-nine people are injured and 91 arrested in an early-morning clash between police and demonstrators at the Univ. of California at Berkeley. The face-off is one in a series of incidents as protest against South Africa's apartheid policy of racial separation swells among U.S. college students. At issue in the Berkeley clash is the estimated $2.4 bil. the university invested in U.S. companies that do business in South Africa.		Astronomers find what they believe to be the most distant object ever seen. Reporting in the British journal *Nature*, an international team of astronomers says that it has found a quasar, a starlike object radiating immense amounts of energy, more than 12.4 bil. light years from Earth. . . . The Dept. of Agriculture suspends a commercial license for field testing what would have been the first live, genetically altered virus released into the environment. The virus, developed by Biologics, was intended as a vaccine to immunize swine against pseudo-rabies. . . . Astronauts tell the presidential commission, which is investigating the explosion of the space shuttle *Challenger* Jan. 28, of their concern over safety problems confronting the shuttle program. There is a chronic problem with shuttle brake systems and there is concern about night landings, outdated training equipment, and intensive training pressure just prior to the launch date.	Sir Peter Pears, 75, renowned British tenor for whom composer Benjamin Britten created some of the most notable roles in 20th-century opera, dies of heart attack in Aldeburgh, England. In such works as *Peter Grimes, Billy Budd* and *Death in Venice*, Pears was Britten's personal and professional partner from the 1930s until the composer's death in 1976. He was also an outstanding interpreter of music by other 20th-century British composers and of music by classical masters.	April 3
					April 4
				"Instruction on Christian Freedom and Liberation," a new Vatican paper on the theology of liberation, views service to the poor as a paramount duty for Christians and approves, in "the extreme case," armed struggle to escape oppressive political and economic systems.	April 5
A Southern, regional presidential "superprimary" in 1988 becomes a reality, as the last of nine Southern states moves the date of its presidential primary to the second Tuesday in March, just two weeks after the New Hampshire primary that traditionally kicks off the primary season. The states are: Alabama, Florida, Georgia, Kentucky, Maryland, Mississippi, Missouri, Oklahoma, and Tennessee.			The virus that causes acquired immune deficiency syndrome has been found for the first time in women's genital secretions, according to two U.S. studies reported in the British medical journal *Lancet*. The discovery increases evidence that the fatal disease could be spread sexually from women to men.		April 6
		Pres. Reagan signs a bill designed to shave $18 bil. off the federal budget deficit over three years. . . . The Reagan administration unveils a plan designed to protect materials patented or copyrighted in the United States from infringement overseas.		Leonid V. Kantorovich, 74, Soviet economist and mathematician who shared the 1975 Nobel Memorial Prize in economic science with Yale Univ. economist Tjalling Koopmans, dies. . . . The Major League baseball season opens after an offseason dominated by friction between players and owners. In the most notable labor developments, teams voluntarily begin the season with 24-man squads (down from 25), and no blue-chip free agents were able to win contracts with new clubs. . . . French novelist Marguerite Duras receives the $50,000 Ritz Paris Hemingway Award for her autobiographical novel *L'Amant* (The Lover).	April 7

F	G	H	I	J
Includes elections, federal-state relations, civil rights and liberties, crime, the judiciary, education, health care, poverty, urban affairs and population.	*Includes formation and debate of U.S. foreign and defense policies, veterans' affairs and defense spending. (Relations with specific foreign countries are usually found under the region concerned.)*	*Includes business, labor, agriculture, taxation, transportation, consumer affairs, monetary and fiscal policy, natural resources, and pollution.*	*Includes worldwide scientific, medical and technological developments, natural phenomena, U.S. weather, natural disasters, and accidents.*	*Includes the arts, religion, scholarship, communications media, sports, entertainments, fashions, fads and social life.*

	World Affairs	Europe	Africa & the Middle East	The Americas	Asia & the Pacific
April 8		Sir Clive Sinclair, founder of Sinclair Research Ltd., is reported to have sold his company for $7.3 mil. to Amstrad Consumer Electronics PLC. Sinclair Research, once worth 136 million pounds sterling, was the world pioneer of low-cost home computers, while Amstrad, considered one of Britain's fastest growing companies, entered the market only two years ago.			The Japanese government approves a package of incentives intended to stimulate the economy in the face of a downturn caused by the strengthened yen.
April 9		In France, rightist Premier Jacques Chirac makes his first major policy statement in the National Assembly and outlines plans to denationalize more than 50 state-owned banks and corporations.		The Canadian Wheat Board slashes the prices it will pay western farmers for wheat, barley, and oats. The move could cost the already hard-pressed growers $723 mil. in income in 1986.	
April 10		The British purchaser of a Goya masterwork announces in London that the painting will go back to Spain. Christie's, the London art house, planned to auction the work today for a price thought likely to top the world record for a painting of $10 mil. But Spain insisted the work was taken out of the country illegally in 1983. . . . As many as 20 people are reported to have died in Italy since March 18 after drinking Italian wine poisoned by methyl alcohol, also known as wood alcohol.			Benazir Bhutto, the exiled leader of the opposition Pakistan People's Party, returns to Pakistan from London and is greeted by thousands of supporters. The daughter of Zulfikar Ali Bhutto, the prime minister executed in 1979, Benazir Bhutto is widely seen to pose the most serious challenge to Gen. Muhammad Zia ul-Haq, the Pakistani president. . . . In Australia, Chris Hurford, minister for immigration and ethnic affairs, announces that the country will accept 95,000 immigrants in 1986-87. Australia had planned to accept 84,000 immigrants during 1985-86 but exceeded that number by an estimated 4,000 people.
April 11				Disclosures March 16 and this day that Nicaraguan Contras are suspected of involvement in gunrunning and drug smuggling in the U.S. sparks demands in Congress that the charges be investigated.	

A	B	C	D	E
Includes developments that affect more than one world region, international organizations and important meetings of major world leaders.	Includes all domestic and regional developments in Europe, including the Soviet Union, Turkey, Cyprus and Malta.	Includes all domestic and regional developments in Africa and the Middle East, including Iraq and Iran and excluding Cyprus, Turkey and Afghanistan.	Includes all domestic and regional developments in Latin America, the Caribbean and Canada.	Includes all domestic and regional developments in Asia and Pacific nations, extending from Afghanistan through all the Pacific Islands, except Hawaii.

U.S. Politics & Social Issues	U.S. Foreign Policy & Defense	U.S. Economy & Environment	Science, Technology & Nature	Culture, Leisure & Life Style	
Actor Clint Eastwood is elected mayor of Carmel, Calif., a small seaside tourist town on the Monterey Peninsula.					April 8
Following the victory of two of his followers in Illinois statewide primaries, ultra-right political organizer Lyndon H. LaRouche Jr. says increasing numbers of voters see him "as the guy who is going to stick it to them in Washington."		In a nationally televised news conference, Pres. Reagan says he is "very adamant" in rejecting any compromise on defense spending or taxes.... The sharp drop in interest rates over the last few months is likely to save the federal government as much as $12 bil. in the current fiscal year and as much as $12 bil. in FY1987, beginning October 1. This is the conclusion of many economic analysts inside and outside the government, cited in a *New York Times* story.... National Steel Corp. and the United Steelworkers of America settle on a 39-month labor contract that features job security and profit sharing for the workers and reduced wages and work rules for the company.		McDonald's Corp. announces that it will begin serving the Classic Coke version of Coca-Cola Co.'s soft drink beginning at the end of the month. The move means that McDonald's, the nation's largest fountain service user of Coke products, will be abandoning the so-called New Coke, which the beverage company introduced in 1985.	April 9
The House of Representatives votes by wide margin to ease firearms restrictions with passage of the Firearms Owners Protection Act (FOPA). The House measure, together with a similar bill passed by the Senate in 1985, will make the first significant changes in the landmark Gun Control Act of 1968.	The United States conducts its second underground nuclear test of the year.	Some 200 banks and insurance companies sell a $487.9 mil. block of shares of Navistar International Corp. The transaction is the largest block trade in New York Stock Exchange history.		It is reported that Barney Rosset has been removed as president and chief executive officer of Grove Press, the avant-garde book publishing company he founded in 1951 and sold in 1985 to British publisher Lord Weidenfeld and Weidenfeld's American partner, Anne Getty.... *Big Deal* opens on Broadway, a musical set in Chicago in the 1930s. It is written, directed, and choreographed by Bob Fosse, who goes on to win the Tony Award for his choreography of the show.	April 10
The U.S. Civil Rights Comm. votes to send back to staff a controversial report urging a one-year halt to programs under which some federal contracts were set aside for businesses owned by minorities or women. On April 10, the White House had publicly stated its support for such programs.... Two federal agents are killed and five wounded in a shootout in Miami, Fla. The incident, one of the bloodiest in the history of the Federal Bureau of Investigation, takes place before neighborhood residents and passersby during an operation to halt a string of armed robberies in the area. Two men thought to be the robberies' sole perpetrators were both killed.... Pres. Reagan and his wife Nancy paid $122,703 in federal income tax on a 1985 gross income of $394,492, according to their tax return, which the White House disclosed.		The government's producer price index fell a seasonally adjusted 1.1% in March, the Labor Dept. reports. The 12.4% annualized decline in the index during the first quarter is the largest in any quarter since the index was first calculated in 1947.		*Broken Rainbows* is released in New York City. The Academy Award-winning documentary about the displacement by the government of Navajo Indians is directed by Victoria Mudd.	April 11

F	G	H	I	J
Includes elections, federal-state relations, civil rights and liberties, crime, the judiciary, education, health care, poverty, urban affairs and population.	Includes formation and debate of U.S. foreign and defense policies, veterans' affairs and defense spending. (Relations with specific foreign countries are usually found under the region concerned.)	Includes business, labor, agriculture, taxation, transportation, consumer affairs, monetary and fiscal policy, natural resources, and pollution.	Includes worldwide scientific, medical and technological developments, natural phenomena, U.S. weather, natural disasters, and accidents.	Includes the arts, religion, scholarship, communications media, sports, entertainments, fashions, fads and social life.

	World Affairs	Europe	Africa & the Middle East	The Americas	Asia & the Pacific
April 12			Sudan holds its first election in 18 years; voting took place over the last 12 days to fill seats in a national assembly that is to run the country while writing a new constitution.		China's nominal parliament, the National People's Congress, concludes meetings to approve the nation's seventh five-year economic plan, for 1986 through 1990
April 13			After a week-long crisis, Israel's national unity coalition government once again narrowly avoids collapse with an agreement to reshuffle two cabinet portfolios and remove Likud-member Yitzhak Modai from his position as finance minister. Modai has been increasingly critical of Labor Party P.M. Shimon Peres.		
April 14		The 12 European Community foreign ministers meet in The Hague and agree to restrict the movements of Libyan diplomats, reduce their numbers, and demand stricter visa requirements of Libyan nationals. While the ministers' joint statement goes further than any previous one in identifying Libya as "implicated in supporting terrorism," it falls short of ordering the closure of Libyan embassies, as the United States and Britain have urged.	In a two-pronged attack, American warplanes bomb what the United States calls "terrorist-related" targets in Tripoli and Benghazi, Libya. Pres. Reagan says he ordered the air attacks in retaliation for the April 5 bombing of a West Berlin discotheque in which an American serviceman was killed, and to deter future Libyan-directed terrorist attacks. He warns of further military action unless Libyan leader Muammar el-Qaddafi stops his alleged support for anti-American terrorism.		
April 15			Libya fires two missiles at a U.S. Coast Guard installation on the tiny Italian island of Lampedusa, about 200 miles off the Libyan coast. Libya's official press agency says the site is "totally destroyed" in retaliation for yesterday's U.S. air raid, but the missiles apparently fell into the sea well short of their intended target. Italy strongly protests the attack.		
April 16					In the Philippines, supporters of ousted president Ferdinand E. Marcos stage a series of marches and rallies over the last four days demanding his reinstatement as president.... The Philippine government charges former Pres. Ferdinand E. Marcos and 25 others with embezzlement. Also charged are his wife Imelda, the couples' three children and 21 associates. The 26 are accused of misappropriating at least $5 bil. in U.S. military aid, foreign loans, and other funds.

A	B	C	D	E
Includes developments that affect more than one world region, international organizations and important meetings of major world leaders.	Includes all domestic and regional developments in Europe, including the Soviet Union, Turkey, Cyprus and Malta.	Includes all domestic and regional developments in Africa and the Middle East, including Iraq and Iran and excluding Cyprus, Turkey and Afghanistan.	Includes all domestic and regional developments in Latin America, the Caribbean and Canada.	Includes all domestic and regional developments in Asia and Pacific nations, extending from Afghanistan through all the Pacific Islands, except Hawaii.

U.S. Politics & Social Issues	U.S. Foreign Policy & Defense	U.S. Economy & Environment	Science, Technology & Nature	Culture, Leisure & Life Style	
Federal investigations of the political organization of ultra-right Lyndon H. LaRouche Jr. are under way in several localities, according to the *New York Times*.... Student writing skills in 1984 are no better than they were in 1974, the National Assessment of Education Progress reports. The group says gains made in the late 1970s have done nothing more than recover ground lost earlier in the decade.				Breyten Breytenbach, regarded as the Afrikaans language's most accomplished poet and writer, returns to South Africa after four years of self-imposed exile to receive his country's top literary award, the Rapport Prize. He won the award for a volume of poetry written while serving a seven-year prison sentence, from 1975 to 1982, for violating South Africa's terrorism laws.	**April 12**
	During a visit to the United States, Japan's Pres. Yasuhiro Nakasone meets with Pres. Reagan. At the end of the talks Nakasone says he expects Japan's trade surplus with the United States to decline by the autumn.			Pope John Paul II pays an unprecedented visit to a Jewish synagogue. In the first known visit by a pope to a synagogue, John Paul embraces Elio Roaff, Rome's chief rabbi, on the steps of Rome's main synagogue, which represents the oldest community in the Jewish diaspora. ... Jack Nicklaus, 46, wins the Masters golf tournament for an unprecedented sixth time.	**April 13**
The *Detroit News* and the *Detroit Free Press* end an old and expensive rivalry with the announcement that they will merge all operations except for news gathering and editing. The newspapers, two of the largest in the country, have vied for the lead in the Detroit market for some 30 years.		Outstanding consumer installment credit grew a seasonally adjusted $4.97 bil. in February, or at an annual rate of 11%, the Federal Reserve Board reports.		Simone De Beauvoir, 78, French author and leftist intellectual, dies in Paris. Her best-selling *The Second Sex* (1949), which condemned marriage as an "obscene bourgeois institution" that kept women from attaining their true individuality, was a literary cornerstone of the contemporary feminist movement. Her other works include several novels, four volumes of autobiography, and *The Coming of Age* (1970), an exhaustive study of the social treatment of the aged in many cultures.... After an absence of 61 years, legendary Russian-born pianist Vladimir Horowitz returns to the Soviet Union to perform two recitals, one in Moscow and one in Leningrad.	**April 14**
	A public opinion poll shows that the majority of Americans oppose Pres. Reagan's request for aid to the Nicaraguan Contras. However, the poll shows that less than half of those surveyed knew either the political orientation of the Sandinista government or which side the United States supports in the conflict.			Jean Genet, 75, dramatist, novelist, and poet who was one of the most important and controversial figures in postwar French literature, dies in Paris of throat cancer. The illegitimate child of a prostitute, he took to a life of beggary, theft, and homosexual prostitution and spent much of his youth and early adulthood in reformatories and prisons. His novels include: *Our Lady of the Flowers*, *The Thief's Journal* and *Miracle of the Rose*. His plays *Deathwatch*, *The Maids*, *The Balcony*, *The Blacks*, and *The Screens* are all considered classic examples of the theater of the absurd.	**April 15**
	Pres. Reagan and his top advisers meet at the White House to discuss continued adherence to the second Strategic Arms Limitation Treaty (SALT II). The administration in 1985 announced that it would abide by the treaty, which technically expired on December 31 of that year. The U.S. Senate has never ratified the pact.... Republicans in the House of Representatives use a surprise parliamentary maneuver to force a delay in a vote on Pres. Reagan's request for $100 mil. in aid to the Nicaraguan Contras. The tactic scuttles a Democratic maneuver to attach the Contra aid vote to a $1.7 bil. supplemental spending bill. The spending bill contains a number of provisions that Reagan opposes, and the president is thought likely to veto it.	Businesses plan to increase their capital spending in 1986 by only 0.9% from 1985 levels after accounting for inflation, according to a Commerce Dept. survey.		Svetlana Alliluyeva, daughter of the late Soviet leader Joseph Stalin, returns to the United States from the Soviet Union. Alliluyeva, 59, had been in the Soviet Union in late 1984 with her American-born daughter, Olga Peters, after 15 years in the United States and two in Great Britain. Olga Peters returns to Britain to resume her studies.... *Billboard*'s best-selling albums for the week are: *Whitney Houston*, Whitney Houston; *Heart*, Heart; *5150*, Van Halen; *Promise*, Sade; and *Falco 3*, Falco.	**April 16**

F	G	H	I	J
Includes elections, federal-state relations, civil rights and liberties, crime, the judiciary, education, health care, poverty, urban affairs and population.	Includes formation and debate of U.S. foreign and defense policies, veterans' affairs and defense spending. (Relations with specific foreign countries are usually found under the region concerned.)	Includes business, labor, agriculture, taxation, transportation, consumer affairs, monetary and fiscal policy, natural resources, and pollution.	Includes worldwide scientific, medical and technological developments, natural phenomena, U.S. weather, natural disasters, and accidents.	Includes the arts, religion, scholarship, communications media, sports, entertainments, fashions, fads and social life.

	World Affairs	Europe	Africa & the Middle East	The Americas	Asia & the Pacific
April 17					
April 18		Marcel (born Marcel Bloch) Dassault, 94, French aircraft designer and manufacturer, dies in Paris. A major figure in aviation history, he designed and built civil and military aircraft, including the best known of his planes, the Mirage fighter jet. His aircraft company was twice nationalized by left-wing French governments, and he was, as a Jew, stripped of his business interests during World War II and imprisoned in the Buchenwald concentration camp. Dassault was one of the richest men in Paris and the oldest member of the French parliament.	South Africa's Pres. Pieter W. Botha announces that the pass laws that severely control the movement of blacks will be rescinded. In a speech to Parliament, Botha says that blacks who have been convicted of violating the laws, one of the most hated aspects of the apartheid system of racial separation, and those in jail awaiting trial will be freed.		Vietnam says that because of the April 14 U.S. attack on Libya, it is suspending talks on American servicemen missing in action in the Vietnam War.... Australia's P.M. Bob Hawke concludes four days of talks with Pres. Reagan and other officials in the United States. Hawke's main objective was to gain assurances that Australian agricultural exports will not be damaged by U.S. farm policy, specifically the Export Enhancement Program.
April 19	The central banks of the United States and Japan each reduce by half a percentage point the interest rate they charge to member financial institutions. The widely expected cuts follow similar actions by France, Belgium, and several other smaller nations. The reductions mark the second round of coordinated rate cuts in six weeks.				
April 20			The public commission of inquiry into Israel's 1983 bank shares collapse issues its long-awaited report. It calls for sweeping changes in the country's capital markets and recommends that the governor of Israel's central bank and the heads of the country's four largest commercial banks resign or face dismissal in 30 days.		At least 300 people die after a double-decker ferry sinks on the Dhaleswari River in Bangladesh.... As many as 100 people are reported killed and as many as 20,000 families left homeless after a reservoir in northeastern Sri Lanka bursts its earthen embankment, releasing five billion cubic feet of water.

A	B	C	D	E
Includes developments that affect more than one world region, international organizations and important meetings of major world leaders.	Includes all domestic and regional developments in Europe, including the Soviet Union, Turkey, Cyprus and Malta.	Includes all domestic and regional developments in Africa and the Middle East, including Iraq and Iran and excluding Cyprus, Turkey and Afghanistan.	Includes all domestic and regional developments in Latin America, the Caribbean and Canada.	Includes all domestic and regional developments in Asia and Pacific nations, extending from Afghanistan through all the Pacific Islands, except Hawaii.

U.S. Politics & Social Issues	U.S. Foreign Policy & Defense	U.S. Economy & Environment	Science, Technology & Nature	Culture, Leisure & Life Style	
The U.S. Court of Appeals for the Third Circuit rules that package warning labels shielded tobacco companies from charges that customers have not been alerted to health hazards. By federal law, all cigarette and cigar packages carry such warnings.... The Rev. Jesse L. Jackson launches a new coalition of liberal activists, elected officials, labor leaders, and farmers that, he says, will become a permanent "progressive force" within the Democratic Party. The organization will be called the National Rainbow Coalition, a term Jackson first coined during his unsuccessful run for the 1984 Democratic presidential nomination.... The Federal Election Committee rejects proposals initiated by the self-styled citizens' lobby Common Cause to regulate the use of "soft money" in political campaigns.	U.S. military officials, examining intelligence gained from satellites and reconnaissance planes say that four of the five main Libyan targets bombed April 14 were hit and substantially damaged.... Americans overwhelmingly support the April 14 bombing of Libya, according to a *New York Times*/CBS News poll. The poll shows that 77% of the public approved of the raid and 14% disapproved. But 43% felt the raid would lead to more terrorism, and 30% thought it will lead to less.	The gross national product increased at an inflation-adjusted 3.2% annual rate for the first quarter, the Commerce Dept. reports. The inflation rate was 2.2%, the lowest since 1972.... The House approves by a 229-173 vote a bill to prohibit union construction contractors from setting up nonunion subsidiaries. The majority includes 29 Republicans, who support 200 Democrats in passing the legislation. The measure, viewed as a test of support for labor, will prevent a company from creating a nonunion subsidiary to transfer work away from a collective bargaining agreement, a practice known as "double breasting."		The 70th annual Pulitzer Prizes are awarded: biography, Elizabeth Frank, *Louise Bogan: A Portrait*; general nonfiction, Joseph Lelyveld, *Move Your Shadow: South Africa Black and White*, and J. Anthony Lucas, *Common Ground: A Turbulent Decade in the Lives of Three American families*; history, Walter A. McDougall, *...the Heavens and the Earth: A Political History of the Space Age*; music, George Perle, *Wind Quintet IV*; Fiction, Larry McMurtry, *Lonesome Dove*; poetry, Henry Taylor, *The Flying Change*; and public service, the *Denver Post* for its study of missing children.... The eighth annual, $100,000 Pritzker Architecture Prize is presented to Gottfried Boehm, a 66-year-old West German architect based in Cologne, West Germany.	**April 17**
		Americans' total personal income rose 0.2%, or $6 bil., in March to a seasonally adjusted annual rate of $3.407 trillion, according to the Commerce Dept. March consumer spending gains an adjusted 0.3%. ... The U.S. Synthetic Fuels Corp. officially ends its existence. Synfuels Corp. began as an ambitious attempt to help free the United States from dependence on foreign oil, an attempt soon beset by management mishaps, failed projects, charges of impropriety, and congressional protests over spending. Created in a time of soaring oil and gas prices, the project became a prime target for budget-cutting as energy costs fell and the federal deficit rose.	A Titan 34-D launch rocket and its secret military payload explode five seconds after lift-off from Vandenberg Air Force Base in California. The payload is reported to be a photographic reconnaissance satellite expected to be put into polar orbit around the Earth.		**April 18**
			The National Aeronautics and Space Admin. announces that the remains of each of the seven *Challenger* astronauts have been recovered from the Atlantic Ocean.	Michael Spinks defends his International Boxing Federation heavyweight title with a split decision over Larry Holmes.... *Arms and the Man*, a revival of George Bernard Shaw's classic antiwar comedy, opens at the Pasadena Playhouse in Pasadena, Calif. Directed by Nikos Psachoropoulos, with John Rubinstein, Richard Thomas, Carole Shelley, and Lisa Eichhorn, this production marks the reopening of one of the most celebrated regional theaters in the United States, which had declared bankruptcy in 1969 and had been dark ever since.	**April 19**
		Trade in agricultural products, long a source of a significant surplus for the United States, continues to deteriorate in early 1986, according to a report in the *New York Times*. Farm products make up only 14% of U.S. exports, the lowest percentage since 1940, according to the Commerce Dept.			**April 20**

F	G	H	I	J
Includes elections, federal-state relations, civil rights and liberties, crime, the judiciary, education, health care, poverty, urban affairs and population.	*Includes formation and debate of U.S. foreign and defense policies, veterans' affairs and defense spending. (Relations with specific foreign countries are usually found under the region concerned.)*	*Includes business, labor, agriculture, taxation, transportation, consumer affairs, monetary and fiscal policy, natural resources, and pollution.*	*Includes worldwide scientific, medical and technological developments, natural phenomena, U.S. weather, natural disasters, and accidents.*	*Includes the arts, religion, scholarship, communications media, sports, entertainments, fashions, fads and social life.*

	World Affairs	Europe	Africa & the Middle East	The Americas	Asia & the Pacific
April 21		In Britain Queen Elizabeth II celebrates her 60th birthday. Despite warnings of possible terrorist attacks, she remains true to her custom of mingling among her subjects on ceremonial occasions . . . In Spain, the socialist government of Premier Felipe Gonzalez announces that it will dissolve parliament and hold general elections, four months ahead of schedule. Political analysts say that the ruling socialists want to maintain the momentum of their recent victory in the referendum on continued membership in the North Atlantic Treaty Org. . . . The 11th Congress of the Socialist Unity (Communist) Party of East Germany concludes in East Berlin's Palace of the Republic. The congress is held once every five years.			
April 22	A seven-day meeting in Geneva of ministers from the Org. of Petroleum Exporting Countries adjourns after reaching agreement to limit production but without setting output quotas for individual nations. The long, acrimonious meeting, at which the ministers again sought means to firm up or reverse falling oil prices, is generally viewed as a minor success.	King Juan Carlos of Spain pays the first visit to Britain by a Spanish monarch since the king's grandfather, Alfonso XIII, came to England in 1905. The king and Queen Sofia are staying at the royal palace at Windsor during their three-day visit. During his visit the king will address a joint session of the House of Lords and the House of Commons.	Ahmed Mestiri, leader of Tunisia's main opposition party, the Social Democratic Movement, is jailed for his part in organizing a demonstration against the U.S. raid on Libya in March.		
April 23				A motion to prohibit comprehensive free-trade talks between the United States and Canada ends in a 10-10 vote in the U.S. Senate Finance Committee. The tie vote technically disapproves the motion, thus allowing the so-called "fast-track" negotiations to proceed.	The rise in the value of the Japanese yen against the dollar accelerates in mid-April with the Japanese currency hitting record highs against the dollar in four straight trading days during which the value of the dollar fell 4.2%; the dollar is now worth 167.98 yen.

A	B	C	D	E
Includes developments that affect more than one world region, international organizations and important meetings of major world leaders.	Includes all domestic and regional developments in Europe, including the Soviet Union, Turkey, Cyprus and Malta.	Includes all domestic and regional developments in Africa and the Middle East, including Iraq and Iran and excluding Cyprus, Turkey and Afghanistan.	Includes all domestic and regional developments in Latin America, the Caribbean and Canada.	Includes all domestic and regional developments in Asia and Pacific nations, extending from Afghanistan through all the Pacific Islands, except Hawaii.

U.S. Politics & Social Issues	U.S. Foreign Policy & Defense	U.S. Economy & Environment	Science, Technology & Nature	Culture, Leisure & Life Style	
A U.S. Census Bureau study finds 13% of adults living in the United States to be illiterate in English, the *New York Times* reports.... The Supreme Court rules, 5-4, that a person suing a news organization for libel must prove that damaging statements are false "on matters of public concern."	The White House announces that Pres. Reagan has made a "tentative" decision to stay within the limits of the second Strategic Arms Limitation Treaty (SALT II).	Today's Dow Jones Industrial Average closing of 1855.90 sets a record high.		Rob de Castella of Australia wins the 90th Boston Marathon in a time of 2:7:51. The time is the best ever for the Boston Marathon and the third fastest on record. Ingrid Kristiansen of Norway is the first woman to finish the marathon in a time of 2:24:55.	**April 21**
The Supreme Court rules that police need no more stringent justification for a warrant to seize pornographic videocassettes than for a warrant to seize other materials, such as weapons or drugs.... David Livingston Funchess, 39, is electrocuted in Starke, Fla. The Vietnam War veteran, diagnosed as suffering from post-traumatic stress disorder stemming from his service in Vietnam, stabbed two people to death while trying to hold up a Jacksonville bar in 1974. Funchess was convicted in 1975, five years before the disorder was recognized as a legal defense, and he is the first veteran with that diagnosis to be executed.... National Broadcasting Co. (NBC) enjoyed the highest prime-time viewership of the three television networks for the 1985-86 season, according to viewer ratings released by A. C. Nielsen Co. The last time NBC was the undisputed ratings leader was the 1954-55 season.... A New York federal grand jury indicts 17 people, including a retired Israeli general, in connection with a plot to sell Iran more than $2 bil. in U.S.-made weapons.		The Republican-controlled Senate overwhelmingly rejects Pres. Reagan's proposals to eliminate a wide array of domestic programs. The vote comes on an amendment to the bipartisan budget voted out of the Senate Budget Committee a month earlier. The amendment would have killed 43 of the 44 domestic programs whose termination was sought by the president. ... The government's consumer price index (CPI) fell a seasonally adjusted 0.4% in March, according to the Labor Dept. The CPI also fell an adjusted 0.4% in February, and the consecutive declines are the first since mid-1965, and the 1.9% annualized decline for the first quarter is the biggest since 1954. ... *The Triumph of Politics: Why the Reagan Revolution Failed*, former White House Budget Dir. David A. Stockman's account of Pres. Reagan's tax-cut program of 1981, is published. The book describes Stockman's conflicts with administration officials after he concluded that supply-side economics—"Reaganomics"—would not work. ... Air pollution remains a "serious public health problem" in the United States, the Environmental Protection Agency warns in a report on air quality for 1984.	The Dept. of Agriculture lifts its two-week ban on the sale of a live genetically engineered virus designed as a vaccine against a costly swine infection, pseudorabies. The department says its review shows that the virus poses virtually no danger to human beings or the environment.	Mircea Eliade, 79, Romanian-born historian of religions who came to be regarded as perhaps the world's foremost authority on spiritual myths and symbolism and perhaps the foremost Western interpreter of Eastern religions, dies in Chicago. Long associated with the Univ. of Chicago, he was the author of more than 50 books, including several novels, as well as such landmarks as the definitive three-volume *A History of Religious Ideas* (1979-85).	**April 22**
Five weeks after winning the Illinois Democratic gubernatorial primary, Adali E. Stevenson III resigns as the party's candidate and files a federal lawsuit to enable him to run as an independent. Stevenson took the drastic step in an effort to separate himself from two candidates who are followers of the ultra-right political organizer Lyndon H. LaRouche Jr. The two beat Stevenson's hand-picked candidates to gain the nominations for lieutenant governor and secretary of state.		James C. Fletcher, head of the National Aeronautics and Space Admin. (NASA) from 1971 to 1977, faces tough questioning at a Senate confirmation hearing on his reappointment as NASA administrator. The *New York Times* reports that federal audits show that NASA wasted billions of dollars through bad management and that Fletcher was far off the mark in projecting costs of the shuttle program.		Harold (born Hyman Arluck) Arlen, 81, composer active on Broadway and in Hollywood, dies in New York City. He created some of the most enduring tunes in American popular music, including "Get Happy," "I Love a Parade" and "Stormy Weather," written in collaboration with lyricist Ted Koehler. In 1938, he collaborated with E.Y. Harburg on the songs for *The Wizard of Oz*, and won an Oscar in 1939 for "Over the Rainbow." Among his other hits were "Blues in the Night" and "That Old Black Magic." ... Otto Ludwig Preminger, 80, motion picture producer and director with a reputation as a tempestuous tyrant and who achieved great success in the film industry while operating largely outside the Hollywood studio structure, dies. The Supreme Court ruled that local censorship boards could not halt the showing of his film, *The Moon is Blue* (1953). Other notable Preminger films include *Laura* (1944), *The Man with the Golden Arm* (1955), and *Anatomy of a Murder* (1959).	**April 23**

F	G	H	I	J
Includes elections, federal-state relations, civil rights and liberties, crime, the judiciary, education, health care, poverty, urban affairs and population.	Includes formation and debate of U.S. foreign and defense policies, veterans' affairs and defense spending. (Relations with specific foreign countries are usually found under the region concerned.)	Includes business, labor, agriculture, taxation, transportation, consumer affairs, monetary and fiscal policy, natural resources, and pollution.	Includes worldwide scientific, medical and technological developments, natural phenomena, U.S. weather, natural disasters, and accidents.	Includes the arts, religion, scholarship, communications media, sports, entertainments, fashions, fads and social life.

	World Affairs	Europe	Africa & the Middle East	The Americas	Asia & the Pacific
April 24		Fearing terrorist reprisals in the wake of the April 14 U.S. air raid on Libya, Western European governments are reported to have increased security measures and tightened curbs on Libyan diplomats and other nationals over the last week. . . . The European Community Comm. imposes a total of $56.24 mil. in fines on 15 petrochemical concerns for price fixing and market-sharing in polypropylene. The violations are found to have occurred between 1977 and 1983.	Nigerian pop music star Fela Anikulapo Kuti, who has a wide following in Europe and North America as well as Africa, is released from prison. A public critic of military rule and corruption in Nigeria, Fela was sentenced to five years' imprisonment on foreign currency trafficking charges in November 1984.		
April 25		The 12 farm ministers of the European Community reach agreement on an agriculture budget for 1986. The package includes what is described as a virtual price freeze on agricultural products. . . . A car bomb explodes in central Madrid killing five members of the paramilitary police corps, the Guardia Civil, and wounding eight other people, including four civil guards. Police focus their investigations on the Basque separatist group Euskadi ta Askatasuna.	Some 300 Libyan civilian aviation students in Britain are barred from flying and will have to leave the country within a few weeks, as the result of an order by Transportation Sec. Nicholas Ridley under the Aviation Security Act. . . . Prince Makhosetive Diamini is installed as King Mswati III of Swaziland in a secret tribal rite near Mbabane. The 18-year-old king has been attending a boarding school in England. He was chosen by the nation's supreme council in 1982 to succeed his father, King Sobhuza II, who died after a 61-year reign.	Nicaraguan Contra leader Adolfo Chamorro is arrested on his arrival in San Jose, Costa Rica from Miami April 22. He is deported to the United States this day.	
April 26			Qatari helicopters strafe the Fasht al-Dibal coral reef in the Persian Gulf, where a Dutch company is building a coast guard station for Bahrain. There are no injuries in the raid; Qatar also seizes 30 foreigners working at the site.		
April 27		Domingo Iturbe Abasolo, suspected leader of the military arm of Euskadi ta Askatasuna, is arrested by French police at a highway roadblock near the Spanish border. Known as "Txomin," Iturbe disappeared in February 1985 from Tours in central France, where he was under house arrest.		Air Canada begins a three-month, experimental ban on smoking on half of its Rapidair shuttle flights between Montreal, Toronto, and Ottawa. The earlier announcement of the experiment provoked a furor among tobacco companies, antismoking groups and the federal government.	

A	B	C	D	E
Includes developments that affect more than one world region, international organizations and important meetings of major world leaders.	Includes all domestic and regional developments in Europe, including the Soviet Union, Turkey, Cyprus and Malta.	Includes all domestic and regional developments in Africa and the Middle East, including Iraq and Iran and excluding Cyprus, Turkey and Afghanistan.	Includes all domestic and regional developments in Latin America, the Caribbean and Canada.	Includes all domestic and regional developments in Asia and Pacific nations, extending from Afghanistan through all the Pacific Islands, except Hawaii.

U.S. Politics & Social Issues	U.S. Foreign Policy & Defense	U.S. Economy & Environment	Science, Technology & Nature	Culture, Leisure & Life Style	
		An independent counsel is named to investigate criminal allegations that former Assist. Attorney Gen. Theodore B. Olson misled Congress during its confrontation with the Reagan administration in 1983 over access to environmental documents.		Two British parachutists jump off the 86th floor observation deck of New York City's Empire State Building and land safely a minute later two blocks away. They are Michael R.P. McCarthy, 25, and Alisdair Boyd, 28, both Londoners. McCarthy's chute got tangled in a traffic light and he was arrested. Boyd got away in a taxi. The two men are the first people to parachute from the landmark building since it was built 55 years earlier. . . . Wallis Warfield Simpson, Duchess of Windsor, 89, American divorcee who was at the heart of a British constitutional crisis in 1936, dies in Paris. When it became known that the newly crowned bachelor King Edward VIII wanted to marry Simpson and have her crowned queen, the combined opposition of his family, the government, and the Church of England led to his abdication in December 1936, and his being given the title the Duke of Windsor. They were married in 1937 and spent many years of self-imposed exile from Britain, but were mainstays of the international social circuit.	April 24
	Pres. Reagan leaves Washington on the first leg of a 13-day trip to the Far East for talks with Southeast Asian foreign ministers in Indonesia and to attend an economic summit of industrialized nations in Tokyo.		The National Aeronautics and Space Admin. (NASA) responds to an April 23 New York Times article, calling it "inaccurate" and "misleading" and outdated. The article, based largely on federal audits, said that NASA had wasted billions of dollars in past years through bad management and that spending on safety programs had been cut back sharply because of budgetary pressures.	Publisher Weekly's hardback fiction best-sellers for the week are: The Bourne Supremacy, Robert Ludlum; Lie Down with Lions, Ken Follett; Lake Wobegon Days, Garrison Keillor; The Mammoth Hunters, Jean M. Auel; and Break In, Dick Francis.	April 25
An alliance of moderate Republicans holds its first meeting in Chicago and charges that leading Republicans have been scared away by conservative threats. The self-styled Republican Mainstream Committee was founded by Rep. Jim Leach (Iowa) and other Republican moderates to counter conservative influence in the party.				Broderick Crawford, 74, stage, screen, and television actor, dies in Rancho Mirage, Calif., after a stroke. Noted for his large frame, raspy voice and gruff manner, in 1937 he created the role of Lennie in John Steinbeck's Of Mice And Men on Broadway, and in 1949 won an Academy Award for his performance in All the King's Men. He appeared in the classic 1950 comedy Born Yesterday with Judy Holliday and William Holden. He was known throughout America as the star of the television series "Highway Patrol" in the 1950s.	April 26
Mid-western Democrats begin a three-week advertising campaign on 180 radio stations in nine farm states, charging that farmers have been abandoned by the Reagan administration.					April 27

F	G	H	I	J
Includes elections, federal-state relations, civil rights and liberties, crime, the judiciary, education, health care, poverty, urban affairs and population.	Includes formation and debate of U.S. foreign and defense policies, veterans' affairs and defense spending. (Relations with specific foreign countries are usually found under the region concerned.)	Includes business, labor, agriculture, taxation, transportation, consumer affairs, monetary and fiscal policy, natural resources, and pollution.	Includes worldwide scientific, medical and technological developments, natural phenomena, U.S. weather, natural disasters, and accidents.	Includes the arts, religion, scholarship, communications media, sports, entertainments, fashions, fads and social life.

	World Affairs	Europe	Africa & the Middle East	The Americas	Asia & the Pacific
April 28		A serious accident at a nuclear power plant in the Soviet Ukraine spews clouds of radiation that eventually spread over the other nations in Europe. The accident involves the No. 4 reactor at the Chernobyl nuclear power plant, located in the town of Pripyat, about 60 miles north of Kiev.... Sweden is the first country outside of the USSR to learn of the Chernobyl accident. The discovery comes when workers at the Forsmark nuclear plant, located on the Baltic coast, detect unusually high levels of radiation. Forsmark is about 800 miles from the accident site.			
April 29	Passenger flights between the United States and the Soviet Union resume after a suspension of nearly five years.				On the occasion of Emperor Hirohito's 85th birthday, Japan holds celebrations to mark his 60-year reign.
April 30		In Norway, the three-party minority coalition government led by Conservative Premier Kaare Willoch collapses after losing a vote of confidence on a proposal to increase petroleum taxes.			Chen Bao-chung, a Chinese Air Force pilot who flew his MiG-19 to South Korea on February 21 and asked for political asylum in a third country, arrives in Taiwan and receives $1.7 mil. in gold as a reward for taking his plane out of China.... In India, central government commandos and paramilitary police seize the Golden Temple in Amritsar from Sikh extremists. The raid touches off renewed unrest in Punjab state. The Golden Temple is the Sikh religion's holiest site. In 1984 government forces reclaimed the temple from extremists in a bloody raid that outraged Sikhs, intensified separatist violence, and led to the assassination of P.M. Indira Gandhi.
May 1					At the request of Premier Prem Tinsulanonda, Thailand's King Bhumibol Adulyadej dissolves the national assembly after the government loses a parliamentary vote on a bill to raise taxes on gas- and diesel-powered vehicles.

A	B	C	D	E
Includes developments that affect more than one world region, international organizations and important meetings of major world leaders.	*Includes all domestic and regional developments in Europe, including the Soviet Union, Turkey, Cyprus and Malta.*	*Includes all domestic and regional developments in Africa and the Middle East, including Iraq and Iran and excluding Cyprus, Turkey and Afghanistan.*	*Includes all domestic and regional developments in Latin America, the Caribbean and Canada.*	*Includes all domestic and regional developments in Asia and Pacific nations, extending from Afghanistan through all the Pacific Islands, except Hawaii.*

U.S. Politics & Social Issues	U.S. Foreign Policy & Defense	U.S. Economy & Environment	Science, Technology & Nature	Culture, Leisure & Life Style	
Former Reagan aide Michael K. Deaver asks for the appointment of an independent counsel to investigate allegations that his lobbying activities violated federal conflict-of-interest laws.		The federal budget deficit for the first six months of FY1986—Oct. 1, 1985-March 31, 1986—reaches $136.34 bil., the Treasury Dept. reports. . . . Productivity among the nation's nonfarm businesses rose at a seasonally adjusted annual rate of 3.4% during the first quarter of 1986, according to the Labor Dept.		The Soviet Union defeats Sweden, 3-2, in Moscow to win the World Hockey Championships for a record 20th time.	April 28
Allies of Chicago Mayor Harold Washington (D) win runoff elections for two disputed city council seats, ending domination of the council by the forces of Washington's chief political rival, Cook County Democratic Chairman Edward R. Vrdolyak. . . . As many as 45% of the volumes stored in the Los Angeles Central Library are destroyed or damaged in a six-hour fire that hit the 60-year-old structure. Fire damage is estimated at about $20 mil.		The government's index of leading economic indicators rose 0.5% in March, the Commerce Dept. reports.		Running back Bo Jackson of Auburn is the first college player selected in the National Football League's annual draft of college players.	April 29
The Supreme Court rules, 7-2, that exclusion of blacks and other minorities from juries by prosecutors on the basis of race violates the 14th Amendment guarantee of "equal protection of the laws." . . . A poll by the nongovernment education research group, National Center for Education Information, finds that 90% of teachers surveyed say that they enjoy their work. Job dissatisfaction and fatigue among teachers (so-called burn-out) has in recent years been painted as a real problem for U.S. schools.	Republican members of the House of Representatives fail to obtain the 218 signatures needed to force a new vote on Pres. Reagan's request for $100 mil. in aid to the Nicaraguan Contras.	The U.S. deficit on merchandise trade increased in March to $14.52 bil., the Commerce Dept. reports. . . . Prices received by farmers for their raw agricultural goods fell 1.6% in April, the Agriculture Dept. reports, to their lowest levels since late 1978. . . . The Dow Jones Industrial Average closes down 41.91 points, in the largest single-day decline on record. In percentage terms the Dow fell 2.3%.	The failure of a safety seal on the space shuttle *Challenger* was almost inevitable because of the combination of cold weather at the launch site Jan. 28 and serious design flaws, the *New York Times* reports on the basis of recent tests.	Robert Stevenson, 81, British-born film director, dies in Santa Barbara, Calif. While at Walt Disney Productions (1956-77), he directed a number of fantasy and adventure films for younger viewers, including *Mary Poppins* (1964). His pre-Disney movies include *King Solomon's Mines* (1937) and *Jane Eyre* (1943).	April 30
The black community of Indianola, Miss., calls off a five-week boycott of local white-owned businesses, after the town's Consolidated School District Board appoints the protesters' candidate as school superintendent. . . . A federal jury in Tucson, Ariz., convicts eight Christian church activists of smuggling or harboring illegal immigrants from El Salvador and Guatemala into the United States.			After the April 28 Chernobyl accident at a nuclear power plant, Moscow contends that the situation at Chernobyl is under control, saying that radiation levels in the area are down by 33%-50%. However, the government does not say how high the radiation was to begin with, or when the decline took place. . . . Five men and one woman of an eight-member expedition led by Will Steger and Paul Schurke become the first explorers since Adm. Robert Peary in 1909 to reach the North Pole assisted only by dogs. They are also the first to have their position at the North Pole confirmed by satellite reading and overflying aircraft. The other team members are Geoff Carroll, Brent Boddy, Richard Weber and Ann Bancroft.	An exhibition of 41 landmark Impressionist and modern paintings on loan from the Soviet Union opens at the National Gallery of Art in Washington, D.C.	May 1

F	G	H	I	J
Includes elections, federal-state relations, civil rights and liberties, crime, the judiciary, education, health care, poverty, urban affairs and population.	*Includes formation and debate of U.S. foreign and defense policies, veterans' affairs and defense spending. (Relations with specific foreign countries are usually found under the region concerned.)*	*Includes business, labor, agriculture, taxation, transportation, consumer affairs, monetary and fiscal policy, natural resources, and pollution.*	*Includes worldwide scientific, medical and technological developments, natural phenomena, U.S. weather, natural disasters, and accidents.*	*Includes the arts, religion, scholarship, communications media, sports, entertainments, fashions, fads and social life.*

	World Affairs	Europe	Africa & the Middle East	The Americas	Asia & the Pacific
May 2	Australia-born Salvation Army officer Eva Burrows, 56, is elected the first woman general of the Salvation Army worldwide in nearly half a century.			Expo 86, the 1986 world's fair, opens in Vancouver, British Columbia, with representation from more than 50 nations and 40 corporations. Expo officials expect about 20 million visitors before it closes October 31.	
May 3					
May 4		Kurt Waldheim, the former UN secretary general, narrowly fails to win an outright majority in Austria's presidential elections. A runoff between Waldheim, running as an independent with the backing of the opposition People's Party, and Kurt Steyrer, the candidate of the ruling Socialist Party, is scheduled for June 8. A controversy over accusations that Waldheim had links to the Nazis during World War II has dominated the campaign.			Babrak Karmal, who was installed as leader of Afghanistan when Soviet troops intervened in the country in 1979, resigns as secretary general of the ruling Communist Party.
May 5					UN-mediated talks between Afghanistan and Pakistan resume in Geneva. The resumption of talks is thought to be linked to yesterday's announced change in leadership in Afghanistan.

A	B	C	D	E
Includes developments that affect more than one world region, international organizations and important meetings of major world leaders.	Includes all domestic and regional developments in Europe, including the Soviet Union, Turkey, Cyprus and Malta.	Includes all domestic and regional developments in Africa and the Middle East, including Iraq and Iran and excluding Cyprus, Turkey and Afghanistan.	Includes all domestic and regional developments in Latin America, the Caribbean and Canada.	Includes all domestic and regional developments in Asia and Pacific nations, extending from Afghanistan through all the Pacific Islands, except Hawaii.

U.S. Politics & Social Issues	U.S. Foreign Policy & Defense	U.S. Economy & Environment	Science, Technology & Nature	Culture, Leisure & Life Style	
		The nation's unemployment rate fell to a seasonally adjusted level of 7.0% of the work force in April, the Labor Dept. reports.... Pres. Reagan signs emergency legislation enabling the Federal Housing Admin. (FHA) to resume insuring mortgages. The bill, which passed the House and Senate April 30, also will allow the Government National Mortgage Assoc. (Ginnie Mae) to resume insuring privately issued securities backed by FHA and Veterans Admin. mortgages. ... The Republican-controlled Senate adopts a $1 trillion federal budget for FY1987. The plan, which has won strong bipartisan support, includes more than $10 bil. in tax increases and a rise in defense spending that is only half the amount sought by Pres. Reagan.	The journal *Science* reports that new tests have established the genuineness of one of science's most famous fossils, Archaeopteryx, a transitional form between dinosaurs and modern birds, which was publicly questioned in 1985 by scientists.	August Wilson's *Joe Turner's Come and Gone* opens at the Yale Repertory Theater in New Haven, Conn. Set in 1911 Pittsburgh, the play concerns a black ex-con who shatters the calm of a boarding house when he arrives with his daughter in search of his wife. The play is directed by Lloyd Richards and stars Charles S. Dutton and Ed Hall.	May 2
As 100 national democratic leaders meet in Atlanta over two days on policy issues, a rival group of more than 1,000 party activists convenes in Washington, D.C., in an attempt to check what they see as a rightward shift by the party's national leadership.			An unmanned National Aeronautics and Space Admin. Delta rocket loses power about 70 seconds after lift-off at Cape Canaveral, Fla., veers out of control and is destroyed by remote signal from an Air Force range safety officer. It is the third consecutive failure of a major space launch, following the loss of the space shuttle *Challenger* Jan. 28 and the explosion on April 18 of a Titan 34-D launch rocket.	Ferdinand, a 17-1 longshot wins the 112th Kentucky Derby at Churchill Downs, with 54-year-old Bill Shoemaker in the saddle.... Heavyweight Mike Tyson wins a unanimous 10-round decision over James (Quick) Tillis. The decision breaks Tyson's record streak of 19 consecutive knockouts at the beginning of a career.	May 3
				In tennis, Steffi Graf of West Germany wins the women's and Andres Gomez of Ecuador wins the men's U.S. Open Clay Court Championship.	May 4
		Personal income in the United States rose an average of 5.3% in 1985, according to the Commerce Dept. The increase, which is not adjusted for inflation, brings per capita income in the United States to $13,451.... First Boston Corp. says it has settled an insider trading case brought against it by the federal Securities and Exchange Comm. The securities firm gave up profits of $132,138 and agrees to pay a $264,276 fine, said to be the largest yet levied under the Insider Trading Sanctions Act of 1984.			May 5

F	G	H	I	J
Includes elections, federal-state relations, civil rights and liberties, crime, the judiciary, education, health care, poverty, urban affairs and population.	*Includes formation and debate of U.S. foreign and defense policies, veterans' affairs and defense spending. (Relations with specific foreign countries are usually found under the region concerned.)*	*Includes business, labor, agriculture, taxation, transportation, consumer affairs, monetary and fiscal policy, natural resources, and pollution.*	*Includes worldwide scientific, medical and technological developments, natural phenomena, U.S. weather, natural disasters, and accidents.*	*Includes the arts, religion, scholarship, communications media, sports, entertainments, fashions, fads and social life.*

	World Affairs	Europe	Africa & the Middle East	The Americas	Asia & the Pacific
May 6	In Tokyo, leaders of the seven major industrial democracies—the United States, Britain, West Germany, Italy, Canada, Japan, and France (the latter represented by both Socialist Pres. Francois Mitterrand and rightist Premier Jacques Chirac)—conclude their 12th annual summit with a tough statement denouncing terrorism and an agreement on the need to follow prudent, free-market oriented economic policies and to increase economic policy coordination. . . . Most participants at Tokyo depict the meeting as one of the most successful of its kind to date.		The military council that has ruled Sudan since overthrowing Pres. Gaafar el-Nimeiry in April 1985 keeps its promise to step down after a one-year transitional period and officially hands over power to a civilian coalition government. . . . Israel becomes the third U.S. ally to join the Strategic Defense Initiative. Britain joined in December 1985 and West Germany in March 1986.	Peru agrees to repay to the International Monetary Fund $110 mil. it owes in overdue interest, by August 15. Peru also agrees to repay a further $76 mil. that will fall due on that date.	Led by Malaysia's only Christian state chief minister, Joseph Pairin Kitingan, Party Bersatu Sabah wins a sweeping victory in state elections held in Sabah over the last two days. . . . Political opponents of South Korea's Pres. Chun Doo Hwan continue their campaign to press for reforms in the constitution. But protests by students demanding an end to Chun's regime grow increasingly violent, culminating in the deaths of two police officers, killed in clashes between students and police. . . . In India, the Lok Sabha (lower house) passes legislation that effectively frees Moslem husbands from paying alimony to their divorced wives. The 372-54 vote follows hours of angry debate and a walkout by many members of the opposition.
May 7		Technical experts of the European Community recommend a temporary ban on food and animal imports from Eastern Europe that might have been contaminated in the April 28 Chernobyl disaster. . . . Gaston Defferre, 75, veteran French socialist politician and vigorous anticommunist, dies after suffering head injuries in a fall yesterday at his home. A hero of the French Resistance in World War II, he played a major role in the regrowth of France's Socialist Party and was mayor of Marseilles for 33 years. As minister for France overseas in 1956, he was the architect of a law that gave autonomy to the African colonies and paved the way for their independence, and as Pres. Mitterrand's minister of the interior (1981-82) he worked to decentralize some powers from Paris to the regions.			Two U.S.-built F-16 fighter jets of Pakistan's air force shoot down one of four Afghan warplanes that penetrated several miles into Pakistani airspace. A second Afghan jet is damaged and is chased back across the border along with the other two planes.
May 8		The crisis at Chernobyl nuclear power plant in the Soviet Ukraine continues, as reports indicate that the core of the stricken reactor is still burning, following the April 28 accident. Soviet accounts and Western satellite surveillance suggest that the crisis had abated as of May 1, but there are new indications that the trouble persists and might worsen. . . . Lord (Emanuel) Shinwell, 101, combative, sharp-tongued veteran of the British trade union movement who became a leading Labour politician and held three successive cabinet posts in the Labour government headed by P.M. Clement Attlee, dies in London from complications from pneumonia. He gave up his seat in the House of Commons in 1970 and entered the House of Lords as a life peer. He was the first centenarian to address either house of Parliament. . . . In Britain, the ruling Conservative Party is set back in local elections and parliamentary by-elections. The party loses hundreds of local council seats and the previously safe parliamentary seat in Ryedale.		Oscar Arias Sanchez, 45, is sworn in as Costa Rica's 47th, and youngest, president. Arias, leader of the National Liberation Party, won the presidential election in February.	

A	B	C	D	E
Includes developments that affect more than one world region, international organizations and important meetings of major world leaders.	Includes all domestic and regional developments in Europe, including the Soviet Union, Turkey, Cyprus and Malta.	Includes all domestic and regional developments in Africa and the Middle East, including Iraq and Iran and excluding Cyprus, Turkey and Afghanistan.	Includes all domestic and regional developments in Latin America, the Caribbean and Canada.	Includes all domestic and regional developments in Asia and Pacific nations, extending from Afghanistan through all the Pacific Islands, except Hawaii.

U.S. Politics & Social Issues	U.S. Foreign Policy & Defense	U.S. Economy & Environment	Science, Technology & Nature	Culture, Leisure & Life Style	
Vice Pres. George Bush and his wife Barbara release their federal tax return for 1985. The document lists Bush's salary of $97,900 and investment earnings of $70,171, for a total income of $168,071. The Bushs paid $31,039, or 18.5% of their income, in federal taxes.		The financially ailing Farm Credit System, a network of 37 banks that forms the nation's biggest farm lender, reports a first-quarter loss of $206 mil. The system, for which Congress had passed emergency backing in 1985, posted losses of nearly $2.7 bil. in 1985.	Mary D. Gohlke, 50, the fourth person in history to undergo a combination heart and lung transplant, dies in Scottsdale, Ariz., of internal bleeding apparently caused by a fall. Gohlke had survived the operation for five years. . . . Two Soviet cosmonauts aboard a Soyuz T-15 transfer from one orbiting space station, *Mir*, to another, the *Salyut-7*, to become the first astronauts to perform such a feat. The transfer, which took 28 hours, began yesterday.	Taking its first major step toward creating a fourth television network, Rupert Murdoch's Fox Broadcasting Co. announces that comedian Joan Rivers will star in a new, one-hour, late-night entertainment program that will begin in the fall and will compete with the first half-hour of "The Tonight Show" hosted by Johnny Carson. . . . The Rev. Donald E. Pelotte, a 41-year-old Abenaki Indian from the Algonquin nation in Maine, becomes the first Native American to be ordained a bishop of the Roman Catholic Church.	**May 6**
	One day after the Senate voted 72-22, the House votes 356-62 to reject a Reagan administration plan to sell $354 mil. in advanced missiles to Saudi Arabia. The decisive margins of the votes are called "veto-proof" by opponents of the sale and appear to reflect a rising tide of anti-Arab sentiment on Capitol Hill.	Democrat and Republican members of the Senate Finance Committee triumphantly celebrate their unanimous approval of what is described as the most sweeping overhaul and simplification of the nation's tax code in decades.			**May 7**
Gov. Mark White (D) announces that 96.7% of Texas teachers passed a competency test administered by the state in March. . . . U.S. District Judge Robert L. Carter in New York City holds two major organizations of the Roman Catholic Church, the National Conf. of Catholic Bishops and the U.S. Catholic Conf., in contempt of court for refusing to divulge documents sought in a lawsuit over the church's tax-exempt status. The case was brought by Abortion Rights Mobilization and 20 other pro-choice groups and individuals.	A House Foreign Affairs subcommittee investigating possible misuse of $27 mil. in U.S. humanitarian aid to the Nicaraguan Contra rebels votes unanimously to subpoena U.S. bank records of Contra suppliers and brokers.	The House passes a $1.7 bil. emergency supplemental spending bill for fiscal 1986 that had been locked up by jurisdictional struggles among several committees and by Pres. Reagan's request for aid to the Nicaraguan rebels. However, Pres. Reagan threatens to veto it, chiefly because it would strip the president of some authority to defer previously authorized spending. . . . The Treasury Dept. over the last four days sold a record $27.03 bil. worth of notes and bonds at its regular quarterly refinancing auction. Interest rate yields resulting from the auction are the lowest since the mid-1970s.	A major study of cancer statistics published in the *New England Journal of Medicine* concludes that Americans' chances of dying of cancer have significantly increased over the last three decades.		**May 8**

F	G	H	I	J
Includes elections, federal-state relations, civil rights and liberties, crime, the judiciary, education, health care, poverty, urban affairs and population.	Includes formation and debate of U.S. foreign and defense policies, veterans' affairs and defense spending. (Relations with specific foreign countries are usually found under the region concerned.)	Includes business, labor, agriculture, taxation, transportation, consumer affairs, monetary and fiscal policy, natural resources, and pollution.	Includes worldwide scientific, medical and technological developments, natural phenomena, U.S. weather, natural disasters, and accidents.	Includes the arts, religion, scholarship, communications media, sports, entertainments, fashions, fads and social life.

	World Affairs	Europe	Africa & the Middle East	The Americas	Asia & the Pacific
May 9		The new Norwegian cabinet contains eight women, including Labor Party Premier Gro Harlem Brundtland. The *Times* of London says that the eight women out of a total of 18 cabinet positions constitute "what is thought to be a world record" for the representation of women.		Six of the top military commanders under Nicaraguan Contra leader Eden Pastora Gomez cut their ties with him and join the U.S.-backed United Nicaraguan Opposition (UNO). The movement caps three years of bitter disagreement within Pastora's Democratic Revolutionary Alliance (Arde). The group split in 1984, leaving Pastora in control of a small faction. More recently, his followers reportedly complained that he was militarily inept and unable to raise funds.	
May 10				The Nicaraguan government charges two U.S. military officers attached to the embassy in Managua with spying.	
May 11					
May 12					U.S. District Judge John F. Keenan rules in New York that Indian and not U.S. courts should hear the lawsuits arising from the 1984 disaster at Union Carbide Corp.'s chemical plant in Bhopal, India.
May 13					

A	B	C	D	E
Includes developments that affect more than one world region, international organizations and important meetings of major world leaders.	Includes all domestic and regional developments in Europe, including the Soviet Union, Turkey, Cyprus and Malta.	Includes all domestic and regional developments in Africa and the Middle East, including Iraq and Iran and excluding Cyprus, Turkey and Afghanistan.	Includes all domestic and regional developments in Latin America, the Caribbean and Canada.	Includes all domestic and regional developments in Asia and Pacific nations, extending from Afghanistan through all the Pacific Islands, except Hawaii.

U.S. Politics & Social Issues	U.S. Foreign Policy & Defense	U.S. Economy & Environment	Science, Technology & Nature	Culture, Leisure & Life Style	
				UBS Switzerland, a 24.3-m (80-ft.) sloop, crosses the finish line near Portsmouth, England, to win the Whitbread round-the-world yacht race. The Swiss sloop, skippered by Pierre Fehlmann, won the 43,000-km (27,000-mi.) race in 117 days, 14 hours, and 31 minutes more than 2½ days faster than the previous record.	**May 9**
A New Orleans jury acquits Louisiana Gov. Edwin W. Edwards (D) of all charges in his second trial for fraud and racketeering. The first trial ended in December 1985 with a hung jury.					**May 10**
	In his weekly radio address Pres. Reagan emphatically endorses the sweeping tax overhaul measure approved by the Senate Finance Committee May 7.		Both Soviet and foreign experts from the International Atomic Energy Agency have asserted over the last three days that the immediate crisis at Chernobyl has ended; the nuclear accident occurred there April 28.	Fritz (Frederick Douglas) Pollard, 92, legendary black American football player and coach, dies in Silver Spring, Md. In 1916, after a sensational season as a halfback for Brown Univ., he became the first black to be named to an all-America college football team. He was also the only black ever to be a head coach in the National Football League (NFL), of the then-NFL Hammond, Ind., team, in 1924.	**May 11**
		H. Robert Heller, an economist for Bank of America, will be nominated to fill the vacant seat on the Federal Reserve Board, the White House announces. Heller will complete the unexpired term of Preston Martin, whose resignation becomes effective at the end of April.... Outstanding consumer installment credit grew a seasonally adjusted $3.71 bil. in March, or at an annual rate of 8.1% the Federal Reserve Board reports. The increase in consumer borrowing is the smallest since May 1983.... In federal court in New York City, the Securities and Exchange Comm. charges Dennis B. Levine, a managing director of the Wall Street securities firm Drexel, Burnham, Lambert, Inc., in what the agency describes as its largest insider trading case ever.		Elisabeth Bergner, 85, Austrian-born Jewish actress who was an international stage and screen star for four decades, dies in London. Her portrayal of Saint Joan in Max Reinhardt's 1924 Berlin production of George Bernard Shaw's play made her name known throughout the German-speaking world. In the early 1930s she settled in London and won acclaim there and in New York City, in 1936 appearing in the London production of Sir James Barrie's last play, *The Boy David*. She returned to the stage in West Germany and Austria in the 1950s. She also made a number of films in France and England.	**May 12**
			The inspector general of National Aeronautics and Space Admin. is investigating whether agency officials played a role in the reassignment of two Morton Thiokol Inc. engineers who testified that they opposed the disastrous launch of the space shuttle *Challenger* in January. The transfer of Allan McDonald and Roger Boisjoly became known May 10 when the presidential commission investigating the loss of the *Challenger* and its crew of seven released testimony taken at a closed hearing on May 2.... The Environmental Protection Agency grants a permit for a second outdoor experiment to test genetically altered bacteria designed to prevent frost damage in crop plants. The permit is issued to Steven Lindow of the Univ. of California.		**May 13**

F	G	H	I	J
Includes elections, federal-state relations, civil rights and liberties, crime, the judiciary, education, health care, poverty, urban affairs and population.	*Includes formation and debate of U.S. foreign and defense policies, veterans' affairs and defense spending. (Relations with specific foreign countries are usually found under the region concerned.)*	*Includes business, labor, agriculture, taxation, transportation, consumer affairs, monetary and fiscal policy, natural resources, and pollution.*	*Includes worldwide scientific, medical and technological developments, natural phenomena, U.S. weather, natural disasters, and accidents.*	*Includes the arts, religion, scholarship, communications media, sports, entertainments, fashions, fads and social life.*

	World Affairs	Europe	Africa & the Middle East	The Americas	Asia & the Pacific
May 14		Soviet leader Mikhail S. Gorbachev ends 18 days of public silence on the Chernobyl nuclear plant accident, which occurred on April 28. Gorbachev addressed the crisis in a 25-minute speech carried nationally on Soviet television. He said the accident started with a surge of power during maintenance on Chernobyl's No. 4 reactor. The surge produced steam and hydrogen that led to an explosion in the reactor building. . . . In Britain, the government-owned British Shipbuilders announce the closure of three shipyards with the loss of 3,500 jobs. At the same time the government says it will spend $15 mil. to help areas in which layoffs will occur.		Canada and the United States agree on the framework of a joint effort to clean up toxic chemicals in the Niagara River. The accord is announced in Washington, D.C., by Thomas McMillan, the Canadian environment minister, and Lee M. Thomas, the administrator of the Environmental Protection Agency.	In Indonesia the Jakarta High Court reduces the prison sentence imposed on retired Indonesian Lt. Col. Hartono Rekso Dharsono from 11 to seven years. Dharsono was convicted and sentenced for subversion in January.
May 15		Sinan Hasani becomes the president of Yugoslavia, succeeding Radovan Vlajkovic in the one-year post. Under the system in place since 1980, eight of the nine-member collective presidency takes turns as the titular head of state. The eight represent Yugoslavia's six constituent republics and two autonomous provinces. (The ninth seat of the leadership group is reserved for the president of the Central Committee Presidium, who does not become head of state.)			Australia's federal government and the state government of Western Australia announce a joint program to purchase land for thousands of Western Australian Aborigines. The program is intended to give Aborigines on many reserves and church mission stations the title to the land they live on.
May 16		The French government of rightist Premier Jacques Chirac scores its first major victory, winning the right to implement by decree its privatization program and some other economic initiatives. The government's "enabling bill" allowing nearly all state-owned enterprises to be sold by 1991 entered the National Assembly April 22.		The Supreme Military Council of Argentina's armed forces sentences Gen. Leopoldo Galtieri and two other members of the military junta that led Argentina into the Falkland (Malvinas) Islands war with Britain in 1982 to prison terms ranging from eight to 14 years. The men were found guilty of negligence in losing the war. . . . Eden Pastora Gomez, the leader of the Democratic Revolutionary Alliance (Arde) Contra group, declares that he is ending his fight against the Nicaraguan government, and crosses into Costa Rica where he asks for political asylum. Pastora says he will convert his rebel army into a political party in exile.	
May 17					

A	B	C	D	E
Includes developments that affect more than one world region, international organizations and important meetings of major world leaders.	Includes all domestic and regional developments in Europe, including the Soviet Union, Turkey, Cyprus and Malta.	Includes all domestic and regional developments in Africa and the Middle East, including Iraq and Iran and excluding Cyprus, Turkey and Afghanistan.	Includes all domestic and regional developments in Latin America, the Caribbean and Canada.	Includes all domestic and regional developments in Asia and Pacific nations, extending from Afghanistan through all the Pacific Islands, except Hawaii.

U.S. Politics & Social Issues	U.S. Foreign Policy & Defense	U.S. Economy & Environment	Science, Technology & Nature	Culture, Leisure & Life Style	
More than two years before the 1988 presidential elections, V.P. George Bush and Sen. Gary Hart (D, Colo.) are the voters' favorites, according to a Gallup Poll. Hart is the choice of 46% of respondents and Bush the choice of 44%.... The Senate takes a step toward controlling a politically embarrassing issue of how much mail lawmakers can send to constituents for free. The Senate unanimously adopts a resolution to restrict use of the so-called "free franking" privilege by senators for the remainder of fiscal 1986.... A federal appeals panel sets aside a lower court decision that requires the National Weather Service to pay $1.25 mil. in damages to the families of three lobstermen who died in a storm because they trusted an erroneous forecast.		The General Accounting Office reports to Congress that federal monitoring of airline safety is faulty and that the Federal Aviation Admin. "cannot say with assurance that airlines are complying with safety regulations."	The National Aeronautics and Space Admin. unveils a new draft of its $8 bil. manned space station that it plans to assemble in orbit in the 1990s in conjunction with other nations.	The *Pride of Baltimore*, a reproduction of a 19th-century Baltimore clipper ship, sinks in a violent storm in the Atlantic Ocean about 240 miles north of Puerto Rico. Four of the crew of 12 are drowned; the survivors are rescued by a Norwegian freighter May 19.... *Variety's* top-grossing films for the week are: *Short Circuit, Jo Jo Dancer, Your Life Is Calling, Blue City, Fire with Fire* and *Wise Guys*.... Dutch historians unveil a new, definitive edition of the diary of Anne Frank in which the Jewish girl recorded 26 months of hiding from the Nazi occupation forces with her family and other Jews.... *Chess*, a musical about a world chess championship marked by East-West political maneuvering, opens in London, with lyrics by Tim Rice, music by Benny Andersson and Bjorn Ulvaeus, and directed by Trevor Nunn.	May 14
			At a Moscow press conference, an international team of medical specialists reveal that 35 people are suffering from serious radiation poisoning as a result of the Chernobyl nuclear plant accident. The victims, 33 men and two women, were near the stricken reactor during the first hours of the crisis. All are being treated at a hospital in Moscow.... Scientists from around the world report on their findings from the historic space probes that passed by Halley's comet in March. In 38 articles in the British journal *Nature*, researchers for the first time offer a detailed picture of the comet's structure.	T(heodore) H(arold) White, 71, one of the most influential U.S. journalists of his time, dies in New York City, following a stroke. His book *The Making of the President 1960*, a chronicle of the dramatic presidential race between Richard Nixon and John F. Kennedy, a seminal work of modern political reporting, was a huge best-seller and garnered White the Pulitzer Prize for general nonfiction. He wrote similar accounts about the presidential elections of 1964, 1968, and 1972, as well as *Breach of Faith: The Fall of Richard Nixon* and a personal memoir, *In Search of History*. White first won recognition covering China for the *Manchester Guardian*, *Boston Globe* and *Time* magazine, and his first book, *Thunder Out of China* (1946) was also a best-seller.	May 15
A federal district judge in Chicago rejects a bid by Adlai E. Stevenson III (D) to run as an independent candidate for governor of Illinois. Stevenson challenged the Illinois election law, which set a December 1985 filing deadline for independents, before the regular party primaries and months before the filing deadline for third parties.... A federal district judge in Washington, D.C., rules that Pres. Reagan has no legal authority to withhold spending appropriated by Congress and approved by the president. The administration had angered members of both parties in Congress by attempting to pare 1986 spending by withholding monies already appropriated.... Nevada District Judge Harry Claiborne, 68, arrives at the federal prison camp at Maxwell Air Force Base in Montgomery, Ala., to begin a two-year sentence for tax evasion, thus becoming the first sitting federal judge in history to be incarcerated for offenses committed while serving on the bench.				*Top Gun* is released in New York. The film stars Tom Cruise, who portrays a pilot in the Navy's elite Fighter Weapons School, where he falls in love with his female astrophysics instructor, played by Kelly McGillis.	May 16
			Steve Wozniak, 35, the computer wizard who cofounded Apple Computer, Inc., the firm that launched the desktop computer industry and made Wozniak a multimillionaire, finally graduates from college, receiving an undergraduate degree from the Univ. of California at Berkeley.	In horse racing, Snow Chief wins the 111th running of the Preakness Stakes in Baltimore. Ferdinand, long-shot winner of the Kentucky Derby, finishes second.	May 17

F	G	H	I	J
Includes elections, federal-state relations, civil rights and liberties, crime, the judiciary, education, health care, poverty, urban affairs and population.	includes formation and debate of U.S. foreign and defense policies, veterans' affairs and defense spending. (Relations with specific foreign countries are usually found under the region concerned.)	Includes business, labor, agriculture, taxation, transportation, consumer affairs, monetary and fiscal policy, natural resources, and pollution.	Includes worldwide scientific, medical and technological developments, natural phenomena, U.S. weather, natural disasters, and accidents.	Includes the arts, religion, scholarship, communications media, sports, entertainments, fashions, fads and social life.

	World Affairs	Europe	Africa & the Middle East	The Americas	Asia & the Pacific
May 18					
May 19			South African ground and air forces strike at alleged guerrilla strongholds of the African National Congress in and around the capitals of neighboring Zimbabwe, Botswana, and Zambia. The raids provoke an international outrage and threaten to wreck an ongoing Commonwealth peace initiative.		
May 20		The Soviet Union appoints its chief delegate to the UN, Yuri Vladimirovich Dubinin, to succeed Anatoly F. Dobrynin as the ambassador to the United States. Dobrynin left the post to join the Secretariat of the Communist Party.			China and Taiwan hold three days of face-to-face talks on the return of a Taiwanese Boeing 747 cargo plane hijacked to China by its pilot May 3. The talks are the first since the communists took power in China in 1949.
May 21		British, West German, and Italian investigators are reported to be probing possible Syrian involvement in three terrorist incidents: the foiled attempt to blow up an Israeli El Al jetliner in London April 17, a bombing in West Berlin April 5, and the Rome airport massacre on Dec. 27, 1985. Growing evidence of Syrian involvement has begun to overshadow Libya's purported sponsorship of terrorism and prompts fears of a new war between Syria and Israel. . . . In the Netherlands, the center-right coalition of P.M. Ruud Lubbers scores an unexpected victory in the general election and retains its parliamentary majority. Pre-election polls had predicted that the coalition would be unseated by a slim margin.	A furor erupts in Israel over a highly critical internal report on the state of the Israeli Defense Forces (IDF). The academic study, drawn up in 1982-83 at the request of Chief of Staff Gen. Moshe Levy and in response to Israel's failures in the war in Lebanon, claims the IDF had lost much of its qualitative edge over its Arab enemies. The uproar results from the fact that the report was apparently largely ignored and suppressed by the high command.	In Guatemala, Pres. Vinicio Cerezo Arevalo announces that he has formally asked the United States for part of the $10 mil. in military aid authorized for Guatemala by the U.S. Congress in 1985. Cerezo requested less than $1 mil. for nonlethal equipment, including medicine and spare parts for trucks and helicopters. Military aid has been suspended since 1977 when the Carter administration tied such aid to improvements in human rights.	In Bangladesh, the pro-government Jatiya Party emerges as the winner of controversial parliamentary elections held May 7, according to results released today. The elections were marked by violence and charges of fraud, and the vote count was delayed briefly, prompting further charges of vote rigging.

A	B	C	D	E
Includes developments that affect more than one world region, international organizations and important meetings of major world leaders.	Includes all domestic and regional developments in Europe, including the Soviet Union, Turkey, Cyprus and Malta.	Includes all domestic and regional developments in Africa and the Middle East, including Iraq and Iran and excluding Cyprus, Turkey and Afghanistan.	Includes all domestic and regional developments in Latin America, the Caribbean and Canada.	Includes all domestic and regional developments in Asia and Pacific nations, extending from Afghanistan through all the Pacific Islands, except Hawaii.

U.S. Politics & Social Issues	U.S. Foreign Policy & Defense	U.S. Economy & Environment	Science, Technology & Nature	Culture, Leisure & Life Style	
				John (born John William Sublett) Bubbles, 84, inventor of the rhythm style of tap dancing, which involves the use of the heels to make a syncopated sound with the toes, dies in Los Angeles. He and Ford (Buck) Washington formed the dance team of "Buck and Bubbles," which became one of the most celebrated acts during the heyday of vaudeville. Bubbles also originated the role of Sportin' Life in George Gershwin's opera *Porgy and Bess.* . . . *Cuba and His Teddy Bear* a drama about a Cuban-American drug dealer and his teen-age son on New York City's Lower East Side, opens in New York City at the Public Theater. The play is written by Reinaldo Povod, directed by Bill Hart, with Robert De Niro and Ralph Macchio.	May 18
The Supreme Court rejects by a 5-4 vote, an affirmative action plan under which black schoolteachers in Jackson, Mich. retain their jobs while some whites with more seniority are laid off. The court's majority says the layoffs violate the white teachers' 14th Amendment right to "equal protection of the laws." . . . In a 5-4 decision the Supreme Court sees no constitutional impediment to aerial surveillance of private property by government investigators without warrants. . . . Pres. Reagan signs into law the Firearms Owners Protection Act, the first significant loosening of the firearms curb contained in the landmark Gun Control Act of 1968.		Gannett Co. announces that it has agreed to buy the *Louisville Courier-Journal* and *Louisville Times*. The newspapers had been put up for sale after prolonged feuding within the Bingham family, which owned the two papers. . . . In a nationally televised news conference, Pres. Reagan firmly rejects an increase in taxes, even one that would be used to fund his military build-up, as was urged by Senate and House budget conferees. He also reiterates his determination to fight for a balanced budget amendment to the Constitution.		The 39th annual international film festival in Cannes, France, awards its top prize, the Golden Palm, to *The Mission*, a British film directed by Roland Joffe.	May 19
The Senate Special Committee on Aging issues a staff report condemning conditions in the country's skilled nursing homes. Committee chairman, Sen. John Heinz (R, Pa.), asserts that too many of the homes "more closely resemble 19th-century asylums than modern health care facilities."		The gross national product rose 3.7% in the first quarter of 1986, according to a revised estimate released by the Commerce Dept. . . . After-tax profits of U.S. corporations fell a seasonally adjusted 4.9% in the first quarter of 1986, the Commerce Dept. reports, in the sharpest drop since the first quarter of 1982.	Helen Brooke Taussig, 87, American physician recognized as the founder of pediatric cardiology, dies in West Chester, Pa., of injuries sustained in an automobile accident. In the 1940s she and Dr. Alfred Blalock developed the first successful "blue baby" operation, a surgical procedure for children born with congenital heart defects that causes their skin to turn blue because of lack of oxygen. In 1959 she was the first woman to become a full professor at the Johns Hopkins Medical School, and in 1965 she became the first woman to be elected president of the American Heart Assoc.	After a final, 12-hour assault, Canadian climbers Sharon Wood, 28, and Dwayne Congdon, 29, both of Canmore, Alberta, reach the top of Mt. Everest at twilight. With the conquest, Wood becomes the first North American woman to scale the world's tallest mountain.	May 20
Pres. Reagan remarks that lack of information, and not government policy, is to blame for any hunger in America. Poverty activists and experts on hunger assail his remarks. A Harvard School of Public Health task force reports today that the number of poor grew by 4 million from 1980 to 1985.	Pres. Reagan vetoes a congressional resolution blocking a scaled-down sale of advanced U.S. missiles to Saudi Arabia. The Senate postpones a vote on overriding or sustaining the veto until after the two-week Memorial Day recess.	Jackie Presser, president of the Teamsters union, indicted on federal racketeering charges May 16, is overwhelmingly reelected for five more years as president of the union. . . . The government's consumer price index fell a seasonally adjusted 0.3% in April, according to the Labor Dept. . . . Americans' total personal income rose 1.2%, or $35 bil., in April to a seasonally adjusted annual rate of $3.447 trillion, according to the Commerce Dept.		*Billboard's* best-selling albums for the week are: *Whitney Houston*, Whitney Houston; *5150*, Van Halen; *Like a Rock*, Bob Seger & the Silver Bullet Band; *Parade*, Prince and the Revolution; and *Pretty in Pink* (movie soundtrack). . . . After performing in Vancouver as part of Expo '86, Leningrad's Kirov Ballet makes its first U.S. appearance in 22 years in Pasadena, Calif. The Kirov's North American tour ends in Canada June 14.	May 21

F	G	H	I	J
Includes elections, federal-state relations, civil rights and liberties, crime, the judiciary, education, health care, poverty, urban affairs and population.	*Includes formation and debate of U.S. foreign and defense policies, veterans' affairs and defense spending. (Relations with specific foreign countries are usually found under the region concerned.)*	*Includes business, labor, agriculture, taxation, transportation, consumer affairs, monetary and fiscal policy, natural resources, and pollution.*	*Includes worldwide scientific, medical and technological developments, natural phenomena, U.S. weather, natural disasters, and accidents.*	*Includes the arts, religion, scholarship, communications media, sports, entertainments, fashions, fads and social life.*

	World Affairs	Europe	Africa & the Middle East	The Americas	Asia & the Pacific
May 22		At a meeting in Brussels, the defense ministers of North Atlantic Treaty Org. approve a U.S. plan to resume the production of chemical weapons.	In South Africa, right-wing white extremists storm and take over a meeting hall in the Transvaal city of Pietersburg, preventing a political rally by the ruling National Party. . . . In an interview in Damascus, Syria, Massoud Barzani claims that guerrillas of the Kurdish Democratic Party have made major gains in their fight for autonomy against the Iraqi government.	In the opening round of the so-called "fast-track" trade talks between the United States and Canada, held in Ottawa, both sides emphasize that the objective of the negotiations is an elimination of bilateral trade barriers. At the same time, Pres. Reagan announces a 35% import duty on Canadian cedar wood products, provoking widespread dismay in Canada. . . . In Mexico, the government raises the price of tortillas, the mainstay of the Mexican diet, more than 75% to 80 pesos a kilogram from 45 pesos. The move is part of an effort to reduce government subsidies.	
May 23		Soviet leader Mikhail S. Gorbachev realigns the nation's foreign policy in a closed-door conference with the nation's senior diplomatic officials. Few details of the meeting are made public, but sources contacted by the Western press maintain that unquestioned control over foreign policy has been given to the international department of the Communist Party Central Committee.	A new round of fighting erupts between Lebanese and Shiite Moslem militiamen and Palestinian guerrillas in three Beirut refugee districts.		
May 24			Margaret Thatcher becomes the first British prime minister to visit Israel when she arrives for a three-day visit. The visit appears to ease some previous tensions in relations between London and Jerusalem.		
May 25				The presidents of Costa Rica, El Salvador, Guatemala, Honduras and Nicaragua conclude a two-day summit at Esquipulas, Guatemala, to discuss a regional peace treaty. A June 6 deadline is set for the signing of a treaty sponsored by the Contadora Group, made up of Colombia, Mexico, Panama, and Venezuela. . . . Virgilio Barco Vargas, 64, wins a landslide victory in Colombia's presidential elections. The victory of the Liberal Party candidate was widely predicted.	Afghan rebels recapture their base at Zhawar six days after it fell to Soviet-backed government forces at the height of a three-week offensive by the Afghan Army.
May 26				In the Dominican Republic, former president Joaquin Balaguer of the Social Christian Reform Party is provisionally declared the winner of presidential elections held 10 days earlier. Balaguer, age 78 and blind, was president for three terms between 1966 and 1978.	

A	B	C	D	E
Includes developments that affect more than one world region, international organizations and important meetings of major world leaders.	Includes all domestic and regional developments in Europe, including the Soviet Union, Turkey, Cyprus and Malta.	Includes all domestic and regional developments in Africa and the Middle East, including Iraq and Iran and excluding Cyprus, Turkey and Afghanistan.	Includes all domestic and regional developments in Latin America, the Caribbean and Canada.	Includes all domestic and regional developments in Asia and Pacific nations, extending from Afghanistan through all the Pacific Islands, except Hawaii.

U.S. Politics & Social Issues	U.S. Foreign Policy & Defense	U.S. Economy & Environment	Science, Technology & Nature	Culture, Leisure & Life Style	
	Attorney Gen. Edwin Meese III apologizes for harsh criticisms about Mexico's handling of drug trafficking, illegal immigration, and a weak economy in congressional hearings May 13. Tensions between the two countries remains high as the officials who testified at the hearings stand by their remarks.	The House passes wide-ranging trade legislation designed to reverse trends that have contributed to record U.S. trade deficits in each of the last four years. Pres. Reagan calls the legislation "rankly political" and warns that its enactment "could plunge the world into a trade war." . . . The Environmental Protection Agency authorizes use of a pesticide containing dichlorodiphenyl-trichloro-ethane (DDT), banned in 1972, in limited amounts.	A space program for the early years of the 21st century is unveiled by the National Comm. on Space, a 15-member panel headed by Thomas O. Paine, who served as National Aeronautics and Space Admin. administrator during the Apollo program. The commission's report envisions a new generation of space vehicles in the immediate future, a return to the moon by 2005, and colonization there by small groups of about 20 people, eventually expanding the effort to mining, manufacturing, and scientific bases.		May 22
	The United States orders the expulsion of Brig. Alexander Potgeiter, South Africa's senior military attache in Washington, D.C. The move comes in response to Pretoria's May 19 military strikes against three black-ruled neighboring states.			Sterling (born Sterling Relyea Walter) Hayden, 70, strapping actor who won critical acclaim for his performances in such Hollywood films as *The Asphalt Jungle* (1950), *Johnny Guitar* (1954) and *The Killing* (1956), dies of cancer in Sausalito, Calif. One of his most compelling roles was that of Jack D. Ripper, the mad U.S. Air Force general in *Dr. Strangelove* (1964). He also wrote two successful books, *Wanderer* (1963) and *Voyage: a Novel of 1896*.	May 23
			According to a *Washington Post*/ABC News poll released, opposition to nuclear energy has risen to record levels in the United States following the Soviet Chernobyl nuclear reactor accident in April. Of 1,506 people interviewed, 78% say they oppose building new nuclear plants and 41% say they would like to see existing plants phased out.	The Montreal Canadiens win the National Hockey League's Stanley Cup championship with a 4-3 win over the Calgary Flames.	May 24
More than five million Americans hold hands in a human chain that stretches across virtually all of the United States. The event, known as Hands Across America, was organized to put a national spotlight upon the problems of poverty and homelessness. . . . Chester Bliss Bowles, 85, U.S. public official who held high posts in four Democratic administrations and personified the liberal wing of the Democratic Party in the 1950s and 1960s, dies in Essex, Conn. The founding partner of the advertising agency originally known as Benton & Bowles, he was elected governor of Connecticut in 1948, and he was twice ambassador to India (1951-53 and 1963-69). He authored several books, including *Ambassador's Report* (1954) about his first diplomatic tour of India.				Sport Aid, a week-long series of events staged to raise money for African famine relief, ends today with a group of sponsored mass runs. An estimated 20 million people in 78 countries and 300 cities take part in the so-called Race Against Time, a sequel to 1985's Live Aid concert spectacular.	May 25
	On Memorial Day, a ceremony at the Vietnam Veterans Memorial in Washington, D.C., honors 110 deceased servicemen whose names are added to the list of the war dead and missing engraved on the monument's black granite wall.	Bethlehem Steel Corp. and the United Steelworkers of America reach agreement on a 37-month labor contract that calls for major pay concessions and a profit-sharing plan for the employees.		In cricket, India wins the Texaco Trophy in the second of two one-day internationals in England. The first match was held May 24.	May 26

F	G	H	I	J
Includes elections, federal-state relations, civil rights and liberties, crime, the judiciary, education, health care, poverty, urban affairs and population.	Includes formation and debate of U.S. foreign and defense policies, veterans' affairs and defense spending. (Relations with specific foreign countries are usually found under the region concerned.)	Includes business, labor, agriculture, taxation, transportation, consumer affairs, monetary and fiscal policy, natural resources, and pollution.	Includes worldwide scientific, medical and technological developments, natural phenomena, U.S. weather, natural disasters, and accidents.	Includes the arts, religion, scholarship, communications media, sports, entertainments, fashions, fads and social life.

	World Affairs	Europe	Africa & the Middle East	The Americas	Asia & the Pacific
May 27	The United States and Japan announce that they have reached an agreement to share information on investigations of securities fraud. The agreement comes as an increasing amount of American money is being invested in Japanese securities.				Japan becomes the world's largest net creditor nation in 1985, according to a report by the Japanese finance ministry. The report estimates the country's net assets abroad at $129.8 bil. in 1985, a $55.5 bil. jump over the $74.3 bil. reported for 1984. . . . In an unprecedented move, Thailand's Premier Prem Tinsulanonda dismisses the army commander in chief, Gen. Arthit Kamlangek. Although no reason is given, government officials the next day say he had been suspected of "hatching a plot" to overthrow Prem.
May 28				In Barbados, the opposition Democratic Labour Party led by former prime minister Errol Barrow wins a landslide victory in general elections, gaining 24 of 27 seats in parliament.	Indonesia and Papua New Guinea hold two days of talks in Jakarta on a friendship and cooperation treaty. The meeting ends a day earlier than scheduled and without final agreement.
May 29		The European Community imposes permanent standards for acceptable radiation levels in food. The new rules replace a ban on food imports from Eastern Europe enacted following the Chernobyl nuclear plant accident in the Soviet Union on April 28. The new restrictions will apply to food shipments as well as to food imported from other areas.			Australia's tiny Democratic Party agree to a modified version of the government's proposed tax on fringe benefits, which are opposed especially by businesses and the automobile industry, in exchange for implementation of tax cuts by December 1.
May 30					The Japanese government adopts a series of measures to help offset the impact of the strong yen on the economy. The yen gained about 30% against the U.S. dollar since the Group of Five in September 1985 agreed to cooperate in bringing down the value of the dollar against other major currencies.

A	B	C	D	E
Includes developments that affect more than one world region, international organizations and important meetings of major world leaders.	Includes all domestic and regional developments in Europe, including the Soviet Union, Turkey, Cyprus and Malta.	Includes all domestic and regional developments in Africa and the Middle East, including Iraq and Iran and excluding Cyprus, Turkey and Afghanistan.	Includes all domestic and regional developments in Latin America, the Caribbean and Canada.	Includes all domestic and regional developments in Asia and Pacific nations, extending from Afghanistan through all the Pacific Islands, except Hawaii.

U.S. Politics & Social Issues	U.S. Foreign Policy & Defense	U.S. Economy & Environment	Science, Technology & Nature	Culture, Leisure & Life Style	
Michigan kicks off the earliest presidential campaign ever, as thousands of Republicans file petitions for the state's Republican primary. The primary is the first step in picking Republican National Convention delegates for 1988.	Pres. Reagan affirms a tentative decision to stay within the limits of the 1979 Strategic Arms Limitation Treaty (SALT II) by dismantling two Poseidon ballistic submarines. However, the president and some of his top aides take a hard line on future compliance.	The Supreme Court rules that the Federal Communications Comm. does not have the authority to regulate rate-making for interstate telephone service.	National Aeronautics and Space Admin. administrator James C. Fletcher reports that 44 potentially serious safety problems have been picked out by the agency for remedy before shuttle flights can be resumed.		**May 27**
		A federal appeals court in Philadelphia rules that Wheeling-Pittsburgh Steel Corp. was not justified in using the federal Bankruptcy Code to break a collective bargaining agreement with the United Steelworkers of America in 1985. . . . The Environmental Protection Agency denies a permit for Chemical Waste Management Inc. to conduct an experimental burning of toxic wastes aboard an incinerator ship off the New Jersey coast. . . . Energy Sec. John S. Herrington reports that the government's list of possible sites for a high-level nuclear waste repository has been narrowed to three locations: Yucca Mountain, Nev., Deaf Smith Co., Tex., and Hanford, Wash.	A live telecast of a space walk by two cosmonauts who changed space stations May 6 is broadcast in the Soviet Union. . . . Uganda becomes the first African nation to openly acknowledge an acquired immune deficiency syndrome epidemic and launches a mass public education campaign to fight its spread. The disease first came to light there in 1982.	Larry Bird of the Boston Celtics is named the National Basketball Assoc.'s most valuable player for the third year in a row.	**May 28**
New York lawyer Whitney North Seymour Jr. is named independent counsel to investigate conflict-of-interest and influence-peddling charges against former Reagan aide Michael K. Deaver.		Pres. Reagan delivers a major policy speech on the issue of trade in which he describes the House trade bill passed May 22 as "kamikaze legislation." Reagan's remarks are made at a meeting of the National Assoc. of Manufacturers in Washington, D.C. . . . The Dow Jones Industrial Average closes at a record high of 1882.35. . . . The government's index of leading economic indicators rose 1.5% in April, the Commerce Dept. reports. . . . The government's producer price index fell a seasonally adjusted 0.6% in April, the Labor Dept. reports.		Jon Pennington, an eighth-grader from Shiremanstown, Pa., wins the 59th annual Scripps-Howard National Spelling Bee in Washington, D.C. Pennington, 13, won by correctly spelling "odontalgia," a fancy word for "toothache." . . . The spate of recent terrorist attacks and the media attention focused on them has caused many Americans to change their plans for foreign travel, particularly in the wake of the U.S. raid on Libya. An estimated 1.8 mil. Americans have canceled overseas trips or changed their itineraries, according to reports over the last six weeks. A U.S. State Dept. survey estimates that there would be a 25% decline in U.S. tourism in Western Europe and a 50% drop in Greece and Egypt.	**May 29**
		The U.S. deficit on merchandise trade dropped in April to $12.07 bil., the Commerce Dept. reports. . . . Prices received by farmers for their raw agricultural goods rose 2.5% in May, the Agriculture Dept. reports.	Shortly after lift-off from the Kourou Space Center in French Guiana, Western Europe's Ariane-2 rocket fails and is destroyed by remote control, along with a $50 mil. telecommunications satellite it is carrying into orbit.	*Publisher Weekly*'s hardback fiction best-sellers for the week are: *I'll Take Manhattan*, Judith Krantz; *A Perfect Spy*, John Le Carre; *The Bourne Supremacy*, Robert Ludlum; *The Mammoth Hunters*, Jean M. Auel; and *Lake Wobegon Days*, Garrison Keillor. . . . Pope John Paul II issues an encyclical on the Holy Spirit. "The Lord and Giver of Life" includes a denunciation of Marxist materialism and atheism, and warnings against the arms race, wars, and terrorism, poverty, famine, and abortion. . . . Perry Ellis, 46, top U.S. fashion designer who referred to his trademark casual style of sportswear as the "slouch look," dies in New York. His name label, launched in 1978, was expected to gross $250 mil. in 1986. His cause of death is officially listed as viral encephalitis.	**May 30**

F	G	H	I	J
Includes elections, federal-state relations, civil rights and liberties, crime, the judiciary, education, health care, poverty, urban affairs and population.	*Includes formation and debate of U.S. foreign and defense policies, veterans' affairs and defense spending. (Relations with specific foreign countries are usually found under the region concerned.)*	*Includes business, labor, agriculture, taxation, transportation, consumer affairs, monetary and fiscal policy, natural resources, and pollution.*	*Includes worldwide scientific, medical and technological developments, natural phenomena, U.S. weather, natural disasters, and accidents.*	*Includes the arts, religion, scholarship, communications media, sports, entertainments, fashions, fads and social life.*

	World Affairs	Europe	Africa & the Middle East	The Americas	Asia & the Pacific
May 31		In Poland the government announces the arrest of Zbigniew Bujak, the most-wanted fugitive in the underground leadership of the outlawed Solidarity labor movement. Lech Walesa, Solidarity's leader, praises Bujak as "one of the most outspoken and bravest fighters for citizens' rights and for the cause of Solidarity." . . . The members of the International Monetary Fund (IMF) vote to admit Poland. The action climaxes a six-year effort by Warsaw to gain IMF membership.			
June 1	The UN General Assembly concludes a special six-day session on resolving Africa's economic crisis, with unanimous agreement on a document that calls for African governments to make major reforms in their devastated economies, and that pledges Western donor nations to "provide sufficient resources" to aid the continental recovery program.			In Ecuador, the government of Pres. Leon Febres Cordero suffers a major setback in mid-term elections and in a referendum on constitutional reform. The elections were originally scheduled for January, but the president delayed them despite a ruling by the constitutional tribunal that the postponement was invalid.	
June 2		The Soviet Union announces that "more than 200" of its citizens will be allowed to immigrate to the United States, mainly to be reunited with relatives and spouses. . . . The state oil company of Norway announces an agreement to sell an estimated $60 bil. worth of natural gas to a consortium of six major Western European buyers beginning in 1993. The gas, the price of which will be pegged to that of crude oil, will come primarily from the North Sea's Sleipner and Troll fields.		The U.S. International Trade Comm. (ITC) rules that Canada caused financial harm to U.S. companies by "dumping" certain steel products on the U.S. market at below manufacturing costs. The ITC imposes penalty duties of up to 41% on Canadian steel products used in oil and natural gas drilling. . . . Canada's P.M. Brian Mulroney announces a retaliatory measure to counter a U.S. 35% import duty on Canadian cedar products. The retaliation takes the form of import duties on a range of U.S. products, including a revival of previously abandoned tariffs on some types of U.S. books and periodicals, semiconductors and computer parts, and higher tariffs on a range of other products.	In the Philippines, a 48-member constitutional commission begins drafting a new charter a little more than a week after Pres. Corazon Aquino named the panel. Aquino suspended the previous constitution, drafted by former Pres. Ferdinand E. Marcos, in March, and currently rules under an interim "freedom constitution." . . . Despite objections by the opposition and bitter infighting in his own Liberal Democratic Party, Japan's Premier Yasuhiro Nakasone dissolves the House of Representatives to make way for elections in both houses of the Diet.
June 3		West Germany's Chancellor Helmut Kohl announces that he is setting up the nation's first ministry of the environment, nature conservation and reactor safety. The move follows widespread criticism of the government's commitment to nuclear energy in the aftermath of the Soviet nuclear accident at Chernobyl.		Leftist rebels in El Salvador formally accept a government offer to resume peace talks that have been stalled since 1984. Pres. Jose Napoleon Duarte made the offer June 1.	

A	B	C	D	E
Includes developments that affect more than one world region, international organizations and important meetings of major world leaders.	Includes all domestic and regional developments in Europe, including the Soviet Union, Turkey, Cyprus and Malta.	Includes all domestic and regional developments in Africa and the Middle East, including Iraq and Iran and excluding Cyprus, Turkey and Afghanistan.	Includes all domestic and regional developments in Latin America, the Caribbean and Canada.	Includes all domestic and regional developments in Asia and Pacific nations, extending from Afghanistan through all the Pacific Islands, except Hawaii.

U.S. Politics & Social Issues	U.S. Foreign Policy & Defense	U.S. Economy & Environment	Science, Technology & Nature	Culture, Leisure & Life Style	
	Pres. Reagan calls on the U.S. Senate to ratify a pending extradition treaty with Britain. The treaty seeks to make it easier for Britain to win extradition of Irish Republican Army members wanted for crimes in the United Kingdom.		Dr. James Rainwater, 68, winner in 1975 of the Nobel Prize in physics, dies in Yonkers, N.Y. He shared the award with two colleagues for demonstrating that, contrary to theory, some atomic nuclei take asymmetrical shapes. His awards and honors also include the title of professor emeritus at Columbia Univ.	The 13th World Cup soccer tournament finals open in Mexico City. Teams representing 24 nations are separated into six different groups in the preliminary round of the month-long tournament. . . . Bobby Rahal wins the 70th Indianapolis 500 race with a record average speed of 170.722 miles per hour. The race also features the closest three-car finish in Indy history, with Kevin Cogan finishing 1.4 seconds behind, and Rick Mears 1.8 seconds behind Rahal.	May 31
				The Mystery of Edwin Drood wins the Antoinette (Tony) Perry Awards for best musical, director (Wilford Leach), and lead actor (George Rose); Bernadette Peters (*Song & Dance*) wins for best actress in a musical. Herb Gardner's *I'm Not Rappaport* wins for best play and lead actor (Judd Hirsch); best actress goes to Lily Tomlin (*Signs of Intelligent Life in the Universe*); and Jerry Zaks wins best director for *The House of Blue Leaves*. . . . Pat Bradley wins the Ladies Professional Golf Assoc. Championship and becomes the first player to win all four major women's tournaments. . . . The team of Derek Bell of Britain, Hans Stuck of West Germany, and Al Holbert of the United States wins the Le Mans 24-hour endurance race in France.	June 1
The Supreme Court rules unanimously that the First Amendment's protection of free speech applies to cable television. But the court declines to set forth specifics and says the protection must be balanced against "competing societal interests." . . . The Supreme Court rules unanimously that the Dept. of Health and Human Services can be sued by 10,000 or more mentally disabled New York residents who were denied disability benefits between 1978 and 1983, when the department secretly changed eligibility criteria. . . . The Senate begins a six-week experiment with live television broadcasts of its proceedings on the Cable Satellite Public Affairs Network. The Senate will vote in late July on whether to make the arrangement permanent.				A permanent reconstruction of one of the most important buildings of modern times is officially unveiled in Barcelona, Spain. The pavilion, designed by Ludwig Miles van der Rohe, was part of the German exhibit at the 1929 World's Fair, and is widely thought to have ushered in the so-called international style of architecture. The Reconstruction is in honor of the legendary architect, who died in 1969 and whose centenary is being celebrated in 1986. . . . A bitter and highly public battle over the $500 mil. estate of the late J. Seward Johnson, heir to the Johnson & Johnson pharmaceutical fortune, ends in an out-of-court settlement. Johnson's six grown children and an oceanographic research institute sued in New York surrogate court to contest a will that left the estate almost totally to Johnson's third wife, Barbara Piasecka Johnson.	June 2
The senate votes to extend the Higher Education Act of 1965 for another five years. The measure will raise the ceiling on student loans and grants but also set stricter standards for eligibility and give the government new powers to crack down on student loan defaulters. The vote is the first ever televised from the Senate chambers.				Dame Anna (born Florence Marjorie Robinson) Neagle, 81, actress who was regarded as the first lady of British cinema from the late 1930s through the early 1950s, dies in Surrey, England. She was married to the late film producer Herbert Wilcox, who produced nearly all her films, among them two in which she portrayed Queen Victoria: *Victoria the Great* and *Sixty Glorious Years*. She also starred in *Nell Gwyn*, *The Lady with a Lamp* (about Florence Nightingale), and *Odette* (1950), in which she portrayed the World War II French Resistance heroine of that name.	June 3

F	G	H	I	J
Includes elections, federal-state relations, civil rights and liberties, crime, the judiciary, education, health care, poverty, urban affairs and population.	*Includes formation and debate of U.S. foreign and defense policies, veterans' affairs and defense spending. (Relations with specific foreign countries are usually found under the region concerned.)*	*Includes business, labor, agriculture, taxation, transportation, consumer affairs, monetary and fiscal policy, natural resources, and pollution.*	*Includes worldwide scientific, medical and technological developments, natural phenomena, U.S. weather, natural disasters, and accidents.*	*Includes the arts, religion, scholarship, communications media, sports, entertainments, fashions, fads and social life.*

	World Affairs	Europe	Africa & the Middle East	The Americas	Asia & the Pacific
June 4		The West German statistics office reports a record monthly trade surplus of 10 bil. deutsche marks (DM) during April, up from DM 8.5 bil. in March and eclipsing the previous record, which was set in October 1984.			In a televised address marking her first 100 days in office, Philippines Pres. Corazon Aquino assesses her government's performance and warns Filipinos not to take their newly won liberties for granted. She urges self-reliance and sacrifice to overcome the nation's serious economic difficulties.
June 5		Soviet sources reveal that in the wake of the nuclear plant accident, areas outside the Chernobyl danger zone have been found to be contaminated, necessitating the evacuation of thousands more people. A total of 92,000 people have been evacuated from the original danger zone, which encompassed an area 20 miles around the Ukrainian town of Pripyat, where the plant was located.			
June 6		Unemployment in West Germany falls to 8.5% of the work force in May, down from 9% in March.			Some 200 African students march through Beijing to protest what they describe as racial discrimination in China. The protest stems from a fracas May 24 at Tianjin Univ. when some 400 Chinese students besieged for five hours a group of Africans at a party celebrating African Liberation Day.
June 7				At the end of a two-day meeting in Panama City, the Contadora Group presents to the five Central American nations a new draft of its proposed treaty. The Contadora Group, which includes Mexico, Panama, Venezuela, and Colombia, calls the draft their "last version." . . . In an attempt to curb growing political tensions in Haiti, the government announces that presidential elections will be held in November 1987.	

A	B	C	D	E
Includes developments that affect more than one world region, international organizations and important meetings of major world leaders.	Includes all domestic and regional developments in Europe, including the Soviet Union, Turkey, Cyprus and Malta.	Includes all domestic and regional developments in Africa and the Middle East, including Iraq and Iran and excluding Cyprus, Turkey and Afghanistan.	Includes all domestic and regional developments in Latin America, the Caribbean and Canada.	Includes all domestic and regional developments in Asia and Pacific nations, extending from Afghanistan through all the Pacific Islands, except Hawaii.

U.S. Politics & Social Issues	U.S. Foreign Policy & Defense	U.S. Economy & Environment	Science, Technology & Nature	Culture, Leisure & Life Style	
	Jonathan Jay Pollard, a former U.S. Navy intelligence analyst, pleads guilty to participating in an espionage conspiracy against the United States on Israel's behalf. He could face up to life in prison and a $500,000 fine. His wife, Anne Henderson Pollard, pleads guilty to lesser charges involving conspiracy to receive embezzled government property and to possession of national defense documents. She could be sentenced to as many as 10 years in prison and fined as much as $500,000.	The Office of Management and Budget announces that the federal government recovered $135 mil. in unpaid loans by withholding individuals' income tax refunds. The experimental approach was launched in January under the Deficit Reduction Act of 1984.... Exxon Corp. reports that 6,200 workers accepted the company's offer of financial incentives for retirement or resignation.... Owen F. Bieber is reelected president of the United Auto Workers at the union's convention in Anaheim, Calif. Bieber, 56, was unopposed for a second three-year term.			June 4
The Senate Judiciary Committee rejects Pres. Reagan's nomination of Jefferson B. Sessions III. to be a federal district judge in Alabama. It is the first total rejection of a judicial nominee by the committee in six years, and only the second in the last 48 years. Sessions came under attack from civil rights groups because of his prosecution in 1985 of three Alabama civil rights activists on voter fraud. The three were latter acquitted by a federal court jury.	Pres. Reagan narrowly averts a major foreign policy defeat as the Senate fails by one vote to override his veto of a congressional resolution barring a scaled-down arms sale to Saudi Arabia.	The Federal Housing Admin. (FHA) stops insuring mortgages for single-family homes because its operating authority has run out. This shutdown is the FHA's sixth since October 1985.... Dennis B. Levine pleads not guilty in New York City to federal charges stemming from alleged insider trading. He also settles a record suit brought against him by the Securities and Exchange Comm. by agreeing to forfeit $11.6 mil. he made in profits.		Short-story writer Peter Taylor is presented with the $5,000 PEN/ Faulkner award for the best work of fiction published in 1985, his latest collection of short stories, *The Old Forest and Other Stories*.... Major international airlines and some U.S. travel agents claim that Americans are recovering from their fears of terrorism and that bookings to Europe have increased in the previous weeks, the *New York Times* reports.	June 5
Pres. Reagan signs a measure updating the federal retirement system enacted by Congress in May.		The Senate passes a $3.9 bil. supplemental spending bill for fiscal 1986. The bill was passed only after the chairmen of the Armed Services Committee and the Appropriations Committee's defense subcommittee settled a jurisdictional battle over some $6.5 bil. in future military spending for specific programs that exceed amounts authorized by the Armed Services Committee.... Outstanding consumer credit grew a seasonally adjusted $4.16 bil. in April, or at an annual rate of 9%, the Federal Reserve Board reports.... The nation's unemployment rate rose to a seasonally adjusted level of 7.2% of the work force in May, the Labor Dept. reports.	A woman gives birth in Los Angeles to a boy who is the first baby in the United States to be born from a frozen embryo. The technique was developed in Australia.... The UN World Health Org. estimates that at least 50,000 Africans have probably contracted acquired immune deficiency syndrome since 1980. The report estimates that at least 1 million to 2 million Africans have been infected with the disease.	The National Institute for Occupational Safety finally wins approval from the White House Office of Management and Budget to begin a study of possible health hazards for workers who use video display terminals (VDTs).... The poet Adrienne Rich is presented with the first annual $25,000 Ruth Lilly Poetry Prize. Endowed by a descendant of drug company founder Eli Lilly, the award is the largest offered to poets.	June 6
				In tennis, Chris Evert Lloyd of the United States wins the women's French Open title, beating Martina Navratilova of the United States 2-6, 6-3, 6-3.	June 7

F	G	H	I	J
Includes elections, federal-state relations, civil rights and liberties, crime, the judiciary, education, health care, poverty, urban affairs and population.	Includes formation and debate of U.S. foreign and defense policies, veterans' affairs and defense spending. (Relations with specific foreign countries are usually found under the region concerned.)	Includes business, labor, agriculture, taxation, transportation, consumer affairs, monetary and fiscal policy, natural resources, and pollution.	Includes worldwide scientific, medical and technological developments, natural phenomena, U.S. weather, natural disasters, and accidents.	Includes the arts, religion, scholarship, communications media, sports, entertainments, fashions, fads and social life.

	World Affairs	Europe	Africa & the Middle East	The Americas	Asia & the Pacific
June 8		Hu Yaobang, general secretary of China's Communist Party, begins a two-week tour of Britain, West Germany, France, and Italy. His trip to Western Europe is the fist by a Chinese Communist Party chief since the 1949 revolution. China in recent years has stressed its support for a united Western Europe as a stabilizing force in the rivalry between the United States and the Soviet Union. . . . Former UN Sec. Gen. Kurt Waldheim is elected president of Austria in a runoff election against socialist candidate Kurt Steyrer. Waldheim, representing the conservative opposition People's Party, overcomes charges concerning his activities in the German Army during World War II to become the first non-socialist elected to the Austrian presidency since the end of the war.			
June 9				The Canadian branch of the U.S.-based United Auto Workers (UAW) union completes its separation from the UAW. In a special national convention in Toronto, delegates approve an agreement with the UAW that gives the Canadian union $32 mil. in strike funds, properties, mortgages, and interest. The delegates approve a new name, the Canadian Auto Workers.	
June 10		A jury in London finds a Belfast man, Patrick J. Magee, guilty of planting the bomb that killed five people attending the Conservative Party conference at the Grand Hotel in Brighton in October 1984. P.M. Margaret Thatcher and most of the British cabinet were at the hotel. The Provisional Irish Republican Army claimed credit for the blast.		Nicaraguan Contras free eight West German nationals they have held prisoner since May 17. The incident has caused tensions between West Germany and the United States, which is backing Contra groups fighting to overthrow the Nicaraguan government. . . . The U.S. International Trade Comm. holds a hearing on a complaint that the U.S. lumber industry is being injured by subsidized Canadian softwood imports. The hearing is the latest development in the bitter trade dispute between the two countries.	

A	B	C	D	E
Includes developments that affect more than one world region, international organizations and important meetings of major world leaders.	Includes all domestic and regional developments in Europe, including the Soviet Union, Turkey, Cyprus and Malta.	Includes all domestic and regional developments in Africa and the Middle East, including Iraq and Iran and excluding Cyprus, Turkey and Afghanistan.	Includes all domestic and regional developments in Latin America, the Caribbean and Canada.	Includes all domestic and regional developments in Asia and Pacific nations, extending from Afghanistan through all the Pacific Islands, except Hawaii.

U.S. Politics & Social Issues	U.S. Foreign Policy & Defense	U.S. Economy & Environment	Science, Technology & Nature	Culture, Leisure & Life Style	
A group of black Republicans is demanding an overhaul of party rules that they say discriminate against minorities and large states, the *Washington Post* reports. The only two blacks now on the 153-member Republican National Committee represent the predominantly black U.S. Virgin Islands.				In tennis, Ivan Lendl of Czechoslovakia wins the men's French Open title beating Mikael Pernfors of Sweden 6-3, 6-2, 6-4.... The Boston Celtics win their 16th National Basketball Assoc. title with a 114-97 victory over the Houston Rockets. Larry Bird is named the most valuable player of the finals.	June 8
The National Org. for Women seeks a nationwide injunction against antiabortion activists who allegedly travel around the country to organize harassment of abortion clinics. The group files its lawsuit in federal district court in Wilmington, Del.... The Supreme Court invalidates the Reagan administration's so-called "Baby Doe" rule, which requires hospitals to treat and feed severely handicapped infants. The administration instituted the rule in 1983, basing it on a 1973 law that prohibits facilities receiving federal funds from discriminating against the handicapped.			The annual meeting of the International Whaling Comm. opens in Malmo, Sweden, with a call for Norway, the Soviet Union, and Japan to stop violating the commission's moratorium, which was set in 1982 and became effective this year.... The report of the presidential shuttle commission severely criticizes the National Aeronautics and Space Admin. (NASA) for its negligence in the January 28 *Challenger* disaster. The accident resulted from a leak of superhot gases from a faulty seal in the shuttle's right-side booster rocket, which failed because of cold weather. The commission says NASA and booster contractor Morton Thiokol, Inc., "first failed to recognize [the faulty seal] as a problem, then failed to fix it, and finally treated it as an acceptable flight risk."	Retiring Yale Univ. Pres. A. Bartlett Giamatti is elected president of Major League Baseball's National League by the league's team owners.	June 9
	A federal bankruptcy judge in Washington, D.C., approves the plan of Mario Vazquez Rana to bring United Press International out of bankruptcy, then giving the Mexican publisher control of the news service. The ruling officially ends almost 14 months of bankruptcy for the service.		A 16-day-old baby receives a new heart in an operation at Loma Linda Univ. Medical Center, in California. The hospital had caused a national stir by initially turning away the child, known as Baby Jesse, who suffers from hypoplastic heart syndrome.	The Rev. Adrian P. Rogers is elected president of the Southern Baptist Convention. The convention meeting in Atlanta chose Rogers, a fundamentalist pastor, over the Rev. W. Winfred Moore, leader of the church's moderate faction. ... Merle Miller, 67, American novelist and biographer who was the author of best-selling biographies of Presidents Harry S. Truman and Lyndon B. Johnson, dies in Danbury, Conn. of complications following an appendectomy. In 1971, he attracted wide attention for an autobiographical article written for the *New York Times Magazine* entitled "What It Means to Be a Homosexual." That article, written in the early days of the gay liberation movement, became the basis for his book, *On Being Different.*	June 10

F	G	H	I	J
Includes elections, federal-state relations, civil rights and liberties, crime, the judiciary, education, health care, poverty, urban affairs and population.	Includes formation and debate of U.S. foreign and defense policies, veterans' affairs and defense spending. (Relations with specific foreign countries are usually found under the region concerned.)	Includes business, labor, agriculture, taxation, transportation, consumer affairs, monetary and fiscal policy, natural resources, and pollution.	Includes worldwide scientific, medical and technological developments, natural phenomena, U.S. weather, natural disasters, and accidents.	Includes the arts, religion, scholarship, communications media, sports, entertainments, fashions, fads and social life.

	World Affairs	Europe	Africa & the Middle East	The Americas	Asia & the Pacific
June 11		The leaders of the Warsaw Pact nations conclude a two-day summit in Budapest. Soviet leader Mikhail S. Gorbachev, visiting Hungary for the first time since coming to power in 1985, leads the discussion. . . . Moscow introduces a proposal for the reduction of strategic weapons at the U.S.-Soviet disarmament talks in Geneva. In keeping with past policy, the details of the offer are not made public by either side.			
June 12		The British government announces the dissolution of the Stormont Parliament, the assembly for Northern Ireland. The widely expected move is announced in the House of Commons by Sec. of State for Northern Ireland Tom King. The assembly at Stormont was created in 1982	South Africa's white minority government declares a nationwide state of emergency, giving virtually unlimited powers to the security forces and reimposing severe restrictions on media coverage of unrest. More than 1,000 people are detained in this first day of the decree, which the government says is needed to forestall violent protests by blacks on June 16, the 10th anniversary of the Soweto uprising.	According to information gathered by U.S. intelligence sources, Panama's army commander, Gen. Manuel Antonio Noriega, who is effectively leader of the country, is deeply involved in a number of illegal activities, including drug trafficking and the supply of arms to Colombian rebels.	
June 13		The Greek parliament passes a law permitting abortion in the first 12 weeks of pregnancy. In the case of rape, incest or when the mother's life is endangered, pregnancies can be terminated up to the 24th week. . . . Britain's seasonally adjusted jobless rate rose to 13.3% in May, according to Dept. of Employment statistics. But inflation in May hit its lowest level since January 1968, according to retail price index data released; falling oil prices and mortgage rates helped hold price increases to 0.2%, or a compounded 2.8% annual rate.	In South Africa, Bishop Desmond Tutu, one of the most prominent black spokesmen and critics of apartheid meets with Pres. Pieter W. Botha in Cape Town. It is the first meeting between the two men in six years and the first private talk between them ever.	V.P. George Bush and Canada's P.M. Brian Mulroney hold a closed-door discussion in Ottawa. Bush later acknowledges that trade was the central topic of the meeting.	

A	B	C	D	E
Includes developments that affect more than one world region, international organizations and important meetings of major world leaders.	Includes all domestic and regional developments in Europe, including the Soviet Union, Turkey, Cyprus and Malta.	Includes all domestic and regional developments in Africa and the Middle East, including Iraq and Iran and excluding Cyprus, Turkey and Afghanistan.	Includes all domestic and regional developments in Latin America, the Caribbean and Canada.	Includes all domestic and regional developments in Asia and Pacific nations, extending from Afghanistan through all the Pacific Islands, except Hawaii.

U.S. Politics & Social Issues	U.S. Foreign Policy & Defense	U.S. Economy & Environment	Science, Technology & Nature	Culture, Leisure & Life Style	
The Supreme Court reaffirms its 1973 decision, *Roe* v. *Wade*, establishing a woman's right to abortion. By a 5-4 ruling, the court strikes down a Pennsylvania law as an unconstitutional restraint against abortion.	An Army initiative to curb smoking among personnel is reported. The new policy says smoking is prohibited in "Dept. of Army-occupied space except for designated smoking areas that are necessary to avoid undue inconvenience to persons who desire to smoke."	A House subcommittee questions managers of the Tennessee Valley Authority (TVA) on safety and management problems that have plagued the TVA's nuclear power program. All five nuclear power plants operated by the TVA in Tennessee and Alabama have been closed because of safety problems since 1985. . . . Congressional budget negotiations recess indefinitely. With the White House refusing to entertain any talk of compromise on taxes, House and Senate conferees are deadlocked over how to make FY1987 spending fit within the limits of the Gramm-Rudman balanced budget law.	Scientists at the California Institute of Technology announce that they have developed the first automated instrument to analyze the structure of DNA (deoxyribonucleic acid), the basic genetic material. The development is expected to accelerate the already rapid pace of genetic research. . . . Canadian astronomers find evidence of planets circling four sunlike stars relatively close to Earth. The discovery is reported by Bruce Campbell at the Canadian Astronomical Society's annual meeting. . . . Scientists at the National Institutes of Health refute a widespread belief that genital herpes, a virus infection, can be transmitted to sexual partners only when there are visible sores or other overt symptoms. As many as 50 million Americans are estimated to be infected with the virus.	The Presbyterian Church (U.S.A.) names the Rev. Benjamin Weir, 62, moderator of its denomination during the church's 198th General Assembly, in Minneapolis. Weir, who served 35 years as a missionary in Beirut, was held hostage by Shiite Moslems in Lebanon for 16 months.	June 11
The Public Health Service releases a report projecting that by 1991 there will be a tenfold increase in deaths from acquired immune deficiency syndrome and in total number of cases in the United States. Government health officials discussed the findings in a Washington, D.C., news conference.	The Reagan administration creates widespread confusion with contradictory statements about whether it will abide by the 1979 Strategic Arms Limitation Treaty (SALT II). Comments over the last two days by top U.S. officials, including Pres. Reagan himself, leave many observers puzzled with regard to the administration's position on SALT II future compliance.	The House passes a comprehensive public housing bill that will require more federal money to be spent on rehabilitation of existing housing than on new construction.			June 12
The National Org. of Women opens its 19th annual convention in Denver. No contenders in the 1988 presidential election are invited to address the three-day meeting. . . . Carmine Persico, the alleged leader of the Colombo organized crime group is convicted with eight associates on racketeering-conspiracy charges in New York City. U.S. Attorney Rudolph W. Giuliani, whose office prosecuted the case, says the federal jury verdict "crushed the top leadership of the Colombo Mafia family."		The Occupational Safety and Health Admin. tightens standards governing exposed asbestos at job sites. Exposure to asbestos fibers loose in the atmosphere is a known cause of asbestosis, a lung disease, and other ailments. . . . Industrial production in May fell a seasonally adjusted 0.6%, the Federal Reserve Board reports. The May output drop follows a revised increase of 0.4% in April and a revised 0.9% drop in March. . . . The government's producer price index rose a seasonally adjusted 0.6% in May, the Labor Dept. reports.	The incidence of tuberculosis is rising among the same groups of people that are at high risk of developing acquired immune deficiency syndrome, according to public health officials quoted in the *Wall Street Journal*. Those groups include intravenous drug users and homosexual males.	Benny (Benjamin David) Goodman, 77, bandleader and clarinetist who for some five decades was known as "The King of Swing," dies of cardiac arrest in New York City. Born in Chicago, he began playing the clarinet at age nine, and by 16 was playing with Chicago's best jazz groups. An August 1935 concert by his first band (formed the year before in New York City) at the Palomar Ballroom in Los Angeles is credited with ushering in the age of swing. Goodman was the first major white bandleader to front an integrated group. He later ventured to perform classical music, and he commissioned works for the clarinet by Bela Bartok and Aaron Copland.	June 13

F	**G**	**H**	**I**	**J**
Includes elections, federal-state relations, civil rights and liberties, crime, the judiciary, education, health care, poverty, urban affairs and population.	*Includes formation and debate of U.S. foreign and defense policies, veterans' affairs and defense spending. (Relations with specific foreign countries are usually found under the region concerned.)*	*Includes business, labor, agriculture, taxation, transportation, consumer affairs, monetary and fiscal policy, natural resources, and pollution.*	*Includes worldwide scientific, medical and technological developments, natural phenomena, U.S. weather, natural disasters, and accidents.*	*Includes the arts, religion, scholarship, communications media, sports, entertainments, fashions, fads and social life.*

	World Affairs	Europe	Africa & the Middle East	The Americas	Asia & the Pacific
June 14			A powerful car bomb explodes outside a restaurant on a seafront boulevard in Durban, South Africa. Two white women are killed immediately, and more than 60 other people, many of them white, are wounded.		
June 15		A poll conducted by the Harris Research Center and reported in the *Observer* shows that 51% of Britons think that their nation should impose economic sanctions against South Africa. That figure is up from 44% in a similar survey in November 1985. . . . West German Chancellor Helmut Kohl's Christian Democratic Union prevails in a key state parliamentary election in Lower Saxony. The vote, coming only seven months before the next federal election, is widely viewed as a referendum on Kohl's leadership.			
June 16		East Germany begins issuing identity cards to foreign diplomats for travel between East Berlin and West Berlin. The action eases, but does not resolve, an East-West dispute over checkpoint controls in the divided city.	Millions of South African blacks stage a one-day strike to mark the 10th anniversary of the 1967 Soweto uprising. The government claims that the national state of emergency it declared June 12 succeeded in preventing black nationalist guerrillas from setting off a mass insurrection; but racial violence continues to mount around the country.		A two-day meeting in Paris of foreign aid donors results in aid commitments to India of $4.5 bil. for the 1986-87 fiscal year.

A	B	C	D	E
Includes developments that affect more than one world region, international organizations and important meetings of major world leaders.	*Includes all domestic and regional developments in Europe, including the Soviet Union, Turkey, Cyprus and Malta.*	*Includes all domestic and regional developments in Africa and the Middle East, including Iraq and Iran and excluding Cyprus, Turkey and Afghanistan.*	*Includes all domestic and regional developments in Latin America, the Caribbean and Canada.*	*Includes all domestic and regional developments in Asia and Pacific nations, extending from Afghanistan through all the Pacific Islands, except Hawaii.*

U.S. Politics & Social Issues	U.S. Foreign Policy & Defense	U.S. Economy & Environment	Science, Technology & Nature	Culture, Leisure & Life Style	
The 13th annual convention of the National Right to Life Committee concludes three days of meetings in Denver. The speakers include an array of leading Republican politicians.				Marlin (Richard) Perkins, 81, zoologist and zookeeper who hosted the television show "Wild Kingdom," for 23 years, dies of lymphatic cancer in suburban St. Louis. In 1949, while serving as director of Chicago's Lincoln Park Zoo, he began his television career as the narrator of "Zoo Parade," which ran for eight years. "Wild Kingdom," for which he and his assistants roamed the globe in search of animals, was first broadcast in 1963. Perkins was also director of the St. Louis Zoo. . . . Alan Jay Lerner, 67, lyricist and playwright whose greatest successes were the product of a long collaboration with the composer Frederick Loewe, dies of lung cancer in New York City. Their Broadway musicals include *Brigadoon* (1947), *Paint Your Wagon* (1951), and *Camelot* (1960). Their greatest success was *My Fair Lady*, which opened in March 1956 and ran for more than 2,700 performances. . . . Jorge Luis Borges, 68, Argentine short story writer, poet, and essayist, dies of liver cancer in Geneva, Switz. One of Latin America's most acclaimed authors and a perennial Nobel Prize candidate, his work was informed by a unique combination of fantastical elements with seemingly realistic details. Collections of his stories include *Fictions*, *The Aleph and Other Stories*, and *Labyrinths*. The victim of a congenital eye disorder, Borges was almost totally blind for three decades.	June 14
The American Medical Assoc.'s House of Delegates adopts a report calling for curbs on the supply of new doctors. The vote comes at the group's annual meeting, which will convene for five days. . . . The International Theater Institute's two-week festival opens in Baltimore amid controversy over the elimination of a production by Britain's National Theater based on *Animal Farm*, George Orwell's 1945 satire of totalitarianism, at the request of the Soviet Union. . . . Public approval of Pres. Reagan's performance is at its highest level ever, according to a Gallup poll in which 68% of respondents say they approve of his handling of his job.				Nigel Mansell of Britain wins the Canadian Grand Prix in Montreal. . . . Ray Floyd wins the U.S. Open golf tournament on the Shinnecock Hills course in Southampton, N.Y.	June 15
The Supreme Court declines to block a plan to end busing of children to desegregate elementary schools in Norfolk, Va.	Pres. Reagan meets with a visiting delegation of Afghan rebel leaders, headed by Burhanuddin Rabbani. While Reagan tells them he has an "unshakable commitment to their cause," he turns down their plea that the United States sever diplomatic relations with the Soviet-backed Afghan regime and extend official recognition to the Moslem resistance forces. Such a move, he says, is "premature."	The Federal Trade Comm. charges that an advertisement run by R.J. Reynolds Tobacco Co. illegally distorts research findings about the health risks of smoking. The ad in question, "Of Cigarettes and Science," ran from March to June in leading national newspapers and magazines.		Lady Diana (born Diana Olivia Winifred Maud Manners) Cooper, the Dowager Viscountess Norwich, 93, legendary beauty and glittering social personality of British high society in the 1920s and 1930s, dies in London. After a brief career in silent films, she was offered the part of the Madonna in Max Reinhardt's theatrical pageant *The Miracle*. Her income enabled her to further the political ambitions of her husband, Alfred Duff Cooper, whom she married in 1919, and who died in 1954.	June 16

F	G	H	I	J
Includes elections, federal-state relations, civil rights and liberties, crime, the judiciary, education, health care, poverty, urban affairs and population.	*Includes formation and debate of U.S. foreign and defense policies, veterans' affairs and defense spending. (Relations with specific foreign countries are usually found under the region concerned.)*	*Includes business, labor, agriculture, taxation, transportation, consumer affairs, monetary and fiscal policy, natural resources, and pollution.*	*Includes worldwide scientific, medical and technological developments, natural phenomena, U.S. weather, natural disasters, and accidents.*	*Includes the arts, religion, scholarship, communications media, sports, entertainments, fashions, fads and social life.*

	World Affairs	Europe	Africa & the Middle East	The Americas	Asia & the Pacific
June 17		Norway's Storting approves a package of tax increases and spending cuts designed to save the government $421 mil. The vote is a victory for the minority coalition government led by Labor Party Premier Gro Harlem Brundtland. The previous conservative government of Kaare Willoch was ousted after a defeat in the Storting over its austerity proposals.	In South Africa, stringent media controls enacted in emergency decrees June 12 are further tightened. New orders ban reports from all black townships and restrict any information about security force activities to that provided by the Bureau of Information, a newly created government body.	Mexico's Finance Min. Jesus Silva Herzog resigns unexpectedly at a critical point in months-long negotiations with Mexico's international creditors on its $98 bil. foreign debt.	In Australia, the federal government orders the expulsion of an official at the South African Embassy in Canberra, Australia, who beat a woman protesting South Africa's apartheid policy of racial separation.
June 18				In Peru, the military stages assaults on three prisons after inmates, members of the Maoist Sendero Luminoso (Shining Path) rebel group, attempt to take over the facilities.	South Korea rejects a North Korean proposal for high-level defense talks between the two nations.
June 19					
June 20	Delegates from 132 nations conclude five-days of meetings in Paris and call for mandatory, comprehensive sanctions against South Africa. The conference was organized by the UN Special Committee Against Apartheid, along with the Org. for African Unity and the Nonaligned Movement. The U.S., British, and West German governments boycotted the meeting.	Bulgaria killed hundreds of ethnic Turks in its drive to make them adopt Slavic names, according to a report by Helsinki Watch, a human rights organization. The report estimates that from 300 to 1,500 ethnic Turks have been killed by security forces since the end of 1984.	Two tough new security bills are forced into law by South Africa's white leaders. The measures will enable the government to detain suspects for six months without trial and to declare "unrest areas" where police will have sweeping powers similar to those pertaining under the current nationwide state of emergency.	The International Monetary Fund agrees to provide Bolivia with a $57 mil. standby loan; the first payment of $15.4 mil. is made today. . . . In Canada, the Ontario legislature passes a law banning physicians from extra-billing, or charging their patients fees higher than the rates allowed by the provincial health insurance plan. The passage comes a week after Ontario doctors began a strike over the extra-billing issue.	
	A	**B**	**C**	**D**	**E**
	Includes developments that affect more than one world region, international organizations and important meetings of major world leaders.	*Includes all domestic and regional developments in Europe, including the Soviet Union, Turkey, Cyprus and Malta.*	*Includes all domestic and regional developments in Africa and the Middle East, including Iraq and Iran and excluding Cyprus, Turkey and Afghanistan.*	*Includes all domestic and regional developments in Latin America, the Caribbean and Canada.*	*Includes all domestic and regional developments in Asia and Pacific nations, extending from Afghanistan through all the Pacific Islands, except Hawaii.*

U.S. Politics & Social Issues	U.S. Foreign Policy & Defense	U.S. Economy & Environment	Science, Technology & Nature	Culture, Leisure & Life Style	
The Education Dept. endorses the use of mobile vans for remedial education classes as a way for parochial schools to circumvent a 1985 Supreme Court decision that bars public school teachers from conducting federal remedial education programs in parochial schools.... Pres. Reagan announces the retirement of Warren E. Burger, 78, as the chief justice of the United States. At the same time, the president announces his intention to elevate Assoc. Justice William H. Rehnquist to be the new chief justice and to name federal appeals court Judge Antonin Scalia to the vacant seat on the high court.		New housing starts dropped 7.4% in May to a seasonally adjusted rate of 1.89 million units, the Commerce Dept. reports.	The Soviet Union holds an "almost frightening" lead over the United States in its space program according to an authoritative British publication, *Jane's Spaceflight Directory.*	Louisiana's Gov. Edwin W. Edwards decides not to commute the life sentence of Wilbert Rideau, who gained national attention as the editor of the *Angolite,* a prize-winning newspaper published bimonthly at the Louisiana State Penitentiary in Angola. Louisiana's pardon board voted, 3-2, in favor of parole. Rideau, a 45-year-old black man, has served 25 years for murdering a white woman in Lake Charles, La., in the course of a 1961 bank robbery.... Brad Daugherty, a forward from North Carolina State, is the first player chosen in the National Basketball Assoc.'s annual draft of college players.... Kate Smith, 79, American singer whose rendition of Irving Berlin's "God Bless America" (which he had rejected as "too saccharine" for a 1918 musical) made her a symbol of U.S. patriotism, dies of respiratory arrest, in Raleigh, N.C. She recorded more than 3,000 songs, including her theme "When the Moon Comes Over the Mountain."	June 17
	In a surprise move, the House of Representatives passes a far-reaching measure that would impose a complete trade embargo on South Africa and require all American companies and citizens to divest themselves of their holdings in that country.		Pres. Reagan signs a comprehensive package of rules, definitions, and guidelines to regulate the growing genetic engineering industry. The rules which have been under development for two years, take effect immediately. Under the guidelines, the National Institutes of Health will continue to set standards and monitor genetic engineering research at the nation's universities.	*Variety*'s top-grossing films of the week are *Back to School, Ferris Bueller's Day Off, Top Gun, Raw Deal* and *Cobra.... Billboard*'s best-selling albums for the week are *Whitney Houston*, Whitney Houston; *Winner in You,* Patti La Belle; *Control,* Janet Jackson; *Like a Rock,* Bob Seger & the Silver Bullet Band; and *5150,* Van Halen.	June 18
The Supreme Court upholds a Pennsylvania law providing a five-year mandatory minimum sentence for anyone who possesses a firearm while committing certain crimes. The law requires judges to impose the sentence if they find by a "preponderance of evidence" that the defendant possessed a gun.... The Supreme Court rules unanimously that states cannot withdraw their state and local government employees from the Social Security System.... The Supreme Court rules unanimously that sexual harassment of an employee by a supervisor violates the federal law against discrimination in the workplace and that a company can be liable for sexual harassment even if the company did not know about a supervisor's actions.	Former Federal Bureau of Investigation (FBI) agent Richard W. Miller is convicted in Los Angeles of six charges of bribery and espionage. Miller is the first FBI agent to be charged with espionage.... Speaking at a high school graduation in Glassboro, N.J., Pres. Reagan credits the Soviet Union with making a "serious effort" to negotiate reductions in nuclear weapons.	Legislation to strengthen protection of the nation's drinking water is signed by Pres. Reagan. Under the bill, the Environmental Protection Agency is required to set national limits within three years on 83 potential contaminants of drinking water.... Americans' total personal income dropped 0.1% or $4 bil. in May, to a seasonally adjusted annual rate of $3.445 trillion, according to the Commerce Dept. May consumer spending rose an adjusted 0.9%.	The American Medical Assoc. says that public schools should be open to children with acquired immune deficiency syndrome (AIDS). Doctors believe that AIDS can be spread only by semen or an exchange of blood, not by the kind of casual contact found in the classroom.	Len Bias, 22, the second player chosen in the National Basketball Assoc.'s (NBA) annual draft of college players, collapses in his dorm room at the Univ. of Maryland and dies from cocaine intoxication. He had been drafted by the NBA champion Boston Celtics.... Coluche (Michel Colucci), 41, French comedian known for his irreverent, often vulgar treatment of authority figures, is killed in a motorcycle accident near Grasse in Southern France. In 1981 he staged a mock candidacy for the presidency of France, he withdrew before the actual voting, but not before opinion polls showed that some 10% of the electorate supported him. He became a major spokesman of the emerging antiracism movement and sponsored a food distribution centers for the unemployed.	June 19
U.S. Tobacco Co. is found not liable in the cancer death of a teenage athlete who used the company's Copenhagen brand snuff. A federal district court in Oklahoma City, Okla., takes less than six hours to arrive at its finding.... Pres. Reagan has two small benign polyps removed from his large intestine. Doctors at Bethesda Naval Medical Center in Maryland discovered and removed the growths during what was described as a routine examination to check for recurrence of colon cancer. In 1985, Reagan underwent major surgery to remove a cancer from his large intestine.		Bristol-Meyers Co. ends the sale of all nonprescription capsule products. The move is brought on by the deaths of two people who took cyanide-laced capsules of the company's Extra-Strength Excedrin painkiller.... The government's consumer price index rose a seasonally adjusted 0.2% in May, according to the Labor Dept.	The British government announces a three-week ban on the slaughter or transport of sheep in parts of North Wales and Cumbria after tests show significant radiation levels in some of the livestock. On May 2 and 3 the regions suffered torrential rains thought to be contaminated with radioactive dust from the April 28 Chernobyl nuclear disaster in the Soviet Union.		June 20

F	G	H	I	J
Includes elections, federal-state relations, civil rights and liberties, crime, the judiciary, education, health care, poverty, urban affairs and population.	*Includes formation and debate of U.S. foreign and defense policies, veterans' affairs and defense spending. (Relations with specific foreign countries are usually found under the region concerned.)*	*Includes business, labor, agriculture, taxation, transportation, consumer affairs, monetary and fiscal policy, natural resources, and pollution.*	*Includes worldwide scientific, medical and technological developments, natural phenomena, U.S. weather, natural disasters, and accidents.*	*Includes the arts, religion, scholarship, communications media, sports, entertainments, fashions, fads and social life.*

	World Affairs	Europe	Africa & the Middle East	The Americas	Asia & the Pacific
June 21					
June 22		The Socialist Workers Party, led by Premier Felipe Gonzalez, retains its parliamentary majority in national elections in Spain.	Seven people convicted of plotting to overthrow Ghanaian leader Jerry Rawlings are executed by firing squad, Accra radio reports. The coup plot, foiled in late 1985, is one of at least a dozen since Rawlings seized power in 1981.		
June 23			In a major policy shift, Britain invites African National Congress president Oliver Tambo to talk with a British government official on the situation in South Africa.		The foreign ministers of the Assoc. of Southeast Asian Nations (ASEAN) attend the organization's 19th annual two-day meeting in Manila, the Philippines. The other member nations of ASEAN are: Brunei, Indonesia, Malaysia, Singapore, and Thailand.
June 24		The United States awards Britain its first major contracts for work on the Strategic Defense Initiative ("Star Wars").	The conflict in Israel between ultraorthodox religious Jews and secular, nonreligious Jews explodes into open vandalism and violence, shocking the Israeli public and threatening the nation with the specter of widening civil strife. The immediate cause is advertising billboards showing women in bathing suits.		Sec. of State George Shultz signs an agreement to give the Philippines $200 mil. in expedited aid. Shultz is in the Philippines as part of a week long tour of Asia. The funds were authorized by Congress in previous years but were not given to then-Pres. Ferdinand E. Marcos because of disputes over how it should be spent. . . . Japan's Economic Planning Agency reports that gross national product (GNP) declined 0.5% in real (inflation-adjusted) terms in the first quarter of 1986. It is the first such drop in GNP since 1975.
June 25			The chief of Israel's secret domestic security agency, the Shin Bet, resigns in exchange for immunity from prosecution for the 1984 deaths of two captured Palestinian bus hijackers. The action causes a political and public uproar in Israel and is challenged by the nation's Supreme Court.	Brazil announces that it has resumed ties with Cuba. Diplomatic relations between the two nations were broken off in 1964 following a right-wing military coup in Brazil.	

A	B	C	D	E
Includes developments that affect more than one world region, international organizations and important meetings of major world leaders.	Includes all domestic and regional developments in Europe, including the Soviet Union, Turkey, Cyprus and Malta.	Includes all domestic and regional developments in Africa and the Middle East, including Iraq and Iran and excluding Cyprus, Turkey and Afghanistan.	Includes all domestic and regional developments in Latin America, the Caribbean and Canada.	Includes all domestic and regional developments in Asia and Pacific nations, extending from Afghanistan through all the Pacific Islands, except Hawaii.

U.S. Politics & Social Issues	U.S. Foreign Policy & Defense	U.S. Economy & Environment	Science, Technology & Nature	Culture, Leisure & Life Style	
				Membership in religious congregations in the United States rose almost 1% in 1984, according to statistics available from the National Council of Churches.... Heisman Trophy winner Bo Jackson announces he will play baseball with the Kansas City Royals and not sign a contract reportedly worth $7 mil. with the Tampa Bay Buccaneers of the National Football League (NFL). Jackson was the first pick in the NFL draft.	June 21
				The June 13 death of pop star Dean Reed, 47, may have been the result of foul play, according to the Sunday *Times* of London. Reed, an American-born singer and actor, had lived in East Germany since 1972. Although little known in the United States, his recordings and films and vocal anti-Americanism made him a superstar in Eastern Europe.	June 22
The Justice Dept. says federal civil rights laws do not forbid the arbitrary firing of employees afflicted with acquired immune deficiency syndrome.				Sir Moses (known as M.I. Finley) Finley, 72, classical historian whose work includes *The World of Odysseus* (1954), *The Ancient Greeks* (1963), and *Ancient Slavery and Modern Ideology* (1980), dies. The U.S.-born scholar moved to England in the 1950s after being fired from an academic post at Rutgers Univ. for refusing to respond to charges that he once was a communist. He became a British national in 1962, was named professor of ancient history at Cambridge in 1970, and was knighted in 1979.	June 23
Roy M. Cohn, the lawyer who became famous as the communist-hunting counsel for Sen. Joe McCarthy's committee in the 1950s, is disbarred by the Appellate Division of the New York State Supreme Court for unethical behavior.... New York Gov. Mario Cuomo (D) and party leaders in the state legislature reach agreement on insurance reforms including restrictions on liability insurers, a compromise on increases in medical malpractice rates, and allowing people harmed by toxic substances to sue after the statute of limitations has expired.		After more than 100 hours of debate spanning 16 days, the Senate approves, 97-3, a bill that will represent the most radical overhaul of the nation's tax code in decades. The bill is virtually identical to the measure reported out of the Senate Finance Committee more than a month earlier.	Workers at the Chernobyl nuclear power plant in the Soviet Ukraine complete construction on a concrete slab under the ruined No.4 reactor. The completion of the slab is a major step in a plan to encase the reactor in an impenetrable "coffin" to cut off the release of radioactivity.		June 24
The Supreme Court rules that libel suits brought in federal courts by public officials and public figures should be dismissed before trial in the absence of "clear and convincing" evidence of malice.	In a major foreign policy victory for Pres. Reagan, the House of Representatives votes to approve his request for $100 mil. in aid for the Contras fighting to overthrow the Nicaraguan government.				June 25

F	G	H	I	J
Includes elections, federal-state relations, civil rights and liberties, crime, the judiciary, education, health care, poverty, urban affairs and population.	Includes formation and debate of U.S. foreign and defense policies, veterans' affairs and defense spending. (Relations with specific foreign countries are usually found under the region concerned.)	Includes business, labor, agriculture, taxation, transportation, consumer affairs, monetary and fiscal policy, natural resources, and pollution.	Includes worldwide scientific, medical and technological developments, natural phenomena, U.S. weather, natural disasters, and accidents.	Includes the arts, religion, scholarship, communications media, sports, entertainments, fashions, fads and social life.

	World Affairs	Europe	Africa & the Middle East	The Americas	Asia & the Pacific
June 26	A 26-day strike against American Telephone and Telegraph Co. by the Communications Workers of America ends as negotiators reach a new contract.	Voters in Ireland vote by more than a three-to-two margin, 935,843 to 528,279, against a proposal that would have ended the nation's constitutional ban on divorce. The defeat of the amendment is a setback for the coalition government headed by P.M. Garret FitzGerald of the Fine Gael Party.		In a blow to the political opposition in Nicaragua, the government closes indefinitely the nation's only independent newspaper, *La Prensa*.	
June 27	The International Court of Justice (the World Court) at The Hague rules that the United States violated international law and Nicaraguan sovereignty in supporting the Contras fighting to overthrow the Sandinista government. Nicaragua brought its suit against the United States in April 1984. The United States, which said in 1985 it would not accept the judgment of World Court, assails today's verdict.	Soviet sources tell Western journalists that Glavlit, the government agency responsible for the censorship of the print in media the Soviet Union, is to be disbanded.... A summit meeting of European Community leaders in The Hague, Neth., reaches a compromise agreement on South African policy that stops short of imposing economic sanctions.		Peru's Pres. Alan Garcia Perez confirms that national police executed more than 100 Maoist rebels during a prison mutiny June 18 and 19. The rebel inmates, members of the Sendero Luminoso (Shining Path) group, had attempted to take over three prisons but were overwhelmed by police and the military.	Sec. of State George P. Shultz tells New Zealand's P.M. David Lange that the United States will no longer promise to defend New Zealand. The statement comes during a 40-minute meeting in Manila that fails to resolve any of the countries' differences.
June 28		The 13th congress of the League of Communists of Yugoslavia concludes four days of meetings in Belgrade. The last party congress was held in 1982.			In India, the country's governing Congress (I) Party wins all 30 seats it contested in elections to the Rajya Sabha (the upper house of India's parliament), easily maintaining its majority in the 244-seat chamber.
June 29					
June 30	Pope John Paul II visits Colombia. He is greeted in Bogota by Pres. Belisario Betancur and his cabinet. It is John Paul's 30th trip abroad as pope and his seventh trip to Latin America.... As a result of talks aimed at bettering relations between the French and Iranian governments, an Iranian dissident group is expelled from France and two French hostages in Lebanon are freed. But French officials insist that their support for Iraq in the Persian Gulf war will not change.	Soviet Leader Mikhail S. Gorbachev assails U.S. arms control policies in a speech to the Polish party congress. The speech follows a series of Soviet moves on a meeting concerning the 1979 Strategic Arms Limitation Treaty (SALT II) and on a parley of U.S. and Soviet aides in connection with a 1986 summit.	The five remaining U.S. oil companies in Libya officially close all operations there. Pres. Reagan set the deadline and said he would enforce it by executive order if necessary; the House backed him in a June 9 vote. Reagan had cut economic ties with Libya in January as a punishment for its alleged support of terrorism.		Japan's current account surplus with the United States in calendar year 1985 is a record $41.73 bil., according to a preliminary report by the finance ministry. That represents 85% of Japan's overall current account surplus of $49.17 bil.

A	B	C	D	E
Includes developments that affect more than one world region, international organizations and important meetings of major world leaders.	*Includes all domestic and regional developments in Europe, including the Soviet Union, Turkey, Cyprus and Malta.*	*Includes all domestic and regional developments in Africa and the Middle East, including Iraq and Iran and excluding Cyprus, Turkey and Afghanistan.*	*Includes all domestic and regional developments in Latin America, the Caribbean and Canada.*	*Includes all domestic and regional developments in Asia and Pacific nations, extending from Afghanistan through all the Pacific Islands, except Hawaii.*

U.S. Politics & Social Issues	U.S. Foreign Policy & Defense	U.S. Economy & Environment	Science, Technology & Nature	Culture, Leisure & Life Style	
The Supreme Court rules, 5-4, that execution of a criminal who is insane is not permissible under the constitutional ban against cruel and unusual punishments.... A special panel for the Republican National Committee dismisses complaints from a group of black Republicans that the party's rules discriminate against blacks and other minorities. A spokesperson for the black Republicans disagrees with the findings and says the group is considering a lawsuit. ... Florida Gov. Bob Graham (D) signs a sweeping law that will temporarily roll back commercial, property, and liability insurance premiums by 40% and limit damage awards in liability suits.		The House and Senate pass a compromise FY1987 federal budget with projected outlays of $995.0 bil.			June 26
Radical lawyer Stephen Bingham is acquitted of murder and conspiracy charges in connection with the 1971 Black Panther's fatal attempt to break out of San Quentin (Calif.) prison. A Marin County, Calif., Superior Court jury arrived at the verdict in San Rafael.		The deficit on merchandise trade grew in May to $14.21 bil., the Commerce Dept. reports.	The human gene mapping project, a proposal to map and define the entire human genetic structure, still in the early discussion stages, is arousing intense interest and debate among molecular biologists, according to the journal *Science*, and other news accounts. ... Scientists are struggling to explain a growing and potentially alarming seasonal depletion of the ozone layer in the atmosphere above Antarctica, according to an article in the journal *Science* and other news accounts. An unusual expedition is being launched to collect new evidence during the Antarctic night in August.	*Publishers Weekly*'s hardback fiction best-sellers for the week are: *I'll Take Manhattan*, Judith Krantz; *Last of the Breed*, Louis L'Amour; *The Bourne Supremacy*, Robert Ludlum; *The Eighth Commandment*, Lawrence Sanders; and *A Perfect Spy*, John Le Carre.	June 27
			The second International Conf. on acquired immune deficiency syndrome (AIDS) begins six days of meetings in Paris, largely under the auspices of the World Health Org. Some 2,500 scientists gather to compare research findings on AIDS.		June 28
John P. East, 55, conservative Republican from North Carolina and a member of the U.S. Senate from 1981, is found dead of carbon monoxide poisoning in the garage of his home in Greenville, N.C. The political protege of Jesse Helms, North Carolina's archconservative senior senator, had been confined to a wheelchair since contracting polio as a young adult. He had been undergoing treatment for hypothyroidism and in September 1985 had announced he would not seek reelection to the Senate.				Argentina's soccer team wins the World Cup tournament in Mexico with a 3-2 victory over West Germany.	June 29
The Supreme Court rules that the secretary of commerce is not required to certify that Japan is in violation of the whale harvesting quotas of the international whaling conservation program. Such a finding under U.S. law would trigger automatic sanctions against Japan.		New labor contracts with the copper industry are negotiated as the old pacts expire. A coalition of 14 unions reach agreement with Kennecott Corp. after days of almost continuous bargaining.... Prices received by farmers for their raw agricultural goods dropped 1.6% in June, the Agriculture Dept. reports.	William R. Graham, acting head of the National Aeronautics and Space Admin. at the time of the *Challenger* shuttle disaster in January, is named by Pres. Reagan as his chief science adviser. As such, he will head the White House Office of Science and Technology Policy.	Declining attendance forces the closure of the last three Playboy Clubs directly owned by Playboy Enterprises Inc.; the clubs are in Chicago, New York, and Century City, Los Angeles. Launched in 1960, the men's club chain reached a peak national membership of almost 1 million in the mid-1970s.	June 30

F	G	H	I	J
Includes elections, federal-state relations, civil rights and liberties, crime, the judiciary, education, health care, poverty, urban affairs and population.	Includes formation and debate of U.S. foreign and defense policies, veterans' affairs and defense spending. (Relations with specific foreign countries are usually found under the region concerned.)	Includes business, labor, agriculture, taxation, transportation, consumer affairs, monetary and fiscal policy, natural resources, and pollution.	Includes worldwide scientific, medical and technological developments, natural phenomena, U.S. weather, natural disasters, and accidents.	Includes the arts, religion, scholarship, communications media, sports, entertainments, fashions, fads and social life.

	World Affairs	Europe	Africa & the Middle East	The Americas	Asia & the Pacific
July 1		The official death toll from the Chernobyl nuclear plant accident in the Soviet Union in April is 26 people. It reached that total June 5.			
July 2		Norway announces it will end commercial whaling in 1987, although it will continue catching whales for "scientific" purposes. Earlier in the year, Norway announced that it would take 350 minke whales for the season, in defiance of the moratorium on whaling called for by the International Whaling Comm.... To avert a trade war over agricultural products, the United States and the European Community agree to a six-month suspension of increased tariffs.			
July 3		The British government announces that it will delay the sell-off of the nation's 10 regional water authorities. Although Environmental Sec. Nicholas Ridley says in a written reply that the sell-off will be undertaken "as soon as practicable," it is widely assumed that the sale will not occur before the next general election.		Chileans stage a two-day general strike to demand a return to democracy. At least six people are shot to death during the strike, and a Chilean-born resident of the United States who is set on fire, Rodrigo Rojas de Negri, later died of his burns.	
July 4		Turkish Premier Turgut Ozal concludes a visit to the self-proclaimed Turkish republic of Northern Cyprus. Ozal's visit to the island of Cyprus, the first by a Turkish head of government since the declaration of the breakaway republic in 1983, prompts international criticism.	Former Pres. Jimmy Carter, the guest of honor at a diplomatic reception in Harare, Zimbabwe, walks out after a cabinet minister uses what was meant as a toast to deliver a stinging attack on U.S. policy toward South Africa. The incident causes the Reagan administration to suspend its aid program to Zimbabwe pending an apology from the government of P.M. Robert Mugabe.	The Nicaraguan government expels the second most important figure in the Roman Catholic Church in Nicaragua, Pablo Antonio Vega Mantilla, charging that he supports the anti-Sandinista Contras. Vega, vice president of the Nicaraguan Bishop's Conf., is forced to leave Nicaragua for Honduras, where he is granted political asylum.... Canada's P.M. Brian Mulroney formally opens his drive to have Quebec sign the constitution. The drive is to be spearheaded by a cabinet-level committee. Quebec was the only province to refuse to sign the constitution when it was repatriated from Britain in 1981.	

A	B	C	D	E
Includes developments that affect more than one world region, international organizations and important meetings of major world leaders.	Includes all domestic and regional developments in Europe, including the Soviet Union, Turkey, Cyprus and Malta.	Includes all domestic and regional developments in Africa and the Middle East, including Iraq and Iran and excluding Cyprus, Turkey and Afghanistan.	Includes all domestic and regional developments in Latin America, the Caribbean and Canada.	Includes all domestic and regional developments in Asia and Pacific nations, extending from Afghanistan through all the Pacific Islands, except Hawaii.

U.S. Politics & Social Issues	U.S. Foreign Policy & Defense	U.S. Economy & Environment	Science, Technology & Nature	Culture, Leisure & Life Style	
In a 5-4 ruling the Supreme Court upholds the right of government to curb truthful advertising in the interest of regulating an undesirable product or activity.	An experimental airship combining a blimp and helicopters crashes during testing at the U.S. Naval Engineering Center in Lakehurst, N.J. One crew member is killed and three injured. The famous 1937 explosion of the German zeppelin *Hindenburg* occurred at the same site.	The Environmental Protection Agency issues new standards to tighten protection against leaks from hazardous-waste tanks. . . . U.S. companies raised nearly as much money through stock and bond offerings in the first half of 1986 as they did in all of 1985, the *Wall Street Journal* reports. For the first six months of 1986, companies raised $165 bil., compared with $171 mil. in all of 1985. . . . The government's index of leading economic indicators rose 0.2% in May, the Commerce Dept. reports.			July 1
In Tucson, Federal District Judge Earl H. Carroll places on probation eight church workers convicted May 1 of illegally smuggling Central American aliens into the United States as part of the Sanctuary Movement. The judge could have imposed sentences of five to 25 years in prison. . . . In two 6-3 rulings, the Supreme Court upholds affirmative action as a remedy for past job discrimination.	Pres. Reagan signs into law a bill reforming the military retirement system. The Senate approved the legislation June 25 and the House June 26.	Pres. Reagan signs a $1.7 bil. supplemental spending bill for FY1986, while complaining that it undercuts executive-branch powers. The bill provides funds for a variety of agencies and programs through September 30, the end of FY1986. . . . The Dow Jones Industrial closes at a record high of 1909.03.		A Los Angeles Superior Court jury awards ventriloquist Paul Winchell a $17.8 mil. verdict in his decade-long fight against Metromedia Inc., which Winchell claims destroyed the tapes of his "Winchell Mahoney Time" children's television series—starring his dummies Jerry Mahoney and Knucklehead Smiff—in a dispute over syndication rights.	July 2
Jonathan Brewster Bingham, 72, liberal New York City Democrat who served nine terms in the House of Representatives (1965-83), dies in New York City of pneumonia and related complications. A leading congressional opponent of the Vietnam War, he was also the chief author of the Nuclear Nonproliferation Act of 1978.		The nation's unemployment rate dropped to a seasonally adjusted 7% of the work force in June, the Labor Dept. reports.		Rudy (born Hubert Prior Vallee) Vallee, 84, American singing idol and movie star of the 1920s and 1930s for whom the term "crooner" was coined, dies in Los Angeles of an apparent heart attack. Famous for his "heigh-ho, everybody" signature greeting and for singing through a megaphone to amplify his nasal voice, he made his first film *The Vagabond Lover* in 1929. A successful radio personality, he enjoyed a resurgence of popularity in the 1960s on Broadway and in film as the tycoon J.B. Biggley in *How to Succeed in Business Without Really Trying*. . . . Barry Douglas, a 26-year-old pianist from Belfast, Northern Ireland, is awarded the gold medal in the main piano section of the quadrennial International Tchaikovsky Music Competition in Moscow. Douglas is the first Westerner to take the top-prize outright since American pianist Van Cliburn triumphed in the first Tchaikovsky competition in 1958. . . . Pres. Reagan ceremonially relights the torch of the Statue of Liberty to mark the beginning of a four-day celebration of the Statue's 100th anniversary.	July 3
		A five-week strike by two unions against the Aluminum Co. of America ends with approval of a new three-year contract with givebacks. The new pact cuts hourly benefits 95 cents and freezes wages. . . . A new contract between Caterpillar Inc. and the United Auto Workers focuses on job security. Wages are frozen over the length of the contract, 28 months, at an average of about $13.60 an hour, although cost-of-living increments will continue to be paid.	According to a new analysis of data from the Voyager 2 spacecraft reported in the journal *Science*, the rings around Saturn and Uranus may be transitory phenomena formed by the relatively recent breakup of a moon or an earlier ring rather than dating from the formation of the solar system, some 4.5 billion years ago.		July 4

F	G	H	I	J
Includes elections, federal-state relations, civil rights and liberties, crime, the judiciary, education, health care, poverty, urban affairs and population.	*Includes formation and debate of U.S. foreign and defense policies, veterans' affairs and defense spending. (Relations with specific foreign countries are usually found under the region concerned.)*	*Includes business, labor, agriculture, taxation, transportation, consumer affairs, monetary and fiscal policy, natural resources, and pollution.*	*Includes worldwide scientific, medical and technological developments, natural phenomena, U.S. weather, natural disasters, and accidents.*	*Includes the arts, religion, scholarship, communications media, sports, entertainments, fashions, fads and social life.*

	World Affairs	Europe	Africa & the Middle East	The Americas	Asia & the Pacific
July 5		The Soviet Communist Party newspaper *Pravda* criticizes bureaucrats for slowing down the effort to resettle the 135,000 people evacuated from areas around the Chernobyl nuclear power plant following the environmental disaster there in April.	Three men armed with AK-47 assault rifles drive through two townships south of Johannesburg and kill five black municipal officials whom many blacks viewed as collaborators with apartheid. Two of the gunmen are killed by police and one escapes.		In an effort to improve the nation's poor trade performance, the Chinese government devalues its currency by 15.8%. China also allows the issuing and discounting of commercial paper by bank branches in 10 cities in an attempt to bail out enterprises facing credit squeezes.
July 6					Two Australians convicted of heroin trafficking are hanged in Kuala Lumpur amid international protests. The executions follow a string of legal appeals by the defendants as well as personal pleas on the part of Australia's P.M. Bob Hawke and Britain's P.M. Margaret Thatcher. . . . Premier Yasuhiro Nakasone's Liberal Democratic Party wins a landslide victory in elections to Japan's Diet, regaining the parliamentary majority it lost in the house of representatives in 1963. The win bolsters Nakasone's chances of changing party rules to allow him to run for a third term as party leader and therefore as premier.
July 7	Agreeing to terms mediated by Javier Perez de Cuellar, secretary-general of the UN, France announces that it and New Zealand have settled their differences over France's role in the bombing of the Greenpeace protest vessel *Rainbow Warrior* in July 1985.		Jordan orders the closure of all 25 offices of Yasir Arafat's Al Fatah, the largest faction within the Palestine Liberation Org.	In Canada, a secret federal study recommends that many federal environmental protection programs be turned over to the provinces. The study was commissioned by Erik Nielsen when he was deputy prime minister. A draft of the report was obtained by the *Toronto Globe and Mail.*	P.M. Bob Hawke wins a crucial vote of support for his economic policies during the Australian Labor Party's 37th national conference, held in Hobart, Tasmania. . . . In the Philippines, a bid by backers of former Pres. Ferdinand E. Marcos to set up a rebel government under Arturo Tolentino, Marcos's running mate in the February elections, fails. Troops supporting Tolentino surrender, and Tolentino abandons the rebellion after learning that they do not have the support of military leaders.
July 8		British women earned only 73% to 74% of the average hourly earnings of men from 1977 through April 1985, according to a report published by the government's Equal Opportunity Comm. . . . The European Court of Human Rights in Strasbourg, France, rules against several British shipbuilding and aircraft companies that claim shareholders were not fairly compensated when company operations were nationalized in 1977 by the British Labour government of James Callaghan.	Tunisia's Pres. Habib Bourguiba dismisses his premier and designated successor, Mohammed Mzali, whom the ailing Bourguiba had confirmed as his successor as recently as June 19. He replaces Mzali with Economy Min. Rachid Sfar.		

A	B	C	D	E
Includes developments that affect more than one world region, international organizations and important meetings of major world leaders.	*Includes all domestic and regional developments in Europe, including the Soviet Union, Turkey, Cyprus and Malta.*	*Includes all domestic and regional developments in Africa and the Middle East, including Iraq and Iran and excluding Cyprus, Turkey and Afghanistan.*	*Includes all domestic and regional developments in Latin America, the Caribbean and Canada.*	*Includes all domestic and regional developments in Asia and Pacific nations, extending from Afghanistan through all the Pacific Islands, except Hawaii.*

U.S. Politics & Social Issues	U.S. Foreign Policy & Defense	U.S. Economy & Environment	Science, Technology & Nature	Culture, Leisure & Life Style	
				At Wimbledon, Martina Navratilova defeats Hana Mandlikova, 7-6, 6-3, to win the women's single tennis title.... The Statue of Liberty is officially opened to the public in a ceremony featuring First Lady Nancy Reagan. The landmark has been closed for restoration since June 23, 1985.	July 5
The country's two chief teachers' organizations vote July 4 and today on aspects of a landmark report issued two months before by the Carnegie Forum on Education and the Economy. The National Educational Assoc. and the American Federation of Teachers both endorse the proposals in the report, the latter more fully than the former. The report asserts "We do not believe the education system needs repairing; we believe it must be rebuilt."				The British national crew Nautilus defeats the Univ. of Pennsylvania in the Grand Challenge Cup for eight-man crews at the Henley Royal Regatta in England.... In tennis, Boris Becker of West Germany wins Wimbledon's men's single title.	July 6
The Supreme Court upholds the authority of school officials to discipline a high school student for giving a "vulgar" and "inappropriate" speech to a school assembly. The term has been marked by an agressive attempt to attain decisions bolstering its conservative ideological philosophy, and the Reagan administration scored points most notably in the area of criminal law.		McDonald's Corp. announces that for the first time it will make available a booklet listing the ingredients of its fast food. The company plans to distribute 100 of the booklets to each of its 7,500 U.S. outlets.... In a 7-2 decision, the Supreme Court says the Gramm-Rudman-Hollings budget-balancing law's mechanism for automatic spending cuts violates the principle of the separation of powers because it vests executive authority in the comptroller general, a legislative-branch officer. ... The dollar plummets to postwar record lows against the Japanese yen in trading on the Tokyo market. The dollar rallies later in the day to close in New York at 162.03 yen to the dollar after hitting 158.20.			July 7
Pres. Reagan signs a measure extending the period of daylight savings time so that clocks are set ahead one hour on the first Sunday of April rather than on the last Sunday of April, as current law provides.... In a 7-0 ruling, the New York State Court of Appeals reinstates charges of attempted murder and assault against Bernhard H. Goetz, "the subway vigilante." ... A Johns Hopkins Univ. study finds that an experimental sexual education program in Baltimore public schools that includes free contraceptives and discussions of the students' personal feelings about sex, finds that participants are more likely to seek contraceptives, less likely to become pregnant, and refrain longer from sex.	Hyman George Rickover, 86, U.S. naval officer who was regarded as the father of the nuclear Navy, dies in Arlington, Va. A Russian immigrant and graduate of the U.S. Naval Academy, he directed the planning and construction of the world's first atomic powered submarine, USS Nautilus, launched in 1954. His abrasive personality and distaste for protocol did little to endear him to Navy brass. Following his retirement in 1982, he called for the outlawing of both nuclear weapons and nuclear power.	The Securities and Exchange Comm. (SEC) votes to prohibit bids for a company's shares that are not open to all shareholders; such limited offers are known as exclusionary tender offers. The SEC also votes a "best price" rule requiring that a bidder for a company pay all shareholders the same price.... The Food and Drug Admin. bans the use of sulfite preservatives in fresh vegetables and fruits. Sulfites have been linked to 13 deaths and various ailments, primarily among people with asthma.... Seafirst Corp., a Seattle bank holding company, reaches agreement with five of its former executives to settle a lawsuit resulting from the huge losses Seafirst incurred after the collapse of Oklahoma's Penn Square in 1982.... U.S. Steel Corp. announces that it will change its name to USX Corp. and restructure the company's assets.	A federal judge in New York dismisses a suit filed by the Pasteur Institute in Paris against the U.S. government over who discovered the virus that causes acquired immune deficiency syndrome. French and American researchers who had once shared information both claim independent credit for the discovery, and the dispute has become rancorous.... Southern California experiences its strongest earthquake since 1979. The quake, which measures 5.9 on the Richter open-ended scale of ground motion, leaves some 40 people injured and causes an estimated $5.75 mil. in damages.		July 8

F	G	H	I	J
Includes elections, federal-state relations, civil rights and liberties, crime, the judiciary, education, health care, poverty, urban affairs and population.	Includes formation and debate of U.S. foreign and defense policies, veterans' affairs and defense spending. (Relations with specific foreign countries are usually found under the region concerned.)	Includes business, labor, agriculture, taxation, transportation, consumer affairs, monetary and fiscal policy, natural resources, and pollution.	Includes worldwide scientific, medical and technological developments, natural phenomena, U.S. weather, natural disasters, and accidents.	Includes the arts, religion, scholarship, communications media, sports, entertainments, fashions, fads and social life.

	World Affairs	Europe	Africa & the Middle East	The Americas	Asia & the Pacific
July 9				After two days of talks in Mexico City, Cuba and the United States fail to reach agreement on reviving a 1984 immigration pact. Under the 1984 agreement, the United States said it would accept Cuban political prisoners and a certain number of immigrants if Cuba took back 2,746 so-called undesirable Cubans who traveled to the United States in the Mariel boatlift in 1980. Cuba suspended the immigration agreement after the United States began broadcasts to Cuba on Radio Marti.	
July 10		An Italian court convicts 11 of the 15 men charged with involvement in the October 1985 hijacking of the *Achille Lauro* cruise ship. The trial opened June 18 in Genoa.... The European Community reaches a new compromise budget for 1986; the new spending plan was made necessary when the European Court of Justice struck down the budget drafted by the European Parliament in December 1985.		Brazil's Pres. Jose Sarney meets with Pope John Paul II at the Vatican and receives the pontiff's endorsement of land reform in Brazil. Sarney's critics in Brazil fault him for moving too slowly on land redistribution, and the government blames activist church members for urging peasants to seize the land.	Le Duan, 78, secretary-general of Vietnam's Communist Party, dies in Hanoi of lung and kidney ailments. One of the prime architects of Hanoi's victory in the Vietnam War, he was the ranking Vietnamese communist since the death of Ho Chi Minh in September 1969.
July 11		*Krasnaya Zvezda* (Red Star), the newspaper of the Soviet defense ministry, reports that the sons of some well-connected Soviet officials are being shielded from fighting in Afghanistan.			China formally applies to rejoin the General Agreement on Tariffs and Trade (GATT). One of GATT's original members in 1947, China withdrew in 1950 after the communist takeover.
July 12		Members of the Protestant majority in Northern Ireland march to commemorate a Protestant victory over Roman Catholics at the 1690 battle of the Boyne and to protest the eight-month-old Anglo-Irish accord. The Orange Day parades, marking the height of the Protestants' so-called marching season, goes off without violence.	In Guinea-Bissau, a military court convicts 56 people of plotting a coup in November 1985 against the government of Pres. Joao Bernardo Vieira; 12 of them are sentenced to death.		
July 13	Canada's P.M. Brian Mulroney attempts to convince British P.M. Margaret Thatcher to join the Commonwealth in imposing tough sanctions on South Africa.	Soviet Foreign Min. Eduard A. Shevardnadze visits Britain as part of an apparent Soviet diplomatic initiative to improve relations with Western Europe.			Mick Young is named president of the federal Australian Labor Party (ALP). The 49-year-old former sheep-shearer adds the post to his positions as special minister of state and chairman of the ALP's National Campaign Committee.
July 14		In the Netherlands, the new cabinet of Dutch Premier Ruud Lubbers is sworn in after almost two months of negotiations between the premier's Christian Democrats and the coalition's junior partner, the Liberal Party.... French Socialist Pres. Francois Mitterrand announces that he will not sign decrees allowing the conservative government to denationalize 65 state-owned companies.... The Bastille Day parade in Paris is France's largest military parade since World War II.			Truong Chinh, an ideological hardliner, is elected to succeed Le Duan as secretary general of Vietnam's Communist Party. Le Duan, who succeeded Ho Chi Minh as effective leader of the party in 1969, died July 10.

A	B	C	D	E
Includes developments that affect more than one world region, international organizations and important meetings of major world leaders.	Includes all domestic and regional developments in Europe, including the Soviet Union, Turkey, Cyprus and Malta.	Includes all domestic and regional developments in Africa and the Middle East, including Iraq and Iran and excluding Cyprus, Turkey and Afghanistan.	Includes all domestic and regional developments in Latin America, the Caribbean and Canada.	Includes all domestic and regional developments in Asia and Pacific nations, extending from Afghanistan through all the Pacific Islands, except Hawaii.

U.S. Politics & Social Issues	U.S. Foreign Policy & Defense	U.S. Economy & Environment	Science, Technology & Nature	Culture, Leisure & Life Style	
The Attorney Gen.'s Comm. on Pornography releases the final draft of a report claiming that violent pornography probably leads to sexual violence. The report calls for a crackdown on obscenity by federal, state, and local authorities.	The transcript of a House subcommittee hearing inadvertently identifies 20 foreign U.S. Air Force bases at which nuclear weapons are stored. The government's standard practice is to keep secret the locations of nuclear-armed bases.		It is "essential" that blood banks adopt improved tests for acquired immune deficiency syndrome (AIDS), a panel of health experts reports in Washington, D.C. Panel members say the chance of catching AIDS through a transfusion is "substantially less than one in 10,000," but that more sensitive tests are required.	*Variety*'s top-grossing films for the week are: *Ruthless People, Under the Cherry Moon, Back to School, The Karate Kid Part II* and *Running Scared*.	July 9
The National Institute on Drug Abuse reports that the number of Americans killed each year in cocaine-related deaths rose from 185 in 1981 to at least 563 in 1985. The number of cocaine users is thought to be stable.		Economic growth between 1981 and 1985 was largely confined to 15 East Coast states and California, which posted an annual growth rate of 4%, according to a study released by Rep. Davis Obey (D, Wis.). The rest of the country had annual growth of 1.4%, and gross national product grew 2.3% annually. . . . The Federal Reserve Board cuts the discount rate, the interest rate it charges on loans to financial institutions, to 6%, the lowest level since October 1977.			July 10
	An Air Force pilot is killed in a jet crash in central California. The mishap results in a security clampdown, leading to speculation that the crash plane was an experimental radar-evading fighter.	The government's producer price index was unchanged in June, the Labor Dept. reports. Over the first six months of 1986, the index fell at an annual rate of 6.5%, the steepest rate of decline since 1949.			July 11
					July 12
			For the first time since it sank in 1912, the ocean liner *Titanic* is viewed by human eyes as Dr. Robert Ballard and a team of scientists from the Woods Hole (Mass.) Oceanographic Institute explore the ship's wreckage on an expedition sponsored by the U.S. Navy.	In auto racing, Nigel Mansell becomes the first Englishman to win the British Grand Prix since 1964.	July 13
A weekend gathering of white supremacists and anti-Semites in Hayden Lake, Idaho, is reported. The two-day Aryan Nations World Congress is North America's first such gathering since 10 members of the Order, a neo-Nazi group, were convicted in December 1985 of racketeering.	Richard W. Miller is sentenced to two life terms plus 50 years in prison for spying for the Soviet Union. Miller, 49, is the first Federal Bureau of Investigation agent convicted of espionage.	Raymond Fernand Loewy, 92, founding father of American industrial design, dies in Monaco. Regarded as having pioneered the "streamlined" look, which drastically altered the appearance of thousands of objects from toothpaste containers to automobiles to airplanes, perhaps his single best known design is the Coca-Cola bottle. In 1945 he founded Raymond Loewy Associates, which became the world's largest industrial design firm and helped design the interior of the Skylab space orbiter. . . . Federal bank regulators close First National Bank and Trust Co. of Oklahoma City. The bank failure is the second-largest in U.S. history. The bank is acquired a few hours after the closing by First Interstate Bancorp of Los Angeles and reopens.	National Aeronautics and Space Admin. officials announce that the space shuttle flight schedule has been moved back from July 1987 to early 1988.	Jane Geddes wins the U.S. Women's Golf Open in Kettering, Ohio.	July 14

F	G	H	I	J
Includes elections, federal-state relations, civil rights and liberties, crime, the judiciary, education, health care, poverty, urban affairs and population.	Includes formation and debate of U.S. foreign and defense policies, veterans' affairs and defense spending. (Relations with specific foreign countries are usually found under the region concerned.)	Includes business, labor, agriculture, taxation, transportation, consumer affairs, monetary and fiscal policy, natural resources, and pollution.	Includes worldwide scientific, medical and technological developments, natural phenomena, U.S. weather, natural disasters, and accidents.	Includes the arts, religion, scholarship, communications media, sports, entertainments, fashions, fads and social life.

	World Affairs	Europe	Africa & the Middle East	The Americas	Asia & the Pacific
July 15				U.S. administration officials announce that U.S. Army personnel and equipment were sent yesterday to Bolivia to help in the war on drug traffickers.	
July 16	The White House confirms reports that U.S. and Soviet officials will meet in Geneva later in the month to discuss a comprehensive ban on nuclear testing. Washington initially rejected a March call from Moscow for such talks.	Hungary becomes the first country to sign a nuclear power pact with the Soviet Union since the April accident at the nuclear plant in Chernobyl. The pact calls for the Soviet Union to supply two VVER 1000-megawatt nuclear reactors for Hungary's Paks plant. The plant, Hungary's only nuclear power station, already has two Soviet VVER-440 reactors.		The former head of Haiti's secret police is sentenced to death July 16 on charges of murder. The trial of Luc Desyr, 61, began July 15. He was the chief of police under Francois Duvalier and his son, Jean Claude Duvalier, who succeeded him. The younger Duvalier fled the country in February.	
July 17					
July 18		In a 35-minute nationally televised speech, Soviet leader Mikhail S. Gorbachev announces that Moscow's year-old moratorium on nuclear testing will be extended until Jan. 1, 1987.	An 11-man delegation from the International Confederation of Free Trade Unions visits South Africa to show solidarity with the country's black union movement and to seek the release of more than 200 union leaders detained under the state of emergency imposed in June.		

A	B	C	D	E
Includes developments that affect more than one world region, international organizations and important meetings of major world leaders.	Includes all domestic and regional developments in Europe, including the Soviet Union, Turkey, Cyprus and Malta.	Includes all domestic and regional developments in Africa and the Middle East, including Iraq and Iran and excluding Cyprus, Turkey and Afghanistan.	Includes all domestic and regional developments in Latin America, the Caribbean and Canada.	Includes all domestic and regional developments in Asia and Pacific nations, extending from Afghanistan through all the Pacific Islands, except Hawaii.

U.S. Politics & Social Issues	U.S. Foreign Policy & Defense	U.S. Economy & Environment	Science, Technology & Nature	Culture, Leisure & Life Style	
		Industrial production in June fell a seasonally adjusted 0.5%, the Federal Reserve Board reports.	Systemization of the country's arrangements for organ transplants is urged in a report issued by a federal advisory committee. The panel says the federal government should oversee a network to locate organ donors, and should also guarantee that "inability to pay" will not keep any American in need from receiving a heart or liver transplant.	The American League wins Major League baseball's annual All-Star game, 3-2, over the National League.	July 15
Parents who had tried to keep 14-year-old Ryan White, who has been diagnosed with acquired immune deficiency syndrome, out of their children's public school classes say they will no longer oppose White's attendance. Earlier today, the Indiana Court of Appeals dismissed the parents' request to overturn a judge's decision allowing White to return to class.		Bank-America reports a loss of $640 mil. for the second quarter of 1986. The loss is the second-largest quarterly loss ever incurred by a U.S. bank.	Soviet cosmonauts Col. Leonid D. Kizim and Vladimir A. Solovyov return safely to Earth after a 125-day mission in space. The cosmonauts land the Soyuz T-15 spacecraft in a field in the republic of Kazakhstan about 33 miles northeast of the city of Arkalyk. . . . Jerrold Reinach Zacharias, 81, American nuclear physicist who directed the engineering division of the Manhattan Project, which developed the first atomic bomb during World War II, dies in Belmont, Mass., of a heart ailment. As director of the Massachusetts Institute of Technology's Laboratory of Nuclear Science after the war, he designed the world's first atomic clock, and in 1956 he formed the Physical Science Study Committee, which revolutionized the teaching of high school physics in the United States.	*Billboard*'s best selling albums for the week are: *Winner in You*, Patti LaBelle; *Control*, Janet Jackson; *So*, Peter Gabriel; *Top Gun* (soundtrack); and *Invisible Touch*, Genesis. . . . In auto racing, Nigel Mansell of Great Britain wins the French Grand Prix.	July 16
	The Senate ratifies a new extradition treaty with Britain, the primary purpose of which is to facilitate the extradition from the United States of members of the outlawed Provisional Irish Republican Army accused of terrorist acts aimed at ending British rule over the six counties that make-up Northern Ireland.	Congress overwhelmingly reaffirms the first $11.7 bil. round of spending cuts made in March under the Gramm-Rudman balanced budget law. The action comes as Congress grapples with the larger question of what to do with the budget process now that the Supreme Court has invalidated a key part of the law's deficit-cutting mechanism. . . . Citizens for Tax Justice, a tax-reform advocacy group, releases a study claiming that 42 large and profitable U.S. companies paid no taxes from 1982 to 1985. . . . House and Senate conferees begin final work on a comprehensive package of tax changes that will represent the most sweeping overhaul of the nation's tax system in decades.	Medical researchers, using elaborate and experimental techniques, report having produced long-term, disease-free survival in nearly half of a group of terminal leukemia patients. The technique combines chemotherapy with extracting and cleansing the patient's own bone marrow.		July 17
		The House Energy and Commerce subcommittee on health and the environment holds hearings on proposed legislation that would ban all tobacco advertising and promotion. According to the federal government, the tobacco industry spent $2.1 bil. on advertising and promotion in 1984. . . . New housing starts dropped 0.8% in June to a seasonally adjusted annual rate of 1.85 million units, the Commerce Dept. reports.		*Publishers Weekly*'s hardback fiction best-sellers for the week are: *Last of the Breed*, Louis L'Amour; *Act of Will*, Barbara Taylor Bradford; *The Bourne Conspiracy*, Robert Ludlum; *The Eighth Commandment*, Lawrence Sanders; and *I'll Take Manhattan*, Judith Krantz.	July 18

F	G	H	I	J
Includes elections, federal-state relations, civil rights and liberties, crime, the judiciary, education, health care, poverty, urban affairs and population.	Includes formation and debate of U.S. foreign and defense policies, veterans' affairs and defense spending. (Relations with specific foreign countries are usually found under the region concerned.)	Includes business, labor, agriculture, taxation, transportation, consumer affairs, monetary and fiscal policy, natural resources, and pollution.	Includes worldwide scientific, medical and technological developments, natural phenomena, U.S. weather, natural disasters, and accidents.	Includes the arts, religion, scholarship, communications media, sports, entertainments, fashions, fads and social life.

	World Affairs	Europe	Africa & the Middle East	The Americas	Asia & the Pacific
July 19		Employees of the French press agency Agence France-Presse (AFP), end a four-day strike after management agrees to delay staff cuts resulting from a reorganization plan. The strike shut down almost all of the agency's domestic and international services.... Italian Pres. Francesco Cossiga asks five-time Christian Democratic premier, Giulio Andreotti, to form a new government in the wake of the resignation of socialist Premier Bettino Craxi. Craxi, who headed Italy's longest-lasting postwar government, resigned June 27 after losing a key parliamentary vote.		Two-thirds of the underground waste dumps in Ontario, Canada, pose a threat to human health, according to a report made public today by the provincial environment ministry.	
July 20		The Sunday *Times* of London and other media report that Britain's Queen Elizabeth II is concerned about the survival of the Commonwealth, which is split over P.M. Margaret Thatcher's refusal to impose sanctions against South Africa.... West German Foreign Min. Hans Dietrich Genscher visits Moscow for talks with the Soviet leadership. His invitation appears to be part of a Kremlin initiative to strengthen Soviet ties with Western Europe.			
July 21		As the 30th anniversary of the Hungarian uprising approaches, the Hungarian government is reported to have ordered a crackdown on dissidents, including curbs on travel and publishing.	Israeli P.M. Shimon Peres flies to Morocco for secret talks with King Hassan II. The surprise summit, initiated by an offer from Hassan, is the first official, high-level contact between an Israeli and an Arab leader since the series of meetings inaugurated by the late Egyptian Pres. Anwar El-Sadat's historic 1977 visit to Jerusalem.	A Venezuelan judge acquits Cuban exile Orlando Bosch of charges that he planned the 1976 bombing of a Cuban Airlines jet in which 73 people died.	
July 22	The Standing Consultative Comm., made up of U.S. and Soviet nuclear arms experts, opens a special round of talks in Geneva to discuss Washington's threat to abrogate the 1979 Strategic Arms Limitation Treaty (SALT II).	The Movement of Socialist Renewal publicizes "To the Citizens of the USSR," a 17-page manifesto urging democratic reforms of the Soviet political and economic systems. The movement is thought to be comprised of officials of the government and Communist Party who wish to remain anonymous.		After months of negotiations Mexico signs an agreement with the International Monetary Fund for a $1.6 bil. loan.	The Japanese Diet overwhelmingly reappoints Yasuhiro Nakasone as premier; Nakasone immediately forms a new cabinet in which only he and Chief Cabinet Sec. Masaharu Gotoda retain their positions.
July 23		Albania failed to meet the target set in its most recent five-year economic plan (1981-85). The official government newspaper, *Bashkimi*, states that national income, a measure similar to gross national product, rose 16% over that achieved under the 1976-80 plan, but at a rate that was only half of the 1981-85 goal.... In France, the conservative government of Premier Jacques Chirac replaces the chairmen of 12 large state-owned companies. Twelve other chairmen are reconfirmed. The cabinet simultaneously approves legislation designed to privatize 65 state companies.		Former Honduran armed forces chief of staff Gen. Jose Bueso Rosa is sentenced in Florida to five years in prison for his part in a failed 1984 plot to assassinate then-president of Honduras, Roberto Suazo Cordova.... In Peru, a civilian judge orders the arrest of army Gen. Jorge Rabanal in connection with the June execution of more than 100 prisoners in Lurigancho prison.	John F. Burns, Beijing bureau chief of the *New York Times*, is expelled from China after being detained for almost a week on suspicion of espionage, "entering an area forbidden to foreigners and gathering intelligence information." The charges relate to a motorcycle trip Burns took through the Chinese countryside, accompanied by a U.S. lawyer and a Chinese national.

A	B	C	D	E
Includes developments that affect more than one world region, international organizations and important meetings of major world leaders.	Includes all domestic and regional developments in Europe, including the Soviet Union, Turkey, Cyprus and Malta.	Includes all domestic and regional developments in Africa and the Middle East, including Iraq and Iran and excluding Cyprus, Turkey and Afghanistan.	Includes all domestic and regional developments in Latin America, the Caribbean and Canada.	Includes all domestic and regional developments in Asia and Pacific nations, extending from Afghanistan through all the Pacific Islands, except Hawaii.

U.S. Politics & Social Issues	U.S. Foreign Policy & Defense	U.S. Economy & Environment	Science, Technology & Nature	Culture, Leisure & Life Style	
				Caroline Bouvier Kennedy, the 28-year-old daughter of Jacqueline Kennedy Onassis and the late Pres. John F. Kennedy, marries Edwin A. Schlossberg, the president of a New York City company specializing in the design of museum interiors and exhibitions.	**July 19**
				Tim Witherspoon successfully defends his World Boxing Assoc. heavyweight title over British challenger Frank Bruno in the 11th round.... The U.S. team wins the World Basketball championship with an 87-85 defeat of the Soviet Union in the final round.... Australia's Greg Norman wins the British Open golf tournament.	**July 20**
A committee of experts convened by the National Institutes of Health reports that patients suffering from pain are likely to be treated with either too much or too little medication.				Barbara Palacios Teyde of Venezuela is chosen Miss Universe.	**July 21**
The city of Philadelphia reaches a tentative agreement with its blue-collar employees two days after the workers vote to end their 20-day strike against the city. More than 15,000 city workers—members of the American Federation of State, County and Municipal Employees (AFSCME) union—went on strike July 1; the white-collar segment settled July 11.... The House votes unanimously to impeach U.S. District Judge Harry E. Claiborne of Las Vegas, who is serving a two-year sentence for tax evasion.	A space-based antimissile shield will cost as much as $770 bil. to build and maintain for 10 years, according to a private study prepared by defense analysts Barry M. Blechman and Victor A. Utgoff of the Johns Hopkins Foreign Policy Institute. It is believed to be the first attempt to quantify the costs of the Strategic Defense Initiative ("Star Wars") using unclassified data.	State officials estimate that Southern farmers stand to lose at least $1 bil. because of a string of record-setting high temperatures that began July 6. This follows a severe drought three months before.... The nation's gross national product increased at an inflation-adjusted rate of 1.1% in the second quarter, the Commerce Dept. reports. The slow economic growth was accompanied by an annual inflation rate of 2.1%, the lowest since 1967.... In a policy speech on South Africa, Pres. Reagan urges the white minority government to negotiate an end to the apartheid system of racial segregation. But he strongly reemphasizes his opposition to new economic sanctions, saying they would be a "historic act of folly."		Eight months after the dissolution of the Oregon commune of Indian guru Baghwan Shree Rajneesh, 54, his former secretary, Ma Anand Sheela, 36, pleads guilty in Portland, Ore., to a variety of state and federal charges, including attempted murder, electronic eavesdropping, immigration fraud, and engineering a food-poisoning epidemic. She is sentenced to a total of 69 years in prison but is expected to serve about four-and-a-half.	**July 22**
The chairman of the Equal Employment Opportunity Comm. (EEOC), Clarence Thomas, says the federal agency will resume the use of hiring goals and timetables, which the EEOC dropped in February, to fight job discrimination. Thomas says the reversal was inspired by the Supreme Court's recent decision giving qualified backing to affirmative action.... The Senate certifies Pres. Reagan's appointment of Daniel A. Manion to the 7th U.S. Circuit Court of Appeals by a vote of 50 to 49. V.P. George Bush cast a vote in support of Manion to break a 49-49 tie, although the tie itself was sufficient to assure nomination.		The government's consumer price index rose a seasonally adjusted 0.5% in June, according to the Labor Dept.... Americans' total personal income rose 0.1% in June to a seasonally adjusted annual rate of $3.479 trillion, the Commerce Dept. reports. Consumer spending in June rose an adjusted 0.6%.... Paul A. Volcker, chairman of the Federal Reserve Board, tells the Senate Banking Committee that coordinated international action is needed to boost economic growth in the United States and abroad. Volcker says that further cuts in U.S. interest rates will not help the economy because of the rising trade deficit.	The Food and Drug Admin. approves commercial production of the first vaccine developed through genetic engineering. The vaccine is intended to protect against the hepatitis B virus, a major cause of liver disease.	Prince Andrew, second son of Britain's Queen Elizabeth II and fourth in line to the British throne, marries Sarah Ferguson in a ceremony at Westminster Abbey in London.	**July 23**

F	G	H	I	J
Includes elections, federal-state relations, civil rights and liberties, crime, the judiciary, education, health care, poverty, urban affairs and population.	*Includes formation and debate of U.S. foreign and defense policies, veterans' affairs and defense spending. (Relations with specific foreign countries are usually found under the region concerned.)*	*Includes business, labor, agriculture, taxation, transportation, consumer affairs, monetary and fiscal policy, natural resources, and pollution.*	*Includes worldwide scientific, medical and technological developments, natural phenomena, U.S. weather, natural disasters, and accidents.*	*Includes the arts, religion, scholarship, communications media, sports, entertainments, fashions, fads and social life.*

	World Affairs	Europe	Africa & the Middle East	The Americas	Asia & the Pacific
July 24		In Poland, an amnesty program begins with the release of 369 prisoners. Government authorities plan to release 20,000 common criminals and most political prisoners under the program, which is set to run until mid-September. . . . A report by the Select Committee on Defense of the British House of Commons criticizes several of P.M. Margaret Thatcher's top aides over the "disreputable" leak to the press of a confidential letter critical of then-Defense Sec. Michael Heseltine in the Westland PLC helicopter affair on January 6. While the leak was made without Thatcher's "direct authority," the report says, the prime minister's defense of her aides was "flimsy to say the least." Heseltine resigned in the wake of the leak.		In Argentina, three months of strike action by the metalworkers' union over pay ends early in July. The strike action contributed to sagging sales and output of automobiles in June. . . . Mexico is admitted to the General Agreement on Tariffs and Trade in time to participate in the September meeting at Punta del Este, Uruguay.	
July 25				A report prepared by Environment Canada and the Ontario environment ministry finds that nearly one-half of the companies surveyed dumped toxic chemicals into the Great Lakes in 1984 in violation of provincial regulations.	
July 26		In England, nine people die as the result of a collision between a truck and a British Rail train carrying some 200 passengers. The crash occurred at an unmanned crossing at Lockington, Humberside.	Rev. Lawrence Martin Jenco, an American priest held hostage for more than 18 months by Shiite Moslem extremists in Lebanon is released by his kidnappers in the eastern Bekaa Valley. Although unharmed, he is in apparently frail health.		
July 27		West Germany's Foreign Min. Hans-Dietrich Genscher says that his country will proceed with plans for a controversial nuclear reprocessing plant in the southern state of Bavaria "without pause for thought." The plant attracted widespread domestic protest and sparked a dispute between the Bavarian state government and the federal government in neighboring Austria.	According to an estimate by the Geneva-based World Council of Churches, more than 10,000 people have been detained by the South African government since the state of emergency was imposed in June.		
July 28		Speaking in the Pacific port city of Vladivostok, Soviet leader Mikhail S. Gorbachev announces that the USSR will withdraw six regiments from Afghanistan by the end of 1986 and calls for a reduction in Western support for the Moslem resistance forces. He also invites China to cooperate on space exploration and in strengthening trade ties.			

A	B	C	D	E
Includes developments that affect more than one world region, international organizations and important meetings of major world leaders.	Includes all domestic and regional developments in Europe, including the Soviet Union, Turkey, Cyprus and Malta.	Includes all domestic and regional developments in Africa and the Middle East, including Iraq and Iran and excluding Cyprus, Turkey and Afghanistan.	Includes all domestic and regional developments in Latin America, the Caribbean and Canada.	Includes all domestic and regional developments in Asia and Pacific nations, extending from Afghanistan through all the Pacific Islands, except Hawaii.

U.S. Politics & Social Issues	U.S. Foreign Policy & Defense	U.S. Economy & Environment	Science, Technology & Nature	Culture, Leisure & Life Style	
		The Interstate Commerce Comm. surprises all sides by rejecting the long-anticipated merger of the Santa Fe and Southern Pacific railroads.	Fritz Albert Lipmann, 87, German-born biochemist who shared the 1953 Nobel Prize in medicine for the discovery of coenzyme A, a substance that aids transformation of food into energy, dies in Poughkeepsie, N.Y. His findings were said to have paved the way to current understanding of bioenergetics, the study of energy exchanges betweeen living things and their environments.	The Commonwealth Games open in Edinburgh, Scotland, with 31 of 58 nations boycotting the event to protest the British government's refusal to impose tough economic sanctions on the government of South Africa because of its apartheid system of racial segregation.	July 24
	Pres. Reagan reiterates his stand that the United States will not curb the Strategic Defense Initiative ("Star Wars") in exchange for Soviet arms concessions. In his weekly radio address, the president asserts that a workable space-based defense against missiles will enhance the U.S. position in negotiations with Moscow.... Pres. Reagan sends a letter to Soviet leader Mikhail S. Gorbachev detailing a formal response to Moscow's latest arms-control proposals. According to administration sources, the key Reagan proposal is a delay of five to seven years in deployment of the U.S. Strategic Defense Initiative ("Star Wars").	A six-week strike by more than 6,200 loggers and sawmill workers against Weyerhaeuser Co. in the Northwest ends with approval of a contract cutting wages more than 20%.		*Heartburn*, a film version of Nora Ephron's 1983 best-selling comic novel about the breakdown of a marriage, is released in New York. Directed by Mike Nichols, the screenplay is by Nora Ephron, and the film stars Meryl Streep and Jack Nicholson.... Vincente Minnelli, 76, Hollywood director known for such innovations as his skillful use of color, dies in Los Angeles. He directed such well-loved musicals as *Meet Me in St. Louis* and *Gigi*, the latter film gained him an Academy Award for best director in 1958. He and his first wife, Hollywood legend Judy Garland, are the parents of movie star Liza Minnelli.	July 25
After three years of improving crime statistics, the Federal Bureau of Investigation releases figures showing that the number of reported crimes rose 4.6% in 1985. ... William Averell Harriman, 94, adviser to Democratic presidents from Franklin D. Roosevelt to Lyndon Johnson, dies in Yorktown, N.Y. of kidney failure complicated by pneumonia. The patrician railroad heir was ambassador to Moscow during World War II and America's Vietnam peace negotiator in 1968.		The share of total family wealth held by the richest 0.5% of households grew to 35% in 1983 from 25% in 1963, it is reported. Democratic staff members of Congress's Joint Economic Committee release the report, which is based on a survey conducted in 1983 for the Federal Reserve Board and a similar survey 20 years earlier.			July 26
			The Soviet Union is reported to be building the world's biggest atom smasher at the Institute of High Energy Physics at Serpukhov, south of Moscow.	In auto racing, Nelson Piquet of Brazil wins the German Grand Prix. ... In bicycle racing, Greg LeMond of the United States becomes the first non-European to win the Tour de France.	July 27
		The Environmental Protection Agency announces an agreement with Phelps Dodge Corp. to sharply reduce air pollution levels at the company's Douglas, Ariz., copper smelter and to close the plant by Jan. 15, 1987.	The National Aeronautics and Space Admin. discloses that *Challenger* pilot Michael J. Smith spoke one last phrase—"uh-oh"—an instant before the doomed space shuttle broke up on January 28. It was previously assumed that the disaster happened instantly and without forewarning to the astronauts.	John Alcott, 55, British-born cinematographer, dies of natural causes while vacationing in the south of France. Best known for his work on all of director Stanley Kubrick's color films, including *2001: A Space Odyssey, A Clockwork Orange, The Shining*, and *Barry Lyndon*, he won the 1976 Academy Award for cinematography for the latter.	July 28

F	G	H	I	J
Includes elections, federal-state relations, civil rights and liberties, crime, the judiciary, education, health care, poverty, urban affairs and population.	Includes formation and debate of U.S. foreign and defense policies, veterans' affairs and defense spending. (Relations with specific foreign countries are usually found under the region concerned.)	Includes business, labor, agriculture, taxation, transportation, consumer affairs, monetary and fiscal policy, natural resources, and pollution.	Includes worldwide scientific, medical and technological developments, natural phenomena, U.S. weather, natural disasters, and accidents.	Includes the arts, religion, scholarship, communications media, sports, entertainments, fashions, fads and social life.

	World Affairs	Europe	Africa & the Middle East	The Americas	Asia & the Pacific
July 29		The 10th congress of the United Workers' (Communist) Party of Poland is held at the Palace of Culture in Warsaw. . . . N. Fomin, the chief engineer at the Chernobyl power plant at the time of the nuclear accident there in April, is expelled from the Communist Party; he lost his job in June.	British Foreign Sec. Sir Geoffrey Howe winds up a week-long peace mission to southern Africa on behalf of the European Community. After his last meeting with Howe, South Africa's Pres. Pieter W. Botha says his government would not allow "direct interference in our internal affairs." He rejects demands that Pretoria unconditionally negotiate with its black opponents, saying such a course will lead to "national suicide."	In Jamaica, Michael Manley's opposition People's National Party wins a landslide victory in local elections, prompting calls for an early general election.	Yesterday's speech by Soviet Gen. Sec. Mikhail S. Gorbachev in Vladivostok is carried on the front page of the *People's Daily*, China's Communist Party newspaper.
July 30	U.S. and Soviet arms-control experts end a special session of the Standing Consultative Comm. without an agreement on the future of the 1979 Strategic Arms Limitation Treaty (SALT II). The parley is held in Geneva.			After years of rivalry and dissension on trade and economic cooperation, Brazil and Argentina sign a package of economic accords during a visit to Argentina by Brazil's Pres. Jose Sarney.	
July 31	Trade representatives from the United States and Japan reach final agreement to resolve a bitter trade dispute involving computer chips. Japan agrees to let U.S. semiconductor manufacturers gain a large share of its market and says it will prevent Japanese producers from engaging in predatory pricing.	In the High Court in London, Justice Stuart Smith issues an injunction prohibiting regular picketing by more than six persons at the News International PLC plant in Wapping, East London. The plant has been the focus of an intense labor dispute between News International, owned by Rupert Murdoch, and some 5,500 print workers who lost their jobs when Murdoch moved the headquarters of his operation to Wapping from Fleet Street in mid-July.			
Aug. 1	Representatives of 54 nations announce the signing of a five-year extension of the Multi-Fiber Arrangement. The treaty forms the framework under which developed nations can negotiate textile import limitations with major textile producers.	In a speech to Communist Party local officials and plant managers in the eastern industrial city of Khabarovsk, Soviet leader Mikhail S. Gorbachev strongly criticizes the lag in fully implementing his program of economic and social reforms. . . . The month-long Italian government crisis ends when Socialist Bettino Craxi is sworn in as Italy's premier. Craxi reassumes the leadership of a five-party coalition government after agreeing with Christian Democratic Party leaders that he would step aside as premier in March 1987 in favor of a Christian Democrat.	Israeli Army Maj. Gen. Amos Yaron, who was criticized and stripped of his command for failing to alert his superiors about the 1982 Beirut Palestinian massacre, is appointed to the prestigious post of Israeli military attache to the United States. Yaron was reportedly on "study leave" for the two previous years. . . . A series of legal challenges brought in the last several weeks by South African community groups and trade unions succeeds in curbing some of the sweeping powers granted to the security forces under the latest state of emergency. But Pres. Pieter W. Botha amends the seven-week-old decree, reinforcing its provisions and circumventing the court decisions that briefly made some restrictions invalid.		

A	B	C	D	E
Includes developments that affect more than one world region, international organizations and important meetings of major world leaders.	Includes all domestic and regional developments in Europe, including the Soviet Union, Turkey, Cyprus and Malta.	Includes all domestic and regional developments in Africa and the Middle East, including Iraq and Iran and excluding Cyprus, Turkey and Afghanistan.	Includes all domestic and regional developments in Latin America, the Caribbean and Canada.	Includes all domestic and regional developments in Asia and Pacific nations, extending from Afghanistan through all the Pacific Islands, except Hawaii.

U.S. Politics & Social Issues	U.S. Foreign Policy & Defense	U.S. Economy & Environment	Science, Technology & Nature	Culture, Leisure & Life Style	
Health care in 1985 cost a total of $425 bil., the Dept. of Health and Human Services reports, and accounted for 10.7% of gross national product, the largest share of any industrial nation.... The Senate votes, 78-21, to make gavel-to-gavel television coverage of its floor proceedings permanent.				A federal grand jury in New York City finds the National Football League liable for one of six civil charges that it violated antitrust laws. The antitrust suit was brought by the rival United States Football League (USFL). The jury awarded the USFL nominal damages of $1, which would be trebled under anti-trust law; the USFL had sought $1.69 mil. in damages.	July 29
		The Senate votes to modify the Gramm-Rudmann balanced bud-get law to restore an automatic spending cut mechanism. The revised law cedes further power to the White House Office of Manage-ment and Budget.... Productivity among the nation's nonfarm busi-nesses rose at a seasonally adjusted annual rate of 1.7% in the second quarter of 1986, according to the Labor Dept.... The Dow Jones Industrial Average closes at a record high of 1892.72.... The deficit on merchandise trade in June was $14.17 bil., the Com-merce Dept. reports.	Federal health officials determine that heterosexual contact accounted for 862 cases of acquired immune deficiency syn-drome, or 4% of the U.S. total, and not 379, or 2%, as previously reported.		July 30
		Prices received by farmers for their raw agricultural goods rose 2.5% in July, the Agriculture Dept. reports.		Teddy (Theodore) Wilson, 73, black jazz pianist, dies in New Brit-ain, Conn., after a long illness. After playing with Louis Armstrong for several years, Wilson became famous in the mid-1930s as part of the Benny Goodman Trio (with Gene Krupa on drums), which helped break the color barrier in popular music. In the late 1930s he made a series of memorable recordings with Mildred Bailey and Billie Holiday, and he continued to perform until the early 1980s.... Stanley Ellin, 69, American mystery writer whose novels and short sto-ries were translated into many lan-guages, dies in New York City, fol-lowing a heart attack. In some countries, including France, Ellin was considered a major literary fig-ure, and in 1981, the Mystery Writ-ers of America honored him with their Grand Master Award for life-time achievement.	July 31
The Senate Judiciary Committee concludes four days of hearings on the nomination of Supreme Court Associate Justice William H. Rehn-quist to be chief justice of the U.S. Supreme Court.		The United Steelworkers of America strike against USX Corp. when negotiators fail to reach agreement on a new contract despite seven weeks of bargaining. ... The Agriculture Dept. says it will provide farmers in drought-stricken Southeastern states with up to $1 bil. in financial relief.... The government's index of leading economic indicators rose 0.3% in June, the Commerce Dept. reports. ... The nation's unemployment rate drops to a seasonally adjusted 6.8% of the work force in July, the Labor Dept. reports.... Pres. Rea-gan decides that the United States will subsidize exports of up to 4 mil-lion metric tons of wheat to the Soviet Union.			Aug. 1

F	G	H	I	J
Includes elections, federal-state rela-tions, civil rights and liberties, crime, the judiciary, education, health care, poverty, urban affairs and population.	Includes formation and debate of U.S. foreign and defense policies, veterans' affairs and defense spending. (Relations with specific foreign countries are usually found under the region concerned.)	Includes business, labor, agriculture, tax-ation, transportation, consumer affairs, monetary and fiscal policy, natural resources, and pollution.	Includes worldwide scientific, medical and technological developments, natural phenomena, U.S. weather, natural disas-ters, and accidents.	Includes the arts, religion, scholarship, communications media, sports, enter-tainments, fashions, fads and social life.

	World Affairs	Europe	Africa & the Middle East	The Americas	Asia & the Pacific
Aug. 2		Ireland's currency, the punt, is devalued by 8% against the other currencies of the European Monetary System. The Irish government takes the move in an attempt to boost the competitiveness of Irish exports, particularly those going to England and the United States.	In the latest incident in the Iran-Iraq war, Iraq conducts its first long-range air strike against the distant Iranian oil port at Sirri Island, near the mouth of the Persian Gulf.		
Aug. 3			A poll of South Africans conducted for the *Sunday Times* of London indicates that the proportion of whites unhappy with apartheid is 45%, up from 32% a year ago, and that 56% think imprisoned African National Congress leader Nelson Mandela should be freed, up from 40%. Although 88% of blacks are unhappy with apartheid, 55% of them do not think violence is justified to change it.		In China, an instruments factory in the northeastern city of Shenyang becomes the first firm to go bankrupt since the 1949 revolution. The declaration of bankruptcy is described in the Western press as a victory for economic reformers over hard-liners in the Communist Party. . . . Malaysia's P.M. Mahathir Mohamad beat off a challenge from Muslim fundamentalists to win a landslide victory in elections over two days. In returning his 13-party National Front coalition government to power, the electorate deals an unexpectedly severe setback to the Pan Malaysian Islamic Party.
Aug. 4	Ministers of the Org. of Petroleum Exporting Countries break a long deadlock and agree to cut their combined oil production by more than 3 million barrels per day for two months. News of the pact boosts oil prices by as much as 50% in subsequent days.				South Korea agrees to impose a limit of 0.8% growth on its textile exports to the United States over the next four years. The agreement follows similar pacts with Taiwan and Hong Kong to cut back textile exports. The pacts are negotiated within the framework of the recently extended Multi-Fiber Arrangement.
Aug. 5	The United States and Soviet Union reach agreement on 13 bilateral cultural, scientific, and educational exchanges. The announcement is made by the U.S. Information Agency in Washington. . . . At the conclusion of a four-day summit of seven Commonwealth heads of state representing Zambia, Zimbabwe, Canada, Bahamas, India, and Australia, Britain's P.M. Margaret Thatcher agrees to impose two limited economic sanctions against South Africa, but resists calls from the other six leaders for more forceful actions.				The British Army dismisses 111 Gurkha soldiers in a May 25 incident in which two officers were said to have suffered broken ribs and other injuries during a brawl after a party following joint U.S.-British exercises in Hawaii. Gurkhas, from Nepal, have been recruited for special British Army units since 1816. . . . Following elections July 27, Thailand's King Bhumibol Adulyadej reappoints Prem Tinsulanonda, 65, as Thailand's premier. The Democratic Party, which gained the most parliamentary seats in the elections, agrees to join the coalition government and nominate Prem for a third term.

A	B	C	D	E
Includes developments that affect more than one world region, international organizations and important meetings of major world leaders.	*Includes all domestic and regional developments in Europe, including the Soviet Union, Turkey, Cyprus and Malta.*	*Includes all domestic and regional developments in Africa and the Middle East, including Iraq and Iran and excluding Cyprus, Turkey and Afghanistan.*	*Includes all domestic and regional developments in Latin America, the Caribbean and Canada.*	*Includes all domestic and regional developments in Asia and Pacific nations, extending from Afghanistan through all the Pacific Islands, except Hawaii.*

U.S. Politics & Social Issues	U.S. Foreign Policy & Defense	U.S. Economy & Environment	Science, Technology & Nature	Culture, Leisure & Life Style	
Roy Marcus Cohn, 59, controversial New York City trial attorney dies at the National Institutes of Health, in Bethesda, Md., of cardiopulmonary arrest and acquired immune deficiency syndrome-related complications. Cohn played a key role in the prosecution of Julius and Ethel Rosenberg as spies, was chief counsel to Sen. Joseph McCarthy (R, Wis.) during his hearings on communist subversion, and later specialized in sensational divorce cases, estate battles, and large-scale criminal proceedings.					Aug. 2
The average cost of a year of college will increase by 6% in the 1986-87 academic year, the College Board reports. It is the sixth consecutive time the group's yearly survey finds costs growing faster than inflation.			At the opening session of the International Congress of Mathematicians at the Univ. of California at Berkeley, three mathematicians, Gerd Faltings, Michael Freedman, and Simon Donaldson, are named winners of the Field Medal, the closest thing in mathematics to a Nobel Prize. The prize is awarded every four years by the International Mathematical Union to "young" mathematicians, traditionally defined as under 40.	Beryl Markham, 83, aviation pioneer who in 1936 became the first person to fly solo across the Atlantic Ocean from east to west, dies in Nairobi, after surgery for a broken leg. Born in Britain, she grew up in Kenya and became a bush pilot. Her historic flight was described at length in her memoirs *West with the Night* (1942), which was reissued to critical acclaim in 1983. She was also a professional horse trainer, with six Kenya Derby winners.... Willie McCovey, Bobby Doerr, and the late Ernie Lombardi are inducted into the Baseball Hall of Fame in Cooperstown, N.Y.	Aug. 3
Pres. Reagan declares a "national mobilization" against illegal drugs, a problem that in the past few months has become a top national concern. In a bow to his wife's highly publicized campaign against drug abuse, Reagan says "starting today, Nancy's crusade to deprive drug peddlers and suppliers of their customers becomes America's crusade."	The State Dept. confirms that the foreign ministers of the United States and the USSR will meet in September to lay the groundwork for a second summit between Pres. Reagan and Soviet leader Mikhail S. Gorbachev.	In its quarterly survey of after-tax earnings, the *Wall Street Journal* reports that second-quarter profits on continuing operations for 476 major corporations fell 8% compared with the second quarter of 1985; net income of companies declined 5%, following a 2% decline in the first quarter of 1986. ... A 19-day strike by 7,000 Detroit municipal employees ends with settlement of a new three-year contract calling for pay increases totaling 8% over the life of the pact.		The United States Football League announces that it is calling off its 1986 season. Just six days ago, the league was awarded only nominal damages in its $1.69 bil. antitrust suit against the National Football League.	Aug. 4
	Four former officers of the failed Penn Square Bank agree to an out-of-court settlement in a $138.5 mil. lawsuit filed by the Federal Deposit Insurance Corp. ... The South, traditionally the lowest-income region of the United States, in 1984 climbed past the Midwest in average after-tax household income, the Census Bureau reports. In the nation as a whole, the average household had after-tax income of $21,564 in 1984 after paying an average $6,400 in income, property, and Social Security taxes.		The space shuttle *Columbia* was within 31 seconds of launch last January 6 without the proper amount of fuel to reach orbit, according to the presidential space shuttle commission. The finding is among staff appendices to the commission's report issued in June on the January 28 explosion of the space shuttle *Challenger*.		Aug. 5

F	**G**	**H**	**I**	**J**
Includes elections, federal-state relations, civil rights and liberties, crime, the judiciary, education, health care, poverty, urban affairs and population.	*includes formation and debate of U.S. foreign and defense policies, veterans' affairs and defense spending. (Relations with specific foreign countries are usually found under the region concerned.)*	*Includes business, labor, agriculture, taxation, transportation, consumer affairs, monetary and fiscal policy, natural resources, and pollution.*	*Includes worldwide scientific, medical and technological developments, natural phenomena, U.S. weather, natural disasters, and accidents.*	*Includes the arts, religion, scholarship, communications media, sports, entertainments, fashions, fads and social life.*

	World Affairs	Europe	Africa & the Middle East	The Americas	Asia & the Pacific
Aug. 6		Albania becomes part of the European railroad network, with the inauguration of a 30-mile rail line linking the northern Albanian city of Shkoder with Titograd, the capital of the southwestern Yugoslavian republic of Montenegro. . . . The 903 work stoppages occurring in Britain in 1985 is the lowest total since 883 stoppages in 1938, the Employment Dept. reports. The number of working days lost to strikes is 6.4 million, down from the 1965-84 average of 10 million days per year.			
Aug. 7		The deputy leader of the hard-line Protestant Democratic Unionist Party in Northern Ireland is arrested by Irish Republican authorities after a group of Protestant "loyalists" cross the border from Northern Ireland into the Republic of Ireland town of Clontibret in County Monaghan for a demonstration. The loyalists, some in military dress, drill in the town, attack two policemen, and paint slogans on a school before returning to County Armagh in the North.		Virgilio Barco Vargas is inaugurated as Colombia's president. In his inaugural speech, Barco pledges to focus on combating "absolute poverty" and ending the violence that has gripped the nation for decades.	
Aug. 8					The 17th meeting of the South Pacific Forum is held. One of the chief items of business is the situation in the French territory of New Caledonia, where many forum members think France is taking too long to end colonial rule.
Aug. 9	Signaling the thaw in relations between Moscow and Beijing, China signs a consular treaty with neighboring Mongolia, which is dominated economically and politically by the Soviet Union and which must seek the approval of the Kremlin before signing the treaty.			In Canada, the national surplus in merchandise balance of trade declines to $260 mil. in July, down from $653 mil. in June, according to Statistics Canada. It is the sixth consecutive month of decline in the trade surplus.	
Aug. 10		Negotiators for the United States and the European Community (EC) announce that they have reached a provisional settlement of a simmering dispute over trade in citrus fruits and pasta. Under the agreement, the United States will roll back tariffs imposed on imports of pasta from Europe. The tariffs were imposed in retaliation for low EC tariffs on citrus products from Mediterranean countries. . . . Food prices in Belgrade, Yugoslavia, have risen by as much as 180% over the last two days. The sudden price hikes appear to have caught the government unawares. In June, the government instituted an anti-inflation rule requiring all companies to obtain approval 120 days in advance of a price increase.			

A	B	C	D	E
Includes developments that affect more than one world region, international organizations and important meetings of major world leaders.	Includes all domestic and regional developments in Europe, including the Soviet Union, Turkey, Cyprus and Malta.	Includes all domestic and regional developments in Africa and the Middle East, including Iraq and Iran and excluding Cyprus, Turkey and Afghanistan.	Includes all domestic and regional developments in Latin America, the Caribbean and Canada.	Includes all domestic and regional developments in Asia and Pacific nations, extending from Afghanistan through all the Pacific Islands, except Hawaii.

U.S. Politics & Social Issues	U.S. Foreign Policy & Defense	U.S. Economy & Environment	Science, Technology & Nature	Culture, Leisure & Life Style	
Vice Pres. George Bush claims a clear victory in the Republicans' precinct delegate elections, held August 5, which marks the opening of the 1988 presidential nominating process. Rep. Jack F. Kemp (R, N.Y.) and television evangelist Rev. Pat Robertson both claim second place. . . . Senate hearings on the nomination of Judge Antonin Scalia to the Supreme Court unfold calmly over two days with no major controversy in view.		An administrative law judge in Washington, D.C., dismisses a Federal Trade Comm. (FTC) complaint against R.J. Reynolds Tobacco Co. The FTC charged that Reynolds had distorted medical research in a 1985 advertisement on the health effects of smoking. . . . The federal budget deficit for FY1986 will be a record $230.2 bil., according to the annual midyear budget forecast by the White House Office of Management and Budget. The figure is $18 bil. above 1985's record deficit of $212 bil. . . . The House votes, 276-149, to uphold Pres. Reagan's veto of a bill that would have placed strict limits on textile imports, primarily from Asian countries.	William J. Schroeder, 54, retired union organizer who in November 1984 became the second recipient of the Jarvik-7 permanent artificial heart, dies at the Humana Hospital Audobon in Louisville, Ky., after the latest in a series of strokes. . . . Iceland announces that it will go ahead with plans to kill up to 120 whales a year and use 51% of the whale meat domestically. Under pressure from the United States, Iceland July 28 abandoned plans to take up to 120 whales for what is described as "scientific purposes." Iceland, which had renounced commercial whaling two years ago, angrily protested July 29 what it construed as an ultimatum from the United States for the island to stop whaling or face a U.S. boycott of Icelandic fish products.		**Aug. 6**
The Federal Communications Comm. adopts rules that require any large- or medium-sized cable television system to carry some of the broadcast stations that operate in the area the cable system serves.		Outstanding consumer installment credit grew a seasonally adjusted $5.07 bil. in June, or at an annual rate of 10.8%, the Federal Reserve Board reports. . . . The Soviet news agency Tass announces that Edward Lee Howard, a former Central Intelligence Agency operative, has been granted political asylum in the Soviet Union. Howard, 34, eluded the Federal Bureau of Investigation in New Mexico in September 1985. . . . The Treasury Dept. sells a record $28.06 bil. worth of notes and bonds at its regular quarterly refinancing auction over three days. Interest rates for the long-term bonds are higher than expected while short-term T-note rates are slightly lower.	In France Pres. Francois Mitterrand surveys by plane areas in southern France that were devastated by forest and brush fires. More than 40,000 acres of forest and hundreds of properties were destroyed during the dry summer according to the Sunday *Times* of London August 3.		**Aug. 7**
A federal magistrate in Alexandria, Va., fines political organizer Lyndon H. LaRouche Jr. $2,000 for failing to answer questions about his personal finances. The information is sought by National Broadcasting Co., which is trying to collect a $202,000 court judgment against LaRouche.				The future of the American National Theater (ANT) at Washington, D.C.'s Kennedy Center for the Performing Arts is thrown into doubt when it is disclosed that ANT's 28-year-old director, Peter Sellars, will be taking a year's sabbatical and that ANT's operations will cease and its staff of six be let go during his year's absence.	**Aug. 8**
		The Senate clears a bill that will raise the national debt ceiling by $244 bil., to $2.323 trillion. Attached to the bill is an amendment that will restore an automatic spending-cut mechanism to the Gramm-Rudman balanced budget law.			**Aug. 9**
				Me and My Girl, the Broadway revival of a 1936 English musical, opens on Broadway. The musical goes on to win three Tony Awards, for best actor and actress in a musical (Robert Lindsay and Maryann Plunkett) and best choreography (Gillian Gregory).	**Aug. 10**

F	G	H	I	J
Includes elections, federal-state relations, civil rights and liberties, crime, the judiciary, education, health care, poverty, urban affairs and population.	*Includes formation and debate of U.S. foreign and defense policies, veterans' affairs and defense spending. (Relations with specific foreign countries are usually found under the region concerned.)*	*Includes business, labor, agriculture, taxation, transportation, consumer affairs, monetary and fiscal policy, natural resources, and pollution.*	*Includes worldwide scientific, medical and technological developments, natural phenomena, U.S. weather, natural disasters, and accidents.*	*Includes the arts, religion, scholarship, communications media, sports, entertainments, fashions, fads and social life.*

	World Affairs	Europe	Africa & the Middle East	The Americas	Asia & the Pacific
Aug. 11	U.S. and Soviet arms control experts hold two days of special talks in Moscow. In addition to reviewing arms issues, they prepared for September pre-summit talks between Sec. of State George P. Shultz and Soviet Foreign Min. Eduard A. Shevardnadze.	In Poland, Adam Michnik a senior activist in the outlawed Solidarity labor movement, is released from prison under the government's limited amnesty program. Fellow leader Bogdan Lis was freed on July 31.		In Canada, the 27th annual provincial premiers conference opens for two days of meetings in Edmonton. Observers at the meeting note an atmosphere of unusual harmony, even on such a divisive issue as Quebec's constitutional role.	
Aug. 12				In Mexico, a former federal police commander is sentenced to four years in prison for accepting a bribe from a reputed drug dealer accused in the 1985 murder of a U.S. Drug Enforcement Admin. agent, Enrique Camarena Salazar.	
Aug. 13		The French National Assembly ends its first parliamentary session under the conservative government of Premier Jacques Chirac. The session is conducted under the historic situation of cohabitation: Chirac's conservative government is serving at the same time that Francois Mitterrand, a socialist, holds the presidency.... East Germany commemorates the 25th anniversary of the start of construction on the Berlin Wall. The 13-foot-high wall isolates West Berlin in East Germany with about 100 miles of heavily guarded concrete and barbed-wire fencing. East Germany regards the barrier as a means of halting potential Western invasion through West Berlin. The West holds that the wall was built to stem the flow of East Germans into West Berlin.	South Africa's ruling National Party concludes a rare two-day federal congress in Durban. Pres. Pieter W. Botha and other top officials make hard-line speeches in what is described as a "stock-taking exercise" to consolidate white support and prepare the party's Afrikaner faithful to face a new round of international sanctions.		
Aug. 14		European Community market managers approve a plan to release 950,000 metric tons of surplus wheat for export. In the past, surpluses have been held back from the export market until November to prevent them from undercutting wheat sales from the fall harvest.... The former head of nuclear safety and the first deputy minister of power and electrification are ousted from the Soviet Communist Party in connection with the Chernobyl nuclear power plant disaster in April.... Unemployment in Britain continued to rise in July to a seasonally adjusted total of 3,224,000, or 11.7% of the work force, according to the Dept. of Employment.		Bolivia's government requests a $100-mil. emergency loan from the United States to compensate for the crippling economic effects of a month-old, joint antidrug operation.	In Pakistan, Benazir Bhutto is arrested, one day after a sweep in which virtually all the top opposition leaders were seized. Bhutto is the 33-year-old daughter of Zulfikar Ali Bhutto, the charismatic prime minister who was overthrown and executed in 1979 by the current president, Gen. Muhammad Zia ul-Haq.

A	B	C	D	E
Includes developments that affect more than one world region, international organizations and important meetings of major world leaders.	*Includes all domestic and regional developments in Europe, including the Soviet Union, Turkey, Cyprus and Malta.*	*Includes all domestic and regional developments in Africa and the Middle East, including Iraq and Iran and excluding Cyprus, Turkey and Afghanistan.*	*Includes all domestic and regional developments in Latin America, the Caribbean and Canada.*	*Includes all domestic and regional developments in Asia and Pacific nations, extending from Afghanistan through all the Pacific Islands, except Hawaii.*

U.S. Politics & Social Issues	U.S. Foreign Policy & Defense	U.S. Economy & Environment	Science, Technology & Nature	Culture, Leisure & Life Style	
Delivering the state of the judiciary address at the annual meeting of the American Bar Assoc., outgoing Chief Justice Warren E. Burger urges the profession to hold fast to traditional standards and guard against "becoming more and more like a common trade in the marketplace."	The Defense Dept. announces that it is withholding a "significant portion" of the monthly progress payments to Lockheed Corp. because of lax security at its Burbank, Calif., plant. The plant is believed to manufacturing the radar-eluding stealth jet fighter.			Bob Tway wins the 68th Professional Golfers Assoc. Championship at the Inverness course in Toledo, Ohio.	**Aug. 11**
A House subcommittee votes unanimously to ask the independent counsel investigating former White House aide Michael K. Deaver to examine possible perjury by Deaver in his hearings before the subcommittee.					**Aug. 12**
	Pres. Reagan wins a major foreign policy victory when the Senate votes to approve his request for $100 mil. in aid to Nicaraguan Contras fighting to overthrow the Sandinista government. A further $300 mil. in economic aid will be given to four of Nicaragua's Central American neighbors, Costa Rica, El Salvador, Guatemala, and Honduras. The House approved an identical aid measure in June.	The National Academy of Sciences issues a report urging the federal government to ban smoking on all domestic commercial flights.	Japan conducts a successful first launch of a new rocket with a Japanese-built second-stage engine and inertial guidance system. The launch from Japan's space center on an island off Kyushu, put two satellites in orbit 938 miles above Earth.	*Billboard*'s best-selling albums for the week are: *True Blue*, Madonna; *Top Gun* (soundtrack); *So*, Peter Gabriel; *Invisible Touch*, Genesis; and *Control*, Janet Jackson.	**Aug. 13**
The Senate Judiciary Committee votes 13-5 to recommend confirmation of Associate Justice William H. Rehnquist as chief justice of the United States and unanimously endorses Judge Antonin Scalia to succeed him as an associate justice of the Supreme Court.	Rear Adm. Grace Hopper, 79, reports to Boston Harbor for a farewell ceremony aboard the USS *Constitution*, ending her tenure as America's oldest active-duty officer. with 43 years in the service. A mathematician by training, Hopper became the Navy's foremost expert on computer languages.	The Environmental Protection Agency sets a cautionary safety standard for the presence of radon gas in residences. The standard, four picocuries per liter of air, is equivalent in health terms to smoking half a pack of cigarettes daily, it is estimated.			**Aug. 14**

F	G	H	I	J
Includes elections, federal-state relations, civil rights and liberties, crime, the judiciary, education, health care, poverty, urban affairs and population.	*Includes formation and debate of U.S. foreign and defense policies, veterans' affairs and defense spending. (Relations with specific foreign countries are usually found under the region concerned.)*	*Includes business, labor, agriculture, taxation, transportation, consumer affairs, monetary and fiscal policy, natural resources, and pollution.*	*Includes worldwide scientific, medical and technological developments, natural phenomena, U.S. weather, natural disasters, and accidents.*	*Includes the arts, religion, scholarship, communications media, sports, entertainments, fashions, fads and social life.*

	World Affairs	Europe	Africa & the Middle East	The Americas	Asia & the Pacific
Aug. 15	Ten F-4 warplanes of the Turkish Air Force cross into Iraq and bomb suspected hideouts of Kurdish separatist guerrillas. The raid is in retaliation for the August 12 Kurdish ambush of an army truck near the Iraqi border in which 12 Turkish soldiers were killed.	The Danish government will show a budget surplus in 1986 estimated at $39 mil. for the first time since 1974. The turnaround is attributed to the stabilization of spending, higher taxes, and greater revenues derived from strong economic expansion.		The International Monetary Fund announces a $115.1 mil. loan package for Ecuador to help offset an expected shortfall in export earnings in 1986 because of the drop in oil prices. . . . The International Monetary Fund declares Peru ineligible for new loans until it pays off some $158 mil. in arrears to the fund.	
Aug. 16			A Sudanese airliner is shot down by the Sudan People's Liberation Army shortly after taking off from the southern town of Malakal, killing 60 people aboard.	Joaquin Balaguer, 78, is sworn in for his fifth term as president of the Dominican Republic. Balaguer is head of the Social Christian Reform Party.	
Aug. 17					
Aug. 18	Soviet and Israeli representatives meet in Helsinki, Finland, to discuss the possible resumption of consular links. It is the first official diplomatic contact between the two nations in 19 years.	A scandal involving millions of French francs missing from Le Carrefour du Development (African Crossroads) a government agency encouraging African development, has proven to be an embarrassment to the French Socialist Party according to press reports over the last six weeks.		Ottawa confirms a plan to sell Canadair Ltd., the government-owned aircraft manufacturer, to Bombardier Inc. of Montreal. The sale price is $86 mil.	

A	B	C	D	E
Includes developments that affect more than one world region, international organizations and important meetings of major world leaders.	Includes all domestic and regional developments in Europe, including the Soviet Union, Turkey, Cyprus and Malta.	Includes all domestic and regional developments in Africa and the Middle East, including Iraq and Iran and excluding Cyprus, Turkey and Afghanistan.	Includes all domestic and regional developments in Latin America, the Caribbean and Canada.	Includes all domestic and regional developments in Asia and Pacific nations, extending from Afghanistan through all the Pacific Islands, except Hawaii.

U.S. Politics & Social Issues	U.S. Foreign Policy & Defense	U.S. Economy & Environment	Science, Technology & Nature	Culture, Leisure & Life Style	
	The Senate votes, 84-14, to impose economic sanctions on South Africa to pressure it to dismantle its apartheid racial system. Thirty-seven Republicans join with all 47 Democrats to form a strong bipartisan majority.	The National Highway Traffic Safety Admin. (NHTSA) announces that it has ended an eight-year investigation of about 60 million automobiles produced by General Motors Corp. Sudden acceleration in some of the cars is alleged to have caused 761 accidents and 31 fatalities. The NHTSA says that its investigators failed to find any common problem that accounts for the accidents attributed to sudden acceleration. . . . Industrial production in July fell a seasonally adjusted 0.1%, the Federal Reserve Board reports. The July decline in output was the third consecutive monthly drop in the index. . . . The government's producer price index declined a seasonally adjusted 0.4% in July, according to the Labor Dept. . . . The House approves defense authorization bills for FY1987; the Senate gave similar approval on August 9. Both measures set military spending at levels below the $320.3 bil. requested by Pres. Reagan.	The White House announces that Pres. Reagan has asked the National Aeronautics and Space Admin. to build a fourth space shuttle to replace the lost *Challenger*.		Aug. 15
		The House and Senate approve an interim increase in the national debt limit of $32.3 bil. to allow the Treasury to continue to borrow money through September. A larger rise in the debt ceiling is stalled because of wrangling between the House and Senate over how to restore an automatic spending-cut mechanism to the Gramm-Rudman balanced budget law. . . . House and Senate conferees approve a sweeping measure to undertake by far the most extensive restructuring of the federal tax system since World War II.	The National Science Foundation selects the State Univ. of New York at Buffalo as the home of a new center for earthquake research.		Aug. 16
A Colorado law to protect home owners causes charges to be dropped against a man who shot and killed a neighbor. The law stipulates that "any occupant of a dwelling. . .shall be immune from criminal prosecution" if he or she injures or kills an illegal intruder whom the occupant reasonably suspects of wrongdoing, or who uses "any physical force, no matter how slight, against any occupant." The measure, passed in 1984, was nicknamed the "Make My Day" law after the famous catchphrase of movie star Clint Eastwood in the film *Dirty Harry*.	Five former U.S. administration officials urge the Reagan administration to limit the Strategic Defense Initiative ("Star Wars"). The five are former defense secretaries Harold R. Brown, Melvin R. Laird, and James R. Schlesinger, Cyrus R. Vance, a former secretary of state, and Brent Scowcroft, a former national security adviser.			Photographer Lee Friedlander, 52, becomes the 27th recipient of the MacDowell Colony Medal for lifetime achievement in the arts. . . . The U.S. team wins the women's World Basketball Championships in Moscow with a 108-88 victory over the Soviet Union.	Aug. 17
				Rev. Charles E. Curran is notified that the Vatican finds him neither "suitable nor eligible" to teach theology at the Catholic Univ. of America in Washington, D.C., because of his dissenting views on sexual matters. The Vatican says Curran has dissented from official church teachings on divorce, abortion, masturbation, artificial contraception, premarital intercourse, and homosexual acts. Curran, a tenured professor of moral theology, has taught at the university since 1965.	Aug. 18

F	G	H	I	J
Includes elections, federal-state relations, civil rights and liberties, crime, the judiciary, education, health care, poverty, urban affairs and population.	*Includes formation and debate of U.S. foreign and defense policies, veterans' affairs and defense spending. (Relations with specific foreign countries are usually found under the region concerned.)*	*Includes business, labor, agriculture, taxation, transportation, consumer affairs, monetary and fiscal policy, natural resources, and pollution.*	*Includes worldwide scientific, medical and technological developments, natural phenomena, U.S. weather, natural disasters, and accidents.*	*Includes the arts, religion, scholarship, communications media, sports, entertainments, fashions, fads and social life.*

	World Affairs	Europe	Africa & the Middle East	The Americas	Asia & the Pacific
Aug. 19	After a five-year break in diplomatic ties, Britain and Guatemala renew consular relations. The break occurred over Guatemala's claim to neighboring Belize, a British colony that gained independence in 1981.... The 35-nation Conf. on Confidence- and Security-Building Measures and Disarmament in Europe begins its final round of talks in Stockholm, Sweden. The talks, which include the United States, Canada, and every nation in Europe except Albania, began in January 1984.				Shooting breaks out across the demilitarized zone separating North and South Korea. North Korea blames the South for starting the firing, but the United Nations command in South Korea accuses North Korean soldiers of setting off the exchange. No injuries are reported.... Papua New Guinea's parliament votes without debate to delay the introduction of television into the country. Under the statutes, anyone caught operating a television station before January 1988 could be fined up to $1 mil.... The Australian Labor Party government unveils its budget for the FY1986-87. The budget contains an unexpectedly low deficit that is engineered to bolster Australia's sinking position in international trade.
Aug. 20		French unemployment rose 1.4% to a record, seasonally adjusted 2.47 million workers in July, according to government figures released. The jobless total represents 10.5% of the force.	Tanzania reaches agreement with the International Monetary Fund (IMF) for a standby facility of about $77 mil., the first such loan in six years, the *Financial Times* of London reports. The pact ends a long-standing dispute and years of desultory talks between the IMF and the financially strapped east African nation, which has a foreign debt of $2.4 bil.		
Aug. 21		A government youth program to clean up litter around Britain gets underway with a trial cleaning of London's Trafalgar Square. The government's U.K. 2,000 environment program, which will eventually employ some 5,000 unemployed young people for up to one year, is a cooperative effort of the government, the private sector, and volunteer organizations.... The Soviet Union formally issues a 382-page report on the Chernobyl disaster. The study is made public at a Moscow news conference called by Andronik M. Petrosyants, chairman of the State Committee for the Peaceful Uses of Atomic Energy. The panel concludes that the accident was the result of human error, specifically stemming from an unauthorized test conducted by the operators of Chernobyl unit No. 4 on April 25-26.	An eruption of poisonous gas from a volcanic lake, Lake Nios, near the town of Wum, in the central African nation of Cameroon, kills more than 1,700 people.... The government of Rwanda issues an international arrest warrant for U.S. researcher Richard MacGuire for the December 1985 murder of American gorilla expert Dian Fossey at her remote Rwandan research center. Friends and associates of the two say the government is motivated by a desire to implicate a non-Rwandan in the internationally embarrassing case.		
Aug. 22		John Stalker, who was removed as head of a controversial investigation of Northern Ireland's police force, is cleared to resume his duties as deputy chief constable of Greater Manchester, England. His reinstatement follows an investigation of alleged misconduct by Stalker unrelated to the Ulster probe.		Canada's annual inflation rate jumped to 4.2% in July, the highest in six months. The annual rate of inflation had dropped to 3.7% in June from 4.1% in May.	

A	B	C	D	E
Includes developments that affect more than one world region, international organizations and important meetings of major world leaders.	Includes all domestic and regional developments in Europe, including the Soviet Union, Turkey, Cyprus and Malta.	Includes all domestic and regional developments in Africa and the Middle East, including Iraq and Iran and excluding Cyprus, Turkey and Afghanistan.	Includes all domestic and regional developments in Latin America, the Caribbean and Canada.	Includes all domestic and regional developments in Asia and Pacific nations, extending from Afghanistan through all the Pacific Islands, except Hawaii.

U.S. Politics & Social Issues	U.S. Foreign Policy & Defense	U.S. Economy & Environment	Science, Technology & Nature	Culture, Leisure & Life Style	
		After-tax profits of U.S. corporations rose a seasonally adjusted 4.1% in the second quarter of 1986 from the previous quarter, the Commerce Dept. reports.... The nation's gross national product increased at an inflation-adjusted annual rate of 0.6% in the second quarter, according to revised figures released by the Commerce Dept.... Congressional Budget Office and White House officials present their joint estimate of the FY1987 federal deficit. Their grim projections show a deficit of $163.4 bil., or $19.4 bil. above the target allowed by the Gramm-Rudman balanced budget law.		In Australia, Melbourne police recover Pablo Picasso's painting, *Weeping Woman*, which was stolen August 2 by a group calling itself the Australian Cultural Terrorists (ACT), which threatened to destroy the painting if the state of Victoria did not upgrade its "niggardly funding of the fine arts" and improve the "clumsy, unimaginative stupidity" of the funds' administration.	Aug. 19
A Rand Corp. study rleased today finds that 15% of patients who subscribe to health maintenance organizations are dissatisfied with their health care, as against only 10% of patients of traditional health services.... Part-time mail carrier Patrick Henry Sherrill opens fire in the Edmond, Okla., post office where he works. After a 10-minute rampage that leaves 14 people dead and six others wounded, Sherrill kills himself with a bullet to the head.		The Labor Dept. proposes to further loosen a 43-year-old ban on home manufacture of many types of clothing and jewelry. The home-based enterprises will have to be certified by the Labor Dept., which requires that payment for goods meet minimum-wage and overtime requirements of federal law.... Americans' personal income rose 0.5% in July to a seasonally adjusted annual rate of $3.503 trillion, the Commerce Dept. reports. Consumer spending rose 0.2% in July.... New housing starts declined 1.8% in July to a seasonally adjusted annual rate of 1.82 mil. units, the Commerce Dept. reports.... The Federal Reserve Board reduces the so-called discount rate to 5.5%, the lowest rate charged on loans to financial institutions since September 1977.	Lt. Gen. Forrest S. McCartney, 55, commander of the Air Force Space Command, is appointed director of National Aeronautics and Space Admin. Kennedy Space Center at Cape Canaveral, Fla., effective October 1. McCartney will replace Richard G. Smith, who is retiring to take a position in private business.	*Variety's*, top grossing films for the week are: *The Fly, Aliens, Nothing in Common, Armed and Dangerous,* and *Heartburn.*... Milton Acorn, 63, itinerant Canadian carpenter-poet who won a Governor-General's Award in 1976 for *The Island Means Minago,* a folk history of his native Prince Edward Island, dies in Charlottetown, P.E.I. of complications from a heart condition and diabetes.... Thad Jones, 63, self-taught jazz drummer, cornetist, and composer, dies of cancer in Copenhagen, Denmark. Known for the harmonic and rhythmic complexity of his arrangements, he had lived in Denmark since the late 1970s.	Aug. 20
		The Pennsylvania Labor and Industry Dept. rules that the work stoppage at USX Corp. steel mills in Pennsylvania is a lockout and that the idled workers, members of the United Steelworkers union, are entitled to unemployment benefits. The benefits have not been paid to strikers, who began their action August 1.... Treasury Dept. officials say that a study on the concentration of wealth in the United States released July 26 is wrong and that the richest 0.5% of households in 1983 held only 26.9% of the nation's wealth, up from 25% in 1963.... The government's consumer price index is unchanged in July, according to the Labor Dept.			Aug. 21
Kerr-McGee Corp. agrees to pay the estate of the late Karen Silkwood $1.38 mil. to settle a 10-year-old lawsuit against the Oklahoma City-based energy company. Under the out-of-court settlement, the company admits no blame for the plutonium contamination of Silkwood, which occurred in 1974 while she was working as a laboratory technician at a Kerr-McGee plant in Crescent, Okla. Silkwood, 28, was killed in a car crash in November 1974 while on her way to meet a reporter to discuss alleged safety violations at the plant. Her story was the subject of the 1983 film *Silkwood.*	Pres. Reagan orders measures to tighten the 26-year-old trade embargo against Cuba. The measures are aimed at preventing Cuba from circumventing the embargo to obtain U.S. dollars and goods. Henceforth, companies operating in foreign countries will be prevented from providing U.S. goods and technology to Cuba.	Norfolk Southern Corp. announces that it is withdrawing its $1.9 bil. bid for the government's 85% stake in Conrail, the freight line operating throughout the Northeast and the Midwest.... Pan American World Airways agrees to pay a $1,950,000 fine for alleged federal safety violations, the Federal Aviation Admin. announces.			Aug. 22
F	G	H	I	J	
Includes elections, federal-state relations, civil rights and liberties, crime, the judiciary, education, health care, poverty, urban affairs and population.	*Includes formation and debate of U.S. foreign and defense policies, veterans' affairs and defense spending. (Relations with specific foreign countries are usually found under the region concerned.)*	*Includes business, labor, agriculture, taxation, transportation, consumer affairs, monetary and fiscal policy, natural resources, and pollution.*	*Includes worldwide scientific, medical and technological developments, natural phenomena, U.S. weather, natural disasters, and accidents.*	*Includes the arts, religion, scholarship, communications media, sports, entertainments, fashions, fads and social life.*	

	World Affairs	Europe	Africa & the Middle East	The Americas	Asia & the Pacific
Aug. 23	China's foreign ministry confirms that Chinese and Soviet troops exchanged fire along the Sino-Soviet border. A Japanese newspaper reported that the shootout occurred July 12. The foreign ministry statement calls the clash an "isolated incident" and says the Chinese "made a representation to the Soviet side."			The Salavadoran government announces that long-awaited peace talks with leftist rebels have been set for September 19 in the eastern town of Sesori. The rebels in June accepted an offer to renew the peace talks, which broke off in 1984. Since then, however, there have been disputes on the location and date and on security arrangements.	
Aug. 24			Cameroon's Pres. Paul Biya visits the region of Lake Nios, near the remote town of Wum, where on August 21 an eruption of poisonous gas from a volcanic lake killed 1,700 people.		
Aug. 25					
Aug. 26			South African police kill at least 20 blacks and wound nearly 100 others in Soweto, the huge black township near Johannesburg. Black tenants had banded together to resist eviction by government authorities who were trying to break a rent boycott by blacks.... According to U.S. officials cited in the *Washington Post*, China has become Iran's largest supplier of arms, reportedly delivering at least $300 mil. worth of missiles and other military equipment over the previous six months. U.S. officials fear that the new weapons will give Iran a significant advantage in the Iran-Iraq war.	In Canada, the federal government and the province of Nova Scotia sign a $161 mil. agreement aimed at increasing the province's share of wealth from offshore drilling and natural gas.	
Aug. 27		West Germany's Chancellor Helmut Kohl announces steps that his government will take to stem the growing tide of refugees seeking political asylum in that country. West Germany, one of the last European states with liberal asylum laws and accessible frontiers, has received record numbers of requests for asylum from refugees over the past two years.			

A	B	C	D	E
Includes developments that affect more than one world region, international organizations and important meetings of major world leaders.	*Includes all domestic and regional developments in Europe, including the Soviet Union, Turkey, Cyprus and Malta.*	*Includes all domestic and regional developments in Africa and the Middle East, including Iraq and Iran and excluding Cyprus, Turkey and Afghanistan.*	*Includes all domestic and regional developments in Latin America, the Caribbean and Canada.*	*Includes all domestic and regional developments in Asia and Pacific nations, extending from Afghanistan through all the Pacific Islands, except Hawaii.*

U.S. Politics & Social Issues	U.S. Foreign Policy & Defense	U.S. Economy & Environment	Science, Technology & Nature	Culture, Leisure & Life Style	
The nation's governors vow a "Second wave of reform in American public education." They propose a program offering greater educational choices for local school districts, coupled with the threat of state takeovers of districts that fail to meet toughened minimum standards. The program is presented on the eve of the National Governors' Assoc. meeting. It is the product of a year-long effort by seven association task forces.	The Federal Bureau of Investigation says it has arrested a Soviet employee of the UN on a subway platform in the Queens borough of New York City as he exchanged money for three classified documents.			The Tainan City team from Taiwan wins the finals of the Little League World Series, 12-0, over Tucson, Ariz.	Aug. 23
The National Governor's Assoc. convenes for three days of meetings at which there is widespread concern that the tax overhaul legislation now before Congress could have far-reaching impact on state governments.					Aug. 24
A federal district judge in New York rules that a 36-year campaign of harassment by the Federal Bureau of Investigation against the Socialist Workers Party, a small Trotskyite party, is illegal and "patently unconstitutional."		Western lumber workers reach agreement on new two-year contracts with Willamette Industries Inc. and Boise Cascade Corp., the *Wall Street Journal* reports.	A conference of nuclear-power experts convenes in Vienna under the auspices of the International Atomic Energy Agency. The purpose of the symposium is a study of the causes and likely effects of the April accident at the Chernobyl nuclear power plant in the Soviet Ukraine.		Aug. 25
		The Census Bureau reports that the median income of U.S. families in 1985 rose 1.3%, to $27,735, only half of 1984's gain of 2.8%. Median income has increased for three consecutive years. The Census Bureau also reports that the U.S. poverty rate declined in 1985 to 14% from 14.4% in 1984. The decline in 1985 marked the second consecutive annual decline in the rate. However, the percentage of households with incomes below the poverty line remains significantly higher than at any point during the 1971-80 period, when it averaged 12.6%.... Most major banks cut their prime lending rates to 7.5% from 8%. The reduction, which brings prime rates to their lowest level since 1977, follows an August 20 cut by the Federal Reserve Board in the discount rate, to 5.5%.	The American Assoc. of Blood Banks urges the adoption of new guidelines for testing donations for non-A, non-B hepatitis, an as yet untreatable form of hepatitis that recently inspired growing concern.		Aug. 26
		Productivity among the nation's nonfarm businesses dropped at a seasonally adjusted annual rate of 0.5% in the second quarter of 1986, according to revised figures released by the Labor Dept.		It is reported that some 18 to 20 hours of lost footage from *It's All True*, a legendary unfinished 1942 semi-documentary on Brazil by Orson Welles, was unearthed in 1984 at Paramount Studios' stock footage vault. Wells, who died in October 1985, never saw any of the recovered footage.	Aug. 27

F	G	H	I	J
Includes elections, federal-state relations, civil rights and liberties, crime, the judiciary, education, health care, poverty, urban affairs and population.	Includes formation and debate of U.S. foreign and defense policies, veterans' affairs and defense spending. (Relations with specific foreign countries are usually found under the region concerned.)	Includes business, labor, agriculture, taxation, transportation, consumer affairs, monetary and fiscal policy, natural resources, and pollution.	Includes worldwide scientific, medical and technological developments, natural phenomena, U.S. weather, natural disasters, and accidents.	Includes the arts, religion, scholarship, communications media, sports, entertainments, fashions, fads and social life.

	World Affairs	Europe	Africa & the Middle East	The Americas	Asia & the Pacific
Aug. 28		West Germany posted a new record trade surplus in July, the government reports. The surplus of 10.9 bil. marks eclipses the previous record of 10 bil. marks set in April.		The Bolivian government imposes a state of siege in an effort to curb unrest among workers protesting the austerity measures of Pres. Victor Paz Estenssoro.	
Aug. 29		A Soviet health official warns of long-term, life-threatening dangers from the April accident at the Chernobyl nuclear power plant. It is the first public admission of such dangers by a government official.		The government of Argentina announces new measures to fight inflation, including a further devaluation of the austral to a total of 12% for August. The annual rate of inflation was reduced dramatically under the June 1985 Austral Plan, but in July and August 1986 it reached the highest levels since the plan was instituted.	Unemployment in Japan rose to a seasonally adjusted 2.9% of the work force in July, matching the post-World War II record set in April, according to government figures released today. Some 1.7 million people were unemployed in July. Unemployment in June was 2.7%.
Aug. 30		An American reporter is detained by Soviet authorities under suspicion of espionage. Nicholas S. Daniloff, the Moscow correspondent of *U.S. News & World Report* magazine is arrested by the KGB (the internal security and intelligence agency) in the Lenin Hills, a wooded section of Moscow.			In the Philippines, two communist leaders freed from prison in a government amnesty in March, launch a new political party, the People's Party. . . . In Pakistan, the National People's Party is formed at a convention near Lahore in Punjab province. A moving force behind the new opposition is Ghulam Mustafa Jatoi, a former leader of Benazir Bhutto's Pakistan People's Party.
Aug. 31		Urho Kaleva Kekkonen, 85, dominant figure in Finnish politics for five decades and Finland's president from 1956 to 1981, dies in Helsinki. He served as prime minister five times before becoming president. He is regarded as the chief architect of his nation's special brand of neutrality, which evolved after World War II in response to Finland's need to maintain cordial relations with the Soviet Union while pursuing ties with the West.			

A	B	C	D	E
Includes developments that affect more than one world region, international organizations and important meetings of major world leaders.	Includes all domestic and regional developments in Europe, including the Soviet Union, Turkey, Cyprus and Malta.	Includes all domestic and regional developments in Africa and the Middle East, including Iraq and Iran and excluding Cyprus, Turkey and Afghanistan.	Includes all domestic and regional developments in Latin America, the Caribbean and Canada.	Includes all domestic and regional developments in Asia and Pacific nations, extending from Afghanistan through all the Pacific Islands, except Hawaii.

U.S. Politics & Social Issues	U.S. Foreign Policy & Defense	U.S. Economy & Environment	Science, Technology & Nature	Culture, Leisure & Life Style	
	Jerry A. Whitworth, 47, is sentenced to 365 years in prison and fined $410,000 for his role in an espionage ring that provided U.S. naval secrets to the Soviet Union.	General Motors Corp. (GMC) announces that it will offer a 2.9% annual interest rate on new three-year car loans. The incentive program, which offers the lowest rate in GMC's history, prompts other car makers to match or undercut it. . . . Robert C. Wright is named to replace Grant Tinker as the National Broadcasting Co. (NBC) television network's chief executive. Tinker is stepping down after five years as head of NBC during which time he lead the network to first place among the three major networks. . . . The government's index of leading economic indicators rose 1.1% in July, the Commerce Dept. reports. . . . Frontier Airlines, the 15th-largest in the United States, files for protection from creditors under Chapter 11 of the federal bankruptcy code, four days after being shut down by its parent company, People Express Inc.			**Aug. 28**
A funeral for Felix Wayne Mitchell in Oakland, Calif., draws national attention. Mitchell, 32, was kingpin of a California heroin ring and a folk hero among poor blacks in Oakland. Mitchell was serving a life sentence at the federal prison in Leavenworth, Kans., when he was stabbed to death August 22 by a fellow inmate.		Prices received by farmers for their raw agricultural goods are unchanged in August, the Agriculture Dept. reports. Farm prices increased 2.5% in July. . . . The U.S. deficit on merchandise trade in July is a record $18.04 bil., the Commerce Dept. reports. . . . The Agriculture Dept. increases by $2 per metric ton the subsidy on wheat offered for export to the Soviet Union.	The International Atomic Energy Agency ends a Vienna conference on the causes and effects of the Chernobyl nuclear plant accident in the Soviet Ukraine.	Three Lutheran denominations agree to a merger that will form a 5.3 million-member Evangelical Lutheran Church in America. The new unit will be the fourth-largest Protestant body in the nation. . . . *Publishers Weekly*'s hardback fiction best-sellers for the week are: *Red Storm Rising*, Tom Clancy; *Wanderlust*, Danielle Steel; *A Matter of Honor*, Jeffrey Archer; *Last of the Breed*, Louis L'Amour; and *I'll Take Manhattan*, Judith Krantz.	**Aug. 29**
					Aug. 30
At least 82 people are killed as the result of a collision between an Aeromexico airliner and a small private airplane over Los Angeles.		Federal Reserve Board Chairman Paul A. Volcker calls the record $18.04 bil. U.S. trade deficit announced Aug 29 "simply unsuitable," and he warns that it could lead to global economic instability.	An earthquake centered in Romania causes damage in neighboring Moldavia, a republic of the USSR. The official Soviet press says the quake killed one person, damaged some 49,500 buildings and forced 528 people to seek medical help. The Romanian government acknowledges that an earthquake occurred but says nothing about casualties or damage. The earthquake measured 6.5 on the open-ended Richter scale of ground motion.	Henry (Spencer) Moore, 88, leading 20th-century sculptor and one of Britain's most acclaimed artists, dies in Much Hadham, England. During World War II he became widely known for his images of the Blitz, and he went on to become the most successful sculptor of his age, his most characteristic sculptural subject is the female reclining figure. Hundreds of his works decorate parks, public squares and buildings around the world. . . . British track and field athletes put on one of their best performances ever in the European Track and Field Championships, winning eight gold medals, two silver, and five bronzes.	**Aug. 31**

F	G	H	I	J
Includes elections, federal-state relations, civil rights and liberties, crime, the judiciary, education, health care, poverty, urban affairs and population.	*Includes formation and debate of U.S. foreign and defense policies, veterans' affairs and defense spending. (Relations with specific foreign countries are usually found under the region concerned.)*	*Includes business, labor, agriculture, taxation, transportation, consumer affairs, monetary and fiscal policy, natural resources, and pollution.*	*Includes worldwide scientific, medical and technological developments, natural phenomena, U.S. weather, natural disasters, and accidents.*	*Includes the arts, religion, scholarship, communications media, sports, entertainments, fashions, fads and social life.*

	World Affairs	Europe	Africa & the Middle East	The Americas	Asia & the Pacific
Sept. 1		A British cabinet committee headed by P.M. Margaret Thatcher approves new immigration measures that will require citizens of India, Pakistan, Bangladesh, Ghana, and Nigeria to obtain visas when visiting Britain. The new measures are harshly criticized by opposition politicians and representatives of some of the nations involved.... In the Soviet Union, as many as 398 people are reported killed as a result of the collision of the Soviet freighter *Pyotr Vasev* and cruise ship *Admiral Nakhimov* on the Black Sea, some eight miles outside the port of Novorossisk.	In Tripoli, Libyan leader Col. Muammer el-Qaddafi celebrates the 17th anniversary of the coup that brought him to power. Qaddafi has rarely been seen in public since the U.S. air strikes on Libya in April, and reports have circulated that he was ill and losing his grip on power.		In the Philippines, Justice Dept. Min. Neptali Gonzales drops rebellion charges against Arturo Tolentino in connection with a revolt in July aimed at taking over the government. Tolentino was former Pres. Ferdinand Marcos's running mate in elections in February.
Sept. 2		In Czechoslovakia, the leaders of the Jazz Section, the jazz musicians' wing of the national musicians'union, are arrested in a crackdown on dissidents. The section, which claims 7,000 members, publishes a weekly newsletter and sponsors jazz concerts that the government views as forums for pro-Western attitudes.... Voest-Alpine, Austria's state-owned steel and engineering group announces that the company will cut its 38,000-strong work force by about one-quarter over the next four years. About one-third of the job cuts will come through attrition, but direct layoffs and early retirement programs will also be used, according to company Chairman Herbert Lewinsky.		The London-based human rights organization Amnesty International charges in a report that the military government of Chile's Pres. Augusto Pinochet Ugarte has used death squads to kidnap, torture, and kill political opponents.... An opinion poll appears to show that a majority of Canadians are unhappy with the performance of P.M. Brian Mulroney. A total of 59% of those surveyed wish to see Mulroney replaced as prime minister, and 56% say they want Mulroney's Progressive Conservative Party out of power in the federal government.	
Sept. 3		The British government issues $4 bil. worth of floating-rate notes on the European market. The issue, designed to boost Britain's foreign exchange reserves, is the largest ever on the Eurobond market.		In Canada, about 5,500 public employees resume an illegal strike against the government of Newfoundland. The strikers returned to work April 7 under a labor truce after a month-long walkout. The central issue is wage parity between the strikers, mainly transportation and clerical workers, and other members of bargaining units of the Newfoundland Assoc. of Public Employees.	
Sept. 4				In Canada, 700 grain handlers are locked out in a wage dispute at the Thunder Bay, Ontario, grain terminals on Lake Superior, one day after 500 grain handlers went on strike. Thunder Bay, with six giant terminals, is Canada's largest port for grain export. The terminals employ about 1,200 handlers.	Indonesia withdraws landing rights for the aircraft of the Royal Australian Air Force. The move is said to be in protest of references to Indonesian Pres. Suharto in the recently published book *Indonesia: The Rise of Capital*, by an Australian, Richard Robison.
Sept. 5		West Germany's gross national product in the second quarter is up 3.3% from a year earlier after adjusting for inflation, the government reports.... The Trades Union Congress, the British umbrella trade union organization, concludes what may be its last annual conference before general elections if elections are called early. Trade union chiefs and Labour Party leader Neil Kinnock tried to form an alliance that could help defeat the current conservative government of P.M. Margaret Thatcher.			Pres. Corazon Aquino meets with a Moslem separatist chieftain and agrees to begin peace talks to end a 14-year-old insurgency.... Four Arab terrorists posing as airport security guards storm aboard a Pan American Airways jumbo jet filled with nearly 400 passengers in Karachi, Pakistan. After a 16-hour standoff on the ground, the gunmen, fearing a rescue raid by Pakistani commandos, open fire on their hostages, killing or fatally wounding 21 people. All four hijackers are taken alive.

A	B	C	D	E
Includes developments that affect more than one world region, international organizations and important meetings of major world leaders.	Includes all domestic and regional developments in Europe, including the Soviet Union, Turkey, Cyprus and Malta.	Includes all domestic and regional developments in Africa and the Middle East, including Iraq and Iran and excluding Cyprus, Turkey and Afghanistan.	Includes all domestic and regional developments in Latin America, the Caribbean and Canada.	Includes all domestic and regional developments in Asia and Pacific nations, extending from Afghanistan through all the Pacific Islands, except Hawaii.

U.S. Politics & Social Issues	U.S. Foreign Policy & Defense	U.S. Economy & Environment	Science, Technology & Nature	Culture, Leisure & Life Style	
		Customer balloting to choose a long-distance telephone carrier ends two years after it was launched in 1984 in order to bring more competition to the field. More than 70% of U.S. phone costumers were included in the balloting.			**Sept. 1**
Norfolk, Va., elementary school students walk to neighborhood schools for the first time in 15 years. The school board voted unanimously in April that the city's elementary schools had become racially integrated and no longer required a busing program. Busing will continue for grades six through 12.	The United States announces that it is cutting off economic aid to Zimbabwe because of that nation's "unwillingness to conduct its relations with us according to accepted norms of diplomatic civility and practice." The United States suspended its aid program after former Pres. Jimmy Carter walked out of a July 4 reception in Harare in response to stinging criticism of U.S. foreign policy by a Zimbabwean cabinet minister.	Prices for platinum deliverable in September hit a record high $663.20 per ounce, an increase of $38.40 from the previous day.		Three Dutch adventurers complete a transatlantic crossing by balloon in the record time of 51 hours, 14 minutes, more than 30 hours faster than the old record set in 1984 by a solo American balloonist. The three set out from Newfoundland in their 15-story-high craft *Dutch Viking*.	**Sept. 2**
Harvard Univ., the country's oldest institution of higher learning, celebrates the 350th anniversary of its founding with four days of fireworks, concerts, academic symposia, and other events. Graduates of the Cambridge, Mass., university include six U.S. presidents and 29 Nobel Prize winners.		World Airways Inc. says that it will end scheduled commercial airline service September 15 and fire 1,500 of its 2,600 employees.		The Moiseyev Dance Co., the popular Soviet folk ballet troupe, opens at New York's Metropolitan Opera House after 12 year absence from the United States.	**Sept. 3**
Former Democratic senator from Massachusetts Paul Tsongas is reported to be in good condition after undergoing a bone-marrow transplant at the Dana-Farber Cancer Institute in Boston. Tsongas, 45, had decided not to run for reelection in 1984 after learning he had a form of cancer known as non-Hodgkins lymphoma.		The Dow Jones Industrial Average closes at a record high of 1919.71, after a one-day jump of 38.38.		Hank (Henry Benjamin) Greenberg, 75, baseball player who led the American League in home runs five times with the Detroit Tigers, dies in Beverly Hills, Calif. The American League's most valuable player in 1935 and 1940, he had a lifetime batting average of .313 and 331 career home runs. In 1956 he became the first Jewish player elected to the Baseball Hall of Fame.	**Sept. 4**
	The Defense Dept. and the National Aeronautics and Space Admin. (NASA) conduct a successful test related to the Strategic Defense Initiative ("Star Wars") using an unmanned NASA Delta rocket launched from Cape Canaveral.	California's Gov. George Deukmejian signs a bill that will allow multinational corporations an alternative to the state's controversial unitary tax system under which corporate profits are taxed on the proportion of its sales, payroll, and real estate within California, regardless of the amount of profit generated in the state. The new bill will allow corporations to be taxed based primarily on the share of U.S. profits generated in California. . . . Gold prices hit a three-year high, closing at $422.80 an ounce on the Commodity Exchange in New York. The price of gold is the highest since a close of $425.20 on Aug. 23, 1985. . . . The nation's unemployment rate dropped to a seasonally adjusted 6.7% of the work force in August, the Labor Dept. reports.			**Sept. 5**

F	G	H	I	J
Includes elections, federal-state relations, civil rights and liberties, crime, the judiciary, education, health care, poverty, urban affairs and population.	*Includes formation and debate of U.S. foreign and defense policies, veterans' affairs and defense spending. (Relations with specific foreign countries are usually found under the region concerned.)*	*Includes business, labor, agriculture, taxation, transportation, consumer affairs, monetary and fiscal policy, natural resources, and pollution.*	*Includes worldwide scientific, medical and technological developments, natural phenomena, U.S. weather, natural disasters, and accidents.*	*Includes the arts, religion, scholarship, communications media, sports, entertainments, fashions, fads and social life.*

	World Affairs	Europe	Africa & the Middle East	The Americas	Asia & the Pacific
Sept. 6	The 41st annual UN General Assembly opens at UN headquarters in New York City. The opening, which coincides with the annual commemoration of the UN International Day of Peace, is dominated by anxiety over the organization's growing financial crisis. The UN's projected expenditures for 1986 are about $840 mil., and there are no surplus funds in the organization's treasury.	Greek Premier Andreas Papandreou says that his government will stand by the austerity program that it introduced in October 1985 despite the potential political consequences. . . . Two Arab terrorists kill 21 Jewish worshipers and then themselves in an attack on a synagogue in Istanbul, Turkey. Four other Jews are wounded, one of them critically.		Brazil's creditor banks complete the signing of an agreement to restructure more than $31 bil. of the nation's $105 bil. in foreign debt.	Takako Doi, 57, becomes the first woman to lead a Japanese political party when she is elected chairman of the opposition Japan Socialist Party.
Sept. 7	The 101 members of the Nonaligned Movement (NAM) conclude their eighth summit in Harare, Zimbabwe, a site chosen to highlight international tensions in southern Africa. The conference is dominated by the issue of sanctions against South Africa and wide-ranging criticism of U.S. foreign policy. NAM is made up of 99 nations and two guerrilla movements, the Palestine Liberation Org. (PLO) and the South West Africa People's Org.	U.S. Trade Rep. Clayton Yeutter agrees to unblock a stalled agreement on U.S. imports of steel from European Community (EC) nations. The agreement was reached in July, but the United States held it up to force EC approval of a separate pact giving U.S. almond and citrus fruit growers access to European markets. Upon receiving assurances that the EC will finalize the citrus pact "within a couple of weeks," Yeutter put the steel pact in place.	Bishop Desmond Tutu, winner of the 1984 Nobel Prize for peace and leading antiapartheid figure, is enthroned as the archbishop of Cape Town. He becomes the first black to lead the 3-million-strong Anglican Church in southern Africa.	Chile's president, Gen. Augusto Pinochet Ugarte, survives an assassination attempt and hours later imposes a state of siege that expands the more limited restrictions already in place under a state of emergency. Opponents of the government are arrested and restrictions are imposed on the press.	
Sept. 8				Canada's Energy Min. Marcel Masse announces that the federal wellhead energy tax will be ended October 1. The move is widely regarded as a concession to Alberta and other western energy producing provinces. The Petroleum Gas and Revenue Tax is a federal 10% levy on oil and natural gas production.	In Pakistan, opposition leader Benazir Bhutto, who was seized in an August crackdown on dissidents, is released from detention.
Sept. 9		Twenty-six British soccer fans are formally indicted for their alleged part in the 1985 riot at Heysel Stadium in Brussels that left 39 people dead. Belgian authorities are seeking the extradition of the 26. . . . Danish Premier Poul Schluter says that his government will seek curbs on immigration when the Folketing (parliament) convenes in October. Following West Germany's August 27 announcement to slow the flood of refugees, Denmark was the last European nation with liberal immigration laws.			The Japanese government agrees in principle to participate in the U.S. Strategic Defense Initiative ("Star Wars") program. The action allows private Japanese companies and government research facilities to take part in Strategic Defense Initiative research.

A	B	C	D	E
Includes developments that affect more than one world region, international organizations and important meetings of major world leaders.	*Includes all domestic and regional developments in Europe, including the Soviet Union, Turkey, Cyprus and Malta.*	*Includes all domestic and regional developments in Africa and the Middle East, including Iraq and Iran and excluding Cyprus, Turkey and Afghanistan.*	*Includes all domestic and regional developments in Latin America, the Caribbean and Canada.*	*Includes all domestic and regional developments in Asia and Pacific nations, extending from Afghanistan through all the Pacific Islands, except Hawaii.*

U.S. Politics & Social Issues	U.S. Foreign Policy & Defense	U.S. Economy & Environment	Science, Technology & Nature	Culture, Leisure & Life Style	
				International Boxing Federation heavyweight champion Michael Spinks retains his title with a fourth round knockout of European champion Steffen Tangstad of Norway. ... The Malibu, Calif., estate of entertainer Barbra Streisand is the scene of a political benefit that reportedly raised $1.5 mil. for Democratic senatorial candidates and the Hollywood Women's Political Committee. ... Blanche (Sarah) Sweet, 90, American actress who starred in many films made by pioneering silent film director D.W. Griffith, including his 1913 *Judith of Bethulia*, one of the first feature length films made in the United States, dies in New York City, after a stroke.	Sept. 6
		The Federal Savings and Loan Insurance Corp. (FSLIC) sues 27 former officers of the failed Sunrise Savings and Loan Assoc. in Boynton Beach, Fla., for more than $250 mil. FSLIC charges the officers with unsound banking practices.	Federal sponsorship of basic scientific research at universities soared in the first six years of the Reagan administration, according to figures reported in the *New York Times*. The increase of 61% since 1981, to more than $4 bil. in FY1986, is the largest since the early 1960s, when U.S. spending surged in the wake of the Soviet Union's launching of the first artificial satellite, Sputnik.	Nelson Piquet of Brazil wins the Italian Grand Prix in Monza. ... Martina Navratilova beat Helena Sukova and Ivan Lendl beat Miloslav Mecir to win the women's and men's titles respectively at the U.S. Open tennis tournament in Queens, N.Y.	Sept. 7
		Treasury Sec. James A. Baker III strikes the first gold coin ever minted by the U.S. government specifically for investment purposes. The coin, called the American Eagle, is intended to give investors an alternative to the South African Krugerrand, the sale of which is banned in the United States.			Sept. 8
Women score major victories in several primaries on "superprimary day." In Maryland, Rep. Barbara Mikulski and Linda Chavez capture the Democratic and Republican senatorial primaries, respectively. Julie Belaga (R) of Connecticut, Carolyn Warner (D) of Arizona, and Patty Cafferata (R) of Nevada win the respective gubernatorial nominations. By "superprimary day," six other women had already won major-party gubernatorial nominations for the first time; two more women are incumbents.		Home mortgage rates fell below 10% for the first time since early May, according to a survey by the Federal Home Loan Mortgage Corp. The average interest rate on 30-year conventional fixed-rate mortgages is 9.9%, down from 10.4% a month earlier. ... Outstanding consumer installment credit grew a seasonally adjusted $5.38 bil. in July, or at an annual rate of 11.4%, the Federal Reserve Board reports.			Sept. 9

F	G	H	I	J
Includes elections, federal-state relations, civil rights and liberties, crime, the judiciary, education, health care, poverty, urban affairs and population.	*Includes formation and debate of U.S. foreign and defense policies, veterans' affairs and defense spending. (Relations with specific foreign countries are usually found under the region concerned.)*	*Includes business, labor, agriculture, taxation, transportation, consumer affairs, monetary and fiscal policy, natural resources, and pollution.*	*Includes worldwide scientific, medical and technological developments, natural phenomena, U.S. weather, natural disasters, and accidents.*	*Includes the arts, religion, scholarship, communications media, sports, entertainments, fashions, fads and social life.*

	World Affairs	Europe	Africa & the Middle East	The Americas	Asia & the Pacific
Sept. 10		French Finance Min. Edouard Balladur names the three state-owned companies that will be the first to be sold to the public by France's conservative government: Saint-Gobain S.A., a glass and material construction concern; Compagnie Financiere de Paribas, a financial holding company; and Assurances Generales de France (AGF), the second-largest French insurance company. . . . The representatives of nine North Atlantic Treaty Org. countries arrive in Czechoslovakia to observe military exercises by 25,000 Warsaw Pact troops. The rare invitation from the Eastern alliance to observe maneuvers at close hand is a good faith effort aimed at bolstering the 35-nation Conf. on Confidence- and Security-Building Measures and Disarmament meeting in Stockholm, Sweden. . . . The French government announces measures that will reduce the influence of English-language music in that country. The measures will require French subtitles on all foreign-language pop music video clips played on state-owned television and would require French public radio stations to devote more than half of their musical air time to French music.		Canadian Agriculture Min. John Wise and Employment Min. Benoit Bouchard unveil a $33.5 mil. program to aid farmers who have been forced off their land by economic difficulties.	
Sept. 11		The British government announces it will offer state-owned British Airways for sale in the first weeks of 1987. The planned privatization is facilitated by a new agreement on air travel between the United States and the United Kingdom.			Japan's Premier Yasuhiro Nakasone wins a one-year extension as president of the Liberal Democratic Party (LDP) when the LDP members of the Diet vote unanimously to change the party rules. Under the old rules, an LDP president could serve only two consecutive terms.
Sept. 12		American reporter Nicholas S. Daniloff, detained by the Soviet Union since Aug. 30 on espionage charges, is given over to the custody of the U.S. Embassy in Moscow. Simultaneously, Gennadi F. Zakharov, a jailed Soviet accused of spying in the United States, is released into the custody of the Soviet ambassador in Washington.	Joseph James Cicippio is kidnapped in Moslem west Beirut, three days after the abduction of compatriot Frank Reed. They are the first U.S. citizens abducted in Lebanon in more than a year. . . . Egyptian Pres. Hosni Mubarak and Israeli P.M. Shimon Peres meet in Alexandria, Egypt, for the first summit meeting between the two nations in five years.		Indonesia devalues its currency, the rupiah, by 31% against the U.S. dollar in an effort to counter the effects of low oil prices. The new price of the currency is 1,644 rupiah to the U.S. dollar, down from 1,134. . . . Communist negotiators in the Philippines reject a proposal by Pres. Corazon Aquino for an immediate 30-day cease-fire.
Sept. 13		At least 19 people are killed in an earthquake that hits the Greek port of Kalamata. The earthquake measures 6.2 on the Richter open-ended scale of ground motion.			In Bangladesh, the government says that the presidential elections scheduled for October 15 will be delayed. Bangladesh's chief opposition groups had threatened to disrupt the election. . . . Philippine Pres. Corazon Aquino forms a truce with the Cordillera People's Liberation Army, which is led by a renegade former Roman Catholic priest, Conrado Balweg.
Sept. 14		Greece's Premier Andreas Papandreou declares a state of emergency in the port of Kalamata as a result of an earthquake that hit the area yesterday. The quake damaged 70% of the buildings in Kalamata and virtually leveled nearby villages.		Leftist rebels in El Salvador say they have called off peace talks with the Salvadoran government, scheduled for September 19, in a dispute over proposed security arrangements. The rebels say they have offered to meet with the government within 10 days to remove obstacles to the negotiations.	A bomb explodes in the arrivals hall at Kimpo International Airport in Seoul, South Korea, killing five people and wounding more than 30. Officials blame North Korea or leftists instigated by North Korea for the blast, which is seen as an attempt to sabotage the Asian Games scheduled to begin in Seoul on September 20.

A	B	C	D	E
Includes developments that affect more than one world region, international organizations and important meetings of major world leaders.	Includes all domestic and regional developments in Europe, including the Soviet Union, Turkey, Cyprus and Malta.	Includes all domestic and regional developments in Africa and the Middle East, including Iraq and Iran and excluding Cyprus, Turkey and Afghanistan.	Includes all domestic and regional developments in Latin America, the Caribbean and Canada.	Includes all domestic and regional developments in Asia and Pacific nations, extending from Afghanistan through all the Pacific Islands, except Hawaii.

U.S. Politics & Social Issues	U.S. Foreign Policy & Defense	U.S. Economy & Environment	Science, Technology & Nature	Culture, Leisure & Life Style	
		Two units of American Electric Power Co. are indicted on charges of operating a Michigan nuclear power plant in violation of federal fire regulations and of lying about it to the Nuclear Regulatory Comm. . . . Thomas H. Wyman resigns as chairman and president of CBS Inc. Company founder William S. Paley is named acting chairman while the post of acting chief executive goes to Laurence A. Tisch, the company's largest shareholder.	The Lawrence Livermore National Laboratory in Livermore, Calif., announces the resignation of one of its most brilliant scientists, Peter Hagelstein, 32, whose nuclear-powered X-ray laser was seen as a potentially crucial element in Pres. Reagan's Strategic Defense Initiative. Hagelstein is reported to have said he wanted to develop an X-ray laser for medical purposes when he came to Livermore in 1975, but got "trapped" into working on weapons. He is to become an associate professor at Massachusetts Institute of Technology.		Sept. 10
The House approves a sweeping legislative package targeting the problem of illegal drugs. Backed by both the Democratic and Republican leadership, the bill passes, 392-16.		A panel representing eight southeastern states votes to designate North Carolina as the repository for the region's low-level nuclear waste. North Carolina will select the sight of the actual dump, which will operate for 20 years beginning in 1993. . . . Stock prices on all markets plunge in the busiest trading day in the history of the New York Stock Exchange. The Dow Jones Industrial average fell a record 86.61 points, or 4.61%, closing at 1792.89.	Henry DeWolf Smyth, 88, Princeton Univ. physicist, dies of a heart attack in Princeton, N.J. His involvement in atom bomb research during World War II enabled him to write the U.S. government's report on the development of the bomb, *Atomic Energy for Military Purposes*, popularly known as the Smyth Report, published in 1945, shortly after the bombings at Hiroshima and Nagasaki.	The Pittsburgh Symphony announces the appointment of Lorin Maazel to a four-year term as music director.	Sept. 11
The Hands Across America poverty benefit has raised $32 mil. to date, according to a report filed by the event's organizers, USA for Africa, with the city of Los Angeles. The report says that, after expenses, some $15 mil. will be left to help the poor.		The government's producer price index rose a seasonally adjusted 0.3% in August, according to the Labor Dept. . . . A record 240.49 million shares are traded today on the New York Stock Exchange. . . . A long, bitter, divisive meatpackers strike against Geo. A. Hormel & Co.'s main plant in Austin, Minn., comes to an end by a vote of 1,060 to 440, when workers approve a new contract that restores wage cuts effected in 1984. The strike began Aug. 17, 1985.		Burdened with a $900,000 debt, the Oakland (Calif.) Symphony files to liquidate under federal bankruptcy laws. The symphony was founded in 1933. . . . Jacques-Henri Lartigue, 92, French photographer, dies in Nice. He was little known until 1963, when a retrospective at New York City's Museum of Modern Art led to his being recognized as a major 20th-century photographer, whose work provides a matchless chronicle of Parisian high society.	Sept. 12
	Pres. Jose Sarney of Brazil concludes a four-day visit to the United States, the first by a civilian president of Brazil in more than 30 years.				Sept. 13
Pres. Reagan and his wife Nancy broadcast a television and radio appeal for a "national crusade" against drug abuse. It is the first time Reagan and his wife have delivered a joint television address during Reagan's presidency.					Sept. 14

F	G	H	I	J
Includes elections, federal-state relations, civil rights and liberties, crime, the judiciary, education, health care, poverty, urban affairs and population.	*Includes formation and debate of U.S. foreign and defense policies, veterans' affairs and defense spending. (Relations with specific foreign countries are usually found under the region concerned.)*	*Includes business, labor, agriculture, taxation, transportation, consumer affairs, monetary and fiscal policy, natural resources, and pollution.*	*Includes worldwide scientific, medical and technological developments, natural phenomena, U.S. weather, natural disasters, and accidents.*	*Includes the arts, religion, scholarship, communications media, sports, entertainments, fashions, fads and social life.*

	World Affairs	Europe	Africa & the Middle East	The Americas	Asia & the Pacific
Sept. 15	A forum on U.S.-Soviet relations convenes in Jurmala, a resort town on the Baltic coast of Soviet Latvia. Sponsored by the Chautauqua Institution of Jamestown, N.Y., the forum is attended by 2,000 Soviets and 220 Americans.	The French cabinet approves a budget for 1987 that calls for reductions in personal and corporate taxes as well as in government spending. The spending and revenue plans set by the new budget would cut the budget deficit to 2.5% of gross domestic product, down from 3% in 1986.			
Sept. 16		The Dutch government announces an austerity budget for FY1987 that calls for the first reduction in government spending in 30 years. The budget also contains tax increases intended to offset revenues lost because of falling prices for oil and natural gas.... Foreign ministers of the 12 European Community nations meeting in Brussels agree to a package of economic sanctions against South Africa, because of its apartheid system of racial segregation, that is weaker than a group of measures threatened in June. The ministers decide to ban imports from South Africa of iron, steel and gold coins. A prohibition against new investment in South Africa is also agreed to.	In South Africa, a fire in the Kinross gold mine in the Transvaal results in the deaths of 177 miners, while another 235 are reported injured. The accident is said to be the worst gold mine disaster in South Africa's history, and the country's worst mine disaster since 1960.		Stocks on the Tokyo Stock Exchange record the sharpest drop ever when the Nikkei stock average plunges 637.33 points, or 3.5%, to 1,7463.19.
Sept. 17		Five explosions in Paris between September 8 and today have killed eight people, caused some 170 injuries, and disrupted life in the French capital. Each blast is either claimed by or attributed to the Lebanese-based group Committee for Solidarity with Arab and Middle Eastern Political Prisoners, which seeks the release of one of its leaders from a French prison.	At the UN General Assembly Angola's Foreign Min. Afonso Van Dunem calls for a top-level meeting between the United States and Angolan officials as a prelude to the reestablishment of diplomatic ties between the two nations. The United States and South Africa are the only major nations not to recognize the Marxist regime of Luanda. Instead they support the antigovernment rebels of the National Union for the Total Independence of Angola, led by former Marxist Jonas Savimbi.	Mexico's first-half trade surplus fell to $1.58 bil., down 60% from the same period in 1985, according to Bank of Mexico figures.	The appellate division of Palau's supreme court rules invalid a 50-year Compact of Free Assoc. with the United States; it is said to conflict with a provision of the Palau constitution that bans nuclear weapons for the country's territory. The United States had hoped to use the pact to end its trusteeship over Palau while still having the advantages of the small country's strategic location in the western Pacific.
Sept. 18	The General Agreement on Tariffs and Trade (GATT) meeting being held in Uruguay rejects a request by the Soviet Union to participate in GATT meetings.... The sixth round of the U.S.-Soviet disarmament talks begins in Geneva.	A retired West German Army officer is shot to death by Czechoslovakian border guards as the guards attempt to stop two Poles from fleeing into West Germany. The West German was apparently not involved in the escape.	The French military attache in Lebanon is shot to death in Christian east Beirut. The killing appears to be linked to an ongoing terrorist bombing campaign in France.	Canadian Finance Min. Michael Wilson discloses that the projected federal deficit will be about $23 bil. by March 31, 1987 (the end of fiscal 1987) higher than anticipated in February, when he presented the FY1986-87 budget.	

A	B	C	D	E
Includes developments that affect more than one world region, international organizations and important meetings of major world leaders.	*Includes all domestic and regional developments in Europe, including the Soviet Union, Turkey, Cyprus and Malta.*	*Includes all domestic and regional developments in Africa and the Middle East, including Iraq and Iran and excluding Cyprus, Turkey and Afghanistan.*	*Includes all domestic and regional developments in Latin America, the Caribbean and Canada.*	*Includes all domestic and regional developments in Asia and Pacific nations, extending from Afghanistan through all the Pacific Islands, except Hawaii.*

U.S. Politics & Social Issues	U.S. Foreign Policy & Defense	U.S. Economy & Environment	Science, Technology & Nature	Culture, Leisure & Life Style	
Sixty-seven former political prisoners and 37 of their relatives arrive in the United States from Cuba. They are admitted to the United States after a dispute within the Reagan administration on whether to bar them as a means of putting pressure on Cuba's Pres. Fidel Castro to resume an immigration agreement he broke off in May 1985. Castro's action was in protest of broadcasts to Cuba by the U.S.-sponsored Radio Marti. . . . Pres. Reagan signs an executive order requiring that federal employees who hold "sensitive" posts be tested for use of illegal drugs. He also unveils his package of proposed legislation for fighting the nation's narcotics problem.	Philippine Pres. Corazon Aquino arrives in the United States at the start of a nine-day visit aimed at winning political and economic support for her government.	Texas Air Corp. agrees to acquire People Express Inc., together with the assets of its bankrupt and closed Frontier Airlines, for a total of about $298 mil.			**Sept. 15**
Former Delaware Gov. Pierre S. Du Pont IV (R) becomes the first person to announce his candidacy for the 1988 presidential nomination.		The U.S. balance of payments on current account shows a record deficit of $34.73 bil. in the second quarter, the Commerce Dept. reports. The gap surpasses a revised current account deficit of $34.04 bil. in the first quarter. The first quarter was originally reported as $33.67 bil., unchanged from the fourth quarter of 1985.			**Sept. 16**
New housing starts rose 0.4% in August to a seasonally adjusted annual rate of 1.82 million units, the Commerce Dept. reports. . . . Political extremist Lyndon H. LaRouche Jr. pays $256,451.26 to settle a disputed harassment judgment won by the National Broadcasting Co. in a countersuit to a failed libel action by LaRouche. The settlement lifts a court order aimed at forcing the political organizer to disclose his finances. . . . The Rev. Pat Robertson, the religious broadcaster, says he will run for the Republican nomination for president if, over the next year, 3 million Americans sign petitions supporting his candidacy. . . . The Senate confirms Antonin Scalia as the newest associate justice of the Supreme Court by a vote of 98-0. . . . The Senate confirms William H. Rehnquist as the 16th Chief Justice of the United States by a vote of 65-33.	The House passes and sends to Pres. Reagan a bill that reorganizes the Pentagon's command structure. The Senate approved the legislation September 16. . . . The House refuses to cut off a $15 mil. Central Intelligence Agency covert military aid program for Jonas Savimbi's National Union for the Total Independence of Angola rebels, who are fighting to overthrow the Angolan government. The vote by the Democrat-controlled House is considered a victory for the Reagan administration.			The New York Mets win baseball's National League East Division title. . . . *Variety*'s top-grossing films for the week are: *Stand By Me, The Fly, Avenging Force, Aliens* and *Nothing in Common*. . . . *Billboard*'s best-selling albums for the week are: *Top Gun*, (soundtrack); *True Blue*, Madonna; *Raising Hell*, Run-D.M.C.; *Back in the Highlife*, Steve Winwood; and *Dancing on the Ceiling*, Lionel Ritchie.	**Sept. 17**
Congress renews for four years the bulk of federal nonentitlement antipoverty programs. The measure authorizes more than $15 bil. for such programs as Head Start, Community Service Block Grants, and the Low Income Home Energy Assistance Program. . . . Attorney Gen. Edwin Meese announces an interim agreement with the British Caribbean colony of Turks and Caicos—known as a money-laundering center for drug traffickers—that will give U.S. prosecutors access to previously secret bank records. . . . A federal district judge rules in Newark, N.J., that mandatory drug testing of government employees violates the Constitution's ban on unreasonable search and seizure.		The U.S. Court of Appeals for the District of Columbia dismisses a lawsuit brought by seven northeastern states requesting federal action to curb air pollution causing acid rain. . . . After-tax profits of U.S. corporations rose a seasonally adjusted 2.1% in the second quarter, rather than 4.1% as originally reported, the Commerce Dept. reports.		Harry J.W. (Jimmy) Belvin, 85, principal chief of the Choctaw Nation for 27 years (1949-76), dies in Durant, Okla. He helped persuade the Interior Dept. to grant his and other Oklahoma tribes more autonomy than they had previously had.	**Sept. 18**

F	G	H	I	J
Includes elections, federal-state relations, civil rights and liberties, crime, the judiciary, education, health care, poverty, urban affairs and population.	Includes formation and debate of U.S. foreign and defense policies, veterans' affairs and defense spending. (Relations with specific foreign countries are usually found under the region concerned.)	Includes business, labor, agriculture, taxation, transportation, consumer affairs, monetary and fiscal policy, natural resources, and pollution.	Includes worldwide scientific, medical and technological developments, natural phenomena, U.S. weather, natural disasters, and accidents.	Includes the arts, religion, scholarship, communications media, sports, entertainments, fashions, fads and social life.

	World Affairs	Europe	Africa & the Middle East	The Americas	Asia & the Pacific
Sept. 19		In the wake of the April Chernobyl nuclear plant disaster, the Swedish government forbids the sale of uninspected reindeer meat.			The Japanese government introduces a package of economic measures designed to provide a boost to Japan's sagging economy. The package is the third in 1986 aimed at offsetting the adverse economic effects of the strong yen.
Sept. 20	Trade ministers from 74 of the 92 member nations of the General Agreement on Tariffs and Trade reach agreement on an agenda for a new round of trade talks, scheduled to begin in 1987 at Punta del Este, Uruguay. . . . Soviet Foreign Min. Eduard A. Shevardnadze meets with Sec. of State George Shultz in Washington, D.C., and holds an unscheduled parley with Pres. Reagan.				Japan continues to record huge trade surpluses with other nations. Its overall surplus in August was $7.5 bil., down from a record $8.22 bil. in July. The trade surplus with the United States was $4.42 bil. in August, compared with $4.52 bil. in July, when exports to the United States rose 28.5%.
Sept. 21			South Africa's national police force confirms that it hired 1,000 blacks, gave them a three-week course, and sent them back to black townships with guns and full police powers to control racial unrest.		
Sept. 22	The 35-nation Conf. on Confidence- and Security-Building Measures and Disarmament in Europe formally adopts a historic final document on reducing the risk of war. The accord, which deals with conventional forces rather than nuclear weapons, is widely hailed as the first major arms control agreement since the 1979 Strategic Arms Limitation Treaty (SALT II). The action ends 32 months of negotiations in Stockholm, Sweden. . . . Israel's P.M. Shimon Peres and Soviet Foreign Min. Eduard A. Shevardnadze meet at the New York City headquarters of the UN to begin a dialogue on the resumption of diplomatic ties between Israel and the Soviet Union. Both men are attending the 41st session of the General Assembly. . . . Addressing the UN General Assembly, Pres. Reagan speaks optimistically of the prospects for meaningful arms control agreements in the near future. In noting his exchange of letters with Soviet leader Mikhail S. Gorbachev, Reagan credits Moscow with making a "serious effort" to respond to Washington's goal of a 50% overall reduction in nuclear weapons.				Japan's Premier Yasuhiro Nakasone causes a furor in the United States when he is reported to have said that the presence of minority groups in the United States has lowered the intellectual achievemnt of the United States.

A	B	C	D	E
Includes developments that affect more than one world region, international organizations and important meetings of major world leaders.	Includes all domestic and regional developments in Europe, including the Soviet Union, Turkey, Cyprus and Malta.	Includes all domestic and regional developments in Africa and the Middle East, including Iraq and Iran and excluding Cyprus, Turkey and Afghanistan.	Includes all domestic and regional developments in Latin America, the Caribbean and Canada.	Includes all domestic and regional developments in Asia and Pacific nations, extending from Afghanistan through all the Pacific Islands, except Hawaii.

U.S. Politics & Social Issues	U.S. Foreign Policy & Defense	U.S. Economy & Environment	Science, Technology & Nature	Culture, Leisure & Life Style	
		The Federal Aviation Admin. plans to require airlines to equip their planes with a device that warns of aircraft approaching on a potential collision course.... The House approves the first major revision of the Federal Insecticide and Rodenticide Act in 14 years by a 329-4 vote.... The Securities and Exchange Comm. tests a new New York Stock Exchange rule designed to curb the volatility of stock prices on the four Fridays each year when stock options, stock index options, and stock index futures contracts all expire at once.	Federal health officials announce at a Washington, D.C., news conference that tests of the drug azidothymidine (AZT) have proven successful in relieving symptoms in cases of acquired immune deficiency syndrome (AIDS). The drug is the "first therapeutic agent which seems to hold promise for some AIDS patients," says Dr. Robert E. Windom, assistant secretary of health and human services.	David Lynch's *Blue Velvet* opens in New York City. The film noir, in which the discovery of a severed human ear leads to a psychopathic sadist and eventually murder, stars Kyle MacLachlan, Isabella Rossellini, Dennis Hopper, and Laura Dern.	**Sept. 19**
A report titled "New Choices in America" is widely reported in the press a week before its formal release by the Democratic National Committee. In the midterm policy paper, the Democratic Party stakes out an internationalist foreign policy posture that is strongly critical of the Soviet Union, and advocates a collection of "pragmatic" domestic programs stressing business investment and commitment to family values.					**Sept. 20**
		Americans' total personal income rose 0.4% in August, to a seasonally adjusted annual rate of $3.505 trillion, and consumer spending rose 1.1%, the Commerce Dept. reports.		At the 38th annual Emmy Awards, "Cagney and Lacey" wins for best drama series and best actress in a drama (Sharon Gless); "The Golden Girls" for best comedy series and best actress in a comedy (Betty White); William Daniels wins for best actor in a drama series, "St. Elsewhere"; Michael J. Fox for best actor in a comedy ("Family Ties"). "Peter the Great" is named best miniseries, and "Love Is Never Silent," best comedy or drama special.	**Sept. 21**
According to the College Entrance Examination Board, results of the 1986 Scholastic Aptitude Test are the same as those in 1985, 431 verbal and 475 math, while those on the American College Test (ACT) show a slight improvement; the average composite score rose to 18.8, on a scale of 1 to 36, up from 18.6 in 1985.... A federal judge in Los Angeles accepts a city council redistricting plan that will increase Hispanic representation on the 15-member council from one to two.... The Rev. Pat Robertson says he is giving up his role as host of the popular religious television talk show, "The 700 Club," because of the political demands resulting from his contemplated run for the Republican presidential nomination.		A federal judge rules that copyright laws apply to the internal design of computer chips. The decision is considered a significant boost for Intel Corp. and Motorola Corp., the leading companies in the manufacture of microprocessors, the tiny circuits that serve as the "brains" of computers and other automated equipment.... U.S. District Court Judge William J. Skinner announces that W.R. Grace & Co. has reached an out-of-court settlement on suits charging that the company's pollution of drinking water supplies in Woburn, Mass., caused six leukemia deaths and numerous illnesses.	The six recipients of the Albert Lasker Medical Research and Public Service Awards are, in clinical/medical research, Dr. Robert Gallo, Dr. Luc Montagnier, and Dr. Myron Essex for acquired immune deficiency syndrome research; in basic medical research, Dr. Rita Levi-Montalcini and Dr. Stanley Cohen for their discovery of natural chemicals known to control cell growth; and in public service, Dr. Ma Haide for the "legendary conquest of venereal disease and the eradication of leprosy in China."		**Sept. 22**

F	**G**	**H**	**I**	**J**
Includes elections, federal-state relations, civil rights and liberties, crime, the judiciary, education, health care, poverty, urban affairs and population.	*Includes formation and debate of U.S. foreign and defense policies, veterans' affairs and defense spending. (Relations with specific foreign countries are usually found under the region concerned.)*	*Includes business, labor, agriculture, taxation, transportation, consumer affairs, monetary and fiscal policy, natural resources, and pollution.*	*Includes worldwide scientific, medical and technological developments, natural phenomena, U.S. weather, natural disasters, and accidents.*	*Includes the arts, religion, scholarship, communications media, sports, entertainments, fashions, fads and social life.*

	World Affairs	Europe	Africa & the Middle East	The Americas	Asia & the Pacific
Sept. 23	Financial regulators from the United States and Britain announce that they have reached an agreement to help each other in investigations of securities fraud cases. Under the agreement, regulators will exchange information as needed in investigations of insider trading, stock and commodities fraud, and other securities fraud.... In an address to the UN General Assembly, Soviet Foreign Min. Eduard A. Shevardnadze denounces Pres. Reagan's UN speech, yesterday, as "propaganda," but nevertheless holds out the prospect for better U.S.-Soviet relations.	The new head of British Coal, Sir Robert Haslam, meets with National Union of Mineworkers (NUM) president Arthur Scargill and the union's executive committee. The meeting is the first between NUM's full executive committee and the management of British Coal (formerly the National Coal Board) since May 1984. The National Coal Board experienced a bitter strike in 1984-85.... The 35-nation Conf. on Security and Cooperation in Europe convenes a two-week meeting in Vienna to lay the groundwork for a November conference.	A force of about 50 dissidents infiltrates Lome, Togo, from nearby Ghana, and attempts to topple the government of Pres. Gnassingbe Eyadema. They are defeated in an all-night street battle with security forces.		
Sept. 24	The World Bank and the International Monetary Fund hold their joint meeting in Washington, D.C. The highlight is the World Bank's announcement that it will increase assistance to the poorest Third World nations by 14%.	Inflation in the European Community (EC) fell for the first time on record in July, the EC announces. Inflation rose only in Spain and Portugal during the month.... Despite income tax reductions effected by British P.M. Margaret Thatcher's government, the share of national income taken in taxes rose to 38.58% in 1985 from 35.33% in 1980, according to a survey undertaken by the Org. for Economic Cooperation and Development. The survey takes into account direct and indirect taxes and other compulsory payments.			
Sept. 25		Representatives of the European Community and the Council of Mutual Economic Assistance, the Soviet-bloc trading organization, conclude three-days of trade talks in Geneva. Generally characterized as a hopeful beginning to long negotiations, the talks are the first between the parties in more than five years.		In Argentina, the trial begins of two former Buenos Aires police chiefs and five others on charges of human rights abuses in the so-called "Dirty War" of the 1970s.	
Sept. 26		The first installment of $50 mil. in U.S. aid pledged to Northern Ireland is presented at the U.S. State Dept. in Washington, D.C., to the British and Irish ambassadors.		Eight Nicaraguan Contras and three mercenaries from Britain, Costa Rica, and France are sentenced by a Costa Rican court for "hostile acts against a foreign government."	Malaysia bans sales of the *Asian Wall Street Journal* for three months and orders two of its reporters to leave the country for writing articles critical of the government.... China's first stock market since the 1949 revolution opens on an experimental basis in the city of Shanghai.
Sept. 27		The City of London conducts a rehearsal of trading in government bonds in anticipation of changes that will come once the markets are liberalized in the so-called Big Bang on October 27.			

A	B	C	D	E
Includes developments that affect more than one world region, international organizations and important meetings of major world leaders.	Includes all domestic and regional developments in Europe, including the Soviet Union, Turkey, Cyprus and Malta.	Includes all domestic and regional developments in Africa and the Middle East, including Iraq and Iran and excluding Cyprus, Turkey and Afghanistan.	Includes all domestic and regional developments in Latin America, the Caribbean and Canada.	Includes all domestic and regional developments in Asia and Pacific nations, extending from Afghanistan through all the Pacific Islands, except Hawaii.

U.S. Politics & Social Issues	U.S. Foreign Policy & Defense	U.S. Economy & Environment	Science, Technology & Nature	Culture, Leisure & Life Style	
		A group of about 200 air traffic controllers meets in Chicago to form the nucleus of a new union aiming to represent the country's 14,484 controllers working for the Federal Aviation Admin. A predecessor union, Professional Air Traffic Controllers Org. was stripped of bargaining rights after an illegal strike in 1981, when Pres. Reagan fired 11,400 controllers. The new group, the National Air Traffic Controllers Assoc. (NATCA), pledges not to go on strike. . . . Federal Home Loan Bank Board chairman Edwin Gray acknowledges that the Federal Savings and Loan Insurance Corp. is far short of funds to protect depositors at the thrifts it expects to fail in 1986 and 1987. . . . Texas Gov. Mark White signs a bill that will allow out-of-state financial institutions to acquire Texas banks. . . . The government's consumer price index rose 0.2% in August, according to the Labor Dept.	The Chinese government signs contracts for a $4 bil. nuclear power station at Daya Bay in southern China, some 30 miles from Hong Kong.		Sept. 23
		The Senate passes a four-year, $52.3 bil. highway construction bill, 99-0. The authorization bill, which carries an amendment to allow states to raise the speed limit to 65 miles per hour on most interstate highways, is sent to conference with the House, which approved a five-year, $91 bil. bill by a 345-34 vote on August 15.			Sept. 24
A measure to extend the 1965 Higher Education Act for another five years clears Congress after a Senate voice vote. The House approved it yesterday, 385-25.	Pres. Corazon Aquino returns to the Philippines from a nine-day visit to the United States. Aquino departed from San Francisco proclaiming that she was "overwhelmed" by the warm reception she had received.	The House narrowly passes a $562 bil. dollar spending bill to fund government operations through fiscal 1987, which begins October 1. . . . The House overwhelmingly approves sweeping legislation that represents the most radical overhaul of the nation's tax code in at least 40 years. The measure passes the House, 292-136, with a majority of representatives of both parties voting for it.	Nikolai N. Semyonov (also rendered Semenov), 90, Soviet scientist, dies. His work on the mechanism of chemical reactions led to his being named, with Britain's Sir Cyril Hinshelwood, winner of the Nobel Prize for chemistry in 1956; he was the first Soviet scientist to receive a Nobel Prize.	The Houston Astros win baseball's National League West Division title.	Sept. 25
William Hubbs Rehnquist is installed as the nation's 16th chief justice, and Antonin Scalia is seated as the 103rd member of the Supreme Court.	Pres. Reagan vetoes a South African sanctions bill passed overwhelmingly by Congress on September 12. Congressional leaders, including Republicans, insist that they have the votes to easily override the veto.	According to a study undertaken for the American Federation of State, County and Municipal Employees, in the first five years of the Reagan administration federal grants to the states and social service programs shrank by $114.8 bil. below what they would have been under rules in effect when Reagan took office.	The Soviet Union joins 49 other nations in Vienna in signing two International Atomic Energy Agency accords on nuclear accident safeguards. The pacts were spurred by the April accident at the Chernobyl nuclear plant.	The California Angels win baseball's American League West Division title. . . . "Crocodile" Dundee is released in New York City. The film, about an Australian whose outback skills serve him in good stead in New York City's urban wilderness, is directed by Peter Faiman and written by Paul Hogan, who stars with Linda Kozlowski. . . . Publishers Weekly's hardback fiction best-sellers for the week are: It, Stephen King; Red Storm Rising, Tom Clancy; Wanderlust, Danielle Steel; A Matter of Honor, Jeffrey Archer; and Last of the Breed, Louis L'Amour.	Sept. 26
Voter turnout in the 1986 primary elections is the lowest in more than 20 years, according to a study that examined 24 of the most closely contested statewide primaries. The study is released by the Committee for the Study of the American Electorate, a nonpartisan Washington, D.C., research organization.		After only two days of debate, the Senate gives final approval, 74-23, to a sweeping overhaul of the nation's tax code. The bill cuts the number of income brackets for individuals and businesses and lowers the maximum tax rates. Offsetting the lower basic rates, it ends a wide variety of deductions, credits, and incentives.			Sept. 27

F	G	H	I	J
Includes elections, federal-state relations, civil rights and liberties, crime, the judiciary, education, health care, poverty, urban affairs and population.	Includes formation and debate of U.S. foreign and defense policies, veterans' affairs and defense spending. (Relations with specific foreign countries are usually found under the region concerned.)	Includes business, labor, agriculture, taxation, transportation, consumer affairs, monetary and fiscal policy, natural resources, and pollution.	Includes worldwide scientific, medical and technological developments, natural phenomena, U.S. weather, natural disasters, and accidents.	Includes the arts, religion, scholarship, communications media, sports, entertainments, fashions, fads and social life.

	World Affairs	Europe	Africa & the Middle East	The Americas	Asia & the Pacific
Sept. 28		The Greens, West Germany's environmentalist and anti-establishment party, vote to unconditionally support a coalition with the nation's mainstream leftist party, the Social Democratic Party, if elections in January 1987 result in a combined majority of the two parties.... By-elections for 11 seats in the Turkish parliament result in losses current Premier Turgut Ozal's party, and significant gains for the party affiliated with former Premier Suleyman Demirel, who is banned from government activity.... In a by-election for the National Assembly, France's rightist coalition increases its share of the vote and increases its majority in the largely ceremonial Senate.			In China, the Communist Party Central Committee meets and issues a code of conduct that reaffirms China's commitment to the "open door" economic policies of Deng Xiaoping, the nation's paramount leader.
Sept. 29			John Demjanjuk, the retired American auto worker extradited to Israel in February, is formally charged with being the notorious Nazi death camp guard known as "Ivan the Terrible." His trial is not expected to begin until the end of year or early 1987.		
Sept. 30	Soviet UN employee Gennadi F. Zakharov is freed and sent home one day after the release of American reporter Nicholas S. Daniloff by Soviet authorities. The two men faced espionage trials by the Soviet Union and the United States, respectively.			After weeks of tough negotiations, Mexico and its 15 leading creditor banks announce agreement on $6 bil. in loans, part of a $12 bil. package put together by the International Monetary Fund. The remaining $6 bil. will be provided by governments and international lending agencies.	The arrest of a top communist leader, Rodolfo Salas, prompts warnings that peace cannot be achieved in the Philippines if he is not freed. The government of Pres. Corazon Aquino began peace negotiations with the communists in April.... Poland's Gen. Wojciech Jaruzelski concludes a series of meetings in China, in the first substantial sign of a reconciliation between Beijing and the Soviet bloc nations.
Oct. 1		According to reports in the Soviet weekly newspaper *Ekonomicheskaya Gazeta*, the population of the Soviet Union has risen to 280.9 million.		Canada's parliament begins a new session with a Speech from the Throne read by Queen Elizabeth II's representative in Canada, Gov. Gen. Jeanne Sauve. The speech outlines the policy goals of the second half of P.M. Brian Mulroney's term in office.	
Oct. 2				Soviet Foreign Min. Eduard A. Shevardnadze concludes a three-day visit to Ottawa, Canada. It is the first trip to Canada by a Soviet foreign minister in 11 years.	India's P.M. Rajiv Gandhi is unharmed when a lone assailant fires upon him in Old Delhi. The shooting wounds several members of his party but none severely.

A	B	C	D	E
Includes developments that affect more than one world region, international organizations and important meetings of major world leaders.	Includes all domestic and regional developments in Europe, including the Soviet Union, Turkey, Cyprus and Malta.	Includes all domestic and regional developments in Africa and the Middle East, including Iraq and Iran and excluding Cyprus, Turkey and Afghanistan.	Includes all domestic and regional developments in Latin America, the Caribbean and Canada.	Includes all domestic and regional developments in Asia and Pacific nations, extending from Afghanistan through all the Pacific Islands, except Hawaii.

U.S. Politics & Social Issues	U.S. Foreign Policy & Defense	U.S. Economy & Environment	Science, Technology & Nature	Culture, Leisure & Life Style	
				Sir Robert (Murray) Helpmann, 77, dancer, choreographer, actor, and director, whose career spanned more than five decades, dies in Sydney, Australia. From 1934 to 1950, he was the leading male dancer with London's Sadler's Wells Ballet and a frequent partner of Margot Fonteyn, and starred with Moira Shearer in the classic English film *The Red Shoes* (1948), which he also choreographed.... In baseball's American League East Division, the Boston Red Sox win the championship.	**Sept. 28**
			The government's top genetic engineering advisory panel proposes a relaxation of national safety guidelines affecting recombinant DNA research, which involves the deletion of a single gene or minor rearrangements of the sequence of an organism's genetic material.		**Sept. 29**
Pres. Reagan signs the Human Services Reauthorization Act of 1986, which extends a number of federal nonentitlement antipoverty programs.... Opening arguments begin in the fraud trial of former Sec. of Labor Raymond J. Donovan. He and eight codefendants appear before a New York State Supreme Court jury in New York City. The nine men are accused of defrauding the New York City Transit Authority of $4.7 mil., largely by means of falsely passing off a business as minority owned.... With action on final spending legislation for FY1987 still snarled, Congress approves a stopgap continuing resolution that extends financing of federal activities through the first week of the new fiscal year beginning October 1. Failure to approve the stopgap spending would have meant a shutdown of the federal government.	The Reagan administration's offer to sell 3.85 million metric tons of subsidized hard wheat to the Soviet Union expires. Instead of acting on the offer, the Soviet Union September 26 purchased about 1 million metric tons of soft wheat from the European Community for $80 a metric ton. The U.S. wheat prices averaged about $91 a metric ton with the subsidy. ... Pres. Reagan announces that he will meet Soviet leader Mikhail S. Gorbachev in Reykjavik, Iceland, October 11-12, to establish a framework for a possible summit in the United States.	The National Labor Relations Board bars Boston Univ. faculty members from union membership on the grounds that they are managerial employees and not entitled to collective bargaining rights under federal law.... Pres. Reagan signs a bill reauthorizing the Federal Housing Admin. home mortgage guarantee program and renewing the Farmers Home Admin. and federal flood and crime insurance.... Prices received by farmers for their raw agricultural goods dropped 2.4% in September, the Agriculture Dept. reports. ... The government's index of leading economic indicators dropped 0.2% in August, the Commerce Dept. reports.... The U.S. deficit on merchandise trade in August was $13.32 bil., the Commerce Dept. reports.	Astronomer and author Carl Sagan is among the 139 people arrested in Mercury, Nev., while demonstrating against continued underground testing of nuclear weapons by the United States in the face of a Soviet moratorium. While the protest is under way the Energy Dept. sets off its 10th (announced) underground test of 1986 some 40 miles to the north.	(Margaret) Storm Jameson (Mrs. Guy Chapman), 95, British novelist, critic, and pioneering feminist, dies. As president of the English section of PEN (Poets, Essayists and Novelists) from 1938 to 1944, she rescued and assisted writers from Nazi-occupied Europe. Her novels include *Cousin Honore*, *Europe to Let*, and *Cloudless May*.	**Sept. 30**
Former Pres. Jimmy Carter's new presidential library and museum is dedicated in Atlanta, Ga.	State Dept. officials announce that the Reagan administration has offered Honduras more advanced jet fighters, either Northrop F-5Es or Israeli-built Kfirs, to upgrade its squadron of warplanes, which dates from the 1950s.				**Oct. 1**
The Census Bureau says that between 2.7 million and 11.5 million Americans would no longer be classified as poor if noncash benefits such as food stamps, housing subsidies, and medical assistance were counted as income; counting noncash benefits would reduce the number of people considered poor by 8%, to 35%, depending on the method used to measure the value of the benefits. However, any standard, the bureau says, poverty has increased and was higher in 1985 than in 1979.	According to an exclusive story in the *Washington Post*, the Reagan administration in August launched a secret campaign designed to convince Libyan leader Col. Muammar el-Qaddafi that he would be hit with another retaliatory strike by U.S. bombers and ousted in a coup. The revelation of the deception strategy, and the unwitting role the American press played in it, causes an uproar.... Congress affirms legislation imposing strict economic sanctions against South Africa when the Senate votes, 78-21, to override a presidential veto; the House voted to override the veto by a vote of 313 to 83 on September 29.	The National Highway Traffic Safety Admin. reduces the fuel efficiency requirement for passenger cars from 27.5 to 26 miles per gallon. The reduced requirements for 1987 and 1988 model-year cars pleases Ford Motor Corp., which had lobbied for the change, and frustrates Chrysler Corp., which had expected to achieve the higher standard.		Baseball is approved as an official sport in the Soviet Union, the news agency Tass reports. Tass says that specialists from Cuba and Nicaragua will teach the game to Soviet athletes.	**Oct. 2**

F	G	H	I	J
Includes elections, federal-state relations, civil rights and liberties, crime, the judiciary, education, health care, poverty, urban affairs and population.	*Includes formation and debate of U.S. foreign and defense policies, veterans' affairs and defense spending. (Relations with specific foreign countries are usually found under the region concerned.)*	*Includes business, labor, agriculture, taxation, transportation, consumer affairs, monetary and fiscal policy, natural resources, and pollution.*	*Includes worldwide scientific, medical and technological developments, natural phenomena, U.S. weather, natural disasters, and accidents.*	*Includes the arts, religion, scholarship, communications media, sports, entertainments, fashions, fads and social life.*

	World Affairs	Europe	Africa & the Middle East	The Americas	Asia & the Pacific
Oct. 3		In Poland, the government declares illegal an attempt by the outlawed Solidarity labor movement to operate openly. Solidarity had decided to test the tolerance of the regime of Gen. Wojciech Jaruzelski in the wake of a sweeping amnesty that began July 24 and was completed September 15.... Under the leadership of Neil Kinnock, the British Labour Party conference is widely regarded as the most unified since the party lost control of the government in the 1979 elections.		The *Times* of London reports that the Soviet Union signs an economic cooperation pact with Nicaragua; the package is believed to be worth some $250 mil.	In response to pressure from the United States, Japan agrees to eliminate its 26% tariff on imported cigarettes. The move will make U.S. cigarettes more competitive in Japan.
Oct. 4		Joining a chorus of European nations, the chief of Sweden's immigration board, Thord Palmlund, says that his nation is "at the limit" of its ability to grant asylum to refugees. The majority of the 1,700 people per month seeking asylum in Sweden are said to be from Iran. ... Queen Beatrix of the Netherlands dedicates the Oosterschelde, the largest and most technologically advanced dike in the Dutch system used to regulate the North Sea.			
Oct. 5			The Sunday *Times* of London reports that Israel has been secretly manufacturing atomic weapons in a hidden underground factory in the Negev Desert for 20 years.		
Oct. 6				In Canada, a settlement of the dispute between the Newfoundland provincial government and 5,000 members of the Newfoundland Assoc. of Public Employees is announced. The employees returned to work September 29, while negotiations continued.	

A	B	C	D	E
Includes developments that affect more than one world region, international organizations and important meetings of major world leaders.	*Includes all domestic and regional developments in Europe, including the Soviet Union, Turkey, Cyprus and Malta.*	*Includes all domestic and regional developments in Africa and the Middle East, including Iraq and Iran and excluding Cyprus, Turkey and Afghanistan.*	*Includes all domestic and regional developments in Latin America, the Caribbean and Canada.*	*Includes all domestic and regional developments in Asia and Pacific nations, extending from Afghanistan through all the Pacific Islands, except Hawaii.*

U.S. Politics & Social Issues	U.S. Foreign Policy & Defense	U.S. Economy & Environment	Science, Technology & Nature	Culture, Leisure & Life Style	
		Congress clears and sends to the president a bill requiring schools to inspect for asbestos hazards and to take steps to protect against any health risks detected. Widely used as an insulation in building materials, asbestos has been found to cause cancer or serious respiratory illnesses over a period of time if its fibers are inhaled. . . . The nation's unemployment rate rose to a seasonally adjusted 6.9% of the work force in September, the Labor Dept. reports. . . . The Senate passes a comprehensive spending bill for FY1987. It is the largest spending measure ever considered by Congress, with $557.7 bil. in direct appropriations and an estimated $16.8 bil. in expected support payments to farmers.	A shuttle launch schedule released by the National Aeronautics and Space Admin. calls for 46 flights between February 1988 and the end of 1994. The new official schedule, the first since the *Challenger* disaster on January 28, is drastically scaled down from the 145 shuttle flights by 1992 envisioned by the agency prior to the disaster.	*Children of a Lesser God*, a film version of Mark Medoff's 1980 Broadway play about a student and her teacher at a school for the deaf, is released in New York City. Directed by Randa Haines, screenplay by Hesper Anderson, the film stars William Hurt and Marlee Matlin, who wins the Academy Award for best actress for her performance.	Oct. 3
			Moscow sends out an alert that a fire has broken out aboard one of its nuclear submarines about 550 miles east of Bermuda.	CBS News anchorman Dan Rather is beaten by two men under mysterious circumstances in New York City. According to Rather, one of them asked him "Kenneth, what is the frequency?" Rather replied, "You have the wrong guy." The man then punched him in the face, knocking him to the pavement.	Oct. 4
				Dancing Brave wins the Prix de l'Arc de Triomphe at Longchamp race track in Paris. . . . Athletes from China and South Korea collect the most medals at the Asian Games, which conclude today in Seoul, South Korea. The Chinese win 94 golds and a total of 222 medals. The South Koreans win 93 golds and 224 medals overall. . . . Hal B. (Harold Brent) Wallis, 88, film producer, dies in Rancho Mirage, Calif. He was involved with many Hollywood classics, including *Little Caesar* (1930), *The Maltese Falcon* (1941), *Casablanca* ¡1942), and *True Grit* (1969).	Oct. 5
Ten individuals and five organizations associated with political extremist Lyndon H. LaRouche Jr. are indicted in Boston on federal fraud and conspiracy charges. At the same time, nearly 300 armed officers from various federal and Virginia state agencies—bearing search warrants—raid two LaRouche offices in Leesburg, Va., looking for related evidence. . . . The Supreme Court begins its 1986-87 term, its first under Chief Justice William H. Rehnquist. The court also includes one new member, Antonin Scalia.	A bill authorizing intelligence operations in fiscal 1987 clears Congress and is sent to the White House for the president's signature. The legislation contains a provision barring the Central Intelligence Agency from using its contingency fund to give aid to the Nicaraguan "Contra" guerrilla forces.	Home mortgage rates rose past 10% in late September, according to the Federal Home Loan Mortgage Corp. The average rate on 30-year conventional fixed-rate mortgages is 10.08%, slightly higher than the 9.9% rate reported a month earlier. . . . BankAmerica Corp., the nation's second-largest bank holding company, receives a $2.78 bil. takeover proposal from California rival First Interstate Bancorp. . . . Investor Carl C. Icahn offers to acquire USX Corp. (formerly U.S. Steel) for approximately $8 bil., heightening speculation as to the fate of the troubled steel and energy company.	A Soviet nuclear-powered Yankee-class balistic submarine sinks in the Atlantic Ocean, three days after it was crippled by an on-board explosion. The boat went down in international waters, about 600 miles east of Bermuda. Three men died in the fire, but the remainder of the crew were evacuated by rescue vessels before it sank.	After a five-year study, the National Geographic Society announces that Christopher Columbus probably first landed in the Americas on the tiny, remote island of Samana Cay, about 65 miles from San Salvador, where most historians thought Columbus landed. Both islands are part of the Bahamas archipelago. . . . Abram Hill, 76, founder of the American Negro Theater, dies in New York City. Founded in New York City in the 1940s, the theater provided a springboard for the careers of black actors such as Harry Belafonte, Ruby Dee, and Sidney Poitier. The theater achieved a major triumph with Hill's own transformation of *Anna Lucasta*, Philip Yordan's play about a Polish family, into a story about blacks; beginning in August 1944 the production ran 900 performances on Broadway.	Oct. 6

F	G	H	I	J
Includes elections, federal-state relations, civil rights and liberties, crime, the judiciary, education, health care, poverty, urban affairs and population.	*Includes formation and debate of U.S. foreign and defense policies, veterans' affairs and defense spending. (Relations with specific foreign countries are usually found under the region concerned.)*	*Includes business, labor, agriculture, taxation, transportation, consumer affairs, monetary and fiscal policy, natural resources, and pollution.*	*Includes worldwide scientific, medical and technological developments, natural phenomena, U.S. weather, natural disasters, and accidents.*	*Includes the arts, religion, scholarship, communications media, sports, entertainments, fashions, fads and social life.*

	World Affairs	Europe	Africa & the Middle East	The Americas	Asia & the Pacific
Oct. 7		In Britain, *The Independent*, a so-called quality newspaper, goes on sale for the first time and sells out the 650,000 copies produced. *The Independent*, which emphasizes its political neutrality, is the first quality paper introduced in Britain since the *Financial Times* was founded in 1888.		In a report on post-Duvalier Haiti, Americas Watch says that government-sponsored slayings of dissidents and economic misery still exist and that the government has taken "few steps to transcend the Duvalier legacy of terror, cronyism and corruption.". . . The Nicaraguan government charges that the Central Intelligence Agency is responsible for a Contra supply plane shot down over southern Nicaragua October 5. A U.S. Marine veteran survived the crash after parachuting from the plane and was captured yesterday; two other Americans died when the plane was shot down.	
Oct. 8		British companies spent a record £6 bil. purchasing U.S. companies in 1986, according to a study published by the British stockbroking firm of Hoare Govett. . . . Waterford Glass Group of Ireland agrees to purchase Wedgewood PLC of Britain in a cash and stock deal valued at $360 mil. The merger will combine Wedgewood's centuries-old fine china manufacture with Waterford's historic glassware operations, which is one of the largest industrial facilities in Ireland. . . . Premier Jacques Chirac's antiterrorist policy is questioned during an emergency debate in the French National Assembly held amid worries of a resumption of the mid-September Paris bombing campaign that has claimed 10 lives to date.	On the eve of Israeli P.M. Shimon Peres's scheduled rotation of power with Foreign Min. Yitzhak Shamir, considerable optimism is expressed regarding the state of the Israeli economy, the *Financial Times* of London reports. Previously rampant inflation was slashed to an annual rate of about 15%. In July, the inflation rate fell to zero for the first time in over a decade.	In Chile, Pres. Augusto Pinochet Ugarte replaces the army member of the four-man military junta and retires nine army generals in a move apparently aimed at strengthening his control of the military. . . . A lockout of 3,700 dock workers in British Columbia that has shut down nearly all of Canada's West Coast ports over the last three days, is lifted in a temporary labor truce.	
Oct. 9	The UN Sec. Gen. Javier Perez de Cuellar is elected to a second five-year term by unanimous votes in the General Assembly and Security Council.	Irina Ratushinskaya, a Soviet dissident poet, is released from prison. Ratushinskaya, 32, was sentenced in 1983 to seven years' hard labor and five years internal exile for antistate activities.			In Indonesia, a military spokesman confirms that in recent weeks nine communists convicted of helping to lead a 1965 attempted coup against then Pres. Sukarno have been executed.
Oct. 10		Britain's P.M. Margaret Thatcher closes the Conservative Party conference by stressing her party's commitment to Britain's nuclear defense and attacking the disarmament proposals of her Labour Party opponents.			

A	B	C	D	E
Includes developments that affect more than one world region, international organizations and important meetings of major world leaders.	Includes all domestic and regional developments in Europe, including the Soviet Union, Turkey, Cyprus and Malta.	Includes all domestic and regional developments in Africa and the Middle East, including Iraq and Iran and excluding Cyprus, Turkey and Afghanistan.	Includes all domestic and regional developments in Latin America, the Caribbean and Canada.	Includes all domestic and regional developments in Asia and Pacific nations, extending from Afghanistan through all the Pacific Islands, except Hawaii.

U.S. Politics & Social Issues	U.S. Foreign Policy & Defense	U.S. Economy & Environment	Science, Technology & Nature	Culture, Leisure & Life Style	
The Democratic Party files a $10 mil. lawsuit against the Republican National Committee, charging that a Republican program to purge ineligible voters from the rolls is really an attempt to "harass, intimidate and improperly challenge" black voters.	Pres. Reagan affirms his commitment to make human rights a key issue at the upcoming talks in Iceland with Soviet leader Mikhail S. Gorbachev, and at the formal summit that could result from those talks. . . . A volley of denials of responsibility is issued by U.S. and Salvadoran officials in the wake of the October 5 downing of a U.S. plane by Nicaragua. Sec. of State George Shultz asserts that the flights are organized by private U.S. citizens. The Central Intelligence Agency denies that the downed plane had any direct link to the U.S. government. However, a spokesman refuses to deny that the agency had no knowledge of the operation.	U.S. District Court Judge James B. Moran in Chicago approves the settlement of a longstanding dispute between United Airlines and female flight attendants. The class action suit involves 1,725 employees who were forced to resign when they married. The subsequent protest by the workers, who charged that their civil rights were violated by sex discrimination, dates back 20 years. . . . The Environmental Protection Agency bans the use of three pesticides— diazinon, dicofol, and dinoseb— and tightens the rules pertaining to use of a top herbicide, alachlor.		Pres. Reagan signs into law a measure designating the rose as the "national floral emblem" of the United States. The ceremony took place in the Rose Garden of the White House. . . . Cheryl Crawford, 84, veteran theatrical producer whose many Broadway shows included *Brigadoon, Sweet Bird of Youth, Paint Your Wagon,* and *One Touch of Venus,* dies in New York City. Before becoming an independent producer, she was involved with the Group Theater, one of the most influential drama groups of the 1930s, which she cofounded in 1931. In 1947 she founded the Actors Studio with Elia Kazan and Robert Lewis.	Oct. 7
	Asst. Sec. of State for Public Affairs Bernard Kalb resigns as the State Dept.'s chief spokesman. He says his action is in protest of what he calls "the reported disinformation program" regarding Libya.	Citing safety violations, the Energy Dept. orders the shutdown of two nuclear plants at the Hanford Nuclear Reservation near Richland, Wash. The two government-owned facilities produce most of the nation's weapons-grade plutonium. The incident that caused the shutdown occurred September 29, when workmen violated rules intended to prevent the accumulation in a container of enough plutonium to begin a nuclear reaction.		The film *Peggy Sue Got Married,* in which a woman is given the opportunity to go back in time 25 years and reassess her choice of a husband, is released in New York City. Directed by Francis Ford Coppola, and with screenplay by Jerry Leichtling and Arlene Sarner, the film stars Kathleen Turner.	Oct. 8
Use of most drugs except cocaine either held steady or declined, according to a federal study entitled the *National Institute on Drug Abuse Household Survey.* . . . The House votes, 230 to 166, to approve a comprehensive measure to reform immigration laws. Until a few days earlier, the bill appeared dead following a House vote September 26 not to bring the bill to the floor. The Senate approved the immigration bill in 1985. A conference committee will work out the difference between the two bills. . . . The Senate votes to convict U.S. District Judge Harry E. Claiborne on three of the four articles of impeachment that he faces. The conviction automatically removes him from office. Claiborne is the 14th federal official to be impeached and the fifth that the Senate has actually convicted.				*Phantom of the Opera,* a musical based on a 1911 thriller by Gaston Leroux, opens in London. With music by Andrew Lloyd Webber, lyrics by Charles Hart and Richard Stilgoe, and directed by Harold Prince, the musical stars Michael Crawford and Sarah Brightman. . . . At the conclusion of a 24-game match against countryman Anatoly Karpov that began July 28, Gary Kasparov of the Soviet Union retains his world chess title.	Oct. 9
	Vice Pres. George Bush and a Bush aide, Donald Gregg, are linked to a private supply operation to provide arms to anti-Sandinista Contras in Nicaragua. The operation came to light after Sandinista troops shot down a U.S. supply plane over southern Nicaragua October 5. Bush denies he had any connection with the flight or its crew.	The government's producer price index rose a seasonally adjusted 0.4% in September, the Labor Dept. reports.	In El Salvador, hundreds of people die as a result of an earthquake that hit San Salvador shortly before noon. The quake, which measures 7.5 on the Richter open-ended scale of ground motion, kills 976 people, injures 8,176 and leaves 31,000 families homeless.		Oct. 10

F	G	H	I	J
Includes elections, federal-state relations, civil rights and liberties, crime, the judiciary, education, health care, poverty, urban affairs and population.	Includes formation and debate of U.S. foreign and defense policies, veterans' affairs and defense spending. (Relations with specific foreign countries are usually found under the region concerned.)	Includes business, labor, agriculture, taxation, transportation, consumer affairs, monetary and fiscal policy, natural resources, and pollution.	Includes worldwide scientific, medical and technological developments, natural phenomena, U.S. weather, natural disasters, and accidents.	Includes the arts, religion, scholarship, communications media, sports, entertainments, fashions, fads and social life.

	World Affairs	Europe	Africa & the Middle East	The Americas	Asia & the Pacific
Oct. 11		In Lebanon, the Revolutionary Justice Org. frees two French hostages. Premier Jacques Chirac meets the men at Orly Airport in Paris and thanks Syria, Saudi Arabia, and Algeria as "those who made this liberation possible." The freed men are Marcel Coudari and Camille Sontag; they were held for six and nine months respectively. . . . The remains of 833 French soldiers killed during the 1945-54 Indochina War are returned to France from Vietnam.			Defense Sec. Caspar Weinberger concludes a visit to China. During his trip an agreement for three U.S. Navy ships to visit a Chinese port is confirmed; this will be the first U.S. port call since the communist takeover in 1949.
Oct. 12	Pres. Reagan and Soviet leader Mikhail S. Gorbachev conclude two days of meetings in Reykjavik, Iceland, for what were to have been discussions to set the agenda for a true summit in the United States. Although the two sides reach broad understandings on arms control, human rights, and other issues, the parley falls apart in a vehement disagreement over the U.S. Strategic Defense Initiative, just as the superpowers appeared on the verge of concluding a pact on the substantial reduction of offensive nuclear weapons.	In West Germany, the conservative Christian Social Union of Bavarian Premier Franz Josef Strauss wins the land (state) elections in Bavaria, but the radical environmentalist Green Party for the first time earns enough votes to win representation in the Bavarian parliament.			A commission set up in May to write a new constitution for the Philippines approves the final draft after 12 months of bitter debate. Soon after taking office in March, Pres. Corazon Aquino abolished the Philippines constitution written under her predecessor, Ferdinand Marcos, and since then has ruled under an interim "freedom charter."
Oct. 13		France's Pres. Francois Mitterrand says that he does not think he will run for reelection. The next presidential election will have to be held by spring 1988, when Mitterrand will be 72 years old. . . . At a meeting in Brussels of the foreign ministers of the North Atlantic Treaty Org., Sec. of State George Shultz briefs America's primary allies on the Iceland talks between Pres. Reagan and Soviet leader Mikhail S. Gorbachev.		Expo '86, the 1986 world's fair in Vancouver, Canada, closes. More than 22 million people visited the fair since its opening in May, far exceeding the organizers expectations of between 13 million and 20 million visitors. Despite the high attendance, Expo '86 lost money.	
Oct. 14	Elie Wiesel, American author and human rights activist, is named the winner of the 1986 Nobel Prize for peace. A Romanian-born Jew who survived two Nazi concentration camps, he is honored for what is described as his role as "a messenger to mankind: his message is one of peace, atonement and human dignity."	The Bank of England induces a one-percentage-point increase in bank lending rates in an effort to support the value of the British pound. The pound has lost about 10% of its value since early July against a trade-weighted basket of currencies, including a 4% drop in September.			
Oct. 15	A five-day World Congress meeting on peace convenes in Copenhagen, Denmark. Some 2,500 delegates to the conference represent 136 countries, according to the *Times* of London.	West Germany's Bundesbank (central bank) reports that the country's net holdings of foreign assets more than doubled between the end of 1983 and mid-1986, to the equivalent of $83 bil. By way of comparison, the Bundesbank says that, owing to its huge current account deficits, the United States went from having $89 bil. in foreign assets at the end of 1983 to being in a net debtor position of $107 bil. at the end of 1985.			Pres. Hossein Mohammed Ershad comes away with an overwhelming majority of votes in the presidential election in Bangladesh. All major opposition parties boycotted the contest, and independent analysts report abundant signs of vote fraud by the government. . . . After months of rumors, the standing central committee of Taiwan's ruling National Party has approved a plan to lift martial law, the government announces. Martial law has been in effect since 1949.

A	B	C	D	E
Includes developments that affect more than one world region, international organizations and important meetings of major world leaders.	*Includes all domestic and regional developments in Europe, including the Soviet Union, Turkey, Cyprus and Malta.*	*Includes all domestic and regional developments in Africa and the Middle East, including Iraq and Iran and excluding Cyprus, Turkey and Afghanistan.*	*Includes all domestic and regional developments in Latin America, the Caribbean and Canada.*	*Includes all domestic and regional developments in Asia and Pacific nations, extending from Afghanistan through all the Pacific Islands, except Hawaii.*

U.S. Politics & Social Issues	U.S. Foreign Policy & Defense	U.S. Economy & Environment	Science, Technology & Nature	Culture, Leisure & Life Style	
			Bernadette Chayrez, 40, the only person to receive two artificial heart implants, dies at the Univ. Medical Center in Tucson, Ariz., during surgery to replace the second implant with a human heart.		Oct. 11
					Oct. 12
		The Commerce Dept. lowers minimum prices for computer chips exported to the United States by Japanese semiconductor makers. The new "fair market values" are said to be about 40% lower than the prices first assigned after the United States and Japan reached a pricing agreement in July. The agreement prevents Japanese manufacturers from undercutting U.S. semiconductor companies by selling chips for less than they cost to make.	The Nobel Prize for medicine or physiology is shared by Dr. Stanley Cohen, an American biochemist, and Dr. Rita Levi-Montalcini, a developmental biologist who holds both Italian and U.S. citizenship. The two are honored for their discovery of "cell growth factors."		Oct. 13
		For the second year in a row, Forbes magazine's list of the 400 richest Americans is headed by Sam Moore Walton, founder of Wal-Mart stores, estimated to be worth $4.5 bil. The next richest Americnas are John Kluge, principal owner of Metromedia Inc, and H. Ross Perot, founder of Electronic Data Systems Corp., both of whom are estimated to be worth at least $2.5 bil.... First Boston Corp. issues $4 bil. worth of bonds backed by low-interest automobile loans from General Motors Corp. The offering is the largest ever in the United States and matches a $4 bil. bond offering by the British government in September for the international record.		The International Olympic Committee decides to stagger the schedules for the Winter and Summer games. After 1992 the winter competition will be held again in 1994, and every four years after that. The Summer Games will remain on their current four-year cycle. The 1988 games are set for Seoul, South Korea, and the Winter Games for Calgary, Canada.	Oct. 14
	The Senate confirms the nominations of 18 ambassadors. A long-standing stalemate over the matter is broken when the Reagan administration's choice for envoy to Belize, James L. Malone, asks that his nomination be temporarily set aside.... Congress clears a $291.8 bil. military authorization bill for fiscal 1987.		The Nobel Prize for physics is shared by three scientists. Winner of half the prize is Ernst Ruska, the German scientist credited with the invention of the electron microscope in 1931. The other half of the prize goes to two scientists at the International Business Machines Zurich Research Laboratory: Gerd Binner, a West German, and Heinrich Rohrer, a Swiss, who designed an electron microscope that allows scientists to "see" individual atoms.... The Nobel Prize for chemistry is shared by Dudley Herschbach, Harvard Univ., Yuan T. Lee, Univ. of California, Berkeley, and John C. Polanyi, Univ. of Toronto, for developing ways to track chemical reactions.	The New York Mets clinch the National League pennant with a 7-6 victory over the Houston Astros in the 16th inning of game six, which is the longest game in the history of post-season baseball. ... The Boston Red Sox win the American League pennant with a decisive 8-1 victory over the California Angels in the seventh and last game of the series.	Oct. 15

F	G	H	I	J
Includes elections, federal-state relations, civil rights and liberties, crime, the judiciary, education, health care, poverty, urban affairs and population.	*Includes formation and debate of U.S. foreign and defense policies, veterans' affairs and defense spending. (Relations with specific foreign countries are usually found under the region concerned.)*	*Includes business, labor, agriculture, taxation, transportation, consumer affairs, monetary and fiscal policy, natural resources, and pollution.*	*Includes worldwide scientific, medical and technological developments, natural phenomena, U.S. weather, natural disasters, and accidents.*	*Includes the arts, religion, scholarship, communications media, sports, entertainments, fashions, fads and social life.*

	World Affairs	Europe	Africa & the Middle East	The Americas	Asia & the Pacific
Oct. 16			An Israeli warplane is shot down during an attack on Palestinian guerrilla bases near the port city of Sidon in southern Lebanon. It is the first Israeli plane to be shot down in almost three years. One of two crewmen is rescued by the Israelis, but the other is missing.	The Commerce Dept. finds that Canada is subsidizing its softwood lumber exports and imposes a 15% countervailing duty on the product.	
Oct. 17		The number of French jobless fell in September by a seasonally adjusted 3.5% to 2.473 million. The decline is attributed to a government job creation scheme.... Denmark's parliament passes legislation designed to cut the nation's intake of refugees by one-half.			
Oct. 18		The Soviet Union ends its secrecy on grain harvests. The government figures on the 1985 grain crop, the first such data made public in five years, shows that 191.6 million metric tons were harvested, about 48 million metric tons short of the target for the year.... A proclamation signed by 122 leading dissidents from Budapest, Prague, Warsaw, and East Berlin urges Eastern Europe to remember the Hungarian uprising, which began 30 years ago on October 23, 1956. Soviet troops crushed the uprising after invading Hungary on Nov. 4, 1956.	Nicaragua's Pres. Daniel Ortega Saavedra accuses Pres. Reagan of being an "international outlaw" and "the world's chief sponsor of terrorism" for approving military aid to the Contras. Pres. Reagan signs a bill today approving $100 mil. in aid to the Nicaraguan Contras.		Queen Elizabeth II concludes the first state visit to China by a British monarch. The groundwork for the visit, which began October 12, was laid by Britain's agreement in late 1984 to give China sovereignty over Hong Kong in 1997. British diplomats say the trip will "set the seal" on improving Sino-British relations.
Oct. 19			Mozambique's Pres. Samora M. Machel is killed when a plane carrying him home from a meeting in Zambia crashes just outside the border of South Africa. Thirty-three other people, including several senior Mozambican government officials, die in the crash. There are 10 survivors. Machel, 53, led his country since guiding it to independence from Portugal in 1975, and was the first major figure in the growing conflict between the black-ruled states of southern Africa and white-ruled South Africa.		

A	B	C	D	E
Includes developments that affect more than one world region, international organizations and important meetings of major world leaders.	Includes all domestic and regional developments in Europe, including the Soviet Union, Turkey, Cyprus and Malta.	Includes all domestic and regional developments in Africa and the Middle East, including Iraq and Iran and excluding Cyprus, Turkey and Afghanistan.	Includes all domestic and regional developments in Latin America, the Caribbean and Canada.	Includes all domestic and regional developments in Asia and Pacific nations, extending from Afghanistan through all the Pacific Islands, except Hawaii.

U.S. Politics & Social Issues	U.S. Foreign Policy & Defense	U.S. Economy & Environment	Science, Technology & Nature	Culture, Leisure & Life Style	
	Four U.S. war veterans who conducted a hunger strike on the steps of the Capitol to protest U.S. aid to the Nicaraguan Contras end their fast.	Industrial production in September rose a seasonally adjusted 0.1%, the Federal Reserve Board reports. Industrial production also gained 0.1% in August. Revised figures for July indicate that output increased by 0.5% for the month, rather than 0.3%, as reported earlier.... The Senate, passes and sends to Pres. Reagan an $18 bil. renewal of the Clean Water Act; the House approved the bill yesterday.... The Nobel Prize for economics is awarded to American economist James McGill Buchanan of George Mason Univ. for his work in "public choice theory," the application of economic principles to political decision making.		Nigerian playwright, poet, novelist, and essayist Wole Soyinka becomes the first African writer, and the first black writer of any nationality, to win the Nobel Prize for literature. His works include the memoir *Ake: The Years of Childhood* (1981) and *A Shuttle in the Crypt* (1967), which he wrote while in prison with Ibo rebels after the outbreak of civil war in Nigeria in 1967.	Oct. 16
House Speaker Thomas P. (Tip) O'Neill Jr. (D, Mass.) puts down the gavel for the last time after 10 years in the post. O'Neill, 73, is retiring after 38 years in the House of Representatives.... Congress clears a major revision of the nation's immigration law. After five years of arduous effort, the legislation finally passes the Senate by a 63-24 vote; the House voted 238-173 on October 15. The bill prohibits the hiring of illegal aliens and offers amnesty and legal residency to millions of illegal aliens now living in the United States.		Pres. Reagan signs the Higher Education Amendment of 1986.... Congress clears a bill authorizing $16.5 bil. for a variety of water projects across the nation. It is the first omnibus water projects authorization approved by Congress in more than a decade.... New housing starts drop 7.6% in September to a seasonally adjusted annual rate of 1.68 million units, the Commerce Dept. reports.... Despite repeated threats of a veto, Pres. Reagan signs a $9 bil., five-year Superfund toxic waste cleanup bill.		*The Color of Money*, in which Paul Newman plays Fast Eddie Felson (a pool hustler he originated in the 1961 film *The Hustler*), opens in New York. Newman is lured back to the game as the manager-mentor of an up-and-coming young hustler played by Tom Cruise. Directed by Martin Scorsese, with a screenplay by Richard Price based on a novel by Walter Tevis, the movie garners Paul Newman his first Academy Award.... *Sid and Nancy*, which recreates the doomed affair between British punk rocker Sid Vicious of the Sex Pistols and his American girlfriend Nancy Spungen, is released in New York City. Directed by Alex Cox, the film stars Gary Oldman and Chloe Webb.... The International Olympic Committee selects Barcelona, Spain, as the site of the 1992 Summer Olympic Games and Albertville in the French Alps as the site of the 1992 Winter Games.	Oct. 17
A broad package of health legislation passes both houses of Congress without dissent. The last bill to be approved by the 99th Congress, it faces a possible veto by Pres. Reagan.... All funding for federal programs for fiscal 1987 (which began October 1), except for Social Security, is included in a $576 bil. omnibus spending bill signed by Pres. Reagan. (Because of a clerical error that omitted two pages of the bill, Pres. Reagan has to sign a corrected version October 31.)	Pres. Reagan signs an omnibus appropriations bill, including $13.37 bil. in foreign aid for fiscal 1987, approved by Congress yesterday. The funding represents the second consecutive year of cutbacks.		Both houses of Congress approve and send to the White House a bill authorizing $7.8 bil. in fiscal 1987 for the National Aeronautics and Space Admin. (NASA). The measure provides authority for NASA to build a new space shuttle to replace *Challenger*, which exploded January 28.		Oct. 18
		General Motors Corp. scraps a billion-dollar project to build a plastic sports car because the venture proves too costly, the *Detroit News* reports.		Moses Asch, 81, record producer who founded Folkways Records in 1947 and had run the company ever since, dies of a heart attack in New York City. Folkways recordings of such artists as Leadbelly, Woody Guthrie, and Brownie McGhee helped spark the U.S. folk music and blues revivals of the 1950s and 1960s. The Folkways catalog, which Asch never allowed to go out of print, also included international folk music as well as albums ranging from *Electronic Agitprop* to *Sounds of North American Frogs*.... Australia wins the World Cup field hockey tournament, defeating England.	Oct. 19

F	G	H	I	J
Includes elections, federal-state relations, civil rights and liberties, crime, the judiciary, education, health care, poverty, urban affairs and population.	Includes formation and debate of U.S. foreign and defense policies, veterans' affairs and defense spending. (Relations with specific foreign countries are usually found under the region concerned.)	Includes business, labor, agriculture, taxation, transportation, consumer affairs, monetary and fiscal policy, natural resources, and pollution.	Includes worldwide scientific, medical and technological developments, natural phenomena, U.S. weather, natural disasters, and accidents.	Includes the arts, religion, scholarship, communications media, sports, entertainments, fashions, fads and social life.

	World Affairs	Europe	Africa & the Middle East	The Americas	Asia & the Pacific
Oct. 20		Interior ministers of the 12 European Community nations agree in London to new immigration measures designed to combat terrorism and drug trafficking.	Yitzhak Shamir is sworn in as Israel's new prime minister, replacing outgoing Shimon Peres, who takes over Shamir's former post as foreign minister. The job swap takes place in accordance with a power rotation agreement reached after the 1984 elections, from which neither Peres's center-left Labor Party nor Shamir's right-wing Likud bloc emerged with enough votes to form a government.	The trial of Eugene Hasenfus, an ex-Marine shot down October 5 while airlifting military supplies to the anti-Sandinista Contras, begins in the Popular Anti-Somocista Tribunal. Hasenfus is charged with terrorism, association to commit illicit acts, and violation of the public security law. Each of the three charges carries a maximum prison term of 30 years.	
Oct. 21	The UN General Assembly passes, 115-21 with 13 abstentions, a resolution calling on Vietnam to withdraw its forces from Cambodia.		One day after General Motors Corp. made a similar announcement, International Business Machines says it will sell its South African subsidiaries to local interests. The arrangements mean that both companies' products will continue to be available in South Africa.		
Oct. 22		The United States and the Soviet Union trade diplomatic expulsions in a dispute that costs the United States the services of 260 Soviet nationals employed at its Moscow Embassy and Leningrad consulate. The dispute began after the Soviet Union accused American reporter Nicholas S. Davidoff of spying. On September 17 the United States expelled 25 members of the Soviet mission to the UN who were identified by the Reagan administration as intelligence agents.			Sixteen South Pacific states reach tentative agreement with the United States over that country's tuna fishing in the region. Under a draft treaty initialed in Nuku'alofa, Tonga, the United States will pay for fishing rights with five annual payments of $12 mil. . . . Ye Jianying (Yeh Chien-ying), 90, veteran Chinese communist army officer and survivor of the Long March of 1934-35, dies in Beijing. The most renowned survivor of the military old guard, his retirement as head of state in 1983 was widely seen as buttressing the faction led by Deng Xiaoping. . . . U.S. Surgeon Gen. C. Everett Koop issues a report calling for education of school children "at the lowest grade possible" about sex and the fatal disease acquired immune deficiency syndrome.
Oct. 23			A threatened plague of grasshoppers and locusts has been brought under control in western and eastern Africa, according to the UN's Food and Agriculture Org. . . . Former self-proclaimed "Emperor" Jean-Bedel Bokassa is promptly arrested and jailed when he unexpectedly returns to the Central African Republic from exile in France.		Australia's Bureau of Statistics announces that there has been a 2.6% increase in the consumer price index during the fiscal quarter ending in September.

A	B	C	D	E
Includes developments that affect more than one world region, international organizations and important meetings of major world leaders.	Includes all domestic and regional developments in Europe, including the Soviet Union, Turkey, Cyprus and Malta.	Includes all domestic and regional developments in Africa and the Middle East, including Iraq and Iran and excluding Cyprus, Turkey and Afghanistan.	Includes all domestic and regional developments in Latin America, the Caribbean and Canada.	Includes all domestic and regional developments in Asia and Pacific nations, extending from Afghanistan through all the Pacific Islands, except Hawaii.

U.S. Politics & Social Issues	U.S. Foreign Policy & Defense	U.S. Economy & Environment	Science, Technology & Nature	Culture, Leisure & Life Style	
The Republican National Committee agrees to drop a controversial program to challenge the eligibility of voters in heavily Democratic districts. Democrats charged the program was designed to harass and intimidate black voters.		The United States is losing its edge in high-technology manufacturing and faces a potential trade deficit for fiscal 1986 of $2.6 bil. in computers, scientific instruments, aircraft, and specialty chemicals, according to a report released by House Democrats on the Joint Economic Committee.	A scientific team reports from Antarctica that a sharp seasonal drop in the atmosphere's protective ozone layer over that continent appears to be caused by a chemical mechanism.		Oct. 20
		A deficit reconciliation bill is signed by Pres. Reagan. The bill, which passed Congress October 17, brings overall federal revenue and spending levels into line with the requirements of the Gramm-Rudman balanced budget act, at least on paper. The measure is designed to make the federal deficit meet the $154 bil. ceiling set by Gramm-Rudman and the congressional budget resolution, and is intended to reduce the overall federal deficit by $11.7 bil.	Three separate teams of scientists finally witness one of the fundamental theoretical events of physics, the quantum jump. The discoveries were recently reported independently by teams at the Univ. of Washington, the Univ. of Hamburg, West Germany, and the National Bureau of Standards.		Oct. 21
A federal district judge in Washington, D.C., orders four former agents of the Federal Bureau of Investigation to pay a total of more than $51,000 to four political activists of the 1960s and a Washington, D.C., peace group. A new policy would allow the government to pay the damages of employees sued for actions done in the line of duty.	West Germany's Chancellor Helmut Kohl concludes two days of meetings with Pres. Reagan and other U.S. officials in Washington. Kohl is the first Western European leader to be briefed directly by Reagan since the October 11 meeting with Soviet leader Mikhail S. Gorbachev in Reykjavik, Iceland.	The nation's gross national product increased at an inflation-adjusted 2.4% annual rate in the third quarter, the Commerce Dept. reports. . . . Pres. Reagan signs into law the most sweeping overhaul of the nation's tax code in 40 years. . . . Ministers of the Org. of Petroleum Exporting Countries end a contentious 17-day meeting in Geneva agreeing to limit oil output for another two months, until December 31.	Albert Szent-Gyorgyi, 93, Hungarian-born biochemist who won the 1937 Nobel Prize for medicine for his isolation of Vitamin C, dies of kidney failure in Woods Hole, Mass. He came to the United States in 1947 and assumed the post of director of research at the Institute of Muscle Research, Marine Biological Laboratories, Woods Hole, Mass. In 1954 he won an Albert Lasker award for his research on heart muscle contraction.	Variety's top-grossing films for the week are: The Color of Money, "Crocodile" Dundee, Peggy Sue Got Married, Jumpin' Jack Flash and Children of a Lesser God. . . . Billboard's best-selling albums for the week are: Slippery When Wet, Bon Jovi; Fore!, Huey Lewis & the News; Third Stage, Boston; Top Gun (soundtrack); and Dancing on the Ceiling, Lionel Richie. . . . British author Kingsley Amis is named the winner of the Booker Prize, Britain's most prestigious award for fiction. He wins the prize for his novel The Old Devils.	Oct. 22
Beginning what he describes as his "last campaign," Pres. Reagan in Missouri launches a 12-day, 13-state whirlwind tour of behalf of 14 key Republican senatorial and gubernatorial candidates.		The federal budget deficit in fiscal 1986 reaches $220.7 bil., according to the Office of Management and Budget. It is the fourth record deficit in the past five years. . . . Americans' total personal income rose 0.3% in September, to a seasonally adjusted annual rate of $3.511 trillion, the Commerce Dept. reports. Consumer spending rose 1.6% in September. . . . The government's consumer price index rose 0.3% in September, according to the Labor Dept.	Blacks account for 25% and Hispanics for 15% of U.S. cases of acquired immune deficiency syndrome, the federal Centers for Disease Control (CDC) reports; 12% of the general population is black and 6% Hispanic. The CDC says intravenous drug use could explain much of the higher risk of infection the minority groups suffer. . . . Adelbert Edward Doisy, 92, biochemist who in 1938 isolated Vitamin K, an achievement for which he shared the 1943 Nobel Prize for medicine with Henrik Dam of Denmark, dies of heart disease in St. Louis. Doisy, who also isolated the female sex hormones estrone and estradiol, was for many years chairman of the biochemistry deptartment at St. Louis Univ.'s School of Medicine.		Oct. 23

F	G	H	I	J
Includes elections, federal-state relations, civil rights and liberties, crime, the judiciary, education, health care, poverty, urban affairs and population.	Includes formation and debate of U.S. foreign and defense policies, veterans' affairs and defense spending. (Relations with specific foreign countries are usually found under the region concerned.)	Includes business, labor, agriculture, taxation, transportation, consumer affairs, monetary and fiscal policy, natural resources, and pollution.	Includes worldwide scientific, medical and technological developments, natural phenomena, U.S. weather, natural disasters, and accidents.	Includes the arts, religion, scholarship, communications media, sports, entertainments, fashions, fads and social life.

	World Affairs	Europe	Africa & the Middle East	The Americas	Asia & the Pacific
Oct. 24			A British jury convicts Jordanian-born Palestinian Nezar Hindawi of the unsuccessful April 17 plot to use his unwitting Irish girlfriend to smuggle a bomb aboard an Israeli El Al airliner flying from London to Tel Aviv. Citing "conclusive evidence" of links between Hindawi and the Syrian government, Britain breaks diplomatic ties with Damascus. Syria denies the charges and responds by cutting ties with London.		The International Monetary Fund approves $519.4 mil. in loans to the Philippines to boost to its economy and help attract further international trade.
Oct. 25	As a protest against apartheid, the International Committee of the Red Cross bars the South African delegation from attending the group's 25th international conference in Geneva.	The military governor of the Spanish Basque province of Giupuzcoa, Gen. Rafael Garrido Gil, is killed by a bomb placed atop his car while it was stopped at a traffic light in San Sebastian. Garrido's wife, Isabel Velasco, and their son Daniel are also killed by the blast, which authorities blame on the Basque separatist organization Euskadi ta Askatasuna.			It is reported today that rebels seeking the overthrow of Lt. Col. Desi Bouterse, the head of government of Suriname, have moved beyond their stronghold in the east and are closing in on the capital, Paramaribo. From July to October the rebels have escalated hit-and-run strikes against military targets.
Oct. 26		The deregulation, authorized by 1984 legislation, of Britain's bus industry goes into effect. Deregulation is resulting in a move away from traditional-size double- and single-decked buses toward more efficient 16-to 21-passenger minibuses, according to the *Financial Times*.			Erich Honecker of East Germany concludes a visit to China. The visit helps restore China's links with the Soviet bloc, which were ruptured during the Sino-Soviet ideological rift of the 1960s.... In the Philippines, a public rift between Pres. Corazon Aquino and Defense Min. Juan Ponce Enrile, the only minister held over from the Marcos administration, threatens stability of the government. Enrile's harshest and most defiant attack on Aquino comes at a rally of supporters of former Pres. Ferdinand E. Marcos, who was ousted in February.
Oct. 27		The European Community (EC) formally approves a settlement of the long running dispute with the United States over trade in citrus fruit. The United States and EC both agree to roll back retaliatory tariffs imposed in the dispute.... A massive deregulation of the London Stock Exchange takes effect. The event, three years in the making, is widely known as the "Big Bang." Among the changes are the opening of the stock exchange to foreign concerns, the reduction of barriers between different financial and trading functions, the further move toward round-the-clock trading of securities and other instruments, and a major increase in competition and workloads on brokerage companies.			

A	B	C	D	E
Includes developments that affect more than one world region, international organizations and important meetings of major world leaders.	Includes all domestic and regional developments in Europe, including the Soviet Union, Turkey, Cyprus and Malta.	Includes all domestic and regional developments in Africa and the Middle East, including Iraq and Iran and excluding Cyprus, Turkey and Afghanistan.	Includes all domestic and regional developments in Latin America, the Caribbean and Canada.	Includes all domestic and regional developments in Asia and Pacific nations, extending from Afghanistan through all the Pacific Islands, except Hawaii.

U.S. Politics & Social Issues	U.S. Foreign Policy & Defense	U.S. Economy & Environment	Science, Technology & Nature	Culture, Leisure & Life Style	
U.S. District Court Judge Thomas G. Hull, in Greenville, Tenn., rules that the Hawkins County public schools violated the First Amendment rights of certain pupils to exercise freedom of religion by using books that assert beliefs contrary to the pupils' religious, fundamentalist Christian beliefs. The students' parents brought suit against the use of a basic reading series approved by the state for grades one through eight. Among the selections objected to by the parents are readings from the *Diary of Anne Frank* and the *Wizard of Oz*.	Pres. Reagan signs an executive order to disburse $100 mil. in aid to the Nicaraguan Contras and also signs a national security directive detailing the aid program. The funds were contained in an omnibus spending bill passed by Congress October 17 and signed by Reagan October 18.	The Federal Trade Comm. issues rules requiring makers of smokeless tobacco to include health warnings in their advertising and on packages of the product. . . . Eleven days before an election in which several Midwestern Senate seats hang in the balance, the Agriculture Dept. announces a program to pay farmers not to grow corn, sorghum, barley, and oats in 1987 because of mounting crop surpluses. Democrats say the plan is a political tactic. . . . The Energy Dept. releases documents showing that during the 1940s the Hanford Nuclear Reservation near Richmond, Wash., routinely discharged radioactive iodine into the environment in amounts equivalent to what would be considered a major nuclear accident today.			Oct. 24
					Oct. 25
				Jackson Scholz, 89, once considered the world's fastest human, dies in Delray Beach, Calif. In 1924 he earned a gold medal for the United States in the 200-meter run in the Paris Olympic Games, but lost to runner Harold Abrahams in the 100-meter run. The contest between Scholz and Abrahams was depicted in the film *Chariots of Fire*. . . . In auto racing, Alain Prost of France wins the Australian Grand Prix and captures the season Grand Prix driving title.	Oct. 26
Sherman (Llewellyn) Adams, 87, New Hampshire politician who from 1953 to 1958 was special assistant to Pres. Dwight D. Eisenhower, dies in Hanover, New Hampshire of kidney failure and respiratory arrest. Wielding such day-to-day power that he came to be thought of as "assistant president," he resigned under fire in 1958 after a scandal in which he admitted accepting gifts, including a vicuna coat from his friend Bernard Goldfine, a Boston industrialist. . . . Pres. Reagan signs into law a sweeping $1.7 bil. measure designed to address all aspects of the war against illegal drugs.			Figures released by the Soviet Union on infant mortality show that the number of Soviet infant deaths is about twice the Western norm; these are the first such figures released by the Soviets since 1974.	A day-long pray-in for peace at Assisi, Italy, draws 150 religious leaders and representatives of 12 of the world's major religions. A worldwide cease-fire, called for the day by Pope John Paul II, who invited the religious assemblage, is partially successful, according to most reports. . . . The New York Mets of the National League win baseball's World Series, coming from behind to defeat the American League's Boston Red Sox, 8-5, in the seventh and deciding game. The Met's third baseman Ray Knight is named the series' most valuable player.	Oct. 27

F	G	H	I	J
Includes elections, federal-state relations, civil rights and liberties, crime, the judiciary, education, health care, poverty, urban affairs and population.	*Includes formation and debate of U.S. foreign and defense policies, veterans' affairs and defense spending. (Relations with specific foreign countries are usually found under the region concerned.)*	*Includes business, labor, agriculture, taxation, transportation, consumer affairs, monetary and fiscal policy, natural resources, and pollution.*	*Includes worldwide scientific, medical and technological developments, natural phenomena, U.S. weather, natural disasters, and accidents.*	*Includes the arts, religion, scholarship, communications media, sports, entertainments, fashions, fads and social life.*

	World Affairs	Europe	Africa & the Middle East	The Americas	Asia & the Pacific
Oct. 28	The United States vetoes for the second time a UN Security Council resolution demanding that the United States comply with an order by the International Court of Justice (World Court) to halt aid to the Nicaraguan Contras.	A dispute arising from Belgium's status as a nation divided between French and Flemish speakers threatens the government of Premier Wilfried Martens during October but fails to topple it after a vote of no confidence in Martens' center-right coalition government is avoided and the dispute is set aside, at least temporarily. . . . West Germany's Chancellor Helmut Kohl and France's Pres. Francois Mitterrand meet in Frankfurt, West Germany. The two-day "cultural summit" is dominated by a discussion about the October 11 summit in Iceland between Pres. Reagan and Soviet leader Mikhail S. Gorbachev.		The Soviet Union substantially increased arms shipments to the Nicaraguan government in the first 10 months of 1986, a U.S. Pentagon spokesperson says. The Soviets are said to have delivered 18,800 metric tons of military equipment.	
Oct. 29		British Foreign Sec. Sir Geoffrey Howe announces that Britain will enforce a 150-mile fishing conservation zone around the Falkland (Malvinas) Islands. Argentina, which lost a war with Britain over the islands in 1983, condemns the British action as "unacceptable" and begins a diplomatic campaign against the move.	King Fahd of Saudi Arabia dismisses Sheik Ahmed Zaki Yamani as the nation's oil minister, the official Saudi Press Agency announces. He served as minister for nearly 25 years and was one of the most influential figures in the Org. of Petroleum Exporting Countries.		
Oct. 30		A pay dispute involving Sweden's public-sector unions that resulted in a month of job actions by hundreds of thousands of Swedes is settled. The primary issue, on which the unions were ultimately defeated, was pay parity with the private sector. The strikes and other job actions had far-reaching effects in Sweden because the nation's public sector accounts for about 60% of the gross national product and 38% of the work force.			
Oct. 31				In Canada, the government sparks a political controversy when it formally awards a fighter aircraft maintenance contract to a consortium led by a Quebec-based company. Officials in Western Canada view the award as a blatant move by P.M. Brian Mulroney to shore up the declining political popularity of the Tories in Quebec.	The United States and Japan announce a broad agreement to coordinate their economic policies and bolster both economies. As the first step of the agreement, Japan's central bank cuts its discount rate, which is the interest rate charged to financial institutions, to 3% from 3.5%. The United States, in return, agrees to cease its efforts to shrink the U.S. deficit in merchandise trade by driving down the value of the dollar against the yen. . . . The president of Laos, Prince Souphanouvong, steps down for health reasons, according to Laotian state radio. Deputy Premier Phoumi Vongvichit is named as interim president. Souphanouvong, 77, became president in 1977, when he lead the communist Pathet Lao to power.
Nov. 1		In Bulgaria, an explosion and fire at a chemical plant kills 17 people and injures 19 others. The plant is located at Devnya, near the Black Sea port city of Varna. . . . A warehouse near Basel, Switzerland, causes a chemical spill in the Rhine River that many believe is the gravest nonnuclear environmental disaster in Europe in a decade. . . . Eleven European Community foreign ministers vote for a package of sanctions against Syria for its alleged participation in a plot to blow up an El Al jetliner in April. Greece dissents, arguing that the measure will isolate Syria from Middle East peace efforts.			

A	B	C	D	E
Includes developments that affect more than one world region, international organizations and important meetings of major world leaders.	Includes all domestic and regional developments in Europe, including the Soviet Union, Turkey, Cyprus and Malta.	Includes all domestic and regional developments in Africa and the Middle East, including Iraq and Iran and excluding Cyprus, Turkey and Afghanistan.	Includes all domestic and regional developments in Latin America, the Caribbean and Canada.	Includes all domestic and regional developments in Asia and Pacific nations, extending from Afghanistan through all the Pacific Islands, except Hawaii.

U.S. Politics & Social Issues	U.S. Foreign Policy & Defense	U.S. Economy & Environment	Science, Technology & Nature	Culture, Leisure & Life Style	
Officials of the Centers for Disease Control are weighing changes in the government's definition of acquired immune deficiency syndrome (AIDS). A proposed broadening of the definition requires further review and ultimate approval by the White House Office of Management and Budget. The current definition requires a depressed immune system and the presence of a variety of specific illnesses linked to AIDS.		Sears Roebuck & Co. says that it will close the domestic operations of its troubled Sears World Trade unit, formed in 1982 to compete with giant Japanese trading firms such as Mitsubishi International Corp. and Mitsui Co. Management problems and the poor climate for U.S. exports has prevented the division from posting a profit in any quarter since it was founded. . . . Dealers in government securities will be more tightly regulated by the Securities and Exchange Comm. under a bill signed by the president.		John (Gerard) Braine, 64, English author who achieved his first and greatest success with his first novel, *A Room at the Top* (1957), dies in London of a ruptured stomach ulcer. A film version of the novel was released in 1959.	Oct. 28
		Productivity among the nation's nonfarm businesses rose at a seasonally adjusted annual rate of 0.2% in the third quarter of 1986, according to the Labor Dept.			Oct. 29
		An omnibus bill naming parts of five rivers for inclusion in the National Wild and Scenic Rivers System, is signed by Pres. Reagan. . . . General Motors Corp. concedes that its Saturn Corp. project in Tennessee will fall short of the levels of production and employment goals, producing 200,000 to 250,000 cars annually rather than 500,000. . . . The U.S. trade deficit on merchandise trade in September was $12.56 bil., the Commerce Dept. reports.			Oct. 30
		The Treasury Dept. reduces the minimum guaranteed interest rate for new U.S. savings bonds to 6% from 7.5%. . . . Prices received by farmers for their raw agricultural goods dropped 0.8% in October, the Agriculture Dept. reports. . . . The government's index of leading economic indicators rose 0.4% in September, the Commerce Dept. reports.	Robert Sanderson Mulliken, 90, Univ. of Chicago chemist and physicist, dies in Arlington, Va. Mulliken's 1928 molecular orbit theory bridged the gap between the atom and the molecule and provided the first detailed picture of how electrons behave when atoms combine to form molecules. His achievement earned him the nickname "Mr. Molecule" and the 1966 Nobel Prize in chemistry.	The film *The Mission* about a Jesuit mission to the Guarani Indians in a mid-18th-century South America threatened by outside political forces, is released in New York City. Directed by Roland Jaffe, screenplay by Robert Bolt, the film stars Robert De Niro and Jeremy Irons. . . . *Publishers Weekly*'s hardback fiction best-sellers for the week are: *It*, Stephen King; *Red Storm Rising*, Tom Clancy; *Hollywood Husbands*, Jackie Collins; *Wanderlust*, Danielle Steel; and *Foundation and Earth*, Isaac Asimov.	Oct. 31
				Sippie (born Beulah Thomas) Wallace dies on her 88th birthday, in Detroit. Known as the "Texas Nightingale," she was one of the leading blues shouters of the 1920s, a contemporary of Ma Rainey and Bessie Smith, and the creator of such earthy blues songs as "Women Be Wise" and "Mighty Tight Woman." . . . In horse racing Skywalker wins the Breeders' Cup Classic at Santa Anita Park in Arcadia, Calif. Other Breeders' Cup winners are Lady Secret (in the Distaff), Manila (Turf race), Capote (Juvenile), Brave Raj (Juvenile Fillies), Smile (Spring), and Last Tycoon (Sprint).	Nov. 1

F	G	H	I	J
Includes elections, federal-state relations, civil rights and liberties, crime, the judiciary, education, health care, poverty, urban affairs and population.	Includes formation and debate of U.S. foreign and defense policies, veterans' affairs and defense spending. (Relations with specific foreign countries are usually found under the region concerned.)	Includes business, labor, agriculture, taxation, transportation, consumer affairs, monetary and fiscal policy, natural resources, and pollution.	Includes worldwide scientific, medical and technological developments, natural phenomena, U.S. weather, natural disasters, and accidents.	Includes the arts, religion, scholarship, communications media, sports, entertainments, fashions, fads and social life.

	World Affairs	Europe	Africa & the Middle East	The Americas	Asia & the Pacific
Nov. 2		Sinn Fein, the political wing of the Irish Republican Army, votes to take any seats it wins in elections for Ireland's Dail. The move, taken by a two-thirds majority vote at the party's annual conference in Dublin, marks a reversal of a Sinn Fein policy in place since 1922.	David P. Jacobsen, an American held hostage for more than 17 months by Shiite Moslem extremists, is freed in Beirut.		
Nov. 3		The ninth congress of the Albanian Workers (Communist) Party is held in Tirana. A congress is held once every five years. The 1986 congress is the first in the party's history without Enver Hoxha, the Albanian president and party first secretary who died in 1985.	The news of covert dealings between Washington and Teheran is broken in the pro-Syrian Beirut magazine *Al Shiraa*. Quoting senior Iranian sources, it reports that former U.S. national security adviser Robert McFarlane secretly visited Teheran in October to discuss a cessation of Iranian support for terrorist groups and security guarantees for the Arab states of the Persian Gulf in exchange for U.S. military spare parts.	Everett Ellis Briggs arrives in Honduras to take up the post vacated in July by Ambassador John Ferch, dismissed reportedly because the administration felt he was not doing enough to encourage cooperation between Honduras and the Nicaraguan Contras.	
Nov. 4		The Hungarian government commemorates the 30th anniversary of the end of the Hungarian uprising with muted ceremony in the town of Szolnok, 30 miles southeast of Budapest. Soviet troops invaded Hungary on Nov. 4, 1956, crushing the uprising.... In Vienna, the foreign ministers of the 35-nation Conf. on Security and Cooperation in Europe convene the third full-scale review of the 1975 Helsinki Final Act.			Am array of Indian parliamentary speakers denounce the United States for its tentative decision to sell Airborne Warnings and Control Systems (AWACS) radar planes to Pakistan. The dispute blunts recent U.S. attempts to improve relations with India.
Nov. 5	For the eighth straight year, the UN General Assembly passes a resolution calling for a negotiated solution to the Afghan conflict. The vote is 122 to 22, with 11 abstentions.				Five days of ethnic rioting in Karachi and Hyderabad, Pakistan, claim 51 lives and leave 400 people wounded. The violence began with a gun battle between Muhajirs and residents of a mostly Pathan district in Karachi.... In the Philippines, Pres. Corazon Aquino announces that a plebiscite on the new constitution will be held Feb. 2, 1987, and that national legislative elections will be held May 11.
Nov. 6					The Australian Council of Trade Unions tentatively approves a two-tier system of worker pay increases, in a marked change in the accord between the powerful union group and the country's Australian Labor Party government.

A	B	C	D	E
Includes developments that affect more than one world region, international organizations and important meetings of major world leaders.	Includes all domestic and regional developments in Europe, including the Soviet Union, Turkey, Cyprus and Malta.	Includes all domestic and regional developments in Africa and the Middle East, including Iraq and Iran and excluding Cyprus, Turkey and Afghanistan.	Includes all domestic and regional developments in Latin America, the Caribbean and Canada.	Includes all domestic and regional developments in Asia and Pacific nations, extending from Afghanistan through all the Pacific Islands, except Hawaii.

U.S. Politics & Social Issues	U.S. Foreign Policy & Defense	U.S. Economy & Environment	Science, Technology & Nature	Culture, Leisure & Life Style	
The Carnegie Foundation for the Advancement of Teaching issues a report calling for an array of reforms in the "flawed institution" of U.S. undergraduate education. The report is entitled "College: The Undergraduate Experience in America."				*The Colored Museum*, a set of satirical sketches about blacks in America by George C. Wolfe, directed by L. Kenneth Richardson, opens at the Public Theater in New York City.... Greta Waitz of Norway wins her eighth New York City Marathon in nine tries in a time of 2:28:06. Gianni Poli of Italy is the winner of the men's competition, with a time of 2:11:06.... Dale Earnhardt wins the Atlanta Journal 500 National Assoc. for Stock Car Racing (NASCAR) event to clinch his second NASCAR Winston Cup season championship.	Nov. 2
The Supreme Court rules that Arizona cannot deny state aid to private family-planning organizations because they provide abortions and abortion counseling.			Edward Cuyler Hammond, 74, biologist and epidemiologist who in 1952, while serving as director of the statistical research section of the American Cancer Society, published the results of a landmark study linking cigarette smoking to lung cancer, dies of cancer in New York City. He later linked cigarette smoking to other cancers, as well as to heart disease, and did other major research demonstrating the cancer-causing effects of asbestos and vinyl chloride.		Nov. 3
Democrats gain control of both houses of Congress for the first time since Pres. Reagan took office in 1981, with a 55-45 majority in the Senate and 258-177 majority in the House.... Republicans post a net loss of two state legislatures, to control only nine, according to preliminary figures issued by the National Conf. of State Legislatures.... Peter MacDonald, from 1970 to 1982 chairman of the Navajo nation, the largest American Indian tribe in the United States, defeats incumbent chairman Peterson Zah to regain leadership of the tribe.		A three-judge federal appeals court panel rules that the Securities and Exchange Comm. (SEC) cannot regulate banks that set up discount brokerage subsidiaries. An SEC rule had required such banks to register with the agency as broker-dealers of securities.	Passive smoking poses a real health risk for children and adults, a committee of the National Academy of Sciences reports. Passive smoking is the inhalation by nonsmokers of the fumes from their neighbors' pipes, cigarettes, and cigars.		Nov. 4
Arizona's Gov.-elect Evan Mecham (R) stirs a political storm when he announces plans to rescind a state holiday honoring slain civil rights leader Martin Luther King Jr.		The Treasury Dept. auctions $9.85 bil. worth of 10-year notes at an average annual yield of 7.25%. The yield is down from 7.47% at the previous auction and is the lowest since the government began selling 10-year notes in 1976.	The National Aeronautics and Space Admin. announces a revision of its command structure designed to tighten communications and management and to eliminate flaws found by investigators following the *Challenger* disaster in January.		Nov. 5
Saying it is "the most comprehensive reform of our immigration laws since 1952," Pres. Reagan signs a landmark immigration bill at a White House ceremony.	John Anthony Walker Jr., the confessed ringleader of an espionage operation said to have been one of the most damaging in U.S. history, is sentenced to life in prison. Michael Lance Walker, his son, is sentenced to 25 years in prison for his role in the ring.... The *New York Times* and *Washington Post* cite informed U.S. intelligence sources in reporting that former U.S. national security adviser Robert McFarlane's visit to Teheran in October was part of a series of secret talks between U.S. and Iranian officials that took place for more than a year both in Iran and in European cities.	General Motors Corp. announces that it will close 11 plants in four states as the first phase of a plan intended to replace obsolete facilities with modern plants. The closings will affect 26,000 hourly workers and 3,000 salaried employees beginning in 1987. The closings are to be completed by 1990.... Outstanding consumer credit grew a seasonally adjusted $8.37 bil. in September, the Federal Reserve Board reports.... Acting by pocket veto to kill an $18 bil. bill to subsidize sewer projects and clean up waterways, Pres. Reagan says the bill provides triple the funds that he requested.			Nov. 6

F	**G**	**H**	**I**	**J**
Includes elections, federal-state relations, civil rights and liberties, crime, the judiciary, education, health care, poverty, urban affairs and population.	*Includes formation and debate of U.S. foreign and defense policies, veterans' affairs and defense spending. (Relations with specific foreign countries are usually found under the region concerned.)*	*Includes business, labor, agriculture, taxation, transportation, consumer affairs, monetary and fiscal policy, natural resources, and pollution.*	*Includes worldwide scientific, medical and technological developments, natural phenomena, U.S. weather, natural disasters, and accidents.*	*Includes the arts, religion, scholarship, communications media, sports, entertainments, fashions, fads and social life.*

	World Affairs	Europe	Africa & the Middle East	The Americas	Asia & the Pacific
Nov. 7				Revenue Canada makes a preliminary finding that the United States is subsidizing corn exports. The department imposes a provisional 67% countervailing duty on U.S. corn imports.	In India, the northern state of Jammu and Kashmir returns to home rule exactly eight months after New Delhi removed the state government from power.... In the Philippines, fears of a coup by members of the military loyal to Defense Min. Juan Ponce Enrile reach a peak. Public utilities and broadcast stations are put under guard during the crisis, and there are reports that a takeover attempt was narrowly avoided.
Nov. 8		Artur London, 71, deputy foreign minister in the early days of the communist regime in Czechoslovakia and one of the leading officials imprisoned for "revisionism" during a Stalinist-style purge of the early 1950s, dies in Prague. Rehabilitated and released from prison in 1956, London published *L'Aveu* (The Confession; 1969), a graphic account of the tortures inflicted upon him by his Czechoslovak jailers in order to get a confession. The book served as the basis for a 1970 film starring Yves Montand and Simone Signoret.... Vyacheslav M(ikhailovich) Molotov, 96, one of Joseph Stalin's closest aides and a member of the Soviet leadership from 1921 to 1957, dies in Moscow. As Soviet premier from 1930 to 1941 he oversaw industrial and agricultural development and helped implement a policy of forced collectivization of farms that lead to a famine in which millions died, especially in the Ukraine. He also played a key role in the political purges of the 1930s. Named foreign minister in 1939, he negotiated the Soviet-German nonaggression pact that year and helped found the United Nations. Molotov was expelled from the Politburo in 1957 after failing to oust Khrushchev as Communist Party leader, he was expelled from the party altogether in 1962, but in 1984 his membership was quietly restored.		Costa Rica says it is boycotting meetings of the Contadora Group until Nicaragua withdraws a suit from the International Court of Justice (World Court) accusing Honduras of aiding the Nicaraguan Contras; Honduras made a similar announcement on October 31.	Japan's Premier Yasuhiro Nakasone visits China. Bilateral trade is the central issue in talks between Nakasone and Chinese leaders.
Nov. 9		Saboteurs sink two of Iceland's four whaling ships and wreck a plant for processing whale oil and bonemeal. Responsibility for the raids is claimed by the Sea Shepherd Conservation Society, an international antiwhaling group.		In Peru, the governing left-of-center American Popular Revolutionary Alliance wins a solid victory in municipal elections. The results are widely interpreted as a vote of confidence in the government of Pres. Alan Garcia Perez.	
Nov. 10				Canada's Defense Min. Perrin Beatty announces that women in the Canadian Forces will be allowed to hold combat-support roles.	Bangladesh's Pres. Hossein Mohammed Ershad ends martial law and revives the country's constitution, but says the military will still have a say in running the country. Ershad instituted military rule upon taking power in 1982, and ended it only after passage of a bill that protected his regime against legal penalties for actions taken under martial law.... Despite rumors of a military coup, Pres. Corazon Aquino goes ahead with a four-day visit to Japan to seek aid for, and urge more investment in, the Philippines.

A	B	C	D	E
Includes developments that affect more than one world region, international organizations and important meetings of major world leaders.	Includes all domestic and regional developments in Europe, including the Soviet Union, Turkey, Cyprus and Malta.	Includes all domestic and regional developments in Africa and the Middle East, including Iraq and Iran and excluding Cyprus, Turkey and Afghanistan.	Includes all domestic and regional developments in Latin America, the Caribbean and Canada.	Includes all domestic and regional developments in Asia and Pacific nations, extending from Afghanistan through all the Pacific Islands, except Hawaii.

U.S. Politics & Social Issues	U.S. Foreign Policy & Defense	U.S. Economy & Environment	Science, Technology & Nature	Culture, Leisure & Life Style	
		The nation's unemployment rate is a seasonally adjusted 6.9% in October, the same rate as in September, the Labor Dept. reports.			Nov. 7
					Nov. 8
					Nov. 9
	A plaque commemorating the service of American Indians in the Vietnam War is dedicated at the Arlington (Va.) National Cemetery. An estimated 43,000 Native Americans served in Vietnam.	Greyhound Lines Inc. and the Amalgamated Transit Union, representing 7,500 of Greyhound's bus drivers and other employees, reach agreement on a new two-year contract with reported wage and benefit concessions of more than $30 mil.... In its quarterly survey of after-tax earnings, the *Wall Street Journal* reports that profits from continuing operations for 507 major corporations rose 4% compared with the third quarter of 1985. The increase is the first as measured by the *Journal*'s year-earlier comparison since the fourth quarter of 1984.		A painting by Jasper Johns entitled *Out the Window* fetches $3,630,000 at auction at Sotheby's in New York. The price is a world record for a work by a living artist at auction.	Nov. 10

F	G	H	I	J
Includes elections, federal-state relations, civil rights and liberties, crime, the judiciary, education, health care, poverty, urban affairs and population.	Includes formation and debate of U.S. foreign and defense policies, veterans' affairs and defense spending. (Relations with specific foreign countries are usually found under the region concerned.)	Includes business, labor, agriculture, taxation, transportation, consumer affairs, monetary and fiscal policy, natural resources, and pollution.	Includes worldwide scientific, medical and technological developments, natural phenomena, U.S. weather, natural disasters, and accidents.	Includes the arts, religion, scholarship, communications media, sports, entertainments, fashions, fads and social life.

	World Affairs	Europe	Africa & the Middle East	The Americas	Asia & the Pacific
Nov. 11	A UN human rights report estimates that more than 100 Afghan villages were bombed by Soviet and Afghan forces and that 10,000 to 12,000 civilians have been killed in the last nine months.... The leaders of the member nations of the Council for Mutual Economic Assistance (Comecon) gather in Moscow. The first formal summit since June 1984 is hosted by Soviet leader Mikhail S. Gorbachev.				Three U.S. Navy warships visit the port of Qingdao, China, in the first U.S. naval port call to China since the communist takeover in 1949.
Nov. 12	The United States and Soviet Union end the sixth round of bilateral disarmament talks in Geneva. The seventh round is set to begin Jan. 15, 1987.	Britain's Queen Elizabeth II opens a new session of Parliament with the traditional Speech from the Throne to a joint session of the Houses of Lords and Commons. While delivered by the queen, the speech is actually an outline of the legislative plans of the current government for the coming Parliament. ... Environment ministers of the four Rhine-side nations meet in Zurich, Switz. They are joined by representatives of Luxembourg and the European Community. At the meeting, Swiss Pres. Alfons Egli, who is also interior minister, says that his nation will be responsible for paying some compensation as a result of the November 1 spill, which resulted from a fire at a chemical warehouse near Basel and seriously polluted the Rhine River.			
Nov. 13		A Guardian-Marplan Index poll shows that the British Conservatives have reversed Labour's lead in public opinion. The Marplan poll is one of several polls in the previous month to show the Conservatives leading Labour.			In the Philippines, Rolando Olalia, chairman of the new leftist People's Party and head of the May First Movement, the nation's largest labor union, is found slain. Members of the People's Party immediately blame the military for the murder of Olalia and his driver. In recent weeks party members complained of threats and incidents of harassment.... Pres. Corazon Aquino of the Philippines concludes a visit to Japan with promises of increased aid and trade.
Nov. 14	A team of U.S. and Soviet scientists chooses three U.S. sites from which it plans to monitor nuclear tests. The scientists are under the auspices of an agreement between the National Resources Defense Council, a private American environmental organization, and the Soviet Academy of Sciences.	The Soviet Union announces that it has withdrawn medium-range nuclear missiles from the Kola Peninsula, near Finland, and is prepared to withdraw ballistic-missile submarines from the Baltic Sea.		The Org. of American States holds its 16th annual general assembly in Guatemala City. Two main items on the agenda are the continuing dispute between Britain and Argentina over the Falkland (Malvinas) Islands and the conflict in Central America.	The United States and Japan reach agreement on cutbacks in Japanese textile exports to the United States. The pact is similar to those reached over the summer between the United States and Hong Kong, South Korea, and Taiwan. Under the pact, Japan would limit growth in its textile exports to the United States to 0.8% a year through 1989.

A	B	C	D	E
Includes developments that affect more than one world region, international organizations and important meetings of major world leaders.	Includes all domestic and regional developments in Europe, including the Soviet Union, Turkey, Cyprus and Malta.	Includes all domestic and regional developments in Africa and the Middle East, including Iraq and Iran and excluding Cyprus, Turkey and Afghanistan.	Includes all domestic and regional developments in Latin America, the Caribbean and Canada.	Includes all domestic and regional developments in Asia and Pacific nations, extending from Afghanistan through all the Pacific Islands, except Hawaii.

U.S. Politics & Social Issues	U.S. Foreign Policy & Defense	U.S. Economy & Environment	Science, Technology & Nature	Culture, Leisure & Life Style	
	The Reagan administration denies that the United States is set to exceed the limits of the 1979 Strategic Arms Limitation Treaty (SALT II). The denial is in response to a *Washington Post* report November 9 that the treaty would be abrogated on or around November 11.			The second Grawemeyer Award is presented to composer Gyorgy Ligeti; he wins the award for his Etudes for solo piano. . . . The National League Cy Young award goes to Houston Astro pitcher Mike Scott.	Nov. 11
				Variety's top-grossing films for the week are: *"Crocodile" Dundee, The Color of Money, Soul Man, Peggy Sue Got Married,* and *52 Pick-Up.*	Nov. 12
	Pres. Reagan acknowledges for the first time that the United States secretly sent "defensive weapons and spare parts" to Iran, but denies that the shipments are part of the deal for the release of American hostages held by Muslim extremists in Lebanon. In a nationally televised speech, Reagan says that he sought to improve relations with Iran because of its strategic importance to the United States and that he has sent arms "to convince Teheran that our negotiators are acting with my authority."			Roger Clemens of the Boston Red Sox is named the winner of the Cy Young award as the American League's top pitcher. . . . The National Conf. of Catholic Bishops concludes a four-day meeting in Washington, D.C., and ponders the growing "disaffection" between the Vatican and the American branch of the Roman Catholic Church. The bishops also approve a final version of a pastoral letter on "economic justice" that immediately draws dissent from within the American branch itself.	Nov. 13
The Univ. of Notre Dame names Rev. Edward A. Malloy, currently the university's associate provost, to succeed the Rev. Theodore M. Hesburgh as its 16th president. Malloy will assume the presidency in May 1987. . . . Pres. Reagan signs an omnibus health bill although he has "serious reservations" about one provision that established a no-fault compensation program for children injured by vaccines. The program will be financed by a new excise tax on the vaccines.	The White House acknowledges that the Central Intelligence Agency (CIA) was also involved in the Iranian arms shipments. It had been previously reported that the administration used only the National Security Council (NSC), to avoid the requirement of notifying congressional intelligence committees. The *Washington Post* reports that Reagan ordered CIA Dir. William Casey in writing not to notify the committees, despite the agency's involvement.	The industrial production index is unchanged in October, according to the Federal Reserve Board. . . . The government's producer price index rose a seasonally adjusted 0.3% in October, the Labor Dept. reports. . . . The Security and Exchange Comm. announces that arbitrager Ivan F. Boesky has agreed to pay $100 mil. in fines for insider trading. Boesky will plead guilty to one unspecified criminal charge and is barred for life from securities trading.	In a report described in news accounts October 28 and today, five top acquired immune deficiency syndrome experts warn that the disease has become "a major health threat to all Africans." The report asserts that "educational programs and blood bank screening must become an immediate public health priority." . . . Pres. Reagan vetoes a fiscal 1987 authorization bill for National Aeronautics and Space Admin. (NASA). The president objects to a provision that would create a National Aeronautics and Space Council to advise the president on civilian space issues. The veto does not affect funding for NASA, which already received its fiscal 1987 appropriations from other legislation.	*The Decline of the American Empire,* a comedy in which eight people associated with a Montreal university discuss their sex lives at length, is released in New York City. The film is written and directed by Denys Arcand.	Nov. 14

F	G	H	I	J
Includes elections, federal-state relations, civil rights and liberties, crime, the judiciary, education, health care, poverty, urban affairs and population.	*Includes formation and debate of U.S. foreign and defense policies, veterans' affairs and defense spending. (Relations with specific foreign countries are usually found under the region concerned.)*	*Includes business, labor, agriculture, taxation, transportation, consumer affairs, monetary and fiscal policy, natural resources, and pollution.*	*Includes worldwide scientific, medical and technological developments, natural phenomena, U.S. weather, natural disasters, and accidents.*	*Includes the arts, religion, scholarship, communications media, sports, entertainments, fashions, fads and social life.*

	World Affairs	Europe	Africa & the Middle East	The Americas	Asia & the Pacific
Nov. 15				The last of the U.S. troops sent to Bolivia in July to aid in the war against drug trafficking leave. The U.S. presence was extended beyond the 60 days originally planned.... Pres. Jose Sarney's center-left Brazilian Democratic Movement Party wins a sweeping victory in congressional and state elections. The win provides the president with a strong endorsement of his anti-inflation and social programs.... Eugene Hasenfus, a U.S. citizen shot down while airlifting arms to the Nicaraguan Contra rebels, is convicted by a government tribunal and sentenced to 30 years in prison for violating Nicaragua's security law. The verdict was widely expected.	Japan agrees to limit its textile and apparel exports to the United States to a growth rate of 0.8% annually through 1989.
Nov. 16		Moscow proposes special meetings between U.S. and Soviet arms-control experts. According to unidentified sources in the Reagan administration, the White House agrees to a special three-day disarmament meeting in Geneva in early December and is considering a Soviet request for a similar gathering in Moscow in January 1987.			
Nov. 17		George Besse, the head of Renault, France's state-owned auto maker, is shot dead in front of his Paris house. The left-wing terrorist group Direct Action claims responsibility.		Argentina offers to end formal hostilities with Britain if Britain drops its 150-mile "military protection zone" around the Falkland (Malvinas) Islands.... Stolen government files on 16 million taxpayers are turned over to the Royal Canadian Mounted Police. The theft was not revealed until the files were recovered. The confidential files, made up of about 2,000 small plastic microfiche cards, had been missing from the Toronto regional office of Revenue Canada since October 30.	
Nov. 18		Britain rejects Argentina's offer to end formal hostilities in exchange for a reduction in Britain's 150-mile protection zone around its South Atlantic colony of the Falkland (Malvinas) Islands.		A bill extending government services in French is passed by the Ontario legislature and receives royal assent. The legislation, known as Bill 8, requires the province to offer government services in both English and French in areas of Ontario heavily populated by French speakers.... The Canadian Radio-Television and Telecommunications Comm., November 14 and today, warns broadcasting companies to increase their amount of domestically produced programming or risk losing their licenses.	In the Philippines, the retrial of 24 people acquitted in the 1983 murder of opposition leader Benigno Aquino, husband of Pres. Corazon Aquino, begins in Manila.

A	B	C	D	E
Includes developments that affect more than one world region, international organizations and important meetings of major world leaders.	Includes all domestic and regional developments in Europe, including the Soviet Union, Turkey, Cyprus and Malta.	Includes all domestic and regional developments in Africa and the Middle East, including Iraq and Iran and excluding Cyprus, Turkey and Afghanistan.	Includes all domestic and regional developments in Latin America, the Caribbean and Canada.	Includes all domestic and regional developments in Asia and Pacific nations, extending from Afghanistan through all the Pacific Islands, except Hawaii.

U.S. Politics & Social Issues	U.S. Foreign Policy & Defense	U.S. Economy & Environment	Science, Technology & Nature	Culture, Leisure & Life Style	
	Pres. Reagan and British P.M. Margaret Thatcher agree on those arms-control issues that should be given priority in the wake of the October Reykjavik summit between Reagan and Soviet leader Mikhail S. Gorbachev. The accord comes in discussions at the presidential retreat in Camp David, Md.		Workers have completed the entombment of the stricken No. 4 reactor at the Chernobyl nuclear power plant in the Soviet Ukraine. The reactor fwas the site of a nuclear accident in April.... Two early morning earthquakes strike Taiwan less than two hours apart, resulting in 14 deaths and at least 41 injuries. The first measured 6.8 and the second 6.3 on the Richter open-ended scale of motion.	Gian Carlo Menotti's latest opera, *Goya*, premieres at the Kennedy Center in Washington, D.C.	Nov. 15
				Repentance, a fictionalized account of repression under Soviet leader Joseph Stalin in the 1930s and 1940s, long a forbidden topic in the country, is the most popular and controversial film in the Soviet Union.	Nov. 16
Eight members of the Colombo crime group are sentenced in New York City on racketeering conspiracy charges stemming from a scheme to extort money from New York concrete construction contractors.... The Supreme Court rules, 8-1, that employers should make a "reasonable" effort to accommodate an employee's religion. But employers "need not further show," Chief Justice William H. Rehnquist wrote for the court, "that each of the employee's alternative accommodations" are unreasonable in order to reject them.	Northrop Corp. announces that it is halting work on its F-20 Tigershark fighter. The decision follows the loss of a crucial Air Force contract.	Legislation setting up a National Scenic Area along 85 miles of the Columbia River between Oregon and Washington is signed into law by Pres. Reagan, although he expresses "grave doubts as to the constitutionality" of parts of the measure.... Pres. Reagan signs a bill authorizing $12 bil. in dam, waterway, and harbor projects.		The Goncourt, France's most coveted literary prize, is awarded to Michel Host for his novel *Valet de Nuit* (Night Valet).... The seventh annual American Book Awards are presented. E.L. Doctorow's novel *World's Fair* wins for fiction and Barry Lopez's *Arctic Dreams* wins for nonfiction.	Nov. 17
	According to nationwide polls conducted over the last four days, only one in five Americans believes that Pres. Reagan's statements on Iran are "essentially true," while 82% disagree with his decision to sell arms to Teheran, which the administration acknowledged November 13.			Roger Clemens, ace pitcher of the Boston Red Sox, is named the most valuable player in the American League.	Nov. 18

F	G	H	I	J
Includes elections, federal-state relations, civil rights and liberties, crime, the judiciary, education, health care, poverty, urban affairs and population.	Includes formation and debate of U.S. foreign and defense policies, veterans' affairs and defense spending. (Relations with specific foreign countries are usually found under the region concerned.)	Includes business, labor, agriculture, taxation, transportation, consumer affairs, monetary and fiscal policy, natural resources, and pollution.	Includes worldwide scientific, medical and technological developments, natural phenomena, U.S. weather, natural disasters, and accidents.	Includes the arts, religion, scholarship, communications media, sports, entertainments, fashions, fads and social life.

	World Affairs	Europe	Africa & the Middle East	The Americas	Asia & the Pacific
Nov. 19			The government of Brunei yesterday took over the Bank of Brunei and today arrested its chairman and two others for allegedly using unsecured loans to companies related to the bank chairman's family.	The International Monetary Fund approves a $1.68 bil. 18-month standby loan to Mexico as part of a $12 bil. package negotiated with Mexico's foreign creditors in July.	
Nov. 20		The French government has ordered a temporary halt to crude oil imports from the Soviet Union, a French official confirms. The move is a protest against France's trade deficit with the Soviet Union, which is expected to be about $750 mil. in 1986, or about one-third of French exports to the Soviet Union.		Over the objections of human rights groups, the World Bank's executive board approves a $250 mil. structural adjustment loan for Chile.	Babrak Karmal, Afghanistan's top leader for more than six years, completes his departure from power by resigning as the country's president and as a member of the Communist Party's Politburo.... Japan agrees to cut back its large share of the U.S. market for machine tools.
Nov. 21		Britain's P.M. Margaret Thatcher and France's Pres. Francois Mitterrand conclude a meeting in Paris by stressing that France and Britain are "closer than ever" in their positions on arms control. Shared stances call for a 50% reduction in U.S. and Soviet strategic weapons over five years, a ban on chemical weapons, and call for agreements on intermediate- and short-range missiles.... Britain's Sec. of State for Social Services Norman Fowler announces that the Health Education Council will be reconstituted and placed in charge of a $30 mil. public education campaign against acquired immune deficiency syndrome.			

A	B	C	D	E
Includes developments that affect more than one world region, international organizations and important meetings of major world leaders.	*Includes all domestic and regional developments in Europe, including the Soviet Union, Turkey, Cyprus and Malta.*	*Includes all domestic and regional developments in Africa and the Middle East, including Iraq and Iran and excluding Cyprus, Turkey and Afghanistan.*	*Includes all domestic and regional developments in Latin America, the Caribbean and Canada.*	*Includes all domestic and regional developments in Asia and Pacific nations, extending from Afghanistan through all the Pacific Islands, except Hawaii.*

U.S. Politics & Social Issues	U.S. Foreign Policy & Defense	U.S. Economy & Environment	Science, Technology & Nature	Culture, Leisure & Life Style	
A federal grand jury in New York City convicts five defendants on charges linked to a so-called commission of organized crime groups. Prosecutors portrayed the commission as the "board of directors" of the Mafia. Praising the verdict, U.S. attorney Rudolph W. Giuliani says the jury succeeded in dismantling the ruling council of La Cosa Nostra.	The Central Intelligence Agency has been sponsoring covert operations in Iran for seven years, since the latter days of the Carter administration, the *Washington Post* reports. . . . In nationally broadcast news conference, devoted exclusively to questions about U.S.-Iranian dealings, Pres. Reagan strongly defends his administration's November 13 disclosure of a policy of selling weapons to Iran but says that no further arms will be sent. Both Democratic and Republican lawmakers appear to find Reagan's comments confusing and misleading. Sen. Sam Nunn (D, Ga.) says "I counted at least seven major contradictions from what I previously had been informed by top officials. . .We have a foreign policy that's in serious disarray now."	The Environmental Protection Agency issues final rules setting air pollution allowances under the so-called "bubble" policy. Under this policy, air pollution content is figured on a regional basis that permits air pollution increases from one source so long as equivalent reductions are made elsewhere within the confines of the so-called bubble. . . . After-tax profits of U.S. corporations rose a seasonally adjusted 4.3% in the third quarter, the Commerce Dept. reports. . . . Housing starts drop 0.2% in October to a seasonally adjusted annual rate of 1.648 million units, the Commerce Dept. reports.		Third baseman Mike Schmidt of the National Leagues' Philadelphia Phillies wins his third most valuable player award.	Nov. 19
Proposals to provide coverage for so-called catastrophic illnesses are unveiled by Dr. Otis R. Bowen, the secretary of health and human services, in a report entitled "Catastrophic Illness Expenses." . . . Sen. Robert C. Byrd (D, W.Va.) is named by the Democrats as the new Senate majority leader for the 100th congress.		All states should forbid the sale of tobacco to anyone less than 18 years old, according to a report issued by the Dept. of Health and Human Services. Currently, 12 states have no age limit for sales and 14 set the purchase age below 18 years. . . . Consumer spending dropped 2% in October—the largest decline since the department began keeping records in 1959—while personal income rose 0.4%, the Commerce Dept. reports.	A team of British scientists confirms for the first time that the Earth's climate is getting warmer, and at the rate expected because of the "greenhouse" effect. Greenhouse theory holds that carbon dioxide and atmospheric pollutants, released into the atmosphere by industry and other human activities, will produce a gradual warming of the Earth's climate by inhibiting the radiation of heat from the Earth's surface back into space, much as the glass in a greenhouse does. . . . In a news conference at UN headquarters, in New York, the director of the World Health Org. announces a top-priority drive against acquired immune deficiency syndrome.		Nov. 20
Two Chicago aldermen are among seven men indicted by a federal grand jury on charges arising from a two-and-a-half-year federal corruption investigation dubbed "Operation Incubator." Aldermen Clifford Kelly and Wallace Davis are charged with accepting payments from Michael Raymond, a convicted swindler who served as an undercover federal informer in the probe.			The Japanese volcano Mount Mihara unleashes a powerful and unexpected eruption, the volcano's first since 1947 and its largest in two centuries. One death is blamed on the eruption, although there are no other injuries reported.	*Publishers Weekly*'s hardback fiction best-sellers for the week are: *Whirlwind*, James Clavell; *It*, Stephen King; *Red Storm Rising*, Tom Clancy; *Hollywood Husbands*, Jackie Collins; and *The Prince of Tides*, Pat Conroy.	Nov. 21

F	G	H	I	J
Includes elections, federal-state relations, civil rights and liberties, crime, the judiciary, education, health care, poverty, urban affairs and population.	Includes formation and debate of U.S. foreign and defense policies, veterans' affairs and defense spending. (Relations with specific foreign countries are usually found under the region concerned.)	Includes business, labor, agriculture, taxation, transportation, consumer affairs, monetary and fiscal policy, natural resources, and pollution.	Includes worldwide scientific, medical and technological developments, natural phenomena, U.S. weather, natural disasters, and accidents.	Includes the arts, religion, scholarship, communications media, sports, entertainments, fashions, fads and social life.

	World Affairs	Europe	Africa & the Middle East	The Americas	Asia & the Pacific
Nov. 22		Adolf G. Tolkachev, who was accused of spying for the Central Intelligence Agency (CIA), is executed for high treason in the Soviet Union. He was arrested in September 1985 on information from Edward Lee Howard, a renegade CIA agent who defected to the Soviet Union at about the time of Tolkachev's arrest.			The government of India says it will seek damages of at least $3 bil. in its suit against Union Carbide Corp. for the 1984 disaster at the company's chemical plant in Bhopal, India. The leak of poisonous gas at the plant is considered the worst industrial accident in history.
Nov. 23		Romanian voters in a national referendum approve a decision by Pres. Nicolae Ceausescu to unilaterally reduce Romania's armed forces and military spending by 5%.... Austria's Socialist Party retains its role as the country's leading party in national elections; but small parties on the right and left make dramatic gains at the expense of the conservative People's Party, which places second in the voting.			Korean Air Lines pilot Park Yong Man releases his assessment that an on-board navigation computer caused KAL Flight 007 to stray into Soviet Pacific airspace on Sept. 1, 1983. The jumbo jet was shot down by a Soviet interceptor, killing 269 people. Park's theory is similar to one by American investigative reporter Seymour Hersh, contained in the August 26 issue of *Atlantic Monthly* magazine.... In the face of further threats of a coup by young military officers loyal to Defense Min. Juan Ponce Enrile, Philippines Pres. Corazon Aquino dismisses her entire cabinet and immediately replaces Enrile with Gen. Rafael Ileto, the deputy defense minister. At the same time she warns communist insurgents that if they do not accept a cease-fire within seven days, "all further negotiation" will be terminated.
Nov. 24		Barclays Bank PLC, Britain's second-largest bank, announces that it has sold its remaining 40% stake in its South African associate, Barclays National Bank Ltd. of South Africa, for the equivalent of $116 mil. It is the first such disinvestment by a major European company in South Africa.... East German guards shoot to death an unidentified man attempting to scale the Berlin Wall in East Berlin. His is the 58th documented death in an escape attempt at the wall.		Canada's External Affairs Min. Joe Clark formally discloses that Canada has granted asylum to five Soviet soldiers who deserted from the war in Afghanistan.	

A	B	C	D	E
Includes developments that affect more than one world region, international organizations and important meetings of major world leaders.	Includes all domestic and regional developments in Europe, including the Soviet Union, Turkey, Cyprus and Malta.	Includes all domestic and regional developments in Africa and the Middle East, including Iraq and Iran and excluding Cyprus, Turkey and Afghanistan.	Includes all domestic and regional developments in Latin America, the Caribbean and Canada.	Includes all domestic and regional developments in Asia and Pacific nations, extending from Afghanistan through all the Pacific Islands, except Hawaii.

U.S. Politics & Social Issues	U.S. Foreign Policy & Defense	U.S. Economy & Environment	Science, Technology & Nature	Culture, Leisure & Life Style	
				Mike Tyson, 20, becomes the youngest fighter to win a world heavyweight boxing title when he scores a second-round technical knockout over Trevor Berbick in Las Vegas, for the championship of the World Boxing Council. . . . Scatman (Benjamin Sherman) Crothers, 76, character actor in films and television, dies of cancer in Van Nuys, Calif. A musician and singer whose 1930s traveling band helped break the color bar in Midwestern clubs, Crothers starred in the television comedy series ''Chico and the Man'' and had memorable roles in *The Shining* and *The Shootist*. . . . *Billboard*'s best-selling albums for the week are: *Third Stage*, Boston; *Slippery When Wet*, Bon Jovi; *Fore!*, Huey Lewis & the News; *True Colors*, Cyndi Lauper; and *Dancing on the Ceiling*, Lionel Richie. . . . William Bradford Huie, 76, Alabama author, journalist, and civil rights crusader, dies in Guntersville, Ala., of an apparent heart attack. His 20 books include *The Execution of Private Slovik*, *The Americanization of Emily*, and *He Slew the Dragon*, a controversial biography of Rev. Martin Luther King Jr.'s assassin, James Earl Ray.	Nov. 22
Philadelphia's former Mayor Frank Rizzo all but formally launches a campaign to win back his job from Mayor Wilson Goode (D).			Dr. Robert Gale, the U.S. physician who aided radiation victims of the April Chernobyl nuclear accident, reveals that blood tests of some of the victims show evidence of genetic mutations.		Nov. 23
		The Interior Dept. releases a preliminary proposal to open the Arctic National Wildlife Refuge to oil and natural gas exploration and development.		Relief pitcher Todd Worrell of the St. Louis Cardinals wins the National League's rookie of the year award.	Nov. 24

F	G	H	I	J
Includes elections, federal-state relations, civil rights and liberties, crime, the judiciary, education, health care, poverty, urban affairs and population.	Includes formation and debate of U.S. foreign and defense policies, veterans' affairs and defense spending. (Relations with specific foreign countries are usually found under the region concerned.)	Includes business, labor, agriculture, taxation, transportation, consumer affairs, monetary and fiscal policy, natural resources, and pollution.	Includes worldwide scientific, medical and technological developments, natural phenomena, U.S. weather, natural disasters, and accidents.	Includes the arts, religion, scholarship, communications media, sports, entertainments, fashions, fads and social life.

	World Affairs	Europe	Africa & the Middle East	The Americas	Asia & the Pacific
Nov. 25	The UN General Assembly votes 116-4 with 34 abstentions, in favor of a resolution calling on Britain and Argentina to reopen talks on "all aspects" of the Falkland (Malvinas) Islands dispute, including sovereignty.			Following on the heels of a landslide victory in congressional and gubernatorial elections, Brazil's Pres. Jose Sarney adjusts his anti-inflation Cruzado Plan in an effort to cool down the overheated economy.	A treaty that will protect the South Pacific from nuclear and other pollution is approved in Noumea, New Caledonia, by delegates from 16 countries. These include about half of the tiny island nations scattered across the South Pacific, as well as New Zealand, Australia, the United States, and France.
Nov. 26		A West German court convicts two Palestinians of carrying out the bombing of an Arab social club in West Berlin March 29 and rules that evidence linking Syria to the attack is "credible." . . . The French cabinet agrees to do away with most of the nation's remaining price controls by the end of the year. The action will fulfill a pledge made earlier by the conservative coalition government of Premier Jacques Chirac.	The Israeli government for the first time confirms its involvement in the secret shipment of U.S. arms to Iran, but it denies any role in the siphoning off of profits for the Nicaraguan rebels.		
Nov. 27		Britons are stunned by the revelation that the physician of the terminally ill King George V injected the monarch, Queen Elizabeth II's grandfather, with separate doses of morphine and cocaine to hasten his death in 1936. The disclosure comes in an article in the journal *History*. . . . French Health Min. Michelle Barzach announces a stepped-up campaign against acquired immune deficiency syndrome (AIDS). The campaign, expected to cost 50 mil. francs in 1987, is part of a program that will designate 1987 as "AIDS Year." About 1,050 AIDS cases have been reported in France.	Mounting revelations of Syrian involvement in sponsoring international terrorism, as well as the disclosure of U.S. arms sales to Iran, have deeply embarrassed the Syrian government, the *New York Times* reports.	The government of Brazil's Pres. Jose Sarney is shaken by the first riots in the 26-year history of the capital, Brasilia. The riots are sparked by the government's decision to start lifting a nine-month-old price freeze as part of the anti-inflation Cruzado Plan.	The government of the Philippines signs a 60-day cease-fire with communist insurgents, to take effect December 10. Talks on substantive issues aimed at ending the 17-year-old war are set to begin 30 days after the truce takes effect.
Nov. 28		Soviet leader Mikhail S. Gorbachev calls today's U.S. violation of SALT II a "major mistake" and a demonstration of Washington's "contempt" for arms control.			Soviet leader Mikhail S. Gorbachev visits India. It is his first visit to India as the leader of the USSR and the first such by a Soviet leader since 1980. . . . The Australian dollar September 15 trades at $0.625, its highest level against the U.S. dollar in almost a month. Australia's dollar continues to gain during the following nine months, closing at $0.65 today.

A	B	C	D	E
Includes developments that affect more than one world region, international organizations and important meetings of major world leaders.	Includes all domestic and regional developments in Europe, including the Soviet Union, Turkey, Cyprus and Malta.	Includes all domestic and regional developments in Africa and the Middle East, including Iraq and Iran and excluding Cyprus, Turkey and Afghanistan.	Includes all domestic and regional developments in Latin America, the Caribbean and Canada.	Includes all domestic and regional developments in Asia and Pacific nations, extending from Afghanistan through all the Pacific Islands, except Hawaii.

U.S. Politics & Social Issues	U.S. Foreign Policy & Defense	U.S. Economy & Environment	Science, Technology & Nature	Culture, Leisure & Life Style	
Bronx County Democratic boss Stanley M. Friedman and three other defendants are convicted on federal racketeering, conspiracy, and mail fraud charges stemming from a New York City corruption scandal. The scandal began in the city's parking violations bureau and the Queens County Democratic organization, but has since spread to other city departments and other boroughs.	The State Dept. announces that Pres. Reagan has given the department full control of U.S. policy toward Iran, effective "immediately," thus ending the secret initiative run by the White House. . . . Following the disclosure that $10 mil. to $30 mil. in profits from the Israeli-brokered sale of American arms to Iran was secretly diverted to help the Contra rebels fighting the Nicaraguan government, Pres. Reagan says that he was not informed about this aspect of his Iranian policy. He also accepts the resignation of national security adviser Vice Adm. John M. Poindexter and fires a key aide, Lt. Col. Oliver L. North. . . . Officials note that the skimming off of Iranian arms profits for the Contras could partly explain how the rebels have been able to finance their resupply operation in the two years since U.S. aid was cut off. It is suggested that, at least since early 1986, the Iranian funds paid for a large part of the resupply effort, which involves hundreds of covert cargo drops over Nicaragua.	Organized labor and Ohbayashi Corp. of Japan reach an agreement opening the way for work rules and pay scales as established by collective bargaining in construction of Toyota Motor Corp.'s car assembly complex in Georgetown, Ky. . . . The government's consumer price index rose 0.2% in October, according to the Labor Dept.		The award for American League rookie of the year goes to Jose Canseco.	Nov. 25
Pres. Reagan appoints three members to a National Security Council review board to review that agency's involvement in the Iran affair. They are John G. Tower, a former Republican senator from Texas, Edmund S. Muskie, a former Democratic senator from Maine who served as Sec. of State in the Carter administration, and Brent Scowcroft, a former national security deputy and adviser in the Nixon and Ford administrations.		The International Typographical Union, the oldest union in the nation, founded in 1852, approves a merger with the Communications Workers of America. . . . The U.S. deficit on merchandise trade in October is $12.06 bil., the Commerce Dept. reports.	Large-scale oil spills into the oceans and seas dropped off sharply after 1983, according to a report available from the Center for Short Lived Phenomena, based in Cambridge, Mass. The decline is attributed in large part to stricter standards for oil transportation and to decreased demand for oil.		Nov. 26
Foreign Service applicants, officers, and their dependents will be tested for signs of acquired immune deficiency syndrome, the State Dept. discloses. Those who test positive will not be posted abroad. . . . Reagan administration officials say that Lt. Col. Oliver L. North, purportedly the "only person" with complete knowledge of the Iran-Contra fund transfer, destroyed documents from the National Security Council files over the weekend of November 22-23.					Nov. 27
	The U.S. breaches the 1979 Strategic Arms Limitation Treaty (SALT II) by deploying a B-52 bomber capable of carrying cruise missiles. The bomber becomes officially operational when it arrives at Carswell Air Force Base near San Antonio, Tex., to join the Strategic Air Command's 7th Bomber Wing.	A new study indicates an incidence of asbestos-related lung diseases among U.S. merchant seaman. About 35% of 2,500 former and current ship workers inspected test positive for asbestos exposure. . . . The prices farmers received for their raw agricultural goods rose 3.3% in November, the Agriculture Dept. reports.	Four out of five middle-aged men risk premature death from heart disease because of unhealthy levels of cholesterol in the blood, according to a landmark study reported in the *Journal of the American Medical Assoc.*		Nov. 28

F	G	H	I	J
Includes elections, federal-state relations, civil rights and liberties, crime, the judiciary, education, health care, poverty, urban affairs and population.	Includes formation and debate of U.S. foreign and defense policies, veterans' affairs and defense spending. (Relations with specific foreign countries are usually found under the region concerned.)	Includes business, labor, agriculture, taxation, transportation, consumer affairs, monetary and fiscal policy, natural resources, and pollution.	Includes worldwide scientific, medical and technological developments, natural phenomena, U.S. weather, natural disasters, and accidents.	Includes the arts, religion, scholarship, communications media, sports, entertainments, fashions, fads and social life.

	World Affairs	Europe	Africa & the Middle East	The Americas	Asia & the Pacific
Nov. 29		The Soviet Communist Party newspaper *Pravda* urges Albania to normalize relations with the Soviet Union. The paper asserts that Moscow's policies have changed significantly since 1961, when the two countries severed ties over ideological differences.			Tens of thousands of riot police are mobilized in Seoul, South Korea, to block an opposition rally banned by the government as a threat to public security. The opposition New Korea Democratic Party called for a new series of rallies against the government because months of talks on revising the constitution have failed to bring decisive results.
Nov. 30					Sikh militants in Punjab state, India, ignite renewed outrage when they shoot and kill 22 bus passengers. The massacre is said to be the bloodiest attack in the three-year wave of communal violence that has plagued the state.
Dec. 1					Pope John Paul II concludes a two-week trip that includes visits to Singapore, Fiji, New Zealand, Australia, and the Seychelles.
Dec. 2				At the closing session of the Cuban Communist Party's third congress, Pres. Fidel Castro warns delegates that economic hardships lie ahead for the population and calls on the party to promote labor discipline and eliminate corruption.... The Inter-American Development Bank approves a $319.3 mil. loan to Chile.... An Argentine court convicts and sentences retired Gen. Ramon Camps, former chief of the Buenos Aires provincial police to 25 years in prison for human rights abuses in the 1970s. Four others are also convicted and sentenced. ... Canada's economy in the third quarter grew at its slowest pace in nearly four years, according to Statistics Canada.	A proposed Compact of Free Assoc. with the United States fails in Palau voting for the fourth time in as many years.... Philippine authorities in Manila announce that they are holding two suspects in the November murder of leftist labor leader and politician Rolando Olalia.

A	B	C	D	E
Includes developments that affect more than one world region, international organizations and important meetings of major world leaders.	*Includes all domestic and regional developments in Europe, including the Soviet Union, Turkey, Cyprus and Malta.*	*Includes all domestic and regional developments in Africa and the Middle East, including Iraq and Iran and excluding Cyprus, Turkey and Afghanistan.*	*Includes all domestic and regional developments in Latin America, the Caribbean and Canada.*	*Includes all domestic and regional developments in Asia and Pacific nations, extending from Afghanistan through all the Pacific Islands, except Hawaii.*

U.S. Politics & Social Issues	U.S. Foreign Policy & Defense	U.S. Economy & Environment	Science, Technology & Nature	Culture, Leisure & Life Style	
Documents linked to weapons shipments in Central America are stolen from the Washington, D.C., office of the International Center for Development Policy, a group that has investigated U.S. activities in Latin America. The group is led by a former ambassador to El Salvador, Robert E. White.				In college football, defensive tackle Jason Buck of Brigham Young Univ. is named the winner of the Outland Trophy as the nation's outstanding lineman.... Cary Grant (born Archibald Alexander Leach), 82, actor, dies, in Davenport, Iowa, of a stroke during a rehearsal of his one-man traveling show, *A Conversation with Cary Grant.* The personification of elegance, wit, and ageless romantic charm, his most popular films include *Bringing Up Baby* (1938), *His Girl Friday* (1940), *The Philadelphia Story* (1940), *Notorious* (1946), and *North by Northwest* (1959).	Nov. 29
				The Hamilton Tiger-Cats win the Canadian Football League's Grey Cup.	Nov. 30
A federal jury in San Francisco convicts Larry John Layton of charges stemming from his part in the 1978 ambush death of Rep. Leo Ryan (D, Calif.) and defectors trying to flee the Guyana jungle compound of Rev. Jim Jones and the Peoples Temple cult. Layton's first trial ended in a hung jury in 1981.... The National Archives makes public the first 1.5 million of some 40 million pages of White House documents from the presidency of Richard Nixon that have been tied up in 12 years of court battles.... A panel of the National League of Cities passes two toughly worded resolutions complaining of the federal government's enactment of new standards for local governments to enforce and simultaneous cutting federal funds for urban programs. ... The Senate probe of the Iran-Contra fund transfer officially gets under way when Lt. Col. Oliver L. North and ex-national security adviser Robert C. McFarlane are questioned in closed-door hearings.		General Motors Corp. (GMC) ousts Texas billionaire H. Ross Perot from its board after Perot stepped up his criticism of GMC's Chairman Roger B. Smith. Perot has been the auto maker's largest individual shareholder since 1984, when GMC acquired the computer services company Perot founded, Electronic Data Systems Corp.	The United States urges an international conference to freeze and ultimately eliminate worldwide production of chlorofluorocarbons (CFCs) and other chemical compounds believed to deplete the ozone layer. The recommendations are submitted to a conference in Geneva sponsored by the UN Environmental Program.	The Musee d'Orsay, a dazzling new exhibition space for French Impressionist and Postimpressionist art, is opened by French Pres. Francois Mitterrand in Paris.... The Associated Press poll of sports writers ranks the Univ. of Miami number one in football.... The Soviet Union wins the 27th Chess Olympiad by the surprisingly thin margin of half a point over runner-up England.	Dec. 1
The U.S. attorney for the Southern District of New York, Rudolph W. Giuliani, is granted a 10-day court delay to "reassess"—in light of the recent disclosures about the Reagan administration's secret arms dealings with Iran—the case against 18 men charged with conspiring to smuggle $2 bil. in weapons to Iran.... Pres. Reagan asks for the appointment of an independent counsel to investigate charges of illegality in his administration's sale of arms to Iran and the diversion of profits to the Nicaraguan Contra rebels. He also names Frank Carlucci to be his new national security adviser; he succeeds Vice Adm. John M. Poindexter, who resigned over his role in the Iran-Contra scandal.		The Environmental Protection Agency proposes $41.2 mil. in penalties against four companies for alleged violation of federal limits on lead in gasoline.... Andrew Solomon and Robert Salsbury, two young Wall Street professionals, draw lenient sentences for their roles in an insider trading case. Both are sentenced to probation, and Solomon is also fined $10,000 and sentenced to 250 hours of community service.... Teamsters union president Jackie Presser's role as an informer for the Federal Bureau of Investigation is officially admitted by the Justice Dept.... The government's index of leading economic indicators rose 0.6% in October, the Commerce Dept. reports.		The United Press International poll of coaches ranks Univ. of Miami number one in football.... Desi Arnaz (born Desiderio Alberto Arnaz y de Acha III), 69, Cuban-born entertainer, dies of lung cancer in Del Mar, Calif. With his first wife, Lucille Ball, he designed, starred in, and produced the comedy series "I Love Lucy" for six seasons (1951-57). The two were divorced in 1960 and Arnaz later devoted himself to raising thoroughbreds.	Dec. 2

F	G	H	I	J
Includes elections, federal-state relations, civil rights and liberties, crime, the judiciary, education, health care, poverty, urban affairs and population.	*Includes formation and debate of U.S. foreign and defense policies, veterans' affairs and defense spending. (Relations with specific foreign countries are usually found under the region concerned.)*	*Includes business, labor, agriculture, taxation, transportation, consumer affairs, monetary and fiscal policy, natural resources, and pollution.*	*Includes worldwide scientific, medical and technological developments, natural phenomena, U.S. weather, natural disasters, and accidents.*	*Includes the arts, religion, scholarship, communications media, sports, entertainments, fashions, fads and social life.*

	World Affairs	Europe	Africa & the Middle East	The Americas	Asia & the Pacific
Dec. 3					The directors of the Herald & Weekly Times Ltd., Australia's largest media group, say they have accepted a $1.18 bil. "purchase" bid by Rupert Murdoch, "in the absence of a more attractive offer." Murdoch controls an international media empire, with interests in newspapers, television, and radio.
Dec. 4		West Germany's gross national product grew in the third quarter at an annual rate of just 1% from the second quarter, the federal statistics office reports. The unemployment rate in November rose to 8.3% from 8.1% in the previous month.... Hundreds of thousands of French students take to the streets to protest educational reforms proposed by the conservative government of Premier Jacques Chirac that would allow France's more than 70 state-run universities to have greater choice in selecting students, to differentiate diplomas by institution, and to raise tuition by as much as 100%.			In Grenada, after a seven-month trial, 14 people accused of the 1983 murder of P.M. Maurice Bishop and 10 other people are found guilty and sentenced to hang. Bishop's murder led to the U.S. invasion of the Caribbean nation the same year.
Dec. 5		At the end of a two-day meeting in Brussels, the defense ministers of the North Atlantic Treaty Org. countries endorse Washington's goals of reducing U.S. and Soviet strategic weapons by 50%, with separate accords on medium-range tactical nuclear missiles.... U.S. and Soviet arms negotiators conclude four days of meetings in Geneva for a special round of informal talks. The negotiating teams hold 17 sessions but fail to narrow their differences.		The longest and most costly strike in British Columbia history comes to an end when forest companies and lumber workers reach agreement on a new two-year contract. The strike, by 21,000 members of the B.C. branch of the International Woodworkers of America, began July 23.	After weeks of tough negotiations, Japan's ruling Liberal Democratic Party approves a plan for the most extensive reform of the tax system in more than 35 years.
Dec. 6		Leaders of the 12 European Community nations hold their semiannual summit in London.			In a surprisingly strong showing, Taiwan's recently formed Democratic Progressive Party wins 23 of the 44 so-called supplementary seats it contested in elections to Taiwan's legislature.
Dec. 7				Honduran aircraft strike against Nicaraguan troops on the border between the two countries after Nicaraguan Army troops penetrate Honduran territory in an operation against Contras based in that country. The Sandinista government charges that the aircraft also bombed two Nicaraguan villages.	
Dec. 8		Soviet dissident Anatoly T. Marchenko dies in prison, where he was about half-way through a 10-year prison sentence for antistate activities. Marchenko, 48, had spent a total of 20 years in labor camps, prisons, or internal exile.... A Soviet deputy foreign minister, Alexander A. Bessmertnykh, tells reporters in Moscow that the scandal surrounding the U.S. arms shipments to Iran has made Washington suspect in its arms-control negotiations with the Soviet Union.	The South African government admits for the first time that children between the ages of 11 and 15 are being detained under the emergency decree issued June 12. It put the number held at 256.	Unarmed U.S. military helicopters ferry Honduran troops to a staging point near a battle area on the Honduran-Nicaraguan border after yesterday's clash. The U.S. military plays no role in the fighting to push back Nicaraguan troops.	

A	B	C	D	E
Includes developments that affect more than one world region, international organizations and important meetings of major world leaders.	Includes all domestic and regional developments in Europe, including the Soviet Union, Turkey, Cyprus and Malta.	Includes all domestic and regional developments in Africa and the Middle East, including Iraq and Iran and excluding Cyprus, Turkey and Afghanistan.	Includes all domestic and regional developments in Latin America, the Caribbean and Canada.	Includes all domestic and regional developments in Asia and Pacific nations, extending from Afghanistan through all the Pacific Islands, except Hawaii.

U.S. Politics & Social Issues	U.S. Foreign Policy & Defense	U.S. Economy & Environment	Science, Technology & Nature	Culture, Leisure & Life Style	
Most U.S. students are "unable to write adequately except in response to the simplest of tasks," according to a report released by the National Assessment of Education Progress. The findings follow a study on the same subject released in April. . . . Vice Pres. George Bush, in his first detailed public comment on the Iran-Nicaragua affair, gives a carefully worded speech in which he voices support for Pres. Reagan while at the same time trying to distance himself from the scandal. His remarks, before the American Enterprise Institute, are televised nationally.	The Air Force announces that it is withholding more than $250 mil. in progress payments from companies that produce systems for the B-1B strategic bomber. The Air Force began deploying the bomber in October.				Dec. 3
				Broadway Bound, the third play in Neil Simon's autobiographical trilogy, (after *Brighton Beach Memoirs* and *Biloxi Blues*), opens in New York City. Directed by Gene Saks, the play stars Linda Lavin, who goes on to win the Tony for best actress in a play. . . . The American Academy of Arts and Letters announces the election of two new members, composer Milton Babbitt and painter Robert Motherwell. The academy is limited to 50 members drawn from the 250-member National Institute of Arts and Letters.	Dec. 4
The U.S. Appeals Court in Washington, D.C. gives the green light for the trial of a 14-year-old lawsuit against Nixon administration aides for warrantless wiretapping of Morton H. Halperin's home telephone. Halperin was a former National Security Council staff member, and the wiretapping was part of a program initiated by the Nixon administration in 1969 to discover the sources of leaks of government secrets to the press.	The Soviet Union announces that it will comply with the 1979 Strategic Arms Limitation Treaty (SALT II) "for the time being." The United States violated the treaty November 28 with the deployment of a B-52 bomber capable of carrying cruise missiles.	Federal agencies will be required to provide their workers with a "reasonably smoke-free environment" as of February 1987, the General Services Admin. announces. . . . Outstanding consumer credit grew a seasonally adjusted $6.78 bil., or at an annual rate of 13.9%, in October, the Federal Reserve Board reports. . . . The nation's unemployment rate held steady for the third consecutive month at a seasonally adjusted 6.9% in November, the Labor Dept. reports.			Dec. 5
In his weekly radio address Pres. Reagan concedes that the "execution" of his Iran policies was "flawed, and mistakes were made."		New contracts between the International Longshoreman's Assoc., the New York Shipping Assoc., and the Council of North Atlantic Shipping Assoc. are wrapped up for all East Coast ports, the *AFL-CIO News* reports.		Miami quarterback Vinny Testaverde is named the winner of the Heisman Trophy as the nation's best college football player.	Dec. 6
				The Society of West End Theater's Olivier awards are presented in London. Winners are, for best play, *Les Liaisons Dangereuses*; best musical, *Phantom of the Opera*; best comedy *When We Are Married*; best actress, Lindsay Duncan (*Les Liaisons Dangereuses*); best actor, Albert Finney, (*Orphans*).	Dec. 7
The government of Broward County, Fla., agrees to rehire and pay $196,000 in back pay and other expenses to Todd Shuttleworth, an employee it fired because he had acquired immune deficiency syndrome (AIDS). The county also agrees to consider AIDS-afflicted employees as being under the protection of the 1973 Rehabilitation Act. . . . House Democrats elect Jim Wright (D, Texas) to be the new House speaker in the 100th Congress, succeeding retired Speaker Thomas P. (Tip) O'Neill Jr. (D, Mass).	Testifying before the House Foreign Affairs Committee, Sec. of State George P. Shultz reveals that the White House, without informing him, opened secret communications with the U.S. ambassador to Lebanon to gain his cooperation in the Iranian arms shipments.	Raymark Industries Inc. announces tentative arrangements to establish a $42 mil. fund to settle as many as 15,000 asbestos injury cases pending against it.	The National Cancer Institute's annual review of cancer statistics finds a decline in cancer death rates for Americans under age 55 in 1984, the last year for which data are available. . . . Harrison (Scott) Brown, 69, American chemist who played a key role in producing plutonium for the first atomic bombs, dies of a lung ailment in Albuquerque, N.M. Brown later emerged as a major opponent of nuclear weapons development; he was a professor of geochemistry at the California Institute of Technology from 1951 to 1977.		Dec. 8

F	G	H	I	J
Includes elections, federal-state relations, civil rights and liberties, crime, the judiciary, education, health care, poverty, urban affairs and population.	Includes formation and debate of U.S. foreign and defense policies, veterans' affairs and defense spending. (Relations with specific foreign countries are usually found under the region concerned.)	Includes business, labor, agriculture, taxation, transportation, consumer affairs, monetary and fiscal policy, natural resources, and pollution.	Includes worldwide scientific, medical and technological developments, natural phenomena, U.S. weather, natural disasters, and accidents.	Includes the arts, religion, scholarship, communications media, sports, entertainments, fashions, fads and social life.

	World Affairs	Europe	Africa & the Middle East	The Americas	Asia & the Pacific
Dec. 9		A West German cabinet minister confirms that his country obtained the release of more than 2,500 East German political prisoners in 1985 through payments to the East German government.... France's Premier Jacques Chirac delays parliamentary action on his legislative program in the face of mass student protests. Chirac's action comes after protests directed against his conservative government's planned university reforms turn violent. One student died after an altercation with the police.		P.M. Brian Mulroney announces that Canada's hard-pressed grain farmers will be given a $720 mil. federal cash subsidy.	
Dec. 10				The presidents of Argentina and Brazil sign 20 economic agreements that they describe as the basis for a Latin American common market.	The official Phnom Penh radio announces a major shuffle of Cambodia's cabinet. Premier Hun Sen is stripped of his positions as foreign minister and chairman of the Communist Party's foreign affairs commission, and two ministers are dropped from the cabinet.
Dec. 11	The Soviet Union and Iran hold their first high-level economic talks since the 1979 Islamic revolution. The two nations sign an economic cooperation protocol, and it is agreed that Soviet technicians withdrawn in 1985 because of Iraqi air raids will return.	In Britain, after nearly 24 hours of continuous debate, the House of Commons passes without alteration the government's Teacher's Pay and Conditions Bill, which overhauls the system for negotiating teacher's pay.	The South African government imposes new rules that considerably tighten the state of emergency imposed in June to combat black unrest. The new measures include near-total censorship of news reports about the crisis over the apartheid system of racial segregation, and a ban on most remaining forms of political opposition in the country.... At least 10 towns in Zambia's central copper belt region are hit by three days of rioting after the government ends subsidies and more than doubles the price of cornmeal, the country's staple food.		

A	B	C	D	E
Includes developments that affect more than one world region, international organizations and important meetings of major world leaders.	Includes all domestic and regional developments in Europe, including the Soviet Union, Turkey, Cyprus and Malta.	Includes all domestic and regional developments in Africa and the Middle East, including Iraq and Iran and excluding Cyprus, Turkey and Afghanistan.	Includes all domestic and regional developments in Latin America, the Caribbean and Canada.	Includes all domestic and regional developments in Asia and Pacific nations, extending from Afghanistan through all the Pacific Islands, except Hawaii.

U.S. Politics & Social Issues	U.S. Foreign Policy & Defense	U.S. Economy & Environment	Science, Technology & Nature	Culture, Leisure & Life Style	
Personality and policy clashes beset a top federal laboratory assigned to investigate acquired immune deficiency syndrome, the National Academy of Sciences reports.... According to a report released by a panel of the National Academy of Sciences, adolescents should not be forced to seek parental consent for abortion and should have easy access to contraceptives.		Six workers at a Virginia nuclear power plant are burned, four fatally, when a pipe carrying "superheated" steam and water ruptures. ... The Supreme Court curbs the effort of companies to challenge mergers by competitors on antitrust grounds. In a 6-2 decision, the court rejects a challenge based merely on the ground that the complainant is "faced with a threat of losses from increased competition, or that the merger would harm small businesses in the industry."			Dec. 9
The Supreme Court rules that independent voters cannot constitutionally be barred from participating in a political party's primary election if the party allows such activity. ... In an effort avoid being set up as scapegoats by the Reagan administration, Israeli government officials leak details about the origins and development of the U.S. arms sales to Iran and their relationship to the American hostages in Lebanon.... U.S. investigators and media begin focusing on the role of Swiss bank accounts in funneling Iranian arms payments to the Contras. A key role is attributed to the Geneva-based Compagnie de Services Fiduciaries S.A., a company with ties to retired U.S. Air Force Maj. Gen. Richard V. Secord, who is thought to have been brought into the arms deal by fired Security Council official, Lt. Col. Oliver North.				Los Angeles's Museum of Contemporary Art (MOCA), designed by Japanese architect Arata Isosaki, opens with "Individuals: A Select History of Contemporary Art, 1945-1986," an exhibition tracing pivotal developments in the postwar era.... The librarian of Congress Daniel J. Boorstin announces that he will leave the post in June 1987 to devote more time to writing. Boorstin is the author of *The Discoverers* (1983), a panoramic history of the sciences.	Dec. 10
Central Intelligence Agency (CIA) Dir. William J. Casey testifies before the House Foreign Affairs Committee in a two-day closed session. Casey reportedly said that "serious errors of judgment" were committed by senior CIA officials who allowed Lt. Col. Oliver North to use the agency's resources for arms shipments to Iran.		The nation's state insurance regulators approve model guidelines that will bar insurance applicants from being asked whether they are homosexual. Insurers want to guard against applicants with acquired immune deficiency syndrome, and it is feared they might discriminate against homosexuals to do so.... A tentative settlement is reached in San Francisco to end a seven-week strike by the Service Employees International Union against the Kaiser Permanente Medical Care Program, the largest private health care system in the country.... The Securities and Exchange Comm. discloses that it has allowed Ivan F. Boesky to reduce his partnership's debt by about $1.32 bil. before announcing the record penalty he agreed to pay for insider trading. ... The Nuclear Regulatory Comm. says that officials of its own southwestern regional office have intimidated other agency inspectors into modifying inspection reports on the Comanche Peak nuclear power plant in Texas.			Dec. 11

F	G	H	I	J
Includes elections, federal-state relations, civil rights and liberties, crime, the judiciary, education, health care, poverty, urban affairs and population.	*Includes formation and debate of U.S. foreign and defense policies, veterans' affairs and defense spending. (Relations with specific foreign countries are usually found under the region concerned.)*	*Includes business, labor, agriculture, taxation, transportation, consumer affairs, monetary and fiscal policy, natural resources, and pollution.*	*Includes worldwide scientific, medical and technological developments, natural phenomena, U.S. weather, natural disasters, and accidents.*	*Includes the arts, religion, scholarship, communications media, sports, entertainments, fashions, fads and social life.*

	World Affairs	Europe	Africa & the Middle East	The Americas	Asia & the Pacific
Dec. 12		North Atlantic Treaty Org. foreign ministers meeting in Brussels endorse a proposal to seek a new forum on the reduction of conventional forces in Europe, from the Atlantic Ocean to the Ural Mountains.		Canada's deputy prime minister, Donald Mazankowski, informs the House of Commons that Ottawa has begun an investigation into the alleged involvement of Canadians in the Iran arms scandal. The probe is being conducted by the Royal Canadian Mounted Police.	The International Monetary Fund approves a $717 mil. loan to China to help correct its balance-of-payments problems.
Dec. 13			Iraqi aircraft bomb Teheran, the Iranian capital, hitting an antiaircraft site and a power station.	As rebels in Suriname seeking to overthrow the government of Lt. Col. Desi Bouterse advance on Paramaribo, Bouterse seeks popular support by reiterating his promise to hold nationwide elections by March 1988.	
Dec. 14				A bitter strike at Gainers Inc. meatpacking plant in Edmonton, Canada, comes to an end when strikers vote to accept a new four-year contract. Over 1,000 workers walked out June 1, in a wage dispute.	
Dec. 15		The Swiss bank Cridit-Suisse freezes at least two accounts believed to have been used by ex-Security Council aide Lt. Col. Oliver North, retired Maj. Gen. Richard Secord, and businessman Albert Hakim in the funneling of Iran arms sales profits to the Nicaraguan Contra rebels.		In Trinidad, the People's National Movement of P.M. George Chambers is swept out of office in general elections ending the party's 30-year political dominance. Final results show the opposition four-party coalition, the National Alliance for Reconstruction, won 33 of 36 seats contested in the House of Representatives.	Tensions among ethnic groups in Karachi, Pakistan, explode in two days of rioting that claim at least 150 lives and leave hundreds of buildings in ruins.

A	B	C	D	E
Includes developments that affect more than one world region, international organizations and important meetings of major world leaders.	Includes all domestic and regional developments in Europe, including the Soviet Union, Turkey, Cyprus and Malta.	Includes all domestic and regional developments in Africa and the Middle East, including Iraq and Iran and excluding Cyprus, Turkey and Afghanistan.	Includes all domestic and regional developments in Latin America, the Caribbean and Canada.	Includes all domestic and regional developments in Asia and Pacific nations, extending from Afghanistan through all the Pacific Islands, except Hawaii.

U.S. Politics & Social Issues	U.S. Foreign Policy & Defense	U.S. Economy & Environment	Science, Technology & Nature	Culture, Leisure & Life Style	
Harry Winston, 75, chairman since 1966 of the Communist Party, U.S.A., dies in Moscow, where he had gone from his home in New York City for treatment of a brain tumor. The son of Mississippi sharecroppers, he joined the party in 1933 and was convicted in 1949 under the Smith Act of conspiring to teach and advocate the forcible overthrow of the U.S. government. He did not surrender until 1956, whereupon he was jailed; he went blind before winning his release in 1961. . . . A Reagan administration report urges that the states be given leeway to mount a range of experiments in reforming the welfare system. . . . Facing the worst crisis of his presidency in the Iran arms scandal, Pres. Reagan finds himself under growing pressure to replace top administration officials or take more decisive action on the crisis.		The government's producer price index rose a seasonally adjusted 0.2% in November, the Labor Dept. reports. . . . The Energy Dept. announces that the "N" reactor at the Hanford nuclear complex near Richland, Wash., a key source of weapons-grade plutonium, will be shut down for six months for safety improvements. The controversial reactor's design is similar to that of the Soviet Union's Chernobyl reactors and there have been persistent reports of serious safety violations.	The *Journal of the American Medical Assoc.* harshly criticizes treatment of cancer with the experimental drug interleukin-2, which was widely characterized as a breakthrough only a year before.	*Crimes of the Heart*, a film based on Beth Henley's 1981 Pulitzer Prize-winning comedy, opens in New York. Directed by Bruce Beresford, it stars Diane Keaton, Jessica Lange, Sissy Spacek, and Sam Shepard. . . . James (Bonecrusher) Smith wins the World Boxing Assoc. heavyweight title when he knocks out Tim Witherspoon in the first round.	Dec. 12
Ella Baker, 83, civil rights activist whose talents as an organizer led to her becoming director of the New York City branch of the National Assoc. for the Advancement of Colored People during World War II, dies in New York City. She set up the national office of the Southern Christian Leadership Conf. in 1957 and served as its executive director, and she also organized the conference that created the Student Nonviolent Coordinating Committee. . . . Burglars steal files from the Cupertino, Calif., lawyer of Albert Hakim, a businessman who has been linked to the diversion of profits from U.S. arms sales to Iran to the Contras fighting the Nicaraguan government.	The United States conducts its 13th announced underground nuclear test of the year in Nevada. The test is the first since a Soviet warning that Moscow's unilateral moratorium will not be extended.				Dec. 13
			The experimental aircraft *Voyager* takes off from Edwards Air Force Base, near Los Angeles, in an attempt to be the first plane to fly around the world without stopping or refueling.		Dec. 14
The Supreme Court strikes down as unconstitutional a federal regulation prohibiting direct political expenditures by nonprofit, issue-oriented corporations. . . . A special commission recommends that top federal officials be given substantial pay increases of 60% to 80%, to offset inflation since 1969, beginning in 1987. . . . The office of Vice Pres. George Bush issues a chronology of contacts that suggests that the Reagan administration knew more about the Contra supply operation than it previously admitted. . . . The *New York Times* reports that Oliver L. North helped a political action committee headed by Carl Channell campaign against congressional opponents of military aid to the Contras. . . . Central Intelligence Agency director William J. Casey suffers a "minor cerebral seizure" one day before he is to testify before the House Foreign Affairs Committee.	Fifty-seven senators urge Pres. Reagan to return to compliance with the 1979 Strategic Arms Limitation Treaty (SALT II). The United States violated the pact in November. . . . The *Washington Post* reports that the Central Intelligence Agency has been sharing secret military intelligence with Iraq for nearly two years. The information includes sensitive U.S. satellite photography that aids Iraq in its air raids on Iranian oil terminals and industrial targets.	Wedtech Corp. files for protection under Chapter 11 of the federal bankruptcy code in New York City. In its petition, the New York-based military contractor says possible financing has dried up as the result of a "continuing barrage" of publicity over such matters as its ties to federal officials. . . . The industrial production index rose a healthy 0.6% in November, the Federal Reserve Board says. . . . Trans World Airways announces that it has reached agreement with its pilots union to extend their contract until February 1992.		New York City's landmark Carnegie Hall reopens after a seven-month shutdown for a $50 mil. remodeling. . . . Serge Lifar, 81, Russian born dancer, choreographer, director, and dance historian, dies in Lausanne, Switzerland. The last world-famous dancer to emerge under the tutelage of Serge Diaghilev, Lifar created a number of roles in early ballets of George Balanchine, most notably *Prodigal Son* and *Apollo*; he was a prolific author of books on dance theory and dance history.	Dec. 15

F	G	H	I	J
Includes elections, federal-state relations, civil rights and liberties, crime, the judiciary, education, health care, poverty, urban affairs and population.	*Includes formation and debate of U.S. foreign and defense policies, veterans' affairs and defense spending. (Relations with specific foreign countries are usually found under the region concerned.)*	*Includes business, labor, agriculture, taxation, transportation, consumer affairs, monetary and fiscal policy, natural resources, and pollution.*	*Includes worldwide scientific, medical and technological developments, natural phenomena, U.S. weather, natural disasters, and accidents.*	*Includes the arts, religion, scholarship, communications media, sports, entertainments, fashions, fads and social life.*

	World Affairs	Europe	Africa & the Middle East	The Americas	Asia & the Pacific
Dec. 16		European Community agriculture ministers reach agreement aimed at reducing the community's huge surplus of dairy and beef products.		The International Monetary Fund announces approval of $128 mil. in loans to Bolivia to support its three-year economic adjustment program begun in 1985.... Sec. of State George Shultz expresses "grave concern" over reports of "gross violations" of human rights by Surinamese soldiers fighting insurgents. According to State Dept. officials, between 50 and 180 people were killed between November 28 and December 4.	
Dec. 17		The number of unemployed workers in Spain reaches a record 2,867,033 in November, it is reported.... Anti-Russian riots break out in the central Asian city of Alma Ata, one day after the removal of the head of the Communist Party of the republic of Kazakhstan. Alma Ata [Almaty] is the capital of the Soviet Republic of Kazakhstan.		In anticipation of continued low income from oil exports, Venezuela says it has asked its creditors to revise a $21.2 bil. debt rescheduling pact signed in February. Venezuela wants to extend the repayment schedule to the year 2000 and reduce the interest rate. ... Nicaragua's National Assembly grants a request from Pres. Daniel Ortega Saavedra to pardon Eugene Hasenfus, a U.S. cargo handler recently sentenced to a 30-year prison term for supplying the Contras with weapons. Hasenfus leaves for Guatemala on the first leg of his journey home.	Eight of 11 men convicted in New York in September of federal crimes involving the Bamboo Gang are sentenced to prison terms ranging from 10 to 25 years.
Dec. 18		Journalists vote to suspend an eight-day strike against Agence France-Presse, after chairman Henri Pegeat Pigeat resigns; Pigeat's restructuring plan included cutting 300 jobs.... French railway workers strike the national rail company, SNCF, to protest government plans to introduce a merit-based promotion system.... Unemployment in Britain fell to 11.7% in November, according to government figures.... The Soviet Union announces that its unilateral moratorium on nuclear testing will end when the United States conducts its first nuclear test in 1987. ... Soviet dissident poet Irina Ratushinskaya, released from prison in October, arrives in London for treatment of a heart problem.	U.S. wildlife researcher Wayne Richard MacGuire is convicted in absentia by a Rwandan court for the 1985 murder in Rwanda of gorilla expert Dian Fossey. In Los Angeles, MacGuire denies any involvement in Fossey's death and calls the murder charge "outrageous." The United States has no extradition treaty with Rwanda.		Vietnam holds its Sixth Communist Party Congress, at which new leaders are elected in the most dramatic political change in the party's 56-year history.
Dec. 19	In an effort to ease the UN's financial crisis, the General Assembly unanimously adopts sweeping resolutions to reform the organization's budget process.	The Soviet ambassador to the United States, Yuri V. Dubinin, tells reporters in Washington, D.C., that U.S. scientists will be allowed to monitor underground nuclear explosions when the USSR resumes testing.... The Soviet Union announces that the dissident couple Andrei D. Sakharov and Dr. Yelena Bonner have been released from internal exile in the city of Gorky. The announcement also says that Sakharov, a renowned physicist, will be permitted to resume his work at the Soviet Academy of Sciences.			
Dec. 20	Concluding ten days of meetings in Geneva, ministers of the Org. of Petroleum Exporting Countries agree to cut their combined oil production by about 1 million barrels per day, from the current level of about 16.6 million barrels per day. The output cuts will take effect Jan. 1, 1987.	In a victory for French Premier Jacques Chirac, the National Assembly passes controversial legislation intended to ease restrictions on working hours. Passage comes after Pres. Francois Mitterrand had earlier blocked a decree that would have effected the change.			In Shanghai as many as 35,000 students march through the streets in the largest rally since 1976.

A	B	C	D	E
Includes developments that affect more than one world region, international organizations and important meetings of major world leaders.	*Includes all domestic and regional developments in Europe, including the Soviet Union, Turkey, Cyprus and Malta.*	*Includes all domestic and regional developments in Africa and the Middle East, including Iraq and Iran and excluding Cyprus, Turkey and Afghanistan.*	*Includes all domestic and regional developments in Latin America, the Caribbean and Canada.*	*Includes all domestic and regional developments in Asia and Pacific nations, extending from Afghanistan through all the Pacific Islands, except Hawaii.*

U.S. Politics & Social Issues	U.S. Foreign Policy & Defense	U.S. Economy & Environment	Science, Technology & Nature	Culture, Leisure & Life Style	
Senate leaders name Sen. Daniel K. Inouye (D, Hawaii) to head the select committee that will investigate the Iran arms deal. . . . The Justice Dept.'s internal inspector opens an investigation into why the department in October asked the Federal Bureau of Investigation to briefly delay its probe of private arms shipments to the Nicaraguan Contras, the *Washington Post* reports. . . . Pres. Reagan proposes that the Senate Intelligence Committee give limited immunity to former National Security Council officials Oliver L. North and John M. Poindexter, to compel them to testify about the Iran arms affair.	Former National Security Agency employee Ronald Pelton is sentenced to three life prison terms plus ten years for having sold military secrets to the Soviet Union.	The U.S. balance of payments on current account showed a record deficit of $36.28 bil. in the third quarter, the Commerce Dept. reports. The gap surpasses the previous record of payments deficit of $34.41 bil. according to revised figures in the second quarter. . . . Housing starts dropped 1.8% in November, to a seasonally adjusted annual rate of 1.598 million units, the Commerce Dept. reports.	U.S. Surgeon Gen. C. Everett Koop issues a report urging the formulation of tough rules against so-called passive smoking.		Dec. 16
House leaders name Rep. Lee Hamilton (D, Ind.), outgoing head of the Intelligence Committee, as head of a committee to investigate the Iran arms deal. . . . The White House announces that Pres. Reagan will enter the Bethesda Naval Hospital for surgery on an enlarged prostate gland that is causing "mild recurring discomfort." . . . A federal jury in Detroit acquits John Z. De Lorean of embezzling $8.5 mil. from the now defunct De Lorean Motor Co. The former auto maker was found innocent of cocaine dealing in 1984.		The nation's gross national product increased at an inflation-adjusted 2.8% in the third quarter, rather than 2.9%, the Commerce Dept. reports.	Surgeons at Papworth Hospital in Cambridge, England, perform what is believed to be the world's first triple-organ transplant, replacing the heart, lungs, and liver of a 35-year-old Yorkshire woman, Davina Thompson.	*Billboard*'s best-selling albums for the week are: *Bruce Springsteen & the E Street Band*, Bruce Springsteen; *Slippery When Wet*, Bon Jovi; *Third Stage*, Boston; *The Way It Is*, Bruce Hornsby & the Range; and *Fore!*, Huey Lewis & the News.	Dec. 17
The execution of Richard Andrade in Florida brings to 17 the total number of prisoners executed in the United States during 1986. A total of 67 executions have been carried out since a Supreme Court decision reinstated the death penalty in 1976. . . . Central Intelligence Agency Dir. William J. Casey, undergoes surgery at Georgetown Univ. Hospital in Washington, D.C., where doctors remove a tumor from the left side of his brain. Casey was scheduled to testify December 16 before the intelligence panel and the House Foreign Affairs Committee.		U.S. Bankruptcy Judge Burton K. Lifland approves as "fair and equitable" a reorganization plan filed by Manville Corp. under the federal bankruptcy code. Manville applied for bankruptcy protection in 1982 when faced with more than 15,000 lawsuits charging health and property damage from the company's asbestos products. . . . Consumer spending rose 1.1% in November, while personal income rose 0.3%, the Commerce Dept. reports. . . . USX Corp. and the United Steelworkers of America agree to have a mediator assist in seeking a settlement of their five-month-old dispute.	French researchers announce successful tests of an experimental birth-control drug, RU 486, that can cause relatively simple and safe abortions in at least 85% of women who take it within 10 days of missing a menstrual period.	One of the most important private collections of English literature is presented to the New York Public Library. The Pforzheimer Foundation's gift of the Pforzheimer Collection, known to scholars as "Shelley and his Circle," contains about 8,000 manuscripts and 13,000 printed volumes that document the creative and personal lives of Percy Bysshe Shelley and other English Romantic poets.	Dec. 18
Attorney Gen. Edwin Meese reportedly tells the White House Intelligence Committee that he discovered the diversion of funds to the Contras when Justice Dept. officials found an undated memo in Lt. Col. Oliver L. North's files proposing the idea. . . . A special panel of three federal judges selects Lawrence E. Walsh as the independent counsel in the Iran arms scandal. The panel gives Walsh a broader mandate than Attorney Gen. Edwin Meese had requested.		The volume of shares traded on New York Stock Exchange, 244.68 million, is the highest ever. . . . The government's consumer price index rose 0.3% in November, the Labor Dept. reports.		*Platoon* a film about the Vietnam War as experienced by a single infantry platoon in 1967, opens in New York. The film, which goes on to win two Academy Awards, including best film, is directed and written by Oliver Stone (best director) and stars Charlie Sheen, Tom Berenger, and Willem Dafoe.	Dec. 19
Michael Griffith, a 23-year-old black man, is hit by a car and killed while fleeing a mob of white New York City teenagers. Described as a "racial lynching" by Mayor Edward I. Koch, the incident shocks the city and draws national notice.					Dec. 20

F	G	H	I	J
Includes elections, federal-state relations, civil rights and liberties, crime, the judiciary, education, health care, poverty, urban affairs and population.	*Includes formation and debate of U.S. foreign and defense policies, veterans' affairs and defense spending. (Relations with specific foreign countries are usually found under the region concerned.)*	*Includes business, labor, agriculture, taxation, transportation, consumer affairs, monetary and fiscal policy, natural resources, and pollution.*	*Includes worldwide scientific, medical and technological developments, natural phenomena, U.S. weather, natural disasters, and accidents.*	*Includes the arts, religion, scholarship, communications media, sports, entertainments, fashions, fads and social life.*

	World Affairs	Europe	Africa & the Middle East	The Americas	Asia & the Pacific
Dec. 21		The Italian senate gives final approval to a 1987 budget that will reduce the nation's deficit to 100,000 bil. lire from 110,000 bil. in 1986. The 1986 deficit represents about 15% of Italy's gross national product.			India and Pakistan announce an agreement to have their border security officials work together more closely. India has long accused Pakistan of harboring and aiding Sikh terrorists, a charge Pakistan denies.
Dec. 22				Uruguay's Pres. Julio Maria Sanguinetti signs into law a controversial amnesty for soldiers accused of human rights abuses under military rule from 1973 to 1985.... In Canada, the Quebec Court of Appeal upholds a 1985 ruling that struck down a provincial ban on the use of languages other than French on public signs.	Shanghai police ban unauthorized demonstrations in the city after several days of protests by students demanding greater democracy.
Dec. 23				Adolfo Calero, leader of the Nicaraguan Democratic Force, reports that the first group of Nicaraguan Contras to receive training in the United States under Pres. Reagan's $100 mil. aid program have graduated.... Argentina's Congress adopts legislation that will put an end to the prosecutions of military personnel for human rights abuses in the 1970s "Dirty War" against leftists.	The Philippines government and communist rebels begin talks aimed at ending the 17-year-old communist insurgency.... Students in Beijing, China, for the first time join in protests for greater democracy.... Indexation of wages to inflation is officially declared at an end in Australia by the Conciliation and Arbitration Comm.
Dec. 24			Aurel Cornea, a French sound technician abducted in Beirut nine months ago, is released in that city by the Revolutionary Justice Org.	Brazil's total foreign debt rises to $108.8 bil., the central bank announces. Brazil is the Third World's most indebted nation.	
Dec. 25		The Soviet Union discloses a full-scale investigation of the December 17-18 nationalist riots in Alma Ata [Almaty], the capital of the Soviet Republic of Kazakhstan.	Iran says its forces have launched a new offensive at the southern end of the Iran-Iraq battle front.... An Iraqi Airways passenger jet en route from Baghdad to Amman, Jordan, crashes during an emergency landing near Arar in northwest Saudi Arabia, apparently after being hijacked. Sixty-seven of the 107 people aboard the plane die.		
Dec. 26				Argentina's Pres. Raul Alfonsin signs into law a measure setting a deadline for prosecution of military personnel for human rights abuses committed in the 1970s.	

A	B	C	D	E
Includes developments that affect more than one world region, international organizations and important meetings of major world leaders.	Includes all domestic and regional developments in Europe, including the Soviet Union, Turkey, Cyprus and Malta.	Includes all domestic and regional developments in Africa and the Middle East, including Iraq and Iran and excluding Cyprus, Turkey and Afghanistan.	Includes all domestic and regional developments in Latin America, the Caribbean and Canada.	Includes all domestic and regional developments in Asia and Pacific nations, extending from Afghanistan through all the Pacific Islands, except Hawaii.

U.S. Politics & Social Issues	U.S. Foreign Policy & Defense	U.S. Economy & Environment	Science, Technology & Nature	Culture, Leisure & Life Style	
	The *Miami Herald* reports that Lt. Col. Oliver L. North routinely passed classified information on Nicaragua to the State Dept.'s office of public diplomacy, which then leaked it to the television networks.				Dec. 21
A Senate Democratic unit is being established within the Senate Judiciary Committee to screen Pres. Reagan's judicial nominations more closely.					Dec. 22
Justice Dept. spokesman Terry Eastland says that the Federal Bureau of Investigation is halting for at least 26 days a probe of arms-smuggling to the Contra rebels in Nicaragua.		Greyhound Corp. agrees to sell its U.S. bus operation for more than $350 mil. to an investor group led by Fred G. Currey, a former chief executive officer of Trailways Inc. . . . The Transportation Dept. asks Volkswagen of America Inc. to recall as many as 30,000 Audi 5000S cars built since 1978. The agency says that a possible defect caused "unwanted, high-power sudden acceleration incidents."	Piloted by Dick Rutan and Jeanna Yeager, the *Voyager* touches down at Edwards Air Force Base to become the first round-the-world flight made without stopping or refueling. The 1,000-lb. experimental aircraft travelled the 25,012 miles in 9 days, 3 minutes and 44 seconds.		Dec. 23
The American Medical Assoc. (AMA) files suit against a new law penalizing Medicare recipients who pay more for health care than the government recommends. The AMA files its suit, naming Sec. of Health and Human Services Otis R. Bowen, in U.S. District Court in Lubbock, Tex.... The *New York Times* reports that, in a memo written at the beginning of the U.S. arms sales to Iran, Central Intelligence Agency Dir. William Casey described the program explicitly as a trade of weapons for hostages. The disclosure contradicts Reagan's assertion that he approved the arms sales only as part of a broader initiative to improve relations with Iran.	The Reagan administration decides to offer Egypt, Israel, and 36 other countries a debt-relief plan that will give them the opportunity to defer part of their interest payments on military loans.... According to a Reagan administration official, some $10 mil. in contributions for the Contra rebels opposed to the government of Nicaragua has been traced to the sultan of Brunei, Sir Mudah Hassanal Bolkiah.			*Variety*'s top-grossing films for the week are: *The Golden Child*, *Star Trek IV: The Voyage Home*, *Little Shop of Horrors*, *Three Amigos*, and *Heartbreak Ridge*.	Dec. 24
	The *New York Times* reports that the U.S. ambassador to Costa Rica, Lewis Tambs, helped secure permission from Costa Rica to build a secret airstrip for the Contra supply operation and oversaw its use early in the year. The airstrip has since been sealed off.				Dec. 25
Chicago Democrats loyal to Mayor Harold Washington (D) oust Alderman Edward Vrdolyak from his post as city Democratic chairman after he files for the 1987 mayoral election as a third-party candidate.... The White House announces that it is creating a special group to coordinate the Reagan administration's responses and strategies in the Iran-Contra arms scandal.				Elsa Lanchester (born Elizabeth Sullivan), 84, British-born actress who after a successful stage career in London became one of Hollywood's outstanding character actresses, dies of pneumonia in Woodland Hills, Calif. She scored a triumph in *The Bride of Frankenstein* (1935) playing both the bride and Frankenstein's creator, Mary Shelley. She married actor Charles Laughton in 1929, with whom she appeared in a number of films, including *Witness for the Prosecution*.... *Publishers Weekly*'s hardback fiction best-sellers for the week are: *It*, Stephen King; *Red Storm Rising*, Tom Clancy; *Whirlwind*, James Clavell; *Hollywood Husband*, Jackie Collins; and *Flight of the Intruder*, Stephen Coonts.	Dec. 26

F	G	H	I	J
Includes elections, federal-state relations, civil rights and liberties, crime, the judiciary, education, health care, poverty, urban affairs and population.	*Includes formation and debate of U.S. foreign and defense policies, veterans' affairs and defense spending. (Relations with specific foreign countries are usually found under the region concerned.)*	*Includes business, labor, agriculture, taxation, transportation, consumer affairs, monetary and fiscal policy, natural resources, and pollution.*	*Includes worldwide scientific, medical and technological developments, natural phenomena, U.S. weather, natural disasters, and accidents.*	*Includes the arts, religion, scholarship, communications media, sports, entertainments, fashions, fads and social life.*

	World Affairs	Europe	Africa & the Middle East	The Americas	Asia & the Pacific
Dec. 27			In an unusual setback for South African security forces, a captured African National Congress guerrilla being transported in the northern Transvaal breaks free, seizes a weapon, and kills two white police officers before escaping.		Sri Lankan government negotiators meet with representatives of the separatist Tamil rebel movement for the first time since August 1985.
Dec. 28			The *London Observer* reports that South Africa plans to build a runway on Marion Island in the South Atlantic Ocean; it is widely suspected that South Africa intends to use the remote site as a secret base for testing nuclear missiles.		
Dec. 29	The United Kingdom and Guatemala reestablish diplomatic relations after having restored consular relations in August. Guatemala had broken off full ties in 1963 when Britain granted self-government to Belize, then known as British Honduras, which Guatemala claimed as its own territory.... The United States and Iran resume negotiations in The Hague over the release of about $500 mil. in Iranian funds that have been frozen in U.S. banks since 1981.	Maurice Harold MacMillan, Earl of Stockton, 92, a member of the House of Commons for 40 years and Britain's prime minister from 1957 to 1963, dies of pneumonia at Birch Grove, his family home in Sussex, England. A scion of the MacMillan publishing family, following his resignation from politics he wrote six volumes of memoirs and devoted increased attention to his duties as chancellor of the Univ. of Oxford, a post to which he was elected in 1960.... Fifty Soviet emigres, some of them Jews, arrive in Moscow from the United States. Their return is highly publicized by the Soviet media.			The Supreme People's Assembly reelects Kim Il Sung as president of North Korea.... The Philippines government files a $750 mil. suit in Manila against former Pres. Ferdinand E. Marcos, seeking the recovery of four buildings in New York City allegedly owned by Marcos and his wife, Imelda.
Dec. 30		The Soviet Union rejects a U.S. proposal that Pres. Reagan and Soviet leader Mikhail Gorbachev exchange televised New Year's messages in 1987 as they did in 1986.	Exxon Corp. announces that it is selling its South African affiliates to an independent trust that will channel future profits to employees and continue to finance social programs for blacks.	Canadian and U.S. trade representatives settle a dispute over the export of Canadian softwood lumber. The settlement, reached after two months of negotiations, heads off a U.S. contervailing duty on the product.	Japan's cabinet adopts a $340 bil. draft budget for the fiscal year beginning April 1, 1987. The budget, approved earlier by the ruling Liberal Democratic Party, abandons a 10-year policy of limiting military spending to 1% of the gross national product.
Dec. 31			Chadian officials have reported that Libyan air and ground forces are using carpet bombing and shelling, napalm and toxic gas to carry out "genocidal" attacks in the north. The Chadian rebels are said to have used Libyan-supplied SA-7 missiles to shoot down three Libyan warplanes.	Nicaragua's Pres. Daniel Ortega Saavedra reports that 1,019 government soldiers died in the war with the Contras in 1986 and that the Contras suffered some 4,000 fatalities.... Chile's Pres. Augusto Pinochet Ugarte announces that a state of siege imposed in September after an attempt on his life will not be renewed when it expires in January 1987. He also announces most Chilean exiles will be allowed to return and that a law legalizing non-marxist political parties will be in force early in 1987.	

A	B	C	D	E
Includes developments that affect more than one world region, international organizations and important meetings of major world leaders.	*Includes all domestic and regional developments in Europe, including the Soviet Union, Turkey, Cyprus and Malta.*	*Includes all domestic and regional developments in Africa and the Middle East, including Iraq and Iran and excluding Cyprus, Turkey and Afghanistan.*	*Includes all domestic and regional developments in Latin America, the Caribbean and Canada.*	*Includes all domestic and regional developments in Asia and Pacific nations, extending from Afghanistan through all the Pacific Islands, except Hawaii.*

U.S. Politics & Social Issues	U.S. Foreign Policy & Defense	U.S. Economy & Environment	Science, Technology & Nature	Culture, Leisure & Life Style	
				George Dangerfield, 82, British-born historian who spent much of his life in the United States, dies of leukemia in Santa Barbara, Calif. *The Strange Death of Liberal England*, widely regarded as his masterpiece, was first published in the United States in 1935. After World War II, he wrote extensively on American history, and his *Era of Good Feelings* won both the Pulitzer Prize and the Bancroft Prize in 1953. . . . Philippines' Pres. Corazon Aquino is named *Time* magazine's Woman of the Year.	Dec. 27
Federal loans to college students tripled over the past 10 years, according to a study by the Joint Economic Committee of Congress.				John D. MacDonald, 70, American author who in a 40-year writing career wrote dozens of books, most of them mysteries, dies after complications from coronary bypass surgery in Milwaukee. . . . In tennis, Australia wins the 28th Davis Cup.	Dec. 28
	The Defense Dept. asks Congress for $2.8 bil. above the funds already provided for the military in the fiscal 1987 budget. Some $500 mil. of the supplemental request is slated for research on the Strategic Defense Initiative ("Star Wars").	The Consumer Federation of America reports that the average consumer's telephone bill has risen by 20% since American Telephone and Telegraph Co. divested its Bell regional units in 1984.	The Justice Dept. announces a settlement with the families of four of the seven astronauts killed in the explosion of the space shuttle *Challenger* January 28. The agreement is made with the families of Francis R. Scobee, Ellison S. Onizuka, Gregory B. Jarvis, and civilian teacher Christa McAuliffe.		Dec. 29
		The Federal Communications Comm. orders American Telephone and Telegraph Co. to reduce its interstate long-distance rates by about half again as much as the company proposed the month before. . . . The National Highway Safety Admin. reopens its probe of sudden acceleration in about 2.3 million J-cars manufactured by General Motors Corp. between 1982 and 1985. The agency's decision to drop the probe in August was widely criticized by consumer groups. . . . The Reagan administration announces that it will impose 200% duties on imports of certain cheese, white wine, liquors, and other agricultural products from the European Community in retaliation for Spain's increased tariffs on corn and sorghum. . . . The government's index of leading economic indicators rose 1.2% in November, the Commerce Dept. reports.			Dec. 30
		Prices farmers receive for their raw agricultural goods decline 2.4% in December, the Agriculture Dept. reports. . . . The U.S. deficit on merchandise trade expanded dramatically in November, reaching a record $19.2 bil. the Commerce Dept. reports.			Dec. 31

F	G	H	I	J
includes elections, federal-state relations, civil rights and liberties, crime, the judiciary, education, health care, poverty, urban affairs and population.	*Includes formation and debate of U.S. foreign and defense policies, veterans' affairs and defense spending. (Relations with specific foreign countries are usually found under the region concerned.)*	*Includes business, labor, agriculture, taxation, transportation, consumer affairs, monetary and fiscal policy, natural resources, and pollution.*	*Includes worldwide scientific, medical and technological developments, natural phenomena, U.S. weather, natural disasters, and accidents.*	*Includes the arts, religion, scholarship, communications media, sports, entertainments, fashions, fads and social life.*

1987

Frantic work by traders on the floor of the New York Stock Exchange reflected the crashing of the Dow Jones Industrial Average on Monday, October 19, 1987.

	World Affairs	Europe	Africa & the Middle East	The Americas	Asia & the Pacific
Jan.	Bank regulators from the United States and Great Britain propose a joint regulation that would set a common standard for evaluating a bank's ratio of capital to assets.	Soviet leader Mikhail S. Gorbachev opens a plenary session of the Communist Party Central Committee with a stunning call for major political reforms including "democratization."	Iranian forces sustain thousands of casualties in an offensive against Basra that is one of bloodiest and most sustained operations of the Persian Gulf War.	Nicaragua's Pres. Daniel Ortega Saavedra signs into law a new constitution but suspends many of the liberties granted in the charter by extending a state of emergency through 1987.	Hu Yaobang resigns as general secretary of the Chinese Communist Party's Central Committee after admitting to major "mistakes"; he is replaced by Premier Zhao Ziyang.
Feb.	Finance ministers from six of the seven major industrial democracies announce an agreement to stabilize the relative values of their currencies at present levels.	The Soviet foreign ministry announces the release from prisons and labor camps of 140 dissidents, the largest release of political prisoners in the USSR since 1956.	Kidnappers of three Americans and one Indian in Beirut extend "until further notice" a threat to kill their hostages unless their demands are met	In a move that threatens the international financial system, Brazil's government suspends interest payments to foreign commercial banks.	India and Pakistan complete the withdrawal of 150,000 troops from their common border in a first step to defuse flaring military tensions between the two nations.
March	The UN Commission on Human Rights rejects U.S.- and Cuban-sponsored resolutions each of which condemned the other for human rights violations.	Soviet leader Mikhail S. Gorbachev calls for the United States and USSR to reach an independent accord on the elimination of medium-range nuclear missiles in Europe.	Col. Muammer el-Qaddafi sustains a major setback when the oasis town of Faya-Largeau, Libya's last major stronghold in Chad, is retaken by government forces.	Haitian voters overwhelmingly approve a new constitution in a referendum.	In China, the 2,719 delegates to the National People's Congress gather in Beijing's Great Hall of the People to begin the annual session of the legislature.
April	The first anniversary of the Chernobyl nuclear plant accident in the Soviet Ukraine is marked by antinuclear protests around the world.	Sec. of State George P. Shultz visits Moscow and comes away with an offer from Soviet leader Mikhail S. Gorbachev to eliminate shorter-range intermediate nuclear forces in Europe.	A six-week-old walkout by black South African railway workers turns violent when police kill at least six blacks in clashes following the dismissal of 16,000 strikers.	Some 25,000 students and opposition politicians march through streets of Caracas, Venezuela, in the biggest antigovernment demonstration in recent years.	Japan's Premier Yasuhiro Nakasone confers with Pres. Reagan in Washington, D.C., on the escalating trade tensions between their two countries.
May	Ministers from the major democratic nations meet in Paris to forge tighter links in the battle against international terrorism.	The United States offers the Soviet Union a draft treaty on the reduction of strategic offensive weapons.	The Navy frigate USS *Stark* is accidentally struck by missiles fired by an Iraqi warplane while on patrol in the Persian Gulf; 37 U.S. sailors are killed in the incident.	Argentina's Pres. Raul Alfonsin presents Congress with a bill freeing most middle- and lower-ranking officers from prosecution for human rigts abuses during the dirty war in the 1970s.	Fijian military authorities announce a compromise settlement of a military coup, but Fiji's deposed civilian leader, of Indian descent, later refuses to accept the arrangement.
June	The 13th summit meeting of the leaders of the world's major industrial democracies, held in Venice, is viewed as satisfactory but yields few initiatives.	Britain's Conservative P.M. Margaret Thatcher becomes the first British leader in 160 years to be elected to a third consecutive term as prime minister.	Lebanon's Premier Rashid Karami is assassinated when a bomb explodes aboard a military helicopter in which he was traveling. There is no firm indication of who is responsible.	Panama's government imposes a 10-day "state of urgency" after the head of the Panama Defense Forces is accused of electoral fraud and involvement in the murder of a political opponent.	South Korea is wracked by student riots, and opposition leader Kim Young Sam rejects Pres. Chun Doo Hwan's offer to allow debate over the national constitution.
July	Morocco's Foreign Min. Abdellatif Filali delivers a letter to the president of the European Community's foreign affairs council indicating Morocco's intention to apply for membership in the EC.	Soviet leader Mikhail S. Gorbachev says the USSR is willing to accept a worldwide elimination of intermediate nuclear forces and offers to withdraw INF warheads from Soviet Asia.	Thousands of Iranian pilgrims clash with Saudi police near the Grand Mosque in Mecca, Islam's holiest city; 275 Iranians, 85 Saudi police and 42 other pilgrims are killed.	Some 174 illegal Indian immigrants are taken into custody by local authorities after landing in lifeboats on the sparsely populated south shore of Nova Scotia.	The chief Tamil rebel group says it will not abide by a peace agreement between Sri Lanka and India designed to end the four-year-old rebellion by Sri Lanka's Tamil minority.
Aug.	Oil prices fall to below $20 a barrel in the biggest one-day drop in more than a year, apparently due to overproduction by the Org. of Petroleum Exporting Countries nations.	West Germany offers to dismantle its 72 Pershing IA missiles if the United States and the Soviet Union implement an agreement on a global ban on intermediate nuclear forces.	An estimated 230,000 to 340,000 black miners in South Africa's gold and coal mining industries strike for higher wages and improved benefits.	The presidents of five Central American nations sign a preliminary peace agreement calling for cease-fires, democratic reforms, and political amnesty in the region.	Against a background of mounting labor unrest, South Korea's ruling and opposition parties agree on a draft constitution clearing the way for direct presidential elections.
Sept.	Representatives of 24 countries sign a treaty designed to reduce the production of chlorofluorocarbons, which destroy the Earth's protective ozone layer.	Erich Honecker becomes the first East German head of state to visit West Germany in what is widely viewed as setting the stage for improved relations between the two Germanys.	A U.S. helicopter seizes an Iranian naval vessel that is allegedly laying mines in the Persian Gulf.	Nicaragua's Pres. Daniel Ortega Saavedra announces that Sandinista troops will withdraw from some 1,500 square miles of territory in northern and central Nicaragua.	UN-mediated talks between Afghanistan and Pakistan end with no significant progress toward setting a timetable for the withdrawal of 115,000 Soviet troops from Afghanistan.
Oct.	World stock markets turn downward following the October 19 collapse of stock prices in the United States, with London and Tokyo hardest hit by the crash.	Premier Zbigniew Messner unveils a package of major reforms aimed at invigorating Poland's stagnant economy, subject to a national referendum on the "rate and degree" of reform.	An Iranian Silkworm missile hit a U.S.-flagged oil tanker in Kuwaiti waters, injuring 18 crewmen; U.S. warships bombard an Iranian oil rig being used as a base for gunboats.	Costa Rica's Pres. Oscar Arias Sanchez, the main architect of a Central American peace plan signed in Guatemala in August, is awarded the Nobel Peace Prize.	Premier Yasuhiro Nakasone chooses former finance minister Noboru Takeshita to succeed him as president of the ruling Liberal Democratic Party.
Nov.	The UN opens its secret files on suspected World War II war criminals; compiled by the UN War Crimes Commission, the files have been available only to governments.	Soviet leader Mikhail S. Gorbachev criticizes Joseph Stalin but stops short of a complete denunciation of the former leader.	Arab leaders at an emergency Arab League summit express unanimous support for Iraq in the Iran-Iraq War and clear the way for Arab states to resume diplomatic relations with Egypt.	Election officials call off what would have been Haiti's first free elections in 30 years amid a wave of terror unleashed by loyalists of deposed Pres. Jean-Claude Duvalier.	The Chinese Communist Party's first national congress since 1982, and its 13th ever, heralds the rise to power of a new generation of Chinese leaders.
Dec.	At a Washington, D.C., summit, Pres. Reagan and Soviet leader Mikhail S. Gorbachev sign a bilateral treaty eliminating intermediate-range nuclear forces.	The leaders of the 12 European Community nations adjourn a two-day summit without agreeing on key farm and budget questions; a crisis meeting to resolve the issue is called for February 1988.	Israeli security forces quell two weeks of violent demonstrations by Palestinians in the occupied territories; Israeli Arabs staged a massive general strike in solidarity.	Mexico, the United States and Morgan Guaranty Trust Co. announce a plan to ease the Mexican debt crisis by swapping as much as $10 bil. in discounted Mexican debt for Treasury bonds.	Ruling Democratic Justice Party candidate Roh Tae Woo wins South Korea's first direct presidential election in 16 years as opposition challengers split the antigovernment vote.

A	B	C	D	E
Includes developments that affect more than one world region, international organizations and important meetings of major world leaders.	*Includes all domestic and regional developments in Europe, including the Soviet Union, Turkey, Cyprus and Malta.*	*Includes all domestic and regional developments in Africa and the Middle East, including Iraq and Iran and excluding Cyprus, Turkey and Afghanistan.*	*Includes all domestic and regional developments in Latin America, the Caribbean and Canada.*	*Includes all domestic and regional developments in Asia and Pacific nations, extending from Afghanistan through all the Pacific Islands, except Hawaii.*

U.S. Politics & Social Issues	U.S. Foreign Policy & Defense	U.S. Economy & Environment	Science, Technology & Nature	Culture, Leisure & Life Style	
The 100th Congress convenes with Democrats controlling both houses for the first time in the Reagan presidency.	The Senate Intelligence Committee votes not to make public a report of its December 1986 closed hearings on the Iran-Contra arms scandal.	Pres. Reagan submits to Congress a $1.024 trillion federal budget for FY1988. It is the first trillion-dollar budget ever submitted.	A panel of medical advisers to the federal Food and Drug Admin. votes to recommend the licensing of the anti-AIDS drug AZT (azidothymidine) for commercial sale.	Robert A. Gottlieb, president and editor in chief of Alfred A. Knopf, is named to succeed William Shawn as editor of *The New Yorker*. Shawn was editor for 35 years.	Jan.
The nonprofit Washington, D.C.-based Children's Defense Fund releases a report showing that the U.S. infant mortality rate is one of the highest in the industrialized world.	The Tower Commission concludes that Pres. Reagan was misled by dishonest staffers who used the profits from the arms-for-hostages deals to fund the Nicaraguan Contras.	Congress enacts the Clean Water Act in the seventh override of a veto by Pres. Reagan.	The number of countries reporting cases of AIDS to the UN World Health Org. has more than doubled in a year to a total of 91, a U.S. official of the agency says.	*Stars & Stripes*, the U.S. yacht skippered by Dennis Conner, returns the America's Cup to the United States with a win over Australia's *Kookaburra III*.	Feb.
A Bergen Co. (N.J.) Superior Court Judge rules that a surrogate mother contract is "constitutionally protected" and awards custody of "Baby M" to her biological father.	Pres. Reagan acknowledges that his administration swapped arms for hostages and concludes that "it was a mistake."	Pres. Reagan announces that the United States has decided to impose duties that will double the import prices of a wide range of popular electronic products imported from Japan.	Prince Louis De Broglie, 94, French Nobel-winning physicist honored for his work leading to the development of wave mechanics, a form of quantum mechanics, dies in Paris.	Rev. Jim Bakker, one of many popular television evangelists in the United States, resigns his ministry after admitting an extramarital sexual encounter seven years ago.	March
Former Sen. Gary Hart (D, Colo.) declares his candidacy for the presidency.	Austria's Pres. Kurt Waldheim is effectively barred from the United States because of his suspected participation in Nazi war crimes during World War II.	Despite an all-out effort by the president to have his veto sustained, Congress overrides Pres. Reagan to enact an $87.5 bil. highway and mass transit bill.	The U.S. government says it is clearing the way for inventors to patent new forms of life created through genetic engineering.	Pres. Reagan nominates Russian scholar James H. Billington, 57, to replace Daniel J. Boorstin as head of the Library of Congress.	April
Thousands of illegal immigrants flood Immigration and Naturalization Service offices nationwide seeking amnesty under the Immigration Reform and Control Act of 1986.	House and Senate committees investigating the Iran-Contra arms scandal open their joint public hearings. Former CIA Dir. William J. Casey, 74, dies of pneumonia and cancer.	Pres. Reagan signs a bill temporarily raising the U.S. national debt limit by about $20 bil., to $2.32 trillion, to enable the government to continue borrowing through July 17.	The National Academy of Sciences urges the Environmental Protection Agency to establish standardized rules to reduce the risks from cancer-causing pesticide residues in food.	Alysheba, with Chris McCarron aboard, wins the 113th Kentucky Derby at Churchill Downs in Louisville, Ky.	May
The Supreme Court strikes down a Louisiana law that requires public schools teaching evolution to teach "creation science" as well.	Congressional hearings into the Iran-Contra arms scandal continue with testimony from Asst. Sec. of State Elliott Abrams and businessman Albert Hakim.	The Supreme Court refuses to hear an appeal by eight northeastern states, the Canadian province of Ontario and environmental groups for federal action to reduce acid-rain pollution.	Canadian geologists say they have identified a vast impact crater on the floor of the North Atlantic Ocean formed by a meteor or asteroid crashing into the Earth 50 million years ago.	Fred (born Frederick Austerlitz) Astaire, 88, one of the great dancers of the 20th century, whose grace and elegance thrilled several generations of moviegoers, dies of pneumonia in Los Angeles.	June
Pres. Reagan proposes new regulations that would bar federal funding for family planning programs that offer abortion counseling.	Sec. of State George P. Shultz testifies before Congress that his opposition to the Iran arms sales sparked a "battle royal" within the White House.	An group of development experts and Third World political leaders issue an urgent call for action to reverse the continuing loss of the world's tropical forests.	The National Science Foundation announces that scientists have found strong evidence that two nearby galaxies have black holes at their centers.	John Hammond, 76, record producer, jazz and blues aficionado, and legendary musical talent scout who numbered among his finds Bessie Smith, Billie Holiday, Benny Goodman and Count Basie, dies in New York City; in later years, he signed up Aretha Franklin, Bob Dylan and Bruce Springsteen.	July
A fire of suspicious origin destroys the Arcadia, Fla., home of a couple whose three hemophiliac sons are known to have been exposed to the virus that causes AIDS.	In a nationally broadcast address, Pres. Reagan asserts that he "was stubborn in pursuit of a policy that went astray" in selling arms to Iran.	Congress passes a comprehensive banking bill that will allow the insolvent Federal Savings and Loan Insurance Corp. to raise $10.8 bil. by issuing long-term bonds.	Gov. Mario Cuomo announces that New York State health officials will test the blood of more than 100,000 people to measure the spread of the virus that causes AIDS.	John Huston, 81, film director, writer and actor, dies in Middletown, R.I., of complications of emphysema. He directed 41 films, many of them film classics, for example, *The Maltese Falcon* (1941) and *The African Queen* (1951).	Aug.
The Senate Judiciary Committee completes its hearings on the nomination of Judge Robert H. Bork to the Supreme Court, as the battle over the appointment increases in intensity.	Amid an ongoing congressional dispute over the Reagan administration's policy in the Persian Gulf, the Senate votes unanimously for a ban on all imports from Iran.	The Federal Deposit Insurance Corp. agrees to provide $970 mil. to save the severely troubled First City Bancorp. of Houston, in the second largest FDIC-approved bailout ever.	Half the states in the United States have filed applications with the Energy Dept. to be the site of the Superconducting Super Collider, the largest atom smasher ever built.	After decades of deliberate neglect by Soviet authorities, the art of the late Russian-born painter Marc Chagall is given a full-scale exhibition in his native land.	Sept.
The Senate rejects Pres. Reagan's nomination of Judge Robert H. Bork to the Supreme Court by a 58-42 vote after one of the most contentious struggles for the post in memory.	Pres. Reagan announces that he and Soviet leader Mikhail S. Gorbachev will hold a summit meeting in Washington, D.C., beginning December 7.	In panicked selling, the Dow Jones industrial average falls an astounding 508.32 points on Monday, October 19, jolting financial markets worldwide.	The Nobel Prize for physiology or medicine is awarded to Japanese molecular biologist Susumu Tonegawa for his research into the body's immune system.	Joseph Campbell, 83, U.S. author of many books on mythology and folklore, the best-known of which is *The Hero with a Thousand Faces* (1949), dies in Honolulu, after a brief illness.	Oct.
U.S. Appeals Court Judge Douglas H. Ginsburg withdraws as Pres. Reagan's nominee to the Supreme Court following his disclosure that he had smoked marijuana in the past.	The House and Senate committees investigating the Iran-Contra arms scandal blame Pres. Reagan for policies that hinged on "secrecy, deception and disdain for the law."	American Airlines had the best on-time performance in September—84.5%—in the Transportation Dept.'s first monthly ranking of service provided by the major airlines.	Western European representatives to the 13-nation European Space Agency agree to pursue three major projects related to manned space flight.	Vincent van Gogh's *Irises* (1889) fetches a record $53.9 mil. at auction at Sotheby's in New York City.	Nov.
A federal jury in Washington, D.C., finds former top White House aide Michael K. Deaver guilty on three counts of perjury for lying under oath about his lobbying activities.	The Defense Dept. announces that the armed services have met their recruitment goals for FY1987 for the eighth consecutive fiscal year of an all-volunteer military.	Pres. Reagan signs two bills embodying a compromise agreement on the FY1988 federal budget and ends a year's worth of legislative labor and frustration.	A six-year joint U.S.-Japanese study of World War II atomic bomb survivors confirms that previous estimates of radiation doses suffered by bomb victims were too high.	Soviet leader Mikhail S. Gorbachev is named *Time* magazine's Man of the Year.	Dec.

F	G	H	I	J
Includes elections, federal-state relations, civil rights and liberties, crime, the judiciary, education, health care, poverty, urban affairs and population.	Includes formation and debate of U.S. foreign and defense policies, veterans' affairs and defense spending. (Relations with specific foreign countries are usually found under the region concerned.)	Includes business, labor, agriculture, taxation, transportation, consumer affairs, monetary and fiscal policy, natural resources, and pollution.	Includes worldwide scientific, medical and technological developments, natural phenomena, U.S. weather, natural disasters, and accidents.	Includes the arts, religion, scholarship, communications media, sports, entertainments, fashions, fads and social life.

	World Affairs	Europe	Africa & the Middle East	The Americas	Asia & the Pacific
Jan. 1		Radio Moscow broadcasts an edited recording of a message to the Soviet people by Pres. Reagan. About one-third of the full message aired on the Voice of America Dec. 31, 1986, was rendered inaudible by Soviet electronic jamming.		Bolivia introduces a new currency, the boliviano, removing six zeros from the value of the old currency, the peso. The boliviano is worth 1 mil. pesos (almost 50 U.S. cents).	Students in Beijing, China stage a rally in defiance of new regulations governing the holding of demonstrations. More than 2,000 students attend the rally in Tiananmen Square, recently declared off-limits to protesters.
Jan. 2					
Jan. 3			Chad's Pres. Hissene Habre announces that a mobile column of army troops captured the oasis town of Fada, in northeastern Chad, after a fierce battle with the 1,000 Libyan troops garrisoned there.		
Jan. 4		West Germany's Chancellor Helmut Kohl creates a political stir when he tells a party rally in Dortmund that East Germany holds 2,000 German "countrymen" as political prisoners in "concentration camps." His remarks prompt denials from East German officials and charges from Kohl's political opponents that he is seeking to win the votes of right-wing extremists.			The Filipino government and Moslem rebels sign a pact under which the Moslems agreed to give up their demands for a separate state, beginning a process to end the 14-year insurgency in which more than 60,000 people have been killed.
Jan. 5		Ireland's 1986 budget deficit of $2 bil. amounted to 8.5% of gross national product, it is reported. The government target was 7.4%.... The 30 terrorist incidents in Italy in 1986 was the smallest number of any year since 1969, according to the interior ministry.		A British Columbia supreme court judge upholds a 1983 law that allows the provincial government to control the supply of physicians in the province by restricting the distribution of billing numbers to physicians. Without a billing number, a doctor cannot seek reimbursement for services rendered under the provincial health plan.	
Jan. 6		Charter 77, Czechoslovakia's leading human rights organization, marks its 10th anniversary. Some members of the group hold a news conference at a Prague apartment and distribute a manifesto critical of the "sterile rigidity" of the government's political and economic systems.... Soviet Internal Affairs Min. Alexander Vlasov admits that there is a growing problem with drug addiction in the Soviet Union. In an interview published in the Communist Party newspaper *Pravda*, Vlasov says that there are 46,000 registered addicts in the country.			Indian politicians loyal to the late P.M. Indira Gandhi form a new political party, the Rashtriya Samajwadi Congress (National Socialist Congress).... Portuguese leaders are reported to have agreed to return Macao to China in 1999, ending four centuries of Portuguese rule.... Indonesia's Pres. Suharto unveils a stringent draft austerity budget for the year beginning April 1. The 22.7 trillion rupiah budget is down 2.6% from the current fiscal year.
Jan. 7		Officials from Finland and the Soviet Union sign a protocol that sets trade between the two nations for 1987 at $5.6 bil. to $6.7 bil. The agreement is signed in Helsinki during a state visit by Soviet Premier Nikolai Ryzhkov.			

A	B	C	D	E
Includes developments that affect more than one world region, international organizations and important meetings of major world leaders.	Includes all domestic and regional developments in Europe, including the Soviet Union, Turkey, Cyprus and Malta.	Includes all domestic and regional developments in Africa and the Middle East, including Iraq and Iran and excluding Cyprus, Turkey and Afghanistan.	Includes all domestic and regional developments in Latin America, the Caribbean and Canada.	Includes all domestic and regional developments in Asia and Pacific nations, extending from Afghanistan through all the Pacific Islands, except Hawaii.

U.S. Politics & Social Issues	U.S. Foreign Policy & Defense	U.S. Economy & Environment	Science, Technology & Nature	Culture, Leisure & Life Style	
				Oklahoma trounces Arkansas, 42-8, in the Orange Bowl; Arizona State downs Michigan, 22-15, in the Rose Bowl; Ohio State beats Texas A&M, 28-12, in the Cotton Bowl; and Nebraska bests Louisiana State, 30-15, in the Sugar Bowl.	Jan. 1
The National Republican Senatorial Committee is reported to have awarded bonuses totaling $225,250 to 87 staff members and consultants the day after the party lost control of the Senate in the November 1986 election.... The Congressional Budget Office reports that the federal budget deficit for FY1987 will be $174.5 bil. if Congress and the president take no action to change current law.				Penn State wins the national college football championship with a 14-10 upset victory over Miami in the Fiesta Bowl.	Jan. 2
The United States and Japan issue separate assessments of each other's systems of edcuation. The U.S. study dwells on the discipline and "hard work" expected of Japanese students, but the as yet untranslated Japanese study reportedly found that cultural differences made it impossible to draw lessons from the United States.				David (Peter) Maysles, 54, filmmaker, dies in New York City, following a stroke. Maysles and his brother Albert played a key role in the development of the documentary genre known as cinema verite, which uses hand-held cameras and no scripts or staged sets. Among their best known films are *Salesman* (1969), *Gimme Shelter* (1970), and *Grey Gardens* (1975).	Jan. 3
The *Washington Post* reports some fellow Republicans are distributing "Recall Ev" buttons to protest Arizona Gov. Evan Mecham's decision to rescind state observance of a January 19 holiday honoring the birthday of Rev. Martin Luther King Jr.				The National Society of Film Critics names *Blue Velvet* and David Lynch as best film and best director of 1986; best actor goes to Bob Hoskins for *Mona Lisa*, and best actress to Chloe Webb for *Sid and Nancy*.	Jan. 4
The busing of children to achieve racially balanced schools counted markedly fewer opponents in 1986 than in 1976, according to Harris Survey findings. In 1986, 53% of respondents opposed busing and 41% favored it, as against 78% against and 14% for busing in 1976.	The Senate Intelligence Committee votes, 7-6, not to make public a 150-page report of the closed hearings it conducted in December 1986 on the Iran-Contra arms scandal. The White House urged that the report be released, but Sen. William S. Cohen (R, Maine) is the only Republican to join the committee's six Democrats in voting to withhold the document.	Pres. Reagan submits to Congress a $1.024 trillion federal budget for FY1988. It is the first trillion-dollar budget ever submitted.	The Soviet Union offers several bargains in seeking to attract customers for its space-launching facilities. In an interview with the official Soviet news agency Tass, Premier Nikolai Ryzhkov says foreign technicians will be allowed to accompany their spacecraft to the Soviet launch site without customs examination.	Margaret Laurence (born Jean Margaret Wemys), 60, one of the leading Canadian novelists of her generation, dies of lung cancer in Lakefield, Ontario. Four novels and a book of short stories set in the fictional town of Manawaka, Manitoba, firmly established her reputation. Many parents campaigned to have *The Diviners* (1974) removed from school reading lists because of its explicit description of an abortion.	Jan. 5
The Justice Dept. announces that it will return to judging election plans by their results and will no longer demand proof that local officials intended to discriminate against minority voters.... The 100th Congress convenes, with Democrats controlling both houses for the first time in the Reagan presidency. Senate Democratic leader Robert C. Byrd (W.Va.) resumes the post of majority leader. The House speaker is Rep. James C. Wright Jr. (Tex.). The Republican minority leaders are Sen. Bob Dole (Kans.) and Rep. Bob Michel (Ill.).		A study by the National Research Council charges that the Nuclear Regulatory Comm.'s program to improve the safety of commercial nuclear reactors is "in dire need of reform." The council is an arm of the National Academy of Sciences.			Jan. 6
Two days after stepping down as Arizona's governor, Bruce Babbitt (D) establishes a presidential campaign committee and names a dozen top campaign staffers. His filing with the Federal Election Comm. makes him the first Democratic candidate eligible for federal matching funds.		As a precautionary measure, the Environmental Protection Agency lowers the level of the chemical daminozide allowed on fruit and vegetables to 20 parts per million from 30 parts per million. The chemical is mostly used to assure that apples ripen at the same time.			Jan. 7

F	G	H	I	J
Includes elections, federal-state relations, civil rights and liberties, crime, the judiciary, education, health care, poverty, urban affairs and population.	*Includes formation and debate of U.S. foreign and defense policies, veterans' affairs and defense spending. (Relations with specific foreign countries are usually found under the region concerned.)*	*Includes business, labor, agriculture, taxation, transportation, consumer affairs, monetary and fiscal policy, natural resources, and pollution.*	*Includes worldwide scientific, medical and technological developments, natural phenomena, U.S. weather, natural disasters, and accidents.*	*Includes the arts, religion, scholarship, communications media, sports, entertainments, fashions, fads and social life.*

	World Affairs	Europe	Africa & the Middle East	The Americas	Asia & the Pacific
Jan. 8	Bank regulators from the United States and Great Britain propose a joint regulation to set a common standard for evaluating a bank's ratio of capital to assets. The agreement marks a significant step toward making banking the first industry to be regulated on a worldwide basis.			The federal government imposes a 15% export tax on Canadian softwood lumber bound for the United States. The levy is part of the settlement of a U.S. trade complaint. Canada annually exports about $3 bil. in softwood to the United States. The tax is expected to generate $438 mil. a year in revenues.	African students march through Beijing to protest against racism in China. The march is spurred by a letter containing racial insults that had circulated in the capital, as well as dissatisfaction with their treatment by the government and Chinese students.
Jan. 9		East Germany's national income—a measurement equivalent to the West's gross national product, minus services—reportedly rose 4.3% in 1986, 0.1 percentage point under the target of the 1986-90 economic plan.	Fighting between Libyan and Chadian troops and rebel forces allied with both sides has heated up over the last week. In response to setbacks on the ground, Libyan jets raided targets in southern Chad, and France responded with an air strike in the north.	Canadian unemployment averaged 9.6% in 1986, according to Statistics Canada, down from 10.5% in 1985. . . . Nicaragua's Pres. Daniel Ortega Saavedra signs into law a new constitution but immediately reimposes a state of emergency in effect since 1982, suspending many of the liberties granted in the charter.	
Jan. 10		A study by independent Swiss technical experts of the Swiss Polytechnical Institute, reports that environmental damage from the 1986 Rhine River chemical spill might not have been as severe as first estimated. The study says that "the regeneration of invertebrate micro-organisms by (spring 1987) is not impossible. And with this, the river would once again be able to support fish, or water life."			
Jan. 11		Strikes that have caused a crisis atmosphere in France for several weeks begin to wind down. The government of conservative Premier Jacques Chirac, whose anti-inflation wage restraint program was challenged by the strikes, appears to have weathered the walkouts.			
Jan. 12		The value of the U.S. dollar fell sharply against other major currencies in the first two weeks of 1987, declining nearly 5% against the West German deutsche mark. The mark also registered record highs against the British pound; and today, its strength against the French franc forced realignment of the European Monetary System.		Argentina announces details of an agreement with the International Monetary Fund (IMF) on a new $1.35 bil. standby loan for the 15 months ending March 1988. Argentina will also receive $480 mil. in compensatory financing to offset an expected loss of revenue from exports of meat and wheat.	
Jan. 13				Mexico's secretary of urban development and economy, Manuel Camacho Solis, announces 100 steps to be implemented in 1987 and 1988 in Mexico City and elsewhere. Mexico City, the world's largest metropolitan area, suffers one of the world's worst smog problems, exacerbated by the city's high altitude. . . . Investigators in Puerto Rico arrest two hotel employees said to be responsible for the fatal New Year's Eve blaze at San Juan's luxurious Dupont Plaza Hotel in which 96 people died.	

A	B	C	D	E
Includes developments that affect more than one world region, international organizations and important meetings of major world leaders.	Includes all domestic and regional developments in Europe, including the Soviet Union, Turkey, Cyprus and Malta.	Includes all domestic and regional developments in Africa and the Middle East, including Iraq and Iran and excluding Cyprus, Turkey and Afghanistan.	Includes all domestic and regional developments in Latin America, the Caribbean and Canada.	Includes all domestic and regional developments in Asia and Pacific nations, extending from Afghanistan through all the Pacific Islands, except Hawaii.

U.S. Politics & Social Issues	U.S. Foreign Policy & Defense	U.S. Economy & Environment	Science, Technology & Nature	Culture, Leisure & Life Style	
Pres. Reagan returns to the White House after undergoing prostate surgery and a full battery of tests to check for a recurrence of intestinal cancer. White House officials say they expect the president to ease back into a normal workload during the typical recovery period of six weeks.	In San Francisco, Federal Judge Marilyn Hall Patel orders the Veterans Admin. (VA) to pay more than $100,000 for destroying documents sought by litigants against the agency. Patell finds the VA in contempt for ignoring a court-approved request for documents related to the thousands of compensation claims by veterans exposed to atomic-test radiation.	A record 11.4 million cars were sold in the United States in 1986, according to the *Wall Street Journal*. The total number of cars and trucks sold in 1986 was an estimated 16 million, also a record. . . . The Dow Jones Industrial Average closes at a record 2002.25, the first time ever over the 2000 mark.			Jan. 8
The Justice Dept. is reported to have suspended three grand jury investigations into a private supply network for the Contras fighting the Nicaraguan government while Iran-Contra special prosecutor Lawrence E. Walsh reviews the probes.	The White House releases the text of Pres. Reagan's Jan. 17, 1986, intelligence finding formally authorizing arms sales to Iran, and a cover memo prepared by Lt. Col. Oliver L. North recommending that Reagan sign the finding.	The nation's unemployment rate dropped two-tenths of a percentage point in December 1986 to a six-year low of 6.6%, the Labor Dept. reports. . . . The government's producer price index fell 2.5% in 1986, the Labor Dept. reports. It is the largest drop since 1949 and the first since 1963. . . . Outstanding consumer credit grew a seasonally adjusted $4.02 bil. in November 1986, the Federal Reserve Board reports.	The National Aeronautics and Space Admin. names an experienced five-man crew to man the next shuttle mission, scheduled for February 1988. It will be the first crew in the history of the shuttle program without a rookie.		Jan. 9
Three reports on the poor showing by U.S. students in international tests of mathematics skill are issued by the Mathematical Sciences Research Board, a division of the National Academy of Sciences.	The Defense Dept.'s sixth annual report on the state of the U.S. military discloses that the Joint Chiefs of Staff, the secretaries of the armed services, and military theater commanders have been directed to focus on the use of high technology to counter the Soviet advantage in defense spending, personnel, and materiel.				Jan. 10
	Defense Sec. Caspar W. Weinberger forms a special panel to draft guidelines on defense technology and long-term military strategy.			The New York Giants and the Denver Broncos advance to the National Football League's Super Bowl. The Giants win the National Football Conf. 17-0 over the Washington Redskins. The Broncos win the American Football Conf. over the Cleveland Browns, 30-23.	Jan. 11
The Supreme Court declines to review a ruling that says congressionally mandated health warnings on cigarette packages and advertising provide manufacturers with liability from certain lawsuits.				The National Book Critics Circle names Reynolds Price's *Kate Vaidan* as the best work of American fiction published in 1986; general nonfiction goes to John Dower's *War Without Mercy: Race and Power in the Pacific War*; biography, Theodore Rosengarten's *Tombee: Portrait of a Cotton Planter*; poetry, Edward Hirsch's *Wild Gratitude*; and criticism, Joseph Brodsky's *Less Than One: Selected Essays*.	Jan. 12
The Supreme Court upholds, 6-3, a California law that requires employers to give women disability leave for pregnancy and childbirth and to guarantee them reinstatement to their jobs. . . . To break a deadlock in the Howard Beach racial attack case, New York's Gov. Mario Cuomo names a special prosecutor, Charles J. Hynes, to take over the case.		The new tax code enacted in 1985 will bring in $15.7 bil. less over the next five years than the law it replaced, according to new Treasury Dept. estimates. A central goal of the new law had been that it should neither increase nor decrease tax collections.		A study released by the Census Bureau gives college-educated women who are still single at age 30 a 58% chance of marrying. The study also predicts that at least 17% of college-educated women who were still single at 40 would eventually marry. . . . Kazuro Ishiguro wins Britain's richest book prize, the $26,200 Whitbread Book of the Year Award, for his novel *An Artist of the Floating World*. . . . New York Giants outside linebacker Lawrence Taylor is named the National Football League's most valuable player.	Jan. 13

F	G	H	I	J
Includes elections, federal-state relations, civil rights and liberties, crime, the judiciary, education, health care, poverty, urban affairs and population.	Includes formation and debate of U.S. foreign and defense policies, veterans' affairs and defense spending. (Relations with specific foreign countries are usually found under the region concerned.)	Includes business, labor, agriculture, taxation, transportation, consumer affairs, monetary and fiscal policy, natural resources, and pollution.	Includes worldwide scientific, medical and technological developments, natural phenomena, U.S. weather, natural disasters, and accidents.	Includes the arts, religion, scholarship, communications media, sports, entertainments, fashions, fads and social life.

	World Affairs	Europe	Africa & the Middle East	The Americas	Asia & the Pacific
Jan. 14		A coalition government of Austria's two largest parties is formed in a return to the "Grand Coalition" that had governed the nation from 1947 to 1966. The coalition was formed after the November 1986 general elections had left no party with a majority.	Sec. of State George P. Shultz completes a tour of six pro-Western, black African nations during which he praised the region's trend toward free-market economics and defended U.S. policy. Overall U.S. aid to sub-Saharan Africa has been cut by 34% in the current fiscal year.		
Jan. 15	West German authorities arrest a Lebanese suspected of being one of the two men who hijacked a Trans World Airlines jet and held hostage 39 passengers for 17 days in June 1985.	The seventh round of disarmament talks between the United States and the Soviet Union opens in Geneva.		Jamaica reaches agreement with the International Monetary Fund on a 15-month, $132.8 mil. standby loan.... In Canada the Nunavut Constitutional Forum, representing the Inuit eastern part of the Northwest Territories, and the Western Constitutional Forum, representing the Dene Indians, Metis (persons of mixed Indian and white ancestry), and whites of the west, reach an agreement on the partition of the region into two separate territories.	Rejecting a January 1 cease-fire proposal by Afghan leader Najibullah—the first in the Soviet-backed government's seven-year-old war against Moslem resistance forces—as a "trap," there are reports of continued fighting in some parts of the country as the truce begins.
Jan. 16		The European Community (EC) will open a full-time representative office in China during 1987.... The Soviet Union and the European Community hold talks in Brussels aimed at establishing diplomatic relations.		In Ecuador renegade air force troops seize Pres. Leon Febres Cordero and 30 members of his military staff and hold them hostage for 12 hours. The president is released after agreeing to free an air force general jailed for an attempted rebellion in 1986.	David Wilson is knighted and named governor of the British territory of Hong Kong. Wilson led the negotiating team that sealed the 1984 agreement under which Hong Kong will be returned to Chinese rule in 1997.... Hu Yaobang, 71, resigns as general secretary of the Chinese Communist Party's Central Committee after admitting to major "mistakes." Premier Zhao Ziyang, 67, is appointed acting general secretary.
Jan. 17				The Los Angeles Times reports that the Central Intelligence Agency has recalled its station chief in Costa Rica following allegations that he supplied the Nicaraguan Contras with military and logistical advice for the private airlift of weapons at a time when U.S. military aid to the Contras was banned.	
Jan. 18	Following the kidnapping of two West German nationals in Lebanon, the Justice Dept. agrees not to seek the death penalty for Mohammed Ali Hamadei who is currently in West German custody awaiting extradition to the United States to stand trial for the 1985 hijacking of a Trans World Airlines jet and the murder of an American serviceman.				
Jan. 19		The Central Statistical Board reports that the population of the Soviet Union was 281.7 million people at the end of 1986 and is expected to rise to 300 million by the year 2000. Soviets born in 1986 have a life expectancy of 69 years, compared with 70 years for those born in 1970.		A diplomatic mission to Central America apparently fails to bring any progress toward peace in the region. The mission was undertaken by the foreign ministers of the Contadora Group nations, their so-called support group, and the secretaries general of the UN and the Org. of American States.	

A	B	C	D	E
Includes developments that affect more than one world region, international organizations and important meetings of major world leaders.	Includes all domestic and regional developments in Europe, including the Soviet Union, Turkey, Cyprus and Malta.	Includes all domestic and regional developments in Africa and the Middle East, including Iraq and Iran and excluding Cyprus, Turkey and Afghanistan.	Includes all domestic and regional developments in Latin America, the Caribbean and Canada.	Includes all domestic and regional developments in Asia and Pacific nations, extending from Afghanistan through all the Pacific Islands, except Hawaii.

U.S. Politics & Social Issues	U.S. Foreign Policy & Defense	U.S. Economy & Environment	Science, Technology & Nature	Culture, Leisure & Life Style	
Issuing the National Urban League's 12th annual "State of Black America," league president John E. Jacob asserts that "Black Americans enter 1987 besieged by the resurgence of raw racism, persistent economic depression and the continued erosion of past gains." . . . The Supreme Court rules, 8-0, that a bank-owned brokerage office is not a branch bank, thereby allowing the establishment of discount brokerage services by national banks across state lines.	The Supreme Court dismisses, 6-2, a challenge to Pres. Reagan's "pocket veto" of a 1983 bill conditioning military aid to El Salvador on human rights progress there. . . . The *Washington Post* cites administration and congressional sources who say that on Jan. 6, 1986, Pres. Reagan signed a top secret intelligence order authorizing the Central Intelligence Agency to provide intelligence advice, training, and equipment to the Nicaraguan Contras.	Long Island Lighting Co. files a federal lawsuit to block New York Gov. Mario Cuomo's plan to prevent the utility from opening the long-delayed Shoreham nuclear power plant.		Outfielder Billy Williams and pitcher Jim (Catfish) Hunter are elected to the baseball Hall of Fame. Each earned the necessary 75% of votes cast by baseball sportswriters to enter the hall.	Jan. 14
	A Trident II intercontinental ballistic missile is flight tested by the Navy at Cape Canaveral, Fla. The Trident II (also known as the D-5 missile) is 44 feet long and weighs 65 tons. It is capable of carrying 10 independently targetable nuclear warheads with a projected range of 11,100 miles.	The Commerce Dept. lifts controls on the export to the Soviet Union of oil-drilling equipment imposed in 1978 by Pres. Jimmy Carter. . . . Audi of America Inc. says it will comply with a government request to recall about 250,000 Audi 5000 series cars to correct a possible defect that caused some of the cars to accelerate suddenly.	The British journal *Nature* publishes a long-awaited study of research fraud that concludes that errors and falsification of data in scientific reports might be more widespread than was generally believed.	Ray (Raymond Wallace) Bolger, 83, loose-limbed dancer and comic who played the Scarecrow in *The Wizard of Oz* (1939), dies of cancer in Los Angeles. Among his many Broadway productions, the most successful was *Where's Charley* (1948), in which he created the song-and-dance number, "Once in Love with Amy."	Jan. 15
		A report by the General Accounting Office (GAO) criticizes the Environmental Protection Agency for mismanaging a program authorized by Congress to ensure safe handling of toxic wastes. The agency has set controls on less than 10% of the 5,000 types of waste identified as potentially harmful. . . . The industrial production index increased 0.5% in December 1986, the Federal Reserve Board reports.	Officials of the International Atomic Energy Agency tentatively endorse the safety measures carried out in and near the Chernobyl nuclear power plant in the Soviet Ukraine. . . . New computer simulations suggest that an all-out nuclear war would probably not result in the complete extinction of the human race, according to an article in the journal *Science*. . . . A Food and Drug Admin. advisory panel votes to recommend the licensing of AZT (azidothymidine) for commercial sale. The drug is the first to show significant results in treatment of acquired immune deficiency syndrome, although it cannot cure the disease.		Jan. 16
		This day's 54.14 increase in the Dow Jones Industrial Average is the largest in history. . . . Tentative agreement on a new labor contract between USX Corp. and the United Steelworkers of America union is reached, subject to ratification vote by union members. A settlement would end the longest steel labor dispute—170 days—in the nation's history.			Jan. 17
A jury in Somerville, N.J., convicts Thomas W. Manning, an avowed revolutionary, of murder while in the commission of felonies in the shooting of state trooper Philip Lamonaco in 1981. Manning, 40, was linked to a left-wing group known as the United Freedom Front.					Jan. 18
	A report prepared by the staff of the Senate Intelligence Committee to summarize its probe of the Iran-Contra arms scandal is published by the *New York Times* despite a committee vote not to publish the report.			The American Library Assoc. awards Sid Fleischman the John Newbery Medal for the best children's book of 1986 for *The Whipping Boy*. The Randolph Caldecott Medal for the best illustrations in an American picture-book for children goes to Richard Egielski for *Hey, Al*.	Jan. 19

F	G	H	I	J
Includes elections, federal-state relations, civil rights and liberties, crime, the judiciary, education, health care, poverty, urban affairs and population.	Includes formation and debate of U.S. foreign and defense policies, veterans' affairs and defense spending. (Relations with specific foreign countries are usually found under the region concerned.)	Includes business, labor, agriculture, taxation, transportation, consumer affairs, monetary and fiscal policy, natural resources, and pollution.	Includes worldwide scientific, medical and technological developments, natural phenomena, U.S. weather, natural disasters, and accidents.	Includes the arts, religion, scholarship, communications media, sports, entertainments, fashions, fads and social life.

	World Affairs	Europe	Africa & the Middle East	The Americas	Asia & the Pacific
Jan. 20		Sir Henry Plumb is elected president of the European Parliament, the first Briton to hold the post.			
Jan. 21	The value of the U.S. dollar continues to drop in world currency markets, even after Treasury Sec. James A. Baker III and Japan's Finance Min. Kiichi Miyazawa meet to discuss the decline.		Shiite Moslem extremists in Lebanon kidnap the second West German businessman in four days. The abductions are apparently meant to dissuade the Bonn government from extraditing to the United States a suspect in the 1985 hijacking of a Trans World Airlines jet. . . . Iranian forces have reportedly made some gains in a new offensive around the Iraqi port of Basra begun January 9. The offensive is one of the bloodiest and most sustained actions of the six-year-old Persian Gulf war.	A group of Brazil's creditor governments agrees to reschedule some $4.1 bil. in loan payments. In its agreement with the Club of Paris, a committee made up of representatives of creditor governments, Brazil won eased terms on repayment of arrears, $2.5 bil. in principal and $780 mil. in interest, accumulated in 1985 and 1986.	
Jan. 22		Sweden's 1986 inflation rate is reported at 3.3%, the lowest in 18 years. . . . In the Soviet Union, the government announces that oil exports will be reduced by 7%. The move comes following consultations in Moscow with Hisham Nazer, Saudi Arabia's oil minister. . . . West Germany announces that it will match Japan by cutting its discount rate to 3%. The U.S. discount rate was 5.5%.		Rightist businessmen in El Salvador call a strike to protest a new tax package but also aimed at forcing Pres. Jose Napoleon Duarte's ouster, according to some business leaders. . . . Canada's population edged over the 25 million mark in June 1986, according to preliminary data released by Statistics Canada. The preliminary data set Canada's population at 25,116,102, a 3.2% increase over the 24,343,181 recorded in 1981 in the previous census.	
Jan. 23		A wave of Arctic air that brought Europe its coldest temperatures in many decades begins to abate. Deaths related to the cold and snow number in the hundreds, with one estimate as high as 265.		The UN Economic Comm. for Latin America and the Caribbean concludes five days of meetings in Mexico City. The commission says that Latin America's $380 bil. foreign debt will "never be paid" and urges changes to the international economic system to avoid unilateral withholding of payments.	In Japan, the cabinet formally decides that defense spending no longer has to be less than 1% of the gross national product. The ceiling was set in 1976 to still fears that Japan might return to its past militarism. . . . Citing an alleged buildup of Pakistani military forces along the border of the two countries, India places its army and air force on maximum alert and seals 200 miles of the Indo-Pakistani border.
Jan. 24			In Lebanon, gunmen posing as police abduct three American teachers and an Indian professor from a west Beirut campus. The kidnappings bring to eight the number of Americans believed held in Lebanon and heighten tensions surrounding the hostage crisis.	U.S. marshals in Foster City, Calif., arrest Carlos Guillermo Suarez Mason, a fugitive Argentine general wanted in connection with the torture and killing of thousands of Argentines in the war against the left in the 1970s.	
Jan. 25		The center-right coalition of West Germany's Chancellor Helmut Kohl is returned to power in general elections, although Kohl's conservative coalition sees its backing fall to the lowest level since the establishment of the German Federal Republic in 1949.			

A	B	C	D	E
Includes developments that affect more than one world region, international organizations and important meetings of major world leaders.	Includes all domestic and regional developments in Europe, including the Soviet Union, Turkey, Cyprus and Malta.	Includes all domestic and regional developments in Africa and the Middle East, including Iraq and Iran and excluding Cyprus, Turkey and Afghanistan.	Includes all domestic and regional developments in Latin America, the Caribbean and Canada.	Includes all domestic and regional developments in Asia and Pacific nations, extending from Afghanistan through all the Pacific Islands, except Hawaii.

U.S. Politics & Social Issues	U.S. Foreign Policy & Defense	U.S. Economy & Environment	Science, Technology & Nature	Culture, Leisure & Life Style	
The Federal Bureau of Investigation says it has captured Silas Bissell, a member of the Weather Underground sought in connection with the bombing of an Air Force Reserve Officer Training Corps building at the Univ. of Washington in Seattle in 1970.... Preliminary rules issued by the Immigration and Naturalization Service will require employers to ascertain the citizenship or immigration status of new workers within 24 hours of their hiring.		A three-judge federal appeals court in Washington, D.C., rules that the president does not have the power to defer for fiscal reasons the spending of money appropriated by Congress.... The nonpartisan Congressional Budget Office says that Pres. Reagan's proposed budget for FY1988 will create a deficit some $27 bil. to $32 bil. larger than the administration claims.	Scientist Peter Hagelstein whose nuclear-powered X-ray laser inspired Pres. Reagan's call for a Strategic Defense Initiative, will return to work at Lawrence Livermore National Laboratory. Revulsion for weapons work prompted the scientist to quit Livermore, to which he now plans to return as a consultant for nonmilitary research.	Sixty-one paintings and sculptures from the private collection of Pablo Picasso are being reluctantly returned to France after Spain decides it cannot keep them, it is reported. The works were lent to Spain by Picasso's widow, Jacqueline, who later told Spanish officials that Spain could keep them.	Jan. 20
The Supreme Court disallows an annexation proposal of an Alabama city because of the potential dilution of the black vote. The court ruled, 6-3, that the proposal would put the city in violation of the 1965 Civil Rights Act.	The Reagan administration informs Congress that it plans to sell 12 F-16 jet fighters to Bahrain and 200 Bradley Fighting Vehicles to Saudi Arabia for $500 mil., according to news reports. It would be the first sale of F-16s to a Persian Gulf Arab state, and the first sale abroad of the controversial Bradley armored personnel carrier.	The House passes, 401-20, a five-year, $91 bil. bill for highway and mass transit programs, despite the threat of a veto because the funding levels exceed Pres. Reagan's budget proposals.... Congress clears a $20 bil. Clean Water Act identical to one Pres. Reagan pocket-vetoed in 1986.... Housing starts surged 13.7% in December 1986, reaching a seasonally adjusted annual rate of 1.8 million units, the Commerce Dept. reports. For all of 1986, housing starts rose 3.7% to 1.807 million units. The consumer price index rose just 1.1% in 1986, the Labor Dept. reports, the lowest annual increase since 1961.		Variety's top-grossing films for the week are: Critical Condition; Platoon; Star Trek IV: The Voyage Home; The Golden Child; and Wanted Dead or Alive.	Jan. 21
The special Senate committee investigating the Iran-Contra arms scandal names Arthur L. Liman III to be its chief counsel.		The Dow Jones Industrial Average jumps a record 51.6 points to close at 2145.67, a new high.... The nation's real gross national product (GNP) grew at a 1.7% annual rate in the fourth quarter of 1986, the Commerce Dept. reports; GNP growth for all of 1986 was 2.5%.			Jan. 22
The Republican National Committee approves New Orleans as the site of the party's Aug. 15-18, 1988, nominating convention. The Democrats had also been favoring the city, but Mayor Sidney Barthelemy (D) clinched the GOP choice by signing a contract giving the Republicans six weeks of unlimited access to the New Orleans Superdome in July and August, effectively barring the city from also hosting the Democratic convention in July.	The Reagan administration solicited aid for the Nicaraguan Contras from at least six countries—including Israel, Singapore, South Korea, Taiwan, Brunei, and Saudi Arabia—in recent years, according to information provided to congressional committees probing the Iran-Contra affair.	Personal spending in December 1986 rose 2%, the largest gain since 1975, the Commerce Dept. reports.... Americans' total personal income rose a nominal 5.2% in 1986, according to the Commerce Dept. Adjusted for inflation, income rose 3% for the year.		Publishers Weekly's fiction hardback best-sellers for the week are: Red Storm Rising, Tom Clancy; It, Stephen King; Whirlwind, James Clavell; Flight of the Intruder, Stephen Coonts; Night of the Fox, Jack Higgins.	Jan. 23
The Supreme Court rules, 5-4, that defendants accused of child abuse had no constitutional right to examine confidential records of state child protective agencies for information helpful to their defense.... The Supreme Court upholds by a 6-3 ruling the use of evidence that was obtained improperly by police through an "honest" mistake.... Some 15,000 to 20,000 demonstrators march through Cumming, Ga., the seat of all-white Forsyth County, to protest racism.	Lawrence Walsh, the independent counsel probing the Iran arms scandal, asks Rep. Lee Hamilton (D, Ind.), who chairs the House committee probing the scandal, not to offer immunity to witnesses in exchange for their testimony.			Hana Mandlikova, a Czechoslovak who has applied for Australian citizenship, upsets top-ranked Martina Navratilova in the women's tennis finals, 7-5, 7-6, to win her second Australian Open.	Jan. 24
A New York Times/CBS News nationwide telephone poll finds that former Sen. Gary Hart (D, Colo.) and Vice Pres. George Bush (R) are the current front-runners for their parties' 1988 presidential nominations.				Stefan Edberg of Sweden wins the Australian Open with a 6-3, 6-4, 3-6, 5-7, 6-3 victory over Australian Pat Cash.... The New York Giants win their first National Football League title since 1956 when they down the Denver Broncos in Super Bowl XXI, 39-20.	Jan. 25
F	G	H	I	J	
Includes elections, federal-state relations, civil rights and liberties, crime, the judiciary, education, health care, poverty, urban affairs and population.	Includes formation and debate of U.S. foreign and defense policies, veterans' affairs and defense spending. (Relations with specific foreign countries are usually found under the region concerned.)	Includes business, labor, agriculture, taxation, transportation, consumer affairs, monetary and fiscal policy, natural resources, and pollution.	Includes worldwide scientific, medical and technological developments, natural phenomena, U.S. weather, natural disasters, and accidents.	Includes the arts, religion, scholarship, communications media, sports, entertainments, fashions, fads and social life.	

	World Affairs	Europe	Africa & the Middle East	The Americas	Asia & the Pacific
Jan. 26			The Org. of the Islamic Conf. holds its fifth summit in Kuwait. The meeting is held despite being boycotted and threatened by Iran, which objects to Kuwait's support for Iraq in the Persian Gulf war.	After talks on wage increases broke down, Argentina's General Confederation of Labor call the eighth nationwide strike to protest the economic policies of Pres. Raul Alfonsin's government.	
Jan. 27	The United States and Mongolia establish diplomatic relations. The move climaxes 15 years of sporadic talks on creating ties.		Fears mount that Anglican Church envoy Terry Waite, who was in Beirut trying to win the release of Western hostages, has himself become a hostage. Waite went underground to meet with the kidnappers and has not been seen since Jan. 20.		Japan announces that it will extend its voluntary curbs on auto exports to the United States for a seventh year, through Mar. 31, 1988. Exports will be held to 2.3 million units for the year. . . . Bangladesh's Pres. Hossein Mohammed Ershad declares a state of emergency following more than two weeks of civil unrest during which at least 10 people have been killed and 1,500 arrested.
Jan. 28		Britain's current account balance fell into deficit in 1986 for the first time since 1979, according to figures released today. Britain's surplus of trade in oil products shrank to £4.14 bil., owing to lower oil prices.			Deposed Pres. Ferdinand Marcos is foiled in a plan to return from exile in the United States to the Philippines, where dissident soldiers attempted a coup January 27.
Jan. 29		The State Dept. lifts an advisory against tourist travel to Kiev, in the Soviet Ukraine, in place since the Chernobyl nuclear power plant accident of 1986; Kiev is about 60 miles from the plant.	Iranian Revolutionary Guards divisions have reportedly captured about 60 square miles of Iraqi territory east of Basra and the Shatt al-Arab waterway, and have overran Basra's outer defensive lines to come within six miles of the key southern Iraqi city.	A third worker is arrested on charges of murder and arson in the New Year's Eve fire that killed 96 people at San Juan's luxurious Dupont Plaza Hotel. The suspect, Jose Francisco Rivera Lopez, 40, a bartender, is charged in San Juan Superior Court with 96 counts of murder, arson, conspiracy and destruction of property.	China's Premier Zhao Ziyang says that the current campaign against "bourgeois liberalization" will be limited and will not interfere with ongoing economic reforms and the opening of China to foreign investment. He spoke in Beijing's Great Hall of the People before senior leaders of the military and the Chinese Communist Party.
Jan. 30			South Africa's Pres. Pieter W. Botha announces that elections for the white house of parliament will be held on May 6. White progressives, prepare to use the vote to challenge the government on the slow pace of apartheid reform.		
Jan. 31					

A	B	C	D	E
Includes developments that affect more than one world region, international organizations and important meetings of major world leaders.	Includes all domestic and regional developments in Europe, including the Soviet Union, Turkey, Cyprus and Malta.	Includes all domestic and regional developments in Africa and the Middle East, including Iraq and Iran and excluding Cyprus, Turkey and Afghanistan.	Includes all domestic and regional developments in Latin America, the Caribbean and Canada.	Includes all domestic and regional developments in Asia and Pacific nations, extending from Afghanistan through all the Pacific Islands, except Hawaii.

U.S. Politics & Social Issues	U.S. Foreign Policy & Defense	U.S. Economy & Environment	Science, Technology & Nature	Culture, Leisure & Life Style	
	Pres. Reagan is interviewed for about 75 minutes by the special commission that he appointed to study the operations of the National Security Council. The White House announced after the meeting that Reagan answered all the commission's questions about his knowledge of U.S. arms sales to Iran.	The Amalgamated Transit Union reaches agreement on a labor contract with the prospective new owners of Greyhound Lines Inc., the *Wall Street Journal* reports.			**Jan. 26**
Pres. Reagan delivered his sixth State of the Union message to Congress and a national television audience.... House Speaker James C. Wright Jr. (D, Tex.) and Senate Majority Leader Robert C. Byrd (D, W.Va.), broadcast a Democratic response to Pres. Reagan's address. Wright speaks chiefly about trade and domestic policy, and Byrd about foreign policy issues.		Wage and salary increases averaged 3.5% in 1986, a drop from 4.4% in 1985, the Labor Dept. reports.... The federal budget deficit for the first three months of FY1987 was $64.34 bil., the Treasury Dept. announces, down 14% from the $75.13 bil. deficit reported in the same quarter a year earlier.		Otto Nathan, 93, German-born Princeton Univ. economist, dies of heart failure in New York City. An executor and co-trustee of the estate of physicist Albert Einstein, in 1957 Nathan won acquittal on a contempt of Congress charge stemming from a confrontation with the House Un-American Affairs Committee.... Seven players are inducted into the Pro Football Hall of Fame: Don Maynard, Larry Csonka, John Henry Johnson, Len Dawson, Joe Greene, Jim Langer, and Gene Upshaw.	**Jan. 27**
	In reaction to the January 24 kidnapping of three Americans, the State Dept. bars U.S. citizens from traveling to Lebanon. The estimated 1,500 Americans still in Lebanon are given 30 days to leave.... African National Congress (ANC) Pres. Oliver Tambo meets with Sec. of State George P. Shultz in Washington, D.C., in the first meeting between a secretary of state and a leader of the ANC, the main anti-apartheid group in South Africa.	W.R. Grace & Co. is indicted by a federal grand jury in Boston on charges of making false statements to the Environmental Protection Agency during a 1982 investigation.... Faced with lawsuits, the Energy Dept. announces that it will postpone until 2003 the opening of its first permanent repository for highly radioactive nuclear waste. The dump was scheduled to open in 1998.	Memorial services for the lost *Challenger* crew are held at Arlington National Cemetery and at other sites around the country.	*Billboard*'s best-selling albums for the week are: *Slippery When Wet*, Bon Jovi; *Different Light*, Bangles; *Third Stage*, Boston; *Night Songs*, Cinderella; and *The Way It Is*, Bruce Hornsby & the Range.	**Jan. 28**
	The Senate Intelligence Committee makes public a 65-page report based on its investigation in 1986 of U.S. shipments of arms to Iran and the diversion of funds from the arms sales to the Nicaraguan rebels known as Contras.	The Reagan administration rescinds plans to impose 200% duties on agricultural products from European Community (EC) nations after winning trade concessions from the EC.		American author J.D. Salinger, best known for his novel *The Catcher in the Rye*, wins a major round in a court fight to block publication of an unauthorized biography by Ian Hamilton. Reversing a lower court ruling, a two-judge panel rules that *J.D. Salinger: A Writing Life* draws excessively on Salinger's unpublished letters, to which Hamilton had gained access at various university libraries.	**Jan. 29**
According to the *New York Times*, at least seven criminal investigations into the Nicaraguan Contras and their backers are under way, this in addition to inquiries by two congressional committees.		Prices received by farmers for their raw agricultural products fell 1.7% in January, the Agriculture Dept. says.... The deficit on merchandise trade plunged 44% in December 1986, to $10.66 bil., the Commerce Dept. reports.	Energy Sec. John S. Herrington says Pres. Reagan has formally approved construction of the world's largest atomic particle accelerator. A request for funding of the mammoth project, projected to cost $6 bil. by the time it is completed in 1996, will be submitted to Congress shortly.	In horse racing's Eclipse Award, winners are named: Snow Chief, in the three-year-old colt category; Turkoman, in the older male class; trainer, D. Wayne Lukas; and jockey, Pat Day. Lady's Secret is named Horse of the Year.	**Jan. 30**
	U.S. and Soviet negotiators at the Geneva disarmament talks agree to set up a special working group on the 1972 anti-ballistic missile (ABM) treaty, to review the testing and development of ABM systems including the U.S. Strategic Defense Initiative.	The United Steelworkers of America ratifies a new four-year contract with USX Corp., ending a 184-day work stoppage that idled 25 USX facilities in nine states.		At the 44th annual Golden Globe the award for best dramatic film goes to *Platoon*; best motion picture comedy or musical, *Hannah and Her Sisters*; best foreign film, *The Assault*. The award for best dramatic series on television goes to "L.A. Law," and the award for best television musical or comedy series goes to "The Golden Girls."	**Jan. 31**

F	G	H	I	J
Includes elections, federal-state relations, civil rights and liberties, crime, the judiciary, education, health care, poverty, urban affairs and population.	*Includes formation and debate of U.S. foreign and defense policies, veterans' affairs and defense spending. (Relations with specific foreign countries are usually found under the region concerned.)*	*Includes business, labor, agriculture, taxation, transportation, consumer affairs, monetary and fiscal policy, natural resources, and pollution.*	*Includes worldwide scientific, medical and technological developments, natural phenomena, U.S. weather, natural disasters, and accidents.*	*Includes the arts, religion, scholarship, communications media, sports, entertainments, fashions, fads and social life.*

	World Affairs	Europe	Africa & the Middle East	The Americas	Asia & the Pacific
Feb. 1		Police raid the Scottish offices of the British Broadcasting Corp. and seize material relating to a planned television series including a banned program about a secret British spy satellite. P.M. Margaret Thatcher insists that the decision to undertake the raids was made by police officials and not by her government.		Brazil's new 559-member National Congress convenes for the first time. The body, which was elected in November 1986, will serve as a constituent assembly to write a new constitution for Brazil.... A 150-mile fishing protection zone set by the British government comes into force around the Falkland (Malvinas) Islands. Argentina claims a 200-mile territorial limit, extending from its mainland, that includes an area that penetrates 50 miles into a segment of the zone claimed by Britain.	
Feb. 2			The International Monetary Fund announces its approval of an $825 mil. loan for Nigeria. The decision is a key element in a complex Nigerian effort to reschedule its $20 bil. foreign debt.	The value of the Canadian dollar reaches a two-year high against the U.S. dollar. The action occurred roughly one year after the Canadian dollar had slumped to a historic low against its U.S. counterpart.	Filipino voters overwhelmingly approve a draft constitution that would provide the legal underpinnings for Pres. Corazon Aquino's fledgling government. The massive majority won by the charter is seen by Aquino enemies and supporters alike as a crucial vote of confidence in her presidency.
Feb. 3		Albania's official ATA news agency reports that only one voter out of more than 1.8 million cast an invalid ballot in the February 1 election. The rest supported the single-slate tickets of the Communist Party. Turnout is said to be 100%. ... For the first time, trade with the European Community (EC) in 1986 accounted for half of Britain's overall trade, the *Times* of London reports.	The Arabian American Oil Co. reports that it has agreed to long-term contracts to buy oil from Saudi Arabia at $18 a barrel. The deal indicates that Saudi Arabia and the other members of the Org. of Petroleum Exporting Countries have succeeded in stabilizing oil prices at $18 a barrel.		
Feb. 4		A group of American foreign policy experts, including some prominent former U.S. public officials, meets with Soviet leader Mikhail S. Gorbachev in Moscow. The visit is sponsored by the private, New York City-based Council on Foreign Relations. ... Spanish negotiators reject a U.S. proposal on troop reductions at U.S. bases in Spain. After two days of talks in Madrid, Sec. Gen. of Foreign Affairs Maximo Cajal says the latest U.S. proposal is welcome but does not include "indispensable components" sought by Spain.	In Teheran, Gerald F. Seib, Middle East correspondent for the *Wall Street Journal*, is released from jail, turned over to the Swiss Embassy, which handles U.S. interests in Iran, and ordered expelled. Seib was seized by elements of the Iranian government on January 31.	A former captain in the Chilean secret police confesses to involvement in the 1976 murder of Orlando Letelier, a former Chilean ambassador to Washington. ... Colombian police and military personnel capture Carlos Enrique Lehder Rivas, 37, the billionaire reputed leader of the world's largest drug trafficking ring, and immediately extradite him to the United States. Lehder is considered one of the world's most violent and successful drug traffickers.	
Feb. 5		Italian judicial officials reveal that antiterrorist prosecutor Domenico Sica has completed a year-long probe into the December 1985 Rome airport massacre. The investigation finds that the attack was planned in Syria and carried out by the renegade Palestinian terrorist group led by Abu Nidal (Sabry al-Banna).		Speaking at the Univ. of Toronto, Defense Min. Perrin Beatty announces that women in the Canadian Forces will be eligible for combat duty.... Brazil's government virtually ends a 12-month-old price freeze that was a key element of the Cruzado Plan, an economic package that has failed to reduce inflation as intended.	

A	B	C	D	E
Includes developments that affect more than one world region, international organizations and important meetings of major world leaders.	Includes all domestic and regional developments in Europe, including the Soviet Union, Turkey, Cyprus and Malta.	Includes all domestic and regional developments in Africa and the Middle East, including Iraq and Iran and excluding Cyprus, Turkey and Afghanistan.	Includes all domestic and regional developments in Latin America, the Caribbean and Canada.	Includes all domestic and regional developments in Asia and Pacific nations, extending from Afghanistan through all the Pacific Islands, except Hawaii.

U.S. Politics & Social Issues	U.S. Foreign Policy & Defense	U.S. Economy & Environment	Science, Technology & Nature	Culture, Leisure & Life Style	
	The Central Intelligence Agency used an abandoned air base in southern Zaire to secretly funnel military aid to antigovernment rebels in Angola in 1986, the *New York Times* reports. The story appears to confirm charges made by Angolan and other African leaders.	A five-month work stoppage by 12,200 members of the United Auto Workers at 13 Deere & Co. plants in Illinois and Iowa ends when the union members overwhelmingly approve terms of a new contract.		The American Football Conf. wins the National Football League's Pro Bowl all-star game in Honolulu, 10-7. National Football Conf. lineman Reggie White of Philadelphia is named the game's most valuable player.... In auto racing, the team of Al Holbert, Al Unser Jr., Derek Bell, and Chip Robinson wins the 24 Hours of Daytona (Fla.) endurance race.	Feb. 1
The Children's Defense Fund, a nonprofit child advocacy group based in Washington, D.C., releases a report that categorizes the U.S. infant mortality rate as one of the highest in the industrialized world.	The United States says it will not renew an agreement that gives New Zealand priority access to U.S.-made military equipment. The move is in retaliation for New Zealand's ban on port visits by U.S. nuclear-powered ships or those that carry nuclear arms.... The White House announces the resignation of William J. Casey as director of the Central Intelligence Agency and Pres. Reagan's nomination of career intelligence analyst Robert M. Gates to succeed him.	In a setback to American Telephone & Telegraph Co. (AT&T), the Justice Dept. recommends that the regional telephone companies created in the 1984 breakup of AT&T be permitted to compete in long distance, computer services, and other businesses.... Productivity among the nation's nonfarm businesses dropped at a 1.7% annual rate in the fourth quarter of 1986, the Labor Dept. reports. Productivity for all of 1986 grew only 0.7%.		The World Cup ski racing season ends, and Pirmin Zurbriggen of Switzerland wins the giant slalom, super giant slalom, downhill, and overall titles.... Alistair (Stuart) MacLean, 64, British author who wrote novels of intrigue and wartime adventure, dies of heart failure in West Munich. His novels, which include *The Guns of Navarone*, *Where Eagles Dare*, and *Ice Station Zebra*, sold millions of copies and were often made into movies.	Feb. 2
Federal health officials concerned about halting the spread of acquired immune deficiency syndrome in the United States say that they are considering expanding use of the acquired immune deficiency syndrome blood test to all patients admitted to hospitals, women seeking prenatal care, and couples applying for marriage licenses.	The United States conducts its first underground nuclear test of the year, at a Nevada site about 86 miles northwest of Las Vegas. The blast apparently takes place ahead of schedule, thwarting the efforts of peace activists and congressional Democrats to block the test.	The government's index of leading economic indicators rose 2.1% in December 1986, the Commerce Dept reports. Much of the increase is attributed to one-time influences, notably the new tax law that took effect January 1.			Feb. 3
By voice vote the House accepts the Senate's version of a bill to channel $50 mil. in federal disaster relief funds to aid the homeless. The bill passed the House January 27 by a vote of 296 to 79 and had passed the Senate with a few amendments January 29 by a vote of 77 to 6.		Congress enacts the Clean Water Act in the seventh override of a Reagan veto. In announcing the Jan. 30 veto, his 60th, Reagan called the bill a "budget-buster...loaded with waste and larded with pork."	Carl Ransom Rogers, 85, extremely influential American psychologist known for developing the client-centered approach to psychotherapy, dies in La Jolla, Calif., of a heart attack after surgery for a broken hip. A founder of humanistic psychology, Rogers was instrumental in the encounter group movement that emerged in the 1960s; his 1961 book *On Becoming a Person* became a bible for the human potential movement.	*Stars & Stripes*, the U.S. yacht skippered by Dennis Conner, wins the America's Cup yachting trophy by completing a four-race sweep of the Australian yacht *Kookaburra III*. ... Liberace (born Wladziu Valentino Liberace), 67, American pianist and entertainer whose flamboyant showmanship, lavish costumes, and giant candelabra helped win him fame, fortune, and a legion of fans during the 1950s, dies in Palm Springs, Calif.	Feb. 4
				Five former players elected to the Basketball Hall of Fame are: Walt Frazier, Pete Maravich, Rick Barry, Bobby Wanzer, and Bob Houbregs.	Feb. 5

F	G	H	I	J
Includes elections, federal-state relations, civil rights and liberties, crime, the judiciary, education, health care, poverty, urban affairs and population.	*Includes formation and debate of U.S. foreign and defense policies, veterans' affairs and defense spending. (Relations with specific foreign countries are usually found under the region concerned.)*	*Includes business, labor, agriculture, taxation, transportation, consumer affairs, monetary and fiscal policy, natural resources, and pollution.*	*Includes worldwide scientific, medical and technological developments, natural phenomena, U.S. weather, natural disasters, and accidents.*	*Includes the arts, religion, scholarship, communications media, sports, entertainments, fashions, fads and social life.*

	World Affairs	Europe	Africa & the Middle East	The Americas	Asia & the Pacific
Feb. 6		The *New York Times* reports it has learned that Soviet Communist Party leaders were briefed on acquired immune deficiency syndrome February 3 by a leading Soviet virologist, Dr. Viktor M. Zhdanov. Zhdanov disclosed the first Soviet cases of acquired immune deficiency syndrome in December 1985.			
Feb. 7			Rumors regarding the fate of Anglican Church envoy Terry Waite continued to circulate over the last week. He disappeared in Beirut January 20 while trying to contact Islamic Jihad and negotiate the release of Western hostages.	Haiti marks the first anniversary of the ouster of Pres. Jean-Claude Duvalier. In a speech to the nation, Lt. Gen. Henri Namphy, the head of the provisional government, appeals to the populace for unity and asks Haitians to support efforts to bring about full democracy.	
Feb. 8			With coordinated air, tank, artillery, and infantry attacks, Iraqi forces are reported to have won back about a third of the territory captured by Iranian troops. Iraq's Pres. Saddam Hussein February 1 claimed his troops had "broken the back" of Iran's offensive.		In the Philippines, a cease-fire between the government and communist rebels ends after the communists rule out an extension of the 60-day truce. Government officials had hoped that the truce and accompanying peace talks in Manila could open the way toward a settlement of the 18-year insurgency by the New People's Army.
Feb. 9		In the West German state of Hesse, the 14-month-old governing coalition of the Social Democratic Party and the Greens collapses with the dismissal of the Greens' only cabinet member, Hesse Environment Min. Joschka Fischer, over the question of nuclear power.	Kidnappers in Beirut who threatened to kill their three American and one Indian hostages by midnight unless their demands were met, relent as the deadline passes and say it will be extended "until further notice." The development comes as the United States attempts to downplay speculation that it is preparing to launch a military attack on Lebanon.	The London-based human rights organization Amnesty International accuses Peruvian authorities of "gross human rights violations" in the crushing of simultaneous rebellions at three prisons in 1986. Some 250 inmates, most of them members of the Sendero Luminoso (Shining Path) Maoist guerrilla group, died when prison guards and the military stormed the prisons.	
Feb. 10		The national death rate among Soviet citizens of working age has decreased by 15% since 1984, according to government mortality figures, the first made public since the 1970s.... The Soviet foreign ministry announces that 140 dissidents have been released from prisons and labor camps through legislative pardons in what is believed the largest release of political prisoners in the USSR since 1956, when the regime of Nikita S. Khrushchev freed thousands of people imprisoned under the regime of Joseph Stalin.	Iran's supreme leader, Ayatollah Ruhollah Khomeini, makes his first public speech in nearly three months, delivered on the eve of the eighth anniversary of the Islamic revolution. His absence had led to rumors that the 86-year-old leader was in poor health.		

A	B	C	D	E
Includes developments that affect more than one world region, international organizations and important meetings of major world leaders.	*Includes all domestic and regional developments in Europe, including the Soviet Union, Turkey, Cyprus and Malta.*	*Includes all domestic and regional developments in Africa and the Middle East, including Iraq and Iran and excluding Cyprus, Turkey and Afghanistan.*	*Includes all domestic and regional developments in Latin America, the Caribbean and Canada.*	*Includes all domestic and regional developments in Asia and Pacific nations, extending from Afghanistan through all the Pacific Islands, except Hawaii.*

U.S. Politics & Social Issues	U.S. Foreign Policy & Defense	U.S. Economy & Environment	Science, Technology & Nature	Culture, Leisure & Life Style	
The U.S. Court of Appeals for the District of Columbia orders the Labor Dept. to set field sanitation standards for farm workers that will guarantee the availability of drinking water and toilet facilities on the job.... Calling it a "doozy" of a mistake, Senate Finance Committee Chairman Lloyd Bentsen (D, Tex.), announces that he is disbanding a $10,000 breakfast club for lobbyists and will return all their contributions.		Outstanding consumer credit grew a seasonally adjusted $105 mil. in December 1986, the Federal Reserve Board reports.... The nation's unemployment rate was unchanged in January at 6.6%, the Labor Dept. reports.	A *Journal of the American Medical Association* study finds that it is relatively easy for husbands or wives to transmit acquired immune deficiency syndrome to their spouses through sexual intercourse, but it appears unlikely that the disease can be transmitted through casual family contact.... Two Soviet cosmonauts are launched toward the *Mir* space station, in orbit since February 1986 and last manned in 1986 by two cosmonauts who spent 125 days in space and taxied between *Mir* and another Soviet space station, Salyut-7.	*The Assault*, a Dutch film about a middle-aged man haunted by memories of the night his family was killed during the Nazi occupation of the Netherlands, is released in New York. Directed and produced by Fons Rademakers, with a screenplay by Gerard Soeteman based on the novel by Harry Mulisch, it wins the Academy Award for best foreign film.	Feb. 6
	Contradicting White House assertions that the Iran arms deal was part of an effort to reach moderate elements in that country, an aide to Vice Pres. George Bush asserts that an Israeli official told him in July 1986 that "we are dealing with the most radical elements" in Iran. Donald Gregg says that the United States turned to anti-Western radicals because contacts with moderates had failed.			Jill Trenary comes from behind to upset defending champion Debi Thomas and win the women's title at the U.S. Figure Skating Championships. Thomas is second and Caryn Kadavy third.	Feb. 7
			Two Soviet cosmonauts successfully dock their Soyuz spacecraft with the orbiting space station, *Mir*, Tass reported. The cosmonauts were launched February 6.	The Western Conf. wins the National Basketball Assoc. All-Star Game 154-149 over the Eastern Conf. Tom Chambers of the Seattle Supersonics is named most valuable player.	Feb. 8
	The *Washington Post* reports that the inspector general's office of the Central Intelligence Agency is examining the agency's 1985-86 covert operations in support of the Nicaraguan Contras to determine if they contravened a congressional ban on military assistance.... Former national security adviser Robert C. McFarlane is hospitalized after taking an overdose of the tranquilizer Valium. McFarlane was scheduled to meet today with the special commission appointed by Pres. Reagan to study the workings of the National Security Council.			Jonathan Schell, one of the *New Yorker* magazine's best-known staff writers, resigns from the magazine in the wake of longtime editor William Shawn's stormy replacement. Schell, a 20-year veteran of the magazine, is the author of *The Fate of the Earth*, a controversial book about nuclear war originally serialized in the *New Yorker*.	Feb. 9
Twelve white teenagers are indicted on charges ranging from second-degree murder to rioting in connection with a Dec. 20, 1986, racial attack in the Howard Beach section of New York City that left a 23-year-old black man, Michael Griffith, dead.... The Democratic Party announces that it has chosen Atlanta as the site of its July 18-21, 1988, presidential nominating convention. Party chairman Paul G. Kirk Jr. reportedly pushed hard for the choice, and he tells reporters that it signals the party's intent "to be competitive in the southern part of this country."		Housing starts declined 0.1% in January, the Commerce Dept. reports.		Stanley Kunitz is named winner of the Bollingen Prize in poetry of the Yale Univ. Library, awarded biennially since 1965 to one or more living American poets.	Feb. 10

F	G	H	I	J
Includes elections, federal-state relations, civil rights and liberties, crime, the judiciary, education, health care, poverty, urban affairs and population.	*Includes formation and debate of U.S. foreign and defense policies, veterans' affairs and defense spending. (Relations with specific foreign countries are usually found under the region concerned.)*	*Includes business, labor, agriculture, taxation, transportation, consumer affairs, monetary and fiscal policy, natural resources, and pollution.*	*Includes worldwide scientific, medical and technological developments, natural phenomena, U.S. weather, natural disasters, and accidents.*	*Includes the arts, religion, scholarship, communications media, sports, entertainments, fashions, fads and social life.*

	World Affairs	Europe	Africa & the Middle East	The Americas	Asia & the Pacific
Feb. 11					In the Philippines, Pres. Corazon Aquino declares the new national constitution to be in "full force" after its landslide ratification in a referendum nine days before.
Feb. 12		West German gross national product showed no real growth in the fourth quarter of 1986, according to Bundesbank figures. The flat growth is attributed to a worsening balance of trade owing to the strong German mark.		The government of Chile says 390 political exiles will be allowed to return to Chile, among them two prominent members of the government of the late Pres. Salvador Allende Gossens, Jorge Godoy, the former labor minister, and Carlos Jorquera, who was Allende's press secretary.	
Feb. 13		The Org. for Economic Cooperation and Development (OECD) says that inflation in OECD member states in 1986 was 2.8%, the lowest level since 1964.			
Feb. 14	The Soviet Union hosts an international forum on peace at the Grand Kremlin Palace in Moscow. The forum, the theme of which is "A Nonnuclear World for the Survival of Mankind," is attended by over 700 artists, scientists, business executives, and public officials from 80 nations.				
Feb. 15				Students at the National Autonomous Univ. of Mexico vote to end an 18-day strike after the authorities bow to demands to set aside a package of academic reforms.	
Feb. 16		Spanish students demanding improved and more widely available education, won some concessions from the socialist government before student strikes were suspended today. Strikes and demonstrations by the students sparked several violent confrontations with police in January and February.	John Demjanjuk, an American auto worker accused of being the sadistic Nazi death camp guard known as "Ivan the Terrible," goes on trial in Jerusalem. It is only the second Nazi war crimes trial to be held in Israel, the first having been that of Adolf Eichmann, who was convicted in 1961 and hanged the following year. The trial of Demjanjuk, who could also face the death penalty if found guilty, is expected to last three to six months.	After a long and bitter leadership battle, Adolfo Calero Portocarrero resigns under pressure as a director of the United Nicaraguan Opposition (UNO), a U.S.-backed Contra alliance. Calero will remain as leader of the Nicaraguan Democratic Force (FDN), the largest of the Contra groups within UNO.	

A	B	C	D	E
Includes developments that affect more than one world region, international organizations and important meetings of major world leaders.	Includes all domestic and regional developments in Europe, including the Soviet Union, Turkey, Cyprus and Malta.	Includes all domestic and regional developments in Africa and the Middle East, including Iraq and Iran and excluding Cyprus, Turkey and Afghanistan.	Includes all domestic and regional developments in Latin America, the Caribbean and Canada.	Includes all domestic and regional developments in Asia and Pacific nations, extending from Afghanistan through all the Pacific Islands, except Hawaii.

U.S. Politics & Social Issues	U.S. Foreign Policy & Defense	U.S. Economy & Environment	Science, Technology & Nature	Culture, Leisure & Life Style	
Lawrence Walsh, the special prosecutor appointed to look into the Iran-Contra affair, assumes control of at least three Justice Dept. inquiries into the private Contra supply network, federal officials report.	An Air Force Titan 3-B rocket is successfully launched from Vandenberg Air Force Base in California. The nature of the payload is not disclosed, although it is assumed to be some sort of intelligence satellite.... Pres. Reagan has postponed indefinitely a decision on whether to reinterpret the 1972 antiballistic missile treaty with regard to the Strategic Defense Initiative, according to the *Washington Post*.				Feb. 11
Pres. Reagan signs a bill providing emergency aid for the homeless. The bill also contains a provision blocking pay increases recommended by Pres. Reagan for Congress and top federal officials, but the raises will stand because the House voted after the expiration of a 30-day statutory limit for passing a joint resolution of disapproval.... A federal jury in Mobile, Ala. awards $7 mil. in damages against the United Klans of America in the 1981 lynching of a black man, Michael Donald. Included in the judgment are six past and present members of the Ku Klux Klan, including Henry Francis Hays, who is on death row, and James Llewellyn Knowles, who is serving a life sentence.		A three-judge appeals court panel in Texas affirm $8.53 bil. of a $10.53 bil. judgment against Texaco Inc. A Texas jury in 1985 ruled in favor of Pennzoil Co. in its suit charging that Texaco had interfered with Pennzoil's tentative agreement to buy Getty Oil Co.	The United States and its space allies reaffirm in a statement "their intention to cooperate on the basis of genuine partnership" in the venture to operate a space station in the mid-1990s.	Tass, the official Soviet news agency, announces that *Dr. Zhivago*, the internationally acclaimed novel by Soviet author Boris Pasternak, will be published in the Soviet Union in 1988.	Feb. 12
		The industrial production index increased 0.4% in January, according to the Federal Reserve Board.... The government's producer price index rose 0.6% in January, the Labor Dept. reports.	The number of countries reporting cases of acquired immune deficiency syndrome to the UN World Health Org. more than doubled in the past year, to a total of 91. Dr. Jonathan Mann, the American director of the agency's acquired immune deficiency syndrome program in Geneva, says the increase in the number of countries reporting acquired immune deficiency syndrome reflects "a growing awareness in the world that this is a disease which has to be reported and which cannot be swept under the carpet."	In Quebec City, Canada, the Soviet national hockey team beats a National Hockey League (NHL) all-star team, 5-3, to split a two-game "Rendez-Vouz '87" contest. The NHL team won the opening game February 11 by a score of 4-3.	Feb. 13
					Feb. 14
After almost three months of internal White House debate, Pres. Reagan announces that he will propose legislation to expand the Medicare system to help cover the costs of catastrophic illness.				Chi Chi Rodriguez wins the Professional Golfers Assoc. Seniors tournament in Palm Beach Gardens, Fla. Rodriguez finishes at 282, six under par, for 72 holes.... Bill Elliott wins the Daytona 500 stock car race.	Feb. 15
			Researchers announce the completion of a crude map of markers along the entire sequence of genetic material of the common intestinal bacterium *Escherichia coli*. The achievement is the first such genetic mapping of a whole organism. ... Researchers have reportedly developed a compound that loses all resistance to electricity when cooled to the temperature of liquid nitrogen. It is one of several recent breakthroughs in what is turning into an international scientific race to achieve superconductivity, zero resistance to electricity, at ever higher temperatures.		Feb. 16

F	G	H	I	J
Includes elections, federal-state relations, civil rights and liberties, crime, the judiciary, education, health care, poverty, urban affairs and population.	*Includes formation and debate of U.S. foreign and defense policies, veterans' affairs and defense spending. (Relations with specific foreign countries are usually found under the region concerned.)*	*Includes business, labor, agriculture, taxation, transportation, consumer affairs, monetary and fiscal policy, natural resources, and pollution.*	*Includes worldwide scientific, medical and technological developments, natural phenomena, U.S. weather, natural disasters, and accidents.*	*Includes the arts, religion, scholarship, communications media, sports, entertainments, fashions, fads and social life.*

	World Affairs	Europe	Africa & the Middle East	The Americas	Asia & the Pacific
Feb. 17		General elections in Ireland result in defeat for P.M. Garrett Fitz-Gerald. But opposition party leader Charles Haughey, who will succeed FitzGerald, falls short of winning an absolute parliamentary majority for his Fianna Fail party.		Ecuador fails to make its January interest payment due on the national debt, the government confirms. According to Economic Planning Min. Oswaldo Davila, the failure to make the January payment was "not due to any premeditated strategy but to a real impossibility of meeting the obligations." He cites economic problems resulting from the drop in oil prices; oil accounts for some 70% of Ecuador's export earnings.	In Vietnam, sweeping changes among top government personnel are announced by Radio Hanoi. The reshuffle follows an even more drastic overhaul of the country's Communist Party leadership in December 1986. The two shake-ups both favor younger officials considered to be technocrats and economic reformers.
Feb. 18				Some 4,000 Peruvian police stage unprecedented raids on five university campuses in search of leftist guerrillas. Universities in Peru are traditionally autonomous and off-limits to police, and the raids are authorized under a yearlong state of emergency.	
Feb. 19			Fighting erupts February 15 between Shiite Amal militiamen and a Druse-led leftist alliance for the control of Moslem west Beirut. It quickly develops into the fiercest clashes seen in the Lebanese capital in four years; by this day the intensity of the violence lessens somewhat as a shaky Syrian-backed truce goes into effect.		India and Pakistan complete the withdrawal of 150,000 troops from their common border in the first of a series of planned pullbacks intended to lessen military tensions between the two nations.
Feb. 20	The United States and Great Britain veto a UN Security Council resolution that would have imposed mandatory economic sanctions against South Africa similar to those enacted by the United States in 1986. West Germany also votes against the measure, while France and Japan abstain.	The Soviet Union frees jailed Jewish dissident Iosif Z. Begun whose plight had gained international attention and embarrassed Soviet officials before and during the Moscow peace conference currently under way.	The executions of nine men were shown on Libyan television according to the British Broadcasting Corp.'s overseas monitoring service. A Libyan official said most of the men had been convicted of membership in a group called al-Jihad, which was "hostile to the people's authority" and had plotted assassinations of Soviet experts.	The government announces a series of new regulations to stem the flow into Canada of immigrants claiming refugee status. Some 18,282 people claimed refugee status in Canada in 1986, an increase of 118% over 1985.... A Salvadoran national, Frank Varelli, testifies before the House Judiciary subcommittee that he was hired by the Federal Bureau of Investigation (FBI) to investigate Committee in Solidarity with the People of El Salvador (CISPES) branches nationwide, and claims that FBI agents told him of their break-in at a CISPES office in Dallas.	The Bank of Japan announces that its basic interest rate will be reduced half a point, to 2.5%, an all-time low. It is the fifth time since January 1986 that the central bank has lowered the interest rate.... Industrial growth in China dropped to a rate of 9% during calendar year 1986, the state statistical bureau reports. The bureau says average annual income for China's 800 million rural inhabitants reached $115 in 1986, up from $107 the year before.
Feb. 21				Nicaragua's Pres. Daniel Ortega Saavedra expresses his government's willingness to consider a new regional peace plan proposed in January by Costa Rica's Pres. Oscar Arias Sanchez. Under the plan, democratic nations in Europe and Latin America would press the Nicaraguan government to hold new elections and agree to a cease-fire and amnesty for the Contras.	

A	B	C	D	E
Includes developments that affect more than one world region, international organizations and important meetings of major world leaders.	Includes all domestic and regional developments in Europe, including the Soviet Union, Turkey, Cyprus and Malta.	Includes all domestic and regional developments in Africa and the Middle East, including Iraq and Iran and excluding Cyprus, Turkey and Afghanistan.	Includes all domestic and regional developments in Latin America, the Caribbean and Canada.	Includes all domestic and regional developments in Asia and Pacific nations, extending from Afghanistan through all the Pacific Islands, except Hawaii.

U.S. Politics & Social Issues	U.S. Foreign Policy & Defense	U.S. Economy & Environment	Science, Technology & Nature	Culture, Leisure & Life Style	
Sixteen associates of political extremist Lyndon H. LaRouche Jr. are indicted by a Virginia grand jury on charges of securities fraud and selling securities as unregistered agents. The indictments allege that the accused and five LaRouche-affiliated organizations cheated thousands of individuals out of as much as $30 mil. through fraudulent fund-raising.		The building and construction trades department of the AFL-CIO signs an agreement with the National Constructors Assoc. committing the unions to flexible work rules and a no-strike policy.		Miss Texas, Michelle Renee Royer, wins the 1987 Miss USA crown. Just hours before the broadcast, pageant officials agreed to clothe contestants in fake furs to keep host Bob Barker, an animal rights activist, from pulling out of the show.	Feb. 17
Lane Kirkland, president of the American Federation of Labor and Congress of Industrial Orgs. announces that labor's endorsement for the presidential nomination is available to candidates of both major parties. . . . Republican and Democratic Party officials announce the creation of a bipartisan commission to sponsor presidential debates in the 1988 election campaign.	Robert M. Gates, acting director of the Central Intelligence Agency, completes two days of questioning by the Senate Select Committee on Intelligence about the agency's activities in the Iran arms deal and secret diversion of funds to the Nicaraguan Contras. . . . In the wake of revelations about the diversion of funds to the Nicaraguan Contras from the sale of U.S. arms to Iran, the Senate Foreign Relations Committee votes, 11-9, to halt aid to the Contras.			*Variety*'s top-grossing films for the week are: *Platoon*; *Outrageous Fortune*; *Black Widow*; *Mannequin*; and *Over the Top*. . . . *Billboard*'s best-selling albums for the week are: *Slippery When Wet*, Bon Jovi; *Licensed to Ill*, Beastie Boys; *Night Songs*, Cinderella; *The Way It Is*, Bruce Hornsby & the Range; and *Different Light*, Bangles.	Feb. 18
The Reagan administration announces specifics of a sweeping drug-detecting program that would require more than a million federal workers to submit urine samples under strict controls to prevent cheating. The guidelines are being issued to carry out an executive order signed by Pres. Reagan in 1986.	Pres. Reagan lifts the remaining economic sanctions against Poland. The sanctions were imposed following the 1981 declaration of martial law in Poland.	Federal Reserve Board Chairman Paul Volcker tells a congressional committee that the Federal Reserve Board will no longer set a target range for growth in the basic measure of money supply, known as M1. . . . Rollins Environmental Services Inc. agrees to pay the state of Louisiana $1.25 mil. to settle pollution charges involving the company's waste disposal plant at Baton Rouge, and it will spend $2.5 mil. to $5 mil. to clean up contaminated ground water at the site.			Feb. 19
Rabbi Meir Kahane, who founded the Jewish Defense League in the United States before immigrating to Israel in the early 1970s, wins restoration of his U.S. citizenship. A federal judge in New York City rules that the U.S. government failed to prove that Kahane intended to relinquish his citizenship by becoming a member of the Israeli Knesset in 1984.	A special commission looking into the workings of the National Security Council (NSC) is examining several boxes of messages from the NSC's computer system that contain new revelations about the Iran-Contra arms scandal. According to unidentified sources familiar with the material, the computer tapes and transcripts reveal "serious discrepancies" and are likely to result in criminal prosecutions.	Consumer spending dropped a record 2% in January, the Commerce Dept. reports, the sharpest decline since the department began keeping records in 1959.	Scientists report locating a gene that causes a form of Alzheimer's disease, a degenerative condition in middle-aged and elderly people that is characterized by profound mental deterioration. In the journal *Science*, Dr. Peter H. St. George Hyslop reports identifying a small area of chromosome 21 that appears to contain the gene causing familial Alzheimer's disease.		Feb. 20
The National Governors Assoc. holds its four-day winter conference in Washington, D.C., at which members endorse an ambitious plan to overhaul the welfare system, emphasizing job training and work requirement for those receiving aid.				Andy Warhol (born Andrew Warhola), 58 or 59, artist and filmmaker who was the best-known figure to emerge from the Pop Art movement of the 1960s, dies in New York City of a heart attack following gall bladder surgery. His work includes silk-screen images of Campbell's soup cans and such pop icons as Elvis Presley and Marilyn Monroe, and underground films, including *Chelsea Girls* (1966). His New York City art studio, "the Factory," was a legendary hangout, and as publisher of *Interview* magazine he tried to ensure that his dictum—"In the future, everybody will be famous for 15 minutes"—would come true.	Feb. 21

F	G	H	I	J
Includes elections, federal-state relations, civil rights and liberties, crime, the judiciary, education, health care, poverty, urban affairs and population.	Includes formation and debate of U.S. foreign and defense policies, veterans' affairs and defense spending. (Relations with specific foreign countries are usually found under the region concerned.)	Includes business, labor, agriculture, taxation, transportation, consumer affairs, monetary and fiscal policy, natural resources, and pollution.	Includes worldwide scientific, medical and technological developments, natural phenomena, U.S. weather, natural disasters, and accidents.	Includes the arts, religion, scholarship, communications media, sports, entertainments, fashions, fads and social life.

	World Affairs	Europe	Africa & the Middle East	The Americas	Asia & the Pacific
Feb. 22	In a broadly worded statement released after a meeting in Paris, finance ministers from the United States and five major allies agree to stabilize the relative values of their currencies at present levels.		Ethiopia's leader Lt. Col. Mengistu Haile Mariam announces that a new constitution was approved by 81% of the voters in a February 1 referendum and that the nation would henceforth be known as the People's Democratic Republic of Ethiopia. The new constitution endorses a Soviet-style, civilian communist government.	In Argentina, a deadline for prosecuting military officials in connection with human rights abuses in the 1970s passes, with some 150 summonses having been issued under a 60-day time limit. In advance of the prosecution deadline, 11 human rights groups filed more than 1,000 criminal charges against some 650 people, most of them military and police officials, for torturing and murdering thousands of Argentines during the so-called "Dirty War."	
Feb. 23		After 12 weeks of bargaining, Spanish Socialist Party leaders agree to form a coalition government with the Basque Nationalist Party (PNV) in the Basque region. The PNV lost its long-held, dominant position in the region in the November 1986 election following a fissure within the party.	Thousands of Syrian troops enter Moslem west Beirut in an effort to halt a week of fighting between rival militias that killed about 300 people and wounded 1,300.		In India, a judicial commission report made public has proclaimed the "total passivity, callousness and indifference" shown by New Delhi police in the face of violent anti-Sikh riots that erupted in the wake of the assassination of P.M. Indira Gandhi in 1984. The victim's son and successor, P.M. Rajiv Gandhi, quickly accepts the panel findings.
Feb. 24		After prolonged negotiations, West Germany's governing coalition partners agree to a tax reform plan totaling $24 bil. The plan is announced by Finance Min. Gerhard Stoltenberg of the Free Democratic Party (FDP), who worked it out with leaders of Chancellor Helmut Kohl's Christian Democratic Union (CDU) and the CDU's Bavarian sister party, the Christian Social Union.		Worried about the rapid spread of acquired immune deficiency syndrome in Brazil, the nation's health ministry begins a preventive campaign featuring newspaper and magazine advertisements as well as late-night television spots recommending the use of condoms and disposable hypodermic needles.	In India, the finance ministry's annual economic Survey of 1986-87 reports 5.5% growth in gross national product during 1985-86.
Feb. 25				According to a report by a private U.S. human rights group, Witness for Peace, and released by Rep. David Bonior (D, Mich.) and Bishop Thomas Gumbleton of Detroit, Nicaraguan Contras have killed, injured, and abused hundreds of civilians in Nicaragua over the past six months.... Argentina's Economics Min. Juan Sourrouille announces a four-month freeze on wages and prices and a devaluation of the currency as part of a set of measures aimed at curbing inflation.	Filipinos celebrate Freedom Day, the culmination of four days of festivities marking the anniversary of the peaceful 1986 overthrow of former Pres. Ferdinand Marcos. Troops, placed on alert beginning February 22, are stationed about Manila to forestall a rumored coup attempt by disgruntled soldiers.

A	B	C	D	E
Includes developments that affect more than one world region, international organizations and important meetings of major world leaders.	Includes all domestic and regional developments in Europe, including the Soviet Union, Turkey, Cyprus and Malta.	Includes all domestic and regional developments in Africa and the Middle East, including Iraq and Iran and excluding Cyprus, Turkey and Afghanistan.	Includes all domestic and regional developments in Latin America, the Caribbean and Canada.	Includes all domestic and regional developments in Asia and Pacific nations, extending from Afghanistan through all the Pacific Islands, except Hawaii.

U.S. Politics & Social Issues	U.S. Foreign Policy & Defense	U.S. Economy & Environment	Science, Technology & Nature	Culture, Leisure & Life Style	
				David (Howard) Susskind, 66, television, motion picture and theater producer and one of America's earliest and best-known TV talk-show hosts, dies in New York City of a heart ailment. By the late 1950s he was producing more live television than the three networks combined. In 1958, Susskind began "Open End," talk show without set time limits; in 1967, this became "The David Susskind Show," a two-hour program that remained on the air until 1986.	**Feb. 22**
Rep. Richard A. Gephardt (D, Mo.) becomes the first official candidate for the 1988 Democratic presidential nomination.				Jackie Joyner-Kersee, the world record holder in the women's heptathlon, is named the winner of the James E. Sullivan Memorial Award as the top amateur athlete in the United States. Joyner-Kersee is the eighth woman to win the award in its 57-year history.	**Feb. 23**
Mayor Harold Washington wins a narrow victory in Chicago's Democratic mayoral primary, beating back a challenge from former Mayor Jane M. Byrne.	Lt. Col. Oliver L. North, a key figure in the Iran-Contra arms scandal, files suit against the special prosecutor in the case, Lawrence E. Walsh, and Attorney Gen. Edwin Meese III. North's suit charges that the federal law permitting the appointment of a special prosecutor is unconstitutional.	In one of the largest banking acquisitions to date, Rainier Bancorp. agrees to be acquired by Security Pacific Corp. in a stock swap valued at $1.1 bil.	An astronomer in Chile discovers a massive supernova, or exploding star, in the southern skies. The star is estimated to be 160,000 light years from Earth, meaning that the cosmic event occurred 160,000 years ago, while the light it generated is only now reaching the Earth.	At the 29th annual Grammy Awards, Paul Simon's *Graceland* is named album of the year; song of the year is "That's What Friends Are For," by Burt Bacharach and his wife Carol Bayer Sager (and which raised $750,000 for acquired immune deficiency syndrome research); Steve Winwood wins best pop male vocalist record of the year and for his single "Higher Love"; best male rock vocalist is Robert Palmer for "Addicted to Love"; best female rock vocalist, Tina Turner for "Back Where You Started" single; and best female pop vocalist, Barbra Streisand for *The Broadway Album*. Top new artist of the year is Bruce Hornsby and the Range.	**Feb. 24**
E(dgar) D(aniel) Nixon, 87, pioneering U.S. civil rights leader, dies in Montgomery, Ala., of respiratory and heart ailments. In the 1920s he and A. Philip Randolph helped organize the Brotherhood of Sleeping Car Porters, America's first successful black union, and in 1955 he chose the Rev. Martin Luther King Jr. to lead the Montgomery, Ala., bus boycott, one of the turning points of the civil rights movement. . . . Participants in a federally sponsored forum on the control of acquired immune deficiency syndrome reach broad agreement on the need for the wider use of blood tests to detect exposure to the acquired immune deficiency syndrome virus, but oppose a Centers for Disease Control proposal to expand mandatory acquired immune deficiency syndrome blood testing in the United States to a variety of groups. . . . The Supreme Court rules that states may not deny unemployment benefits to employees who are dismissed for refusing to work on their Sabbath. . . . The Supreme Court upholds by a 5-4 decision an affirmative action program in Alabama that provides for promotions of equal numbers of black and white state troopers.	The State Dept. announces that Washington will not join an initiative to create a nuclear-free zone in the South Pacific. The South Pacific Forum, an informal association of 13 Pacific nations including Australia and New Zealand, began the initiative in 1984.	The Federal Savings and Loan Insurance Corp. is presently operating at a deficit, according to an audit by the General Accounting Office (GAO). The GAO has not determined the extent of the deficit, but it estimates that the fund, which insures accounts at savings and loan associations for up to $100,000, is between $6 bil. and $8 bil. in the red.		The National Collegiate Athletic Assoc. announces a package of sanctions against Southern Methodist Univ.'s (SMU) football program, including cancellation of the school's 1987 football season. The penalties come after SMU players were found to have been illegally paid by school officials at a time when the Dallas, Tex., school was on probation for separate infractions.	**Feb. 25**

F	G	H	I	J
Includes elections, federal-state relations, civil rights and liberties, crime, the judiciary, education, health care, poverty, urban affairs and population.	Includes formation and debate of U.S. foreign and defense policies, veterans' affairs and defense spending. (Relations with specific foreign countries are usually found under the region concerned.)	Includes business, labor, agriculture, taxation, transportation, consumer affairs, monetary and fiscal policy, natural resources, and pollution.	Includes worldwide scientific, medical and technological developments, natural phenomena, U.S. weather, natural disasters, and accidents.	Includes the arts, religion, scholarship, communications media, sports, entertainments, fashions, fads and social life.

	World Affairs	Europe	Africa & the Middle East	The Americas	Asia & the Pacific
Feb. 26		In connection with the 1982 collapse of Banco Ambrosiano, Italian justice ministry officials confirm that an arrest warrant has been issued by magistrates in Milan for the head of the Vatican Bank, Archbishop Paul Marcinkus. . . . The Soviet Union conducts an underground nuclear test in the republic of Kazakhstan. The detonation formally ends Moscow's 18-month unilateral moratorium on testing, which began officially on Aug. 6, 1985. . . . Terrorist killings in Northern Ireland in 1986 rose to 61 from 54 in 1985, according to the *Times* of London. The number of injured rose to 1,450 from 916, and the incidence of shootings, explosions, and armed robberies all rose.		Chile reaches agreement with its bank advisory committee to restructure some $10.6 bil. of the nation's foreign debt and extend $1.7 bil. of short-term trade credits.	
Feb. 27			Israel denies that it once offered military instructors to aid the Nicaraguan Contras, as asserted in a White House memorandum contained in the Tower Comm.'s report on the Iran-Contra affair. The Tower report cites a May 1986 memo written by former National Security Council staffer Lt. Col. Oliver L. North and describing a purported Israeli offer to send military instructors to Nicaragua.		
Feb. 28		A seven-magistrate panel in Paris sentences to life in prison 35-year-old Georges Ibrahim Abdallah, for involvement in three attacks on foreign diplomats. Abdallah is believed to be the leader of the Lebanese Armed Revolutionary Faction. . . . In a statement issued by the official Soviet news agency, Soviet leader Mikhail S. Gorbachev calls for the United States and USSR to reach an accord on the elimination of medium-range nuclear missiles in Europe that would be separate from any other arms control matter.			South Korea holds groundbreaking ceremonies for its so-called Peace Dam, a project intended to guard against possible harm from a North Korean dam already under construction only a few miles across the demilitarized zone separating the two countries. . . . India's P.M. Rajiv Gandhi presents parliament with his government's $48 bil. budget for FY1987-88. Under the budget, defense spending will increase by 23%.
March 1					Pakistan has developed a nuclear bomb, according to an interview reportedly conducted with Dr. Abdul Qadir Khan, head of the country's nuclear research program, and published in the Indian and British press. Khan quickly disavows the report, which nonetheless renews suspicions, growing since late 1986, that Pakistan has achieved nuclear capability.
March 2		In Britain, the Teachers' Pay and Conditions Act goes into effect, allowing Education Sec. Kenneth Baker to impose a pay deal on the 400,000 teachers in England and Wales. Teachers from Britain's two largest education unions later stage half-day strikes to protest the imposition of the Conservative government's pay and working conditions pact.		Led by Boris N. Yeltsin, four members of the Presidium of the Supreme Soviet visit Nicaragua to inspect state development projects. It is the highest-ranking Soviet delegation ever to visit Nicaragua. Yeltsin is the city of Moscow's Communist Party secretary and a candidate (alternate) member of the Politburo.	Japan announces that the official national unemployment rate reached 3% in January, the highest such rate since monthly reporting began in 1953. . . . In the Philippines, some 100,000 people visit Malacanang Palace to view the treasure trove of goods left behind by the fleeing family of former Pres. Ferdinand E. Marcos.

A	B	C	D	E
Includes developments that affect more than one world region, international organizations and important meetings of major world leaders.	Includes all domestic and regional developments in Europe, including the Soviet Union, Turkey, Cyprus and Malta.	Includes all domestic and regional developments in Africa and the Middle East, including Iraq and Iran and excluding Cyprus, Turkey and Afghanistan.	Includes all domestic and regional developments in Latin America, the Caribbean and Canada.	Includes all domestic and regional developments in Asia and Pacific nations, extending from Afghanistan through all the Pacific Islands, except Hawaii.

U.S. Politics & Social Issues	U.S. Foreign Policy & Defense	U.S. Economy & Environment	Science, Technology & Nature	Culture, Leisure & Life Style	
In a closely watched case, a San Diego judge rules that Pamela Rae Stewart, 28, cannot be charged with criminal neglect of her unborn child. Prosecutors had alleged that Stewart, who was diagnosed with placenta previa, contributed to her son's death by ignoring the advice of her doctor to refrain from using street drugs, to avoid sexual intercourse, and to immediately seek medical attention if she began bleeding.	In a report on the National Security Council released today, the Tower Comm. says that a confused and unaware Pres. Reagan allowed himself to be misled by dishonest staff members who organized the trade of arms to Iran for hostages held in Lebanon and pursued a secret war against the Nicaraguan government.			The general synod of the Church of England votes to proceed with church legislation to allow the ordination of women priests. However, Archbishop of Canterbury Robert Runcie says that the vote is not a decisive one and that final approval for female clergy will not come to a vote before 1991.	Feb. 26
Pres. Reagan accepts the resignation of White House chief of staff Donald T. Regan and immediately names former Senate Majority Leader Howard H. Baker Jr. (R, Tenn.) as his replacement. The moves come one day after the president received the report of the Tower Comm.'s investigation National Security Council staff in the Iran-Contra arms scandal. The report condemned Regan for the "chaos" in the White House that ensued after the Iran policy was disclosed.		Prices received by farmers for their raw agricultural products were unchanged in February, the Agriculture Dept. reports.... The government's consumer price index rose 0.7% in January, the sharpest increase in more than four years, according to the Labor Dept. ... The U.S. deficit on merchandise trade rose in January to $14.78 bil., the Commerce Dept. reports.		*Publishers Weekly's* hardback fiction best-sellers for the week are: *Windmills of the Gods*, Sidney Sheldon; *The Eyes of the Dragon*, Stephen King; *Red Storm Rising*, Tom Clancy; *Night of the Fox*, Jack Higgins; *It*, Stephen King.	Feb. 27
					Feb. 28
				Bertrand DeJouvenel, 83, French political philosopher and economist who as a young man had an affair with his stepmother, the novelist Colette, dies in Paris.	March 1
The so-called "Pizza Connection" trial ends in New York City with the convictions of a former Sicilian Mafia chief and 16 other men as part of a ring that distributed tons of drugs through a network of pizza parlors.		Apple Computer Corp. introduces two new models in its popular Macintosh line. The new models feature color graphics, expandability and, with a special circuit card, compatibility with the personal computers sold by International Business Machines Corp.		(George) Randolph Scott, 89, rugged Hollywood star for more than three decades, dies of heart and lung ailments in Los Angeles. Best known for a series of Westerns made late in his career, including *Seven Men from Now* (1956), *Comanche Station* (1960) and *Ride the High Country* (1962), his last film, he was considered one of the richest men in Hollywood; his oil and real estate holdings alone were estimated to be at least $100 mil.	March 2
F	G	H	I	J
Includes elections, federal-state relations, civil rights and liberties, crime, the judiciary, education, health care, poverty, urban affairs and population.	*Includes formation and debate of U.S. foreign and defense policies, veterans' affairs and defense spending. (Relations with specific foreign countries are usually found under the region concerned.)*	*Includes business, labor, agriculture, taxation, transportation, consumer affairs, monetary and fiscal policy, natural resources, and pollution.*	*Includes worldwide scientific, medical and technological developments, natural phenomena, U.S. weather, natural disasters, and accidents.*	*Includes the arts, religion, scholarship, communications media, sports, entertainments, fashions, fads and social life.*

	World Affairs	Europe	Africa & the Middle East	The Americas	Asia & the Pacific
March 3		Italy's Premier Bettino Craxi resigns his post, thus ending the longest tenure of any Italian leader since World War II—three years, seven months. The resignation, which sets off a new round of bargaining to choose a leader from the five-party governing coalition, is announced by the socialist premier in the Italian Senate.			Philippine Pres. Corazon Aquino announces that as a first step toward financing land reform, the government will sell companies sequestered from allies of ousted Pres. Ferdinand Marcos. Communist insurgents and leftist groups tolerated by the government have long made land reform a key demand.... The massive deployment of South Korean police prevents protests in Seoul and half a dozen other cities planned in memory of Park Chong Chol, a 21-year-old student activist slain by police.
March 4		West Germany's trade with East Germany fell 9% in 1986, the first decline since 1979, the West German economics ministry reports. Exports fell 9%, to 7.8 bil. marks, and imports dropped 10%, to 7.3 bil. marks.	Unofficial reports say at least 100 people are killed as 30 Turkish warplanes bomb suspected Kurdish rebel targets inside Iraq in retaliation for a Kurdish attack in eastern Turkey 10 days before that left 14 villagers dead, most of them women and children.... State Dept. officials report that the U.S. Agency for International Development is sending 17 financial experts to Liberia to help manage its debt-ridden economy. Under the plan, which Liberia has accepted as the price for continued American aid, the team will exercise "joint authority" over Liberia's exports and imports, the budget, tax collection, customs, foreign exchange, and the central bank.		
March 5		Britain surpassed France as the world's third-leading arms dealer in 1986, according to the *Financial Times*. Over the period 1982-85, the United States accounted for 36% of world arms sales, followed by the Soviet Union (19%), France (13%), and Britain (7%).		Haiti formally asks a court in Grasse, France, to order deposed Pres. Jean-Claude Duvalier to pay back $120 mil. he allegedly looted from the nation during his 15 years in office. Duvalier fled Haiti in February 1986 and has lived in France since then.	Sec. of State George P. Shultz concludes a visit to China. The trip came as the Reagan administration was struggling with the Iran arms scandal and shortly after the Chinese leadership's ouster of Hu Yaobang as general secretary of the Chinese Communist Party. Hu fell in a purge of reformers thought to be too influenced by the West.
March 6		The British ferry *Herald of Free Enterprise* capsizes shortly after setting out for Dover, England, from the Belgian port of Zeebrugge. Although 409 of 543 passengers and crew are brought ashore in a remarkably efficient rescue operation, the probable death toll of 134 (including 82 passengers missing and presumed dead) makes the mishap the worst peacetime disaster in the history of English Channel shipping.		At least 300 people are reported dead as a series of earthquakes strikes the remote northeastern jungle region of Ecuador. The quakes, the strongest of which measure 7.3 on the Richter scale of ground motion, are centered in the Andes about 70 miles northeast of Quito, the capital. Damage to the country's main oil pipeline forces a halt oil production and exports.	

A	B	C	D	E
Includes developments that affect more than one world region, international organizations and important meetings of major world leaders.	Includes all domestic and regional developments in Europe, including the Soviet Union, Turkey, Cyprus and Malta.	Includes all domestic and regional developments in Africa and the Middle East, including Iraq and Iran and excluding Cyprus, Turkey and Afghanistan.	Includes all domestic and regional developments in Latin America, the Caribbean and Canada.	Includes all domestic and regional developments in Asia and Pacific nations, extending from Afghanistan through all the Pacific Islands, except Hawaii.

U.S. Politics & Social Issues	U.S. Foreign Policy & Defense	U.S. Economy & Environment	Science, Technology & Nature	Culture, Leisure & Life Style	
The socialist mayor of Burlington, Vt., Bernard Sanders, easily wins reelection to a fourth two-year term. He is believed to be the nation's only socialist mayor.... Drawing attention to the plight of America's homeless, a number of well-known actors and politicans take part in the "Grate American Sleep-Out," sleeping out on heating grates in Washington, D.C., a protest organized by homeless advocate Mitch Snyder and actor Martin Sheen.... The Supreme Court rules that a 1973 law barring discrimination against the handicapped in federally aided programs protects those suffering from contagious diseases. The ruling involved an elementary school teacher with tuberculosis but is construed as applying as well to people suffering from acquired immune deficiency syndrome or other contagious diseases.... In the wake of the February 26 Tower Comm. report on the Iran-Contra covert arms scandal, Pres. Reagan's approval rating drops to a four-year low, according to a CBS News/New York Times poll.	Robert M. Gates withdraws as Pres. Reagan's nominee to be director of the Central Intelligence Agency, and the president names a new nominee, William H. Webster, director of the Federal Bureau of Investigation.	The government's index of leading economic indicators fell 1% in January, the Commerce Dept. reports.		Baseball's Hall of Fame Committee on Veterans elects former Negro Leagues third baseman Ray Dandridge to membership in the Cooperstown, N.Y., shrine. Dandridge is the 11th inductee to win election primarily for play in the Negro Leagues.... Nora Kaye (born Nora Koreff), 67, first American dramatic ballerina with an international reputation, dies of cancer in Santa Monica, Calif. Among two dozen ballets created for her are Antony Tudor's *Pillar of Fire* (1942) and Agnes de Mille's *Fall River Legend* (1948). She collaborated on several dance films, including *The Turning Point* (1977), with her husband director-choreographer Herbert Ross.... Danny Kaye (born David Daniel Kaminski), 74, a comedian and entertainer, dies in Los Angeles of heart failure brought on by internal bleeding and hepatitis. His films include *Up in Arms* (1944), *The Secret Life of Walter Mitty* (1947), and *Hans Christian Andersen* (1952). In the 1960s, he hosted "The Danny Kaye Show" on television. His comic performances raised millions of dollars for the UN International Children's Emergency Fund.	March 3
U.S. District Judge W. Brevard Hand in Mobile, Ala., bans more than 40 textbooks on social studies, history, and home economics, from Alabama public schools on the grounds that they promote the "religion" of "secular humanism" and that they are thus in violation of the constitutional prohibition against government establishment of a religion.... Pres. Reagan denounces as "despicable fiction" published reports that his wife Nancy played a major role in the February 27 dismissal of chief of staff Donald T. Regan and other key government decisions.	Testifying before a federal grand jury investigating the sale of U.S. arms to Iran and the diversion of profits to the Contras, Adolfo Calero Portocarrero hands over financial records of his Nicaraguan Democratic Force Contra army to special prosecutor Lawrence Walsh.... Jonathan Jay Pollard is sentenced to life in prison for spying for Israel. His wife, Anne Henderson Pollard, is sentenced to five years in prison as an accessory.... Pres. Reagan acknowledges for the first time that his administration swapped arms for hostages and concludes that "it was a mistake." The president's 13-minute, nationally televised speech is in response to the Tower Comm.'s highly critical report, which said the president had allowed his staff to engineer arms sales to Iran and private assistance to the Nicaraguan Contra rebels.			At the annual Alfred I. duPont-Columbia Univ. Awards for excellence in broadcast journalism, Bill Moyers is presented with a gold baton for a program he prepared "CBS Reports: The Vanishing Family–Crisis in Black America." ... Maria Jolas (born Maria McDonald), 94, U.S.-born translator who was one of the last survivors of novelist James Joyce's Paris circle, dies in Paris, France. During the 1920s she and her husband, Eugene Jolas, published the literary quarterly *transition*, in which excerpts from what eventually became Joyce's *Finnegans Wake* first appeared.	March 4
				The Templeton Prize for Progress in Religion is awarded to the Rev. Stanley L. Jaki, a Benedictine monk who holds a doctorate in physics, for his work in "bridging the gap between science and religion."	March 5
A federal district judge in Washington, D.C., rules that the National Archives, in arranging for the release of former Pres. Richard M. Nixon's official papers, does not automatically have to withhold documents over which Nixon claims executive privilege.				In the Philippines, Archbishop of Manila Jaime Cardinal Sin is reported to have bowed to Vatican edicts against involvement of the clergy in politics. The reform-minded prelate had played a sizable role in mobilizing public opinion against former Pres. Ferdinand Marcos.	March 6

F	G	H	I	J
Includes elections, federal-state relations, civil rights and liberties, crime, the judiciary, education, health care, poverty, urban affairs and population.	Includes formation and debate of U.S. foreign and defense policies, veterans' affairs and defense spending. (Relations with specific foreign countries are usually found under the region concerned.)	Includes business, labor, agriculture, taxation, transportation, consumer affairs, monetary and fiscal policy, natural resources, and pollution.	Includes worldwide scientific, medical and technological developments, natural phenomena, U.S. weather, natural disasters, and accidents.	Includes the arts, religion, scholarship, communications media, sports, entertainments, fashions, fads and social life.

	World Affairs	Europe	Africa & the Middle East	The Americas	Asia & the Pacific
March 7					
March 8		Joblessness in the European Community (EC) reaches a record level of 17.1 million in January, the EC reports.	Iran concludes an offensive begun March 4 in Iraq's northern Kurdistan region, seizing snow-covered mountain heights northeast of the key oil city of Kirkuk. The Iranian success is verified by a *Washington Post* reporter.		Japan's ruling Liberal Democratic Party loses a parliamentary by-election in which the opposition candidate ran almost solely against Premier Yasuhiro Nakasone's unpopular call for a 5% sales tax.
March 9		Leading British banks cut their base lending rates by half a percentage point to 10.5%. The cut, prompted by action from the Bank of England, comes as somewhat of a surprise because the central bank had been resisting a rate cut. A major impetus for the rate reduction was the strength of the pound.		The Honduran Air Force shoots down a C-47 cargo plane over western Honduras after the pilot refuses repeated requests to identify himself. Three or four people are reported killed. Honduran authorities say they suspect that the plane, downed near the borders of El Salvador and Guatemala, was on a drug smuggling mission. No illegal cargo was found in the wreckage.	
March 10		Charles Haughey of Fianna Fail becomes Ireland's prime minister when the Dail elects him to the post by a margin of a single vote. Haughey's party won 81 Dail seats in the February general election, three short of an absolute majority in the 166-member parliament.		In Brazil, heavily armed troops occupy the 10 oil refineries owned by the state oil company, Petrobras, to prevent a threatened strike.... In Peru, three Andean peasants are found guilty of the 1983 massacre of eight journalists and sentenced to prison terms ranging from six to 10 years. The journalists were slain in the hamlet of Uchuraccay by villagers who claimed to have believed they were rebels belonging to the Maoist Sendero Luminoso (Shining Path) group.	Australia's top federal labor relations board formally establishes a two-tier system for wage increases. The new structure replaces the indexing of wage rises to inflation, an approach abandoned in late 1986 by the Australian Council of Trade Unions and the Australian Labor Party government.
March 11	Meeting in Geneva, the UN Comm. on Human Rights rejects a U.S. resolution condemning Cuba for human rights violations. A similar resolution by Cuba charging that the United States violates the rights of Indians, blacks, and Puerto Ricans is also defeated.	West Germany's Chancellor Helmut Kohl is formally reelected to his post by a vote of the Bundestag, West Germany's lower parliamentary house.... A judge in Prague, Czechoslovakia, convicts five leaders of the Jazz Section cultural dissident organization of participating in illegal business activities.		In the aftermath of the March 5-6 earthquakes in northeastern Ecuador, officials report that 4,000 people have been officially declared missing, and at least 20,000 are believed homeless. The effects of the quakes were greatly magnified by mudslides and flooding.	

A	B	C	D	E
Includes developments that affect more than one world region, international organizations and important meetings of major world leaders.	Includes all domestic and regional developments in Europe, including the Soviet Union, Turkey, Cyprus and Malta.	Includes all domestic and regional developments in Africa and the Middle East, including Iraq and Iran and excluding Cyprus, Turkey and Afghanistan.	Includes all domestic and regional developments in Latin America, the Caribbean and Canada.	Includes all domestic and regional developments in Asia and Pacific nations, extending from Afghanistan through all the Pacific Islands, except Hawaii.

U.S. Politics & Social Issues	U.S. Foreign Policy & Defense	U.S. Economy & Environment	Science, Technology & Nature	Culture, Leisure & Life Style	
				Waldo Salt, 72, screenwriter, dies of lung cancer in Los Angeles. Blacklisted in Hollywood in the 1950s and early 1960s, Salt went on to win two Academy Awards, for *Midnight Cowboy* (1970) and *Coming Home* (1979). . . . Mike Tyson, World Boxing Council champion, takes the World Boxing Assoc. heavyweight title with a 12-round unanimous decision over James "Bonecrusher" Smith in Las Vegas.	March 7
				The first world indoor track and field championships conclude after three days in Indianapolis. Some 490 athletes from 90 nations participated, and six world records were set. The Soviet Union, East Germany, and the United States led the overall medals table, winning 35 of the 72 medals awarded.	March 8
Liberal economist Lester Thurow is named dean of the Sloan School of Management at the Massachusetts Institute of Technology. . . . The Supreme Court upholds the use of evidence obtained by police under a law found to be unconstitutional, as long as the police reasonably believed that the law was constitutional. . . . The Supreme Court rules that aliens seeking political asylum do not have to prove a "clear probability" that they will be killed, tortured, or otherwise persecuted for their beliefs if returned to their homeland. The Reagan administration had argued the contrary position in the case.	Carl R. Channell, a fund-raiser for conservative causes, releases audits of his nine tax-exempt foundations to show that he did not receive any money from the sale of weapons to Iran. An 1986 report in the Lowell (Mass.) *Sun* charged that Channell used about $5 mil. from the arms sales to subsidize commercials linking congressional Democrats to communist leaders and Iran's Ayatollah Ruhollah Khomeini.	The average rate on 30-year, conventional fixed-rate mortgages was 9.08% in early March, the lowest since January 1978, the Federal Home Loan Mortgage Corp. reports. . . . Outstanding consumer credit grew a seasonally adjusted $536 mil. in January, the Federal Reserve Board reports. . . . The nation's unemployment rate held steady in February at 6.6% for the third consecutive month, according to the Labor Dept.	Dr. Joseph G. Perpich, a 45-year-old psychiatrist, lawyer, and authority on the ethical aspects of biomedical research, is named to head a new program at the Howard Hughes Medical Inst. With assets of $5.2 bil., the institute is one of the leading private sources of money for biomedical research. . . . Scientists testifying before the health and environment subcommittee of the House Energy and Commerce Committee say there has been an alarming depletion of the protective atmospheric ozone layer, which absorbs harmful ultraviolet radiation from the sun, in the last 10 years.		March 9
According to results of a 1986 survey of 290,249 freshmen at 552 colleges and universities, 7% said they were interested in becoming elementary or secondary school teachers. It is the fourth yuear in a row that the number of college freshmen interested in teaching has increased. . . . Former Gov. Bruce Babbitt (D, Ariz.) formally declares his candidacy for the 1988 Democratic presidential nomination. A relative unknown, Babbitt's attention-getting proposals on such issues as Social Security and foreign trade break with popular Democratic positions.	In his annual report to Congress, Pres. Reagan accuses the Soviet Union of violating six current arms control treaties and voices his administration's "deep and continuing concerns about Soviet noncompliance" with the 1972 antiballistic missile treaty. His report cites in particular the Soviet early warning radar facility near Krasnoyarsk, as well as smaller radar stations under construction in the USSR.	General Dynamics Corp. was the nation's largest defense contractor in FY1986, according to the Defense Dept.		In a major statement of the Roman Catholic Church's position on birth technologies, the Vatican condemns virtually all forms of artificial fertilization and generation of human life outside the body, including any medical or scientific interference in procreation except that which assists married couples who engage in "normal" intercourse.	March 10
Under strong advice not to respond to impromptu queries, Pres. Reagan evades reporters' questions at White House photo sessions by feigning laryngitis. Asked about recent polls showing his credibility damaged by the Iran-Contra covert arms scandal, Reagan replies several times in a whisper, but with a broad grin, "I've lost my voice."	Congressional committees investigating the Iran-Contra arms scandal grant limited immunity to Iranian-born businessman Albert Hakim in an effort to gain access to his financial records. Hakim was a partner of Richard V. Secord, who was involved in shipping arms to Iran and funnelling private aid to the Nicaraguan Contras. . . . The House of Representatives votes, 230-196, to suspend further aid to the Nicaraguan Contras unless Pres. Reagan provides an accounting of funds the Contras have received from the United States and elsewhere within 180 days.			An exhibit of three generations of Wyeth family artists opens at the Soviet Academy of the Arts in Leningrad, the first Soviet show to include American art in nearly eight years. The show, "An American Vision: Three Generations of Wyeth Art," contains works by N.C. Wyeth (1882-1945), his son Andrew, 69, and Andrew's son James, 40.	March 11

F	G	H	I	J
Includes elections, federal-state relations, civil rights and liberties, crime, the judiciary, education, health care, poverty, urban affairs and population.	Includes formation and debate of U.S. foreign and defense policies, veterans' affairs and defense spending. (Relations with specific foreign countries are usually found under the region concerned.)	Includes business, labor, agriculture, taxation, transportation, consumer affairs, monetary and fiscal policy, natural resources, and pollution.	Includes worldwide scientific, medical and technological developments, natural phenomena, U.S. weather, natural disasters, and accidents.	Includes the arts, religion, scholarship, communications media, sports, entertainments, fashions, fads and social life.

	World Affairs	Europe	Africa & the Middle East	The Americas	Asia & the Pacific
March 12		The European Court of Justice rules that a 470-year-old German law controlling the legal contents of beer cannot be used to exclude the importation of foreign beer that does not fit the description. . . . The Soviet Union conducts its second underground nuclear test of the year in the republic of Kazakhstan. Moscow's first detonation of 1987, conducted February 26, ended an 18-month unilateral moratorium on testing. . . . U.S. negotiators in Geneva offer a package of verification measures in concert with the U.S. draft treaty on the removal of medium-range nuclear missiles from Europe.		Canada's Justice Min. Ramon Hnatyshyn presents to the House of Commons the main part of a federal report on the presence in Canada of suspected Nazi war criminals. The study, ordered in 1985, was prepared by a special commission headed by Justice Jules Deschenes of the Quebec Superior Court.	Australian income from tourism increased 23.2% during 1986, according to figures released by the Org. for Economic Cooperation and Development, which says that this is the largest such increase for any developed nation during the year.
March 13		An Australian judge rules against the British government's request to prevent publication of the memoirs of a former leading member of MI5, the British counterintelligence service. Britain's P.M. Margaret Thatcher, however, confirms that Britain will appeal the verdict, meaning that publication of the book will be delayed further.	A week of rioting between Moslems and Christians in Northern Nigeria leaves at least 15 people dead and dozens of churches and mosques burned. The federal military government quells the unrest with curfews, mass arrests, and shoot-to-kill orders to troops.		
March 14		Roy Jenkins, a former president of the European Community and a founder of the Social Democratic Party of Great Britain, is elected chancellor of Oxford Univ., becoming the first non-Conservative to be elected to the post since 1834. The position of chancellor, a lifetime appointment, is largely ceremonial.	Iran heightens its threat to the flow of oil from the Persian Gulf by setting up large, land-based antiship missiles near the Straits of Hormuz, according to U.S. intelligence sources cited in the *New York Times*.		
March 15		A large crowd of demonstrators marches through Budapest calling for democracy in Hungary. Western observers estimated the crowd at 1,500-2,000 people, making it one of the largest unofficial public gatherings in Hungary since 1956. On this date in 1848, Hungarian nationalists began an unsuccessful revolution against Austrian rule.			Ramon Diaz, chairman of the Presidential Comm. on Good Government, reports that some $400 mil. of former Philippine Pres. Ferdinand E. Marcos' wealth has been recovered. Diaz says the panel has also sequestered shares in at least 286 companies owned by Marcos or his cronies.
March 16		Finnish parliamentary elections result in strong gains for the conservative Kokoomus Party. The party's showing could mean a place for Kokoomus in the Finnish government for the first time in 20 years. Pres. Mauno Koivisto will choose a party leader to form a new government. Negotiations to form a coalition are expected to take weeks.		In its first-ever official protest filed with the United States, Costa Rica demands clarification of U.S. statements on the use of a secret Costa Rican airstrip by a private U.S. plane supplying aid to the Nicaraguan Contras.	

A	B	C	D	E
Includes developments that affect more than one world region, international organizations and important meetings of major world leaders.	*Includes all domestic and regional developments in Europe, including the Soviet Union, Turkey, Cyprus and Malta.*	*Includes all domestic and regional developments in Africa and the Middle East, including Iraq and Iran and excluding Cyprus, Turkey and Afghanistan.*	*Includes all domestic and regional developments in Latin America, the Caribbean and Canada.*	*Includes all domestic and regional developments in Asia and Pacific nations, extending from Afghanistan through all the Pacific Islands, except Hawaii.*

U.S. Politics & Social Issues	U.S. Foreign Policy & Defense	U.S. Economy & Environment	Science, Technology & Nature	Culture, Leisure & Life Style	
	A federal district judge in Washington, D.C., dismisses two lawsuits brought by Lt. Col. Oliver L. North that sought to block the investigation of the Iran-Contra arms deal by a special prosecutor. The judge, Barrington D. Parker, authorized the prosecutor to continue his investigation.			Brian Orser of Canada wins the men's world figure skating championship in Cincinnati. Brian Boitano of the United States finishes second after failing to complete the first quadruple spin jump ever in competition, and Alexander Fadeyev of the Soviet Union is third.... Woody (Wayne Woodrow) Hayes, 74, fiery football coach at Ohio State from 1951 to 1978, dies in Upper Arlington, Ohio, of an apparent heart attack. With Hayes's emphasis on the running game, the Buckeyes compiled a 205-61-10 record.	March 12
At the conclusion of a seven-month trial and seven days of jury deliberations, reputed Mafia boss John Gotti and six of his alleged Gambino crime family lieutenants are acquitted of federal racketeering and conspiracy charges in New York City.		The industrial production index rose 0.5% in February, according to the Federal Reserve Board.... The producer price index rose a seasonally adjusted 0.1% in February, the Labor Dept. reports.			March 13
				Katarina Witt of East Germany wins the women's world figure skating championship in Cincinnati. Defending Champion Debi Thomas of the United States is second, and Caryn Kadavy of the United States is third.	March 14
The nation's teachers are reported to have enjoyed pay raises well above inflation from 1983 through 1986, with salary increases nationwide of 7.8% in 1983-84, 8.4% in 1984-85, and 7% in 1985-86.				The National Football League announces that it has reached a $1.428 bil. agreement on a three-year package for television coverage, including, for the first time, cable rights for ESPN.... *Starlight Express*, a hit London musical that features an assortment of trains depicted by cast members on roller skates, opens at the Gershwin Theater in New York City. Written by Andrew Lloyd Webber, with lyrics by Richard Stilgoe, and directed by Trevor Nunn, the musical stars Greg Mowry, Reva Rice, Robert Torti, and Braden Danner.	March 15
The Democratic race for the 1988 presidential nomination widens when Massachusetts Gov. Michael S. Dukakis announces the formation of a campaign committee and his intention to officially enter the race in May.... Rep. Mario Biaggi (D) of New York, and Meade Esposito, former Democratic leader of the borough of Brooklyn, are indicted on federal charges of bribery, fraud, and conspiracy involving attempts to help an ailing ship-repair company. The government also charges Biaggi with obstruction of justice.		An independent advisory panel of five medical experts recommends that the federal Food and Drug Admin. (FDA) grant approval for the first time to a remedy for baldness. The recommendation for approval of the remedy, developed by Upjohn Co., is expected to be adopted by the FDA, which could put the drug on the U.S. market within a year.			March 16

F	G	H	I	J
Includes elections, federal-state relations, civil rights and liberties, crime, the judiciary, education, health care, poverty, urban affairs and population.	Includes formation and debate of U.S. foreign and defense policies, veterans' affairs and defense spending. (Relations with specific foreign countries are usually found under the region concerned.)	Includes business, labor, agriculture, taxation, transportation, consumer affairs, monetary and fiscal policy, natural resources, and pollution.	Includes worldwide scientific, medical and technological developments, natural phenomena, U.S. weather, natural disasters, and accidents.	Includes the arts, religion, scholarship, communications media, sports, entertainments, fashions, fads and social life.

	World Affairs	Europe	Africa & the Middle East	The Americas	Asia & the Pacific
March 17		The Soviet Union calls for the creation of an international agency to prevent the deployment of weapons in space. The proposal is made at the 40-nation Geneva Committee disarmament talks in Switzerland. . . . The European Community (EC) reportedly posted its first trade surplus in 1986. Despite a 10% decline in exports, to 340 bil. ECUs, against a rise of only 7% in import volume, import costs fell 17% due to the falling dollar and lower oil prices. . . . Portugual's gross domestic product grew 4% in 1986, up from 3.3% in 1985, according to a central bank data report. The solid growth was boosted by Portugal's entry into the European Community. Inflation in the Iberian nation fell to 11.9% in 1986 from 29.3% two years earlier.		Canada's Fisheries Min. Thomas Siddon announces that Canadian ports have been indefinitely closed to French fishing vessels. Siddon says the move was prompted by evidence of French vessels exceeding the limit on cod catches in a disputed fishing zone near Newfoundland.	Japan's gross national product (GNP) grew by just 2.5% (adjusted for inflation) during the 1986 calendar year, the Economic Planning Agency reports. That is the country's smallest expansion of GNP during any calendar year since 1974. Analysts blame the harm done to exports by the runaway appreciation of the yen.
March 18			Israel's cabinet decides to downgrade its military and other ties with South Africa's white minority government. Israeli officials admit they are acting in response to pressure from the U.S. Congress and the American Jewish community.	Responding to pressure from Canada, Pres. Reagan renews his commitment to a $5 bil. program to fight acid rain. In a 1986 agreement with Canada, the Reagan administration endorsed a five-year program under which Washington and U.S. industry would each contribute $2.5 bil. to develop new technologies to burn coal more cleanly.	
March 19		The number of unemployed workers in Britain fell by a record 44,000 in February, the Employment Dept. reports. The decline brought the seasonally adjusted number of jobless to 3.074 million.			Australia's defense ministry issues a policy statement outlining its plans for transforming Australia into a significant regional military power.
March 20		French officials say that six people charged as spies two days earlier are suspected of having passed secrets about the Ariane European space rocket for the Soviet bloc. . . . Britain's inflation held steady at an annual rate of 3.9% in February, the Employment Dept. reports. The new retail price index report incorporates statistical changes and moves the base period to January 1987 from January 1974.		Mexico and some 360 creditor banks begin signing an agreement to provide up to $7.7 bil. in new loans. The loans are part of a package put together by banks and multilateral lending agencies in 1986 to promote development and economic growth.	

A	B	C	D	E
Includes developments that affect more than one world region, international organizations and important meetings of major world leaders.	Includes all domestic and regional developments in Europe, including the Soviet Union, Turkey, Cyprus and Malta.	Includes all domestic and regional developments in Africa and the Middle East, including Iraq and Iran and excluding Cyprus, Turkey and Afghanistan.	Includes all domestic and regional developments in Latin America, the Caribbean and Canada.	Includes all domestic and regional developments in Asia and Pacific nations, extending from Afghanistan through all the Pacific Islands, except Hawaii.

U.S. Politics & Social Issues	U.S. Foreign Policy & Defense	U.S. Economy & Environment	Science, Technology & Nature	Culture, Leisure & Life Style	
The Judicial Conf. of the United States, a panel of 27 federal judges, recommends that Congress consider impeachment proceedings against U.S. District Judge Alcee L. Hastings of Miami. . . . Under pressure from Congress, the White House drops a plan to tighten government control over information in electronic databases.		Pres. Reagan signs the National Appliance Energy Conservation Act of 1987, legislation that requires the Energy Dept. to set energy efficiency standards for household electrical appliances. . . . Housing starts rose 2.6% in February, the Commerce Dept. reports. . . . The U.S. balance of payments on current account shows a record deficit of $36.84 bil. in the fourth quarter of 1986 and $140.57 bil. for all of 1986, also a record, the Commerce Dept. reports.			**March 17**
Former White House aide Michael K. Deaver is indicted on five counts of perjury for lying to a federal grand jury and to Congress about his lobbying activities. . . . San Francisco agrees to a "comparable pay" agreement under which $35.4 mil. will be paid in special raises to women and members of minority groups whose wages are lower than those of men in jobs of comparable worth. The agreement calls for a raise of 4.5% in 1987 and 5% in 1988 for more than 12,000 city and county workers.	The Senate votes, 52-48, to defeat a resolution that would have blocked payment to the Nicaraguan Contras of $40 mil. in aid remaining from a $100 mil. package approved in 1986. The House earlier approved a six-month delay of further aid. . . . House and Senate committees investigating the Iran-Contra arms scandal vote to merge their staffs, share evidence, and hold joint hearings beginning May 5. The committees also set a timetable for granting immunity from prosecution to Lt. Col. Oliver L. North and Vice Adm. John M. Poindexter.	Fleet Financial Corp. of Providence, R.I., announces that it will acquire Norstar Bancorp. of Albany, N.Y., in a July 1988 stock swap valued at $1.3 bil. It is the most expensive bank merger ever planned. . . . The Commerce Dept.'s estimate of growth in the nation's gross national product in the fourth quarter of 1986 is revised downward for a second time, to a meager 1.1% annual rate. . . . After-tax profits of U.S. corporations rose a seasonally adjusted 6.1% in the fourth quarter of 1986, the Commerce Dept. reports. For all of 1986, profits rose 1.9%.		The ninth annual $100,000 Pritzger Architecture Prize is presented to Japanese architect and urban planner Kenzo Tange. . . . *Variety*'s top-grossing films for the week are: *Lethal Weapon, A Nightmare on Elm Street, Part 3: Dream Warriors, Tin Men, Angel Heart* and *Platoon.*	**March 18**
The Rev. Jesse Jackson takes a step toward seeking the Democratic nomination for president by opening an Iowa office for his exploratory committee. Iowa is the site of the first statewide delegate caucus.	Pres. Reagan defends his decision to sell arms to Iran but assures reporters that he "would not go down that same road again." The president fields reporters' questions on the Iran-Contra arms scandal and other topics in his first nationally broadcast news conference in four months.	Consumer spending rose 1.7% in February after a sharp decline the previous month, the Commerce Dept. says. . . . The House Budget Committee begins drafting a budget resolution for FY1988. The 1985 Gramm-Rudman balanced-budget law requires a reduction of the deficit to about $108 bil., some $50 bil. to $60 bil. less than 1987. . . . Boyd L. Jefferies agrees to plead guilty to two felony counts of securities law violations in connection with the insider-trading scandal on Wall Street. Jefferies was the founding chairman of the controversial brokerage house, Jefferies Group Inc., which pioneered off-market stock trading. . . . William Gates becomes the personal computer industry's first billionaire. Gates, a Harvard dropout, is the founder and chairman of Microsoft Corp.	Prince Louis (Victor Pierre Raymond) De Broglie, 94, French scientist, dies in Paris. In 1929 he won the Nobel Prize for physics for his 1924 hypothesis that particles should also exhibit certain wavelike properties, a prediction that led to the development of wave mechanics. . . . The federal Centers for Disease Control says that physicians should consider recommending a blood test for the acquired immune deficiency syndrome virus infection to some people who received transfusions of blood and blood products between 1978 and the spring of 1985, when mandatory testing of donated blood was introduced.	Television evangelist the Rev. Jim Bakker resigns his ministry after admitting an extramarital sexual encounter seven years ago. Bakker subsequently charges that he was blackmailed as part of a "diabolical plot" to gain control of his PTL (Praise the Lord) enterprise, which reported $129 mil. in revenues in 1986.	**March 19**
					March 20

F	G	H	I	J
Includes elections, federal-state relations, civil rights and liberties, crime, the judiciary, education, health care, poverty, urban affairs and population.	Includes formation and debate of U.S. foreign and defense policies, veterans' affairs and defense spending. (Relations with specific foreign countries are usually found under the region concerned.)	Includes business, labor, agriculture, taxation, transportation, consumer affairs, monetary and fiscal policy, natural resources, and pollution.	Includes worldwide scientific, medical and technological developments, natural phenomena, U.S. weather, natural disasters, and accidents.	Includes the arts, religion, scholarship, communications media, sports, entertainments, fashions, fads and social life.

	World Affairs	Europe	Africa & the Middle East	The Americas	Asia & the Pacific
March 21		Alan Dukes is elected in Dublin as leader of Ireland's Fine Gael opposition party. The 41-year-old economist succeeds Garret Fitz-Gerald, the former prime minister who stepped down following Fine Gael's defeat in the February elections.			Philippine Pres. Corazon Aquino tells reporters in Manila that she resents criticism by Asst. Sec. of Defense for International Security Affairs Richard L. Armitage who said March 17 that the Aquino government trusted in "symbolic political acts" to stop communist rebels, and that it had "regrettably failed" to develop a comprehensive counterinsurgency program.
March 22					In the Philippines, Pres. Corazon Aquino tells graduating military cadets that military victory and not compromise will end the country's communist insurgency and the rebellions by other extremist forces. The president asserts that the "answer to the terrorism of the left and the right is not social and economic reform but police and military action."
March 23		Former West German Chancellor Willy Brandt resigns as chairman of the Social Democratic Party (SPD). Brandt, who has held the party post for 23 years, steps aside amid pressure stemming from a controversial appointment for party spokesperson.	The Islamic Jihad for the Liberation of Palestine, a group that has kidnapped four Beirut Univ. College teachers, warns that one of the hostages, American Alann Steen, is gravely ill and in danger of dying "in 10 days," but says it will free him in exchange for 100 Arab prisoners held by Israel. . . . An apparent coup attempt against the government of Sierra Leone's Pres. Joseph Momoh is foiled. The revolt, allegedly led by senior police officers, was quelled by the country's paramilitary forces after a gun battle in Freetown.	Canada's Fisheries Min. Thomas Siddon announces that the government will permit the resumption of the commercial seal hunt from ships off the East Coast. International protests and a European boycott of Canadian seal pelts had effectively ended large-scale hunts in the early 1980s. . . . Control of the Inter-American Development Bank's (IDB) $3 bil.-a-year lending program is the focus of the IDB's annual meeting, and the IDB's annual report warns that Latin American nations will be unable to sustain economic growth without new investment in production capacity.	
March 24		France's Premier Jacques Chirac signs a contract with Walt Disney Productions Inc. for the creation of Europe's first Disneyland amusement park. The park, to be built on undeveloped land at Marne-la-Vallee on the eastern outskirts of Paris, is scheduled to open in 1992.			Japan's cabinet approves the country's first comprehensive package of measures to combat the spread of acquired immune deficiency syndrome, previously considered a problem of foreigners. Following the January death of a prostitute in Kobe, acquired immune deficiency syndrome information hotlines have received almost a million calls, and attendance at the country's normally thriving hostess bars and other sex emporia has plummeted.
March 25		The European Community's (EC) 30th anniversary is marked by ceremonies in Rome. A March 19 poll in the *Financial Times* showed that two-thirds of the EC's citizens want the community to develop into a "United States of Europe." . . . Swedish economic growth in 1986 was only 1.3%, the smallest gain since 1982, according to figures from the nation's central statistical office.		Ecuadoran workers stage a general strike to protest austerity measures imposed by the government March 14 in the wake of a series of devastating earthquakes March 5-6. At least 11 people are reported wounded by gunfire or gasoline bombs during the 24-hour strike, and 83 arrests are made.	In China, the 2,719 delegates to the National People's Congress gather in Beijing's Great Hall of the People to begin the annual 16-day session of the legislature.

A	B	C	D	E
Includes developments that affect more than one world region, international organizations and important meetings of major world leaders.	*Includes all domestic and regional developments in Europe, including the Soviet Union, Turkey, Cyprus and Malta.*	*Includes all domestic and regional developments in Africa and the Middle East, including Iraq and Iran and excluding Cyprus, Turkey and Afghanistan.*	*Includes all domestic and regional developments in Latin America, the Caribbean and Canada.*	*Includes all domestic and regional developments in Asia and Pacific nations, extending from Afghanistan through all the Pacific Islands, except Hawaii.*

U.S. Politics & Social Issues	U.S. Foreign Policy & Defense	U.S. Economy & Environment	Science, Technology & Nature	Culture, Leisure & Life Style	
				Robert Preston (born Robert Preston Meservey), 68, versatile Tony Award-winning actor best known for his stage-and-screen portrayal of confidence man Prof. Harold Hill in *The Music Man*, dies of lung cancer in Santa Barbara, Calif. Preston received an an Oscar nomination for his portrayal of a master of ceremonies at a transvestite nightclub in the 1982 film *Victor/Victoria*.... *Serious Money*, a comedy about insider trading on the London stock exchange, opens at London's Royal Court Theater. Written by Caryl Churchill, with songs by Ian Dury, the play is directed by Max Stafford-Clark and stars Gary Oldman, Alfred Molina, Lesley Manville, and Linda Bassett.	**March 21**
The number of blacks holding senior policymaking and managerial positions in the federal government has dropped since Pres. Reagan took office, according to an analysis of government data by the *New York Times*.				The British Academy of Film and Television Arts names *A Room with a View* best picture of 1986. Maggie Smith wins best actress honors for her role in that film, and Bob Hoskins is named best actor for *Mona Lisa*.	**March 22**
The Supreme Court lets stand an affirmative action plan for promotion of blacks in the Cincinnati fire department. The court, without comment, refuses to hear a challenge to the plan by white firefighters and their union. The plan provides for the promotion of at least one black for every six whites promoted to lieutenant from 1984 to 1986.		The Interior Dept. proposes to bring more fragile coastal areas under federal protection of the National Coastal Barrier Resources System. The system, established in 1982, makes development within its confines expensive and risky by prohibiting federal assistance for such things as roads, bridges, sewers, or flood insurance.			**March 23**
Former Sec. of State Alexander M. Haig Jr. formally launches his campaign for the 1988 Republican presidential nomination.	Defense Sec. Caspar W. Weinberger presents the sixth annual edition of the booklet *Soviet Military Power*. As in previous editions, the 159-page booklet warns of an aggressive buildup by Moscow.		India's second-generation space rocket fails shortly after takeoff from Sirharikota and falls into the Bay of Bengal with its payload, a 330-pound satellite.		**March 24**
Legislation to gradually raise the minimum hourly wage from the current $3.35 to $4.65 by 1990 is introduced in Congress. After 1990, the minimum rate would be set annually at no less than half the average national wage, which is currently $8.88 an hour.... In its first ruling on affirmative action for women, the Supreme Court rules, 6-3, that an employer may act voluntarily to remedy a "manifest imbalance" in the work force, as long as the rights of other workers are not "unnecessarily trammeled."	Senate Republicans succeed in turning back an attempt by Democratic leaders to end a filibuster and force a vote on a bill cutting off further aid to the Nicaraguan Contras.... The House Appropriations Committee attaches two arms control amendments to a supplemental appropriations bill for FY1987. One amendment would cut off funding for deployment of weapons that exceed the limits set by the 1979 Strategic Arms Treaty.	Comprehensive trade legislation clears three congressional committees and moves to the House floor. The bulk of the bill is a measure that will require presidential retaliation against specific unfair trade practices.	The 1986 nuclear disaster at the Soviet Union's Chernobyl nuclear power plant will result in more than 1,000 additional cases of cancer in the 12 European Community (EC) nations, according to a report for the EC by the British National Radiological Protection Board. Hardest hit will be West Germany (an estimated 384 cases), Italy (346), and Greece (108).	Pope John Paul II issues an encyclical stressing the role of the Virgin Mary in the Roman Catholic faith. The encyclical, the sixth of Pope John Paul II's eight-year papacy, points to Mary as a source of unity among all Christians because she was the "common mother." The document is particularly aimed at strengthening Rome's ties with Christians of the eastern churches, where Marian devotion is prominent.	**March 25**

F	G	H	I	J
Includes elections, federal-state relations, civil rights and liberties, crime, the judiciary, education, health care, poverty, urban affairs and population.	*Includes formation and debate of U.S. foreign and defense policies, veterans' affairs and defense spending. (Relations with specific foreign countries are usually found under the region concerned.)*	*Includes business, labor, agriculture, taxation, transportation, consumer affairs, monetary and fiscal policy, natural resources, and pollution.*	*Includes worldwide scientific, medical and technological developments, natural phenomena, U.S. weather, natural disasters, and accidents.*	*Includes the arts, religion, scholarship, communications media, sports, entertainments, fashions, fads and social life.*

	World Affairs	Europe	Africa & the Middle East	The Americas	Asia & the Pacific
March 26		In Yugoslavia, a nationwide wave of protest strikes ends. The unrest was prompted by a government decree, effective March 1, that placed emergency controls on wages in an effort to ease the nation's economic crisis.... The seventh round of U.S.-Soviet arms talks in Geneva adjourns with the two sides apparently far apart on the removal from Europe of medium-range missiles.		The provinces of New Brunswick and British Columbia decide to fully participate in the Canada Health Act, it is reported. They were the last two holdout provinces in the nation.	In Beijing, Chinese and Portuguese negotiators initial a joint declaration that will restore Macao to mainland rule as of Dec. 20, 1999. The Portuguese-administered enclave on the Chinese coast south of Hong Kong was the first European settlement in China in 1557, and will be the last colonial territory to revert to Chinese rule.
March 27		A joint study prepared by the Central Intelligence Agency and the Defense Intelligence Agency finds that the Soviet economy grew by 4.2% in 1986, double the average growth rate over the past 10 years. The report attributes the strong performance to a good grain harvest and to increased time put in by factory workers.	Chad announces that its army has retaken the oasis town of Faya-Largeau, two days after French military sources reported that Libyan forces were withdrawing from what had been their last major stronghold in northern Chad. The development is considered a severe setback to the ambitions of Libyan leader Col. Muammar el-Qaddafi.	In Canada, a constitutional conference on native self-government fails to produce an agreement. At issue is a long-standing proposal, backed by P.M. Brian Mulroney, to amend the constitution to include self-government for Indians, Inuit (Eskimos), Metis (persons of mixed Indian and white descent), and nonstatus Indians (persons who have lost their Indian legal status through marriage or otherwise).	
March 28		A flare-up of tensions over oil rights in the Aegean Sea threatens a military confrontation between Greece and Turkey, but conciliatory acts by both governments defuse the situation. The easing of the situation is widely characterized as a freeze in the conflict over Aegean oil, not a resolution of it.	In South Africa the black National Union of Mineworkers (NUM) begins a pilot "sleep-in" protest against the migrant labor system under which blacks work in the mines while their wives and children live in distant tribal "homelands."		
March 29				Haitian voters overwhelmingly approved a new constitution in a referendum. Preliminary results from more than half the 1,500 polling places show that 99% of the 742,000 votes so far counted back the constitution. Almost 3 million voters are eligible to vote, but accurate estimates of how many turned out for the referendum are not immediately available.	Philippine Pres. Corazon Aquino tells a campaign crowd in Davao City that unarmed vigilante groups are a legitimate example of the "people power" that helped propel her into office. The campaign for her national senate slate has brought the president to the southern city, site of a recent struggle for power between communist rebels and vigilantes armed by the military.

A	B	C	D	E
Includes developments that affect more than one world region, international organizations and important meetings of major world leaders.	*Includes all domestic and regional developments in Europe, including the Soviet Union, Turkey, Cyprus and Malta.*	*Includes all domestic and regional developments in Africa and the Middle East, including Iraq and Iran and excluding Cyprus, Turkey and Afghanistan.*	*Includes all domestic and regional developments in Latin America, the Caribbean and Canada.*	*Includes all domestic and regional developments in Asia and Pacific nations, extending from Afghanistan through all the Pacific Islands, except Hawaii.*

U.S. Politics & Social Issues	U.S. Foreign Policy & Defense	U.S. Economy & Environment	Science, Technology & Nature	Culture, Leisure & Life Style	
In an effort to put the Iran-Contra affair behind him and end four months of political isolation, Pres. Reagan makes his first political trip since the 1986 elections. He travels to Columbia, Mo., for appearances that his aides hope will focus on education and other policy issues.		The Dow Jones Industrial Average closes at a record high of 2372.59. The previous record closing of 2244.09 was set February 19.	An Atlas-Centaur rocket carrying a Navy communications satellite goes out of control shortly after lift-off from Cape Canaveral and is blown up by safety officials.	Dave Brubeck and his jazz quartet play to a sold-out Soviet audience of some 2,500 noisily cheering fans at his Moscow debut in a concert hall off Red Square. . . . Southern Mississippi wins basketball's National Invitation Tournament finals in New York City, 84-80, over La Salle. Randolph Keys is named most valuable player. . . . A three-day meeting of a council set up to study the Holy See's economic status reports that the Vatican is facing a record budget deficit of about $63 mil. for 1987.	March 26
A three-judge panel of the 11th Circuit Court of Appeals in Atlanta, Ga., suspends a federal district court order removing certain textbooks from Alabama public schools because they promote the "religion" of "secular humanism." Acting on a request by the Alabama Board of Education and a dozen parents, the court allows the books to be returned to the pupils pending consideration of the appeal.		The Senate approves, 79-11, a comprehensive banking bill that will impose a one-year moratorium on banks offering new securities, insurance, or real estate services, and allow the insolvent Federal Savings and Loan Insurance Corp. to borrow as much as $7.5 bil. over two years. . . . The government's consumer price index rose 0.4% in February, the Labor Dept. reports. . . . Pres. Reagan announces that the United States has decided to impose duties that will double the import prices of a wide range of popular electronic products from Japan. The action is a response to Tokyo's alleged failure to live up to a 1986 agreement barring Japanese companies from selling semiconductor chips in the United States for less than a "fair market value" determined by the United States.	Physicists at Wayne State Univ. in Detroit say they have identified a material that achieved superconductivity at a temperature vastly higher than any previously reported. Superconductivity, the absence of electrical resistance, has become one of the most explosive areas of physical research, with more gains reported in the past year than in the previous half-century.	Publishers Weekly's hardback fiction best-sellers for the week are: Windmills of the Gods, Sidney Sheldon; The Eyes of the Dragon, Stephen King; Fine Things, Danielle Steel; Red Storm Rising, Tom Clancy; and Bolt, Dick Francis.	March 27
		Citing "management deficiencies" that threaten safety, the Energy Dept. halts four research reactors at its Oak Ridge, Tenn., atomic complex. . . . In response to a warning from a National Academy of Sciences panel that the plants are operating beyond the capacity of their cooling systems, the Energy Dept. orders its three weapons-production nuclear reactors in South Carolina to reduce to half-power.		North Dakota beats Michigan State, 5-3, to win the National Collegiate Athletic Assoc. hockey championship in Detroit. Tony Hrkac, who one day earlier was named the nation's outstanding hockey player during the season, wins the award as the tournament's most valuable player. . . . Billboard's best-selling albums for the week are: Licensed to III, Beastie Boys; Slippery When Wet, Bon Jovi; The Way It Is, Bruce Hornsby & the Range; Graceland, Paul Simon; and Invisible Touch, Genesis.	March 28
According to the results of a weigh-in conducted over the last six days at more than 200 sites throughout the state, about 5,600 residents of New Mexico shed 34,000 pounds in the first stage of the first state-wide program in the United States to increase health awareness and reduce the risk of heart disease.				The Lady Volunteers of Tennessee win the National Collegiate Athletic Assoc. women's basketball title, 67-44, over Louisiana Tech in the tournament finals. Tennessee freshman Tonya Edwards is named the tournament's most valuable player.	March 29

F	G	H	I	J
Includes elections, federal-state relations, civil rights and liberties, crime, the judiciary, education, health care, poverty, urban affairs and population.	Includes formation and debate of U.S. foreign and defense policies, veterans' affairs and defense spending. (Relations with specific foreign countries are usually found under the region concerned.)	Includes business, labor, agriculture, taxation, transportation, consumer affairs, monetary and fiscal policy, natural resources, and pollution.	Includes worldwide scientific, medical and technological developments, natural phenomena, U.S. weather, natural disasters, and accidents.	Includes the arts, religion, scholarship, communications media, sports, entertainments, fashions, fads and social life.

	World Affairs	Europe	Africa & the Middle East	The Americas	Asia & the Pacific
March 30		Some 40 defendants go on trial in Madrid for their roles in selling adulterated vegetable oil believed to have caused the death of some 600 Spaniards from 1981 through 1985. Billed in Spain as the "trial of the century," the proceedings are expected to last several months. . . . In Spain, the socialist government of Premier Felipe Gonzalez easily survives a no-confidence vote in parliament; but continued labor unrest threatens his government's austerity program.			In an interview published in *Time* magazine, Pakistan's Pres. Muhammad Zia ul-Haq frankly acknowledges that his country can build a nuclear bomb.
March 31		France's Premier Jacques Chirac wins assurance from Pres. Reagan that the United States will take into account European fears over Soviet short-range missiles during negotiations on intermediate-range nuclear forces. . . . In Ireland, the 1987 budget of the new Fianna Fail government of P.M. Charles Haughey is presented. The austerity budget cuts government spending by some $440 mil. in an effort to reduce the budget deficit and restore faith in the nation's ailing economy.		The *Miami Herald* reports that only 28 of 2,027 eligible political exiles have accepted an offer by the Chilean government of Pres. Augusto Pinochet Ugarte to return to their country. . . . In El Salvador, leftist rebels of the Farabundo Marti National Liberation Front attack a major military base and kill more than 60 soldiers, including an American military adviser, in their most successful operation in recent years. . . . Suriname's National Assembly approves a draft constitution that paves the way for elections later in the year. The draft is to be submitted to a referendum in September; if it is approved, an election to bring a return to civilian rule will take place November 25.	
April 1		Turkey's economy grew 8% in 1986, the best figure in a decade, the State Institute of Statistics reports. The gain compares with a 5% increase in 1985.		The Chilean Comm. on Human Rights reports that a prison hunger strike has grown to include 348 of the country's 511 political prisoners. . . . Six weeks after Brazil suspended interest payments on its medium- and long-term debt, three major U.S. banking companies announce that they have placed certain loans to Brazil on nonaccrual status. . . . In Bolivia, trade union leaders ordered the suspension of a 12-day hunger strike by 5,000 workers and students who have been fasting to protest the government's economic policies. The protest is ended to enable leaders of the Bolivian Workers' Central (COB) to meet with the government.	

A	B	C	D	E
Includes developments that affect more than one world region, international organizations and important meetings of major world leaders.	Includes all domestic and regional developments in Europe, including the Soviet Union, Turkey, Cyprus and Malta.	Includes all domestic and regional developments in Africa and the Middle East, including Iraq and Iran and excluding Cyprus, Turkey and Afghanistan.	Includes all domestic and regional developments in Latin America, the Caribbean and Canada.	Includes all domestic and regional developments in Asia and Pacific nations, extending from Afghanistan through all the Pacific Islands, except Hawaii.

U.S. Politics & Social Issues	U.S. Foreign Policy & Defense	U.S. Economy & Environment	Science, Technology & Nature	Culture, Leisure & Life Style	
Disturbed by "the large numbers of graduates of leading business and law schools who have become convicted felons," outgoing Securities and Exchange Comm. Chairman John S.R. Shad announces a $30 mil. gift to establish an ethics program at Harvard Business School.		Currency and stock markets react swiftly and decisively to retaliatory tariffs imposed by the United States on Japanese electronic goods on March 27 as the U.S. dollar drops to 144.70 yen to the dollar, its lowest point against the yen since World War II.		At the 59th annual Academy Awards, *Platoon* wins four Oscars, including best picture and director (Oliver Stone). Best actor goes to Paul Newman (*The Color of Money*); best actress, Marlee Matlin (*Children of a Lesser God*); best supporting actor and actress are Michael Caine and Dianne Wiest, respectively, for their roles in *Hannah and Her Sisters*. The Dutch film *The Assault* is named best foreign-language feature. *Down and Out in America* and *Artie Shaw: Time Is All You've Got* share honors for best documentary feature. . . . Indiana wins the the National Collegiate Athletic Assoc. championship of college basketball by defeating Syracuse, 74-73. Indiana's Keith Smart is named the tournament's most valuable player. . . . Vincent Van Gogh's *Sunflowers* (1889), the largest of seven versions of the subject painted by the Dutch artist in Arles, France, during the final burst of creativity that ended with his suicide in 1890, fetches $39.9 mil. at Christie's in London. The price is by far the highest ever paid for a work of art at auction.	March 30
The Supreme Court upholds the right of public employers to search offices for evidence of wrongdoing and the right of public employees to some privacy in the workplace. . . . In the first U.S. test of the legality of a surrogate mother contract, Bergen County (N.J.) Superior Court Judge Harvey R. Sorkow rules that the contract in question is "constitutionally protected" and awards custody of "Baby M" to her biological father, William Stern, and terminates all parental rights for surrogate mother Mary Beth Whitehead.		The Nuclear Regulatory Comm. (NRC) orders the Peach Bottom nuclear power plant at Delta, Pa., shut down after operators are found sleeping at the controls. The action against the Philadelphia Electric Co. plant is the NRC's first immediate shutdown order in eight years. . . . In a surprise move, Citibank and Chase Manhattan Bank raise their prime lending rates to 7.75% from 7.5%, the first increase in their base rate on corporate loans since 1984. . . . The government's index of leading economic indicators rose 0.7% in February, the Commerce Dept. reports.	In Australia, a Queensland rock painting is the first such painting found outside of Europe that depicts an Ice Age animal. Found in a rock shelter north of Cairns, the painting depicts a rhinoceros-sized marsupial known as the diprotodon. The creature was the largest of all marsupials and has been extinct for 6,000 years.	Former world chess champion Anatoly Karpov of the Soviet Union defeats countryman Andrei Sokolov to earn a title match against world champion Soviet Gary Kasparov.	March 31
Making his first extensive public comments on acquired immune deficiency syndrome, Pres. Reagan endorses acquired immune deficiency syndrome education in the schools but insists that such programs should remain under local control and teach sexual abstinence and fidelity. Speaking before the College of Physicians of Philadelphia, which is celebrating its 200th birthday, the president calls acquired immune deficiency syndrome "public health enemy No. 1."		The House Budget Committee sends to the floor a $1.038 trillion FY1988 budget that is sharply at odds with Pres. Reagan's requests. The budget is adopted on a 21-14 party-line vote. It proposes $18 bil. in new taxes and a defense budget that is $15.9 bil. below Pres. Reagan's request.	Pres. Reagan and France's Premier Jacques Chirac announce settlement of a long-standing dispute over who discovered the virus that causes acquired immune deficiency syndrome. Credit for the discovery involves not only professional pride and the race for a possible Nobel Prize but also millions of dollars in royalties for acquired immune deficiency syndrome screening tests developed to detect exposure to the virus.		April 1

F	G	H	I	J
Includes elections, federal-state relations, civil rights and liberties, crime, the judiciary, education, health care, poverty, urban affairs and population.	Includes formation and debate of U.S. foreign and defense policies, veterans' affairs and defense spending. (Relations with specific foreign countries are usually found under the region concerned.)	Includes business, labor, agriculture, taxation, transportation, consumer affairs, monetary and fiscal policy, natural resources, and pollution.	Includes worldwide scientific, medical and technological developments, natural phenomena, U.S. weather, natural disasters, and accidents.	Includes the arts, religion, scholarship, communications media, sports, entertainments, fashions, fads and social life.

	World Affairs	Europe	Africa & the Middle East	The Americas	Asia & the Pacific
April 2			Ian Smith, prime minister of white-ruled Rhodesia before it became black-ruled Zimbabwe, is suspended from the Zimbabwean Parliament for one year. He is being penalized for a speech he made in February to white businessmen in Johannesburg, South Africa, urging them to fight the "blackmail" of international economic sanctions against South Africa.	Brazil's Finance Min. Dilson Funaro unveils a five-year plan that will permit economic growth of 7% a year by limiting the payment of funds to Brazil's creditors.	
April 3		The Greek parliament passes legislation authorizing the government to take over most land held by the Greek Orthodox Church and distribute it to farm cooperatives. The legislation, strongly opposed by the church, will also place urban church holdings under the administration of lay-dominated committees.		Marcial Samaniego, vice president of Paraguay's Chamber of Deputies, says the government will not renew the 33-year-old state of siege in Asuncion that has been extended virtually every three months since Pres. Alfredo Stroessner came to power in 1954.... In Canada, the national homicide rate fell to a 15-year low in 1986, according to preliminary data released by Statistics Canada. The data indicate that there were 561 killings in Canada in 1986, a 20% drop from 1985.	
April 4				Since February the Nicaraguan government has conscripted thousands of new recruits into the reserves and undertaken maneuvers to improve Managua's defenses. The moves reflect, in large part, a reported concern expressed by Pres. Daniel Ortega Saavedra that the United States might invade.	
April 5		Voters in Switzerland overwhelmingly approve a referendum to tighten rules on immigration and political asylum.	Chief Leabua Jonathan, 73, prime minister of Lesotho for more than 20 years before his ouster in a military coup in January 1986, dies of stomach cancer in Pretoria, South Africa.... Western creditor governments known as the Club of Paris have agreed in principle on a debt relief plan for sub-Saharan Africa calling for rescheduling government-to-government debt repayments over a 15- to 20-year span, with lengthy grace periods and substantially reduced interest.	Pres. Reagan visits Ottawa for his third annual summit with Canada's P.M. Brian Mulroney. The issues of acid rain and free trade dominate the discussions.	
April 6				Pope John Paul II concludes a six-day visit to Chile. The Pope's stay is marred by an outbreak of violence and fighting when police and demonstrators clash during an outdoor mass in Santiago April 3.	
April 7					A package of "extraordinary and urgent" measures aimed at stimulating Japan's economy is outlined by the ruling Liberal Democratic Party. Domestic interests and Japan's trading partners have pressed for such a move.

A	B	C	D	E
Includes developments that affect more than one world region, international organizations and important meetings of major world leaders.	Includes all domestic and regional developments in Europe, including the Soviet Union, Turkey, Cyprus and Malta.	Includes all domestic and regional developments in Africa and the Middle East, including Iraq and Iran and excluding Cyprus, Turkey and Afghanistan.	Includes all domestic and regional developments in Latin America, the Caribbean and Canada.	Includes all domestic and regional developments in Asia and Pacific nations, extending from Afghanistan through all the Pacific Islands, except Hawaii.

U.S. Politics & Social Issues	U.S. Foreign Policy & Defense	U.S. Economy & Environment	Science, Technology & Nature	Culture, Leisure & Life Style	
In a move hailed by some as the first step toward a complete overhaul of the nation's welfare system, the Senate votes, 99-0, to approve legislation amending the Job Training Partnership Act. The bill authorizes bonus payments to states that develop and implement programs to move long-term welfare recipients into private sector jobs.	Jack F. Matlock Jr. takes over as the U.S. ambassador to Moscow. He succeeds Arthur A. Hartman. . . . In the wake of a spy scandal in which two former U.S. Marine Corps embassy guards are alleged to have aided Soviet spies, the State Dept. announces that the head of security at the U.S. Embassy in Moscow has been recalled "temporarily" for consultations.	Congress overrides a presidential veto to enact an $87.5 bil. highway and mass transit bill. . . . The Environmental Protection Agency proposes rules to safeguard against leaks from underground storage tanks holding oil products or chemicals.	The International Business Machines Corp. unveils its long-awaited second generation of personal computers. . . . The New England Journal of Medicine reports on a new surgical technique that offers the prospect of significant relief from Parkinson's disease, a progressive nervous disorder involving loss of muscle control, through transplanting tissue from the adrenal glands to the brain.	Buddy (Bernard) Rich, 69, jazz musician often hailed as "the world's greatest drummer," dies in Los Angeles of respiratory and cardiac failure while undergoing treatment for a brain tumor. From his vaudeville beginnings as Baby Traps, he later played with Artie Shaw and Tommy Dorsey before starting his own band after World War II. After touring with trumpeter Harry James, in 1966 he again formed his own band, with which he worked on and off for the rest of his life.	April 2
		White House Budget Dir. James C. Miller III calls for major changes that would give the administration increased control over the congressional budget process and urges Congress to make the congressional budget resolution subject to presidential veto. . . . The nation's unemployment rate declined in March to 6.5% from February's 6.6%, according to the Labor Dept. . . . The increase in the Dow Jones Industrial Average, 69.89 points, is the largest on record.	Pres. Reagan approves a scaled-down version of the proposed space station, which is encountering serious financial and political problems. The project is being divided into two phases. Construction of the first phase is projected to begin in mid-1994, with permanent manning planned by early 1996.	The fabled jewelry collection of the Duchess of Windsor, who died in April 1986, is auctioned in Geneva along with a host of personal effects. The total of the two-day sale, conducted by Sotheby's, is $50,281,887, a record for a jewelry sale and seven times Sotheby's presale estimate.	April 3
		The General Accounting Office says Pres. Reagan has illegally deferred $265 mil. that Congress appropriated for other purposes to give pay increases to government employees. But the agency concedes that it does not have "authority to compel release of the funds."			April 4
					April 5
Rep. Jack Kemp (R, N.Y.) formally declares his candidacy for the 1988 Republican presidential nomination.		The Supreme Court removes a lower federal court protection for Texaco Inc. against having to post a crippling $12 bil. appeals bond in its court fight with Pennzoil Co. The decision puts Texaco under intense pressure to settle the complicated litigation with Pennzoil, and brings back an imminent threat of a bankruptcy filing.		Sugar Ray Leonard, who has fought only one bout in five years, upsets middleweight champion Marvelous Marvin Hagler in a 12-round split decision to win the World Boxing Council middleweight title. . . . Author Peter Taylor is named winner of the $50,000 Ritz Paris Hemingway Award for his novel A Summons to Memphis.	April 6
Mayor Harold Washington (D) of Chicago decisively wins reelection to a second four-year term; Washington supporters win control of the city council for the first time. . . . Political action committees contributed a record $84.6 mil. to House candidates in the 1986 general election, according to a report by the self-styled citizens' lobby Common Cause.	Pres. Reagan orders a study of security at the U.S. Embassy compound under construction in Moscow. The move comes in the wake of allegations that U.S. Marine guards aided Soviet spies to penetrate the current embassy. The new embassy complex, which has cost $100 mil. thus far, is scheduled for completion in 1989.	Outstanding consumer credit grew a seasonally adjusted $1.77 bil. in February, the Federal Reserve Board reports.			April 7

F	G	H	I	J
Includes elections, federal-state relations, civil rights and liberties, crime, the judiciary, education, health care, poverty, urban affairs and population.	Includes formation and debate of U.S. foreign and defense policies, veterans' affairs and defense spending. (Relations with specific foreign countries are usually found under the region concerned.)	Includes business, labor, agriculture, taxation, transportation, consumer affairs, monetary and fiscal policy, natural resources, and pollution.	Includes worldwide scientific, medical and technological developments, natural phenomena, U.S. weather, natural disasters, and accidents.	Includes the arts, religion, scholarship, communications media, sports, entertainments, fashions, fads and social life.

	World Affairs	Europe	Africa & the Middle East	The Americas	Asia & the Pacific
April 8	Finance officials from the seven biggest industrial countries reaffirm their commitment to stabilize the U.S. dollar and reduce trade imbalances.	The known death toll from the March 6 capsizing of the British ferry *Herald of Free Enterprise* off Zeebrugge, Belgium, has risen to 184—50 more than originally reported—as divers continue to recover bodies trapped amid debris in the boat's upper deck.		In El Salvador, the rightist National Conciliation Party (PCN) agrees that, effective this day, it will end a three-month strike during which it has refused to participate in legislative debates or votes. Rafael Moran Castaneda of the PCN says his party will end the boycott even if its ally, the Nationalist Republican Alliance (ARENA), refuses to do so.	In South Korea, the unofficial leaders of the opposition New Korea Democratic Party (NKDP) leave the party to form a group of their own. The two men, Kim Dae Jung and Kim Young Sam, claim that elements of the NKDP have fallen under the sway of the government.
April 9	Yesterday's announcement by finance officials from the Group of Seven confirming their commitment to stabilize the U.S. dollar and reduce trade imbalances, pushes the dollar to new lows against the Japanese yen. . . . A sharp increase in the number of Soviet Jews allowed to emigrate from the USSR and renewed contacts between Soviet and Israeli officials in recent weeks are reported.	Ireland's supreme court rules that ratification of the Single European Act would violate the Irish constitution. The 1986 act, designed to create even closer bonds among the 12 European Community (EC) members, has now been signed by all EC nations except Ireland.			
April 10		The Dutch parliament is the latest European governing body to tighten immigration rules. Under the new provisions, refugees attempting to enter the Netherlands who had previously passed through or sought asylum in any other Western nation will be turned back.	Kuwait declines a U.S. offer to provide escorts for its oil tankers, which have come under frequent attack by Iran because of Kuwait's support for Iraq in the Iran-Iraq war. . . . Egypt's ruling National Democratic Party has reportedly retained its commanding majority in parliamentary elections held April 6, but an alliance that includes Islamic fundamentalists succeeded in significantly strengthing the opposition.		
April 11		Soviet leader Mikhail S. Gorbachev ends a three-day visit to Czechoslovakia, a trip widely viewed as an important test of unity in the Soviet bloc. Relations between Moscow and Prague have been strained over the resistance of the Czechoslovak leadership to emulating the reforms initiated by Gorbachev in the Soviet Union.		Some 25,000 students and opposition politicians march through the streets of Caracas, Venezuela, in the biggest antigovernment demonstration in recent years. The government of Pres. Jaime Lusinchi in past weeks has faced worsening student violence, and Venezuelans are said to be concerned that the president is losing his grip on power as he grapples with mounting economic and political pressures.	
April 12					The Alliance Party looses power in Fiji parliamentary elections held over the last nine days. The victorious coalition of two opposition parties pledges to ban nuclear weapons from Fijian territory and to pursue a foreign policy of nonalignment, but opposes establishment of a Soviet Embassy in Fiji.

A	B	C	D	E
Includes developments that affect more than one world region, international organizations and important meetings of major world leaders.	Includes all domestic and regional developments in Europe, including the Soviet Union, Turkey, Cyprus and Malta.	Includes all domestic and regional developments in Africa and the Middle East, including Iraq and Iran and excluding Cyprus, Turkey and Afghanistan.	Includes all domestic and regional developments in Latin America, the Caribbean and Canada.	Includes all domestic and regional developments in Asia and Pacific nations, extending from Afghanistan through all the Pacific Islands, except Hawaii.

U.S. Politics & Social Issues	U.S. Foreign Policy & Defense	U.S. Economy & Environment	Science, Technology & Nature	Culture, Leisure & Life Style	
Federal Bureau of Investigation Dir. William H. Webster admits that he might have been "negligent" in not following up on an early warning of possible criminal violations in the Iran-Contra affair by Lt. Col. Oliver L. North. Webster makes the admission in testimony before the Senate Intelligence Committee during confirmation hearings on his nomination to become director of the Central Intelligence Agency.	The White House agrees to review Pres. Reagan's personal notes and turn over relevant excerpts to the congressional committees investigating the Iran-Contra arms scandal. The review would cover entries in Reagan's diary dating back to January 1984, and all references to Iran or to the Nicaraguan rebels will be noted. Reagan will retain final discretion over what passages to reveal to the committee.				April 8
Sen. Paul Simon (D, Ill.) reverses himself and announces that he will make a formal declaration of his candidacy for the presidency in May. Simon earlier tried to persuade Arkansas Sen. Dale Bumpers (D) to run.		After decisively rejecting Pres. Reagan's proposed budget for FY1988, the House approves a trillion-dollar budget plan that freezes or increases funding for most domestic programs and keeps military spending below the amount needed to keep pace with inflation.		In a ceremony that coincides with the biennial Jerusalem International Book Fair, South African novelist J.M. Coetzee receives the $5,000 Jerusalem Prize for the Freedom of the Individual in Society.	April 9
	James H. Webb Jr. takes over as secretary of the Navy succeeding the retired John F. Lehman Jr. The Senate had confirmed Webb by voice vote April 9.	The producer price index rose a seasonally adjusted 0.4% in March, the Labor Dept. reports.			April 10
		Warming of the Earth's atmosphere due to the buildup of carbon dioxide and other gases can be curbed by government actions, according to a study by the World Resources Institute report. The study says the warming can be significantly limited by more efficient use of energy, restoring deforested tropical areas, and reducing chlorofluorocarbon emissions.		Erskine Caldwell, 83, author whose earthy tales of the American South include two of the best-selling novels of all time, *Tobacco Road* (1932) and *God's Little Acre* (1933), dies of lung cancer in Paradise Valley, Ariz. Though tame by contemporary standards, several of his books were banned. . . . Primo Levi, 67, Italian Jewish author whose autobiographical writings drew on his experiences as a concentration camp survivor and as a chemist, dies in Turin, after falling down stairs at his home. During World War II, he served in the Italian resistance before being deported to Auschwitz in 1943, an experience recounted in his 1947 memoir *If This Is a Man*.	April 11
	The Defense Dept. announces that a total of 11 Marine Corps guards are being recalled from two U.S. diplomatic outposts as part of the growing investigation stemming from the Moscow Embassy spy scandal.	Texaco Inc. becomes the largest U.S. company to file for bankruptcy after attempts to settle its legal dispute with Pennzoil Co. collapse.	Soviet cosmonauts assist in the successful docking of a new unmanned space module with the orbiting station *Mir* after two earlier efforts at docking failed.	Larry Mize wins the 51st Masters golf tournament in Augusta, Ga. . . . France's Alain Prost wins the season-opening Formula One event, the Brazilian Grand Prix in Rio de Janeiro.	April 12

F	G	H	I	J
Includes elections, federal-state relations, civil rights and liberties, crime, the judiciary, education, health care, poverty, urban affairs and population.	*Includes formation and debate of U.S. foreign and defense policies, veterans' affairs and defense spending. (Relations with specific foreign countries are usually found under the region concerned.)*	*Includes business, labor, agriculture, taxation, transportation, consumer affairs, monetary and fiscal policy, natural resources, and pollution.*	*Includes worldwide scientific, medical and technological developments, natural phenomena, U.S. weather, natural disasters, and accidents.*	*Includes the arts, religion, scholarship, communications media, sports, entertainments, fashions, fads and social life.*

	World Affairs	Europe	Africa & the Middle East	The Americas	Asia & the Pacific
April 13		Amid record trade deficits with Japan, the European Community (EC) warns Japan that the trade situation between the two parties is becoming intolerable. Figures released by the EC show that Japan had run a record surplus of $2.13 bil. with the EC in March.	Low-level fighting continues in northern Chad between the advancing Chadian Army and retreating Libyan forces, according to reports over the last two weeks. Meanwhile, Chad exhibits a vast array of military equipment abandoned by Libya and estimated to be worth $500 mil. to $1 bil.	Argentina reaches agreement with its bank advisory committee on a new loan and refinancing package worth some $30 bil. With a foreign debt of $52 bil., Argentina is the third-largest debtor in the Third World, after Brazil ($108 bil.) and Mexico ($100 bil.).	Japan's stock market, with total capitalization of an estimated $2.688 trillion, has overtaken the U.S. market, with $2.672 trillion, as the largest in the world, according to an analysis by Morgan Stanley & Co.... South Korea's Pres. Chun Doo Hwan suspends the country's debate over constitutional reform and says his successor will be chosen by an electoral college, a method thought to all but guarantee victory for the government's chosen candidate.... In South Korea, Kim Dae Jung and Kim Young Sam, formerly the unofficial leaders of the dissident New Korea Democratic Party (NKDP), formally organize their new party, the Party for Reunification and Democracy.
April 14		Turkey formally applies to become a full member of the European Community (EC). Turkey's chances for admission are clouded by its ongoing feud with EC member Greece, which has vowed to block Turkish membership.			
April 15		Sec. of State George P. Shultz leaves Moscow with an offer from Soviet leader Mikhail S. Gorbachev to eliminate shorter-range intermediate nuclear forces in Europe. ... The *New York Times* reports that the Hungarian capital of Budapest has erected a statue in honor of Raoul Wallenberg, the Swedish diplomat who saved thousands of Hungarian Jews during World War II and then disappeared after his arrest by Soviet authorities. The statue was donated by former U.S. Ambassador Nicolas M. Salgo.	The first anniversary of the U.S. bombing raid on Libya is marked at a rally held in Tripoli from 11:30 p.m. to 2:30 a.m. attended by several hundred foreign "peace delegates" and journalists. Col. Muammar el-Qaddafi appears for less than two minutes and then abruptly leaves, after which his 14-year-old son addresses the crowd, denouncing the U.S. raid as an act of terrorism over which Libya has been victorious.	An Argentine army major accused of human rights abuses in the 1970s refuses to appear before a civilian court and takes refuge at an army base in Cordoba. The action by the rebellious officer, who is backed by sympathetic middle-ranking officers, sparks the worst crisis of civilian Pres. Raul Alfonsin's three-year-old administration.	
April 16	The governments of seven nations disclose an agreement to limit the export of large missiles and related missile technology. The pact is designed to curtail the spread of nuclear weapons. The participating nations are the United States, Great Britain, France, West Germany, Italy, Canada, and Japan.				

A	B	C	D	E
Includes developments that affect more than one world region, international organizations and important meetings of major world leaders.	*Includes all domestic and regional developments in Europe, including the Soviet Union, Turkey, Cyprus and Malta.*	*Includes all domestic and regional developments in Africa and the Middle East, including Iraq and Iran and excluding Cyprus, Turkey and Afghanistan.*	*Includes all domestic and regional developments in Latin America, the Caribbean and Canada.*	*Includes all domestic and regional developments in Asia and Pacific nations, extending from Afghanistan through all the Pacific Islands, except Hawaii.*

U.S. Politics & Social Issues	U.S. Foreign Policy & Defense	U.S. Economy & Environment	Science, Technology & Nature	Culture, Leisure & Life Style	
Former Sen. Gary Hart (D, Colo.) declares his candidacy for the presidency with a speech at Red Rocks Park outside Denver. . . . A federal commission releases sentencing guidelines for federal judges that details 43 levels of sentences, from no imprisonment to a life term.					**April 13**
The White House makes public the 1986 tax returns of President and Mrs. Reagan. The Reagans paid $92,460 in federal taxes, 27.5% of their adjusted gross income of $336,640.		The U.S. deficit on merchandise trade rose in February to $15.06 bil., the Commerce Dept. reports. . . . A federal judge rejects government efforts to fine General Motors Corp. $4 mil. and force it to recall its 1980 X-cars for an alleged brake defect. . . . A dramatic decline of lead emissions into the atmosphere shows up in the Environmental Protection Agency's annual report on air pollution. The report, assessing air pollution conditions in 1985, shows a 48% drop in lead emissions to the atmosphere, primarily through motor vehicle exhaust, to a total of 23.2 million tons, from 44.2 million tons in 1984.			**April 14**
In a *Washington Post*/ABC News poll, 65% of those questioned say they think Pres. Reagan is not telling the public the truth about the Iran-Contra arms scandal. In a poll taken a month earlier, 49% had said they doubted the president.		The industrial production index dropped a seasonally adjusted 0.3% in March, according to the Federal Reserve Board.	Stanford Univ. physicists unveil the Stanford Linear Collider, a new atom smasher. Developed under the direction of Nobel laureate Burton Richter, the device uses new and relatively low-cost technology to achieve high-energy particle collisions.	*Variety*'s top-grossing films for the week are: *The Secret of My Success, Police Academy 4: Citizens on Patrol, Blind Date, Lethal Weapon,* and *Platoon.*	**April 15**
The Federal Communications Comm. adopts major new restrictions on the broadcast of obscene and offensive material and warns radio and television station owners that they face fines or loss of their licenses if they broadcast sexually explicit language or song lyrics. . . . Former White House political director Lyn Nofziger, a longtime adviser to Pres. Reagan, is indicted by a federal grand jury for his lobbying activities on behalf of the Wedtech Corp., a Bronx, N.Y.-based military contractor.		Housing starts dropped 3.2% in March to a seasonally adjusted annual rate of 1.774 million units, the Commerce Dept. says.	The government says it is clearing the way for inventors to patent new forms of life created through genetic engineering. The announcement says the policy will formally be published by the Commerce Dept.'s Patent and Trademark Office next week.	Columbia Univ. presents the 71st annual Pulitzer Prizes. The award for fiction goes to Peter Taylor's *A Summons to Memphis*; history, Bernard Bailyn's *Voyagers to the West: A Passage in the Peopling of America on the Eve of the Revolution*; biography, David J. Garrow's *Bearing the Cross: Martin Luther King Jr. and the Southern Christian Leadership Conference*; general nonfiction, David K. Shipler's *Arab and Jew: Wounded Spirits in a Promised Land*; poetry, Rita Dove's *Thomas and Beulah*; music, John Harbison's *The Flight into Egypt*; public service, Andrew Schneider and Matthew Brelis of the *Pittsburgh Press* for a series documenting drug use and other medical problems that went undetected in screenings of airline pilots.	**April 16**

F	G	H	I	J
Includes elections, federal-state relations, civil rights and liberties, crime, the judiciary, education, health care, poverty, urban affairs and population.	Includes formation and debate of U.S. foreign and defense policies, veterans' affairs and defense spending. (Relations with specific foreign countries are usually found under the region concerned.)	Includes business, labor, agriculture, taxation, transportation, consumer affairs, monetary and fiscal policy, natural resources, and pollution.	Includes worldwide scientific, medical and technological developments, natural phenomena, U.S. weather, natural disasters, and accidents.	Includes the arts, religion, scholarship, communications media, sports, entertainments, fashions, fads and social life.

	World Affairs	Europe	Africa & the Middle East	The Americas	Asia & the Pacific
April 17			In a surprise announcement, P.M. Robert Mugabe says that his ruling Zimbabwe African National Union has broken off unity talks with opposition leader Joshua Nkomo's Zimbabwe African People's Union, saying they "served no useful purpose." Nkomo later says the setback is only temporary.		
April 18		In Italy, Christian Democrat Amintore Fanfani is sworn in as the premier of Italy's 46th government since World War II. Fanfani's rise to the premiership temporarily solves a seven-week Italian government crisis. His minority government is widely expected to be voted down by parliament, thus clearing the way for early general elections.			In the Philippines, forces loyal to the government swiftly crush an attempt by military rebels to free soldiers imprisoned for a failed January coup.
April 19				In Argentina, a rebellion triggered by an army officer who refused to appear before a civilian court April 15 to answer charges of human rights abuses ends peacefully after Pres. Raul Alfonsin personally persuaded the remaining 130 officers to surrender.	Deputies to Vietnam's National Assembly are chosen under election procedures that are generally agreed to be the most open that Vietnam has enjoyed under communist rule. Although the Communist Party of Vietnam is still the country's only legal party and all candidates must profess communism and have the approval of the quasi-governmental Vietnam Fatherland Front, all were nominated at public meetings and faced questions and criticism at public forums.
April 20					
April 21					More than 100 people are killed in a bombing attack by Tamil rebels in Colombo, Sri Lanka. The explosion, only four days after the murder of 118 Sinhalese by Tamils disguised as soldiers, renews fears of an escalation of the civil war between the island nation's Tamil minority and Sinhalese majority.

A	B	C	D	E
Includes developments that affect more than one world region, international organizations and important meetings of major world leaders.	Includes all domestic and regional developments in Europe, including the Soviet Union, Turkey, Cyprus and Malta.	Includes all domestic and regional developments in Africa and the Middle East, including Iraq and Iran and excluding Cyprus, Turkey and Afghanistan.	Includes all domestic and regional developments in Latin America, the Caribbean and Canada.	Includes all domestic and regional developments in Asia and Pacific nations, extending from Afghanistan through all the Pacific Islands, except Hawaii.

U.S. Politics & Social Issues	U.S. Foreign Policy & Defense	U.S. Economy & Environment	Science, Technology & Nature	Culture, Leisure & Life Style	
	Washington announces that the United States and Soviet Union have agreed in principle to conduct underground nuclear tests at each other's test sites as a first step on verification. The announcement is made by Kenneth L. Adelman, the head of the U.S. Arms Control and Disarmament Agency.	The United States imposes 100% tariffs on Japanese electronics imports worth about $300 mil. annually. The tariffs are in retaliation for various alleged unfair trade practices. The tariffs will apply to imports of laptop and desktop personal computers, color televisions with 18-, 19- and 20-inch screens, and home power tools.	Though women still account for only a small percentage of cases of acquired immune deficiency syndrome (AIDS) in the United States, the percentage of women who contracted AIDS via sex with men more than doubled between 1982 and 1986, according to a study published in the *Journal of the American Medical Association*. The research focuses on nearly 2,000 reported cases of AIDS in women.	Richard Wilbur, poet, translator, and critic, is named as the second poet laureate of the United States. Wilbur, 66, succeeds Robert Penn Warren, 81, who is stepping down after one year because of poor health. . . . Pres. Reagan nominates Russian scholar James H. Billington, 57, currently director of the Woodrow Wilson International Center for Scholars in Washington, D.C., to replace Daniel J. Boorstin as head of the Library of Congress. . . . Willi Smith, 39, fashion designer who created sportswear for both men and women, dies in New York City of generalized cryptococcal fungal infection, which is a manifestation of acquired immune deficiency syndrome. One of the world's foremost black designers, in 1986 his company, WilliWear, had gross sales of more than $25 mil.	April 17
				Carlos Baker, 77, Princeton Univ. English professor who was novelist Ernest Hemingway's official biographer, dies in Princeton, N.J. Baker's *Ernest Hemingway: A Life Story* appeared in 1969. He was the Woodrow Wilson Professor of Literature at Princeton before he retired from teaching in 1977.	April 18
An internal White House review of covert operations concludes that almost a third of the missions authorized by Pres. Reagan should be ended, according to the *Washington Post*. Reagan ordered the review in November 1986, when the Iran-Contra arms scandal first broke. The report refers only to active covert operations, not secret missions designed only to gather information.	Gen. Maxwell D(avenport) Taylor, 85, who during World War II commanded the 101st Airborne Division on D-Day and through some of the fiercest fighting in Europe, dies in Washington, D.C., of amyotrophic lateral sclerosis (Lou Gehrig's disease). In Korea, he led field troops as commander of the Eighth Army, and from 1962 to 1964 was chairman of the Joint Chiefs of Staff, after which and he served as U.S. ambassador to Saigon, from 1964 to 1965.		The last California condor in the wild is captured by biologists at the Bitter Creek National Wildlife Refuge 40 miles southwest of Bakersfield.	Antony Tudor (born William Cook), 78 or 79, British-born choreographer who revolutionized ballet through the introduction of psychologically revealing gestures (reflecting the influence of Freudian thought), dies in New York City after a heart attack. He produced his early masterpiece *Jard in aux Lilas* in 1936 and came to the United States in 1939, at the invitation of the Ballet Theater (later known as American Ballet Theater), with which he remained closely associated for the rest of his career. His *Pillar of Fire* (1942) made American dancer Nora Kaye an international star. Other notable Tudor ballets include *Dark Elegies* (1937), *Undertow* (1945), and *Echoing of Trumpets* (1963).	April 19
		Interior Sec. Donald Hodel recommends to Congress opening the coastal plain of Alaska's Arctic National Wildlife Refuge to oil drilling.		Japan's Toshihiko Seko wins the Boston marathon in 2:11:50. Rosa Mota of Portugal wins the women's race in 2:25:21.	April 20
The Supreme Court rules that defendants who played a major role in a crime that resulted in murder may be sentenced to death if they displayed a "reckless indifference" to life. The 5-4 decision written by Justice Sandra Day O'Connor sanctions the death penalty in such cases even if the defendant was not the actual killer nor had intended to kill anyone.	The Second U.S. Circuit Court of Appeals in New York generally confirms the $220 mil. class-action settlement in the Agent Orange case under which seven chemical companies that produced Agent Orange, a herbicide used in the Vietnam War, agreed to pay $180 mil. to settle claims of injury from the chemical brought by about 15,000 veterans and their families. Since 1984 the fund has grown to more than $220 mil., including interest.	The Supreme Court upholds, 6-3, state regulation of corporate takeovers. The court upholds an Indiana law that imposes restrictions against hostile offers for companies incorporated in that state. . . . Congressional committees investigating the Iran-Contra arms scandal vote to grant limited immunity from prosecution to former national security adviser Rear Adm. John M. Poindexter. . . . According to Treasury Dept. figures released today, the federal budget deficit totaled $121.93 bil. for the first half of FY1987 (Oct. 1, 1986, through Mar. 31, 1987). That figure is down more than $15 bil. from the deficit of $136.34 bil. posted in the same period of FY1986.		Soviet Jewish pianist Vladimir O. Feltsman gives his first Moscow recital in more than eight years at Tchaikovsky Hall, one of the Soviet capital's main auditoriums. Feltsman had been barred from giving public concerts in Moscow and Leningrad since seeking, and being denied, permission to emigrate in 1979.	April 21

F	G	H	I	J
Includes elections, federal-state relations, civil rights and liberties, crime, the judiciary, education, health care, poverty, urban affairs and population.	Includes formation and debate of U.S. foreign and defense policies, veterans' affairs and defense spending. (Relations with specific foreign countries are usually found under the region concerned.)	Includes business, labor, agriculture, taxation, transportation, consumer affairs, monetary and fiscal policy, natural resources, and pollution.	Includes worldwide scientific, medical and technological developments, natural phenomena, U.S. weather, natural disasters, and accidents.	Includes the arts, religion, scholarship, communications media, sports, entertainments, fashions, fads and social life.

	World Affairs	Europe	Africa & the Middle East	The Americas	Asia & the Pacific
April 22		The union for some 1.5 million West German metalworkers reaches an agreement with its employers group that will reduce the working week by 90 minutes, to 37 hours, by 1990. The agreement, which affects West Germany's motor and engineering industries and is widely seen as a victory for the union, averts a nationwide strike.	A six-week-old walkout by black railway workers in South Africa erupts into violence in Johannesburg, when police open fire and kill at least six blacks in clashes that followed the dismissal of 16,000 strikers. It is one of the worst days of unrest since the latest state of emergency was declared in June 1986.		
April 23		U.S. and Soviet negotiators return to Geneva to reopen discussions on intermediate nuclear forces (INF). Although negotiations on strategic and space weapons are not scheduled to reopen until May 5, the INF talks have been given new impetus by the offer from Soviet leader Mikhail S. Gorbachev to remove from Europe shorter-range missiles in addition to longer-range systems.			After removing the sales tax proposal on which Premier Yasuhiro Nakasone had staked much of his political capital, the lower house of Japan's Diet approves the long-delayed FY1987 budget.... The Vietnamese government announces a package of reforms aimed at reducing central control of the economy and giving more leeway to the profit motive. . . . Indonesia's quasi-governmental Golkar group attains a record majority in national elections. But the campaign's greatest excitement is generated by the massive crowds drawn to rallies for the tiny Indonesian Democratic Party (PDI).
April 24					Malaysia's P.M. Mahathir Mohamad retains political power and his post as president of the United Malays National Org. despite an internal party struggle of an intensity not seen before in Malaysian politics.
April 25		In general elections in Iceland, the center-right coalition government of Premier Steingrimur Hermannsson fails to win enough seats in parliament to hold power and negotiations to form a new government are expected to take weeks or months. In the election, the nation's feminist party nearly doubles its previous share of the vote.	South African Army commandos raid targets in the southern Zambian city of Livingstone, killing four people and critically wounding one. Pretoria says the dead were African National Congress (ANC) "terrorists," while Zambian officials and witnesses maintain that all the victims were Zambian civilians with no connection to the ANC.	Citing his nation's severe economic crisis, El Savaldor's Pres. Jose Napoleon Duarte appeals to Pres. Reagan April 10 for an exception to the new U.S. immigration law for Salvadorans living illegally in the United States. Duarte's appeal is disclosed by the *New York Times* in a story this day.	
April 26		The Soviet Union proposes that the top defense officials of the United States and USSR meet to discuss the anti-ballistic missile treaty with regard to Star Wars testing.	Feuding factions of the Palestine Liberation Org. (PLO) conclude a formal six-day meeting in Algeria with an apparent reconciliation between radicals and moderates under the undisputed leadership of PLO chairman Yasir Arafat, but with the adoption of a more hard-line stance on Arab-Israeli peace issues that damages the PLO's relations with Egypt, Jordan, and Morocco.		

A	B	C	D	E
Includes developments that affect more than one world region, international organizations and important meetings of major world leaders.	*Includes all domestic and regional developments in Europe, including the Soviet Union, Turkey, Cyprus and Malta.*	*Includes all domestic and regional developments in Africa and the Middle East, including Iraq and Iran and excluding Cyprus, Turkey and Afghanistan.*	*Includes all domestic and regional developments in Latin America, the Caribbean and Canada.*	*Includes all domestic and regional developments in Asia and Pacific nations, extending from Afghanistan through all the Pacific Islands, except Hawaii.*

U.S. Politics & Social Issues	U.S. Foreign Policy & Defense	U.S. Economy & Environment	Science, Technology & Nature	Culture, Leisure & Life Style	
The Supreme Court rejects, 5-4, a general racial challenge to the death penalty as insufficient proof that the defendant in the case under review is a victim of discrimination. . . . Joe Hunt, the leader of a Santa Monica, Calif., group that called itself the Billionaire Boys Club, is convicted of the murder of reputed Beverly Hills con man Ronald G. Levin.		Testifying before the Senate Banking Committee, U.S. Attorney Rudolph Giuliani urges Congress to toughen securities fraud laws, impose more stringent sentencing, and establish a firm definition of insider trading. . . . The Environmental Protection Agency proposes regulations for monitoring asbestos building materials in schools and for sealing off or removing those that are hazardous. The rules, required by legislation enacted in 1986, call for inspections and any handling of such materials by certified and trained workers.			April 22
The trustees of the Ronald Reagan Presidential Foundation say they have abandoned a plan to build a library honoring Pres. Reagan on the campus of Stanford Univ. The decision comes after three years of resistance from students and faculty.		Stock speculator Ivan F. Boesky pleads guilty to one count of conspiracy to file false documents with the federal government, a charge that carries a maximum sentence of five years in prison and a $250,000 fine. . . . The nation's gross national product grew at a 4.3% annual rate in the first quarter, after adjustment for inflation, the Commerce Dept. reports. . . . The Dow Jones Industrial Average closes at a new high of 2405.54, and a seat on the New York Stock Exchange is sold for a record $1 mil.	Six stories of a high-rise apartment building under construction in downtown Bridgeport, Conn., collapse, trapping dozens of construction workers under tons of rubble.		April 23
		The government's consumer price index rose 0.4% in March, the same increase as in February, the Labor Dept. reports. . . . Consumer spending rose 0.3% in March, and Americans' total personal income increased 0.2%, the Commerce Dept. says. . . . The House passes a $9 bil. supplemental appropriations bill for the remainder of FY1987, the current fiscal year. The bill supplies extra money for various programs through the end of the fiscal year on September 30. . . . The Dept. of Housing and Urban Development abruptly delays an auction of $410 mil. worth of mortgages on low-cost housing after members of Congress and advocacy groups protest.	The first authorized outdoor test of genetically engineered bacteria called Frostban occurs in a strawberry patch in northern California, about three-and-a-half years after its sponsor first asked for government permission. The test is conducted by Advanced Genetic Sciences Inc. of Oakland, Calif.	*Publishers Weekly*'s hardback fiction best-sellers for the week are: *Fine Things*, Danielle Steel; *Windmills of the Gods*, Sidney Sheldon; *The Eyes of the Dragon*, Stephen King; *Red Storm Rising*, Tom Clancy; and *Destiny*, Sally Beauman.	April 24
Backers of leading Republican presidential candidates agree to hold Michigan's presidential nominating convention Jan. 29-30, 1988, more than a week before the Iowa caucuses that traditionally start the nominating season, it is reported.				*Billboard*'s best-selling albums for the week are: *The Joshua Tree*, U2; *Licensed to Ill*, Beastie Boys; *Slippery When Wet*, Bon Jovi; *Look What the Cat Dragged In*, Poison; and *Graceland*, Paul Simon.	April 25
		An agreement between management and television news writers, editors, and other employees at the American Broadcasting Co. (ABC) brings to an end two months of labor unrest at ABC and at CBS, which settled April 16. The new contracts call for modest salary increases for employees, while the network wins more flexibility in hiring temporary employees, ignoring seniority in layoffs, and using managers and on-air reporters to write stories.	The first anniversary of the Chernobyl nuclear plant accident in the Soviet Ukraine is marked by antinuclear protests around the world. The accident began Apr. 26, 1986, when the No. 4 reactor at Chernobyl went out of control during an unauthorized power experiment. An explosion and fire in the reactor's core spewed clouds of radiation over the Soviet Union and Europe.		April 26

F	G	H	I	J
Includes elections, federal-state relations, civil rights and liberties, crime, the judiciary, education, health care, poverty, urban affairs and population.	Includes formation and debate of U.S. foreign and defense policies, veterans' affairs and defense spending. (Relations with specific foreign countries are usually found under the region concerned.)	Includes business, labor, agriculture, taxation, transportation, consumer affairs, monetary and fiscal policy, natural resources, and pollution.	Includes worldwide scientific, medical and technological developments, natural phenomena, U.S. weather, natural disasters, and accidents.	Includes the arts, religion, scholarship, communications media, sports, entertainments, fashions, fads and social life.

	World Affairs	Europe	Africa & the Middle East	The Americas	Asia & the Pacific
April 27		Soviet negotiators in Geneva offer a draft treaty on the removal from Europe of intermediate nuclear forces (INF), but insist that there can be no agreement on shorter-range INF weapons without the elimination nuclear-capable Pershing IA missiles based in West Germany.... The British government initiates contempt of court proceedings against three newspapers for printing stories based on *Spycatcher*, the controversial memoirs of former British counterintelligence agent Peter Wright, whose most damaging assertion is that in 1974 "30 MI5 [counterintelligence] officers were engaged in a politically motivated plot to hound Harold Wilson from office as prime minister."		Canada's Agriculture Min. John Wise announces that a 19-month moratorium on foreclosures by the federal Farm Credit Corp. will be lifted on May 1. The agency suspended foreclosures in September 1985, when 670 farmers faced immediate foreclosure. (An estimated 14,800 agency accounts are in arrears, including 6,000 farmers who have not made debt payments in two or more years.)	
April 28		Italy's Pres. Francesco Cossiga dissolves the parliament and calls early elections for June after the 10-day-old government of Christian Democrat Amintore Fanfani loses a vote of confidence. Fanfani will stay on as caretaker premier.... Britain's leading banks cut their base lending rates by half a percentage point, to 9.5%, the lowest level since January 1985.... Portuguese Pres. Mario Soares dissolves his nation's parliament and calls elections for July, two years ahead of schedule. The action follows an April 3 censure vote that brought down the conservative minority government of Premier Anibal Cavaco Silva. Cavaco Silva will stay on as caretaker premier until the election.	Two South African court decisions, one April 24, the other today, overturn key censorship powers that the government gave itself under the ongoing nationwide state of emergency.... For the first time in their modern history, mainstream Sudanese are openly considering the possibility of allowing Sudan's war-wracked south to secede from the rest of the country, the *Washington Post* reports.		In Australia, the Liberal Party formally decides to end its 38-year alliance with the National Party. The split comes three months after National Party politician Sir Johannes Bjelke-Petersen launched his maverick campaign to divide the two conservative opposition parties.
April 29		The West German first-quarter trade surplus reaches a record $15.5 bil., according to statistics released.			Premier Yasuhiro Nakasone of Japan arrives in Washington, D.C., to confer with Pres. Reagan on the escalating trade tensions between their two countries. Japan has amassed a record overall trade surplus of $101.4 bil. during FY1986. That is by far the largest trade surplus of any nation.
April 30		West German and West Berlin officials lead a celebration of the 750th anniversary of the founding of Berlin.... Finland's first conservative-led government since World War II is sworn in. The new four-party government will be led by Premier Harri Holkeri of the conservative Kokoomus Party.		Canada's P.M. Brian Mulroney and the premiers of the 10 provinces reach a unanimous agreement designed to bring Quebec into the constitution. The key provision of the Meech Lake agreement calls for the recognition of Quebec as a "distinct society" within Canada. ... Former president of the Dominican Republic, Salvador Jorge Blanco, asks for asylum at the home of the Venezuelan ambassador. A warrant for his arrest on charges of corruption was issued April 29.	

A	B	C	D	E
Includes developments that affect more than one world region, international organizations and important meetings of major world leaders.	Includes all domestic and regional developments in Europe, including the Soviet Union, Turkey, Cyprus and Malta.	Includes all domestic and regional developments in Africa and the Middle East, including Iraq and Iran and excluding Cyprus, Turkey and Afghanistan.	Includes all domestic and regional developments in Latin America, the Caribbean and Canada.	Includes all domestic and regional developments in Asia and Pacific nations, extending from Afghanistan through all the Pacific Islands, except Hawaii.

U.S. Politics & Social Issues	U.S. Foreign Policy & Defense	U.S. Economy & Environment	Science, Technology & Nature	Culture, Leisure & Life Style	
"Subway vigilante" Bernhard H. Goetz goes on trial in New York City. Goetz, who acquired his nickname after shooting four black youths in a New York City subway car in December 1984, faces 13 criminal charges, including four for attempted murder.	Austria's Pres. Kurt Waldheim is effectively barred from the United States because of his suspected participation in Nazi war crimes during World War II. The Justice Dept. says that "the evidence collected establishes a prima facie case that Kurt Waldheim assisted or otherwise participated in the persecution of persons because of race, religion, national origin or political opinion."	Reversing itself, the Justice Dept. argues that the regional telephone companies created in the breakup of American Telephone & Telegraph Co. should not be allowed to expand into long-distance service. . . . The Interior Dept. sends Congress a five-year plan for opening millions of acres of the outer continental shelf—including part of the Georges Bank off Cape Cod, the Florida Keys, the Pacific Coast, and Norton Sound off Alaska—to oil and gas exploration. . . . Chrysler Corp. says that its net income dropped 24% in the first quarter, to $269.7 mil. Chrysler blames the slippage on the costs of retooling plants as well as expensive sales incentive programs.	A report issued by the World Comm. on Environment and Development after three years of study warns that proliferating pollution and depletion of natural resources are "making survival ever more difficult and uncertain."		April 27
Independent counsel Lawrence E. Walsh says that there is "ample basis" for a broad criminal investigation of the Iran-Contra arms scandal. . . . The Supreme Court upholds a federal law classifying certain foreign government films as "political propaganda" and under which three Canadian films on acid rain and nuclear war were banned.		The Labor Dept. issues long-awaited rules requiring provision of drinking water and sanitation facilities for farm workers. The court-ordered rules apply to farms with 11 or more workers—an estimated 471,600 farm workers, about a third of the nation's farmhands. About a fourth of the workers covered are migrant field hands. . . . The federal government charges Browning-Ferris Industries Inc. with illegal handling of hazardous industrial wastes at a Livingston, La., facility. The Justice Dept., in a suit filed in federal court in Baton Rouge on behalf of the Environmental Protection Agency, accuses the company of a multitude of serious violations over a period of years.		At a news conference, the Rev. Jerry Falwell announces that the Rev. Jim Bakker's ministry at PTL (Praise the Lord), a television evangelistical empire Baker founded, "ceased" after a meeting of the PTL board of directors. . . . Quarterback Vinny Testaverde, the 1986 Heisman Trophy winner, is selected by the Tampa Bay Buccaneers as the first player in the National Football League draft of college players.	April 28
Conservative fund-raiser Carl R. Channell pleads guilty in Washington, D.C., to conspiracy to defraud the government for his role in funding the Nicaraguan Contra rebels. Channell's conviction marks the first criminal case in the Iran-Contra arms scandal. . . . Massachusetts Gov. Michael S. Dukakis declares his candidacy for the 1988 Democratic presidential nomination. . . . The Senate Rules Committee approves legislation that will establish a system of voluntary public financing for Senate campaigns. Candidates who opt for federal financing will have to accept a ceiling on their overall spending and tight limits on what they can raise from private individuals and political action committees.	Retired Air Force Maj. Gen. Richard V. Secord will testify voluntarily, without immunity from prosecution, before congressional committees investigating the Iran-Contra arms scandal, it is reported. Secord is scheduled to be the first witness when public hearings commence May 5. Secord helped both to arrange the shipments of arms to Iran and to set up the funding network for aid to the Contras.	The government's index of leading economic indicators rose 0.4% in March, propelled mostly by higher stock prices, the Commerce Dept. reports. . . . Merrill Lynch & Co. says that it has sustained a loss of about $250 mil. before taxes, largely because of unauthorized trading in mortgage securities by a senior trader. Wall Street sources agree that the trading setback is, in the words of a rival, "a new world record." . . . Ford Motor Co. emerges as the most profitable U.S. corporation in the first quarter of 1987. Ford reports a net income of $1.49 bil., more than double its earnings a year earlier, on sales of $18.14 bil.			April 29
	The House of Representatives passes a bill requiring the president to order retaliation against trade partners that do not open up their markets to U.S. products. . . . Testifying at a congressional hearing on his nomination to head the Central Intelligence Agency, Federal Bureau of Investigation (FBI) Dir. William H. Webster reports that in 1985 the FBI questioned Lt. Col. Oliver L. North about efforts to fund the Contra rebels in Nicaragua.	Agriculture Sec. Richard E. Lyng announces that the Soviet Union has agreed to buy 4 million metric tons of subsidized American wheat. The tonnage, which is equivalent to about one-half of the annual Kansas wheat crop, represents 14% of total U.S. wheat sales for 1986-87.	American space experts report the apparent failure of a Soviet Proton rocket launch designed to loft navigation satellites into proper orbit.	The Evangelical Lutheran Church in America comes into being with the formal merger of three American branches of Lutheranism. The new unit constitutes the nation's fourth largest Protestant body, with 5.3 million members. It is formed from the 2.9 million-member Lutheran Church in America (LCA), the 2.3 million-member American Lutheran Church (ALC), and the 110,000-member Assoc. of Evangelical Lutheran Churches (AELC). The 2.6 million-member Lutheran Church-Missouri Synod remains outside the merged group.	April 30

F	G	H	I	J
Includes elections, federal-state relations, civil rights and liberties, crime, the judiciary, education, health care, poverty, urban affairs and population.	*Includes formation and debate of U.S. foreign and defense policies, veterans' affairs and defense spending. (Relations with specific foreign countries are usually found under the region concerned.)*	*Includes business, labor, agriculture, taxation, transportation, consumer affairs, monetary and fiscal policy, natural resources, and pollution.*	*Includes worldwide scientific, medical and technological developments, natural phenomena, U.S. weather, natural disasters, and accidents.*	*Includes the arts, religion, scholarship, communications media, sports, entertainments, fashions, fads and social life.*

	World Affairs	Europe	Africa & the Middle East	The Americas	Asia & the Pacific
May 1		A law giving Soviet citizens the right to engage in limited private-sector business activities takes effect. The "Law on Individual Labor Activity" allows Soviets to obtain local licenses to sell their skills for profit in 40 categories of business.			In South Korea, the newly formed Party for Reunification and Democracy selects Kim Young Sam as its leader at a convention in Seoul. Kim formed the party with fellow opposition leader Kim Dae Jung (currently under house arrest) after a split in their New Korea Democratic Party. The new group is not recognized by the ruling Democratic Justice Party.
May 2					
May 3		In West Germany, the radical "fundis," or fundamentalists, emerge from the Greens' Party congress with control of the party's leadership. The gains came at the expense of the "realos," or pragmatists, who led the Greens toward greater cooperation with West Germany's traditional left.			
May 4			King Hassan II of Morocco and Algerian Pres. Chadli Benjedid meet briefly in the Moroccan town of Oujda to discuss the 11-year-old war in the Western Sahara, where Algerian-backed guerrillas of the Polisario Front continue to contest Morocco's control of the territory.		
May 5					

A	B	C	D	E
Includes developments that affect more than one world region, international organizations and important meetings of major world leaders.	Includes all domestic and regional developments in Europe, including the Soviet Union, Turkey, Cyprus and Malta.	Includes all domestic and regional developments in Africa and the Middle East, including Iraq and Iran and excluding Cyprus, Turkey and Afghanistan.	Includes all domestic and regional developments in Latin America, the Caribbean and Canada.	Includes all domestic and regional developments in Asia and Pacific nations, extending from Afghanistan through all the Pacific Islands, except Hawaii.

U.S. Politics & Social Issues	U.S. Foreign Policy & Defense	U.S. Economy & Environment	Science, Technology & Nature	Culture, Leisure & Life Style	
Justice Sandra Day O'Connor cancels a scheduled "private briefing" for a group of Republican contributors after a press report that such a meeting violates legal ethics.... A Cincinnati jury finds Detroit automobile worker Ronald Ebens not guilty of a federal civil rights charge stemming from the 1982 beating death of a young man of Chinese ancestry, Vincent Chin.	Two U.S. lawmakers are seeking a congressional audit of the Central Intelligence Agency's deliveries of sophisticated, shoulder-fired antiaircraft missiles to rebel movements in Angola and Afghanistan, the *Washington Post* reports. The move follows a report that some Stinger missiles were seized from a group of arms-trafficking bandits arrested in Zambia.	Major banks increase the prime rate to 8% from 7.75%. The prime rate has traditionally been the rate charged by banks to their biggest and most reliable borrowers. Those borrowers are now often charged less than the prime rate, but the rate is still closely watched as a benchmark figure.		*My Life as a Dog*, a film about a crucial year in the life of a young boy, is released in New York. Made in Sweden and directed by Lasse Hallstrom, the screenplay is based on a novel by Reidar Jonsson.	May 1
	A former U.S. ambassador for Costa Rica, Lewis Tambs, asserts that senior U.S. government officials directed his actions in support of the Nicaraguan Contras during his time in San Jose. Tambs resigned amid allegations that he improperly aided the Contras.			Alysheba, with Chris McCarron aboard, wins the 113th Kentucky Derby at Churchill Downs in Louisville, Ky.... A glittering international audience including Queen Sofia of Spain and Princess Caroline of Monaco attends the gala opening performance of a $10-mil. production of Giuseppe Verdi's opera *Aida* at the Temple of Luxor in Egypt. Placido Domingo sings Radames to Maria Chiara's Aida. ... Tea remains the most-favored beverage in Britain, according to an annual study of the Tea Council. Eighty percent of Britons drink tea, and of the 8.25 cups of beverages consumed daily by the average British citizen 3.7 cups are tea.	May 2
	Pres. Reagan launches a new appeal for aid to the Nicaraguan Contras, two days before congressional hearings are due to open on the Iran-Contra arms scandal. In a shift of strategy, he focuses not on the military conflict with the Sandinistas, but on diplomacy, the democratic goals of the Contras, and economic assistance for Central America.			Nigel Mansell of Great Britain wins the San Marino Grand Prix in Mola, Italy.... Davey Allison wins the Winston 500 NASCAR (National Assoc. for Stock Car Racing) event in Talladega, Ala.... Sweden wins the world ice hockey championship in Vienna. Sweden's 9-0 thrashing of Canada on the last day of competition gave it the title on goal differential over the defending champion Soviet Union.	May 3
The Supreme Court rules unanimously that states may require private, all-male public service clubs to admit women as members.... The Supreme Court rules that one of its three standing tests for obscene material should be based on a national standard upon which reasonable people would agree. Whether the material appeals to "prurient interest" or depicts sex in a "patently offensive" way is based on community standards.		Productivity among the nation's nonfarm businesses rose at a 1.7% annual rate in the first quarter, the Labor Dept. says.		Pope John Paul II concludes a six-day visit to West Germany. His activities stir memories of Hitler's Nazi era and draw criticism from Jewish groups.	May 4
Thousands of illegal immigrants come to Immigration and Naturalization Service (INS) offices around the nation to take advantage of the amnesty program under the Immigration Reform and Control Act of 1986. Some 50,000 persons pick up applications at 107 special legalization offices set up for the event; the INS estimates that 3.9 million illegal immigrants are eligible for amnesty under the new law.	House and Senate committees investigating the Iran-Contra arms scandal open their joint public hearings. The committees devote the first week to the testimony of retired Air Force Maj. Gen. Richard V. Secord.... The State Dept. announces that U.S. and Soviet negotiators in Geneva have reached agreement on a draft accord to lessen the danger of an accidental war through the exchange of information on military exercises, missile tests, and other activities covered under current arms agreements.				May 5

F	G	H	I	J
Includes elections, federal-state relations, civil rights and liberties, crime, the judiciary, education, health care, poverty, urban affairs and population.	Includes formation and debate of U.S. foreign and defense policies, veterans' affairs and defense spending. (Relations with specific foreign countries are usually found under the region concerned.)	Includes business, labor, agriculture, taxation, transportation, consumer affairs, monetary and fiscal policy, natural resources, and pollution.	Includes worldwide scientific, medical and technological developments, natural phenomena, U.S. weather, natural disasters, and accidents.	Includes the arts, religion, scholarship, communications media, sports, entertainments, fashions, fads and social life.

	World Affairs	Europe	Africa & the Middle East	The Americas	Asia & the Pacific
May 6		East Germany cancels its invitation to West Berlin Mayor Eberhard Diepgen to attend an official celebration in East Berlin. Diepgen had been invited for the celebration of the 750th anniversary of the founding of Berlin, but in a speech April 30 he condemned East Germany for using deadly force against people trying to cross the Berlin Wall into West Berlin.	South Africa's Pres. Pieter W. Botha's Nationalist Party government is returned to power with a slightly increased majority in South Africa's whites-only parliamentary elections.		
May 7					
May 8	The United States offers the Soviet Union a draft treaty on the reduction of strategic (long-range) offensive weapons in a meeting between Ronald F. Lehman, the U.S. chief negotiator on strategic arms, and his Soviet counterpart, Lem Masterkov.	A bystander and eight members of the outlawed Provisional Irish Republican Army (IRA) are ambushed and killed by British security forces after bombing a police station in Loughgall, County Armagh, Northern Ireland, in what is described as the most serious military setback for the IRA since the 1920s.			China accuses a Japanese reporter of illegally obtaining "national intelligence" and orders him to leave the country within 10 days. The journalist, Shuitsu Henmi of the Kyodo news agency, is the third foreign reporter to be expelled from China in 11 months and the fourth in three years.
May 9		A Polish Ilyushin-62 jetliner bound for New York City crashes in a forest on the outskirts of Warsaw, killing all 183 passengers and crew. The crew reported engine difficulties shortly after the plane took off from Warsaw's Okecie Airport. . . . In Malta's general elections the conservative Nationalist Party is returned to power after 16 years of Labour Party rule. The victory for the Nationalists will mean closer ties between Malta and the West, particularly with the European Community.			
May 10				Amnesty International, the London-based human rights organization, issues a report on human rights in Guatemala in which the group calls for an urgent investigation into abuses of "staggering proportions" committed in the 20 years of military rule prior to 1986.	

A	B	C	D	E
Includes developments that affect more than one world region, international organizations and important meetings of major world leaders.	Includes all domestic and regional developments in Europe, including the Soviet Union, Turkey, Cyprus and Malta.	Includes all domestic and regional developments in Africa and the Middle East, including Iraq and Iran and excluding Cyprus, Turkey and Afghanistan.	Includes all domestic and regional developments in Latin America, the Caribbean and Canada.	Includes all domestic and regional developments in Asia and Pacific nations, extending from Afghanistan through all the Pacific Islands, except Hawaii.

U.S. Politics & Social Issues	U.S. Foreign Policy & Defense	U.S. Economy & Environment	Science, Technology & Nature	Culture, Leisure & Life Style	
Casting a critical eye on the Constitution, Supreme Court Justice Thurgood Marshall says the document was "defective from the start, requiring several amendments, a civil war, and momentous social transformation to attain the system of constitutional government, and its respect for the individual freedoms and human rights, we hold as fundamental today." . . . Richard R. Miller, a public relations executive, pleads guilty to a felony charge filed by Lawrence E. Walsh, the independent counsel in the Iran-Contra arms probe.	William J. Casey, 74, director of the Central Intelligence Agency (CIA) from 1981 until ill-health forced his resignation in January, dies of pneumonia and cancer in Glen Cove, N.Y. He oversaw one of the biggest peacetime buildups in the American intelligence community, but his last days as director were overshadowed by the widening Iran-Contra arms scandal and questions about his involvement in it. Casey was chief of secret intelligence in Europe for the Office of Strategic Services (which became the CIA) during World War II; he later became a multimillionaire businessman.	Most major airlines in the United States are operating without enough experienced air traffic controllers on hand, the General Accounting Office reports.	Jane Smith, widow of Challenger pilot Michael J. Smith, files a $1.5 bil. lawsuit against the U.S. government, Morton Thiokol Inc., and former space agency engineer Lawrence B. Mulloy. The suit, filed in U.S. District Court in Orlando, Fla., seeks $500 mil. in damages jointly from the defendants for alleged negligence in the shuttle accident, which killed all seven crew members in 1986.	The Rev. Jim Bakker and the Rev. Richard Dortch are dismissed as ministers of the Assemblies of God for "conduct unbecoming to a minister," it is announced. The Rev. G. Raymond Carlson, general superintendent of the church, says Bakker's dismissal is based in particular on an admitted "sexual encounter" with a church secretary, Jessica Hahn, and "his alleged misconduct involving bisexual activity."	May 6
		Outstanding consumer credit contracted by a seasonally adjusted $63 mil. in March, the first drop since July 1982, the Federal Reserve Board says. . . . Over the last three days the Treasury Dept. sells $29 bil. of notes and bonds at rates sharply higher than the previous quarterly refinancing. . . . The Democratic-controlled Senate approves a trillion-dollar federal budget for FY1988 that will avoid a cut in military spending, but only if Pres. Reagan accepts $18.3 bil. in new taxes. The vote was 56-42, along party lines, with Republican Sens. Lowell P. Weicker Jr. (Conn.), Robert T. Stafford (Vt.), and John H. Chafee (R.I.) joining 53 Democrats in support.	The wife and children of Ronald E. McNair, an astronaut killed in the Challenger disaster in 1986, reach a settlement of their lawsuit against Morton Thiokol. Terms of the settlement were not disclosed. . . . The Food and Drug Admin. approves expanded use of cancer therapy with the experimental drug interleukin-2, or IL-2. Touted as a potential breakthrough in 1985, the drug has high risks and potentially devastating side effects. . . . Even moderate drinking of alcoholic beverages significantly increases the risk of breast cancer in women, according to research published in the *New England Journal of Medicine*.	At the end of the BOC Challenge race, Frenchman Philippe Jeantot sails into Newport, R.I., aboard his 60-foot sloop *Credit Agricole III* to complete a 27,000-mile, solo circumnavigation of the world in the record time of 134 days, 5 hours, 23 minutes, and 56 seconds.	May 7
Only five days after a newspaper revelation that he apparently spent part of a weekend at his home with a 29-year-old woman who is not his wife, former Sen. Gary Hart of Colorado goes from being the Democratic presidential frontrunner for 1988 to being an ex-candidate. Hart announces that he is abandoning his quest for the presidency.		The nation's unemployment rate dropped in April to 6.2%, the Labor Dept. reports, the lowest recorded since March 1980.			May 8
Campaign spending in House and Senate races totals $450 mil. in 1986, more than double the amount in 1978, according to figures released by the Federal Election Comm.				At the Folger Shakespeare Library in Washington, D.C., novelist Richard Wiley is presented with the PEN/Faulkner Award for fiction, for his novel *Soldiers in Hiding*.	May 9
				Hiromi Taniguchi of Japan wins the London Marathon in 2:9:50. Ingrid Kristiansen of Norway wins the women's division, for the third time, in 2:22:48 seconds.	May 10

F	G	H	I	J
Includes elections, federal-state relations, civil rights and liberties, crime, the judiciary, education, health care, poverty, urban affairs and population.	*Includes formation and debate of U.S. foreign and defense policies, veterans' affairs and defense spending. (Relations with specific foreign countries are usually found under the region concerned.)*	*Includes business, labor, agriculture, taxation, transportation, consumer affairs, monetary and fiscal policy, natural resources, and pollution.*	*Includes worldwide scientific, medical and technological developments, natural phenomena, U.S. weather, natural disasters, and accidents.*	*Includes the arts, religion, scholarship, communications media, sports, entertainments, fashions, fads and social life.*

	World Affairs	Europe	Africa & the Middle East	The Americas	Asia & the Pacific
May 11		The trial of Klaus Barbie, 73, the SS lieutenant who headed the German Gestapo in Lyons in World War II, opens in Lyons. Barbie came to be known as the Butcher of Lyons for his particularly sadistic treatment of Jewish and French Resistance prisoners.			The cabinet of India's P.M. Rajiv Gandhi votes to bring the strife-torn state of Punjab under central government rule. The decision marks the end of Gandhi's two-year effort to conciliate the state's Sikh majority and defuse a terrorist campaign for independence.... Early returns from what is generally held to be the Philippines' freest and most honest national election since at least 1971 indicate that candidates endorsed by Pres. Corazon Aquino will form a comfortable majority in both chambers of the new national legistlature.
May 12		In Malta, Eddie Fenech Adami of the Nationalist Party is sworn in as premier of the Mediterranean island nation.		Bahamian P.M. Lynden O. Pindling dissolves parliament and announces that a general election will be held June 19. The announcement comes amid renewed charges that the prime minister and members of his Progressive Liberal Party have received payoffs from international drug smugglers.	
May 13	Ministers from the 24 member nations of the Org. for Economic Cooperation and Development adjourn a two-day meeting with a call to reduce national farm subsidies.		Israel's deadlocked inner cabinet fails to endorse a plan to convene an international Middle East peace conference. In a victory for P.M. Yitzhak Shamir, Foreign Min. Shimon Peres is unable to follow through on his threat to break up the coalition government, although it is left virtually paralyzed.	Argentina's Pres. Raul Alfonsin presents to the congress a bill that would free from prosecution hundreds of officers at the rank of lieutenant colonel or below in connection with abuses in the so-called "dirty war" against leftists in the 1970s.... Nicaraguan Contras meeting in Miami announce the appointment of six members of a seven-member directorate for the Nicaraguan Resistance, a new rebel organization formed May 6 after months of bickering among leaders of the old United Nicaraguan Opposition (UNO).	Japanese officials disclose that Premier Yasuhiro Nakasone's controversial plan for a 5% sales tax has been abandoned.... The Australian Labor Party government unveils an economic statement that promises a 2% reduction in federal outlays (after inflation) for FY1987-88, the greatest such reduction in decades.
May 14					In Fiji, P.M. Timoci Bavadra and his 11-member cabinet are taken prisoner, just 31 days after assuming office. The coup is the first in the history of Fiji, which has enjoyed a democratic parliamentary government since gaining independence from Britain in 1970.
May 15		The Nuclear Planning Group of the North Atlantic Treaty Org. (NATO) calls for the global elimination of all U.S. and Soviet longer-range intermediate nuclear forces. Although unanimous, the position does not represent a formal posture by the alliance as a whole.... In Britain, royal assent is given to 52 bills passed during the session of Parliament that is to be dissolved today.... Inflation as measured by the retail price index stood at an annualized 4.2% rate in April, the government reports.	Following a series of reforms, the International Monetary Fund (IMF) officially agrees to loan Egypt $327 mil. over the next 18 months. Egypt March 15 reached agreement with the IMF on a $327 mil. loan after taking measures to satisfy some of the conditions that the fund had set under a new reform plan.		

A	B	C	D	E
Includes developments that affect more than one world region, international organizations and important meetings of major world leaders.	Includes all domestic and regional developments in Europe, including the Soviet Union, Turkey, Cyprus and Malta.	Includes all domestic and regional developments in Africa and the Middle East, including Iraq and Iran and excluding Cyprus, Turkey and Afghanistan.	Includes all domestic and regional developments in Latin America, the Caribbean and Canada.	Includes all domestic and regional developments in Asia and Pacific nations, extending from Afghanistan through all the Pacific Islands, except Hawaii.

U.S. Politics & Social Issues	U.S. Foreign Policy & Defense	U.S. Economy & Environment	Science, Technology & Nature	Culture, Leisure & Life Style	
Attorney Gen. Edwin Meese III requests that an independent counsel undertake a criminal investigation of his ties to Wedtech Corp., a New York-based defense contractor that is the subject of a number of federal and state inquiries.... A.H. Robins Co. offers a revised proposal for compensating the 320,000 women seeking compensation for pelvic infections, sterility, and other problems caused by the company's Dalkon Shield intrauterine birth control device in the 1970s.	The House and Senate select committees investigating the Iran-Contra affair hear testimony from Robert C. McFarlane, White House national security adviser from 1983 to 1985. McFarlane was in a position to judge the degree of Pres. Reagan's involvement in the Iranian arms initiative and the effort to resupply the Nicaraguan Contra rebels after such aid was barred by Congress. However, a combination of incomplete or evasive answers by McFarlane and a lack of probing follow-up questions by lawmakers leaves specific details about Reagan's role still unclear.	The Mine Safety and Health Admin. set a record $111,470 in fines against the owner and former operator of a Utah coal mine where 27 workers died in a fire in 1984. The civil penalty is the largest imposed by the Labor Dept. agency in its 10-year history.	The National Aeronautics and Space Admin. (NASA) is sharply criticized for the loss of an Atlas-Centaur rocket and payload in an electrical storm on March 26. "The Air Force missed the call on the weather, and NASA wasn't able to recognize that error," said Jon R. Busse in summarizing the findings of a board of inquiry that he had directed.		**May 11**
		The United States will sell advanced fighter planes to Honduras over a two-year period, the White House announces. The United States in late 1986 offered to sell Honduras more advanced jets to upgrade its squadron of dated warplanes. The proposed sale is part of the U.S. effort to bolster Honduran defenses against neighboring Nicaragua.		Film director Woody Allen appears before a Senate subcommittee to protest the computerized coloring of black-and-white movies, a practice he calls "sinful." In videotaped testimony, ailing director John Huston, an early and vocal opponent of what has come to be known as "colorization," calls the coloring of his classic film *The Maltese Falcon* "bushwhacking."	**May 12**
	Pres. Reagan sends to Congress two new legal studies in support of the idea that the United States is free to adopt a permissive interpretation of the 1972 antiballistic missile treaty. A broader interpretation of the treaty will permit accelerated testing, and perhaps an early deployment, of elements of the U.S. Strategic Defense Initiative ("Star Wars").			Richard Ellmann, 69, literary scholar whose 1959 biography of James Joyce became the definitive work on the Irish novelist, dies of pneumonia in Oxford, England. The American-born Ellmann taught at a number of U.S. universities before joining the faculty of Oxford Univ. in 1970, where he was Goldsmiths' professor emeritus of English literature. He suffered from amyotrophic lateral sclerosis, or Lou Gehrig's Disease.	**May 13**
The office of Vice Pres. George Bush discloses that a chronology of his contacts with Felix I. Rodriguez, a Bay of Pigs veteran who worked with the Nicaraguan Contras, omitted a June 1986 meeting between Rodriguez and Bush aide Col. Samuel J. Watson; the chronology was released in December 1986.	Pres. Reagan turns down a request from El Salvador's Pres. Jose Napoleon Duarte to exempt thousands of Salvadorans from a new U.S. immigration law under which employers could be penalized for hiring illegal aliens.	The U.S. deficit on merchandise trade shrank in March to $13.63 bil., the Commerce Dept. says.... According to a White House budget office analysis reported in the *Wall Street Journal*, the budget deficit in Pres. Reagan's proposed FY1988 budget is $27 bil. higher than the $108 bil. deficit target mandated by the Gramm-Rudman balanced budget law.		Rita Hayworth (born Margarita Carmen Cansino), 68, one of the most popular U.S. film stars of the 1940s, dies in New York City of complications from Alzheimer's disease. Her first starring roles were in films that highlighted her lush beauty, but her screen persona was perhaps best realized in the 1946 film *Gilda*. Her five husbands included Orson Welles, who directed her in *The Lady from Shanghai*, and Prince Aly Khan.	**May 14**
After months of denying that he knew specifics about private efforts to aid the Nicaraguan Contra rebels, Pres. Reagan tells a group of journalists that he was regularly briefed on Contra aid because it was "my idea to begin with."... The Comm. on Civil Rights rejects, 5-3, a staff report strongly condemning the Supreme Court's March 25 decision upholding job preferences for women.	A Marine Corps general directs military prosecutors to proceed with a court-martial of Sgt. Clayton J. Lonetree, a former guard at the current U.S. Embassy in Moscow. Lonetree was one of two principal suspects in the embassy spy scandal.	The producer price index rose a seasonally adjusted 0.7% in April, according to the Labor Dept.... The industrial production index fell 0.4% in April, the Federal Reserve Board reports.... Major banks, led by Chase Manhattan Bank, increase their prime lending rate to 8.25% from 8%. The increase is the third in less than two months. The prime is a reference rate to which many bank loans to businesses and consumers are linked. ... Pres. Reagan signs a bill temporarily raising the U.S. national debt limit by about $20 bil., to $2.32 trillion. The increase enables the government to continue borrowing through July 17.		Comedienne Joan Rivers bows out as permanent host of Fox Broadcasting Co.'s eight-month-old late-night talk show amid evidence that she might not appear on the show again, despite Fox's reported offer of occasional guest spots.	**May 15**

F	G	H	I	J
Includes elections, federal-state relations, civil rights and liberties, crime, the judiciary, education, health care, poverty, urban affairs and population.	*Includes formation and debate of U.S. foreign and defense policies, veterans' affairs and defense spending. (Relations with specific foreign countries are usually found under the region concerned.)*	*Includes business, labor, agriculture, taxation, transportation, consumer affairs, monetary and fiscal policy, natural resources, and pollution.*	*Includes worldwide scientific, medical and technological developments, natural phenomena, U.S. weather, natural disasters, and accidents.*	*Includes the arts, religion, scholarship, communications media, sports, entertainments, fashions, fads and social life.*

	World Affairs	Europe	Africa & the Middle East	The Americas	Asia & the Pacific
May 16		At the conclusion of a three-day trip to the Soviet Union, France's Premier Jacques Chirac reflects on the recent deterioration in relations between the two nations. Franco-Soviet tensions have been heightened by the recent Ariane spy affair and by Soviet opposition to France's plan to modernize its independent nuclear deterrent.			
May 17	(Karl) Gunnar Myrdal, 88, Swedish economist, social scientist, and social reformer, dies in Stockholm. His seminal work, *An American Dilemma: The Negro Problem and Modern Democracy* (1944), was an insightful commentary on U.S. race relations. In Sweden, he helped draft many social and economic programs, and as a UN official he was an early promoter of East-West detente. He was cowinner of the 1974 Nobel Prize in economics. (His late wife, Alva, was cowinner of the 1982 Nobel Prize for peace.)	Several polls undertaken in West Germany show that Soviet leader Mikhail Gorbachev is a somewhat more popular leader than Pres. Reagan, the *New York Times* reports.	The frigate USS *Stark* is struck by missiles fired by an Iraqi warplane while on patrol in the Persian Gulf. Thirty-seven U.S. sailors are killed in the apparently accidental attack. The United States protests the attack but accepts Iraq's apologies and its claim that the strike was inadvertent.		
May 18				Amid growing demands for early national elections, Brazil's Pres. Jose Sarney says he is willing to leave office in 1990 rather than in 1991, when his term officially expires. There is growing dissatisfaction with Sarney in Brazil, exacerbated by the recent disclosure of corruption involving the construction of a $2.5 bil. railroad.	
May 19		Soviet leader Mikhail S. Gorbachev says that the USSR will remove its SS-20 medium-range missiles targeted on Asia if the United States agrees to certain conditions. . . . An estimated 15,000-20,000 European farmers protest peacefully in Brussels against planned cuts in European Community farm subsidies. Farm ministers have not yet given final approval to the cuts, which are contained in a package intended to save the EC $5 bil. in subsidies over two years.			In Australia, P.M. Bob Hawke orders the immediate closing of the Libyan people's bureau (embassy) in Canberra. In April, Hawke accused the North African nation of aiming to spread terrorism and revolt among Australia's Pacific neighbors.
May 20		Lt. Col. Otelo Saraiva de Carvalho, a hero of the 1974 revolution that ended 50 years of right-wing rule in Portugal, is found guilty of running a secret left-wing terrorist organization. He is sentenced to 15 years in prison for his association with the Popular Forces of April 25 (FP-25), which is suspected in the assassinations of at least 15 businessmen and landowners and in bomb attacks on foreign targets.	The main questions about the May 17 attack by Iraq on a U.S. Navy frigate center on why the ship involved, the USS *Stark*, did not defend itself from Iraqi missiles. According to U.S. officers, the *Stark* did not view the approaching Iraqi jet as an enemy, and the ship's advanced electronic equipment somehow failed to detect the firing of the French-made, sea-skimming Exocet missiles.		

A	B	C	D	E
Includes developments that affect more than one world region, international organizations and important meetings of major world leaders.	Includes all domestic and regional developments in Europe, including the Soviet Union, Turkey, Cyprus and Malta.	Includes all domestic and regional developments in Africa and the Middle East, including Iraq and Iran and excluding Cyprus, Turkey and Afghanistan.	Includes all domestic and regional developments in Latin America, the Caribbean and Canada.	Includes all domestic and regional developments in Asia and Pacific nations, extending from Afghanistan through all the Pacific Islands, except Hawaii.

U.S. Politics & Social Issues	U.S. Foreign Policy & Defense	U.S. Economy & Environment	Science, Technology & Nature	Culture, Leisure & Life Style	
		The 6,000-mile voyage of the barge *Mobro 4,000*, loaded with 3,168 tons of trash from Islip, N.Y., ends in frustration at Gravesend Bay off Brooklyn, N.Y. Towed by the tugboat *Break of Dawn*, the *Mobro 4,000*'s travels in search of a dump began on March 22, when an Islip landfill refused the gigantic load.	The Soviet Union announces the successful test launch from the Baikonur space center in Kazakhstan of a "new generation" rocket with a 100-ton payload capacity. The two-stage rocket, dubbed Energia (Energy), is powered by eight liquid hydrogen engines, four of them strapped to the rocket body.	Alysheba captures the second leg of U.S. thoroughbred horse racing's triple crown with a victory in the 112th running of the Preakness at Pimlico race track in Baltimore.	**May 16**
					May 17
The Supreme Court interprets a 121-year-old civil rights law barring racial discrimination as a protection in general against ethnic discrimination.... The Supreme Court rules, 6-3, that a union can discipline members who work as supervisors for companies with which the union does not have a contract. ... Sen. Paul Simon (D, Ill.) becomes the latest announced candidate for the 1988 Democratic presidential nomination.	The Supreme Court extends a ban against suing the government for negligence involving military personnel to include cases where the negligence originates with a civilian employee.			Los Angeles Laker Earvin (Magic) Johnson becomes the first guard in 23 years to win the National Basketball Assoc.'s most valuable player award.	**May 18**
The Senate confirms the nomination of William H. Webster as director of the Central Intelligence Agency by a 94-1 vote.... Philadelphia's Mayor W. Wilson Goode wins renomination by a substantial margin in Democratic mayoral primary. Former Mayor Frank L. Rizzo, who switched parties, wins the Republican primary decisively.	The Justice Dept. announces a decision to end its investigation of General Dynamics Corp. for suspected contract fraud. The department says that a successful prosecution was questionable due to insufficient evidence. The investigation stemmed from allegations that General Dynamics' Electric Boat Division had deliberately underbid on a Navy contract to build SSN-688 attack submarines, and then had submitted false claims on cost overruns.	Citicorp, the largest U.S. bank, announces that it will add $3 bil. to its reserves to cover anticipated losses, mainly on foreign loans. The bank says that the write-off will result in a $2.5 bil. loss in the second quarter of 1987.... Housing starts dropped 2.9% in April to a seasonally adjusted annual rate of 1.699 million units, the Commerce Dept. says.		Alice Sheldon, 71, critically acclaimed science fiction author who wrote under the pseudonym James Tiptree Jr., dies in McLean, Va., of a self-inflicted gunshot wound after fatally shooting her 84-year-old ailing husband. The two had apparently entered into a suicide pact.... The 40th annual international film festival in Cannes, France, awards its top prize, the Golden Palm, to French director Maurice Pialat's *Under Satan's Sun*.	**May 19**
The keys to the door and the deed to the national headquarters of the United Klans of America near Tuscaloosa, Ala., are turned over to a 67-year-old black woman from Mobile, Ala., three months after a federal jury in Mobile awarded Beulah Mae Donald and her family $7 mil. in damages against the Ku Klux Klan group in connection with the 1981 murder of her teenage son.	The House passes a $289 bil. defense authorization bill for FY1988. The measure is approved on a 239-177 vote largely along partisan lines. Twelve Republicans voted for the bill, while 18 Democrats opposed it.		A report published by the National Academy of Sciences urges a standardized rule to reduce the risks from cancer-causing pesticide residues in food. The report, prepared by a blue-ribbon academic panel, urges the Environmental Protection Agency to establish a "negligible risk" standard that would permit approval of pesticides only if their tumor-causing incidence was less than one in every million people exposed.	*Variety*'s top-grossing films for the week are: *Ishtar, The Gate, The Secret of My Success, Creepshow 2*, and *Gardens of Stone*.	**May 20**

F	G	H	I	J
Includes elections, federal-state relations, civil rights and liberties, crime, the judiciary, education, health care, poverty, urban affairs and population.	Includes formation and debate of U.S. foreign and defense policies, veterans' affairs and defense spending. (Relations with specific foreign countries are usually found under the region concerned.)	Includes business, labor, agriculture, taxation, transportation, consumer affairs, monetary and fiscal policy, natural resources, and pollution.	Includes worldwide scientific, medical and technological developments, natural phenomena, U.S. weather, natural disasters, and accidents.	Includes the arts, religion, scholarship, communications media, sports, entertainments, fashions, fads and social life.

	World Affairs	Europe	Africa & the Middle East	The Americas	Asia & the Pacific
May 21					The first three U.S. lawyers allowed to practice in Japan under a recent law are accredited by the justice ministry. The United States had pressed for Japan to open its legal-services market to foreigners since 1982.... In Singapore, 16 people are arrested and jailed for their involvement in "a Marxist conspiracy to subvert the existing social and political system" that sought to turn Singapore into a communist state through "manipulation of religious and other organizations," most notably the Roman Catholic Church.... North Korea's Pres. Kim Il Sung arrives in Beijing for his first official visit to China since 1982.
May 22		The Soviet Union announces that it is giving up commercial whaling and that its whaling fleet is returning from its final hunting season in the Antarctic. The flagship of the whaling fleet is destined to be converted to a fisheries ship, according to the announcement on Moscow radio.	China announces that it has increased its military forces stationed on the Indian border. It also gives the first official confirmation of growing friction between the two countries' border forces, but denies news and eyewitness reports that there have been actual skirmishes.		
May 23					Riots break out in Seoul, South Korea, over charges of a cover-up in the January slaying by police of a student activist.
May 24			The Israeli Supreme Court rules that the Shin Bet, Israel's secret domestic intelligence and countert-errorist agency, used harsh interrogation methods and false testimony to wrongly convict a Moslem officer in the Israeli Army of espionage. It is the second major scandal to rock the Shin Bet in the past year.		Fiji's deposed civilian leader, Timoci Bavadra, says he refuses to accept a compromise settlement of a recent military coup announced by military authorities on May 21. The coup was staged May 14 by ethnic Fijian Army officers opposed to the government giving significant political power to citizens of Indian descent.
May 25				At the start of a five-day state visit, France's Pres. Francois Mitterrand addresses a joint session of the Canadian parliament. The visit appears to usher in a new era of Franco-Canadian relations, which have been cool for 20 years over France's support for Quebec separatism.... Canada's Health Min. Jake Epp unveils a five-year, $156 mil. federal program aimed at curbing the abuse of alcohol, illegal drugs, and legal medications through treatment centers, research, and education.	In Japan, the government lists 56 financial concerns, 39 domestic and 17 foreign, that will be licensed to manage investments in the Japanese financial market. Under legislation introduced several months before, the concerns were newly required to seek licenses.

A	B	C	D	E
Includes developments that affect more than one world region, international organizations and important meetings of major world leaders.	Includes all domestic and regional developments in Europe, including the Soviet Union, Turkey, Cyprus and Malta.	Includes all domestic and regional developments in Africa and the Middle East, including Iraq and Iran and excluding Cyprus, Turkey and Afghanistan.	Includes all domestic and regional developments in Latin America, the Caribbean and Canada.	Includes all domestic and regional developments in Asia and Pacific nations, extending from Afghanistan through all the Pacific Islands, except Hawaii.

U.S. Politics & Social Issues	U.S. Foreign Policy & Defense	U.S. Economy & Environment	Science, Technology & Nature	Culture, Leisure & Life Style	
	In the third week of congressional hearings on the Iran-Contra arms scandal, the House and Senate committees hear further testimony from Robert W. Owen, who describes himself as a "foot soldier" in the secret Contra aid effort; Adolfo Calero, head of the largest Contra faction; and retired Maj. Gen. John K. Singlaub, chairman of the World Anticommunist League.		A gene that causes an extremely rare nerve disease has been linked with the development of breast cancer, according to a study published in the *New England Journal of Medicine*. Although the study does not actually prove that the gene causes breast cancer, "the association is statistically very strong," according to the principal author, Dr. Michael Swift of the Univ. of North Carolina.		May 21
Two hundred years after delegates from the 13 original states gathered in Philadelphia to frame the U.S. Constitution, the city hosts a variety of festivities marking the event and kicking off six months of bicentennial celebrations around the United States.	Austria's Chancellor Franz Vranitzky concludes an official three-day visit to the United States. He is unsuccessful in his attempt to have the United States reverse its recent action barring Austria's Pres. Kurt Waldheim from the United States because of his alleged role in Nazi war crimes during World War II.	After-tax profits of U.S. corporations fell 5.5% in the first quarter, the Commerce Dept. says.			May 22
				Billboard's best-selling albums for the week are: *The Joshua Tree*, U2; *Slippery when Wet*, Bon Jovi; *Look What the Cat Dragged In*, Poison; *Licensed to Ill*, Beastie Boys; and *Graceland*, Paul Simon.	May 23
Some 250,000 people crowd onto San Francisco's Golden Gate Bridge for its 50th anniversary. More than 500,000 other people packing the bridge approaches are denied access by engineers worried about whether the span can support the weight.... Six days after the National Institute of Mental Health concluded that Stephen E. Breuning, a prominent researcher into the use of psychoactive drugs with the mentally retarded, had fabricated many of his results, federal officials begin seeking his prosecution.				Al Unser Sr. wins the Indianapolis 500 auto race to become only the second driver to capture the race four times.... Jane Geddes wins the Ladies Professional Golf Assoc. Championship in Kings Island, Ohio.... Hermione Gingold, 89, English-born comedienne whose stage and screen career spanned more than 70 years, dies in New York City. She became known to London theatergoers in the 1940s for her work in revues, most notably *Sweet and Low*, her most notable U.S. stage success was in the Broadway revue *John Murray Anderson's Almanac* (1953-54). Her movie credits include *Gigi* (1958) and *The Music Man* (1962).	May 24
A New York State Supreme Court jury in New York City acquits former Labor Sec. Raymond J. Donovan of the larceny and fraud charges that forced him from office in March 1985. Donovan was the only sitting cabinet member ever to be indicted. "The question is, should this indictment have ever been brought?" says Donovan. "Which office do I go to to get my reputation back? Who will reimburse my company for the economic jail it's been in for two-and-a-half years?"		The government's consumer price index rose 0.4% in April, the same increase as in the previous two months, the Labor Dept. reports. ... Consumer spending rose 0.6% in April, despite the sharpest drop in after-tax personal income in nearly 12 years, the Commerce Dept. says.		Johns Hopkins beats Cornell, 11-10, to win the National Collegiate Athletic Assoc. Division I lacrosse championship.... In cricket, England wins the Texaco Trophy in a three-match series of one-day internationals against the touring Pakistan side.	May 25

F	G	H	I	J
Includes elections, federal-state relations, civil rights and liberties, crime, the judiciary, education, health care, poverty, urban affairs and population.	*Includes formation and debate of U.S. foreign and defense policies, veterans' affairs and defense spending. (Relations with specific foreign countries are usually found under the region concerned.)*	*Includes business, labor, agriculture, taxation, transportation, consumer affairs, monetary and fiscal policy, natural resources, and pollution.*	*Includes worldwide scientific, medical and technological developments, natural phenomena, U.S. weather, natural disasters, and accidents.*	*Includes the arts, religion, scholarship, communications media, sports, entertainments, fashions, fads and social life.*

	World Affairs	Europe	Africa & the Middle East	The Americas	Asia & the Pacific
May 26		Irish voters back ratification of the Single European Act in a referendum necessitated by an Irish supreme court ruling in April that foreign policy aspects of the act violate the Irish constitution. . . . In Greenland's fourth general election since it achievd home rule from Denmark in 1979, the governing center-left coalition of the social democratic Siumut Party and Inuit Ataqatigiit Party, are expected to return to power, although they lose votes to parties on the left and right.	Two official investigations into the Jonathan Pollard spy affair are released. Both criticize the Israeli government's role but find no evidence that the top leadership possessed direct knowledge of the espionage operation, which seriously damaged Israel's relations with the United States.		In India, the official death toll in about a week of Hindu-Moslem rioting is 93, a news account says. The bulk of the fighting has been in Meerut, Uttar Pradesh state, where 84 people were killed, and in Old Delhi, where nine have died. . . . Japan owned a record $180.35 bil. in net overseas assets during 1986, 39% more than in 1985, the finance ministry reports. It is the second year in a row that Japan has been the world's top creditor nation.
May 27		North Atlantic Treaty Org. (NATO) defense ministers conclude a two-day meeting. As expected, the ministers use the opportunity to discuss the proposed removal of intermediate nuclear force (INF) missiles from Europe. Much of the talk centers on ways of bolstering NATO's nuclear deterrent in the absence of the INF weapons.			
May 28	Ministers from the major democratic nations meet in Paris to forge tighter links in the battle against international terrorism. No new concrete plan of action emerges from the meeting, which is held amid extremely tight security. Nonetheless, officials such as Attorney Gen. Edwin Meese hail the meeting as the first in a series of steps toward increased cooperation.		The Ivory Coast, long viewed as one of black Africa's few economic success stories, announces that it can no longer service its external debt. The nation tells its creditors in the so-called Clubs of Paris and London (made up of Western governments and commercial banks, respectively) that the payments crisis is due to the collapse of coffee and cocoa prices.	Argentina's Congress gives final approval of a plan to move the capital of Argentina from Buenos Aires to the Patagonian twin cities of Viedma and Carmen de Patagones. . . . Brig. Gen. Rafael del Pino Diaz, the highest-ranking Cuban to defect to the United States since the 1959 revolution, flies a Cessna 402 plane to a U.S. Navy base in Florida. . . . In El Salvador, leftist rebels offer a new peace plan to the government, but Pres. Jose Napoleon Duarte rejects it the same day, demanding instead that the rebels lay down their arms and join the democratic process.	During FY1986, direct overseas investments by Japanese companies reach a record $22.32 bil., the finance ministry reports. Investments in the United States accounted for 45.5% of the total.

A	B	C	D	E
Includes developments that affect more than one world region, international organizations and important meetings of major world leaders.	Includes all domestic and regional developments in Europe, including the Soviet Union, Turkey, Cyprus and Malta.	Includes all domestic and regional developments in Africa and the Middle East, including Iraq and Iran and excluding Cyprus, Turkey and Afghanistan.	Includes all domestic and regional developments in Latin America, the Caribbean and Canada.	Includes all domestic and regional developments in Asia and Pacific nations, extending from Afghanistan through all the Pacific Islands, except Hawaii.

U.S. Politics & Social Issues	U.S. Foreign Policy & Defense	U.S. Economy & Environment	Science, Technology & Nature	Culture, Leisure & Life Style	
The Supreme Court upholds, 6-3, the practice of "preventive detention" before trial if a federal court determines that the suspect is a danger to the public. . . . The Immigration and Naturalization Service defers for a month enforcement of the sanctions on employers of illegal aliens. The sanctions—including penalties of up to six months in jail and fines of $10,000 for each illegal alien hired—were scheduled to take effect June 1. . . . The Supreme Court says an illegal deportation cannot be used to bar an alien's reentry to the United States. In *United States* v. *Mendoza-Lopez* the court rules, 5-4, that the original deportation proceeding in the case of two Mexicans was unfair because the aliens had not been advised fully of their right to counsel and to apply for suspension of deportation.	William H. Webster is sworn in as director of the Central Intelligence Agency.			Arthur M(itchell) Sackler, 73, research psychiatrist who made a fortune in medical advertising and trade publications, and the manufacture of over-the-counter drugs, dies of a heart attack in New York City. A philanthropist and arts patron, Sackler gave 1,000 pieces of Asian and Near Eastern art for the Smithsonion Institution's Arthur M. Sackler Gallery. . . . In an interview on ABC's "Nightline" television program, the Rev. Jim Bakker, whose extramarital affair with a 19-year-old church secretary led to his departure from his PTL television empire, accuses the Rev. Jerry Falwell of attempting to "steal Heritage USA [an evangelical theme park] and my ministry."	May 26
			John H(oward) Northrop, 95, U.S. scientist who shared the 1946 Nobel prize in chemistry with two other Americans for their work on the purification and crystallization of enzymes, dies in Wickenberg, Ariz. He was a life member of the Rockefeller Institute for Medical Research, now known as Rockefeller Univ.	In soccer, Porto of Portugal earns the European Champions Cup, 2-1, over Bayern Munich of West Germany in Vienna. . . . Writer Alice Munro receives her third Governor General's Literary Award, one of Canada's top literary prizes, for her collection of short stories, *The Progress of Love*. Writer Yvon Rivard receives the award for French-language fiction.	May 27
Another quarter-million pages of documents from former Pres. Richard M. Nixon's White House are opened to public view. One document in particular seems to show the genesis of the Watergate scandal. It is a Jan. 14, 1971, memo from Nixon to chief of staff H.R. Haldeman about then-Democratic Party chairman Lawrence F. O'Brien and O'Brien's one-time service to billionaire Howard Hughes.	Top Reagan administration officials tell Congress that a U.S. plan to protect Kuwaiti oil tankers from Iranian attack will be delayed for several weeks. The new policy, which will expand U.S. military involvement in the Persian Gulf, has drawn strong criticism from both Republicans and Democrats following the May 17 Iraqi missile attack that killed 37 sailors aboard the frigate USS *Stark*.			A team of U.S. amateurs wins golf's Walker Cup in match-play competition in Britain. . . . Hundreds of celebrities converge on the Far Hills, N.J., estate of multi-millionaire publisher Malcolm Forbes to celebrate the 70th anniversary of *Forbes* magazine, which was founded by his father. . . . Stephanie Petit, an eighth-grader from Bethel Park, Pa., wins the 60th annual Scripps-Howard National Spelling Bee in Washington, D.C. Petit wins by correctly spelling "staphylococci," a kind of bacteria. . . . *Talk Radio*, a play that focuses on a late-night radio show host who savages his callers, opens at the Public Theater in New York City. Written by Eric Bogosian, based on an original idea by Tad Savinar, the play is directed by Frederick Zollo and stars Bogosian and Robyn Peterson.	May 28

F	G	H	I	J
Includes elections, federal-state relations, civil rights and liberties, crime, the judiciary, education, health care, poverty, urban affairs and population.	Includes formation and debate of U.S. foreign and defense policies, veterans' affairs and defense spending. (Relations with specific foreign countries are usually found under the region concerned.)	Includes business, labor, agriculture, taxation, transportation, consumer affairs, monetary and fiscal policy, natural resources, and pollution.	Includes worldwide scientific, medical and technological developments, natural phenomena, U.S. weather, natural disasters, and accidents.	Includes the arts, religion, scholarship, communications media, sports, entertainments, fashions, fads and social life.

	World Affairs	Europe	Africa & the Middle East	The Americas	Asia & the Pacific
May 29		Warsaw Pact leaders end a two-day summit in East Berlin with a call for direct talks with the North Atlantic Treaty Org. . . . Mathias Rust, a 19-year-old pilot from Munich, West Germany, lands his single-engine Cessna 172 in Moscow's Red Square after an unauthorized flight from Helsinki, Finland, across 400 miles of Soviet airspace. Although spotted by Soviet interceptors, Rust was not challenged.	In Japan, the cabinet approves a $43 bil. plan for spending to stimulate the domestic economy. The package totals some $9 bil. more than was expected. Many observers have reservations about the plan, but overall response is favorable.	In a rare display of public criticism, Chinese authorities fire Forestry Min. Yang Zhong "for serious dereliction of duty and bureaucratic mismanagement" for his handling of the biggest forest fire in China's recent history. . . . Cuban authorities free Roberto Martin Perez Rodriguez, 53, the longest-serving political prisoner in Cuba, apparently at the request of Panama's Gen. Manuel Antonio Noriega. He had served 27 years and 10 months of a 30-year sentence following his conviction for plotting to overthrow Pres. Fidel Castro.	Japan's five chief steelmakers all post losses for FY1986. The strong yen is blamed for the hampering of exports.
May 30					Joaquim Pinto Machado resigns as governor of Macao, the Portuguese-administered territory in China. He had encountered hostile civil servants and widespread corruption after his appointment in 1986. . . . The 18th meeting of the South Pacific Forum concludes in Apia, the capital of Western Samoa. The chief issue before the group is the recent coup in Fiji, the caretaker regime of which declined to send a representative after Australia and New Zealand indicated they would object.
May 31				The prime ministers of the seven island nations in the Org. of Eastern Caribbean States are reported to have voted to create a single nation, pending national referendums. The new English-speaking federation will include St. Vincent and the Grenadines, St. Lucia, Montserrat, Dominica, Grenada, Antigua and Barbuda, and St. Christopher and Nevis, with a total population of some 600,000 and a combined gross domestic product of $620 mil.	
June 1		West Germany's coalition government announces a qualified acceptance of a Soviet proposal to rid Europe of medium-range nuclear missiles. The announcement comes after more than a month of indecision in Bonn. The government says that it will support the so-called "double-zero option," under which both shorter-and longer-range intermediate nuclear forces will be removed from Europe.	Lebanon's Premier Rashid Karami is assassinated when a bomb explodes aboard a military helicopter in which he is traveling. There are no firm indications of who is responsible, and Lebanese leaders from across the political spectrum condemn the slaying.	Public services and unionized private businesses in British Columbia are idled by a massive 24-hour general strike called by the British Columbia Federation of Labor to protest a proposed sweeping revision of the province's labor laws. . . . The prime minister of Barbados, Errol W. Barrow, dies. Erskine Sandiford, deputy prime minister, minister of education, and leader of the House of Assembly, is sworn in to succeed him.	

A	B	C	D	E
Includes developments that affect more than one world region, international organizations and important meetings of major world leaders.	*Includes all domestic and regional developments in Europe, including the Soviet Union, Turkey, Cyprus and Malta.*	*Includes all domestic and regional developments in Africa and the Middle East, including Iraq and Iran and excluding Cyprus, Turkey and Afghanistan.*	*Includes all domestic and regional developments in Latin America, the Caribbean and Canada.*	*Includes all domestic and regional developments in Asia and Pacific nations, extending from Afghanistan through all the Pacific Islands, except Hawaii.*

U.S. Politics & Social Issues	U.S. Foreign Policy & Defense	U.S. Economy & Environment	Science, Technology & Nature	Culture, Leisure & Life Style	
In response to a question from a *Boston Globe* reporter, Rep. Barney Frank (D, Mass.) acknowledges that he is a homosexual. "I don't think my sex life is relevant to my job," Frank says. "But on the other hand I don't want to leave the impression that I'm embarrassed by my life."	Congressional committees investigating the Iran-Contra arms scandal hear testimony from: Robert C. Dutton, who managed the Contra airlift while on the payroll of Maj. Gen. Richard V. Secord; Felix Rodriguez, a veteran Central Intelligence Agency (CIA) operative in Latin America; Lewis Tambs, who as U.S. ambassador to Costa Rica in 1985 and 1986 tried to open a "southern front" against the Sandinista government from Costa Rica; and Joe Fernandez, former CIA station chief in Costa Rica.	The Federal Reserve Board says that it spent $4.06 bil. in the first quarter of 1987 to bolster the dollar in international currency markets. ... The government's index of leading economic indicators dropped 0.6% in April, the Commerce Dept. reports. ... California State Superior Court Judge Ira A. Brown rules in San Francisco that insurers, not manufacturers, are liable for claims from victims of asbestos-related diseases. The ruling is made in a consolidated trial involving four former asbestos makers and more than 20 insurers.		*Publishers Weekly*'s hardback fiction best-sellers for the week are: *Fine Things*, Danielle Steel; *The Haunted Mesa*, Louis L'Amour; *The Ladies of Missalonghi*, Colleen McCullough; *Windmills of the Gods*, Sidney Sheldon; and *Texasville*, Larry McMurtry. ... A Los Angeles Superior Court jury finds director John Landis and four associates innocent of involuntary manslaughter in connection with the 1982 deaths of actor Vic Morrow and two children on the set of the *Twilight Zone* film when the use of a special-effects explosive led to the crash of a helicopter during the filming of a Vietnam War scene. ... In Turin, Italy, Said Aouita of Morocco sets a world record in the two-mile run of 8 minutes, 13.45 seconds. ... Donna Shalala, president since 1980 of the Hunter College division of the City Univ. of New York, is reported to have accepted an appointment as chancellor of the Univ. of Wisconsin's central campus at Madison. The post is the university's highest and one of the premier jobs in public education. Shalala will be the first woman chancellor in the university's 139-year history.	May 29
				Mike Tyson retains his World Boxing Council and World Boxing Assoc. heavyweight titles with a sixth-round technical knockout of Pinklon Thomas.	May 30
Saying that acquired immune deficiency syndrome is "spreading surreptitiously through our population" and that "we have a moral obligation not to endanger others," Pres. Reagan calls for a wide range of acquired immune deficiency syndrome (AIDS) testing at the federal and state levels. The president's remarks were made at a benefit dinner sponsored by the American Foundation for AIDS Research (AmFAR).				The Edmonton Oilers capture the National Hockey League's Stanley Cup with a 3-1 victory over the Philadelphia Flyers. Flyers goalie Ron Hextall wins the Conn Smythe Trophy as the most valuable player in the Stanley Cup.	May 31
The Supreme Court upholds, 5-4, a Maine law requiring employers to provide severance pay to workers laid off by plant closings or relocations. Maine's law, which is said to be unique among the states, requires a one-time severance payment equal to one week's pay for each year of employment.	Pres. Reagan signs legislation to make permanent a new "GI Bill" program that was set up on a three-year basis in 1984. The program provides qualified veterans with $300 a month in educational benefits, to a maximum of $10,800.		The Third International Conf. on acquired immune deficiency syndrome meets in Washington, D.C. More than 6,000 scientists and health professionals from 50 countries attended, making it the largest scientific meeting ever devoted exclusively to the disease. In the nearly 250 formal presentations, no major breakthroughs are reported, only significant small steps.		June 1

F	G	H	I	J
Includes elections, federal-state relations, civil rights and liberties, crime, the judiciary, education, health care, poverty, urban affairs and population.	*Includes formation and debate of U.S. foreign and defense policies, veterans' affairs and defense spending. (Relations with specific foreign countries are usually found under the region concerned.)*	*Includes business, labor, agriculture, taxation, transportation, consumer affairs, monetary and fiscal policy, natural resources, and pollution.*	*Includes worldwide scientific, medical and technological developments, natural phenomena, U.S. weather, natural disasters, and accidents.*	*Includes the arts, religion, scholarship, communications media, sports, entertainments, fashions, fads and social life.*

	World Affairs	Europe	Africa & the Middle East	The Americas	Asia & the Pacific
June 2					In Australia, the Northern Territory's government gives Michael and Lindy Chamberlain a complete pardon and a public apology for the convictions stemming from the 1980 death of their daughter. But the government also explicitly states that the couple has not been exonerated.
June 3				Canada's P.M. Brian Mulroney and the 10 provincial premiers sign the Meech Lake Agreement that brings Quebec into the constitution. The accord, which fundamentally changes the concept of federalism in Canada, must be ratified by parliament and the provincial legislatures.... The World Bank and Inter-American Development Bank suspend loans to Peru because of overdue debt payments. In July 1985, Pres. Alan Garcia Perez announced a policy of limiting foreign debt payments to 10% of exports. The International Monetary Fund cut off credit to Peru in 1986.	
June 4			In response to the May 28 arrest and beating of the second-ranking British diplomat in Teheran, Britain closes an Iranian consulate. A complete break between the two nations is seen as a growing possibility.		India takes a direct hand in Sri Lanka's ethnic civil war when it undertakes an airlift of food and medicine to the Jaffna Peninsula in northern Sri Lanka. India is responding to a fierce military campaign against Tamil rebels in retaliation for the slaughter of hundreds of Sinhalese civilians by the rebels in April.... New Zealand's ban on nuclear weapons and nuclear-powered vessels becomes law when parliament approves, 39-29, the Nuclear Free Zone, Disarmament and Arms Control Bill.... The Philippine government suffers a setback when a U.S. appeals court rules that the United States does not have jurisdiction over the billions of dollars that former Pres. Ferdinand E. Marcos is believed to have stolen from the Philippines.
June 5				Canada's Defense Min. Perrin Beatty unveils a study that calls for, among other things, the purchase of a fleet of nuclear-powered attack submarines. The white paper is Canada's first comprehensive review of military policy in 16 years.	Both houses of Australia's parliament are dissolved, as the nation's political parties prepare for a July 11 general election.

A	B	C	D	E
Includes developments that affect more than one world region, international organizations and important meetings of major world leaders.	Includes all domestic and regional developments in Europe, including the Soviet Union, Turkey, Cyprus and Malta.	Includes all domestic and regional developments in Africa and the Middle East, including Iraq and Iran and excluding Cyprus, Turkey and Afghanistan.	Includes all domestic and regional developments in Latin America, the Caribbean and Canada.	Includes all domestic and regional developments in Asia and Pacific nations, extending from Afghanistan through all the Pacific Islands, except Hawaii.

U.S. Politics & Social Issues	U.S. Foreign Policy & Defense	U.S. Economy & Environment	Science, Technology & Nature	Culture, Leisure & Life Style	
The Senate approves a $9.4 bil. FY1987 supplemental appropriations bill that includes a requirement that would-be immigrants be screened for acquired immune deficiency syndrome (AIDS). The Senate measure will now have to be reconciled with a bill that passed the House in April with no AIDS amendment. Fiscal 1987 expires Sept. 30.	In congressional hearings into the Iran-Contra arms scandal, Asst. Sec. of State for Inter-American Affairs Elliott Abrams denies that the order to open a "southern front" against Nicaragua originated with a three-man Restricted Interagency Group consisting of Lt. Col. Oliver L. North, Alan D. Fiers, and Abrams. He also admits that his November 1986 appearance before the Senate Intelligence Committee was misleading, but insists that his statements were technically correct.	Pres. Reagan announces that Paul A. Volcker has decided to step down as chairman of the Federal Reserve Board when his second term ends Aug. 6. Reagan, who says he offered Volcker a third term, nominates economist Alan Greenspan to succeed him.		Andres Segovia, 94, Spanish classical guitarist whose career spanned nearly eight decades, dies of a heart attack in Madrid. Regarded as the most important performer and teacher in the history of the guitar, he was largely responsible for the resurgence of interest in classical guitar music. . . . Sammy Kaye, 77, leader of one of the U.S.'s most popular "sweet bands" of the swing era, dies of cancer in Ridgewood, N.J. A bandleader for some 50 years, he had more than 100 hit records; his band was particularly popular during World War II, when it performed live on Kaye's long-running radio show "Sunday Serenade."	June 2
A federal grand jury in New York City accuses Rep. Mario Biaggi (D, N.Y.) and six other men of violating federal antiracketeering laws in taking bribes and extorting payments from the scandal-ridden Wedtech Corp. . . . Congressional hearings into the Iran-Contra arms scandal continue with testimony from Albert Hakim, the business partner of retired Maj. Gen. Richard V. Secord, and the person considered most familiar with the intricate financial arrangements behind the scandal. Testifying under a limited grant of immunity, Hakim details the disposition of the profits left over from the sale of U.S. arms to Iran that were not diverted to the Contras.		Transportation Sec. Elizabeth Dole informs Congress of plans to increase the nation's air traffic manpower by 955 controllers, supervisors, and managers, in light of a predicted 5% to 6% increase in air traffic in 1988. . . . The Environmental Protection Agency announces new air quality standards for particulate matter. The new standards limit the total daily particulate content to 150 micrograms per cubic meter of air, down from the current 260 micrograms. . . . The Rev. Leon H. Sullivan, author of an influential antidiscrimination code of conduct for U.S. companies operating in South Africa, known as the Sullivan Principles, calls for a complete corporate pullout from that nation within nine months. He also urges the U.S. government to break diplomatic relations with the white minority regime and impose total economic sanctions until it dismantles the apartheid racial system.		The Untouchables is released in New York. Based loosely on a 1960s TV series, U.S. Treasury agent Eliot Ness teams up with an incorruptible cop to bring down the Chicago Prohibition empire of Al Capone. The film is written by David Mamet, directed by Brian De Palma, and stars Kevin Costner, Robert De Niro, and Sean Connery, who wins the Academy Award for best supporting actor for his performance.	June 3
The Federal Election Comm. rules that former Sen. Gary Hart (D, Colo.) is not eligible to receive federal matching funds for his aborted 1988 presidential campaign. The bipartisan commission says Hart was no longer a candidate when he submitted his application for federal funds May 18. Hart withdrew from the presidential race May 8 after a scandal erupted over his alleged involvements with women other than his wife.	A House Foreign Affairs panel effectively clears the way for the sale of 12 F-5 jets to Honduras when it votes, 6-6, on a resolution to block the sale. Tied votes lose in Congress.				June 4
		The nation's unemployment rate was unchanged in May at 6.2%, the Labor Dept. reports. . . . Outstanding consumer credit expanded by a seasonally adjusted $2.93 bil. in April, the Federal Reserve Board reports.	The National Aeronautics and Space Admin. (NASA) names 15 new astronaut candidates, including Mae C. Jemison, 30, a medical doctor from Glendale, Calif., and the first black woman to enter the program. Lt. Cmdr. Bruce E. Melnick, 37, of Traverse City, Mich., is the first Coast Guard officer named to the astronaut program.		June 5

F	G	H	I	J
Includes elections, federal-state relations, civil rights and liberties, crime, the judiciary, education, health care, poverty, urban affairs and population.	Includes formation and debate of U.S. foreign and defense policies, veterans' affairs and defense spending. (Relations with specific foreign countries are usually found under the region concerned.)	Includes business, labor, agriculture, taxation, transportation, consumer affairs, monetary and fiscal policy, natural resources, and pollution.	Includes worldwide scientific, medical and technological developments, natural phenomena, U.S. weather, natural disasters, and accidents.	Includes the arts, religion, scholarship, communications media, sports, entertainments, fashions, fads and social life.

	World Affairs	Europe	Africa & the Middle East	The Americas	Asia & the Pacific
June 6	An official row between Iran and Britain continues when Iran expells five British diplomats from Teheran in retaliation for the "unjustified" closing of Iran's Manchester consulate two days before.	According to a telephone poll conducted for the U.S. Information Agency (USIA), Western Europeans credit the Soviet Union more than the United States on arms control. The survey was conducted in Great Britain, France, and West Germany by Western European polling services under contract to USIA.	Kuwait's State Security Court sentences six Kuwaitis to hang for pro-Iranian sabotage and subversion. In all, 16 Kuwaiti citizens, four of them still being sought, are charged with firebombing the emirate's oil facilities in June 1986 and January 1987.	Nicaragua's Pres. Daniel Ortega Saavedra announces that prices and wages are to be raised as part of a package of economic measures aimed at strengthening the nation's failing economy. The president also announces that the government is cutting oil consumption by 5%, although the army and other vital branches of the economy will be guaranteed gasoline supplies.	
June 7		France's gross domestic product (GDP) grew just 0.1% in the first quarter and 2.2% for all of 1986, the government reports. The report is the first on GDP issued by France since mid-1986, owing to a revision of the bases on which the data were calculated.			
June 8	Leaders of the seven major non-communist industrial nations hold their 13th annual economic summit in Venice, Italy; though the meeting is viewed as satisfactory, few new initiatives emerge from the conference. The leaders meeting at the Venice summit are Pres. Ronald Reagan, Italy's Premier Amintore Fanfani, Britain's P.M. Margaret Thatcher, France's Pres. Francois Mitterrand, West Germany's Chancellor Helmut Kohl, Japan's Premier Yasuhiro Nakasone, and Canada's P.M. Brian Mulroney.		Meir Kahane, the U.S.-born rabbi who won election to the Israeli Knesset in 1984 as leader of the ultranationalist Kach movement, is banned from the floor of the Knesset for refusing to pledge allegiance to the state of Israel. Kahane, 54, substituted a religious oath for the prescribed loyalty oath, something he had also done in 1984. This time Kahane's version of the oath is declared invalid by the speaker of the Knesset, Shlomo Hillel.	Argentina's Pres. Raul Alfonsin signs into law a bill legalizing divorce. Under the law, civil marriages can be dissolved by mutual consent after three years, and couples can be legally separated after two years of marriage. After three years of legal separation, either partner can apply for a divorce. Remarriage is permitted under the law.	
June 9		The Soviet Union expresses a willingness to open its nuclear test sites to mandatory international inspections as part of a comprehensive ban on testing. Vladimir F. Petrovsky, a Soviet deputy foreign minister, proposes the test-ban program at the opening of the summer session of the 40-nation Geneva Committee disarmament talks in Switzerland.			

A	B	C	D	E
Includes developments that affect more than one world region, international organizations and important meetings of major world leaders.	Includes all domestic and regional developments in Europe, including the Soviet Union, Turkey, Cyprus and Malta.	Includes all domestic and regional developments in Africa and the Middle East, including Iraq and Iran and excluding Cyprus, Turkey and Afghanistan.	Includes all domestic and regional developments in Latin America, the Caribbean and Canada.	Includes all domestic and regional developments in Asia and Pacific nations, extending from Afghanistan through all the Pacific Islands, except Hawaii.

U.S. Politics & Social Issues	U.S. Foreign Policy & Defense	U.S. Economy & Environment	Science, Technology & Nature	Culture, Leisure & Life Style	
				In horse racing, Bet Twice wins the 119th Belmont Stakes in Elmont, New York. Alysheba, who won the first two legs of thoroughbred horse racing's triple crown, finished a disappointing fourth, missing out on a $5 mil. bonus that would have gone to a triple crown winner.... Steffi Graf of West Germany wins tennis's French Open women's title defeating top-ranked Martina Navratilova of the United States.	June 6
The Ku Klux Klan stages its first march and rally in Greensboro, N.C., since 1979, when five leftist demonstrators were shot to death in a "death to the Klan" rally. The shootout had led to three trials, the most recent in 1985. The march by some 150 Klan members carrying Confederate flags and chanting "KKK" is held amid tight security.	Lt. Col. Oliver L. North begins his long awaited testimony before congressional committees investigating the Iran-Contra arms scandal. He admits deceiving Congress and justifies the misuse of funds from the arms sales on the grounds of national security and the safety of his family. North says he believes that all his activities as a member of the National Security Council staff were authorized by his superiors, including the preparation of a chronology in November 1986 that contained several falsehoods.			In tennis, Czechoslovakia's Ivan Lendl wins the French Open men's title for the third time in four years. ... Stanford Univ. wins the National Collegiate Athletic Assoc. baseball title, 9-5, over Oklahoma State ... The 41st annual (Antoinette Perry) Tony Awards are presented. *Les Miserables* captures eight Tonys, including best musical, and best director, John Caird. August Wilson's *Fences* wins four, including best play; director, Lloyd Richards; and performance by a leading actor, James Earl Jones. *Me and My Girl* wins Tonys for best performances by a leading actor and actress in a musical, Robert Lindsay and Maryann Plunkett. Best leading actress in a play is Linda Lavin for *Broadway Bound*.	June 7
The Supreme Court upholds, 6-3, a Social Security regulation that has severely cut back the number of successful applicants for Social Security disability benefits in recent years. Before the regulation was issued in 1978, about 8% of some 2 million claims made annually were rejected because of insufficient medical severity; under the regulations in force, the number of rejections rose to 40%, or about 800,000 claims per year.	The head of a State Dept. special panel calls for an overhaul of the chancery building of the new U.S. Embassy in Moscow in order to rid the facility of eavesdropping devices planted by the Soviets.	The Supreme Court refuses to hear an appeal for federal action to reduce so-called acid-rain pollution. The appeal by eight states, Ontario, and environmental groups sought to force the Reagan administration to adhere to a commitment allegedly made by the Carter administration to take regulatory action to reduce the pollution.... BankAmerica Corp. adds $1.1 bil. to its reserve, a move that will result in a $1 bil. loss in the second quarter.... Silver, gold, and oil offered the best returns on investment in the year ending June 1, according to an annual tally by Salomon Brothers Inc., with returns of 40%, 29%, and 27%, respectively.	Advanced Genetic Sciences Inc. announces that its Frostban bacteria successfully protected strawberries from subfreezing temperatures. The experiment by the Oakland, Calif., firm is the first outdoor test of a genetically engineered bacterium.	Pope John Paul II begins a seven-day visit to his native Poland.	June 8
Sen. Joseph R. Biden Jr. (D, Del.) officially announces his candidacy for the 1988 Democratic presidential nomination.... California tax crusader Paul Gann tells a Sacramento news conference that he contracted acquired immune deficiency syndrome (AIDS) from blood transfusions during surgery in 1982. One of the most vigorous supporters of Proposition 13, the 1978 statewide property tax limit, Gann says he will devote the rest of his life to promoting universal testing for AIDS.	Congressional committees investigating the Iran-Contra arms scandal hear two days of testimony from Fawn Hall, Lt. Col. Oliver L. North's secretary at the National Security Council, who describes altering four memos on Nov. 21, 1986. All the memos were from North to Robert C. McFarlane and were written in 1985. One of the memos originally proposed that the Contras try to destroy a ship carrying weapons from Asia to the Nicaraguan government, while the others referred to Guatemalan, Saudi Arabian, and private efforts to aid the Contras.	Citing the Fifth Amendment's requirement that "just compensation" be paid whenever government "takes" private property, the Supreme Court rules, 6-3, that local governments can be liable for damages if their zoning or other regulations deprived landowners of the use of their land even temporarily. ... Justice Dept. officials confirm their plans to bring suit against the national leadership of the Teamsters union and to put the union under court-appointed trusteeship. The effort is focusing on use of the Racketeer Influenced and Corrupt Organizations Act.			June 9

F	G	H	I	J
Includes elections, federal-state relations, civil rights and liberties, crime, the judiciary, education, health care, poverty, urban affairs and population.	Includes formation and debate of U.S. foreign and defense policies, veterans' affairs and defense spending. (Relations with specific foreign countries are usually found under the region concerned.)	Includes business, labor, agriculture, taxation, transportation, consumer affairs, monetary and fiscal policy, natural resources, and pollution.	Includes worldwide scientific, medical and technological developments, natural phenomena, U.S. weather, natural disasters, and accidents.	Includes the arts, religion, scholarship, communications media, sports, entertainments, fashions, fads and social life.

	World Affairs	Europe	Africa & the Middle East	The Americas	Asia & the Pacific
June 10	East Germany's Socialist Unity (Communist) Party restores formal relations with the Chinese Communist Party. The ties between the two parties were suspended in the 1960s during the ideological rift between China and the Soviet Union. East German leader Erich Honecker visited China in 1986, a sign that possible reconciliation was near.		South Africa's Pres. Pieter W. Botha extends the nation's 12-month-old state of emergency for another year. In a speech to parliament and a subsequent televised address to the nation, Botha says that "the background of violence and unrest" that led to the promulgation of the decree in 1986 "still exists."		The nomination of a sucessor to Pres. Chun Doo Hwan by South Korea's ruling Democratic Justice Party (DJP) is followed by the worst street violence that Seoul has suffered in years. The DJP nominee is Roh Tae Woo, chief of the party and a close friend of Pres. Chun. Roh's election, due in December 1987, is all but assured by the country's indirect voting system, and critics maintain that he will serve simply as a more personable frontman for Chun and his military regime.
June 11		Conservative P.M. Margaret Thatcher becomes the first British leader in 160 years to be elected to a third consecutive term as prime minister.... Unemployment in the European Community (EC) declined to 16.3 million in April from 16.7 million in March, the EC reports. The unemployment rate in nine EC nations declined to 11.2% from 11.5%. Data from Spain, Greece, and Portugal was difficult to merge with that of the other EC countries.		The government of Panama imposes a 10-day "state of urgency" following three days of antigovernment protests. The protests began after Col. Roberto Diaz Herrera, the former second-in-command of the Panama Defense Forces, accused the chief of the force, Gen. Manuel Antonio Noriega, with electoral fraud and involvement in the murder of a political opponent in 1985.	
June 12		Foreign ministers of the North Atlantic Treaty Org. endorse the U.S. idea of a global ban on American and Soviet medium-range missiles. In accepting the U.S. plan, the allies also conditionally endorse the Soviet "double-zero option" on Euromissiles.... In a speech at the Brandenburg Gate in West Berlin, Pres. Reagan issues a challenge to Soviet leader Mikhail Gorbachev to "tear down" the Berlin Wall separating East and West Berlin.	The South African government releases 1,000 detainees, some of whom have been held for up to a year without charges under the emergency decree. Meanwhile, candlelight vigils are held in black townships and bells are tolled in Anglican churches for the thousands who remain in detention.... Jean-Bedel Bokassa, the former self-proclaimed emperor of the Central African Republic, is convicted and sentenced to death in Bangui criminal court for ordering the murders of at least 20 real and imagined opponents during his 14-year rule.	In Argentina, a federal judge overturns a military amnesty law, signed by Pres. Raul Alfonsin June 8, that ended the prosecutions of most military officers for human rights abuses committed in the 1970s "dirty war" against the left.... The Brazilian government announces emergency measures to help stop spiraling inflation and pay interest on the nation's foreign debt. The measures include a wage and price freeze for up to 90 days and a 10.56% devaluation of the cruzado.	
June 13		Britain's P.M. Margaret Thatcher unveils the cabinet for the beginning of her third term in office. Among the most notable developments are the reemergence of scandal-tainted former minister Cecil Parkinson and the resignation from the cabinet of Conservative Party Chairman Norman Tebbit.			
June 14		In West Germany, Hans-Jochen Vogel wins the formal backing of the Social Democratic Party to be its chairman. He will succeed elder statesman Willy Brandt, who announced his resignation in March after a controversy over a political appointment.			

A	B	C	D	E
Includes developments that affect more than one world region, international organizations and important meetings of major world leaders.	*Includes all domestic and regional developments in Europe, including the Soviet Union, Turkey, Cyprus and Malta.*	*Includes all domestic and regional developments in Africa and the Middle East, including Iraq and Iran and excluding Cyprus, Turkey and Afghanistan.*	*Includes all domestic and regional developments in Latin America, the Caribbean and Canada.*	*Includes all domestic and regional developments in Asia and Pacific nations, extending from Afghanistan through all the Pacific Islands, except Hawaii.*

U.S. Politics & Social Issues	U.S. Foreign Policy & Defense	U.S. Economy & Environment	Science, Technology & Nature	Culture, Leisure & Life Style	
The *New York Daily News* agrees on damages it will pay four black journalists who won a landmark race discrimination suit against the New York City newspaper in April. The settlement is reached days before a federal jury was to have ruled on damages in the second phase of the trial.				Elizabeth Hartman, 45, actress who was nominated for an Academy Award for best actress in 1966 for her role in the film *A Patch of Blue*, dies in Pittsburgh, in a fall from her fifth-floor apartment that police listed as a possible suicide. She enjoyed sudden success as a film actress following *A Patch of Blue*, but her career declined in succeeding years.... Isabel Rogers is elected to lead the Presbyterian Church (USA).	June 10
The House of Representatives passes a $16 bil. measure to reauthorize federal housing and community development programs for the FY1988. The bill passes by a vote of 285-120, with 49 Republicans joining the majority, despite White House threats to veto any bill that authorizes more than the $11 bil. that Pres. Reagan designated for housing in his FY1988 budget request.	Pres. Reagan announces that he is "temporarily" withdrawing a proposal to sell 1,600 Maverick air-to-ground missiles to Saudi Arabia. The White House makes the decision after it becomes clear that Congress will veto the sale.	The nation's air traffic controllers vote overwhelmingly to form a new union, the National Air Traffic Controllers Assoc. Their previous union collapsed in 1981 after Pres. Reagan fired 11,400 striking controllers.... In separate rulings, the Nuclear Regulatory Comm. (NRC) denies requests by the Public Service Co. of New Hampshire to operate its Seabrook plant at low power and by the Long Island Lighting Co.'s request to run its Shoreham plant at 25% power. Local and state officials oppose the emergency evacuation plans for the respective beachfront communities near the plants.			June 11
	Saying that it lacks the evidence to prosecute him, the Marine Corps dismisses espionage charges against Cpl. Arnold Bracy in the Moscow Embassy scandal. U.S. officials quoted by the press admit that the United States is not certain whether Soviet agents had entered the current U.S. Embassy in Moscow, or to what extent security had been compromised if the penetration did in fact take place.	The U.S. deficit on merchandise trade shrank in April to $13.3 bil., the Commerce Dept. says.... The producer price index rose a seasonally adjusted 0.3% in May, according to the Labor Dept.... Three months after the departure of its founder, the Rev. Jim Bakker, who had disclosed an extramarital liaison with a church secretary, the PTL (Praise the Lord) ministry files for court protection from its creditors under Chapter 11 of the federal bankruptcy laws. PTL has substantial real estate and other assets estimated to be far in excess of its liabilities, but its cash needs are enormous.		Pope John Paul II's pilgrimage to his native Poland is marred by violence when some of the estimated 15,000 people assembled to hear the pontiff at an open-air mass in Gdansk march to the Lenin Shipyards where a melee with police breaks out.... The film *Predator*, about U.S. military operatives who run into a murderous extraterrestrial in the jungles of Central America, is released in New York. Directed by John McTiernan and written by Jim Thomas and John Thomas, the film stars Arnold Schwarzenegger.	June 12
In Nashville for the 55th annual meeting of the Conf. of Mayors, mayors of both parties lament the plight of the cities under the Reagan administration. The conference became a presidential showcase as most of the Democratic hopefuls and two Republicans (former Delaware Gov. Pierre S. Du Pont IV and the Rev. Pat Robertson) put in appearances.				Geraldine Page, 62, one of the leading stage actresses of her generation, dies of a heart attack in New York City. Her biggest stage success was in Tennessee Williams's *Sweet Bird of Youth* (1959), opposite Paul Newman. She received the first of seven Academy Award nominations for her first screen appearance, in the 1953 western, *Hondo*, and won an Oscar in 1986 for her role as an elderly widow in *The Trip to Bountiful*. She won two Emmys and at the time of her death she was starring in a revival of Noel Coward's *Blithe Spirit*.	June 13
				The Los Angeles Lakers win the National Basketball Assoc. (NBA) title with a home-court, 81-68 victory over the defending champion Boston Celtics in the sixth game of the best-of-seven NBA finals. Lakers guard Earvin (Magic) Johnson is named the most valuable player in the finals.... In auto racing, a team led by Derek Bell of Britain wins the Le Mans (France) 24-hour endurance race.... The Greek national team upsets the Soviet Union, 103-101, to win the European Basketball Championship.	June 14

F	G	H	I	J
Includes elections, federal-state relations, civil rights and liberties, crime, the judiciary, education, health care, poverty, urban affairs and population.	Includes formation and debate of U.S. foreign and defense policies, veterans' affairs and defense spending. (Relations with specific foreign countries are usually found under the region concerned.)	Includes business, labor, agriculture, taxation, transportation, consumer affairs, monetary and fiscal policy, natural resources, and pollution.	Includes worldwide scientific, medical and technological developments, natural phenomena, U.S. weather, natural disasters, and accidents.	Includes the arts, religion, scholarship, communications media, sports, entertainments, fashions, fads and social life.

	World Affairs	Europe	Africa & the Middle East	The Americas	Asia & the Pacific
June 15		General elections over two days in Italy result in setbacks for the Communist Party and gains for the Christian Democrats and the Socialists. The results appear to pave the way for the return of the five-party coalition that has governed Italy almost continuously since 1981, but negotiations to form a government are expected to be long and difficult.	Umaru Dikko, the former Nigerian transport minister who was the subject of a bungled 1984 kidnapping plot, is granted temporary asylum by a British immigration tribunal. The judgment overturns a 1985 decision that Dikko be sent back to Nigeria to face fraud and corruption charges. . . . At a meeting in Lagos, Nigeria, the UN Economic Comm. for Africa finds that at least 25 of the 45 black-ruled nations of sub-Saharan Africa have begun substantial structural reforms, most emphasising free-market agricultural policies.		
June 16				Panama City, Panama, appears to be returning to normal after a series of protests sparked by accusations that Gen. Manuel Antonio Noriega, the chief of the Panama Defense Forces, is involved in murder and corruption. The charges were made last week by Col. Roberto Diaz Herrera, after he was forcibly retired as chief of the general staff.	Japan's gross national product grew by just 2.6% (adjusted for inflation) during FY1986, the government's Economic Planning Agency says. The showing marks an improvement over the decline registered in FY1985, but is still the slowest expansion the economy has achieved since 1975.
June 17			Sheik Sultan bin Mohammed Al Qasimi of Sharjah, one of the seven sheikdoms that make up the United Arab Emirates (UAE), is overthrown by his older brother, Sheik Abdel-Aziz bin Mohammed Al Qasimi, in a bloodless palace coup.	Meeting with Costa Rica's Pres. Oscar Arias Sanchez in Washington, D.C., Pres. Reagan expresses reservations about the perceived leniency toward Nicaragua in a peace plan put forward by Arias in February and tells Arias that the military effort by the Contras is the only way to pressure the Sandinistas.	
June 18	In its semiannual economic report, the Org. for Economic Cooperation and Development (OECD) revises downward its estimates for overall growth in the 24 OECD nations. The Paris-based organization of democratic industrial nations urges the largest industrial nations to act quickly to implement their pledges to cooperate to increase world growth.	In May, the number of unemployed in Britain fell below 3 million for the first time since July 1984, the Employment Dept. reports. The drop in joblessness is the 11th consecutive monthly decline and is also the largest drop on record.		Canada's National Energy Board blocks a plan by Quebec to export electric power to New England states. Hydro-Quebec, a provincially owned utility, signed a contract in 1985 for the sale of energy to the New England Power Pool (Nepool), a consortium of 93 U.S. utilities.	Central Seoul is thrown into turmoil as rioting South Korean students battle police. The outburst in the capital climaxes eight days of nationwide street fighting and protests directed at South Korea's military regime. . . . Vietnam's Pres. Truong Chinh and Premier Pham Van Dong, the last associates of the late Ho Chi Minh to hold high office in Vietnam, are removed from office as part of a reform-oriented sweep of the Vietnamese leadership.

A	B	C	D	E
Includes developments that affect more than one world region, international organizations and important meetings of major world leaders.	Includes all domestic and regional developments in Europe, including the Soviet Union, Turkey, Cyprus and Malta.	Includes all domestic and regional developments in Africa and the Middle East, including Iraq and Iran and excluding Cyprus, Turkey and Afghanistan.	Includes all domestic and regional developments in Latin America, the Caribbean and Canada.	Includes all domestic and regional developments in Asia and Pacific nations, extending from Afghanistan through all the Pacific Islands, except Hawaii.

U.S. Politics & Social Issues	U.S. Foreign Policy & Defense	U.S. Economy & Environment	Science, Technology & Nature	Culture, Leisure & Life Style	
Pres. Reagan defends his Persian Gulf policy and his performance at the previous week's Venice economic summit, and he challenges Congress to join him in reforming the federal budget process. . . . The Supreme Court rules, 5-4, against the use of "victim impact statements" at sentencing hearings of a capital case. The court says such statements concerning the effect of a crime on the victim or victim's family violate, in death-penalty cases, the Eighth Amendment's prohibition on cruel and unusual punishments. . . . The city of Los Angeles opens its first "urban campground" for the homeless on part of a 45-acre site owned by the Southern California Rapid Transit District.		Walter W(olfgang) Heller, 71, U.S. economist who headed the Council of Economic Advisers under John F. Kennedy and Lyndon B. Johnson, dies in Silverdale, Wash., after a heart attack. Heller was the architect of the historic tax cut of 1964 that stimulated unprecedented growth in the U.S. economy and he helped develop the theory of revenue sharing, under which state and local governments were deemed more efficient spenders of federal tax revenues than the federal government itself.			June 15
The Justice Dept. says that it considers the Ethics in Government Act, under which special prosecutors are appointed to probe wrongdoing by government officials, unconstitutional and recommends that Pres. Reagan veto any extension of the act when it expires in January 1988. . . . A New York State Supreme Court jury acquits "subway vigilante" Bernhard H. Goetz, who is white, of the attempted murder of four black youths on a New York City subway train in December 1984. Acquitted of assault, reckless endangerment, and weapons-possession charges, he is convicted of carrying a loaded, unlicensed weapon in a public place.	U.S. negotiators in Geneva formally propose the elimination of American and Soviet intermediate nuclear forces (INF) worldwide. The proposal exceeds both the U.S. "zero option" plan, under which longer-range INF weapons would be removed from Europe, or the Soviet "double-zero option," under which both shorter- and longer-range Euromissiles would be removed. . . . Pres. Reagan nominates Lt. Gen. Alfred M. Gray Jr. to succeed Gen. P.X. Kelley as commandant of the Marine Corps. Kelley is preparing to retire at the end of his four-year term on the Joint Chiefs of Staff.	The U.S. balance of payments on current account narrowed to $37.12 bil. in the first quarter, the Commerce Dept. says. . . . The Federal Reserve Board reports that its industrial production index rose 0.5% in May. . . . Housing starts dropped 2.7% in May, at an adjusted annual pace of 1.62 million, their lowest level since December 1984, the Commerce Dept. says.		The Southern Baptists' 130th annual convention in St. Louis reelects the Rev. Dr. Adrian Rogers as president.	June 16
	Lawyers for Lt. Col. Oliver L. North inform congressional investigators that the former National Security Council staffer will refuse to answer questions in private about his role in the Iran-Contra arms scandal. . . . Pres. Reagan rejects a Soviet proposal for high-level talks on the 1972 antiballistic missile treaty. The Soviets' April proposal calls for top defense officials on both sides to discuss the language of the treaty with regard to the testing of antimissile systems.	The nation's gross national product grew at a robust annual pace of 4.8% in the first quarter, the Commerce Dept. says in releasing revised figures. . . . Pres. Reagan names Northwestern Univ. law professor David S. Ruder to head the Securities and Exchange Comm.	Two Canadian geologists say they have identified on the floor of the North Atlantic Ocean a vast impact crater formed by a meteor.	*Variety*'s top-grossing films for the week are: *The Untouchables, Predator, The Witches of Eastwick, Beverly Hills Cop II*, and *The Believers*.	June 17
The Senate fails for the third time to end a filibuster by Republicans that is blocking passage of a campaign reform bill. The measure will provide federal financing of Senate elections and impose spending limits on candidates. The Senate also attempted to end the filibuster on June 9 and June 16.		A House-Senate conference committee approves a compromise budget for FY1988 that puts Congress on a collision course with Pres. Reagan. The $1 trillion budget allows Pres. Reagan an increase in military spending only in exchange for $19.3 bil. in tax increases. . . . Consumer spending edged up 0.1% in May, while personal income rose 0.2%, the Commerce Dept says.	Scientists announce the first "clear evidence" that a reduction in cholesterol in the bloodstream can slow, or even reverse, the formation of fatty deposits in the arteries. Such deposits clog arteries and contribute to heart attacks.		June 18

F	G	H	I	J
Includes elections, federal-state relations, civil rights and liberties, crime, the judiciary, education, health care, poverty, urban affairs and population.	Includes formation and debate of U.S. foreign and defense policies, veterans' affairs and defense spending. (Relations with specific foreign countries are usually found under the region concerned.)	Includes business, labor, agriculture, taxation, transportation, consumer affairs, monetary and fiscal policy, natural resources, and pollution.	Includes worldwide scientific, medical and technological developments, natural phenomena, U.S. weather, natural disasters, and accidents.	Includes the arts, religion, scholarship, communications media, sports, entertainments, fashions, fads and social life.

	World Affairs	Europe	Africa & the Middle East	The Americas	Asia & the Pacific
June 19		The Basque terrorist organization ETA (Basque Homeland and Liberty) claims responsibility for a car bombing in a parking garage that kills 17 people and injures some 40 others at a Barcelona, Spain, supermarket.		In the Bahamas, the ruling Progressive Liberal Party (PLP) wins a general election by a wide margin, giving P.M. Lynden O. Pindling his sixth term in office. The PLP wins despite widespread allegations that government members are involved in drug trafficking.	
June 20		A raid on the Turkish village of Pinarcik near the Turkish-Syrian border kills 31 people, including 16 children. The attack is claimed by a previously unknown Kurdish separatist group called the Peoples' Army for the Liberation of Kurdistan (ARGK), which is thought to be a breakaway faction of the Kurdish Workers' Party (PKK).	Iraq ends a month-long lull in the Persian Gulf shipping war with a jet attack on a tanker carrying Iranian oil. Baghdad had observed an unofficial cease-fire in the shipping war since the May 17 attack on the USS *Stark*, and Teheran followed suit. . . . After several days of tense uncertainty, the United Arab Emirates' Supreme Council reinstates Sheik Sultan bin Mohammed Al Qasimi as the ruler of the emirate of Sharjah. Sultan's brother, Sheik Abdel-Aziz bin Mohammed Al Qasimi, who seized power on July 17, is named crown prince with powers still to be determined.		
June 21		The Soviet Union for the first time holds elections in which in some races there are more than one candidate for each office. Gen. Sec. Mikhail S. Gorbachev called for such a system in his "democratization" speech in January. Voters went to the polls to elect 52,000 Communist Party soviets (local councils) around the nation.			The London-based human rights group Amnesty International charges that more than 500 Tamils have vanished after being arrested by Sri Lankan authorities and that it has also found evidence of systematic torture and arbitrary killings by government forces.
June 22		After adjustment for inflation, Britain's gross domestic product rose 3.3% in the first quarter of 1987 from the year-earlier quarter and 1.3% from the fourth quarter of 1986, the Central Statistical Office reports. Those figures are the average of three measures of economic activity: output, income, and expenditures.			Australia and the United States reaffirm the strength of their partnership in a joint statement issued at the close of ministerial talks held in Canberra. The daylong series of meetings is officially considered the annual conference of the Anzus pact military alliance, from which the third Anzus member, New Zealand, was suspended in 1986.

A	B	C	D	E
Includes developments that affect more than one world region, international organizations and important meetings of major world leaders.	Includes all domestic and regional developments in Europe, including the Soviet Union, Turkey, Cyprus and Malta.	Includes all domestic and regional developments in Africa and the Middle East, including Iraq and Iran and excluding Cyprus, Turkey and Afghanistan.	Includes all domestic and regional developments in Latin America, the Caribbean and Canada.	Includes all domestic and regional developments in Asia and Pacific nations, extending from Afghanistan through all the Pacific Islands, except Hawaii.

U.S. Politics & Social Issues	U.S. Foreign Policy & Defense	U.S. Economy & Environment	Science, Technology & Nature	Culture, Leisure & Life Style	
The Supreme Court strikes down, 8-2, a Louisiana law requiring public schools teaching evolution to teach "creation science" as well. . . . The Supreme Court rules, 6-3, that a defendant in a child-molesting case does not have a constitutional right to attend a pretrial hearing to determine the child's competency to testify. In *Kentucky* v. *Stincer*, Associate Justice Harry A. Blackmun writes that the defendant has "the opportunity for full and effective cross-examination" of the witnesses during trial. . . . The Supreme Court affirms, 6-3, lower court decisions that a labor union violates civil rights law by deliberately refusing to press discrimination claims, even if the union leadership holds no bias against minorities.	Citing "lack of confidence in their performance" following the May 17 Iraqi missile attack in the Persian Gulf that killed 37 sailors, the Navy announces that the captain and two other officers of the USS *Stark* are being relieved of duty. . . . A federal judge in Los Angeles dismisses criminal fraud charges against General Dynamics Corp. related to the defunct Army DIVAD (division air defense) Sergeant York mobile antiaircraft weapon. The Pentagon canceled DIVAD production in August 1985.			After months of debate surrounding the "colorization" process, the U.S. Copyright Office of the Library of Congress rule that computer-colored films will be granted copyright status if the tinted versions reveal a certain degree of human creativity and are produced by existing computer-coloring technology. . . . *Roxanne*, a contemporary adaptation of Edmond Rostand's romantic drama *Cyrano de Bergerac*, is released in New York. Directed by Fred Schepisi and with a screenplay by Steve Martin, the film stars Martin and Daryl Hannah.	**June 19**
				New Zealand beats France, 29-9, to win the World Cup of rugby.	**June 20**
			The Food and Drug Admin. is reported to have put a controversial experimental drug for Alzheimer's disease on a "fast track" toward potential licensing. The fast track authorizes tests of the drug, tetrahydroaminoacridine, or THA, on more than 300 patients at 17 medical centers. Alzheimer's disease is a degenerative condition in middle-aged and elderly people that is characterized by profound mental deterioration.	Scott Simpson wins the $150,000 first prize at the U.S. Open golf championship. Tom Watson finishes second by one stroke when his try for a birdie on the 72nd and final hole came up just inches short.	**June 21**
The Supreme Court rules, 6-3, that mandatory death penalties violate the Eighth and Fourteenth Amendments. A mandatory death sentence had been imposed on Raymond W. Shuman in Nevada for murdering a fellow prisoner while serving time on a previous murder conviction. . . . Three hotel workers arrested in connection with the New Year's Eve fire that killed 97 people at the luxurious Dupont Plaza Hotel in San Juan, Puerto Rico, are sentenced to prison terms ranging from 75 to 99 years. All three defendants pleaded guilty April 24 to federal charges of arson.		The Environmental Protection Agency reaches agreement with a number of companies to share costs of cleaning up an 11-acre toxic waste dump in La Marque, Tex., near Galveston, that ranks 27th on the list of the most hazardous waste sites in the nation. . . . The House approves by voice vote a bill placing security of computer files in the hands of the Commerce Dept.'s National Bureau of Standards. The Defense Dept. will retain control over classified national security information.		David Robinson, a basketball center from the Naval Academy, goes to the San Antonio Spurs as the first player selected in the National Basketball Assoc. draft of college players. . . . Fred Astaire (born Frederick Austerlitz), 88, one of the great dancers of the 20th century, whose grace and elegance thrilled several generations of moviegoers, dies of pneumonia in Los Angeles. Between 1933 and 1968 he starred in more than 30 film musicals, 10 costarring Ginger Rogers, including *Top Hat* (1935) and *Follow the Fleet* (1936).	**June 22**

F	G	H	I	J
Includes elections, federal-state relations, civil rights and liberties, crime, the judiciary, education, health care, poverty, urban affairs and population.	*Includes formation and debate of U.S. foreign and defense policies, veterans' affairs and defense spending. (Relations with specific foreign countries are usually found under the region concerned.)*	*Includes business, labor, agriculture, taxation, transportation, consumer affairs, monetary and fiscal policy, natural resources, and pollution.*	*Includes worldwide scientific, medical and technological developments, natural phenomena, U.S. weather, natural disasters, and accidents.*	*Includes the arts, religion, scholarship, communications media, sports, entertainments, fashions, fads and social life.*

	World Affairs	Europe	Africa & the Middle East	The Americas	Asia & the Pacific
June 23				Quebec's National Assembly is the first provincial legislature to ratify the so-called Meech Lake agreement designed to bring Quebec into the constitution.... Saying that it has no jurisdiction in the case, a court in Grasse, France, refuses to hear a case brought by the Haitian government against deposed Pres. Jean-Claude Duvalier accusing him of embezzling millions of dollars during his 15 years in office.... Argentina's Supreme Court upholds a law exempting from prosecution hundreds of military officers accused of human rights abuses in the 1970s. The amnesty law was declared unconstitutional in two federal courts earlier in the month.	
June 24		The West German government confirms reports that it has decided not to extradite Mohammed Ali Hamadei, a suspect in the 1985 hijacking of a Trans World Airlines jet to the United States, and will instead try him in West Germany for air piracy and murder. Washington expresses satisfaction with Bonn's decision in the sensitive case, which has caused strains between the two allies.		A study by a U.S.-based economist concludes that Canada ranks behind only the United States as the world's largest debtor nation. The study was conducted by Shafiqul Islam, a visiting fellow at the Institute for International Economics in Washington, D.C.	South Korea's Pres. Chun Doo Hwan offers once again to allow debate over the national constitution. But Kim Young Sam, a top leader of the political opposition, rejects the concession and holds out little hope for an end to the riots and demonstrations plaguing the country. The exchange takes place in a private meeting brought about by the country's two-week surge of unrest.
June 25	The International Whaling Comm. approves, by a 19-6 vote, a U.S. proposal putting restrictions on the group's provision allowing some killing of whales for scientific purposes. The commission has no enforcement power for its resolutions, but most of the 32 countries attending the conference speak disapprovingly of the so-called research killing of whales as a pretext for commercial killing.	Britain's Queen Elizabeth II opens a new session of Parliament with the traditional Speech from the Throne to a joint session of the Houses of Lords and Commons. ... Soviet leader Mikhail S. Gorbachev calls for a "radical reorganization of economic management" to be in place in the USSR by the end of the 1980s. He offers a package of guidelines at the opening session of a two-day plenum of the Communist Party Central Committee.		The Supreme Court of Canada rules unanimously that Ontario's program of extended public funding for Roman Catholic schools is constitutional. Under the controversial Bill 30, Ontario began funding church schools beyond Grade 10 in 1985.... Colombia's Supreme Court declares unconstitutional a law ratifying a 1979 extradition treaty with the United States. The court ruled in December 1986 that the treaty was unconstitutional, but Pres. Virgilio Barco Vargas immediately wrote it back into law.	
June 26		In Yugoslavia, the Central Committee of the ruling League of Communists meets in Belgrade to discuss growing ethnic tensions in Kosovo province. Kosovo is an autonomous province in the Yugoslav republic of Serbia. Ethnic Albanians, who are the majority in Kosovo, control the provincial administration. Serbs and Montenegrins, who make up about 13% of Kosovo's population, repeatedly complain of mistreatment by the majority.		The U.S. Senate June 26 passes a resolution, 84-2, calling for free elections in Panama. It also urges Gen. Manuel Antonio Noriega to step down while an independent investigation is undertaken to probe charges that the general is involved in political murder, drug trafficking, and election fraud. Those charges were leveled earlier in June by Noriega's former second-in-command.	Protesting the group's "constant vote against Japan," Tatsuo Saito of Japan resigns as a member of the International Whaling Comm. The action is taken after the commission, meeting in Bournemouth, England, adopts resolutions condemning whaling for scientific research by Japan, Iceland, and South Korea.

A	B	C	D	E
Includes developments that affect more than one world region, international organizations and important meetings of major world leaders.	Includes all domestic and regional developments in Europe, including the Soviet Union, Turkey, Cyprus and Malta.	Includes all domestic and regional developments in Africa and the Middle East, including Iraq and Iran and excluding Cyprus, Turkey and Afghanistan.	Includes all domestic and regional developments in Latin America, the Caribbean and Canada.	Includes all domestic and regional developments in Asia and Pacific nations, extending from Afghanistan through all the Pacific Islands, except Hawaii.

U.S. Politics & Social Issues	U.S. Foreign Policy & Defense	U.S. Economy & Environment	Science, Technology & Nature	Culture, Leisure & Life Style	
The Supreme Court upholds, 7-2, the authority of Congress to require states to raise the drinking age to 21 or lose federal highway aid.... At its annual meeting in Chicago, the American Medical Assoc. (AMA) adopts a policy that is more selective in who should be tested for the virus that causes acquired immune deficiency syndrome than are the Reagan administration proposals. The American Medical Assoc. governing board rejects testing of hospital patients or marriage license applicants but recommends that doctors urge people in these two groups to be tested if their family history or life-style places them in a high-risk category.	Congressional committees probing the Iran-Contra arms scandal resume public hearings. A series of present and former officials from the Central Intelligence Agency, and the State, Justice, and Defense departments discussed their small roles in various aspects of the affair.	The government's consumer price index rose a modest 0.3% in May, the Labor Dept. reports.... The difference between the amount of U.S. assets held by foreigners and the amount of foreign assets held by U.S. investors more than doubled in 1986, to $263.65 bil., the Commerce Dept. reports. As recently as 1982, the United States was the world's largest creditor nation.			June 23
The Supreme Court affirms, 5-4, the First Amendment right of a public employee to slur Pres. Reagan in private remarks without punishment. Ardith McPherson, a 19-year-old clerk in a county constable's office related the assassination attempt on Reagan to the administration's cuts in welfare and other programs and said, "If they go for him again, I hope they get him." ... The Supreme Court upholds an exemption for religious groups from the federal law barring discrimination in employment based on religion.... The *New York Times* reports that Veterans Admin. (VA) doctors are strenuously opposed to a Reagan administration proposal that all people admitted to VA hospitals be routinely tested for infection with the acquired immune deficiency syndrome virus.	Congressional committees probing the Iran-Contra arms scandal announce an agreement with Lt. Col. Oliver L. North's lawyer in exchange for assurances that North will testify beginning July 7. The committees will limit the private interrogation to one day and one topic, Reagan's knowledge of the diversion of funds to the Contras. North earlier had appeared willing to risk being cited for contempt of Congress if he were not granted several concessions.	The Supreme Court restricts use of the mail-fraud law to protection of property rights. In a 7-2 decision written by Associate Justice Byron R. White, the court rules out use of the law to protect "intangible rights, such as the right to have public officials perform their duties honestly." ... The Senate approves a $1 trillion budget resolution for FY1988. The resolution passed the House June 20. Adoption of the joint resolution sets Congress in direct opposition to the White House.... The Environmental Protection Agency (EPA) announces final standards limiting the presence of eight hazardous chemicals including vinyl chloride, benzene, and carbon tetrachloride, in drinking water. The standards, to go into effect Dec. 31, 1988, are issued in compliance with the Safe Drinking Water Act of 1986.		Jackie (Herbert John) Gleason, 71, rotund comedian, actor, and musician, dies of cancer in Fort Lauderdale, Fla. A leading show business figure of the 1950s and 1960s, his "Jackie Gleason Show," a comedy-variety program on CBS television, ran from 1952 to 1959 and from 1962 to 1970. His 1950s comedy series, "The Honeymooners," is a classic of the medium. He won an Oscar nomination for his portrayal of pool shark Minnesota Fats in *The Hustler* (1961), and he won a Tony for his performance in the 1959 Broadway musical *Take Me Along*.	June 24
The Supreme Court affirms the authority of the U.S. Olympic Committee to bar a homosexual rights group from using "Gay Olympics" as the title of its athletic games.... The Supreme Court rules, 6-3, that law enforcement officers are immune from liability when they conduct an illegal, warrantless search if they believe, and it is reasonable to believe, that the search was legal.... The Supreme Court upholds a 1984 federal law reducing welfare costs by deducting child support payments in some households.	The Supreme Court rules out damage suits by military personnel against the government or superior officers, even for violations of constitutional rights. The court also approves the court-martial of military personnel for crimes occurring off-base and unrelated to their service.... Congressional committees probing the Iran-Contra arms scandal reach an agreement with the government of Israel to obtain information from that country's probe of the arms sales to Iran.	The Dow Jones closings set a record high of 2451.05.		Pope John Paul II holds a 35-minute audience with Austria's president and former UN sec. gen. Kurt Waldheim. The meeting draws intense criticism from the international Jewish community because of Waldheim's link to Nazi war crimes in World War II.	June 25
At the conclusion of the Supreme Court's 1986-87 term, Associate Justice Lewis F. Powell Jr. retires from the bench. Appointed to the court by Pres. Nixon in 1971, Powell was a pragmatist who was considered conservative on business and criminal-law issues and liberal on social issues like civil rights, civil liberties, and separation of church and state.... The Supreme Court lets stand a ruling upholding the Customs Service's impoundment of a multimillion-dollar planeload of jewelry, cash, and other valuables seized from former Philippine Pres. Ferdinand Marcos after he fled to Hawaii in 1986. The goods are in dispute between Marcos and the new Philippine administration of Pres. Corazon Aquino.	Former Defense Sec. James R. Schlesinger issues a formal report on the security problems at the new U.S. Embassy in Moscow. In his report, prepared on behalf of the State Dept., Schlesinger maintains that America overestimated its ability to counteract Soviet espionage efforts with "superior U.S. technology and ingenuity." He concludes that Washington's confidence was "misplaced."	The Supreme Court strikes down a California law requiring public access to beaches as a condition for obtaining a building permit. In a 5-4 decision written by Justice Antonin Scalia, the court rules that the California Coastal Comm.'s requirement constitutes a "taking" under the Fifth and Fourteenth Amendments for which the state must compensate landowners.... Arthur F. Burns (born Arthur Frank Burnzeig), 83, economist, dies in Baltimore of complications stemming from triple-bypass heart surgery in April. A university professor, in 1953 he was named to head Pres. Dwight D. Eisenhower's Council of Economic Advisers, served as president of the National Bureau of Economic Research, and chairman of the Federal Reserve Board 1970-78.		*Full Metal Jacket*, which follows an 18-year-old Marine recruit from boot camp to combat during the 1968 Tet offensive in Vietnam, is released in New York. Directed by Stanley Kubrick and with a screenplay by Kubrick, Michael Herr, and Gustav Hasford, the film is based on Hasford's novel *The Short Timers* and stars Matthew Modine, Lee Ermey, and Vincent D'Onofrio.... *Jean de Florette*, the first part of a two-part film adaptation of a Marcel Pagnol epic novel of peasant life in the Midi region of France in the 1920s, is released in New York. Directed by Claude Berri and with a screenplay by Berri and Gerard Brach, the film stars Yves Montand, Gerard Depardieu, Elisabeth Depardieu, and Daniel Auteuil.	June 26

F	G	H	I	J
Includes elections, federal-state relations, civil rights and liberties, crime, the judiciary, education, health care, poverty, urban affairs and population.	Includes formation and debate of U.S. foreign and defense policies, veterans' affairs and defense spending. (Relations with specific foreign countries are usually found under the region concerned.)	Includes business, labor, agriculture, taxation, transportation, consumer affairs, monetary and fiscal policy, natural resources, and pollution.	Includes worldwide scientific, medical and technological developments, natural phenomena, U.S. weather, natural disasters, and accidents.	Includes the arts, religion, scholarship, communications media, sports, entertainments, fashions, fads and social life.

	World Affairs	Europe	Africa & the Middle East	The Americas	Asia & the Pacific
June 27			In South Africa, more than 2,000 hard-liners walk out of a meeting called to discuss the liberalization of the Dutch Reformed Church, the influential establishment religion of the Afrikaner community, which has in the past provided theological justifications for apartheid. The right-wing dissidents vote to form a new all-white church in reaction to the church's recent criticisms of apartheid and efforts to open its membership to all races.		A delegation of Japanese cabinet ministers visits China in an effort by the two nations to smooth their worsening relations.
June 28	Ministers of the Org. of Petroleum Exporting Countries (OPEC), meeting for three days in Vienna, Austria, agree to limit their nations' combined oil production to 16.6 million barrels a day through the end of 1987. That is slightly higher than OPEC's current daily production ceiling of 15.8 million barrels, but it represents a cut from the 18.3-million-barrel daily output that OPEC had tentatively planned for the fourth quarter of 1987.				
June 29	Noncommunist industrialized nations provided $37 bil. in aid to developing nations in 1986, according to a study by the Org. for Economic Cooperation and Development (OECD). While that figure is up from $29.4 bil. in 1985, it represents an increase of just 2.5% after adjusting for inflation and the effects of a weaker dollar, the OECD said.	Leaders of the 12 European Community (EC) nations meet in Brussels for their semiannual summit. The leaders make modest progress on reforming the EC's Common Agriculture Policy, and all nations except Britain agree to broad guidelines on budget reform.	The October 1986 air crash that killed Mozambique's Pres. Samora Machel and 34 others was caused by the ineptitude of the plane's Soviet flight crew, an international investigative commission says. The board of inquiry says there is "not a shred of evidence" to back Soviet and Mozambican claims that South Africa had in effect assassinated Machel by deliberately luring his plane off course with a decoy navigational beacon.		
June 30		The Supreme Soviet, the USSR's nominal parliament, enacts a law that will allow state enterprises to become self-sustaining, a proposal that is at the core of Gen. Sec. Mikhail S. Gorbachev's new economic reforms.		The House of Commons defeats a motion to restore capital punishment in Canada. The death penalty was abolished in 1976. . . . In Panama, the government lifts a state of emergency that has been in effect since June 11.	Australia and China agree to joint development of a new iron ore mine in Western Australia. The agreement, signed in Beijing by representatives of the two countries, forms an operating partnership between China Metallurgical Import and Export Corp. and Hamersley Iron Ltd.
July 1		The number of asylum-seekers in West Germany has dropped sharply in 1987 from 1986, the interior ministry reports. Only 20,000 people sought asylum in the first five months of 1987, and only 60,000 are expected to do so in all of 1987, compared with 100,000 in 1986, the ministry says. . . . Italy's gross domestic product shrank 0.4% in the first quarter of 1987 from the last quarter of 1986, according to a government report.	Nigeria's president, Maj. Gen. Ibrahim Babangida, unveils detailed plans for returning the nation to civilian rule, but pushes back until 1992 the date when he and other military leaders will return to the barracks. . . . Rabbi Meir Kahane regains his privileges as a member of the Israeli Knesset by taking the loyalty oath required of Knesset members. Knesset speaker Shlomo Hillel had stripped Kahane of his privileges in June for refusing to take the oath.	Brazil announces that it is suspending repayment of $1.05 bil. in principal that is due to be paid in 1987 to the Club of Paris, a group of Western creditor governments. Brazil will continue to pay interest due on the loans amounting to $242 mil.	Two days after his top political ally backed opposition demands for reform, South Korea's Pres. Chun Doo Hwan follows suit and says his military government will permit election of the next president by direct popular vote. The announcement apparently ends the political crisis that has gripped South Korea since June 10. Word of the impending shift has already helped bring quiet to the nation's streets after almost three weeks of massive riots and demonstrations.

A	B	C	D	E
Includes developments that affect more than one world region, international organizations and important meetings of major world leaders.	*Includes all domestic and regional developments in Europe, including the Soviet Union, Turkey, Cyprus and Malta.*	*Includes all domestic and regional developments in Africa and the Middle East, including Iraq and Iran and excluding Cyprus, Turkey and Afghanistan.*	*Includes all domestic and regional developments in Latin America, the Caribbean and Canada.*	*Includes all domestic and regional developments in Asia and Pacific nations, extending from Afghanistan through all the Pacific Islands, except Hawaii.*

U.S. Politics & Social Issues	U.S. Foreign Policy & Defense	U.S. Economy & Environment	Science, Technology & Nature	Culture, Leisure & Life Style	
				Billboard's best-selling albums for the week are: *Whitney*, Whitney Houston; *Girls, Girls, Girls*, Motley Crue; *The Joshua Tree*, U2; *Whitesnake*, Whitesnake; and *Slippery When Wet*, Bon Jovi.	June 27
		After-tax household income adjusted for inflation averaged $22,650 in 1985, 0.9% higher than the previous year, the Census Bureau says.			June 28
Sen. Albert Gore Jr. (D, Tenn.) formally launches his campaign for the 1988 Democratic presidential nomination with a speech in his hometown of Carthage, Tenn.		The Environmental Protection Agency warns 14 municipal areas that they face a ban on new construction of any heavily polluting facility because of failure to meet clean-air standards. The areas included Los Angeles, Chicago, Cleveland, Denver, Atlanta, and the four California counties of Sacramento, Ventura, Kern, and Fresno.			June 29
A letter by David H. Martin, director of the office of Government Ethics, says a "limited blind partnership" in which Attorney Gen. Edwin Meese III invested $60,000 in 1985 did not comply with federal ethics regulations.... Congress's controversial 1987 pay raises are allowed to stand when U.S. District Court Judge Louis F. Oberdorfer dismisses a lawsuit by six members of Congress who contended that Congress acted unconstitutionally. The raises, included in recommendations submitted by Pres. Reagan, took effect automatically when Congress failed to disapprove them within 30 days. Congress had waited until the 31st day to pass legislation purporting to block the increases.	Pres. Reagan rejects suggestions by congressional leaders that he delay his administration's plans for the U.S. reflagging and naval escort of 11 Kuwaiti oil tankers in the Persian Gulf. The implementation of the plan is set for mid-July, despite the renewal of the "tanker war" between Iran and Iraq, new Iranian threats against the United States, and the discovery of mines moored in the shipping lanes to Kuwait.	The Senate votes to ban the sale of Toshiba Corp. products in the United States in protest of the illegal sale of militarily useful technology to the Soviet Union by a subsidiary of the giant Japanese company.... The government's index of leading economic indicators rose 0.7% in May, the Commerce Dept. reports.... The U.S. Treasury Dept. announces that it will cancel a 32-year-old treaty that exempts investments in the Netherlands Antilles from almost all taxes. The Caribbean islands have been one of the world's most lucrative tax havens, with 60 banks and more than 24,000 corporations registered in the autonomous Dutch territory of 200,000 people.	Scientists at a conference in Rochester, N.Y., say experiments will soon begin that will involve transplanting fetal tissue from humans or animals into the brains of Parkinson's disease victims.	Patrik Sjoberg of Sweden high-jumps 7 feet, 11 and one-quarter inches (2.42 m) to set a new world record in the event.... The 1.7 million-member United Church of Christ adopts a declaration acknowledging the continuing religious validity of the Jewish faith and affirming that Judaism has not been "superseded" by Christianity. The declaration, the first such statement by a major U.S. Protestant denomination, is approved at the church's national convention in Cleveland.	June 30
U.S. Appeals Court Judge Robert H. Bork is nominated by Pres. Reagan to succeed Supreme Court Associate Justice Lewis F. Powell, who is retiring. Bork, 60, is a leading conservative jurist and former Nixon administration official.... Seven Democratic presidential hopefuls for 1988 hold a low-key televised debate in Houston that largely focuses on criticism of the Reagan administration's handling of the economy.	The Senate agrees to a compromise with the House of Representatives on the issue of security at the new U.S. Embassy in Moscow. The move clears the way for approval of a delayed supplemental spending bill. The Moscow facility, which was nearing completion, was found to be riddled with electronic eavesdropping devices planted by the Soviet workers.	The Senate gives final approval to a long-delayed supplemental appropriations bill for FY1987, the current fiscal year. The bill passed the House June 30. The main force driving the bill was the need to extend funding for farm-support programs, which ran out in May. However, a variety of disagreements slowed the bill's progress through the Senate and a House-Senate conference.			July 1

F	G	H	I	J
Includes elections, federal-state relations, civil rights and liberties, crime, the judiciary, education, health care, poverty, urban affairs and population.	*Includes formation and debate of U.S. foreign and defense policies, veterans' affairs and defense spending. (Relations with specific foreign countries are usually found under the region concerned.)*	*Includes business, labor, agriculture, taxation, transportation, consumer affairs, monetary and fiscal policy, natural resources, and pollution.*	*Includes worldwide scientific, medical and technological developments, natural phenomena, U.S. weather, natural disasters, and accidents.*	*Includes the arts, religion, scholarship, communications media, sports, entertainments, fashions, fads and social life.*

	World Affairs	Europe	Africa & the Middle East	The Americas	Asia & the Pacific
July 2			The *Times* of London reports that the government of Somalia has begun a secret military campaign to lay waste to an area along the northwest border in an effort to "obliterate" Ethiopian-backed rebels operating among the country's Isaaq clans. Details of the plan were contained in a confidential report submitted to Pres. Mohamed Siad Barre earlier in the year. A copy of the report, judged authentic by analysts, was leaked by dissident Somali emigres in Norway.		The Chinese government signs an agreement permitting it to televise 52 films from the library of Twentieth Century Fox Film Corp., according to the *Financial Times*. The deal will also enable the U.S. film company to sell six minutes of advertising time in each broadcast. A Fox executive says the agreement marks "the first time American films will be regularly available on the Chinese national television network."
July 3		The Yugoslav government announces that it has been granted an extension on the repayment of $245 mil. in debt principal owed to Western commercial banks.			
July 4		Klaus Barbie is found guilty by a court in Lyons, France, of crimes against humanity and is sentenced to life in prison. The specific counts on which he was found guilty charged Barbie with deportations of 842 people that resulted in the deaths of more than 370 Jews and French Resistance fighters during World War II.			
July 5					In Pakistan, peaceful protest rallies are held to mark the 10th anniversary of Muhammad Zia ul-Haq's seizure of power. The government permits the so-called Black Day protests, and no incidents are reported. . . . In China, more than 1 million students have reportedly been assigned to compulsory work in the countryside for the summer recess. The move follows massive pro-democracy protests mounted by students in December 1986.
July 6					The Reagan administration formally proposes that all nations cease all subsidies for agriculture by the year 2000. The proposal is welcomed warily by delegates to the General Agreement on Tariffs and Trade in Geneva, where it is presented, but is opposed by many members of Congress.

A	B	C	D	E
Includes developments that affect more than one world region, international organizations and important meetings of major world leaders.	*Includes all domestic and regional developments in Europe, including the Soviet Union, Turkey, Cyprus and Malta.*	*Includes all domestic and regional developments in Africa and the Middle East, including Iraq and Iran and excluding Cyprus, Turkey and Afghanistan.*	*Includes all domestic and regional developments in Latin America, the Caribbean and Canada.*	*Includes all domestic and regional developments in Asia and Pacific nations, extending from Afghanistan through all the Pacific Islands, except Hawaii.*

U.S. Politics & Social Issues	U.S. Foreign Policy & Defense	U.S. Economy & Environment	Science, Technology & Nature	Culture, Leisure & Life Style	
Political extremist Lyndon H. LaRouche Jr. is indicted on charges of conspiring to block a federal investigation of a million-dollar credit card fraud. . . . Eighteen young Mexican men locked in a steel-wall boxcar are found dead of suffocation and dehydration by border patrol agents in the small town of Sierra Blanca, Tex., 90 miles southeast of El Paso. A 19th man, identified as Miguel Tostado Rodriguez, 21, survives and provides authorities with details of the tragedy. . . . House Democratic Whip Rep. Tony Coelho (D, Calif.) and the Democratic Congressional Campaign Committee admit having violated campaign finance laws by accepting the use of a yacht and an airplane for political events in 1985-86.		The nation's unemployment rate fell in June, to 6% from 6.2% in May, the Labor Dept. reports. . . . The Interstate Commerce Comm. gives permission to Greyhound Lines Inc., the nation's largest bus line, to buy its main competitor, Trailways Corp. Greyhound, which expressed its intent to make the purchase June 19, takes over temporary operation of Trailways immediately.		Michael Bennett (born Michael Bennett Di Figlia), 44, Broadway choreographer and director who drew on his early experiences as a chorus dancer for the musical *A Chorus Line*, the longest-running show in Broadway history, dies in Tucson, of lymphoma related to acquired immune deficiency syndrome. He won eight Tony Awards. . . . The producers of the hit London musical *The Phantom of the Opera* and the Actors' Equity Assoc. reach agreement to allow British actress Sarah Brightman to recreate her starring role in the show on Broadway. The producers agree to hire an American actor for a major London production sometime within the next three years.	July 2
		Frequently invoking the spirit of Thomas Jefferson, Pres. Reagan calls for an "Economic Bill of Rights" which, he says, will force government to "live within its means and balance its budget." Reagan returns to familiar themes in a speech that is designed to set the tone for his budget confrontation with Congress. . . . A rule change by the Federal Trade Comm. that makes it more difficult for so-called corporate raiders to launch surprise takeover bids for publicly held companies takes effect today.	An international group of development experts and Third World political leaders issues an urgent call for action to reverse the continuing loss of the world's tropical forests, which are diminishing by an area roughly the size of Maryland every year.		July 3
The *New York Times* reports that Operation PUSH Inc., the civil rights group founded by possible democratic presidential candidate the Rev. Jesse Jackson, is in a financial shambles and uncertain of survival. An audit covering 1985 was filed with Illinois officials June 30, a year later than required, and a statement from the auditor says the 1984 audit could not be completed "because of major inadequacies in the organization's accounting records."				In tennis, Martina Navratilova beats Steffi Graf of West Germany to win a record sixth consecutive singles title at Wimbledon, in England. . . . Delegates attending the 70th international convention of Lions Club International in Taipei, Taiwan, vote to abolish immediately the organization's 70-year-old ban on female members. The Lions are a service club with more than 1.3 million members in more than 150 countries. . . . Poet Philip Levine is awarded the second annual, $25,000 Ruth Lilly Poetry Prize.	July 4
				Australian Pat Cash upset tennis's top-seeded Ivan Lendl of Czechoslovakia to earn his first Wimbledon title. . . . In auto racing, Nigel Mansell of Britain wins his second consecutive French Grand Prix in Le Castellet. . . . Crews from the Soviet Union dominate the Henley (England) Royal Regatta, winning five finals. It is the first time the Soviets have competed in the event since 1974.	July 5
A federal judge bars the Dept. of Housing and Urban Development from selling $536 mil. of mortgages on low-income rental housing, blocking the sale of 311 mortgages until a pending lawsuit challenging the sale is resolved. . . . Opponents of Arizona's Gov. Evan Mecham (R), who rescinded a state holiday honoring slain civil rights leader Martin Luther King Jr., launch a petition drive to force a recall election. A "boycott Arizona" campaign by convention planners and performers has cost the state some $18 mil.		Chrysler Corp. agrees to pay $1.6 mil. to settle federal charges of job health and safety violations at its Newark, Del., assembly plant. The penalty is the largest ever imposed by the Labor Dept.'s Occupational Safety and Health Admin.	A National Academy of Sciences panel reports that the proposed space station will cost an estimated $10 bil. more than the most recent estimate by the National Aeronautics and Space Admin. (NASA). The scientific panel, asked by NASA to review the projected costs, came up with $27.5 bil.—$21 bil. for the first phase of the program and $6.5 bil. for the second phase. NASA's latest estimate was $14 bil. for phase one and a total of $17.9 bil. to complete the project.		July 6

F	G	H	I	J
Includes elections, federal-state relations, civil rights and liberties, crime, the judiciary, education, health care, poverty, urban affairs and population.	Includes formation and debate of U.S. foreign and defense policies, veterans' affairs and defense spending. (Relations with specific foreign countries are usually found under the region concerned.)	Includes business, labor, agriculture, taxation, transportation, consumer affairs, monetary and fiscal policy, natural resources, and pollution.	Includes worldwide scientific, medical and technological developments, natural phenomena, U.S. weather, natural disasters, and accidents.	Includes the arts, religion, scholarship, communications media, sports, entertainments, fashions, fads and social life.

	World Affairs	Europe	Africa & the Middle East	The Americas	Asia & the Pacific
July 7					In India, a total of 72 people die in attacks mounted over two days by Sikh separatists. More people die in these assaults than in any other incident of the terrorist campaign to break Indian rule of Punjab. The latest attacks began July 6 when gunmen commandeered a bus traveling the main highway between New Delhi and Chandigarh, the capital of Punjab. The hijackers opened fire with a spray of bullets that killed 37 Hindu passengers and one of the gunmen.
July 8		In Iceland, Thorsteinn Palsson, leader of the conservative Independence Party, assumes control of a new coalition government. His coalition also includes the centrist Progressives and the left-of-center Social Democrats.	The Israeli Knesset narrowly defeats several bills that sought to bar non-Orthodox Jewish converts from winning automatic Israeli citizenship under the nation's Law of Return. U.S. Jewish groups, most associated with the Reform and Conservative branches of Judaism, which are not recognized by Israel's Orthodox establishment, warned that passage of the legislation would seriously harm world Jewish unity as well as American Jewish support for Israel.		
July 9		Attacks by Kurdish rebels kill 28 Turkish villagers, many of them women and children. The attacks on the villages of Pecenek and Yuvali near the Syrian border come less than a month after 31 people were killed in similar raids in the village of Pinarcik. The recent attacks are said to be claimed by the Kurdistan People's Party, a wing of the Kurdish Workers' Party.			A little more than a week after the nation's military regime promised a transition to democracy, South Koreans gather by the hundreds of thousands to honor Lee Han Yol, a student activist slain by riot police at the start of the protests that pushed the government to promise reform.... Carlos Melancia is sworn in as governor of Macao, the Portuguese colony in China.... According to tape recordings played during U.S. congressional hearings, Ferdinand Marcos has been plotting once again to take over the Philippines. It is the second time that the deposed Philippine president has been publicly revealed to be plotting a return to power from exile in Hawaii.
July 10				The Panama Defense Forces prevent antigovernment demonstrators from holding a rally to call for the ouster of Gen. Manuel Antonio Noriega, de facto leader of Panama. Pres. Eric Arturo Delvalle earlier banned all mass demonstrations warning of "the imminent danger" posed by the rallies.	

A	B	C	D	E
Includes developments that affect more than one world region, international organizations and important meetings of major world leaders.	Includes all domestic and regional developments in Europe, including the Soviet Union, Turkey, Cyprus and Malta.	Includes all domestic and regional developments in Africa and the Middle East, including Iraq and Iran and excluding Cyprus, Turkey and Afghanistan.	Includes all domestic and regional developments in Latin America, the Caribbean and Canada.	Includes all domestic and regional developments in Asia and Pacific nations, extending from Afghanistan through all the Pacific Islands, except Hawaii.

U.S. Politics & Social Issues	U.S. Foreign Policy & Defense	U.S. Economy & Environment	Science, Technology & Nature	Culture, Leisure & Life Style	
The chairmen of the two major parties announce that all the current Democratic and Republican presidential candidates have agreed to take part in party-sponsored election debates should they win their party's nomination.		A federal appeals court in Washington, D.C., rules that bank holding companies can operate brokerage subsidiaries that trade securities and give investment advice. The decision is a victory for banks and another step in the gradual disintegration of the limits placed on banks by the Glass-Steagall Act.			July 7
In a speech to the National Press Club in Washington, D.C., Eleanor Smeal formally announces her intention to leave the presidency of the National Org. for Women in order to concentrate on a "feminization of power" drive for the 1988 election.... Katharine (Kitty) Dukakis, the wife of Gov. Michael S. Dukakis (D, Mass.), reveals that she was addicted to amphetamine diet pills for 26 years.... Attorney Gen. Edwin Meese announces that the Reagan administration is easing immigration rules for some 150,000-200,000 Nicaraguans currently living illegally in the United States.... Peter Hiam resigns as Massachusetts State insurance commissioner to protest a proposed state regulation allowing life and disability insurers (but not health insurers) to test for acquired immune deficiency syndrome.	At the Iran-Contra hearings, Lt. Col. Oliver L. North testifies that Sec. of State George P. Shultz, Asst. Sec. of State Elliott Abrams, Central Intelligence Agency official Alan Fiers, and the late Vice Adm. Arthur Moreau all knew about his network of assistance to the Nicaraguan Contras. His testimony calls into question the general perception that Shultz was detached from the Iran-Contra activities.			*Variety*'s top-grossing films for the week are: *Dragnet, Spaceballs, The Untouchables, The Witches of Eastwick*, and *Innerspace*.	July 8
Appearing before the Senate government affairs oversight subcommittee to answer questions about his financial arrangements with W. Franklyn Chinn, a former official of the Wedtech Corp., which is the subject of a number of federal and state criminal probes, Attorney Gen. Edwin Meese III says he knew as early as 1985 that Chinn had ties to Wedtech, but that his dealings with Chinn never posed a conflict of interest.	At the Iran-Contra hearings, Lt. Col. Oliver L. North tells Senate counsel Arthur Liman that under a "fall-guy plan" created by the Reagan administration, he was to be the "scapegoat," shielding his superiors, including Pres. Reagan, from blame for the Iran-Contra operation. North also portrays the late Central Intelligence Agency Dir. William J. Casey as the driving force in the effort to aid the Contras and to deceive Congress about that assistance.	The Senate refuses, by a 60-40 vote, to eliminate from an omnibus trade bill a provision requiring employers to give employees prior notice of plant closings. The provision was attached to the measure by voice vote the day before. It will require companies with 100 employees or more to give workers 60 days' prior notice of plant closings or mass layoffs.			July 9
	On his fourth day of congressional testimony, Lt. Col. Oliver L. North tells Arthur L. Liman, the counsel to the Senate committee investigating the Iran-Contra scandal, that William J. Casey, the late Central Intelligence Agency director, planned to use profits from the Iranian arms sales to fund a self-sustaining covert network free of congressional oversight and appropriations processes.			John Hammond, 76, record producer, jazz and blues aficionado, and legendary musical talent scout who "discovered" Bessie Smith, Billie Holiday, Benny Goodman, Count Basie, Aretha Franklin, Bob Dylan, and Bruce Springsteen, among others, dies in New York City. An heir to the Vanderbilt fortune, Hammond subsidized recordings by such artists as Fletcher Henderson and Chick Webb and he also helped bring about jazz's first racially integrated group, the Benny Goodman Trio.	July 10

F	G	H	I	J
Includes elections, federal-state relations, civil rights and liberties, crime, the judiciary, education, health care, poverty, urban affairs and population.	*Includes formation and debate of U.S. foreign and defense policies, veterans' affairs and defense spending. (Relations with specific foreign countries are usually found under the region concerned.)*	*Includes business, labor, agriculture, taxation, transportation, consumer affairs, monetary and fiscal policy, natural resources, and pollution.*	*Includes worldwide scientific, medical and technological developments, natural phenomena, U.S. weather, natural disasters, and accidents.*	*Includes the arts, religion, scholarship, communications media, sports, entertainments, fashions, fads and social life.*

	World Affairs	Europe	Africa & the Middle East	The Americas	Asia & the Pacific
July 11	Matej Gaspar, a boy born in Zagreb, Yugoslavia, is visited in the hospital immediately after his birth by UN Sec. Gen. Javier Perez de Cuellar, who proclaims the infant the world's five billionth person. No one knows for sure who that person is, but the UN Fund for Population Activities predicted that global population would reach 5 billion at about the time Matej was born.	Answering U.S. State Dept. spokesman Charles E. Redman's complaints that the Soviet Union appears to be "drawing back" from a "constructive or positive approach to addressing some of the tough issues" on arms control, Soviet Premier Nikolai I. Ryzhkov asserts that Moscow has shown a "maximum willingness to compromise" and has "also tried to consicer the wishes of the U.S.A. and its allies."		In Canada, the federal government and British Columbia sign an agreement under which the South Moresby region of the Queen Charlotte Islands, off the B.C. coast, will become a national park. The islands have been the center of a dispute between lumber companies and the Haida Indians.	P.M. Bob Hawke leads the Australian Labor Party (ALP) to victory in national elections. Claiming to be the party best suited to steer Australia through its difficult economic straits, the ALP succeeds for the first time in winning three general elections in a row.
July 12			A large group of dissident Afrikaners, members of South Africa's dominant white community, conclude four days of ground-breaking talks in Dakar, Senegal, with exiled black leaders of the African National Congress rebel movement. The conference ends with a broad outline of agreement between the two sides on the necessity of replacing South Africa's apartheid system with a nonracial democracy. . . . The first group of Soviet diplomats to visit Israel in 20 years arrives quietly in Tel Aviv.	Some 174 illegal Indian immigrants land in lifeboats on the sparsely populated south shore of Nova Scotia. The ailens try to claim refugee status and insist they have traveled directly to Canada from India, but Canadian authorities conclude that the port of origin was somewhere in Western Europe.	
July 13		The European Community ends its nine-month-old ban on high-level exchanges with Syria. The decision, in part a response to the expulsion of the Abu Nidal terrorist cperations from Syria, comes at a foreign ministers meeting in Copenhagen, Denmark, after Britain drops its opposition to ending the ban.			In a move to help pave the way for upcoming elections promised by the military regime, South Korea's Pres. Chun Doo Hwan accepts the resignations of all cabinet members who belong to his Democratic Justice Party. . . . Ramaswami Venkataraman is elected president of India with the backing of P.M. Rajiv Gandhi.
July 14					Two car bombs detonated in Karachi, Pakistan, kill at least 72 people and wound as many as 300 others. The twin blasts are attributed to the Soviet-backed regime in neighboring Afghanistan. Pakistan has long supported anti-Marxist Afghan guerrillas. . . . After 48 years, martial law is officially lifted in Taiwan. The island's government describes the step as a "new milestone" on the road to democracy and part of a liberalization program initiated by Pres. Chiang Ching-kuo in March 1986. . . . Australia suffered an annual inflation rate of 9.8% during calendar 1986, the Australian Bureau of Statistics reports.
July 15				Brazil's Pres. Jose Sarney visits Argentina where he and Argentine Pres. Raul Alfonsin sign 10 accords relating to the mutual integration and development pact agreed upon in 1986 during his three-day visit.	The Taiwanese government eases stringent 38-year-old foreign-exchange controls that helped Taiwan build up one of the world's largest reserves of foreign currency. Investments abroad will no longer require the approval of Taiwan's Central Bank of China, except when an investor wants to place more than $5 mil. overseas in a given year. Foreign exchange earned by Taiwanese will no longer have to be converted into Taiwanese currency, and there will be no limit on payments for imports.

A	B	C	D	E
Includes developments that affect more than one world region, international organizations and important meetings of major world leaders.	Includes all domestic and regional developments in Europe, including the Soviet Union, Turkey, Cyprus and Malta.	Includes all domestic and regional developments in Africa and the Middle East, including Iraq and Iran and excluding Cyprus, Turkey and Afghanistan.	Includes all domestic and regional developments in Latin America, the Caribbean and Canada.	Includes all domestic and regional developments in Asia and Pacific nations, extending from Afghanistan through all the Pacific Islands, except Hawaii.

U.S. Politics & Social Issues	U.S. Foreign Policy & Defense	U.S. Economy & Environment	Science, Technology & Nature	Culture, Leisure & Life Style	
	According to a CBS News/New York Times poll, 43% of Americans view Lt. Col. Oliver L. North favorably after the first two days of his testimony before the congressional panels investigating the Iran-Contra arms scandal, while only 14% had an unfavorable opinion of North. In a similar poll taken in February, North's favorable rating was 6%, against 35% who viewed him unfavorably.				July 11
		The producer price index rose a seasonally adjusted 0.2% in June, according to the Labor Dept.		In auto racing, Nigel Mansell of Britain wins the British Grand Prix.	July 12
Nearly four years after initial complaints that children were being molested at the Virgina McMartin Pre-School in Manhattan Beach, Calif., the two remaining defendants in the case go on trial in Los Angeles Superior Court. The case, which has cost more than $6 mil. to date has been marked by months of preliminary hearings, the dismissal of charges against five defendants, the defection of a prosecutor, and the death of a key witness.		The House approves a ban on cigarette smoking on airline flights of two hours or less. The ban is attached by amendment to a $26.8 bil. transportation spending bill for FY1988.			July 13
	Robert C. McFarlane, who testified before the congressional panels investigating the Iran-Contra arms scandal in May, returns to contradict several of Lt. Col. Oliver L. North's assertions of July 7, particularly North's claim that "every single activity that I conducted, I conducted with the authority of my superiors."	The President's Task Force on Regulatory Relief recommends wider use of methanol and ethanol as a way to meet federal air quality goals and reduce the nation's dependence on imported oil.		The National League wins Major League baseball's annual All-Star Game, 2-0, in 13 innings at the Oakland Coliseum. Tim Raines of the Montreal Expos is named the game's most valuable player.	July 14
	Rear Adm. John M. Poindexter, national security adviser from late 1985 through November 1986, tells congressional panels that he never told Pres. Reagan about the diversion of funds from arms transactions with Iran to the Contra rebels fighting the Nicaraguan government. Poindexter says that he authorized the diversion and deliberately kept Reagan in the dark in order to "provide some future deniability for the President if it ever leaked out."	The U.S. deficit on merchandise trade expanded in May to $14.4 bil., the Commerce Dept reports. ... The Federal Reserve Board reports that its industrial production index rose 0.2% in June.			July 15

F	G	H	I	J
Includes elections, federal-state relations, civil rights and liberties, crime, the judiciary, education, health care, poverty, urban affairs and population.	Includes formation and debate of U.S. foreign and defense policies, veterans' affairs and defense spending. (Relations with specific foreign countries are usually found under the region concerned.)	Includes business, labor, agriculture, taxation, transportation, consumer affairs, monetary and fiscal policy, natural resources, and pollution.	Includes worldwide scientific, medical and technological developments, natural phenomena, U.S. weather, natural disasters, and accidents.	Includes the arts, religion, scholarship, communications media, sports, entertainments, fashions, fads and social life.

	World Affairs	Europe	Africa & the Middle East	The Americas	Asia & the Pacific
July 16		Seasonally adjusted unemployment in Britain declined for the 12th consecutive month in June, the Employment Dept. reports.		Bolivia signs an agreement with its private bank creditors to use funds donated by foreign governments and administered by the International Monetary Fund to buy back its almost $1 bil. in debt to commercial banks at a substantial discount of 15 U.S. cents on the dollar. . . . Nicaraguan Contras stage their biggest raids in six years, on three northern towns, including the site of a key military base. U.S. military experts who recommended against the attacks say they produce no military gains.	
July 17		The government of France breaks off diplomatic relations with Iran after an Iranian sought for questioning by French officials takes refuge in the Iranian Embassy in Paris. . . . Italy's highest court annuls arrest warrants for Archbishop Paul Marcinkus, chairman of the Institute for Religious Works—the Vatican bank—and two other officials. . . . The East German government announces a program of amnesty for prisoners, including those convicted of political offenses, and abolishes the death penalty.			China registered a trade deficit of $2 bil. for the first half of calendar 1987, according to figures from China's customs bureau. This is well below the figure the bureau reported for the same period in 1986. The improvement is traced to government controls that helped lower imports by 6% and to a boom in textile exports.
July 18		It is reported that nearly 2,000 youths have been punished in connection with the nationalist riots in Alma-Ata, the capital of the Soviet republic of Kazakhstan, in December 1986.	In Mozambique, antigovernment rebels massacre 386 civilians and wound 76 in and around the town of Homoine, the official Mozambican news agency reports. South Africa denies Mozambique's charge that it is responsible for the atrocity because of its alleged role in supplying the rebels. The death toll is the worst for a single incident in Mozambique's 10-year-old civil war.	Gilberto Freyre, 87, internationally known Brazilian sociologist, dies in Recife, Brazil, of a brain hemorrhage. His best-known work, *Masters and Slaves* (1933), examined the relationship between Brazil's Portuguese colonizers and their African slaves.	
July 19		The Social Democratic Party of Portugal's Premier Anibal Cavaco Silva wins a majority of the popular vote and control of parliament in elections. The results will give Portugal its first majority government since democracy was restored in the bloodless 1974 revolution. . . . Martial law is lifted in the in the provinces of Diyarbakir, Mardin, Siirt, and Hakkari in southeastern Turkey, after eight-and-a-half years.			
July 20		Morocco indicates its intention to apply for membership in the European Community (EC). The action by the North African nation comes in the form of a letter delivered by Foreign Min. Abdellatif Filali to the current president of the EC's foreign affairs council, Uffe Elleman-Jensen of Denmark. . . . In Hungary, prices on selected consumer goods and services are raised in the first step of a national austerity program. The prices of flour and bread rise by 19%, cigarettes by 20%, fuel oil by 29%, diesel oil by 10%, heating gas by 17%, and electricity by 18%.		Argentina's Economy Min. Juan Sourrouille unveils a set of economic measures aimed at slowing inflation by reducing the budget deficit. Argentina's budget deficit is reported to be equivalent to 6.5% of gross national product, and inflation is running at about 8% a month.	In the Micronesian island group of Palau, an appeals court orders acquittals for the three men convicted of the 1986 killing of Pres. Haruo I. Remelik, according to a news report. Palau is administered by the United States as part of the UN Trust Territory of the Pacific Islands.

A	B	C	D	E
Includes developments that affect more than one world region, international organizations and important meetings of major world leaders.	Includes all domestic and regional developments in Europe, including the Soviet Union, Turkey, Cyprus and Malta.	Includes all domestic and regional developments in Africa and the Middle East, including Iraq and Iran and excluding Cyprus, Turkey and Afghanistan.	Includes all domestic and regional developments in Latin America, the Caribbean and Canada.	Includes all domestic and regional developments in Asia and Pacific nations, extending from Afghanistan through all the Pacific Islands, except Hawaii.

U.S. Politics & Social Issues	U.S. Foreign Policy & Defense	U.S. Economy & Environment	Science, Technology & Nature	Culture, Leisure & Life Style	
More than 200 members of the 100th Congress gather in Philadelphia to celebrate the bicentennial of the Great Compromise, the creation of the United States's bicameral legislature. The compromise, equal representation for all states in the Senate and representation in the House based on population, resolved a constitutional dispute among the nation's founders over how to apportion representation fairly for the populous and sparsely populated states. The compromise was adopted by a majority of one vote on July 16, 1787. . . . A federal judge postpones the perjury trial of former White House aide Michael K. Deaver for at least three months.	Japan promises to work harder at keeping militarily useful technology out of the hands of communist countries, U.S. aides say. The Japanese government made the assurances because of U.S. anger over Toshiba Machine Co.'s illegal dealings with the Soviet Union. The U.S. Senate recently voted to bar the imports of Toshiba Corp., Toshiba Machine's parent.	*USA Today*, the national newspaper launched by Gannett Co. in 1982, reports an operating profit for May of $1.1 mil., its first ever profits. . . . The administration moves to stop Congress from implementing a $7.2 bil. deficit-cutting maneuver for the FY1988 budget, it is reported. The cut is part of a package of $37 bil. in planned savings contemplated by the House and Senate. . . . White House Budget Dir. James C. Miller III estimates that the federal budget deficit for FY1987 will shrink by $66 bil., to $155 bil. The target for the year under the Gramm-Rudman balanced-budget law is $144 bil., plus or minus $10 bil.			July 16
In a rare instance of taking sides by a sitting member of the Supreme Court, Associate Justice John Paul Stevens publicly praises the qualifications of Judge Robert H. Bork as Pres. Reagan's nominee for the empty seat on the court.		Housing starts dropped 0.7% in June, to a seasonally adjusted annual rate of 1.59 million units, the Commerce Dept. says.		*Publishers Weekly*'s hardback fiction best-sellers for the week are: *Misery*, Stephen King; *Mesa*, Louis L'Amour; *Presumed Innocent*, Scott Turow; *Weep No More My Lady*, Mary Higgins Clark; and *Dirk Gently's Holistic Detective Agency*, Douglas Adams.	July 17
At a three-day convention in Philadelphia, the National Org. for Women elects Molly Yard as its new president.					July 18
				In golf, Nick Faldo of Britain wins the 116th British Open.	July 19
					July 20

F	G	H	I	J
Includes elections, federal-state relations, civil rights and liberties, crime, the judiciary, education, health care, poverty, urban affairs and population.	*Includes formation and debate of U.S. foreign and defense policies, veterans' affairs and defense spending. (Relations with specific foreign countries are usually found under the region concerned.)*	*Includes business, labor, agriculture, taxation, transportation, consumer affairs, monetary and fiscal policy, natural resources, and pollution.*	*Includes worldwide scientific, medical and technological developments, natural phenomena, U.S. weather, natural disasters, and accidents.*	*Includes the arts, religion, scholarship, communications media, sports, entertainments, fashions, fads and social life.*

	World Affairs	Europe	Africa & the Middle East	The Americas	Asia & the Pacific
July 21			Amnesty International issues a report charging the Kenyan government with trying to stamp out political opposition by torture, unlawful detention, and unfair trials. The report backs allegations that caused an international stir in March when they first appeared in the *Washington Post*. . . . Israel is reported to have test-fired a new intermediate-range ballistic missile of a type that can be armed with nuclear warheads.		The Philippine government's Presidential Comm. on Good Government has filed seven civil suits against deposed Pres. Ferdinand Marcos since July 16. The suits are filed in a special anti-graft court in Manila, and seek a total of some $30 bil. after a U.S. court rules that the United States does not have jurisdiction over the fortune Marcos is thought to have stolen upon fleeing the Philippines.
July 22		Soviet leader Mikhail S. Gorbachev says that the Kremlin is willing to accept a worldwide elimination of intermediate nuclear forces (INF), and he offers to drop Moscow's insistence on keeping INF warheads in Soviet Asia. . . . Boosted by its recent acquisition of Alfa Romeo, Fiat S.p.A. of Italy led in Western European car sales in the first half of 1987 with a 15% market share, followed by Volkswagen AG (14.8%), Ford Motor Co. (11.8%), Peugeot-Citroen-Talbot (11.6%), General Motors Corp. (10.9%), and Renault (10.4%).	Three U.S. Navy warships escort two U.S.-flagged Kuwaiti oil tankers through the Strait of Hormuz and into the Persian Gulf, where the convoy is joined by a fourth American warship.	The Canadian government begins releasing the illegal-alien Indians who landed in Nova Scotia July 12. The migrants have been held at the Canadian Forces base in Halifax. Immigration officials decided that the majority could remain in Canada in the care of citizen sponsors who are required to post a bond of $3,765 per illegal.	Pres. Corazon Aquino decrees that the Philippines' large agricultural estates should be broken up and the land distributed among peasant farmers. But the long-awaited decree leaves key details uncertain, and draws complaints from both landowners and peasant activists.
July 23		The Soviet Union replies to the July 21 Israeli announcement that Israel test-fired a new intermediate-range ballistic missile with a series of warnings, telling Israel that deployment of the missile can lead to "consequences that it could not possibly handle."		The International Monetary Fund (IMF) is reported to have signed a letter of intent to provide Bolivia with a three-year, $173.3 mil. loan. In the letter, the IMF says Bolivia's economy will grow by 2.2% in 1987, which will be the first growth in seven years. In less than two years in office, the government of Pres. Victor Paz Estenssoro has reduced the federal budget deficit to 3.5% of gross domestic product (GDP) from 30%, raised revenues from taxes to 14% of GDP from 1%, and slashed inflation to around 10% from 24,000% in 1985.	
July 24		Hussein Ali Mohammed Hariri hijacks an Air Afrique jetliner and kills a French passenger before being overpowered by the flight crew at the airport in Geneva, Switz. The Lebanese Hariri seeks the release of two suspected terrorists held in West Germany. . . . The March capsizing of the British North Sea ferry *Herald of Free Enterprise*, in which 188 people died, resulted from carelessness by the crew and "the disease of sloppiness" that "infected" the operating company "from top to bottom," according to a board of inquiry report.			In Japan, the upper house of the Diet gives final approval to a supplementary budget already approved by the lower house July 14. The budget will allow the government to spend $14 bil. as the first stage in a plan for disbursing some $43 bil. to stimulate the economy.

A	B	C	D	E
Includes developments that affect more than one world region, international organizations and important meetings of major world leaders.	*Includes all domestic and regional developments in Europe, including the Soviet Union, Turkey, Cyprus and Malta.*	*Includes all domestic and regional developments in Africa and the Middle East, including Iraq and Iran and excluding Cyprus, Turkey and Afghanistan.*	*Includes all domestic and regional developments in Latin America, the Caribbean and Canada.*	*Includes all domestic and regional developments in Asia and Pacific nations, extending from Afghanistan through all the Pacific Islands, except Hawaii.*

U.S. Politics & Social Issues	U.S. Foreign Policy & Defense	U.S. Economy & Environment	Science, Technology & Nature	Culture, Leisure & Life Style	
Texas Gov. Bill Clements (R), who was elected to office on a pledge to veto "any and all" tax increases, signs the largest tax increase in U.S. history, $5.7 bil.... After months of behind-the-scenes negotiations, Sen. Daniel Patrick Moynihan (D, N.Y.), chairman of the Senate Finance Committee's subcommittee on family policy, introduces a welfare reform bill that will likely serve as the basis for Senate efforts to overhaul the welfare system.	Closing four days of testimony before Congressional committees investigating the Iran-Contra arms scandal, Rear Adm. John M. Poindexter, Pres. Reagan's former national security adviser, defends his actions but provides little new information.... Japan becomes the fifth country to formally agree to participate in research on the space-based antimissile Strategic Defense Initiative.	The Senate approves, 71-27, broad trade legislation that will pressure the president to retaliate against unfair trade practices. Pres. Reagan has threatened to veto the bill.... The U.S. Postal Service reaches agreement with the two largest postal unions covering 579,000 employees on a new 40-month contract. The settlement calls for average wage increases of between $1,700 and $1,866.... The Occupational Safety and Health Admin. proposes a $2.59 mil. fine against IBP Inc. for deliberately concealing worker injuries and illnesses at a Dakota City, Nebr., beefpacking plant.			July 21
The House approves by a 302-127 vote a bill to expand the Medicare program to protect elderly and disabled persons against "catastrophic" medical costs. Yesterday, the White House warned that Pres. Reagan will veto the bill, which is a much larger version than an administration proposal put forth by Sec. of Health and Human Services Otis R. Bowen.... Pres. Reagan signs a bill authorizing more than $1 bil. in emergency aid for the nation's homeless over the next two years.		The government's consumer price index rose 0.4% in June, the Labor Dept. reports.		*Billboard*'s best-selling albums for the week are: *Whitney*, Whitney Houston; *The Joshua Tree*, U2; *Girls, Girls, Girls*, Motley Crue; *Whitesnake*, Whitesnake; and *Bad Animals*, Heart.	July 22
Pres. Reagan appoints a 13-member commission to advise him on combating acquired immune deficiency syndrome (AIDS).... Senate Judiciary Committee Chairman Joseph R. Biden Jr. (D, Del.) says that the Senate should consider Judge Robert H. Bork's judicial philosophy and ideology in deciding whether to confirm his appointment to the Supreme Court. Senate Republican Leader Bob Dole (Kans.) replies that consideration of Bork's views on "specific political and social issues" would "offend common sense [and] be horribly shortsighted."... The Republican National Committee agrees to obtain federal court clearance for its "ballot security programs." The Democratic National Committee had brought a $10 mil. lawsuit contending that the Republicans' systematic challenges to voter eligibility intimidates and harasses black voters.	Sec. of State George P. Shultz tells Congressional committees investigating the Iran-Contra affair that he strongly opposed the secret arms sales to Iran and that former administration officials William Casey, Robert McFarlane, and Rear Adm. John Poindexter withheld information from Pres. Reagan in order to continue the Iranian initiative.... The United States has suspended military and economic aid to Panama and downgraded its contacts with the head of the Panama Defense Forces, Gen. Manuel Antonio Noriega, as a sign of its dissatisfaction with the military-controlled government, the *Washington Post* reports.	Its position at the top of the Big Three automakers now solid, Ford Motor Co. is once again the most profitable U.S. corporation, reporting record earnings in the second quarter of $1.5 bil., up 39% from a year earlier.... General Motors Corp. reports a 3.7% decline in earnings, to $980.3 mil., fourth-highest among all U.S. companies.	A report by an independent panel praises the National Aeronautics and Space Admin. (NASA) for "going in the right direction" in trying to get the space shuttle program back on track. But the panel also prods NASA to get its safety review process into a finer mold where individuals make the final decision.		July 23
Pres. Reagan names U.S. District Judge William S. Sessions of San Antonio as his choice to be director of the Federal Bureau of Investigation.... A New York Times/CBS News Poll reports that 62% of those people surveyed think the Senate should attach a great deal of importance to a Supreme Court nominee's positions on constitutional issues in deciding how to vote on confirmation.		The nation's gross national product grew at a 2.6% annual rate in the second quarter, after adjustment for inflation, the Commerce Dept. reports.... Union Carbide Corp. agrees to pay $408,500 to settle federal charges of violations of health and safety rules at chemical plants in Institute and South Charleston, West Virginia. The Occupational Safety and Health Admin. in 1986 cited 556 instances of violations against the chemical company, for which it sought penalties of $1,377,300.			July 24

F	G	H	I	J
Includes elections, federal-state relations, civil rights and liberties, crime, the judiciary, education, health care, poverty, urban affairs and population.	Includes formation and debate of U.S. foreign and defense policies, veterans' affairs and defense spending. (Relations with specific foreign countries are usually found under the region concerned.)	Includes business, labor, agriculture, taxation, transportation, consumer affairs, monetary and fiscal policy, natural resources, and pollution.	Includes worldwide scientific, medical and technological developments, natural phenomena, U.S. weather, natural disasters, and accidents.	Includes the arts, religion, scholarship, communications media, sports, entertainments, fashions, fads and social life.

	World Affairs	Europe	Africa & the Middle East	The Americas	Asia & the Pacific
July 25					India's P.M. Rajiv Gandhi makes himself his government's fifth foreign minister in the latest reshuffle of his cabinet.
July 26					
July 27		The North Atlantic Treaty Org. (NATO) presents a detailed plan for a new forum for East-West negotiations on reducing conventional forces in Europe. The plan is offered in Vienna at exploratory talks that began in February between NATO and the Warsaw Pact.	The Org. of African Unity (OAU) holds its 23rd annual summit conference in Addis Ababa, Ethiopia. Disputes between radical and more moderate nations prevent the OAU from arriving at a consensus on the issue of foreign debt payments.		The Philippines' newly formed Congress formally convenes in Manila in ceremonies that mark the end of unchecked presidential domination of the national government. The country's new constitution provides for a system of checks and balances under which the chief executive will lose the power of decree that then-Pres. Ferdinand Marcos had assumed after his 1972 coup.
July 28		In a speech to a Communist Party (CP) Central Committee plenum in Sofia, Bulgaria's CP leader Todor Zhivkov calls for broad political and economic reforms and envisions a system under which the party would play a reduced role in running the government and the economy. . . . Crimean Tatars have staged a series of unprecedented large-scale demonstrations in Moscow over the last five days. As many as 1,000 Tatars came to Moscow to campaign for the restoration of their autonomous homeland in the Crimea, a peninsula on the Black Sea.		The opposition National Civil Crusade continues its pressure on Panama's military and civilian leaders with a general strike that paralyzes the capital and other cities. On the first day of the two-day strike, security forces arrest Robert Diaz Herrera, a leading critic of Panama Defense Forces chief and de facto head of Panama, Gen. Manuel Antonio Noriega.	

A	B	C	D	E
Includes developments that affect more than one world region, international organizations and important meetings of major world leaders.	Includes all domestic and regional developments in Europe, including the Soviet Union, Turkey, Cyprus and Malta.	Includes all domestic and regional developments in Africa and the Middle East, including Iraq and Iran and excluding Cyprus, Turkey and Afghanistan.	Includes all domestic and regional developments in Latin America, the Caribbean and Canada.	Includes all domestic and regional developments in Asia and Pacific nations, extending from Afghanistan through all the Pacific Islands, except Hawaii.

U.S. Politics & Social Issues	U.S. Foreign Policy & Defense	U.S. Economy & Environment	Science, Technology & Nature	Culture, Leisure & Life Style	
At the outset of its four-day annual meeting, the National Governors' Assoc. outlines new proposals for improving America's economic competitiveness abroad and for reducing disparities in prosperity among regions at home.... Todd Shuttleworth, 34, a Florida man who gained national attention by fighting to get his job back when he was fired by Broward County in 1984 after contracting acquired immune deficiency syndrome (AIDS), dies in San Francisco, of AIDS-related complications.		Commerce Sec. Malcolm Baldrige dies after being crushed by a horse that reared and fell over backward on him. The accident occurred as Baldrige, a champion rodeo rider, was practicing for a calf-roping competition to be held tonight at the Contra Costa County fairgrounds in Walnut Creek, Calif. Born in Omaha in 1922, the son of a one-term Republican congressman, he joined the Reagan administration in 1981 as its original commerce secretary.	The Soviet Union launches a huge radar satellite for "remote sensing" of the Earth's surface. The launch is not announced by Tass, the official Soviet news agency, until August 2.		July 25
	The *Washington Post* alleges in a news story that Pres. Reagan "actively led the initial effort last November to conceal the essential details of his secret arms-for-hostages program." The story is based on notes taken in a White House meeting Nov. 10, 1986, by then-deputy national security adviser Alton G. Keel Jr.		Scientists have found strong evidence that two nearby galaxies have black holes at their centers, the National Science Foundation announces. Black holes are predicted by the theory of relativity but cannot be observed directly. A black hole is a mass of matter so dense that its gravity is strong enough to prevent the escape of any mass or energy, even light, and scientists suspect that they are responsible for the vast amounts of energy at the centers of galaxies.	In auto racing, Nelson Piquet of Brazil wins the West German Grand Prix.... In cycling, Stephen Roche, racing for the Italian-based Carrera team, wins the Tour de France, becoming the first Irish winner in the history of the event. ... Hugh Wheeler, 75, English-born three-time Tony award winner for his books for the musicals *A Little Night Music* (1973), *Candide* (1974), and *Sweeney Todd* (1978), dies in Pittsfield, Mass., of lung and heart failure. A novelist (under the pseudonym Patrick Quentin, among others) and screenwriter, he wrote the screenplays for *Travels with My Aunt, Cabaret, A Little Night Music* and *Nijinski* and won Edgar Allan Poe mystery-writing awards in 1961 and 1973.	July 26
	The Navy says it will not court-martial the captain and chief weapons officer of the USS *Stark* for failing to take defensive measures against an allegedly accidental Iraqi missile attack May 17 in which 37 U.S. sailors were killed. Capt. Glenn R. Brindel and Lt. Basil Moncrief instead receive letters of reprimand for command errors during the incident and are allowed to resign their commissions.	T. Allan McArtor is sworn in as head of the Federal Aviation Admin. and serves notice to all certified carriers and crew members that flights must be operated safely or certification will be taken away. ... A surge in auto sales helped push consumer spending up 0.7% in June, the Commerce Dept. reports; personal income rose 0.4% in June.... A protracted strike at IBP Inc.'s flagship Dakota City, Nebr., meatpacking plant ends with ratification of a new four-year contract, it is announced. The dispute dates back to Dec. 14, 1986.			July 27
	White House spokesman Marlin Fitzwater announces that the United States has formally agreed at the Geneva arms talks that all missiles and warheads covered by a U.S.-Soviet treaty on intermediate-range nuclear forces should be destroyed.	The Occupational Safety and Health Admin. fines a New Haven, Conn., company $480,840 for violation of worker safety rules. Uretek Inc., a fabric-coating company, is accused of exposing employees to harmful chemical solvents, especially dimethylformamide, a toxin to the liver.... Pres. Reagan unveils a broad federal program to help U.S. business develop the commercial potential of superconductors, materials that have no resistance to electrical currents.		Britain's Laura Davies wins the U.S. Women's Open golf championship.... Carlton Fredericks (born Harold Carlton Caplan), 76, radio commentator for nearly half a century and writer on nutrition and health, dies of a heart attack in Yonkers, N.Y.	July 28

F	G	H	I	J
Includes elections, federal-state relations, civil rights and liberties, crime, the judiciary, education, health care, poverty, urban affairs and population.	Includes formation and debate of U.S. foreign and defense policies, veterans' affairs and defense spending. (Relations with specific foreign countries are usually found under the region concerned.)	Includes business, labor, agriculture, taxation, transportation, consumer affairs, monetary and fiscal policy, natural resources, and pollution.	Includes worldwide scientific, medical and technological developments, natural phenomena, U.S. weather, natural disasters, and accidents.	Includes the arts, religion, scholarship, communications media, sports, entertainments, fashions, fads and social life.

	World Affairs	Europe	Africa & the Middle East	The Americas	Asia & the Pacific
July 29	The Soviet negotiators at the Geneva arms talks present a draft treaty on curtailing weapons in space. The document, Moscow's most detailed proposal on such weapons, restates Moscow's insistence that the United States adhere to the 1972 antiballistic missile treaty, a demand Washington views as an attempt by the Soviets to curb the development of the Star Wars program.	Giovanni Goria, a Christian Democrat and former treasury minister, is sworn in as premier of Italy's 47th government since the end of World War II. Goria will lead a coalition of the same five parties that composed the government of the Socialist Party premier Bettino Craxi.... Six former officials of the Chernobyl nuclear power plant in the Soviet Ukraine are sentenced for their roles in the 1986 disaster at the facility after a three-week trial in the town of Chernobyl, 20 kilometers from the power plant. ... In Paris, Britain's P.M. Margaret Thatcher and France's Pres. Francois Mitterrand exchange ratified copies of a treaty formally setting the stage for the construction of a tunnel under the English Channel.		In Port-au-Prince, Haiti, at least eight persons are killed and 15 injured when soldiers fire into a crowd of some 2,500 people protesting against the Tontons Macoutes, also known as the Volunteers for National Security, the private militia of deposed Pres. Jean-Claude Duvalier.	Sri Lanka and India sign a peace agreement, designed to end the four-year-old armed rebellion of Sri Lanka's Tamil minority, under which India is to deploy 3,000 troops in the troubled Jaffna Peninsula in northern Sri Lanka. But the chief Tamil rebel group says it will not abide by the agreement, and news of the accord provokes protests, arson, rioting and looting among the Sinhalese majority. Some 40 people die, about half of them protesters shot dead by police in Colombo; the government orders a nationwide curfew.
July 30		The Law Lords, Britain's highest court, further restrict British press coverage of *Spycatcher*, a controversial book by a former member of MI5, the counterintelligence service. Leading media figures and opposition politicians criticize the decision as repressive.... Local rates (property taxes) in England will be replaced by a community charge, or poll tax, over a four-year period beginning in 1990, according to a plan approved by P.M. Margaret Thatcher's cabinet.		In Colombia, Camila Michelsen Nino, 22, the daughter of financier Jaime Michelsen Uribe, is freed by the April 19 (M-19) rebel group after nearly two years in captivity. Her father reportedly paid $500,000 in ransom and reimbursed 6,000 depositors who lost money in the collapse, reportedly due to fraud, of his Grand Colombian Financial Group. Michelsen Nino was kidnapped in September 1985.	In Pakistan, opposition leader Benazir Bhutto announces that she has agreed to marry Asif Zardari, a man picked for her by her family. Her intended husband comes from a wealthy family in Bhutto's home province of Sind. Avowedly apolitical, he is 34 years old, a building contractor, and a noted polo player. In a departure from tradition, Bhutto, also 34, has been able to meet him and approve him as a choice.
July 31		The Soviet negotiators at the Geneva arms talks present a draft treaty on reducing strategic (long-range) nuclear weapons. The move comes two months after the United States offered its version of an accord on strategic arms. Moscow continues to explicitly link an agreement on long-range weapons to curbs on the U.S. Strategic Defense Initiative, the so-called Star Wars program.	Thousands of Iranian pilgrims stage a protest and fight with Saudi police near the Grand Mosque in Mecca, Islam's holiest city. The Saudi government reports the next day that 402 people died in the riot: 275 Iranians, 85 Saudi policemen, and 42 pilgrims of other nationalities. Hospital reports listed 649 people as injured, including 303 Iranians.		Japan suffers an unemployment rate of 3.1% during the first six months of calendar 1987, the statistical bureau of the premier's office announces. That is the highest unemployment rate to be recorded in the 34 years of the survey's existence. The surge was blamed on the appreciation of the yen.
Aug. 1					Vietnam's Foreign Min. Nguyen Co Thach negotiates with a U.S. delegation on the issue of the more than 2,400 U.S. servicemen listed as missing in action in Indochina.
Aug. 2				Social Democrat Louis Eugene Athis, considered a likely presidential candidate in Haiti's November elections, is hacked to death with two colleagues at a meeting of peasants in Leogane.	

A	B	C	D	E
Includes developments that affect more than one world region, international organizations and important meetings of major world leaders.	Includes all domestic and regional developments in Europe, including the Soviet Union, Turkey, Cyprus and Malta.	Includes all domestic and regional developments in Africa and the Middle East, including Iraq and Iran and excluding Cyprus, Turkey and Afghanistan.	Includes all domestic and regional developments in Latin America, the Caribbean and Canada.	Includes all domestic and regional developments in Asia and Pacific nations, extending from Afghanistan through all the Pacific Islands, except Hawaii.

U.S. Politics & Social Issues	U.S. Foreign Policy & Defense	U.S. Economy & Environment	Science, Technology & Nature	Culture, Leisure & Life Style	
	Testifying before House and Senate committees investigating the Iran-Contra arms scandal, Attorney Gen. Edwin Meese III defends his own brief probe of the affair, which led to his Nov. 25, 1986, announcement that funds from arms sales to Iran had been diverted to the Nicaraguan Contra rebels. But he admits that he failed to ask some critical questions of key participants.	A consumer group issues a report challenging the effectiveness of a device installed by Audi of America Inc. to prevent sudden, unintended acceleration in Audi's 5000 series cars. The New York Public Interest Research Group says that 125 incidents of sudden acceleration have been reported since January in cars in which a shift-lock mechanism have been installed.		A handwritten working draft of the Bill of Rights, the only such document known to exist, has been found and identified in the Library of Congress, the *New York Times* reports. James C. Hutson, chief of the library's manuscript division, tells the *Times* he found the document in 1985 but has only recently finished authenticating it.	July 29
Speaking to a group of antiabortion advocates at the White House, Pres. Reagan proposes a new set of regulations that will bar federal funding for family planning programs that offer abortion counseling. . . . The nation's poverty rate declined to 13.6%—or 32.4 million Americans—in 1986 from 14%, the Census Bureau reports. It is the third straight year in which the percentage of Americans living below the official poverty line has shrunk.	Kenneth L. Adelman announces that he will step down as director of the U.S. Arms Control and Disarmament Agency by the end of 1987. . . . Former White House chief of staff Donald T. Regan testifies before the Congressional committees investigating the Iran-Contra arms scandal that, when no hostages were released following a February 1986 shipment of arms to Iran, Pres. Reagan felt that "we'd been had." Regan said he told the president that "we'd been snookered again, and how many times do we have to put up with this rug merchant type of stuff?"	Pres. Reagan signs a short-term increase in the national debt limit to $2.32 trillion, enough to continue funding the federal government until August 6. . . . The government's index of leading economic indicators rose 0.8% in June, the Commerce Dept. reports. . . . Median family income in 1986 was $29,460, 4.2% higher than the 1985 figure even after the 1.9% adjustment for inflation, according to the Census Bureau. Median income has now increased for four straight years. There are as many families with incomes above median income as below the median income.	An ailing Soviet cosmonaut, aloft since February 6 and orbiting Earth in the space station Mir, is replaced on the space station and returned to the Soviet Union.		July 30
Pres. Reagan has a small skin cancer removed from his nose. It is the third operation on the president's face and the second on his nose. . . . A federal judge orders the government to expunge records resulting from an illegal wiretap that the Nixon administration placed on the home telephone of *New York Times* reporter Hedrick Smith in 1969.	Defense Sec. Caspar W. Weinberger testifies before the congressional committees investigating the Iran-Contra arms scandal that he repeatedly tried to stop the arms sales to Iran and that he thought he had succeeded each time, only to discover that White House officials had deceived him in order to keep the operation going.	The Dow Jones Industrial Average closes at a record high 2572.07, surpassing the previous high close of 2451.05 on June 25. . . . Prices received by farmers for their raw agricultural products fell 2.3% in July, the Agriculture Dept. reports.		Joseph E(dward) Levine, 81, movie mogul who became wealthy distributing such Italian-made beefcake epics as *Hercules* and *Hercules Unchained*, dies in Greenwich, Conn., after a short illness. Through his company, Embassy Pictures, he also produced such prestigious films as *The Graduate, Carnal Knowledge* and *The Lion in Winter*. Over the course of his career he was involved as producer, distributor, or backer in some 500 films.	July 31
	Pres. Reagan says that throughout the House and Senate hearings on the Iran-Contra arms scandal, "I haven't heard a single word that indicated in any of the testimony that laws were broken." He sidesteps a direct question about whether he will consider pardoning former aides Rear Adm. John M. Poindexter and Lt. Col. Oliver L. North. . . . Mary R. Stout, a 43-year-old former U.S. Army nurse, is elected president of the Vietnam Veterans of America, a 35,000-member group with just 300 female members. Stout, who spent a year working in a surgical hospital in Vietnam, is thought to be the first woman to lead a national veterans' organization.			Mike Tyson wins a unanimous 12-round decision over Tony Tucker to unify boxing's heavyweight title for the first time since Leon Spinks defeated Muhammad Ali in 1978. . . . Pola Negri (born Barbara Apollonia Chalupiec), at least 87, Polish-born actress became one of the most flamboyant Hollywood stars of the silent film era, dies of pneumonia in San Antonio, Tex. Known for portraying fatally alluring women, she had off-screen romances with such stars as Charlie Chaplin and Rudolph Valentino.	Aug. 1
In a poll of 405 state and federal judges on the nomination of Justice Robert H. Bork to the Supreme Court, conducted by the *National Law Journal*, about half say they would vote to confirm Bork to the high court. Twenty-four percent are opposed and the rest offer no opinion.		First Fidelity Bancorp, the second-largest bank holding company in New Jersey, and Fidelcor Inc., which has the biggest depositor base in Philadelphia, announce plans to merge. With an indicated value of $1.34 bil., the stock swap will be the largest such merger to date, and will create the nation's 18th-largest bank.			Aug. 2
F Includes elections, federal-state relations, civil rights and liberties, crime, the judiciary, education, health care, poverty, urban affairs and population.	**G** Includes formation and debate of U.S. foreign and defense policies, veterans' affairs and defense spending. (Relations with specific foreign countries are usually found under the region concerned.)	**H** Includes business, labor, agriculture, taxation, transportation, consumer affairs, monetary and fiscal policy, natural resources, and pollution.	**I** Includes worldwide scientific, medical and technological developments, natural phenomena, U.S. weather, natural disasters, and accidents.	**J** Includes the arts, religion, scholarship, communications media, sports, entertainments, fashions, fads and social life.	

	World Affairs	Europe	Africa & the Middle East	The Americas	Asia & the Pacific
Aug. 3	The seventh quadrennial session of the UN Conf. on Trade and Development (UNCTAD VII) concludes in Geneva. UNCTAD is the principal forum for the discussion of so-called North-South issues, or economic matters involving the industrialized and developing nations.				
Aug. 4	West Germany exported a greater value of goods than any other nation in 1986, according to figures released by the International Monetary Fund, thus displacing the United States as the world's largest exporter despite having a population only one-fourth as large. West Germany's growth is due in part to the decline in the value of the U.S. dollar during 1986, which increased the dollar value of exports from countries other than the United States.			P.M. Brian Mulroney unveils a $900 mil. program to aid economic growth in Western Canada. The Western Diversification Initiative is aimed at broadening the economic base of the Western provinces through the expansion of small- and medium-sized businesses.	In Palau, voters in a referendum approve an end to the country's ban on nuclear weapons. The move is expected to clear the way for approval of a proposed accord with the United States. . . . In Papua New Guinea, P.M. Paias Wingti is returned to power when he puts together a 54-member plurality in the country's 109-seat legislature.
Aug. 5					Officers of the Liberation Tigers of Tamil Eelam, a group seeking autonomy for the Tamil minority in northern Sri Lanka, begin handing over their weapons to authorities near Jaffna. In exchange, the Sri Lankan government extends a general amnesty to 5,400 Tamils held or sought as political offenders or terrorism suspects. . . . South Korea's Democratic Justice Party (DJP) formally elects as its president Roh Tae Woo, the party's chairman and its candidate for president of the country.
Aug. 6		The Bank of England engineers a surprise increase in banks' base lending rates to 10%. The one-point increase reverses two half-point cuts made in April and May.	South Africa and Mozambique agree to renew a joint security commission established as part of the 1984 Nkomati nonaggression pact. The commission will investigate Mozambique's charge that Pretoria was indirectly responsible for the July massacre of hundreds of Mozambicans in the town of Homoine by right-wing antigovernment rebels.		In Australia, Liberal Party leader John Howard announces the revival of the political coalition with the National Party. The two parties formally ended their 38-year alliance in April. Howard was able to convince wavering parliamentarians within his party that the political split had been a key factor in the opposition Labour Party victory in the federal elections in July.

A	B	C	D	E
Includes developments that affect more than one world region, international organizations and important meetings of major world leaders.	Includes all domestic and regional developments in Europe, including the Soviet Union, Turkey, Cyprus and Malta.	Includes all domestic and regional developments in Africa and the Middle East, including Iraq and Iran and excluding Cyprus, Turkey and Afghanistan.	Includes all domestic and regional developments in Latin America, the Caribbean and Canada.	Includes all domestic and regional developments in Asia and Pacific nations, extending from Afghanistan through all the Pacific Islands, except Hawaii.

U.S. Politics & Social Issues	U.S. Foreign Policy & Defense	U.S. Economy & Environment	Science, Technology & Nature	Culture, Leisure & Life Style	
	At the conclusion of three months of public hearings into the Iran-Contra arms scandal, Senate panel chairman Sen. Daniel K. Inouye (D, Hawaii) criticizes the "flawed policy kept alive by a secret White House junta, despite repeated warnings and signs of failure." Ranking House Republican Rep. Dick Cheney (Wyo.) seeks to place the scandal in the context of the "traditional struggle between the president and Congress over policy-making and implementation." . . . A document released by the committees investigating the Iran-Contra arms scandal appears to contradict the claim of Vice Pres. George Bush that his contacts with Felix Rodriguez (alias Max Gomez) concerned aiding only the government of El Salvador, not the Contra rebels in Nicaragua.	By a vote of 91-2, the Senate approves the nomination of economist Alan Greenspan to head the Federal Reserve Board. . . . Productivity among the nation's non-farm businesses rose at an annual rate of 1.4% in the second quarter, the Labor Dept. reports.			**Aug. 3**
The Federal Communications Comm. (FCC) votes, 4-0, to abolish an unconstitutional restriction of free speech, the "fairness doctrine" that for 38 years has required radio and television broadcasters to present balanced coverage of controversial issues. . . . Jesse (Marvin) Unruh, 64, Democratic politician, dies of cancer in Marina del Rey, Calif. As speaker of the California assembly from 1961 to 1968, he was one of the most influential and progressive state legislators in the United States. In 1974 he was elected state treasurer, which office he turned into a major source of financial and political power.	Rep. Les AuCoin (D, Ore.) faults a Central Intelligence Agency report on the slaying of a U.S. volunteer by Contras in Nicaragua for failing to question the Contras on the exact circumstances of the killing. The slain American, Benjamin Linder, was killed in April during a Contra attack on a work crew near San Jose de Bocay in northern Nicaragua. . . . Pres. Reagan unveils what he calls a "renewed diplomatic initiative" toward Nicaragua that offers a cease-fire in exchange for changes in Nicaraguan policy. Liberal Democrats call it a ploy to win further military aid for the U.S.-backed Nicaraguan Contra rebels, and conservative Republicans call it a setback to the Contra cause.	The Senate passes the Competitive Equality Banking Act of 1987, a comprehensive banking bill that will allow the insolvent Federal Savings and Loan Insurance Corp. to raise $10.8 bil. by issuing long-term bonds. . . . More than a fifth of homes tested in a 10-state survey contain unsafe levels of radon, a radioactive gas that causes lung cancer, the Environmental Protection Agency reports. . . . A federal appeals court rules that the Nuclear Regulatory Comm. (NRC) cannot consider the cost of safety equipment in deciding whether plants must have the equipment.	New York state health officials will test the blood of more than 100,000 people to measure more accurately the spread of the virus that causes acquired immune deficiency syndrome (AIDS), Gov. Mario Cuomo (D) announces. The test will be the largest study undertaken by any state to determine if the AIDS virus is spreading beyond the two groups considered at greatest risk, sexually active gay men and intravenous drug users.		**Aug. 4**
Gary Hart, who dropped out of the Democratic presidential race in May in the face of scandal over his personal life, is still the top choice of Democratic voters, according to a Gallup poll commissioned by *The Nation* magazine. . . . The *Wall Street Journal* reports that George A. Mallick, a business partner of House Speaker James C. Wright Jr. (D, Tex.), has received federal aid for a project to redevelop the historic Fort Worth stockyards area at Wright's instigation.	Vice Pres. George Bush tells the *Washington Post* that he has been vindicated by the Iran-Contra hearings. Bush was apparently present at some of the high-level White House meetings on the transactions with Iran, but he has not emerged as a major player in either the Central American or the Middle Eastern operation.	The House of Representatives rejects, 261-160, a measure that will bar the Nuclear Regulatory Comm. from relaxing licensing procedures for two controversial nuclear power plants in New Hampshire and New York.			**Aug. 5**
		Members of the United Steelworkers of America at LTV Corp. approve a contract calling for supplemental pension benefits for retirees. The company will restore about 92% of the supplemental pension benefits for employees who agree to retire early, in the face of plant shutdowns.			**Aug. 6**

F	G	H	I	J
Includes elections, federal-state relations, civil rights and liberties, crime, the judiciary, education, health care, poverty, urban affairs and population.	Includes formation and debate of U.S. foreign and defense policies, veterans' affairs and defense spending. (Relations with specific foreign countries are usually found under the region concerned.)	Includes business, labor, agriculture, taxation, transportation, consumer affairs, monetary and fiscal policy, natural resources, and pollution.	Includes worldwide scientific, medical and technological developments, natural phenomena, U.S. weather, natural disasters, and accidents.	Includes the arts, religion, scholarship, communications media, sports, entertainments, fashions, fads and social life.

	World Affairs	Europe	Africa & the Middle East	The Americas	Asia & the Pacific
Aug. 7			During the first large-scale maneuvers by the recently built-up naval arm of the Revolutionary Guards in the Persian Gulf, Iran warns foreign warships to stay away or face "severe retaliation." . . . Camille Nimer Chamoun, 87, powerful Maronite Christian leader who served as president of Lebanon from 1952 to 1958, dies of a heart attack in Beirut. A wealthy businessman, politician, and lawyer, he was an outspoken critic of Syria, the Palestine Liberation Org., and pro-Iranian Shiite Moslem militia factions, and survived at least three major assassination attempts.	In Guatemala City, Guatemala, the presidents of Costa Rica, Guatemala, Nicaragua, El Salvador, and Honduras sign a preliminary agreement calling for cease-fires in the region's many conflicts. . . . After announcing the nationalization of Peru's private banks July 28, the government agrees to abide by a court ruling that suspends the takeover of 33 banks, investment agencies, and insurance companies. . . . The Canadian government releases a heavily censored version of a study on official complicity and the presence in Canada of ex-Nazis and former collaborators after World War II. . . . In Colombia, it is reported that escalating clashes between government troops and left-wing rebels resulted in more than 1,600 deaths in the year ending July 31.	Nobosuke Kishi, 90, premier of Japan from 1957 to 1960, dies of a heart ailment in Tokyo. The dominant figure in pre-war Japanese industrial planning, he was minister of commerce and industry during World War II, after which he was imprisoned for war crimes until 1948. Prime minister from 1957 to 1960, he continued to exercise considerable influence over the long-ruling Liberal Democratic Party.
Aug. 8			Chad reports that its army has overrun the Aozou strip, the last swath of Chadian territory occupied by Libyan troops.	A Gallup poll shows that 75% of Panamanians believe that Gen. Manuel Antonio Noriega, the de facto leader of Panama, should resign. More than 50% believe that Pres. Eric Arturo Delvalle and his government should step down.	Sri Lanka's Finance Min. Ronnie de Mel is reported to have made an appeal for massive international aid to repair the damage caused by four years of civil war. De Mel says property damage could total $515 mil.
Aug. 9			Black miners in South Africa's gold and coal mining industries begin a strike for higher wages and improved benefits. Estimates of the number of striking workers run from 230,000 to 340,000, making it the largest, legal contract-related job action in South African history.	A 33-year-old territorial dispute between Venezuela and Colombia flares up after a Colombian warship enters an area of the Gulf of Venezuela claimed by Venezuela.	
Aug. 10		France rejects an appeal from Chad to provide air cover for its forces, which are reportedly being subjected to heavy retaliatory bombardment by Libyan warplanes, in the dispute over the Aozou airstrip.			
Aug. 11				Following the discovery of a boatload of Indian aliens in Nova Scotia in July, Canada's P.M. Brian Mulroney convenes an emergency session of the House of Commons to deal with the influx of illegal aliens. . . . The cabinet of the Dominican Republic's Pres. Joaquin Balaguer resigns so that he can restructure the government. The move comes two weeks after a general strike in which at least one person died.	

A	B	C	D	E
Includes developments that affect more than one world region, international organizations and important meetings of major world leaders.	Includes all domestic and regional developments in Europe, including the Soviet Union, Turkey, Cyprus and Malta.	Includes all domestic and regional developments in Africa and the Middle East, including Iraq and Iran and excluding Cyprus, Turkey and Afghanistan.	Includes all domestic and regional developments in Latin America, the Caribbean and Canada.	Includes all domestic and regional developments in Asia and Pacific nations, extending from Afghanistan through all the Pacific Islands, except Hawaii.

U.S. Politics & Social Issues	U.S. Foreign Policy & Defense	U.S. Economy & Environment	Science, Technology & Nature	Culture, Leisure & Life Style	
In an effort to head off a call for stricter intelligence oversight laws, Pres. Reagan sends a letter to leaders of the House and Senate intelligence committees announcing new procedures for reporting covert operations to Congress.... According to a *Washington Post*/ABC News poll, Lt. Col. Oliver L. North was the most popular and the most believable of the last six witnesses in the Iran-Contra investigation, and Rear Adm. John M. Poindexter the least popular and least believable.	Law enforcement sources in the United States confirm published reports that a U.S. federal grand jury in Miami is investigating Gen. Manuel Antonio Noriega, head of the Panama Defense Forces, for his alleged involvement in drug trafficking.	The nation's unemployment rate fell in July to 5.9%, the Labor Dept. reports.... Outstanding consumer credit rose by a seasonally adjusted $3.46 bil., an annual rate of 7.6%, in June, the Federal Reserve Board reports.... The Securities and Exchange Comm. (SEC) proposes a formal definition of illegal insider trading in stocks. The definition is contained in a five-page proposal to Congress of language to use in new legislation governing securities transactions. ... The *Wall Street Journal* finds that net income at 524 large corporations it surveys quarterly fell 21% in the second quarter from the same period a year earlier.		Lynne Cox swims from Little Diomede Island, Alaska, to Big Diomede Island, USSR, a distance of 2.7 miles in the first-ever feat of this kind in the frigid waters of the Bering Strait.	**Aug. 7**
Two Democratic presidential hopefuls, Gov. Michael S. Dukakis (Mass.) and Rep. Richard A. Gephardt (Mo.) meet in a debate in Des Moines, Iowa. Dukakis issued the challenge after Gephardt derided him for taking credit for Massachusetts's economic recovery.	Commenting on the Guatemala City agreement of the day before, Pres. Reagan is cautious in his support. He says he welcomes the commitment to peace and democracy but adds that there is a long way to go before the plan is successful. Pres. Reagan says his administration's acceptance depends on U.S. interests and those of the "Nicaraguan resistance."			Football stars Don Maynard, Larry Csonka, Jim Langer, Joe Greene, Gene Upshaw, John Henry Johnson, and Len Dawson are inducted into the Pro Football Hall of Fame in Canton, Ohio.	**Aug. 8**
				Composer and conductor Leonard Bernstein becomes the 28th recipient of the MacDowell Colony Medal for lifetime achievement in the arts.... Larry Nelson parred the first hole of a sudden-death playoff with Lanny Wadkins to win the 69th Professional Golfers Assoc. Championship.	**Aug. 9**
		Pres. Reagan nominates C. William Verity Jr. to be secretary of commerce, succeeding Malcolm Baldrige, who died July 25.... Pres. Reagan signs another in a series of temporary increases in the national debt limit passed by Congress August 7, just before a month-long recess.... I(orwith) W(ilbur) Abel, 78, labor leader who helped found the United Steelworkers of America and served as the union's third president from 1965 to 1977, dies of cancer in Malvern, Ohio. Under his presidency, union membership rose dramatically, the union amassed a strike fund of more than $85 mil., and the union concluded an historic no-strike agreement to end production and stockpiling swings.		Patrick Aloysius Cardinal O'Boyle, 91, first Roman Catholic archbishop of Washington, D.C., dies in Washington, D.C., of pneumonia and kidney failure after an operation for a broken hip. Appointed arhbishop when the new archdiocese split off from the archdiocese of Baltimore in 1948, he was elevated to cardinal in 1967. A liberal on social issues, he ordered the desegregation of Catholic schools in the archdiocese in 1949. On doctrinal matters, he was a staunch conservative and an outspoken defender of the Vatican's stance on birth control.	**Aug. 10**
Sen. Joseph R. Biden Jr. (D, Del.), chairman of the Senate Judiciary Committee, says he does not believe he can vote to approve the nomination of Judge Robert H. Bork to the Supreme Court unless Bork "fundamentally" changes his views on a number of issues.... In a Federal Bureau of Investigation (FBI) "sting" operation that swept across New York state, 44 current or former municipal officials—most of them highway officials—are charged with taking bribes or kickbacks from an undercover FBI agent.	The Reagan administration has prepared a new version of a controversial secrecy pledge for government personnel with access to classified information, the *Washington Post* reports. Since its introduction in January, the agreement has been signed by an estimated 2 million employees. Those who signed it promised not to disclose either "classified" or "classifiable" information under penalty of losing their security clearances and likely their jobs.	The Environmental Protection Agency announces that Velsicol Chemical Corp. has agreed to stop selling chlordane and heptachlor, two leading termite-control chemicals, until it can demonstrate that they can be used safely to protect houses.			**Aug. 11**

F	G	H	I	J
Includes elections, federal-state relations, civil rights and liberties, crime, the judiciary, education, health care, poverty, urban affairs and population.	*Includes formation and debate of U.S. foreign and defense policies, veterans' affairs and defense spending. (Relations with specific foreign countries are usually found under the region concerned.)*	*Includes business, labor, agriculture, taxation, transportation, consumer affairs, monetary and fiscal policy, natural resources, and pollution.*	*Includes worldwide scientific, medical and technological developments, natural phenomena, U.S. weather, natural disasters, and accidents.*	*Includes the arts, religion, scholarship, communications media, sports, entertainments, fashions, fads and social life.*

	World Affairs	Europe	Africa & the Middle East	The Americas	Asia & the Pacific
Aug. 12		East Germany and West Germany swap a total of five people convicted of espionage. Western observers believe the swap was facilitated by East German leader Erich Honecker's planned visit to West Germany.	The scope of the international crisis over the Persian Gulf continues to widen following deadly rioting in Mecca, Saudi Arabia, the previous week. A U.S.-owned supertanker hit a mine in an area just outside the gulf, leading Britain and France to dispatch minesweepers to the region and eliciting new threats from Iran. Iraq has resumed air attacks against Iran, the United States is conducting a surprise escort of reflagged Kuwaiti tankers, and it is revealed that a U.S. warplane has fired on at an Iranian jet.		
Aug. 13		The Law Lords, who constitute Britain's highest court, uphold temporary injunctions barring British newspapers from publishing *Spycatcher*, the memoirs of former counterintelligence (MI5) agent Peter Wright, which is a best-seller in the United States. . . . The number of Britain's unemployed workers declined in July, to 10.4%, for the 13th straight month, the Dept. of Employment reports.		Breaking with tradition, Mexico's ruling Institutional Revolutionary Party (PRI) discloses the names of six possible candidates for the party's presidential nomination. Elections for a successor to Pres. Miguel de la Madrid Hurtado are scheduled for July 1988. The PRI nominee is virtually assured the presidency. The party has been in power since 1929 and has never lost a major election. . . . A federal jury in Wilmington, N.C., finds Samuel Alberto Escruceria-Delgado, a Colombian senator, guilty of 32 drug trafficking charges.	
Aug. 14	A standoff involving the besieged French and Iranian embassies in Teheran and Paris continues through the week. The crisis goes on amid controversial press reports about earlier secret agreements between conservative Premier Jacques Chirac and the governments of Iran and Iraq.				
Aug. 15					Australian police and Aborigines clash in Brewarrina, New South Wales, following the funeral of Lloyd James Boney, an Aborigine who was found dead by hanging in his cell in the local jail. Boney is the 17th Aborigine to die in police custody since April 1986, and the 44th since 1980. . . . In New Zealand, the Labour government of P.M. David Lange is reelected to a second term. Lange is the first Labour prime minister to win reelection in New Zealand since Walter Nash in 1938.
Aug. 16					In Australia, an official of the town of Brewarrina, in New South Wales, accuses the Australian Broadcasting Corp. of inciting Aborigines to riot. Aborigines and police clashed in the town August 15.

A	B	C	D	E
Includes developments that affect more than one world region, international organizations and important meetings of major world leaders.	*Includes all domestic and regional developments in Europe, including the Soviet Union, Turkey, Cyprus and Malta.*	*Includes all domestic and regional developments in Africa and the Middle East, including Iraq and Iran and excluding Cyprus, Turkey and Afghanistan.*	*Includes all domestic and regional developments in Latin America, the Caribbean and Canada.*	*Includes all domestic and regional developments in Asia and Pacific nations, extending from Afghanistan through all the Pacific Islands, except Hawaii.*

U.S. Politics & Social Issues	U.S. Foreign Policy & Defense	U.S. Economy & Environment	Science, Technology & Nature	Culture, Leisure & Life Style	
State and local tax collections amounted to $370.8 bil. during the year ending June 1986, Commerce Clearing House Inc. reports. The total is 7% higher than the previous 12-month period. The states collected a total of $227.7 bil., a 6.1% increase for the period. Localities took in $143.1 bil., a rise of 8.5%.	In a nationally broadcast response to the recently concluded House and Senate hearings on the Iran-Contra arms scandal, Pres. Reagan asserts that he "was stubborn in pursuit of a policy that went astray" in selling arms to Iran.... Sen. George J. Mitchell (D, Maine) presents the official Democratic response to Reagan, with a forceful and direct: "Obey the law."	An administrative law judge of the Federal Communications Comm. (FCC) rules that because of offenses that include lying to the FCC, overbilling advertisers, and falsifying records, RKO General Inc. is disqualified from holding licenses for 12 radio and two television stations the company operates in nine cities around the United States.		Alessandro Andrei of Italy breaks the world record in the shot put three times in a meet in Viareggio, Italy. Andrei's final and longest throw is 75 feet, 2 inches.... *Variety*'s top-grossing films for the week are *The Living Daylights*, *Stakeout*, *The Lost Boys*, *La Bamba* and *Robocop*.	**Aug. 12**
A spokesman for the Rev. Jesse Jackson announces that the Democrat has raised more than $520,000 for his planned 1988 presidential race. Jackson has not yet declared his candidacy and has not filed official disclosure forms. ... Joan B. Kroc, widow of the founder of McDonald's Corp., has given the Democratic Party $1 mil., the largest single contribution in the party's history, it is announced. An advocate of nuclear disarmament, Kroc says she is alarmed at the Reagan administration policies. ... A nationwide opinion poll commissioned by the National Women's Political Caucus finds that more than half the nation's voters say that a woman could do as well or better than a man as president.	Senior Reagan administration officials are reported as saying that the White House plans to go through with a request for $150 mil. in aid in September if the current peace talks in Central America do not progress. The administration is concerned about providing the Contras with money after September 30, when current funding expires, but before November 7, when the 90-day deadline set out in the Guatemala agreement expires.	Over the last four days the Treasury Dept. has sold $28.1 bil. of notes and bonds at rates significantly higher than at the previous quarterly refinancing auction.			**Aug. 13**
A nationally televised debate among the Republican presidential contenders October 28 will have to do without Vice Pres. George Bush, it is reported. The debate, intended to complement one held by Democratic contenders in July, has been postponed twice because of objections by Bush and Sen. Robert Dole (R, Kans.), the two frontrunners.		The U.S. Forest Service announces a pact with environmentalists and loggers to protect 1,000 miles of rivers in the East and Midwest. The agreement covers 112 rivers and 301,000 acres of national forest within a quarter of a mile of the banks of the rivers in 11 states.		Officials of the U.S. Postal Service and the Bureau of Engraving and Printing disclose that an unauthorized Star of David, invisible to the naked eye, was etched into the die of a $1 postage stamp by government engraver Kenneth Kipperman. It is reportedly the first time a symbol has been etched surreptitiously on a U.S. stamp.	**Aug. 14**
					Aug. 15
		The U.S. deficit on merchandise trade surges in June to $15.71 bil., the Commerce Dept. reports.... The producer price index rose a seasonally adjusted 0.2% in July, according to the Labor Dept.... The Federal Reserve Board reports that its industrial production index rose a strong 0.8% in July.		Attempting to ward off global disaster, thousands of believers in "harmonic convergence" assemble at a number of sacred sites around the world to meditate, hold hands, and "resonate" by humming. The event is the inspiration of Jose Arguelles, a Boulder, Colo., art history teacher and author of a book on Mayan cosmology.... On the 10th anniversary of the death of singer Elvis Presley, thousands of fans gather at Memphis (Tenn.) State Univ. for a three-hour memorial service.	**Aug. 16**

F	G	H	I	J
Includes elections, federal-state relations, civil rights and liberties, crime, the judiciary, education, health care, poverty, urban affairs and population.	Includes formation and debate of U.S. foreign and defense policies, veterans' affairs and defense spending. (Relations with specific foreign countries are usually found under the region concerned.)	Includes business, labor, agriculture, taxation, transportation, consumer affairs, monetary and fiscal policy, natural resources, and pollution.	Includes worldwide scientific, medical and technological developments, natural phenomena, U.S. weather, natural disasters, and accidents.	Includes the arts, religion, scholarship, communications media, sports, entertainments, fashions, fads and social life.

	World Affairs	Europe	Africa & the Middle East	The Americas	Asia & the Pacific
Aug. 17	Oil prices decline to below $20 a barrel in the biggest one-day drop in more than a year. The price drop comes in response to apparent overproduction by member nations of the Org. of Petroleum Exporting Countries.	(Walter Richard) Rudolf Hess, 93, onetime deputy to Nazi Party and German leader Adolf Hitler and the last survivor of the 19 German officials convicted by the Nuremberg war crimes tribunal in 1946, dies in West Berlin's British Military Hospital, apparently by his own hand. In May 1941, Hess flew from Germany to England, where he was imprisoned until war's end. Sentenced to life imprisonment at Nuremberg, since 1966 he had been the only occupant of Spandau Prison in West Berlin.		In El Salvador, in what is reported to be their worst assault in several months, leftist rebels ambush a military convoy near San Isidro and kill at least nine soldiers. The ambush takes place just two days before a meeting of Central American foreign ministers in El Salvador to discuss a regional peace plan signed in Guatemala City August 7.	
Aug. 18		In a move to catch the socialist opposition off-guard and to capitalize on the still-vital Danish economy before an expected downturn in the fall, Denmark's Premier Poul Schluter calls for general elections to be held September 8, four months before the term of his conservative government is scheduled to end.	American journalist Charles Glass, kidnapped June 16 in south Beirut by Shiite Moslem gunmen, manages to flee to freedom. Although he maintains that his escape was genuine, U.S. officials and Arab sources suggest that Glass's captors may have let him get away in response to pressure by Iran and Syria.		One legislator is killed and 15 are injured in a grenade attack on Sri Lanka's parliament hours after the Tamil Tigers, announced that it will surrender all its weapons to an Indian Army peacekeeping force. . . . Australia had a trade deficit of $286 mil. in July, according to the government. The July figure is a sharp reversal from June, when Australia enjoyed a trade surplus of $113 mil. Taken together, the figures reflect a swing of $399 mil. over a one-month period.
Aug. 19				The foreign ministers of five Central American nations meet in El Salvador to discuss the regional peace plan signed in Guatemala City August 7. The Guatemala Pact calls for the foreign ministers to meet as an executive committee within 15 days to regulate and promote the terms agreed upon in the plan.	
Aug. 20	Relations between the Soviet Union and Japan appear to worsen when the two countries trade expulsions based on accusations of military and industrial espionage. Some Western observers believe that the rift has its roots in a May controversy, when Japan announced that it had broken up a Soviet spy ring in Tokyo. Four Soviet diplomats were forced to leave Japan in the wake of that dispute.				

A	B	C	D	E
Includes developments that affect more than one world region, international organizations and important meetings of major world leaders.	*Includes all domestic and regional developments in Europe, including the Soviet Union, Turkey, Cyprus and Malta.*	*Includes all domestic and regional developments in Africa and the Middle East, including Iraq and Iran and excluding Cyprus, Turkey and Afghanistan.*	*Includes all domestic and regional developments in Latin America, the Caribbean and Canada.*	*Includes all domestic and regional developments in Asia and Pacific nations, extending from Afghanistan through all the Pacific Islands, except Hawaii.*

U.S. Politics & Social Issues	U.S. Foreign Policy & Defense	U.S. Economy & Environment	Science, Technology & Nature	Culture, Leisure & Life Style	
	Senior U.S. envoys to the five Central American nations meet at the State Dept. in Washington, D.C., to evaluate the peace plan known as the Guatemala Pact. The envoys reportedly are told to convey the Reagan administration's concern about the plan to its allies in Central America.		A U.S. space policy study team headed by astronaut Sally Ride recommends that the United States get its space program back on track by undertaking a detailed probing of the Earth from space while at the same time preparing to return to the moon and eventually to visit Mars.	Carlos Drummond de Andrade, 84, Brazilian poet and a leader of Brazil's modernist movement in literature, dies in Rio de Janeiro after a heart attack. One of the foremost Portuguese-language poets of the 20th century, he was also considered "perhaps the most successful humorous poet of really major stature in this century." . . . Clarence Brown, 97, U.S. film director who was a six-time Academy Award nominee, dies of kidney failure in Santa Monica, Calif. His 1927 silent film *Flesh and the Devil launched Greta Garbo, with whom he worked on six more films, including Anna Christie.* His other films include *National Velvet* (1944) and *The Yearling* (1946).	Aug. 17
Twenty people are indicted in Brooklyn, N.Y., on charges of labor racketeering in the construction industry. The charges involve rigging of bids, manipulating the awarding of contracts, bribery, extortion, collusion, and fraud.		Housing starts rose 0.9% in July following four consecutive monthly declines, the Commerce Dept. reports.	Plans for the first human trials in the United States of an experimental vaccine against acquired immune deficiency syndrome are announced by U.S. health officials and by MicroGeneSys Inc., the West Haven, Conn.-based company that developed the vaccine. . . . A panel of the National Academy of Sciences concludes that there is no evidence that organisms created by the technique of genetic engineering pose any "unique" risks to the environment.	Washington, D.C., art historian and portrait painter Charles Merrill Mount, 59, is arrested in connection with what federal authorities say is one of the largest thefts of historic U.S. documents, including a 1904 letter signed by novelist Henry James that is missing from the Library of Congress. . . . Peter Schidlof, 65, Austrian-born violist who fled to England as a refugee from the Nazis in 1938, dies of a heart attack in Cumbria, England. He was a founding member of the Amadeus Quartet in 1948, which was one of the leading exponents of the standard repertory for string quartet.	Aug. 18
	A heavily edited transcript of testimony given by Central Intelligence Agency agent Duane R. (Dewey) Clarridge shows that, in early 1984, U.S. officials approved a plan by which South Africa would provide money to train and arm the Contra rebels fighting the government of Nicaragua. Clarridge testified in closed session to members of House and Senate committees investigating the Iran-Contra arms scandal on August 4.	The AFL-CIO and Adolph Coors Co. announce an agreement to end their bitter, decade-long dispute. The union federation says it will call off its consumer boycott of Coors beer, which began in 1977 in a labor dispute at the company's only brewery in Golden, Colo. . . . The Labor Dept. announces regulations extending a requirement that workers be notified of the possibility of exposure to hazardous chemicals on the work site. . . . The White House announces that Pres. Reagan has signed legislation restricting air tours over three national parks, the Grand Canyon (Ariz.), Yosemite (Calif.), and Haleakala (Hawaii).			Aug. 19
Switzerland's highest court orders Swiss banks to turn over confidential documents regarding funds from the Iran arms deals to special prosecutor Lawrence E. Walsh. Simultaneously, a panel of U.S. appeals court judges upholds the authority of Walsh's investigation. . . . The five declared candidates for the 1988 Democratic presidential nomination appear before the three-day meeting of the National Women's Political Caucus, but as-yet-undeclared candidate Rep. Patricia Schroeder (D, Colo.), stirs the most interest.		Citing a potential health hazard, the Agriculture Dept. blocks the sale of about 30 million pounds of processed beef from Australia. Australia fears that the United States is edging toward a total cutoff of beef imports from that nation.			Aug. 20

F	G	H	I	J
Includes elections, federal-state relations, civil rights and liberties, crime, the judiciary, education, health care, poverty, urban affairs and population.	Includes formation and debate of U.S. foreign and defense policies, veterans' affairs and defense spending. (Relations with specific foreign countries are usually found under the region concerned.)	Includes business, labor, agriculture, taxation, transportation, consumer affairs, monetary and fiscal policy, natural resources, and pollution.	Includes worldwide scientific, medical and technological developments, natural phenomena, U.S. weather, natural disasters, and accidents.	Includes the arts, religion, scholarship, communications media, sports, entertainments, fashions, fads and social life.

	World Affairs	Europe	Africa & the Middle East	The Americas	Asia & the Pacific
Aug. 21			Zimbabwe's House of Assembly votes, 78-0, to abolish the 20 seats reserved for whites since Zimbabwe achieved independence as a black-ruled nation in 1980. The bill will become law in September after it receives the approval of the Senate, which is assured. The remaining 80 assembly members will then form an electoral college and select people to fill the vacated seats until the next general election in 1990.	In a meeting with El Salvador's Pres. Jose Napoleon Duarte, Nicaraguan Contra leaders formally accept the peace agreement, known as the Guatemala Pact.... Argentina and its creditor banks sign a debt restructuring agreement worth $34.7 bil. In the deal, $29.5 bil. of public and private sector debt is rescheduled, and Argentina receives $1.95 bil. in new funds. The package also includes a trade credit maintenance facility and a $2 bil. standby money market facility.	In a major victory for South Korean workers, Hyundai Group, the nation's largest industrial company, bows to government pressure and agrees to recognize a new independent trade union. For the past four weeks, South Korean workers have staged widespread strikes and other protests, some violent, demanding higher wages, improved working conditions, and better unions.
Aug. 22					In South Korea, a young shipyard worker dies in a clash with riot police on the southern island of Koje. The protester, Lee Sok Kyu, is apparently killed by fragments of a tear gas canister as 3,000 workers protesting a lockout by Daewoo Shipyard and Machinery Ltd. clash with 2,000 riot police.
Aug. 23		Thousands of people march through the streets of the capital cities of the Soviet Baltic republics, Latvia, Lithuania, and Estonia. Large public protests in the region are the latest sign of a resurgence of nationalism within the Soviet Union.			
Aug. 24	A UN conference on the arms race opens in New York City. The United States boycotts the parley, which is scheduled to last three weeks. The stated purpose of the Conf. on the Relationship Between Disarmament and Development is to discuss the possible effect of disarmament on international economic development, particularly in the Third World.	In Britain, members of the National Union of Mineworkers (NUM) vote overwhelmingly to support industrial action against a new British Coal code of conduct. The support for industrial action is seen as a significant victory for controversial NUM Pres. Arthur Scargill. . . . The body of Rudolf Hess, the former deputy to Nazi German leader Adolf Hitler who died August 17, is secretly buried in a private ceremony designed to thwart attempts by neo-Nazi groups to use the burial as a rallying platform.	U.S. Navy warships completing an escort of reflagged Kuwaiti tankers out of the Persian Gulf fire warning shots across the bows of two small fishing craft and challenge an Iranian Navy ship.		
Aug. 25	U.S. negotiators at the bilateral Geneva arms talks offer a new package of proposals on verifying the removal of medium-range missiles. The State Dept. insists that the proposals will simplify, but not soften, the Reagan administration's original stance on intermediate-range nuclear forces verification.	The Soviet government adopts a new law that requires suspected carriers of the virus that causes acquired immune deficiency syndrome to undergo testing, the official news agency Tass reports.			

A	B	C	D	E
Includes developments that affect more than one world region, international organizations and important meetings of major world leaders.	Includes all domestic and regional developments in Europe, including the Soviet Union, Turkey, Cyprus and Malta.	Includes all domestic and regional developments in Africa and the Middle East, including Iraq and Iran and excluding Cyprus, Turkey and Afghanistan.	Includes all domestic and regional developments in Latin America, the Caribbean and Canada.	Includes all domestic and regional developments in Asia and Pacific nations, extending from Afghanistan through all the Pacific Islands, except Hawaii.

U.S. Politics & Social Issues	U.S. Foreign Policy & Defense	U.S. Economy & Environment	Science, Technology & Nature	Culture, Leisure & Life Style	
	Pres. Reagan meets in Los Angeles with military and political leaders of the Nicaraguan Contras to reassure them of U.S. support. The Contras ask the president to request new military and nonlethal aid from Congress, and suggest that the military portion be be used for arms only if the Nicaraguan government fails to comply with the terms of the Guatemala Pact by the November 7 deadline.	The government's consumer price index rose a slight 0.2% in July, the Labor Dept. reports. . . . The nation's gross national product rose at an annual rate of 2.3% in the second quarter, the Commerce Dept. reports. . . . After-tax profits of U.S. corporations rose a healthy 4.2% in the second quarter, the Commerce Dept. says.		*Dirty Dancing*, a musical love story set in an upstate New York mountain resort in the 1960s, is released in New York. The film stars Patrick Swayze and Jennifer Grey. . . . A $15 mil. civil suit brought by convicted murderer Jeffrey R. MacDonald against Joe McGinniss, author of *Fatal Vision*, ends with a deadlocked jury. McDonald contends that McGinniss led him to believe he was sympathetic to his case in order to interview him.	**Aug. 21**
				Billboard's best-selling albums for the week are: *Whitney*, Whitney Houston; *Whitesnake*, Whitesnake; *Bad Animals*, Heart; *Bigger and Deffer*, L.L. Cool J; and *The Joshua Tree*, U2. . . . Joseph P. Lash, 77, author whose long friendship with Eleanor Roosevelt led to his selection as her official biographer, dies in Boston, while being treated for a heart ailment. *Eleanor and Franklin*, the first installment in his two-volume biography of Mrs. Roosevelt, earned Lash the 1972 Pulitzer Prize for biography.	**Aug. 22**
In the Democratic presidential race, Massachusetts Gov. Michael S. Dukakis receives most of the fire from his rivals at a televised debate in Des Moines, Iowa. Recognizing that the attacks imply front-runner status, Dukakis says afterward, "I enjoyed it."				The 10th Pan American Games conclude in Indianapolis. Athletes from the United States win the most medals of any nation, but the athletic accomplishments at the games are partially overshadowed by the performances of a large delegation of Cuban athletes and by protests against their appearance. The games began August 8.	**Aug. 23**
A federal appeals court in Cincinnati reverses a lower court ruling requiring the Hawkins County, Tenn., public schools to excuse certain children from reading classes because the textbooks are offensive to their religious beliefs. . . . Bayard Rustin, 75 or 77, civil rights leader and principal organizer of the 1963 Washington, D.C., rally at which the Rev. Martin Luther King Jr. delivered his "I have a dream" speech, dies of cardiac arrest after surgery for a ruptured appendix in New York City. A socialist, pacifist, and Quaker, Rustin achieved social change through alliances with labor, white liberals, Jews, and other minorities. The openly gay Rustin also urged black leaders to adopt a more active role in the struggle against acquired immune deficiency syndrome.	A jury of eight U.S. Marine Corps officers sentences Marine Sgt. Clayton J. Lonetree to 30 years in prison for spying for the Soviet Union. The court-martial, conducted at the Quantico (Va.) Marine base, began July 22. Lonetree, who did not testify, was convicted August 21.	Defying economists' predictions that consumer spending would slow down, U.S. consumers increased their spending by 0.9% in July, according to the Commerce Dept. The increase in spending is more than double the 0.4% rise in personal income.			**Aug. 24**
Vice Pres. George Bush says he has now decided to take part in a nationally televised Republican presidential debate on the "Firing Line" TV program October 28. Bush was criticized by most of his rivals for twice forcing the event's postponement.		The Dow Jones Industrial Average closings set a record high 2722.42, surpassing the previous record closing of 2572.07 July 31. . . . The Commerce Dept. imposes a civil penalty of $381,000 on NCR Corp. for violations by the computer maker of a law prohibiting cooperation with an Arab boycott of Israel. The fine is the largest ever levied under the 1977 law.			**Aug. 25**

F	G	H	I	J
Includes elections, federal-state relations, civil rights and liberties, crime, the judiciary, education, health care, poverty, urban affairs and population.	Includes formation and debate of U.S. foreign and defense policies, veterans' affairs and defense spending. (Relations with specific foreign countries are usually found under the region concerned.)	Includes business, labor, agriculture, taxation, transportation, consumer affairs, monetary and fiscal policy, natural resources, and pollution.	Includes worldwide scientific, medical and technological developments, natural phenomena, U.S. weather, natural disasters, and accidents.	Includes the arts, religion, scholarship, communications media, sports, entertainments, fashions, fads and social life.

	World Affairs	Europe	Africa & the Middle East	The Americas	Asia & the Pacific
Aug. 26		West Germany offers to dismantle its 72 Pershing IA missiles if the United States and Soviet Union implement an agreement on a global ban on intermediate-range nuclear forces (INF). The aging missiles are the key obstacle to a superpower INF pact.		One of the longest strikes in the history of Mexico's automobile industry ends when workers at Volkswagen de Mexico S.A. accept a 78% pay increase. Ten thousand Volkswagen workers went on strike July 1 to press for a 100% pay increase plus a 23% "emergency increase" tied to a minimum wage raise that goes into effect immediately.	Despite an announcement by Philippine Pres. Corazon Aquino that she would partially roll back fuel price increases she announced August 14, labor groups go ahead with strikes and demonstrations planned to protest the price increase.... Australia's national economy grew 2% in the 1986-87 fiscal year, according to the government.
Aug. 27					
Aug. 28			Libya recaptures from Chadian troops the main outpost in the Aozou strip, a disputed stretch of desert territory along the border between the two countries.	In Canada, a bill aimed at ending a national railroad strike is passed by both houses of parliament and given royal assent. Similar back-to-work legislation was needed to halt Canada's last national rail strike, in 1973. The Associated Railway Unions, an organization with a total of 50,000 members, has been on strike against CP Rail and Canadian National Railways since August 23.	A revolt by mutinous Philippine soldiers against the government of Pres. Corazon Aquino begins in Manila but is put down by loyal government troops within the next 24 hours. The uprising is the most serious since the Aquino government came to power.... Benigno S. Aquino III, the only son of the Philippine president, is shot and three of his bodyguards are killed near the Malacanang Palace after he stops to talk to soldiers who turn out to be rebels.
Aug. 29			Iraq breaks a 45-day lull in the Persian Gulf shipping war with aerial attacks on Iranian tankers and offshore oil installations.		
Aug. 30			A three-week strike by more than 250,000 black workers in South Africa's gold and coal mining industry ends when the union accepts an offer from management that it rejected four days earlier. In the face of mass firings of strikers, the miners end their walkout without the wage gains they sought.		

A	B	C	D	E
Includes developments that affect more than one world region, international organizations and important meetings of major world leaders.	Includes all domestic and regional developments in Europe, including the Soviet Union, Turkey, Cyprus and Malta.	Includes all domestic and regional developments in Africa and the Middle East, including Iraq and Iran and excluding Cyprus, Turkey and Afghanistan.	Includes all domestic and regional developments in Latin America, the Caribbean and Canada.	Includes all domestic and regional developments in Asia and Pacific nations, extending from Afghanistan through all the Pacific Islands, except Hawaii.

U.S. Politics & Social Issues	U.S. Foreign Policy & Defense	U.S. Economy & Environment	Science, Technology & Nature	Culture, Leisure & Life Style	
Former Nevada Sen. Paul Laxalt announces that he is dropping out of the race for the 1988 Republican presidential nomination.... A federal appeals court in Atlanta overturns a federal district court decision banning 44 textbooks from public schools in Alabama because they promote the "religion" of "secular humanism." ... U.S. prosecutors in New York City unveil a new tactic in their war against organized crime by filing a civil suit against the Bonanno crime organization. The suit is the first to use a civil complaint against a Mafia family under the Racketeer Influenced and Corrupt Orgs. Act (RICO).	In a speech on U.S.-Soviet relations to the Town Hall of California, a speakers' forum in Los Angeles, Pres. Reagan calls for the Soviet Union to expand the concept of glasnost (openness) both in its domestic reforms and in its foreign policy.	General Motors Corp. (GMC) closes down its 64-year-old assembly plant in Norwood, Ohio, as part of a massive reorganization move spurred by the inroads of foreign competition. The plant-closing is the first of 11 in four states planned by GMC through 1990; the closings will affect a total of 29,000 jobs.	Georg Wittig, 90, professor emeritus of organic chemistry at the Univ. of Heidelberg, West Germany, dies in Heidelberg. A 1979 Nobel laureate in chemistry, he was honored for demonstrating a method of linking carbon and phosphorus that made possible new ways to synthesize biologically active substances.		Aug. 26
Sen. William Proxmire (D, Wis.) tells reporters that he will not run for reelection in 1988 because he will be "too old," 79, when his next term ends.... A federal appeals court in St. Paul strikes down a 1981 Minnesota law that requires women under 18 either to inform both parents or to obtain court approval before getting an abortion.	Edited transcripts of private testimony from two former Central Intelligence Agency (CIA) officials, Claire George and Alan Fiers, and a former aide to Lt. Col. Oliver L. North, shed light on the role of the late CIA chief William J. Casey in the Iran-Contra program and on the efforts by the Iranian government to keep the arms deals going after they were revealed. The testimony has been released over the last three days by congressional committees investigating the Iran-Contra arms scandal.	The Environmental Protection Agency reproves Dr. Gary Strobel of Montana State Univ. for undertaking an unauthorized experiment with a genetically altered microbe and injecting it into American elm trees to see if they could be made resistant to Dutch elm disease.... Environmental groups file suit against the Interior Dept.'s plan to open the outer continental shelf to oil and gas exploration. The plan, which went into effect July 2, will open for exploration millions of acres, including areas off the West Coast, the Florida Keys, and the Georges Bank near Massachusetts.			Aug. 27
The Arcadia, Fla., home of a couple whose three sons are hemophiliacs known to have been exposed to the virus that causes acquired immune deficiency syndrome is destroyed in a fire of suspicious origins. The fire caps a week of bomb and death threats against Clifford and Louise Ray, and their daughter and three sons, as well as a boycott of local schools prompted by the return to school of the three boys after a year's absence.				John Huston, 81, film director, writer, and actor who was one of the most honored figures in world cinema, dies in Middletown, R.I., of complications of emphysema. His 41 films include *The Maltese Falcon* (1941), *The Treasure of the Sierra Madre* (1948), for which he won Oscars for best writer and director, and *The African Queen* (1951). Huston directed Oscar-winning performances by his father Walter in *The Treasure of the Sierra Madre* and by his daughter Anjelica in *Prizzi's Honor* (1985).	Aug. 28
The Dept. of Health and Human Services proposes rules to tighten restrictions on abortion-related activities of all family-planning clinics that receive federal funding. The rule changes are designed to carry out Pres. Reagan's abortion policy, first outlined in a July 30 speech to antiabortion advocates.				Lee Marvin, 63, Hollywood "tough guy" who appeared in more than 50 films, including *The Man Who Shot Liberty Valance* (1962), *The Dirty Dozen* (1967) and, most notably, *Cat Ballou* (1965), for which he won an Oscar for best actor, dies of a heart attack in Tucson, Ariz. In 1979 he was the defendant in a landmark "palimony" suit filed by his former mistress, Michelle Triola Marvin. Her right to sue was upheld, but she was awarded far less money than she sought.	Aug. 29
A *Des Moines Register* poll of likely Democratic presidential voters finds Rep. Richard A. Gephardt (Mo.) first with 18%, followed by Gov. Michael S. Dukakis (Mass.) at 14%, Sen. Paul Simon (Ill.) at 13%, Sen. Joseph R. Biden (Del.) at 10%, and the Rev. Jesse Jackson and former Gov. Bruce Babbitt (Ariz.) at 9%. The gap among the top three is within the poll's stated 5% margin of error. The most popular choice is "undecided," with 20%.			A redesigned booster rocket to help propel the American space shuttle into orbit is tested, apparently successfully, in the foothills of the Wasatch Mountains near Brigham City, Utah.	Wade Hampton McCree Jr., 67, former federal judge and the U.S. solicitor general in the Carter administration, dies in Detroit after a heart attack while being treated for heart ailments and cancer. He was the first black to sit as a judge on a Michigan court. After stepping down as solicitor general in 1981, he was a professor at the Univ. of Michigan Law School.... Ben Johnson of Canada shatters the world record in the 100-meter dash to win the gold medal at the World Track & Field Championships in a time of 9.83 seconds.	Aug. 30

F	G	H	I	J
Includes elections, federal-state relations, civil rights and liberties, crime, the judiciary, education, health care, poverty, urban affairs and population.	*Includes formation and debate of U.S. foreign and defense policies, veterans' affairs and defense spending. (Relations with specific foreign countries are usually found under the region concerned.)*	*Includes business, labor, agriculture, taxation, transportation, consumer affairs, monetary and fiscal policy, natural resources, and pollution.*	*Includes worldwide scientific, medical and technological developments, natural phenomena, U.S. weather, natural disasters, and accidents.*	*Includes the arts, religion, scholarship, communications media, sports, entertainments, fashions, fads and social life.*

	World Affairs	Europe	Africa & the Middle East	The Americas	Asia & the Pacific
Aug. 31		A Soviet military official hints that his country is willing to make a key, broad concession on nuclear test verification, but only if the United States agrees to negotiate a test ban. The statement comes from Col. Gen. Nikolai F. Chervov, the head of the arms control directorate of the Soviet general staff.	Iran begins responding to Iraq's stepped up aerial attacks, which began August 29, with speedboat attacks on Arab tankers and freighters.		South Korea's ruling and opposition parties agree on a draft of a new constitution that clears the way for the direct election of a new president. The agreement is reached against a background of mounting labor unrest and continuing agitation for democratic reform.
Sept. 1		West Germany's gross national product grew 1.5% in the second quarter of 1987 from the previous quarter, the Federal Statistics Office reports.... The Austrian government has reportedly convened a panel of six military historians to examine possible war crimes committed by Pres. Kurt Waldheim while in the German Army during World War II.		Mexico's Pres. Miguel de la Madrid gives his state of the nation address. The president says the government's economic austerity measures are beginning to succeed in bringing the nation out of its severest crisis in modern times.	
Sept. 2	The five permanent members of the UN Security Council—the United States, USSR, Britain, France, and China—approve a proposed peace mission to the Persian Gulf by Sec. Gen. Javier Perez de Cuellar for the following week.				
Sept. 3			The president of the tiny central African country of Burundi, Col. Jean-Baptiste Bagaza, is overthrown in a bloodless military coup while he is attending a summit of French-speaking nations in Canada.		
Sept. 4	The leaders and representatives of 37 French-speaking nations attend the second annual francophone summit held over three days in Quebec City, Canada. The summit is formally organized under the aegis of La Francophonie, a newly formed organization that is the French-speaking equivalent of the Commonwealth of Nations. The talks are dominated by the issue of Third World debt.	According to data compiled by the Central Statistical Office the average net wealth of private individuals in Britain increased nearly fourfold between 1976 and 1986, while the cost of living increased by a factor of just 2.4.... The Soviet Supreme Court in Moscow sentences Mathias Rust to four years in a labor camp. In May, the 19-year-old West German flew a light plane from Helsinki, Finland, to land in Moscow's Red Square.		Brazil's Pres. Jose Sarney announces that Brazilian scientists have succeeded in enriching uranium, but reaffirms his nation's commitment not to use the material to construct a nuclear bomb.... In Bangladesh, a week of devastating floods has left over 24 million people either homeless or without food. The floods are attributued to monsoon rains that fell in the northern high country in late July.	
Sept. 5			Kuwait expels five of seven Iranian diplomats amid reports that a total of three long-range surface-to-surface missiles, apparently Iranian, have been fired at Kuwait over the previous three days.		Burma's government demonetizes the national currency, the kyat, with the exception of small-denomination bank notes in a move that renders 80% of the currency valueless and disrupts Burma's economy.

A	B	C	D	E
Includes developments that affect more than one world region, international organizations and important meetings of major world leaders.	Includes all domestic and regional developments in Europe, including the Soviet Union, Turkey, Cyprus and Malta.	Includes all domestic and regional developments in Africa and the Middle East, including Iraq and Iran and excluding Cyprus, Turkey and Afghanistan.	Includes all domestic and regional developments in Latin America, the Caribbean and Canada.	Includes all domestic and regional developments in Asia and Pacific nations, extending from Afghanistan through all the Pacific Islands, except Hawaii.

U.S. Politics & Social Issues	U.S. Foreign Policy & Defense	U.S. Economy & Environment	Science, Technology & Nature	Culture, Leisure & Life Style	
The American Civil Liberties Union forsakes a long-standing neutrality policy and announces opposition to Pres. Reagan's nomination of Judge Robert H. Bork to the Supreme Court.		Prices received by farmers for their raw agricultural products declined 2.3% in August, according to the Agriculture Dept.		A federal judge in New York City dismisses a lawsuit brought against the General Services Admin. (GSA) by sculptor Richard Serra, who filed the suit in late 1986 to prevent removal of his controversial sculpture *Tilted Arc* from Federal Plaza in lower Manhattan and to collect $30 mil. in damages. The judge rules that "even if *Tilted Arc* is (free) speech," the artist's rights have to be "balanced against the authority and mission of the GSA," which owns the sculpture.	Aug. 31
An attempt by antiwar protesters to block the movement of arms at the Concord (Calif.) Naval Weapons Center ends in tragedy when a weapons train plows into a group of demonstrators, critically injuring S. Brian Willson, a 45-year-old Vietnam veteran and longtime peace activist. Willson was struck by the train, which dragged him 25 feet, fracturing his skull and severing his right leg below the knee. Surgeons later amputated his other leg below the knee.		Coca-Cola Co. announces that it plans to spin off its entertainment division, which includes Columbia Pictures Inc., and combine it with Tri-Star Pictures Inc., to create Columbia Pictures Entertainment Inc., in which it will retain a 49% stake.... The Labor Dept. issues new regulations to curb worker exposure to benzene, a cancer-causing derivative of petroleum. A federal study in 1976 showed a fivefold increase in the incidence of leukemia among workers exposed to the chemical.	The Food and Drug Admin. approves marketing of lovastatin, described as the most effective drug yet devised for lowering cholesterol in the bloodstream. High blood cholesterol levels have been linked with arterial disease and heart attacks, and an estimated 20 million Americans have cholesterol levels that put them at risk of heart attacks.	Pope John Paul II meets with nine Jewish leaders to hear their concerns over his recent audience with Austria's Pres. Kurt Waldheim and other issues. The Pope, acting to ease Jewish-Catholic tensions prior to a visit to the United States later in September, announces that the church is preparing an official document on the Holocaust and that the Jewish-Roman Catholic dialogue on sensitive issues will be reinvigorated.	Sept. 1
The Transportation Dept. orders major airlines to begin regular reporting of lost luggage and flight delays for the benefit of passengers.			Half the states in the United States have filed applications with the Energy Dept. to be the site of the largest atom smasher ever built; today is the deadline set by the Energy Dept. for such applications.	After decades of deliberate neglect by Soviet authorities, the art of the late Russian-born painter Marc Chagall, who died in 1985, is given a full-scale exhibition in his native land. More than 250 paintings, prints, and drawings drawn from private collections and from Soviet museum storerooms are exhibited at the Pushkin Museum in Moscow in a show marking the centenary of Chagall's birth.	Sept. 2
		Gary Strobel cuts down and destroys 14 young American elm trees that he has been using for genetic tests of altered microbes. Strobel, a plant pathologist at Montana State Univ., had injected the trees with genetically modified bacteria in an attempt to combat Dutch elm disease. Strobel was mildly disciplined by the Environmental Protection Agency for conducting the experiment, which introduced altered genes into the environment without approval.			Sept. 3
		The Federal Reserve Board raises the interest rate it charges on loans to financial institutions—the discount rate—to 6% from 5.5%. Major banks follow by increasing their prime rate to 8.75% from 8.25%.... The nation's unemployment rate was unchanged in August at 5.9%, the Labor Dept. says.... Outstanding consumer credit rose by a seasonally adjusted $3.46 bil. in July, the Federal Reserve Board says, at an annual rate of 7.1%.			Sept. 4
					Sept. 5

F	G	H	I	J
Includes elections, federal-state relations, civil rights and liberties, crime, the judiciary, education, health care, poverty, urban affairs and population.	Includes formation and debate of U.S. foreign and defense policies, veterans' affairs and defense spending. (Relations with specific foreign countries are usually found under the region concerned.)	Includes business, labor, agriculture, taxation, transportation, consumer affairs, monetary and fiscal policy, natural resources, and pollution.	Includes worldwide scientific, medical and technological developments, natural phenomena, U.S. weather, natural disasters, and accidents.	Includes the arts, religion, scholarship, communications media, sports, entertainments, fashions, fads and social life.

	World Affairs	Europe	Africa & the Middle East	The Americas	Asia & the Pacific
Sept. 6		Turks vote by the narrowest of margins to allow some 200 banned politicians, including two former premiers, to return to political activity. In a surprise move, Premier Turgut Ozal announces, before the results of the referendum are clear, that parliamentary elections will be held in November 1987, a year before they are due.	Chadian forces respond to Libya's retaking of the Aozou strip August 28 by crossing into Libya for the first time and razing Matan as Sarra, a key air base.	In Argentina, Pres. Raul Alfonsin's Radical Civic Union (UCR) suffers a major defeat in mid-term elections. The Justicialist Party (Peronists) take advantage of popular discontent with the government over the state of the economy to make a comeback.	
Sept. 7		Erich Honecker becomes the first East German head of state to visit West Germany. Honecker's five-day visit includes 12 hours of talks with West Germany's Chancellor Helmut Kohl. The talks produce only modest results, but the symbolism of the trip is widely regarded as setting the stage for improved relations between the two Germanys.	In Maputo, Mozambique, the Pretoria government frees 133 Angolan prisoners of war and two Europeans accused of aiding South african rebels in exchange for one South African soldier held by Angola.... A Libyan bomber is shot down by French forces as it tries to raid the Chadian capital of Ndjamena in response to yesterday's raid by Chad on a Libyan air base.	Reversing a recent decision to cut back oil supplies to Nicaragua, the Soviet Union agrees to provide the Sandinistas with an additional 100,000 tons of oil in 1987. The supply will carry Nicaragua through until the end of the year.	
Sept. 8				Chile's military government authorizes the return of 31 left-wing exiles as part of a program announced in December 1986.	
Sept. 9		Twenty-five British soccer fans are flown to Belgium to face charges related to 39 deaths during a riot at a soccer game in Brussels' Heysel Stadium in 1985.		Brazil scraps a controversial plan to gain debt relief by converting half the nation's $67 bil. commercial debt to discounted bonds. The plan, strongly opposed by commercial bankers and the Reagan administration, would have converted the $67 bil. in medium- and long-term debt to foreign banks into tradable, fixed-interest, below-market-rate bonds with a maturity of about 35 years.	Australia's P.M. Bob Hawke defends his plan to introduce a national identity card. Parliament twice rejected legislation to establish the card. Under the new plan, all Australians will be required to carry a so-called Australia Card. The card will have the owner's photograph and an ID number linked to a federal computerized data bank.
Sept. 10		Denmark's Premier Poul Schluter presents his new government to Queen Margrethe II. Schluter was given the mandate to form a new government despite setbacks for his four-party coalition in September 8 elections. Schluter's coalition will now hold only 70 seats in the 179-seat parliament.	Ethiopian strongman Lt. Col. Mengistu Haile Mariam is elected Ethiopia's first "civilian" president by the country's new parliament. The provisional military council which has governed the nation since the 1974 revolution is formally dissolved, and the government becomes a Soviet-style people's republic.		Four days of UN-mediated talks between Afghanistan and Pakistan end with no significant progress toward setting a timetable for the withdrawal of 115,000 Soviet troops from Afghanistan. Pakistan currently shelters more than 3 million Afghan refugees and is a major conduit for arms going to the Afghan rebels.

A	B	C	D	E
Includes developments that affect more than one world region, international organizations and important meetings of major world leaders.	Includes all domestic and regional developments in Europe, including the Soviet Union, Turkey, Cyprus and Malta.	Includes all domestic and regional developments in Africa and the Middle East, including Iraq and Iran and excluding Cyprus, Turkey and Afghanistan.	Includes all domestic and regional developments in Latin America, the Caribbean and Canada.	Includes all domestic and regional developments in Asia and Pacific nations, extending from Afghanistan through all the Pacific Islands, except Hawaii.

U.S. Politics & Social Issues	U.S. Foreign Policy & Defense	U.S. Economy & Environment	Science, Technology & Nature	Culture, Leisure & Life Style	
				In auto racing, Nelson Piquet of Brazil wins the Italian Grand Prix at Monza.... Stephen Roche of Ireland wins cycling's World Professional Road Championship in Austria.	Sept. 6
The Rev. Jesse Jackson, who came in third for the Democratic presidential nomination in 1984, declares that he will be a candidate for president in 1988. He becomes the sixth active and declared candidate in the Democratic field.					Sept. 7
A majority of an American Bar Assoc. panel rates Judge Robert H. Bork "well qualified" for the Supreme Court.... In a highly unusual public criticism of a sitting president from a member of the Supreme Court, Associate Justice Thurgood Marshall confirms that he told syndicated columnist Carl T. Rowan that Pres. Reagan ranks at "the bottom" of U.S. presidents in terms of rights for blacks.	According to testimony just released, Donald P. Gregg, a key adviser to the Vice Pres., George Bush knew as early as August 1986 that National Security Council staff member Lt. Col. Oliver L. North was helping provide weapons to the Nicaraguan Contras.... Three members of Congress returning from a surprise visit to a controversial Soviet radar facility question whether it is part of an elaborate system to guard against nuclear missile attacks as the Reagan administration has asserted in arguing for the Strategic Defense Initiative.				Sept. 8
The presidential advisory commission on acquired immune deficiency syndrome (AIDS) holds its first full-scale meeting in Washington, D.C. During the two-day meeting, the 13-member panel is briefed by federal AIDS officials from more than a dozen different departments and agencies. Citing reports that more and more doctors and other health workers are refusing to treat AIDS patients, Surgeon Gen. C. Everett Koop warns that "the ethical foundations of health care itself" are threatened by a "fearful and irrational minority."		The Federal Deposit Insurance Corp. (FDIC) agrees to provide $970 mil. to save the severely troubled First City Bancorp. of Houston. The bailout is the second-largest ever approved by the FDIC. ... Ford Motor Co. recalls 4.3 million cars, light trucks, and vans to correct a problem in their fuel systems that has produced 230 engine fires. The repair effort is not expected to be costly but could hurt Ford's effort to be seen as the industry leader in quality workmanship and innovative design.		The 44th Venice Film Festival awards its top prize, the Golden Lion, to French director Louis Malle's *Au Revoir, les Enfants* (So Long, Children).... *Variety*'s top-grossing films for the week are: *Stakeout*; *No Way Out*; *Dirty Dancing*; *The Big Easy*; and *The Fourth Protocol*.	Sept. 9
The Hispanic population has increased 30% since 1980, five times as fast as the rest of the population, the Census Bureau reports. Hispanics now total 18.8 million, or 7.9% of the U.S. population, according to the bureau, up 4.3 million from 1980.	Sec. of State George Shultz confirms that the Reagan administration plans to ask Congress for $270 mil. in aid for the Contras after current funding expires September 30. The $270 mil. is far more than the sum the administration had previously indicated it would request.	A federal judge refuses to lift regulations that prohibit regional telephone companies from providing long-distance service and manufacturing phone equipment. However, the so-called Baby Bells, spun off in the break-up of American Telephone & Telegraph Co., will be allowed to expand into the transmission of electronic information services.		Pope John Paul II arrives in Miami to begin a 10-day, nine-city tour of the United States. In addition to Miami, the Pope is to visit Columbia, S.C., New Orleans, San Antonio, Phoenix, Los Angeles, Monterey, Calif., San Francisco, and Detroit before going briefly to Canada.	Sept. 10

F	G	H	I	J
Includes elections, federal-state relations, civil rights and liberties, crime, the judiciary, education, health care, poverty, urban affairs and population.	*Includes formation and debate of U.S. foreign and defense policies, veterans' affairs and defense spending. (Relations with specific foreign countries are usually found under the region concerned.)*	*Includes business, labor, agriculture, taxation, transportation, consumer affairs, monetary and fiscal policy, natural resources, and pollution.*	*Includes worldwide scientific, medical and technological developments, natural phenomena, U.S. weather, natural disasters, and accidents.*	*Includes the arts, religion, scholarship, communications media, sports, entertainments, fashions, fads and social life.*

	World Affairs	Europe	Africa & the Middle East	The Americas	Asia & the Pacific
Sept. 11		France has the highest tax rates among the Group of Five nations, according to a report by the Org. for Economic Cooperation and Development. Taxes account for 45% of gross domestic product in France, compared with slightly less than 40% in West Germany and Britain and less than 30% in the United States and Japan.	Chad and Libya accept a cease-fire in their border war over the Aozou Strip. The pact is brokered by Zambia's Pres. Kenneth Kaunda, the chairman of the Org. of African Unity. The conflict escalated sharply in August and early September, and both sides have suffered heavy casualties.		
Sept. 12		Yugoslav Vice Pres. Hamdija Pozderac resigns from the government following the disclosure of a multimillion-dollar financial scandal in Yugoslavia.			
Sept. 13		In a surprise move, the Bank of Italy and the Italian government announce new measures to bolster the lira. The action comes after the central Bank of Italy was forced to spend an estimated $7 bil. in international currency markets to bolster the sagging currency in August and early September.			Residents of the French Pacific territory of New Caledonia vote overwhelmingly to retain their territorial ties to the French Republic. The results of the referendum, however, are condemned by the indigenous Kanak population, who seek independence, as well as by leaders in neighboring South Pacific states.
Sept. 14					
Sept. 15	The 42nd annual UN General Assembly opens. Peter Florin, 65, East Germany's deputy foreign minister, is unanimously elected to the one-year post of General Assembly president. He succeeds Humayun Rashid Choudhoury of Bangladesh.				

A	B	C	D	E
Includes developments that affect more than one world region, international organizations and important meetings of major world leaders.	Includes all domestic and regional developments in Europe, including the Soviet Union, Turkey, Cyprus and Malta.	Includes all domestic and regional developments in Africa and the Middle East, including Iraq and Iran and excluding Cyprus, Turkey and Afghanistan.	Includes all domestic and regional developments in Latin America, the Caribbean and Canada.	Includes all domestic and regional developments in Asia and Pacific nations, extending from Afghanistan through all the Pacific Islands, except Hawaii.

U.S. Politics & Social Issues	U.S. Foreign Policy & Defense	U.S. Economy & Environment	Science, Technology & Nature	Culture, Leisure & Life Style	
	The Senate begins floor debate on a $303 bil. FY1988 defense authorization bill. The House passed a $295 bil. defense authorization May 20.	The U.S. deficit on merchandise trade surged to $16.5 bil. in July, setting a new record and confounding expectations that the trade gap is stabilizing, the Commerce Dept. says. . . . The average interest rate on 30-year, conventional fixed-rate mortgages was 10.9% during the second week of September, the Federal Home Loan Mortgage Corp. reports, a full percentage point above the average a year ago.	The rate of cigarette smoking in the United States continued to decline in 1986, reaching an all-time low of 26.5% of adults, according to a survey by the federal Centers for Disease Control.	Peter Tosh, 42, reggae singer and founding member of Bob Marley's Wailers, the Jamaican group that popularized reggae internationally, is fatally shot by armed robbers at his home in Kingston, Jamaica. After leaving the Wailers in 1973, Tosh formed his own group. . . . Lorne Greene, 72, Canadian-born stage, screen and television actor, dies in Santa Monica, Calif., of pneumonia contracted after surgery for a perforated ulcer. Best known for his role as Ben Cartwright, patriarch of the Ponderosa ranch in NBC-TV's "Bonanza" (1959-73), as a radio news announcer for the Canadian Broadcasting Corp. during World War II, he was known as "the voice of Canada."	Sept. 11
The Rev. Marion G. (Pat) Robertson shook his Republican rivals with a well organized victory in an Iowa Republican straw poll. It follows a similar triumph in Michigan caucuses in 1986 and strong challenges to mainstream Republican organizations in other states such as South Carolina.				In tennis, Martina Navratilova wins the singles championship at the U.S. Open.	Sept. 12
				Singer Michael Jackson begins his first solo world tour, performing before a sold-out crowd of 38,000 packed into a Tokyo baseball stadium. . . . Mervyn LeRoy, 86, Hollywood director, dies in Beverly Hills, Calif.; he had Alzheimer's disease. His 75 films over 40 years included *Little Caesar* (1930), *Quo Vadis* (1951), *Waterloo Bridge* (1940), and *Mr. Roberts* (1955).	Sept. 13
The executive director of the presidential advisory commission on acquired immune deficiency syndrome, Linda Sheaffer, is ousted by commission chairman Dr. W. Eugene Mayberry.		RJR Nabisco Inc. says it has been developing a cigarette that will produce little smoke, no ash, and no tobacco smoke odor. . . . Transportation Sec. Elizabeth Hanford Dole submits her resignation, effective October 1, to join the presidential campaign of her husband, Sen. Robert J. Dole (R, Kans.).	A National Research Council panel cautions that a proposed U.S. project to build a space station would be difficult, dangerous, and much more costly than presented thus far. A council committee concludes after a four-month study that the design of the project is "reasonable" on a short-term basis but that a longer-range purpose should be ascertained before the commitment is made to initiate the project.	Ivan Lendl wins the men's singles tennis championship at the U.S. Open. . . . Kaye Lani Rae Rafko, 24, is crowned Miss America in Atlantic City, N.J. Rafko, who competed as Miss Michigan, is a registered nurse. . . . Soviet-affairs scholar James H. Billington, 58, is sworn in as the 13th Librarian of Congress, succeeding social historian Daniel J. Boorstin, 72. . . . A.C. Nielsen Co. scraps its 20-year-old "diary-meter" system of determining U.S. television show ratings and begins to rely exclusively on its new audience-measuring method known as "people meters."	Sept. 14
The Senate Judiciary Committee launches its hearings on the nomination of Judge Robert H. Bork to the Supreme Court. In his testimony, Bork describes his judicial philosophy as within the mainstream of the current court. . . . An arbitration panel orders International Business Machines (IBM) Corp. and Fujitsu Ltd. to share a vast amount of crucial software that IBM has developed. The order settles a bitter, secret five-year dispute between the two companies.	Reacting to "terrorism committed and supported by organizations and individuals affiliated with the PLO," the State Dept. announces that it has ordered the Palestine Information Office in Washington, D.C., to close within 30 days.	The U.S. balance of payments on current account rose in the second quarter to a record deficit of $41.1 bil., the Commerce Dept. says. . . . The Federal Reserve Board reports that its industrial production index rose just 0.3% in August.	An Ariane-3 rocket successfully launches two telecommunications satellites into orbit from Kourou, French Guiana. The launch by the European Space Agency is its first since the failure of a blast-off in May 1986, 16 months ago.		Sept. 15

F	G	H	I	J
Includes elections, federal-state relations, civil rights and liberties, crime, the judiciary, education, health care, poverty, urban affairs and population.	*Includes formation and debate of U.S. foreign and defense policies, veterans' affairs and defense spending. (Relations with specific foreign countries are usually found under the region concerned.)*	*Includes business, labor, agriculture, taxation, transportation, consumer affairs, monetary and fiscal policy, natural resources, and pollution.*	*Includes worldwide scientific, medical and technological developments, natural phenomena, U.S. weather, natural disasters, and accidents.*	*Includes the arts, religion, scholarship, communications media, sports, entertainments, fashions, fads and social life.*

	World Affairs	Europe	Africa & the Middle East	The Americas	Asia & the Pacific
Sept. 16	A UN special panel chaired by former U.S. Attorney Gen. Elliot L. Richardson, issues a report on the world body's ability to deal with international crises. The report concedes that the UN has often failed in its response to crises around the world.	France's Finance Min. Edouard Balladur presents the government's budget for 1988. Balladur's plan seeks to reduce both the budget deficit and income tax rates. . . . Arthur Christopher John Lord Soames, 66, British soldier and diplomat, dies in Hampshire, England, following surgery for an abdominal obstruction. Married to Mary Churchill in 1947, he held office under five Conservative prime ministers.	UN Sec. Gen. Javier Perez de Cuellar returns to New York after visits to Iran and Iraq in a bid to end the seven-year-old Persian Gulf war. There is little indication that his mission was successful. . . . After observing a tacit truce while UN Sec. Gen. Javier Perez de Cuellar was in the region, Iraq resumes air raids on Iranian industrial targets and oil tankers, and Iran responds with attacks of its own.	In the wake of the ruling Radical Civic Union's defeat in mid-term elections September 6, Argentina's Pres. Raul Alfonsin announces replacements for five of the eight ministers whose resignations he accepted.	North Korea and its Western creditor banks reach agreement on rescheduling the nation's unpaid foreign debt. A group of 140 Western commercial banks August 17 notified North Korea that it was in formal default on $770 mil. in outstanding loans.
Sept. 17	Vietnam applies to establish diplomatic relations with the European Community.	Albania and West Germany agree to establish diplomatic relations. Earlier in the year, Albania established diplomatic ties with Canada, Spain, and Bolivia, and formally ended its 40-year-old state of war with Greece. . . . Unemployment in Britain fell in August to the lowest level in more than four years, the Employment Dept. reports. The decline in joblessness in August is the 14th consecutive monthly drop.		The Canadian Auto Workers union ends a two-day strike against Chrysler Canada Ltd., a unit of Chrysler Corp. of the United States. . . . Foreign ministers from Costa Rica, El Salvador, Guatemala, Honduras, and Nicaragua hold talks with representatives from the Contadora Group, the Org. of American States, and the UN, and agree to the creation of committees to supervise various aspects of the Central American peace accord.	France's Premier Jacques Chirac visits New Caledonia and calls for talks between the French territory's indigenous Kanaks and the Caldoches of European heritage. . . . Philippine Pres. Corazon Aquino caps a week of government reorganization when she removes her closest adviser, Executive Sec. Joker Arroyo. The military has pressed for the removal of Arroyo.
Sept. 18		Pres. Reagan announces that the United States and Soviet Union have tentatively agreed on a treaty for the global elimination of medium-range nuclear missiles. Neither the United States nor the Soviet Union gives specific details of the tentative accord.		Venezuela reaches agreement with its bank creditors on the rescheduling of $20.34 bil. of its estimated $35 bil. foreign debt.	
Sept. 19		Hungary's parliament debates additional steps in the national austerity plan instituted in July. At the end of the four-day session, new measures, including a value-added tax, are approved.			
Sept. 20				Costa Rica's Pres. Oscar Arias Sanchez begins an eight-day visit to the United States to promote the Central American peace accord signed in August. . . . The Nicaraguan government announces that the opposition newspaper *La Prensa* can resume publishing immediately, free of censorship.	
Sept. 21	The period of general debate at the 42nd UN General Assembly begins with a series of addresses by world leaders and foreign ministers. The speeches focus chiefly on the Persian Gulf crisis and arms control.	Britain's gross domestic product (GDP), adjusted for inflation and seasonal variations, was 3.7% higher in the second quarter of 1987 than in the second quarter of 1986, according to an average measure by the Central Statistics Office. By the same measure GDP was up 0.5% from the first quarter of 1987.	South Africa's Pres. Pieter Botha says his government, which is suspected of having nuclear weapons capabilities, is prepared to sign the Nuclear Nonproliferation Treaty. Pretoria has previously refused to join the accord, which has been signed by 134 nations. . . . American forces seize an Iranian naval vessel that is allegedly laying mines in the Persian Gulf.	Bolivia will lose $8.7 mil. in U.S. aid because of its failure to substantially reduce the nation's coca crop, the State Dept. says. In 1986 Congress set coca crop eradication requirements as a condition for U.S. aid.	

A	B	C	D	E
Includes developments that affect more than one world region, international organizations and important meetings of major world leaders.	*Includes all domestic and regional developments in Europe, including the Soviet Union, Turkey, Cyprus and Malta.*	*Includes all domestic and regional developments in Africa and the Middle East, including Iraq and Iran and excluding Cyprus, Turkey and Afghanistan.*	*Includes all domestic and regional developments in Latin America, the Caribbean and Canada.*	*Includes all domestic and regional developments in Asia and Pacific nations, extending from Afghanistan through all the Pacific Islands, except Hawaii.*

U.S. Politics & Social Issues	U.S. Foreign Policy & Defense	U.S. Economy & Environment	Science, Technology & Nature	Culture, Leisure & Life Style	
U.S. District Judge Russell Clark orders an increase in property and income taxes to pay for improvements designed to erase racial discrimination in the Kansas City, Mo., school system.		The House approves by a vote of 263 to 156 a measure aimed at protecting the U.S. textile, apparel, and shoe industries. The margin by which the bill passed will not be sufficient to override an almost certain veto by Pres. Reagan.	Representatives of 24 countries sign a treaty designed to preserve the protective ozone layer in the Earth's atmosphere by reducing the production of chlorofluorocarbons, ozone-destroying chemicals with a variety of industrial uses as refrigerants, aerosol propellants, and solvents.	Johannesburg's Market Theater, a showcase for multiracial drama in South Africa since its founding in 1976, introduces the first professional South African production of William Shakespeare's *Othello* with a black in the title role, John Kani, winner of a 1975 Tony Award for his Broadway role in Athol Fugard's *Sizwe Banzi Is Dead*.	Sept. 16
The House of Representatives approves $1.2 bil. in reparations for the 66,000 Japanese-Americans held in detention centers in World War II and still living.... Philadelphia holds a 15-hour gala celebration for the bicentennial of the signing of the U.S. Constitution. Pres. Reagan delivers the keynote address at Independence Hall.	Fawaz Younis, a suspected Lebanese Shiite Moslem terrorist, is arraigned in U.S. District Court in Washington, D.C., on charges of having led the hijacking of a Jordanian airliner in 1985. Fawaz was flown to the United States after being arrested in international waters in the Mediterranean by agents of the Federal Bureau of Investigation.	A midway accounting of a $300 mil., 10-year research effort by the Reagan administration's National Acid Precipitation Assessment Program says relatively few U.S. lakes and streams have become acidified and damage to crops, forests, and human health is negligible.... Ford Motor Co. and the United Auto Workers (UAW) union tentatively agree on a new three-year contract that guarantees employment for Ford's 104,000 UAW workers.		The International Olympic Committee (IOC) sends invitations to 167 nations to join in the 1988 Summer Olympic Games in Seoul, South Korea. IOC president Juan Antonio Samaranch says that IOC officials have won "assurances" that Soviet-bloc athletes will not boycott the games. The question of a boycott arose over demands by North Korea to host some of the events at the games.	Sept. 17
	Defense Sec. Caspar W. Weinberger approves six preliminary tests of antiballistic missile components related to the Strategic Defense Initiative ("Star Wars").		U.S. space agency officials report that the recent test-firing of the redesigned space shuttle booster rocket was completely successful. A crack found in the steel casing of the rocket after the test and reported September 4 was attributed to the failure of a water spray system used to cool the rocket after the test firing. In an actual blast-off, the rocket cools itself during its drop-off into the ocean.	*Fatal Attraction*, a movie about a casual extramarital fling with murderous consequences, is released in New York. The film, directed by Adrian Lyne, stars Michael Douglas, Glenn Close, and Anne Archer. ... *Sarcophagus*, a play about the 1986 Chernobyl nuclear disaster set in a ward for terminal radiation patients, opens simultaneously at the Yale Repertory Theater in New Haven, Conn., and at the Los Angeles Theater Center. Written by Vladimir Gubaryev, the play is directed by David Chambers and stars David Brisbin and Betty Miller.	Sept. 18
Teachers in Detroit ratify a new three-year contract, ending a 20-day walkout. The school system's 190,000 pupils return to classes September 22.... Judge Robert H. Bork concludes an unprecedented five days of testimony before the Senate Judiciary Committee by reaffirming his belief that his role as a Supreme Court justice would be "to interpret the law and not make it."				*Billboard*'s best-selling albums for the week are: *La Bamba* (soundtrack); *Whitney*, Whitney Houston; *Whitesnake*, Whitesnake; *Hysteria*, Def Leppard; and *Bad Animals*, Heart.	Sept. 19
		Forbes magazine releases its first list of foreign billionaires. Heading the list is Yoshiaki Tsutsumi, the head of Japan's Seibu Railway Group, and worth an estimated $20 bil. Yesterday *Fortune* magazine released a rival list that differs considerably from the *Forbes* list. Heading the *Fortune* list is the sultan of Brunei, Sir Mudah Hassanal Bolkiah, who *Fortune* says is worth $25 bil.		At the 39th annual Emmy Awards, the award for best comedy series goes to "The Golden Girls"; outstanding drama series, "L.A. Law"; best miniseries, "A Year in the Life"; "Promise" wins for best comedy or drama special. The awards for best lead actor and actress in a drama series go to Bruce Willis, "Moonlighting," and Sharon Gless, "Cagney & Lacey;" for best actor and actress in a comedy series, to Michael J. Fox, "Family Ties," and Rue McClanahan, "The Golden Girls."	Sept. 20
Illinois's Gov. James R. Thompson (R) signs into law a broad range of bills aimed at fighting acquired immune deficiency syndrome (AIDS), thus becoming the first U.S. governor to approve sweeping AIDS legislation.	A report by the Senate Foreign Relations Committee cautions the Reagan administration against attempting to unilaterally reinterpret the 1972 antiballistic missile treaty. Pres. Reagan in May sent Congress two legal studies purporting to show that the United States could legally adopt a broad interpretation of the treaty that would facilitate plans for an early deployment of the Strategic Defense Initiative.	Car purchases helped pushed consumer spending up 1.5% in August, while personal income rose 0.5%, the Commerce Dept. says.	The recipients of the 1987 Albert Lasker Medical Research Awards are molecular biologists Susumu Tonegawa of the Massachusetts Inst. of Technology, Dr. Philip Leder of the Harvard Medical School, and Dr. Leroy Hood of the California Inst. of Technology, and psychiatrist Dr. Mogens Schou, director of psychopharmacology research at Aarhus Univ. Psychiatric Institute in Riskov, Denmark.	An arbitrator for Major League baseball rules that team owners conspired against free agent players following the 1985 season. The arbitrator sustained a grievance brought by the Major League Players Assoc. claiming that the owners violated a section of Article XVIII of the 1976 basic agreement, which reads "Clubs shall not act in concert with other clubs" on the issue of free agency.	Sept. 21

F	G	H	I	J
Includes elections, federal-state relations, civil rights and liberties, crime, the judiciary, education, health care, poverty, urban affairs and population.	*Includes formation and debate of U.S. foreign and defense policies, veterans' affairs and defense spending. (Relations with specific foreign countries are usually found under the region concerned.)*	*Includes business, labor, agriculture, taxation, transportation, consumer affairs, monetary and fiscal policy, natural resources, and pollution.*	*Includes worldwide scientific, medical and technological developments, natural phenomena, U.S. weather, natural disasters, and accidents.*	*Includes the arts, religion, scholarship, communications media, sports, entertainments, fashions, fads and social life.*

	World Affairs	Europe	Africa & the Middle East	The Americas	Asia & the Pacific
Sept. 22				Nicaragua's Pres. Daniel Ortega Saavedra formally announces that the government is preparing to declare a unilateral cease-fire in unspecified areas of the country. The announcement marks the latest in a series of steps taken by the government to comply with the Central American peace plan signed in Guatemala in August. Under the plan, democratic reforms are to be in place by November 7.	The strikes and unrest that have beset South Korean business and industry since July had less of an effect on the economy than was originally forecast, according to trade figures released by the Bank of Korea. Exports in August were up 20% from a year earlier, and the nation's current account surplus for the month was $468 mil., down $100 mil. from August 1986.
Sept. 23				Leftist rebels in El Salvador agree to meet with the government October 4 to begin negotiations on peace. A spokesman for the Democratic Revolutionary Front, the political arm of the rebel movement, says the rebels want to negotiate a cease-fire.... Canada abruptly breaks off talks with the United States on a comprehensive trade agreement. The two sides have been struggling since May 1986 to meet a U.S. congressional deadline on having an agreement in place by Oct. 5, 1987.	
Sept. 24		French and West German troops conclude five days of joint war games in West Germany. The exercise symbolizes growing military cooperation between the two nations.... France's Finance Min. Edouard Balladur announces the government's plan to sell its holdings in four state-controlled companies with a total market value of about $16 bil.... The average prison population in England and Wales during 1986 was a record 46,900, up from 46,300 in 1985, according to a Prison Service report.	Zimbabwe's Finance Min. Bernard Chidzero discloses that, faced with mounting economic woes, African nations are considering freezing interest payments on their combined $180 bil. foreign debt. He says a proposal on the subject has been drafted by a 15-nation steering committee and will be considered at a meeting of the Org. of African Unity in December.		
Sept. 25		West Germany's trade surplus hit a two-year low in August, the government reports. The smaller August surplus of $3.57 bil. will help West German officials argue at the upcoming international economic meetings that their economy does not need further stimulation.		Brazil presents a new plan to reschedule its foreign debt, but the proposal is given a cool reception by Brazil's leading international bank creditors.	Indian and Pakistani troops clash over two days in the disputed border area of Kashmir, Indian military officials announce. The officials say a Pakistani battalion attempted to dislodge Indian troops from the strategic Siachen Glacier but was repulsed and lost 150 men. The Indian military does not release its own casualty figures. Pakistan has no comment on the Indian report. The two countries have clashed in three wars since 1947.
Sept. 26			Egypt's Pres. Hosni Mubarak and France's Premier Jacques Chirac inaugurate the Cairo Metro, Africa's first subway. Modeled after the famous Paris Metro, the project cost more than $400 mil., most of it financed with long-term, easy-credit loans from the French government. It was built by a consortium of 17 French companies, which began construction in 1982.	The Nicaraguan government continues to make moves to comply with the terms of the Central American peace plan signed in Guatemala in August. It opens the border with Honduras to allow reunions between families separated by the war.	

A	B	C	D	E
Includes developments that affect more than one world region, international organizations and important meetings of major world leaders.	*Includes all domestic and regional developments in Europe, including the Soviet Union, Turkey, Cyprus and Malta.*	*Includes all domestic and regional developments in Africa and the Middle East, including Iraq and Iran and excluding Cyprus, Turkey and Afghanistan.*	*Includes all domestic and regional developments in Latin America, the Caribbean and Canada.*	*Includes all domestic and regional developments in Asia and Pacific nations, extending from Afghanistan through all the Pacific Islands, except Hawaii.*

U.S. Politics & Social Issues	U.S. Foreign Policy & Defense	U.S. Economy & Environment	Science, Technology & Nature	Culture, Leisure & Life Style	
Rep. Mario Biaggi (D, N.Y.), the senior member of New York City's congressional delegation, is convicted of federal charges involving illegal gratuities, but is acquitted of more serious counts of bribery and conspiracy. His codefendant, Meade Esposito, the former Democratic leader of the Brooklyn borough of New York City, is also acquitted of bribery and conspiracy.		The increase in the Dow Jones Industrial Average on this day, 75.23 points, is the highest on record, surpassing the previous record one-day increase of 69.89 points, set April 3.		The National Football League Players Assoc. goes on strike after the second week of regular season games. The players' general agreement with the owners expired at the end of August, and the players set today's strike deadline on September 7. The primary dispute between the parties is the issue of free agency, the ability of a player to change teams without restriction once his contract with a particular team has expired.	Sept. 22
Sen. Joseph R. Biden Jr. (Del.) drops out of the race for the 1988 Democratic presidential nomination following revelations that he had overstated his academic credentials, relied on the unattributed use of other politicians' speeches—notably those of British Labour Party chief Neil Kinnock—and been penalized in a plagiarism incident in law school.	The House of Representatives approves $3.5 mil. in nonlethal aid to the Nicaraguan Contras for a 40-day period beginning October 1. The compromise aid amendment was negotiated by House Speaker Jim C. Wright, Jr. (D, Tex.) and House minority leader Robert Michel (R, Ill.).	Antitrust officials from the Justice Dept. urge disapproval of a joint operating agreement between Detroit's two major newspapers, the *Detroit News* and the *Detroit Free Press*. . . . Setrag Mooradian, former chief accountant for a company controlled by arbitrager Ivan F. Boesky, reportedly receives immunity from prosecution in exchange for his help in the Securities and Exchange Comm.'s probe of insider trading. . . . The House approves a spending bill to keep the federal government funded through November 20.		Bob (Robert Louis) Fosse, 60, Broadway director and choreographer, dies of a heart attack in Washington, D.C., just as a revival of *Sweet Charity* is opening at the National Theater. One of the most honored directors on Broadway, in 1973 he won two Tony awards for *Pippin*, an Oscar for the film version of *Cabaret*, and an Emmy award for a television special. . . . *Publishers Weekly*'s hardback fiction bestsellers for the week are: *Presumed Innocent*, Scott Turow; *Patriot Games*, Tom Clancy; *Legacy*, James Michener; *Sarum*, Edward Rutherford; and *Misery*, Stephen King.	Sept. 23
The *Washington Post* reports that over the past two years House Speaker James C. Wright Jr. (D, Tex.) has received almost $55,000 in royalties on a book published by a longtime friend who gave Wright $3.25 for every $5.95 copy sold, more than five times the conventional royalty rate. Under a provision of House ethics rules that Wright himself suggested in 1977, royalties are not counted against members' outside-earnings limits.				Mary Astor (born Lucile Langhanke), 81, actress who made her screen debut at age 14 in the silent film era and went on to make more than 100 films over more than four decades, dies of complications of emphysema in Woodland Hills, Calif. Best remembered as the treacherous heroine of John Huston's *The Maltese Falcon* (1941), in 1949 she was placed in a sanatorium for alcoholics. She later resumed her acting career and launched a second career as a writer.	Sept. 24
The Senate votes, 90-0, to confirm William S. Sessions as director of the Federal Bureau of Investigation.	According to *U.S. News & World Report*, Bob Woodward's forthcoming *Veil: The Secret Wars of the CIA, 1981-1987* says the late Central Intelligence Agency director William J. Casey confessed from his death bed to having known about the diversion of Iran arms sales profits to the Nicaraguan Contra rebels. . . . Congress declines to extend a six-year waiver exempting Pakistan from U.S. nuclear proliferation restrictions.		(George) Emlyn Williams, 81, Welsh actor and playwright who wrote many hit plays, including *Night Must Fall* (1935) and *The Corn Is Green* (1938), both of which he starred in, dies in London, after cancer surgery. Later in his career, he did notable solo performances of the works of Charles Dickens and Dylan Thomas, and he also appeared in a number of films.	In a moot court set up in a Washington, D.C., church, a three-member panel of Supreme Court associate justices rules unanimously that the plays and sonnets attributed to William Shakespeare were actually written by Shakespeare, and not by Edward de Vere, the 17th Earl of Oxford. The justices, William J. Brennan Jr., Harry A. Blackmun, and John Paul Stevens, issue their ruling after hearing competing arguments for Shakespeare and de Vere from two American Univ. law professors.	Sept. 25
					Sept. 26

F	G	H	I	J
Includes elections, federal-state relations, civil rights and liberties, crime, the judiciary, education, health care, poverty, urban affairs and population.	Includes formation and debate of U.S. foreign and defense policies, veterans' affairs and defense spending. (Relations with specific foreign countries are usually found under the region concerned.)	Includes business, labor, agriculture, taxation, transportation, consumer affairs, monetary and fiscal policy, natural resources, and pollution.	Includes worldwide scientific, medical and technological developments, natural phenomena, U.S. weather, natural disasters, and accidents.	Includes the arts, religion, scholarship, communications media, sports, entertainments, fashions, fads and social life.

	World Affairs	Europe	Africa & the Middle East	The Americas	Asia & the Pacific
Sept. 27				Soldiers based on the outskirts of Buenos Aires, Argentina, lock themselves in their barracks to protest the replacement of their commander Lt. Col. Dario Fernandez Maguer, who in April refused to help put down a rebellion by army officers supporting a colleague summoned to face human rights abuse charges.	
Sept. 28			Mehdi Hashemi, a Shiite Moslem cleric who helped expose the secret U.S. arms sales to Iran, is executed by firing squad in Teheran, according to the official Iranian news agency. Hasehemi, a key aide to the designated successor to Iran's Ayatollah Ruhollah Khomeini, was tried and convicted in mid-August of "corruption on Earth," the most serious crime under Iran's system of Islamic law.		India and Sri Lanka's most powerful Tamil guerrilla group, the Liberation Tigers of Tamil Eelam, agree to an accord that gives the Tigers a majority on the council that will administer the semi-autonomous northern and eastern provinces of Sri Lanka.
Sept. 29	The World Bank and the International Monetary Fund hold their annual joint meeting in Washington, D.C. The conferees agree to increase the capital of the World Bank and consider a proposal to stabilize currency exchange rates by linking them to an index of commodity prices. Various approaches to the Third World debt crisis are also discussed, with no apparent resolution.			Peru's Congress approves a controversial law to nationalize the nation's financial system. The law will place under state control Peru's 10 banks, 17 insurance companies, and six finance companies.	Australia's P.M. Bob Hawke drops his plan to introduce a national identity card after opposition parties find a technicality enabling them to block the legislation in the Senate. The so-called Australia Card, which has been rejected twice by parliament, is intended to help reduce tax evasion and welfare cheating. Critics oppose the plan as an invasion of privacy.
Sept. 30		The Soviet Union flight tests an intercontinental ballistic missile (ICBM) that ends with a splashdown of the missile's dummy warheads about 500 miles northwest of the Hawaiian Islands. The missile, an upgraded version of the SS-18 ICBM, is launched from Tyuratam, in central Siberia. The target site is closer to U.S. soil than in any previous Soviet test.		Nicaragua's Pres. Daniel Ortega Saavedra announces that at midnight, October 6, Sandinista troops will begin withdrawing from some 1,500 square miles of territory in northern Jinotega and Nueva Segovia provinces and in Nueva Guinea in central Nicaragua. . . . In Ecuador, the government says it has temporarily suspended oil exploration in the Aguarico region of the Amazon, where members of the primitive Red Feet tribe of Huaorani, or Auca (killer) Indians, killed two missionaries, the Roman Catholic bishop of Aguarico and a nun, in July.	
Oct. 1		Soviet leader Mikhail S. Gorbachev calls for talks between the Warsaw Pact and North Atlantic Treaty Org. on a "military detente" in Europe's northern seas. Speaking in the Soviet's Arctic port city of Murmansk, the general secretary urges a curtailment of military activity in the Baltic, North, Greenland, and Norwegian seas.		Nicaragua's opposition newspaper *La Prensa* resumespublishing after a 15-month ban. . . . The electoral commission in Suriname says that 93.8% of the ballots from a September 30 referendum favor a new constitution, which will clear the way for elections in November. The National Assembly approved the draft constitution in March.	

A	B	C	D	E
Includes developments that affect more than one world region, international organizations and important meetings of major world leaders.	Includes all domestic and regional developments in Europe, including the Soviet Union, Turkey, Cyprus and Malta.	Includes all domestic and regional developments in Africa and the Middle East, including Iraq and Iran and excluding Cyprus, Turkey and Afghanistan.	Includes all domestic and regional developments in Latin America, the Caribbean and Canada.	Includes all domestic and regional developments in Asia and Pacific nations, extending from Afghanistan through all the Pacific Islands, except Hawaii.

U.S. Politics & Social Issues	U.S. Foreign Policy & Defense	U.S. Economy & Environment	Science, Technology & Nature	Culture, Leisure & Life Style	
	According to an account of the origins of the Iran arms scandal by Michael Ledeen, in its eagerness to win the release of U.S. hostages held in Lebanon, the Reagan administration preferred a straight arms-for-hostages trade and ignored a genuine opportunity to establish friendly contact in Iran. Ledeen is a former consultant to the National Security Council whose extensive contacts in the Middle East were influential in the early arms transactions with Iran.			For the first time in the history of the 60-year-old biennial Ryder Cup, a team of European golfers wins the event in the United States. The European team outscored the U.S. team, 15-13, in the three-day match-play competition.	Sept. 27
Rep. Patricia Schroeder (D, Colo.) announces that she will not enter the race for the Democratic presidential nomination in 1988.... The U.S. First Circuit Court of Appeals rescinds a landmark 1974 district court ruling ordering the use of racial guidelines in assigning students to Boston's schools. The panel indicates that the Boston School Committee is in compliance with desegregation standards set in 1974.					Sept. 28
	The Senate votes, 98-0, for a ban on all American imports from Iran. The unanimous vote comes amid a continuing congressional dispute over the Reagan administration's policy in the Persian Gulf and follows news reports that U.S. purchases of Iranian oil have climbed dramatically in recent months.	Pres. Reagan reluctantly signs into law a bill that will impose automatic reductions in federal spending if Congress and the president cannot reach annual targets set out in the legislation. Reagan says he is signing the bill only because it is attached to a measure raising the nation's debt ceiling.... Henry Ford II, 70, industrialist who led the automobile company founded by his grandfather and namesake from 1945 to 1970, dies in Detroit of pneumonia complicated by kidney failure and a blood infection. After the 1967 Detroit race riots, Ford supported the hiring of blacks and masterminded the construction of the Renaissance Center, a massive redevelopment project.		The third Grawemeyer Award, for musical composition, is formally presented to British composer Harrison Birtwistle at a special concert in his honor at the Univ. of Louisville, in Kentucky.	Sept. 29
The presidential campaign of Massachusetts Gov. Michael S. Dukakis (D) is jolted when his two top aides, John Sasso and Paul Tully, resign after acknowledging they provided reporters with a videotape that derailed the candidacy of Democratic rival Sen. Joseph R. Biden Jr. (Del.).	A report to Congress by the congressional Office of Technology Assessment concludes that a large-scale study of the effects of Agent Orange on ground troops in Vietnam cannot be conducted because too few troops were exposed to the toxic chemical, according to a New York Times report.	The government's index of leading economic indicators rose 0.6% in August, the Commerce Dept. reports.... Prices received by farmers for their raw agricultural products rose 1.6% in September, the Agriculture Dept. reports.... Pres. Reagan signs stopgap continuing appropriation that will fund government activities through November 10. The measure was approved by the House September 23 and by the Senate September 25 as it became apparent that the gulf between Pres. Reagan and Congress over spending priorities could not be bridged in the time remaining in the fiscal year.	Depletion of the protective ozone layer in the atmosphere over Antarctica is the worst recorded since measurements began in the 1970s, researchers report.		Sept. 30
From the steps of a tenement in the Bedford-Stuyvesant neighborhood of Brooklyn, N.Y., the Rev. Marion G. (Pat) Robertson, a Southern Baptist television evangelist, announces his bid for the Republican presidential nomination. Robertson says there is a need for the nation to "restore fundamental moral values."		The House authorizes $18.6 bil. in spending for airport and air traffic control improvements over the next five years.... Fiscal 1988 begins without enactment of any of the 13 appropriation bills needed to fund the federal government's activities.	A severe earthquake rocks the Los Angeles area causing at least six deaths (including at least three from heart attacks) and dozens of injuries. Measuring 6.1 on the Richter scale, the quake strikes at 7:42 a.m. At least 16 aftershocks measuring 3.0 or more on the Richter scale are felt in the next three hours.		Oct. 1

F	G	H	I	J
Includes elections, federal-state relations, civil rights and liberties, crime, the judiciary, education, health care, poverty, urban affairs and population.	Includes formation and debate of U.S. foreign and defense policies, veterans' affairs and defense spending. (Relations with specific foreign countries are usually found under the region concerned.)	Includes business, labor, agriculture, taxation, transportation, consumer affairs, monetary and fiscal policy, natural resources, and pollution.	Includes worldwide scientific, medical and technological developments, natural phenomena, U.S. weather, natural disasters, and accidents.	Includes the arts, religion, scholarship, communications media, sports, entertainments, fashions, fads and social life.

	World Affairs	Europe	Africa & the Middle East	The Americas	Asia & the Pacific
Oct. 2		An international tribunal orders France to pay $8.1 mil. in damages to Greenpeace for its controversial sinking of the environmental group's ship *Rainbow Warrior* in New Zealand's Auckland harbor in 1985.	Lloyd's of London says that a total of 375 vessels have been damaged or attacked by either Iraq or Iran since the Persian Gulf war began in 1980; 107 of the incidents have occurred thus far in 1987. Iraq is thought responsible for most of the attacks. Lloyd's estimates that its insurance companies have paid more than $1.65 bil. in damages since the war began. . . . Tunisia's autocratic and pro-Western Pres. Habib Bourguiba fires his premier and designated successor, who has been in office for little over a year, and replaces him with an army general.	Five Central American vice presidents sign an accord agreeing to the creation of a Central American parliament, as provided for in the regional peace plan signed in August. Under the plan Guatemala, Costa Rica, Honduras, Nicaragua, and El Salvador will each have 20 delegates to the parliament, representing different political parties. The parliament will meet for one month each year in Guatemala City.	Japan's Defense Dir. Gen. Yuko Kurihara announces that Japan is dropping a plan to design and build a new jet fighter plane. Instead, he says, Japan will make multiple purchases of a modified version of one of two U.S. planes.
Oct. 3		Vice Pres. George Bush concludes a high-profile visit to Poland and five members of the North Atlantic Treaty Org. (NATO). Bush reassures NATO leaders that a U.S.-Soviet treaty eliminating medium-range nuclear missiles will in no way lessen America's commitment to defend Western Europe. . . . The Soviet Union opens a top-secret chemical weapons complex at Shikhany to an informal inspection by visitors from 45 countries.		The United States and Canada reach agreement on a comprehensive bilateral trade pact, subject to approval by the U.S. Congress and the Canadian parliament. . . . Miskito Indian leader Uriel Vanegas announces that his group has agreed to end its fight against the Nicaraguan government. Appearing with Nicaraguan Interior Min. Tomas Borge, Vanegas says he is not surrendering but that his group will "support the Sandinista project if it defends Indian rights."	
Oct. 4				Ending months of intense speculation, Mexico's ruling Institutional Revolutionary Party (PRI) names Planning and Budget Min. Carlos Salinas de Gortari as its candidate to run for the presidency in the July 1988 election.	
Oct. 5		In Romania, Ion Dinca, a first deputy premier, informs a plenary session of the Communist Party Central Committee that Romania is in a state of energy emergency. Romania has undergone severe energy shortages every year since 1982. Under the last state of emergency, declared in 1985, military units were assigned to run half of the country's power stations.	Egypt's Pres. Hosni Mubarak is reelected to a second six-year term in an unopposed referendum.		The Chinese Air Force shoots down a Vietnamese fighter plane that entered Chinese air space, the official New China News Agency reports. The report maintains that the Vietnamese plane, a MiG-21, flew 20 miles into Chinese territory, over Guangxi Zhuang Autonomous Region in southern China.
Oct. 6	Japanese and U.S. officials say that Japan will help develop and pay for a new "precision navigation" system to help ships of all nations avoid mines in the region in the Persian Gulf. Japan has also pledged to increase its foreign aid to some Arab governments and assume a greater share of the cost of supporting the U.S. military presence in Japan.			Twenty hours of talks between leftist rebels and the Salvadoran government produce an agreement to form two commissions to negotiate a cease-fire and execute other terms of the Guatemala peace plan signed August 7. . . . Nicaraguan troops begin withdrawing from war zones in three provinces in preparation for a cease-fire that goes into effect tomorrow. Contra leaders say they will not respect the cease-fire, declared unilaterally by the government. . . . Brazil's foreign ministry issues an urgent appeal for foreign specialists to help treat at least 240 people contaminated by radioactive cesium 137 found by scavengers in an abandoned radiotherapy institute in Goias State.	Fiji's army chief Lt. Col. Sitiveni Rabuka formally proclaims Fiji a republic, 11 days after he seized power in his second coup in less than five months. Rabuka promises a new constitution guaranteeing indigenous Fijians political power over the islands' Indians, who make up 49% of Fiji's population of 725,000. Indigenous Fijians, who are of Melanesian descent, make up 46% of the population.

A	B	C	D	E
Includes developments that affect more than one world region, international organizations and important meetings of major world leaders.	*Includes all domestic and regional developments in Europe, including the Soviet Union, Turkey, Cyprus and Malta.*	*Includes all domestic and regional developments in Africa and the Middle East, including Iraq and Iran and excluding Cyprus, Turkey and Afghanistan.*	*Includes all domestic and regional developments in Latin America, the Caribbean and Canada.*	*Includes all domestic and regional developments in Asia and Pacific nations, extending from Afghanistan through all the Pacific Islands, except Hawaii.*

U.S. Politics & Social Issues	U.S. Foreign Policy & Defense	U.S. Economy & Environment	Science, Technology & Nature	Culture, Leisure & Life Style	
	The Senate passes a $303 bil. defense authorization bill for the 1988 fiscal year. The figure includes funds for the Energy Dept.'s nuclear weapons programs. . . . Pres. Reagan submits a report to Congress in which he says that one year of American economic sanctions against South Africa has failed to achieve any positive results and rejects the idea of imposing any new punitive measures against the white minority regime there.	The nation's unemployment rate dropped to 5.8% in September from 5.9% the month before, the Labor Dept. says.	Sir Peter (Brian) Medawar, 72, British zoologist dies in London. A co-winner of the 1960 Nobel Prize for medicine or physiology for his work paving the way for organ transplantation, Medawar was director of Great Britain's National Institute for Medical Research from 1962 to 1971 and a renowned author and philosopher of science. . . . Experimental trials begin in Britain of a French drug that could induce abortion. The drug, RU486, works by blocking progesterone receptors in the lining of the uterus, allowing the menstrual cycle to continue normally.	Madeleine Carroll (born Marie-Madeleine Bernadette O'Carroll), 81, British-born actress who by the early 1930s was a star of British cinema, dies near Marbella, Spain. Cast as the leading lady in two early Alfred Hitchcock thrillers made in England, *The 39 Steps* (1935) and *Secret Agent* (1936), she also appeared in a number of Hollywood films, including *The Prisoner of Zenda* (1937).	Oct. 2
			A new study of homosexual men in Finland finds that some who become infected with the virus that causes acquired immune deficiency syndrome (AIDS) do not form antibodies against the virus for more than a year. The finding raises questions about the effectiveness of the common AIDS tests, which detect the presence of antibodies in the bloodstream, and about proposals for mass screening programs.	Jean Anouilh, 77, French dramatist who was one of the most widely performed playwrights of his age, dies of a heart attack in Lausanne, Switzerland. Among his best-known works are *Antigone* (1944), a modern version of the Sophocles tragedy, *The Lark* (1953), and *Becket* (1959).	Oct. 3
The Chicago Teachers Union approves a new two-year contract, ending the school system's longest strike ever. The new contract includes a 4% pay hike in each of the two years. classes will begin October 6. . . . According to a Roper Org. poll published in the *Atlanta Journal and Constitution*, the Rev. Jesse Jackson is the leading Democratic presidential candidate, and Vice Pres. George Bush holds a commanding lead among Republicans.	The Reagan administration violates congressional restrictions when it uses federal funds to finance propaganda on behalf of the Nicaraguan Contra forces, a report by the General Accounting Office says. Congress has barred the use of taxpayer money for "publicity and propaganda purposes not authorized by the Congress."		Issuing an appeal for more funds in the global battle against acquired immune deficiency syndrome (AIDS), Zambia's Pres. Kenneth Kaunda reveals that the death in December 1986 of his fifth son at the age of 30 was caused by AIDS. "It does not need my son's death to appeal to the international community to treat the question of AIDS as a world problem," Kaunda told a news conference in the Zambian capital of Lusaka.	The Major League baseball season ends with four teams advancing to the National and American league championship series. The St. Louis Cardinals win the National League (NL) Eastern Division and will play the San Francisco Giants, winners of the NL West. In the American League championship series, the Eastern Division champion Detroit Tigers will play the Western Division champion Minnesota Twins.	Oct. 4
The trial of reputed Colombian drug boss Carlos Enrique Lehder Rivas opens in Jacksonville, Fla. Lehder, who was arrested in February and extradited to the United States the same day, faces an 11-count federal indictment.		The Environmental Protection Agency sets new water pollution controls for three major industries: plastics, synthetic fibers, and organic chemicals.	Warning that 40 million Americans have blood cholesterol levels that put them at high risk for heart disease, a panel convened by the National Heart, Lung, and Blood Institute, a federal agency, issues the United States's first comprehensive guidelines for the screening and treatment of high cholesterol.		Oct. 5
The Senate Judiciary Committee votes, 9-5, to reject the nomination of Robert H. Bork to the Supreme Court. The vote sends the nomination to the full Senate with a recommendation against approval. . . . The Education Dept. issues *AIDS and the Education of Our Children: A Guide for Parents and Teachers*, a handbook for teachers and parents urging them to tell young people that the best way to avoid acquired immune deficiency syndrome is to practice abstinence.		The House votes to provide $2.5 bil. in federal assistance for the beleaguered Farm Credit System and to create a secondary market for farm real estate loans.			Oct. 6

F	G	H	I	J
Includes elections, federal-state relations, civil rights and liberties, crime, the judiciary, education, health care, poverty, urban affairs and population.	*Includes formation and debate of U.S. foreign and defense policies, veterans' affairs and defense spending. (Relations with specific foreign countries are usually found under the region concerned.)*	*Includes business, labor, agriculture, taxation, transportation, consumer affairs, monetary and fiscal policy, natural resources, and pollution.*	*Includes worldwide scientific, medical and technological developments, natural phenomena, U.S. weather, natural disasters, and accidents.*	*Includes the arts, religion, scholarship, communications media, sports, entertainments, fashions, fads and social life.*

	World Affairs	Europe	Africa & the Middle East	The Americas	Asia & the Pacific
Oct. 7	The UN General Assembly approves a resolution expressing its "firmest support" for the peace plan signed August 7 in Guatemala. The resolution is sponsored by Costa Rica, El Salvador, Guatemala, Honduras, and Nicaragua, the five signatories of the plan, and by the eight Latin American nations of the Contadora Group and Lima Group that back the peace process.		The punishing Iraqi attacks on tankers carrying Iranian oil are apparently having an effect. According to the Cyprus-based *Middle East Economic Survey* newsletter, Iran's exports averaged 2.2 million barrels a day in September, down from the 2.8 million barrels a day that it was able to export during a de facto cease-fire in August. Iran has also reportedly been forced to charter 14 extra tankers, effectively doubling its fleet.	The Guatemalan government and leftist rebels open the first peace talks in 26 years of political violence. The exploratory talks are held in compliance with the August Central American peace plan.... In Chile, the National Workers Command calls a strike to press workers' demands for higher wages. Three people are killed during clashes with police, one of them a two-year-old boy.	The Chinese government cuts off communications and increases security forces in Tibet's capital city of Lhasa in an effort to prevent protests on the 37th anniversary of China's military takeover of the region.... The exiled Dalai Lama encourages peaceful protest against conditions in Tibet but declines to say that he still favors independence for the region.
Oct. 8		The jury of a coroner's inquest into the 188 deaths in the March 1987 sinking of the *Herald of Free Enterprise* rules that all but one of the dead were victims of unlawful killing and not of accidental death.... Soviet negotiators at the U.S.-Soviet arms talks in Geneva back away from a September compromise excluding 72 West Germany-based Pershing IA missiles from a U.S.-Soviet treaty on eliminating their intermediate nuclear forces.	U.S. forces in the Persian Gulf capture two Iranian vessels that yield evidence that Iran possesses American-made, shoulder-fired antiaircraft Stinger missiles.... The Reagan administration reaches a compromise with Senate opponents in an effort to win approval of a planned sale of U.S. arms to Saudi Arabia.	Nicaragua's Pres. Daniel Ortega Saavedra, addressing the UN General Assembly, offers to meet with Pres. Reagan or other U.S. officials after the Central American peace plan, signed in August, is implemented. He suggests December 10 as a date for such a meeting.	U.S. Ambassador John Gunther Dean signs an agreement in principle that will allow India to buy an advanced supercomputer from a U.S. company. India says it intends to use the computer for weather research.
Oct. 9				Peace talks between the Guatemalan government and leftist rebels end in Spain with a communique expressing support for peace and democracy but giving no indication of progress or that further meetings will take place.	
Oct. 10		Poland's Premier Zbigniew Messner unveils a package of major reforms aimed at invigorating the country's stagnant economy. The proposals are endorsed by the ruling United Workers' (Communist) Party.... The Italian Chamber of Deputies approves a compromise agreement on the teaching of religion in public schools. The pact is widely seen as a victory for the Roman Catholic Church.			Australia'a P.M. Bob Hawke meets with Sec. of State George Shultz near San Francisco to discuss trade relations between the two nations. Hawke also briefs Shultz on the political situation in Fiji in the aftermath of that nation's second coup in less than five months.
Oct. 11				In a move opposed by El Salvador's Pres. Jose Napoleon Duarte, some 4,500 refugees return home from the Mesa Grande camp in neighboring Honduras. The Central American peace pact signed in August requires governments in the region to facilitate the repatriation and resettlement of refugees.	

A	B	C	D	E
Includes developments that affect more than one world region, international organizations and important meetings of major world leaders.	Includes all domestic and regional developments in Europe, including the Soviet Union, Turkey, Cyprus and Malta.	Includes all domestic and regional developments in Africa and the Middle East, including Iraq and Iran and excluding Cyprus, Turkey and Afghanistan.	Includes all domestic and regional developments in Latin America, the Caribbean and Canada.	Includes all domestic and regional developments in Asia and Pacific nations, extending from Afghanistan through all the Pacific Islands, except Hawaii.

U.S. Politics & Social Issues	U.S. Foreign Policy & Defense	U.S. Economy & Environment	Science, Technology & Nature	Culture, Leisure & Life Style	
Dr. W. Eugene Mayberry, chief executive officer of the Mayo Clinic in Rochester, Minn., resigns as chairman of Pres. Reagan's 13-member AIDS advisory commission. The panel's vice chairman, Dr. Woodrow A. Myers Jr., announces his own resignation as well. Myers says that their departure is prompted by a "lack of support" from the Reagan administration and "significant" clashes of personality and ideology within the commission that have rendered it unable "to move the agenda forward."	Charging that the Central American peace plan signed in Guatemala in August does not address U.S. security concerns in the region, Pres. Reagan renews his commitment to seek $270 mil. in aid for the Nicaraguan Contras.	Major banks raise their prime lending rates to 9.25% from 8.75%. The increase is the fifth in 1987 and brings the rate to its highest level in more than a year and a half.... Outstanding consumer credit rose to a seasonally adjusted $4.66 bil. in August, the Federal Reserve Board says.			Oct. 7
In his first official filing as a presidential candidate, former television evangelist Pat Robertson confirms that he misrepresented his marriage date to conceal the fact that his first child was conceived out of wedlock.... Massachusetts Gov. Michael S. Dukakis names Harvard Law School professor Susan R. Estrich to manage his campaign. ... The Immigration and Naturalization Service eases its amnesty rules to allow children not eligible for amnesty to remain with their parents.		Pres. Reagan names James H. Burnley IV to succeed Elizabeth Hanford Dole as head the Transportation Dept.... Negotiators for General Motors Corp. and the United Auto Workers reach agreement on a new three-year contract. The agreement is said to be similar to the pact reached in September with Ford Motor Co.		The Rev. Jerry Falwell resigns as chairman of the PTL (Praise the Lord) ministry; he is joined in his action by the entire board of directors. Falwell abruptly severs ties with the PTL after a bankruptcy court permits an alternate reorganization plan to be submitted by a group aligned with defrocked evangelist Jim Bakker.	Oct. 8
Judge Robert H. Bork declares that he will not withdraw his nomination to the Supreme Court, despite an announced majority of senators opposed to his seating on the court.				Clare Boothe Luce, 84, editor, playwright, politician and diplomat, dies of cancer in Washington, D.C. Married to *Time* magazine founder and media mogul Henry R. Luce in 1935, she was editor of *Vanity Fair* magazine (1933-34), authored hit plays, including *The Women* (1936), served two terms as a Republican congresswoman from Connecticut (1943-47), and as ambassador to Italy (1953-57), and was a member of Pres. Reagan's unpaid Foreign Intelligence Advisory Board.	Oct. 9
The Rev. Jesse Jackson formally launches his campaign for the 1988 Democratic presidential nomination.					Oct. 10
An AIDS awareness march in Washington, D.C., draws between 200,000 and 500,000 participants. Marchers began by unfurling a 7,000-pound patchwork quilt bearing the names of more than 1,900 people who have died of acquired immune deficiency syndrome. Most of those commemorated in the quilt are men, many remembered only by their first names.					Oct. 11

F	G	H	I	J
Includes elections, federal-state relations, civil rights and liberties, crime, the judiciary, education, health care, poverty, urban affairs and population.	Includes formation and debate of U.S. foreign and defense policies, veterans' affairs and defense spending. (Relations with specific foreign countries are usually found under the region concerned.)	Includes business, labor, agriculture, taxation, transportation, consumer affairs, monetary and fiscal policy, natural resources, and pollution.	Includes worldwide scientific, medical and technological developments, natural phenomena, U.S. weather, natural disasters, and accidents.	Includes the arts, religion, scholarship, communications media, sports, entertainments, fashions, fads and social life.

	World Affairs	Europe	Africa & the Middle East	The Americas	Asia & the Pacific
Oct. 12		A telephone poll of 1,000 citizens in the Soviet capital city of Moscow reveals that 53% favor the withdrawal of Soviet troops from Afghanistan, while 27% oppose such a move. The remaining 20% of those polled offer no opinion. The survey was conducted jointly by Soviet and French researchers.			
Oct. 13	The Soviet Union joins 38 other countries in voting in favor of a General Assembly resolution challenging the acceptance of Israel's UN membership credentials. The anti-Israel forces fall far short of the two-thirds majority (106 nations) required for passage of the resolution.			Costa Rica's Pres. Oscar Arias Sanchez, the main architect of a Central American peace plan signed in Guatemala in August, is awarded the Nobel Prize for peace. ... Gunmen identified by witnesses as plainclothes police beat and shoot to death Haitian presidential candidate Yves Volel as he is making a speech outside police headquarters in Port-au-Prince.	
Oct. 14				After consultation with political, business, and union leaders, the government of Argentina announces a set of austerity measures—including a wage and price freeze—designed to curb inflation, reduce the public sector deficit, stimulate exports, and attract private investment. . . . Peru's paramilitary police seize the nation's two largest private banks, two days after a controversial law went into effect nationalizing Peru's financial system. Pres. Alan Garcia Perez first proposed the nationalization in July.	Taiwan's ruling Nationalist Party (Kuomintang) announces that Taiwanese residents will be allowed to travel to China to visit relatives "by blood or marriage." Civil servants and military personnel, however, will still be restricted from such visits.
Oct. 15		The Soviet Union announces that it will repay all of its outstanding debts to the UN. The announcement, by Deputy Foreign Min. Vladimir F. Petrovsky, indicates a new interest by Moscow in the world body.	Capt. Thomas Sankara is overthrown as the leader of Burkina Faso in a violent military coup led by his former friend and chief adviser, Capt. Blaise Compaore. Sankara and 12 other officials are executed and buried on the next morning outside Ouagadougou, the capital, an official source tells the Associated Press and Reuters news agencies.		In Fiji, Sir Penaia Ganilau resigns as governor general after a military coup September 25 challenged his authority to rule. Queen Elizabeth II accepts the resignation, thereby severing Fiji's last official ties to the Commonwealth.
Oct. 16	The fragile agreement limiting oil production by members of the Org. of Petroleum Exporting Countries is threatened by reports that Saudi Arabia is planning secret price discounts to the companies that participate in the Arabian-American Oil Co. (Aramco).		An Iranian Silkworm missile hits the *Sea Isle City*, a U.S.-flagged oil tanker in Kuwaiti waters, injuring 18 crewmen.	Canada and the United States conclude a draft agreement on bilateral efforts to clean up pollution in the Great Lakes. The pact is designed to bolster the 1978 Great Lakes Water Quality Agreement, under which the two countries are pledged to eliminate toxic discharges into the waters.	

A	B	C	D	E
Includes developments that affect more than one world region, international organizations and important meetings of major world leaders.	*Includes all domestic and regional developments in Europe, including the Soviet Union, Turkey, Cyprus and Malta.*	*Includes all domestic and regional developments in Africa and the Middle East, including Iraq and Iran and excluding Cyprus, Turkey and Afghanistan.*	*Includes all domestic and regional developments in Latin America, the Caribbean and Canada.*	*Includes all domestic and regional developments in Asia and Pacific nations, extending from Afghanistan through all the Pacific Islands, except Hawaii.*

U.S. Politics & Social Issues	U.S. Foreign Policy & Defense	U.S. Economy & Environment	Science, Technology & Nature	Culture, Leisure & Life Style	
Vice Pres. George Bush formally launches his campaign for the 1988 Republican presidential nomination. . . . Alf(red) M(ossman) Landon, 100, Republican governor of Kansas (1933-37) who lost the 1936 presidential election in a landslide, dies in Topeka. Although he never again ran for political office, he was regarded as the Republican Party's elder statesman and in 1978 his daughter, Nancy Landon Kassebaum, became the first Kansas woman elected to the U.S. Senate.		For the third consecutive year, retailer Sam Moore Walton, 69, tops the *Forbes* magazine list of the 400 richest Americans with an estimated worth of $8.5 bil. Media mogul John Kluge, 73, is worth $3 bil., and Texas investor H. Ross Perot, 57, worth $2.9 bil. . . . Salomon Brothers Inc. announces a major retrenchment, under which it will completely abandon the municipal bond underwriting business in which it attained the largest market share of any Wall Street firm.	A Soviet research satellite jeopardized when a monkey freed its left arm from a restraining cuff and fiddled with everything in reach five days into the flight, returns to Earth on schedule. . . . The Nobel Prize for medicine goes to Susumu Tonegawa, a Japanese molecular biologist working at the Massachusetts Institute of Technology.	The Minnesota Twins beat the Detroit Tigers in the American League Championship series. They will advance to the World Series. . . . The *New York Times* lists the following current fiction bestsellers: *Firestarter*, Stephen King; *The Key to Rebecca*, Ken Follett; *The Fifth Horseman*, Larry Collins and Dominique Lapierre; *Rage of Angels*, Sidney Sheldon; and *Fanny*, Erica Jong.	Oct. 12
More than 600 gay rights activists, including a number of people with acquired immune deficiency syndrome, are arrested on the steps of the U.S. Supreme Court while attempting to enter the court to protest its 1986 ruling upholding a Georgia law that makes sodomy a crime.			Walter Houser Brattain, 85, physicist, dies in Seattle of complications of Alzheimer's disease. In 1956 he and fellow Bell Telephone Laboratories research scientists John Bardeen and William Shockley shared the Nobel Prize in physics for their invention of the transistor.	*The Mahbharata*, a marathon stage production based on the Indian epic, opens at the Brooklyn Academy of Music in New York. Written by Jean-Claude Carriere, the play is adapted into English and directed by Peter Brook, and stars Miriam Goldschmidt and Jeffery Kissoon.	Oct. 13
The Columbia Univ. graduate school of business rescinds the offer of a $100,000 finder's fee made by corporate raider and adjunct professor Asher Edelman to any student who could find a company for him to buy. Edelman's students had voted, 14-1, in favor of his right to make the offer. . . . The First U.S. Circuit Court of Appeals rules, 2-1, that the Boston Symphony Orchestra violated the civil rights of actress Vanessa Redgrave when it canceled a series of concerts she was to narrate in 1982 for fear that performances would be disrupted because of her support for the Palestine Liberation Org.		The U.S. deficit on merchandise trade declined only slightly in August to $15.7 bil., the Commerce Dept. says. The smaller-than-expected decline triggers a three-day plunge in the stock market that brings the Dow Jones Industrial Average down a total of 235.48 points for the week.	Two American scientists, Charles J. Pedersen and Donald J. Cram, and a Frenchman, Jean-Marie Lehn, are awarded the Nobel Prize for chemistry for discovering how to make relatively simple molecules that mimic the functions of much more complex molecules produced by living cells. . . . The Nobel Prize for physics goes to J. Georg Bednorz and K. Alex Mueller of the IBM Zurich Research Laboratory, for their 1986 discovery of superconductivity in a new class of ceramics at temperatures higher than previously thought possible.	The St. Louis Cardinals win the National League pennant with a 6-0 victory over the San Francisco Giants. The Cardinals advance to baseball's World Series against the Minnesota Twins. . . . *Burn This*, a play by Lanford Wilson about the relationship between a female choreographer and the brother of her artistic mentor, a gay man who died in a boating accident, opens in New York City at the Plymouth Theater. Directed by Marshall W. Mason, it stars Joan Allen, John Malkovich, Jonathan Hogan, and Lou Liberatore.	Oct. 14
John A. Zaccaro is acquitted of charges that he tried to extort a $1 mil. bribe from a cable-TV company seeking to do business with the Queens borough of New York City. Zaccaro is the husband of 1984 Democratic vice presidential candidate Geraldine A. Ferraro, who contends that he came under scrutiny only because of her own prominence.		The House passes, 225-186, a bill requiring that workers whose jobs expose them to the risk of occupational diseases be so informed. The bill establishes a review board to identify such workers, who will be entitled to company-paid medical monitoring and testing, and transfer to other positions if necessary. . . . Public Service Co. of New Hampshire skips a $37.5 mil. interest payment on its bonds. The utility owns the largest stake in Seabrook, a nuclear power plant that remains in limbo while federal officials debate whether the plant will be allowed to open.		The National Football League Players Assoc. calls off its 24-day-old strike despite failing to win a new collective bargaining contract or a back-to-work agreement with the team owners. Although the end of the strike is seen as a defeat for the union, management's hard-line stance is seen as possibly strengthening the union's chance of winning an antitrust suit against the league.	Oct. 15
Sec. of Health and Human Services Otis R. Bowen says he is issuing an administrative order to prevent the Social Security Admin. from implementing a new policy that would reduce welfare benefits under the Supplemental Security Income (SSI) Program. Some 4.3 million elderly, blind, and disabled Americans with little or no income from other sources receive funds under the program.		The Dow Jones Industrial Average plummets a record 108.35 points, bringing the Dow's three-day loss to a total of 261.43 points. . . . The producer price index rose 0.3% in September, after seasonal adjustment, the Labor Dept. reports. . . . The Federal Reserve Board says that its industrial production index rose a modest 0.2% in September.	An infant boy diagnosed in utero as suffering from a fatal heart malformation becomes the world's youngest heart transplant patient. The child, Paul Holc, undergoes the surgery at Loma Linda (Calif.) Univ. Medical Center just two-and-a-half hours after his delivery by cesarean section.	Eighteen-month-old Jessica McClure, trapped 22 feet underground in an abandoned well shaft in Midland, Tex., is rescued after workers spend two-and-a-half days drilling through hardpan rock to reach her. . . . *Hope and Glory*, in which director John Boorman recalls his boyhood in England during World War II, is released in New York. Produced and written by Boorman, the film stars Sebastian Rice Edwards, Sarah Miles, and Sammi Davis.	Oct. 16

F	G	H	I	J
Includes elections, federal-state relations, civil rights and liberties, crime, the judiciary, education, health care, poverty, urban affairs and population.	*Includes formation and debate of U.S. foreign and defense policies, veterans' affairs and defense spending. (Relations with specific foreign countries are usually found under the region concerned.)*	*Includes business, labor, agriculture, taxation, transportation, consumer affairs, monetary and fiscal policy, natural resources, and pollution.*	*Includes worldwide scientific, medical and technological developments, natural phenomena, U.S. weather, natural disasters, and accidents.*	*Includes the arts, religion, scholarship, communications media, sports, entertainments, fashions, fads and social life.*

	World Affairs	Europe	Africa & the Middle East	The Americas	Asia & the Pacific
Oct. 17	The leaders of the Commonwealth conclude their five-day annual Heads of Government Conf. in Vancouver, Canada. Britain's P.M. Margaret Thatcher stands alone at the conference in opposing tougher economic sanctions against the white-minority government of South Africa.	Turkey's parliament approves a new election law that sets November 29 as the date for general elections. The action was made necessary when Turkey's Constitutional Court October 9 struck down a hastily passed election law enacted in early September.		Canadian indoor postal workers end a 17-day walkout after the federal government enacts back-to-work legislation. It is Canada's second nationwide postal strike in four months. A job action by letter carriers and mail truck drivers was settled in July.	
Oct. 18	Federico Mayor Zaragoza of Spain in nominated to succeed Amadou-Mahtar M'Bow of Senegal as the director general of the UN Educational, Scientific and Cultural Org. (UNESCO). Mayor's nomination must be confirmed by UNESCO's general conference.	Results of the Swiss general election return the governing centrist coalition to power. Environmentalist Green parties gain seats in the 200-member National Chamber, but not as many as were expected. Only 49% of Swiss voters go to the polls, about the same as during the last general election in 1983.		In Canada, a strike by 265 Great Lakes marine engineers ends with the announcement of a contract settlement. The engineers began the strike against the Canadian Lake Carriers Assoc. on September 28.	
Oct. 19			In retaliation for the October 16 attack by an Iranian missile on a U.S.-flagged oil tanker, U.S. warships bombard an offshore Iranian oil rig that is being used as a base for Iranian gunboats.		Kim Young Sam, head of South Korea's opposition Reunification Democratic Party, calls for a national convention November 5 to nominate an opposition presidential candidate. The rival opposition leader, Kim Dae Jung, opposes the idea.
Oct. 20	One day after the New York Stock Exchange posts its biggest-ever loss, world stock markets follow suit. The London exchange experiences record declines over the last two days, and the Tokyo market suffers a record 14.9% loss. RN 16634				Japan's Premier Yasuhiro Nakasone chooses Noboru Takeshita, a former finance minister, to succeed him as president of the ruling Liberal Democratic Party, virtually assuring Takeshita's being named premier.... Pres. Corazon Aquino warns that the Philippine government will use force if necessary to break a series of nationwide strikes that are disrupting the Philippine economy.
Oct. 21		Belgium's Premier Wilfried Martens presents to King Baudouin a caretaker government of the same four center-right parties he led prior to his resignation two days ago. The coalition will serve until new general elections, which are expected before the end of 1987. The government crisis results from longstanding disputes over language and culture that divide Belgium's Flemish (Dutch) speakers and French speakers.			
Oct. 22			Iran responds to the October 19 bombardment of an Iranian oil rig by a U.S. warship by firing another missile into Kuwait's main offshore oil loading platform.... According to a variety of reports, Ethiopia is faced with the prospect of its second devastating famine in three years. An unexpected drought has led to crop failures ranging from 70% to 100% in the northern provinces of Eritrea and Tigre, putting an estimated 5 million people at risk of starvation.	In Panama, the ministry of the presidency closes the office of Vice Pres. Roderick Esquivel, who is visiting Nicaragua. Esquivel has recently called for an investigation into allegations that Panama's de facto leader Gen. Manuel Antonio Noriega is involved in election fraud, drug trafficking, and political murders.... The Bank of Canada lowers its lending rate to 8.26% from 9.83%, the largest drop in the 52-year history of the central bank.	Indian troops have reportedly killed more than 600 Tamil rebels in 12 days of heavy fighting around the northern Sri Lanka city of Jaffna, an Indian military official claims, and at least 129 Indian soldiers have also died.... During a speech to delegates at a meeting of the General Agreement on Tariffs and Trade in Geneva, P.M. Bob Hawke pledges to eliminate all of Australia's protective trade measures, including tariffs, if such a move will help open world trade markets.

A	B	C	D	E
Includes developments that affect more than one world region, international organizations and important meetings of major world leaders.	*Includes all domestic and regional developments in Europe, including the Soviet Union, Turkey, Cyprus and Malta.*	*Includes all domestic and regional developments in Africa and the Middle East, including Iraq and Iran and excluding Cyprus, Turkey and Afghanistan.*	*Includes all domestic and regional developments in Latin America, the Caribbean and Canada.*	*Includes all domestic and regional developments in Asia and Pacific nations, extending from Afghanistan through all the Pacific Islands, except Hawaii.*

U.S. Politics & Social Issues	U.S. Foreign Policy & Defense	U.S. Economy & Environment	Science, Technology & Nature	Culture, Leisure & Life Style	
First Lady Nancy Reagan undergoes surgery for removal of her left breast after a biopsy reveals cancerous cells. The 50-minute operation, a modified radical mastectomy, is performed at Bethesda Navy Medical Center in suburban Maryland by a team of four surgeons headed by Drs. Oliver Beahrs and Donald McIlrath of the Mayo Clinic in Rochester, Minn.					Oct. 17
					Oct. 18
Bernhard H. Goetz is sentenced to six months in prison for illegal weapons possession. Goetz was acquitted in June of the attempted murder of four youths on a New York City subway train in December 1984.... The Senate's most senior member, Sen. John C. Stennis (D, Miss.), announces that he will not run for a seventh term in 1988.... The Supreme Court divides evenly, 3-3, on the Reagan administration's refusal to grant visas to foreigners affiliated with communist organizations who have been invited to speak in the United States.... The Los Angeles Unified School District board votes, 4-3, to rescind an earlier decision to adopt year-round scheduling for all the city's public schools.	Sec. of State George P. Shultz concludes a four-day visit to the Middle East. He reports no diplomatic gains on the brief trip, which leaves the United States with little prospect of forcing any breakthroughs in the Arab-Israeli peace process during the remainder of the Reagan administration.	In frenzied, panicked selling, the Dow Jones Industrial Average falls an astounding 508.32 points. The crash marks the end of a bull market during which the Dow rose steadily from 776.92 in August 1982 to a high of 2722.42 in August 1987.... Analysts worldwide attribute the collapse of the Dow to threats by Treasury Sec. James A. Baker III that the United States would allow the dollar to fall against the West German mark, coupled with the perception that policy coordination among the major economic powers is weakening.		Jacqueline Du Pre, 42, English cellist who came to be recognized as one of the world's leading exponents of her instrument, dies in London. In the 1960s, she and her husband, pianist and conductor Daniel Barenboim, were hailed as the golden young couple of classical music, but her career was cut short in the early 1970s by the onset of multiple sclerosis. She continued to teach, and her story became the basis for a play, *Duet for One*, a film version of which was released in 1987.	Oct. 19
The Democratic Congressional Campaign Committee sues the Federal Election Comm. for not acting on the committee's complaint against a conservative fund raiser.	India's P.M. Rajiv Gandhi meets with Pres. Reagan in Washington, D.C., to discuss ways to improve ties between the United States and India. Talks focus on U.S. military and economic assistance to Pakistan, with which India has foughtd three wars since 1947.	The Reagan administration takes the first step to impose $23 bil. in automatic, across-the-board federal spending cuts required under the revised Gramm-Rudman balanced-budget law.... Housing starts increased by a surprising 4.4% in September, the Commerce Dept. says.	The Environmental Protection Agency (EPA) announces that it has approved a Monsanto experiment to release a gene-altered microbe that will help scientists learn how other genetically engineered organisms might disperse in the environment. The approval is the first granted under the Toxic Substances Control Act for a field test of a genetically engineered organism by the EPA.		Oct. 20
	The Senate approves a resolution that requires Pres. Reagan to report to Congress within 30 days on his administration's Persian Gulf policies, but avoids invoking the controversial War Powers Act. Instead, the proposal puts off until late 1987 or early 1988 any specific consideration of the U.S. policy of escorting reflagged Kuwaiti tankers.		Merck & Co. announces that it has developed a drug to treat river blindness and will distribute it free to countries that request it. River blindness, or onchocerciasis, a debilitating disease that affects an estimated 18 million people in Africa, the Middle East, and Latin America, is caused by a parasitic worm spread by the bite of the black fly, which breeds in rivers.	The winner of the Nobel Prize in economic science is Robert M. Solow, a 63-year-old professor at the Massachusetts Institute of Technology, and a leading proponent of Keynesian economics, which favors government intervention in economic markets, for his contributions to the theory of economic growth.... *Variety*'s top-grossing films for the week are: *Fatal Attraction*; *The Princess Bride*; *Like Father Like Son*; *Someone to Watch Over Me*; and *Baby Boom*.	Oct. 21
	The Reagan administration announces that it will restrict exports of certain high-technology products to China in retaliation for China's alleged sale of Silkworm missiles to Iran, which is believed to have used them against U.S. and Kuwaiti targets in the Persian Gulf. ... The federal Comm. on Fine Arts votes, 4-1, to reject a proposal to add a statue of a woman to the Vietnam Veterans Memorial in Washington, D.C.	Apparently conceding that he will consider increased taxes as a way of dealing with the budget deficit, Pres. Reagan says in a press conference that he will negotiate with Congress and that he is putting "everything on the table with the exception of Social Security." ... A St. Clair County Circuit Court jury in Belleville, Ill., finds Monsanto Co. liable for $16.2 mil. in punitive damages for a toxic chemical spill in January 1979 in Sturgeon, Mo.		The Nobel Prize for literature is awarded to Joseph Brodsky, an exiled Soviet-born poet and essayist who writes in both Russian and English.	Oct. 22
F	G	H	I	J	
Includes elections, federal-state relations, civil rights and liberties, crime, the judiciary, education, health care, poverty, urban affairs and population.	Includes formation and debate of U.S. foreign and defense policies, veterans' affairs and defense spending. (Relations with specific foreign countries are usually found under the region concerned.)	Includes business, labor, agriculture, taxation, transportation, consumer affairs, monetary and fiscal policy, natural resources, and pollution.	Includes worldwide scientific, medical and technological developments, natural phenomena, U.S. weather, natural disasters, and accidents.	Includes the arts, religion, scholarship, communications media, sports, entertainments, fashions, fads and social life.	

	World Affairs	Europe	Africa & the Middle East	The Americas	Asia & the Pacific
Oct. 23		Disclosure of an apparent extramarital affair between Greek Premier Andreas Papandreou and a 33-year-old television interviewer weakens the Papandreou government, according to press reports over the past week. The alleged affair with Dimitra Liani comes at a time when Papandreou's popularity has been hurt by other factors including the government's continued austerity program and problems with the environment.		Peru's Pres. Alan Garcia Perez announces delayed wage increases of between 20% and 30% and an increase in the minimum wage, to $52 per month from $40.	
Oct. 24					
Oct. 25		Yugoslavia's federal government sends a special paramilitary police unit to Kosovo to quell ethnic unrest in that province. Kosovo, an autonomous region in the republic of Serbia, is the site of ongoing strife between a majority made up of ethnic Albanians and a minority population of Serbs and Montenegrins.			The Chinese Communist Party begins its 13th national congress in Beijing. The congress heralds the rise of a new generation of Chinese leaders and reaffirms the course of economic reform adopted by China's paramount ruler, Deng Xiaoping. . . . After 16 days of fighting with Tamil separatists, the Indian Army peacekeeping force in Sri Lanka takes control of the northern city of Jaffna, a stronghold of the Liberation Tigers of Tamil Eelam.
Oct. 26				In Canada, the House of Commons votes, 242-16, to approve the so-called Meech Lake constitutional agreement. The pact will give Quebec the constitutionally protected status of a "distinct society" within Canada. It will also make fundamental changes in the balance of power between the federal government and the 10 provinces.	
Oct. 27		Representatives of the seven nations forming the Western European Union formally adopted a "Platform on European Security Interests." The action marks the latest step in a series of moves designed to strengthen cooperation on defense matters among Western European nations.		El Salvador's National Assembly approves, 45-0, an amnesty that applies to leftist guerrillas, military members accused of massacres, and rightist death squads. . . . Central American foreign ministers meet in San Jose, Costa Rica, in the last session before regional cease-fires take effect. Under the terms of the regional peace agreement signed in August, the cease-fires are due to come into force November 5.	South Korea's rewritten constitution is overwhelmingly approved in a popular referendum. About 93% of the votes cast are in favor of ratifying the new charter. Election officials claim that 20 million people, 78% of the electorate, turned out to vote.

A	B	C	D	E
Includes developments that affect more than one world region, international organizations and important meetings of major world leaders.	Includes all domestic and regional developments in Europe, including the Soviet Union, Turkey, Cyprus and Malta.	Includes all domestic and regional developments in Africa and the Middle East, including Iraq and Iran and excluding Cyprus, Turkey and Afghanistan.	Includes all domestic and regional developments in Latin America, the Caribbean and Canada.	Includes all domestic and regional developments in Asia and Pacific nations, extending from Afghanistan through all the Pacific Islands, except Hawaii.

U.S. Politics & Social Issues	U.S. Foreign Policy & Defense	U.S. Economy & Environment	Science, Technology & Nature	Culture, Leisure & Life Style	
The Senate rejects Pres. Reagan's nomination of Robert H. Bork to the Supreme Court by a 58-42 vote. Opposition to the nominee sprang largely out of concern that Bork was not in the mainstream of judicial interpretation of the Constitution, and that he could upset or thwart a number of recent landmark decisions, especially on the issues of abortion, civil rights, and women's rights.		At the end of a hectic week on Wall Street, the Dow Jones Industrial Average posts a net loss of 295.95 points to close at 1950.76.... The nation's gross national product grew at an inflation-adjusted 3.8% annual rate in the third quarter, the Commerce Dept. reports.... The government's consumer price index rose a slight 0.2% in September, the Labor Dept. reports.		*Publishers Weekly*'s hardback fiction best-sellers for the week are: *Presumed Innocent*, Scott Turow; *Leaving Home: A Collection of Lake Wobegon Stories*, Garrison Keillor; *Heaven and Hell*, John Jakes; *Patriot Games*, Tom Clancy; and *Beloved*, Toni Morrison.	Oct. 23
		The AFL-CIO executive board approves the readmittance of the Teamsters Union after 30 years. ... The Labor Dept. imposes a record $5.1 mil. in fines against contractors for a Bridgeport, Conn., apartment complex that collapsed in April killing 28 workers.... A 17-week strike against the National Broadcasting Co. by technicians, writers, producers, and editors ends with acceptance of a new three-year contract.		*Billboard*'s best-selling albums for the week are: *Bad*, Michael Jackson; *Whitesnake*, Whitesnake; *A Momentary Lapse of Reason*, Pink Floyd; *Dirty Dancing* (soundtrack); and *Hysteria*, Def Leppard.	Oct. 24
			Doctors believe a St. Louis teenager who died in 1969 was infected with the virus that caused acquired immune deficiency syndrome (AIDS) a decade before the first AIDS cases surfaced among male homosexuals in New York City, the *Chicago Tribune* reports.	The American League's Minnesota Twins win baseball's World Series with a 4-2 victory over the St. Louis Cardinals in game seven. Twins pitcher Frank Viola is named most valuable player of the series.... In auto racing, Dale Earnhardt wins the Winston Cup title for the NASCAR (National Assoc. for Stock Car Racing) season.... In the first-ever meeting between a Soviet national team and a team from the National Basketball Assoc., the Milwaukee Bucks beat the Soviets, 127-100, in Milwaukee.	Oct. 25
	Reacting to Iran's "increasingly bellicose behavior" in the Persian Gulf and its "unprovoked attacks" on American military forces and merchant ships, Pres. Reagan announces an embargo on all U.S. imports from Iran and extends the list of "militarily useful" items the export of which to Iran is banned. ... Accused of lying about his Nazi past when he entered the United States in the 1950s, Reinhold Kulle is deported to West Germany after Associate Supreme Court Justice John Paul Stevens refuses an emergency appeal.	Declining auto sales drove consumer spending down 0.5% in September, while personal income gained 0.7%, the Commerce Dept. says.... Congressional leaders of both parties meet with Pres. Reagan and administration officials to lay the groundwork for discussions on cutting the federal budget deficit.... A distraught Miami investor who apparently lost millions of dollars in the stock market crash shoots and kills one broker and critically wounds another before shooting himself, at a suburban Miami branch of Merrill Lynch & Co.	A successful Titan 34D rocket launched from Vandenberg Air Force Base in California carries a secret military payload, believed to be a spy satellite, into orbit. The the Air Force launch is the first successful U.S. launch of a major payload in two years.		Oct. 26
The Senate approves by an 86-11 vote a bill to expand the Medicare program to protect the elderly and disabled against "catastrophic" medical costs. The House passed a similar bill in July.				*Lettice and Lovage*, a play in which two women plot the destruction of London's postwar architecture, opens at the Globe Theater in London. Written by Peter Shaffer and directed by Michael Blakemore, the play stars Maggie Smith, Margaret Tyzack, and Richard Pearson.	Oct. 27

F	G	H	I	J
Includes elections, federal-state relations, civil rights and liberties, crime, the judiciary, education, health care, poverty, urban affairs and population.	*Includes formation and debate of U.S. foreign and defense policies, veterans' affairs and defense spending. (Relations with specific foreign countries are usually found under the region concerned.)*	*Includes business, labor, agriculture, taxation, transportation, consumer affairs, monetary and fiscal policy, natural resources, and pollution.*	*Includes worldwide scientific, medical and technological developments, natural phenomena, U.S. weather, natural disasters, and accidents.*	*Includes the arts, religion, scholarship, communications media, sports, entertainments, fashions, fads and social life.*

	World Affairs	Europe	Africa & the Middle East	The Americas	Asia & the Pacific
Oct. 28				The nuclear accident that exposed residents of Goiania, Brazil, to radioactive cesium 137 in September has claimed four victims in the last five days. . . . Ecuadoran workers stage a one-day general strike to demand the resignation of Interior Min. Luis Robles Plaza, who was impeached and convicted by Congress in connection with the violation of the rights of criminals and guerrillas in police custody.	Kim Dae Jung, one of the two main opposition leaders in South Korea, formally declares his candidacy for president. His decision confirms a split with rival opposition leader Kim Young Sam, who announced his candidacy October 10.
Oct. 29		The British government announces that it will go ahead with a plan to sell to the public its 31.5% stake in British Petroleum Co. (BP), despite the depressed state of world securities markets. In announcing the decision to proceed with the record $12.2 bil. offering, Chancellor of the Exchequer Nigel Lawson pledges that the Bank of England will support the BP share price through a buy-back offer.		Leftist rebels in El Salvador pull out of peace talks to protest what they say is government involvement in the death of prominent human rights activist Herbert Ernesto Anaya Sanabria, shot and killed by two unidentified gunmen October 26. . . . Nicaragua's ruling Sandinista National Liberation Front declares "that there will never, at any time or in any place, be any direct or indirect political dialogue with the counterrevolutionary leadership" of the Contras.	Over two days in Malaysia, as many as 80 opposition leaders and critics of the ruling administration are arrested in a government crackdown. The government also closes four newspapers and bans public rallies.
Oct. 30	World stock markets continue to slide, following the October 19 crash. This week began with huge declines on the Asian markets, particularly in Hong Kong, where selling pressure had been pent up the previous week while the market was closed.				Kim Dae Jung announces in Seoul, South Korea, that he is forming a new political party to support his presidential campaign. Kim is unanimously elected chairman of the new party, which is named the Party for Peace and Democracy.
Oct. 31			Syria's Premier Abdel Rauf al-Kassem resigns after the parliament censures four of his cabinet ministers accused of incompetence and negligence relating to the country's continuing economic stagnation. . . . Julius Nyerere, Tanzania's president from 1961 to 1985, is overwhelmingly reelected to another five-year term as chairman of the ruling Chama Cha Mapinduzi (Revolutionary Party), Tanzania's sole political party.		
Nov. 1			In the wake of yesterday's resignation by Premier Abdel Rauf al-Kassem, Syria's Pres. Hafez al-Assad names parliament speaker Mahmoud Zubi premier and shuffles the cabinet, bringing in technical experts in an attempt to deal with the nation's declining agricultural and industrial sectors. No shifts in foreign policy are expected.	Rene Levesque, 65, provincial premier of Quebec from 1976 to 1985, dies of a heart attack in Montreal, Canada. Expelled from the Liberal Party in 1967 over the issue of Quebec sovereignty, he formed the Parti Quebecois and led the party to power in the 1976 election. In 1979, he pushed through a highly controversial law formalizing the status of French as Quebec's only official language.	
Nov. 2		Soviet leader Mikhail S. Gorbachev criticizes Joseph Stalin but falls short of a complete denunciation of the former leader. Gorbachev's nationally televised speech is the keynote address of celebrations on the eve of the 70th anniversary of the Bolshevik Revolution.		Haiti's Provisional Electoral Council is the target of a number of violent incidents after the council bars 12 candidates from the November 29 presidential election because of their close association with deposed Pres. Jean-Claude Duvalier and his late father, Pres. Francois Duvalier.	

A	B	C	D	E
Includes developments that affect more than one world region, international organizations and important meetings of major world leaders.	Includes all domestic and regional developments in Europe, including the Soviet Union, Turkey, Cyprus and Malta.	Includes all domestic and regional developments in Africa and the Middle East, including Iraq and Iran and excluding Cyprus, Turkey and Afghanistan.	Includes all domestic and regional developments in Latin America, the Caribbean and Canada.	Includes all domestic and regional developments in Asia and Pacific nations, extending from Afghanistan through all the Pacific Islands, except Hawaii.

U.S. Politics & Social Issues	U.S. Foreign Policy & Defense	U.S. Economy & Environment	Science, Technology & Nature	Culture, Leisure & Life Style	
Republican presidential candidates Vice Pres. George Bush, former Delaware Gov. Pierre S. DuPont IV, Rep. Jack F. Kemp (N.Y.), former Sec. of State Alexander M. Haig Jr., the Rev. Pat Robertson, and Senate Minority Leader Bob Dole (Kans.) hold their first televised debate, hosted by William F. Buckley Jr. . . . Candidates for the 1988 presidential election had already spent $55 mil. by September 30, according to Federal Election Comm. documents. The candidates have raised $70 mil. to date.	In compliance with the Central American peace plan signed in August, Guatemala's Congress approves an amnesty law that will take effect November 5 and under which rebels who lay down their arms within 180 days will be pardoned.	A stock market rally is snuffed out when it becomes apparent that the world's central banks are allowing the dollar to fall further against major currencies, following the October 19 crash. . . . The Senate approves a bill to increase authorized spending for airport improvement. Funding is authorized for more air-traffic controllers, and for broadening safety requirements for small planes.			Oct. 28
Pres. Reagan names U.S. Court of Appeals Judge Douglas H. Ginsburg, 41, as his new nominee to sit on the Supreme Court. . . . A five-year legal battle between a white Mormon couple and a Navajo Indian woman over custody of the woman's son is settled in a tribal courtroom in the Navajo capital of Window Rock, Ariz. Michael Carter, now 10, will become the permanent ward of the couple. . . . The Senate approves a smoking ban on airline flights of 90 minutes or less.		The Environmental Protection Agency orders school systems to inspect their buildings for asbestos and have it removed or quarantined to protect children and workers from the cancer-causing fibers. . . . Clearing the way to license the controversial Seabrook and Shoreham nuclear plants in New Hampshire and New York, the Nuclear Regulatory Comm. decides to consider licensing nuclear power plants even if community officials refuse to approve evacuation plans.		Woody (Woodrow Charles) Herman, 74, jazz clarinetist and big band leader, dies in Los Angeles of congestive heart failure, emphysema, and pneumonia. In a career that spanned five decades, he led a series of ensembles in a wide range of styles that reflected the continually changing character of popular music. . . . Thomas Hearns wins the World Boxing Council middleweight title in a fight with Argentine Juan Roldan. He is the first fighter to win world titles in four different weight classes. . . . British author Penelope Lively is named winner of Britain's Booker Prize for her novel *Moon Tiger*.	Oct. 29
A special federal prosecutor says a grand jury, after an unannounced inquiry, has voted not to indict former Labor Sec. Raymond J. Donovan on allegations that he lied about seeking a $250,000 kickback while in private business. Donovan and seven associates in May were acquitted of unrelated fraud charges in a New York state court.	Pres. Reagan announces that he and Soviet leader Mikhail S. Gorbachev will hold a summit in Washington, D.C., beginning December 7.	The government's index of leading economic indicators declined 0.1% in September, the Commerce Dept. says.	Pres. Reagan signs legislation authorizing $9.57 bil. for the National Aeronautics and Space Admin. in FY1988.	Joseph Campbell, 83, author of many books on mythology and folklore, dies in Honolulu after a brief illness. Among his better known works are *The Hero with a Thousand Faces* (1949), which filmmaker George Lucas says provided him with the inspiration for *Star Wars*, and the four-volume *Masks of God* (1959-67); he taught at Sarah Lawrence College for nearly four decades.	Oct. 30
				In tennis, U.S. women win their ninth straight victory over their British counterparts for the Wightman Cup. The final score in the competition was five matches to two.	Oct. 31
Douglas H. Ginsburg's Supreme Court nomination hits a snag with the disclosure that he led a Justice Dept. effort to win First Amendment protection for cable television operators when he had a large sum invested in a cable company. . . . A federal appeals court in San Francisco rules that the Orange County, Calif., Dept. of Education had no grounds to reassign Vincent Chalk to a desk job because he suffers from acquired immune deficiency syndrome.				In auto racing, Nelson Piquet of Brazil clinches the Formula One title when top rival Nigel Mansell of Great Britain is forced out of the Japanese Grand Prix because of an injury sustained in a crash October 30. . . . Ibrahim Hussein of Kenya and Priscilla Welch of Britain win the men's and women's division of the New York Marathon in 2:11:1 and 2:30:17, respectively.	Nov. 1
Organizers of a four-month drive to force a recall of Arizona's Gov. Evan Mecham (R) file nearly twice as many petition signatures as needed. . . . The *Wall Street Journal* reports that as currently performed in the United States, the Pap smear used to detect cancer of the uterine cervix fails to detect about one in four cases of cancer or precursor cell abnormalities.		The Texas Supreme Court refuses to hear Texaco Inc.'s request that it throw out Pennzoil Co.'s $10.3 bil. judgment against Texaco. Without issuing an opinion, Texas's highest court flatly rejects Texaco's case, which cites 130 errors allegedly made by lower courts.			Nov. 2

F	G	H	I	J
Includes elections, federal-state relations, civil rights and liberties, crime, the judiciary, education, health care, poverty, urban affairs and population.	Includes formation and debate of U.S. foreign and defense policies, veterans' affairs and defense spending. (Relations with specific foreign countries are usually found under the region concerned.)	Includes business, labor, agriculture, taxation, transportation, consumer affairs, monetary and fiscal policy, natural resources, and pollution.	Includes worldwide scientific, medical and technological developments, natural phenomena, U.S. weather, natural disasters, and accidents.	Includes the arts, religion, scholarship, communications media, sports, entertainments, fashions, fads and social life.

	World Affairs	Europe	Africa & the Middle East	The Americas	Asia & the Pacific
Nov. 3		Aleksandr N. Yakovlev, a member of the Soviet Politburo, confirms Western reports of a dispute over economic reform between Boris N. Yeltsin, head of the Moscow Communist Party (CP), and Yegor K. Ligachev, CP ideologist and number two figure in the Kremlin hierarchy... Presenting the government's annual economic statement, Great Britain's Chancellor of the Exchequer, Nigel Lawson asserts that the economic program has prepared the nation to "weather any storm" caused by the sharp decline in world stock prices.	One day after a U.S. Navy warship in the Persian Gulf fired on a suspected Iranian gunboat after the vessel allegedly threatened a U.S. tanker and refused to heed warnings, it is learned that the vessel was an unarmed Arab fishing craft; one Indian crewman was killed.... South Africa's Pres. Pieter W. Botha and Zulu Chief Mangosuthu Gatsha Buthelezi meet in Durban to launch a multiracial advisory body for Natal province.		In Malaysia, police arrested at least 12 opposition political figures and antigovernment critics over the last several days. The latest arrests raise to 93 the number of people who have been jailed in a week-long government crackdown.
Nov. 4		The Nuclear Planning Group of the North Atlantic Treaty Org. (NATO) gives its support to a proposed treaty banning intermediate nuclear forces. The group is made up of NATO's defense ministers.			In Hong Kong, the government reports that a majority of the public favors establishing direct elections for the territory's legislative council, but only a minority supported introducing such elections in 1988.
Nov. 5			The South African government frees veteran black activist Govan Mbeki, a 77-year-old former chairman of the banned African National Congress, who has been in prison for 23 years. His unconditional release leads to speculation that Pretoria is weighing the release of ANC leader Nelson Mandela.	The Central American peace plan signed in Guatemala in August goes into effect. Regional foreign ministers earlier declared today the beginning of the peace plan compliance process rather than the deadline for putting the plan into effect.... Rejecting a unilateral cease-fire declared by the Salvadoran government earlier in the day, the Farabundo Marti National Liberation Front accuses government troops of deploying in rebel-dominated areas despite the truce.	
Nov. 6	The UN opens to public scrutiny its secret files on thousands of suspected World War II war criminals. The files were compiled by the UN War Crimes Comm., which was disbanded in 1948.... Despite the instability in world currency markets, stock markets around the world steady. The Dow Jones Industriual Average closes the week at 1959.05, down 34.49 from October 30.			Brazil and its leading creditor banks reach preliminary agreement on a short-term plan under which Brazil will resume interest payments on its foreign debt and seek an economic program with the International Monetary Fund ... U.S. Trade Rep. Clayton K. Yeutter and Mexico's Commerce and Industry Sec. Hector Hernandez Cervantes sign a long-awaited bilateral trade "understanding" under which the two nations agree to negotiate trade disputes.... Canada's national unemployment rate fell to 8.4% in October, the lowest since November 1981, according to Statistics Canada.	Noboru Takeshita is elected premier of Japan, succeeding Yasuhiro Nakasone. Takeshita immediately forms a new cabinet that includes several people who support the outgoing premier in key positions.
Nov. 7		A three-hour military parade in Moscow's Red Square marks the climax of the Soviet Union's week-long celebration of the 70th anniversary of the Bolshevik Revolution.	After only a little more than a month in office, Tunisia's Premier Zine el-Abidine Ben Ali overthrows Pres. Habib Bourguiba on the grounds that the aging leader is senile and unable to govern. The uncontested coup is reportedly greeted with relief in Tunisia, as well as in Algeria, Libya, France, and the United States.		

A	B	C	D	E
Includes developments that affect more than one world region, international organizations and important meetings of major world leaders.	Includes all domestic and regional developments in Europe, including the Soviet Union, Turkey, Cyprus and Malta.	Includes all domestic and regional developments in Africa and the Middle East, including Iraq and Iran and excluding Cyprus, Turkey and Afghanistan.	Includes all domestic and regional developments in Latin America, the Caribbean and Canada.	Includes all domestic and regional developments in Asia and Pacific nations, extending from Afghanistan through all the Pacific Islands, except Hawaii.

U.S. Politics & Social Issues	U.S. Foreign Policy & Defense	U.S. Economy & Environment	Science, Technology & Nature	Culture, Leisure & Life Style	
Incumbent Mayor B. Wilson Goode (D), Philadelphia's first black mayor, wins a narrow reelection victory over former Mayor Frank Rizzo (R). But Rizzo refuses to concede defeat, and Goode's 14,000-vote victory margin (out of roughly 650,000 votes cast) is subject to the counting of absentee ballots and a possible recount.		Pres. Reagan announces the appointment of Ann Dore McLaughlin to his cabinet as secretary of labor. She will succeed William E. Brock III, who resigned to head the presidential effort of Sen. Robert Dole (R, Kans.).		The Rev. Jerry Falwell announces his resignation as president of the Moral Majority, the group he founded to bring fundamentalist Christian influence to bear on electoral politics. . . . Baseball's rookie of the year award goes to Oakland A's first baseman Mark McGwire of the American League.	Nov. 3
Sec. of Education William J. Bennett unveils a plan to tighten eligibility requirements for colleges, universities, and trade schools receiving federal student aid. . . . The House votes, 254-158, to prohibit most employers from using lie detectors to test workers. The bill does not apply to federal, state, and local governments.		The Labor Dept. fines the Bath (Maine) Iron Works Corp. a record $4.2 mil. for job-safety violations. The shipyard, a major Navy contractor, is cited by the department's Occupational Safety and Health Admin. for more than 3,000 violations.	Earthquake scientists report that the October 1 earthquake and aftershocks that struck Los Angeles might have been caused by a previously unrecognized geological fault running beneath some of the most heavily populated sections of the city. . . . Genentech Inc. wins a broad U.S. patent covering basic techniques of genetic engineering. The award is thought to mean that other biotechnology concerns will have to get a license from Genentech to continue operating in the field.	The National League's Rookie of the Year award goes to San Diego Padre catcher Benito Santiago.	Nov. 4
	In a lavish ceremony in the White House Rose Garden, Pres. Reagan accepts Defense Sec. Caspar W. Weinberger's resignation, and praises his role in the administration's military build-up. Reagan also nominates White House national security adviser Frank C. Carlucci to succeed Weinberger as secretary of defense and names Lt. Gen. Colin L. Powell to succeed Carlucci. Powell will be the first black to hold the national security post.	The U.S. dollar tumbles to new lows against major currencies amid indications by the Reagan administration that supporting the sliding dollar is not a high priority. . . . The Senate ratifies, 93-0, an international pact to ban ocean dumping of plastics. The agreement requires nations to provide port facilities for dumping the debris, which is a grave threat to ocean wildlife.		The Rev. Patricia Ann McClurg, a 48-year-old Presbyterian minister from Plainfield, N.J., is the first female minister elected to head the National Council of Churches. . . . *Into the Woods*, a fairy tale musical by Stephen Sondheim, opens in New York City at the Martin Beck Theater. Directed by James Lapine and starring Bernadette Peters, Joanna Gleason, Chip Zien, Tom Aldredge, and Robert Westenberg, the musical wins three Tony awards.	Nov. 5
		The nation's unemployment rate rose to 5.9% in October, the Labor Dept. says. . . . Outstanding consumer debt rose a sharp $6.06 bil. in September, the Federal Reserve Board says.			Nov. 6
U.S. Appeals Court Judge Douglas H. Ginsburg withdraws as Pres. Reagan's nominee to the Supreme Court because of the "clamor" aroused over disclosure that he smoked marijuana in the past. His withdrawal comes just 15 days after the Senate rejected Reagan's initial nominee, Judge Robert H. Bork.					Nov. 7

F	G	H	I	J
Includes elections, federal-state relations, civil rights and liberties, crime, the judiciary, education, health care, poverty, urban affairs and population.	Includes formation and debate of U.S. foreign and defense policies, veterans' affairs and defense spending. (Relations with specific foreign countries are usually found under the region concerned.)	Includes business, labor, agriculture, taxation, transportation, consumer affairs, monetary and fiscal policy, natural resources, and pollution.	Includes worldwide scientific, medical and technological developments, natural phenomena, U.S. weather, natural disasters, and accidents.	Includes the arts, religion, scholarship, communications media, sports, entertainments, fashions, fads and social life.

	World Affairs	Europe	Africa & the Middle East	The Americas	Asia & the Pacific
Nov. 8		At a wreath-laying ceremony on Britain's Remembrance Day for slain veterans, a bomb planted by the outlawed Provisional Irish Republican Army kills 11 people and injures more than 60 others in Enniskillen, County Fermanagh, Northern Ireland.... Italians vote in favor of five referendum propositions dealing with nuclear energy, parliamentary oversight, and judicial accountability. Turnout for the two-day vote is just 62.5%.	Arab leaders at an emergency summit of the Arab League, in Amman, Jordan, unanimously condemn Iran and express support for Iraq in the Persian Gulf war. The resolution also clears the way for Arab states to resume diplomatic relations with Egypt, broken off in 1979 when Cairo signed a peace treaty with Israel.		
Nov. 9		U.S. and Soviet delegations begin formal negotiations in Geneva on banning underground nuclear tests. The talks were agreed upon by Sec. of State George P. Shultz and Soviet Foreign Min. Eduard A. Shevardnadze during discussions in Washington in September.			India's parliament passes a measure extending central government rule over the strife-torn northern state of Punjab for an additional six months. The state's Sikh majority is waging a violent campaign to establish an independent homeland in the region.
Nov. 10		Spain formally notifies the United States that the current agreement covering U.S. bases in Spain will not be extended past the May 14, 1988, expiration date. Negotiations are continuing in an attempt to reach a compromise agreement that will retain a U.S. military presence in Spain.	Niger's Pres. Seyni Kountche dies in Paris of a brain tumor. A few hours before his death, Col. Ali Seybou, the army chief of staff and a cousin of Kountche, is named acting president.		
Nov. 11		The Soviet Communist Party Central Committee dismisses Boris N. Yeltsin as the head of the Moscow city party organization. He is the first senior party official to be removed after attaining power under Soviet leader Mikhail S. Gorbachev.	South Africa acknowledges for the first time that its troops clashed with Cuban and Soviet forces in southern Angola. Pretoria says it intervened on behalf of the National Union for the Total Union of Angola (UNITA) rebels after they routed an Angolan Army offensive, drawing the Cuban soldiers and Soviet advisers directly into the fighting.		
Nov. 12		Britain's Employment Dept. reports that the unemployment rate in October fell below 10% for the first time in five years.	Iran responds to the November 8 condemnation by Arab leaders by denouncing the Arab rulers as stooges of the United States and promising a new offensive against the "aggressor Baghdad regime."	Amid stepped-up efforts to negotiate a cease-fire in Nicaragua, Pres. Daniel Ortega Saavedra proposes immediate negotiations with the Contras, to take place in the United States and be mediated by Miguel Cardinal Obando y Bravo.... Under an amnesty enacted as part of the Central American peace plan, Salvadoran military judges order the release of five leftist rebels involved in two murders in El Salvador in 1983 and 1985.... The Canadian Life and Health Insurance Assoc. Inc. announces that purchasers of large policies will have to submit to testing for acquired immune deficiency syndrome.	In Dhaka, Bangladesh, at least six people are killed and hundreds arrested during three days of clashes between police and antigovernment protesters seeking the ouster of Pres. Hussein Mohammed Ershad.... Sri Lanka's parliament passes, 136-11, legislation giving the nation's Tamil minority limited autonomy in a unified district in the northern and eastern provinces.... An Australian government commission begins an inquiry into the cases of 64 Aborigines who have died in jail or in police custody since 1980. Police have classified most of the deaths as suicides.

A	B	C	D	E
Includes developments that affect more than one world region, international organizations and important meetings of major world leaders.	*Includes all domestic and regional developments in Europe, including the Soviet Union, Turkey, Cyprus and Malta.*	*Includes all domestic and regional developments in Africa and the Middle East, including Iraq and Iran and excluding Cyprus, Turkey and Afghanistan.*	*Includes all domestic and regional developments in Latin America, the Caribbean and Canada.*	*Includes all domestic and regional developments in Asia and Pacific nations, extending from Afghanistan through all the Pacific Islands, except Hawaii.*

U.S. Politics & Social Issues	U.S. Foreign Policy & Defense	U.S. Economy & Environment	Science, Technology & Nature	Culture, Leisure & Life Style	
In a CBS News/*New York Times* poll taken the day after Judge Douglas H. Ginsburg withdrew his nomination to the Supreme Court, 58% of the respondents do not think having "ever smoked marijuana" should disqualify someone from serving on the Supreme Court; of those who say it should, an additional 21% say it should not be a disqualifier if the candidate "only smoked it in college." Almost identical numbers apply to presidential candidates.				In Calcutta, India, Australia defeats England to win the World Cup in cricket.	Nov. 8
Emphasizing his roots in the Republican heartland, Sen. Robert J. Dole (R, Kans.) officially declares his candidacy for the 1988 Republican presidential nomination.		Texas Eastern Transmission Corp. comes to an agreement with federal officials to clean up toxic deposits of polychlorinated biphenyls along 10,000 miles (16,000 km) of natural gas pipeline between Texas and New Jersey.		The National Book Awards are presented. Larry Heinemann's *Paco's Story* wins for fiction, and Richard Rhodes's *The Making of the Atomic Bomb* wins for nonfiction. The awards date back to 1950 but have undergone several changes of format; from 1980 through 1986, they were known as the American Book Awards.	Nov. 9
The Supreme Court rules, 6-0, that the Internal Revenue Service does not have to provide data requested under the Freedom of Information Act even if identification of individual taxpayers is removed.		In the Transportation Dept.'s first monthly ranking of major airlines by on-time performance and baggage return service, American Airlines posts the best on-time record, 84.5%, for September.... The Labor Dept. announces final settlement of its 10-year-old lawsuit against the Teamsters union pension fund. The fund will remain under court supervision, probably until the year 2007.... The poorest one-tenth of Americans will pay federal taxes at a 20% higher rate in 1988 than they did in 1977, and the richest one-hundredth will pay at a rate almost 20% less than they did a decade ago, according to the Congressional Budget Office.	Western European representatives to the 13-nation European Space Agency (ESA) agree to pursue three major projects related to manned space flight. The decision is made without support from Britain, which does not consider development of a Western European manned-space capability commercially feasible. The other ESA ministers, however, approve development of the Columbus manned space laboratory, the Hermes space mini-shuttle, and the Ariane-Five launcher.		Nov. 10
Pres. Reagan announces that federal Judge Anthony Kennedy of California will be his new nominee to the Supreme Court. Kennedy was passed over by a divided White House just two weeks before in favor of U.S. Appeals Court Judge Douglas H. Ginsburg, who withdrew his nomination November 7.				Vincent van Gogh's *Irises* (1889) fetches a record $53.9 mil. at auction at Sotheby's in New York City. The previous record for a work sold at auction, $39.9 mil., was set in March by another van Gogh painting, *Sunflowers*.... In baseball, Boston Red Sox righthander Roger Clemens is named the American League's Cy Young award for the second consecutive year.... *Variety*'s top-grossing films for the week are: *Fatal Attraction*; *Hello Again*; *Fatal Beauty*; *Baby Boom*; and *The Hidden*.	Nov. 11
A federal district judge in Baltimore overturns convictions that sent former Gov. Marvin Mandel of Maryland and five associates to prison in 1977 on mail fraud and racketeering charges.... An ethics panel of the American Medical Assoc. issues detailed guidelines informing doctors of their moral obligation to treat patients infected with the acquired immune deficiency syndrome virus.		The U.S. deficit on merchandise trade declines in September to $14.08 bil., from $15.71 bil. in August, the Commerce Dept. says.	A major Finnish study offers the latest support for the theory that there are good and bad forms of cholesterol. But the theory is undermined by results of another major study announced at almost the same time, a joint U.S.-Soviet study.		Nov. 12

F	G	H	I	J
Includes elections, federal-state relations, civil rights and liberties, crime, the judiciary, education, health care, poverty, urban affairs and population.	*Includes formation and debate of U.S. foreign and defense policies, veterans' affairs and defense spending. (Relations with specific foreign countries are usually found under the region concerned.)*	*Includes business, labor, agriculture, taxation, transportation, consumer affairs, monetary and fiscal policy, natural resources, and pollution.*	*Includes worldwide scientific, medical and technological developments, natural phenomena, U.S. weather, natural disasters, and accidents.*	*Includes the arts, religion, scholarship, communications media, sports, entertainments, fashions, fads and social life.*

	World Affairs	Europe	Africa & the Middle East	The Americas	Asia & the Pacific
Nov. 13		Britain's inflation data, as reported by the Employment Dept., shows a 0.5% gain in the retail price index for the month and 4.5% inflation over the previous 12 months. While the price increase is greater than the 4.2% annual rate in September, the government is reported to still be confident that inflation will decline by year's end.		Nicaragua's Pres. Daniel Ortega Saavedra presents an 11-point proposal for a cease-fire in Nicaragua that requires the U.S.-backed Contras to lay down their arms and accept a political amnesty.	
Nov. 14		In Poland, the government announces that consumer prices will rise an average of 40% in 1988. The price hike, an offshoot of the economic reform plan unveiled in October, is intended to "heal the market . . . and to arrest inflation," the government says.			
Nov. 15		In Yugoslavia, the federal government sharply increases prices and imposes a retroactive general wage freeze. The measures are to remain in effect until June 1988. . . . Thousands of industrial workers in Brasov, Romania, stage a violent protest against shortages caused by the latest energy crisis. Regulations to tighten the rationing of energy were announced November 11.		A key committee draws up a new constitution for Brazil, dealing Pres. Jose Sarney a blow by backing a four-year presidential term. Sarney had sought a five-year term. The committee also votes for a parliamentary system to be set up on Mar. 15, 1988, to replace the presidential system.	
Nov. 16					South Korea's Pres. Chun Doo Hwan officially opens the nation's presidential campaign and announces that elections will be held December 16. Seven candidates formally register to run for president.
Nov. 17					
Nov. 18		Boris N. Yeltsin, ousted as Communist Party (CP) chief of Moscow November 11 after criticizing the pace of economic reforms in the USSR, is given an important government post, according to the official Soviet news agency Tass. . . . In the capital of the Soviet republic of Latvia, hundreds of police, militiamen, and civilian vigilantes block an attempted nationalist protest on the anniversary of Latvian independence from the Soviet Union in 1918.		In an effort to preserve the nation's foreign currency reserves, Mexico's central bank stops supporting the peso against the dollar on the open market, a move that sends the value of the peso plummeting.	

A	B	C	D	E
Includes developments that affect more than one world region, international organizations and important meetings of major world leaders.	Includes all domestic and regional developments in Europe, including the Soviet Union, Turkey, Cyprus and Malta.	Includes all domestic and regional developments in Africa and the Middle East, including Iraq and Iran and excluding Cyprus, Turkey and Afghanistan.	Includes all domestic and regional developments in Latin America, the Caribbean and Canada.	Includes all domestic and regional developments in Asia and Pacific nations, extending from Afghanistan through all the Pacific Islands, except Hawaii.

U.S. Politics & Social Issues	U.S. Foreign Policy & Defense	U.S. Economy & Environment	Science, Technology & Nature	Culture, Leisure & Life Style	
Beech-Nut Nutrition Corp., the second-largest maker of baby-food products in the United States, pleads guilty to 215 federal felony counts of intentionally shipping millions of jars of bogus apple juice for babies.		Pres. Reagan announces punitive tariffs on some $105 mil. in imports from Brazil in retaliation for Brazil's import restrictions on U.S. computer software.... The government's producer price index declined 0.2% in October, the Labor Dept. says.	The Food and Drug Admin. gives clearance to Genentech Inc., of South San Francisco, Calif., to begin marketing tissue plasminogen activator (TPA), a genetically engineered blood clot dissolver, as an emergency heart attack medication. The drug will be marketed under the brand name Activase.		Nov. 13
The Senate Judiciary Committee schedules confirmation hearings, beginning December 14, on Anthony Kennedy's nomination to the Supreme Court.				For the first time since he defected from the Soviet Union in 1961, ballet star Rudolf Nureyev, the 49-year-old head of the Paris Opera Ballet, returns to his homeland. He is granted an unusual two-day visa to visit his ailing mother at her home in Ufa, the Tatar capital of the Bashkir Republic in the Urals.	Nov. 14
A Des Moines Register poll finds Sen. Robert J. Dole (Kans.) at the head of the Republican presidential field for the Feb. 8, 1988, Iowa precinct caucuses that kick off the presidential race. Dole is the choice of 36% of Iowa republicans and Vice Pres. George Bush of 30%; no other GOP candidate posted more than 10%. In the Democratic standings, Sen. Paul Simon (Ill.) leads with 24%, followed by Massachusetts Gov. Michael S. Dukakis with 18%, Rep. Richard A. Gephardt (Mo.) with 14%, and the Rev. Jesse L. Jackson, 11%.	A bipartisan congressional caucus charges that the Salvadoran military and ruling party are misusing American aid to conduct a war against leftist rebels. The caucus also says that the unstable economic situation in El Salvador has jeopardized efforts for peace.			Gerhard Berger wins the Australian Grand Prix in Adelaide.	Nov. 15
The Supreme Court upholds the convictions of former Wall Street Journal reporter R. Foster Winans and two others in connection with a scheme to profit from advance information on daily stock tips published by the newspaper.	The Supreme Court lets stand a ruling allowing Vietnam veterans access to corporate research data on the controversial herbicide Agent Orange. Litigation on the issue—in which veterans claim health impairments from exposure during the Vietnam War to the herbicide, which contains the toxic chemical dioxin—was resolved in a settlement in 1984, and company documents on the suit were to be returned on the ground that they contained "proprietary information."	The Federal Reserve Board says that its industrial production index rose a solid 0.6% in October.		Moroccan author Tahar Ben Jelloun wins the Goncourt Prize, France's most coveted literary award, for his novel La Nuit Sacree (The Sacred Night).	Nov. 16
The Senate votes to block the first broad housing legislation to reach it in final form in seven years.... A federal jury in Denver convicts two white supremacists and acquits two others of civil rights violations in the 1984 machine-gun slaying of Denver radio personality Alan Berg.... The House approves, 305-112, a revision of the 1939 Hatch Act, which restricts partisan political activities by federal employees.	The White House and Congress reach a compromise on arms control provisions in the FY1988 defense authorization. The various aspects of the compromise are incorporated into the authorization. ... The House votes, 399-17, to approve legislation that will grant cabinet-level status to the Veterans Admin.... In a ceremony at the Pentagon, Pres. Reagan awards retiring Defense Sec. Caspar W. Weinberger the presidential Medal of Freedom.	The Environmental Protection Agency asks for a delay in implementing clean-air deadlines on reduction of ozone and carbon monoxide pollution. Some 50 to 60 cities may fail to meet a December 31 deadline for reducing the pollutants below levels designated dangerous to public health. Failure to meet the deadlines would lead to sanctions on construction of new industrial plants.		In baseball, Toronto Blue Jay outfielder George Bell wins the American League's most valuable player award.	Nov. 17
	House and Senate committees that held hearings on the Iran-Contra arms scandal through the summer issue their final report. The 690-page document chronicles the many questions that remain unanswered about the affair, but places blame firmly on the shoulders of Pres. Reagan for policies in Iran and Central America that hinged on "secrecy, deception and disdain for the law."	Housing starts fell 8.2% in October to their lowest level since April 1983, the Commerce Dept. reports.		Outfielder Andre Dawson of the Chicago Cubs is voted the National League's most valuable player.	Nov. 18

F	G	H	I	J
Includes elections, federal-state relations, civil rights and liberties, crime, the judiciary, education, health care, poverty, urban affairs and population.	Includes formation and debate of U.S. foreign and defense policies, veterans' affairs and defense spending. (Relations with specific foreign countries are usually found under the region concerned.)	Includes business, labor, agriculture, taxation, transportation, consumer affairs, monetary and fiscal policy, natural resources, and pollution.	Includes worldwide scientific, medical and technological developments, natural phenomena, U.S. weather, natural disasters, and accidents.	Includes the arts, religion, scholarship, communications media, sports, entertainments, fashions, fads and social life.

	World Affairs	Europe	Africa & the Middle East	The Americas	Asia & the Pacific
Nov. 19				Nicaraguan Contra leaders say that they have rejected a cease-fire proposal put forward by Pres. Daniel Ortega Saavedra three days earlier. Alfonso Robelo, a director of the Nicaraguan Resistance, says the proposal is "a propaganda act" offering little more than "a way to surrender."	At the UN General Assembly, a report prepared for the UN Human Rights Comm. claims that progress has been made in the protection of basic human rights in Afghanistan. But the Independent Counsel on International Human Rights harshly criticizes both the Afghan government and the Soviet occupation forces.
Nov. 20		A U.S. official announces that the United States and Soviet Union will conduct joint underground nuclear tests in 1988 to calibrate monitoring gear for the purpose of future verification.		In the latest of a series of debt reschedulings with international creditors over the previous year, Jamaica is reported to have signed a $50 mil. agreement with Club of Paris creditors. The deal covers all the principal and 85% of the interest that falls due to the Club of Paris between the end of 1986 and Mar. 31, 1988. It also covers Jamaican loans from the U.S. Agency for International Development and the U.S. Defense Dept.	Commerce Sec. C. William Verity criticizes Japan's refusal to open its construction projects to U.S. companies and warns of possible congressional retaliation. . . . Sixty-two labor groups merge to form Japan's largest union, the Japanese Private Sector Trade Union Confederation, which boasts a membership of 5.6 million workers.
Nov. 21				Colombian highway police arrest Jorge Luis Ochoa Vasquez, reputed to be one of two top chiefs of the Medellin Cartel, a drug consortium reportedly responsible for 80% of the cocaine entering the United States each year. . . . In Paraguay, a convention of the ruling Colorado Party unanimously nominates Pres. Alfredo Stroessner, 75, as its candidate for the 1988 presidential election.	
Nov. 22		French historian Emmanuel Le Roy Ladurie is appointed director of the Bibliotheque Nationale, France's national library. Regarded as one of the world's most influential historians, Le Roy Ladurie is a leader of the "Annales" school, centered in Paris, which places greater emphasis on the lives of ordinary people than on the deeds of their leaders.		El Salvador's Pres. Jose Napoleon Duarte accuses rightist political leader Roberto D'Aubuisson of responsibility for the 1980 murder of Oscar Arnulfo Romero, archbishop of San Salvador. . . . To show compliance with the regional peace plan signed in Guatemala in August, Nicaragua frees 985 pardoned political prisoners.	
Nov. 23	The United States pledges to pay at least $90 mil. to the UN in December to head off a possible UN budget crisis. The promise is in response to appeals from Sec. Gen. Javier Perez de Cuellar.			Two exiled left-wing civilian rebel leaders returned to El Salvador November 21 and this day to test the political opening provided for under the terms of the Central American peace agreement signed in August.	In the Philippines, a communist rebel group claims responsibility for a series of attacks near Clark Air Base October 28 in which three U.S. servicemen were killed. . . . Indian troops in Sri Lanka resume operations against Tamil guerrillas following a two-day cease-fire. India claims that the Liberation Tigers of Tamil Eelam separatist group has failed to respond "positively" to the cease-fire. . . . In Japan, the cabinet approves a proposed FY1988 budget that includes a 4.8% spending hike, the largest in six years.

A	B	C	D	E
Includes developments that affect more than one world region, international organizations and important meetings of major world leaders.	Includes all domestic and regional developments in Europe, including the Soviet Union, Turkey, Cyprus and Malta.	Includes all domestic and regional developments in Africa and the Middle East, including Iraq and Iran and excluding Cyprus, Turkey and Afghanistan.	Includes all domestic and regional developments in Latin America, the Caribbean and Canada.	Includes all domestic and regional developments in Asia and Pacific nations, extending from Afghanistan through all the Pacific Islands, except Hawaii.

U.S. Politics & Social Issues	U.S. Foreign Policy & Defense	U.S. Economy & Environment	Science, Technology & Nature	Culture, Leisure & Life Style	
		The Federal Savings and Loan Insurance Corp. pledges $1.3 bil. to salvage Vernon Savings & Loan Assoc., a Texas thrift that federal regulators closed in March, when 96% of its loans were found to be in default. . . . Saying that the forests are endangered by a "broad array" of pollutants, not just the sulfur dioxide and nitrogen oxides linked to acid rain, the American Forestry Assoc. urges Congress to tighten air pollution laws to protect the nation's forests. . . . Tax revenues taken in by state and local governments increased 5.9% in 1986, to a total of $382.5 bil., Commerce Clearing House reports.			Nov. 19
The District of Columbia Court of Appeals upholds, 5-2, the authority of the district government to require equal treatment of homosexual student groups at Georgetown Univ., but says the Roman Catholic institution does not have to "officially recognize" such groups.	The State Dept. announces that the United States and Cuba have agreed to reactivate a 1984 immigration pact that calls for Cuba to take back more than 2,000 "undesirables" who traveled to the United States in the 1980 Mariel boatlift; in exchange the United States will accept Cuban political prisoners and more than 20,000 Cuban immigrants a year. . . . The Senate votes, 91-1, to confirm Frank C. Carlucci as the new secretary of defense.	White House and congressional negotiators announce an agreement on a plan to reduce the federal budget deficit by $30 bil. in FY1988 and by $46 bil. in the following year. . . . The government's consumer price index rose 0.4% in October, the Labor Dept. reports. . . . The Labor Dept. tightens regulations to protect workers from exposure to formaldehyde, a widely used industrial chemical that causes serious eye, skin, and lung irritations.		Publishers Weekly's hardback fiction best-sellers for the week are: Kaleidoscope, Danielle Steel; Presumed Innocent, Scott Turow; Leaving Home: A Collection of Lake Wobegon Stories, Garrison Keillor; Patriot Games, Tom Clancy; and Heaven and Hell, John Jakes. . . . The Last Emperor, an epic of 20th-century China centered on the life of Pu Yi, China's last emperor, is released in New York. Directed by Bernardo Bertolucci, with a screenplay by Mark Peploe and Bertolucci, the film stars John Lone, Joan Chen, and Peter O'Toole.	Nov. 20
				Billboard's best-selling albums for the week are: Dirty Dancing (soundtrack); Tunnel of Love, Bruce Springsteen; Bad, Michael Jackson; Whitesnake, Whitesnake; and A Momentary Lapse of Reason, Pink Floyd. . . . Ferdinand, the 1986 Kentucky Derby winner, edges Alysheba, the 1987 Derby victor, to win horse racing's Breeders' Cup Classic. Very Subtle wins the Sprint; Theatrical, the Turf; Success Express, Juvenile; Epitome, the Juvenile Fillies; Miesque, the Mile; and Sacahuista, the Distaff.	Nov. 21
	Sec. of State George P. Shultz and Soviet Foreign Min. Eduard A. Shevardnadze finalize the schedule for the December summit between Pres. Reagan and Soviet leader Mikhail S. Gorbachev.			West Germany's Steffi Graf wins the Virginia Slims Championship and finishes the year as the top-ranked women's tennis player. In 77 matches during 1987, Graf lost only twice, to Martina Navratilova in the finals of both Wimbledon and the U.S. Open. . . . North Carolina wins the National Collegiate Athletic Assoc. women's soccer championship, 1-0, over Massachusetts in Amherst, Mass.	Nov. 22
				After a brief court proceeding in Los Angeles, convicted murderer Jeffrey R. MacDonald agrees to settle for $325,000 his $15-mil. civil suit against author Joe McGinniss. The case went to trial before a jury, but that trial ended in a mistrial with the jury deadlocked.	Nov. 23

F	G	H	I	J
Includes elections, federal-state relations, civil rights and liberties, crime, the judiciary, education, health care, poverty, urban affairs and population.	Includes formation and debate of U.S. foreign and defense policies, veterans' affairs and defense spending. (Relations with specific foreign countries are usually found under the region concerned.)	Includes business, labor, agriculture, taxation, transportation, consumer affairs, monetary and fiscal policy, natural resources, and pollution.	Includes worldwide scientific, medical and technological developments, natural phenomena, U.S. weather, natural disasters, and accidents.	Includes the arts, religion, scholarship, communications media, sports, entertainments, fashions, fads and social life.

	World Affairs	Europe	Africa & the Middle East	The Americas	Asia & the Pacific
Nov. 24					The standing committee of the National People's Congress appoints Li Peng acting premier. Li's appointment continues the changing of the guard within the Chinese leadership that began earlier in November. Li is expected to be officially confirmed as premier at a meeting of the full congress in 1988.
Nov. 25	The UN Security Council unanimously demands that South Africa unconditionally withdraw all of its troops from Angola, where they are fighting alongside National Union for the Total Independence of Angola (UNITA) rebels against Soviet- and Cuban-backed government forces.	Ministers of eight Northern European nations reach an agreement in London to reduce pollution levels in the North Sea. The pact will reduce the incineration of toxic wastes there by 1991 and end it by 1994, and ban the dumping of harmful industrial wastes beginning in 1990.	A Palestinian guerrilla flies a motorized hang glider from Lebanon into northern Israel and attacks an army base, killing six Israeli soldiers and wounding seven others before being shot dead.	In a rebuff to the military, Surinamese voters hand a three-party opposition coalition a landslide victory in the country's first national elections in 10 years. Official results show the coalition Front for Democracy and Development (FDD) winning 85% of the vote. The recently formed National Democratic Party (NDP) of Cmdr. Desi Bouterse, the head of government, takes 9%, according to the official figures.	Hundreds of people are killed when Typhoon Nina strikes the central Philippines with winds of more than 120 miles an hour.
Nov. 26		Greek Economy Min. Costas Simitis resigns to protest Premier Andreas Papandreou's retraction of an anti-inflationary incomes policy. Simitis announced the policy, part of his anti-inflationary stabilization program, on November 24. Papandreou retracted it the next day following trade union protests and strike threats.		Eight Latin American presidents gather in Acapulco, Mexico, for the first such summit without the participation of the United States. Latin America's foreign debt of almost $400 bil. is the focus for the so-called Group of Eight, which discusses peace in Central America, regional economic integration, and Cuba's role in hemispheric affairs. The countries participating in the talks are Argentina, Brazil, Colombia, Mexico, Panama, Peru, Uruguay, and Venezuela.	
Nov. 27		A public offering for shares in Eurotunnel, the Anglo-French consortium building a rail tunnel under the English Channel, closes today with 20% of the shares offered in Britain still unsubscribed. . . . Ireland's most wanted guerrilla suspect is captured in a shootout in Urlingford, County Kilkenny. The "border fox" is wanted in connection with the kidnapping of a Dublin dentist and as many as 30 murders, most of which occurred during the late 1970s.	Antigovernment rebels in Zimbabwe massacre 16 white members of a Christian missionary group, most of them women and children, in Matabeleland province south of Bulaway.	Air Canada, the government-owned airline, suspends service and locks out its striking ground workers. The airline last halted service in 1978 in response to wildcat strikes by ground workers.	Deng Xiaoping, China's paramount leader and chairman of the Central Military Comm., replaces the nation's top three military staff officers. The change of command appears to be part of the Communist Party's move to replace aging veterans in the military and the party with younger, more reform-minded leaders.
Nov. 28		In Britain, the government publishes its controversial bill to reform education policy. The bill is met by a chorus of opposition from the Labour Party and union groups involved in education.	The Zimbabwean press asserts that South Africa is indirectly responsible for the November 26-27 massacre in southeast Zimbabwe because of its alleged support of the Matabeleland dissidents as a way of destabilizing the Mugabe government. . . . In Mozambique, the Mozambique National Resistance continues to carry out massacres of civilians; 373 people have died in ambushes of convoys on the highway north of Maputo in the last six weeks, according to the state-run news agency.		
Nov. 29	In a series of moves over three days, two of five French hostages remaining in Lebanon are released, and France and Iran allow diplomats effectively under arrest in their Paris and Teheran embassies to go home. The actions taken by France, including the announcement that negotiations are proceeding on money owed by France to Iran, are being criticized by British and U.S. officials.	Turkey's Premier Turgut Ozal easily wins reelection in a general election. Thanks to new electoral laws and a divided opposition, Ozal's conservative Motherland Party will hold nearly two-thirds of the seats in the new 450-member parliament despite winning just over 36% of the vote.		Election officials call off what would have been Haiti's first free elections in 30 years amid a wave of terror unleashed by loyalists of deposed Pres. Jean-Claude Duvalier.	South Korea's presidential campaign is marked by harsh criticism of ruling Democratic Justice Party (DJP) candidate Roh Tae Woo. Opposition leaders condemn Roh for his role in the 1979 military coup and accuse the DJP of widespread campaign violations.

A	B	C	D	E
Includes developments that affect more than one world region, international organizations and important meetings of major world leaders.	Includes all domestic and regional developments in Europe, including the Soviet Union, Turkey, Cyprus and Malta.	Includes all domestic and regional developments in Africa and the Middle East, including Iraq and Iran and excluding Cyprus, Turkey and Afghanistan.	Includes all domestic and regional developments in Latin America, the Caribbean and Canada.	Includes all domestic and regional developments in Asia and Pacific nations, extending from Afghanistan through all the Pacific Islands, except Hawaii.

U.S. Politics & Social Issues	U.S. Foreign Policy & Defense	U.S. Economy & Environment	Science, Technology & Nature	Culture, Leisure & Life Style	
		After-tax profits of U.S. corporations rose at a seasonally adjusted annual rate of 5.2% in the third quarter, the Commerce Dept. reports.	An unusual earthquake swarm strikes southern California's Imperial Valley, over two days. The strongest of the tremors, measuring 6.3 on the Richter scale, follows by less than 12 hours one with a magnitude of 6.0, according to the National Geological Survey.	The United States and Soviet Union announce that the last major obstacle to a treaty on eliminating intermediate-range nuclear forces has been resolved.	Nov. 24
Chicago's Mayor Harold Washington (D) dies after suffering a heart attack at his city hall desk. The city's first black mayor, Washington finally won undisputed control of the city council in April, and the 65-year-old mayor said frequently that he intended to be mayor for the next 20 years.				*Three Men and a Baby*, a U.S. remake of the 1986 French farce *3 Men and a Cradle*, is released in New York. The film is directed by Leonard Nimoy and stars Tom Selleck, Steve Guttenberg, and Ted Danson.	Nov. 25
		Consumer spending in October remained largely unchanged from a revised 0.3% drop in September, the Commerce Dept. reports.... The Environmental Protection Agency announces plans to complete the cleanup of the Love Canal neighborhood in Niagara Falls, N.Y. The area, contaminated by seepage from a toxic waste dump, was declared a federal environmental emergency in 1980.			Nov. 26
					Nov. 27
			Choh Hao Li, 74, biochemist who in 1971 synthesized the human pituitary growth hormone, which he discovered in the 1950s, dies of cancer in Berkeley, Calif. Born in China, he spent more than 50 years in the Univ. of California system; since 1983 he had been director of UC-San Francisco's laboratory of molecular endocrinology. His last major achievement was the discovery in 1978 of beta-endorphin, a powerful pain-killing substance produced in the brain.		Nov. 28
Cuban inmates end an eight-day siege at a federal detention center in Oakdale, La., and release their remaining 26 hostages after reaching a settlement with federal negotiators.	The United States announces the suspension of all nonhumanitarian aid to Haiti, after scheduled elections were called off this day in Haiti.			The Edmonton Eskimos win the Canadian Football League's Grey Cup Championship over the Toronto Argonauts.	Nov. 29

F	G	H	I	J
Includes elections, federal-state relations, civil rights and liberties, crime, the judiciary, education, health care, poverty, urban affairs and population.	Includes formation and debate of U.S. foreign and defense policies, veterans' affairs and defense spending. (Relations with specific foreign countries are usually found under the region concerned.)	Includes business, labor, agriculture, taxation, transportation, consumer affairs, monetary and fiscal policy, natural resources, and pollution.	Includes worldwide scientific, medical and technological developments, natural phenomena, U.S. weather, natural disasters, and accidents.	Includes the arts, religion, scholarship, communications media, sports, entertainments, fashions, fads and social life.

	World Affairs	Europe	Africa & the Middle East	The Americas	Asia & the Pacific
Nov. 30		The Polish government acknowledges that it has failed to win the support of sufficient numbers of voters to implement a proposed program of economic and political reforms. The measures were voted upon in a national referendum November 29.		Canada's Solicitor Gen. James F. Kelleher announces a pending reorganization of the Canadian Security Intelligence Service. The shake-up is to include new curbs on domestic wiretapping and on the use of informants.	Afghanistan's Pres. Najibullah declares that all Soviet troops will withdraw from Afghanistan within 12 months, if the United States and Pakistan stop supplying aid to rebels fighting the Soviet-backed Afghan government.... Laos and China formally agree to normalize diplomatic relations, severed following the Vietnamese invasion of Cambodia in December 1978. China has clashed repeatedly with Vietnam since 1979.
Dec. 1	The USSR and Third World nations join with the United States, Britain, and other Western countries at the UN General Assembly to defeat a provocative Syrian-proposed resolution on terrorism.	Prince Charles attacks architects, developers, and planners for ruining the London skyline with modernist designs, and likens their destruction to that caused by Nazi Germany's bombing raids during World War II. His verbal assault comes during a speech at the annual Planning and Communications Committee Dinner at the Mansion House.	To mark its 75th anniversary, the African National Congress (ANC) holds its first international conference, a parley in Arusha, Tanzania, that brings together antiapartheid groups from around the world. The ANC is the main group fighting to overthrow South Africa's white minority regime.		In India, the government files homicide charges against Union Carbide Corp. for the 1984 disaster at the company's chemical plant in Bhopal, India.
Dec. 2		The West German government announces a $12.8 bil. program to increase commercial lending, but the package draws criticism from business, banking and opposition political leaders for being insufficient.		Two civilian rebel leaders, who returned to El Salvador from exile in November to test the political openness in their homeland, end their visits November 29 and this day. Ruben Zamora, vice president of the Democratic Revolutionary Front (FDR), a political front allied with the Farabundo Marti National Liberation Front (FMLN) rebel army, leaves El Salvador three days after FDR president Guillermo Ungo.	
Dec. 3		The central banks of West Germany and six other European nations reduce key interest rates to stem the continuing fall in value of the U.S. dollar. The West German Bundesbank reduces its discount rate to 2.5%, the lowest in the bank's 110-year history.... The British government obtains a High Court injunction barring the broadcast of a British Broadcasting Corp. (BBC) radio program on British security services. The action is the latest in a series that have prompted charges of censorship against P.M. Margaret Thatcher.		Canada's Health Min. Jack Epp unveils a $4.1 bil. national childcare plan.	Japan blocks the adoption of a General Agreement on Tariffs and Trade (GATT) ruling ordering Tokyo to lift import quotas on 10 categories of agricultural products after the United States and other GATT members refuse to accept a Japanese offer to remove restrictions on eight of the 10 product areas.... A Vietnamese court in Ho Chi Minh City convicts 17 people of high treason and banditry for their roles in an attempted guerrilla invasion.
Dec. 4		The Conservative government of Britain's P.M. Margaret Thatcher publishes as legislation its plan to overhaul the system of property taxes (rates) in England and Wales and replace it with a community charge, or poll tax. The Local Government Finance Bill is widely viewed as the most controversial legislation facing the current session of Parliament.		Two days of indirect peace talks between the Nicaraguan government and the U.S.-backed Contra rebels ends in deadlock. Each side rejects cease-fire proposals put forward by the other, and government negotiators also reject a truce proposal offered by mediator Miguel Cardinal Obando y Bravo.... In compliance with provisions of the Central American peace treaty signed in August, Honduras's Pres. Jose Azcona Hoyo announces a general amnesty, to take effect December 11.	At the end of ten days of meetings, former Cambodian leader Prince Norodom Sihanouk and Premier Hun Sen, head of the Vietnamese-backed Cambodian government, announce an agreement to work toward a peaceful solution to the nation's political problems.... In Japan, the Economic Planning Agency reports that the gross national product for the second quarter of FY1987 rose 2% over the previous quarter.

A	B	C	D	E
Includes developments that affect more than one world region, international organizations and important meetings of major world leaders.	Includes all domestic and regional developments in Europe, including the Soviet Union, Turkey, Cyprus and Malta.	Includes all domestic and regional developments in Africa and the Middle East, including Iraq and Iran and excluding Cyprus, Turkey and Afghanistan.	Includes all domestic and regional developments in Latin America, the Caribbean and Canada.	Includes all domestic and regional developments in Asia and Pacific nations, extending from Afghanistan through all the Pacific Islands, except Hawaii.

U.S. Politics & Social Issues	U.S. Foreign Policy & Defense	U.S. Economy & Environment	Science, Technology & Nature	Culture, Leisure & Life Style	
The College Board announces that U.S. students received a total of about $20.5 bil. in aid from federal, state, and local governments as well as from the colleges themselves during the 1986-87 school year. The total amount of aid is $535 mil. more than students received in 1985-86.	The National Broadcasting Co. (NBC) of the United States airs a one-hour interview in prime time with Soviet leader Mikhail S. Gorbachev. It is the first one-on-one interview of the Soviet leader by a U.S. television network. (The interview, taped at the Kremlin, was conducted November 29.)	In New York, the dollar closes at post World War II lows of 1.6396 West German marks and 132.24 Japanese yen. The dollar has lost about 50% of its value against those currencies since peaking in March of 1985. . . . Prices received by farmers for their raw agricultural products rose 3.1% in November, the Agriculture Dept. reports. . . . The Senate votes, 74-0, to confirm James H. Burnley IV as transportation secretary. Burnley has been deputy transportation secretary since 1983.		James (Arthur) Baldwin, 63, author who explored the plight of oppressed blacks in 20th-century America in a variety of literary forms, dies of stomach cancer in St. Paul de Vence, France. A novelist and playwright, it was as an essayist that he achieved his reputation as the foremost literary spokesman of the black struggle for civil rights in the 1950s and 1960s. His three most important collections of essays are *Notes of a Native Son* (1955), *Nobody Knows My Name* (1961), and *The Fire Next Time* (1963). His novels include *Go Tell It on the Mountain* (1953), *Giovanni's Room* (1956), and *Another Country* (1962). Baldwin lived mostly in France since the late 1940s.	Nov. 30
The Supreme Court refuses to rule on a New Jersey law requiring a daily "moment of silence" in public school classrooms "for quiet and private contemplation and introspection." . . . All 12 Republican and Democratic presidential candidates meet in a televised debate presented by NBC News and moderated by NBC anchor Tom Brokaw. . . . The Senate approves, 97-1, a broad elementary and secondary education bill that could cost up to $7.4 bil.		The government's index of leading economic indicators declined 0.2% in October, the Commerce Dept. says. . . . The Supreme Court upholds, 8-0, the right of citizens to bring suit under the Clean Water Act against polluters on the basis of "either continuous or intermittent violation." . . . The Environmental Protection Agency announces plans for a phased reduction in use of chemicals that are causing depletion of the protective ozone layer in the stratosphere.	The National Aeronautics and Space Admin. names its prime contractors for construction of a multibillion-dollar space station, the nation's first permanent outpost in space. The contracts are assigned to Boeing Co., McDonnell Douglas Corp., General Electric Co., and Rockwell International Corp.		Dec. 1
Alderman Eugene Sawyer (D), 53, the longest-serving black member of the city council, is selected acting mayor of Chicago after days of political infighting and a tumultuous all-night city council session. He succeeds Harold Washington who died November 25.	Pres. Reagan's annual report to Congress on Soviet compliance with arms treaties accuses the Soviets of a technical violation of the 1972 antiballistic missile treaty. . . . The U.S. Agriculture Dept. announces the sale to the Soviet Union of an additional 500,000 metric tons of subsidized wheat, to be delivered through 1988, the final year of the current U.S.-Soviet grain pact.				Dec. 2
The National Education Assoc. (NEA) decides to postpone endorsing a candidate for president in 1988. The decision is made by the organization's political action committee at the request of NEA president Mary Hatwood Futrell, who says that while there is "strong support for a multiple endorsement" of several Democratic candidates, she is concerned that it might hamper eventual support for a front-runner if one emerges.	Pres. Reagan, in a joint interview with four TV news anchors, says conservative critics of his intermediate-range nuclear force arms reduction treaty do not understand the treaty, which is expected to be signed at a coming summit between Reagan and Soviet leader Mikhail S. Gorbachev.	Shearson Lehman Brothers Holdings Inc. announces a definitive agreement to purchase E.F. Hutton Group Inc. for $960 mil. in cash and debt securities. The combination will rival Merrill Lynch & Co. as the largest company on Wall Street. . . . Federal and state regulators close a record nine banks, bringing the nationwide total for the year to 173.	Luis Federico Leloir, 81, Argentine chemist who won the Nobel Prize for chemistry in 1970 for his research into the metabolism and storage of sugars, dies in Buenos Aires.		Dec. 3
An 11-day siege at a federal penitentiary in Atlanta ends with the release of 89 remaining hostages.	Pres. Reagan signs a bill authorizing $296 bil. for defense-related programs in FY1988.	Salomon Inc. announces that it is withdrawing from a $1 bil. office and residential building complex to be constructed at New York City's Columbus Circle. The investment company, which says it will take a $51 mil. charge against its fourth-quarter earnings related to the project, had pledged financing for the plan and had agreed to rent space there.		Rouben (Zachary) Mamoulian, 90, Russian-born U.S. film and stage director, dies in Los Angeles. Acclaimed for such inventive early sound films as *Dr. Jekyll and Mr. Hyde* (1932), *Queen Christina* (1933), and *Becky Sharp* (1935), the first major feature in three-color Technicolor, he also directed major Broadway musical productions including *Porgy and Bess* (1935), *Oklahoma!* (1943), and *Carousel* (1945). . . . The 50-member American Academy of Arts and Letters announces the election of three new members: poet James Dickey, novelist William Styron, and scholar Joseph Campbell.	Dec. 4

F	G	H	I	J
Includes elections, federal-state relations, civil rights and liberties, crime, the judiciary, education, health care, poverty, urban affairs and population.	*Includes formation and debate of U.S. foreign and defense policies, veterans' affairs and defense spending. (Relations with specific foreign countries are usually found under the region concerned.)*	*Includes business, labor, agriculture, taxation, transportation, consumer affairs, monetary and fiscal policy, natural resources, and pollution.*	*Includes worldwide scientific, medical and technological developments, natural phenomena, U.S. weather, natural disasters, and accidents.*	*Includes the arts, religion, scholarship, communications media, sports, entertainments, fashions, fads and social life.*

	World Affairs	Europe	Africa & the Middle East	The Americas	Asia & the Pacific
Dec. 5		The leaders of the 12 European Community nations adjourn a two-day summit in Copenhagen without reaching agreement on key farm and budget questions and a crisis summit meeting is called for February 1988.... The Mutual and Balanced Force Reduction talks in Vienna end another year with little progress toward cutting conventional forces in Europe. The discussions have been going on for 14 years.			In Fiji, Brig. Sitiveni Rabuka steps down as acting head of state and government, and appoints Sir Penaia Ganilau the first president of the new republic of Fiji. Ganilau is the nation's former governor general.
Dec. 6				Nicaraguan soldiers shoot down a small plane near San Juan del Norte and capture its pilot, an American said to have links to the Contras fighting the government. The plane, a Cessna 172 flown by James Jordan Denby, 57, is hit by rifle fire and forced to make an emergency landing on Nicaragua's Caribbean coast close to the Costa Rican border.	Bangladesh's Pres. Hossein Mohammed Ershad dissolves parliament in the face of widespread, opposition-led strikes and protests.... In the Seychelles a new four-year parliament is elected. All 36 candidates for the 25 seats are members of the ruling Seychelles People's United Party.
Dec. 7	Pope John Paul II and Ecumenical Patriarch Dimitrios I of Constantinople sign a joint declaration in Rome expressing hope that "the progress of dialogue" will help Roman Catholics and Eastern Orthodox Christians "to grow in better reciprocal awareness."			Alberta becomes the third province (after Quebec and Saskatchewan) to ratify the so-called Meech Lake constitutional accord which gives Quebec the constitutionally protected status of a "distinct society" within Canada.... U.S. and Canadian negotiators in Ottawa reach agreement on the final text of a comprehensive bilateral trade agreement.	
Dec. 8	In a ceremony attended by Vice Pres. George Bush, members of the Reagan cabinet, U.S. congressional leaders, and Soviet officials, Pres. Reagan and Gen. Sec. Mikhail Gorbachev sign the intermediate-range nuclear forces treaty in the East Room of the White House on the first day of a three-day summit in Washington, D.C.	The signing of the U.S.-Soviet treaty to eliminate intermediate-range nuclear forces is well received in Western Europe, but political leaders are quick to caution that the agreement is just one step in a process to improve European security.... Poland and its Club of Paris creditor nations sign an agreement to reschedule $9 bil. of Poland's more than $22 bil. n debt to Club of Paris nations.		A plane carrying Peru's top soccer team crashes in the Pacific Ocean off Lima, killing 37 people connected with the team and five crew members.... The International Monetary Fund disburses to Argentina $165.5 mil. in special drawing rights under the fund's standby facility.	
Dec. 9		According to West German officials cited by the *Washington Post*, East Germany has ordered its border guards not to shoot at people attempting to cross the Berlin Wall.		Canada's Supreme Court votes 7-1, to void a provision in the federal Criminal Code on so-called "constructive murder," thus throwing into doubt hundreds of convictions.... In Haiti, the Provisional Council of Government led by Lt. Gen. Henri Namphy announces that national elections will be held on Jan. 17, 1988.... In Argentina, the General Confederation of Workers stages its 10th general strike against the government of Pres. Raul Alfonsin. The strike halts public transportation in and around Buenos Aires, and most factories close.	Japan's Defense Agency says that a Japanese fighter plane fired warning shots at a Soviet bomber that was violating Japanese airspace. The incident marks the first time since the end of World War II that Japanese planes fired warning shots at an aircraft from another nation.

A	B	C	D	E
Includes developments that effect more than one world region, international organizations and important meetings of major world leaders.	*Includes all domestic and regional developments in Europe, including the Soviet Union, Turkey, Cyprus and Malta.*	*Includes all domestic and regional developments in Africa and the Middle East, including Iraq and Iran and excluding Cyprus, Turkey and Afghanistan.*	*Includes all domestic and regional developments in Latin America, the Caribbean and Canada.*	*Includes all domestic and regional developments in Asia and Pacific nations, extending from Afghanistan through all the Pacific Islands, except Hawaii.*

U.S. Politics & Social Issues	U.S. Foreign Policy & Defense	U.S. Economy & Environment	Science, Technology & Nature	Culture, Leisure & Life Style	
Supporters of the Rev. Pat Robertson pack a Virginia state party conference for a nonbinding straw poll to give their candidate 83% of the vote, against only 8% for Vice Pres. George Bush. On the same day, state GOP officials reject proposals that would link state presidential delegate selection to the result of Virginia's Mar. 8, 1988, primary. Instead, delegates will be chosen through a series of meetings and caucuses as Robertson prefers.				Wide receiver and kick returner Tim Brown is named the winner of the Heisman Trophy as the nation's top collegiate football player.	Dec. 5
An ABC News/Washington Post poll in the United States gives the Soviet leader Mikhail S. Gorbachev a 59% "favorable" rating, only four points lower than that of Reagan. The poll is made public two days before the Washington summit between the two leaders.	According to the contents of a declassified congressional transcript reported by the *Washington Post*, the United States had a total stockpile of 23,400 nuclear warheads at the start of 1987.			Clemson wins the National Collegiate Athletic Assoc. soccer championship with a 2-0 victory over San Diego State.	Dec. 6
At 53.58%, the United States has the lowest voter turnout rate of 28 countries studied by the Library of Congress's Congressional Research Service. That was the percentage of citizens of voting age who voted in the 1984 U.S. presidential election.		Outstanding consumer debt rose by a noticeable $3.74 bil. in October, the Federal Reserve Board reports. The increase, at an annual rate of 7.4%, brings outstanding credit to a total of $608.75 bil.		Gareth Bennett, a conservative priest and theologian prominent in the Church of England, commits suicide amid a controversy over an anonymous written attack on the church's liberal leadership. . . . The *New York Times* lists the following current fiction best-sellers: *The Covenant*, James A. Michener; *The Key to Rebecca*, Ken Follett; *Come Pour the Wine*, Cynthia Freeman; *Firestarter*, Stephen King; and *The Fifth Horseman*, Larry Collins and Dominique Lapierre.	Dec. 7
Populist state Assemblyman Art Agnos wins a stunning 70%-30% victory in San Francisco's nonpartisan mayoral election over veteran city Supervisor John Molinari. . . . Coretta Scott King, the widow of slain civil rights leader Dr. Martin Luther King Jr., files suit against Boston Univ., where Dr. King received his doctorate, demanding that the school relinquish thousands of documents he deposited there in 1964, four years before his death.					Dec. 8
Stella Nickell, 44, of Auburn, Wash., is indicted by a federal grand jury in Seattle on charges that in June of 1986 she caused the deaths of her husband and another Auburn resident by lacing Extra-Strength Excedrin capsules with cyanide. Officials say it is the first time anyone in the United States has been charged in a fatal drug tampering.				Chad Hennings of the Air Force Academy wins football's Outland Trophy as the nation's top interior lineman.	Dec. 9

F	G	H	I	J
Includes elections, federal-state relations, civil rights and liberties, crime, the judiciary, education, health care, poverty, urban affairs and population.	Includes formation and debate of U.S. foreign and defense policies, veterans' affairs and defense spending. (Relations with specific foreign countries are usually found under the region concerned.)	Includes business, labor, agriculture, taxation, transportation, consumer affairs, monetary and fiscal policy, natural resources, and pollution.	Includes worldwide scientific, medical and technological developments, natural phenomena, U.S. weather, natural disasters, and accidents.	Includes the arts, religion, scholarship, communications media, sports, entertainments, fashions, fads and social life.

	World Affairs	Europe	Africa & the Middle East	The Americas	Asia & the Pacific
Dec. 10	Central bankers from 12 leading non-communist industrial nations announce an agreement aimed at unifying regulatory standards. At the heart of the agreement is the stated aim of increasing the central banks' capital to 8% of assets within five years.... Costa Rica's Pres. Oscar Arias Sanchez urges the superpowers to stop intruding in Central American affairs. He makes his plea in Oslo, Norway, in his speech accepting the Nobel Prize for peace, which he was awarded for his authorship of a Central American peace plan signed in Guatemala in August.		Ayatollah Ruhollah Khomeini, the supreme Iranian leader, summons other top officials to his home to receive his new "political-divine will and testament," exactly five years after he made his previous will.	Brazil formally suspends a 10-month payment moratorium on its foreign debt by paying $357 mil. in overdue interest. In addition, foreign commercial banks turn over to Brazil's creditors $715 mil. as payment on overdue interest, for a total of $1.072 bil.	Japan's finance ministry announces that Japan's overall trade surplus with other nations fell 36% in November, to $4.74 bil. from $7.4 bil. one year earlier. November was the seventh month in a row in which the trade surplus declined from 1986 figures. The overall trade surplus for the first 11 months of calendar 1987 stood at $71.22 bil.
Dec. 11		The allies of the United States and the Soviet Union endorse the treaty to eliminate intermediate-range nuclear forces. The foreign ministers of the North Atlantic Treaty Org. back the treaty at a meeting in Brussels after a briefing by Sec. of State George P. Shultz, and the heads of the Warsaw Pact nations gather in East Berlin for a briefing by Soviet leader Mikhail S. Gorbachev.			
Dec. 12			After a year-long trial, a South Yemen court condemns former Pres. Ali Nasser Mohammed al-Hasani to death in absentia on charges of treason, terrorism, and sabotage. Thirty-four of his followers are also sentenced, 18 of them in absentia. Others among the 108 defendants receive prison terms of between five and 15 years, while a few are acquitted or amnestied.	Nicaragua's Defense Min. Humberto Ortega Saavedra says that the Soviet Union has agreed to back a major military buildup in Nicaragua. The minister says that the Soviets will supply the Sandinista government with advanced MiG fighter jets, missiles, and artillery and that 600,000 Nicaraguans will be under arms by 1995.	
Dec. 13		According to East Germany's official press agency ADN, the government has inaugurated an amnesty program under which 24,621 convicted inmates have been released from prison and 1,753 suspects set free while awaiting trial in an amnesty program.... Belgian voters deal a general election setback to Premier Wilfried Martens and his Christian Democratic grouping.			
Dec. 14	The Org. of Petroleum Exporting Countries ends an arduous six-day meeting in Vienna by extending its widely ignored benchmark price of $18 a barrel and equally flouted production quotas totaling 16.6 million barrels a day.	Some 5,000 officials discuss Romania's economic problems at a three-day Communist Party conference in Bucharest. In addition to an energy crisis, the nation is plagued with chronic food shortages, stagnant productivity, and growing unrest.	Border clashes break out between Kenya and Uganda, and Kenya responds by expelling Uganda's ambassador and stopping border traffic between the two economically interdependent East African nations.	Mexico's central bank devalues the official peso by 18% to relieve pressure on the currency. A month earlier, the government halted support for the free-market peso, causing an unexpectedly sharp decline in its value.	Leaders of the six member states of the Assoc. of Southeast Asian Nations (ASEAN) meet in the Philippine capital city of Manila. The ASEAN countries are Brunei, Indonesia, Malaysia, Philippines, Singapore, and Thailand.
Dec. 15		Poland's Premier Zbigniew Messner announces a revision of the plan to impose sharp price rises in 1988. The plan was rejected by voters in a national referendum in November.		Canada's P.M. Brian Mulroney announces a $2.1 bil. federal aid package for farmers. It was the largest single assistance package ever offered to Canadian growers. ... The World Bank approves a $250 mil. loan to Chile to support economic reform, including trade liberalization measures.	

A	B	C	D	E
Includes developments that affect more than one world region, international organizations and important meetings of major world leaders.	Includes all domestic and regional developments in Europe, including the Soviet Union, Turkey, Cyprus and Malta.	Includes all domestic and regional developments in Africa and the Middle East, including Iraq and Iran and excluding Cyprus, Turkey and Afghanistan.	Includes all domestic and regional developments in Latin America, the Caribbean and Canada.	Includes all domestic and regional developments in Asia and Pacific nations, extending from Afghanistan through all the Pacific Islands, except Hawaii.

U.S. Politics & Social Issues	U.S. Foreign Policy & Defense	U.S. Economy & Environment	Science, Technology & Nature	Culture, Leisure & Life Style	
		The U.S. deficit on merchandise trade rose to a record $17.63 bil. in October, the Commerce Dept. reports.		Jascha Heifetz, 86, one of the most renowned violinists of the 20th century, dies in Los Angeles, from injuries received in a fall. Born in Lithuania, he achieved great success as a child prodigy in Europe. His October 1917 debut at New York City's Carnegie Hall became the stuff of musical legend, and he performed regularly around the world until retiring from the concert stage in 1972.... The 50-member administrative board of the U.S. Catholic Conf., the organization that represents the nation's 300 bishops, releases a position paper entitled *The Many Faces of AIDS: A Gospel Response.*	Dec. 10
A federal judge in Richmond, Va., orders A.H. Robins Co. to set aside $2.475 bil. in its bankruptcy reorganization plan to compensate women who claim to have been injured by the company's Dalkon Shield intrauterine birth control device.... The Senate votes, 94-0, to confirm the nomination of Ann Dore McLaughlin as labor secretary. She will succeed William E. Brock III, who resigned in October to join the presidential campaign of Sen. Robert Dole (R, Kans.).	Pres. Reagan launches his fight to have the Senate ratify the U.S.-Soviet treaty to end intermediate-range nuclear forces. The president urges support for the treaty at a closed-door meeting with congressional leaders at the White House.	The government's producer price index remained unchanged for November, the Labor Dept. says. ... A three-member panel of the U.S. Court of Appeals for the District of Columbia voids Federal Communications Comm. rules requiring large- or medium-size cable television systems to carry some broadcast stations on their channels.	In Canada, the federal government orders the recall and destruction of live and cooked mussels, clams, oysters, and quahogs from the Atlantic Coast provinces and issues a public health warning of the possible toxic contamination of the mollusks.	The film *Wall Street*, about an ambitious young Wall Street broker who falls under the dangerous influence of a veteran corporate raider, is released in New York. Directed by Oliver Stone and written by Stone and Stanley Weiser, the film stars Michael Douglas, who wins the Oscar for best actor, Charlie Sheen, Daryl Hannah, Martin Sheen, Hal Holbrook, and Terence Stamp.	Dec. 11
A conservative coalition led by supporters of the Rev. Pat Robertson and Rep. Jack F. Kemp (R, N.Y.) narrowly wins a Republican Party rules showdown in Michigan, as the GOP state committee votes, 52-48, to change the party's delegate selection rules to bar a group of officeholders thought to be predominantly supporters of Vice Pres. George Bush.					Dec. 12
	White House national security adviser Lt. Gen. Colin L. Powell reveals on a television news program that the Reagan administration is insisting that the Soviets destroy or modify their radar facility at Krasnoyarsk before any new understandings can be reached on the antiballistic missile treaty.				Dec. 13
		The Bank of Boston Corp. announces that it is writing off $200 mil. of its $1 bil. in loans to Third World nations.... In the wake of the October stock market crash, Merrill Lynch & Co. freezes most salaries, and cuts bonuses and commissions for its securities sales people. The cutbacks are an attempt to save $370 mil. in costs in 1988.... The Federal Reserve Board says that its industrial production index rose 0.4% in November.			Dec. 14
Former Sen. Gary Hart (D, Colo.), who abandoned his six-year quest for the presidency in May, stuns the political world by announcing that he is rejoining the Democratic race for the presidency.... Despite "very strong doubt about its constitutionality," Pres. Reagan signs legislation authorizing appointment of independent prosecutors to investigate alleged wrongdoing by high-level executive branch officials.		The deficit in the U.S. balance of payments on current account in the third quarter is a record $43.38 bil., up from a revised record $41.19 bil. in the second quarter, the Commerce Dept. reports.... The Environmental Protection Agency sanctions continued use of the herbicide alachlor, perhaps the most widely used commercial weed killer in the United States, despite the risk that it could cause cancer and contaminate drinking-water supplies.			Dec. 15
F	G	H	I	J	
Includes elections, federal-state relations, civil rights and liberties, crime, the judiciary, education, health care, poverty, urban affairs and population.	*Includes formation and debate of U.S. foreign and defense policies, veterans' affairs and defense spending. (Relations with specific foreign countries are usually found under the region concerned.)*	*Includes business, labor, agriculture, taxation, transportation, consumer affairs, monetary and fiscal policy, natural resources, and pollution.*	*Includes worldwide scientific, medical and technological developments, natural phenomena, U.S. weather, natural disasters, and accidents.*	*Includes the arts, religion, scholarship, communications media, sports, entertainments, fashions, fads and social life.*	

	World Affairs	Europe	Africa & the Middle East	The Americas	Asia & the Pacific
Dec. 16	Thirty-three leading economists from 13 nations issue a report warning of dire economic problems if the leading industrial economies do not act quickly to address international imbalances. The recommendations laid out in the paper are similar to those accepted in recent years as necessary by economists and world leaders but which the leaders have not been able to put into place.	Amid an ongoing controversy over the Conservative government's health program, Britain's Health Min. Tony Newton pledges an immediate $180 mil. infusion for the National Health Service.... The largest Mafia trial ever ends in Palermo, Sicily, with the conviction of 338 of 452 defendants, including the notorious Michele "the Pope" Greco, who is sentenced to life in prison.			Roh Tae Woo, the candidate of the ruling Democratic Justice Party, wins South Korea's first direct presidential election in 16 years. Opposition leaders Kim Dae Jung and Kim Young Sam split most of the antigovernment vote.... The Tokyo Stock Exchange agrees to admit 16 more foreign securities firms, bringing to 22 the total number of foreign concerns seated on the exchange. The first six foreign firms were admitted in 1985.
Dec. 17		Gustav Husak resigns as the secretary general of the Czechoslovakian Communist Party (CP). He is succeeded by Milos Jakes, a member of the CP Central Committee Presidium (politburo).... In Britain, the seasonally adjusted unemployment rate fell to 9.5% in November, the Dept. of Employment announces. The rate is the lowest since 1982 and marks the 17th consecutive monthly decline.	According to Lloyd's Maritime Information Services, both Iraq and Iran carried out 21 attacks in the Persian Gulf tanker war in October and November. There have been 163 attacks on shipping thus far in 1987, and a total of 421 since 1981.		A Bhopal, India, district court judge orders Union Carbide Corp. to pay $270 mil. in interim relief for victims of the 1984 gas leak at the company's chemical plant in Bhopal.
Dec. 18		The British economy expanded by 5% in the year to September, the fastest rate of growth in 14 years, according to figures released by the Central Statistical Office.... The European Community (EC) agrees to suspend special trade benefits for South Korean exporters. The move is in retaliation for South Korea's refusal to grant EC exporters the same legal protection against patent infringement that U.S. companies receive.	At least 17 Palestinians have been killed and many more wounded in an unprecedented wave of Palestinian unrest that began December 9 in the Israeli-occupied Gaza Strip and the West Bank.	Air Canada resumes service two days after settling a labor dispute with its 8,500 ground workers. The government-owned airline suspended service November 27.	In Pakistan, opposition leader Benazir Bhutto, 34, is married to Asif Ali Zardari, also 34, in a traditional Moslem ceremony. The marriage was arranged by the parents of the bride and groom.
Dec. 19		Britain's Queen Elizabeth II uses her Christmas message to speak out against the violence in Northern Ireland for the first time.... Italy's gross domestic product is up 2.5% in the third quarter from year-earlier levels, and 0.5% above the second-quarter level, according to government figures.		In Canada, the federal government fires the two top executives of the troubled Farm Credit Corp. The government-owned corporation has an accumulated deficit of over $260 mil.	
Dec. 20				On the eve of cease-fire talks in the Dominican Republic, the Contras fighting the Nicaraguan government launch what they describe as their biggest attack of the six-year war, assaulting three gold-mining towns in a remote region of Zelaya province in northeastern Nicaragua.	More than 1,600 people are missing and presumed dead in a collision of a Philippine inter-island ferry, the *Dona Paz*, and a Phillipine oil tanker, the *Victor*, in the waters of the Tablas Strait some 110 miles south of Manila.
Dec. 21	The UN General Assembly ends its fall session by approving a total budget for 1988 and 1989 of $1.77 bil. Israel is the only nation to vote against the budget. The United States, Australia, and Japan abstain in protest of the spending amount.	High Court Justice Richard R.F. Scott rejects the British government's request for a permanent injunction against press reports on the book *Spycatcher*, the memoirs of former MI5 (counterintelligence) agent Peter Wright.	There is rioting in Jerusalem December 19, and Israel's Arab citizens stage a massive general strike this day in sympathy with the Palestinians in the occupied territories.		

A	B	C	D	E
Includes developments that affect more than one world region, international organizations and important meetings of major world leaders.	Includes all domestic and regional developments in Europe, including the Soviet Union, Turkey, Cyprus and Malta.	Includes all domestic and regional developments in Africa and the Middle East, including Iraq and Iran and excluding Cyprus, Turkey and Afghanistan.	Includes all domestic and regional developments in Latin America, the Caribbean and Canada.	Includes all domestic and regional developments in Asia and Pacific nations, extending from Afghanistan through all the Pacific Islands, except Hawaii.

U.S. Politics & Social Issues	U.S. Foreign Policy & Defense	U.S. Economy & Environment	Science, Technology & Nature	Culture, Leisure & Life Style	
A federal jury in Washington, D.C., finds former top White House aide Michael K. Deaver guilty on three counts of perjury for lying under oath about his lobbying activities. . . . The House votes, 230-194, to approve the Family Welfare Reform Act, designed to get welfare recipients into the work force. . . . The U.S. Conf. of Mayors reports that despite economic improvements the demand for emergency shelter in 26 major cities rose 21% in 1987; demand for food assistance rose 18%.		Housing starts climb 7.5% in November, the Commerce Dept. says.		*Broadcast News*, a comedy about the Washington bureau of a national television network, opens in New York. Directed, written, and produced by James L. Brooks, the film stars William Hurt, Albert Brooks, and Holly Hunter. . . . The movie *Moonstruck*, a romantic comedy set in an Italian-American neighborhood of New York City, opens in New York. Directed by Norman Jewison and written by John Patrick Shanley, the movie stars Cher, Olympia Dukakis, and Nicolas Cage.	Dec. 16
Ann Dore McLaughlin is sworn in as secretary of labor; she succeeds Bill Brock.	A previously undisclosed White House computer memorandum found after the conclusion of a congressional investigation into the Iran-Contra affair describes Vice Pres. George Bush as a "solid" supporter of the White House's Iranian arms-for-hostages deal. . . . The Defense Dept. announces a resumption of the production of chemical weapons. Production of such arms was halted in 1969.	Traffic fatalities rose by more than 50% on highways where the speed limit has been increased to 65 miles per hour, the Transportation Dept. reports from a survey of data from 22 states.	A U.S. satellite and two balloon-borne detectors are reported to have detected the first gamma ray emissions from a supernova sighted in the southern skies in February.	*The Dead*, a film adaptation of James Joyce's *Dubliners* short story, opens in New York. Directed by John Huston, it is written by Tony Huston and stars Anjelica Huston and Donal McCann. . . . Marguerite Yourcenar (born Marguerite de Crayencour), 84, novelist, playwright, poet, classicist, and translator, dies in Northeast Harbor, Me., following a stroke. The Belgian-born author grew up in France but moved to the United States in the 1940s and became a naturalized U.S. citizen. She is best known for her 1951 novel *Memoirs of Hadrian*.	Dec. 17
A federal judge in New York City sentences stock speculator Ivan F. Boesky to three years in prison for conspiring to file false stock trading records.		The government's consumer price index rose 0.3% in November, the Labor Dept. reports. . . . Congress clears legislation authorizing $10.2 bil. in spending for airport and air-traffic control improvements over the next five years.	According to an article in the journal *Science*, a six-year joint U.S.-Japanese study of World War II atomic bomb survivors confirms what began to be suspected in the mid-1970s, that previous estimates of the radiation doses inflicted on the bomb victims were high.	The film *Ironweed*, about an aging derelict who tries to come to grips with his past as he roams Depression-era Albany, N.Y., is released in New York. Based on the novel by William Kennedy, who wrote the screenplay, the movie is directed by Hector Babenco and stars Jack Nicholson and Meryl Streep.	Dec. 18
		Congress passes and sends to Pres. Reagan a package that will supply $4 bil. to the ailing Farm Credit System, a network of 37 institutions that supplies credit exclusively to farmers. . . . Texaco Inc. and Pennzoil Co. announce a settlement of their four-year legal battle over Texaco's 1984 purchase of Getty Oil Co. Under the agreement, Texaco will pay Pennzoil $3 bil.		Gary Kasparov of the Soviet Union retains the world chess championship in a 24-game match that began October 12 against countryman Anatoly Karpov.	Dec. 19
	A report by the General Accounting Office accuses Northrop Corp. of failing to properly test a key guidance component of the air-launched cruise missile. The report is made public by the House Armed Services Committee.	A congressional report sharply attacks the Nuclear Regulatory Comm. as having an "unhealthy empathy for the needs of the nuclear industry to the detriment of the safety of the American people." . . . Sales of three-wheeled all-terrain vehicles (ATVs), which have been linked to about 900 deaths since their introduction in the early 1980s, will be banned under an agreement worked out by the ATV industry, the Justice Dept., and the Consumer Product Safety Comm.		Sweden beats India, 5-0, to win tennis's Davis Cup.	Dec. 20
Three white teenagers are convicted of manslaughter in connection with the racial attack in the Howard Beach section of New York City that, a year and a day earlier, left a 23-year-old black man, Michael Griffith, dead after he fled onto a highway and was struck by a car.	Sec. of the Navy James H. Webb Jr. announces steps to open more jobs to women and to curb sexual harassment in the service.		Seventeen days after having been pronounced clinically dead upon arrival at a Fargo, N. Dak. hospital, Alvaro Garza Jr., 11, returns to his Moorhead, Minn., home with no signs of permanent brain damage. Garza was submerged for about 45 minutes after falling through ice and his body temperature was only 80 degrees Fahrenheit when rescued.	Hungary and East Germany become the first Soviet-bloc nations formally to accept invitations to the 1988 Summer Olympics in Seoul, South Korea.	Dec. 21

F	G	H	I	J
Includes elections, federal-state relations, civil rights and liberties, crime, the judiciary, education, health care, poverty, urban affairs and population.	*Includes formation and debate of U.S. foreign and defense policies, veterans' affairs and defense spending. (Relations with specific foreign countries are usually found under the region concerned.)*	*Includes business, labor, agriculture, taxation, transportation, consumer affairs, monetary and fiscal policy, natural resources, and pollution.*	*Includes worldwide scientific, medical and technological developments, natural phenomena, U.S. weather, natural disasters, and accidents.*	*Includes the arts, religion, scholarship, communications media, sports, entertainments, fashions, fads and social life.*

	World Affairs	Europe	Africa & the Middle East	The Americas	Asia & the Pacific
Dec. 22	The Org. for Economic Cooperation and Development (OECD) releases a report predicting lower world growth rates as a result of the October 19 stock market crash. The Paris-based OECD reduced its estimate of economic growth for its 24 member nations by half a percentage point to 2.25%.	European Community industry ministers reach a revised compromise pact to phase out steel quotas over the next six months to three years.		According to a report by the UN Economic Comm. for Latin America and the Caribbean, the region's economy has worsened in 1987, with average inflation of 187% and a combined debt of some $409.8 bil. . . . Two days after being sentenced to five years in prison for crimes against Panama's state security, Col. Roberto Diaz Herrera is pardoned and permitted to leave for Venezuela where he is granted political asylum. . . . Cease-fire talks in the Dominican Republic between the Nicaraguan government and U.S.-backed Contras are suspended indefinitely.	South Korean president-elect Roh Tae Woo asserts that he will urge the nation's various intelligence agencies to focus on external threats and refrain from interfering in domestic politics.
Dec. 23					The chairman of Sri Lanka's ruling United National Party and three of his aides are shot to death in the Wellawatta district, six miles south of downtown Colombo. The gunmen are believed to be Sinhalese extremists.
Dec. 24		Interior Min. Karl Blecha becomes the highest ranking Austrian official to urge Pres. Kurt Waldheim to resign because of his record in the German Army in World War II.	Journalist Terry A. Anderson, the longest-held American hostage in Lebanon, appears on a videotape released in Beirut by his captors, the pro-Iranian Islamic Jihad (Holy War) group.		Marudur Gopalan Ramachandran, the chief minister of the state of Tamil Nadu, India, dies of a heart attack at his home in the southeastern city of Madras. Ramachandran, 70, was India's leading ethnic Tamil politician. . . . Indonesia's government announces a broad package of economic reforms aimed at stimulating trade and investment in the country.
Dec. 25			A crackdown by Israeli security forces over the three preceding days succeeds in at least temporarily quelling two weeks of violent demonstrations by Palestinians in the occupied West Bank and Gaza Strip. . . . Syrian soldiers arrest scores of Christians in northern Lebanon on suspicion of involvement in attacks on Syrian peacekeeping troops in Moslem west Beirut over the past five weeks; but a Sunni Moslem cleric claims that he leads the group responsible.		Japan's national unemployment rate remains 2.7% (seasonally adjusted) in November, unchanged from October, the government reports.
Dec. 26		The Soviet foreign ministry reports that the USSR has about 50,000 tons of chemical weapons. It is the first time that the Soviets have indicated the size of their chemical arms stockpile.	The six conservative Arab states of the Persian Gulf meet in Riyadh, Saudi Arabia, and urge the UN Security Council to impose sanctions on Iran for its refusal to accept a cease-fire in its war with Iraq.		
Dec. 27		In Poland, fourteen members of the dissident organization Freedom and Peace end a hunger strike in Warsaw. The 12 men and two women fasted for two weeks to protest the plight of nine members of the organization who were jailed for draft resistance.	Israeli military courts begin trials of Palestinian activists accused of fomenting the widespread riots that wracked the occupied West Bank and Gaza Strip for weeks before being quelled by an Israeli crackdown.		

A	B	C	D	E
Includes developments that affect more than one world region, international organizations and important meetings of major world leaders.	Includes all domestic and regional developments in Europe, including the Soviet Union, Turkey, Cyprus and Malta.	Includes all domestic and regional developments in Africa and the Middle East, including Iraq and Iran and excluding Cyprus, Turkey and Afghanistan.	Includes all domestic and regional developments in Latin America, the Caribbean and Canada.	Includes all domestic and regional developments in Asia and Pacific nations, extending from Afghanistan through all the Pacific Islands, except Hawaii.

U.S. Politics & Social Issues	U.S. Foreign Policy & Defense	U.S. Economy & Environment	Science, Technology & Nature	Culture, Leisure & Life Style	
Pres. Reagan signs a pair of bills embodying a compromise agreement on the FY1988 federal budget.... Congress sends to Pres. Reagan a $30.3 bil., two-year housing authorization bill, the first passed since 1981. The president is expected to sign the legislation. ... A federal grand jury in New York City indicts two associates of Attorney Gen. Edwin Meese III on charges of extracting bribes from the Wedtech Corp. in order to influence Meese and other federal officials to obtain military contracts for the company.	Spending authority for defense in FY1988 totals $291.5 bil., including $8.1 mil. for the Nicaraguan Contras through Feb. 29, 1988. Other provisions could raise the total package for the Contras to more than $14 mil.... Pres. Reagan signs legislation authorizing $4.1 bil. for FY1988 and $4.3 bil. for the following year for the State Dept. ... The Defense Dept. announces that all of the armed services met their recruitment goals for FY1987, the eighth consecutive year of successful recruiting in the all-volunteer military.	The FY1988 deficit reconciliation bill is a package of measures designed to reduce the federal budget deficit $33.4 bil. below the level projected for FY1988, and by another $42.7 bil. in FY1989.	Scientists report discovery of a gene that strongly appears to determine whether a fetus develops into a boy or a girl. The study, led by David C. Page of the Whitehead Institute for Biomedical Research in Cambridge, Mass., is published in the journal *Cell*.... The FY1988 federal budget includes $904.5 mil. to fight acquired immune deficiency syndrome, $427.3 mil. more than in FY1987.	Henry Strater, 91, realist painter who was part of the "lost generation" of American artists in Paris after World War I, dies in Palm Beach, Fla. He illustrated Ezra Pound's *Cantos* and was the basis for a character in Fitzgerald's novel *This Side of Paradise*.	Dec. 22
Soviet Ambassador Yuri V. Dubinin presents a $5,000 check to homeless advocate Mitch Snyder, who led the "Grate American Sleep-Out" in March.... Claus von Bulow confirms that he has reached an out-of-court settlement with his two stepchildren, Annie-Laurie Kneissl and Alexander von Auersperg, in the battle over the estate of his wife, Martha "Sunny" von Bulow, who has been in a coma for seven years.		The Reagan adminstration lowers its estimate of 1988 gross national product growth to 2.4% from the 3.5% predicted during the summer, due to the anticipated effects of the October stock market crash and rising interest rates and tighter monetary policy.		*Good Morning, Vietnam*, a tragicomedy centered on the life of a manic Armed Forces Radio disk jockey broadcasting from Saigon during the Vietnam War, is released in New York. Directed by Barry Levinson and written by Mitch Markowitz, the film stars Robin Williams and Forest Whitaker.... *Variety*'s top-grossing films for the week are: *Eddie Murphy Raw*; *Throw Momma from the Train*; *Three Men and a Baby*; *Wall Street*; and *Planes, Trains and Automobiles*.	Dec. 23
The Federal Communications Comm. (FCC) votes, 4-0, to permit radio and television stations to broadcast "indecent" programming between midnight and six a.m. without fear of FCC action. At all other times, the agency says, such programming will be prohibited.		The Federal Communications Comm. orders local telephone companies to reduce the access fees they charge long-distance companies. The reduction is to go into effect Jan. 1, 1988.			Dec. 24
Some 40 hours after her escape from the Federal Correctional Institution for Women in Alderson, W. Va., Lynette (Squeaky) Fromme is recaptured, walking along a country road about two miles from the prison. The follower of imprisoned cult leader Charles Manson, Fromme is serving a life sentence for a 1975 assassination attempt on Pres. Gerald Ford.					Dec. 25
				Soviet leader Mikhail S. Gorbachev is named *Time* magazine's Man of the Year, some three weeks after the Washington, D.C., summit at which he and Pres. Reagan signed a bilateral treaty on the global elimination of intermediate-range nuclear forces.... *Billboard*'s best-selling albums for the week are: *Dirty Dancing* (soundtrack); *Bad*, Michael Jackson; *Faith*, George Michael; *Whitesnake*, Whitesnake; and *Tiffany*, Tiffany.	Dec. 26
				Anthony West, 73, Anglo-American novelist and critic who was a long-time staff writer for the *New Yorker* magazine, dies in Stonington, Conn. The illegitimate son of H.G. Wells and Dame Rebecca West; his novel *The Heritage* is a thinly disguised account of his stormy relationship with his parents.	Dec. 27
F	G	H	I	J	
Includes elections, federal-state relations, civil rights and liberties, crime, the judiciary, education, health care, poverty, urban affairs and population.	Includes formation and debate of U.S. foreign and defense policies, veterans' affairs and defense spending. (Relations with specific foreign countries are usually found under the region concerned.)	Includes business, labor, agriculture, taxation, transportation, consumer affairs, monetary and fiscal policy, natural resources, and pollution.	Includes worldwide scientific, medical and technological developments, natural phenomena, U.S. weather, natural disasters, and accidents.	Includes the arts, religion, scholarship, communications media, sports, entertainments, fashions, fads and social life.	

	World Affairs	Europe	Africa & the Middle East	The Americas	Asia & the Pacific
Dec. 28		Swiss chemical maker Sandoz AG says that it will pay between $39 mil. and $45 mil. for damages caused by the 1986 Rhine River chemical spill. In addition, the company has set up a fund for environmental safeguards on the Rhine.	Kenya's Pres. Daniel arap Moi and Uganda's Pres. Yoweri Museveni met for two hours at the Kenyan border town of Malaba and agreed on a series of steps to ease the growing tensions between their two countries.		South Korea's gross national product grew an inflation-adjusted 12.2% during 1987, only slightly down from the 12.5% growth rate recorded in 1986, according to a preliminary report from the Bank of Korea.
Dec. 29	The International Monetary Fund announces the creation of an $8.4 bil. pool for nominal-interest lending to the world's poorest nations, primarily in sub-Saharan Africa. Funding for the plan will come largely from the Group of Seven industrial nations, with the exception of the United States.	The Soviet Union, the world's largest oil producer, produced 4.57 million barrels of oil, a domestic record, in 1987, exceeding its previous record of 4.51 million barrels in 1983.		A plan to ease the Mexican debt crisis by swapping as much as $10 bil. in discounted Mexican debt for U.S. Treasury bonds is announced. The plan is put together by Mexico, the United States, and Morgan Guaranty Trust Co.... A national moment of silence is observed in Peru as a demonstration against the terrorism that has wracked the country since 1980, when Maoist insurgents began a war against the government.	
Dec. 30		The Yugoslav federal parliament for the first time ends a legislative year without approving a budget for the coming year. Since the legislators fail to agree on spending for 1988, Yugoslavia will enter the new year with its 1987 budget still in effect.	The government of the nominally independent tribal South African "homeland" of Transkei is ousted in the second military coup in three months, led by Maj. Gen. Bantu Holomisa.	Argentina's central bank devalues the currency, the austral, by 6.7% against the U.S. dollar, raising the exchange rate to 3.75 australs to the dollar from 3.5.... In Canada, the government reimposes a ban on the offshore commercial hunting of harp seal pups. Blueback hooded seals are also placed on a protected list.... A judge in Medellin, Colombia, frees Jorge Luis Ochoa Vasquez, reputed to be one of two top chiefs of the Medellin Cartel, a drug consortium reportedly responsible for 80% of the cocaine entering the United States.	Thirteen days after Soviet and Afghan government troops launched an offensive against rebel forces surrounding the besieged garrison town of Khost, 15 miles from the Pakistan border, a convoy carrying food and supplies reaches the town.
Dec. 31		France suspends most aid to Haiti, saying the situation there is "too confused to continue our cooperation." France gave Haiti some $35 mil. in aid in 1987 and had intended to double that figure in 1988.	Zimbabwe's P.M. Robert Mugabe is sworn in as the country's first executive president, thus paving the way for Mugabe's long-stated goal of turning Zimbabwe from a parliamentary democracy into a one-party socialist state.		Sixty-five Amerasian children—Vietnamese fathered by Americans during the Vietnam War—and 91 of their relatives arrive in Bangkok, Thailand, from Vietnam, en route to the United States.

A	B	C	D	E
Includes developments that affect more than one world region, international organizations and important meetings of major world leaders.	*Includes all domestic and regional developments in Europe, including the Soviet Union, Turkey, Cyprus and Malta.*	*Includes all domestic and regional developments in Africa and the Middle East, including Iraq and Iran and excluding Cyprus, Turkey and Afghanistan.*	*Includes all domestic and regional developments in Latin America, the Caribbean and Canada.*	*Includes all domestic and regional developments in Asia and Pacific nations, extending from Afghanistan through all the Pacific Islands, except Hawaii.*

U.S. Politics & Social Issues	U.S. Foreign Policy & Defense	U.S. Economy & Environment	Science, Technology & Nature	Culture, Leisure & Life Style	
The Federal Election Comm. votes unanimously that Democratic presidential candidate Gary Hart is eligible for an initial $100,000 in federal matching funds now that he has reactivated his presidential campaign.... Ronald Gene Simmons, a 47-year-old retired Air Force master sergeant, allegedly kills 16 people in and around the small town of Dover, Ark., in the Ozark foothills.		An expected sharp decline in U.S. Christmas holiday retail buying does not materialize. According to the New York Times, sales were up about 3% over 1986, less than the level of inflation but not the sharp drop that some analysts had feared.			Dec. 28
At a Washington, D.C., news conference, Sec. of Education William J. Bennett outlines what he says will be the ideal curriculum for U.S. high schools. Bennett has long urged the nation's secondary schools to adopt a tougher core curriculum of required classes.	The White House national security adviser, Lt. Gen. Colin L. Powell, says in a letter that the Strategic Defense Intiative could destroy a U.S.-Soviet treaty on strategic weapons.	Legislation banning dumping of plastics at sea is signed by Pres. Reagan. The bill also extends for two years the international fishery agreement between the United States and Japan, and reauthorizes the Sea Grant College Program to provide funds for research in maritime industries.... Five people are killed in a fire and explosion that destroys part of the Morton Thiokol Inc. plant near Brigham City, Utah, where the first stage of the four-stage MX intercontinental ballistic missile is built.	Col. Yuri V. Romanenko returns to the Soviet Union from the space station Mir after spending a record 326 days in orbit. "I feel terrific," Romanenko says on a television interview minutes after emerging from the spacecraft in Soviet Kazakhstan.		Dec. 29
Republican candidate Alexander M. Haig Jr. announces that he is dropping out of the Republican presidential race in Iowa.		The government's index of leading economic indicators declined 1.7% in November, the Commerce Dept. says.... An administrative law judge in Detroit rejects the application of Detroit's two daily newspapers—the Detroit News and the Detroit Free Press—to combine their business operations.			Dec. 30
Pres. Reagan signs an executive order effecting pay raises of 2% for 2.1 million federal civilian workers and 2.2 million military personnel. The raises were authorized by Congress in the recently enacted omnibus spending bill for FY1988.		The U.S. dollar closes out the year at record postwar lows against the Japanese yen and West German mark, down 23% against the yen and 18% against the mark.... Waste Management Inc. announces that it has abandoned plans to burn toxic wastes on incinerator ships off the U.S. coast.... The Federal Savings and Loan Insurance Corp. aids in the mergers of four failing thrifts, bringing to 48 the number of savings and loans rescued or liquidated in 1987.			Dec. 31

F	G	H	I	J
Includes elections, federal-state relations, civil rights and liberties, crime, the judiciary, education, health care, poverty, urban affairs and population.	Includes formation and debate of U.S. foreign and defense policies, veterans' affairs and defense spending. (Relations with specific foreign countries are usually found under the region concerned.)	Includes business, labor, agriculture, taxation, transportation, consumer affairs, monetary and fiscal policy, natural resources, and pollution.	Includes worldwide scientific, medical and technological developments, natural phenomena, U.S. weather, natural disasters, and accidents.	Includes the arts, religion, scholarship, communications media, sports, entertainments, fashions, fads and social life.

1988

A bomb aboard Pan Am Flight 103 detonated over Lockerbie, Scotland, in December 1988. Policemen guarded the site following reports that the dead passengers had been looted.

	World Affairs	Europe	Africa & the Middle East	The Americas	Asia & the Pacific
Jan.	China rejects a Soviet offer of a summit until the USSR reduces its forces on the Chinese border, withdraws from Afghanistan, and ends its support of Vietnam's occupation of Cambodia.	Soviet Foreign Min. Eduard A. Shevardnadze says the Soviet Union hopes to withdraw all its troops from Afghanistan by the end of 1988.	Defying international opinion, Israel expels four Palestinian activists charged with instigating the riots that wracked the occupied West Bank and Gaza Strip for more than a month.	Representatives of the Nicaraguan government and the Contra rebels in Costa Rica hold the first face-to-face talks in the six-year civil war.	Pres. Chiang Ching-kuo, 77, son of the Chinese Nationalist leader Chiang Kai-shek, dies of a heart attack in Taipei. His death ends nearly 40 years of family rule over Taiwan.
Feb.	The International Monetary Fund had a $5.9 bil. repayment surplus in 1987. The world's lender of last resort, the IMF provides short-term liquidity to debtor nations.	An international panel finds that Austria's Pres. Kurt Waldheim knew war crimes were committed by his German Army units in World War II and that he concealed and misrepresented his record.	The South African government restricts the activities of 17 leading black opposition groups and bars the country's largest labor federation from engaging in political action.	The Justice Dept. unseals two indictments charging Panama's military leader and de facto ruler, Gen. Manuel Antonio Noriega, with involvement in international drug trafficking.	Laos and Thailand agree to a truce aimed at ending an armed border conflict that erupted between the two countries in November 1987.
March	The UN General Assembly votes in favor of two resolutions opposing a U.S. plan to close the New York City office of the Palestine Liberation Org.	Leaders of the 16 North Atlantic Treaty Org. nations meet in Brussels to reach an agreement on NATO's defense posture in light of the U.S.-Soviet treaty to eliminate intermediate-range nuclear forces.	Iraq kills hundreds and possibly thousands of its own Kurdish citizens when it bombs a northeastern Iraqi border town with chemical weapons after its capture by Iranian forces.	The Nicaraguan government and Contra leaders sign a cease-fire pact in an attempt to end a civil war that has resulted in some 25,000 deaths since 1981.	Bangladesh's ruling Jatiya Party wins an overwhelming majority in parliamentary elections disrupted by violence and boycotted by the country's main opposition groups.
April	The World Court rules unanimously against a U.S. effort to close the Palestine Liberation Org.'s observer mission to the UN.	The Kremlin's No. 2 figure, Yegor K. Ligachev, has been demoted at a special session of the Politburo, according to the Western press.	U.S. Navy warships and planes sink or cripple six Iranian naval vessels in a series of clashes in the Persian Gulf prompted by mine damage to a U.S. ship.	The United States sends an additional 1,300 troops to Panama to beef up the security of American bases there.	Afghanistan and Pakistan sign agreements providing for the withdrawal of Soviet troops from Afghanistan, creation of a neutral Afghanistan, and the repatriation of Afghan refugees.
May	Ministers from the 24 members of the Org. for Economic Cooperation and Development conclude their annual meeting with an uneasy compromise on the issue of reducing farm subsidies.	Janos Kadar is removed as general secretary of Hungary's Socialist Workers' (Communist) Party at a national party conference in Budapest; he is replaced by Premier Karoly Grosz.	Representatives from the United States, Angola, Cuba and South Africa meet for the first time to discuss the future of Angola and Namibia (South-West Africa).	Panama's military strongman Gen. Manuel Antonio Noriega rejects a U.S. proposal to leave the country in exchange for the United States dropping drug-trafficking charges against him.	The Soviet Union officially begins to withdraw its estimated 115,000 troops from Afghanistan under the terms of the four-party peace accords signed in Geneva in April.
June	Leaders of the seven major industrial democracies express satisfaction with the state of the world economy and agree to measures aimed at keeping the world economy growing.	The 19th All-Union Conference of the Soviet Communist Party—the first since 1941—opens in Moscow to decide the pace and direction of Soviet leader Mikhail S. Gorbachev's reforms.	South African blacks stage a massive strike to protest proposed new labor laws and the government's ban on political activity by trade unions and other antiapartheid groups.	In Haiti, Lt. Gen. Henri Namphy proclaims himself president following the ouster of civilian Pres. Leslie F. Manigat.	Philippine Pres. Corazon Aquino signs a bill providing for the redistribution of large tracts of government-owned and private farmland.
July	The World Bank warns that the global economy faces the possibility of a worldwide recession unless industrial countries address unsolved budget and trade imbalances.	The legislature of the Nagorno-Karabakh Autonomous Region votes to secede from the Soviet Azerbaijan Republic and reunify with the Soviet Armenian Republic.	The frigate USS *Vincennes* shoots down an Iranian commercial airliner over the Persian Gulf after mistaking it for an F-14 fighter jet. All 290 people aboard the plane are killed.	Carlos Salinas de Gortari is proclaimed the winner of Mexico's presidential election although by the smallest majority in his party's 59-year history.	Ne Win announces his resignation as chairman of Burma's ruling Burma Socialist Program Party after 26 years; he is succeeded by hard-liner Sein-Lwin.
Aug.	UN Sec. General Javier Perez de Cuellar announces a cease-fire between Iran and Iraq and says the two countries have agreed to discuss a Persian Gulf War peace settlement.	Thousands of anti-Soviet demonstrators in Prague mark the 20th anniversary of the Soviet-led invasion of Czechoslovakia.	Morocco and the Polisario Front tentatively agree to accept a joint UN-Org. of African Unity plan to end the 13-year-old war over the former Spanish colony of Western Sahara.	The human rights organization Americas Watch reports that human rights in Central America are in a "dismal" condition, especially in Guatemala and El Salvador.	Pakistani Pres. Muhammad Zia ul-Haq and U.S. Amb. Arnold L. Raphel are killed when their plane explodes and crashes in eastern Pakistan shortly after takeoff.
Sept.	The 1988 Nobel Peace Prize is awarded to the UN peacekeeping forces; some 10,000 UN peacekeeping troops and observers are currently on duty in seven regions around the world.	In Yugoslavia, the Serbian republic sends a police unit to the autonomous province of Kosovo to reinforce federal paramilitary police in containing ethnic unrest.	Taking advantage of the Persian Gulf War cease-fire to crush the Kurdish guerrilla movement, Iraqi forces use chemical weapons in a major drive against Kurdish rebels in the north.	Noncommissioned officers ousted Haiti's Pres. Henri Namphy; Lt. Gen. Prosper Avril, former aide to presidents Francois Duvalier and Jean-Claude Duvalier, is named president.	Burma's Defense Min. and armed forces chief of staff Gen. Saw Maung ousts civilian Pres. Maung Maung in a military coup.
Oct.	Amnesty International charges 135 nations with having human rights violations in 1987. The figure is the largest since the group's first annual survey in 1961.	Yugoslavia's Pres. Raif Dizdarevic warns that continued nationalist and economic unrest could lead to the imposition of a state of emergency.	South Africa holds its first multiracial, nationwide, municipal elections open to all races, but most blacks stay away from the polls.	Facing international criticism of Brazil's environmental policies, Pres. Jose Sarney announces measures designed to check the rapid destruction of the Amazon rain forests.	The United States and the Philippines sign an interim accord covering U.S. use of six military facilities in the Philippines through 1991.
Nov.	The central banks of 11 industrial nations mount a massive and coordinated intervention in foreign-exchange markets to support the plunging U.S. dollar.	Nationalist and ethnic ferment in the Soviet republics tests the limits of Moscow's tolerance for *glasnost* and "democratization," especially in the Baltic and Transcaucasus regions.	The Palestine Liberation Org. proclaims an independent Palestinian state and votes for the first time to accept key UN resolutions implicitly recognizing Israel.	P.M. Brian Mulroney of Canada's Progressive Conservative Party becomes the first Conservative prime minister in the 20th century to win reelection to a consecutive term.	Benazir Bhutto's opposition Pakistani People's Party emerges as the victor in Pakistan's first open elections in more than a decade.
Dec.	A midterm review in Montreal of the Uruguay Round of the General Agreement on Tariffs and Trade breaks down when the United States and the European Community fail to agree on agriculture trade reform.	A Pan Am jetliner flying from London to New York City explodes in midair. All 259 passengers and crew are killed, and 11 residents of Lockerbie, Scotland, are reported dead or missing.	Angola, Cuba and South Africa sign a U.S.-mediated agreement providing for the independence of Namibia (South-West Africa) and the withdrawal of Cuban troops from Angola.	A mutiny to protest the imprisonment of officers convicted of human rights abuses and other issues ends when rebellious Argentine soldiers surrender to loyal government troops.	Benazir Bhutto becomes the first woman in modern history to lead a predominantly Moslem nation when she is named prime minister of Pakistan by acting Pres. Ghulam Ishaq Khan.

A	B	C	D	E
Includes developments that affect more than one world region, international organizations and important meetings of major world leaders.	Includes all domestic and regional developments in Europe, including the Soviet Union, Turkey, Cyprus and Malta.	Includes all domestic and regional developments in Africa and the Middle East, including Iraq and Iran and excluding Cyprus, Turkey and Afghanistan.	Includes all domestic and regional developments in Latin America, the Caribbean and Canada.	Includes all domestic and regional developments in Asia and Pacific nations, extending from Afghanistan through all the Pacific Islands, except Hawaii.

U.S. Politics & Social Issues	U.S. Foreign Policy & Defense	U.S. Economy & Environment	Science, Technology & Nature	Culture, Leisure & Life Style	
The Supreme Court rules that censorship of a student newspaper by public school officials is not unconstitutional if it is "reasonably related to legitimate pedagogical concerns."	The Senate Foreign Relations Committee opens hearings on the ratification of the U.S.-Soviet treaty to eliminate intermediate-range nuclear forces.	A Presidential Task Force on Market Mechanisms report on the October 1987 stock-market crash calls for radical changes in the regulation of U.S. capital markets.	The atmosphere's protective ozone layer has diminished worldwide, not just over Antarctica, according to a report in the journal *Science*.	The National Society of Film Critics selects *The Dead*, John Huston's last film, as the best film of 1987.	Jan.
The Senate votes to confirm Judge Anthony M. Kennedy as an associate justice of the Supreme Court, to fill the vacancy left by the retirement of Justice Lewis F. Powell Jr.	A Senate Foreign Relations subcommittee holds hearings on Panama's Gen. Manuel Antonio Noriega, recently indicted by two Florida federal grand juries on drug charges.	The Energy Dept. says that it will not reopen its plutonium-producing nuclear reactor, known as the N reactor, at the Hanford nuclear site near Richland, Wash.	Richard Feynman, 69, Nobel Prize-winning physicist who played a key role in the production of the atom bomb at Los Alamos, N.Mex., dies of abdominal cancer in Los Angeles.	The 15th Olympic Winter Games open in Calgary, Alberta; a record number of athletes, more than 1,750, from a record 57 nations, are attending the games.	Feb.
V.P. George Bush wins all 16 Republican primaries on "Super Tuesday" to finish the day with well over half the 1,139 votes needed to capture the Republican presidential nomination.	The Senate Foreign Relations Committee votes to approve the U.S.-Soviet treaty on intermediate-range nuclear forces.	In an unusual display of bipartisan support for a budget measure, the House approves a $1.2 trillion budget plan for FY1989.	The Senate unanimously votes to ratify an international treaty to curb global use of ozone-depleting chlorofluorocarbons (CFCs) widely used as cooling agents.	New York City's Metropolitan Opera commissions composer Philip Glass to create *The Voyage* for the 500th anniversary of Christopher Columbus's voyage to America in 1992.	March
The Arizona Senate convicts Gov. Evan Mecham (R) on two charges of official misconduct and removes him from office.	Senate Majority Leader Robert C. Byrd (D, W.Va.) tells reporters that the Senate will not "rush to judgment" in ratifying the U.S.-Soviet treaty on intermediate-range nuclear forces.	Defying all expectations, the U.S. deficit on merchandise trade grew to $13.83 bil. in February, the Commerce Dept. reports, sending stock and bond markets downward.	A mouse with a genetically engineered susceptibility to cancer is the subject of the world's first patent for an animal life form.	The Univ. of Kansas beats Oklahoma, 83-79, to win the National Collegiate Athletic Association basketball title.	April
Gov. Michael S. Dukakis (D, Mass.) wins landslide victories in Democratic presidential primaries in Ohio and Indiana, moving a giant step closer to the Democratic nomination.	The Senate ratifies the U.S.-Soviet treaty eliminating intermediate-range nuclear forces, the first arms-control agreement since the 1972 SALT I to receive Senate approval.	Pres. Reagan vetoes comprehensive trade legislation and calls for "prompt action on a second bill after the Congress sustains my veto."	U.S. Surgeon Gen. C. Everett Koop reports that cigarettes and other tobacco products are "addicting in the same sense as are drugs such as heroin and cocaine."	Chet Baker, 58, trumpeter and vocalist, dies; as part of the Gerry Mulligan Quartet, he helped define West Coast "cool jazz" in the 1950s.	May
Gov. Michael S. Dukakis (Mass.) clinches the Democratic presidential nomination with a four-state primary sweep in New Jersey, Montana, New Mexico and California.	A massive Pentagon fraud scandal is revealed, when agents of the Federal Bureau of Investigation and the Naval Investigative Service conduct searches of homes and offices in 12 states.	The Agriculture Dept. says that half of the nation's agricultural counties have been designated as drought disaster areas after the driest spring since 1934.	A Japanese mathematician retracts his claim to have discovered a proof of Fermat's last theorem six weeks after it was first announced.	The Los Angeles Lakers beat the Detroit Pistons, 108-105, becoming the first team in 19 years to win back-to-back National Basketball Assoc. championship titles.	June
Attorney Gen. Edwin Meese III abruptly announces his resignation, claiming that he has been "completely vindicated" of wrongdoing by an independent prosecutor's report.	Pres. Reagan announces that the United States will pay compensation to the families of the 290 victims of the Iranian Airbus shot down by the Navy July 3.	The nation's unemployment rate in June fell to 5.2%, the Labor Dept. says, bringing unemployment to its lowest level since 1974.	Surgeon General C. Everett Koop releases a report calling on Americans to cut the amount of fat in their diets, saying dietary fat is a major national health problem.	West Germany's Steffi Graf wins the women's singles title at Wimbledon by downing six-time defending champion Martina Navratilova. Sweden's Stefan Edberg wins the men's singles title.	July
The House impeaches U.S. Dist. Judge Alcee L. Hastings of Florida for high crimes and misdemeanors and forwards the proceedings to the Senate.	The House approves sweeping new economic sanctions against South Africa, banning almost all U.S. investment in South Africa and almost all trade between the two countries.	The Federal Home Loan Bank Board says it has spent $1.9 bil. in taking over and reorganizing 14 insolvent Oklahoma thrifts into six regional institutions.	The World Health Org. estimates that 5 million to 10 million people are infected with the AIDS virus worldwide, and that there are 200,000 to 250,000 active cases of the disease.	The *Last Temptation of Christ*, a film version of the life of Jesus, opens to street protests in seven U.S. cities and in Montreal and Toronto.	Aug.
Presidential nominees George Bush and Michael S. Dukakis hold their first televised debate, which ranges over the candidates' records, taxes, abortion, and the Iran-contra scandal.	Two Pershing II missile engines are the first U.S. weapons components eliminated under the U.S.-Soviet treaty on intermediate-range nuclear forces.	The Securities and Exchange Comm. charges Drexel Burnham Lambert Inc., Michael R. Milken and several others with insider trading, stock manipulation and other crimes.	A two-man Soviet space crew returns safely to Earth after being stuck in orbit with a dwindling air supply for 25 hours.	West Germany's Steffi Graf becomes the fifth player to win tennis's Grand Slam when she wins the U.S. Open in New York City.	Sept.
The two vice presidential nominees, Sen. Lloyd M. Bentsen Jr. (D, Texas) and Sen. Dan Quayle (R, Ind.), meet in a TV debate.	A federal grand jury in New York City indicts former Philippine Pres. Ferdinand E. Marcos, his wife and eight associates on racketeering charges.	The federal budget deficit totals $155.1 bil. in FY1988, the Treasury Dept. reports.	Radiocarbon testing of the Shroud of Turin dates the venerated cloth to about 1280 A.D., Anastasio Cardinal Ballestrero, Roman Catholic archbishop of Turin, announces.	Naguib Mahfouz, author of 40 novels and short story collections about ancient and modern Egypt, becomes the first Arabic-language writer to win the Nobel Prize for literature.	Oct.
V.P. George Herbert Walker Bush (R) is elected to be the 41st president of the United States, defeating Massachusetts Gov. Michael S. Dukakis (D) in a 54%-46% victory.	Citing his "associations with terrorism," the State Dept. denies Palestine Liberation Org. chairman Yasir Arafat permission to visit New York to address the UN General Assembly.	The Farmers Home Admin. says over 80,000 farmers hold delinquent loans and face foreclosure. Kohlberg Kravis Roberts & Co. acquires RJR Nabisco Inc. for a record $25.07 bil.	The New York City Health Dept. begins distributing sterile needles to drug abusers. The controversial plan is part of an effort to halt the spread of AIDS.	Pablo Picasso's *Acrobat and Young Harlequin* (1905) is sold at auction for a record $38.5 mil., the highest price yet paid for a work of 20th-century art.	Nov.
Pres. Reagan says his administration has a "duty" to withhold certain classified documents that Iran-Contra defendant, Oliver L. North, wants to use in his defense if he is brought to trial.	Sec. of State George P. Shultz announces that Pres. Reagan has authorized the opening of a "substantive dialogue" with the Palestine Liberation Org.	The Federal Home Loan Bank Board ends 1988 with a week of frenetic activity culminating in the sale of savings and loan institutions with assets totaling $18.58 bil.	The Soviet republic of Armenia is devastated by an earthquake registering 6.9 on the Richter scale; an estimated 18,000 people in the town of Spitak are killed.	Three paintings by Dutch artist Vincent van Gogh are stolen from the Kroller-Muller National Museum in Otterlo, the Netherlands.	Dec.

F	G	H	I	J
Includes elections, federal-state relations, civil rights and liberties, crime, the judiciary, education, health care, poverty, urban affairs and population.	*Includes formation and debate of U.S. foreign and defense policies, veterans' affairs and defense spending. (Relations with specific foreign countries are usually found under the region concerned.)*	*Includes business, labor, agriculture, taxation, transportation, consumer affairs, monetary and fiscal policy, natural resources, and pollution.*	*Includes worldwide scientific, medical and technological developments, natural phenomena, U.S. weather, natural disasters, and accidents.*	*Includes the arts, religion, scholarship, communications media, sports, entertainments, fashions, fads and social life.*

	World Affairs	Europe	Africa & the Middle East	The Americas	Asia & the Pacific
Jan. 1	Pres. Reagan and Soviet leader Mikhail S. Gorbachev exchange televised New Year's greetings. A previous exchange of such messages took place on Jan. 1, 1986.	In Britain, government papers from 1957 released Dec. 31, 1987, are reported to show that the British government did not disclose the true severity of an October 1957 fire at the Windscale atomic plant. The government of Conservative P.M. Harold Macmillan suppressed the information so as to avoid jeopardizing nuclear cooperation with the United States.	The Israeli Army stages a huge show of force, saturating the West Bank, Gaza, and Jerusalem with troops and successfully muzzling Palestinian attempts to mark the 23rd anniversary of the first military operation against Israel by Yasir Arafat's Fatah guerrillas.	Canada begins to deregulate its transportation sector. Under federal guidelines, controls on civil aviation, railroads, merchant shipping, and interprovincial trucking are immediately loosened.	
Jan. 2			Lebanese police report that Israeli warplanes, helicopters and gunboats struck Palestinian targets in southern Lebanon, killing 21 people and wounding 14. . . . Pres. Robert Mugabe completes a recent remodeling of the Zimbabwean government by naming an expanded 27-member cabinet that includes former opposition leader Joshua Nkomo. The reshuffle consolidates the December 1987 merger of Nkomo's Zimbabwe African People's Union with Mugabe's ruling Zimbabwe African National Union (Patriotic Front).	Pres. Reagan and Canada's P.M. Brian Mulroney sign the final text of the U.S.-Canadian trade accord at separate locations. The federal legislatures of both nations still must approve the accord before the date it is scheduled to come into force—Jan. 1, 1989.	
Jan. 3		On her 3,167th day in office, P.M. Margaret Thatcher becomes the longest-serving British prime minister in the 20th century; she has served more than eight and two-thirds years since winning election in 1979.	Ignoring U.S. opposition, Israel announces that it will permanently deport nine Palestinian activists charged with instigating the severe rioting that broke out in the occupied Gaza Strip and West Bank last month.		
Jan. 4		Portugal's unemployment rate fell in the third quarter of 1987 to 8%, the lowest in four years, according to the National Statistical Institute. The UGT, Portugal's largest trade union, claims that the rate, which represents 370,000 people out of work, is misrepresentative because a large number of people counted as employed are enrolled in short-term job training programs.			In Australia, Gerry Hand, the minister for Aboriginal affairs, announces that he will boycott all ceremonies commemorating the nation's bicentennial. The government has planned a yearlong celebration to mark the 200th anniversary of the settlement of Australia by white Europeans.
Jan. 5		The rate of savings in Britain fell to 5% of disposable (after-tax) income, a 29-year low, during the third quarter of 1987, according to data from the Central Statistical Office. . . . The Soviet Union granted exit visas to 8,155 Jews in 1987, according to the National Conf. of Soviet Jewry. The figure is believed to be the highest total since 1981 and nine times the total in 1986.		El Salvador's Pres. Jose Napoleon Duarte announces that leftist rebels were responsible for the October 1987 slaying of human rights activist Herbert Ernesto Anaya Sanabria, who was president of the Salvadoran Human Rights Comm., a nongovernmental group. His death sparked protests and accusations that the government was responsible. The leftist rebels fighting the government called off a scheduled round of peace talks after the murder.	

A	B	C	D	E
Includes developments that affect more than one world region, international organizations and important meetings of major world leaders.	Includes all domestic and regional developments in Europe, including the Soviet Union, Turkey, Cyprus and Malta.	Includes all domestic and regional developments in Africa and the Middle East, including Iraq and Iran and excluding Cyprus, Turkey and Afghanistan.	Includes all domestic and regional developments in Latin America, the Caribbean and Canada.	Includes all domestic and regional developments in Asia and Pacific nations, extending from Afghanistan through all the Pacific Islands, except Hawaii.

U.S. Politics & Social Issues	U.S. Foreign Policy & Defense	U.S. Economy & Environment	Science, Technology & Nature	Culture, Leisure & Life Style	
Supreme Court Chief Justice William H. Rehnquist warns that the federal judiciary is facing "a serious dilemma" because Congress is restricting funding at a time when work loads are increasing and there is a shortage of judges and other court personnel.			According to a report in the journal *Science*, the atmosphere's protective ozone layer has diminished worldwide, and not just over Antarctica. A sharp depletion of the ozone shield over Antarctica in recent years has triggered global concern.	Miami defeats Oklahoma 20-14 in the Orange Bowl; Auburn ties Syracuse 16-16 in the Sugar Bowl; Michigan State edges out Univ. of Southern California 20-17 in the Rose Bowl; and Texas A&M trounces Notre Dame 35-10 in the Cotton Bowl.	Jan. 1
		The collapse of an Ashland Oil Co. storage tank spills nearly a million gallons of diesel fuel into the Monongahela River about 20 miles upriver from Pittsburgh. The accident, one of the largest inland fuel spills in U.S. history, endangers water supplies for thousands of people and businesses and destroys or jeopardizes fish, fowl, and other wildlife along the Monongahela and Ohio Rivers.	According to an announcement by the Centers for Disease Control, in 1986 the United States experienced its first substantial increase in tuberculosis (TB) cases among Americans in 33 years of record-keeping. There were 22,768 cases of TB in 1986, up 2.6% from the 22,201 cases reported in 1985.		Jan. 2
				The Univ. of Miami is ranked the top college football team in the Associated Press and United Press International polls. . . . The National Society of Film Critics selects director John Huston's last film, *The Dead*, based on a story by James Joyce, best film of 1987. John Boorman is named best director for *Hope and Glory*; Steve Martin, best actor for *Roxanne*; and Emily Lloyd, best actress for *Wish You Were Here*.	Jan. 3
The first 1988 presidential campaign matching funds authorized by the Federal Election Comm. are paid out to Republicans—Vice Pres. George Bush, $5,761,540; the Rev. Pat Robertson, $4,495,607; Sen. Robert J. Dole (Kans.), $4,338,141; Rep. Jack F. Kemp (N.Y.), $3,012,949; former Gov. Pierre S. (Pete) du Pont IV (Del.), $1,868,762; and former Sec. of State Alexander M. Haig Jr., $274,850—and to Democrats Gov. Michael S. Dukakis (Mass.), $3,493,418; Rep. Richard A. Gephardt (Mo.), $1,737,216; Sen. Albert Gore Jr. (Tenn.), $1,556,401; Sen. Paul Simon (Ill.), $1,390,137; former Gov. Bruce Babbitt (Ariz.), $719,235; and former Sen. Gary Hart (Colo.), $100,000.		White House Budget Dir. James C. Miller III sends Congress a letter saying it is impossible to meet that day's legal deadline for submitting the fiscal 1989 federal budget.			Jan. 4
				Pete Maravich, 40, the greatest scorer in the history of National Collegiate Athletic Assoc. basketball, dies after collapsing during a pickup game in Pasadena, Calif.; his death is attributed to congenital heart defects. At Louisiana State Univ., 1968-70, he scored a record 3,667 points for a career average of 44.2 points. In 10 years in the National Basketball Assoc., he averaged 24.2 points a game and led the league in scoring in the 1977 season. He was inducted into the Basketball Hall of Fame in 1987.	Jan. 5

F	G	H	I	J
Includes elections, federal-state relations, civil rights and liberties, crime, the judiciary, education, health care, poverty, urban affairs and population.	Includes formation and debate of U.S. foreign and defense policies, veterans' affairs and defense spending. (Relations with specific foreign countries are usually found under the region concerned.)	Includes business, labor, agriculture, taxation, transportation, consumer affairs, monetary and fiscal policy, natural resources, and pollution.	Includes worldwide scientific, medical and technological developments, natural phenomena, U.S. weather, natural disasters, and accidents.	Includes the arts, religion, scholarship, communications media, sports, entertainments, fashions, fads and social life.

	World Affairs	Europe	Africa & the Middle East	The Americas	Asia & the Pacific
Jan. 6		Soviet Foreign Min. Eduard A. Shevardnadze says the Soviet Union hopes to withdraw all its troops from Afghanistan by the end of 1988.... Turkish inflation in 1987 was 55.1%, according to the State Institute of Statistics. That is up from 24% in 1986 and is the highest in seven years. Turkey's treasury estimates wholesale price inflation at 59.2% and says that the cost of living in Istanbul is up 67.3% for the year.... The Soviet Bank of Foreign Economic Affairs is reported to have issued $78 mil. in 10-year, 5% Eurobonds, in what is believed to be the first public bond offering by an enterprise incorporated solely in the USSR.			Australia's national teachers' union instructs its members to boycott any school activities that celebrate the country's 200th birthday without considering the plight of the Aborigines.
Jan. 7		France's socialist Pres. Francois Mitterrand continues to lead public opinion polls in the run-up to the spring presidential election, according to U.S. press reports. He maintains the lead despite his not having announced whether he will be a candidate.			Taiwan's overall trade surplus rose 22%, from $15.61 bil. in 1986 to a record $19.03 bil. in 1987, the government reports. The surplus with the United States, Taiwan's largest trading partner, also increased, to $16 bil. from $13.5 bil., according to the trade report issued by the Directorate Gen. of Budget, Accounting and Statistics.
Jan. 8			Britain's P.M. Margaret Thatcher ends a five-day trip to Africa during which she repeatedly stresses her opposition to tougher economic sanctions against the white minority-ruled government of South Africa.		
Jan. 9			Egypt's Pres. Hosni Mubarak arrives in Saudi Arabia to begin a tour of the six nations of the Gulf Cooperation Council. The trip comes on the heels of the Arab League move in November 1987 to end Cairo's eight-year diplomatic isolation over its separate peace with Israel, a decision prompted by the Gulf states' desire to have Egypt as a military counterweight to Iran should it succeed in defeating Iraq.		
Jan. 10		Unemployment in West Germany rose to 9.2% of the work force in December 1987 from 8.5% in November and 8.9% in December 1986, the government reports. The December 1987 figure represented 2.31 million people out of work.	The Israeli-occupied Gaza Strip is hit by two days of the most intense rioting to date, according to witnesses. More than 50 people are reported wounded by Israeli gunfire, and street battles continued into the night.		

A	B	C	D	E
Includes developments that affect more than one world region, international organizations and important meetings of major world leaders.	Includes all domestic and regional developments in Europe, including the Soviet Union, Turkey, Cyprus and Malta.	Includes all domestic and regional developments in Africa and the Middle East, including Iraq and Iran and excluding Cyprus, Turkey and Afghanistan.	Includes all domestic and regional developments in Latin America, the Caribbean and Canada.	Includes all domestic and regional developments in Asia and Pacific nations, extending from Afghanistan through all the Pacific Islands, except Hawaii.

U.S. Politics & Social Issues	U.S. Foreign Policy & Defense	U.S. Economy & Environment	Science, Technology & Nature	Culture, Leisure & Life Style	
A federal grand jury in Los Angeles indicts nine people in connection with the 1985 slaying of Drug Enforcement Admin. agent Enrique Camarena Salazar and his pilot, Alfredo Zavala Avelar, in Mexico. . . . Pres. Reagan signs a bill to prop up the sagging Farm Credit System with up to $4 bil. in government-backed bonds.		The performance record of domestic airlines fell off sharply in November 1987, the Transportation Dept. reports. The data, a new monthly record required by the department and aimed at improving service, shows that only 76% of airline flights arrived within 15 minutes of schedule in November, down from 80% in October 1987.	In Canada, the federal government partially lifts a ban on the sale of Atlantic Coast hinged-shell mollusks. The ban was imposed Dec. 11, 1987, because of evidence of toxic contamination. However, the prohibition remains in effect with regard to mollusks from Prince Edward Island, the eastern and northern coasts of New Brunswick, Quebec's Gaspe Peninsula and lower North Shore of the Gulf of St. Lawrence, and part of the north shore of Nova Scotia along the Bay of Fundy.		Jan. 6
Robert Streetman in Huntsville, Tex., is put to death by lethal injection, becoming the first inmate executed in the United States in 1988. The 27-year-old high-school dropout killed an elderly woman in Kountze, Tex., during a 1982 burglary that netted $1. . . . New York City Mayor Edward I. Koch (D) signs into law the city's first comprehensive antismoking bill. The measure was approved by the city council, 30-1, with one abstention, on Dec. 23, 1987, and takes effect on April 6, 1988.		Outstanding consumer debt rose $2.22 bil. in November 1987, the Federal Reserve Board reports, at an annual rate of 4.4%, to a total of $610.11 bil. . . . Pres. Reagan names James M. Stephens to succeed Donald L. Dotson as chairman of the National Labor Relations Board. Dotson left the board on Dec. 16, 1987, when his term expired.	Doctors in Mexico City report having transplanted tissue from an aborted fetus into the brains of two victims of Parkisnon's disease, a chronic progressive nervous disease. The leader of the medical team, Dr. Ignacio Madrazo, reports the procedure in the New England Journal of Medicine.	Trevor Howard, 71, British actor who began his career in the theater but from 1944 concentrated on the cinema, dies of influenza and bronchitis in Bushey, England. He appeared in more than 70 films and starred in such classics as Brief Encounter (1946), The Third Man (1950), and the 1962 remake of Mutiny on the Bounty.	Jan. 7
Arizona's Gov. Evan Mecham (R), already facing a recall election, is indicted on six felony counts, including perjury and filing a false campaign finance report.		The Presidential Task Force on Market Mechanisms' report on the October 1987 stock-market crash concludes that "the financial system approached breakdown" on Tuesday, Oct. 20, 1987, and calls for radical changes in the regulation of the nation's capital markets to prevent a repetition of the near-meltdown of October 19. . . . The nation's unemployment rate fell to 5.7% in December 1987, the Labor Dept. reports.	The Journal of the American Medical Assoc. publishes an essay purporting to be a first-person account of the mercy-killing by a young physician of a 20-year-old terminal cancer patient. The essay, titled "It's Over, Debbie," sparks a furious debate over euthanasia and triggers criminal inquiries.		Jan. 8
		The massive oil spill moving down the Ohio River forces city officials in Wheeling, W.Va., to declare an emergency situation. The emergency is lifted January 11 as the slick begins to dilute.		In the National Football League playoffs, the Minnesota Vikings beat the San Francisco 49ers, 36-24, in the National Football Conf., and in the American Football Conf., the Cleveland Browns beat the Indianapolis Colts, 38-21. . . . Brian Boitano wins his fourth consecutive U.S. men's figure skating competition, and Debi Thomas wins her second national women's title.	Jan. 9
				In the National Football League playoffs, the Washington Redskins beat the Chicago Bears 21-17 in the National Football Conf., and the Denver Broncos beat the Houston Oilers 34-10 in the American Football Conf.	Jan. 10

F	G	H	I	J
Includes elections, federal-state relations, civil rights and liberties, crime, the judiciary, education, health care, poverty, urban affairs and population.	Includes formation and debate of U.S. foreign and defense policies, veterans' affairs and defense spending. (Relations with specific foreign countries are usually found under the region concerned.)	Includes business, labor, agriculture, taxation, transportation, consumer affairs, monetary and fiscal policy, natural resources, and pollution.	Includes worldwide scientific, medical and technological developments, natural phenomena, U.S. weather, natural disasters, and accidents.	Includes the arts, religion, scholarship, communications media, sports, entertainments, fashions, fads and social life.

	World Affairs	Europe	Africa & the Middle East	The Americas	Asia & the Pacific
Jan. 11			Sec. of State George P. Shultz and Canada's External Affairs Min. Joe Clark sign an accord on the traffic of U.S. ships through Arctic waters. The signing takes place during a one-day visit to Ottawa by Shultz.	A survey by the *Toronto Globe and Mail* finds that over 10,000 Canadians are infected with acquired immune deficiency syndrome (AIDS). As of mid-November 1987, there were 1,364 diagnosed cases of AIDS in Canada. Approximately one-half of the diagnosed victims have died.	Australia's population rose by 230,500 (1.4%) during the year ending June 30, 1987, to a total of 16,248,000. The report, prepared by the Australian Bureau of Statistics, shows that 55% of the increase came through births, with the balance attributed to immigration. . . . Sony Corp., which touched off the home-video cassette recorder revolution in 1975 with the introduction of its Betamax model, but then lost the market to the rival VHS recording system, announces in Tokyo that it will begin selling VHS models in Europe, starting in the spring.
Jan. 12		In Yugoslavia, the federal parliament breaks a budget stalemate by approving spending for 1988. The 1988 budget sets spending at $4.37 bil. That figure is $84.9 mil. less than the spending proposal that had been blocked in parliament in December 1987.	Two days after it is reported that Iran had snubbed Syria's latest proposals to end the Iran-Iraq war, the peace bid is apparently further derailed when Iraq breaks a nine-day, tacit truce in the shipping war with new air attacks on Iranian oil tankers.	Three days before a meeting of Central American presidents to review the regional peace agreement signed in August 1987, Costa Rican Pres. Oscar Arias Sanchez orders three Nicaraguan Contra leaders to give up their armed struggle against the Nicaraguan government or leave Costa Rica. . . . In a further step toward the restoration of democracy in Suriname, the National Assembly elects former Agriculture Min. Ramsewak Shankar, 50, as the nation's new president.	The Chinese foreign ministry rejects a request by Soviet leader Mikhail S. Gorbachev for a summit meeting. In the longtime rift between the two nations, China has repeatedly cited three conditions for a normalization of relations: a reduction of Soviet forces on the Chinese border; a Soviet withdrawal from Afghanistan; and an end of Soviet support for the Vietnamese occupation of Cambodia.
Jan. 13		France rescinds its expulsion of Iranian dissidents in the face of hunger strikes by some of the dissidents and their supporters in Paris. Seventeen members of the People's Mujahadeen, most from Iran, were expelled from France in December 1987 in a move apparently related to the release of French hostages from Lebanon. . . . West Germany's gross national product grew by an inflation-adjusted 1.7% in 1987, down from 2.5% in 1986, according to a preliminary report. . . . In Spain, unemployment in December 1987 topped 3 million, or 21% of the work force, the labor ministry reports.	Defying international opinion, Israel expels four Palestinian activists who were part of a group of nine men charged with instigating the rioting that has wracked the occupied West Bank and Gaza Strip for more than a month. The four are flown by an army helicopter into Lebanon and dropped off at a mountain pass near Hasbaya, just north of Israel's self-proclaimed security zone in southern Lebanon.	In Nicaragua, an American whose plane was downed there in December 1987 is arraigned before a tribunal on charges of violating the nation's security laws. James Jordan Denby is accused of being a "mercenary pilot" with "links with the war of aggression against Nicaragua."	Taiwan's Vice Pres. Lee Teng-hui, Chiang Ching-kuo's designated successor, is sworn in as president immediately after Chiang's death.

A	B	C	D	E
Includes developments that affect more than one world region, international organizations and important meetings of major world leaders.	Includes all domestic and regional developments in Europe, including the Soviet Union, Turkey, Cyprus and Malta.	Includes all domestic and regional developments in Africa and the Middle East, including Iraq and Iran and excluding Cyprus, Turkey and Afghanistan.	Includes all domestic and regional developments in Latin America, the Caribbean and Canada.	Includes all domestic and regional developments in Asia and Pacific nations, extending from Afghanistan through all the Pacific Islands, except Hawaii.

U.S. Politics & Social Issues	U.S. Foreign Policy & Defense	U.S. Economy & Environment	Science, Technology & Nature	Culture, Leisure & Life Style	
Vice Pres. George Bush is questioned under oath by the staff of the special prosecutor in the Iran-Contra affair, Lawrence E. Walsh. A statement from Bush's office says Bush testified "voluntarily," but a *Washington Post* story says the terms of his appearance were the subject of intense negotiation.		District Judge Frank McGarr in Chicago assesses Amoco Corp. $85.2 mil. for the oil spill from the *Amoco Cadiz* supertanker off the coast of Brittany in 1978.	I(sidor) I(saac) Rabi, 89, U.S. physicist born in Austria-Hungary and long associated with Columbia Univ., dies in New York City. He won the 1944 Nobel Prize for physics for his discovery and measurement of the radio-frequency spectrum of atomic nuclei whose magnetic spin had been disturbed, work that led to the development of atomic clocks and nuclear magnetic resonance imaging techniques for medical diagnosis. He played a major role in the development of radar during World War II and later championed nuclear arms control.	The National Book Critics Circle names Philip Roth's *The Counterlife* the best work of U.S. fiction published in 1987; general nonfiction goes to Richard Rhodes's *The Making of the Atomic Bomb*; biography, Donald R. Howard's *Chaucer: His Life, His Work, His World*; criticism, Edwin Denby's *Dance Writings*; and poetry, C.K. Williams' *Flesh and Blood*. Robert Giroux, the 73-year-old editor in chief of Farrar, Straus & Giroux, is honored with a special citation for "his distinguished contribution to the enhancement of American literary and critical standards." . . . The American Library Assoc. awards the 1987 John Newbery Medal for the best U.S. children's book to Russell Friedman's *Lincoln: A Photobiography*. The Randolph Caldecott Medal for best illustrations in a picture-book for children goes to C. John Schoenherr, who illustrated Jane Yolen's *Owl Moon*.	**Jan. 11**
	A blue-ribbon advisory panel on future defense strategy delivers its report to Pres. Reagan. The Comm. on Integrated Long-Term Strategy was formed in 1987 by then-Defense Sec. Caspar W. Weinberger.		New York State health officials release the results of a statewide study in which the blood of every infant born during a month-long period beginning in late November 1987 was tested for antibodies to the virus that causes acquired immune deficiency syndrome. The study, performed on 19,157 infants throughout the state, showed 164 positive tests for antibodies, one in every 117 babies. . . . The United States and Soviet Union sign an accord on scientific cooperation. The pact replaces and expands the U.S.-Soviet science agreement concluded at the 1985 Geneva summit. RN18077 . . . The National Institutes of Health concludes that Montana State Univ. researcher Gary Strobel did break the agency's rules for genetic research when he introduced gene-altered bacteria into a group of elm trees in 1987. The decision does not affect sanctions leveled against Strobel by the Environmental Protection Agency, which has its own rules for genetic research.	Willie Stargell, a powerful slugger who played his entire 21-year career with the Pittsburgh Pirates, is elected to the Baseball Hall of Fame in Cooperstown, N.Y.	**Jan. 12**
The Supreme Court rules, 5-3, that censorship of a student newspaper by public school officials is not unconstitutional as long as it is "reasonably related to legitimate pedagogical concerns" and has a "valid educational purpose." . . . For the first time in 13 years, the use of cocaine by high school seniors in 1987 declined from the previous year's level, according to a survey by the Univ. of Michigan's Institute of Social Research. Use of marijuana and hashish, which peaked in 1978, is found to be at the lowest levels in the survey's 13-year history. The survey, however, finds that alcohol use among high school seniors has more or less stabilized since 1984 and that cigarette smoking has shown little or no decline since 1984.					**Jan. 13**

F	G	H	I	J
Includes elections, federal-state relations, civil rights and liberties, crime, the judiciary, education, health care, poverty, urban affairs and population.	*Includes formation and debate of U.S. foreign and defense policies, veterans' affairs and defense spending. (Relations with specific foreign countries are usually found under the region concerned.)*	*Includes business, labor, agriculture, taxation, transportation, consumer affairs, monetary and fiscal policy, natural resources, and pollution.*	*Includes worldwide scientific, medical and technological developments, natural phenomena, U.S. weather, natural disasters, and accidents.*	*Includes the arts, religion, scholarship, communications media, sports, entertainments, fashions, fads and social life.*

	World Affairs	Europe	Africa & the Middle East	The Americas	Asia & the Pacific
Jan. 14		French consumer prices rose 3.1% in 1987, up from a 2.1% gain in 1986, the government reports. But the finance ministry points out that, excluding energy costs, 1987 inflation was the lowest in 15 years.	Meeting in London, a majority of Nigeria's commercial creditors vote to accept a controversial plan under which their promissory notes covering $3.2 bil. in unpaid and uninsured trade debts will be repaid by Nigeria at below-market interest rates over a 22-year period. However, a group of disgruntled creditors move to challenge the acceptance of the debt plan.	Miguel Angel Pavon, vice president of the independent Honduran Human Rights Defense Committee, is murdered in San Pedro Sula, Honduras.	
Jan. 15		The United States and Spain formally announce that the United States, at Spain's request, will withdraw 72 F-16 fighter-bombers based at the Torrejon air base near Madrid over the next three years. The agreement on the F-16s, rumored for a month, paves the way for a comprehensive pact that will preserve a U.S. military presence in Spain. . . . Sean MacBride, 83, Irish jurist, diplomat, human rights activist, and Nobel laureate, dies of pneumonia in Dublin. Active in the Irish Republican Army for 20 years, he was the most successful trial lawyer in Dublin. In 1946 he founded the radical nationalist party, Clann na Poblachta, which two years later helped oust the ruling Fianna Fail Party. He was foreign minister in the coalition government of 1948-51, under which Ireland became an independent republic. A cofounder of Amnesty International in 1961, he was secretary general of the International Comm. of Jurists from 1963 to 1970, and shared the Nobel Prize for peace with Japanese statesman Eisaku Sato in 1974 and was awarded its Soviet equivalent, the Lenin Prize, in 1977. . . . Soviet leader Mikhail S. Gorbachev meets in Moscow with physicist Andrei D. Sakharov in what is apparently the first face-to-face discussion between Gorbachev and a major Soviet dissident. Gorbachev freed Sakharov and his wife, Dr. Yelena G. Bonner, from internal exile in 1986.	Guerrillas of the Eritrean People's Liberation Front (EPLF) ambush a convoy in northern Ethiopia that is carrying food for famine victims. The attack is not revealed by relief officials until five days later. . . . The Angolan government says its army is battling 6,000 South African troops, backed by artillery, armored vehicles, and aircraft, around the strategic southeastern garrison town of Cuito Cuanavale.		
Jan. 16			Nabih Berri, leader of the Shiite Moslem Amal militia, announces that his men will end their nearly three-year-old blockade of Palestinian refugee camps in Lebanon as a gesture of solidarity toward the current Palestinian uprising in the Israeli-occupied West Bank and Gaza Strip.	In a dramatic reversal, Nicaragua's Pres. Daniel Ortega Saavedra announces a number of concessions at a summit meeting of Central American presidents convened to discuss the progress of the regional peace agreement signed in August 1987. The pledge of concessions receives only a tepid response from Nicaraguan Contra leaders.	
Jan. 17				Haiti's government-appointed electoral council names Leslie Manigat, a conservative university professor who spent 23 years in exile, as the winner of the controversial January 17 presidential election. A previous poll, in November 1987, was called off after thugs, aided by soldiers, unleashed a wave of terror against voters that resulted in 34 deaths, according to official figures.	

A	B	C	D	E
Includes developments that affect more than one world region, international organizations and important meetings of major world leaders.	Includes all domestic and regional developments in Europe, including the Soviet Union, Turkey, Cyprus and Malta.	Includes all domestic and regional developments in Africa and the Middle East, including Iraq and Iran and excluding Cyprus, Turkey and Afghanistan.	Includes all domestic and regional developments in Latin America, the Caribbean and Canada.	Includes all domestic and regional developments in Asia and Pacific nations, extending from Afghanistan through all the Pacific Islands, except Hawaii.

U.S. Politics & Social Issues	U.S. Foreign Policy & Defense	U.S. Economy & Environment	Science, Technology & Nature	Culture, Leisure & Life Style	
Judge Robert H. Bork's resignation from the federal appellate court in the District of Columbia is accepted by Pres. Reagan. Bork's Supreme Court nomination was rejected by the Senate in October 1987 after a bitter confirmation fight.		Retail sales rose a healthy 0.7% in December 1987, the Commerce Dept. says. This gain, the largest since August, follows a 0.1% November increase and a 0.9% October drop. Auto sales fueled the increase, rising 2.4% in December after a 0.7% drop the previous month. This increase is attributed to dealer and manufacturer incentives.			Jan. 14
Pres. Reagan is pronounced "in excellent health" by White House physician John Hutton. The president's annual physical reveals no recurrence of colon cancer and no intestinal polyps.	Pres. Reagan signs a waiver permitting the United States to renew aid to Pakistan. The waiver, which exempts Pakistan from U.S. nuclear nonproliferation laws until April 1, 1990, certifies that a cutoff in aid would jeopardize U.S. security interests.	The deficit on merchandise trade fell 25% in November 1987 to $13.22 bil., down from the October 1987 record trade deficit, the Commerce Dept. reports. . . . The government's producer price index declined 0.3% in December 1987, the Labor Dept. reports.			Jan. 15
					Jan. 16
	The Justice Dept. says it has withdrawn an arrest warrant issued in 1986 for Mohammed Abul Abbas, the accused mastermind of the 1985 hijacking of the Italian cruise ship *Achille Lauro*. Abbas is the leader of the Palestine Liberation Front, a small faction within the Palestine Liberation Org. The warrant is being dropped because a review determined that the United States does not have the evidence necessary to convict Abbas in an American court.			The Washington Redskins defeat the Minnesota Vikings, 17-10, to win the National Football Conf. title, and the Denver Broncos take the American Football Conf. title with a 38-33 win over the Cleveland Browns. The Redskins and the Broncos will play each other in the Super Bowl.	Jan. 17

F	G	H	I	J
Includes elections, federal-state relations, civil rights and liberties, crime, the judiciary, education, health care, poverty, urban affairs and population.	Includes formation and debate of U.S. foreign and defense policies, veterans' affairs and defense spending. (Relations with specific foreign countries are usually found under the region concerned.)	Includes business, labor, agriculture, taxation, transportation, consumer affairs, monetary and fiscal policy, natural resources, and pollution.	Includes worldwide scientific, medical and technological developments, natural phenomena, U.S. weather, natural disasters, and accidents.	Includes the arts, religion, scholarship, communications media, sports, entertainments, fashions, fads and social life.

	World Affairs	Europe	Africa & the Middle East	The Americas	Asia & the Pacific
Jan. 18	At the end of 1987 the world's debtor nations owed an estimated $1.19 trillion, according to a World Bank report. In 1987, the debtor countries made $29 bil. more in debt repayments than they received in new loans, down marginally from a $30.7 bil. net repayment figure in 1986.	A prominent West German nuclear fuels company announces a management shake-up amid charges that the company illegally shipped fissionable nuclear material to Libya and Pakistan.... Western European car sales rose 6% in volume, to 12.37 million units in 1987, according to preliminary industry estimates reported. The Volkswagen group remains the leading producer with a 15% market share, followed by the Fiat group (14.2%), the Peugeot group (12.1%), Ford (12.0%), and General Motors Corp. (10.7%). The combined market share of all Japanese manufacturers fell to 11.3% from 11.6% in 1986.... Spain's gross domestic product grew an estimated 4.5% in 1987, up from 3.3% growth in 1986, the Bank of Spain reports.		In Argentina, the second military rebellion in nine months to be led by army Lt. Col. Aldo Rico ends when Rico surrenders unconditionally to troops loyal to the government. Rico was charged with organizing a revolt in April 1987 that forced the government to grant amnesty to hundreds of military personnel involved in the so-called "Dirty War" against Argentine leftists in the late 1970s and early 1980s.	About 80% of the registered voters in 62 of the Philippines' 73 provinces go to the polls to vote in the country's first free local elections since 1971.
Jan. 19			In a new tactic, Israeli security forces have begun widespread beatings of Palestinian protesters in the occupied West Bank and Gaza Strip. Palestinians and foreign relief officials say the beatings have been going on for more than a week before the issue began being discussed by Israeli officials and covered by the Israeli press.		Japan's overall trade surplus declined in 1987 for the first time in five years, the finance ministry reports. The surplus dropped to $79.83 bil. during the year, down 3.5% from the 1986 record high of $82.74 bil.... China's cabinet, the state council, reimposes price controls on most basic raw materials and services. The move suspends a two-year-old program under which the government attempted to reduce the role of central planning within the economy in favor of letting the marketplace set prices.
Jan. 20		Italy's balance of payments showed a surplus of 1,637 bil. lira in 1987, reversing a 1986 deficit of 2.965 bil. lira, the Bank of Italy reports.		The environment committee of Canada's House of Commons issues a report calling for a halt in the construction of nuclear power plants. Canada has 19 operating nuclear reactors. They are regulated by the Atomic Energy Control Board, which is under the jurisdiction of the Dept. of Energy, Mines and Resources.... The Canadian dollar rose above US$0.78 for the first time in four years. Aided by the slumping U.S. dollar and moderate intervention by the Bank of Canada, the Canadian dollar surged to a high of 78.03 cents in international currency trading.	Two U.S. congressmen report that Vietnam's Foreign Min. Nguyen Co Thach has agreed in principle to allow all Amerasian children—Vietnamese fathered by Americans during the Vietnam War—and their family members to immigrate to the United States within two years.... Abdul Ghaffar Khan, 98, a Pathan tribesman and one of the leaders of India's struggle for independence from Great Britain, dies in Peshawar, Pakistan. A Moslem, Ghaffar Khan supported Mohandas Gandhi and Jawaharlal Nehru, both Hindus. Having helped India gain independence, he opposed the establishment of the separate state of Pakistan. He was unsuccessful in his struggle to create an autonomous Pathan state that would have combined Pathan lands in Pakistan and Afghanistan.
Jan. 21		In an interview published in the Communist Party newspaper Pravda, a Soviet official predicts that 3 million bureaucrats will lose their jobs by 1990 because of economic reforms.			Philippine Pres. Corazon Aquino appoints armed forces chief of staff Gen. Fidel Ramos to replace Defense Min. Rafael Ileto, who resigns today.... Premier Hun Sen, head of the Vietnamese-backed government of Cambodia, proposes a 24-month timetable for the withdrawal of Vietnamese troops from the country. Hun Sen makes the offer during meetings with Cambodian resistance leader Prince Norodom Sihanouk in the French village of St. Germain-en-Laye, near Paris.

A	B	C	D	E
Includes developments that affect more than one world region, international organizations and important meetings of major world leaders.	Includes all domestic and regional developments in Europe, including the Soviet Union, Turkey, Cyprus and Malta.	Includes all domestic and regional developments in Africa and the Middle East, including Iraq and Iran and excluding Cyprus, Turkey and Afghanistan.	Includes all domestic and regional developments in Latin America, the Caribbean and Canada.	Includes all domestic and regional developments in Asia and Pacific nations, extending from Afghanistan through all the Pacific Islands, except Hawaii.

U.S. Politics & Social Issues	U.S. Foreign Policy & Defense	U.S. Economy & Environment	Science, Technology & Nature	Culture, Leisure & Life Style	
All six Republican presidential candidates will be eligible to win delegates in the March 8, Texas primary election, state GOP Chairman George Strake announces. A federal investigation of fraudulent signatures on the petitions of two candidates, Sen. Robert J. Dole (Kans.) and former Sec. of State Alexander M. Haig Jr., began January 8. Those of two others, Pierre S. (Pete) du Pont IV and Rep. Jack F. Kemp (N.Y.), were later questioned.				The president of the International Olympic Committee, Juan Antonio Samaranch, announces that a record 161 of the 167 nations invited to the 1988 Summer Olympic Games in Seoul, South Korea, have agreed to attend. The games are scheduled to be held September 17 through October 2.	**Jan. 18**
A 40-year-old former secretary, Joyce Brown, who became a test case for a New York City policy of forcibly hospitalizing homeless individuals judged to be mentally ill, is released from Bellevue Hospital after a state judge rules that she cannot be given antipsychotic medication against her will.				Christopher Nolan is named winner of Britain's Whitbread Book of the Year Award, for *Under the Eye of the Clock.*	**Jan. 19**
A committee of the Arizona House of Representatives begins hearings to consider the impeachment of Gov. Evan Mecham (R). A special counsel appointed by the legislature reported back January 15 with a toughly worded statement recommending the governor's impeachment on three charges. ... The Supreme Court rules out removal of disruptive emotionally disturbed pupils from classrooms without permission of the parents or a court. The 6-2 decision, *Honig v. Doe*, is based on the Education of the Handicapped Act of 1975.		The government's consumer price index rose 4.4% in 1987, the Labor Dept. reports.... Housing starts fell 16.2% in December 1987, the Commerce Dept. reports.... The National Transportation Safety Board formally cites marijuana use by Conrail engineer Ricky L. Gates as a prime cause of the January 1987 collision of an Amtrak passenger train and a string of Conrail locomotives near Baltimore. Sixteen Amtrak passengers died, and Gates was indicted on 16 counts of manslaughter in May; he is to be tried in Baltimore in February 1988.		*Variety*'s top-grossing films for the week are: *Good Morning, Vietnam, Moonstruck, Three Men and a Baby, Broadcast News* and *For Keeps.*	**Jan. 20**
A Justice Dept. study finds that half to three-quarters of the men arrested for serious crimes in a dozen cities used illegal drugs shortly before their arrest. The study, sponsored by the National Institute of Justice, the research arm of the Justice Dept., is reportedly the first national study to test criminal suspects for drug use at the time of arrest.				After saying for years that his extensive art collection will eventually be donated to the Los Angeles County Museum of Art, Occidental Petroleum Corp. chairman Armand Hammer, 89, announces plans to build a $30-mil. private museum to house the collection, valued at $250 mil.	**Jan. 21**

F	G	H	I	J
Includes elections, federal-state relations, civil rights and liberties, crime, the judiciary, education, health care, poverty, urban affairs and population.	*Includes formation and debate of U.S. foreign and defense policies, veterans' affairs and defense spending. (Relations with specific foreign countries are usually found under the region concerned.)*	*Includes business, labor, agriculture, taxation, transportation, consumer affairs, monetary and fiscal policy, natural resources, and pollution.*	*Includes worldwide scientific, medical and technological developments, natural phenomena, U.S. weather, natural disasters, and accidents.*	*Includes the arts, religion, scholarship, communications media, sports, entertainments, fashions, fads and social life.*

	World Affairs	Europe	Africa & the Middle East	The Americas	Asia & the Pacific
Jan. 22		U.S. negotiators in Geneva present their Soviet counterparts a draft antimissile-defense treaty to supplement the 1972 anti-ballistic missile treaty. The draft is the first formal U.S. proposal in Geneva related to the Strategic Defense Initiative ("Star Wars").... France and West Germany formally establish joint councils on defense and economic issues. Agreements establishing the councils are signed in Paris by French Pres. Francois Mitterrand and West German Chancellor Helmut Kohl during celebrations on the 25th anniversary of a friendship treaty signed by Charles de Gaulle and Konrad Adenauer.			Philippine Pres. Corazon Aquino reaffirms her general support for land reform, but declines to offer congress any specific recommendations toward enacting legislation on the issue.... China's ministry of foreign economic relations and trade announces that the nation recorded an overall surplus of $1.9 bil. on trade of $67.3 bil. during 1987, reversing a three-year string of deficits.
Jan. 23				Nicaraguan soldiers down a DC-6 cargo plane carrying supplies to the Contras. The plane is shot down near Nueva Guinea in Zelaya department, near the Costa Rican border. One survivor is captured the next day, and four bodies found.	
Jan. 24			Following widespread international criticism and reports January 19-20 of excessive brutality by soldiers, the Israeli Army issues stricter guidelines on its policy of beating Palestinian demonstrators in the occupied West Bank and Gaza Strip. The military authorities also lift curfews on all but one refugee camp in Gaza.		In Bangladesh, at least eight people are killed and 100 injured when police open fire on protesters marching in the southeastern city of Chittagong. The incident is the most violent confrontation between the police and antigovernment demonstrators since a series of strikes and riots began Nov. 10, 1987.

A	B	C	D	E
Includes developments that affect more than one world region, international organizations and important meetings of major world leaders.	Includes all domestic and regional developments in Europe, including the Soviet Union, Turkey, Cyprus and Malta.	Includes all domestic and regional developments in Africa and the Middle East, including Iraq and Iran and excluding Cyprus, Turkey and Afghanistan.	Includes all domestic and regional developments in Latin America, the Caribbean and Canada.	Includes all domestic and regional developments in Asia and Pacific nations, extending from Afghanistan through all the Pacific Islands, except Hawaii.

U.S. Politics & Social Issues	U.S. Foreign Policy & Defense	U.S. Economy & Environment	Science, Technology & Nature	Culture, Leisure & Life Style	
A federal appeals court panel in the District of Columbia overturns by a 2-1 vote the law authorizing independent counsels to investigate alleged wrongdoing by high-ranking federal officials. The court says the law "seriously weakens constitutional structures that serve to protect individual liberty." . . . A federal judge in New York City declares a mistrial in the federal racketeering and drug trial of reputed mobster Gene Gotti and nine codefendants. The trial has been under way for nine months in Eastern District Court in the borough of Brooklyn. The mistrial was sought by the prosecution, which alleged that the jury had been tampered with.		Chevron USA agrees to pay a $1.5 mil. penalty to settle federal charges of polluting Santa Monica Bay. . . . An arbitrator for Major League Baseball grants immediate free agency to seven of the 62 players involved in a 1985 collusion case brought against team owners by the Major League Players Assoc.	A study reported in the *Journal of the American Medical Assoc.* says that a prescription cream designed for fighting acne seems to reverse some of the effects of sun induced facial wrinkles. It remains unknown how Retin-A works and what its long-term side effects are. . . . The 1986 disaster at the Chernobyl nuclear power plant in the Soviet Ukraine caused no noticeable increase in radiation risks in Western nations, according to a study by the nuclear agency of the Org. for Economic Cooperation and Development.	Undisputed heavyweight champion Mike Tyson successfully defends his title against former champion Larry Holmes.	**Jan. 22**
		The Enrico Fermi II nuclear power plant near Detroit goes into commercial operation, 14 years behind schedule and about $4 bil. over budget.		Steffi Graf of West Germany wins the Australian Open women's singles tennis title. . . . *Billboard*'s best-selling albums for the week are: *Tiffany*, Tiffany; *Faith*, George Michael; *Dirty Dancing* (soundtrack); *Bad*, Michael Jackson; *Whitesnake*, Whitesnake. . . . The 45th annual Golden Globe awards are presented; four awards go to *The Last Emperor*, including that for best dramatic film. The award for best movie comedy or musical goes to *Hope and Glory*. The Swedish film *My Life as a Dog* is named best foreign film.	**Jan. 23**
				Swede Mats Wilander wins the Australian Open men's singles tennis title. . . . Novelist Toni Morrison, 56, is the subject of an unusual statement signed by 48 black writers and critics and published in the *New York Times Book Review*. The statement is both a "testament of thanks" to Morrison for her "life work" and a protest aimed at the mainstream U.S. literary community over the fact that she has yet to win "the keystone honors of the National Book Award or the Pulitzer Prize." . . . In London, the Society of West End Theater presents its annual Laurence Olivier awards. Honored as best play of the year is Caryl Churchill's *Serious Money*; best comedy, a revival of George Abbott and John Cecil Holm's classic farce *Three Men on a Horse*; a revised version of Stephen Sondheim and James Goldman's musical *Follies* wins the award for best musical.	**Jan. 24**

F	**G**	**H**	**I**	**J**
Includes elections, federal-state relations, civil rights and liberties, crime, the judiciary, education, health care, poverty, urban affairs and population.	*Includes formation and debate of U.S. foreign and defense policies, veterans' affairs and defense spending. (Relations with specific foreign countries are usually found under the region concerned.)*	*Includes business, labor, agriculture, taxation, transportation, consumer affairs, monetary and fiscal policy, natural resources, and pollution.*	*Includes worldwide scientific, medical and technological developments, natural phenomena, U.S. weather, natural disasters, and accidents.*	*Includes the arts, religion, scholarship, communications media, sports, entertainments, fashions, fads and social life.*

	World Affairs	Europe	Africa & the Middle East	The Americas	Asia & the Pacific
Jan. 25		The Senate Foreign Relations Committee opens hearings on the ratification of the U.S.-Soviet treaty to eliminate intermediate-range nuclear forces. The treaty was signed by Pres. Reagan and Soviet leader Mikhail S. Gorbachev on Dec. 8, 1987, but will not take effect until ratified by the Senate. . . . Britain's Attorney Gen. Sir Patrick Mayhew announces that the government will not seek to prosecute policemen in Northern Ireland for their roles in an alleged "shoot to kill" policy against suspected terrorists in 1982. . . . British farm income declined by 1.5% in 1987 from 1986, according to a government white paper.	Egypt's Pres. Hosni Mubarak begins five days of official visits to Britain and the United States, where his talks with high government officials concentrate on trying to restart the Arab-Israeli peace process in the wake of the ongoing Palestinian uprising in the Israeli-occupied territories.	In Colombia, drug traffickers in Medellin kidnapped Attorney Gen. Carlos Mauro Hoyos Jimenez; his bullet-riddled, blindfolded, and handcuffed body was found hours later in the nearby village of El Retiro. Hoyos had been investigating the December 1987 release from prison of Medellin cocaine baron Jorge Luis Ochoa Vasquez, whose extradition had been sought by the United States. . . . Ramsewak Shankar is sworn in as president of Suriname, ending almost eight years of military rule. Shankar was elected president by the National Assembly earlier in January. At his inauguration he called for a "renewed. . .working relationship" with the Netherlands (former colonial ruler) and improved economic ties with the United States. Both those nations had cut off aid to Suriname after the military authorities in 1982 killed 15 civilian opposition leaders.	
Jan. 26					As many as 2 million people crowd Sydney harbor to celebrate Australia Day, the 200th anniversary of the landing of the country's first European settlers, who came to Australia to establish a penal colony.
Jan. 27		Production of North Sea oil averaged a record 3.65 million barrels per day in 1987, up 2.8% from 1986, according to a report by a London brokerage house, James Capel. Britain's output fell to 2.47 million barrels per day from 2.54 million in 1986; but that decline is more than offset by a 17.3% increase in Norwegian production to 1.02 million barrels per day.	Gunmen in Syrian-controlled west Beirut abduct a West German resident of Lebanon. The kidnapping appears to be linked to the ongoing trial in Dusseldorf, West Germany, of Abbas Ali Hamadei, an accused Lebanese terrorist.		The Thai government begins officially turning away Vietnamese refugees who are fleeing Vietnam by boat through Cambodia to Thailand. . . . In Australia, a government commission headed by former Supreme Court Justice James Muirhead begins hearings into the deaths in police custody of scores of Aborigines since 1980.

A	B	C	D	E
Includes developments that affect more than one world region, international organizations and important meetings of major world leaders.	Includes all domestic and regional developments in Europe, including the Soviet Union, Turkey, Cyprus and Malta.	Includes all domestic and regional developments in Africa and the Middle East, including Iraq and Iran and excluding Cyprus, Turkey and Afghanistan.	Includes all domestic and regional developments in Latin America, the Caribbean and Canada.	Includes all domestic and regional developments in Asia and Pacific nations, extending from Afghanistan through all the Pacific Islands, except Hawaii.

U.S. Politics & Social Issues	U.S. Foreign Policy & Defense	U.S. Economy & Environment	Science, Technology & Nature	Culture, Leisure & Life Style	
In his seventh State of the Union message, Pres. Reagan pledges a vigorous final year of his presidency, "right to the finish line." The president delivers the nationally broadcast speech before a joint session of Congress.... The Democrats' assessment of America is "tougher than the President's," Senate Majority Leader Robert C. Byrd (D, W.Va.) says in the party's follow-up rebuttal to Reagan's State of the Union speech. "The dark side of the Reagan years has only begun to loom," Byrd says.... Vice Pres. George Bush and CBS, Inc. news anchor Dan Rather engage in a live interview that quickly turns into a shouting match concerning Bush's involvement in the Iran-Contra affair.... After a two-year battle over a federal desegregation order that polarized the city of Yonkers, N.Y., local officials and the plaintiffs agree on a plan to build low-income housing in mainly white neighborhoods. The order was issued in November 1985 in New York City by District Court Judge Leonard B. Sand.... The Justice Dept. and the Equal Employment Opportunity Comm. are reported to have found that Federal Bureau of Investigation (FBI) agent Donald Rochon was shunned and humiliated by his colleagues in the FBI's Omaha office in 1983 and 1984 because he was black.... Reza Eslaminia and Arben Dosti, two members of a former Los Angeles business and social organization that called itself the Billionaire Boys Club, are convicted in California of kidnapping and murdering Eslamina's father.		Campeau Corp. of Canada launches a hostile $4.2 bil. offer for Federated Department Stores Inc. of the United States. The bid of $47 a share comes little more than a year after Campeau, a Toronto-based real estate developer, entered retailing by acquiring Allied Stores Corp. of the United States.			Jan. 25
			A single aspirin tablet taken every other day could cut the rate of heart attack in men nearly in half, according to results of a mammoth study reported in the *New England Journal of Medicine*.		Jan. 26
	Pres. Reagan submits to Congress a request for $36.25 mil. in aid to the Contras fighting the Nicaraguan government. Of the total, $3.6 mil. will be for military aid to be held in escrow until March 31. It will be freed (after consultation with Costa Rica, El Salvador, Guatemala and Honduras) if the Nicaraguan government and the Contras have not by then reached agreement on a cease-fire.	The nation's gross national product grew at a 4.2% annual rate in the fourth quarter of 1987, the Commerce Dept. reports.... The Federal Reserve Board votes, 5-1, to accept in principle compromise international capital requirements for banks. The move follows a December 1987 agreement with the central banks of 11 other, major industrial nations aimed at increasing financial institutions' capital levels to 8% of assets by 1992.		Ferdinand, trained by Charlie Whittingham, is named winner of the Eclipse Awards Horse of the Year title for 1987.	Jan. 27

F	G	H	I	J
Includes elections, federal-state relations, civil rights and liberties, crime, the judiciary, education, health care, poverty, urban affairs and population.	*Includes formation and debate of U.S. foreign and defense policies, veterans' affairs and defense spending. (Relations with specific foreign countries are usually found under the region concerned.)*	*Includes business, labor, agriculture, taxation, transportation, consumer affairs, monetary and fiscal policy, natural resources, and pollution.*	*Includes worldwide scientific, medical and technological developments, natural phenomena, U.S. weather, natural disasters, and accidents.*	*Includes the arts, religion, scholarship, communications media, sports, entertainments, fashions, fads and social life.*

	World Affairs	Europe	Africa & the Middle East	The Americas	Asia & the Pacific
Jan. 28		Britain's Court of Appeal upholds the convictions of six Irish nationals for the November 1974 pub bombings in Birmingham that killed 21 people and injured 160. The case was reopened amid public pressure and the emergence of new evidence. . . . Britain's balance of payments in 1987 showed its largest deficit in 13 years, according to figures released by the Dept. of Trade and Industry.		Representatives of the Nicaraguan government and the Contra rebels in Costa Rica hold the first face-to-face talks in the six-year civil war. In the two days of talks, no apparent progress is made in arranging a cease-fire, although both sides agree to meet again in two weeks' time in Guatemala. . . . The Supreme Court of Canada votes, 5-2, to strike down as unconstitutional federal curbs on abortion. In effect, the ruling legalizes abortion on demand in Canada. . . . In Peru, a general strike to protest economic conditions turns violent as protesters go on a rampage, throwing firebombs and clashing with police. One person is killed and more than 40 are injured, and scores of arrests are made.	
Jan. 29		U.S. and Soviet experts conclude visits to the principal nuclear weapons test sites in each other's country. A team of 20 Americans toured the Soviet test site at Semipalatinsk in Central Asia January 11-14. Twelve Soviets toured the U.S. test site in Nevada January 26-29. The visits are aimed at familiarizing the experts with the facilities in preparation for joint underground nuclear tests sometime in 1988.	In Angola, the rebel National Union for the Total Independence of Angola claims that its guerrillas have forced government troops and their Soviet and Cuban military advisers to withdraw from the town of Cuito Cuanavale after a month-long siege. Even as the fighting rages, Asst. Sec. of State for African Affairs Chester A. Crocker visits Luanda for another round of talks on negotiating a Cuban troop withdrawal from Angola and independence for South African-occupied Namibia.		Japan's ministry of international trade and industry announces that it will continue to impose a quota of 2.3 million units on auto exports to the United States in the fiscal year beginning April 1.
Jan. 30					
Jan. 31		The premiers of Greece and Turkey meeting in Davos, Switzerland, agree to work toward solving the long-standing problems between their two nations.		In Ecuador, left-of-center presidential candidates Rodrigo Borja Cevallos, of the Democratic Left Party, and Abdala Bucaram Ortiz, of the Roldosista Party, are the leading vote-getters in elections; since neither wins an absolute majority, they must face each other in a runoff election May 8.	India's P.M. Rajiv Gandhi dissolves the state government of Tamil Nadu and institutes presidential rule, following a violent melee in the state assembly between opposing political factions of the same party. The melee erupted January 28 on the floor of the assembly between rival members of the state's ruling party, the All-India Anna Dravida Munnetra Kazhagam (ADMK).

A	B	C	D	E
Includes developments that affect more than one world region, international organizations and important meetings of major world leaders.	Includes all domestic and regional developments in Europe, including the Soviet Union, Turkey, Cyprus and Malta.	Includes all domestic and regional developments in Africa and the Middle East, including Iraq and Iran and excluding Cyprus, Turkey and Afghanistan.	Includes all domestic and regional developments in Latin America, the Caribbean and Canada.	Includes all domestic and regional developments in Asia and Pacific nations, extending from Afghanistan through all the Pacific Islands, except Hawaii.

U.S. Politics & Social Issues	U.S. Foreign Policy & Defense	U.S. Economy & Environment	Science, Technology & Nature	Culture, Leisure & Life Style	
The Senate passes civil rights legislation that will reverse the impact of a 1984 Supreme Court ruling that narrowed the scope of federal civil rights laws. The Senate measure requires any institution that receives federal aid to obey antibias laws in all its programs and activities.		Increased auto sales drove consumer spending up 0.5% in December 1987, while personal income gained 0.7%, the Commerce Dept. reports. For all of 1987, spending grew 5.9%.... Public Service Co. of New Hampshire files an anticipated plea for protection from creditors under Chapter 11 of the federal bankruptcy code. The utility, heavily laden with debt from the controversial Seabrook nuclear power plant, is the first major public utility to file for bankruptcy-law protection since the Depression.... Import prices surged 14.8% in 1987, the Labor Dept. reports. The 1987 increase follows a 1986 drop of 8.6%. Import prices in the fourth quarter of 1987 rose 2%, up from a 1.6% increase in the third quarter.... A federal grand jury in Boston indicts Ocean Spray Cranberries Inc. on felony and misdemeanor charges of pollution. The indictment, bringing the first felony charges under the Clean Water Act as amended in 1987, accuses the Plymouth, Mass.-based cooperative of violating clean-water laws by dumping pollutants into a town sewage system.	(Emil) Klaus (Julius) Fuchs, 76, German-born physicist who passed crucial nuclear secrets to the Soviet Union, dies. Active in the anti-Nazi underground, he fled Germany in the early 1930s. During World War II, he worked on the development of the atom bomb in Britain and the United States and later helped direct nuclear research in Britain. Arrested for espionage in February 1950, he pleaded guilty and was sentenced to 14 years in prison; Julius and Ethel Rosenberg were implicated in the same nuclear espionage ring. Released in 1959, Fuchs became deputy director of East Germany's nuclear research institute and a member of the central committee of the East German Communist Party.... Delegates from nearly 150 nations at a World acquired immune deficiency syndrome (AIDS) summit in London call for "urgent action by all governments and people" to combat AIDS, including educational efforts and medical and social support. The conference was organized jointly by the World Health Org. and the British government.	The Alfred I. duPont-Columbia Univ. Awards for excellence in broadcast journalism are presented; a golden baton, the top duPont honor, is awarded to "Eyes on the Prize," a public television documentary series about the civil rights movement.	Jan. 28
The Dept. of Health and Human Services issues new rules that will bar federally funded family planning clinics from engaging in abortion-related activities. The new rules are the final version of a policy formulated by the department in August 1987 at the behest of Pres. Reagan.	The U.S. government announces that it will end special trade privileges for Hong Kong, Singapore, South Korea, and Taiwan. The action, which takes effect Jan. 2, 1989, will remove the four countries from the Generalized System of Preferences, under which some 140 lesser developed countries are allowed to export many products to the United States duty-free.			*Publishers Weekly*'s hardback fiction best-sellers for the week are: *The Bonfire of the Vanities*, Tom Wolfe; *The Tommyknockers*, Stephen King; *Kaleidoscope*, Danielle Steel; *Presumed Innocent*, Scott Turow; and *Patriot Games*, Tom Clancy.	Jan. 29
Vice Pres. George Bush scores a victory at Michigan's statewide Republican convention that is expected to win him nearly half of the state's 77 delegates to the Republican National Convention in August. However, virtually all the delegates face challenges.	Spurred by the continuing Palestinian unrest in the Israeli-occupied territories, the United States moves to launch a new Middle East peace initiative, and Pres. Reagan sends special envoy Philip C. Habib to Jordan for a day of talks with King Hussein.	Prices received by farmers for their raw agricultural product rose 2.4% in January, the Agriculture Dept. reports.			Jan. 30
			New York State officials announce that they have given permission to New York City health authorities to begin distributing hypodermic syringes free to drug addicts in an attempt to curtail the spread of acquired immune deficiency syndrome. Infection through shared needles has made intravenous drug users one of the chief risk groups for the blood-borne virus.	A Jaguar driven by Raul Boesel of Brazil, John Nielsen of Denmark, and Martin Brundle of Great Britain wins the Daytona 24-Hours race. ... The Washington Redskins win Super Bowl XXII, 42-10, over the Denver Broncos. Redskins quarterback Doug Williams is named the Super Bowl's most valuable player. ... CBS, Inc.'s broadcast of Super Bowl XXI receives a Nielsen rating of 48.3.	Jan. 31

F	G	H	I	J
Includes elections, federal-state relations, civil rights and liberties, crime, the judiciary, education, health care, poverty, urban affairs and population.	*Includes formation and debate of U.S. foreign and defense policies, veterans' affairs and defense spending. (Relations with specific foreign countries are usually found under the region concerned.)*	*Includes business, labor, agriculture, taxation, transportation, consumer affairs, monetary and fiscal policy, natural resources, and pollution.*	*Includes worldwide scientific, medical and technological developments, natural phenomena, U.S. weather, natural disasters, and accidents.*	*Includes the arts, religion, scholarship, communications media, sports, entertainments, fashions, fads and social life.*

	World Affairs	Europe	Africa & the Middle East	The Americas	Asia & the Pacific
Feb. 1		Finland's Pres. Mauno Koivisto is the top vote-getter in a two-day presidential election. Koivisto, a Social Democrat, fails to win a majority of the popular vote, but he is widely expected to win reelection when the electoral college convenes in mid-February. . . . The Soviet foreign ministry announces the death, sometime in January, of Georgi Maximilianovich Malenkov, 86, who succeeded Josef Stalin as premier in March 1953. Malenkov's premiership was marked by a more conciliatory attitude toward the West and by attempts to step up production of consumer goods and curb the role of the secret police. Ousted in 1955, he was later banished to Kazakhstan, where he lived in obscurity for more than 30 years. . . . The Bank of England engineers a one-half percentage point increase in banks' base lending rates. The increase brings the benchmark rate to 9%. . . . In Poland, prices of about half of the nation's goods and services rise an average of 27% under the government's economic reform plan, which goes into effect today. The increases are the steepest since 1982. The cost of basic foods increases 40%, tobacco products rise by 40%, alcoholic beverages by 46%, train and bus fares by 50%, and diesel fuel by 60%. Rents also escalate sharply. . . . Unemployment in the European Community (EC) in December 1987 rose to 16.3 million workers, Eurostat reports. For 1987 as a whole, the unemployment rate in nine EC nations (excluding Spain, Portugal, and Greece) averaged 11%, down from 11.1% in 1986.			
Feb. 2			A special Commonwealth committee meets for two days in Lusaka, Zambia, to discuss how to pressure South Africa into racial reform. The only concrete measure adopted is a call for international banks to refuse to reschedule the repayment of loans made to Pretoria. The group is made up of eight foreign ministers and headed by Canada's External Affairs Min. Joe Clark.		The Japanese government officially accepts a ruling by the General Agreement on Tariffs and Trade (GATT) in Geneva ordering Japan to remove import quotas on 10 categories of agricultural goods. But the Japanese declare that they will implement the GATT ruling only on eight of the 10 product groups and will retain quotas on the other two categories, starches and evaporated milk.

A	B	C	D	E
Includes developments that affect more than one world region, international organizations and important meetings of major world leaders.	Includes all domestic and regional developments in Europe, including the Soviet Union, Turkey, Cyprus and Malta.	Includes all domestic and regional developments in Africa and the Middle East, including Iraq and Iran and excluding Cyprus, Turkey and Afghanistan.	Includes all domestic and regional developments in Latin America, the Caribbean and Canada.	Includes all domestic and regional developments in Asia and Pacific nations, extending from Afghanistan through all the Pacific Islands, except Hawaii.

U.S. Politics & Social Issues	U.S. Foreign Policy & Defense	U.S. Economy & Environment	Science, Technology & Nature	Culture, Leisure & Life Style	
	Defense Sec. Frank C. Carlucci testifies before the Senate Foreign Relations Committee as that panel begins its second week of hearings on ratifying the U.S.-Soviet treaty on intermediate-range nuclear forces.	The Senate ratifies two conventions of the International Labor Org. (ILO). The ratification, the first such action by the Senate in 35 years, brings to nine the number of ILO conventions approved by the United States. The ILO, an adjunct of the UN, has 162 conventions in all.... A 12-year, $1 bil. plan to clean up a hazardous waste site at the federally owned Rocky Mountain Arsenal near Denver is filed in federal court in Denver. Under the plan, Shell Oil Co. will help the Army finance the cleanup, paying $330 mil. to $380 mil. of the total cost, estimated at $750 mil. to $1 bil. or more. The agreement settles a federal lawsuit brought against Shell in 1983 under the federal Superfund law.... The Commodity Futures Trading Comm. releases its report on the October 1987 stock market crash. The 200-page report recommends better coordination between regulators and exchange officials, including joint efforts against the practice of so-called intermarket front-running, in which investment banks buy stock-index futures in anticipation of corporate stock buybacks.		The family of artist Marc Chagall agrees to donate more than 450 of his works to France in lieu of inheritance taxes owed by the Chagall estate, the French finance ministry announces. The agreement gives France the largest and most important collection of modern paintings since a similar settlement was reached with the heirs of Pablo Picasso in 1972. Chagall, a native of Russia, had been a French citizen for nearly five decades when he died in 1985.	Feb. 1
The Federal Bureau of Investigation defends a lengthy and extensive surveillance effort against hundreds of American citizens and groups opposed to the Reagan administration's policies in Central America. The effort became known January 27 when a New York civil rights group, the Center for Constitutional Rights, released documents obtained from the bureau under the Freedom of Information Act.... The Senate Judiciary Committee takes the Reagan administration to task for failing to appoint members of minorities and women to federal judgeships.		The government's index of leading economic indicators declines 0.2% in December 1987, the Commerce Dept. reports.... The nation's leading banks lower their prime lending rate to 8.5%. The cut is the first since November 1987, when the rate was lowered to 8.75% from 9%.... San Francisco savings and loan executive Anthony M. Frank is named postmaster general. Frank succeeds Preston R. Tisch, who announced earlier his intention to return to private business.... The Securities and Exchange Comm. (SEC) releases its report on the October 1987 stock market crash. The SEC's report concludes that futures trading and strategies involving the use of futures were largely responsible for speed and depth of the stock market collapse.... The Federal Home Loan Bank Board announces a plan to rescue 143 ailing savings and loan associations in Texas. The plan targets 104 insolvent Texas thrifts and 39 others on the edge of insolvency.	The number of new cases of most major forms of cancer in the United States is continuing to increase about 1% a year, according to the annual report of the National Cancer Institute. Scientists have no specific explanation for the rise, though current speculation focuses on environmental causes such as exposure to industrial wastes and industrial chemicals, radon gas, diesel exhausts, and various dietary factors.	Minnesota Vikings defensive tackle Alan Page, Chicago Bears tight end (and now coach) Mike Ditka, Oakland Raiders wide receiver Fred Belitnikoff, and Pittsburgh Steelers linebacker Jack Ham are elected to the Pro Football Hall of Fame in Canton, Ohio.	Feb. 2

F	G	H	I	J
Includes elections, federal-state relations, civil rights and liberties, crime, the judiciary, education, health care, poverty, urban affairs and population.	Includes formation and debate of U.S. foreign and defense policies, veterans' affairs and defense spending. (Relations with specific foreign countries are usually found under the region concerned.)	Includes business, labor, agriculture, taxation, transportation, consumer affairs, monetary and fiscal policy, natural resources, and pollution.	Includes worldwide scientific, medical and technological developments, natural phenomena, U.S. weather, natural disasters, and accidents.	Includes the arts, religion, scholarship, communications media, sports, entertainments, fashions, fads and social life.

	World Affairs	Europe	Africa & the Middle East	The Americas	Asia & the Pacific
Feb. 3	The International Monetary Fund (IMF) had a $5.9 bil. repayment surplus in 1987. The IMF acts as the world's lender of last resort, conditionally providing short-term liquidity to debtor nations.	A U.S. envoy says that American economic aid to Poland will not be revived until Warsaw's economic reforms prove successful and are accepted by a "broad spectrum of Polish society."			
Feb. 4				Mexico's trade surplus in 1987 increased more than 83% from a year earlier, to $8.43 bil. Exports for the year are valued at $20.65 bil., up 28%, and imports are $12.2 bil. Almost two-thirds of the export growth is accounted for by manufactured goods.	In Malaysia, the Kuala Lumpur high court declares that the nation's ruling party, the United Malays National Org. (UMNO), is illegal because a number of its branches had failed to properly register under the country's Societies Act.
Feb. 5		The Soviet Union announces the posthumous rehabilitation of Nikolai I. Bukharin and 19 other disgraced Bolsheviks, many of whom were executed following the 1938 show trials during the regime of Soviet leader Joseph Stalin. They were all convicted of various forms of treason.	The *Washington Post* reports that Kenya has made a number of moves to improve its human rights image, which was badly battered in 1987 by accusations of police torture of political dissidents. The changes indicate that Pres. Daniel arap Moi is moving to appease Western donor governments, which have expressed concern about the Kenyan abuses.	Alfonso Robelo Callejas, one of the six directors of the Nicaraguan Resistance Contra organization, resigns rather than leave Costa Rica. Costa Rica's Pres. Oscar Arias Sanchez said in January that Contra leaders residing in his country had to end their armed struggle against Nicaragua or leave Costa Rica.	
Feb. 6		West Germany's Chancellor Helmut Kohl tells a seminar on Western security that he opposes the idea of eliminating all tactical weapons from Europe. However, he calls for negotiations between the North Atlantic Treaty Org. and the Warsaw Pact to reduce and set equal ceilings on such arms.			India plans to send 15,000 more troops to Sri Lanka in an effort to quash Tamil guerrilla resistance to the 1987 peace accord, Sri Lankan government officials report. India is estimated to have 40,000 to 55,000 soldiers already deployed in Sri Lanka.

A	B	C	D	E
Includes developments that affect more than one world region, international organizations and important meetings of major world leaders.	*Includes all domestic and regional developments in Europe, including the Soviet Union, Turkey, Cyprus and Malta.*	*Includes all domestic and regional developments in Africa and the Middle East, including Iraq and Iran and excluding Cyprus, Turkey and Afghanistan.*	*Includes all domestic and regional developments in Latin America, the Caribbean and Canada.*	*Includes all domestic and regional developments in Asia and Pacific nations, extending from Afghanistan through all the Pacific Islands, except Hawaii.*

U.S. Politics & Social Issues	U.S. Foreign Policy & Defense	U.S. Economy & Environment	Science, Technology & Nature	Culture, Leisure & Life Style	
The Senate votes, 97-0, to confirm Judge Anthony M. Kennedy as an associate justice of the U.S. Supreme Court. The unanimous vote ends a bitter seven-month battle over the seat vacated in June 1987 by Associate Justice Lewis F. Powell Jr.... The New Jersey Supreme Court rules that surrogate motherhood contracts involving payment are illegal. The court, however, allows custody of 22-month-old Melissa Stern, the child at the center of the "Baby M" case, to remain with her biological father, William Stern, and his wife, Elizabeth.... Hector Escudero Aponte, a maintenance worker who admitted setting the fire that killed 97 people at the DuPont Plaza Hotel in San Juan, Puerto Rico, on New Year's Eve 1986, is sentenced to 30 years in prison. Three other members of his union local are arrested and charged in the case.	The House of Representatives votes, 219-211, to reject Pres. Reagan's request for at least $36.25 mil. in aid to the Nicaraguan Contras.			The National Religious Broadcasters vote to make compliance with their new code of ethics a requirement for membership in the organization. The code was drawn up by the group's board of directors in September 1987 and circulated to members for guidance; compliance was voluntary.	**Feb. 3**
Former television evangelist the Rev. Pat Robertson wins an overwhelming victory in Republican presidential voting in Hawaii. Republicans vote in a straw poll of presidential preferences and also elect about 1,700 delegates to the state's May GOP convention, where the state's 20 delegates to the national convention will be chosen.... The Immigration and Naturalization Service abandons its much publicized effort to deport author Margaret Randall, a U.S.-born citizen of Mexico who has been threatened with deportation since 1986 because of her writings in praise of leftist revolutions.		The board of the New York Stock Exchange votes unanimously to forbid the use of its electronic order system for a form of program trading whenever the Dow Jones industrial average rises or falls 50 points or more on a single day.... Productivity among the nation's nonfarm businesses fell at an annual rate of 0.2% in the fourth quarter of 1987, the Labor Dept. reports. For all of 1987, productivity rose a scant 0.8%.... Chrysler Corp. reports that its fourth-quarter net earnings rose to $350.2 mil., up 8% from a year earlier. The number-three carmaker's net income for all of 1987 dropped 7%, to $1.29 bil., due to a one-time gain in 1986. Chrysler subsequently paid a flat $500 in profit-sharing to each of some 100,000 workers.		Three former players—Bullet Wes Unseld, Kansas center Clyde Lovellette, and Bobby McDermott—and Oregon State coach Ralph Miller are elected to the Basketball Hall of Fame in Springfield, Mass.	**Feb. 4**
The Republican-controlled Arizona House of Representatives votes, 46-14, to impeach the state's Republican governor, Evan Mecham. Mecham will be tried before the state senate on charges of "high crimes, misdemeanors and malfeasance in office." ... Pres. Reagan signs the first major housing legislation passed during his administration. It will provide $15 bil. for housing and community development in FY1988 (which began Oct. 1, 1987) and $15.3 bil. for FY1989.	The Justice Dept. unseals two indictments charging Gen. Manuel Antonio Noriega, Panama's military leader and de facto ruler, with involvement in international drug trafficking.	The nation's unemployment rate remained unchanged at 5.7% in January, the Labor Dept. reports. ... Outstanding consumer debt rose $4.45 bil. in December 1987, the Federal Reserve Board reports, at an annual rate of 8.8%, to a total of $612.57 bil.		*The Unbearable Lightness of Being*, a film based on Milan Kundera's love story set in Czechoslovakia around the time of the Soviet military invasion of 1968, is released in New York. Directed by Philip Kaufman, with a screenplay by Jean-Claude Carriere and Kaufman, the film stars Daniel Day Lewis, Juliette Binoche, and Lena Olin.	**Feb. 5**
					Feb. 6

F	G	H	I	J
Includes elections, federal-state relations, civil rights and liberties, crime, the judiciary, education, health care, poverty, urban affairs and population.	*Includes formation and debate of U.S. foreign and defense policies, veterans' affairs and defense spending. (Relations with specific foreign countries are usually found under the region concerned.)*	*Includes business, labor, agriculture, taxation, transportation, consumer affairs, monetary and fiscal policy, natural resources, and pollution.*	*Includes worldwide scientific, medical and technological developments, natural phenomena, U.S. weather, natural disasters, and accidents.*	*Includes the arts, religion, scholarship, communications media, sports, entertainments, fashions, fads and social life.*

	World Affairs	Europe	Africa & the Middle East	The Americas	Asia & the Pacific
Feb. 7				Leslie F. Manigat is sworn in as Haiti's new president two years to the day after Pres. Jean-Claude Duvalier fled into exile. Manigat was elected January 17 in a vote widely viewed as tainted.	
Feb. 8		Soviet leader Mikhail S. Gorbachev declares that if a settlement is reached in March during UN-sponsored peace talks between Afghanistan and Pakistan, Soviet troops will begin to leave Afghanistan on May 15, and will complete their withdrawal within 10 months.	Government troops in northern Ethiopia open fire on a crowd of famine victims, killing 20 and wounding many more, when they refuse to board trucks bound for a resettlement site.	An American pilot shot down over Nicaragua in late 1987 and released by the government in January 1988 is acquitted of the charges against him. The trial of the American, James Jordan Denby, continued after he was freed and returned to the United States.	In South Korea, Kim Young Sam resigns as president of the Reunification Democratic Party, the nation's largest opposition group. At a news conference in Seoul, Kim says that he is stepping down in an attempt to help unify the two main opposition parties, which have been in disarray following their defeat in the December 1987 presidential elections.... The government of Taiwan lowers import tariffs by an average of 50% on 3,500 items in an effort to open Taiwanese markets and reduce the nation's trade surplus. Taiwan's overall trade surplus jumped 22% in 1987, to a record $19.03 bil.
Feb. 9	A report by an international panel of historians formally finds that Austria's Pres. Kurt Waldheim had known of war crimes being committed by his units during his World War II service in the German Army, but that he himself did not commit any crimes. The panel says that Waldheim, who was formerly secretary general of the UN, had concealed and misrepresented his war record.			Haiti's National Assembly unanimously approves Pres. Leslie Manigat's choice of Martial Celestin, a 75-year-old lawyer, to be premier.	The Australian ministry of foreign affairs and trade announces the resumption of economic aid to Fiji. Australia's aid program was suspended to protest a military coup in Fiji in September 1987.
Feb. 10		Italy's Premier Giovanni Goria submits his resignation to Pres. Francesco Cossiga after losing key votes on his 1988 budget. The president reserves judgment over whether to accept the resignation and asks Goria to stay on to lead a caretaker government.	South Africa sends troops and police into the nominally independent tribal homeland of Bophuthatswana to quell a military coup, which 15 hours earlier ousted the black territory's president, Lucas Mangope. Five people were reported killed in the initial coup and the South African intervention.		In Bangladesh, more than 100 people are killed and hundreds of others wounded in violent clashes throughout the country during local elections.... The government of Hong Kong proposes limited electoral reforms for the British colony's legislature but indicates that only minor changes will be introduced before 1991. China is to take over the administration of Hong Kong in 1997.

A	B	C	D	E
Includes developments that affect more than one world region, international organizations and important meetings of major world leaders.	Includes all domestic and regional developments in Europe, including the Soviet Union, Turkey, Cyprus and Malta.	Includes all domestic and regional developments in Africa and the Middle East, including Iraq and Iran and excluding Cyprus, Turkey and Afghanistan.	Includes all domestic and regional developments in Latin America, the Caribbean and Canada.	Includes all domestic and regional developments in Asia and Pacific nations, extending from Afghanistan through all the Pacific Islands, except Hawaii.

U.S. Politics & Social Issues	U.S. Foreign Policy & Defense	U.S. Economy & Environment	Science, Technology & Nature	Culture, Leisure & Life Style	
			Following torrential rains that caused the Quitandinha River to overflow its banks, two days of floods and mud slides have claimed at least 127 lives in Rio de Janeiro state, according to a Brazilian civil defense spokesman. Officials say 102 deaths have been confirmed in Petropolis, a mountain resort some 40 miles north of the city of Rio de Janeiro. Meanwhile, rescue workers continue searching for victims beneath tons of mud and rock.	The Eastern Conf. wins the National Basketball Assoc. All-Star game, 139-133, over the Western Conf. Bulls Guard Michael Jordan wins the Most Valuable Player award for the game. . . . The American Football Conf. defeats the National Football Conf., 15-6, in the National Football League Pro Bowl all-star game.	**Feb. 7**
Sen. Robert J. Dole (R, Kans.) and Rep. Richard A. Gephardt (D, Mo.) finish first in their respective parties' Iowa presidential caucuses. The major surprise is a second-place finish on the Republican side by former television evangelist the Rev. Pat Robertson. Robertson relegated Vice Pres. George Bush, the early Republican favorite, to third place.	A Senate Foreign Relations subcommittee begins three days of hearings on the activities of Panama's military leader, Gen. Manuel Antonio Noriega, who days earlier was indicted by two Florida federal grand juries on drug charges.				**Feb. 8**
Sec. of Education William J. Bennett sends Congress a report harshly criticizing the nation's for-profit trade schools. Bennett asserts that such institutions, known as proprietary schools, are guilty of "exploitative and deceitful practices" that defraud students.				The Wales Conf. beats the Campbell Conf. in the National Hockey League All-Star Game, 6-5.	**Feb. 9**
Sec. of Education William J. Bennett declares that six states—Delaware, Florida, Georgia, Missouri, Oklahoma, and Virginia—have still failed to fully comply with a 1964 federal law barring racial segregation in public colleges and universities receiving federal funds. . . . The Justice Dept. says that it has decided not to request appointment of a special prosecutor to review conflict-of-interest allegations against Judge Douglas H. Ginsburg. The allegations arose after Pres. Reagan nominated Ginsburg to the Supreme Court.	The ongoing dispute between Senate Democrats and the Reagan administration over interpretation of the 1972 antiballistic missile treaty took a new turn in the last week to include the new treaty on intermediate-range nuclear forces. . . . Commerce Sec. C. William Verity declares Japan in violation of an international whaling ban and invokes U.S. laws authorizing sanctions for such offenses. . . . A federal three-judge appellate panel in San Francisco votes, 2-1, to overturn as unconstitutional an Army ban on homosexuals. In handing down the ruling, the U.S. Ninth Circuit Court of Appeals becomes the first court to prohibit an armed service from discriminating against persons on the basis of sexual orientation. . . . The State Dept. issues its annual report to Congress on international human rights. The 1,300-page document covers conditions in 170 nations during calendar 1987. A key highlight of the report is the improvement in human rights conditions in the Soviet Union.	The American Stock Exchange announces that as much as $1 mil. will be refunded to customers who traded stock-index options on Oct. 20, 1987, the day after the stock market crashed.		Kirk Varnedoe, a 42-year-old professor of art history at New York Univ.'s Institute of Fine Arts, is named to succeed William S. Rubin as director of painting and sculpture at New York City's Museum of Modern Art.	**Feb. 10**

F	G	H	I	J
Includes elections, federal-state relations, civil rights and liberties, crime, the judiciary, education, health care, poverty, urban affairs and population.	Includes formation and debate of U.S. foreign and defense policies, veterans' affairs and defense spending. (Relations with specific foreign countries are usually found under the region concerned.)	Includes business, labor, agriculture, taxation, transportation, consumer affairs, monetary and fiscal policy, natural resources, and pollution.	Includes worldwide scientific, medical and technological developments, natural phenomena, U.S. weather, natural disasters, and accidents.	Includes the arts, religion, scholarship, communications media, sports, entertainments, fashions, fads and social life.

	World Affairs	Europe	Africa & the Middle East	The Americas	Asia & the Pacific
Feb. 11		Two reports on the performance of the London Stock Exchange during the stock market crash of October 1987 are relatively laudatory. The first report was issued yesterday by the exchange itself and the second, this day, by the central Bank of England.	Four U.S. doctors from Physicians for Human Rights, a Boston-based monitoring group, accuse the Israeli Army and police of unleashing "an unrestrained epidemic of violence" against Palestinian civilians. They say the conditions in hospitals and clinics in the territories are "appalling," and that many of the wounded might suffer permanent injury because of lack of proper care.		The Vietnamese government unveils a sweeping amnesty program affecting more than 9,000 prisoners and detainees, including about 1,000 officials of the former South Vietnamese government.
Feb. 12		Two U.S. warships are bumped by Soviet naval vessels in the Black Sea. No serious injuries or damage is reported. The incident took place about nine miles off the southern coast of the Soviet Crimean Peninsula, where the USSR's Black Sea Fleet is based. . . . An Italian court convicts Palestinian gunmen Ibrahim Mohammed Khaled and sentences him to 30 years in prison for the December 1985 Rome airport massacre. Two other defendants, fugitive Palestinian terrorist leader Abu Nidal (Sabry al-Banna) and his associate Rashid al-Hamieda, are sentenced in absentia to life imprisonment for organizing the raid.			
Feb. 13		An emergency summit of European Community (EC) leaders in Brussels produces sweeping agreements on agricultural policy, aid to poorer member nations, and overall EC funding. Agreement is announced at the conclusion of the three-day meeting after Britain's P.M. Margaret Thatcher ends her dissent on farm reform.		Pres. Reagan and Mexico's Pres. Miguel de la Madrid Hurtado hold their sixth summit. Meeting in Mazatlan, the two countries sign a textile agreement that will widen the access of Mexican textiles and garments to U.S. markets.	
Feb. 14		A fire at the main library of the Soviet Academy of Sciences, in Leningrad, destroys 400,000 books and damages more than 3 million others. The facility, founded by Czar Peter the Great in 1714, is regarded as one of the world's great libraries, housing over 17 million volumes, some dating back to the 17th century.		Nicaragua's Pres. Daniel Ortega Saavedra announces the introduction of a new currency, the new cordoba, effectively revaluing the currency against the U.S. dollar. Beginning February 15, Nicaraguans can exchange their old cordobas for new ones at the rate of 1,000 to one. . . . Gen. Alfredo Stroessner, 75, is elected to an eighth term as president of Paraguay. Official results show that Stroessner and candidates from his Colorado Party won 88.6% of the vote. The government reports 92.6% turnout overall, with some parts of the country reporting turnout as high as 98%.	

A	B	C	D	E
Includes developments that affect more than one world region, international organizations and important meetings of major world leaders.	Includes all domestic and regional developments in Europe, including the Soviet Union, Turkey, Cyprus and Malta.	Includes all domestic and regional developments in Africa and the Middle East, including Iraq and Iran and excluding Cyprus, Turkey and Afghanistan.	Includes all domestic and regional developments in Latin America, the Caribbean and Canada.	Includes all domestic and regional developments in Asia and Pacific nations, extending from Afghanistan through all the Pacific Islands, except Hawaii.

U.S. Politics & Social Issues	U.S. Foreign Policy & Defense	U.S. Economy & Environment	Science, Technology & Nature	Culture, Leisure & Life Style	
A federal jury in Washington, D.C., finds former White House political director Lyn Nofziger guilty of illegally lobbying senior White House aides on behalf of Wedtech Corp., a scandal-ridden defense contractor, and two other clients after leaving the government in January 1982.... Federal Railroad Admin. (FRA) regulations mandating drug and alcohol testing for rail workers after major accidents are declared unconstitutional by a federal appeals court in San Francisco. In a 2-1 vote, the Ninth Circuit Court of Appeals says that the FRA rules violate the Fourth Amendment ban against unreasonable searches because they allow testing without evidence that a worker is drug- or alcohol-impaired.	According to declassified U.S. intelligence documents, Soviet commandos are believed to have made covert visits to the U.S.-owned St. Lawrence Island. The island is part of the state of Alaska and lies about 40 miles from the Soviet coast, in the Bering Strait. The large, sparsely populated island has no significant military facilities, according to the Defense Dept.	The Occupational Safety and Health Admin. (OSHA) fines a lead-smelting plant at Herculaneum, Mo., $2.8 mil. for health and record-keeping violations. The fine, the third-largest of its kind ever set, was proposed after a six-month inspection that uncovered violations of "virtually every section of the OSHA lead standard," officials report.	The Reagan administration sets forth a revised space program featuring a greatly enhanced role for the private sector. Under the new program, the administration proposes to spend about $700 mil. over five years to lease space on a commercial space station.... The National Aeronautics and Space Admin. announces it has successfully tested a redesigned booster rocket seal at the joint that failed and led to the destruction of the shuttle *Challenger* on Jan. 28, 1986, and the death of its seven astronauts.... The National Academy of Sciences endorses a massive and controversial $3 bil. project to map all the genetic material in the human body. It releases a report urging Congress to appropriate an additional $200 mil. a year (about 3% more than current biomedical research funding) for 15 years to complete the project.		**Feb. 11**
Former Sec. of State Alexander Haig abandons his campaign for the Republican presidential nomination four days before the New Hampshire primary and emphatically endorses Sen. Robert Dole (Kans.).		The deficit on merchandise trade fell to $12.2 bil. in December 1987, the Commerce Dept. reports. The improvement follows the November 1987 decrease in the trade deficit to $13.22 bil. and brought the deficit to its lowest monthly total since January 1987.... The trade deficit for all of 1987 rose to a record $171.22 bil., 9.6% larger than the $156.16 bil. deficit in 1986, according to the Commerce Dept. Exports increased 11.4%, to $252.87 bil. Imports also increased, by 10.7%, to $424.08 bil.... The government's producer price index rose 0.4% in January, the Labor Dept. reports.		Louis Malle's *Au Revoir les Infants*, a film about a Jesuit boarding school during the Nazi occupation of France, is released in New York City.	**Feb. 12**
				The 15th Olympic Winter Games open in Calgary, Alberta. The Canadian city is hosting a record number of athletes, more than 1,750, from a record 57 nations.	**Feb. 13**
				Bobby Allison wins the Daytona 500 stock car race.... Frederick Loewe, 86, composer who with longtime lyricist partner Alan Jay Lerner created such hit Broadway musicals as *Brigadoon* (1947), *Paint Your Wagon* (1951), and *My Fair Lady* (1956), dies in Palm Springs, Calif. Lerner and Loewe's last major collaborations were the movie musical *Gigi* (1959) and the Broadway musical *Camelot* (1960); Lerner died in 1986.	**Feb. 14**

F	G	H	I	J
Includes elections, federal-state relations, civil rights and liberties, crime, the judiciary, education, health care, poverty, urban affairs and population.	*Includes formation and debate of U.S. foreign and defense policies, veterans' affairs and defense spending. (Relations with specific foreign countries are usually found under the region concerned.)*	*Includes business, labor, agriculture, taxation, transportation, consumer affairs, monetary and fiscal policy, natural resources, and pollution.*	*Includes worldwide scientific, medical and technological developments, natural phenomena, U.S. weather, natural disasters, and accidents.*	*Includes the arts, religion, scholarship, communications media, sports, entertainments, fashions, fads and social life.*

	World Affairs	Europe	Africa & the Middle East	The Americas	Asia & the Pacific
Feb. 15		Finland's electoral college reelects Pres. Mauno Koivisto to a second six-year term. Koivisto earned reelection by winning 189 of the electoral college's 301 votes. . . . French gross domestic product grew 0.4% in the fourth quarter of 1987 and 2.1% for the year, the National Statistics Institute reports.	A ferry chartered by the Palestine Liberation Org. for a protest voyage to Israel is damaged in Limassol, Cyprus, by an underwater explosion reportedly caused by a limpet mine attached to the ship's hull. Israeli officials, while not openly admitting responsibility, expressed satisfaction at the disabling of the ferry. . . . Fighting between rival political factions of Zulus in South Africa's Natal province continues to escalate, according to reports. More than 100 blacks were killed in January, the highest one-month toll in the conflict so far, bringing the total number of dead to more than 400 since early 1987.		More than 22 million babies were born in China during 1987, up about 1 million from 1986, the government's family planning director announces; China's total population increased to 1.07 billion during the year. . . . A spokesman for the U.S. Embassy in Bangkok, Thailand, reports that a total of 604 Amerasians (Vietnamese fathered by Americans during the Vietnam War) and their relatives have been accepted for resettlement in the United States in the previous 17 days.
Feb. 16					
Feb. 17		In the Soviet Union, the Communist Party Central Committee begins a two-day plenary meeting. The session ends with an announcement of changes on the policy-making Politburo.	A U.S. Marine officer in charge of a UN truce observer group in Lebanon is abducted while driving near the southern port city of Tyre. Lt. Col. William Richard Higgins, 43, becomes the ninth American hostage currently being held in Lebanon; altogether, more than 20 foreign captives are being held by a variety of groups.		Laos and Thailand agree to a truce aimed at ending an armed border conflict that erupted between the two countries in November 1987.
Feb. 18		It is announced that Boris N. Yeltsin, the controversial former Communist Party chief for Moscow, has been removed as a candidate (nonvoting) member of the Politburo.			

A	B	C	D	E
Includes developments that affect more than one world region, international organizations and important meetings of major world leaders.	Includes all domestic and regional developments in Europe, including the Soviet Union, Turkey, Cyprus and Malta.	Includes all domestic and regional developments in Africa and the Middle East, including Iraq and Iran and excluding Cyprus, Turkey and Afghanistan.	Includes all domestic and regional developments in Latin America, the Caribbean and Canada.	Includes all domestic and regional developments in Asia and Pacific nations, extending from Afghanistan through all the Pacific Islands, except Hawaii.

U.S. Politics & Social Issues	U.S. Foreign Policy & Defense	U.S. Economy & Environment	Science, Technology & Nature	Culture, Leisure & Life Style	
			Richard P(hillips) Feynman, 69, Nobel Prize-winning U.S. physicist widely regarded as one of the most creative scientists of his time, dies of abdominal cancer in Los Angeles. He played a key role in the production of the atom bomb, and his later work on quantum electrodynamics won him a Nobel Prize in 1965, which he shared with two other scientists. A leader in subatomic particle research, his 1985 autobiography, *Surely You're Joking, Mr. Feynman*, was a bestseller. In 1986, he served on the presidential panel investigating the *Challenger* space shuttle disaster and publicly demonstrated that a piece of the critical rocket booster O-ring seal lost virtually all resiliency when dipped in ice water. . . . The Georgia Institute of Technology shuts down its nuclear reactor because of a troubled operating situation. On orders of the Nuclear Regulatory Comm., irradiation experiments are suspended following a mishap and apparent spread of contamination in the reactor building in the summer of 1987.		**Feb. 15**
Vice Pres. George Bush scores a desperately needed victory in the New Hampshire Republican presidential primary election, while Massachusetts Gov. Michael S. Dukakis wins an easy and expected victory in the Democratic race.		The Energy Dept. says that it is not reopening its plutonium-producing nuclear reactor, known as the N reactor, at the Hanford nuclear site near Richland, Wash.			**Feb. 16**
A group of minority students at the Univ. of Massachusetts at Amherst ends a peaceful six-day occupation of a school building after university administrators agree to address a list of racial grievances raised by the students.		Emissions of lead into the atmosphere declined dramatically in 1986 for a second consecutive year, the Environmental Protection Agency reports. The 59% decline in 1986 followed one of 48% recorded for 1985. The dramatic drops are attributed largely to a lowering of the permissible lead concentration of gasoline. . . . The Federal Reserve Board reports that its industrial production index rose 0.2% in January. . . . Housing starts fell 1.9% in January, the Commerce Dept. reports.		*Variety*'s top-grossing films for the week are: *Good Morning, Vietnam, Moonstruck, Shoot to Kill, The Serpent and the Rainbow*, and *Action Jackson*.	**Feb. 17**
Former Arizona Gov. Bruce Babbitt (D) ends his campaign for the Democratic presidential nomination. . . . Former Delaware Gov. Pierre S. (Pete) du Pont IV (R) announces the end of his campaign for the Republican presidential nomination. . . . Anthony M. Kennedy is sworn in as an associate justice of the Supreme Court. The court is brought to its full nine-seat membership for the first time since Associate Justice Lewis F. Powell Jr. retired on June 26, 1987.	Defense Sec. Frank C. Carlucci unveils the seventh annual report on the state of the U.S. military. The six previous documents were issued by his predecessor, Caspar W. Weinberger. The newest report focuses on the budget constraints set by Congress in 1987.	Pres. Reagan submits to Congress a $1.09 trillion budget for FY1989 that conforms to the general course set forth in the deficit-reduction agreement reached with Congress late in 1987. . . . The Federal Reserve Board announces that it is liberalizing restrictions on U.S. banks involved in swaps of Third World debt for equity. The change relaxes guidelines issued in August 1987 that authorized U.S. banks to swap debt only for shares in state-owned companies being privatized. . . . Ford Motor Co., the nation's second-largest auto maker, reports record fourth-quarter earnings of $932 mil., up 19% from a year earlier. For all of 1987, Ford reports a $4.6 bil. profit, a 39.4% increase from $3.3 bil. in 1986 and the best earnings ever for an auto company.	The Soviet news agency Tass reports a Proton rocket launch failure and the loss of three satellites. The satellites were designed "to test elements and equipment of a space navigation system," Tass says, but failure of the rocket's fourth stage prevents them from attaining the desired orbit. . . . French and Israeli scientists writing in the journal *Nature* conclude that fossils found in an Israeli cave demonstrate that anatomically modern humans were living about 92,000 years ago, more than twice the 35,000-40,000-year estimate currently accepted. The conclusions are based on human remains from the Qafzeh cave in Israel that were tested with a new technique called thermoluminescence.		**Feb. 18**

F	G	H	I	J
Includes elections, federal-state relations, civil rights and liberties, crime, the judiciary, education, health care, poverty, urban affairs and population.	*Includes formation and debate of U.S. foreign and defense policies, veterans' affairs and defense spending. (Relations with specific foreign countries are usually found under the region concerned.)*	*Includes business, labor, agriculture, taxation, transportation, consumer affairs, monetary and fiscal policy, natural resources, and pollution.*	*Includes worldwide scientific, medical and technological developments, natural phenomena, U.S. weather, natural disasters, and accidents.*	*Includes the arts, religion, scholarship, communications media, sports, entertainments, fashions, fads and social life.*

	World Affairs	Europe	Africa & the Middle East	The Americas	Asia & the Pacific
Feb. 19		The Spanish government announces that it will open talks with the Basque separatist group Euskadi ta Askatasuna (ETA). The agreement comes four weeks after ETA proposed a truce aimed at ending its campaign of violence for a Basque homeland.		In Nicaragua, cease-fire talks between the Sandinista government and the U.S.-backed Contras are abruptly broken off by the mediator, Cardinal Miguel Obando y Bravo.	
Feb. 20					
Feb. 21		George Vassiliou, a 56-year-old millionaire businessman running as an independent, is elected president of Cyprus in a runoff election against rightist Glafkos Clerides. Spyros Kyprianou, the incumbent president, was eliminated one week earlier after finishing third in the first round of voting.			
Feb. 22	The executive directors of the World Bank agree on a $74.8 bil. general capital increase. The increase, the bank's third since 1959, will bring its total capital base to $171 bil. Under the plan, the capital is to be pledged by all 151 member nations by Sept. 30, 1993.	West Germany's trade surplus with the United States shrank 14.7% in 1987 from 1986 levels, the federal statistics office reports.			
Feb. 23		The foreign ministers of the six Balkan nations meet in Belgrade. It is believed to be the first high-level conference of the Balkan states since World War II. The envoys in attendance are Reis Malile of Albania, Petur Mladenov of Bulgaria, Karolos Papoulias of Greece, Ioan Totu of Romania and Mesut Yilmaz of Turkey. The host is Yugoslavia's Foreign Min. Budimir Loncar.		Brazilian officials report that heavy rainstorms that began February 19 have left some 275 residents of Rio de Janeiro dead.	China's gross national product increased 9.4% in 1987, to $292.9 bil. A report, issued by the state statistical bureau, also shows an increase in inflation. Retail prices rose 9.1% during the year, but wages increased at a significantly slower pace. Average real wages for urban workers increased only 1.7%, while agricultural wages rose 5.3%.
Feb. 24		Sweden's gross national product grew 2.5% to 2.7% in 1987, but is expected to slow to between 1.2% and 1.4% in 1988.	The South African government severely restricts the activities of 17 leading black opposition groups and bars the country's largest labor federation from engaging in any political action. The sweeping ban effectively eliminates the country's few remaining outlets for nonviolent, extraparliamentary opposition to the apartheid system of racial separation.		According to Laotian and Western sources quoted by United Press International, Vietnam has withdrawn about half of the 40,000 troops it is estimated to have deployed in neighboring Laos.

A	B	C	D	E
Includes developments that affect more than one world region, international organizations and important meetings of major world leaders.	Includes all domestic and regional developments in Europe, including the Soviet Union, Turkey, Cyprus and Malta.	Includes all domestic and regional developments in Africa and the Middle East, including Iraq and Iran and excluding Cyprus, Turkey and Afghanistan.	Includes all domestic and regional developments in Latin America, the Caribbean and Canada.	Includes all domestic and regional developments in Asia and Pacific nations, extending from Afghanistan through all the Pacific Islands, except Hawaii.

U.S. Politics & Social Issues	U.S. Foreign Policy & Defense	U.S. Economy & Environment	Science, Technology & Nature	Culture, Leisure & Life Style	
		Pres. Reagan and his Council of Economic Advisers release their annual economic reports. The reports criticize the monetary policy pursued by the Federal Reserve Board in 1987 as restrictive and blame the Fed in part for the current economic slowdown.	Andre F(rederic) Cournand, 92, French-born physician and physiologist, dies of pneumonia in Great Barrington, Mass. A professor of medicine at Columbia Univ., Cournand teamed with Dickinson Richards in researching the practical uses of the heart catheter, invented by Werner Forssmann of Germany in 1929; the three men shared the 1956 Nobel Prize for medicine.	Pope John Paul II deplores the superpower military rivalry between East and West as diverting the resources of the world away from development of the Third World, and curbing poverty and injustice.	Feb. 19
		The *New York Post*, one of North America's oldest newspapers, with an unbroken history of publishing since 1801, escapes oblivion as owner Rupert Murdoch and the newspaper's labor unions agree to labor cost cuts of $22 mil. The last-minute agreement, the result of 16 hours of hard negotiations, clears the way for the sale of the financially ailing tabloid to New York City real-estate developer Peter Kalikow for $37.6 mil.		The 15th Olympic Winter Games in Calgary, Alberta, end. Athletes from the Soviet Union win the most medals of any nation, 29, including 11 gold. East German athletes win 25 medals, nine of them gold. The United States wins six medals, two of them gold.... *Billboard*'s best-selling albums for the week are *Faith*, George Michael; *Dirty Dancing* (soundtrack); *Tiffany*, Tiffany; *Kick*, INXS; and *Bad*, Michael Jackson.	Feb. 20
				Television evangelist Jimmy Swaggart admits to an unspecified "sin" in a tearful confession to an overflow crowd of more than 6,000 at his ministry's Family Worship Center in Baton Rouge, La.	Feb. 21
	James H. Webb Jr. resigns as secretary of the Navy in an angry protest over the defense budget. He assumed the post in April 1987.	The *Wall Street Journal* finds that net income at 487 large corporations it surveys quarterly surged 51% in the fourth quarter from the same period a year earlier.		On his first visit to the United States, world chess champion Gary Kasparov of the Soviet Union plays 59 simultaneous games against New York City schoolchildren. None of the youngsters is able to beat the 24-year-old champion, but two manage to play him to a draw.	Feb. 22
Sen. Robert Dole (Kans.) wins solid victories in the Republican presidential primary in South Dakota and in caucuses in Minnesota. Democrat Rep. Richard Gephardt (Mo.) wins a convincing victory in South Dakota with 44% of the vote over Massachusetts Gov. Michael S. Dukakis, who won 31%. In Minnesota, Dukakis wins with 34% of the vote and the Rev. Jesse Jackson takes second with 20%.... The Supreme Court upholds, 5-3, the right of Mississippi and other coastal states to control lands under non-navigable tidal waters, such as wetlands, marshes, and drainage ditches.	The White House announces that Pres. Reagan has chosen William L. Ball III to succeed James Webb, who resigned yesterday, as secretary of the Navy.	The Supreme Court rules, 8-0, that the interior secretary exceeded his authority in 1982 by consigning water from the Oahe Reservoir in South Dakota to a proposed coal slurry pipeline from Wyoming to the Gulf Coast.	The chairman of Pres. Reagan's acquired immune deficiency syndrome (AIDS) advisory commission, retired Adm. James D. Watkins, issues a report calling for a $2 bil. increase in annual public spending to expand drug treatment programs and improve health care services to fight the spread of AIDS.		Feb. 23
The Supreme Court unanimously reaffirms and extends the constitutional protection of criticism of public figures. The ruling overturns a jury's $200,000 award to the Rev. Jerry Falwell for "emotional distress" over a *Hustler* magazine parody that depicted him as an incestuous drunk.... The Supreme Court rejects by a 6-2 vote a challenge by landlords to a San Jose, Calif., rent control law. The law provides, among other things, for the city to consider "hardship" to the tenant before approving rent increases requested by landlords.		Federal Reserve Board chairman Alan Greenspan publicly warns the Reagan administration to stop pressuring the nation's central bank to lower interest rates and boost the nation's money supply.		*Money* magazine publishes a list of the 200 wealthiest people in Great Britain. The top five are: Queen Elizabeth II, estimated worth of $5.89 bil.; Sir John Moores, founder of the Littlewoods football pools and mail order empire, $3 bil.; food magnate Garry Weston, $2.65 bil.; the property-owning Duke of Westminster, $2.47 bil.; and financier Sir James Goldsmith, $1.76 bil.	Feb. 24

F	G	H	I	J
Includes elections, federal-state relations, civil rights and liberties, crime, the judiciary, education, health care, poverty, urban affairs and population.	*Includes formation and debate of U.S. foreign and defense policies, veterans' affairs and defense spending. (Relations with specific foreign countries are usually found under the region concerned.)*	*Includes business, labor, agriculture, taxation, transportation, consumer affairs, monetary and fiscal policy, natural resources, and pollution.*	*Includes worldwide scientific, medical and technological developments, natural phenomena, U.S. weather, natural disasters, and accidents.*	*Includes the arts, religion, scholarship, communications media, sports, entertainments, fashions, fads and social life.*

	World Affairs	Europe	Africa & the Middle East	The Americas	Asia & the Pacific
Feb. 25		The Soviet Union removes its SS-12 medium-range nuclear missiles from two bases in East Germany and places them on military trains bound for the USSR. The missiles are removed in spite of the fact that the U.S.-Soviet treaty on intermediate-range nuclear forces has not yet been ratified by the U.S. Senate. The treaty will not take formal effect until ratification.	Sec. of State George P. Shultz arrives in Jerusalem in an effort to revive the moribund Arab-Israeli peace process. After a week of shuttling between Israel, Egypt, Jordan and Syria he appears to have little to show for his efforts.		The Indian government successfully tests a surface-to-surface missile with a range of at least 150 miles, P.M. Rajiv Gandhi announces. The missile, known as Prithvi (Hindi for "Earth"), was launched into the Bay of Bengal from the Sriharikota space center on India's southeast coast. . . . Roh Tae Woo is sworn in as president in South Korea's first peaceful transition of power since independence in 1948. Roh succeeds Pres. Chun Doo Hwan, a former army general who assumed power in early 1980 following a military coup the previous year.
Feb. 26	The State Dept. announces that Romania has relinquished its most-favored-nation trade status with the United States. Bucharest notified Washington of the decision through diplomatic channels. The move is an apparent response to U.S. complaints about the state of human rights in Romania. . . . The volume of world trade grew 4% in 1987 and is expected to expand "at least as rapidly" in 1988, the General Agreement on Tariffs and Trade reports.	After several weeks of demonstrations by ethnic Armenians, an official statement from Soviet leader Mikhail S. Gorbachev calls for a restoration of order. "The Communist Party Central Committee has been disturbed by this turn of events, [which] is fraught with serious consequences." The protests are the latest flare-up of nationalism in the Soviet Union. . . . Britain's "Big Four" clearing (commercial) banks issue their 1987 year-end financial reports February 18-26. Owing to huge provisions the four banks made in 1987 to protect against problem loans to the Third World, two of the institutions suffered losses and the other two posted sharply lower profits. The four banks are: Lloyds Bank PLC, Midland Bank PLC, National Westminster Bank PLC, and Barclays PLC.		Panama's National Assembly votes to oust Pres. Eric Arturo Delvalle after Delvalle announces that he is firing the head of the Panama Defense Forces, Gen. Manuel Antonio Noriega. Noriega, the de facto leader of Panama, refuses to step down. The National Assembly names a new president, but the United States and most Latin American nations pledge support for Delvalle as the legitimate head of government in Panama.	
Feb. 27		Protest leaders in Yerevan, in the Soviet republic of Armenia, agree to suspend nationalist demonstrations for one month. The move comes one day after Soviet leader Mikhail S. Gorbachev met privately with two ethnic Armenian writers at the Kremlin and offered assurances he would devote personal attention to Armenian grievances.			
Feb. 28			Senegalese voters cast ballots in presidential and legislative elections and return Pres. Abdou Diouf for another five-year term.		
Feb. 29		Bulgaria holds its first elections since World War II—with more than one candidate for a political post. Under a new law, 66,582 candidates sought 55,426 posts in municipal and regional elections. BTA, the official Bulgarian news service, reports a 98.4% turnout of eligible voters.		In Panama, a general strike called by opponents of Gen. Manuel Antonio Noriega begins. According to an estimate by Horacio Icaza, a director of the Panama City Chamber of Commerce, some 70% of all industries and commercial businesses in the capital are closed. Noriega's newly chosen president, Solis Palma, puts the effectiveness at only 40% in the capital. . . . U.S. Trade Rep. Clayton K. Yeutter announces that the United States will delay the imposition of $105 mil. in trade sanctions against Brazil because of "recent progress" in a dispute over Brazilian import restrictions on U.S. computer software.	Finance Min. Narayan Datt Tiwari unveils the Indian government's $56.3 bil. budget for fiscal 1988-89, which begins April 1. The budget stresses increased government aid for poor sections of the country, including a number of measures designed to alleviate the effects of the severe summer drought of 1987.

A	B	C	D	E
Includes developments that affect more than one world region, international organizations and important meetings of major world leaders.	Includes all domestic and regional developments in Europe, including the Soviet Union, Turkey, Cyprus and Malta.	Includes all domestic and regional developments in Africa and the Middle East, including Iraq and Iran and excluding Cyprus, Turkey and Afghanistan.	Includes all domestic and regional developments in Latin America, the Caribbean and Canada.	Includes all domestic and regional developments in Asia and Pacific nations, extending from Afghanistan through all the Pacific Islands, except Hawaii.

U.S. Politics & Social Issues	U.S. Foreign Policy & Defense	U.S. Economy & Environment	Science, Technology & Nature	Culture, Leisure & Life Style	
The 1987 results for the Scholastic Aptitude Test (SAT) and the American College Test (ACT) show little change from 1986, according to a report by the Education Dept. Nationally, the average SAT score remained 906 in 1987, the same level as the previous year. The SAT, which is administered by the College Entrance Examination Board, is based on a scale of 400 to 1,600.... A report by the National Assessment of Educational Progress asserts that many elementary and secondary school students are unable to interpret and evaluate the material that they read. The federally funded panel, which is administered by the non-profit Educational Testing Service, based its study on a comprehensive reading exam given in 1986 to 36,000 students in grades three, seven, and 11.		Median family income climbed from 1970 to 1986, while family income inequalities widened, the Congressional Budget Office (CBO) reports. The CBO study challenges other studies that have shown family incomes as virtually unchanged since 1970 and states that "median adjusted family income" has risen 20% since 1970.		The Vatican has an operating deficit of $56,723,375 for 1986, the National Conf. of Catholic Bishops discloses in Washington, D.C. The information is disclosed, for the first time in history, to stimulate contributions from the faithful, it is reported.... The Chicago City Council approves an ordinance that will allow the Chicago Cubs to install lights for night games at Wrigley Field. The Cubs have played only daytime baseball there for 72 years.	**Feb. 25**
		The government's consumer price index rose 0.3% in January, the Labor Dept. reports.... Consumer spending and personal income both rose 0.3% in January, the Commerce Dept. reports.... The 8th U.S. Circuit Court of Appeals rules that corporations cannot pass along pollution cleanup costs to their insurers under a standard commercial liability policy. The court finds that such policies were written to cover suits relating to property damage or third-party liability and do not apply to suits seeking recovery of the cost of cleanup of hazardous waste sites.		*Publishers Weekly*'s hardback fiction best-sellers for the week are: *The Bonfire of the Vanities*, Tom Wolfe; *The Tommyknockers*, Stephen King; *Presumed Innocent*, Scott Turow; *Kaleidoscope*, Danielle Steel; and *Lightning*, Dean R. Koontz.... The movie *Hairspray* is released in New York, a satirical comedy set in early 1960s Baltimore, where teenagers vie to become celebrities on a local dance show; directed and written by John Waters, with Divine, Ricki Lake, Debbie Harry, Sonny Bono, Jerry Stiller, and Pia Zadora.	**Feb. 26**
				American Broadcasting Co. (ABC), which paid $309 mil. for the rights to telecast the Olympic Winter Games, is expected to lose about $75 mil. on the venture, according to the *Financial Times* newspaper. In the United States, the average ratings for ABC's telecasts were 19.3% of the 88.6 million American television households; on average, 30% of all television sets that were on at any one time were tuned in to the games.	**Feb. 27**
					Feb. 28
A grand jury is empaneled in Poughkeepsie, N.Y., by New York State Attorney Gen. Robert Abrams to investigate the alleged abduction and sexual assault of a black teenager, Tawana Brawley, by six white men. Brawley, 16, is a resident of the nearby Dutchess County, N.Y., community of Wappingers Falls.		Prices received by farmers for their raw agricultural products dropped 0.8% in February, the Agriculture Dept reports.... The Dow Jones industrial average closes at 2071.62, its highest level since the Oct. 19, 1987, stock market collapse, surpassing the previous post-crash high set January 7.... The Environmental Protection Agency warns Congress that an estimated one in five commercial and public buildings could have asbestos problems. But the agency's report to Congress declines to offer any immediate plan to cope with the problems.			**Feb. 29**

F	G	H	I	J
Includes elections, federal-state relations, civil rights and liberties, crime, the judiciary, education, health care, poverty, urban affairs and population.	*Includes formation and debate of U.S. foreign and defense policies, veterans' affairs and defense spending. (Relations with specific foreign countries are usually found under the region concerned.)*	*Includes business, labor, agriculture, taxation, transportation, consumer affairs, monetary and fiscal policy, natural resources, and pollution.*	*Includes worldwide scientific, medical and technological developments, natural phenomena, U.S. weather, natural disasters, and accidents.*	*Includes the arts, religion, scholarship, communications media, sports, entertainments, fashions, fads and social life.*

	World Affairs	Europe	Africa & the Middle East	The Americas	Asia & the Pacific
March 1					The New Zealand government abruptly cancels the planned sale of its 70% stake in Petroleum Corp. of New Zealand Ltd. Richard Prebble, the minister for state-owned enterprises, says the deal collapsed after representatives from British Gas insisted that New Zealand officials agree to a list of legal provisions "which the government considered to be unacceptable." ... The official New China News Agency says that Prince Norodom Sihanouk has decided to remain as head of Cambodia's three-party antigovernment coalition. Sihanouk had announced in January that he was resigning from the coalition.
March 2	The UN Gen. Assembly votes, 143-1, in favor of two resolutions opposing a U.S. plan to close the New York City office of the Palestine Liberation Org. (PLO), which is the headquarters of the PLO's permanent observer mission to the UN.				
March 3	Borrowing on international capital markets was steady for all of 1987, the Org. for Economic Cooperation and Development (OECD) reports. In its latest Financial Market Trends Report, a survey issued three times a year, the OECD reports that borrowing on international capital markets for all of 1987 was $383.8 bil., down slightly from $389.5 bil. in 1986.	The leaders of the 16 nations of the North Atlantic Treaty Org. (NATO) meet in Brussels over two days. The last such NATO summit was held in 1982. The aim of the 1988 summit is to reach agreement on NATO's defense posture in light of the U.S.-Soviet treaty to eliminate intermediate-range nuclear forces.		Eighteen months of direct rule by Britain ends after a general election in the Caribbean colony of Turks and Caicos Islands. The People's Democratic Movement of Oswaldo Skippings wins 11 of the 13 Legislative Council seats. The remaining two seats go to members of the Progressive National Party.	In Bangladesh, the ruling Jatiya Party wins an overwhelming majority of seats in parliamentary elections marred by violence and boycotted by the country's main opposition groups. The elections were held to choose a new 300-member parliament to replace the previous legislature, which was dissolved in December 1987 by Pres. Hossein Mohammed Ershad, the Jatiya Party leader.

A	B	C	D	E
Includes developments that affect more than one world region, international organizations and important meetings of major world leaders.	Includes all domestic and regional developments in Europe, including the Soviet Union, Turkey, Cyprus and Malta.	Includes all domestic and regional developments in Africa and the Middle East, including Iraq and Iran and excluding Cyprus, Turkey and Afghanistan.	Includes all domestic and regional developments in Latin America, the Caribbean and Canada.	Includes all domestic and regional developments in Asia and Pacific nations, extending from Afghanistan through all the Pacific Islands, except Hawaii.

U.S. Politics & Social Issues	U.S. Foreign Policy & Defense	U.S. Economy & Environment	Science, Technology & Nature	Culture, Leisure & Life Style	
As expected, Massachusetts Gov. Michael S. Dukakis (D) and Vice Pres. George Bush (R) win their parties' respective primaries in Maine, yesterday, and Vermont today.		The government's index of leading economic indicators fell 0.6% in January, the Commerce Dept. reports. . . . State and local tax collections amounted to $398.4 bil. during the year ending June 1987, Commerce Clearing House Inc. reports. The total is 7.4% higher than in the previous 12-month period. The states collected a total of $246.6 bil., up 8.2% for the year. Localities took in $151.9 bil., a rise of 6.1%.		The chairman of Olympiques Calgary Olympics, the organizing committee of the 15th Winter Olympics, estimates that the games will turn a profit of $25.4 mil. . . . For the first time since it was formed in 1956, the veterans committee of baseball's Hall of Fame does not select any candidates for the hall. The committee reportedly considered 29 candidates. . . . Miss Texas, Courtney Gibbs, is crowned Miss USA. Gibbs is the fourth consecutive Miss Texas to win the Miss USA title. The television broadcast is hosted for the first time by television personality Alan Thicke, who replaces longtime host Bob Barker. Barker, a crusader for animal rights, dropped out because a mink coat had been included as one of the prizes.	March 1
The House of Representatives votes, 315-98, in favor of legislation that would overturn a 1984 Supreme Court ruling that limits the scope of federal law prohibiting discrimination on the basis of sex, race, age, or physical handicap. The legislation was approved by the Senate in January by a vote of 75-14. . . . The Rev. Pat Robertson wins almost half the delegates in Alaska's Republican presidential precinct caucuses. Early figures give him 47% of the total. . . . J. Saunders Redding, 81, author and historian who was one of the founders of the academic discipline of Afro-American studies, dies in Ithaca, N.Y. In 1949, he became one of the first blacks to teach at an Ivy League institution when he was appointed a visiting professor of English at Brown Univ. In 1970, he became the first black professor on Cornell Univ.'s faculty of arts and sciences. . . . The results of an international science study show that U.S. students perform poorly compared with students in many other countries. The study by the International Assoc. for the Evaluation of Educational Achievement shows the United States finished eighth out of 15 nations.				The 30th annual Grammy Awards are presented. U2's *Joshua Tree* is named album of the year and wins for best rock performance by a duo or group; record of the year, Paul Simon's *Graceland*; song of the year, James Horner, Barry Mann, and Cynthia Weil's "Somewhere Out There" for the animated film *An American Tail*; best female pop vocalist award, Whitney Houston for *I Wanna Dance With Somebody*; best male pop vocalist, Sting for *Bring on the Night* album. Best rock vocalist, Bruce Springsteen for the *Tunnel of Love* album. Unlike in past years, male and female entries for the rock vocal award were combined. Top new artist of the year is Jody Watley. . . . For his work as a proponent of Islamic unity who helped bring together world religious leaders, Inamullah Khan, the secretary general of the World Moslem Congress, is named the 1988 winner of the Templeton Prize for Progress in Religion.	March 2
The Senate approves a bill to restrict use of polygraphs, or lie detectors, to test employees or prospective employees in private industry. The bill is sent to conference with the House, which passed a more restrictive version in November 1987. Leslye Arsht, deputy White House press secretary, says Pres. Reagan is willing to work with Congress to come up with a version he can sign. . . . The Reagan administration suspends its effort to prevent federally funded family planning clinics from engaging in abortion-related activities. Rules barring such activities were to have gone into effect today. The administration acts hours after a federal judge in Boston issues a nationwide injunction permanently prohibiting enforcement of the new policy.	In a setback for Speaker James C. Wright Jr. (D, Tex.), the House of Representatives votes, 216-208, to reject a Democratic plan to provide $30.8 mil. in nonlethal aid to the Nicaraguan Contras fighting the Sandinista government.		Sewall Wright, 98, geneticist widely regarded as the foremost U.S. evolutionary theorist of the 20th century, dies in Madison, Wis. With R.A. Fisher and J.B.S. Haldane of Britain, Wright developed field population genetics, providing a mathematical underpinning for the 19th-century theories of Charles Darwin and Gregor Mendel. His four-volume magnum opus, *Evolution and the Genetics of Populations*, was completed in 1968.		March 3

F	G	H	I	J
Includes elections, federal-state relations, civil rights and liberties, crime, the judiciary, education, health care, poverty, urban affairs and population.	Includes formation and debate of U.S. foreign and defense policies, veterans' affairs and defense spending. (Relations with specific foreign countries are usually found under the region concerned.)	Includes business, labor, agriculture, taxation, transportation, consumer affairs, monetary and fiscal policy, natural resources, and pollution.	Includes worldwide scientific, medical and technological developments, natural phenomena, U.S. weather, natural disasters, and accidents.	Includes the arts, religion, scholarship, communications media, sports, entertainments, fashions, fads and social life.

	World Affairs	Europe	Africa & the Middle East	The Americas	Asia & the Pacific
March 4		The Soviet Union reveals that 31 people died in ethnic clashes in the Soviet republic of Azerbaijan February 28 in what is believed to be the most serious outbreak of nationalist violence in the USSR since the anti-Russian riots in the central Asian city of Alma-Ata in December 1986.... Greece's Premier Andreas Papandreou and Turkey's Premier Turgut Ozal meet in Brussels after a North Atlantic Treaty Org. summit. The meeting, their second this year, marks continued progress in easing tensions between the traditional rivals. The two leaders announce that Ozal will visit Greece in mid-June.		Faced with a cash crisis, Panama's government orders the nation's banks to close. The move follows a decree issued March 1 by Eric Arturo Delvalle freezing Panamanian assets abroad and urging a boycott of all payments to the regime of military leader Gen. Manuel Antonio Noriega. Delvalle was president of Panama until forced out by a vote of the Noriega-controlled National Assembly in late February. Latin American countries and the United States continue to back Delvalle.... In its latest effort to settle its medium- and long-term debt, Brazil reaches a tentative agreement with its major bank creditors to reschedule $62 bil. of foreign debt.	
March 5			An Iranian diplomat privately hands an unsigned statement to the UN Security Council saying that Teheran accepts the cease-fire resolution passed by the council in July 1987, the *New York Times* reports.		Western news reports say that as many as nine people are killed when police clash with hundreds of Buddhist monks and several thousand other pro-independence demonstrators in the Tibetan capital city of Lhasa.
March 6		Three unarmed Irish terrorist suspects are slain in Gibraltar by British security forces. British and Spanish authorities say that the three, two men and a woman, had been planning a car bomb attack.	South Africa's Defense Min. Magnus Malan says that his government is prepared to deal directly with the Soviet Union in an effort to end Angola's 13-year-old civil war. Citing Moscow's recent offer to withdraw Soviet troops from Afghanistan, Malan says that a similar arrangement for a "free, nonaligned and neutral" Angola would be acceptable to Pretoria.		
March 7	Industrial nations increased their reserve holdings in 1987, the International Monetary Fund (IMF) reports. According to the IMF, Japan became the world's largest holder of non-gold reserves, with $81.1 bil. at the end of 1987, overtaking West Germany, which became the world's second-largest holder with $78.3 bil. in reserves.			In Canada, the chief justice of the Supreme Court of British Columbia, Allan McEachern, strikes down a provincial regulation that curbed public funding for abortions.	
March 8		Kurt Georg Kiesinger, 83, chancellor of West Germany from 1966 to 1969, dies of heart failure in Tubingen, West Germany. A Christian Democrat, he headed a government formed by a "grand coalition" of Christian Democrats and Social Democrats. His past as a minor Nazi official brought him much negative attention when he became a candidate for chancellor, and in a widely publicized incident Nazi hunter Beate Klarsfeld slapped him in the face at a conference in West Berlin in November of 1968. He lost the 1969 election to Willy Brandt but remained a member of the Bundestag until 1980.... At least eight Soviet soldiers have died in battles with Azerbaijanis to restore order in the Azerbaijan Republic city of Sumgait, according to an Armenian nationalist leader, Ambartsum Galestyan. The Soviet government has made no mention of fighting or troop casualties.		Almost three weeks of protests against economic conditions in the Dominican Republic result in seven deaths, it is reported. The unrest stems from a complaint by residents of Couti about pollution of a nearby river by a state-owned mining company. That grew into nationwide strikes and demonstrations over the rising cost of living in which protesters clashed with police and soldiers.	

A	B	C	D	E
Includes developments that affect more than one world region, international organizations and important meetings of major world leaders.	*Includes all domestic and regional developments in Europe, including the Soviet Union, Turkey, Cyprus and Malta.*	*Includes all domestic and regional developments in Africa and the Middle East, including Iraq and Iran and excluding Cyprus, Turkey and Afghanistan.*	*Includes all domestic and regional developments in Latin America, the Caribbean and Canada.*	*Includes all domestic and regional developments in Asia and Pacific nations, extending from Afghanistan through all the Pacific Islands, except Hawaii.*

U.S. Politics & Social Issues	U.S. Foreign Policy & Defense	U.S. Economy & Environment	Science, Technology & Nature	Culture, Leisure & Life Style	
		The Labor Dept. reports a drop in the nation's unemployment rate in February, to 5.6% from 5.7%.... The Federal Reserve Bank of New York says it purchased $4.14 bil. of U.S. currency in the foreign exchange market in the last two months of 1987 and the first month of 1988. The intervention by the Fed was designed to prevent the U.S. currency from plunging further against the Japanese yen and the West German mark.		*Babette's Feast*, a Danish film about a mysterious Frenchwoman who works as a housekeeper for two unmarried daughters of a Danish clergyman and is revealed to be a brilliant chef as she prepares a sumptuous feast, opens in New York. Directed by Gabriel Axel, who also wrote the screenplay, the movie is based on a novella by Isak Dinesen. The film will win the Academy Award for best foreign film.	March 4
Vice Pres. George Bush wins the South Carolina Republican primary. (The Democratic caucus will be held a week later.)					March 5
					March 6
A federal judge dismisses a $35 mil. libel suit brought by the Rev. Pat Robertson, the former television evangelist and current Republican presidential candidate, against a former congressman who claimed that Robertson pulled strings to shirk combat duty in the Korean War.	China's Foreign Min. Wu Xueqian meets in Washington, D.C., with Pres. Reagan and Sec. of State George P. Shultz for talks concerning trade between the two countries and China's relationship with Iran. The two sides agree on a number of issues, including Chinese support for an arms embargo against Iran, an end to recent U.S. sanctions on the sale of high-technology goods to China, and Beijing's acceptance of American Peace Corps volunteers.	Outstanding consumer debt rose $5.42 bil. in January, the Federal Reserve Board reports.	The federal government and Morton Thiokol Inc. provide a total of $7.7 mil. in annuities to settle legal claims by families of four of the astronauts killed in the explosion of the space shuttle *Challenger* in January 1986.	Divine (born Harris Glenn Milstead), 42, hefty female impersonator who starred in many films made by Baltimore-based filmmaker John Waters, dies of a heart attack in Los Angeles. Winning acclaim for his role in the infamous underground classic *Pink Flamingos* (1972), he had starred most recently in Waters's more mainstream release *Hairspray* (1988).	March 7
Vice Pres. George Bush wins all 16 Republican presidential primaries held today, "Super Tuesday." With an unprecedented cluster of state contests, most in Southern states, Bush wins more than 700 delegates; 1,139 are needed to capture the Republican nomination. Gov. Michael S. Dukakis (Mass.) is the big winner on the Democratic side and now leads the overall count with about 500 of the 2,082 delegates needed for the Democratic nomination.					March 8

F	G	H	I	J
Includes elections, federal-state relations, civil rights and liberties, crime, the judiciary, education, health care, poverty, urban affairs and population.	Includes formation and debate of U.S. foreign and defense policies, veterans' affairs and defense spending. (Relations with specific foreign countries are usually found under the region concerned.)	Includes business, labor, agriculture, taxation, transportation, consumer affairs, monetary and fiscal policy, natural resources, and pollution.	Includes worldwide scientific, medical and technological developments, natural phenomena, U.S. weather, natural disasters, and accidents.	Includes the arts, religion, scholarship, communications media, sports, entertainments, fashions, fads and social life.

	World Affairs	Europe	Africa & the Middle East	The Americas	Asia & the Pacific
March 9	A Soviet spokesman spurns South Africa's March 6 offer to deal directly with the USSR in an effort to end Angola's 13-year-old civil war.	France's 1987 current account moved into a deficit of 27.2 bil. francs from a surplus of 20.2 bil. in 1986, the government reports.	One day after about 40 canoe-borne, armed rebels attacked the police headquarters of the tiny West African island nation of Sao Tome and Principe March 8 in an abortive coup attempt, forces loyal to Pres. Manuel Pinto da Costa defeat the raiders, killing two and capturing most of the others.	Contra rebels free an American volunteer kidnapped during an offensive action in northern Nicaragua. The American, construction worker Richard Boren, is affiliated with Witness for Peace, a Washington-based religious group that opposes aid to the Contras. He was seized during a Contra raid on Mancotal in Jinotega province March 1. Four people reportedly died in the attack, 11 were wounded and 12 were abducted.	
March 10		Austria marks the 50th anniversary of the *Anschluss* when, under threat of invasion, Austria formed a union with Adolf Hitler's Nazi Germany in 1938. At the center of the commemorations is an examination of Austria's role as both a victim and a perpetrator of Nazism.			Indonesia's People's Consultative Assembly reelects Pres. Suharto to serve a fifth five-year term. The election is largely ceremonial, since the 66-year-old president is the only candidate for the country's top office and his ruling Golongan Karya (Golkar) Party controls about 900 of the 1,000 seats in the electoral assembly.
March 11		Italy's Premier Giovanni Goria resigns his post after a dispute over nuclear power; he had been scheduled to step down March 17.	Iran and Iraq have resumed their "war of the cities" over the past two weeks, with each country firing barrages of missiles into the other's capital, killing hundreds of civilians.		
March 12	Crisis talks at the International Cocoa Org. in London collapse without an agreement on actions to stop a slide in cocoa prices.				

A	B	C	D	E
Includes developments that affect more than one world region, international organizations and important meetings of major world leaders.	Includes all domestic and regional developments in Europe, including the Soviet Union, Turkey, Cyprus and Malta.	Includes all domestic and regional developments in Africa and the Middle East, including Iraq and Iran and excluding Cyprus, Turkey and Afghanistan.	Includes all domestic and regional developments in Latin America, the Caribbean and Canada.	Includes all domestic and regional developments in Asia and Pacific nations, extending from Afghanistan through all the Pacific Islands, except Hawaii.

U.S. Politics & Social Issues	U.S. Foreign Policy & Defense	U.S. Economy & Environment	Science, Technology & Nature	Culture, Leisure & Life Style	
					March 9
Rep. Jack F. Kemp (N.Y.) drops out of the race for the Republican presidential nomination. . . . In Alaska's Democratic Party precinct caucuses the Rev. Jesse Jackson narrowly edges out Dukakis, 35% to 31%. The caucuses are the first step toward selecting the state's 12 convention delegates. . . . Four white students at Dartmouth College who were accused of harassing a black professor are punished by the school's disciplinary review board. The four are all staffers of the *Dartmouth Review*, a politically conservative off-campus newspaper whose members had been involved in a number of racial controversies since the paper's founding in 1980. . . . John Larry (Johnny) Spain, a former Black Panther convicted of murder for his role in the bloody 1971 attempt to free San Quentin Prison inmate George Jackson, is released on $350,000 bond from the California Medical Facility at Vacaville after 21 years in prison. Spain is awaiting retrial on murder and conspiracy charges stemming from the 1971 incident.		The Dept. of Energy confirms that a plan to bury radioactive waste in New Mexico salt beds has been sharply curtailed after reports of water leaks in the repository.	A major step toward an effective vaccine against malaria is reported by Colombian scientists writing in the British journal *Nature*. The experimental vaccine, tested in a small number of volunteers in South America, is considered significant because it is the first to attack malaria parasites at the stage in their life cycle when they multiply and begin to attack the red blood cells, producing symptoms of the disease.	Glenn Cunningham, 78, top U.S. miler of the 1930s, dies in Menifee, Ark., of an apparent heart attack. In meets at New York City's Madison Square Garden he set six world records for the mile and the 1,500 meters and another at 1,000 yards; in 1979, he was named the greatest track athlete in the history of the Garden.	**March 10**
Former Sen. Gary Hart (Colo.) drops out of the race for the Democratic presidential nomination. . . . Robert C. McFarlane, Pres. Reagan's national security adviser from October 1983 through December 1985, pleads guilty in U.S. District Court in Washington, D.C., to four misdemeanor counts of withholding information from Congress in connection with the Iran-Contra scandal. In exchange for his plea McFarlane agrees to cooperate fully with independent counsel Lawrence E. Walsh's ongoing investigation. . . . The government's producer price index fell 0.2% in February, the Labor Dept. reports.	Attorney Gen. Edwin Meese III formally orders the Palestine Liberation Org.'s (PLO) New York office closed by March 21. The order comes in a letter from Meese to Zehdi L. Terzi, the PLO's UN representative. Meese tells Terzi that he will go to court, if necessary, to ensure compliance with the order.		The European Space Agency successfully launches two telecommunications satellites from its Kourou space center in French Guiana. The agency's Ariane-3 rocket put the satellites into orbit.		**March 11**
The Rev. Jesse Jackson handily wins the South Carolina Democratic primary with about 54% of the vote. Although a Chicago resident, Jackson is a "favorite son" in South Carolina, having been born in Greenville. Vice Pres. George Bush won the state's Republican primary the week before.				Romare (Howard) Bearden, 75, artist best known for his vivid, intricate collages in which he sought to capture the rich diversity of black life in America, dies in New York City, following a stroke.	**March 12**

F	G	H	I	J
Includes elections, federal-state relations, civil rights and liberties, crime, the judiciary, education, health care, poverty, urban affairs and population.	*Includes formation and debate of U.S. foreign and defense policies, veterans' affairs and defense spending. (Relations with specific foreign countries are usually found under the region concerned.)*	*Includes business, labor, agriculture, taxation, transportation, consumer affairs, monetary and fiscal policy, natural resources, and pollution.*	*Includes worldwide scientific, medical and technological developments, natural phenomena, U.S. weather, natural disasters, and accidents.*	*Includes the arts, religion, scholarship, communications media, sports, entertainments, fashions, fads and social life.*

	World Affairs	Europe	Africa & the Middle East	The Americas	Asia & the Pacific
March 13			South Africa's churches, in the last two weeks, have moved defiantly to fill the void created by the white government's February 24 banning of political activity by 18 predominantly black organizations. Clerics are leading protest marches and services in support of peaceful civil disobedience, while Pretoria responds by banning the new church-led antiapartheid movement.		The Seikan train tunnel, connecting the main Japanese island of Honshu with the northern island of Hokkaido, is officially opened. The 33.46-mile tunnel is the longest in the world to date. . . . Bangladesh's Pres. Hossein Mohammed Ershad declares that his country has officially ceased to be a secular state and will be transformed into an Islamic republic. Ershad says the country's constitution will be adapted to conform to the law of the Koran, the sacred book of Islam.
March 14					Chinese and Vietnamese warships exchange fire in the South China Sea in a dispute over the Spratly Islands. Both countries claim the archipelago, situated about 200 miles east of Vietnam, as part of their territory and each accuses the other of provoking the clash.
March 15		Britain's Chancellor of the Exchequer Nigel Lawson presents a budget for 1988-89 that includes an overhaul of the nation's income tax system. The controversial plan prompts unprecedented protest in the House of Commons from opposition politicians. . . . A Soviet government official, in a newspaper interview, compares the ethnic violence in the Azerbaijan Republic city of Sumgait to the "pogroms" of old. Pogrom, a Russian word meaning an organized persecution of a minority group, is historically associated with massacres of Jews in czarist Russia.			

A	B	C	D	E
Includes developments that affect more than one world region, international organizations and important meetings of major world leaders.	Includes all domestic and regional developments in Europe, including the Soviet Union, Turkey, Cyprus and Malta.	Includes all domestic and regional developments in Africa and the Middle East, including Iraq and Iran and excluding Cyprus, Turkey and Afghanistan.	Includes all domestic and regional developments in Latin America, the Caribbean and Canada.	Includes all domestic and regional developments in Asia and Pacific nations, extending from Afghanistan through all the Pacific Islands, except Hawaii.

U.S. Politics & Social Issues	U.S. Foreign Policy & Defense	U.S. Economy & Environment	Science, Technology & Nature	Culture, Leisure & Life Style	
The board of trustees at Gallaudet Univ., the nation's only liberal arts college for the deaf, names a deaf man, Irving King Jordan Jr., president of the university. Jordan, a Gallaudet graduate who has been dean of the university's college of arts and sciences since 1986, becomes the school's first non-hearing president.				Entertainers Frank Sinatra, Sammy Davis Jr., and Dean Martin open their nationwide "Rat Pack" reunion tour to a sell-out crowd at the Oakland (Calif.) Coliseum. The three performers first appeared together in 1960.	March 13
The superintendent of the Los Angeles school system abandons a plan to put the city's public schools on a year-round schedule.		The Senate votes, 83-0, to ratify an international treaty to curb global use of ozone-depleting chemicals. . . . The National Oceanic and Atmospheric Admin. fines three Japanese companies a total of $100,000 for fishing illegally in U.S. waters off Alaska in early January. The three companies received the maximum civil penalty, a fine of $25,000 for each vessel involved in the incident.			March 14
Sen. Paul Simon (Ill.) scores a critically needed win in his home-state Democratic presidential primary election. The other Illinois "favorite son," the Rev. Jesse Jackson, a longtime Chicago resident, takes a strong second place. . . . The Senate approves, 88-4, a bill revising immigration quotas to increase the flow of professionals and skilled workers into the United States. The bill, which still requires House action, is the second phase of immigration reform begun in 1986 with enactment of the basic law to prevent illegal immigration. . . . Convicted killer Willie Jasper Darden, 54, is executed by electrocution at the Florida State Prison at Starke. Darden spent 14 years on Florida's death row since being convicted of fatally shooting Lakeland furniture store owner James Turman in September 1973 after Turman walked into the store and found his wife being robbed of $15. . . . Darden's execution follows by hours that of 38-year-old Vietnam veteran Wayne Robert Felde in Louisiana. Felde, convicted of the 1978 murder of a Shreveport policeman, is electrocuted just after midnight at the state penitentiary at Angola. . . . The Carnegie Foundation for the Advancement of Teaching issues a report that says the recent educational reform movement in the United States has "largely bypassed" schools in the nation's big cities. The report is entitled, "An Imperiled Generation: Saving Urban Schools."	The Senate passes a bill to require the president to inform Congress of covert operations within 48 hours of their inception. The House of Representatives is considering a similar measure.	Federal Reserve Board Chairman Alan Greenspan warns that stronger economic growth in 1988 could lead to renewed inflation and vows again to put the economy first in determining Fed interest rate policy. . . . The U.S. balance of payments on current account shows a record $160.68 bil. deficit in 1987, the Commerce Dept. reports. The current-account deficit for 1987 increased 13%, surpassing the $141.35 bil. 1986 record. It is the sixth straight annual current-account deficit, and leaves the United States once again the world's leading debtor nation.	A U.S. study finds that there has been a significant decline in the atmosphere's ozone layer over the Northern Hemisphere over the previous two decades.		March 15

	World Affairs	Europe	Africa & the Middle East	The Americas	Asia & the Pacific
March 16				Denying that Nicaraguan troops have invaded Honduras, Nicaragua's Pres. Daniel Ortega invites observers from the UN and the Org. of American States to visit the border area.	
March 17		The Bank of England engineers a one-half-percentage-point cut in commercial bank interest rates. The move comes amid a surge in the value of the British pound and a dispute between P.M. Margaret Thatcher and Chancellor of the Exchequer Nigel Lawson over whether to stem the surge. . . . Joblessness in Britain falls to a seasonally adjusted level of 2.531 million workers in February, the lowest total since February 1982. The decline of 33,400 is the 19th consecutive monthly drop and brings the unemployment rate to 9.1%.	Six South African blacks sentenced to be hanged are given a one-month reprieve by a Pretoria Supreme Court judge, 15 hours before their scheduled execution. The five men and one woman, known as the "Sharpeville Six," were convicted of involvement in the lynch-mob killing of a black councillor in the township of Sharpeville in September 1984.		Japan's gross national product grew 4.2% (adjusted for inflation) during calendar 1987, up from 2.4% the previous year, the Economic Planning Agency reports.
March 18		Soviet leader Mikhail S. Gorbachev ends a four-day visit to Yugoslavia. Yugoslavia was ousted from the Soviet bloc in 1948 during a bitter dispute between Yugoslav leader Josip Broz Tito and Soviet leader Joseph Stalin. Since that time, Belgrade has pursued a policy of nonalignment. . . . Gross domestic product growth during 1987 in Britain was the highest since 1973, according to data from the Central Statistical Office. Inflation-adjusted growth of 4.4%, an average of three separate gross domestic product measures, is the strongest showing since a 7.3% gain 14 years earlier.		Panama slides deeper into crisis in this week as street demonstrations spread to government workers demanding to be paid by the government, and the Panama Defense Forces put down a coup attempt apparently aimed at ousting the military leader, Gen. Manuel Antonio Noriega.	The Australian government's Bureau of Mineral Resources announces that it has lowered its estimates of future crude oil yields. The bureau's median estimate of yields for the year 2000 from oil fields currently undiscovered was reduced to 81,000 barrels per day from a 1986 estimate of 208,000 barrels per day. The median estimate is judged by the bureau to have a 50% chance of being accurate.
March 19		Two British soldiers are assaulted by a mob at an Irish Republican Army funeral in West Belfast and then taken away and shot dead. The two men, armed but not in uniform, met their deaths after apparently blundering into the funeral procession.	The radio of the Eritrean People's Liberation Front (EPLF) reports that a major rebel offensive begun March 17 has destroyed three divisions of the Ethiopian Army. The guerrillas advanced from their trenches near the town of Nakfa and captured the strategic garrison town of Afabet, which is about 60 miles north of Asmara, the provincial capital of Eritrea. Afabet served as the army's main storage depot in northern Eritrea for the past decade.		In Colombia, police report that the pro-Cuban National Liberation Army (ELN) has released a Canadian engineer, Richard Paulson, who was kidnapped in 1987. Paulson worked for Occidental Petroleum Corp. The ELN demanded a multimillion-dollar ransom for Paulson, but it is not immediately known if any money was paid for his release.

A	B	C	D	E
Includes developments that affect more than one world region, international organizations and important meetings of major world leaders.	Includes all domestic and regional developments in Europe, including the Soviet Union, Turkey, Cyprus and Malta.	Includes all domestic and regional developments in Africa and the Middle East, including Iraq and Iran and excluding Cyprus, Turkey and Afghanistan.	Includes all domestic and regional developments in Latin America, the Caribbean and Canada.	Includes all domestic and regional developments in Asia and Pacific nations, extending from Afghanistan through all the Pacific Islands, except Hawaii.

U.S. Politics & Social Issues	U.S. Foreign Policy & Defense	U.S. Economy & Environment	Science, Technology & Nature	Culture, Leisure & Life Style	
Former National Security Council staff member Lt. Col. Oliver L. North, former national security adviser Rear Adm. John M. Poindexter, retired Air Force Major Gen. Richard V. Secord and Iranian-American businessman Albert Hakim are indicted by a federal grand jury in Washington, D.C., on charges of conspiring to defraud the U.S. government by secretly providing funds and supplies to the Contra rebels fighting the government of Nicaragua. . . . Pres. Reagan vetoes legislation designed to restore civil-rights protections invalidated by the Supreme Court's 1984 ruling in *Grove City College* v. *Bell*. The legislation was approved by the Senate in January and by the House of Representatives earlier in March. Both houses of Congress gave the bill enough support to override a presidential veto. . . . A Taiwanese gang member, Tung Kuei-sen, is convicted by a Redwood City, Calif., jury of first-degree murder for the 1984 killing in the United States of Henry Liu, an author of books and articles critical of the government of Taiwan. Tung claims that the Taiwanese government ordered the killing.	Charging that Nicaragua has invaded Honduras, Pres. Reagan orders 3,200 U.S. troops sent to Honduras in a show of support for the Honduran government of Pres. Jose Azcona Hoyo.	The Federal Reserve Board reports that its industrial production index rose 0.2% in February. . . . Housing starts surged 8.9% in February, the Commerce Dept. reports, to an adjusted annual rate of 1.494 million units.		New York City's Metropolitan Opera commissions minimalist composer Philip Glass to create a full-length work for the 1992 celebration marking the 500th anniversary of Christopher Columbus's discovery of America. The work, entitled *The Voyage*, will premiere in October 1992. . . . *Variety*'s top-grossing films for the week are: *Masquerade, Moonstruck, Frantic, Good Morning, Vietnam* and *Vice Versa*.	March 16
		The deficit on merchandise trade grew to $12.44 bil. in January, the Commerce Dept. reports. . . . Apple Computer Inc. files a copyright-infringement suit against industry rivals Microsoft Corp. and Hewlett-Packard Co. The suit accuses the two companies of copying elements of Apple's Macintosh software programs.		Susan Butcher wins her third consecutive Iditarod Trail dogsled race, the 1,150-mile Alaskan race from Anchorage to Nome.	March 17
		The Dow Jones industrial average closes at 2087.37, its highest level since the Oct. 19, 1987, stock market collapse. . . . The Federal Home Loan Bank Board announces that the nation's savings and loan associations lost a record $6.8 bil. in 1987. The loss, which follows a net profit of $132 mil. for the industry in 1986, is 50% greater than the previous $4.6 bil. record loss in 1981. . . . The Federal Home Loan Bank Board (FHLBB) announces that it will guarantee all depositors and general creditors of the American Savings & Loan Assoc. The FHLBB move follows the disclosure by Financial Corp. of America that American Savings, its savings and loan unit, had a negative net worth of $106 mil. at the end of 1987.		The Japanese Yomiuri Giants down the Hanshin Tigers, 9-4, in the inaugural baseball game at the Tokyo Dome, Japan's first domed stadium. Nicknamed the Big Egg, the dome cost $280 mil. to build and is modeled after Minneapolis's Metrodome. . . . *Stand and Deliver*, a film based on the true story of an inspirational math teacher at an East Los Angeles high school, is released in New York. Directed by Ramon Menendez and written by Menendez and Tom Musca, the film stars Edward James Olmos and Lou Diamond Phillips.	March 18
In Democratic caucuses in Kansas, Gov. Michael S. Dukakis (Mass.) wins 39% of local delegates selected, followed by the Rev. Jesse Jackson's 27%. National delegates will be selected at district conventions April 23. . . . In South Dakota, the Democratic Party allots nine delegates to Rep. Richard A. Gephardt (Mo.) and six to Gov. Michael S. Dukakis (Mass.) on the basis of the results of a nonbinding primary held February 23. Nine more delegates will be decided later.				*Billboard*'s best-selling albums for the week are: *Dirty Dancing* (soundtrack); *Faith*, George Michael; *Kick*, INXS; *Bad*, Michael Jackson; and *Tiffany*, Tiffany.	March 19

F	G	H	I	J
Includes elections, federal-state relations, civil rights and liberties, crime, the judiciary, education, health care, poverty, urban affairs and population.	Includes formation and debate of U.S. foreign and defense policies, veterans' affairs and defense spending. (Relations with specific foreign countries are usually found under the region concerned.)	Includes business, labor, agriculture, taxation, transportation, consumer affairs, monetary and fiscal policy, natural resources, and pollution.	Includes worldwide scientific, medical and technological developments, natural phenomena, U.S. weather, natural disasters, and accidents.	Includes the arts, religion, scholarship, communications media, sports, entertainments, fashions, fads and social life.

	World Affairs	Europe	Africa & the Middle East	The Americas	Asia & the Pacific
March 20				In El Salvador, the Christian Democratic Party of Pres. Jose Napoleon Duarte suffers a serious defeat in elections for the National Assembly and municipal offices. The rightist Nationalist Republican Alliance (ARENA) wins more than 80% of the municipal elections, and it could replace the Christian Democrats as the majority party in the 60-seat National Assembly.	The Indian military has secretly stockpiled a number of low-yield atomic bombs that could be delivered by combat aircraft, according to unidentified U.S. intelligence sources quoted in a United Press International report.... As many as 28 people have been killed in the past week during riots in Burma, according to unconfirmed accounts in Western news reports. The accounts say that government troops clashed with student protesters at several university campuses in Rangoon. About 50 students are reported injured and hundreds arrested.
March 21			Reports that Iraq killed hundreds and possibly thousands of its own Kurdish citizens March 16, when it bombed a northeastern Iraqi border town with chemical weapons after it was captured by Iranian forces, are confirmed today when Iran brings Western reporters to the town of Halabja, where they photographed scores of corpses sprawled in the streets.... Kenya holds its first parliamentary elections since 1983. Some of those who lose their seats raise charges of ballot-rigging and bribery. Kenya is a one-party state, and parliament is widely viewed as a rubber stamp for Pres. Daniel arap Moi, who wields uncontested power.	The board of the International Monetary Fund endorses an economic austerity plan adopted by the Argentine government, paving the way for the disbursement of more than $1 bil. in government and bank loans for the country.	
March 22				Brazil's Constituent Assembly, which is drafting a new national constitution, approves an amendment upholding the presidential system of government. The vote is considered a major political victory for incumbent Pres. Jose Sarney, whose opponents had pushed for adoption of a parliamentary system under which executive power would have been divided between the president and a premier.	A Tokyo district court judge finds Toshiba Machine Co. guilty of illegally selling sophisticated technology to the Soviet Union. The company is fined $15,750 and two former Toshiba executives are given suspended prison terms.... The Chinese government for the first time begins accepting bids from foreigners for the purchase of long-term leases of land-use rights in Shanghai. Previously, the communist government had not allowed foreigners to control any land in China.

A	B	C	D	E
Includes developments that affect more than one world region, international organizations and important meetings of major world leaders.	Includes all domestic and regional developments in Europe, including the Soviet Union, Turkey, Cyprus and Malta.	Includes all domestic and regional developments in Africa and the Middle East, including Iraq and Iran and excluding Cyprus, Turkey and Afghanistan.	Includes all domestic and regional developments in Latin America, the Caribbean and Canada.	Includes all domestic and regional developments in Asia and Pacific nations, extending from Afghanistan through all the Pacific Islands, except Hawaii.

U.S. Politics & Social Issues	U.S. Foreign Policy & Defense	U.S. Economy & Environment	Science, Technology & Nature	Culture, Leisure & Life Style	
The Rev. Jesse Jackson wins the nonbinding Democratic presidential primary in Puerto Rico with about 32% of the vote; the outcome has no bearing on the allocation of the island's 56 Democratic delegates. V.P George Bush wins 98% of the Republican vote, picking up all 14 convention delegates.				Gil (born Ian Ernest Gilmore) Evans, 75, Canadian-born U.S. composer, arranger, and bandleader whose collaboration with trumpeter Miles Davis gave rise to some of the most influential jazz albums of the 1950s and 1960s, dies of peritonitis in Cuernavaca, Mexico, where he had gone to recover from prostate surgery. Evans is widely regarded as the most important post-World War II jazz composer and orchestrator, after Duke Ellington. In later years, Evans embraced rock with as much vigor as he had once embraced bebop.... The British Academy of Film and Television Arts names the French film *Jean de Florette* best picture; Sean Connery, best actor for *The Name of the Rose*; and Anne Bancroft, best actress for *84 Charing Cross Road*. ... David Henry Hwang's *M. Butterfly* opens on Broadway; the play is based on the true story of a French foreign service officer convicted of espionage after a 20-year affair he had with a Beijing Opera diva whom he seemingly did not realize was actually a man. Directed by John Dexter, the play stars John Lithgow and B.D. Wong.	March 20
			The Senate clears the way for implementation of a U.S.-Japanese nuclear cooperation agreement signed by the United States and Japan in 1987. Under the 30-year agreement, scheduled to take effect April 24, Japan will receive the right to reprocess spent nuclear fuel and to recover plutonium from the fuel without a case-by-case approval from the United States, which provides the fuel for Japan's nuclear plants.... U.S. scientists have secretly achieved nuclear fusion in tiny hydrogen fuel pellets, the *New York Times* reports. The success, a goal whose practical pursuit has already cost some $2 bil., has been kept secret since its accomplishment about two years before at the government's nuclear test site in Nevada, the *Times* says.... Patrick (Christopher) Steptoe, 74, British obstetrician and gynecologist who with Cambridge Univ. physiologist Robert Edwards pioneered the first *in vitro* ("test-tube") fertilization procedure, dies of cancer in Canterbury, England. Steptoe delivered the world's first test-tube baby by cesarean section, at Oldham, England, in 1978.... China's ministry of public health announces that a total of 292,301 cases of hepatitis-A have been reported in Shanghai since January. Eleven people are said to have died from the disease.	Undisputed heavyweight champion Mike Tyson knocks out Tony Tubbs in the second round of a bout in Tokyo to retain his title.	March 21
Congress, as expected, overrides Pres. Reagan's veto of legislation designed to restore civil rights protections invalidated by the Supreme Court's 1984 ruling in *Grove City College* v. *Bell*. ... Gov. Michael S. Dukakis (Mass.) wins the Democrats Abroad primary, held in London, England. Dukakis receives 42% of the vote to the Rev. Jesse Jackson's 15%, but all but one of the nine delegates remain uncommitted.	The Justice Dept. files a lawsuit aimed at forcing closure of the Palestine Liberation Org.'s office in New York City. The suit is brought in federal district court in the city.	Four of the nation's largest insurers—Hartford Fire Insurance Co., Allstate Insurance Co., Aetna Life & Casualty Co., and Cigna—and Lloyd's of London Insurance Service Office Inc. are accused by seven states of violating antitrust laws in a conspiracy to manipulate the availability and cost of commercial liability coverage.... The Justice Dept. files suit against the St. Louis metropolitan sewer district to prohibit it from dumping raw and improperly treated wastes into the Mississippi River.		Writer-director Jean-Claude Lauzon's film *Un Zoo la Nuit* (Night Zoo) dominates Canada's Genie Awards, winning best picture and 12 other awards, including best director and best screenplay, Lauzon, and best actor, Roger Le Bel. Sheila McCarthy is voted best actress for *I've Heard the Mermaids Singing*.	March 22

F	G	H	I	J
Includes elections, federal-state relations, civil rights and liberties, crime, the judiciary, education, health care, poverty, urban affairs and population.	Includes formation and debate of U.S. foreign and defense policies, veterans' affairs and defense spending. (Relations with specific foreign countries are usually found under the region concerned.)	Includes business, labor, agriculture, taxation, transportation, consumer affairs, monetary and fiscal policy, natural resources, and pollution.	Includes worldwide scientific, medical and technological developments, natural phenomena, U.S. weather, natural disasters, and accidents.	Includes the arts, religion, scholarship, communications media, sports, entertainments, fashions, fads and social life.

	World Affairs	Europe	Africa & the Middle East	The Americas	Asia & the Pacific
March 23		Soviet leader Mikhail S. Gorbachev calls for a revival of the nation's cooperative farms. The general secretary's comments are made in Moscow to a national congress of collective farmers. It is the first such congress to be held since 1969.		The Sandinista government of Nicaragua and the leaders of the Contra rebel forces sign a cease-fire pact in an attempt to end a civil war that has resulted in some 25,000 deaths since 1981. The 60-day truce is signed in the Nicaraguan town of Sapoa near Nicaragua's southern border with Costa Rica after three days of face-to-face talks between the leftist government and Contra leaders.	India's parliament passes a constitutional amendment giving the government of P.M. Rajiv Gandhi the power to suspend some civil liberties in the strife-torn northern state of Punjab. The legislation also extends central government rule over the state for three years. ... The Chinese government revokes the passport of a prominent Chinese graduate student in the United States and dismisses him from his academic post because of his membership in a dissident political group, the Chinese Embassy in Washington confirms. The student, Hu Ping, is chairman of the Chinese Alliance for Democracy, a New York-based organization that promotes democratic reform in China. He is also editor of *China Spring*, a magazine published by the alliance.
March 24		Joe Bossano of the Gibraltar Socialist Labour Party wins a landslide election as Gibraltar's new chief minister. His victory ends 40 years of rule by the center-right Assoc. for the Advancement of Civil Rights (AACR) in the British colony on the southern tip of Spain.	Mordechai Vanunu, the former nuclear technician who revealed details of Israel's secret atomic weapons program to the *Sunday Times* of London, is convicted of treason and espionage in a Jerusalem court.		
March 25	A panel of the General Agreement on Tariffs and Trade (GATT) rules that Japanese monitoring of the price of microchip exports to countries other than the United States constitutes a violation of GATT regulations. The ruling, which requires the approval of the full GATT council, upholds a complaint filed by the European Community charging that provisions of a 1986 U.S.-Japanese semiconductor trade pact that allow Japan to monitor the prices of microchips exported to third countries amount to unfair price-fixing.	The first full meeting of the Anglo-Irish conference in five months is held in London. Representatives from both sides emerge from the six-hour meeting with optimistic pronouncements on the future of Anglo-Irish relations. ... According to government figures released today, Britain posted another large balance of payments deficit in February. ... In Czechoslovakia, an unauthorized demonstration by about 2,000 Roman Catholics in Bratislava, the capital of the predominantly Catholic state of Slovakia, is broken up by police.			The National People's Congress, China's nominal parliament, holds its annual legislative session in Beijing's Great Hall of the People. The 20-day session is attended by 2,978 delegates. ... South Korea's gross national product grew 12% in real terms during 1987, to $118.6 bil., the Bank of Korea announces.
March 26		A scheduled nationalist mass demonstration in Yerevan, the capital of Soviet Armenia, is thwarted by the heavy presence of soldiers and KGB (secret police) agents.			

A	B	C	D	E
Includes developments that affect more than one world region, international organizations and important meetings of major world leaders.	Includes all domestic and regional developments in Europe, including the Soviet Union, Turkey, Cyprus and Malta.	Includes all domestic and regional developments in Africa and the Middle East, including Iraq and Iran and excluding Cyprus, Turkey and Afghanistan.	Includes all domestic and regional developments in Latin America, the Caribbean and Canada.	Includes all domestic and regional developments in Asia and Pacific nations, extending from Afghanistan through all the Pacific Islands, except Hawaii.

U.S. Politics & Social Issues	U.S. Foreign Policy & Defense	U.S. Economy & Environment	Science, Technology & Nature	Culture, Leisure & Life Style	
	The Reagan administration announces that by March 28 it will begin pulling out the more than 3,000 troops sent to Honduras the previous week. That announcement is in line with a March 18 assertion by Defense Sec. Frank Carlucci that the troops would remain in Honduras only 10 days. . . . Pres. Reagan announces that he will visit Moscow May 29-June 2 for his next summit with Soviet leader Mikhail S. Gorbachev. The announcement is made in the White House Rose Garden with Soviet Foreign Min. Eduard A. Shevardnadze at the president's side.	The government's consumer price index rose 0.2% in February, the Labor Dept. reports. . . . Honda of America Manufacturing Inc. agrees to pay $6 mil. in settlement of federal job-bias charges against blacks and women. . . . The House approves a $1.2 trillion budget plan for fiscal 1989. The plan, a nonbinding resolution outlining congressional spending decisions, is based on the budget agreement worked out with the White House in 1987 after the October stock-market crash. . . . Northwest Airlines announces it is imposing a no-smoking rule on its domestic routes and nearby international routes. The policy will go into effect on April 23, the same day a federal regulation takes effect banning smoking on domestic flights lasting two hours or less. . . . After-tax profits of U.S. corporations rose a seasonally adjusted 1.6% in the fourth quarter of 1987, the Commerce Dept. reports. Profits increased by a revised 5.5% in the third quarter. For all of 1987, profits rose 8.4%.			March 23
The four criminal defendants in the Iran-Contra arms scandal, Lt. Col. Oliver L. North, Rear Adm. John M. Poindexter, Maj. Gen. Richard V. Secord (ret.) and Albert Hakim, are arraigned in U.S. District Court in Washington, D.C., before Judge Gerhard A. Gesell. All four plead not guilty. The next hearing in the case is set for April 12.	A New York Times/CBS News poll shows that 52% of Americans surveyed believe the United States should not have sent troops to Honduras March 16 after reports of a Nicaraguan incursion; 35% agree with the decision to send them.	Consumer spending rose 0.7% in February, according to the Commerce Dept., to a seasonally adjusted annual rate of $3.067 trillion. Personal income increased 0.9%. . . . E.I. Du Pont de Nemours & Co. announces plans to phase out production of chlorofluorocarbons (CFCs) because of evidence linking them to the depletion of the protective ozone layer in the stratosphere. . . . Ivan F. Boesky begins to serve a three-year prison term for securities fraud, nearly six years after he began to trade illegally on inside stock information.		Michela Figini of Switzerland clinches skiing's World Cup overall women's title.	March 24
Pres. Reagan says he does not believe that former White House aide Lt. Col. Oliver L. North and former national security adviser Rear Adm. John M. Poindexter are guilty of any criminal offense in the Iran-Contra arms scandal. . . . Robert E. Chambers Jr. pleads guilty to first-degree manslaughter in the death of Jennifer Levin during a sexual encounter in New York City's Central Park, behind the Metropolitan Museum of Art.				*Publishers Weekly*'s hardback fiction best-sellers for the week are: *The Icarus Agenda*, Robert Ludlum; *The Bonfire of the Vanities*, Tom Wolfe; *Hot Money*, Dick Francis; *Presumed Innocent*, Scott Turow; and *Treasure*, Clive Cussler. . . . Brian Boitano of the United States wins the men's title at the World Figure Skating Championships in Budapest, Hungary. . . . Robert (born Abdullah Jaffa Bey Khan) Joffrey, 57, choreographer and founder and artistic director of the Joffrey Ballet, the first major American ballet company to commission modern-dance choreographers, dies in New York of liver, renal and respiratory failure. Among the best known of his 15 ballets are *Pas de Deesses* (1954) and *Astarte* (1967), a mixed-media rock ballet that put the company on the cover of *Time* magazine.	March 25
The Rev. Jesse Jackson scores an overwhelming victory in Michigan's Democratic presidential caucuses, shattering an effort by Massachusetts Gov. Michael S. Dukakis to create a sense of unstoppable momentum for his own nomination. The victory brings Jackson neck and neck with Dukakis in the national delegate count, and forces Democratic officials to grapple with the possibility that Jackson could go into the Democratic convention with the largest number of delegates and a moral claim to the nomination.				Kenya's John Ngugi wins the men's cross-country world championship in Auckland, New Zealand. Ingrid Kristiansen of Norway takes the women's title. . . . Katarina Witt of East Germany March 26 wins her fourth women's title at the World Figure Skating Championships in Budapest. . . . In skiing, Pirmin Zurbriggen of Switzerland wins the World Cup overall men's title in the season's last slalom race in Saalbach, Austria.	March 26

F	G	H	I	J
Includes elections, federal-state relations, civil rights and liberties, crime, the judiciary, education, health care, poverty, urban affairs and population.	Includes formation and debate of U.S. foreign and defense policies, veterans' affairs and defense spending. (Relations with specific foreign countries are usually found under the region concerned.)	Includes business, labor, agriculture, taxation, transportation, consumer affairs, monetary and fiscal policy, natural resources, and pollution.	Includes worldwide scientific, medical and technological developments, natural phenomena, U.S. weather, natural disasters, and accidents.	Includes the arts, religion, scholarship, communications media, sports, entertainments, fashions, fads and social life.

	World Affairs	Europe	Africa & the Middle East	The Americas	Asia & the Pacific
March 27		Protest strikes have virtually paralyzed Nagorno-Karabakh, a predominantly Armenian autonomous region in the Soviet republic of Azerbaijan, according to the Soviet press. The press does not say when the strikes began, but does indicate that they started when railroad workers refused to unload freight in Stepanakert, the region's capital.			The *Star* and the *Sunday Star*, two English-language newspapers in Malaysia, resume publication after being shut down for five months by the Malaysian government. Two other papers in the country remain closed.
March 28			The Israeli army announces that it is sealing off the entire West Bank and Gaza Strip for three days in order to smother planned Palestinian protests. It is the first time such a step has been taken since Israel occupied the territories in 1967. The move shows the government's mounting frustration with its inability to stop the Arab uprising, now almost four months old.	Nicaraguan government and Contra negotiators resume two days of talks that the previous week led to a 60-day cease-fire agreement. The negotiators agree that Contra fighters will assemble in five cease-fire zones around the country and remain in the zones until May, during which time the two sides will hold political talks.... The 3,200 U.S. soldiers sent to Honduras March 16, as a show of force after reports of a Nicaraguan incursion, begin returning to the United States.... A band of about 20 white settlers armed with rifles and shotguns ambushes a group of 120 unarmed Tikuna Indians in Brazil's northwest state of Amazonas, near the Colombian border, killing at least four, injuring 25, and leaving 10 missing. The attack takes place just before authorities are due to begin evicting white squatters from Indian lands.	
March 29					
March 30			Three Iranian gunboats fire on a Kuwaiti military outpost on the island of Bubiyan in the northern Persian Gulf. Kuwait, which supports Iraq in its war with Iran, says two of its men were killed or wounded and that its forces fired back.		

A	B	C	D	E
Includes developments that affect more than one world region, international organizations and important meetings of major world leaders.	Includes all domestic and regional developments in Europe, including the Soviet Union, Turkey, Cyprus and Malta.	Includes all domestic and regional developments in Africa and the Middle East, including Iraq and Iran and excluding Cyprus, Turkey and Afghanistan.	Includes all domestic and regional developments in Latin America, the Caribbean and Canada.	Includes all domestic and regional developments in Asia and Pacific nations, extending from Afghanistan through all the Pacific Islands, except Hawaii.

U.S. Politics & Social Issues	U.S. Foreign Policy & Defense	U.S. Economy & Environment	Science, Technology & Nature	Culture, Leisure & Life Style	
	The Senate votes, 93-5, to ratify the U.S.-Soviet treaty on eliminating intermediate-range nuclear forces (INF). A two-thirds majority was needed for ratification. The INF pact is the first arms-control agreement since the 1972 Strategic Arms Limitation Treaty (SALT I) to receive Senate approval.			August Wilson's *Joe Turner's Come and Gone*, a play about black residents of a Pittsburgh boardinghouse in 1911 reflecting on their passage from the South to the North, opens on Broadway. Directed by Lloyd Richards, the play stars Mel Winkler, L. Scott Caldwell, Ed Hall, and Raynor Scheine.	**March 27**
Rep. Richard A. Gephardt (D, Mo.) folds up his presidential campaign the day before the deadline for registering as a candidate for reelection to Congress.... Special prosecutor Lawrence E. Walsh and the Israeli government announce that they have reached an agreement under which Israel will cooperate with Walsh's Iran-Contra investigation.... The president of Dartmouth College, James O. Freedman, accuses the *Dartmouth Review*, a politically conservative off-campus newspaper, of "poisoning the intellectual environment of our campus." Earlier in March, four students affiliated with the paper were punished by Dartmouth for harassing a black professor.				The Ritz Paris Hemingway Award, presented annually to the best novel published in English, is not awarded in 1988 because none of the three books nominated—Toni Morrison's *Beloved*, Nadine Gordimer's *A Sport of Nature*, and Michael Ondaatje's *In the Skin of a Lion*—received the necessary six votes out of 10 to qualify for the prize.	**March 28**
Gov. Michael S. Dukakis wins in the Connecticut primary, completing a sweep of the New England states. Vice Pres. George Bush comes closer to wrapping up the Republican nomination with an overwhelming win in Connecticut; Bush's father had represented the state in Congress as a senator.... Sen. Robert J. Dole (Kans.) formally drops out of the race for the Republican presidential nomination.... Two top Justice Dept. officials abruptly quit their posts in protest of Attorney Gen. Edwin Meese III's continuing legal entanglements.	Japanese and U.S. negotiators reach an agreement in Washington, D.C., that will open Japanese public works projects to U.S. construction firms. The accord resolves a two-year-old trade dispute that has become a major point of contention between Tokyo and Washington.	The government's index of leading economic indicators climbs 0.9% in February, the Commerce Dept. reports.... A federal appeals court in Washington, D.C., rejects the Reagan administration's contention that former presidents have a broad right to prevent the release of the records of their presidencies. The administration made its contention in support of former Pres. Richard M. Nixon, who has carried on a 14-year legal effort to block the National Archives' release of papers and White House tape recordings from his administration. ... A federal appeals court panel for the District of Columbia strikes down as unconstitutional a law barring publisher Rupert Murdoch from ownership of both newspapers and television stations in New York and Boston.... The Senate shelves a bill requiring warnings to workers exposed to disease-causing hazards in the workplace. The measure, one of organized labor's priority bills, fails to surmount a filibuster by conservative Republicans. The House had passed similar legislation in 1987.		The national leadership of the Assemblies of God bars the Rev. Jimmy Swaggart from preaching from the pulpit or on his television show for at least a year while he is rehabilitated from "moral failure." ... Ted Kluszewski, 63, home-run hitting first baseman who led the National League in home runs in 1954 with 49, dies in Cincinnati after suffering a heart attack. Over 15 seasons, 11 of them with the Cincinnati Reds, he batted .298 and hit 279 home runs.	**March 29**
As of today, the Federal Election Comm. has distributed $48.1 mil. in matching funds to presidential candidates. The payments, funded by a voluntary income-tax checkoff, match every contribution of $250 or less raised by a qualifying candidate from individuals. Total matching funds of eligible Republican candidates are the Rev. Pat Robertson, $8.5 mil.; Vice Pres. George Bush, $7.4 mil.; and Sen. Robert J. Dole (Kans.), $7.1 mil. Eligible Democrats are Gov. Michael S. Dukakis (Mass.), $5.9 mil.; Sen. Paul Simon (Ill.), $2.8 mil.; Sen. Albert A. Gore Jr. (Tenn.), $2.7 mil.; Rep. Richard A. Gephardt (Mo.), $2.6 mil.; the Rev. Jesse Jackson, $1.5 mil.	The Senate Foreign Relations Committee votes, 17-2, to approve the U.S.-Soviet treaty on intermediate-range nuclear forces. Republican Senators Jesse A. Helms (N.C.) and Larry Pressler (S.Dak.) vote against the pact and vow to take their fight to the Senate floor. ... William L. Ball III is sworn in as the secretary of the Navy succeeding James H. Webb Jr. The Senate confirmed Ball's nomination on a unanimous vote March 23.	The Senate approves legislation that will lift many of the barriers that have blocked commercial banks from underwriting securities. The bill, approved 94-2, will allow banks to own and operate securities firms and will set the stage for securities firms to enter the banking business. The legislation requires approval by the House of Representatives, where passage of a bill as broad as the Senate measure is uncertain.... Prices received by farmers for their raw agricultural products were unchanged in March, the Agriculture Dept. reports.		The Univ. of Connecticut wins basketball's National Invitation Tournament with a 72-67 triumph over Ohio State. Connecticut guard Phil Gamble earns most valuable player honors.... *Beetlejuice*, a comedy directed by Tim Burton, is released in New York. With a screenplay by Michael McDowell and Warren Skaaren, based on a story by McDowell and Larry Wilson, the film stars Adam Baldwin, Geena Davis, and Michael Keaton.	**March 30**
F	**G**	**H**	**I**	**J**	
Includes elections, federal-state relations, civil rights and liberties, crime, the judiciary, education, health care, poverty, urban affairs and population.	*Includes formation and debate of U.S. foreign and defense policies, veterans' affairs and defense spending. (Relations with specific foreign countries are usually found under the region concerned.)*	*Includes business, labor, agriculture, taxation, transportation, consumer affairs, monetary and fiscal policy, natural resources, and pollution.*	*Includes worldwide scientific, medical and technological developments, natural phenomena, U.S. weather, natural disasters, and accidents.*	*Includes the arts, religion, scholarship, communications media, sports, entertainments, fashions, fads and social life.*	

	World Affairs	Europe	Africa & the Middle East	The Americas	Asia & the Pacific
March 31				The People's Democratic Movement wins a landslide victory in the general election in the British colony of Turks and Caicos Islands. An interim advisory council has ruled the Caribbean island state since July 1986.	
April 1					The Japanese government begins for the first time in 25 years to tax the interest on personal savings. Previously, under a system known as *maruyu*, Japanese savers were allowed to keep up to $72,000 in tax-free bank or postal accounts.
April 2				In El Salvador, the central electoral council issues official results for the March 20 legislative elections showing that the Nationalist Republican Alliance (ARENA) did not win an absolute majority in the Legislative Assembly, as preliminary results showed. . . . Canada's chartered banks raise their prime rate to 10.25%, an increase of one-half a percentage point. The prime rate is the interest charged by the banks on loans to their most credit-worthy customers.	
April 3			Sec. of State George P. Shultz begins six days of shuttle diplomacy between Middle Eastern capitals in his second such visit to the region in five weeks. At the end, he appears to have little to show for his effort to convince Israel and its Arab neighbors to join the peace plan he has proposed.		

A	B	C	D	E
Includes developments that affect more than one world region, international organizations and important meetings of major world leaders.	Includes all domestic and regional developments in Europe, including the Soviet Union, Turkey, Cyprus and Malta.	Includes all domestic and regional developments in Africa and the Middle East, including Iraq and Iran and excluding Cyprus, Turkey and Afghanistan.	Includes all domestic and regional developments in Latin America, the Caribbean and Canada.	Includes all domestic and regional developments in Asia and Pacific nations, extending from Afghanistan through all the Pacific Islands, except Hawaii.

U.S. Politics & Social Issues	U.S. Foreign Policy & Defense	U.S. Economy & Environment	Science, Technology & Nature	Culture, Leisure & Life Style	
The Faculty Senate at Stanford Univ. votes to replace a Western culture course required of freshmen with a similar course that will also examine non-Western cultures and issues regarding race, ethnicity, class and gender. The current yearlong "Western Civilization" course will be replaced during the fall 1989 semester with the new course called "Cultures, Ideas and Values."	The House of Representatives yesterday and the Senate today approve $47.9 mil. in humanitarian aid for the Nicaraguan Contras and children injured in the war. The votes come a week after the Contras and the Nicaraguan government signed a 60-day cease-fire agreement.	The Teamsters union reaches tentative agreement with the nation's largest trucking companies on a new three-year labor contract. The agreement, covering about 200,000 drivers and warehouse workers, reportedly calls for pay increases totaling about 8% over the life of the contract.		Columbia Univ. presents the 72nd Pulitzer Prizes. The award for fiction goes to Toni Morrison's *Beloved*; drama, Alfred Uhry's *Driving Miss Daisy*; history, Robert V. Bruce's *The Launching of Modern American Science, 1846-1876*; biography, David Herbert Donald's *Look Homeward: A Life of Thomas Wolfe*; general nonfiction, Richard Rhodes's *The Making of the Atomic Bomb*; poetry, William Meredith's *Partial Accounts: New and Selected Poems*; music, William Bolcom's *12 New Etudes for Piano* public service, the *Charlotte Observer* for its coverage of the scandal surrounding the ministry of Jim and Tammy Bakker.	March 31
James C. McKay, the independent prosecutor investigating Attorney Gen. Edwin Meese III, announces that, "based on the evidence developed to date," he does not plan to seek an indictment of the attorney general. . . . Ending two years as a fugitive, a reputed major Mexican drug trafficker, Jose Contreras Subias, is arrested in the United States. Contreras escaped in 1985 from a Mexican prison, where he was being held in connection with the murder of a federal police officer. He is also a suspect in the 1985 murder in Mexico of Drug Enforcement Admin. agent Enrique Camarena Salazar and his pilot.		The nation's unemployment rate in March fell to 5.5%, the Labor Dept. reports. . . . Underwriters continue to recover from the October 1987 stock market collapse as the amount of new corporate debt and equity offerings rose to $67.9 bil. in the first quarter. . . . On Wall Street, Merrill Lynch & Co. is reported to have surpassed Salomon Brothers as the leading U.S. underwriter in the first quarter.		Douglas Edwards, 70, the first nightly television news anchorman in the United States, ends his 46-year career as a broadcast journalist when he signs off after an edition of *CBS Newsbreak* at noon.	April 1
The Rev. Jesse Jackson wins the Democratic presidential caucus in the U.S. Virgin Islands with 634 votes to 37 for Gov. Michael S. Dukakis (Mass.), the only other candidate on the ballot.				Lake Superior State College of Michigan wins the National Collegiate Athletic Assoc. Division I ice hockey title with a 4-3 victory against St. Lawrence. Laker goalie Bruce Hoffort earns the tournament's most valuable player award.	April 2
	The *Washington Post* reports a proposal to establish a U.S.-secured headquarters in the former Panama Canal Zone for Panama's ousted Pres. Eric Arturo Delvalle. These recommendations, and others proposing military action, reportedly come from Sec. of State George Shultz and Deputy Sec. of State for Latin American Affairs Elliott Abrams. U.S. officials refuse to comment on the reports.			Louisiana Tech wins the women's National Collegiate Athletic Assoc. basketball tournament title, 56-54, over Auburn. Lady Techster Erica Westbrooks is named the tournament's most valuable player. . . . In auto racing, Alain Prost of France wins the Brazilian Formula One Grand Prix, the opening event of the Formula One season, in Rio de Janeiro.	April 3

F	G	H	I	J
Includes elections, federal-state relations, civil rights and liberties, crime, the judiciary, education, health care, poverty, urban affairs and population.	*Includes formation and debate of U.S. foreign and defense policies, veterans' affairs and defense spending. (Relations with specific foreign countries are usually found under the region concerned.)*	*Includes business, labor, agriculture, taxation, transportation, consumer affairs, monetary and fiscal policy, natural resources, and pollution.*	*Includes worldwide scientific, medical and technological developments, natural phenomena, U.S. weather, natural disasters, and accidents.*	*Includes the arts, religion, scholarship, communications media, sports, entertainments, fashions, fads and social life.*

	World Affairs	Europe	Africa & the Middle East	The Americas	Asia & the Pacific
April 4	Industrial production in the industrial countries expanded for the fifth straight year in 1987, the International Monetary Fund reports. Industrial output grew 3.6%, following a 0.9% increase in 1986.			The conflict over language rights in Canada is revived when legislation is introduced in the province of Saskatchewan aimed at restricting francophone rights. About 25,000 of Saskatchewan's 1 million residents are French-speaking.... The International Monetary Fund approves a $65 mil. standby loan for Costa Rica, even though Costa Rica has not yet agreed on a debt-rescheduling package with its commercial bank creditors. The nation has a foreign debt of $4.4 bil.	Sec. of Defense Frank C. Carlucci begins a five-day visit to India and Pakistan and announces separate agreements to provide the two countries, which are hostile rivals of one another, with advanced American military equipment.... An Indian state appeals court judge orders Union Carbide Corp. to pay $193 mil. in interim damages for victims of the 1984 gas leak at the company's chemical plant in Bhopal, India. More than 2,000 people were killed by the gas leak, the world's worst industrial disaster. ... The Japanese government charges two Tokyo-based trading companies with illegally selling sophisticated electronic measuring equipment to China. According to officials of Japan's ministry for trade and industry, the sales were in violation of regulations of the international Coordinating Committee for Multilateral Export Controls (Cocom), which bars the transfer of certain types of high-technology products to communist countries.
April 5			Arabic-speaking gunmen, presumed to be Shiite Moslem extremists, hijack a Kuwait Airways jet with 112 people aboard and divert it to Iran. The flight was en route from Bangkok, Thailand, to Kuwait.		
April 6			The disputed death of a 15-year-old Israeli girl, killed April 6 while hiking in the occupied West Bank with a group of teenage Jewish settlers, stirs a major controversy. She is initially reported to have been stoned to death by angry Arabs, but it later develops that she was apparently shot to death accidentally by an Israeli guard during a confrontation in which two Palestinians were also killed.		The Vietnamese government returns to the United States what are believed to be the remains of 27 American servicemen listed as missing in action during the Vietnam War. Another three sets of remains, reported to be those of ethnic Asians thought to be Americans killed during the war, are also turned over to U.S. authorities.
April 7			As of today, Iraq has fired 142 long-range surface-to-surface missiles at Teheran and other Iranian cities, and Iran has responded by launching 65 missiles at Iraqi urban centers, particularly Baghdad, since the missile duel began February 29. The duel was stopped briefly by a Turkish-mediated truce March 11, but Iraq resumed the strikes two days later, claiming that Teheran violated the truce by shelling civilian areas in its Kurdish offensive; Iran replied in kind on March 14.		Prices on the Tokyo stock market soar to a new record high, making it the first stock market in the world to surpass a peak reached before the October 1987 world stock market collapse. The Nikkei average closes at 26,769.22, rising above the previous 26,646.43 record set Oct. 14, 1987.... Sales of imported cars in Japan jumped 41.1% during fiscal 1987, to a record 104,340 units, the Japan Automobile Importers Assoc. announces. Import sales in 1986 totaled 73,924.

A	B	C	D	E
Includes developments that affect more than one world region, international organizations and important meetings of major world leaders.	Includes all domestic and regional developments in Europe, including the Soviet Union, Turkey, Cyprus and Malta.	Includes all domestic and regional developments in Africa and the Middle East, including Iraq and Iran and excluding Cyprus, Turkey and Afghanistan.	Includes all domestic and regional developments in Latin America, the Caribbean and Canada.	Includes all domestic and regional developments in Asia and Pacific nations, extending from Afghanistan through all the Pacific Islands, except Hawaii.

U.S. Politics & Social Issues	U.S. Foreign Policy & Defense	U.S. Economy & Environment	Science, Technology & Nature	Culture, Leisure & Life Style	
Massachusetts Gov. Michael S. Dukakis wins a narrow victory over the Rev. Jesse Jackson in the first round of Colorado's Democratic presidential caucuses. On the Republican side, Vice Pres. George Bush scores another massive win.... The Arizona Senate convicts Gov. Evan Mecham (R) on two charges of official misconduct and removes him from office. Mecham is the first governor to be impeached and removed from office in nearly 60 years. Acting Arizona Gov. Rose Mofford (D), the former secretary of state, is sworn in as governor the following day.				The Univ. of Kansas beats the Univ. of Oklahoma to win the 50th National Collegiate Athletic Assoc. basketball title, 83-79. Univ. of Kansas forward Danny Manning is voted the tournament's most valuable player.	April 4
Massachusetts Gov. Michael S. Dukakis wins a solid victory in Wisconsin's Democratic presidential primary, putting a dent in the Rev. Jesse Jackson's recently acquired claim to front-runner status. On the Republican side, Vice Pres. George Bush scores another victory, taking 84% of the vote.... U.S. students are familiar with basic computer parts but have little or no knowledge of the most important computer applications and programs, according to a report issued by the National Assessment of Educational Progress. Based on a nationwide survey conducted in 1986 of 24,000 students in grades three, seven, and 11, the report focused on three areas of computer literacy: knowledge of computer technology, understanding of computer applications, and understanding of computer programming.		The on-time arrival performance of major airlines in the United States improved in February over the previous month, the Transportation Dept. reports.... Japanese investors purchased a record $12.7 bil. of U.S. real estate during 1987, boosting their total holdings to $26.34 bil., the *Los Angeles Times* reports. The *Times* report is based on an advance copy of a study conducted by Kenneth Leventhal & Co., a Los Angeles-based accounting and consulting firm.			April 5
Former television evangelist the Rev. Pat Robertson announces that he is ending active campaigning for the Republican presidential nomination.... A New Jersey Superior Court judge grants Mary Beth Whitehead-Gould visitation rights one day a week (up to six hours) to see Melissa Stern, the two-year-old child Whitehead-Gould had borne under a surrogacy contract for William and Elizabeth Stern.... Pres. Reagan denies Japan fishing privileges in U.S. waters because of that country's continued slaughter of whales.		Curbs on computerized program trading on the New York Stock Exchange are triggered for the first time.	The World Wildlife Fund reports that Chinese authorities have arrested 203 people for illegally hunting giant pandas, which are in danger of extinction; they recovered 146 pelts.		April 6
Sen. Paul Simon (Ill.) "suspends" active campaigning for the Democratic presidential nomination but does not drop out of the race or release his delegates to other candidates. Simon currently has about 170 delegates.... A federal jury in Fort Smith, Ark., acquits 13 white supremacists of charges that they conspired to overthrow the government and kill a federal judge and a Federal Bureau of Investigation agent.					April 7

F	G	H	I	J
Includes elections, federal-state relations, civil rights and liberties, crime, the judiciary, education, health care, poverty, urban affairs and population.	Includes formation and debate of U.S. foreign and defense policies, veterans' affairs and defense spending. (Relations with specific foreign countries are usually found under the region concerned.)	Includes business, labor, agriculture, taxation, transportation, consumer affairs, monetary and fiscal policy, natural resources, and pollution.	Includes worldwide scientific, medical and technological developments, natural phenomena, U.S. weather, natural disasters, and accidents.	Includes the arts, religion, scholarship, communications media, sports, entertainments, fashions, fads and social life.

	World Affairs	Europe	Africa & the Middle East	The Americas	Asia & the Pacific
April 8			One day after about half of the hostages from the April 5 hijacking of a Kuwait Airways jet are released in Mashad, Iran, and after an unsuccessful attempt to land in Beirut, Lebanon, the plane flies to Cyprus. Kuwait continues to reject the hijackers' demand that it free 17 convicted Shiite terrorists.	Eight hundred Marines arrive in Panama for a previously scheduled three-week jungle training program, the day after a three-day airlift of an additional 1,300 troops to beef up security at American bases there. The United States emphasizes that the Marines' training program is unrelated to recent U.S. pressure to force the ouster of Panama's de facto leader, Gen. Manuel Antonio Noriega, who is the chief of the Panama Defense Forces. . . . The Honduran government declares a state of emergency in the nation's two largest towns after anti-American rioting erupts to protest the April 5 capture of Juan Ramon Matta Ballesteros, a reputed major drug trafficker who is said to be worth billions of dollars and to have ties to the Medellin cocaine cartel in Colombia. He was flown to the United States. Five people died in the riots.	Japanese investors purchased the most foreign equities in 1987, adding $16.9 bil. to their portfolios, while the British, the largest net buyers of foreign equities in 1986, sold $16.8 bil. in 1987. U.S. investors liquidated $1.5 bil. in non-U.S. equities in 1987.
April 9		Following its worst year ever, the Eurobond market shook off the effects of the October 1987 stock market collapse in the first quarter of 1988, it is reported. The volume of new issues in all currencies in the first quarter is $45 bil., only $5 bil. less than in the year-earlier quarter and over double that of the fourth quarter of 1987.	Palestine Liberation Org. Chairman Yasir Arafat meets with Soviet leader Mikhail Gorbachev in Moscow.		
April 10					The Seto Ohashi bridge complex, the longest road and rail bridge in the world to date, opens for traffic. The six-mile complex connects the main island of Honshu with the island of Shikoku.
April 11		Widespread and controversial reforms in Britain's complex social security system go into effect. The changes grew out of the 1986 Social Security Act. The reforms are described as the most far reaching since the British social security system was launched by Lord Beveridge more than 40 years ago.		El Salvador's Pres. Jose Napoleon Duarte denies amnesty to three leftists charged in the 1985 slaying of four U.S. Marines and eight civilians in San Salvador. The decision not to free the three under a new amnesty law overturns a January 26 appeals court, which ruled that amnesty applied in the case because the slaying was a political crime that had a military objective.	Japan's overall trade surplus declined during fiscal 1987 for the first time in six years, dropping about 15% to $76.02 bil. from $89.74 bil. the previous fiscal year, the finance ministry announces.

A	B	C	D	E
Includes developments that affect more than one world region, international organizations and important meetings of major world leaders.	Includes all domestic and regional developments in Europe, including the Soviet Union, Turkey, Cyprus and Malta.	Includes all domestic and regional developments in Africa and the Middle East, including Iraq and Iran and excluding Cyprus, Turkey and Afghanistan.	Includes all domestic and regional developments in Latin America, the Caribbean and Canada.	Includes all domestic and regional developments in Asia and Pacific nations, extending from Afghanistan through all the Pacific Islands, except Hawaii.

U.S. Politics & Social Issues	U.S. Foreign Policy & Defense	U.S. Economy & Environment	Science, Technology & Nature	Culture, Leisure & Life Style	
Former White House political director Lyn Nofziger, 63, is sentenced to 90 days in prison, fined $30,000, and given two years' probation for illegally lobbying the White House after his return to private life in 1982. Nofziger was convicted February 11 on three felony counts under the 1978 Ethics in Government Act. After sentencing Nofziger, U.S. District Court Judge Thomas Flannery stays execution of the sentence pending an appeal and releases Nofziger on his own recognizance.... According to Pres. Reagan's tax returns, the Reagans have an adjusted gross income of $345,359, on which they were liable for $86,638 in federal taxes. Their 1987 returns included income of $59,943 from the president's blind trust and deductions for $25,407 in charitable contributions.	Pres. Reagan invokes the Emergency Economic Powers Act of 1977 to bar U.S. companies and individuals from making any payments to the Panamanian government. Reagan declares a national emergency in order to impose the sanctions, citing "the unusual and extraordinary threat posed by the actions of Manuel Antonio Noriega and Manuel Solis Palma [who replaced Eric Arturo Delvalle as president in February] to challenge the duly constituted authorities of the government of Panama."	Outstanding consumer debt rose $5.3 bil. in February, the Federal Reserve Board reports, at an annual rate of 10.3%, to a total of $619.19 bil.		The Knights of Malta, an ancient Roman Catholic charitable order, elect their first British leader since the 13th century. Andrew Bertie, a descendant of Britain's royal Stuart family, is elected grand master of the order at a secret conclave of 36 electors at the group's villa in Rome. (The results of the election are not announced until April 11, following approval by Pope John Paul II.)... Television evangelist Jimmy Swaggart is defrocked as a minister of the Assemblies of God for refusing to accept disciplining by the church leadership. In March, the national leadership of the Pentecostal denomination ordered Swaggart to stop preaching for a year after he confessed to "moral failure" and having committed an unspecified sin.	April 8
				In horse racing, Rhyme 'N' Reason wins the Grand National Steeplechase at Aintree, England, with Brendan Powell aboard.	April 9
				Sandy Lyle of Scotland birdies the 72nd and final hole of the Masters golf tournament to earn a one-shot victory over Mark Calcavecchia.	April 10
The Dept. of Housing and Urban Development says it will need only $9.2 bil. to repair and modernize the nation's 1.3 million public housing units, less than half the amount a congressionally commissioned study estimated.				A draft report by a panel of U.S. Roman Catholic bishops calls for expanding women's role in church leadership in all areas except the priesthood. The paper, entitled "Partners in the Mystery of Redemption: A Pastoral Response to Women's Concerns," is being circulated prior to consideration at a national conference of bishops in November 1989.... The 60th annual Academy Awards are presented. *The Last Emperor* wins nine Oscars, including best picture and best director, Bernardo Bertolucci. Best actor is Michael Douglas for *Wall Street*; best actress, Cher, *Moonstruck*; best supporting actor, Sean Connery, *The Untouchables*; best supporting actress, Olympia Dukakis, *Moonstruck*; best original screenplay, John Patrick Shanley, *Moonstruck*; best foreign-language feature, *Babette's Feast* (Denmark); and best documentary, *The 10-Year Lunch: The Wit and Legend of the Algonquin Round Table.*	April 11

F	G	H	I	J
Includes elections, federal-state relations, civil rights and liberties, crime, the judiciary, education, health care, poverty, urban affairs and population.	*Includes formation and debate of U.S. foreign and defense policies, veterans' affairs and defense spending. (Relations with specific foreign countries are usually found under the region concerned.)*	*Includes business, labor, agriculture, taxation, transportation, consumer affairs, monetary and fiscal policy, natural resources, and pollution.*	*Includes worldwide scientific, medical and technological developments, natural phenomena, U.S. weather, natural disasters, and accidents.*	*Includes the arts, religion, scholarship, communications media, sports, entertainments, fashions, fads and social life.*

	World Affairs	Europe	Africa & the Middle East	The Americas	Asia & the Pacific
April 12				In El Salvador, the Nationalist Republican Alliance (ARENA) formally challenges the April 2 election results announced by the central electoral council. ARENA claims to have won 31 seats, and thus a majority, in the 60-seat assembly.... Argentina's trade surplus plunged 77% in 1987, to $490 mil. from $2.13 bil. in 1986. Exports fell 8.4% during the year, to $6.275 bil. from $6.853 bil. the previous year, while imports jumped 22.5% to $5.785 bil. from $4.723 bil.	Bangladesh's Pres. Hossein Mohammed Ershad lifts the state of emergency that was imposed on the country in November 1987 during a period of civil unrest. Opposition leaders dismiss the lifting of the ban as a superficial move and vow to continue their campaign to force Ershad from office.
April 13	The seven leading industrial nations—the United States, Japan, West Germany, France, Italy, Great Britain, and Canada—reaffirm their commitment to a stable U.S. dollar and a coordinated economic policy, promising again "to cooperate closely on exchange markets" to support that commitment.	The leader of the Christian Democratic Party, Ciriaco De Mita, is sworn in as premier of Italy's 48th government since World War II. De Mita, who formed his government after weeks of tough negotiations, will lead a coalition comprising the same five parties that have governed Italy since 1981.... Soviet leader Mikhail S. Gorbachev turns back a strong challenge from the Kremlin's number two figure, Yegor K. Ligachev, according to unconfirmed reports cited by the *New York Times*. Ligachev is the Communist Party's chief ideologist, a member of the two top party organs, the Politburo and Secretariat, and is regarded as the head of the Kremlin's conservative faction.	The odyssey of Kuwait Airways Flight 422, hijacked April 5 by Shiite Moslem terrorists, continues. After negotiations with Cypriot and Palestine Liberation Org. officials, the gunmen release 12 passengers and the refueled jet flies to Algiers (with about 32 hostages still aboard) where hopes for a quick end to the drama prove unfounded. The hijackers killed two Kuwaiti hostages, on April 9 and 11, as the plane sat on the ground in Larnaca, Cyprus.		

A	B	C	D	E
Includes developments that affect more than one world region, international organizations and important meetings of major world leaders.	Includes all domestic and regional developments in Europe, including the Soviet Union, Turkey, Cyprus and Malta.	Includes all domestic and regional developments in Africa and the Middle East, including Iraq and Iran and excluding Cyprus, Turkey and Afghanistan.	Includes all domestic and regional developments in Latin America, the Caribbean and Canada.	Includes all domestic and regional developments in Asia and Pacific nations, extending from Afghanistan through all the Pacific Islands, except Hawaii.

U.S. Politics & Social Issues	U.S. Foreign Policy & Defense	U.S. Economy & Environment	Science, Technology & Nature	Culture, Leisure & Life Style	
The Arizona Supreme Court orders cancellation of a special May 17 recall election that was to have decided the fate of Gov. Evan Mecham (R). Mecham was removed from office April 4, upon his conviction in an impeachment trial. Former Sec. of State Rose Mofford (D) became acting governor during Mecham's impeachment trial and succeeded to the governorship upon his conviction. The court's decision means that Mofford will serve out Mecham's term through 1990.... Senate Majority Leader Robert C. Byrd (D, W.Va.) announces that he will step down from the Democratic leadership post, a position he has held since 1977.... The *Washington Post* reports that the presidential campaign committee of the Rev. Pat Robertson (R), the former television evangelist, turned over 1986 fund-raising and financial records to the Internal Revenue Service (IRS) April 4. The IRS won a court order for the records as part of a long-running investigation into whether Robertson illegally channelled millions of dollars from his tax-exempt Christian Broadcasting Network into his political campaign.				Alan Paton, 85, South African author and political leader, dies in Durban, South Africa, of throat cancer. His 1948 novel *Cry, the Beloved Country* sold over 15 million copies in 20 languages and dramatized the nature of South African apartheid and the conditions of the black majority under white minority rule. He served as head of the multiracial Liberal Party until the party was outlawed in 1968.	April 12
A minor furor engulfs the White House and the Washington press corps after Larry Speakes, Pres. Reagan's press secretary for nearly six years, admits in a book that he more than once fed the press concocted quotes that he attributed to Reagan. Pres. Reagan comments for the first time today, saying he was unaware of the statements made in his name by his personal spokesman.... Puerto Rico's Gov. Rafael Hernandez Colon and Senate Pres. Miguel Hernandez Agosto endorse the presidential candidacy of Gov. Michael S. Dukakis (D, Mass.), who now has the backing of all but two of the island's delegates. The Rev. Jesse Jackson won the island's nonbinding primary in March.... The problems besieging Attorney Gen. Edwin Meese III and his stewardship of the Justice Dept. continue when a new conflict-of-interest controversy surfaces involving Meese's wife Ursula. The controversy involves a $40,000-a-year job Ursula Meese got with the Multiple Sclerosis Society after working there as an unpaid volunteer. The salary came out of a grant to the society from the Howard Bender real estate interests in Washington.					April 13

F	G	H	I	J
Includes elections, federal-state relations, civil rights and liberties, crime, the judiciary, education, health care, poverty, urban affairs and population.	Includes formation and debate of U.S. foreign and defense policies, veterans' affairs and defense spending. (Relations with specific foreign countries are usually found under the region concerned.)	Includes business, labor, agriculture, taxation, transportation, consumer affairs, monetary and fiscal policy, natural resources, and pollution.	Includes worldwide scientific, medical and technological developments, natural phenomena, U.S. weather, natural disasters, and accidents.	Includes the arts, religion, scholarship, communications media, sports, entertainments, fashions, fads and social life.

	World Affairs	Europe	Africa & the Middle East	The Americas	Asia & the Pacific
April 14			The U.S. frigate *Samuel B. Roberts* strikes an underwater mine in international waters in the central Persian Gulf; it was returning to Bahrain after having escorted a U.S.-flagged Kuwaiti oil tanker as part of the Navy's ongoing convoy operation.	Colombia's Pres. Virgilio Barco Vargas declares a state of emergency in the Uraba banana-growing region of Antioquia department following the massacre of more than 40 peasants between March 4 and April 11. The massacres occurred in a region where leftist politicians and rebels have a strong influence.	Afghanistan and Pakistan sign three UN-mediated agreements providing for the withdrawal of Soviet troops from Afghanistan, the creation of a neutral Afghan state, and the voluntary repatriation of millions of Afghan refugees. In a separate pact, the United States and the Soviet Union pledged to serve as guarantors of the agreements.
April 15	In two days of meetings the International Monetary Fund and the World Bank set several changes in their lending procedures designed to lessen the burden of debtor nations. The Contingency Financing Mechanism and Extended Fund Facility will increase the amount of cash available to developing nations and the length of time over which the loans can be repaid.	Unemployment in Britain fell in March to a seasonally adjusted level of 2.5 million, the Dept. of Employment reports. The jobless decline in March was the 20th consecutive monthly fall and brought joblessness to its lowest level since December 1981.		The Canadian dollar closes at 81.12 cents (U.S.) on international currency markets, its highest level since October 1983. The continued weakness of the U.S. dollar has led to a steady rise in the value of Canada's currency. The Canadian dollar hit 81 cents (U.S.) March 31, the first time in five years it has reached that level.	
April 16		A court in Palermo, Sicily, convicts 53 of 79 defendants in the second so-called maxi-trial of alleged members of the Sicilian Mafia. The trial was held in the same heavily fortified jailhouse courtroom as the first maxi-trial, in which 338 of 452 defendants were convicted in December 1987.	The military chief of the Palestine Liberation Org. is gunned down in his home in Tunisia. Initial evidence indicates that the assassination was carried out by Israeli commandos. The Israeli government's refusal to deny responsibility, and a barrage of leaks from official sources, virtually confirms that Israel is in fact responsible.	Nicaraguan Contra directors travel to Managua to open three days of cease-fire talks with the government. The talks, originally scheduled to begin April 6, end without much progress, but the two sides agree to further negotiations April 28-30.	
April 17		Albania and Greece sign their first postwar agreement to encourage trade across their 154-mile border. The pact, which represents another step for Albania away from its traditional isolationism, is signed in Athens.... A Soviet newspaper article reported in the West suggests the policies and purges of former leader Joseph Stalin killed as many as 50 million people. A nationwide campaign to discredit the former leader is flourishing, spurred in part by an anti-Stalin speech in November 1987 by Communist Party Gen. Sec. Mikhail S. Gorbachev.		Mexico's government reduced its budget deficit to an annual rate of 2.5%-3% of gross domestic product in the first quarter of 1988, finance officials report.	American evangelist Billy Graham gives his first sermon in China. Graham spoke for 50 minutes to an audience of more than 1,000 Chinese Christians at a church in Beijing.... The upper house of the Japanese Diet approves the national budget for fiscal 1988, which began April 1. The budget, totaling $450.4 bil., was approved by the lower house March 10. The cabinet had passed the budget measure in December 1987.

A	B	C	D	E
Includes developments that affect more than one world region, international organizations and important meetings of major world leaders.	*Includes all domestic and regional developments in Europe, including the Soviet Union, Turkey, Cyprus and Malta.*	*Includes all domestic and regional developments in Africa and the Middle East, including Iraq and Iran and excluding Cyprus, Turkey and Afghanistan.*	*Includes all domestic and regional developments in Latin America, the Caribbean and Canada.*	*Includes all domestic and regional developments in Asia and Pacific nations, extending from Afghanistan through all the Pacific Islands, except Hawaii.*

U.S. Politics & Social Issues	U.S. Foreign Policy & Defense	U.S. Economy & Environment	Science, Technology & Nature	Culture, Leisure & Life Style	
		Defying all expectations, the deficit on merchandise trade grew to $13.83 bil. in February, the Commerce Dept. reports.... The Senate adopts a $1 trillion budget plan for fiscal 1989 that differs from an agreement reached with the White House and a version approved by the House of Representatives. The Senate plan, voted 69-26 and headed for conference with the House, conforms in the main to the accord with the White House that was negotiated following the stock-market crash in October 1987. The Senate shifts to more spending and higher tax receipts, primarily necessitated by a new antidrug effort.... New York real estate and hotel magnate Harry B. Helmsley and his wife, Leona, are indicted in New York City for failing to report as income over $4 mil. in luxury personal expenses allegedly billed as tax-deductible business expenses. Both enter pleas of not guilty.			April 14
The Senate votes to impose economic sanctions on Mexico for failing to do enough to combat narcotics trafficking, but rejects similar penalties for the Bahamas. After rejecting sanctions against the Bahamas by a vote of 54-40, the Senate votes, 63-27, to penalize Mexico despite objections from the White House and the Justice Dept. ... A nationally known drug researcher is indicted in federal court in Baltimore for falsifying medical research. The researcher, Stephen E. Breuning, 35, is the author of several influential studies that purport to show that the drugs Ritalin and Dexedrine are more effective than other drugs in controlling hyperactive retarded children. Prosecutors say they believe Breuning's indictments are the first such charges in a federal court.		The government's producer price index climbed 0.6% in March, the Labor Dept. reports.... The Federal Reserve Board reports that its industrial production index rose 0.1% in March.	The Reagan administration bars researchers at the National Institutes of Health from performing any experiments involving human fetal tissue until the legal and ethical issues can be studied by an expert committee.... A committee sponsored by the National Academy of Sciences and funded by the Dept. of Agriculture affirms that Americans consume too much dietary fat. It says one key solution to the problem is to lower the fat content of farm animals through breeding, changes in animal feed, and genetic engineering.	Opposition to Pres. Reagan's Strategic Defense Initiative (Star Wars) proposal is under study by the American Roman Catholic bishops, according to a report in the New York Times.	April 15
Gov. Michael S. Dukakis (D, Mass.) wins the first round of the Arizona Democratic presidential caucuses, capturing about 54% of the 38,000 votes cast to 38% for the Rev. Jesse Jackson.					April 16
				Henryk Jorgensen of Denmark and Ingrid Kristiansen of Norway are the winners of the London Marathon.... Louise Nevelson, 88, pioneer creator of environmental sculpture who became one of the world's foremost women artists, dies in New York, after several months of poor health. Known above all for her wall sculptures, which she created for 30 years before making her first sale, she achieved her first recognition as a major artist with her white-on-white Dawn's Wedding Feast in 1959; this was followed by her Holocaust memorial Homage to the 6,000,000 in 1964.	April 17

F	G	H	I	J
Includes elections, federal-state relations, civil rights and liberties, crime, the judiciary, education, health care, poverty, urban affairs and population.	Includes formation and debate of U.S. foreign and defense policies, veterans' affairs and defense spending. (Relations with specific foreign countries are usually found under the region concerned.)	Includes business, labor, agriculture, taxation, transportation, consumer affairs, monetary and fiscal policy, natural resources, and pollution.	Includes worldwide scientific, medical and technological developments, natural phenomena, U.S. weather, natural disasters, and accidents.	Includes the arts, religion, scholarship, communications media, sports, entertainments, fashions, fads and social life.

	World Affairs	Europe	Africa & the Middle East	The Americas	Asia & the Pacific
April 18		The Conservative government of Britain's P.M. Margaret Thatcher wins a key vote in the House of Commons on its plan to overhaul the nation's local tax system, known as the poll tax. But 38 Conservative members of Parliament vote against the government in one of the most significant parliamentary rebuffs to the prime minister since she took office in 1979.	U.S. Navy warships and planes sink or cripple six Iranian naval vessels in a daylong series of clashes across the southern Persian Gulf. The battle starts after U.S. forces destroy two Iranian oil platforms in retaliation for an April 14 incident in which a U.S. ship was damaged by a mine allegedly laid by Iran. . . . Iraq claims to have driven Iranian forces from the strategic southern peninsula at the disused Iraqi oil port of Fao. Iran's capture of Fao in early 1986 was considered one of Iraq's most ignominious defeats in the seven-and-a-half-year-old Persian Gulf war. Thus, its recapture was seen as a major military and psychological victory for the regime of Iraqi Pres. Saddam Hussein. . . . After a 14-month trial, an Israeli court in Jerusalem convicts John Demjanjuk of being the notorious "Ivan the Terrible," a sadistic killer at the Nazi death camp of Treblinka in Poland in 1942-43, where 850,000 Jews were murdered.	In Canada, about 85% of Quebec province loses electrical power, apparently after a freak ice storm damages the Arnaud substation of Hydro-Quebec, the provincially owned utility. Power is not restored until the next day.	
April 19		A West German court in Dusseldorf convicts Abbas Ali Hamadei, a Lebanese Shiite Moslem, of complicity in the kidnapping of two West Germans in Beirut, Lebanon, in 1987. He is given an unexpectedly stiff sentence of 13 years in prison. . . . Denmark's Premier Poul Schluter calls a snap general election for May 10. The action is prompted by an April 14 vote of the Folketing approving a resolution to tighten the nation's policy against port visits by ships with nuclear weapons. The resolution is a defeat for Schluter's center-right minority coalition government and poses problems for Denmark's membership in the North Atlantic Treaty Org.		The United States begins delivering food to Nicaraguan Contras in Honduras under a program approved by Congress in March. Congress approved $47.9 mil. in aid to the Contras and to Nicaraguan children injured in the war.	Queen Elizabeth II and Prince Philip begin a three-week tour of Australia in celebration of the former British colony's bicentennial. . . . In Singapore, the government rearrests eight former prisoners who signed a letter April 18 in which they repudiated confessions they made in 1987 and charged that they were tortured while in police custody.

A	B	C	D	E
Includes developments that affect more than one world region, international organizations and important meetings of major world leaders.	Includes all domestic and regional developments in Europe, including the Soviet Union, Turkey, Cyprus and Malta.	Includes all domestic and regional developments in Africa and the Middle East, including Iraq and Iran and excluding Cyprus, Turkey and Afghanistan.	Includes all domestic and regional developments in Latin America, the Caribbean and Canada.	Includes all domestic and regional developments in Asia and Pacific nations, extending from Afghanistan through all the Pacific Islands, except Hawaii.

U.S. Politics & Social Issues	U.S. Foreign Policy & Defense	U.S. Economy & Environment	Science, Technology & Nature	Culture, Leisure & Life Style	
			The National Institutes of Health (NIH) establishes an Office of Acquired Immune Deficiency Syndrome (AIDS) Research reporting directly to NIH Dir. James B. Wyngaarden, in an effort to strengthen and centralize coordination of the research effort into AIDS.	Kenya's Ibrahim Hussein wins the men's division of the 92nd Boston Marathon; his time of 2:08:43 is second fastest in Boston history. Rosa Mota of Portugal is the women's winner in 2:24:30.	April 18
Marred by divisiveness and controversy, the New York Democratic presidential primary ends with a strong victory—51%—for Massachusetts Gov. Michael S. Dukakis. The Rev. Jesse Jackson finishes a solid second with 37% after weathering scathing personal attacks from New York City Mayor Edward I. Koch (D). . . . In New York, Vice Pres. George Bush pulls to within a few delegates of clinching the Republican nomination by winning about 95% of the vote in the Republican primary. Bush wins almost all the 134 Republican convention delegates. . . . The Senate approves a bill to extend federal lobbying restrictions to members of Congress and their top aides after they leave government service. The bill is sent by voice vote to the House, where similar legislation is in the works. . . . The Supreme Court, 5-3, upholds the right to build a federal road across a site used for at least 200 years by American Indians for religious rituals.		Housing starts rose 1.9% in March, the Commerce Dept. reports, to an adjusted annual rate of 1.543 million. . . . Federal inspectors propose fines totaling $1.6 mil. against Asarco Inc. for alleged violations of lead, arsenic, and other chemical health standards at its East Helena, Mont., lead smelter.			April 19

F	G	H	I	J
Includes elections, federal-state relations, civil rights and liberties, crime, the judiciary, education, health care, poverty, urban affairs and population.	*Includes formation and debate of U.S. foreign and defense policies, veterans' affairs and defense spending. (Relations with specific foreign countries are usually found under the region concerned.)*	*Includes business, labor, agriculture, taxation, transportation, consumer affairs, monetary and fiscal policy, natural resources, and pollution.*	*Includes worldwide scientific, medical and technological developments, natural phenomena, U.S. weather, natural disasters, and accidents.*	*Includes the arts, religion, scholarship, communications media, sports, entertainments, fashions, fads and social life.*

	World Affairs	Europe	Africa & the Middle East	The Americas	Asia & the Pacific
April 20		The Kremlin's number two figure, Yegor K. Ligachev, is demoted at a special session of the Politburo, according to the Western press. Ligachev was earlier rumored to have bluntly challenged the leadership of Communist Party Gen. Sec. Mikhail S. Gorbachev.	The hijacking of a Kuwaiti Airways jet that began April 5 ends when the hijackers, under an agreement negotiated by Algerian officials, release their remaining 31 hostages in Algiers and are allowed free passage out of the country. The pro-Iranian Shiite Moslem terrorists are believed to have traveled to Beirut, Lebanon, by way of Syria. . . . The State Dept. issues a report charging that antigovernment rebels in Mozambique waged a systematic campaign of terror and massacre against civilians, killing at least 100,000 of them over the last two years.	Relations between Canada and France have soured in the past week in the latest episode of the long-standing dispute over fishing rights in waters claimed by both countries. The disputed waters are south and west of Newfoundland. France's claim is based on the fact that two small islands south of Newfoundland, St.-Pierre and Miquelon, are French owned.	The government of Thailand reaches an agreement in Bangkok with a UN agency that will allow Vietnamese refugees arriving by sea to remain in Thailand. The agreement officially ends a three-month-old government policy of forcibly turning away Vietnamese boat people from Thailand's shores.
April 21			Israel begins a three-day holiday celebrating the 40th anniversary of its existence as an independent Jewish state.		

A	B	C	D	E
Includes developments that affect more than one world region, international organizations and important meetings of major world leaders.	Includes all domestic and regional developments in Europe, including the Soviet Union, Turkey, Cyprus and Malta.	Includes all domestic and regional developments in Africa and the Middle East, including Iraq and Iran and excluding Cyprus, Turkey and Afghanistan.	Includes all domestic and regional developments in Latin America, the Caribbean and Canada.	Includes all domestic and regional developments in Asia and Pacific nations, extending from Afghanistan through all the Pacific Islands, except Hawaii.

U.S. Politics & Social Issues	U.S. Foreign Policy & Defense	U.S. Economy & Environment	Science, Technology & Nature	Culture, Leisure & Life Style	
The Rev. Jesse Jackson emerges virtually tied with Gov. Michael S. Dukakis (D, Mass.) in Vermont's Democratic presidential town caucuses. On the Republican side, Vice Pres. George Bush wins about 90% of the state convention delegates. . . . One day after Senate Democrats selected 43 of their members to be so-called "superdelegates" to the Democratic National Convention, House Democrats choose 207 superdelegates. . . . The House approves a seven-month extension of the amnesty program for undocumented immigrants to apply for legal residence. The current deadline for immigrants who have been in the United States since at least 1982 to register with impunity is May 4. The bill would extend the program through November 30. . . . The Senate approves by voice vote a bill extending federal education programs for the next five years. The legislation, passed the House of Representatives April 19. The entire package is sent to the White House for Pres. Reagan's signature. . . . The Senate approves legislation to offer a national apology and compensation to Japanese-Americans interned in World War II. The bill is sent to conference with the House, which passed similar legislation earlier. The Reagan administration opposes the legislation and has threatened to veto it, largely because of the more than $1 bil. in cost for compensation.	The Supreme Court upholds the Veterans Admin.'s view of alcoholism as coming from "willful misconduct" rather than as a disease, in determining eligibility for certain benefits. . . . The Air Force announces that the top-secret B-2 Stealth strategic bomber will make its official maiden flight sometime in the fall of 1988. The Stealth, designed to evade enemy radar detection, has been one of the military's most shadowy projects.	Pushed by a record increase in apparel prices, the government's consumer price index climbed 0.5% in March, the Labor Dept. reports. . . . Overcoming several unexpected obstacles, First City Bancorp. of Texas completes its long-delayed $1.5 bil. bailout. The Federal Deposit Insurance Corp.-assisted bailout is the second largest in banking history, after the $4.5 bil. bailout of Continental Illinois Corp. in 1984.		*Variety*'s top-grossing films for the week are: *Colors, Beetlejuice, Above the Law, Biloxi Blues* and *Moonstruck*.	**April 20**
Sen Albert Gore (D, Tenn.) ends his active campaign for the Democratic presidential nomination. . . . Vice Pres. George Bush and his wife, Barbara, paid $86,396 in federal income tax on an adjusted gross income of $308,396, according to a copy of their return. Bush reported $114,681 from his job as vice president. Other income is mostly from his blind trust, including $31,264 in interest and dividends, $26,075 in capital gains, and $112,261 in supplemental income. The Bushes claimed $53,314 in itemized deductions, including $12,225 in charitable contributions. . . . Gov. Michael S. Dukakis (D, Mass.) signs a landmark universal health-care bill that guarantees health insurance to all residents of the state. Dukakis has frequently promoted his health proposals on the presidential campaign trail.	Sec. of State George P. Shultz confers with top Soviet officials in Moscow in the latest of a series of high-level contacts between the two superpowers.	Disregarding an April 19 veto threat by Pres. Reagan, the House of Representatives overwhelmingly passes comprehensive trade legislation aimed at forcing the United States to take tougher action to open up foreign markets and retaliate against unfair trade practices. The bill will now go to the Senate. . . . General Motors Corp. (GMC) reports that its first-quarter earnings rose 18% from the year-earlier period to $1.09 bil. GMC's quarterly profits climbed due to accounting changes that allowed the world's largest auto maker to defer certain manufacturing expenses until a vehicle was sold rather than made. Without the changes, profits at the nation's largest auto maker would have dropped 6%.	A mouse with a genetically engineered susceptibility to cancer is the subject of the world's first patent for an animal life form. The U.S. Patent Office, which issued the patent under a new policy announced in 1987, calls the action a "singularly historic event."	Spain's Cervantes Prize for literature is presented to Carlos Fuentes, the Mexican novelist known for such books as *The Death of Artemio Cruz* and *Our Land.* . . . I.A.L. Diamond, 67, Hollywood screenwriter and longtime collaborator of director Billy Wilder, dies in Beverly Hills of multiple myeloma. Diamond is best known for films made with Wilder such as *Love in the Afternoon, Some Like It Hot, Irma la Douce, Kiss Me, Stupid, The Private Life of Sherlock Holmes* and *The Apartment*, for which he won an Academy Award.	**April 21**

F	G	H	I	J
Includes elections, federal-state relations, civil rights and liberties, crime, the judiciary, education, health care, poverty, urban affairs and population.	*Includes formation and debate of U.S. foreign and defense policies, veterans' affairs and defense spending. (Relations with specific foreign countries are usually found under the region concerned.)*	*Includes business, labor, agriculture, taxation, transportation, consumer affairs, monetary and fiscal policy, natural resources, and pollution.*	*Includes worldwide scientific, medical and technological developments, natural phenomena, U.S. weather, natural disasters, and accidents.*	*Includes the arts, religion, scholarship, communications media, sports, entertainments, fashions, fads and social life.*

	World Affairs	Europe	Africa & the Middle East	The Americas	Asia & the Pacific
April 22					The Taiwanese government begins freeing 6,000 prisoners and reduces the sentences of another 16,000 in a mass amnesty to mark the 100th day since the death of former Pres. Chiang Ching-kuo. Nineteen political prisoners are released under the amnesty, while 11 others have their sentences cut.
April 23				Human rights abuses in Panama are on the increase, according to a report issued by the U.S.-based rights group Americas Watch. The report says that the Panama Defense Forces have beaten and intimidated protesters and vandalized their property since Gen. Manuel Antonio Noriega, head of the forces, has come under pressure to step down.	
April 24		France's Socialist Pres. Francois Mitterrand leads all other candidates in the first round of the French presidential elections with 34.04% of the vote. He will face conservative Premier Jacques Chirac, the runner-up, in the run-off election May 8. The other major development in the election is the surprisingly strong showing of right-wing National Front leader Jean-Marie Le Pen.			

A	B	C	D	E
Includes developments that affect more than one world region, international organizations and important meetings of major world leaders.	*Includes all domestic and regional developments in Europe, including the Soviet Union, Turkey, Cyprus and Malta.*	*Includes all domestic and regional developments in Africa and the Middle East, including Iraq and Iran and excluding Cyprus, Turkey and Afghanistan.*	*Includes all domestic and regional developments in Latin America, the Caribbean and Canada.*	*Includes all domestic and regional developments in Asia and Pacific nations, extending from Afghanistan through all the Pacific Islands, except Hawaii.*

U.S. Politics & Social Issues	U.S. Foreign Policy & Defense	U.S. Economy & Environment	Science, Technology & Nature	Culture, Leisure & Life Style	
	Defense Sec. Frank C. Carlucci and Adm. William J. Crowe, chairman of the Joint Chiefs of Staff, inform Congress that the administration has decided to expand the Navy's rules of engagement in the Persian Gulf to permit U.S. warships to protect non-U.S.-flag merchant shipping from armed attack in certain unspecified circumstances.	General Motors Corp. (GMC) announces that it will reduce its auto production capacity to correspond to current sales. The retreat, which will involve the permanent closing of several of GMC's 25 car assembly plants in the United States and Canada, will significantly shrink the world's largest industrial concern for the first time in its 80-year history. . . . The Internal Revenue Service revokes the tax-exempt status of the PTL (Praise the Lord) television ministry and Heritage USA religious-theme park founded by Jim and Tammy Faye Bakker. Bakker resigned from the organization in March 1987 after disclosures of a sexual escapade with a former church secretary. PTL subsequently filed for protection from its creditors under Chapter 11 of the federal bankruptcy code.			April 22
				Greek cycling champion Kanellos Kanellopoulos sets three new world records for human-powered flight, pedaling the *Daedalus 88* across 74 miles of the Aegean Sea from Crete to a crash landing just off the Greek island of Santorini. The flight, which lasted three hours 54 minutes, breaks the distance record for human-powered flight, and duration and straight-line distance records. . . . *Billboard*'s best-selling albums for the week are: *Dirty Dancing* (soundtrack); *Bad*, Michael Jackson; *More Dirty Dancing* (soundtrack); *Faith*, George Michael; *Kick*, INXS. . . . Arthur Michael Ramsey, 83, archbishop of Canterbury, dies in Oxford, England, of bronchial pneumonia following a brief illness. Spiritual head of the Church of England and leader of the worldwide Anglican Church from 1961 to 1974, Ramsey was a progressive social activist. In 1966 he met with Pope Paul VI in Rome, in what was the first official visit to a pope by a head of the Anglican Church in 400 years. Upon his retirement in 1974, he was made a life peer and took the title of Lord Ramsey of Canterbury.	April 23
Sec. of Education William J. Bennett declares in a report that the U.S. educational system is "still at risk" despite five years of improvement. The report is an evaluation of the nation's schools on the fifth anniversary of the release of "A Nation at Risk," the landmark 1983 report published by the government's National Comm. on Excellence in Education.	The Office of Technology Assessment, the research arm of Congress, concludes that the Strategic Defense Initiative ("Star Wars") will probably "suffer a catastrophic failure" in its "first (and presumably only)" use.			The National Football League holds its annual draft of college players. Aundray Bruce, Auburn linebacker, is selected by the Atlanta Falcons as the first player in the draft.	April 24

F	G	H	I	J
Includes elections, federal-state relations, civil rights and liberties, crime, the judiciary, education, health care, poverty, urban affairs and population.	*Includes formation and debate of U.S. foreign and defense policies, veterans' affairs and defense spending. (Relations with specific foreign countries are usually found under the region concerned.)*	*Includes business, labor, agriculture, taxation, transportation, consumer affairs, monetary and fiscal policy, natural resources, and pollution.*	*Includes worldwide scientific, medical and technological developments, natural phenomena, U.S. weather, natural disasters, and accidents.*	*Includes the arts, religion, scholarship, communications media, sports, entertainments, fashions, fads and social life.*

	World Affairs	Europe	Africa & the Middle East	The Americas	Asia & the Pacific
April 25	The International Court of Justice at The Hague rules unanimously against the U.S. effort to close the UN observer mission of the Palestine Liberation Org. The advisory opinion by the tribunal, which is also known as the World Court, was sought by the UN Gen. Assembly.		Palestine Liberation Org. (PLO) Chairman Yasir Arafat and Syria's Pres. Hafez al-Assad meet in Damascus for the first time since 1983, when Syria fomented a mutiny within the PLO in Lebanon and expelled Arafat to Tunisia.		
April 26			Saudi Arabia announces that it is breaking diplomatic relations with Iran and gives Iranian diplomats and their dependents a week to leave the country. The Saudi government says it is acting in response to the 1987 riot by Iranian pilgrims in Mecca in which over 400 people died, the subsequent attack on the Saudi Embassy in Teheran, and Iran's continuing raids on commercial shipping in the Persian Gulf as part of its war with Iraq.		The ruling Democratic Justice Party fails to win a majority of seats in a general election for South Korea's National Assembly, marking the first time in the country's history that a ruling party has lost control of the legislature.
April 27		The Conservative government of Britain's P.M. Margaret Thatcher announces concessions that will increase spending on social security by $187 mil.		Canada's P.M. Brian Mulroney visits Washington, D.C., for his fourth annual summit with Pres. Reagan. The chief topics of the summit are acid rain and the U.S.-Canada trade accord.... A federal judge in San Francisco rules that a former Argentine Army general, Carlos Guillermo Suarez Mason, should be extradited to Argentina to face murder charges in connection with the torture and killing of thousands of Argentine civilians during the 1970s.... In Panama, the government arrests at least 12 opposition leaders in a sweep apparently aimed at thwarting street protests against Gen. Manuel Antonio Noriega, the country's de facto ruler, planned for April 28.	
April 28	The World Bank announces that a proposed $74.8 bil. general capital increase has become effective. The capital boost, supported by 133 of the 151 member nations, will now occur whether or not the U.S. Congress approves.	Against the wishes of the British government, Thames Television broadcasts an investigatory program, "Death on the Rock," on the March killings of three Provisional Irish Republican Army members by British security forces in the colony of Gibraltar.... In Britain, in an important test case, the Law Lords uphold the right of a former British soldier to sue the government for damages that he claims were suffered during British nuclear weapons tests in the late 1950s.			The Chinese government releases the first draft of the Basic Law, or constitution, under which Hong Kong is to be governed after British rule over the colony ends in 1997.

A	B	C	D	E
Includes developments that affect more than one world region, international organizations and important meetings of major world leaders.	*Includes all domestic and regional developments in Europe, including the Soviet Union, Turkey, Cyprus and Malta.*	*Includes all domestic and regional developments in Africa and the Middle East, including Iraq and Iran and excluding Cyprus, Turkey and Afghanistan.*	*Includes all domestic and regional developments in Latin America, the Caribbean and Canada.*	*Includes all domestic and regional developments in Asia and Pacific nations, extending from Afghanistan through all the Pacific Islands, except Hawaii.*

U.S. Politics & Social Issues	U.S. Foreign Policy & Defense	U.S. Economy & Environment	Science, Technology & Nature	Culture, Leisure & Life Style	
Gov. Michael S. Dukakis (D, Mass.) wins about 70% of the vote and a large majority of the delegates in Utah's Democratic presidential caucuses. That percentage will translate into 19 of Utah's 23 convention delegates, to four for the Rev. Jesse Jackson, who had 16% of the vote. A planned nonbinding Republican straw vote is cancelled because Vice Pres. George Bush has virtually locked up the nomination. . . . A bitterly divided Supreme Court votes, 5-4, to review a major 1976 decision that prohibits private schools from discriminating on the basis of race. The 1976 rule often is cited as precedent and applied to many other cases to prohibit discrimination in housing, education and other areas.	The Senate passes and sends to the House a bill that will make eligible for disability benefits veterans who have been exposed to nuclear radiation in the course of military service. . . . Pres. Reagan extends for a further 12 months a three-year-old trade embargo against Nicaragua. He reports to Congress that the Sandinista government poses an "unusual and extraordinary threat" to the United States. . . . Defense Sec. Frank C. Carlucci overrules the commandant of the Marine Corps, Gen. Alfred M. Gray Jr., on the matter of widening the role of women in the Marines. A Pentagon task force report recommends that the armed services crack down on sexual harassment and open up noncombat job opportunities for servicewomen.			By bidding $4.94 mil. at a literary auction in New York City, Warner Books wins the right to publish the sequel to Margaret Mitchell's novel *Gone with the Wind*. The sequel will be written by Virginia-based author Alexandra Ripley.	April 25
Vice Pres. George Bush clinches the Republican presidential nomination with an overwhelming win in the Pennsylvania primary. Running all but unopposed, Bush wins 79% of the vote. On the Democratic side, Massachusetts Gov. Michael S. Dukakis wins the Pennsylvania primary, taking 67% of the vote to 27% for the Rev. Jesse Jackson. . . . The Supreme Court hears arguments on the constitutionality of the 1978 law authorizing appointment of an independent prosecutor to investigate alleged crimes by high government officials.		The nation's gross national product, adjusted for inflation, grew at a 2.3% annual rate in the first quarter, the Commerce Dept. reports. . . . A new, reform-style water-projects bill is approved by the Senate by voice vote. Designed to avoid the "pork barrel" classification, it is the "first non-controversial water resources development act in a quarter century," according to Sen. Daniel Patrick Moynihan (D, N.Y.).			April 26
The National Low Income Housing Preservation Committee issues a study warning that as many as 543,000 privately owned, federally subsidized housing units are likely to be lost to low-income residents by 2002 without U.S. government action.		The Senate passes comprehensive trade legislation aimed at opening up foreign markets and expanding U.S. trade. But the 63-36 vote leaves its supporters short of the two-thirds majority needed to override a threatened presidential veto. The House cleared the trade bill by a vote of 312 to 107 last week. The margin in the House is more than 20 votes over the two-thirds majority that would be needed to override a veto. . . . Consumer spending rose 0.7% and personal income rose 0.8% in March, the Commerce Dept. reports. . . . Chrysler Corp. reports that its first-quarter net earnings fell to $183.7 mil., down 32% from $269.4 mil. a year earlier. The nation's number-three auto maker blames the drop on a one-time charge for plant closings.			April 27
		Among the Big Three auto makers, Ford Motor Co. is once again the most profitable. The nation's second-largest auto maker reports record first-quarter earnings of $1.62 bil. The 9% increase in profit from the first quarter of 1987 gives Ford the highest single-quarter earnings ever in the history of the auto industry. A 132% increase in Ford's overseas earnings was largely responsible for the gain, outweighing a 9% decrease in the auto company's U.S. profits.			April 28

F	G	H	I	J
Includes elections, federal-state relations, civil rights and liberties, crime, the judiciary, education, health care, poverty, urban affairs and population.	*Includes formation and debate of U.S. foreign and defense policies, veterans' affairs and defense spending. (Relations with specific foreign countries are usually found under the region concerned.)*	*Includes business, labor, agriculture, taxation, transportation, consumer affairs, monetary and fiscal policy, natural resources, and pollution.*	*Includes worldwide scientific, medical and technological developments, natural phenomena, U.S. weather, natural disasters, and accidents.*	*Includes the arts, religion, scholarship, communications media, sports, entertainments, fashions, fads and social life.*

	World Affairs	Europe	Africa & the Middle East	The Americas	Asia & the Pacific
April 29		Britain's balance of payments deficit narrowed sharply to $475 mil. in March, the government reports. . . . In Britain, the government-appointed Kingman Committee releases its report on the teaching of the English language. The study group, led by Sir John Kingman of Bristol Univ., finds that the teaching of standard English should be stressed relative to the use of the spoken language of everyday life.			Thailand's Premier Prem Tinsulanonda dissolves his cabinet and parliament after the main party in his coalition government is fractured by a dispute over a bill to protect U.S. copyrights. New elections are scheduled for July 24, official Radio Thailand announces. . . . The United States and Taiwan end four days of trade talks in Taipei without reaching any agreements. During the talks, U.S. negotiators pressed Taiwan to liberalize trade restrictions on a number of goods and services, including agricultural products, intellectual property, financial services, and cigarette and alcohol sales.
April 30	The turnover of stocks as a percentage of total stock market capitalization is highest in 1987 on the Frankfurt stock market. According to a study by Morgan Stanley Capital International, stocks valued at 91% of Frankfurt's year-end market capitalization of $207 bil. were traded in 1987. On Wall Street, 85% of a total market capitalization of $2.2 trillion were traded in 1987. In Tokyo, the world's largest stock market, turnover was 59% of an end-of-1987 market capitalization of $3.0 trillion. In London, only 41% of the market's year-end capitalization of $664 bil. were traded in 1987.			Nicaraguan government and Contra representatives conclude three days of talks in Managua, but the top-level peace talks fail to reach agreement.	
May 1		Poland's official May Day celebrations are met with Solidarity-led demonstrations in 15 cities. At least 100 arrests are reported. Solidarity called for the demonstrations as a show of public opposition to the government's economic policies and as a show of support for the striking workers at the Lenin Steel Mill near Krakow.		In a continuing dispute over the results of legislative elections held in March, El Salvador's main political parties install two legislative assemblies.	The UN Border Relief Operation halts its food deliveries to a Cambodian refugee camp in eastern Thailand after the Khmer Rouge guerrilla army refuses to allow the UN agency access to the camp to monitor distribution of the food. UN officials suspect that food supplies sent to the camp, known as Huay Chan, are ending up in the hands of Khmer Rouge soldiers fighting the Vietnamese-backed Cambodian government.
May 2	Oil ministers of the Org. of Petroleum Exporting Countries (OPEC) postpone a decision on a proposal for a joint production-cutting effort with non-OPEC oil producers. The decision not to take immediate action is made after four nights of deliberations in Vienna and pushes the issue onto the agenda for the group's regularly scheduled meeting in June. . . . The aggregate trade deficit of industrial countries in nominal U.S. dollar terms expands to $85.4 bil. in 1987, the International Monetary Fund reports. The industrial country trade deficit in 1987 is considerably higher than the $66.1 bil. 1986 deficit but remains lower than the $99.1 bil. 1985 deficit.				

A	B	C	D	E
Includes developments that affect more than one world region, international organizations and important meetings of major world leaders.	Includes all domestic and regional developments in Europe, including the Soviet Union, Turkey, Cyprus and Malta.	Includes all domestic and regional developments in Africa and the Middle East, including Iraq and Iran and excluding Cyprus, Turkey and Afghanistan.	Includes all domestic and regional developments in Latin America, the Caribbean and Canada.	Includes all domestic and regional developments in Asia and Pacific nations, extending from Afghanistan through all the Pacific Islands, except Hawaii.

U.S. Politics & Social Issues	U.S. Foreign Policy & Defense	U.S. Economy & Environment	Science, Technology & Nature	Culture, Leisure & Life Style	
Federal District Judge David Kenyon in Los Angeles upholds the right of Salvadorans detained by federal authorities for deportation to seek political asylum and to have legal representation.	Defense Sec. Frank C. Carlucci presents the seventh annual edition of *Soviet Military Power*. The 1988 book states that the United States and Soviet Union were roughly equal in military spending in calendar 1987. The Congress appropriated $289.5 bil. for defense programs for fiscal 1987.	The government's index of leading economic indicators climbed 0.8% in March, the Commerce Dept. reports. . . . Prices received by farmers for raw agricultural products in April were unchanged, the Agriculture Dept. reports.		*Publishers Weekly*'s hardback fiction best-sellers for the week are: *The Icarus Agenda*, Robert Ludlum; *The Bonfire of the Vanities*, Tom Wolfe; *Treasure*, Clive Cussler; *Rock Star*, Jackie Collins; and *Hot Money*, Dick Francis.	April 29
					April 30
				Phil Parsons wins the Winston 500 National Assoc. for Stock Car Racing event in Talladega, Ala. . . . Ayrton Senna of Brazil wins the San Marino (Italy) Grand Prix.	May 1
The day after officially retiring from the U.S. Marine Corps, Oliver L. North receives a hero's welcome at the Lynchburg, Va., campus of Liberty Univ., whose founder, the Rev. Jerry Falwell, invited the former National Security Council aide to deliver the 1988 commencement address.		The Supreme Court eases the antitrust standard to allow manufacturers to drop discount dealers to protect other retailers from price competition. The court rules, 6-2, that an agreement between a manufacturer and a retailer to terminate a discounter, who sells at lower prices, is not automatically illegal under federal antitrust law unless there is an explicit effort to fix prices. . . . Productivity among the nation's nonfarm businesses rose at an annual rate of 0.9% in the first quarter, the Labor Dept. reports.		At an auction at Sotheby's, *210 Coca-Cola Bottles*, a 1962 painting by Andy Warhol, who died in 1987, sells for $1.43 mil. At that same auction, a Jackson Pollock painting called *Search* is purchased for $4.8 mil., an auction record for the artist and for any post-World War II artwork. . . . Delegates to the United Methodist General Conf. reaffirm the church's view that homosexual behavior is "incompatible with Christian teaching." The quadrennial conference votes, 676-293, to retain the church's ban on ordination of "self-avowed practicing homosexuals." The ban was adopted in 1984.	May 2

F	G	H	I	J
Includes elections, federal-state relations, civil rights and liberties, crime, the judiciary, education, health care, poverty, urban affairs and population.	*Includes formation and debate of U.S. foreign and defense policies, veterans' affairs and defense spending. (Relations with specific foreign countries are usually found under the region concerned.)*	*Includes business, labor, agriculture, taxation, transportation, consumer affairs, monetary and fiscal policy, natural resources, and pollution.*	*Includes worldwide scientific, medical and technological developments, natural phenomena, U.S. weather, natural disasters, and accidents.*	*Includes the arts, religion, scholarship, communications media, sports, entertainments, fashions, fads and social life.*

	World Affairs	Europe	Africa & the Middle East	The Americas	Asia & the Pacific
May 3			A four-power, two-day conference on the issues of Angola and Namibia (South-West Africa) begins in London. The meeting, which ends on a note of restrained optimism, brings together for the first time representatives of the United States, Angola, Cuba, and South Africa.		The New Zealand government announces that it plans to deregulate the country's oil industry. The move, which takes effect May 9, ends wholesale and retail price controls and lifts restrictions prohibiting the importation into New Zealand of refined petroleum products.
May 4	The Council of the General Agreement on Tariffs and Trade (GATT) rules that the 1986 U.S.-Japan bilateral semiconductor agreement violates GATT rules. The council also rejects a U.S. request that a dispute panel be formed to investigate subsidies on European Community (EC) oilseed subsidies, and postpones a decision on an EC request for retaliation against a U.S. oil tax that GATT previously ruled as discriminatory.		Three Frenchmen who have been held hostage in Lebanon for three years are released to French representatives in Beirut. Their release comes just four days before the final round of the French presidential elections pitting incumbent socialist Pres. Francois Mitterrand against conservative Premier Jacques Chirac. . . . Two days after moving into Israel's self-declared security zone in southern Lebanon in a hunt for Palestinian guerrillas, most of the Israeli force withdraws after failing to find any Palestinians but engaging in a fierce battle for a fortified Shiite Moslem village north of the security zone, in which 40 Lebanese and three Israelis are killed.		Philippine Pres. Corazon Aquino announces that former Pres. Ferdinand E. Marcos will not be allowed to return to the Philippines to attend the funeral of his mother, Josefa Edralin Marcos, who died earlier today. . . . Fang Lizhi, China's most prominent dissident, makes his first political address since his ouster from the Communist Party in January 1987. Speaking to an audience of about 500 students at Beijing Univ., Fang calls for "more democracy in China" and urges the Communist Party to "recognize the concept of human rights above all."
May 5		Polish paramilitary riot police stage a predawn raid on the Lenin Steel Mill, forcing an end to a nine-day strike at the plant. The mill, located in Nowa Huta, near Krakow, is Poland's largest and most modern industrial facility. At least 15,000 of the plant's 32,000 workers participated in the strike.		Uruguay's supreme court upholds a controversial 1986 law granting amnesty to soldiers accused of human rights abuses under military rule from 1973 to 1985. The court rules, 3-2, that the law "coincides perfectly with constitutional principles."	French commandos attack a cave on the New Caledonian island of Ouvea and free 23 French hostages held captive by a group of Melanesian separatists. The dawn assault results in the deaths of 15 separatists and two French commandos. . . . In Australia, a report to the federal government on new means of funding higher education is released by the three-member Wran Committee. The highlight of the report is a proposal to institute a special tax on the income of all former college students to help offset the costs of their higher education.
May 6				Canada's unemployment rate in April declined to the lowest point in nearly seven years, according to Statistics Canada. The April jobless rate was 7.7%, down from 7.8% in both February and March. The April figure is the lowest since the 6.8% rate in August 1981.	

A	B	C	D	E
Includes developments that affect more than one world region, international organizations and important meetings of major world leaders.	Includes all domestic and regional developments in Europe, including the Soviet Union, Turkey, Cyprus and Malta.	Includes all domestic and regional developments in Africa and the Middle East, including Iraq and Iran and excluding Cyprus, Turkey and Afghanistan.	Includes all domestic and regional developments in Latin America, the Caribbean and Canada.	Includes all domestic and regional developments in Asia and Pacific nations, extending from Afghanistan through all the Pacific Islands, except Hawaii.

U.S. Politics & Social Issues	U.S. Foreign Policy & Defense	U.S. Economy & Environment	Science, Technology & Nature	Culture, Leisure & Life Style	
Gov. Michael S. Dukakis (D, Mass.) wins landslide victories in Democratic presidential primaries in Ohio and Indiana, capturing nearly 200 delegates and moving a giant step closer to the Democratic nomination. His Democratic rival, the Rev. Jesse L. Jackson, wins the primary in the District of Columbia by a similarly lopsided margin. . . . Vice Pres. George Bush wins all three Republican primaries—Ohio, Indiana, and the District of Columbia—and all 153 Republican delegates at stake. Bush clinched the Republican nomination the week before in Pennsylvania.			A plague of billions of locusts, the worst in 30 years, is threatening to wreck crops in North Africa and plunge sub-Saharan Africa into another devastating famine, according to reports during the preceding several months. Desert locust swarms first sighted in early 1987 along the Red Sea coast have since migrated all the way across the continent.	A vast assortment of objects amassed by the late pop artist Andy Warhol is auctioned at Sotheby Parke Burnet in New York City over the last two weeks. The auction is one of the most extensive estate sales in history and one of the most highly publicized. The collection of 10,000 items fetches $25.3 mil., $10 mil. above estimates, with the proceeds (less Sotheby's 10% commission) going to the Andy Warhol Foundation for the Visual Arts, established in the artist's will. . . . A work by artist Jasper Johns, a painting called *Diver*, fetches $4.18 mil. at auction at Christie's in New York, a record for a work by a living artist. . . . David Mamet's *Speed-the-Plow*, a play about a Hollywood producer and studio executive who scheme to get their "buddy film" project made, while the exec's secretary backs a moralistic script by an "Eastern sissy writer," opens on Broadway. The play is directed by Gregory Mosher and stars Joe Mantegna, Ron Silver, and Madonna.	**May 3**
The nation's historic amnesty program for illegal aliens expires in a frenzy of last-minute applications. More than 100,000 applicants jammed legalization centers around the country on the last day of the program. It is expected that nearly 1.4 million illegal immigrants have sought amnesty by claiming residence in the United States since Jan. 1, 1982; if their claims are verified, the aliens achieve legal status leading to citizenship. . . . A federal judge in Boston declares a mistrial in the fraud and obstruction of justice trial of political organizer Lyndon H. LaRouche Jr., six of his followers, and five affiliated organizations.		The United Auto Workers union and Chrysler Corp. reach agreement on a new contract comparable with those negotiated in 1987 with Ford Motor Co. and General Motors Corp. . . . LTV Corp. outlines to various creditors its plan to emerge from bankruptcy and pay back about $6.2 bil. in debt in its attempt to end the second largest bankruptcy in U.S. history after that of Texaco Inc.	The Norwegian government confirms that some 15 metric tons of heavy water, a material that could be used to make nuclear weapons, has been lost. The material, in one large shipment, was apparently diverted in 1983.		**May 4**
The Los Angeles Unified School District board approves a new plan to provide bilingual education to non-English-speaking students in the city's public schools. Under the plan students will be taught in their own language until they have mastered English.					**May 5**
		The nation's unemployment rate in April fell to 5.4%, the Labor Dept. reports. . . . Outstanding consumer debt rose $4.46 bil. in March, the Federal Reserve Board reports, at an annual rate of 8.6%, to a total of $620.9 bil.		A 30-day suspension of Cincinnati Reds baseball manager Pete Rose is upheld by the executive committee of the National League. The suspension and a $10,000 fine were imposed May 2 by National League Pres. A. Bartlett Giamatti after Rose twice pushed first base umpire Dave Pallone after a key call in the ninth inning of an April 30 game in Cincinnati against the New York Mets. The Mets won the game, 6-5.	**May 6**

F	G	H	I	J
Includes elections, federal-state relations, civil rights and liberties, crime, the judiciary, education, health care, poverty, urban affairs and population.	*Includes formation and debate of U.S. foreign and defense policies, veterans' affairs and defense spending. (Relations with specific foreign countries are usually found under the region concerned.)*	*Includes business, labor, agriculture, taxation, transportation, consumer affairs, monetary and fiscal policy, natural resources, and pollution.*	*Includes worldwide scientific, medical and technological developments, natural phenomena, U.S. weather, natural disasters, and accidents.*	*Includes the arts, religion, scholarship, communications media, sports, entertainments, fashions, fads and social life.*

	World Affairs	Europe	Africa & the Middle East	The Americas	Asia & the Pacific
May 7		A group of Soviet dissidents meets in Moscow to form an independent political party, the Democratic Union. Under the Soviet constitution, the Communist Party is the USSR's only legal political entity.			
May 8			Israel's Foreign Min. Shimon Peres pays a two-day surprise official visit to Budapest, Hungary. It is the first visit by a senior Israeli leader to any of the communist countries that broke relations with Israel after the 1967 war.	Rodrigo Borja Cevallos of the Democratic Left (ID) Party is elected president of Ecuador, defeating Abdala Bucaram Ortiz, of the Roldosista Party, in a runoff election.	
May 9		Christian Democrat Wilfried Martens is sworn in as premier of Belgium, ending a five-month political impasse resulting from inconclusive elections in December 1987.			
May 10		An eight-day protest strike by workers at the Lenin Shipyard in Gdansk ends without agreement. The end of the Gdansk strike brings Poland its first calm since the start of the nationwide labor unrest, April 25.			A report commissioned by Union Carbide Corp. and released by a U.S. consulting firm asserts that the 1984 gas leak at Union Carbide's chemical plant in Bhopal, India, was the result of employee sabotage. More than 3,000 people were killed by the gas leak, the world's worst industrial disaster.
May 11	The increase in the U.S. prime rate today comes as world stock markets tumbled on fears of increasing interest rates worldwide. The Dow Jones industrial average drops 37.80 points to 1965.85, its lowest level since February 11, after sharp stock market drops in London and Tokyo.	H(arold) A(drian) R(ussell) (Kim) Philby, 76, Soviet double agent who was head of the anti-Soviet section of the British Secret Intelligence Service (SIS), dies in Moscow. At one time SIS liaison officer with the Central Intelligence Agency, he was later revealed as the "third man" in a spy ring involving fellow Cambridge Univ. graduates Guy Burgess and Donald Maclean. Philby's activities were not fully exposed until his own defection in 1963.	Five days after fierce fighting between rival Lebanese Shiite Moslem militias erupted in Beirut's southern suburbs, a cease-fire goes into effect. At least 172 people have been killed and more than 600 wounded, and the fundamentalist pro-Iranian Hizballah (Party of God) appears to have won a victory over the more mainstream, Syrian-backed Amal militia.	An attempted rebellion led by two army officers against Guatemala's civilian government fails, and the unidentified officers are arrested.	

A	B	C	D	E
Includes developments that affect more than one world region, international organizations and important meetings of major world leaders.	*Includes all domestic and regional developments in Europe, including the Soviet Union, Turkey, Cyprus and Malta.*	*Includes all domestic and regional developments in Africa and the Middle East, including Iraq and Iran and excluding Cyprus, Turkey and Afghanistan.*	*Includes all domestic and regional developments in Latin America, the Caribbean and Canada.*	*Includes all domestic and regional developments in Asia and Pacific nations, extending from Afghanistan through all the Pacific Islands, except Hawaii.*

U.S. Politics & Social Issues	U.S. Foreign Policy & Defense	U.S. Economy & Environment	Science, Technology & Nature	Culture, Leisure & Life Style	
	The *New York Times* challenges Vice Pres. George Bush's assertions that he had no knowledge of drug trafficking by Panama's military leader, Gen. Manuel Antonio Noriega, until Noriega was indicted in the United States in February. Citing Reagan administration officials, the *Times* says that then U.S. ambassador to Panama Everett Briggs told Bush of Noriega's involvement in drug smuggling at a meeting in 1985.			Winning Colors wins the 114th running of the Kentucky Derby at Churchill Downs in Louisville, Ky., with Gary Stevens aboard.... Pope John Paul II returns to Latin America for a 12-day tour of Uruguay, Bolivia, Paraguay, and Peru on his 37th foreign trip during his papacy and his ninth visit to Latin America.	May 7
				Robert A(nson) Heinlein, 80, one of the world's most popular and prolific writers of science fiction, dies in Carmel, Calif. He won an unprecedented four Hugo Awards for best novel, for *Double Star* (1956), *Starship Troopers* (1959), *Stranger in a Strange Land* (1961), and *The Moon Is a Harsh Mistress* (1966). In 1975, Heinlein was the first recipient of the Science Fiction Writers of America grand master Nebula Award, given for lifetime achievement.	May 8
A memoir by former White House chief of staff Donald Regan reveals that astrology influenced the scheduling of major presidential events. That disclosure, which Regan calls "the most closely guarded secret of the Reagan White House," is contained in his book, *For the Record: From Wall Street to Washington*.... Mayor Edward Koch proposes a record $25.2 bil. operating budget for New York City for the year beginning July 1. The mayor's combination of property tax increases and service cuts draws dour remarks from within the city council, which will vote on the budget.... Sec. of Education William J. Bennett announces that he will resign from his cabinet post in mid-September.		The *Wall Street Journal* finds that net income at 509 major corporations it surveys quarterly surged 24% in the first quarter from the same period a year earlier. The first-quarter increase was less than the 51% surge in the fourth quarter of 1987 and the 33% gain in the third.			May 9
Gov. Michael S. Dukakis (D, Mass.) and Vice Pres. George Bush (R) win their respective parties' West Virginia and Nebraska presidential primaries, reaping most of the delegates at stake for their parties' nomination at national conventions in the summer.		Reacting to increasing pressure from clients and regulators, five large Wall Street securities firms temporarily suspend the most commonly used form of program trading, stock-index arbitrage, for their own accounts.		Beverly Sills announces that she will step down as general director of the New York City Opera effective Jan. 1, 1989. Sills, the opera company's star soprano in the 1960s and 1970s, took charge of the company in 1979, a year before retiring from the stage.... The National Basketball Assoc. names guard Mark Jackson of the New York Knicks as the rookie of the year for the 1987-88 season.	May 10
Pres. Reagan endorses the presidential bid of Vice Pres. George Bush, telling guests at a Republican fund-raising dinner that he will do "all he can" to elect Bush in November.		The nation's leading banks raise their prime lending rate to 9% from 8.5%. The increase in the prime is the first since October 1987, and follows three separate prime rate cuts.... Thrifts insured by the Federal Savings and Loan Insurance Corp. lost $3.3 bil. in capital in the first quarter of 1988, the Federal Home Loan Bank Board reports. The loss, second only to the $4.5 bil. drop in the fourth quarter of 1987, is caused largely by write-downs of real estate loans and properties in the depressed Southwest.		Scores of show business luminaries converge on New York City's Carnegie Hall to pay tribute to songwriter Irving Berlin on the occasion of his 100th birthday. Among those performing at the gala are singers Frank Sinatra, Willie Nelson, Rosemary Clooney, and Ray Charles, dancer Tommy Tune, and composer-conductor Leonard Bernstein. Berlin did not attend.... Tabatha Foster, 3, the world's longest survivor of a five-organ transplant, dies at Childrens' Hospital of Pittsburgh, of "multisystem failure" brought on by a blood infection.	May 11

F	G	H	I	J
Includes elections, federal-state relations, civil rights and liberties, crime, the judiciary, education, health care, poverty, urban affairs and population.	Includes formation and debate of U.S. foreign and defense policies, veterans' affairs and defense spending. (Relations with specific foreign countries are usually found under the region concerned.)	Includes business, labor, agriculture, taxation, transportation, consumer affairs, monetary and fiscal policy, natural resources, and pollution.	Includes worldwide scientific, medical and technological developments, natural phenomena, U.S. weather, natural disasters, and accidents.	Includes the arts, religion, scholarship, communications media, sports, entertainments, fashions, fads and social life.

	World Affairs	Europe	Africa & the Middle East	The Americas	Asia & the Pacific
May 12				Argentina's Supreme Court rules that the so-called Law of Due Obedience, which exempts military officers from prosecution for alleged human rights abuses committed during the 1970s, applies to two generals and a colonel, as well as to lower-ranking officers.... The provincial government of Quebec, Canada, offers families a cash incentive to have children. The plan is part of the provincial budget. Quebec's fertility rate is 1.4 children for each woman of child-bearing age. The fertility rate for industrialized nations is 2.1, and for Canada as a whole, 1.7.	The government of Vietnam issues a written appeal for international emergency aid after declaring that more than 3 million Vietnamese people are "at the edge of starvation." The appeal says that 8 million people in 12 northern provinces, including the city of Hanoi, are "seriously short of food." The government states that 108,000 tons of rice and grain are needed to feed people in the stricken provinces until the next harvest, in June or July.
May 13		Britain and the Republic of Ireland announce a compromise to enable extradition of terrorist suspects to Britain from Ireland. Neither nation, however, admits backing down in the dispute, and details of the compromise are not clear.		Brazil celebrates a national holiday, marking the 100th anniversary of the abolition of slavery. Slavery was banned in the country after Princess Isabel of Brazil signed the Golden Law on May 13, 1888, freeing 780,000 slaves.	
May 14		France's Pres. Francois Mitterrand announces the dissolution of the National Assembly and sets a two-round parliamentary election for June 5 and June 12. The action comes less than a week after Mitterrand easily won election to a second seven-year term.... Willem Drees, 101, premier of the Netherlands from 1948 to 1958 (the longest premiership in Dutch history) and the architect of the nation's comprehensive welfare system, dies in The Hague. Under his stewardship, the Netherlands recovered from five years of German occupation during World War II. Drees, who helped found the Dutch Labor Party after the war, quit the party in the early 1970s because he felt it was moving too far to the left.	Iraqi warplanes carry out a long-range bombing raid on the Iranian offshore oil terminal at Larak Island, near the mouth of the Persian Gulf. Five supertankers are set afire and seriously damaged, and up to 22 crew members are dead or missing.	The Nicaraguan government imposes new curbs on the media. Radio news programs are barred from insulting government leaders, and restrictions are placed on reports on military recruitment, which has stepped up in recent weeks.	
May 15		Yugoslavia's Vice Pres. Raif Dizdarevic succeeds Pres. Lazar Mojsov in the one-year post. Under the system in place since 1980, eight members of the nine-member collective presidency take turns as the titular head of state. The eight represent Yugoslavia's six constituent republics and two autonomous provinces. (The ninth seat of the leadership group is reserved for the head of the Central Committee Presidium of the League of Communists, who does not become head of state.)			The Soviet Union officially begins to withdraw its estimated 115,000 troops from Afghanistan under the terms of the four-party peace accords signed in Geneva in April. The accords mandate that half the Soviet contingent be out by August 15, and the remainder by Feb. 15, 1989.... Afghan rebel forces seize a key Afghan army outpost in the eastern town of Jaji, on the Pakistani border. Large stocks of weapons and ammunition left behind by the retreating government troops are captured by the rebels.... The Chinese government removes price controls on certain basic foodstuffs in Beijing and Shanghai as part of its effort to wean the nation from an economy dominated by central planning in favor of one governed by free market forces.

A	B	C	D	E
Includes developments that affect more than one world region, international organizations and important meetings of major world leaders.	Includes all domestic and regional developments in Europe, including the Soviet Union, Turkey, Cyprus and Malta.	Includes all domestic and regional developments in Africa and the Middle East, including Iraq and Iran and excluding Cyprus, Turkey and Afghanistan.	Includes all domestic and regional developments in Latin America, the Caribbean and Canada.	Includes all domestic and regional developments in Asia and Pacific nations, extending from Afghanistan through all the Pacific Islands, except Hawaii.

U.S. Politics & Social Issues	U.S. Foreign Policy & Defense	U.S. Economy & Environment	Science, Technology & Nature	Culture, Leisure & Life Style	
		Over three days, the Treasury Dept. sells $26.02 bil. of notes and bonds at rates that are the highest in over two years. . . . The Federal Communications Comm. proposes a new method of regulating long-distance telephone rates that it says could save consumers $1.6 bil. over the next four years.	After sponsoring nearly $240 mil. of artificial heart research since 1964, the National Institutes of Health announces that the federal government will no longer finance research aimed at developing full-scale artificial hearts.	Paul Osborn, 86, screenwriter and prolific Broadway playwright of the 1930s, '40s, and '50s, dies in New York City. He had hit runs on Broadway with such adaptations as *A Bell for Adano* (1944-45, from John Hersey's novel) and *The World of Susie Wong* (1958-59, from Richard Mason's novel). His screenwriting credits include *The Yearling* (1947), *East of Eden* (1955), and *South Pacific* (1958). In 1980, he won his first Tony Award for a revival of his 1939 play *Mornings at Seven*.	May 12
		The government's producer price index rose 0.4% in April, the Labor Dept. reports.	Biologists report discovering a second genetic code that directs one of the steps in protein synthesis within living cells. The discovery is announced by scientists at the Massachusetts Institute of Technology writing in the British journal *Nature*. The discovery, sought for two decades, clarifies the last step in the multistep process by which information coded in molecules of DNA (deoxyribonucleic acid) is translated into unique proteins within the cell.		May 13
				Chet (Chesney) Baker, 58, jazz trumpeter and vocalist who helped set the standard for West Coast "cool jazz" in the early 1950s, dies after falling from the window of an Amsterdam hotel; a police spokesman said he had taken heroin just before he fell. Baker was one of the original members of the revolutionary, pianoless Gerry Mulligan Quartet, but his career was blighted by heroin addiction, and after a 1968 beating in which he lost most of his teeth, he did not play again for several years. . . . Novelist T. Coraghessan Boyle is presented with the 1988 PEN/Faulkner Award for Fiction for his third novel, *World's End*.	May 14
				Alain Prost of France wins the Monaco Grand Prix in Monte Carlo.	May 15

F	G	H	I	J
Includes elections, federal-state relations, civil rights and liberties, crime, the judiciary, education, health care, poverty, urban affairs and population.	*Includes formation and debate of U.S. foreign and defense policies, veterans' affairs and defense spending. (Relations with specific foreign countries are usually found under the region concerned.)*	*Includes business, labor, agriculture, taxation, transportation, consumer affairs, monetary and fiscal policy, natural resources, and pollution.*	*Includes worldwide scientific, medical and technological developments, natural phenomena, U.S. weather, natural disasters, and accidents.*	*Includes the arts, religion, scholarship, communications media, sports, entertainments, fashions, fads and social life.*

	World Affairs	Europe	Africa & the Middle East	The Americas	Asia & the Pacific
May 16	Consumer prices in the world's developing countries rose 40.1% in 1987, the International Monetary Fund reports, about 10 percentage points greater than in 1986 but well beneath the 1985 high of 46.9%.		Algeria and Morocco announce that they are restoring diplomatic relations 12 years after breaking them over the issue of the Western Sahara, where Algerian-backed guerrillas of the Polisario Front continue to fight Moroccan forces.		
May 17		The Bank of England initiates a reduction in commercial banks' base lending rates to 7.5% from 8.0%. The cut in the benchmark lending rate follows reports of a renewed feud over monetary policy between P.M. Margaret Thatcher and Chancellor of the Exchequer Nigel Lawson. . . . The overseer of a West German fund to compensate Jews for the Nazi genocide of World War II says that the fund is missing millions of dollars apparently stolen by his predecessor. Though the precise amount of missing funds has not been determined, reports estimate the total at as much as $20 mil.			
May 18				Canada's opposition parties in the House of Commons withhold unanimous consent on a motion to have a free vote on an abortion resolution introduced by the ruling Progressive Conservative Party. Canada has been without an abortion law since January, when the nation's Supreme Court struck down restrictions on the procedure.	At least 46 people, most of them Sikh militants, are reported killed over the past 10 days during a siege by Indian government troops of the Golden Temple at Amritsar, the holiest Sikh shrine.
May 19	Ministers from the 24 member nations of the Org. for Economic Cooperation and Development conclude their annual meeting with an uneasy compromise on the issue of reducing farm subsidies.	Seasonally adjusted unemployment in Britain fell below 2.5 million in April, the first time in more than six-and-a-half years, the government reports. The 2.455 million jobless workers represent 8.8% of the work force.			

A	B	C	D	E
Includes developments that affect more than one world region, international organizations and important meetings of major world leaders.	Includes all domestic and regional developments in Europe, including the Soviet Union, Turkey, Cyprus and Malta.	Includes all domestic and regional developments in Africa and the Middle East, including Iraq and Iran and excluding Cyprus, Turkey and Afghanistan.	Includes all domestic and regional developments in Latin America, the Caribbean and Canada.	Includes all domestic and regional developments in Asia and Pacific nations, extending from Afghanistan through all the Pacific Islands, except Hawaii.

U.S. Politics & Social Issues	U.S. Foreign Policy & Defense	U.S. Economy & Environment	Science, Technology & Nature	Culture, Leisure & Life Style	
The Rev. Pat Robertson, the former television evangelist, withdraws from the Republican presidential race and endorses Vice Pres. Bush.		The Federal Reserve Board reports that its industrial production index rose 0.7% in April. . . . The Supreme Court upholds, 8-0, an antitrust award of $2.2 mil. won by a surgeon against a hospital peer-review panel. The surgeon contends that the panel, which had criticized his work and tried to terminate his services, acted against him because he was a competitor. . . . The Reagan administration's working group on the October 1987 stock market crash releases its report, proposing only one major change in the nation's financial markets. The sole major change proposed is the establishment of coordinated trading halts, or circuit breakers.	Surgeon Gen. C. Everett Koop declares, in a massive report, that cigarettes and other tobacco products are "addicting in the same sense as are drugs such as heroin and cocaine."	Howard Nemerov is named poet laureate of the United States, becoming the third person to hold the post since it was created in 1985. He will succeed Richard Wilbur. While holding the laureateship, Nemerov, 68, will continue to teach at Washington Univ. in St. Louis, where he is a professor of English.	May 16
Massachusetts Gov. Michael S. Dukakis wins Oregon's Democratic presidential primary with 56% of the vote to 38% for his remaining rival, the Rev. Jesse L. Jackson. Vice Pres. George Bush, who has already clinched the Republican nomination, wins the Republican primary with 73% of the vote and takes all 32 GOP convention delegates.		The U.S. deficit on merchandise trade dropped 30% in March, to $9.75 bil., the Commerce Dept. reports, bringing the trade deficit to its lowest level in three years.	The Office of Technology Assessment reports that Americans spent $1 bil. on medical efforts to combat infertility in 1987, but that only about half of those who underwent treatment for infertility succeeded in bearing a child.		May 17
	The Senate votes, 91-6, to rebuff an attempt by hardcore conservatives to block ratification of the U.S.-Soviet treaty on intermediate-range nuclear forces.	Housing starts rose 0.5% in April, the Commerce Dept. reports, to an adjusted annual rate of 1.561 million. . . . The Federal Home Loan Bank Board says it will provide $2 bil. to merge four insolvent Texas thrifts into the healthy Southwest Savings Assoc. of Dallas. The sum is the largest ever provided by the bank board's Federal Savings and Loan Insurance Corp. in a merger case.		*Variety*'s top-grossing films for the week are: *Friday the 13th Part VII—The New Blood, Colors, Salsa, Beetlejuice,* and *Shakedown.*	May 18
Trial-heat polls matching the likely presidential nominees, reported May 17 and today, give Massachusetts Gov. Michael S. Dukakis (D) a large early lead over Vice Pres. George Bush (R).		The Teamsters union leadership declares a tentative contract submitted to the membership accepted and in effect, despite a "no" vote against it by nearly 64% of the members voting on the settlement. Under a provision of the union's constitution, the general executive board can declare an agreement ratified if less than two-thirds of those voting oppose it. This is the first time that the provision has been invoked for a master freight agreement since the clause was written into the constitution in 1961.			May 19

F	G	H	I	J
Includes elections, federal-state relations, civil rights and liberties, crime, the judiciary, education, health care, poverty, urban affairs and population.	Includes formation and debate of U.S. foreign and defense policies, veterans' affairs and defense spending. (Relations with specific foreign countries are usually found under the region concerned.)	Includes business, labor, agriculture, taxation, transportation, consumer affairs, monetary and fiscal policy, natural resources, and pollution.	Includes worldwide scientific, medical and technological developments, natural phenomena, U.S. weather, natural disasters, and accidents.	Includes the arts, religion, scholarship, communications media, sports, entertainments, fashions, fads and social life.

	World Affairs	Europe	Africa & the Middle East	The Americas	Asia & the Pacific
May 20					More than 200 people are injured in Taipei when a government-sanctioned march by Taiwanese farmers protesting the country's agricultural policies degenerates into a riot. The incident is the most violent protest in Taiwan since 1947, when army troops from mainland China suppressed a rebellion by native Taiwanese, news reports say.... In Japan, the National Land Agency declares that the total value of land in the metropolitan Tokyo area has increased to 10 times the national budget. In its annual report on land utilization, the agency says the value of land in Tokyo at the end of 1986 increased to $4.48 trillion, more than 10 times the national budget of $450 bil. for fiscal 1988, which began April 1.
May 21				Gov. Gen. Jeanne Sauve formally opens the new, permanent home of the National Gallery of Canada in Ottawa. Since the 1880s, Canada's primary art museum had been housed in a series of temporary locations.	
May 22		Janos Kadar is removed as the general secretary of Hungary's Socialist Workers' (Communist) Party at the national party conference in Budapest. He is replaced by Premier Karoly Grosz. The two-day conference, which is extensively covered by the Hungarian media, is perhaps the most open gathering ever held by an Eastern European communist party. Debate among the delegates is vigorous and often critical of the Socialist Workers' Party leadership.		Some 80,000 peasants demanding land and the nationalization of foreign oil companies begin marches on six Colombian cities. The peasants are also protesting what they say is government neglect of rural areas and demanding an end to the army's "dirty war" against them.	
May 23		In Britain, the Conservative government's controversial community charge proposal, the Poll Tax, easily wins a key vote in the House of Lords. The government's efforts to bring in enough votes to defeat an amendment to the bill proposed by Conservative Lord Chelwood results in a House of Lords turnout that is the second-largest on record.... Britain's gross domestic product, adjusted for inflation and seasonal factors, grew 0.25% from the previous quarter and was up 4.6% from the year-earlier period, the government reports.	Israeli military authorities reopened Arab elementary schools in the occupied West Bank after a months-long shutdown caused by the Palestinian uprising. Both sides claim the development as a victory.		A new wave of student demonstrations erupts in South Korea over the past week, following the protest suicide May 15 of a college student in Seoul. The disturbances are the largest to hit the country since the summer of 1987, when mass street protests forced the government to adopt sweeping democratic reforms.... The Japanese government publishes a five-year economic development plan covering fiscal 1988 through 1992. The plan forecasts an annual rate of increase in domestic demand of 4.25% over the five-year period, while predicting a drop in external demand. Overall, the economy is expected to grow at an annual rate of 3.75% under the plan.

A	B	C	D	E
Includes developments that affect more than one world region, international organizations and important meetings of major world leaders.	*Includes all domestic and regional developments in Europe, including the Soviet Union, Turkey, Cyprus and Malta.*	*Includes all domestic and regional developments in Africa and the Middle East, including Iraq and Iran and excluding Cyprus, Turkey and Afghanistan.*	*Includes all domestic and regional developments in Latin America, the Caribbean and Canada.*	*Includes all domestic and regional developments in Asia and Pacific nations, extending from Afghanistan through all the Pacific Islands, except Hawaii.*

U.S. Politics & Social Issues	U.S. Foreign Policy & Defense	U.S. Economy & Environment	Science, Technology & Nature	Culture, Leisure & Life Style	
	Pres. Reagan signs into law three major bills related to military veterans. One of the measures mandates disability benefits for so-called "atomic vets," or people who contracted cancer following exposure to radiation while in the service after World War II; the second provides job training and employment counseling for veterans; and the third is an omnibus health-care measure.	The government's consumer price index rose 0.4% in April, the Labor Dept. reports.			May 20
			In a major policy change, the National Cancer Institute is now urging that all women who have had breast cancer surgery should follow up with drug or hormone therapy whether or not there is evidence that the cancer has spread.	Risen Star, ridden by Eddie Delahoussaye, wins the 113th running of the Preakness Stakes at Pimlico Race Course in Baltimore. . . . *Billboard*'s best-selling albums for the week are: *Faith*, George Michael; *Dirty Dancing* (soundtrack); *More Dirty Dancing* (soundtrack); *Bad*, Michael Jackson; *The Hardline According to Terence Trent D'Arby*, Terence Trent D'Arby.	May 21
				Sweden wins the World Team Cup in Tennis. . . . Ulf Timmermann of East Germany sets a world record in the shot put with a toss of 75 feet, eight inches.	May 22
Two months after the Coast Guard and the Customs Service, under a new Reagan administration policy known as "zero tolerance," began seizing boats, cars, and other vehicles in which small amounts of illegal drugs were found, the White House says that the government will no longer seize boats in international waters merely because they are found to be carrying minute quantities of drugs.			The Food and Drug Admin. approves a contraceptive device known as the cervical cap for availability by prescription to U.S. women. The cap, which resembles a large rubber thimble, is fitted by a physician to cover the base of the uterine cervix. After the initial fitting, the device is removed and reinserted by the user.	The 41st annual Cannes film festival in France awards its top prize, the Golden Palm, to Danish director Bille August's *Pelle the Conqueror*.	May 23

F	G	H	I	J
Includes elections, federal-state relations, civil rights and liberties, crime, the judiciary, education, health care, poverty, urban affairs and population.	*Includes formation and debate of U.S. foreign and defense policies, veterans' affairs and defense spending. (Relations with specific foreign countries are usually found under the region concerned.)*	*Includes business, labor, agriculture, taxation, transportation, consumer affairs, monetary and fiscal policy, natural resources, and pollution.*	*Includes worldwide scientific, medical and technological developments, natural phenomena, U.S. weather, natural disasters, and accidents.*	*Includes the arts, religion, scholarship, communications media, sports, entertainments, fashions, fads and social life.*

	World Affairs	Europe	Africa & the Middle East	The Americas	Asia & the Pacific
May 24		Israel's Foreign Min. Shimon Peres meets with European Community (EC) foreign ministers in Brussels. He urges his counterparts to seek the approval by the European Parliament of a trade protocol that was rejected in March. Relations are already strained by Israel's handling of the Palestinian uprising, which has been strongly criticized by the EC.	The Org. of African Unity holds its 24th annual summit and marks its 25th anniversary in Addis Ababa, Ethiopia. More than 30 African heads of state attend the conference.		Pakistan is reported to have successfully tested a medium-range surface-to-surface missile capable of carrying a nuclear warhead. The *New York Times* report quotes unidentified officials of the Reagan administration and the Pakistani government who say that Pakistan launched the missile April 25 at a test range in the Thar Desert in the southern part of the country.
May 25	The Soviet Union reveals for the first time its official casualty figures for the Afghan war. As of May 1, a high-ranking aide in the defense ministry says, 13,310 Soviet soldiers were killed and 35,478 wounded during eight-and-a-half years of combat in Afghanistan. In addition, 311 soldiers are listed as missing in action.		The bloody strife between rival Lebanese Shiite Moslem militias in Beirut's southern suburbs continues as Syria delays on making good its threat to deploy troops to restore order. The delay follows objections from Iran, and is also linked to concerns over the fate of the Western hostages believed to be held in south Beirut. . . . In a surprise attack, Iraq drives Iranian forces from their positions in the marshy Shalamcheh area east of Basra, a foothold that Iran won at great expense in January 1987. The Iraqi victory is the latest and clearest sign that the battlefield initiative in the more than seven-and-a-half-year-old Persian Gulf conflict has shifted to Iraq, and that popular enthusiasm for the war among Iranians seems to be waning. . . . Libya's leader Col. Muammer el-Qaddafi declares an end to his nation's long-standing armed dispute with neighboring Chad. Qaddafi says that Libya, as a "present" to Africa on the 25th anniversary of the Org. of African Unity, will recognize the Chadian government.	In an embarrassing defeat for U.S. policy in Panama, talks on ousting military strongman Gen. Manuel Antonio Noriega collapse. Noriega rejects a U.S. proposal to give up power and leave the country temporarily, in return for which the United States will drop drug-trafficking indictments against him. . . . The Canadian Human Rights Comm. issues regulations that prohibit most employers from requiring workers or prospective employees to submit to mandatory acquired immune deficiency syndrome testing.	
May 26	A New York Times/CBS News telephone poll of 939 Muscovites, indicates strong support for Gen. Sec. Gorbachev's overall program of reforms, particularly in the spheres of democratization and openness. The poll was conducted for the U.S. news organizations by the Soviet Institute for Sociological Research.		Syria and Iran reach agreement on a plan for deploying Syrian troops in Beirut's southern suburbs. The Syrian move into the area on the following day ends three weeks of vicious fighting between rival Lebanese Shiite Moslem militias; at least 300, and possibly more than 400, people are reported killed in the fighting.		The chief of staff of the Soviet armed forces, Marshal Sergei F. Akhromeyev, announces in Moscow that the Soviet Union had 100,300 troops in Afghanistan at the start of the formal withdrawal period earlier in May. Previous Western estimates had put Soviet troop strength at about 115,000. . . . The Vietnamese government formally announces in Hanoi that it will withdraw 50,000 of its soldiers from Cambodia by the end of 1988. The exit is set to begin in June. . . . The Japanese Diet approves a U.S.-Japanese nuclear cooperation pact that will allow Japan to ship spent nuclear fuel to Western Europe from the United States for reprocessing. The agreement cleared the U.S. Senate in March.

A	B	C	D	E
Includes developments that affect more than one world region, international organizations and important meetings of major world leaders.	Includes all domestic and regional developments in Europe, including the Soviet Union, Turkey, Cyprus and Malta.	Includes all domestic and regional developments in Africa and the Middle East, including Iraq and Iran and excluding Cyprus, Turkey and Afghanistan.	Includes all domestic and regional developments in Latin America, the Caribbean and Canada.	Includes all domestic and regional developments in Asia and Pacific nations, extending from Afghanistan through all the Pacific Islands, except Hawaii.

U.S. Politics & Social Issues	U.S. Foreign Policy & Defense	U.S. Economy & Environment	Science, Technology & Nature	Culture, Leisure & Life Style	
New Jersey's education commissioner Saul Cooperman moves to have the state seize control of a city school system that he says has "reached a state of managerial bankruptcy." Cooperman begins the takeover process after finding that the Jersey City, N.J., school district had failed to correct chronic and pervasive problems discovered by three separate investigative teams that had monitored the district since 1984. The city's school system is the state's second largest, with a total enrollment of 28,865 students. . . . Vice Pres. George Bush (R) and Massachusetts Gov. Michael S. Dukakis (D) easily win the Idaho presidential primaries, Bush with 82% of the vote and Dukakis with 73%. The Democratic event was a nonbinding "beauty contest."		Pres. Reagan vetoes comprehensive trade legislation and calls for "prompt action on a second bill after the Congress sustains my veto." The House of Representatives immediately votes, 308-113, to override the veto, but Senate Democrats admit that it is unlikely they can muster the two-thirds majority needed to override the veto.	Australians have the third-longest life expectancy rates in the world. As of 1986, a study presented to the country's health ministers shows that life expectancy for Australian males had reached 72.77 years, and for females 79.13 years. Only residents of Iceland and Japan have longer life spans, the report says.	Thailand's Porntip Nakhirunkanok is crowned Miss Universe in Taipei, Taiwan. . . . CBS, Inc. wins the bidding for the U.S. rights to televise the 1992 Winter Olympics in Albertville, France. The $243 mil. offered by CBS exceeds the International Olympic Committee's expectations of $200 mil. and outbids National Broadcasting Co. by $68 mil. . . . The 10th annual Pritzger Architecture Prize, presented at the Art Institute of Chicago, is shared by Gordon Bunshaft of the United States and Oscar Niemeyer of Brazil.	May 24
				Michael Jordan, the Chicago Bulls guard who led the National Basketball Assoc. in scoring during the season, is named the league's most valuable player.	May 25
The government begins distributing to all American households a bluntly worded eight-page booklet on acquired immune deficiency syndrome. The booklet was prepared under the direction of Surgeon Gen. C. Everett Koop and the Centers for Disease Control. The government expects to mail 114 million copies by June 30, at a cost of $17 mil. . . . Rep. Dan Rostenkowski (D, Ill.) led all House members in speaking fees in 1987, collecting $245,000 for 51 speeches, according to House financial disclosure statements. Rostenkowski donated all but $26,000 of the money to stay within legal limits.		The House approves the fiscal 1989 budget plan by a 201-181 vote. The plan projects a $135.3 bil. deficit for the year, which begins October 1. The figure is under the $146 bil. trigger that would automatically impose across-the-board spending cuts, known as a "sequester."	The Food and Drug Admin. announces that it has ordered the manufacturer of the anti-acne prescription drug Accutane to adopt unprecedented new measures to prevent its use by pregnant women. The drug, made by Roche Laboratories, a division of Hoffmann-La Roche Inc. of Nutley, N.J., has been linked to serious birth defects, including mental retardation and misplaced facial features.	The Edmonton Oilers win their fourth National Hockey League Stanley Cup in five years when they complete a four-game sweep of the Boston Bruins.	May 26

F	G	H	I	J
Includes elections, federal-state relations, civil rights and liberties, crime, the judiciary, education, health care, poverty, urban affairs and population.	Includes formation and debate of U.S. foreign and defense policies, veterans' affairs and defense spending. (Relations with specific foreign countries are usually found under the region concerned.)	Includes business, labor, agriculture, taxation, transportation, consumer affairs, monetary and fiscal policy, natural resources, and pollution.	Includes worldwide scientific, medical and technological developments, natural phenomena, U.S. weather, natural disasters, and accidents.	Includes the arts, religion, scholarship, communications media, sports, entertainments, fashions, fads and social life.

	World Affairs	Europe	Africa & the Middle East	The Americas	Asia & the Pacific
May 27		Britain's current account deficit in April was $971 mil., the government reports.... European venture capital funds raised more money than their U.S. counterparts for the first time ever in 1987. European venture capitalists raised $5 bil. in 1987, more than twice the amount raised in 1986, according to a study by KPMG Peat Marwick for the European Venture Capital Assoc., a Brussels trade group. By comparison, U.S. venture capitalists raised $4.9 bil., up from $4.5 bil. in 1986.	Consumer spending was flat while personal income rose 0.1% in April, the Commerce Dept. reports.		Afghanistan's Pres. Najibullah chooses Mohammed Hassan Sharq to become the new Afghan premier, replacing Soltan Ali Keshtmand.
May 28				In the third round of peace talks in Managua, the Nicaraguan government unexpectedly offers to make political reforms. Contra leaders characterize the offer as vague and limited but say it improves the prospects for a settlement.	
May 29	Pres. Reagan and Soviet leader Mikhail S. Gorbachev meet in Moscow for their fourth summit. It is the president's first visit to the Soviet Union. During the summit, Reagan, known for his hard-line anti-Soviet stance, noticeably softens his views.		Siaka (Probyn) Stevens, 82, leader of the West African nation of Sierra Leone for 17 years, dies in Freetown, Sierra Leone; he had suffered a crippling stroke in December 1987. He became prime minister in 1968 after a military coup and assumed the presidency in April 1971, two days after Sierra Leone became a republic. He retired as president in late 1985, becoming one of only a handful of black African leaders ever to give up power voluntarily.		Declaring that law and order in Pakistan has "broken down to an alarming extent," Pres. Muhammad Zia ul-Haq dissolves the country's National Assembly and dismisses P.M. Muhammad Khan Junejo and his 33-member cabinet.
May 30					India's population tops the 800 million mark, government officials report. The new level is 20 million higher than recent estimates and represents an increase of 120 million since the 1980 census. India currently adds about 16 million people a year to its population, news reports say.
May 31				Canada's federal government offers a $10 mil. emergency assistance program to farmers in the drought-stricken Prairie Provinces where grasslands have dried up for lack of rain.	Customs officials in Sydney, Australia, uncover 12 tons of weapons that apparently were being smuggled to Fiji from the Middle East. The illegal shipment contains enough weapons for 1,000 men, news reports say, giving rise to speculation that the arms were intended for antigovernment factions planning an uprising in Fiji.... Direct overseas investments by Japanese companies increase by 49.5% during fiscal 1987, to a record $33.36 bil. from $22.32 bil. the previous year, the finance ministry reports.

A	B	C	D	E
Includes developments that affect more than one world region, international organizations and important meetings of major world leaders.	Includes all domestic and regional developments in Europe, including the Soviet Union, Turkey, Cyprus and Malta.	Includes all domestic and regional developments in Africa and the Middle East, including Iraq and Iran and excluding Cyprus, Turkey and Afghanistan.	Includes all domestic and regional developments in Latin America, the Caribbean and Canada.	Includes all domestic and regional developments in Asia and Pacific nations, extending from Afghanistan through all the Pacific Islands, except Hawaii.

U.S. Politics & Social Issues	U.S. Foreign Policy & Defense	U.S. Economy & Environment	Science, Technology & Nature	Culture, Leisure & Life Style	
Trailing in the national polls, Vice Pres. George Bush meets with his top political and economic advisers to map a turnaround. The latest ABC News/Washington Post poll shows Dukakis leading Bush by 53%-40%, although support for both candidates is regarded as "soft."	The Senate passes a $299.5 bil. defense authorization bill for fiscal 1989 by voice vote. On May 11 the House passed a defense authorization with an identical funding ceiling. The $299.5 bil. figure, which is what Pres. Reagan requested in February, includes money for such defense-related projects as the Energy Dept.'s nuclear weapons programs.	New York State and Long Island Lighting Co. (Lilco) reach an "agreement in principle" to close the controversial Shoreham nuclear power station.	The journal *Science* reports that, in the air over the Arctic regions, scientists have gathered the first evidence of the chlorofluorocarbon (CFC) chemicals that have been linked to the destruction of the ozone over Antarctica.	*Publishers Weekly*'s hardback fiction best-sellers for the week are: *Zoya*, Danielle Steel; *The Icarus Agenda*, Robert Ludlum; *The Bonfire of the Vanities*, Tom Wolfe; *Love in the Time of Cholera*, Gabriel Garcia Marquez; and *Rock Star*, Jackie Collins. . . . Sy (Melvin James) Oliver, 77, jazz composer, arranger, trumpeter, and vocalist, dies of lung cancer in New York City. His work with the Jimmie Lunceford and Tommy Dorsey orchestras made him one of the most influential figures of the big band era. He formed his own nine-piece band in the early 1970s, appearing with it at the Rainbow Room in New York City from 1974 until his retirement in 1984.	May 27
					May 28
				Pope John Paul II names 25 new cardinals of the Roman Catholic Church, bringing the membership of the College of Cardinals to 161. The new cardinals come from 18 countries; by region, 10 are from Western Europe, four from Asia, three each from Africa, South America, and North America, and two from Eastern Europe. . . . Rick Mears wins his third Indianapolis 500 and the seventh for cars driven for the racing team of Roger Penske.	May 29
				Syracuse Univ. wins the National Collegiate Athletic Assoc. Division I lacrosse championship with a 13-8 win over Cornell Univ.	May 30
		Prices received by farmers for raw agricultural products in May climb 3.1%, the Agriculture Dept. reports. . . . The Supreme Court upholds, 5-4, the practice of importing into the United States so-called "gray-market" goods, or brand-name goods marketed through unauthorized channels without the approval of the owners of the trademarks for those goods. . . . An agreement to start cleaning up the Stringfellow Acid Pits near Riverside, Calif., is reached between state and federal environmental officials and representatives of 16 companies that dumped toxic chemicals and metals at the site, a 20-acre rock quarry. . . . W.R. Grace & Co. pleads guilty to lying to the Environmental Protection Agency about the amount of toxic chemicals used at its plant in Woburn, Mass.			May 31

F	G	H	I	J
Includes elections, federal-state relations, civil rights and liberties, crime, the judiciary, education, health care, poverty, urban affairs and population.	Includes formation and debate of U.S. foreign and defense policies, veterans' affairs and defense spending. (Relations with specific foreign countries are usually found under the region concerned.)	Includes business, labor, agriculture, taxation, transportation, consumer affairs, monetary and fiscal policy, natural resources, and pollution.	Includes worldwide scientific, medical and technological developments, natural phenomena, U.S. weather, natural disasters, and accidents.	Includes the arts, religion, scholarship, communications media, sports, entertainments, fashions, fads and social life.

	World Affairs	Europe	Africa & the Middle East	The Americas	Asia & the Pacific
June 1		West Germany's economy showed solid growth during the first quarter of 1988, according to a government report. The report predicts that growth for the year could exceed the 2% rate that has been forecast.		Angry Mohawk Indians living on the 5,000-resident Kahnawake reserve, south of Montreal, begin a one-day blockade of a Montreal-area highway and bridge in response to a raid on their reserve by the Royal Canadian Mounted Police. . . . Brazil's Constituent Assembly, which is drafting a new national constitution, approves 497-10, a provision that will protect the land rights of the country's native Indians. The provision will give the Indians permanent possession of their traditional tribal areas and will protect them from outside commercial interests.	
June 2	Total borrowing on international capital markets is a record $118.2 bil. in the first quarter of 1988, the Org. of Economic Cooperation and Development reports.		Iran's supreme leader Ayatollah Ruhollah Khomeini names parliament speaker Hojatolislam Ali Akbar Hashemi Rafsanjani to be commander in chief of Iran's overall military effort. The unexpected announcement makes Rafsanjani the most powerful man in Iran after Khomeini and Khomeini's likely successor.	Brazil's Constituent Assembly votes, 328-222, to grant Pres. Jose Sarney a five-year term in office. The decision will allow Sarney, who assumed the presidency in March 1985, to remain in office until March 1990.	A panel commissioned to review Hong Kong's securities markets in the wake of the October 1987 worldwide stock market crash releases a report listing numerous faults with the industry and proposes major reforms. The commission cites a number of factors as contributing to the near collapse of the securities markets, including poor management at the stock exchange and the Hong Kong Futures Exchange, as well as insufficient regulatory control by the government. . . . After six years of negotiations, Antarctic Treaty nations agree on a far-reaching convention that will permit commercial mining on the southern continent and in its surrounding seas. The agreement is signed by the 33 governments represented at month-long talks held in Wellington, New Zealand. It will become binding when ratified by 16 of the 20 nations that signed the Antarctica Treaty of 1959.
June 3					
June 4		The Soviet Communist Party publishes a final list of the 5,000 delegates attending the national party conference scheduled to begin June 28 in Moscow. The conference is to debate party policies and practices, including the economic, political, and social reforms initiated by Gen. Sec. Mikhail S. Gorbachev.			

A	B	C	D	E
Includes developments that affect more than one world region, international organizations and important meetings of major world leaders.	Includes all domestic and regional developments in Europe, including the Soviet Union, Turkey, Cyprus and Malta.	Includes all domestic and regional developments in Africa and the Middle East, including Iraq and Iran and excluding Cyprus, Turkey and Afghanistan.	Includes all domestic and regional developments in Latin America, the Caribbean and Canada.	Includes all domestic and regional developments in Asia and Pacific nations, extending from Afghanistan through all the Pacific Islands, except Hawaii.

U.S. Politics & Social Issues	U.S. Foreign Policy & Defense	U.S. Economy & Environment	Science, Technology & Nature	Culture, Leisure & Life Style	
An unexpected and serious dwindling of state revenues has begun to occur in certain key states, notably California, New York, and Massachusetts, the *Wall Street Journal* reports.		The government's index of leading economic indicators climbed 0.2% in April, the Commerce Dept. reports, encouraging fears of increased inflation.... Despite huge losses in the October 1987 stock market crash, New York Stock Exchange specialist firms in 1987 had their most profitable year ever. The 54 market makers earned a pre-tax total of $369.3 mil. in 1987.	U.S. Army researchers report that the virus causing acquired immune deficiency syndrome has been found in unusual cases to remain hidden within certain cells of the body, undetectable by standard blood antibody tests.		June 1
The chairman of the presidential commission on acquired immune deficiency syndrome (AIDS), retired Adm. James D. Watkins, urges Pres. Reagan to issue an executive order prohibiting discrimination on the basis of AIDS and urges adoption of legislation to prohibit such bias.				The winner of the 61st annual Scripps-Howard National Spelling Bee is Rageshree Ramachandran, a 13-year-old girl from Carmichael, Calif. The eighth-grader won by correctly spelling "elegiacal."	June 2
		The nation's unemployment rate in May rose to 5.5%, the Labor Dept. says.... The standard of living improved far more slowly between 1972 and 1987 in the United States than in other industrialized countries. According to an index designed by the U.S. Council on Competitiveness, U.S. living standards have "essentially stagnated over the past 15 years," growing "only one-fourth as fast as the average of other industrial nations." In the same period, West Germany achieved a higher standard of living than the United States, and Japan a standard nearly as high.	The journal *Science* reports that Japanese mathematician Yoichi Miyaoka retracted his proof of Fermat's last theorem less than six weeks after it first became publicly known, when other mathematicians discovered a central flaw. The January announcement of the theorem, which has been the "Holy Grail" for mathematicians since it was postulated by Pierre Fermat in 1637, had caused a stir in the scientific community.... The Centers for Disease Control predicts for the first time that the acquired immune deficiency syndrome (AIDS) virus will eventually kill almost all those it infects unless a cure is developed. The conclusion, published in the journal *Science*, comes from a long-term study of more than 6,000 homosexual and bisexual men who enrolled at a San Francisco clinic for studies of hepatitis B between 1978 and 1980, before AIDS was even recognized.	The Ruth Lilly Poetry Prize goes to Anthony Hecht.... *Big*, a film about a boy (played by Tom Hanks) who is transformed into a man, is released in New York. Directed by Penny Marshall, with a screenplay by Gary Ross and Anne Spielberg, the film also stars Elizabeth Perkins.	June 3
				Steffi Graf of West Germany wins the women's title at the French Open tennis championships.	June 4

F	G	H	I	J
Includes elections, federal-state relations, civil rights and liberties, crime, the judiciary, education, health care, poverty, urban affairs and population.	Includes formation and debate of U.S. foreign and defense policies, veterans' affairs and defense spending. (Relations with specific foreign countries are usually found under the region concerned.)	Includes business, labor, agriculture, taxation, transportation, consumer affairs, monetary and fiscal policy, natural resources, and pollution.	Includes worldwide scientific, medical and technological developments, natural phenomena, U.S. weather, natural disasters, and accidents.	Includes the arts, religion, scholarship, communications media, sports, entertainments, fashions, fads and social life.

	World Affairs	Europe	Africa & the Middle East	The Americas	Asia & the Pacific
June 5		French voters go to the polls in the first round of a two-stage general election for deputies to the National Assembly. The Socialist Party of Pres. Francois Mitterrand does not do as well as preelection opinion polls had predicted, but it retains a good chance of winning an absolute majority in the National Assembly in the second round of voting to be held June 12.		John Cardinal O'Connor confirms that Cuba's Pres. Fidel Castro has agreed to release most of the political prisoners his government acknowledges are being held in Cuba's prisons. O'Connor, the Roman Catholic archbishop of New York, visited Cuba April 18-22 and personally appealed for the release.	
June 6		In Britain, the base rate, a benchmark interest rate for lending, is raised for the second time in four days, to 8.5%. As of June 2, the base rate stood at 7.5%, the lowest in a decade, before it was raised to 8% in a bid to stabilize the falling pound.		Mexico holds elections for the presidency and national legislatures. Voting results, which the governing Institutional Revolutionary Party (PRI) promises to release tonight, are not released. The delay in reporting the figures is widely believed to have arisen because of a stunning decline for the PRI, which has governed Mexico for 59 years.	Immigration surpassed births in 1987 as the principle source of population growth in Australia for the first time since 1950, the Australian Bureau of Statistics reports. . . . In a move that threatens the U.S. military presence in the Philippines, the Philippine senate approves, 19-3, a bill that will ban nuclear weapons from the country. Similar legislation is still pending in the house. . . . In a series of raids against suspected dissidents, security forces in Fiji arrest 43 ethnic Indians, including two former cabinet ministers, and uncover hundreds of buried weapons in seven villages in the predominantly Indian western section of the main island, Viti Levu.
June 7		Three days after Denmark's Queen Margrethe II swears in a new cabinet headed by conservative Premier Poul Schluter, Schluter announces that a compromise has been reached on Denmark's opposition to port visits by ships with nuclear weapons, the issue that prompted general elections four weeks earlier. . . . Sweden's Justice Min. Anna-Greta Leijon resigns her post after it is disclosed that she authorized a secret investigation into the unsolved 1986 assassination of Olof Palme.	The Arab League holds an emergency three-day summit in Algiers to discuss the six-month-old Palestinian uprising in the Israeli-occupied territories. The resolution approved at the conference vows "all possible support by all possible means" for the uprising, but does not make a public pledge of financial aid, as sought by the Palestine Liberation Org.	El Salvador's Pres. Jose Napoleon Duarte, 62, is confirmed to be terminally ill with cancer, after exploratory surgery in the United States in which doctors removed a malignant tumor from his stomach. . . . In Mexico, the Institutional Revolutionary Party's presidential candidate, Carlos Salinas de Gortari, claims victory in the June 6 election, but his claim is challenged by his two major opponents, each of whom quotes partial election returns showing himself to be leading in the vote.	Bangladesh's parliament approves a constitutional amendment making Islam the state religion. The amendment declares that "the state religion of the republic is Islam, but other religions may be practiced in peace and harmony." About 87% of the country's total population of 105 million people are Moslems. . . . The Indian Army begins withdrawing some of its estimated 50,000 troops from Sri Lanka. Indian officials will not reveal the number of soldiers being pulled out, but Western news reports put the figure at between 3,000 and 5,000. India deployed troops in Sri Lanka under the terms of a peace accord signed by the two countries in 1987.

A	B	C	D	E
Includes developments that affect more than one world region, international organizations and important meetings of major world leaders.	*Includes all domestic and regional developments in Europe, including the Soviet Union, Turkey, Cyprus and Malta.*	*Includes all domestic and regional developments in Africa and the Middle East, including Iraq and Iran and excluding Cyprus, Turkey and Afghanistan.*	*Includes all domestic and regional developments in Latin America, the Caribbean and Canada.*	*Includes all domestic and regional developments in Asia and Pacific nations, extending from Afghanistan through all the Pacific Islands, except Hawaii.*

U.S. Politics & Social Issues	U.S. Foreign Policy & Defense	U.S. Economy & Environment	Science, Technology & Nature	Culture, Leisure & Life Style	
				Sweden's Mats Wilander wins the men's title at the French Open tennis championships.... The 42nd annual Tony (Antoinette Perry) Awards are presented. Andrew Lloyd Webber's *The Phantom of the Opera* wins seven awards, including best musical; best director, Harold Prince; and best leading actor, Michael Crawford. Stephen Sondheim's *Into the Woods* wins for best original score (Sondheim), best book of a musical, James Lapine, and best leading actress, Joanna Gleason. David Henry Hwang's *M. Butterfly* wins the award for best play and best director, John Dexter. Joan Allen is named best actress for *Burn This*; and Ron Silver, best actor for *Speed-the-Plow*. The Cole Porter musical *Anything Goes* is named for best revival.... The Russian Orthodox Church celebrates the 1,000th anniversary of the introduction of Christianity into medieval Russia. The church has over 40 million followers, most living in the Soviet Union. The week-long celebration has the full support of the Kremlin, which appears anxious to shed its reputation of violent hostility to religion.	June 5
A former aide to House Speaker Jim Wright (D, Tex.) says Wright assigned him to help write a book that earned Wright almost $55,000 in royalties. The book, *Reflections of a Public Man*, is part of the controversy surrounding the speaker because its publisher, Carlos Moore, was paid more than $250,000 by Wright's campaign committee while Moore was paying royalties on the book at a lavish 55% rate to Wright.		The Senate clears a compromise $1.1 trillion congressional budget resolution for the 1989 fiscal year beginning October 1. The nonbinding spending plan, which calls for no new taxes and is widely seen as a postponement of tough deficit-reduction decisions, is approved by a 58-29 vote.... The Supreme Court unanimously upholds, 9-0, the right of union employees, under state law, to sue employers over dismissal even if their contract provides a grievance procedure and other remedies.		Iran Barkley wins the World Boxing Council middleweight title in his bout against champion Thomas Hearns.	June 6
Massachusetts Gov. Michael S. Dukakis clinches the Democratic presidential nomination with a four-state primary sweep in New Jersey, Montana, New Mexico, and California, in the traditional finale to the presidential primary season. (One Republican primary remains, in North Dakota June 14.) ... U.S. elementary and secondary school students have a poor grasp of all but the most basic math skills, according to a report released by the National Assessment of Educational Progress. The assessment panel based its study on exams given in 1985-86 to 17,000 students aged nine, 13, and 17, and 34,980 students in grades three, seven, and 11.... In California, voters approve two conflicting proposals on public financing of state election campaigns. By a 58%-42% margin, voters approve a measure that sets limits on campaign fund raising but that explicitly prohibits public financing of state campaigns.		Outstanding consumer debt rose $3.65 bil. in April, the Federal Reserve Board reports, at an annual rate of 7%, to a total of $626.85 bil.			June 7

F	G	H	I	J
Includes elections, federal-state relations, civil rights and liberties, crime, the judiciary, education, health care, poverty, urban affairs and population.	*Includes formation and debate of U.S. foreign and defense policies, veterans' affairs and defense spending. (Relations with specific foreign countries are usually found under the region concerned.)*	*Includes business, labor, agriculture, taxation, transportation, consumer affairs, monetary and fiscal policy, natural resources, and pollution.*	*Includes worldwide scientific, medical and technological developments, natural phenomena, U.S. weather, natural disasters, and accidents.*	*Includes the arts, religion, scholarship, communications media, sports, entertainments, fashions, fads and social life.*

	World Affairs	Europe	Africa & the Middle East	The Americas	Asia & the Pacific
June 8			South Africa's black workers end a massive three-day strike to protest the white government's proposed new labor law and its February banning of political activity by trade unions and other antiapartheid groups. Although the three-day strike lost some momentum in its last two days, up to 2 million blacks stayed away from their jobs the first day, reportedly making it the biggest strike in South African history.	Canadian and French negotiators meet in Paris to discuss a formal resumption of talks over North American fishing rights. Ottawa suspended the talks May 6, when France seized a Newfoundland trawler.	
June 9			The South African government renews the two-year-old nationwide state of emergency for another year.	In Nicaragua, the fourth round of peace talks in Managua between the Sandinista government and the Contras ends with no progress toward a settlement.	
June 10				Mexico's 1987 economic solidarity pact among government, labor, and business continues to help reduce inflation, with the rate for May falling to 1.9%, the government reports. That figure represents the lowest monthly rise in prices since November 1981.	Philippine Pres. Corazon Aquino signs into law a bill providing for the redistribution of large tracts of government-owned and private farmland. The legislation is passed June 7 by the Philippine senate and June 8 by the house of representatives.
June 11	The Org. of Petroleum Exporting Countries meets in Vienna for four days to find some way to prop up weak oil prices, but decides in the end to maintain the current production quotas for the next six months.	Giuseppe Saragat, 89, president of Italy from 1964 to 1971 and a prominent figure in the history of Italian socialism, dies of heart disease in Rome. He founded his own party, the Socialist Party of Italian Workers, which later became the Social Democratic Party, before his 1964 election as Italy's first socialist president. Saragat served as foreign minister in the center-left administration headed by Christian Democrat Aldo Moro.			

A	B	C	D	E
Includes developments that affect more than one world region, international organizations and important meetings of major world leaders.	Includes all domestic and regional developments in Europe, including the Soviet Union, Turkey, Cyprus and Malta.	Includes all domestic and regional developments in Africa and the Middle East, including Iraq and Iran and excluding Cyprus, Turkey and Afghanistan.	Includes all domestic and regional developments in Latin America, the Caribbean and Canada.	Includes all domestic and regional developments in Asia and Pacific nations, extending from Afghanistan through all the Pacific Islands, except Hawaii.

U.S. Politics & Social Issues	U.S. Foreign Policy & Defense	U.S. Economy & Environment	Science, Technology & Nature	Culture, Leisure & Life Style	
The judge in the Iran-Contra conspiracy case rules that former National Security Council staff member Oliver L. North, former national security adviser John M. Poindexter, retired Air Force Maj. Gen. Richard V. Secord, and Iranian-American businessman Albert Hakim will have to be tried separately in order to ensure that their constitutional rights are protected. The ruling is a setback for special prosecutor Lawrence E. Walsh, who sought to try the four defendants together on charges that they conspired to defraud the U.S. government by secretly providing funds and supplies to the Contra rebels fighting the government of Nicaragua. . . . The Senate gives final approval to a bill that will expand the Medicare program to protect the elderly and disabled against "catastrophic" medical costs. The House passed the legislation June 2. Pres. Reagan is expected to sign the legislation. . . . The House of Representatives passes, 328-78, legislation aimed at restricting the commercialization of children's television. The bill will limit commercial time during children's shows to a total of 10.5 minutes an hour on weekends and 12 minutes an hour on weekdays. The legislation now moves to the Senate.		The Senate fails to override Pres. Reagan's veto of comprehensive trade legislation, and congressional leaders immediately begin efforts to introduce a second bill. The House successfully voted to override the veto in May. . . . Monsanto Co. agrees to a $1.5 mil. settlement of a chemical poisoning case filed by more than 170 former plant workers. The settlement calls for payments of $200,000 each to six retired employees who contracted bladder cancer they say was caused by exposure to a rubber additive at the company's plant in Nitro, W.Va., near Charleston.		The International Skating Union votes at a meeting in Davos, Switzerland, to drop compulsory figures from international skating competitions effective July 1, 1990. The figures will also be reduced in dance programs. . . . Pittsburgh Penguin Mario Lemieux is named the winner of the Hart Trophy as the National Hockey League's most valuable player.	June 8
			A community health clinic in Portland, Oreg., announces that it will start distributing clean hypodermic needles to drug addicts in an effort to stem the spread of acquired immune deficiency syndrome (AIDS). Contaminated needles are one of the main pathways for transmission of the AIDS virus. Similar proposals in New York City and Boston, among other cities, have been put on the shelf because of political sensitivities.		June 9
The House Ethics Committee votes unanimously to investigate allegations concerning House Speaker James C. Wright Jr. (D, Tex.).		The government's producer price index rose 0.5% in May, the Labor Dept. reports.		Louis (Dearborn) L'Amour, 80, prolific author of best-selling westerns, dies of lung cancer in Los Angeles. It is believed that his 101 books are all in print, with sales nearing 200 million worldwide. *Hondo* (1953), his first novel and perhaps his best-known, was made into a film starring John Wayne. Many of his other works were also adapted as feature films or television productions. He is the only novelist to have been honored with both a congressional gold medal (1983) and a presidential Medal of Freedom (1984).	June 10
				Risen Star wins the 120th Belmont Stakes in Belmont, N.Y. . . . Harvard Univ. wins the national collegiate rowing championship for the second year in a row, edging out Northeastern Univ. in the Cincinnati regatta. . . . In the most spectacular event of its kind since the 1985 Live Aid famine relief concert, 72,000 fans and 70 performers converge on Wembley Stadium outside London for a 10-hour pop music celebration of the 70th birthday of jailed South African black nationalist leader Nelson Mandela.	June 11

F	G	H	I	J
Includes elections, federal-state relations, civil rights and liberties, crime, the judiciary, education, health care, poverty, urban affairs and population.	*Includes formation and debate of U.S. foreign and defense policies, veterans' affairs and defense spending. (Relations with specific foreign countries are usually found under the region concerned.)*	*Includes business, labor, agriculture, taxation, transportation, consumer affairs, monetary and fiscal policy, natural resources, and pollution.*	*Includes worldwide scientific, medical and technological developments, natural phenomena, U.S. weather, natural disasters, and accidents.*	*Includes the arts, religion, scholarship, communications media, sports, entertainments, fashions, fads and social life.*

	World Affairs	Europe	Africa & the Middle East	The Americas	Asia & the Pacific
June 12		Neither the Socialist Party of France's Pres. Francois Mitterrand nor the country's rightist coalition is able to secure a majority in France's second and final round of voting for deputies to the National Assembly. The election marks the first time since the Fifth Republic was founded in 1958 that French voters have failed to install an absolute assembly majority.			
June 13	International bank lending increased 39% to $732 bil. in 1987, the International Monetary Fund reports. Bank lending to industrial countries rose 28% to $527 bil., with $223 bil. lent to Japanese residents and $96 bil. lent to U.S. residents.	European Community (EC) finance ministers agree to remove all restrictions on the movement of capital within the 12-nation trading bloc by 1992. The capital liberalization agreement, reached after a compromise with France and Denmark, will allow citizens of EC-member countries to open bank accounts throughout the Community. The move thus represents a major breakthrough in the EC's effort to remove all internal trade barriers by 1992.	In the Persian Gulf war, Iran says its Revolutionary Guards have driven into southern Iraq and inflicted heavy casualties in Iran's first major offensive after a recent series of military setbacks. Iraq claims it crushed the Iranian attack.		The *People's Daily*, the official Communist Party newspaper in China, reports that as many as 30 million workers in China's urban labor force of 130 million have no real jobs and spend their working hours playing cards or watching television. One government official is quoted as saying that such overstaffing costs the state about $16.2 bil. a year in wages and benefits, or about half the revenues generated by state-owned industries.
June 14		The Kremlin acknowledges that Soviet leader Joseph Stalin unjustly deported thousands of Latvians during and after World War II. Following the Soviet annexation of Latvia in 1940, Stalin ordered more than 31,000 Latvian nationalists and dissidents sent to Siberia and other remote parts of the USSR. The deportations continued through 1949.		Nicaragua's Pres. Daniel Ortega Saavedra announces that wage and price controls are being lifted and credit and imports curbed in an effort to revive Nicaragua's floundering economy.	A committee of Japan's ruling Liberal Democratic Party (LDP) unveils the details of a sweeping overhaul of the country's tax system. The reform plan, published by the LDP's Tax System Research Council after months of internal party debate, is to be taken up by the Diet during a special 120-day legislative session scheduled to begin in mid-July.
June 15		The Supreme Soviet (parliament) of the USSR's Armenian Republic passes a resolution urging a reunification with the Nagorno-Karabakh Autonomous Region of the neighboring Soviet Azerbaijan Republic. Nagorno-Karabakh is predominantly Armenian and Christian, while Azerbaijan is overwhelmingly Shiite Moslem. The Kremlin placed Nagorno-Karabakh under Azerbaijan jurisdiction in 1923.			In South Korea, antigovernment protests begun in mid-May by radical students continue to rock the country, culminating in a series of violent clashes between police and protesters who are attempting to march to the truce village of Panmunjom for a meeting with North Korean students to discuss national reunification. . . . The Dalai Lama, the exiled spiritual leader of Tibetan Buddhists, proposes a plan under which China would grant Tibet limited autonomy but would retain the right to control the region's foreign affairs and station troops there.

A	B	C	D	E
Includes developments that affect more than one world region, international organizations and important meetings of major world leaders.	Includes all domestic and regional developments in Europe, including the Soviet Union, Turkey, Cyprus and Malta.	Includes all domestic and regional developments in Africa and the Middle East, including Iraq and Iran and excluding Cyprus, Turkey and Afghanistan.	Includes all domestic and regional developments in Latin America, the Caribbean and Canada.	Includes all domestic and regional developments in Asia and Pacific nations, extending from Afghanistan through all the Pacific Islands, except Hawaii.

U.S. Politics & Social Issues	U.S. Foreign Policy & Defense	U.S. Economy & Environment	Science, Technology & Nature	Culture, Leisure & Life Style	
			Meeting for the last time, the U.S. presidential commission on acquired immune deficiency syndrome narrowly approves, 6-5, an antibias proposal that its chairman, retired Adm. James D. Watkins, calls "the key issue in the [commission's] entire [final] report," which is due to be delivered to the White House June 24.... Leading world researchers and health authorities on acquired immune deficiency syndrome (AIDS) convene a five-day conference in Stockholm. More than 6,000 AIDS experts from 125 countries attend the Fourth International Conf. on AIDS.	In auto racing, the team of Jan Lammers of the Netherlands and Andy Wallace and Johnny Dumfries of Britain wins the Le Mans (France) 24-hour endurance race.	June 12
A federal jury in Newark, N.J., finds a tobacco company partly to blame for the death of a cigarette smoker, the first such ruling in more than 300 tobacco liability lawsuits dating back to 1954.... The Supreme Court agrees to review the constitutionality of a new sentencing code for federal crimes that went into effect in November 1987. In the eight months since it went into effect, 59 federal judges have struck down the code as unconstitutional while 44 have upheld it, according to a count by the San Diego Federal Defenders program as reported by the *Wall Street Journal*.		The Supreme Court lets stand the Federal Reserve Board's approval for commercial bank affiliates to underwrite three kinds of securities: commercial paper, municipal revenue bonds and securities backed by mortgages or consumer debt.			June 13
White House chief of staff Howard H. Baker Jr. announces that he will leave his post July 1 rather than serve out the last seven months of Pres. Reagan's term.... Convicted murderer Edward R. Byrne Jr., 28, is put to death by electrocution in Angola, La., becoming the 100th person to be executed since the Supreme Court reinstated the death penalty in 1976.	A massive Pentagon fraud scandal is revealed, when agents of the Federal Bureau of Investigation and the Naval Investigative Service conduct searches of homes and offices in 12 states. Based on government statements, press accounts, and hearsay, the scandal involves the possibility that defense contractors, acting through middlemen, bribed Defense Dept. aides to steer lucrative military contracts their way.	The U.S. deficit on merchandise trade dropped to a seasonally adjusted $9.89 bil. in April, the Commerce Dept. reports.... New York State's Suffolk County legislature enacts a law regulating use of video-display terminals (VDTs) in the workplace. It is believed to be the first such law enacted in the United States. Similar legislation has been introduced in at least 25 states, and is pending in six. In Suffolk County, it is backed by labor leaders and condemned by business leaders.		The Rev. Jerry Vines of Jacksonville is elected president of the Southern Baptist Convention. Vines, 50, is on the fundamentalist side of the Southern Baptist schism between conservatives and moderates, or liberals.	June 14
	The Supreme Court rules, 6-2, that national security agencies are not immune from suits by fired employees protesting violation of constitutional rights.	The Federal Reserve Board reports that its industrial production index rose 0.4% in May.... The U.S. balance of payments on current account widened 18.6% in the first quarter, the Commerce Dept. reports. The current-account deficit rose to a seasonally adjusted $39.75 bil. from a revised $33.52 bil. deficit in the fourth quarter of 1987, but it is less than the record $41.97 bil. recorded in the third quarter of that year.	The European Space Agency successfully launches a new generation of Ariane rocket from Kourou, French Guiana. The new Ariane-4 is capable of orbiting payloads of up to 4.6 tons, compared with the 2.8 tons maximum capacity of the previous generation.	*Variety*'s top-grossing films for the week are: *Big, Crocodile Dundee II, Big Business, The Presidio*, and *Rambo III*.... *Bull Durham*, a film about a romantic triangle set in the world of minor-league baseball, is released in New York. Directed and written by Ron Shelton, the film stars Susan Sarandon, Kevin Costner, and Tim Robbins.	June 15

F	G	H	I	J
Includes elections, federal-state relations, civil rights and liberties, crime, the judiciary, education, health care, poverty, urban affairs and population.	*Includes formation and debate of U.S. foreign and defense policies, veterans' affairs and defense spending. (Relations with specific foreign countries are usually found under the region concerned.)*	*Includes business, labor, agriculture, taxation, transportation, consumer affairs, monetary and fiscal policy, natural resources, and pollution.*	*Includes worldwide scientific, medical and technological developments, natural phenomena, U.S. weather, natural disasters, and accidents.*	*Includes the arts, religion, scholarship, communications media, sports, entertainments, fashions, fads and social life.*

	World Affairs	Europe	Africa & the Middle East	The Americas	Asia & the Pacific
June 16	France and Iran formally restore diplomatic relations after an 11-month break. The move comes five weeks after secret talks between Paris and Teheran brought about the release of the last three French hostages being held by pro-Iranian extremists in Lebanon.				Australia's federal cabinet votes to endorse some form of tax on university graduates to help offset the costs of higher education. The minister for employment, education, and training, John Dawkins, is instructed to refine the basic plan proposed in May by the Wran Committee, which calls for a special 2% tax to be levied on university graduates once they begin earning more than $16,900 a year.... Japan's Economic Planning Agency says that its gross national product grew by 4.9% (adjusted for inflation) during fiscal 1987.
June 17		An unauthorized international seminar on peace and human rights, held in Prague, is disrupted by the police. The gathering, known as Prague '88, is cohosted by Charter 77, Czechoslovakia's dissident human rights organization, and the newly formed Czechoslovak Independent Peace Assoc.			
June 18		Turkey's Premier Turgut Ozal is wounded slightly by a gunman while addressing a convention of his governing Motherland Party in Ankara.			
June 19	Leaders of the seven major industrial democracies meet for three days in Toronto for their 14th annual summit on world economic issues. Expressing broad satisfaction with the state of the world economy and their own policy coordinating process, the seven heads of state congratulate themselves for their economic accomplishments and agree to several measures aimed at keeping the world economy growing.				

A	B	C	D	E
Includes developments that affect more than one world region, international organizations and important meetings of major world leaders.	Includes all domestic and regional developments in Europe, including the Soviet Union, Turkey, Cyprus and Malta.	Includes all domestic and regional developments in Africa and the Middle East, including Iraq and Iran and excluding Cyprus, Turkey and Afghanistan.	Includes all domestic and regional developments in Latin America, the Caribbean and Canada.	Includes all domestic and regional developments in Asia and Pacific nations, extending from Afghanistan through all the Pacific Islands, except Hawaii.

U.S. Politics & Social Issues	U.S. Foreign Policy & Defense	U.S. Economy & Environment	Science, Technology & Nature	Culture, Leisure & Life Style	
The Senate adopts a comprehensive revision of the nation's welfare program with a major emphasis on work requirements. The legislation is sent to conference with the House, which passed a differing measure in December 1987. The House bill does not contain a work requirement. The Reagan administration considers neither version acceptable because of the lack of emphasis on a work program.... Former Arizona Gov. Evan Mecham (R) is found not guilty of deliberately concealing a $350,000 campaign loan during his 1986 run for the governorship. Also acquitted is Mecham's brother and campaign treasurer, Willard. Mecham was impeached and removed as governor April 4 on charges that originally included the campaign loan. The state Senate dropped the loan from among the impeachment charges because Mecham was under indictment.... The judge in the Iran-Contra conspiracy case formally denies a key defense motion to dismiss the case on the grounds that the prosecution made improper use of the testimony some defendants gave Congress under grants of limited immunity. Three of the four defendants in the case, former National Security Council staff member Oliver L. North, former national security adviser John M. Poindexter, and Albert Hakim, an Iranian-American businessman, were granted immunity in 1987 to testify before the select congressional committees investigating the arms scandal. The fourth defendant, Richard V. Secord, a retired Air Force major general, testified voluntarily.		The General Accounting Office (GAO) estimates that the Agriculture Dept.'s Commodity Credit Corp. lost $1.5 bil. on two credit guarantee programs aimed at expanding farm exports. The GAO blames lax management for the loss, and charges that bad-risk countries continued to receive credit guarantees despite their uncreditworthiness.... The House of Representatives approves a $44.1 bil. appropriation to fund the Agriculture Dept. and federal nutrition and rural development programs for the fiscal year beginning October 1. Overall, spending in the measure is set at $12 bil. less than present levels and $2.5 bil. less than the Reagan administration had sought.			June 16
		Housing starts plunged 12.2% in May, the Commerce Dept. reports, to an adjusted annual rate of 1.384 million.... The Superfund cleanup program to detoxify toxic waste sites is condemned as "largely ineffective" because of poor management and an inadequate work force, according to a report by the Office of Technology Assessment, a nonpartisan scientific agency reporting to Congress.			June 17
In the presidential race, Massachusetts Gov. Michael S. Dukakis (D) makes a three-day Southern swing, picking up the endorsement of former presidential rival Sen. Albert Gore Jr. (D, Tenn.) and touching down in Florida, South Carolina, Alabama, Mississippi, and Louisiana as well. At most stops he talks tough about issues such as drugs and crime.				*Billboard*'s best-selling albums for the week are: *Faith*, George Michael; *Open Up and Say...Ahh!*, Poison; *Hysteria*, Def Leppard; *Dirty Dancing* (soundtrack); and *OU812*, Van Halen.	June 18
	Australia's P.M. Bob Hawke begins an eight-day visit to the United States for the fifth time in five years, stopping in Washington, D.C., and several other cities for meetings with Pres. Reagan, Congress, and a number of nongovernment organizations. The agenda for much of the trip focuses on U.S.-Australian trade relations.				June 19

F	G	H	I	J
Includes elections, federal-state relations, civil rights and liberties, crime, the judiciary, education, health care, poverty, urban affairs and population.	Includes formation and debate of U.S. foreign and defense policies, veterans' affairs and defense spending. (Relations with specific foreign countries are usually found under the region concerned.)	Includes business, labor, agriculture, taxation, transportation, consumer affairs, monetary and fiscal policy, natural resources, and pollution.	Includes worldwide scientific, medical and technological developments, natural phenomena, U.S. weather, natural disasters, and accidents.	Includes the arts, religion, scholarship, communications media, sports, entertainments, fashions, fads and social life.

	World Affairs	Europe	Africa & the Middle East	The Americas	Asia & the Pacific
June 20		The Peoples Front of Estonia, a nationalist political organization, is accorded official recognition by the Estonian Republic of the USSR. The front is believed to be the first large-scale non-communist political group to be recognized by a Soviet republic and, by extension, the Kremlin itself.		Lt. Gen. Henri Namphy, head of an interim military-led government that ruled Haiti until a civilian administration was restored in February, names himself president after the military ousts Pres. Leslie F. Manigat.	The Australian dollar closes at 82.1 U.S. cents, its highest level since January 1985. The Australian dollar has risen more than 20% against most major currencies since hitting a low of 67 U.S. cents in the wake of the October 1987 worldwide stock market crash. . . . Japan's Premier Noboru Takeshita signs a pact with Pres. Reagan that establishes guidelines for cooperation between the United States and Japan on a wide range of scientific research projects. The pact replaces a similar accord reached in 1980.
June 21		The West German Bundesbank increases a key refinancing rate in an attempt to restrain the rising U.S. dollar, check money supply growth, and hold down inflation at home. . . . Unions representing writers and cultural figures in Soviet Latvia call on the Kremlin to grant the republic the status of a "sovereign state" within the USSR. The call, in the form of a proclamation published in Latvian newspapers, is perhaps the boldest nationalist appeal ever made by state-supervised organizations.		Mexico's public and private foreign debt fell 2.9% to $103.9 bil. in the first quarter of 1988, the central bank reports. The decline is the first significant quarterly reduction in the nation's total foreign debt for three years.	The governments of Australia and New Zealand agree to remove all tariffs between their two countries by July 1, 1990. The decision is announced at the end of the two-day talks between Australia's trade negotiations minister, Michael Duffy, and New Zealand's overseas trade minister, Mike Moore.
June 22	The Org. for Economic Cooperation and Development reports that capital flow to the developing world from industrialized countries dropped about 10% after adjustment for inflation and exchange rates in 1987.	The Bank of England prompts a rise in commercial bank base lending rates to 9% from 8.5%. The move is the seventh U.K. base rate change in three-and-a-half months, and the fourth increase.	Arab militants in the six-month-old Palestinian uprising are increasingly turning to firebombs and arson in their fight against the Israeli military occupation of the West Bank and Gaza Strip, according to reports over the last two days.	In Canada, the House of Commons votes, 200-7, to give final approval to the so-called Meech Lake Accord, which is designed to bring Quebec into the constitutional process. The vote completes federal ratification of the accord. All 10 provinces had to approve the agreement by the spring of 1990.	In Vietnam, the National Assembly elects Do Muoi, the third-ranking member of the country's politburo, to be the new premier; he replaces Pham Hung, who died in March. Western analysts consider Do, 71, a conservative on economic and defense issues.
June 23		In France, Socialist Premier Michel Rocard is formally reappointed as premier. Also this day, the Communists join the Socialists to elect former Socialist Premier Laurent Fabius as president of the National Assembly.		A U.S. judge dismisses a $24 mil. damage suit filed on behalf of two American journalists against 29 people in connection with a 1984 bombing in Nicaragua. The lawsuit was filed on behalf of cameraman Tony Avirgan and his wife, Martha Honey, a freelance writer, by the Washington, D.C.-based Christic Institute, a public policy group.	

A	B	C	D	E
Includes developments that affect more than one world region, international organizations and important meetings of major world leaders.	Includes all domestic and regional developments in Europe, including the Soviet Union, Turkey, Cyprus and Malta.	Includes all domestic and regional developments in Africa and the Middle East, including Iraq and Iran and excluding Cyprus, Turkey and Afghanistan.	Includes all domestic and regional developments in Latin America, the Caribbean and Canada.	Includes all domestic and regional developments in Asia and Pacific nations, extending from Afghanistan through all the Pacific Islands, except Hawaii.

U.S. Politics & Social Issues	U.S. Foreign Policy & Defense	U.S. Economy & Environment	Science, Technology & Nature	Culture, Leisure & Life Style	
The federal grand jury investigating the Iran-Contra arms scandal indicts former Central Intelligence Agency official Joseph F. Fernandez on criminal charges stemming from his alleged role in helping funnel weapons and supplies to the Contra rebels fighting the government of Nicaragua.... The Supreme Court unanimously upholds a New York City law that bars discrimination by private, business-oriented clubs. The force of the law serves to open up many private men's clubs to women and minorities.		Carl C. Icahn concedes defeat in his proxy fight for five seats on the board of Texaco Inc., after Kohlberg Kravis Roberts & Co. announces it has cast its 4.9% Texaco stake in favor of management, conclusively ending the bitter proxy battle.		Curtis Strange defeats Nick Faldo of England in an 18-hole playoff to win the 88th U.S. Open golf championship.... Chicago architect Thomas H. Beeby, dean of the Yale School of Architecture since 1985, is named winner of a competition to design a $140 mil. building that is to be Chicago's new central library. The library will be named after the late Mayor Harold Washington. The new central library is to be built at the corner of State and Van Buren Streets in downtown Chicago and is scheduled to open in mid-1991. With an area of about half a million square feet, it will be the largest municipal library ever built in the United States.	June 20
Massachusetts Gov. Michael S. Dukakis (D) continues to lead Vice Pres. George Bush (R) in the polls. The latest *Washington Post* trial-heat presidential poll has Dukakis leading, 51%-39%, compared with 53%-40% a month earlier.		The government's consumer price index rose 0.3% in May, the Labor Dept. reports.... The Federal Home Loan Bank Board announces that the nation's savings and loan associations lost $3.78 bil. in the first quarter. The deficit follows a revised $3.81 bil. loss for the thrift industry in the fourth quarter of 1987 and a revised $7.6 bil. loss for the year. The industry recorded a $100 mil. profit in the first quarter of 1987.		The Los Angeles Lakers become the first team in 19 years to win back-to-back National Basketball Assoc. (NBA) titles when they defeat the Detroit Pistons, 108-105, in game seven of the NBA championship series. Laker forward James Worthy is named most valuable player in the NBA finals.	June 21
				Who Framed Roger Rabbit, a film combining live action and animation, is released in New York. Set in 1940s Hollywood, the movie concerns a private detective (who's live) hired by Roger Rabbit (who's animated). Directed by Robert Zemeckis with a screenplay by Jeffrey Price and Peter S. Seaman, the movie is based on Gary K. Wolf's book *Who Censored Roger Rabbit?*. Starring Bob Hoskins, Christopher Lloyd, and Joanna Cassidy, the movie becomes the top-grossing film in the United States in 1988 and wins Academy Awards for editing, sound effects editing, visual effects, and a special award for chief animator Richard Williams.	June 22
		The Reagan administration raises its estimate of 1988 gross national product to 3% from the 2.9% projected in February.... The Agriculture Dept. says that half of the nation's agricultural counties have been designated as drought disaster areas after the driest spring since the dust bowl year of 1934. ... After-tax profits of U.S. corporations fell 1.1% in the first quarter, the Commerce Dept. reports, to an annual rate of $144.2 bil.	James E. Hansen of the National Aeronautics and Space Admin.'s Goddard Institute of Space Studies tells a Senate panel that the Earth is warmer than at any time in at least a century, and that it is now virtually certain that the warming is due to man-made pollutants in the atmosphere. Mathematical models have long predicted that the atmospheric buildup of carbon dioxide and other byproducts of human activity will trigger a so-called "greenhouse effect" in which heat from the sun will be prevented from radiating back into space by a blanket of atmospheric gases.... As many as 300 people are feared dead in northeastern Turkey after thousands of tons of mud and rock cascade down a rain-soaked mountain and smash into the Turkish village of Catak in the Black Sea province of Trabzon. The mudslide hit at 2 a.m., burying buses, cars, two restaurants, a school, and homes.		June 23

F	G	H	I	J
Includes elections, federal-state relations, civil rights and liberties, crime, the judiciary, education, health care, poverty, urban affairs and population.	*Includes formation and debate of U.S. foreign and defense policies, veterans' affairs and defense spending. (Relations with specific foreign countries are usually found under the region concerned.)*	*Includes business, labor, agriculture, taxation, transportation, consumer affairs, monetary and fiscal policy, natural resources, and pollution.*	*Includes worldwide scientific, medical and technological developments, natural phenomena, U.S. weather, natural disasters, and accidents.*	*Includes the arts, religion, scholarship, communications media, sports, entertainments, fashions, fads and social life.*

	World Affairs	Europe	Africa & the Middle East	The Americas	Asia & the Pacific
June 24		Canada's Defense Min. Perrin Beatty announces that one 600-man infantry battalion will be deployed in Norway, from West Germany, in the event of a military crisis in Europe. In effect, the move means that Canada is further reducing its commitment to defend the northern flank of the North Atlantic Treaty Org.	Officials from the governments of Angola, Cuba, South Africa, and the United States meet in Cairo, Egypt, in a second round of formal four-power talks aimed at bringing an end to fighting in Angola and bringing independence to Namibia (South-West Africa).		Australia's minister for primary industries and energy, John Kerin, and Japan's agriculture minister, Takashi Sato, sign an agreement liberalizing Japan's restrictions on the import of Australian beef. Japan signed a similar bilateral agreement June 20 with the United States.
June 25	The UN announces that it will send $9.1 mil. in food to Vietnam to help offset severe shortages plaguing 12 northern provinces.				
June 26	The third UN Gen. Assembly special session on disarmament ends with the 159 delegates unable to agree on a revision of the first UN disarmament declaration, drafted in 1978.				French Premier Michel Rocard achieves the first major success of his premiership when he announces that negotiations over New Caledonia have produced an accord between representatives of the indigenous Melanesian population and French settlers. The agreement concerning the administration of the troubled Pacific colony comes less than two months after 21 people were killed when French commandos stormed a cave where Melanesian, or Kanak, separatists were holding some 20 French captives.... The official Laotian news agency reports that about 47% of the population cast ballots in the first nationwide elections since the communist takeover in 1975. The voting is held to fill 2,410 seats on local district councils.
June 27		Hungarians stage a massive anti-Romania protest in Budapest. According to differing estimates, 30,000 to 50,000 people take part, making it the largest unofficial demonstration in Hungary since the 1956 uprising against communist rule.... Britain's current account deficit set a one-month record in May, the government reports. The report shows a deficit in May of 1.21 bil. pounds up from 728 mil. in April and surpassing the previous record of 1.16 bil. set in January.			

A	B	C	D	E
Includes developments that affect more than one world region, international organizations and important meetings of major world leaders.	Includes all domestic and regional developments in Europe, including the Soviet Union, Turkey, Cyprus and Malta.	Includes all domestic and regional developments in Africa and the Middle East, including Iraq and Iran and excluding Cyprus, Turkey and Afghanistan.	Includes all domestic and regional developments in Latin America, the Caribbean and Canada.	Includes all domestic and regional developments in Asia and Pacific nations, extending from Afghanistan through all the Pacific Islands, except Hawaii.

U.S. Politics & Social Issues	U.S. Foreign Policy & Defense	U.S. Economy & Environment	Science, Technology & Nature	Culture, Leisure & Life Style	
According to figures from the first 15 months of the 1988 election cycle, reported in the newspaper *USA Today*, the top 10 defense contractors gave $689,329 to congressional leaders and members with oversight over defense spending.		Consumer spending grew 0.5% and personal income rose 0.3% in May, the Commerce Dept. reports.		*Publishers Weekly*'s hardback fiction best-sellers for the week are: *Zoya*, Danielle Steel; *The Icarus Agenda*, Robert Ludlum; *People Like Us*, Dominick Dunne; *Love in the Time of Cholera*, Gabriel Garcia Marquez; and *The Bonfire of the Vanities*, Tom Wolfe.	June 24
The Democratic Party adopts a brief, thematic platform for the fall campaign. The chief contending forces are those of Gov. Michael S. Dukakis (D, Mass.), who has clinched the nomination, and the Rev. Jesse L. Jackson, his remaining active challenger.				At their seminannual meeting, the nation's Roman Catholic bishops issue a report disapproving deployment of the Strategic Defense Initiative, the space-based missile-defense system known as "Star Wars."	June 25
					June 26
The Supreme Court affirms the right of local government to ban picketing in front of a person's home. In a 6-3 ruling, the court upholds an ordinance passed by Brookfield, Wisc., after antiabortion demonstrators picketed the home of a local doctor who performed abortions as part of his practice in several clinics. . . . Michigan's Gov. James J. Blanchard (D) signs a bill making Michigan the first state to outlaw commercial surrogate motherhood contracts. The law, which will bar payment to the natural mother beyond actual medical bills, is to go into effect September 1.		The Supreme Court extends protection to government contractors from lawsuits arising from defects in their products. The case concerned a Marine helicopter pilot who died in a crash off Virginia Beach when he could not get out an escape hatch that opened out, instead of in, and was trapped by water pressure. . . . Driven by the worsening drought, prices of corn, wheat, and soybean futures have soared to historically high levels at the Chicago Board of Trade this month. The drought sends the Commodity Research Bureau index to 270.52, its highest level since June 29, 1984, when it stood at 271.00, and 20% above its February 1988 low. . . . In the second-largest insider trading case ever brought, the Securities and Exchange Comm. charges Stephen Sui-Kuan Wang Jr., a Morgan Stanley & Co. mergers and acquisitions analyst, and Fred C. Lee, a Taiwanese businessman, with participation in a scheme that allegedly reaped more than $19 mil. in illegal insider-trading profits.		Undisputed heavyweight boxing champion Mike Tyson knocks out challenger and former champion Michael Spinks just 91 seconds into the first round of a 12-round bout; it is the fourth-shortest in heavyweight history. . . . U.S. Roman Catholic bishops vote to rewrite a controversial policy statement on acquired immune deficiency syndrome (AIDS) adopted unanimously by the bishops' 50-member administrative board in December 1987. That statement expressed qualified endorsement for an education program that included information about condoms to prevent the spread of AIDS.	June 27

F	G	H	I	J
Includes elections, federal-state relations, civil rights and liberties, crime, the judiciary, education, health care, poverty, urban affairs and population.	*Includes formation and debate of U.S. foreign and defense policies, veterans' affairs and defense spending. (Relations with specific foreign countries are usually found under the region concerned.)*	*Includes business, labor, agriculture, taxation, transportation, consumer affairs, monetary and fiscal policy, natural resources, and pollution.*	*Includes worldwide scientific, medical and technological developments, natural phenomena, U.S. weather, natural disasters, and accidents.*	*Includes the arts, religion, scholarship, communications media, sports, entertainments, fashions, fads and social life.*

	World Affairs	Europe	Africa & the Middle East	The Americas	Asia & the Pacific
June 28	Tokyo remains the world's most expensive city for the third year in a row in 1987, with Osaka second and Teheran third. According to *Business International*, Los Angeles is the most expensive city in the United States (but ranks only 30th worldwide) followed by Washington, D.C. (31st), and New York, Chicago, and San Francisco (tied for 33rd). The most expensive city in Europe is Oslo (7th worldwice), followed by Zurich (9th) and Geneva (10th).	The 19th All-Union Conf. of the Soviet Communist Party opens at the Kremlin Palace of Congresses in Moscow. The last national party conference was held in 1941. The chief purpose of the four-day meeting is to decide the pace and direction of the economic, political, and social reforms initiated by Soviet leader Mikhail S. Gorbachev. . . . In France, a new cabinet led by Socialist Premier Michel Rocard is sworn in. As in his previous short-lived government, senior members of the Socialist Party fill the major cabinet positions, while centrists and independents are given some lesser portfolios. . . . France's economic growth in 1987 is 2.2%, according to the national statistical institute. The inflation-adjusted growth is up slightly from 2.1% in 1986.			
June 29		The British government presents its long-awaited white paper (policy document) on reform of the Official Secrets Act. The proposed legislative outline will specify six types of information that it will be illegal to cisclose or receive.			

A	B	C	D	E
Includes developments that affect more than one world region, international organizations and important meetings of major world leaders.	Includes all domestic and regional developments in Europe, including the Soviet Union, Turkey, Cyprus and Malta.	Includes all domestic and regional developments in Africa and the Middle East, including Iraq and Iran and excluding Cyprus, Turkey and Afghanistan.	Includes all domestic and regional developments in Latin America, the Caribbean and Canada.	Includes all domestic and regional developments in Asia and Pacific nations, extending from Afghanistan through all the Pacific Islands, except Hawaii.

U.S. Politics & Social Issues	U.S. Foreign Policy & Defense	U.S. Economy & Environment	Science, Technology & Nature	Culture, Leisure & Life Style	
		The Justice Dept. files suit to oust the national leadership of the Teamsters union and have a trustee appointed to run the union until new officers are selected in a "free and fair" election.	The next flight of a U.S. space shuttle, scheduled for August 22 from Kennedy Space Center in Florida, is delayed until September 4, the National Aeronautics and Space Admin. announces. The slippage is attributed to minor problems.		June 28
The Supreme Court upholds, 7-1, the validity of a law providing for special prosecutors to investigate suspected wrongdoing by high-ranking federal officials. The court firmly and totally rejects Reagan administration arguments that the 1978 law, arising from the Watergate scandal, encroaches on the presidency and trespasses on the constitutional doctrine of separation of powers among the branches of government.... The Supreme Court widens the challenge for women and minorities to protest discrimination in hiring or promotions. In a unanimous decision, with Associate Justice Anthony M. Kennedy not participating, the court says that women and minorities need not prove intentional discrimination in cases where employers base their decisions on subjective criteria.... The Supreme Court upholds federal funding for religious groups to counsel teenagers against premarital sex. The 5-4 decision says the 1981 law authorizing such counseling does not on its face violate the constitutional requirement for separation of church and state. ... The Supreme Court strikes down an Iowa law designed to protect child victims of sex abuse by allowing them to testify behind screens rather than confront their alleged abusers. In a 6-2 decision, the court says use of the screen violates the Sixth Amendment right of defendants to confront witnesses against them.... The Supreme Court rules out, 5-3, imposition of the death penalty for juveniles under the age of 16. But the court leaves open the possibility that states could adopt new laws providing for such executions.... The House of Representatives passes a long-stalled fair-housing bill that will expand protection against housing discrimination and expedite review of complaints. The bill now goes to the Senate, where approval is expected.		Prices received by farmers for raw agricultural products in June surge 7.3%, the Agriculture Dept. reports.... The government's index of leading economic indicators fell 0.1% in May, the Commerce Dept. reports.			June 29

F	G	H	I	J
Includes elections, federal-state relations, civil rights and liberties, crime, the judiciary, education, health care, poverty, urban affairs and population.	*Includes formation and debate of U.S. foreign and defense policies, veterans' affairs and defense spending. (Relations with specific foreign countries are usually found under the region concerned.)*	*Includes business, labor, agriculture, taxation, transportation, consumer affairs, monetary and fiscal policy, natural resources, and pollution.*	*Includes worldwide scientific, medical and technological developments, natural phenomena, U.S. weather, natural disasters, and accidents.*	*Includes the arts, religion, scholarship, communications media, sports, entertainments, fashions, fads and social life.*

	World Affairs	Europe	Africa & the Middle East	The Americas	Asia & the Pacific
June 30					In South Korea, the government releases 46 people imprisoned for political crimes, including Kim Keun Tae, South Korea's most prominent dissident, and 453 other convicts. Justice ministry officials maintain that after the amnesty fewer than 100 political prisoners will remain in custody. Opposition leaders insist that the true number is more than 600.... Vietnam withdraws its top military leaders from Cambodia as part of its plan to pull 50,000 troops from the country by the end of the year. Gen. Le Ngoc Hien, head of the Vietnamese military forces in Cambodia, and 300 of his officers fly to Hanoi from Phnom Penh after turning over control of their troops to Cambodian commanders.
July 1		The 19th All-Union Conf. of the Soviet Communist Party ends at the Palace of Congresses in Moscow. The conference, which opened June 28, featured debate that was often blunt and unrestrained, and the openness of the gathering stunned many Soviet citizens, millions of whom were mesmerized by the television and newspaper coverage of the event.			China's ministry of foreign affairs proposes a settlement plan designed to end the conflict in Cambodia between the Vietnamese-backed regime of Heng Samrin and the country's three-party antigovernment guerrilla coalition.... Officials of the Japan Teachers Union accuse the government of censoring elementary and secondary school textbooks in order to downplay Japan's role as an aggressor during World War II and magnify the status of the emperor.... Japan's finance ministry reports that the government posted a record $14.2 bil. surplus in its FY1987 budget. Officials say the surplus is largely the result of higher than expected personal income and corporate tax revenues.
July 2					
July 3			The USS *Vincennes* shoots down an Iranian commercial airliner over the southern Persian Gulf after mistaking it for an attacking F-14 fighter jet. All 290 people aboard the plane are killed, making it the sixth-worst aviation disaster in history.... Iranian officials and radio condemn the United States for its "barbaric massacre" and warn, "We will not leave the crimes of America unanswered."	Seventeen peasants, including five children, are slain in Meta department in eastern Colombia. Their assassins, calling themselves the Fascist Red Army, admit, two days later, that the intended target was the mayor of El Castillo, a member of the leftist Patriotic Union (UP).	
July 4		The Soviet Union declares that it will grant amnesty to any of its soldiers who deserted their units in Afghanistan. The Soviet prosecutor general, the country's chief legal officer, makes the announcement at a press conference in Moscow.		The 13-member Caribbean Community and Common Market (Caricom) holds its annual five-day summit in Antigua.	Australia's embassy in the United States reports that the government achieved a record surplus of $1.84 bil. in the 1987-88 fiscal year, which ended June 30. The surplus is about twice the amount predicted as recently as May.... Papua New Guinea's P.M. Paias Wingti is forced to resign after he loses a no-confidence vote in parliament. Wingti, the third prime minister removed by the legislature since Papua New Guinea's independence in 1975, is replaced by Rabbie Namaliu, the Pangu Pati leader who succeeded Michael Somare as head of the opposition less than one week earlier.

A	B	C	D	E
Includes developments that affect more than one world region, international organizations and important meetings of major world leaders.	Includes all domestic and regional developments in Europe, including the Soviet Union, Turkey, Cyprus and Malta.	Includes all domestic and regional developments in Africa and the Middle East, including Iraq and Iran and excluding Cyprus, Turkey and Afghanistan.	Includes all domestic and regional developments in Latin America, the Caribbean and Canada.	Includes all domestic and regional developments in Asia and Pacific nations, extending from Afghanistan through all the Pacific Islands, except Hawaii.

U.S. Politics & Social Issues	U.S. Foreign Policy & Defense	U.S. Economy & Environment	Science, Technology & Nature	Culture, Leisure & Life Style	
		The United States remained the world's largest debtor nation at the end of 1987, the Commerce Dept. reports. The value of foreigners' assets in the United States exceeds U.S. assets overseas by $368.23 bil. at the end of 1987.		The Vatican excommunicates Archbishop Marcel Lefebvre and formally recognizes the first schism in the Roman Catholic Church in more than a century. The church acts after the renegade conservative archbishop, in open defiance of Pope John Paul II, consecrated four bishops for his Fraternity of St. Pius X at Econe, Switzerland. The bishops are automatically excommunicated, or excluded from the church.	June 30
Pres. Reagan signs legislation expanding the Medicare program to protect the elderly and disabled against "catastrophic" medical costs. The legislation cleared Congress June 8.					July 1
New national polls show Vice Pres. George Bush (R) closing the gap against his all-but-certain presidential opponent, Gov. Michael S. Dukakis (D, Mass.). A Gallup poll puts Bush within striking distance, trailing Dukakis by only 46%-41%. An ABC News/Money magazine poll also finds the governor's lead, which had once been as high as 53%-40%, shrinking.			The National Institutes of Health (NIH), yielding to congressional pressure, reverses its decision, announced in May, to suspend its funding of research aimed at developing a self-contained artificial heart, according to NIH director Dr. James Wyngaarden, who confirms the shift.	West German Steffi Graf wins the women's singles tennis title at Wimbledon for the first time by downing six-time defending champion Martina Navratilova.	July 2
	In a brief statement Pres. Reagan says he is "saddened" to report that "in a proper defensive action" the U.S. Navy's cruiser *Vincennes* today shot down an Iranian airliner.			In auto-racing Alain Prost of France wins the French Grand Prix in La Catellet.	July 3
				Stefan Edberg of Sweden wins the men's Wimbledon singles title, defeating West German Boris Becker.... The United States is chosen as the host nation for the 15th World Cup soccer tournament in 1994. The United States, which will host the event for the first time, is selected by a meeting of the International Federation of Football Associations in Zurich over rival bids from Brazil and Morocco.	July 4

F	G	H	I	J
Includes elections, federal-state relations, civil rights and liberties, crime, the judiciary, education, health care, poverty, urban affairs and population.	Includes formation and debate of U.S. foreign and defense policies, veterans' affairs and defense spending. (Relations with specific foreign countries are usually found under the region concerned.)	Includes business, labor, agriculture, taxation, transportation, consumer affairs, monetary and fiscal policy, natural resources, and pollution.	Includes worldwide scientific, medical and technological developments, natural phenomena, U.S. weather, natural disasters, and accidents.	Includes the arts, religion, scholarship, communications media, sports, entertainments, fashions, fads and social life.

	World Affairs	Europe	Africa & the Middle East	The Americas	Asia & the Pacific
July 5					Two senior Chinese officials warn that the country faces the possibility of "upheaval" and "turmoil" as economic and political reforms continue to alter the structure of Chinese society, the official New China News Agency reports. The two leaders, Premier Li Peng and Public Security Min. Wang Fang, make the remarks in Beijing during a national conference of state security officials.
July 6	The World Bank warns that the world economy faces the possibility of a worldwide recession unless industrial countries address unsolved budget and trade imbalances. In its annual World Development Report, the bank says that without changed policies among industrialized nations the continued world economic growth essential to improving the growth prospects of developing countries will be jeopardized.	A series of devastating explosions rocks the Piper Alpha oil platform in the North Sea. Some 166 workers, many from Scotland, are feared killed in the oil rig disaster, the worst in the North Sea since operations began there in 1968.			Aides to a number of top Japanese politicians, including Premier Noboru Takeshita and his predecessor, Yasuhiro Nakasone, are reported to be involved in a growing stock-trading scandal.
July 7		Joblessness in the European Community (EC) in the year through May averages 15.5 million, down 2.5%, or 400,000 workers, according to figures released by the EC.		Canada's House of Commons votes to approve a bill designed to strengthen the rights of French-speaking Canadians; the measure is sent to the Senate. Bill C-72, formally known as "An Act on the Status and Use of Official Languages in Canada," was introduced by the government in June 1987. The legislation moves toward fulfilling a long-standing promise by P.M. Brian Mulroney to revise the 19-year-old federal Official Languages Act to give French an equal status with English nationwide.	In a major shift in policy, South Korea's Pres. Roh Tae Woo announces that he wants to end the decades-old posture of confrontation between the two Koreas and will seek to improve ties with the North. The president outlines the new policy in his first nationally televised speech since his inauguration in February.
July 8			Over the previous two weeks Palestine Liberation Org. (PLO) guerrillas loyal to Yasir Arafat are driven from their last strongholds in south Beirut by the Syrian-backed PLO dissident faction led by Col. Saed Musa (Abu Musa). The last few hundred pro-Arafat fighters are evacuated from the flattened refugee camps of Shatila and Bourj al Barajneh to the Ain Hilwe district outside the southern Lebanese port city of Sidon.	In Haiti, Lt. Gen. Henri Namphy, who came to power in June after a military coup, scraps the constitution that was approved overwhelmingly in a referendum in March 1987. He says a new charter will be written soon.	
July 9					The UN mediator in the Afghan civil war calls for a cease-fire between the Soviet-backed regime in Kabul and the country's anticommunist guerrillas. The mediator, Diego Cordovez, also urges that a transitional "government of peace and reconstruction" be established in Afghanistan by September 1.

A	B	C	D	E
Includes developments that affect more than one world region, international organizations and important meetings of major world leaders.	Includes all domestic and regional developments in Europe, including the Soviet Union, Turkey, Cyprus and Malta.	Includes all domestic and regional developments in Africa and the Middle East, including Iraq and Iran and excluding Cyprus, Turkey and Afghanistan.	Includes all domestic and regional developments in Latin America, the Caribbean and Canada.	Includes all domestic and regional developments in Asia and Pacific nations, extending from Afghanistan through all the Pacific Islands, except Hawaii.

U.S. Politics & Social Issues	U.S. Foreign Policy & Defense	U.S. Economy & Environment	Science, Technology & Nature	Culture, Leisure & Life Style	
Attorney Gen. Edwin Meese III abruptly announces his resignation, claiming that he has been "completely vindicated" of wrongdoing by an independent prosecutor's report. The announcement comes only hours after independent prosecutor James C. McKay files an 830-page report on his 14-month criminal investigation of Meese with a federal court in the District of Columbia. The report remains under court seal at this time.	U.S. District Judge Jack B. Weinstein releases the disbursement plan for the $240 mil. settlement arranged with seven chemical companies for Vietnam veterans claiming illness from exposure to the herbicide Agent Orange.	The Senate overwhelmingly approves a bill requiring companies to give workers advance notice of layoffs and plant closings. The vote, 72-23, is five votes more than necessary to override a presidential veto. A similar measure attached to the trade bill was the pretext cited by Pres. Reagan in vetoing the legislation in May. Clearance of the plant-closing provision separately will open the way to reconsideration of the trade bill. Both bills are pending in the House. . . . Eight of the 12 regional banks for cooperatives of the Farm Credit System vote to merge into a single national bank with $9.3 bil. in assets. The new consolidated bank, the National Bank for Cooperatives, will rank as the nation's 15th largest business lender, with a portfolio of $6.6 bil. in loans outstanding.	The Food and Drug Admin. warns consumers against the indiscriminate use of the anti-acne drug Retin-A to erase wrinkles. Sales of the drug soared after it was found to produce some lessening of facial wrinkles.		July 5
		Ashland Oil Inc. and the federal government reach agreement on a cleanup of a massive oil spill that occurred in January when a 4-million-gallon tank ruptured at the firm's plant near Pittsburgh. Under part of the agreement Ashland agrees to reimburse the government $680,000 for costs incurred for the cleanup of the Monongahela and Ohio Rivers.			July 6
		The Federal Home Loan Bank Board (FHLBB) says that the probable cost of rescuing the nation's insolvent savings and loan associations will be twice as high as it was previously estimated. FHLBB Chairman M. Danny Wall tells the House Banking Committee that merging or closing 117 bankrupt Texas thrifts will cost $15.2 bil., over twice the $7 bil. estimated only six weeks before. . . . The Securities and Exchange Comm. votes a "one share, one vote" rule banning public corporations from issuing dual classes of stock that diminish the voting power of existing shareholders.		After a lengthy journey from the United States to Hungary, the remains of Hungarian composer Bela Bartok are given a state burial in Budapest. Bartok, one of the giants of 20th-century music, was 64 years old when he died in New York City in 1945, five years after he immigrated to the United States in despair over the rise of fascism. The transfer of his remains was made at the request of his two sons, Bela Jr., 77, who lives in Hungary, and Peter, 64, who lives in the United States.	July 7
Judge Gerhard A. Gesell in the Iran-Contra conspiracy case orders former National Security Council staff member Oliver L. North to stand trial September 20, and demands that the prosecution turn over to the defense any secret documents that show that North acted with approval from his superiors.		The nation's unemployment rate in June fell to 5.2%, the Labor Dept. says. . . . Outstanding consumer debt rose $2.42 bil. in May, the Federal Reserve Board reports, at an annual rate of 4.6%, to a total of $631.8 bil.			July 8
		Jackie Presser, 61, president of the International Brotherhood of Teamsters, the largest U.S. labor union since 1983, dies in Lakewood, Ohio; he had a heart ailment and had been suffering from cancer. He had been charged with using union funds to pay organized crime figures for work they had not performed, but the trial was postponed because of his poor health; in June of this year, the Justice Dept. filed suit to have the Teamsters' leaders replaced by a court-appointed trustee.			July 9

F	G	H	I	J
Includes elections, federal-state relations, civil rights and liberties, crime, the judiciary, education, health care, poverty, urban affairs and population.	Includes formation and debate of U.S. foreign and defense policies, veterans' affairs and defense spending. (Relations with specific foreign countries are usually found under the region concerned.)	Includes business, labor, agriculture, taxation, transportation, consumer affairs, monetary and fiscal policy, natural resources, and pollution.	Includes worldwide scientific, medical and technological developments, natural phenomena, U.S. weather, natural disasters, and accidents.	Includes the arts, religion, scholarship, communications media, sports, entertainments, fashions, fads and social life.

	World Affairs	Europe	Africa & the Middle East	The Americas	Asia & the Pacific
July 10				Some 3,000 protestors organized by the Democratic Coordinator, an opposition coalition of business groups, unions, and political parties, gather in a town south of Managua, Nicaragua, to demonstrate against economic conditions and demand that the government stand down, to be replaced by a "government of national salvation."	
July 11	Concessions by the West German Bundesbank allow central bankers from 12 leading industrial countries to agree on minimum international capital requirements for banks. At a meeting in Basel, the central bankers sign the final version of an accord agreed upon in December 1987. It requires banks to have capital equivalent to 8% of their risk-weighted assets by the end of 1992. . . . Confronted with small but increasing delinquencies on its loans for the first time in its history, the World Bank discreetly increases its provisions for loan losses to $500 mil. from $100 mil. The move comes with a record number of eight countries—Nicaragua, Guyana, Liberia, Syria, Peru, Sierra Leone, Zambia, and Panama—over six months in arrears on repayments to the bank. Together they owe $3.24 bil., or 3.6% of the bank's $89.9 bil. of disbursed loans outstanding at the end of 1987.			The Nicaraguan government orders the U.S. ambassador and seven other American diplomats to leave the country within 72 hours. Foreign Min. Miguel d'Escoto accuses Ambassador Richard H. Melton and the other diplomats of inciting rebellion against the Sandinista government. The move follows the July 10 opposition rally. . . . Pres. Jose Napoleon Duarte, who for six weeks has been receiving treatment in the United States for terminal cancer, returns to El Salvador. Duarte says he intends to resume his duties as president. Under the nation's constitution, as long as the president is in the country he cannot delegate power. Thus, should Duarte become too ill or weak to work, he will have to leave the country or resign in order to delegate his responsibilities to anyone else.	The chief justice of the Australian High Court reverses his previous opposition to a national bill of rights and becomes one of the first federal judges to urge serious consideration of the matter. Previous calls for a bill of rights, heard in the 1970s and again soon after P.M. Bob Hawke took office, had been widely opposed by the Australian judicial establishment.
July 12		The legislature of the Nagorno-Karabakh Autonomous Region votes to secede from the Soviet Azerbaijan Republic and unify with the Soviet Armenian Republic. The vote provides more fuel for the violent ethnic tensions in the southern Caucasus region of the USSR.			

A	B	C	D	E
Includes developments that affect more than one world region, international organizations and important meetings of major world leaders.	Includes all domestic and regional developments in Europe, including the Soviet Union, Turkey, Cyprus and Malta.	Includes all domestic and regional developments in Africa and the Middle East, including Iraq and Iran and excluding Cyprus, Turkey and Afghanistan.	Includes all domestic and regional developments in Latin America, the Caribbean and Canada.	Includes all domestic and regional developments in Asia and Pacific nations, extending from Afghanistan through all the Pacific Islands, except Hawaii.

U.S. Politics & Social Issues	U.S. Foreign Policy & Defense	U.S. Economy & Environment	Science, Technology & Nature	Culture, Leisure & Life Style	
				In auto racing, Ayrton Senna of Brazil wins the rain-soaked British Grand Prix.	July 10
	Pres. Reagan announces that the United States will pay compensation to the families of the 290 victims of the Iranian Airbus shot down by the USS *Vincennes* July 3.		Barbara (Frances) (Baroness Wootton of Abinger) Wootton, 91, dies. British social scientist who challenged conventional wisdom in fields ranging from economics to sociology to criminology, her experiences as a lay magistrate for nearly half a century and as chairman of juvenile courts in London for 16 years formed the basis for her seminal work *Social Science and Social Pathology* (1959). She was a member of four royal commissions and was one of the four women among the first life peers created in 1958.		July 11
After a search that took more than a month, Gov. Michael S. Dukakis (D, Mass.) names Sen. Lloyd Bentsen (D, Tex.) as his vice presidential running-mate. The choice is announced less than a week before the opening of the Democratic National Convention in Atlanta, where Dukakis is expected to receive the party's presidential nomination.... Pres. Reagan names former Pennsylvania Gov. Richard Thornburgh (R) to succeed Edwin Meese III as attorney general.		In its first major assessment of the effects of this year's drought, the Agriculture Dept. predicts a 26% plunge in 1988 corn production, to 5.2 billion bushels.... The Senate approves a $10.6 bil. spending bill for transportation programs for the fiscal year beginning October 1. The bill provides $1.8 bil. more than the Reagan administration sought but $240 mil. less than the amount adopted earlier by the House.		The American League wins Major League Baseball's annual All-Star Game, 2-1. Oakland Athletics' catcher Terry Steinbach drives in both American League runs, one with a home run, to earn the game's most valuable player award.... Joshua (Lockwood) Logan, 79, stage and screen director, dies in New York City; he had been suffering from a debilitating disorder known as supranuclear palsy. He staged such memorable Broadway shows as *Annie Get Your Gun* (1946) and *Picnic* (1953), and *Mr. Roberts* (1948) and *South Pacific* (1949), which he also coauthored and coproduced. His screen credits include such hits as *Bus Stop* (1956), *Sayonara* (1957), and *Paint Your Wagon* (1969).	July 12

F	G	H	I	J
Includes elections, federal-state relations, civil rights and liberties, crime, the judiciary, education, health care, poverty, urban affairs and population.	*Includes formation and debate of U.S. foreign and defense policies, veterans' affairs and defense spending. (Relations with specific foreign countries are usually found under the region concerned.)*	*Includes business, labor, agriculture, taxation, transportation, consumer affairs, monetary and fiscal policy, natural resources, and pollution.*	*Includes worldwide scientific, medical and technological developments, natural phenomena, U.S. weather, natural disasters, and accidents.*	*Includes the arts, religion, scholarship, communications media, sports, entertainments, fashions, fads and social life.*

	World Affairs	Europe	Africa & the Middle East	The Americas	Asia & the Pacific
July 13			Angolan, South African, Cuban, and U.S. officials in New York City conclude the third round of a recent series of four-power talks on ending the fighting in Angola and bringing independence to Namibia. Asst. Sec. of State Chester A. Crocker, who is mediating the negotiations, says that the participants have reached a tentative agreement on the "principles for a peaceful settlement in southwestern Africa."	After a week-long delay, Mexico's Federal Electoral Comm. announces final returns for the July 6 presidential election, giving victory to the candidate of the ruling Institutional Revolutionary Party (PRI), Carlos Salinas de Gortari. Salinas received 50.36% of the vote, the lowest share ever recorded by a PRI candidate in the party's 59-year history.	Taiwan's ruling Nationalist Party (Kuomintang, or KMT) concludes its week-long 13th congress at a secluded retreat on Yang Ming Shan mountain outside of Taipei. The congress, the first in seven years, is said by Western observers to be the most open and democratic in the party's 94-year history.
July 14	The World Bank reports that it took in $3.4 bil. more from debtor nations than it lent in the year ending June 30. The bank says it took in $1.2 bil. more than it lent to the world's 15 most indebted nations.	British Rail Corp. announces plans for a 180-mile-per-hour line between London and the forthcoming Eurotunnel on the southeastern coast of Kent. The high-speed train lines and a new London terminal are expected to cost between $1.3 bil. and $2 bil. and are slated to be open by 1998.			
July 15		The leaders of the Warsaw Pact nations meet for two days in Warsaw. The meeting is chaired by Soviet leader Mikhail S. Gorbachev and is held behind closed doors, but at its conclusion the leaders make public four separate resolutions on arms control they have adopted.	In South Africa, the authorities ban all events celebrating imprisoned African National Congress leader Nelson Mandela's 70th birthday on July 18. In protest, Mandela's wife, Winnie, rejects a government offer of a six-hour family reunion in prison.		
July 16		Soviet leader Mikhail S. Gorbachev concludes a six-day visit to Poland. The general secretary chairs a Warsaw Pact summit during his last two days in Poland.		At a rally in Mexico City, opposition leader Cuauhtemoc Cardenas kicks off a national campaign to protest the results of the recent presidential election. Carlos Salinas de Gortari, candidate of the ruling Institutional Revolutionary Party (PRI), was named the winner of the July 6 election by the PRI-dominated Federal Electoral Comm. Cardenas, candidate of the National Democratic Front, a coalition of leftist parties, placed second and alleges that the PRI won through widespread fraud.	

A	B	C	D	E
Includes developments that affect more than one world region, international organizations and important meetings of major world leaders.	Includes all domestic and regional developments in Europe, including the Soviet Union, Turkey, Cyprus and Malta.	Includes all domestic and regional developments in Africa and the Middle East, including Iraq and Iran and excluding Cyprus, Turkey and Afghanistan.	Includes all domestic and regional developments in Latin America, the Caribbean and Canada.	Includes all domestic and regional developments in Asia and Pacific nations, extending from Afghanistan through all the Pacific Islands, except Hawaii.

U.S. Politics & Social Issues	U.S. Foreign Policy & Defense	U.S. Economy & Environment	Science, Technology & Nature	Culture, Leisure & Life Style	
The Senate passes legislation that will provide $59.1 bil. for the Housing and Urban Development Dept. and various other federal agencies in fiscal 1989. It is $633.4 mil. lower than the $59.7 bil. House version passed June 22 and $409.7 mil. more than has been requested by the Reagan administration.		The House of Representatives overwhelmingly passes a revised version of comprehensive trade legislation aimed at opening up foreign markets and expanding U.S. trade. The bill will now go to the Senate, where passage is expected. . . . The House passes a bill requiring advance notice of plant closings by a 286-136 vote, four votes more than the two-thirds majority needed to override a veto. The bill, already approved by the Senate with enough support to survive a veto, is sent to the White House. Pres. Reagan opposes the legislation, and vetoed an earlier trade bill largely because the plant-closing provision was attached to it. . . . Federal Reserve Board Chairman Alan Greenspan signals that an interest-rate increase is likely in order to slow the growth of the nation's economy and prevent a surge of inflation. During his semiannual testimony to the Senate Finance Committee, Greenspan warns that the economy is nearing the limits of capacity and says that the Fed "at this juncture might be well advised to err more on the side of restrictiveness rather than stimulus."	An 80-foot Indian space rocket fails shortly after takeoff and falls into the Bay of Bengal with its payload, a 330-pound satellite. The cause of the launch failure, the second in 15 months, is unknown.	Variety's top-grossing films for the week are: Coming to America, Who Framed Roger Rabbit, Big, Bull Durham, and Arthur 2 on the Rocks.	July 13
The Senate Judiciary Committee rejects the nomination of Bernard Siegan to the Court of Appeals for the Ninth Circuit. The nomination, pending since February 1987, is defeated by an 8-6 vote along party lines. A Republican proposal to send the nomination to the full Senate without a recommendation also loses, 7-7, with one Democrat, Sen. Dennis DeConcini (Ariz.), joining the panel's six Republicans.	Prompted by an Atlanta Journal-Constitution series called "The Famine Weapon in the Horn of Africa," Democrats angrily question Reagan administration officials about their Sudanese policy during hearings by the House Select Committee on Hunger.	The nation's leading banks raise their prime lending rate to 9.5% from 9%. The increase in the prime is the second in 1988 to date, bringing the rate to its highest level since March 1986.			July 14
The Teamsters union's general executive board elects William J. McCarthy, an international vice president of the union for New England, to be president of the union for the remaining three years of the term of Jackie Presser, who died July 9.		The U.S. deficit on merchandise trade widened to a seasonally adjusted $10.93 bil. in May, the Commerce Dept. reports. . . . The government's producer price index rose 0.4% in June, the Labor Dept. reports. . . . The Federal Reserve Board reports that its industrial production index rose 0.4% in June.		The movie Die Hard, a film about a New York City cop who undertakes to rescue a group of hostages being held in a Los Angeles office tower, is released in New York. Directed by John McTiernan with screenplay by Jeb Stuart and Steven E. de Souza, based on the novel by Roderick Thorp, the movie stars Bruce Willis, Bonnie Bedelia, and Alan Rickman. . . . A Fish Called Wanda, an English comedy about four misfits who go to great lengths to double-cross each other after robbing a London jeweler, is released in New York. Directed by Charles Crichton and written by John Cleese, the film stars Cleese, Jamie Lee Curtis, Michael Palin, Tom Georgeson, and Kevin Kline, who wins the Academy Award for best supporting actor for his performance.	July 15
				Billboard's best-selling albums for the week are: OU812, Van Halen; Hysteria, Def Leppard; Faith, George Michael; Dirty Dancing (soundtrack); Appetite for Destruction, Guns N' Roses. . . . Florence Griffith Joyner shatters the world record in the women's 100-meter dash at the U.S. Olympic Track and Field Trials with a time of 10.49 seconds.	July 16

F	G	H	I	J
Includes elections, federal-state relations, civil rights and liberties, crime, the judiciary, education, health care, poverty, urban affairs and population.	Includes formation and debate of U.S. foreign and defense policies, veterans' affairs and defense spending. (Relations with specific foreign countries are usually found under the region concerned.)	Includes business, labor, agriculture, taxation, transportation, consumer affairs, monetary and fiscal policy, natural resources, and pollution.	Includes worldwide scientific, medical and technological developments, natural phenomena, U.S. weather, natural disasters, and accidents.	Includes the arts, religion, scholarship, communications media, sports, entertainments, fashions, fads and social life.

	World Affairs	Europe	Africa & the Middle East	The Americas	Asia & the Pacific
July 17		Industrial disputes involving air traffic controllers in Greece and France cause a weekend of long delays for European air travelers. The problem is exacerbated by a combination of steady growth in air travel over the previous years, the peak summer holiday season, and the use of outdated communications between air-traffic control systems in different nations.		In Honduras, six U.S. soldiers are wounded when assailants fire at them and hurl grenades as they leave a disco in San Pedro Sula. The leftist Cinchonero People's Liberation Movement claims responsibility in a call to a local radio station the following day.	The Industrial Bank of Japan publishes an unprecedentedly critical report on U.S. industry, arguing that American corporate culture is largely responsible for America's loss of international competitiveness. Surveying the performance of 23 U.S. industries from 1980 to 1986, the study argues that U.S. companies tended to ignore long-term goals for short-term financial results, focusing on domestic rather than overseas markets.
July 18			In a surprise announcement, Iran says it accepts a UN Security Council peace plan to end the Persian Gulf War, which has lasted nearly eight years and killed an estimated 1 million people.	In Canada, the federal government and Newfoundland sign a multibillion-dollar preliminary agreement with an energy consortium to develop the Hibernia offshore oil field. It will be the largest energy project in Atlantic Canada. Hibernia is located in the Atlantic Ocean's Grand Banks area, about 195 miles southeast of St. John's, Newfoundland. . . . The assembly of the Nicaraguan Resistance elects the Contras' top military commander, Col. Enrique Bermudez, to one of seven posts in the group's new directorate.	
July 19	Ranked by deposits, the world's 10 largest banks at the end of 1987 were all Japanese. According to an annual survey published by *American Banker*, Dai-Ichi Kangyo Bank Ltd. remains the world's largest bank, with $275.3 bil. in deposits. For the first time in the 31-year history of the survey no U.S. banks are among the top 25. The largest U.S. bank, Citibank, ranks 28th with $104.9 bil. in deposits. The survey attributes the increased dominance of Japanese banks to the appreciation of the yen against the U.S. dollar and to the deregulation of interest rates on large deposits in Japan.			Nicaragua's Pres. Daniel Ortega Saavedra extends through August the cease-fire that has been in effect since March.	China's inflation rate has reached its highest level in nearly 40 years, according to the state statistical bureau; retail prices in June were up 19% from the same month in 1987, the largest increase since 1949.
July 20	The collective outstanding debt of developing countries increased to $1.2 trillion by the end of 1987, the Org. for Economic Cooperation and Development reports, up 3%. Interest payments by developing countries fell to $64 bil., increasing slightly in sub-Saharan Africa but declining "significantly" in Latin America.			In Mexico, Cuauhtemoc Cardenas, the presidential candidate of the National Democratic Front in the elections of July 6, kicks off a post-election campaign to drum up support against president-elect Carlos Salinas de Gortari's ratification. Salinas was the candidate of the ruling Institutional Revolutionary Party.	Pakistan's Pres. Muhammad Zia ul-Haq announces that elections will be held November 16 to choose new members for the National Assembly. The previous assembly, which acted as the lower house of the Pakistani parliament, was dismissed by the president in May.
July 21					

A	B	C	D	E
Includes developments that affect more than one world region, international organizations and important meetings of major world leaders.	Includes all domestic and regional developments in Europe, including the Soviet Union, Turkey, Cyprus and Malta.	Includes all domestic and regional developments in Africa and the Middle East, including Iraq and Iran and excluding Cyprus, Turkey and Afghanistan.	Includes all domestic and regional developments in Latin America, the Caribbean and Canada.	Includes all domestic and regional developments in Asia and Pacific nations, extending from Afghanistan through all the Pacific Islands, except Hawaii.

U.S. Politics & Social Issues	U.S. Foreign Policy & Defense	U.S. Economy & Environment	Science, Technology & Nature	Culture, Leisure & Life Style	
					July 17
The three-day Democratic National Convention opens in Atlanta, Ga. Texas state treasurer Ann Richards gives the keynote address. . . . Independent prosecutor James C. McKay says in a report just made public that Attorney Gen. Edwin Meese III "probably violated the criminal law" in four instances while in office, but that prosecution is not warranted because of the absence of self-gain, corrupt intention, or a pattern of past malpractice.				Severiano Ballesteros of Spain wins golf's British Open in the final round.	**July 18**
In a late-night address at the Democratic National Convention, the Rev. Jesse L. Jackson stirs the crowd with a fervent speech that closes with personal recollections of his impoverished childhood and the repeated exhortation to "Keep hope alive." . . . The 1988 Democratic platform is adopted at the party's national convention. Although it restates Democratic commitment to such principles as equal rights for women, it is essentially a broad, thematic, and unspecific document developed by a Dukakis-dominated party committee the previous month. . . . An estimated 240,000 people left the land in 1987, dropping the nation's farm population to its lowest level since the 1850s. The survey, released annually by the Census Bureau and the Agriculture Dept., reports that an average of 4.986 million people lived on farms in 1987, or just 2% of the total U.S. population of 243.4 million. That compares with 5.226 million in 1986, or 2.2% of the national population of 241.1 million.		Housing starts increased 5.1% in June, the Commerce Dept. reports, to an adjusted annual rate of 1.454 million.			**July 19**
Gov. Michael S. Dukakis of Massachusetts clinches the Democratic presidential nomination with a final vote total of 2,876.25 delegate votes to 1,218.5 for the Rev. Jesse L. Jackson. It is then moved that his nomination be accepted unanimously.	The State Dept. rejects an offer by the Soviet Union to dismantle a controversial radar complex in return for U.S. concessions on the 1972 antiballistic missile treaty.	The Environmental Protection Agency proposes four options to control emissions of benzene, a byproduct of oil refining and chemical manufacturing that can cause leukemia.			**July 20**
Gov. Michael S. Dukakis of Massachusetts accepts the Democratic nomination for president, pledging to depart from the "cramped ideals and limited ambitions of the Reagan era" and lead the nation to "the next American frontier." Dukakis declares, "My friends, if anyone tells you that the American dream belongs to the privileged few and not to all of us, you tell them that the Reagan era is over. . .and a new era is about to begin."		General Motors Corp. (GMC) reports its second-quarter earnings rose 54% from the year-earlier period to $1.51 bil. GMC's quarterly profits climb is due to higher sales, better production management, and a significant accounting change.			**July 21**
F	G	H	I	J
Includes elections, federal-state relations, civil rights and liberties, crime, the judiciary, education, health care, poverty, urban affairs and population.	Includes formation and debate of U.S. foreign and defense policies, veterans' affairs and defense spending. (Relations with specific foreign countries are usually found under the region concerned.)	Includes business, labor, agriculture, taxation, transportation, consumer affairs, monetary and fiscal policy, natural resources, and pollution.	Includes worldwide scientific, medical and technological developments, natural phenomena, U.S. weather, natural disasters, and accidents.	Includes the arts, religion, scholarship, communications media, sports, entertainments, fashions, fads and social life.

	World Affairs	Europe	Africa & the Middle East	The Americas	Asia & the Pacific
July 22		Britain's P.M. Margaret Thatcher names Leon Brittan as the senior British commissioner to the European Community's seven-member commission for the four-year term beginning in 1989.	Having responded to Iran's July 18 acceptance of a UN peace plan to end the Persian Gulf War by launching new attacks, Iraq demands direct talks with Teheran as a precondition for accepting a formal truce. UN Sec. Gen. Javier Perez de Cuellar moves quickly to try to work out a compromise between the two antagonists.		
July 23				In Canada, the Council of Yukon Indians, representing the territory's 12 bands, approves most of a major land-claims settlement offer. Under the settlement, negotiated by the council and the territorial and federal governments, the Yukon's 5,500 Indians will receive full title to about 10,000 square miles of land and more than $167 mil. in compensation. In return, the Indians will relinquish their ancestral claim to lands that encompass virtually the entire Yukon.	Ne Win, who has led Burma for 26 years, announces his resignation as chairman of the nation's ruling Burma Socialist Program Party. He says he is stepping down in response to student-led rioting in March and June that "showed the lack of trust and confidence in the government." . . . Michio Watanabe, chairman of the policy affairs council of Japan's ruling Liberal Democratic Party, angers U.S. blacks when he suggests in a speech at a party conference that many blacks do not mind going into bankruptcy.
July 24					
July 25					The warring factions in the 10-year-old Cambodian conflict hold their first face-to-face peace talks. The four-day parley brings together representatives from Vietnam, the Vietnamese-backed Cambodian regime of Heng Samrin, and the country's three antigovernment guerrilla groups. . . . A group of some 700 Aborigines riot in Geraldton, Western Australia, following the funeral of an Aboriginal man who died in police custody. . . . The government of Vanuatu expels from parliament five members of the opposition, including P.M. Father Walter Lini's chief rival, former cabinet minister Barak Sope. The five are accused of inciting antigovernment riots.
July 26					The central committee of Burma's Socialist Program Party chooses Sein Lwin, a retired army general who is currently the party's joint secretary general and head of the council of state, to replace Ne Win, who resigned July 23 as party chairman.

A	B	C	D	E
Includes developments that affect more than one world region, international organizations and important meetings of major world leaders.	Includes all domestic and regional developments in Europe, including the Soviet Union, Turkey, Cyprus and Malta.	Includes all domestic and regional developments in Africa and the Middle East, including Iraq and Iran and excluding Cyprus, Turkey and Afghanistan.	Includes all domestic and regional developments in Latin America, the Caribbean and Canada.	Includes all domestic and regional developments in Asia and Pacific nations, extending from Afghanistan through all the Pacific Islands, except Hawaii.

U.S. Politics & Social Issues	U.S. Foreign Policy & Defense	U.S. Economy & Environment	Science, Technology & Nature	Culture, Leisure & Life Style	
		The government's consumer price index rose 0.3% in June, the Labor Dept. reports.... Pres. Reagan orders the imposition of trade sanctions against Brazil in retaliation for its failure to protect U.S. pharmaceutical patents.			July 22
A Federal Election Comm. study finds that political action committees were much more generous to congressional candidates in 1988 than they were in the previous election cycle.... The Food and Drug Admin. announces that it will allow people affected by acquired immune deficiency syndrome or other diseases to import drugs for their own personal use that have not been approved for sale in the United States.				*Publishers Weekly*'s hardback fiction best-sellers for the week are: *Alaska*, James Michener; *To Be the Best*, Barbara Taylor Bradford; *Zoya*, Danielle Steel; *The Bonfire of the Vanities*, Tom Wolfe; and *The Icarus Agenda*, Robert Ludlum.	July 23
The city of Chicago enacts restrictions that prohibit smoking in enclosed public spaces such as meeting rooms or taxicabs, require restaurants and transportation facilities to provide nonsmoking sections, and oblige employers to set aside nonsmoking areas if employees request it.				Pedro Delgado of Spain wins the 21-day Tour de France bicycle race.... Liselotte Neumann of Sweden wins the U.S. Women's Open golf championship by three strokes over Patty Sheehan.	July 24
		Pres. Reagan formally submits to Congress legislation to implement the U.S.-Canada trade accord. Members of Congress, even those who are not enthusiastic about the trade accord, predict that it will be given swift approval. Under the so-called "fast-track" rules in effect for the accord, which was signed in January, Congress has 90 legislative days to either approve or reject the legislation.		A New York state judge rules that boats from New Zealand and the United States should contest for the America's Cup yachting trophy in September. The decision ends a legal battle that began late last year when a New Zealand syndicate challenged the American holders of the cup to a race at less than the traditional four-year interval.	July 25
The House Ethics Committee unanimously votes to hire Chicago lawyer Richard T. Phelan as its special counsel to investigate House Speaker James C. Wright Jr. (D, Tex.).... Two former top Justice Dept. officials testify before the Senate Judiciary Committee on their refusal to continue working at the department under Attorney Gen. Edwin Meese III. One of them, William F. Weld, former head of the department's criminal division, says he believes that Meese's conduct in office was prosecutable. The other, Arnold I. Burns, who was deputy attorney general, describes the department under Meese as "a world of Alice in Wonderland, a world of illusion."					July 26

F	G	H	I	J
Includes elections, federal-state relations, civil rights and liberties, crime, the judiciary, education, health care, poverty, urban affairs and population.	*Includes formation and debate of U.S. foreign and defense policies, veterans' affairs and defense spending. (Relations with specific foreign countries are usually found under the region concerned.)*	*Includes business, labor, agriculture, taxation, transportation, consumer affairs, monetary and fiscal policy, natural resources, and pollution.*	*Includes worldwide scientific, medical and technological developments, natural phenomena, U.S. weather, natural disasters, and accidents.*	*Includes the arts, religion, scholarship, communications media, sports, entertainments, fashions, fads and social life.*

	World Affairs	Europe	Africa & the Middle East	The Americas	Asia & the Pacific
July 27			After Iraq continues to insist on direct negotiations with Iran, UN Sec. Gen. Javier Perez de Cuellar suspends two days of separate talks with the foreign ministers of Iran and Iraq aimed at ending the eight-year-old Persian Gulf War.	Brazil's Constituent Assembly votes to approve the draft of a new constitution and send it on to a second and final round of voting, scheduled for September.	Thailand's Premier Prem Tinsulanonda, who has served as the nonelected head of the Thai government for nearly eight-and-a-half years, declines an offer to remain in his post for another term. The acting deputy premier, Chatichai Choonhavan, is named Prem's successor. Chatichai, 66, is a retired army major general and one of Prem's closest political supporters.
July 28			Fighting between Iran and Iraq continues over the last few days, despite the beginnings of UN-negotiated peace talks, as Iraq seeks to strengthen its hand at the bargaining table by capturing more Iranian prisoners. . . . Human rights groups blame the Khartoum government for Sudan's civil war. Militias have massacred thousands of ethnic Dinkas and dislocated hundreds of thousands of others in what a Human Rights Watch official has compared to genocide.	In Canada, the House of Commons debates the abortion issue over two days without reaching a consensus on legislation to replace the law struck down by the Supreme Court of Canada in January. The debate is spurred by a new motion on abortion introduced by the government.	
July 29		In Great Britain, two of the Conservative government's most controversial legislative proposals, the Education Reform Bill and Local Government Finance Bill (poll tax), become law when they receive Royal Assent.		The Inter-American Court of Human Rights finds Honduras guilty in the 1981 disappearance and presumed murder of Angel Manfredo Velasquez Rodriguez, a 35-year-old Honduran student leader. Human rights groups blame the military for his disappearance.	Japan's unemployment rate dropped to 2.4% in June, the lowest level in more than five years.
July 30					The human rights group Asia Watch releases a report—the second this year—claiming that "a minimum of several hundred" Tibetans are being detained by the Chinese as a result of unrest in late 1987 and early 1988.
July 31			King Hussein of Jordan announces that his government will cut its legal and administrative ties to the Israeli-occupied West Bank, surrendering its claims to the territory to the Palestine Liberation Org.		

A	B	C	D	E
Includes developments that affect more than one world region, international organizations and important meetings of major world leaders.	Includes all domestic and regional developments in Europe, including the Soviet Union, Turkey, Cyprus and Malta.	Includes all domestic and regional developments in Africa and the Middle East, including Iraq and Iran and excluding Cyprus, Turkey and Afghanistan.	Includes all domestic and regional developments in Latin America, the Caribbean and Canada.	Includes all domestic and regional developments in Asia and Pacific nations, extending from Afghanistan through all the Pacific Islands, except Hawaii.

U.S. Politics & Social Issues	U.S. Foreign Policy & Defense	U.S. Economy & Environment	Science, Technology & Nature	Culture, Leisure & Life Style	
The Office of Government Ethics announces that a review of former Attorney Gen. Edwin Meese III's conduct in office is underway and will "be handled with dispatch." ... The Washington, D.C.-based National Geographic Society reports that young adults in the United States scored lower than their counterparts in eight other countries in an international test of geographic knowledge; American adults ranked sixth.	Pres. Reagan signs a finding authorizing covert activities aimed at ousting Panama's military leader, Gen. Manuel Antonio Noriega, the *Washington Post* reports, citing administration and congressional sources.	The nation's gross national product grew at a 3.1% annual rate in the second quarter, the Commerce Dept. reports. ... The Environmental Protection Agency reports that 87% of the nation's municipal sewage plants have met a July 1 deadline requiring removal of at least 85% of the bacteria and pollutants from industrial and household waste. ... A congressional research report warns that the nation's air traffic control system must be modernized to cope safely with the continuing growth of commercial air traffic. ... Among the Big Three auto makers, Ford Motor Co. again remains the most profitable. The nation's second-largest auto maker reports second-quarter earnings of $1.66 bil.	Surgeon Gen. C. Everett Koop releases a report describing dietary fat as a major national health problem and calling on Americans to cut the amount of fat in their diets. The 712-page report, officially "The Surgeon General's Report on Fitness and Health," is billed by Koop as the most comprehensive report on nutrition and health ever presented by the government.		July 27
An NBC News/Wall Street Journal poll of citizens likely to vote gives Democratic presidential nominee Gov. Michael S. Dukakis a 51% to 34% lead over Republican candidate Vice Pres. George Bush. A similar Gallup poll gives Dukakis a 55%-38% lead.	The United States reveals the number and location of plants involved in the production of chemical weapons. The disclosure is made by Max L. Friedersdorf, the head of the U.S. delegation to the 40-nation UN Conf. on Disarmament in Geneva.	The House of Representatives and the Senate approve separate but similar drought relief bills. Both measures will now go to a conference committee that will reconcile differences and reduce costs for deficit-related reasons. ... Consumer spending increased 1% and personal income 0.7% in June, the Commerce Dept. reports. ... The Senate passes a bill to renew the Endangered Species Act. The bill is sent to conference with the House, which approved a similar bill seven months earlier. Opposition to the bill by western mountain-state senators collapses in the face of an election-year enthusiasm for the environmental measure, which is designed to protect animals, plants, and marine life. ... Chrysler Corp. reports its second-quarter net earnings fell to $320.4 mil., down 24% from the 1987 second quarter. The number-three auto maker blames the decline on its pursuit of increased market share through lower auto prices.	According to a new study, about 31% of all conceptions end in miscarriage, usually in the early months of pregnancy and often before women know they are pregnant. There are not usually any lasting effects on fertility.		July 28
		Prices received by farmers for raw agricultural products climb 3.6% in July, the Agriculture Dept. reports. ... The Senate approves a $47.3 bil. appropriations bill to fund the Agriculture Dept. and federal nutrition and rural development programs for fiscal 1989. Overall, the Senate measure is $3.2 bil. more than a similar House measure and $645 mil. more than the Reagan administration sought. ... A Washington, D.C., federal appeals court panel rejects a Federal Communications Comm. (FCC) ruling that limits "indecent" programming to broadcasts between midnight and 6 a.m. The panel votes, 3-0, that the FCC has not shown that such a limitation is necessary to protect children.			July 29
After sending more conflicting signals about what his role in the fall campaign will be, the Rev. Jesse L. Jackson returns to the stump, campaigning for the first time for the Democratic presidential nominee, Massachusetts Gov. Michael S. Dukakis.				Mike Ditka, Jack Ham, Fred Biletnikoff, and Alan Page are inducted into the Pro Football Hall of Fame in Canton, Ohio.	July 30
				Willie Stargell is inducted into baseball's Hall of Fame in Cooperstown, N.Y.	July 31
F Includes elections, federal-state relations, civil rights and liberties, crime, the judiciary, education, health care, poverty, urban affairs and population.	**G** Includes formation and debate of U.S. foreign and defense policies, veterans' affairs and defense spending. (Relations with specific foreign countries are usually found under the region concerned.)	**H** Includes business, labor, agriculture, taxation, transportation, consumer affairs, monetary and fiscal policy, natural resources, and pollution.	**I** Includes worldwide scientific, medical and technological developments, natural phenomena, U.S. weather, natural disasters, and accidents.	**J** Includes the arts, religion, scholarship, communications media, sports, entertainments, fashions, fads and social life.	

	World Affairs	Europe	Africa & the Middle East	The Americas	Asia & the Pacific
Aug. 1		The Soviets dynamite four SS-12 missiles at the Saryozek missile range in the Central Asian republic of Kazakhstan. They are the first weapons destroyed under the U.S.-Soviet treaty on intermediate-range nuclear forces. The destruction coincides with the visit to the Soviet Union of Defense Sec. Frank C. Carlucci, although he is not present at the range.	Following a summer of protests by the media, environmentalists, and West African governments over the unregulated dumping of toxic waste from Europe and the United States in poor, ill-equipped African countries, West African regimes from Morocco to the Congo cancel all known contracts and arrest dozens of officials. While several of the instances involved illegal dumping, others entailed formal contracts with African governments.		The Japanese finance ministry reports a record $14.23 bil. budget surplus for fiscal 1987, the largest increase recorded by the government since World War II.
Aug. 2	World merchandise trade grew 5% in volume in 1987, according to the secretariat of the General Agreement on Tariffs and Trade. In value, world merchandise trade grew 16.5%, to $2.475 trillion. West Germany exported more than the United States for the second straight year.				South Korea's four leading auto makers plan production increases that will double the number of vehicles they produce to more than 3.4 million a year by 1993, government and industry officials announce.
Aug. 3	The price committee of the Org. of Petroleum Exporting Countries (OPEC) decides not to call an extraordinary meeting of OPEC's ministers despite the depressed state of oil prices to about $5 below the group's reference price of $18 a barrel.	Mathias Rust, the 20-year-old West German pilot who landed his light plane in Moscow's Red Square in May 1987, is released from a Soviet prison and flown to Frankfurt from Moscow after being officially expelled by the Soviets. He served less than one year of a four-year sentence.			
Aug. 4		In Yugoslavia, the price of electricity rises about 40%, railway fares as much as 70%, and cooking oil by 66% as the government lifts certain price controls as part of an austerity program adopted May 15. Controls on wages and government spending remain in place.		Human rights in Central America are in a "dismal" condition, according to a report by the U.S. human rights organization Americas Watch. The group says military and paramilitary forces continue to carry out political murders on a wide scale in Guatemala and El Salvador, and to a lesser extent in Honduras.	

A	B	C	D	E
Includes developments that affect more than one world region, international organizations and important meetings of major world leaders.	Includes all domestic and regional developments in Europe, including the Soviet Union, Turkey, Cyprus and Malta.	Includes all domestic and regional developments in Africa and the Middle East, including Iraq and Iran and excluding Cyprus, Turkey and Afghanistan.	Includes all domestic and regional developments in Latin America, the Caribbean and Canada.	Includes all domestic and regional developments in Asia and Pacific nations, extending from Afghanistan through all the Pacific Islands, except Hawaii.

U.S. Politics & Social Issues	U.S. Foreign Policy & Defense	U.S. Economy & Environment	Science, Technology & Nature	Culture, Leisure & Life Style	
		The Environmental Protection Agency sets production quotas for chemicals linked to depletion of the Earth's protective ozone layer. The chemicals, chlorofluorocarbons (CFCs), are widely used as refrigerants and cleaning agents and in the production of plastic foam.		Swimming is the most popular participant sport in the United States, according to a survey by the National Sporting Goods Assoc., which measures participation by persons over seven years old. For some categories (swimming, exercise walking, bicycling, and others) participants were counted only if they took part in the sport six or more times; one time was sufficient for other sports, such as softball or basketball.	Aug. 1
Pres. Reagan issues an "action plan" against acquired immune deficiency syndrome (AIDS) that sidesteps the key recommendations of his own advisory commission's report released June 17, including passage of a federal law barring discrimination against individuals infected with the disease.... The Senate passes fair-housing legislation that will expand protection against housing discrimination and expedite review of complaints. The bill will now go back to the House, which passed a housing bill slightly varied from the Senate measure. Pres. Reagan is expected to sign the legislation into law.... U.S. District Judge Leonard B. Sand holds Yonkers, N.Y., in contempt of a desegregation order and calls the New York suburb "a national symbol of defiance to civil rights." The court imposes an accumulating fine against the city that could force bankruptcy within 22 days.	The New York Times and ABC News report that the U.S. Navy's investigation of the July 3 shooting down of an Iranian passenger plane over the Persian Gulf blames the tragedy on errors by the crew of the cruiser USS Vincennes. Defense Dept. officials familiar with the inquiry say that the military investigators found no fault with the U.S. ship's advanced Aegis radar system but instead attribute the mistakes to the nervousness and lack of combat experience of the Vincennes's crew.	Pres. Reagan announces that he will not veto a bill requiring notice of plant closings and will allow the politically popular measure to become law without his signature. It is the first time during his presidency that Reagan allows a bill to become law by taking no action on it within the 10-day period of consideration allowed the president. ... The government's index of leading economic indicators rises 1.4% in June, the Commerce Dept. reports.	The Indian government reports that at least 215 people in New Delhi have died and another 11,000 required medical treatment as the result of a month-long epidemic of cholera that began during the country's annual monsoon season.	Raymond Carver, 50, short-story writer and poet widely regarded as the laureate of America's working poor, dies at his home in Port Angeles, Wash., of cancer. Writing in short, declarative sentences, among his most highly regarded works are his 1976 short-story collection Will You Please Be Quiet, Please?, his 1984 collection Cathedral, his 1981 collection What We Talk About When We Talk About Love, and his 1983 Fires, a collection of poems, essays, and short stories. He spent much of his life struggling with alcohol and persistent poverty.	Aug. 2
Gov. Michael S. Dukakis (D, Mass.), the Democratic presidential nominee, orders his personal physician to release a detailed health summary. The report says Dukakis has had "no significant illnesses during his lifetime and has been in excellent health...He has had no psychological symptoms, complaints or treatment." ... The House impeaches U.S. District Judge Alcee L. Hastings of Florida for high crimes and misdemeanors. The House votes overwhelmingly, 413-3, to adopt 17 articles of impeachment against Hastings, who becomes the 15th federal official, and 11th judge, to be impeached by the House since 1787. The proceedings will go next to the Senate, which has the sole power under the Constitution "to try all impeachments."	Pres. Reagan vetoes a $299.6 bil. defense authorization bill for fiscal 1989 in what is widely viewed as a politically motivated action. "The bill would signal a basic change in the future direction of our national defense, away from strength and proven success and back toward the weakness and accommodation of the 1970s," Reagan says at a White House press briefing.... Democrats in the Senate reach agreement on a plan to provide the Contras fighting the Nicaraguan government with $27 mil. in nonlethal aid. The agreement, backed by liberal and conservative Democrats alike, is spurned by the White House as "totally unacceptable."	The Senate overwhelmingly passes a revised version of comprehensive trade legislation aimed at opening up foreign markets and expanding U.S. trade. The House cleared the bill one month ago. The bill now goes to Pres. Reagan, who is expected to sign it.... The Environmental Protection Agency announces a $33.1 mil. settlement with 48 parties for cleanup of four hazardous waste sites in Massachusetts and New Hampshire. A lawsuit is also filed in federal district court in Boston for additional sharing of the cleanup costs from 25 other "recalcitrant parties that refused government offers to settle."			Aug. 3
Rep. Mario Biaggi (D, N.Y.) and five other individuals are convicted in a five-month racketeering trial involving Wedtech Corp., a Bronx, N.Y., contractor that was once hailed by Pres. Reagan as a symbol of how minority group members could achieve success through entrepreneurship.	Defense Sec. Frank C. Carlucci concludes a four-day visit to the Soviet Union. Carlucci, the first U.S. defense secretary to visit the USSR not in the company of a U.S. president, was invited by Soviet Defense Min. Gen. Dmitri T. Yazov.	Productivity among the nation's nonfarm businesses fell at an annual rate of 1.7% in the second quarter, the Labor Dept. reports.			Aug. 4

F	G	H	I	J
Includes elections, federal-state relations, civil rights and liberties, crime, the judiciary, education, health care, poverty, urban affairs and population.	Includes formation and debate of U.S. foreign and defense policies, veterans' affairs and defense spending. (Relations with specific foreign countries are usually found under the region concerned.)	Includes business, labor, agriculture, taxation, transportation, consumer affairs, monetary and fiscal policy, natural resources, and pollution.	Includes worldwide scientific, medical and technological developments, natural phenomena, U.S. weather, natural disasters, and accidents.	Includes the arts, religion, scholarship, communications media, sports, entertainments, fashions, fads and social life.

	World Affairs	Europe	Africa & the Middle East	The Americas	Asia & the Pacific
Aug. 5					A UN report issued in Geneva accuses Australia of disregarding the rights of the nation's 160,000 Aborigines and calls for improvements in the living conditions of the minority group. The report, by a subcommission of the UN Human Rights Comm., claims that most Aborigines, Australia's native inhabitants, are destitute and out of work.
Aug. 6		Among major industrialized countries, Switzerland had the highest labor costs in 1987. According to a Union Bank of Switzerland study, labor costs in Switzerland averaged $18.36 an hour.			In India, the leader of the Gurkha National Liberation Front, Subash Ghising, formally announces an end to his movement's two-year insurgency against authorities in West Bengal state, the United News of India reports. On July 25 Ghising reached an agreement with the Indian and West Bengal governments under which the Gurkhas were granted limited autonomy within the West Bengal district of Darjeeling.
Aug. 7					Seven opposition parties in India form a coalition aimed at defeating P.M. Rajiv Gandhi in general elections due before the end of 1989. The new National Front is to be led by former Gandhi cabinet minister Vishwanath Pratap Singh.
Aug. 8		The Duchess of York, the former Sarah Ferguson, gives birth to a daughter, Beatrice Elizabeth Mary (Princess Beatrice of York), the first child for her and her husband, Prince Andrew, Duke of York.	UN Sec. Gen. Javier Perez de Cuellar announces that a cease-fire between Iran and Iraq will take effect August 20 and that both countries have agreed to open talks five days later in Geneva to discuss the terms of a final peace settlement in the Persian Gulf war. . . . Angola, Cuba, and South Africa issue a joint statement declaring that "a de facto cessation of hostilities is now in effect" in the conflict in Angola and the neighboring territory of Namibia (South-West Africa). The agreement was hammered out in a series of talks mediated by the United States, the latest of which ended August 5.		

A	B	C	D	E
Includes developments that affect more than one world region, international organizations and important meetings of major world leaders.	*Includes all domestic and regional developments in Europe, including the Soviet Union, Turkey, Cyprus and Malta.*	*Includes all domestic and regional developments in Africa and the Middle East, including Iraq and Iran and excluding Cyprus, Turkey and Afghanistan.*	*Includes all domestic and regional developments in Latin America, the Caribbean and Canada.*	*Includes all domestic and regional developments in Asia and Pacific nations, extending from Afghanistan through all the Pacific Islands, except Hawaii.*

U.S. Politics & Social Issues	U.S. Foreign Policy & Defense	U.S. Economy & Environment	Science, Technology & Nature	Culture, Leisure & Life Style	
In the Iran-Contra conspiracy case, Judge Gerhard A. Gesell postpones the trial of the most prominent defendant, former National Security Council staff member Oliver L. North, at least until after the November presidential elections. Gesell says he is pushing back the trial date (originally set for September 20) in order to give both the prosecuting and defense attorneys more time to sort through the hundreds of thousands of classified government documents related to the case.		The nation's unemployment rate in July rose to 5.4%, the Labor Dept. reports. . . . Outstanding consumer debt surged $5.43 bil. in June, the Federal Reserve Board reports, at an annual rate of 10.2%, to a total of $638.57 bil. . . . Pres. Reagan accepts the resignation of Treasury Sec. James A. Baker III and names Nicholas F. Brady to succeed him. Baker is stepping down effective August 17 to manage the presidential campaign of Vice Pres. George Bush. . . . Pres. Reagan agrees to freeze emission levels of nitrogen oxide at the 1987 amount for at least the next seven years. In taking the action, the president authorizes the State Dept. to continue negotiations with other nations that endorse a protocol to reduce acid rain. The U.S. action is a policy reversal for the administration, which in 1985 refused to be a party to a similar protocol, accepted by 16 nations, to cut emissions of sulfur dioxide, another major ingredient of acid rain.	Two days of torrential rains devastate Khartoum, Sudan, with the worst flooding in this century. The city's telephone and telex links are cut until August 8, by which time at least a quarter of Khartoum's 4 million people are homeless.		Aug. 5
				Ballerina Natalia Makarova, who defected from the Soviet Union in 1970, rejoins her former troupe, the Kirov ballet company, for a performance in London. The event marks the first time that Moscow has allowed a Soviet dancer to rejoin his or her former company after defecting. Makarova danced Odette in Tchaikovsky's *Swan Lake*.	Aug. 6
The average cost of a year of college will rise by 7% in the upcoming academic year, the College Board reports, faster than inflation for the eighth consecutive year. Bennington College is the most expensive school in the country, with a total annual cost of $20,540.		A 22-week strike by 9,000 movie and television writers ends with ratification of a new four-year contract with producers. The strike, the third longest in Hollywood history, disrupts fall television programming and poses a threat to studio and network revenues. Layoffs in allied services are widespread. . . . Rupert Murdoch's News Corp. agrees to purchase Triangle Publications Inc. for $3 bil. in the largest transaction ever in the publishing industry. The purchase of Triangle, the publisher of *TV Guide, Seventeen*, and the *Daily Racing Form*, will end the involvement of Walter Annenberg and his family in publishing after nearly a century. Annenberg, 80, was chairman of Triangle, a private company closely held by him, family members, and related foundations.			Aug. 7
		The Senate approves a bill to revise federal regulation of the commercial nuclear power industry and to standardize designs of new plants. The measure calls for creation of a Nuclear Safety Agency to replace the five-member Nuclear Regulatory Comm. The bill is headed for consultation with the house. . . . The *Wall Street Journal* finds that net income at 487 major corporations it surveyed surged 101% in the second quarter from the same period in 1987, while after-tax earnings from continuing operations surged 103%.		The Chicago Cubs play their first night game ever at Wrigley Field in the middle of their 73rd season. The Cubs have a 3-1 lead over the Philadelphia Phillies by the fourth inning, but the game is rained out after a delay of more than two hours.	Aug. 8

F	G	H	I	J
Includes elections, federal-state relations, civil rights and liberties, crime, the judiciary, education, health care, poverty, urban affairs and population.	*Includes formation and debate of U.S. foreign and defense policies, veterans' affairs and defense spending. (Relations with specific foreign countries are usually found under the region concerned.)*	*Includes business, labor, agriculture, taxation, transportation, consumer affairs, monetary and fiscal policy, natural resources, and pollution.*	*Includes worldwide scientific, medical and technological developments, natural phenomena, U.S. weather, natural disasters, and accidents.*	*Includes the arts, religion, scholarship, communications media, sports, entertainments, fashions, fads and social life.*

	World Affairs	Europe	Africa & the Middle East	The Americas	Asia & the Pacific
Aug. 9		In a West German court, Mohammed Ali Hamadei unexpectedly confesses to involvement in the June 1985 hijacking of a Trans World Airlines plane, but he denies that he killed an American passenger. The Lebanese defendant claims he "pleaded" with his accomplice not to shoot the hostage, U.S. Navy diver Robert Dean Stethem.			
Aug. 10				Costa Rica's president, Oscar Arias Sanchez, meets with Cuba's Pres. Fidel Castro and asks for assistance in reviving the stalled Central American peace plan signed in 1987. Arias won a Nobel Peace Prize for his role as architect of that plan.... Rodrigo Borja Cevallos is inaugurated as president of Ecuador in a ceremony in the capital city, Quito. Borja, a social democrat, won election in May, succeeding Leon Febres Cordero, an arch-conservative.	The human rights group Amnesty International publishes a report criticizing the Indian government for failing to investigate allegations that police and security forces have illegally killed scores of Sikh militants since the beginning of 1987.
Aug. 11					A rocket attack by Afghan rebels on the Soviet base at Kilagay, which houses Afghanistan's main fuel and munitions dump, touches off a huge explosion, killing as many as 800 Soviet soldiers and civilians.

A	B	C	D	E
Includes developments that affect more than one world region, international organizations and important meetings of major world leaders.	Includes all domestic and regional developments in Europe, including the Soviet Union, Turkey, Cyprus and Malta.	Includes all domestic and regional developments in Africa and the Middle East, including Iraq and Iran and excluding Cyprus, Turkey and Afghanistan.	Includes all domestic and regional developments in Latin America, the Caribbean and Canada.	Includes all domestic and regional developments in Asia and Pacific nations, extending from Afghanistan through all the Pacific Islands, except Hawaii.

U.S. Politics & Social Issues	U.S. Foreign Policy & Defense	U.S. Economy & Environment	Science, Technology & Nature	Culture, Leisure & Life Style	
A Gallup poll shows Democratic presidential nominee Gov. Michael S. Dukakis's lead dwindling to 49%-42%. Vice Pres. George Bush is expected to get the same sort of ''lift'' from next week's Republican convention that Dukakis got from the Democratic convention three weeks ago.... According to a survey released by the American Council on Education, 43% of college students who graduated in 1984 were in debt for education expenses when they finished school; the average debt was $5,470 per student, $6,350 for private college students and $4,970 for public college students.... New Jersey's Education Dept. imposes a partial takeover of the Jersey City school system that will give the state control over the local district's financial and personnel operations.		The House of Representatives approves, 366-40, the U.S.-Canada free trade agreement, and the Senate Finance Committee endorses the pact unanimously, readying it for consideration by the full chamber.... The Federal Reserve Board raises the discount rate, the interest rate on loans it charges to financial institutions, to 6.5% from 6%. The increase, the first since September 1987, leaves the discount rate at its highest level since July 1986.... The Senate passes a bill to bar dumping of sewage sludge into the ocean by January 1992. The measure will also make dumping of medical waste into the ocean a federal crime.			**Aug. 9**
Pres. Reagan signs into law a bill offering the nation's apology and reparations to Japanese-Americans interned during World War II. The final version of the measure was adopted by the Senate July 27, by voice vote, and by the House August 4, by a vote of 257-156.	The Senate votes, 49-47, to approve a Democratic plan to provide the Nicaraguan Contras with $27 mil. in nonlethal aid. The vote comes after a Republican proposal for military and nonlethal aid was rejected, as expected.	The House passes, 307-98, a bill authorizing purchase of land near the Manassas National Battlefield Park in Virginia to prevent development of a shopping mall on the site. The 542-acre site is the place where Confederate Gen. Robert E. Lee established headquarters during the Second Battle of Manassas (known also as the Second Battle of Bull Run) in 1862. The bill is sent to the Senate.... The Environmental Protection Agency proposes regulations to limit the levels of hazardous lead in drinking water. The major proposal is to have suppliers control the acidity of their water in order to reduce tainting by lead from corrosion in pipes and solder in plumbing, the major source of lead in drinking water.	The space shuttle *Discovery*'s three big engines are successfully test fired on a launch pad at Cape Canaveral, Fla.	*Clean and Sober*, a movie about a yuppie businessman (played by Michael Keaton) who checks into a detox center to avoid prosecution for embezzlement, is released in New York. The film, which also stars Kathy Baker, is directed by Glenn Gordon Caron and written by Tod Carroll.	**Aug. 10**
	The Senate passes, 90-4, a $282.6 bil. spending bill for the Pentagon for the fiscal year beginning October 1. The Senate attached provisions to the bill to tighten regulation of defense consultants and to get U.S. allies to bear a larger share of allied defense costs. The bill is sent to conference with the House.... The House of Representatives approves a sweeping new set of economic sanctions against South Africa to pressure it to end its apartheid policy of racial separation. The bill will ban almost all trade between the two countries and require all American corporations and citizens to end their investments in South Africa. However, there is Senate resistance to the bill, which Pres. Reagan has vowed to veto.	The United States's leading banks raise their prime lending rate to 10% from 9.5%. The increase, the third in 1988 thus far, brings the prime to its highest level since June 1985.... Following swift congressional reconciliation and approval, Pres. Reagan signs a compromise $3.9 bil. drought relief bill to aid farmers and ranchers afflicted by the nation's worst drought since the dust bowl years of the 1930s. ... Mortgage rates surge to their highest point thus far in 1988 in response to the surprise decision of the Federal Reserve Board to raise the discount rate by half a point. The rate on 30-year fixed-rate loans purchased by the Federal Home Loan Mortgage Corp. climbs to 10.82%, up from 10.50% the previous day. Adjustable-rate mortgages linked to short-term indexes climb to 10.62% following the rate hike, compared with 10.35% at the beginning of August.	A study published in the *New England Journal of Medicine* finds that coronary bypass surgery improves the chances for survival of heart disease in high risk patients; but the difference in survival rates diminishes after five years.		**Aug. 11**

F	G	H	I	J
Includes elections, federal-state relations, civil rights and liberties, crime, the judiciary, education, health care, poverty, urban affairs and population.	Includes formation and debate of U.S. foreign and defense policies, veterans' affairs and defense spending. (Relations with specific foreign countries are usually found under the region concerned.)	Includes business, labor, agriculture, taxation, transportation, consumer affairs, monetary and fiscal policy, natural resources, and pollution.	Includes worldwide scientific, medical and technological developments, natural phenomena, U.S. weather, natural disasters, and accidents.	Includes the arts, religion, scholarship, communications media, sports, entertainments, fashions, fads and social life.

	World Affairs	Europe	Africa & the Middle East	The Americas	Asia & the Pacific
Aug. 12		The European Community's guaranteed farm price levels average 150% above prevailing prices on world markets in July, according to figures from Britain's ministry of agriculture.			Sein Lwin, Burma's president and ruling party leader, steps down after less than three weeks in power. His resignation culminates a week of widespread unrest in the country during which at least 95 people were killed. Sein Lwin succeeded Burmese leader Ne Win after the latter abruptly resigned July 23 as head of the Burma Socialist Program Party, the country's sole political organization. . . . India's P.M. Rajiv Gandhi signs a peace accord with leaders of a tribal movement in Tripura state, which borders eastern Bangladesh. The accord is aimed at ending an anti-government insurgency that has claimed 2,000 lives since 1980.
Aug. 13					Andreas Kohlschutter, a spokesman for the UN's Afghan relief effort, is quoted in a report in the New York Times as saying that the UN has undertaken "the largest mine-clearing operation the world has ever faced." He reports that 25,000 people have been killed by mines in the war in Afghanistan, and that another 30 to 50 casualties are reported each week. Soviet and Afghan military forces deployed millions of mines throughout Afghanistan during years of war.
Aug. 14		The commander of the Soviet military forces in Afghanistan announces that half of the Soviet contingent of more than 100,000 troops have been withdrawn from the country in accordance with the terms of the four-party peace accords signed in Geneva in April. . . . In Poland, police and pro-Solidarity demonstrators clash in the Baltic port city of Gdansk. The demonstrators are marking the eighth anniversary of the protests that led to the creation of the banned Solidarity union.			
Aug. 15		A Belgian budget for 1989 of 1,963 bil. Belgian francs with receipts targeted at 1,564 bil. francs is unveiled; the budget reflects the government's aim of reducing the budget deficit to 7% of gross national product.	Thirteen Canadian military observers arrive in Baghdad as part of a UN force to monitor a truce in the Iran-Iraq war. Canada is to provide a total of 15 observers, 370 military communications personnel and 110 support-staff members to the 24-nation UN truce force.	In Paraguay, Pres. Alfredo Stroessner is sworn in for an eighth term in office.	
Aug. 16					

A	B	C	D	E
Includes developments that affect more than one world region, international organizations and important meetings of major world leaders.	Includes all domestic and regional developments in Europe, including the Soviet Union, Turkey, Cyprus and Malta.	Includes all domestic and regional developments in Africa and the Middle East, including Iraq and Iran and excluding Cyprus, Turkey and Afghanistan.	Includes all domestic and regional developments in Latin America, the Caribbean and Canada.	Includes all domestic and regional developments in Asia and Pacific nations, extending from Afghanistan through all the Pacific Islands, except Hawaii.

U.S. Politics & Social Issues	U.S. Foreign Policy & Defense	U.S. Economy & Environment	Science, Technology & Nature	Culture, Leisure & Life Style	
Richard Lewis Thornburgh, 56, is sworn in as the nation's 76th attorney general, replacing Edwin Meese III. Meese announced in July his intention to resign.		The government's producer price index rose 0.5% in July, the Labor Dept. reports.		The movie *Last Temptation of Christ*, based on the novel by Nikos Kazantzakis, opens to street protests in seven U.S. cities and in Montreal and Toronto. The film version of the life of Jesus is the subject of an international controversy, from July through September, that combines the issues of artistic freedom, the sanctity of religious beliefs, and anti-Semitism.	Aug. 12
			A study in the British journal the *Lancet* shows that heart attack victims given a combination of aspirin and the clot-dissolving drug streptokinase within four hours of a heart attack are more than twice as likely to survive as are those who receive routine hospital care.	In soccer, the U.S. national team routs Jamaica, 5-1, in St. Louis to advance to a final qualifying tournament for the 1990 World Cup.	Aug. 13
Congress sends to the White House August 11 a so-called "dire emergency" supplemental spending measure providing an additional $672 mil. for fiscal 1988 programs; Pres. Reagan signs the bill this day.				Jeff Sluman wins the Professional Golfers Assoc. Championship tournament at the Oak Tree Golf Club in Edmond, Okla.	Aug. 14
The four-day Republican National Convention opens in New Orleans. Pres. Reagan is given center stage on opening night for a sentimental farewell to the party he has led for eight years.		Increasing fears of inflation, the Federal Reserve Board reports that its industrial production index rose 0.8% in July.			Aug. 15
Vice Pres. George Bush announces his selection of Sen. James Danforth Quayle III (R, Ind.) as his vice presidential running mate.... The keynote address at the Republican National Convention is given by New Jersey Gov. Tom Kean.... The Republican National Convention approves the party's platform for the 1988 election without audible dissent. The document, prepared by the conservative-dominated platform committee, incorporates Bush's recent proposal for a child-care tax credit, pledges not to increase taxes and to cut capital gains taxes, and contains less harsh criticism of the Soviet Union than recent party platforms have.		The U.S. deficit on merchandise trade widened 28.5% to a seasonally adjusted $12.54 bil. in June, the Commerce Dept. reports.... The Federal Reserve Board reports that U.S. industry operated at 83.5% of capacity in July, its highest operating rate in eight years. U.S. factories, mines and utilities are now operating closer to full capacity than they have since March 1980, when industry operated at 83.7% of capacity.			Aug. 16

F	G	H	I	J
Includes elections, federal-state relations, civil rights and liberties, crime, the judiciary, education, health care, poverty, urban affairs and population.	Includes formation and debate of U.S. foreign and defense policies, veterans' affairs and defense spending. (Relations with specific foreign countries are usually found under the region concerned.)	Includes business, labor, agriculture, taxation, transportation, consumer affairs, monetary and fiscal policy, natural resources, and pollution.	Includes worldwide scientific, medical and technological developments, natural phenomena, U.S. weather, natural disasters, and accidents.	Includes the arts, religion, scholarship, communications media, sports, entertainments, fashions, fads and social life.

	World Affairs	Europe	Africa & the Middle East	The Americas	Asia & the Pacific
Aug. 17			The banned African National Congress (ANC) accepts responsibility for a series of bombings in which scores of South African civilians have been killed and wounded. ANC officials say they have taken steps to end such attacks.		Pakistan's Pres. Muhammad Zia ul-Haq and U.S. Ambassador Arnold L. Raphel are killed when their plane explodes in midair and crashes in eastern Pakistan shortly after takeoff. Twenty-eight other people, including several senior Pakistani Army officers and the chief American military attache to Pakistan, also die in the crash. There are no survivors.... Queen Elizabeth II announces in London that Australia's Foreign Min. Bill Hayden will serve as the country's next governor general. The governor general serves as the deputy to the British monarch, who is technically Australia's head of state. The post is largely ceremonial.... In Singapore, the government dissolves parliament and announces that new elections will be held on September 3, about 16 months before the end of the current parliamentary term. In a related development, the government July 16 frees Francis T. Seow, a former solicitor general who was detained for alleged subversive activities, reportedly to allow him to run in the upcoming elections.
Aug. 18		In Britain, joblessness fell in July for the 24th consecutive month, by a seasonally adjusted 58,500 to 2.3 million, the government reports. The figure, the lowest in seven years, represents 8.2% of the work force.	South Africa's Pres. Pieter W. Botha today hints that an understanding might be reached whereby African National Congress leader Nelson Mandela will not have to return to prison. The 70-year-old black nationalist leader was hospitalized April 12 in Cape Town, suffering from tuberculosis. Mandela has been in jail for a quarter-century on charges of conspiring to overthrow South Africa's white minority government. But he has spurned Botha's offers to free him if he renounces violence.	Amnesty International accuses the Peruvian army of killing hundreds of people and torturing or abducting thousands of others since 1983 and says that killings and disappearances have increased significantly in the past two years.	The Politburo of China's Communist Party approves a five-year plan aimed at reforming the country's system of wages and prices, the official New China News Agency reports.
Aug. 19		The British government reports that inflation was 4.8% for the 12 months ending July, the highest level for two-and-a-half years. Recent increases in mortgage rates are expected to push inflation even higher in coming months.			Burma's ruling party appoints Attorney Gen. Maung Maung the nation's new leader. He replaces Sein Lwin, a former army general who resigned August 12 after only 17 days in office. Sein Lwin's resignation was spurred by a week of widespread and bloody student-led protests that left the country virtually paralyzed.... Talks between North and South Korea begin; they are the first between the two Koreas since a previous dialogue was suspended by the North in January 1986. A new round of negotiations is scheduled for mid-October.

A	B	C	D	E
Includes developments that affect more than one world region, international organizations and important meetings of major world leaders.	Includes all domestic and regional developments in Europe, including the Soviet Union, Turkey, Cyprus and Malta.	Includes all domestic and regional developments in Africa and the Middle East, including Iraq and Iran and excluding Cyprus, Turkey and Afghanistan.	Includes all domestic and regional developments in Latin America, the Caribbean and Canada.	Includes all domestic and regional developments in Asia and Pacific nations, extending from Afghanistan through all the Pacific Islands, except Hawaii.

U.S. Politics & Social Issues	U.S. Foreign Policy & Defense	U.S. Economy & Environment	Science, Technology & Nature	Culture, Leisure & Life Style	
Vice Pres. George Bush introduces his selection for vice president, Sen. Dan Quayle (R, Ind.), at a joint news conference saying Quayle has shown "strong appeal to young people and to women voters in his state." However, questions about Quayle's military service in the Indiana National Guard and about whether he used family connections to avoid the draft at the height of the Vietnam War crop up immediately.... A bill authorizing more funds for the outgoing and incoming presidents in the transition between administrations is approved by the House and Senate earlier and signed this day by Pres. Reagan. The next president and vice president will receive $3.5 mil. for transition expenses, up from the $2 mil. currently supplied. The outgoing leaders will get $1.5 mil., instead of $1 mil.	The White House is reported to have ordered the State Dept. and Central Intelligence Agency not to cooperate with a congressional investigation into illegal activities by Panama's military leader, Gen. Manuel Antonio Noriega.	Federal Judge Joyce Hens Green blocks a joint operating agreement between Detroit's two main newspapers, the *Detroit Free Press* and the *Detroit News.* In temporarily blocking the agreement, which was approved August 8 by outgoing Attorney Gen. Edwin Meese III, Green rules that Meese might have acted in a manner that was "arbitrary, capricious and...contrary to the law." A hearing on the papers' bid for antitrust exemption is set for September.... The Food and Drug Admin. gives final approval for Upjohn Co. to market its antibaldness drug minoxidil as a prescription treatment. The drug will be sold under the trade name Rogaine.... Housing starts increase 2.4% in July, the Commerce Dept. reports, to an adjusted annual rate of 1.489 million.	U.S. and Soviet scientists conduct the first joint nuclear test by the superpowers. Some 43 Soviet scientists are present when the United States detonates a 150-kiloton nuclear device (the equivalent of 150,000 tons of TNT) 2,000 feet (600 m) underground at the Nevada Test Site.		Aug. 17
Vice Pres. George Bush accepts the Republican nomination for president, pledging to "keep America moving forward, always forward." Earlier in the evening, Bush's chosen running mate, Sen. Dan Quayle (R, Ind.), is nominated by acclamation.				Sir Frederick Ashton, 83, one of the greatest classical choreographers of the 20th century and a director of Britain's Royal Ballet from 1963 to 1970, dies in his sleep in Sussex, England. Inspired to become a dancer as a boy after seeing Anna Pavlova dance, he helped develop a distinctively British balletic style marked by elegance, lyricism, and grace. His best-known works include *Enigma Variations, Symphonic Variations, La Fille Mal Gardee, Cinderella, Romeo and Juliet, Daphnis and Chloe* and *The Dream.*	Aug. 18
Pres. Reagan signs a bill providing $59.4 bil. in fiscal 1989 for the Dept. of Housing and Urban Development, the National Aeronautics and Space Admin., the Environmental Protection Agency, the Veterans Admin., and various other agencies.... Pres. Reagan signs a bill reauthorizing programs providing temporary care for disabled children who are at risk of abuse. Disabled children often are at risk of abuse because of the unrelenting demand for constant care. It was passed by the House July 26 and Senate August 9.... Pres. Reagan signs a bill to provide devices and services for the handicapped to aid them at home and on the job. The measure was approved by the Senate August 2 and by the House August 8.... A federal appeals court panel upholds a district judge's 1987 ruling ordering an increase in local property taxes to help pay for extensive improvements designed to erase racial discrimination in the Kansas City, Mo., school system.	The Pentagon releases the results of a Navy investigation into the July 3 downing of Iran Air Flight 655 by the USS *Vincennes.* The report finds that human error caused the crew to mistake the passenger plane for a hostile F-14 fighter.	Pres. Reagan signs into law an energy and water development bill designating $17.8 bil. in spending for energy-research projects, dams, harbors and irrigation canals.	Dutch scientists announce that an epidemic that killed 9,000 seals in the North and Baltic Seas—about 70% of the local population—was caused by the canine distemper virus or a close relative.		Aug. 19

F	G	H	I	J
Includes elections, federal-state relations, civil rights and liberties, crime, the judiciary, education, health care, poverty, urban affairs and population.	*includes formation and debate of U.S. foreign and defense policies, veterans' affairs and defense spending. (Relations with specific foreign countries are usually found under the region concerned.)*	*Includes business, labor, agriculture, taxation, transportation, consumer affairs, monetary and fiscal policy, natural resources, and pollution.*	*Includes worldwide scientific, medical and technological developments, natural phenomena, U.S. weather, natural disasters, and accidents.*	*Includes the arts, religion, scholarship, communications media, sports, entertainments, fashions, fads and social life.*

	World Affairs	Europe	Africa & the Middle East	The Americas	Asia & the Pacific
Aug. 20		Eight British soldiers are killed and 28 injured when the bus they are riding in is rocked by a bomb blast near Omagh, County Tyrone, in Northern Ireland. The attack, claimed by the outlawed Provisional Irish Republican Army, brings the number of Ulster-related British military fatalities in 1988 to 26, more than the previous five years combined and the most since 1979.	Iran and Iraq officially begin a UN-brokered cease-fire, ending at least temporarily the nearly eight-year-old Persian Gulf war.		French officials and the leaders of contending ethnic groups on the South Pacific colony of New Caledonia reach a revised agreement designed to prevent a renewal of unrest there. The same parties reached a pact in June, but negotiators for the indigenous Melanesian (Kanak) population were not able to win support for the draft plan from a convention of the Kanak Socialist Nationalist Liberation Front (FLNKS) separatist group.... Lazarus Salii, president of the western Pacific island republic of Palau, is found shot to death at his home in the capital city of Koror. Vice Pres. Thomas Remengesau is sworn in as acting president.
Aug. 21		Thousands of anti-Soviet demonstrators in Prague mark the 20th anniversary of the Soviet-led invasion of Czechoslovakia. Warsaw Pact troops entered Czechoslovakia August 20-21, 1968, to overthrow the "Prague Spring" reformist regime of Communist Party leader Alexander Dubcek, who was formally removed from power in 1969.			
Aug. 22		A new law in England and Wales allows pubs to stay open between 3:00 and 5:30 p.m., and to remain open an extra hour on Sundays, until 3:00 p.m. The changes reverse a 1915 law instituted to discourage drinking by factory workers in World War I.	The government of the central African nation of Burundi says that at least 5,000 people have been killed in ethnic violence that began August 14 between the ruling minority Tutsi tribe and the majority Hutu tribe. Witnesses from among the 35,000 refugees who have fled to neighboring Rwanda report that Burundian army troops massacred thousands of defenseless Hutu civilians.		
Aug. 23		West Germany reports a merchandise trade surplus for June of $7.45 bil. The surplus is a one-month record.			In Australia, Federal Treasurer Paul Keating presents parliament with the government's budget package for fiscal 1988-89, which began June 30. The package forecasts a record surplus of $4.4 bil., a reduction in the current account deficit to $7.6 bil., and stabilization of external debt at a level equal to about 30.5% of the gross domestic product.
Aug. 24		The president of Cyprus and the leader of the breakaway Turkish community on the Mediterranean island conclude two days of talks in Geneva. The two men, Pres. George Vassiliou, who governs the island's Greek Cypriots, and Rauf Denktash, leader of the Turkish Republic of Northern Cyprus, characterize their talks as productive and promise to resume negotiations for a comprehensive peace beginning in September.			

A	B	C	D	E
Includes developments that affect more than one world region, international organizations and important meetings of major world leaders.	*Includes all domestic and regional developments in Europe, including the Soviet Union, Turkey, Cyprus and Malta.*	*Includes all domestic and regional developments in Africa and the Middle East, including Iraq and Iran and excluding Cyprus, Turkey and Afghanistan.*	*Includes all domestic and regional developments in Latin America, the Caribbean and Canada.*	*Includes all domestic and regional developments in Asia and Pacific nations, extending from Afghanistan through all the Pacific Islands, except Hawaii.*

U.S. Politics & Social Issues	U.S. Foreign Policy & Defense	U.S. Economy & Environment	Science, Technology & Nature	Culture, Leisure & Life Style	
A federal jury in New York City finds that three of the Hunt brothers of Dallas conspired with a group of other investors to corner the world silver market in 1979 and 1980. Nelson Bunker Hunt, William Herbert Hunt, Lamar Hunt and the other defendants are ordered to pay over $130 mil. in damages to Minpeco S.A., a commodities company owned by the Peruvian government. In its civil lawsuit, Minpeco claims that it incurred losses of $151 mil. during the period in which the Hunts manipulated the market.					**Aug. 20**
United Farm Workers Pres. Cesar Chavez ends a 36-day fast at a mass in Delano, Calif., attended by thousands of supporters backing his boycott of California table grapes. He began the fast July 17 to protest use of pesticides on table grapes and to dramatize the union's boycott launched in 1984.			A major earthquake rocks the Himalayas along the India-Nepal border, killing at least 650 people and injuring thousands. The quake, the region's strongest since 1934, measures 6.7 on the Richter scale of ground motion.		**Aug. 21**
Vice Pres. George Bush, the Republican presidential nominee, overtakes Democratic nominee Gov. Michael S. Dukakis for the first time in a CBS News poll. Bush surged to a 46% to 40% lead over Dukakis.			Morton Thiokol Inc., maker of the booster rocket blamed for the 1986 *Challenger* explosion, reaches a tentative settlement of a wrongful-death suit brought against it by the widow of *Challenger* pilot, Navy Capt. Michael J. Smith. Families of the other six *Challenger* victims settled earlier.		**Aug. 22**
		Easing fears of inflation, the government's consumer price index rose 0.4% in July, the Labor Dept. reports, at a 5.2% compound annual rate.... Pres. Reagan signs into law a revised version of comprehensive trade legislation aimed at opening foreign markets and expanding U.S. trade.	The World Health Org. estimates that 5 million to 10 million people are infected with the acquired immune deficiency syndrome (AIDS) virus worldwide, and that there are 200,000 to 250,000 active cases of the disease. The agency has received 108,176 reports of confirmed AIDS cases as of July 30.		**Aug. 23**
The American Federation of Labor-Congress of Industrial Organizations gives its endorsement to the Democratic presidential nominee, Massachusetts Gov. Michael S. Dukakis.		The Environmental Protection Agency proposes minimum standards for municipal trash dumps. The rules are designed to prevent toxic leakage from the nation's 6,000 municipal landfills. Monitoring procedures for possible leakage into groundwater supplies are to be established, and controls over odor, fires, and rodents required.		The 32nd general council of the United Church of Canada votes in favor of a resolution allowing practicing homosexuals to be ordained as ministers. The United Church, with about 900,000 members, is Canada's largest Protestant denomination.	**Aug. 24**

F	G	H	I	J
Includes elections, federal-state relations, civil rights and liberties, crime, the judiciary, education, health care, poverty, urban affairs and population.	*Includes formation and debate of U.S. foreign and defense policies, veterans' affairs and defense spending. (Relations with specific foreign countries are usually found under the region concerned.)*	*Includes business, labor, agriculture, taxation, transportation, consumer affairs, monetary and fiscal policy, natural resources, and pollution.*	*Includes worldwide scientific, medical and technological developments, natural phenomena, U.S. weather, natural disasters, and accidents.*	*Includes the arts, religion, scholarship, communications media, sports, entertainments, fashions, fads and social life.*

	World Affairs	Europe	Africa & the Middle East	The Americas	Asia & the Pacific
Aug. 25		West German officials report the arrest of a former U.S. Army sergeant and seven other persons in Western Europe on suspicion of operating a major espionage ring passing secret North Atlantic Treaty Org. military documents to Soviet-bloc agents. Existence of the spy ring is first reported by the *New York Times*. . . . Britain's economy continued to grow in July but at the expense of a record trade deficit and higher inflation. In an attempt to rein in the economy, Chancellor of the Exchequer Nigel Lawson engineers the eighth increase in bank lending rates this summer. . . . In Portugal, a fire destroys Lisbon's historic Chiado district, killing one person and leaving 300 people without homes. The fire, which began at about 3:45 a.m. on the third floor of a department store, causes an estimated $260 mil. in damage and destroys more than 40 businesses in the 17th- and 18th-century quarter.			Japan's Premier Noboru Takeshita announces that Japan will provide China with a loan package worth about $6 bil., to be paid out between 1990 and 1995.
Aug. 26		In a major reversal of government policy, Poland's Interior Min. Gen. Czeslaw Kiszczak announces publicly that the government seeks the involvement of the Solidarity union in resolving a two-week-old strike. Tens of thousands of Polish workers have stayed off their jobs since August 15 in a renewal of the labor unrest that paralyzed the nation in April and May. The government has used force to break some of the strikes but is also relying on mediation by the Roman Catholic Church to restore a semblance of peace.	One day after UN-mediated peace talks between Iran and Iraq open in Geneva, Iraq insists that it be ceded full control of the disputed Shatt al-Arab waterway between the two countries. The demand is considered a major obstacle to achieving a permanent end to the Persian Gulf War.		Delegates from North and South Korea adjourn their talks in the truce village of Panmunjom after failing to reach agreement on a number of key issues.
Aug. 27				Canada's P.M. Brian Mulroney defers any action by his Progressive Conservative Party on the abortion issue and says he will introduce no abortion legislation until Canada's Supreme Court decides a case on the rights of the fetus.	Philippine Vice Pres. Salvador H. Laurel announces the formation of a new opposition coalition to challenge Pres. Corazon Aquino. The Union for National Action, comprising six right-wing factions, is the first significant opposition group since Aquino was swept to power in February 1986.
Aug. 28	Chinese and Soviet officials meet in Beijing for a series of talks on the Cambodian conflict. No concrete agreements are announced at the conclusion of the five-day talks, but both sides hailed the conference as a positive development.	Hungary's Premier Karoly Grosz meets with Romania's Pres. Nicolae Ceausescu in an attempt to reach agreement on the issues dividing their countries. Hungary has accused Romania of persecuting its ethnic-Hungarian population.			

A	B	C	D	E
Includes developments that affect more than one world region, international organizations and important meetings of major world leaders.	Includes all domestic and regional developments in Europe, including the Soviet Union, Turkey, Cyprus and Malta.	Includes all domestic and regional developments in Africa and the Middle East, including Iraq and Iran and excluding Cyprus, Turkey and Afghanistan.	Includes all domestic and regional developments in Latin America, the Caribbean and Canada.	Includes all domestic and regional developments in Asia and Pacific nations, extending from Afghanistan through all the Pacific Islands, except Hawaii.

U.S. Politics & Social Issues	U.S. Foreign Policy & Defense	U.S. Economy & Environment	Science, Technology & Nature	Culture, Leisure & Life Style	
The number of medical school applications and enrollments declined in the 1987-88 academic year, the American Medical Assoc. reports. U.S. medical schools received 28,123 applications in 1987-88, down about 10% from the 31,323 received in 1986-87, the association's report says.... An administrative law judge in Trenton, N.J., rules that the state's system of funding public education is unconstitutional because it discriminates against low-income urban school districts.	Former White House staffer Barbara Honegger says the 1980 Reagan-Bush campaign made a secret "October surprise" deal with Iran under which U.S. hostages in Teheran were held until after the election to ensure Pres. Jimmy Carter's defeat, in return for which the Reagan administration approved arms deliveries to Iran, via Israel, beginning in January 1981.		A group of 23 leading American science and engineering societies release a letter urging the presidential candidates to strengthen the role of the White House science adviser in the next administration.		Aug. 25
Twenty men accused by the government of constituting the entire membership of the Lucchese organized crime family in New Jersey are acquitted by a federal jury in Newark of 77 counts against them. The verdicts, reached after just 14 hours of deliberations, end a trial that lasted 21 months.		Consumer spending increased 0.5% and personal income 0.6% in July, the Commerce Dept. reports.		*Publishers Weekly*'s hardback fiction best-sellers for the week are: *The Cardinal of the Kremlin*, Tom Clancy; *Till We Meet Again*, Judith Krantz; *Alaska*, James Michener; *To Be the Best*, Barbara Taylor Bradford; and *Doctors*, Erich Segal.... *The Thin Blue Line*, a docudrama based on the true story of a controversial murder conviction, opens in New York. The movie is directed and written by Errol Morris and stars the principals in the case and Adam Goldfine and Derek Horton.	Aug. 26
				The Tai Chung team from Taiwan defeats Pearl City, Hawaii, 10-0, to win the 42nd Little League World Series, in Williamsport, Pa. Tai Chung's victory in the tournament is the fifth straight by a team from the Far East.... *Billboard*'s best-selling albums for the week are: *Tracy Chapman*, Tracy Chapman; *Hysteria*, Def Leppard; *Roll with It*, Steve Winwood; *Appetite for Destruction*, Guns N' Roses; and *He's the D.J., I'm the Rapper*, D.J. Jazzy Jeff & the Fresh Prince.	Aug. 27
				Ayrton Senna of Brazil wins his fourth consecutive Formula One auto race, the Belgian Grand Prix in Spa-Francorchamps.... Rosie Jones wins the Ladies Professional Golf Assoc. World Championship in Buford, Ga.... The 40th annual Emmy Awards, the first in which cable networks are allowed to compete, are presented. "Thirtysomething" wins for outstanding drama series; "The Wonder Years," best comedy series; "The Murder of Mary Phagan," best miniseries; "Inherit the Wind," best comedy or drama special; Michael J. Fox ("Family Ties") and Bea Arthur ("The Golden Girls"), for best actor and actress, respectively, in a comedy series; Richard Kiley ("A Year in the Life") and Tyne Daly ("Cagney & Lacey"), best actor and actress, respectively, in a drama series; and Jason Robards ("Inherit the Wind") and Jessica Tandy ("Foxfire") for best actor and actress, respectively, in the limited series or special category.	Aug. 28

F	G	H	I	J
Includes elections, federal-state relations, civil rights and liberties, crime, the judiciary, education, health care, poverty, urban affairs and population.	*Includes formation and debate of U.S. foreign and defense policies, veterans' affairs and defense spending. (Relations with specific foreign countries are usually found under the region concerned.)*	*Includes business, labor, agriculture, taxation, transportation, consumer affairs, monetary and fiscal policy, natural resources, and pollution.*	*Includes worldwide scientific, medical and technological developments, natural phenomena, U.S. weather, natural disasters, and accidents.*	*Includes the arts, religion, scholarship, communications media, sports, entertainments, fashions, fads and social life.*

	World Affairs	Europe	Africa & the Middle East	The Americas	Asia & the Pacific
Aug. 29					
Aug. 30			Morocco and the Polisario Front tentatively agree to accept a joint UN-Org. of African Unity plan to end the 13-year-old war over the Western Sahara. The plan calls for a UN-supervised cease-fire followed by a referendum on the disputed territory's future independence or integration into Morocco.	Chile's ruling military junta nominates Pres. Augusto Pinochet Ugarte, who has ruled the country for 15 years, as sole candidate in a presidential plebiscite scheduled for October 5, setting the stage for the country's 7.3 million registered voters to choose whether to return Pinochet Ugarte to office for another eight years.	The United States for the first time formally accuses the Soviet Union of violating the Geneva accords on Afghanistan by sending bombers from Soviet territory to strike Afghan rebel positions near the northern city of Kunduz.
Aug. 31		Lech Walesa, founder of Poland's outlawed Solidarity trade union, meets with Interior Min. Gen. Czeslaw Kiszczak to discuss the nation's continuing labor unrest. After the talks, thought to be the first direct contact between Solidarity and the government since 1982, Walesa issues a statement urging an end to the nationwide strikes that began August 15.		Canada's House of Commons votes to approve implementation of the free-trade accord with the United States. The legislation now goes to the Senate, where the opposition Liberal Party has vowed to block it until a general election is called.	The Japanese construction ministry reports that housing starts declined in July from the same month in 1987, the first such drop in 27 months.
Sept. 1			A UN team that spent about two weeks visiting prisoner of war camps in Iran and Iraq issues its report. The team finds that Iran has used a form of "spiritual guidance" and "indoctrination" that is "indistinguishable from mental pressure" to turn about 20% of its estimated 70,000 Iraqi prisoners into militants loyal to Ayatollah Khomeini and hostile to Iraq's Pres. Saddam Hussein. Among the 35,000 Iranian prisoners in Iraq, the team finds "no proof of systematic indoctrination" but some evidence of "psychological pressure."		
Sept. 2	The UN Conf. on Trade and Development urges commercial banks to write off 30% of the debt owed them by the world's 15 most heavily indebted nations in order to release needed foreign exchange and break the vicious circle of overindebtedness and stagnation.		The white South African government withdraws a package of legislation aimed at strengthening the Group Areas Act segregation laws after the "colored" (mixed-race) and Indian houses of the tricameral parliament blocked consideration of the five bills by boycotting all debate.... Iran accuses Iraq of violating the August 20 cease-fire more than 60 times, and Iraq claims that Iran committed 74 violations. None of the supposed violations are apparently very serious.		
Sept. 3		Poland's nationwide strikes end as about the last 200 striking coal miners at the Manifest Lipcowy (July Manifesto) coal complex in Silesia leave the facility after lengthy meetings with dissident labor leader Lech Walesa.		In Canada, the federal budget deficit for the 1987-88 fiscal year stands at $22.69 bil., according to a Finance Dept. report. The report states that the fiscal 1987-88 deficit was 5.1% of the gross domestic product, a decline of 3.5 percentage points from fiscal 1984-85.	The People's Action Party of Singapore's P.M. Lee Kuan Yew wins a resounding victory in general elections for parliament. The ruling party wins 80 of the 81 seats in the legislature.... Australian voters reject by a 2-1 margin four proposed amendments to the country's constitution concerning the length of parliamentary terms, the size of constituencies, the status of local government, and certain constitutional rights and freedoms.

A	B	C	D	E
Includes developments that affect more than one world region, international organizations and important meetings of major world leaders.	*Includes all domestic and regional developments in Europe, including the Soviet Union, Turkey, Cyprus and Malta.*	*Includes all domestic and regional developments in Africa and the Middle East, including Iraq and Iran and excluding Cyprus, Turkey and Afghanistan.*	*Includes all domestic and regional developments in Latin America, the Caribbean and Canada.*	*Includes all domestic and regional developments in Asia and Pacific nations, extending from Afghanistan through all the Pacific Islands, except Hawaii.*

U.S. Politics & Social Issues	U.S. Foreign Policy & Defense	U.S. Economy & Environment	Science, Technology & Nature	Culture, Leisure & Life Style	
	The Justice Dept. announces an end to the Reagan administration's effort to shut down the UN observer mission of the Palestine Liberation Org. in New York City.	A California condor chick, the product of the first captive mating by the nearly extinct species, is hatched in an incubator at the San Diego Wild Animal Park. The hatching brings to 28 the number of California condors known to be extant.			Aug. 29
Democratic presidential nominee Gov. Michael S. Dukakis unveils what is billed as a new, aggressive style, launching a broadside at Vice Pres. George Bush that is loaded with references to the Iran-Contra affair and the state of the economy.		The government's index of leading economic indicators plunged 0.8% in July, the Commerce Dept. reports.... Prices received by farmers for raw agricultural products climbed 2.1% in August, the Agriculture Dept. reports.... District Court Judge Barrington D. Parker sanctions Eastern Airlines' plan to drop 12% of its flights but says the carrier cannot eliminate the 4,000 jobs affected without negotiating the issue with its unions.			Aug. 30
Cordis Corp., a Miami, Fla., manufacturer, pleads guilty to federal charges that from 1980 to 1985 it sold pacemakers with defective batteries and filed false quality-assurance reports with the Food and Drug Admin.	At the close of a review of the 1972 antiballistic missile treaty, the United States announces that it will not conclude any arms-control treaties with the Soviet Union unless Moscow agrees to dismantle its phased-array radar complex near Krasnoyarsk, in Siberia....	Continuing the acceleration of its merger program, the Federal Home Loan Bank Board announces it has provided $1.9 bil. in financial assistance for the reorganization of 14 insolvent Oklahoma thrifts into six larger regional institutions.... Real family income rose 1% in 1987 to a record high while the poverty rate remained nearly flat at 13.5%, the Census Bureau reports. Inflation-adjusted median family income grew for the fifth straight year to $30,850, surpassing the record $30,820 set in 1973.		Variety's top-grossing films for the week are: A Nightmare on Elm Street 4: The Dream Master, Betrayed, Die Hard, A Fish Called Wanda, and Married to the Mob.	Aug. 31
		The Federal Communications Comm. announces unanimous approval of initial technical guidelines for high-definition television (HDTV) that will gradually bring the new technology to the market by the early 1990s.	Luis W. Alvarez, 77, winner of the 1968 Nobel Prize in physics for his use of bubble chambers to detect new subatomic particles, dies of cancer in Berkeley, Calif. A member of the team that developed the atomic bomb, he recently supported his son Walter's theory that asteroid impacts eliminated the dinosaurs and thousands of other species 65 million years ago.		Sept. 1
Gov. Michael S. Dukakis tries to revitalize his flagging presidential campaign by rehiring former campaign manager John Sasso, who resigned after publicizing the fact that Dukakis rival Sen. Joseph R. Biden Jr. (D, Del.) plagiarized a speech by British Labour Party leader Neil Kinnock.				A world rock tour to benefit the human rights organization Amnesty International opens at London's Wembley Stadium. The featured performers include Bruce Springsteen, Sting, Peter Gabriel, Tracy Chapman, and Senegalese singer Youssou N'Dour. The tour is scheduled to visit at least 13 countries before winding up in mid-October.	Sept. 2
					Sept. 3

F	G	H	I	J
Includes elections, federal-state relations, civil rights and liberties, crime, the judiciary, education, health care, poverty, urban affairs and population.	Includes formation and debate of U.S. foreign and defense policies, veterans' affairs and defense spending. (Relations with specific foreign countries are usually found under the region concerned.)	Includes business, labor, agriculture, taxation, transportation, consumer affairs, monetary and fiscal policy, natural resources, and pollution.	Includes worldwide scientific, medical and technological developments, natural phenomena, U.S. weather, natural disasters, and accidents.	Includes the arts, religion, scholarship, communications media, sports, entertainments, fashions, fads and social life.

	World Affairs	Europe	Africa & the Middle East	The Americas	Asia & the Pacific
Sept. 4		Lech Walesa, founder of the dissident Solidarity trade union, defends his role in ending Poland's latest round of labor unrest. He has been criticized for using his influence to get the strikers back to work in exchange for the government's promise to hold "round table" discussions with the opposition.		Bolivia's Planning Min. Gonzalo Sanchez de Lozada is nominated as the presidential candidate of the country's ruling National Revolutionary Movement (MNR) in general elections scheduled for May 1989. Sanchez is credited with cutting Bolivia's inflation rate from 24,000% in 1985 to around 10% in 1987.	
Sept. 5				Canada's P.M. Brian Mulroney signs historic agreements-in-principle to transfer government land to the Dene (Indians) and Metis (persons of mixed Indian and white ancestry) of the Northwest Territories, and give the territory more control over its energy resources.	
Sept. 6		West Germany's gross national product grew at an inflation-adjusted annual rate of 3.9% in the first half of 1988 and was up 3.4% in the second quarter from the year-earlier period, the government reports.		Peru's new Min. of Economy and Finance Abel Salinas unveils a package of austerity measures aimed at reducing inflation and bolstering reserves of hard currency. Among the new measures is the institution of a single exchange rate of 250 intis to the U.S. dollar.	
Sept. 7					
Sept. 8			The Iraqi Army has unleashed a major drive, including the widespread use of poison gas, against Kurdish rebels in northern Iraq, according to reports over the last two weeks. More than 100,000 refugees have fled across the border into Turkey as Iraq takes advantage of the cease-fire in the Persian Gulf war to try to crush the Kurdish guerrilla movement once and for all.		South Korea has improved its human rights record recently, but is still holding about 600 political prisoners, according to a report by Amnesty International, the London-based human rights organization. The report disputes the government's claim that nearly 1,300 political prisoners have been freed since 1987. Amnesty asserts that the actual number is about 400.

A	B	C	D	E
Includes developments that affect more than one world region, international organizations and important meetings of major world leaders.	Includes all domestic and regional developments in Europe, including the Soviet Union, Turkey, Cyprus and Malta.	Includes all domestic and regional developments in Africa and the Middle East, including Iraq and Iran and excluding Cyprus, Turkey and Afghanistan.	Includes all domestic and regional developments in Latin America, the Caribbean and Canada.	Includes all domestic and regional developments in Asia and Pacific nations, extending from Afghanistan through all the Pacific Islands, except Hawaii.

U.S. Politics & Social Issues	U.S. Foreign Policy & Defense	U.S. Economy & Environment	Science, Technology & Nature	Culture, Leisure & Life Style	
				The National Football League opens its season with the Washington Redskins seeking to become the first team to win consecutive Super Bowls since the Pittsburgh Steelers, who won Super Bowls XIII and XIV in 1979 and 1980.	Sept. 4
At a Labor Day rally in Detroit, Democratic presidential nominee Gov. Michael S. Dukakis reaches out to the middle class, saying that the Reagan administration serves the "privileged few" while the vast majority of middle-class Americans "are getting squeezed." Republican nominee, Vice Pres. George Bush, opens his campaign by appealing to Americans to "protect the gains we've made in jobs and peace" and not let Dukakis "take it away from you."		The nation's unemployment rate rose to 5.5% in August, the Labor Dept. reports. . . . The Federal Home Loan Bank Board (FHLBB) announces that the Robert M. Bass Group Inc. has agreed to acquire American Savings & Loan Assoc. of Stockton, Calif., the nation's largest insolvent thrift, with about $2 bil. in federal assistance. It is the most costly rescue of a single failed savings and loan and the fourth $1 bil.-plus rescue by the FHLBB in the past three weeks.			Sept. 5
The Drug Enforcement Admin.'s chief administrative law judge, Francis L. Young, recommends making marijuana available as a prescribed drug for the treatment of the nausea associated with chemotherapy. Young says the drug "is one of the safest therapeutically active substances known to man."			The National Weather Service concludes that the summer of 1988 was the hottest on record since 1936, *USA Today* reports. The weather service's report is based on a review of high temperatures for June, July, and August in 95 cities across the country. Above-average temperatures are recorded in 86 of the 95 cities. The heat was produced by a shift in the jet stream, the upper-atmosphere steering current, that also caused the United States to suffer its worst drought in 44 years. . . . Widespread flooding that began August 19 has left three-quarters of Bangladesh under water and more than 25 million people homeless. The government's official death toll is listed as 490, but newspaper reports put the total at 1,154; the total number of casualties will not be known for several weeks, as communications throughout Bangladesh have been severely disrupted.		Sept. 6
		Revealing the extent of its efforts to check the summer rise of the dollar, the Federal Reserve Bank of New York says it has sold $2.93 bil. of U.S. currency in foreign exchange markets from May to July. . . . The Securities and Exchange Comm. (SEC) charges Drexel Burnham Lambert Inc., Drexel's junk-bond department head, Michael R. Milken, and several others with insider trading, stock manipulation, and other securities violations. The charges are the most sweeping brought against a major Wall Street firm in the 54-year history of the SEC.	Soviet cosmonauts Col. Vladimir Lyakhov and Capt. Abdul Ahad Mohmand, the first Afghan cosmonaut, land safely in Kazakhstan after a tense, 25-hour drama in the Soyuz TM5 space capsule as they returned from a mission to the orbiting space station *Mir*.	Sheelah Ryan, a 63-year-old real estate broker, presents her winning ticket to claim a record $55.16 mil. prize in the Florida lottery, the largest jackpot to date in a state lottery.	Sept. 7
Gov. Michael S. Dukakis's campaign staffers agree to Vice Pres. George Bush's demands that there be only two presidential debates. Negotiations continue over the length of the debates and the number of moderators or panelists.	The United States destroys two Pershing II missile engines, the first American weapons components eliminated under the U.S.-Soviet treaty on intermediate-range nuclear forces (INF). The USSR began destroying its INF missiles in August.	Outstanding consumer debt rose $2.57 bil. in July, the Federal Reserve Board reports, at an annual rate of 4.8%, to a total of $645.6 bil.	An Ariane rocket launches two U.S. communications satellites from the European Space Agency site at Kourou, French Guiana.	Leading players in the America's Cup competition agree to a pact that will govern the race in future years. The pact is agreed to by the only three entities ever to have run the regattas: the New York Yacht Club, the Royal Perth Yacht Club of Australia, and the San Diego Yacht Club. These "trustees" are joined in the agreement by another dozen possible future participants. . . . A. Bartlett Giamatti, president of the National League, is named the next commissioner of Major League Baseball. Giamatti, a former Yale Univ. professor and president, will succeed Peter Ueberroth.	Sept. 8
F	**G**	**H**	**I**	**J**	
Includes elections, federal-state relations, civil rights and liberties, crime, the judiciary, education, health care, poverty, urban affairs and population.	*Includes formation and debate of U.S. foreign and defense policies, veterans' affairs and defense spending. (Relations with specific foreign countries are usually found under the region concerned.)*	*Includes business, labor, agriculture, taxation, transportation, consumer affairs, monetary and fiscal policy, natural resources, and pollution.*	*Includes worldwide scientific, medical and technological developments, natural phenomena, U.S. weather, natural disasters, and accidents.*	*Includes the arts, religion, scholarship, communications media, sports, entertainments, fashions, fads and social life.*	

	World Affairs	Europe	Africa & the Middle East	The Americas	Asia & the Pacific
Sept. 9					
Sept. 10				Mexico's Chamber of Deputies, sitting as the electoral college, certifies Carlos Salinas de Gortari as the nation's president-elect. Salinas was the candidate of the ruling Institutional Revolutionary Party in elections held July 6.	Burma's ruling party announces plans to hold multiparty general elections, ending 26 years of one-party rule in the country. The decision comes after more than a month of nationwide protests against the government and is considered a victory for the swelling ranks of the opposition.... The government of Sri Lanka announces that the northern and eastern provinces, home to most of the country's ethnic Tamil minority, will be merged into one.
Sept. 11		Britain and France voice qualms about the European Community's (EC) plan for harmonizing value-added tax (VAT) rates. VAT rates in the 12 EC nations currently range from 12% in Spain and Portugal to 25% in Ireland.		Weeks of violence in the capital of Haiti culminate in an attack by some 50 or more thugs armed with machetes, truncheons, knives, and guns on the congregation of St. Jean Bosco Church in Port-au-Prince. At least 13 people die and more than 70 are wounded. The Rev. Jean Bertrand Aristide, a vocal critic of the government who is saying mass at the time of the attack, escapes injury.	
Sept. 12		The Italian government appropriates $1.1 bil. for the clean-up of Venice lagoon. Changes in water levels in the city's canal are to be moderated with the use of 80 huge underwater dams, known by the Italian acronym Moses, to be installed over the next six years.	The last West German hostage in Lebanon, Rudolf Cordes, is freed in west Beirut after 20 months in captivity.	The French foreign ministry announces that talks with Canada over North American fishing rights have been suspended indefinitely and calls for international mediation because it is "impossible to reach an agreement through bilateral negotiations."	
Sept. 13	In a major policy reversal by Washington, the United States pledges to restore its share of UN funding, including payments that have been long withheld. The UN, which is facing financial collapse, relies on the United States for 25% of its total funding.... The governments of South Korea and Hungary announce that they will exchange permanent diplomatic missions. The move marks the first time South Korea has established official ties with a communist country.	Oscar Fernandez-Mell, Cuba's ambassador to Britain, and embassy official Carlos Medina Perez leave London for Prague, Czechoslovakia, after being ordered out of Britain. The expulsions stem from a shooting incident involving Western intelligence operatives and Medina Perez.... Finland's 1989 budget includes income tax reductions for individuals; the top marginal rate falls to 44%, and the basic rate to 37%. Tax reductions will be offset by tax hikes on businesses and benefits and a reduction on allowances.	The UN-mediated peace talks between Iran and Iraq on ending the Persian Gulf war end without progress but with a proposal that they resume the following week.		The Japanese government announces that it will lift diplomatic sanctions imposed on North Korea in January in retaliation for the bombing of a South Korean airliner. The sanctions are lifted four days before the start of the 1988 Summer Olympic Games in Seoul, South Korea.

A	B	C	D	E
Includes developments that affect more than one world region, international organizations and important meetings of major world leaders.	Includes all domestic and regional developments in Europe, including the Soviet Union, Turkey, Cyprus and Malta.	Includes all domestic and regional developments in Africa and the Middle East, including Iraq and Iran and excluding Cyprus, Turkey and Afghanistan.	Includes all domestic and regional developments in Latin America, the Caribbean and Canada.	Includes all domestic and regional developments in Asia and Pacific nations, extending from Afghanistan through all the Pacific Islands, except Hawaii.

U.S. Politics & Social Issues	U.S. Foreign Policy & Defense	U.S. Economy & Environment	Science, Technology & Nature	Culture, Leisure & Life Style	
Democratic presidential nominee, Massachusetts Gov. Michael S. Dukakis, hits back at his opponent, Vice Pres. George Bush, after weeks of attacks implicitly questioning Dukakis's patriotism.... A federal jury in St. Paul, Minn., finds G.D. Searle & Co. negligent in testing its Copper-7 birth control device and awards $8.75 mil. to a woman who says the device made her sterile.		The government's producer price index rose 0.6% in August, the Labor Dept. reports.... The Senate approves a bill to restrict imports of textiles, apparel, and shoes, but with less than the two-thirds majority needed to override a threatened presidential veto. The bill now goes to a House-Senate conference to be reconciled.	At least 30 separate forest fires, some of which began in June, are burning out of control in seven Western states and Alaska.	The 55-foot U.S. catamaran *Stars & Stripes* skippered by Dennis Conner wins the second of two races against the 90-foot monohull *New Zealand*, skippered by David Barnes, to retain the America's Cup for the United States. The competition, held off the coast of San Diego, is the 27th—and most contentious—challenge for the 137-year-old cup.	Sept. 9
On the brink of bankruptcy from court-ordered fines, the city of Yonkers, N.Y., consents to a housing desegregation plan and brings an end to a bitter and protracted battle with the Justice Dept. and the National Assoc. for the Advancement of Colored People.				Steffi Graf of West Germany wins the U.S. Open. That title, added to her earlier 1988 victories in the Australian and French Opens and at Wimbledon, makes her only the fifth player ever, and the first since 1970, to win tennis's Grand Slam. ... Miss Minnesota, Gretchen Elizabeth Carlson, 22, is crowned Miss America in Atlantic City, N.J.	Sept. 10
				Mats Wilander of Sweden wins the men's U.S. Open tennis title.... Gerhard Berger of Austria wins auto racing's Italian Grand Prix.	Sept. 11
The Office of Government Ethics takes former Attorney Gen. Edwin Meese III to task for using his position to benefit a friend and for disregarding a commitment to divest himself of stock that posed a potential conflict of interest.		The Agriculture Dept.'s drought damage estimate is a 31% plunge in 1988 grain production to 191 million metric tons.... The Environmental Protection Agency issues a national health advisory on radon, recommending testing of homesites for the presence of the cancer-causing gas. Radon, which is invisible and radioactive, is produced by the natural decay of uranium in soil.			Sept. 12
Pres. Reagan signs far-reaching housing legislation that will expand protection against housing discrimination and expedite review of complaints.		The deficit in the U.S. balance of payments on current account shrank 9.8% in the second quarter, the Commerce Dept. reports.... The Energy Dept. announces that it is indefinitely postponing opening a nuclear waste repository in New Mexico. The repository, the Waste Isolation Pilot Plant (WIPP) 26 miles east of Carlsbad, was scheduled to open in October.... A group of nine large personal-computer (PC) makers join forces to develop their own standard PC in a direct challenge to industry leader International Business Machines Corp. and its Personal Systems/2 line of computers.			Sept. 13

F	G	H	I	J
Includes elections, federal-state relations, civil rights and liberties, crime, the judiciary, education, health care, poverty, urban affairs and population.	*Includes formation and debate of U.S. foreign and defense policies, veterans' affairs and defense spending. (Relations with specific foreign countries are usually found under the region concerned.)*	*Includes business, labor, agriculture, taxation, transportation, consumer affairs, monetary and fiscal policy, natural resources, and pollution.*	*Includes worldwide scientific, medical and technological developments, natural phenomena, U.S. weather, natural disasters, and accidents.*	*Includes the arts, religion, scholarship, communications media, sports, entertainments, fashions, fads and social life.*

	World Affairs	Europe	Africa & the Middle East	The Americas	Asia & the Pacific
Sept. 14		U.S. and Soviet scientists conduct an underground nuclear test at the Soviet test range near Semipala-tinsk, in the republic of Kazakhstan. It is the second test in a two-test program of joint monitoring.			
Sept. 15		In Yugoslavia, the federal government gives special powers to the paramilitary police to deal with Kosovo province's ethnic unrest. . . . Economic data for August continues to paint a picture of a booming British economy but with rising inflation, and August unemployment figures showed joblessness declining for the 25th consecutive month.	Zimbabwe's Pres. Robert Mugabe is awarded the Hunger Project prize, which recognizes African leaders who work to end hunger. The director of the U.S.-based project says Mugabe has turned Zimbabwe into Africa's "agricultural success story."		A three-judge panel of the court of appeals in the Northern Territory, Australia, overturns the murder conviction of Lindy Chamberlain and says she and her husband Michael are innocent in the death of their baby daughter, whom authorities now believe to have been killed by a dingo, or wild dog.
Sept. 16		Organs of the official Soviet press reverse their previous stand by criticizing the Polish government and supporting compromise between Warsaw and Poland's opposition elements. . . . Gen. Sec. Mikhail S. Gorbachev expands his 1986 initiative on peace and security in the Asia-Pacific region. The Soviet leader says that the USSR will be willing to give up its naval base at Cam Ranh Bay in Vietnam if the United States abandons its military bases in the Philippines.	The Defense Dept. recommends that the Navy halt its full-time escort operation for reflagged Kuwaiti tankers and other U.S.-registered vessels in the Persian Gulf, Reagan administration officials report. Because there have been no significant shipping attacks in two months, the Pentagon is planning a new "zone defense" in which merchant vessels will always be fairly close to a U.S. warship but not travel in a convoy.		
Sept. 17				In Haiti, noncommissioned officers oust Pres. Henri Namphy. Lt. Gen. Prosper Avril, a former aide to Presidents Francois Duvalier and Jean-Claude Duvalier, is named president the next day.	

A	B	C	D	E
Includes developments that affect more than one world region, international organizations and important meetings of major world leaders.	Includes all domestic and regional developments in Europe, including the Soviet Union, Turkey, Cyprus and Malta.	Includes all domestic and regional developments in Africa and the Middle East, including Iraq and Iran and excluding Cyprus, Turkey and Afghanistan.	Includes all domestic and regional developments in Latin America, the Caribbean and Canada.	Includes all domestic and regional developments in Asia and Pacific nations, extending from Afghanistan through all the Pacific Islands, except Hawaii.

U.S. Politics & Social Issues	U.S. Foreign Policy & Defense	U.S. Economy & Environment	Science, Technology & Nature	Culture, Leisure & Life Style	
A CBS News/New York Times poll suggests that Vice Pres. George Bush has bested Democratic presidential nominee Gov. Michael S. Dukakis. Only 32% of respondents view Dukakis favorably, as against 25% who view him unfavorably. Although Dukakis stresses competence as an issue, respondents feel Bush is more competent by a margin of 51% to 34%.... A CBS News/New York Times poll shows that only one-third of the electorate feel that Bush running mate Sen. Dan Quayle (R, Ind.) is qualified to be president.... The Bush and Dukakis forces reach final agreement on the ground rules for their two debates, on September 25 and either October 13 or 14. The vice presidential candidates, Bentsen and Quayle, will debate October 5. ... William S. Sessions, director of the Federal Bureau of Investigation, announces that he disciplined six bureau supervisors for serious mistakes in conducting a domestic surveillance campaign targeted on opponents of the Reagan administration's policies in Central America. The group targeted was the Committee in Solidarity with the People of El Salvador, or CISPES.		The merchandise trade deficit shrank to a seasonally adjusted $9.53 bil. in July, its lowest level since December 1984, the Commerce Dept. reports.... The Federal Reserve Board reports that its industrial production index rose 0.2% in August.... The House unanimously approves legislation raising penalties for insider trading. The maximum penalty for insider trading rises to $2.5 mil. from $500,000 for firms and to $1 mil. from $100,000 for individuals; the maximum prison term is doubled to 10 years.... The United States calls for an end to the differential treatment in trade given to developing countries during most of the post-1945 period.			Sept. 14
	As the international furor over charges that Iraq used chemical weapons against Kurdish insurgents continues to mount, the Senate votes to impose punitive sanctions on Iraq. Iraq and Turkey say they will not cooperate with a proposed UN investigation.	The Senate confirms Nicholas F. Brady as treasury secretary. Brady, who is sworn in later in the day, replaces James A. Baker III, who resigned in August to head Vice Pres. George Bush's presidential campaign.... Ashland Oil Inc. is indicted by a federal grand jury in Pittsburgh on two criminal misdemeanor counts of violating environmental laws in the January oil spill that sent a massive oil slick down the Ohio River.		The International Olympic Committee votes to hold the 1994 Winter Olympic Games in the town of Lillehammer, Norway.	Sept. 15
			An advisory committee of the National Institutes of Health concludes that it is ethically acceptable to use human fetal tissue obtained from legal abortions for medical research and therapy.		Sept. 16
			Hurricane Gilbert, the biggest storm ever recorded in the Western Hemisphere, ends an eight-day, 2,500-mile sweep across the Caribbean and the Gulf of Mexico, during which it caused at least 260 deaths and billions of dollars in damage.	The XXIV Summer Olympic Games begin in Seoul, South Korea, with opening ceremonies in front of nearly 100,000 spectators at Olympic Stadium. A record number of more than 9,600 athletes from a record 160 countries are scheduled to participate in the games.	Sept. 17

F	G	H	I	J
Includes elections, federal-state relations, civil rights and liberties, crime, the judiciary, education, health care, poverty, urban affairs and population.	Includes formation and debate of U.S. foreign and defense policies, veterans' affairs and defense spending. (Relations with specific foreign countries are usually found under the region concerned.)	Includes business, labor, agriculture, taxation, transportation, consumer affairs, monetary and fiscal policy, natural resources, and pollution.	Includes worldwide scientific, medical and technological developments, natural phenomena, U.S. weather, natural disasters, and accidents.	Includes the arts, religion, scholarship, communications media, sports, entertainments, fashions, fads and social life.

	World Affairs	Europe	Africa & the Middle East	The Americas	Asia & the Pacific
Sept. 18		The Social Democratic Party of Sweden's Premier Ingvar Carlsson is returned to power in general elections. The environmentalist Green Party wins parliamentary representation for the first time, but not enough to hold the balance of power as polls had predicted.	In its first official casualty count, Iran says that it has lost 123,220 soldiers and 11,000 civilians in its eight-year war with Iraq. Another 60,711 troops are listed as missing in action, but many of them are believed to be prisoners in Iraq. The death toll is well below the estimates of Western analysts, who have put the number of Iranian dead at about 300,000.		The leader of Burma's armed forces seizes control of the government in a military coup. The move marks the nation's fourth change of government in less than two months. The coup, led by the minister of defense and armed forces chief of staff, Gen. Saw Maung, ousts civilian Pres. Maung Maung after only a month in office. . . . An article in the *Bulletin of the Atomic Scientists* claims that Japan used chemical weapons and poisons against the Chinese and other prisoners of war in World War II and that the U.S. government covered up evidence of Japan's chemical warfare capabilities after the war.
Sept. 19		Poland's Premier Zbigniew Messner and his entire 19-member cabinet resign amid widespread discontent over the state of the economy. Messner was in office for less than three years.	Iraq rules out resumption of the UN-mediated peace talks with Iran in New York City. The talks ended September 13 and were scheduled to resume in New York this week.	The Nicaraguan government and Contra representatives meeting in Guatemala City fail to reach agreement on the resumption of peace talks broken off in June. The Contras say they are willing to start full negotiations September 26.	Emperor Hirohito, Japan's reigning monarch since 1925, falls seriously ill after vomiting blood from an intestinal hemorrhage.
Sept. 20	The 43rd annual session of the UN Gen. Assembly opens at UN headquarters in New York City. Argentina's Foreign Min. Dante Caputo is elected in a secret ballot to the one-year post of Gen. Assembly president. He succeeds Peter Florin of East Germany.	Britain's P.M. Margaret Thatcher outlines her vision of a European Community that stresses "cooperation between independent sovereign states." The strong tone of her speech at the College of Europe in Bruges, Belgium, prompts criticism from Europeans who hold visions of a more unified Europe. . . . The Netherlands' 1989 budget will both reduce taxes and ease fiscal austerity. Value-added and corporate-income taxes will be pared and the fiscal deficit will narrow to 5.4% of gross national product.			
Sept. 21		A draft national economic plan for 1989 calls for the USSR to shift toward the manufacture of consumer goods and away from the traditional emphasis on heavy industries. The plan envisions 6.7% growth in consumer goods production, compared with 2.5% growth in other manufacturing.	Dissident Kenyan lawyer Gibson Kamau Kuria is awarded the Robert F. Kennedy Human Rights Award. An outspoken critic of abuses by the Kenyan government, Kuria was imprisoned in 1987 after he represented victims of police brutality. . . . A staff report by the Senate Foreign Relations Committee says there is "overwhelming evidence" of Iraqi poison gas attacks on Kurdish guerrillas and civilians.		

A	B	C	D	E
Includes developments that affect more than one world region, international organizations and important meetings of major world leaders.	*Includes all domestic and regional developments in Europe, including the Soviet Union, Turkey, Cyprus and Malta.*	*Includes all domestic and regional developments in Africa and the Middle East, including Iraq and Iran and excluding Cyprus, Turkey and Afghanistan.*	*Includes all domestic and regional developments in Latin America, the Caribbean and Canada.*	*Includes all domestic and regional developments in Asia and Pacific nations, extending from Afghanistan through all the Pacific Islands, except Hawaii.*

U.S. Politics & Social Issues	U.S. Foreign Policy & Defense	U.S. Economy & Environment	Science, Technology & Nature	Culture, Leisure & Life Style	
					Sept. 18
The College Entrance Examination Board releases the 1988 results of the Scholastic Aptitude Test (SAT) and the American College Test (ACT). The average SAT score nationally is 904, based on a scale of 400 to 1600. The average ACT score nationally is 18.8, based on a scale of 1 to 36. Scores on the SAT drop from 1987, while those on the ACT show a slight improvement.		The Senate votes to give final passage to the measure implementing the U.S. part of the U.S.-Canada trade accord. The House approved the legislation in August. Pres. Reagan is expected to sign the measure.	Israel becomes the eighth nation capable of launching a satellite when it hoists an experimental craft aloft to collect data on solar energy and the Earth's magnetic field. It is expected to remain in orbit about a month.	Pope John Paul II concludes his fourth trip to Africa, having visited the five independent black African states bordering South Africa: Zimbabwe, Botswana, Lesotho, Swaziland, and Mozambique.	**Sept. 19**
	House Speaker Jim Wright (D, Tex.) alleges that "clear testimony from CIA people" shows that the Central Intelligence Agency (CIA) backed activities by the Nicaraguan opposition in the hope of provoking the Nicaraguan government into taking repressive measures. . . . Richard Williams announces that he has formally presented his credentials as the first U.S. ambassador to the government of the Mongolian People's Republic. The two countries established official diplomatic relations in January 1987.	After-tax profits of U.S. corporations in the second quarter surged 8.9%, to an annual rate of $162.7 bil., the Commerce Dept. reports.			**Sept. 20**
By September 21, both presidential campaign organizations, those of Vice Pres. George Bush (R) and Gov. Michael S. Dukakis (D, Mass.), are limiting campaign appearances by the candidates to focus on briefings and rehearsals for their first televised debate on September 25. . . . The percentage of Americans holding high school diplomas and college degrees reached a record high in 1987, the Census Bureau reports. A total of 76.5% of all Americans 25-years-old and over graduated high school and 19.9% completed at least four years of college as of March 1987. The respective figures for 1986 had been 74.7% and 19.4%. . . . The College Board announces that students received a record total of more than $24.5 bil. in financial aid from federal, state, and local sources as well as from academic institutions during the 1987-88 school year.		The government's consumer price index rose 0.4% in August, the Labor Dept. reports, at a 5.2% compound annual rate. . . . Consumer spending increased 0.5% and personal income 0.2% in August, the Commerce Dept. reports. . . . Housing starts dropped 3.3% in August, the Commerce Dept. reports, to an adjusted annual rate of 1.436 million units.	A Swedish study finds no increase in the number of birth defects or miscarriages stemming from the 1986 nuclear disaster at Chernobyl in the Soviet Union. The study covers over 250,000 births.	*Variety*'s top-grossing films for the week are: *Crossing Delancey, A Fish Called Wanda, Die Hard, Moon over Parador,* and *Betrayed.*	**Sept. 21**

F	G	H	I	J
Includes elections, federal-state relations, civil rights and liberties, crime, the judiciary, education, health care, poverty, urban affairs and population.	Includes formation and debate of U.S. foreign and defense policies, veterans' affairs and defense spending. (Relations with specific foreign countries are usually found under the region concerned.)	Includes business, labor, agriculture, taxation, transportation, consumer affairs, monetary and fiscal policy, natural resources, and pollution.	Includes worldwide scientific, medical and technological developments, natural phenomena, U.S. weather, natural disasters, and accidents.	Includes the arts, religion, scholarship, communications media, sports, entertainments, fashions, fads and social life.

	World Affairs	Europe	Africa & the Middle East	The Americas	Asia & the Pacific
Sept. 22			Just minutes before his six-year term expires at midnight, Lebanon's Pres. Amin Gemayel appoints an interim military government headed by a Christian general to rule Lebanon after parliament once again fails to convene to elect a successor.... Meeting with South Africa's Pres. Pieter Botha, UN Sec. Gen. Javier Perez de Cuellar promises the UN will be impartial in working for Namibia's transition to independence. Botha agrees to allow a UN technical team into Namibia to plan the deployment of UN civilian and military peacekeeping forces.	Haiti's new president, Lt. Gen. Prosper Avril, is reported to be gaining control over unrest in the military after five days in which noncommissioned officers at military barracks throughout the country ousted their superiors.... The Canadian government announces that it will pay about $238 mil. in compensation for the internment of Japanese-Canadians in World War II. Some 21,000 Japanese-Canadians were interned and their businesses, farms, and personal property confiscated by the government.	In Hong Kong, liberal candidates suffer a major setback in indirect elections for Hong Kong's Legislative Council, the territory's lawmaking body, as moderate and conservative candidates win a majority of the 13 contested seats.
Sept. 23					
Sept. 24	Finance ministers and central bankers of the Group of Seven nations—the United States, Japan, West Germany, France, Italy, Great Britain, Canada—reaffirm their commitment to exchange-rate stability.		In west Beirut, Moslem members of the old "national unity" cabinet, led by acting Premier Selim al-Hoss, refuse to recognize the regime appointed by Christian leader Amin Gemayel and instead insist that they still hold power. The move follows the failure of a U.S.-Syrian effort to find a presidential candidate acceptable to both sides, raising fears that a formal partition will replace the nation's de facto sectarian divisions and plunge the country into renewed, large-scale communal violence after a three-year lull.		Three of Burma's most prominent opposition figures announce the formation of the broad-based League for Democracy, a coalition of the country's various antigovernment factions, including students, workers, and Buddhist monks.
Sept. 25		Britain's Social and Liberal Democratic Party—the consolidated successor to the former Liberal Party and Social Democratic Party—holds its inaugural fall conference. The parties joined forces as the Alliance in the last two general elections.		Bypassing the International Monetary Fund, the World Bank announces it has agreed to a four-part, $1.25 bil. loan to Argentina in return for structural economic reforms.	

A	B	C	D	E
Includes developments that affect more than one world region, international organizations and important meetings of major world leaders.	Includes all domestic and regional developments in Europe, including the Soviet Union, Turkey, Cyprus and Malta.	Includes all domestic and regional developments in Africa and the Middle East, including Iraq and Iran and excluding Cyprus, Turkey and Afghanistan.	Includes all domestic and regional developments in Latin America, the Caribbean and Canada.	Includes all domestic and regional developments in Asia and Pacific nations, extending from Afghanistan through all the Pacific Islands, except Hawaii.

U.S. Politics & Social Issues	U.S. Foreign Policy & Defense	U.S. Economy & Environment	Science, Technology & Nature	Culture, Leisure & Life Style	
The scientific skills of U.S. elementary and secondary school students remain "distressingly low" despite recent efforts by educators to boost standards, according to a study by the National Assessment of Educational Progress.		The House passes a $2.1 bil. anti-drug bill that calls for expansion of drug education and treatment programs and interdiction of incoming shipments and local law enforcement provisions, many of which liberals consider unconstitutional. . . . The Federal Home Loan Bank Board says that the nation's savings and loan associations lost $7.5 bil. in the first half of 1988.			Sept. 22
The House adopts an acquired immune deficiency syndrome (AIDS) policy bill that is sent to conference with the Senate, which earlier approved its own AIDS policy bill. The House bill calls for AIDS testing; the Senate bill focuses primarily on research and education. . . . Former Reagan aide Michael K. Deaver is given a three-year suspended sentence for his conviction on charges of lying under oath about his lobbying activities after leaving the White House.	Soviet Foreign Min. Eduard A. Shevardnadze concludes a three-day trip to Washington for talks on arms control with Sec. of State George P. Shultz. The central subject is the strategic arms limitation talks (START) negotiations in Geneva. The talks are moving forward, but at a pace that makes it unlikely that a treaty will be reached before a new U.S. president takes office.	Pres. Reagan signs legislation to provide a 4.1% pay increase for most federal civilian workers. The bill does not apply to members of Congress, federal judges, cabinet secretaries, or the president. It is the largest federal pay raise since 1981, when a 4.8% figure was approved. . . . The House clears legislation to test and promote use of alternative fuels—especially methanol (wood alcohol), ethanol (grain alcohol), and natural gas—in automobiles, buses, and trucks. The bill passed the Senate September 20.		The film *Dead Ringers*, a horror fantasy about a pair of twin gynecologists and the woman who breaks the bond between them, sending them on a descent into drug addiction and violence, is released in New York. Directed by David Cronenberg, the film stars Jeremy Irons and Genevieve Bujold. . . . *Gorillas in the Mist*, a film about Dian Fossey (Sigourney Weaver), a naturalist who spent 18 years studying gorillas in Africa before her mysterious murder in 1985, is released in New York. Directed by Michael Apted, the film also stars Bryan Brown and Julie Harris.	Sept. 23
				Billboard's best-selling albums for the week are: *Appetite for Destruction*, Guns N' Roses; *Hysteria*, Def Leppard; *Tracy Chapman*, Tracy Chapman; *He's the D.J., I'm the Rapper*, D.J. Jazzy Jeff & the Fresh Prince; and *Roll with It*, Steve Winwood. . . . The Rev. Barbara C. Harris, 58, is elected a bishop of the Episcopal Church, becoming the first woman to be elected a bishop in the history of the 70-million-member Anglican communion, of which Episcopalians are a part.	Sept. 24
The 1988 presidential nominees, Vice Pres. George Bush (R) and Massachusetts Gov. Michael S. Dukakis (D), meet head-to-head for the first time in a televised debate. The event covers a wide range of issues ranging from the candidates' records to abortion, taxes, and the Iran-Contra scandal. It produces sharp attacks and sometimes acrimonious exchanges but no real surprises.				French climber Marc Batard sets a record when he scales Mt. Everest, the world's highest mountain at 29,028 feet, in 22 hours, 30 minutes from his base camp at 17,400 feet. . . . William Alton (Billy) Carter III, 51, younger brother of former Pres. Jimmy Carter, who achieved celebrity and notoriety following his brother's election in 1976, dies in Plains, Ga. of pancreatic cancer. A gas station owner and peanut farmer, with the family business in a blind trust during his brother's presidency, he found himself without an occupation. Following two trips to Libya as the guest of Muammer el-Qaddafi, the revelation that he received a $220,000 loan from the Libyan regime (for which he became a registered agent) led to a Senate investigation. Its report, issued one month before the 1980 presidential election, charged Pres. Carter with negligence in not disassociating himself from Billy's activities.	Sept. 25

F	G	H	I	J
Includes elections, federal-state relations, civil rights and liberties, crime, the judiciary, education, health care, poverty, urban affairs and population.	*Includes formation and debate of U.S. foreign and defense policies, veterans' affairs and defense spending. (Relations with specific foreign countries are usually found under the region concerned.)*	*Includes business, labor, agriculture, taxation, transportation, consumer affairs, monetary and fiscal policy, natural resources, and pollution.*	*Includes worldwide scientific, medical and technological developments, natural phenomena, U.S. weather, natural disasters, and accidents.*	*Includes the arts, religion, scholarship, communications media, sports, entertainments, fashions, fads and social life.*

	World Affairs	Europe	Africa & the Middle East	The Americas	Asia & the Pacific
Sept. 26	Pres. Reagan gives a farewell address to the Gen. Assembly. In his seventh speech to the UN, the president praises the world body for its peacekeeping operations in the Persian Gulf and Afghanistan, and he hails UN Sec. Gen. Javier Perez de Cuellar for his "persistence, patience and unyielding will" in working for peace in the troubled regions.	Turkey's Premier Turgut Ozal says he will not resign despite a setback in yesterday's national referendum on when to hold municipal elections, now scheduled for March 1989. Ozal wanted them moved up to November 1988.			
Sept. 27	Soviet Foreign Min. Eduard A. Shevardnadze addresses the UN Gen. Assembly. Shevardnadze touches on three disparate issues, Afghanistan, a controversial Soviet radar facility, and the environment, all of which he links to the matter of world peace.... The International Monetary Fund and the World Bank hold their annual, joint two-day meeting in West Berlin. The two institutions reaffirm U.S.-supported policies in both international monetary policy and developing-country debt.	Poland's Sejm confirms Mieczyslaw Rakowski as the nation's new premier. The Central Committee of the United Workers' (Communist) Party chose Rakowski for the post yesterday. He succeeds Zbigniew Messner, who resigned with his entire cabinet September 19.... Britain's balance of payments deficit shrank in August from record levels in July, according to government figures.			
Sept. 28		The signing of a new agreement governing U.S. bases in Spain is immediately criticized by opposition Spanish politicians who say that Spain's ban against nuclear weapons on its territory might be violated by the agreement.	Kuwait dispatches a three-man team of diplomats to reopen its embassy in Teheran, in what is seen as an effort by Kuwait to achieve balance in its relations with its two giant neighbors, Iran and Iraq.		
Sept. 29	The Norwegian Nobel Committee awards the 1988 Nobel Prize for peace to the UN peacekeeping forces. At the time of the award, some 10,000 UN peacekeeping troops and observers are on duty in seven regions around the world.	An Austrian budget for 1989 is presented that seeks to cut the budget deficit to 4% of gross domestic product, a reduction of one-half a percentage point, partly by selling state-owned industries. Spending is targeted at $40 bil.	An international panel in Geneva rules for Egypt and against Israel in a long-running territorial dispute over the Sinai beach resort of Taba, claimed by both sides but occupied by Israel since the 1967 war.		

A	B	C	D	E
Includes developments that affect more than one world region, international organizations and important meetings of major world leaders.	Includes all domestic and regional developments in Europe, including the Soviet Union, Turkey, Cyprus and Malta.	Includes all domestic and regional developments in Africa and the Middle East, including Iraq and Iran and excluding Cyprus, Turkey and Afghanistan.	Includes all domestic and regional developments in Latin America, the Caribbean and Canada.	Includes all domestic and regional developments in Asia and Pacific nations, extending from Afghanistan through all the Pacific Islands, except Hawaii.

U.S. Politics & Social Issues	U.S. Foreign Policy & Defense	U.S. Economy & Environment	Science, Technology & Nature	Culture, Leisure & Life Style	
		The Environmental Protection Agency calls for a worldwide halt in the use of chlorofluorocarbons (CFCs) to prevent further deterioration of the protective ozone layer in the stratosphere. . . . Congress clears a bill to revise and renew for five years the 1973 Endangered Species Act prohibiting possession or commerce in endangered or threatened species or in products made from such wildlife. . . . Ending a bitter dispute with the United Auto Workers union and Wisconsin officials, Chrysler Corp. agrees to pay over $250 mil. to avert a legal battle over the company's January decision to close its Kenosha, Wis., assembly plant.			Sept. 26
Congress clears the fiscal 1989 appropriations bill for the commerce, justice and state departments, the federal judiciary, and some 20 related agencies.	The House votes, 388-16, to bar the export of arms and sensitive technology to Iraq to punish it for using chemical weapons.	The Commerce Dept. warns that debt-burdened developing nations such as Mexico and Brazil face obstacles to restored creditworthiness if the United States reduces its trade deficit by import reduction and protectionist trade policies. . . . Pres. Reagan signs a bill appropriating $9.9 bil. for fiscal 1989 operation of the Interior Dept. and related agencies. The measure was approved by both houses of Congress September 8. The total value of U.S. mergers reaches a record $129.4 bil. in the first half of 1988. The previous record was set in the first half of 1985, when companies spent $100 bil. on deals.			Sept. 27
A federal jury in Los Angeles finds three Mexicans guilty in the 1985 torture and murder of Enrique Camarena Salazar, a Drug Enforcement Admin. agent, and Alfredo Zavala Avelar, his pilot, in Guadalajara, Mexico. The trial ends with the conviction of the three men over three days, September 22, 26, and 28. . . . A federally funded study by the Harvard School of Public Health recommends that Medicare payments to doctors be restructured; under the proposed changes, family doctors would receive more money and specialists would receive less.		Pres. Reagan vetoes a bill that will restrict imports of textiles, apparel, and shoes. . . . Pres. Reagan signs into law the bill implementing the U.S. end of the U.S.-Canada trade accord. . . . A $10.8 bil. fiscal 1989 spending bill for the Transportation Dept. and related agencies clears Congress. . . . The Senate clears a bill to accelerate the safety evaluation of pesticides by the Environmental Protection Agency. The House passed the bill September 20.			Sept. 28
In an out-of-court settlement, the DeSoto County (Fla.) School District agrees to pay $1.1 mil. to the family of Clifford and Louise Ray, whose three sons are infected with the acquired immune deficiency syndrome virus. The Rays accused school officials in Arcadia, Fla., of abuse of power, depriving their sons of their rights, and helping to create an atmosphere of hatred against the boys.	The House votes to authorize the United States to contribute $420 mil. to the World Bank over six years. The authorization is incorporated into a fiscal 1989 foreign aid appropriations bill. . . . Pres. Reagan signs a $299.5 bil. defense authorization for fiscal 1989. The measure, which includes the Energy Dept.'s nuclear weapons programs, replaces the authorization vetoed by Reagan in August.	Prices received by farmers for raw agricultural product rose 0.7% in September, the Agriculture Dept. reports. The drought-related increase kept farm prices at their highest level since July 1984. Prices rose a revised 2.1% in August and 3.6% in July.	The space shuttle *Discovery* blasts off from Cape Canaveral, Fla., carrying five astronauts and successfully achieves orbit for the beginning of a four-day mission. It is the first shuttle launch since Jan. 28, 1986, when the shuttle *Challenger* exploded 73 seconds after lift-off in a disaster in which all seven astronauts were killed.	Charles Addams, 76, cartoonist whose black humor graced the pages of the *New Yorker* magazine for half a century, dies in New York City of a heart attack. His 1946 cartoon showing the residents of a ghoulish-looking Victorian house preparing to greet Christmas carolers by dousing them with what appeared to be boiling oil inspired the television series "The Addams Family."	Sept. 29

F	G	H	I	J
Includes elections, federal-state relations, civil rights and liberties, crime, the judiciary, education, health care, poverty, urban affairs and population.	*Includes formation and debate of U.S. foreign and defense policies, veterans' affairs and defense spending. (Relations with specific foreign countries are usually found under the region concerned.)*	*Includes business, labor, agriculture, taxation, transportation, consumer affairs, monetary and fiscal policy, natural resources, and pollution.*	*Includes worldwide scientific, medical and technological developments, natural phenomena, U.S. weather, natural disasters, and accidents.*	*Includes the arts, religion, scholarship, communications media, sports, entertainments, fashions, fads and social life.*

	World Affairs	Europe	Africa & the Middle East	The Americas	Asia & the Pacific
Sept. 30		The Soviet Communist Party Central Committee approves a sweeping shake-up at the highest levels of the Kremlin. The reorganization further consolidates the power of Gen. Sec. Mikhail S. Gorbachev. The purge is designed to bolster *perestroika*, Gorbachev's program of economic, social, and political reform, by replacing older or obstructionist officials with reform-minded allies of Gorbachev.			In an attempt to rein in the country's overheated economy, China's Communist Party leadership calls for new anti-inflationary measures and postpones the lifting of state price controls in an abrupt slowing of the economic reform program adopted in the late 1970s. . . . Burmese Army troops rout two guerrilla groups in the Moon Yang region, about 20 miles from the Chinese border, after two weeks of intense fighting during which more than 200 guerrillas and 47 soldiers have been killed.
Oct. 1		Continuing the sweeping shake-up in the party leadership begun at the behest of Communist Party Gen. Sec. Mikhail S. Gorbachev, the Supreme Soviet confirms Gorbachev as president of the Soviet Union.	Lebanese kidnappers calling themselves the Islamic Jihad for the Liberation of Palestine say they will release one captive as a gesture to gain U.S. support for the Palestinian uprising in Israeli-occupied territory.	Canada's P.M. Brian Mulroney makes his long-expected decision to call a federal election. The balloting is to be held on November 21.	
Oct. 2		At the annual conference of Britain's Labour Party, party leader Neil Kinnock overwhelmingly wins reelection to his post, but he suffers several setbacks in his attempts to move the party toward the political center. . . . At the close of a two-day organizing congress, the Popular Front of Estonia, the first independent nationalist/political organization recognized by the Kremlin, demands that Moscow give Estonia more autonomy over its economy and culture.			In Pakistan, at least 225 people have been killed in three days of ethnic violence between native Sindhis and Mohajir Moslem immigrants, which began when Sindhis began attacks in Moslem neighborhoods in Hyderabad.
Oct. 3		Franz Josef Strauss, 73, premier of the West German state of Bavaria and a leading politician of post-1945 West Germany, dies in Regensburg, Bavaria, of heart failure. He cofounded the conservative Christian Social Union, which he led for the last 25 years. Defense minister from 1956 to 1962, he was the architect of West German rearmament until forced to resign in 1962. He later served as finance minister from 1966 to 1969 under the "grand coalition" of the left and right.	Lebanese kidnappers calling themselves the Islamic Jihad for the Liberation of Palestine release Mithileshwar Singh, an Indian educator who has been held hostage in Beirut along with three Americans for more than 20 months. . . . Libya and Chad resume diplomatic relations and say they will seek a peaceful settlement of their territorial dispute over the Aouzou strip. The joint communique brings a formal end to the long desert war between the two nations.		A majority of state workers—between 80% and 95%—in Rangoon, Burma, return to work after two months of strikes in support of democratic reforms.
Oct. 4	Amnesty International charges 135 nations with rights violations in 1987. The figure represents more than 80% of the 159 countries belonging to the UN and is the largest recorded since the group issued its first annual survey in 1961.			Eight Canadians who filed suit over 1950s brainwashing experiments funded by the Central Intelligence Agency reach a tentative out-of-court settlement with the agency.	

A	B	C	D	E
Includes developments that affect more than one world region, international organizations and important meetings of major world leaders.	*Includes all domestic and regional developments in Europe, including the Soviet Union, Turkey, Cyprus and Malta.*	*Includes all domestic and regional developments in Africa and the Middle East, including Iraq and Iran and excluding Cyprus, Turkey and Afghanistan.*	*Includes all domestic and regional developments in Latin America, the Caribbean and Canada.*	*Includes all domestic and regional developments in Asia and Pacific nations, extending from Afghanistan through all the Pacific Islands, except Hawaii.*

U.S. Politics & Social Issues	U.S. Foreign Policy & Defense	U.S. Economy & Environment	Science, Technology & Nature	Culture, Leisure & Life Style	
Congress passes a major revision of the nation's welfare system, the first overhaul in 53 years. In one provision, the measure will require states to establish education and training programs in order to receive federal funds for welfare. . . . District Judge Lucius D. Bunton of Midland, Tex., finds the Federal Bureau of Investigation guilty of discrimination against Hispanic agents in promotions and working conditions and of retaliating against an Hispanic agent for filing a discrimination complaint.		The government's index of leading economic indicators rose 0.4% in August, the Commerce Dept. reports. . . . Chronic failures at the Savannah River Plant in South Carolina that supplied fuel for the nation's nuclear weapons are publicized for the first time at a joint hearing of the Senate Governmental Affairs Committee and the House Government Operations subcommittee on environment, energy, and natural resources. The plant's last active reactor was shut down in August. . . . The U.S. auto industry ends its 1988 model year with sales of all vehicles above 15.4 million for the fourth year in a row. Consumers continue to trade cars for minivans and sport utility vehicles. Vehicles built in the United States by foreign-based companies continue to expand market share, while sales of imported cars continue to drop due to the weakened U.S. dollar. . . . Pres. Reagan signs the Dept. of Transportation and Related Agencies Appropriations Act of 1989.		*Publishers Weekly's* hardback fiction best-sellers for the week are: *The Cardinal of the Kremlin*, Tom Clancy; *Till We Meet Again*, Judith Krantz; *Spock's World*, Diane Duane; *Alaska*, James Michener; and *Demon Lord of Karanda*, David Eddings. . . . In a statement upholding the dignity of women and defining their role in the Roman Catholic Church and society, Pope John Paul II refers to the traditional dominance exercised by men over women as an "evil inheritance" and says overcoming the tradition is "the task of every human being, whether woman or man."	Sept. 30
	Pres. Reagan signs a $14.3 bil. foreign aid bill cleared yesterday by Congress. The bill is the last of the regular fiscal 1989 appropriations bills to be processed, and final action is taken at 11:59 p.m., just before the start of the new fiscal year.		Nobel laureate James Watson becomes the part-time head of the National Institutes of Health's newly created Office for Human Genome Research, the goal of which is to map the complete sequence of genes in the human genetic makeup.		Oct. 1
				Baseball's New York Mets win the National League's Eastern Division and will play the Los Angeles Dodgers, champions of the West. The American League Championship Series will match the Boston Red Sox, the Eastern Division champs, against the Western champion Oakland Athletics. . . . The XXIV Summer Olympic Games in Seoul, South Korea, conclude. The games were attended by athletes from a record 160 nations. Top medal winners are the Soviet Union, with 132 (55 gold); East Germany, 102 (37 gold); and the United States, 94 (36 gold). . . . Italian horse Tony Bin, with John Reid aboard, wins the 67th running of the Prix de l'Arc de Triomphe in Paris.	Oct. 2
		Saying that stricter standards cost U.S. jobs and aid foreign manufacturers, Transportation Sec. James Burnley lowers gasoline mileage requirements for 1989 model passenger cars to 26.5 miles per gallon from the congressionally set standard of 27.5 mpg.	The space shuttle *Discovery's* four-day mission is hailed as "an absolute, stunning success" by Rear Adm. Richard H. Truly, head of the shuttle program for the National Aeronautics and Space Admin.		Oct. 3
The House extends the Civil Rights Act of 1964 to give basic protection against discrimination based on race, color, national origin, religion, sex, handicap, or age to the 12,137 people who work on the House payroll.		For the second time, the House fails to override Pres. Reagan's veto of legislation restricting textile, apparel, and shoe imports. . . . Reinvigoration of the 1970 Clean Air Act is abandoned by its chief sponsor, Sen. George Mitchell (D, Maine), who says "the reality is that there will be no action on clean-air legislation this year."			Oct. 4

F	G	H	I	J
Includes elections, federal-state relations, civil rights and liberties, crime, the judiciary, education, health care, poverty, urban affairs and population.	Includes formation and debate of U.S. foreign and defense policies, veterans' affairs and defense spending. (Relations with specific foreign countries are usually found under the region concerned.)	Includes business, labor, agriculture, taxation, transportation, consumer affairs, monetary and fiscal policy, natural resources, and pollution.	Includes worldwide scientific, medical and technological developments, natural phenomena, U.S. weather, natural disasters, and accidents.	Includes the arts, religion, scholarship, communications media, sports, entertainments, fashions, fads and social life.

	World Affairs	Europe	Africa & the Middle East	The Americas	Asia & the Pacific
Oct. 5		According to Royal Ulster Constabulary (RUC) records, 2,699 people have died, including 254 members of the RUC and 410 members of the British Army, in the 20 years since the latest round of violence began in Northern Ireland.		In a plebiscite, Chileans vote against a new eight-year term for Pres. Augusto Pinochet Ugarte, paving the way for new elections and a new president by 1990. Pinochet will remain commander in chief of the armed forces for four years.... Brazil's National Congress puts into effect a new constitution that guarantees basic civil and labor rights and provides for the country's first popular presidential election in nearly 30 years.	Pakistan's supreme court rules that the late Pres. Muhammad Zia ul-Haq's dissolution of the National Assembly and the cabinet at the end of May was unconstitutional, but says the caretaker administration appointed by Zia should remain in power until general elections scheduled for November 16.
Oct. 6		In Yugoslavia, the politburo of the ruling League of Communists in the self-governing Vojvodina province resigns following a proposal by Slobodan Milosevic, the Serbian party leader, that Vojvodina be annexed by Serbia.	The government of Algeria's Pres. Chadli Benjedid declares a state of siege two days after mass rioting by disenchanted youths breaks out in Algiers. The unrest quickly spread to the nation's other cities.		
Oct. 7				In Canada, the national unemployment rate declined to 7.8% in September from 8% in August, according to Statistics Canada. The 7.8% figure is 0.1 percentage point above the six-year low of 7.7% recorded in April.	The Indian government imposes a ban on *Satanic Verses*, a new novel by best-selling author Salman Rushdie, claiming that certain passages offend the country's Moslem leaders.
Oct. 8		Otto Lambsdorff is elected the new leader of West Germany's centrist Free Democratic Party, the junior partner in the coalition government of Christian Democratic Chancellor Helmut Kohl. Four years ago Lambsdorff resigned as economics minister in a political scandal.		Canadian corporate profits rose to $3.11 bil. in the second quarter of 1988, according to a *Wall Street Journal* survey of 214 companies.	
Oct. 9		Pres. Raif Dizdarevic warns Yugoslavia that continued nationalist and economic unrest could lead to the imposition of a state of emergency. Rising Serbian nationalism, coupled with widespread discontent over the troubled economy, has plunged Yugoslavia into its most difficult period since World War II.	Negotiators from Angola, Cuba, South Africa, and the United States conclude three days of "informal consultations" mediated by Asst. Sec. of State Chester A. Crocker. The meeting ends with a compromise under which all 50,000 Cuban troops in Angola will leave within a 24- to 30-month period.		
Oct. 10	Addressing the UN Gen. Assembly, Bangladesh's Foreign Min. Humayun Rashid Chowdhury calls for an international effort to control his country's annual flood problem. His plea is aimed especially at India, Nepal, China, and Bhutan.	In a sign of the worsening internal security situation, Yugoslavia's Pres. Raif Dizdarevic cancels all army leaves.... During a two-day meeting of the Central Committee plenum, Czechoslovakia's Premier Lubomir Strougal resigns, in an apparent victory for the conservative leadership of the Czechoslovak Communist Party. He had been in office since 1970. He is replaced the following day by Ladislav Adamec.			
Oct. 11		Soviet foreign ministry chief spokesman Gennadi I. Gerasimov says the Kremlin has no intention of interfering in either Yugoslavia or Czechoslovakia and that the situations in both countries are "internal problems" from the Kremlin's point of view.			Four leading Indian opposition groups join to form a "national alternative" to P.M. Rajiv Gandhi's ruling Congress (I) Party. The Janata Dal (People's Party) is inaugurated in a formal ceremony in the southern state of Karnataka.

A	B	C	D	E
Includes developments that affect more than one world region, international organizations and important meetings of major world leaders.	Includes all domestic and regional developments in Europe, including the Soviet Union, Turkey, Cyprus and Malta.	Includes all domestic and regional developments in Africa and the Middle East, including Iraq and Iran and excluding Cyprus, Turkey and Afghanistan.	Includes all domestic and regional developments in Latin America, the Caribbean and Canada.	Includes all domestic and regional developments in Asia and Pacific nations, extending from Afghanistan through all the Pacific Islands, except Hawaii.

U.S. Politics & Social Issues	U.S. Foreign Policy & Defense	U.S. Economy & Environment	Science, Technology & Nature	Culture, Leisure & Life Style	
During a television debate vice presidential candidate Sen. Dan Quayle (R, Ind.) asserts that he is as experienced in government as John F. Kennedy was when he ran for the presidency in 1960. Sen. Lloyd M. Bentsen Jr. (D, Tex.) replies, "Senator, I served with Jack Kennedy. I knew Jack Kennedy. Jack Kennedy was a friend of mine. Senator, you're no Jack Kennedy."		The nation's unemployment rate fell to 5.3% in September, the Labor Dept. reports. . . . Federal Home Loan Bank Board Chairman M. Danny Wall says that the probable cost of rescuing the nation's insolvent thrift institutions will be $45 bil.-$50 bil.			Oct. 5
A state grand jury in Poughkeepsie, N.Y., concludes that black teenager Tawana Brawley lied when she claimed to have been kidnapped and raped by a gang of white men in 1987. . . . The Justice Dept. reverses its previous position and rules that acquired immune deficiency syndrome (AIDS) patients and those infected with the AIDS virus are covered by a federal law that bars discrimination against handicapped people.	The Defense Dept. unveils a plan to substantially cut back the initial phase of deployment of the Strategic Defense Initiative ("Star Wars") from $115 bil. to $69 bil.				Oct. 6
A Parental and Medical Leave Act dies in the Senate when an attempt to cut off debate fails. The partisan struggle lasted nine days and saw the fashioning of a Democratic "pro-family package" to gain passage of the parental leave measure. . . . A trust fund set up to handle claims against A.H. Robins Co.'s Dalkon Shield intrauterine device begins making payments to injured women.		Outstanding consumer debt rose $5.44 bil. in August, the Federal Reserve Board reports. The increase, at an annual rate of 10.1%, brings outstanding credit to a total of $654.78 bil. Borrowing grew at a 6.7% annual rate in July and a 15.2% rate in June.			Oct. 7
Atlanta police have arrested more than 400 people at a series of antiabortion protests sponsored by Operation Rescue in the last five days. Most of the arrests are for obstructing clinic entrances and blocking streets near clinics.				Columbia Univ. snaps a 44-game losing streak in football with a 16-13 victory over Princeton Univ. in New York City.	Oct. 8
The Supreme Court opens its 1988-89 term with 23 new cases on the docket, including one that focuses on the question of whether Consolidated Rail Corp. (Conrail) is required to bargain with workers over drug testing. . . . The Bureau of Justice Statistics of the Justice Dept. reports that the national crime rate rose 1.8% in 1987. The increase marks the end of a five-year decline in the crime rate.				Completing a four-game sweep, the Oakland Athletics beat the Boston Red Sox, 4-1, winning the American League pennant and a trip to the World Series. Oakland reliever Dennis Eckersley wins the most valuable player award.	Oct. 9
		Forbes magazine's annual list of the 400 richest people in the United States ranks retailer Sam Moore Walton first with total assets valued at $6.7 bil., followed by media mogul John Kluge, $3.2 bil., and Texas investor H. Ross Perot, $3 bil.			Oct. 10
A federal grand jury charges Bank of Credit & Commerce International Holdings S.A. (BCCI), two of its units, and nine BCCI executives with conspiring to launder over $32 mil. in profits from alleged U.S. cocaine sales by the Medellin drug cartel of Colombia.			An international group of mathematicians announces that it has succeeded in the first factoring of a 100-digit number. The number, $10^{104} + 1$, was selected for its difficulty. Factoring consists of finding the prime numbers that divide the number evenly, a process that is largely trial-and-error.		Oct. 11
F	**G**	**H**	**I**	**J**	
Includes elections, federal-state relations, civil rights and liberties, crime, the judiciary, education, health care, poverty, urban affairs and population.	*Includes formation and debate of U.S. foreign and defense policies, veterans' affairs and defense spending. (Relations with specific foreign countries are usually found under the region concerned.)*	*Includes business, labor, agriculture, taxation, transportation, consumer affairs, monetary and fiscal policy, natural resources, and pollution.*	*Includes worldwide scientific, medical and technological developments, natural phenomena, U.S. weather, natural disasters, and accidents.*	*Includes the arts, religion, scholarship, communications media, sports, entertainments, fashions, fads and social life.*	

	World Affairs	Europe	Africa & the Middle East	The Americas	Asia & the Pacific
Oct. 12			Algeria's Pres. Chadli Benjedid lifts the emergency decree imposed after unrest that erupted October 4 and promises a national referendum on democratic political reforms. Unofficial estimates put the death toll at more than 200.	Brazil's Pres. Jose Sarney announces a series of measures designed to check the rapid destruction of the Amazon rain forests, hundreds of thousands of square miles of which have been cleared in the previous two decades.	
Oct. 13					
Oct. 14		Delegates to the annual conference of Britain's Conservative Party greet P.M. Margaret Thatcher's closing speech with cries of "10 more years." The confident Tories have held power for nine years.... Britain's annual inflation rate in the 12 months through September rose to a three-year high of 5.9%, the government reports.		In Canada, the national consumer price index, the measure of inflation, rose 4.1% in the 12 months through September, up from a 4.0% reading in August, according to Statscan. The inflation rate has been hovering in the 4% range for most of the year.	
Oct. 15					
Oct. 16					An official report by Pakistani investigators asserts that "a criminal act or sabotage" caused the plane crash in August that killed Pres. Muhammad Zia ul-Haq, U.S. Ambassador Arnold L. Raphel, and 28 others.

A	B	C	D	E
Includes developments that affect more than one world region, international organizations and important meetings of major world leaders.	Includes all domestic and regional developments in Europe, including the Soviet Union, Turkey, Cyprus and Malta.	Includes all domestic and regional developments in Africa and the Middle East, including Iraq and Iran and excluding Cyprus, Turkey and Afghanistan.	Includes all domestic and regional developments in Latin America, the Caribbean and Canada.	Includes all domestic and regional developments in Asia and Pacific nations, extending from Afghanistan through all the Pacific Islands, except Hawaii.

U.S. Politics & Social Issues	U.S. Foreign Policy & Defense	U.S. Economy & Environment	Science, Technology & Nature	Culture, Leisure & Life Style	
		Billionaire real estate developer Donald Trump agrees to buy the Eastern Airlines shuttle service (which serves Washington, D.C., New York, and Boston) from Texas Air Corp. for $365 mil. The Eastern pilots union opposes the sale and says it will fight the deal.... The Environmental Protection Agency says it will allow use of new pesticides that may cause cancer so that farmers and food processors will stop using older, higher-risk pesticides given clearance before the government required complete carcinogenic data.		The Los Angeles Dodgers win the National League pennant, 6-0, over the New York Mets in the concluding game of their seven-game play-off series. In the World Series, the Dodgers will face the Oakland Athletics. Dodgers Pitcher Orel Hershiser is named the series' most valuable player.	Oct. 12
A poll taken immediately after the second and final presidential debate between Vice Pres. George Bush (R) and Gov. Michael S. Dukakis (D, Mass.) finds that 49% of respondents consider Bush the winner, as against only 33% who thought Dukakis won.... Congress clears a compromise bill on acquired immune deficiency syndrome that provides for a $1 bil. program of testing, counseling, research, and home health care, but does not clear the provisions for ensuring confidentiality of testing sought by the bill's chief sponsors.... A Florida state judge in West Palm Beach rules that state statutes protecting lawyer-client confidentiality allow a lawyer to withold his client's identity, even if the client might have committed a homicide.... Pres. Reagan signs into law a welfare reform bill, or Family Support Act, revising the major welfare programs to focus on training and jobs for reentry into the work force.		The U.S. merchandise trade deficit climbed to a seasonally adjusted $12.18 bil. in August, the Commerce Dept. reports.	The *New England Journal of Medicine* reports that a U.S. military program to test all members of the armed forces for the acquired immune deficiency syndrome virus has recorded only one false positive test out of more than 135,000 recruits tested, proving far more accurate than predicted.	Anastasio Cardinal Ballestrero, Roman Catholic archbishop of Turin, Italy, announces that radiocarbon testing of the Shroud of Turin dates the venerated cloth to about 1280 a.d. The shroud, bearing the blood-stained image of a crucified man, has been venerated for centuries as the sheet in which Jesus was buried.... Naguib Mahfouz, an Egyptian novelist, playwright and screenwriter, becomes the first Arabic-language writer to win the Nobel Prize for literature. Mahfouz, 77, has written 40 novels and short story collections about ancient and modern Egypt.	Oct. 13
Political extremist Lyndon H. LaRouche Jr. and six associates are indicted in federal court in Alexandria, Va., on 13 counts of mail fraud, conspiracy to commit mail fraud, and conspiracy to defraud the Internal Revenue Service.	Pres. Reagan issues a statement in which he admits that his administration cannot win enough votes in Congress to free $16.3 mil. in military aid for the Nicaraguan Contra rebels that has been held up since 1985.	The government's producer price index rose 0.4% in September, the Labor Dept. reports.... The Federal Reserve Board reports that its industrial production index was unchanged in September.... Pres. Reagan signs a bill to test and facilitate use of alternative fuels in automobiles, buses, and trucks.		*The Accused*, a film about an assistant district attorney who decides to prosecute witnesses who encouraged a gang rape in a crowded barroom, is released in New York. Inspired by a true case, the film is directed by Jonathan Kaplan and stars Kelly McGillis and Jodie Foster, who wins an Oscar for best actress for her performance.	Oct. 14
			E.I. DuPont de Nemours & Co. announces that it will market in 1989 a strain of genetically engineered mice. DuPont's mice are the first animals developed through genetic engineering that have ever received a U.S. patent.	The world rock tour to benefit Amnesty International ends with a concert in Buenos Aires, Argentina. The six-week tour featured performances by Bruce Springsteen, Sting, Peter Gabriel, Tracy Chapman, and Senegalese singer Youssou N'Dour and visited 19 cities on five continents, attracting more than 1 million people.	Oct. 15
Two surveys by the Alan Guttmacher Institute of New York City indicate that abortion is common among all racial, economic and religious groups in the United States. Nearly 3% of American women of childbearing age had an abortion in 1987. The rate is 2.3% for white women, 4.3% for Hispanics, and 5.3% for nonwhites.		The Office of Management and Budget announces that Congress met the October 15 deadline on the Gramm-Rudman deficit reduction law; the budget deficit was $145.45 bil., $545 mil. shy of the $146 bil. called for by Gramm-Rudman.			Oct. 16

F	G	H	I	J
Includes elections, federal-state relations, civil rights and liberties, crime, the judiciary, education, health care, poverty, urban affairs and population.	Includes formation and debate of U.S. foreign and defense policies, veterans' affairs and defense spending. (Relations with specific foreign countries are usually found under the region concerned.)	Includes business, labor, agriculture, taxation, transportation, consumer affairs, monetary and fiscal policy, natural resources, and pollution.	Includes worldwide scientific, medical and technological developments, natural phenomena, U.S. weather, natural disasters, and accidents.	Includes the arts, religion, scholarship, communications media, sports, entertainments, fashions, fads and social life.

	World Affairs	Europe	Africa & the Middle East	The Americas	Asia & the Pacific
Oct. 17		An emergency two-day session of the Central Committee of Yugoslavia's ruling League of Communists fails to come up with solutions to the country's drastic economic and political problems, especially growing Serbian nationalism. . . . Queen Elizabeth II begins the first state visit to Spain by a reigning British monarch. She is greeted by her third cousin, King Juan Carlos.		The United States says it will grant Mexico a short-term loan of up to $3.5 bil. The bridging loan is to tide Mexico over until it obtains longer-term financing from multilateral lending agencies. The Mexican government and president-elect Carlos Salinas de Gortari agree to extend economic reforms in return for the funds.	The United States and the Philippines sign an interim accord covering American use of six military facilities in the Philippines, including strategically important Clark Air Base and Subic Bay Naval Base, through 1991.
Oct. 18			Estimates of the minimum number of Palestinians killed during the Palestinian uprising, or *intifada*, in the occupied West Bank and Gaza Strip since December 1987 range from 265 to more than 300, with an additional 7,000 people injured by gunfire, tear gas, and beatings.	Pres. Raul Alfonsin announces that Argentina's presidential elections will be held May 14, 1989. Calling the coming elections "a victory for democracy," he hails what will be Argentina's first peaceful transition of power from one civilian president to another since 1928.	
Oct. 19	Representatives of both North Korea and South Korea offer tentative proposals for the reunification of their divided country during successive addresses, over two days, before the UN Gen. Assembly in New York City.	The British government bans television or radio broadcasts of statements by officials of 11 Northern Ireland organizations, including Sinn Fein, the political wing of the outlawed Provisional Irish Republican Army.		The Honduran foreign ministry announces suspension of negotiations with the United States on a new military agreement, reportedly because of Honduras's concern over the future of U.S.-backed Contra rebels based in Honduras.	
Oct. 20		The Italian government October 14, and a consortium of British banks today, reach separate agreements providing the Soviet Union with a total of $3 bil. in trade credits.		In Canada, a five-day blockade by Indians of an oil-rich area of northern Alberta is broken by the Royal Canadian Mounted Police. Twenty-seven people are arrested.	

A	B	C	D	E
Includes developments that affect more than one world region, international organizations and important meetings of major world leaders.	*Includes all domestic and regional developments in Europe, including the Soviet Union, Turkey, Cyprus and Malta.*	*Includes all domestic and regional developments in Africa and the Middle East, including Iraq and Iran and excluding Cyprus, Turkey and Afghanistan.*	*Includes all domestic and regional developments in Latin America, the Caribbean and Canada.*	*Includes all domestic and regional developments in Asia and Pacific nations, extending from Afghanistan through all the Pacific Islands, except Hawaii.*

U.S. Politics & Social Issues	U.S. Foreign Policy & Defense	U.S. Economy & Environment	Science, Technology & Nature	Culture, Leisure & Life Style	
The Teamsters union endorses Vice Pres. George Bush for president. The Teamsters supported Ronald Reagan in both 1980 and 1984, but the Reagan Justice Dept. has moved to take over the union because of its ties to organized crime. . . . Rep. Patrick L. Swindall (R, Ga.) is indicted by a federal grand jury on 10 counts of perjury for his testimony in a federal money-laundering investigation. Swindall asked that the grand jury indict him October 3 so that he could clear his name in a trial before the November 8 election. . . . In what is believed to be the first ruling of its kind at the federal court level, a Providence, R.I., judge orders a state hospital to remove a feeding tube from a comatose patient, Marcia V. Gray, or transfer her to an institution that will comply with her family's wishes.		American Telephone & Telegraph Co. says it will reduce long-distance rates an average of 3.8% in a move that would save businesses and consumers $697 mil. a year.	The Nobel Prize for physiology or medicine is shared by American researchers George H. Hitchings and Gertrude B. Elion, and a Briton, Sir James W. Black, for work that led to the introduction of drugs widely used to treat heart disease, ulcers, and leukemia.	Pres. Reagan awards the Presidential Medal of Freedom to entertainer Pearl Bailey, former labor leader Irving Brown, former Supreme Court Chief Justice Warren E. Burger, economist Milton Friedman, Jean Faircloth MacArthur (the widow of former Army Gen. Douglas MacArthur), former Deputy Defense Sec. David Packard and, postuhmously, former Commerce Sec. Malcolm Baldrige and J. Willard Marriott Sr., founder of the Marriott hotel and restaurant chain.	Oct. 17
On the heels of the second presidential debate October 13 a Wall Street Journal/NBC News poll gives Vice Pres. George Bush (R) a 55%-38% lead in the public preference over his rival, Massachusetts Gov. Michael S. Dukakis (D). . . . Speaking at Westminster College in Fulton, Mo., where in 1946 Britain's P.M. Winston Churchill coined the term "Iron Curtain" to describe Soviet hegemony over Eastern Europe, Vice Pres. George Bush says the Russian Revolution is now "losing its luster." . . . Massachusetts Gov. Michael S. Dukakis works to solidify traditional Democratic support, rousing a blue-collar crowd in Saginaw, Mich., with a populist us-against-them theme. "George Bush wants to help the people who already have it made," Dukakis says. "I want to help every American family make it."			Maurice Allais wins the Nobel Prize in economics. Cited primarily for his research in market theory, he is also noted for the implications of his work for state-run monopolies.		Oct. 18
The Senate clears and sends to the White House a bill to restrict commercials broadcast to children and to make children's television fare a factor in license renewal. The House approved the measure in June. . . . The Food and Drug Admin. adopts a new policy on drug approval. The change is designed to promote quicker access to new drugs for patients suffering from life-threatening illnesses such as acquired immune deficiency syndrome.	Congress clears legislation making genocide a crime and establishing penalties for it, thus putting into effect a 1948 UN treaty signed by Pres. Harry S Truman in 1949 but not ratified by the Senate until 1986.	Housing starts rose 1.5% in September, the Commerce Dept. reports, to an adjusted annual rate of 1.453 million units. . . . Congress completes action on a bill to curb ocean pollution by ending all dumping of sewage sludge after 1991, and sends it to Pres. Reagan. . . . On the anniversary of the 1987 stock market collapse, the Dow Jones Industrial Average drops 43 points on a rumor that Vice Pres. George Bush has a mistress. The market rebounds to close down only 22.58 points after the story is denied.	West Germans Hartmut Michel, Robert Huber and Johann Deisenhofer win the Nobel Prize for chemistry for their efforts in mapping the structure of protein molecules essential in photosynthesis. . . . The Nobel Prize for physics is awarded to Americans Leon Lederman, Melvin Schwartz, and Jack Steinberger for their experiments with the subatomic neutrino particle in the early 1960s.	Variety's top-grossing films for the week are: The Accused, Alien Nation, Punchline, Gorillas in the Mist and Crossing Delancey.	Oct. 19
Legislation authorizing aid to the homeless is approved by the Congress and sent to Pres. Reagan. The bill authorizes $1.3 bil. over the next two years for a variety of programs including shelter, food, job training, physical and mental health care, and counseling for alcohol or drug problems.		RJR Nabisco Inc. management says that it has begun to develop a $17 bil. takeover offer for the food and tobacco giant that would take the company private. . . . Lamar Hunt agrees to a $17 mil. settlement with Peruvian commodities company Minpeco S.A. The settlement relieves Hunt of the burden of any portion of the $130 mil. judgment against him and his two brothers and other defendants in the silver-market conspiracy case.			Oct. 20

F	G	H	I	J
Includes elections, federal-state relations, civil rights and liberties, crime, the judiciary, education, health care, poverty, urban affairs and population.	Includes formation and debate of U.S. foreign and defense policies, veterans' affairs and defense spending. (Relations with specific foreign countries are usually found under the region concerned.)	Includes business, labor, agriculture, taxation, transportation, consumer affairs, monetary and fiscal policy, natural resources, and pollution.	Includes worldwide scientific, medical and technological developments, natural phenomena, U.S. weather, natural disasters, and accidents.	Includes the arts, religion, scholarship, communications media, sports, entertainments, fashions, fads and social life.

	World Affairs	Europe	Africa & the Middle East	The Americas	Asia & the Pacific
Oct. 21					
Oct. 22	Leading oil ministers of the Org. of Petroleum Exporting Countries (OPEC) stick to the status quo in production levels despite chronic oversupply and depressed prices. The next OPEC meeting is scheduled for November.		Palestine Liberation Org. (PLO) chairman Yasir Arafat, Jordan's King Hussein, and Egypt's Pres. Hosni Mubarak meet in an effort to narrow the split between the PLO and Jordanian leaders.		
Oct. 23			An attempt by Israel to keep Soviet Jews with Israeli visas from immigrating to the United States and other Western countries fails due to a lack of international cooperation, it is reported. Some 90% of Soviet Jews with Israeli visas use the visas to enter the United States and other Western countries.		
Oct. 24		West Germany's Chancellor Helmut Kohl visits Moscow for four days of talks with Soviet Pres. Mikhail S. Gorbachev, who tells reporters that the "ice has been broken" in West German-Soviet relations.			
Oct. 25				Argentina's former Pres. Isabel Martinez de Peron returns to her homeland from Spain where she has lived since 1981. A former leader of the Peronist movement, Peron is thought to support Alfonsin's Radical Civic Union more than the opposition Justicialist Party (Peronists).	
Oct. 26	The UN Gen. Assembly elects five new nonpermanent members of the Security Council: Canada, Finland, Malaysia, Ethiopia, and Colombia.	The European Court of Human Rights rules that the Irish government must do away with its hundred-year-old laws against homosexuality.		Amnesty International says the killing of civilians and other human rights abuses in El Salvador by right-wing death squads have increased dramatically over the past 18 months.	

A	B	C	D	E
Includes developments that affect more than one world region, international organizations and important meetings of major world leaders.	Includes all domestic and regional developments in Europe, including the Soviet Union, Turkey, Cyprus and Malta.	Includes all domestic and regional developments in Africa and the Middle East, including Iraq and Iran and excluding Cyprus, Turkey and Afghanistan.	Includes all domestic and regional developments in Latin America, the Caribbean and Canada.	Includes all domestic and regional developments in Asia and Pacific nations, extending from Afghanistan through all the Pacific Islands, except Hawaii.

U.S. Politics & Social Issues	U.S. Foreign Policy & Defense	U.S. Economy & Environment	Science, Technology & Nature	Culture, Leisure & Life Style	
A federal grand jury in New York City indicts former Philippine Pres. Ferdinand E. Marcos, his wife, and eight associates on six counts that constitute a "pattern of racketeering" activities since 1972. . . . Congress clears legislation that will extend federal lobbying restrictions for the first time to former members of Congress and their top aides. . . . Congress clears an immigration measure allowing more visas for Irish citizens to enter the United States.	The Senate passes a bill to create a privately funded memorial in honor of the 10,000 women who served in the Vietnam War. If signed into law, the measure will override a 1987 decision by the federal Comm. on Fine Arts rejecting such a memorial.	The government's consumer price index rose 0.3% in September, the Labor Dept. reports. The September increase in the index, at a 4.1% compound annual rate, follows a 0.4% rise in August. . . . Following record highs on October 10, October 18, and October 20, the Dow Jones Industrial Average reaches a new post-crash high of 2183.50. The previous post-crash high of 2158.61 was set July 5. . . . Congress reauthorizes the Patent and Trademark Office for three years. The bill ensures public access to information held by the office and also says that the refusal to license use of a patented item is not misuse of the patent.	Congress completes action on a bill authorizing fiscal 1989-91 funding for the National Aeronautics and Space Admin. with $2 bil. authorized for a manned space station in 1990, and $3 bil. in 1991.	*Publishers Weekly*'s hardback fiction best-sellers for the week are: *The Cardinal of the Kremlin*, Tom Clancy; *Breathing Lessons*, Anne Tyler; *Till We Meet Again*, Judith Krantz; *Spock's World*, Diane Duane; and *Alaska*, James Michener. . . . *Little Dorrit*, a screen adaptation of the Charles Dickens novel, is released in New York. Directed and written by Christine Edzard, the two-part, six-hour film stars Derek Jacobi, Alec Guinness, Sarah Pickering, Joan Greenwood, Miriam Margolyes, Eleanor Bron, and Michael Elphink.	Oct. 21
The 100th Congress adjourns an activist and productive session. Among the last measures passed are a major antidrug bill that allows the death penalty for drug-related murders and imposes a civil fine of up to $10,000 for possession of even small amounts of such illegal drugs as marijuana and cocaine; a tax bill with numerous changes in the tax code, and a taxpayer "bill of rights"; and a bill increasing penalties for insider trading.			Hurricane Joan has lashed the Caribbean Basin over the last five days causing at least 186 deaths and leaving hundreds of thousands of people homeless in five countries.	The Los Angeles Dodgers complete a four-games-to-one victory in the 85th World Series over the heavily favored Oakland Athletics. Dodgers' pitcher Orel Hershiser earns the series' most valuable player award.	Oct. 22
	The *Boston Globe* publishes the first investigative report in the mainstream press into the so-called "October surprise" theory that the 1980 Reagan-Bush campaign made a deal with Iran to hold the 52 U.S. hostages in Teheran until after the election to ensure Pres. Jimmy Carter's defeat.				Oct. 23
Democratic presidential hopeful Gov. Michael S. Dukakis accuses the Bush camp of "running a campaign based on distortions and distractions and outright lies." Bush defends his advertising and says Dukakis is trying to "run from the facts of his record."					Oct. 24
Two Ku Klux Klan groups and 12 individuals are ordered to pay about $1 mil. to 53 civil rights marchers injured in a demonstration in Forsyth County, Ga., in 1987.	Pres. Reagan signs a bill creating a cabinet-level Dept. of Veterans Affairs. The conference report was cleared by the Senate in a voice vote October 18. It was passed in a House voice vote October 6.	Pres. Reagan signs a pesticide review bill for safety evaluation of ingredients in pesticides.	Typhoon Ruby pounds the Philippines, killing several hundred people and leaving approximately 100,000 homeless.		Oct. 25
Pres. Reagan pocket vetoes the Whistleblower bill, a bill to protect federal workers who expose waste, fraud, and abuse. The move offends Congress, which passed the legislation without one negative vote in either house.		The nation's gross national product grew at a 2.2% annual rate in the third quarter, the Commerce Dept. reports. . . . Testifying before the Senate Banking Committee, Federal Reserve Board Chairman Alan Greenspan expresses concern about the growing volume of leveraged buyout debt and warns that borrowing to finance multibillion-dollar corporate takeovers carries "risks. . .for lenders and the economy."	Roussel Uclaf S.A. announces it will suspend distribution of RU 486, an abortion-inducing drug approved for use in France and China. The French company says the action comes "in the face of emotion on the part of public opinion in France and abroad."	Anglo-Australian author Peter Carey wins the Booker Prize, Britain's most prestigious fiction award, for his *Oscar and Lucinda*, a tragicomic historical novel set mainly in England and Australia in 1865.	Oct. 26

F	G	H	I	J
Includes elections, federal-state relations, civil rights and liberties, crime, the judiciary, education, health care, poverty, urban affairs and population.	Includes formation and debate of U.S. foreign and defense policies, veterans' affairs and defense spending. (Relations with specific foreign countries are usually found under the region concerned.)	Includes business, labor, agriculture, taxation, transportation, consumer affairs, monetary and fiscal policy, natural resources, and pollution.	Includes worldwide scientific, medical and technological developments, natural phenomena, U.S. weather, natural disasters, and accidents.	Includes the arts, religion, scholarship, communications media, sports, entertainments, fashions, fads and social life.

	World Affairs	Europe	Africa & the Middle East	The Americas	Asia & the Pacific
Oct. 27		Finance Min. Boris I. Gostev discloses that the Soviet Union will have a budget deficit of $58 bil. in 1988 and also acknowledges that the government kept deficits hidden for several years.	The results of South Africa's first municipal elections open to voters of all races are announced. Only 30% of the 1.5 million registered black voters in contested wards cast ballots, and among whites, the ruling National Party retained control of most major city councils, while the far-right Conservative Party made strong gains in rural and industrial areas. . . . Aid groups accuse both the Sudanese government and rebel forces of blocking international relief efforts to bring aid to areas in the southern Sudan where war-related famine has reached devastating proportions.		The official New China News Agency publicizes details of a number of economic policy changes advocated by Zhao Ziyang, China's Communist Party leader, aimed primarily at controlling the country's record inflation rate.
Oct. 28				A poll of 811 eligible Canadian voters concludes that Liberal Party leader John Turner "won" the two debates held October 24 and 25, with 46% of those polled favoring Turner's performance, 19% that of P.M. Brian Mulroney, and 10% that of New Democratic Party leader Edward Broadbent. . . . A former Mexican policeman is sentenced in Los Angeles to 240 years plus life in prison for the 1985 torture-slaying of Drug Enforcement Admin. agent Enrique Camarena Salazar and his pilot Alfredo Zavala Avelar.	
Oct. 29					
Oct. 30					World Expo 88, one of the highlights of Australia's bicentennial celebration, officially closes. Some 18.3 million visitors attended the Brisbane fair during its six-month run.
Oct. 31			The kidnappers of Terry A. Anderson, the longest-held American hostage in Lebanon, release a videotape in which the Associated Press correspondent faults the U.S. government and appeals to the next president to end "this terrible impasse."	Leaders of the leftist Farabundo Marti National Liberation Front conclude a two-week tour of Latin America in an unprecedented diplomatic effort to promote support for a negotiated end to the war in El Salvador. . . . The Nicaraguan government extends for a further month a cease-fire that has been in effect since March, and Contra leaders in Miami agree to observe the cease-fire. Both sides reserve the right to carry out defensive actions.	

A	B	C	D	E
Includes developments that affect more than one world region, international organizations and important meetings of major world leaders.	Includes all domestic and regional developments in Europe, including the Soviet Union, Turkey, Cyprus and Malta.	Includes all domestic and regional developments in Africa and the Middle East, including Iraq and Iran and excluding Cyprus, Turkey and Afghanistan.	Includes all domestic and regional developments in Latin America, the Caribbean and Canada.	Includes all domestic and regional developments in Asia and Pacific nations, extending from Afghanistan through all the Pacific Islands, except Hawaii.

U.S. Politics & Social Issues	U.S. Foreign Policy & Defense	U.S. Economy & Environment	Science, Technology & Nature	Culture, Leisure & Life Style	
The Educational Testing Service announces that it will replace its national teachers' examination with a more comprehensive three-part test. The current exam is taken by 200,000 teaching candidates in 30 states and the District of Columbia.		Consumer spending remained unchanged while personal income rose 0.5% in September, the Commerce Dept. reports.			Oct. 27
		The federal budget deficit for fiscal 1988 totaled $155.1 bil., the Treasury Dept. reports, up from the $149.66 bil. level recorded for fiscal 1987. The 1988 figure was helped by a Social Security surplus of $38.8 bil., compared with $19.57 bil. in 1987.... The Occupational Safety and Health Admin. announces a record $4.3 mil. fine against John Morrell & Co. for "egregious" and "willful" health and safety violations at the meat-packer's Sioux Falls, S.Dak., plant. ... Pres. Reagan signs legislation requiring that plastic ring "six-pack holders" be degradable to prevent harm to marine animals. The same legislation also provides for expansion of the San Francisco Bay National Wildlife Refuge.	The French health ministry orders Roussel-Uclaf S.A. to resume distribution of RU 486, a recently developed pill to induce abortion. The action comes just two days after Roussel withdrew the drug because of international protests.		Oct. 28
A survey by *Editor & Publisher* magazine finds that Vice Pres. George Bush (R) has been endorsed by 195 of the nation's dailies and Gov. Michael Dukakis (D, Mass.) by 51; 63% of those surveyed had endorsed neither candidate as of October 24.		Pres. Reagan signs a bill to deal with detecting and protecting homes from radon, a radioactive gas that seeps into structures from decaying uranium deposits in soil. The problem is considered a threat in as many as 8 million homes in the United States.		*Billboard*'s best-selling albums for the week are: *New Jersey*, Bon Jovi; *Appetite for Destruction*, Guns N' Roses; *Cocktail* (soundtrack); *Hysteria*, Def Leppard; and *Simple Pleasures*, Bobby McFerrin.	Oct. 29
				John (born Jacques Haussmann) Houseman, 86, actor and producer, dies of spinal cancer in Malibu, Calif. In the 1930s he teamed with Orson Welles in a series of projects, including the 1938 radio production *War of the Worlds* and later helped establish the Juilliard drama school and the Acting Co. repertory group. In 1973 he won an Oscar for best supporting actor in *The Paper Chase*.	Oct. 30
Imelda Marcos, the wife of former Philippine Pres. Ferdinand E. Marcos, pleads not guilty in federal court in New York City to charges that she and her husband stole more than $100 mil. from the Philippine government.	Less than two weeks after Pres. Reagan assured South Korea's Pres. Roh Tae Woo he would attempt to ease tensions between the United States and North Korea, the State Dept. announces that it is relaxing some restrictions on diplomatic contact, travel, and trade with North Korea.	Prices received by farmers for raw agricultural products are unchanged in October from September, the Agriculture Dept. reports. Prices were unchanged in September after rising 2.1% in August.... Sears, Roebuck & Co. announces an extensive restructuring aimed at bolstering its financial performance. The Chicago-based company plans to sell its 110-story Sears Tower in Chicago and buy back up to 40 million shares, or about 10% of its common stock, at an estimated cost of $1.6 bil.... Pres. Reagan signs the 1886 Berne Convention Implementation Act, making the United States the 77th nation to join the Berne Convention for the Protection of Literary and Artistic Works.		Ayrton Senna of Brazil clinches the season Formula One Grand Prix title with a victory in the Japan Grand Prix in Suzuka.	Oct. 31

F	G	H	I	J
Includes elections, federal-state relations, civil rights and liberties, crime, the judiciary, education, health care, poverty, urban affairs and population.	*Includes formation and debate of U.S. foreign and defense policies, veterans' affairs and defense spending. (Relations with specific foreign countries are usually found under the region concerned.)*	*Includes business, labor, agriculture, taxation, transportation, consumer affairs, monetary and fiscal policy, natural resources, and pollution.*	*Includes worldwide scientific, medical and technological developments, natural phenomena, U.S. weather, natural disasters, and accidents.*	*Includes the arts, religion, scholarship, communications media, sports, entertainments, fashions, fads and social life.*

	World Affairs	Europe	Africa & the Middle East	The Americas	Asia & the Pacific
Nov. 1		Britain's Chancellor of the Exchequer Nigel Lawson presents his annual Autumn Economic Statement to the House of Commons. Lawson says that government spending in fiscal 1988-1989, which ends in March 1989, will total $271.4 bil. . . . Iceland's 1989 budget includes tax increases and spending cuts aimed at producing a budget surplus of 1.1 bil. Icelandic krona, or 0.5% of gross domestic product.	Israelis go to the polls in record numbers to cast votes in their first national parliamentary election since 1984. The Labor Party and its allies win 48 seats as against 46 for the Likud bloc and its allies. . . . South Africa's Home Affairs Min. Stoffel Botha bans the *Weekly Mail*, the country's most prominent "alternative" newspaper, for one month, calling it a threat to public safety due to its crusading antiapartheid stories.		
Nov. 2		At the start of a two-day visit to Poland, Britain's P.M. Margaret Thatcher finds herself in the middle of a dispute between the Polish government and the Solidarity trade union, whose negotiations on proposed "round-table" talks have broken down.		Final arrangements are completed on a debt settlement accord between Brazil and its leading creditor banks. The agreement reschedules $62 bil. of foreign bank debt and provides Brazil with a new $5.2 bil. loan package.	
Nov. 3		Representatives of the European Community and the Soviet Union meet in Brussels to discuss closer economic ties. The two sides appear to remain far apart on basic issues.			A coup attempt in the island republic of the Maldives is thwarted when, at Pres. Maumoon Abdul Gayoom's request, India dispatches 1,600 paratroopers and three gunboats to repel a force made up largely of foreign mercenaries.
Nov. 4		Alexander A. Bessmertnykh, a Soviet deputy foreign minister, announces that his country is temporarily suspending withdrawal of its troops from Afghanistan because of the deteriorating military situation there.	The Algerian government claims an 83% voter turnout and a 92% "yes" vote in yesterday's referendum on constitutional reforms proposed by Pres. Chadli Benjedid in response to mass rioting in October.		
Nov. 5					
Nov. 6		A national referendum that could lead to independence for the French colony of New Caledonia is approved by 80% of French voters casting ballots, but only 37% of the electorate voted, the lowest for a referendum since World War II. . . . West German joblessness slipped in October to a six-year low of 8%, the government reports.		Col. Jean-Claude Paul, 49, commander of Haiti's most powerful army battalion, dies at his home in Port-au-Prince in what a police spokesman says the following day is a suspected poisoning.	

A	B	C	D	E
Includes developments that affect more than one world region, international organizations and important meetings of major world leaders.	Includes all domestic and regional developments in Europe, including the Soviet Union, Turkey, Cyprus and Malta.	Includes all domestic and regional developments in Africa and the Middle East, including Iraq and Iran and excluding Cyprus, Turkey and Afghanistan.	Includes all domestic and regional developments in Latin America, the Caribbean and Canada.	Includes all domestic and regional developments in Asia and Pacific nations, extending from Afghanistan through all the Pacific Islands, except Hawaii.

U.S. Politics & Social Issues	U.S. Foreign Policy & Defense	U.S. Economy & Environment	Science, Technology & Nature	Culture, Leisure & Life Style	
The Health and Human Services Dept. begins implementation of a Medicare reimbursement policy for unusually long or costly hospital visits. Hospitals will be reimbursed after 24 days of a patient's stay, rather than after 18 days.		The government's index of leading economic indicators fell 0.1% in September, the Commerce Dept. reports.	Under an agreement signed in Sofia, Bulgaria, 25 industrialized nations pledge to freeze the rate of emission of nitrogen oxides, a major source of acid rain and smog.	A $60.9 mil. California lottery prize, believed to be the largest jackpot in the world, will be shared by two groups who pooled their entries—25 Sears Roebuck & Co. workers in Sacramento and 15 employees of Fallbrook Hospital in San Diego County—and Ron Smith, an oil company production supervisor. Each of the three winning tickets will receive about $20.3 mil. over 20 years.... The Cincinnati Reds' Chris Sabo is named as the Jackie Robinson National League rookie of the year.	Nov. 1
		Productivity among the nation's nonfarm businesses increased at a 1.3% annual rate in the third quarter, the Labor Dept. reports.... Pres. Reagan signs legislation for tracking disposal of medical wastes and providing penalties for violation of health rules. The legislation was sparked by recent incidents of medical waste washing up on Northeast and Great Lakes beaches during the past summer.		Conductor Zubin Mehta announces that he will resign as music director of the New York Philharmonic once his current contract expires in 1991.... Shortstop Walt Weiss of the Oakland Athletics is named the American League's rookie of the year.	Nov. 2
		The White House announces Pres. Reagan's pocket veto of a bill to protect 1.4 million acres in Montana as wilderness areas. Reagan says he acted to protect jobs in the economically strapped state.... More than 6,000 computers across the country shut down over two days after being sabotaged by a computer "virus" in the worst incident of computer tampering reported to date.... An RJR Nabisco Inc. management group launches a $21.16 bil. takeover offer for the food and tobacco giant following the breakdown of talks with rival bidder Kohlberg Kravis Roberts & Co.	The outgoing director of the Soviet Institute of Space Research, Roa Z. Sagdeyev, warns that the Soviet Union is in danger of losing its lead in space because of an entrenched scientific bureaucracy.		Nov. 3
At the inaugural of Johnetta B. Cole, Spelman College's first black woman president, Bill Cosby announces that he and his wife, Camille, will donate $20 mil. to the predominantly black women's institution; it is the largest individual contribution ever to a historically black school.... Pres. Reagan signs a bill providing for a $1 bil. program of testing, counseling, research, and home health care for victims of acquired immune deficiency syndrome.	Pres. Reagan signs legislation making genocide a crime under U.S. law. The action implements a 1948 UN treaty, the United States becoming one of almost 100 countries that are party to the pact.	The nation's unemployment rate fell to 5.2% in October, the Labor Dept. reports.			Nov. 4
Pres. Reagan vetoes a bill that would have limited advertising during children's television programs and that would also have made programming for children a factor in renewing a station's license.				Alysheba, a four-year-old colt, wins the Breeders' Cup Classic at Louisville's Churchill Downs. Personal Ensign wins the Distaff, Is It True takes the Juvenile, and Open Mind the Juvenile Fillies; Gulch wins the Sprint, Miesque takes the Mile for the second year in a row, and Great Communicator wins the Turf.	Nov. 5
			A powerful earthquake hits a remote region in southwest China near the Burmese border. Some 16 counties are affected by the quake, which measures 7.6 on the Richter scale and is blamed for 938 deaths.	Grete Waitz of Norway, 35, wins the women's division of the New York City Marathon for the ninth time, finishing in 2:28:7. Steve Jones of Wales wins the men's race in 2:08:20.	Nov. 6

F	G	H	I	J
Includes elections, federal-state relations, civil rights and liberties, crime, the judiciary, education, health care, poverty, urban affairs and population.	Includes formation and debate of U.S. foreign and defense policies, veterans' affairs and defense spending. (Relations with specific foreign countries are usually found under the region concerned.)	Includes business, labor, agriculture, taxation, transportation, consumer affairs, monetary and fiscal policy, natural resources, and pollution.	Includes worldwide scientific, medical and technological developments, natural phenomena, U.S. weather, natural disasters, and accidents.	Includes the arts, religion, scholarship, communications media, sports, entertainments, fashions, fads and social life.

	World Affairs	Europe	Africa & the Middle East	The Americas	Asia & the Pacific
Nov. 7		The British government presents a long-awaited plan for deregulating television and radio broadcasting in what is described as the most radical change to the industry since independent companies were allowed in 1954.			
Nov. 8				In Canada, the Council of Yukon Indians approves an agreement that will provide the territory's 12 bands with hundreds of millions of dollars and an area of land nearly the size of the province of Nova Scotia.	In Cambodia, two days of peace talks involving the head of the Vietnamese-backed Cambodian regime and the leaders of two antigovernment guerrilla factions end without significant agreements.
Nov. 9			The last Belgian minesweeper leaves the Persian Gulf only four days after the Italian government announced it would withdraw its naval forces by the end of the year. The U.S. Navy has also scaled back its presence in recent months.		In South Korea, the opposition-controlled National Assembly holds two days of televised hearings into allegations of corruption surrounding former Pres. Chun Doo Hwan.
Nov. 10		The rate of unemployment in the European Community (EC) fell to 10.2% in September, down from 13% a year ago, the largest year-to-year decline since 1983 according to Eurostat; 15.6 million people in the EC are unemployed.		In Canada, two voter polls, one reported November 7 and the other this day, agree that the Liberal Party is leading in the election campaign.	In the western Pacific island republic of Palau, Ngiratkel Etpison is declared the winner in the presidential election held November 2, defeating his strongest challenger, Roman Tmetuchl, by 31 votes out of 9,000 cast.

A	B	C	D	E
Includes developments that affect more than one world region, international organizations and important meetings of major world leaders.	Includes all domestic and regional developments in Europe, including the Soviet Union, Turkey, Cyprus and Malta.	Includes all domestic and regional developments in Africa and the Middle East, including Iraq and Iran and excluding Cyprus, Turkey and Afghanistan.	Includes all domestic and regional developments in Latin America, the Caribbean and Canada.	Includes all domestic and regional developments in Asia and Pacific nations, extending from Afghanistan through all the Pacific Islands, except Hawaii.

U.S. Politics & Social Issues	U.S. Foreign Policy & Defense	U.S. Economy & Environment	Science, Technology & Nature	Culture, Leisure & Life Style	
The Supreme Court strikes down as racially discriminatory a zoning ordinance that restricts private construction of multifamily housing projects to areas of town where most of the town's minorities reside.... The New York City Health Dept. begins distributing sterile needles to drug abusers. The controversial plan is part of an effort to halt the spread of acquired immune deficiency syndrome.... Pres. Reagan signs the Homeless Assistance Act.... Judge Gerhard A. Gesell dismisses a charge that Oliver L. North, a key figure in the Iran-Contra conspiracy case, obstructed justice by allegedly attempting to hide the fact that a $13,800 security fence installed at his Virginia home was paid for by arms dealer Richard V. Secord.		Outstanding consumer debt rose $1.88 bil. in September, the Federal Reserve Board reports. The increase, at a 3.5% annual rate, is the smallest since November 1987 and follows a revised $5.32 bil. (9.9%) in August.... A *Wall Street Journal* survey finds that net income at 490 major corporations rose 12% in the third quarter to $24.97 bil., while after-tax earnings from continuing operations rose 14%.		Sugar Ray Leonard knocks out Donny Lalonde of Canada, becoming World Boxing Council (WBC) light heavyweight and WBC super middleweight champion.	Nov. 7
Vice Pres. George Herbert Walker Bush (R) is elected the 41st president of the United States, defeating Massachusetts Gov. Michael S. Dukakis (D). Bush takes 53% of the popular vote with a 426-112 victory in the electoral vote.... The Democrats make a net gain of one Senate seat in the election, with the new Senate to be made up of 55 Democrats and 45 Republicans. Many incumbents run uneventful races, and only four are defeated. ... Democrats also pick up three seats in the House, where there are now 260 Democrats to 175 Republicans.... Democratic incumbents are reelected in Washington, North Dakota, and Vermont; Republican incumbents are reelected in Delaware, Missouri, North Carolina, Rhode Island, and Utah; West Virginia and Indiana elect Democrats; and a Republican wins in Montana.				Indian-born author Salman Rushdie wins Britain's Whitbread Prize for his novel *Satanic Verses*.	Nov. 8
President-elect George Bush picks his campaign chairman, James A. Baker III, to be secretary of state, in his first appointment to his new cabinet.... John Newton Mitchell, 75, attorney general from 1969 to 1972 and a major figure in the Watergate scandal, dies following a heart attack in Washington. He served 19 months in a federal prison for his conviction for conspiracy, obstruction of justice, and perjury, after which he returned to private life in Washington.		The U.S. dollar plunges to a 10-month low on the news that Vice Pres. George Bush won the presidential election. In late New York trading, the dollar stood at 1.7637 marks and 124.07 yen, down from 1.7890 marks and 125.73 yen the day before. The British pound climbed to $1.7922 from $1.7700.		In Major League Baseball, Frank Viola of the Minnesota Twins is named winner of the American League's Cy Young Award as the league's outstanding pitcher.	Nov. 9
Pres. Reagan signs the Undetectable Firearms Act of 1988, a measure designed to prevent the use of plastic firearms to evade detection by metal detectors or X-ray machines at airports and public buildings.		The government's producer price index held steady in October, the Labor Dept. reports.... The Labor Dept. announces regulations that will lift a 45-year-old federal ban on the commercial home manufacture of gloves and mittens, buttons and buckles, embroidery, handkerchiefs, and jewelry. The regulations are quickly denounced by organized labor.... The Dept. of Energy announces that Texas will be the home of a $4.4 bil. Superconducting Super Collider, a project bid on by half the states. The device will be the world's largest and most expensive scientific instrument.	At the conclusion of a week of discussions in Washington, U.S. and Soviet space scientists announce an agreement to cooperate in a planned exploration of Mars.	In Major League Baseball, Orel Hershiser of the Los Angeles Dodgers is named the unanimous winner of the National League's Cy Young Award as the league's outstanding pitcher.	Nov. 10

F	G	H	I	J
Includes elections, federal-state relations, civil rights and liberties, crime, the judiciary, education, health care, poverty, urban affairs and population.	*Includes formation and debate of U.S. foreign and defense policies, veterans' affairs and defense spending. (Relations with specific foreign countries are usually found under the region concerned.)*	*Includes business, labor, agriculture, taxation, transportation, consumer affairs, monetary and fiscal policy, natural resources, and pollution.*	*Includes worldwide scientific, medical and technological developments, natural phenomena, U.S. weather, natural disasters, and accidents.*	*Includes the arts, religion, scholarship, communications media, sports, entertainments, fashions, fads and social life.*

	World Affairs	Europe	Africa & the Middle East	The Americas	Asia & the Pacific
Nov. 11		Philipp Jenninger, president of the West German parliament, resigns the morning after delivering a controversial speech on the 50th anniversary of *Kristallnacht*, a 1938 pogrom against Jews in Germany and Austria.			
Nov. 12			Palestine Liberation Org. Chairman Yasir Arafat opens the Palestine National Council with an appeal to president-elect George Bush to formulate a new U.S. policy of "justice" and "fairness" toward Palestinians.		Americans Donna Long and James Copp, arrested in Laos in early October while searching for U.S. servicemen missing in action since the Vietnam War, are released after paying a $1,500 administrative fine.
Nov. 13				In an interview published in the *Washington Post*, Nicaragua's Economics Min. Luis Carrion Cruz says Hurricane Joan caused more than $900 mil. in damage in October.	
Nov. 14		Spain and Portugal are formally admitted into the Western European Union, a defense organization. The other seven nations in the alliance are Great Britain, France, West Germany, Belgium, the Netherlands, Luxembourg, and Italy.	Following an agreement between P.M. Yitzhak Shamir's right-wing Likud bloc and religious parties that made a strong showing in national elections November 1, Israel's Pres. Chaim Herzog nominates Shamir to form a new government.	The Org. of American States' 18th general assembly convenes in San Salvador. The organization's financial crisis is a focus of discussion; member nations are about $45 mil. in arrears in their contributions, with the United States owing some $30 mil.	
Nov. 15	The Org. for Economic Cooperation and Development reports that economic policy officials of the leading industrial countries expect world economic growth to continue, employment opportunities to expand, and inflation to remain at low levels.		The legislative body of the Palestine Liberation Org. proclaims the establishment of an independent Palestinian state and votes to accept key UN resolutions that implicitly recognize Israel, Resolutions 242 and 338.... Negotiators for Angola, Cuba, South Africa and the United States in Geneva reach agreement on a timetable for the withdrawal of Cuban troops from Angola and the independence of South African-controlled Namibia.		An Indian municipal court judge issues arrest warrants for former Union Carbide Corp. chairman Warren Anderson and two other company officials in connection with the 1984 gas leak at Union Carbide's chemical plant in Bhopal. India's Industry Min. Vengala Rao puts the total death toll at 3,289. About 2,000 people were killed in the immediate aftermath of the gas leak; the others died later from injuries suffered in the disaster.
Nov. 16		The Estonian Supreme Soviet, the republic's legislature, asserts the right to unilaterally veto national laws affecting the republic, a direct challenge to Moscow's authority with implications for the whole Baltic region.			Benazir Bhutto's opposition Pakistani People's Party emerges as the victor in Pakistan's first open elections in more than a decade, with 92 of 205 contested National Assembly seats, nearly twice as many as any other faction.... The lower house of the Japanese Diet hands Premier Noboru Takeshita a major political victory in approving a sweeping overhaul of the country's tax system. Passage of the reform bill in the upper house is considered likely.

A	B	C	D	E
Includes developments that affect more than one world region, international organizations and important meetings of major world leaders.	Includes all domestic and regional developments in Europe, including the Soviet Union, Turkey, Cyprus and Malta.	Includes all domestic and regional developments in Africa and the Middle East, including Iraq and Iran and excluding Cyprus, Turkey and Afghanistan.	Includes all domestic and regional developments in Latin America, the Caribbean and Canada.	Includes all domestic and regional developments in Asia and Pacific nations, extending from Afghanistan through all the Pacific Islands, except Hawaii.

U.S. Politics & Social Issues	U.S. Foreign Policy & Defense	U.S. Economy & Environment	Science, Technology & Nature	Culture, Leisure & Life Style	
A panel of physicians and medical school faculty organized by the New York Academy of Medicine recommends that medical training in the United States be radically revised and that there be more emphasis on training physicians to be socially conscious and skilled in doctor-patient relationships.		The Farmers Home Admin. says it will begin to notify over 80,000 farmers whose loans are delinquent that they face the possibility of foreclosure.... Pres. Reagan signs into law the tax code revision, including a Bill of Rights for the taxpayer in dealings with the Internal Revenue Service. The bill also provides for extension of the Manassas National Battlefield Park in Virginia.... The Dow Jones Industrial Average slides 47.66 points, to 2067.03, as the dollar plunges to 40-year lows against the Japanese yen. The decline of the dollar after the election victory of Vice Pres. George Bush forces the Dow down 78.77 points this week in the steepest election-week decline since 1948.			Nov. 11
		Former Apple Computer Inc. chairman Steve Jobs launches the Next computer, an ultrafast machine that features object-oriented programming in which programs that perform complex tasks can be assembled from programming modules.			Nov. 12
				Alain Prost of France wins the Australian Formula One Grand Prix.... Antal Dorati, 82, Hungarian-born conductor, dies in Bern, Switzerland. He served as principal conductor for more than a dozen orchestras in Europe and the United States, and led the National Symphony in the inaugural concert of the John F. Kennedy Center for the Performing Arts in Washington in 1971. His recordings of the Haydn symphonies were particularly praised.	Nov. 13
The Transportation Dept. announces plans for random testing for drug use of nearly 4 million transportation workers in the private sector.					Nov. 14
President-elect George Bush announces that he will name Treasury Sec. Nicholas F. Brady to stay on in that post in the Bush administration.... The *New York Times* reports that the Social Security Admin. (SSA) is proposing to tighten regulations used in appeals for retirement, Supplemental Security Income, and Medicare benefits, in the first effort to restrict the appeals process since the SSA was created in 1946.... Pres. Reagan signs the Immigration Amendments of 1988, allowing more visas for Irish citizens to enter the United States.	Pres. Reagan signs authorization for a Vietnam Women's Memorial in the District of Columbia or environs.	The Federal Reserve Board reports that its industrial production index rose 0.4% in October.	The Soviet Union successfully orbits its first space shuttle, *Buran*. The unmanned craft, whose name means snowstorm, completes two orbits in a flight lasting three hours and 25 minutes.... Pres. Reagan signs the Commercial Space Launch Act Amendments of 1988, to back up insurance protection for private space launchings.	In Major League Baseball, Los Angeles Dodger left fielder Kirk Gibson is named the National League's most valuable player.	Nov. 15
		The U.S. merchandise trade deficit shrinks to a seasonally adjusted $10.46 bil. in September, the Commerce Dept. reports.... The Federal Reserve Board reports that the nation's factories, mines and utilities operated at 84% of capacity in October, the highest rate since February 1980; 85% is the threshold widely considered to signal increased inflation.... Pres. Reagan signs a bill modifying the nation's basic trademark law.... Pres. Reagan signs the Washington Park Wilderness Act of 1988.	Albert Lasker Medical Research Awards are given to molecular biologists Thomas R. Cech (Univ. of Colorado) and Phillip A. Sharp (Massachusetts Institute of Technology), for their work on the role of ribonucleic acid (RNA); Dr. Vincent P. Dole is cited for his discovery that methadone could be used to treat heroin addiction; and Sen. Lowell P. Weicker Jr. is cited for public service.	Jose Canseco, the right fielder of the Oakland Athletics, is named the most valuable player in Major League Baseball's American League.	Nov. 16

F	G	H	I	J
Includes elections, federal-state relations, civil rights and liberties, crime, the judiciary, education, health care, poverty, urban affairs and population.	*Includes formation and debate of U.S. foreign and defense policies, veterans' affairs and defense spending. (Relations with specific foreign countries are usually found under the region concerned.)*	*Includes business, labor, agriculture, taxation, transportation, consumer affairs, monetary and fiscal policy, natural resources, and pollution.*	*Includes worldwide scientific, medical and technological developments, natural phenomena, U.S. weather, natural disasters, and accidents.*	*Includes the arts, religion, scholarship, communications media, sports, entertainments, fashions, fads and social life.*

	World Affairs	Europe	Africa & the Middle East	The Americas	Asia & the Pacific
Nov. 17	The Federal Reserve Bank and the central banks of 10 other industrial nations mount a massive and coordinated intervention in foreign-exchange markets to support the plunging U.S. dollar.	The British government reports that seasonally adjusted unemployment fell in October to 2.16 million, down 31,500 from September. The decline in unemployment, the 27th straight monthly fall, brings the jobless rate for Britain to 7.7%. . . . Annual earnings in Britain continued their strong rise in September, with earnings up 9.25% for the 12 months ending September; there was a 7.4% increase in productivity over the same period.	A spokesman for the South-West African People's Org. (SWAPO) says that, in the wake of the November 15 agreement on Angola, SWAPO is ready to sign a formal cease-fire with South Africa to end the 23-year-old war in Namibia.		Representatives from North and South Korea agree to the basic format for parliamentary talks aimed at improving relations between the two countries: Each side will be limited to a delegation of 50 people, and their national assemblies will meet only at the opening and closing of the talks.
Nov. 18		In Britain, the government reports that inflation in the 12 months through October totaled 6.4%, the highest level since July 1985.	The Angolan and Cuban governments give their formal approval to the regional peace accord announced November 15. . . . A landmark treason trial, one of the longest in South African history, ends in Pretoria with four of 19 black activists convicted of treason, seven others convicted of terrorism, and eight defendants acquitted.	A Nicaraguan judge rules that 16 of more than 30 people arrested after an opposition rally in the city of Nandaime in July are innocent and orders their release from prison; nine others are released on condition that they return if charges against them are renewed.	Soviet Pres. Mikhail S. Gorbachev visits India where he reassures that country of the Soviet Union's continued desire for close ties, as well as to discuss regional issues, including the Afghan conflict and relations with China.
Nov. 19		Hundreds of thousands of Serbs march through Belgrade, Yugoslavia, to protest the alleged persecution of Serbs by ethnic Albanians in Kosovo province. Serbian party leader Slobodan Milosevic is at the head of the marchers.	Jonas Savimbi, leader of the National Union for the Total Independence of Angola (UNITA), says he welcomes the November 15 accord but that UNITA will engage government forces until the Cuban withdrawal is complete and the Marxist regime in Luanda agrees to form a government of national reconciliation with UNITA.		Benazir Bhutto's opposition Pakistan People's Party (PPP) suffers a setback in regional elections, winning in only one of the country's four provinces. The conservative nine-party Islamic Democratic Alliance (IDA), headed by Nawar Sharif, emerges as the victor in the other three provinces.
Nov. 20					The human rights organization Asia Watch issues a report on political and civil rights in Indonesia, particularly in the former Portuguese colony East Timor, where there have been some improvements although the Timorese people still live in "a climate of fear."

A	B	C	D	E
Includes developments that affect more than one world region, international organizations and important meetings of major world leaders.	*Includes all domestic and regional developments in Europe, including the Soviet Union, Turkey, Cyprus and Malta.*	*Includes all domestic and regional developments in Africa and the Middle East, including Iraq and Iran and excluding Cyprus, Turkey and Afghanistan.*	*Includes all domestic and regional developments in Latin America, the Caribbean and Canada.*	*Includes all domestic and regional developments in Asia and Pacific nations, extending from Afghanistan through all the Pacific Islands, except Hawaii.*

U.S. Politics & Social Issues	U.S. Foreign Policy & Defense	U.S. Economy & Environment	Science, Technology & Nature	Culture, Leisure & Life Style	
President-elect George Bush names outgoing New Hampshire Gov. John H. Sununu (R) as his White House chief of staff.		Housing starts surge 7.2% in October, the Commerce Dept. reports, to a seasonally adjusted annual rate of 1.554 million. . . . Attempting to ensure some progress at the upcoming meeting of the General Agreement on Tariffs and Trade, Pres. Reagan modifies his position that all nations end export-related agricultural subsidies by the year 2000 and calls instead for "flexible adjustment" to ease the shock of eliminating farm aid.		Sheila (born Lily Shiel) Graham, 84, former gossip columnist, dies of congestive heart failure in Palm Beach, Fla. With Louella Parsons and Hedda Hopper, Graham was one of the "unholy trio" of Hollywood's most powerful gossip writers. Her affair with novelist F. Scott Fitzgerald (who died in her arms) was the inspiration for her first book, *Beloved Infidel* (1958). She was Fitzgerald's model for Kathleen, the heroine of his unfinished novel *The Last Tycoon*.	Nov. 17
Pres. Reagan signs legislation to curb use of illegal drugs and broaden orientation and treatment programs. The measure also establishes the cabinet-level office of a federal drug "czar," a position requiring confirmation by the Senate. . . . The Dept. of Health and Human Services reports that spending on health care services in the United States rose to $500 bil. in 1987, an increase of 9.8% over 1986 and more than double the rate of inflation for the same period.	Pres. Reagan signs a bill to provide a special court to review cases on benefit claims by veterans.	Pres. Reagan signs a bill to ban ocean dumping of sewage sludge and industrial waste after 1991.			Nov. 18
Sen. George J. Mitchell (Maine) wins a three-way contest for the post of majority leader being vacated by Sen. Robert J. Byrd (W.Va.). The choice of Mitchell is seen as affirming the Democratic Party's traditional values while sharpening its public image. . . . Nicodemo Scarfo, the reputed head of organized crime in Philadelphia and Atlantic City, is convicted of murder and other charges in Philadelphia together with 16 of his associates. . . . Pres. Reagan signs the Major Fraud Act of 1988, a bill making "procurement fraud" against the federal government a crime by itself.		The House gives final approval to a bill designating as wilderness 1.7 million acres within three national park areas—Olympic National Park, Mount Rainier National Park and North Cascades National Park—in Washington State. . . . Pres. Reagan signs a bill authorizing funds for the Patent and Trademark Office and clarifying the doctrine of patent misuse.			Nov. 19
		The worst forest fire season in the United States since the 1920s is declared over, leaving behind 6 million acres of burned woodland. Some 30,000 professional firefighters, Army and Marine troops and temporary workers were employed to battle the blazes; 10 people died in the line of duty. . . . More than 70 tornadoes touch down in parts of the South and Midwest over the previous six days, killing nine people and destroying homes, businesses, and automobiles.		Bill Elliott clinches the Winston Cup season title of the National Assoc. for Stock Car Racing circuit with his 11th-place finish in the Atlanta Journal 500. . . . The Univ. of North Carolina wins its seventh National Collegiate Athletic Assoc. women's soccer title in eight years with a 4-1 victory over North Carolina State. . . . Pope John Paul II beatifies Mother Katharine Drexel, a Philadelphia nun who devoted her life to creating schools for American Indians and blacks and who died in 1955. The beatification brings her one step closer to sainthood.	Nov. 20

F	G	H	I	J
Includes elections, federal-state relations, civil rights and liberties, crime, the judiciary, education, health care, poverty, urban affairs and population.	*Includes formation and debate of U.S. foreign and defense policies, veterans' affairs and defense spending. (Relations with specific foreign countries are usually found under the region concerned.)*	*Includes business, labor, agriculture, taxation, transportation, consumer affairs, monetary and fiscal policy, natural resources, and pollution.*	*Includes worldwide scientific, medical and technological developments, natural phenomena, U.S. weather, natural disasters, and accidents.*	*Includes the arts, religion, scholarship, communications media, sports, entertainments, fashions, fads and social life.*

	World Affairs	Europe	Africa & the Middle East	The Americas	Asia & the Pacific
Nov. 21				The ruling Progressive Conservative Party, led by P.M. Brian Mulroney, wins the Canadian general election. Mulroney, 49, is the first Conservative prime minister in the 20th century to win reelection to a consecutive term.	
Nov. 22		Queen Elizabeth II opens a new session of Britain's Parliament with the Speech from the Throne to a joint session of the houses of Lords and Commons. The speech outlines the latest legislative plans of the government of conservative P.M. Margaret Thatcher.	South Africa gives its formal approval to a regional peace accord with Angola and Chad announced November 15.		Australia's P.M. Bob Hawke announces that the United States and Australia have signed a new 10-year agreement covering two sensitive American military facilities used to collect intelligence data on the Soviet Union.
Nov. 23		Sweden's Finance Min. Kjell Feldt outlines the Social Democratic government's plan for a major reform of the Swedish tax system. While details are lacking, press reports indicate that personal income taxes could be halved.... Talks between Pres. George Vassiliou of Cyprus and Rauf Denktash, head of the island's breakaway Turkish republic, have bogged down over issues of Turkish involvement in Cypriot affairs and on right of free settlement on the island.	South Africa's Pres. Pieter W. Botha reprieves the "Sharpeville Six," five men and a woman sentenced to death for their involvement in the 1984 lynching of a black township official. Botha also commutes the death sentences of three other blacks convicted of murder and four white policemen convicted of killing blacks.		Apologizing publicly to the South Korean people for corruption and human rights abuses committed during his eight years in power, former Pres. Chun Doo Hwan takes full "responsibility for the wrongdoings and mistakes during my tenure."
Nov. 24		Mounted police break up protests by thousands of students in central London after a march denouncing the government's planned student loan program. Sixty people are arrested and 16, including three policemen, are injured.... Hungary's parliament confirms Miklos Nemeth as premier. He was picked for the post by the Central Committee of the ruling Socialist Workers' (Communist) Party November 23.			An Indian government official reports that at least 1,786 Indian brides were slain in 1987, many of them burned alive, for failure to provide a sufficient dowry—a practice officially outlawed in 1961—for their husband or his family.

A	B	C	D	E
Includes developments that affect more than one world region, international organizations and important meetings of major world leaders.	Includes all domestic and regional developments in Europe, including the Soviet Union, Turkey, Cyprus and Malta.	Includes all domestic and regional developments in Africa and the Middle East, including Iraq and Iran and excluding Cyprus, Turkey and Afghanistan.	Includes all domestic and regional developments in Latin America, the Caribbean and Canada.	Includes all domestic and regional developments in Asia and Pacific nations, extending from Afghanistan through all the Pacific Islands, except Hawaii.

U.S. Politics & Social Issues	U.S. Foreign Policy & Defense	U.S. Economy & Environment	Science, Technology & Nature	Culture, Leisure & Life Style	
President-elect George Bush announces two appointments: Attorney Gen. Richard L. Thornburgh and Education Sec. Lauro F. Cavazos. Both are holdovers from the Reagan Admin.... Rep. Robert Garcia (D, N.Y.) is indicted in New York City on federal bribery and extortion charges involving the scandal-ridden Wedtech Corp.... Surrounded by old friends, Pres. Reagan breaks ground in Simi Valley, Calif., for the library that will house his presidential documents. The $43-mil. library will be built with private funds but operated by the National Archives.... An Associated Press canvass of all 50 states finds that the final, unofficial popular vote totals for the November 8 election are 48,138,478 votes, or 53.44%, for Vice Pres. George Bush (R), and 41,114,068, or 45.64%, for Gov. Michael S. Dukakis (D, Mass).		Nine states file legal action against the Environmental Protection Agency seeking publication of a 1981 finding that sulfur dioxide emissions from coal-burning plants in the United States harm Canada with acid-rain fallout.	The Food and Drug Admin. approves the use of alpha interferon for treatment of Kaposi's sarcoma, a skin cancer often found in acquired immune deficiency syndrome. Alpha interferon is a disease-fighting substance produced naturally in humans that can also be reproduced in quantity through gene-splicing techniques.	The United States and the Soviet Union sign an agreement to monitor drug use by each other's athletes. The pact is viewed as an important step in the fight against the use of performance-enhancing drugs by athletes.... Syndicated humor columnist Art Buchwald files a $5 mil. lawsuit in Los Angeles, claiming that Paramount Pictures based the movie *Coming to America* on a treatment he sold to Paramount in 1983 titled "King for a Day." The studio claims the movie is based on an idea by the film's star, comedian Eddie Murphy.... Carl Owen Hubbell, 85, baseball Hall of Famer, dies of injuries sustained in an automobile crash in Arizona. He played for the New York Giants from 1928 to 1943 and was twice named the National League's most valuable player. In the 1934 All-Star Game, he struck out in succession Babe Ruth, Lou Gehrig, Jimmie Foxx, Al Simmons, and Joe Cronin.	Nov. 21
Hundreds of people gathered in Washington, D.C., to mark the 25th anniversary of the assassination of Pres. John F. Kennedy, who was murdered in Dallas in 1963.		The Reagan administration projects that the gross national product will expand 3.5% in 1989.... The government's consumer price index rose 0.4% in October, the Labor Dept. reports. The increase, at a compound annual rate of 5.1%, follows a 0.3% increase in September and a 0.4% rise in August.... In a landmark accord, the Energy Dept. agrees to clean up toxic waste in the soil and water at the Portsmouth Uranium Enrichment Complex at Piketon, Ohio. The plant produces fuel for nuclear power plants and submarine reactors.... The Census Bureau reports that the federal contribution to state and local government revenues in 1987 was 13.6 cents per dollar of revenue. The high was 18.7 cents in 1978; the previous low was 13.5 cents in 1966.	Raymond Arthur Dart, 95, Australian-born anatomist who revolutionized the study of human origins, dies in Johannesburg, reportedly of complications from a cerebral hemorrhage. In 1924 he discovered a 3-million-year-old fossil skull, *Australopithecus africanus*, that he described as the "missing link" between apes and humans, a theory not widely accepted until Louis Leakey confirmed the African origin of humankind after World War II.		Nov. 22
Pres. Reagan announces that he will veto a bill that extends federal lobbying restrictions to former lawmakers and top congressional aides, for the first time, and tightens the limits on former administration officials.... Pres. Reagan completes his consideration of legislation sent to him by the second session of the 100th Congress.	President-elect George Bush chooses arms control specialist Brent Scowcroft for his national security adviser.	Major airlines discontinue discount air fares used by 50% of their passengers. The move, contingent upon its staying power, signals to analysts an end to the fare wars that have characterized the industry since deregulation a decade ago.			Nov. 23
Three former Drug Enforcement Admin. agents are charged in Los Angeles with laundering money from narcotics trafficking. John Anthony Jackson and Wayne Countryman are under arrest, but Darnell Garcia remains a fugitive.			A study reported by Burroughs Wellcome Co., the manufacturer of AZT (azidothymidine or zidovudine), shows that the drug prolongs the lives of patients suffering from acquired immune deficiency syndrome.		Nov. 24

F	G	H	I	J
Includes elections, federal-state relations, civil rights and liberties, crime, the judiciary, education, health care, poverty, urban affairs and population.	*Includes formation and debate of U.S. foreign and defense policies, veterans' affairs and defense spending. (Relations with specific foreign countries are usually found under the region concerned.)*	*Includes business, labor, agriculture, taxation, transportation, consumer affairs, monetary and fiscal policy, natural resources, and pollution.*	*Includes worldwide scientific, medical and technological developments, natural phenomena, U.S. weather, natural disasters, and accidents.*	*Includes the arts, religion, scholarship, communications media, sports, entertainments, fashions, fads and social life.*

	World Affairs	Europe	Africa & the Middle East	The Americas	Asia & the Pacific
Nov. 25		Britain's balance of payments deficit reached a record high in October, the government reports. The announcement prompts action by the Bank of England, which engineers a one-percentage-point increase in bank lending rates. . . . The West German parliament passes a health care reform package aimed at saving $8.2 bil. per year by placing more of the costs on individuals; it is an effort to ease health care and pension financing problems posed by the country's aging population.		The human rights group Americas Watch reports that Guatemalan government forces are responsible for a serious increase in human rights abuses, including a majority of the 621 political murders in the first nine months of the year.	
Nov. 26	Sec. of State George P. Shultz denies Palestine Liberation Org. chairman Yasir Arafat permission to address the UN Gen. Assembly in New York because of his "associations with terrorism." The decision sparks an international uproar, and Arab nations immediately move to shift the UN meeting to Geneva.		More than 50 nations (almost none of which recognize Israel) have recognized the Palestine Liberation Org.'s November 15 declaration of independence for the Israeli-occupied West Bank, Gaza Strip, and East Jerusalem. . . . South Africa unconditionally releases, on "medical-humanitarian grounds," Zephania Mothopeng, 75, a founder of the Pan-Africanist Congress (PAC), and Harry Gwala, 69, a trade unionist and African National Congress organizer.		
Nov. 27		Portugal's draft 1989 budget foresees a reduction in the deficit to 7.8% of gross domestic product, from 8.7% in 1988. Spending is set at $14.4 bil.		In the Dominican Republic, former Pres. Salvador Jorge Blanco and two business executives are convicted in absentia of corruption during his administration of 1982-86; they are sentenced to 20 years each in prison and fined a total of $17.3 mil.	
Nov. 28	The Org. of Petroleum Exporting Countries agrees on new production targets designed to push up the price of petroleum by about $6 a barrel in the first half of 1989.	Romania's leader Nicolae Ceausescu reaffirms his determination to reshape the nation's agricultural sector by razing rural villages and resettling their inhabitants by force, a program known as *sistematizarea* (systemization) that calls for the destruction of over 7,000 peasant communities. Romania began implementing the plan in August. . . . U.S. and Soviet negotiators sign a new grain trade agreement lasting through the end of 1990. The pact replaces one that formally expired at the end of September.			
Nov. 29	The European Court of Human Rights rules that four complainants from Northern Ireland held in 1984 for periods ranging from four days to nearly seven days were denied their rights to be brought "promptly" before a judicial authority under the 1950 European Convention.	Hungary's hard-currency debt at the end of September fell to $16.6 bil.; Hungary has the highest per capita debt of any country in Eastern Europe, and about 45% of the nation's hard-currency earnings is devoted to debt repayment.		The Canadian government begins land-claim negotiations with the Lubicon Lake Cree Indian band of northern Alberta. Lubicons and their supporters pressed the Indians' land claim by blockading an oil-rich area of Alberta in October. . . . Latin American leaders of the Group of Eight (from which Panama was expelled in February) call for a summit with president-elect George Bush in early 1989 to discuss economic development, foreign debt, and other regional issues.	

A	B	C	D	E
Includes developments that affect more than one world region, international organizations and important meetings of major world leaders.	Includes all domestic and regional developments in Europe, including the Soviet Union, Turkey, Cyprus and Malta.	Includes all domestic and regional developments in Africa and the Middle East, including Iraq and Iran and excluding Cyprus, Turkey and Afghanistan.	Includes all domestic and regional developments in Latin America, the Caribbean and Canada.	Includes all domestic and regional developments in Asia and Pacific nations, extending from Afghanistan through all the Pacific Islands, except Hawaii.

U.S. Politics & Social Issues	U.S. Foreign Policy & Defense	U.S. Economy & Environment	Science, Technology & Nature	Culture, Leisure & Life Style	
			An earthquake hits southeastern Canada and the northeastern United States. The quake, which was centered in Chicoutimi, about 90 miles north of Quebec City, measures 6.0 on the Richter scale. ... Archaeologists in Tibooburra, 530 miles northwest of Sydney, New South Wales, announce the discovery of hundreds of thousands of crude stone tools at an ancient tool "factory" used by native Aborigines some 2,000 years ago.	*Publishers Weekly*'s hardback fiction best-sellers for the week are: *The Sands of Time*, Sidney Sheldon; *The Queen of the Damned*, Anne Rice; *The Cardinal of the Kremlin*, Tom Clancy; *One*, Richard Bach; and *Anything for Billy*, Larry McMurtry.	Nov. 25
				Billboard's best-selling albums for the week are: *Bad Medicine*, Bon Jovi; *Baby, I Love Your Way/Freebird Medley*, Will to Power; *Desire*, U2; *How Can I Fall?*, Breathe; and *Kissing a Fool*, George Michael.	Nov. 26
				John (born Richmond Reed Carradine) Carradine, 82, actor best known for his character roles, dies in a hospital in Milan, Italy, of heart, kidney, and lung ailments. He specialized in playing villains, mad scientists, and other eccentrics in Westerns and horror movies. Among his most highly praised roles were the gambler Hatfield in *Stagecoach* (1939) and the reformed preacher Casey in John Ford's film version of *The Grapes of Wrath* (1940).	Nov. 27
The Office of Management and Budget proposes that Medicare and Medicaid payments be allowed to grow by $7 bil. less than had been projected for FY1990. Doctors, hospitals, and legislators criticize the plan.		Leading banks raise their prime lending rate by half a percentage point to 10.5%. The increase, the fourth in 1988 to date, brings the prime to its highest level since May 1985.	Two tornado systems sweep through Raleigh, N.C., killing four people and injuring at least 157; more than 500 people are left homeless.	A 1905 painting by Pablo Picasso titled *Acrobat and Young Harlequin* sets a record when it sells at Christie's auction house in London for $38.5 mil. The price is the highest yet paid for a work of 20th-century art.	Nov. 28
Judge Gerhard A. Gesell dismissed the charge of wire fraud against Oliver L. North, a key figure in the Iran-Contra conspiracy case because, he says, given the broader conspiracy count against North, it would likely cause "substantial confusion in the minds of jurors." ... The Supreme Court rules, 6-3, to uphold a conviction despite police negligence in failing to preserve evidence that might have exonerated the defendant. "Unless a criminal defendant can show bad faith on the part of the police," Chief Justice William H. Rehnquist writes for the majority, "failure to preserve potentially useful evidence does not constitute a denial of due process of law." ... The Supreme Court upholds, 8-1, the right of indigent defendants to have legal representation on appeal of conviction.		Independent arbitrators order Fujitsu Ltd. of Japan to pay a total of $833.2 mil. to International Business Machines Corp., settling a six-year-old software copying dispute between the two companies. ... After-tax profits of U.S. corporations rose 0.2% in the third quarter, the Commerce Dept. reports, to an annual rate of $163.1 bil.	A cyclone devastates coastal areas of Bangladesh and eastern India. At least 800 people are killed and hundreds of thousands left homeless. ... The Food and Drug Admin. approves test kits for screening blood for the presence of HTLV-1, a rare virus that causes a form of leukemia and a type of brain disease called tropical spastic paraparesis.	The 1988 National Book Awards are presented. Pete Dexter wins the fiction prize for his novel *Paris Trout*, and Neil Sheehan wins the nonfiction award for *A Bright Shining Lie: John Paul Vann and America in Vietnam*.	Nov. 29

F	G	H	I	J
Includes elections, federal-state relations, civil rights and liberties, crime, the judiciary, education, health care, poverty, urban affairs and population.	*Includes formation and debate of U.S. foreign and defense policies, veterans' affairs and defense spending. (Relations with specific foreign countries are usually found under the region concerned.)*	*Includes business, labor, agriculture, taxation, transportation, consumer affairs, monetary and fiscal policy, natural resources, and pollution.*	*Includes worldwide scientific, medical and technological developments, natural phenomena, U.S. weather, natural disasters, and accidents.*	*Includes the arts, religion, scholarship, communications media, sports, entertainments, fashions, fads and social life.*

	World Affairs	Europe	Africa & the Middle East	The Americas	Asia & the Pacific
Nov. 30					
Dec. 1		At the end of a three-day session, the Supreme Soviet, the USSR's nominal parliament, approves changes in the Soviet constitution that will reorganize the nation's political structure in 1989.... *Pravda*, the Communist Party newspaper, reports that clashes between Christian Armenians and Shiite Moslem Azerbaijanis in the Transcaucasus have left 28 people dead; Soviet officials confirm that over 100,000 people have left their homes because of the violence.... U.S. and Italian authorities arrest 79 people believed to be involved in a major Sicilian-based narcotics smuggling operation. An additional 129 suspects, 23 in the United States and 106 in Italy, are still being sought.		In his inaugural address, Mexico's Pres. Carlos Salinas de Gortari calls for immediate renegotiation of the country's $104 bil. foreign debt. Mexico's annual debt payments now account for about 5% of gross national product.	Benazir Bhutto is named prime minister of Pakistan by acting Pres. Ghulam Ishaq Khan. The ascension of Bhutto, the first woman in modern history to lead a predominantly Moslem nation, is heralded by her supporters as a sign that democracy has returned to Pakistan after 11 years of military rule.
Dec. 2	The U.S. Navy is primarily to blame for the shooting down of Iran Air Flight 655 over the Persian Gulf in July, according to a probe by the International Civil Aviation Org. (ICAO) reported by the Canadian Press news service.		Four armed Soviet hijackers peacefully surrender to Israeli authorities after their plane lands at a military airfield near Tel Aviv. The hijackers are returned to the USSR under guard the following day.		
Dec. 3		At the close of a two-day, semiannual summit meeting in Rhodes, Greece, leaders of the 12 European Community nations say that about half the necessary legislation to implement the goal of an internal open market by 1992 is now in place.			
Dec. 4				Carlos Andres Perez, 66, of the governing Democratic Action (AD) Party, is elected president of Venezuela. Perez, a former president, defeats Eduardo Fernandez, 48, secretary general of the Christian Social Party (Copei), and more than 20 other candidates from smaller parties.	Pakistan's newly elected P.M. Benazir Bhutto forms a cabinet made up of 10 ministers and eight ministers of state. Bhutto announces she will hold the portfolios of defense, finance, and information.
Dec. 5			Charles Bester, an 18-year-old white South African, is sentenced to six years in prison for refusing conscription into the South African Defense Force (SADF). A committed pacifist and devout Christian, Bester argues he cannot serve in an institution that perpetuates the "evil" of apartheid.		Senior Soviet officials hold three days of unprecedented talks with representatives of the anticommunist Afghan guerrilla alliance in the first direct diplomatic contact between them since the Soviet invasion in 1979.

A	B	C	D	E
Includes developments that affect more than one world region, international organizations and important meetings of major world leaders.	*Includes all domestic and regional developments in Europe, including the Soviet Union, Turkey, Cyprus and Malta.*	*Includes all domestic and regional developments in Africa and the Middle East, including Iraq and Iran and excluding Cyprus, Turkey and Afghanistan.*	*Includes all domestic and regional developments in Latin America, the Caribbean and Canada.*	*Includes all domestic and regional developments in Asia and Pacific nations, extending from Afghanistan through all the Pacific Islands, except Hawaii.*

U.S. Politics & Social Issues	U.S. Foreign Policy & Defense	U.S. Economy & Environment	Science, Technology & Nature	Culture, Leisure & Life Style	
Republican senators reelect their leadership team, including Minority Leader Robert J. Dole (Kans.) and Minority Whip Alan K. Simpson (Wyo.). . . . The Dept. of Health and Human Services will begin cutting Medicare funds for professionally assisted home dialysis treatments on Jan. 1, 1989, arguing that Congress never intended Medicare to pay for home dialysis requiring help from medical staff.	Officials of U.S.-financed Radio Liberty and its sister station, Radio Free Europe, say that the Soviet Union has stopped electronic jamming of its broadcasts for the first time in 35 years.	Kohlberg Kravis Roberts & Co. is declared the winner in the contest for RJR Nabisco Inc., agreeing to acquire the food and tobacco giant for a record $25.07 bil. . . . Personal income climbed 1.8% and consumer spending rose 0.8% in October, the Commerce Dept. reports. . . . Prices received by farmers for raw agricultural products fell 0.7% in November, the Agriculture Dept. reports. Farm prices fell a revised 0.7% in October. The two straight monthly declines are the first since February.	The National Hurricane Center reports that the 1988 hurricane season, which officially ends today, was the worst in history; six hurricanes and five tropical storms killed more than 500 people and caused more than $5 bil. in damages in the Caribbean and in Central and South America. . . . Following the suicide of his lawyer, Dov Eitan, the day before, a hearing to appeal the death sentence of accused Nazi war criminal John Demjanjuk is postponed for six months.	*Variety*'s top-grossing films for the week are: *Scrooged, The Land Before Time, Child's Play, Cocoon: The Return,* and *Oliver and Company.*	Nov. 30
Pres. Reagan declares that his administration has a "duty" to withhold certain highly classified government documents that Oliver L. North, a key figure in the Iran-Contra conspiracy case, wants to use in his defense if he is brought to trial. . . . The Dept. of Health and Human Services publishes the first annual government study of all nursing homes in the United States. It finds broad compliance with health and safety standards, but many homes do not follow proper procedures in drug dispensing and food service.	The White House announces that Lt. Gen. Colin L. Powell, Pres. Reagan's national security adviser, will be nominated for the rank of full general (four stars) and will take over the Army's Forces Command in 1989.	Continuing its recent seesaw pattern, the government's index of leading economic indicators rose 0.1% in October, the Commerce Dept. reports.		The National Broadcasting Co. wins the rights for U.S. television coverage of the 1992 Summer Olympic Games in Barcelona; the network is expected to sell some coverage to cable television to help reduce the costs of its $401 mil. bid for the rights.	Dec. 1
President-elect George Bush meets with Massachusetts Gov. Michael S. Dukakis, the defeated Democratic presidential nominee, and with Dukakis's running mate, Sen. Lloyd M. Bentsen (D, Tex.). . . . The United States deports to Cuba five Cuban convicts who traveled to the United States in the 1980 boatlift from Mariel.			A panel of experts appointed by the National Institutes of Health concludes that a scientific paper coauthored by Nobel laureate David Baltimore contains "serious errors of misstatement and omission" but no deliberate fraud.		Dec. 2
Social Security Admin. Commissioner Dorcas R. Hardy rejects a proposal to revise the Social Security appeals process, saying the proposed changes do not meet suitable standards of equity, compassion, and efficiency.				Barry Sanders, a junior tailback from Oklahoma State Univ., is named the recipient of the 1988 Heisman Trophy awarded to college football's top player. . . . Olympic sprinter Florence Griffith Joyner is named the winner of the 1988 Jesse Owens Award as the outstanding U.S. track and field athlete of the year.	Dec. 3
		Aluminum Co. of America and Reynolds Metals Co. announce tentative 43-month labor agreements with the Aluminum, Brick & Glass Workers and the United Steelworkers unions. The contracts will supersede current pacts, due to expire May 31, 1989, and will cover 22,300 union members at 32 plants nationwide.		The Univ. of Indiana wins the National Collegiate Athletic Assoc. Division I soccer title with a victory in the tournament finals over Howard Univ., 1-0.	Dec. 4
A federal grand jury in Charlotte, N.C., indicts defrocked television evangelist Jim Bakker, 48, a former PTL Club president, on charges of fraud in connection with the sale of partnerships in vacation lodgings. . . . The House Democratic Caucus unanimously nominates Speaker Jim Wright (D, Tex.) for another two-year term. His election when the 101st Congress convenes in January 1989 is viewed as a formality.		The economy generated 463,000 new payroll jobs in November while the unemployment rate rose from 5.2% to 5.3%, the Labor Dept. reports. . . . American Express Co., Dow Chemical Co., Pfizer Inc., and Sara Lee Corp. unveil an unprecedented plan to convert as much as $5.6 bil. of their common stock into a hybrid package of debt and equity securities, called Unbundled Stock Units, in an effort to raise the market value of their shares.	West Germany's Environment Min. Klaus Toepfer confirms that a serious incident caused the closure of a nuclear power plant near Frankfurt in December 1987, as reported publicly in the U.S. journal *Nucleonics Week.*		Dec. 5

F	G	H	I	J
Includes elections, federal-state relations, civil rights and liberties, crime, the judiciary, education, health care, poverty, urban affairs and population.	*Includes formation and debate of U.S. foreign and defense policies, veterans' affairs and defense spending. (Relations with specific foreign countries are usually found under the region concerned.)*	*Includes business, labor, agriculture, taxation, transportation, consumer affairs, monetary and fiscal policy, natural resources, and pollution.*	*Includes worldwide scientific, medical and technological developments, natural phenomena, U.S. weather, natural disasters, and accidents.*	*Includes the arts, religion, scholarship, communications media, sports, entertainments, fashions, fads and social life.*

	World Affairs	Europe	Africa & the Middle East	The Americas	Asia & the Pacific
Dec. 6	The International Monetary Fund projects economic growth of 4.25% in the Group of Seven nations in 1988. Managing Dir. Michel Camdessus says the growth rate, the strongest since the early 1970s, offers "a window of opportunity" for developing countries to dismantle trade barriers.			Rebellious Argentine Army soldiers surrender to loyal government troops after staging a five-day mutiny—the army's third in 20 months—to protest the imprisonment of military officers convicted of human rights abuses and to demand an increase in military spending.	
Dec. 7	Following a private meeting with UN Sec. Gen. Javier Perez de Cuellar and Gen. Assembly Pres. Dante Caputo, Mikhail S. Gorbachev becomes the first Soviet leader to address the UN Gen. Assembly in New York since 1960.	The parliament of the republic of Estonia reaffirms its November declaration of sovereignty and ignores a ruling by the Presidium (executive council) of the national Supreme Soviet that the November declaration is unconstitutional.	Palestine Liberation Org. (PLO) chairman Yasir Arafat concludes a two-day meeting with American Jews in Sweden by declaring explicitly that the PLO accepts Israel and condemns terrorism; U.S. and Israeli officials immediately fault Arafat's statement as inadequate.... Imprisoned African National Congress leader Nelson Mandela is moved from a Cape Town clinic to a guarded house on the grounds of a prison farm in what appears to be a South African government strategy of releasing Mandela in stages.	A Nicaraguan judge orders the release of the 10 remaining prisoners jailed for participating in an antigovernment protest in Nandaime in July, after giving them suspended sentences.	
Dec. 8		On the first day of a two-day meeting in Brussels, the foreign ministers of the North Atlantic Treaty Org. (NATO) propose a sharp reduction in the number of main battle tanks in the European arsenals of NATO and the Warsaw Pact.	Seaborne Israeli troops raid a Palestinian guerrilla base near Beirut in their deepest ground attack inside Lebanon since 1983. Israel calls the operation a success, but it draws swift international and domestic criticism.		
Dec. 9	A midterm review of the Uruguay Round of the General Agreement on Tariffs and Trade breaks down when the United States and the European Community fail to agree on agriculture trade reform.	A motion of censure by the rightist Rally for the Republic against the government of France's socialist Premier Michel Rocard, which has been plagued by public sector strikes in recent weeks, fails.			
Dec. 10	Political figures and human rights activists from around the world gather in Paris to mark the 40th anniversary of the UN Universal Declaration on Human Rights.	The European Community (EC) says a ban on the importation of U.S. meat from hormone-fed cattle will go into effect Jan. 1, 1989. Originally set to take effect Jan. 1, 1988, the ban will affect about $150 mil. of U.S. meat exports to the EC annually.			
Dec. 11		The Soviet Council of Ministers (cabinet) adopts a resolution calling for the national currency, the ruble, to be devalued by 50% on Jan. 1, 1990. The plan is part of a program to attract foreign investment and facilitate trade.... Norway's final 1989 budget is submitted to parliament by the Labor government. The budget predicts a lower surplus than previously expected, because of lower oil export revenues.	An effort by South Africa's Conservative Party (CP) to reintroduce "petty apartheid" in towns under its control following municipal elections in October, backfires as blacks effectively boycott white-owned shops, panicking white merchants and leading them to repudiate the CP moves.		

A	B	C	D	E
Includes developments that affect more than one world region, international organizations and important meetings of major world leaders.	Includes all domestic and regional developments in Europe, including the Soviet Union, Turkey, Cyprus and Malta.	Includes all domestic and regional developments in Africa and the Middle East, including Iraq and Iran and excluding Cyprus, Turkey and Afghanistan.	Includes all domestic and regional developments in Latin America, the Caribbean and Canada.	Includes all domestic and regional developments in Asia and Pacific nations, extending from Afghanistan through all the Pacific Islands, except Hawaii.

U.S. Politics & Social Issues	U.S. Foreign Policy & Defense	U.S. Economy & Environment	Science, Technology & Nature	Culture, Leisure & Life Style	
President-elect George Bush names Houston businessman Robert A. Mosbacher Sr. as commerce secretary, Stanford Univ. economist Michael J. Boskin as chairman of the White House Council of Economic Advisers, Washington lawyer Carla Hills as U.S. trade representative, and career diplomat Thomas R. Pickering as U.S. ambassador to the UN. William H. Webster will remain director of central intelligence.... The Supreme Court rules that the Labor Dept. improperly denied disability benefits to about 100,000 miners afflicted with black-lung disease, but the court restricts any remedy from its ruling only to those cases still pending.... In an address to the American Medical Assoc.'s House of Delegates meeting in Dallas, Asst. Attorney Gen. Charles R. Rule warns the nation's doctors that price fixing is a violation of anti-trust laws.	Soviet leader Mikhail S. Gorbachev visits New York City for two days of brief talks with Pres. Reagan and president-elect George Bush.	An Energy Dept. report lists 155 instances of contamination at the 16 nuclear weapons production plants in the United States. The assessment of environmental problems at the nation's vast nuclear arms complex confirms that they are more serious than officially revealed heretofore.	The space shuttle *Atlantis* successfully completes a secret four-day mission during which it is widely reported to have placed in orbit a $500 mil. advanced radar reconnaissance satellite to monitor most of the Soviet Union.	Roy Orbison, 52, singer and songwriter who was one of the world's most popular recording artists in the early 1960s, dies of a heart attack in Nashville. Between 1960 and 1964 he was the top-selling male singer in the world with such songs as "Only the Lonely, Running Scared, Crying, Blue Bayou," and "Oh, Pretty Woman." After several personal tragedies he began a successful comeback effort in 1987.	Dec. 6
		Outstanding consumer debt rose $3.56 bil. in October, the Commerce Dept. reports. The increase, at an annual rate of 6.5%, is attributed to both continued strength in credit-card purchases and increased auto sales.... The Federal Aviation Admin. (FAA) fines 29 airlines more than $1.6 mil. for security lapses at passenger checkpoints through which undercover FAA agents carried mock weapons hidden in carry-on baggage or on their person.		Auburn Univ. defensive tackle Tracy Rocker is named the winner of the Outland Trophy as the nation's top interior lineman in college football.	Dec. 7
			A National Aeronautics and Space Admin. official at the Marshall Space Flight Center reports that hot gases improperly penetrated insulation in five of the 10 nozzle joints in the shuttle *Discovery* during launch in September.		Dec. 8
			At a spirited meeting of the American Geophysical Union, a team that recently proclaimed Isaac Newton's Law of Gravity in need of revision concedes that its measurements do not prove the case.	*Mississippi Burning*, a film about two Federal Bureau of Investigation agents confronting racism in Mississippi as they probe the disappearance of three civil-rights workers in 1964, is released in New York. The movie is directed by Alan Parker and stars Gene Hackman, Willem Dafoe, and Frances McDormand.	Dec. 9
			Western Europe's Ariane-4 rocket is launched from Kourou, French Guiana, and deploys two telecommunications satellites, one for television broadcasts to Europe and the other for British military communications.		Dec. 10
					Dec. 11

F	G	H	I	J
Includes elections, federal-state relations, civil rights and liberties, crime, the judiciary, education, health care, poverty, urban affairs and population.	Includes formation and debate of U.S. foreign and defense policies, veterans' affairs and defense spending. (Relations with specific foreign countries are usually found under the region concerned.)	Includes business, labor, agriculture, taxation, transportation, consumer affairs, monetary and fiscal policy, natural resources, and pollution.	Includes worldwide scientific, medical and technological developments, natural phenomena, U.S. weather, natural disasters, and accidents.	Includes the arts, religion, scholarship, communications media, sports, entertainments, fashions, fads and social life.

	World Affairs	Europe	Africa & the Middle East	The Americas	Asia & the Pacific
Dec. 12		The last person known to have been convicted of "anti-Soviet agitation," Vasif Melyanov, is freed after eight years of internal exile.	The kidnappers of U.S. Marine Lt. Col. William R. Higgins, head of the UN Truce Supervision Org. in Lebanon, say that they decided to "execute" him after he confessed to spying for Israel and the Central Intelligence Agency.	The 34th Canadian parliament opens with Queen Elizabeth II's Speech from the Throne, read by Gov. Gen. Jeanne Sauve as the representative of the British monarch. P.M. Brian Mulroney recalled parliament before the end of 1988 to achieve swift passage of the enabling legislation related to the U.S.-Canada trade pact. . . . The government of Mexico's newly installed Pres. Carlos Salinas de Gortari announces an economic package that eases a year-old anti-inflation program under which wages and prices were frozen.	Pakistan's acting president, Ghulam Ishaq Khan, who assumed power in August after the death of longtime Pakistani leader Muhammad Zia ul-Haq, is elected to a five-year presidential term. P.M. Benazir Bhutto wins a mandatory vote of confidence in the National Assembly less than two weeks after taking office.
Dec. 13		Ireland's Attorney Gen. John Murray announces that Ireland will not extradite suspected terrorist Patrick Ryan to Great Britain because of doubts that he will receive a fair trial. The decision provokes an angry response from Britain's P.M. Margaret Thatcher.	Palestine Liberation Org. chairman Yasir Arafat proposes a three-point peace plan in an address to the UN Gen. Assembly in Geneva, where it reconvened after the United States refused him a visa to visit New York. . . . Meeting in Brazzaville, Congo, representatives from Angola, Cuba, and South Africa sign a U.S.-mediated agreement providing for the independence of Namibia (South-West Africa) and the withdrawal of Cuban troops from Angola.		
Dec. 14		Nearly 8 million Spanish workers stay off their jobs in what is described as the widest general strike in that nation since 1934. The one-day job action is in protest of the socialist government's economic policies. . . . Swedish police arrest a suspect in suburban Stockholm in connection with the unsolved 1986 slaying of Premier Olof Palme. Press reports identify the accused as Carl Gustav Christer Pettersson. . . . The East German government liberalizes rules governing travel abroad; East Germans are now allowed to leave the country for funerals of aunts, uncles, and in-laws, rather than only for a member of the immediate family.			

A	B	C	D	E
Includes developments that affect more than one world region, international organizations and important meetings of major world leaders.	Includes all domestic and regional developments in Europe, including the Soviet Union, Turkey, Cyprus and Malta.	Includes all domestic and regional developments in Africa and the Middle East, including Iraq and Iran and excluding Cyprus, Turkey and Afghanistan.	Includes all domestic and regional developments in Latin America, the Caribbean and Canada.	Includes all domestic and regional developments in Asia and Pacific nations, extending from Afghanistan through all the Pacific Islands, except Hawaii.

U.S. Politics & Social Issues	U.S. Foreign Policy & Defense	U.S. Economy & Environment	Science, Technology & Nature	Culture, Leisure & Life Style	
In an address billed as his farewell speech on domestic policy, Pres. Reagan blames the growth and persistence of federal budget deficits on what he calls an "iron triangle" of Congress, the press, and special interest groups. . . . The Supreme Court rules, 5-4, that the National Collegiate Athletic Assoc. did not violate Univ. of Nevada-Las Vegas basketball coach Jerry Tarkanian's constitutional rights when it disciplined him for recruiting and other violations. . . . A government report warns that a growing shortage of registered nurses could erode hospital care in the United States and recommends that federal funds be used to recruit and train new nurses and provide better pay for practicing nurses. . . . In an attempt to defuse tensions arising from his description of the Indian lifestyle as "primitive," Pres. Reagan holds his first meeting with American Indian leaders since he took office. Reagan also told a Soviet audience in May that the United States had probably erred in "humoring" Indians by allowing them to remain on reservations. . . . The *Wall Street Journal* reports that the supporters of Vice Pres. George Bush (R) and Gov. Michael S. Dukakis (D, Mass) each spent more than $100 mil., making 1988 the most expensive presidential campaign on record.		The National Forest Service announces that it will bar logging in parts of national forests in Oregon and Washington to protect the spotted owl, whose only habitat is the aged forests of the Pacific Northwest.			Dec. 12
A presidential advisory commission unanimously recommends that the salaries of members of Congress, judges, and top executive-branch officials be increased by 50% or more. In exchange for congressional increases to $135,000 (from $89,500), the commission recommends that members give up speaking fees and restrict travel paid for by private interests.		The deficit in the U.S. balance of payments on current account narrowed 8.4% in the third quarter, the Commerce Dept. reports.	The *New York Times* reports that scientists designing the world's biggest atom smasher, the Superconducting Super Collider, have encountered problems making the giant magnets that are to be the driving force of the machine. . . . The Food and Drug Admin. approves the sale of a test that takes only five minutes to screen for the presence of the acquired immune deficiency syndrome virus. Previous tests required a minimum of three hours.		Dec. 13
(William) Stuart Symington, 87, Democratic senator from Missouri from 1953 to 1976, dies of a heart ailment in New Canaan, Conn. He entered government service in 1945 when Pres. Harry S Truman appointed him chairman of the Surplus Property Admin. He was later assistant secretary of war for air and, when the Air Force was formed in 1947, was named its first secretary. During the Army-McCarthy hearings of 1954, he emerged as a strong opponent of Sen. Joseph R. McCarthy, and from the 1960s he was a vocal critic of military spending and the U.S. presence in Vietnam.	In a major shift in U.S. Middle East policy, Sec. of State George P. Shultz announces that Pres. Reagan has authorized the opening of a "substantive dialogue" with the Palestine Liberation Org.	The U.S. merchandise trade deficit shrank to a seasonally adjusted $10.35 bil. in October, the Commerce Dept. reports. . . . The Federal Reserve Board reports that U.S. factories, mines, and utilities operated at 84.2% of capacity in November. The increase brings capacity utilization to its highest level since November 1979. . . . The Federal Reserve Board reports that its industrial production index rose 0.5% in November. . . . President-elect George Bush names Clayton K. Yeutter, the Reagan administration's trade representative, to be his secretary of agriculture.		CBS, Inc. wins the rights to broadcast Major League Baseball games for four years beginning in 1990. The $1.1 bil. CBS bid tops ones by American Broadcasting Co. and National Broadcasting Co., which have shared network broadcasting rights since 1975.	Dec. 14

F	G	H	I	J
Includes elections, federal-state relations, civil rights and liberties, crime, the judiciary, education, health care, poverty, urban affairs and population.	Includes formation and debate of U.S. foreign and defense policies, veterans' affairs and defense spending. (Relations with specific foreign countries are usually found under the region concerned.)	Includes business, labor, agriculture, taxation, transportation, consumer affairs, monetary and fiscal policy, natural resources, and pollution.	Includes worldwide scientific, medical and technological developments, natural phenomena, U.S. weather, natural disasters, and accidents.	Includes the arts, religion, scholarship, communications media, sports, entertainments, fashions, fads and social life.

	World Affairs	Europe	Africa & the Middle East	The Americas	Asia & the Pacific
Dec. 15		Foreign rescue teams begin leaving the Soviet republic of Armenia, bringing an end to significant efforts to locate survivors of the earthquake that struck December 7. The earthquake has left several cities in ruins, including Spitak, where 90% of the 20,000 inhabitants are dead.... Unemployment in Britain fell in November for the 28th consecutive month, according to government figures. A total of 2.11 million people were unemployed, the lowest number since April 1981.... The U.S.-Soviet talks on banning underground nuclear tests conclude their third and final scheduled round in Geneva. The two nations are unable to reach agreement.... The British government publishes a bill aimed at reducing job discrimination against Roman Catholics in Northern Ireland. Unemployment among Catholic men in Ulster is 17%, compared with 7% among their Protestant counterparts.		Canada's Supreme Court votes, 5-0, to strike down a controversial section of Bill 101, the 1977 Quebec law that made French the official language of the province and that is the centerpiece of francophone nationalism in Quebec.... The Salesian order of the Roman Catholic Church says it has expelled Haitian Rev. Jean Bertrand Aristide, an activist priest, for using religion to incite hatred and violence. The order had directed Aristide to leave Haiti by October 17, but he did not.	The human rights organization Amnesty International says that a "pattern of torture" has reemerged in the Philippines as a result of the government's increased efforts to crush a communist insurgency.
Dec. 16		European Community Comm. Pres. Jacques Delors announces the commissioners in the new 17-member group, which will serve from early January through 1992, the target date for the barrier-free internal European market.... The British government publishes its Social Security Bill 1988-89. The bill is aimed at cutting the unemployment benefits of those not actively seeking work or those who refuse a job because of low wages.	United Nations-brokered peace talks in Geneva between Iran and Iraq on reaching a permanent end to the Persian Gulf war are postponed indefinitely.... In South Africa, a gathering of far-right white separatists draws a much larger crowd than the official ceremony addressed by Pres. Pieter W. Botha during celebrations of the 150th anniversary of the Great Trek, the most sacred Afrikaner holiday.		
Dec. 17			In Tunis, Palestine Liberation Org. chairman Yasir Arafat vows to do his best to curb terrorism; at the same time he accuses Israel of "state terrorism" for its killing of Palestinians in the occupied territories.	Pres. Alan Garcia resigns as head of Peru's ruling American Popular Revolutionary Alliance (APRA). His political rival, Sen. Luis Alva Castro, gains control of the party three days later when he is voted secretary general.	
Dec. 18	The World Bank issues a report calling for the development of a new developing-country debt strategy that emphasizes voluntary reduction by lenders of existing privately held debt.	Under growing criticism for a banking scandal, a decision to free a terrorist suspect, and his public appearances with his mistress, Greece's Premier Andreas Papandreou wins a crucial parliamentary vote on his 1989 budget.... Denmark's 1989 budget includes reductions of about $1.5 bil. in health and welfare spending. The budget totals $31 bil.		Diplomats and officials cited in today's *New York Times* say that a UN team visiting Cuba in September found 121 long-term political prisoners held there, but little evidence of torture or inhumane conditions.	Soviet Foreign Min. Eduard A. Shevardnadze begins a tour of Asia with a visit to Japan, his first in nearly three years, to hold talks aimed at improving relations between the two countries.

A	B	C	D	E
Includes developments that affect more than one world region, international organizations and important meetings of major world leaders.	*Includes all domestic and regional developments in Europe, including the Soviet Union, Turkey, Cyprus and Malta.*	*Includes all domestic and regional developments in Africa and the Middle East, including Iraq and Iran and excluding Cyprus, Turkey and Afghanistan.*	*Includes all domestic and regional developments in Latin America, the Caribbean and Canada.*	*Includes all domestic and regional developments in Asia and Pacific nations, extending from Afghanistan through all the Pacific Islands, except Hawaii.*

U.S. Politics & Social Issues	U.S. Foreign Policy & Defense	U.S. Economy & Environment	Science, Technology & Nature	Culture, Leisure & Life Style	
Saying that such a policy could result in poor care for Medicare patients, the General Accounting Office criticizes health maintenance organizations for giving financial rewards to doctors who hold down costs.... The National Center for Health Statistics reports that in 1987 the life expectancy of black Americans decreased, while that for white Americans increased.			The 13-nation European Space Agency agrees to support Horizon 2000, a 20-year program to mount astronomy satellites and unmanned probes around the solar system.		Dec. 15
President-elect George Bush names former Sen. John Tower (R, Tex.) as secretary of defense. Although Bush aides indicated his preference for Tower more than a month ago, the appointment was delayed while a background check was completed and unflattering rumors circulated about the appointee.... In the Iran-Contra conspiracy case, independent counsel Lawrence E. Walsh appoints San Francisco attorney John Keker to be the chief prosecutor at Oliver L. North's trial. ... A federal jury in Alexandria, Va., convicts political extremist Lyndon H. LaRouche Jr. and six associates of conspiracy and mail fraud involving $34 mil. in loans solicited by the LaRouche organization between 1983 and 1987.... The *Los Angeles Times* reports that gang violence in Los Angeles reached a record level in 1988, with at least 236 gang killings as of this date, 15% more than in all of 1987.		The government's producer price index rose 0.3% in November, the Labor Dept. reports.... Housing starts climbed 1.4% in November, the Commerce Dept. reports, to a seasonally adjusted annual rate of 1.563 million.	A treaty to protect Earth's ozone shield comes into force with formal endorsement by the European Community, whose 12 members and the United States (which has also ratified) represent more than two-thirds of world production areas.	*Rain Man*, about a Los Angeles car salesman and his autistic brother who come to know each other on a cross-country trip, opens in New York. The film wins the Academy Award for best picture, director (Barry Levinson), and original screenplay (Ronald Bass and Barry Morrow), and stars Dustin Hoffman (best actor) and Tom Cruise.	Dec. 16
A Committee for the Study of the American Electorate study finds that 1988 voter turnout was the lowest in a presidential election since 1924, with only 91,602,291 Americans, or 50.16% of those eligible to vote, casting ballots.					Dec. 17
				In tennis West Germany upsets defending champion Sweden, four matches to one, in Goteborg, Sweden, to win the 1988 Davis Cup.	Dec. 18

F	G	H	I	J
Includes elections, federal-state relations, civil rights and liberties, crime, the judiciary, education, health care, poverty, urban affairs and population.	*Includes formation and debate of U.S. foreign and defense policies, veterans' affairs and defense spending. (Relations with specific foreign countries are usually found under the region concerned.)*	*Includes business, labor, agriculture, taxation, transportation, consumer affairs, monetary and fiscal policy, natural resources, and pollution.*	*Includes worldwide scientific, medical and technological developments, natural phenomena, U.S. weather, natural disasters, and accidents.*	*Includes the arts, religion, scholarship, communications media, sports, entertainments, fashions, fads and social life.*

	World Affairs	Europe	Africa & the Middle East	The Americas	Asia & the Pacific
Dec. 19			Israel's P.M. Yitzhak Shamir agrees to form a coalition government with his own right-wing Likud Party and the center-left Labor Party, led by longtime rival Shimon Peres. The accord ends political haggling and governmental paralysis that followed Israel's indecisive November 1 general elections. . . . Egyptian police round up 300 suspects and three militants are killed during a major crackdown on Islamic fundamentalists that began after the stabbing death of a high-ranking security agent in a Cairo suburb in early December.	In Canada, Manitoba Premier Gary Filmon stuns the political community by announcing that he will not push for ratification of the Meech Lake constitutional accord until Quebec changes its language policy.	Voters in Sri Lanka go to the polls in the first presidential election since 1982. The balloting follows three months of election-related violence that has all but crippled the country and left hundreds of people dead.
Dec. 20	The UN Security Council votes unanimously to send a 70-man unarmed observer force to Angola to oversee the withdrawal of Cuban troops. . . . Forty-three nations in Vienna sign a UN convention on drug trafficking and abuse that calls for extradition of suspected drug traffickers among signatory countries and backs the right to confiscate assets. . . . A United Nations Children's Fund report estimates that 500,000 children have died in the past year from the deceleration or reversal of development programs in less developed countries caused by onerous external debt burdens. . . . The Org. for Economic Cooperation and Development's *World Economic Outlook* calls economic conditions in its 24 industrialized member countries "more buoyant than at any time since the early 1970s," and projects that real gross national product in the industrialized world will expand 3.25%.		The International Committee of the Red Cross in Lebanon withdraws its 17-member staff after they receive death threats. It is the first time in its 125-year history that the Red Cross has suspended operations to protect its workers. . . . The Sudanese government of P.M. Sadiq al-Mahdi declares a state of emergency in Khartoum following reports of an attempted coup. The following day 25 supporters of former Pres. Gaafar el-Nimeiry are arrested.		
Dec. 21	The UN Gen. Assembly approves spending plans for the years 1988 through 1991. Under new procedures championed by the United States, the budgets are approved by consensus.	A Pan Am jetliner flying from London to New York City breaks apart and crashes into the village of Lockerbie, Scotland. All 244 passengers and 15 crew members on board are killed in the crash. As of December 23, at least 11 residents of Lockerbie will also be reported dead, or missing and believed dead.			Five days after Vanuatu's Pres. George Sokomanu ordered P.M. Father Walter Lini to dissolve the parliament, Lini orders security forces to arrest Pres. Sokomanu, and charges him with sedition and inciting a mutiny. . . . The South Korean government implements an amnesty program for 2,015 people who had been convicted or accused of "politically motivated" crimes.

A	B	C	D	E
Includes developments that affect more than one world region, international organizations and important meetings of major world leaders.	*Includes all domestic and regional developments in Europe, including the Soviet Union, Turkey, Cyprus and Malta.*	*Includes all domestic and regional developments in Africa and the Middle East, including Iraq and Iran and excluding Cyprus, Turkey and Afghanistan.*	*Includes all domestic and regional developments in Latin America, the Caribbean and Canada.*	*Includes all domestic and regional developments in Asia and Pacific nations, extending from Afghanistan through all the Pacific Islands, except Hawaii.*

U.S. Politics & Social Issues	U.S. Foreign Policy & Defense	U.S. Economy & Environment	Science, Technology & Nature	Culture, Leisure & Life Style	
President-elect George Bush selects Rep. Jack Kemp (R, N.Y.) to head the Dept. of Housing and Urban Development.... Electors of the Electoral College cast their ballots for president and vice president. Vice Pres. George Bush (R) earned 426 presidential electoral votes to 112 for his rival Gov. Michael S. Dukakis (D, Mass.) in the November 8 election.... The National Assoc. for the Advancement of Colored People Legal Defense and Educational Fund reports that only 11 prisoners were executed in 1988, down from 25 in 1987 and 18 per year in 1985 and 1986.	A Ford Foundation panel of civilian and military defense experts cochaired by Defense Secretaries Harold Brown and James R. Schlesinger finds that the two-year effort to reform the Defense Dept.'s procurement practices has failed.	A jury finds Shell Oil Co. responsible for cleaning up toxic waste on land it leased from the Army at Rocky Mountain Arsenal near Denver. Previously it had been determined that Shell would split the cleanup costs with the U.S. Army.	The National Aeronautics and Space Admin. makes public long-range plans that include a base on the Moon and a manned expedition to Mars.		Dec. 19
		The government's consumer price index rose 0.3% in November, the Labor Dept. reports. The increase, at a compound annual rate of 4.4%, follows a 0.4% rise in October.... Leading U.S. stock indexes end the year at levels considerably higher than expected in the aftermath of the October 1987 stock market collapse; but stock markets remain at levels well beneath precrash highs.... The Farmers Home Admin. lost $22 bil. in fiscal 1987, leaving the lending agency with a cumulative deficit of $36 bil., according to a General Accounting Office audit.	Computer scientists at Concordia Univ. in Montreal prove that a type of finite geometry known as a projective plane of order 10 cannot exist; it has been described as one of the "top 10" problems in combinatorial analysis.		Dec. 20
The judge in the Iran-Contra conspiracy case announces in Washington, D.C., that the trial of former National Security Council staff member Oliver L. North is to begin Jan. 31, 1989.	Pres. Reagan says the United States and its allies are "discussing" the possibility of taking military action against a Libyan facility suspected of being a chemical weapons factory.... Eric Arturo Delvalle, who was ousted as president of Panama in February, arrives in the United States for talks with American officials, who still recognize Delvalle as president though he lives in hiding in Panama.	Drexel Burnham Lambert Inc. agrees to plead guilty to six felony violations of federal securities law and to pay penalties of $650 mil. The agreement, on criminal charges of wire, mail, and securities fraud, comes after a two-year investigation of the investment bank.... Personal income fell 0.2% in November while consumer spending rose 0.6%, the Commerce Dept. reports.... According to a forecast by the Battelle Memorial Institute, U.S. research and development (R&D) spending is expected to rise just 3.4% in 1989, to $129.2 bil., as against a 6% rise in 1988. Most of the slowdown is expected to be in government—primarily defense—spending.	Soviet cosmonauts Vladimir Titov and Musa Manarov return to Earth after spending a record 366 days in space.... Nikolaas Tinbergen, 81, Dutch-born British zoologist, dies in Oxford, England, after suffering a stroke. He gained prominence in the late 1930s as one of the founders of ethology, a branch of biology that studies animal behavior. In 1973 he became the first behavioralist to win the Nobel Prize for medicine or physiology.	The film *Dangerous Liaisons*, a drama of seduction and betrayal in 18th-century France, is released in New York. Directed by Stephen Frears with a screenplay by Christopher Hampton adapted from the novel *Les Liaisons Dangereuses* by Choderlos de Laclos, the film stars Glenn Close, John Malkovich, Michelle Pfeiffer, and Swoosie Kurtz.... The Danish film *Pelle the Conqueror*, about the experiences of a Swedish boy and his widowed father as farm laborers in turn-of-the-century Denmark, opens in New York. Directed and written by Bille August, based on a novel by Martin Andersen Nexo and starring Max von Sydow and Pelle Hvenegaard, the film goes on to win the Academy Award for best foreign film.... The film *Working Girl*, a comedy about a secretary who takes on the identity of her aggressive boss when the boss breaks her leg, opens in New York. Directed by Mike Nichols and written by Kevin Wade, the film stars Melanie Griffith, Sigourney Weaver, and Harrison Ford.	Dec. 21

F	G	H	I	J
Includes elections, federal-state relations, civil rights and liberties, crime, the judiciary, education, health care, poverty, urban affairs and population.	*Includes formation and debate of U.S. foreign and defense policies, veterans' affairs and defense spending. (Relations with specific foreign countries are usually found under the region concerned.)*	*Includes business, labor, agriculture, taxation, transportation, consumer affairs, monetary and fiscal policy, natural resources, and pollution.*	*Includes worldwide scientific, medical and technological developments, natural phenomena, U.S. weather, natural disasters, and accidents.*	*Includes the arts, religion, scholarship, communications media, sports, entertainments, fashions, fads and social life.*

	World Affairs	Europe	Africa & the Middle East	The Americas	Asia & the Pacific
Dec. 22			Meeting under U.S. auspices in New York City, the foreign ministers of Angola, Cuba, and South Africa sign two accords providing for the independence of Namibia (South-West Africa) and the withdrawal of 50,000 Cuban troops from Angola over a 27-month period.	Francisco Mendes Filho (known as Chico Mendes) is shot to death at his home in the northeastern village of Xapuri, Brazil. An outspoken opponent of the destruction of Brazil's Amazon rain forests, he received the 1987 UN Global 500 ecology prize for his work to save the forests. He was also president of the Xapuri rural workers union, an organization of itinerant rubber tappers.	
Dec. 23	The Polish Sejm passes two laws lifting restrictions on private business. The passage of the new legislation marks the end of a year-long battle over the reforms within the government and Communist Party.... A deputy premier of the Soviet Armenian republic announces an end of efforts to locate any more survivors of the December 15 Armenian earthquake. By an official count, about 18,000 people were found alive in the rubble. Some 8,000 of that number later died.	In an effort to reassure the UN that it will not intimidate voters in the Namibian (South-West African) elections, South Africa has agreed to reduce the territory's police force by over 1,000 men and to disband Koevoet (crowbar), a 3,000-man paramilitary force.... Amal and Palestine Liberation Org. guerrillas loyal to Yasir Arafat agree to end their long feud in southern Lebanon and announce a disengagement of forces and exchange visits in their respective strongholds in Sidon and Tyre.	A Colombian judge is reported to have been granted asylum in the United States after being kidnapped and threatened with death for prosecuting members of Colombia's powerful drug cartels. The judge was granted asylum in November after traveling to the United States in 1986.... Cuba's central planning board chief Antonio Rodriguez Maurell tells the National People's Assembly that the nation's economy will grow by 1.5% to 2.5% in 1989.	India's P.M. Rajiv Gandhi concludes a five-day visit to China. The trip is the first to China by an Indian leader since Gandhi's grandfather, P.M. Jawaharlal Nehru, visited in 1954, and the first summit meeting between the two countries since 1960.... Real estate values in Japan jumped 20.2% in fiscal 1987, the largest such increase in 14 years.	
Dec. 24		In the Soviet Union the Communist Party commission appointed to oversee relief efforts in the wake of the December 15 Armenian earthquake estimates that reconstruction will cost $10.9 bil.			The upper house of the Japanese Diet enacts the country's first major tax reform plan in 40 years. Passage of the six separate bills is considered an important political victory for Premier Noboru Takeshita.
Dec. 25			Egypt's Pres. Hosni Mubarak says he is willing to pay his first visit to Israel if it will help revive the Middle East peace process. Israel's P.M. Yitzhak Shamir and the United States warmly greet the prospect.		In the past 10 days, Vietnam has withdrawn six infantry divisions, totaling 18,000 troops, from Cambodia as part of its pledge to halve its military contingent there by the end of the year.
Dec. 26		Britain's North Sea oil output is cut by 10% when a floating oil collection platform, the supertanker Medora, breaks loose from its moorings over the weekend, forcing the closing of three oil fields.	In black townships near Pietermaritzburg, Natal, South Africa, 12 people are reported killed in two days of violence between the conservative Inkatha organization and radical Congress of South African Trade Unions. The killings come despite a September truce between the two Zulu groups.		
Dec. 27		The Italian cabinet decrees a package of tax changes including a reduction in income tax for salaried employees and a partial amnesty for self-employed tax evaders. The 1989 budget deficit is targeted at $91.4 bil. but the actual gap is expected to be greater.	Morocco's King Hassan II agrees to meet with the Polisario Front, a rebel movement, for talks aimed at ending the war over the disputed Western Sahara.		Chinese police remove African students to the security of a private guesthouse 50 miles outside Nanjing following a violent confrontation with Chinese students at a dance at Hehai Univ. on December 24.

A	B	C	D	E
Includes developments that affect more than one world region, international organizations and important meetings of major world leaders.	Includes all domestic and regional developments in Europe, including the Soviet Union, Turkey, Cyprus and Malta.	Includes all domestic and regional developments in Africa and the Middle East, including Iraq and Iran and excluding Cyprus, Turkey and Afghanistan.	Includes all domestic and regional developments in Latin America, the Caribbean and Canada.	Includes all domestic and regional developments in Asia and Pacific nations, extending from Afghanistan through all the Pacific Islands, except Hawaii.

U.S. Politics & Social Issues	U.S. Foreign Policy & Defense	U.S. Economy & Environment	Science, Technology & Nature	Culture, Leisure & Life Style	
Vice Pres. George Bush appoints Louis W. Sullivan as secretary of health and human services; Samuel K. Skinner, secretary of transportation; Rep. Manuel Lujan Jr. (R, N.M.), secretary of the interior; former Rep. Edward J. Derwinski (R, Ill.), secretary of veterans affairs; and William K. Reilly, administrator of the Environmental Protection Agency.... In a television interview, Pres. Reagan says many homeless people "make it their own choice" not to seek shelter and that a "large percentage" are "retarded" people who voluntarily leave institutions in which they are placed.... New York City Mayor Edward I. Koch establishes a five-member commission to investigate allegations of corruption and other misdeeds in the city's public school system.... District Judge Stephen V. Wilson rules that key provisions of the 1952 McCarran-Walter Act are unconstitutional because they deprive immigrants of rights to free speech and make aliens subject to deportation for advocating communism or totalitarianism.		The Federal Aviation Admin. reports that the U.S. government alerted airlines, airports, and embassies in Europe of a possible attack on an airliner after a caller told the U.S. Embassy in Finland December 5 that a Pan Am plane flying from Frankfurt to the United States would be the target of a bombing attempt within the next two weeks.... A federal grand jury in Santa Cruz, Calif., indicts 25-year-old computer hacker Kevin D. Mitnick on charges that he stole computer programs via telephone link-ups and by using unauthorized long-distance service codes.	Citing unexpected findings following the 1986 *Challenger* disaster, a National Research Council panel urges the National Aeronautics and Space Admin. to renew efforts to improve the space shuttle booster rocket.		Dec. 22
				Publishers Weekly's hardback fiction best-sellers for the week are: *The Sands of Time*, Sidney Sheldon; *The Cardinal of the Kremlin*, by Tom Clancy; *The Queen of the Damned*, Anne Rice; *One*, Richard Bach; *Alaska*, James Michener.	Dec. 23
	Vice Pres. George Bush chooses former Reagan cabinet secretary Elizabeth H. Dole to be his secretary of labor.				Dec. 24
					Dec. 25
					Dec. 26
In its first comprehensive effort to calculate the economic well-being of Americans, the Census Bureau reports that federal government programs have done more than employment or taxes to reduce inequality of household income.				A poll of international news agencies in 36 nations conducted by the Soviet press agency Tass names U.S. sprinter Florence Griffith Joyner the top athlete of 1988.... Hal Ashby, 59, film director, dies of liver and colon cancer in Malibu, Calif. His many popular movies included *Shampoo*, *Coming Home*, *The Last Detail*, and *Being There* as well as the cult hit *Harold and Maude*. In 1968, he won an Academy Award for editing the film *In the Heat of the Night*.	Dec. 27

F	G	H	I	J
Includes elections, federal-state relations, civil rights and liberties, crime, the judiciary, education, health care, poverty, urban affairs and population.	Includes formation and debate of U.S. foreign and defense policies, veterans' affairs and defense spending. (Relations with specific foreign countries are usually found under the region concerned.)	Includes business, labor, agriculture, taxation, transportation, consumer affairs, monetary and fiscal policy, natural resources, and pollution.	Includes worldwide scientific, medical and technological developments, natural phenomena, U.S. weather, natural disasters, and accidents.	Includes the arts, religion, scholarship, communications media, sports, entertainments, fashions, fads and social life.

	World Affairs	Europe	Africa & the Middle East	The Americas	Asia & the Pacific
Dec. 28		Leaders of the 12 European Community nations conclude a two-day summit in Hanover, West Germany, in an air of relative harmony. On the most contentious issue facing the summit, the leaders establish a high-level group to study how the community can move toward a common currency, perhaps overseen by a common central bank. . . . British investigators confirm that the crash of Pan Am Flight 103 in Lockerbie, Scotland, on December 21 was caused by a powerful explosive device. . . . A report released by the advocacy group Shelter says that there were 370,000 people in Britain recognized as homeless by local authorities as of 1987, the latest year for which figures are complete. The group estimates that the total number of homeless might be as high as 1 million.		Canada's Immigration Min. Barbara McDougall announces that the government will not grant amnesty to, or relax its screening process for, immigrants claiming refugee status.	An Australian government commission investigating the deaths of Aborigines in police custody issues an interim report that calls for a number of changes in police procedures regarding Aborigine prisoners. . . . Japan's Nikkei average, the main index of the Tokyo Stock Exchange, rises 108.07 points to end 1988 at a record high 30,159.00. . . . South Korea's Premier Kang Young Hoon announces that South Korea has agreed to hold high-level political and military talks with North Korea in an effort to ease tensions between the two countries.
Dec. 29			More than a year after their yacht was seized, allegedly by the Abu Nidal Palestinian terrorist group, two French girls are freed; the girls' mother and five Belgians remain in captivity in Lebanon.	Mexico's congress votes its approval of the government's 1989 budget. All 170 opposition members present vote against the bill, protesting that the 60% of the budget destined for foreign debt payments is excessive.	India's P.M. Rajiv Gandhi and the newly elected prime minister of Pakistan, Benazir Bhutto, meet for the first time in Islamabad, Pakistan, at the fourth annual summit of the seven-nation South Asian Assoc. for Regional Cooperation.
Dec. 30		Yugoslavia's Premier Branko Mikulic and his cabinet resign in an economic dispute with the parliament. It is the first time that a Yugoslav government has fallen since the communists came to power in 1945. . . . The London Stock Market's Financial Times-Stock Exchange index of 100 stocks closes the year at 1793.1, up 4.7% for the year. A high for the year of 1892.2 was reached on June 23.		Two days after final passage in the House of Commons by a 141-111 vote, Bill C-2 implementing the Canadian end of the U.S.-Canada trade accord receives royal assent. The trade agreement is to take effect on Jan. 1, 1989. . . . Colombia says it has suspended payment on its $16.5 bil. foreign debt until the government can obtain $1.7 bil. in new financing, expected in three months' time. . . . In a surprise move, Venezuela says it will suspend payments on its foreign debt. The move is reportedly necessitated by rising international interest rates and depressed oil prices.	
Dec. 31				Brazil's annual inflation rate reaches a record high of 934% in 1988. The figure is nearly three times the previous record of 366% recorded in 1987, according to preliminary data released by the Brazilian Statistical Institute.	

A	B	C	D	E
Includes developments that affect more than one world region, international organizations and important meetings of major world leaders.	Includes all domestic and regional developments in Europe, including the Soviet Union, Turkey, Cyprus and Malta.	Includes all domestic and regional developments in Africa and the Middle East, including Iraq and Iran and excluding Cyprus, Turkey and Afghanistan.	Includes all domestic and regional developments in Latin America, the Caribbean and Canada.	Includes all domestic and regional developments in Asia and Pacific nations, extending from Afghanistan through all the Pacific Islands, except Hawaii.

U.S. Politics & Social Issues	U.S. Foreign Policy & Defense	U.S. Economy & Environment	Science, Technology & Nature	Culture, Leisure & Life Style	
The Boston school committee agrees in principle to a plan under which parents could choose from a number of nearby public schools when deciding where to send their children.... A majority of high school students tested in a national survey do not understand basic economic terms and principles, according to a study by the private, nonprofit Joint Council on Economic Education.	Pres. Reagan extends the territorial waters of the United States from three to 12 miles; the United States is the 105th nation to proclaim the 12-mile limit under the authority of 1982 UN Convention on the Law of the Sea.... Vice Pres. George Bush causes some controversy by appointing Robert M. Gates, a career intelligence officer, as his deputy national security adviser.... A Pentagon advisory panel recommends the closing of 86 domestic military bases as a money-saving measure.	Claiming it has suffered "heavy and growing financial injury," the American Telephone & Telegraph Co. files antidumping complaints against 12 leading Japanese, Taiwanese, and South Korean manufacturers of small-business telecommunications equipment. ... U.S. businesses plan to increase spending on new plant and equipment 6% in 1989, the Commerce Dept. reports, far less than the 10.4% rise in business spending estimated for 1988, which was the largest in five years.	Researchers at Edinburgh Univ. in Scotland find that some cancers involve the loss of cancer-suppressing genes that are normally present.	*Variety*'s top-grossing films for the week are: *Rain Man, Twins, Working Girl, The Naked Gun: From the Files of Police Squad*, and *Dirty Rotten Scoundrels*.	**Dec. 28**
The *Washington Post* reports that Washington, D.C., Mayor Marion S. Barry (D) was in the hotel room of a drug suspect when police detectives were about to attempt to make an undercover purchase from the suspect.		The Federal Aviation Admin. announces new security rules on U.S. airlines operating in Western Europe and the Middle East. All luggage checked on board will be inspected, either by hand or by X ray, beginning December 31.... The Federal Deposit Insurance Corp. says it has managed 200 bank failures and provided assistance to 21 other troubled banks with total assets of $53.8 bil., a record in the 55-year history of the federal agency.... U.S. industry is expected to expand for the seventh straight year in 1989, driven by continued export growth and an increased demand for services, the Commerce Dept. reports.			**Dec. 29**
Political appointees of the Reagan administration are reminded to submit their resignations, subject to the pleasure of their cabinet secretary so that incoming Bush cabinet members will not be faced with half-empty offices when they take over.... Pres. Reagan and Vice Pres. George Bush receive subpoenas to testify as defense witnesses in the pending Iran-Contra conspiracy trial of former National Security Council staff member Oliver L. North.... Television evangelist and former presidential candidate the Rev. Pat Robertson agrees to pay $25,000 in fines for election-law violations, the Federal Election Comm. announces.		Gross national product grew at a revised 2.5% annual rate in the third quarter, the Commerce Dept. reports. The current final report is the last of two revisions.... The U.S. dollar ends the year against most major currencies above end-of-1987 levels. The dollar closes the year at 124.95 Japanese yen and 1.7700 West German marks, up about 4% and 13.4%, respectively, since the start of 1988.... The government's index of leading economic indicators drops 0.2% in November, the Commerce Dept. reports.... Prices received by farmers for raw agricultural goods rose 0.7% in December, the Agriculture Dept. reports. The December increases leave average prices received by farmers about 14% greater than in December 1987. Farm prices rose a revised 0.7% in November and fell 0.7% in October.... The Court of Appeals for the District of Columbia orders an environmental review of the Interior Dept.'s five-year plan for leasing offshore oil and gas.		Isamu Noguchi, 84, sculptor, dies of heart failure in New York City. With their combination of Oriental and contemporary sensibilities, his works bridged the gap between Eastern and Western aesthetics. Although he occasionally experimented with modern materials, he preferred clay, wood, and stone. His works ranged from small, delicate pieces to large, public sculpture gardens, and he also created stage settings for dance works by Martha Graham, George Balanchine, and Merce Cunningham.	**Dec. 30**
		The Federal Home Loan Bank Board (FHLBB) ends 1988 with a week of selling savings and loan institutions with assets totaling $18.58 bil. for which the FHLBB agrees to provide more than $4.8 bil. in financial assistance.		*Billboard*'s best-selling albums for the week are: *Giving You the Best That I Got*, Anita Baker; *Rattle and Hum*, U2; *Cocktail* (soundtrack); *Appetite for Destruction*, Guns N' Roses (Geffen); and *New Jersey*, Bon Jovi.	**Dec. 31**

F	G	H	I	J
Includes elections, federal-state relations, civil rights and liberties, crime, the judiciary, education, health care, poverty, urban affairs and population.	*Includes formation and debate of U.S. foreign and defense policies, veterans' affairs and defense spending. (Relations with specific foreign countries are usually found under the region concerned.)*	*Includes business, labor, agriculture, taxation, transportation, consumer affairs, monetary and fiscal policy, natural resources, and pollution.*	*Includes worldwide scientific, medical and technological developments, natural phenomena, U.S. weather, natural disasters, and accidents.*	*Includes the arts, religion, scholarship, communications media, sports, entertainments, fashions, fads and social life.*

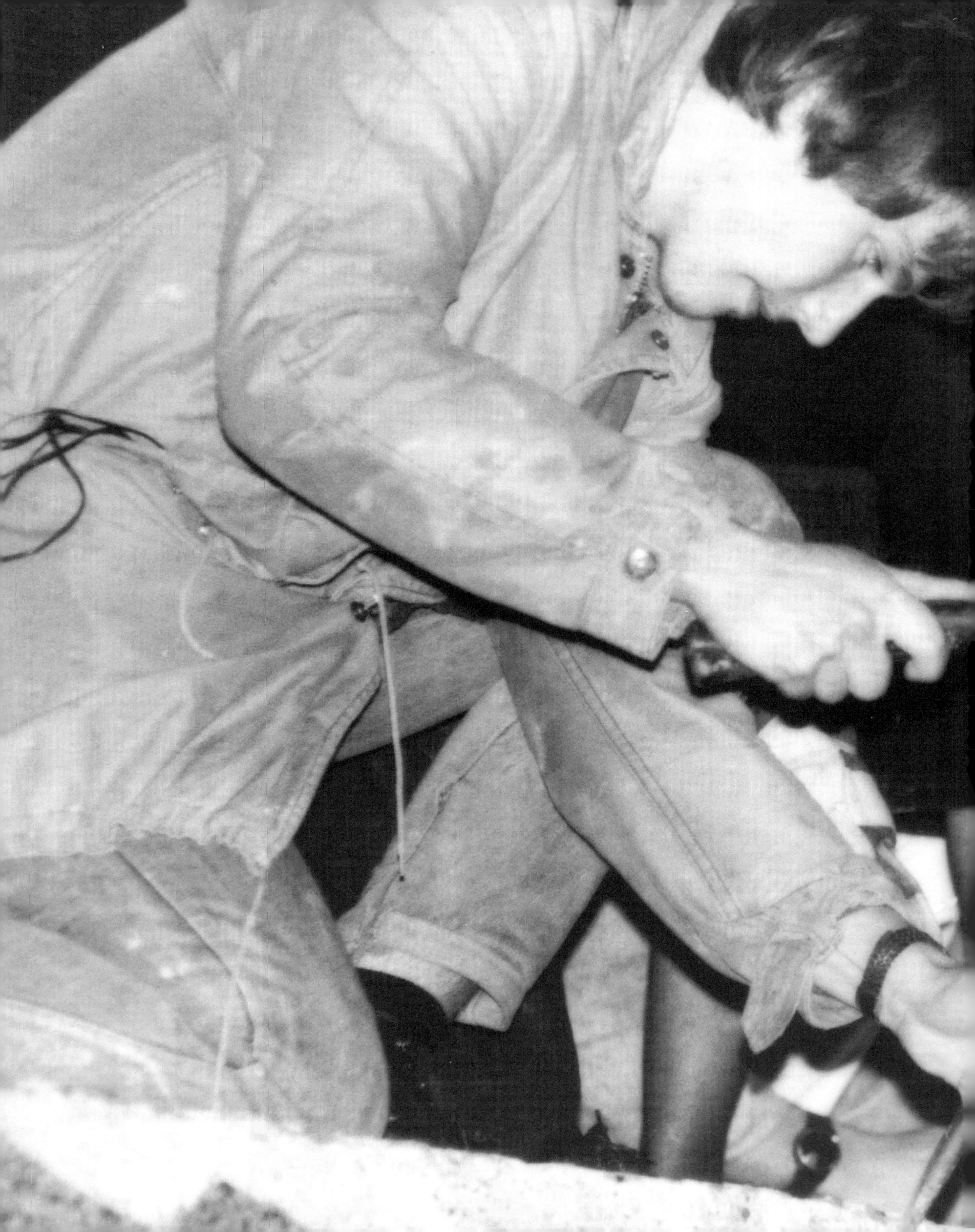

1989

A Berliner chips away at the top of the Berlin Wall erected between East and West Berlin in 1961.

	World Affairs	Europe	Africa & the Middle East	The Americas	Asia & the Pacific
Jan.	A Paris conference of 149 nations called by France's Pres. Francois Mitterrand to give impetus to the UN Conference on Disarmament condemns the use of chemical weapons.	The European Community imposes a ban on all imports of beef from hormone-treated cattle, and the United States retaliates by imposing 100% tariffs on $100 mil. of imported EC food products.	Two U.S. Navy F-14 fighters shoot down two Libyan MiG-23 fighters in a clash over international waters in the Gulf of Sidra off the Libyan coast.	The government of Argentina announces several emergency measures designed to offset a severe electricity shortage that has left the country in danger of a national blackout.	Fearing a breakdown in security as Soviet troops withdraw from the country, the major Western-allied nations begin closing their embassies in Afghanistan.
Feb.	Iran's Ayatollah Ruhollah Khomeini pronounces a death sentence on British author Salman Rushdie and the publishers of his "blasphemous" novel, The Satanic Verses.	The prominent dissident Czechoslovak playwright Vaclav Havel is convicted on charges connected to January protests and is sentenced to nine months in jail.	South Africa's antiapartheid organizations disown Winnie Mandela, wife of jailed black nationalist leader Nelson Mandela, saying she has "abused the trust" of the black community.	Gen. Alfredo Stroessner, Paraguay's president for 34 years, is overthrown in a military coup led by second-ranking officer Gen. Andes Rodriguez that leaves scores of people dead.	The Indian Supreme Court orders U.S.-based Union Carbide Corp. to pay $470 mil. in compensation to victims of a 1984 gas leak at the company's chemical plant in Bhopal, India.
March	More than 100 nations agree on a treaty to control the export of hazardous wastes across national borders, a pact designed to curb the dumping of toxic waste in developing countries.	The Conventional Forces in Europe talks designed to facilitate cuts in non-nuclear forces, from the Atlantic Ocean to the USSR's Ural Mountains, formally opens.	The Bush administration unveils proposals it hopes will lessen tension between Israel and the Palestine Liberation Org. in the Israeli-occupied West Bank and Gaza Strip.	Alfredo Cristiani, 41, candidate of the right-wing Nationalist Republican Alliance, defeats Christian Democrat Fidel Chavez Mena in presidential elections in El Salvador.	The first major battle in the Afghan war since the withdrawal of Soviet troops in February begins when rebel forces launch an offensive against the eastern city of Jalalabad.
April	The International Monetary Fund and World Bank broadly endorse a new U.S. developing-country debt-reduction plan and pledge to provide resources to facilitate its implementation.	In keeping with a pledge by Soviet leader Mikhail S. Gorbachev to reduce Soviet forces deployed in Eastern Europe, the Soviet Union begins a formal withdrawal of forces from Hungary.	Over 450 people die as tensions between Senegal and Mauritania erupt into communal riots. An international airlift repatriates 50,000 people from both countries.	Nicaragua's Pres. Daniel Ortega Saavedra signs an electoral reform and media laws, as required under a regional agreement reached by five Central American presidents.	Vietnam announces that it will withdraw all its troops from Cambodia by September 30, nearly 11 years after invading the country to oust Pol Pot's Khmer Rouge regime.
May	The U.S. dollar rises to a 29-month high on currency markets despite intervention by the U.S. Federal Reserve and at least nine other central banks.	The Congress of People's Deputies, the new Soviet parliament, opens with 2,250 deputies in attendance, the majority of them workers and academicians chosen through direct elections.	Frederik W. de Klerk, widely expected to become South Africa's president in September, vows to pursue constitutional and social reforms but rejects the idea of black majority rule.	In Argentina, the Peronist movement returns to power after 13 years when Justicialist Party candidate Carlos Saul Menem wins decisively in the presidential election.	Mikhail S. Gorbachev's state visit to China for the first Sino-Soviet summit in 30 years is eclipsed by massive pro-democracy demonstrations led by Chinese university students.
June	Ali Akbar Hashemi Rafsanjani, speaker of the Iranian parliament, travels to the Soviet Union in a trip that marks a pronounced warming of relations between the two nations.	Poland's communist regime suffers a humiliating defeat as candidates endorsed by the independent trade union Solidarity all but sweep parliamentary elections.	Ayatollah Ruhollah Khomeini, the catalyst of the Iranian revolution against Shah Mohammed Riza Pahlevi, dies; Pres. Ali Khamenei is chosen as the nation's leader.	Argentine Pres. Raul Alfonsin announces that he will resign and allow Peronist president-elect Carlos Saul Menem to assume office five months early.	Tens of thousands of Chinese Army troops crush student-led pro-democracy protests in Beijing that began in mid-April. General Sec. Zhao Ziyang and other top officials are ousted.
July	Leaders of the seven major industrial democracies pledge to cooperate on preserving the global environment and to support the U.S. developing-country debt initiative.	Janos Kadar, 77, Hungarian leader who ruled from the 1956 uprising against Soviet domination until 1988, dies of pneumonia and circulatory ailments in Budapest.	A Lebanese group issues a videotape showing that it has hanged Marine Lt. Col. William R. Higgins after Israeli commandos abduct a Shiite Moslem sheik from southern Lebanon.	In Cuba, former army major general Arnaldo Ochoa Sanchez and three other officers are executed following their convictions for drug smuggling and other criminal activities.	In parliamentary elections, Japan's Liberal Democratic Party suffers a stunning defeat, losing its majority in the upper house of the Diet for the first time since 1955.
Aug.	Banca Nazionale del Lavoro, Italy's largest state-owned bank, discloses that it is under investigation by U.S. and Italian authorities for "procedurally improper practices."	Poland's Sejm confirms Solidarity activist Tadeusz Mazowiecki as the country's new premier in the first known democratic transfer of power away from a ruling communist party.	South Africa's Pres. Pieter W. Botha resigns following a bitter showdown with his cabinet. Ruling National Party leader Frederick W. de Klerk is sworn in as acting president.	Colombia's Pres. Virgilio Barco imposes a curfew in 10 cities, including Medellin, as the government intensifies its crackdown on drug traffickers.	Former Education Min. Toshiki Kaifu is elected premier of Japan, replacing Sosuke Uno, who resigned amid scandal after barely two months in office.
Sept.	In an address to the UN General Assembly, Soviet Foreign Min. Eduard A. Shevardnadze urges the elimination of superpower chemical-arms stockpiles and a ban on production.	More than 13,000 East Germans leave Hungary for West Germany via Austria in the largest exodus of East Germans to the West since the construction of the Berlin Wall in 1961.	Egypt's Pres. Hosni Mubarak and Israel's Defense Min. Yitzhak Rabin discuss Egypt's plan to break a stalemate over Palestinian elections in the Israeli-occupied territories.	Presidential appointee Francisco Rodriguez is sworn in as president of Panama. Opposition candidate Guillermo Endara is believed to have won the election by a three-to-one margin.	Vietnam completes the withdrawal of its troops from Cambodia, 10 years and nine months after invading the country to topple the Khmer Rouge regime of Pol Pot and install a pro-Vietnamese government.
Oct.	The Nobel Peace Prize is awarded to the Dalai Lama, the exiled religious and political leader of Tibet, for his efforts to free his homeland from Chinese rule using nonviolent means.	The Hungarian Socialist Workers' (Communist) Party renounces Marxism, renames itself the Hungarian Socialist Party, and embraces democratic socialism as its guiding doctrine.	South African authorities release Walter Sisulu and seven senior members of the outlawed African National Congress, which holds a technically illegal rally in Soweto.	Officers of the Panamanian Defense Forces attempt to overthrow Gen. Manuel Antonio Noriega in an unsuccessful coup thought to have been backed by the United States.	China celebrates the 40th anniversary of Communist Party rule with a day of parades and fireworks staged amid extremely tight security in Beijing's Tiananmen Square.
Nov.	Org. of Petroleum Exporting Countries sets new oil production quotas in an agreement that signals a willingness to base quota allotments on the production capacities of individual members.	Czechoslovakia's Communist Party leadership is replaced and the new regime hastens to make concessions on reform in the face of mounting opposition led by the Civic Forum.	Namibian voters give the leftist South-West African People's Org. a majority, but not the two-thirds majority needed for it to write its own constitution for the territory.	In El Salvador, government troops are widely believed responsible for the murder of six Jesuits and two female employees.	India's P.M. Rajiv Gandhi announces his resignation after it becomes clear that his ruling Congress (I) party has lost its majority in parliament in general elections.
Dec.	At a shipboard summit with Pres. Bush in Marsaxlokk Bay, Malta, Soviet Pres. Mikhail S. Gorbachev declares an end to the Cold War. Pres. Bush adopts a more cautious attitude.	Communist regimes in Czechoslovakia, Hungary, Poland, Romania, and East Germany, collapse, the Berlin Wall falls, and Lithuania proclaims its independence from the USSR.	South Africa's Pres. F. W. de Klerk meets for the first time with jailed African National Congress leader Nelson Mandela to discuss the political future of South Africa.	Following a U.S. invasion of Panama, military strongman Gen. Manuel Antonio Noriega takes refuge in the Vatican's diplomatic mission in Panama City.	The leader of India's opposition National Front, Vishwanath Pratap Singh, is sworn in as prime minister of a minority government.

A	B	C	D	E
Includes developments that affect more than one world region, international organizations and important meetings of major world leaders.	Includes all domestic and regional developments in Europe, including the Soviet Union, Turkey, Cyprus and Malta.	Includes all domestic and regional developments in Africa and the Middle East, including Iraq and Iran and excluding Cyprus, Turkey and Afghanistan.	Includes all domestic and regional developments in Latin America, the Caribbean and Canada.	Includes all domestic and regional developments in Asia and Pacific nations, extending from Afghanistan through all the Pacific Islands, except Hawaii.

U.S. Politics & Social Issues	U.S. Foreign Policy & Defense	U.S. Economy & Environment	Science, Technology & Nature	Culture, Leisure & Life Style	
In his inaugural address, Pres. Bush calls on Americans "to make kinder the face of the nation and gentler the face of the world."	Defense Sec. Frank C. Carlucci endorses the recommendations of his Commission on Base Realignment and Closure regarding 91 domestic military bases.	Federal Bureau of Investigation agents posing as commodity traders accumulate evidence of widespread criminal fraud at the Chicago Board of Trade and the Chicago Mercantile Exchange.	Surgeon Gen. C. Everett Koop informs Pres. Reagan that he will not issue a planned report on the health risks of abortion, because the scientific data is inconclusive.	Salvador Dali, 84, Spanish-born Surrealist who was one of the best-known artists of his day, dies in Spain of heart disease and pneumonia.	Jan.
In opening arguments in the Iran-Contra trial of Oliver L. North, John W. Keker portrays North as a chronic liar who placed himself "above the law."	The Senate Armed Services Committee votes to reject John G. Tower as Pres. Bush's nominee as secretary of defense.	Treasury Sec. Nicholas F. Brady says the total cost of rescuing insolvent U.S. savings and loan institutions will likely reach an estimated $157.6 bil.	The Food and Drug Admin. announces that it will allow wider availability of the experimental drug, pentamidine, used to prevent a form of pneumonia common in AIDS patients.	Barbara Wertheim Tuchman, 77, Pulitzer Prize-winning historian whose books include The Guns of August and A Distant Mirror, dies after a stroke in Greenwich, Conn.	Feb.
A Harvard Business Review article proposing that women in managerial positions choose either a "career primary" or so-called "mommy track" career path sparks controversy.	Pres. Bush and leaders of Congress sign a bipartisan accord on Central America that includes continued humanitarian aid for the Nicaraguan Contras.	The Exxon Valdez supertanker spills 200,000 barrels of oil into the Gulf of Alaska after running aground in Prince William Sound 25 miles from the port of Valdez.	The space shuttle Discovery completes a near-perfect five-day flight with a flawless landing at Edwards Air Force Base, California.	Property developers in London grant permission for archaeologists to work on the site of the Rose Theater, where works by William Shakespeare and other playwrights were originally performed.	March
The House Ethics Committee releases a report accusing Speaker James C. Wright Jr. (D, Tex.) of violating House rules on the acceptance of gifts and outside income.	Forty-seven sailors are killed in an explosion inside a gun turret aboard USS Iowa while the battleship is taking part in naval exercises 300 miles north of Puerto Rico.	A Senate bill that would boost the minimum wage to $4.55 an hour by 1991 is sent to conference with the House; Pres. Bush has threatened a veto of the bill.	The Centers for Disease Control reports that 90,990 cases of AIDS have been reported in the United States; some 52,435 patients, or 58%, have died.	Lucille Desiree Ball, 77, one of television's most popular comediennes and star of "I Love Lucy," dies in a hospital in Los Angeles following emergency heart surgery.	April
House Speaker James C. Wright Jr. says he will resign from Congress for violating ethics rules. Oliver L. North is found guilty on three counts in the Iran-Contra arms scandal.	Sec. of State James A. Baker III calls on Israel to renounce any designs on the occupied territories and begin a serious dialogue with its Palestinian foes.	Congress gives final approval to a compromise $1.2 trillion budget plan for FY1990 based on a deficit reduction agreement worked out with the Bush administration.	Eighty nations represented at a meeting in Helsinki, Finland, call for an end to the production of ozone-damaging chlorofluorocarbons (CFCs), by the year 2000.	Pablo Picasso's 1901 self-portrait, Yo Picasso, is sold to an unidentified buyer for a record $47.85 mil.	May
A scandal involving mismanagement and corruption at the Dept. of Housing and Urban Development grows amid revelations about misconduct at both the federal and local level.	The House gives conditional approval for an agreement between the United States and Japan on the joint development of a new Japanese fighter plane, the FSX.	The United States remains the world's largest debtor nation at the end of 1988 as its net debt widens 40% to $532.5 bil., the Commerce Dept. reports.	A report in the New England Journal of Medicine finds the AIDS virus can lie dormant in humans for up to three years before it is detected with standard blood tests.	The Corcoran Gallery of Art in Washington, D.C., cancels a planned exhibit of the works of controversial photographer Robert Mapplethorpe, who died in March of AIDS.	June
The Supreme Court upholds a Missouri abortion law and sets the stage for dismantling of Roe v. Wade, the 1973 decision recognizing a constitutional right to abortion.	Pres. Bush travels to Eastern Europe to show U.S. support for political and economic reforms in Poland and Hungary.	Pres. Bush sends Congress proposals to tighten controls against air pollution by utilities, automobile manufacturers and other manufacturing facilities and small businesses.	An Energy Dept. panel concludes that there is scant evidence for so-called "cold fusion," the popular name for nuclear fusion produced with a tabletop apparatus.	Laurence Olivier, 82, the most renowned film and stage actor and director of the century, dies in his sleep at his home in Steyning, England.	July
Documents from former Housing and Urban Development secretary, Samuel R. Pierce Jr., expose widespread political favoritism at the scandal-ridden department.	Pres. Bush nominates Army Gen. Colin L. Powell as chairman of the Joint Chiefs of Staff. If confirmed, Powell would be the first black ever to head the Joint Chiefs.	Pres. Bush signs thrift industry bailout legislation that will provide some $166 bil.—three-quarters of it from taxpayers—over 10 years to close or merge insolvent thrifts.	Climaxing a 12-year mission, the Voyager 2 spacecraft passes within 3,000 miles of Neptune and generates striking images and startling discoveries about the distant planet.	Pitcher Nolan Ryan of Major League Baseball's Texas Rangers becomes the first man to strike out 5,000 batters.	Aug.
The murder of a black teenager answering a newspaper advertisement for a used car in a predominantly white neighborhood in Brooklyn, N.Y., inflames racial tensions throughout the city.	The Central Intelligence Agency has reportedly dismissed the intelligence officer responsible for supplying U.S. military aid to the Afghan rebels due to complaints about mismanagement of the supply program.	In a significant legislative victory for the president, the House rejects a Democratic alternative to a capital gains tax cut backed by Pres. Bush.	Hurricane Hugo rips through the Caribbean from Guadeloupe to the southeast United States, causing billions of dollars in damage and leaving tens of thousands of people homeless.	Irving Berlin, 101, Russian-born American songwriter whose classics include God Bless America and White Christmas, dies in his sleep at home in New York City.	Sept.
Pres. Bush vetoes a spending bill that includes a provision allowing the use of Medicaid funds to pay for abortions for poor women who are victims of rape or incest.	Pres. Bush holds separate talks at the White House with Zaire's Pres. Mobutu Sese Seko and Angolan rebel leader Jonas Savimbi in an effort to end Angola's civil war.	Pres. Bush orders $16.1 bil. in automatic, across-the-board spending cuts when the government fails to meet the Gramm-Rudman deficit reduction deadline.	An earthquake measuring 7.1 on the Richter scale strikes northern California, killing 67 people and destroying buildings and roadways in the San Francisco Bay area.	Spain's Camilo Jose Cela, 73, antifascist publisher and author of the novel The Family of Pascual Duarte among other works, wins the Nobel Prize in literature.	Oct.
The Senate Ethics Committee votes to hire an outside counsel to investigate six senators involved in the failed Lincoln Savings and Loan Assoc.	The United States agrees to return $567 mil. in Iranian assets frozen since 1979 in a move described as unconnected to the issue of U.S. hostages in Lebanon.	Congress clears and Pres. Bush signs legislation raising the federal government's debt ceiling to $3.123 trillion for the current fiscal year.	Astronomers discern an enormous sheet of scattered galaxies arrayed almost in a plane, the largest structure ever discovered, at the farthest reaches of the universe.	National Endowment for the Arts Chairman John E. Frohnmayer suspends a $10,000 federal grant for a "political" art exhibit about AIDS, but reverses himself under pressure from the arts community.	Nov.
A federal judge in Washington, D.C., orders former Pres. Ronald Reagan to submit documents to the court to see if they are relevant to the Iran-Contra trial of John M. Poindexter.	State Dept. officials say the United States will not soon return to the UN Educational, Scientific and Cultural Org., from which it withdrew in 1984 because of its anti-Western bias.	Pres. Bush signs a $14.7 bil. deficit reduction bill designed to lower the federal deficit to the $100 bil. maximum allowed under the Gramm-Rudman balanced budget law for FY1990.	The National Academy of Sciences reports that exposure to low levels of radiation is three to four times more likely to cause fatal cancer than has been previously assumed.	Samuel Beckett, 83, Irish-born Nobelist whose plays, including Waiting for Godot, had a major impact on 20th-century drama, dies of a respiratory ailment in Paris.	Dec.

F	G	H	I	J
Includes elections, federal-state relations, civil rights and liberties, crime, the judiciary, education, health care, poverty, urban affairs and population.	Includes formation and debate of U.S. foreign and defense policies, veterans' affairs and defense spending. (Relations with specific foreign countries are usually found under the region concerned.)	Includes business, labor, agriculture, taxation, transportation, consumer affairs, monetary and fiscal policy, natural resources, and pollution.	Includes worldwide scientific, medical and technological developments, natural phenomena, U.S. weather, natural disasters, and accidents.	Includes the arts, religion, scholarship, communications media, sports, entertainments, fashions, fads and social life.

	World Affairs	Europe	Africa & the Middle East	The Americas	Asia & the Pacific
Jan. 1		The European Community (EC) imposes a ban on imports of beef from hormone-treated cattle, which affects $130 mil. of U.S. exports. The United States retaliates by imposing 100% tariffs on $100 mil. of EC food products.	Israel's Finance Min. Shimon Peres unveils a new austerity plan calling for budget cuts of $550 mil., $220 mil. in reductions of government subsidies for food and gasoline, and the elimination of thousands of government jobs.	As Cuba celebrates the 30th anniversary of the revolution that brought Pres. Fidel Castro to power, Castro reaffirms his commitment to the fundamentals of Marxism-Leninism.	India announces that it will withdraw two battalions of peacekeeping troops from Sri Lanka within a week. Various news reports estimate the number of troops involved at between 2,000 and 4,000.
Jan. 2				Brazil's foreign debt dropped by 5.2% in 1988, to $114.9 bil., according to the country's central bank. Despite the decrease, Brazil remains the Third World's largest debtor.	Tibetan exiles in India are dismayed by a recent statement signed by Indian P.M. Rajiv Gandhi recognizing Chinese sovereignty over the disputed autonomous region of Tibet, according to a spokesman for the Dalai Lama, the spiritual leader of more than 1.5 million Tibetans worldwide.
Jan. 3		New statistics released by the Italian state statistical agency show that Italy remains the noncommunist world's sixth-leading economic power, behind the United States, Japan, West Germany, France, and Britain.... Amnesty International releases a report saying that "torture, deaths in custody, political imprisonment and unfair trials" continue to infest the Turkish justice system.... Poland's Defense Min. Florian Siwicki says that "tens of thousands" of the nation's military personnel will be demobilized as an economic measure.		In Canada, the total number of diagnosed cases of AIDS reached 2,292 by the end of 1988, according to the Federal Center for AIDS.	
Jan. 4		Turkey's Foreign Min. Mesut Yilmaz has reportedly agreed to open Turkish files dating back to the Ottoman Empire and concerning the alleged genocide of 1.5 million Armenians in 1915.	Claiming "self-defense" in the face of "hostile intent," two U.S. Navy F-14 fighters shoot down two Libyan MiG-23 fighters in a clash over international waters off the Libyan coast. Libya says its aircraft were unarmed victims of a "premeditated attack." ... Morocco's King Hassan II holds direct talks with leaders of the Polisario Front, the guerrilla movement that has waged a 13-year war against Moroccan troops for control of the Western Sahara.		
Jan. 5	European Community (EC) ambassadors approve a European Commission proposal to impose 100% duties on $96.6 mil. worth of imported U.S. walnuts and dried fruits in response to U.S. punitive tariffs on EC goods.	Britain's savings rate fell to just 1.3% of disposable income in the third quarter of 1988, its lowest level since the 1940s, according to government figures.			Chinese authorities release 45 African students who were confined to the Yangzhou guesthouse for 10 days as a result of racial unrest between African and Chinese students. Three Africans and three Chinese remain in detention.... African students in Hangzhou, China end a 10-day boycott of classes after the university president agrees to publish an open letter declaring that none of the students is infected with Acquired Immune Deficiency Syndrome as a university receptionist had told callers.
Jan. 6					Despite a flurry of last-minute appeals for clemency, Satwant Singh and Kehar Singh are hung at the Tihar central jail in New Delhi for their involvement in the 1984 assassination of P.M. Indira Gandhi.... Cambodia's Pres. Heng Samrin announces that Vietnam will complete the withdrawal of its troops from Cambodia by September pending a negotiated end to Vietnam's 10-year occupation of the country.

A	B	C	D	E
Includes developments that affect more than one world region, international organizations and important meetings of major world leaders.	Includes all domestic and regional developments in Europe, including the Soviet Union, Turkey, Cyprus and Malta.	Includes all domestic and regional developments in Africa and the Middle East, including Iraq and Iran and excluding Cyprus, Turkey and Afghanistan.	Includes all domestic and regional developments in Latin America, the Caribbean and Canada.	Includes all domestic and regional developments in Asia and Pacific nations, extending from Afghanistan through all the Pacific Islands, except Hawaii.

U.S. Politics & Social Issues	U.S. Foreign Policy & Defense	U.S. Economy & Environment	Science, Technology & Nature	Culture, Leisure & Life Style	
In his annual report on the state of the federal judiciary, Chief Justice William H. Rehnquist urges Congress to create 73 new federal judgeships and raise salaries of federal judges. . . . The population of the United States has reached 246.9 million—2.3 million higher than in 1988—according to Census Bureau estimates.					**Jan. 1**
				In the Rose Bowl, the Univ. of Michigan beats the Univ. of Southern California 22-14; in the Orange Bowl, the Univ. of Miami routs Nebraska 23-3; in the Sugar Bowl, Florida State takes Auburn 13-7; and in the Cotton Bowl, UCLA bests Arkansas 17-3.	**Jan. 2**
House Speaker Jim Wright (D, Tex.) and Minority Leader Robert H. Michel (R, Ill.) announce they will name a bipartisan panel to undertake the first comprehensive review of House ethics rules in more than a decade.		The amount of new corporate debt and equity offerings remained virtually unchanged in 1988, rising only 0.4% to $273.4 bil. Bonds dominated 1988 offerings as the number of new stock issues plunged.	A report by a presidential advisory panel urges that the United States develop consortia of universities, government laboratories, and industry to develop superconducting materials and create marketable products from the new technology.	Following its 34-21 victory over West Virginia in yesterday's Fiesta Bowl, Notre Dame is voted the nation's number-one college football team by the Associated Press and United Press International.	**Jan. 3**
At the official recording of presidential ballots of the Electoral College from the 1988 presidential election, Vice Pres. George H.W. Bush receives 426 votes, Massachusetts Gov. Michael S. Dukakis (D) 111, and Dukakis running mate, Sen. Lloyd M. Bentsen Jr. (Tex.) one. . . . A federal judge in Miami denies a motion by lawyers for Panama's military leader, Gen. Manuel Antonio Noriega, to dismiss charges against him of drug trafficking and racketeering.	The Justice Dept. drops all charges against a retired Israeli general and 10 international businessmen accused in April 1986 of conspiring to sell more than $2 bil. in U.S.-made weapons to Iran.	The Congressional Budget Office projects a federal budget deficit of $141 bil. for FY1990, compared with a $125 bil. figure estimated by the White House Office of Management and Budget. . . . The estimated cost of cleaning up and renovating the nation's 45 nuclear defense facilities will be several hundred billion dollars over several decades, according to an Energy Dept. study.		Alysheba wins horse racing's Eclipse Award as Horse of the Year for 1988.	**Jan. 4**
In the Iran-Contra conspiracy case, independent counsel Lawrence E. Walsh moves to dismiss the two central charges against Oliver L. North because of the Reagan administration's refusal to release documents North insists are necessary for his defense. . . . Pres. Reagan approves a recommendation by a bipartisan presidential advisory commission to increase the salaries of members of Congress, federal judges, and top executive-branch officials by 50% or more.	Defense Sec. Frank C. Carlucci endorses the recommendations of his Commission on Base Realignment and Closure which had earlier submitted a list of 91 domestic military bases to be either closed or partially shut down.		Two studies published in the *Journal of the American Medical Association* show that cigarette smokers are increasingly likely to be poor, members of a minority group, and of limited education. . . . Declaring the "future welfare of human society" at risk, the National Academy of Sciences urges president-elect George H.W. Bush to put the threat of rising global temperatures high on his agenda		**Jan. 5**
	A federal grand jury in Alexandria, Va., returns the first indictment in the Pentagon procurement scandal, which allegedly involves dozens of contractors, Pentagon employees, and private consultants.	Unemployment in December 1988 fell to 5.3%, a 14-year low, the Labor Dept. reports. The average 1988 jobless rate was 5.5%.			**Jan. 6**

F	G	H	I	J
Includes elections, federal-state relations, civil rights and liberties, crime, the judiciary, education, health care, poverty, urban affairs and population.	*Includes formation and debate of U.S. foreign and defense policies, veterans' affairs and defense spending. (Relations with specific foreign countries are usually found under the region concerned.)*	*Includes business, labor, agriculture, taxation, transportation, consumer affairs, monetary and fiscal policy, natural resources, and pollution.*	*Includes worldwide scientific, medical and technological developments, natural phenomena, U.S. weather, natural disasters, and accidents.*	*Includes the arts, religion, scholarship, communications media, sports, entertainments, fashions, fads and social life.*

	World Affairs	Europe	Africa & the Middle East	The Americas	Asia & the Pacific
Jan. 7				In an attempt to stem runaway inflation, Peru devalues the inti by 28.5% against the U.S. dollar. The new exchange rate is 700 intis to the dollar.... Darly Alves da Silva, a wealthy Brazilian rancher suspected of conspiracy in the December 1988 murder of labor leader and environmentalist Francisco Mendes Filho, surrenders to police in Acre state; he denies any involvement in the killing.	Emperor Hirohito, 87, Japan's longest-reigning monarch, dies in Tokyo of cancer. Hirohito, who ruled for 62 years, is succeeded by his only son, Crown Prince Akihito.
Jan. 8					
Jan. 9		Belgium's parliament approves a series of measures aimed at transferring power from the central government to three regions: French-speaking Wallonia in the south, Dutch-speaking Flanders in the north, and Brussels.			
Jan. 10		The Swedish government of Social Democratic Premier Ingvar Carlsson unveils its 1989-90 budget, which is designed to show a surplus for the first time since 1962.	The withdrawal of Cuban troops from Angola begins with the departure of 450 soldiers on three planes; 50,000 Cubans are to leave by July 1991.	Inflation in Mexico in 1988 fell by two-thirds to 51.7%, the government announces. The decline is attributed to an economic package that fixed the exchange rate of the peso against the U.S. dollar, and froze wages and prices.	Japan's ministry of international trade and industry announces that it will continue to impose a quota of 2.3 million units on auto exports to the United States in the fiscal year beginning April 1.
Jan. 11	A conference of 149 nations in Paris condemns the use of chemical weapons; the conference is part of an effort to push the UN Conf. on Disarmament in Geneva to achieve an international curb on chemical arms.... The United States, Britain, and France veto a UN Security Council resolution deploring the January 4 downing of two Libyan military jets by U.S. Navy fighters.	Hungary's parliament approves bills legalizing freedom of assembly and freedom of association.... In the Yugoslav republic of Montenegro, protesters force the resignation of Montenegro's collective presidency and the republic's representative in the federal collective presidency.... West Germany's gross national product grew at an inflation-adjusted 3.4% in 1988, according to preliminary figures.			
Jan. 12		The official Soviet news agency Tass reports that the disputed Nagorno-Karabakh Autonomous Region—an ethnic-Armenian enclave within the Azerbaijan republic—will be placed under "special administration."		Following two days of secret talks between presidential adviser Rafael Pardo and rebel leader Carlos Pizarro Leongomez, the government of Colombia signs a peace pact with the leftist April 19 Movement (M-19).	

A	B	C	D	E
Includes developments that affect more than one world region, international organizations and important meetings of major world leaders.	*Includes all domestic and regional developments in Europe, including the Soviet Union, Turkey, Cyprus and Malta.*	*Includes all domestic and regional developments in Africa and the Middle East, including Iraq and Iran and excluding Cyprus, Turkey and Afghanistan.*	*Includes all domestic and regional developments in Latin America, the Caribbean and Canada.*	*Includes all domestic and regional developments in Asia and Pacific nations, extending from Afghanistan through all the Pacific Islands, except Hawaii.*

U.S. Politics & Social Issues	U.S. Foreign Policy & Defense	U.S. Economy & Environment	Science, Technology & Nature	Culture, Leisure & Life Style	
					Jan. 7
		The U.S. Export-Import Bank says it is suspending new direct lending to U.S. exporters because of a Reagan administration budget proposal to eliminate the bank's lending authority. The action does not affect its $10.2 bil. loan-guarantee program.		The Cincinnati Bengals win the National Football League's American Conference Championship with a 21-10 victory over the Buffalo Bills. The San Francisco 49ers beat the Chicago Bears, 28-3, for the National Football Conference title.	**Jan. 8**
The Supreme Court agrees to review a Missouri abortion law, which could open to review the high court's landmark 1973 *Roe* v. *Wade* ruling recognizing a woman's right to an abortion. . . . Surgeon Gen. Dr. C. Everett Koop, a long-time abortion opponent, surprises both liberals and conservatives by informing Pres. Reagan that he will not issue a planned report on the health risks of abortion because the scientific data are inconclusive.	A federal district judge in Brownsville, Tex., issues a temporary restraining order suspending a 1988 immigration policy that has left hundreds of Central American immigrants living in primitive camps at their point of entry until their applications for political asylum can be processed.	Pres. Reagan proposes a $1.15 trillion budget for FY1990 that will increase defense spending 2% faster than inflation and bring the deficit below the $100 bil. target set by the Gramm-Rudman law. . . . Outstanding consumer debt rose $4.48 bil. in November 1988, at an annual rate of 8.2%, the Federal Reserve Board reports.		Boston Red Sox left fielder Carl Yastrzemski and Cincinnati Reds catcher Johnny Bench are elected to the Baseball Hall of Fame. . . . The American Library Assoc. awards the John Newbery Medal for best children's book to Paul Fleischman's *Joyful Noise: Poems for Two Voices*; the Randolph Caldecott Medal for best illustrated children's book goes to Stephen Gammell for Karen Ackerman's *Song and Dance Man*. . . . The National Book Critics Circle award for fiction goes to Bharati Mukherjee for *The Middleman and Other Stories*; nonfiction, to the late Richard Ellmann for his biography *Oscar Wilde*.	**Jan. 9**
The Labor Dept. announces that Harris Trust & Savings Bank of Chicago has agreed to pay $14 mil. in back pay to women and minority employees hired between 1973 and 1988, in settlement of a long-standing federal discrimination suit.		Housing starts fell 2.2% in December 1988, the Commerce Dept. reports. The total number of housing units started in 1988 fell to 1.487 million. . . . House Banking Committee members have their first look at the details of the 34 thrift transactions arranged by the Federal Home Loan Bank Board in December 1988 in which $4 bil. in tax breaks were guaranteed to the buyers of insolvent institutions.			**Jan. 10**
In what he says will be his last speech from the Oval Office, Pres. Reagan delivers a farewell address to the nation. . . . According to a Labor Dept. survey of 7,502 business and factory locations employing 4.5 million workers, less than 1% of the nation's work force was subjected to drug testing during a 15-month period in 1987-88.		The Supreme Court rules, 8-1, that states have broad power to bar utilities from billing consumers for the costs of planning and constructing facilities canceled before they were put in use.	In a report issued on the 25th anniversary of the first surgeon general's report on smoking, Surgeon Gen. C. Everett Koop reports that cigarette smoking has caused more deaths than previously believed.	In Canada, a federal inquiry into drug use in amateur sports opens in Toronto. The inquiry is triggered by the scandal surrounding sprinter Ben Johnson, who was stripped of an Olympic gold medal after testing positive for steroids.	**Jan. 11**
President-elect George Bush names former Education Sec. William J. Bennett to the newly created cabinet-level post of "drug czar" to coordinate the war on drugs. . . . A Louis Harris survey conducted for the National Association for the Advancement of Colored People Legal Defense and Educational Fund indicates that whites think blacks are better off than blacks themselves do.		President-elect George Bush names retired Adm. James D. Watkins to the post of secretary of energy. . . . The National Air Traffic Controllers Assoc. reaches tentative agreement with the Federal Aviation Admin. in the controllers' first labor pact since the Professional Air Traffic Controllers Org. was dissolved in 1981.	Sixteen leading U.S. electronics manufacturers agree to work together to develop high-definition television (HDTV) technology that will enable them to capture a major share of the potentially huge U.S. HDTV market.	The Sadler's Wells Royal Ballet will move its operations from London to Birmingham as of August.	**Jan. 12**

F	G	H	I	J
Includes elections, federal-state relations, civil rights and liberties, crime, the judiciary, education, health care, poverty, urban affairs and population.	*Includes formation and debate of U.S. foreign and defense policies, veterans' affairs and defense spending. (Relations with specific foreign countries are usually found under the region concerned.)*	*Includes business, labor, agriculture, taxation, transportation, consumer affairs, monetary and fiscal policy, natural resources, and pollution.*	*Includes worldwide scientific, medical and technological developments, natural phenomena, U.S. weather, natural disasters, and accidents.*	*Includes the arts, religion, scholarship, communications media, sports, entertainments, fashions, fads and social life.*

	World Affairs	Europe	Africa & the Middle East	The Americas	Asia & the Pacific
Jan. 13		The Soviet Union's Council of Ministers orders government ministries, managers, and the nation's republics to take "drastic measures" to cut spending to alleviate chronic shortages and rising inflation that threaten *perestroika*, Mikhail S. Gorbachev's program of reforms.			The *Times* of London reports that Australia's Great Barrier Reef is in danger of being destroyed by millions of crown-of-thorns starfish that have already eaten away as much as a third of the reef.
Jan. 14	Belgium's Premier Wilfried Martens says Belgium will halt all new development plans in Zaire after Pres. Mobutu Sese Seko's government announces that it is suspending payments on Belgian loans and scrapping cooperation agreements with Belgium.	Paul Vanden Boeynants, the 69-year-old former premier of Belgium, is kidnapped in Brussels; several revolutionary groups subsequently claim responsibility for the abduction.		In Canada, housing starts declined 10% in 1988, according to Canada Mortgage and Housing Corp. preliminary figures.	
Jan. 15		The Conf. on Security and Cooperation in Europe review of the 1975 Helsinki Final Act culminates in a human rights accord many regard as the most important rights document since the Helsinki agreement itself.... Police in Leipzig, East Germany, arrest 190 people in an unauthorized civil rights demonstration, and in Prague, Czechoslovakia, riot police use force to drive 2,000 protesters from Wenceslas Square.		The government of Brazil's Pres. Jose Sarney introduces a new currency and imposes a freeze on wages and prices in an effort to stem the country's runaway inflation, which soared to a record 934% in 1988.	Two senior Soviet officials reaffirm Moscow's plans to complete the withdrawal of its troops from Afghanistan by mid-February under the terms of the Afghan peace accords signed in Geneva in 1988.
Jan. 16		Home Sec. Douglas Hurd announces that the cases of the "Guildford 4," who were convicted of the fatal October 1974 bombing of a pub in Guildford, south of London, will be reviewed by Britain's Court of Appeal.... France's 1988 inflation rate was 3.1%.		The Panamanian Defense Forces Benevolent Society opens its own bank in Panama City in what many see as a move by Gen. Manuel Antonio Noriega to expand his control over the economy and to launder drug money.	Diplomats from China and Vietnam begin four days of high-ranking talks on Cambodia for the first time in nine years. The talks, taking place in Beijing, are cloaked in secrecy.
Jan. 17		Yugoslavia's 1988 inflation rate was 251%. Social output, a broad measure of economic production, fell by 2%.	Nigeria's Pres. Ibrahim Babangida announces an easing of restrictions on foreign investment, a long debated move intended to accelerate the government's privatization and debt-conversion programs.		Western diplomats report that Soviet forces began withdrawing their remaining 50,000 troops from Afghanistan in early or mid-January.

A	B	C	D	E
Includes developments that affect more than one world region, international organizations and important meetings of major world leaders.	Includes all domestic and regional developments in Europe, including the Soviet Union, Turkey, Cyprus and Malta.	Includes all domestic and regional developments in Africa and the Middle East, including Iraq and Iran and excluding Cyprus, Turkey and Afghanistan.	Includes all domestic and regional developments in Latin America, the Caribbean and Canada.	Includes all domestic and regional developments in Asia and Pacific nations, extending from Afghanistan through all the Pacific Islands, except Hawaii.

U.S. Politics & Social Issues	U.S. Foreign Policy & Defense	U.S. Economy & Environment	Science, Technology & Nature	Culture, Leisure & Life Style	
New York City "subway vigilante" Bernhard H. Goetz is sentenced to a one-year prison term for possessing the unlicensed gun with which he shot four youths on a subway train in December 1984.		The Occupational Safety and Health Admin. restricts the use of 376 toxic and hazardous substances in the workplace in its first major overhaul of standards since the agency's formation in 1971.... The government's producer price index rose 4% in 1988, the Labor Dept. reports.... Retail sales climbed 6.7% in 1988 to a record $1.61 trillion, the Commerce Dept. reports.		Sterling Allen Brown, 87, poet, critic, and teacher of black American literature at Howard Univ., dies of leukemia in Takoma Park, Md. His students included writers Amiri Baraka and Toni Morrison, psychologist Kenneth B. Clark, and actor Ossie Davis.	Jan. 13
In his final Saturday radio broadcast to the nation, Pres. Reagan says the "economy is booming," that domestic problems are being dealt with, and that the "Soviet menace shows some signs of relenting."... Alabama's state prisons are returned to state jurisdiction after 13 years under federal control. In 1975, U.S. District Judge Frank M. Johnson Jr. ruled that the "jungle atmosphere" in the prisons exceeded "any current definition of cruel and unusual punishment."					Jan. 14
The American Council on Higher Education issues a study showing that the number of black men at U.S. colleges and universities declined from 470,000 in 1976 to 436,000 in 1986; the enrollment of black women rose from 563,000 to 645,000 in the same period.				Richard Roud, 59, American film historian, dies of a heart attack in Nimes, France. In 1963, Roud created the New York Film Festival, a major vehicle for introducing U.S. audiences to foreign films.	Jan. 15
On the birthday of slain civil rights leader Martin Luther King Jr., president-elect George H.W. Bush pledges that his administration will pursue equality for black Americans.... The predominantly black Overtown section of Miami erupts into rioting after a black motorcyclist is killed by an Hispanic police officer.					Jan. 16
An internal Justice Dept. report finds that former Attorney Gen. Edwin Meese III committed serious breaches of ethics that would have required disciplinary action had he not resigned his post in 1988.... The Senate Ethics Committee votes unanimously to hire a special counsel to investigate allegations of improprieties against five senators connected with the failed Lincoln Savings and Loan Assoc., and against Sen. Alfonse M. D'Amato (R, N.Y.), who has been linked to the Dept. of Housing and Urban Development scandal.... The Supreme Court upholds a 1982 California congressional redistricting plan by which the legislature solidified Democratic control of all 45 congressional districts.... A young gunman armed with a semiautomatic rifle and two pistols opens fire on a group of schoolchildren in Stockton, Calif., killing five pupils and wounding 29—all Southeast Asian refugees—before killing himself.		In anticipation of a single internal market in the European Community in 1992 and despite the weak dollar, U.S. businesses nearly tripled their acquisitions in Europe in 1988, to $3.6 bil.... The value of publicly reported Japanese acquisitions in the United States doubled in 1988, to a record $12.7 bil., and Japanese companies took part in 130 U.S. takeovers.			Jan. 17

F	G	H	I	J
Includes elections, federal-state relations, civil rights and liberties, crime, the judiciary, education, health care, poverty, urban affairs and population.	Includes formation and debate of U.S. foreign and defense policies, veterans' affairs and defense spending. (Relations with specific foreign countries are usually found under the region concerned.)	Includes business, labor, agriculture, taxation, transportation, consumer affairs, monetary and fiscal policy, natural resources, and pollution.	Includes worldwide scientific, medical and technological developments, natural phenomena, U.S. weather, natural disasters, and accidents.	Includes the arts, religion, scholarship, communications media, sports, entertainments, fashions, fads and social life.

	World Affairs	Europe	Africa & the Middle East	The Americas	Asia & the Pacific
Jan. 18			South Africa's Constitutional Development Min. Chris Heunis is sworn in as acting president after Pres. Pieter W. Botha suffers a mild stroke.... Former Ugandan dictator Idi Amin Dada is reportedly sent back to exile in Saudi Arabia, 15 days after he slipped into Zaire on a false passport apparently en route to Uganda a decade after he was deposed.	The volume of shares traded on Canada's five stock exchanges—Toronto, Vancouver, Alberta, Montreal, and Winnipeg—fell 26.7%, to 11 billion shares, in 1988.	Japan's overall trade surplus declined 2.9%, to $77.39 bil., in 1988 for the second year in a row, the finance ministry reports.
Jan. 19		Yugoslavia's collective presidency names as premier Ante Markovic, a member of the League of Communists' Central Committee and past president and premier of the republic of Croatia.... Britain's unemployment rate fell to a seasonally adjusted 7.2% in December 1988, according to government figures.			The Japanese finance ministry unveils its proposed budget for FY1989 and a supplementary budget for 1988. Under the 1989 budget, government spending for the fiscal year beginning April 1 will total $491 bil.
Jan. 20					
Jan. 21		A report published by *Izvestia*, the Soviet government newspaper, paints a gloomy portrait of 1988 Soviet economic performance and projects a budget deficit of at least $160 bil. by 1990.	Fearing a breakdown in security as Soviet troops withdraw and leave the Afghan Army to defend itself against the anticommunist mujaheddin rebels, Western allies begin closing their embassies in Kabul.		India's P.M. Rajiv Gandhi suffers a major setback when his Congress (I) Party finishes third in legislative elections held in the key southern state of Tamil Nadu.
Jan. 22					
Jan. 23		More than 800 people are reported arrested in six days of human rights protests in Czechoslovakia honoring the anniversary of the death of Jan Palach, who killed himself to protest the Soviet occupation in 1968.... East German leader Erich Honecker announces an impending cutback in his country's armed forces, which he characterizes as a "constructive contribution to disarmament."	Israel redoubles its efforts to crush the year-old Palestinian *intifada* or uprising, in the occupied West Bank and Gaza Strip.	El Salvador's Farabundo Marti National Liberation Front releases details of a proposal under which its member groups would agree to take part in presidential elections and abide by the results; in exchange, the rebels ask for security guarantees and a six-month postponement of the voting.	An earthquake hits the Soviet Central Asian republic of Tadzhikistan, killing more than 200 people. It is the second major earthquake in the USSR in two months. In December 1988 about 25,000 people died in an earthquake in Soviet Armenia.

A	B	C	D	E
Includes developments that affect more than one world region, international organizations and important meetings of major world leaders.	*Includes all domestic and regional developments in Europe, including the Soviet Union, Turkey, Cyprus and Malta.*	*Includes all domestic and regional developments in Africa and the Middle East, including Iraq and Iran and excluding Cyprus, Turkey and Afghanistan.*	*Includes all domestic and regional developments in Latin America, the Caribbean and Canada.*	*Includes all domestic and regional developments in Asia and Pacific nations, extending from Afghanistan through all the Pacific Islands, except Hawaii.*

U.S. Politics & Social Issues	U.S. Foreign Policy & Defense	U.S. Economy & Environment	Science, Technology & Nature	Culture, Leisure & Life Style	
The Supreme Court upholds, 8-1, the constitutionality of a revision of federal sentencing rules designed to reduce disparities in sentencing for similar crimes and to stiffen penalties for white-collar crimes. . . . According to a New York Times/CBS News poll, Pres. Reagan leaves office with a 68% approval rating, the highest of any American president at the end of his term since World War II. . . . Public Citizen's Congress Watch reports that nearly 200 House members have accumulated a total of more than $39 mil. in leftover campaign funds that will be available for personal use after retirement.	Defense Sec. Frank C. Carlucci sends his final annual report to Congress on the state of the military, which urges Congress not to make deep cuts in spending. "It is imperative that we resume a commitment to stable, moderate growth in defense funding," it says.	British companies reportedly purchased a record $33.5 bil. worth of U.S. companies and their assets in 1988. . . . Further eroding the barriers erected by the Glass-Steagall Act of 1933, the Federal Reserve Board says it will allow banks to underwrite a limited amount of corporate debt issues. . . . The Environmental Protection Agency announces an "action plan" to stem the loss of wetlands to developers and farmers.		Pres. Ronald Reagan issues presidential pardons for New York Yankees baseball owner George M. Steinbrenner III and nine others. Steinbrenner was convicted in 1974 for an illegal contribution to Pres. Richard M. Nixon's 1972 re-election campaign. . . . The fourth annual Rock and Roll Hall of Fame inductions are announced: the Rolling Stones, Dion, Otis Redding, the Temptations, and Stevie Wonder. In addition, the Ink Spots, Bessie Smith, and the Soul Stirrers are honored as early influences on rock and roll. Producer/songwriter Phil Spector is named in the nonperforming category. . . . Prima ballerina Natalia Makarova returns to the USSR for the first time in 18 years and performs with her old company, the Kirov Ballet of Leningrad.	Jan. 18
	Pres. Reagan modifies U.S. trade sanctions against Libya so that five American oil companies can resume operations there. The decision is meant to prevent Libya from reaping "the significant financial windfall" it enjoys by selling the companies' oil. . . . The Reagan administration issues a report saying that it has found no evidence of American prisoners of war in Vietnam after 1973.	The government's consumer price index rose 4.4% in 1988, equaling the 1987 increase, the Labor Dept. reports.			Jan. 19
George Herbert Walker Bush is sworn in as the 41st president of the United States and in his inaugural address calls on Americans "to make kinder the face of the nation and gentler the face of the world."		Exxon Corp.'s Imperial Oil Ltd. of Canada agrees to acquire Texaco Canada Inc. for $4.15 bil. Under the terms, Imperial agrees to pay $34.36 a share, or $3.24 bil., for Texaco Inc.'s 78% stake in Texaco Canada.		Beatrice Gladys Lillie (Lady Peel), 94, Canadian-born actress and comedienne known as "the funniest woman in the world," dies in Henley-on-Thames, England. She appeared in numerous plays, musicals, and films, including *Auntie Mame, Around the World in Eighty Days,* and *Thoroughly Modern Millie.* She won a Tony Award in 1953 for her one-woman show *An Evening with Beatrice Lillie.*	Jan. 20
David Duke, a former leader of the Ku Klux Klan, places first out of a field of seven contenders in a special primary election to fill a vacancy in the Louisiana State house of representatives.					Jan. 21
				The San Francisco 49ers come from behind to win the National Football League's Super Bowl championship game, 20-16, over the Cincinnati Bengals; 49ers wide receiver Jerry Rice is named most valuable player.	Jan. 22
Addressing the antiabortion March for Life in Washington, D.C., via telephone, Pres. Bush says he will work to repeal the 1973 Supreme Court decision legalizing abortion. . . . Miami police officer William E. Lozano is arrested and charged with manslaughter in the fatal shooting of a black motorcyclist January 16. . . . John Gotti, the reputed head of the nation's largest organized-crime group, the Gambino crime family, is arrested in New York City on charges that he ordered the shooting of a carpenters' union official.		The Supreme Court invalidates a Richmond, Va., program setting aside 30% of the city's public works funds for minority-owned construction companies.		Salvador (Salvador Domingo Felipe Jacinto Dali Domenech Cusi y Farres) Dali, 84, outspoken Spanish-born surrealist who explored the subconscious mind in paintings, films, plays, ballets, and other artistic media, dies in Spain of heart disease and pneumonia.	Jan. 23

F	G	H	I	J
Includes elections, federal-state relations, civil rights and liberties, crime, the judiciary, education, health care, poverty, urban affairs and population.	Includes formation and debate of U.S. foreign and defense policies, veterans' affairs and defense spending. (Relations with specific foreign countries are usually found under the region concerned.)	Includes business, labor, agriculture, taxation, transportation, consumer affairs, monetary and fiscal policy, natural resources, and pollution.	Includes worldwide scientific, medical and technological developments, natural phenomena, U.S. weather, natural disasters, and accidents.	Includes the arts, religion, scholarship, communications media, sports, entertainments, fashions, fads and social life.

	World Affairs	Europe	Africa & the Middle East	The Americas	Asia & the Pacific
Jan. 24		An Amnesty International report criticizes East Germany's record on human rights, especially for holding nonpublic trials under vaguely defined laws.		At least 36 people are killed and dozens more wounded in two days of fighting between heavily armed Argentine civilian rebels who seized control of a military base outside Buenos Aires and police and army troops.	The Japanese cabinet approves the FY1989 budget after increasing the original spending proposals for foreign aid to developing nations and defense to 5.9% and 7.8%, respectively.
Jan. 25		A Carmelite convent at Auschwitz, a former Nazi death camp in Poland, will be moved outside the camp grounds, Roman Catholic officials announce. Jewish groups protested the presence of the convent, which was established in 1984.		Jose Miguel Barros, Chile's ambassador to the United States in the late 1970s, testifies that he was told the 1976 assassination of former Chilean Amb. Orlando Letelier was ordered by the country's military intelligence chief. . . . El Salvador's Pres. Jose Napoleon Duarte rejects the January 23 offer by the Farabundo Marti National Liberation Front to take part in presidential elections and abide by the results.	Soviet foreign ministry spokesman Gennadi I. Gerasimov officially confirms that the final "withdrawal process" of Soviet troops from Afghanistan has started.
Jan. 26	Officials of six members of the Org. of Petroleum Exporting Countries (OPEC) and eight non-OPEC oil producers end a two-day meeting by agreeing to push oil prices toward an $18-a-barrel target.	In Britain, an independent report largely approves "Death on the Rock," a 1988 Thames Television program on the killing in Gibraltar of three Irish Republican Army operatives by British security forces to whom two of the three were reportedly trying to surrender.			
Jan. 27		Poland's government and the banned Solidarity trade union announce that talks will begin February 6 in a breathrough apparently prompted by Solidarity's conditional acceptance of the regime's offer of legalization. . . . Sir Thomas Octave Murdoch Sopwith, 101, British aircraft pioneer, dies near Winchester, England. He designed the World War I Sopwith Camel fighter plane and later helped found Hawker Aircraft Co., which produced the Hawker Harrier, the world's first vertical-take-off-and-landing aircraft.			
Jan. 28	U.S., Soviet, and Cuban officials who were involved in the Cuban missile crisis (Oct. 13-28, 1962) hold a two-day conference in Moscow to review the events of that time.		The New York Times reports that Iran used companies in the United States, West Germany, and other countries to illegally import chemicals needed for making poison gas, in response to Iraq's extensive use of these weapons in the Iran-Iraq War.		

A	B	C	D	E
Includes developments that affect more than one world region, international organizations and important meetings of major world leaders.	Includes all domestic and regional developments in Europe, including the Soviet Union, Turkey, Cyprus and Malta.	Includes all domestic and regional developments in Africa and the Middle East, including Iraq and Iran and excluding Cyprus, Turkey and Afghanistan.	Includes all domestic and regional developments in Latin America, the Caribbean and Canada.	Includes all domestic and regional developments in Asia and Pacific nations, extending from Afghanistan through all the Pacific Islands, except Hawaii.

U.S. Politics & Social Issues	U.S. Foreign Policy & Defense	U.S. Economy & Environment	Science, Technology & Nature	Culture, Leisure & Life Style	
Sentenced to death for the 1978 kidnap and murder of a 12-year-old and the murder of two Florida State Univ. students, Theodore (Ted) Bundy is electrocuted at the Florida State Prison in Starke.		Drexel Burnham Lambert Inc. enters an interim plea of not guilty to six felony counts of mail and securities fraud. Drexel also faces civil charges brought by the Securities and Exchange Comm.... The Agriculture Dept. says that 36,028 farmers failed to meet a 45-day Farmers Home Admin. deadline to declare their interest in restructuring overdue debt to the government.		Pittsburgh Steelers quarterback Terry Bradshaw and cornerback Mel Blount, Oakland and Los Angeles Raider offensive tackle Art Shell, and Green Bay Packer defensive back and kick return specialist Willie Wood are voted into the Pro Football Hall of Fame.	Jan. 24
Pres. Bush appoints an eight-member commission to recommend a code of ethics for government officials in all three branches of government.... The Senate unanimously confirms James A. Baker III as secretary of state, Richard G. Darman as director of the Office of Management and Budget, and Elizabeth H. Dole as labor secretary.				First-time novelist Paul Sayer wins Britain's Whitbread Book of the Year Prize for *The Comforts of Madness*, a novel set in the mind of a catatonic hospital patient.... *Variety*'s top-grossing films for the week are: *Rain Man*, *Twins*, *Beaches*, *Working Girl*, and *The Accidental Tourist*.	Jan. 25
The National Academy of Sciences issues a paper calling for sweeping reforms in the way mathematics is taught in the United States.... Virginia's Lieutenant Gov. L. Douglas Wilder (D) launches a campaign to succeed Gov. Gerald L. Baliles (D), who is barred by law from seeking a second consecutive term.		The Federal Home Loan Bank Board says it has filed suits against three of the largest U.S. accounting firms for issuing clean financial statements to insolvent thrifts.		Former Pres. Ronald Reagan signs a contract—reportedly worth between $1 mil. and $5 mil.—with Simon & Schuster to produce a collection of his speeches and a memoir of his eight-year presidency.... The so-called Cologne Declaration by 163 European Roman Catholic theologians criticizes Pope John Paul II for authoritarianism and for acting "in a way that does not conform with his office."	Jan. 26
In his first official news conference, Pres. Bush stresses ethics in government, reassures savings and loan depositors, and supports a tax cut for capital investments and a 50% pay hike for members of Congress.				*Publishers Weekly*'s hardback fiction best-sellers for the week are: *The Sands of Time*, Sidney Sheldon; *The Cardinal of the Kremlin*, Tom Clancy; *Breathing Lessons*, Anne Tyler; *One*, Richard Bach; and *A Season in Hell*, Jack Higgins.	Jan. 27
			The Argentine ship *Bahia Paraiso* runs aground and capsizes near Antarctica's Palmer Peninsula, spilling diesel fuel that threatens a wide variety of wildlife in the Bransfield Strait near Palmer Station. The 316 passengers and crew are rescued.	Steffi Graf wins the Australian Open women's singles title, her fifth consecutive grand slam championship.... Alysheba is named the winner of the 1988 Eclipse Award for thoroughbred racing's horse of the year.... The 46th annual Golden Globe awards are presented to *Working Girl*, for best musical or comedy film; *Rain Man*, dramatic film; Denmark's *Pelle the Conqueror*, foreign film. In the television categories: "thirtysomething" wins for best dramatic series and "The Wonder Years" musical or comedy series.	Jan. 28

F	G	H	I	J
Includes elections, federal-state relations, civil rights and liberties, crime, the judiciary, education, health care, poverty, urban affairs and population.	Includes formation and debate of U.S. foreign and defense policies, veterans' affairs and defense spending. (Relations with specific foreign countries are usually found under the region concerned.)	Includes business, labor, agriculture, taxation, transportation, consumer affairs, monetary and fiscal policy, natural resources, and pollution.	Includes worldwide scientific, medical and technological developments, natural phenomena, U.S. weather, natural disasters, and accidents.	Includes the arts, religion, scholarship, communications media, sports, entertainments, fashions, fads and social life.

	World Affairs	Europe	Africa & the Middle East	The Americas	Asia & the Pacific
Jan. 29					
Jan. 30	Appealing for broader participation in church activity by lay Roman Catholics, Pope John Paul II takes men to task for participating only sporadically in church activity and "abdicating their proper church responsibilities, allowing them to be fulfilled only by women."		Syria and Iran impose a peace settlement on rival Lebanese Shiite Moslem militias, ending a month of bitter fighting.	Pres. Daniel Ortega Saavedra announces austerity measures—including cutting the national budget by 44% and discharging as many as 35,000 public employees and security personnel—in an effort to shore up Nicaragua's battered economy.	
Jan. 31		The British government proposes an overhaul of the National Health Service that would continue free medical treatment and give doctors and hospitals more control over the allocation of medical resources. . . . Some 25,000 victims of Soviet leader Joseph Stalin's purges are rehabilitated when the Communist Party Central Committee passes a resolution authorizing the mass reversal of purge convictions.	Israel's Finance Min. Shimon Peres presents the Knesset with a $28.8 bil. budget for the fiscal year beginning in April. Debt service will take up 40% of spending, with defense receiving 22%, leaving a little over a third of the budget for all other expenditures.		Prosecutors in Seoul, South Korea, investigating charges of corruption by the government of former Pres. Chun Doo Hwan assert there is no evidence that Chun extorted money or engaged in other fundraising irregularities.
Feb. 1			Iran celebrates the 10th anniversary of the "10 Days of Dawn," when the return of Ayatollah Ruhollah Khomeini from exile precipitated the collapse of the government associated with the late Shah Mohammed Riza Pahlevi.	Canada's Defense Min. William McKnight annouces approval of a U.S. request to test an advanced version of the cruise missile over northwest Canada.	
Feb. 2			South Africa's Pres. Pieter W. Botha resigns as leader of the ruling National Party (NP). He is replaced by conservative Transvaal NP boss Education Min. Frederik W. de Klerk.	In his inauguration speech, Venezuela's Pres. Carlos Andres Perez focuses on the need for economic and government reform, and for cooperation among nations in the Western Hemisphere and among members of the Org. of Petroleum Exporting Countries.	UN relief officials report on plans for an emergency airlift to supply food and fuel to Afghan cities besieged by antigovernment forces. . . . In its first electoral test since assuming power in December 1988, the Pakistan People's Party of P.M. Benazir Bhutto is dealt a setback in parliamentary by-elections.
Feb. 3	The Group of Seven leading industrial nations reaffirms its commitment to stable exchange rates and economic policy coordination and expresses confidence that international trade imbalances will diminish in 1989.			Alfredo Stroessner, Paraguay's president for 34 years, is overthrown in a military coup that leaves scores of soldiers and civilians dead. The coup is led by Gen. Andres Rodriguez, the second-ranking officer in Paraguay's armed forces.	Japan's surplus on its current account, which measures trade in goods and services, fell in 1988 for the first time in seven years, the finance ministry reports.
Feb. 4	Soviet Foreign Min. Eduard A. Shevardnadze becomes the first Soviet foreign minister in 30 years to set foot on Chinese soil, and the first ever to make an official state visit to China.			In a policy shift, Brazil's foreign ministry says Brazil will accept international funds—including so-called debt-for-nature swaps—to protect Amazon rain forests as long as conservation projects remain in Brazilian hands.	

A	B	C	D	E
Includes developments that affect more than one world region, international organizations and important meetings of major world leaders.	Includes all domestic and regional developments in Europe, including the Soviet Union, Turkey, Cyprus and Malta.	Includes all domestic and regional developments in Africa and the Middle East, including Iraq and Iran and excluding Cyprus, Turkey and Afghanistan.	Includes all domestic and regional developments in Latin America, the Caribbean and Canada.	Includes all domestic and regional developments in Asia and Pacific nations, extending from Afghanistan through all the Pacific Islands, except Hawaii.

U.S. Politics & Social Issues	U.S. Foreign Policy & Defense	U.S. Economy & Environment	Science, Technology & Nature	Culture, Leisure & Life Style	
		Gross national product grew at a 2% annual rate in the fourth quarter of 1988, the Commerce Dept. reports.		Ivan Lendl wins the Australian Open men's singles title and regains the world's top ranking among men.... The National Conf. downs the American Conf., 34-3, in the National Football League's annual Pro Bowl. Philadelphia Eagle quarterback Randall Cunningham, the first black starting quarterback in Pro Bowl history, is named the game's most valuable player.... *Billboard*'s best-selling albums for the week are: *Don't Be Cruel*, Bobby Brown; *Appetite for Destruction*, Guns N' Roses; *Traveling Wilburys*, Traveling Wilburys; *Hysteria*, Def Leppard; and *Open Up and Say...Ahh!*, Poison.	Jan. 29
In New York City, former criminal lawyer Joel B. Steinberg is convicted of first-degree manslaughter for the beating death of his six-year-old illegally adopted daughter, Lisa.... A private commission of health-care experts and policy makers proposes a comprehensive plan to insure health coverage for all citizens by augmenting, but not replacing, private health insurance provided by employers.		Personal income rose 7.5% to $4.063 trillion in 1988, while consumer spending increased 7.1% to $3.226 trillion, the Commerce Dept. reports.		Conductor Daniel Barenboim is named to succeed Sir Georg Solti as music director of the Chicago Symphony Orchestra beginning with the 1991-92 season.	Jan. 30
The trial of former National Security Council staff member Oliver L. North—the first defendant to face a criminal trial in connection with the Iran-Contra affair—opens in federal district court in Washington, D.C.... General Motors Corp. (GMC) settles a class-action lawsuit charging that it discriminated against black employees.		The Senate confirms Robert Mosbacher as commerce secretary, Carla Hills as U.S. special trade representative, and Samuel K. Skinner as transportation secretary.... Prices received by farmers for raw agricultural products rose 1.4% in January, the Agriculture Dept. reports.	U.S. students aged 13 placed last in an international comparison of mathematics and science skills, according to a report released by the Educational Testing Service.		Jan. 31
	In his first diplomatic mission of the Bush administration, Vice Pres. J. Danforth Quayle visits Venezuela and El Salvador, carrying a message of "democracy, democracy, and more democracy."	The government's index of leading economic indicators climbed 0.6% in December 1988, the Commerce Dept. reports.	A National Institutes of Health panel absolves Nobel Prize winner David Baltimore and several colleagues of charges of research fraud in a paper published in 1986. ... The Environmental Protection Agency says it plans to ban daminozide (trade name Alar), a suspected cancer-causing chemical sprayed on apples, but will not do so for at least 18 months.	In the absence of a collective bargaining contract, National Football League team owners institute a free agency policy for more than 600 players.	Feb. 1
	The Senate Armed Services Committee postpones a vote on the confirmation of former Sen. John G. Tower as secretary of defense pending further probes of Tower's personal life.	The Senate confirms Manuel Lujan Jr. as interior secretary, Jack F. Kemp as secretary of housing and urban development, and William K. Reilly as Environmental Protection Agency director.... The General Accounting Office releases a report criticizing five accounting firms for failing to report fraud and mismanagement at several insolvent Texas thrifts.		In the World Alpine Ski Championships, Tamara McKinney wins the women's combined slalom and downhill event, earning the first medal for a U.S. skier in a world championship or Olympics since 1985.	Feb. 2
Ruling that New York state discriminates against girls by awarding scholarships solely on the basis of Scholastic Aptitude Test results, a federal judge orders the state education department to award merit scholarships on the basis of test scores and high school grades.		The U.S. unemployment rate rose one-tenth of a percentage point to 5.4% in January, the Labor Dept. reports.	The average global temperature in 1988 was the highest in the 130 years since reliable record keeping began, according to scientists from the British Meteorological Office and the Univ. of East Anglia.	John Cassavetes, 59, actor, screenwriter, and director, dies of complications from cirrhosis of the liver in Los Angeles. Nominated for Academy Awards for *Faces* (1968) and *A Woman Under the Influence* (1974), he also starred in *Rosemary's Baby*, *The Dirty Dozen*, and *Edge of the City*.	Feb. 3
				Marlon Starling wins the World Boxing Council welterweight championship in his bout with title-holder Lloyd Honeyghan.	Feb. 4

F	G	H	I	J
Includes elections, federal-state relations, civil rights and liberties, crime, the judiciary, education, health care, poverty, urban affairs and population.	Includes formation and debate of U.S. foreign and defense policies, veterans' affairs and defense spending. (Relations with specific foreign countries are usually found under the region concerned.)	Includes business, labor, agriculture, taxation, transportation, consumer affairs, monetary and fiscal policy, natural resources, and pollution.	Includes worldwide scientific, medical and technological developments, natural phenomena, U.S. weather, natural disasters, and accidents.	Includes the arts, religion, scholarship, communications media, sports, entertainments, fashions, fads and social life.

	World Affairs	Europe	Africa & the Middle East	The Americas	Asia & the Pacific
Feb. 5				Paraguay's deposed Pres. Alfredo Stroessner is flown into exile in Brazil. Stroessner, 76, was the longest-ruling head of state in the Western Hemisphere.	As Soviet news media report the withdrawal of all Soviet forces from the Afghan capital of Kabul, Soviet Foreign Min. Eduard A. Shevardnadze flies to Islamabad, Pakistan, in a list-ditch effort to negotiate a peaceful settlement to the Afghan civil war.
Feb. 6		A UN Human Rights Commission report notes that the Soviet Union has taken major steps toward religious freedom and cites the greater availability of Bibles and release of religious dissidents.... The opening of round-table talks among the Polish government, the Solidarity labor union, intellectuals, and church leaders in Warsaw is nationally televised.		Paraguay's Gen. Andres Rodriguez announces that new presidential and congressional elections will be held May 1 and will be open to all political parties except the Communist Party.	At a news conference in Islamabad, Pakistan, Soviet Foreign Min. Eduard A. Shevardnadze says that "up to 15,000 Soviet troops" have been killed in Afghanistan since the Soviet invasion on Dec. 27, 1979.
Feb. 7					
Feb. 8					
Feb. 9		Demanding higher wages, about 5,000 miners stage a four-day wildcat strike at the Belchatow coal mine, which supplies Poland's largest power generating station.		In Jamaica, former prime minister Michael Manley of the People's National Party defeats incumbent P.M. Edward Seaga of the Jamaica Labour Party in national elections. ... P.M. John Swan's United Bermuda Party wins 50% of the popular vote in the British colony of Bermuda's general election.	
Feb. 10			In a document prepared at the request of Pope John Paul II, the Vatican condemns racism as sinful and urges strong action against apartheid, South Africa's system of racial separation.		
Feb. 11		The Central Committee of Hungary's ruling Socialist Workers' (Communist) Party approves the creation of independent political parties.		The unemployment rate in Canada was 7.8% in 1988, according to Statistics Canada data, one percentage point less than in 1987.	South Korea's current account surplus reached $14.27 bil. in 1988, more than double the figure recorded in 1987.
Feb. 12					

A	B	C	D	E
Includes developments that affect more than one world region, international organizations and important meetings of major world leaders.	Includes all domestic and regional developments in Europe, including the Soviet Union, Turkey, Cyprus and Malta.	Includes all domestic and regional developments in Africa and the Middle East, including Iraq and Iran and excluding Cyprus, Turkey and Afghanistan.	Includes all domestic and regional developments in Latin America, the Caribbean and Canada.	Includes all domestic and regional developments in Asia and Pacific nations, extending from Afghanistan through all the Pacific Islands, except Hawaii.

U.S. Politics & Social Issues	U.S. Foreign Policy & Defense	U.S. Economy & Environment	Science, Technology & Nature	Culture, Leisure & Life Style	
				The team of Derek Bell of Britain, Bob Wollek of France, and John Andretti of the United States wins the Daytona 24 Hours endurance race.	Feb. 5
The Southern Poverty Law Center in Atlanta reports that the white supremacist movement has been revitalized by the emergence of violent, neo-Nazi skinhead youth groups.		Pres. Bush unveils a $126.2 bil. thrift industry rescue plan that will close or sell 350 ailing savings and loan institutions and overhaul the thrift regulatory system.... Productivity among the nation's non-farm businesses increased 1.4% in 1988, the Labor Dept. reports.	The Food and Drug Admin. announces that it will exand the availability of pentamidine, an experimental aerosol drug used to prevent a form of pneumonia often found in patients afflicted with AIDS.	Barbara Wertheim Tuchman, 77, historian whose best-selling books focused on war and the lives of men involved in war, dies after a stroke in Greenwich, Conn. She won Pultzer Prizes for *The Guns of August* (1962) and *Stilwell and the American Experience in China, 1911-45* (1971).	Feb. 6
Congress rejects a pay increase of 50% or more for legislators, federal judges, and top executive branch officials. Pres. Bush, who publicly supported the proposed increases, signs the disapproval resolution.	The State Dept.'s annual human rights review criticizes Israel for a "substantial increase in human rights violations" in the occupied West Bank and Gaza Strip, and charges Brazil with human rights violations in connection with massacres in rural land disputes.	The Federal Deposit Insurance Corp. and Federal Home Loan Bank Board seize control of four insolvent thrifts with total assets of $5.6 bil. Regulators plan to seize 224 insolvent thrifts by the end of February.... Outstanding consumer debt rose $5.4 bil. in December 1988, at an annual rate of 9.9%, the Commerce Dept. reports.		The Campbell Conference wins the National Hockey League All-Star Game in Edmonton, Alberta, 9-6, over the Wales Conference. Los Angeles King center Wayne Gretzky wins the most valuable player award.	Feb. 7
	The Senate unanimously confirms Clayton K. Yeutter as agriculture secretary.			A controversy breaks out in Spain over the apparent increase in the "shaving" of the horns of bulls used in bullfighting. A study by the National Health Academy finds that 82 of the 262 bulls tested had had their horns blunted before fighting. The practice is illegal.	Feb. 8
Addressing a joint session of Congress, Pres. Bush calls for new initiatives in education, child care, the environment, drug abuse, homelessness, and science and space research, among other areas.... Commenting on Pres. Bush's budget address, House Speaker Jim Wright (D, Tex.) pledges Democratic cooperation in achieving a "kinder, gentler America."		In its three-part quarterly refinancing, the Treasury Dept. over two days sells $28.75 bil. of new notes and bonds.			Feb. 9
Ronald H. Brown, a Washington, D.C., lawyer with close ties to liberal Democrats, is elected chairman of the Democratic National Committee, becoming the first black ever to head a major U.S. political party.	Pres. Bush confers with Canada's P.M. Brian Mulroney in Ottawa. It is Bush's first trip to a foreign country since taking office in January.	The government's producer price index climbed 1% in January, the Labor Dept. reports.... Leading banks raise their prime lending rate by half a percentage point to 11%; it is the fifth increase in the past 12 months.		William (Pop) Gates and players-turned-coaches K. Jones and Lenny Wilkens are elected to the Pro Basketball Hall of Fame.... The pairs figure skating competition is won by Kristi Yamaguchi and Rudi Galindo, qualifing for the world championships.	Feb. 10
In Boston, the Rev. Barbara Clementine Harris becomes the first woman consecrated as a bishop in the Episcopal Church.	Sec. of State James A. Baker III begins a get-acquainted tour of 15 North Atlantic Treaty Org. nations at a time when the reform policies of Soviet Pres. Mikhail S. Gorbachev are increasingly admired by the Western Europe public.	U.S. District Court Judge Jack B. Weinstein dismisses a racketeering lawsuit against the Long Island Lighting Co., which was earlier found guilty of lying to state regulators to obtain rate increases.			Feb. 11
				The sloop *Thursday's Child* sails from Sandy Hook, N.J., to San Francisco by way of Cape Horn, at the tip of South America, in 81 days, 20 hours—8 days and 12 hours faster than the record set by the American clipper ship *Flying Cloud* in 1854.... The Western Conf. wins the National Basketball Assoc.'s All-Star Game in Houston, 143-134. Karl Malone of the Utah Jazz is named most valuable player.	Feb. 12

F	G	H	I	J
Includes elections, federal-state relations, civil rights and liberties, crime, the judiciary, education, health care, poverty, urban affairs and population.	Includes formation and debate of U.S. foreign and defense policies, veterans' affairs and defense spending. (Relations with specific foreign countries are usually found under the region concerned.)	Includes business, labor, agriculture, taxation, transportation, consumer affairs, monetary and fiscal policy, natural resources, and pollution.	Includes worldwide scientific, medical and technological developments, natural phenomena, U.S. weather, natural disasters, and accidents.	Includes the arts, religion, scholarship, communications media, sports, entertainments, fashions, fads and social life.

	World Affairs	Europe	Africa & the Middle East	The Americas	Asia & the Pacific
Feb. 13		One month after his abduction from the garage of his Brussels apartment building, former Belgian Premier Paul Vanden Boeynants is freed in the French city of Tournai after his family pays kidnappers a ransom.		In Canada, a confidential 1986 government study made public by the *Toronto Globe and Mail* concludes that federal law enforcement agencies are hampered by rivalry, incompetence, and poor management.	Government prosecutors arrest four businessmen, including the founder and former chairman of Recruit Co., on bribery charges in the first major arrests in Japan's ongoing stock trading scandal.
Feb. 14		Speaking at a special Kremlin gathering, Soviet Gen. Sec. Mikhail Gorbachev rejects the idea of renouncing the one-party state as "politically and theoretically unsound." . . . The Soviet interior ministry reveals that overall crime jumped by 17.8% in 1988, including a 14.1% increase in murder, to 16,710. . . . Britain's Office of Population Census and Survey estimates that 1.6% of English and Welsh men of the generation currently around 30 years old will die from AIDS.	Iranian leader Ayatollah Ruhollah Khomeini urges Moslems throughout the world to execute Salman Rushdie, Indian-born British author of the novel *The Satanic Verses*, perceived as blasphemous to Islam. . . . In response to a request by Ivory Coast Pres. Felix Houphouet-Boigny, who is trying to mediate an end to Angola's 13-year-old civil war, rebel leader Jonas Savimbi suspends the annual offensive against the Angolan Army.	The presidents of five Central American nations meeting in El Salvador agree on a draft plan to disarm and repatriate Honduras-based Nicaraguan Contra rebels in return for open elections in Nicaragua.	A Soviet foreign ministry spokesman says that 30,000 mujaheddin have massed outside the Afghan capital of Kabul, and another 15,000 around Jalalabad, in anticipation of the final withdrawal of Soviet troops. . . . India's Supreme Court orders U.S.-based Union Carbide Corp. to pay $470 mil. in compensation to victims of a 1984 gas leak at the company's chemical plant in Bhopal, India.
Feb. 15		The West German government acknowledges that its intelligence service warned as early as 1980 that Libya was considering building a chemical weapons plant at Rabata with the aid of East and West German sources.	The reputation of Winnie Mandela in South Africa's antiapartheid movement is severely damaged by reports of a Soweto boy's death, allegedly at the hands of Mandela's bodyguards.	Pres. Jose Sarney's latest anti-inflation plan suffers a setback when Brazil's congress rejects a proposal to privatize loss-making state industries and delays the planned closure of five ministries. . . . Chile's Roman Catholic human rights group, the Vicariate of Solidarity, refuses to turn over to a military court medical records showing the names of people treated by the church group for injuries incurred in antigovernment protests.	The Soviet Union withdraws its last troops from Afghanistan, ending a decade of intervention in a civil war between the Soviet-supported Marxist regime in Kabul and a broad coalition of Muslim rebel groups. . . . Sri Lanka's ruling United National Party emerges as the victor in the country's first parliamentary elections since 1977.
Feb. 16		The number of unemployed workers in Britain fell in January to below 2 million for the first time in eight years, according to official unemployment statistics. . . . Some 1,000 people attend the founding convention of the Social Democratic Union of Slovenia, the first self-proclaimed opposition political party in Yugoslavia since World War II.	South Africa's major antiapartheid organizations formally denounce and disown Winnie Mandela, wife of jailed black nationalist leader Nelson Mandela, saying she has "abused the trust" of the black community.	The Bank of Canada raises its lending rate to 11.70%, a three-year high, and the nation's chartered banks raise their prime rates one-half a percentage point, to 12.75%.	
Feb. 17		Britain's inflation rate rose to 7.5% in January, the government reports. The rate is the highest in six years, and the highest among the seven leading democratic industrial powers.	At the conclusion of a two-day summit Algeria, Libya, Mauritania, Morocco, and Tunisia proclaim the formation of a common market for the region, to be called the Arab Maghreb Union. . . . Iran's Pres. Ali Khamenei tells worshipers in Teheran that "this wretched man [Salman Rushdie] has no choice but to die because he has confronted a billion Moslems" with his book *Satanic Verses*.		
Feb. 18		The United States and the European Community (EC) agree to a 75-day truce in the unresolved trade war over meat from hormone-treated cattle. . . . The Soviet Union's Communist Party Politburo has reportedly approved measures that will expand the republics' economic independence and give them greater leeway on environmental policies.			Afghanistan's Pres. Najibullah declares a nationwide state of emergency.
Feb. 19		Italy is reportedly suffering a severe winter drought, with losses to farmers owing to the lack of rainfall estimated at $1.5 bil., and losses to ski resorts of $1.3 bil. from the lack of snow.			

A	B	C	D	E
Includes developments that affect more than one world region, international organizations and important meetings of major world leaders.	Includes all domestic and regional developments in Europe, including the Soviet Union, Turkey, Cyprus and Malta.	Includes all domestic and regional developments in Africa and the Middle East, including Iraq and Iran and excluding Cyprus, Turkey and Afghanistan.	Includes all domestic and regional developments in Latin America, the Caribbean and Canada.	Includes all domestic and regional developments in Asia and Pacific nations, extending from Afghanistan through all the Pacific Islands, except Hawaii.

U.S. Politics & Social Issues	U.S. Foreign Policy & Defense	U.S. Economy & Environment	Science, Technology & Nature	Culture, Leisure & Life Style	
					Feb. 13
Seeking to become New York City's first black mayor, Manhattan borough president David Dinkins announces a bid to unseat three-term incumbent Mayor Edward I. Koch in the Democratic primary in the fall.... The National Assessment of Educational Progress reports that although U.S. students have improved their basic knowledge over the past 20 years, few are able to apply that knowledge in real-life situations.	The Army reportedly failed to meet its recruitment goal for the first quarter of 1988; it is the first time it has fallen short since 1980.	General Motors Corp. reports record annual profits in 1988 after three years of low earnings. Net income surged 37% to $4.86 bil., surpassing the previous record of $4.5 bil. set in 1984.			**Feb. 14**
		The Federal Reserve Board reports that U.S. factories, mines, and utilities operated at 84.4% of capacity in January, its highest level since October 1979.... The Federal Reserve Board reports that its industrial production index rose 0.3% in January.			**Feb. 15**
Pres. Bush says that he will not support legislation to ban the import or sale of semiautomatic weapons.		Under foreign pressure, the Treasury Dept. rules that most imported minivans and sports utility vehicles will still be classified as cars rather than trucks, and thus subject to tariffs of 2.5% rather than 25%.... For the third straight year, Ford Motor Co. out-earns General Motors and reports record earnings, as 1988 profit surged to $5.3 bil., the highest full-year profit in the history of the auto industry.			**Feb. 16**
According to findings published in the *Journal of the American Medical Association*, the spread of AIDS among intravenous drug users in New York City has slowed in the past four years, stabilizing at about 55% to 60%.		The merchandise trade deficit shrank in 1988 for the first time in eight years to $137.34 bil., the Commerce Dept. reports.	Researchers report finding over the Arctic high concentrations of chlorofluorocarbons, which are believed to be causing a "hole" in the atmosphere's protective ozone layer over the Antarctic.	Vernon (Lefty) Gomez, 80, pitcher with the New York Yankees in the 1930s, dies of congestive heart failure in a hospital in Larkspur, Calif. In 14 major league seasons, the Hall of Famer had a won-lost record of 189-102, his best season being 26-5 in 1934.... "What Is the Proper Way to Display a U.S. Flag?" an Art Institute of Chicago exhibit by Scott Tyler, sparks intense controversy. Viewers are intended to write their impressions of the exhibit in a ledger that can be reached only by stepping on a flag mounted on the floor.	**Feb. 17**
David Duke, a former Grand Wizard of the Knights of the Ku Klux Klan, is narrowly elected to the Louisiana state legislature from the predominantly white New Orleans suburb of Metairie.	The Defense Advisory Committee on Women in the Services reports that U.S. servicewomen stationed in Southern Europe were subject to constant sexual harassment by fellow servicemen and foreign nationals.				**Feb. 18**
		Housing starts soared 8% in January, the Commerce Dept. reports.			**Feb. 19**

F	G	H	I	J
Includes elections, federal-state relations, civil rights and liberties, crime, the judiciary, education, health care, poverty, urban affairs and population.	Includes formation and debate of U.S. foreign and defense policies, veterans' affairs and defense spending. (Relations with specific foreign countries are usually found under the region concerned.)	Includes business, labor, agriculture, taxation, transportation, consumer affairs, monetary and fiscal policy, natural resources, and pollution.	Includes worldwide scientific, medical and technological developments, natural phenomena, U.S. weather, natural disasters, and accidents.	Includes the arts, religion, scholarship, communications media, sports, entertainments, fashions, fads and social life.

	World Affairs	Europe	Africa & the Middle East	The Americas	Asia & the Pacific
Feb. 20				Eleven Amazonian Indian tribes begin gathering in Altamira, Brazil, to protest the construction of a hydroelectric dam on the Xingu River in Para State that would flood more than 15 million acres of virgin forest and displace more than 35,000 Indians.	Afghanistan's Premier Mohammed Hassan Sharq resigns and a supreme military council assumes control of most government functions in the wake of the withdrawal of Soviet troops from the country.
Feb. 21	Representatives of countries that are not members of the Org. of Petroleum Exporting Countries (OPEC) agree to reduce their output by up to 300,000 barrels per day in support of OPEC efforts to stabilize world oil markets and achieve the $18-a-barrel target.	The prominent Czechoslovak playwright Vaclav Havel is convicted on charges connected to January protests in Prague and is sentenced to nine months in jail.... Britain's gross domestic product grew an estimated 4.5% in 1988, according to figures released by the Central Statistics Office.		Rebels in El Salvador offer to cease hostilities and join "the nation's political life" if the government undertakes a major restructuring of the military and postpones elections scheduled for March.... Facing one of its worst crises in five years, the government of Argentina's Pres. Raul Alfonsin closes all foreign-exchange operations and announces further measures to reduce inflation and stimulate exports.	
Feb. 22		Amnesty International criticizes Bulgaria for failing to provide information on an estimated 150 ethnic Turks jailed since 1984 for resisting the regime's campaign to force the Turkish minority to adopt Slavic names and Slavic culture.... France's 1988 gross domestic product grew 3.6% in 1988, the government reports.	Midway through his Mideast tour in the Soviet Union's most comprehensive Arab-Israeli peace initiative in recent years, Foreign Min. Eduard A. Shevardnadze meets with Israel's Foreign Min. Moshe Arens in Cairo.		
Feb. 23			Soviet Foreign Min. Eduard Shevardnadze concludes a 10-day tour of the Middle East with visits to Iraq and Iran, and has a rare audience with Iran's supreme leader, Ayatollah Ruhollah Khomeini.		Moderate Sibghatullah Mojaddidi and Islamic fundamentalist Abdul Rasul Sayyaf are named president and premier, respectively, of an interim Afghan government that will take power if the Soviet-backed regime in Kabul collapses.
Feb. 24	European nations recall their diplomats from Teheran after Iran's Ayatollah Ruhollah Khomeini reiterates his death threat against Salman Rushdie, the British author of the novel *The Satanic Verses*.	A proposed merger between two of Spain's largest banks, Banco Espanol de Credito (Banesto) and Banco Central, falls apart after feuding erupts among the financiers involved in the deal.	In yesterday's referendum, 73% of Algerian voters are reported to have favored a new constitution that drops all references to socialism and clears the way for a multi-party system.		Emperor Hirohito, Japan's longest-reigning monarch and the last of the major leaders of the World War II era, is buried in a day-long funeral ceremony attended by some 700 foreign dignitaries.... Union Carbide Corp. sends $465 mil. to the Indian Supreme Court as compensation for victims of the 1984 gas leak at the company's chemical plant in Bhopal, India.
Feb. 25		In Poland, police clash with young anticommunist demonstrators in several cities over two days. It is believed to be Poland's worst political violence in nearly a year.... Poland's Premier Mieczyslaw Rakowski attends the Warsaw reopening of *Protest*, a play by Czechoslovak dissident playwright Vaclav Havel who was sentenced to nine months in prison on February 21.			During international meetings occasioned by the gathering of leaders for the funeral of Japan's Emperor Hirohito, Indonesia and China announce that they will normalize relations after a 22-year break.

A	B	C	D	E
Includes developments that affect more than one world region, international organizations and important meetings of major world leaders.	Includes all domestic and regional developments in Europe, including the Soviet Union, Turkey, Cyprus and Malta.	Includes all domestic and regional developments in Africa and the Middle East, including Iraq and Iran and excluding Cyprus, Turkey and Afghanistan.	Includes all domestic and regional developments in Latin America, the Caribbean and Canada.	Includes all domestic and regional developments in Asia and Pacific nations, extending from Afghanistan through all the Pacific Islands, except Hawaii.

U.S. Politics & Social Issues	U.S. Foreign Policy & Defense	U.S. Economy & Environment	Science, Technology & Nature	Culture, Leisure & Life Style	
The Immigration and Naturalization Service announces plans to detain Central Americans seeking asylum without proper papers, in a tent city near Brownsville, Tex.					Feb. 20
In opening arguments, associate independent counsel John W. Keker attempts to portray Oliver L. North as a chronic liar who deliberately misled congressional and presidential inquiries into the Iran-Contra affair and placed himself ''above the law.''... Rep. Bill Grant, a conservative Democrat from the Florida Panhandle, announces that he is switching to the Republican Party in a move that gives the GOP a majority of the state's House delegation.... The Supreme Court rules unanimously that an antiracketeering law cannot be used to close an adult bookstore without a prior court determination that the materials for sale are obscene.		A *Wall Street Journal* survey of 645 major corporations finds that net income rose 20% in the 1988 fourth quarter from the year-earlier period; after-tax earnings from continuing operations rose 22%.			Feb. 21
The Supreme Court rules, 6-3, that local officials are not liable under the Constitution for failure to protect a child from physical harm by a parent.		The consumer price index surged 0.6%, at a 7.2% compound annual rate, in January, the Labor Dept. reports.		Grammy awards go to George Michael's *Faith*, album of the year; best song, record, and pop male vocalist, Bobby McFerrin, *Don't Worry, Be Happy*; best new artist and pop female vocalist, Tracy Chapman, *Fast Car*; top rock male vocalist, Robert Palmer, *Simply Irresistible*; and top rock female vocalist, Tina Turner, *Tina Live in Europe*.... *Variety*'s top-grossing films for the week are: *The 'Burbs, Rain Man, The Fly II, Cousins,* and *Bill & Ted's Excellent Adventure*.	Feb. 22
The Rev. Timothy S. Healy, president of Georgetown Univ. in Washington, D.C., is named president and chief executive officer of the New York Public Library.... Candidates for the 101st Congress spent a total of more than $457 mil. in campaign funds in 1987-88, according to a report released by the Federal Election Commission.	The Senate Armed Services Committee votes, 11-9, to reject John G. Tower's nomination as secretary of defense. Opponents cite allegations of Tower's drinking, sexual misbehavior, and financial ties to the defense industry.	Treasury Sec. Nicholas F. Brady discloses that the total cost of rescuing insolvent U.S. savings and loan institutions will likely reach an estimated $157.6 bil.		Hans Helmut Kirst, 74, one of West Germany's most popular novelists, dies of heart failure in Bremen, West Germany. His books, which were highly popular in the United States and Great Britain, include *The Lieutenant Must Be Mad* (1951), *Night of the Generals* (1962), and the trilogy *08/15*.	Feb. 23
	A court-martial board at the United States' Subic Bay Naval Base in the Philippines reprimands Capt. Alexander G. Balian for failing to rescue Vietnamese refugees on the high seas.	The Federal Reserve Board raises the discount rate by half a percentage point, to 7%, its highest level in nearly three years.		*Publishers Weekly*'s hardback fiction best-sellers for the week are *Midnight*, Dean R. Koontz; *The Sands of Time*, Sidney Sheldon; *Rivals*, Janet Dailey; *The Cardinal of the Kremlin*, Tom Clancy; and *Mutation*, Robin Cook.	Feb. 24
				Undisputed world heavyweight boxing champion Mike Tyson retains his title with a fifth-round technical knockout of Britain's Frank Bruno.... *Billboard*'s best-selling albums for the week are: *Don't Be Cruel*, Bobby Brown; *Appetite for Destruction*, Guns N' Roses; *Traveling Wilburys*, Traveling Wilburys; *Shooting Rubberbands at the Stars*, Edie Brickell & New Bohemians; and *Electric Youth*, Debbie Gibson.	Feb. 25

F	G	H	I	J
Includes elections, federal-state relations, civil rights and liberties, crime, the judiciary, education, health care, poverty, urban affairs and population.	Includes formation and debate of U.S. foreign and defense policies, veterans' affairs and defense spending. (Relations with specific foreign countries are usually found under the region concerned.)	Includes business, labor, agriculture, taxation, transportation, consumer affairs, monetary and fiscal policy, natural resources, and pollution.	Includes worldwide scientific, medical and technological developments, natural phenomena, U.S. weather, natural disasters, and accidents.	Includes the arts, religion, scholarship, communications media, sports, entertainments, fashions, fads and social life.

	World Affairs	Europe	Africa & the Middle East	The Americas	Asia & the Pacific
Feb. 26		France's 1988 trade deficit grew to $5.3 bil., the government reports. France's deficit in industrial trade quadrupled, while its surplus in farm and food trade increased and its deficit in energy products declined.			
Feb. 27	The volume of world merchandise trade expanded 8.5% in 1988, and the value of trade expanded 14%, to a record $2.84 trillion, the General Agreement on Tariffs and Trade reports. West Germany and the United States are the world's top two exporters.	Yugoslavia's collective presidency sends troops to Kosovo province, a predominantly Albanian self-governing region of the Serbian republic that has been torn by ethnic strife.		Canada's P.M. Brian Mulroney and nine of the 10 provincial premiers hold an informal first ministers' meeting in Ottawa on the subject of the Meech Lake constitutional accord. The issue remains at an impasse. . . . Chief Min. Emile Gumbs and his Anguilla National Alliance are reelected, but a dispute with British Gov. Geoffrey Whittaker immediately following the election leaves Anguilla without a parliament.	The Australian dollar falls sharply in trading in Sydney and New York, at one point prompting intervention by the U.S. Federal Reserve to halt the decline.
Feb. 28			Amnesty International charges that the Iraqi government of Pres. Saddam Hussein has imprisoned, tortured, and executed hundreds and perhaps thousands of children of political dissidents over the past several years.		The Chinese government made little progress in its fight against inflation in 1988, according to figures released by the state statistical bureau; inflation rate reached 27% in December 1988.
March 1		Britain posted a current account deficit of 1.7 bil. pounds sterling in January, the third worst deficit on record.	The final obstacles blocking the process by which Namibia is to gain its independence from South Africa clear the UN General Assembly.	In Venezuela, at least 300 people are killed in three days of rioting sparked by government-imposed increases in transportation fares and gasoline prices and the imposition of martial law. . . . Canada's gross domestic product grew 4.5% in 1988, according to Statistics Canada. . . . Characterizing it as a "publicity maneuver," Salvadoran rebels reject the military's February 28 unilateral truce declaration.	
March 2					Malaysia's hereditary rulers elect Sultan Azlan Shah of Perak state to be the country's ninth king; the office of king rotates every five years among the nine sultans. . . . Talks between representatives of North and South Korea aimed at setting up a meeting between the two nations' premiers are suspended following a dispute over a joint U.S.-South Korean military exercise.
March 3	Japan drops plans to finance the construction of a paved highway through the Amazon rain forests in western Brazil.	The minority Socialist government of Norway formally unveils an $800 mil. plan to combat growing unemployment, which has reached 4%.			India's P.M. Rajiv Gandhi unveils several proposals—including release of militant Sikhs detained since 1984, a key demand of Sikh leaders—aimed at restoring peace in the strife-torn northern state of Punjab.
March 4				Edward Broadbent resigns as the national leader of Canada's New Democratic Party. He held the post for 14 years and led the party in four general elections.	

A	B	C	D	E
Includes developments that affect more than one world region, international organizations and important meetings of major world leaders.	Includes all domestic and regional developments in Europe, including the Soviet Union, Turkey, Cyprus and Malta.	Includes all domestic and regional developments in Africa and the Middle East, including Iraq and Iran and excluding Cyprus, Turkey and Afghanistan.	Includes all domestic and regional developments in Latin America, the Caribbean and Canada.	Includes all domestic and regional developments in Asia and Pacific nations, extending from Afghanistan through all the Pacific Islands, except Hawaii.

U.S. Politics & Social Issues	U.S. Foreign Policy & Defense	U.S. Economy & Environment	Science, Technology & Nature	Culture, Leisure & Life Style	
A New York Times/CBS News public opinion poll report shows that Pres. Bush has a 61% approval rating after his first month in office.			The National Weather Service reports that tornadoes killed 32 people in the United States in 1988. The average number of fatalities due to tornadoes is 99.	(David) Roy Eldridge, 78, flamboyant and innovative jazz trumpeter, dies in a hospital in Valley Stream, N.Y. Regarded as the link between Louis Armstrong's pioneering trumpet solos of the 1920s and Dizzy Gillespie's bebop style of the 1950s, he played with Gene Krupa, Artie Shaw, and Benny Goodman, among others.	Feb. 26
			Konrad Zacharias Lorenz, 85, Austrian scientist who pioneered the study of animal behavior known as ethology, dies of kidney failure in Altenburg, Austria. A Nobel laureate, Lorenz held that behavioral patterns such as aggression and maternal bonding are inherited. . . . The U.S. Geological Survey reports that nearly three times as many people died in earthquakes around the world in 1988 as in an average year.		Feb. 27
Cook County State's Attorney Richard M. Daley defeats acting Mayor Eugene Sawyer in Chicago's Democratic mayoral primary election. . . . The use of illegal drugs—including, for the first time, crack cocaine—among high school seniors continued to fall in 1988, according to an annual survey.		New York Gov. Mario M. Cuomo (D) and the Long Island Lighting Co. sign a new agreement to close the $5.5 bil. Shoreham nuclear power plant. . . . Sears Roebuck & Co. closes all 824 of its retail stores while employees spend 42 hours manually tagging 50,000 items to reflect price reductions of up to 50%.		Second baseman and manager Red Schoendienst, who played from 1945 to 1963 and managed the St. Louis Cardinals from 1965 to 1976, and Al Barlick, a National League umpire for more than 27 seasons beginning in 1940, are elected to the Baseball Hall of Fame.	Feb. 28
Dr. Louis W. Sullivan is confirmed by the Senate as secretary of health and human services. . . . Ruling that prosecutors suppressed evidence and knowingly used perjured testimony to convict Randall Dale Adams, whose case was the subject of a documentary, *The Thin Blue Line*, a Texas appeals court overturns his conviction.	According to a report by the State Dept., worldwide production of coca leaf, marijuana, opium, and hashish increased sharply in 1988, despite U.S. efforts to eradicate drug cultivation.	Retired Adm. James D. Watkins is confirmed by the Senate as secretary of energy. . . . Personal income rose 1.8% to a $4.282 trillion annual rate in January, and consumer spending increased just 0.1% to $3.457 trillion, the Commerce Dept. reports.			March 1
A federal appeals court in Philadelphia upholds the 1987 conviction of a group of antiabortion demonstrators under the federal Racketeering Influenced and Corrupt Organizations Act.	Former Rep. Edward J. Derwinski (R, Ill.) is confirmed by the Senate as the nation's first secretary of veterans' affairs.		A National Academy of Sciences panel calls for broad changes in American eating habits, including a diet that is lower in fat and higher in vegetables and carbohydrates. . . . Environment ministers from the 12 European Community nations agree to halt production of chlorofluorocarbons by the end of the century.		March 2
A federal judge in Washington, D.C., sentences former Reagan administration aide Robert C. McFarlane to two years' probation and fines him $20,000 for his role in the Iran-Contra arms scandal.		The government's index of leading economic indicators rose 0.6% in January, the Commerce Dept. reports.		Property developers in London give archaeologists another 10 weeks to work on a site where Elizabethan London's major theaters were located, including the 16th-century Rose Theater.	March 3
Despite a judge's ban on a planned concert by neo-Nazi rock and roll bands, about 100 members of white supremacist groups gather in Napa County, Calif., for what is billed as an "Aryan Woodstock."		Striking machinists, supported by pilots and flight attendants, close down 90% of Eastern Airlines' flight operations. . . . Time Inc. and Warner Communications Inc. agree to a merger that will create the largest media and entertainment group in the world, with a stock market value of $15.3 bil. and annual revenues of over $10 bil.			March 4

F	G	H	I	J
Includes elections, federal-state relations, civil rights and liberties, crime, the judiciary, education, health care, poverty, urban affairs and population.	Includes formation and debate of U.S. foreign and defense policies, veterans' affairs and defense spending. (Relations with specific foreign countries are usually found under the region concerned.)	Includes business, labor, agriculture, taxation, transportation, consumer affairs, monetary and fiscal policy, natural resources, and pollution.	Includes worldwide scientific, medical and technological developments, natural phenomena, U.S. weather, natural disasters, and accidents.	Includes the arts, religion, scholarship, communications media, sports, entertainments, fashions, fads and social life.

	World Affairs	Europe	Africa & the Middle East	The Americas	Asia & the Pacific
March 5		Led by poet Yevgeny Yevtushenko, about 2,000 people gathered in Moscow to remember the victims of leader Joseph Stalin begin chanting in favor of Boris Yeltsin's candidacy for the Congress of People's Deputies.		The Venezuelan government lifts a nighttime curfew in half the country's 20 states and reopens elementary schools; the curbs were imposed following last week's riots over price increases.	
March 6		The Conventional Forces in Europe talks, a new East-West arms-control forum designed to facilitate cuts in nonnuclear forces between the Atlantic Ocean and the Ural Mountains, formally open in Vienna.		Workers in Trinidad stage a general strike to protest an economic austerity program imposed to meet the requirements for a $128 mil. standby loan from the International Monetary Fund.	The first major battle in the Afghan war since the withdrawal of Soviet troops in mid-February begins when rebel forces launch a much-heralded offensive against the eastern city of Jalalabad.
March 7	Iran formally breaks diplomatic relations with Britain after the British government fails to satisfy Iran's demand that it denounce author Salman Rushdie and his novel *The Satanic Verses*.			Responding to international criticism, the Brazilian government unveils a comprehensive environmental program for the Amazon region.	After three days of rioting in Lhasa, Tibet, in which at least 16 people were reported to have died, the Chinese government imposes martial law for the first time since the 1959 uprising in Tibet.
March 8					As many as 130 Vietnamese refugees are believed to have drowned after their small fishing boat overturned in a collision with a Japanese supertanker.
March 9		The UN Commission on Human Rights approves a resolution, co-sponsored by Hungary, to investigate Romania, in what is thought to be the first time that a Soviet-bloc country has urged the investigation of an ally for rights violations.... The Conf. on Confidence- and Security-Building Measures talks (formerly the Conf. on Confidence- and Security-Building Measures and Disarmament in Europe), involving 35 nations, opens in Europe.	The government of Sudan is reportedly on the edge of collapse as the army demands that P.M. Sadiq al-Mahdi either resign or take immediate steps to end the nation's debilitating civil war.	Canada's Supreme Court refuses to decide whether fetuses are entitled to constitutional protections, including a right to life.... The Inter-American Development Bank suspends credit to Peru because it is more than six months behind in debt payments. The World Bank and the International Monetary Fund suspended credit to Peru in 1986.	
March 10		The West German Social Democratic Party and the environmentalist Alternative List finalize an agreement to form a coalition government in West Berlin.			
March 11			The Bush administration unveils a set of proposals that it hopes to press upon Israel and the Palestine Liberation Org. as a means of laying the groundwork for regional peace negotiations.		
March 12			A two-day conference on peace in the Mideast at Columbia Univ. in New York City brings together members of the Palestine Liberation Org. and members of Israel's Knesset and the Peace Now movement.	The Salvadoran military acknowledges that soldiers are responsible for the September 1988 massacre of 10 unarmed civilians in the hamlet of San Francisco and says it is turning over two officers to the courts.	

A	B	C	D	E
Includes developments that affect more than one world region, international organizations and important meetings of major world leaders.	Includes all domestic and regional developments in Europe, including the Soviet Union, Turkey, Cyprus and Malta.	Includes all domestic and regional developments in Africa and the Middle East, including Iraq and Iran and excluding Cyprus, Turkey and Afghanistan.	Includes all domestic and regional developments in Latin America, the Caribbean and Canada.	Includes all domestic and regional developments in Asia and Pacific nations, extending from Afghanistan through all the Pacific Islands, except Hawaii.

U.S. Politics & Social Issues	U.S. Foreign Policy & Defense	U.S. Economy & Environment	Science, Technology & Nature	Culture, Leisure & Life Style	
The daily television news program Channel One begins broadcasting to classrooms nationwide despite widespread criticism of the show's being supported by commercial advertisements.			Reversing a long-held position, the American Academy of Pediatrics says that the circumcision of male infants has medical benefits in protecting against kidney and urinary infections.		March 5
The Supreme Court strkes down a Michigan law requiring that 7% of state contracts be awarded to minority-owned businesses and 5% to businesses owned by women.... The Supreme Court rules unanimously that the right to a jury trial is not guaranteed for drunk-driving defendants.	A federal judge in Los Angeles fines Rockwell International Corp. $5.5 mil. for defrauding the Air Force in what is thought to be the largest criminal penalty ever levied against a defense contractor.				March 6
Republican National Committee chairman Lee Atwater resigns from the board of trustees of predominantly black Howard Univ. in Washington, D.C., following four days of student protests against his appointment.		The Commerce Dept. imposes a preliminary 2.72% antidumping duty on imported Canadian steel rails to settle a complaint of unfair trade practices filed by Bethlehem Steel Corp. against two Canadian firms.	An international conference in London ends with a call for speeding up plans to phase out the chemicals believed to be destroying the ozone layer in the Earth's upper atmosphere.	The John M. Templeton Prize for Progress in Religion is awarded to the Very Reverend Lord MacLeod, founder of the Iona community in Scotland, and Carl Friedrich von Weizsaecker, who has studied the relationship between physics, cosmology, and theology.	March 7
The Harvard Business Review publishes a controversial article by Felice N. Schwartz in which she suggests that women in managerial positions be considered as either "career primary" or "career-and-family."		A bill to raise the minimum wage to $4.65 an hour over three years is approved by a committee in the Senate. The minimum wage has been $3.35 an hour since 1981.	Health and Human Services Sec. Louis W. Sullivan says that his department will support programs to supply hypodermic needles to drug addicts in an effort to halt the spread of AIDS among intravenous drug users.	American Roman Catholic archbishops visit the Vatican for an unprecedented four-day dialogue with Pope John Paul II and top Vatican officials on certain divergences from the orthodox course prescribed by Rome.	March 8
William J. Bennett is confirmed by the Senate to serve as the first director of the cabinet-level Office of National Drug Control Policy.		Eastern Airlines, the nation's seventh-largest airline, files for protection under Chapter 11 of the federal bankruptcy code.... U.S. District Judge Gustave Diamond fines Ashland Oil Inc. $2.25 mil. for a January 1988 oil spill that polluted the Monongahela and Ohio Rivers and threatened drinking water supplies in three states.	The New England Journal of Medicine reports that the surgical procedure of balloon angioplasty used in conjunction with clot-dissolving drugs, is no more effective in the treatment of heart attacks than prompt treatment with the drugs alone.	Robert Mapplethorpe, 42, photographer whose starkly elegant, often homoerotic work generated widespread admiration and controversy, dies in New York City, of Acquired Immune Deficiency Syndrome.... The Heidi Chronicles, a play about the life and loves of a feminist who grows up in the period 1965-1989, opens in New York. The play is written by Wendy Wasserstein and directed by Daniel Sullivan.	March 9
Pres. Bush's panel on ethics in government recommends a ban on all honoraria for government officials and a uniform limit on other outside earned income.... A federal grand jury has filed new charges against former Philippine Pres. Ferdinand E. Marcos and others in connection with the illegal transfer and embezzlement of $77 mil. for their private use.	Sharon Rogers, wife of Capt. Will C. Rogers III, whose frigate USS Vincennes shot down an Iranian jetliner in July 1988, narrowly escapes injury when a bomb explodes in her van while she is driving to work in San Diego, Calif.	In a major shift in U.S. developing-country debt policy, the Treasury Dept. unveils the outline of a revised U.S. debt strategy that endorses voluntary debt reduction by commercial banks.... The unemployment rate dropped to 5.1% in February, the Labor Dept. reports, lower than at any time since May 1974.	Scientists report that they have found that there is only one type of receptor in human cells to which the more than 100 different rhinoviruses that cause the common cold attach.		March 10
	John J(ay) McCloy, 93, lawyer and diplomat, dies in Stamford, Conn. U.S. high commissioner in Germany (1949-52), he oversaw the creation of a civilian government and supervised the disbursement of $1 bil. in aid to the war-ravaged economy. He was also president of the World Bank, chairman of Chase Manhattan Bank and the Ford Foundation, and consultant to presidents Kennedy, Johnson, Nixon, and Ford.		At an environmental summit conference in The Hague, leaders and ranking envoys of 24 nations call for a new organization with special enforcement powers to protect the planet's atmosphere.		March 11
				Maurice Evans, 87, British-born actor and producer best known for Shakespearean roles in the 1930s and 1940s, dies in a nursing home in Brighton, England. His abbreviated version of Hamlet for troops in the South Pacific during World War II became known as "G.I. Hamlet." His film credits include Rosemary's Baby (1968) and The Planet of the Apes (1968).	March 12
F	G	H	I	J	
Includes elections, federal-state relations, civil rights and liberties, crime, the judiciary, education, health care, poverty, urban affairs and population.	Includes formation and debate of U.S. foreign and defense policies, veterans' affairs and defense spending. (Relations with specific foreign countries are usually found under the region concerned.)	Includes business, labor, agriculture, taxation, transportation, consumer affairs, monetary and fiscal policy, natural resources, and pollution.	Includes worldwide scientific, medical and technological developments, natural phenomena, U.S. weather, natural disasters, and accidents.	Includes the arts, religion, scholarship, communications media, sports, entertainments, fashions, fads and social life.	

	World Affairs	Europe	Africa & the Middle East	The Americas	Asia & the Pacific
March 13		In Romania, a group of retired senior officials are reported to have been arrested after sending an open letter to Pres. Nicolae Ceausescu criticizing his iron rule.	Foreign ministers of the Org. of the Islamic Conference meeting in Riyadh, Saudi Arabia, condemn Salman Rushdie as an apostate but refuse to endorse Iran's death sentence against the British author.	Venezuela replaces its dual exchange rate with a single floating rate, in effect devaluing its currency, the bolivar, as part of the government's economic adjustment strategy announced a month earlier.	The six members of the Assoc. of Southeast Asian Nations adopt new restrictions on Vietnamese refugees, who must now prove they face religious or political persecution to qualify for asylum.
March 14	Kerstin Ekman and Lars Gyllensten resign their life memberships in Sweden's Academy of Letters, which awards the Nobel Prize for literature, over its failure to condemn Iran's death sentence against Salman Rushdie.	Greece's Premier Andreas Papandreou survives a motion of no confidence against his Socialist government. The vote was prompted by a continuing scandal over misappropriated funds from the Bank of Crete.			
March 15		The economy ministers of the six Balkan states meeting in Ankara, Turkey, for the region's first economic summit agree to several proposals, including the creation of a Balkan Chamber of Commerce, aimed at easing regional trade barriers and facilitating economic contacts.	Israel returns the Sinai beach resort of Taba, on the Gulf of Aqaba, marking the end of a long-running territorial dispute that came to represent the "cold peace" between the two nations.		
March 16		The Communist Party (CP) Central Committee endorses a sweeping plan to revitalize the Soviet Union's stagnant agricultural sector.			
March 17			South Africa's Pres. Pieter W. Botha unexpectedly returns to work after having suffered a stroke in January. It is a move that pits him against his own National Party, the majority of which want him to step aside in favor of Frederik W. de Klerk.	The Inter-American Development Bank approves a $26.5 bil. capital increase that will allow it to triple lending to Latin America over the next four years and assume a larger role in resolving the region's debt crisis.	Japan's gross national product grew at an inflation-adjusted 5.7% in calendar 1988, the Economic Planning Agency reports, higher than at any time since 1973, when the economy grew 7.9%.
March 18		An estimated 200,000 people march in Bilbao, Spain, calling on Basque extremists to extend a cease-fire that has been in effect since January. The cease-fire, offered by the ETA (Basque Homeland and Liberty) military group, is due to expire on Easter Sunday, March 26.			

A	B	C	D	E
Includes developments that affect more than one world region, international organizations and important meetings of major world leaders.	Includes all domestic and regional developments in Europe, including the Soviet Union, Turkey, Cyprus and Malta.	Includes all domestic and regional developments in Africa and the Middle East, including Iraq and Iran and excluding Cyprus, Turkey and Afghanistan.	Includes all domestic and regional developments in Latin America, the Caribbean and Canada.	Includes all domestic and regional developments in Asia and Pacific nations, extending from Afghanistan through all the Pacific Islands, except Hawaii.

U.S. Politics & Social Issues	U.S. Foreign Policy & Defense	U.S. Economy & Environment	Science, Technology & Nature	Culture, Leisure & Life Style	
The Teamsters union reaches agreement with the Justice Dept. on election reform and a watchdog review board, as part of a settlement of federal racketeering charges brought against the union. . . . The California State Assembly votes to prohibit the sale, possession or manufacture of semiautomatic assault weapons. If signed into law, the bill will make the state the first in the country to enact such a ban.		After two weeks of a machinists' strike supported by pilots and flight attendants, Eastern Airlines is flying only 10% of its regularly scheduled 1,040 daily flights.			March 13
In a major policy change, the Bush administration announces that it will ban imports of semiautomatic assault rifles indefinitely.	A federal jury convicts Lebanese Shiite Moslem militiaman Fawaz Younis in the June 1985 hijacking of a Jordanian airliner in Beirut in the first application of U.S. "long-arm" statutes that make terrorist attacks against U.S. citizens anywhere in the world a crime.	The deficit in the balance of payments on current account shrank 12.1% in 1988, the Commerce Dept. reports.	Two days of record monsoon rainfalls are reported in Australia; the highest reported reading is in Motpena, South Australia, where 10.8 inches of rain, twice the yearly average, falls in a 24-hour period.		March 14
In order to be "consistent with U.S. government policy," Colt Industries announces that it will stop sales to civilians of its AR-15 semiautomatic rifle. . . . Pres. Bush submits to Congress a proposal for tax credits to help low-income families pay for child care.		The merchandise trade deficit shrank to a seasonally adjusted $9.49 bil. in January, the Commerce Dept. reports.		Joe Runyan wins Alaska's 1,168-mile Iditarod dog sled race to snap the three-year winning streak of Susan Butcher, who finished second.	March 15
		The Federal Reserve Board reports that its industrial production index held steady in February.	To stem concern about the use of the ripener daminozide (brand name Alar), the Food and Drug Admin., the Environmental Protection Agency and the Dept. of Agriculture say that eating apples is safe. . . . The British journal *Nature* reports the estimated median incubation time of the virus that causes Acquired Immune Deficiency Sydrome (AIDS) at 9.8 years.	Kurt Browning of Canada wins the men's Figure Skating title at the World Championships.	March 16
	The Senate confirms Rep. Dick Cheney (R, Wyo.) as secretary of defense by a vote of 92-0. Cheney's confirmation finally rounds out the Bush cabinet, almost two months after Bush's inauguration.	The government's producer price index climbed 1% in February, the Labor Dept. reports. . . . Southern California regional authorities adopt a stern new code of regulations in a long-range program to reduce air pollution. The three-phase plan ranges from banning gasoline-powered lawn mowers to ending the use of gasoline in automobiles by the year 2007.	The Food and Drug Admin. (FDA) over the last five days quarantines all fruit imported from Chile after U.S. government investigators discover traces of cyanide in two Chilean seedless red grapes. The FDA move leads U.S. produce wholesalers and retailers to pull all Chilean fruit from the market until today, when the ban on Chilean grapes is lifted.		March 17
		A bill to raise the minimum wage to $4.65 an hour over three years is approved by a committee in the House. The minimum wage has been $3.35 an hour since 1981.	The space shuttle *Discovery* completes a near-perfect five-day flight with a flawless landing at Edwards Air Force Base in California.	Midori Ito of Japan wins the women's World Figure Skating title at the World Championships after performing the first successful triple axel jump by a woman in a world championship. . . . Pete Weber becomes only the third man to win bowling's triple crown when he wins the Professional Bowlers Association National Championship. Weber won the two other legs of the triple crown, the Tournament of Champions and the U.S. Open, in 1987 and 1988, respectively.	March 18

F	G	H	I	J
Includes elections, federal-state relations, civil rights and liberties, crime, the judiciary, education, health care, poverty, urban affairs and population.	*Includes formation and debate of U.S. foreign and defense policies, veterans' affairs and defense spending. (Relations with specific foreign countries are usually found under the region concerned.)*	*Includes business, labor, agriculture, taxation, transportation, consumer affairs, monetary and fiscal policy, natural resources, and pollution.*	*Includes worldwide scientific, medical and technological developments, natural phenomena, U.S. weather, natural disasters, and accidents.*	*Includes the arts, religion, scholarship, communications media, sports, entertainments, fashions, fads and social life.*

	World Affairs	Europe	Africa & the Middle East	The Americas	Asia & the Pacific
March 19		Thousands of Muscovites hold public demonstrations over the last two weeks in support of the parliamentary candidacy of Boris N. Yeltsin. Yeltsin, a former head of the Moscow city Communist Party, is seeking the city's at-large seat in the elections for the new Congress of People's Deputies. The elections were set for March 26.... Several thousand Greek-Cypriot women and their supporters march into Turkish-controlled northern Cyprus to protest the continued division of the island nation. The women's group, Women Walk Home, meets with violence from Turkish police guards at the town of Lymbia, in the UN buffer zone. Nine are reported injured there, and 32 arrested.		Alfredo Cristiani, 41, candidate of the right-wing Nationalist Republican Alliance (ARENA), is elected president of El Salvador, defeating Fidel Chavez Mena of the Christian Democratic Party. He will succeed Christian Democratic President Jose Napoleon Duarte June 1.	
March 20					South Korean Pres. Roh Tae Woo announces that he is postponing indefinitely a vote of confidence on his rule that he promised during his 1987 election campaign. Roh says he is delaying the vote, which was expected to be held in April, to avoid "the repetition of the confusion and violence" that accompanied the 1987 contest.... The National People's Congress, China's nominal parliament, begins its annual legislative session in Beijing. In stark contrast to the previous year's session, the somber and guarded assembly emphasizes tighter central control over politics and economics.
March 21				P.M. Kennedy Simmonds is reelected to a third consecutive term in general elections in St. Christopher (St. Kitts) and Nevis.... Ousted Panamanian Pres. Eric Arturo del Valle, still recognized by the U.S. as Panama's leader, announces that he has made his permanent home in Miami.	Three days of peace talks among the warring factions in the Cambodian conflict end with no significant progress reported. The talks mark the second time the four main factions in the 10-year-old war have assembled for face-to-face negotiations. The first series of meetings occurred in July 1988.
March 22	More than 100 nations reach agreement in Basel, Switzerland on a treaty to control the exporting of hazardous wastes across national borders. The pact, designed to curb the dumping of toxic waste in developing countries, requires an exporting country to obtain prior written permission from the government of a recipient country before such wastes can be shipped.		The Palestine Liberation Org., in its first substantive meeting with the Bush administration, in Tunis, rejects a U.S. request that it help ease the violence of the intifada (uprising) in the Israeli-occupied West Bank and Gaza Strip.		

A	B	C	D	E
Includes developments that affect more than one world region, international organizations and important meetings of major world leaders.	Includes all domestic and regional developments in Europe, including the Soviet Union, Turkey, Cyprus and Malta.	Includes all domestic and regional developments in Africa and the Middle East, including Iraq and Iran and excluding Cyprus, Turkey and Afghanistan.	Includes all domestic and regional developments in Latin America, the Caribbean and Canada.	Includes all domestic and regional developments in Asia and Pacific nations, extending from Afghanistan through all the Pacific Islands, except Hawaii.

U.S. Politics & Social Issues	U.S. Foreign Policy & Defense	U.S. Economy & Environment	Science, Technology & Nature	Culture, Leisure & Life Style	
		Housing starts plunged 11.4% in February as a result of colder weather and higher mortgage rates, the Commerce Dept. reports.		Kenya's John Ngugi wins his fourth consecutive world cross-country championship. Ngugi's time was 39 minutes, 42 seconds. Kenya also wins the team title. . . . The British Academy of Film and Televison Arts names Bernardo Bertolucci's *The Last Emperor* best film; French director Louis Malle, best director for *Au Revoir les Enfants*; John Cleese, best actor for *A Fish Called Wanda*; and Maggie Smith, best actress for *The Lonely Passion of Judith Hearne. Death on the Rock*, about the killing of three suspected Provisional Irish Republican Army terrorists in Gibraltar, wins the award for best broadcast documentary.	March 19
The Supreme Court lifts a stay against the merger of non-editorial functions by Detroit's two daily newspapers, the *Detroit News* and the *Detroit Free Press*.					March 20
The Supreme Court upholds federal drug-testing programs for workers in jobs involving public safety and health. The court upholds Federal Railroad Admin. regulations for testing railroad crews after accidents. . . . Randall Dale Adams, whose conviction for murdering a Dallas police officer in 1976 was overturned in the wake of widespread publicity generated by a 1988 documentary *The Thin Blue Line*, is released on a personal recognizance bond after serving more than 12 years in prison.	In one of his first significant foreign policy decisions since assuming office, Pres. Bush announces that he has decided to proceed with plans for joint development of a new Japanese fighter plane, the FSX.	The consumer price index rose 0.4% in February, the Labor Dept. reports.	A team of California chemists creates a new state of matter in which individual chemical molecules are imprisoned within larger molecules, it is reported. The discovery is reported by a team led by Donald J. Cram of the Univ. of California at Los Angeles, co-winner of the 1987 Nobel Prize in chemistry.		March 21
The Supreme Court rules, 9-0, that New York City's major governing body, the Board of Estimate, is unconstitutional because it violates the principle of one person, one vote. The court upholds a 1987 appeals court decision that the board is unconstitutional in that the five borough presidents have equal votes despite a vast population difference between the lowest-populated borough, Staten Island (350,000 people), and the highest-populated borough, Brooklyn (2.2 million people). . . . House Republicans elect Rep. Newt Gingrich of Georgia to the number-two post of party whip. He replaces former Rep. Dick Cheney (R, Wyo.), who resigned to become secretary of defense. . . . Leon King, who was convicted of beating a man to death during a robbery attempt in 1978, is executed by means of a lethal injection in Huntsville, Texas.		Millions of pounds of toxic chemicals are being emitted into the atmosphere in every state of the union, according to a survey by the House Energy and Commerce Committee's subcommittee on health and the environment.		The Genie awards are presented by the Canadian Academy of Cinema and Television. *Dead Ringers* wins 10 awards, including best picture, best director, David Cronenberg, and best actor, Jeremy Irons. Jackie Burroughs, is best actress for *A Winter Tan*.	March 22

F	G	H	I	J
Includes elections, federal-state relations, civil rights and liberties, crime, the judiciary, education, health care, poverty, urban affairs and population.	*Includes formation and debate of U.S. foreign and defense policies, veterans' affairs and defense spending. (Relations with specific foreign countries are usually found under the region concerned.)*	*Includes business, labor, agriculture, taxation, transportation, consumer affairs, monetary and fiscal policy, natural resources, and pollution.*	*Includes worldwide scientific, medical and technological developments, natural phenomena, U.S. weather, natural disasters, and accidents.*	*Includes the arts, religion, scholarship, communications media, sports, entertainments, fashions, fads and social life.*

	World Affairs	Europe	Africa & the Middle East	The Americas	Asia & the Pacific
March 23		Britain's annual inflation rate rose to 7.8% in February, the highest rate since August 1982, the Dept. of Employment reports. February inflation was up from a 7.5% rate in January. Rising mortgage rates are blamed for much of the increase.		Argentine Pres. Carlos Saul Menem promises pardons for certain military officers and guerrillas involved in the nation's "dirty war" of the 1970s and for some government officials jailed for mishandling the 1982 war with Great Britain over the Falkland Islands (Malvinas).	
March 24				Pres. Bush and congressional leaders sign a bipartisan accord on Central America that includes continued humanitarian aid for the Contras fighting the Nicaraguan government.	The first major battle in the Afghan war since the withdrawal of Soviet troops in mid-February begins March 6 when rebel forces launch an offensive against the eastern city of Jalalabad. After some early gains, however, the rebel advance bogs down, and by this day foreign observers say the battle has settled into a stalemate. . . . More than 600 people are killed or injured in unrest in Tibet during the previous 18 months, the Chinese press reports. Major General Zhang Shaosong, political commissar of the Chinese Army contingent in Tibet, is quoted by the official New China News Agency as saying there have been 21 outbreaks of violence in the disputed region, resulting in "more than 600 casualties," since September 1987.
March 25			Egypt's Pres. Hosni Mubarak, Jordan's King Hussein, and Palestine Liberation Org. chairman Yasir Arafat meet in Ismailia, Egypt, to coordinate their approaches to the Arab-Israeli peace process.		
March 26		The Soviet Union holds its first nationwide multicandidate parliamentary elections since 1917 in a step toward Western-style democracy that has unexpectedly embarrassing results for the Communist Party leadership.			In Laos's first national elections—for the 79 seats in the Supreme People's Assembly—since the communists came to power in 1975, only 47% of the electorate are reported to have participated in the voting.
March 27					A previously secret Indian government report released to parliament says that Rajendra Kumar Dhawan, a top aide to the late P.M. Indira Gandhi and a key adviser to current P.M. Rajiv Gandhi, is suspected of complicity in the former's assassination.
March 28			In what is seen as part of a purge of moderates and pragmatists led by Ayatollah Ruhollah Khomeini himself, Ayatollah Hussein Ali Montazeri quits under pressure as the designated successor to Khomeini.		

A	B	C	D	E
Includes developments that affect more than one world region, international organizations and important meetings of major world leaders.	Includes all domestic and regional developments in Europe, including the Soviet Union, Turkey, Cyprus and Malta.	Includes all domestic and regional developments in Africa and the Middle East, including Iraq and Iran and excluding Cyprus, Turkey and Afghanistan.	Includes all domestic and regional developments in Latin America, the Caribbean and Canada.	Includes all domestic and regional developments in Asia and Pacific nations, extending from Afghanistan through all the Pacific Islands, except Hawaii.

U.S. Politics & Social Issues	U.S. Foreign Policy & Defense	U.S. Economy & Environment	Science, Technology & Nature	Culture, Leisure & Life Style	
		Gross national product grew at a 2.4% annual rate in the fourth quarter of 1988, the Commerce Dept. reports.... After-tax profits of U.S. corporations rose 2.8% in the fourth quarter of 1988, to an annual rate of $173.9 bil., the Commerce Dept. reports.	Two scientists, Stanley Pons of the Univ. of Utah and Martin Fleischmann of the Univ. Southampton, in England, announce that they have achieved a controlled nuclear fusion reaction at room temperature. The achievement, if confirmed, would represent a monumental breakthrough in energy production. But much of the scientific world remains skeptical until the unorthodox claims can be confirmed.	Television host Dick Clark will retire from the TV show "American Bandstand"; he hosted the popular rock-and-roll dance program for 33 years.	March 23
Disbarred lawyer Joel B. Steinberg is sentenced in a New York City court following his conviction for manslaughter in the beating death of his six-year-old illegally adopted daughter, Lisa. Steinberg receives the maximum sentence of eight-and-a-third to 25 years in prison.		Loaded with 1,260,000 barrels of crude oil, the supertanker *Exxon Valdez* runs aground on Bligh Reef in Prince William Sound, 25 miles from Valdez, Alaska, the southern terminal of the Alyeska pipeline.... Personal income surged 1% to a $4.315 trillion annual rate in February while consumer spending increased 0.5% to a $3.38 trillion rate, the Commerce Dept. reports.	A Delta rocket launches a $140 mil. satellite as an orbiting sensor in space for research on the Strategic Defense Initiative space-based anti-missile defense.		March 24
	Bush administration officials have reportedly asked Afghan rebel leaders in Afghanistan to restrict the production and sale of opium, which can be converted into heroin, in areas under their control.			Oxford Univ. wins the annual University Boat Race against Cambridge on the Thames River in London. The race marks the first time that both crews used women coxswains.... *Billboard*'s best-selling albums for the week are: *Electric Youth*, Debbie Gibson; *Don't Be Cruel*, Bobby Brown; *Appetite for Destruction*, Guns N' Roses; *Forever Your Girl*, Paula Abdul; and *Traveling Wilburys*, Traveling Wilburys.	March 25
				Nigel Mansell of Britain wins the opening race of the Formula One Grand Prix season, the *Brazilian Grand Prix*.	March 26
Alarmed by the high crime in Washington, D.C., which had the highest murder rate of any major U.S. city in 1988, the Bush administration reportedly plans to make the city the showpiece of its effort to fight drugs and drug-related crime.	The United States agrees to accept an Iraqi offer to pay $27.3 mil. in compensation to the families of 37 American sailors killed in a May 1987 attack on the Navy frigate USS *Stark*.			Malcolm Cowley, 90, writer, editor, and critic, dies of a heart attack in New Milford, Conn. As an editor at the *New Republic* magazine in the 1930s and at Viking Press (1944-85), he championed the cause of such writers as William Faulkner and John Dos Passos. His own essays and profiles also celebrated the so-called Lost Generation of American writers.	March 27
		Alaska's Lt. Gov. Stephen McAlpine says that he is "severely disappointed" in the Exxon Corp.'s response to the March 24 *Exxon Valdez* oil spill.	The official Soviet news agency Tass reports that radio contact with the Soviet unmanned spacecraft Phobos 2 has been lost just as the craft was to enter orbit around the Martian moon Phobos.	A New York State judge rules that the San Diego Yacht Club's successful 1988 defense of the America's Cup was the result of an intentionally "gross mismatch" and orders the cup forfeited to the New Zealand challenger.	March 28

F	G	H	I	J
Includes elections, federal-state relations, civil rights and liberties, crime, the judiciary, education, health care, poverty, urban affairs and population.	*Includes formation and debate of U.S. foreign and defense policies, veterans' affairs and defense spending. (Relations with specific foreign countries are usually found under the region concerned.)*	*Includes business, labor, agriculture, taxation, transportation, consumer affairs, monetary and fiscal policy, natural resources, and pollution.*	*Includes worldwide scientific, medical and technological developments, natural phenomena, U.S. weather, natural disasters, and accidents.*	*Includes the arts, religion, scholarship, communications media, sports, entertainments, fashions, fads and social life.*

	World Affairs	Europe	Africa & the Middle East	The Americas	Asia & the Pacific
March 29	Abdullah al-Ahdal, spiritual leader of Belgium's Muslim community, and an associate are assassinated in Brussels, apparently because of their criticism of Iran's death threat against the author Salman Rushdie.	Clashes in Yugoslavia's Kosovo province between paramilitary riot police and thousands of ethnic Albanians have claimed at least 23 lives over the previous six days.			
March 30	The Ministerial Monitoring Committee of the Org. of Petroleum Exporting Countries concludes its quarterly meeting in Vienna with plans to increase oil production in the summer of 1989 if prices remain strong.			Canada's External Affairs Min. Joe Clark announces an end to a decade-old ban on Canadian high-level diplomatic contacts with the Palestine Liberation Org. . . . At least seven people are killed during a five-day siege at El Pavon maximum security prison in Guatemala following a failed mass breakout March 26 by about 100 of the prison's 1,300 inmates.	Speaking before the Japanese Diet, Premier Noboru Takeshita issues Japan's first formal apology to North Korea for its subjugation of the Korean peninsula from 1910 to 1945.
March 31					
April 1		Empress Zita of Austria, who ruled with her husband, Karl, from 1916 until their exile in 1918, is laid to rest in Vienna. The empress was the last monarch of the 600-year-old Habsburg dynasty.	Iraqis go to the polls to elect a new 250-member National Assembly in what is billed as an exercise in democracy and political liberalization following the end of the Persian Gulf War and two decades of rule by Pres. Saddam Hussein and his Baath Party. . . . Namibia's UN-monitored transition to independence is disrupted as armed guerrillas of the South-West African People's Org. infiltrating en masse from Angola clash with South African security forces.		In Japan, a controversial 3% sales tax passed by the Diet in December 1988 is implemented. Confusion about various provisions of the new levy has caused chaos among businesses and retailers in recent weeks.
April 2			In what is considered Tunisia's freest election in over 30 years of independence, the ruling party of Pres. Zine el-Abidine Ben Ali wins a landslide victory despite a strong challenge from Islamic fundamentalists.	Soviet leader Mikhail S. Gorbachev visits Cuba for his first extensive talks with Fidel Castro since 1986. The last Soviet leader to visit Cuba was Leonid Brezhnev, in 1974. . . . In Haiti, an attempted coup by members of an elite military battalion seeking to oust Pres. Prosper Avril fails.	

A	B	C	D	E
Includes developments that affect more than one world region, international organizations and important meetings of major world leaders.	Includes all domestic and regional developments in Europe, including the Soviet Union, Turkey, Cyprus and Malta.	Includes all domestic and regional developments in Africa and the Middle East, including Iraq and Iran and excluding Cyprus, Turkey and Afghanistan.	Includes all domestic and regional developments in Latin America, the Caribbean and Canada.	Includes all domestic and regional developments in Asia and Pacific nations, extending from Afghanistan through all the Pacific Islands, except Hawaii.

U.S. Politics & Social Issues	U.S. Foreign Policy & Defense	U.S. Economy & Environment	Science, Technology & Nature	Culture, Leisure & Life Style	
Housing and Urban Development Sec. Jack F. Kemp announces that he will exempt the state of Virginia from federal administrative rules governing tenant evictions in a policy designed to make it easier to evict drug dealers and users from public housing projects.		A federal grand jury in New York indicts Michael R. Milken and two other Drexel Burnham Lambert Inc. employees on 98 counts of racketeering, securities fraud, insider trading, and other criminal charges. ... The government's index of leading economic indicators fell 0.3% in February, the Commerce Dept. reports.		At the 61st annual Academy Awards, *Rain Man* wins awards for best picture, actor (Dustin Hoffman), director (Barry Levinson), and original screenplay. Best actress is Jodie Foster (*The Accused*); supporting actor, Kevin Kline (*A Fish Called Wanda*), and supporting actress, Geena Davis (*The Accidental Tourist*). The Danish film *Pelle the Conqueror* wins for best foreign film. *Who Framed Roger Rabbit*, the top-grossing film for 1988, wins for editing, sound effects editing and visual effects. ... In basketball, St. John's Univ. wins a record fifth National Invitational Tournament championship with a 73-65 victory over St. Louis. ... *Variety*'s top-grossing films for the week are: *Fletch Lives*, *Dead Bang*, *Lean on Me*, *Leviathan*, and *Chances Are*.	March 29
		Prices received by farmers for raw agricultural products rose 0.7% in March, the Agriculture Dept. reports.	A study in the *New England Journal of Medicine* reports that the $80-per-dose streptokinase (TPA) and $2,250-a-dose tissue plasminogen activator are equally effective in treating heart attacks.	The 73rd annual Pulitzer Prize in fiction goes to Anne Tyler, *Breathing Lessons*; drama, Wendy Wasserstein, *The Heidi Chronicles*; history, Taylor Branch, *Parting the Waters: America in the King Years, 1954-63*, and James M. McPherson, *Battle Cry of Freedom: The Civil War Era*; biography, the late Richard Ellmann for *Oscar Wilde*; general monfiction, Neil Sheehan, *A Bright Shining Lie: John Paul Vann and America in Vietnam*; poetry, Richard Wilbur, *New and Collected Poems*; music, Roger Reynolds, *Whispers Out of Time*. In journalism, *The Anchorage Daily News* wins the public service award for its series about alcoholism among Native Americans in Alaska.	March 30
The Bush administration grants a request from 13 senators to transfer $5 mil. in federal funds to a program that provides the drug AZT (azidothymidine, or zidovudine) to AIDS patients who cannot afford it. ... A federal appeals court in Washington, D.C., rules that a Federal Communications Comm. 1978 policy designed to promote minority ownership of radio and television stations is unconstitutional.		The sale of Eastern Airlines' East Coast shuttle to developer Donald Trump is cleared by negotiators, and next has to be approved by the bankruptcy court.		*Publishers Weekly*'s hardback fiction best-sellers for the week are: *The Satanic Verses*, Salman Rushdie; *Star*, Danielle Steel; *The Edge*, Dick Francis; *Billy Bathgate*, E. L. Doctorow; and *Midnight*, Dean R. Koontz.	March 31
				Harvard Univ. wins the National Collegiate Athletic Association ice hockey title with a 4-3 overtime victory over the Univ. of Minnesota.	April 1
A Dept. of Justice study released today finds that more than 60% of all inmates released from state prisons are arrested again for committing a serious crime within three years.				The Univ. of Tennessee Lady Volunteers defeat Auburn, 76-60, to win the National Collegiate Athletic Assoc. Division I women's basketball title. Tennessee forward Bridgette Gordon is named most valuable player.	April 2

F	G	H	I	J
Includes elections, federal-state relations, civil rights and liberties, crime, the judiciary, education, health care, poverty, urban affairs and population.	*Includes formation and debate of U.S. foreign and defense policies, veterans' affairs and defense spending. (Relations with specific foreign countries are usually found under the region concerned.)*	*Includes business, labor, agriculture, taxation, transportation, consumer affairs, monetary and fiscal policy, natural resources, and pollution.*	*Includes worldwide scientific, medical and technological developments, natural phenomena, U.S. weather, natural disasters, and accidents.*	*Includes the arts, religion, scholarship, communications media, sports, entertainments, fashions, fads and social life.*

	World Affairs	Europe	Africa & the Middle East	The Americas	Asia & the Pacific
April 3	The International Monetary Fund and World Bank broadly endorse the new U.S. developing-country debt-reduction plan and pledge to provide resources to facilitate its implementation.		After meeting wth Egypt's Pres. Hosni Mubarak in Washington, D.C., Pres. Bush says Egypt and the United States "share the goals of security for Israel, the end of the occupation and achievement of Palestinian political rights."		Australia's gross domestic product grew 4.2% in calendar 1988, according to figures released by the bureau of statistics.
April 4			Israel's P.M. Yitzhak Shamir arrives in New York City at the start of a 10-day tour during which he will meet with Pres. Bush and Sec. of State James A. Baker III.		China's National People's Congress passes a law under which citizens can sue the government in what Chinese officials and Western observers say marks an important step in the development of China's legal system.
April 5		In Poland, talks between government and opposition leaders close with accords on broad political and economic reform that place Poland on a par with Hungary in terms of democratic reform in Eastern Europe. . . . Soviet leader Mikhail S. Gorbachev begins an official three-day visit to Britain.	The *Financial Times* reports that Iraq's chief Western creditors privately reached an informal accord on rescheduling Baghdad's wartime debt at a meeting of the Paris Club of industrialized countries.	Ruling that a lower court had no authority to order the arrests, a Venezuelan military tribunal orders the release of 15 soldiers and police officers accused in the October 1988 massacre of 14 fishermen.	Vietnam announces that it will unconditionally withdraw all its troops from Cambodia by September 30, nearly 11 years after invading the country to oust the Khmer Rouge government of Pol Pot. . . . A former head of the National Safety Council of Australia, the world's largest private search and rescue organization, is arrested near Perth in connection with the apparent theft of $33 mil. in council funds.
April 6				Brazil's Pres. Jose Sarney announces a $358 mil., five-year program to protect and develop the Brazilian Amazon region as part of the "Our Nature" initiative launched in October 1988.	
April 7		Tass, the official Soviet news agency, reports that 42 of 69 crew members died when a Soviet nuclear submarine caught fire and sank in international waters off Norway. . . . After a seven-year investigation magistrates in Milan, Italy, announce the indictments of 35 people in connection with the $1.3 bil. collapse of Banco Ambrosiano in 1982.			Indian government investigators formally charge five Sikhs, one of whom is dead, with conspiracy in the assassination of P.M. Indira Gandhi in 1984.
April 8	Clearing the way for the resumption of the Uruguay Round of trade negotiations, representatives of the General Agreement on Tariffs and Trade agree on negotiating guidelines in agriculture, textiles, intellectual property, and import safeguards.	In France, former Premier Jacques Chirac's neo-Gaullist Rally for the Republic holds a special meeting of its National Council to deal with a growing challenge to the party's leadership from younger members.		Mexican federal agents in Guadalajara arrest Miguel Angel Felix Gallardo, reputed to be one of the world's top drug traffickers.	
April 9		At least 16 people are killed in a clash between Soviet troops and nationalist demonstrators in Tbilisi, the capital of the republic of Georgia.	Citing Kurdish sources, British newspapers report that Iraqi troops have given the 100,000 Kurdish inhabitants of Diza 17 days to leave before razing the city. The Kurds fear being relocated to Iraq's southern desert.		

A	B	C	D	E
Includes developments that affect more than one world region, international organizations and important meetings of major world leaders.	Includes all domestic and regional developments in Europe, including the Soviet Union, Turkey, Cyprus and Malta.	Includes all domestic and regional developments in Africa and the Middle East, including Iraq and Iran and excluding Cyprus, Turkey and Afghanistan.	Includes all domestic and regional developments in Latin America, the Caribbean and Canada.	Includes all domestic and regional developments in Asia and Pacific nations, extending from Afghanistan through all the Pacific Islands, except Hawaii.

U.S. Politics & Social Issues	U.S. Foreign Policy & Defense	U.S. Economy & Environment	Science, Technology & Nature	Culture, Leisure & Life Style	
		The Supreme Court upholds a New Jersey corporate tax law that bars companies from deducting from income their federal windfall profits tax payments.		The Univ. of Michigan wins the National Collegiate Athletic Assoc. Division I men's basketball title, 80-79, over Seton Hall. Michigan forward Glen Rice is named most valuable player.	April 3
Richard M. Daley (D), a three-term Cook County state's attorney, is elected mayor of Chicago, the same post his father had held for 21 years.					April 4
Pres. Bush presents Congress with a $441 mil. plan to promote academic excellence, but it is immediately assailed by educators and congressional Democrats who say it is inadequate and will do little to improve the quality of education across the country.... The House votes, 238-154, to establish 9:00 p.m. Eastern Standard Time—8:00 p.m. Central Time and 7:00 p.m. Mountain Time and Pacific coast states—as the uniform poll-closing time in the continental United States for presidential elections. ... Nicodemo Scarfo, the reputed head of organized crime in Philadelphia and southern New Jersey, is convicted together with seven associates of the first-degree murder of reputed mobster Frank D'Alfonso.		Joseph Hazelwood, fugitive captain of the supertanker *Exxon Valdez*, surrenders to authorities in New York and is jailed on charges including being drunk when the tanker ran aground on March 24.	In the sixth and largest debt-for-nature swap, the World Wildlife Fund and Nature Conservancy agree to absorb $9 mil. in Ecuadoran debt and to spend a comparable local-currency amount to preserve rain forests in western Ecuador.		April 5
A government document released by Oliver L. North's defense attorneys shows that both Pres. Bush and then-president Ronald Reagan played significant roles in efforts to secure third-country aid for the Nicaraguan Contras at a time when U.S. assistance to the rebels had been barred by Congress.... Federal prosecutors in New York City say that former Philippine Pres. Ferdinand E. Marcos is too ill to stand trial and they seek to have the criminal charges filed against him temporarily suspended.		An agreement to sell strike-bound Eastern Airlines to an investors' group led by former baseball commissioner Peter V. Ueberroth is announced by Frank Lorenzo, chairman of the parent Texas Air Corp.... Outstanding consumer debt expanded $4.22 bil. in February, at a 7.5% annual rate, the Commerce Dept. reports.			April 6
		Pres. Bush pledges federal assistance—including military troops and equipment—to clean up the 240,000-barrel crude oil spill resulting from the March 24 grounding of the tanker *Exxon Valdez* in Alaska. ... The unemployment rate drops to 4.9% in March, the Labor Dept. reports, its lowest level since December 1973.		The International Basketball Federation votes to allow professional basketball players to compete in the Olympics beginning with the 1992 games in Barcelona. Surveys show that 50% to 60% of U.S. National Basketball Assoc. players are interested in playing in the games.	April 7
					April 8
The Dept. of Justice releases preliminary figures showing that personal and household crime rose 1.8% in 1988, the second consecutive year that crime has increased, following a five-year decline.				Nick Faldo of England wins the Masters golf tournament in Augusta, Ga.	April 9

F	G	H	I	J
Includes elections, federal-state relations, civil rights and liberties, crime, the judiciary, education, health care, poverty, urban affairs and population.	Includes formation and debate of U.S. foreign and defense policies, veterans' affairs and defense spending. (Relations with specific foreign countries are usually found under the region concerned.)	Includes business, labor, agriculture, taxation, transportation, consumer affairs, monetary and fiscal policy, natural resources, and pollution.	Includes worldwide scientific, medical and technological developments, natural phenomena, U.S. weather, natural disasters, and accidents.	Includes the arts, religion, scholarship, communications media, sports, entertainments, fashions, fads and social life.

	World Affairs	Europe	Africa & the Middle East	The Americas	Asia & the Pacific
April 10				Haiti's Pres. Prosper Avril appears to have established his control over the armed forces two days after an attempted coup, although Avril declines to pronounce the rebellion over.... The Chilean Army issues declares its support for Pres. Augusto Pinochet and expresses "profound unease" at suggestions that he resign as commander in chief when a democratically elected government assumes power in March 1990.	Six people have been killed in the last five days in a wave of unrest on the Papua New Guinean island of Bougainville. Two of the dead are soldiers, reported to be the first ever killed in action.
April 11		*Pravda*, the Soviet Communist Party newspaper, offers a front-page editorial condemning all nationalist movements in the USSR as efforts to "undermine" the state.		Mexico announces tentative agreement with the International Monetary Fund for a $3.64 bil. loan to support the country's economic adjustment program, including the reduction of Mexico's $104 bil. foreign debt.	In an attempt to end a political crisis that has all but paralyzed his government, Japan's Premier Noboru Takeshita appears before the Diet to answer questions about his involvement in the Recruit stock trading scandal.
April 12		The Basque separatist military group Euskadi Ta Askatasuna (ETA) takes credit for two days of terrorist attacks in Spain following the breakdown of talks in Algiers between the ETA and the Spanish government.... Pres. Nicolae Ceausescu tells the Communist Party Central Committee that Romania has repaid its foreign debt ahead of schedule. At the end of 1988, the country's gross foreign debt was $3.2 bil., down from $10 bil. in 1981.			
April 13			An Israeli border police raid on an Arab village near Bethlehem in the occupied West Bank, kills at least four Palestinian youths and wounds more than 20 others.		
April 14			The cabinet and ruling party of Zimbabwe's Pres. Robert Mugabe is shaken by a corruption scandal that has lead to the resignations of six top government officials during the previous six weeks.	In Ottawa, Canada, Indians protest, against a government plan to cut back a university education assistance program under which the federal government pays for Indians' and Inuits' post-secondary education.	China's population has reached a record 1.1 billion, the Chinese government reports. The figure, considered low by some Chinese researchers, is more than double that recorded in 1949 and represents about 22% of the world's total population.... The former president of Vanuatu, George Sokomanu, and Barak Sope, are released from prison after an appeals court overturns their March convictions on sedition charges after attempting to stage a constitutional coup in the island nation.
April 15	Ninety-five British soccer fans are killed and nearly 200 injured when several thousand fans surge into already crowded stands in the opening minutes of a Football Association Cup semifinal game between Liverpool and Nottingham Forest in Sheffield, South Yorkshire.				Hu Yaobang, 73, former general secretary and chairman of the Chinese Communist Party, dies of a heart attack in Beijing. Purged during the Cultural Revolution of 1966, he was rehabilitated in 1973 and named to the top post of the Communist Party in 1980. He resigned in disgrace after students took to the streets to demand greater democracy in December 1986.

A	B	C	D	E
Includes developments that affect more than one world region, international organizations and important meetings of major world leaders.	Includes all domestic and regional developments in Europe, including the Soviet Union, Turkey, Cyprus and Malta.	Includes all domestic and regional developments in Africa and the Middle East, including Iraq and Iran and excluding Cyprus, Turkey and Afghanistan.	Includes all domestic and regional developments in Latin America, the Caribbean and Canada.	Includes all domestic and regional developments in Asia and Pacific nations, extending from Afghanistan through all the Pacific Islands, except Hawaii.

U.S. Politics & Social Issues	U.S. Foreign Policy & Defense	U.S. Economy & Environment	Science, Technology & Nature	Culture, Leisure & Life Style	
Pres. Bush signs the Whistleblower Protection Act, legislation designed to shield federal employees from retaliation if they disclose fraud and abuse in their agencies. . . . The Bush administration's plans to fight drugs and drug-related crime in Washington, D.C., center on transfering 250 prisoners from the city to federal prisons and the eventual construction of two new prisons.					April 10
Following an election campaign that generated little public interest, voters in Los Angeles return Mayor Tom Bradley (D) to office for an unprecedented fifth term. . . . In a complaint to the House Ethics Committee, Rep. Newt Gingrich (R, Ga.) is cited for violating House rules on the acceptance of gifts and outside income in the promotion of his book *Window of Opportunity*.			The National Research Council, a working group of the National Academy of Sciences, recommends against federal support for a privately developed orbital space station.		April 11
Pres. Bush proposes a series of measures aimed at tightening ethical standards for members of Congress, the executive branch, and the federal judiciary. . . . Pres. Bush and his wife, Barbara, paid $62,106 in federal taxes on an adjusted gross income of $287,171 in 1988, according to tax returns released by the White House. . . . Vice Pres. Dan Quayle and his wife, Marilyn, paid $24,314 in federal income taxes on an adjusted gross income of $156,546 in 1988.		The Senate approves, 62-37, a bill that will boost the minimum wage to $4.55 an hour by late 1991. The measure is sent to conference with the House, which passed a similar bill March 23. . . . The proposed sale of Eastern Airlines to an investment group headed by Peter V. Ueberroth collapses in a continuing stalemate between Eastern's striking unions and Frank Lorenzo, chairman of Eastern's Texas Air Corp. . . . SmithKline Beckman Corp. and Beecham Group PLC of Great Britain agree to a merger that will create the second-largest pharmaceutical company in the world with total capitalization of $16.4 bil. and annual sales of $6.7 bil.	Pres. Bush chooses Rear Adm. Richard Truly to head the National Aeronautics and Space Admin. (NASA), replacing James C. Fletcher, who led the agency after the *Challenger* disaster in 1986.	Abbott (Abbie) Hoffman, 52, radical protest leader of the 1960s, anti-Vietnam War activist and founder of the Yippies (Youth International Party), is found dead at his home in New Hope, Pa. He rose to national prominence as a defendant in the raucous Chicago Seven Trial of 1969-70; his conviction was later overturned on appeal. . . . Walker Smith "Sugar Ray" Robinson, 67, five-time world champion middleweight boxer, dies in Culver City, Calif. He suffered from Alzheimer's disease and diabetes. In a career that lasted from 1940 to 1965 he posted a record 175 wins (with 110 knockouts) and 19 losses (with only one knockoout).	April 12
A report by the Senate Foreign Relations subcommittee on terrorism, narcotics, and international operations says that the Reagan administration repeatedly undercut efforts to curb the illegal narcotics trade in pursuing its foreign policy goals.	Congress approves $49.8 mil. in humanitarian aid to the Nicaraguan Contra rebels.	Settling civil charges brought by the Securities and Exchange Comm., Drexel Burnham Lambert Inc. agrees to give federal regulators unprecedented control over its operations.			April 13
		After a month of closed-door negotiations, Pres. Bush announces an agreement with congressional leaders on the broad outlines of budget policy to meet the mandated FY1990 deficit target of $100 bil. . . . The merchandise trade deficit expanded sharply to a seasonally adjusted $10.5 bil. in February, the Commerce Dept. reports. . . . The government's producer price index increased 0.4% in March, the Labor Dept. reports. . . . The Federal Reserve Board reports that its industrial production index held steady in March.			April 14
					April 15

F	G	H	I	J
Includes elections, federal-state relations, civil rights and liberties, crime, the judiciary, education, health care, poverty, urban affairs and population.	*Includes formation and debate of U.S. foreign and defense policies, veterans' affairs and defense spending. (Relations with specific foreign countries are usually found under the region concerned.)*	*Includes business, labor, agriculture, taxation, transportation, consumer affairs, monetary and fiscal policy, natural resources, and pollution.*	*Includes worldwide scientific, medical and technological developments, natural phenomena, U.S. weather, natural disasters, and accidents.*	*Includes the arts, religion, scholarship, communications media, sports, entertainments, fashions, fads and social life.*

	World Affairs	Europe	Africa & the Middle East	The Americas	Asia & the Pacific
April 16		To ease public dissatisfaction over severe domestic shortages, the Soviets are reportedly importing massive amounts of Western and Japanese consumer goods ranging from razor blades and detergent to pantyhose.		Uruguayans vote to retain an amnesty granted in 1986 to the armed forces and police for human rights violations allegedly committed during the 1973-85 military dictatorship.	More than 1,000 students in Shanghai, China, march and sing national songs in honor of the late Hu Yaobang, whose refusal to crack down on student unrest made him a hero to liberal reformers and intellectuals.
April 17		In Poland, a three-judge panel in Warsaw legalizes the outlawed Solidarity trade union, which has been banned since 1982. . . . The central banks of the 12 European Community nations unveil a plan for full economic and monetary union, including a unified monetary policy, a single currency, and procedures for national budgets and other macroeconomic policy.			
April 18		The founder of Poland's Solidarity trade union, Lech Walesa, holds private discussions with Poland's Pres. Wojciech Jaruzelski in Warsaw for the first time since before martial law began in 1981. . . . The Grand Duchy of Luxembourg celebrates the 150th anniversary of the signing of the Treaty of London, which gave the small nation independence from the rule of King William of the Netherlands.		A 24-hour general strike called by United Workers Central, Chile's largest labor confederation, to protest the continued incarceration of union president Manuel Bustos, ends in violence that leaves two people dead.	
April 19				El Salvador's Attorney Gen. Roberto Garcia Alvarado is killed when a bomb placed on top of his armored car explodes. Garcia, 53, was a supporter of the rightist Nationalist Republican Alliance (ARENA).	
April 20		The 100th anniversary of the birth of German Nazi dictator Adolf Hitler passes with little fanfare. Police seal off Braunau, Austria, where Hitler was born, because of threats against Mayor Gerhard Skiba because of an antifascist monument recently erected in front of the house where Hitler was born.	Jordan's King Hussein comes away from two days of talks with top U.S. leaders in Washington, D.C., expressing partial support for Israeli P.M. Yitzhak Shamir's plan for Palestinian elections in the occupied West Bank and Gaza Strip. . . . Ten people are reported killed and more than 30 injured after three days of clashes between protesters and security forces in southern Jordan over recent price increases. . . . Maurice Nyagumbo, 64, Zimbabwe's fourth-ranking cabinet minister and number three in the Zimbabwe African National Union-Patriotic Front politburo, dies in a Harare hospital of poisoning, apparently a suicide. Implicated in a corruption scandal that has shaken the government, Nyagumbo resigned hours before his death was reported.		

A	B	C	D	E
Includes developments that affect more than one world region, international organizations and important meetings of major world leaders.	Includes all domestic and regional developments in Europe, including the Soviet Union, Turkey, Cyprus and Malta.	Includes all domestic and regional developments in Africa and the Middle East, including Iraq and Iran and excluding Cyprus, Turkey and Afghanistan.	Includes all domestic and regional developments in Latin America, the Caribbean and Canada.	Includes all domestic and regional developments in Asia and Pacific nations, extending from Afghanistan through all the Pacific Islands, except Hawaii.

U.S. Politics & Social Issues	U.S. Foreign Policy & Defense	U.S. Economy & Environment	Science, Technology & Nature	Culture, Leisure & Life Style	
					April 16
The House Ethics Committee releases a report accusing Speaker James C. Wright Jr. (D, Tex.) of five counts of violating House rules on the acceptance of gifts and outside income.	In the wake of agreements in Warsaw on political and economic liberalization, Pres. Bush announces an eight-point package of economic aid for Poland.	The House votes, 297-90, to remove many of the restrictions of the Hatch Act of 1939, which bars federal and postal employees from engaging in partisan political activity.		Abebe Mekonnen of Ethiopia wins the 93rd running of the Boston Marathon, with a time of 2:9:6. Ingrid Kristiansen of Norway is the first woman finisher, with a time of 2:24:33. . . . Czechoslovakia's state publishing house, Odeon, is reportedly planning to issue the works of famed Czechoslovak writer Franz Kafka, whose work was banned in Czechoslovakia following the communist take-over in 1948.	April 17
Rejecting their claim that they did not seek medical treatment for their daughter because of their religious beliefs, a Sarasota, Fla., jury convicts the parents of a seven-year-old girl of third-degree murder and child abuse in connection with the girl's death from diabetes.	Clearing the way for 91 domestic military facilities to be partially or completely shut down, the House defeats a resolution to reject the recommendations of the Defense Dept.'s Comm. on Base Realignment and Closure.	The consumer price index climbed 0.5% in March as energy prices continued to surge, the Labor Dept. reports. . . . Housing starts dropped 5.4% in March, the Commerce Dept. reports. . . . The Supreme Court upholds state laws allowing those who suffer indirect financial losses—such as those who purchase their goods from retailers or wholesalers—as a result of violations of state antitrust law to sue the violators.		The three major broadcast television networks lost viewers during the 1988-89 season—the sixth straight—according to figures released by the A.C. Nielsen Co.	April 18
Several hundred thousand people march in Washington, D.C., to demonstrate in support of "safe and legal" abortion and to urge the Supreme Court not to overturn the 1973 Roe v. Wade decision recognizing a woman's right to an abortion. . . . A 28-year-old Wall Street investment banker jogging in New York City's Central Park is beaten unconscious and raped by a group of youths. The woman's name is being withheld by the major news media.	At least 47 sailors are killed in an explosion inside a gun turret on the battleship USS Iowa during a naval exercise in the Atlantic Ocean about 300 miles north of Puerto Rico.	The Senate overwhelmingly approves landmark thrift industry bailout legislation, agreeing to spend $157 bil. over the next 10 years to close or merge over 500 insolvent savings and loan institutions.	A large asteroid passed within half a million miles of Earth on March 23, astronomers announce. The occurrence, undetected until afterward, is said to be the closest such approach since the asteroid Hermes passed about the same distance from Earth in 1937.	Daphne Du Maurier, 81, best-selling Gothic novelist and short story writer, dies in Cornwall, England, the setting for many of her novels. Alfred Hitchcock directed movie versions of her novels Jamaica Inn (1939) and Rebecca (1940) and short story The Birds. Her other works include Frenchman's Creek and My Cousin Rachel; in 1969, she was made a Dame Commander of the British Empire.	April 19
U.S. District Judge Gerhard A. Gesell sends the case of former National Security Council staff member Oliver L. North to the jury and says that "neither the president nor any of the defendant's superiors had the legal authority to order anyone to violate the law."			In an article published in the British journal Nature, Australian researcher John A. Talent presents evidence that many fossil specimens that Panjab Univ.'s Viswa Jit Gupta claims to have discovered in the Himalayas must actually have come from elsewhere in the world.		April 20

F	G	H	I	J
Includes elections, federal-state relations, civil rights and liberties, crime, the judiciary, education, health care, poverty, urban affairs and population.	Includes formation and debate of U.S. foreign and defense policies, veterans' affairs and defense spending. (Relations with specific foreign countries are usually found under the region concerned.)	Includes business, labor, agriculture, taxation, transportation, consumer affairs, monetary and fiscal policy, natural resources, and pollution.	Includes worldwide scientific, medical and technological developments, natural phenomena, U.S. weather, natural disasters, and accidents.	Includes the arts, religion, scholarship, communications media, sports, entertainments, fashions, fads and social life.

	World Affairs	Europe	Africa & the Middle East	The Americas	Asia & the Pacific
April 21		Moscow reports that wages in the first quarter of 1989 grew at an annualized rate of 9.4%, while productivity in the same period rose only 4.5%.			A U.S. military adviser to the Philippine Army, Lt. Col. James N. Rowe, is shot to death while being driven to work in a Manila suburb. Communist rebels later claim responsibility for the attack.
April 22		The poor results of economic reform have forced Soviet leader Mikhail S. Gorbachev to change the pace and direction of *perestroika*, according to a U.S. intelligence report. The report says that the Soviet economy grew only 1.5% in 1988, about the same as in 1987.		Nicaragua's Pres. Daniel Ortega Saavedra signs an electoral reform law and a media law, as required under a regional agreement reached by five Central American presidents in February. The February agreement requires the Nicaraguan government to have in place by April 25 reforms that will bring about conditions for a free and fair election by February 1990.	In defiance of the Chinese government's warning, more than 100,000 students and supporters filled Tiananmen Square over two days for a huge pro-democracy rally timed to coincide with the official Communist Party memorial service for former Communist Party leader Hu Yaobang, who died April 15.
April 23					A major offensive by Afghan rebel forces against the eastern city of Jalalabad is ordered by senior officials of the Pakistani government during a meeting that is also attended by the U.S. ambassador to Pakistan, the *New York Times* reports. . . . Pakistani foreign ministry officials say there is "no truth" in the *Times* report. "Afghans, including the Afghan mujaheddin, are very independent people," an unidentified official says. "They do not take orders from anyone regarding their own affairs, much less about the conduct of fighting in their country."
April 24			Jordanian Premier Zaid al-Rifai resigns in the wake of the previous week's rioting over price increases imposed under an agreement with the International Monetary Fund. . . . In a landmark verdict in South Africa, a judge ends an 18-month trial by acquitting five black activists charged with subversion and sedition for having set up "alternative people's structures" and staged rent boycotts in Johannesburg's Alexandria township during the 1984-86 period of unrest. Those acquitted include Moses Mayekiso, general secretary of the National Union of Metalworkers of South Africa. Judge P. J. van der Walt rules that the defendants were justified in trying to improve the township's bleak living conditions.		

A	B	C	D	E
Includes developments that affect more than one world region, international organizations and important meetings of major world leaders.	Includes all domestic and regional developments in Europe, including the Soviet Union, Turkey, Cyprus and Malta.	Includes all domestic and regional developments in Africa and the Middle East, including Iraq and Iran and excluding Cyprus, Turkey and Afghanistan.	Includes all domestic and regional developments in Latin America, the Caribbean and Canada.	Includes all domestic and regional developments in Asia and Pacific nations, extending from Afghanistan through all the Pacific Islands, except Hawaii.

U.S. Politics & Social Issues	U.S. Foreign Policy & Defense	U.S. Economy & Environment	Science, Technology & Nature	Culture, Leisure & Life Style	
				James Kirkwood, 64, novelist, actor and playwright, who in 1976 won a Tony Award and a Pulitzer Prize as the coauthor (with Nicholas Dante) of the book to the long-running Broadway musical *A Chorus Line*, dies of cancer in New York City. As an actor, he appeared in the films *Oh, God! Book II* (1980) and *Mommie Dearest* (1981). His novels include *There Must be a Pony!* and *P.S. Your Cat Is Dead.* . . . The film *Field of Dreams*, a fable about an Iowa farmer whose dream of building a baseball field and seeing the 1919 Chicago White Sox play on it comes true, is released in New York. Directed and written by Phil Alden Robinson and based on the book *Shoeless Joe* by W.P. Kinsella, the film stars Kevin Costner, Amy Madigan, Ray Liotta, James Earl Jones, and Burt Lancaster.	April 21
			Emilio Gino Segre, 84, nuclear physicist at the Univ. of California at Berkeley and cowinner of the 1959 Nobel Prize in physics for confirming the existence of the antiproton, dies of a heart attack in Lafayette, Calif. The antiproton was the first such antiparticle discovered and lent support to theories concerning the possibility of antimatter, matter composed entirely of antiparticles.		April 22
				Quarterback Troy Aikman of the Univ. of California at Los Angeles was the first player chosen in the National Football League's annual draft of college players in New York City. He was selected by the Dallas Cowboys. . . . In auto racing, Ayrton Senna of Brazil wins the San Marino Grand Prix.	April 23
A federal grand jury in Alexandria, Va., indicts former Central Intelligence Agency station chief Joseph F. Fernandez on two criminal counts of obstructing the 1987 Tower Commission inquiry into the Iran-Contra arms scandal and two counts of lying to federal investigators. . . . Richard M. Daley is sworn in as mayor of Chicago. Daley, a Democrat, becomes the city's 45th mayor. He was elected earlier in the month to serve the final two years of the late Mayor Harold Washington's second term.	Pres. Bush leads a 45-minute memorial service for the 47 sailors killed in the gun-turret explosion on the battleship USS *Iowa* April 19. The Navy April 20 revealed that 11 sailors in the doomed No. 2 turret gun crew had escaped the blast unharmed.				April 24

F	G	H	I	J
Includes elections, federal-state relations, civil rights and liberties, crime, the judiciary, education, health care, poverty, urban affairs and population.	*Includes formation and debate of U.S. foreign and defense policies, veterans' affairs and defense spending. (Relations with specific foreign countries are usually found under the region concerned.)*	*Includes business, labor, agriculture, taxation, transportation, consumer affairs, monetary and fiscal policy, natural resources, and pollution.*	*Includes worldwide scientific, medical and technological developments, natural phenomena, U.S. weather, natural disasters, and accidents.*	*Includes the arts, religion, scholarship, communications media, sports, entertainments, fashions, fads and social life.*

	World Affairs	Europe	Africa & the Middle East	The Americas	Asia & the Pacific
April 25		Soviet leader Mikhail S. Gorbachev engineers a sweeping purge of the Central Committee, the Communist Party's supreme representative body, and of the Central Auditing Comm., the party's fiscal watchdog agency. The changes come at a Central Committee plenum. The purge appears to further consolidate Gorbachev's power and remove a portion of the conservative opposition to his reform program.... Starting with Hungary, the Soviet Union begins a formal withdrawal of some of its forces from Eastern Europe. The withdrawals are consistent with a pledge by Soviet leader Mikhail S. Gorbachev to reduce Soviet forces deployed in Hungary, East Germany and Czechoslovakia by a total of 50,000 troops and 10,000 main battle tanks by the end of 1991.			Japan's Premier Noboru Takeshita announces that he plans to resign "to take responsibility" for the spread of public distrust caused by his involvement in the Recruit scandal. The Recruit affair, which surfaced in 1988 as a stock trading scandal, mushroomed in recent months to become what many analysts consider the worst scandal in post war Japan.... In South Korea, the Seoul district court sentences to death a young woman who pleaded guilty to planting a bomb that destroyed a Korean Air Lines passenger jet, killing all 115 people aboard, in November 1987. The woman, 27-year-old Kim Hyon Hui, admitted that she and a 70-year-old male accomplice planted the bomb on orders from the North Korean government. Kim's accomplice committed suicide when the couple was captured several days after the bombing.
April 26			Following a violent clash April 7 between Islamic fundamentalists and police, Egyptian authorities launched the latest in a series of crackdowns and arrested 1,500 alleged Moslem militants, according to reports in the *New York Times*. Among those reported seized by police is Sheik Omar Abdel Rahman, a blind theologian considered the spiritual leader of Jihad (Holy War), the underground extremist group blamed for assassinating Egypt's Pres. Anwar el-Sadat in 1981.... Arab League ministers meeting in Tunis agree on a truce plan that calls for a three-month cease-fire and the reopening of Moslem ports, the international airport and all crossing points between east and west Beirut. A pan-Arab observer force is to monitor the truce.		Sultan Azlan Shah of Perak state is sworn in as the ninth king of Malaysia in a ceremony at the national palace in Kuala Lumpur. He replaces Sultan Mahmood Iskandar of Johore.

A	B	C	D	E
Includes developments that affect more than one world region, international organizations and important meetings of major world leaders.	Includes all domestic and regional developments in Europe, including the Soviet Union, Turkey, Cyprus and Malta.	Includes all domestic and regional developments in Africa and the Middle East, including Iraq and Iran and excluding Cyprus, Turkey and Afghanistan.	Includes all domestic and regional developments in Latin America, the Caribbean and Canada.	Includes all domestic and regional developments in Asia and Pacific nations, extending from Afghanistan through all the Pacific Islands, except Hawaii.

U.S. Politics & Social Issues	U.S. Foreign Policy & Defense	U.S. Economy & Environment	Science, Technology & Nature	Culture, Leisure & Life Style	
	Defense Sec. Richard B. Cheney presents Congress with $10 bil. in proposed Pentagon budget cuts for FY1990. The reductions will trim former Pres. Ronald Reagan's FY1990 authorization request to $295.6 bil. from $305.6 bil., excluding funds earmarked for the Energy Dept.'s nuclear weapons programs. Cheney aims at bringing the budget into line with Pres. Bush's desire for zero growth (factored for inflation) in the defense budget for the fiscal year.	U.S. copyright holders ask U.S. Trade Representative Carla A. Hills to target 12 countries as pirates of films, music, books and computer software. The International Intellectual Property Alliance says piracy by the 12 mainly Asian countries costs the United States $1.3 bil. in annual sales, and is largely government condoned. The copyright holders say U.S. industry lost another $95 mil. annually because of trade barriers in the specified countries.	A strong earthquake strikes Mexico City, killing one person, injuring 350 others and damaging several buildings. The quake, which measured about 7.0 on the Richter scale, is centered 40 miles east of Acapulco. The tremors set off a panic among residents who remembered the earthquake of September 1985, which killed about 10,000 people.... The International Maritime Org. agrees on new operating procedures to deal with environmental disasters at sea. Meeting in London, representatives of 66 countries decided on a plan to pay salvage companies the expenses of their salvage work plus an additional payment of 30% of those costs.	The fourth Grawemeyer Award for large-scale orchestral composition is awarded to Cambodian-American composer Chinary Ung.	**April 25**
The father of a comatose 16-month-old boy is arrested in a Chicago hospital and charged with murder after he unplugs the child's respirator and allows him to die. Witnesses say that the man, Rodolfo Linares, cradled his son for 20 minutes until the boy was dead, while holding police officers and hospital staff workers at bay with a pistol. He then surrendered the gun and collapsed in sobs, according to reports.		The Fish and Wildlife Service announces a decision to list the spotted owl as a threatened species in federally managed forests in the Northwest. If implemented, the status would bar logging in about half of federal "old-growth" forest land in that area.... Gross national product grew at a 5.5% annual rate in the first quarter of 1989, the Commerce Dept. reports.	A tornado hit central Bangladesh killing at least 1,000 people and injuring 12,000. Government officials report that more than 20 villages have been destroyed and that at least 30,000 people are homeless. The tornado is accompanied by heavy rains that bring a small degree of relief to the region, which has been suffering from a severe drought.	Lucille Desiree Ball, 77, who starred in the sitcom "I Love Lucy" (1951-57), which featured her as the wife of a Cuban band leader (played by her real-life husband Desi Arnaz), dies in a hospital in Los Angeles, one week after undergoing emergency heart surgery. "I Love Lucy" was the most popular television program in the United States and the first show filmed in front of a live audience. ... *Variety*'s top-grossing films for the week are: *Pet Sematary, Major League, Say Anything, The Dream Team* and *See You in the Morning*.	**April 26**

F	**G**	**H**	**I**	**J**
Includes elections, federal-state relations, civil rights and liberties, crime, the judiciary, education, health care, poverty, urban affairs and population.	*Includes formation and debate of U.S. foreign and defense policies, veterans' affairs and defense spending. (Relations with specific foreign countries are usually found under the region concerned.)*	*Includes business, labor, agriculture, taxation, transportation, consumer affairs, monetary and fiscal policy, natural resources, and pollution.*	*Includes worldwide scientific, medical and technological developments, natural phenomena, U.S. weather, natural disasters, and accidents.*	*Includes the arts, religion, scholarship, communications media, sports, entertainments, fashions, fads and social life.*

	World Affairs	Europe	Africa & the Middle East	The Americas	Asia & the Pacific
April 27		West German Chancellor Helmut Kohl reaffirms his government's call for early negotiations aimed at reducing short-range nuclear weapons in Europe. That position puts him at odds with the United States and Great Britain and is creating a major rift within the North Atlantic Treaty Org. in the run-up to celebrations in May of the 40th anniversary of the alliance.... A leading Soviet toxicologist confirms that troops used a form of poison gas to subdue nationalist demonstrators in Tbilisi, the capital of the Georgian republic, April 9. The confirmation is published in Georgia's regional newspaper, *Zarya Vostoka*. As of April 20, the official death toll from the Tbilisi clash reached 20. Over 120 demonstrators remain hospitalized, some in critical condition.	Israel's P.M. Yitzhak Shamir's proposal for Palestinian elections in the occupied West Bank and Gaza Strip have caused a ferment of interest, according to reports during the previous three weeks. Palestine Liberation Org. officials, along with local Palestinian leaders, criticize the Shamir plan but do not reject it out of hand, and hint they are ready to compromise.	In Brazil, the government of Pres. Jose Sarney announces tough measures aimed at ending a wave of strikes involving some two million workers. During a three-week period in April, workers shut ports, crippled the banking system, blocked garbage collection, paralyzed public transportation and halted production in key manufacturing sectors, including the motor industry. The strikers are protesting a government-imposed wage and price freeze program.	A series of pro-democracy protests and rallies begun by Chinese students in Beijing April 15 after the death of former Communist Party leader Hu Yaobang, swells by this day into one of the largest popular demonstrations against the government since the communists came to power in 1949. In the largest rally since the start of the unrest, between 100,000 and 150,000 demonstrators, cheered on by as many as half a million workers and other onlookers, march through Beijing for more than 12 hours.... Konosuke Matsushita 94, founder of Japan's Matsushita Electric Industrial Co., the world's largest producer of consumer electronic goods, dies of pneumonia in Osaka, Japan. Born in poverty, Matsushita was often regarded as the pioneer of the modern Japanese corporation, with its emphasis on 'maruga-kae,' or strong social ties between the company and its employees. By the 1980s the company had sales of about $41 bil. and produced everything from electric rice cookers to video cassette recorders, many of which are sold under the brand name Panasonic.... A special commission appointed in January by Premier Noboru Takeshita in response to the Recruit stock trading scandal issues a report urging a number of political reforms. The 12-member panel proposes that cabinet ministers and their deputies be barred from buying or selling stocks or real estate; that all political candidates be required to disclose their income and assets upon taking office; and that all officials who reaped profits from the Recruit affair be forced to return the money to the public coffers.
April 28		A Belgian judge finds 14 British soccer fans guilty of manslaughter in connection with the 1985 riot at Heysel Stadium that resulted in 39 deaths. Ten other British fans are acquitted and two face separate action. The fans were all supporters of Liverpool, which had been facing Juventus of Italy in the 1985 European Cup final at Heysel, in Brussels. Thirty-six of those who died in the melee were Italians.... The latest Soviet census data places the nation's population at 286.7 million, a 9.3% increase from 1979. The highest birthrate is in predominantly Moslem Central Asia, and ethnic Russians make up 51% of the population, down from 56% in 1959.	Mobil Corp., the largest U.S. company remaining in South Africa, announces that it is selling its holdings there after 91 years of operations. Mobil Chairman Allen Murray says the move is based on economic considerations and is not taken in response to pressures from shareholders or antiapartheid groups.		Japan's ruling Liberal Democratic Party, ignoring an opposition boycott, rams the government's $470 bil. budget for FY1989 through the lower house of the Diet without debate. The budget, which has been stalled in the Diet since mid-March, moves to the upper house, where approval is considered a formality.... Japan's surplus on its current account, measuring trade in goods and services, dropped for the second year in a row in FY1988, the finance ministry reports. The surplus fell 8.9% during the fiscal year, which ended March 31, 1989, to $76.97 bil. from $84.47 bil.

A	B	C	D	E
Includes developments that affect more than one world region, international organizations and important meetings of major world leaders.	*Includes all domestic and regional developments in Europe, including the Soviet Union, Turkey, Cyprus and Malta.*	*Includes all domestic and regional developments in Africa and the Middle East, including Iraq and Iran and excluding Cyprus, Turkey and Afghanistan.*	*Includes all domestic and regional developments in Latin America, the Caribbean and Canada.*	*Includes all domestic and regional developments in Asia and Pacific nations, extending from Afghanistan through all the Pacific Islands, except Hawaii.*

U.S. Politics & Social Issues	U.S. Foreign Policy & Defense	U.S. Economy & Environment	Science, Technology & Nature	Culture, Leisure & Life Style	
Black teenager Tawana Brawley admits to a former boyfriend that she made up her story of rape and abduction by a gang of white men in Wappingers Falls, New York in November 1987. In an interview published in *New York Newsday*, the friend, Daryl Rodriguez, says that Brawley recently told him that she invented the story with the help of her mother to avoid being punished by her stepfather for running away from home.	The Vietnamese government returns to the United States what are believed to be the remains of 21 American servicemen killed in the Vietnam War. Some 1,730 Americans are still listed as missing in action in Vietnam, and another 634 are listed as missing in Cambodia, Laos and China.	Personal income rose 0.8% to a $4.350 trillion annual rate in March while consumer spending rose 0.2% to $3.495 trillion, the Commerce Dept. reports.	The three-member crew of the Soviet space station, *Mir*, returns safely to Earth after an eight-month mission.... The Food and Drug Admin. says it has approved human testing of the experimental anti-AIDS drug GLQ223. The drug represents a highly purified form of the plant extract trichosanthin, derived from the root of a Chinese cucumber plant. The root is used in China to induce abortion and to treat some forms of cancer.		April 27
The Center for Women Policy Studies, an advocacy group, charges that the Scholastic Aptitude Test (SAT) is biased against women. Calling the widely used college admissions test "a defective product," the center's executive director, Leslie R. Wolfe, calls on the Educational Testing Service of Princeton, New Jersey, which administers the test, to eliminate questions that favor one gender over the other.... Pres. Bush and Vice Pres. Quayle hold a meeting to discuss the circumstances under which Quayle would assume the presidency if Bush were to become incapacitated, the *Washington Post* reports. The meeting, which took place in the Oval Office of the White House on April 18, is attended by First Lady Barbara Bush, White House counsel C. Boyden Gray and the president's chief physician, Burton Lee II, the Post report says.	U.S. Trade Representative Carla A. Hills says the United States will retaliate against Japan for restricting U.S. access to its telecommunications market unless "Japanese authorities act immediately to remedy the practices at issue."	The government's index of leading economic indicators dropped 0.7% in March, the Commerce Dept. reports.... Prices received by farmers for raw agricultural products dropped 2% in April, the Agriculture Dept. reports.		*Publishers Weekly*'s hardback fiction best-sellers of the week are: *The Satanic Verses*, Salman Rushdie; *A Prayer for Owen Meany*, John Irving; *Star*, Danielle Steel; *Billy Bathgate*, E. L. Doctorow; and *We Are Still Married: Stories and Letters*, Garrison Keillor.	April 28

F	G	H	I	J
Includes elections, federal-state relations, civil rights and liberties, crime, the judiciary, education, health care, poverty, urban affairs and population.	*Includes formation and debate of U.S. foreign and defense policies, veterans' affairs and defense spending. (Relations with specific foreign countries are usually found under the region concerned.)*	*Includes business, labor, agriculture, taxation, transportation, consumer affairs, monetary and fiscal policy, natural resources, and pollution.*	*Includes worldwide scientific, medical and technological developments, natural phenomena, U.S. weather, natural disasters, and accidents.*	*Includes the arts, religion, scholarship, communications media, sports, entertainments, fashions, fads and social life.*

	World Affairs	Europe	Africa & the Middle East	The Americas	Asia & the Pacific
April 29		Yugoslavia's inflation is running at an annual rate of 490.1%. The newest figure is 92.6 percentage points higher than the March rate. The rate in April 1988 was 152%.	Racial and economic tensions between the West African nations of Senegal and Mauritania, sparked by an April 9 border incident, erupt into five days of communal riots that kill at least 450 people.		In China, one week after a string of demonstrations culminated in a massive protest march in Beijing involving as many as 150,000 people, government officials meet with a group of hand-picked student leaders to hear their demands, but the meeting is later dismissed by many students as inadequate. Forty-five students from 16 universities meet in Beijing with Yuan Mu, a spokesman for the State Council, He Dongchang, a vice minister on the state education commission, and other officials.
April 30		A rift within the North Atlantic Treaty Org. over West Germany's call for early negotiations on battlefield nuclear weapons continues. West German Chancellor Helmut Kohl meets in Deidesheim, West Germany, with British P.M. Margaret Thatcher. Following three hours of talks, Thatcher, who with the United States is leading the opposition in NATO to talks with the Soviets on reducing the short-range missiles, stresses that NATO nations are bound by policy decisions made at previous summit meetings.	In Zimbabwe, political maverick Edgar Tekere, a former ally of Zimbabwe's Pres. Robert Mugabe, announces the formation of a new party to challenge the ruling Zimbabwe African National Union (Patriotic Front) in the 1990 general elections.		
May 1				Three months after seizing power in a military coup, General Andres Rodriguez is overwhelmingly elected to a four-year term as president of Paraguay. The election is the freest and cleanest in Paraguay since 1926. It follows eight barely contested elections since 1954, won by deposed Pres. Alfredo Stroessner, who was overthrown by Rodriguez in February. . . . A Venezuelan judge orders a number of arrests in a corruption scandal involving the alleged misappropriation of public funds. In the scam, some $3 bil. to $4 bil. was apparently stolen under a now-defunct program to allocate foreign currency at favorable exchange rates for essential imports.	
May 2		Yasir Arafat, chairman of the Palestine Liberation Org., pays his first official visit to France. He meets with Pres. Francois Mitterrand and declares that the 25-year-old Palestine National Charter, which calls for Israel's destruction, has been "superseded." . . . The center-right coalition government of Dutch Premier Ruud Lubbers resigns after a split over funding for an ambitious environmental plan. The break between Lubbers's Christian Democrats and their junior coalition partner, the People's Party for Freedom and Democracy (Liberals), marks the end of a seven-year rule for the coalition. Lubbers is asked by Queen Beatrix to head a caretaker government until new elections, which are moved up to September 1989 from May 1990. . . . Hungary begins to dismantle the barbed-wire fence along its border with neutral Austria, becoming the first Soviet-bloc country to open a border with Western Europe. The fence, 150 miles long, was erected in 1969 to replace minefields set up by Hungary in 1949. The barrier is scheduled to be completely torn down in 1990.		Canada's P.M. Brian Mulroney visits the United States. The three-day trip features a meeting with Pres. Bush.	

A	B	C	D	E
Includes developments that affect more than one world region, international organizations and important meetings of major world leaders.	Includes all domestic and regional developments in Europe, including the Soviet Union, Turkey, Cyprus and Malta.	Includes all domestic and regional developments in Africa and the Middle East, including Iraq and Iran and excluding Cyprus, Turkey and Afghanistan.	Includes all domestic and regional developments in Latin America, the Caribbean and Canada.	Includes all domestic and regional developments in Asia and Pacific nations, extending from Afghanistan through all the Pacific Islands, except Hawaii.

U.S. Politics & Social Issues	U.S. Foreign Policy & Defense	U.S. Economy & Environment	Science, Technology & Nature	Culture, Leisure & Life Style	
				In hockey, the Soviet Union clinches the title in the World Championships in Stockholm when it beats Canada, 5-3. . . . *Billboard*'s best-selling albums for the week are: *Like A Prayer*, Madonna; *Loc-Ed After Dark*, Tone Loc; *Don't Be Cruel*, Bobby Brown; *Electric Youth*, Debbie Gibson; and *G N' R Lies*, Guns N' Roses.	April 29
			Researchers discover 17 industrial accidents in the United States over the past 25 years in which deadly chemicals were released that exceeded in toxicity the lethal accident that killed 3,000 people in Bhopal, India in 1984, according to a *New York Times* report.	Sergio Leone, 67, Italian film director regarded as the father of the "spaghetti westerns," dies of a heart attack in Rome. His low-budget films helped revive the western, and made an international star of actor Clint Eastwood, who starred in Leone's *A Fistful of Dollars* (1964), *For a Few Dollars More* (1965), and *The Good, the Bad and the Ugly* (1966).	April 30
The Supreme Court puts the burden of proof on employers to justify their decisions on hiring and promoting, once a woman presents direct evidence that sex discrimination played a part. The court, in a 6-3 decision, says that in such cases, the employer must prove by a preponderance of the evidence that the same decision would have been made even if gender had not been taken into account.		In an unusually strong statement, the chairman of the Bush administration's Council of Economic Advisers, Michael Boskin, warns that U.S. retaliation against unfair foreign trading practices could trigger "a worldwide recession."	The first U.S. patient to have human fetal cells implanted into his brain as a treatment for Parkinson's disease is showing small but steady improvement, his doctor says. Parkinsonism is a degenerative condition of the brain.	The 11th annual Pritzker Architecture Prize is presented to Los Angeles-based architect Frank O. Gehry.	May 1
An Oregon man accused of beating a black Ethiopian immigrant to death with a baseball bat pleads guilty in a Portland courtroom. The accused killer, Kenneth M. Mieske, pleads guilty in the murder of the Ethiopian, Mulugeta Seraw, in Portland on November 13, 1988. Police charge that Mieske and several friends attacked Seraw outside the Ethiopian's apartment and that Mieske smashed Seraw's skull with a baseball bat. . . . Few public school systems around the country are doing enough to teach teenagers how to avoid pregnancy, according to the Alan Guttmacher Institute, a nonprofit group that studies reproductive issues. The institute bases its report on three 1988 studies of sex education: a survey of policy in all 50 states, a review of 162 large school districts and a poll of 4,241 public school teachers who provided sex education in grades seven through 12.		Pres. Bush approves the subsidized sale to the USSR of 1.5 mil. tons of wheat. The value of the grain on the world market is between $240 mil. and $270 mil., according to the Agriculture Dept. . . . The U.S. International Trade Comm. (ITC) ends a sweeping investigation of unfair trading practices, ruling that imports of antifriction bearings from Western Europe and Asia injured U.S. producers. The ITC ruling will allow the imposition of U.S. antidumping duties against three kinds of ball bearings imported from West Germany, France, Italy, Sweden, Great Britain, Romania, Japan, Singapore and Thailand.	A declaration calling for an end to the production of ozone-damaging chemicals by the year 2000 is adopted by consensus of 80 nations represented at a meeting in Helsinki, Finland. The declaration specifically cites chlorofluorocarbons (CFCs) to be phased out "as soon as possible, but not later than 2000," and it calls for a phase-out of other ozone-damaging substances such as halon gas, which is used in fire extinguishers, "as soon as feasible."		May 2

F	G	H	I	J
Includes elections, federal-state relations, civil rights and liberties, crime, the judiciary, education, health care, poverty, urban affairs and population.	*Includes formation and debate of U.S. foreign and defense policies, veterans' affairs and defense spending. (Relations with specific foreign countries are usually found under the region concerned.)*	*Includes business, labor, agriculture, taxation, transportation, consumer affairs, monetary and fiscal policy, natural resources, and pollution.*	*Includes worldwide scientific, medical and technological developments, natural phenomena, U.S. weather, natural disasters, and accidents.*	*Includes the arts, religion, scholarship, communications media, sports, entertainments, fashions, fads and social life.*

	World Affairs	Europe	Africa & the Middle East	The Americas	Asia & the Pacific
May 3		The European Community (EC) issues its annual report detailing U.S. trade barriers to EC exports, including tariffs, antidumping provisions, export supports, and import quotas.	Egyptian author Naguib Mahfouz, winner of the 1988 Nobel Prize for literature, is under police protection after receiving death threats from Islamic fundamentalists, according to reports during the week. In February, Mahfouz called Iran's Ayatollah Khomeini a "terrorist" for his death edict against Salman Rushdie, author of *The Satanic Verses*.	The military government of Chilean Pres. Augusto Pinochet withdraws its 19-point constitutional reform offer after the 17-member opposition Coalition of Parties for Democracy rejects the proposals as insufficient. "In the face of this rejection . . . there is no room for any reform," says Interior Min. Carlos Caceres. "The opposition has closed all possibility of achieving the necessary consensus."	Prince Norodom Sihanouk, the president of Cambodia's three-party guerrilla coalition, concludes a two-day meeting in Jakarta, Indonesia with Cambodian Premier Hun Sen, head of the Vietnamese-backed regime in Phnom Penh. The latest meeting, the fourth since the two leaders began a dialogue in 1987, was scheduled for September but was moved up after Vietnam announced an advanced timetable for the withdrawal of its troops from Cambodia. . . . In South Korea six riot policemen are killed during an attempt to rescue five colleagues being held hostage by student protesters at a university in the southern city of Pusan. The death toll is by far the highest for police in a single incident in recent years, government officials say. . . . The 45,000 Indian peacekeeping troops deployed in Sri Lanka are to be withdrawn by the end of 1989, a top Sri Lankan official announces. Ranjan Wijeratne, Sri Lanka's minister of defense and foreign affairs, says some 20,000 Indian troops will be pulled out by July, and the remaining 25,000 will leave by the end of the year.
May 4		Conservative British P.M. Margaret Thatcher marks the completion of 10 years in office. She becomes the first British prime minister since 1822 to hold office for a decade. Thatcher herself seeks to play down the significance of the anniversary and to focus on the future. In an early morning meeting with the press at her 10 Downing Street residence, she vowed that there would be "no slowing down" and that the next 10 years would be very exciting.		In Canada, CP Rail formally opens the Rogers Pass Tunnel, the largest tunnel in the Western Hemisphere. The tunnel runs 22 miles through the Selkirk Mountains in British Columbia's Glacier National Park.	A crowd of at least 100,000 Chinese students and workers stages a march in Beijing to demand democratic reforms. The rally, one of the largest in modern Chinese history, comes one week after a string of similar demonstrations culminated in a massive protest march in the nation's capital involving as many as 150,000 people. The latest demonstration occurs on the 70th anniversary of the founding of the May 4 Movement of 1919, an early nationalistic and democratic movement that was led by students.
May 5			An international six-day airlift repatriates over 50,000 people from Senegal and Mauritania following five days of ethnic violence that is the worst the region has seen in recent years.		
May 6					In China, students at Beijing University, the nation's largest educational institution, vote to continue their two-week-old boycott of classes. The vote comes after students at a number of other universities in the capital began returning to classes May 5. At the height of the boycott, more than 70,000 university students in Beijing stayed away from class.

A	B	C	D	E
Includes developments that affect more than one world region, international organizations and important meetings of major world leaders.	*Includes all domestic and regional developments in Europe, including the Soviet Union, Turkey, Cyprus and Malta.*	*Includes all domestic and regional developments in Africa and the Middle East, including Iraq and Iran and excluding Cyprus, Turkey and Afghanistan.*	*Includes all domestic and regional developments in Latin America, the Caribbean and Canada.*	*Includes all domestic and regional developments in Asia and Pacific nations, extending from Afghanistan through all the Pacific Islands, except Hawaii.*

U.S. Politics & Social Issues	U.S. Foreign Policy & Defense	U.S. Economy & Environment	Science, Technology & Nature	Culture, Leisure & Life Style	
An annual government assessment concluded that educational progress had been 'stagnant' despite increases in school spending. The report found nationwide student achievement "merely average."	In a 7-4 ruling, the U.S. Court of Appeals for the Ninth Circuit in San Francisco decides that Perry Watkins, an admitted homosexual, can reenlist in the Army because the Army was aware of his homosexuality when it allowed him to reenlist in the past.	Productivity among the nation's nonfarm businesses increased at a 0.5% annual rate in the first quarter, the Labor Dept. reports.		Christine (born George Jorgensen) Jorgensen, 62, the first U.S. transsexual to announce that she had undergone a sex change operation, dies of cancer in San Clemente, Calif. Following the operation, which took place in Denmark in 1952, she was the focus of intense tabloid newspaper interest. She later starred in a nightclub act that featured her theme song, "I Enjoy Being a Girl."	May 3
In the Iran-Contra arms scandal, former National Security Council staff member Oliver L. North is found guilty of aiding and abetting the obstruction of Congress, destroying government documents and receiving illegal gratuity; he is acquitted on nine other counts. . . . Surgeon Gen. C. Everett Koop announces that he will resign his post effective July 13. Koop, whose term is not due to expire until November, makes the announcement in a letter to Pres. Bush. . . . Aubrey Adams Jr., a former state prison guard, is executed in the electric chair in Starke, Fla. Adams was sentenced to death for killing an eight-year-old girl, Trisa Gail Thornley, in 1978.		The leader of the most prominent Melanesian group seeking independence for the French colony of New Caledonia, Jean-Marie Tjibaou, is assassinated with his chief deputy, Yeiwene Yeiwene. The suspects in the case are described as Melanesian, or Kanak, extremists. Tjibaou was the leader of the Kanak Socialist National Liberation Front (FLNKS). . . . The California Supreme Court unanimously upholds Proposition 103, a sweeping insurance reform that will slash property and casualty insurance rates by 20% throughout the state. The decision stuns the insurance industry, which stands to lose up to $4 bil. in annual revenue in California as a result of the reform. The law will impose strict regulation on the state insurance industry, the largest and one of the least regulated in the United States.	The space shuttle Atlantis successfully deploys the unmanned Magellan spacecraft toward a rendezvous with the planet Venus in 1990. Starting Magellan on its 15-month trip to Venus, where it is to compile a radar map during an eight-month orbiting period, is the major task of the four-day flight, which began from Cape Canaveral, Fla. .		May 4
A suit filed in mid-April by 10 news organizations seeking access to an intelligence summary used as an exhibit in the criminal trial of former National Security Council staff member Oliver L. North is settled, after the Justice Dept. agrees to release a heavily edited version of the document. . . . U.S. District Judge Lucius Bunton III in El Paso, Texas, requires the Federal Bureau of Investigation to end its "unsystematic, excessively subjective" method of promoting special agents. The judge orders the bureau to reform its promotion system and eliminate discrimination against Hispanic agents.		The unemployment rate rose three-tenths of a percentage point to 5.2% in April, the Labor Dept. reports. . . . Outstanding consumer debt expanded $5.37 bil. in March, at a 9.4% annual rate, the Commerce Dept. reports. . . . Bethlehem Steel Corp. reaches agreement with the United Steelworkers of America on a 50-month contract restoring wage concessions made during leaner times seven years earlier.			May 5
Dallas Mayor Annette Strauss (D) easily wins reelection to a second two-year term. Voters in San Antonio return former Mayor Lila Cockrell to office for a two-year term. Cockrell, who held office from 1975 to 1981, replaces Mayor Henry Cisneros, who declined to seek a fifth term in the face of problems with his son's health and his marriage.				Pope John Paul II ends a pilgrimage to Africa. The nine-day journey takes him to Madagascar, the French island of Reunion, Zambia and Malawi. . . . In horse racing, Sunday Silence upsets odds-on favorite Easy Goer to win the 115th running of the Kentucky Derby at Churchill Downs in Louisville.	May 6

F	G	H	I	J
Includes elections, federal-state relations, civil rights and liberties, crime, the judiciary, education, health care, poverty, urban affairs and population.	Includes formation and debate of U.S. foreign and defense policies, veterans' affairs and defense spending. (Relations with specific foreign countries are usually found under the region concerned.)	Includes business, labor, agriculture, taxation, transportation, consumer affairs, monetary and fiscal policy, natural resources, and pollution.	Includes worldwide scientific, medical and technological developments, natural phenomena, U.S. weather, natural disasters, and accidents.	Includes the arts, religion, scholarship, communications media, sports, entertainments, fashions, fads and social life.

	World Affairs	Europe	Africa & the Middle East	The Americas	Asia & the Pacific
May 7				In Panama's presidential elections, the candidate of the coalition backed by Panama's military strongman and de facto leader, General Manuel Antonio Noriega, claims victory. But foreign observers and the Roman Catholic Church agree that the opposition has won overwhelmingly and that the Noriega regime is attempting to steal the election.... In Bolivia, Gonzalo Sanchez de Lozada of the ruling National Revolutionary Movement (MNR) and former military dictator Hugo Banzer Suarez of the Nationalist Democratic Action party (ADN) both declare victory in the presidential election. Because neither candidate wins an absolute majority, the new Congress will have to select the 77th Bolivian president when it convenes in August.... Peruvian Premier Armando Villanueva del Campo resigns following an intensification of violence and terror by leftist guerrillas that leaves two congressmen dead. "My irrevocable resignation has been accepted by the president," says Villanueva. "Now it will be someone else's turn to face what our country is going through."	
May 8		The Central Committee of the ruling Socialist Workers' (Communist) Party forces former Hungarian leader Janos Kadar into retirement. Kadar, 76, was ousted as party general secretary in May 1988 and handed the honorary post of party president. In today's action, Kadar is relieved of the honorary post as well as his seat on the Central Committee.... Serbian party leader Slobodan Milosevic is elected president of the Yugoslav republic of Serbia. Milosevic, the head of the Serbian nationalist movement, is to relinquish his party post.... West Germany's unemployment rate fell in April to the lowest level in six-and-a-half years according to government figures.		An Argentine appeals court in Buenos Aires orders former air force commander Brigadier General Orlando Ramon Agosti released from jail. A member of the ruling military junta in 1976, Agosti was sentenced to four-and-a-half years in prison in December 1985 on charges of torturing political prisoners in the 1970s.	
May 9			Guatemalan Air Force officers and soldiers stage an abortive coup, the second such rebellion in a year. The coup bid is apparently aimed against the defense minister, Major General Hector Alejandro Gramajo Morales, a moderate officer, and not against the government of Pres. Vinicio Cerezo.		The Indian government disburses the first payments to heirs of the more than 2,000 adults killed in the 1984 gas leak at the Union Carbide Corp. chemical plant in Bhopal, India. Descendants of the adult victims of the disaster are to receive monthly checks of about $50 in government funds until legal appeals surrounding the $470 mil. settlement agreed to by Union Carbide are resolved.... The Afghan Army is reported to have broken a four-month siege of the eastern city of Jalalabad in a six-day offensive against antigovernment rebel forces. The offensive is considered a major psychological victory for the army, which Western analysts predicted would collapse soon after the withdrawal of Soviet troops from the country earlier in the year.

A	B	C	D	E
Includes developments that affect more than one world region, international organizations and important meetings of major world leaders.	Includes all domestic and regional developments in Europe, including the Soviet Union, Turkey, Cyprus and Malta.	Includes all domestic and regional developments in Africa and the Middle East, including Iraq and Iran and excluding Cyprus, Turkey and Afghanistan.	Includes all domestic and regional developments in Latin America, the Caribbean and Canada.	Includes all domestic and regional developments in Asia and Pacific nations, extending from Afghanistan through all the Pacific Islands, except Hawaii.

U.S. Politics & Social Issues	U.S. Foreign Policy & Defense	U.S. Economy & Environment	Science, Technology & Nature	Culture, Leisure & Life Style	
More than 200 people are arrested in the previous two weeks during a series of protests relating to an ongoing dispute that pits the rights of native American Indians against those of fishing enthusiasts in northern Wisconsin. Under treaties signed by native Chippewa tribes and the U.S. government in 1837 and 1842, the Chippewa retain the right to harvest fish in land they ceded to the United States. Since 1985, the Chippewa have exercised that right by spearing spawning walleye in northern Wisconsin lakes, thereby depleting the local stock, according to sport fishers.				In auto racing, Ayrton Senna of Brazil wins the Monaco Grand Prix in Monte Carlo. . . . Davey Allison wins the National Assoc. for Stock Car Racing Winston 500 event in Talladega, Alabama.	**May 7**
		The *Wall Street Journal* reports that net income at 644 major corporations it surveyed rose 10% in the first quarter from the year-earlier period, while after-tax earnings from continuing operations rose 11%.			**May 8**
Pres. Bush draws fire from some civil rights groups in the previous weeks over his choice of William Lucas, a black Detroit lawyer, to head the Justice Dept.'s civil rights division. . . . Bowing to pressure from people with Acquired Immune Deficiency Syndrome (AIDS), the National Institutes of Health announces that it is establishing a toll-free telephone hot line through which AIDS victims can learn whether they are eligible for experimental treatment programs around the country. The new number, 1-800-TRIALS-A, will supplement the existing general-information AIDS hot line, 1-800-342-AIDS.			Scientists B. Stanley Pons of the Univ. of Utah and Martin Fleischmann of the Univ. of Southampton in England, who in March announced the potentially revolutionary discovery of "cold fusion," nuclear fusion at room temperatures, address criticism of their work at a conference. The encounter does little to dispel growing skepticism in the scientific community over their claims.	The most expensive painting sold at the semi-annual Impressionist and contemporary art sales at the auction houses of Christie's and Sotheby's is Pablo Picasso's 1901 self-portrait *Yo Picasso*, which is sold today to an unidentified buyer for $47.85 mil.	**May 9**

F	G	H	I	J
Includes elections, federal-state relations, civil rights and liberties, crime, the judiciary, education, health care, poverty, urban affairs and population.	*Includes formation and debate of U.S. foreign and defense policies, veterans' affairs and defense spending. (Relations with specific foreign countries are usually found under the region concerned.)*	*Includes business, labor, agriculture, taxation, transportation, consumer affairs, monetary and fiscal policy, natural resources, and pollution.*	*Includes worldwide scientific, medical and technological developments, natural phenomena, U.S. weather, natural disasters, and accidents.*	*Includes the arts, religion, scholarship, communications media, sports, entertainments, fashions, fads and social life.*

	World Affairs	Europe	Africa & the Middle East	The Americas	Asia & the Pacific
May 10		Sec. of State James A. Baker III makes his first visit to the USSR for talks with the Soviet leadership. U.S.-Soviet relations have been at a virtual standstill since Pres. Bush took office in January.... In West Germany, the chairman of the company believed to have played a prominent role in the construction of a controversial Libyan chemical plant is arrested by authorities. The executive, Jurgen Hippenstiel-Imhausen, is arrested at the Bochum headquarters of Gesellschaft fuer Automation, a unit of Imhausen-Chemie GmbH.		The Panamanian government annuls the May 7 presidential elections, charging foreign interference. The main opposition candidates for president and for the two vice presidential positions are severely beaten by supporters of Noriega. The United States strongly condemns the election as fraudulent.... A teachers' strike that closed half of Mexico's grammar and high schools and vocational institutions ends when some 8,000 teachers vote to approve a 25% increase in wages and benefits. The agreement also includes reforms in the election of union officials.	
May 11				Delegates at a two-day international conference in Stockholm on Nicaragua's economic situation pledge $50 mil. in aid to Managua. That is short of the $250 mil. that Nicaragua's Pres. Daniel Ortega says Nicaragua needs to implement its economic austerity program. However, the participants say they will consider additional funding to support the nation's economic recovery.... Citibank of the United States says it has seized $80 mil. of Ecuadoran deposits to set against a trade credit it granted the country. The seizure by the commercial bank is believed to be only the third of its kind since the onset of the developing-country debt crisis in 1982.	Pres. Ranasinghe Premadasa opens peace talks with representatives of Sri Lanka's largest and most powerful ethnic Tamil guerrilla group. The talks are aimed at ending a six-year-old civil war between Sri Lanka's Tamil minority and Sinhalese majority.
May 12			Frederik W. de Klerk, who is widely expected to become South Africa's next president in September, vows to pursue new constitutional and social reforms but rejects the idea of black majority rule. His speech to the House of Assembly, the white chamber of parliament, is his first major policy address since becoming leader of the ruling National Party (NP) in February.		
May 13					In China, 1,000 students begin a hunger strike. The strikers demand, among other things, a televised meeting with China's leaders to discuss political reforms.... Two reports released recently by separate human rights organizations accuse Indian peacekeeping troops in Sri Lanka of torturing and killing local civilians, according to a New York Times article. One report is compiled by London-based Amnesty International, and the other is put together by the Jaffna Univ. Teachers for Human Rights group in Sri Lanka.

A	B	C	D	E
Includes developments that affect more than one world region, international organizations and important meetings of major world leaders.	Includes all domestic and regional developments in Europe, including the Soviet Union, Turkey, Cyprus and Malta.	Includes all domestic and regional developments in Africa and the Middle East, including Iraq and Iran and excluding Cyprus, Turkey and Afghanistan.	Includes all domestic and regional developments in Latin America, the Caribbean and Canada.	Includes all domestic and regional developments in Asia and Pacific nations, extending from Afghanistan through all the Pacific Islands, except Hawaii.

U.S. Politics & Social Issues	U.S. Foreign Policy & Defense	U.S. Economy & Environment	Science, Technology & Nature	Culture, Leisure & Life Style	
The House votes, 417-0, to impeach U.S. District Judge Walter L. Nixon, who is serving a five-year sentence for perjury to a federal grand jury and federal investigators. Nixon, who refused to resign his judgeship in the Southern District of Mississippi and is still drawing his $89,500 annual salary, is the 16th federal official in U.S. history to be impeached. He is only the second judge in U.S. history to be convicted of a crime while still on the bench. . . . In a widely reported gaffe, Vice Pres. Dan Quayle garbles the slogan of the United Negro College Fund in a speech to the group. In place of the actual slogan: "A mind is a terrible thing to waste," the vice president says: "What a waste it is to lose one's mind, or not to have a mind. How true that is."		Alaskan officials and Exxon Co. officials dispute the pace and effectiveness of the cleanup of the *Exxon Valdez* oil spill in Prince William Sound.			May 10
Independent counsel Lawrence E. Walsh announces that a federal grand jury in Washington, D.C., has indicted retired Air Force Major General Richard V. Secord for perjury during his 1987 testimony before the congressional Iran-Contra investigating committees. . . . A Ford Foundation study concludes that the social welfare programs in the United States are failing and recommends a broad range of initiatives that it says will add $29 bil. a year to the current $500 bil. that the federal government spends on social and medical programs.	The Veterans Affairs Dept. announces that it plans to reconsider disability claims by Vietnam veterans based on exposure to the defoliant Agent Orange. Veterans Affairs Sec. Edward J. Derwinski says the department will not appeal a federal court ruling made public May 8 that the government had applied too strict a standard in determining whether exposure to Agent Orange caused particular health problems.	In its three-part quarterly refinancing, the Treasury Dept., over three-days, sells $28.75 bil. of new notes and bonds.	Kenya reverses its policy and calls for a worldwide ban on the trade of ivory, seeking to save its dwindling elephant population from extinction at the hands of poachers. The day before, the Interior Dept. urged a ban as well, and began considering whether to designate the African elephant as an "endangered" species under U.S. law, rather than merely a 'threatened' one.		May 11
	In his first major address on U.S.-Soviet relations, Pres. Bush says that it is "time to move beyond containment" and instead "seek the integration of the Soviet Union into the community of nations." The president's comments come in a commencement speech at Texas A & M Univ., in College Station, Texas.	The government's producer price index increased in April by 0.4% for the second straight month, the Labor Dept. reports.	The Bush administration reverses itself and says it will work toward an international treaty to curb global warming. Negotiators at a UN-sponsored meeting in Geneva, Switzerland are currently seeking to draft a treaty to deal with the so-called greenhouse effect, a trend to global warming triggered by a build-up of pollutants in the atmosphere.		May 12
			Although the number of cases of Acquired Immune Deficiency Sydrome reported in the United States continues to rise, the rate of increase has been declining, the Centers for Disease Control (CDC) reports. The CDC says that 90,990 cases of AIDS were reported in the United States as of its latest count. Of that total, some 52,435 patients, or 58%, have died.	James Salter is presented with the ninth annual PEN/Faulkner Award for fiction for *Dusk & Other Stories* at the Folger Shakespeare Library in Washington, D.C.	May 13

F	G	H	I	J
Includes elections, federal-state relations, civil rights and liberties, crime, the judiciary, education, health care, poverty, urban affairs and population.	Includes formation and debate of U.S. foreign and defense policies, veterans' affairs and defense spending. (Relations with specific foreign countries are usually found under the region concerned.)	Includes business, labor, agriculture, taxation, transportation, consumer affairs, monetary and fiscal policy, natural resources, and pollution.	Includes worldwide scientific, medical and technological developments, natural phenomena, U.S. weather, natural disasters, and accidents.	Includes the arts, religion, scholarship, communications media, sports, entertainments, fashions, fads and social life.

	World Affairs	Europe	Africa & the Middle East	The Americas	Asia & the Pacific
May 14				Justicialist Party (Peronist) candidate Carlos Saul Menem wins a decisive victory in the Argentine presidential election, sweeping the Peronist movement into power for the first time since 1976. . . . Mexico's foreign ministry issues an unusual statement blasting Panama's Noriega for his unsavory "moral and ethical reputation." It says his leadership is "discredited" and accuses him of having made sure his "personal interests prevail over those of the Panamanian people." The statement says Panama is "lamentably distanced. . .from Latin America's democratic community." However, Mexico reiterates its commitment to the principle of nonintervention.	
May 15	Soviet leader Mikhail S. Gorbachev concludes a four-day visit to China, the first Sino-Soviet summit in 30 years. But the historic trip is eclipsed by massive pro-democracy demonstrations led by Chinese university students. At the height of the unrest during the summit, more than one million people will demonstrate peacefully in Beijing on May 17.	In Yugoslavia, Janez Drnovsek of Slovenia succeeds Raif Dizdarevic in the one-year post of federal president.		The government unveils a liberalization of Mexico's foreign investment rules as part of an effort to make the economy more competitive and increase capital flows into Mexico. The old rules barred foreign investment in some industries and limited foreigners to minority partnerships in most others.	
May 16			Artillery exchanges between Lebanon's Christian-led forces and Syrian-led Moslem forces continue to batter Beirut through mid-May, despite two truces negotiated by the Arab League. The violence is punctuated by the April 16 death amid heavy shelling of the Spanish ambassador and today's car-bomb murder of the religious leader of Lebanon's Sunni Moslems.	Soviet leader Mikhail S. Gorbachev tells the United States that the Soviet Union is halting shipments of arms to Nicaragua because the United States has shifted to a diplomatic tack in its Central America policy, the White House says.	The semiofficial China News Service reveals that some 320,000 Chinese troops fought in the Vietnam War against South Vietnam and the United States. The report says that more than 4,000 Chinese soldiers were killed in the war. The United States has repeatedly accused China of direct involvement in the war, but Beijing has denied the allegations. The revelation of Chinese participation in the conflict comes one month after a military newspaper in the Soviet Union made the first public acknowledgment of a Soviet combat role in the war.
May 17		A court in Frankfurt, West Germany, convicts Lebanese Mohammed Ali Hamadei of hijacking a Trans World Airlines jet and murdering U.S. Navy diver Robert Dean Stethem in June 1985. Hamadei is sentenced to life in prison. . . . In Czechoslovakia dissident playwright Vaclav Havel is released from prison on parole. Within hours of being set free, he vows to continue his human rights activism and calls for the Czechoslovak authorities to release other political prisoners.		The Org. of American States holds an emergency meeting and adopts a resolution condemning abuses by Panama's military strongman, General Manuel Antonio Noriega, and calls for the "peaceful transfer of power" to a democratically elected government. The meeting takes place a week after the Noriega regime annulled elections that, by most accounts, were won by the opposition, and after Noriega supporters severely beat three opposition candidates.	Over one million Chinese gather in Beijing's central square to call for democratic reforms and demand that Deng Xiaoping, China's paramount leader, and the rest of the nation's leadership step down.

A	B	C	D	E
Includes developments that affect more than one world region, international organizations and important meetings of major world leaders.	Includes all domestic and regional developments in Europe, including the Soviet Union, Turkey, Cyprus and Malta.	Includes all domestic and regional developments in Africa and the Middle East, including Iraq and Iran and excluding Cyprus, Turkey and Afghanistan.	Includes all domestic and regional developments in Latin America, the Caribbean and Canada.	Includes all domestic and regional developments in Asia and Pacific nations, extending from Afghanistan through all the Pacific Islands, except Hawaii.

U.S. Politics & Social Issues	U.S. Foreign Policy & Defense	U.S. Economy & Environment	Science, Technology & Nature	Culture, Leisure & Life Style	
				A group of about 300 actors and other theater supporters hold an all-night vigil at the site of the Elizabethan-era Rose Theater in London. The group is protesting plans to erect an office building on the site. The demonstration ends after a deal is struck with the developer, under which construction will be delayed for one month while architects consider plans that will allow the building to be constructed around the preserved remains of the theater.	**May 14**
Pres. Bush sets forth the details of a $1.2 bil. federal anticrime package. The most significant provisions of the plan are two proposals restricting the use of firearms. . . . The Supreme Court rules unanimously that a challenge to police use of force against a suspect should be determined on the basis of "objective reasonableness" rather than the intent of the officers, whether they acted in "good faith" or with malicious intent to harm.		Overrruling a 1953 decision, the Supreme Court rules, 5-4, that arbitration agreements to resolve disputes over the purchase of securities are binding. . . . The apple industry announces that it is asking growers to discontinue use of the controversial chemical Alar, which is blamed for a 20% drop in sales because of reports that Alar poses a cancer risk to children. . . . The United States and the state of Washington enter into a 30-year agreement to clean up radioactive and hazardous waste at the Hanford nuclear reservation.			**May 15**
Seattle voters approve a citizen initiative to limit downtown real estate development. By a margin of better than two to one, Seattle residents favor limiting the amount of office space to be added and the height of new buildings. . . . A federal judge in Washington, D.C., strikes down several key provisions of the 1988 Child Protection and Obscenity Enforcement Act. The act required anyone who produced, distributed or copied books, magazines, films or videotapes with "explicit sexual content" to take steps to verify that all nude models pictured in the material were at least 18 years old and to keep records on the models involved.	The Senate hands Pres. Bush a significant foreign policy victory when it votes down, 52-47, a motion to block an agreement on joint U.S.-Japanese development of a new Japanese fighter plane, the FSX.	Housing starts dropped in April for the third consecutive month to their lowest level in six years, the Commerce Dept. reports. . . . Denver voters approve a plan for a $2.3 bil. airport to replace 60-year-old Stapleton International Airport. A final environmental-impact statement and funding for the project have to be obtained.			**May 16**
	Congress clears and sends to the White House a bill to increase the minimum wage to $4.55 an hour by 1991. The bill faces a veto threat by Pres. Bush, who is insisting on a lower base wage and a subminimum training wage unacceptable to Democrats.	Transportation Sec. Samuel K. Skinner sets 1990-model gas mileage standards at 27.5 miles per gallon as an incentive to "develop better engines and get better mileage." . . . The merchandise trade deficit shrinks to a seasonally adjusted $8.86 bil. in March, the Commerce Dept. reports.		The Sejm (parliament) approves a package of laws giving the Roman Catholic Church legal status in Poland. The move clears the way for diplomatic relations between Warsaw and the Vatican. Poland is the first Soviet-bloc nation to extend legal recognition to the church.	**May 17**

F	G	H	I	J
Includes elections, federal-state relations, civil rights and liberties, crime, the judiciary, education, health care, poverty, urban affairs and population.	*Includes formation and debate of U.S. foreign and defense policies, veterans' affairs and defense spending. (Relations with specific foreign countries are usually found under the region concerned.)*	*Includes business, labor, agriculture, taxation, transportation, consumer affairs, monetary and fiscal policy, natural resources, and pollution.*	*Includes worldwide scientific, medical and technological developments, natural phenomena, U.S. weather, natural disasters, and accidents.*	*Includes the arts, religion, scholarship, communications media, sports, entertainments, fashions, fads and social life.*

	World Affairs	Europe	Africa & the Middle East	The Americas	Asia & the Pacific
May 18	The 24-nation Org. for Economic Cooperation and Development agrees to liberalize cross-border capital movements by mid-1990, including mergers, underwritings, and short-term capital investments.			The Bank of Canada lowers its lending rate 20 basis points, to 12.30%. It marks the third consecutive week of decline in the central bank rate.... In the first such action by Venezuelan workers in 30 years, the Confederation of Venezuelan Workers stages a general strike in protest of the government's austerity measures.	
May 19		Britain's inflation rate rose to 8% in April, the highest rate in seven years, the government reports. The rate of retail price inflation is up from 7.9% in March and is the highest since April 1982.			In China, in what amounts to a popular uprising against the current leadership of the Chinese Communist Party, hundreds of thousands of students and workers defying martial law continue to stage hunger strikes and massive pro-democracy protests in the heart of Beijing.
May 20		After a 25-month trial, a court in Madrid finds that 600-700 deaths from ''toxic syndrome'' since 1981 are attributable to adulterated cooking oil; two of the 37 defendants receive significant prison sentences.	Ethiopia's Pres. Mengistu Haile Mariam appears to have regained firm control of the country four days after top military officers launched a coup while he was visiting East Germany.		
May 21		Reformists within Hungary's ruling Socialist Workers' Party issue a manifesto calling for Hungarian neutrality, talks on transition to a multiparty system, and a radical transformation of the economy, among other things.... As many as 100 ethnic Turks in Bulgaria are reported to have been killed in two days of protests against the government's forced assimilation policy.			
May 22	The U.S. dollar rises to a 29-month high of 2.0123 West German marks and 142.05 Japanese yen despite intervention by the Federal Reserve and at least nine other central banks.				
May 23		Richard von Weizsaecker is reelected as West Germany's president by a vote of the Bundesversammlung (Federal Assembly) in Bonn. Weizsaecker becomes only the third president in the republic's 40 years to be reelected.	An emergency summit of the Arab League in Casablanca, Morocco, to deal with the Palestinian question and the crisis in Lebanon opens dramatically with the return of Egypt after a 10-year absence, but it ends with a stalemate over Lebanon, where Syria and Iraq are locked in a bitter proxy war.	Ending more than a week of speculation, Argentina's Pres. Alfonsin says he will not transfer power to president-elect Carlos Saul Menem before the constitutionally mandated date of December 10.	In China, the internal struggle for the leadership of the Communist Party begins to overshadow the ongoing massive demonstrations in Beijing's Tiananmen Square.

A	B	C	D	E
Includes developments that affect more than one world region, international organizations and important meetings of major world leaders.	Includes all domestic and regional developments in Europe, including the Soviet Union, Turkey, Cyprus and Malta.	Includes all domestic and regional developments in Africa and the Middle East, including Iraq and Iran and excluding Cyprus, Turkey and Afghanistan.	Includes all domestic and regional developments in Latin America, the Caribbean and Canada.	Includes all domestic and regional developments in Asia and Pacific nations, extending from Afghanistan through all the Pacific Islands, except Hawaii.

U.S. Politics & Social Issues	U.S. Foreign Policy & Defense	U.S. Economy & Environment	Science, Technology & Nature	Culture, Leisure & Life Style	
A grand jury in Cook Co., Ill., refuses to indict Rodolfo Linares of murder charges. Linares had unplugged his comatose 15-month-old son's respirator and allowed the boy to die.		Congress gives final approval to a compromise $1.2 trillion budget plan for FY1990. . . . The consumer price index climbed 0.7% in April as energy costs recorded their largest monthly gains ever, the Labor Dept. reports. . . . The Federal Aviation Admin. orders airlines to make extensive repairs to their aging planes. The order for certain Boeing models will cost an estimated $142 mil. in repairs.	The World Health Org. predicts that the number of cases of Acquired Immune Deficiency Syndrome worldwide will increase from 450,000 to 5 million in the year 2000, and the number of people infected with the AIDS virus will increase from between 5 and 10 million to between 15 and 30 million people. . . . An article in the journal *Science* by two Univ. of Toronto scientists says that the water level in the world's oceans appears to have risen 2.4 millimeters per year over the past century. . . . The National Aeronautics and Space Admin. names former astronaut William Lenoir to head the $30 bil. space station program in a move that many see as indicative of the agency's intention to fight for full funding.		May 18
		The Dow Jones industrial average surpasses the 2500 mark for the first time since the October 1987 stock market crash, reaching a post-crash high of 2501.10.			May 19
Warren Grant Magnuson, 84, Washington State Democratic representative (1937-44) and senator (1944-80), dies of congestive heart failure and diabetes in Seattle. President pro tempore of the Senate and chair of the Commerce and Appropriations committees, he sponsored important bills on health policy and safety standards.		Week-long National Transportation Safety Board hearings in Anchorage, Alaska, reveal that alcohol, risky navigation, illegal procedures, and lax supervision played key roles in the *Exxon Valdez* oil spill.		Two weeks after winning the Kentucky Derby, Sunday Silence wins the Preakness Stakes, the second leg of thoroughbred racing's Triple Crown, at Pimlico Race Course in Baltimore.	May 20
		The General Accounting Office estimates that the Bush administration's plan to bail out the savings and loan industry will cost taxpayers $285.4 bil. over 30 years.		Nancy Lopez wins the Ladies Professional Golf Assoc. Championship.	May 21
A House Ways and Means Committee study shows that average U.S. family income increased from $27,917 in 1979 to $29,487 in 1987, and that the gap between the nation's richest and poorest citizens widened. . . . The *New York Times* reports that episodes of racist graffiti, jokes, brawls, and anonymous hate letters have been reported at 175 colleges and universities nationwide since 1986.			An American College Health Assoc.-sponsored study of anonymous blood samples from 16,861 students finds that 0.2% of U.S. college students are infected with the virus that causes Acquired Immune Deficiency Syndrome.	The Los Angeles Lakers' Magic Johnson is named the National Basketball Assoc.'s most valuable player for the 1988-89 season.	May 22
A federal jury in Anchorage convicts two former advisers to North Slope Borough Mayor Eugene Brower of extortion, racketeering, and fraud for seeking to extort as much as $18 mil. during the North Slope construction boom of the early 1980s.			The International Business Machines Corp., American Telephone and Telegraph Co. and the Massachusetts Institute of Technology agree to form the Consortium for Superconducting Electronics to research and develop applications for high-temperature superconductivity.	The 42nd annual film festival in Cannes, France, awards its top prize, the Palme d'Or (Golden Palm), to director Steven Soderbergh's *sex, lies and videotape*.	May 23

F	G	H	I	J
Includes elections, federal-state relations, civil rights and liberties, crime, the judiciary, education, health care, poverty, urban affairs and population.	Includes formation and debate of U.S. foreign and defense policies, veterans' affairs and defense spending. (Relations with specific foreign countries are usually found under the region concerned.)	Includes business, labor, agriculture, taxation, transportation, consumer affairs, monetary and fiscal policy, natural resources, and pollution.	Includes worldwide scientific, medical and technological developments, natural phenomena, U.S. weather, natural disasters, and accidents.	Includes the arts, religion, scholarship, communications media, sports, entertainments, fashions, fads and social life.

	World Affairs	Europe	Africa & the Middle East	The Americas	Asia & the Pacific
May 24	The International Monetary Fund says it will set aside 25%-30% of extended or standby loans from existing resources to support debt-principal reduction by developing countries under the initiative launched by U.S. Treasury Sec. Nicholas F. Brady.	France's most-wanted war crimes suspect, 74-year-old Paul Touvier, is arrested at a Roman Catholic priory in Nice. Touvier is charged with crimes against humanity for his collaboration with the Nazis to fight the French Resistance and persecute Jews during World War II. . . . Hungary and Czechoslovakia agree to form a bilateral commission of experts to study the environmental impact of the joint Danube River dam project.	Students in Benin City, Nigeria, begin protests against the government's economic austerity measures. The demonstrations spread quickly and turn violent, prompting the government to close universities and ban political activity in some areas.	The Canadian government issues guidelines on the deadly disease Acquired Immune Deficiency Syndrome (AIDS) with regard to employment in the federal civil service. The guidelines prohibit the harassment of federal employees with AIDS and guarantee the secrecy of all AIDS-related government records.	In Taiwan, Pres. Lee Teng-hui appoints Lee Huan, the secretary general of the ruling Nationalist Party (Kuomintang, or KMT), to be the nation's new premier.
May 25		The Soviet Union's new Congress of People's Deputies opens with 2,250 deputies in attendance, most of them chosen for the parliament through direct elections and the majority of them workers and academicians. . . . Irish P.M. Charles Haughey calls for a general election June 15.		The Nicaraguan government orders two U.S. diplomats to leave the country, accusing them of fomenting strikes by Nicaraguan teachers.	China's paramount leader Deng Xiaoping and hard-line Premier Li Peng have reportedly emerged as the victors in an internal Communist Party power struggle triggered by the pro-democracy protests in Beijing.
May 26					
May 27					Wan Li, chairman of China's National People's Congress, signals his support for Premier Li Peng in an internal Communist Party power struggle triggered by the pro-democracy protests in Beijing. . . . In China, 3,000 pro-democracy strikers end their nine-day fast, reportedly to regain their strength for the expected confrontation with the military.
May 28		France confirms that it received covert U.S. technical assistance for its nuclear weapons program even after suspending a bilateral nuclear arms cooperation agreement in 1966 when it quit the military structure of the North Atlantic Treaty Org.			
May 29		At a 40th anniversary summit meeting in Brussels, Pres. Bush offers the North Atlantic Treaty Org. (NATO) a detailed proposal on reducing East-West conventional forces in Europe, and NATO reaches a compromise on East-West talks on short-range nuclear forces.			Special prosecutors in Tokyo conclude their eight-month criminal investigation of the so-called Recruit scandal, which led to the arrest or indictment of the former chairmen of the Recruit Co. and Nippon Telegraph & Telephone Corp. and 17 other politicians and government officials.

A	B	C	D	E
Includes developments that affect more than one world region, international organizations and important meetings of major world leaders.	Includes all domestic and regional developments in Europe, including the Soviet Union, Turkey, Cyprus and Malta.	Includes all domestic and regional developments in Africa and the Middle East, including Iraq and Iran and excluding Cyprus, Turkey and Afghanistan.	Includes all domestic and regional developments in Latin America, the Caribbean and Canada.	Includes all domestic and regional developments in Asia and Pacific nations, extending from Afghanistan through all the Pacific Islands, except Hawaii.

U.S. Politics & Social Issues	U.S. Foreign Policy & Defense	U.S. Economy & Environment	Science, Technology & Nature	Culture, Leisure & Life Style	
Gov. George Deukmejian (R) signs two bills that make California the first state in the nation to restrict the sale and possession of assault weapons. . . . The Univ. of California, Berkeley, announces that it is changing its admissions policy to raise academic standards and to add more students from racially and economically diverse groups.				The film *Indiana Jones and the Last Crusade* is released in New York. The third (and, according to director Steven Spielberg, the final) installment of the Indiana Jones adventure series stars Harrison Ford, Sean Connery, Denholm Elliott, Alison Doody, John Rhys-Davies, Julian Glover and River Phoenix.	May 24
Teachers in Los Angeles vote for an agreement ending a 10-day strike that crippled the nation's second-largest school system. The pact calls for a 24% pay increase over three years and gives teachers a larger role in school management.		In the first use of the so-called Super 301 provision of the 1988 Omnibus Trade Act, Pres. Bush identifies Japan, Brazil, and India as unfair trading partners . . . After-tax profits of U.S. corporations fell 1.7% to a $171.6 bil. annual rate in the first quarter, the Commerce Dept. reports.		The Calgary Flames win the National Hockey League Stanley Cup, with a 4-2 victory over the Montreal Canadiens in the sixth game of the series. Calgary defenseman Al MacInnis wins the Conn Smythe Trophy as the most valuable player.	May 25
In a surprise announcement, Rep. Tony Coelho (D, Calif.) declares that he will step down as majority whip and give up his seat in the House to avoid a prolonged congressional investigation into his financial dealings. . . . A Columbus, Ohio, jury convicts Rep. Donald E. "Buz" Lukens (R) of contributing to the delinquency and unruliness of a minor for having sex with a 16-year-old girl. . . . A Washington Post/ABC News poll shows that 59% of those surveyed rate congressional ethics as "not so good" or "poor," compared with 39% who rate Congress as "good" or "excellent."		Consumer spending rose 1.1% to a $3.53 trillion annual rate in April, while personal income rose 0.4% to $4.369 trillion, the Commerce Dept. reports. . . . National Steel Corp. announces an accord with the United Steelworkers of America on a 50-month contract providing for immediate restoration of wage concessions made in 1986.		*Publishers Weekly*'s hardback fiction best-sellers for the week are: *The Satanic Verses*, Salman Rushdie; *The Negotiator*, Frederick Forsyth; *While My Pretty One Sleeps*, Mary Higgins Clark; *Star*, Danielle Steel; and *The Temple of My Familiar*, Alice Walker.	May 26
	Sec. of State James A. Baker III meets with South Africa's Foreign Min. Roelof F. Botha, in Rome, for the first high-level contact between the Bush administration and the Pretoria government.			*Billboard*'s best-selling albums for the week are *Like A Prayer*, Madonna; *The Raw and the Cooked*, Fine Young Cannibals; *GN'R Lies*, Guns N' Roses; *Beaches* (soundtrack); and *Loc-Ed After Dark*, Tone Loc.	May 27
		The American Telephone & Telegraph Co. reaches agreement with two unions on new three-year contracts marked by innovative family-care benefits. The pacts call for better child-care benefits, more leave to cope with family problems, and reimbursement of adoption costs.		Emerson Fittipaldi of Brazil wins the Indianapolis 500 auto race. . . . In tennis, West Germany wins the World Team Cup tournament in Duesseldorf, West Germany, two matches to one, in the finals over Argentina. . . . Donni Leaycraft of Louisiana State Univ. wins the National Collegiate Athletic Assoc. men's tennis singles title, 6-1, 4-6, 6-3, over Steven Jung of Nebraska.	May 28
					May 29

F	G	H	I	J
Includes elections, federal-state relations, civil rights and liberties, crime, the judiciary, education, health care, poverty, urban affairs and population.	Includes formation and debate of U.S. foreign and defense policies, veterans' affairs and defense spending. (Relations with specific foreign countries are usually found under the region concerned.)	Includes business, labor, agriculture, taxation, transportation, consumer affairs, monetary and fiscal policy, natural resources, and pollution.	Includes worldwide scientific, medical and technological developments, natural phenomena, U.S. weather, natural disasters, and accidents.	Includes the arts, religion, scholarship, communications media, sports, entertainments, fashions, fads and social life.

	World Affairs	Europe	Africa & the Middle East	The Americas	Asia & the Pacific
May 30				Mexico reaches agreement with its foreign government creditors on a $2.5 bil. debt restructuring plan.	The Bank of Japan raises its official discount rate by three-quarters of a percentage point, to 3.25%.
May 31				The United States retaliates against Nicaragua's May 25 expulsion of two U.S. diplomats by ordering the expulsion of two Nicaraguan envoys. The two countries engaged in a similar trading of expulsions in 1988.... In Canada, net farm income in 1988 declined by 11% due to the long drought, according to Statistics Canada.... A UN-sponsored conference on Central American refugees adopts a $380 mil., three-year plan to help an estimated 146,400 registered and 893,000 illegal refugees in Central America and Mexico.	Australia's foreign debt tops the A$100 bil. mark for the first time, the government's bureau of statistics reports. The nation's net foreign debt for the first quarter of 1989 was A$103.2 bil. (US$77 bil.).
June 1	Ministers of the 24 member countries of the Org. for Economic Cooperation and Development conclude their annual meeting with a communique indirectly criticizing the U.S. decision to designate Japan, Brazil, and India as unfair traders under the Super 301 provision of the 1988 Omnibus Trade Act.	The Portuguese parliament approves a package of constitutional reforms that do away with the primary vestiges of Marxist ideology embedded in the 1976 constitution.		Alfredo Cristiani, 41, of the right-wing Nationalist Republican Alliance (ARENA), is sworn in as president of El Salvador in the nation's first transfer of power from one civilian government to another. ...Canada's gross domestic product (GDP) fell 0.3% in March, according to Statistics Canada data, in what many view as the start of a long-anticipated economic slowdown in Canada.	Sri Lanka's Pres. Ranasinghe Premadasa touches off a diplomatic dispute with India when he demands that the 45,000 Indian peacekeeping troops stationed in Sri Lanka be withdrawn before the end of July.
June 2		Komsomolskaya Pravda, the newspaper of the Communist Party youth organization, confirms the 1962 massacre of striking workers in Novocherkassk, an incident that has been hidden from the Soviet public for decades.			Japan's Foreign Min. Sosuke Uno is elected premier, replacing Noboru Takeshita, who resigned over his involvement in the so-called Recruit scandal.
June 3		In the Soviet Union, a gas pipeline explosion engulfs two passing railway trains in flames near the town of Ufa in the Ural Mountains. At least 190 people are killed, 720 hospitalized, and 270 missing.			Tens of thousands of Chinese Army troops sweep into Beijing to crush a student-led pro-democracy movement that began in mid-April. The bloody crackdown provokes antigovernment sentiment in numerous Chinese cities, and is harshly condemned by nations around the world.

A	B	C	D	E
Includes developments that affect more than one world region, international organizations and important meetings of major world leaders.	Includes all domestic and regional developments in Europe, including the Soviet Union, Turkey, Cyprus and Malta.	Includes all domestic and regional developments in Africa and the Middle East, including Iraq and Iran and excluding Cyprus, Turkey and Afghanistan.	Includes all domestic and regional developments in Latin America, the Caribbean and Canada.	Includes all domestic and regional developments in Asia and Pacific nations, extending from Afghanistan through all the Pacific Islands, except Hawaii.

U.S. Politics & Social Issues	U.S. Foreign Policy & Defense	U.S. Economy & Environment	Science, Technology & Nature	Culture, Leisure & Life Style	
A federal court-appointed official recommends that a unified governing board be set up to oversee desegregation at all colleges and universities within the Louisiana state university system.... Rep. Claude Denson Pepper, 88, liberal Democrat from Florida who was the oldest member of the Congress, dies of cancer in Walter Reed Army Medical Center in Washington, D.C. A senator from 1937 to 1951, he returned to the House in 1962 as representative of a congressional district in Miami. On May 25 he was awarded the Medal of Freedom by Pres. Bush.		Foreign investors spent a record $65 bil. to acquire or establish U.S. businesses in 1988, the Commerce Dept. reports.		The League of American Theaters and Producers reports that Broadway set a box office record of $262 mil. in 1988-89, although attendance fell and a record-low 30 new productions opened during the season.	May 30
Following a year-long ordeal over charges that he violated House ethics rules, Speaker James C. Wright Jr. (D, Tex.) announces that he will resign his seat in Congress. ... Federal District Judge W. Arthur Garrity approves a plan that will allow parents in Boston to choose the public school they want their children to attend.... In his last press conference before leaving office, Surgeon General C. Everett Koop proposes a major campaign to fight alcohol abuse and drunken driving, including restrictions on alcohol advertising, tougher drunk-driving laws, and higher taxes on beer, wine and liquor.		Federal District Judge David Edelstein names three attorneys as overseers of the Teamsters union to guard against corruption or influence by organized crime.... The government's index of leading economic indicators rose 0.8% in April, the Commerce Dept. reports.... Prices received by farmers for raw agricultural products rose 2.7% in May, the Agriculture Dept. reports.		*Variety*'s top-grossing films for the week are: *Indiana Jones and the Last Crusade*, *See No Evil, Hear No Evil*, *Field of Dreams*, *Road House*, and *Pink Cadillac*.	May 31
Education Sec. Lauro F. Cavazos announces a series of measures designed to penalize trade schools and other institutions that have high student loan default rates, which currently cost the federal government about $1.8 bil. a year. ... Housing and Urban Development Sec. Jack F. Kemp announces that his department has overhauled the Section 8 Moderate Rehabilitation Program and that funding applications will be selected on the basis of such factors as overcrowding and poverty in the local community.			A study in the *New England Journal of Medicine* finds that the virus that causes Acquired Immune Deficiency Syndrome (AIDS) can lie dormant in humans for up to three years before it is detected with standard blood tests.	Scott Isaacs, 14, an eighth-grade student from Littleton, Colo., wins the 62nd annual Scripps-Howard National Spelling Bee, topping a field of 222 contenders by correctly spelling the word "spoliator."	June 1
American Bar Assoc. evaluations of federal judicial nominees will be resumed under an agreement with the Justice Dept.		The unemployment rate fell one-tenth of a percentage point to 5.1% in May, the Labor Dept. reports.		The fourth annual Ruth Lilly Poetry Prize is awarded to Mona Van Duyn, author of six books of poetry and cofounder of the literary quarterly *Perspective*.... *Dead Poets Society*, a film about an iconoclastic teacher at a private boys' school in the late 1950s, is released in New York City. Directed by Peter Weir, the film stars Robin Williams and Robert Sean Leonard.	June 2
		Thousands of demonstrators rally at Hampton Beach, N.H., to protest preparations for the first low-power testing of the nearby Seabrook nuclear power plant.		The Skydome, a $416 mil. retractable-domed stadium, opens in Toronto, replacing Exhibition Stadium as the home of Major League Baseball's Toronto Blue Jays and the Canadian Football League's Toronto Argonauts.	June 3

F	G	H	I	J
Includes elections, federal-state relations, civil rights and liberties, crime, the judiciary, education, health care, poverty, urban affairs and population.	Includes formation and debate of U.S. foreign and defense policies, veterans' affairs and defense spending. (Relations with specific foreign countries are usually found under the region concerned.)	Includes business, labor, agriculture, taxation, transportation, consumer affairs, monetary and fiscal policy, natural resources, and pollution.	Includes worldwide scientific, medical and technological developments, natural phenomena, U.S. weather, natural disasters, and accidents.	Includes the arts, religion, scholarship, communications media, sports, entertainments, fashions, fads and social life.

	World Affairs	Europe	Africa & the Middle East	The Americas	Asia & the Pacific
June 4		In Poland's first open elections in 40 years, the communist regime suffers a humiliating defeat as Solidarity-backed candidates all but sweep the parliamentary elections.	The death of Iran's Ayatollah Ruhollah Khomeini shortly before midnight is announced early today. The catalyst of the Iranian revolution against Shah Mohammed Riza Pahlevi, he ruled as Iran's supreme religious and political leader since returning from exile in February 1979. The nation's senior Shiite Moslem clergymen chose Pres. Ali Khamenei as Khomeini's successor. Khomeini was believed to be 87 or 89.		In China, an all-out military assault against the pro-democracy protesters in Beijing's Tiananmen Square begins about midnight; hundreds are reported killed after the military opens fire in the square.
June 5			The Iranian news agency reports that eight people are crushed to death and hundreds of others injured as hundreds of thousands of Iranians turn out to view Ayatollah Ruhollah Khomeini's body as it lies in state in a refrigerated glass coffin on a hilltop north of Teheran.		
June 6				Driven by a trade surplus that increased to $613 mil. from $582.4 mil. the year before, the Chilean economy expanded at a 9.4% annual rate in the first quarter.	Three days of torrential rains have reportedly triggered the worst floods and landslides in Sri Lanka in 40 years. Government officials say the floods killed at least 310 people and left more than 100,000 homeless.
June 7	The Org. of Petroleum Exporting Countries agrees on a higher production ceiling, about 19.5 million barrels a day, for the second half of 1989, which it hopes will hold oil prices at about $18 a barrel.	East German security police arrest 120 young people during an East Berlin sit-in to protest alleged fraud in local government elections. All 273,344 candidates were pre-approved by the ruling Socialist Unity (Communist) Party, with many running under an official "Unity List."		A Suriname Airways jetliner crashes while attempting to land near Paramaribo, the capital of Suriname, killing 169 of the 182 people aboard.	
June 8					Australian military air traffic controllers assume direction of commercial flights approaching Sydney Airport after a quarter of the regular-duty civilian controllers refuse to report for work in a job action.... Speculation surrounding the Chinese leadership is relaxed when Premier Li Peng appears on national television praising a group of army soldiers in the Great Hall of the People, apparently for their efforts in support of the crackdown on the student-led pro-democracy movement.
June 9		At the close of the first session of the Soviet Union's Congress of People's Deputies, Premier Nikolai I. Ryzhkov publicly reveals the Soviet Union's foreign debt figure, $56 bil.... European Community environment ministers adopt antipollution standards for small cars similar to those in the United States, effective July 1, 1992, for new cars, and Dec. 12, 1992, for existing models.		Jose Antonio Rodriguez Porth, the top civilian adviser to El Salvador's Pres. Alfredo Cristiani, is assassinated as he leaves his home in San Salvador. He is the first cabinet minister killed in the nine-year-old war with leftist rebels.... The biggest stock market collapse in Brazilian history is triggered when market speculator Naji Robert Nahas writes $31.1 mil. in bad checks to brokerage firms to partially cover some $239 mil. in stock, options, and futures debt.	The Chinese government announces that an undisclosed number of "thugs" and "hooligans" have been arrested for suspected involvement in the pro-democracy demonstrations of the last few weeks.
June 10					

A	B	C	D	E
Includes developments that affect more than one world region, international organizations and important meetings of major world leaders.	*Includes all domestic and regional developments in Europe, including the Soviet Union, Turkey, Cyprus and Malta.*	*Includes all domestic and regional developments in Africa and the Middle East, including Iraq and Iran and excluding Cyprus, Turkey and Afghanistan.*	*Includes all domestic and regional developments in Latin America, the Caribbean and Canada.*	*Includes all domestic and regional developments in Asia and Pacific nations, extending from Afghanistan through all the Pacific Islands, except Hawaii.*

U.S. Politics & Social Issues	U.S. Foreign Policy & Defense	U.S. Economy & Environment	Science, Technology & Nature	Culture, Leisure & Life Style	
			At the Fifth International Conference on Acquired Immune Deficiency Syndrome (AIDS), some progress in research toward a vaccine against the disease is reported, especially a study by polio vaccine pioneer Dr. Jonas Salk, but the primary focus is on social issues such as AIDS prevention, transmission, and testing.	At the 43rd annual Antoinette Perry (Tony) Awards, *Jerome Robbins's Broadway* wins for best musical, director (Jerome Robbins), lead actor (Jason Alexander). Ruth Brown is named best actress (*Black and Blue*). *Lend Me a Tenor* wins for best director (Jerry Zaks) and actor (Philip Bosco). Best play is Wendy Wasserstein's *The Heidi Chronicles*; and best actress, Pauline Collins (*Shirley Valentine*).	June 4
Altering a longstanding interpretation of the Civil Rights Act of 1964, the Supreme Court rules, 5-4, that minority workers must prove racial discrimination in employment discrimination lawsuits.		Leading U.S. banks cut their prime lending rate by half a percentage point to 11%, the first reduction in the prime since February 1988.	Dr. Ian Craft, director of the in-vitro fertilization unit at London's Humana Wellington Hospital, reports in the medical journal *The Lancet* that a woman aged 48 and in early menopause has given birth to twins conceived from eggs donated by a younger woman.		June 5
Rep. Thomas S. Foley (D, Wash.) is elected speaker of the House of Representatives, replacing Rep. James C. Wright Jr. (D, Tex.), who resigned amid allegations that he violated House ethics rules.	The Justice Dept. discloses that it has begun a criminal investigation of the government's illegal disposal of radioactive waste and concealment of hazardous contamination at the Rocky Flats Nuclear Weapons Plant near Denver.	Sacramento County voters in California approve a proposal to close the Rancho Seco nuclear power plant in the first closure of an operating U.S. nuclear power plant by popular vote.			June 6
		A Senate-approved $3.3 bil. supplemental spending bill for FY1989 drops $822 mil. intended for a federal antidrug program passed earlier by the House but opposed by the White House.... Net withdrawals from federally insured thrifts dropped to $5.4 bil. in April, the Federal Home Loan Bank Board reports. April is the 12th straight monthly net withdrawal for the savings and loan industry.		Wayne Gretzky of the Los Angeles Kings is named the winner of the Hart Trophy as the National Hockey League's most valuable player for a record ninth time.	June 7
Ruling 5-1 that the state's public school system is unconstitutional because of wide disparities in spending between rich and poor districts, the Kentucky Supreme Court orders the state legislature to devise a system that will distribute education funds more evenly.... Harvard Univ. alumni elect to the university's 30-member board of overseers South African Anglican Archbishop Desmond Tutu, actor John Lithgow, and Labor Sec. Elizabeth Dole, among others.	Developments in China dominate Pres. Bush's first formal, prime-time, nationally televised news conference from the White House.			In game two of the National Basketball Assoc. Championship finals the Detroit Pistons beat the Los Angeles Lakers, 108-105.	June 8
		The government's producer price index climbed 0.9% in May, the Labor Dept. reports.	A study published in *Science* shows that federal estimates of cases of Acquired Immune Deficiency Syndrome (AIDS) in the United States might have "substantially" underestimated the extent of the disease among whites and in the Midwest.... George Wells Beadle, 85, geneticist and president of the Univ. of Chicago from 1961 to 1968, dies of Alzheimer's disease in Pomona, Calif. He shared the 1958 Nobel Prize in physiology or medicine with Edward L. Tatum and Joshua Lederberg for work demonstrating how genes control basic chemical processes in living cells.		June 9
Saying it has accomplished its goal of getting conservative Christians involved in politics, the Rev. Jerry Falwell announces the disbanding of the Moral Majority, the conservative religious and political organization he founded in 1979.	Pakistan's P.M. Benazir Bhutto ends a six-day visit to the United States during which she met with Pres. Bush for talks on the Afghan civil war, which has forced some 3.5 million Afghan refugees into Pakistan.			In tennis, the women's singles champion of the French Open is Arantxa Sanchez of Spain.... Easy Goer wins the Belmont Stakes and denies Sunday Silence's bid for the Triple Crown of thoroughbred racing.	June 10
F	G	H	I	J	
Includes elections, federal-state relations, civil rights and liberties, crime, the judiciary, education, health care, poverty, urban affairs and population.	*Includes formation and debate of U.S. foreign and defense policies, veterans' affairs and defense spending. (Relations with specific foreign countries are usually found under the region concerned.)*	*Includes business, labor, agriculture, taxation, transportation, consumer affairs, monetary and fiscal policy, natural resources, and pollution.*	*Includes worldwide scientific, medical and technological developments, natural phenomena, U.S. weather, natural disasters, and accidents.*	*Includes the arts, religion, scholarship, communications media, sports, entertainments, fashions, fads and social life.*	

	World Affairs	Europe	Africa & the Middle East	The Americas	Asia & the Pacific
June 11				Contra rebel leader Alfredo Cesar, a director of the Nicaraguan Resistance Movement, returns to Nicaragua after seven years in exile and joins the centrist Social Democratic Party.	
June 12		Soviet Pres. Mikhail S. Gorbachev is given an enthusiastic reception as he begins his first state visit to West Germany, the centerpiece of which is the signing of a declaration pledging closer ties between Moscow and Bonn. . . . Soviet Premier Nikolai I. Ryzhkov visits Uzbek SSR to survey the damage of nine days of ethnic violence, the worst ethnic strife in the USSR since Mikhail S. Gorbachev came to power in 1985.		Argentina's Pres. Raul Alfonsin announces that he will resign and allow Peronist president-elect Carlos Saul Menem to assume office five months early. . . . In an effort to bolster its anti-inflation plan and to protect workers' basic wages, the Nicaraguan government announces a package of economic measures that includes a devaluation of the cordoba.	
June 13	A 60-nation, UN-sponsored conference adopts a so-called Comprehensive Plan of Action in an attempt to stanch the flow of refugees fleeing Vietnam for Hong Kong and other countries in Southeast Asia.	Amid a continuing rift over whether Britain should become a full member of the European Monetary System, P.M. Margaret Thatcher says that Chancellor of the Exchequer Nigel Lawson has her "full and unequivocal and generous backing." . . . The Hungarian regime and leading opposition factions begin formal talks on a transition to a multiparty political system.		Mexico's Jose Antonio Zorrilla Perez, the former head of a now defunct federal police agency, is arrested in connection with the 1984 slaying of Mexico's best-known journalist and columnist, Manuel Buendia.	
June 14				Cuban authorities arrest Gen. Arnaldo Ochoa Sanchez on charges of drug trafficking in what some view as a shake-up stemming from dissent in the top ranks. . . . Amnesty International charges Guatemalan right-wing death squads with the disappearance of 222 people since 1986. . . . Formally abandoning the anti-inflation Summer Plan, Brazil reinstates full indexation of the economy and daily currency devaluations.	

A	B	C	D	E
Includes developments that affect more than one world region, international organizations and important meetings of major world leaders.	Includes all domestic and regional developments in Europe, including the Soviet Union, Turkey, Cyprus and Malta.	Includes all domestic and regional developments in Africa and the Middle East, including Iraq and Iran and excluding Cyprus, Turkey and Afghanistan.	Includes all domestic and regional developments in Latin America, the Caribbean and Canada.	Includes all domestic and regional developments in Asia and Pacific nations, extending from Afghanistan through all the Pacific Islands, except Hawaii.

U.S. Politics & Social Issues	U.S. Foreign Policy & Defense	U.S. Economy & Environment	Science, Technology & Nature	Culture, Leisure & Life Style	
				In tennis, Michael Chang of the United States wins the men's singles championship at the French Open.... Soviet pianist Aleksei Sultanov, 19, wins the quadrennial Van Cliburn International Piano Competition in Fort Worth, Tex.... Driving a Mercedes, West Germans Joachen Mass and Manuel Reuter and Swede Stanley Dickens cover 3,271 miles to win the Le Mans 24 Hour race.	**June 11**
The Supreme Court rules, 5-4, that white workers claiming unfair treatment as a result of affirmative action settlements can seek redress under civil rights legislation.... The Court also declines, 5-4, to override a ban against use of "victim impact statements" by prosecutors to persuade juries to impose the death penalty in murder cases.... Rep. Julian C. Dixon (D, Calif.), chairman of the House Ethics Committee, reveals that his wife earned more than $100,000 in 1988 on an investment in two gift shops at Los Angeles International Airport.	The United States and Soviet Union sign an agreement barring the use of military force in the event of an accidental confrontation or misunderstanding.	Pres. Bush presents proposals for a sweeping revision of the Clean Air Act, setting goals for major reductions of smog, acid rain, and toxic industrial emissions.... The U.S. Semiconductor Industry Assoc. and the Electronic Industries Assoc. of Japan announce the formation of a consumer electronics task force to help expand U.S. computer-chip market share in Japan.		At a Canadian government inquiry into drug use by athletes, sprinter Ben Johnson admits that he used anabolic steroids and lied about it. Johnson was stripped of a gold medal at the 1988 Summer Olympics in Seoul after testing positive for stanozolol.... Sugar Ray Leonard retains his World Boxing Council super-middleweight title after fighting Thomas Hearns to a draw.	**June 12**
Massachusetts Gov. Michael S. Dukakis (D) signs legislation authorizing Boston Univ. to have full administrative control over the Chelsea, Mass., public school system for 10 years.		Saying the excessive increase would cost young people jobs, Pres. Bush vetoes a bill to raise the minimum wage to $4.55 an hour, from $3.35, over three years.... The Federal Home Loan Bank Board says U.S. thrift industry losses reached $3.4 bil. in the first quarter of 1989.... The deficit in the balance of payments on current account rose to a seasonally adjusted $30.69 bil. in the first quarter, the Commerce Dept. reports.		The Detroit Pistons complete a four-game sweep of the Los Angeles Lakers in the National Basketball Assoc. championship finals. Pistons shooting guard Joe Dumars is named the series most valuable player. The game is the last in the 20-year career of 42-year-old Lakers' center Kareem Abdul-Jabbar.... Honor Lilbush Wingfield Tracy, 75, Anglo-Irish travel writer, columnist, and author whose writings satirized Irish and English society, dies of unreported causes at a nursing home in Oxford, England. Among her best-known books are *Mind You, I've Said Nothing!* (1953), *The Deserters* (1954), and *The Straight and Narrow Path* (1956).... The Corcoran Gallery of Art in Washington, D.C., cancels a planned retrospective of the work of the late photographer Robert Mapplethorpe, whose starkly elegant black-and-white photographs often feature homoerotic or sadomasochistic images. The exhibit has appeared in Philadelphia and Chicago; it was set to open in Washington, D.C., on July 1.	**June 13**
House Democrats elect Rep. Richard A. Gephardt (Mo.) to the post of majority leader and Rep. William H. Gray III (Pa.) to be majority whip, completing an overhaul of the party's top three House leadership posts.			The Senate Energy and Natural Resources Committee hears a controversial Dept. of Energy proposal to redirect the nation's nuclear fusion research into a new technology called inertial confinement fusion.		**June 14**

F	G	H	I	J
Includes elections, federal-state relations, civil rights and liberties, crime, the judiciary, education, health care, poverty, urban affairs and population.	*Includes formation and debate of U.S. foreign and defense policies, veterans' affairs and defense spending. (Relations with specific foreign countries are usually found under the region concerned.)*	*Includes business, labor, agriculture, taxation, transportation, consumer affairs, monetary and fiscal policy, natural resources, and pollution.*	*Includes worldwide scientific, medical and technological developments, natural phenomena, U.S. weather, natural disasters, and accidents.*	*Includes the arts, religion, scholarship, communications media, sports, entertainments, fashions, fads and social life.*

	World Affairs	Europe	Africa & the Middle East	The Americas	Asia & the Pacific
June 15			In response to appeals from Libya's Col. Muammer el-Qaddafi and mediation by terrorist Abu Nidal's Fatah Revolutionary Council, Belgian doctor Jan Cools is freed unharmed after 13 months in captivity in Lebanon.		In the first imposition of capital punishment against protesters seized during the recent unrest, three young workers in Shanghai, China, are sentenced to death for setting fire to a train last week.
June 16		In solemn memorial ceremony in Budapest, Hungary reburies the remains of Premier Imre Nagy and his four closest aides—long reviled as counterrevolutionaries for their role in the 1956 uprising against Soviet domination.... Youths in Kazakh SSR go on a rampage directed against non-Kazakh migrant workers; the unrest is blamed on high unemployment and deteriorating living conditions.... The official Soviet news agency confirms a 1957 explosion of radioactive wastes at a weapons plant in the Ural Mountains, an accident hidden from the Soviet public for decades.			In a key speech published in the West today, China's paramount leader, Deng Xiaoping, says that the Communist Party leadership was forced to crush the pro-democracy movement to prevent its own downfall.
June 17		Poland and its commercial bank creditors reach an interim agreement on rescheduling about $200 mil. in 1989-90 debt.		Canada's Liberal Party national council postpones the party's leadership convention until mid-1990 in a move that raises the possibility that the Liberals will have to function under an interim leader until then.	
June 18		In a defeat for Greece's scandal-tainted Socialist Premier Andreas Papandreou the conservative New Democracy Party comes out ahead in general elections, but fails to win a parliamentary majority.... Left-of-center parties win a majority in the European Parliament. Socialists, the largest single group, communists, and Green environmental groups could muster 260 of the 518 seats as a bloc.		Mexico's Pres. Carlos Salinas de Gortari announces an eight-month extension of wage, price, and currency controls due to expire July 31.	
June 19		The U.S.-Soviet strategic (long-range nuclear) arms reduction talks (START) resume after a seven-month recess, the 11th round of START talks since 1982.			Burma's military government changes the country's official English name to the Union of Myanmar, and that of the capital city from Rangoon to Yangon.... Australia's deficit on current account, which measures trade in goods and services, is $1.37 bil. in May, the highest monthly figure ever recorded.

A	B	C	D	E
Includes developments that affect more than one world region, international organizations and important meetings of major world leaders.	*Includes all domestic and regional developments in Europe, including the Soviet Union, Turkey, Cyprus and Malta.*	*Includes all domestic and regional developments in Africa and the Middle East, including Iraq and Iran and excluding Cyprus, Turkey and Afghanistan.*	*Includes all domestic and regional developments in Latin America, the Caribbean and Canada.*	*Includes all domestic and regional developments in Asia and Pacific nations, extending from Afghanistan through all the Pacific Islands, except Hawaii.*

U.S. Politics & Social Issues	U.S. Foreign Policy & Defense	U.S. Economy & Environment	Science, Technology & Nature	Culture, Leisure & Life Style	
The Supreme Court reaffirms a landmark 1976 civil rights decision implementing an 1866 rights law providing protection against private, as well as government, discrimination.		The Supreme Court rules, 5-4, that states can be sued by private parties to recover the costs of cleanup of hazardous-waste sites under the federal Superfund law.... The merchandise trade deficit shrank to a seasonally adjusted $8.26 bil. in April, the Commerce Dept. reports. ... The Federal Reserve Board reports that its industrial production index was unchanged in May.	The Food and Drug Admin. approves the aerosol pentamidine, a drug used to prevent Pneumocystis carinii pneumonia, a form of pneumonia that is the leading cause of death in people with Acquired Immune Deficiency Syndrome (AIDS).... A study by Northwestern Univ.'s Annenberg Washington Program says that Americans' reluctance to commit organs and tissues for transplantation after death prevents thousands of patients from receiving life-saving organ transplants each year.		June 15
As a scandal involving long-term mismanagement and political corruption at the Dept. of Housing and Urban Development (HUD) widens, HUD Inspector Gen. Paul A. Adams offers testimony concerning the embezzlement of federal funds by local escrow agents.	Denying a Chilean extradition request, the U.S. government releases Chilean leftist guerrilla leader Sergio Buschmann Silva. Officials concluded that the charges were not covered by the 1900 U.S.-Chile extradition treaty.	The consumer price index climbed 0.6% in May, the Labor Dept. reports.			June 16
					June 17
		The House Energy and Commerce Committee says the Reagan administration and former Energy Sec. John S. Herrington masked health and safety problems at the nation's 17 nuclear weapons facilities and left "a crisis of the highest order" to the Bush administration.		I(sidore) F(einstein) Stone, 81, iconoclastic journalist, and author, dies in a hospital in Boston after suffering a heart attack. In his muckraking newsletter, *I.F. Stone's Weekly* (1953-68), he decried McCarthyism, racism, the nuclear arms race, and American involvement in the Vietnam war, and uncovered examples of government malfeasance. His *Trial of Socrates* (1988), which took the Greek philosopher to task for preaching against Athenian democracy, was a best-seller.... Curtis Strange becomes the first golfer to win two consecutive U.S. Open tournaments since Ben Hogan in 1950-51.	June 18
Attorney Gen. Richard L. Thornburgh announces details of a controversial plan to dismantle the Justice Dept.'s 14 regional organized crime strike forces and merge them with local U.S. attorneys' offices.... The nonprofit Carnegie Corp.'s *Turning Points: Preparing American Youth for the 21st Century*, warns that U.S. schools are doing a poor job of educating students between the ages of 10 and 15.					June 19

F	G	H	I	J
Includes elections, federal-state relations, civil rights and liberties, crime, the judiciary, education, health care, poverty, urban affairs and population.	Includes formation and debate of U.S. foreign and defense policies, veterans' affairs and defense spending. (Relations with specific foreign countries are usually found under the region concerned.)	Includes business, labor, agriculture, taxation, transportation, consumer affairs, monetary and fiscal policy, natural resources, and pollution.	Includes worldwide scientific, medical and technological developments, natural phenomena, U.S. weather, natural disasters, and accidents.	Includes the arts, religion, scholarship, communications media, sports, entertainments, fashions, fads and social life.

	World Affairs	Europe	Africa & the Middle East	The Americas	Asia & the Pacific
June 20	Energy demand in developing and communist countries has more than doubled since the oil shortage of 1973-74 induced by the Org. of Petroleum Exporting Countries.	Britain's gross domestic product in the first quarter grew only 0.3%, after adjustment for inflation, the Central Statistics Office reports.	Soviet-Iranian relations thaw as Ali Akbar Hashemi Rafsanjani, speaker of the Iranian parliament, signs economic agreements worth over $6 bil. during a four-day trip to the Soviet Union.		Sri Lanka's Pres. Ranasinghe Premadasa reimposes a nation-wide state of emergency to counter the militant Sinhalese People's Liberation Front, which is blamed for the deaths of 1,700 people since the new year.
June 21	The U.S. threat to take unilateral action against trading partners under Section 301 of the 1988 Omnibus Trade Act violates GATT principles and is criticized at the semiannual meeting of the General Agreement on Tariffs and Trade.				Chinese authorities report the arrest of more than 500 students and workers over six days as the campaign against pro-democracy activists continues. At least 1,500 people have been detained since the crackdown began.
June 22		P&O European Ferries (formerly Townsend Thoresen), operators of the *Herald of Free Enterprise*, which capsized in March 1987 with the loss of 193 lives, is charged with corporate manslaughter.	Angola's Pres. Jose Eduardo dos Santos and Jonas Savimbi, head of the National Union for the Total Independence of Angola, unexpectedly agree to a formal truce in their 14-year-old civil war.		
June 23	An Org. for Economic Cooperation and Development report shows that member countries increased their official aid to developing countries by 6.7% in 1988, from $41.5 bil. in 1987 to $47.6 bil. in 1988.			Colombia signs a $1.7 bil. loan agreement with its creditor banks. The majority of the funds will be used for renegotiating debt payments falling due in 1988 and 1989.	
June 24		Hungary's Reformist State Economic Affairs Min. Rezso Nyers is named to head the new four-man Presidium (party collective presidency) established by the ruling Socialist Workers' Party.		A study prepared for Nicaragua's Pres. Daniel Ortega Saavedra and reported in the *New York Times* says that the country's economy has shrunk so much that it may now rank as the poorest in the Western Hemisphere.	China's Communist Party ousts General Sec. Zhao Ziyang and other top officials in a widely expected leadership shuffle in the wake of the student-led pro-democracy movement that has rocked the country.
June 25		An estimated 40,000 people gather in Kishinyov, Moldavian SSR, to protest the 1940 creation of the republic after it was ceded to the USSR by Romania, and demanding autonomy and unification with Bukovina, a formerly Romanian area of the Soviet Ukraine.			Afghanistan's Pres. Najibullah appoints Mahmoud Baryalai, brother of former president Babrak Karmal (ousted in 1986), to serve as first deputy premier.
June 26	Sec. of State James A. Baker III proposes the establishment of a "pan-Pacific entity" to facilitate the free flow of goods, services, capital, technology, and ideas among the United States, Japan, Australia, New Zealand and the newly industrialized economies of East Asia.	An accident aboard a Soviet nuclear submarine in the Norwegian Sea forces the vessel to shut down its reactors, surface, and use diesel power to limp to Murmansk, headquarters of the Soviet Northern Fleet.		An Ontario Supreme Court judge in Toronto rules that Canada's war-crimes law, which allows people to be tried for crimes committed outside of Canadian jursdiction, does not violate the Charter of Rights and Freedoms.	

A	B	C	D	E
Includes developments that affect more than one world region, international organizations and important meetings of major world leaders.	Includes all domestic and regional developments in Europe, including the Soviet Union, Turkey, Cyprus and Malta.	Includes all domestic and regional developments in Africa and the Middle East, including Iraq and Iran and excluding Cyprus, Turkey and Afghanistan.	Includes all domestic and regional developments in Latin America, the Caribbean and Canada.	Includes all domestic and regional developments in Asia and Pacific nations, extending from Afghanistan through all the Pacific Islands, except Hawaii.

U.S. Politics & Social Issues	U.S. Foreign Policy & Defense	U.S. Economy & Environment	Science, Technology & Nature	Culture, Leisure & Life Style	
A federal jury in Atlanta finds former Rep. Patrick L. Swindall (R, Ga.) guilty on nine counts of perjury for his testimony in a federal money-laundering investigation. ... The Florida state legislature passes a bill mandating strict penalties for parents or other gun owners whose weapons are used accidentally by children under age 17.	The Senate Foreign Relations Committee votes, 12-7, to approve the nomination of former Central Intelligence Agency official Donald P. Gregg as ambassador to South Korea.	A United Mine Workers strike that began April 5 in Virginia and West Virginia has spread to eight other states and involves an estimated 27,000 miners.			June 20
The Supreme Court rules, 5-4, that burning the American flag as a political protest is protected by the First Amendment guarantee of free speech.... Ruling that sanctions can rarely be applied to the press for publishing truthful information obtained legally about matters of public interest, the Court overturns a $100,000 damage award against a newspaper for publishing the name of a rape victim in violation of a state law.	The Vietnamese government returns to the United States what are believed to be the remains of 28 American servicemen killed in the Vietnam War and says it will return another 16 sets of remains at a later date.... Chairman of the Joint Chiefs of Staff Adm. William J. Crowe Jr. completes a 10-day tour of the USSR, the first ever by a chairman of the Joint Chiefs.	Owen F. Bieber wins by acclamation a third three-year term as president of the United Auto Workers.	Seven leading U.S. computer and semiconductor firms say they are forming U.S. Memories Inc., a consortium to build a plant to produce dynamic random access memory chips (DRAMs).	Ballet dancer Mikhail Baryshnikov announces that he will resign his post as artistic director of the American Ballet Theater in New York City as of July 1990.	June 21
The Census Bureau reports that fertility among U.S. women in their 30s is rising, and 33% of babies born between July 1987 and July 1988 were born to women in their 30s, compared with only 19% in 1976.... The Supreme Court, 5-4, rules out use of the Civil Rights Act of 1866 to bring damage suits against state or local governments for racial discrimination.					June 22
The Supreme Court strikes down a 1988 law banning "indecent" speech on obscene and indecent telephone messages for commercial purposes.... The Supreme Court rules, 5-4, that indigent inmates on death row do not have a constitutional right to a lawyer to assist them in a second round of state court appeals.... The Illinois state legislature rescinds a 1988 law requiring mandatory Acquired Immune Deficiency Syndrome (AIDS) tests for all couples seeking a marriage license.		Consumer spending rose 0.3% to a $3.544 trillion annual rate in May while personal income rose 0.3% to $4.39 trillion, the Commerce Dept. reports.... The Commerce Dept. announces an agreement to monitor the use of drift nets by Japanese fishing fleets in the North Pacific in compliance with the Drift Net Act of 1987.			June 23
		Three major oil spills occur within 12 hours, in Rhode Island, Delaware, and Texas, only 12 weeks after the nation's worst-ever oil spill in Alaska's Prince William Sound.		*Billboard*'s best-selling albums for the week are: *The Raw and the Cooked*, Fine Young Cannibals; *Beaches* (soundtrack); *Don't Be Cruel*, Bobby Brown; *Like A Prayer*, Madonna; and *Full Moon Fever*, Tom Petty.	June 24
				A county judge in Cincinnati temporarily blocks a scheduled hearing by the commissioner of Major League Baseball into allegations that Cincinnati Reds manager Pete Rose gambled on baseball games.	June 25
The Supreme Court rules that the Constitution's ban on "cruel and unusual punishment" does not prohibit execution either of mentally retarded or juvenile criminals.... The Supreme Court rules that the federal Racketeer Influenced and Corrupt Organizations law is not limited to organized crime activities and can be invoked on evidence of a single, continuing fraud scheme.		Pres. Bush signs a bill removing the last price controls on natural gas for the first time since 1954, when the Supreme Court ruled such controls legal.		An investigative report prepared for the baseball commissioner A. Bartlett Giamatti says that "the documentary evidence" shows that Cincinnati Reds manager Pete Rose bet on baseball and on Reds games.	June 26

F	G	H	I	J
Includes elections, federal-state relations, civil rights and liberties, crime, the judiciary, education, health care, poverty, urban affairs and population.	Includes formation and debate of U.S. foreign and defense policies, veterans' affairs and defense spending. (Relations with specific foreign countries are usually found under the region concerned.)	Includes business, labor, agriculture, taxation, transportation, consumer affairs, monetary and fiscal policy, natural resources, and pollution.	Includes worldwide scientific, medical and technological developments, natural phenomena, U.S. weather, natural disasters, and accidents.	Includes the arts, religion, scholarship, communications media, sports, entertainments, fashions, fads and social life

	World Affairs	Europe	Africa & the Middle East	The Americas	Asia & the Pacific
June 27	The European Community announces sanctions against China to protest the "brutal repression" of pro-democracy activists.	The Supreme Soviet, the new standing legislature, rejects six nominees to the 71-member Council of Ministers, the nation's super-cabinet, and Premier Nikolai I. Ryzhkov is forced to withdraw their nominations.... Britain's balance of payments deficit in May narrows to a seasonally adjusted $2.05 bil., the Dept. of Trade and Industry reports. The May figure is about 25% below the average monthly gap for the first four months of the year.			Australia P.M. Bob Hawke's approval rating has dropped to 34%, its lowest level yet recorded, according to a public opinion poll published by the *Sydney Australian* newspaper.
June 28		Britain's National Union of Railwaymen stages its second one-day strike in eight days. The strikes are the most prominent in several months of job actions by workers in a variety of industries and government.		The government of Argentina's Pres. Raul Alfonsin formally ends a 30-day state of emergency imposed in response to rioting and looting that occurred throughout Argentina in May.	Observers and unofficial Chinese sources say the Chinese foreign ministry is recalling all the nation's ambassadors for consultations.... The Sri Lankan government and the largest ethnic Tamil guerrilla group, the Liberation Tigers of Tamil Eelam, announce that they have agreed to a cease-fire in the country's six-year-old civil war.
June 29		Charter 77, the Czechoslovak rights organization, begins national circulation of a seven-point petition calling for democratic reforms and religious freedom in Czechoslovakia.		Nicaragua's Pres. Daniel Ortega Saavedra says that fighting between government and Contra forces from January to May caused 559 Sandinista casualties, including 153 dead, and 638 Contra casualties, including 355 dead.	
June 30			Mid-level officers led by Brig. Gen. Omar Hassan al-Bashir overthrow the civilian government of Sudan's P.M. Sadiq al-Mahdi. The new regime imposes a state of emergency and abolishes the constitution.... Accusing the rebels of violating the recent cease-fire by cutting power lines and ambushing civilian convoys, Angola's government suspends talks with the National Union for the Total Independence of Angola.	Bolivia's Interior Ministry announces the arrest of eight members of the Zarate Willka Armed Liberation Front, a terrorist group responsible for the murder of two Mormon missionaries and an August 1988 assassination attempt on Sec. of State George P. Shultz in La Paz.	China raises the official civilian death toll in the June 3-4 military suppression of the pro-democracy movement in Beijing to over 200, including a number of doctors and other innocent bystanders.
July 1		Tzanis Tzannetakis of Greece's conservative New Democracy Party is sworn in as the nation's premier, ending the nearly eight-year rule of Socialist Andreas Papandreou.... In a prerecorded evening address on nationwide television, Soviet Pres. Mikhail S. Gorbachev warns that ethnic violence and nationalism pose an "enormous danger" to the USSR.			An estimated 15,000 leftist activists from 170 nations gather in Pyongyang, North Korea, for political discussions at the 13th World Festival of Youth and Students.
July 2		Andrei Andreyevich Gromyko, 79, Soviet diplomat, dies following an apparent stroke in Moscow. Ambassador to the United States (1943-46) and foreign minister from 1957 to 1985, he played leading roles in the conduct of Soviet foreign policy in the post-World War II era and the rise of Pres. Mikhail Gorbachev.		For the first time in its 60-year history, Mexico's Institutional Revolutionary Party concedes defeat in a gubernatorial election, held in the state of Baja California Norte.	

A	B	C	D	E
Includes developments that affect more than one world region, international organizations and important meetings of major world leaders.	Includes all domestic and regional developments in Europe, including the Soviet Union, Turkey, Cyprus and Malta.	Includes all domestic and regional developments in Africa and the Middle East, including Iraq and Iran and excluding Cyprus, Turkey and Afghanistan.	Includes all domestic and regional developments in Latin America, the Caribbean and Canada.	Includes all domestic and regional developments in Asia and Pacific nations, extending from Afghanistan through all the Pacific Islands, except Hawaii.

U.S. Politics & Social Issues	U.S. Foreign Policy & Defense	U.S. Economy & Environment	Science, Technology & Nature	Culture, Leisure & Life Style	
Responding to a recent Supreme Court ruling that burning the American flag is protected as free speech under the First Amendment, Pres. Bush calls for a constitutional amendment barring desecration of the flag.... A federal appeals court overturns the conviction of former Reagan administration aide Lyn Nofziger for illegally lobbying top White House officials after he left government.		Saying he is ''not proud or pleased'' with what he's found since taking office, Energy Sec. James D. Watkins pledges to ''chart a new course for the department toward full accountability in the areas of environment, safety and health.''		Sir A(lfred) J(ules) Ayer, 78, British philosopher, dies in London from a respiratory ailment. A leading proponent of logical positivism, which holds that statements that cannot be verified by experience are meaningless, he wrote *Language, Truth and Logic* (1936), which is considered the basic English-language work on the subject.	June 27
		The House adopts a bill to provide $18.5 bil. for energy and water projects, including funds for construction of a Superconducting Super Collider and cleanup of toxic wastes at nuclear weapons plants. ... The Federal Deposit Insurance Corp. announces that it has awarded the 20 insolvent Texas banks owned by MCorp to Banc One Corp. of Columbus, Ohio. Officials estimate that the rescue will cost $2 bil.... The government's index of leading economic indicators fell 1.2% in May, the Commerce Dept. reports.	A national survey shows that as many as 25 million Americans, or 16% of the U.S. population over age 15, might be infected with the sexually transmitted herpes simplex Type II virus.... The National Institutes of Health, which awards about $7 bil. in research grants annually, is investigating 77 cases of alleged fraud or scientific misconduct in federally funded research.	*Variety*'s top-grossing films for the week are: *Batman*, *Ghostbusters II*, *Honey, I Shrunk the Kids*, *Indiana Jones and the Last Crusade*, and *Dead Poets Society*.	June 28
Housing and Urban Development Sec. Jack F. Kemp announces the termination of a much abused $500 mil. loan guarantee program originally intended to spur development of affordable housing.... Pres. Bush unveils a ''sweeping system of reform'' to significantly alter the way national political campaigns are funded.... House Republicans introduce a proposed constitutional amendment to prohibit the burning of the American flag.	The House of Representatives votes, 418-0, to impose new sanctions on China for its crackdown on the pro-democracy movement. The package will write into law the sanctions previously announced by Pres. Bush as well as a number of additional restrictions.	The United States remained the world's largest debtor nation at the end of 1988 as its net debt grew 40% to $532.5 bil., the Commerce Dept. reports.... Prices received by farmers for raw agricultural products fell 2% in June, the Agriculture Dept. reports.			June 29
''Sex and Morality in the U.S.,'' a 19-year-old survey of American sexual attitudes, is released by the Kinsey Institute.... The Justice Dept. announces that a federal grand jury investigation of racial harassment of a black Federal Bureau of Investigation agent ended without an indictment.		The Energy Dept. agrees to pay at least $73 mil. to settle thousands of claims of people who lived near a nuclear weapons plant in Fernald, Ohio, that leaked uranium into the water and air.	Researchers pinpoint a set of genes whose presence appears to render some families uncommonly susceptible to multiple sclerosis, a debilitating nerve disease.	*Publishers Weekly*'s hardback fiction best-sellers for the week are: *The Russia House*, John le Carre; *The Negotiator*, Frederick Forsyth; *While My Pretty One Sleeps*, Mary Higgins Clark; *Red Phoenix*, Larry Bond; *The Temple of My Familiar*, Alice Walker.... *Do the Right Thing*, a film about black-white relations in one block of the Bedford-Stuyvesant section of Brooklyn, N.Y., opens in New York City. The film is directed and written by Spike Lee and stars Lee, Danny Aiello, Ossie Davis, and Ruby Dee.	June 30
The Federal Election Comm. fines Sen. Alan Cranston's (D, Calif.) 1984 presidential campaign committee $50,000. Cranston exceeded the limit on personal donations to his own campaign, and received illegal donations and letters of credit.					July 1
	Admiral William J. Crowe Jr. announces that he will not serve a third two-year term as chairman of the Joint Chiefs of Staff. Crowe's second term is set to expire September 30.			A series of U.S. movie box office records are broken May 24-July 2 with the release of three blockbuster films: *Indiana Jones and the Last Crusade*, *Ghostbusters II*, and *Batman*.	July 2

F	G	H	I	J
Includes elections, federal-state relations, civil rights and liberties, crime, the judiciary, education, health care, poverty, urban affairs and population.	*Includes formation and debate of U.S. foreign and defense policies, veterans' affairs and defense spending. (Relations with specific foreign countries are usually found under the region concerned.)*	*Includes business, labor, agriculture, taxation, transportation, consumer affairs, monetary and fiscal policy, natural resources, and pollution.*	*Includes worldwide scientific, medical and technological developments, natural phenomena, U.S. weather, natural disasters, and accidents.*	*Includes the arts, religion, scholarship, communications media, sports, entertainments, fashions, fads and social life.*

	World Affairs	Europe	Africa & the Middle East	The Americas	Asia & the Pacific
July 3	The International Coffee Org. (ICO) Council suspends export quotas and price controls after ICO delegates reject two proposals for extending the International Coffee Agreement beyond September 1989.			Novelist Mario Vargas Llosa announces that he will reenter the Peruvian presidential race as the candidate of the center-right Democratic Front (Fredemo) coalition for the March 1990 election.	The Japanese media report that newly installed Liberal Democratic Party Premier Sosuke Uno has carried on extramarital affairs with several geishas, or paid female escorts. . . . Commonwealth of Nations Sec. Gen. Sir Shridath Ramphal informs Pakistan's P.M. Benazir Bhutto that all 48 members of the Commonwealth have agreed to the readmittance of Pakistan to the organization.
July 4		A Soviet MiG-23 fighter jet crashes into a house near the French-Belgian border and kills a 19-year-old man. The jet had flown on autopilot after the pilot bailed out over Poland. . . . Poland's new bicameral parliament convenes. The 260 legislators from the Solidarity trade union are the first formal political opposition in a Soviet-bloc government in the post-World War II period.			Britain's Foreign Sec. Sir Geoffrey Howe completes a visit to Hong Kong in an attempt to reassure local citizens of Britain's concern for the future of the colony in the wake of China's violent suppression of a pro-democracy movement in Beijing.
July 5		An official of the ruling United Workers' Party confirms that Poland's parliament will not choose a president until after a July 9 visit to Poland by Pres. Bush.	Agreeing to hard-line conditions opposed by Palestinians and the United States, Israel's P.M. Yitzhak Shamir wins right-wing Likud Party support for his proposed Middle East peace initiative. . . . Jailed African National Congress leader Nelson Mandela meets secretly with Pres. Pieter W. Botha in Cape Town in an unexpected and unprecedented meeting that stuns South Africans of all races.		A multinational economic aid plan for the Philippines is unveiled at a two-day World Bank-sponsored conference of 19 Western and Asian nations and seven international financial institutions. . . . The Australian armed forces announce a restructuring of the top command of the three service branches that will eliminate roughly 15% of senior officer and civilian staff positions in Canberra.
July 6		Janos Kadar, 77, Hungarian leader who came to power in the wake of the 1956 uprising against Soviet domination, dies of pneumonia and circulatory ailments in Budapest. Initially an ally of reformist Premier Imre Nagy, he later negotiated in secret with Moscow to be installed as premier, a post he held until last year. . . . Hungary's Supreme Court posthumously rehabilitates Imre Nagy, the former premier executed in 1958, declaring the innocence of Nagy and eight associates convicted of treason after the 1956 uprising.		In Canada, nine militant Indian bands sign a mutual-defense treaty by which they pledge to support one another in confrontations between any band and government authorities and to cooperate in bringing Indian-rights complaints before the UN.	
July 7		Amid increased signs of disunity within the Soviet bloc, leaders of the seven Warsaw Pact nations hold their annual summit in Bucharest, Romania.		Closing the biggest political scandal to hit Cuba since Pres. Fidel Castro's revolution in 1959, a Cuban military court in Havana sentences former Maj. Gen. Arnaldo Ochoa Sanchez and three other officers to death for drug smuggling and other criminal activities.	Aborigines in the Maralinga region of South Australia seek the release of a government report detailing the extent of plutonium contamination from British atomic weapons tests in the area in the 1950s and 1960s.
July 8		A U.S. delegation inspects a Soviet cruise missile and visits two secret military facilities under the auspices of the Soviet Academy of Sciences and the Natural Resources Defense Council, a New York-based environmental group.		Carlos Saul Menem is sworn in as president of Argentina in the first transfer of power from one democratically elected civilian president to another in Argentina in 61 years.	In China, two men convicted of arson during antigovernment demonstrations in June in Chengdu, the capital of Sichuan province, are put to death.

A	B	C	D	E
Includes developments that affect more than one world region, international organizations and important meetings of major world leaders.	Includes all domestic and regional developments in Europe, including the Soviet Union, Turkey, Cyprus and Malta.	Includes all domestic and regional developments in Africa and the Middle East, including Iraq and Iran and excluding Cyprus, Turkey and Afghanistan.	Includes all domestic and regional developments in Latin America, the Caribbean and Canada.	Includes all domestic and regional developments in Asia and Pacific nations, extending from Afghanistan through all the Pacific Islands, except Hawaii.

U.S. Politics & Social Issues	U.S. Foreign Policy & Defense	U.S. Economy & Environment	Science, Technology & Nature	Culture, Leisure & Life Style	
The Supreme Court upholds, 5-4, a restrictive Missouri abortion law, apparently setting the stage for overturning *Roe* v. *Wade*, the 1973 decision recognizing a constitutional right to abortion.... The Supreme Court rules unconstitutional a Nativity scene displayed in the Allegheny Co., Pa., courthouse but upholds a display of a Hanukkah menorah on the steps of the Pittsburgh city hall a block away.				Peter Koech of Kenya breaks the world record in the 3,000 meter steeplechase with a time of 8:05.35 in the DN Galan meet in Stockholm, Sweden.	July 3
				The Rev. George A. Stallings Jr. is suspended as a Roman Catholic priest after holding a July 2 mass for his own African-American Catholic Congregation, or Imani Temple, at Howard Univ. in Washington, D.C. ... Alexander I. Solzhenitsyn, the exiled Nobel Prize-winning novelist, is reported to have been reinstated to membership in the Soviet Writers' Union.	July 4
A landmark San Francisco city ordinance granting legal recognition to "domestic partnerships" of heterosexual and homosexual unmarried couples is suspended after a petition for a referendum on the issue is presented to the city registrar.	A U.S. Army study finds that the hand-held Stinger antiaircraft missile "immediately changed the terms of combat" in Afghanistan and was "the war's decisive weapon," accounting for 269 planes in 340 attempts, according to rebel accounts.				July 5
Housing and Urban Development (HUD) Sec. Jack F. Kemp announces that he is suspending the Retirement Service Center program, which provides mortgage insurance for communal housing projects for the elderly.	Sec. of State James A. Baker III explicitly endorses the ongoing Cambodian peace talks between Premier Hun Sen, head of the Vietnamese-backed regime in Phnom Penh, and Prince Norodom Sihanouk, a key figure in Cambodia's resistance coalition.... Arguing that a jail term "would only harden" the retired Marine's "misconceptions" about government service, U.S. District Judge Gerhard A. Gesell give former National Security Council staff member Oliver L. North a three-year suspended sentence and fines him $150,000.	Environmental Protection Agency Administrator William K. Reilly announces that the United States will prohibit production and importation of nearly all asbestos products by 1997, except a few where substitutes are unavailable or minimal health risk is posed.... Deloitte, Haskins & Sells and Touche Ross & Co., the two smallest of the "Big Eight" accounting firms, agree in principle to merge, and Arthur Andersen & Co. and Price Waterhouse & Co. say they will formally explore a merger over the next 60 days.		Pres. Bush presents the Presidential Medal of Freedom to retired Air Force Gen. James Doolittle; diplomats C. Douglas Dillon and George Kennan; former Sen. Margaret Chase Smith (R, Maine); and the late comedienne Lucille Ball.	July 6
Pres. Bush asks Congress for pay raises ranging from 8% to 25% for senior executive branch officials and even larger salary increases for highly skilled government specialists such as doctors and scientists.... Gene Gotti, the brother of reputed Gambino crime family boss John Gotti, and John Carneglia are sentenced to 50 years in prison and fined $75,000 each following their conviction on racketeering and drug trafficking charges.	According to reports over the past two weeks the United States has succeeded in pressuring West Germany and India to stop companies from selling a shipment of chemicals to Iran that could be used to make poison gas.	The unemployment rate rose one-tenth of a percentage point to 5.2% in June, the Labor Dept. reports. ... Outstanding consumer debt expanded $3.6 bil. in May, at a 6.2% annual rate, the Federal Reserve Board reports.... The federal funds rate, the interest rate charged on overnight loans between banks, drops sharply to close at 8.875%.	More than one-third of all American adults, about 60 million people over age 20, need to lower their blood cholesterol, according to a study published in the *Journal of the American Medical Association*.		July 7
		A group of federal health officials, AIDS activists, doctors, and drug company representatives meet in New York City to discuss new ways of testing experimental anti-AIDS drugs.			July 8

F	G	H	I	J
Includes elections, federal-state relations, civil rights and liberties, crime, the judiciary, education, health care, poverty, urban affairs and population.	Includes formation and debate of U.S. foreign and defense policies, veterans' affairs and defense spending. (Relations with specific foreign countries are usually found under the region concerned.)	Includes business, labor, agriculture, taxation, transportation, consumer affairs, monetary and fiscal policy, natural resources, and pollution.	Includes worldwide scientific, medical and technological developments, natural phenomena, U.S. weather, natural disasters, and accidents.	Includes the arts, religion, scholarship, communications media, sports, entertainments, fashions, fads and social life.

	World Affairs	Europe	Africa & the Middle East	The Americas	Asia & the Pacific
July 9			Amid widespread violence in Mogadishu, Somalia, Roman Catholic Bishop Salvatore Colombo is assassinated on the steps of his cathederal.		
July 10		Britain's Sec. of State for Trade and Industry Lord Young of Graffham announces plans to require brewers owning more than 2,000 pubs to allow the sale of other brands of beer in certain of their pubs.	The leadership of Israel's Labor Party recommends withdrawing from the coalition government with the Likud Party because of the hard-line conditions P.M. Yitzhak Shamir has agreed to put on his fledgling peace initiative.	Canada's Federal Defense Min. William McKnight and Sarcee Nation Chief Roy Whitney agree to set up a joint committee to study the military's use of Indian land in Alberta.	
July 11		Pres. Bush lunches at the home of the Solidarity founder Lech Walesa in Gdansk, Poland, and addresses workers at the Lenin Shipyard in Gdansk, birthplace of the independent trade union Solidarity.			The Chinese leadership is reported to have stepped up its attacks on pro-democracy activists and their supporters, and ousted party chief Zhao Ziyang could face a trial for his "counterrevolutionary" activities.
July 12		The Irish Dail elects Charles Haughey to his fourth term as premier after Haughey agrees to a coalition between his Fianna Fail Party and the Progressive Democrats, who broke with Fianna Fail four years ago.		Argentina's Pres. Carlos Saul Menem says he will be willing to declare a formal end to hostilities with Great Britain over the Falkland (Malvinas) Islands if Britain opens its 150-mile exclusion zone around the islands.	
July 13		At the Conventional Forces in Europe talks, the North Atlantic Treaty Org. presents a comprehensive U.S. proposal calling for a limit of 5,700 combat aircraft and 1,900 helicopters on each side.			

A	B	C	D	E
Includes developments that affect more than one world region, international organizations and important meetings of major world leaders.	Includes all domestic and regional developments in Europe, including the Soviet Union, Turkey, Cyprus and Malta.	Includes all domestic and regional developments in Africa and the Middle East, including Iraq and Iran and excluding Cyprus, Turkey and Afghanistan.	Includes all domestic and regional developments in Latin America, the Caribbean and Canada.	Includes all domestic and regional developments in Asia and Pacific nations, extending from Afghanistan through all the Pacific Islands, except Hawaii.

U.S. Politics & Social Issues	U.S. Foreign Policy & Defense	U.S. Economy & Environment	Science, Technology & Nature	Culture, Leisure & Life Style	
		Yoshiaki Tsutsumi, head of Japan's Seibu Railway Group, leads *Forbes* magazine's list of the world's richest individuals with a net worth of $15 bil., followed by Taikichiro Mori, $14.2 bil., and Sam Moore Walton, $8.7 bil.		West Germans Steffi Graf and Boris Becker win the singles titles at Wimbledon's All-England Lawn Tennis and Croquet Club. . . . Alain Prost of France wins auto racing's French Grand Prix.	July 9
			The National Inst. of Allergy and Infectious Diseases announces that AZT (azidothymidine, or zidovudine) will be given to pregnant women infected with the AIDS virus in an effort to determine whether it can protect newborns from infection.	Mel(vin Jerome) Blanc, 81, actor who provided the voices for such famous cartoon characters as Bugs Bunny, Daffy Duck, Porky Pig, Elmer Fudd, and Woody Woodpecker, dies of heart disease and emphysema in Los Angeles. In a career that spanned more than 60 years, he did voices for 800 Warner Bros. cartoons and the animated television series "The Bugs Bunny Show" and "The Flintstones." . . . Paula Ivan of Romania sets a new record in the women's mile, clocking a time of 4:15.61 seconds at a grand prix meet in Nice, France.	July 10
Testifying before a House committee, Housing and Urban Development Sec. Jack F. Kemp acknowledges that the department's scandals are "a discredit to the previous administration," and faults the efforts of his predecessor, Samuel R. Pierce Jr.				Lord (Laurence Kerr) Olivier, 82, British actor, director, and producer, considered the greatest actor of his generation, dies at his home in Steyning, England. A gifted stage actor, he was the first director of Britain's National Theatre. His film roles included portrayals of Shakespeare's Hamlet and Henry V, and he starred in such films as *Wuthering Heights* (1939) and *Rebecca* (1940). . . . The American League wins Major League Baseball's 60th annual All-Star Game, 5-3. Kansas City Royal outfielder Bo Jackson is named most valuable player.	July 11
		A panel of Energy Dept. experts concludes that there is scant evidence for so-called "cold fusion," the name attached to claims made by two chemists that they produced nuclear fusion in a table-top apparatus.		Sidney Hook, 86, American philosopher, social critic, and teacher, dies of congestive heart failure in Stanford, Calif. A socialist and "secular humanist" his books include *Toward the Understanding of Karl Marx: A Revolutionary Interpretation* (1933), *The Hero in History* (1943), and *Pragmatism and the Tragic Sense of Life* (1974). He taught at New York Univ. (1927-69), and was later a senior research fellow at the Hoover Institute at Stanford Univ. . . . The House of Representatives votes to cut $45,000 from the $171.4 mil. appropriation for the National Endowment for the Arts (NEA) as a reaction to two controversial NEA-sponsored photographic exhibits. . . . The film *When Harry Met Sally. . .*, about a pair of New York friends who gradually fall in love, is released in New York City. The romantic comedy directed by Rob Reiner stars Billy Crystal and Meg Ryan.	July 12
The Senate approves an immigration bill extending more visas to Western Europeans and to skilled workers without family ties in the United States.	Pres. Bush completes a five-day trip to Eastern Europe the primary aim of which was to show support for the political and economic reforms in Poland and Hungary. . . . The Defense Dept. conducts the first space test of a neutral particle beam, a potential component of a Strategic Defense Initiative antimissile shield.				July 13

F	G	H	I	J
Includes elections, federal-state relations, civil rights and liberties, crime, the judiciary, education, health care, poverty, urban affairs and population.	Includes formation and debate of U.S. foreign and defense policies, veterans' affairs and defense spending. (Relations with specific foreign countries are usually found under the region concerned.)	Includes business, labor, agriculture, taxation, transportation, consumer affairs, monetary and fiscal policy, natural resources, and pollution.	Includes worldwide scientific, medical and technological developments, natural phenomena, U.S. weather, natural disasters, and accidents.	Includes the arts, religion, scholarship, communications media, sports, entertainments, fashions, fads and social life.

	World Affairs	Europe	Africa & the Middle East	The Americas	Asia & the Pacific
July 14	At their 15th annual summit, leaders of the seven major industrial democracies endorse existing economic policies, and pledge to cooperate on preserving the environment and to support the U.S. developing-country debt initiative.	France's celebration of the 200th anniversary of the 1789 Revolution climaxes with the so-called Festival of the Planet's Tribes to commemorate the 1789 storming of the Bastille prison.	The day following the arrest of several Moslem leaders in connection with the July 9 assassination in Mogadishu of Somalia's Roman Catholic archbishop, police fire on rioting crowds protesting outside a mosque.		
July 15					Chinese officials dismiss Lee Tze Chung, editor in chief of the traditionally procommunist *Wen Wei Po* newspaper in Hong Kong, who has become an outspoken critic of the crackdown in Beijing.
July 16		An estimated 100,000 to 150,000 ethnic Turks are reported to have fled Bulgaria for Turkey between late May and mid-July, because of government attempts to force the assimilation of the Turkish minority.	A second round of peace talks resumes between Angola's government and National Union for the Total Independence of Angola rebels. The government suspended the talks in June.		
July 17		Austria formally applies for membership in the European Community. The main stumbling block is expected to be its desire, explicitly stated in its application, to remain militarily neutral.		In an attempt to stem monthly inflation of 200%, 300 leading Argentine industrial companies sign an accord with the government under which they agree to fix prices at July 15 levels for 90 days.	
July 18	The United States and Soviet Union have reached agreement on some provisions of a proposed international treaty to ban chemical weapons.		Kenya's Pres. Daniel arap Moi lights a bonfire of some 2,500 elephant tusks confiscated from poachers over the past four years.		
July 19	Switzerland extradites Saudi Arabian businessman Adnan M. Khashoggi to the United States to stand trial on charges of aiding former Philippine Pres. Ferdinand E. Marcos and his wife, Imelda, in stealing money and artwork from the Philippines.	The Polish parliament elects the nation's leader, Gen. Wojciech Jaruzelski, as Poland's executive-style president. The sole candidate, Jaruzelski receives the minimum number of votes needed.		Nicaragua celebrates the 10th anniversary of the arrival in Managua of the leaders of the Sandinista National Liberation Front two days after Pres. Anastasio Somoza Debayle fled into exile.	U.S. and South Korean intelligence analysts have clear evidence that North Korea is developing the means to produce nuclear weapons at a site north of Pyongyang, the *Wall Street Journal* reports.
July 20			The Mauritanian government, dominated by lighter-skinned Moors, has reportedly expelled as many as 40,000 black Mauritanian citizens, claiming they were nationals of neighboring Senegal.	Brazilian authorities order the preventive arrest of two men charged with market manipulation and fraud related to the worst stock market collapse in Brazilian history.	Myanmar's military regime has reportedly placed Aung San Suu Kyi, secretary general of the League for Democracy and the nation's leading opposition figure, under house arrest.

A	B	C	D	E
Includes developments that affect more than one world region, international organizations and important meetings of major world leaders.	Includes all domestic and regional developments in Europe, including the Soviet Union, Turkey, Cyprus and Malta.	Includes all domestic and regional developments in Africa and the Middle East, including Iraq and Iran and excluding Cyprus, Turkey and Afghanistan.	Includes all domestic and regional developments in Latin America, the Caribbean and Canada.	Includes all domestic and regional developments in Asia and Pacific nations, extending from Afghanistan through all the Pacific Islands, except Hawaii.

U.S. Politics & Social Issues	U.S. Foreign Policy & Defense	U.S. Economy & Environment	Science, Technology & Nature	Culture, Leisure & Life Style	
	To protest China's crackdown on pro-democracy activists, the Senate votes to impose new sanctions, including suspending a federally funded private investment program and the sale of police equipment and civilian nuclear materials.	The government's producer price index dropped 0.1% in June, the Labor Dept. reports.... The Federal Reserve Board reports that its industrial production index fell 0.2% in June.... The U.S. Court of Appeals for the District of Columbia rules that companies causing oil spills are liable for the full cost of restoring the environment to its condition before the pollution.			July 14
				Leading heavyweight contender Evander Holyfield knocks out Brazilian Adilson Rodrigues in the second round; the victory raises Holyfield's record to 22-0 with 18 knockouts.	July 15
		Members of the United Steelworkers of America ratify separate four-year contracts with National Steel Corp. and Inland Steel Industries Inc. over the weekend.		Herbert von Karajan, 81, Austrian conductor and one of the foremost figures in 20th-century music, dies after suffering a heart attack at his home in Anif, Austria. During a 35-year tenure with the Berlin Philharmonic he conducted more than 800 recordings, especially works by Mozart, Beethoven, Wagner, and Bruckner.... In golf, Betsy King wins the U.S. Women's Open four shots over Nancy Lopez.	July 16
The National Board for Professional Teaching Standards announces that it has prepared guidelines to be used in the nation's first general school teacher certification program.... The Census Bureau agrees to undertake a special survey and prepare the groundwork for possible adjustment of the 1990 census to compensate for undercounting of minority groups.	The State Dept. announces that it has offered to pay compensation of $100,000 to $250,000 to the families of each of the 290 people killed aboard the Iranian Airbus shot down by the USS *Vincennes* in July 1988.	In its first full semiannual economic forecast, the Bush administration projects that the U.S. economy will expand 2.7% in 1989 and 2.6% in 1990.... The Office of Technology Assessment says that even aggressive use of current technology over the next decade will not clean the air in about half of the 81 cities currently failing the smog standard.		Poland becomes the only country in Eastern Europe, other than nonaligned Yugoslavia, to have formal diplomatic relations with the Holy See. Poland's communist leaders broke with the Vatican in 1945.	July 17
		The merchandise trade deficit widened to a seasonally adjusted $10.24 bil. in May, the Commerce Dept. reports.... The United States lifts export restrictions on a broad range of desktop personal computers and clears the way for their sale to the Soviet Union and Eastern bloc countries.			July 18
Police in Tucson, Ariz., arrest John Bardo and charge him with the murder, yesterday, of actress Rebecca Schaeffer, at her home in Los Angeles. Officials decribe the man as an "obsessive fan" of Schaeffer.		Ending a four-month slide to their lowest level since 1982, housing starts rose 7% in June as interest rates fell, the Commerce Dept. reports.... The consumer price index climbed 0.2% in June, the Labor Dept. reports.			July 19
		Testiftying before Congress, Federal Reserve Board Chairman Alan Greenspan says the U.S. economy will slow substantially in the coming months, but adds that he still believes a recession remains avoidable.	On the 20th anniversary of the Apollo 11 mission to the Moon, the House adopts a $65.1 bil. appropriations bill that includes a 15% increase for the federal space program.... Pres. Bush calls for the United States to commit itself to completing an orbiting space station, establishing a base on the Moon, and sending a manned mission to Mars.... The report of a major study published in the *New England Journal of Medicine* confirms that an aspirin tablet every other day reduces the risk of heart attack in men over age 50.	An exhibit of photographs by the late Robert Mapplethorpe, opens at the Washington (D.C.) Project for the Arts. The Corcoran Gallery of Art cancelled the same show for fear that some of the pictures would spark a political controversy in Congress.	July 20

F	G	H	I	J
Includes elections, federal-state relations, civil rights and liberties, crime, the judiciary, education, health care, poverty, urban affairs and population.	Includes formation and debate of U.S. foreign and defense policies, veterans' affairs and defense spending. (Relations with specific foreign countries are usually found under the region concerned.)	Includes business, labor, agriculture, taxation, transportation, consumer affairs, monetary and fiscal policy, natural resources, and pollution.	Includes worldwide scientific, medical and technological developments, natural phenomena, U.S. weather, natural disasters, and accidents.	Includes the arts, religion, scholarship, communications media, sports, entertainments, fashions, fads and social life.

	World Affairs	Europe	Africa & the Middle East	The Americas	Asia & the Pacific
July 21		East Germany enjoyed a 4% growth in national income (the equivalent of gross national product, minus services) in the first half of 1989, according to government data reported in the West.		The Inter-American Court of Human Rights, an arm of the Org. of American States, orders Honduras to pay $695,000 to the families of two men the court found to have been killed by army death squads. . . . The Senate approves $16 mil. for FY1990 and $13 mil. in FY1992 to fund TV Marti, which will broadcast news and entertainment programs to Cuba.	
July 22		Running under the banner of the Democratic Forum, the Rev. Gabor Roszik, a Lutheran minister, wins a parliamentary by-election to become Hungary's first noncommunist deputy since 1947.	Mozambique's Pres. Joaquim Chissano says a delegation of government officials and churchmen are prepared to meet with the right-wing Mozambique National Resistance rebel group.	Three Haitian Army officers detained by the Immigration and Naturalization Service since arriving in the United States after an unsuccessful coup against Pres. Prosper Avril in April agree to end a hunger strike and travel to Venezuela.	
July 23		Giulio Andreotti, a Christian Democrat, is sworn in as premier of Italy's 49th post war government; he assumes the premiership for the sixth time.	Israel's coalition government averts a possible collapse when it votes, 21-4, to reaffirm its support for P.M. Yitzhak Shamir's peace plan for Palestinian elections in the occupied West Bank and Gaza Strip. . . . Israeli officials confirm reports that the Palestine Liberation Org. has offered a list of conditions under which it might approve of P.M. Shamir's plan for Palestinian elections in the occupied territories.	Mexico reaches an agreement to reduce its $54 bil. in medium- and long-term commercial bank debt, becoming the first country to do so under the U.S. developing-country debt strategy launched in March. . . . American John Hull, who was arrested in Costa Rica in January on suspicion of trafficking in drugs and weapons for the Nicaraguan Contras, has apparently fled the country.	Japan's ruling Liberal Democratic Party suffers a stunning defeat in parliamentary elections, losing its majority in the upper house of the Diet for the first time since coming to power in 1955. . . . The leaders of India's 12 opposition parties announce the resignation of all 106 opposition members of the lower house of parliament to protest P.M. Rajiv Gandhi's refusal to resign over the Bofors arms scandal.
July 24		In a surprise move, Britain's P.M. Margaret Thatcher promotes John Major to succeed Geoffrey Howe as foreign secretary, and there is widespread speculation that he is being groomed as a successor to Thatcher.			After yesterday's stunning defeat of Japan's ruling Liberal Democratic Party in parliamentary elections, newly installed Premier Sosuke Uno announces that he will resign to take the blame for the loss.
July 25		Spanish Socialist Enrique Baron Crespo is elected president of the European Parliament at the first full assembly meeting of the new parliament.	The small Indian Ocean island nation of Mauritius officially launches itself as Africa's first offshore banking center, with tax and duty incentives to attract foreign banks.	A state of emergency is declared in Manitoba, Canada, as over 200 forest fires rage out of control in the northern part of the province. . . . In Suriname, Army Commander Desi Bouterse rejects a peace accord signed by the three-party civilian government of Pres. Ramsewak Shankar and the leaders of a three-year-old guerrilla insurgency.	In Australia, workers in a wide range of industries and businesses throughout New South Wales stay off the job in what is billed by union leaders as a "day of outrage" against the state government.
July 26		Soviet coal miners end a series of wildcat strikes begun July 10 after the government pledges major concessions. . . . In Poland, Solidarity's parliamentary caucus votes against joining the United Workers' Party in the government.		National Reconstruction Party candidate Fernando Collor de Mello, an obscure former state governor, emerges the front-runner in Brazil's upcoming presidential election with the support of 41%-44% of the electorate.	In Australia, thousands of workers throughout Victoria participate in a 24-hour walkout over government reforms to the state's worker compensation plan, known as WorkCare.

A	B	C	D	E
Includes developments that affect more than one world region, international organizations and important meetings of major world leaders.	Includes all domestic and regional developments in Europe, including the Soviet Union, Turkey, Cyprus and Malta.	Includes all domestic and regional developments in Africa and the Middle East, including Iraq and Iran and excluding Cyprus, Turkey and Afghanistan.	Includes all domestic and regional developments in Latin America, the Caribbean and Canada.	Includes all domestic and regional developments in Asia and Pacific nations, extending from Afghanistan through all the Pacific Islands, except Hawaii.

U.S. Politics & Social Issues	U.S. Foreign Policy & Defense	U.S. Economy & Environment	Science, Technology & Nature	Culture, Leisure & Life Style	
At a meeting of the American Federation of Teachers (AFT), federation Pres. Albert Shanker calls on his union to embrace popular school reform proposals before the changes are forced on them.... The AFT's annual survey of teacher salaries finds that the average teacher salary in the 1988-89 school year was $29,629; the average starting salary was $19,598.	The State Dept. acknowledges that senior U.S. diplomat Felix S. Bloch has been videotaped passing a briefcase to a Soviet intelligence agent and is under investigation for "illegal activities."... The Congress approves legislation in support of a Bush administration plan to provide covert aid to two non-communist Cambodian resistance groups.... The House approves, 329-69, a foreign aid bill worth $14.3 bil., about $400 mil. less than Pres. Bush requested. Military and economic aid to key U.S. allies would be cut by some $700 mil.	Pres. Bush sends to Congress his clean-air proposals to tighten controls against pollution by utilities, automobile manufacturers, and other manufacturing facilities and small businesses.		Undisputed heavyweight champion Mike Tyson retains his title when his bout against Carl (The Truth) Williams is stopped only 93 seconds into the first round.	July 21
					July 22
			Italy's northern Adriatic coast is being plagued by a vast glutinous mass of algae. The yellow scum is believed to be caused by a combination of climatic factors and pollution from Italy's rivers.	Donald Barthelme, 58, critically acclaimed short story writer and novelist, dies of cancer at a hospital in Houston. Known for their innovative style and wry humor, his works ranged from the novel *Snow White* (1967), a parody of the Walt Disney film, to the children's book *The Slightly Irregular Fire Engine*, for which he won a National Book Award in 1972.... Greg LeMond of the United States wins the 23-day Tour de France bicycle race.... Carl Yastrzemski, Johnny Bench, Red Schoendienst, and Al Barlick are inducted into the Baseball Hall of Fame.	July 23
William M. Taylor, a prominent Florida Republican, admits that he was paid more than $500,000 in cash and property interests for lobbying the Dept. of Housing and Urban Development on behalf of developers.		Time Inc. acquires Warner Communications Inc. for $70 a share, or $14 bil., after the Delaware Supreme Court clears the transaction and Paramount Communications Inc. withdraws its hostile bid for Time.... Exxon Corp. estimates the cost of cleaning up the 500-mile-long *Exxon Valdez* oil spill at $1.28 bil., making the March 24 accident one of the most expensive industrial accidents in history.			July 24
House Minority Whip Newt Gingrich (R, Ga.) is reported to have given temporary raises to congressional staffers who worked on his 1986 and 1988 campaigns in violation of federal law and House rules. ... At the request of independent counsel Lawrence E. Walsh, U.S. District Judge Harold H. Greene dismisses two of the most serious charges against former national security adviser John M. Poindexter.		Ending a months-long dispute within his administration, Pres. Bush says he will extend U.S. steel quotas for another two-and-a-half years but that he will negotiate for open world steel markets during that time.	As over 200 forest fires rage in Manitoba, Canada, nearly 21,000 residents have been evacuated to safety. About 1,600 firefighters are battling the fires, which have burned 2.2 million acres of woodland.		July 25
		Congress approves a moratorium on leasing and drilling for offshore oil as part of the FY1990 spending bill for the Interior Dept. and related agencies.	The Justice Dept. reports that Cornell Univ. graduate student Robert Tappan Morris has been indicted on a felony count under the Computer Fraud and Abuse Act in connection with the release of a computer virus that shut down a nationwide computer network in November 1988.	The Senate votes to cut funding for the National Endowment for the Arts and approves restrictions that prohibit any federal funding of "obscene or indecent" art works. ... *Variety*'s top-grossing films for the week are: *Lethal Weapon II*, *When Harry Met Sally...*, *Batman*, *Licence to Kill*, and *Honey, I Shrunk the Kids*.	July 26

F	G	H	I	J
Includes elections, federal-state relations, civil rights and liberties, crime, the judiciary, education, health care, poverty, urban affairs and population.	*Includes formation and debate of U.S. foreign and defense policies, veterans' affairs and defense spending. (Relations with specific foreign countries are usually found under the region concerned.)*	*Includes business, labor, agriculture, taxation, transportation, consumer affairs, monetary and fiscal policy, natural resources, and pollution.*	*Includes worldwide scientific, medical and technological developments, natural phenomena, U.S. weather, natural disasters, and accidents.*	*Includes the arts, religion, scholarship, communications media, sports, entertainments, fashions, fads and social life.*

	World Affairs	Europe	Africa & the Middle East	The Americas	Asia & the Pacific
July 27		After a five week trial, a court in Stockholm convicts Carl Gustav Christer Pettersson, a substance abuser and petty criminal, in the 1986 assassination of Swedish Premier Olof Palme. An appeal is expected.... The Supreme Soviet, the USSR's standing legislature, approves a resolution in support of plans by the Baltic republics of Lithuania and Estonia to develop autonomous free-market economic systems.... The official death toll stands at 19 after two weeks of violence between Soviet Georgians and Abkhazians in Transcaucasian communities along the Black Sea.			
July 28	Some 500 Chinese students representing more than 150,000 Chinese students studying overseas hold a three-day conference in Chicago to discuss ways to keep the pro-democracy movement alive.		Israeli commandos abduct a pro-Iranian Shiite Moslem sheik from southern Lebanon in an effort to force the release of captured Israeli soldiers.... Hojatolislam Ali Akbar Hashemi Rafsanjani, speaker of the Iranian parliament, wins a landslide victory in Iran's presidential elections. He succeeds Pres. Ali Khamenei.		The governments of Sri Lanka and India defuse a seven-week-old diplomatic confrontation with an agreement on the start of a withdrawal of Indian peacekeeping troops from Sri Lanka.
July 29		Honoring a preelection promise, newly elected Polish Pres. Wojciech Jaruzelski resigns as the general secretary of the United Workers' Party.			
July 30	A 19-nation conference seeking an end to the war in Cambodia opens in Paris.			Chilean voters overwhelmingly approve 54 reforms to the 1980 constitution aimed at easing the nation's transition to democracy after 16 years of military rule. Voter turnout is reported to have been 93%.	
July 31			A Lebanese extremist group responds to Israel's abduction of a pro-Iranian Shiite cleric by issuing a videotape purporting to show that it has hung Lt. Col. William R. Higgins, a U.S. Marine attached to the UN Truce Supervision Org.... Mozambique's ruling Frelimo Party endorses Pres. Joaquim Chissano's peace moves but insists that the Mozambique National Resistance rebel group renounce violence and recognize Mozambique's constitutional system.		
Aug. 1		As part of its economic restructuring the Polish government lifts price controls on nearly all food items. Despite widespread complaints, no organized protests are reported.			Japan's booming economy has caused the highest ratio of vacancies to job seekers since 1974, with 134 jobs available for every 100 applicants in June, according to government figures. Unemployment was 2.2%.

A	B	C	D	E
Includes developments that affect more than one world region, international organizations and important meetings of major world leaders.	Includes all domestic and regional developments in Europe, including the Soviet Union, Turkey, Cyprus and Malta.	Includes all domestic and regional developments in Africa and the Middle East, including Iraq and Iran and excluding Cyprus, Turkey and Afghanistan.	Includes all domestic and regional developments in Latin America, the Caribbean and Canada.	Includes all domestic and regional developments in Asia and Pacific nations, extending from Afghanistan through all the Pacific Islands, except Hawaii.

U.S. Politics & Social Issues	U.S. Foreign Policy & Defense	U.S. Economy & Environment	Science, Technology & Nature	Culture, Leisure & Life Style	
A report by the National Academy of Sciences finds that economic and social gains by black Americans stagnated during the 1970s and 1980s and that blacks remain "separated from the mainstream of national life under conditions of great inequality."	The House passes a FY1990 defense authorization bill that is significantly at odds with the spending priorities set by Pres. Bush and Defense Sec. Richard B. Cheney.	The United Auto Workers lose a key representation vote at the Nissan Motor Corp. assembly plant in Smyrna, Tenn. The union has failed to organize any of the four Japanese-owned auto plants in the United States.... Gross national product grew at a 1.7% annual rate in the second quarter, the Commerce Dept. reports.... In passing the FY1990 agriculture spending bill the Senate accepts a Bush administration request to remove a cap on commodity export subsidies; the House set a cap of $770 mil. for the fiscal year.			July 27
		William Stevens, president of Exxon Co. U.S.A., tells a congressional panel that his company will comply with "any reasonable request" to complete cleanup of the *Exxon Valdez* oil spill.... Consumer spending held steady at a $3.441 trillion annual rate in June, while personal income rose 0.3% to a $4.407 trillion rate, the Commerce Dept. reports.	Deaths from lung cancer continue to rise sharply among American women according to the Centers for Disease Control in Atlanta, up 44% from 1979 to 1986, compared with a rise of only 7% among men.	*Publishers Weekly*'s hardback fiction best-sellers for the week are: *The Russia House*, John le Carre; *Polar Star*, Martin Cruz Smith; *Red Phoenix*, Larry Bond; *While My Pretty One Sleeps*, Mary Higgins Clark; and *Day of the Cheetah*, Dale Brown.	July 28
				Javier Sotomayor of Cuba becomes the first person to high jump eight feet when he accomplishes the feat at the Caribbean Championships in San Juan, Puerto Rico.... *Billboard*'s best-selling albums for the week are: *Batman* (soundtrack), Prince; *The Raw and the Cooked*, Fine Young Cannibals; *Hangin' Tough*, New Kids on the Block; *Don't Be Cruel*, Bobby Brown; and *Girl You Know It's True*, Milli Vanilli.	July 29
The National Governors' Assoc. conference concludes with an invitation by Pres. Bush to meet with the 50 state governors at an "education summit" to be held September 27-28.				In auto racing, Ayrton Senna of Brazil wins the German Grand Prix.	July 30
A 1988 survey sponsored by the National Institute on Drug Abuse finds that casual drug use in the United States has declined over the past three years, though use of cocaine and crack cocaine has increased.	Following the apparent execution of U.S. Marine Lt. Col. William R. Higgins by Lebanese extremists the Bush administration launches a diplomatic campaign to prevent the threatened execution of a second U.S. hostage.... The House votes, 382-29, to pass an $8.7 bil. military construction appropriations bill for FY1990, including $500 mil. for funding military base closings and realignments cleared by Congress in April.... Pres. Bush vetoes a bill putting restrictions on the joint development by the United States and Japan of a new Japanese fighter plane, known as the FSX.	Farm prices drop 0.7% in July, the Agriculture Dept. reports.		Michael Harrington, 61, cochairman of the Democratic Socialists of America organization, dies of cancer in Larchmont, N.Y. With its assertion of an underclass of poor Americans living below the poverty line and ignored by government and society, his book *The Other America: Poverty in the United States* (1962) sparked a national debate on poverty and is credited with inspiring the War on Poverty programs of the 1960s.	July 31
On a 7-7 vote, the Senate Judiciary Committee rejects the nomination of William C. Lucas as assistant attorney general for civil rights.... The House votes, 399-18, to approve a bill that will waive the Sherman Antitrust Act to allow broadcast and cable television representatives to meet and discuss voluntary guidelines to curb violent programming.		Energy Sec. James D. Watkins outlines a five-year, $19.5 bil. plan to clean up pollution, repair equipment, and improve procedures at the nation's atomic weapons plants.			Aug. 1

F	G	H	I	J
Includes elections, federal-state relations, civil rights and liberties, crime, the judiciary, education, health care, poverty, urban affairs and population.	Includes formation and debate of U.S. foreign and defense policies, veterans' affairs and defense spending. (Relations with specific foreign countries are usually found under the region concerned.)	Includes business, labor, agriculture, taxation, transportation, consumer affairs, monetary and fiscal policy, natural resources, and pollution.	Includes worldwide scientific, medical and technological developments, natural phenomena, U.S. weather, natural disasters, and accidents.	Includes the arts, religion, scholarship, communications media, sports, entertainments, fashions, fads and social life.

	World Affairs	Europe	Africa & the Middle East	The Americas	Asia & the Pacific
Aug. 2					
Aug. 3			As the Bush administration indicates that it is exploring all channels to free American hostages but that it will not negotiate with terrorists, Lebanese Shiite Moslem kidnappers lift their threat to execute an American hostage.... The World Wildlife Fund and U.S. Agency for International Development announce a $3 mil. debt-for-nature swap with Madagascar to promote conservation and provide debt relief for the island nation.	Nicaragua's Pres. Daniel Ortega Saavedra announces that the Sandinista government will suspend conscription into the armed services from September 1 until after the February 1990 elections.... The number of diagnosed cases of Acquired Immune Deficiency Syndrome (AIDS) in Canada reached 2,853 by mid-July, according Dr. Alastair Clayton, the head of the Federal Centre for AIDS. Over 57% of those with AIDS have died of the disease.	
Aug. 4		An interim report on the April tragedy that killed 95 soccer fans at a stadium in Sheffield, England, places the primary blame for the incident on the police.		Canada's unemployment rate rose to 7.5% in July from 7.3% in June, according to Statistics Canada.	Japan's Emperor Akihito, accompanied by his wife, Empress Michiko, holds his first press conference since assuming the Chrysanthemum Throne in January.
Aug. 5		Two candidates running under the banner of the Democratic Forum, the nation's most prominent opposition group, in Hungary's parliamentary by-elections beat the ruling Socialist Workers Party candidates.			
Aug. 6				Jaime Paz Zamora is inaugurated as president of Bolivia following a power-sharing deal with former military dictator Hugo Banzer Suarez.	
Aug. 7			A small plane carrying Rep. Mickey Leland (D, Tex.) and 15 other people is reported missing in western Ethiopia after it fails to arrive at a refugee camp near the Sudanese border.	Five Central American presidents agree on a December 5 deadline for dismantling Nicaraguan Contra rebel camps in Honduras and repatriating some 10,000 to 12,000 Contras and their families.	Citing ill health, New Zealand's P.M. David Lange announces that he will resign tomorrow. The move follows the ruling Labour Party's vote to reinstate his political rival, Roger Douglas, as finance minister.... Australia's Industrial Relations Comm. announces wage increases of about 6.5% for the nation's labor force. In exchange, workers must accept job changes aimed at boosting productivity.

A	B	C	D	E
Includes developments that affect more than one world region, international organizations and important meetings of major world leaders.	Includes all domestic and regional developments in Europe, including the Soviet Union, Turkey, Cyprus and Malta.	Includes all domestic and regional developments in Africa and the Middle East, including Iraq and Iran and excluding Cyprus, Turkey and Afghanistan.	Includes all domestic and regional developments in Latin America, the Caribbean and Canada.	Includes all domestic and regional developments in Asia and Pacific nations, extending from Afghanistan through all the Pacific Islands, except Hawaii.

U.S. Politics & Social Issues	U.S. Foreign Policy & Defense	U.S. Economy & Environment	Science, Technology & Nature	Culture, Leisure & Life Style	
A federal jury in Washington, D.C., finds the crew of a Korean Air Lines jet shot down by a Soviet fighter in 1983 guilty of "willful misconduct" because they knowingly flew into Soviet air space.	The Senate passes a FY1990 defense authorization bill that generally supports the spending priorities of Pres. Bush but differs substantially from the House defense authorization.	After a two-and-a-half-year probe of the Chicago futures markets, the Justice Dept. announces the indictment of 46 traders at the Chicago Board of Trade and Chicago Mercantile Exchange.... Efforts to devise a deficit-reduction package for FY1990 end when House Democrats split over the issue of a capital-gains tax cut proposed by House Ways and Means Committee chairman Rep. Dan Rostenkowski (D, Ill.).		Musical theater composer Stephen Sondheim, whose credits range from *West Side Story* to *A Little Night Music*, is named the first visiting professor of drama and musical theater at Oxford Univ.	Aug. 2
Documents from the files of former Housing and Urban Development Sec. Samuel R. Pierce Jr. implicate Pierce and others in the widespread political favoritism at the scandal-ridden department.... The House votes, 238-189, to approve a $3.4 bil. spending bill for the District of Columbia for FY1990.	The United States signs an agreement to provide Haiti with $10 mil. of food aid, resuming economic assistance that was cut after abortive presidential elections in 1987.	The Public Citizen Health Research Group accuses the Food and Drug Admin. of negligence for not enforcing a law requiring makers of medical devices to notify the agency of malfunctions that could cause death or serious injury.... The government's index of leading economic indicators dropped 0.1% in June, the Commerce Dept. reports.... Productivity among the nation's nonfarm businesses increases at a 0.2% annual rate in the second quarter, the Labor Dept. reports.	A U.S. government study finds that AZT (azidothymidine, or zidovudine) significantly slows the progress of Acquired Immune Deficiency Syndrome (AIDS) in people who show early symptoms of the disease.... A Swedish study of 23,244 women reported in the *New England Journal of Medicine* indicates that combination therapy with female hormones to treat symptoms of menopause may increase the risk of breast cancer.	A federal judge in Indianapolis rules that Peg L. Goldberg must return to a Greek Orthodox church in Cyprus a set of sixth-century mosaics purchased from a Turkish art dealer for $1.1 mil. in 1988.	Aug. 3
The Senate Ethics Committee announces it has found that Sen. David Durenberger (R, Minn.) may have violated Senate rules in connection with a book publishing arrangement and that it has retained outside counsel to investigate the matter.	The House votes, 312-105, to pass a $286.4 bil. defense appropriation for FY1990 and again rejects key priorities of the Bush administration.	The Senate passes, 99-0, comprehensive oil-spill legislation that focuses on prevention of future accidents, improving cleanup procedures, and affixing liability. ... A bill raising the federal debt limit to $2.87 trillion through October 31 is cleared by Congress.... The unemployment rate remained at 5.2% in July, the Labor Dept. reports.	According to a study reported in the journal *Science*, a new drug called deprenyl appears to slow the progress of Parkinson's disease, a degenerative brain disorder.	*sex, lies and videotape*, a film about a woman, her husband, her sister and an old friend of her husband's who become involved in a series of intricate sexual liaisons, is released in New York. Directed and written by Steven Soderbergh, the film stars Andie MacDowell and James Spader.	Aug. 4
			At least 150 people are reported killed and more than 100,000 forced from their homes after two weeks of torrential rains trigger heavy flooding in Bangladesh.		Aug. 5
The Federal Bureau of Investigation's annual *Uniform Crime Reports* shows that violent crime in the United States increased in 1988 by 5.5% and that property crime rose by 2.8%.... At the National Urban League's annual conference in Washington, D.C., there is much discussion about the impact of recent Supreme Court decisions on affirmative action.		The Communication Workers of America begin a strike against NYNEX Corp., the parent company of New York Telelphone, Bell Atlantic Corp., and Pacific Telesis Group; health care is the crucial issue.			Aug. 6
A report by the National Conference of State Legislatures says 30 states raised taxes in 1989, 11 states reduced them, and the remainder kept them at about the same level as in 1988.		The *Wall Street Journal* quarterly earnings review shows that net income for the second quarter at 643 major corporations registered a 4% gain over the year-earlier period; after-tax earnings rose 5%. ... Pres. Bush signs into law a bill setting a temporary federal debt limit of $2.87 trillion.			Aug. 7

F	G	H	I	J
Includes elections, federal-state relations, civil rights and liberties, crime, the judiciary, education, health care, poverty, urban affairs and population.	*Includes formation and debate of U.S. foreign and defense policies, veterans' affairs and defense spending. (Relations with specific foreign countries are usually found under the region concerned.)*	*Includes business, labor, agriculture, taxation, transportation, consumer affairs, monetary and fiscal policy, natural resources, and pollution.*	*Includes worldwide scientific, medical and technological developments, natural phenomena, U.S. weather, natural disasters, and accidents.*	*Includes the arts, religion, scholarship, communications media, sports, entertainments, fashions, fads and social life.*

	World Affairs	Europe	Africa & the Middle East	The Americas	Asia & the Pacific
Aug. 8		Bonn closes its permanent mission in East Berlin to all visitors after hundreds of East Germans seeking political asylum take refuge in three West German diplomatic facilities.	Representatives of South Africa's Zulu Inkatha Freedom Party and African National Congress are reportedly trying to negotiate an end to feuding that has killed more than 2,000 blacks in the past two years.	The Supreme Court of Canada lifts an injunction aimed at preventing a 21-year-old Quebec woman from obtaining an abortion. The court does so without addressing the volatile issue of fetal rights.... Canada's Dept. of National Health and Welfare announces that people with early symptoms of the deadly disease Acquired Immune Deficiency Syndrome (AIDS) can be treated with the experimental drug AZT (azidothymidine, or zidovudine).	
Aug. 9		An estimated 20,000 ethnic Russian residents of Estonia walk off their jobs to protest a law that would restrict the political rights of non-Estonians.			Japan's former Education Min. Toshiki Kaifu is elected premier of Japan, replacing Sosuke Uno, who resigned amid scandal after barely two months in office.
Aug. 10		The Roman Catholic Church scraps plans to move a convent out of the former Nazi death camp of Auschwitz in Poland, as controversy over the religious center flares anew.		Argentina's gross domestic product contracted 3.1% in 1988 from the previous year, the government reports. Industrial production was down 7% and construction plunged 14.5% for the year.	
Aug. 11		The independent trade union Solidarity leads tens of thousands of workers in a one-hour "warning strike" in the Baltic cities of Gdansk and Gdynia. Demands include higher wages and a rollback of food prices.			
Aug. 12					Amid increased concern in South Korea over illegal contacts with North Korea, government prosecutors disclose that they are investigating alleged links between opposition leader Kim Dae Jung and the North.... Nearly 100 people have been killed in violent clashes between the ethnic Assamese majority and the minority Bodo tribe in India's Assam state, and 20,000 people have fled to refugees camps or neighboring states.
Aug. 13			Syrian troops and their Lebanese Moslem allies launch the first ground offensive against Christian positions since the current round of fighting began in Lebanon five months ago.... After a six-day search in western Ethiopia, wreckage of the plane carrying Rep. Mickey Leland and 15 others which crashed en route to a refugee camp near Sudan is found on a remote mountainside; there are no survivors.		
Aug. 14		The 20th anniversary of the stationing of British troops in Northern Ireland passes in relative calm.... About 150,000 workers stage a one-day walkout and protest rally in Baku, the capital of Azerbaijan SSR, to call for autonomy and an end to Moscow's administration of the disputed Nagorno-Karabakh region.	South Africa's Pres. Pieter W. Botha resigns following a bitter showdown with his cabinet.... Ayatollah Ali Khamenei, Iran's supreme religious leader, bitterly attacks the United States and rejects negotiations on the issue of Americans held hostage in Lebanon by pro-Iranian extremists.		Sixteen people are sentenced to death and another 59 receive jail sentences for their roles in an unsuccessful 1988 coup attempt in the Indian Ocean nation of Maldives Republic.

A	B	C	D	E
Includes developments that affect more than one world region, international organizations and important meetings of major world leaders.	Includes all domestic and regional developments in Europe, including the Soviet Union, Turkey, Cyprus and Malta.	Includes all domestic and regional developments in Africa and the Middle East, including Iraq and Iran and excluding Cyprus, Turkey and Afghanistan.	Includes all domestic and regional developments in Latin America, the Caribbean and Canada.	Includes all domestic and regional developments in Asia and Pacific nations, extending from Afghanistan through all the Pacific Islands, except Hawaii.

U.S. Politics & Social Issues	U.S. Foreign Policy & Defense	U.S. Economy & Environment	Science, Technology & Nature	Culture, Leisure & Life Style	
A federal district court jury convicts E. Robert Wallach of racketeering in connection with the Wedtech Corp. corruption and bribery scandal; Wallach is an old friend of former Attorney Gen. Edwin Meese III.		Outstanding consumer debt expanded $2.99 bil. in June, at a 5.1% annual rate, the Federal Reserve Board reports.	A European Space Agency Ariane-4 rocket is launched from Kourou, French Guiana, carrying two satellites, one a scientific satellite programmed to measure distances between stars, the other a West German vehicle for direct broadcasting.		Aug. 8
The College Board estimates that the average cost for a year of college will rise by 6% to 9% in the 1989-90 school year, the ninth straight year that the price of college has risen faster than the rate of inflation. . . . A pro-choice candidate defeats an anti-abortion candidate in the Republican primary for a seat in the California legislature.		Pres. Bush signs landmark thrift industry legislation to launch the largest federal rescue in U.S. history. The package provides $166 bil. over 10 years to close or merge insolvent thrifts.	A federal study published in the *Journal of Pediatrics* shows that babies conceived through in vitro fertilization—so-called test-tube babies—are as healthy and mentally alert as those conceived normally.		Aug. 9
State tax collections rose 7% in the fiscal year ending June 30, 1988, the Commerce Dept. reports. The total is $264 bil., compared with $246 bil. in the previous fiscal year. . . . Federal drug agents in New York City arrest Humberto Sanchez Butiago, identified as the chief chemist of Colombia's powerful Medellin drug cartel, who was lured to the United States by undercover agents.	Pres. Bush nominates Army Gen. Colin L. Powell to replace Admiral William J. Crowe Jr. as chairman of the Joint Chiefs of Staff. If confirmed, Powell would be the first black ever to head the Joint Chiefs.	Environmental officials from eight Northeastern states announce an agreement to put rules into place to restrict toxic emissions of automobiles and light trucks, beginning with the 1993 model year. . . . Releasing a listing of what it considers to be the nation's top 500 offenders, the National Wildlife Federation warns that "Toxic chemical pollution has reached epic proportions."		In his first start since a cancerous tumor was removed from his pitching arm 10 months ago, San Francisco Giants pitcher Dave Dravecky goes eight innings and allows only four hits against the Cincinnati Reds.	Aug. 10
		The government's producer price index dropped 0.4% in July, the Labor Dept. reports.			Aug. 11
			William Bradford Shockley, 79, physicist and professor emeritus of electrical engineering at Stanford Univ., dies of prostate cancer in Stanford, Calif. Cowinner of the 1956 Nobel Prize for physics with John Bardeen and Walter H. Brattain, for their invention of the transistor, Shockley later alienated his colleagues and the public with his assertions that blacks were genetically inferior to whites.	The World Cup ski season opens with the first World Cup events ever held in Australia. The races are held in Thredbo in the Snowy Mountains.	Aug. 12
			The U.S. space shuttle *Columbia* successfully completes a secret military mission with a five-man crew after a flight that lasted five days, one hour and 56 minutes.	Payne Stewart wins the Professional Golfers Assoc. championship.	Aug. 13
Edward K. O'Brien, staff coordinator at the Drug Enforcement Admin.'s headquarters in Arlington, Va., is arrested at Logan International Airport in Boston and charged with cocaine trafficking.		Robert Bernerd Anderson, 79, businessman and political appointee, dies following surgery for cancer in New York City. Secretary of the Navy and of the treasury under Dwight Eisenhower, in 1987 he was sentenced to prison after pleading guilty to tax evasion and other charges and spent one month in federal prison and five months under house arrest.			Aug. 14

F	G	H	I	J
Includes elections, federal-state relations, civil rights and liberties, crime, the judiciary, education, health care, poverty, urban affairs and population.	*Includes formation and debate of U.S. foreign and defense policies, veterans' affairs and defense spending. (Relations with specific foreign countries are usually found under the region concerned.)*	*Includes business, labor, agriculture, taxation, transportation, consumer affairs, monetary and fiscal policy, natural resources, and pollution.*	*Includes worldwide scientific, medical and technological developments, natural phenomena, U.S. weather, natural disasters, and accidents.*	*Includes the arts, religion, scholarship, communications media, sports, entertainments, fashions, fads and social life.*

	World Affairs	Europe	Africa & the Middle East	The Americas	Asia & the Pacific
Aug. 15			National Party leader Frederick W. de Klerk is sworn in as acting president of South Africa just three weeks before elections in which the party faces its toughest challenge since coming to power in 1948.		
Aug. 16					Australia's trade deficit hit a record $1.3 bil. in July, the first month of FY1989, the government reports.
Aug. 17	Banca Nazionale del Lavoro, Italy's largest state-owned bank, discloses that it is under investigation by U.S. and Italian authorities for "procedurally improper practices."	Poland's Pres. Wojciech Jaruzelski accepts a proposal for a Solidarity-led coalition government, and the government announces the resignation of Premier Czeslaw Kiszczak after only 15 days on the job.		Canada posted its lowest quarterly merchandise trade surplus in 12 years in the second quarter of 1989, according to Statistics Canada.	
Aug. 18	Negotiators for Britain and Argentina agree to hold talks aimed at reestablishing diplomatic relations and to set aside temporarily the divisive issue of the sovereignty of the Falkland (Malvinas) Islands.			The front-runner in Colombia's upcoming May 1990 presidential election, Liberal Party candidate Luis Carlos Galan, is assassinated by Medellin cartel drug traffickers at a campaign rally in a Bogota suburb.	
Aug. 19					
Aug. 20		Fifty-six people are believed killed when the dredger *Bowbelle* rams the chartered party boat *Marchioness* on the River Thames in central London after midnight; about 140 people were aboard the party boat.	British conservationist George Adamson, whose work returning captive and orphaned lions to the wild was popularized in the book and film *Born Free*, is shot to death by bandits near his remote bush camp in northeastern Kenya.		
Aug. 21		Five hundred representatives of nationalist groups from throughout the Soviet Union meet in Riga, Latvian SSR, to discuss independence issues. . . . About 3,000 protesters gather in Prague to mark the 21st anniversary of the Soviet-led invasion of Czechoslovakia. The banned demonstration is broken up by security police, and there are 370 arrests.	In Harare, Zimbabwe, the Org. of African Unity endorses the new African National Congress blueprint for negotiations with South Africa's white minority government.	At the premiers' conference in Quebec City, Canada's provincial premiers issue a communique opposing the proposed federal 9% value-added tax on goods and services, due to take effect on January 1, 1991.	
Aug. 22		The Turkish government stops further immigration of ethnic Turks from Bulgaria, more than 300,000 of whom have fled Bulgaria's persecution of those who practice Turkish and Islamic customs.	The government of Angola's Pres. Jose Eduardo dos Santos and rebels of Jonas Savimbi's National Union for the Total Independence of Angola blame each other for the failure of a two-month-old truce.		

A	B	C	D	E
Includes developments that affect more than one world region, international organizations and important meetings of major world leaders.	Includes all domestic and regional developments in Europe, including the Soviet Union, Turkey, Cyprus and Malta.	Includes all domestic and regional developments in Africa and the Middle East, including Iraq and Iran and excluding Cyprus, Turkey and Afghanistan.	Includes all domestic and regional developments in Latin America, the Caribbean and Canada.	Includes all domestic and regional developments in Asia and Pacific nations, extending from Afghanistan through all the Pacific Islands, except Hawaii.

U.S. Politics & Social Issues	U.S. Foreign Policy & Defense	U.S. Economy & Environment	Science, Technology & Nature	Culture, Leisure & Life Style	
		Atlantic Richfield Co. announces that it will introduce a low-emission regular gasoline to the Southern California market September 1 as a replacement for its leaded regular gasoline.	In a reversal of previous policy, the Gay Men's Health Crisis of New York, the city's largest private AIDS organization, announces that it will endorse widespread voluntary testing for the AIDS virus.	International Boxing Federation middleweight champion Michael Nunn retains his title with a majority decision in 12 rounds over Iran Barkley. ... San Francisco Giants pitcher Dave Dravecky's comeback ends today when he breaks a bone in his arm while throwing a pitch in the sixth inning against the Montreal Expos.	**Aug. 15**
		The United States in July imported more than 50% of the oil it consumed for the first time since 1977. ... The Food and Drug Admin. says it is conducting its own analysis of the 30 top-selling generic drugs in the United States to determine whether they are safe and effective.... Housing starts rise 0.8% in July to a seasonally adjusted annual rate of 1.43 million units, the Commerce Dept. reports.	Nursing mothers who drink appear to transfer enough alcohol to their infants to impair muscle coordination, according to a study by Sterling K. Clarren in the *New England Journal of Medicine*.		**Aug. 16**
		The Congressional Budget Office warns that the federal deficit will reach $127 bil. for FY1991 — almost double the $64 bil. set by Gramm-Rudman—even if Congress honors its April budget agreement with the White House. ... The merchandise trade deficit fell to a seasonally adjusted $8.17 bil. in June, the Commerce Dept. reports.	U.S. health officials announce that the drug AZT (azidothymidine, or zidovudine) could delay the onset of Acquired Immune Deficiency Syndrome (AIDS) in people infected with the disease but who have shown no symptoms of it.		**Aug. 17**
		Easing recession fears, the consumer price index rose 0.2% for the second straight month in July, the Labor Dept. reports.	A study published in the *Journal of the American Medical Association* estimates that only about 20% of the 10 million Americans afflicted with depression are getting treatment.		**Aug. 18**
	The General Accounting Office says that sanctions against Pretoria have been weak because the State Dept. did not give the Customs Service a list of South African goods barred from entering the country.		In Britain, some 150 tons of heavy crude oil spills into the River Mersey from an underground pipeline owned by the Shell UK unit of the Royal Dutch/Shell Co., which could face criminal charges over the spill.		**Aug. 19**
				Said Aouita of Morocco breaks the oldest major individual running record in track when he runs the 3,000 meters in a time of 7:20.45.	**Aug. 20**
					Aug. 21
Huey Percy Newton, 47, black activist, is shot to death in Oakland; there is no known suspect or motive. A cofounder of the Black Panther Party, Newton was a charismatic symbol of black anger in the late 1960s. Convicted in 1968 of voluntary manslaughter in the death of an Oakland policeman, "Free Huey" became a rallying cry among radicals and college students; his conviction was overturned in 1970.		The Environmental Protection Agency files 13 civil lawsuits charging violation of asbestos-removal rules at schools, restaurants, apartments, and other facilities in 10 states.	At a conference in Pasadena, Calif., Prof. Valery Barsukov of the Vernadsky Institute of Geochemistry and Analytical Chemistry in Moscow outlines Soviet plans to visit Mercury and a Martian moon.	Diana Dalziel Vreeland, legendary fashion arbiter and editor, dies of a heart attack in New York City; she is believed to have been in her late 80s. Editor of *Harper's Bazaar* (1939-62) and *Vogue* (1962-71), she later mounted historical exhibits for the Metropolitan Museum of Art's Costume Institute.... Texas Rangers pitcher Nolan Ryan becomes the first man to strike out 5,000 batters when he fans Rickey Henderson of the Oakland Athletics in the fifth inning of a game in Arlington, Tex.	**Aug. 22**

F	G	H	I	J
Includes elections, federal-state relations, civil rights and liberties, crime, the judiciary, education, health care, poverty, urban affairs and population.	*Includes formation and debate of U.S. foreign and defense policies, veterans' affairs and defense spending. (Relations with specific foreign countries are usually found under the region concerned.)*	*Includes business, labor, agriculture, taxation, transportation, consumer affairs, monetary and fiscal policy, natural resources, and pollution.*	*Includes worldwide scientific, medical and technological developments, natural phenomena, U.S. weather, natural disasters, and accidents.*	*Includes the arts, religion, scholarship, communications media, sports, entertainments, fashions, fads and social life.*

	World Affairs	Europe	Africa & the Middle East	The Americas	Asia & the Pacific
Aug. 23		Estonia, Latvia, and Lithuania SSR mark the 50th anniversary of the 1939 Hitler-Stalin pact that brought the Baltic republics into the Soviet sphere with massive demonstrations and calls for independence.	In the third week of a civil disobedience campaign against the three-year-old state of emergency, South African police in Cape Town open fire with rubber bullets and tear gas on a rally by schoolchildren.		
Aug. 24		Poland's Sejm confirms Solidarity activist Tadeusz Mazowiecki as the country's new premier. The momentous vote represents the first known democratic transfer of power away from a ruling Communist Party.... Britain's balance of payments deficit for July reached £2.1 bil., the second-worst monthly total on record, according to Central Statistical Office figures.		A senior official of Brazil's central bank confirms that the government has prohibited indefinitely the transfer abroad of all foreign companies' profits and dividends.	Australian domestic airline service stops after 1,600 pilots resign in a labor dispute that sets the stage for a showdown with the government, which is attempting to hold the line on wage increases.
Aug. 25				Stressing education and scientific research and development, P.M. Brian Mulroney outlines his "vision for Canada" in a speech to the Progressive Conservative Party convention in Ottawa.	South Korean opposition leader Kim Dae Jung and two members of his Party for Peace and Democracy are indicted in connection with an illegal 1988 visit to North Korea by party member Suh Kyong Won, who has been charged with espionage.
Aug. 26		According to a public opinion poll in the *Sunday Times* of London, Britain's Conservative Party has made gains on the Labour Party opposition, boosting their backing by four percentage points to 40%.			
Aug. 27		Poland's Roman Catholic primate, Cardinal Jozef Glemp, speaks out strongly against a 1987 accord to move a Catholic convent from the grounds of the Nazi World War II death camp at Auschwitz, Poland.			A spokesman for Cambodia's Prince Norodom Sihanouk announces that the prince has resigned as head of the Cambodian resistance coalition. No motive is given for the move, which is not unprecedented.
Aug. 28			More than half of the 277 foreign companies that have pulled out of South Africa since 1984 are U.S. firms, according to a study prepared for a UN commission examining the activities of transnational corporations in South Africa and Namibia.		The Chinese government announces that "too many" privately owned companies have been set up in recent years and that large numbers of them will be forced to close in the near future. ... Feuding among rival Afghan rebel groups has reportedly escalated into open conflict, and Western diplomats are beginning to doubt whether the rebels can overcome the Soviet-backed Afghan government anytime soon.

A	B	C	D	E
Includes developments that affect more than one world region, international organizations and important meetings of major world leaders.	Includes all domestic and regional developments in Europe, including the Soviet Union, Turkey, Cyprus and Malta.	Includes all domestic and regional developments in Africa and the Middle East, including Iraq and Iran and excluding Cyprus, Turkey and Afghanistan.	Includes all domestic and regional developments in Latin America, the Caribbean and Canada.	Includes all domestic and regional developments in Asia and Pacific nations, extending from Afghanistan through all the Pacific Islands, except Hawaii.

U.S. Politics & Social Issues	U.S. Foreign Policy & Defense	U.S. Economy & Environment	Science, Technology & Nature	Culture, Leisure & Life Style	
The shooting death of black teen-ager Yusuf K. Hawkins in a predominantly white neighborhood in New York City where he had gone to answer a advertisement for a used car inflames racial tensions throughout the city.			R(onald) D(avid) Laing, 61, British psychiatrist renowned for his unorthodox theories about mental illness, particularly schizophrenia, dies of a heart attack in St. Tropez, France. In the 1960s he experimented with alternative approaches including the use of psychedelic drugs, but he grew disenchanted with much of his early thinking and later admitted many of his treatment methods had failed.	Victoria Brucker, a first baseman for San Pedro, Calif., becomes the first girl to play for an American team in the concluding rounds of the Little League tournament.... CBS Inc. wins the U.S. broadcasting rights for the 1994 Winter Olympics in Lillehammer, Norway with a bid of $300 mil.	Aug. 23
		Shaking the stigma of the October 1987 stock market crash, the Dow Jones industrial average surges 56.53 points to a record high of 2734.64. The previous record of 2722.42 was set exactly two years earlier.... The Commodity Exchange announces that it has fined gold and silver broker Preston H. Semel and his firm a total of $550,000 for "fraudulent conduct" on the world's major gold trading market.	The Voyager 2 spacecraft, launched Aug. 20, 1977, passes within about 3,000 miles of the planet Neptune. The fly-by produces a multitude of striking images and startling discoveries about the distant planet.... Canadian and U.S. researchers at Sick Children's Hospital in Toronto and the Univ. of Michigan's Howard Hughes Medical Institute announce that they have isolated and cloned the gene responsible for causing cystic fibrosis.	Major League Baseball Commissioner A. Bartlett Giamatti says Cincinnati Reds manager Pete Rose will be permanntly banned from baseball for betting on Major League games, including those involving the Reds.	Aug. 24
The Federal Election Comm. reports that the 16 leading candidates in the 1988 presidential primary campaign raised $213.8 mil. and spent $210.7 mil.; 66% came from donations by individuals, 31% from federal matching funds, and 2% from political action committees.				*Publishers Weekly*'s hardback fiction best-sellers for the week are: *The Russia House*, John le Carre; *Polar Star*, Martin Cruz Smith; *Red Phoenix*, Larry Bond; *Blessings*, Belva Plain; and *The Joy Luck Club*, Amy Tan.	Aug. 25
		The United Auto Workers union ratifies a contract with Diamond-Star Motors Corp.—a joint venture of Chrysler Corp. and Japan's Mitsubishi Motors Corp.—that guarantees jobs except in the face of imminent corporate collapse.		A team from Trumbull, Conn., downs Kaohsiung of Taiwan, 5-2, to win the Little League World Series. The win is the first for a team from the United States since 1983.... Irving (born Irving Tennenbaum) Stone, 86, author who pioneered the genre known as the biographical novel, dies in Los Angeles, after a heart attack. His works include *Lust for Life* (1934), based on the life of Dutch painter Vincent van Gogh, and *The Agony and the Ecstasy* (1961), based on the life of Michelangelo.... *Billboard*'s best-selling albums for the week are: *Batman* (movie soundtrack); *Repeat Offender*, Richard Marx; *Hangin' Tough*, New Kids on the Block; *Forever Your Girl*, Paula Abdul; *Steel Wheels*, Rolling Stones; and *Full Moon Fever*, Tom Petty.	Aug. 26
			In the first orbital launching of a privately owned rocket in the history of the space program, the McDonnell Douglas Space Systems Co. launches a Delta rocket carrying a television broadcasting satellite for a British company.	In auto racing, Ayrton Senna of Brazil wins the Belgian Grand Prix.	Aug. 27
Joseph Wright Alsop Jr., 78, Washington, D.C.-based journalist whose nationally syndicated political column "The Capital Parade" (later "Matter of Fact") was known for its pessimistic outlook on foreign affairs and fierce support for the U.S. military in Vietnam, dies of lung cancer and emphysema in Washington, D.C.			Astronomers say that according to current theory a giant disk of slowly rotating hydrogen gas about 65 million light years from Earth (and first detected in 1988) is a galaxy in the early stages of formation.		Aug. 28

F	G	H	I	J
Includes elections, federal-state relations, civil rights and liberties, crime, the judiciary, education, health care, poverty, urban affairs and population.	Includes formation and debate of U.S. foreign and defense policies, veterans' affairs and defense spending. (Relations with specific foreign countries are usually found under the region concerned.)	Includes business, labor, agriculture, taxation, transportation, consumer affairs, monetary and fiscal policy, natural resources, and pollution.	Includes worldwide scientific, medical and technological developments, natural phenomena, U.S. weather, natural disasters, and accidents.	Includes the arts, religion, scholarship, communications media, sports, entertainments, fashions, fads and social life.

	World Affairs	Europe	Africa & the Middle East	The Americas	Asia & the Pacific
Aug. 29					Mitsui Bank Ltd., the ninth-largest commercial bank in Japan, and Taiyo Kobe Bank Ltd., Japan's 12th largest, announce plans to merge April 1, 1990, a move that will create the second-largest bank in the world.
Aug. 30				A curfew is imposed in 10 Colombian cities including Medellin, the center of the nation's narcotics trade, as the government of Pres. Virgilio Barco intensifies its crackdown on drug traffickers.	An international conference on Cambodia ends without any progress toward ending the decade-old conflict, due largely to the lack of agreement on a role for the Khmer Rouge guerrillas in a postwar government.... Amnesty International releases a report accusing the Central Committee of the Chinese Communist Party of ordering the secret execution of dissidents seized in June.... At least 11 people are killed and 350 injured when violence erupts during a one-day nationwide strike called by Indian opposition groups to protest alleged government corruption.
Aug. 31	A panel of the UN Human Rights Comm. passes a resolution criticizing the Chinese government for its June crackdown on a student-led pro-democracy movement in Beijing and other major cities.	In England, Buckingham Palace announces that Princess Anne, Queen Elizabeth II's daughter, and her husband, Captain Mark Phillips, will separate after 15 years of marriage.	South Africa's Supreme Court rules against the Carletonville municipal council's bid to bar blacks from the town's parks after white merchants facing a black consumer boycott sued to overturn the rule.	At a special session of the Org. of American States, the United States asserts that Panama's military strongman Gen. Manuel Antonio Noriega continues to play a part in drug trafficking and money laundering.... The lower house of Argentina's legislature approves Pres. Carlos Menem's economic emergency bill, although it allows for only a 50% reduction in government subsidies to privately owned companies.... In Cuba, a military tribunal sentences former Interior Min. Gen. Jose Abrantes Fernandez to 20 years in prison for abuse of authority, improper use of government funds and negligence in his duties.	The Vietnamese Communist Party says that the national leader Ho Chi Minh died on Sept. 2, 1969, not Sept. 3 as originally reported, because the party didn't want the date of his death to coincide with National Day.
Sept. 1		Poland, West Germany, and East Germany hold separate observances of the 50th anniversary of the outbreak of World War II, which began with the shelling of the Polish fort of Westerplatte by the German battleship *Schleswig-Holstein* at 4:45 a.m. on Sept. 1, 1939.... Scotland Yard puts the final death toll for the August sinking of the Thames River party boat *Marchioness* at 51; 86 people survived the sinking.... Spanish Premier Felipe Gonzalez dissolves the Cortes (parliament) and sets general elections for October 29.		Francisco Rodriguez, appointed to succeed outgoing Pres. Manuel Solis Palma, is sworn in as president of Panama. A government tribunal had annulled May elections won by opposition candidate Guillermo Endara.	
Sept. 2				A Nicaraguan opposition coalition chooses Violeta Barrios de Chamorro, publisher of the opposition newspaper *La Prensa*, as its candidate in presidential elections scheduled for February 1990.	In an apparent effort to diminish the extent of Western influence in China, education officials say they plan to limit the number of graduate students who will be permitted to study in the West.... One man is killed and as many as 15 others are injured during a riot at a Vietnamese refugee camp in Hong Kong in the second major disturbance at the Sek Kong detention center in little more than a month.

A	B	C	D	E
Includes developments that affect more than one world region, international organizations and important meetings of major world leaders.	Includes all domestic and regional developments in Europe, including the Soviet Union, Turkey, Cyprus and Malta.	Includes all domestic and regional developments in Africa and the Middle East, including Iraq and Iran and excluding Cyprus, Turkey and Afghanistan.	Includes all domestic and regional developments in Latin America, the Caribbean and Canada.	Includes all domestic and regional developments in Asia and Pacific nations, extending from Afghanistan through all the Pacific Islands, except Hawaii.

U.S. Politics & Social Issues	U.S. Foreign Policy & Defense	U.S. Economy & Environment	Science, Technology & Nature	Culture, Leisure & Life Style	
Florida Republican Ileana Ros-Lehtinen becomes the first Cuban-American elected to Congress when she wins a special election for the House seat left empty by the death of Democrat Claude Pepper in May.		The National Park Service attributes between 40% and 70% of winter haze over the Grand Canyon to a coal-fired power plant in Arizona.... After-tax profits of U.S. corporations declined 5.4% to a $164.3 bil. annual rate in the second quarter, the Commerce Dept. reports.... To help monitor futures transactions, the Commodities Futures Trading Comm. proposes to collect traders' record cards more often and to require more detailed information to be entered on them.		At its first legislative assembly, in Rosemont, Ill., the newly merged Evangelical Lutheran Church in America adopts a neutral stance on abortion and a compassionate stand on the fatal disease Acquired Immune Deficiency Syndrome (AIDS).	Aug. 29
A longtime friend of Washington, D.C., Mayor Marion S. Barry Jr. (D) tells federal investigators that he smoked crack cocaine with the mayor in December 1988.... A federal district court jury convicts New York hotel owner Leona Helmsley of 33 counts of income tax evasion, fraud, and conspiracy but acquits her of extorting kickbacks from suppliers and contractors.		Consumer spending rose 0.7% to a $3.482 trillion annual rate in July while personal income also rose 0.7% to a $4.449 trillion rate, the Commerce Dept. reports.... The Federal Aviation Admin. orders the installation of new bomb detectors designed to screen out all types of bombs at major airports in the United States and overseas.		Dorothy Schiff, 86, owner of the *New York Post* for 37 years, dies of cancer in New York City. Heiress to an investment banking fortune, she bought the *Post* in 1939 and transformed it into one of the country's most liberal daily newspapers before selling it in 1976 to Australian newpaper magnate Rupert Murdoch.... *Variety*'s top-grossing films for the week are: *Parenthood*, *Uncle Buck*, *The Abyss*, *When Harry Met Sally...*, and *Lethal Weapon 2*.	Aug. 30
Judge Robert Potter commits television evangelist Jim Bakker to a mental institution for psychiatric evaluation after he is reportedly found cowering in a fetal position in his lawyer's office and suffering from hallucinations.		In a move opposed by the airline pilots union and the National Transportation Safety Board, the Federal Aviation Admin. relaxes rules for recreational pilot licenses while limiting their use to rural areas.... Farm prices drop 1.4% in August, the Agriculture Dept. reports. The monthly decline is the third straight for American agricultural products.... The Labor Dept. issues new "lockout/tagout" rules requiring employers to install locks on equipment to guard against inadvertent operation of equipment during maintenance.		Arbitrator Thomas Roberts orders Major League Baseball's 26 owners to pay a total of more than $10 mil. to compensate players harmed by the owner's collusion against free agency after the 1985 season.	Aug. 31
	Saying that Panama is "without any legitimate government," Pres. Bush says his administration will neither recognize nor have diplomatic contact with the government of Panama.	The Environmental Protection Agency calls for an end to the use of the chemical Alar (a ripener and crisper) in apples and other foods, as of May 31, 1991.... The Dow Jones industrial average closes at an all-time record high 2752.09. The previous record close, 2743.36, was posted Aug. 28.... The government's index of leading economic indicators rose 0.2% in July, its first gain in two months, the Commerce Dept. reports.	A study reported in the *Journal of the American Medical Association* finds that people with symptoms of depression have no higher incidence of cancer than people who are not depressed.	A(ngelo) Bartlett Giamatti, 51, professor of literature, former president of Yale Univ., and commissioner of Major League Baseball, dies of a heart attack at his summer home on Martha's Vineyard, Mass. The youngest person ever named president of Yale, in 1978, he was named president of the National League in 1986 and commissioner of baseball in 1988.	Sept. 1
As about 300 demonstrators march through the streets of Bensonhurst, N.Y., to protest the August 23 murder of Yusuf K. Hawkins, local residents yell taunts such as "Nigger, go home" and "You savages."					Sept. 2

F	G	H	I	J
Includes elections, federal-state relations, civil rights and liberties, crime, the judiciary, education, health care, poverty, urban affairs and population.	*Includes formation and debate of U.S. foreign and defense policies, veterans' affairs and defense spending. (Relations with specific foreign countries are usually found under the region concerned.)*	*Includes business, labor, agriculture, taxation, transportation, consumer affairs, monetary and fiscal policy, natural resources, and pollution.*	*Includes worldwide scientific, medical and technological developments, natural phenomena, U.S. weather, natural disasters, and accidents.*	*Includes the arts, religion, scholarship, communications media, sports, entertainments, fashions, fads and social life.*

	World Affairs	Europe	Africa & the Middle East	The Americas	Asia & the Pacific
Sept. 3			Arab and Western sources cited by the *New York Times* say that Libya has recently moved to cut back its funding and support for terrorist and guerrilla movements around the world.	Some 150 people are killed when a Cubana Airlines jet carrying Italian tourists crashes on takeoff from Havana's Jose Marti airport.	
Sept. 4		Hungary's Interior Min. Istvan Horvath says that no East German refugees can be allowed to leave Hungary for West Germany until East Germany and Hungary reach a definitive agreement on emigration policy.... At the annual conference of Britain's Trades Union Congress (TUC) labor federation, more women are promoted to the TUC's general council and a defense plank calling for multilateral nuclear disarmament is adopted.	After months of increasing inter-Arab violence, the leadership of the Palestinian intifada urges Arab militants to avoid indiscriminate killings of fellow Arabs suspected of collaborating with Israel.	George Price of the People's United Party is elected prime minister of Belize. Price held power for 30 years before losing the 1984 election by a landslide to Manuel Esquivel of the United Democratic Party.	
Sept. 5				Some 40,000 nurses represented by the Quebec Federation of Nurses begin an illegal strike for a 10% wage increase for 1989 and a contract guarantee that future wages will be indexed to inflation.	
Sept. 6		In the Netherlands, the Christian Democratic Party wins a plurality in general elections and Premier Ruud Lubbers, who has governed since 1982, is widely expected to lead the next government.	South Africa's ruling National Party retains its majority in white parliamentary elections but loses substantial ground to the far right Conservative Party and the new Democratic Party on the left.... Hundreds of thousands of black workers and students observe a two-day general strike to protest their exclusion from South Africa's parliamentary elections.	Eduardo Martinez Romero, accused of money laundering for the Medellin drug cartel, is the first Colombian extradited to the United States since Pres. Virgilio Barco reinstated the Colombian-U.S. extradition treaty.	
Sept. 7	The 102-member Nonaligned Movement concludes its ninth summit in Belgrade, Yugoslavia, with the adoption of a policy declaration that is more moderate and less anti-United States than those in the past.		The Ethiopian government is reported to have opened peace talks with Eritrean rebels in the United States over the last two weeks.		The trial in absentia of former Philippine Pres. Ferdinand E. Marcos and his wife, Imelda, opens in Manila. The Marcoses are charged with the "plunder of the nation's wealth" for allegedly embezzling millions of dollars in government funds.
Sept. 8		With promises of legal aid in their bid to emigrate, 116 East Germans leave the West German mission in East Berlin.... Hungarian leader Reszo Nyers proposes demilitarizing Hungary's borders with neutral Austria and nonaligned Yugoslavia, with a pullback of troops and offensive weapons from the two borders by the end of 1990.			
Sept. 9			After delays in political and economic reforms promised in October 1988, Algeria's Pres. Chadli Benjedid dismisses Premier Kasdi Merbah and names Mouloud Hamrouche to form a new government.		

A	B	C	D	E
Includes developments that affect more than one world region, international organizations and important meetings of major world leaders.	Includes all domestic and regional developments in Europe, including the Soviet Union, Turkey, Cyprus and Malta.	Includes all domestic and regional developments in Africa and the Middle East, including Iraq and Iran and excluding Cyprus, Turkey and Afghanistan.	Includes all domestic and regional developments in Latin America, the Caribbean and Canada.	Includes all domestic and regional developments in Asia and Pacific nations, extending from Afghanistan through all the Pacific Islands, except Hawaii.

U.S. Politics & Social Issues	U.S. Foreign Policy & Defense	U.S. Economy & Environment	Science, Technology & Nature	Culture, Leisure & Life Style	
					Sept. 3
	The Central Intelligence Agency has reportedly dismissed the intelligence officer responsible for supplying U.S. military aid to the Afghan rebels due to complaints about mismanagement of the supply program.			Georges Simenon, 86, popular Belgian novelist who created the well-known Paris police detective Inspector Maigret, dies of unreported causes in Lausanne, Switzerland. Simenon wrote 84 Maigret mysteries, 136 other novels, more than 1,000 articles and short stories, and 200 pseudonymous novellas; more than 600 million copies of his books have been sold in 47 languages.	Sept. 4
The Chicago school system begins the school year under a plan that will shift control to parent-led councils at each of the city's 540 schools in what is thought to be the most radical school decentralization plan ever.... Pres. Bush outlines the details of an administration plan to combat drug use and drug trafficking.		The Commerce Dept. announces requirements for commercial shrimp fishermen to use nets equipped with trapdoor devices to allow turtles—many species of which are threatened with extinction—to escape drowning.			Sept. 5
Lawyers for former national security adviser John M. Poindexter charge that then-president Ronald Reagan authorized him to give false answers to congressional committees investigating the Iran-Contra affair in mid-1986.... The 1989-90 school year in Chelsea, Mass., begins with the city's public schools under the control of Boston Univ. in the first instance of a private organization assuming control of a public school system.	In response to threats by Lebanese Christians, the United States closes its embassy in Beirut and evacuates its entire staff for the first time since Lebanon's civil war began in 1975.		A Harvard Univ. School of Public Health study reported in the *Journal of the National Cancer Institute* finds no evidence of higher cancer risk among women who started taking birth-control pills in their mid-20s.		Sept. 6
The Senate, 76-8, approves major legislation to prohibit discrimination against handicapped people in employment and in access to public accommodations, transportation, and communications.	The Energy Dept. says it will resume production of tritium, a component of nuclear weapons, at its Savannah River Site nuclear reactor in South Carolina in 1990. It also announces the closure of the site's three-year-old uranium plant, which makes nuclear fuel for U.S. Navy ships.	A coalition of environmental groups, religious organizations, and investors proposes a code of environmental conduct by corporations to be known as the Valdez Principles, after the *Exxon Valdez*.			Sept. 7
The U.S. Court of Appeals unanimously rejects independent counsel James C. McKay's request to reconsider a ruling by a court panel overturning the conviction of former Reagan administration aide Lyn Nofziger.		Consumer debt declined $280 mil. in July, at an annual rate of 0.5%, the Federal Reserve Board reports.			Sept. 8
				West Germany's Steffi Graf wins the women's singles championship at the U.S. Open tennis tournament. The Open also marks the last tournament for six-time champion Chris Evert.	Sept. 9

F	G	H	I	J
Includes elections, federal-state relations, civil rights and liberties, crime, the judiciary, education, health care, poverty, urban affairs and population.	Includes formation and debate of U.S. foreign and defense policies, veterans' affairs and defense spending. (Relations with specific foreign countries are usually found under the region concerned.)	Includes business, labor, agriculture, taxation, transportation, consumer affairs, monetary and fiscal policy, natural resources, and pollution.	Includes worldwide scientific, medical and technological developments, natural phenomena, U.S. weather, natural disasters, and accidents.	Includes the arts, religion, scholarship, communications media, sports, entertainments, fashions, fads and social life.

	World Affairs	Europe	Africa & the Middle East	The Americas	Asia & the Pacific
Sept. 10		Citing the more than 5,000 East Germans in refugee camps and 60,000 others on vacation in Hungary, Budapest drops a 20-year agreement with East Germany that prevented the transmigration of East Germans to the West. . . . The Ukrainian Popular Movement for Perestroika, or Ruk, concludes its founding congress, attended by more than 1,000 delegates and foreign guests. . . . As many as 161 of 179 passengers drown when a Romanian pleasure boat sinks after colliding with a Bulgarian barge on the Danube River about 150 miles northeast of Bucharest.	A State Dept. report says that the Somali Army "purposely murdered" at least 5,000 unarmed civilians between May 1988 and March 1989 during a northern campaign aganist Somali National Movement rebels.		
Sept. 11		One day before the confirmation of a new Solidarity-led cabinet, the Polish government devalues the national currency, the zloty, by 18.5% against the U.S. dollar; it is the 10th large devaluation of 1989. . . . In Norway's general elections, Premier Gro Harlem Brundtland's Labor Party wins the most votes, but the rightist Progress Party makes the most substantial gains.			
Sept. 12		Poland's Sejm, or lower house of parliament, confirms Premier Tadeusz Mazowiecki's 23-member coalition cabinet; 402 of 415 deputies present back the confirmation, and 13 abstain. . . . East Germany files a diplomatic protest against Hungary and demands that Budapest immediately halt the exodus of East Germans to West Germany through Hungary.	Namibia's UN-supervised transition to independence from South Africa enters a critical phase as a senior official of the South-West African People's Org. (SWAPO) guerrilla movement is assassinated and SWAPO leader Sam Nujoma returns from nearly 30 years in exile.	Quebec's nurses begin returning to their jobs after one week on strike. . . . Colombian authorities arrest suspected drug trafficker Guillermo Bueno Delgado and money launderer Bernardo Pelaez Roldan. The United States says it will file extradition requests for both.	
Sept. 13	Japan had the lowest rate of inflation—1%—among industrialized countries in 1988, according to International Labor Org. statistics, while Peru had the highest rate, at 1,722%. U.S. inflation was 4.4%.			Mexico and its major creditor banks agree on details of a plan announced in July for reducing the country's $53 bil. commercial bank debt.	The State Dept. declares that it has received numerous "credible, first-hand reports" that the military regime in Myanmar tortures antigovernment activists.
Sept. 14	A report by the General Agreement on Tariffs and Trade says the nearly 40% growth of international merchandise trade in the period 1983 to 1988 is greater than at any time since the early 1970s.	In the face of congressional pressure, the Bush administration reverses itself and says it will double the amount of food aid for Poland to $100 mil. in the next fiscal year. . . . Italy's largest state-owned bank, Banca Nazionale del Lavoro, is shaken by disclosures that its branch in Atlanta, Ga., has made as much as $3 bil. in unauthorized loan commitments to Iraq. . . . More than 13,000 East Germans have left Hungary for West Germany via Austria in the last four days in the largest exodus of East Germans to the West since the construction of the Berlin Wall in 1961.	F. W. de Klerk is officially elected to a five-year term as state president of South Africa by the electoral college of parliament, which includes whites, coloreds, and Indians, but no blacks.	Public services in Quebec are in turmoil, as at least 225,000 provincial employees are on strike. The walkouts disrupt schools, health-care facilities, government offices and social-service agencies.	The UN High Commissioner for Refugees reports that more than 61,000 Vietnamese boat people are reported to have fled their homeland between January and August, more than the total for any full year since 1981.

A	B	C	D	E
Includes developments that affect more than one world region, international organizations and important meetings of major world leaders.	Includes all domestic and regional developments in Europe, including the Soviet Union, Turkey, Cyprus and Malta.	Includes all domestic and regional developments in Africa and the Middle East, including Iraq and Iran and excluding Cyprus, Turkey and Afghanistan.	Includes all domestic and regional developments in Latin America, the Caribbean and Canada.	Includes all domestic and regional developments in Asia and Pacific nations, extending from Afghanistan through all the Pacific Islands, except Hawaii.

U.S. Politics & Social Issues	U.S. Foreign Policy & Defense	U.S. Economy & Environment	Science, Technology & Nature	Culture, Leisure & Life Style	
				West German Boris Becker wins the men's singles championship at the U.S. Open tennis tournament. . . . Alain Prost of France wins the Italian Grand Prix in Monza.	Sept. 10
The College Entrance Examination Board reports that the average score on the 1989 Scholastic Aptitude Test fell from 904 to 903 (on a scale of 400 to 1,600) and on the American College Test from 18.8 to 18.6 (on a scale of 1 to 36).		Drexel Burnham Lambert Inc. pleads guilty to six counts of fraud and pays more than $500 mil. in fines and restitution in a record Wall Street criminal settlement. . . . In its largest enforcement action to date, the Commodity Futures Trading Comm. charges the International Trading Group Ltd. and Siegel Trading Co. with fraud for failure to disclose the high risks in trading commodity futures options.		*Fortune* magazine's annual list of the world's billionaires includes 157 individuals and families. The top five are the Sultan of Brunei ($25 bil.), King Fahd of Saudi Arabia ($18 bil.), candy magnate Forrest Mars ($12.5 bil.), Britain's Queen Elizabeth II ($10.9 bil.) and publishers Samuel and Donald Newhouse ($10 bil.).	Sept. 11
In response to a Supreme Court June decision saying that burning the flag is constitutionally protected free speech, the House passes, 380-38, a bill barring physical desecration of the American flag. . . . The House Ethics Committee votes to open a preliminary inquiry to determine whether Rep. Barney Frank (D, Mass.) violated House rules by hiring a male prostitute as a personal aide.		The deficit in the balance of payments on current account increased 2% in the second quarter, to a seasonally adjusted $30.99 bil., the Commerce Dept. reports. . . . A General Accounting Office report recommends that the Fish and Wildlife Service consider closing those of the nation's 452 wildlife refuges that cannot be adequately protected from human despoilation.		An international spelling bee by the polling firm Gallup International finds that Americans are the worst spellers in the English-speaking world. Australians are the best, followed by Canadians and British.	Sept. 12
	The Senate falls one vote short of the two-thirds majority needed to override Pres. Bush's veto of congressional restrictions on U.S.-Japanese joint development of a new Japanese fighter plane, the FSX.	An explosion of methane gas at a coal mine in Wheatcroft, Ky., kills 10 miners. The cause of the explosion is not immediately known.	After seven years of development, the Univ. of Minnesota Press releases a new version of the Minnesota Multiphasic Personality Inventory, the world's most widely used psychological assessment test first published in 1942.	Francis T. (Fay) Vincent is named to succeed the late A. Bartlett Giamatti as commissioner of Major League Baseball. He is elected unanimously by the major league's 26 owners at a special meeting in Milwaukee. . . . Lincoln Kirstein announces that he will retire as general director of the New York City Ballet and as president of the School of American Ballet, both of which he cofounded with the late George Balanchine.	Sept. 13
Law enforcement agents in Hawaii and elsewhere are reportedly alarmed about the widespread availability of "ice," a smokeable form of methamphetamine that produces a longer high than cocaine-based crack. . . . The Education Dept. reports that the high school dropout rate in 1988 was 12.9%—12.7% for white students, 14.9% for blacks, and 35.8% for Hispanics. All told, 4.2 million students dropped out of high school.		The House Ways and Means Committee approves a capital gains tax cut in a defeat for committee Chairman Dan Rostenkowski (D, Ill.). Liberal Democrats view the cut as primarily benefiting the wealthy. . . . The Senate approves a permanent smoking ban on all domestic airline flights in the United States. . . . The California Air Resources Board unanimously adopts a new antismog measure that mandates computerized warning systems—which do not yet exist—in new cars by 1994.	The British journal *Nature* reports that scientists have found a distinctive protein linked to Alzheimer's disease outside the brain, fueling hope that a laboratory test for the disease can be developed.		Sept. 14

F	**G**	**H**	**I**	**J**
Includes elections, federal-state relations, civil rights and liberties, crime, the judiciary, education, health care, poverty, urban affairs and population.	Includes formation and debate of U.S. foreign and defense policies, veterans' affairs and defense spending. (Relations with specific foreign countries are usually found under the region concerned.)	Includes business, labor, agriculture, taxation, transportation, consumer affairs, monetary and fiscal policy, natural resources, and pollution.	Includes worldwide scientific, medical and technological developments, natural phenomena, U.S. weather, natural disasters, and accidents.	Includes the arts, religion, scholarship, communications media, sports, entertainments, fashions, fads and social life.

	World Affairs	Europe	Africa & the Middle East	The Americas	Asia & the Pacific
Sept. 15	Finance officials from 15 of the world's richest countries meet in Paris to begin coordinated action against the international flow of profits from illegal drug operations.	France's suicide rate continues to grow sharply, according to ministry of health statistics, and it is the fastest-growing cause of death among people 15 to 24 years old.		Representatives of the Farabundo Marti National Liberation Front and the rightist government of El Salvador's Pres. Alfredo Cristiani agree to begin formal peace negotiations October 16-17 in Costa Rica.	
Sept. 16					China's paramount leader, Deng Xiaoping, 85, appears in public for the first time in more than three months. His reappearance quells rumors that he is seriously ill or has already died.
Sept. 17				A spokesman for the Royal Canadian Mounted Police asserts that five heavily armed Latin Americans arrested in New Brunswick were planning to free two Colombians arrested on suspicion of drug smuggling. . . . Americas Watch and the National Coalition for Haitian Refugees criticize Lt. Gen. Prosper Avril's government for failing to end widespread political violence in Haiti and for not moving to restore democracy.	
Sept. 18	Government and chemical-industry officials from 67 nations gather in Canberra, Australia, for a four-day conference on chemical weapons sponsored by the U.S. government in consultation with Australia. . . . The failure of the International Cocoa Org. to agree on price support measures sends cocoa prices to a 14-year low.	Britain's Min. for Health David Mellors says the government will fund use of the drug AZT (azidothymidine or zidovudine) for treatment of Acquired Immune Deficiency Syndrome (AIDS) if it proves effective in delaying the onset of the disease.	Meeting in Cairo, Egypt's Pres. Hosni Mubarak and Israel's Defense Min. Yitzhak Rabin discuss Egypt's new 10-point plan to break a stalemate over proposed Palestinian elections in the West Bank and Gaza Strip.		India and Sri Lanka sign an agreement providing for the withdrawal of an estimated 42,000 Indian peacekeeping troops from Sri Lanka by the end of the year.
Sept. 19	A panel of the General Agreement on Tariffs and Trade rules that Canada must end its system of import controls on some dairy products in a ruling that threatens Canada's entire system of farm marketing boards.	A new East German umbrella opposition group, New Forum, is formed to challenge the communist political monopoly. . . . The Vatican offers to help finance the construction of an ecumenical center to house Carmelite nuns currently occupying a controversial convent in Poland at the World War II Auschwitz death camp.	A French DC-10 jetliner flying from the Congo to Paris with 171 people aboard explodes in midair over Niger, probably due to a bomb, after a stopover in Chad. There are no survivors. . . . In Burkina Faso, four men are executed by firing squad for trying to overthrow head of state Capt. Blaise Compaore. The dead include Defense Min. Jean-Baptiste Boukari Lengani and the minister of economic promotions, Captain Henri Zongo.	Hurricane Hugo rips through the Caribbean islands of Guadeloupe, Montserrat, the Virgin Islands, and Puerto Rico over the previous four days, causing billions of dollars in property damage, leaving tens of thousands of people homeless, and killing at least 20 people.	
Sept. 20		Soviet Pres. Mikhail S. Gorbachev engineers a purge of the Communist Party's Politburo at a two-day closed plenary session of the Central Committee ostensibly called to debate nationalism and ethnic strife. . . . The European Community (EC) announces that it will take Britain to court for failing to meet EC standards for drinking water.			

A	B	C	D	E
Includes developments that affect more than one world region, international organizations and important meetings of major world leaders.	Includes all domestic and regional developments in Europe, including the Soviet Union, Turkey, Cyprus and Malta.	Includes all domestic and regional developments in Africa and the Middle East, including Iraq and Iran and excluding Cyprus, Turkey and Afghanistan.	Includes all domestic and regional developments in Latin America, the Caribbean and Canada.	Includes all domestic and regional developments in Asia and Pacific nations, extending from Afghanistan through all the Pacific Islands, except Hawaii.

U.S. Politics & Social Issues	U.S. Foreign Policy & Defense	U.S. Economy & Environment	Science, Technology & Nature	Culture, Leisure & Life Style	
Former Housing and Urban Development Sec. Samuel R. Pierce Jr. refuses to testitify before a House Government Operations subcommittee because his team of lawyers has not had sufficient time to prepare him.		With the approach of winter, Exxon Corp. halts its billion-dollar effort to mop up the 11-million-gallon *Exxon Valdez* oil spill in Prince William Sound.... The Interior Dept. postpones the prospective sale of oil and gas leases in the Atlantic Ocean between Rhode Island and North Carolina and out 200 miles offshore from September 1990 until July 1991.... The Federal Reserve Board reports that its industrial production index increased 0.3% in August.... The government's producer price index dropped 0.4% in August, the Labor Dept. reports.		Robert Penn Warren, 84, Pulitzer Prize-winning author, dies of cancer at his summer home in Stratton, Vt. Winner of Pulitzer Prizes for his novel *All the King's Men* (1946) and for poetry (1957 and 1979), he was the first poet laureate of the United States. He also coauthored two seminal works of literary criticism, *Understanding Poetry* and *Understanding Fiction*.... *Sea of Love* is released in New York. Directed by Harold Becker and starring Al Pacino, Ellen Barkin, and John Goodman, the film is about a police detective who becomes involved with the chief suspect in a murder investigation.	Sept. 15
				Miss Missouri, Debbye Turner, is crowned Miss America at the annual Atlantic City, N.J., pageant. Turner, 23, a senior at the Univ. of Missouri veterinary school, is the third black Miss America.	Sept. 16
				The 41st annual Emmy Awards are presented to "L.A. Law" for best drama; "Cheers," comedy; "The Tracey Ullman Show," variety, music, or comedy program; "War and Remembrance," mini-series; and "Day One" and "Roe v. Wade" tie for best drama or comedy special. Carroll O'Connor wins for best actor in a drama ("In the Heat of the Night"); Richard Mulligan, comedy actor ("Empty Nest"); James Woods, mini-series or special actor ("My Name is Bill W"); Dana Delany, drama actress ("China Beach"); Candice Bergen, comedy actress ("Murphy Brown"); Holly Hunter, mini-series or special actress, "Roe v. Wade".	Sept. 17
Burroughs-Wellcome Co. announces that it has agreed to cut by 20% the price of its anti-viral drug AZT (azidothymidine, or zidovudine), the only drug currently licensed to treat the fatal Acquired Immune Deficiency Syndrome (AIDS). A year's supply of AZT costs up to $8,000.					Sept. 18
		The merchandise trade deficit fell to a seasonally adjusted $7.58 bil. in July, the Commerce Dept. reports.... The consumer price index holds steady in August, the first time in three years it has not risen according to Labor Dept. statistics reported.... Housing starts fell 5% in August to a seasonally adjusted annual rate of 1.35 million units, the Commerce Dept. reports.	Martin Delaney, director of a private study of tricosanthin (known as Compound Q or GLQ223), a controversial anti-AIDS drug derived from the root of Chinese cucumber plants, says the study has produced promising results. The Food and Drug Admin. August 9 asked Delany to stop the study after one death and several cases of dementia were reported among the participants.	A New York appeals court overrules a lower court and returns the America's Cup yachting trophy to the San Diego Yacht Club. In 1989 a New York judge awarded the cup to the New Zealand club.	Sept. 19
Miami-Dade Co., Fla., school superintendent Joseph A. Fernandez is named schools chancellor of the New York City public school system, the nation's largest.		A House subcommittee kills a Bush administration proposal that would have allowed car makers to meet emission standards by averaging the amount of emissions from all models rather than applying them to each car.		*A Dry White Season*, a film about a white South African schoolteacher who becomes involved in the anti-apartheid struggle when his black gardener is killed while in police custody, is released in New York. Directed by Euzhan Palcy and based on Andre Brink's novel, the film stars Donald Sutherland, Janet Suzman, Zakes Mokae, and Marlon Brando.	Sept. 20

F	G	H	I	J
Includes elections, federal-state relations, civil rights and liberties, crime, the judiciary, education, health care, poverty, urban affairs and population.	Includes formation and debate of U.S. foreign and defense policies, veterans' affairs and defense spending. (Relations with specific foreign countries are usually found under the region concerned.)	Includes business, labor, agriculture, taxation, transportation, consumer affairs, monetary and fiscal policy, natural resources, and pollution.	Includes worldwide scientific, medical and technological developments, natural phenomena, U.S. weather, natural disasters, and accidents.	Includes the arts, religion, scholarship, communications media, sports, entertainments, fashions, fads and social life.

	World Affairs	Europe	Africa & the Middle East	The Americas	Asia & the Pacific
Sept. 21	The 44th annual session of the UN General Assembly opens at UN headquarters in New York City. Nigeria's UN representative, Joseph Namvan Garba, is elected in a secret ballot to the one-year post of General Assembly president. He succeeds Dante Caputo of Argentina.	Greece's 1989 public sector borrowing requirement (budget deficit) will be $11.4 bil., according to reports.	Saudi Arabia publicly beheads 16 Kuwaiti Shiite Moslems for planting bombs in the Islamic holy city of Mecca during the annual pilgrimage in July. The condemned men confess and claim that Iran was behind the bombings.		Australia's August trade deficit was $2 bil., a new record for that month, the government reports.
Sept. 22		The Provisional Irish Republican Army claims responsibility for a blast that kills 10 British military bandsmen and injures 22 at the Royal Marines School of Music in the English Channel town of Deal, Kent.			
Sept. 23	Britain's P.M. Margaret Thatcher concludes a six-day trip to Japan and Moscow. Her trip to Japan was dominated by trade issues, and that to Moscow by her warm praise for Pres. Mikhail S. Gorbachev's reforms. . . . Saying the dollar's increasing strength is "inconsistent with longer-run economic fundamentals." Group of Seven economics ministers vow to cooperate in holding down the value of the U.S. currency.		Michel Aoun, Lebanon's Christian army leader, reluctantly accepts an Arab League plan to end the latest round of fighting in the Lebanese civil war in preparation for an Arab-sponsored peace conference.		
Sept. 24		Britain's Green Party concludes its annual four-day conference with unprecedented press coverage, attributed to its 15% share of the vote in June elections for the European Parliament. . . . A Harris poll shows that the Greens, with 7% support, have retaken third place among British parties from the Social and Liberal Democrats.		Colombia's Justice Min. Monica de Greiff resigns after Pres. Virgilio Barco Vargas accused her of "dragging her feet" in signing an extradition order the constitutionality of which she had questioned. . . . Calling the government's drug policy "myopic," a number of Colombian justice ministry officials quit and some 4,500 judges threaten to strike unless the ministry provides them with better protection. . . . The military government of Haiti's Pres. Prosper Avril announces that legislative elections will be held in July and August of 1990 and presidential elections in October and November.	
Sept. 25	Addressing the UN General Assembly, Pres. Bush offers an 80% reduction in the U.S. stockpile of chemical weapons in exchange for deep cuts in the Soviet arsenal. Soviet Foreign Min. Eduard A. Shevardnadze urges an immediate elimination of superpower chemical-arms stockpiles and a ban on production.			Speaking before the General Assembly, Argentina's Pres. Carlos Saul Menem presses his nation's claim to the Falkland (Malvinas) Islands. . . . In Canada, the ruling Quebec Liberal Party handily defeats the rival Parti Quebecois (PQ) in provincial elections, capturing 92 of the 125 seats in the provincial legislature to the PQ's 29 seats.	

A	B	C	D	E
Includes developments that affect more than one world region, international organizations and important meetings of major world leaders.	Includes all domestic and regional developments in Europe, including the Soviet Union, Turkey, Cyprus and Malta.	Includes all domestic and regional developments in Africa and the Middle East, including Iraq and Iran and excluding Cyprus, Turkey and Afghanistan.	Includes all domestic and regional developments in Latin America, the Caribbean and Canada.	Includes all domestic and regional developments in Asia and Pacific nations, extending from Afghanistan through all the Pacific Islands, except Hawaii.

U.S. Politics & Social Issues	U.S. Foreign Policy & Defense	U.S. Economy & Environment	Science, Technology & Nature	Culture, Leisure & Life Style	
Ruling that "human life begins at the moment of conception," Tennessee State Court Judge W. Dale Young awards temporary custody of seven frozen embryos to a divorced woman, Mary Sue Davis, rather than to her ex-husband, Junior Davis, who sought to prevent their being used. . . . The Federal Bureau of Investigation says it will not appeal a May 5 federal court order to reform its promotion system and eliminate discrimination against Hispanic agents.	A Washington, D.C., meeting between Soviet Foreign Min. Eduard A. Shevardnadze and Pres. Bush leads to a possible breakthrough in the conflict over the U.S. Strategic Defense Initiative. . . . The Senate confirms Army Gen. Colin L. Powell as the chairman of the Joint Chiefs of Staff. He succeeds retiring Adm. William J. Crowe Jr. October 1.	Rather than violate federal environmental laws on storage and disposal of hazardous waste, Rockwell International Corp. sues the U.S. government over operation of the Rocky Flats nuclear weapons plant in Colorado as required under contract with the Energy Dept.	Hurricane Hugo hits Charleston, S.C., late in the evening with winds of 135 miles per hour, setting off a 17-foot tidal surge that sweeps into Charleston Harbor.	Author Werner Aspenstrom becomes the third member of the Swedish Royal Academy's Nobel Prize selection committee to resign in protest of the academy's failure to condemn death threats against Salman Rushdie.	Sept. 21
Arizona Gov. Rose Mofford (D) signs legislation restoring January 19 as a state holiday honoring the birthday of slain civil rights leader Rev. Martin Luther King Jr.		Consumer spending rose 0.9% to a $3.508 trillion annual rate in August, while personal income rose 0.4% to a $4.466 trillion annual rate, the Commerce Dept. reports. . . . The Energy Dept. announces a mutual agreement with Rockwell International Corp. to terminate the company's contract as operator of the department's Rocky Flats nuclear weapons plant near Denver.	Hurricane Hugo heads north from Charleston, S.C., through the Carolinas before dissipating over Virginia, West Virginia, Ohio, Pennsylvania, and New York.	Irving (born Israel Baline) Berlin, 101, Russian-born American songwriter, dies in his sleep at his home in New York City. His 18 movie scores and 19 Broadway musicals account for only some of his 1,500 songs, including "Alexander's Ragtime Band," "White Christmas," "Puttin' On the Ritz," "Cheek to Cheek," and "There's No Business Like Show Business." In 1954, he assigned the royalties from "God Bless America" to a public fund, for which he received a congressional gold medal.	Sept. 22
					Sept. 23
		About 1 billion people—most of them in developing nations of Africa, Asia, and Latin America—suffer from disease, malnourishment, or poor health, according to a report issued by the UN's World Health Org., and some 11 million Third World children die each year from preventable or treatable diseases.		A team of 12 European golfers retains the Ryder Cup after a three-day match-play contest against the United States ends in a tie, 14-14. As holders of the cup and as a result of the tie, they keep possession.	Sept. 24
Dr. Elizabeth Morgan, a plastic surgeon who has spent more than two years in jail on contempt charges for refusing to reveal the whereabouts of her daughter in a custody battle with her ex-husband, is released after a law designed to free her passes Congress. . . . The *St. Louis Sun*, the country's first major newspaper since the debut of the *Washington Times* in 1982, begins publication.					Sept. 25

F	G	H	I	J
Includes elections, federal-state relations, civil rights and liberties, crime, the judiciary, education, health care, poverty, urban affairs and population.	Includes formation and debate of U.S. foreign and defense policies, veterans' affairs and defense spending. (Relations with specific foreign countries are usually found under the region concerned.)	Includes business, labor, agriculture, taxation, transportation, consumer affairs, monetary and fiscal policy, natural resources, and pollution.	Includes worldwide scientific, medical and technological developments, natural phenomena, U.S. weather, natural disasters, and accidents.	Includes the arts, religion, scholarship, communications media, sports, entertainments, fashions, fads and social life.

	World Affairs	Europe	Africa & the Middle East	The Americas	Asia & the Pacific
Sept. 26	About 20 nations, including the United States and Soviet Union, either possess chemical weapons or are acquiring them, according to a Western intelligence assessment reported by the *Times* of London. ... The International Monetary Fund and the World Bank resume their April discussions on the pressing issue of debt reduction in the Third World and discuss their own future funding needs.	British trade figures for August showed a $3.2 bil. current account deficit.		The Colombian government and the April 19 Movement (M-19) reach an accord under which the rebels agree to disarm and become incorporated into political life provided the government grants amnesty for M-19 members by the end of October.	Vietnam completes the withdrawal of its troops from Cambodia, 10 years and nine months after invading the country to topple the Khmer Rouge regime of Pol Pot and install a pro-Vietnamese government.
Sept. 27	Org. of Petroleum Exporting Countries ministers sanction an increase in the official production ceiling from 19.5 million to 20.5 million barrels a day.	The parliament of Slovenia defies Yugoslavia's central government by amending the republic's constitution to allow Slovenia to secede from Yugoslavia.	Public buses, swimming pools, and recreation centers in Johannesburg, South Africa, are formally opened to all races one day after the city council voted to approve the desegregation measure.	Argentina's Pres. Carlos Saul Menem announces that the International Monetary Fund has agreed to loan his country $1.5 bil. Menem makes the announcement in Washington, D.C., after meeting with Pres. Bush.	Chinese and British negotiators open discussions on the transfer of Hong Kong's sovereignty to China in 1997. The meetings are reportedly dominated by debate over China's right to station regular army troops in Hong Kong.
Sept. 28		The Greek parliament charges Andreas Papandreou, Greece's socialist premier from 1981 until June 1989, and seven others with corruption and abuses of power and orders them to stand trial.			Ferdinand E. Marcos, 72, president of the Philippines from 1965 to 1985, dies in a hospital in Honolulu. Elected president in 1965, he imposed martial law in 1972. His fall from power began after the 1983 assassination of Benigno S. Aquino Jr.; he was forced into exile after he declared himself the winner of a fraudulent election over Aquino's widow, Corazon in 1985. ... North Korea's Foreign Min. Kim Young Nam and Deputy Foreign Min. Kang Sok Ju unveil a plan for a new round of reunification talks with the South in early 1990.
Sept. 29					
Sept. 30		The Yugoslav republic of Montenegro reburies the remains of exiled former King Nicholas I, Queen Milena, and their two daughters in what is believed to be the first time that the remains of an exiled monarch have been returned to a communist country.	At an Arab-sponsored conference in Saudi Arabia, members of Lebanon's parliament begin talks to hammer out a permanent peace settlement.		

A	B	C	D	E
Includes developments that affect more than one world region, international organizations and important meetings of major world leaders.	Includes all domestic and regional developments in Europe, including the Soviet Union, Turkey, Cyprus and Malta.	Includes all domestic and regional developments in Africa and the Middle East, including Iraq and Iran and excluding Cyprus, Turkey and Afghanistan.	Includes all domestic and regional developments in Latin America, the Caribbean and Canada.	Includes all domestic and regional developments in Asia and Pacific nations, extending from Afghanistan through all the Pacific Islands, except Hawaii.

U.S. Politics & Social Issues	U.S. Foreign Policy & Defense	U.S. Economy & Environment	Science, Technology & Nature	Culture, Leisure & Life Style	
Former Housing and Urban Development (HUD) Sec. Samuel R. Pierce Jr. refuses to appear before a congressional panel investigating influence-peddling at HUD.... A New York Times/CBS News poll finds that Pres. Bush enjoys a higher approval rating—69%— than any of the previous four presidents at the same point in their terms.					Sept. 26
Pres. Bush meets with the nation's governors in Charlottesville, Va., in an effort to devise a plan to improve the nation's schools.... Testifying before a Senate banking subcommittee, General Accounting Office Comptroller Gen. Charles A. Bowsher says that the Federal Housing Admin.'s mortgage programs lost a record $4.2 bil. in 1988.	The Defense Dept.'s eighth annual edition of *Soviet Military Power* tones down descriptions of the Soviet menace.	Japan's Sony Corp. agrees to buy Columbia Pictures Entertainment Inc. for $3.4 bil. in the biggest foreign acquisition to date by any Japanese company.	The Albert Lasker Medical Research Award for public service is made to Dr. Lewis Thomas, author of *Lives of a Cell*, "for opening the wonders of 20th-century medical research and practice to the average person."	*Variety*'s top-grossing films for the week are: *Sea of Love, Black Rain, Parenthood, When Harry Met Sally...*, and *sex, lies and videotape.*	Sept. 27
		The House votes, 239-190, to reject a Democratic alternative to a capital gains tax cut backed by Pres. Bush. The vote is a galling wound for the new House Democratic leadership, which saw 64 party members defect to join 175 Republicans in supporting the tax cut.... Insurance industry analysts say that Hurricane Hugo September 21-22 is the costliest storm ever to hit the U.S. mainland, with total damages estimated at $4 bil.		Meeting in Philadelphia, the Episcopal Church's House of Bishops reaffirms the church's decision to ordain women, but it notes that opposition remains "a recognized theological position" within the church.	Sept. 28
Federal and local law enforcement agents in Los Angeles seize at least 22 tons of cocaine, with a street value of $6 bil. to $7 bil., and $10 mil. in cash in what officials describe as the largest seizure of illegal drugs in history.		NWA Inc. agrees to reduce KLM Royal Dutch Airlines's 70% equity stake in Northwest Airlines, which KLM obtained by investing $400 mil. in Alfred A. Checchi's June takeover of NWA, Northwest's corporate parent.... Pres. Bush signs a $18.56 bil. energy and water bill that includes $1.1 bil. for water projects, $1.66 bil. for cleanup of the nation's nuclear weapons plants; and $225 mil. in start-up costs for a superconducting supercollider in north-central Texas.		The Senate votes to confirm John E. Frohnmayer as chairman of the National Endowment for the Arts. ... Dancer Mikhail Baryshnikov abruptly resigns as artistic director of the American Ballet Theater in New York City, one year earlier than Baryshnikov's planned departure.... *Publishers Weekly*'s hardback fiction best-sellers for the week are: *Clear and Present Danger*, Tom Clancy; *The Pillars of the Earth*, Ken Follett; *California Gold*, John Jakes; *The Russia House*, John le Carre; and *The Old Silent*, by Martha Grimes.	Sept. 29
				Virgil Garnett Thomson, 92, Kansas-born composer and music critic, dies at his home in New York City. He collaborated with Gertrude Stein on the operas *Four Saints in Three Acts* (1934) and *The Mother of Us All* (1947), and won a Pulitzer Prize in music for the score of the documentary film *Louisiana Story* (1949). Chief music critic for the *New York Herald Tribune* from 1940, his *Virgil Thomson Reader* won a 1982 National Book Critics Circle Award.... *Billboard*'s best-selling albums for the week are: *Girl You Know It's True*, Milli Vanilli; *Hangin' Tough*, New Kids on the Block; *Forever Your Girl*, Paula Abdul; *Steel Wheels*, Rolling Stones; and *Repeat Offender*, Richard Marx.	Sept. 30

F	G	H	I	J
Includes elections, federal-state relations, civil rights and liberties, crime, the judiciary, education, health care, poverty, urban affairs and population.	*Includes formation and debate of U.S. foreign and defense policies, veterans' affairs and defense spending. (Relations with specific foreign countries are usually found under the region concerned.)*	*Includes business, labor, agriculture, taxation, transportation, consumer affairs, monetary and fiscal policy, natural resources, and pollution.*	*Includes worldwide scientific, medical and technological developments, natural phenomena, U.S. weather, natural disasters, and accidents.*	*Includes the arts, religion, scholarship, communications media, sports, entertainments, fashions, fads and social life.*

	World Affairs	Europe	Africa & the Middle East	The Americas	Asia & the Pacific
Oct. 1	Pakistan rejoins the Commonwealth of Nations, 17 years after withdrawing to protest the organization's recognition of the newly independent nation of Bangladesh.	At its annual conference in Brighton, Sussex, the British Labour Party adopts a major package of reforms—including an end to its call for unilateral British nuclear disarmament—intended to move the party toward the political center.			China celebrates the 40th anniversary of communist rule with a day of parades and fireworks in Beijing's Tiananmen Square staged amid extremely tight security. . . . In the wake of a summer of scandals and electoral setbacks that have left Japan's ruling Liberal Democratic Party staggering, the party wins a by-election for a seat in the upper house of the Diet.
Oct. 2		Yugoslavia's federal government reports that inflation rose to 1,181% in September, up from 893.8% in August and 217% in September 1988.			
Oct. 3	The price of raw coffee falls in major international markets to a 14-year low when Brazil, the world's largest producer, dashes hopes of a new International Coffee Agreement. Export quotas were suspended in July.	East Germany suspends unrestricted travel to Czechoslovakia, effectively closing its border with that country, in a move aimed at stemming the flow of would-be emigres from East Germany to West Germany. . . . The European Community approves a plan to regulate television transmissions beginning in October 1991. Belgium and Denmark oppose the measure.		The government of Panama's Gen. Manuel Antonio Noriega accuses the United States of backing a failed coup attempt during which Noriega was briefly held by officers of the Panamanian Defense Forces. . . . In Washington, D.C., Pres. Bush and Mexico's Pres. Carlos Salinas de Gortari sign an agreement intended to expand bilateral trade and investment with the United States.	Tokyo's district court upholds the constitutionality of a decision by the education ministry to censor passages in a textbook describing Japanese brutality during Japan's invasion of China in the 1930s.
Oct. 4	A Washington, D.C., federal judge sentences convicted Lebanese hijacker Fawaz Younis to 30 years in prison for the 1985 seizure of a Royal Jordanian Airlines plane in Beirut.	More than 17,000 East German refugees have immigrated to West Germany from Czechoslovakia and Poland over the last four days with the permission of the East German government. . . . Eighteen East Germans who sought asylum yesterday at the U.S. Embassy in East Berlin leave the facility after receiving an East German promise that they would be allowed to immigrate to West Germany.			The Khmer People's National Liberation Front, one of three rebel factions fighting the Vietnamese-backed government of Cambodia, launches a "general offensive" against Vietnam-backed Cambodian Army troops.
Oct. 5	The Nobel Peace Prize is awarded to Tibet's exiled religious and political leader, the Dalai Lama, for his efforts to free his homeland from Chinese rule using nonviolent means.		Jonas Savimbi, Angola's rebel leader, agrees to resume cease-fire talks with Zaire's Pres. Mobutu Sese Seko.	According to the Canadian Centre for Justice Statistics, there were 575 homicides nationwide in 1988, 10% fewer than in 1987 and well under the average of 647 killings a year over the past 10 years.	The Australian government announces that it is deferring for one year a decision on whether to allow the reopening of an abandoned mine in a mineral-rich region near Kakadu National Park.
Oct. 6		East Germany celebrates its 40th anniversary amid escalating opposition protests and the continuing flow of East German refugees to West Germany.	Israel's divided coalition cabinet rejects Egyptian Pres. Hosni Mubarak's Middle East peace initiative, at least temporarily, amid some confusion about a proposed American compromise.	P.M. Brian Mulroney nominates Ramon Hnatyshyn to succeed Jeanne Sauve as the 24th governor general of Canada, the representative of the reigning British monarch, who is Canada's head of state. . . . The number of divorces in Canada rose 11% in 1987 over the previous year, according to a Statistics Canada report. There were 86,985 divorces nationwide in 1987, compared with 78,160 in 1986.	

A	B	C	D	E
Includes developments that affect more than one world region, international organizations and important meetings of major world leaders.	Includes all domestic and regional developments in Europe, including the Soviet Union, Turkey, Cyprus and Malta.	Includes all domestic and regional developments in Africa and the Middle East, including Iraq and Iran and excluding Cyprus, Turkey and Afghanistan.	Includes all domestic and regional developments in Latin America, the Caribbean and Canada.	Includes all domestic and regional developments in Asia and Pacific nations, extending from Afghanistan through all the Pacific Islands, except Hawaii.

U.S. Politics & Social Issues	U.S. Foreign Policy & Defense	U.S. Economy & Environment	Science, Technology & Nature	Culture, Leisure & Life Style	
					Oct. 1
The Texas Supreme Court rules unanimously that the state's school financing system is unconstitutional because of "glaring disparities" in spending between rich and poor districts.		A House subcommittee votes unanimously to apply nationwide California's strict standards on car exhaust, which have also been approved by eight Northeastern states.		The Most Reverend Robert Runcie, Archbishop of Canterbury, ends a four-day visit to the Vatican, where he conferred with Pope John Paul II on possible reunification of the Roman Catholic and Anglican churches.	Oct. 2
Former Mayor Maynard Jackson, a Democrat, wins a landslide victory in Atlanta's nonpartisan mayoral election with 79% of the vote, easily defeating five rivals led by City Councilman Hosea Williams. . . . Two black Democrats—City Council Pres. George L. Forbes and Ohio State Sen. Michael R. White—place first and second in Cleveland's nonpartisan mayoral primary, ahead of three white candidates. . . . Housing and Urban Development Sec. Jack F. Kemp announces a series of reforms designed to end the mismanagement and political influence-peddling that flourished under his predecessor, Samuel R. Pierce Jr.					Oct. 3
The House of Representatives votes, 360-66, to repeal the Medicare Catastrophic Care Act, an addition to the Medicare program providing payment for "catastrophic" medical costs signed into law in 1988.		The United Mine Workers union applies for reaffiliation with the AFL-CIO after 42 years. Under John L. Lewis, the UMW withdrew from the American Federation of Labor in a dispute over the Taft-Hartley Act. . . . A strike by 55,000 machinists of the International Assoc. of Machinists severely crimps Boeing Co.'s production of commercial aircraft; 85% of its members rejected the company's contract offer. . . . Federal Deposit Insurance Corp. Chairman L. William Seidman predicts that the cost of rescuing insolvent thrift institutions could exceed the $50 bil. approved by Congress.			Oct. 4
The New Jersey State government takes control of the Jersey City school system because of the district's failure to meet minimum educational standards.	After denying any U.S. involvement in the failed coup attempt in Panama, senior Bush aides admit that U.S. troops blocked two routes the rebels believed loyalist troops would use to come to the defense of Gen. Manuel Antonio Noriega.	The House passes a $10.9 bil. budget reconciliation bill designed to reduce the federal budget deficit to its 1990 target of $110 bil.	An American Red Cross study shows that the risk of infection with the human immunodeficiency virus through a blood transfusion is dropping by more than 30% each year and is now less than one in 28,000.		Oct. 5
Refusing to follow the House in repealing the Medicare Catastrophic Coverage Act of 1988, the Senate unanimously adopts a scaled-down version of the act, which insures the elderly against catastrophic medical costs.		Pres. Bush formally designates Richard C. Breeden as chairman of the Securities and Exchange Comm. . . . A probe of the Rocky Flats nuclear arms plant near Denver finds dangerous accumulations of plutonium in various exhaust ducts in manufacturing buildings. . . . The nation's unemployment rate rose to 5.2% in September, the Labor Dept. reports. . . . Consumer debt rose $3.48 bil. in August, at an annual 6.0% rate, the Federal Reserve Board reports.		Bette (born Ruth Elizabeth Davis) Davis, 81, legendary Hollywood movie star, dies of breast cancer at a hospital in Neuilly-sur-Seine, France. Her more than 80 films include *Dark Victory* (1941), *All About Eve* (1950), and *What Ever Happened to Baby Jane?* (1962). She won Academy Awards for best actress in *Dangerous* (1935) and *Jezebel* (1938).	Oct. 6

F	G	H	I	J
Includes elections, federal-state relations, civil rights and liberties, crime, the judiciary, education, health care, poverty, urban affairs and population.	*Includes formation and debate of U.S. foreign and defense policies, veterans' affairs and defense spending. (Relations with specific foreign countries are usually found under the region concerned.)*	*Includes business, labor, agriculture, taxation, transportation, consumer affairs, monetary and fiscal policy, natural resources, and pollution.*	*Includes worldwide scientific, medical and technological developments, natural phenomena, U.S. weather, natural disasters, and accidents.*	*Includes the arts, religion, scholarship, communications media, sports, entertainments, fashions, fads and social life.*

	World Affairs	Europe	Africa & the Middle East	The Americas	Asia & the Pacific
Oct. 7		Renaming itself the Hungarian Socialist Party, the ruling Hungarian Socialist Workers' Party becomes the first communist party to renounce Marxism and embrace democratic socialism as its guiding doctrine.... Congress' FY1990 appropriations bill for the Interior Dept. and related agencies contains, for the first time ever, a restriction limiting arts grants on the basis of content.		Argentina's Pres. Carlos Saul Menem pardons 277 military personnel and civilians, including three former ruling military junta members, in a controversial effort at "national reconciliation."	Two Burmese students who yesterday hijacked an airliner with 83 people aboard in an effort to publicize human rights abuses by the military government in Myanmar release their hostages and surrender to Thai authorities.
Oct. 8		Twenty-eight members of the Ulster Defense Regiment are arrested during an early morning sweep by police in Northern Ireland as part of a probe into leaks of sensitive documents by Ulster security forces to Protestant paramilitaries.			Singapore's long-time P.M. Lee Kuan Yew announces that he plans to step down before the end of 1990 and hand over power to his designated successor, Deputy P.M. Goh Chok Tong.
Oct. 9		The Soviet Union's standing legislature, the Supreme Soviet, approves a bill giving workers the legal right to strike, though under severely restricted conditions, for the first time since 1917.			
Oct. 10		With the 10-year-old government of P.M. Margaret Thatcher trailing the Labour Party by 10 percentage points in the polls due to the country's economic problems, Britain's Conservative Party holds its annual conference in Blackpool.	South Africa's Pres. F. W. de Klerk announces the pending unconditional release of Walter Sisulu and seven other black political prisoners, not including African National Congress leader Nelson Mandela.		China's Communist Party Gen. Sec. Jiang Zemin has been chosen to act as the "core" of a new generation of leaders, according to the official party newspaper, *People's Daily*, thus becoming the heir apparent to paramount leader Deng Xiaoping.
Oct. 11	The Nobel Prize for economics is awarded to Trygve Haavelmo, a Norwegian professor honored for his pioneering work in econometrics in the 1940s. Professor emeritus at the Univ. of Oslo, Haavelmo devised mathematical statistical methods for testing economic data to determine the accuracy of the underlying theory.	Yannis Grivas, the president of Greece's Supreme Court, is appointed caretaker premier until a general election November 5. Premier Tzannis Tzannetakis resigned on October 7.	The head of the UN Transition Assistance Group in Namibia says the group cannot verify charges that the South-West African People's Org. guerrilla movement detained, tortured, or killed hundreds of suspected spies over the past decade.	Citing the increasing health risk from accumulating toxic pollution for the 35 million people living in the Great Lakes basin, Canadian and U.S. officials issue an urgent call to clean up the Great Lakes. ... Amnesty International, the London-based human rights organization, releases a report charging that sectors of the military, acting with paramilitary groups and often with drug traffickers, have executed thousands of Colombians in the 17 months through May.	
Oct. 12		A Swedish appeals court overturns the conviction of Carl Gustav Christer Pettersson, convicted of the 1986 assassination of Premier Olof Palme.... Poland's Solidarity-led government unveils a detailed program to create a free-market economy modeled on that of highly developed economies and providing for a degree of normalcy in people's everyday lives.	In spite of international protests, the Iraqi Army has succeeded in gaining military control of Iraq's northern Kurdish region, the *Financial Times* reports.		

A	B	C	D	E
Includes developments that affect more than one world region, international organizations and important meetings of major world leaders.	Includes all domestic and regional developments in Europe, including the Soviet Union, Turkey, Cyprus and Malta.	Includes all domestic and regional developments in Africa and the Middle East, including Iraq and Iran and excluding Cyprus, Turkey and Afghanistan.	Includes all domestic and regional developments in Latin America, the Caribbean and Canada.	Includes all domestic and regional developments in Asia and Pacific nations, extending from Afghanistan through all the Pacific Islands, except Hawaii.

U.S. Politics & Social Issues	U.S. Foreign Policy & Defense	U.S. Economy & Environment	Science, Technology & Nature	Culture, Leisure & Life Style	
				Pope John Paul II begins a 10-day visit to South Korea, Indonesia, East Timor, and Mauritius. It is the 44th world trip of his papacy and his fourth visit to Asia.	Oct. 7
Speaking to the National Federation of Republican Women, Pres. Bush says his administration has appointed 139 women to senior positions, more in nine months than any administration has appointed in a given year.... A Gallup Organization Inc. poll initiated by the National Endowment for the Humanities finds that many American college students have only a limited knowledge of history and literature.				The Oakland Athletics win the American League pennant over the Toronto Blue Jays. Oakland left fielder Rickey Henderson wins the American League Championship Series' most valuable player award.... Carroll House wins the Prix de l'Arc de Triomphe in Paris, Europe's richest horse race.	Oct. 8
State and local tax collections rose 7.2% to a total of $428.3 bil. during the year ending June 1988, Commerce Clearing House Inc. reports; state revenues were up 5.9% from the year before and local revenues up 9.4%.			The Nobel Prize for physiology or medicine is awarded to American medical researchers Dr. J. Michael Bishop and Dr. Harold E. Varmus, of the Univ. of California at San Francisco, for their discovery of how normal cell growth can go awry and cause cancer.	The San Francisco Giants win the National League pennant over the Chicago Cubs. Giants first baseman Will Clark wins the most valuable player award in the National League Championship Series	Oct. 9
Meeting in a two-day special session, the Florida state legislature votes down a series of measures proposed by Gov. Bob Martinez (R) that would have restricted access to abortion.					Oct. 10
The House of Representatives narrowly votes to restore Medicaid funds to pay for abortions in cases of rape or incest. Pres. Bush has pledged to veto any bill easing restrictions on federal funding of abortions.... The National Academy of Sciences says that obstetricians are declining to deliver babies because of skyrocketing malpractice costs. The number of doctors and nurse-midwives willing to assist a normal delivery has dropped by 20% in the past five years.		A House Energy subcommittee rejects a key provision of the Bush administration's clean-air plan requiring the production of 1 million automobiles fueled by a clean-burning gasoline alternative for sale in the nation's dirtiest cities.			Oct. 11
The House votes final approval for a bill to prohibit the physical desecration of the American flag before sending the bill to the White House for Pres. Bush's signature.... Lyphomed Inc. announces that it will distribute pentamidine, which is used to prevent pneumonia in people with Acquired Immune Deficiency Syndrome (AIDS), free to health care providers for dispensing to uninsured patients.	The Bush administration is reportedly preparing guidelines for American officials in Panama. The administration has been criticized for not playing an active role in the October 3 coup, despite Pres. Bush's professed support for Gen. Manuel Antonio Noriega's overthrow.... Pres. Bush reportedly sends Congress certification that Pakistan does not possess nuclear weapons. The certification is required annually by U.S. law to allow the release of American aid to Pakistan.	The American Stock Exchange announces that former Democratic Rep. James R. Jones of Oklahoma will be its new chairman.... Several major U.S. banks including Chemical New York Corp., Bank of New York Co., and Chase Manhattan Corp. report heavy third-quarter losses caused by reserve increases to cover loans to Third World countries and domestic businesses.	The Nobel Prize for chemistry is awarded to Sidney Altman, Yale Univ., and Thomas Cech, Univ. of Colorado, for their independent discoveries concerning the nature of the genetic material RNA (ribonucleic acid).... The Nobel Prize for physics is shared by Norman F. Ramsey, Harvard Univ., for research that led to the development of the atomic clock, and by Hans Dehmelt, Univ. of Washington, Seattle, and Wolfgang Paul, Univ. of Bonn, West Germany, for developing methods of isolating atoms and subatomic particles for prolonged study.... National Aeronautics and Space Admin. researchers say that the concentration of ozone over the South Pole is at the lowest level ever recorded.		Oct. 12

F	G	H	I	J
Includes elections, federal-state relations, civil rights and liberties, crime, the judiciary, education, health care, poverty, urban affairs and population.	*Includes formation and debate of U.S. foreign and defense policies, veterans' affairs and defense spending. (Relations with specific foreign countries are usually found under the region concerned.)*	*Includes business, labor, agriculture, taxation, transportation, consumer affairs, monetary and fiscal policy, natural resources, and pollution.*	*Includes worldwide scientific, medical and technological developments, natural phenomena, U.S. weather, natural disasters, and accidents.*	*Includes the arts, religion, scholarship, communications media, sports, entertainments, fashions, fads and social life.*

	World Affairs	Europe	Africa & the Middle East	The Americas	Asia & the Pacific
Oct. 13		In Britain inflation ran at a 7.6% rate for the 12 months ending September, according to government statistics. Inflation and interest rates are the highest of any major Western industrialized nation.		A decision by the Royal Canadian Mounted Police to allow Sikh officers to wear traditional turbans, retain their traditional beards and carry Sikh ceremonial daggers while on duty causes a furor.	
Oct. 14			The *Washington Post* reports that Nelson Mandela, South Africa's preeminent prisoner and acknowledged head of the African National Congress, negotiated the release of Walter Sisulu and others after months of secret negotiations with South African officials.	Less than two weeks after Colombia's Supreme Court upheld the extradition of drug suspects, the government flies three reputed cocaine traffickers to the United States to face trial.	
Oct. 15			Shortly after their dawn release by South African authorities, Walter Sisulu and seven senior members of the African National Congress (ANC) hold a news conference in Soweto that appears to mark the de facto unbanning of the ANC.		With Filipino opinion split about whether the body of Ferdinand E. Marcos should be buried in his native province of Ilocos Norte, the deposed president is buried in Honolulu, Hawaii.
Oct. 16	Tokyo's stock exchange, the first major market to open after Wall Street's October 13 sell-off, falls 647.33 points, to 34,468.69. The London market index closes down 70.5 points, at 2163.4.	The minority center-right coalition government of Norway's Premier Jan Syse is sworn in. Socialist Premier Gro Harlem Brundtland resigned October 13 after inconclusive elections in September.	The 103-nation Convention on International Trade in Endangered Species votes to ban all trade in ivory in an effort to save Africa's dwindling elephant herds from further decimation at the hands of poachers.... Libya's Col. Muammer el-Qaddafi and Egypt's Pres. Hosni Mubarak hold discussions marking a new stage in Qaddafi's efforts to ease his government's international isolation.		
Oct. 17	On the Tokyo stock exchange, the Nikkei index rises to close at 34,996.08, but the London market does not respond positively to Wall Street's recovery, and closes down at 2135.5.	Amnesty International praises the Soviet Union for dramatic improvements in human rights, particularly in the drop in political arrests and the increased numbers of prisoners released from psychiatric hospitals.			In a surprise decision, P.M. Rajiv Gandhi calls for parliamentary elections to be held in India in late November, two months ahead of schedule. The national elections will be India's first since 1984.
Oct. 18	The UN General Assembly elects five new nonpermanent members to the Security Council. Cuba, Romania, and South Yemen are considered hard-line Marxist countries resistant to Soviet Pres. Mikhail S. Gorbachev's reforms. The other countries are Zaire and Ivory Coast.... Chinese dissident physicist Fang Lizhi, who has been confined to the U.S. Embassy in Beijing since June, is named the winner of the sixth annual Robert F. Kennedy Human Rights Award.	The Central Committee of East Germany's Socialist Unity Party removes Erich Honecker as the nation's leader after 18 years and replaces him with Politburo member Egon Krenz.... The Hungarian National Assembly makes 94 changes to the nation's 1949 constitution to pave the way for multiparty free elections in 1990. The amended constitution will remain in effect only until the new National Assembly is seated, when a new constitution will be drafted.		In San Jose, Costa Rica, little progress is reported in peace talks between the leftist rebels of the Farabundo Marti National Liberation Front and the rightist Salvadoran government.	A series of strong earthquakes hits northern China, leaving at least 29 people dead and destroying between 5,000 and 8,000 houses, the official New China news agency reports.

A	B	C	D	E
Includes developments that affect more than one world region, international organizations and important meetings of major world leaders.	*Includes all domestic and regional developments in Europe, including the Soviet Union, Turkey, Cyprus and Malta.*	*Includes all domestic and regional developments in Africa and the Middle East, including Iraq and Iran and excluding Cyprus, Turkey and Afghanistan.*	*Includes all domestic and regional developments in Latin America, the Caribbean and Canada.*	*Includes all domestic and regional developments in Asia and Pacific nations, extending from Afghanistan through all the Pacific Islands, except Hawaii.*

U.S. Politics & Social Issues	U.S. Foreign Policy & Defense	U.S. Economy & Environment	Science, Technology & Nature	Culture, Leisure & Life Style	
Common Cause asks the Senate Ethics Committee and the Justice Dept. to open inquiries into Senators Alan Cranston (D, Calif.), John Glenn (D, Ohio), John McCain (R, Ariz.), Donald Riegle (D, Mich.) and Dennis DeConcini (D, Ariz.), who intervened with federal regulators on behalf of the Lincoln Savings and Loan Assoc. and its owner Charles H. Keating.	At a White House news conference, Pres. Bush defends his administration's response to the recent Panama coup attempt and reiterates his wish to see Panamanian military leader Gen. Manuel Antonio Noriega removed from power.	The Dow Jones industrial average drops 190 points, its biggest plunge since the October 1987 market crash.... The government's producer price index rose 0.9% in September, the Labor Dept. reports.	Scientists at the rival Stanford Linear Accelerator Center in Palo Alto and the European Center for Nuclear Research in Geneva, Switzerland, announce that they have now established that the universe contains no more than three fundamental kinds of matter.	Archaeologists report the discovery of the remains of the Globe Theater, where many of William Shakespeare's plays were first performed, at a site just south of the River Thames near London's Southwark Bridge.	Oct. 13
					Oct. 14
					Oct. 15
	In one of several steps by the West to support reform in the USSR, Poland, and Hungary, the United States offers to provide the Soviet Union with advisers to help that country restructure its beleaguered economy.	E. Robert Wallach is sentenced in New York City to six years in prison following his conviction on racketeering charges connected with the scandal-ridden Wedtech Corp. Codefendants W. Franklyn Chinn and Rusty Kent London are also sentenced.... The Dow Jones industrial average rises 88 points, easing fears of more turmoil in the financial markets following the 190-point drop of October 13.... Pres. Bush signs an order imposing $16.1 bil. in automatic spending cuts across the board because the government failed to meet the Gramm-Rudman deficit-reduction law deadline.			Oct. 16
Bush administration officials announce that the president has chosen Dr. Antonia Novello, deputy director of the National Institute of Child Health and Human Development, to succeed Dr. C. Everett Koop as surgeon general.		The Federal Reserve Board reports that its industrial output index declined 0.1% in September. ... The Fed reports that factories, mines, and utilities operated at 83.6% of capcity in September.... The House Banking Committee begins hearings into the collapse of Lincoln Savings and Loan Assoc. in Irvine, Calif. The cost of the federal bailout is reportedly $2.5 bil., more than any thrift failure to date.	An earthquake initially calculated as 6.9 on the open-ended Richter scale of ground motion destroys buildings and roadways in the San Francisco Bay area and surrounding regions. The quake's epicenter is located near Loma Prieta peak in the Santa Cruz Mountains, about 75 miles south of San Francisco. ... The World Psychiatric Assoc. votes to readmit the Soviet Union after a public acknowledgement by the Soviets of earlier abuses of psychiatry for political reasons.		Oct. 17
Settling the first of four cases involving sexual misconduct pending before the committee, the House Ethics Committee disciplines Rep. Jim Bates (D, Calif.) for sexually harassing his female staff members.		The Census Bureau reports that the median U.S. family income fell from $32,251 in 1987 to $32,191 in 1988; the poverty rate edged down from 13.4% to 13.1%.... According to an analysis by Robert Greenstein of the nonprofit Center on Budget Priorities, the gap between the nation's richest and poorest families widened to an all-time record.	The space shuttle *Atlantis* carries the Galileo spacecraft into orbit on a six-year journey to the planet Jupiter. The $1.4 bil. robot spacecraft is to probe the Jovian atmosphere and tour the Jovian moons beginning in 1995. Its photographs are expected to be 1,000 times as sharp as those returned by the Voyager spacecraft in 1979.		Oct. 18

F	G	H	I	J
Includes elections, federal-state relations, civil rights and liberties, crime, the judiciary, education, health care, poverty, urban affairs and population.	*Includes formation and debate of U.S. foreign and defense policies, veterans' affairs and defense spending. (Relations with specific foreign countries are usually found under the region concerned.)*	*Includes business, labor, agriculture, taxation, transportation, consumer affairs, monetary and fiscal policy, natural resources, and pollution.*	*Includes worldwide scientific, medical and technological developments, natural phenomena, U.S. weather, natural disasters, and accidents.*	*Includes the arts, religion, scholarship, communications media, sports, entertainments, fashions, fads and social life.*

	World Affairs	Europe	Africa & the Middle East	The Americas	Asia & the Pacific
Oct. 19	After three days of talks in Madrid, British and Argentine negotiators announce that the two nations will reestablish consular relations, broken off by the 1982 war over the Falkland (Malvinas) Islands.	Following a long campaign to free the "Guildford Four," the British Court of Appeal voids the convictions of Patrick Armstrong, Paul Hill, Gerard Conlon, and Carole Richardson for the 1974 bombings of pubs in Guildford and Woolwich that killed seven people and injured almost 90. . . . Hungary's National Assembly formally legalizes Hungary's opposition political parties and abolishes the authority of the ruling Socialist Party to base party organizing committees at workplaces.			
Oct. 20					
Oct. 21			With grain harvests in parts of Ethiopia only 15% the normal yield, the World Food Program calls for donations of 240,000 tons of food relief to prevent a famine that could affect 1.7 million people by March 1990.	A Honduran jetliner carrying 146 people crashes into the side of a mountain in Las Mesitas, Honduras, killing 131 people. The crash is believed to be the worst air disaster in Central American history. . . . Pres. Bush signs a $9 mil. aid package to assist opposition parties challenging the ruling Sandinista National Liberation Front in Nicaraguan elections scheduled for February 1990.	
Oct. 22	The Commonwealth Heads of Government meeting in Malaysia call for continued economic sanctions against South Africa, but Britain's P.M. Margaret Thatcher is criticized for issuing Britain's own statement on South Africa just half an hour after the group's official communique.		After weeks of negotiations in Saudi Arabia, Christian and Moslem members of Lebanon's parliament agree in principle on a new national charter. Christian and Moslem militia leaders in Lebanon condemn the accord.		
Oct. 23		Addressing the Supreme Soviet, Soviet Foreign Min. Eduard A. Shevardnadze says his country's 1979 military intervention in Afghanistan was illegal and that the Krasnoyarsk radar complex violates the 1972 antiballistic missile treaty. . . . Hungary marks the 33rd anniversary of the 1956 uprising with a "day of national reconciliation" during which acting Pres. Matyas Szuros proclaims Hungary a free republic.		The results of a nationwide public opinion poll indicate that four out of five Canadians oppose the proposed 9% federal value-added tax on goods and services, scheduled to take effect in 1991.	The communist Khmer Rouge, largest of the three resistance factions battling Cambodia's Vietnamese-backed government, announces that it has seized the key western town of Pailin from government troops.
Oct. 24	Noting that the United States regularly deports illegal immigrants from Haiti and Mexico, P.M. Margaret Thatcher criticizes U.S. condemnation of Britain's policy of deporting Vietnamese refugees from Hong Kong.	Two days before a Warsaw Pact summit in Poland, a Polish government editorial says "We see [the USSR] as the main guarantor of our security. But we want to arrange our internal affairs in a sovereign way."			The New York Times reports that U.S. officials are increasingly concerned that North Korea is developing the capability to produce nuclear weapons. . . . In South Korea, 36 students are sentenced to prison terms of from 30 months to life for their involvement in a May protest at Dongui Univ. during which seven riot policemen died; 35 others receive suspended sentences.

A	B	C	D	E
Includes developments that affect more than one world region, international organizations and important meetings of major world leaders.	Includes all domestic and regional developments in Europe, including the Soviet Union, Turkey, Cyprus and Malta.	Includes all domestic and regional developments in Africa and the Middle East, including Iraq and Iran and excluding Cyprus, Turkey and Afghanistan.	Includes all domestic and regional developments in Latin America, the Caribbean and Canada.	Includes all domestic and regional developments in Asia and Pacific nations, extending from Afghanistan through all the Pacific Islands, except Hawaii.

U.S. Politics & Social Issues	U.S. Foreign Policy & Defense	U.S. Economy & Environment	Science, Technology & Nature	Culture, Leisure & Life Style	
The Senate approves, 67-31, a $157.6 bil. spending bill for the Education, Labor, and Health and Human Services departments. The bill also reinstates federal funding for Medicaid abortions in cases of rape or incest.... Only a week after Congress approved a legislative statute aimed at outlawing desecration of the American flag without altering the Constitution, the Senate rejects a constitutional amendment to bar desecration of the American flag.	The House of Representatives votes, 345-47, to approve an $837.5 mil. aid package for Poland and Hungary. The bill is sent to the Senate.	The merchandise trade deficit rose to a seasonally adjusted $10.77 bil. in August, the Commerce Dept. reports.... The consumer price index rose 0.2% in September, the Labor Dept. reports.		The Nobel Prize for literature is awarded to Spanish author Camilo Jose Cela. He has written 10 novels, including *The Family of Pascual Duarte* (1942), and *The Hive* (1951), and published the literary magazine *Papeles de Son Armadans*, which printed articles by opposition figures during the fascist regime of Gen. Francisco Franco.	Oct. 19
The Senate convicts U.S. District Judge Alcee L. Hastings of Florida of eight impeachment articles and removes him from office.... A New York City jury convicts Rep. Robert Garcia (D, N.Y.) and his wife, Jane Lee Garcia, of extortion and conspiracy for their role in the Wedtech Corp. bribery and corruption scandal.			Thirty-nine Antarctic Treaty signatories agree to a special round of negotiations in 1990 on a "comprehensive protection system" for Antarctica.		Oct. 20
Pres. Bush vetoes an appropriations bill that includes a provision allowing the use of Medicaid funds to pay for abortions for poor women who are the victims of rape or incest.... The Food and Drug Admin. approves the distribution DDI, or dideoxyinosine, an experimental drug that has been shown to help stop the multiplication in the body of the virus that causes Acquired Immune Deficiency Syndrome (AIDS).	The Defense Dept. has reportedly rejected a Pentagon study urging the military to consider easing its ban on homosexual personnel.				Oct. 21
				In auto racing, Alain Prost clinches the season Formula One driving title.... World chess champion Gary Kasparov of the Soviet Union easily wins two games in New York City against the world's top chess computer, Deep Thought, which recently beat several grandmasters.	Oct. 22
		Pres. Bush signs into law a FY1990 appropriations bill for the Interior Dept. and related agencies.	The *Atlantis* successfully completes the space shuttle program's 31st mission, during which it launched the Galileo spacecraft on a six-year journey to Jupiter.		Oct. 23
The Pennsylvania House votes overwhelmingly to approve a series of restrictions on abortion that would make Pennsylvania's abortion laws among the strictest in the nation.... Television evangelist Jim Bakker is sentenced to 45 years in prison and fined $500,000 for fraud and conspiracy convictions in connection with the PTL television ministry scandal.					Oct. 24

F	G	H	I	J
Includes elections, federal-state relations, civil rights and liberties, crime, the judiciary, education, health care, poverty, urban affairs and population.	Includes formation and debate of U.S. foreign and defense policies, veterans' affairs and defense spending. (Relations with specific foreign countries are usually found under the region concerned.)	Includes business, labor, agriculture, taxation, transportation, consumer affairs, monetary and fiscal policy, natural resources, and pollution.	Includes worldwide scientific, medical and technological developments, natural phenomena, U.S. weather, natural disasters, and accidents.	Includes the arts, religion, scholarship, communications media, sports, entertainments, fashions, fads and social life.

	World Affairs	Europe	Africa & the Middle East	The Americas	Asia & the Pacific
Oct. 25		Defying the government, more than 100 members of the Czechoslovak official press sign a petition demanding the release of two editors of the leading dissident newspaper *Lidove Noviny* (People's News).			South Korea agrees to purchase 120 advanced jet fighter planes from the United States at an estimated cost of $2 bil.... Standard & Poor's Corp. drops Australia's credit rating for the second time in three years. Australia's deficit on current account, which measures trade in goods and services, rose to $1.38 bil. in September.
Oct. 26		Chancellor of the Exchequer Nigel Lawson, Britain's top economic official, resigns over policy differences with P.M. Margaret Thatcher, who names Foreign Sec. John Major as his successor.... The foreign ministers of the seven Warsaw Pact nations meet in Warsaw in the first meeting of the alliance in Poland since the Solidarity-led government came to power.	Israel is reported to have secretly aided a South African program to develop an intermediate-range ballistic missile capable of carrying a nuclear warhead, in exchange for which South Africa provided uranium for Israel's own atomic weapons program.		Australia's consumer price index rose 2.3% in the three months through September, or at an annual rate of 8%, the government reports.
Oct. 27		The East German government announces an amnesty for those who have fled the country and for those who have been jailed or are facing prosecution for demonstrating.		P.M. Brian Mulroney announces that Canada will join the Org. of American States (OAS). Canada's formal entry is to take place at an OAS meeting scheduled for November.... Costa Rica reaches agreement with its commercial bank creditors on a proposal to reduce the nation's $1.8 bil. foreign debt by about $1 bil.	
Oct. 28		Riot police use clubs to break up a 10,000-strong pro-democracy protest in Prague, Czechoslovakia.			Former Pres. Ronald Reagan and his wife, Nancy, visit Japan as guests of the Fujisankei Communications Group, a leading media conglomerate that reportedly paid Reagan $2 mil. to give two 20-minute speeches.... Chinese authorities announce that army troops stationed in Beijing to enforce martial law since May 20 will be withdrawn from the capital and replaced with local police forces.
Oct. 29		Spain's Premier Felipe Gonzalez is reelected to a third four-year term when his Socialist Workers Party earns a one-seat majority in the Spanish Cortes.	In one of the largest political gatherings ever held in South Africa, nearly 70,000 people attend a rally for the African National Congress, which is still officially banned, at a soccer stadium near Soweto.		
Oct. 30		Turkey and Bulgaria hold talks in Kuwait on the issue of Bulgaria's ethnic Turks, some 300,000 of whom migrated to Turkey during the summer because of fear of persecution by the Bulgarian government.			The government of Japan, which imports 40% of the world's ivory supply, announces a total ban on the import of ivory in accordance with action by the Convention on International Trade in Endangered Species.

A	B	C	D	E
Includes developments that affect more than one world region, international organizations and important meetings of major world leaders.	*Includes all domestic and regional developments in Europe, including the Soviet Union, Turkey, Cyprus and Malta.*	*Includes all domestic and regional developments in Africa and the Middle East, including Iraq and Iran and excluding Cyprus, Turkey and Afghanistan.*	*Includes all domestic and regional developments in Latin America, the Caribbean and Canada.*	*Includes all domestic and regional developments in Asia and Pacific nations, extending from Afghanistan through all the Pacific Islands, except Hawaii.*

U.S. Politics & Social Issues	U.S. Foreign Policy & Defense	U.S. Economy & Environment	Science, Technology & Nature	Culture, Leisure & Life Style	
The House falls 51 votes short of the two-thirds majority needed to override Pres. Bush's veto of a bill that included provisions for the use of Medicaid funds to pay for abortions in certain instances.... Rep. Bill Alexander (D, Ark.) files eight new charges accusing House Minority Whip Newt Gingrich (R, Ga.) of violating congressional rules and federal statutes. Alexander filed a 10-count complaint in April.	Declaring that Nicaragua still poses ''an unusual and extraordinary threat to the national security and foreign policy of the United States,'' Pres. Bush extends 1985 trade sanctions against Nicaragua.			Mary Therese McCarthy, 77, novelist, critic, and one of America's preeminent literary figures for five decades, dies of cancer in New York City. Much of her work, including *Memories of a Catholic Girlhood* (1957) and the novel *The Group* (1963), are autobiographical.... *Variety*'s top-grossing films for the week are: *Look Who's Talking*, *The Fabulous Baker Boys*, *Sea of Love*, *Next of Kin*, and *Black Rain*.	Oct. 25
The federal government enacts a $4.15 bil. aid package for quake-stricken northern California; the official death toll stands at 63, with some 3,000 people injured and 14,000 made homeless.... The Food and Drug Admin. agrees to allow the use of AZT (zidovudine, or azidothymidine) in children who have Acquired Immune Deficiency Syndrome (AIDS), and Burroughs Wellcome Co. says it plans to distribute AZT free to children with AIDS.		Environmentalists say that a Bush administration proposal to revise the nation's pesticide laws would ease standards for cancer risk from pesticides in foods and prevent states from setting more stringent standards.... The nation's three major auto companies report reduced operating profits for the third quarter, and all show losses on U.S. automobile manufacturing. ... Gross national product grew at a 2.5% annual rate in the third quarter, the Commerce Dept. reports.	Officials put the death toll from the October 17 Loma Prieta earthquake that hit San Francisco at 63.	The owners of National Football League teams elect Washington, D.C., lawyer Paul Tagliabue as the league's new commissioner. He succeeds Pete Rozelle who was commissioner for 30 years.... Britain's most prestigious fiction award, the Booker Prize, is awarded to Japanese-born author Kazuo Ishiguro for his third novel, *The Remains of the Day*.	Oct. 26
Pres. Bush vetoes an appropriations bill for the District of Columbia because of his objection to a provision that allows the use of federal or district funds for abortions.... Appearing a second time before a House Government Operations subcommittee, former Housing and Urban Development Sec. Samuel R. Pierce Jr. refuses to answer questions from the panel.... Two days of rioting at the Pennsylvania State Correctional Institution at Camp Hill leave more than 120 people injured and damage or destroy 14 of the prison's 31 buildings.	After several months of negotiations with the Senate Intelligence Committee, Pres. Bush agrees to notify Congress in advance or within ''a few days'' of nearly all the government's covert actions.	Consumer spending rose 0.2%, to a $3.526 trillion annual rate in September, while personal income rose 0.3%, to a $4.469 trillion annual rate, the Commerce Dept. reports.		Jane Pauley announces that she will quit as co-host of NBC's morning ''Today'' show in January, reportedly because the network hired news anchorwoman Deborah Norville two months before.... *Publishers Weekly*'s hardback fiction best-sellers for the week are: *Clear and Present Danger*, Tom Clancy; *The Pillars of the Earth*, Ken Follett; *California Gold*, John Jakes; *Jimmy Stewart and His Poems*, Jimmy Stewart; and *Star Trek: The Lost Years*, J. M. Dillard.	Oct. 27
	Former Pres. Richard M. Nixon travels to China for six days of talks with senior Chinese leaders. Nixon is the most prominent American to visit the country since the collapse of the student-led democracy movement.			After an 11-day delay caused by the October 17 Loma Prieta earthquake, the Oakland Athletics complete a four-game sweep of the San Francisco Giants to win the World Series. Oakland pitching ace Dave Stewart is named most valuable player.... *Billboard*'s best-selling albums for the week are: Janet Jackson's *Rhythm Nation 1814*, Janet Jackson; *Girl You Know It's True*, Milli Vanilli; *Dr. Feelgood*, Motley Crue; *Steel Wheels*, Rolling Stones; and *Forever Your Girl*, Paula Abdul.	Oct. 28
Personal and household crime rose by 3.1% in 1988, according to final figures from the Justice Dept.'s annual National Crime Survey. The number of personal crimes (including robbery, rape, assault and personal theft) increased by more than 600,000 from 1987, to a total of about 20 million. The number of household crimes (including burglary and motor vehicle theft) remained at about 15.8 million.					Oct. 29
		Mitsubishi Estate Co. of Japan pays $846 mil. to acquire a 51% stake in Rockefeller Center Group, thereby getting a controlling interest in New York City's Rockefeller Center/Radio City Music Hall complex.... The Food and Drug Admin. is drafting new rules to help curb health claims on packaged food, the White House announces.		Singer Bette Midler wins a $400,000 federal court jury verdict in Los Angeles against the advertising agency Young & Rubicam for using a ''sound-alike'' singer in a television commercial.	Oct. 30
F	G	H	I	J	
Includes elections, federal-state relations, civil rights and liberties, crime, the judiciary, education, health care, poverty, urban affairs and population.	*Includes formation and debate of U.S. foreign and defense policies, veterans' affairs and defense spending. (Relations with specific foreign countries are usually found under the region concerned.)*	*Includes business, labor, agriculture, taxation, transportation, consumer affairs, monetary and fiscal policy, natural resources, and pollution.*	*Includes worldwide scientific, medical and technological developments, natural phenomena, U.S. weather, natural disasters, and accidents.*	*Includes the arts, religion, scholarship, communications media, sports, entertainments, fashions, fads and social life.*	

	World Affairs	Europe	Africa & the Middle East	The Americas	Asia & the Pacific
Oct. 31		Hungary's National Assembly votes to hold a national referendum on a method of choosing a president. The referendum will be held November 26, when Hungarians were to have picked a president by popular vote.... Turkey's parliament elects Turgut Ozal, premier since 1983, to a seven-year term as the nation's president. Opposition parties boycott the election process.			
Nov. 1		East Germany reopens its border with Czechoslovakia, spurring a huge new movement of refugees to West Germany. The Czechoslovak border has been closed since October 3 to quell the flow of would-be emigres.		Amid a barrage of criticism, Nicaragua's Pres. Daniel Ortega Saavedra announces an end to a 19-month unilateral cease-fire against the Contra rebels.	Pakistan's P.M. Benazir Bhutto wins a narrow victory in a no-confidence vote in the National Assembly called by the opposition Islamic Democratic Alliance.... The UN General Assembly unanimously passes a resolution calling for an end to armed conflict in Afghanistan between the communist government in Kabul and anticommunist Moslem guerrillas.
Nov. 2				Accusing the Salvadoran government of involvement in the October 31 bombing of a labor federation headquarters in which 10 people died, the Farabundo Marti National Liberation Front withdraws from peace talks that opened the previous month.... Ernesto Ruffo Appel of the National Action Party is sworn in as governor of Baja California Norte, becoming the first opposition governor in Mexico in 60 years. Elections were held in the state July 2.	
Nov. 3	The United States and Soviet Union announce their first cosponsorship of a resolution in the UN General Assembly, for all nations to honor "the principles of sovereign equality, political independence amd nonintervention in internal affairs."	Eco-Glasnost, an environmental group, leads what is believed to be the largest pro-democracy demonstration in Bulgaria's postwar history. An estimated 9,000 people in Sofia call for free elections and other democratic reforms.		Canada's federal government introduces an abortion bill that makes abortion punishable by up to two years in prison, but allows any woman to obtain an abortion if a physican agrees that her mental or physical health would be impaired by carrying the fetus to term.	
Nov. 4		In what is believed to be the biggest protest in East German history, more than 500,000 pro-democracy demonstrators march peacefully in East Berlin.... According to a recent poll, 90% of Soviet citizens consider the country's economic situation bad or critical, 44% think that government bureaucracy hinders economic reform, and 24% think Pres. Mikhail S. Gorbachev's policies will never succeed.	In an indication of their support for the Nigerian government's economic austerity program, Western donor governments approve more than $600 mil. in concessional aid for Nigeria.		

A	B	C	D	E
Includes developments that affect more than one world region, international organizations and important meetings of major world leaders.	*Includes all domestic and regional developments in Europe, including the Soviet Union, Turkey, Cyprus and Malta.*	*Includes all domestic and regional developments in Africa and the Middle East, including Iraq and Iran and excluding Cyprus, Turkey and Afghanistan.*	*Includes all domestic and regional developments in Latin America, the Caribbean and Canada.*	*Includes all domestic and regional developments in Asia and Pacific nations, extending from Afghanistan through all the Pacific Islands, except Hawaii.*

U.S. Politics & Social Issues	U.S. Foreign Policy & Defense	U.S. Economy & Environment	Science, Technology & Nature	Culture, Leisure & Life Style	
	Pres. Bush announces that he and Soviet Pres. Mikhail S. Gorbachev will hold an "interim, informal" summit on ships in the Mediterranean Sea December 2-3.	Congress clears and sends to Pres. Bush a $67 bil. appropriations bill that includes the first funds for construction of a planned orbiting space station and key changes to the federal mortgage market.... Federal and state investigators testify before the House Banking Committee that they discovered evidence of criminal violations by Lincoln Savings and Loan Assoc. officials in 1988.... Sales of new houses dropped 14% in September, to a seasonally adjusted annual rate of 618,000 units, the Commerce Dept. reports.			Oct. 31
	Court documents filed by attorneys for Pan American World Airways suggest that the U.S. government had prior warnings about a possible terrorist attack on Pan Am Flight 103 but failed to act.	The Labor Dept.'s Occupational Safety and Health Admin. proposes record fines of $7.3 mil. against USX Corp. for health and safety violations at two Pennsylvania plants.	The Bush administration extends a ban on federal financing of research using transplanted fetal tissues.... A congressional panel recommends opening for use two small repositories for radioactive waste from the nation's nuclear power plants until a permanent repository at Yucca Mountain, Nev., opens.		Nov. 1
Pres. Bush dismisses speculation that he plans to dump Vice Pres. Dan Quayle as his running mate for the 1992 presidential election.... The *Los Angeles Herald-Examiner* publishes its last edition, leaving the nation's second-largest city with only one major daily newspaper, the *Los Angeles Times*.... The Senate votes, 78-17, to revise a federal law that would allow Oliver L. North to receive his $1,900-a-month Navy pension despite his conviction for shredding government documents.	House and Senate conferees approve a $305 bil. defense authorization for FY1990, which began October 1. The bill awaits final passage in the two houses.	Pres. Bush and congressional Republicans abandon their drive to attach a capital gains tax cut to deficit-reduction legislation or to a bill to raise the federal debt ceiling in the current session of Congress. ... KLM Royal Dutch Airlines announces that it will reduce to 21% from 57% its equity stake in NWA Inc., parent company of Northwest Airlines, in order to comply with an earlier Transportation Dept. demand to do so.... Productivity among the nation's nonfarm businesses increased at a 2.1% annual rate in the third quarter, the Labor Dept. reports.			Nov. 2
For the second time in two weeks, and only the seventh time in U.S. history, the Senate convicts a federal judge, Walter L. Nixon Jr. of Biloxi, Miss., on impeachment articles and removes him from office.		The nation's unemployment rate remained at 5.2% in October, the Labor Dept. reports.... Pres. Bush signs an $18.4 bil. appropriations bill for the Treasury, the Executive Office of the President, the Postal Service and other independent agencies.		According to a fitness study published in the *Journal of the American Medical Association*, even modest amounts of physical exercise can substantially reduce a person's risk of dying of heart disease, cancer and other causes.	Nov. 3
				In horse racing, Sunday Silence wins the Breeders' Cup Classic; other winners are Rhythm (Juvenile); Go For Wand (Juvenile Fillies); Dancing Spree (Sprint); Steinlen (Mile); Bayakoa (Distaff); and Prized (Turf).	Nov. 4

F	G	H	I	J
Includes elections, federal-state relations, civil rights and liberties, crime, the judiciary, education, health care, poverty, urban affairs and population.	*Includes formation and debate of U.S. foreign and defense policies, veterans' affairs and defense spending. (Relations with specific foreign countries are usually found under the region concerned.)*	*Includes business, labor, agriculture, taxation, transportation, consumer affairs, monetary and fiscal policy, natural resources, and pollution.*	*Includes worldwide scientific, medical and technological developments, natural phenomena, U.S. weather, natural disasters, and accidents.*	*Includes the arts, religion, scholarship, communications media, sports, entertainments, fashions, fads and social life.*

	World Affairs	Europe	Africa & the Middle East	The Americas	Asia & the Pacific
Nov. 5		For the second time in five months, Greek elections fail to produce a majority government. The conservative New Democracy party leads in the voting, but fell three seats short of an overall majority.	Lebanese parliamentarians elect Syrian-backed moderate Christian Rene Moawad president and ratify an Arab League-sponsored plan to end Lebanon's civil war. Christian army commander Gen. Michel Aoun and other Christian hard-liners reject Moawad and the accord.		
Nov. 6				For the first time since peace negotiations broke down in June 1988, Nicaraguan officials and Contra rebels open direct talks at the UN in New York City.... The Canadian government announces its acceptance of a U.S.-Canada free-trade ruling against a Canadian fisheries practice concerning the processing of salmon and herring.	
Nov. 7		On the 72nd anniversary of the Soviet Union's Bolshevik Revolution, nationalist and pro-democracy demonstrators stage unprecedented nationwide protests.			
Nov. 8		The Central Committee of East Germany's ruling Socialist Unity Party removes half the remaining full (voting) members of the Politburo in a move believed to have been at the behest of party leader Egon Krenz.... The *Moscow News* reports that more than 250 people who worked at the Chernobyl, Ukraine, nuclear power station or who participated in the subsequent cleanup, have died since the April 1986 catastrophe.	Jordanians go to the polls in the kingdom's first general election in 22 years.		
Nov. 9		East Germany announces a relaxation of restrictions on the travel and immigration of its citizens to the West. "The Berlin Wall no longer divides Berliners," says West Berlin Mayor Walter Momper, and within hours, thousands of jubilant East Germans and West Germans meet at the Berlin Wall for an impromptu celebration that lasts into the next day.		The Nicaraguan Contras replace their seven-member directorate with a new four-member, military-civilian commission that transfers power to younger, less politically involved military commanders.... Amnesty International issues a report stating that Nicaraguan soldiers have summarily executed dozens of peasants in the war against the Contras over the previous three years.	China's paramount leader, Deng Xiaoping, steps down as chairman of the Central Military Commission, his last formal position in the Communist Party leadership.

A	B	C	D	E
Includes developments that affect more than one world region, international organizations and important meetings of major world leaders.	Includes all domestic and regional developments in Europe, including the Soviet Union, Turkey, Cyprus and Malta.	Includes all domestic and regional developments in Africa and the Middle East, including Iraq and Iran and excluding Cyprus, Turkey and Afghanistan.	Includes all domestic and regional developments in Latin America, the Caribbean and Canada.	Includes all domestic and regional developments in Asia and Pacific nations, extending from Afghanistan through all the Pacific Islands, except Hawaii.

U.S. Politics & Social Issues	U.S. Foreign Policy & Defense	U.S. Economy & Environment	Science, Technology & Nature	Culture, Leisure & Life Style	
The first memorial to the civil rights movement in the United States is dedicated at a ceremony in Montgomery, Ala. Commissioned by the Southern Poverty Law Center, the memorial is designed by Maya Lin.				Vladimir Samoylovich Horowitz, 86, Russian-born piano virtuoso, noted for his speed, power, and technical brilliance, dies of an apparent heart attack at his home in New York City. His performances of such Romantic composers as Tchaikovsky and Rachmaninoff were dazzling; many of his more than 150 records were classical best-sellers and he won more than 20 Grammy Awards. In 1933 he married Wanda Toscanini, daughter of conductor Arturo Toscanini. . . . Juma Ikangaa of Tanzania wins the New York City Marathon in a record time of 2:08:01. Ingrid Kristiansen of Norway is the first woman across the line in 2:25:30.	Nov. 5
Testifying as part of a plea-bargain agreement, Charles Lewis, a former friend of Washington, D.C., Mayor Marion S. Barry Jr. (D), testifies that he gave Barry crack cocaine on "more than one occasion."	The United States agrees to return $567 mil. in Iranian assets frozen since 1979. Although the two issues are not related, Pres. Bush later says he hopes Iran will use its influence to help free American hostages in Lebanon.	The *Wall Street Journal* quarterly earnings review report shows that corporate net income in the third quarter at 645 major corporations was down 18% over the year before; after-tax earnings fell 21%. . . . Braniff Inc. suspends operations and puts itself up for sale. The Kansas City-based airline has been operating since September 28 under Chapter 11 bankruptcy protection.		The 300-member National Conference of Catholic Bishops unanimously rules out the so-called pro-choice position as an option for Catholics.	Nov. 6
Democrats sweep three key races in general elections: Virginia's L. Douglas Wilder becomes the first black elected state governor in U.S. history; David N. Dinkins is elected New York City's first black mayor; and Rep. James J. Florio is elected governor of New Jersey. . . . Voters in New York City approve a major revision of the city charter under which the Board of Estimate, ruled unconstitutional, will be dissolved and its power redistributed to the mayor, the City Council, and the Planning Comm.	Philippine Pres. Corazon Aquino visits the United States to meet with Pres. Bush and other officials for talks on economic aid and the future of U.S. military facilities in the country.	Consumer debt increased $606 mil. in September, at a 1% annual rate, the Federal Reserve Board reports. . . . Congress clears legislation raising the federal government's debt ceiling to $3.123 trillion for the current fiscal year, which began Oct. 1. The last-minute action averts financial default by the government.	An international conference on climate change adopts a compromise resolution to stabilize carbon dioxide emissions believed to contribute to atmospheric warming, or the "greenhouse effect."	Baltimore Orioles relief pitcher Gregg Olson is named the American League's top rookie of the year.	Nov. 7
Former Air Force Maj. Gen. Richard V. Secord pleads guilty to one count of making a false statement to congressional investigators probing the Iran-Contra arms scandal; 11 other charges against Secord are dropped. . . . The Senate sends to the White House a $17.2 bil. appropriations bill for the departments of Commerce, Justice and State and the federal judiciary, and that also provides for reparations to Japanese-Americans held in World War II internment camps.		The Senate passes, 89-8, legislation that increases the minimum wage from $3.35 to $4.25 an hour by 1991, and that sets a lower minimum wage for teenagers.		The National League's top rookie honors goes to Chicago Cubs center fielder Jerome Walton. . . . *Henry V*, a screen adaptation of William Shakespeare's play about the British king who defeated the French at the battle of Agincourt in 1415, is released in New York. Directed and adapted by Kenneth Branagh, the film stars Branagh, Derek Jacobi, Ian Holm, Judi Dench, Paul Scofield, and Emma Thompson.	Nov. 8
The California Board of Education unanimously adopts new textbook guidelines that support the teaching of evolution. With the largest school system in the nation, California purchases 10% of all school textbooks in the United States. . . . House and Senate conferees reach agreement on a $1.75 bil. measure to expand federal aid for child care. The compromise extends the Head Start program to provide all-day care for children from poor families. . . . The Senate clears a $1.97 bil. FY1990 appropriations bill for the legislative branch. The final version allots some $100 mil. for franking privileges, a dispute over which has dogged the bill's path.		The government's producer price index rose 0.4% in October, the Labor Dept. reports. . . . The House approves, 375-5, oil-spill legislation calling for double hulls on tankers and assigning liability for cleanup. . . . Pres. Bush signs into law a FY1990 appropriations bill for space, housing, environmental, and veterans programs.			Nov. 9

F	G	H	I	J
Includes elections, federal-state relations, civil rights and liberties, crime, the judiciary, education, health care, poverty, urban affairs and population.	*Includes formation and debate of U.S. foreign and defense policies, veterans' affairs and defense spending. (Relations with specific foreign countries are usually found under the region concerned.)*	*Includes business, labor, agriculture, taxation, transportation, consumer affairs, monetary and fiscal policy, natural resources, and pollution.*	*Includes worldwide scientific, medical and technological developments, natural phenomena, U.S. weather, natural disasters, and accidents.*	*Includes the arts, religion, scholarship, communications media, sports, entertainments, fashions, fads and social life.*

	World Affairs	Europe	Africa & the Middle East	The Americas	Asia & the Pacific
Nov. 10		Todor Zhivkov, the longest-serving leader in the Soviet bloc, unexpectedly resigns as Bulgaria's president after 18 years and as secretary general of the Communist Party, which he directed since 1954. Foreign Min. Petar Mladenov is named his successor as secretary general.	In Jordan, King Hussein's hopes for a loyalist, conservative majority in parliament are thwarted by unexpected gains by Muslim fundamentalists, leftist, and Arab nationalist candidates in the November 11 elections.	Canada's P.M. Brian Mulroney and the 10 provincial premiers agree to try to rescue the Meech Lake constitutional accord. Manitoba and New Brunswick have not ratified the accord, the deadline for which is June 1990.	
Nov. 11			Polls in Namibia close after four days of a closely monitored, UN-supervised election to determine the future of what is known as Africa's last colony.		
Nov. 12		Dolores Gomez Ibarruri, 93, Spanish communist, dies of pneumonia and a heart ailment in Madrid. Known as "La Pasionaria" for her impassioned oratory in defense of the republican cause during the Spanish Civil War, in 1939 she fled to the USSR. Upon her return in 1977 she was elected to the Spanish parliament.... *Pravda*, the official newspaper of the Soviet Union's ruling Communist Party says, "There are no other public forces in this country apart from the party of Communists" capable of leading reforms.	Palestinian terrorist leader Abu Nidal is reported to have killed most of the leaders of his Fatah Revolutionary Council (FRC) and buried them in concrete.	The Salvadoran government declares a state of siege two days after the leftist Farabundo Marti National Liberation Front launched the heaviest urban offensive of the 10-year-old civil war.	
Nov. 13		East Germany's Volkskammer (people's chamber, or parliament) confirms the reform-minded Dresden party leader Hans Modrow to replace Willi Stoph as premier. Meanwhile, an estimated 200,000 people hold a pro-democracy rally in Leipzig.... The Soviet Union's 1,400 top economists and managers hold an unprecedented three-day conference in Moscow to debate the future course of Soviet Pres. Mikhail S. Gorbachev's economic reform policies.			
Nov. 14		During a visit by France's visiting Foreign Min. Roland Dumas, Soviet Pres. Mikhail S. Gorbachev warns the West against exploiting the turmoil in Eastern Europe.	According to final results of elections in Namibia, the South-West African People's Org. failed to win the two-thirds margin necessary for it to draft its own constitution for the territory, which is expected to gain independence from South Africa in 1990.		
Nov. 15	At the end of a three-day Vatican conference on Acquired Immune Deficiency Syndrome (AIDS), Pope John Paul II calls for "a global plan to combat AIDS and drug addiction," urges help for AIDS sufferers, and denounces "every form of discrimination" against them.	The East German government announces that nearly 3 million of its citizens have visited West Berlin and that it has issued 7.7 million travel visas to East Germans since the borders opened November 9.	Palestinians in the Israeli-occupied West Bank and Gaza Strip celebrate the first anniversary of the Palestine National Council's declaration of a Palestinian state.	In El Salvador, the military launches heavy counterattacks and routs rebels of the Farabundo Marti National Liberation Front from the "liberated territories" in the suburbs of San Salvador.... Fernando Collor de Mello and Luis Inacio da Silva are the top two vote-getters in the first round of Brazil's first presidential elections in 29 years. A run-off election is scheduled for December 17.... The government of Bolivia's Pres. Jaime Paz Zamora declares a state of siege in response to an increasingly violent national teachers' strike.	Amnesty International asserts that the military government in Myanmar has detained more than 3,000 political prisoners—100 of whom have been sentenced to death—since a crackdown on dissent began in late July.

A	B	C	D	E
Includes developments that affect more than one world region, international organizations and important meetings of major world leaders.	*Includes all domestic and regional developments in Europe, including the Soviet Union, Turkey, Cyprus and Malta.*	*Includes all domestic and regional developments in Africa and the Middle East, including Iraq and Iran and excluding Cyprus, Turkey and Afghanistan.*	*Includes all domestic and regional developments in Latin America, the Caribbean and Canada.*	*Includes all domestic and regional developments in Asia and Pacific nations, extending from Afghanistan through all the Pacific Islands, except Hawaii.*

U.S. Politics & Social Issues	U.S. Foreign Policy & Defense	U.S. Economy & Environment	Science, Technology & Nature	Culture, Leisure & Life Style	
Pres. Bush unveils a housing initiative that he says is designed to "bring basic shelter and affordable housing within reach of millions of Americans."			A report in the journal *Science* says that two experiments that seemed to offer evidence of a postulated "fifth force" in nature have been withdrawn.	*My Left Foot*, the true story of Christy Brown, a working-class Irish boy who overcomes cerebral palsy to become a painter and writer, is released in New York. The film is based on the book by Brown and stars Daniel Day-Lewis and Brenda Fricker, who win Oscars for best actor and supporting actress, respectively.	Nov. 10
			Archaeologists from the Univ. of Chicago have unearthed a mass grave at the site of an Indian civilization that flourished in Bolivia between 300 b.c. and 1200 a.d.		Nov. 11
A series of demonstrations by abortion rights supporters is held in some 150 cities across the United States. The largest—estimated at between 150,000 and 300,000—takes place in Washington, D.C.					Nov. 12
		The Supreme Court upholds, 4-4, a joint operating agreement for a partial merger of the *Detroit News* and the *Detroit Free Press*, which was accorded an antitrust exemption under the Newspaper Preservation Act of 1970.		*The Fabulous Baker Boys*, about two piano-playing brothers (Jeff Bridges and Beau Bridges) who revitalize their tired nightclub act by hiring a sultry female singer (Michelle Pfeiffer), is released in New York.... *Crimes and Misdemeanors*, a film about a hypocritical New York ophthalmologist and obnoxious television producer who prosper while a sincere documentary film maker and compassionate rabbi suffer, opens in New York. Directed and written by Woody Allen, it stars Martin Landau, Anjelica Huston, Alan Alda, and Mia Farrow.	Nov. 13
Republican legislators Lynn Martin (Ill.), Claudine Schneider (R.I.), Nancy L. Johnson (Conn.), and Olympia J. Snowe (Maine) urge Pres. Bush to demonstrate more flexibility regarding the abortion issue.... The Bush administration endorses a Senate bill that would give Puerto Rico the right to decide its future.		The Federal Reserve Board reports that its industrial production index declined 0.7% in October. ... Retail sales fell by 1% in October, to a seasonally adjusted $144.5 bil., the Commerce Dept. reports.	The evidence linking excess blood cholesterol to heart disease is "overwhelming," according to a joint statement by the American Heart Assoc. and the government's National Heart, Lung and Blood Institute.	The National League's Cy Young Award goes to San Diego Padre reliever Mark Davis.	Nov. 14
	The Senate votes, 91-8, to clear a $305 bil. defense authorization.	The Federal Reserve Board reports that capacity utilization fell to 82.8% in October.		Kansas City Royals pitcher Bret Saberhagen is named the American League's Cy Young Award winner.... *The Little Mermaid*, an animated musical version of the Hans Christian Andersen tale about a mermaid who falls in love with a human prince, is released in New York.	Nov. 15

F	G	H	I	J
Includes elections, federal-state relations, civil rights and liberties, crime, the judiciary, education, health care, poverty, urban affairs and population.	Includes formation and debate of U.S. foreign and defense policies, veterans' affairs and defense spending. (Relations with specific foreign countries are usually found under the region concerned.)	Includes business, labor, agriculture, taxation, transportation, consumer affairs, monetary and fiscal policy, natural resources, and pollution.	Includes worldwide scientific, medical and technological developments, natural phenomena, U.S. weather, natural disasters, and accidents.	Includes the arts, religion, scholarship, communications media, sports, entertainments, fashions, fads and social life.

	World Affairs	Europe	Africa & the Middle East	The Americas	Asia & the Pacific
Nov. 16				The murder of six Jesuit priests and two female employees in El Salvador draws widespread condemnation and revives acrimonious debate in Congress over further military aid to the Salvadoran government.... Canada's Supreme Court rules unanimously that a father of a fetus does not have a legal basis for seeking a civil injunction to prevent a woman from obtaining an abortion.	The UN General Assembly approves a resolution calling for creation of a four-way interim government in Cambodia including representatives of the Phnom Penh regime and the three antigovernment resistance groups.
Nov. 17					
Nov. 18		Meeting to discuss the rapid pace of political change in Eastern Europe, leaders of the 12 European Community nations pledge economic aid to countries embracing democracy.			
Nov. 19		Fired by a rumor that a university student was beaten to death by riot police November 17, more than 10,000 people hold a pro-democracy demonstration in Prague, Czechoslovakia.	Pretoria dismisses allegations by three former South African security police who claim they worked with covert police "hit squads" that assassinated opponents of the apartheid government over the years.		
Nov. 20	The UN General Assembly adopts the Convention on the Rights of the Child, the first treaty of its kind. The pact outlines standards on education, adoption, protection from sexual abuse, and other issues.	The Supreme Soviet rejects legislation that would have granted some economic autonomy to all 15 Soviet republics; deputies feel the legislation does not loosen central government control over the republics' economies enough.	One of South Africa's most highly decorated soldiers, retired Col. Jan Breytenbach, claims that National Union for the Total Independence of Angola rebels have slaughtered thousands of elephants for ivory to finance the movement's war effort.	P.M. Brian Mulroney leads a delegation of more than 200 Canadian government and business executives in the first official visit to the USSR by a Canadian prime minister in 18 years.	

A	B	C	D	E
Includes developments that affect more than one world region, international organizations and important meetings of major world leaders.	*Includes all domestic and regional developments in Europe, including the Soviet Union, Turkey, Cyprus and Malta.*	*Includes all domestic and regional developments in Africa and the Middle East, including Iraq and Iran and excluding Cyprus, Turkey and Afghanistan.*	*Includes all domestic and regional developments in Latin America, the Caribbean and Canada.*	*Includes all domestic and regional developments in Asia and Pacific nations, extending from Afghanistan through all the Pacific Islands, except Hawaii.*

U.S. Politics & Social Issues	U.S. Foreign Policy & Defense	U.S. Economy & Environment	Science, Technology & Nature	Culture, Leisure & Life Style	
	A federal district judge approves a subpoena requiring former president Ronald Reagan to provide private notes and testimony for the Iran-Contra trial of former national security adviser John M. Poindexter.	Congress approves a $39.5 bil. appropriations bill for the Agriculture Dept. and related agencies. . . . The merchandise trade deficit fell to a seasonally adjusted $7.94 bil. in September, the Commerce Dept. reports.	A wave of violent weather sweeping across much of the eastern United States spawns a series of tornadoes that kills 29 people and leaves 1,000 homeless.	In the face of widespread criticism, National Endowment for the Arts chairman John E. Frohnmayer reverses his November 8 decision to suspend a $10,000 federal grant for an exhibit on the subject of Acquired Immune Deficiency Syndrome (AIDS). . . . A revival of *Gypsy*, the musical about stage mother Mama Rose and her attempts to make stars out of her daughters Baby June (who became actress June Havoc) and Louise (stripper Gypsy Rose Lee), opens on Broadway.	Nov. 16
		Housing starts rose 12% in October to a seasonally adjusted annual rate of 1.42 million units, the Commerce Dept. reports. . . . Pres. Bush signs into law a minimum wage increase approved by Congress November 8.	In a report published in the journal *Science*, astronomers mapping the farthest reaches of the universe describe an enormous sheet of scattered galaxies arrayed almost in a plane—the largest structure ever discovered—which its discoverers dub the "Great Wall."		Nov. 17
Pennsylvania bans most abortions at public hospitals, prohibits almost all abortions after 24 weeks of gestation, and requires prior notification of the spouse, counseling on alternatives and a 24-hour waiting period. . . . The House clears and sends to the president legislation increasing the pay of members of Congress, federal judges, and top officials of the executive branch.			A cosmic background explorer satellite is launched from Vandenberg Air Force Base, Calif., to search for lingering traces from the Big Bang, the cosmic event most scientists believe to have started the universe.		Nov. 18
		Congress sends to the president a bill authorizing up to $26 mil. a year to buy wetlands in the United States, Canada, and Mexico to preserve habitats of whooping cranes and other endangered waterfowl.	Scientists at the California Institute of Technology say they have identified the oldest and most distant object yet discovered, a quasar close to the edge of the observable universe.	The Rev. Leonid Kishkovsky of the Orthodox Church of America is installed as president of the National Council of Churches, becoming the first Orthodox clergyman to head the largely Protestant liberal council. . . . The United States downs Trinidad & Tobago, 1-0, to win a berth in the final round of the World Cup soccer competition for the first time since 1950. . . . Rusty Wallace wins the NASCAR (National Assoc. for Stock Car Racing) Winston Cup season title. . . . The Univ. of North Carolina downs Colorado College, 2-0, to win its fourth consecutive National Collegiate Athletic Assoc. Division I women's soccer title.	Nov. 19
Genetic tests show that 10-year-old Kimberly Michelle Mays is the daughter of Ernest and Regina Twigg, who maintain that she was switched at birth for a baby whom they raised as their own and who died last year. . . . The Congress clears and sends to Pres. Bush legislation reauthorizing through 1993 domestic government volunteer programs including ACTION, VISTA, VISTA Literacy Corps, and the Older American Volunteer Programs.		The International Trade Comm. rules that Matsushita Electric Industrial Co., Toshiba Corp., and the Taiwanese subsidiary of Nitsuko Ltd. have competed unfairly with U.S. makers of telecommunications equipment by dumping their goods in U.S. markets.	Two studies, by the Economic Policy Institute and the National Advisory Committee on Semiconductors, urge full government support for the electronics industry's efforts to develop semiconductors and telecommunications networks.	Milwaukee Brewer center fielder Robin Yount wins the American League's most valuable player award for the second time.	Nov. 20

F	G	H	I	J
Includes elections, federal-state relations, civil rights and liberties, crime, the judiciary, education, health care, poverty, urban affairs and population.	*Includes formation and debate of U.S. foreign and defense policies, veterans' affairs and defense spending. (Relations with specific foreign countries are usually found under the region concerned.)*	*Includes business, labor, agriculture, taxation, transportation, consumer affairs, monetary and fiscal policy, natural resources, and pollution.*	*Includes worldwide scientific, medical and technological developments, natural phenomena, U.S. weather, natural disasters, and accidents.*	*Includes the arts, religion, scholarship, communications media, sports, entertainments, fashions, fads and social life.*

	World Affairs	Europe	Africa & the Middle East	The Americas	Asia & the Pacific
Nov. 21	In a report urging steps to reverse sub-Saharan Africa's dire economic problems, the World Bank emphasizes grassroots development policies and greater accountability by African governments.	Faced with widespread strikes and pro-democracy protests, Czechoslovakia's hard-line Premier Ladislav Adamec begins talks with representatives of a new opposition group, Civic Forum.... Greece's three major political parties agree to form a coalition government headed by Xenophon Zolotas, the 85-year-old former head of the Bank of Greece.... The debate on the Queen's Speech, listing the legislation the Conservative government seeks to pass in Parliament, is the first House of Commons proceedings ever to be broadcast live on television.		Direct negotiations in New York City between Nicaraguan officials and Contra leaders end when the two sides fail to reach agreement on a cease-fire.	
Nov. 22			Lebanon's Pres. Rene Moawad is assassinated after only 17 days in office when a powerful bomb explodes next to his motorcade in Moslem west Beirut. The blast kills 23 other people and deals a severe blow to the fledgling Arab League peace plan.		
Nov. 23		Former Czechoslovak leader Alexander Dubcek, architect of the doomed 1968 "Prague Spring" reform movement and now a retired forestry clerk, addresses a crowd of about 70,000 pro-democracy demonstrators in Bratislava.		Canada's federal government closes indefinitely seven large commercial fishing zones between Prince Rupert and Vancouver Island, British Columbia, due to evidence of contaminated shellfish. ... Lucia Barrera de Cerna, who reported seeing some 30 or 40 men dressed as soldiers kill six Jesuit priests and two female employees at the Jose Simeon Canas Univ. of Central America November 16, is flown from El Salvador to the United States amid heavy security.	Settling charges of bid-rigging for projects at a U.S. naval base in Japan, some 100 Japanese construction companies agree to pay $32.6 mil. in damages to the United States.... The Victoria Supreme Court rules that the Australian Federation of Air Pilots is liable for as much as $7.8 mil. in damages for its role in directing a work slowdown of domestic pilots in mid-August.... Australia recorded a $1.75.bil. trade deficit in October, the government announces.
Nov. 24		Gen. Sec. Milos Jakes and 12 other members of the policy-making Presidium of Czechoslovakia's Communist Party resign en masse at an emergency session of the Central Committee.... The 14th Congress of Romania's Communist Party unanimously reelects Pres. Nicolae Ceausescu to his sixth five-year term as general secretary.	Two days after the assassination of Rene Moawad, Lebanon's parliament elects to the presidency Elias Hrawi, a moderate Maronite Catholic who is on good terms with Syria.... South Africa announces the creation of four "free opening areas" open to all races for integrated residential living. They are the only areas in which the Group Areas Act no longer applies.		
Nov. 25			Lebanon's Pres. Elias Hrawi reappoints Selim al-Hoss as premier and approves a 14-member cabinet equally divided between Christians and Moslems. Hoss is also named foreign minister.		Church officials in New York announce that New Zealand Episcopalians have elected Penelope Ann Bansall Jamieson as bishop of Dunedin. Jamieson, 47, is the first woman elected to head an Episcopal diocese.
Nov. 26		In the first nationwide free vote in Hungary for more than 40 years, a referendum determines that Hungary's next president will be chosen by parliament following free parliamentary elections in 1990.... Swiss voters vote by nearly a two-to-one ratio to maintain the nation's army, but 35.6% of voters back a proposed constitutional amendment that simply says, "Switzerland has no army."	Comoros Pres. Ahmed Abdallah Abderemane is assassinated by rebels led by a disgruntled former army commander. Supreme Court head Said Mohamed Djohar will head an interim government of the Indian Ocean island nation.	Luis Alberto Lacalle of the National Party is elected president of Uruguay when Lacalle and two other National Party candidates win a 38% plurality of the vote in the 12-man race.... Accusing the Sandinista government of supplying arms to the leftist Farabundo Marti National Liberation Front, El Salvador's Pres. Alfredo Cristiani suspends diplomatic and commercial ties with Nicaragua.	An estimated 55% to 60% of India's 498 million registered voters in 24 states and seven districts voted in the election of 525 members of the 545-seat Lok Sabha.

A	B	C	D	E
Includes developments that affect more than one world region, international organizations and important meetings of major world leaders.	Includes all domestic and regional developments in Europe, including the Soviet Union, Turkey, Cyprus and Malta.	Includes all domestic and regional developments in Africa and the Middle East, including Iraq and Iran and excluding Cyprus, Turkey and Afghanistan.	Includes all domestic and regional developments in Latin America, the Caribbean and Canada.	Includes all domestic and regional developments in Asia and Pacific nations, extending from Afghanistan through all the Pacific Islands, except Hawaii.

U.S. Politics & Social Issues	U.S. Foreign Policy & Defense	U.S. Economy & Environment	Science, Technology & Nature	Culture, Leisure & Life Style	
Iranian-American arms dealer Albert Hakim pleads guilty in federal court to one misdemeanor charge—supplementing the salary of former National Security Council staff member Oliver L. North—in connection with the Iran-Contra arms scandal.... Testifying before a Senate Judiciary subcommittee, former White House press secretary James S. Brady urges the panel to approve legislation requiring a seven-day waiting period on the purchase of handguns.	Pres. Bush signs a $14.6 bil. foreign aid appropriations bill including a major aid package for Poland and Hungary, which have both taken steps toward dismantling their one-party communist systems.... Pres. Bush signs a $285.8 bil. defense appropriations bill for FY1990.	Ashland Oil Inc. agrees to pay Pennsylvania $4.6 mil. in costs and penalties stemming from the collapse of a storage tank near Pittsburgh that spilled 750,000 gallons of diesel fuel into the Monongahela River.... A 48-day strike against the Boeing Co. ends when machinists approve a new three-year contract wrapped in holiday cash bonuses.... Pres. Bush signs an $11.97 bil. transportation spending bill with a $3.18 bil. rider for anti-drug programs.		Left fielder Kevin Mitchell of the San Francisco Giants is named the National League's most valuable player.... Ballet dancer Rudolf Nureyev resigns as director of the Paris Opera Ballet.	Nov. 21
In a nationally televised Thanksgiving Eve address, Pres. Bush hails the emergence of a "new Europe" and says "America believes that liberty is an idea whose time has come in Eastern Europe."... The Senate by voice vote acts to repeal the Medicare Catastrophic Coverage Act of 1988, which provides insurance against catastrophic medical costs for the elderly.		The Senate passes a deficit reduction bill designed to produce $14.6 bil. in savings and new revenues from taxes and increased licensing fees.... Congress extends through March 1992 voluntary restraint agreements limiting steel imports from trading partners with subsidized steel industries.... Trade Rep. Carla Hills says that negotiations on unfair Japanese practices in the construction industry have progressed enough to delay U.S. retaliatory action under the Omnibus Trade and Competitiveness Act.	Simple blood tests that can detect 60% to 70% of fetuses with Down's syndrome, the main cause of mental retardation, are reported to have been introduced over the past few months.		Nov. 22
		Eastern Airlines pilots and flight attendants end their nine-month strike against the carrier. Members of the machinists union, which initiated the strike in March, remain on strike.			Nov. 23
A federal judge dismisses all four Iran-Contra criminal charges against former Central Intelligence Agency station chief Joseph F. Fernandez after the Bush administration bars the release of classified information that Fernandez says is necessary for his defense.... U.S. consumption of hard liquor reached its lowest level in 27 years, according to statistics in a report by the federal Centers for Disease Control released today.			The British government announces that beginning in 1990 some blood taken from anonymous hospital and clinic patients will be tested for AIDS and the data broken down by age group, sex, and geographical location.		Nov. 24
					Nov. 25
					Nov. 26

F	G	H	I	J
Includes elections, federal-state relations, civil rights and liberties, crime, the judiciary, education, health care, poverty, urban affairs and population.	Includes formation and debate of U.S. foreign and defense policies, veterans' affairs and defense spending. (Relations with specific foreign countries are usually found under the region concerned.)	Includes business, labor, agriculture, taxation, transportation, consumer affairs, monetary and fiscal policy, natural resources, and pollution.	Includes worldwide scientific, medical and technological developments, natural phenomena, U.S. weather, natural disasters, and accidents.	Includes the arts, religion, scholarship, communications media, sports, entertainments, fashions, fads and social life.

	World Affairs	Europe	Africa & the Middle East	The Americas	Asia & the Pacific
Nov. 27			A Hercules transport plane chartered by the Central Intelligence Agency to ferry arms to the National Union for the Total Independence of Angola crashes in southern Angola.	All 107 people on board an Avianca Airlines Boeing 727-100 passenger jet bound from Bogota for Cali, Colombia, die when the plane explodes in midair and crashes a few minutes after takeoff.... In Honduras, opposition presidential candidate Rafael Leonardo Callejas claims victory in the November 26 presidential election.	
Nov. 28	Showing a new willingness to base quota allotments on the production capacities of individual members, the Org. of Petroleum Exporting Countries sets new production quotas for individual member nations.	In an address to the Bundestag, West Germany's Chancellor Helmut Kohl outlines a plan to produce a confederation of East and West Germany. The plan is criticized in East Germany and the Soviet Union.... In an effort to head off possible legislative action, editors of Britain's 20 leading newspapers agree to a code of conduct and a system to pursue the interests of persons possibly wronged by the papers.... The Supreme Soviet votes, 348-5, to disband a Kremlin commission that has administered the disputed enclave of Nagorno-Karabakh since January and to return control of the region to Azerbaijan SSR.	South Africa's Pres. F. W. de Klerk announces the dismantling of the National Security Management System which superceded civilian authority, particularly in black areas, and which critics likened to a shadow government and a "creeping coup d'etat."	Haiti's deficit tripled to $60 mil. in 1988-89, the first fiscal year under the government of Pres. Prosper Avril. The nation's foreign debt was $800 mil., more than three times the annual budget.	Share prices on the Taiwan stock exchange plunge 547.98 points, or 5.7%, to 9,040.09. It marks the largest one-day drop in the exchange's history.
Nov. 29	The World Jewish Congress releases a copy of a Central Intelligence Agency document showing that it knew for more than 40 years that Austria's Pres. Kurt Waldheim was an intelligence officer in the German Army in World War II and not a law student as he once claimed.	The southern Yugoslav republic of Serbia severs economic relations with the northern republic of Slovenia, effectively halting trade between the two regions.			India's P.M. Rajiv Gandhi announces his resignation after it becomes clear that his ruling Congress (I) Party has lost its majority in Parliament in last week's general elections.
Nov. 30		The Czechoslovak government announces it will open its borders and remove all restrictions on travel to the West, and high-ranking officials meet with Civic Forum to allay their fears of a military coup.		The United States and Canada agree to about $5 bil. in tariff cuts on a range of goods, including pharmaceuticals, electric motors, and scientific instruments, to take effect April 1, 1990.	
Dec. 1		Soviet Pres. Mikhail S. Gorbachev meets with Pope John Paul II at the Vatican. The meeting is the first ever between a leader of the Soviet Union and the head of the Roman Catholic Church.			A military uprising in the Philippines begins shortly after midnight as rebel soldiers attack military positions in suburban Manila, including the Cavite naval base and Villamor and Sangley Point air force bases.

A	B	C	D	E
Includes developments that affect more than one world region, international organizations and important meetings of major world leaders.	Includes all domestic and regional developments in Europe, including the Soviet Union, Turkey, Cyprus and Malta.	Includes all domestic and regional developments in Africa and the Middle East, including Iraq and Iran and excluding Cyprus, Turkey and Afghanistan.	Includes all domestic and regional developments in Latin America, the Caribbean and Canada.	Includes all domestic and regional developments in Asia and Pacific nations, extending from Afghanistan through all the Pacific Islands, except Hawaii.

U.S. Politics & Social Issues	U.S. Foreign Policy & Defense	U.S. Economy & Environment	Science, Technology & Nature	Culture, Leisure & Life Style	
The Supreme Court's lack of acceptance of any new cases after a two-week Thanksgiving recess highlights a relatively light docket shaping up for the new term.	The U.S. space shuttle *Discovery* successfully completes a secret, six-day military mission the primary task of which is reported to have been to launch a spy satellite into orbit.		Alyssa Smith, a 21-month-old girl, becomes the first U.S. recipient of a liver transplant from a living donor when she receives a section of her mother's liver in a 12-hour operation at Wyler's Children's Hospital in Chicago.		Nov. 27
		Energy Dept. officials announce that the proposed nuclear waste dump at Yucca Mountain, Nev., will not be ready until at least 2010. The site was originally scheduled to open in 1998 and then in 2003.			Nov. 28
		After-tax profits of U.S. corporations declined 7.2%, to a $149.5 bil. annual rate in the third quarter, the Commerce Dept. reports. . . . In a compromise Interior Sec. Manuel Lujan Jr. announces that long-term water supply contracts with California farmers will be renewed and assessed afterward for environmental impact.		Romanian gymnast Nadia Comaneci, who stunned the world in 1976 when, at age 14, she won the first perfect 10s ever awarded in Olympic competition, defects via Hungary. . . . *Variety*'s top-grossing films for the week are: *Back to the Future Part II*, *Harlem Nights*, *The Little Mermaid*, *Steel Magnolias*, and *Look Who's Talking*.	Nov. 29
	Pres. Bush rejects a bill that would have permitted all Chinese citizens currently in the United States on student visas to remain in the country until at least June 1990.	In an effort to reduce toxic emissions from incinerators by 90% by 1994, the Environmental Protection Agency proposes that municipal waste incinerators be required to recycle at least 25% of the waste they now burn. . . . Consumer spending fell 0.2%, to a $3.630 trillion annual rate in October, while personal income rose 0.9% to a $4.510 trillion annual rate, the Commerce Dept reports. . . . Farm prices rose 1.4% in November the Agriculture Dept. reports.			Nov. 30
		Visiting the Rocky Flats nuclear weapons plant, Energy Sec. James D. Watkins says plutonium operations will not be resumed until inspection and a review of procedures proves it is "safe." . . . The index of leading economic indicators fell 0.4% in October, the Commerce Dept. reports.		Alvin Ailey, 58, dancer, choreographer, and director, dies of a blood disorder at a hospital in New York City. His Alvin Ailey American Dance Theater, founded in 1958 and exclusively black until 1963, was one of the leading international modern dance troupes, blending elements of classical ballet, jazz, Afro-Caribbean dance, and the modern dance of Martha Graham and Lester Horton. . . . *Publishers Weekly*'s hardback fiction best-sellers for the week are: *Daddy*, Danielle Steel; *The Dark Half*, Stephen King; *Clear and Present Danger*, Tom Clancy; *Caribbean*, James A. Michener; and *Foucault's Pendulum*, Umberto Eco.	Dec. 1

F	G	H	I	J
Includes elections, federal-state relations, civil rights and liberties, crime, the judiciary, education, health care, poverty, urban affairs and population.	Includes formation and debate of U.S. foreign and defense policies, veterans' affairs and defense spending. (Relations with specific foreign countries are usually found under the region concerned.)	Includes business, labor, agriculture, taxation, transportation, consumer affairs, monetary and fiscal policy, natural resources, and pollution.	Includes worldwide scientific, medical and technological developments, natural phenomena, U.S. weather, natural disasters, and accidents.	Includes the arts, religion, scholarship, communications media, sports, entertainments, fashions, fads and social life.

	World Affairs	Europe	Africa & the Middle East	The Americas	Asia & the Pacific
Dec. 2	In their first meeting since Pres. Bush took office, Pres. Bush and Soviet Pres. Mikhail S. Gorbachev hold two days of talks in a shipboard summit in the Mediterranean island republic of Malta.				Vishwanath Pratap Singh, leader of India's opposition National Front, is sworn in as prime minister of a minority government. It is only the second time since 1947 that Congress (I) has not led the government.... Taiwanese voters go to the polls to choose some 300 national legislators, mayors and local officials in the first elections since 1949 in which opposition candidates are legally allowed to participate.... The Communist Party of Malaya signs a peace agreement with the governments of Malaysia and Thailand, bringing a formal end to a 41-year-old guerrilla war.
Dec. 3		In a move unprecedented in the Eastern bloc, the entire leadership of East Germany's ruling Socialist Unity Party resigns, and all 163 members of the Central Committee resign.		The Mexican government extends until July 31, 1990, an anti-inflation economic solidarity pact with business and labor under which wages and prices were controlled; the pact has been in effect since December 1987.	
Dec. 4		Warsaw Pact leaders meeting in Moscow condemn the 1968 invasion of Czechoslovakia. Pres. Mikhail Gorbachev called the meeting to brief his allies on his summit with Pres. Bush.... Following UN Sec. Gen. Javier Perez de Cuellar's meetings with Greek Cypriot Pres. George Vassiliou and with Turkish Cypriot leader Rauf Denktash, Denktash says he is ready to renew tripartite negotiations.	King Hussein names Mudar Badran to replace Sharif Zeid bin Shaker as Jordan's premier.		
Dec. 5			Israeli troops kill five heavily armed Arab gunmen who crossed the border from Egypt, reportedly intending to carry out terrorist attacks on the second anniversary of the Palestinian intifada.... Diplomatic and Palestinian sources in Tripoli, Libya, report that Palestinian terrorist leader Abu Nidal is neither ill nor under house arrest as has been reported.	Colombian authorities determine that the November 27 jet crash that killed all 107 people was caused by a bomb, probably planted by Colombian drug smugglers.	
Dec. 6	Following a U.S. threat to halt all UN funding, the UN General Assembly drops a proposed resolution to upgrade the status of the Palestine Liberation Org. from an observer organization to nonmember state.... The Drug Enforcement Admin. reports that the United States, Luxembourg, Britain, Switzerland, and Austria have frozen $61.8 mil. in funds belonging to Medellin drug boss Jose Gonzalo Rodriguez Gacha.		Lebanon's Pres. Elias Hrawi remains locked in a stand-off with renegade Christian army commander Gen. Michel Aoun, who says Hrawi's election, like that of his predecessor Rene Moawad, was unconstitutional.... The United States says that Egypt has formally accepted the five-point plan proposed by Sec. of State James A. Baker III for Israeli-Palestinian talks.... Jordan's premier Mudar Badran announces a new cabinet that excludes members of the fundamentalist Moslem Brotherhood, which won the largest parliamentary bloc in the country's recent elections.	In the Colombia drug cartels' continuing war against the government, at least 52 people are killed and more than 600 wounded when a massive truck bomb explodes outside the headquarters of the security and intelligence agency in Bogota.	Philippine Pres. Corazon Aquino imposes a nationwide state of emergency in response to the December 1 coup attempt.

A	B	C	D	E
Includes developments that affect more than one world region, international organizations and important meetings of major world leaders.	Includes all domestic and regional developments in Europe, including the Soviet Union, Turkey, Cyprus and Malta.	Includes all domestic and regional developments in Africa and the Middle East, including Iraq and Iran and excluding Cyprus, Turkey and Afghanistan.	Includes all domestic and regional developments in Latin America, the Caribbean and Canada.	Includes all domestic and regional developments in Asia and Pacific nations, extending from Afghanistan through all the Pacific Islands, except Hawaii.

U.S. Politics & Social Issues	U.S. Foreign Policy & Defense	U.S. Economy & Environment	Science, Technology & Nature	Culture, Leisure & Life Style	
			A bipartisan report released by the House Government Operations Committee recommends that the government lift its ban on funding research into in vitro fertilization, which is opposed by antiabortion groups.... The Solar Maximum Mission satellite's nine-year study of the Sun ends when it falls from orbit over the Indian Ocean. Solar Max was in service for nearly a complete solar cycle, from peak turbulence through subsidence and back to peak activity.	Andre Ware, the Univ. of Houston quarterback, is named the winner of the Heisman Trophy as the nation's top college player.	Dec. 2
The General Accounting Office reports that the federal prison population has doubled since 1980, from 24,162 to 48,017 inmates. Designed to hold 30,860 prisoners, the federal system is now 56% over capacity.			Cindy Martin, 26, becomes the world's first recipient of a transplanted heart, liver, and kidney in an operation performed by Dr. Thomas Starzl and Dr. John Armitage at Presbyterian-Univ. Hospital in Pittsburgh.	The universities of Virginia and Santa Clara share the National Collegiate Athletic Assoc. Division I championship after playing to a 1-1 tie in the finals.	Dec. 3
Attorney Gen. Richard Thornburgh announces that the Justice Dept. is investigating allegations of perjury and conspiracy against former Housing and Urban Development Sec. Samuel R. Pierce Jr.	Briefing North Atlantic Treaty Org. members on the Malta summit, Pres. Bush pledges a continued U.S. military presence in Europe and urges further integration of the European Community.... The Navy successfully conducts an underwater launch of an unarmed Trident II (D5) ballistic missile. It is the fourth test launching at sea. Two of the previous three tests have failed.	M. Danny Wall resigns as head of the Office of Thrift Supervision amid criticism of his handling of the U.S. thrift industry crisis and especially the collapse of the Lincoln Savings and Loan Assoc.... The Environmental Protection Agency proposes to ban most uses of ethylene bisdithiocarbamate, a carcinogenic fungicide known as EBDC and used on about one-third of U.S. fruit and vegetable crops. ... About 40,000 employees of Nynex Corp., the parent of New York Telephone and New England Telephone and Telegraph Co., return to work after settlement of their four-month-old strike.			Dec. 4
In its first report, the National Commission on Acquired Immune Deficiency Syndrome (AIDS) charges that the federal government has failed to respond adequately to the AIDS crisis.... The Supreme Court rules, 6-3, that a local government can be sued for damages for interfering improperly in labor negotiations.		International Business Machines Corp. announces a restructuring plan aimed at substantially cutting costs and including a cut of 10,000 people from its payroll through attrition and a buy-back of up to $4 bil. of its own stock.... Pres. Bush signs into law the Nevada wilderness area bill setting aside 733,000 acres of land for the state's first wilderness area.		Mohammed Elewonibi, a guard for Brigham Young Univ. who is a native of Nigeria, is named the winner of college football's Outland trophy as the nation's top lineman.	Dec. 5
		Office of Thrift Supervision regulations aimed at forcing savings and loan institutions to adopt sounder fiscal practices mandate new capital-to-asset ratios.	Scientists report that the Voyager 2 spacecraft detected winds of 1,500 miles per hour, the strongest in the solar system, around Neptune's great dark spot, a vast cyclonic storm in its atmosphere.		Dec. 6

F	G	H	I	J
Includes elections, federal-state relations, civil rights and liberties, crime, the judiciary, education, health care, poverty, urban affairs and population.	Includes formation and debate of U.S. foreign and defense policies, veterans' affairs and defense spending. (Relations with specific foreign countries are usually found under the region concerned.)	Includes business, labor, agriculture, taxation, transportation, consumer affairs, monetary and fiscal policy, natural resources, and pollution.	Includes worldwide scientific, medical and technological developments, natural phenomena, U.S. weather, natural disasters, and accidents.	Includes the arts, religion, scholarship, communications media, sports, entertainments, fashions, fads and social life.

	World Affairs	Europe	Africa & the Middle East	The Americas	Asia & the Pacific
Dec. 7	State Dept. officials say the United States does not plan to return to the United Nations Educational, Scientific and Cultural Org., which it quit in 1984 because of its fiscal mismanagement and anti-Western bias.	Ladislav Adamec resigns as Czechoslovakia's premier amid a political crisis over power-sharing after 14 months in office. Pres. Gustav Husak chooses Communist Marian Calfa as Adamec's successor. . . . Lithuania defies the central Soviet government when the Lithuanian Supreme Soviet votes to remove from the constitution a provision guaranteeing the Communist Party's monopoly on power in Lithuania. . . . Britain's Conservative government publishes legislation to reform the broadcasting industry.	Israel cautiously welcomes Egypt's acceptance, yesterday, of a five-point plan proposed by Sec. of State James A. Baker III for Israeli-Palestinian talks. . . . Gunmen from the Syrian-backed Shiite Amal militia and the pro-Iranian, fundamentalist Hizballah (Party of God) clash in west Beirut. Ten people die before Syrian troops end the fighting. . . . Nigeria's military government announces the postponement until late 1990 of local government elections originally scheduled for late December 1989. The government still plans to return to civilian rule in 1992.	Manitoba agrees to supply Ontario with hydroelectric power for $11 bil., the largest inter-provincial energy sale in Canadian history.	A week-long coup attempt by rebel Philippine Army soldiers in Manila collapses. The coup attempt is the sixth and most serious against Pres. Corazon Aquino since she assumed power in February 1986.
Dec. 8			The Palestine Liberation Org. says it will insist on a more direct role in the peace process than is outlined in Sec. of State James A. Baker III's proposed five-point plan for Israeli-Palestinian talks. . . . Faced with widespread public disillusionment, Benin's Pres. Mathieu Kerekou says the nation will abandon its Marxist-Leninist ideology in favor of political reforms and the promotion of private enterprise.	In Canada, the national unemployment rate rose slightly to 7.6% in November from 7.4% in October, according to Statistics Canada.	
Dec. 9		With the party's former leadership facing criminal prosecution for alleged corruption, East Germany's ruling Socialist Unity Party elects liberal lawyer Gregor Gysi to the new post of party chairman.	As the Palestinian intifada against Israeli occupation enters its third year, two Palestinians are shot to death by soldiers during a West Bank protest.		Two top Bush administration officials make a surprise visit to Beijing to meet with Chinese leaders in an apparent effort to repair deteriorating Sino-U.S. relations. . . . Rebel Philippine Army troops relinquish control of a key military airport in Cebu, bringing to an end a nine-day uprising against the government of Pres. Corazon Aquino.
Dec. 10		Immediately after swearing in a 21-member coalition cabinet with the Communist Party in a minority role, Czechoslovak Pres. Gustav Husak resigns. The government is still led by a communist, Premier Marian Calfa. . . . Dissident playwright Vaclav Havel and former Czechoslovak leader Alexander Dubcek announce their respective candidacies for president. Parliament has 14 days to choose a successor to Pres. Husak.		The presidents of five Central American nations start a summit meeting in San Jose, Costa Rica, aimed at bringing an end to the fighting in El Salvador and continuing the demobilization of the Nicaraguan Contras. . . . One person is killed and more than 20 others are injured when a riot breaks out at an opposition rally in Masatepe, Nicaragua. Bipartisan American observers say pro-Sandinista mobs began the attacks.	
Dec. 11	An international team of six explorers using dog sleds and skis and led by Will Steger of Minnesota reaches the South Pole after a trek of more than 1,900 miles that began on July 27.	An estimated 200,000 demonstrators in Leipzig, East Germany, gathering to celebrate the gains of the pro-democracy movement, begin a mass call for reunification with West Germany. . . . West Germany's Interior Ministry reports that more than 650,000 immigrants have entered the country since January, including 317,548 from East Germany, 225,000 from Poland and 87,000 from the Soviet Union.			Chinese authorities have reportedly begun secret trials of six students from a foreign affairs institute who are accused of participating in the pro-democracy uprising in June.
Dec. 12		Opening the second session of the Congress of People's Deputies, Soviet Pres. Mikhail S. Gorbachev says that reforms must be introduced to restructure the Soviet Union but puts off debate over the preeminent role of the Communist Party in the constitution.			Hong Kong authorities deport 51 Vietnamese refugees from a refugee detention center, initiating a controversial program of forced repatriation advocated by the British government.

A	B	C	D	E
Includes developments that affect more than one world region, international organizations and important meetings of major world leaders.	Includes all domestic and regional developments in Europe, including the Soviet Union, Turkey, Cyprus and Malta.	Includes all domestic and regional developments in Africa and the Middle East, including Iraq and Iran and excluding Cyprus, Turkey and Afghanistan.	Includes all domestic and regional developments in Latin America, the Caribbean and Canada.	Includes all domestic and regional developments in Asia and Pacific nations, extending from Afghanistan through all the Pacific Islands, except Hawaii.

U.S. Politics & Social Issues	U.S. Foreign Policy & Defense	U.S. Economy & Environment	Science, Technology & Nature	Culture, Leisure & Life Style	
Miami police officer William Lozano is convicted of manslaughter in the deaths of two black motorcycle riders in January that set off three days of rioting in the Overtown section of Miami.		Consumer debt increased $3.34 bil. in October, at a 5.7% annual rate, the Federal Reserve Board reports.		Sugar Ray Leonard wins a unanimous decision over Roberto Duran in a 12-round bout, retaining his World Boxing Council middleweight title.	Dec. 7
		The nation's unemployment rate increased to 5.3% in November, the Labor Dept. reports.	*Science* magazine reports that researchers at Tulane Univ.'s Delta Regional Primate Research Center have developed a vaccine that protects monkeys against a simian version of the virus that causes Acquired Immune Deficiency Syndrome (AIDS).		Dec. 8
	Boris Yeltsin, Soviet reformer and outspoken critic of Pres. Mikhail Gorbachev, opens an eight-day U.S. visit with a meeting with national security adviser Brent Scowcroft and, briefly, Pres. Bush.			The draw for the 1990 World Cup soccer tournament, to be held in Italy, is finalized at a lavish ceremony in Rome featuring actress Sophia Loren and opera tenor Luciano Pavarotti.	Dec. 9
Police arrest 111 of an estimated 4,500 demonstrators gathered outside St. Patrick's Cathedral in New York City to protest John Cardinal O'Connor's statements on Acquired Immune Deficiency Syndrome (AIDS), homosexuality, and abortion. Several dozen demonstrators enter the church and noisily disrupt the service.				Yevgeny Pasternak, son of the late Soviet author Boris Pasternak, receives his father's Nobel Prize for literature medal at a ceremony in Stockholm. Soviet authorities forced Pasternak, author of the novel *Dr. Zhivago*, to decline the prize in 1958. His works have recently been reissued under Soviet leader Mikhail S. Gorbachev's policy of openness.	Dec. 10
				City of Angels, a musical comedy about a novelist's attempt to turn his book into a respectable movie in 1940s Hollywood, opens on Broadway. The musical, which wins six Tony Awards, has a book by Larry Gelbart, music by Cy Coleman, lyrics by David Zippel, and stars Gregg Edelman, Dee Hoty and James Naughton.	Dec. 11
Billionaire hotel owner Leona Helmsley is sentenced to four years in prison for her conviction on tax evasion charges; she is also ordered to pay $8.9 mil. in fines and back taxes and to perform 750 hours of community service.	Testifying before the Senate Budget Committee, former Defense Sec. Robert S. McNamara and former Asst. Defense Sec. Lawrence J. Korb say that given the reduced Soviet military threat, the Pentagon can afford to cut its budget in half by the year 2000. . . . In a speech in West Berlin, Sec. of State James A. Baker III gives the most specific outline to date of the U.S. position on changes in Europe being sparked by reforms in the Soviet bloc.	The Bush administration announces accords with 18 nations to phase out most subsidies to domestic steel industries even as it announces new steel quotas for major trading partners. . . . Pres. Bush signs legislation to expand Everglades National Park in Florida and to improve the natural flow of water into the area. The bill provides for a 107,600-acre expansion of the park in cooperation with the state of Florida.		*Grand Hotel*, a musical version of the 1932 film about life in a an elegant Berlin hotel in 1928, opens on Broadway. The musical, which wins five Tony awards, is directed and choreographed by Tommy Tune, based on a novel by Vicki Baum and stars Liliane Montevecchi, David Carroll, Jane Krakowski and Michael Jeter.	Dec. 12

F	G	H	I	J
Includes elections, federal-state relations, civil rights and liberties, crime, the judiciary, education, health care, poverty, urban affairs and population.	*Includes formation and debate of U.S. foreign and defense policies, veterans' affairs and defense spending. (Relations with specific foreign countries are usually found under the region concerned.)*	*Includes business, labor, agriculture, taxation, transportation, consumer affairs, monetary and fiscal policy, natural resources, and pollution.*	*Includes worldwide scientific, medical and technological developments, natural phenomena, U.S. weather, natural disasters, and accidents.*	*Includes the arts, religion, scholarship, communications media, sports, entertainments, fashions, fads and social life.*

	World Affairs	Europe	Africa & the Middle East	The Americas	Asia & the Pacific
Dec. 13			South Africa's Pres. F. W. de Klerk meets for the first time with jailed African National Congress leader Nelson Mandela to discuss the political future of South Africa.... At a special two-day session on apartheid the UN General Assembly adopts a declaration setting out general guidelines for the peaceful transformation of South Africa into a nonracial democracy.	Shunning reforms currently under way in Eastern bloc nations, Pres. Fidel Castro says Cuba faces a "tense economic situation" that coincides with "the worsening problems in socialist countries."	
Dec. 14	The General Agreement on Tariffs and Trade (GATT) criticizes certain aspects of U.S. trade policy, especially its reliance on bilateral trade agreements to avoid GATT jurisdiction, but says the United States maintains generally free-trade practices.	Italy's Treasury Min. Guido Carli says that employees at the Banca Nazionale del Lavoro are being investigated in connection with the bank's extension of $2.9 bil. in unauthorized credit to Iraq through its Atlanta, Ga., branch.... Andrei Dmitrievich Sakharov, 68, Soviet nuclear physicist and a leading Soviet dissident, dies of an apparent heart attack in Moscow. A codeveloper of the Soviet Union's hydrogen bomb, he won the 1975 Nobel Peace Prize for his human rights efforts and was exiled to the closed city of Gorky from 1980 to 1987 for criticizing the Soviet invasion of Afghanistan.... In Britain, the number of people claiming jobless benefits declined for the 40th straight month in November, the government reports.		Christian Democratic opposition leader Patricio Aylwin wins Chile's first presidential election since 1970. Aylwin's victory signals the end of the authoritarian rule of Gen. Augusto Pinochet Ugarte, who came to power in a coup in 1973.	The Philippine Senate approves a bill granting Pres. Corazon Aquino special emergency powers for six months. Similar legislation was passed yesterday by the House of Representatives.... Amnesty International reports that more than 1,000 people a month have been killed by guerrillas and government security forces in Sri Lanka since the government reimposed a state of emergency in June.
Dec. 15		In Timisoara, Romania, a rally to prevent the arrest and deportation to Hungary of the Rev. Laszlo Tokes, a popular Protestant minister active in promoting the rights of ethnic Hungarians, is reported to have blossomed into a full-scale pro-democracy rally.... The mayor of Pisa, Italy, orders the "leaning tower" to be temporarily closed for repairs after a scientific commission established by the government in Rome warns that the landmark is in danger of toppling. The 179-foot-high tower, construction on which began in 1173, leans about 17 feet off perpendicular.... A report by West German federal and Jewish officials finds that the late Werner Nachmann, former chairman of the Central Council of Jews in Germany, embezzled nearly $16 mil. from government funds intended for Holocaust survivors.	South Africa's highest court reverses the controversial 1988 convictions of 11 black activists on treason and terrorism charges in the so-called Delmas trial.... The government of the Comoros returns to civilian control when French troops force the departure of European mercenaries who had ruled the Indian Ocean island nation since the assassination of Pres. Ahmed Abdallah Abderemane November 26.	Panama's National Assembly of Representatives, a 510-member body appointed by Gen. Manuel Antonio Noriega in October, approves a resolution stating that "the Republic of Panama is declared to be in a state of war" with the United States as long as United States "aggression," in the form of economic sanctions imposed in 1988, continues.... In Colombia, the number-two man in the Medellin drug cartel, Jose Gonzalo Rodriguez Gacha, is killed in a shoot-out with a force of some 300 commandos and soldiers at a ranch near Tolu.	A federal jury in Seattle orders the estate of the late Philippine ruler Ferdinand E. Marcos and his widow, Imelda, to pay more than $15 mil. to the families of Silme Domingo and Gene Viernes after the Marcoses are found liable in connection with the 1981 murders of the anti-Marcos activists.
Dec. 16				Marine Lt. Robert Paz is killed when Panama Defense Forces (PDF) troops open fire on him and three other unarmed, off-duty U.S. servicemen as they try to drive their private car away from a crowd of civilians and soldiers at a roadblock outside PDF headquarters in Panama City.	
Dec. 17		At the concluding session of an extraordinary two-part congress, East Germany's ruling Socialist Unity Party continues to ready itself for free elections now set for May 6, 1990.		Brazilian voters go to the polls in their nation's first direct presidential election since 1960.	

A	B	C	D	E
Includes developments that affect more than one world region, international organizations and important meetings of major world leaders.	Includes all domestic and regional developments in Europe, including the Soviet Union, Turkey, Cyprus and Malta.	Includes all domestic and regional developments in Africa and the Middle East, including Iraq and Iran and excluding Cyprus, Turkey and Afghanistan.	Includes all domestic and regional developments in Latin America, the Caribbean and Canada.	Includes all domestic and regional developments in Asia and Pacific nations, extending from Afghanistan through all the Pacific Islands, except Hawaii.

U.S. Politics & Social Issues	U.S. Foreign Policy & Defense	U.S. Economy & Environment	Science, Technology & Nature	Culture, Leisure & Life Style	
The Justice Dept. approves a revised New York City charter and clears the way for implementation of the remodeled city government beginning Jan. 1, 1990.			A UN General Assembly committee reaches agreement on a resolution to end the use of drift nets in fishing after June 1992. The United States and New Zealand had sought a resolution on an immediate ban. Japan, with fishing fleets that make extensive use of the giant nets, announced earlier in the week that it would end the practice in 1992.	*Driving Miss Daisy*, a film about a Southern Jewish widow's friendship with her black chauffeur, is released in New York. The Oscar-winning film directed by Bruce Beresford stars Jessica Tandy, Morgan Freeman, and Dan Aykroyd.	Dec. 13
Three members of Congress ask the General Accounting Office to determine whether women are now being adequately represented in government-funded medical research.		American Express Co. approves a plan to inject nearly $900 mil. into its securities subsidiary, Shearson Lehman Hutton Holdings Inc.	The Redoubt Volcano in southern Alaska erupts, spewing volcanic ash seven miles into the air at Cook Inlet. The volcano, which last erupted in 1966, is located 115 miles southwest of Anchorage.	*Tru*, a one-man drama about writer Truman Capote, opens on Broadway. Written and directed by Jay Presson Allen, it stars Robert Morse, who wins the Tony for best actor. . . . *Glory*, an account of the exploits of the 54th Massachusetts Regiment—one of the first black regiments to fight for the North in the Civil War—is released in New York. Directed by Edward Zwick, the film stars Matthew Broderick, Cary Elwes, Morgan Freeman, and Denzel Washington, who wins the Oscar for best supporting actor.	Dec. 14
		The merchandise trade deficit rose to a seasonally adjusted $10.20 bil. in October, the Commerce Dept. reports. . . . BASF Corp. and the Oil, Chemical and Atomic Workers Union reach agreement on a new three-year contract that will end one of the longest management lockouts in U.S. labor history.			Dec. 15
A report prepared by the House Government Operations Committee finds that the Public Health Service and the Dept. of Health and Human Services censor research on abortion. . . . Federal Appeals Court Judge Robert S. Vance is killed in Birmingham, Alabama, in a bombing that is believed to be racially motivated. Vance served on the U.S. Court of Appeals for the 11th Circuit, which has recently ruled in favor of school desegregation and against the Ku Klux Klan.	The seven-month federal investigation of veteran diplomat Felix S. Bloch on suspicion of espionage has been scaled back for lack of evidence, federal officials say.		Carbon dioxide emissions have grown faster in the United States since 1986 than in the rest of the world, according to statistics compiled by the World Resources Institute.		Dec. 16
	The *Sunday Times* of London reports that the Central Intelligence Agency has concluded that Pres. Mikhail S. Gorbachev's hold on power remains strong despite the recent setbacks for his economic reforms.	Plagued by bad real estate loans, the Bank of New England Corp.—with assets of $32 bil. the second-largest bank in New England—increases its loan loss reserves by $700 mil.		West Germany clinches its second straight Davis Cup tennis title when Boris Becker routs Mats Wilander of Sweden, 6-2, 6-0, 6-2.	Dec. 17

F	G	H	I	J
Includes elections, federal-state relations, civil rights and liberties, crime, the judiciary, education, health care, poverty, urban affairs and population.	Includes formation and debate of U.S. foreign and defense policies, veterans' affairs and defense spending. (Relations with specific foreign countries are usually found under the region concerned.)	Includes business, labor, agriculture, taxation, transportation, consumer affairs, monetary and fiscal policy, natural resources, and pollution.	Includes worldwide scientific, medical and technological developments, natural phenomena, U.S. weather, natural disasters, and accidents.	Includes the arts, religion, scholarship, communications media, sports, entertainments, fashions, fads and social life.

	World Affairs	Europe	Africa & the Middle East	The Americas	Asia & the Pacific
Dec. 18		The Soviet Union and the European Community sign a 10-year trade agreement that provides for technical cooperation and increased ties in banking, tourism, nuclear power, petroleum and natural gas, and insurance.... Saying that Turkey's treatment of workers, citizens, and minority rights falls short of European Community (EC) standards, an EC commission effectively rejects Turkey's application for membership.	The results of Iran's parliamentary by-elections held December 15 are reported today. Moderate supporters of Pres. Ali Akbar Hashemi Rafsanjani's pragmatic economic policies make the most gains.... In the wake of an intensification of a civil war in the south, the military regime of Sudan'a Gen. Omar Hassan al-Bashir is reported to be cracking down hard on civilian opponents in Khartoum.	The Farabundo Marti National Liberation Front acknowledges that 401 of its fighters have died in the current offensive against the government of El Salvador.	
Dec. 19		During a goodwill trip to Brussels, Soviet Foreign Min. Eduard A. Shevardnadze becomes the first envoy of a Warsaw Pact nation to visit the headquarters of the North Atlantic Treaty Org.	Jordan's Premier Mudar Badran announces the end of martial law, which has been in effect in the country for 22 years.... The ruling Zimbabwe African National Union-Patriotic Front of Pres. Robert Mugabe merges with its former rival, Joshua Nkomo's Zimbabwe African People's Union.	Canada's Finance Min. Michael Wilson announces that the government has decided to lower its proposed value-added tax on goods and services from 9% to 7%.... An immigration appeals panel in Canada determines that a group of 174 illegal Indian immigrants, most of them Sikhs, can claim refugee status in applying for permanent residence on the grounds that they suffer repression from Indian authorities because of their religion.	The Japanese government announces that it is beginning deportation of 1,668 Chinese refugees who are reported to have entered Japan disguised as Vietnamese boat people.... The Philippine Senate and House of Representatives passes a joint bill giving Pres. Corazon Aquino special emergency powers for six months.
Dec. 20		In an unprecedented move, the Lithuanian Communist Party declares itself independent of the Soviet national Communist Party. It is the first regional branch of the ruling party ever to proclaim sovereignty.... Britains's Conservative government publishes its Environmental Protection Bill, designed to tighten environmental regulation by placing responsibility for most pollution control under Her Majesty's Inspectorate of Pollution.... Hungary's Premier Miklos Nemeth resigns from the 24-member Presidium of the ruling Socialist Party to protest parliament's refusal to support his proposals for the 1990 national budget.	After a month of discussions Namibia's newly elected Constituent Assembly agrees in principle to a Western-style constitution that includes a declaration of rights, a multiparty democratic state with an elected parliament, and an independent judiciary.	Pres. Bush dispatches 12,000 U.S. troops to join 12,000 already stationed in Panama in an effort to overthrow the government of Panama's military strongman Gen. Manuel Antonio Noriega. U.S. forces capture major sites around Panama City, but Noriega himself eludes capture.... Francisco Collor de Mello of the conservative National Reconstruction Party is named the winner of Brazil's December 17 presidential election over Luis Inacio da Silva, of the leftist Worker's Party.	The British government announces that it will grant full citizenship to as many as 225,000 Hong Kong residents before the colony reverts to Chinese rule in 1997.
Dec. 21		Romanian television captures a stunned look on Pres. Nicolae Ceausescu's face as his speech from a balcony of the Royal Palace is drowned out by the jeers of thousands of people chanting pro-democracy slogans.			The new minority government of India's P.M. Vishwanath Pratap Singh wins a mandatory vote of confidence in the Indian Parliament after the opposition Congress (I) Party announces that it will abstain.
Dec. 22		Hungary's acting Pres. Matyas Szuros announces that free parliamentary elections will be held Mar. 25, 1990.	A four-day conference of Pres. Robert Mugabe's Zimbabwe African National Union-Patriotic Front ends with a declaration that its goal remains the creation of a one-party, Marxist-Leninist, socialist state.	Pres. Bush orders an additional 2,000 troops sent to Panama to join the 22,500 already there, to help reestablish control.	

A	B	C	D	E
Includes developments that affect more than one world region, international organizations and important meetings of major world leaders.	Includes all domestic and regional developments in Europe, including the Soviet Union, Turkey, Cyprus and Malta.	Includes all domestic and regional developments in Africa and the Middle East, including Iraq and Iran and excluding Cyprus, Turkey and Afghanistan.	Includes all domestic and regional developments in Latin America, the Caribbean and Canada.	Includes all domestic and regional developments in Asia and Pacific nations, extending from Afghanistan through all the Pacific Islands, except Hawaii.

U.S. Politics & Social Issues	U.S. Foreign Policy & Defense	U.S. Economy & Environment	Science, Technology & Nature	Culture, Leisure & Life Style	
Robert E. Robinson, a black lawyer and alderman in Savannah, Ga., is killed by a pipe bomb sent to his office in what seems to be part of a series of racially motivated bombings.	The United States announces that National Security Advisor Brent Scowcroft and Deputy Sec. of State Lawrence S. Eagleburger, who traveled to China earlier in December, also visited secretly in July, just after the government's suppression of the pro-democracy uprising in Beijing.		The National Aeronautics and Space Admin. announces that the launch of the next space shuttle, originally scheduled for December 21, has been postponed until January 1990.	Christina Orr-Cahall, director of the Corcoran Gallery of Art in Washington, D.C., resigns amid criticism of her cancellation of a planned exhibit of the work of the late, controversial photographer Robert Mapplethorpe.	Dec. 18
		Pres. Bush signs the $14.7 bil. deficit-reduction bill designed to lower the federal deficit to the $100 bil. maximum allowed under the Gramm-Rudman balanced-budget law for FY1990.... The Environmental Protection Agency reports that it has obtained commitments from polluters to pay $1 bil. for cleanups. Nearly $150 mil. of the settlements came after cleanup orders were issued.... Housing starts fell 4.7% in November to a seasonally adjusted annual rate of 1.36 million units, the Commerce Dept. reports.	Exposure to low levels of radiation are at least three to four times more likely to cause fatal cancer than had previously been assumed, according to a report by the National Academy of Sciences.		Dec. 19
	Pres. Bush says the United States has invaded Panama to safeguard U.S. lives, defend democracy in Panama, combat drug trafficking, and protect the integrity of the Panama Canal Treaty.... The State Dept. announces that it has decided to tear down its unfinished embassy building in Moscow and to construct a newer, more secure facility.... A National Academy of Sciences report advises the Energy Dept. to postpone and possibly cancel plans for new plants to process plutonium for bombs.			*Born on the Fourth of July*, the true story of a young Marine who is paralyzed while fighting in Vietnam and who becomes an outspoken opponent of the war, is released in New York. Directed by Oliver Stone and based on the book by Ron Kovic, the film stars Tom Cruise, Kyra Sedgwick, and Raymond J. Barry.... Modern dancer and choreographer Judith Jamison is chosen to succeed the late Alvin Ailey as director of the Alvin Ailey American Dance Theater. Jamison danced with the company between 1964 and 1980.	Dec. 20
U.S. District Judge Harold H. Greene orders former Pres. Ronald Reagan to submit excerpts of his diaries and notes to the court to see whether they are relevant to Poindexter's trial defense.... Truck driver Larry W. Mahoney is found guilty on 27 accounts of manslaughter in connection with the May 1988 collision of his pickup truck and a church bus near Carrollton, Ky.		Consumer spending rose 0.7%, to a $3.64 trillion annual rate in November, while personal income rose 0.8% to a $4.54 trillion annual rate, the Commerce Dept. reports.	According to data from the Meteorological Office, the mean temperature for central England for the year was 10.7 degrees Celsius, besting the record 10.61 degrees set in 1949 and the highest since records were first kept in 1659.		Dec. 21
The Senate Ethics Committee says it has begun formal inquiries into allegations of impropriety by Sens. Alan Cranston (D, Calif.), John Glenn (D, Ohio), John McCain (R, Ariz.), Donald W. Riegle Jr. (D, Mich.), and Dennis DeConcini (D, Ariz.), in connection with the collapse of the Lincoln Savings and Loan Assoc., and Sen. Alfonse M. D'Amato (R, N.Y.) for his involvement with the scandal-tainted Dept. of Housing and Urban Development.... Circuit Court Judge John P. Corderman is injured in the explosion of a mail bomb sent to his home in Hagerstown, Md.			Participants at a meeting of the American Geophysical Union revise their predictions of the rise in ocean levels by the year 2050 to 12 inches rather than the three feet or more predicted earlier.... A study reported in the *Journal of the American Medical Association* says that results of tests for Lyme disease, a tick-borne bacterial infection, vary among different laboratories and even within the same laboratory.	Samuel Barclay Beckett, 83, Irish-born playwright and novelist who won the 1969 Nobel Prize for literature, dies of a respiratory ailment at a hospital in Paris. His "theater of the absurd" plays include *Waiting for Godot* (1953), *Endgame* and *Krapp's Last Tape*. His other works include the novel trilogy *Molloy*, *Malone Dies*, and *The Unnamable*. He wrote most of his works in French, which he then translated into English.... *Publishers Weekly*'s hardback fiction bestsellers for the week are: *Daddy*, Danielle Steel; *The Dark Half*, Stephen King; *Caribbean*, James A. Michener; *Clear and Present Danger*, Tom Clancy; and *Foucault's Pendulum*, Umberto Eco.	Dec. 22

F	G	H	I	J
Includes elections, federal-state relations, civil rights and liberties, crime, the judiciary, education, health care, poverty, urban affairs and population.	*Includes formation and debate of U.S. foreign and defense policies, veterans' affairs and defense spending. (Relations with specific foreign countries are usually found under the region concerned.)*	*Includes business, labor, agriculture, taxation, transportation, consumer affairs, monetary and fiscal policy, natural resources, and pollution.*	*Includes worldwide scientific, medical and technological developments, natural phenomena, U.S. weather, natural disasters, and accidents.*	*Includes the arts, religion, scholarship, communications media, sports, entertainments, fashions, fads and social life.*

	World Affairs	Europe	Africa & the Middle East	The Americas	Asia & the Pacific
Dec. 23		Polish officials sign a letter of intent committing the government to meeting International Monetary Fund targets on controlling inflation and cutting spending and clearing the way for Poland to receive a $725 mil. standby loan.		In Colombia, the leftist April 19 Movement (M-19) rebel group says it has suspended a peace pact with the government because of congress's failure to approve key points of the peace plan agreed to earlier.	
Dec. 24		The Congress of People's Deputies adopts a resolution condemning the 1939 Soviet-German Nonaggression Treaty under which Soviet authorities illegally conspired with Nazi Germany to occupy independent nations in Eastern Europe including Latvia, Lithuania and Estonia.		Panama's Gen. Manuel Antonio Noriega takes refuge at the Vatican's diplomatic mission in Panama City after evading capture in an intense manhunt by U.S. troops. Virtually all remaining resistance to U.S. forces quickly collapses at the news.	
Dec. 25		Romania's president and Communist Party leader, Nicolae Ceausescu, and his wife and second in command, Elena, are executed by a military firing squad following a secret trial.	Iran says it has released 50 ailing or disabled Iraqi prisoners of war as a goodwill gesture. An earlier attempt to arrange a swap collapsed after only 400 men were freed. UN officials estimate that both sides hold 100,000 POWs between them.	The Associated Press reports that U.S. officials believe that Cuba is sending weapons to the Farabundo Marti National Liberation Front rebels in El Salvador via Mexico, and Guatemala.... Brazil's Globo Television reports that Fernando Collor de Mello received 53.03% of the vote in the final tally of Brazil's presidential election.	
Dec. 26		Following yesterday's execution of Romanian Pres. Nicolae Ceausescu, the National Salvation Front names former party official Ion Iliescu as interim president and vows to hold free elections in April 1990.... At an emergency meeting of the Communist Party Central Committee in Moscow, Soviet Pres. Mikhail S. Gorbachev condemns the Lithuanian Communist Party's decision to break with the national party.... The Yugoslav Central Committee of the ruling League of Communists supports a recommendation that the party relinquish its monopoly on political power. The move is to be debated at a party congress in January 1990.	Israeli forces mount air and ground raids deep into Lebanon against Lebanese Communist Party bases from which attacks against Israeli troops and their south Lebanon army militia allies have been launched.... According to an interview with Renamo (Mozambique National Resistance) rebel leader Afonso Dhlakama in the *Washington Post*, the proposed peace process in Mozambique remains deadlocked over the rebels' refusal to recognize the Frelimo government's constitution and laws.		Saman Piyasiri Fernando, the fourth and last surviving leader of the radical Sinhalese People's Liberation Front, dies during a shootout while in police custody in a suburb of Colombo. The group's other leaders also died while in police custody.
Dec. 27		Bulgaria's Communist Party and the opposition Union of Democratic Forces agree to begin detailed power-sharing talks in January 1990.	The UN Food and Agriculture Org. says Ethiopia will need more than 1 million tons of food if it is to avoid a repetition of its 1984-85 famine.	Amid a nationwide wave of violence by leftist rebels and right-wing extremists, the offices of the International Red Cross in Guatemala are seriously damaged when a grenade is thrown from a passing car.	The *Washington Post* reports that China's communist leadership has circulated criticism of Soviet Pres. Mikhail S. Gorbachev's reform policies and blamed them for the "subversion of socialism in Eastern Europe."
Dec. 28		Following the lead of neighboring Lithuania, the parliament of the Latvian SSR repeals the Communist Party's constitutionally protected role in the republic's government.			Japan's Ministry of Trade and Industry proposes measures to boost imports over the next decade; highlights include new tax credits for companies that import foreign goods and the elimination of tariffs on more than 1,000 imports.... Philippine officials report that they have uncovered evidence linking opposition leader Sen. Juan Ponce Enrile to this month's coup attempt against the government of Corazon Aquino.

A	B	C	D	E
Includes developments that affect more than one world region, international organizations and important meetings of major world leaders.	Includes all domestic and regional developments in Europe, including the Soviet Union, Turkey, Cyprus and Malta.	Includes all domestic and regional developments in Africa and the Middle East, including Iraq and Iran and excluding Cyprus, Turkey and Afghanistan.	Includes all domestic and regional developments in Latin America, the Caribbean and Canada.	Includes all domestic and regional developments in Asia and Pacific nations, extending from Afghanistan through all the Pacific Islands, except Hawaii.

U.S. Politics & Social Issues	U.S. Foreign Policy & Defense	U.S. Economy & Environment	Science, Technology & Nature	Culture, Leisure & Life Style	
					Dec. 23
		An explosion at an Exxon Corp. refinery in Baton Rouge—the second-largest in the United States—ignites five tanks full of heating oil, killing one person and injuring seven. The refinery tanks hold 3.6 million gallons of oil, about 3% of the nation's heating oil reserves.			Dec. 24
				Alfred Manuel (Billy) Martin, 61, baseball player and manager, dies of injuries after a traffic accident at his home near Binghamton, N.Y. A New York Yankees second baseman in the 1950s, he tied the record for the highest batting average (.500) in a six-game World Series. He managed the Yankees five times between 1975 and 1988, winning the 1976 American League pennant and 1977 World Series, and managed the Minnesota Twins, Detroit Tigers, and Oakland Athletics.... *Billboard*'s best-selling albums for the week are: *Girl You Know It's True*, Milli Vanilli; *Janet Jackson's Rhythm Nation 1814*, Janet Jackson; *Storm Front*, Billy Joel; *Steel Wheels*, Rolling Stones; and *Forever Your Girl*, Paula Abdul.	Dec. 25
					Dec. 26
	Military officials report that 23 U.S. soldiers and three civilians have been killed since the invasion of Panama began a week ago; 297 members of the Panama Defense Force and at least 400 Panamanian civilians have also died.				Dec. 27
		Eastern Airlines announces plans to lay off 600 management and nonunion employees and cut wages for about half its work force.	At least 11 people are killed and more than 120 injured when an earthquake measuring 5.5 on the open-ended Richter scale of ground motion strikes the city of Newcastle in New South Wales, Australia.	*Variety*'s top-grossing films for the week are: *The War of the Roses*, *National Lampoon's Christmas Vacation*, *Back to the Future Part II*, *We're No Angels*, and *Family Business*.... The five top-grossing films of 1989 are: *Batman*, $251.2 mil.; *Indiana Jones and the Last Crusade*, $195.7 mil.; *Lethal Weapon 2*, $147.3 mil.; *Honey, I Shrunk the Kids*, $129.9 mil.; and *Ghostbusters II*, $112.5 mil.	Dec. 28

F	G	H	I	J
Includes elections, federal-state relations, civil rights and liberties, crime, the judiciary, education, health care, poverty, urban affairs and population.	Includes formation and debate of U.S. foreign and defense policies, veterans' affairs and defense spending. (Relations with specific foreign countries are usually found under the region concerned.)	Includes business, labor, agriculture, taxation, transportation, consumer affairs, monetary and fiscal policy, natural resources, and pollution.	Includes worldwide scientific, medical and technological developments, natural phenomena, U.S. weather, natural disasters, and accidents.	Includes the arts, religion, scholarship, communications media, sports, entertainments, fashions, fads and social life.

	World Affairs	Europe	Africa & the Middle East	The Americas	Asia & the Pacific
Dec. 29		Vaclav Havel is the first noncommunist elected president of Czechoslovakia by the Federal Assembly in more than 40 years. Following his swearing-in, Havel pledges to lead the country to free elections.... The Financial Times-Stock Exchange 100 share index finishes the year up 35.1% to close at 2,422.7, less than 21 points below the index's record high set in July 1987.		In an effort to bolster Panama's economy, badly damaged by U.S. sanctions imposed in 1988, the Bush administration flies $50 mil. in cash to Panama, part of a total of $188 mil. due primarily for Panama Canal fees and U.S. military installations in Panama.	
Dec. 30		Poland's senate approves economic reform legislation that will give Poland the most market-oriented economic system in the Soviet bloc. The economic restructuring is a condition for further International Monetary Fund assistance.... The Communist Party newspaper *Pravda* publishes its first criticism of V. I. Lenin in what seems to mark the newspaper's entry into a historical debate about the Soviet Union's founder.	Angola's Pres. Jose Eduardo dos Santos outlines peace proposals that implicitly provide for the right-wing National Union for the Total Independence of Angola rebels to participate in national elections but rule out a multiparty political system.		
Dec. 31	Stock markets in the world's financial centers generally advanced in 1989, as capitalism chalked up major political victories. European markets were up 27.7% for the year, while the Tokyo exchange, the world's largest, expanded 18.6%.		Israel's government is confronted by a new crisis when P.M. Yitzhak Shamir fires Science Min. Ezer Weizman from the cabinet for allegedly meeting with Palestine Liberation Org. officials.		South Korea's former president Chun Doo Hwan appears before the National Assembly to testify about alleged corruption and abuses of power during his eight years in office.

A	B	C	D	E
Includes developments that affect more than one world region, international organizations and important meetings of major world leaders.	*Includes all domestic and regional developments in Europe, including the Soviet Union, Turkey, Cyprus and Malta.*	*Includes all domestic and regional developments in Africa and the Middle East, including Iraq and Iran and excluding Cyprus, Turkey and Afghanistan.*	*Includes all domestic and regional developments in Latin America, the Caribbean and Canada.*	*Includes all domestic and regional developments in Asia and Pacific nations, extending from Afghanistan through all the Pacific Islands, except Hawaii.*

U.S. Politics & Social Issues	U.S. Foreign Policy & Defense	U.S. Economy & Environment	Science, Technology & Nature	Culture, Leisure & Life Style	
		The Dow Jones industrial average closes the year at 2753.20, up 584.63 points from the 1988 year-end close of 2168.67. The year's gain, equal to 27%, occurs despite an October panic sell-off of 190 points and end-of-the-year recession fears. . . . The U.S. dollar defies some predictions of steep declines in 1989 to end the year ahead against most major currencies, though down from peaks reached in June and September.			Dec. 29
				Billboard's best-selling albums for the week are: Girl You Know It's True, Milli Vanilli; Storm Front, Billy Joel; Janet Jackson's Rhythm Nation 1814, Janet Jackson; . . .But Seriously, Phil Collins; and Forever Your Girl, Paula Abdul.	Dec. 30
					Dec. 31

F	G	H	I	J
Includes elections, federal-state relations, civil rights and liberties, crime, the judiciary, education, health care, poverty, urban affairs and population.	Includes formation and debate of U.S. foreign and defense policies, veterans' affairs and defense spending. (Relations with specific foreign countries are usually found under the region concerned.)	Includes business, labor, agriculture, taxation, transportation, consumer affairs, monetary and fiscal policy, natural resources, and pollution.	Includes worldwide scientific, medical and technological developments, natural phenomena, U.S. weather, natural disasters, and accidents.	Includes the arts, religion, scholarship, communications media, sports, entertainments, fashions, fads and social life.

NAME INDEX

The index is arranged alphabetically letter-by-letter. Entries are arranged both alphabetically and chronologically. Every index entry contains the year, month, day and column location (e.g., Allen, Woody 1988 Feb 7J). The year is 1986, the month is February, the day is 7 and the column is J.

A

Aaron, Hank 1982 Aug 1J
Abbas, Ferhat 1985 Dec 24C
Abbas, Mohammed Abul 1985 Oct 30B; 1988 Jan 17G
Abbott, George 1988 Jan 24J
Abbott, Jack Henry 1981 Sep 23F; 1982 Jan 21J/Apr 15J
Abdallah, Georges Ibrahim 1987 Feb 28B
Abdallah Abderemane, Ahmed 1985 Nov 7C; 1989 Nov 26C/Dec 15C
Abdul, Paula 1989 Mar 25J/Aug 26J/Sep 30J/Oct 28J/Dec 25J/Dec 30J
Abdul-Jabbar, Kareem 1980 May 29J; 1984 Apr 5J; 1985 Jun 9J; 1989 Jun 13J
Abdullah, Farouk 1984 Jan 14E
Abdullah, Sheik Mohammed 1982 Sep 8E
Abel, I(orwith) W(ilbur) 1987 Aug 10H
Abell, George 1983 Oct 7I
Abraham, F. Murray 1984 Sep 19J; 1985 Mar 25J
Abrahams, Harold 1986 Oct 26J
Abram, Morris B. 1983 Dec 6F
Abramowitz, Morton 1983 Jan 12G
Abrams, Elliott 1981 Oct 30G; 1987 Jun 2G/Jul 8G; 1988 Apr 3G
Abrams, Robert 1988 Feb 29F
Abrantes Fernandez, Jose 1989 Aug 31D
Abu Eain, Ziad 1981 Dec 13G; 1983 Dec 13C
Abuhazira, Aharon 1982 Apr 23C
Abu Musa Abu Majdi see Musa, Saed
Abu Nader, Fuad 1984 Oct 9C
Abu Nidal 1982 Nov 9C; 1984 Jun 8C; 1987 Feb 5B; 1988 Feb 12B; 1989 Jun 15C/Nov 12C/Dec 5C
Abu Rabia, Hammad 1981 Jan 12C
Abu Sharif 1980 Jun 17E
Ackerman, Karen 1989 Jan 9J
Acorn, Milton 1986 Aug 20J
Adair, Donald 1986 Feb 8J
Adair, Paul ("Red") 1983 Jul 31C
Adamec, Ladislav 1988 Oct 10B; 1989 Nov 21B/Dec 7B
Adams, Ansel 1984 Apr 22J; 1985 Mar 5J
Adams Jr., Aubrey 1989 May 4F
Adams, Bryan 1985 Jul 27J/Aug 24J
Adams, Douglas 1985 Feb 8J; 1987 Jul 17J
Adams, Gerry 1984 Mar 14B
Adams, Harriet 1982 Mar 27J
Adams, John Michael Geoffrey (Tom) 1985 Mar 11D
Adams, Lane 1985 Nov 22I
Adams, Paul A. 1989 Jun 16F
Adams, Randall Dale 1989 Mar 1F/Mar 21F
Adams, Robert 1984 Sep 17J
Adams, Sherman (Llewellyn) 1986 Oct 27F
Adamson, George 1989 Aug 20C
Adamson, Joy 1981 Aug 28J
Addams, Charles 1988 Sep 29J

Adelman, Kenneth L. 1983 Jan 12G/Apr 14G; 1987 Apr 17G/Jul 30G
Adenauer, Konrad 1988 Jan 22B
Adler, Bill 1983 Dec 18J; 1984 Jan 20J/Mar 23J
Adler, Luther 1984 Dec 8J
Affatigato, Marco 1980 Aug 6B
Agca, Mehmet Ali 1981 May 13J/Jul 22J; 1982 Feb 16B
Aggett, Neil 1982 Feb 5C/Dec 21C
Agnew, Spiro T. 1981 Apr 27F; 1982 Nov 28F; 1983 Jan 4F
Agnos, Art 1987 Dec 8F
Agosti, Orlando Ramon 1989 May 8D
Aguirre Lanari, Juan 1983 Jan 3D/Jan 9D
Ahdal, Abdullah al- 1989 Mar 29A
Ahidjo, Ahmadou 1982 Nov 6C
Ahmed, Manzur 1981 Jun 1E/Jun 2E
Aiello, Danny 1989 Jun 30J
Aiello, Stephen R. 1980 Jan 3F
Aikman, Troy 1989 Apr 23J
Ailey, Alvin 1989 Dec 1J/Dec 20J
Aivazov, Todor Stoyanov 1982 Dec 18B
Aka, Ghol 1980 Jun 22B
Akhromeyev, Sergei F. 1985 Oct 22B; 1988 May 26B
Akihito, Emperor (Japan) 1989 Jan 7E/Aug 4E
Akin, Susan 1985 Sep 14J
Albanese, Alfredo 1980 May 12B
Albaret, Celeste 1984 Apr 25J
Albee, Edward 1984 May 3J
Albert, Carl 1982 Nov 28F
Albert, Stephen 1985 Apr 24J
Albright, Ivan le Lorraine 1983 Nov 18J
Alcott, Amy 1980 Jul 13J; 1985 Aug 18J
Alcott, John 1986 Jul 28J
Alda, Alan 1989 Nov 13J
Alder, Bill 1984 Feb 10J
Aldredge, Tom 1987 Nov 5J
Aldrich, Robert 1983 Dec 5J
Alekseyeva, Lisa 1981 Dec 10B
Alemann, Roberto 1982 May 5D
Alex, Janet 1982 Jul 25J
Alexander, Bill 1982 Aug 18F; 1989 Oct 25F
Alexander, Jason 1989 Jun 4J
Alexandrov, Alexandr 1983 Nov 23I
Alexandrov, Grigori 1983 Dec 19J
Alfonsin, Raul
    civil strife: state of siege 1985 Oct 25D/Dec 9D
    economic policy: labor/tax reform 1983 Dec 17D; Austral Plan 1985 Jun 14D; wage hikes 1985 Dec 30D; strikes 1989 Feb 21D
    foreign policy: Brazil accords 1987 Jul 15D
    government: presidential elections 1983 Oct 30D; 1985 Nov 3D; 1988 Oct 18D; inauguration 1983 Dec 9D-10D; cabinet/military shifts 1984 Jul 5D; 1985 Feb 18D; 1987 Sep 16D; federal capital relocation 1987 Mar 25D; divorce legalization 1987 Jun 8D; Menem power play 1989 May 23D; resignation 1989 Jun 12D

human rights: military junta trials 1983 Dec 13D; 1984 Feb 14D/Sep 20D; 1985 Apr 22D; 1986 Dec 26D; 1987 Apr 19D/May 13D/Jun 12D
Alford, Steve 1986 Mar 1J
Algren, Nelson 1981 May 9J
Ali, Kamal Hassan 1982 Jun 17C; 1985 Jan 8C/Sep 4C
Ali, Muhammad 1980 Jan 13J/Jan 31J/Oct 2J/Feb 2H; 1984 Sep 20J
Alia, Ramiz 1985 Apr 13B
Alibi, Chedi 1985 Feb 3B
Alice, Mary 1985 May 3J
Allain, Bill 1985 Nov 28J
Allais, Maurice 1988 Oct 18J
Allen Jr., Charles R. 1984 Jan 26G
Allen, Jay Presson 1989 Dec 14J
Allen, Joan 1987 Oct 14J; 1988 Jun 5J
Allen, Lew 1981 Jun 30G; 1982 Jun 21G
Allen, Marcus 1981 Dec 5J
Allen, Richard V.
    foreign policy: labels PLO terrorists 1981 Mar 26A
    government service: foreign policy post resignations 1980 Sep 30F; 1982 Jan 4F; intelligence advisors named 1981 Oct 10G; Haig feud 1981 Nov 3F
    political payments: from Japan 1981 Nov 13F/Nov 24F/Nov 29F/Dec 1F/Dec 23F
Allen, Woody 1986 Feb 7J/Mar 16J; 1987 May 12J; 1989 Nov 13J
Allende, Salvador 1981 Sep 11D
Alliluyeva, Svetlana 1986 Apr 16J
Allin, John M. 1985 Sep 10J
Allison, Bobby 1988 Feb 14J
Allison, Davey 1987 May 3J; 1989 May 7J
Allison, Fran 1985 Dec 6J
Allon, Yigal 1980 Feb 29C
Alsop Jr., Joseph Wright 1989 Aug 28F
Altman, Sidney 1989 Oct 12I
Alunni, Corrado 1980 Apr 28B
Alva Castro, Luis 1988 Dec 17D
Alvarez, Luis (police officer) 1985 Jul 22F
Alvarez, Luis W. (physicist) 1980 Jan 1I; 1988 Sep 1I
Alvarez, Walter 1988 Sep 1I
Alvarez Martinez, Gustavo 1982 Apr 1D; 1983 Jun 9D; 1984 Mar 31D
Alves da Silva, Darly 1989 Jan 7D
Aly Khan, Prince 1987 May 14J
Amaro da Costa, Adelino 1980 Dec 4B
Ameche, Don 1986 Mar 24J
Amin, Hafizullah 1980 Jan 21E
Amin Dada, Idi 1980 Oct 7C/Oct 15C; 1981 Nov 19F; 1989 Jan 18C
Amis, Kingsley 1986 Oct 22J
Anaya Sanabria, Herbert Ernesto 1987 Oct 29D; 1988 Jan 5D
Anderson, Hesper 1986 Oct 3J
Anderson, Jack 1980 Apr 21F/Aug 16G
Anderson, John B.
    presidential campaign (1980): debates 1980 Jan 5F/Sep 9F/Sep 21F; primaries 1980 Mar 4F/Mar

18F/Apr 1F; candidacy 1980 Apr 24F; polls 1980 Jun 23F/Aug 19F; GOP nomination vote 1980 Jul 16F; press conference 1980 Jul 31F; Urban League address 1980 Aug 6F; running mate 1980 Aug 25F; endorsements 1980 Sep 6F; election results 1980 Nov 4F
    presidential campaign (1984): 1983 Nov 7F; 1984 Apr 26F/Aug 28F
Anderson, Robert Bernerd 1989 Aug 14H
Anderson, Sparky 1984 Oct 18J
Anderson, Terry A. 1985 Mar 16C; 1987 Dec 24C; 1988 Oct 31C
Anderson, Warren M. 1981 Sep 30H; 1984 Dec 7E; 1988 Nov 15E
Andersson, Benny 1986 May 14J
Andrade, Richard 1986 Dec 18F
Andrei, Alessandro 1987 Aug 12J
Andreotti, Giulio 1986 Jul 19B; 1989 Jul 23B
Andretti, John 1989 Feb 5J
Andretti, Mario 1981 May 25J; 1985 May 26J
Andrew, Prince (Great Britain) 1986 Mar 18J/Jul 23G; 1988 Aug 8B
Andropov, Yuri V.
    arms control: European limits 1982 Dec 21B; intermediate range missiles 1983 Jan 31B/Aug 26B/Nov 24B; Reagan plan 1983 Feb 1B; space weapons ban 1983 Apr 27I/Aug 18B; nuclear free zones 1983 Jun 6B
    economic policy: 1982 Nov 22B; 1983 Feb 23B/Aug 15B
    foreign policy: detente 1982 Nov 22B; Finland 1983 Jun 6B; U.S. 1982 Nov 15A; 1983 Jul 22A; West Germany 1983 Jun 4B; 1984 Feb 13B
    government: Soviet state and party posts 1982 May 24B/Nov 12B/Nov 23B; 1983 Jun 16B
    personal issues: illness 1983 Nov 5B/Dec 29B; death 1984 Feb 9B; funeral 1984 Feb 14B
Andrus, Cecil 1980 Feb 12H
Andrzejewski, Jerzy 1983 Apr 20J
Angell, Wayne D. 1985 Oct 19H
Anne, Princess (Great Britain) 1989 Aug 31B
Annenberg, Walter 1981 Feb 26J; 1988 Aug 7H
Anouilh, Jean 1987 Oct 3J
Anthony, Douglas 1982 Nov 10E
Antonioni, Michelangelo 1984 Feb 12J
Antonov, Serge Ivanov 1982 Nov 25B
Aoki, Isao 1980 Jun 15J
Aouita, Said 1985 Jul 27J; 1987 May 29J; 1989 Aug 20J
Aoun, Michel 1989 Sep 23C/Nov 5C/Dec 6C
Apel, Hans 1981 Mar 7B
Apted, Michael 1988 Sep 23J
Aquino Jr., Benigno Simeon
    assassination: 1983 Aug 21E/Aug 23E-24E/Aug 27E/Aug 30E; fu-

neral 1983 Aug 31E; investigation (civilian) 1983 Sep 12E/Oct 22E/Dec 28D; 1984 Jan 4E/Oct 23E/Oct 24E; investigation (military) 1983 Sep 17E; 1984 Jan 4E; indictments 1984 Nov 5E; 1985 Jan 23E; trial 1985 Feb 22E/May 2E/Dec 3E; 1986 Nov 18E
    government opposition: freed 1980 Apr 8E; coalition formed 1982 Feb 14E; movements monitored 1983 Nov 17E
Aquino III, Benigno 1987 Aug 28E
Aquino, Corazon
    civil strife: communist insurgency 1986 Mar 5E/Sep 12E-13E/Nov 23E; 1987 Mar 3E/Mar 21E/Mar 22E; Moslem insurgency 1986 Sep 5E; vigilante groups 1987 Mar 29E
    economic policy: trade 1986 Nov 10E/Nov 13E; land reform 1987 Mar 3E/Jul 22E; 1988 Jan 22E/Jun 10E; strikes 1987 Aug 26E/Oct 20E
    foreign policy: Japan visit 1986 Nov 10E/Nov 13E; U.S. visits 1986 Sep 15G/Sep 25G; 1989 Nov 7G
    government: anti-Marcos rally 1983 Sep 22E; military support 1986 Feb 22E; constitutional issues 1986 Mar 25E/Jun 2E/Oct 12E/Nov 5E; 1987 Feb 2E/Feb 11E; address to nation 1986 Jun 4E; opposition 1986 Oct 26E; 1988 Aug 27E; cabinet shakeup 1986 Nov 23E; 1987 Sep 17E; 1988 Jan 21E; legislative elections 1987 May 11E; Marcos bar 1988 May 4E; emergency powers 1989 Dec 6E/Dec 14E/Dec 19E; coup attempts 1989 Dec 7E
    personal issues: Time "Woman of the Year" 1986 Dec 27J
    presidential elections: 1985 Dec 3E/Dec 11E; 1986 Feb 7E/Feb 13E/Feb 16E/Feb 25E
Aquino, Ramon C. 1985 Nov 19E
Arafat, Yasir
    Arab-Israeli policy: Egypt 1983 Dec 22C/Dec 22G; 1988 Oct 22C; 1989 Mar 25C; Jordan 1982 Oct 13C/Nov 30C; 1983 Apr 5C/Apr 10C; 1984 Mar 1C; 1985 Oct 29C; 1986 Feb 19C; 1988 Oct 22C; 1989 Mar 25C; Lebanon 1982 Jun 27C/Jul 3C/Aug 30C/Sep 16C; 1983 Sep 18G/Dec 20C; Libya 1980 Jan 5C; occupied territories 1982 Sep 15C; 1983 Jan 20C; 1984 Feb 28C; Syria 1983 May 30C/Jun 23C-24C/Jul 19C; 1988 Apr 25C; UN 1985 Oct 14A; 1988 Nov 26A/Dec 13C
    foreign policy: China 1984 May 7A; France 1981 Aug 30C; 1989 May 2B; India 1980 Apr 9A; Japan 1981 Oct 14A; Soviet Union 1981

Oct 20A; 1988 Apr 9C; Vatican 1982 Sep 15A

PLO leadership: supporters of 1983 Jan 17C/Aug 4C; 1984 Nov 29C; 1987 Apr 26C; rebellion against 1983 May 19C/May 21C-22C/Jun 1C/Jun 18C/Jun 24C/Nov 3C/Nov 9C/Nov 16C/Nov 23C; terrorism opposed 1985 Nov 7C; 1988 Dec 17C

U.S. policy: 1980 Dec 5A; 1982 Jul 25C; 1988 Nov 12C/Nov 26A/Dec 7C

Arcand, Denys 1986 Nov 14J

Archer, Anne 1987 Sep 18J

Archer, Jeffrey

best-sellers: *First Among Equals* 1984 Aug 24J/Oct 19J; *Kane and Abel* 1980 Aug 17J; *Matter of Honor* 1986 Aug 29J/Sep 26J; *Prodigal Daughter* 1982 Jul 11J/Aug 8J/Sep 12J

Ardakani, Ali Shams 1983 Apr 3C

Ardant, Fanny 1981 Oct 11J

Ardebeli, Ayatollah Moussavi 1981 Aug 31C/Sep 18C

Ardito Barletta Vallarina, Nicolas 1984 May 7D/May 16B/Oct 11D; 1985 Sep 28E

Arens, Moshe 1981 Dec 26C; 1983 Feb 11C/Apr 13C/Jul 26C/Aug 16C; 1984 May 28C; 1989 Feb 22C

Argov, Shlomo 1982 Jun 3C/Jun 4C

Argue, Hazen 1980 Jul 24D/Nov 20D

Arguelles, Jose 1987 Aug 16J

Arguello, Alexis 1982 May 22J/Jul 31J/Nov 12J

Arias Madrid, Arnulfo 1984 May 7D/May 16B

Arias Sanchez, Oscar

Central American peace plan: 1987 Feb 21D/Jun 17D/Sep 20D/Dec 10H; 1988 Jan 12D/Feb 5D/Aug 10D

Nobel peace prize: 1987 Oct 13D/Dec 10H

presidential elections: 1986 Feb 2D; inauguration 1986 May 8D

Arieti, Silvano 1981 Aug 7I

Aristide, Jean Bertrand 1988 Sep 11D/Dec 15D

Arlen, Harold (Hyman Arluck) 1986 Apr 23J

Armada Comyn, Alfonso 1981 Feb 25B

Armitage, John 1989 Dec 3I

Armitage, Richard L. 1987 Mar 21E

Armstrong, Herbert W. 1986 Jan 15J

Armstrong, Louis 1983 Apr 22J; 1986 Jul 31J; 1989 Feb 26J

Armstrong, Patrick 1989 Oct 19B

Arnaz, Desi 1986 Dec 2J; 1989 Apr 26J

Arnold, R.C. 1983 Nov 28H

Aronson, Boris 1980 Nov 16J

Arosemena Gomez, Otto 1980 Sep 30D

Arquette, Rosanna 1985 Mar 29J

Arron, Henck A.E. 1980 Feb 25D

Arroyo, Joker 1987 Sep 17E

Arsht, Leslye 1988 Mar 3F

Arthit Kamlang-ek 1986 May 27E

Arthur, Bea 1988 Aug 28J

Artigas, Joseph 1983 Dec 25J

Artis, John 1985 Nov 7F

Artukovic, Andrija 1986 Feb 15B

Asch, Moses 1986 Oct 19J

Ashbery, John 1985 Jan 15J

Ashby, Hal 1988 Dec 27J

Ashcroft, John 1985 Apr 10H

Ashcroft, Peggy 1985 Mar 25J; 1986 Mar 16J

Ashe, Arthur 1980 Sep 7J; 1985 Jul 13J

Ashford, Emmet 1980 Mar 1J

Ashley, Laura 1985 Sep 17J

Ashton, Frederick 1988 Aug 18J

Ashton-Warner, Sylvia 1984 Apr 28J

Asimov, Isaac 1982 Dec 12J; 1983 Jan 16J; 1986 Oct 31J

Askew, Reubin 1983 Jul 10F; 1984 Jan 3G/Jan 15F/Feb 11F/Mar 1F

Asner, Ed 1980 Sep 7J

Aspenstrom, Werner 1989 Sep 21J

Aspin, Les 1983 Nov 23I; 1985 Jan 4G/Oct 6G

Assad, Hafez-al

Arab-Israeli policy: Israel 1981 Apr 11C; Jordan 1985 Dec 31C; Lebanon 1981 Apr 11C; 1982 Jul 15C; 1983 May 7C; 1984 Apr 20C; 1985 Mar 23C; PLO 1981 Mar 15J/Mar 24C; 1988 Apr 25C

government: purge 1980 Jan 1C; assassination attempt 1980 Jun 26C; opposition slaying 1980 Jul 21C; coup attempts 1982 Jan 30C/Mar 7C; premier named 1987 Nov 1C

U.S. policy: Habib meeting 1981 May 14C; accusations against 1982 Mar 7C; Reagan request rejected 1982 Jul 15C; Shultz meetings 1983 May 7C/Jul 6C; flier released 1984 Jan 3C/Jan 4C

Astaire, Fred 1987 Jun 22J

Astor, Mary 1987 Sep 24J

Astorga, Nora 1984 Mar 22G/Apr 18A

Atanasov, Georgi 1986 Mar 21B

Athanassiadis, Tzortzis 1983 Mar 19B

Athis, Louis Eugene 1987 Aug 2D

Athulathmudali, Lalith 1985 Jun 18E

Atkins, Chet 1983 Oct 20J

Atkins, Doug 1982 Aug 7J

Atkins, Humphrey 1981 Feb 12B; 1982 Apr 5B

Atkins, Richard 1982 Apr 5B

Atkins, Thomas I. 1983 May 20F

Atkinson, Brooks 1984 Jan 13J

Atkinson, Eugene 1981 Oct 14F

Attas, Haydar Bakr al- 1986 Jan 25C

Attlee, Clement 1986 May 8B

Atwa, Ali 1985 Oct 17G

Atwater, Lee 1989 Mar 7F

Atwood, Margaret 1986 Mar 28J

Aucoin, Les 1987 Aug 4G

Auel, Jean M.

best-sellers: *Mammoth Hunters* 1985 Dec 20J; 1986 Jan 31J/Feb 28J/Mar 28J/Apr 25J/May 30J; *Valley of Horses* 1982 Sep 12J/Oct 17J/Nov 14J/Dec 12J; 1983 Jan 16J/Feb 13J

August, Bille 1988 May 23J/Dec 21J

Aung San Suu Kyi 1989 Jul 20E

Austin, Hudson 1983 Oct 20D/Oct 30D

Austin, Tracy 1981 Sep 12J

Auteuil, Daniel 1987 Jun 26J

Autry, James D. 1983 Oct 5F/Oct 31F

Averof-Tossizza, Evanghelos 1980 May 8B

Avirgan, Tony 1988 Jun 23D

Avril, Prosper 1988 Sep 17D/Sep 22D; 1989 Apr 2D/Apr 10D/Jul 22D/Sep 17D/Sep 24D/Nov 28D

Awad, Musa 1983 Jun 1C

Axel, Gabriel 1988 Mar 4J

Ay, Omer 1982 Feb 16B

Ayer, A(lfred) J(ules) 1989 Jun 27J

Aykroyd, Dan 1989 Dec 13J

Aylwin, Patricio 1989 Dec 14B

Azcona Hoyo, Jose 1985 Dec 23D; 1986 Jan 27D; 1987 Dec 4D; 1988 Mar 16G

Aziz, Tariq 1980 Sep 25C; 1982 Dec 29C; 1984 Nov 26G

Azlan Shah ibni Sultan Yusuf Izzudin 1989 Mar 2E/Apr 26E

B

Babangida, Ibrahim 1985 Aug 27C/Dec 20C; 1986 Feb 24C; 1987 Jul 1C; 1989 Jan 17C

Babbitt, Bruce 1987 Jan 7F/Mar 10F/Aug 30F; 1988 Jan 4F/Feb 18F

Babbitt, Milton 1986 Dec 4J

Babcock, Barbara 1981 Sep 13J

Babenco, Hector 1985 Jul 26J; 1987 Dec 18J

Babiuch, Edward 1980 Aug 24B

Baby Jane Doe 1983 Nov 16F

Baby Jesse 1986 Jun 10I

Baby M (Melissa Stern) 1987 Mar 31F; 1988 Feb 3F

Baby Moses 1985 Nov 20I

Bach, Johann Sebastian 1984 Dec 19J

Bach, Richard 1988 Nov 25J/Dec 23J; 1989 Jan 27J

Bacharach, Burt 1987 Feb 24J

Bader, Douglas 1982 Sep 5B

Badran, Mudar 1989 Dec 4C/Dec 6C/Dec 19C

Baez, Joan 1986 Jan 25J

Bagaza, Jean-Baptiste 1987 Sep 3C

Bahonar, Jad 1981 Aug 30C

Bailey, Mildred 1986 Jul 31J

Bailey, Pearl 1988 Oct 17J

Bailyn, Bernard 1987 Apr 16J

Baker, Anita 1988 Dec 31J

Baker, Bobby 1980 Jun 15F

Baker, Buddy 1985 May 5J

Baker, Carlos 1987 Apr 18J

Baker, Chet (Chesney) 1988 May 14J

Baker, Ella 1986 Dec 13F

Baker Jr., Howard H.

economic policy: tax proposals 1982 Jun 22H

foreign policy: China arms sales 1982 Jun 1E; El Salvador aid 1981 Feb 25G; Saudi arms sales 1981 Apr 26G; terrorism 1983 Oct 24G

government service: Senate majority leader 1980 Dec 2F; Senate retirement 1983 Jan 21F; White House staff chief 1987 Feb 27F; 1988 Jun 14F

presidential elections: 1980 Jan 5F/Feb 17F/Mar 4F

Baker III, James A.

foreign policy: Cambodia peace talks 1989 Jul 6G; Europe 1989 Dec 12G; Israel 1989 Apr 4C; Israeli-Palestinian talks 1989 Dec 6C-8C; NATO nation tour 1989 Feb 11G; pan-Pacific region 1989 Jun 26A; Saudi AWACS deal 1981 Oct 29G; South Africa 1989 May 27G; Soviet Union 1989 May 10B

government service: treasury secretary 1985 Jan 8F/Jan 29H; 1988 Aug 5H; economic council 1985 Apr 11F; state secretary 1988 Nov 9F; 1989 Jan 25F

monetary and fiscal policy: tax plan hearings 1985 Jun 11H; dollar value decline 1985 Jul 25H; 1987 Jan 21A/Oct 19H; debtor nation aid plan 1985 Oct 11A/Dec 17D; 1986 Jun 29H; gold coin minting 1986 Sep 8H

Baker, Josephine 1984 Jan 31J

Baker, Kathy (actress) 1988 Aug 10J

Baker, Kathy (golfer) 1985 Jul 14J

Baker, Kenneth 1987 Mar 2B

Baker, Russell 1983 Apr 18J

Baker, Susan 1985 Aug 5J

Bakhtiar, Shahpur 1980 Jul 8C

Bakker, Jim

PTL scandal: ministry ends 1987 Mar 19J/Apr 28J/May 6J; Falwell

Babangida accused 1987 May 26J; ministry reorganization 1987 Oct 8J; ministry tax status revoked 1988 Apr 22H; indictment 1988 Dec 5F; mental breakdown 1989 Aug 31F; sentencing 1989 Oct 24F

TV revenues: 1980 Feb 25J

Bakker, Tammy Faye 1988 Mar 31J/Apr 22H

Bakkoush, Abdul Hamid 1984 Nov 17C

Balaguer, Joaquin 1986 May 26D/Aug 16D; 1987 Aug 11D

Balanchine, George 1983 Mar 16J/Apr 30J; 1984 Oct 9J; 1986 Dec 15J; 1988 Dec 30J; 1989 Sep 13J

Baldrige, Malcolm 1980 Dec 11F; 1982 Aug 2H; 1983 May 25E/Jul 21A; 1987 Jul 25H; 1988 Oct 17J

Baldwin, Adam 1988 Mar 30J

Baldwin, James (Arthur) 1987 Nov 30J

Baldwin, Roger 1981 Aug 26F

Balian, Alexander G. 1989 Feb 24G

Baliles, Gerald L. 1989 Jan 26F

Ball, Lucille 1986 Dec 2J; 1989 Apr 26J/Jul 6J

Ball III, William L. 1988 Feb 23G/Mar 30G

Balladur, Edouard 1986 Sep 10B; 1987 Sep 16B/Sep 24B

Ballard, Robert D. 1985 Sep 1J; 1986 Jul 13I

Ballesteros, Severiano 1980 Apr 13J; 1983 Apr 11J; 1984 Jul 22J; 1988 Jul 18J

Ballestrero, Anastasio Cardinal 1988 Oct 13J

Baltimore, David 1988 Dec 2I; 1989 Feb 1I

Balweg, Conrado 1986 Sep 13E

Bancroft, Ann (explorer) 1986 May 1I

Bancroft, Anne (actress) 1988 Mar 20J

Bane, Frank B. 1983 Jan 23F

Bang, Frederik Barry 1981 Oct 3I

Bani-Sadr, Abolhassan

government: as Iranian president 1980 Jan 25C; 1981 Jun 22; as Revolutionary Council head 1980 Feb 7C; as commander in chief 1980 Feb 19C; 1981 Jun 10C; Khomeini criticizes 1980 Jun 29C; premier appointed 1980 Jul 26C; power struggle 1981 Jan 31C/Feb 4C/Mar 8C/Mar 9C/Mar 16C/May 27C/Jun 7C; aide arrested 1981 May 19C; in hiding 1981 Jun 26C/Jul 5C; France grants asylum 1981 Jul 29C

Iran-Iraq War: 1980 Sep 20C/Oct 1A/Oct 12C; 1981 Jan 5C/Mar 2C

U.S. policy: shah 1980 Feb 13C/Apr 16C/Jun 4C; hostage crisis 1980 Feb 13C/Apr 16C/Jun 28C; 1981 Jan 26C

Banks, Dennis 1984 Sep 13F

Banks, Willie 1985 Jun 16J

Banzer Suarez, Hugo 1985 Jul 15D; 1989 May 7D/Aug 6D

Baraka, Amiri 1989 Jan 13J

Barber, Samuel 1981 Jan 23J

Barbera, Margaret 1982 Jun 16J

Barbie, Klaus

war crimes: extradition request 1983 Jan 15D/Jan 27B; arrest 1983 Jan 25D; expulsion 1983 Feb 4B; trial 1983 Feb 5B; 1987 May 11B/Jul 4B; U.S. postwar dealings 1983 Feb 8B/Mar 15G/Aug 16B; 1985 Jun 28G

Barco Vargas, Virgilio 1986 May 25D/Aug 7D; 1987 Jun 25D; 1988 Apr 14D; 1989 Aug 30D/Sep 6D/Sep 24D

Bardeen, John 1987 Oct 13I; 1989 Aug 12I

Bardo, John 1989 Jul 19F

Barenboim, Daniel 1987 Oct 19J; 1989 Jan 30J

Barfield, Margie Velma 1984 Nov 2F

Barilla, Paolo 1985 Jun 16J

Barish, Leora 1985 Mar 29J

Barker, Bob 1987 Feb 17J; 1988 Mar 1J

Barker, Len 1981 May 15J

Barkin, Ellen 1989 Sep 15J

Barkley, Iran 1988 Jun 6J; 1989 Aug 15J

Bar-Kochba, Moshe 1984 Jun 1C

Barlick, Al 1989 Feb 28J/Jul 23J

Barnes, David 1988 Sep 9J

Barnes, Michael D. 1984 May 9G

Barnett, David 1980 Oct 29G

Barnett, Marilyn 1981 May 1J

Barnum, P.T. 1980 Apr 30J

Baroni, Geno C. 1984 Aug 27F

Barr Jr., Alfred Hamilton 1981 Aug 15J

Barr, Stringfellow 1982 Feb 3J

Barrantes Lingan, Alfonso 1985 Apr 14D/Jun 1D

Barre de Nanteuil, Luc de la 1984 Feb 15A

Barrera de Cerna, Lucia 1989 Nov 23D

Barrett, Emma ("Sweet Emma") 1983 Jan 28J

Barrie, James 1986 May 12J

Barrionuevo Pena, Jose 1984 Jun 15B

Barros, Jose Miguel 1989 Jan 25D

Barrow, Errol W. 1986 May 28D; 1987 Jun 1D

Barrows, Sydney Biddle 1985 Jul 19J

Barry Jr., Marion S. 1984 Aug 28F; 1988 Dec 29F; 1989 Aug 30F/Nov 6F

Barry, Raymond J. 1989 Dec 20J

Barry, Rick 1987 Feb 5J

Barsukov, Valery 1989 Aug 22I

Barszcz, Edward 1981 May 24B

Barthelemy, Sidney 1987 Jan 23F

Barthelme, Donald 1989 Jul 23J

Barthes, Roland 1980 Mar 25J

Bartok, Bela 1986 Jun 13J; 1988 Jul 7J

Bartok Jr., Bela 1988 Jul 7J

Bartok, Peter 1988 Jul 7J

Baryalai, Mahmoud 1989 Jun 25E

Baryshnikov, Mikhail 1982 Jun 3J; 1989 Jun 21J/Sep 29J

Barzach, Michelle 1986 Nov 27B

Barzani, Massoud 1986 May 22C

Barzel, Rainer 1984 Oct 25B

Barzini, Luigi 1984 Mar 30J

Bashir, Omar Hassan Ahmed al- 1989 Jun 30C/Dec 18C

Basie, Count (William James) 1983 May 23J; 1984 Apr 26J; 1987 Jul 10J

Bass, Dick 1985 Apr 30J

Bass, Ronald 1988 Dec 16J

Bassett, Linda 1987 Mar 21J

Batard, Marc 1988 Sep 25J

Bates, Jim 1989 Oct 18F

Bates, Kathy 1983 Apr 1J

Bateson, Gregory 1980 Jul 4I

Baudouin, King (Belgium) 1981 Dec 17B; 1983 Sep 25J; 1985 Jul 16B; 1987 Oct 21B

Bauer, Charita 1985 Feb 28J

Baum, Vicki 1989 Dec 12J

Baum, William Cardinal 1980 Jan 15J

Bavadra, Timoci 1987 May 14E/May 24E

Baxter, Anne 1985 Dec 12J

Baxter, William 1981 Aug 26H; 1982 Jan 8H/Jun 17H

Bayer, Herbert 1985 Sep 30J

Bayne, Beverly 1982 Aug 29J

Baz, Osama el- 1982 Mar 22C

Bazargan, Mehdi 1984 May 28C

Beadle, George Wells 1989 Jun 9I

Beahrs, Oliver 1987 Oct 17F

Bean, Andy 1983 Jul 17J

Beard, James Andrews 1985 Jan 23J

Bearden, Romare (Howard) 1988 Mar 12J

Beaton, Cecil 1980 Jan 18J

Beatrice of York, Princess (Beatrice Elizabeth Mary) (Great Britain) 1988 Aug 8B
Beatrix, Queen (Beatrix Wilhelmina Amgard) (Netherlands) 1980 Jan 31B; 1981 Sep 2B; 1986 Oct 4B; 1989 May 2B
Beatty, Perrin 1986 Nov 10D; 1987 Feb 5D/Jun 5D; 1988 Jun 24B
Beatty, Warren 1982 Mar 29J
Beauman, Sally 1987 Apr 24J
Beavogui, Louis Lansana 1984 Mar 27C
Beck, Julian 1985 Sep 14J
Becker, Boris 1985 Jul 7J; 1986 Jul 6J; 1988 Jul 4J; 1989 Jul 9J/Sep 10J/Dec 17J
Becker, Harold 1989 Sep 15J
Beckett, Samuel Barclay 1984 May 3J; 1989 Dec 22J
Beckwith, Charles 1980 May 1C
Bedelia, Bonnie 1988 Jul 15J
Bednorz, J. Georg 1987 Oct 14I
Beeby, Thomas H. 1988 Jun 20J
Beggs, James 1981 Jun 18I; 1982 Jun 24I; 1983 Jul 18I
Begin, Aliza 1983 Jun 29C
Begin, Menachem
Arab-Israeli policy: Palestinian autonomy talks 1980 Jan 10C/Apr 16C/Aug 3C/Aug 9C; 1981 Aug 26C; Saudi Arabia 1980 May 27C; 1981 Apr 22C/Sep 13C/Nov 1C; EC fact-finding mission 1980 Jul 31A; Egypt 1980 Aug 15C; 1981 Jun 4C; Syria 1981 May 21C/May 24C; Iraq reactor bombing 1981 Jun 9C; UN speech 1982 Jun 18A
government: Jerusalem office move 1980 Jun 22C; parliamentary elections 1981 Jan 18C/Jun 30C; confidence votes 1981 Aug 5C/Dec 2C; 1982 Oct 19C; protests 1981 Nov 22C; coalition enlarged 1982 Jul 23C; resignation urged 1982 Sep 19C; Peres attacks 1983 Feb 14C; address to nation 1983 Apr 17C; resignation announced 1983 Aug 28C
Lebanese policy: Soviet role 1981 May 24C; Christian ties 1981 Jun 3C; U.S. role 1981 Jul 19A; 1982 Jun 6C/Jun 9G/Jun 13C/Jun 15G/Aug 4G; 1983 Jul 7C; PLO 1982 Jun 29C/Jul 17C; Gemayel assassination 1982 Sep 15C; Beirut refugee camp massacre 1982 Sep 19C-20C/Sep 22G/Sep 25C/Sep 29C/Nov 6C/Nov 14/Nov 18/Nov 24C
occupation policy: Gaza Strip 1981 Oct 15C; West Bank 1981 Oct 15C; 1982 May 3C; territorial concessions 1982 Apr 27C; Jewish settlements 1982 May 2C; 1983 Apr 17C
personal issues: ill health 1980 Jun 30C; 1983 Jun 29C
U.S. policy: Palestinian autonomy talks 1980 Apr 16C; Saudi arms sales 1981 Apr 22C/Sep 13C; criticism 1981 Jul 22C/Aug 31G/Dec 20C; Reagan meetings 1981 Sep 10G; 1982 Jun 21G; Beirut massacre 1982 Sep 22G
Begin, Monique 1983 Dec 12D
Begun, Iosif Z. 1987 Feb 20B
Beheshti, Ayatollah Mohammed 1981 Jun 28C
Beikman, Charles 1980 Apr 8D
Belafonte, Harry 1986 Oct 6J
Belaga, Julie 1986 Sep 9F
Belaunde Terry, Fernando 1980 May 18D/Jul 28D; 1983 May 31D; 1984 Apr 9D; 1985 Jul 28D
Bel Geddes, Barbara 1986 Jan 14J
Bell, Buddy 1980 Dec 6J
Bell, Derek 1986 Feb 2J/Jun 1J; 1987 Feb 1J/Jun 14J; 1989 Feb 5J
Bell, George 1987 Nov 17J
Bell, Terrel H. 1981 Jan 7F/Feb 2F; 1982 Aug 3F/Sep 29F/Dec 6H; 1985 Jan 10F
Bellow, Saul 1982 Mar 7J/Apr 11J
Belushi, John 1983 Mar 18J; 1986 Mar 5J
Belvin, Harry J.W. ("Jimmy") 1986 Sep 18J
Benacerraf, Baruj 1980 Oct 10I
Ben Ali, Zine el-Abidine 1987 Nov 7C; 1989 Apr 2C
Benatar, Pat
best-sellers: *Crimes of Passion* 1980 Oct 8J/Dec 3J; 1981 Jan 7J/Feb 11J/Mar 4J; *Get Nervous* 1982 Nov 17J/Dec 15J; 1983 Jan 5J; *Precious Time* 1981 Aug 5J/Sep 9J
Ben Bella, Ahmed 1980 Oct 30C
Bench, Johnny 1989 Jan 9J/Jul 23J
Benchley, Nathaniel 1981 Dec 14J
Benchley, Peter 1981 Dec 14J
Benchley, Robert 1981 Dec 14J
Benelissar, Eliahu 1980 Feb 23C
Benirschke, Rolf 1982 Jan 2J
Benitez, Wilfred 1982 Dec 4J
Benjedid, Chadli 1983 Feb 26C; 1984 Jan 12C; 1987 May 4C; 1988 Oct 12C/Nov 4C; 1989 Sep 9C
Ben Jelloun, Tahar 1987 Nov 16J
Benn, Tony 1981 Sep 27B; 1982 Oct 27B
Bennett, Don 1982 Jul 18J
Bennett, Gareth 1987 Dec 7J
Bennett, John C. 1980 May 4J
Bennett, Michael 1981 Dec 20J; 1987 Jul 2J
Bennett, William J.
"drug czar": appointment 1989 Jan 12F; confirmation 1989 Mar 9F
education secretary: appointment 1985 Jan 10F; confirmation 1985 Feb 6H; budget cuts 1985 Feb 11F; bilingualism 1985 Sep 26F; voucher system 1985 Nov 13F; effective teaching 1986 Mar 4F; eligibility rules 1987 Nov 4F; ideal curriculum 1987 Dec 29F; trade schools 1988 Feb 9F; segregation 1988 Feb 10F; system "at risk" 1988 Apr 24F; resignation 1988 May 9F
Benoit, Joan 1984 Aug 5J
Benson, Ezra Taft 1985 Nov 11J
Benton, Robert 1980 Apr 14J; 1984 Sep 21J
Bentsen Jr., Lloyd M. 1986 Jan 7F; 1987 Feb 6F; 1988 Jul 12F/Sep 14F/Oct 5F/Dec 2F; 1989 Jan 4F
Benvenisti, Meron 1985 Feb 9C
Benyahia, Muhammad 1982 May 3C
Berbick, Trevor 1986 Mar 23J/Nov 22J
Berenger, Tom 1986 Dec 19J
Beresford, Bruce 1983 Mar 4J; 1986 Dec 12J; 1989 Dec 13J
Berezovoy, Anatoly 1982 Aug 20I,1982 Nov 14I
Berg, Alan 1984 Jun 18F/Oct 18F; 1985 Apr 15F; 1987 Nov 17F
Berg, Alban 1981 Feb 25J
Berg, Paul 1980 Oct 14I
Bergen, Candice 1989 Sep 17J
Berger, Gerhard 1987 Nov 15J; 1988 Sep 11J
Bergland, Bob 1980 Feb 29H
Bergman, Ingmar 1983 Jun 17J
Bergman, Ingrid 1982 Aug 29J
Bergner, Elisabeth 1986 May 12J
Bergstroem, Sune K. 1982 Oct 11I
Berlin, Irving (Israel Baline) 1984 Feb 15J; 1986 Jun 17J; 1988 May 11J; 1989 Sep 22J
Berlinguer, Enrico 1984 Jun 12J
Bermudez, Enrique 1988 Jul 18D
Bernardin, Joseph L. Cardinal 1982 Jul 10J; 1983 Feb 2J
Bernbach, William 1982 Oct 2J
Berne, Eric 1985 Jan 13J
Bernstein, Leonard 1987 Aug 9J; 1988 May 11J
Berri, Claude 1987 Jun 26J
Berri, Nabih 1984 Feb 24C/Mar 14C/May 10C/Sep 12C; 1985 Jun 26C; 1988 Jan 16C
Berrigan, Daniel 1985 Nov 22F
Berrigan, Philip 1985 Nov 22F
Berrigan, Ted 1983 Jul 4J
Berry, Chuck 1986 Jan 23J
Berry, Mary Frances 1983 Dec 16F
Berry, Walter 1986 Mar 1J
Bertie, Andrew 1988 Apr 8J
Bertolucci, Bernardo 1987 Nov 20J; 1988 Apr 11J; 1989 Mar 19J
Bertrand, Maurice 1985 Sep 30A
Bespalov, Ivan P. 1985 Mar 22B
Besse, Georges 1986 Nov 17B
Bessie, Alvah 1985 Jul 21J
Bessmertnykh, Alexander A. 1986 Dec 8B; 1988 Nov 4B
Bester, Charles 1988 Dec 5C
Bestiamanova, Natalya 1986 Mar 21J
Betancourt, Romulo 1981 Sep 28D
Betancourt de Liski, Regina 1980 Mar 9D
Betancur Cuartas, Belisario
civil strife: amnesty 1982 Dec 5D; regional talks 1983 Oct 5D; state of siege 1984 May 1D; Justice palace assault 1985 Nov 13D
foreign policy: Reagan meets 1982 Dec 3D; papal visit 1986 Jun 30A
government: presidential elections 1982 May 31D; inauguration 1982 Aug 7D; nationalizations 1986 Jan 19D
Betjeman, John 1984 Dec 19J
Bettis, Valerie 1982 Sep 26J
Beuys, Joseph 1986 Jan 23J
Beveridge, Lord 1988 Apr 11B
Bhave, Vinoba Acharya 1982 Nov 15E
Bhindranwale, Jarnail Singh 1984 Jun 6E/Jun 7E
Bhumibol Adulyadej, King (Thailand) 1986 May 1E/Aug 5E
Bhutto, Benazir
foreign policy: Commonwealth readmittance 1989 Jul 3E; India 1988 Dec 29E; U.S. visit 1989 Jun 10G
government: elections 1988 Nov 16E/Nov 19E; 1989 Feb 2E; as Pakistani prime minister 1988 Dec 1E; cabinet formed 1988 Dec 4E; parliament confidence vote 1988 Dec 12E; 1989 Nov 1E
personal issues: brother's death 1985 Aug 22E/Aug 29E/Nov 4E; marriage 1987 Jul 30E/Dec 18E
political opposition: release from detention 1984 Jan 10E; 1986 Sep 8E; return to Pakistan 1985 Aug 22E; 1986 Apr 10E; brother's death 1985 Aug 22E/Aug 29E/Nov 4E; arrest 1986 Aug 14E
Bhutto, Shahnawaz 1985 Aug 22E/Aug 29E/Nov 4E
Biaggi, Mario 1987 Mar 16F/Jun 3F/Sep 22F; 1988 Aug 4F
Bias, Len 1986 Mar 1J/Jun 19J
Biden Jr., Joseph R.
plagiarism incident: 1987 Sep 23F/Sep 30F; 1988 Sep 2F
politics: intelligence information limits 1982 Mar 16F; Bork Supreme Court nomination 1987 Jul 23F/Aug 11F
presidential campaign: candidacy 1987 Jun 9F; polls 1987 Aug 30F
Bieber, Owen F. 1983 May 18F; 1984 Oct 4H; 1986 Jun 4H; 1989 Jun 21H
Bignone, Reynaldo Benito Antonio
government: presidency 1982 Jun 22D-23D/Jul 1D; political parties 1982 Jul 16D/Aug 3D; elections 1982 Dec 1D; 1983 Feb 28D; arrest 1984 Jan 10D
Biko, Steven 1980 Jun 29C
Biletnikoff, Fred 1988 Feb 2J/Jul 30J
Billington, James H. 1987 Apr 17J/Sep 14J
Binaisa, Godfrey 1980 May 11C
Bingham Sr., Barry 1986 Jan 9H
Bingham, Jonathan Brewster 1986 Jul 3F
Bingham, Stephen 1986 Jun 27F
Binner, Gerd 1986 Oct 15I
Binoche, Juliette 1988 Feb 5J
Biondi, Matt 1985 Aug 7J/Aug 17J/Aug 18J
Bird, Henry ("Professor Longhair") 1980 Jan 30J
Bird, Junius Bouton 1982 Apr 2I
Bird, Larry 1985 Jun 3J; 1986 May 28J/Jun 8J
Birendra, King (Nepal) 1985 Jun 20E
Birtwistle, Harrison 1987 Sep 29J
Bishop, J. Michael 1989 Oct 9I
Bishop, Maurice 1980 Jun 20D; 1983 Oct 19D/Oct 30D; 1984 Feb 22D/Oct 16D; 1986 Dec 4E
Bissell, Silas 1987 Jan 20F
Bitar, Salah el- 1980 Jul 21C
Bitov, Oleg 1984 Sep 18B
Bitterman III, Chester Allen 1981 Mar 7D
Biya, Paul 1982 Nov 6C; 1986 Aug 24C
Bjelke, Erik 1982 Sep 11I
Bjelke-Petersen, Johannes 1980 Nov 29E; 1981 Jul 20E; 1987 Apr 28E
Black, Barbara Aronstein 1986 Jan 2F
Black, James W. 1988 Oct 17I
Black, Stephen Don 1981 Jun 20D
Blackmun, Harry A. 1984 Sep 18F/Oct 10F; 1985 Feb 28F; 1987 Jun 19F/Sep 25J
Blaize, Herbert Augustus 1984 Dec 3D
Blake, Eubie 1983 Feb 7J/Feb 12J
Blakemore, Michael 1987 Oct 27J
Blalock, Alfred 1986 May 20I
Blanc, Mel(vin Jerome) 1989 Jul 10J
Blanchard, James J. 1985 Nov 8F; 1988 Jun 27F
Blanco, Salvador Jorge 1982 May 16D/Aug 16D; 1987 Apr 30D; 1988 Nov 27D
Blecha, Karl 1987 Dec 24B
Blechman, Barry M. 1986 Jul 22G
Blewett, Neal 1984 Feb 1E; 1985 Mar 27E
Bloch, Felix (physicist) 1983 Sep 10I
Bloch, Felix S. (diplomat) 1989 Jul 21G/Dec 16G
Block, John R.
agricultural policy: foreclosures 1982 Jan 21H; grain cuts 1982 Jan 29H; price supports 1982 May 5H; 1986 Jan 13H; surplus food distribution 1982 Jun 1H; farm bill 1985 Feb 22H; farm credit system 1985 Dec 19H
government service: agriculture post resignation 1986 Jan 7H
grain sales: Algeria 1985 Jun 4H; El Salvador 1983 Aug 6G; Soviet Union 1985 Aug 30A
Bloembergen, Nicolaas 1981 Oct 19I
Bloomfield, Michael 1981 Feb 15J
Blount, Mel 1989 Jan 24J
Bluford, Guion S. 1983 Sep 5I
Blum, Norbert 1982 Oct 5B
Blume, Judy 1984 Mar 23J/Apr 20J/Dec 3J
Blumenthal, Richard 1980 Feb 11F
Blunt, Anthony 1980 Aug 18J; 1981 Nov 1B; 1983 Mar 26B
Bobo, Willie 1983 Sep 15J
Boddy, Brent 1986 May 1I
Bodine, Geoff 1986 Feb 16J
Boehm, Gottfried 1986 Apr 17J
Boehm, Karl 1981 Aug 14J
Boesel, Raul 1988 Jan 31J
Boesky, Ivan F. 1986 Nov 14H/Dec 11H; 1987 Apr 23H/Sep 23H/Dec 18F; 1988 Mar 24H
Bogosian, Eric 1987 May 28J
Boisjoly, Roger 1986 May 13I
Boitano, Brian 1985 Feb 1J; 1986 Feb 8J/Mar 21J; 1987 Mar 12J; 1988 Jan 9J/Mar 25J
Bok, Derek C. 1984 Apr 19F
Bokassa, Jean-Bedel 1986 Oct 23C; 1987 Jun 12C
Boland, Edward P. 1983 Apr 13G
Bolcom, William 1988 Mar 31J
Bolger, Ray (Raymond Wallace) 1987 Jan 15J
Bolger, William 1980 Apr 21H
Boll, Heinrich Theodore 1985 Jul 16J
Bolling, Richard 1982 Apr 29F
Bolt, Robert 1986 Oct 31J
Bonanno Sr., Joseph 1980 Sep 2F; 1985 Sep 6F
Bond, Larry 1989 Jun 30J/Jul 28J/Aug 25J
Boney, Lloyd James 1987 Aug 15E
Bonior, David 1987 Feb 25D
Bonker, Don 1983 Nov 9G
Bonner, Neville 1983 Jun 15E
Bonner, Yelena G. 1980 Jan 22B; 1982 Apr 8B; 1984 May 2B/Aug 23B; 1985 Oct 28B/Dec 6A; 1986 Dec 19B
Bono, Sonny 1988 Feb 26J
Bontempo, Michael A. 1982 Oct 21F
Boorman, John 1987 Oct 16J; 1988 Jan 3J
Boorstin, Daniel J. 1986 Dec 10J; 1987 Apr 17J/Sep 14J
Bordaberry, Juan Maria 1985 Mar 1C
Bordonaro, Vincent 1983 May 12F/May 27F
Boren, Richard 1988 Mar 9D
Borg, Bjorn 1980 Jun 8J/Jul 6J/Sep 7J; 1981 Jun 7J/Jul 4J/Sep 13J
Borge, Tomas 1985 Jun 28D; 1987 Oct 3D
Borges, Jorge Luis 1981 May 12D; 1986 Jun 14J
Borisov, Vladimir 1980 Mar 29B
Borja Cevallos, Rodrigo 1984 Jan 28D/May 6D; 1988 Jan 31D/May 8D/Aug 10D
Bork, Robert H.
federal appeals court rulings: 1981 Dec 7F; 1987 Jul 28H; 1988 Jan 14F
Supreme Court nomination: 1987 Jul 1F/Oct 9F; support 1987 Jul 17F/Jul 23F/Sep 8F; opposition 1987 Jul 23F/Aug 11F/Aug 31F; polls 1987 Aug 2F; testimony 1987 Sep 15F/Sep 19F; Senate votes 1987 Oct 6F/Oct 23F
Bormann, Martin 1984 Sep 21I
Borusewicz, Bogdan 1986 Jan 11B
Bosch, Orlando 1986 Jul 21D
Boschwitz, Rudy 1983 Mar 3H
Bosco, Philip 1989 Jun 4J
Boskin, Michael J. 1988 Dec 6F; 1989 May 1H
Bossano, Joe 1988 Mar 24B
Botha, Pieter W.
apartheid: homelands 1980 Aug 8C; 1985 Sep 11C; political prisoner amnesty 1985 Feb 28C; church leadership meeting 1985 Aug

19C; Mandela imprisonment 1986 Jan 31C; 1988 Aug 18C; pass laws 1986 Jan 31C/Apr 18C; Tutu meeting 1986 Jun 13C; Buthelezi meeting 1987 Nov 3C; death sentences commuted 1988 Nov 23C; Great Trek ceremony 1988 Dec 16C; Mandela meeting 1989 Jul 5C

arms control: nuclear weapons curb 1987 Sep 21C

foreign policy: EC mission 1986 Jul 29C; Taiwan 1980 Oct 13A; UN 1985 Jul 29C; 1988 Sep 22C; Western Europe tour 1984 Jun 14A; Zambia 1982 Apr 30C

government: parliamentary elections 1981 Jan 28C/Apr 30C; 1985 Oct 30C; 1987 Jan 30C/May 6C; party members expelled 1982 Mar 3C; constitution endorsed 1983 Nov 2A; elected South African president 1984 Sep 5C; cabinet announced 1984 Sep 15C; speeches 1985 Aug 15C/Sep 30C; state of emergency 1986 Mar 7C/Aug 1C; 1987 Jun 10C; party congress 1988 Aug 13C; resignation as party leader 1989 Feb 2C; return to presidency 1989 Mar 17C; resignation as president 1989 Aug 14C

Namibia: 1980 Jun 13C; 1984 Jun 9C; 1985 Apr 18C; 1988 Sep 22C

personal issues: ill health 1989 Jan 18C

Botha, Roelof ("Pik") 1981 May 15C; 1982 Nov 28C; 1989 May 27G

Botha, Stoffel 1988 Nov 1C

Bouchard, Benoit 1986 Sep 10D

Boudin, Kathy 1981 Oct 20F/Oct 22F; 1984 May 3F

Boulez, Pierre 1981 Feb 25J

Boult, Adrian 1983 Feb 23J

Boumedienne, Houari 1980 Oct 30C

Bourassa, Robert 1983 Oct 15D; 1986 Jan 20D

Bourdeaux, Michael 1984 May 15J

Bourgeois, Louise 1983 Feb 19J

Bourguiba, Habib 1984 Jan 6C; 1986 Jul 8C; 1987 Oct 2C/Nov 7C

Bouterse, Desi 1982 Nov 3D; 1986 Oct 25E/Dec 13D; 1987 Nov 25D; 1989 Jul 25D

Boutsen, Thierry 1985 Feb 3J

Bowdon, Mark 1983 Mar 18I

Bowen, Billy 1982 Sep 27J

Bowen, Lionel 1983 Aug 12E

Bowen, Otis R. 1985 Nov 7F/Dec 12F; 1986 Nov 20F/Dec 24F; 1987 Jul 22F/Oct 16F

Bowie, David 1983 May 11J/Jun 15J

Bowles, Chester Bliss 1986 May 25F

Bowsher, Charles A. 1989 Sep 27F

Boyce, Christopher 1981 Aug 21G

Boyd, Alisdair 1986 Apr 24J

Boyd, William C. 1983 Feb 19I

Boyle, Richard 1986 Mar 5J

Boyle, T. Coraghessan 1988 May 14J

Boyle, Tony (William Anthony) 1985 May 31F

Brach, Gerard 1987 Jun 26J

Bracy, Arnold 1987 Jun 12G

Brademas, John 1980 Dec 8F

Bradford, Barbara Taylor 1983 May 15J; 1985 Jun 14J/Jul 19J; 1986 Jul 18J; 1988 Jul 23J/Aug 26J

Bradford, Robert 1981 Nov 14B/Nov 23B

Bradley, Bill 1986 Jun 29H

Bradley, James 1985 Dec 15D/Dec 17D

Bradley, Jenny 1983 Jun 3J

Bradley, Melvin L. 1982 Apr 19F

Bradley, Omar 1981 Apr 8G

Bradley, Pat 1981 Jul 26J; 1986 Jun 1J

Bradley, Tom 1985 Apr 9F; 1989 Apr 11F

Bradshaw, Terry 1989 Jan 24J

Brady, James S. 1981 Mar 24F/Mar 30F; 1989 Nov 21F

Brady, Nicholas F. 1982 Apr 12F; 1988 Aug 5H/Sep 15H/Nov 15F; 1989 Feb 23H/May 24A

Brailovsky, Viktor 1980 Nov 13B

Braine, John (Gerard) 1986 Oct 28J

Branagh, Kenneth 1989 Nov 8J

Branch, Taylor 1989 Mar 30J

Brando, Marlon 1983 Nov 18J; 1989 Sep 20J

Brandstetter, Wanda 1980 Nov 7F

Brandt Jr., Edward N. 1983 May 24I

Brandt, Willy 1983 Feb 9A; 1987 Mar 23B/Jun 14B; 1988 Mar 8B

Brassaï (Gyula Halasz) 1984 Jul 8J

Brattain, Walter Houser 1987 Oct 13I; 1989 Aug 12I

Braudel, Fernand (Paul Achille) 1985 Nov 28J

Brautigan, Richard 1984 Oct 25J

Brawley, Tawana 1988 Feb 29F/Oct 6F; 1989 Apr 27F

Braxton, Dwight 1983 Mar 18J

Brecht, Bertolt 1984 May 3J

Breeden, Richard C. 1989 Oct 6H

Brelis, Matthew 1987 Apr 16J

Brennan Jr., William J. 1980 Oct 24F; 1984 Oct 29G; 1985 Jul 1F/Oct 12F/Oct 25F; 1987 Sep 25J

Brett, George 1980 Nov 18J; 1985 Oct 16J

Breuning, Stephen E. 1987 May 24F; 1988 Apr 15F

Breytenbach, Breyten 1986 Apr 12J

Breytenbach, Jan 1989 Nov 20C

Brezhnev, Leonid I.

agriculture: 1980 Oct 21B; 1981 Nov 16B; 1982 May 24B

arms control: Persian Gulf demilitarization 1980 Dec 11A; 1982 Apr 6A; European missile deployment 1981 Apr 3B/Nov 25B/Dec 2B; 1982 Feb 3A/Mar 16B-16G/Mar 27A; U.S. talks 1981 Jun 23A; preemptive nuclear strike bar 1981 Nov 2A; nuclear freeze proposal 1982 May 18A/Jun 15A/Oct 28G

foreign policy: China 1982 Mar 24A/Sep 26A; France 1980 May 19B; Lebanon 1982 Jul 20A; Middle East 1981 May 22A; 1982 Sep 15C; Persian Gulf 1980 Dec 9A/Dec 11A; Poland 1981 Apr 7B/Apr 8B/Apr 14B/Jul 21B/Aug 15B/Dec 23G; 1982 Aug 16B; West Germany 1980 Jul 1B; 1981 Apr 3B/Nov 25B/Dec 2B

government: Politburo reelected 1981 Mar 3B; retirement 1982 Sep 4B

Olympic Games: 1980 May 7J

personal issues: ill health 1982 Apr 2B/Apr 22B/May 1B; retirement 1982 Sep 4B; death 1982 Nov 10B; funeral 1982 Nov 15B

U.S. policy: 1981 Feb 23A/Mar 10A/Jun 23A/Sep 7A/Dec 23G; 1982 Apr 19A/Sep 15C/Oct 27A

Bricchetti, Renato 1983 Aug 28B

Bricktop (Ada Beatrice Queen Victoria Louise Virginia Smith) 1984 Jan 31J

Bridges, Beau 1989 Nov 13J

Bridges, Jeff 1989 Nov 13J

Briggs, Charles H. 1984 Jul 1G

Briggs, Everett Ellis 1986 Nov 3D; 1988 May 7G

Brightman, Sarah 1986 Oct 9J; 1987 Jul 2J

Brindel, Glenn R. 1987 Jul 27G

Brink, André 1989 Sep 20J

Brink, David R. 1982 Apr 28F

Brinkley, David 1981 Sep 18J

Brisbin, David 1987 Sep 18J

Brisson, Frederick 1984 Oct 8J

Brittan, Leon 1985 Jun 25B/Jul 10B/Dec 19B; 1986 Jan 24B; 1988 Jul 22B

Britten, Benjamin 1986 Apr 3J

Britten, Terry 1985 Feb 26J

Britz, Jerilyn 1981 Jun 14J

Broadbent, Edward 1984 Aug 15D; 1988 Oct 28D; 1989 Mar 4D

Brock, Lou 1985 Jan 7J/Jul 28J

Brock III, William E.

government service: named labor secretary 1985 Mar 20H/Apr 26H

labor policy: affirmative action 1985 Jun 27F; farm workers 1985 Sep 11H

politics: Carter policy attack 1980 Jan 1G; Dole campaign 1987 Nov 3H

trade policy: Japan import laws 1983 May 13E; copper imports 1984 Sep 6H; EC pipe/tube imports 1985 Jan 11A

Brocka, Lino 1983 May 17E

Broderick, Matthew 1985 Mar 28J; 1989 Dec 14J

Brodsky, Joseph 1987 Jan 12J/Oct 22J

Brokaw, Tom 1987 Dec 1F

Bron, Eleanor 1988 Oct 21J

Brook, Peter 1987 Oct 13J

Brooks, Albert 1987 Dec 16J

Brooks Jr., Charles 1982 Dec 7F

Brooks, James L. 1983 Nov 23J; 1984 Apr 9J; 1987 Dec 16J

Brooks, Louise 1985 Aug 8J

Brower, Eugene 1989 May 23F

Brown, Bobby 1989 Jan 29J/Feb 25J/Mar 25J/Apr 29J/Jun 24J/Jul 29J

Brown, Bryan 1988 Sep 23J

Brown, Christy 1989 Nov 10J

Brown, Clarence 1987 Aug 17J

Brown, Dale 1989 Jul 28J

Brown, Douglas J. 1986 Jan 19F

Brown, Harold R.

defense policy: China talks 1980 Jan 13E/May 29G; military posture 1980 Jan 29G; armed forces recruitment 1980 Jun 11G; Saudi arms deal 1980 Oct 5C; Japan talks 1980 Dec 12G; SDI limits urged 1986 Aug 17G; procurement practices 1988 Dec 19G

Brown, Harrison (Scott) 1986 Dec 8I

Brown, Ira A. 1987 May 29H

Brown, Irving 1988 Oct 17J

Brown, Jackson 1980 Sep 10J

Brown, James 1986 Jan 23J

Brown Jr., Jerry (Edmund) 1980 Jan 12F/Feb 10F; 1981 Jul 10H

Brown, Joyce 1988 Jan 19F

Brown, Michael S. 1985 Oct 14I/Nov 22I

Brown, Ronald H. 1989 Feb 10F

Brown, Ruth 1989 Jun 4J

Brown, Sterling Allen 1989 Jan 13J

Brown, Tim 1987 Dec 5J

Browne, Jackson 1980 Aug 13J

Browning, Edmond L. 1985 Sep 10J

Browning, Kurt 1989 Mar 16J

Brubeck, Dave 1987 Mar 26J

Bruce, Aundray 1988 Apr 24J

Bruce, Robert V. 1988 Mar 31J

Bruce, Virginia 1982 Feb 24J

Brucker, Victoria 1989 Aug 23J

Bruhn, Erik 1986 Apr 1J

Brundle, Martin 1988 Jan 31J

Brundtland, Gro Harlem 1981 Feb 4B; 1986 May 9B/Jun 17B; 1989 Sep 11B/Oct 16B

Bruno, Frank 1986 Jul 20J; 1989 Feb 25J

Brutus, Dennis 1983 Sep 6F

Bryant, Paul ("Bear") 1982 Dec 15J/Dec 29J; 1983 Jan 26J

Brynner, Yul 1985 Jun 30J/Oct 10J

Brzezinski, Zbigniew 1980 Sep 6G/Sep 17F; 1981 Feb 20F/Aug 12G

Bua, Nicholas J. 1982 Oct 5I; 1985 Aug 1H

Buback, Siegfried 1980 Jul 31B

Bubbles, John (John William Sublett) 1986 May 18J

Bubka, Sergei 1985 Jul 13J

Bucaram, Assad 1980 Apr 11D

Bucaram Ortiz, Abdala 1988 Jan 31D/May 8D

Buchanan, James McGill 1986 Oct 16H

Buchwald, Art 1988 Nov 21J

Buck, Jason 1986 Nov 29J

Buck, Marilyn Jean 1985 May 11F

Buckley, Esther Gonzales-Arroyo 1983 Dec 6F

Buckley, James L. 1982 Mar 20A; 1985 Dec 17F

Buckley, William F. (CIA agent) 1984 Mar 16C/Oct 2C; 1985 Jan 28C/Oct 4C

Buckley Jr., William F. (political commentator) 1982 Feb 7J/Mar 7J; 1987 Oct 28F

Budd, Zola 1984 Aug 19J; 1986 Mar 23J

Buendia, Manuel 1989 Jun 13D

Bueno Delgado, Guillermo 1989 Sep 12D

Bueso Rosa, Jose 1985 Nov 20D; 1986 Jul 23D

Buettner-Janusch, John 1980 Jul 16F/Nov 13F

Bufman, Zev 1983 Mar 10J

Buhari, Mohammed 1983 Dec 31C; 1984 Jan 3C/May 7C; 1985 Aug 27C

Bujak, Zbigniew 1982 Aug 1B; 1986 May 31B

Bujold, Genevieve 1988 Sep 23J

Bukharin, Nikolai I. 1988 Feb 5B

Bukin, Andrei 1986 Mar 21J

Bumpers, Dale 1983 Jan 15F; 1987 Apr 9F

Bundy, Ted (Theodore) 1989 Jan 24F

Bunker, Ellsworth 1984 Sep 27G

Bunshaft, Gordon 1988 May 24J

Bunting, Basil 1985 Apr 17J

Bunton III, Lucius D. 1988 Sep 30F; 1989 May 5F

Bunuel, Luis 1983 Jul 30J

Bunzel, John H. 1983 Dec 6F

Burcham, Jack C. 1985 Apr 24I

Burford, Anne McGill Gorsuch

EPA Superfund controversy: 1982 Dec 16F; 1983 Feb 3H/Feb 7H/Mar 3H-4H/Mar 9H/Mar 16/Aug 11H/Sep 28H

government service: EPA administrator 1981 Feb 21H; 1983 Mar 9H; coastal panel appointment controversy 1984 Jul 2H/Aug 1H

Burger, Warren E.

bicentennial commission: 1985 Jun 25F

ceremonial duties: O'Connor sworn 1981 Sep 25F; Reagan sworn 1985 Jan 20F

judicial issues: violent crime penalties 1981 Feb 8F; Nixon improper talks 1981 Dec 10F; legal arbitration 1982 Jan 24F; court workload 1982 Nov 18F; 1984 Jan 2F/Dec 30F; 1985 Feb 17F; prison reform 1983 Jan 2F; legal profession 1984 Feb 14F/Aug 5F; traditional standards 1986 Aug 11F

personal issues: retirement 1986 Jun 17F; Medal of Freedom 1988 Oct 17J

Supreme Court rulings: A-plant licensing 1984 Aug 21H; Sabbath work laws 1985 Jun 26F

Burgess, Guy 1983 Mar 6B/Mar 26B; 1988 May 11B

Burke, Kelly 1982 Apr 22G

Burnet, (Frank) Macfarlane 1985 Aug 31I

Burnett, Carol 1981 Mar 27J

Burnham, Forbes 1980 Oct 6D; 1984 Jul 5A/Aug 11D; 1985 Aug 6D

Burnley IV, James H. 1987 Oct 8H/Nov 30H; 1988 Oct 3H

Burns, Arnold I. 1988 Jul 26F

Burns, Arthur F. 1987 Jun 26H

Burns, John F. 1986 Jul 23E

Burroughs, Jackie 1989 Mar 22J

Burroughs, William 1983 Feb 19J

Burrows, Abe 1985 May 17J

Burrows, Eva 1986 May 2A

Burton, Charles 1982 Aug 29I

Burton, Phillip 1983 Apr 10F/Apr 12H

Burton, Richard (Richard Jenkins) 1983 Mar 10J; 1984 Aug 5J

Burton, Tim 1988 Mar 30J

Buryatia, Boris 1982 Mar 5B

Buscetta, Tommaso 1984 Oct 18B/Oct 25B

Buschmann Silva, Sergio 1989 Jun 16G

Bush, Barbara 1985 Apr 12H; 1986 May 6F; 1988 Apr 21F; 1989 Apr 12F/Apr 28F

Bush, George Herbert Walker

appointments and resignations

cabinet and subcabinet: Baker (state) 1988 Nov 9F; Brady (treasury) 1988 Sep 15H/Nov 15F; Cavazos (education) 1988 Nov 21F; Derwinski (VA) 1988 Dec 22F; Dole (labor) 1988 Dec 24H; Kemp (HUD) 1988 Dec 19F; Koop (surgeon general) 1989 May 4F; Lujan (interior) 1988 Dec 22F; Lucas (civil rights) 1989 May 9F; Mosbacher (commerce) 1988 Dec 6F; Novello (surgeon general) 1989 Oct 17F; Reilly (EPA) 1988 Dec 22F; Skinner (transportation) 1988 Dec 22F; Sullivan (HHS) 1988 Dec 22F; Thornburgh (attorney general) 1988 Nov 21F; Tower (defense) 1988 Dec 16F; Watkins (energy) 1989 Jan 12H

councils, commissions and agencies: Bennett (drug czar) 1989 Jan 12F; Boskin (CEA) 1988 Dec 6F; Breeden (SEC) 1989 Oct 6H; Gates (NSC) 1988 Dec 28G; Hills (trade representative) 1988 Dec 6F; Scowcroft (NSC) 1988 Nov 23G; Truly (NASA) 1989 Apr 12I; Webster (CIA) 1988 Dec 6F

diplomatic and military: Pickering (UN ambassador) 1988 Dec 6F; Powell (joint chiefs) 1989 Aug 10G

judicial: Manion (appeals court) 1986 Jul 23F

white house: Sununu (staff chief) 1988 Nov 17F

awards and honors: 1989 Jul 6J

banks and banking: regulatory reform 1984 Jan 31H; thrift bailout 1989 Jan 27F/Feb 6H/Aug 9H

congressional relations: 1989 Jan 27F/Feb 9F/Apr 14H/Oct 27G

constitutional amendments: 1989 Jun 27F

crime and law enforcement: gun control 1989 Feb 16F/May 15F; narcotics 1989 Sep 5A/Nov 21H

defense and armed forces: 1989 Apr 24G-25G/Jul 27G/Nov 9H/Nov 21G

disarmament and arms control: intermediate-range missiles 1983 Jan

31B; 1987 Oct 3B; chemical weapons 1984 Apr 4A/Apr 18A; 1989 Sep 25A; INF treaty signing 1987 Dec 8A; conventional forces in Europe 1989 May 29B; short-range nuclear forces 1989 May 29B

economy: budget and deficit issues 1985 May 10H; 1989 Apr 14H/Aug 7H/Oct 16H/Oct 23H/Nov 2H-3H/Dec 19H; Dow Jones average 1988 Oct 19H/Nov 9H/Nov 11H

education: 1989 Apr 5F/Jul 30F/Sep 27F

energy and power: 1989 Jun 26H/Sep 29H

environment and pollution: 1989 Apr 7H/Jun 12H/Jul 21H/Sep 29H/Nov 9H/Dec 5H/Dec 12H

foreign aid: 1989 Jul 21G/Nov 21G

foreign policy: Afghanistan 1989 Jun 10G; Africa 1982 Nov 23C; 1985 Mar 11C; Argentina 989 Sep 27D; Brazil 1989 May 25H; Canada 1986 Jun 13D; 1989 Feb 10G/May 2D; China 1985 Oct 18E; 1989 Jun 8G/Nov 30G; Eastern Europe 1989 Jul 13G/Nov 22F; Egypt 1989 Apr 3C; Europe 1983 Jan 31B/Jun 24G; 1987 Oct 3B; France 1981 Jun 24B; Hungary 1989 Jul 13G/Nov 21G; India 1989 May 25H; Iran 1989 Nov 6G; Israel 1989 Apr 4C; Japan 1982 Apr 23E; 1989 Mar 21G/May 16G/May 25H/Jul 31G; Latin America 1989 Mar 24D; Lebanon 1989 Nov 6G; Mexico 1989 Oct 3D; NATO 1989 May 29B/Dec 4G; Nicaragua 1989 Mar 24D/Oct 21D/Oct 25G; Pakistan 1989 Jun 10G/Oct 12G; Palestinians 1988 Nov 12C; Panama 1988 May 7G; 1989 Sep 1G/Oct 13G/Dec 20D-20G/Dec 22D; Philippines 1989 Nov 7G; Poland 1989 Apr 17G/Jul 5B/Jul 11B/Jul 13G/Nov 22G; Soviet Union 1982 Nov 15A; 1988 Oct 18F/Dec 6G; 1989 May 2H/May 12G/Sep 21G/Oct 31G/Dec 2A/Dec 9G; United Nations 1985 Mar 11C; West Germany 1983 Jun 25B

foreign trade: unfair trading 1989 May 25H; steel quotas 1989 Jul 25H

housing: 1989 Nov 9H/Nov 10F

intelligence issues: 1989 Oct 27G

Iran-Contra arms scandal: 1986 Oct 10G/Dec 15F/Dec 3F; 1987 May 14F/Sep 8G/Aug 3G/Aug 5G/Dec 17G; 1988 Jan 11F/Dec 30F; 1989 Apr 6F

labor and employment: AFL-CIO attack on 1982 Feb 16H; government workers 1989 Feb 7F/Apr 10F/Jul 7F; minimum wage 1989 Jun 13H/Nov 17H

medicine and health care: abortion 1984 Sep 11F; 1989 Jan 23F/Oct 11F/Oct 21F/Oct 27F/Nov 14F; Medicaid 1989 Oct 17F

minority issues: Black Americans 1983 Jul 15F; 1989 Jan 16F; civil rights 1983 Jul 15F; 1989 May 9F

personal issues: income tax returns 1984 Sep 26F; 1985 Apr 12H; 1986 May 6F; 1988 Apr 21F; 1989 Apr 12F; Rather shouting match 1988 Jan 25F

politics: Haig feud 1981 Mar 24F; conservative leadership defeat 1985 Mar 2F; ethics issues 1989 Jan 25F/Jan 27F/Mar 10F/Apr 12F; polls 1989 Feb 26F/Sep

26F; campaign financing 1989 Jun 29F

presidential campaign (1980)
debates: 1980 Jan 5F
primaries: Alabama 1980 Mar 11F; Arkansas 1980 Feb 16F; Connecticut 1980 Mar 25F; Florida 1980 Mar 11F; Georgia 1980 Mar 11F; Indiana 1980 May 6F; Iowa 1980 Jan 21F; Kansas 1980 Apr 1F; Louisiana 1980 Apr 5F; Maryland 1980 May 13F; Massachusetts 1980 Mar 4F; Michigan 1980 May 20F; Nebraska 1980 May 13F; New Hampshire 1980 Feb 26F; New York 1980 Mar 25F; North Carolina 1980 May 6F; Oregon 1980 May 20F; Pennsylvania 1980 Apr 22F; Puerto Rico 1980 Feb 17F; Tennessee 1980 May 6F; Texas 1980 May 3F; Vermont 1980 Mar 4F; Washington, D.C. 1980 May 6F; Wisconsin 1980 Apr 1F
quits race: 1980 May 26F
vice-presidential nomination: 1980 Jul 17F

presidential campaign (1984): polls 1984 Jul 31F/Sep 26F; vice-presidential nomination 1984 Aug 22F; debates 1984 Sep 17F/Oct 11F; election results 1985 Jan 7F; inauguration 1985 Jan 21F

presidential campaign (1988)
candidacy: 1987 Oct 12F
convention: precinct delegate elections 1986 Aug 6F; delegate selection rules 1987 Dec 5F/Dec 12F; party platform 1988 Aug 16F; Quayle joins ticket 1988 Aug 16F/Aug 17F; nomination 1988 Aug 18F
debates: 1987 Aug 14F/Aug 25F/Oct 28F; 1988 Sep 8F/Sep 14F/Sep 21F/Sep 25F
election results: 1988 Nov 8F/Nov 21F/Dec 19F; 1989 Jan 4F
endorsements: 1988 May 11F/May 16F/Oct 17F/Oct 29F
finances: 1988 Jan 4F/Mar 30F/Dec 12F
inauguration: 1989 Jan 20F
media: 1988 Aug 30F/Sep 5F/Sep 9F/Oct 24F
polls: 1986 Feb 1F/May 14F; 1987 Jan 25F/Oct 4F/Nov 15F; 1988 May 19F/May 27F/Jun 21F/Jul 2F/Jul 28F/Aug 9F/Aug 22F/Sep 14F/Oct 13F/Oct 18F
primaries: Colorado 1988 Apr 4F; Connecticut 1988 Mar 29F; Idaho 1988 May 24F; Indiana 1988 May 3F; Iowa 1988 Feb 8F; Maine 1988 Mar 1F; Michigan 1988 Jan 30F; Nebraska 1988 May 10D; New Hampshire 1988 Feb 16F; New York 1988 Apr 19F; Ohio 1988 May 3F; Oregon 1988 May 17F; Pennsylvania 1988 Apr 26F; Puerto Rico 1988 Mar 20F; South Carolina 1988 Mar 5F; Super Tuesday 1988 Mar 8F; Utah 1988 Apr 25F; Vermont 1988 Mar 1F/Apr 20F; Washington, D.C. 1988 May 3F; West Virginia 1988 May 10D; Wisconsin 1988 Apr 5F
staff: 1988 Aug 5H

transition: 1988 Dec 2F/Dec 30F
presidential campaign (1992): 1989 Nov 2F
presidential succession: 1981 Mar 30F; 1985 Jul 13F; 1989 Apr 28F
religion: 1983 Mar 7G
science and technology: 1989 Jan 5I/Sep 29H; space flight 1989 Apr 12I/Jul 20I/Nov 9H
state and local issues: 1981 Jul 19F; 1989 Jul 30F/Sep 27F
taxes: 1982 May 19F; 1989 Jan 27F/Mar 15F/Nov 2H
transportation: 1989 Nov 21H
welfare: 1989 Mar 15F
women: 1989 Oct 8F

Busse, Jon R. 1987 May 11I
Bussey, Charles 1981 Nov 25F
Bustos, Manuel 1985 Dec 23D; 1989 Apr 18D
Butcher, Susan 1986 Mar 13J; 1988 Mar 17J; 1989 Mar 15J
Buthelezi, Mangosuthu Gatsha 1980 May 10C; 1987 Nov 3C
Butterfield, Fox 1983 Apr 28J
Butterfield, Lyman Henry 1982 Apr 25J
Butts, Vernon Robert 1981 Jan 11F
Byrd, Robert C.
foreign policy: Saudi arms sales 1981 Oct 22G; Gorbachev meeting 1985 Sep 3B
politics: open convention endorsement 1980 Aug 2F; minority leader post 1984 Dec 12F; Reagan speech rebuttals 1985 Apr 24H; 1987 Jan 27F; 1988 Jan 25F; majority leader post 1986 Nov 20F; 1987 Jan 6F; party post resignation 1988 Apr 12F
Byrne Jr., Edward R. 1988 Jun 14F
Byrne, Jane M. 1983 Feb 22H; 1987 Feb 24F

C

Cabral, Luis de Almeida 1980 Nov 14C
Caceres, Carlos 1989 May 3D
Cadavid, Marco Fidel 1985 Mar 16F
Caesar, Adolph 1984 Sep 14J
Cafferata, Patty 1986 Sep 9F
Cage, Nicolas 1987 Dec 16J
Cagney, James 1986 Mar 30J
Caine, Michael 1986 Feb 7J; 1987 Mar 30J
Caird, John 1981 Oct 4J; 1987 Jun 7J
Cajal, Maximo 1987 Feb 4B
Calcavecchia, Mark 1988 Apr 10J
Caldwell, Erskine 1984 Dec 7J; 1987 Apr 11J
Caldwell, L. Scott 1988 Mar 27J
Caldwell, Taylor 1981 Feb 8J/Mar 8J; 1985 Aug 30J
Caldwell, Zoe 1982 Jun 6J
Calero Portocarrero, Adolfo 1983 Jul 20D; 1986 Dec 23D; 1987 Feb 16D/Mar 4G/May 21G
Calfa, Marian 1989 Dec 7B/Dec 10B
Califano Jr., Joseph A. 1982 Jul 26F/Dec 14F
Callaghan, James 1986 Jul 8B
Callejas, Rafael Leonardo 1989 Nov 27D
Callister, Marion 1981 Dec 23F
Calvi, Roberto 1983 Feb 18B
Calvino, Italo 1985 Sep 19J
Calvo Sotelo, Leopoldo 1981 Feb 10B/Feb 26B/Aug 24B/Nov 13B/Aug 27B
Camacho Solis, Manuel 1987 Jan 13D
Camarena Salazar, Enrique
kidnap: 1985 Feb 7D
murder: 1985 Mar 6D; arrests 1985 Mar 14D/Apr 4D/Apr 30D; 1986 Aug 12D; 1988 Apr 1F; indict-

ments 1988 Jan 6F; trial 1988 Sep 28F/Oct 28D
Camdessus, Michel 1988 Dec 6A
Campbell, Bruce 1986 Jun 11I
Campbell, Earl 1980 Jan 9J
Campbell, Joseph 1987 Oct 30J/Dec 4J
Camps, Ramon 1986 Dec 2D
Canaday, John Edwin 1985 Jul 19J
Canetti, Elias 1981 Oct 15J
Cannon, Howard M. 1981 May 22H; 1983 Jan 20J
Canseco, Jose 1986 Nov 25J; 1988 Nov 16J
Caponi, Donna 1981 Jun 14J
Caponnetto, Antonio 1985 Nov 9B
Capote, Truman (Truman Streckfus Persons) 1984 Aug 25J; 1989 Dec 14J
Capra, Frank 1982 Mar 4J; 1983 Oct 11J; 1985 Aug 1J; 1986 Jan 14J
Capucci, Hilarion 1980 May 6C
Caputo, Dante 1984 Nov 29D; 1988 Sep 20A/Dec 7A; 1989 Sep 21A
Cara, Irene 1983 Jun 15J
Caramanlis, Constantine 1980 May 5B; 1985 Mar 9B
Cardenas, Cuauhtemoc 1988 Jul 16D/Jul 20D
Cardonas Ramirez, Blandina 1983 Dec 16F
Carew, Rod 1985 Aug 4J
Carey, Hugh L. 1980 Apr 11H/May 5F; 1982 Jan 15F
Carey, Peter 1988 Oct 26J
Carey, Rick 1985 Aug 18J
Carli, Guido 1989 Dec 14B
Carlin, Paul N. 1986 Jan 6H
Carlson, G. Raymond 1987 May 6J
Carlson, Gretchen Elizabeth 1988 Sep 10J
Carlsson, Ingvar 1986 Mar 12B; 1988 Sep 18B; 1989 Jan 10B
Carlton, Steve 1982 Oct 26J
Carlucci, Frank C.
armed forces: annual report 1988 Feb 18G; 1989 Jan 18G; women's role 1988 Apr 25G; military bases 1989 Jan 5G
defense and disarmament policy: INF treaty 1988 Feb 1G; Honduras troop exit 1988 Mar 23G; India, Pakistan arms sales 1988 Apr 4E; Persian Gulf 1988 Apr 22G; Soviet Union 1988 Apr 29G/Aug 1B/Aug 4G
government service: national security adviser 1986 Dec 2F; defense secretary 1987 Nov 5G/Nov 20G

Carmichael, Hoagy 1981 Dec 27J
Carneglia, John 1989 Jul 7F
Carnes, Kim 1981 Jul 8J
Carney, Patricia 1985 Oct 31D
Caroline, Princess (Monaco) 1987 May 2J
Caron, Glenn Gordon 1988 Aug 10J
Caro Quintero, Rafael 1985 Apr 4D
Carpenter, David 1985 Jun 24H
Carpenter, Karen 1983 Feb 4J
Carpenter, Richard 1983 Feb 4J
Carpio Nicolle, Jorge 1985 Nov 3D
Carradine, John (Richmond Reed Carradine) 1988 Nov 27J
Carranza, Nicolas 1984 Mar 21G
Carriere, Jean-Claude 1987 Oct 13J; 1988 Feb 5J
Carrillo, Elpedia 1986 Mar 5J
Carrillo, Santiago 1982 Jun 9B
Carrington, Lord 1980 Jan 26A/Mar 14B/May 22B; 1981 Jul 6A/Nov 3A; 1982 Apr 5B
Carrion Cruz, Luis 1988 Nov 13D
Carroll, David 1989 Dec 12J
Carroll, Earl H. 1986 Jul 2F
Carroll, Geoff 1986 May 1I
Carroll, Madeleine 1987 Oct 2J
Carroll, Tod 1988 Aug 10J

Carron, Owen 1981 Aug 21B; 1982 Jan 21A
Carson, Johnny 1986 May 6J
Carter III, Billy (William Alton)
Libyan scandal: registers as agent 1980 Jul 14F; Senate probe 1980 Jul 24F/Jul 30F/Aug 1F/Aug 4F/Aug 6F/Aug 22G/Sep 17F/Oct 2F/Oct 29F; 1981 Apr 21F
obituary: 1988 Sep 25J
Carter, Helena Bonham 1986 Mar 7J
Carter, Jimmy
agriculture: 1980 Jul 28H
appointments and resignations: Aiello (ethnic affairs) 1980 Jan 3F; Muskie (state) 1980 Apr 29G; Sawhill (synthetic fuels) 1980 Sep 10F
budget and deficit issues: 1980 Jan 28H/Feb 27H/Mar 31H/May 2H/Jul 8G/Oct 1H; 1981 Jan 15H
business and industry: Chrysler bailout 1980 Jan 7H; auto industry 1980 Apr 17H/May 14H/Jul 8H; steel industry 1980 Sep 30H; railroad deregulation 1980 Oct 14H
cities: 1980 Jun 1F/Jun 10F/Aug 6F
crime and law enforcement: Miami riots 1980 May 19F/Jun 9F
defense and armed forces: draft registration 1980 Feb 8G/Mar 6G/Jun 27G/Jul 2G; budget 1980 Apr 27G; nuclear weapons 1980 Jun 16G/Aug 8G/Oct 1H; Vietnam War memorial 1980 Jul 1G; veterans' hospitals 1980 Aug 26F
disarmament and arms control: SALT II 1980 Mar 14G
economy: projections 1980 Jan 28H/Apr 17H/Jul 21H; anti-inflation program 1980 Mar 14H; dollar value 1980 Mar 17A; banking reserves 1980 Mar 31H; tax cuts 1980 Aug 28H; State of Union message 1981 Jan 16F; Reagan charges denied 1982 Sep 30F
education: refugees 1980 Oct 10F; school busing 1980 Dec 4F
energy and power: Alaska oil pipeline 1980 Jan 17H; oil supply routes 1980 Jan 23G/Feb 1G/Feb 12G/Sep 24A; oil windfall profits tax 1980 Apr 2H; oil import fee 1980 May 13H/Jun 5F/Jun 6F/Jun 19H; synthetic fuel 1980 Jun 26H; nuclear fusion research 1980 Oct 7H
environment and pollution: nuclear waste storage sites 1980 Feb 12I; Love Canal aid 1980 May 21H/Oct 1H; Alaska lands conservation 1980 Dec 2H
farewell address: 1981 Jan 14F
foreign policy: Afghanistan 1980 Feb 15G; Africa 1980 Jan 31J; Algeria 1980 Nov 2C; China 1980 Jul 10E; 1981 Sep 3E; Egypt 1980 Apr 9A/Apr 16C/Jun 18A/Aug 3C; 1981 Oct 6A/Oct 10A; European Community 1980 Apr 10A; India 1980 Jan 16E-16I/Jun 19I; Israel 1980 Mar 3G/Apr 9A/Apr 16C/Apr 24C/Jun 18A/Aug 3C; Japan 1980 Jul 10E; Jordan 1980 Jun 18A; Middle East conference 1983 Nov 6A; Nicaragua 1980 Jul 8G/Sep 12D; Pakistan 1980 Jan 16E-16G; Palestinians 1980 Apr 9A/Apr 16C/Jun 18A/Aug 3C; 1981 Oct 11G; Persian Gulf 1980 Jan 23G/Jan 25G/Jan 29C/Feb 1G/Feb 12G/Sep 24A; Poland 1980 Aug 29G/Sep 12B/Dec 2G; Portugal 1980 Jun 26B; Saudi Ara-

bia 1980 Jul 8C; Soviet Union 1980 Dec 2G; 1981 Jan 16F; Spain 1980 Jun 25B; Taiwan 1981 Sep 3E; United Nations 1980 Mar 3G; West Germany 1980 Jun 16G/Nov 20G; Yugoslavia 1980 Jun 24B; Zimbabwe 1986 Jul 4C/Sep 2G

foreign trade: uranium sales to India 1980 May 16I/Jun 19I; arms sales to Saudi Arabia 1980 Jul 8C; grain sales to Poland 1980 Sep 12B

grain embargo: 1980 Jan 4A/Jan 30F/Jul 4F/Nov 20D

human rights: 1980 Nov 17G

immigration and refugees: 1980 May 5D-6F/May 14D/Jun 7F/Oct 10F

intelligence issues: security leaks 1980 Jul 17F

Iran hostage crisis: approval rating 1980 Jan 10F; commission of inquiry 1980 Feb 13A; Khomeini letter 1980 Mar 29A; sanctions 1980 Apr 1G/Apr 10A/Apr 13G/Apr 17G; Iranian protests 1980 Jun 6C/Aug 2C; town meetings 1980 Jul 4F; parliament OKs release 1980 Nov 2C; hostages greeted on return 1981 Jan 21G; Supreme Court rules on release terms 1981 Jul 2F; "October surprise" theory 1988 Aug 25G/Oct 23G

labor and employment: 1980 Jan 10F-10H

Moscow Olympics boycott: 1980 Jan 20J/Jan 31J/Mar 21J/Apr 12J/May 15J

personal issues: post-presidency plans 1980 Nov 12F/Nov 12J

politics: 1980 Jan 1G/Apr 10G

presidential campaign (1980)
convention: 1980 May 5F/Jul 28F; nomination 1980 Aug 14F

debates: 1980 Sep 9F/Sep 21F/Sep 25F/Oct 28F

election results: 1980 Nov 4F

endorsements: 1980 May 9G/Jun 5F/Aug 5F/Aug 20F

investigations: 1981 Oct 23J; 1983 Jun 30F/Jul 19F

party platform: 1980 Jun 24F/Aug 12F-13F

polls: 1980 Jan 8F-9F/Apr 18F/Jun 23F/Aug 19F

primaries: Alabama 1980 Mar 11F; Arkansas 1980 May 27F; California 1980 Jun 3F; Connecticut 1980 Mar 25F; Florida 1980 Mar 11F; Georgia 1980 Mar 11F; Illinois 1980 Mar 18F; Iowa 1980 Jan 21F; Kansas 1980 Apr 1F; Kentucky 1980 May 27F; Louisiana 1980 Apr 5F; Maine 1980 Feb 10F; Maryland 1980 May 13F; Massachusetts 1980 Mar 4F; Michigan 1980 Apr 26F; Montana 1980 Jun 3F; Nebraska 1980 May 13F; Nevada 1980 May 27F; New Hampshire 1980 Feb 26F; New Jersey 1980 Jun 3F; New Mexico 1980 Jun 3F; New York 1980 Mar 25F; Ohio 1980 Jun 3F; Oregon 1980 May 20F; Pennsylvania 1980 Apr 22F; Rhode Island 1980 Jun 3F; South Dakota 1980 Jun 3F; Texas 1980 May 3F; Vermont 1980 Mar 4F; West Virginia 1980 Jun 3F; Wisconsin 1980 Apr 1F

transition: 1980 Nov 17F

presidential library: 1986 Oct 1F

State of Union messages: 1980 Jan 23G; 1981 Jan 16F

Carter, Michael 1987 Oct 29F
Carter, Robert L. 1986 May 8F
Carter, Rubin ("Hurricane") 1985 Nov 7F
Carton, Marcel 1985 Mar 22C
Carver, Raymond 1988 Aug 2J
Cary, Frank T. 1980 Dec 21H
Casas Vila, Enrique 1984 Feb 23B/Feb 24B
Casey, Albert V. 1986 Jan 6H
Casey, Aloysius G. 1985 Aug 23G
Casey, Martha 1985 Jun 26H
Casey, William J.
covert actions: freedom of information exemption 1981 Sep 24G; El Salvador rebel aid 1982 Mar 8D; foreign agents act abuses 1982 Apr 8G; Iran intelligence unit 1983 Aug 23G; Nicaraguan waters mining 1984 Apr 11G/Apr 26G; House panel "debategate" report 1984 May 23F; guerrilla warfare manual 1984 Nov 14G/Dec 2G

government service: CIA director 1980 Dec 11F; personnel changes 1984 Jul 1G; resignation 1987 Feb 2G

Iran-Contra arms scandal: 1986 Nov 14G/Dec 11F/Dec 24F; 1987 Jul 9G/Jul 10G/Jul 23G/Aug 27G/Sep 25G

personal issues: private business ruling 1981 May 19F; resignation urged 1981 Jul 23F; Senate committee probe 1981 Jul 29G/Dec 2G; financial statement 1981 Jul 30G; ill health 1986 Dec 15F/Dec 18F; death 1987 May 6G; Woodward book 1987 Sep 25G

Cash, Pat 1983 Dec 28J; 1987 Jan 25J/Jul 5J
Cassatt, Mary 1983 May 17J
Cassavetes, John 1989 Feb 3J
Cassidy, Joanna 1988 Jun 22J
Casson, Hugh 1984 Dec 19J
Castaneda, Jorge 1980 Mar 27D; 1981 Nov 23D
Castellano, Paul 1984 Mar 30F; 1985 Dec 16F; 1986 Mar 5F
Castillo Arriola, Eduardo 1983 Jan 8D
Castle, Jerome 1980 Apr 7H
Castro, James Emilio 1984 Jul 12J
Castro Ruz, Fidel
economic policy: 1985 Aug 3D; 1986 Dec 2D; 1989 Dec 13D

foreign policy: French trade accord 1980 Apr 1D; in Soviet Union 1989 Apr 2D

government: ministries shuffled 1980 Jan 11D; 1986 Feb 7D; revolution anniversary 1989 Jan 1D

human rights: Peruvian embassy asylum seekers 1980 Apr 6D; political prisoners 1986 Sep 15F; 1987 May 29D; 1988 Jun 5D

Latin policy: Central American peace efforts 1983 Jul 23D; 1988 Aug 10D; Colombia 1981 Apr 3D; Costa Rica 1988 Aug 10D; Havana debt conference 1985 Aug 3D; Mexico 1983 Jul 23D; Nicaragua 1983 Jul 28D; 1985 Jan 10D; Panama 1987 May 29D; Peru 1980 Apr 6D

U.S. policy: 1981 Sep 16G; 1984 Jan 2D; 1985 Jan 25D/Feb 3D; 1986 Sep 15F

Cather, Willa 1984 Aug 11J
Cato, R. Milton 1984 Jul 25D
Caulkins, Tracy 1982 Apr 18J
Cavaco Silva, Anibal 1987 Apr 28B/Jul 19B

Cavallo, Domingo 1982 Aug 24D
Cavanagh, Thomas Patrick 1984 Dec 18G; 1985 May 23G
Cavazos, Lauro F. 1988 Nov 21F; 1989 Jun 1F
Ceausescu, Elena 1989 Dec 25B
Ceausescu, Nicolae
economic policy: Danube-Black Sea canal 1984 May 26B; defense spending cuts vote 1986 Nov 23B; agricultural resettlement 1988 Nov 28B; foreign debt 1989 Apr 12B

foreign policy: Poland 1980 Oct 21B; 1982 Feb 13B; Hungary 1988 Aug 28B

government: critics arrested 1989 Mar 13B; reelected Romania general secretary 1989 Nov 24B; protests against 1989 Dec 21B; executed 1989 Dec 25B

U.S. policy: 1982 Feb 13B

Cebrian, Juan Luis 1980 May 9B
Cech, Thomas R. 1988 Nov 16I; 1989 Oct 12I
Cecil, Lord (Edward Christian) David (Gascoyne) 1986 Jan 1J
Cela, Camilo Jose 1989 Oct 19J
Celenk, Bekir 1982 Dec 18B
Celeste, Richard 1985 Mar 15H/Mar 25H
Celestin, Martial 1988 Feb 9D
Cerezo Arevalo, Marco Vinicio 1985 Nov 3D/Dec 8D; 1986 May 21D; 1989 May 9D
Ceron Ortega, Daniel 1982 Dec 13D
Cesar, Alfredo 1989 Jun 11D
Chafee, John H. 1987 May 7H
Chagall, Marc (Moyshe Shagal) 1985 Mar 28J; 1987 Sep 2J; 1988 Feb 1J
Chalk, Vincent 1987 Nov 1F
Chamberlain, Azaria 1986 Feb 7E
Chamberlain, Lindy 1985 Nov 12E; 1986 Feb 7E; 1987 Jun 2E; 1988 Sep 15E
Chamberlain, Michael 1987 Jun 2E; 1988 Sep 15E
Chamberlain, Wilt 1984 Apr 5J
Chambers, David 1987 Sep 18J
Chambers, George 1986 Dec 15D
Chambers Jr., Robert E. 1988 Mar 25F
Chambers, Tom 1987 Feb 8J
Chambers, Whittaker 1984 Mar 26J
Chamorro, Adolfo 1986 Apr 25D
Chamorro, Violeta Barrios de 1980 May 18D; 1989 Sep 2D
Chamoun, Camille Nimer 1987 Aug 7C
Champion, Gower 1980 Aug 25J
Chan, Julius 1980 Mar 11E
Chandernagor, Andre 1981 Oct 13B
Chandler, A.B. ("Happy") 1982 Aug 1J
Chandrasekhar, Subrahmanyan 1983 Oct 19I
Chang, Michael 1989 Jun 11J
Chang Yong Ja 1982 Aug 9E
Channell, Carl R. 1986 Dec 15F; 1987 Mar 9G/Apr 29F
Channing, Stockard 1985 Jun 2J; 1986 Mar 19J
Chan Si 1985 Jan 14E
Chaplin, Charlie 1984 Mar 1J; 1987 Aug 1J
Chapman, Mark David 1980 Dec 8J; 1981 Jun 22J/Aug 24J
Chapman, Tracy 1988 Aug 27J/Sep 2J/Sep 24J/Oct 15J; 1989 Feb 22J
Chappell, Fred 1985 Jan 15J
Charles, Prince (Great Britain)
architectural criticism: 1987 Dec 1B

personal issues: engagement 1981 Feb 24B; marriage 1981 Jul 29B; birth of children 1982 Jun 21B; 1984 Sep 15J

royal travels: Australia visit 1983 Mar 20E; 1985 Oct 27E; U.S. visit 1985 Nov 9J; 1986 Feb 17F

Charles, Mary Eugenia 1980 Jul 21D; 1985 Jul 3D
Charles, Ray 1983 Jul 11J; 1986 Jan 23J; 1988 May 11J
Charleson, Ian 1981 Sep 26J
Charlotte, Grand Duchess (Luxembourg) 1985 Jul 9B
Chase, Lucia (Mrs. Thomas Ewing Jr.) 1986 Jan 9J
Chastain, Thomas 1983 Dec 18J; 1984 Jan 20J/Feb 10J/Mar 23J
Chatichai Choonhavan 1988 Jul 27E
Chaves, Aureliano 1981 Sep 24D
Chavez, Cesar 1988 Aug 21F
Chavez, Linda 1986 Sep 9F
Chavez Mena, Fidel 1989 Mar 19D
Chayefsky, Paddy (Sidney) 1981 Aug 1J
Chayrez, Bernadette 1986 Feb 9I/Oct 11I
Chazov, Yevgeny I. 1985 Oct 11A/Dec 10A
Checchi, Alfred A. 1989 Sep 29H
Cheever, John 1981 Apr 30J; 1982 Jun 19J
Chekhov, Anton 1985 Mar 21J
Chelos, George 1986 Mar 19F
Chelwood, Lord 1988 May 23B
Chen, Joan 1987 Nov 20J
Chen Baochung 1986 Apr 30E
Cheney, Richard B. 1987 Aug 3G; 1989 Mar 17G/Mar 22F/Apr 25G/Jul 27G
Chenoweth, Dean 1982 Jul 31J
Chen Wencheng 1981 Jul 18F
Cher (Cherilyn Sarkisian) 1987 Dec 16J; 1988 Apr 11J
Chernenko, Konstantin U.
arms control: 1984 Sep 1B

foreign policy: France 1984 Jun 23B; Poland 1984 May 4B; West Germany 1984 Mar 12B

government: Soviet state and party posts 1984 Feb 13B/Feb 23B/Apr 11B

personal issues: ill health 1984 Sep 1B/Sep 5B; 1985 Jan 14B/Jan 21B/Feb 5B/Feb 24B; death 1985 Mar 10B

U.S. policy: 1984 Mar 2B-2G/Mar 23A/Jun 14G/Sep 1B

Chervov, Nikolai F. 1987 Aug 31B
Chevenement, Jean-Pierre 1984 Aug 29B
Cheysson, Claude 1981 Aug 30C/Dec 8A; 1982 Jan 14A; 1984 Feb 5C
Chhabiram (bandit) 1982 Mar 5E
Chiang Ching-kuo 1981 Oct 10E; 1984 Mar 21E; 1985 Jan 15E; 1987 Jul 14E; 1988 Jan 13E
Chiang Kai-shek 1982 Mar 10E
Chiara, Maria 1987 May 2J
Chidzero, Bernard 1987 Sep 24C
Chiles, Lawton 1984 Dec 12F
Chin, Larry Wu-Tai 1986 Jan 2G/Feb 7G
Chin, Tiffany 1985 Feb 2J
Chin, Vincent 1984 Sep 19F; 1987 May 1F
Chin A Sen, Henk R. 1980 Aug 13D
Chinn, W. Franklyn 1987 Jul 9F; 1989 Oct 16H
Chirac, Jacques
arms control: intermediate-range nuclear forces 1987 Mar 31B

economic policy: denationalizations 1986 Apr 9B; Tokyo G-7 summit 1986 May 6A; education bill protests 1986 Dec 9B; work-hours decree 1986 Dec 20B; EuroDisney park pact 1987 Mar 24B; AIDS research 1987 Apr 1I; Cairo metro 1987 Sep 26C

foreign policy: New Caledonia visit 1987 Sep 17E; Soviet visit 1987 May 16B

government: French presidential campaign 1981 Feb 7B; 1988 Apr 24B/May 4C; premier 1986 Mar 20B; party meeting 1989 Apr 8B

Mideast policy: anti-terrorist policy 1986 Oct 8B; Lebanon hostages 1986 Oct 11B; Iran-Iraq War 1987 Aug 14A

U.S. policy: 1987 Mar 31B/Apr 1I

Chissano, Joaquim 1989 Jul 22C/Jul 31C
Choh Hao Li 1987 Nov 28I
Choi Kyu Hah 1980 Aug 16E
Chowdhury, Humayun Rashid 1987 Sep 15A; 1988 Oct 10A
Chretien, Jean 1981 Nov 9D; 1983 Apr 11D
Christensen, A. Sherman 1982 Aug 4F; 1983 Nov 23F
Christensen, Lew 1984 Oct 9J
Christo, Javacheff 1983 May 4J
Christopher, Warren 1980 Nov 10C; 1981 Jan 28C
Chu, David S.C. 1984 Aug 19G
Chuikov, Vasily I. 1982 Mar 18B
Chun Doo Hwan
Burma bombing: 1983 Oct 9E-10E/Dec 9E

constitutional reform: 1986 Feb 24E; 1987 Apr 13E/Jun 24E/Jul 1E

corruption scandal: 1982 May 21E; 1988 Nov 9E/Nov 23E; 1989 Jan 31E/Dec 31E

government: Choi Kyu Hah succession 1980 Aug 16E; South Korea president 1980 Aug 27E; 1981 Feb 11E; inaugural address 1980 Sep 1E; cabinet reorganized 1983 Oct 14E; 1987 Jul 13E; protests against 1986 May 6E; 1987 Jun 24E; successor nominated 1987 Jun 10E; presidential campaign 1987 Nov 16E

human rights: political prisoners 1981 Jan 23E; 1983 Aug 12E; martial law 1981 Jan 24E; U.S. report 1981 Feb 2E; political activities ban 1984 Feb 25E

Japan talks: 1984 Sep 8E

Church, Frank F(orrester) 1984 Apr 7F
Church Jr., Samuel 1982 Nov 9H
Ciardi, John Anthony 1986 Mar 30J
Cicippio, Joseph James 1986 Sep 12C
Cimino, Michael 1985 Aug 29J
Cirishin, Viktor 1985 Feb 5B
Cisneros, Henry G(abriel) 1981 Apr 4F; 1986 Mar 10F; 1989 May 6F
Civiletti, Benjamin 1980 Feb 11F/May 19F/Aug 6F
Claiborne, Harry E. 1986 May 16F/Jul 22F/Oct 9F
Clair, Rene 1981 Mar 15J
Clancy, Tom
best-sellers: Cardinal of the Kremlin 1988 Aug 26J/Sep 30J/Oct 21J/Nov 25J/Dec 23J; 1989 Jan 27J/Feb 24J; Clear and Present Danger 1989 Sep 29J/Oct 27J/Dec 1J/Dec 22J; Patriot Games 1987 Sep 23J/Oct 23J/Nov 20J; 1988 Jan 29J; Red Storm Rising 1986 Aug 29J/Sep 26J/Oct 31J/Nov 21J/Dec 26J; 1987 Jan 23J/Feb 27J/Mar 27J/Apr 24J; Hunt for Red October 1985 May 24J/Jun 14J/Jul 19J/Aug 16J/Sep 27J

Clark, Barney B. 1982 Dec 2I/Dec 19I/Dec 27I; 1983 Mar 23I; 1984 Nov 25I
Clark, Dick 1989 Mar 23J
Clark, Ed 1980 Oct 28F
Clark, Joe 1983 Jun 11D; 1985 Jul 8D/Oct 28D; 1986 Nov 24D; 1988 Jan 11C/Feb 2C; 1989 Mar 30D
Clark, Judith 1981 Oct 20F
Clark, Kenneth (historian) 1983 May 21J
Clark, Kenneth B. (psychologist) 1983 Aug 11J; 1989 Jan 13J
Clark, Mamie 1983 Aug 11J
Clark, Mary Higgins 1987 Jul 17J; 1989 May 26J/Jun 30J/Jul 28J
Clark, Ramsey 1980 Jun 4C/Jun 6C
Clark, Russell 1987 Sep 16F
Clark, Will 1989 Oct 9J
Clark, William P. 1982 Jan 4F; 1983 Oct 13H/Oct 17G/Nov 18H; 1984 Aug 8H
Clarke, Arthur C. 1982 Nov 14J/Dec 12J; 1983 Jan 16J/Feb 13J/Mar 13J
Clarke, Kenneth 1983 May 23J
Clarren, Sterling K. 1989 Aug 16I
Clarridge, Duane R. ("Dewey") 1987 Aug 19G
Claude, Albert 1983 May 22I
Clausen, Alden Winship ("Tom") 1981 Jul 1A; 1983 Sep 27A; 1986 Mar 13G
Clavell, James
    best-sellers: Noble House 1981 May 10J/May 24J/Jul 5J/Aug 9J/Sep 6J/Oct 4J/Nov 8J/Dec 6J; 1982 Jan 10J/Feb 7J; Whirlwind 1986 Jan 11J/Nov 21J/Dec 26J; 1987 Jan 23J
Claxton, Tracy 1985 Mar 31J
Clayton, Alastair 1989 Aug 3D
Cleese, John 1988 Jul 15J; 1989 Mar 19J
Clemens, Roger 1986 Nov 13J/Nov 18J; 1987 Nov 11J
Clements, Bill 1987 Jul 21F
Clemon, U.W. 1984 Feb 27A
Clerc, Jose-Luis 1981 Dec 13J
Clerides, Glafkos 1988 Feb 21B
Climaco, Cesar 1984 Nov 14E
Clooney, Rosemary 1988 May 11J
Close, Glenn 1984 Jun 3J; 1987 Sep 18J; 1988 Dec 21J
Clurman, Harold 1980 Sep 9J
Coard, Bernard 1983 Oct 19D/Oct 30D
Cobb, Ty 1984 Apr 13J; 1985 Sep 11J
Cockerell, Mark 1985 Feb 1J
Cockfield, Lord 1983 May 4B
Cockrell, Lila 1989 May 6F
Cody, John P. Cardinal 1981 Sep 10J; 1982 Apr 25F/Jul 10J
Coe, Sebastian 1981 Feb 11J/Aug 28J
Coelho, Tony 1987 Jul 2F; 1989 May 26F
Coetzee, Gerrie 1984 Dec 2J
Coetzee, J.M. 1987 Apr 9J
Cogan, Kevin 1986 May 31J
Cohen, Stanley 1986 Sep 22I/Oct 13I
Cohen, William S. 1987 Jan 5G
Cohn, Roy Marcus 1986 Jun 24F/Aug 2F
Colby, William 1981 Dec 31G
Cole, Carroll E. 1985 Dec 6F
Cole, Johnetta B. 1988 Nov 4F
Cole, Lester 1985 Aug 15J
Cole, Nat King 1984 May 1J
Coleman, Cy 1980 Apr 30J; 1989 Dec 11J
Coleman, Vince 1985 Nov 27J
Coleman, William T. 1982 Apr 19F
Colette (novelist) 1987 Mar 1J
Collett, Alec 1985 Mar 25C
Collins, Jackie
    best-sellers: Hollywood Husbands 1986 Oct 31J/Nov 21J/Dec 26J; Hollywood Wives 1983 Sep 11J/Oct 16J/Nov 13J; Lucky 1985

Sep 27J/Oct 25J; Rock Star 1988 Apr 29J/May 27J
Collins, Larry 1980 Oct 12J/Dec 7J; 1987 Oct 12J/Dec 7J
Collins, Martha Layne 1983 Nov 8F
Collins, Pauline 1989 Jun 4J
Collins, Phil
    best-sellers: ...But Seriously 1989 Dec 30J; No Jacket Required 1985 Mar 30J/Apr 27J/May 25J/Jun 22J/Jul 27J/Aug 24J; 1986 Feb 25J
    Grammy awards: 1985 Feb 26J; 1986 Feb 25J
Collor de Mello, Fernando 1989 Jul 26D/Nov 15D/Dec 20D/Dec 25D
Colombo, Salvatore 1989 Jul 9C
Coltrane, John 1985 Aug 30J
Coluche (Michel Colucci) 1986 Jun 19J
Columbus, Christopher 1986 Oct 6J; 1988 Mar 16J
Comaneci, Nadia 1981 May 31J; 1989 Nov 29J
Commoner, Barry 1980 Apr 13F
Compaore, Blaise 1987 Oct 15C; 1989 Sep 19C
Conable Jr., Barber B. 1986 Mar 13G
Condon, Richard 1985 Jun 14J
Congdon, Dwayne 1986 May 20J
Conlon, Gerard 1989 Oct 19B
Connally, John B. 1980 Jan 5F/Feb 16F/Mar 8F/Mar 9F
Conner, Dennis 1987 Feb 4J; 1988 Sep 9J
Connery, Sean 1987 Jun 3J; 1988 Mar 20J/Apr 11J; 1989 May 29J
Connors, Jimmy 1982 Jul 4J/Sep 12J; 1983 Sep 11J; 1984 Jul 8J
Conover, C. Todd 1984 Oct 15H
Conried, Hans 1982 Jan 5J
Conroy, Pat 1986 Nov 21J
Constantine, King (Greece) 1980 Jul 29C
Conte, Lansana 1985 Jul 4C
Conti, Samuel 1980 Aug 18F
Contreras Subias, Jose 1988 Apr 1F
Coogan, Jackie 1984 Mar 1J
Cook, Robin 1981 Mar 8J/Apr 12J; 1983 Aug 14J; 1989 Feb 24J
Cooke, Jack Kent 1985 Aug 29H
Cooke, Janet 1981 Apr 15J
Cooke, Sam 1986 Jan 23J
Cooke, Terence Cardinal 1983 Oct 6J
Cools, Jan 1989 Jun 15C
Cooney, Gerry 1982 Jun 11J
Coonts, Stephen 1986 Dec 26J; 1987 Jan 23J
Cooper, Alfred Duff 1986 Jun 16J
Cooper, Cecil 1980 Dec 6J
Cooper, Diana (Diana Olivia Winifred Maud Manners) 1986 Jun 16J
Cooperman, Saul 1988 May 24F
Copland, Aaron 1982 Aug 30J; 1986 Jun 13J
Copp, James 1988 Nov 12E
Coppola, Francis Ford 1983 Feb 12J; 1986 Oct 8J
Corderman, John P. 1989 Dec 22F
Cordes, Rudolf 1988 Sep 12C
Cordovez, Diego 1988 Jul 9E
Cori, Ferdinand 1984 Oct 20I
Cori, Gerty T. 1984 Oct 20I
Corn Jr., Ira G. 1982 Apr 28J
Cornea, Aurel 1986 Dec 24C
Correia, Angelo 1982 Feb 13B
Corridan, John M. 1984 Jul 1J
Corsetti, Paul W. 1982 Sep 7J
Cortazar, Julio 1984 Feb 12J
Corterier, Peter 1982 Mar 29B
Cosby, Bill 1985 Nov 19J; 1988 Nov 4F
Cosby, Camille 1988 Nov 4F
Cossiga, Francesco
    government: quits cabinet 1980 Mar 19B; Italian premier 1980 Apr 4B/Sep 27B; cleared in terrorist

tipoff 1980 Jul 27B; inaugurated president 1985 Jun 24B; coalition crises 1986 Jul 19B; 1987 Apr 28B; 1988 Feb 10B
    Japan joint venture: 1980 Sep 20B
Costa Mendez, Nicanor 1982 Mar 6A/Apr 19D/Apr 30D/May 1D/May 25A
Costner, Kevin 1987 Jun 3J; 1988 Jun 15J; 1989 Apr 21J
Coudari, Marcel 1986 Oct 11B
Cougar, John see Mellencamp, John Cougar
Countryman, Wayne 1988 Nov 24F
Cournand, Andre F(rederic) 1988 Feb 19I
Court, Charles 1981 Jul 4E
Couto e Silva, Golbery do 1981 Aug 6D
Coward, Noel 1983 Mar 10J; 1987 Jun 13J
Cowley, Malcolm 1989 Mar 27J
Cox, Alex 1986 Oct 17J
Cox, Archibald 1981 Dec 7F
Cox, Lynne 1987 Aug 7J
Crabbe, Buster (Clarence Linden) 1983 Apr 23J
Craft, Christine 1983 Aug 8F/Oct 31F; 1984 Jan 13J; 1985 Jun 28J
Craft, Ian 1989 Jun 5I
Cram, Donald J. 1987 Oct 14I; 1989 Mar 21I
Cram, Steve 1985 Jul 16J/Jul 27J/Aug 4J
Crane, Philip 1980 Jan 5F
Cranston, Alan
    foreign policy: India, Pakistan A-tests 1987 Apr 27I; Soviet visit 1981 Sep 5A
    "Keating 5" ethics probe: 1989 Oct 13F/Dec 22F
    presidential campaign (1984): California convention 1983 Jan 15F; polls 1983 Jun 11F; women's groups 1983 Jul 10F/Oct 2F; matching funds 1984 Jan 3G; debates 1984 Jan 15F/Feb 11F; withdrawal 1984 Feb 29F; campaign finance violations 1989 Jul 1F
Crawford, Broderick 1986 Apr 26J
Crawford, Cheryl 1986 Oct 7J
Crawford, Michael 1986 Oct 9J; 1988 Jun 5J
Craxi, Bettino
    Achille Lauro incident: 1985 Oct 12A/Oct 17B/Nov 8B
    government: Italian premier 1983 Aug 4B; 1985 Oct 17B; 1986 Jul 19B/Aug 1B; 1987 Mar 3B; parliament confidence vote 1985 Nov 8B
    organized crime: 1984 Oct 3F
    Tokyo G-7 summit: 1986 May 6A
Creighton, Thomas 1985 Mar 8I/Mar 13I
Crenshaw, Ben 1984 Apr 15J
Crespo, Enrique Baron 1989 Jul 25B
Crichton, Charles 1988 Jul 15J
Crimmins, Craig S. 1980 Sep 7F; 1981 Jun 4J/Sep 2F
Crippen, Robert L. 1981 Apr 12I
Cristiani, Alfredo 1989 Mar 19D/Jun 1D/Jun 9D/Sep 15D/Nov 26D
Crocker, Chester A. 1981 Jun 17G; 1984 Dec 3G; 1988 Jan 29C/Jul 13C/Oct 9C
Crohn, Burrill B. 1983 Jul 29I
Cronenberg, David 1988 Sep 23J; 1989 Mar 22J
Cronin, James W. 1980 Oct 14I
Cronin, Joe 1988 Nov 21J
Cronkite, Walter 1980 Feb 15J; 1981 Mar 3G; 1984 Mar 29G
Crosbie, John 1986 Mar 4D
Cross, Ben 1981 Sep 26J
Cross, Christopher 1980 Aug 13J/Sep 10J; 1981 Feb 25J

Crothers, Scatman (Benjamin Sherman) 1986 Nov 22J
Crowe Jr., William J. 1985 Jul 10G/Oct 1G; 1988 Apr 22G; 1989 Jun 21G/Jul 2G/Aug 10G/Sep 21G
Cruise, Tom 1986 May 16J/Oct 17J; 1988 Dec 16J; 1989 Dec 20J
Crystal, Billy 1989 Jul 12J
Csonka, Larry 1987 Jan 27J/Aug 8J
Cukor, George 1983 Jan 24J
Cunningham, Glenn 1988 Mar 10J
Cunningham, Merce 1988 Dec 30J
Cunningham, Randall 1989 Jan 29J
Cuomo, Mario M.
    abortion controversy: 1984 Aug 9F/Sep 13F
    economic policy: insurance reforms 1986 Jun 24F
    health issues: acid rain curbs 1984 Aug 14H; AIDS study 1987 Aug 4I
    Howard Beach racial attack: 1987 Jan 13F
    politics: gubernatorial campaign 1982 Sep 23F; Democratic convention keynote speech 1984 Jul 16F
    Shoreham nuclear power plant: 1983 Dec 14H; 1987 Jan 14H; 1989 Feb 28H
Curley, Germaine 1983 Feb 26F
Curran, Charles E. 1986 Aug 18J
Currey, Fred G. 1986 Dec 23H
Curtin, Jane 1985 Sep 12J
Curtis, Gustavo 1980 Jan 6D
Curtis, Jamie Lee 1988 Jul 15J
Cussler, Clive 1984 Jul 20J; 1986 Feb 28J; 1988 Mar 25J/Apr 29J

D

Dacko, David 1981 Mar 19C/Mar 20C/Sep 1C
Dafoe, Willem 1986 Dec 19J; 1988 Dec 9J
Dagnino Pastore, Jose Maria 1982 Aug 24D
Dahab, Abdel Rahman Siwar el- 1985 Apr 6C/Apr 25C
Dailey, Janet 1989 Feb 24J
Dalai Lama 1987 Oct 7E; 1988 Jun 15E; 1989 Jan 2E/Oct 5A
Dale, Jim 1980 Apr 30J/Jun 8J
Daley, Peter 1983 Aug 10H
Daley, Richard M. 1983 Feb 22H; 1989 Feb 28F/Apr 4F/Apr 24F
D'Alfonso, Frank 1989 Apr 5F
Dali, Salvador (Salvador Domingo Felipe Jacinto Dali Domenech Cusi y Farres) 1983 Jul 30J; 1985 Mar 8J; 1989 Jan 23J
Dalla Chiesa, Carlo Alberto 1982 Sep 3B
Daly, Tyne 1985 Sep 12J; 1988 Aug 28J
Dam, Henrik 1986 Oct 23I
Dam, Kenneth W. 1983 Oct 30G
D'Amato, Alfonse M. 1980 Sep 9F, 1989 Jan 17F; 1989 Dec 22F
Danchev, Vladimir 1983 May 23B
Dandridge, Ray 1987 Mar 3J
Dangerfield, George 1986 Dec 27J
Daniel, Beth 1981 Jul 26J/Aug 23J
Daniels, William 1985 Sep 12J; 1986 Sep 21J
Daniloff, Nicholas S. 1986 Aug 30B/Sep 12B/Sep 30A/Oct 22B
Danner, Braden 1987 Mar 15J
Danson, Ted 1987 Nov 25J
Dante, Nicholas 1989 Apr 21J
Daoudy, Adib 1980 Jun 16A
D'Arby, Terence Trent 1988 May 21J
Darden, Willie Jasper 1988 Mar 15F
Darman, Richard G. 1985 Jan 31H; 1989 Jan 25F
Dart, Raymond Arthur 1988 Nov 22I

Darwin, Charles 1984 Apr 14F; 1988 Mar 3I
Da Silva, Luis Inacio 1981 Feb 25D; 1989 Nov 15D/Dec 20D
Dass, Arjun 1985 Sep 4E
Dassault, Marcel (Marcel Bloch) 1986 Apr 18B
D'Aubuisson, Roberto
    death squads: 1984 Mar 3D; 1985 Sep 29D; U.S. ambassador plot 1984 Jun 22D; 1985 Sep 29D; Romero assassination 1985 Sep 29D; 1987 Nov 22D
    government opposition: arrest demanded 1981 Mar 4G; rebel peace plan rejected 1982 Oct 26D; presidential campaign 1984 Mar 27D/Apr 10D/May 7D-8D/May 11D; Duarte inauguration 1984 Jun 1D; resigns party leadership 1985 Sep 29D
Daugherty, Brad 1986 Jun 17J
Dausset, Jean 1980 Oct 10I
Davies, Laura 1987 Jul 28J
Davila, Oswaldo 1987 Feb 17D
Da Vinci, Leonardo 1980 Jun 16J/Dec 12J
Davis, Al 1980 Jan 18J
Davis, Alvin 1984 Nov 20J
Davis, Bette (Ruth Elizabeth Davis) 1989 Oct 6J
Davis, Brad 1985 Apr 21J
Davis, Clarissa 1986 Mar 30J
Davis, Geena 1988 Mar 30J; 1989 Mar 29J
Davis, Gene B. 1985 Apr 6J
Davis, Junior 1989 Sep 21F
Davis, Mark 1989 Nov 14J
Davis, Marvin 1981 Apr 1J
Davis, Mary Sue 1989 Sep 21F
Davis, Miles 1984 Apr 23J; 1985 Aug 30J; 1988 Mar 20J
Davis, Nathaniel 1984 Feb 8J
Davis, Ossie 1989 Jan 13J/Jun 30J
Davis, Patti 1984 Feb 14F
Davis, Ray E. 1984 Feb 8J
Davis, Sammi 1987 Oct 16J
Davis Jr., Sammy 1984 Dec 24J; 1988 Mar 13J
Davis, Wallace 1986 Nov 21F
Dawkins, John (Australian politician) 1988 Jun 16E
Dawkins, Johnny (basketball player) 1986 Mar 1J
Dawson, Andre 1987 Nov 18J
Dawson, Len 1987 Jan 27J/Aug 8J
Day, Doris 1985 Oct 2J
Day, Dorothy 1980 Nov 29F
Day, Pat 1985 Jan 8J; 1987 Jan 30J
Dayan, Moshe 1980 Mar 9C; 1981 Jun 24C/Oct 16C
Day-Lewis, Daniel 1986 Mar 7J; 1988 Feb 5J; 1989 Nov 10J
Dean, John Gunther 1987 Oct 8E
Deaver, Michael K.
    government service: White House resignation 1981 Dec 20F
    lobbying scandal: investigation 1986 Apr 28F/May 29F/Aug 12F; indictment 1987 Mar 18F; trial 1987 Jul 16F; conviction 1987 Dec 16F; sentencing 1988 Sep 23F
Debakey, Michael 1980 Mar 28C
De Beauvoir, Simone 1986 Apr 14J
Debizet, Pierre 1981 Jul 26B
De Borchgrave, Arnaud 1980 Jul 13J/Aug 17J/Sep 14J
Debreu, Gerard 1983 Oct 17I
De Broglie, Prince Louis (Victor Pierre Raymond) 1987 Mar 19I
Debus, Kurt Heinrich 1983 Oct 10I
Debus, Sigurd 1981 Apr 16B
Debussy, Claude 1983 Nov 7J
De Castella, Rob 1986 Apr 21J

Decker, Mary 1984 Aug 19J; 1985 Jan 19J

Deconcini, Dennis 1988 Jul 14F; 1989 Oct 13F/Dec 22F

Dee, Ruby 1986 Oct 6J; 1989 Jun 30J

Defferre, Gaston 1982 Aug 10B; 1984 Jun 15B; 1986 May 7B

Degas, Edgar 1983 May 18J

De Gaulle, Charles 1981 Jul 18B; 1988 Jan 22B

De Greiff, Monica 1989 Sep 24D

De Grey, Roger 1984 Dec 19J

Dehmelt, Hans 1989 Oct 12I

Deighton, Len 1984 Jan 20J/Feb 10J

Deisenhofer, Johann 1988 Oct 19I

Dejouvenel, Bertrand 1987 Mar 1J

De Klerk, Frederik W.
 government: chosen party leader 1989 Feb 2C; reforms vowed 1989 May 12C; elected South African president 1989 Sep 14C-15C
 peace initiatives: political prisoner releases 1989 Oct 10C; security system scrapped 1989 Nov 28C; Mandela meeting 1989 Dec 13C

De Kooning, Willem 1983 May 10J

De la Espriella, Ricardo 1982 Jul 31D; 1984 Feb 13D

Delahoussaye, Eddie 1988 May 21J

De La Madrid Hurtado, Miguel
 economic policy: 1982 Dec 1D/Dec 27D; 1987 Sep 1D
 government: Mexico presidential elections 1981 Sep 25D; 1982 Jul 4D; 1987 Aug 13D; cabinet named 1982 Nov 30D; inauguration 1982 Dec 1D
 Latin policy: 1983 Jul 23D/Aug 14D; 1984 May 17D
 trade agreements: 1988 Feb 13D
 U.S. policy: 1982 Oct 8D; 1983 Aug 14D; 1984 May 17D; 1986 Jan 3D; 1988 Feb 13D

Delamare, Louis 1981 Sep 4C

Delaney, Martin 1989 Sep 19I

Delany, Dana 1989 Sep 17J

De Larosiere, Jacques 1980 Jan 15D

De la Vega, Jorge 1982 Feb 24D

Delgado, Pedro 1988 Jul 24J

Delillo, Don 1985 Nov 21J

Dellums, Ronald V. 1983 Nov 9G

Del Monaco, Mario 1982 Oct 15J

De Lorean, John Z. 1982 Oct 19B/Oct 19J; 1984 Jul 18B/Aug 16F; 1986 Dec 17F

Delors, Jacques 1984 Jul 19B/Dec 8B; 1988 Dec 16B

Del Pino Diaz, Rafael 1987 May 28D

Del Tredici, David 1980 Apr 14J

Delvalle, Eric Arturo 1985 Sep 28E; 1987 Jul 10D/Aug 8E; 1988 Feb 26D/Mar 4D/Apr 3G/Dec 21G,1989 Mar 21D

Del Valle Alliende, Jaime 1984 Jan 25D/Nov 29D

De Mel, Ronnie 1987 Aug 8E

De Mille, Agnes 1987 Mar 3J

Demirel, Suleyman 1980 Sep 12B/Sep 21B/Oct 11B; 1986 Sep 28B

De Mita, Ciriaco 1988 Apr 13B

Demjanjuk, John 1986 Mar 2C/Mar 19C/Sep 29C; 1987 Feb 16C; 1988 Apr 18C/Nov 30I

Dempsey, Jack 1983 May 31J

Denby, Edwin 1983 Jul 12J; 1988 Jan 11J

Denby, James Jordan 1987 Dec 6D; 1988 Jan 13D/Feb 8D

Dench, Judi 1989 Nov 8J

Deneuve, Catherine 1981 Feb 11J

Deng Xiaoping
 defense and armed forces: 1980 Feb 25E; 1981 Jan 4E; 1984 Dec 29E; 1987 Nov 27E

economic reforms: 1980 Sep 11E; 1982 Sep 1E; 1985 Jan 1E/Sep 24E; 1986 Sep 28E; 1987 Oct 25E
 foreign policy: Hong Kong 1984 May 25E; Taiwan 1982 Jun 1E; U.S. 1982 Jun 1E
 government: party reorganization 1981 Jun 29E/Nov 2E; retirement considered 1986 Mar 25E; protests against 1989 May 17E; power struggle 1989 May 25E; pro-democracy movement 1989 Jun 16E; quits military commission 1989 Nov 9E
 personal issues: ill health rumors 1989 Sep 16E

De Niro, Robert 1980 Nov 14J; 1981 Mar 30J; 1986 May 18J/Oct 31J; 1987 Jun 3J

Denktash, Rauf 1984 Jan 17B; 1985 Mar 1B/Jun 9B/Jun 12B; 1988 Aug 24B/Nov 23B; 1989 Dec 4B

Denny, John 1983 Nov 2J

Dent, Richard 1986 Jan 26J

Denton, Steve 1982 Jan 3J/Dec 13J

De Palma, Brian 1983 Nov 8J; 1987 Jun 3J

Depardieu, Elisabeth 1987 Jun 26J

Depardieu, Gerard 1981 Oct 11J; 1987 Jun 26J

Dern, Laura 1986 Sep 19J

Derwinski, Edward J. 1988 Dec 22F; 1989 Mar 2G/May 11G

Deschenes, Jules 1982 Sep 8D; 1987 Mar 12D

D'Escoto Brockman, Miguel 1983 Jun 6D; 1988 Jul 11D

Desmond, Johnny (Giovanni de Simone) 1985 Sep 6J

De Souza, Steven E. 1983 Jul 15J

Destro, Robert A. 1983 Dec 16F

Desyr, Luc 1986 Jul 16D

Deukmejian, George 1983 Feb 17H; 1985 Sep 26F; 1986 Sep 5H; 1989 May 24F

De Vere, Edward 1987 Sep 25J

Devi, Phoolan 1983 Feb 14E

DeVincenzo, Anthony (Tony Mike) 1983 Nov 18J

Devine, James B. 1983 Aug 3D

Devine, Michael 1981 Aug 20B

Dewey, Thomas 1984 Jul 26F

Dexter, John 1988 Mar 20J/Jun 5J

Dexter, Pete 1988 Nov 29J

Dharsono, Hartono Rekso 1986 May 14E

Dhawan, Rajendra Kumar 1989 Mar 27E

Dhlakama, Afonso 1989 Dec 26C

Diaghilev, Serge 1986 Dec 15J

Diamini, Prince Makhosetive (Swaziland) 1986 Apr 25C

Diamond, Gustave 1989 Mar 9H

Diamond, I.A.L. 1988 Apr 21J

Diamond, Neil 1981 Feb 11J/Mar 4J

Diana, Princess of Wales (Lady Diana Spencer) (Great Britain) 1981 Feb 24B/Jul 29B; 1982 Jun 21B; 1983 Mar 20E; 1984 Sep 15J; 1985 Oct 27E/Nov 9J

Diaz, Ramon 1987 Mar 15E

Diaz Herrera, Roberto 1987 Jun 11D/Jun 16D/Jul 28D/Dec 22D

Dick, Philip K. 1982 Mar 2J

Dickens, Charles 1981 Oct 4J; 1982 Jun 6J; 1985 Dec 2J; 1987 Sep 25I; 1988 Oct 21J

Dickens, Stanley 1989 Jun 11J

Dickey, James 1987 Dec 4J

Diebenkorn, Richard 1985 Dec 15J

Diepgen, Eberhard 1987 May 6B

Dietrich, Paul 1984 Jun 21J

Dietz, Howard 1983 Jul 30J

Dikko, Umaru 1987 Jun 15C

Dillard, J.M. 1989 Oct 27J

Dillon, C. Douglas 1984 May 3H; 1989 Jul 6J

Dillon, Mia 1981 Nov 4J

Dimitrios I (Eastern Orthodox patriarch) 1987 Dec 7A

Din, Hassan Izz al- 1985 Oct 17G

Dinca, Ion 1987 Oct 5B

Dineen, Gerald 1980 Jun 17G

Dinesen, Isak (Karen Blixen) 1985 Dec 18J; 1988 Mar 4J

Dingell, John D. 1983 Mar 1H

Dinh Nho Liem 1980 Feb 8E

Dinkins, David N. 1989 Feb 14F/Nov 7F

Diouf, Abdou 1988 Feb 28C

Dipale, Ernest Moabi 1982 Aug 8C

Dirac, Paul Adrian Maurice 1984 Oct 20I

Dirksen, Everett 1986 Feb 3F

Dith Pran 1984 Nov 2J

Ditka, Mike 1988 Feb 2J/Jul 30J

Dityatin, Alexandr 1980 Jul 25J

Divine (Harris Glenn Milstead) 1988 Feb 26J/Mar 7J

Dixon, Julian C. 1989 Jun 12F

Dizdarevic, Raif 1988 May 15B/Oct 9B/Oct 10B; 1989 May 15B

Djohar, Said Mohamed 1989 Nov 26C

Djuranovic, Veselin 1985 May 15B

Dobrynin, Anatoly F. 1981 Jan 17A; 1984 Jul 1A; 1986 May 20B

Doctorow, E.L. 1981 Jan 11J; 1986 Nov 17J; 1989 Mar 31J/Apr 28J

Dodd, Christopher 1983 Apr 27G

Doe, Samuel K. 1980 Apr 12C; 1981 Jul 17C; 1983 Aug 28C; 1984 Jul 26C; 1985 Apr 1C/Oct 29C; 1986 Jan 6D

Doerr, Bobby 1986 Aug 3J

Doerr, Harriet 1984 Nov 16J

Doherty, Joseph Patrick Thomas 1984 Dec 13A

Doherty, Kieran 1981 Aug 2B

Dohrn, Bernadine 1980 Dec 3F

Doi, Takako 1986 Sep 6E

Doisy, Adelbert Edward 1986 Oct 23I

Dolanc, Stane 1980 Jun 5B

Dole, Elizabeth Hanford 1983 Jan 5H; 1984 Aug 13H; 1985 Sep 19H; 1987 Jun 3H/Sep 14H; 1988 Dec 24H; 1989 Jan 25F/Jun 8F

Dole, Robert J. (Bob)
 budget and spending programs: budget-cutting proposals 1981 Oct 7F; deficit reduction 1981 Nov 3H; bankruptcy measures 1982 Aug 27H
 confirmation issues: Bork 1987 Jul 23F
 minority leadership post: 1984 Nov 28F; 1987 Jan 6F; 1988 Nov 30F
 presidential campaign (1980): 1980 Jan 5F/Mar 15F
 presidential campaign (1988): preview 1985 Jun 29F; debates 1987 Aug 14F/Oct 28F; wife joins 1987 Sep 14H; candidacy declared 1987 Nov 9F; polls 1987 Nov 15F; matching funds 1988 Jan 4F/Mar 30F; signature fraud probe 1988 Jan 18F; primaries 1988 Feb 8F/Feb 23F; endorsements 1988 Feb 12F; withdrawal 1988 Mar 29F

Dole, Vincent P. 1988 Nov 16I

Domenici, Pete 1981 Oct 7F

Domingo, Placido 1987 May 2J

Domingo, Silme 1989 Sep 15E

Domino, Fats 1986 Jan 23J

Do Muoi 1988 Jun 22E

Donald, Beulah Mae 1987 May 20F

Donald, David Herbert 1988 Mar 31J

Donald, Michael 1983 Dec 19F; 1987 Feb 12F

Donaldson, Simon 1986 Aug 3I

Donaldson, Stephen R. 1982 May 9J/Jun 6J; 1983 Apr 10J/May 15J/Jun 1J/Jun 12J

D'Onofrio, Vincent 1987 Jun 26J

Donovan, Raymond J.
 kickback scandal: investigations 1981 Dec 29F; 1982 May 18F/Jun 28H/Aug 25F/Sep 13F; resignation urged 1982 May 20F; indictment 1984 Oct 1F; trial 1985 Mar 15F; 1986 Sep 30F; 1987 May 25F; probe dropped 1987 Oct 30F
 labor secretary: work at home laws 1981 May 1H

Doody, Alison 1989 May 24J

Doolittle, James 1989 Jul 6J

Dorati, Antal 1988 Nov 13J

Dorfman, Albert 1982 Jul 27I

Dorfman, Allen M. 1983 Jan 20J/Mar 30F

Dorsey, Jimmy 1985 Jan 7J

Dorsey, Tommy 1987 Apr 2J; 1988 May 27J

Dortch, Richard 1987 May 6J

Dorticos Torrado, Osvaldo 1983 Jun 23D

Dos Passos, John 1989 Mar 27J

Dos Santos, Jose Eduardo 1989 Jun 22C/Aug 22C/Dec 30C

Dosti, Arben 1988 Jan 25F

Dotson, Donald L. 1988 Jan 7H

Douglas, Barry 1986 Jul 3J

Douglas, Helen Gahagan 1980 Jun 28F

Douglas, Melvyn 1980 Apr 14J

Douglas, Michael 1987 Sep 18J/Dec 11J; 1988 Apr 11J

Douglas, Roger 1989 Aug 7E

Douglas, William O. 1980 Jan 19F

Doumani, Edward 1984 Jun 18J/Aug 15J

Doumani, Fred 1984 Jun 18J/Aug 15J

Dove, Rita 1987 Apr 16J

Dowdy, Wayne 1983 Jan 29H

Dowell, Anthony 1985 Jun 21J

Dower, John 1987 Jan 12J

Dozier, James L. 1981 Dec 17B; 1982 Jan 28B

Dozier, Theresa Knecht 1985 Apr 4F

Drapeau, Jean 1982 Nov 14D

Draper, Morris 1981 Apr 13G

Dravecky, Dave 1989 Aug 10J/Aug 15J

Drees, Willem 1988 May 14B

Dregger, Alfred 1985 Apr 20B

Drew, Richard G. 1980 Dec 7I

Drexel, Katharine 1988 Nov 20J

Drinan, Robert 1980 May 5J; 1981 Jun 27F

Drnovsek, Janez 1989 May 15B

Drummond de Andrade, Carlos 1987 Aug 17J

Duane, Diane 1988 Sep 30J/Oct 21J

Duarte, Jose Napoleon
 civil war: amnesty law 1984 Oct 8D; 1988 Apr 11D; rebel talks 1984 Oct 8D/Oct 9D/Oct 15D/Nov 30D; 1985 May 16G; 1986 Jun 3D; rebel peace plan 1987 May 28D; contra leaders meeting 1987 Aug 21D; refugee repatriation 1987 Oct 11D
 economic policy: 1981 Jul 1D; 1986 Jan 21D
 government: electoral commission 1981 Mar 5D; El Salvador presidential elections 1984 Mar 25D/Mar 27D/Apr 10D/May 7D-8D/May 11D/June 1D; 1989 Jan 25D; cabinet named 1984 May 31D; inauguration 1984 Jun 1D; electoral law veto overruled 1985 Feb 7D; parliamentary elections 1985 Mar 31D; 1988 Mar 20D; rightists press ouster 1987 Jan 22D
 personal issues: daughter kidnapped 1985 Sep 10; ill health 1988 Jun 7D/Jul 11D

political killings: probe panel set 1984 Aug 28D; U.S. Marine '81 deaths 1984 Nov 28D; 1985 Aug 27D; 1988 Apr 11D; ethics investigator's death 1985 Jan 6D; Romero '80 death 1987 Nov 22D; rights commission activist's '87 death 1988 Jan 5D
 U.S. policy: military aid 1981 Apr 20D/Jul 13D; 1984 May 21G-22G; immigration laws 1987 Apr 25D/May 14G

Duarte Duran, Ines Guadalupe 1985 Sep 10D/Sep 25D/Oct 24D

Dubberstein, Waldo H. 1983 Apr 29G

Dubcek, Alexander 1980 Nov 27B; 1988 Aug 21B; 1989 Nov 23B/Dec 10B

Dubinin, Yuri Vladimirovich 1986 May 20B/Dec 19B; 1987 Dec 23F

Dubinsky, David 1982 Sep 17H

Dubos, Rene Jules 1982 Feb 20I

Dubuffet, Jean 1985 May 12J

Dudai, Avi 1982 Nov 17C

Duffy, Michael 1988 Jun 21E

Dukakis, Kitty (Katharine) 1987 Jul 8F

Dukakis, Michael S.
 governorship: health care bill signed 1988 Apr 21F; school legislation 1989 Jun 13F
 gubernatorial campaign (1982): 1982 Sep 14F
 presidential campaign (1988)
  candidacy: 1987 Mar 16F/Apr 29F
  convention: party platform 1988 Jun 25F; Bentsen chosen running mate 1988 Jul 12F; Democratic nomination 1988 Jul 20F-21F
  debates: 1987 Aug 8F/Aug 23F/Sep 8F/Sep 14F/Sep 21F/Sep 25F
  election results: 1988 Nov 8F/Nov 21F/Dec 19F; 1989 Jan 4F
  endorsements: 1988 Apr 13F/Jun 18F/Aug 24F/Oct 29F; Jackson campaigns for 1988 Jul 30F
  finances: matching funds 1988 Jan 4F/Mar 30F; expenditures 1988 Dec 12F
  media: Biden videotape 1987 Sep 30F; personal attacks 1988 Aug 30F/Sep 5F/Sep 9F/Oct 18F/Oct 24F
  personal issues: wife's addiction 1987 Jul 8F; health records 1988 Aug 3F
  polls: 1987 Aug 30F/Nov 15F; 1988 May 19F/May 27F/Jun 21F/Jul 21F/Jul 28F/Aug 9F/Aug 22F/Sep 14F/Oct 13F/Oct 18F/Oct 29F
  primaries: Alaska 1988 Mar 10F; Arizona 1988 Apr 16F; California 1988 Jun 7F; Colorado 1988 Apr 4F; Connecticut 1988 Mar 29F; Idaho 1988 May 24F; Indiana 1988 May 3F; Kansas 1988 Mar 19F; Maine 1988 Mar 1F; Michigan 1988 Mar 26F; Minnesota 1988 Feb 23F; Montana 1988 Jun 7F; Nebraska 1988 May 10D; New Hampshire 1988 Feb 16F; New Jersey 1988 Jun 7F; New Mexico 1988 Jun 7F; New York 1988 Apr 19F; Ohio 1988 May 3F; Oregon 1988 May 17F; overseas 1988 Mar 22F; Pennsylvania 1988 Apr 26F; South Dakota 1988 Feb 23F/Mar 19F; Super Tuesday 1988

Mar 8F; Utah 1988 Apr 25F; Vermont 1988 Mar 1F/Apr 20F; Virgin Islands 1988 Apr 2F; Washington, D.C. 1988 May 3F; West Virginia 1988 May 10D; Wisconsin 1988 Apr 5F

staff: 1987 Sep 30F/Oct 8F; 1988 Sep 2F

transition: 1988 Dec 2F

Dukakis, Olympia 1987 Dec 16J; 1988 Apr 11J

Duke, David 1989 Jan 21F/Feb 18F

Duke, Patty 1985 Nov 5J

Dukes, Alan 1987 Mar 21B

Duk Koo Kim 1982 Nov 13J/Nov 17J

Dumars, Joe 1989 Jun 13J

Dumas, Roland 1989 Nov 14B

Du Maurier, Daphne 1989 Apr 19J

Dumfries, Johnny 1988 Jun 12J

Duncan Jr., Charles 1980 Sep 6H

Duncan, Lindsay 1986 Dec 7J

Dunn, Douglas 1986 Jan 28J

Dunne, Dominick 1988 Jun 24J

Duplantier, Adrian 1985 Jan 10F

Du Pont IV, Pierre S. ("Pete") 1986 Sep 16F; 1987 Jun 13F/Oct 28F; 1988 Jan 4F/Jan 18F/Feb 18F

Du Pre, Jacqueline 1987 Oct 19J

Durack, Peter 1982 May 19A

Duran, Roberto 1980 Sep 20J/Nov 25J/Nov 26J; 1989 Dec 7J

Durant, Ariel 1981 Oct 25J/Nov 8J

Durant, Will 1981 Oct 25J/Nov 8J

Durante, Jimmy 1980 Jan 29J

Duras, Marguerite 1984 Nov 12J; 1986 Apr 7J

Durenberger, David 1989 Aug 4F

Durjanovic, Veselin 1982 May 16B

D'Urso, Giovanni 1980 Dec 12B

Dury, Ian 1987 Mar 21J

Dutton, Charles S. 1986 May 2J

Dutton, Robert C. 1987 May 29G

Duvalier, Francois 1986 Jul 16D; 1987 Nov 2D; 1988 Sep 17D

Duvalier, Jean-Claude

  coup: assassination attempt 1983 Jan 2D; anti-government protests 1986 Jan 8D/Jan 31D; flees Haiti 1986 Feb 7D; refuge sought 1986 Feb 10D; embezzlement suit 1987 Mar 5D/Jun 23D

  government: censorship 1980 Apr 11D; 1984 May 10D; National Assembly elections 1984 Feb 12D; constitutional referendum 1985 Jul 22D; interior minister dismissed 1985 Sep 10D

Duvall, Robert 1983 Mar 4J; 1984 Apr 9J

Duvall, Shelley 1980 May 23J

Dylan, Bob 1986 Jan 25J; 1987 Jul 10J

Dyson, Freeman 1985 Jan 14J

Dzhanibekov, Vladimir 1981 Mar 22I

E

Eads, Gary 1982 Jan 3H

Eagleburger, Lawrence S. 1989 Dec 18G

Eanes, Antonio Ramalho 1980 Oct 19B/Dec 7B; 1981 Aug 11B; 1985 May 23E

Earnhardt, Dale 1980 Nov 15J; 1986 Nov 2J; 1987 Oct 25J

East, John P. 1984 Dec 3G; 1986 Jun 29F

Eastland, James Oliver 1986 Feb 19F

Eastland, Terry 1986 Dec 23F

Eastwood, Clint 1983 Jan 31E; 1986 Apr 8F/Aug 17F; 1989 Apr 30J

Ebens, Ronald 1984 Jun 28F/Sep 19F; 1987 May 1F

Ecevit, Bulent 1980 Oct 11B; 1981 Dec 3B; 1982 Apr 10B

Echeverria Vielman, Guillermo 1983 Jun 8D

Eckersley, Dennis 1988 Oct 9J

Eckstine, Billy 1983 Apr 22J

Eco, Umberto

  best-sellers: *Foucault's Pendulum* 1989 Dec 1J/Dec 22J; *Name of the Rose* 1983 Jul 10J/Aug 14J/Sep 11J/Oct 16J/Nov 13J/Dec 18J; 1984 Jan 20J/Feb 10J

Edberg, Stefan 1985 Dec 9J; 1987 Jan 25J; 1988 Jul 4J

Eddings, David 1988 Sep 30J

Edel, Leon 1986 Feb 17J

Edelman, Asher 1987 Oct 14F

Edelman, Gerald 1985 Sep 6I

Edelman, Gregg 1989 Dec 11J

Edelstein, David 1982 Mar 19H; 1989 May 31H

Edralin Marcos, Josefa 1988 May 4E

Edward VIII, King (Great Britain) 1986 Apr 24J

Edwards, Douglas 1988 Apr 1J

Edwards, Edwin W. 1986 May 10F/Jun 17J

Edwards, James B. 1981 Jul 23F; 1982 Nov 5H

Edwards, Joan 1981 Aug 27J

Edwards, Robert 1988 Mar 21I

Edwards, Sebastian Rice 1987 Oct 16J

Edwards, Tonya 1987 Mar 29J

Edzard, Christine 1988 Oct 21J

Egielski, Richard 1987 Jan 19J

Egli, Alfons 1986 Nov 12B

Ehrlichman, John D. 1980 Jan 19F; 1981 Dec 10F

Eichhorn, Lisa 1986 Apr 19J

Eichmann, Adolf 1987 Feb 16C

Einstein, Albert 1982 Dec 12I; 1983 Sep 10J

Eisenhower, Dwight D. 1986 Oct 27F; 1987 Jun 26H

Eisenstein, Sergei 1983 Dec 19J

Eitan, Dov 1988 Nov 30I

Eizenstat, Stuart 1980 Dec 4F

Ekman, Kerstin 1989 Mar 14A

Elder, Jack 1985 Feb 21F

Eldjarn, Kristjan 1980 Jan 16B

Eldridge, (David) Roy 1989 Feb 26J

Elewonibi, Mohammed 1989 Dec 5J

Elgin, Lord 1983 May 13B

Eliade, Mircea 1986 Apr 22J

Elion, Gertrude B. 1988 Oct 17I

Elizabeth II, Queen (Great Britain)

  foreign issues: Commonwealth survival 1986 Jul 20B; Fiji coup 1987 Oct 15E; Northern Ireland 1987 Dec 19B

  parliament sessions: 1980 Nov 20B; 1984 Nov 6B; 1985 Nov 6B; 1986 Nov 12B; 1987 Jun 25B; 1988 Nov 22B

  personal issues: blanks fired at 1981 Jun 14B; 60th birthday marked 1986 Apr 21B; wealth estimated 1988 Feb 24J; 1989 Sep 11J; Princess Anne separates 1989 Aug 31B

  royal travels: Australia 1986 Feb 17E/Mar 2E; 1988 Apr 19E/Aug 17E; Canada 1982 Apr 17D; 1984 Sep 24J; China 1986 Oct 18E; Nepal 1986 Feb 17E; New Zealand 1986 Feb 17E; Spain 1988 Oct 17B; U.S. 1983 Feb 26G

Elleman-Jensen, Uffe 1987 Jul 20B

Ellin, Stanley 1986 Jul 31J

Ellington, Duke 1984 Jan 31J; 1985 Apr 21J/Sep 15J; 1988 Mar 20J

Elliot, James ("Jumbo") 1981 Mar 22J

Elliot, Osborn 1983 Nov 18J

Elliott, Bill 1985 Feb 17J/May 5J; 1987 Feb 15J; 1988 Nov 20J

Elliott, Denholm 1986 Mar 7J; 1989 May 24J

Ellis, Perry 1986 May 30J

Ellison, James D. 1985 Jul 17F

Ellison, Pervis 1986 Mar 31J

Ellmann, Richard 1987 May 13J; 1989 Jan 9J/Mar 30J

Elphink, Michael 1988 Oct 21J

Elwes, Cary 1989 Dec 14J

Eman, Henny 1986 Jan 1D

Endara, Guillermo 1989 Sep 1D

Enders, John Franklin 1985 Sep 9I

Enders, Thomas O. 1981 Aug 13D; 1982 Mar 10D; 1983 Mar 1G/May 24D

Engel, Morris 1985 Jan 16J

Engen, Donald 1984 Dec 4H

Engle, Joe H. 1981 Nov 12I

Enrile, Juan Ponce 1984 Jan 4E; 1986 Feb 22E/Oct 26E/Nov 7E/Nov 23E; 1989 Dec 28E

Ephron, Nora 1983 Jun 1J/Jun 12J/Jul 10J; 1986 Jul 25J

Epp, Jake (Arthur Jacob) 1987 May 25D/Dec 3D

Epton, Bernard 1983 Apr 12F

Erdrich, Louise 1985 Jan 14J

Erhard, Wernher 1984 Dec 14J

Erim, Nihat 1980 Jul 19B

Erkmen, Hayrettin 1980 Mar 29B

Erlander, Tage 1985 Jun 21B

Ermey, Lee 1987 Jun 26J

Ernst, Jimmy 1983 Feb 19J

Ershad, Hossein Mohammed

  civil strife: martial law 1982 Mar 24E/Mar 27E; 1984 May 12C; 1985 Mar 1E; 1986 Nov 10E; opposition protests 1983 Nov 28E; 1987 Jan 27E/Dec 6E/Nov 12E; state of emergency 1987 Jan 27E; 1988 Apr 12E

  government: ousts Sattar 1982 Mar 24E; military courts set up 1982 Mar 25E; assumes presidency 1983 Dec 11E; political curbs eased 1984 Mar 26E; parliamentary elections 1984 May 12C; 1985 Jan 15E; 1986 Mar 22E; referendum on rule 1985 Mar 1E/Mar 21E; wins presidency 1986 Oct 15E; parliament dissolved 1987 Dec 6E; Islamic republic declared 1988 Mar 13E

  natural disasters: 1985 May 25I

Ertegun, Ahmet 1985 Aug 5J

Ervin Jr., Sam J. 1985 Apr 23F

Erving, Julius ("Dr. J.") 1981 May 27J

Escruceria-Delgado, Samuel Alberto 1987 Aug 13D

Escudero Aponte, Hector 1988 Feb 3F

Eslaminia, Reza 1988 Jan 25F

Espinoza, Julian 1980 Aug 22D

Esposito, Meade 1987 Mar 16F/Sep 22F

Esquivel, Manuel 1984 Dec 14D; 1989 Sep 4D

Esquivel, Roderick 1987 Oct 22D

Essex, Myron 1986 Sep 22I

Estrich, Susan R. 1987 Oct 8F

Eti Alesana, Tofilau 1985 Dec 27E

Etpison, Ngiratkel 1988 Nov 10E

Evans, Bill 1980 Sep 15J

Evans, Gil (Ian Ernest Gilmore) 1985 Aug 30J; 1988 Mar 20J

Evans, Linda (actress) 1985 Oct 31J

Evans, Linda Sue 1985 May 11F

Evans, Maurice 1989 Mar 12J

Evans, Robert 1984 Jun 18J/Aug 15J

Everly Brothers 1986 Jan 23J

Evert Lloyd, Chris

  Australian Open: 1982 Dec 5J; 1985 Dec 8J

  French Open: 1980 Jun 7J; 1985 Jun 8J; 1986 Jun 7J

  Toyota Championships: 1982 Dec 19J

U.S. Open: 1980 Sep 6J; 1982 Sep 11J; 1983 Sep 10J; 1984 Sep 8J; 1989 Sep 9J

  Wimbledon: 1980 Jul 4J; 1981 Jul 3J; 1982 Jul 3J; 1984 Jul 7J

Evren, Kenan 1980 Sep 12B; 1982 May 14B; 1983 Apr 29B/Jun 28B; 1984 Jan 17B

Ewing, Patrick 1985 Sep 18J

Eyadema, Gnassingbe 1980 Apr 8C; 1986 Sep 23C

Eyen, Tom 1981 Dec 20J

Eyskens, Mark 1981 Apr 6B

Eytan, Rafael 1982 May 14C/Nov 14C

F

Fabius, Laurent 1985 Apr 25E/Sep 20B/Sep 25B; 1988 Jun 23B

Fadeyev, Alexander 1987 Mar 12J

Fadlallah, Mohammed Hussein 1983 Oct 26C; 1985 Mar 8C

Fagan, Michael 1982 Jul 9B

Fagoth Muller, Steadman 1982 Feb 23D; 1985 Jan 9D

Fahd, King (Saudi Arabia)

  government: becomes king 1982 Jun 13C; amnesty decreed 1984 Jul 5C; oil minister dismissed 1986 Oct 29C

  Middle East peace plan: 1980 May 27C; 1981 Aug 8C/Nov 2C/Nov 17C/Nov 25A; 1982 Jul 14G

  personal issues: wealth estimated 1989 Sep 11J

  U.S. policy: 1982 Jul 14G; 1983 Jul 4C; 1984 May 21G; 1985 Feb 12G

Faiman, Peter 1986 Sep 26J

Faisal, Saud al- 1983 Jul 4C

Faldo, Nick 1987 Jul 19J; 1988 Jun 20J; 1989 Apr 9J

Fallah, Valiollah 1981 Mar 2C

Falldin, Thorbjorn 1981 May 4B

Fallows, James 1983 Apr 28J

Faltings, Gerd 1983 Jul 23I; 1986 Aug 3I

Falwell, Jerry

  Bakker scandal: PTL ministry 1987 Apr 28J/Oct 8J; Bakker accusations 1987 May 26J

  Jewish prayers controversy: 1980 Oct 11J

  Penthouse damage suit: 1981 Aug 6J; 1988 Feb 24F

  politics: political group formed 1986 Jan 3F; Moral Majority 1987 Nov 3J; 1989 Jun 10F; North commencement speech 1988 May 2F

Fanfani, Amintore 1987 Apr 18B/Apr 28B/Jun 8A

Fang Lizhi 1988 May 4E; 1989 Oct 18A

Farkas, Bertalan 1980 May 26I

Farrar, Margaret 1984 Jun 11J

Farrash, Hussein 1984 Oct 2C

Farrow, Mia 1989 Nov 13J

Fassbinder, Rainer Werner 1981 Jul 10J; 1982 Jun 10J

Fassi, Dena al- 1982 Mar 16J

Fassi, Mohammed al- 1982 Mar 16J

Fast, Howard 1981 Mar 14J

Fauci, Anthony S. 1985 Jul 10I

Faulkner, William 1989 Mar 27J

Faurisson, Robert 1981 Jul 3B

Fayad, Alvaro 1986 Mar 13D

Faylen, Frank 1985 Aug 2J

Febres Cordero Rivadeneira, Leon 1984 Jan 28D/May 6D; 1986 Jan 13G/Jun 1D; 1987 Jan 16D

Fedorchuk, Vitali V. 1982 Dec 17B

Feghall, Jose 1985 Jun 2J

Fehlmann, Pierre 1986 May 9J

Feigen, Richard 1987 Mar 14J

Feinstein, Dianne 1983 Jun 3F/Nov 8F

Fela (Fela Anikulapo-Kuti) 1986 Apr 24C

Felde, Wayne Robert 1988 Mar 15F

Feldman, Trude 1981 Oct 17G

Feldstein, Martin 1983 Mar 25H

Feldt, Kjell 1988 Nov 23B

Felipe, Prince (Spain) 1986 Jan 30B

Felis, Kenneth P. 1985 Jun 24H

Feltsman, Vladimir O. 1987 Apr 21J

Fender, P(ercy) G(eorge) H(enry) 1985 Jun 15J

Fenech Adami, Eddie 1987 May 12B

Fenelon, Fania 1983 Dec 20J

Ferch, John 1986 Nov 3D

Ferguson, Sarah see Sarah, Duchess of York

Ferlinghetti, Lawrence 1982 Jun 6J

Fermat, Pierre 1988 Jun 3I

Fernandez, Eduardo 1988 Dec 4D

Fernandez, Joseph A. 1989 Sep 20F

Fernandez, Joseph F. (Tomas Castillo) 1987 May 29G; 1988 Jun 20F; 1989 Apr 24F/Nov 24F

Fernandez Maguer, Dario 1987 Sep 27D

Fernandez-Mell, Oscar 1988 Sep 13B

Fernando, Enrique 1982 May 10E

Fernando, Saman Piyasiri 1989 Dec 26E

Ferraro, Geraldine A.

  personal issues: financial irregularities, House probe 1984 Aug 7F/Aug 20F/Aug 25F/Sep 12F/Dec 4F; husband acquitted 1987 Oct 15F

  presidential campaign (1984): vice presidential nomination 1984 Jul 12F/Jul 19F; polls 1984 Jul 31F/Sep 26F; on tour 1984 Aug 2F; Aug 9F; personal finances 1984 Aug 20F/Aug 25F; debates 1984 Sep 17F/Oct 11F; media slurs 1984 Sep 21F; election results 1985 Jan 7F

Ferre, Maurice 1985 Nov 5F

Ferreira Aldunata, Wilson 1984 Jun 16D

Ferrier, Johan 1980 Aug 13D

Fetchit, Stepin 1985 Nov 19J

Feynman, Richard P(hillips) 1988 Feb 15I

Fiallos Navarro, Francisco 1982 Dec 12D

Field, Sally 1980 Apr 14J; 1984 Sep 21J; 1985 Mar 25J

Fiennes, Randolph 1982 Aug 29I

Fiers, Alan D. 1987 Jun 2G/Jul 8G/Aug 27G

Fierstein, Harvey 1983 Jun 5J

Figini, Michela 1988 Mar 24J

Figueiredo, Joao Baptista 1980 Feb 5D; 1981 Sep 19D/Sep 24D/Nov 12D/Dec 6D; 1982 May 12D; 1984 Jun 28D

Figueroa, Gustavo 1982 May 10D

Filali, Abdellatif al- 1987 Jul 20B

Filmon, Gary 1988 Dec 19D

Fingers, Rollie 1981 Nov 25J

Finley, Moses (M.I. Finley) 1986 Jun 23J

Finnbogadottir, Vigdis 1985 Oct 24B

Finney, Albert 1986 Dec 7J

Firyubin, Nikolai 1981 Aug 27E

Fischer, Joschka 1987 Feb 9B

Fisher, Bernard 1985 Nov 22I

Fisher, R.A. 1988 Mar 3I

Fitch, Val 1980 Oct 14I

Fittipaldi, Emerson 1989 May 28J

Fitzgerald, A. Ernest 1982 Jun 24F; 1984 Jun 25G

Fitzgerald, F. Scott 1983 Jun 3J; 1984 Jan 31J; 1987 Dec 22J; 1988 Nov 17J

Fitzgerald, Garret

  EC presidency: 1984 Jul 19B/Jul 25B

  foreign policy: Great Britain 1981 Aug 16B/Nov 6B; 1985 Nov 15B; Ulster accord 1985 Nov 15B; U.S. visit 1984 Mar 16G

  government: Irish prime minister 1981 Jun 30B; 1982 Jan 27B/Dec

14B; local elections 1985 Jun 20B; parliamentary elections 1987 Feb 17B
Fitzgerald, James 1984 Nov 30H
Fitzgerald, Robert Stuart 1985 Jan 16J
Fitzsimmons, Frank 1981 May 6H/May 15H
Fitzwater, Marlin 1987 Jul 28G
Flannery, Thomas 1988 Apr 8F
Flanzamaton, Moses 1985 Apr 1C
Fleischman, Paul 1989 Jan 9J
Fleischman, Sid 1987 Jan 19J
Fleischmann, Martin 1989 Mar 23I/May 9I
Fleischmann, Peter F. 1986 Jan 13J
Fletcher, James C. 1986 Mar 1I/Apr 23H/May 27I; 1989 Apr 12I
Florin, Peter 1987 Sep 15A; 1988 Sep 20A
Florio, James J. 1989 Nov 7F
Flory, Paul John 1985 Sep 9I
Floyd, Ray 1982 Aug 8J; 1986 Jun 15J
Flutie, Doug 1984 Dec 1J; 1985 Jan 25J/Mar 8J
Flynn, Errol 1980 Aug 1J
Flynn, William 1981 Jan 13J
Flynt, Larry 1983 Nov 8J
Fo, Dario 1983 Aug 27F; 1984 Nov 15G
Fogelberg, Dan 1980 Mar 5J
Fogerty, John 1985 Feb 23J/Mar 30J/Apr 27J
Foley, Thomas S. 1980 Dec 8F; 1989 Jun 6F
Folkerts, Knut 1980 Jul 31B
Follett, Ken
  best-sellers: *Eye of the Needle* 1981 Jul 24J; *Key to Rebecca* 1980 Oct 12J/Dec 7J; 1981 Jan 11J/Feb 8J/Mar 8J; 1987 Oct 12J/Dec 7J; *Lie Down with Lions* 1986 Feb 28J/Mar 28J/Apr 25J; *Man from St. Petersburg* 1982 Jun 6J/Jul 11J/Aug 8J; *Pillars of the Earth* 1989 Sep 29J/Oct 27J; *Triple* 1980 Jan 13J/Feb 10J
Fomin, N. 1986 Jul 29B
Fonda, Henry 1981 Dec 4J; 1982 Mar 29J/Aug 12J
Fonda, Jane 1981 Dec 4J; 1985 May 6H
Fontaine, Marcel 1985 Mar 22C
Fontanne, Lynn 1983 Jul 30J
Fonteyn, Margot 1986 Sep 28J
Foot, Michael 1980 Nov 10B
Foote, Horton 1983 Mar 4J; 1985 Dec 20J
Forbes, George L. 1989 Oct 3F
Forbes, Malcolm 1987 May 28J
Ford, Gerald R. 1980 Jan 9F/Mar 15F/Jul 17F; 1981 Oct 10A/Oct 11G; 1983 Nov 6A/Nov 17F
Ford, Harrison 1981 Jun 12J; 1985 Feb 8J; 1988 Dec 21J; 1989 May 24J
Ford II, Henry 1987 Sep 29H
Ford, John 1983 Nov 30J; 1984 Sep 7J; 1988 Nov 27J
Foreman, Carl 1984 Jun 26J
Forlani, Arnaldo 1980 Oct 2B/Oct 18B; 1981 May 26B/Jun 10B
Forman, Milos 1984 Sep 19J; 1985 Mar 25J
Forrest, Helen 1983 Jul 6J
Forssmann, Werner 1988 Feb 19I
Forster, E.M. 1986 Mar 7J
Forsyth, Frederick
  best-sellers: *Devil's Alternative* 1980 Feb 10J/Mar 9J/Apr 6J/May 4J/Jun 8J; *Fourth Protocol* 1984 Oct 19J/Dec 14J; 1985 Jan 18J; *Negotiator* 1989 May 26J/Jun 30J
Fortas, Abe 1982 Apr 5F
Fosse, Bob (Robert Louis) 1986 Apr 10J; 1987 Sep 23J
Fossey, Dian 1985 Dec 26I; 1986 Aug 21C/Dec 18C; 1988 Sep 23J
Foster, Andrew ("Rube") 1981 Aug 2J

Foster, Jodie 1981 Apr 2F/Sep 29J; 1988 Oct 14J; 1989 Mar 29J
Foster, Tabatha 1988 May 11J
Foucault, Michel 1984 Jun 25J
Fountain, L.H. 1982 Aug 3I
Fournier, Pierre 1986 Jan 8J
Fowler, Norman 1980 Mar 19B; 1985 Jun 3B; 1986 Nov 21B
Fowler, William A. 1983 Oct 19I
Fox, Michael J. 1986 Sep 21J; 1987 Sep 20J; 1988 Aug 28J
Fox, Terry 1981 Jun 28J
Foxx, Jimmie 1988 Nov 21J
Foyt, A.J. 1985 Feb 3J
Francis, Dick
  best-sellers: *Bolt* 1987 Mar 27J; *Break In* 1986 Apr 25J; *Danger* 1984 Apr 20J/May 11J; *Edge* 1989 Mar 31J; *Hot Money* 1988 Mar 25J/Apr 29J; *Proof* 1985 Apr 19J; *Reflex* 1981 May 24J
Franco, Francisco 1981 Feb 26B; 1982 Dec 15B; 1985 Nov 24B
Franjien, Suleiman 1980 Feb 17C; 1984 Aug 23C
Frank, Anne 1986 May 14J
Frank, Anthony M. 1988 Feb 2H
Frank, Barney 1987 May 29F; 1989 Sep 12F
Frank, Elizabeth 1986 Apr 17J
Frank, James 1981 Jan 13J
Frank, Joseph 1985 Jan 14J
Frank, Leo M. 1986 Mar 11F
Franklin, Aretha 1984 Jul 25J; 1987 Jul 10J
Franklin, Joseph Paul 1981 Sep 28F; 1982 Jun 2F
Franz Josef II, Grand Duke (Liechtenstein) 1984 Aug 26B
Fraser, Douglas 1980 Jan 3D/Jan 13H/May 13H; 1981 Dec 9H; 1983 May 18F; 1984 Oct 4H
Fraser, John A. 1985 Sep 23D
Fraser, Malcolm
  economic policy: tax reforms 1982 Jul 19E; job protests 1982 Oct 26E
  environmental protection: Great Barrier Reef 1980 Jun 10I
  foreign policy: Soviet envoy criticized 1981 Mar 4E
  government: defense spending 1980 Feb 19E; polls 1980 Oct 15E; elections 1980 Oct 18E/Oct 21E; 1983 Mar 5E; Labour plan 1981 Aug 25E; appointments 1982 Oct 11E
  tax fraud scandal: 1982 Sep 28E
Frazier, Marvis 1983 Nov 25J
Frazier, Walt 1987 Feb 5J
Frears, Stephen 1986 Mar 7J; 1988 Dec 21J
Frederick, Pauline 1980 Jul 7J
Fredericks, Carlton 1987 Jul 28J
Freed, Alan 1986 Jan 23J
Freedman, James O. 1988 Mar 28F
Freedman, Michael 1986 Aug 3I
Freeman, Cynthia
  best-sellers: *Come Pour the Wine* 1980 Dec 7J; 1981 Jan 11J/Feb 8J; 1987 Dec 7J; *No Time for Tears* 1981 Dec 6J; *Portraits* 1980 Mar 9J/Apr 6J/May 4J
Freeman, Derek 1983 Jan 31I
Freeman, Morgan 1989 Dec 13J/Dec 14J
Freij, Elias 1982 Jan 22C
Frei Montalva, Eduardo 1982 Jan 22B
Freitas do Amaral, Diogo 1986 Jan 26B/Feb 16B
Frelich, Phyllis 1980 Jun 8J
Freud, Anna 1982 Oct 9I
Freud, Sigmund 1981 Nov 5I; 1982 Oct 9I
Frey, Jim 1984 Oct 17J
Freyre, Gilberto 1987 Jul 18D

Fricker, Brenda 1989 Nov 10J
Fried, Charles 1985 Jul 15H
Friedersdorf, Max L. 1988 Jul 28G
Friedlander, Lee 1986 Aug 17J
Friedman, Benny 1982 Nov 23J
Friedman, Milton 1988 Oct 17J
Friedman, Russell 1988 Jan 11J
Friedman, Stanley M. 1986 Nov 25F
Friedman, Stephen 1982 Jan 20J
Friedman, Thomas L. 1983 Feb 25J
Frisch, Max 1986 Feb 28J
Frischenschlager, Friedhelm 1985 Feb 1B
Frohnmayer, Dave 1983 Oct 6F
Frohnmayer, John E. 1989 Sep 29J/Nov 16J
Fromm, Erich 1980 Mar 18J
Fromme, Lynette ("Squeaky") 1987 Dec 25F
Fuchs, (Emil) Klaus (Julius) 1988 Jan 28I
Fuentes, Carlos 1988 Apr 21J
Fugard, Athol 1980 Nov 17J; 1987 Sep 16J
Fukui, Kenichi 1981 Oct 19I
Fuller, Buckminster R. 1983 Jul 1J
Fuller, Charles 1982 Apr 12J; 1984 Sep 14J
Fullerton, C. Gordon 1982 Mar 22I
Funaro, Dilson 1987 Apr 2D
Funchess, David Livingston 1986 Apr 22F
Funderburk, David 1985 May 15B
Futrell, Mary Hatwood 1985 Jul 3F; 1987 Dec 3F

G

Gabler, Hans Walter 1984 Jun 16J
Gabriel, Peter 1986 Jul 16J/Aug 13J; 1988 Sep 2J/Oct 15J
Gacy, John Wayne 1980 Mar 13F/Mar 13J
Gairy, Eric 1984 Jan 21D
Galan, Luis Carlos 1989 Aug 18D
Gale, Robert 1986 Nov 23I
Galestyan, Ambartsum 1988 Mar 8B
Galindo, Rudi 1989 Feb 10J
Gallardo, Miguel Angel Felix 1989 Apr 8D
Galliner, Peter 1983 Jun 28B
Gallo, Robert C. 1985 Feb 7I; 1986 Sep 22I
Gallup, George H. 1984 Jul 26F
Galman y Dawang, Rolando 1983 Aug 30E/Dec 28D; 1984 Nov 5E
Galtieri, Leopoldo 1981 Dec 11D; 1982 Apr 1A/Apr 11A/Apr 17D/Apr 22D/Jun 17D; 1986 May 16D
Gamble, Phil 1988 Mar 30J
Gammell, Stephen 1989 Jan 9J
Gance, Abel 1981 Nov 11J
Gandhi, Indira
  assassination: 1984 Oct 31E; riots 1984 Nov 1E; funeral 1984 Nov 3E; trial 1985 Feb 11E/May 13E; 1986 Jan 22E; executions 1989 Jan 6E; top aide implicated 1989 Mar 27E; suspects charged 1989 Apr 7E
  civil strife: Assam violence 1983 Feb 25E/Apr 1E; Sikh militancy 1983 Feb 27E/Oct 6E; 1984 Jun 13E
  family planning: 1983 Jul 11E
  foreign policy: Pakistan 1980 Jan 16E-16G; 1981 Aug 19E; Soviet visit 1982 Sep 22A; UN address 1983 Sep 28A
  government: India elections 1980 Jan 6E; 1982 May 19E; 1983 Jan 5E/Feb 23E; 1984 Mar 29E/May 23E; sworn prime minister 1980 Jan 14E; state assemblies dis-

solved 1980 Feb 17E; Tamil Nadu governor fired 1980 Oct 26E; Andhra Pradesh minister resigns 1982 Feb 16E; cabinet revamped 1983 Jan 26E
  U.S. policy: Pakistani military aid 1980 Jan 16E/Jan 16G; 1981 Aug 19E; wheat purchases 1981 Jul 21E; visit 1982 Jul 26E; nuclear fuel dispute 1982 Jul 29A
Gandhi, Mahatma Mohandas K. 1982 Mar 19E/Nov 15E; 1988 Jan 20E
Gandhi, Maneka 1982 Sep 25E; 1984 Aug 8E
Gandhi, Rajiv
  arms control and defense: 1985 Jan 28A; spending 1987 Feb 28E; missiles tested 1988 Feb 25E
  Bhopal gas leak: 1984 Dec 4E
  Bofors arms scandal: 1989 Jul 23E
  civil strife: Gandhi assassination 1984 Nov 1E; 1987 Feb 23E; 1989 Mar 27E; emergency measures 1985 Jul 7E; Sikhs 1985 Jul 24E; 1987 Feb 23E/May 11E; 1989 Mar 3E; Assam accord 1985 Aug 15E; Tamil Nadu 1988 Jan 31E; Tripura accord 1988 Aug 12E
  foreign policy: China 1988 Dec 23E; 1989 Jan 2E; Great Britain meeting 1985 Oct 15B; Pakistan 1985 Dec 17E; 1987 Oct 20G; 1988 Dec 29E; Soviet visit 1985 May 26A; Tibet 1989 Jan 2E; U.S. visits 1985 Jun 15G; 1987 Oct 20G
  government: India elections 1984 Jun 15E; 1984 Dec 28E; 1985 Mar 5E/Dec 16E; 1989 Jan 21E/Oct 17E; prime minister 1984 Oct 31E/Dec 31E; 1989 Nov 29E; party president 1984 Nov 12E; cabinet reorganized 1986 Jan 19E; 1987 Jul 25E; Venkataraman backed 1987 Jul 13E; opposition coalition 1988 Aug 7E/Oct 11E; 1989 Jul 23E
  personal issues: Maneka Gandhi feud 1984 Aug 8E; assassination foiled 1986 Oct 2E
Gandhi, Sanjay 1980 Jun 23E; 1984 Aug 8E
Ganigan, Andrew 1982 May 22J
Ganilau, Penaia 1987 Oct 15E/Dec 5E
Gann, Paul 1987 Jun 9F
Garaicoetxea, Carlos 1980 Mar 9B
Garba, Joseph Namvan 1989 Sep 21A
Garbo, Greta 1987 Aug 17J
Garcia, Darnell 1988 Nov 24F
Garcia, Jane Lee 1989 Oct 20F
Garcia, Robert 1988 Nov 21F; 1989 Oct 20F
Garcia, Romeo Lucas 1982 Mar 23D
Garcia Alvarado, Roberto 1989 Apr 19D
Garcia Marquez, Gabriel 1981 Apr 3D; 1982 Oct 21J; 1983 Feb 12J; 1984 Aug 11J; 1988 May 27J/Jun 24J
Garcia Meza Tejada, Luis 1980 Aug 1D/Sep 10D
Garcia Perez, Alan
  economic policy: foreign debt 1985 Jul 30D; 1987 Jun 3D; bank nationalization 1987 Oct 14D; wage increases 1987 Oct 23D
  government: Peru presidential elections 1985 Apr 14D/Jun 1D; inauguration 1985 Jul 28D/Jul 30D; party post resignation 1988 Dec 17D
  prison mutiny: 1986 Jun 27D
Garcia Robles, Alfonso 1982 Oct 12A
Garcia Rodriguez, Felix 1980 Sep 11A
Gardiner, Lord 1981 Jun 14B
Gardiner, Muriel 1985 Feb 6J
Gardner, Herb 1985 Nov 19J; 1986 Jun 1J

Garland, Judy 1984 May 1J; 1986 Jul 25J
Garland, William ("Red") 1984 Apr 23J
Garn, Jake 1981 Jun 25G
Garner, Peggy Ann 1984 Oct 16J
Garreau, Jacqueline 1980 Apr 29J
Garrido Gil, Rafael 1986 Oct 25B
Garrity Jr., W. Arthur 1985 Sep 3F; 1989 May 31F
Garrow, David J. 1987 Apr 16J
Garwood, Robert 1980 Feb 1G; 1981 Feb 5G
Garza Jr., Alvaro 1987 Dec 21I
Gaspar, Matej 1987 Jul 10J
Gass, William 1983 Feb 19J; 1986 Feb 17J
Gates, Ricky L. 1988 Jan 20H
Gates, Robert M. 1987 Feb 2G/Feb 18G/Mar 3G; 1988 Dec 28G
Gates, William (businessman) 1987 Mar 19H
Gates, William ("Pop") (basketball player) 1989 Feb 10J
Gatski, Frank 1985 Jan 22J
Gaye, Marvin 1984 Apr 1J/Nov 2F
Gaye Sr., Marvin 1984 Nov 2F
Gaynor, Janet 1982 Sep 5J; 1984 Sep 14J
Gayoom, Maumoon Abdul 1988 Nov 3E
Geddes, Jane 1986 Jul 14J; 1987 May 24J
Gehrig, Lou 1988 Nov 21J
Gehry, Frank O. 1989 May 1J
Gelbart, Larry 1989 Dec 11J
Geller, Margaret 1986 Jan 12I
Gemayel, Amin
  civil strife: east Beirut control 1983 Feb 15C; unity urged 1983 Aug 25C; national reconciliation talks 1983 Sep 26C/Oct 31C/Nov 11A; 1984 Feb 1C
  government: Wazan renamed premier 1982 Oct 4C; rule by decree 1982 Nov 3C; resignation urged 1983 Aug 13C; government collapses 1984 Feb 5C; successor sought 1984 Mar 14C; Karami appointed premier 1984 Apr 26C; national unity cabinet 1984 May 10C/Sep 12C; Maronite support 1984 Oct 9C; military government 1988 Sep 22C/Sep 24C
  peace initiatives: UN forces 1982 Oct 18A; U.S. 1982 Oct 19A/Nov 1G; 1983 Dec 2G; France 1982 Oct 20B; 1983 Oct 24C; Saudi plan 1984 Feb 15C; Syria 1984 Apr 20C; 1985 Mar 23C
Gemayel, Bashir 1982 Jan 23C/Aug 23C/Sep 14C/Sep 15C/Oct 1C
Gemayel, Pierre 1982 Sep 15C; 1984 Aug 29C
Gemma, Peter 1981 Jul 7F
Genet, Jean 1986 Apr 15J
Geng Biao 1981 Mar 6E; 1982 Nov 19E
Genscher, Hans-Dietrich
  energy policy: A-plants 1986 Jul 27B
  foreign policy: Iran 1984 Jul 22A; Poland 1982 Jan 6B; Soviet Union 1981 Apr 3B; 1983 Oct 16A; 1986 Jul 20B
  government: West German party leader 1982 Nov 5B; 1984 May 27B
George V, King (Great Britain) 1986 Nov 27B
George, Clair E. 1984 Jul 1G; 1987 Aug 27G
Georgeson, Tom 1988 Jul 15J
Gephardt, Richard A.
  House majority leader: 1989 Jun 14F
  presidential campaign (1988): candidacy declared 1987 Feb 23F; debates 1987 Aug 8F; polls 1987

Aug 30F/Nov 15F; matching funds 1988 Jan 4F/Mar 30F; primaries 1988 Feb 8F/Feb 23F/Mar 19F; withdrawal 1988 Mar 28F

Gerasimov, Gennadi I. 1988 Oct 11B; 1989 Jan 25E

Gernreich, Rudi (Rudolph) 1985 Apr 21J

Gershwin, George 1983 May 1J/Aug 17J; 1985 Aug 24J; 1986 May 18J

Gershwin, Ira 1983 May 1J/Aug 17J; 1985 Aug 24J

Gerulaitis, Vitas 1980 Jun 8J

Geschwind, Norman 1984 Nov 4I

Gesell, Gerhard A. 1988 Mar 24F/Jul 8F/Aug 5F/Nov 7F/Nov 29F; 1989 Apr 20F/Jul 6G

Gestsson, Svavar 1980 Jan 16B

Geter, Lenell 1983 Nov 20F/Dec 14F; 1984 Mar 26F

Getty, Anne 1985 Mar 4J; 1986 Apr 10J

Getty, Gordon P. 1984 Sep 18H; 1985 Mar 4J

Getty, J. Paul 1982 Mar 1J/Mar 16J

Geva, Eli 1982 Jul 25C

Ghaffar Khan, Abdul 1988 Jan 20E

Ghani, Abdul-Jabbar Oman 1983 Apr 16C

Ghising, Subash 1988 Aug 6E

Ghotbzadeh, Sadegh 1980 Mar 7C/Mar 25A/Apr 8C/Apr 30A/Nov 7C/Nov 10C; 1982 Apr 10C/Sep 15C

Giacometti, Alberto 1985 Jul 15J

Giacometti, Diego 1985 Jul 15J

Giamatti, A(ngelo) Bartlett 1985 Dec 10F; 1986 Jun 9J; 1988 May 6J/Sep 8J; 1989 Jun 26J/Aug 24J/Sep 1J/Sep 13J

Gibbs, Courtney 1988 Mar 1J

Gibson, Bob 1981 Aug 2J

Gibson, Debbie 1989 Feb 25J/Mar 25J/Apr 29J

Gibson, Kenneth A. 1982 Oct 21F

Gibson, Kirk 1988 Nov 15J

Gibson, Mel 1983 Jan 21J

Gibson, Phil S. 1984 Apr 28F

Gide, Andre 1983 Jun 3J

Gierek, Edward 1980 Aug 18B/Aug 19B/Sep 6B; 1981 Jan 26B/Jul 15B

Gilbert, David Joseph 1981 Oct 20F

Gilbert, Walter 1980 Oct 14I

Gilchrist, Ellen 1984 Nov 16J

Gillespie, Dizzy 1983 Sep 15J; 1989 Feb 26J

Gilliam, Terry 1985 Dec 14J

Gilmore, Horace 1980 Sep 25F

Giloteaux, Santiago 1982 Sep 2D

Ginastera, Alberto 1983 Jun 25J

Gingold, Hermione 1987 May 24J

Gingrich, Newt 1989 Mar 22F/Apr 11F/Jul 25F/Oct 25F

Ginsberg, Allen 1982 Jun 6J; 1986 Jan 12J

Ginsburg, Douglas H. 1987 Oct 29F/Nov 1F/Nov 7F/Nov 8F; 1988 Feb 10F

Ginzton, Edward 1984 Feb 4I

Girardelli, Marc 1985 Mar 20J; 1986 Mar 23J

Giroux, Robert 1988 Jan 11J

Giscard D'Estaing, Valery
anti-Semitism: 1980 Oct 8B
economic policy: EC expansion slowdown 1980 Jun 5B
foreign policy: Soviet Union 1980 May 19B; West Germany 1980 Jul 7B/Jul 11B
government: French parliamentary elections 1980 Nov 30B; 1984 Sep 23B; candidacy 1981 Mar 2B; presidential elections 1981 Apr 26B/May 10B
nuclear weapons: 1980 Jun 26I/Jul 11B

Githii, George 1982 Jul 21C

Giuliani, Rudolph W. 1986 Jun 13F/Nov 19F/Dec 2F; 1987 Apr 22H

Glass, Charles 1987 Aug 18C

Glass, Philip 1983 Jul 18J; 1988 Mar 16J

Gleason, Jackie (Herbert John) 1985 Jan 26I; 1987 Jun 24J

Gleason, Joanna 1987 Nov 5J; 1988 Jun 5J

Glemp, Jozef Cardinal
Auschwitz convent dispute: 1989 Aug 27B
church developments: named Polish primate 1981 Jul 7J; papal visits 1982 Feb 11B/Jul 21B/Nov 8B; Jasna Gora rites 1982 Aug 15B/Aug 26B; named cardinal 1983 Feb 2J; activist priest transfer 1984 Mar 15B
human rights: strike moratorium plea 1981 Aug 26B; artists, intellectuals petition 1982 Jan 21B; women prisoners' release urged 1982 Apr 18B; Walesa release urged 1982 Aug 26B

Glenn, John
"Keating 5" ethics probe: 1989 Oct 13F/Dec 22F
presidential campaign (1984): California convention 1983 Jan 15F; candidacy 1983 Apr 21F; women's groups 1983 Jul 10F/Oct 2F; primaries 1983 Jul 13F; matching funds 1984 Jan 3G; debates 1984 Jan 15F/Feb 11F; withdrawal 1984 Mar 16F

Gless, Sharon 1986 Sep 21J; 1987 Sep 20J

Glover, Julian 1989 May 24J

Glubb, John Bagot 1986 Mar 17B

Gluck, Jeffrey M. 1984 Jun 21J

Gluck, Louise 1986 Feb 17J

Godfrey, Arthur 1983 Mar 16J

Godfrey, Robert Franklin 1980 May 19F

Godoy, Jorge 1987 Feb 12D

Godoy Reyes, Virgilio 1984 Oct 21D

Godunov, Alexander 1982 Jun 3J

Goetz, Bernhard Hugo
New York City subway vigilante: surrender 1984 Dec 31F; indictment 1985 Jan 25F/Mar 27F; charges 1986 Jan 16F/Jul 8F; trial 1987 Apr 27F/Jun 16F; sentencing 1987 Oct 19F; 1989 Jan 13F

Goh Chok Tong 1989 Oct 8E

Gohlke, Mary D. 1986 May 6I

Gokhale, V.P. 1984 Dec 7E

Goldberg, Dennis 1985 Feb 28C

Goldberg, Peg L. 1989 Aug 3J

Goldfine, Adam 1988 Aug 26J

Goldfine, Bernard 1986 Oct 27F

Golding, William 1983 Oct 6J

Goldman, Gary 1983 Mar 11E

Goldman, James 1988 Jan 24J

Goldmann, Nahum 1982 Aug 29C

Goldschmidt, Miriam 1987 Oct 13J

Goldsmith, James 1988 Feb 24J

Goldsmith, Judy 1982 Oct 10F

Goldstein, Alan 1985 Jul 12F

Goldstein, Joseph L. 1985 Oct 14I/Nov 22I

Goldwater, Barry 1981 Jul 23F/Jul 29G; 1983 Mar 26F/Dec 4G; 1984 Apr 11G

Golovanov, Vladimir 1980 Jun 30C

Gomez, Andres 1986 May 4J

Gomez, Vernon ("Lefty") 1989 Feb 17J

Gomez Fyns, Fernando 1980 Mar 17D

Gomez Ibarruri, Dolores 1989 Nov 12B

Gomulka, Wladyslaw 1982 Sep 1B

Gonsalves, Eric 1981 Apr 17G

Gonzales, Neptali 1986 Sep 1E

Gonzalez, Felipe 1980 Jun 25B; 1982 Oct 28B/Dec 2B; 1986 Jun 22B; 1987 Mar 30B; 1989 Sep 1B/Oct 29B

Gonzalez, Jose Esteban 1981 Mar 19D

Goode, W. Wilson 1983 May 17F/Nov 8F; 1985 Nov 6F; 1986 Mar 6F/Nov 23F; 1987 May 19F/Nov 3F

Gooden, Dwight 1984 Nov 19J; 1985 Aug 25J/Nov 13J

Goodman, Alan Harry 1982 May 7C; 1983 Apr 7C

Goodman, Benny (Benjamin David) 1984 May 1J; 1985 Jan 7J; 1986 Jun 13J/Jul 31J; 1987 Jul 10J; 1989 Feb 26J

Goodman, Hirsh 1982 Sep 24C

Goodman, John 1989 Sep 15J

Goodman Jr., Robert O. 1983 Dec 4C/Dec 25G/Dec 29C/Dec 31C; 1984 Jan 3C/Jan 4C/Jan 4G

Goodman, Steve 1984 Sep 20J

Goolagong, Evonne 1980 Jul 4J

Gorbachev, Mikhail S.
agriculture: 1988 Mar 23B
armed forces: troops exit Eastern Europe 1989 Apr 25B
arms control: INF treaty 1985 Apr 7B; 1987 Feb 28B/Apr 15B/Apr 23B/May 19B/Jul 22B/Dec 8A/Dec 11B; 1988 Jan 25B; A-test moratorium 1985 Jul 29B/Aug 13B; 1986 Mar 13B/Mar 14G/Mar 29B/Jul 18B; Reagan letter exchange 1985 Jul 29G; 1986 Jul 25G/Sep 22A; European talks proposed 1985 Oct 3B; A-test ban proposed 1986 Jan 15B-16B; strategic arms 1986 Jun 30B; SALT II violations 1986 Nov 28B; northern seas 1987 Oct 1B; Warsaw Pact resolutions 1988 Jul 15B
awards and honors: *Time* "Man of the Year" 1987 Dec 26J
Chernobyl A-plant accident: 1986 May 14B
church policy: papal meeting 1989 Dec 1B
economic reforms: 1985 Apr 8B/Jun 11B; 1986 Feb 25B/Aug 1B; 1987 Jun 25B/Jun 30B; 1989 Apr 22B
foreign policy: Afghanistan 1986 Jul 28B; 1988 Feb 8B; China 1986 Jul 28B-29E; 1988 Jan 12E; 1989 May 15A/Dec 27E; Comecon summit 1986 Nov 11A; Cuba 1989 Apr 2D; Czechoslovakia 1986 Mar 28B; 1987 Apr 11B; 1989 Apr 25B; East Germany 1989 Apr 25B; France 1985 Oct 3B; 1989 Nov 14B; Great Britain 1984 Dec 15B; 1985 Oct 3B; 1989 Apr 5B/Sep 23A; Hungary 1986 Jun 11B; 1989 Apr 25B; India 1985 May 26A; 1986 Nov 28E; 1988 Nov 18E; Nicaragua 1989 May 16D; Palestinians 1988 Apr 9C; Philippines 1988 Sep 16B; Poland 1988 Jul 16B; 1989 Jul 15B-16B; 1989 Dec 4B; West Germany 1987 May 17B; 1988 Oct 24B; 1989 Jun 12B; Yugoslavia 1988 Mar 18B
government: Chernenko succession 1984 Feb 16B; 1985 Feb 5B; Soviet state, party posts 1985 Mar 11B; 1988 Oct 1B; power consolidation 1985 Mar 22B/Jul 2B; party congress 1986 Feb 25B; foreign policy realignment 1986 May 23B; polls 1987 May 17B/Dec 6F; 1988 May 26B/Nov 4B; multiple-candidate elections 1987 Jun 21B; Stalin criticism 1987 Nov 2B; 1988 Apr 17B; Yeltsin dismissal 1987 Nov 11B; Ligachev challenge 1988 Apr 13B/Apr 20B; party conference 1988 Jun 4B/Jun 28B; party reorganization 1988 Sep 30B; one-party state 1989 Feb 14B; Central Committee purge 1989 Apr 25B; Politburo purge 1989 Sep 20B; Soviet restructuring 1989 Dec 12B
human rights: Sakharov meeting 1988 Jan 15B
nationalism and separatism: Armenia 1988 Feb 26B-27B; ethnic violence warning 1989 Jul 1B; Lithuania 1989 Dec 26B
U.S. policy: hate campaign 1985 Aug 26B; senators meet 1985 Sep 3B; Jackson meets 1985 Nov 19B; cultural exchanges 1985 Nov 21B; 1986 Jan 8J; New Year's greetings 1986 Jan 1A/Dec 30B; 1988 Jan 1A; test-ban summit snub 1986 Mar 30G; ex-officials meet 1987 Feb 4B; Berlin challenge 1987 Jun 12B; Brokaw TV interview 1987 Nov 30G; Asia-Pacific peace initiative 1988 Sep 16B; Nicaragua arms cutoff 1989 May 16D; CIA power estimate 1989 Dec 17G
U.S. summits: Geneva 1985 Jul 2G/Nov 14G/Nov 21B; Reykjavik 1986 Sep 30G/Oct 7G/Oct 12A-13B; Washington, D.C. 1987 Oct 30G/Nov 22G; Moscow 1988 Mar 23G/May 29A; New York City 1988 Dec 6G; Malta 1989 Oct 31G/Dec 2A

Gorbatko, Viktor F. 1980 Jul 23I

Gordimer, Nadine 1988 Mar 28J

Gordon, Bridgette 1989 Apr 2J

Gordon, Mary 1981 Apr 19J

Gordon, Ruth 1985 Aug 28J

Gordon, Spiver 1985 Nov 14F

Gore Jr., Albert A. 1985 Aug 5J; 1987 Jun 29F; 1988 Jan 4F/Mar 30F/Apr 21F/Jun 18F

Gore, Tipper (Mary Elizabeth) 1985 Aug 5J

Goren, Schlomo 1980 Feb 19C

Goria, Giovanni 1987 Jul 29; 1988 Feb 10B/Mar 11B

Gorman, Paul F. 1984 Aug 8G

Gorsuch, Anne M. see Burford, Anne McGill Gorsuch

Gostev, Boris I. 1988 Oct 27B

Gotoda, Masaharu 1988 Jul 22E

Gotti, Gene 1988 Jan 22F; 1989 Jul 7F

Gotti, John 1987 Mar 13F; 1989 Jan 23F/Jul 7F

Gottschalk, Louis Moreau 1985 Mar 1J

Goukouni Oueddei 1980 Apr 8C; 1981 Oct 29C; 1983 Feb 28C/Jul 20C; 1984 Jan 25C

Gould, Chester 1985 May 11J

Gould, Florence 1985 Apr 24J

Gould, Glenn 1982 Oct 4J; 1983 Feb 23J

Goya, Francisco 1986 Apr 10B

Grable, Betty 1983 Jul 6J

Grace, Princess (Monaco) 1982 Sep 14J

Graf, Steffi
Australian Open: 1988 Jan 23J; 1989 Jan 28J
French Open: 1987 Jun 6J; 1988 Jun 4J
U.S. Open: 1986 May 4J; 1988 Sep 10J; 1989 Sep 9J
Virginia Slims: 1987 Nov 22J
Wimbledon: 1987 Jul 4J; 1988 Jul 2J; 1989 Jul 9J

Graham, Alexander 1981 Aug 25H

Graham, Billy 1988 Apr 17E

Graham, Bob 1980 Dec 6F; 1986 Jun 26F

Graham, David 1981 Jun 21J

Graham, Martha 1985 May 19J; 1988 Dec 30J; 1989 Dec 1J

Graham, Sheila (Lily Shiel) 1988 Nov 17J

Graham, William R. 1986 Jun 30I

Gramajo Morales, Alejandro 1989 May 9D

Gramm, Phil 1982 May 1F; 1983 Jan 5F/Feb 12F

Grant, Bill 1989 Feb 21F

Grant, Cary (Archibald Alexander Leach) 1986 Nov 29J

Granville, Joseph 1981 Jan 9H/Sep 23H/Sep 28H

Grass, Gunter 1980 Apr 11J

Graves, John Earl 1980 Mar 4G

Graves, Robert (von Ranke) 1985 Dec 7J

Gray Jr., Alfred M. 1987 Jun 16G; 1988 Apr 25G

Gray, C. Boyden 1989 Apr 28F

Gray, Edwin 1986 Sep 23H

Gray, Herb 1981 Jun 4E

Gray, Marcia V. 1988 Oct 17F

Gray III, William H. 1983 Jun 25J; 1985 Jan 4F; 1986 Jan 10C; 1989 Jan 14F

Greco, Michele ("The Pope") 1986 Feb 20B; 1987 Dec 16B

Greeley, Andrew M. 1982 May 9J; 1986 Feb 28J

Green, Hubert 1985 Aug 11J

Green, Joyce Hens 1988 Aug 17H

Green, Pincus 1983 Sep 19H/Sep 22G

Greenberg, Hank (Henry Benjamin) 1986 Sep 4J

Greene, Graham 1983 Feb 12J

Greene, Harold H.
AT&T antitrust case: 1981 Jan 16H/Sep 11H; 1982 Jan 21H/Aug 11H/Aug 19H/Aug 24H
Poindexter trial: 1989 Jul 25F/Dec 21F
Reagan campaign probe: 1984 Feb 29F/May 14F

Greene, Joe 1987 Jan 27J/Aug 8J

Greene, Lorne 1987 Sep 11J

Greenspan, Alan 1983 Aug 1H; 1987 Jun 2H/Aug 3H; 1988 Feb 24H/Mar 15H/Jul 13H/Oct 26H; 1989 Jul 20H

Greenstein, Robert 1989 Oct 18H

Greenwood, Joan 1988 Oct 21J

Gregg, Donald P. 1986 Oct 10G; 1987 Feb 7G/Sep 8G; 1989 Jun 20G

Gregory, George J. 1983 May 23H

Gregory, Gillian 1986 Aug 10J

Gregory, Paul 1982 Sep 5J

Gretzky, Wayne
awards and honors: 1980 Jun 6J; 1982 Jun 8J; 1985 May 30J; 1989 Feb 7J/Jun 7J
contracts: 1982 Jan 20J
records and achievements: 1982 Feb 19J/Feb 24J/Mar 17J/Mar 25J; 1989 Jun 7J

Grey, Jennifer 1987 Aug 21J

Griffin, Marvin 1982 Jun 13F

Griffith, D.W. 1986 Sep 6J

Griffith, Melanie 1986 Dec 21J

Griffith, Michael 1986 Dec 20F; 1987 Feb 10F/Dec 21F

Griffiths, Edgar 1980 May 6J

Grimes, Martha 1989 Sep 29J

Gritz, James G. ("Bo") 1983 Jan 31E/Feb 28E/Mar 11E

Grivas, Yannis 1989 Oct 11B

Gromyko, Andrei Andreyevich
arms control: no-first-use pledge 1982 Jun 15A; intermediate-range missiles 1983 Jan 16B/Jan 18B/Apr 2B/Oct 16A; 1985 Jan 8A; strategic arms 1985 Jan 8A
foreign policy: Afghanistan 1981 Jul 6A; China 1982 Nov 16A; France 1980 Apr 25A; 1983 Apr 2B; 1984 Jun 23B; Great Britain 1981 Jul

6A; 1983 Apr 2B; Poland 1981 Jul 5B; UN 1983 Sep 17G; 1984 Sep 27B; West Germany 1983 Jan 16B/Oct 16A
government: named Soviet president 1985 Jul 2B
Korean airline incident: 1983 Sep 7B/Sep 8G
obituary: 1989 Jul 2B
U.S. policy: Muskie meetings 1980 May 16A/Sep 25A; Haig letter, meetings 1981 Feb 11A/Sep 23A; 1982 Jan 26A/Jun 18A; Shultz meetings 1982 Sep 18A/Oct 4A; 1983 Sep 8G; 1985 May 14H; Mondale meetings 1984 Sep 16F/Sep 27G; UN speech criticism 1984 Sep 27B; Reagan meeting 1984 Sep 28G
Gropius, Walter 1985 Sep 30J
Gross, Ariela 1983 Jun 16F
Grossman, Albert B. 1986 Jan 25J
Grosvenor, Melville Bell 1982 Apr 22J
Grosz, Karoly 1988 May 22B/Aug 28B
Grove Jr., Brandon W. 1983 Aug 15C
Gruentzig, Andres 1985 Oct 27I
Guare, John 1986 Mar 19J
Guarnieri, Johnny 1985 Jan 7J
Gubaryev, Vladimir 1987 Sep 18J
Gucwa, Stanislaw 1980 Dec 13B
Gueiler Tejada, Lidia 1980 Jun 9D
Guerrero, Manuel 1985 Mar 30D
Guess, Francis F. 1983 Dec 16F
Guevara, Angel Anibal 1982 Mar 7D
Guillaume, Robert 1985 Sep 12J
Guillen, Ozzie 1985 Nov 25J
Guinness, Alec 1988 Oct 21J
Gulabzoi, Sayed Mohammed 1980 Jan 21E
Gumbleton, Thomas 1987 Feb 25D
Gumbs, Emile 1989 Feb 27D
Gunduz, Orhan 1982 May 4A
Gunn, Wendell Wilkie 1982 Apr 19F
Gupta, Viswa Jit 1989 Apr 20I
Gurragcha, Jugderdemidiyn 1981 Mar 22I
Guthrie, Arlo 1984 Sep 20J
Guthrie, Woody 1986 Oct 19J
Gutierrez, Jaime Abdul 1980 Aug 31D
Guttenberg, Steve 1987 Nov 25J
Guzman Fernandez, Antonio 1982 Jul 4D/Aug 16D
Gwala, Harry 1988 Nov 26C
Gyllensten, Lars 1989 Mar 14A
Gysi, Gregor 1989 Dec 9B

H

Haakmat, Andre 1982 Dec 11D
Haavelmo, Trygve 1989 Oct 11A
Habib, Philip C.
government service: Bechtel ties 1982 Jul 25G; resignation 1983 Jul 22G
Lebanese policy: Syrian missile deployment 1981 May 2C/May 5A/Jun 1C/Jun 9C; meetings held 1981 May 7C; Israeli intervention 1982 Jun 13C/Jul 14C/Aug 15C/Dec 21C; 1983 Mar 1C; PLO withdrawal 1982 Jul 26C/Jul 30C/Aug 6A/Aug 13C
Medal of Freedom: 1982 Sep 7G
Mideast policy: Israel 1981 Jul 19A; 1982 Feb 26C; Jordan 1982 Jul 26C; 1988 Jan 30G; PLO 1982 Feb 26C; shuttle diplomacy 1981 Dec 11G; 1982 Oct 11G/Feb 26C; Syrian meeting 1981 May 14C

Haddad, Saad 1982 Nov 17C; 1983 Feb 14C
Hadzi, Dimitri 1983 Feb 19J
Hagelstein, Peter 1986 Sep 10I; 1987 Jan 20I
Haggerty, Julie 1986 Mar 19J
Hagler, "Marvelous" Marvin 1980 Sep 27J; 1985 Apr 15J; 1986 Mar 10J; 1987 Apr 6J
Hagnes, Helen 1980 Jul 24J/Sep 7F; 1981 Sep 2F
Hahn, Jessica 1987 May 6J
Haidala, Mohammed Khouna Ould 1980 Jan 4C; 1984 Dec 12C
Haig Jr., Alexander M.
arms control: neutron bomb 1981 Feb 5G; intermediate-range missile talks 1981 May 4A/Jul 14G/Sep 14G; NATO A-warning 1981 Nov 4G-5G; first use 1982 Apr 6G; missile tests 1982 Jun 20B
Asian policy: China 1981 Jun 16G; India 1981 Apr 17G; Indochinese refugees 1981 May 20G; Pakistan 1981 Apr 17G; Vietnam 1981 Jun 20G
energy exploration: 1981 Oct 24A
European policy: NATO 1981 Nov 4G-5G; Poland 1981 Apr 11G; 1982 Jan 26A/Feb 13B; Romania 1982 Feb 13B; Turkey 1982 May 14B
Falklands crisis: 1982 Apr 8A/Apr 11A/Apr 13A/Apr 15A/Apr 19A-19D/Apr 22A/Apr 27A
foreign policy: congressional hearings 1981 Mar 18G; UN developing nation speech 1981 Sep 21G
government service: as secretary of state 1981 Jan 21G; 1982 Jun 25G; crisis-management team feud 1981 Mar 24F; "guerrilla campaign" charges 1981 Nov 3F; Nixon administration role 1982 Apr 13F
Iran-Iraq War: 1982 May 26G
Latin policy: Caribbean Basin 1981 Dec 4D; Central America 1981 Dec 4D; 1982 Feb 5G; El Salvador 1981 Mar 4G/Nov 5D; 1982 Feb 2G/Mar 2D; Mexico 1981 Nov 23D; Nicaragua 1981 Feb 27D/Nov 22G/Nov 23D
Mideast policy: Iran 1981 Jan 28G; Israel 1981 Jan 10C/Aug 17G; 1932 Sep 14G; Jordan 1981 Apr 6G; Palestinian autonomy talks 1981 Feb 23G; Saudi Arabia 1981 Apr 8G/Oct 1G; Syria 1981 Apr 9C
presidential campaign (1988): 1987 Mar 24F/Oct 28F/Dec 30F; 1988 Jan 4F/Jan 18F/Feb 12F
Reagan assassination attempt: 1981 Mar 30F
Soviet policy: Gromyko letter 1981 Feb 11A; summit talks 1981 Feb 23G; congressional hearings 1981 Mar 18G/May 9A; White House feud 1981 Aug 11G; chemical weapons 1981 Sep 13G-14B; Gromyko meetings 1981 Sep 23A; 1982 Jan 26A/Jun 18A; missile tests 1982 Jun 20B
Haines, Connie 1983 Jul 6J
Haines, Randa 1986 Oct 3J
Hakim, Albert 1986 Dec 13F/Dec 15B; 1987 Mar 11G/Jun 3G; 1988 Mar 16F/Mar 24F/Jun 8F/Jun 16F; 1989 Nov 21F
Hakim, Nadim 1984 Aug 23C
Halaby, Elizabeth 1981 Jun 10C
Halas, George Stanley ("Papa Bear") 1983 Oct 31J
Haldane, J.B.S. 1988 Mar 3I

Haldeman, H.R. 1987 May 28F
Haley, Bill 1981 Feb 9J
Haley, Leroy 1982 Jun 26J
Halfoul, Mohammed Milhem 1980 May 3C
Hall, Ed 1986 May 2J; 1988 Mar 27J
Hall, Fawn 1987 Jun 9G
Hall, Peter 1981 Jun 7J
Halleck, Charles Abraham 1986 Feb 3F
Hallinan, Hazel Hunkins 1982 May 17F
Halloran, Richard 1983 Feb 25J
Hallstrom, Lasse 1987 May 1J
Halperin, Morton H. 1986 Dec 5F
Ham, Jack 1988 Feb 2J/Jul 30J
Hamad, Abd al-Latif Yusuf al- 1982 Oct 25C
Hamadei, Abbas Ali 1988 Jan 27C/Apr 19B
Hamadei, Mohammed Ali 1985 Oct 17G; 1987 Jan 18A/Jun 24B; 1988 Aug 9B; 1989 May 17B
Hamdun, Walid 1982 Apr 17C
Hamieda, Rashid al- 1988 Feb 12B
Hamilton, Ian 1987 Jan 29J
Hamilton, James 1983 Jul 19F
Hamilton, Lee 1986 Dec 17F; 1987 Jan 24G
Hamilton, Margaret 1985 May 16J
Hamilton Jr., Thomas 1980 Feb 1G
Hammer, Armand 1980 Dec 12J; 1982 Oct 6G; 1988 Jan 21J
Hammer, Michael P. 1985 Jul 3D
Hammett, Dashiell 1984 Jun 30J
Hammond, Edward Cuyler 1986 Nov 3I
Hammond, John 1987 Jul 10J
Hampton, Christopher 1988 Dec 21J
Hampton, David 1983 Nov 18J
Hamrouche, Mouloud 1989 Sep 9C
Hand, Gerry 1988 Jan 4E
Hand, W. Brevard 1987 Mar 4F
Hanika, Sylvia 1981 Jun 6J
Hanks, Tom 1988 Jun 3J
Hanley, Edward J. 1982 Mar 13H
Hanley, James 1985 Nov 11J
Hannah, Daryl 1987 Jun 19J/Dec 11J
Hans Adam, Crown Prince (Liechtenstein) 1984 Aug 26B
Hansen, James E. 1988 Jun 23I
Hansen, Kenneth 1981 Aug 27G
Hanson, Howard 1981 Feb 26J
Harbison, John 1987 Apr 16J
Harburg, Edgar Y. ("Yip") 1981 Mar 5J; 1986 Apr 23J
Hardy, Alister 1985 Feb 27J/May 23J
Hardy, Dorcas R. 1988 Dec 3F
Hardy, Thomas 1980 Dec 12J
Hariri, Hussein Ali Mohammed 1987 Jul 24B
Harnwell, Gaylord P. 1982 Apr 18I
Haroon, Mahmud 1982 Jan 17E
Harper, Ashby 1982 Aug 28J
Harper Jr., James Durward 1983 Oct 15G; 1984 Apr 3F/May 14G
Harrelson, Charles V. 1982 Dec 14F; 1983 Mar 18F
Harriman, William Averell 1986 Jul 26F
Harrington, Michael 1989 Jul 31J
Harris, Barbara Clementine 1988 Sep 24J; 1989 Feb 11F
Harris, Fred 1980 Apr 13F
Harris, Jean 1980 Mar 10J; 1981 Feb 24J
Harris, Julie 1988 Sep 23J
Harris, Ladonna 1980 Aug 13F
Harris, Patricia Roberts 1985 Mar 23F
Harrison, George 1985 Feb 24J
Harrison, Rex 1986 Jan 27J
Harry, Debbie 1988 Feb 26J
Hart, Bill 1986 May 18J
Hart, Charles 1986 Oct 9J
Hart, Frederick 1984 Nov 9G
Hart, Gary
presidential campaign (1984)
California convention: 1983 Jan 15F

candidacy: 1983 Feb 17F; 1984 Jun 6F/Jun 26F
debates: 1984 Jan 15F/Feb 11F/Mar 18F/Mar 28F/Jun 3F
dirty tricks: 1984 Mar 29G
matching funds: 1984 Jan 3G
primaries: Alabama 1984 Mar 13F; Arizona 1984 Apr 14F; California 1984 Jun 5F; Connecticut 1984 Mar 27F; Florida 1984 Mar 13F; Georgia 1984 Mar 13F; Idaho 1984 May 22F; Illinois 1984 Mar 20F; Indiana 1984 May 8F; Maine 1984 Mar 4F; Maryland 1984 May 8F; Massachusetts 1984 Mar 13F; Minnesota 1984 Mar 20F; Nebraska 1984 May 15F; New Hampshire 1984 Feb 28F; New Jersey 1984 Jun 5F; New Mexico 1984 Jun 5F; New York 1984 Apr 3F; North Carolina 1984 May 8F; Ohio 1984 May 8F; Oregon 1984 May 15F; Pennsylvania 1984 Apr 10F; Rhode Island 1984 Mar 13F; South Carolina 1984 Mar 17F; South Dakota 1984 Jun 5F; Tennessee 1984 May 1F; Vermont 1984 Mar 6F; Washington, D.C. 1984 May 1F; West Virginia 1984 Jun 5F; Wisconsin 1984 Apr 3F/Apr 7F
women's groups: 1983 Jul 10F/Oct 2F
presidential campaign (1988): candidacy: 1986 Jan 4F; 1987 Apr 13F/Dec 15F; matching funds: 1987 Jun 4F/Dec 28F; 1988 Jan 4F; polls: 1986 May 14F; 1987 Jan 25F/Aug 5F; withdrawal: 1987 May 8F; 1988 Mar 11F
Hartling, Poul 1985 Sep 7A/Dec 10A
Hartman, Arthur A. 1987 Apr 2G
Hartman, Elizabeth 1987 Jun 10J
Hasani, Ali Nasser Mohammed al- 1980 Apr 23C; 1986 Jan 23C/Jan 25C; 1987 Dec 12C
Hasani, Sinan 1986 May 15B
Hasenfus, Eugene 1986 Oct 20D/Nov 15D/Dec 17D
Hasford, Gustav 1987 Jun 26J
Hashemi, Mehdi 1987 Sep 28C
Haslam, Robert 1986 Sep 23B
Hass, Robert 1985 Jan 14J
Hassan II, King (Morocco)
civil strife: 1984 Jan 22C
Iran-Iraq War: 1980 Sep 23C
Mideast policy: Algeria 1983 Feb 26C; 1987 May 4C; Egypt 1984 Jan 20C; Israel 1986 Jul 21C; Libya 1984 Aug 13C
U.S. policy: 1982 Oct 22C
Western Sahara conflict: 1981 Jun 26C; 1983 Feb 26C; 1985 Oct 23C; 1987 May 4C; 1988 Dec 27C; 1989 Jan 4C
Hassanal Bolkiah Mu'izzaddin Waddaulah, Sir Mudah (Sultan of Brunei) 1984 Feb 23C; 1986 Dec 24G; 1987 Sep 20H; 1989 Sep 11J
Hastings, Alcee L. 1987 Mar 17F; 1988 Aug 3F; 1989 Oct 20F
Hatcher, Richard 1981 May 1F
Hatfield, Mark O. 1982 Mar 30G; 1983 Mar 4G; 1985 Feb 12G
Hatter Jr., Terry J. 1982 Nov 15G
Haughey, Charles 1981 Jun 11B; 1982 Mar 9B/Mar 26B/Nov 4B; 1987 Feb 17B/Mar 10B/Mar 31B; 1989 May 25B/Jul 12B
Hauptman, Herbert A. 1985 Oct 16I
Hauptman, William 1985 Apr 25J
Hauser, Thomas 1984 Feb 8J

Havel, Vaclav 1989 Feb 21B/Feb 25B/May 17B/Dec 10B/Dec 29B
Havens, Richie 1986 Jan 25J
Hawke, Robert (Bob)
aboriginal policy: 1983 Nov 11E/Nov 22E
agriculture: 1986 Apr 18E
arms control: A-tests 1983 Jun 9A
economic policy: currency fall 1985 Feb 20E; tax summit 1985 Jul 4E; wage-price accord 1985 Sep 4E
foreign policy: ANZUS pact 1985 Feb 5G; ASEAN 1983 Nov 22E; Cambodia 1983 Jun 14E/Nov 22E; Fiji 1987 Oct 10E; France 1983 Jun 9A; Libya 1987 May 19E; Malaysia 1986 Jul 6E; Soviet Union 1983 Mar 19E; Vietnam 1983 Jun 14E/Nov 22E
government: Australia elections 1983 Mar 5E; 1984 Oct 8E; 1985 Dec 7E; 1987 Jul 11E; British constitutional links 1986 Mar 2E; party conference 1986 Jul 7E; national identity card 1987 Sep 9E/Sep 29E; bill of rights 1988 Jul 11E; polls 1989 Jun 27F
national parks: 1983 Nov 11E/Nov 22E
trade: 1986 Apr 18E; 1987 Oct 10E/Oct 22E; 1988 Jun 19G
U.S. policy: 1983 Jun 14E; 1985 Feb 5G; 1986 Apr 18E; 1987 Oct 10E; 1988 Jun 19G/Nov 22E
Hawkins, Coleman 1984 Apr 23J
Hawkins, Joe Daniel 1981 Jun 20D
Hawkins, Paula 1984 Jun 25G
Hawkins, Yusuf K. 1989 Aug 23F/Sep 2F
Hayden, Bill (William) 1981 Aug 25E; 1985 Nov 10E; 1988 Aug 17E
Hayden, Sterling (Sterling Relyea Walter) 1986 May 23J
Haydon, Murray P. 1985 Feb 17I
Hayes, Alfred 1985 Aug 14J
Hayes, Woody (Wayne Woodrow) 1987 Mar 12J
Haymes, Dick 1983 Jul 6J
Hays, Henry Francis 1983 Dec 19F; 1987 Feb 12F
Hayworth, Rita 1987 May 14J
Hazam, Louis 1983 Sep 6J
Hazelwood, Joseph 1989 Apr 5H
Head, Edith 1981 Oct 24J
Healey, Denis 1980 Nov 10B; 1981 Sep 27B; 1982 Apr 19B
Healy, Timothy S. 1989 Feb 23F
Hearns, Thomas ("Hit Man") 1981 Sep 16J; 1982 Dec 4J; 1985 Apr 15J; 1987 Oct 29J; 1988 Jun 6J; 1989 Jun 12J
Hearst, Patricia 1980 Aug 25F; 1981 May 3F
Hearstshaw, Gillian Catherine 1981 May 3F
Heath, Mike 1985 Aug 17J
Hebb, Donald Olding 1985 Aug 20I
Hecht, Anthony 1988 Jun 3J
Hecht, Harold 1985 May 25J
Heckler, Margaret M.
government service: named HHS secretary 1983 Jan 12F; named Irish ambassador 1985 Oct 1F
health care policy: disabled 1983 Jun 7F; terminal illness 1983 Jun 14I; 1984 Apr 23I; terminal illness 1983 Aug 17F; aspirin labels 1985 Jan 23I
He Dongchang 1989 Apr 29E
Heep, Danny 1985 Jul 11J
Heidemann, Gerd 1985 Jul 8B
Heiden, Eric 1980 Feb 15J/Feb 16J/Feb 19J/Feb 21J/Feb 23J; 1985 Jun 23J
Heifetz, Jascha 1987 Dec 10J
Heineback, Bo 1983 Mar 12B
Heinemann, Larry 1987 Nov 9J

Heinlein, Robert A(nson) 1988 May 8J
Heinz, John 1986 May 20F
Hekmatyar, Gulbuddin 1984 Aug 27C
Helen, Queen (Romania) 1982 Nov 28B
Heller, H. Robert 1986 May 12H
Heller, Joseph 1984 Oct 19J
Heller, Walter W(olfgang) 1987 Jun 15H
Hellman, Lillian 1981 May 7J; 1984 Jun 30J/Dec 7J; 1985 Feb 6J
Helms, Jesse A.
    abortion: 1981 May 21F; 1982 Sep 8F-9F/Sep 15F
    INF treaty: 1988 Mar 30G
    Mideast policy: Israel 1982 Aug 7G
    politics: party platform 1980 Jul 17F; Supreme Court powers 1982 Aug 18F; Shultz protest 1985 Jul 16F
    school issues: busing 1982 Mar 2F; prayer 1982 Sep 23F
Helmsley, Harry B. 1988 Apr 14H
Helmsley, Leona 1988 Apr 14H; 1989 Aug 30F/Dec 12F
Helpmann, Robert (Murray) 1986 Sep 28J
Hemingway, Ernest 1984 Jan 31J; 1987 Apr 18J
Henderson, Fletcher 1987 Jul 10J
Henderson, Rickey 1989 Aug 22J/Oct 8J
Heng Samrin 1984 Jan 7E; 1985 Oct 18E; 1988 Jul 1E/Jul 25E; 1989 Jun 6E
Henley, Beth 1981 Apr 13J/Nov 4J; 1986 Dec 12J
Henley, Don 1986 Feb 25J
Henmi, Shuitsu 1987 May 8E
Hennings, Chad 1987 Dec 9J
Henry Charles Albert David, Prince (Great Britain) 1984 Sep 15J
Hepburn, Katherine 1981 Dec 4J; 1982 Mar 29J
Herbert, Frank 1981 May 24J/Jul 5J; 1984 Apr 20J/May 11J; 1985 May 24J; 1986 Feb 11J
Herman, Jerry 1983 Aug 21J
Herman, Woody (Woodrow Charles) 1984 May 1J; 1987 Oct 29J
Hermannsson, Steingrimur 1987 Apr 25B
Hernandez Jr., John W. 1983 Mar 25H
Hernandez, Willie 1984 Nov 6J
Hernandez Agosto, Miguel 1988 Apr 13F
Hernandez Cervantes, Hector 1987 Nov 6D
Hernandez Colon, Rafael 1980 Dec 18D; 1988 Apr 13F
Hernu, Charles 1983 Aug 31B/Sep 7C; 1985 Sep 20B/Sep 25B
Herr, Michael 1987 Jun 26J
Herrington, John S. 1985 Jan 10F/Feb 6H/Jun 5H; 1986 May 28H; 1987 Jan 30I; 1989 Jun 18H
Herschbach, Dudley 1986 Oct 15I
Hersey, John 1984 Aug 11J; 1988 May 12J
Hersh, Seymour 1982 Apr 13F; 1986 Nov 23E
Hershiser, Orel 1988 Oct 12J/Oct 22J/Nov 10J
Herzog, Chaim 1983 Mar 22C; 1984 Aug 5C; 1988 Nov 14C
Herzog, Whitey 1982 Oct 25J
Hesburgh, Theodore M. 1986 Nov 14F
Heseltine, Michael 1981 Aug 5B; 1983 Jul 6B; 1986 Jan 9B/Jan 24B/Jul 24B
Hess, (Walter Richard) Rudolf 1987 Aug 17B/Aug 24B
Heunis, Chris 1989 Jan 18C
Hevroni, Moshe 1982 Nov 17C
Hewlett, William R. 1983 Mar 27J
Hextall, Ron 1987 May 31J
Heymann, C. David 1983 Dec 12J
Hiam, Peter 1987 Jul 8F
Hickey, James A. 1983 Mar 7G

Hicks, James L. 1986 Jan 19J
Higgins, Jack 1987 Jan 23J/Feb 27J; 1989 Jan 27J
Higgins, William Richard 1988 Feb 17C/Dec 12C; 1989 Jul 31C/Jul 31G
Higham, Charles 1980 Aug 1J
Hikmatyar, Gulbaddin 1980 Jan 21E
Hill, Abram 1986 Oct 6J
Hill, Paul 1989 Oct 19B
Hill, Ralph Lee 1980 Jun 15F
Hillel, Shlomo 1987 Jun 8C/Jul 1C
Hilleman, Maurice R. 1983 Nov 16I
Hills, Carla A. 1988 Dec 6F; 1989 Jan 31H/Apr 25H/Apr 28G/Nov 22H
Himes, Chester 1984 Nov 12J
Hinault, Bernard 1985 Jul 21J
Hinckley Jr., John W.
    Jodie Foster: 1981 Apr 2F-2J/Apr 8J/Sep 29J
    Reagan assassination attempt: 1981 Mar 30F; psychiatric testing 1981 Apr 3F; suicide attempt 1981 Nov 15F; trial 1982 May 4F/Jun 21F
Hindawi, Nezar 1986 Oct 24C
Hines, Earl ("Fatha") 1983 Apr 22J
Hinshelwood, Cyril 1986 Sep 25I
Hinson, Jon 1981 Mar 16F
Hinton, Deane R. 1982 Mar 28A/Mar 29D/Oct 29G
Hippenstiel-Imhausen, Jurgen 1989 May 10B
Hirabayashi, Gordon 1986 Feb 10G
Hirohito, Emperor (Japan) 1986 Apr 29E; 1988 Sep 19E; 1989 Jan 7E/Feb 24E/Feb 25E
Hirsch, Edward 1987 Jan 12J
Hirsch, Judd 1981 Sep 13J; 1985 Nov 19J; 1986 Jun 1J
Hiss, Alger 1981 Mar 8F; 1984 Mar 26J
Hitchcock, Alfred 1980 Apr 29J; 1985 Mar 21J; 1986 Jan 27J; 1987 Oct 2J
Hitchings, George H. 1988 Oct 17I
Hitler, Adolf 1983 May 6J; 1984 Mar 21B/Sep 21I; 1985 Jul 8B; 1989 Apr 20B
Hnatyshyn, Ramon 1987 Mar 12D; 1989 Oct 6D
Hoareau, Gerard 1985 Nov 29E
Hobbs, Truman 1984 Apr 13F
Hobeika, Elie 1986 Jan 15C
Ho Chi Minh 1986 Jul 10E; 1989 Aug 31E
Hocke, Jean-Pierre 1985 Dec 10A
Hodel, Donald P.
    energy and environmental policy: strategic oil reserves 1984 Mar 6H; irrigation 1985 Mar 28H; oil drilling 1985 Sep 10H; 1987 Apr 20H
    government service: as energy secretary 1982 Nov 5H; as interior secretary 1984 Jan 10F/Feb 6H; Mott to park service 1985 May 1H; Iacocca fired 1986 Feb 12J
Hodges, Margaret 1985 Jan 7J
Hoffman, Abbie (Abbott) 1980 Sep 4F; 1981 Apr 7J/Jun 2F; 1989 Apr 12J
Hoffman, Dustin 1980 Apr 14J; 1988 Dec 16J; 1989 Mar 29J
Hoffman, Ronald 1981 Oct 19I
Hoffort, Bruce 1988 Apr 2J
Hofheinz, Roy Mark 1982 Nov 21F
Hofstadter, Douglas 1980 Apr 14J
Hogan, Ben 1989 Jun 18J
Hogan, Jonathan 1987 Oct 14J
Hogan, Paul 1986 Sep 26J
Hogan, Thomas F. 1983 Dec 30F
Holbert, Al 1986 Feb 2J/Jun 1J; 1987 Feb 1J
Holbrook, Hal 1987 Dec 11J
Holbrook, James R. 1981 Feb 16G
Holc, Paul 1987 Oct 16I
Holden, William 1986 Apr 26J
Holderied, Kristine 1984 May 23G

Holding, Clyde 1985 Mar 14E
Holiday, Billie 1984 Apr 26J; 1986 Jul 31J; 1987 Jul 10J
Holkeri, Harri 1987 Apr 30B
Holland, Andre 1981 Apr 12C
Holland, Leland 1981 Feb 8C
Hollein, Hans 1985 Apr 3J
Holliday, Judy 1986 Apr 26J
Hollings, Ernest F.
    presidential campaign (1984): California convention 1983 Jan 15F; candidacy 1983 Apr 18F; women's group 1983 Jul 10F/Oct 2F; matching funds 1984 Jan 3G; debates 1984 Jan 15F/Feb 11F; withdrawal 1984 Mar 1F
Holloway, Stanley 1982 Jan 30J
Hollowood, Bernard 1981 Mar 28J
Holly, Buddy 1986 Jan 23J
Holm, Ian 1989 Nov 8J
Holm, John Cecil 1988 Jan 24J
Holmes, Larry 1980 Oct 2J; 1982 Jun 11J; 1983 Mar 27J/Nov 25J; 1985 Sep 21J; 1986 Apr 19J; 1988 Jan 22J
Holmes, Rupert 1985 Dec 2J
Holomisa, Bantu 1987 Dec 30C
Holt, John 1985 Sep 14J
Holyfield, Evander 1989 Jul 15J
Honecker, Erich
    armed forces: 1989 Jan 23B
    foreign policy: Bulgaria 1984 Sep 9B; China 1986 Oct 26E; Poland 1980 Oct 8B
    German reunification: 1981 Feb 15B/Dec 11B; 1984 Feb 13B; 1987 Aug 12B/Sep 7B
    government ouster: 1989 Oct 18B
Honegger, Barbara 1983 Aug 22F; 1988 Aug 25G
Honey, Martha 1988 Jun 23D
Honeyghan, Lloyd 1989 Feb 4J
Hood, Leroy 1987 Sep 21I
Hook, Sidney 1989 Jul 12J
Hooks, Benjamin L. 1980 Jul 15F; 1983 May 20F/May 26F/Jun 11F; 1986 Feb 15F
Hopkins, Sam ("Lightnin'") 1982 Jan 30J
Hopper, Dennis 1986 Sep 19J
Hopper, Grace 1986 Aug 14G
Hopper, Hedda 1988 Nov 17J
Horman, Charles 1984 Feb 8J
Hornbeck, William 1983 Oct 11J
Horner, James 1988 Mar 2J
Hornsby, Bruce 1987 Feb 24J
Hornung, Paul 1986 Jan 28J
Horowitz, Vladimir Samoylovich 1986 Apr 14J; 1989 Nov 5J
Horton, Derek 1988 Aug 26J
Horton, Lester 1989 Dec 1J
Horvath, Istvan 1989 Sep 4B
Horwood, Owen 1981 Aug 12C
Hoskins, Bob 1987 Jan 4J/Mar 22J; 1988 Jun 22J
Hosni, Mohammed Salem 1982 Mar 14C
Hoss, Selim al- 1980 Jun 7C/Jul 20C; 1988 Sep 24C; 1989 Nov 25C
Host, Michel 1986 Nov 17J
Hoty, Dee 1989 Dec 11J
Houbregs, Bob 1987 Feb 5J
Houphouet-Boigny, Felix 1985 Oct 28C; 1989 Feb 14C
Houseman, John (Jacques Haussmann) 1988 Oct 30J
Houssay, Bernardo A. 1984 Oct 20I
Houston, Ken 1986 Jan 28J
Houston, Whitney
    best-sellers: I Wanna Dance With Somebody 1988 Mar 2J; Saving All My Love for You 1986 Feb 25J; Whitney 1987 Jun 27J/Jul 22J/Aug 22J/Sep 19J; Whitney Houston 1985 Sep 28J/Oct 26J; 1986 Feb 19J/Mar 22J/Apr 16J/May 21J/Jun 18J

Grammy awards: 1986 Feb 25J; 1988 Mar 2J
Howard, Donald R. 1988 Jan 11J
Howard, Edward Lee 1986 Aug 7H/Nov 22B
Howard, John 1985 Dec 7E; 1987 Aug 6E
Howard, Richard 1983 Feb 19J
Howard, Trevor 1988 Jan 7J
Howe, Geoffrey
    economic policy: 1980 Mar 26B/Nov 24B; 1982 Mar 9B
    foreign policy: East Germany 1985 Apr 9B; Falkland Islands 1986 Oct 29B; Hong Kong 1984 Apr 20A; 1989 Jul 4E; southern Africa peace mission 1986 Jul 29C
    government: British foreign secretary 1983 Jun 11B
Howe, Gordie 1980 Jun 4J
Hoxha, Enver 1985 Apr 11B/Apr 13B; 1986 Nov 3B
Hoyos Jimenez, Carlos Mauro 1988 Jan 25D
Hoyt, Lamarr 1983 Oct 25J; 1985 Jul 16J
Hoyte, Desmond 1984 Aug 11D; 1985 Aug 6D/Dec 11D
Hrawi, Elias 1989 Nov 24C/Nov 25C/Dec 6C
Hrkac, Tony 1987 Mar 28J
Hua Guofeng 1980 Jul 10E/Sep 7E/Sep 10E; 1981 Jan 4E/Feb 6E/Jun 29E; 1982 Sep 12E
Huang, Hanson 1985 May 15E
Huang Hua 1980 Jan 21E; 1982 Nov 16A/Nov 19E
Hubbard, L. Ron 1986 Jan 24J
Hubbell, Carl Owen 1988 Nov 21J
Hubbell, Webster 1981 Nov 25F
Hubel, David H. 1981 Oct 9I
Huberty, James Oliver 1984 Jul 4F
Hudson, Rock (Roy Scherer Jr.) 1985 Jul 25J/Oct 2J/Oct 31J
Huff, Sam 1982 Aug 7J
Hugel, Max 1981 Jul 14G/Jul 23F
Hughes, Francis 1981 May 12B/May 13B
Hughes, Harry 1985 May 14H
Hughes, Howard 1987 May 28F
Hughes, John 1983 Aug 3G
Hughes, Ted 1984 Dec 19J; 1985 Dec 2J
Huie, William Bradford 1986 Nov 22J
Hulce, Tom 1984 Sep 19J
Hull, John 1989 Jul 23D
Hull, Thomas G. 1986 Oct 24F
Hulme, Keri 1985 Oct 31J
Hummel, Arthur 1985 Jul 22G
Humphrey, Doris 1985 May 19J
Hun Sen 1985 Jan 14E; 1986 Dec 10E; 1987 Dec 4E; 1988 Jan 21E; 1989 May 3E/Jul 6G
Hunt Jr., E. Howard 1983 May 14F
Hunt, Joe 1987 Apr 22F
Hunt, Lamar 1980 May 30H; 1988 Aug 20F/Oct 20H
Hunt, Linda 1983 Jan 21J; 1984 Apr 9J
Hunt, Nelson Bunker 1980 Mar 26H/Mar 31H/Apr 1H/May 30H/Oct 21H; 1982 Apr 12H; 1988 Aug 20F
Hunt, Rex 1982 Apr 1D/Jun 26D
Hunt, William Herbert 1980 Mar 31H/Apr 1H/May 30H/Oct 21H; 1982 Apr 12H; 1988 Aug 20F
Hunter, Alberta 1984 Oct 17J
Hunter, Catfish (Jim) 1987 Jan 14J
Hunter, Holly 1987 Dec 16J; 1989 Sep 17J
Hu Ping 1988 Mar 23E
Hurd, Douglas 1984 Sep 10B; 1989 Jan 16B
Hurford, Chris 1986 Apr 10E
Hurley, Ruby 1980 Aug 9F

Hurson, Martin 1981 Jul 13B
Hurt, Mary Beth 1981 Nov 4J
Hurt, William 1984 Jun 21J; 1985 Jul 26J; 1986 Mar 16J/Mar 24J/Oct 3J; 1987 Dec 16J
Hurtado Larrea, Osvaldo 1982 Oct 27D
Husak, Gustav 1980 Oct 9B; 1987 Dec 17B; 1989 Dec 7B/Dec 10B
Hussain, Ghasi 1980 Mar 13C
Hussein, King (Jordan)
    Arab-Israeli policy: Egypt 1984 Dec 1C; 1985 Mar 6C; 1988 Oct 22C; 1989 Mar 25C; Israel 1980 Apr 24C; 1984 Mar 14C/Sep 14C/Oct 1C; 1989 Apr 20C; Syria 1981 Jun 2C; 1985 Dec 31C
    government: East Bank elections 1984 Jan 9C; parliament meets 1984 Jan 9C; Islamic fundamentalism 1985 Dec 27C; parliamentary elections 1989 Nov 10C; premier named 1989 Dec 4C
    Iran-Iraq War: 1980 Sep 23C/Oct 6C/Oct 8C/Oct 27C/Dec 8C; 1982 Jul 20C
    Palestinians: Lebanon fighting 1982 Jul 26C/Aug 6C; Arafat meetings 1982 Oct 13C/Nov 30C; 1983 Apr 5C; 1984 Mar 1C; 1985 Oct 29C; 1988 Oct 22C; 1989 Mar 25C; Israel recognition 1982 Nov 4C; Arafat attack 1983 Apr 10C; 1986 Feb 19C; dialogue 1984 Jan 16C; West Bank ties 1984 Feb 28C; 1988 Jul 31C; West Bank, Gaza elections 1989 Apr 20C
    personal issues: children 1981 Jun 10C
    U.S. policy: Haig meeting 1981 Apr 6G; visits 1981 Nov 3C; 1984 Feb 14G; 1985 May 31G; Reagan peace plan 1982 Sep 13C; 1983 Apr 5C/Apr 8C; interview 1984 Mar 14C; Habib meeting 1988 Jan 30G
Hussein, Abdel Aziz 1980 Jan 25G
Hussein, Ibrahim 1987 Nov 1J; 1988 Apr 18J
Hussein, Saddam
    foreign policy: Jordan 1982 Jul 20C; Soviet Union 1984 Mar 9A; Syria 1982 Apr 17C
    government: opposition bombings 1983 Dec 27C
    Iran-Iraq War: border agreement voided 1980 Sep 17C; peace offers 1980 Sep 28C/Sep 30C/Nov 4C; 1981 Dec 15C; 1983 Feb 23C; holy war declared 1980 Nov 9C; minority aid offer 1981 Mar 24C; A-weapons threat 1981 Jun 23C; military actions 1982 Mar 30C; 1987 Feb 8C; Arab aid asked 1982 Jul 17C; Kharg Island ship threat 1982 Aug 15C; POW camps 1988 Sep 1C
    U.S. policy: 1983 Dec 20C
Huston, Anjelica 1985 Jun 14J; 1986 Mar 24J; 1987 Aug 28J/Dec 17J; 1989 Nov 13J
Huston, John 1983 Mar 3J; 1985 Jun 14J; 1986 Jan 2J; 1987 May 12J/Aug 28J/Dec 17J; 1988 Jan 3J
Huston, Walter 1987 Aug 28J
Hutchison, Mavis 1980 Aug 15J
Hutson, James C. 1987 Jul 29J
Hutton, Barbara 1983 Dec 12J
Hutton, John 1988 Jan 15F
Hutton, Timothy 1981 Mar 30J
Hu Yaobang
    foreign policy: French CP talks 1982 Oct 17A; North Korea visit 1984 May 4E; U.S. 1983 Nov 26E; 1987 Mar 5E
    government ouster: 1987 Jan 16E

Hong Kong: 1986 Jun 8B
   personal issues: 1989 Apr 15E-16E/Apr 22E/Apr 27E
   Taiwan: 1981 Oct 10E; 1983 Nov 26E
Hvenegaard, Pelle 1988 Dec 21J
Hwang, David Henry 1988 Jun 5J
Hyman, Trina Schart 1985 Jan 7J
Hynes, Charles J. 1987 Jan 13F
Hyslop, Peter H. St. George 1987 Feb 20I

I

Iacocca, Lee A. 1983 Jul 13H/Dec 8H; 1984 Oct 4H; 1986 Feb 12J
Icahn, Carl C. 1985 Aug 23H; 1986 Oct 6H; 1988 Jun 20H
Icaza, Horacio 1988 Feb 29D
Ieng Sary 1981 Jul 8E
Ieoh Ming Pei 1983 May 16J
Iglesias, Julio 1984 Oct 27J
Ikangaa, Juma 1989 Nov 5J
Ileto, Rafael 1986 Nov 23E; 1988 Jan 21E
Iliescu, Ion 1989 Dec 26B
Ilyichev, Leonid 1984 Mar 26A
Inge, William 1985 Dec 27J
Inman, Bobby Ray 1982 Apr 21G
Inoue, Takehiro 1983 Dec 21H
Inouye, Daniel K. 1986 Dec 16F; 1987 Aug 3G
Irons, Jeremy 1984 Jun 3J; 1986 Oct 31J; 1988 Sep 23J; 1989 Mar 22J
Irving, John
   best-sellers: Cider House Rules 1985 Jun 14J/Jul 19J/Aug 16J; Hotel New Hampshire 1981 Oct 4J/Nov 8J/Dec 6J; 1982 Jan 10J/Feb 7J; Prayer for Owen Meany 1989 Apr 28J
Irwin, Hale 1983 Jul 17J
Isaac, Rhys L. 1983 Apr 18J
Isaacs, Scott 1989 Jun 1J
Isaacs, Susan 1984 Mar 23J
Isabel, Princess (Brazil) 1988 May 13D
Iselin, John Jay 1983 Nov 18J
Ishaq Khan, Ghulam 1988 Dec 1E/Dec 12E
Isherwood, Christopher (William Bradshaw) 1986 Jan 4J
Ishiguro, Kazuo 1987 Jan 13J; 1989 Oct 26J
Islam, Shafiqul 1987 Jun 24D
Ismail, Abdel Fattah 1980 Apr 23C
Isosaki, Arata 1986 Dec 10J
Israelyan, Viktor 1984 Feb 21B
Istomin, Eugene 1980 Feb 26J
Istomin, Marta Casals 1980 Feb 26J
Ito, Masayoshi 1980 Nov 28E; 1981 May 16E
Ito, Midori 1989 Mar 18J
Iturbe Abasolo, Domingo 1986 Apr 27B
Iturbi, Jose 1980 Jun 28J
Ivan, Paula 1989 Jul 10J
"Ivan The Terrible" (Nazi death camp guard) 1986 Mar 19C/Sep 29C; 1987 Feb 16C
Ivey, Judith 1983 Jun 5J; 1984 Jun 21J
Ivory, James 1986 Mar 7J

J

Jackson, Bo (Vincent) 1985 Dec 7J; 1986 Apr 29J/Jun 21J; 1989 Jul 11J
Jackson, Earl Lloyd 1980 Oct 23F
Jackson, George 1988 Mar 10F
Jackson, Henry M. ("Scoop") 1983 Sep 1F
Jackson, Janet 1986 Jun 18J/Jul 16J/Aug 13J; 1989 Oct 28J/Dec 25J/Dec 30J
Jackson, Jesse L.
   foreign policy: Cuba prisoner release 1984 Jun 28A; Gorbachev meeting 1985 Nov 19B
   Operation PUSH: 1987 Jul 4F
   "peace patrols": 1980 Jul 25F
   presidential campaign (1984)
      candidacy: 1983 Nov 3F
      debates: 1984 Jan 15F/Feb 11F/Mar 18F/Mar 28F/Jun 3F
      Democratic convention: 1984 Apr 23F/Jun 6F
      economic proposals: 1984 Apr 21F
      matching funds: 1984 Jan 3G
      primaries: Arizona 1984 Apr 14F; California 1984 Jun 5F; Connecticut 1984 Mar 27F; Florida 1984 Mar 13F; Georgia 1984 Mar 13F; Idaho 1984 May 22F; Illinois 1984 Mar 20F; Nebraska 1984 May 15F; New Jersey 1984 Jun 5F; New Mexico 1984 Jun 5F; New York 1984 Apr 3F; Oregon 1984 May 15F; Pennsylvania 1984 Apr 10F; Rhode Island 1984 Mar 13F; South Carolina 1984 Mar 17F; South Dakota 1984 Jun 5F; Tennessee 1984 May 1F; Washington, D.C. 1984 May 1F; West Virginia 1984 Jun 5F; Wisconsin 1984 Apr 3F/Apr 7F
   presidential campaign (1988): candidacy 1987 Sep 7F/Oct 10F; Democratic convention 1988 Jul 19F-20F; Dukakis campaigning 1988 Jul 30F; exploratory committee 1987 Mar 19F; funding 1987 Aug 13F; 1988 Mar 30F; party platform 1988 Jun 25F; polls 1987 Aug 30F/Oct 4F/Nov 15F; primaries 1988 Feb 23F/Mar 10F/Mar 12F/Mar 15F/Mar 19F-20F/Mar 22F/Mar 26F/Apr 2F/Apr 4F-5F/Apr 13F/Apr 16F/Apr 19F-20F/Apr 25F-26F/May 3F/May 17F
   Rainbow Coalition: 1986 Apr 17F
   Syrian mission: U.S. flier release 1983 Dec 25G/Dec 29C/Dec 31C; 1984 Jan 3C-4C/Jan 4G
Jackson, Joe 1982 Nov 17J
Jackson, John Anthony 1988 Nov 24F
Jackson, Mark 1988 May 10J
Jackson, Maynard 1989 Oct 3F
Jackson, Michael
   best-sellers: Bad 1987 Oct 24J/Nov 21J/Dec 26J; 1988 Jan 23J/Feb 20J/Mar 19J/Apr 23J/May 21J; Off the Wall 1980 Mar 5J/Apr 2J/Apr 30J; Thriller 1983 Feb 9J/Mar 9J/Apr 13J/May 11J/Jun 15J/Jul 13J/Aug 17J/Sep 14J/Oct 19J/Nov 9J/Dec 14J; 1984 Jan 11J/Jan 21J/Feb 18J/Feb 28J/Mar 24J/Apr 28J/May 20J/May 28J; We Are the World 1986 Feb 25J
   business investments: music publishing company 1985 Aug 15J
   Grammy awards: 1984 Feb 28J; 1986 Feb 25J
   tours: 1984 Dec 9J; 1987 Sep 13J
Jackson, Reggie 1980 Aug 11J; 1984 Sep 17J
Jackson, Thomas Penfield 1987 Jul 16F
Jackson, Tommy ("Hurricane") 1982 Feb 14J
Jackson, Travis 1982 Aug 1J
Jacob, John E. 1982 Aug 1F; 1983 Jan 19F; 1987 Jan 14F
Jacobi, Derek 1985 Jun 2J; 1988 Oct 21J; 1989 Nov 8J
Jacobsen, David P. 1986 Nov 2C
Jaeger, Andrea 1982 Jun 6J; 1983 Jul 2J
Jaffe, Roland 1984 Nov 2J; 1986 Oct 31J
Jakes, John
   best-sellers: California Gold 1989 Sep 29J/Oct 27J; Heaven and Hell 1987 Oct 23J/Nov 20J; Love and War 1984 Dec 14J; 1985 Jan 18J; North and South 1982 Mar 7J/Apr 11J/May 9J/Jun 6J/Jul 11J
Jakes, Milos 1987 Dec 17B; 1989 Nov 24B
Jaki, Stanley L. 1987 Mar 5J
Jakobson, Roman 1982 Jul 18J
James, Harry 1983 Jul 6J; 1987 Apr 2J
James, Henry 1987 Aug 18J
James, P.D. 1980 Jul 13J
Jameson, Mike 1986 Jan 25J
Jameson, (Margaret) Storm 1986 Sep 30J
Jamieson, Penelope Ann Bansall 1989 Nov 25E
Jamison, Judith 1989 Dec 20J
Janka, Les 1983 Oct 31F
Janson, Horst W. 1982 Sep 30J
Jarrell, Tommy (Thomas Jefferson) 1985 Jan 28J
Jaruzelski, Wojciech
   foreign policy: China 1986 Sep 30E; Czechoslovakia 1982 Apr 5B; papal visit 1982 Jul 21B/Nov 8B; 1983 Jun 17B
   government: named Polish premier 1981 Feb 9B; "democratic renewal" 1981 Feb 19B; cabinet shuffles 1981 Jun 12B/Jul 31B; 1982 Oct 9B; anti-Soviet crackdown 1981 Sep 24B; national accord plea 1981 Dec 3B; power consolidation 1981 Dec 15B; 1983 Nov 22B; martial law 1982 Jan 25B/Jul 21B; Politburo backs 1983 May 31B; resigns as premier 1985 Nov 6B; elected president 1989 Jul 19B; resigns as party secretary 1989 Jul 29B; coalition OKd 1989 Aug 17B
   labor unrest: strike plea 1981 Feb 12B; Solidarity 1981 Feb 16B/Apr 10B; 1982 Jan 4B; 1986 Oct 3B; 1989 Aug 17B; work stoppage 1981 Mar 10B; Walesa meeting 1989 Apr 18B
   Soviet policy: Warsaw pact 1981 Aug 8B; anti-Soviet crackdown 1981 Sep 24B; visits 1982 Mar 2B/Aug 16B; 1984 May 4B
   U.S. policy: 1982 Jan 4B/Jan 25B
Jarvis, Gregory B. 1986 Dec 29I
Jatoi, Ghulam Mustafa 1986 Aug 30E
Javits, Jacob Koppel 1980 Sep 9F; 1986 Mar 7F
Jawara, Dawda 1982 May 5C
Jaworski, Leon 1982 Dec 9F
Jayewardene, Junius R. 1982 Oct 21E/Oct 28E; 1984 Jul 2A
Jeantot, Philippe 1987 May 7J
Jefferies, Boyd L. 1987 Mar 19H
Jeffries, Randy Miles 1985 Dec 20G
Jemison, Mae C. 1987 Jun 5I
Jenco, Lawrence Martin 1985 Jan 8C; 1986 Jul 26C
Jenkin, Patrick 1982 Jul 19B
Jenkins, Dan 1984 Dec 14J
Jenkins, Farish 1981 Sep 17I
Jenkins, Gordon 1984 May 1J
Jenkins, Roy 1981 Jun 7B; 1982 Jul 2B; 1987 Mar 14B
Jenninger, Philipp 1988 Nov 11B
Jenrette Jr., John 1980 Feb 2F/Jun 13F/Oct 7F/Dec 10F; 1981 Mar 2J
Jenrette, Rita 1981 Mar 2J
Jerne, Niels K. 1984 Oct 15I
Jessel, George 1981 May 24J
Jessup, Philip Caryl 1986 Jan 31A
Jeter, Michael 1989 Dec 12J
Jewison, Norman 1984 Sep 14J; 1987 Dec 16J
Jhabvala, Ruth Prawer 1986 Mar 7J
Jiang Hua 1983 Jun 9E
Jiang Qing (Chiang Ching) 1980 Nov 20E; 1981 Jan 25E; 1983 Jan 25E/Jun 9E
Jiang Zemin 1989 Oct 10E
Jimenez Gomez, Carlos 1984 Jul 5D
Ji Pengfei 1985 Dec 22E
Jobs, Steven 1986 Jan 17H; 1988 Nov 12H
Joel, Billy 1980 Feb 27J/Apr 2J/Apr 30J/Jun 4J/Jul 9J/Aug 13J; 1989 Dec 25J/Dec 30J
Joffe, Roland 1986 May 19J
Joffrey, Robert (Abdullah Jaffa Bey Khan) 1988 Mar 25J
Johansson, Thomas 1984 Aug 12J
John XXIII, Pope 1985 Jan 25A
Johncock, Gordon 1982 May 30J
John Paul II, Pope
   African policy: 6-nation tour 1980 May 2J; in West Africa 1982 Feb 19A; 7-nation tour 1985 Aug 19J; in southern Africa 1988 Sep 19J; 1989 May 6J; in Mauritius 1989 Oct 7J
   appointments: Vatican education post 1980 Jan 15J; Canton archbishop 1981 Jun 6J; Polish primate 1981 Jul 7J; Chicago archbishop 1982 Jul 10J; cardinals 1983 Feb 2J; 1985 Apr 24J; 1988 May 29J; Knights of Malta 1988 Apr 8J
   Asian and Pacific Rim policy: in Guam/Japan/Philippines 1981 Feb 15J; in South Korea 1984 May 6J; in India 1986 Feb 1J; 5-nation tour 1986 Dec 1E; in East Timor/Indonesia/South Korea 1989 Oct 7J
   assassination attempt: 1981 May 13J; arrests 1981 May 13J; 1982 Feb 16B/Nov 25B; recovery 1981 May 14J/May 18J/Jun 3J/Aug 14J; Agca found guilty 1981 Jul 22J; Portugal try 1982 May 12B; Bulgarians deny 1982 Dec 18B; KGB suspect 1982 Dec 31A; report issued 1984 Jun 9B; indictments 1984 Oct 26B; trial 1985 May 27B; acquittals 1986 Mar 29B
   Banco Ambrosiano scandal: 1982 Nov 26B
   Canadian policy: 1984 Sep 9J
   ecumenical developments: Anglican church 1989 Oct 2J; Eastern Orthodox Church 1987 Dec 7A; Judaism 1986 Apr 13J; 1987 Jun 25J/Sep 1J
   encyclicals: Holy Spirit 1986 May 30J; human misery 1980 Dec 2A; labor-management 1981 Sep 15J; Virgin Mary 1987 Mar 25J
   European policy: in Great Britain 1980 May 9J; 1982 May 23A/May 31B/Jun 2B; in France 1980 Jun 22B; in West Germany 1980 Nov 15J; 1987 May 4J; in Portugal 1982 May 12B; in Spain 1982 Oct 31B/Nov 9B; Soviets charge meddling 1982 Dec 29A-30B; Lithuania bishops visit 1983 Apr 6J; Waldheim meeting 1987 Jun 25J; Lefebvre excommunication 1988 Jun 30J; Gorbachev visit 1989 Dec 1B
   Latin policy: in Argentina 1980 Dec 12A; 1982 Apr 17D/May 23A/Jun 11D; in Bolivia 1988 May 7J; in Brazil 1980 Jun 30J; 1986 Jul 10D; in Central America 1983 Mar 2D/Mar4D/Mar 6D; in Chile 1980 Dec 12A; 1987 Apr 6D; in Colombia 1986 Jun 30A; in Ecuador 1985 Jan 26D/Feb 5J; in El Salvador 1982 Feb 28A; 1983 Mar 6D; in Nicaragua 1983 Mar 4D; in Paraguay 1988 May 7J; in Peru 1985 Jan 26D/Feb 5J; 1988 May 7J; in Trinidad 1985 Jan 26D/Feb 5J; in Uruguay 1988 May 7J; in Venezuela 1985 Jan 26D
   peace initiatives: PLO meeting 1982 Sep 15A; pray-in for peace 1986 Oct 27J; superpower rivalry 1988 Feb 19J
   personal issues: ill health 1981 Jun 20J
   Polish policy: support for 1980 Aug 20B; Walesa meetings 1981 Jan 15J; 1983 Jun 23B-24B; Glemp named Polish primate 1981 Jul 7J; Solidarity support 1982 Jan 1B; Glemp meetings 1982 Feb 11B; tours 1982 Jul 21B/Nov 8B; 1983 May 16B; 1987 Jun 8J/Jun 12J; Jaruzelski meetings 1983 Jun 17B
   social issues: AIDS 1989 Nov 15A; human rights 1985 Jan 12J; racism 1985 Aug 19J; 1989 Feb 10C; women 1988 Sep 30J
   theological issues: canon law revisions 1983 Jan 25J; celibacy 1980 Oct 14J; Holy Spirit encyclical 1986 May 30J; lay participation 1989 Jan 30A; Lefebvre excommunication 1988 Jun 30J; public office 1980 May 4J; theologians criticism 1989 Jan 26J; Vatican II review 1985 Jan 25A; Virgin Mary encyclical 1987 Mar 25J; women's role 1988 Sep 30J
   U.S. policy: Baum appointed to Vatican post 1980 Jan 15J; Reagan meetings 1982 Jun 7B; 1984 May 2A-2G; Bernardin named Chicago archbishop 1982 Jul 10J; tour 1987 Sep 10J; Drexel beatified 1988 Nov 20J; bishops meet 1989 Mar 8J
Johns, Jasper 1986 Nov 10J; 1988 May 3J
Johnson, Barbara Piasecka 1986 Jun 2J
Johnson, Ben 1987 Aug 30J; 1989 Jan 11J/Jun 12J
Johnson, Ernest 1983 Feb 26F
Johnson Jr., Frank M. 1989 Jan 14F
Johnson, J. Seward 1986 Jun 2J
Johnson, John Henry 1987 Jan 27J/Aug 8J
Johnson, Lyndon B. 1981 Sep 20F; 1983 Jan 21F
Johnson, Magic (Earvin) 1980 May 16J; 1981 Jun 26J; 1982 Jun 8J; 1985 Nov 23J; 1987 May 18J/Jun 14J; 1989 May 22J
Johnson, Manuel H. 1985 Oct 19H
Johnson, Nancy L. 1989 Nov 14F
Johnson Jr., Nevell 1985 Jul 22F
Johnson, Norma Holloway 1985 Jul 26H
Johnston, J. Bennett 1982 Mar 2F
Joiner, Charles 1983 May 27F
Jolas, Betsy 1983 Feb 19J
Jolas, Eugene 1987 Mar 4J
Jolas, Maria 1987 Mar 4J
Jolson, Al 1983 Jul 16J
Jonathan, Leabua 1986 Jan 20D; 1987 Apr 5C
Jones, Colin 1983 Mar 19J
Jones, David ("Deacon") 1980 Aug 1J
Jones, David C. 1981 Jan 28G; 1982 Jun 16G
Jones, Herbert 1982 May 30D
Jones, James Earl 1980 Nov 17J; 1985 May 3J; 1987 Jun 7J; 1989 Apr 21J
Jones, James R. 1989 Oct 12H

Jones, Jim 1980 Feb 28J/Apr 8D; 1986 Dec 1F
Jones, Joseph Rudolph ("Philly Joe") 1985 Aug 30J
Jones, K. 1989 Feb 10J
Jones, Owen 1980 Jan 5D
Jones, Ralph Waldo Emerson 1982 Apr 9J
Jones, Rosie 1984 Jul 15J; 1988 Aug 28J
Jones, Stephanie 1980 Apr 8D
Jones, Steve 1988 Nov 6J
Jones, Telery 1980 Jan 5D
Jones, Thad 1986 Aug 20J
Jones, William H. 1982 Nov 23J
Jong, Erica 1980 Sep 14J/Oct 12J; 1987 Oct 12J
Jonsson, Reidar 1987 May 1J
Joplin, Janis 1984 Jul 25J; 1986 Jan 25J
Jordan, Barbara 1980 Jan 1J
Jordan, Hamilton 1980 May 28F
Jordan Jr., Irving King 1988 Mar 13F
Jordan, Michael 1988 Feb 7J/May 25J
Jordan Jr., Vernon E. 1980 May 29F/Jun 1F; 1982 Jun 2F
Jorgensen, Anker 1981 Nov 12B
Jorgensen, Christine (George Jorgensen) 1989 May 3J
Jorgensen, Henryk 1988 Apr 17J
Jorquera, Carlos 1987 Feb 12D
Joyce, James 1983 Jun 3J; 1984 Jun 16J; 1987 Mar 4J/May 13J/Dec 17J; 1988 Jan 3J
Joyner, Florence Griffith 1988 Jul 16J/Dec 3J/Dec 27J
Joyner-Kersee, Jackie 1987 Feb 23J
Juan Carlos, King (Spain) 1981 Feb 10B/Feb 24B/Feb 26B/Nov 17B; 1982 Aug 27B; 1986 Apr 22B; 1988 Oct 17B
Julesberg, Elizabeth 1985 Feb 19J
Julia, Raul 1985 Jul 26J
Juliana, Queen (Netherlands) 1980 Jan 31B
Jumbaz, Hisham 1980 Aug 16C
Jumblat, Walid
  civil strife: Beirut airport operation 1983 Aug 13C/Aug 16C; denies reprisal attack 1983 Dec 4C; talks fail 1984 Feb 1C; U.S. shelling threat 1984 Feb 8C; cease-fire broken 1984 Feb 24C; peace plan 1984 Mar 14C
  government: national unity cabinet 1984 May 10C/Sep 12C
Junejo, Muhammad Khan 1985 Mar 23E/Aug 14E; 1988 May 29E
Jung, Steven 1989 May 28J
Justice, Donald 1980 Apr 14J

K

Kadar, Janos 1988 May 22B; 1989 May 8B/Jul 6B
Kadavy, Caryn 1987 Feb 7J/Mar 14J
Kafka, Franz 1989 Apr 17J
Kahane, Meir 1984 Dec 25C; 1987 Feb 20F/Jun 8C/Jul 1C
Kahl, Gordon 1983 Jun 3H
Kahn, Herman 1983 Jul 7I
Kaifu, Toshiki 1989 Aug 9E
Kalb, Bernard 1986 Oct 8G
Kalb, Marvin 1980 Mar 1J
Kalikow, Peter 1988 Feb 20H
Kaline, Al 1980 Aug 3J
Kampelman, Max M. 1985 Jan 26A
Kandel, Eric R. 1983 Nov 16I
Kane Jr., John L. 1985 Nov 26H
Kanellopoulos, Kanellos 1988 Apr 23J
Kang Sok Ju 1989 Sep 28E
Kang Young Hoon 1988 Dec 28E
Kani, John 1987 Sep 16J
Kania, Stanislaw
  foreign policy: Soviet Union 1980 Oct 30B; 1981 Apr 14B

government: named party leader 1980 Sep 6B; leadership challenge overcome 1981 Jun 11B; re-elected party leader 1981 Jul 18B; dismissed as party leader 1981 Oct 18B
  Solidarity: Walesa meeting 1980 Nov 14B; instigators opposed 1981 Feb 3B; street protests 1981 Aug 11B
Kanin, Garson 1985 Aug 28J
Kantorovich, Leonid V. 1986 Apr 7J
Kapitsa, Pyotr L. 1984 Apr 8I
Kaplan, Henry 1984 Feb 4I
Kaplan, Jonathan 1988 Oct 14J
Kaplan, Robert 1983 Mar 13D
Karajan, Herbert von 1989 Jul 16J
Karami, Rashid 1984 Apr 26C/Jun 12C/Oct 5A; 1985 Apr 17C; 1987 Jun 1C
Karl II, King (Romania) 1982 Nov 28B
Karle, Jerome 1985 Oct 16I
Karmal, Babrak 1980 Mar 11A/Jul 20E; 1986 May 4E/Nov 20E; 1989 Jun 25E
Karoly, Bela 1981 May 31J
Karpov, Anatoly 1985 Feb 15J/Sep 2J/Nov 9J; 1986 Oct 9J; 1987 Mar 31J/Dec 19J
Karpov, Viktor P. 1985 Mar 16B
Karry, Heinz Herbert 1981 May 11B
Kasparov, Gary 1985 Feb 15J/Sep 2J/Nov 9J; 1986 Oct 9J; 1987 Mar 31J/Dec 19J; 1988 Feb 22J; 1989 Oct 22J
Kassebaum, Nancy Landon 1987 Oct 12F
Kassem, Abdul Rauf al- 1981 Oct 31C; 1985 Oct 21C; 1987 Oct 31C/Nov 1C
Kastler, Alfred 1984 Jan 7I
Kaufman, Bob 1986 Jan 12J
Kaufman, George S. 1985 Aug 24J
Kaufman, Henry 1980 Feb 22H; 1981 Apr 22H
Kaufman, Murray ("Murray The K") 1982 Feb 21J
Kaufman, Philip 1988 Feb 5J
Kaunda, Kenneth 1980 Oct 27C; 1982 Apr 30C; 1987 Sep 11C/Oct 4I
Kawasmeh, Fahad 1980 May 3C
Kaye, Danny 1987 Mar 3J
Kaye, Nora 1987 Mar 3J/Apr 19J
Kaye, Sammy 1987 Jun 2J
Kazan, Elia 1986 Oct 7J
Kazantzakis, Nikos 1988 Aug 12J
Kean, Thomas H. 1982 Apr 12F; 1985 Sep 9F/Nov 5F; 1988 Aug 16F
Keating, Charles H. 1989 Oct 13F
Keating, Paul 1988 Aug 23E
Keaton, Diane 1986 Dec 12J
Keaton, Michael 1988 Mar 30J/Aug 10J
Keel Jr., Alton G. 1987 Jul 26G
Keenan, John F. 1986 May 12E
Keillor, Garrison
  best-sellers: Lake Wobegon Days 1985 Sep 27J/Oct 25J/Nov 22J/Dec 20J; 1986 Jan 31J/Feb 28J/Mar 28J/Apr 25J/May 30J; Leaving Home 1987 Oct 23J/Nov 20J; We Are Still Married 1989 Apr 28J
Keitel, Harvey 1984 Jun 21J
Keker, John W. 1988 Dec 16F; 1989 Feb 21F
Kekkonen, Urho Kaleva 1981 Oct 27B; 1986 Aug 31B
Kelleher, James F. 1987 Nov 30D
Kelley, P.X. 1987 Jun 16G
Kelly, Clifford 1986 Nov 21F
Kelly, Pam 1982 Mar 30J
Kelly, Richard 1980 Feb 2F/Jul 15F; 1981 Jan 26F
Kelly, William 1985 Feb 8J
Kemp, Jack F.
  government service: conservative leadership poll 1985 Mar 2F; HUD

secretary 1988 Dec 19F; 1989 Feb 2H
housing policy: tenant eviction rules 1989 Mar 29F; Section 8 overhaul 1989 Jun 1F; loan guarantee program 1989 Jun 29F; retirement program suspension 1989 Jul 6F; predecessor faulted 1989 Jul 11F; reforms announced 1989 Oct 3F
presidential campaign (1988): preview appearance 1985 Jun 29F; precinct delegate elections 1986 Aug 6F; candidacy 1987 Apr 6F; debates 1987 Oct 28F; delegate selection rules 1987 Dec 12F; matching funds 1988 Jan 4F; fraudulent signatures probe 1988 Jan 18F; withdrawal 1988 Mar 10F
Kennan, George F. 1982 Apr 7G; 1989 Jul 6J
Kennedy, Anthony M. 1987 Nov 11F/Nov 14F; 1988 Feb 3F/Feb 18F/Jun 29F
Kennedy, Caroline Bouvier 1986 Jul 19J
Kennedy, David 1980 Jan 22J
Kennedy, Edward M.
  Chappaquiddick incident: 1980 Jan 15F/Mar 12F
  foreign policy: Soviet grain embargo 1980 Jan 30F; A-freeze plan 1982 Mar 30G; Central American aid 1984 Mar 28G; South Africa 1985 Jan 13C
  personal issues: divorce 1981 Jan 21F
  politics: Reagan administration attack 1982 Jul 28F
  presidential campaign (1980)
    candidacy: 1980 Jan 28F
    Carter reconciliation: 1980 Jun 5F/Aug 5F
    debates: 1980 Jan 12F
    Democratic convention: 1980 May 5F/Jul 28F/Aug 11F-12F
    endorsements: 1980 Jul 31F
    party platform: 1980 Jun 24F/Aug 12F
    polls: 1980 Jan 8F
    primaries: Alabama 1980 Mar 11F; Arkansas 1980 May 27F; California 1980 Jun 3F; Connecticut 1980 Mar 25F; Florida 1980 Mar 11F; Georgia 1980 Mar 11F; Illinois 1980 Mar 18F; Indiana 1980 May 6F; Iowa 1980 Jan 21F; Kansas 1980 Apr 1F; Kentucky 1980 May 27F; Louisiana 1980 Apr 5F; Maine 1980 Feb 10F; Maryland 1980 May 13F; Massachusetts 1980 Mar 4F; Michigan 1980 Apr 26F; Montana 1980 Jun 3F; Nebraska 1980 May 13F; Nevada 1980 May 27F; New Hampshire 1980 Feb 26F; New Jersey 1980 Jun 3F; New Mexico 1980 Jun 3F; New York 1980 Mar 25F; North Carolina 1980 May 6F; Ohio 1980 Jun 3F; Oregon 1980 May 20F; Pennsylvania 1980 Apr 22F; Rhode Island 1980 Jun 3F; South Dakota 1980 Jun 3F; Tennessee 1980 May 6F; Texas 1980 May 3F; Vermont 1980 Mar 4F; Washington, D.C. 1980 May 6F; West Virginia 1980 Jun 3F; Wisconsin 1980 Apr 1F
    Urban League address: 1980 Aug 6F
    withdrawal: 1980 Aug 11F
presidential campaign (1984): 1982 Dec 1F

presidential campaign (1988): 1985 Dec 19F
Kennedy, John F. 1980 Jan 4F; 1983 Nov 22F; 1984 Jul 17I; 1988 Oct 5F/Nov 22F
Kennedy II, Joseph P. 1985 Dec 4F
Kennedy Sr., Joseph P. 1980 Oct 13J
Kennedy, Robert F. 1985 Jun 25F; 1986 Mar 4F
Kennedy, William 1984 Apr 16J; 1987 Dec 18J
Kenyon, David 1988 Apr 29F
Kerekou, Mathieu 1984 Aug 1C; 1989 Dec 8C
Kerin, John 1988 Jun 24E
Kerr, Ewing T. 1982 Nov 4H
Kershner, Irvin 1980 May 21J
Kertesz, Andre 1985 Sep 27J
Keshtmand, Soltan Ali 1988 May 27E
Keys, Randolph 1987 Mar 26J
Keyworth, George 1982 Jun 24I
Khaddam, Abdel Halim 1982 Dec 15C; 1983 Jul 19C; 1985 Jun 17C
Khaled, Ibrahim Mohammed 1988 Feb 12B
Khaled, Sheik Hassan 1982 May 6C
Khalid, King (Saudi Arabia) 1980 Jan 1C; 1982 Apr 14A/Jun 13C
Khalifa, Sheik Isa bin Salman al- 1983 Jul 19C
Khalkhali, Ayatollah Sadegh 1980 Dec 7C; 1981 Mar 8C
Khama, Seretse 1980 Jul 13C
Khamenei, Ayatollah Mohammed Ali 1981 Sep 15C/Oct 5C; 1984 May 29C; 1989 Feb 17C/Jun 4C/Aug 14C
Khan, Abdul Qadir 1987 Mar 1E
Khan, Fazlur R. 1982 Mar 27I
Khan, Inamullah 1988 Mar 2J
Khan, Yaqub 1983 Jul 2E
Khashoggi, Adnan M. 1989 Jul 19J
Khieu Samphan 1981 Mar 10E/Sep 4E; 1982 Feb 21E; 1983 May 1E
Khomeini, Ayatollah Ruhollah
  foreign policy: Saudi peace plan 1981 Nov 17C; Soviet Union 1989 Feb 23C
  government: Bani-Sadr as military commander 1980 Feb 19C; 1981 Jun 10C; general amnesty 1980 Mar 18C; Bani-Sadr charges traded 1980 Jun 27C/Jun 29C; Ghotbzadeh release ordered 1980 Nov 10C; Bani-Sadr clerical feud 1981 Feb 4C/Mar 9C/Mar 16C/May 27C; purges 1981 Apr 1C/Jul 9C; 1989 Mar 28C; Bani-Sadr ousted as president 1981 Jun 22C; assembly to choose successor 1982 Oct 12C; 1983 Jul 14C; Montazeri named successor 1985 Nov 23C; Rafsanjani named military commander 1988 Jun 2C; return celebrated 1989 Feb 1C
  Iran-Iraq War: 1980 Apr 8C/Sep 30C/Oct 12C/Oct 19C; 1982 Mar 31C/Jul 14C; 1988 Sep 1C
  personal issues: ill health 1980 Jan 23C; 1987 Feb 10C; will 1987 Dec 10C; death 1989 Jun 4C; funeral 1989 Jun 5C
  Rushdie death threat: 1989 Feb 14C/Feb 24A
  U.S. hostage crisis: 1980 Feb 13C/Mar 10A/Mar 29A/Apr 7C/May 6C/Sep 12C/Sep 15G
Khrushchev, Nikita S. 1984 Aug 8B; 1986 Nov 8B; 1987 Feb 10B
Khrushchev, Nina Petrovna 1984 Aug 8B
Khun Sa 1982 Feb 23E
Kianuri, Nureddin 1983 May 4B
Kiesinger, Kurt Georg 1988 Mar 8B
Kiley, Richard 1988 Aug 28J

Killanin, Lord 1980 Apr 23J/May 7J/May 15J/Jul 16J
Killen, James 1980 Sep 9E
Kimche, David 1983 Feb 27C
Kim Chong Il 1980 Oct 14E
Kim Dae Jung
  government opposition: accusations against 1980 May 22E/May 31E; death sentence 1980 Sep 17E/Nov 3E/Nov 8E/Nov 18E/Nov 28E; 1981 Jan 23E; released from prison 1982 Dec 23E; returns from exile 1985 Feb 8E; party formed 1987 Apr 8E/Apr 13E/Oct 30E; probed 1989 Aug 12E; indicted 1989 Aug 25E
  presidential campaign: 1987 Oct 19E/Oct 28E/Oct 30E/Dec 16E
Kim Hyon Hui 1989 Apr 25E
Kim Il Sung 1980 Jul 18E/Oct 14E; 1982 Feb 10E; 1984 May 4E/May 25A; 1986 Dec 29E; 1987 May 21E
Kim Keun Tae 1988 Jun 30E
Kimto, Fatime 1982 Oct 22C
Kim Young Nam 1989 Sep 28E
Kim Young Sam
  government opposition: detention ended 1981 May 1E; united front formed 1983 Jun 2D; party formed 1987 Apr 8E/Apr 13E/May 1E; constitutional debate 1987 Jun 24E; leadership resignation 1988 Feb 8E
  presidential elections: 1987 Oct 19E/Oct 28E/Dec 16E
King, B.B. 1983 Jul 11J
King, Betsy 1989 Jul 16J
King, Billie Jean 1981 May 1J
King, Coretta Scott 1984 Mar 29G; 1986 Jun 20F; 1987 Dec 8F
King, Edward J. 1980 Dec 7H; 1982 Sep 14F
King, Ignatius (Gong Pinmei) 1985 Jul 3E
King, Leon 1989 Mar 22F
King Jr., Martin Luther
  holiday: federal law 1983 Aug 2F/Oct 19F/Nov 2F; 1986 Jan 20F; Arizona controversy 1986 Nov 5F; 1987 Jan 4F/Jul 6F; 1989 Sep 22F
  personal issues: widow sues Boston U 1987 Dec 8F
  tributes: 1983 Jan 15F/Aug 27F; 1985 Jan 15F/Apr 4F
King Sr., Martin Luther ("Daddy") 1984 Nov 11F
King, Stephen
  best-sellers: Christine 1983 Apr 10J/May 15J/Jun 1J/Jun 12J/Jul 10J/Dec 18J; Cujo 1981 Sep 6J/Oct 4J/Nov 8J/Dec 6J; 1982 Jan 10J; Dark Half 1989 Dec 1J/Dec 22J; Different Seasons 1982 Sep 12J; Eyes of the Dragon 1987 Mar 27J/Apr 24J; Firestarter 1980 Sep 14J/Oct 12J/Dec 7J; 1981 Jan 11J/Feb 8J; 1987 Oct 12J/Dec 7J; It 1986 Sep 26J/Oct 31J/Nov 21J/Dec 26J; 1987 Jan 23J/Feb 27J; Misery 1987 Jul 17J/Sep 23J; Pet Sematary 1983 Nov 13J/Dec 18J; 1984 Jan 20J/Feb 10J/Mar 23J; Shining 1980 May 23J; Skeleton Crew 1985 Jul 19J/Aug 16J/Sep 27J; Talisman 1984 Dec 14J; 1985 Jan 18J/Feb 8J; Thinner 1985 Apr 19J/May 24J; Tommyknockers 1988 Jan 29J/Feb 26J
King, Tom 1986 Jun 12B
Kingman, John 1988 Apr 29B
Kingston, Maxine Hong 1981 Apr 30J
Kinneary, Joseph 1981 Nov 24H/Dec 24H

Kinnell, Galway 1983 Apr 18J
Kinnock, Neil 1983 Oct 2B; 1986 Sep 5B/Oct 3B; 1987 Sep 23F; 1988 Sep 2F/Oct 2B
Kinsella, W.P. 1989 Apr 21J
Kinski, Nastassia 1980 Dec 12J
Kipperman, Kenneth 1987 Aug 14J
Kirchschlager, Rudolph 1980 May 18B
Kirk Jr., Paul G. 1985 Feb 1F/Feb 16F; 1987 Feb 10F
Kirkland, Lane 1981 Sep 26B; 1982 Feb 16H; 1983 Feb 21F; 1985 Oct 28H; 1987 Feb 18F
Kirkpatrick, Jeane J. 1981 Mar 23G/Aug 28G; 1983 Feb 22G/Mar 23G; 1985 Feb 8G
Kirkwood, James 1989 Apr 21J
Kirst, Hans Helmut 1989 Feb 23J
Kirstein, Lincoln 1989 Sep 13J
Kishi, Nobosuke 1987 Aug 7E
Kishkovsky, Leonid 1989 Nov 19J
Kissinger, Henry A. 1982 Apr 13F/Sep 20J/Dec 31A; 1983 Jul 18G/Oct 9D; 1984 Feb 27G
Kissoon, Jeffery 1987 Oct 13J
Kiszczak, Czeslaw 1988 Aug 26B/Aug 31B; 1989 Aug 17B
Kitingan, Joseph Pairin 1986 May 6E
Kittle, Ron 1983 Nov 23J
Kizer, Carolyn 1985 Apr 24J
Kizer, Kenneth W. 1986 Feb 14H
Kizim, Leonid D. 1980 Nov 27I; 1986 Jul 16I
Klarsfeld, Beate 1988 Mar 8B
Klarsfeld, Serge 1983 Feb 8B
Klein, Lawrence R. 1980 Oct 15H
Kleindienst, Richard 1981 Apr 14F
Kline, Kevin 1981 Jun 7J; 1988 Jul 15J; 1989 Mar 29J
Kline, Nathan S. 1983 Feb 11I
Klinghoffer, Leon 1985 Oct 9C/Oct 20J/Nov 18B
Klitzing, Klaus von 1985 Oct 16I
Klug, Aaron 1982 Oct 18I
Kluge, John 1986 Oct 14H; 1987 Oct 12H; 1988 Oct 10H
Kluszewski, Ted 1988 Mar 29J
Kneissl, Annie-Laurie 1987 Dec 23J
Knight, Ray 1986 Oct 27J
Knoll, Hans-Peter 1981 Feb 28B
Knopf, Alfred A. 1984 Aug 11J
Knowles, James Llewellyn 1987 Feb 12F
Koch, Edward I.
  crime: racial violence 1986 Dec 20F; school corruption probe 1988 Dec 22F
  economic policy: transit strike settlement 1980 Apr 11H; highway project 1981 Mar 14H/Sep 7F; budget 1988 May 9F
  health care: AIDS proposal 1985 Oct 2F; antismoking bill 1988 Jan 7F
  Lennon memorial: 1985 Oct 9J
  politics: elections 1981 Sep 22F; 1982 Sep 23F; 1985 Sep 10F/Nov 5F; Jackson attack 1988 Apr 19F
Koech, Peter 1989 Jul 3J
Koehler, George J.F. 1984 Oct 15I
Koehler, Ted 1986 Apr 23J
Koen, Karleen 1985 Aug 28J
Koestler, Arthur 1983 Mar 3J
Koestler, Cynthia 1983 Mar 3J
Kohl, Helmut
  arms control: tactical weapons 1988 Feb 6B; NATO summit 1989 Apr 27B/Apr 30B; short-range A-weapons 1989 May 27B/Apr 30B
  atomic energy: 1986 Jun 3B
  economic policy: student protest 1982 Dec 4B; tax reform plan 1987 Feb 24B
  foreign policy: France 1984 Sep 22B; 1986 Feb 28B/Oct 28B; 1988

Jan 22B; Great Britain 1989 Apr 30B; Soviet Union 1983 Jun 4B; 1988 Oct 24B; Warsaw Pact proposals 1983 Jan 6B; World War I ceremony 1984 Sep 22B
  G-7 summits: 1986 May 6A; 1987 Jun 8A
  German reunification: 1984 Feb 13B; 1987 Jan 4B/Sep 7B; 1989 Nov 28B
  government: elected chancellor 1982 Oct 1B; cabinet sworn 1982 Oct 4B; West German elections 1983 Mar 6B; 1985 May 12B; 1986 Jun 15B; 1987 Jan 25B; asylum laws 1986 Aug 27B; reelected chancellor 1987 Mar 11B
  U.S. policy: 1982 Nov 15A; 1984 Nov 30G; 1986 Oct 22G
Kohlschutter, Andreas 1988 Aug 13C
Koivisto, Mauno 1983 Jun 6B; 1987 Mar 16B; 1988 Feb 1B/Feb 15B
Kokoschka, Oskar 1980 Feb 22J
Kolingba, Andre 1981 Sep 1C
Kolone, Vaai 1985 Dec 27E
Kondrashin, Kiril 1981 Mar 7J
Koontz, Dean R. 1988 Feb 26J; 1989 Feb 24J/Mar 31J
Koop, C. Everett
  surgeon general: abortion 1989 Jan 9F; AIDS 1986 Oct 22E; 1987 Sep 9F; 1988 May 26F; alcohol abuse 1989 May 31F; dietary fat 1988 Jul 27I; sex education 1986 Oct 22E; smoking 1982 Feb 22I; 1983 Nov 17H; 1984 May 23I; 1985 Dec 19I; 1986 Mar 23F/Dec 16I; 1988 May 16I; 1989 Jan 11I; resignation 1989 May 4F
Koopmans, Tjalling 1986 Apr 7J
Kopechne, Mary Jo 1980 Jan 15F/Mar 12F
Korb, Lawrence J. 1989 Dec 12G
Korkala, George Gregory 1981 Nov 19F
Korolev, Yuri 1985 Nov 10J
Kosar, Bernie 1984 Jan 2J
Kostadinov, Penyu B. 1983 Sep 23G
Kostelanetz, Andre 1980 Jan 13J
Kosygin, Alexei 1980 Oct 23B
Kotzwinkle, William 1982 Oct 17J/Nov 14J/Dec 12J
Kountche, Seyni 1987 Nov 10C
Kovalyonok, Vladimir 1981 Mar 13I
Kovic, Ron 1989 Dec 20J
Kozlowski, Linda 1986 Sep 26J
Kraft, Joseph 1986 Jan 10J
Krajger, Sergej 1981 May 15B
Krakowski, Jane 1989 Dec 12J
Kramer, Larry 1985 Apr 21J
Kramer, Stanley 1984 Oct 23J
Kramer, Villagran 1980 Sep 2D
Krantz, Judith
  best-sellers: I'll Take Manhattan 1986 May 30J/Jun 27J/Jul 18J/Aug 29J; Mistral's Daughter 1983 Jan 16J/Feb 13J/Mar 13J/Nov 13J; Princess Daisy 1980 Feb 10J/Mar 9J/Apr 6J/May 4J/Jun 8J; Till We Meet Again 1988 Aug 26J/Sep 30J/Oct 21J
Krasner, Lee 1984 Jun 19J
Kreisky, Bruno 1980 Mar 13C; 1981 Dec 18B; 1982 Dec 28C; 1983 May 24B
Krenz, Egon 1989 Oct 18B/Nov 8B
Kriangsak Chamanand 1980 Feb 19E/Mar 3E; 1985 Sep 17E
Krieger, Henry 1981 Dec 20J
Kriek, Johan 1982 Jan 3J/Dec 13J
Kripalani, Jiwatram Bhagwandas 1982 Mar 19E
Krishnamurti, Jiddu 1986 Feb 17J
Kristiansen, Ingrid 1985 Jul 27J; 1986 Apr 21J; 1987 May 10J; 1988 Mar 26J/Apr 17J; 1989 Apr 17J/Nov 5J

Kroc, Joan B. 1987 Aug 13F
Kroc, Ray A. 1984 Jan 14J
Kroesen, Frederick J. 1980 Apr 23G; 1981 Sep 15G
Krol, John Cardinal 1982 Nov 21A
Krugman, Saul 1983 Nov 16I
Krupa, Gene 1986 Jul 31J; 1989 Feb 26J
Kubasov, Valery 1980 May 26I
Kubrick, Stanley 1980 May 23J; 1983 Dec 8J; 1986 Jul 28J; 1987 Jun 26J
Kudlow, Lawrence 1982 Dec 8H
Kuhn, Bowie 1981 Aug 20J; 1982 Nov 1J; 1984 Oct 1J; 1985 Mar 18J
Kuhn, Rick 1981 Nov 23J
Kujau, Konrad 1985 Jul 8B
Kulikov, Viktor 1981 Jan 14B
Kulle, Reinhold 1987 Oct 26G
Kundera, Milan 1985 Jan 9J; 1988 Feb 5J
Kung, Hans 1980 Feb 5J/Apr 10J
Kunitz, Stanley 1987 Feb 10J
Kureishi, Hanif 1986 Mar 7J
Kuria, Gibson Kamau 1988 Sep 21C
Kurihara, Yuko 1987 Oct 2E
Kuron, Jacek 1982 Sep 3B
Kurosawa, Akira 1986 Jan 2J
Kurtz, Swoosie 1986 Mar 19J; 1988 Dec 21J
Kusturica, Emir 1985 May 20J
Kusumaatmadja, Mochtar 1983 Sep 26E
Kuznets, Simon 1985 Jul 9J
Kyprianou, Spyros 1983 Nov 15B; 1984 Jan 17B; 1985 Mar 1B/Jun 12B/Dec 8B; 1988 Feb 21B
Kyriazides, Nikos 1984 Apr 10J
Kyser, Kay (James King Kern) 1985 Jul 23J

L

LaBelle, Patti 1986 Jun 18J/Jul 16J
Laborde, Anthony 1982 Jan 9F
Lacalle, Luis Alberto 1989 Nov 26D
Laclos, Pierre Ambroise Francois Choderlos de 1988 Dec 21J
Lacoste, Pierre 1985 Sep 20B
La Follette, Suzanne 1983 Apr 23J
Lafontant, Roger 1985 Sep 10D
Lago Roman, Victor 1982 Nov 4B
Laing, R(onald) D(avid) 1989 Aug 23I
Laird, Melvin R. 1986 Aug 17G
Lake, Ricki 1988 Feb 26J
Lalonde, Donny 1988 Nov 7J
Lalonde, Marc 1982 Oct 27D
Lam, Wilfredo 1982 Sep 11J
Lambsdorff, Otto 1988 Oct 8B
Lamizana, Sangoule 1980 Nov 25C
Lamm, Richard D. 1984 Mar 27F
Lammers, Jan 1988 Jun 12J
Lamonaco, Philip 1987 Jan 18F
La Motta, Jake 1980 Nov 14J
L'Amour, Louis (Dearborn)
  best-sellers: Haunted Mesa 1987 May 29J; Jubal Sackett 1985 Jun 14J/Jul 19J; Last of the Breed 1986 Jun 27J/Jul 18J/Aug 29J/Sep 26J; Lonesome Gods 1983 Apr 10J/May 15J; Mesa 1987 Jul 17J; Walking Drum 1984 Jun 15J
  obituary: 1988 Jun 10J
Lamrani, Mohamed Karim 1985 Oct 23C
Lancaster, Burt 1985 May 25J; 1989 Apr 21J
Lance, Bert 1980 Apr 30F/Jun 9F; 1986 Feb 12H
Lanchester, Elsa (Elizabeth Sullivan) 1986 Dec 26J
Landau, Martin 1989 Nov 13J
Landers, Ann (Eppie Lederer) 1985 Nov 22I
Landis, John 1987 May 29J

Landon, Alf(red) M(ossman) 1984 Jul 26F; 1987 Oct 12F
Lang, Harold 1985 Jul 26J
Lange, David 1984 Jul 13A/Jul 14E; 1985 Feb 4B/Feb 19E/Feb 26E; 1986 Jun 27E; 1987 Aug 15E; 1989 Aug 7E
Lange, Jessica 1985 May 6H; 1986 Dec 12J
Lange, Mark A. 1983 Dec 4C
Langer, Bernhard 1981 Jul 19J; 1984 Jul 22J; 1985 Apr 14J
Langer, Jim 1987 Jan 27J/Aug 8J
Langer, Suzanne Katherina 1985 Jul 17J
Langrick, Margaret 1986 Mar 20J
Lanier, Willie 1986 Jan 28J
Lansing, Sherry 1980 Jan 1J
Lansky, Meyer 1983 Jan 15J
Lapierre, Dominique 1980 Oct 12J/Dec 7J; 1987 Oct 12J/Dec 7J
Lapine, James 1984 May 2J; 1985 Apr 24J; 1987 Nov 5J; 1988 Jun 5J
Lara Bonilla, Rodrigo 1984 May 1D
Larkin, Philip (Arthur) 1985 Dec 2J
Larosiere, Jacques de 1983 Sep 27A
Larouche Jr., Lyndon H.
  fundraising scandal: probe 1986 Apr 12F; fine 1986 Aug 8F; NBC suit settlement 1986 Sep 17F; associates indicted 1986 Oct 6F; 1987 Feb 17F; indicted 1987 Jul 2F; 1988 Oct 14F; mistrial declared 1988 May 4F; convicted 1988 Dec 16F
  Illinois primaries: 1986 Mar 18F/Apr 9F/Apr 23F
Larrieu, Francie 1981 Feb 27J
Lartigue, Jacques-Henri 1986 Sep 12J
Lash, Joseph P. 1987 Aug 22J
Laszlo, Ernest 1984 Jan 6J
La Torre, Pio 1982 Apr 30B
Lattimore, Richmond 1984 Feb 26J
Laughton, Charles 1986 Dec 26J
Lauper, Cyndi 1984 Jun 16J; 1985 Feb 26J; 1986 Nov 22J
Laurel, Salvador H. 1982 Feb 14E; 1983 Aug 23E; 1985 Dec 11E; 1988 Aug 27E
Laurence, Margaret 1987 Jan 5J
Lauzon, Jean-Claude 1988 Mar 22J
Lavelle, Rita M.
  "Superfund" scandal: Reagan dismissal 1983 Feb 7H; Senate hearings 1983 Feb 23H; House probes 1983 Mar 1H; contempt citation 1983 May 18H/May 27F; acquittal 1983 Jul 22F; perjury indictment 1983 Aug 4H; conviction 1983 Dec 1H; 1985 Apr 19H; sentence 1984 Jan 9H; 1985 Apr 19H
Lavin, Linda 1986 Dec 4J; 1987 Jun 7J
Lawford, Peter 1984 Dec 24J
Lawler, Richard 1982 Jul 24I
Lawrence, D.H. 1985 Nov 16J
Lawrence, Malcolm 1985 Aug 4F
Lawson, Nigel
  economic policy: spending program cuts 1983 Jul 7B; BP privatization 1983 Jul 25B; 1987 Oct 29B; budget 1984 Mar 13B; 1988 Mar 15B; annual statement 1987 Nov 3B; 1988 Nov 1B; income tax reform 1988 Mar 15B
  government service: resigns Exchequer post 1989 Oct 26B
  monetary policy: coin, bank notes 1984 Nov 12B; bank lending rates 1988 Mar 17B/Aug 25B; European Monetary System 1989 Jun 13B
Laxalt, Paul 1981 Jun 25G; 1982 Nov 6F; 1983 Oct 13G; 1985 Aug 19F/Oct 12G; 1987 Aug 26F
Laya, Jaime 1982 Sep 13E
Layton, Joe 1980 Apr 30J

Layton, Larry John 1981 Sep 26F; 1986 Dec 1F
Lazareva, Natalya 1982 Jul 3B
Leach, Jim 1983 Mar 4G; 1985 Feb 12G; 1986 Apr 26F
Leach, Wilford 1985 Dec 2J; 1986 Jun 1J
Leadbelly 1986 Oct 19J
Leakey, Louis 1988 Nov 22I
Leakey, Richard 1984 Aug 22I
Lear, Norman 1985 Aug 29H
Leary, Timothy 1980 Nov 1J
Leaycraft, Donni 1989 May 28J
Lebedev, Valentin 1982 Aug 20I/Nov 14I; 1983 Aug 16I
Le Bel, Roger 1988 Mar 22J
Le Carre, John
  best-sellers: Little Drummer Girl 1983 Apr 10J/May 15J/Jun 1J/Jun 12J/Jul 10J/Aug 14J; Perfect Spy 1986 May 30J/Jun 27J; Russia House 1989 Jun 30J/Jul 28J/Aug 25J/Sep 29J; Smiley's People 1980 Jan 13J/Feb 10J/Mar 9J/Apr 6J
Ledeen, Michael 1987 Sep 27G
Leder, Philip 1987 Sep 21I
Lederberg, Joshua 1989 Jun 9I
Lederer, Jiri 1980 Sep 2B
Lederer, Raymond 1980 Feb 2F/May 28F; 1981 Jan 9F
Lederman, Leon 1988 Oct 19I
Le Duan 1981 Jul 4E; 1986 Jul 10E/Jul 14E
Lee II, Burton 1989 Apr 28F
Lee, Fred C. 1988 Jun 27H
Lee, Robert E. 1988 Aug 10H
Lee, Spike 1989 Jun 30J
Lee, Yuan T. 1986 Oct 15I
Lee Chul Hee 1982 Aug 9E
Lee Han Yol 1987 Jul 9E
Lee Huan 1989 May 24E
Lee Kuan Yew 1984 Jan 23E/Dec 22E; 1985 Jan 2E/Aug 27E; 1988 Sep 3E; 1989 Oct 8E
Lee Kyu Kwang 1982 Aug 9E
Lee Sok Kyu 1987 Aug 22E
Leestma, David C. 1984 Oct 11I
Lee Teng-hui 1984 Mar 21E; 1988 Jan 13E; 1989 May 24E
Lee Tze Chung 1989 Jul 15E
Lefebvre, Marcel 1980 Apr 7J; 1988 Jun 30J
Lefever, Ernest 1981 Jun 5G
Lehder Rivas, Carlos Enrique 1987 Feb 4D/Oct 5F
Lehman Jr., John F. 1981 Aug 19G/Oct 22G; 1985 May 21G; 1987 Apr 10G
Lehman, Ronald F. 1987 May 8A
Lehn, Jean-Marie 1987 Oct 14I
Lehninger, Albert Lester 1986 Mar 4I
Leichtling, Jerry 1986 Oct 8J
Leijon, Anna-Greta 1988 Jun 7B
Leland, Mickey 1989 Aug 7C/Aug 13C
Leloir, Luis Federico 1987 Dec 3I
Lelyveld, Joseph 1986 Apr 17J
Lemieux, Mario 1988 Jun 8J
Lemond, Greg 1986 Jul 27J; 1989 Jul 23J
Lendl, Ivan
  Australian Open: 1989 Jan 29J
  French Open: 1981 Jun 7J; 1985 Jun 9J; 1986 Jun 8J; 1987 Jun 7J
  U.S. Open: 1982 Sep 12J; 1983 Sep 11J; 1984 Sep 9J; 1985 Sep 8J; 1986 Sep 7J; 1987 Sep 14J
  Wimbledon: 1987 Jul 5J
Lengani, Jean-Baptiste Boukari 1989 Sep 19C
Le Ngoc Hien 1988 Jun 30E
Lenin, Vladimir Ilyich 1989 Dec 30B
Lenkowsky, Leslie 1984 May 15G
Lennon, John

best sellers: *Double Fantasy* 1981 Jan 7J/Feb 11J/Mar 4J; 1982 Feb 24J

Grammy awards: 1982 Feb 24J

personal issues: murder 1980 Dec 8J; 1981 Jun 22J/Aug 24J; FBI surveillance disclosure 1983 Mar 22J; memorial dedication 1985 Oct 9J

Lennon, Sean 1985 Oct 9J

Lenoir, William 1989 May 18I

Lenya, Lotte 1981 Nov 27J

Leonard, Elmore 1985 Mar 15J

Leonard, Robert Sean 1989 Jun 2J

Leonard, Sugar Ray 1980 Sep 20J/Nov 25J/Nov 26J; 1981 Sep 16J; 1982 Nov 9J; 1987 Apr 6J; 1988 Nov 7J; 1989 Jun 12J/Dec 7J

Leone, Sergio 1989 Apr 30J

Leontieff, Wassili 1983 Feb 12J

Leopold III, King (Belgium) 1983 Sep 25J

Le Pen, Jean-Marie 1988 Apr 24B

Lerner, Alan Jay 1986 Jun 14J; 1988 Feb 14J

Leroux, Gaston 1986 Oct 9J

Leroy, Mervyn 1987 Sep 13J

Le Roy Ladurie, Emmanuel 1987 Nov 22B

Letelier, Orlando 1981 May 30A; 1987 Feb 4D; 1989 Jan 25D

Leval, Pierre N. 1983 Oct 14J

Levesque, Rene 1980 Apr 15D; 1982 Apr 16D; 1983 Jun 10D; 1984 Nov 19D/Dec 15D; 1985 Jun 20D; 1987 Nov 1D

Levi, Julian 1982 Feb 28J

Levi, Primo 1987 Apr 11J

Levick, Brian 1985 Mar 15C/Mar 30C

Levi-Montalcini, Rita 1986 Sep 22I/Oct 13I

Levin, Jennifer 1988 Mar 25F

Levin, Jeremy 1984 Oct 2C

Levin, Ronald G. 1987 Apr 22F

Levine, David 1983 Feb 19J

Levine, Dennis B. 1986 May 12H/Jun 5H

Levine, James 1983 Sep 15J

Levine, Joseph E(dward) 1987 Jul 31J

Levine, Philip 1987 Jul 4J

Levinson, Barry 1987 Dec 23J; 1988 Dec 16J; 1989 Mar 29J

Levitas, Elliott 1983 Feb 23H

Levy, David 1982 Nov 3C; 1984 Feb 14C

Levy, Moshe 1982 Jun 8C; 1983 Aug 16C; 1986 May 21C

Lewinsky, Herbert 1986 Sep 2B

Lewis Jr., Andrew L. 1980 Dec 11F

Lewis, Ann 1984 Dec 8F

Lewis, Carl 1984 Aug 11J; 1985 Jan 9J

Lewis, Charles 1989 Nov 6F

Lewis, Chris 1983 Jul 2J

Lewis, Drew 1982 Apr 21H; 1983 Jan 5H

Lewis, Jerry Lee 1980 May 16J; 1986 Jan 23J

Lewis, John L. 1989 Oct 4H

Lewis, Robert 1986 Oct 7J

Lewis, Samuel 1981 Apr 22C

Liani, Dimitra 1987 Oct 23B

Liao Chengzhi 1982 Nov 20E

Libby, Willard F. 1980 Sep 8J

Liberace (Wladziu Valentino Liberace) 1982 Oct 14J; 1983 Oct 16J; 1987 Feb 4J

Liberace, George 1983 Oct 16J

Liberatore, Lou 1987 Oct 14J

Liddy, G. Gordon 1980 Apr 21F

Liendo, Horacio Tomas 1981 Nov 21D

Lifar, Serge 1986 Dec 15J

Lifland, Burton K. 1986 Dec 18H

Ligachev, Yegor K. 1987 Nov 3B; 1988 Apr 13B/Apr 20B

Ligeti, Gyorgy 1986 Nov 11J

Lightfoot, Gordon 1986 Jan 25J

Lillie, Beatrice Gladys 1989 Jan 20J

Lilly, Bob 1980 Aug 1J

Liman III, Arthur L. 1987 Jan 22F/Jul 9G/Jul 10G

Limann, Hilla 1981 Dec 31C

Limon, Rafael ("Bazooka") 1982 May 22J

Lin, Maya 1982 Nov 13G; 1989 Nov 5F

Linares, Rodolfo 1989 Apr 26F/May 18F

Lin Bao (Lin Piao) 1982 Oct 2E; 1983 Apr 30E/Jun 9E

Linder, Benjamin 1987 Aug 4G

Lindow, Steven 1986 May 13I

Lindsay, Robert 1986 Aug 10J; 1987 Jun 7J

Lindsay-Hogg, Michael 1985 Apr 21J

Lini, Walter 1988 Jul 25E/Dec 21E

Linowitz, Sol 1980 Oct 15A/Dec 7A

Liotta, Ray 1989 Apr 21J

Li Peng 1985 May 16A; 1987 Nov 24E; 1988 Jul 5E; 1989 May 25E/May 27E/Jun 8E

Lipmann, Fritz Albert 1986 Jul 24I

Lis, Bogdan 1986 Aug 11B

Lisker, Joel 1980 Jul 30F

List, Eugene 1985 Mar 1J

Lithgow, John 1988 Mar 20J; 1989 Jun 8F

Little, Sally 1980 Jun 8J

Little Richard 1986 Jan 23J

Litynski, Jan 1982 Sep 3B

Liu, Henry 1985 Jan 15E/Feb 27E/Apr 9E/Apr 19E; 1988 Mar 16F

Liuzzo, Viola 1983 May 27F

Lively, Penelope 1987 Oct 29J

Li Xiannian 1983 Jun 18E; 1985 Jul 23G

Llewellyn, Richard 1983 Nov 30J

Lloyd, Christopher 1988 Jun 22J

Lloyd, Danny 1980 May 23J

Lloyd, Emily 1988 Jan 3J

Lloyd Webber, Andrew 1980 Jun 8J; 1986 Oct 9J; 1987 Mar 15J; 1988 Jun 5J

Lo Chengxun 1983 May 15E

Lockridge, Richard 1982 Jun 19J

Loesser, Frank 1985 May 17J

Loewe, Frederick 1986 Jun 14J; 1988 Feb 14J

Loewy, Raymond Fernand 1986 Jul 14H

Logan, Joshua (Lockwood) 1988 Jul 12J

Lombardi, Ernie 1986 Aug 3J

Loncar, Budimir 1988 Feb 23B

London, Artur 1986 Nov 8B

London, George 1985 Mar 24J

London, Rusty Kent 1989 Oct 16H

Lone, John 1987 Nov 20J

Lonetree, Clayton J. 1987 May 15G/Aug 24G

Long, Cathy W. 1985 Mar 30F

Long, Clarence D. 1983 Aug 8G

Long, Donna 1988 Nov 12E

Long, Gillis W. 1985 Jan 20F/Mar 30F

Long, Huey P. 1985 Feb 25F

Long, Leo 1981 Nov 1B

Long, Russell B. 1985 Feb 25F

Longowal, Harchand Singh 1985 Jul 24E/Aug 20E

Loos, Anita 1981 Aug 18J

Lopez, Barry 1986 Nov 17J

Lopez, Nancy 1984 Aug 20J/Aug 22J; 1985 Jun 2J; 1989 May 21J/Jul 16J

Lopez Portillo, Jose 1980 May 28D/Aug 3D/Sep 1D; 1981 Jan 5D/May 12D/Jun 9D; 1982 Feb 21D/Sep 1D

Lopez Sibrian, Rodolfo Isidro 1984 Nov 28D

Lord, Bette Bao 1982 Jan 10J/Feb 7J/Mar 7J

Lord, Winston 1985 Jul 22G

Loren, Sophia 1983 Feb 12J; 1989 Dec 9J

Lorenz, Konrad Zacharias 1989 Feb 27I

Lorenzo, Frank 1989 Apr 6H/Apr 12H

Lorincz, Shlomo 1982 Jul 8C

Loring, Eugene 1982 Aug 30J

Losey, Joseph 1984 Jun 22J

Louganis, Greg 1985 Feb 18J

Louis, Joe 1981 Apr 21J

Lousma, Jack 1982 Mar 22I

Lovellette, Clyde 1988 Feb 4J

Low, George M. 1984 Jul 17I

Lowenstein, Allard K. 1980 Mar 14F

Lown, Bernard 1985 Oct 11A/Dec 10A

Loy, Myrna 1984 Mar 5J

Lozano, William E. 1989 Jan 23F/Dec 7F

Lubbers, Ruud 1985 Nov 1B/Nov 29B; 1986 May 21B/Jul 14B; 1989 May 2B/Sep 6B

Lucas, Deana 1982 Jun 11H

Lucas, George 1980 May 21J/Sep 10J; 1987 Oct 30J

Lucas, J. Anthony 1986 Apr 17J

Lucas, Jeffrey 1982 Jun 11H

Lucas, William C. 1989 May 9F/Aug 1F

Lucas Garcia, Romeo 1981 Feb 17D/May 3D

Luce, Clare Boothe 1987 Oct 9J

Luce, Henry R. 1987 Oct 9J

Lucey, Patrick J. 1980 Aug 25F

Luder, Italo 1983 Dec 6D

Luders, Rolf 1983 Jan 28D/Feb 15D

Ludlum, Robert

  best-sellers: *Aquitaine Progression* 1984 Mar 23J/Apr 20J/May 11J/Jun 15J/Jul 20J/Aug 24J; *Bourne Conspiracy* 1986 Jul 18J; *Bourne Identity* 1980 Mar 9J/Apr 6J/May 4J/Jun 8J/Jul 13J/Aug 17J; *Bourne Supremacy* 1986 Mar 28J/Apr 25J/May 30J/Jun 27J; *Icarus Agenda* 1988 Mar 25J/Apr 29J/May 27J/Jun 24J/Jul 23J; *Parsifal Mosaic* 1982 Apr 11J/May 9J/Jun 6J/Jul 11J/Aug 8J

Ludwig, Klaus 1985 Jun 16J

Luedtke, Kurt 1985 Dec 18J

Luers, William H. 1985 Nov 13J

Lufti, Ali 1985 Sep 4C

Lugar, Richard G. 1982 Dec 2F

Lujan, Jorge 1982 Jan 16J

Lujan Jr., Manuel 1988 Dec 22F; 1989 Feb 2H/Nov 29H

Lukas, D. Wayne 1987 Jan 30J

Lukas, J. Anthony 1985 Nov 21J; 1986 Feb 17J

Lukens, Donald E. ("Buz") 1989 May 26F

Luly, Mohammed Mahmoud Ould 1980 Jan 4C

Lunceford, Jimmie 1988 May 27J

Lund, Mary 1985 Dec 19I; 1986 Jan 2I

Lunt, Alfred 1983 Jul 30J

Lupone, Patti 1980 Jun 8J

Lurie, Alison 1985 Apr 24J

Lusinchi, Jaime 1983 Dec 4D; 1984 Feb 2D/May 27D; 1987 Apr 11D

Luther, Martin 1983 Nov 10J

Lyakhov, Vladimir 1983 Nov 23I; 1988 Sep 7I

Lyle, Graham 1985 Feb 26J

Lyle, Sandy 1985 Jul 21J; 1988 Apr 10J

Lynch, David 1986 Sep 19J; 1987 Jan 4J

Lynch, Kevin 1981 Aug 1B

Lyne, Adrian 1987 Sep 18J

Lyng, Richard E. 1986 Jan 29H/Mar 28H; 1987 Apr 30H

Lynn, Fred 1980 Dec 6J

M

Maazel, Lorin 1986 Sep 11J

MacArthur, Douglas 1988 Oct 17J

MacArthur, Jean Faircloth 1988 Oct 17J

MacArthur, Roderick J. 1984 Dec 15J

MacBride, Sean 1988 Jan 15B

Macchio, Ralph 1986 May 18J

MacDonald, Dwight 1982 Dec 19J

MacDonald, Jeffrey R. 1982 Mar 31J; 1987 Aug 21J/Nov 23J

MacDonald, John D. 1981 May 10J/May 24J/Jul 5J; 1982 Aug 8J; 1986 Dec 28J

MacDonald, Peter 1986 Nov 4F

MacDonald, Ross 1983 Jul 11J

MacDowell, Andie 1989 Aug 4J

MacEachen, Allan J. 1981 Apr 23D; 1982 Jun 28D/Oct 24D

MacGuigan, Mark 1980 Apr 22J; 1981 Jan 22D

MacGuire, Wayne Richard 1986 Aug 21C/Dec 18C

Machel, Samora M. 1980 Mar 18C; 1986 Oct 19C; 1987 Jun 29C

MacInnis, Al 1989 May 25J

MacKay, Lizbeth 1981 Nov 4J

MacKellar, Michael 1981 Feb 14E; 1982 Apr 19E

Mackin, Catherine 1982 Nov 20J

MacLachlan, Kyle 1986 Sep 19J

MacLachlan, Patricia 1986 Jan 20J

MacLaine, Shirley 1983 Nov 23J; 1984 Apr 9J

MacLean, Alistair (Stuart) 1987 Feb 2J

Maclean, Donald 1983 Mar 6B/Mar 26B; 1988 May 11B

MacLeish, Archibald 1982 Apr 20J

MacLeod, Lord 1989 Mar 7J

MacMichael, David 1984 Jun 12G

Macmillan, (Maurice) Harold (Earl of Stockton) 1986 Dec 29B; 1988 Jan 1B

Macomber, William B. 1985 Nov 13J

MacQueen, Robert M. 1985 Sep 20G

MacRae, Gordon 1986 Jan 24J

Madani, Ahmad 1980 Jan 25C

Madani, Ayatollah Assadollah 1981 Sep 11C

Madigan, Amy 1989 Apr 21J

Madonna (Madonna Louise Ciccone)

  as actress: 1985 Mar 29J; 1988 May 3J

  best-sellers: *Like A Prayer* 1989 Apr 29J/May 27J/Jun 24J; *Like a Virgin* 1984 Dec 22J; 1985 Jan 26J/Feb 23J; *True Blue* 1986 Aug 13J/Sep 17J

  personal issues: marriage 1985 Aug 16J

Madrazo, Ignacio 1988 Jan 7I

Magana, Alvaro Alfredo 1982 Apr 29D/May 2D/Oct 28D; 1983 Jun 18G/Aug 19D

Magee, John 1981 Apr 29B

Magee, Patrick (actor) 1982 Aug 14J

Magee, Patrick J. (terrorist) 1986 Jun 10B

Magnuson, Warren Grant 1989 May 20F

Magruder, Jeb Stuart 1983 May 14F

Ma Haide 1986 Sep 22I

Mahathir bin Mohamad 1984 Jul 15E; 1986 Aug 3E; 1987 Apr 24E

Mahdi, Sadiq al- 1988 Dec 20C; 1989 Mar 9C/Jun 30C

Mahfouz, Naguib 1988 Oct 13J; 1989 May 3C

Mahindra, Keshub 1984 Dec 7E

Mahler, Margaret 1985 Oct 2I

Mahmood Iskander, Sultan 1984 Feb 9E

Mahoney, John 1986 Mar 19J

Mahoney, Larry W. 1989 Dec 21F

Mahre, Phil 1982 Jan 24J

Mailer, Norman 1980 Jan 13J/Apr 14J; 1981 Sep 23F; 1983 Feb 12J/Aug 2J; 1984 Dec 7J

Majano, Adolfo Arnoldo 1980 Aug 31D; 1981 Oct 12D

Major, John 1989 Jul 24B/Oct 26B

Makarov, Oleg 1980 Nov 27I

Makarova, Natalia 1982 Dec 18J; 1983 Jun 5J; 1988 Aug 6J; 1989 Jan 18J

Malamud, Bernard 1986 Mar 18J

Malan, Magnus 1988 Mar 6C

Malden, Karl 1984 Jul 1J

Malenkov, Georgi Maximilianovich 1988 Feb 1B

Malile, Reis 1988 Feb 23B

Malina, Judith 1985 Sep 14J

Malkovich, John 1987 Oct 14J; 1988 Dec 21J

Malle, Louis 1987 Sep 9J; 1988 Feb 12J; 1989 Mar 19J

Mallick, George A. 1987 Aug 5F

Malloy, Edward A. 1986 Nov 14F

Malone, James L. 1986 Oct 15G

Malone, James William 1983 Nov 15J; 1985 Sep 15J

Malone, Karl 1989 Feb 12J

Malone, Moses 1983 May 31J

Malraux, Andre 1983 Jun 3J

Maltz, Albert 1985 Apr 26J

Maluf, Paulo Salim 1985 Jan 15D

Mamby, Saul 1982 Jun 26J

Mamet, David 1984 Mar 25J/Apr 16J; 1987 Jun 3J; 1988 May 3J

Mamoulian, Rouben (Zachary) 1987 Dec 4J

Manarov, Musa 1988 Dec 21I

Manatt, Charles T. 1981 May 5F; 1983 Jan 6F; 1984 Apr 23F

Manchester, Melissa 1983 Feb 23J

Mancini, Ray ("Boom Boom") 1982 Nov 13J/Nov 17J; 1985 Aug 22J

Mandel, Marvin 1987 Nov 12F

Mandela, Nelson

  peace initiatives: terms set 1985 Jan 27C; Botha meeting 1989 Jul 5C; de Klerk meeting 1989 Dec 13C

  personal issues: birthday celebrations 1988 Jun 11J/Jul 15C; wife denounced 1989 Feb 16C

  prison release issue: release offer rejected 1985 Feb 28C; demonstrations 1985 Aug 28C; release terms set 1986 Jan 31C; polls 1986 Aug 3C; Mbeki test case 1987 Nov 5C; release hinted 1988 Aug 18C; moved to guarded house 1988 Dec 7C; release negotiated 1989 Oct 14C

Mandela, Winnie 1985 Dec 3C/Dec 22C; 1986 Apr 2C; 1988 Jul 15C; 1989 Feb 15C/Feb 16C

Mandlikova, Hana 1980 Sep 6J; 1981 Jun 6J/Jul 3J; 1982 Sep 11J; 1985 Sep 7J; 1986 Jul 5J; 1987 Jan 24J

Mangope, Lucas 1988 Feb 10C

Manigat, Leslie F. 1988 Jan 17D/Feb 7D/Feb 9D/Jun 20D

Manion, Daniel A. 1986 Jul 23F

Mankiller, Wilma 1985 Dec 14F

Manley, Michael 1980 Jan 15D/Mar 25D/Oct 30D; 1986 Jul 29D; 1989 Feb 9D

Mann, Barry 1988 Mar 2J

Mann, Herbie 1983 Sep 15J

Mann, Jonathan 1987 Feb 13I

Mann, Thomas 1984 Aug 11J

Manning, Danny 1988 Apr 4J

Manning, Thomas W. 1987 Jan 18F

Manotoc, Tommy 1982 Jan 3E/Feb 9E

Mansell, Nigel 1986 Jun 15J/Jul 13J/Jul 16J; 1987 May 3J/Jul 5J/Jul 12J/Nov 1J; 1989 Mar 26J

Mansfield, Mike 1981 Jan 7G

Manson, Charles 1987 Dec 25F

Mantegna, Andrea 1985 Apr 18J

Mantegna, Joe 1988 May 3J

Mantle, Mickey 1985 Mar 18J

Mantovani, Annunzio Paolo 1980 Mar 29J

Manville, Lesley 1987 Mar 21J

Mao Zedong 1980 Aug 11E; 1981 Jun 30E/Aug 20E; 1982 Oct 2E; 1983 Apr 30E/Dec 26E

Mapplethorpe, Robert 1989 Mar 9J/Jun 13J/Jul 20J/Dec 18J

Mara, Sir Kamisese 1982 Jul 10E
Maravich, Pete 1987 Feb 5J; 1988 Jan 5J
Marchais, Georges 1982 Feb 7B
Marchenko, Anatoly T. 1986 Dec 8B
Marcinkus, Paul 1982 Jul 30B; 1984 Apr 1B; 1987 Feb 26B/Jul 17B
Marcos, Ferdinand E.
  Aquino assassination: 1983 Aug 24E/Aug 27E/Sep 12E/Oct 22E; 1985 Dec 2E-3E
  civil strife: rebel priests warned 1982 Nov 28E; terrorism decrees repealed 1983 Aug 5E; Moslem separatists 1983 Oct 8E
  corruption issues
    in Philippines: assets recovery sought 1986 Mar 1E/Dec 29E; embezzlement charged 1986 Apr 16E; partial funds recovery 1987 Mar 15E; suits filed 1987 Jul 21E; trial starts 1989 Sep 7E
    in Switzerland: assets frozen 1986 Mar 25E; Khashoggi extradited to U.S. 1989 Jul 19J
    in U.S.: documents disputed 1986 Mar 13E/Mar 20E; customs seizure upheld 1987 Jun 26F; indicted 1988 Oct 21F; new charges filed 1989 Mar 10F; trial delay sought 1989 Apr 6F; Khashoggi extradited 1989 Jul 19J; liable in '81 murder 1989 Dec 15E
  foreign policy: Chile snubbed 1980 Mar 22A
  government: election fraud 1980 Feb 11E; opposition groups 1980 Aug 29E; 1982 Feb 14E; 1984 Dec 26E; martial law lifted 1981 Jan 17E; legislature opened 1981 Jan 19E; constitutional amendments approved 1981 Apr 7E; re-elected president 1981 Jun 16E; communist party 1982 Feb 28E/Mar 6E; supreme court 1982 May 10E/May 14E; 1985 Nov 19E; death penalty decree 1983 May 16E; opposition demonstrations 1983 Sep 22E-23E/Oct 2E; 1985 Oct 21E; cabinet changes 1984 May 18E/Jun 30E; assembly elections 1984 May 23E; Climaco assassination probe 1984 Nov 14E; impeachment effort 1985 Aug 13E; martial law anniversary 1985 Sep 21E; presidential elections 1985 Nov 3E/Nov14E/Dec 11E; 1986 Feb 7E/Feb 13E/Feb 16E/Feb 22E
  loyalists: demonstrations 1986 Apr 16E/Oct 26E; coup attempts 1986 Jul 7E/Sep 1E; 1987 Jan 28E/Feb 25E/Jul 9E
  monetary policy: IMF loan terms 1984 Oct 13E; 1985 Nov 18E
  ouster and exile: flees 1986 Feb 25E; arrives in U.S. 1986 Feb 26E; return forbidden 1988 May 4E
  personal issues: son-in-law kidnapped 1982 Jan 3E/Feb 9E; death 1989 Sep 28E; funeral 1989 Oct 15E
  U.S. policy: 1985 Oct 12G/Nov 1G
Marcos, Imelda 1983 May 17E; 1984 Jun 30E; 1985 Aug 13E; 1986 Mar 20E/Apr 16E/Dec 29E; 1988 Oct 31F; 1989 Jul 19J/Sep 7E/Dec 15E
Margolies, Irwin M. 1984 May 31F
Margolyes, Miriam 1988 Oct 21J
Margrethe II, Queen (Denmark) 1987 Sep 10B; 1988 Jun 7B
Mariategui, Sandro 1984 Apr 9D/Jun 5D

Marin, Jose 1980 Jun 25D
Marino, Dan 1984 Dec 20J
Maris, Roger 1985 Dec 14J
Markey, Lucille Parker 1982 Jul 25J
Markham, Beryl 1986 Aug 3J
Markovic, Ante 1989 Jan 19B
Markowitz, Mitch 1987 Dec 23J
Marley, Bob 1981 May 11J
Marr, Marvin 1983 Nov 18J
Marriott Sr., J. Willard 1988 Oct 17J
Mars, Forrest 1989 Sep 11J
Marshall, Penny 1988 Jun 3J
Marshall, Ray 1980 Jan 16H/Sep 8H
Marshall, Thurgood 1987 May 6F/Sep 8F
Martens, Wilfried 1980 Mar 24B/Oct 4B; 1981 Dec 17B; 1985 Jul 16B/Nov 28B; 1987 Oct 21B/Dec 13B; 1988 May 9B; 1989 Jan 14A
Martin, Billy (Alfred Manuel) 1989 Dec 25J
Martin, Cindy 1989 Dec 3I
Martin, David H. 1987 Jun 30F
Martin, Dean 1984 Dec 24J; 1988 Mar 13J
Martin, John 1985 May 19J
Martin, Lynn 1989 Nov 14F
Martin, Mary 1982 Sep 5J
Martin, Preston 1983 Jun 1H; 1986 May 12H
Martin, Steve 1987 Jun 19J; 1988 Jan 3J
Martinez, Bob 1989 Oct 10F
Martinez, Eugenio R. 1983 May 14F
Martinez, Julie 1980 Jan 12I
Martinez, Victor 1985 May 2D
Martinez de Hoz, Jose Alfredo 1980 Jul 11D
Martinez Romero, Eduardo 1989 Sep 6D
Martins, Peter 1983 Mar 16J/Dec 6J
Marvin, Lee 1987 Aug 29J
Marvin, Michelle Triola 1987 Aug 29J
Marx, Richard 1989 Aug 26J/Sep 30J
Masire, Quett 1980 Jul 18C
Mason, Curtis 1984 Mar 26F
Mason, Marshall W. 1987 Oct 14J
Mason, Richard 1988 May 12J
Masri, Zafir al- 1986 Mar 2C
Mass, Joachen 1989 Jun 11J
Masse, Marcel 1986 Sep 8D
Masselli, Nathan 1982 Aug 25F
Massera, Emilio 1981 Jul 14D; 1983 Aug 21D
Massey, Raymond 1983 Jul 29J
Massie, Jacques 1981 Jul 18B/Jul 26B
Massing, Hede 1981 Mar 8F
Masson, Jeffrey Moussaieff 1981 Nov 5I
Massoud, Ahmad Shah 1984 Jul 13C/Aug 27C
Masterkov, Lem 1987 May 8A
Masterson, Peter 1985 Dec 20J
Masvidal, Raul 1985 Nov 5F
Mathias, Bob 1980 Jul 26J
Matlin, Marlee 1986 Oct 3J; 1987 Mar 30J
Matlock Jr., Jack F. 1987 Apr 2G
Matlovich, Leonard 1980 Nov 24G
Matsushita, Konosuke 1989 Apr 27E
Matta Ballesteros, Juan Ramon 1988 Apr 8D
Matthias, Charles 1981 Sep 5A
Mattingly, Don 1985 Nov 20J
Mattox, Jim 1983 Oct 31F; 1984 Apr 14F
Matuzok, Vasily Yakovlevich 1984 Nov 23E
Maung Maung 1988 Aug 19E/Sep 18E
Mauroy, Pierre 1981 Jun 23B/Jul 8B; 1982 Feb 11B; 1984 Apr 11B
Maury-Laribiere, Michel 1980 Jul 9B
Maxwell, Cedric ("Cornbread") 1981 May 14J
Mayberry, W. Eugene 1987 Sep 14F/Oct 7F

Mayekiso, Moses 1989 Apr 24C
Mayer, Norman D. 1982 Dec 8G
Mayhew, Patrick 1988 Jan 25B
Maynard, Clement T. 1982 Nov 13D
Maynard, Don 1987 Jan 27J/Aug 8J
Maynard, Robert C. 1983 Apr 30J
Mayor Zaragoza, Federico 1987 Oct 18A
Mays, Benjamin E. 1984 Mar 28J
Mays, Kimberly Michelle 1989 Nov 20F
Mays, Willie 1985 Mar 18J
Maysles, Albert 1987 Jan 3J
Maysles, David (Peter) 1987 Jan 3J
Mazankowski, Donald 1986 Feb 16B/Dec 12D
Mazowiecki, Tadeusz 1989 Aug 24B/Sep 12B
Mazzoli, Romano L. 1982 Mar 17F
Mbeki, Govan 1987 Nov 5C
M'Bow, Amadou-Mahtar 1984 Mar 14A; 1987 Oct 18A
McAlpine, Stephen 1989 Mar 28H
McAnuff, Des 1985 Apr 25J/Jun 2J
McArtor, T. Allan 1987 Jul 27H
McAuliffe, Sharon Christa 1985 Jul 19I; 1986 Dec 29I
McCadam, Scott 1985 Aug 17J
McCain, John 1989 Oct 13F/Dec 22F
McCall, Tom 1983 Jan 8H
McCandless, Bruce 1984 Feb 7I
McCann, Donal 1987 Dec 17J
McCarron, Chris 1987 May 2J
McCarthy, Joseph R. 1983 Jan 31F/Sep 11J; 1986 Jun 24F/Aug 2F; 1988 Dec 14F
McCarthy, Mary Therese 1983 Feb 12J; 1989 Oct 25J
McCarthy, Michael R.P. 1986 Apr 24J
McCarthy, Sheila 1988 Mar 22J
McCarthy, William J. 1988 Jul 15F
McCartney, Forrest S. 1986 Aug 20I
McCartney, Paul 1980 Jul 9J; 1982 Jun 16J; 1985 Feb 24J/Aug 15J
McClanahan, Rue 1987 Sep 20J
McClellan, Irina Astakova 1986 Jan 30F
McClelland, James 1986 Jan 10E
McClintock, Barbara 1983 Oct 10I
McCloskey, Frank 1985 May 1F
McCloskey, Paul 1982 Jul 25C
McCloy, John J(ay) 1989 Mar 11G
McClure, Jessica 1987 Oct 16J
McClurg, Patricia Ann 1987 Nov 5J
McCord, James I. 1986 Feb 26J
McCormack, John 1980 Nov 22F
McCormick, Frank 1982 Nov 21J
McCovey, Willie 1986 Jan 8J/Aug 3J
McCoy, Andre 1980 Mar 14J
McCraw, Thomas K. 1985 Apr 24J
McCree Jr., Wade Hampton 1987 Aug 30J
McCreesh, Raymond 1981 May 21B
McCrory, Milton 1983 Mar 19J
McCullers, Carson 1985 Dec 27J
McCullough, Colleen
  best-sellers: Indecent Obsession 1981 Nov 8J/Dec 6J; 1982 Jan 10J/Feb 7J/Mar 7J/Apr 11J; Ladies of Missalonghi 1987 May 29J
McDermott, Bobby 1988 Feb 4J
McDonald, Allan 1986 May 13I
McDonald, David 1980 Apr 20D
McDonnell Jr., James S. 1980 Aug 22J
McDonnell, Joseph 1981 Jul 10B
McDormand, Frances 1988 Dec 9J
McDougall, Barbara 1988 Dec 28D
McDougall, Walter A. 1986 Apr 17J
McDowell, Michael 1988 Mar 30J
McEachern, Allan 1988 Mar 7D
McElwee, Thomas 1981 Aug 8B
McEnroe, John
  Davis Cup: 1981 Dec 13J
  U.S. Open: 1980 Sep 7J; 1981 Sep 13J; 1984 Sep 9J; 1985 Sep 8J

  Wimbledon: 1980 Jul 6J; 1981 Jul 4J; 1982 Jul 4J; 1983 Jul 2J; 1984 Jul 8J
McFarlane, Robert C.
  government service: national security adviser 1983 Oct 17G; 1985 Dec 4G
  Iran-Contra arms scandal: Teheran visit 1986 Nov 3C/Nov 6G; testimony 1986 Dec 1F; 1987 May 11G/Jul 14G; memos to North 1987 Jun 9G; accusations against 1987 Jul 23G; guilty plea 1988 Mar 11F; sentencing 1989 Mar 3F
  Mideast negotiations: 1983 Jul 22G/Jul 26C/Aug 1C/Aug 4C
  personal issues: suicide attempt 1987 Feb 9G
McFerrin, Bobby 1988 Oct 29J; 1989 Feb 22J
McGarr, Frank 1988 Jan 11H
McGee, Willie 1985 Nov 18J
McGhee, Brownie 1986 Oct 19J
McGill, William J. 1980 Jan 7J
McGillis, Kelly 1985 Feb 8J; 1986 May 16J; 1988 Oct 14J
McGinniss, Joe 1984 Nov 28J; 1987 Aug 21J/Nov 23J
McGlinchey, Dominic 1984 Mar 17B; 1985 Oct 9B/Oct 18B
McGovern, George 1982 Jan 15F; 1983 Oct 2F; 1984 Jan 15F/Feb 11F/Mar 14F
McGovern, Walter T. 1986 Feb 6F
McGrath, J. Paul 1984 Feb 15H
McGuinn, Warner T. 1985 Mar 14J
McGwire, Mark 1987 Nov 3J
McIlrath, Donald 1987 Oct 17F
McInnes, Stewart 1986 Mar 25D
McIntyre, Richard 1985 May 1F
McKay, James C. 1988 Apr 1F/Jul 5F/Jul 18F; 1989 Sep 8F
McKellen, Ian 1981 Jun 7J
McKeown, Charles 1985 Dec 14J
McKeown, Laurence 1981 Sep 6B
McKinley, Robin 1985 Jan 7J
McKinney, Tamara 1989 Feb 22J
McKnight, William 1989 Feb 1D/Jul 10D
McLaughlin, Ann Dore 1987 Nov 3H/Dec 11F/Dec 17F
McMillan, Thomas 1986 May 14D
McMurtry, Larry 1985 Aug 16J; 1986 Apr 17J; 1987 May 29J; 1988 Nov 25J
McNair, Ronald E. 1987 May 7I
McNamara, Robert S. 1980 Oct 3A; 1981 Jul 1A; 1982 Apr 7G; 1989 Dec 12G
McPherson, Ardith 1987 Jun 24F
McPherson, James M. 1989 Mar 30J
McPherson, Peter 1983 Nov 4G
McQueen, Steve 1980 Nov 7J
McTiernan, John 1987 Jun 12J; 1988 Jul 15J
Mead, Margaret 1980 Jul 4I; 1983 Jan 31I
Meany, George 1980 Jan 10H
Mears, Rick 1982 May 15J/May 30J; 1986 May 31J; 1988 May 29J
Mecham, Evan
  King holiday controversy: 1986 Nov 5F; 1987 Jan 4F
  political corruption: recall election 1987 Jul 6F/Nov 2F; 1988 Apr 12F; indicted 1988 Jan 8F; impeached 1988 Jan 20F/Feb 5F; convicted on misconduct 1988 Apr 4F; acquitted on campaign loan 1988 Jun 16F
Mecham, Willard 1988 Jun 16F
Mecir, Miloslav 1986 Sep 7J
Medawar, Peter (Brian) 1985 Aug 31I; 1987 Oct 2I
Medina Perez, Carlos 1988 Sep 13B
Medoff, Mark 1980 Jun 8J; 1986 Oct 3J
Meese III, Edwin A.

  ethics issues: independent counsel 1984 Mar 27F/Sep 20F; government contracts 1985 Jun 3F; legal fees awarded 1985 Jun 7F; Ethics office scores 1987 Jun 30F; 1988 Sep 12F; top aides quit 1988 Mar 29F; independent prosecutor 1988 Apr 1F/Jul 5F/Jul 6F; wife's conflict of interest 1988 Apr 13F; Senate hearings 1988 Jul 26F-27F; Justice report scores 1989 Jan 17F
  foreign policy: Cuba aid warning 1981 Feb 22G; Mexico "drug" apology 1986 May 22G; Turks/Caicos bank pact 1986 Sep 18F; Paris anti-terror meeting 1987 May 28A; Nicaragua immigration rules 1987 Jul 8F; PLO office closing 1988 Mar 11G
  government service: named attorney general 1984 Jan 22F; confirmation hearings 1984 Mar 6F/Dec 18F; 1985 Feb 5F; confirmed 1985 Feb 23F; named domestic council head 1985 Apr 11F; resigns as attorney general 1988 Jul 5F
  Iran-Contra arms scandal: 1986 Dec 19F; 1987 Feb 24G/Jul 29G
  judicial issues: CIA domestic surveillance 1981 Mar 17F; constitutional interpretation 1985 Oct 12F/Oct 25F/Nov 15F; Miranda rule 1985 Oct 14F; antitrust exemption 1988 Aug 17H
  Wedtech scandal: 1987 May 11F/Jun 30F/Jul 9F/Dec 22F; 1989 Aug 8F
Meese, Ursula 1988 Apr 13F
Mehta, Zubin 1988 Nov 2J
Meier, Richard 1983 Feb 19J
Mejia Victores, Oscar Humberto 1983 Aug 7D/Aug 8D/Aug 8G; 1985 Apr 12D
Mekonnen, Abebe 1989 Apr 17J
Melancia, Carlos 1987 Jul 9E
Mellencamp, John Cougar 1982 Aug 18J/Sep 22J/Oct 13J; 1985 Oct 26J/Nov 30J/Dec 21J; 1986 Jan 29J/Mar 22J
Melnick, Bruce E. 1987 Jun 5I
Melton, Richard H. 1988 Jul 11D
Meltzer, Clyde 1984 Dec 17H
Melyanov, Vasif 1988 Dec 12B
Menard, William Henry 1986 Feb 9I
Mendel, Gregor 1988 Mar 3I
Mendes Filho, Francisco 1988 Dec 22D; 1989 Jan 7D
Menem, Carlos Saul
  economic policy: emergency bill 1989 Aug 31D; IMF loan 1989 Sep 27D
  Falklands policy: 1989 Jul 12D/Sep 23D/Sep 25D/Oct 7D
  government: Argentine president 1989 May 14D/May 23D/Jun 12D/Jul 8D; "dirty war" pardons 1989 Sep 23D/Oct 7D
Menendez, Mario Benjamin 1982 Apr 4D/Apr 7D/Jun 14D/Jun 16D
Menendez, Ramon 1988 Mar 18J
Mengele, Josef 1985 Feb 6G/Jun 21A
Mengistu, Haile Mariam 1980 Dec 4C; 1984 Jan 13C; 1987 Feb 22C/Sep 10C; 1989 May 20C
Mennin, Peter 1983 Jun 17J
Menotti, Gian Carlo 1986 Nov 15J
Merbah, Kasdi 1989 Sep 9C
Mercer, Mabel 1984 Jan 31J/Apr 20J
Merchant, Ismail 1986 Mar 7J
Mercouri, Melina 1983 Aug 31J
Meredith, William 1988 Mar 31J
Merman, Ethel 1984 Feb 15J
Merrifield, Robert Bruce 1984 Oct 17I
Messerer, Mikhail 1980 Feb 5J

Messerer, Sulamith 1980 Feb 5J
Messmer, Otto 1983 Oct 28J
Messner, Zbigniew 1985 Nov 6B; 1987 Oct 10B/Dec 15B; 1988 Sep 19B/Sep 27B
Mestiri, Ahmed 1986 Apr 22C
Meyer, Edward C. 1983 Jun 9G
Meyer, Irwin 1982 Jan 20J
Meyer, Mary 1980 Jan 4I
Michael, George
best-sellers: Faith 1987 Dec 26J; 1988 Jan 23J/Feb 20J/Mar 19J/Apr 23J/May 21J/Jun 18J/Jul 16J; 1989 Feb 22J
Michaux, Henri 1984 Oct 18J
Michel, Hartmut 1988 Oct 19I
Michel, Robert H. 1980 Dec 8F; 1983 Dec 29G; 1987 Jan 6F/Sep 23G; 1989 Jan 3F
Michelsen Nino, Camila 1987 Jul 30D
Michelsen Uribe, Jaime 1987 Jul 30D
Michener, James A.
best-sellers: Alaska 1988 Jul 23J/Aug 26J/Sep 30J/Oct 21J/Dec 23J; Caribbean 1989 Dec 1J/Dec 22J; Covenant 1980 Dec 7J; 1981 Jan 11J/Feb 8J/Mar 8J/Apr 12J; 1987 Dec 7J; Legacy 1987 Sep 23J; Poland 1983 Sep 11J/Oct 16J/Nov 13J/Dec 18J; 1984 Jan 20J/Feb 10J; Space 1982 Oct 17J/Nov 14J/Dec 12J; 1983 Jan 16J/Feb 13J/Mar 13J
Texas 1985 Oct 25J/Nov 22J/Dec 20J; 1986 Jan 31J
Michiko, Empress (Japan) 1989 Aug 4E
Michnik, Adam 1981 Jan 8B; 1982 Sep 3B; 1986 Aug 11B
Midler, Bette 1983 Dec 18J; 1989 Oct 30J
Mieske, Kenneth M. 1989 May 2F
Mies van der Rohe, Ludwig 1986 Jun 2J
Mijatovik, Cvijetin 1980 Jun 24B
Mikhailov, Valerian 1984 Apr 19B
Mikulic, Branko 1986 Jan 6B; 1988 Dec 30B
Mikulski, Barbara 1986 Sep 9F
Milena, Queen (Montenegro) 1989 Sep 30B
Miles, Sarah 1987 Oct 16J
Milgram, Stanley 1984 Dec 20I
Milk, Harvey 1985 Oct 21F
Milken, Michael R. 1988 Sep 7H; 1989 Mar 29H
Milland, Ray (Reginald Truscott-Jones) 1986 Mar 10J
Miller, Alice 1985 Jun 2J
Miller, Barry 1985 Mar 28J
Miller, Betty 1987 Sep 18J
Miller, G. William 1980 Feb 8F/Oct 8A/Dec 2H
Miller, George 1985 Feb 12G; 1986 Feb 9F
Miller, Glenn 1985 Sep 6J
Miller, Henry 1980 Jun 7J
Miller III, James C. 1981 Oct 26H; 1982 Mar 18H; 1985 Jul 19H/Dec 12H; 1987 Apr 3H/Jul 16H; 1988 Jan 4H
Miller, Johnny 1981 Apr 12J
Miller, Merle 1986 Jun 10J
Miller, Ralph 1988 Feb 4J
Miller, Richard R. 1987 May 6F
Miller, Richard W. 1984 Oct 3G/Nov 13G; 1986 Jun 19G/Jul 14G
Miller, Roger 1985 Apr 25J
Miller, William G. 1980 May 10H
Millet, Kate 1983 Feb 12J
Mills, Irving 1985 Apr 21J
Milosevic, Slobodan 1988 Oct 6B/Nov 19B; 1989 May 8B
Milosz, Czeslaw 1980 Oct 9J
Milson, Menachem 1982 Mar 26C
Milstein, Cesar 1984 Oct 15I
Minnelli, Liza 1986 Jul 25J
Minnelli, Vincente 1986 Jul 25J

Minter, Alan 1980 Sep 27J
Mintoff, Dom 1981 Dec 12B/Dec 19B; 1984 Oct 4B
Miro, Joan 1983 Dec 25J
Mirsalim, Mostafa 1980 Jul 26C
Mishima, Yukio 1985 Dec 27J
Mitchell, Clarence M. 1984 Mar 18J
Mitchell, Felix Wayne 1986 Aug 29F
Mitchell, George (musician) 1988 Nov 26J
Mitchell, George J. (politician) 1987 Aug 12G; 1988 Oct 4H/Nov 19F
Mitchell, James 1984 Jul 25D
Mitchell, John Newton 1988 Nov 9F
Mitchell, Kevin 1989 Nov 21J
Mitchell, Margaret 1988 Apr 25J
Mitchelson, Marvin M. 1982 Mar 16J
Mitnick, Kevin D. 1988 Dec 22H
Mitscherlich, Alexander 1982 Jun 26I
Mitterrand, Francois
African policy: Chad 1983 Aug 16B/Aug 18G/Aug 25A; 1984 Sep 20A/Nov 16C; Zaire 1982 Oct 8A; 1984 Sep 20A
arms control: neutron bomb 1982 Oct 15B; medium-range A-arms 1983 Jan 20B; A-tests 1983 Jun 9A; intermediate-range A-arms 1983 Sep 28A; West German summit 1986 Feb 28B; UK summit 1986 Nov 21B
Asian and Pacific Rim policy: Australia 1983 Jun 9A
ceremonial duties: D-Day anniversary 1984 Jun 6A; Musee d'Orsay opening 1986 Dec 1J; Riviera fire tour 1986 Aug 7I; World War I ceremony 1984 Sep 22B
economic policy: minimum wage 1981 Jun 3B; growth program 1981 Aug 19B; energy exploration 1981 Oct 24A; austerity policies 1983 Jun 8B; self-criticism 1983 Jul 8B; state-owned companies 1986 Jul 14B; working hours 1986 Dec 20B
English Channel tunnel: 1987 Jul 29B
European policy: Great Britain 1981 Oct 11B; 1986 Nov 21B; 1987 Jul 29B; Napoleon's debt 1984 May 19B; New Caledonia 1985 Jan 19A; Soviet Union 1984 Jun 23B; Switzerland 1984 May 19B; West Germany 1981 Jul 12B; 1982 Jan 13B; 1983 Jan 20B; 1984 Sep 22B; 1986 Feb 28B/Oct 28B; 1988 Jan 22B
foreign policy: Canada 1987 May 25D; developing countries 1981 Sep 1A; G-7 summits 1982 Jun 5B; 1985 May 4A; 1986 May 6A; 1987 Jun 8A; UN 1981 Sep 1A; 1983 Sep 28A
government: presidential nomination 1980 Nov 8B; presidential election 1981 Jun 24B/Apr 26B/May 10B; 1986 Oct 13B; 1988 Jan 7B/Apr 24B; inaugurated French president 1981 May 21B; "cohabitation" with conservatives 1986 Oct 13B; parliamentary elections 1988 May 14B/Jun 5B/Jun 12B
Mideast policy: Egypt 1981 Oct 6A; Israel 1982 Mar 3C/Nov 25C; Lebanon 1982 Oct 20B; 1983 Oct 24C; 1988 May 4C; Libya 1983 Aug 16B; 1984 Nov 16C; PLO 1982 Nov 25C; 1989 May 2B; Sinai 1981 Oct 19A
U.S. policy: 1981 Jun 24B/Oct 18A; 1982 Mar 12A; 1983 May 18B/Aug 18G; 1984 Mar 21G
Miyaoka, Yoichi 1988 Jun 3I
Miyazawa, Kiichi 1987 Jan 21A

Mize, Johnny 1981 Aug 2J
Mize, Larry 1987 Apr 12J
Mladenov, Petar 1988 Feb 23B; 1989 Nov 10B
Moawad, Rene 1989 Nov 5C/Nov 22C/Nov 24C/Dec 6C
Mobutu Sese Seko 1982 May 13C/May 14A/Oct 8A; 1984 Jul 29C/Sep 20A; 1985 Jun 21C; 1989 Jan 14A/Oct 5C
Modai, Yitzhak 1986 Apr 13C
Modigliani, Franco 1985 Oct 15J
Modine, Matthew 1987 Jun 26J
Modrow, Hans 1989 Nov 13B
Modzelewski, Karol 1981 Feb 16B
Moffet, John 1985 Aug 18J
Moffett, D.W. 1985 Apr 21J
Moffett, Toby 1982 Apr 17G
Mofford, Rose 1988 Apr 4F/Apr 12F; 1989 Sep 22F
Mohieddin, Ahmed Fuad 1982 Jan 2C/Feb 20C
Mohmand, Abdul Ahad 1988 Sep 7I
Moi, Daniel T. Arap 1980 Dec 4C; 1982 May 20C/Aug 1C; 1983 May 17C; 1987 Dec 28C; 1988 Feb 5C/Mar 21C/Jul 18C
Mojaddidi, Sibghatullah 1989 Feb 23E
Mojsov, Lazar 1988 May 15B
Mokae, Zakes 1989 Sep 20J
Molina, Alfred 1987 Mar 21J
Molinari, Guy V. 1983 Mar 3H
Molinari, John 1987 Dec 8F
Moloise, Benjamin 1985 Oct 18C
Molotov, Vyacheslav M(ikhailovich) 1986 Nov 8B
Momoh, Joseph 1985 Oct 5C; 1987 Mar 23C
Momper, Walter 1989 Nov 9B
Moncrief, Basil 1987 Jul 27G
Mondale, Walter F.
economic policy: taxes 1984 Aug 4F/Aug 12F; budget plan 1984 Sep 10F
foreign policy: Latin policy attacks 1983 Jun 19F; Gromyko meeting 1984 Sep 16F/Sep 27G
presidential campaign (1980): debates 1980 Jan 12F; renominated vice president 1980 Aug 14F
presidential campaign (1984)
Black Americans: 1983 Jul 15F
California convention: 1983 Jan 15F
campaign trail 1984 Aug 2F/Sep 3F
candidacy: 1983 Feb 21F; 1984 Jan 3G
debates: 1984 Jan 15F/Feb 11F/Mar 18F/Mar 28F/Jun 3F/Sep 17F/Oct 7F-8F/Oct 21F-22F
Democratic convention: delegate majority claimed 1984 Jun 6F; Ferraro joins ticket 1984 Jul 12F; nominated 1984 Jul 18F
election results: 1984 Jan 6F/Dec 21F; 1985 Jan 7F
endorsements: 1983 Jul 13F/Aug 9F/Oct 5G/Dec 10D; 1984 Jun 26F/Aug 19F/Aug 28F/Sep 19H/Oct 28F/Oct 29F
funding: 1984 Jan 3G/Apr 25F/Apr 27F
media: personal attacks 1984 Aug 24F/Sep 6F; post-election accounts 1984 Nov 7F
polls: 1983 Apr 9F/Jun 11F/Oct 1F; 1984 Jul 31F/Sep 12F/Sep 26F/Oct 22F
primaries: Alabama 1984 Mar 13F; Arizona 1984 Apr 14F; California 1984 Jun 5F; Connecticut 1984 Mar 27F; Florida 1984 Mar 13F; Georgia 1984 Mar 13F; Idaho 1984

May 22F; Indiana 1984 May 8F; Iowa 1984 Feb 20F; Maine 1984 Mar 4F-5F; Maryland 1984 May 8F; Massachusetts 1984 Mar 13F; Minnesota 1984 Mar 20F; Nebraska 1984 May 15F; New Hampshire 1984 Feb 28F/Mar 5F; New Jersey 1984 Jun 5F; New Mexico 1984 Jun 5F; New York 1984 Apr 3F; North Carolina 1984 May 8F; Ohio 1984 May 8F; Oregon 1984 May 15F; Pennsylvania 1984 Apr 10F; Rhode Island 1984 Mar 13F; South Carolina 1984 Mar 17F; South Dakota 1984 Jun 5F; Tennessee 1984 May 1F; Vermont 1984 Mar 6F; Washington, D.C. 1984 May 1F; West Virginia 1984 Jun 5F; Wisconsin 1984 Apr 3F/Apr 7F
women's groups: 1983 Oct 10F/Oct 2F; 1984 Jul 1F
Monday, Rick 1981 Oct 19J
Monet, Claude 1985 Oct 27J
Monge, Luis Alberto 1982 Feb 7D/May 8D/May 22D/Dec 4D; 1984 Aug 10D
Mongi, Gregory 1984 Aug 29E
Monk, Thelonius Sphere 1982 Feb 17J
Monroe, Marilyn 1982 Dec 28J; 1987 Feb 21J
Monroe, Marion 1983 Jun 25J
Montagnier, Luc 1985 Feb 7I; 1986 Sep 22I
Montalto, Giangiacomo Ciaccio 1983 Jan 25B
Montand, Yves 1985 Sep 30J; 1986 Nov 8B; 1987 Jun 26J
Montazeri, Ayatollah Hussein Ali 1985 Nov 23C; 1989 Mar 28C
Montenegro, Alejandro 1982 Sep 17D
Monterrosa, Domingo 1984 Oct 23D
Montevecchi, Liliane 1989 Dec 12J
Montilla, Miguel 1982 Mar 21J
Moon, Sun Myung 1981 Oct 15J; 1982 May 5J/May 18J/Jul 16J/Oct 4J
Mooradian, Setrag 1987 Sep 23H
Moore Jr., Arch A. 1986 Jan 1F
Moore, Carlos 1988 Jun 6F
Moore, Henry (Spencer) 1986 Aug 31J
Moore, Jeremy 1982 Jun 14D
Moore, John 1982 Apr 19E
Moore, Mike 1988 Jan 21E
Moore, W. Winfred 1986 Jun 10J
Moorehead, Alan 1983 Sep 29J
Moores, John 1988 Feb 24J
Morales, Pablo 1985 Aug 18J
Moran, James B. 1986 Oct 7H
Moran Castaneda, Rafael 1987 Apr 8D
Morante, Elsa 1985 Nov 25J
Moravia, Alberto 1985 Nov 25J
Mordell, Louis J. 1983 Jul 23I
Moreau, Arthur 1987 Jul 8G
Moretti, Mario 1981 Apr 4B
Morgan, Elizabeth 1989 Sep 25F
Morgan, Harry 1980 Sep 7J
Mori, Taikichiro 1989 Jul 9H
Morial, Ernest N. ("Dutch") 1982 Mar 20F; 1985 Oct 19F
Morin, Claude 1982 Jun 6D
Morison, Samuel Loring 1984 Oct 1G; 1985 Oct 17G
Moro, Aldo 1980 Mar 12B/Mar 28B; 1983 Jan 24B; 1988 Jun 11B
Morrice, Norman 1985 Jun 21J
Morris, Bruce 1985 Feb 7J
Morris, Edmund 1980 Apr 14J
Morris, Errol 1988 Aug 26J
Morris, Robert Tappan 1989 Jul 26I
Morris, Wright 1981 Apr 30J
Morrison, Danny 1982 Jan 21A
Morrison, Toni 1987 Oct 23J; 1988 Jan 24J/Mar 28J/Mar 31J; 1989 Jan 13J

Morrow, Barry 1988 Dec 16J
Morrow, Vic 1987 May 29J
Morse, Robert 1989 Dec 14J
Mortada, Saad 1980 Feb 23C
Morton, Thruston 1982 Aug 14F
Mosbacher Sr., Robert A. 1988 Dec 6F; 1989 Jan 31H
Moscone, George 1985 Oct 21F
Moses, Robert 1981 Jul 29F
Mosher, Gregory 1985 Apr 29J; 1988 May 3J
Moss, Robert 1980 Jul 13J/Aug 17J/Sep 14J
Mota, Rosa 1987 Apr 20J; 1988 Apr 18J
Motherwell, Robert 1985 Aug 18J; 1986 Dec 4J
Mothopeng, Zephania 1988 Nov 26C
Mott Jr., William Penn 1985 May 1H
Mount, Charles Merrill 1987 Aug 18J
Mountcastle Jr., Vernon B. 1983 Nov 16I
Moussavi-Khamenei, Mir Hussein 1983 Apr 13C/Dec 18E; 1984 Nov 24C; 1985 Jan 23G
Mowry, Greg 1987 Mar 15J
Moye, Charles 1980 Jun 9F
Moyers, Bill 1987 Mar 4J
Moynihan, Daniel Patrick 1982 May 30G; 1984 Apr 15G/Apr 26G; 1987 Jul 21F; 1988 Apr 26H
Mozart, Wolfgang Amadeus 1984 Sep 19J
Mswati III, King (Swaziland) 1986 Apr 25C
Mubarak, Hosni
economic policy: Cairo subway opens 1987 Sep 26C
European policy: France 1987 Sep 26C; Great Britain 1988 Jan 25C
government: Egyptian president 1981 Oct 7C/Oct 13C; prime minister named 1982 Jan 2C; 1985 Sep 4C; Sadat brother's trial 1983 Feb 12C; parliamentary elections 1984 May 27C; reelected president 1987 Oct 5C
Mideast policy: Iran 1984 Aug 10C; Iraq 1982 Jul 5C; Israel 1982 Feb 28C/Apr 15C/Jul 15C; 1984 Feb 15C; 1986 Sep 12C; 1988 Dec 25C; 1989 Sep 18C/Oct 6C; Jordan 1984 Sep 25C/Dec 1C; 1985 Mar 6C; 1988 Oct 22C; 1989 Mar 25C; Lebanon 1984 Feb 15C; Libya 1983 Feb 16C; 1984 Aug 10C; 1989 Oct 16C; PLO 1982 Jul 15C/Nov 25C; 1983 Dec 22C-22G; 1988 Oct 22C; 1989 Mar 25C; Sudan 1982 Oct 12C; 1983 Feb 22C
U.S. policy: 1982 Feb 3A; 1983 Feb 16C; 1984 Feb 14G; 1985 Mar 9G; 1988 Jan 25C; 1989 Apr 3C
Mudd, Roger 1980 Jul 1J
Mudd, Victoria 1986 Apr 11J
Mudge, Dirk 1983 Jan 18C
Mueller, K. Alex 1987 Oct 14I
Mugabe, Robert
foreign policy: South Africa 1980 Jun 26C; 1981 Apr 18C; U.S. visit 1980 Aug 27C; aid 1981 Mar 27C
government: presidential elections 1980 Feb 2A/Mar 4C; Zimbabwe prime minister 1980 Mar 11C; one-party rule 1982 Aug 5C; powers expanded 1984 Aug 12C; parliamentary elections 1985 Jul 6C; Zimbabwe president 1987 Dec 31C; cabinet changes 1988 Jan 2C; party merger 1989 Dec 19C; party conference 1989 Dec 22C
Nkomo rivalry: 1980 Jul 26C/Nov 11C; 1981 Jan 10C/Jan 27C; 1982 Feb 17C/Mar 11C; 1987 Apr 17C

personal issues: return from exile 1980 Jan 27C; gets award 1988 Sep 15C

Mugabi, John ("The Beast") 1986 Mar 10J

Muhayshi, Umar Abdullah 1983 Mar 4G

Muirhead, James 1988 Jan 27E

Mukherjee, Bharati 1989 Jan 9J

Muktananda, Swami Paramahansa 1982 Oct 2E

Muldoon, Robert 1981 Dec 9E; 1984 Jul 14E

Mulisch, Harry 1987 Feb 6J

Mullen Jr., Francis M. 1982 Jan 21F

Mulligan, Richard 1989 Sep 17J

Mulliken, Robert Sanderson 1986 Oct 31I

Mulloy, Lawrence B. 1987 May 6I

Mulroney, Brian
  abortion issue: 1988 Aug 27D
  constitutional issues: Quebec accord 1986 Jul 4D/Oct 31D; 1987 Mar 27D; Meech Lake accord 1987 Apr 30D/Jun 3D; 1989 Feb 27D/Nov 10D
  defense policy: radar system 1985 Mar 18D; aircraft contract controversy 1986 Oct 31D
  economic policy: farm aid 1986 Dec 9D; 1987 Dec 15D; regional aid 1987 Aug 4D
  foreign policy: OAS entry 1989 Oct 27D; South Africa sanctions 1986 Jul 13A; Thatcher meeting 1986 Jul 13A; Soviet visit 1989 Nov 20D
  G-7 summits: 1986 May 6A; 1987 Jun 8A
  government: party leadership 1983 Jun 11D; elections 1983 Aug 29D; 1984 Aug 15D/Sep 4D; 1988 Oct 1D/Oct 28D/Nov 21D; Canadian prime minister 1984 Sep 17D; parliament opens 1984 Nov 5D; 1986 Oct 1D; secrecy rules issued 1984 Nov 23D; polls 1986 Sep 2D; Tory convention 1989 Aug 25D; governor general named 1989 Oct 6D
  immigration policy: 1987 Aug 11D
  language issue: 1988 Jul 7D
  native rights: 1985 Apr 18D; 1987 Mar 27D; 1988 Sep 5D
  U.S.-Canada trade pact: 1985 Sep 26D; 1986 Jun 2D; 1988 Jan 2D/Dec 12D
  U.S. policy: SDI support 1985 Feb 1D; Reagan meetings 1985 Mar 18D; 1986 Mar 19D; 1987 Apr 5D; 1988 Apr 27D; Bush meetings 1986 Jun 13D; 1989 Feb 10G/May 2D
  women's status: 1984 Aug 15D

Munro, Alice 1987 May 27J

Murdoch, Rupert
  Australian companies: 1980 Sep 29E; 1986 Dec 3E
  British companies: 1981 Feb 13J; 1982 Feb 8B; 1986 Jul 31B
  U.S. companies: 1982 Dec 20H; 1988 Feb 20H/Mar 29H/Aug 7H

Murphy, Dale 1982 Nov 17J; 1983 Nov 8J

Murphy, Dwayne 1980 Dec 6J

Murphy, Eddie 1988 Nov 21J

Murphy, Ervin 1980 Mar 1F

Murphy, Gerald 1984 Apr 1I

Murphy, John 1980 Feb 2F/Jun 18F/Dec 3F

Murphy, Richard W. 1981 Sep 28C; 1984 Sep 29C; 1985 Aug 18C

Murray, Allen 1989 Apr 28C

Murray, John 1988 Dec 13B

Murtha, John 1980 Feb 2F

Musa, Saed 1983 May 21C/Sep 16C; 1988 Jul 8C

Musca, Tom 1988 Mar 18J

Museveni, Yoweri 1985 Dec 17C; 1986 Jan 29C; 1987 Dec 28C

Muskie, Edmund S.
  arms control: A-strategy shift 1980 Aug 8G
  foreign policy: Soviet Union 1980 May 16A/Sep 25A; 1981 Jan 17A; UN address 1980 Aug 25A
  government service: secretary of state 1980 Apr 29G/May 9G; Iran-Contra review board 1986 Nov 26F
  Iran hostage crisis: 1980 Sep 15G; 1981 Jan 17A
  Iran-Iraq War: 1980 Sep 25A

Mussawi, Hussein 1983 Oct 26C

Mussc, George 1982 Aug 7J

Mussorgsky, Modeste 1985 Mar 24J

Muwanga, Paulo 1980 Dec 11C; 1983 Jun 5C

Mwinyi, Ali Hassan 1984 Apr 19C; 1985 Nov 3C

Myers, Michael 1980 Feb 2F/May 28F/Aug 31F/Oct 2F

Myers Jr., Woodrow A. 1987 Oct 7F

Myrdal, Alva 1982 Oct 12A; 1986 Feb 1A; 1987 May 17A

Myrdal (Karl) Gunnar 1986 Feb 1A; 1987 May 17A

Myrer, Anton 1982 Apr 11J

Mzali, Mohammed 1986 Jul 8C

N

Nachmann, Werner 1989 Dec 15B

Nader, Ralph 1980 Jan 14I; 1982 Aug 18I; 1985 Feb 11H

Nagy, Imre 1989 Jun 16B/Jul 6B

Nahas, Naji Robert 1989 Jun 9D

Naipaul, Shiva 1985 Aug 13J

Naipaul, V.S. 1985 Aug 13J

Nair, C.V. Devan 1985 Mar 28E/Aug 27E

Najibullah 1987 Jan 15E/Nov 30E; 1988 May 27E; 1989 Feb 18E/Jun 25E

Nakasone, Yasuhiro
  corruption issues: Tanaka conviction 1983 Oct 28E/Dec 26E; Recruit scandal 1988 Jul 6E
  defense policy: 1983 Jan 20E/Jan 24E
  economic policy: sales tax 1987 Mar 8E/May 13E; budget 1987 Apr 23E
  foreign policy: in Canada 1986 Jan 12D; in China 1986 Nov 8E
  G-7 summits: 1986 May 6A; 1987 Jun 8A
  government: elected Japan premier 1982 Nov 26E; 1983 Dec 26E; parliamentary elections 1983 Jun 26E; 1986 Jul 6E; 1987 Mar 8E; elected LDP leader 1984 Oct 29E; protests against 1985 Jan 1E; dissolves parliament 1986 Jun 2E; reappointed premier 1986 Jul 22E; LDP term extended 1986 Sep 11E; successor named 1987 Oct 20A
  trade policy: 1982 Dec 7E; 1983 Jan 6E; 1985 Apr 9E
  U.S. policy: defense 1983 Jan 6E/Jan 18E; minorities 1986 Sep 22E; trade 1983 Jan 6E/Jan 18E; 1985 Jan 2A/Apr 2H; 1986 Apr 13G; 1987 Apr 29E

Nakazawa, Kisaburo 1983 Dec 21H

Nakhirunkanok, Porntip 1988 May 24J

Namaliu, Rabbie 1988 Jul 4E

Namath, Joe 1985 Jan 22J

Namphy, Henri 1987 Feb 7D/Dec 9D; 1988 Jun 20D/Jul 8D/Sep 17D

Napoleon Bonaparte 1984 May 19B

Narozniak, Jan 1980 Nov 27B

Nash, Donald 1982 Jun 16J

Nash, Geoffrey 1985 Mar 14C

Nash, Walter 1987 Aug 15E

Nasser, Gamal Abdel 1981 Oct 10A

Nassry, Zia Khan 1982 Nov 6C

Natali, Lorenzo 1985 Feb 28A

Natarajan, Balu 1985 Jun 6J

Nathan, Otto 1987 Jan 27J

Natividad, Irene 1985 Jun 30F

Natshe, Mustapha 1983 Jul 8C

Nattino Allende, Santiago 1985 Mar 30D

Naude, Beyers 1982 Nov 28C

Naughton, James 1989 Dec 11J

Navarrete, Roland 1982 May 22J

Navon, Yitzhak 1980 Feb 23C; 1983 Mar 22C/Apr 17C

Navratilova, Martina
  Australian Open: 1982 Dec 5J; 1985 Dec 8J; 1987 Jan 24J
  awards and honors: 1985 Jan 8J
  French Open: 1982 Jun 6J; 1985 Jun 8J; 1986 Jun 7J; 1987 Jun 6J
  Toyota Championships: 1982 Dec 19J
  U.S. Open: 1981 Sep 12J; 1983 Sep 10J; 1984 Sep 8J; 1985 Sep 7J; 1986 Sep 7J; 1987 Sep 12J
  Wimbledon: 1982 Jul 3J; 1983 Jul 2J; 1984 Jul 7J; 1985 Jul 6J; 1986 Jul 5J; 1987 Jul 4J; 1988 Jul 2J

Nazer, Hisham 1987 Jan 22B

Ndlovu, Moven 1984 Nov 10C/Nov 22C

N'Dour, Youssou 1988 Sep 2J/Oct 15J

Neagle, Anna (Florence Marjorie Robinson) 1986 Jun 3J

Neaher, Edward 1981 Nov 17F

Nearing, Scott 1983 Aug 24J

Neede, Laurens Edward 1980 Feb 25D

Neel, Alice 1984 Oct 13J

Negri, Pola 1987 Aug 1J

Nehemiah, Renaldo 1981 Aug 19J

Nehru, Jawaharlal 1984 Oct 31E; 1988 Jan 20E/Dec 23E

Nelligan, Kate 1981 Jul 24J

Nelson, Alan 1986 Feb 20F

Nelson, Eric Hilliard (Rick) 1985 Dec 31J

Nelson, Larry 1981 Aug 9J; 1987 Aug 9J

Nelson, Willie 1982 Jun 16J/Jul 11J; 1988 May 11J

Nemerov, Howard 1988 May 16J

Nemeth, Miklos 1988 Nov 24B; 1989 Dec 20B

Nenni, Pietro 1980 Jan 1B

Neporozhny, Pyotr S. 1985 Mar 22B

Neumann, Liselotte 1988 Jul 24J

Nevelson, Louise 1988 Apr 17J

Neves, Tancredo de Almeida 1985 Jan 15D/Mar 15D/Mar 20D/Apr 5D/Apr 21D

Newhouse, Donald 1989 Sep 11J

Newhouse Jr., Samuel I. 1985 Mar 8J; 1986 Jan 13J; 1989 Sep 11J

Ne Win 1981 Aug 8E/Nov 9E; 1985 Aug 7E; 1988 Jul 23E

Newman, Paul 1983 Jul 11J; 1986 Oct 17J; 1987 Mar 30J/Jun 13J

Newton, Huey P(ercy) 1989 Aug 22F

Newton, Isaac 1988 Dec 9I

Newton, Tony 1988 Dec 16B

Nexo, Martin Andersen 1988 Dec 21J

Ngor, Haing S. 1984 Nov 2J; 1985 Mar 25J

Ngugi, John 1986 Mar 23J; 1988 Mar 26J; 1989 Mar 19J

Nicholas I, King (Montenegro) 1989 Sep 30B

Nichols, Daniel 1984 Dec 13F; 1985 Jul 12F/Sep 27F

Nichols, Donald 1984 Dec 13F; 1985 Jul 12F/Sep 27F

Nichols, Mike 1984 Jun 3J/Jun 21J; 1986 Jul 25J; 1988 Dec 21J

Nicholson Jr., Arthur D. 1985 Apr 23B

Nicholson, Ben 1982 Feb 6J

Nicholson, Jack 1980 May 23J; 1983 Nov 23J; 1984 Apr 9J; 1985 Jun 14J; 1986 Jan 2J/Jul 25J; 1987 Dec 18J

Nichopoulos, George 1980 Jan 19J/May 16J

Nickell, Stella 1987 Dec 9F

Nicklaus, Jack
  British Open: 1980 Jul 20J
  Masters: 1981 Apr 12J; 1986 Apr 13J
  PGA championship: 1980 Sep 10J; 1983 Aug 7J
  U.S. Open: 1980 Jun 15J; 1982 Jun 20J

Nicks, Stevie 1981 Sep 9J/Sep 30J; 1983 Jul 13J

Nielsen, Erik 1986 Mar 11D/Jul 7D

Nielsen, John 1988 Jan 31J

Niemeyer, Oscar 1988 May 24J

Niemoeller, Martin 1984 Mar 6J

Nimeiry, Mohammed Gaafar el-
  economic policy: 1981 Nov 9C
  government: parliaments dissolved 1981 Oct 5C; state of emergency ended 1984 Sep 29C; opponent hanged 1985 Jan 18C; overthrown 1985 Apr 6C; supporters arrested 1988 Dec 20C
  Mideast policy: PLO haven 1982 Jul 26C; Egypt pact 1982 Oct 12C; Libyan coup plot 1983 Feb 22C
  U.S. policy: AWACS sale 1984 Mar 18C

Nimoy, Leonard 1987 Nov 25J

Niven, David 1983 Jul 29J

Nixon, E(dgar) D(aniel) 1987 Feb 25F

Nixon, Peter 1980 Jun 24E

Nixon, Richard M.
  ceremonial duties: Pahlevi funeral 1980 Jul 29C; Sadat funeral 1981 Oct 10A
  China visit: 1989 Oct 28G
  Watergate and other irregularities: Fitzgerald case 1981 Aug 14F; 1982 Jun 24F; antiwar protest "dirty tricks" 1981 Sep 24F; Burger improper talks 1981 Dec 10F; Lennon FBI surveillance 1983 Mar 22J; White House documents release 1983 Dec 30F; 1986 Dec 1F; 1987 Mar 6F/May 28F; 1988 Mar 29H; wiretap liability 1986 Dec 5F; 1987 Jul 31F

Nixon Jr., Walter L. 1989 May 10F/Nov 3F

Nkomo, Joshua
  government: appointed to cabinet 1981 Jan 27C; 1988 Jan 2C; curfew opposed 1984 Mar 11C; party members accused of murder 1984 Nov 22C; party merger 1989 Dec 19C
  Mugabe rivalry: 1980 Jul 26C/Nov 11C; 1981 Jan 10C; 1982 Feb 17C/Mar 11C; 1987 Apr 17C
  personal issues: returns to Zimbabwe 1980 Jan 13C

Nobari, Ali Riza 1981 Jun 7C

Nofzinger, Lyn 1982 Aug 9F; 1987 Apr 16F; 1988 Feb 11F/Apr 8F; 1989 Jun 27F/Sep 8F

Noguchi, Isamu 1988 Dec 30J

Nolan, Christopher 1988 Jan 19J

Noor, Queen (Jordan) 1981 Jun 10C

Nordland, Rod 1983 Feb 25J

Nordli, Odvar 1981 Feb 4B

Noriega, Manuel Antonio
  arms and drug trafficking: U.S. implicates 1986 Jun 12D; U.S. congressional probes 1987 Jun 26D/Aug 7G; 1988 Feb 5G; indictments 1988 Feb 5G; Bush knowledge dispute 1988 May 7G; U.S. blocks probe 1988 Aug 17G; U.S.

drug charges upheld 1989 Jan 4F/Aug 31D
  economic policy: U.S. suspends aid 1987 Jul 23G; U.S. cuts off payments 1988 Apr 8G; opens bank 1989 Jan 16D
  foreign policy: Cuba frees political prisoner 1987 May 29D; condemns OAS 1989 May 17D
  government: Panama presidential elections 1984 May 10D; 1989 May 7D/May 10D; critic murdered 1985 Sep 14D; polls 1987 Aug 8E; opposition leaders arrested 1988 Apr 27D; U.S. talks collapse 1988 May 25D; U.S. covert activities, coup role 1988 Jul 27G; 1989 Oct 5G/Oct 12G-13G
  unrest: opposition protests 1987 Jun 11D/Jun 16D/Jul 10D; general strikes staged 1987 Jul 28D; 1988 Feb 29D; human rights abuses 1988 Apr 23D
  U.S. invasion: Marines train 1988 Apr 8D; eludes U.S. capture 1989 Dec 20D; in Vatican mission 1989 Dec 24D

Norman, Greg 1984 Jun 18J; 1986 Jul 20J

Norman, Marsha 1983 Apr 1J/Apr 18J

Norris, Mike 1980 Dec 6J

North, Andy 1985 Jun 16J

North, John Ringling 1985 Jun 4J

North, Oliver L.
  Iran-Contra arms scandal
    disclosures and leaks: fired 1986 Nov 25G; documents destroyed 1986 Nov 27F; Swiss bank accounts 1986 Dec 10F/Dec 15B; PAC role charged 1986 Dec 15F; Meese discovery 1986 Dec 19F; classified information 1986 Dec 21G; Reagan intelligence 1987 Jan 9G; Israel denies aid 1987 Feb 27C; Bush knowledge disputed 1987 Sep 8G
    polls: 1987 Jul 11G/Aug 7G
    probes and hearings: congressional testimony 1986 Dec 1F; 1987 Jul 7G-8G/Jul 10G/Jun 2G/Jun 9G/Jul 14G; immunity studied, terms agreed 1986 Dec 1F/Dec 16F; 1987 Mar 18G/Jun 17G/Jun 24G; special prosecutor sued 1987 Feb 24G/Mar 12G; FBI negligence admitted 1987 Apr 8F/Apr 30G; Reagan believes innocent 1987 Aug 1G; 1988 Mar 25F
    trial: indicted 1988 Mar 16F; arraigned 1988 Mar 24F; separated 1988 Jun 8F; dismissal motion denied 1988 Jun 14F; date set 1988 Jul 8F; delayed 1988 Aug 5F; 2 charges dismissed 1988 Nov 7F/Nov 29F; Reagan withholds documents 1988 Dec 1F; chief prosecutor named 1988 Dec 16F; date reset 1988 Dec 21F; Reagan, Bush subpoenaed 1988 Dec 30F; reduced charges sought 1989 Jan 5F; opens 1989 Jan 31F; opening arguments 1989 Feb 21F; jury begins deliberation 1989 Apr 20F; convicted 1989 May 4F; sentenced 1989 Jul 6G

personal issues: commencement address 1988 May 2F; Senate studies pension 1989 Nov 2F

Northrop, John H(oward) 1987 May 27I

Norville, Deborah 1989 Oct 27J

Nott, John 1982 Apr 7A/May 6B/Jun 12D/Jun 13D/Dec 14B

Novello, Antonia 1989 Oct 17F

Nudel, Ida 1982 Mar 27B

Nujoma, Sam 1984 Jun 9C; 1989 Sep 12C

Nunn, Michael 1989 Aug 15J

Nunn, Sam 1984 Oct 22G; 1986 Nov 19G

Nunn, Trevor 1981 Oct 4J; 1983 Jun 5J; 1986 May 14J; 1987 Mar 15J/Jun 7J

Nureyev, Rudolf 1987 Nov 14J; 1989 Nov 21J

Nyagumbo, Maurice 1989 Apr 20C

Nyerere, Julius K. 1980 Oct 26C; 1984 Nov 12C; 1985 Nov 3C; 1987 Oct 31C

Nyers, Rezso 1989 Jun 24B/Sep 8B

Nystrom, Joakim 1983 Dec 28J

O

Obando y Bravo, Miguel Cardinal 1987 Nov 12D/Dec 4D; 1988 Feb 19D

Oberdorfer, Louis F. 1984 Jan 9H; 1985 Sep 30G; 1987 Jun 30F

Obey, Davis 1986 Jul 10H

Obote, Milton 1980 May 27C/Oct 7C; 1981 Apr 10C; 1985 Jul 27C

O'Boyle, Patrick Aloysius Cardinal 1987 Aug 10J

Obregon Cano, Ricardo 1985 Aug 27D

O'Brien, Edward K. 1989 Aug 14F

O'Brien, Lawrence F. 1987 May 28F

O'Brien, Pat 1983 Oct 15J

Ochoa Sanchez, Arnaldo 1989 Jun 14D/Jul 7D

Ochoa Vasquez, Jorge Luis 1987 Nov 21D/Dec 30D; 1988 Jan 25D

O'Connor, Carroll 1989 Sep 17J

O'Connor, John J. Cardinal 1984 Mar 19J; 1988 Jun 5D; 1989 Oct 10F

O'Connor, Sandra Day

  personal issues: cancels GOP meeting 1987 May 1F

  Supreme Court nomination: 1981 Jul 7F/Sep 8F/Sep 16F/Sep 21F/Sep 25F

  Supreme Court rulings: court shift to right 1984 Sep 18F; death penalty 1987 Apr 21F

Odeh, Alex 1985 Oct 11F

Odetta 1986 Jan 25J

Odinga, Odinga 1982 May 20C

O'Flaherty, Liam 1984 Sep 7J

Ogarkov, Nikolai 1980 Jun 22B; 1982 Mar 10B

O'Halloran, Michael 1981 Sep 7B

O'Hara, Patrick 1981 May 21B

Ohira, Masayoshi 1980 May 16E/Jun 12E/Jun 22E/Jul 10E

Ojok, David Oyite 1980 May 11C

O'Keeffe, Georgia 1986 Mar 6J

Okello, Tito 1985 Dec 17C

Olalia, Rolando 1986 Nov 13E/Dec 2E

Oldman, Gary 1986 Oct 17J; 1987 Mar 21J

Olds, Sharon 1985 Jan 14J

O'Leary, Michael 1982 Oct 29B

Olin, Lena 1988 Feb 5J

Oliver, Sy (Melvin James) 1988 May 27J

Olivier, Sir Laurence (Kerr) 1989 Jul 11J

Olmos, Edward James 1988 Mar 18J

Olsen, Merlin 1982 Aug 7J

Olson, Gregg 1989 Nov 7J

Olson, Theodore B. 1986 Apr 24H

Olszewski, Jerzy 1981 May 24B

Olszowski, Stefan 1981 Jan 5B/Sep 22B

Omeliantchik, Oksana 1985 Nov 10J

Onassis, Jacqueline Kennedy 1986 Jul 19J

Ondaatje, Michael 1988 Mar 28J

O'Neill Jr., Thomas P. (Tip)

  budgets: 1981 Jun 16F/Sep 9F; 1982 Apr 28H; 1983 Mar 15F; 1984 Jan 25F

  foreign policy: El Salvador 1983 Mar 10G; 1984 Mar 30G; Grenada 1983 Nov 8G; Lebanon 1983 Oct 24G/Dec 29G; Nicaragua 1985 Apr 4G

  legislation: immigration reform 1983 Oct 4F; War Powers Resolution 1984 Mar 30G

  politics: Reagan administration 1981 Jun 16F; 1982 Oct 23F; 1984 Jan 25F; retires 1986 Oct 17F

Onizuka, Ellison S. 1986 Dec 29I

Ono, Yoko 1981 Jan 7J/Feb 11J/Mar 4J; 1985 Feb 24J/Oct 9J

Opel, John R. 1980 Dec 21H

Oppenheimer, Frank 1985 Feb 3I

Oppenheimer, J. Robert 1985 Feb 3I

Orbison, Roy 1988 Dec 6J

Orff, Carl 1982 Mar 29J

Orkin, Ruth 1985 Jan 16J

Ormandy, Eugene (Jeno Blau) 1985 Mar 12J

Orr, Verne 1985 Mar 28G/Dec 11G

Orrcahall, Christina 1989 Dec 18J

Orrick, William H. 1984 Dec 11H

Orser, Brian 1987 Mar 12J

Ortega Gomez, Eduardo 1982 Sep 8D

Ortega Saavedra, Daniel

  economic policy: 1981 Oct 7A; 1987 Jun 6D; 1988 Feb 14D/Jun 14D; 1989 Jan 30D/May 11D/Jun 24D

  foreign policy: Honduras 1982 Nov 12D; 1988 Mar 16D; Soviet Union 1984 Jun 24A

  government: state of emergency 1984 Jul 19D; 1985 Oct 15D; 1987 Jan 9D; Nicaragua elections 1984 Nov 5D/Nov 14D; sworn president 1985 Jan 10D; electoral reform law 1989 Apr 22D; media law 1989 Apr 22D

  military developments: Cuban advisers 1985 Feb 27D/May 2D; war casualties 1986 Dec 31D; 1989 Jun 29D; conscription 1987 Apr 4D; 1989 Aug 3D

  peace initiatives: arms moratorium 1985 Feb 27D/Jun 13D; cease-fires 1985 Apr 21D; 1987 Sep 22D/Nov 13D/Nov 19D; 1988 Jul 19D; 1989 Nov 1D; Costa Rica peace plan 1985 Nov 11D; 1987 Feb 21D/Sep 22D/Sep 30D; 1988 Jan 16D; troop withdrawals 1987 Sep 30D; contra talks 1987 Nov 12D

  U.S. mercenary capture: helicopter shot down 1984 Jun 12D; Hasenfus pardoned 1986 Dec 17D

  U.S. policy: rebel aid alleged 1983 Apr 25D; Stone meetings 1983 Jun 10D; Shultz meetings 1984 Jun 1D; 1985 Mar 2D; invasion plot charged 1984 Oct 2D; talks deteriorate 1984 Nov 3D; criticism 1985 Oct 21A; 1986 Oct 18C; Reagan meeting offered 1987 Oct 8D

Ortega Saavedra, Humberto 1984 Dec 26D; 1985 Dec 30D; 1987 Dec 12D

Ortiz Mena, Antonio 1980 Nov 1D; 1984 Mar 26D/Mar 28D

Orwell, George 1984 Jan 18J; 1986 Jun 15F

Osborn, Paul 1988 May 12J

Osborne, John 1981 May 2F

Ospina, Ivan 1980 Jun 25D

Ospir, Ivan Maria 1985 Aug 28D

Oswald, Lee Harvey 1981 Oct 4F

O'Toole, Peter 1987 Nov 20J

Oudeh, Mohammed Daoud 1981 Aug 1C

Ouedraogo, Jean-Baptiste 1982 Nov 7C; 1983 Aug 5C

Overton, William Ray 1982 Jan 5F

Ovett, Steve 1981 Aug 28J

Owen, David 1982 Apr 13B

Owen, Johnny 1980 Nov 3J

Owen, Robert B. 1980 Mar 18A

Owen, Robert W. 1987 May 21G

Owens, Jesse 1980 Mar 31J; 1984 Aug 11J

Owings, Nathaniel 1984 Jun 13J

Ozal, Turgut

  foreign policy: Cyprus 1986 Jul 4B; Greece 1988 Mar 4B; U.S. 1985 Apr 6G

  government: appointed Turkish deputy premier 1980 Sep 21B; elected premier 1983 Nov 6B; 1986 Sep 28B; 1987 Sep 6B/Nov 29B; 1988 Sep 26B; referendum 1987 Sep 6B; resignation barred 1988 Sep 26B; elected president 1989 Oct 31B

  personal issues: wounded by gunman 1988 Jun 18B

P

Pabon Pabon, Rosemberg 1982 Dec 5D

Pabst, G.W. 1985 Aug 8J

Pacino, Al 1989 Sep 15J

Packard, David 1983 Mar 27J; 1988 Oct 17J

Packwood, Bob 1982 Dec 2F

Padilla Lorenzo, Heberto 1980 Mar 16D

Padover, Saul 1981 Feb 22J

Page, Alan 1988 Feb 2J/Jul 30J

Page, David C. 1987 Dec 22I

Page, Geraldine 1985 Dec 20J; 1986 Mar 24J; 1987 Jun 13J

Page, Greg 1984 Dec 2J; 1985 Apr 29J

Page, Robert E. 1984 Apr 12J

Pagnol, Marcel 1987 Jun 26J

Pahlevi, Shah Mohammed Riza

  exile: 1980 Jan 17C/Mar 23A/Mar 24A-Mar 25/Apr 16C

  Iranian government claims: 1980 Feb 17A/May 26A/Sep 12C/Nov 2C/Dec 19C; 1983 Jul 1F

  personal issues: surgery 1980 Mar 28C; death 1980 Jul 27C; funeral 1980 Jul 29C

Paige, Satchel (Leroy) 1982 Jul 8J

Paine, Thomas O. 1986 May 22I

Paisley, Ian 1981 Feb 12B/Nov 23B/Dec 21G/Dec 24B

Pak Sae Jik 1981 Aug 6E

Palach, Jan 1989 Jan 23B

Palacios Teyde, Barbara 1986 Jul 21J

Palcy, Euzhan 1989 Sep 20J

Paley, William S. 1982 Sep 9J; 1986 Sep 10H

Palin, Michael 1988 Jul 15J

Pallone, Dave 1988 May 6J

Palma, Sergio 1982 Jan 16J

Palma, Solis 1988 Feb 29D

Palme, Lisbeth 1986 Feb 28B

Palme, Olof

  arms control: 1982 Jun 1A

  assassination: 1986 Feb 28B; 1988 Jun 7B/Dec 14B; 1989 Jul 27B/Oct 12B

  government: elections 1982 Sep 19B; 1985 Sep 15B; sworn Swedish premier 1982 Oct 7B

  Iran-Iraq War mediation: 1980 Nov 24A; 1981 Jan 16A/Feb 19A

Palmer, Lilli (Lilli Marie Peiser) 1986 Jan 27J

Palmer, Robert 1987 Feb 24J; 1989 Feb 22J

Palmieri, Doria 1980 Nov 24J

Palmlund, Thord 1986 Oct 4B

Palsson, Thorsteinn 1987 Jul 8B

Panameno de Garcia, Emelina 1984 Nov 20G

Panetta, Leon E. 1985 Sep 10H

Papandreou, Andreas

  economic policy: 1981 Nov 22B; 1986 Sep 6B/Sep 14B; 1987 Nov 26B; 1988 Dec 18B

  extramarital affair: 1987 Oct 23B

  foreign policy: Cyprus 1982 Mar 1B; Turkey 1988 Mar 4B; U.S. 1981 Nov 22B

  government: sworn Greek premier 1981 Oct 21B; communists return 1982 Dec 25B; elections 1985 Mar 9B/Apr 22B/Jun 2B; 1989 Jun 18B; confidence vote 1989 Mar 14B; corruption charges 1989 Sep 28B

Papon, Maurice 1983 Jan 19B

Papoulias, Karolos 1988 Feb 23B

Papp, Joseph 1982 May 29E

Paputin, Viktor 1980 Jan 3E

Parada, Jose Manuel 1985 Mar 30D

Pardo, Rafael 1989 Jan 12D

Park Chong Chol 1987 Mar 3E

Park Chung Hee 1980 May 18E

Parker, Alan 1988 Dec 9J

Parker, Barrington D. 1985 Jan 17F; 1987 Mar 12G; 1988 Aug 30H

Parker, Charlie 1984 Apr 23J

Parkhurst, Michael 1983 Jan 31H/Feb 10H

Parkinson, Cecil 1987 Jun 13B

Parks, Bert 1980 Jan 4J

Parks, Rosa 1980 Jan 28J

Park Yong Man 1986 Nov 23E

Parnell, Kenneth Eugene 1980 Mar 1F

Parsons, Louella 1988 Nov 17J

Parsons, Phil 1988 May 1J

Pasternak, Boris 1987 Feb 12J; 1989 Dec 10J

Pasternak, Yevgeny 1989 Dec 10J

Pastora Gomez, Eden

  as Nicaragua contra leader: Costa Rica expels 1982 May 22D; goes underground 1983 Apr 15D; U.S. support charged 1983 Apr 25D; fighting renewed 1983 Jul 4D; rebel alliances 1984 Apr 25D; 1986 May 9D; wounded in bombing 1984 May 30D; peace offer 1984 Jul 2D; Costa Rica asylum 1986 May 16D

Pastore, Dagnino 1982 Jul 5D

Patel, Marilyn Hall 1987 Jan 8G

Patinkin, Mandy 1984 May 2J

Patino, Antenor 1982 Feb 2D

Paton, Alan 1988 Apr 12J

Patrick, Ted 1980 Sep 26J

Patterson, Floyd 1982 Feb 14J

Patwari, Prabhudas 1980 Oct 26E

Paul VI, Pope 1988 Apr 23J

Paul, Jean-Claude 1988 Nov 6C

Paul, Wolfgang 1989 Oct 12I

Paulen, Adrian 1980 Jul 31J

Pauley, Jane 1989 Oct 27J

Paulson, Richard 1988 Mar 19E

Pavarotti, Luciano 1989 Dec 9J

Pavlova, Anna 1980 Aug 18J

Pavon, Miguel Angel 1988 Jan 14D

Pawley, Howard 1984 Feb 27D

Paz, Robert 1989 Dec 16D

Paz Barnica, Edgardo 1982 Nov 12D

Paz Estenssoro, Victor 1980 Jul 9D; 1985 Aug 5D; 1986 Aug 28D; 1987 Jul 23D

Paz Garcia, Policarpo 1980 Jul 20D

Paz Zamora, Jaime 1989 Aug 6D/Nov 15D

Peacock, Andrew 1982 Oct 11E

Pearlman, Mark D. 1985 Jul 3D

Pears, Peter 1986 Apr 3J

Pearson, Richard 1987 Oct 27J

Peary, Robert 1986 May 1I

Peckham, Robert 1985 Aug 21H

Peckinpah, Sam 1984 Dec 28J

Pedersen, Charles J. 1987 Oct 14I

Peerce, Jan 1984 Dec 15J

Pei, Wenzhong 1982 Sep 18I

Pelaez Roldan, Bernardo 1989 Sep 12D

Pelotte, Donald E. 1986 May 6J

Pelton, Ronald 1986 Dec 16G

Pendleton Jr., Clarence M. 1983 Mar 20F/Nov 30F; 1985 Mar 5F

Penn, Sean 1985 Aug 16J

Pennington, Jon 1986 May 29J

Penske, Roger 1988 May 29J

Pen Sovan 1981 Dec 5E

Peploe, Mark 1987 Nov 20J

Pepper, Claude Denson 1984 Dec 6F; 1989 May 30J/Aug 29F

Percovich Roca, Luis 1983 May 5D

Percy, Charles H. 1980 Dec 5A/Dec 12A; 1982 May 20G

Pereira, Fernando 1985 Jul 10E

Perenchio, L. Jerrold 1985 Aug 29H

Peres, Shimon

  Arab-Israeli policy: Beirut massacre 1982 Sep 19C; Egypt 1986 Sep 12C; Lebanon 1983 Jun 8C; 1984 Sep 14C; 1985 Dec 26C; Syria 1985 Dec 26C; West Bank 1980 Apr 24C

  economic policy: 1984 Dec 25G; 1986 Feb 23C; 1989 Jan 1C/Jan 31C

  foreign policy: European Community 1988 May 24B; Hungary 1988 May 8C; Morocco 1986 Jul 21C; Soviet Union 1985 Jul 15C; 1986 Sep 22A

  government: Sharon retention attacked 1983 Feb 14C; national unity government 1984 Jul 25C/Aug 5C/Aug 31C/Sep 2C/Sep 14C; Sharon apology 1985 Nov 15C; Shamir leadership rotation 1986 Oct 20C; coalition rule 1987 May 13C; 1988 Dec 19C

  Pollard spy case: 1985 Dec 1C

  U.S. policy: 1980 Apr 24C; 1984 Oct 7G/Dec 25G

Perez, Carlos Andres 1988 Dec 4D; 1989 Feb 2D

Perez, Chalin 1983 Feb 26F

Perez, Danielle 1985 Mar 22C/Mar 31C

Perez, Leander 1983 Feb 26F

Perez de Cuellar, Javier

  Falklands War: 1982 Apr 26A/May 2A/May 17A/May 26A/Jun 2A

  Iran-Iraq War: air raids 1984 Jun 10C; 1987 Sep 16C; peace missions 1985 Apr 9A; 1987 Sep 2A/Sep 16C; chemical weapons 1986 Mar 14C; peace talks 1988 Jul 22C/Jul 27C; cease-fire 1988 Aug 8C

  peace missions: Cambodia/Vietnam conference 1985 Jan 30A; Cyprus talks 1983 Nov 15A; 1984 Jan 17B; 1985 Jun 12B; 1989 Dec 4B; Greenpeace settlement 1986 Jul 7A; Lebanon observers 1982 Aug 3A; Mideast talks 1984 Jan 17C; Poland rights probe 1982 Dec 21A; South Africa visit 1988 Sep 22C

  United Nations secretariat: elected secretary general 1981 Dec 15A; 1986 Oct 9A; peacekeeping reforms 1982 Sep 7A; arms control 1985 Sep 17A; global population 1987 Jul 10J; Gorbachev meeting 1988 Dec 7A

U.S. policy: funds pledged 1987 Nov 23A; peace efforts 1988 Sep 26A

Perez Esquivel, Adolfo 1980 Oct 13A; 1981 Feb 19D

Perez Rodriguez, Roberto Martin 1987 May 29D

Perkins, Carl Dewey 1984 Aug 3F

Perkins, Elizabeth 1988 Jun 3J

Perkins, Marlin (Richard) 1986 Jun 14J

Perle, George 1986 Apr 17J

Pernfors, Mikael 1986 Jun 8J

Peron, Isabel Martinez de (Maria Estela) 1981 Mar 20D/Jul 6D; 1983 Apr 14D/Dec 6D/Dec 9D; 1985 Feb 21D; 1988 Oct 25D

Peron, Juan Domingo 1985 Feb 21D

Perot, H. Ross 1984 Sep 25J; 1985 Oct 15J; 1986 Oct 14H/Dec 1H; 1987 Oct 12H; 1988 Oct 10H

Perpich, Joseph G. 1987 Mar 9I

Perry, Eleanor 1981 Mar 14J

Persico, Carmine 1986 Jun 13F

Pertini, Alessandro 1980 Oct 2B; 1981 Jun 10B; 1982 Jun 7B; 1983 Dec 23B

Peters, Bernadette 1984 May 2J; 1986 Jun 1J; 1987 Nov 5J

Peters, Olga 1986 Apr 16J

Peters, Thomas J. 1983 Aug 14J

Peterson, Peter 1984 May 3H

Peterson, Robyn 1987 May 28J

Peter the Great, Czar (Russia) 1988 Feb 14B

Petit, Stephanie 1987 May 28J

Petri, Elio 1982 Nov 19J

Petrosyants, Andronik M. 1986 Aug 21B

Petrovsky, Vladimir F. 1987 Jun 9B/Oct 15B

Pettersson, Carl Gustav (Christer) 1988 Dec 14B; 1989 Jul 27B/Oct 12B

Petty, Richard 1981 Feb 15J

Petty, Tom 1989 Jun 24J/Aug 26J

Peyrefitte, Alain 1980 Nov 7B

Peyrolles, Gilles 1985 Mar 25C/Apr 1C

Pfeiffer, Michelle 1988 Dec 21J; 1989 Nov 13J

Pflimlin, Pierre 1984 Jul 24B

Phagan, Mary 1986 Mar 11F

Pham Hung 1988 Jun 22E

Pham Tuen 1980 Jul 23I

Pham Van Dong 1987 Jun 18E

Phelan, Richard T. 1988 Jul 26F

Philby, H(arold) A(drian) R(ussell) (Kim) 1983 Mar 26B; 1988 May 11B

Philip II, King (Macedonia) 1982 Sep 1F

Philip, Prince (Great Britain) 1983 Feb 26G; 1986 Feb 17E; 1988 Apr 19E

Phillips, Craig 1986 Feb 1J

Phillips, Duncan 1985 Jun 19J

Phillips, Lou Diamond 1988 Mar 18J

Phillips, Marjorie Acker 1985 Jun 19J

Phillips, Mark 1989 Aug 31B

Phillips, Sam 1986 Jan 23J

Phipps, Susie Guillory 1985 Oct 19J

Phoenix, River 1989 May 24J

Phoumi Vongvichit 1986 Oct 31E

Piaget, Jean 1980 Sep 16I

Pialat, Maurice 1987 May 19J

Picasso, Pablo 1986 Aug 19J; 1987 Jan 20J; 1988 Feb 1J/Nov 28J; 1989 May 9J

Pickens, Slim 1983 Dec 8J

Pickens, T. Boone 1985 May 20H

Pickering, Sarah 1988 Oct 21J

Pickering, Thomas R. 1984 Jun 22D/Aug 8G; 1985 Sep 29D; 1988 Dec 6F

Pierce Jr., Samuel R. 1983 May 19F; 1989 Jul 11F/Aug 3F/Sep 15F/Sep 26F/Oct 3F/Oct 27F/Dec 4F

Pierre, Albert 1986 Feb 26D

Pigeat, Henri 1986 Dec 18B

Pignedoli, Sergio 1980 Jun 15J

Pinckney, Ed 1985 Apr 1J

Pindling, Lynden O. 1982 Jun 10D; 1987 May 12D/Jun 19D

Pinkowski, Josef 1980 Oct 30B/Oct 31E; 1981 Feb 9B

Pinochet Ugarte, Augusto
assassination attempt: 1986 Sep 7D
civil strife: anti-government protests 1980 Aug 27D; 1983 Jun 14D/Jun 17D/Aug 11D/Sep 11D; 1984 Mar 27D/Sep 5D; 1985 Sep 4D; political exiles 1982 Dec 22D; 1984 Feb 13D; 1987 Mar 31D; state of siege 1983 Aug 26D; 1984 Nov 6D/Nov 15D; 1985 Jun 16D; 1986 Sep 7D/Dec 31D; death squads 1985 Mar 30D; 1986 Sep 2D; military strengthened 1986 Oct 8D; 1989 Apr 10D
economic policy: 1983 Feb 15D/Jun 17D
foreign policy: Philippines 1980 Mar 22A
government: constitution 1980 Jul 11D/Sep 11D; political activity ban 1981 Sep 11D; cabinet changes 1982 Apr 22D; 1983 Feb 15D; resignation bar 1984 Sep 11D; presidential term plebiscite 1988 Aug 30D/Oct 5D
human rights: 1982 Mar 10D; 1985 Mar 30D; 1986 Mar 14A/Mar 31D/Sep 2D

Pinter, Harold 1984 May 3J/Jun 22J

Pinto Balsemao, Francisco 1981 Jan 9B/Feb 22B/Aug 11B

Pinto da Costa, Manuel 1988 Mar 9C

Pinto Machado, Joaquim 1987 May 30E

Pintor, Lupe 1980 Nov 3J

Piquet, Nelson 1985 Jul 7J; 1986 Mar 23J/Jul 27J/Sep 7J; 1987 Jul 26J/Sep 6J/Nov 1J

Pizarro Leongomez, Carlos 1989 Jan 12D

Pizzolato, Orlando 1985 Oct 27J

Plain, Belva 1980 Jun 8J/Jul 13J/Aug 17J/Sep 14J; 1982 Jul 11J/Aug 8J; 1984 Oct 19J; 1989 Aug 25J

Planinc, Milka 1982 May 16B; 1984 May 15B; 1985 May 31G; 1986 Jan 6B

Player, Gary 1984 Aug 19J

Plomley, Roy 1985 May 28J

Plumb, Henry 1987 Jan 20B

Plunkett, Maryann 1986 Aug 10J; 1987 Jun 7J

Pohl, Dan 1982 Apr 11J

Poindexter, John M.
government service: national security adviser 1985 Dec 4G; 1986 Nov 25G
Iran-Contra arms scandal: Reagan backs 1986 Dec 16F; 1987 Aug 1G; 1988 Mar 25F; congressional hearings 1987 Mar 18G/Apr 21H/Jul 15G/Jul 21G/Jul 23G; 1989 Sep 6F; credibility poll 1987 Aug 7F; conspiracy trial 1988 Mar 16F/Mar 24F/Jun 8F/Jun 16F; 1989 Jul 25F/Nov 16G/Dec 21F

Poitier, Sidney 1983 Nov 18J; 1985 Nov 19J; 1986 Oct 6J

Polanski, Roman 1980 Dec 12J

Polanyi, John C. 1986 Oct 15I

Poli, Gianni 1986 Nov 2J

Poli, Robert 1981 Aug 25H

Pollack, Sydney 1985 Dec 18J; 1986 Mar 24J

Pollard, Anne Henderson 1986 Jun 4G; 1987 Mar 4G

Pollard, Fritz (Frederick Douglas) 1986 May 11J

Pollard, Jonathan Jay 1985 Nov 21G/Dec 1C; 1986 Jun 4G; 1987 Mar 4G/May 26C

Pollock, Jackson 1984 Jun 19J; 1988 May 2J

Pol Pot 1985 Sep 2E

Polya, George 1985 Sep 7I

Polyakov, Vladimir 1981 Sep 15A

Pons, B. Stanley 1989 Mar 23I/May 9I

Ponselle, Rosa 1981 May 25J

Popieluszko, Jerzy 1984 Oct 30B/Nov 3B/Nov 27B; 1985 Feb 7B

Popov, Leonid 1980 Apr 9I/Oct 11I; 1982 Aug 19I/Aug 27I

Porter, Cole 1984 Jan 31J/Feb 15J; 1988 Jun 5J

Porter, Katherine Anne 1980 Sep 18J

Porter, Robert Rodney 1985 Sep 6I

Potgeiter, Alexander 1986 May 23G

Potter, Peter (William Moore) 1983 Apr 17J

Potter, Robert 1989 Aug 31F

Pound, Ezra 1987 Dec 22J

Povarnitsin, Rudolf 1985 Aug 11J

Povod, Reinaldo 1986 May 18J

Powell, Brendan 1988 Apr 9J

Powell, Colin L. 1987 Nov 5G/Dec 13G/Dec 29G; 1988 Dec 1G; 1989 Aug 10G/Sep 21G

Powell, Jody 1980 Mar 29A

Powell Jr., Lewis F. 1983 May 9F; 1985 Jun 10H; 1986 Jan 8H; 1987 Jun 26F

Powell, William 1984 Mar 5J

Powers, John A. ("Shorty") 1980 Jan 1I

Pozderac, Hamdija 1987 Sep 12B

Prebble, Richard 1988 Mar 1E

Premadasa, Ranasinghe 1989 May 11E/Jun 1E/Jun 20E

Preminger, Otto Ludwig 1986 Apr 23J

Prem Tinsulanonda
government: named Thai premier 1980 Mar 3E; 1983 Apr 30E; 1986 Aug 5E; forms coalition 1983 May 7E; coup foiled 1985 Sep 9E; parliament dissolved 1986 May 1E; army commander dismissed 1986 May 27E; government dissolved 1988 Apr 29E; new term declined 1988 Jul 27E

Presley, Elvis 1980 Jan 19J/May 16J; 1986 Jan 23J; 1987 Aug 16J

Presser, Jackie 1986 May 21H/Dec 2H; 1988 Jul 9H/Jul 15F

Pressler, Larry 1988 Mar 30G

Presthus, Rolf 1982 Oct 6B

Preston, Robert 1987 Mar 21J

Price, George 1984 Jan 20D/Dec 14D; 1989 Sep 4D

Price, Jeffrey 1988 Jun 22J

Price, Leontyne 1984 Dec 31J; 1985 Jan 3J

Price, Melvin 1981 Oct 6G; 1985 Jan 4G

Price, Reynolds 1987 Jan 12J

Price, Richard 1986 Dec 17J

Priestley, John Boynton 1984 Aug 14J

Prime, Geoffrey Arthur 1982 Nov 10B

Prince, Harold 1980 Jun 8J; 1986 Oct 9J; 1988 Jun 5J

Prior, James 1981 Oct 6B; 1982 Apr 5B; 1984 Sep 10B

Pritikin, Nathan 1985 Feb 21I

Pritzker, Abram Nicholas 1986 Feb 8J

Prost, Alain
Australian Grand Prix: 1986 Oct 26J; 1988 Nov 13J
Brazilian Grand Prix: 1985 Apr 7J; 1987 Apr 12J; 1988 Apr 3J
British Grand Prix: 1985 Jul 21J
European Grand Prix: 1985 Oct 6J
Formula One: 1989 Oct 22J
French Grand Prix: 1988 Jul 3J; 1989 Jul 9J
Italian Grand Prix: 1985 Sep 8J; 1989 Sep 10J
Monaco Grand Prix: 1988 May 15J

Proust, Marcel 1984 Apr 25J

Proxmire, William 1980 Feb 8F; 1987 Aug 27F

Pryor, Aaron 1982 Mar 21J/Nov 12J

Pryor, Richard 1980 Jul 25J

Psachoropoulos, Nikos 1986 Apr 19J

Puente, Tito 1983 Sep 15J

Puig, Manuel 1985 Jul 26J

Pujol Garcia, Juan 1984 Jun 3J

Pu Yi 1987 Nov 20J

Puzo, Mario 1984 Dec 14J; 1985 Jan 18J/Feb 8J/Mar 15J

Pym, Francis 1980 Jun 17B; 1982 Apr 22A/May 10B

Q

Qaddafi, Muammer el-
Chad conflict: 1982 Nov 25C; 1983 Feb 28C/Aug 18C; 1984 Nov 16C; 1987 Mar 27C; 1988 May 25C
foreign policy: Austria 1982 Mar 13A; France 1984 Nov 16C
government: opponent assassinated 1980 Apr 11C; coup marked 1986 Sep 1C
international terrorism: Reagan plot 1981 Dec 6C; Tripoli barracks raid 1984 May 8C; Grand Mosque plot 1984 Sep 1C; Berlin discotheque bombing 1986 Apr 5B; Lebanese hostage plea 1989 Jun 15C
Iran-Iraq War: 1980 Oct 10C
Mideast policy: Egypt 1984 Nov 17C; 1989 Oct 16C; Morocco 1984 Aug 13C; Syria 1980 Sep 2C; Tunisia 1982 Feb 27C
U.S. air raids: covert operations 1985 Nov 3G; aircraft carriers moved 1986 Jan 23G; air attacks 1986 Mar 27C/Apr 14C; deception strategy 1986 Oct 2G; anniversary marked 1987 Apr 15C

Qasimi, Abdel-Aziz bin Mohammed al- 1987 Jun 17C/Jun 20C

Qian Qichen 1984 Mar 26A

Qoddousi, Hojatolislam Ali 1981 Sep 5C

Quayle, Dan (James Danforth)
personal issues: income tax returns 1989 Apr 12F
presidential campaign (1988): 1988 Aug 16F/Aug 17F-18F/Sep 14F/Oct 5F; 1989 Apr 28F
as vice president: El Salvador visit 1989 Feb 1G; Venezuela visit 1989 Feb 1G; education gaffe 1989 May 10F; Bush to retain in '92 1989 Nov 2F

Quayle, Marilyn 1989 Apr 12F

Queen, Richard 1980 Jul 11C/Jul 15C

Queffelec, Yann 1985 Nov 18J

Quinlan, Karen Ann 1985 Jun 11J

Quiwonkpa, Thomas 1985 Nov 12C

R

Rabanal, Jorge 1986 Jul 23D

Rabbani, Burhanuddin 1984 Aug 27C; 1986 Jun 16G

Rabe, David 1984 Jun 21J

Rabi, I(sidor) I(saac) 1988 Jan 11I

Rabin, Yitzhak 1981 Jul 22C; 1985 Mar 12C; 1989 Sep 18C

Rabuka, Sitiveni 1987 Oct 6E/Dec 5E

Rademakers, Fons 1987 Feb 6J

Rafael Videla, Jorge 1980 Sep 30D

Rafko, Kaye Lani Rae 1987 Sep 14J

Rafsanjani, Hojatolislam Ali Akbar Hashemi 1980 Aug 17C/Sep 8C; 1981 Aug 31C/Oct 23C; 1988 Jun 2C; 1989 Jun 20C/Jul 28C/Dec 18C

Rahal, Bobby 1986 May 31J

Rahman, Sheik Omar Abdel 1989 Apr 26C

Rahner, Karl 1984 Mar 30J

Raines, Tim 1987 Jul 14J

Rainey, Ma 1986 Nov 1J

Psachoropoulos, Nikos 1986 Apr 19J

Rainier III, Prince (Monaco) 1982 Sep 14J

Rainwater, James 1986 May 31I

Rajai, Mohammed Ali 1980 Oct 5C/Oct 17C/Dec 1C; 1981 Jan 26C/Jul 24C/Aug 30C

Rajavi, Massoud 1981 Jul 29C/Aug 31C

Rajneesh, Bhagwan Shree 1985 Sep 16J/Nov 14F; 1986 Jul 22J

Rakowski, Mieczyslaw 1980 Sep 14B; 1982 Aug 7B; 1988 Sep 27B; 1989 Feb 25B

Rallis, George John 1980 May 8B

Ramachandran, Marudur Gopalan 1980 May 31E; 1987 Dec 24E

Ramachandran, Rageshree 1988 Jun 2J

Ramadan, Mohammed Mustafa 1980 Apr 11C

Rambert, Marie 1982 Jun 12J

Rame, Franca 1983 Aug 27F

Ramgoolam, Seewoosagur 1982 Jun 11C

Ramirez, Raul A. 1985 Sep 3H

Ramirez, Richard 1985 Sep 27F

Ramirez Mercado, Sergio 1982 Mar 9D; 1985 May 1D/May 10D

Ramos, Fidel 1986 Feb 22E; 1988 Jan 21E

Ramos, Julio 1982 Dec 11D

Ramphal, Shridath 1989 Jul 3E

Ramsey, Arthur Michael 1988 Apr 23J

Ramsey, Norman F. 1989 Oct 12I

Ramu ("Wolf Boy") 1985 Feb 18I

Rand, Ayn 1982 Mar 6J

Randall, Margaret 1988 Feb 4F

Randolph, A. Philip 1987 Feb 25F

Rangel, Charles 1983 Jan 15F

Rao, Vengala 1988 Nov 15E

Raphaelson, Samson 1983 Jul 16J

Raphel, Arnold L. 1988 Aug 17E/Oct 16E

Rappaport, Paul 1980 Apr 21J

Rasheed, Hakeem Abdul 1980 Feb 7J

Rasmussen, Leo 1983 Jul 22A

Rather, Dan 1980 Feb 15J; 1986 Oct 4J; 1988 Jan 25F

Ratushinskaya, Irina 1986 Oct 9B/Dec 18B

Rau, Johannes 1985 May 12B

Rauchfuss, Wolfgang 1985 May 16A

Rauda Murcia, Bernardo 1983 Oct 28D

Rauff, Walter Herman Julius 1984 Jan 25D/May 14B

Raulerson, James David 1985 Jan 30F

Ravel, Maurice 1983 Nov 7J

Rawlings, Jerry 1981 Dec 31C; 1982 Jan 2C/Jan 13C/Jan 22E; 1983 Jun 19C; 1986 Jun 22C

Ray, Clifford and Louise 1987 Aug 28F; 1988 Sep 29F

Ray, James Earl 1986 Nov 22J

Raymond, Michael 1986 Nov 21F

Reagan, Nancy
ceremonial duties: Statue of Liberty opened 1986 Jul 5J; drug war 1986 Aug 4F/Sep 14F; Japan visit 1989 Oct 28E
ethics issues: Allen gift probe 1981 Nov 13F
personal issues: son's dance performace 1981 Mar 15J; tax returns 1985 Apr 12H; 1986 Apr 11F; 1987 Apr 14F; government decision-making role 1987 Mar 4F; cancer surgery 1987 Oct 17F

Reagan, Ronald P. ("Ron") 1980 Nov 24J; 1981 Mar 15J

Reagan, Ronald Wilson
abortion and birth control: 1982 Sep 8F/Sep 14F; 1983 Jun 16F; 1984 Jan 30F/Sep 11F; 1985 Jan 22F; 1987 Jul 30F; 1989 Jan 9F
agriculture
subsidies and debt relief: dairy price-supports 1981 Mar 31H;

1983 Nov 29F; drought relief bill 1988 Aug 11H; Farm Credit System bailout 1985 Dec 19H/Dec 23H; 1987 Dec 19H; 1988 Jan 6F; farm debt 1984 Sep 18H; 1985 Mar 6H/Mar 10H; legislation 1985 Dec 18H; payment-in-kind (PIK) program 1982 Dec 9H; 1983 Jan 11H/Mar 11H/Jul 30F; 1984 Apr 10H; Pennsylvania farm visit 1982 May 14H

trade issues: Australian talks 1986 Apr 18E; export subsidies eased 1988 Nov 17H; Soviet grain sales 1982 Mar 22H/Mar 27G/Apr 24G/Jul 30H/Aug 2H/Oct 15H/Oct 18H; 1983 Apr 22A; 1984 Nov 1G; 1986 Aug 1H; sugar import quotas 1982 May 4H

appointments and resignations
cabinet and subcabinet: Abrams (state) 1981 Oct 30G; Baker (treasury) 1985 Jan 8F; 1988 Aug 5H; Baldrige (commerce) 1980 Dec 11F; Bell (EEOC) 1981 Jan 7F; Bennett (education) 1985 Jan 10F/Feb 6H; Block (agriculture) 1980 Dec 23F; Bowen (HHS) 1985 Nov 7F; Brady (treasury) 1988 Aug 5F; Brock (labor) 1985 Mar 20H; Burnley (transportation) 1987 Oct 8H; Carlucci (defense) 1987 Nov 5G; Clark (interior) 1983 Oct 13H; Dole (transportation) 1983 Jan 5H; Donovan (labor) 1980 Dec 16G; Edwards (energy) 1980 Dec 22F; Haig (state) 1980 Dec 16G; 1982 Jun 25G; Heckler (HHS) 1983 Jan 12F; Herrington (energy) 1985 Jan 10F/Feb 6H; Hodel (interior) 1985 Jan 10F/Feb 6H/Nov 5H; Lewis (transportation) 1980 Dec 11F; Lyng (agriculture) 1986 Jan 29H; McLaughlin (labor) 1987 Nov 3H; Meese (attorny general) 1985 Feb 5F/Feb 23F; Pierce (HUD) 1980 Dec 22F; Regan (treasury) 1980 Dec 11F; Schweiker (HHS) 1980 Dec 11F; Shultz (state) 1982 Jun 25G; Smith (attorney general) 1980 Dec 11F; Thornburgh (attorney general) 1988 Jul 12F; Verity (commerce) 1987 Aug 10H; Watt (interior) 1980 Dec 22F; Weinberger (defense) 1980 Dec 11F; 1987 Nov 5G

councils, commissions and agencies: Abram (rights) 1983 Dec 6F; Abramowitz (arms control) 1983 Jan 12G; Adelman (ACDA) 1983 Jan 12G; Allen (NSA) 1980 Oct 30F/Dec 23F; 1982 Jan 4F; Angell (Fed) 1985 Oct 19H; Billington (Library of Congress) 1987 Apr 17J; Bradley (minorities) 1982 Apr 19F; Buckley (state) 1983 Dec 6F; Bunzel (rights) 1983 Dec 6F; Burford (EPA) 1984 Jul 2H/Aug 1H; Burger (bicentennial) 1985 Jun 25F; 1986 Jun 17F; Casey (CIA) 1980 Dec 11F; 1987 Feb 2G; civil rights commission 1983 May 25F; Clark (NSA) 1982 Jan 4F; Conable (World Bank) 1986 Mar 13G; Fletcher (NASA) 1986 Mar 1I; Gates

(CIA) 1987 Feb 2G/Mar 3G; Greenspan (Fed) 1987 Jun 2H; Gunn (trade) 1982 Apr 19F; Lavelle (EPA) 1983 Feb 7H; 1985 Oct 19H; Johnson (Fed) 1985 Oct 19H; Mayberry (AIDS) 1987 Oct 17G; 1985 Dec 4G; McFarlane (NSA) 1983 Oct 17G/Jul 22G; 1985 Dec 4G; Lenkowsky (USIA) 1984 May 15G; Miller (OMB) 1985 Jul 19H; Poindexter (NSA) 1985 Dec 4G; Ruckelshaus (EPA) 1983 Mar 21H; 1984 Nov 29H; Ruder (SEC) 1987 Jun 17H; Seger (Fed) 1984 Jul 3F; Sessions (FBI) 1987 Jul 24F; Stephens (NLRB) 1988 Jan 7H; Stockman (OMB) 1980 Dec 11F; Thomas (EPA) 1984 Nov 29H; Volcker (Fed) 1983 Jun 18H/Jul 27H; 1987 Jun 2H; Webster (CIA) 1987 Mar 3G; Yeutter (trade) 1985 Apr 2H

diplomatic: Habib (Mideast) 1983 Jul 22G; Heckler (Ireland) 1985 Oct 1F; Mansfield (Japan) 1981 Jan 7G; Rumsfeld (Mideast) 1983 Nov 3G; Walters (UN) 1985 Feb 8G

judicial: Bork (appeals court/Supreme Court) 1981 Dec 7F; 1987 Jul 1F/Jul 17F/Aug 31F/Oct 23F; 1988 Jan 14F; Ginsburg (Supreme Court) 1987 Oct 29F/Nov 7F; Kennedy (Supreme Court) 1987 Nov 11F; Manion (appeals court) 1986 Jul 23F; O'Connor (Supreme Court) 1981 Jul 7F; Rehnquist (Supreme Court) 1986 Jun 17F; Scalia (Supreme Court) 1986 Jun 17F; Sessions (district court) 1986 Jun 5F

military: Ball (navy) 1988 Feb 23G; Crowe (joint chiefs) 1985 Jul 10G; Gray (marines) 1987 Jun 16G; Powell (joint chiefs) 1987 Nov 5G; 1988 Dec 1G

white house staff: Baker (staff chief) 1987 Feb 27F; 1988 Jun 14F; Graham (science) 1986 Jun 30I; Laxalt (GOP chairman) 1982 Nov 6F; Regan (staff chief) 1985 Jan 8F; 1987 Feb 27F

armaments: antiballistic missile system 1983 Mar 23G; 1984 Mar 21G; landbased mobile ICBMs 1983 Apr 11G/Apr 19G; MX missiles 1981 Oct 2G/Dec 31G; 1982 May 19G/Nov 22G/Nov 25A/Dec 7H; 1983 Jan 3G/Apr 11G/Apr 19G/May 12G/May 25F; 1984 Dec 3G; 1985 Feb 26G/Mar 12G/Mar 28G; neutron warheads 1981 Aug 10G; nuclear warheads 1982 Mar 29G; strategic weapons policy 1981 Oct 2G/Oct 5G-6G; submarine communications system 1981 Oct 8G; Star Wars study 1988 Apr 15J

arts and culture: 1988 Oct 31H
awards and honors: 1982 Mar 23F/Sep 7G; 1984 Mar 26J; 1987 Nov 17G; 1988 Oct 17J
banks and banking: 1982 Mar 3H/Oct 15H; 1984 Jun 25H
budget and spending programs: '82 cuts planned 1981 Feb 27F; '82 budget submitted 1981 Mar 10H;

'81-84 resolution rejected 1981 Apr 9H; Gramm-Latta resolution 1981 May 7F; '82 funds debated 1981 Jul 31H/Sep 24H/Oct 7F/Nov 10H; '82 cuts signed 1981 Aug 13H; '82 funds vetoed, spending extension signed 1981 Nov 23H; '82-84 projections 1981 Dec 4F; 1982 Jan 6H; '83 proposals criticized 1982 Feb 11F; '83 compromise debated 1982 Mar 16F/Apr 5H/Apr 28H-29F/May 4H/May 24F; '82 supplemental funds 1982 Jun 24H/Jul 18H/Aug 28H/Sep 10H; '84 budget submitted 1983 Jan 31H; '84 budget resolution 1983 Mar 23F/Jun 23H; '83 stopgap funds 1983 Oct 1H/Nov 14F; '85 budget submitted 1984 Feb 1H; '85 compromise 1984 Mar 15H; '85 spending signed 1984 Oct 12H; '86 draft plan 1984 Dec 5H; '86 budget submitted 1985 Feb 4H; '86 compromise debated 1985 Mar 13H/Mar 21H/Mar 27H/Apr 4H/Apr 24H/May 10H/Jul 3H/Aug 31H; '85 stopgap funds 1985 Nov 14F; '87 budget submitted 1986 Feb 5H; '87 compromise debated 1986 Feb 26H/Mar 7H/Mar 13H/Mar 19H/Apr 7H/Apr 22H/May 16F/Oct 18F; '86 supplemental funds 1986 May 8H/Jul 2H; '87 spending signed 1986 Oct 18G; '88 budget submitted 1987 Jan 5H/Apr 1H/Apr 9H; '87 spending deferral barred 1987 Jan 20H; '88 compromise debated 1987 Jun 18H/Jul 3H/Sep 29H-30H/Dec 22F-22G; '89 budget submitted 1988 Feb 18H; '88 supplemental funds 1988 Aug 14F; '88 transition expenses 1988 Aug 17F; '89 compromise debated 1988 Aug 19F/Sep 27H; '90 budget submitted 1989 Jan 9H

business and industry
    investment issues: economic program support 1982 Mar 18F; enterprise zones 1982 Mar 23H; plant closings 1988 Jul 5H/Jul 13H/Aug 2H; productivity committee 1982 Jan 6H; superconductors 1987 Jul 28H

    protection issues: automobiles 1980 Jul 12H/Dec 20H; copyright bill 1982 Jul 13H; lie detectors 1988 Mar 3F; military technology exports 1985 Jul 12G; nuclear fuel reprocessing 1981 Oct 8I; patents and trademarks 1988 Nov 16H/Nov 19H; regulations freeze 1981 Jan 29F; space launch insurance 1988 Nov 15I

cabinet and White House staff: reorganization 1985 Apr 11F; Democratic screening 1986 Dec 22F
cities: 1980 Dec 1H; 1981 Mar 2H/Mar 14H; 1982 Mar 23H/Nov 29F
civil rights: AIDS 1988 Jun 2F/Aug 2F; fair housing 1983 May 19F/Jul 12F; 1988 Aug 2F; Grove City College v. Bell 1988 Mar 16F/Mar 22F; policy defense 1983 Aug 1F; rights commission 1981 Nov 16F; 1982 Sep 12F; 1983 Mar 20F/May 25F/Oct 25F/Nov 30F; school desegregation 1983 Jul 12F; Voting Rights Act 1981 Jan 6F; 1982 Jun 29F
congressional relations: 1981 Apr 28H/Jun 16F; 1982 Mar 9F; 1983

Nov 19G; 1987 Dec 11G; 1988 Nov 23F
constitutional amendments: 1982 May 6F/Jul 19F; 1986 Mar 25H/May 19H
crime and law enforcement: drug trafficking: 1982 Oct 14F; 1986 Aug 4F/Sep 14F/Sep 15F/Oct 27F; 1988 Nov 18F; gun control: 1983 May 6F; 1986 May 19F; 1988 Nov 19F; insider trading: 1988 Nov 19F; legislation: 1982 Sep 13F; 1983 Jan 14F; 1984 Jul 17H/Oct 12F; drinking: 1984 Jul 17H
debt and deficit issues: balanced budget bill 1982 Jul 19F; 1985 Nov 12H/Dec 12H/Dec 18G; 1986 Jan 20H/Feb 5H/Apr 7H/Oct 21H; 1987 Jan 20H; deficit estimates 1982 Jan 6H; 1985 Feb 27H/Aug 8H; 1987 May 14H; deficit summit 1987 Oct 20H/Oct 22H/Oct 26H; foreign debt 1983 Feb 14G; Iron Triangle 1988 Dec 12F; national debt limit 1981 Feb 7H; 1983 Nov 21H; 1984 May 25H; 1987 May 15H/Jul 30H/Aug 10H; spending cuts/taxes 1981 Nov 3H; 1982 Aug 16F
defense and armed forces
    budget issues: authorization bill 1983 Sep 24G; 1987 Dec 4G; 1988 Aug3G/Sep 29G; economic recovery proposals 1981 Feb 18H/Sep 9H/Sep 12G; 1984 Dec 18G
    civil defense: 1982 Mar 29G
    courts: 1983 Nov 18G
    personnel issues: black general promoted 1982 Aug 11G; military retirement system 1986 Jul 2G; Rickover replacement 1981 Nov 13G
    procurment issues: 1983 Aug 20G; 1985 Jun 17G
    reorganization: 1986 Apr 2G/Sep 17G
    strategy and tactics: 1988 Jan 12G; radar defense system 1985 Mar 18D; weapons 1981 Oct 5G
depressed and disaster areas: 1988 Aug 11H
disarmament and arms control
    ABM treaty: 1987 Feb 11G/May 13G/Jun 17G/Sep 21G
    ASAT pact: 1984 Apr 2G/Jul 1A
    European issues: CFE talks 1984 Jan 16G; speech hailed 1981 Nov 18B; Thatcher agreement 1986 Nov 15G
    SALT II: 1982 Apr 17G/1983 Apr 22G; 1984 Jan 23G; 1985 Jun 10G/Dec 23G; 1986 Apr 16G/Apr 21G/May 27G/Jun 12G/Jun 19G/Dec 15G; 1987 Mar 10G
    Soviet issues: A-arms cuts 1981 Nov 18A; 1982 May 9G/Jun 4B; 1986 Feb 24G; A-arms freeze 1982 Apr 1G/Oct 4G; 1983 Mar 31G/Jun 16F; Andropov attacks 1983 Feb 1B; anti-nuclear movement 1983 Oct 22G; A-test ban 1982 Jul 20G; 1986 Mar 29B/Mar 30G; A-test invite 1985 Jul 29G; 1986 Mar 14G; Brezhnev proposals 1982 Mar 16G/May 18A; chemical weapons 1984 Apr 4A; Gorbachev meetings 1986 Oct 12A; intermediate-range nuclear missiles 1983 Jan 31B/Mar 30G/Apr 2B/Jun

Nov 19G; 1987 Dec 11G; 1988 Nov 23F
constitutional amendments: 1982 May 6F/Jul 19F; 1986 Mar 25H/May 19H
crime and law enforcement: drug trafficking: 1982 Oct 14F; 1986 Aug 4F/Sep 14F/Sep 15F/Oct 27F; 1988 Nov 18F; gun control: 1983 May 6F; 1986 May 19F; 1988 Nov 19F; insider trading: 1988 Nov 19F; legislation: 1982 Sep 13F; 1983 Jan 14F; 1984 Jul 17H/Oct 12F; drinking: 1984 Jul 17H

24A; 1984 Jan 16G; 1987 Sep 18B; limited nuclear war 1981 Oct 16G/Oct 20G; Shevardnadze denounces 1986 Sep 23A; zero option 1982 Feb 4A; 1983 Jan 20G
START: 1983 Jun 8G/Oct 4G
Star Wars: 1985 Feb 11G/Sep 17G; 1986 Jul 25G
UN issues: 1982 Apr 6A; 1983 Sep 26A; 1984 Sep 24A; 1986 Sep 22A
economy: advisory board 1981 Feb 10H; economic report 1984 Feb 2H; 1986 Feb 6H; 1988 Feb 19H; national economic emergency 1980 Dec 17H/Dec 28H; 1988 Apr 8G; new federalism 1982 Jan 26H; oil allocation 1982 Mar 20H; program defended 1981 Oct 1H; 1982 Feb 26H/Mar 3H/Apr 3H/Sep 28F/Nov 16F; recession admitted 1981 Oct 18H; recovery promised 1982 Oct 13F; Stockman rebuked 1981 Nov 12F; TV reports criticized 1982 Mar 17F; wage-price council 1981 Jan 29H; World's Fair 1982 May 1I
education
    busing: 1980 Nov 18F
    federal aid: tax-exempt status 1982 Jan 12F/Jan 19F; veterans 1987 Jun 1G
    religious issues: school meetings 1984 Jul 25F/Aug 11F; voluntary prayer 1980 Oct 3J; 1982 May 6F/May 17F; 1983 May 21F
    teachers: convention address 1983 Jul 5F; effectiveness report 1986 Mar 4F; space shuttle 1984 Aug 27I
    tuition and student aid: private school tax credits 1982 Apr 15F; 1983 May 21F; student aid 1982 Apr 10F; 1986 Oct 17H; tax credits 1982 Sep 16F; 1983 Nov 16F
energy and power: alternative fuels 1988 Oct 14H; A-power cooperation 1985 Jul 23G; appropriations bill 1983 Jul 15H; daylight savings time 1986 Jul 8F; Energy Department end 1982 May 24H; energy efficiency standards 1987 Mar 17H; Hoover Dam power 1984 Aug 17H; low-income assistance 1984 Oct 30F; oil and gas drilling 1982 Dec 19F; oil price controls 1981 Jan 28H; research projects 1988 Aug 19H
environment and pollution
    acid rain: 1987 Mar 18D; 1988 Aug 5H
    air and water: Clean Water Act 1986 Oct 16H; 1987 Jan 21H/Feb 4H; drinking water 1986 Jun 19H; nitrogen oxide emissions 1988 Aug 5H; ocean dumping 1987 Dec 29H; 1988 Oct 19H/Nov 18H/Dec 28G; water clean-up 1986 Nov 6H; water development 1986 Nov 17H; 1988 Aug 19H
    EPA Superfund scandal 1983 Feb 16F/Mar 1H/Mar 4H
    pesticides: 1988 Oct 25H
    research: 1982 Oct 22H
    solid waste: hazardous waste 1984 Nov 8H; 1986 Apr 1H/Oct 17H; medical wastes 1988 Nov 2H; radon 1988 Oct 29H; sixpack holders 1988 Oct 28H

wilderness areas: 1984 Oct 9H; 1988 Oct 28H

espionage and intelligence issues: classified information 1982 Apr 2G; covert operations 1981 Dec 4F; 1985 Nov 3G; 1987 Apr 19F; guerrilla warfare manual 1984 Oct 18G; intelligence oversight laws 1987 Aug 7F; lie detector tests 1985 Dec 11G/Dec 20G; Moscow embassy security 1987 Apr 7G

families and family life: 1981 Mar 5F; 1984 Aug 16F/Oct 9F; 1986 Nov 14F; 1988 Aug 19F/Nov 5F

foreign aid: 1983 Dec 7G; 1985 Aug 8G; 1988 Oct 1G

foreign policy
Afghanistan: 1981 Mar 9G/Dec 27G; 1982 Dec 26G; 1986 Nov 18G
Africa: 1985 Jan 3G
Argentina: 1981 Mar 17D; 1982 Apr 1A/Jul 12G; 1983 Dec 10G
Asia: 1986 Apr 25G
Australia: 1985 Feb 5G; 1986 Apr 18E; 1988 Jun 19G
Bahrain: 1983 Jul 19C
Brazil: 1982 May 12D/Nov 30D/Dec 1D-2D; 1986 Mar 17D; 1987 Nov 13G; 1988 Jul 22H
Canada: 1981 Mar 11D; 1985 Mar 18D; 1986 Mar 19D; 1987 Mar 18D/Apr 5D; 1988 Apr 27D
Caribbean: 1981 Jun 9D; 1982 Feb 24D/Apr 8D; 1986 Feb 20D
Central America: 1982 Feb 24D; 1983 Apr 6G/Apr 27G/Jul 18G/Jul 26G/Sep 1G; 1984 Jan 11G/Feb 3G/Feb 17G/May 9G/May 22G
Chad: 1983 Aug 4G/Aug 10G
China: 1982 Jun 1E; 1983 Oct 13G/Nov 26E; 1984 Apr 26A/May 1G; 1985 Jul 23G; 1988 Mar 7G
Colombia: 1982 Dec 3D
Costa Rica: 1982 Dec 4D; 1986 Aug 13G; 1987 Jun 17D
Cuba: 1982 Apr 6G; 1985 Jul 8G; 1986 Jan 2G/Aug 22G
developing nations: 1981 Oct 15A
Ecuador: 1986 Jan 13G
Egypt: 1980 Nov 23C/Dec 7A; 1981 Aug 5C/Oct 6A/Oct 10A; 1984 Feb 14G/Mar 18C
El Salvador: aid requests 1981 Feb 25G; 1983 Feb 28G/Mar 10G/Jun 18G; 1984 Apr 13G; Cronkite interview 1981 Mar 3G; Duarte election hailed 1984 May 22G; Duarte meetings 1985 May 16G; guerrilla talks explored 1983 Jun 20G; House, Senate actions 1981 Mar 2F; 1982 Mar 2G; 1983 Oct 6G; 1984 Mar 14G/May 24G; 1986 Aug 13G; human rights 1983 Jan 20D/Nov 30G; 1984 Jan 4G/Aug 29F; 1987 Jan 14G; immigration law 1987 Apr 25D/May 14G; pocket veto 1984 Aug 29F; 1987 Jan 14G; Schaufelberger assassination 1983 May 27G; travel ban 1984 Nov 1G
European Community: 1982 Aug 12B/Oct 21A; 1985 Oct 16H
Falklands crisis: 1982 Apr 1A
France: 1981 Oct 18A; 1982 Mar 12A; 1983 Aug 10G; 1987 Mar 31B/Apr 1I

G-7 summits: 1985 May 4A; 1986 May 6A; 1987 Jun 8A
Great Britain: 1984 Dec 22G; 1986 May 31G/Nov 15G
Grenada: 1983 Oct 25B/Oct 25D; 1986 Feb 20D
Guatemala: 1986 Aug 13G
Honduras: 1984 Jul 8G; 1985 May 21D; 1986 Aug 13G; 1988 Mar 16G
India: 1982 Jul 29A; 1985 Jun 15G; 1987 Oct 20G
Iran: Airbus tragedy 1988 Jul 3G/Jul 11G; Bahai executions plea 1983 May 22G/May 28C; embargo imposed 1987 Oct 26G; hostage crisis 1980 Dec 24C; 1981 Jan 8G/Jan 27F/Jul 2F; 1985 Jul 8G; 1986 Nov 13G/Nov 19G/Dec 6F/Dec 24F; 1987 Jan 9G/Jan 26G/Mar 4G/Jul 26G
Iraq: 1983 Dec 20C; 1984 Nov 26G
Ireland: 1981 Aug 3G
Israel: Begin cables, letters 1982 Jun 6C/Jun 9G; Begin meetings 1981 Sep 10G; 1982 Jun 15G/Jun 21G; Camp David process 1980 Dec 7A; cluster bombs 1982 Jul 16G/Sep 29G; criticized by 1984 Feb 14C; fighter planes 1981 Aug 17G; 1983 Mar 31G/Mar 13C/May 6G/May 20G; peace proposals 1982 Sep 6C/Sep 8C; Peres meeting 1984 Oct 7G; policy change denied 1982 Feb 16G; settlement freeze 1982 Sep 14G; Shamir meeting 1983 Nov 29A
Italy: 1982 Jun 7B
Japan: automobile export quotas 1985 Mar 1H; aviation agreement 1982 Jun 4E; electronics import duties 1987 Mar 27H; fishing 1987 Dec 29H; 1988 Apr 6F; Mansfield retained 1981 Jan 7G; Nakasone meetings 1983 Jan 18E; 1985 Jan 2A/Apr 2H; 1986 Apr 13G; 1987 Apr 29E; scientific cooperation 1988 Jun 20E; Senate condemns trade practices 1985 Mar 28H; Suzuki meetings 1981 May 8E/May 8G; Takeshita meeting 1988 Jun 20E; visits 1983 Nov 14E
Jordan: 1981 Nov 3C; 1982 Sep 13C; 1983 Apr 7C/Apr 10C; 1984 Feb 14G; 1988 Jan 30G
Kuwait: 1987 Jun 30G/Oct 21G
Lebanon: Beirut refugee camps massacre 1982 Sep 18G; foreign aid 1983 Jun 27G; Gemayel meetings 1982 Oct 19A; 1983 Dec 2G; hostage released 1985 Sep 18C; Israeli invasion 1982 Jun 30G/Aug 4G; 1983 Feb 22C; Marine headquarters bombing 1983 Dec 27G; U.S. troops in 1982 Jul 6G/Aug 20G/Sep 28G/Nov 1G; 1983 Mar 15G/Oct 12G/Oct 23G/Dec 14G/Dec 29G; 1984 Jan 19G/Feb 7G/Feb 8C/Feb 15G/Mar 30C
Libya: air attacks 1986 Apr 14C; called terrorist state 1985 Jul 8G; CIA covert operation 1985 Nov 3G; economic sanctions 1986 Jan 7G; 1989 Jan 19G; military action studied

1988 Dec 21G; Qaddafi denies death plot 1981 Dec 6C; U.S. citizens asked to leave 1981 Dec 10G; 1986 Jan 7G; U.S. fleet leaves 1986 Mar 27C; U.S. oil companies close 1986 Jun 30C
Mexico: 1981 Jan 5D/Jun 9D; 1982 Oct 8D; 1983 Aug 14D; 1984 May 17D; 1986 Jan 3D; 1988 Feb 13D
Middle East: Arab League delegation 1982 Oct 21C-22C; fresh start urged 1982 Sep 1A; Habib mission 1981 Dec 11G; 1982 Jul 25G/Oct 11G
Morocco: Arab League delegation 1982 Oct 22C
Nicaragua: cease-fire plans 1985 Apr 4G/Apr 5D; 1987 Aug 4C; contra aid 1983 Mar 29G; 1985 Apr 18G/Apr 20G/Aug 30G; 1986 Feb 25G/Oct 18C/Oct 24G; 1987 Jan 14G/May 3G/May 15F/Aug 21G/Oct 7G; 1988 Jan 27G/Oct 14G; covert operations 1982 Mar 10G; 1983 Apr 14G; 1985 Jan 23G/Feb 21G/Jul 8G/Dec 14G; 1986 Mar 16G; Guatemala City agreement 1987 Aug 8G; guerrilla warfare manual 1984 Oct 18G; Honduras invasion 1988 Mar 16G; House, Senate actions 1983 Sep 22G; 1984 May 24G/Jun 25G; 1985 Apr 24G/Jun 12G; 1986 Mar 20G/Mar 27G/Apr 16G/Apr 30G/Jun 25G/Aug 13G; 1987 Mar 11G; 1988 Feb 3G; Neutrality Act violations 1983 Nov 3F; Ortega meeting 1987 Oct 8D; polls 1986 Apr 15G; trade embargo 1985 May 1G; 1988 Apr 25G; World Court proceedings 1985 Jan 18G
North Korea: 1985 Jul 8G; 1988 Oct 31G
Pakistan: 1988 Jan 15G
Panama: 1988 Apr 8G/Jul 27G
Philippines: 1985 Oct 12G
PLO: 1981 Oct 17G; 1982 Jul 15C; 1983 Feb 22C/Apr 5C; 1988 Dec 14G
Poland: 1981 Mar 26A/Dec 17G/Dec 23G; 1982 Jan 4B/Oct 9G/Oct 27G; 1987 Feb 19G
Romania: 1982 Feb 21G
Saudi Arabia: AWACS sales 1981 Oct 16G/Oct 28G/Oct 29G; Fahd meetings 1982 Jul 14G; 1985 Feb 12G; foreign minister meeting 1982 Jul 20A; missile sales 1986 May 21G/Jun 5G; 1987 Jun 11G; Saudi peace proposal 1981 Oct 29G; support for 1984 May 21G
South Africa: 1981 May 15C; 1984 Nov 21G/Dec 7G; 1985 Sep 9G; 1986 Jul 22H/Sep 26G; 1987 Oct 2G
South Korea: 1981 Feb 2E; 1983 Sep 5G/Nov 14E; 1985 Oct 16H; 1988 Oct 31G
Soviet Union: ABM treaty violations 1987 Dec 2G; "bombing Russia" joke 1984 Aug 11G; Brezhnev 1981 Feb 23A/Mar 10A; 1982 Apr 19A/Sep 15C/Nov 11G; Chernenko 1984 Mar 23A/Jun 14G; dissidents 1981 May 29B; fishing

ban lifted 1984 Jul 25G; glasnost 1987 Aug 26G; Gorbachev 1985 Jul 2G/Nov 21B; 1986 Aug 4G/Sep 30G/Oct 7G/Oct 12A; 1987 Jun 12B/Oct 30G/Nov 22G; 1988 Mar 23G/May 29A/Dec 6G; grain embargo and sales 1981 Mar 27G/Apr 24G; 1982 Aug 2H/Oct 15H/Oct 18H; 1983 Apr 22A; 1984 Nov 1G; 1986 Aug 1H; Grenada invasion condemned 1983 Oct 25B; Gromyko meeting 1984 Sep 28G; INF treaty 1987 Dec 3G/Dec 8A/Dec 11G; Korean airline incident 1983 Sep 5G; military spending issues 1982 Feb 7A/Mar 31G; 1983 Mar 25G; Moscow embassy security 1987 Apr 7G; New Year's greetings 1986 Jan 1A/Dec 30B; 1987 Jan 1B; 1988 Jan 1A; Olympic Games boycott 1984 May 28J; Poland crisis 1981 Mar 26A/Dec 17G; press criticism 1981 Feb 4A; 1984 Jun 27G; regional peace plan 1985 Oct 24A; sanctions 1981 Dec 23G/Dec 29G/Dec 30B; 1982 Jun 18G/Jul 22B/Jul 24B/Jul 28G/Aug 10G/Aug 12B/Sep 29G/Nov 13G; Shevardnadze meetings 1986 Sep 20A; strategic arms plan 1981 Oct 5A; terrorism 1986 Jan 2G
Spain: 1985 May 6A
Sudan: 1984 Mar 18C
Syria: 1982 Jul 20A; 1984 Jan 4C-4G
Taiwan: 1981 Jun 17E; 1982 Jun 1E/Jul 8F
Turkey: 1985 Apr 6G
United Nations: budget contribution 1985 Aug 16G; human rights 1985 Dec 10G; IMF/World Bank speeches 1981 Sep 29A; 1983 Sep 27G; Law of the Sea treaty 1982 Jul 8G/Dec 30G; speeches 1983 Sep 26A; 1984 Sep 24A; 1985 Oct 24A; 1988 Sep 26A; UNESCO withdrawal 1983 Dec 28A
West Germany: Berlin visit 1982 Jun 11B; 1987 Jun 12B; Bitburg cemetery visit 1985 Apr 11G/Apr 16G/Apr 18G-19G/Apr 20B/Apr 30B/May 5B; Kohl meetings 1982 Nov 15A; 1984 Nov 30G; 1986 Oct 22G; Schmidt meetings 1980 Nov 20G; 1982 Jan 5B
Yugoslavia: 1985 May 31G

foreign trade: Canada 1985 Sep 26D/Dec 10H; 1986 May 22D; 1988 Jan 2D/Jul 25H/Sep 19H/Sep 28H; export controls 1983 Aug 20H/Oct 14H; 1984 Mar 30H; 1985 Jul 12G; exports to protected markets 1985 Sep 7H; export subsidies 1983 Jan 11H; 1988 Nov 17H; import curbs 1982 May 4H/Oct 21A; 1983 Apr 1H; 1984 Sep 18H; 1985 Aug 28H/Aug 31H/Sep 17H/Dec 17H; 1988 Sep 28H; legislation 1986 May 22H/May 29H; 1988 May 24H/Aug 23H; textile agreement 1988 Feb 13D

holidays and special events: Constitution bicentennial 1987 Sep 17F; D-Day anniversary 1984 Jun 6A; Grenada invasion anniversary

1984 Oct 24G; King holiday 1983 Jan 15F/Nov 2F; national floral emblem 1986 Oct 7J; Vietnam War memorial 1984 May 28G

housing: 1982 Mar 29H/Jun 24H; 1983 Jul 12F; 1986 May 2H/Sep 30H; 1988 Feb 5F/Sep 13F

human rights: 1981 Apr 30G; 1985 Dec 10G; 1986 Oct 7G

immigration and refugees: 1986 Nov 6F; 1987 Apr 25D/May 14G; 1988 Nov 15F

inauguration: 1981 Jan 20F; 1985 Jan 20F-21F

Iran-Contra arms scandal
administration stance: 1986 Nov 13G/Nov 19G/Nov 25G/Dec 3F/Dec 6F/Dec 24F; 1987 Jan 9G/Mar 4G/Mar 19G/Mar 26F/Aug 12G
congressional committee hearings: 1987 Apr 8G/May 11G/Jun 24G/Jul 9G/Jul 15G/Jul 23G/Jul 26G/Jul 30G/Nov 18G
independent counsel appointment: 1986 Dec 2F
North role: innocence asserted 1987 Aug 1G; 1988 Mar 25F; limited immunity proposed 1986 Dec 16F; trial 1988 Dec 1F/Dec 30F; 1989 Apr 6F
Poindexter role: innocence asserted 1987 Aug 1G; 1988 Mar 25F; limited immunity proposed 1986 Dec 16F; trial 1989 Sep 6F/Nov 16G/Dec 21F
polls: 1986 Apr 15G/Nov 18G; 1987 Apr 15F
Tower Commission: 1986 Nov 26F; 1987 Jan 26G/Feb 26G

labor and employment
ethics issues: Whistleblower bill vetoed 1988 Oct 26F
jobs: unemployment benefits 1982 Feb 1H; 1983 Mar 24F; unemployment rate 1983 Feb 4H; youth programs 1984 Oct 30F
unions: air traffic controllers 1981 Aug 3H/Dec 9F; railroads 1982 Jul 8H; teachers addressed 1983 Jul 5F; Teamsters meeting 1981 Dec 1H
wages and hours: federal flextime experiment 1982 Mar 26H; federal hiring freeze 1981 Mar 6H; federal pay raises 1987 Feb 12F/Apr 4H/Dec 31F; 1988 Sep 23H; 1989 Jan 5F; federal retirement system 1986 Jun 6F; productivity committee 1982 Jan 6H; time off for overtime 1985 Nov 13F

medicine and health care
Agent Orange: 1984 Oct 24G
AIDS: 1987 Apr 1F/Apr 1I/May 31F/Jul 23F; 1988 Aug 2F/Nov 4F
disabled: 1984 Sep 19F/Oct 9F; 1988 Aug 19F
drugs: medical wastes 1988 Nov 2H; Orphan Drug Act 1985 Aug 11H; prescription drugs 1984 Sep 24H; tobacco warning labels 1986 Feb 27F
funding and research: biomedical research 1985 Nov 20F; hunger report 1984 Jan 10E; omnibus health bill 1986 Nov 14F
Medicare: 1983 Jun 23F; 1987 Feb 15F; 1988 Jul 1F

veterans: 1983 Dec 21G; 1988 May 20G
minorities: Black Americans 1981 Jun 29F; 1982 Jan 3F/Jan 12F/Jan 19F/Mar 11F; 1984 Nov 21G; 1985 Jan 15F; 1987 Sep 8F; 1988 Aug 10F; Jews and Judaism 1983 Apr 17F; 1984 Sep 6F; Native Americans 1983 Jun 1F; 1988 Dec 12F
money and finance: 1980 Nov 5H; 1982 Nov 27H; 1984 Aug 10H
pardons: 1981 Apr 15F; 1983 May 14F; 1989 Jan 18J
parks and recreation areas: air tour restrictions 1987 Aug 19H; battlefield park 1988 Nov 11H; scenic rivers system 1985 Apr 26H; 1986 Oct 30H/Nov 17H; wilderness areas 1983 Jan 14H; 1985 Apr 26H; 1988 Nov 3H/Nov 16H; wildlife refuges 1988 Oct 28H
personal
 assassination attempt: 1981 Mar 30F/Apr 3F/Apr 11F
 ceremonial duties: West Point commencement address 1981 May 27G; Statue of Liberty celebration 1986 Jul 3J; Japan visit 1989 Oct 28E
 family issues: ethnic joke apology 1980 Feb 18F; son married 1980 Nov 24J; son's dance performance 1981 Mar 15J; daughter at anti-nuclear rally 1981 Jul 14F; wife's role in decisions 1987 Mar 4F; book contracts signed 1989 Jan 26J
 health issues: abdominal cancer surgery 1985 Jul 13F/Jul 20F; skin cancer surgery 1985 Aug 1F/Oct 11F; 1986 Jan 18F; 1987 Jul 31F; abdominal benign polyps removed 1986 Jun 20F; prostate surgery 1986 Dec 17F; 1987 Jan 8F; annual physical 1988 Jan 15F
 presidential library: 1987 Apr 23F; 1988 Nov 21F
 security issues: Carter Blair House bugging story 1981 Oct 23J; golf club intruder 1983 Oct 22F
 tax returns: 1983 Apr 15J; 1984 Apr 13F; 1985 Apr 12H; 1986 Apr 11F; 1987 Apr 14F; 1988 Apr 8H
politics: congressional elections 1982 Sep 8F; 1986 Oct 23F; conservatives addressed 1981 Mar 20F; debategate 1983 Jun 30F/Jul 19F; 1984 Feb 29F/May 14F; lobbying restrictions 1988 Nov 23F; Puerto Rico 1982 Jan 12G
polls: 1981 Mar 18F/Jun 20F; 1982 Jan 10F; 1986 Jan 28F/Jun 15F; 1987 Mar 3F/May 17B/Dec 6F; 1989 Jan 18F
presidential campaign (1980)
 campaign issues: style 1980 Feb 5F; economic proposals 1980 Jun 25F/Sep 9F; Urban League address 1980 Aug 6F; Social Security 1980 Sep 7F; Democrats wooed 1980 Oct 2F; women on Supreme Court 1980 Oct 14F
 convention: nominated 1980 Jul 16F; Bush joins ticket 1980 Jul 17F
 debategate: 1983 Jun 30F/Jul 19F; 1984 Feb 29F/May 14F

debates: 1980 Jan 5F/Feb 20F/Sep 9F/Sep 21F/Sep 25F/Oct 28F
election results: 1980 Nov 4F
endorsements: 1980 Apr 14F
finances: funding committees 1980 Jul 1F/Aug 28F; campaign pledges 1980 Oct 19F
polls: 1980 Jan 9F/Jan 11F/Apr 18F/Jun 23F/Aug 19F
primaries: Alabama 1980 Mar 11F; Arkansas 1980 Feb 16F; Connecticut 1980 Mar 25F; Florida 1980 Mar 11F; Georgia 1980 Mar 11F; Illinois 1980 Mar 18F; Indiana 1980 May 6F; Iowa 1980 Jan 21F; Kansas 1980 Apr 1F; Louisiana 1980 Apr 5F; Maryland 1980 May 13F; Massachusetts 1980 Mar 4F; Michigan 1980 May 20F; Nebraska 1980 May 13F; New Hampshire 1980 Feb 26F; New York 1980 Mar 25F; North Carolina 1980 May 6F; Oregon 1980 May 20F; Pennsylvania 1980 Apr 22F; South Carolina 1980 Mar 8F; Tennessee 1980 May 6F; Texas 1980 May 3F; Vermont 1980 Mar 4F; Wisconsin 1980 Apr 1F
transition: 1980 Nov 17F
presidential campaign (1984)
 campaign issues: reelection committee 1983 Oct 13G/Oct 17F; taxes 1984 Aug 4F/Aug 12F; Labor Day 1984 Sep 3F; Jewish group address 1984 Sep 6F; Democratic voter appeal 1984 Sep 13F/Sep 19F; mailing lists 1986 Mar 22F
 candidacy: 1984 Jan 29F/Jan 30F
 convention: nomination 1984 Aug 22F/Aug 23F
 debates: 1984 Feb 11F/Sep 17F/Oct 7F/Oct 21F/Oct 22F
 election results: 1984 Jan 6F/Dec 21F; 1985 Jan 7F
 endorsements: 1984 Oct 28F
 media: 1984 Jul 25F
 polls: 1984 Jul 31F/Sep 12F/Sep 26F/Oct 22F
 post-election accounts: 1984 Nov 7F
presidential campaign (1988): Bush endorsed 1988 May 11F; convention 1988 Aug 15F
press and broadcasting: concocted quotes 1988 Apr 13F; farewell address 1989 Jan 11F; final radio broadcast 1989 Jan 14F; laryngitis feigned 1987 Mar 11F; public broadcast aid bill veto 1984 Aug 29F; TV advertising 1988 Nov 5F; Voice of America speech 1985 Nov 9G
religion
 Bahais: 1983 May 22G/May 28C
 Catholic Church: A-arms opposed 1982 Apr 26G; 1988 Apr 15J; needy aid 1982 Apr 13F; papal meeting 1982 Jun 7B; 1984 May 2A-2G
 politics: 1983 Mar 8F; 1984 Aug 23J
 school issues: student group meetings 1984 Jul 25F/Aug 11F; voluntary school prayer 1980 Oct 3J; 1982 May 6F/May 17F
science and technology: 1981 Oct 27I; 1985 Nov 20F; 1986 Jun 18I; 1987 Jan 30I; 1988 Jun 20E

Social Security: 1980 Sep 7F; 1981 May 12F/May 20F; 1983 Mar 25F/Apr 20F; 1984 Jul 6F/Aug 23H
space and space flights: Challenger disaster 1986 Jan 31F/Feb 3I; launch insurance 1988 Nov 15I; NASA funding 1986 Nov 14I; 1987 Oct 30I; private satellites 1984 Feb 24H; space shuttle 1984 Aug 27I; space station 1987 Apr 3I
sports: 1981 Apr 21J; 1984 May 28J/Jul 28J/Aug 13J
state and local issues: 1981 Jul 30F; 1982 Feb 22F/Mar 15F/May 10F; 1985 Nov 8H/Nov 13F; 1986 Feb 24F
State of the Union address: 1981 Feb 18H; 1982 Jan 26H; 1984 Jan 25F; 1985 Feb 6F; 1986 Feb 4F; 1987 Jan 27F; 1988 Jan 25F
taxes
 as campaign issue: 1980 Jun 25F; 1984 Aug 4F/Aug 12F
 reforms and proposals: tax-cut plan 1981 Jun 4H/Jul 27H/Aug 4H; 1982 Nov 23H; tax increases 1981 Nov 10H/Dec 17H; 1982 Aug 6F/Aug 16F; 1983 May 17H/Dec 14H; 1987 Oct 20H; tuition credits 1982 Apr 15F/Sep 16F; 1983 Nov 16H; flat tax 1982 Jul 6H; interest and dividend witholding 1983 Aug 5H; tax code overhaul 1985 May 7H/May 28H/May 30H/Sep 2H; 1986 May 11H/Oct 22H; 1988 Nov 11H; state unitary tax 1985 Nov 8H
terrorism: 1984 Apr 16G
transportation: automobiles 1980 Jul 12H/Dec 20H; aviation 1981 Aug 3H/Aug 13H/Dec 9F; 1982 Jun 4E; 1987 Aug 19H; budget proposals 1983 Aug 15H; 1988 Sep 30H; intercity bus operators 1982 Sep 20H; railroads 1982 Jul 8H/Sep 22H; roads 1981 Mar 14H/Sep 7F; 1984 Jul 17H; 1985 Mar 13H
veterans: 1983 Dec 21G; 1984 Oct 24G; 1987 Jun 1G; 1988 May 20G/Oct 25G/Nov 15G/Nov 18G
waters, territorial: 1984 Jul 25G; 1987 Dec 29H; 1988 Apr 6F
welfare and poverty: budget and spending programs 1982 Apr 13F; 1983 Jul 30F; 1984 Oct 30F; 1986 Sep 30F; 1988 Oct 13F; hunger 1983 Aug 2F; 1986 May 21F; homelessness 1987 Feb 12F/Jul 22F; 1988 Nov 7F/Dec 22F
 women: 1980 Oct 14F; 1981 Jul 7F; 1982 Jan 3F; 1983 Aug 1F; 1984 Aug 23H
 youth: 1984 Jul 17H/Oct 30F
Real, Manuel 1981 Jun 3H
Redding, J. Saunders 1988 Mar 2F
Redding, Otis 1989 Jan 18J
Reddy, Sanjiva 1982 Jan 25E
Reder, Walter 1985 Jan 23J/Feb 1B
Redford, Robert 1981 Mar 30J
Redgrave, Lynn 1985 Mar 21J
Redgrave, Michael S(cudamore) 1985 Mar 21J
Redgrave, Vanessa 1980 Nov 2J; 1982 Apr 11J; 1983 Dec 20J; 1985 Mar 21J; 1986 Jan 2J; 1987 Oct 14F
Redman, Charles E. 1987 Jul 11B
Reed, Dean 1986 Jun 22J
Reed, Donna 1986 Jan 14J
Reed, Frank 1986 Sep 12C
Reed, Thomas 1984 Aug 30F
Rees, Roger 1982 Jun 6J

Regan, Donald T.
 government service: treasury secretary 1980 Dec 11F; White House staff chief 1985 Jan 8F; 1987 Feb 27F; Reagan astrology 1988 May 9F
 Iran-Contra arms scandal: 1987 Jul 30G
 monetary policy: Fed 1981 Oct 6H; deficits 1981 Oct 30H/Nov 3H; 1982 Jan 6H; prime lending rates 1983 Feb 25H; OPEC oil price cuts 1983 Mar 14H; China taxation treaty 1984 Mar 21A; Argentina loan 1984 Mar 31G
Rehnquist, William Hubbs
 judicial issues: 1988 Jan 1F; 1989 Jan 1F
 personal issues: TV interview 1984 Dec 29F
 Supreme Court nomination: as chief justice 1986 Jun 17F/Aug 1F/Aug 14F/Sep 17F/Sep 26F
 Supreme Court rulings: capital punishment 1981 Apr 27F; caseload 1982 Sep 23F; PAC spending limits 1985 Mar 18F; term begins 1986 Oct 6F; reasonable religious leave 1986 Nov 17F; mishandled evidence conviction 1988 Nov 29F
Reid, John 1988 Oct 2J
Reid, Ptolemy 1984 Aug 11D
Reilly, William K. 1988 Dec 22F; 1989 Feb 2H/Jul 6H
Reiner, Rob 1989 Jul 12J
Reinhardt, Max 1986 May 12J/Jun 16J
Reischauer, Edwin 1981 May 17G
Reiser, Pete 1981 Oct 25J
Remeliik, Haruo I. 1985 Jun 30E/Oct 25E; 1987 Jul 20E
Remengesau, Thomas 1988 Aug 20E
Remini, Robert 1984 Nov 16J
Renault, Gilbert 1984 Jul 29J
Renault, Mary 1983 Dec 13J
Rene, France Albert 1981 Dec 2C
Renoir, Pierre Auguste 1985 Oct 27J
Retton, Mary Lou 1985 Jan 8J
Reuter, Manuel 1989 Jun 11J
Rewald, Ronald 1984 Nov 21F
Rexroth, Kenneth 1982 Jun 6J
Reynolds, Roger 1989 Mar 30J
Reynolds, William Bradford 1985 Jun 27F
Rhine, Joseph 1980 Feb 20I
Rhodes, John 1980 Dec 8F
Rhodes, Richard 1987 Nov 9J; 1988 Jan 11J/Mar 31J
Rhys-Davies, John 1989 May 24J
Ribera, Jose 1985 Mar 14J
Rice, Anne 1988 Nov 25J/Dec 23J
Rice, Glen 1989 Apr 3J
Rice, Jerry 1989 Jan 22J
Rice, Reva 1987 Mar 15J
Rice, Tim 1986 May 14J
Rich, Adrienne 1986 Jun 6J
Rich, Buddy (Bernard) 1987 Apr 2J
Rich, Marc 1983 Sep 19H/Sep 20G/Sep 22G; 1984 Oct 11H
Richardson, Carole 1989 Oct 19B
Richardson, Elliot L. 1987 Sep 16A
Richardson, L. Kenneth 1986 Nov 2J
Richardson, Ralph 1983 Oct 10J
Richardson, Ron 1985 Apr 25J
Richey, Charles R. 1985 Mar 5H/Jun 12H/Aug 19F
Richie, Lionel
 best-sellers: All Night Long 1983 Dec 14J; Can't Slow Down 1983 Nov 9J/Dec 14J; 1984 Jan 21J/Feb 18J/Mar 24J/Apr 28J/May

20J/May 28J/Jun 16J/Jul 21J; 1985 Feb 26J; Dancing on the Ceiling 1986 Sep 17J/Oct 22J/Nov 22J; Lionel Richie 1982 Nov 17J/Dec 15J; 1983 Jan 5J/Feb 9J/Mar 9J; Truly 1983 Feb 23J; We Are the World 1986 Feb 25J
 Grammy awards: 1983 Feb 23J; 1985 Feb 26J; 1986 Feb 25J
Richmond, Frederick W. 1982 Jan 20F/Aug 25F/Nov 10F
Richter, Burton 1987 Apr 15I
Richter, Charles F(rancis) 1985 Sep 30I
Rickman, Alan 1988 Jul 15J
Rickover, Hyman George 1981 Nov 13G; 1986 Jul 8G
Rico, Aldo 1988 Jan 18D
Riddles, Libby 1985 Mar 20J
Ride, Sally 1987 Aug 17I
Rideau, Wilbert 1986 Jun 17J
Ridley, Nicholas 1986 Apr 25C/Jul 3B
Riegle Jr., Donald W. 1989 Oct 13F/Dec 22F
Rifai, Zaid al- 1985 Oct 21C; 1989 Apr 24C
Ringling, John 1985 Jun 4J
Rios Montt, Efrain 1982 Jun 9D/Jun 10D/Jun 30D; 1983 Jan 8D/Jun 8D/Jun 29D/Aug 7D
Ripken Jr., Cal 1982 Nov 24J; 1983 Nov 16J
Ripley, Alexandra 1988 Apr 25J
Ripley, S. Dillon 1984 Sep 17J
Rison, Tyrone 1983 Dec 16F
Ritola, Willie 1982 Apr 24J
Ritter, Samuel 1984 Jun 14F
Ritz, Jimmy 1985 Nov 17J
Rivard, Yvon 1987 May 27J
Rivera Lopez, Jose Francisco 1987 Jan 29D
Rivera y Damas, Arturo 1981 Jul 12D
Rivers, Joan 1985 Jan 18J/Feb 8J/Mar 15J; 1986 May 6J; 1987 May 15J
Rivlin, Alice M. 1982 Feb 25H/Jul 27H
Rizzo, Frank L. 1983 May 17F; 1986 Nov 23F; 1987 May 19F/Nov 3F
Roach, James Terry 1986 Jan 10F
Roach, Janet 1985 Jun 14J
Roach, John R. 1983 Nov 15J
Roaff, Elio 1986 Apr 13J
Robards, Jason 1988 Aug 28J
Robbins, Harold 1981 Jul 5J/Aug 9J
Robbins, Jerome 1985 Jul 26J; 1989 Jun 4J
Robbins, Tim 1988 Jun 15J
Robelo Callejas, Alfonso 1980 Apr 22D/May 18D; 1987 Nov 19D; 1988 Feb 5D
Roberts, John 1980 Jun 23D
Roberts, Oral 1980 Feb 25J
Roberts, Thomas 1989 Aug 31J
Robertson, Marion G. (Pat)
 presidential campaign (1988): precinct delegate elections 1986 Aug 6F; candidacy 1986 Sep 17F; 1987 Oct 1F; mayors addressed 1987 Jun 13F; polls 1987 Sep 12F/Dec 5F; campaign spending/matching funds 1987 Oct 8F; 1988 Jan 4F/Mar 30F; debates 1987 Oct 28F; party rules 1987 Dec 12F; primaries 1988 Feb 4F/Feb 8F/Mar 2F; libel suit dropped 1988 Mar 7F; ends campaign 1988 Apr 6F; election-law violations 1988 Apr 12F/Dec 30F; withdrawal 1988 May 16F
 religious organization: revenues 1980 Feb 25J; talk show 1986 Sep 22F
Robinson Jr., Aubrey E. 1980 May 13H; 1982 Nov 30H
Robinson, Chip 1987 Feb 1J
Robinson, David 1987 Jun 22J
Robinson, Earl 1985 Aug 14J

Robinson, Frank 1982 Aug 1J
Robinson, Jackie 1982 Jul 8J
Robinson, Julia Bowman 1985 Jul 30I
Robinson, Maurice R. 1982 Feb 7J
Robinson, Phil Alden 1989 Apr 21J
Robinson, Robert E. 1989 Dec 18F
Robinson Jr., Roscoe 1982 Aug 11G
Robinson, Sugar Ray (Walker Smith) 1989 Apr 12J
Robison, Richard 1986 Sep 4E
Robles Plaza, Luis 1987 Oct 28D
Robson, Flora 1984 Jul 7J
Roca, Renee 1986 Feb 8J
Rocard, Michel 1988 Jun 23B/Jun 26E/Jun 28B/Dec 9B
Roccaserra, Jean-Paul 1984 Aug 24B
Roche, Stephen 1987 Jul 26J/Sep 6J
Roche, Victoria 1984 Aug 21J
Rochon, Donald 1988 Jan 25F
Rock, John 1984 Dec 4I
Rockefeller, David 1982 Mar 2G; 1986 Jan 13C
Rocker, Tracy 1988 Dec 7J
Rodgers, Bill 1980 Mar 21J
Rodino Jr., Peter W. 1982 May 18F; 1985 Jul 9F
Rodrigues, Adilson 1989 Jul 15J
Rodriguez, Andres 1989 Feb 3D/Feb 6D/May 1D
Rodriguez, Chi Chi 1987 Feb 15J
Rodriguez, Daryl 1989 Apr 27F
Rodriguez, Felix I. 1987 May 14F/May 29G/Aug 3G
Rodriguez, Francisco 1989 Sep 1D
Rodriguez, Lucien 1983 Mar 27J
Rodriguez Gacha, Jose Gonzalo 1989 Dec 6A/Dec 15D
Rodriguez Maurell, Antonio 1988 Dec 23D
Rodriguez Porth, Jose Antonio 1989 Jun 9D
Rodriguez Sahagun, Agustin 1981 Nov 13B
Roe, Allison 1981 Apr 20J/Oct 25J
Roffe, Diann 1985 Feb 6J
Rogers, Adrian P. 1986 Jun 10J; 1987 Jun 16J
Rogers, Bill 1981 Jul 19J
Rogers, Carl Ransom 1987 Feb 4I
Rogers, George 1981 Apr 28J
Rogers, Ginger 1987 Jun 22J
Rogers, Isabel 1987 Jun 10J
Rogers, Kenny 1980 Jan 2J/Dec 3J; 1981 Jan 7J; 1983 Nov 9J
Rogers, Sharon 1989 Mar 10G
Rogers, Will 1985 Nov 19J
Rogers III, Will C. 1989 Mar 10G
Roginski, Arseny 1981 Dec 8B
Rohrer, Heinrich 1986 Oct 15I
Roh Tae Woo 1987 Jun 10E/Aug 5E/Nov 29E/Dec 16E/Dec 22E; 1988 Feb 25E/Jul 7E; 1989 Mar 20E
Rojas de Negri, Rodrigo 1986 Jul 3D
Roldan, Juan 1987 Oct 29J
Roldos Aguilera, Jaime 1980 Apr 11D; 1981 May 24D
Rollins Jr., Howard E. 1984 Sep 14J
Rollins, Sonny (Theodore) 1983 May 23J
Rolon, Ismael 1985 May 5D
Romanenko, Yuri V. 1980 Sep 18I; 1987 Dec 29I
Romanov, Semyon 1983 Sep 4B
Romberg, Alan D. 1983 Oct 3G/Oct 20G/Dec 13G
Romero, Carlos Huberto 1980 May 2D
Romero Barcelo, Carlos 1980 Dec 18D
Romero y Galdamez, Oscar Arnulfo 1980 Mar 24D/Mar 30D; 1984 Aug 28D; 1985 Aug 20D/Sep 29D; 1987 Nov 22D
Ronstadt, Linda 1980 Mar 5J/Apr 2J; 1983 Dec 14J; 1984 Jan 21J
Rooney, Kevin 1982 Jul 31J
Roosevelt, Eleanor 1987 Aug 22J

Roosevelt, Franklin D. 1984 Jul 26F; 1986 Jan 19F
Rosa Chavez, Grigorio 1983 Dec 25D
Rosahn, Eve 1982 Jan 28F
Rosberg, Keke 1982 Oct 25J
Rose, George 1985 Dec 2J; 1986 Jun 1J
Rose, Pete 1984 Apr 13J; 1985 Sep 11J; 1988 May 6J; 1989 Jun 25J/Jun 26J/Aug 24J
Rosenberg, Julius and Ethel 1983 Sep 23F; 1986 Aug 2F; 1988 Jan 28I
Rosenberg, Steven A. 1985 Dec 4I
Rosenberg, Susan Lisa 1984 Nov 29F
Rosengarten, Theodore 1987 Jan 12J
Ros-Lehtinen, Ileana 1989 Aug 29F
Ross, Gary 1988 Jun 3J
Ross, Herbert 1987 Mar 3J
Rossellini, Isabella 1986 Sep 19J
Rosset, Barney 1985 Mar 4J; 1986 Apr 10J
Rossi, Guido 1982 Aug 11B
Rossner, Judith 1983 Aug 14J/Sep 11J/Oct 16J
Rostand, Edmond 1987 Jun 19J
Rostenkowski, Dan 1985 Sep 26H; 1988 May 26F; 1989 Aug 2H/Sep 14H
Rostker, Bernard 1980 Sep 4G
Rostow, Eugene 1983 Jan 12G
Roszik, Gabor 1989 Jul 22B
Roth, Philip 1988 Jan 11J
Rother, Stanley 1981 Jul 28D
Rothko, Mark 1983 Nov 9J
Rothschild, Alain de 1982 Oct 17B
Roud, Richard 1989 Jan 7J
Rourke, Russell A. 1985 Dec 11G
Rowan, Carl T. 1987 Sep 8F
Rowe, James N. 1989 Apr 21E
Royer, Charles 1982 Jul 13F
Royer, Michelle Renee 1987 Feb 17J
Royo Sanchez, Aristedes 1980 Jan 23A; 1982 Jul 30D/Jul 31D
Rozelle, Pete 1980 Jan 18J; 1985 Jan 22J; 1989 Oct 26J
Rozier, Mike 1983 Dec 3J
Ruane, Kevin 1983 Jan 7B
Rubbia, Carlo 1984 Oct 17I
Rubell, Steve 1980 May 28F
Rubens, Peter Paul 1985 Jun 13J
Rubin, William S. 1988 Feb 10J
Rubinstein, Arthur 1982 Dec 20J
Rubinstein, John 1980 Jun 8J; 1986 Apr 19J
Ruckelshaus, William D. 1983 Mar 21H/May 18H/Jun 23H/Jul 26H; 1984 Nov 29H/Dec 11H
Rudenko, Lyudmila 1986 Mar 21J
Ruder, David S. 1987 Jun 17H
Rudolph, Arthur L.H. 1984 Oct 17A
Ruffing, Charles ("Red") 1986 Feb 17J
Ruffo Appel, Ernesto 1989 Nov 2D
Ruiz, Henry 1985 Oct 25B
Ruiz, Rosie 1980 Mar 21J/Apr 29J
Rule, Charles R. 1988 Dec 6F
Rumsfeld, Donald H. 1983 Nov 3G/Dec 20C
Runcie, Robert 1980 May 9J; 1982 May 31B; 1987 Feb 26J; 1989 Oct 2J
Runyan, Joe 1989 Mar 15J
Rurarz, Zdislaw 1981 Dec 24B
Rushdie, Salman 1988 Oct 7E/Nov 8J
    awards and honors: Sweden Academy of Letters protest 1989 Mar 14A/Sep 21J
    best-sellers: Satanic Verses, The 1989 Mar 31J/Apr 28J/May 26J
    death threats: by Khomeini 1989 Feb 14C; by Khamenei 1989 Feb 17C; European diplomats recalled 1989 Feb 24A; Iran breaks ties 1989 Mar 7A; Islamic Conference condemns 1989 Mar 13C; supporter assassinated 1989 Mar 29A
Rushing, Jimmy 1984 Apr 26J
Ruska, Ernst 1986 Oct 15I

Russell, Rosalind 1984 Oct 8J
Rust, Mathias 1987 May 29B/Sep 4B; 1988 Aug 3B
Rustin, Bayard 1987 Aug 24F
Rutan, Dick 1986 Dec 23I
Ruth, Babe 1985 Dec 14J; 1988 Nov 21J
Ruth, Mike 1985 Dec 11J
Rutherford, Edward 1987 Sep 23J
Ruzici, Virginia 1980 Jun 7J
Ryan, Alan 1983 Mar 15G
Ryan, Leo 1986 Dec 1F
Ryan, Meg 1989 Jul 12J
Ryan, Nolan 1981 Sep 26J; 1985 Jul 11J; 1989 Aug 22J
Ryan, Patrick 1988 Dec 13B
Ryan, Sheelah 1988 Sep 7J
Ryle, Martin 1984 Oct 14I
Ryskind, Morrie 1985 Aug 24J
Ryumin, Valery 1980 Apr 9I/Oct 11I
Ryzhkov, Nikolai I. 1987 Jan 5I/Jan 7B/Jul 11B; 1989 Jun 9B/Jun 12B/Jun 27B

S

Sabah, Sheik Jabir al-Ahmad al- 1985 May 25C; 1986 Apr 3C
Sabah, Sheik Salim al- 1984 Jul 11A
Sabato, Ernesto 1985 Apr 23J
Saberhagen, Bret 1985 Nov 11J; 1989 Nov 15J
Sabin, Albert B. 1980 Apr 16I
Sabo, Chris 1988 Nov 1J
Sa Carneiro, Francisco Manuel Lumbrales de 1980 Jun 26B/Oct 5B/Dec 4B; 1981 Jan 9B
Sackler, Arthur M(itchell) 1987 May 26J
Sadat, Anwar el-
    assassination: 1981 Oct 6A,Oct 6C-7C/Oct 9C-10C; trial 1981 Nov 12C/Nov 21C/Dec 29C; 1982 Mar 6C/Apr 15C/May 8C; 1984 Sep 30C
    foreign policy: Soviet Union 1980 Jan 28C; Shah granted asylum 1980 Mar 24A; Afghanistan 1981 Sep 22A
    government: Islamic League meets 1980 Nov 10A; Coptic pope removed, Moslem Brotherhood banned 1981 Sep 5C
    Iran-Iraq War: 1980 Nov 1C; 1981 Mar 31C
    Mideast policy: Israel 1980 Feb 23C/Aug 15C; 1981 May 6C/May 31C/Jun 4C/Oct 6C; Lebanon 1981 May 6C/Jun 4C; Palestinian autonomy talks 1980 Jan 10C/Apr 9A/May 8C/Aug 3C; 1981 Aug 26C; Palestinian government-in-exile 1981 Feb 17C; Syria 1981 May 6C
    U.S. policy: 1980 Apr 9A/Nov 23C; 1981 Jul 27C/Aug 5C/Sep 22A
Sade 1986 Feb 25J/Mar 22J/Apr 16J
Sadr, Imam Moussa 1980 Sep 9C
Sadri, John 1980 Jan 2J
Sagan, Carl 1985 Oct 25J/Nov 22J/Dec 20J; 1986 Jan 31J/Sep 30I
Sagdeyev, Roa Z. 1988 Nov 3I
Sager, Carol Bayer 1987 Feb 24J
Saguy, Yehoshua 1983 Mar 1C
Said, Sultan Qaboos bin 1982 May 8C
Saikia, Hiteswar 1983 Feb 27E
St. John, Bernard 1985 Mar 11D
Saint-Exupery, Antoine De 1983 Jun 3J
Saito, Tatsuo 1987 Jun 26E
Sakharov, Andrei D.
    government opposition: international pressure urged 1980 Jan 2B; internal exile 1980 Jan 22B; 1986 Dec 19B; abuses charged 1980 Jan 28B; UN debate set 1980 Feb 5A;

hunger strike 1981 Dec 10B; 1984 May 2B; medical treatment denied 1982 Apr 8B; letter smuggled out 1986 Feb 15B; Gorbachev meeting 1988 Jan 15B
    personal issues: wife convicted 1984 Aug 23B; wife granted visa 1985 Oct 28B; wife visits U.S. 1985 Dec 6A; death 1989 Dec 14B
Saks, Gene 1983 Jun 5J; 1985 Mar 28J/Jun 2J; 1986 Dec 4J
Sakurauchi, Yoshio 1982 Mar 23E
Salas, Rodolfo 1986 Sep 30E
Salazar, Alberto 1980 Oct 26J; 1981 Oct 25J; 1982 Apr 19J/Oct 24J
Salazar Arguello, Jorge 1980 Nov 17D
Salerno, Anthony ("Fat Tony") 1986 Mar 21F
Salgo, Nicolas M. 1987 Apr 15B
Salieri, Antonio 1984 Sep 19J
Salii, Lazarus 1985 Oct 25E; 1988 Aug 20E
Salinas, Abel 1988 Sep 6D
Salinas de Gortari, Carlos
    economic policy: 1988 Oct 17D/Dec 1D; 1989 Jun 18D
    government: named PRI presidential candidate 1987 Oct 4D; Mexico presidential elections 1988 Jun 7D/Jul 13D/Jul 20D; certified president-elect 1988 Sep 10D; sworn president 1988 Dec 1D
    U.S. policy: 1988 Oct 17D; 1989 Oct 3D
Salinger, J.D. 1987 Jan 29J
Salisbury, Harrison E. 1985 Dec 15J
Salk, Jonas 1989 Jun 4I
Salnikov, Vladimir 1980 Jul 22J
Salsbury, Robert 1986 Dec 2H
Salt, Waldo 1987 Mar 7J
Salter, James 1989 May 13J
Samaniego, Marcial 1987 Apr 3D
Samaranch, Juan Antonio 1980 Jul 16J; 1984 May 31J; 1987 Sep 17J; 1988 Jan 18J
Samoyoa, Salvador 1980 Jan 8D
Sampson, Ralph 1982 Mar 26J
Samuelson, Joan Benoit 1986 Feb 24J
Samuelsson, Bengt I. 1982 Oct 11I
Sanchez Butiago, Humberto 1989 Aug 10F
Sanchez de Lozada, Gonzalo 1988 Sep 4D; 1989 May 7D
Sanchez Vicario, Arantxa 1989 Jun 10J
Sand, Leonard B. 1988 Jan 25F/Aug 2F
Sandalo, Roberto 1980 Jul 27B
Sandberg, Ryne 1984 Nov 13J
Sanders, Barry 1988 Dec 3J
Sanders, Bernard 1987 Mar 3F
Sanders, Lawrence
    best-sellers: Case of Lucy Bending 1982 Sep 12J; Eighth Commandment 1986 Jun 27J/Jul 18J; Fourth Deadly Sin 1985 Aug 16J/Sep 27J; Third Deadly Sin 1981 Aug 9J/Sep 6J/Oct 4J
Sandiford, Erskine 1987 Jun 1D
Sands, Bobby (Robert) 1981 Apr 10B/Apr 23B/Apr 29B/May 5B/May 6B; 1982 May 5B
Sanford, Isabel 1981 Sep 13J
Sanford, Terry 1981 Feb 24F; 1985 Feb 1F
Sanger, Frederick 1980 Oct 14I
Sanguinetti, Julio Maria 1984 Nov 26D; 1985 Mar 1C; 1986 Dec 22D
Sankara, Thomas 1983 Aug 5C; 1987 Oct 15C
Santiago, Benito 1987 Nov 4J
Santmyer, Helen Hooven 1984 Jul 20J/Aug 24J/Oct 19J; 1986 Feb 21J
Sanusi, Muhammad 1985 May 15E
San Yu 1981 Nov 9E; 1983 Oct 10E
Sapielo, Piotr 1980 Nov 27B

Saragat, Giuseppe 1988 Jun 11B
Sarah, Duchess of York (Sarah Ferguson) (Great Britain) 1986 Mar 18J/Jul 23G; 1988 Aug 8B
Saraiva de Carvalho, Otelo 1987 May 20B
Sarandon, Susan 1988 Jun 15J
Sargent, Alvin 1981 Mar 30J
Sarkis, Elias 1980 Jul 20C; 1981 Apr 8C; 1982 Jun 20C/Jun 20C/Jun 25C/Jul 23C
Sarner, Arlene 1986 Oct 8J
Sarney Costa, Jose
    Amazon basin: 1988 Oct 12D; 1989 Apr 6D
    atomic energy: 1987 Sep 4D
    economic policy: land reforms 1985 Oct 10D; anti-inflation plans 1986 Feb 28D/Nov 25D/Nov 27D; 1989 Jan 15D/Feb 15D
    foreign policy: papal meeting 1986 Jul 10D; Argentina 1986 Jul 30D; 1987 Jul 15D; U.S. 1986 Sep 13G
    government: as interim president 1985 Mar 15D/Apr 5D; assumes Brazil presidency 1985 Apr 21D; restores direct vote 1985 May 8D; congress, state elections 1986 Nov 15D; presidential term 1987 May 18D; 1988 Jun 2D; constitutional reform 1987 Nov 15D; 1988 Mar 22D
Saroyan, William 1981 May 18J
Sartawi, Issam 1982 Jul 13C/Jul 14G
Sartre, Jean-Paul 1980 Apr 15J
Sartzetakis, Christos 1985 Apr 22B
Sasso, John 1987 Sep 30F; 1988 Sep 2F
Sassou-Nguesso, Denis 1984 Jul 30C
Sasway, Benjamin H. 1984 Feb 3G
Sato, Eisaku 1988 Jan 15B
Sato, Takashi 1988 Jun 24E
Sattar, Abdus 1981 Nov 15E/Nov 17E; 1982 Mar 24E/Mar 25E
Saude Maria, Victor 1984 Mar 10C
Sauve, Jeanne 1986 Feb 29D; 1984 Jun 21D; 1986 Oct 1D; 1988 May 21D/Dec 12D; 1989 Oct 6D
Savary, Alain 1983 May 5B
Savimbi, Jonas 1986 Feb 8G/Sep 17C/Sep 17G; 1988 Nov 19C; 1989 Feb 14C/Jun 22C/Aug 22C/Oct 5C
Savinar, Tad 1987 May 28J
Savinykh, Viktor 1981 Mar 13I
Savitch, Jessica 1983 Oct 24J
Savitskaya, Svetlana 1982 Aug 19I/Aug 27I; 1984 Jul 25I
Sawhill, John 1980 Sep 10F
Saw Maung 1988 Sep 18E
Sawyer, Eugene 1987 Dec 2F; 1989 Feb 28F
Sax, Steve 1982 Nov 22J
Sayer, Paul 1989 Jan 25J
Sayyaf, Abdul Rasul 1989 Feb 23E
Scalia, Antonin
    Supreme Court nomination: name submitted 1986 Jun 17F; congressional hearings 1986 Aug 6F/Aug 14F; confirmed 1986 Sep 17F; seated 1986 Sep 26F
    Supreme Court rulings: term begins 1986 Oct 6F; beach access 1987 Jun 26H
Scarfo, Nicodemo 1988 Nov 19F; 1989 Apr 5F
Scargill, Arthur 1984 May 30B; 1986 Sep 23B; 1987 Aug 24B
Schaeffer, Rebecca 1989 Jul 19F
Schanberg, Sydney 1984 Nov 2J
Schaufelberger, Albert A. 1983 May 26D/May 27D/May 27G
Schawlow, Arthur 1981 Oct 19I
Scheine, Raynor 1988 Mar 27J
Schell, Jonathan 1987 Feb 9J
Schepisi, Fred 1987 Jun 19J

Schidlof, Peter 1987 Aug 18J
Schiff, Dorothy 1989 Aug 30J
Schlachter, Douglas M. 1982 Jan 6G
Schlesinger, James R. 1986 Aug 17G; 1987 Jun 26G; 1988 Dec 19G
Schlossberg, Edwin A. 1986 Jul 19J
Schluter, Poul 1986 Sep 9B; 1987 Aug 18B/Sep 10B; 1988 Apr 19B/Jun 7B
Schmidt Jr., Benno C. 1985 Dec 10F
Schmidt, Helmut
  arms control: A-weapons deployment 1980 Jun 16G/Jul 15B; 1981 Nov 25B/Dec 2B; A-freeze defeat 1982 Apr 22B
  European policy: East Germany 1981 Dec 11B; France 1980 Jul 11B; 1981 Jul 12B; 1982 Jan 13B/Jul 22B; NATO 1980 Jul 15B; Poland 1982 Jan 5B
  government: Catholic bishops criticism 1980 Sep 13B; parliamentary elections 1980 Oct 5B; ousted 1982 Oct 1B
  Soviet policy: 1980 Jul 1B; 1981 Apr 9B/Nov 25B-26A/Dec 2B; 1982 Jan 5B/Jul 22B
  U.S. policy: 1980 Jun 16G/Nov 20G; 1981 Apr 9B/Nov 18B/Nov 26A
Schmidt, Mike 1980 Nov 26J; 1981 Nov 17J; 1986 Nov 19J
Schnabel, Julian 1983 May 20J
Schneider, Alan (Abram Leopoldovich) 1984 May 3J
Schneider, Andrew 1987 Apr 16J
Schneider, Claudine 1989 Nov 14F
Schneider, Romy 1982 May 29J
Schneider, Vreni 1986 Mar 23J
Schoendienst, Red 1989 Feb 28J/Jul 23J
Schoenherr, C. John 1988 Jan 11J
Scholem, Gershom 1982 Feb 20J
Scholz, Jackson 1986 Oct 26J
Schou, Mogens 1987 Sep 21I
Schrader, Leonard 1985 Jul 26J
Schroeder, Patricia 1987 Aug 20F/Sep 28F
Schroeder, William J. 1984 Nov 25I; 1986 Aug 6I
Schulberg, Budd 1983 Nov 18J
Schulte, Eduard Reinhold Karl 1983 Sep 28A
Schurke, Paul 1986 May 1I
Schwalb Lopez Aldana, Fernando 1984 Apr 9D
Schwartz, Felice N. 1989 Mar 8F
Schwartz, Irving 1983 Sep 6F
Schwartz, Melvin 1988 Oct 19I
Schwarzenegger, Arnold 1987 Jun 12J
Schweiker, Richard S. 1980 Dec 11F; 1982 Oct 6F/Nov 4I; 1983 Jan 10F/Jan 12F
Scobee, Francis R. 1986 Dec 29I
Scofield, Paul 1989 Nov 8J
Scoon, Paul 1983 Oct 29D/Nov 1D/Nov 2D/Nov 9D/Nov 15D
Scorsese, Martin 1980 Nov 14J; 1986 Oct 17J
Scott, Ian 1985 Nov 9D
Scott, Mike 1986 Nov 11J
Scott, (George) Randolph 1987 Mar 2J
Scott, Richard R.F. 1987 Dec 21B
Scotto, Anthony 1980 Jan 22F
Scowcroft, Brent 1983 Apr 18G; 1986 Aug 17G/Nov 26F; 1988 Nov 23G; 1989 Dec 9G/Dec 18G
Seaga, Edward Phillip George 1980 Oct 30D; 1983 Dec 15D; 1989 Feb 9D
Seaman, Peter S. 1988 Jun 22J
Sears, David 1985 Feb 23J
Seaver, Tom 1985 Aug 4J
Sebelius, Keith 1982 Sep 5F
Secord, Richard V.
  Iran-Contra arms scandal: Swiss banks 1986 Dec 10F/Dec 15B; congressional hearings 1987 Apr 29G/May 5G; indicted 1988 Mar 16F; 1989 May 11F; arraigned 1988 Mar 24F; trial 1988 Jun 8F/Jun 16F; North obstruction 1988 Nov 7F; pleads guilty 1989 Nov 8F
Sedgwick, Kyra 1989 Dec 20J
Segal, Erich 1988 Aug 26J
Seger, Martha 1984 Jul 3F
Segovia, Andres 1987 Jun 2J
Segre, Emilio Gino 1989 Apr 22I
Seib, Gerald F. 1987 Feb 4C
Seiberling, John 1983 Feb 1H; 1984 Mar 8H
Seidelman, Susan 1985 Mar 29J
Seidman, L. William 1989 Oct 4H
Seifert, Jaroslav 1984 Oct 11J; 1986 Jan 10J
Sein Lwin 1988 Jul 26E/Aug 12E/Aug 19E
Sejna, Jan 1981 Oct 18A
Seko, Toshihiko 1981 Apr 20J; 1987 Apr 20J
Sekou Toure, Ahmed 1982 May 10C; 1984 Apr 3C
Sellars, Peter 1984 Jun 5J; 1985 Jan 24J; 1986 Aug 8J
Selleck, Tom 1987 Nov 25J
Sellers, Peter 1980 Jul 24J
Semel, Preston H. 1989 Aug 24H
Semyonov, Nikolai N. 1986 Sep 25I
Senna, Ayrton 1988 May 1J/Jul 10J/Aug 28J/Oct 31J; 1989 Apr 23J/May 7J/Jul 30J/Aug 27J
Sennett, Mack 1983 Oct 11J
Seow, Francis T. 1988 Aug 17E
Seraw, Mulugeta 1989 May 2F
Serebrov, Aleksandr 1982 Aug 19I/Aug 27I
Seregni, Liber 1984 Mar 19D
Serra, Richard 1985 May 31J; 1987 Aug 31J
Sert, Josep Lluis 1983 Mar 15J
Sessions III, Jefferson B. 1986 Jun 5F
Sessions, Roger Huntington 1985 Mar 16J
Sessions, William S. 1987 Jul 24F/Sep 25F; 1988 Sep 14F
Sethi, Prakash Chand 1984 Mar 31E
Seurat, Georges 1984 May 2J
Seuss, Dr. (Theodore Seuss Geisel) 1984 Apr 20J/May 11J
Seybou, Ali 1987 Nov 10C
Seymour Jr., Whitney North 1986 May 29F
Sfar, Rachid 1986 Jul 8C
Shacochis, Bob 1985 Nov 21J
Shad, John S.R. 1981 Jul 13H; 1987 Mar 30F
Shaffer, Peter 1981 Jun 7J; 1984 Sep 19J; 1987 Oct 27J
Shagari, Shehu 1983 Aug 6C/Dec 31C; 1984 Jan 3C
Shah, Sultan Idris 1984 Feb 9E
Shahi, Agha 1980 Mar 5G
Shaker, Sharif Zeid bin 1989 Dec 4C
Shakespeare, William 1985 Nov 23J; 1987 Sep 16J/Sep 25J; 1989 Oct 13J
Shalala, Donna 1987 May 29J
Shalamov, Varlam 1982 Jan 30J
Shamir, Yitzhak
  Arab-Israeli policy: Egypt 1988 Dec 25C; Jordan 1989 Apr 20C; Lebanon 1983 Mar 8C; PLO 1983 Jan 3C; 1989 Apr 27C/Jul 23C
  economic policy: 1986 Oct 8C
  government: named Israeli foreign minister 1980 Mar 9C; coalition government 1983 Sep 12C; 1987 May 13C; 1988 Dec 19C; 1989 Jul 10C/Jul 23C; takes office 1983 Oct 10C; national unity government 1984 Jul 25C/Aug 31C/Sep 2C; sworn prime minister 1986 Oct 20C; forms new government 1988 Nov 14C; cabinet minister fired 1989 Dec 31C
  peace initiatives: 1989 Apr 20C/Apr 27C/Jul 5C/Jul 10C/Jul 23C
  U.S. policy: 1981 Feb 23G; 1983 Mar 15C/Jul 26C/Nov 29A; 1989 Apr 4C
Shankar, Ramsewak 1988 Jan 12D/Jan 25D; 1989 Jul 25D
Shanker, Albert 1985 Jul 13F; 1989 Jul 21F
Shanley, John Patrick 1987 Dec 16J; 1988 Apr 11J
Shapiro, Peter 1985 Nov 5F
Shariat Madari, Kazem 1980 Jan 9C
Sharif, Nawar 1988 Nov 19E
Sharon, Ariel
  Arab-Israeli policy: Egypt 1982 Apr 15C; Iran 1982 May 26C; Israeli-occupied territories 1981 Sep 23C; Lebanon 1981 Nov 9C; 1982 Aug 12C/Sep 6C; 1983 Jan 25C
  Beirut massacre: 1982 Sep 19C/Oct 25C/Nov 7C/Nov 18C/Feb 8C; 1983 Feb 10C; 1985 Jan 9F
  government: Bedouins curbed 1981 Dec 26C; resigns as defense minister 1983 Feb 11C; cabinet post retained 1983 Feb 13C-14C; Peres apology 1985 Nov 15C
  personal issues: *Time* libel suit 1983 Feb 28C/Jun 22J
  U.S. policy: 1983 Jan 25C
Sharp, Phillip A. 1988 Nov 16I
Sharq, Mohammed Hassan 1988 May 27E; 1989 Feb 20E
Shatner, William 1983 Jan 31E
Shaw, Artie 1985 Jan 7J; 1987 Apr 2J; 1989 Feb 26J
Shaw, Bernard 1981 May 3F
Shaw, George Bernard 1986 Apr 19J/May 12J
Shaw, Irwin 1984 May 16J
Shawn, William 1987 Feb 9J
Shazli, Saad Eddin al- 1980 Apr 2C
Shcharansky, Anatoly B. 1981 May 29B; 1986 Jan 7E/Feb 11G
Shchelokov, Nikolai A. 1982 Dec 17B
Sheaffer, Linda 1987 Sep 14F
Shearer, Moira 1986 Sep 28J
Shearer, Norma 1983 Jun 12J
Sheehan, Neil 1988 Nov 29J; 1989 Mar 30J
Sheehan, Patty 1988 Jul 24J
Sheehy, Susan 1983 Apr 18J
Sheela, Ma Anand 1986 Jul 22J
Sheen, Charlie 1986 Dec 19J; 1987 Dec 11J
Sheen, Martin 1987 Mar 3F/Dec 11J
Shehu, Mehmet 1985 Feb 28B/Mar 1B
Sheldon, Alice 1987 May 19J
Sheldon, Sidney
  best-sellers: *If Tomorrow Comes* 1985 Feb 8J/Mar 15J/Apr 19J/May 24J/Jun 14J; *Master of the Game* 1982 Sep 12J/Oct 17J/Nov 14J; 1983 Feb 13J/Mar 13J/Aug 14J; *Rage of Angels* 1980 Jul 13J/Aug 17J/Sep 14J/Oct 12J; 1987 Oct 12J; *Sands of Time* 1988 Nov 25J/Dec 23J; 1989 Jan 27J/Feb 24J; *Windmills of the Gods* 1987 Feb 27J/Mar 27J/Apr 24J/May 29J
Shell, Art 1989 Jan 24J
Shelley, Carole 1986 Apr 19J
Shelley, Percy Bysshe 1986 Dec 18J
Shelton, Ron 1988 Jun 15J
Shenouda III (Coptic pope) 1981 Sep 5C; 1985 Jan 6C
Shepard, Sam 1986 Dec 12J
Sherrill, Patrick Henry 1986 Aug 20F
Sherwood, Robert 1983 Jul 29J
Shevardnadze, Eduard A.
  Afghanistan military intervention: 1988 Jan 6B; 1989 Feb 5E-6E
  arms control: Star Wars 1989 Sep 21G; chemical weapons 1989 Sep 25A; Krasnoyarsk radar complex 1989 Oct 23B
  foreign policy: in Canada 1986 Oct 2D; in China 1989 Feb 4A; in Great Britain 1986 Jul 13B; in Iran 1989 Feb 23C; in Iraq 1989 Feb 23C; Israel 1986 Sep 22A; 1989 Feb 22C; in Japan 1986 Jan 19E; 1988 Dec 18E; NATO headquarters 1989 Dec 19B
  UN speeches: 1985 Sep 26A/Oct 24A; 1986 Sep 23A; 1988 Sep 27A
  U.S. policy: 1986 Aug 11A/Sep 20A; 1987 Nov 22G; 1988 Mar 23G/Sep 23G; 1989 Sep 21G
Shin Hyon Hwack 1980 May 20E
Shinwell, Lord (Emanuel) 1986 May 8B
Shipler, David K. 1983 Feb 25J; 1987 Apr 16J
Shockley, William Bradford 1980 Feb 28I; 1987 Oct 13I; 1989 Aug 12I
Shoemaker, Bill 1985 Mar 3J; 1986 May 3J
Sholokhov, Mikhail 1984 Feb 21J
Short, Robert 1982 Nov 20J
Shostakovich, Dmitri 1981 Apr 11J
Shostakovich, Maxim 1981 Apr 11J
Shoushounova, Elena 1985 Nov 10J
Shultz, George P.
  African policy: 6-nation tour 1987 Jan 14C
  Asian and Pacific Rim policy: Cambodia 1983 Jun 25E; China 1983 Feb 2E/Aug 18G/Oct 13G; 1987 Mar 5E; 1988 Mar 7G; India 1983 Jun 30E; Japan 1983 Jan 30E; 1984 Jul 7G; New Zealand 1984 Jul 13A; 1986 Jun 27E; Pakistan 1983 Jul 2E; Philippines 1986 Jun 24E; Thailand 1983 Jun 25E; Vietnam 1984 Sep 11G
  Canadian policy: 1982 Oct 24D; 1985 Oct 28D; 1988 Jan 11C
  European policy: communist bloc 1982 Oct 18G; Great Britain 1982 Dec 17G; NATO 1986 Oct 13B; Spain 1982 Dec 15G; Yugoslavia 1985 May 31G
  G-7 summits: 1983 May 29A
  government service: as secretary of state 1982 Jun 25G/Jul 15F; "ideological purge" 1985 Jul 16F
  Iran-Contra arms scandal: 1986 Dec 8G; 1987 Jul 8G/Jul 23G
  Korean airline incident: 1983 Sep 1G/Sep 8G
  Latin policy: 5-nation tour 1984 Jan 31G; Bolivia 1989 Jun 30D; Catholic bishops criticize 1983 Mar 7G; El Salvador 1983 Feb 28G/Jul 20G; Grenada invasion 1983 Oct 23G/Dec 15G; Haiti 1984 May 14G; Nicaragua 1984 Jun 1D/Nov 12D; 1985 Mar 2D; 1986 Oct 7G; 1987 Sep 10G; OAS address 1982 Nov 17D; Panama 1988 Apr 3G; Suriname 1986 Dec 16D
  Mideast policy: Israel 1982 Oct 16A/Nov 18G; 1983 May 6G/Jul 7C/Jul 26C; 1984 Dec 25G; Jordan 1985 May 31G; Lebanon 1983 May 4C/Jul 5C; Palestinians 1982 Jul 13G; 1985 May 10C; 1988 Nov 26A/Dec 14G; peace plan 1987 Oct 19G; 1988 Feb 25C/Apr 3C; Saudi Arabia 1983 Jul 4C; Syria 1983 May 7C/May 10A/Jul 6C
  personal issues: PEN congress address 1986 Jan 17J; assassination attempt arrests 1989 Jun 30D
Shuman, Raymond W. 1987 Jun 22F
Shuttleworth, Todd 1986 Dec 8F; 1987 Jul 25F
Siad Barre, Mohamed 1987 Jul 2C
Sica, Domenico 1987 Feb 5B
Siddon, Thomas 1987 Mar 17D/Mar 23D
Sidle, Winant 1984 Feb 9F
Sidler, Maren 1980 Jun 14J
Siegan, Bernard 1988 Jul 14F
Siegbahn, Kai M. 1981 Oct 19I
Sierra Torres, Manuel de la 1980 Aug 1B
Signoret, Simone 1985 Sep 30J; 1986 Nov 8B
Silkwood, Karen 1981 Dec 11I; 1983 Jan 19F; 1986 Aug 22F
Sills, Beverly 1988 May 10J
Silva Herzog, Jesus 1982 May 15D/Aug 21D; 1984 Mar 27D; 1986 Jun 17D
Silver, Ron 1988 May 3J/Jun 5J
Silverman, Fred 1981 Jun 30J
Silverman, Kenneth 1985 Apr 24J
Silverman, Leon 1981 Dec 29F; 1982 Jun 28H
Silverman, Mervyn 1984 Apr 9I
Silvers, Phil 1985 Nov 1J
Silverstein, Shel 1985 Jan 13J
Simenon, Georges 1989 Sep 4J
Simitis, Costas 1987 Nov 26B
Simmonds, Kennedy 1984 Jun 20D; 1989 Mar 21D
Simmons, Al 1988 Nov 21J
Simmons, Chet 1985 Jan 15J
Simmons, Ronald Gene 1987 Dec 28F
Simms, Phil 1986 Feb 2J
Simon, Claude 1985 Oct 17J
Simon, Neil 1985 Mar 28J/Jun 2J; 1986 Dec 4J
Simon, Paul (musician) 1987 Feb 24J/Mar 28J/Apr 25J/May 23J; 1988 Mar 2J
Simon, Paul (politician) 1987 Apr 9F/Aug 30F/Nov 15F; 1988 Jan 4F/Mar 15F/Mar 30F/Apr 7F
Simpson, Alan K. 1982 Mar 17F; 1988 Nov 30F
Simpson, O.J. 1985 Jan 22J
Simpson, Scott 1987 Jun 21J
Simpson, Wallis Warfield 1986 Apr 24J
Sims, John Haley ("Zoot") 1985 Mar 23J
Sin, Jaime Cardinal 1983 Aug 27E; 1984 Oct 2E; 1987 Mar 6J
Sinatra, Frank 1983 Jul 6J; 1984 May 1J/Dec 24J; 1988 Mar 13J/May 11J
Sinclair, Clive 1986 Apr 8B
Sindona, Michele 1980 Mar 27H; 1982 Jul 22B; 1985 Mar 15B
Singh, Beant 1985 Feb 11E
Singh, Kehar 1989 Jan 6E
Singh, Malkhan 1982 Jun 17E
Singh, Mithileshwar 1988 Oct 3C
Singh, Satwant 1989 Jan 6E
Singh, Vishwanath Pratap 1988 Aug 7E; 1989 Dec 2E/Dec 21E
Singh, Zail 1982 Jul 12E
Singlaub, John K. 1987 May 21G
Sinha, Ram Dulari 1985 Mar 20E
Sinowatz, Fred 1983 May 24B
Sirhan, Sirhan Bishara 1985 Jun 25F; 1986 Mar 4F
Sirica, John J. 1980 May 4J; 1984 May 16I
Sisulu, Walter 1989 Oct 10C/Oct 14C/Oct 15C
Sital, B. 1980 Feb 25D
Siwicki, Florian 1989 Jan 3B
Sizer, Theodore R. 1983 Oct 19F
Sjoberg, Patrik 1987 Jun 30J
Skaaren, Warren 1988 Mar 30J
Skiba, Gerhard 1989 Apr 20B
Skiles, Scott 1986 Mar 1J
Skinner, Samuel K. 1988 Dec 22F; 1989 Jan 31H/May 17H
Skinner, William J. 1986 Sep 22H
Skippings, Oswaldo 1988 Mar 3E

Slaughter, Enos 1985 Mar 6J/Jul 28J
Slim, Memphis 1983 Jul 11J
Sloane, Eric 1985 Mar 6J
Sluman, Jeff 1988 Aug 14J
Small, Ronald Hugh 1980 Apr 7D
Smart, Keith 1987 Mar 30J
Smeal, Eleanor 1982 Oct 10F; 1987 Jul 8F
Smirnov, Alexander 1981 Jun 3B
Smith, Alyssa 1989 Nov 27I
Smith, Bailey 1980 Sep 18J; 1981 Jun 9J
Smith, Bessie 1986 Nov 1J; 1987 Jul 10J; 1989 Jan 18J
Smith, Bruce 1985 Apr 30J
Smith, Cathy Evelyn 1983 Mar 18J
Smith, Geoff 1985 Apr 15J
Smith, Harold Rossfields 1982 Jan 13J
Smith, Hedrick 1987 Jul 31F
Smith, Ian 1980 Feb 14C/Aug 31C; 1981 Apr 12C; 1987 Apr 2C
Smith, James ("Bonecrusher") 1986 Dec 12J; 1987 Mar 7J
Smith, Jane 1987 May 6I
Smith, John Eldon 1983 Dec 15F
Smith Jr., Joseph 1981 Mar 18J
Smith, Kate 1986 Jun 17J
Smith, Maggie 1986 Mar 7J; 1987 Mar 22J/Oct 27J; 1989 Mar 19J
Smith, Margaret Chase 1989 Jul 6J
Smith, Martin Cruz 1981 May 10J/May 24J/Jul 5J/Aug 9J/Sep 6J/Oct 4J; 1989 Jul 28J/Aug 25J
Smith, Michael J. 1986 Jul 28I; 1987 May 6I; 1988 Aug 22I
Smith, Muriel Burrell 1985 Sep 13J
Smith, Ozzie 1985 Oct 16J
Smith, Red (Walter Wellesley) 1982 Jan 15J
Smith, Richard Craig 1984 Apr 9G/May 13G
Smith, Richard G. 1986 Aug 20I
Smith, Roger B. 1980 Sep 9H; 1986 Dec 1H
Smith, Ron 1988 Nov 1J
Smith, Samantha 1983 Jul 22A; 1985 Aug 26J
Smith, Stuart 1986 Jul 31B
Smith, Willi 1987 Apr 17J
Smith, William French
antibusing legislation: 1982 May 6F
contracts and billing issues: debt collection drive 1981 Apr 20H; Electric Boat overruns 1984 Oct 31G
government service: as attorney general 1980 Dec 11F; 1984 Jan 22F
immigration panel proposals: 1981 May 20G
investigations and inquiries: special prosecutor law 1981 May 21F; FBI drug probe role 1982 Jan 21F; FBI political groups 1983 Mar 6F; Meese 1984 Mar 27F; Carter campaign papers 1984 May 14F; Mengele 1985 Feb 6G
judicial activism: 1981 Oct 29F
personal issues: tax shelter 1982 Jun 1F; finances probed 1982 Jul 21F
Smyth, Henry Dewolf 1986 Sep 11I
Sneath, William 1981 Sep 30H
Snell, George 1980 Oct 10I
Sneva, Tom 1983 May 29J
Snider, Duke 1980 Aug 3J
Snider, Paul 1980 Aug 15J/Sep 15J
Snow, C.P. 1980 Jul 1J
Snowe, Olympia J. 1989 Nov 14F
Snyder, Mitch 1986 Mar 16F; 1987 Mar 3F/Dec 23F
Soames, Lord Arthur Christopher John 1980 Jan 18C/Mar 11C; 1987 Sep 16B
Soares, Mario 1980 Oct 19B; 1983 Jun 9B; 1985 Jun 13B; 1986 Jan 26B/Feb 16B/Mar 9B; 1987 Apr 28B
Soares Carneiro, Antonio 1980 Dec 7B
Sobhuza II, King (Swaziland) 1982 Aug 21C; 1986 Apr 25C
Soderbergh, Steven 1989 May 23J/Aug 4J
Soeteman, Gerard 1987 Feb 6J
Sofia, Queen (Spain) 1986 Apr 22B; 1987 May 2J
Sognnaes, Reidar 1984 Sep 21I
Sokol, Herman 1985 Jun 21I
Sokolov, Andrei 1987 Mar 31J
Sokolov, Valentin 1984 Nov 8J
Sokomanu, George 1988 Dec 21E; 1989 Apr 14E
Solarz, Stephen J. 1980 Jul 18E; 1983 Jan 15G; 1984 Feb 29G
Solh, Takieddin 1980 Jul 20C
Solis Palma, Manuel 1988 Apr 8G; 1989 Sep 1D
Solomon, Andrew 1986 Dec 2H
Solomon, Harold 1980 Jul 12J
Solovyov, Vladimir A. 1986 Jul 16I
Solow, Robert M. 1987 Oct 21J
Solti, Georg 1980 Feb 27J; 1989 Jan 30J
Solzhenitsyn, Alexander I. 1983 Mar 2J; 1985 Jun 5J; 1989 Jul 4J
Somare, Michael 1980 Mar 11E; 1982 Aug 2E; 1985 Nov 21E; 1988 Jul 4E
Somoza Debayle, Anastasio 1980 Jul 19D/Sep 5D/Sep 17D; 1983 Mar 28D; 1984 Apr 25D; 1989 Jul 19D
Sondergaard, Gale 1985 Aug 14J
Sondheim, Stephen 1983 Feb 19J; 1984 Feb 15J/May 2J; 1985 Apr 24J; 1987 Nov 5J; 1988 Jan 24J/Jun 5J; 1989 Aug 2J
Sones Jr., F. Mason 1983 Nov 16I
Sonoda, Sunao 1981 Oct 14A
Son Sann 1981 Sep 4E; 1982 Jul 11E; 1983 May 1E
Sontag, Camille 1986 Oct 11B
Sope, Barak 1988 Jul 25E; 1989 Apr 14E
Sopwith, Thomas Octave Murdoch 1989 Jan 27B
Sorenson, Theodore 1982 Nov 28F
Sorkow, Harvey R. 1987 Mar 31F
Sotomayor, Javier 1989 Jul 29J
Soudarikov, Nikolai 1981 Mar 4E
Souphanouvong, Prince (Laos) 1986 Oct 31E
Sourrouille, Juan 1987 Feb 25D/Jul 20D
Soussoudis, Michael A. 1985 Nov 25A
Sovern, Michael I. 1980 Jan 7J
Soyinka, Wole 1986 Oct 16J
Spacek, Sissy 1985 May 6H; 1986 Dec 12J
Spadafora, Hugo 1985 Sep 14D
Spader, James 1989 Aug 4J
Spadolini, Giovanni 1981 Jun 28B; 1982 Jun 7B/Jul 31B/Aug 7B/Aug 11B/Aug 23B/Nov 13B
Spain, James 1980 Mar 29B
Spain, John Larry (Johnny) 1988 Mar 10F
Spasowski, Romuald 1981 Dec 20B
Speakes, Larry 1982 Jan 13F; 1983 Nov 16G/Nov 30G; 1984 May 8H; 1985 Jan 23H; 1988 Apr 13F
Spector, Phil 1989 Jan 18J
Speer, Albert 1981 Sep 1B
Speidel, Hans 1984 Nov 28B
Spellman, Eugene 1982 Aug 2F
Spellman, John 1982 Apr 7I
Sperry, Roger W. 1981 Oct 9I
Speth, Gus 1980 Feb 19I
Spicer, Richard C. 1984 Oct 19D
Spielberg, Anne 1988 Jun 3J
Spielberg, Steven 1981 Jun 12J; 1985 Dec 18J; 1989 May 24J
Spinks, Leon 1987 Aug 1J
Spinks, Michael 1983 Mar 18J; 1985 Feb 23J/Sep 21J/Oct 9J; 1986 Apr 19J/Sep 6J; 1988 Jun 27J
Spinney, Franklin C. 1984 Aug 19G
Sporkin, Stanley 1985 Dec 17F
Springfield, Rick 1982 May 5J
Springsteen, Bruce
best-sellers: *Born in the U.S.A.* 1984 Jul 21J/Aug 25J/Sep 22J/Oct 27J/Nov 24J/Dec 22J; 1985 Jan 26J/Feb 23J/Mar 30J/Apr 27J/May 25J/Jun 22J/Jul 27J/Sep 28J; *Bruce Springsteen and the E Street Band* 1986 Dec 17J; *Dancing in the Dark* 1985 Feb 26J; *Nebraska* 1982 Oct 13J; *River* 1980 Dec 3J; *Tunnel of Love* 1987 Nov 21J; 1988 Mar 2J
Grammy awards: 1985 Feb 26J; 1988 Mar 2J
tours: 1988 Sep 2J/Oct 15J
Sprizzo, John E. 1984 Dec 13A
Spungen, Nancy 1986 Oct 17J
Ssemogerere, Paul 1980 Dec 10C
Stacy, Hollis 1984 Jul 15J
Stadler, Craig 1982 Apr 11J
Stafford, Robert T. 1987 May 7H
Stafford-Clark, Max 1987 Mar 21J
Stalin, Joseph 1986 Apr 16J/Nov 16J; 1987 Nov 2B; 1988 Apr 17B/Jun 14B; 1989 Jan 31B/Mar 5B
Stalker, John 1986 Aug 22B
Stallings Jr., George A. 1989 Jul 4J
Stamp, Terence 1987 Dec 11J
Standerwick, Lynn 1983 Mar 11E
Stanislavski, Konstantin 1982 Feb 17J
Stankiewicz, Richard 1983 Mar 27J
Stapleton, Maureen 1981 May 7J
Stargell, Willie 1988 Jan 12J/Jul 31J
Starling, Marlon 1989 Feb 4J
Starr, Richard 1983 Jan 12G
Starr, Ringo 1985 Feb 24J
Starzl, Thomas 1989 Dec 3I
Staubach, Roger 1985 Jan 22J
Stayner, Steven 1980 Mar 1F
Stecher, Martin B. 1982 Jan 20F
Steel, Danielle
best-sellers: *Changes* 1983 Oct 16J/Nov 13J; *Crossings* 1982 Oct 17J; *Daddy* 1989 Dec 1J/Dec 22J; *Family Album* 1985 Mar 15J/Apr 19J/May 24J; *Fine Things* 1987 Mar 27J/Apr 24J/May 29J; *Full Circle* 1984 Jun 15J/Jul 20J/Aug 24J; *Kaleidoscope* 1987 Nov 20J; 1988 Jan 29J/Feb 26J; *Secrets* 1985 Nov 22J/Dec 20J; 1986 Jan 31J; *Star* 1989 Mar 31J/Apr 28J/May 26J; *Wanderlust* 1986 Aug 29J/Sep 26J/Oct 31J; *Zoya* 1988 May 27J/Jun 24J/Jul 23J
Steel, David 1982 Sep 24B
Steen, Alann 1987 Mar 23C
Steeples, Lemuel 1980 Mar 14J
Steger, Will 1986 May 1I; 1989 Dec 11A
Stein, Aaron Marc 1985 Aug 29J
Stein, Gertrude 1983 Jun 3J; 1989 Sep 30J
Stein, John H. 1984 Jul 1G
Steinbach, Terry 1988 Jul 12J
Steinbeck, John 1986 Apr 26J
Steinberg, Joel B. 1989 Jan 30F/Mar 24F
Steinberg, Lisa 1989 Jan 30F/Mar 24F
Steinberger, Jack 1988 Oct 19I
Steinbrenner III, George M. 1989 Jan 18J
Steiner, Roswitha 1986 Mar 23J
Stenberg, Leif 1985 Nov 21I
Stennis, John C. 1987 Oct 19F
Stepanov, Andrei 1984 Apr 19B
Stephen, Ninian 1985 Oct 26E
Stephens, James M. 1988 Jan 7H
Stephenson, Jan 1982 Jun 13J; 1983 Jul 31J
Steptoe, Patrick (Christopher) 1988 Mar 21I
Sterling, Wallace E.J. 1985 Jul 1J
Stern, Elizabeth 1988 Feb 3F/Apr 6F
Stern, Melissa 1988 Feb 3F/Apr 6F
Stern, Richard 1985 Mar 23J
Stern, William 1987 Mar 31F; 1988 Feb 3F/Apr 6F
Stethem, Robert Dean 1985 Jun 15C; 1988 Aug 9B; 1989 May 17B
Stevens, Gary 1988 May 7J
Stevens, George 1983 Oct 11J
Stevens, Jimmy 1980 Nov 14E
Stevens, John Paul 1982 Mar 3F; 1985 Oct 25F; 1987 Jul 17F/Sep 25J/Oct 26G
Stevens, Robert T. 1983 Jan 31F
Stevens, Siaka (Probyn) 1985 Oct 5C; 1988 May 29C
Stevens, William 1989 Jul 28H
Stevenson III, Adlai E. 1986 Mar 18F/Apr 23F/May 16F
Stevenson, Robert 1986 Apr 30J
Stevenson, Robert Louis 1984 Dec 27J
Stewart, Dave 1989 Oct 28J
Stewart, Fred Mustard 1981 Apr 12J
Stewart, Ian 1985 Dec 12J
Stewart, Jimmy 1989 Oct 27J
Stewart, Mary 1980 Jan 13J
Stewart, Michael 1985 Nov 24F
Stewart, Pamela Rae 1987 Feb 26F
Stewart, Payne 1989 Aug 13J
Stewart, Potter 1981 Jun 18F; 1985 Jan 21F/Dec 7F
Stewart, Robert 1984 Feb 7I
Steyrer, Kurt 1986 May 4B/Jun 8B
Stieglitz, Alfred 1986 Mar 6J
Stier, Edwin H. 1983 Nov 30H
Stigler, George 1982 Oct 20I
Stilgoe, Richard 1986 Oct 9J; 1987 Mar 15J
Stiller, Jerry 1988 Feb 26J
Sting 1985 Aug 24J/Sep 28J; 1988 Mar 2J/Sep 2J/Oct 15J
Stitt, Sonny 1982 Jul 22J
Stockman, David A.
budget and spending programs: deficit issues 1981 Sep 2H/Sep 9H/Sep 12G/Oct 28H; 1982 Mar 5H; New Federalism 1982 Feb 4F; farm price supports 1985 Feb 5H; military retirement 1985 Feb 5H
government service: OMB director 1980 Dec 11F; 1985 Jul 9H
personal issues: book published 1986 Apr 22H
politics: *Atlantic Monthly* interview 1981 Nov 11H; Reagan criticizes 1981 Nov 12F; Republican senators support 1981 Nov 13F
Stockwell, John 1980 Jun 25J
Stoessel Jr., Walter J. 1982 Mar 8A
Stokes, Louis 1980 Jan 4F; 1983 Nov 9G
Stokowski, Leopold 1985 Mar 12J
Stoltenberg, Gerhard 1987 Feb 24B
Stone, I(sidore) F(einstein) 1989 Jun 18J
Stone, Irving (Irving Tennenbaum) 1989 Aug 26J
Stone, Oliver 1985 Aug 29J; 1986 Mar 5J/Dec 19J; 1987 Mar 30J/Dec 11J; 1989 Dec 20J
Stone, Richard 1984 Oct 18J
Stone, Richard B. 1983 May 25G/Jun 9D-Jun 10D/Jun 12D/Jun 20G/Jul 8D/Jul 10D/Jul 31D/Aug 30D
Stoph, Willi 1989 Nov 13B
Stoppard, Tom 1984 Jun 3J; 1985 Dec 14J
Stout, Mary R. 1987 Aug 1G
Stout, Michael 1985 Mar 8J
Stowe, John 1980 Oct 7F
Strake, George 1988 Jan 18F
Strange, Curtis 1988 Jun 20J; 1989 Jun 18J
Strasberg, Lee 1982 Feb 17J
Strater, Henry 1987 Dec 22J
Stratten, Dorothy 1980 Aug 15J/Sep 15J
Straub, Peter 1983 Mar 13J; 1984 Dec 14J; 1985 Jan 18J/Feb 8J
Strauss, Annette 1989 May 6F
Strauss, Franz Josef 1980 Sep 13B; 1982 Oct 10B; 1986 Oct 12B; 1988 Oct 3B
Stravinsky, Igor 1983 Apr 30J/Jun 23J
Strawberry, Darryl 1983 Nov 21J
Streep, Meryl 1980 Apr 14J; 1986 Jul 25J; 1987 Dec 18J
Streetman, Robert 1988 Jan 7F
Streisand, Barbra
best-sellers: *Broadway Album* 1985 Dec 21J; 1986 Jan 29J/Feb 19J; 1987 Feb 24J; *Guilty* 1980 Oct 8J/Dec 3J; 1981 Jan 7J
Grammy awards: 1987 Feb 24J
political benefit: 1986 Sep 6J
Strekalov, Gennadi 1980 Nov 27I
Strobel, Gary 1987 Aug 27H/Sep 3H; 1988 Jan 12I
Stroessner, Alfredo 1983 Feb 6D; 1984 Aug 15B; 1986 Mar 16D; 1987 Nov 21D; 1988 Feb 14D/Aug 15D; 1989 Feb 3D/Feb 5D/May 1D
Stronge, James 1981 Jan 21B
Stronge, Norman 1981 Jan 21B
Strougal, Lubomir 1988 Oct 10B
Stuart, Jeb 1988 Jul 15J
Stuck, Hans 1986 Jun 1J
Studds, Gerry E. 1982 Feb 2G; 1983 Feb 4G
Styne, Jule 1984 Feb 15J
Styron, William 1980 May 1J; 1987 Dec 4J
Suarez, Xavier 1985 Nov 5F
Suarez Gonzalez, Adolfo 1980 May 7B/Jun 25B/Sep 8B; 1981 Jan 29B
Suarez Mason, Carlos Guillermo 1987 Jan 24D; 1988 Apr 27D
Suave, Jeanne 1984 Nov 5D
Suazo Cordova, Roberto
government: military hands over power 1980 Jul 20D; elected president 1981 Nov 29D; armed forces command assumed 1984 Mar 31D
personal issues: daughter kidnapped 1982 Dec 14D/Dec 23D; assassination plot 1984 Nov 1D; 1985 Nov 20D; 1986 Jul 23D
Reagan visit: 1985 May 21D
Suazo Estrada, Judith Xiomara 1982 Dec 14D/Dec 23D
Subic, Joseph 1980 Apr 10C
Suharto 1985 Jul 5E; 1986 Sep 4E; 1987 Jan 6E; 1988 Mar 10E
Suh Kyong Won 1989 Aug 25E
Sukarno 1985 Jul 5E; 1986 Oct 9E
Sukova, Helena 1986 Sep 7J
Sullivan, Daniel 1989 Mar 9J
Sullivan, Danny 1985 May 26J
Sullivan, John 1984 Aug 28D
Sullivan, John L. 1982 Aug 8G
Sullivan, Kathryn D. 1984 Oct 11I
Sullivan, Leon H. 1987 Jun 3H
Sullivan, Louis W. 1988 Dec 22F; 1989 Mar 1F/Mar 8I
Sullivan, William 1980 Sep 6G
Sultan, Prince (Saudi Arabia) 1982 Feb 9G
Sultanov, Aleksei 1989 Jun 11J
Summer, Donna 1980 Jan 2J/Jan 25J
Sundberg, Jim 1980 Dec 6J
Sununu, John H. 1988 Nov 17F
Surtees, Robert 1985 Jan 5J
Suslov, Mikhail 1981 Apr 23B; 1982 Jan 25B
Susskind, David (Howard) 1987 Feb 22J
Sutcliffe, Peter B. 1981 Jan 5B/Apr 29B
Sutcliffe, Rick 1984 Nov 23J
Sutherland, Donald 1981 Jul 24J; 1989 Sep 20J
Sutton, Hal 1983 Aug 7J

Suzman, Janet 1989 Sep 20J
Suzuki, Zenko
  foreign policy: PLO 1981 Oct 14A; USSR 1981 Apr 28A/Sep 10E
  government: elected premier 1980 Jul 17E; Kuril Islands dispute 1981 Sep 10E; declares fiscal emergency 1982 Sep 16E; resigns as premier 1982 Oct 12E
  U.S. policy: 1980 Dec 12G; 1981 Apr 28A/May 8E/May 8G; 1982 Jun 4E
Swaggart, Jimmy 1988 Feb 21J/Mar 29J/Apr 8J
Swan, John 1989 Feb 9D
Swanson, Gloria 1980 Oct 13J; 1983 Apr 4J
Swayze, Patrick 1987 Aug 21J
Sweeney, Dennis 1980 Mar 14F
Sweet, Blanche (Sarah) 1986 Sep 6J
Swenson, Kari A. 1984 Jul 16F/Dec 13F; 1985 Jul 12F/Sep 27F
Swift, Michael 1987 May 21I
Swigert, Jack 1983 Jan 3F
Swimmer, Ross O. 1985 Dec 14F
Swindall, Patrick L. 1988 Oct 17F; 1989 Jun 20F
Sykes, Roosevelt 1983 Jul 11J
Symington, (William) Stuart 1988 Dec 14F
Symms, Steven D. 1984 Dec 3G
Syse, Jan 1989 Oct 16B
Szabo, Gabor 1982 Feb 26J
Szent-Gyorgyi, Albert 1986 Oct 22I
Szuros, Matyas 1989 Oct 23B/Dec 22B

T

Tabatabai, Ali Akbar 1980 Jul 22F/Jul 23F
Tagliabue, Paul 1989 Oct 26J
Taha, Mahmoud Mohammed 1985 Jan 18C
Tailleferre, Germaine 1983 Nov 7J
Takenaka, Masahisa 1985 Jan 27E
Takeshita, Noboru
  economic policy: tax reform 1988 Nov 16E/Dec 24E
  foreign policy: China loan 1988 Aug 25E; North Korea apology 1989 Mar 30E; U.S. scientific pact 1988 Jun 20E
  government: chosen party leader 1987 Oct 20A; elected Japanese premier 1987 Nov 6E; resigns 1989 Apr 25E
  Recruit stock trading scandal: 1988 Jul 6E; 1989 Apr 11E/Apr 25E/Apr 27E
Talabani, Jalal 1984 Jul 29C
Talent, John A. 1989 Apr 20I
Talmadge, Herman 1980 May 30F
Tamayo Mendez, Arnaldo 1980 Sep 18I
Tambo, Oliver 1985 Jul 23C/Nov 4C; 1986 Jan 9C/Jun 23C; 1987 Jan 28G
Tambs, Lewis 1986 Dec 25G; 1987 May 2G/May 29G
Tamimi, Sheik Raja Bayud 1980 May 3C
Tan, Amy 1989 Aug 25J
Tanaka, Kakuei 1982 Dec 22E; 1983 Oct 12E/Oct 28E/Dec 26E
Tandy, Jessica 1988 Aug 28J; 1989 Dec 13J
Tange, Kenzo 1987 Mar 18J
Tangstad, Steffen 1986 Sep 6J
Tang Yiming, Dominic 1981 Jun 6J
Taniguchi, Hiromi 1987 May 10J
Taniguchi, Masaharu 1985 Jun 17J
Tanner III, Everett 1985 Oct 30J
Tanner, Marion 1985 Oct 30J
Tardencillas Espinosa, Jose 1982 Mar 12G
Tarkanian, Jerry 1988 Dec 12F
Tarkenton, Fran 1986 Jan 28J

Tarnower, Herman 1980 Mar 10J; 1981 Feb 24J
Tarsis, Valery 1983 Mar 3J
Tate, John 1980 Mar 31J
Tati, Jacques 1982 Nov 5B
Tatum, Edward L. 1989 Jun 9I
Taube, Henry 1983 Oct 19I
Taubman, Alfred 1983 Sep 19J
Tauro, Joseph 1985 Aug 12F
Taussig, Helen Brooke 1986 May 20I
Taya, Maaouiya Ould Sid Ahmed 1984 Dec 12C
Taylor, Elizabeth 1981 May 7J; 1983 Mar 10J; 1984 Aug 5J; 1985 Sep 12J
Taylor, Henry 1986 Apr 17J
Taylor, James H. 1984 Jul 1G
Taylor Jr., Johnny 1984 Feb 29F
Taylor, Lawrence 1987 Jan 13J
Taylor, Lee 1980 Nov 13J
Taylor, Maxwell D(avenport) 1987 Apr 19G
Taylor, Peter 1986 Jun 5J; 1987 Apr 6J/Apr 16J
Taylor, William M. 1989 Jul 24F
Teacher, Brian 1981 Jan 4J/Jun 6J
Teale, Edwin Way 1980 Oct 18J
Tebbit, Norman 1987 Jun 13B
Teehankee, Claudio 1986 Feb 25E
Tejero Molina, Antonio 1981 Feb 23B/Feb 24B
Tekere, Edgar 1980 Aug 6C; 1981 Jan 10C; 1989 Apr 30C
Teller, Edward 1984 May 13I
Temple, Shirley 1985 Nov 19J
Teresa, Mother (Agnes Gonxha Bojaxhiu) 1980 Aug 7J
Terkel, Studs 1985 Apr 24J
Terpil, Frank 1981 Sep 22G/Nov 19F
Terry, John 1985 March 29I
Terzi, Zehdi L. 1988 Mar 11G
Teske, Charlotte 1982 Apr 19J
Testaverde, Vinny 1986 Dec 6J; 1987 Apr 28J
Tevis, Walter 1986 Oct 17J
Thach, Nguyen Co 1987 Aug 1E; 1988 Jan 20E
Thackeray, Bal 1984 May 17E
Thalberg, Irving 1983 Jun 12J
Thatcher, Margaret
  African policy: 1988 Jan 8C
  appointments and resignations: Brittan (EC) 1988 Jul 22B; Heseltine (defense) 1986 Jan 9B; Howe (foreign) 1983 Jun 11B; Hurd (Ulster) 1984 Sep 10B; Lawson (Exchequer) 1989 Oct 26B; Major (foreign/Exchequer) 1989 Jul 24B/Oct 26B
  arms control: 1986 Nov 15G/Nov 21B; 1989 Apr 30B
  Asian and Pacific Rim policy: Afghanistan 1981 Oct 8A; Asia visit 1985 Apr 14B; Australia 1986 Jul 6E; 1987 Mar 13B; Japan 1989 Sep 23A; Malaysia 1986 Jul 6E
  civil strife: London bombing 1981 Oct 11B; Brighton bombing 1984 Oct 12B; 1986 Jun 10B; soccer violence 1985 Mar 13B
  Commonwealth policy: 1986 Jul 20B/Aug 5A; 1987 Oct 17A; 1989 Oct 22A; Canada 1983 Sep 26D; 1986 Jul 13A; India 1985 Oct 15B
  economic policy: unemployment 1981 Jul 27B; immigration reform 1986 Sep 1B; poll tax controversy 1987 Jul 30B/Dec 4B; 1988 Apr 18B; monetary policy feud 1988 Mar 17B/May 17B; social security 1988 Apr 27B
  European policy: European Community 1980 Jun 2B; 1988 Feb 13B/Sep 20B; 1989 Jun 13B; Eurotunnel pact 1987 Jul 29B; France 1981 Oct 11B; 1986 Nov 21B; 1987 Jul 29B; Ireland 1981 Aug 16B/Nov 6B; 1985 Nov 15B; 1988 Dec 13B; Northern Ireland 1985 Nov 15B; Poland 1988 Nov 2B; Soviet Union 1989 Sep 23A; West Germany 1989 Apr 30B
  Falklands War: Argentine invasion 1982 Apr 1A; naval force sent 1982 Apr 3B; Commons speech 1982 Apr 14A; negotiations 1982 Apr 19B/May 13B/May 20A; South Georgia recaptured 1982 Apr 26B; troop advance 1982 May 27D; prisoner totals 1982 Jun 17D; sovereignty talks barred 1982 Jun 23B; probe panel named 1982 Jul 6B; visits 1983 Jan 8D-9D
  G-7 summits: 1986 May 6A; 1987 Jun 8A
  government: parliament opened 1980 Nov 20B; 1984 Nov 6B; 1985 Nov 6B; 1988 Nov 22B; cabinet changes 1981 Sep 14B; 1987 Jun 13B; party conferences 1981 Oct 16B; 1986 Oct 10B; 1988 Oct 14B; local elections 1982 May 6B; Liberal leader attacks 1982 Sep 24B; party conventions 1982 Oct 8B; parliamentary elections 1983 Jun 9B; polls 1985 Feb 10B; lawyers' convention address 1985 Jul 15B; censorship 1987 Feb 1B/Dec 3B; as British prime minister 1987 Jun 11B; 1988 Jan 3B; 1989 May 4B
  Mideast policy: Israel 1986 May 24C; PLO 1985 Oct 14C
  Moscow Olympics boycott: 1980 Mar 25J
  personal issues: son rescued in Sahara 1982 Jan 14J
  South Africa sanctions: 1985 Oct 15B; 1986 Jul 13A/Jul 20B/Aug 5A; 1987 Oct 17A; 1988 Jan 8C; 1989 Oct 22A
  U.S. policy: 1981 Nov 18B; 1982 Apr 1A; 1984 Dec 22G; 1986 Nov 15G; 1989 Oct 24A
  Westland scandal: 1986 Jan 9B/Jul 24B
Thatcher, Mark 1982 Jan 14J
Thayer, Paul 1984 Jan 4G
Theismann, Joe 1983 Dec 20J
Thicke, Alan 1988 Mar 1J
Thomas, Clarence 1986 Feb 11F/Jul 23F
Thomas, Debi 1985 Feb 2J; 1986 Feb 8J/Mar 21J; 1987 Feb 7J/Mar 14J; 1988 Jan 9J
Thomas, Dylan 1987 Sep 25I
Thomas, Isiah 1986 Feb 9J
Thomas, Jim 1987 Jun 12J
Thomas, John 1987 Jun 12J
Thomas, Lee M. 1984 Nov 29H; 1986 May 14D
Thomas, Lewis 1989 Sep 27I
Thomas, Lowell 1981 Aug 30J
Thomas, Pinklon 1984 Aug 31J; 1985 Jun 15J; 1986 Mar 23J; 1987 May 30J
Thomas, Richard 1986 Apr 19J
Thompson, Daley 1980 Jul 26J
Thompson, Davina 1986 Dec 17I
Thompson, Emma 1989 Nov 8J
Thompson Jr., Frank 1980 Feb 2F/Jun 18F/Dec 3F
Thompson, James R. 1987 Sep 21F
Thompson, Mark J. 1985 Apr 24J
Thompson, Thomas 1982 May 9J/Jun 6J
Thomson, Meldrim 1980 Apr 14F
Thomson, Virgil Garnett 1989 Sep 30J
Thorn, Gaston 1980 Jul 31A

Thornburgh, Richard Lewis 1988 Jul 12F/Aug 12F/Nov 21F; 1989 Jun 19F/Dec 4F
Thornley, Trisa Gail 1989 May 4F
Thornton, Willie Mae 1984 Jul 25J
Thoroddsen, Gunnar 1980 Feb 8B
Thorp, Roderick 1988 Jul 15J
Thorpe, Jim 1982 Oct 13J
Thorson, Scott 1982 Oct 14J
Thorton, William 1983 Sep 5I
Thurow, Lester 1987 Mar 9F
Tiedge, Hans Joachim 1985 Aug 23B
Tieri, Frank 1980 Jun 30F
Tierno, Galvan Enrique 1986 Jan 20B
Tikhonov, Nikolai 1980 Oct 23B; 1981 Feb 27B; 1984 Nov 31D
Tillis, James ("Quick") 1986 May 3J
Tillstrom, Burr 1985 Dec 6J
Timerman, Jacobo 1984 Jan 7D
Timmermann, Ulf 1988 May 22J
Tinbergen, Nikolaas 1988 Dec 21I
Tinker, Grant 1986 Aug 28H
Tinoco, Victor Hugo 1983 Mar 23D
Tirso, Josip Broz 1980 Jan 20B/Apr 4B; 1988 Mar 18B
Titov, Vladimir 1988 Dec 21I
Tiwari, Narayan Datt 1988 Feb 29E
Tjibaou, Jeanmarie 1989 May 4H
Tmetuchl, Roman 1988 Nov 10E
Tobin, James 1981 Oct 13H
Todhunter, John 1983 Mar 18H
Todorov, Stanko 1981 Jun 16B
Toepfer, Klaus 1988 Dec 5I
Tokes, Laszlo 1989 Dec 15B
Tolbert Jr., William 1980 Apr 12C
Tolentino, Arturo 1986 Jul 7E/Sep 1E
Tolkachev, Adolf G. 1986 Nov 22B
Tomlin, Lily 1985 Sep 26J; 1986 Jun 1J
Tonegawa, Susumu 1987 Sep 21I/Oct 12I
Tonkin, David 1981 Nov 4E
Tooker, George 1983 Feb 19J
Toole, John Kennedy 1981 Apr 13J
Torrelio Villa, Celso 1982 Jul 19D
Torres, Arnoldo 1983 Aug 24F
Torrijos Herrera, Omar 1981 Jul 31D
Torti, Robert 1987 Mar 15J
Toscanini, Arturo 1989 Nov 5J
Toscanini, Wanda 1989 Nov 5J
Tosh, Peter 1987 Sep 11J
Tostado Rodriguez, Miguel 1987 Jul 2F
Totu, Ioan 1988 Feb 23B
Toure, Ahmed 1984 Mar 27C
Touvier, Paul 1989 May 24B
Tower, John G. 1984 Jan 10G; 1986 Nov 26F; 1988 Dec 16F; 1989 Feb 2G/Feb 23G
Tracy, Honor Lilbush Wingfield 1989 Jun 13J
Trammell, Alan 1980 Dec 6J
Traore, Diarra 1985 Jul 4C
Travanti, Daniel J. 1981 Sep 13J
Travis, Merle 1983 Oct 20J
Treen, David 1981 Jul 21F
Trenary, Jill 1987 Feb 7J
Treumann, Andrzej 1982 Oct 22B
Treurnicht, Andries P. 1982 Mar 20C
Trevino, Lee 1984 Aug 19J
Trifa, Valerian 1982 Oct 7F
Trifonov, Yuri 1981 Mar 28J
Trimmer, Lance 1983 Mar 11E
Troisgros, Jean 1983 Aug 8J
Troisgros, Pierre 1983 Aug 8J
Tromp, Felipe 1986 Jan 1D
Trottier, Bryan 1980 May 24J
Trudeau, Pierre Elliott
  Asian and Pacific Rim policy: 1982 Aug 29D; 1983 Jan 19D
  constitutional reform plan: conferences 1980 Jun 9D/Sep 13D; 1981 Sep 23D/Oct 19D; provincial agreement 1980 Jul 6D; parliament recall 1980 Sep 18D; New-

foundland blocks 1981 Mar 31D; Supreme Court arguments 1981 May 4D; opponents deadline 1981 Oct 18D; compromise agreement 1981 Nov 5D; parliament sent plan 1981 Nov 18D; House, Senate approve 1981 Dec 2D/Dec 8D; UK parliament approves 1981 Dec 20; 1982 Jan 18A/Mar 8D/Mar 25A
  economic policy: business 1980 Apr 14D; energy costs 1981 Aug 10D; interest rates 1981 Aug 10D; wage and price guidelines 1982 Jul 7D/Jul 27D/Aug 29D; demonstrations 1982 Aug 19D/Aug 21D
  European policy: French visit 1982 Nov 8A; peace tour 1983 Nov 7A/Dec 5E
  government: reelected Canada prime minister 1980 Feb 18D; Sauve appointed 1980 Feb 29D; starts fourth term 1980 Mar 3D; by-elections 1981 Aug 17D; resignation 1984 Feb 29D
  Latin policy: 1983 Feb 20D
  native peoples: 1984 Mar 9D
  Quebec independence: 1980 May 2D
  U.S. policy: 1981 Mar 11D; 1982 Oct 19D/Oct 24D
Trudell, Bernard 1983 Mar 28I
Truffaut, Francois 1981 Feb 11J/Oct 11J; 1984 Oct 21J/Oct 23J
Truly, Richard H. 1981 Nov 12I; 1988 Oct 3I; 1989 Apr 12I
Truman, Harry S 1983 Mar 7F; 1988 Oct 19G
Trumka, Richard L. 1982 Nov 9H/Dec 22H; 1985 Dec 20H
Trump, Donald 1988 Oct 12H; 1989 Mar 31H
Truong Chinh 1981 Jul 4E; 1986 Jul 14E; 1987 Jun 18E
Tsedenbal, Yumjaagiyn 1984 Aug 23E
Tsongas, Paul 1986 Sep 4F
Tsutsumi, Yoshiaki 1987 Sep 20H; 1989 Jul 9H
Tubb, Ernest 1984 Sep 6J
Tubbs, Tony 1985 Apr 29J; 1988 Mar 21J
Tuchman, Barbara Wertheim 1989 Feb 6J
Tucker, Tony 1987 Aug 1J
Tudor, Antony 1987 Mar 3J/Apr 19J
Tugendhat, Christopher 1984 May 23B
Tully, Paul 1987 Sep 30F
Tune, Tommy 1983 May 1J/Jun 5J; 1988 May 11J; 1989 Dec 12J
Tung Kueisen 1988 Mar 16F
Tunguyan, Mohammed Jawad Baqir 1980 Oct 31C
Turbay Ayala, Julio Cesar 1980 Mar 9D; 1982 Jun 4D
Turkmen, Ilter 1983 Nov 15B
Turman, James 1988 Mar 15F
Turner, Debbye 1989 Sep 16J
Turner, J(oseph) M(allard) W(illiam) 1984 Jul 5J
Turner, John Napier 1984 Mar 20D/Jun 16D/Jun 30D/Aug 15D/Sep 4D; 1988 Oct 28D
Turner, Joseph Vernon ("Big Joe") 1985 Nov 24J
Turner, Kathleen 1985 Jun 14J; 1986 Oct 8J
Turner, Stansfield 1983 May 1G
Turner, Ted 1980 Jun 1J; 1982 Sep 14J
Turner, Tina
  best-sellers: Back Where You Started 1987 Feb 24J; Better Be Good to Me 1985 Feb 26J; One of the Living 1986 Feb 25J; Private Dancer 1984 Aug 25J/Sep 22J/Oct 27J/Nov 24J/Dec 22J;

1985 Mar 30J; *Tina Live in Europe* 1989 Feb 22J
  Grammy awards: 1985 Feb 26J; 1986 Feb 25J; 1987 Feb 24J; 1989 Feb 22J
Turow, Scott
  best-sellers: *Presumed Innocent* 1987 Jul 17J/Sep 23J/Oct 23J/Nov 20J; 1988 Jan 29J/Feb 26J/Mar 25J
Tutu, Desmond 1984 Oct 16A/Dec 7G; 1986 Apr 2C/Jun 13C/Sep 7C; 1989 Jun 8F
Twain, Mark 1985 Mar 14J/Apr 25J
Tway, Bob 1986 Aug 11J
Twigg, Ernest and Regina 1989 Nov 20F
Twiggy (Leslie Hornby) 1983 May 1J
Tworkov, Jack 1982 Sep 4J
Tyler, Anne 1983 Feb 19J; 1985 Oct 25J; 1986 Feb 17J; 1988 Oct 21J; 1989 Jan 27J/Mar 30J
Tyler, Bonnie 1983 Oct 19J
Tyler, Scott 1989 Feb 17J
Tynan, Kenneth 1980 Jul 26J
Tyson, Mike
  title bouts: Berbick 1986 Nov 22J; Bruno 1989 Feb 25J; Holmes 1988 Jan 22J; Jameson 1986 Jan 25J; Smith 1987 Mar 7J; Spinks 1988 Jun 27J; Thomas 1987 May 30J; Tillis 1986 May 3J; Tubbs 1988 Mar 21J; Tucker 1987 Aug 1J; Williams 1989 Jul 21J
Tyzack, Margaret 1987 Oct 27J
Tzannetakis, Tzannis 1989 Jul 1B/Oct 11B

U

Udall, Morris 1981 Aug 18F; 1983 Jan 15F
Ueberroth, Peter V. 1984 Oct 1J; 1985 Mar 18J/May 7J/Sep 24J; 1986 Feb 28J; 1988 Sep 8J; 1989 Apr 6H/Apr 12H
Uhry, Alfred 1988 Mar 31J
Ulam, Stanislaw Marcin 1984 May 13I
Ulloa Elias, Manuel 1982 Dec 10D
Ullsten, Ola 1981 Oct 31B
Ulusu, Bulent 1980 Sep 21B; 1982 May 14B
Ulvaeus, Bjorn 1986 May 14J
Ung, Chinary 1989 Apr 25J
Ungo, Guillermo 1984 Oct 15D; 1987 Dec 2D
Uno, Sosuke 1989 Jun 2E/Jul 3E/Jul 24E/Aug 9E
Unruh, Jesse (Marvin) 1987 Aug 4F
Unseld, Wes 1988 Feb 4J
Unser Jr., Al 1986 Feb 2J; 1987 Feb 1J
Unser Sr., Al 1985 Feb 3J; 1987 May 24J
Unser, Bobby 1981 May 25J
Updike, John 1982 Apr 12J; 1984 Jun 15J/Aug 11J
Upshaw, Gene 1987 Jan 27J/Aug 8J
Urban, Jerzy 1982 Jan 9B
Urban, Matt 1980 Jul 9G
Urey, Harold 1981 Jan 5I
Uris, Leon 1984 May 11J/Jun 15J
Urruchua Durand, Federico 1985 Aug 28D
Usher, Harry 1985 Jan 15J
Ustinov, Dmitri F. 1981 Nov 7B; 1982 Mar 20E/Dec 6B; 1984 Mar 9E/May 20B
Utgoff, Victor A. 1986 Jul 22G

V

Vainio, Martti 1984 Aug 12J
Valentino, Rudolph 1987 Aug 1J

Valenzuela, Fernando 1981 Nov 11J
Vallee, Rudy (Hubert Prior Vallee) 1986 Jul 3J
Van Agt, Andreas 1981 May 26B/Sep 2B/Oct 16B/Nov 5B/Nov 16B; 1982 May 12B
Van Allsburg, Chris 1986 Jan 20J
Van Benthem, Evert 1985 Feb 21J
Van Berg, Jack 1985 Jan 8J
Van Boven, Theo 1982 Feb 10A
Vance, Courtney B. 1985 May 3J
Vance, Cyrus R. 1980 Jan 14J/Mar 4G/Apr 24G/Apr 26G/May 9G; 1986 Aug 17G
Vance, Robert S. 1989 Dec 16F
Van de Kamp, John 1982 Dec 28J
Vanden Boeynants, Paul 1989 Jan 14B/Feb 13B
Van der Lubbe, Marinus 1981 Apr 22B
Van der Meer, Simon 1984 Oct 17I
Van der Walt, P.J. 1989 Apr 24C
Vanderwier, Gerald M. 1983 Dec 1G
Van der Zee, James 1983 May 15J
Van Dunem, Afonso 1985 Jun 12A; 1986 Sep 17C
Van Duyn, Mona 1983 Feb 19J; 1989 Jun 2J
Van Dyke, Willard 1986 Jan 23J
Vane, John R. 1982 Oct 11I
Vanegas, Uriel 1987 Oct 3D
Van Gogh, Vincent 1985 Apr 24J; 1987 Mar 30J/Nov 11J
Van Lieshout, Scott 1984 Oct 19D
Van Niel, Cornelis Bernardus 1985 Mar 10I
Van Slyke, Helen 1980 May 4J/Jun 8J
Vanunu, Mordechai 1988 Mar 24C
Varelli, Frank 1987 Feb 20D
Vargas Llosa, Mario 1983 Feb 5D; 1985 Mar 29J; 1989 Jul 3D
Vargas Pazos, Frank 1986 Mar 14D
Varmus, Harold E. 1989 Oct 9I
Varnedoe, Kirk 1988 Feb 10J
Vasilev, Zhelyo Kolev 1982 Dec 18B
Vassiliou, George 1988 Feb 21B/Aug 24B/Nov 23B; 1989 Dec 4B
Vasyutin, Vladimir 1985 Nov 21I
Vaughan, Arky 1985 Mar 6J/Jul 28J
Vaughan, Sarah 1983 Apr 22J
Vazquez Rana, Mario 1986 Jun 10H
Veeck, Bill 1986 Jan 2J
Vega Mantilla, Pablo Antonio 1986 Jul 4D
Velasquez Rodriguez, Angel Manfredo 1988 Jul 29D
Velyati, Ali Akbar 1983 Feb 23C
Venkataraman, Ramaswami 1981 Sep 16E; 1987 Jul 13E
Ver, Fabian C. 1983 Sep 17E; 1984 Nov 5E; 1985 Jan 23E/Feb 22E/Dec 2E
Verdi, Giuseppe 1987 May 2J
Vergara Campos, Roger 1980 Aug 12D
Verity Jr., C. William 1987 Aug 10H/Nov 20E; 1988 Feb 10G
Vesco, Robert 1980 Apr 1F; 1984 May 6A
Vessey Jr., John W. 1985 Jul 10G
Vetere, Go 1985 Feb 3B
Vicious, Sid 1986 Oct 17J
Vidal, Gore 1981 May 10J; 1984 Jul 20J/Aug 24J
Videla, Jorge Rafael 1984 Aug 2D
Vides Casanova, Carlos Eugenio 1984 Oct 7D
Vidor, King 1982 Nov 1J
Vieira, Joao Bernardo 1980 Nov 14C; 1986 Jul 12C
Viera, Jose Rodolfo 1985 Jul 3D
Viernes, Gene 1989 Dec 15E
Vilas, Guillermo 1980 Jan 2J; 1982 Jun 5J; 1983 Jun 8J
Vildoso Calderon, Guido 1982 Jul 29D/Sep 17D
Viljoen, Constand 1985 Jul 1C

Villanueva del Campo, Armando 1989 May 7D
Vincent, Fay (Francis T.) 1989 Sep 13J
Vines, Jerry 1988 Jun 14J
Vinge, Joan D. 1983 Jun 1J/Jun 12J/Jul 10J/Aug 14J/Sep 11J
Vinogradov, Ivan M. 1983 Mar 20I
Viola, Frank 1985 Aug 4J; 1987 Oct 25J; 1988 Nov 9J
Viola, Roberto Eduardo 1980 Oct 3D; 1981 Mar 17D/Mar 29D/Nov 20D/Nov 21D/Dec 11D
Vitale, John J. 1982 Jun 5H
Vlajkovic, Radovan 1985 May 15B; 1986 May 15B
Vlasov, Alexander 1987 Jan 6B
Vogel, Hans-Jochen 1984 Mar 12B; 1987 Jun 14B
Voinovich, George V. 1985 Mar 25F/Oct 2F
Volcker, Paul A.
  government service: appointed Fed chairman 1983 Jun 18H; confirmed 1983 Jul 27H; resignation 1987 Jun 2H
  Hunt silver bailout: 1980 May 2H
  monetary policy: budget deficits 1981 Aug 20H; 1982 Jan 26H/Feb 10H/Apr 22H/Jul 28H; foreign borrowing 1985 Feb 6G; interest rates 1981 Jul 16H; 1983 Feb 16H/Apr 12H; 1986 Jul 23H; money supply 1980 Jan 2H; 1983 Feb 16H/Jul 14H/Jul 20H; 1984 Jul 25H; 1985 Feb 20H; 1986 Feb 20H; 1987 Feb 19H; trade deficits 1986 Jul 23H/Aug 31H
Volel, Yves 1987 Oct 13D
Von Auersperg, Alexander 1987 Dec 23J
Von Braun, Wernher 1983 Oct 10I
Von Bulow, Claus 1982 Mar 16J; 1984 Oct 1F; 1985 Jun 10F; 1987 Dec 23J
Von Bulow, Sunny (Martha) 1984 Oct 1F; 1985 Jun 10F; 1987 Dec 23J
Vonnegut, Kurt 1980 Jan 13J/Feb 10J; 1985 Nov 22J
Von Sydow, Max 1988 Dec 21J
Vranitzky, Franz 1987 May 22G
Vrdolyak, Edward R. 1986 Mar 18F/Apr 29F/Dec 26F
Vreeland, Diana (Dalziel) 1989 Aug 22J
Vuckovich, Pete 1982 Nov 3J
Vysotsky, Vladimir 1980 Jul 28B; 1982 Jan 18B

W

Wade, Kevin 1988 Dec 21J
Wadkins, Lanny 1984 Aug 19J; 1987 Aug 9J
Wagner, Jane 1985 Sep 26J
Waite, Terry 1985 Feb 5A/Nov 28C; 1987 Jan 27C/Feb 7C
Waitz, Grete 1980 Oct 26J; 1982 Oct 24J; 1984 Aug 5J; 1985 Oct 27J; 1986 Nov 2J; 1988 Nov 6J
Wajda, Andrzej 1983 Apr 20J
Waldheim, Kurt
  presidential elections: 1986 May 4B/Jun 8B
  UN secretary general: Cambodia 1980 Aug 2A; Cyprus 1980 Apr 3B; Egypt 1981 Oct 6A; Iran hostage crisis 1980 Jan 4A/Feb 17A; Iran-Iraq War 1980 Oct 1A/Oct 10A; Israel 1981 Feb 10A; Palestinians 1980 Jul 25A; Thailand 1980 Aug 2A; Vietnam 1980 Aug 2A
  war crimes controversy: 1986 Mar 4B; U.S. bars entry 1987 Apr 27G/May 22G; papal meeting 1987 Jun 25J; panel probe 1987

Sep 1B/Dec 24B; 1988 Feb 9A; CIA disclosure 1989 Nov 29A
Walesa, Bogdan 1983 Dec 10A
Walesa, Danuta 1983 Dec 10A
Walesa, Lech
  foreign issues: East Germans, Czechs attack 1980 Nov 5B/Nov 21B; papal meetings 1987 Jan 15J; 1983 Jun 23B-24B; Bush meeting 1989 Jul 11B
  Nobel peace prize: 1983 Oct 5A/Dec 10A
  political issues: arrested 1981 Dec 13B; detained 1982 Apr 11B/May 27B/Aug 7B/Aug 26B; released 1982 Nov 14B; job reinstatement refused 1983 Jan 14B; police questioning 1983 May 28B; slander trial 1986 Jan 21B/Feb 11B
  Solidarity movement: labor unrest 1980 Aug 28B/Nov 15B; 1981 Jan 29B/Apr7B/Jun 6B/Jun 12B/Oct 25B/Dec 3B; government meetings 1980 Nov 14B; 1988 Aug 31B; leadership struggles 1981 Mar 31B/Sep 10B/Oct 1B/Oct 8B; media access 1981 Sep 13B; talks rejected 1982 Feb 15B; statements denied 1982 Feb 20B; Lenin Shipyard rallies 1983 Mar 17B; May Day protest 1984 May 1B; amnesty 1984 Jul 21B; Gdansk protest 1984 Dec 16B; Bujak praised 1986 May 31B; labor unrest 1988 Sep 3B-4B; Jaruzelski meeting 1989 Apr 18B
Wali, Wali-Shah 1983 Mar 6C
Walken, Christopher 1984 Jun 21J
Walker, Alan 1984 Aug 22I
Walker, Alice 1983 Apr 18J/Apr 28J; 1985 Dec 18J; 1989 May 26J/Jun 30J
Walker, Arthur James 1985 May 29G/Aug 9G/Nov 12G
Walker, Doak 1986 Jan 28J
Walker, Herschel 1982 Dec 4J; 1983 Feb 23J
Walker Jr., John Anthony 1985 May 20G/May 22G/Jun 3G/Aug 9G/Oct 28G/Nov 12G; 1986 Nov 6G
Walker, Joseph 1985 Aug 1J
Walker, Kenny 1986 Mar 1J
Walker, Michael Lance 1985 May 22G/May 29G/Oct 28G; 1986 Nov 6G
Wall, M. Danny 1988 Jul 7H/Oct 5H; 1989 Dec 4H
Wallace, Andy 1988 Jun 12J
Wallace, Dewitt 1984 May 8J
Wallace, Earl W. 1985 Feb 8J
Wallace, George C. 1982 Sep 7F/Sep 28F/Nov 2F
Wallace, Lila Bell Acheson 1984 May 8J
Wallace, Mike 1982 Jan 11J
Wallace, Paul 1985 Aug 17J
Wallace, Rusty 1989 Nov 19J
Wallace, Sippie (Beulah Thomas) 1986 Nov 1J
Wallach, E. Robert 1989 Aug 8F/Oct 16H
Wallenberg, Raoul 1981 Jan 15A/Oct 31B; 1987 Apr 15B
Wallis, Hal B. (Harold Brent) 1986 Oct 5J
Wallop, Malcolm 1984 Oct 22G
Walsh, Lawrence E.
  Iran-Contra arms scandal: named independent counsel 1986 Dec 19F; Justice probes 1987 Jan 9F/Feb 11F; immunity opposed 1987 Jan 24G; North challenges 1987 Feb 24G; records handed over 1987 Mar 4G; criminal probe seen 1987 Apr 28F; Miller pleads guilty 1987 May 6F; Swiss OK bank records access 1987 Aug 20F; McFarlane gets immunity

1988 Mar 11F; Israel in probe agreement 1988 Mar 28F; trials separated 1988 Jun 8F; North prosecutor named 1988 Dec 16F; North dismissal motion 1989 Jan 5F; Secord indictment 1989 May 11F; Poindexter dismissal motion 1989 Jul 25F
Walsh, Sharon 1980 Jan 1J
Walters, Vernon A. 1985 Feb 8G/May 16F
Walton, Jerome 1989 Nov 8J
Walton, Sam Moore 1984 Sep 18H; 1985 Oct 15J; 1986 Oct 14H; 1987 Oct 12H; 1988 Oct 10H; 1989 Jul 9H
Waltrip, Darrell 1985 Nov 17J
Wambaugh, Joseph 1981 Aug 9J/Sep 6J; 1983 Apr 10J
Wang, David Henry 1988 Mar 20J
Wang Jr., Stephen Sui-Kuan 1988 Jun 27H
Wang Bingqian 1984 Mar 21A
Wang Fang 1988 Jul 5E
Wang Hongwen 1980 Nov 20E; 1981 Jan 25E
Wang Zhong 1983 Jan 17E
Wan Li 1980 Apr 16E; 1989 May 27E
Wanzer, Bobby 1987 Feb 5J
Ward, Theodore 1983 May 8J
Ware, Andre 1989 Dec 2J
Warhol, Andy 1987 Feb 21J; 1988 May 2J/May 3J
Waring, Fred 1984 Jul 29J
Warner, Carolyn 1986 Sep 9F
Warner, John W. 1984 Jan 10G/Nov 13G
Warren, Earl 1985 Dec 7F
Warren, Robert Penn 1986 Feb 26J; 1987 Apr 17J; 1989 Sep 15J
Warwick, Kim 1981 Jan 4J/Jun 6J
Washer, Ben 1982 Sep 5J
Washington, Chester L. 1983 Aug 31J
Washington, Denzel 1989 Dec 14J
Washington, Ford ("Buck") 1986 May 18J
Washington, George 1983 Oct 19F; 1984 Sep 21I
Washington, Harold
  government: mayoral primaries 1983 Feb 22H; 1987 Feb 24F; elected Chicago mayor 1983 Apr 12F; 1987 Apr 7F; city council elections 1986 Mar 18F/Apr 29F; 1987 Apr 7F; Vrdolyak ousted 1986 Dec 26F
  personal issues: death 1987 Nov 25F; library named 1988 Jun 20J
Wasserstein, Wendy 1989 Mar 9J/Mar 30J/Jun 4J
Watanabe, Michio 1982 Apr 16E; 1988 Jul 23E
Waterman, Robert H. 1983 Aug 14J
Waters, John 1988 Feb 26J/Mar 7J
Waters, Muddy (McKinley Morganfield) 1983 Apr 30J
Waterston, Sam 1984 Nov 2J
Watkins, James D. 1988 Feb 23I/Jun 2F/Jun 12I; 1989 Jan 12H/Mar 1H/Jun 27H/Aug 1H/Dec 1H
Watkins, Perry 1989 May 3G
Watley, Jody 1988 Mar 2J
Watson, Barbara M. 1983 Feb 17F
Watson, James 1988 Oct 1I
Watson, Samuel J. 1987 May 14F
Watson Jr., Thomas 1980 Jan 2B
Watson, Tom
  British Open: 1980 Jul 20J; 1982 Jul 18J; 1983 Jul 17J; 1984 Jul 22J
  Masters Tournament: 1981 Apr 12J; 1984 Apr 15J
  U.S. Open: 1982 Jun 20J; 1987 Jun 21J
Watt, James G.
  Beach Boys ban: 1983 Apr 7J

energy policy: coastal oil, gas drilling 1982 May 13F; 1985 Jul 26H; federal coal leases 1982 Nov 22H; 1983 May 12H/Sep 20H/Sep 28H; 1984 Feb 8H
government service: Sierra Club ouster drive 1981 Apr 16H; Udall warned 1981 Aug 18F; resigns as interior secretary 1983 Oct 9H
land policy: wilderness areas 1982 Feb 21F/Dec 30H; Native Americans 1982 Dec 8F; 1983 Jan 27F; water rights 1982 Dec 8F; public sales 1983 Jul 28H; private ranchers 1985 Sep 3H
Watts, Glenn 1982 May 20F
Waxman, Henry 1985 Jan 24H
Wayne, John 1988 Jun 10J
Wayte, David A. 1983 Jul 19G; 1985 Sep 10G
Wazan, Shafik al- 1982 Jun 25C/Jul 30C/Oct 4C/Nov 3C; 1983 Sep 26C/Oct 23C; 1984 Feb 5C
Weaver, Mike 1980 Mar 31J; 1985 Jun 15J
Weaver, Sigourney 1984 Jun 21J; 1988 Sep 23J/Dec 21J
Webb, Chick 1987 Jul 10J
Webb, Chloe 1986 Oct 17J; 1987 Jan 4J
Webb, Dan K. 1982 Dec 3F
Webb, Jack 1982 Dec 22J
Webb Jr., James H. 1987 Apr 10G/Dec 21G; 1988 Feb 22G/Feb 23G/Mar 30G
Weber, Pete 1989 Mar 18J
Weber, Richard 1986 May 1I
Weber, Vin 1983 Mar 3H
Webster, William H.
CIA director: nominated 1987 Mar 3G/Apr 8F/Apr 30G; confirmed 1987 May 19F; sworn 1987 May 26G; retains post 1988 Dec 6F
FBI director: Freedom of Information Act 1981 Nov 12F; drug enforcement role 1982 Jan 21F; terrorist plot 1983 Dec 14F
Iran-Contra arms scandal: 1987 Apr 8F/Apr 30G
Wechsler, James A. 1983 Sep 11J
Wee Kim Wee 1985 Aug 27E
Weekly, David Scott 1983 Mar 11E
Weems, Donald 1982 Jan 20F
Weicker Jr., Lowell P. 1987 May 7H; 1988 Nov 16I
Weidenbach, Lisa Larsen 1985 Apr 15J
Weidenbaum, Murray 1981 Aug 30H/Nov 17H/Dec 8H
Weidenfeld, Lord George 1985 Mar 4J; 1986 Apr 10J
Weil, Cynthia 1988 Mar 2J
Weill, Kurt 1981 Nov 27J
Wein, George 1986 Jan 25J
Weinberger, Caspar W.
African policy: Chad 1983 Aug 18G
Asian and Pacific Rim policy: China 1981 Apr 4G; 1983 Sep 29E/Oct 13G; 1986 Oct 11E; Pacific Rim 5-nation tour 1982 Nov 8E
A-war strategy: NATO missile deployment 1981 Apr 7G; 1983 Jun 5B; plan explained 1981 Oct 20G; A-blast warning denied 1981 Nov 5G; plan debated 1982 May 29G/Jun 20G/Aug 9G
Beirut Marine base bombing: 1983 Oct 23G/Oct 29G/Nov 23G; 1984 Jan 16G/Feb 8G
defense budget: Reagan plan 1980 Nov 23F; Carter request 1981 Jan 28G; administration proposals 1981 Sep 9H; 1982 Mar 4G; 1983 Mar 9G; 1984 Feb 1G/May 3G/Dec 18G; 1985 Feb 4G; annual report 1986 Feb 5G
defense contract controversy: spare parts scandal 1983 Jul 18G/Sep

6G; senators criticize Pentagon 1983 Oct 6G; expense claims questioned 1985 Mar 12G; Sergeant York gun cancelled 1985 Aug 27G
European policy: France 1983 Aug 18G; Poland 1981 Apr 4G; Turkey 1981 Dec 5G
government service: named defense secretary 1980 Dec 11F; resignation 1987 Nov 5G; Medal of Freedom 1987 Nov 17G
Iran-Contra arms scandal: 1987 Jul 31G
Latin policy: Central America tour 1983 Sep 6D; El Salvador 1985 Jul 31G; Grenada 1983 Oct 26G
Mideast policy: Israel 1981 Jul 22C; 1983 May 2C; Lebanon 1983 Feb 24G; Saudi Arabia 1982 Feb 9G
military policy: neutron warheads 1981 Aug 10G; strategic weapons policy 1981 Oct 5G; mobilization strategy 1982 Feb 8G; newspaper coverage protest 1982 Aug 23G; high-tech disclosures curb 1984 Nov 7G; strategy outlined 1984 Nov 28G; strategy panel named 1987 Jan 11G
politics: Reagan campaign memo 1984 Oct 3F
Soviet policy: arms control issues 1981 Apr 4G; 1982 Apr 14G/Oct 28G; 1985 Oct 22G; military power assessed 1983 Mar 9G; 1985 Apr 2G; 1987 Mar 24G
Star Wars: 1985 Jan 31G; 1987 Sep 18G
Weinfeld, Edward 1983 Nov 9G
Weinstein, Jack B. 1985 May 28G; 1988 Jul 5G; 1989 Feb 11H
Weir, Benjamin 1985 Sep 18C; 1986 Jun 11J
Weir, Peter 1983 Jan 21J; 1985 Feb 8J; 1989 Jun 2J
Weiser, Stanley 1987 Dec 11J
Weiss, Peter 1982 May 10J/Aug 14J
Weiss, Solomon 1982 Nov 27J
Weiss, Walt 1988 Nov 2J
Weissmuller, Johnny 1982 Apr 18J; 1984 Jan 20J
Weizman, Ezer 1980 May 14C/May 25C/Nov 23C; 1989 Dec 31C
Weizsaecker, Carl Friedrich von 1989 Mar 7J
Weizsaecker, Richard von 1989 May 23B
Welch, Priscilla 1987 Nov 1J
Weld, William F. 1988 Jul 26F
Welles, Orson 1985 Oct 10J; 1986 Aug 27J; 1987 May 14J; 1988 Oct 30J
Wells, H.G. 1985 Oct 10J; 1987 Dec 27J
Welty, Eudora 1983 Apr 28J
Wenders, Wim 1984 May 23J
Werner, Oskar 1984 Oct 23J
West, Anthony 1987 Dec 27J
West, Francis J. 1982 Dec 18A
West, Jessamyn 1984 Feb 25J
West, Mae 1980 Nov 22J
West, Rebecca 1983 Mar 15J; 1987 Dec 27J
Westbrooks, Erica 1988 Apr 3J
Westenberg, Robert 1987 Nov 5J
Westminster, Duke of (Gerald Grosvenor) 1988 Feb 24J
Westmoreland, William C. 1982 Jul 15J/Sep 13J; 1983 Apr 26J/Oct 14J; 1984 Oct 11F; 1985 Feb 18F
Weston, Garry 1988 Feb 24J
Wheeler, Hugh 1987 Jul 26J
Whitaker, Forest 1987 Dec 23J
White, Betty 1986 Sep 21J
White, Byron R. 1983 Oct 5F/Oct 31F; 1985 Jul 1F; 1987 Jun 24H
White, Daniel (Dan) 1985 Oct 21F

White, Frank 1980 Dec 6J
White, Frank D. 1981 Mar 19F
White, Mark 1986 Mar 10F/May 86/May 8F/Sep 23H
White, Michael R. 1989 Oct 3F
White, Reggie 1987 Feb 1J
White, Robert E. 1981 Feb 1F; 1982 Jul 27G; 1986 Nov 29F
White, Ryan 1986 Feb 13F/Feb 21F/Jul 16F
White, Theodore H(arold) 1986 May 15J
White, Timothy Lee 1980 Mar 1F
Whitehead-Gould, Mary Beth 1987 Mar 31F; 1988 Apr 6F
Whitmire, Kathy 1983 Nov 8F
Whitney, John Hay ("Jock") 1982 Feb 8J
Whitney, Roy 1989 Jul 10D
Whittaker, Geoffrey 1989 Feb 27D
Whittingham, Charlie 1988 Jan 27J
Whitworth, Jerry A. 1985 Jun 3G; 1986 Aug 28G
Whitworth, Kathy 1981 Jul 26J
Wickham Jr., John A. 1983 Aug 8G; 1984 Feb 2G
Wiesel, Elie 1986 Oct 14A
Wiesel, Torsten N. 1981 Oct 9I
Wiesenthal, Simon 1985 Sep 27B
Wiest, Dianne 1986 Feb 7J; 1987 Mar 30J
Wijeratne, Ranjan 1989 May 3E
Wilander, Mats 1982 Jun 5J; 1985 Jun 9J; 1988 Jan 24J/Jun 5J/Sep 11J; 1989 Dec 17J
Wilbur, Richard 1987 Apr 17J; 1988 May 16J; 1989 Mar 30J
Wilcox, Herbert 1986 Jun 3J
Wilde, Oscar 1983 Nov 18J
Wilder, Billy 1988 Apr 21J
Wilder, L. Douglas 1989 Jan 26F/Nov 7F
Wildman, John 1986 Mar 20J
Wiley, Richard 1987 May 9J
Wilhelm, Hoyt 1985 Jan 7J/Jul 28J
Wilkens, Lenny 1989 Feb 10J
Wilkerson, Cathlyn Platt 1980 Jul 8F
Wilkins, Roy 1981 Sep 8F
Will, Hubert L. 1985 Feb 14F
William, Prince (William Arthur Philip Louis) (Great Britain) 1982 Jun 21B; 1984 Sep 15J
Williams, Billy 1987 Jan 14J
Williams, Carl ("The Truth") 1989 Jul 21J
Williams, Charles ("Cootie") 1985 Sep 15J
Williams, C.K. 1988 Jan 11J
Williams, Doug 1988 Jan 3J
Williams, (George) Emlyn 1987 Sep 25I
Williams Jr., Harrison A. 1980 Feb 2F/Oct 30F; 1981 May 1F/Aug 24F; 1982 Feb 16F/Mar 11F
Williams, Hosea 1989 Oct 3F
Williams, Joe 1984 Apr 26J
Williams, John 1980 Jan 10J
Williams, John Bell 1983 Mar 26F
Williams, Kit 1981 Mar 8J/Apr 12J/May 10J
Williams, Leroy 1982 Aug 27F
Williams, R. Foster 1985 Jun 24H
Williams, Richard (diplomat) 1988 Sep 20G
Williams, Richard (film animator) 1988 Jun 22J
Williams, Robert Wayne 1983 Dec 15F
Williams, Robin 1987 Dec 23J; 1989 Jun 2J
Williams, Roy Lee 1981 May 15H/May 22H/Jun 4H; 1982 Dec 15H; 1983 Mar 30F
Williams, Shirley 1982 Sep 23B
Williams, Spencer 1982 Jun 3H
Williams, Tennessee 1983 Feb 25J; 1984 Dec 7J; 1985 Dec 27J; 1987 Jun 13J
Williams, Vanessa 1984 Jul 23J

Williams, Wayne B. 1981 Jun 21F; 1982 Feb 27F
Willis, Bruce 1987 Sep 20J; 1988 Jul 15J
Willoch, Kaare 1981 Oct 14B; 1985 Sep 10B; 1986 Apr 30B/Jun 17B
Willson, S. Brian 1987 Sep 1F
Wilson, August 1984 Oct 11J; 1985 May 3J; 1986 May 2J; 1987 Jun 7J; 1988 Mar 27J
Wilson, David 1987 Jan 16E
Wilson, Dennis 1983 Dec 28J
Wilson, Edwin P.
Libya assassination plot: indictment 1983 Feb 16G; acquittal 1983 Mar 4G; trial 1983 Nov 9G; conviction 1984 Nov 29F
Libya export scheme: Justice probe 1981 Sep 22G; arrest 1982 Jun 15G; indictment 1982 Jul 19G; trial 1982 Nov 17G; 1983 Feb 5G/Feb 18G; conviction 1983 Nov 7G
Wilson, Harold 1981 Mar 29B; 1987 Apr 27B
Wilson, Helen Dolan 1982 Apr 25F
Wilson, Kenneth G. 1982 Oct 18J
Wilson, Lanford 1980 Apr 14J; 1987 Oct 14J
Wilson, Larry 1988 Mar 30J
Wilson, Margaret Bush 1983 May 26F/Jun 11F
Wilson, Meredith 1984 Jun 15J
Wilson, Michael 1984 Nov 8D; 1986 Sep 18D; 1989 Dec 19D
Wilson, Stephen V. 1988 Dec 22F
Wilson, Teddy (Theodore) 1986 Jul 31J
Wilson, Willie 1980 Dec 6J
Winans, R. Foster 1984 May 19H; 1987 Nov 16F
Winchell, Paul 1986 Jul 2J
Windom, Robert E. 1986 Sep 19I
Wingti, Paias 1985 Nov 21E; 1987 Aug 4E; 1988 Jul 4E
Winkler, Mel 1988 Mar 27J
Winograd, Garry 1984 Mar 19J
Winston, Harry 1986 Dec 12F
Winter, John 1985 Jun 16J
Winwood, Steve 1981 Apr 8J/May 6J; 1986 Sep 17J; 1987 Feb 24J; 1988 Aug 27J/Sep 24J
Wise, John 1986 Sep 10D; 1987 Apr 27D
Witherspoon, Tim 1984 Aug 31J; 1986 Jul 20J/Dec 12J
Witt, Katarina 1987 Mar 14J; 1988 Mar 26J
Witt, Mike 1984 Sep 30J
Wittig, Georg 1987 Aug 26I
Wittkowski, Michael E. 1984 Sep 3J
Wlosik, Bogdan 1982 Oct 20B
Wolf, Gary K. 1988 Jun 22J
Wolfe, George C. 1986 Nov 2J
Wolfe, Leslie R. 1989 Apr 28F
Wolfe, Tom
American Book Awards: 1980 May 1J
best-sellers: Bonfire of the Vanities 1988 Jan 29J/Feb 26J/Mar 25J/Apr 29J/May 27J/Jun 24J/Jul 23J; Right Stuff 1980 May 1J
Wolff, Tobias 1985 May 11J
Wolfram Jr., Edward P. 1983 Sep 6F
Wollek, Bob 1985 Feb 3J; 1989 Feb 5J
Wonder, Stevie 1985 May 13J/Nov 30J; 1989 Jan 18J
Wong, B.D. 1988 Mar 20J
Wong, George S.K. 1986 Mar 27I
Wood, Audrey 1985 Dec 27J
Wood, Curtis 1984 Oct 19D
Wood Jr., John H. 1982 Dec 14F; 1983 Mar 18F
Wood, Natalie 1981 Nov 29J
Wood, Sharon 1986 May 20J
Wood, Willie 1989 Jan 24J

Woodard, Jeff 1981 Feb 28J
Woodruff, Robert Winship 1985 Mar 7J
Woods, James 1986 Mar 5J; 1989 Sep 17J
Woodward, Bob 1987 Sep 25G
Woo Jung Chien 1982 Oct 16E
Wootton, Barbara (Frances) (Baroness Wootton of Abinger) 1988 Jul 11I
Worrell, Todd 1986 Nov 24J
Worthy, James 1988 Jun 21J
Wouk, Herman 1983 Feb 16J; 1985 Apr 19J
Wozniak, Steve 1986 May 17I
Wright Jr., James C.
ethics issues: federal aid for friend 1987 Aug 5F; book royalties 1987 Sep 24F; 1988 Jun 6F; House committee probe 1988 Jun 10F/Jul 26F; House rules review 1989 Jan 3F; House abuses charged 1989 Apr 17F
foreign policy: Nicaragua 1984 Mar 20G; 1987 Sep 23G; 1988 Mar 3G/Sep 20G
government service: elected House speaker 1986 Dec 8F; renominated House speaker 1988 Dec 5F; resigns House seat 1989 May 31F
politics: Reagan veto criticism 1982 Aug 28H; Congress convenes 1987 Jan 6F; State of Union response 1987 Jan 27F; Bush budget address response 1989 Feb 9F
Wright, Peter 1987 Apr 27B/Aug 13B/Dec 21B
Wright, Richard 1985 Nov 28J
Wright, Robert C. 1986 Aug 28H
Wright, Sewall 1988 Mar 3I
Wujec, Henryk 1982 Sep 3B; 1984 Aug 13B
Wu Xueqian 1982 Nov 19E; 1983 Oct 13G; 1988 Mar 7G
Wyeth, Andrew 1987 Mar 11J
Wyeth, James 1987 Mar 11J
Wyeth, N.C. 1987 Mar 11J
Wyler, William 1981 Jul 27J
Wyman, Thomas H. 1986 Sep 10H
Wyngaarden, James B. 1988 Apr 18I/Jul 2I
Wyszynski, Stefan 1981 May 28B/Jul 7J

X

Xiao Jingguang 1980 Feb 19E
Xu Wenli 1981 Apr 10E

Y

Yablonski, Joseph 1985 May 31F
Yadin, Yigael 1984 Jun 28C
Yakovlev, Aleksandr N. 1987 Nov 3B
Yamaguchi, Kristi 1989 Feb 10J
Yamani, Sheik Ahmed Zaki 1981 Apr 19A/Apr 23C/Sep 8A; 1986 Oct 29C
Yanes, Pedro Rene 1985 Jan 6D
Yang Dechi 1980 Feb 25E
Yang Jing 1981 Apr 10E
Yang Zhong 1987 May 29D
Yao Wenyuan 1980 Nov 20E; 1981 Jan 25E
Yao Yilin 1981 Feb 28E
Yarbrough, Gary Lee 1984 Oct 18F
Yard, Molly 1987 Jul 18F
Yaron, Amos 1982 Nov 7C; 1983 Mar 1C; 1986 Aug 1C
Yastrzemski, Carl 1989 Jan 9J/Jul 23J
Yazov, Dmitri T. 1988 Aug 4G
Yeager, Jeanna 1986 Dec 23I
Yeehankee, Claudio 1985 Nov 19E
Ye Fei 1980 Feb 19E
Yeiwene, Yeiwene 1989 May 4H

Ye Jianying (Yeh Chienying) 1981 Sep 30E; 1986 Oct 22E

Yeltsin, Boris N. 1987 Mar 2D/Nov 3B/Nov 11B/Nov 18B; 1988 Feb 18B; 1989 Mar 5B/Mar 19B/Dec 9G

Yermishkin, Oleg N. 1984 Mar 1J

Yeutter, Clayton K. 1985 Apr 2H; 1986 Sep 7B; 1987 Nov 6D; 1988 Feb 29D/Dec 14H; 1989 Feb 8H

Yevtushenko, Yevgeny 1989 Mar 5B

Yilmaz, Mesut 1988 Feb 23B; 1989 Jan 4B

Yolen, Jane 1988 Jan 11J

Yordan, Philip 1986 Oct 6J

Yoshimura, Wendy 1980 Aug 25F

Young, Andrew J. 1981 Oct 27F; 1983 Aug 1F; 1985 Oct 8F

Young, Coleman A. 1982 Jul 13F; 1985 Sep 10F

Young, Francis L. 1988 Sep 6F

Young, John W. 1981 Apr 12I

Young, Mick 1986 Jul 13E

Young, W. Dale 1989 Sep 21F

Young of Graffham, Lord 1989 Jul 10B

Younis, Fawaz 1987 Sep 17G; 1989 Mar 14G/Oct 4A

Yount, Robin 1982 Nov 9J; 1989 Nov 20J

Yourcenar, Marguerite 1980 Mar 16J; 1987 Dec 17J

Yuan Mu 1989 Apr 29E

Yurchenko, Vitaly 1985 Sep 26B/Nov 4G

Z

Zaccaro, John A. 1984 Aug 25F; 1987 Oct 15F

Zacharias, Jerrold Reinach 1986 Jul 16I

Zacharin, Zeev 1982 Nov 14C

Zadora, Pia 1988 Feb 26J

Zah, Peterson 1982 Nov 2F; 1986 Nov 4F

Zaida, Mohammed Abbas 1985 Oct 12A

Zakharov, Gennadi F. 1986 Sep 12B/Sep 30A

Zaks, Jerry 1986 Mar 19J/Jun 1J; 1989 Jun 4J

Zambrano, Jose Alberto 1980 Jan 19D

Zamora, Ruben 1983 Jan 19D/Jul 31D; 1984 Oct 15D; 1987 Dec 2D

Zaratiegui, Horacio 1982 Sep 20D

Zardari, Asif Ali 1987 Jul 30E/Dec 18E

Zavala Avelar, Alfredo 1985 Mar 6D/Mar 14D/Apr 4D/Apr 30D; 1988 Jan 6F/Sep 28F/Oct 28D

Zebro, Saye 1980 Nov 25C

Zehe, Alfred 1983 Nov 10G

Zemeckis, Robert 1988 Jun 22J

Zerbo, Saye 1982 Nov 7C

Zhang Aiping 1982 Nov 19E

Zhang Chunqiao 1980 Nov 20E; 1981 Jan 25E

Zhang Shaosong 1989 Mar 24E

Zhang Wenjin 1980 Feb 5A

Zhao Ziyang
  economic policy: 1980 Sep 11E; 1981 Nov 30E; 1988 Oct 27E
  foreign policy: Cambodia conflict 1981 Feb 1E; Europe trips 1984 Jun 16E; 1985 Jun 19B; Macao talks 1985 May 23E; Soviet ties 1982 Nov 19A; U.S. trip 1984 Jan 12A
  government: appointed China deputy premier 1980 Apr 16E; premier 1980 Sep 10E; appointed acting general secretary 1987 Jan 16E; ousted 1989 Jun 24E
  pro-democracy movement: "bourgeois liberalization" campaign 1987 Jan 29E; ousted 1989 Jun 24E; trial studied 1989 Jul 11E

Zhdanov, Viktor M. 1987 Feb 6B

Zhivkov, Todor 1981 Jun 16B; 1984 Sep 9B; 1987 Jul 28B; 1989 Nov 10B

Zhou Nan 1984 Sep 7E

Zia ul-Haq, Muhammad
  assassination: 1988 Aug 17E/Oct 16E
  foreign policy: China 1980 Jan 21E; India 1985 Dec 17E; Iran-Iraq War 1980 Oct 1A; U.S. 1981 Aug 28G
  government: democracy transition delayed 1982 Mar 21E; censorship lifted 1983 Mar 27E; protests 1983 Aug 14E; 1987 Jul 5E; referendum on presidency 1984 Dec 19E; elections 1985 Feb 25E; 1988 Jul 20E; martial law ended 1985 Dec 30E; assembly, cabinet dissolved 1988 May 29E/Oct 5E

nuclear capability: 1981 Nov 25E; 1987 Mar 30E

Ziaur Rahman 1981 May 30E/Jun 2E

Zien, Chip 1987 Nov 5J

Zimbalist Jr., Efrem 1985 Feb 22J

Zimbalist Sr., Efrem 1985 Feb 22J

Zimbalist, Stephanie 1985 Feb 22J

Zipori, Mordechai 1982 Nov 18C

Zippel, David 1989 Dec 11J

Zita, Empress (Austria) 1989 Apr 1B

Zoeller, Fuzzy 1981 Aug 9J; 1984 Jun 18J

Zollo, Frederick 1987 May 28J

Zolotas, Xenophon 1989 Nov 21B

Zongo, Henri 1984 Jul 1J; 1989 Sep 19C

Zorrilla Perez, Jose Antonio 1989 Jun 13D

Zubi, Mahmoud 1987 Nov 1C

Zuckerman, Mortimer B. 1984 Jun 11F

Zundel, Ernst 1985 Feb 28D

Zurbriggen, Pirmin 1987 Feb 2J; 1988 Mar 26J

Zwick, Edward 1989 Dec 14J

Zwillich, Ellen Taaffe 1983 Apr 18J

Zworykin, Vladimir 1982 Jul 29I

SUBJECT INDEX

The index is arranged alphabetically letter-by-letter. Entries are arranged both alphabetically and chronologically. Every index entry contains the year, month, day and column location (e.g., adoption 1981 Aug 16D). The year is 1981, the month is August, the day is 16 and the column is D.

A

Aarhus University (Denmark) 1987 Sep 21I

ABA *see* American Bar Association

Abbott Northwestern Hospital (Minneapolis) 1985 Dec 19I; 1986 Jan 2I

ABC *see* American Broadcasting Company

Abenaki Indians 1986 May 6J

Abkhazians (ethnic group) 1989 Jul 27B

ABM *see* antiballistic missiles

Aborigines
  arts and culture: archaeological digs 1988 Nov 25I; sacred sites 1980 May 8E; 1984 May 7E
  crime and law enforcement: imprisonment rates 1981 Mar 9E; legal reforms 1981 Mar 16E
  defense and disarmament: A-test contamination 1985 Dec 5E; 1989 Jul 7E
  government and politics: parliamentary representation 1983 Jun 15E
  health care: death rates 1983 Apr 21I
  human rights: police custody deaths/riots 1987 Aug 15E-16E/Nov 12E; 1988 Jan 6E/Jan 27E/Jul 25E/Dec 28E; UN rights commission role 1980 Sep 3A; 1982 Feb 18E; 1988 Aug 5E; World Council of Churches study 1981 Jul 4E
  land rights: Ayers Rock dispute 1983 Oct 26H/Nov 11E; 1985 Mar 14E/Oct 26E; land titles 1981 Nov 4E; leases 1981 Jul 20E; 1982 Mar 3E; legislation 1985 Apr 17E; 1986 Mar 3E/May 15E; mining 1980 May 8E/Jul 27E; 1982 Mar 1E; 1983 Nov 22E; protests 1982 Oct 4E; 1988 Jan 4E

abortion *see also advocacy groups* (e.g., Operation Rescue)
  crime and law enforcement: abortion clinic owner kidnapped 1982 Aug 20F; RICO Act convictions upheld 1989 Feb 2F
  foreign developments: Australia 1980 May 30E; Canada 1988 Jan 28D/Mar 7D/May 18D/Jul 28D/Aug 27D; 1989 Aug 8D/Nov 3D/Nov 16D; Greece 1986 Jun 13B; Ireland 1983 Sep 7B; Italy 1981 May 18B; Netherlands 1980 Dec 20B; Portugal 1982 Nov 12B; United Nations 1984 Aug 14A; 1985 Jul 10F/Sep 30G; USSR 1981 Jun 3B
  health issues: fetal tissue research 1988 Sep 16I; Medicaid 1980 Jan 15F/Jun 30F/Sep 17F; 1989 Oct 11F/Oct 19F; NAS report 1986 Dec 9F; research censorship 1989 Dec 16F; RU 486 1986 Dec 18I; 1987 Oct 2I; 1988 Oct 26I/Oct

28I; spontaneous 1980 Jan 4I; 1981 Apr 3I
  political and legislative issues: California Republican primary 1989 Aug 9F; GOP platform 1980 Jul 9F; Helms amendment 1981 May 21F; state restrictions 1987 Aug 27F; 1989 Oct 10F/Oct 24F/Nov 18F; U.S. aid ban 1985 Jul 10F
  polls and surveys: 1988 Oct 16F
  religious issues: Catholics 1984 Aug 9F/Sep 13F/Dec 18J; Lutherans 1989 Aug 29J; Presbyterians 1985 Jun 11J
  rights issues: demonstrations 1984 Jan 23F; 1985 Jan 22F; 1986 Mar 9F; 1989 Apr 19F/Nov 12F/Dec 10F; family planning clinics 1982 Aug 20F; 1986 Jun 9F; 1987 Aug 29F; 1988 Jan 29F/Mar 3A/Oct 8F; League of Women Voters support 1983 Jan 19F; NOW seeks injunction 1986 Jun 9F; Virginia in vitro clinic approved 1980 Jan 8I
  Supreme Court developments: federal and state funding 1980 Feb 19F/Jun 30F; 1986 Nov 3F; O'Connor nomination 1981 Jul 7F; picketing ban upheld 1988 Jun 27F; Roe reversal backed by Reagan 1985 Jul 15H; state and local curbs 1981 Mar 23F; 1982 May 24F/Nov 30F; 1983 Jun 15F; 1986 Jun 11F; 1989 Jan 9F/Jul 3F

abortion clinics 1982 Aug 20F; 1986 Jun 9F; 1987 Aug 29F; 1988 Jan 29F/Mar 3A/Oct 8F

abortion pill *see* RU 486

Abortion Rights Mobilization 1986 May 8F

Above the Law (film) 1988 Apr 20J

Abscam scandal
  criminal proceedings: Jenrette Jr., John 1980 Jun 13F/Oct 7F/Dec 10F; Kelly, Richard 1980 Jul 15F; 1981 Jan 26F; Lederer, Raymond 1980 May 28F; 1981 Jan 9F/Aug 13F; 1982 Sep 3F; Murphy, John 1980 Dec 3F; 1981 Aug 13F; 1982 Sep 3F; Myers, Michael 1980 May 28F/Aug 31F/Oct 2F; 1981 Aug 13F; 1982 Sep 3F; Stowe, John 1980 Oct 7F; Thompson Jr., Frank 1980 Jun 18F/Dec 3F; 1981 Aug 13F; 1983 Sep 3F; Williams Jr., Harrison 1981 May 1F/Aug 13F/Aug24F; 1982 Feb 16F/Mar 11F
  sting operation and expose: 1980 Feb 2F/Feb 11F/Aug 20F; 1982 Oct 9F/Dec 16F
  Supreme Court rulings: 1980 Oct 14F; 1981 Jan 19F

Abu Nidal 1985 Dec 27A; 1987 Jul 13B

Abyss, The (film) 1989 Aug 30J

A.C. Nielsen Co. *see* Nielsen ratings

Academy Awards (Oscars) 1980 Apr 14J; 1981 Mar 30J; 1982 Mar 29J;

1984 Apr 9J; 1985 Mar 25J; 1986 Mar 24J; 1987 Mar 30J; 1988 Apr 11J; 1989 Mar 29J

Academy of Television Arts and Sciences *see* Emmy Awards

Accidental Death of an Anarchist (Dario Fo) (book/play) 1984 Nov 15G

Accidental Tourist, The (Anne Tyler) (book/film) 1985 Oct 25J; 1986 Feb 17J; 1989 Jan 25J/Mar 29J

accidents *see specific type* (e.g., airplane crashes); *individual incidents* (e.g., Lockerbie air crash)

Accuracy in Academia 1985 Aug 4F

Accuracy In Media 1985 Jun 26J

Accused, The (film) 1988 Oct 14J/Oct 19J; 1989 Mar 29J

Accutane (drug) 1983 Jul 25I; 1988 May 26I

ACDA *see* Arms Control and Disarmament Agency, U.S.

AC/DC (singing group) 1980 Dec 3J; 1981 Jan 7J/May 6J/May 27J/Jul 8J/Dec 9J; 1982 Jan 20J

Acid from Heaven (film) 1983 Feb 24J

acid rain
  Canadian policy: film documentaries 1983 Feb 24J; parliament urges action 1981 Oct 8D
  environmental impact: conferences 1985 Sep 20A; lakes affected by 1980 Feb 2I; 1981 Jan 5H; 1985 Aug 29H; measurements of 1981 Jan 25H; state sues for federal action 1986 Sep 18H; 1987 Jun 8H
  U.S.-Canada issues: 1980 Jun 23D/Aug 5D; 1982 Jul 26D; 1983 Aug 23D/Oct 16D; 1985 Mar 18D; 1986 Jan 8D/Mar 19D
  U.S. policy: Bush proposals 1989 Jun 12H; Reagan programs 1987 Mar 18D; 1988 Aug 5H

Acid Rain: Requiem or Recovery? (film) 1983 Feb 24J

ACLU *see* American Civil Liberties Union

Acquired Immune Deficiency Syndrome Research, U.S. Office of (NIH) 1988 Apr 18I

Acrobat and Young Harlequin (Pablo Picasso) (painting) 1988 Nov 28J

Acropolis (Athens, Greece) 1983 May 13B/Aug 31J

ACT *see* American College Test

ACTION (volunteer program) 1989 Nov 20F

Action for Children's Television 1983 Oct 11F

Action Jackson (film) 1988 Feb 17J

Activase (drug) 1987 Nov 13I

Act of Will (Barbara Taylor Bradford) (book) 1986 Jul 18J

actors and actresses *see individual artists in the name index* (e.g., Hepburn, Katherine)

ACTWU *see* Amalgamated Clothing and Textile Workers Union

acyclovir (drug) 1982 Mar 30I; 1985 Jan 29I

ADA *see* Americans for Democratic Action

Adam (home computer) 1985 Jan 2H

ADB *see* Asian Development Bank

Addenbrooke Hospital (Cambridge, England) 1980 Jan 10I

Addicted to Love (Robert Palmer) (recording) 1987 Feb 24J

Adirondack Mountains 1980 Feb 2I

Admiral Nakhimov (ship) 1986 Sep 1B

Adolph Coors Co. *see* Coors Co., Adolph

Adolph Rupp Trophy *see* Rupp Trophy (basketball)

adoption 1981 Aug 16D; 1989 May 28H/Nov 20A

Adoration of the Magi (Andrea Mantegna) (painting) 1985 Apr 18J

Adriatic Sea 1989 Jul 23I

adult bookstores 1989 Feb 21F

adultery 1987 Mar 19J/May 26J/Oct 23B; 1989 Jul 3E

Advanced Genetic Sciences Inc. 1985 Nov 14I; 1986 Feb 25H/Mar 24I; 1987 Apr 24I/Jun 8I

advertising
  foreign developments: Brazil 1987 Feb 24D; China 1987 Jul 2E; Israel 1986 Jun 24C
  health care: AIDS 1987 Feb 24D; alcohol 1989 May 31F; doctors 1980 Jul 22I; pain relievers 1983 Jul 13H; tobacco 1983 Jul 21I; 1984 Sep 30H; 1985 Dec 10F; 1986 Jun 16H/Jul 18H/Aug 6H/Oct 24H; 1987 Jan 12F
  media: children's TV programs 1983 Oct 11F; 1988 Nov 5F; 1989 Mar 5F; FTC deceptive ad challenges 1981 Oct 26H; 1982 Mar 18H; 1983 Oct 21F; government limits 1986 Jul 1F; Midler "sound-alike" suit 1989 Oct 30J
  obituaries: Bernbach, William 1982 Oct 2J
  politics: 1986 Apr 27F; 1988 Oct 24F
  religion: 1986 Jun 24C

Advisory Commission on Inter-governmental Relations 1983 May 10H

Aegis (radar system) 1988 Aug 2G

Aegyptopithecus (fossil primate) 1980 Feb 7I

Aeroflot (airline) 1980 Jan 12G/Feb 4B; 1981 Dec 29G; 1982 Feb 6B; 1983 Sep 17G

Aeromexico (airline) 1986 Aug 31F

Aetna Life & Casualty Co. 1988 Mar 22H

AFDC *see* Aid to Families with Dependent Children (AFDC)

affirmative action 1980 Jul 2F; 1981 Nov 16F; 1984 Jun 12F/Aug 2E/Dec 13F; 1985 Jan 19F/Jun 27F/Jul 24F; 1986 May 19F/Jul 2F/Jul 23F; 1987 Feb 25F/Mar 23F/Mar 25F; 1989 Jun 12F/Aug 6F

Afghanistan *see also* Afghanistan War; *individual leaders in the name index* (e.g., Karmal, Babrak)
  economy: food deficit 1982 Mar 8E; land reform 1981 Aug 18E; natural gas 1980 Jan 27E
  foreign relations: embassies closed 1989 Jan 21C
  government and politics: Baryalai appointed deputy premier 1989 Jun 25E; collapse claimed 1981 Oct 18E; interim leaders chosen 1989 Feb 23E; Islamic appeal 1982 Mar 15C; Karmal backers slain 1981 Jul 15E; Karmal centralizes power 1980 Jul 20E; Karmal resigns posts 1986 May 4E/Nov 20E; Najibullah declares state of emergency 1989 Feb 18E; rebel leader bribed 1980 Jan 21E; Sharq serves as premier 1988 May 27E; 1989 Feb 20E
  human rights: 1984 Feb 10G; 1987 Nov 19E
  sports: Olympics withdrawal 1984 May 17J

Afghanistan War
  accidents and disasters: 1982 Nov 3E
  anti-war movement: demonstrations 1980 Feb 21E/May 1E/May 15E/Jun 8E/Dec 27A/Dec 29E; desertions/amnesty 1980 Feb 22E/Jun 20J/Sep 15E/Sep 15A; 1986 Nov 24D; 1988 Jul 4B; dissention 1980 Jan 2B; 1983 May 23B; 1989 Oct 23B
  atrocities and rights violations: 1980 Feb 4A/Feb 4E; 1983 Jan 27A; 1984 Dec 17A; 1986 Nov 11A
  casualties: 1982 Dec 22A; 1985 Nov 3C; 1986 Nov 11A; 1988 May 25B; 1989 Feb 6E
  chemical weapons: 1980 Aug 7G/Aug 21G; 1981 Sep 13G/Sep 14B; 1982 Mar 8A/Mar 22A/Nov 29A
  conscription: 1982 Nov 2E; 1986 Jul 11B
  diplomatic and political developments: Canada 1986 Nov 24D; China 1980 Jan 19A/Jun 6A; 1982 Nov 19A; 1988 Jan 12E; Commonwealth 1980 Sep 8E; Conference of Islamic States 1980 Jan 29A/May 22A; Egypt 1980 Jan 28C; France 1980 Feb 8A; G-7 1980 Jun 22A; Great Britain 1981 Oct 8A; India 1980 Jan 16G; Iran 1980 May 14E; NATO 1980 Jan 15A/May 14A/Jun 26B; nonaligned nations 1981 Feb 13A; Romania 1980 Mar 14B;

United States 1980 Jan 2B/Jan 8A/Feb 4B/Mar 18G; 1981 Dec 27G; 1982 Dec 26G; 1983 May 26E/Jul 2E; 1988 Aug 30E; West Germany 1980 Jul 1B

humanitarian and military aid: 1980 Feb 15G; 1981 Mar 9G/Sep 22A; 1984 Jul 26G/Nov 27G; 1985 Oct 9G; 1987 May 1G; 1989 Feb 2E/Jul 5G/Sep 4G

immigration and refugees: Pakistan 1981 Mar 20E; 1984 Dec 20E; Turkey 1982 Aug 3A

military operations: Ghazni 1980 Jul 28E; Herat 1980 Jan 2E/Aug 11E/Sep 8E; Jaji 1988 May 15E; Jalalabad 1980 Jan 10E; 1989 Mar 6E/Mar 24E/Apr 23E/May 9E; Kabul 1980 Oct 15E; Kabul area military camp 1980 Jul 6E; Kandahar 1980 Aug 11E; Khost 1987 Dec 30E; Kilagay 1988 Aug 11E; Kunar 1980 Feb 29C; mine-clearing 1988 Aug 13C; Pakistan 1980 Feb 23E/Sep 26E; 1986 May 7E; Panjshir Valley 1980 Sep 13E; 1984 Apr 21C/Jul 13C/Nov 12C; Shomali Valley 1983 May 10E/Oct 6E; Zhawar 1986 May 25E

military strategy: cease-fire broken 1987 Jan 15E; retaliation 1980 Jul 9E; stalemate 1980 Apr 4E; 1981 Dec 28C; tactics 1980 Jul 14E

peace initiatives: Afghanistan 1980 May 14E/May 15E; European Community 1981 Jul 6A; Great Britain 1980 Feb 28A/Mar 11A; Pakistan 1988 Apr 14E; USSR 1989 Feb 5E

peace talks: Afghanistan/Pakistan 1982 Jun 16A; 1983 Jun 24A; 1986 May 5E; 1987 Sep 10E; USSR/rebels 1988 Dec 5E; USSR/U.S. 1982 Jul 23A

poll and surveys: 1987 Oct 12B

rebel groups and leaders: 1981 Jul 11E; 1983 May 26E; 1984 Aug 27C; 1986 Jun 16G; 1989 Mar 25G/Apr 23E/Aug 28E

troop reinforcements: 1980 Jan 16E/Jan 19E/Jul 3E; 1981 Apr 1E/Apr 8E

troop withdrawals: 1980 Jun 22B/Jun 27B; 1986 Jul 28B; 1987 Nov 30E; 1988 Jan 6B/Feb 8B/May 15E/May 26E/Aug 14B/Nov 4B; 1989 Jan 15E/Jan 17E/Jan 25E/Feb 14E/Feb 15E

UN peacekeeing role: General Assembly resolutions 1980 Jan 14A/Jan 15A/Nov 20A; 1983 Nov 23A; 1985 Nov 13A; 1986 Nov 5A; 1989 Nov 1E; mediator asks cease-fire 1988 Jul 9E; Security Council resolution 1980 Jan 7A

AFP see Agence France-Presse

Africa see also specific country names (e.g., Kenya)

arts and culture: Nobel Prize 1986 Oct 16J; Olympic Games 1980 Jan 31J; 1984 Jul 1J/Jul 11J

economy: agriculture 1985 Dec 16C; banking 1989 Jul 25C; debt relief plan 1987 Apr 5C; foreign debt 1987 Sep 24C; 1988 Jul 20A; IMF lending pool 1987 Dec 29A; OPEC oil set aside 1980 Nov 9C; performance review 1986 Jan 31C; regional cooperation 1981 Jan 17C; regional development plan 1980 Apr 1C; structural reforms 1987 Jun 15C; subway inauguration 1987 Sep

26C; UN crisis session 1986 Jun 1A; World Bank aid pledge 1985 Feb 1A; World Bank report 1989 Nov 21A

education: illiteracy 1980 Dec 4J; students in China 1986 Jun 6E; 1987 Jan 8E; 1988 Dec 27E; 1989 Jan 5E

environmental issues: drought 1983 Mar 18I; 1985 Feb 23C; elephants 1989 May 11I/Oct 16C; ivory trade 1989 May 11I/Oct 16C; locusts 1986 Oct 23C; 1988 May 3I; toxic waste dumping 1988 Aug 1C

famine: benefit events 1985 Jan 28J/Jul 13J; 1986 May 25J; European Community aid 1985 Feb 28A; Hunger Project award 1988 Sep 15C; UN relief 1985 Sep 7A; U.S. relief 1984 Dec 5G; 1985 Jan 3G; Worldwatch report 1985 Feb 17C

foreign relations: European Community 1986 Jul 29C; Great Britain 1988 Jan 8C; Israel 1983 Aug 28C; nonaligned movement 1985 Apr 25A; United States 1980 Jan 31J; 1981 Jun 2G; 1982 Nov 23C; 1985 Mar 11C; 1987 Jan 14C

health care: 1986 May 28I/Nov 14I; 1987 Oct 4I/Oct 21I; 1989 Sep 24I

immigration and refugees: 1985 Sep 7A

political issues: Chad conflict 1983 Oct 3A; 1984 Feb 5C/Dec 11C; UN Namibia plan 1982 Jul 13A

religion: Jerusalem attack protest 1982 Apr 14A; new cardinals named by pope 1988 May 29J; papal visits 1980 May 2J; 1985 Aug 19J; 1988 Sep 19J; 1989 May 6J

Africa, U.N. Economic Commission for 1987 Jun 15C

African-American Catholic Congregation 1989 Jul 4J

African Methodist Episcopal Churches 1984 Nov 30J

African National Congress (ANC) see also individual leaders in the name index (e.g., Mandela, Nelson)

demonstrations and protests: 1989 Oct 29C

foreign developments: Great Britain 1986 Feb 3C/Jun 23C; United States 1987 Jan 28G

internal developments: conferences 1987 Dec 1C; Inkatha strife 1989 Aug 8C; Tambo interview 1985 Nov 4C

peace initiatives: Pretoria contacts 1985 Aug 31C/Sep 13C/Oct 11C; 1987 Jul 12C; Pretoria talks 1989 Aug 21C

political prisoners: death sentences 1980 Nov 26C; escape 1986 Dec 27C; executions 1983 Jun 9C; 1985 Oct 18C; releases 1985 Feb 28C; 1987 Nov 5C; 1988 Nov 26C; 1989 Oct 15C

terrorism: civilian bombings/raids 1982 Dec 9C; 1983 May 23C-24C; 1984 Mar 16C; 1985 Jun 14C/Jul 23C; 1986 Jan 9C/May 19C; 1987 Apr 25C; 1988 Aug 17C

Afrikaners 1982 Nov 28C; 1986 Apr 12J/Aug 13C; 1987 Jun 27C/Jul 12C; 1988 Dec 16C

AFSCME see American Federation of State, County and Municipal Employees

AFT see American Federation of Teachers

Afterburner (ZZ Top) (recording) 1985 Dec 21J

Agacher border strip (Burkina Faso/Mali) 1985 Dec 25C

Against All Odds (film) 1984 Mar 7J

Against All Odds (Phil Collins) (recording) 1985 Feb 26J

Against the Wind (Bob Seger & the Silver Bullet Band) (recording) 1980 Apr 2J/Apr 30J/Jun 4J/Jul 9J

Agence France-Presse (AFP) 1986 Jul 19B/Dec 18B

Agency for International Development, U.S. (AID) 1983 Jun 10D/Aug 11G/Nov 4G/Nov 12D; 1984 Dec 9C; 1985 Jul 9A/Sep 30G; 1987 Mar 4C/Nov 20D; 1989 Aug 3C

Agent Orange (herbicide)

health risks: manufacturing site contamination 1983 Jun 2H; veterans studies issued 1980 Jan 3I; 1982 Aug 31G/Oct 25G; 1983 Apr 29G; 1987 Sep 30G; Vietnam War warning 1983 Jul 5H

legal issues: chemical companies sued 1983 Aug 6G; 1984 May 7G; 1985 May 28G; 1987 Apr 21G; 1988 Jul 5G; data access upheld by Supreme Court 1987 Nov 16G; government sued 1984 Dec 27G

political issues: disability benefits 1984 Oct 24G; 1989 May 11G; medical care legislation 1981 Jun 18G; veterans lobby formed 1983 Sep 21G

Agent Provocateur (Foreigner) (recording) 1985 Feb 23J

AGF see Assurances Generales de France

Agnes of God (film) 1985 Oct 23J

agriculture see specific country (e.g., France); organization (e.g., European Economic Community); individual crop (e.g., wheat)

Agriculture, U.S. Department of see also specific department head in the name index (e.g., Block, John R.)

appointments and resignations: Block, John 1980 Dec 23F; 1986 Jan 7H; Lyng, Richard 1986 Jan 29H; Yeutter, Clayton 1988 Dec 14H

budget and spending programs: 1985 Oct 8H/Dec 18H; 1988 Jun 16H/Jul 29H; 1989 Nov 16H

credit and debt issues: credit guarantee programs 1988 Jun 16H; family farm debt 1985 Mar 10H; farm value 1985 Jun 11H; Polish feed grain loans 1981 Jul 28G

environmental issues: drought 1983 Sep 2I; 1986 Aug 1H; 1988 Jun 23H/Jul 12H/Sep 12H; wilderness areas 1983 Feb 1H

farm population: 1982 Nov 24H

food stamp program: 1985 Oct 8H

genetic engineering: 1981 Jun 18I; 1986 Apr 3I/Apr 22I

health issues: Alar declared safe 1989 Mar 16I; chickens destroyed 1983 Dec 26H; dietary fat 1988 Apr 15I; Mediterranean fruit flies 1981 Jul 10H

price and production issues: dairy price regulation 1984 Jun 4H; farm subsidies 1982 Apr 20H; 1983 Mar 22H; 1986 Oct 24H; harvest estimates 1982 Nov 29H; 1983 Sep 12H; 1984 Jan 13H; 1985 Aug 12H; storage programs 1981 Oct 6H

school lunch programs: 1985 May 17F

trade issues: Australian beef imports 1987 Aug 20F; EC exports compared 1987 Jul 1H; Soviet grain sales 1984 Nov 1G; 1986 Aug 29H; 1987 Dec 2G; 1989 May 2H

Ahmedis (Moslem sect) 1984 Apr 27E

AID see Agency for International Development, U.S.

Aida (Giuseppe Verdi) (opera) 1985 Jan 3J; 1987 May 2J

AIDS (acquired immune deficiency syndrome)

arts and entertainment issues: Normal heart opens 1985 Apr 21J; NYC arts exhibit 1989 Nov 16J; Sag kissing rule 1985 Oct 31J

budget and spending programs: 1983 Jun 14I; 1987 Jun 2F/Dec 22I; 1988 Sep 23F/Oct 13F; 1989 Mar 31F

civil rights issues: 1985 Aug 14F; 1986 Jun 23F/Dec 8F; 1987 Mar 3F/Nov 1F; 1988 May 25D/Oct 6F; 1989 May 24D

demonstrations and protests: 1987 Oct 11F; 1989 Jan 5E/Dec 1CF

education: Brazil media blitz 1987 Feb 24D; Florida school attendence dispute 1987 Aug 28F; 1988 Sep 29F; NYC school boycott 1985 Sep 9F; school ban opposed by AMA 1986 Jun 19I; school guide issued 1987 Oct 6F; school programs urged by surgeon gen 1986 Oct 22E; UK campaign 1986 Nov 21B

foreign developments: Africa 1986 May 28I/Nov 14I; 1987 Oct 4I; Australia 1984 Nov 15I; 1985 Mar 27E; Brazil 1987 Feb 24D; Canada 1987 Nov 12D; 1988 Jan 11D/May 25D; 1989 Jan 3D/May 24D/Aug 3D; China 1989 Jan 5E; France 1986 Nov 27B; Great Britain 1986 Nov 21B; Japan 1987 Mar 24E; USSR 1987 Feb 6B/Aug 25B

health care issues

drugs: approved treatment 1989 Apr 27I/Jul 8I/Oct 21F; AZT 1986 Sep 19I; 1987 Jan 16I; 1988 Nov 24I; 1989 Mar 31F/Jul 10I/Aug 3I/Aug 8D/Aug 17I/Sep 18B/Sept 18F/Oct 26F; non-approved treatment 1988 Jul 23F

medical ethics: 1987 Nov 12F

medical history: appearance 1982 Jul 17I; early cases 1987 Oct 25I

needle distribution: 1985 Oct 2F; 1988 Jan 31I/Jun 9I/Nov 7F

risks: blood transfusions 1984 Nov 15I; 1986 Jul 9I; 1987 Mar 19I; 1989 Oct 5I; casual transmission ruled out 1986 Feb 6I; pneumonia 1989 Feb 6I/Jun 15I/Oct 12F; tuberculosis 1986 Jun 13I

vaccines: 1987 Aug 18I; 1989 Dec 8I

people: Gann, Paul 1987 Jun 9F; Hudson, Rock 1985 Jul 25J/Oct 31J

political and legislative issues: Social Security benefits 1983 May 18F; state laws 1985 Sep 18F/Sep 26H; 1987 Sep 21F

religious issues: Catholic church 1987 Dec 10J; 1988 Jun 27J; 1989 Nov 15A/Dec 10F; Lutherans 1989 Aug 29J

research

awards: Laskers 1986 Sep 22I

findings: immune system defect 1985 Jul 10I; incubation time 1989 Mar 16I; infection/disease linkage 1986 Mar 21I; nonsexual contact risk 1986 Feb 6I; virus identification 1983 May 20I; 1984 Apr 23I; 1987 Apr 1I; virus protein duplicated 1986 Feb 7I

methodology: CDC laboratory faulted 1986 Dec 9F; Gallo/Montagnier controversy 1985 Feb7I; 1986 Sep 22

studies: heterosexual spread 1985 Oct 18I; 1986 Apr 6I; 1987 Feb 6I/Apr 17I; infection/disease linkage 1986 Mar 21I; NYS population tests 1987 Aug 4I; testing effectiveness 1984 Oct 17I

vaccines: 1987 Aug 18I; 1989 Dec 8I

social issues: bathhouses 1984 Oct 15F/Nov 28F; 1985 Oct 2F; high-risk behavior 1984 Nov 22F; nonsexual contact risk 1986 Feb 6I

statistics

foreign: Canada 1988 Jan 11D; 1989 Jan 3D/Aug 3D; Great Britain 1989 Feb 14B

U.S.: among whites 1989 Jun 9I; college students 1989 May 22I; heterosexual contact 1986 Jul 30I; 1987 Feb 6I; infants 1988 Jan 12I; intravenous drug users 1989 Feb 17F; in Midwest 1989 Jun 9I

testing

applications: Foreign Service 1986 Nov 27F; hospital admission 1987 Feb 3F; insurance 1985 Sep 26H/Nov 1H; 1987 Jul 8F/Nov 12D; marriage licenses 1987 Feb 3F; 1989 Jun 23F; military 1985 Oct 25G; 1987 Jun 24F; 1988 Oct 13I; prenatal care 1987 Feb 3F

commercial tests for: 1985 Mar 2F

effectiveness of: 1984 Oct 17I; 1987 Oct 3I; 1988 Jun 1I; 1989 Jun 1I

as foreign policy: Australia 1985 Mar 27E; Canada 1987 Nov 12D; Great Britain 1989 Nov 24I; USSR 1987 Aug 25B

as U.S. policy: AMA stance 1987 Jun 23F; FDA approval 1988 Dec 13I; gay organizations endorse 1989 Aug 15I; state stance 1985 Sep 18F/Sep 26H

AIDS, Second International Conference on 1986 Jun 28I

AIDS, Third International Conference on 1987 Jun 1I

AIDS, Fourth International Conference on 1988 Jun 12I

AIDS, Fifth International Conference on 1989 Jun 4I

AIDS and the Education of Our Children: A Guide for Parents and Teachers (Education Department) 1987 Oct 6F

AIDS Research, American Foundation for see American Foundation for AIDS Research (AmFAR)

Aid to Families with Dependent Children (AFDC) 1981 May 4F

AIM see American Indian Movement

Air Afrique 1987 Jul 24B

air bags 1982 Aug 3H/Nov 18H; 1984 Jul 11H

Air Canada 1983 Jul 29D; 1986 Apr 27D; 1987 Nov 27D/Dec 18D

air conditioning 1983 Aug 9H

aircraft *see specific types* (e.g., Stealth)

Air Florida 1984 Apr 3H/Sep 26H

Air Force, U.S.
 accidents and disasters: experimental fighter 1986 Jul 11G; Titan 2 missile silo 1980 Sep 19G; Titan missile 1985 Aug 28I
 aircraft: B-2 (Stealth) bomber 1988 Apr 20G; *see also specific planes* (e.g., B-1)
 base issues: nuclear-armed bases identified 1986 Jul 9G; Ramstein base bombed 1981 Aug 31B/Sep 2B
 budget and spending programs: Reagan arms buildup costs study 1983 Feb 3G
 contract and billing issues: General Electric Co. 1985 May 13G; Hughes Aircraft Co. 1984 Aug 22G/Nov 19G; McDonnell Douglas Corp. 1984 Feb 24G; Northrop Corp. 1986 Nov 17G; Rockwell International Corp. 1985 Dec 11G; 1989 Mar 6G
 personnel issues: homosexuality suit dropped 1980 Nov 24G; Rourke sworn secretary 1985 Dec 11G; women 1985 Feb 7G
 space program: antisatellite missiles 1984 Jan 21G; 1985 Sep 13G; Soviet satellite weapons capability 1982 Apr 22G; Space Command creation 1982 Jun 21G; space shuttle launch problems 1984 Aug 21I; Titan launch 1987 Feb 11G/Oct 26I

Air Force Academy, U.S. (Colorado Springs, Colo.) 1980 May 21G; 1981 Feb 3G; 1984 Sep 15G; 1987 Dec 9J

Air Force Reserve Officer Training Corps, U.S. 1987 Jan 20F

Air Force Space Command, U.S. 1986 Aug 20I

Air India 1985 Jun 23A

airline pilots
 age issues: 1983 Aug 17F; 1985 Jan 8F
 business issues: Eastern Airlines bailout 1984 Feb 19H; shuttle service purchase opposed 1988 Oct 12H
 labor issues: Australian work actions 1989 Aug 24E/Nov 23E; contracts 1986 Dec 15H; pilot hiring ordered 1985 Aug 1H; strikes 1985 May 17H/Jun 15H; 1989 Mar 4H/Mar 13H/Nov 23H
 safety issues: air traffic control safety 1981 Aug 18H; recreational pilot licenses 1989 Aug 31H

Air Line Pilots Association 1985 Jun 15H

airlines *see specific companies* (e.g., American Airlines)

Airplane (film) 1980 Aug 6J/Sep 3J

airplane crashes
 Aeroflot (Siberia): 1982 Feb 6B
 Air Force plane (California): 1986 Jul 11G
 Air-India (Atlantic Ocean): 1985 Jun 23A
 Argentine plane (Iran): 1981 Jul 26C
 Avianca Airlines (Colombia): 1989 Nov 27D/Dec 5D
 B-1 bomber (California): 1984 Aug 29G/Oct 1G
 Bennett plane (Anchorage, Alaska): 1980 May 4J
 Benyahia plane (Algeria): 1982 May 3C

British jetliner (Canary Islands): 1980 Apr 25B
 CIA plane (Angola): 1989 Nov 27C
 CIA plane (El Salvador): 1984 Oct 19D
 Colombian airliner (Spain): 1983 Nov 27D
 Cubana Airlines (Cuba): 1989 Sep 3D
 Delta Airlines (Dallas/Fort Worth): 1985 Aug 2H
 experimental airship (Lakehurst, N.J.): 1986 Jul 1G
 Gandhi plane (India): 1980 Jun 23E
 Hakim plane (Lebanon): 1984 Aug 23C
 Honduran jetliner (Honduras): 1989 Oct 21D
 Iran government plane (Iran): 1981 Sep 29C
 Iraqi Airways (Saudi Arabia): 1986 Dec 25C
 Japan Airlines (Japan): 1985 Aug 12E
 Korean Air Lines Flight 007 (USSR): 1983 Sep 1A
 Leland plane (Ethiopia): 1989 Aug 13C
 Machel plane (South Africa): 1986 Oct 19C; 1987 Jun 29C
 Mexicana Airlines (Mexico): 1986 Mar 31D
 Nelson plane (De Kalb, Texas): 1985 Dec 31J
 Nicaraguan helicopter (Nicaragua): 1982 Dec 11D
 Pan Am jet (Lockerbie, Scotland): 1988 Dec 21B/Dec 28B; 1989 Nov 1G
 Pan Am jet (New Orleans): 1982 Jul 9I; 1985 Aug 25H
 Peru airliner (Pacific Ocean): 1987 Dec 8D
 Polish jetliner (Poland): 1980 Mar 14J; 1987 May 9B
 Roldos Aguilera plane (Ecuador): 1981 May 24D
 Salvadoran military plane (El Salvador): 1984 Oct 23D
 Smith plane (Maine): 1985 Aug 26J
 Soviet fighter jet (French-Belgian border): 1989 Jul 4B
 Suriname Airways (Suriname): 1989 Jun 7D
 Twilight Zone helicopter (California): 1987 May 29J
 U.S. Army helicopter (West Germany): 1982 Sep 11G
 U.S. troop transport (Gander, Newfoundland): 1985 Dec 12D
 Vietnam War sites excavation: 1985 Dec 4G
 Yugoslav jetliner (Corsica): 1981 Dec 1B
 Zia ul-Haq plane (Pakistan): 1988 Aug 17E/Oct 16E

air pollution 1980 Dec 22H; 1984 Mar 23H; 1987 Nov 19H; 1989 Mar 17H/Jul 21H; *see also specific kinds of air pollution* (e.g., acid rain)

air quality standards 1987 Jun 3H

air traffic controllers 1985 Sep 19H; 1986 Sep 23H; 1987 May 6H/Jun 3H/Jun 11H/Oct 1H; 1988 Jul 17B

air traffic control system 1986 Mar 6H; 1987 Dec 18H; 1988 Jul 27H

Air Transport Association (ATA) 1981 Aug 26H

AK-47 (assault rifle) 1986 Jul 5C

Alabama

accidents and disasters: rains/floods 1983 Apr 12I
 atomic energy: 1983 Jan 16H; 1986 Jun 11H
 awards and honors: King prize 1980 Jan 28J
 crime and law enforcement: death penalty ruled unconstitutional 1980 Jun 20F; FBI negligence charges 1983 May 27F; judge assassinated 1989 Dec 16F; Ku Klux Klan indictments 1984 May 17F; prisons returned to state jurisdiction 1989 Jan 14F; voting fraud conviction 1985 Nov 14F
 demonstrations and protests: civil rights march 1982 Feb 18F; 1985 Mar 7F
 education: school desegregation suit 1983 Jul 11F/Jul 12F; textbook bannings 1987 Mar 4F/Mar 27F/Aug 26F; voluntary prayer 1985 Jun 4F
 foreign issues: China lawsuit 1984 Feb 27A
 health care: infant mortality rates 1983 Jan 25F
 labor and employment: affirmative action upheld 1987 Feb 25F
 obituaries: Bryant, Paul (Bear) 1983 Jan 26J; Huie, William Bradford 1986 Nov 22J
 politics and government: annexation proposal disallowed by Supreme Court 1987 Jan 21F; primary date changed 1986 Apr 6F; Reagan judicial nominee rejected 1986 Jun 5F; Reagan visit 1982 Mar 15F; Wallace gubernatorial bid 1982 Sep 7F/Sep 28F; election 1982 Nov 2F
 presidential campaigns: Dukakis visit 1988 Jun 18F; primaries and caucuses 1980 Mar 11F; 1984 Mar 13F
 religion: school textbook bannings 1987 Mar 4F/Mar 27F/Aug 26F; school voluntary prayer 1985 Jun 4F
 sports: auto racing 1989 May 7J
 transportation: mass transit system 1981 Mar 1H

Alabama, University of (Tuscaloosa) 1980 Jan 1J/Jan 2J; 1981 Feb 28J; 1982 Jan 1J/Dec 15J/Dec 29J

alachlor (herbicide) 1984 Nov 20H; 1985 Feb 22I; 1986 Oct 7H; 1987 Dec 15H

Alar (chemical ripener) 1989 Feb 1I/Mar 16I/May 15H/Sep 1H

Alaska
 accidents and disasters: Dutch luxury liner fire 1980 Oct 4I; forest fires 1988 Sep 9I; volcanic eruptions 1986 Mar 27I; 1989 Dec 14I
 awards and honors: Pulitzer 1989 Mar 30J
 energy issues: gas pipeline 1982 Apr 20F/Apr 30H; oil and gas exploration 1980 Oct 3H; 1987 Apr 27H; oil export ban end 1983 Jan 23H
 environmental issues: lands bill 1980 Aug 19H/Dec 2H; wildlife refuge oil drilling 1984 Nov 30H; 1987 Apr 20H
 Exxon Valdez oil spill: 1989 Mar 24H/Mar 28H/Apr 5H/Apr 7H/May 10H/May 20H/Jul 24H/Jul 28H/Sep 7H/Sep 15H
 foreign issues: Japan fishing rights 1982 Apr 26G; 1988 Mar 14H; Soviet commando visits 1988 Feb 11G; USSR releases captured

boat 1984 Sep 19B; USSR releases Greenpeace members 1983 Jul 22A
 health care: canned salmon recall 1982 Apr 8I; infant mortality rates 1983 Jan 25F
 presidential campaigns: 1988 Mar 2F/Mar 10F
 sports: Bering Strait swim 1987 Aug 7J; Iditarod dog sled race 1985 Mar 20J; 1986 Mar 13J; 1988 Mar 17J; 1989 Mar 15J
 transportation: railroad ownership 1985 Jan 5H

Alaska (James Michener) 1988 Jul 23J/Aug 26J/Sep 30J/Oct 21J/Dec 23J

Alaska pipeline 1980 Jan 17H; 1982 Apr 7I/Apr 20F/Apr 30H

Alaska Railroad 1985 Jan 5H

Alawite Moslems 1983 Jan 4C

Albania *see also individual leaders in the name index* (e.g., Hoxha, Enver)
 economy: austerity plans 1986 Jul 23B
 foreign relations: Balkan nations conference 1988 Feb 23B; Greece 1985 Jan 12B; 1988 Apr 17B; USSR 1982 Nov 29B; 1986 Nov 29B; West Germany 1987 Sep 17B
 government and politics: Alia chosen party secretary 1985 Apr 13B; election turnout 1987 Feb 3B; party congress 1986 Nov 3B; Premier Shehu killing 1985 Feb 28B/Mar 1B
 obituaries: Hoxha, Enver 1985 Apr 11B
 sports: Olympic Games nonparticipation 1984 Jul 28J
 transportation: European railroad network joined 1986 Aug 6B; Greece/Albania highway opened 1985 Jan 12B

Albanians, ethnic
 Yugoslavia: 1987 Jun 26B/Oct 25B; 1988 Nov 19B; 1989 Feb 27B/Mar 29B

Alberta (Canada) 1981 Mar 1D-2D/May 16D/Sep 1D; 1982 Apr 30D; 1986 Sep 8D; 1987 Dec 7D; 1988 Oct 20D/Nov 29D; 1989 Jul 10D

Alberta Stock Exchange 1989 Jan 18D

Albertville (France) 1986 Oct 17J

alcohol and alcoholism *see also specific alcoholic beverage* (e.g., beer)
 crime and law enforcement: intoxication 1983 Jan 30F
 foreign developments: Australia 1981 Mar 9E; 1986 Jan 4E; Canada 1987 May 25D; France 1980 Dec 10B; Iran 1981 Sep 3C; Norway 1982 Oct 6B; Poland 1988 Feb 1B; Singapore 1985 Mar 28E; USSR 1983 Feb 23B; 1985 May 16B
 health risks: breast cancer 1987 May 7I; genetics 1980 Jun 7I; infant nursing 1989 Aug 16I; pregnancy 1980 Jan 4I; Pulitzer prize expose 1989 Mar 30J; VA policy 1988 Apr 20G
 people: Tower nomination 1989 Feb 23G
 statistics: high school seniors 1988 Jan 13F

Al Dawa Party (Iraq) 1983 Dec 27C

aldicarb (pesticide) 1985 Aug 11H; 1986 Feb 14H

Alexander Howden Group 1982 Sep 8B

Alfa Romeo S.p.A. 1980 Sep 20B

Alfred A. Knopf Inc. *see* Knopf Inc., Alfred A.

algae 1980 Apr 2I; 1989 Jul 23I

Algeria *see also individual leaders in the name index* (e.g., Benjedid, Chadil)
 civil strife: Berber unrest 1980 Apr 19C; state of seige declared 1988 Oct 6C
 foreign relations: Libya summit meeting 1980 Apr 15C; Morocco 1983 Feb 26C; 1987 May 4C; 1988 May 16C; Tunisia coup 1987 Nov 7C
 government and politics: Ben Bella freed 1980 Oct 30C; Benjedid re-elected president 1984 Jan 12C; constitutional referendum 1988 Nov 4C; 1989 Feb 24C; national charter revision 1986 Jan 15C; premier dismissed 1989 Sep 9C; state of emergency declared 1988 Oct 6C
 hijackings: Kuwait Airways Flight 422 1988 Apr 13C/Apr 20C; TWA flight 847 1985 Jun 14A/Jun 15C/Jun 16C
 Iran hostage crisis: 1980 Nov 2C/Nov 10C/Dec 25C; 1981 Jan 3A/Jan 7C/Jan 18A
 obituaries: Abbas, Ferhat 1985 Dec 24C; Benyahia, Muhammad 1982 May 3C
 religion: Islamic fundamentalists 1981 Oct 6C
 trade and aid: common market announced 1989 Feb 17C; oil production set aside 1980 Nov 9C; Spain natural gas contract 1985 Feb 23A; U.S. wheat sales 1985 Jun 4H

Algonquin Indians 1986 May 6J

Alien Nation (film) 1988 Oct 19J

Aliens (film) 1986 Aug 20J/Sep 17J

alimony 1986 May 6E

Alitalia (airline) 1983 Apr 30A

Allied Corp. 1981 May 11H; 1982 Sep 22H/Sep 24H/Dec 22H; 1983 Dec 13H

All Night Long (Lionel Richie) (recording) 1983 Dec 14J

All of Me (film) 1984 Oct 10J

All-Star Game (baseball) 1981 Aug 9J; 1983 Jul 6J; 1984 Jul 10J; 1985 Jul 16J; 1986 Jul 15J; 1987 Jul 14J; 1988 Jul 12J; 1989 Jul 11J

All-Star Game (basketball) 1980 Feb 3J; 1982 Jan 31J; 1983 Feb 13J; 1984 Jan 29J; 1985 Feb 10J/Feb 20J; 1986 Feb 9J; 1987 Feb 8J; 1988 Feb 7J; 1989 Feb 8J

All-Star Game (ice hockey) 1985 Feb 12J; 1988 Feb 9J; 1989 Feb 7J

Allstate Insurance Co. 1982 Jun 11H; 1988 Mar 22H

all-terrain vehicles (ATVs) 1985 Aug 15J; 1987 Dec 20H

All That Jazz (film) 1980 Feb 27J/Apr 23J

almonds 1986 Sep 7B

Almost Paradise (Susan Isaacs) 1984 Mar 23J

Aloha Bowl (football) 1982 Dec 25J

Aloma's Ruler (racehorse) 1982 May 15J

Al Shiraa (Lebanese magazine) 1986 Nov 3C

Altered States (film) 1981 Apr 4J

alternating current synthesizer 1981 Mar 20I

alternative fuels 1988 Sep 23H/Oct 14H

aluminum 1980 Apr 19I; 1983 May 30H

Aluminum, Brick & Glass Workers International Union (AFL-CIO) 1988 Dec 4H

Aluminum Co. of America (ALCOA) 1983 Dec 13H; 1986 Jul 4H; 1988 Dec 4H

Alvenus (ship) 1984 Jul 30H

Alvin Ailey American Dance Theater 1989 Dec 20J

Always on My Mind (Willie Nelson) (recording) 1982 Jun 16J/Jul 11J

Alysheba (racehorse) 1987 May 2J/May 16J/Nov 21J; 1988 Nov 5J; 1989 Jan 4J/Jan 28J

Alzheimer's disease 1984 Aug 31I; 1987 Feb 20I/Jun 21I; 1989 Sep 14I

Al-Zulfikar (the Sword) (Pakistani group) 1982 Jan 17E

AMA *see* American Medical Association

Amadeus (play/film) 1980 Dec 17J; 1981 Jun 7J; 1984 Sep 19J; 1985 Mar 25J

Amal (Shiite Moslem militia) 1983 Aug 28C/Oct 26C; 1985 Apr 1C/Apr 17C/Jun 7C/Jun 17C; 1987 Feb 19C; 1988 Jan 16C/May 11C/Dec 23C; 1989 Dec 7C

Amalgamated Clothing and Textile Workers Union (ACTWU) 1983 Oct 20F

Amalgamated Transit Union (ATU) 1980 Apr 2H; 1983 Dec 3F; 1986 Nov 10H; 1987 Jan 26H

amantadine (drug) 1982 Sep 2I

Amazon Basin 1981 Jan 6D; 1987 Sep 30E; 1988 Oct 12D/Dec 22D; 1989 Feb 4D/Mar 3A/Mar 7D/Apr 6D

AMC *see* American Motors Corp.

Amerasians 1982 Oct 7E; 1984 Sep 11G; 1988 Jan 20E/Feb 15E

American Academy and Institute of Arts and Letters 1983 Feb19J; 1984 Dec 7J; 1985 Mar 23J/Dec 15J; 1986 Dec 4J; 1987 Dec 4J

American Academy of Pediatrics 1989 Mar 5I

American Airlines 1982 Mar 10H; 1987 Nov 10H

American Association for the Advancement of Science 1980 Jan 1I/Jan 4I; 1985 May 29F

American Association of Blood Banks 1986 Aug 26I

American Association of State Colleges and Universities 1985 May 29F/Jun 2F

American Astronomical Society 1986 Jan 12I

American Ballet Theater (New York City) 1982 Jun 3J; 1989 Jun 21J/Sep 29J

American Bandstand (TV show) 1989 Mar 23J

American Bar Association (ABA)
conventions: 1983 Jul 27F; 1984 Feb 14F/Aug 5F; 1985 Jul 15B
court nominee ratings: 1981 Sep 8F; 1987 Sep 8F; 1989 Jun 2F
ethics code: 1983 Aug 2F
legislation: 1982 Jan 25F/Apr 28F
Rosenberg case: 1983 Sep 23F

American Bell Inc. 1982 Jun 10H

American Book Awards 1980 May 1J; 1981 Apr 30J; 1983 Apr 28J; 1984 Nov 16J; 1985 Nov 21J; 1986 Nov 17J

American Breast Cancer Society 1982 Oct 17I

American Broadcasting Company (ABC)
awards: DuPont 1986 Feb 5J; Emmy 1984 Sep 24J
business issues: Capital Cities purchase 1985 Mar 18H; FCC pro-
poses syndication rules revision 1983 Aug 4H; Kissinger signs contract with 1982 Sep 20J; labor contracts 1987 Apr 26H
Nielsen ratings: 1983 Feb 16J/Nov 20J; 1984 Feb 21J; 1985 Jan 20J; 1988 Feb 27J
programming: "Amerika" miniseries to proceed 1986 Jan 22J; baseball broadcasting rights lost 1988 Dec 14J; CIA files complaint against 1984 Nov 21F; Supreme Court documentary 1984 Dec 29F

American Cancer Society 1980 Apr 28I; 1981 Mar 24I; 1983 Aug 2I; 1984 Apr 1I; 1985 Feb 8I/Feb 12F/Nov 22I

American Civil Liberties Union (ACLU) 1982 Oct 9F; 1987 Aug 31F

American College Health Association 1989 May 22I

American College of Obstetricians and Gynecologists 1985 Aug 1C

American Colleges, Association of *see* Association of American Colleges

American College Test (ACT) 1986 Sep 22F; 1988 Feb 25F/Sep 19F; 1989 Sep 11F

American Council of Life Insurance 1985 Nov 1H

American Council on Higher Education 1989 Jan 15F

American Eagle (coin) 1986 Sep 8H

American Electorate, Committee for the Study of the *see* Committee for the Study of the American Electorate

American Electric Power Co. 1986 Sep 10H

American Enterprise Institute 1986 Dec 3F

American Express Co. 1981 Apr 21H/Apr 23H; 1988 Dec 5H; 1989 Dec 14H

American Farm Bureau 1982 Oct 18H

American Federation of Labor and Congress of Industrial Organizations (AFL-CIO) *see also* member unions (e.g., Aluminum, Brick & Glass Workers)
conventions and meetings: 1981 Nov 19H; 1983 Oct 5G; 1985 Oct 28H; 1987 Feb 17H
defense issues: 1982 Feb 16H; 1985 Feb 19H
economic policy: 1983 Feb 21F; 1984 Feb 20H; 1985 May 8H
foreign issues: Solidarity support 1981 Sep 26B
health and safety issues: 1984 Sep 20H
membership: Teamsters 1987 Oct 24H; United Auto Workers 1981 Jul 1H; United Mine Workers 1989 Oct 4H
obituaries: Meany, George 1980 Jan 10H
political endorsements: Carter 1980 Aug 20F; Dem/GOP 1987 Feb 18F; Dukakis 1988 Aug 24F; Mondale 1983 Aug 9F/Oct 5G; 1984 Aug 19F
strikes and settlements: Coors boycott called off 1987 Aug 19H

American Federation of State, County and Municipal Employees (AFSCME) 1984 Feb 20F; 1986 Jul 22F/Sep 26H

American Federation of Teachers (AFT) 1983 Jul 5F; 1984 Feb 14H; 1985 Jul 13F; 1986 Jul 6F; 1989 Jul 21F/Jul 21F

American Federation of Television and Radio Artists 1980 Jul 21J/Sep 7J/Oct 23J

American Film Institute 1982 Mar 4J; 1983 Mar 3J

American Fool (John Cougar) (recording) 1982 Aug 18J/Sep 22J/Oct 13J

American Forestry Association 1987 Nov 19H

American Foundation for AIDS Research (AmFAR) 1987 May 31F

American General Corp. 1982 Apr 16H

American Geophysical Union 1988 Dec 9I; 1989 Dec 22I

American Gigolo (film) 1980 Feb 27J

American Health Foundation 1980 Mar 6I

American Heart Association 1984 Feb 21I/Nov 11I; 1989 Nov 14I

American Indian Movement (AIM) 1984 Sep 13F

American Institute for Free Labor Development 1983 Jul 26D

American Insurance Association 1983 Aug 22H

American Iron and Steel Institute 1982 Dec 31H; 1985 Aug 18H; 1986 Jan 30H

American Jewish Committee 1982 Sep 22C

American Jewish Congress 1982 Sep 22C; 1985 Jul 25J

American League (baseball)
awards: Cy Young 1981 Nov 25J; 1984 Nov 6J; 1985 Nov 11J; 1986 Nov 13J; 1987 Nov 11J; 1988 Nov 9J; 1989 Nov 15J; Golden Glove 1980 Dec 6J; manager of the year 1984 Oct 18J; most valuable player (MVP) 1980 Nov 18J; 1981 Nov 25J; 1983 Nov 16J; 1985 Nov 20J; 1986 Nov 18J; 1987 Nov 17J; 1988 Nov 16J; 1989 Nov 20J; rookie of the year 1983 Nov 23J; 1984 Nov 20J; 1985 Nov 25J; 1986 Nov 25J; 1987 Nov 3J; 1988 Nov 2J; 1989 Nov 7J
division playoffs: 1984 Sep 30J; 1986 Sep 26J/Sep 28J
pennants: 1980 Oct 10J; 1981 Oct 15J; 1982 Oct 10J; 1983 Oct 8J; 1984 Oct 5J; 1985 Oct 16J; 1986 Oct 15J; 1987 Oct 4J/Oct 12J; 1988 Oct 2J/Oct 9J; 1989 Oct 8J

American Library Association 1982 Feb 14J

American Lutheran Church 1987 Apr 30J

American Medical Association (AMA) 1980 Jul 22I; 1983 Jun 23F/Dec 6F; 1985 Dec 10F; 1986 Jun 15F/Jun 19I/Dec 24F; 1987 Jun 23F/Nov 12F; 1988 Aug 25F/Dec 6F

American Medical Colleges, Association of *see* Association of American Medical Colleges

American Motors Corp. (AMC) 1980 Jun 21H/Sep 24H; 1981 Nov 11H; 1982 Apr 18H; 1983 May 5H; 1985 Jun 28H/Jul 12H/Jul 31H

American National Theater 1984 Jun 5J; 1986 Aug 8J

American Nazi Party 1983 Apr 21F; 1984 Apr 13F

American Petroleum Institute (API) 1980 Jan 17H/Mar 12H; 1981 Apr 23H; 1982 Jan 15H/Mar 4H/Apr 9H

American Presbyterians 1983 Jun 10J

American Psychiatric Association 1984 Sep 12F

American Red Cross 1989 Oct 5I

American Savings and Loan Association 1982 Oct 26H; 1988 Mar 18H/Sep 5H

Americans for Change 1980 Jul 1F

Americans for Democratic Action (ADA) 1981 Jun 27F; 1984 Dec 8F

American Society of Travel Agents 1980 Oct 19E

American Stock Exchange (Amex) 1980 Mar 21H; 1983 Feb 15H/Dec 30H; 1988 Feb 10H; 1989 Oct 12H

American Tail, An (film) 1988 Mar 2J

American Telephone and Telegraph Co. (AT&T)
antitrust case: divesture plan 1983 Mar 25H/Jul 8H/Aug 5H/Dec 1H/Dec 12H; 1984 Jan 1H/Dec 14H; Litton suit 1981 Jun 29H; MCI suit 1980 Jun 13H; 1983 Jan 12F; 1985 May 28H; spinoffs OKd 1984 Dec 14H; trial 1981 Jan 16H/Sep 11H; 1982 Jan 8H/Jan 21H/Mar 25H/Aug 11H/Aug 19H/Aug 24H
business issues: antidumping complaints 1988 Dec 28H; deregulation rules 1980 Apr 7H; earnings 1982 Mar 2H; Moody ratings downgrade 1983 Mar 10H; reorganization 1980 Aug 20H; securities issued 1983 Nov 21H; subsidiary approved 1982 Jun 10H; toxic waste cleanup 1985 Aug 5H
labor issues: contracts 1989 May 28H; down sizing 1984 Aug 27H; 1985 Aug 21H; strikes and settlements 1983 Aug 28H; 1986 Jun 26A; technologies unit layoffs 1984 Aug 27H
rate issues: access fees 1983 Dec 1H; billing increases 1986 Dec 29H; 1988 Oct 17H; hookup fees freeze 1984 Mar 28H; long distance rates 1984 May 10H/Nov 21H; 1986 Dec 30H; 1988 Oct 17H
research and development: data processing 1981 Nov 7H; 1984 Mar 27H; satellites 1980 Feb 20I; superconductivity 1989 May 23I
service issues: Beirut attack hotline set up 1983 Oct 27G; local subsidies 1983 Nov 10H

American Trucking Association 1983 Feb 10H

American University (Washington, D.C.) 1985 Dec 15J; 1987 Sep 25J

"American Vision, An: Three Generations of Wyeth Art" (art exhibit) 1987 Mar 11J

American Werewolf in London, An (film) 1981 Sep 2J

American Women: Three Decades of Change (Census Bureau) 1983 Oct 10F

America's Cup (yacht race) 1980 Sep 25J; 1983 Sep 26J; 1987 Feb 4J; 1988 Jul 25J/Sep 8J/Sep 9J; 1989 Mar 28J/Sep 19J

Americas Watch 1982 Nov 23D; 1984 Feb 9G; 1985 Mar 5D; 1986 Oct 7D; 1988 Apr 23D/Aug 4D/Nov 25D; 1989 Sep 17D

Amerika (TV show) 1986 Jan 22J

Amex *see* American Stock Exchange

AmFAR *see* American Foundation for AIDS Research

Amherst College (Amherst, Mass.) 1985 Mar 1J

Amityville II, The Possession (film) 1982 Oct 6J

Amnesty International

benefit rock music tour: 1988 Sep 2J/Oct 15J
national reports: Bulgaria 1989 Feb 22B; Chile 1980 Sep 8D; 1986 Sep 2D; China 1981 Dec 9A; 1984 Sep 25A; 1989 Aug 30E; Colombia 1989 Oct 11D; East Germany 1989 Jan 24B; El Salvador 1984 May 21A; 1988 Oct 26D; Guatemala 1981 Feb 17D; 1982 Oct 11D; 1987 May 10D; 1989 Jun 14D; Haiti 1985 Mar 12D; India 1988 Aug 10E; 1989 May 13E; Indonesia 1985 Jun 25E; Iran 1981 Oct 12C; Iraq 1989 Feb 28C; Kenya 1987 Jul 21C; Myanmar (Burma) 1989 Nov 15E; Nicaragua 1989 Nov 9D; Peru 1985 Jan 22D; 1987 Feb 9D; 1988 Aug 18D; Philippines 1982 Sep 14E; 1988 Dec 15E; South Korea 1989 Sep 8E; Sri Lanka 1987 Jun 21E; 1989 May 13E/Dec 14E; Turkey 1985 Jul 23B; 1989 Jan 3B; United States 1981 Oct 14F/Dec 9A; USSR 1980 Apr 29B; 1981 Dec 9A; 1989 Oct 17B
world reports: 1980 Dec 10A; 1981 May 27A/Dec 9A; 1988 Oct 4A

Amoco Cadiz (ship) 1988 Jan 11H

Amoco Corp. 1988 Jan 11H

amphetamine (drug) 1987 Jul 8F

Amritsar (India) *see* Golden Temple

Amstrad Consumer Electronics PLC 1986 Apr 8B

Amtrak 1988 Jan 20H

anabolic steroids 1983 Aug 28J; 1984 Aug 12J; 1989 Jun 12J

ANC *see* African National Congress

Anchorage Daily News, The 1989 Mar 30J

Andean Pact 1985 Sep 16D

"..And *Ladies of the Club*" (Helen Hooven Santmyer) (book) 1984 Jul 20J/Aug 24J/Sep 14J/Oct 19J

Andrew Jackson and the Course of Democracy, 1833-1845, Vol. III (Robert Remini) (book) 1984 Nov 16J

Andrew W. Mellon Foundation *see* Mellon Foundation, Andrew W.

Andy Warhol Foundation for the Visual Arts *see* Warhol Foundation for the Visual Arts, Andy

Angel Heart (film) 1987 Mar 18J

Angels of September (Andrew M. Greeley) (book) 1986 Feb 28J

Anglican Church
female ordination: 1987 Feb 26J
papacy: archbishop of Canterbury meeting 1980 May 9J; 1982 May 31B; 1989 Oct 2J
personnel: Bennett suicide 1987 Dec 7J; Tutu becomes Cape Town archbishop 1986 Sep 7C
social issues: inner city poverty 1985 Dec 2B; remarriage rules changed 1981 Oct 7J

Anglo-Irish accord (1985) 1985 Nov 27B/Dec 31B; 1986 Jan 23B/Mar 3B/Jul 12B

Angola *see also* individual leaders in the name index (e.g., Savimbi, Jonas)
civil war: rebels turn over hostages 1985 Mar 14C; truce unravels 1989 Aug 22C; UNITA ivory trade claimed 1989 Nov 20C; UNITA military operations 1984 Dec 29C; 1988 Jan 29C; 1989 Feb 14C; Zaire rebel aid 1987 Feb 1G
economy: regional development plan 1980 Apr 1C

peace initiatives: Cuban troop pull-out 1989 Jan 10C; dos Santos offers plan 1989 Dec 30C; government-UNITA talks 1989 Jun 30C/Jul 16C/Oct 5C; government-UNITA truce effected 1989 Jun 22C/Aug 22C; Ivory Coast mediation 1989 Feb 14C; regional accord 1987 Mar 8C/Nov 22C/Dec 13C/Dec 22C; UNITA sets peace terms 1988 Nov 19C; U.S.-mediated regional talks 1982 Nov 28C/Dec 8C; 1983 Dec 15C; 1984 Jan 8C/Feb 16C/Mar 13C; 1985 Nov 27A; 1988 May 3C/Jun 24C/Jul 13C/Aug 8C/Oct 9C/Nov 15C/Dec 20A
South African conflict: Cabinda raid 1985 May 23C/Jun 12A; death toll, arms seizure 1981 Sep 14C; foreign reporters attacked 1981 Sep 6C; peace accord approved 1988 Nov 22C; POW swap 1987 Sep 7C; Pretoria troop exit 1981 Aug 28C/Sep 9C; 1983 Dec 15C; 1984 Jan 8C/Nov 20C; 1985 Apr 17C; Soviet officer captured 1981 Sep 1C; SWAPO bases raided 1980 Jun 13C; 1981 Mar 17C/Aug 24C; 1982 Mar 16C/Mar 20C; 1985 Jul 1C/Sep 22C; UN demands Pretoria pullout 1987 Nov 25A; UNITA claims victory 1987 Nov 11C; 1988 Jan 15C; UN sends peacekeepers 1988 Dec 20A
sports: Olympics boycott 1984 Jun 26J
U.S. relations: 1981 Mar 19G/Aug 18C; 1982 Mar 2G; 1985 Jul 10G/Jul 13C/Dec 10G; 1986 Feb 8G/Sep 17G; 1987 Feb 1G/May 1G; 1988 Jan 29C; 1989 Nov 27C

Angolite (prison newspaper) 1986 Jun 17J

Anguilla 1989 Feb 27D

Animal Farm (George Orwell) (book) 1986 Jun 15F

animal rights 1987 Feb 17J; 1988 Mar 1J

animals 1980 Jan 23I; 1981 Jun 18I; 1984 Nov 15I; 1985 Dec 1B; 1986 May 7B; 1988 Jun 30I; 1988 Apr 15I/Apr 21I/Oct 15I/Oct 28H; see also specific kinds (e.g., dogs)

Annapolis see Naval Academy

Annie (musical/film) 1982 Jan 20J/Jul 7J

anorexia nervosa 1983 Feb 4J

Answer as a Man (Taylor Caldwell) (book) 1981 Feb 8J/Mar 8J

answering machines 1985 Feb 15J

Antarctica 1982 Aug 29I; 1986 Jun 27I; 1987 May 22B; 1988 Jun 2E; 1989 Feb 17I/Oct 12I/Oct 20I/Dec 11A

Antelope (ship) 1982 May 23D

anthrax 1980 Jun 29I; 1982 Jan 14B

anthropology 1984 Aug 22I

anti-abortion movement see abortion

antiballistic missiles (ABMs) 1984 Jun 29B

anti-nuclear movement
foreign developments: Australia 1983 Jul 2I; Belgium 1983 Oct
23B; Canada 1984 Mar 6D; Great Britain 1984 Apr 4B; Japan 1982 Mar 22E/Jun 7G; New Zealand 1985 Feb 4B; Spain 1983 Oct 23B; West Germany 1981 Feb 28B
health and safety issues: A-power plant accidents listed 1980 Jul 14I; 1981 Jul 26I; 1982 Aug 18I; Chernobyl anniversary 1987 Apr 26I; Seabrook plant 1980 May 25F; Shoreham plant 1983 Jun 5I; Three Mile Island anniversary 1980 Mar 28F
people: Berrigan 8 convictions upheld 1985 Nov 22F; Reagan daughter addresses rally 1981 Jul 14F; Reagan radio address 1983 Oct 22G

anti-satellite weapons 1983 Aug 18B; 1984 Jan 21G/Apr 2G/Jun 29B; 1985 Aug 20G/Aug 21B/Sep 13G/Sep 20G

anti-Semitism 1981 Jul 28J; 1986 Jul 14F

Anti-Slavery Society for the Protection of Human Rights 1981 Aug 11C

antitrust actions
commodities: oil 1981 Dec 23H; 1982 Aug 6H; 1984 Apr 26H; steel 1984 Feb 15H
computers see International Business Machines
electronics: television manufacturing 1986 Mar 26H
food and beverages: cereal makers 1982 Jan 15H; citrus processing 1981 Feb 20H
foreign developments: Australia 1982 May 19A; Canada 1984 Sep 17D
health care: doctors 1984 Mar 27F; 1988 May 16H/Dec 6F
insurance: 1988 Mar 22H
political and legislative issues: Baxter conflict of interest 1981 Aug 26H; 1982 Jun 17H; cities granted immunity 1985 Mar 27H; merger challenges curbed 1986 Dec 9H; merger guidelines 1982 Jun 14H; 1984 Jun 14H; state laws upheld 1989 Apr 18H
press and broadcasting: broadcast violence guidelines 1989 Aug 1F; college sports 1984 Jun 27F; Detroit papers merger 1987 Sep 23H; 1988 Aug 17H; 1989 Nov 13H
retail trade: discount dealers 1988 May 2H
sports: college telecasts 1984 Jun 27F; football 1982 May 7J; 1984 Jun 27F/Nov 17J; 1986 Jul 29J; 1987 Oct 15J
telecomunications see American Telephone and Telegraph
transportation: airlines 1984 Aug 13H; automobiles 1985 Apr 15H; railroads 1981 Oct 20H

Anything for Billy (Larry McMurtry) (book) 1988 Nov 25J

Anything Goes (musical) 1988 Jun 5J

Any Which Way You Can (film) 1981 Jan 7J

ANZUS see Australia, New Zealand, U.S. Treaty Organization

Aozou strip (Chad) 1987 Aug 8C/Aug 28C/Sep 6C/Aug 10B; 1988 Oct 3C

AP see Associated Press

Apartheid, U.N. Special Committee Against 1986 Jun 20A

API see American Petroleum Institute

Appalachian State University (Boone, N.C.) 1985 Feb 7J

Appetite for Destruction (Guns N' Roses) (recording) 1988 Jul 16J/Aug 27J/Sep 24J/Oct 29J/Dec 31J; 1989 Jan 29J/Feb 25J/Mar 25J

Apple Computer Inc. 1983 Mar 8I/Aug 30H; 1984 Jan 24I; 1985 May 31H; 1986 Jan 17H/May 17I; 1987 Mar 2H; 1988 Mar 17H

Apple II (personal computer) 1983 Aug 30H

apples 1987 Jan 7H/Nov 13F; 1989 Feb 1I/Mar 16I/May 15H/Sep 1H

appliances 1981 Feb 18H; 1982 Sep 28C; 1987 Mar 17H

April 5 Forum (Chinese dissident magazine) 1981 Apr 10E

April 19 Movement (M-19) (Colombian guerrilla group) see also specific terrorist incident
deaths: 1986 Mar 13D
peace pacts: 1985 Jun 23D; 1989 Jan 12D/Sep 26D/Dec 23D
terrorism and unrest: Cali street fighting 1985 Nov 30D; Corinto siege 1985 Jan 7D; Florencia attack 1984 Mar 14D; kidnappings 1987 Jul 30D; prison escapes 1980 Jun 25D; raids against 1981 Mar 18D; 1986 Mar 13D

Aquitaine Progression, The (Robert Ludlum) (book) 1984 Mar 23J/Apr 20J/May 11J/Jun 15J/Jul 20J/Aug 24J

AR-15 (semiautomatic rifle) 1989 Mar 15F

Arab-American Anti-Discrimination Committee 1985 Oct 11F

Arab and Jew: Wounded Spirits in a Promised Land (David K. Shipler) (book) 1987 Apr 16J

Arab and Middle Eastern Political Prisoners, Committee for Solidarity with see Committee for Solidarity with Arab and Middle Eastern Political Prisoners

Arabian-American Oil Co. (Aramco) 1987 Feb 3C/Oct 16A

Arab League
Iran-Iraq war: 1980 Nov 27C; 1984 May 20C; 1987 Nov 8C
Israel: 1981 Jun 11C; 1982 Sep 9C/Oct 21C
Lebanon: 1989 May 23C/Sep 23C/Nov 5C/Nov 22C
Palestinians: 1982 Sep 9C/Sep 21C; 1988 Jun 7C; 1989 May 23C
Saudi Arabian peace plan: 1981 Nov 25A
United States: 1982 Sep 21C/Oct 21C/Oct 22C

Arab Maghreb Union 1989 Feb 17C

Arabsat-1 (satellite) 1985 Feb 8I

Aramco see Arabian-American Oil Co.

ARC Armored Services of Puerto Rico Inc. 1980 Nov 21D

archaeology
exhibitions: Israeli show rejected by New York museum 1982 Feb 23J
finds: Aborigine tools (Australia) 1988 Nov 25I; Bronze Age shipwreck (Turkey) 1984 Dec 4I; Globe Theater (London) 1989 Oct 13J; Great Wall (China) 1983 Feb 26I; Indian civilization (Bolivia) 1989 Nov 11I; Mayan tomb (Guatemala) 1984 May 15I; Philip II of Macedonia assassination site (Greece) 1982 Sep 1F; Rose Theater (London) 1989 Mar 3J

obituaries: Bird, Junius Bouton 1982 Apr 2I; Wenzhong Pei 1982 Sep 18I; Yadin, Yigael 1984 Jun 28C

Archaeopteryx (fossil) 1986 May 2I

architecture
awards and honors see Pritzker Architecture Prize
buildings and memorials: Chicago central library 1988 Jun 20J; Vietnam War Memorial (Washington, D.C.) 1982 Nov 13G; World's Fair pavilion reconstructed 1986 Jun 2J
criticism: from Prince Charles 1987 Dec 1B
obituaries: Bayer, Herbert 1985 Sep 30J; Khan, Fazlur R. 1982 Mar 27I; Owings, Nathaniel 1984 Jun 13J; Sert, Josep Lluis 1983 Mar 15J; Speer, Albert 1981 Sep 1B

Arc of a Diver (Steve Winwood) (recording) 1981 Apr 8J/May 6J

Arctic Dreams (Barry Lopez) (book) 1986 Nov 17J

Arctic National Wildlife Refuge (Alaska) 1986 Nov 24H; 1987 Apr 20H

Arctic regions 1982 Aug 29I; 1983 May 21I; 1985 Sep 10D; 1986 May 1I; 1988 Jan 11C/May 27I; 1989 Feb 17I; see also Antarctica

Arde (Nicaraguan Contra group) 1984 Apr 25D

Ardent (ship) 1982 May 21D

Arena (Duran Duran) (recording) 1984 Dec 22J; 1985 Jan 26J

Argentina see also individual leaders in the name index (e.g., Alfonsin, Raul)
accidents and disasters: Bahia Paraiso oil spill 1989 Jan 28I
arms control: A-weapons test ban 1985 Jan 28A; space weapons development ban 1985 Jan 28A
arts and culture: Amnesty International benefit rock tour 1988 Oct 15J; Borges awarded Ollin Yoliztli prize 1981 May 12D; National Museum thefts 1980 Dec 25J; Sabato awarded Cervantes Prize 1985 Apr 23J; Timerman returns 1984 Jan 7D
Beagle Channel dispute see Beagle Channel dispute
church developments: papal visit 1982 Jun 11D
demonstrations and protests: 1981 Apr 30D/Nov 10D; 1982 Mar 30D/Dec 16D
economy: 5-year plan 1985 Jan 8D; austerity measures 1981 Dec 31D; 1986 Aug 29D; 1987 Feb 25D/Jul 20D/Oct 14D; 1989 Feb 21D/Jul 17D; banking 1980 Mar 28D/Apr 25D; 1981 Feb 9D; 1985 May 17D; devaluations 1981 Feb 2D/Jun 1D; 1982 Jul 5D; 1987 Feb 25D/Dec 30D; GDP 1989 Aug 10D; inflation rate 1984 Jan 7D; tax cuts, fiscal reform 1980 Jul 11D
Falkland Islands see Falkland Islands
foreign debt: bank loans 1982 Dec 31D; 1983 Aug 16D/Sep 16D; 1984 Mar 31G; 1987 Apr 13D; court actions 1983 Oct 3D/Oct 5D/Oct 8D; debtor nation summits 1984 Jun 21D/Sep 14D; 1985 Feb 8D; 1987 Nov 26D; IDB loans 1984 Mar 27D/Mar 28D; IMF loans 1982 Sep 29D; 1983 Jan 24D/Aug 16D; 1984 Jun 11D/Sep 25D/Dec 28D; 1985 Mar 16D/Jun 11D; 1987 Jan 12D/Dec 8D; 1988 Mar 21D; payments suspended 1983

Mar 7D; restructuring agreements 1987 Apr 13D/Aug 21D; U.S. loans 1985 Jul 8B; 1989 Oct 19A; World Bank loans 1988 Sep 25D
foreign relations: Austria 1981 Jun 19A; Great Britain 1983 Jun 7A; 1985 Jul 8B; 1989 Oct 19A; Group of Eight 1987 Nov 26D; Iran 1981 Jul 26C; Israel 1981 Jul 26C; Italy 1982 Nov 11A; USSR 1980 Jan 12A; 1986 Jan 29A; West Germany 1983 Aug 3D
government and politics: Alfonsin elected president 1983 Oct 30D; Bignone named president 1982 Jun 22D; capital relocation plan 1987 May 28D; central bank director resigns 1982 Sep 2D; democracy restoration urged 1981 Dec 16D; Galtieri resigns as president 1982 Jun 17D; junta delays presidential selection 1980 Sep 30D; junta ex-member house arrest 1981 Jul 14D; Luder nominated by Peronist Party 1983 Dec 6D; Menem elected 1989 May 14D; ministers resign 1982 Aug 24D; Peron corruption conviction 1981 Mar 20D; Peron detention lifted 1980 Dec 24D; Peron house arrest ends 1981 Jul 6D; Peron party president resignation 1985 Feb 21D; Peron political ban lifted 1983 Apr 14D; state of emergency ended 1989 Jun 28D; Viola as president 1980 Oct 3D; 1981 Dec 11D
human rights: Agosti release ordered 1989 May 8D; amnesty for military 1982 Aug 10D; 1983 Aug 19D/Sep 23D; 1986 Dec 23D; 1987 Jun 23D; 1988 May 12D; bodies discovered 1982 Oct 22D; Buenos Aires protest 1981 Apr 30D; demonstrations and protests 1981 Apr 30D; 1983 May 20D; Inter-American Commission for Human Rights 1980 Apr 18D; military rule protested 1984 Mar 30D; military trials 1983 Aug 21D; 1984 Jan 10D/Aug 2D; 1985 Apr 22D/Dec 9D/Dec 21D; 1986 Sep 25D/Dec 2D; 1987 Feb 22D; missing persons list 1983 Jan 13D/Apr 28D; Perez Esquivel awarded Nobel Prize 1980 Oct 13A; police break-up protest 1982 Dec 16D; Timerman returns 1984 Jan 7D
labor issues: Ford factory occupation 1985 Jul 14D; general strikes 1985 May 23D; 1986 Jan 24D/Mar 25D; 1987 Dec 9D; metalworkers' strike 1986 Jul 24D; strike for higher wages 1982 Dec 6D; 1984 Sep 3D
Latin relations: Brazil 1980 May 17D; 1986 Jul 30D/Dec 10D; Ecuador 1981 Mar 6D; Nicaraguan contras 1984 Sep 8D; Peru 1981 Mar 6D
obituaries: Borges, Jorge Luis 1986 Jun 14J; Cortazar, Julio 1984 Feb 12J; Ginastera, Alberto 1983 Jun 25J; Leloir, Luis Federico 1987 Dec 3I
sports: boxing 1982 Jan 16J; 1987 Oct 29J; soccer 1986 Jun 29J; tennis 1980 Jan 2J; 1981 Dec 13J; 1982 Jun 5J; 1983 Jun 8J; 1989 May 28J
terrorism and unrest: army rebellion, mutiny 1987 Sep 27D; 1988 Jan 18D/Dec 6D; 1989 Jan 24D; Peronists, rebels linked 1983 May 20D; rightist terror network 1985

Jun 2D/Aug 27D; Somoza assassination 1980 Sep 17D

trade issues: surplus data 1988 Apr 12D

United Nations policy: 1982 Nov 11A; 1988 Sep 20A

U.S. relations: 1981 Mar 17D; 1982 Jul 12G; 1983 Jan 22D/Aug 3D/Dec 10G; 1984 Feb 10H/Mar 31G/Dec 2D; 1986 Jan 13C; 1987 Jan 24D; 1988 Apr 27D

ARGK see Peoples' Army for the Liberation of Kurdistan

Argus Co. 1981 Jan 20C

Argyle Diamond Mines Joint Venture 1982 Dec 22E

Ariana (Afghan airline) 1980 Sep 15E

Ariane (rocket) 1980 May 23I; 1981 Jun 19I; 1982 Sep 10I; 1983 Jun 16I; 1985 May 6I/Sep 12I; 1987 Mar 20B; 1988 Sep 8I

Ariane-1 (rocket) 1984 Mar 4I

Ariane-2 (rocket) 1986 May 30I

Ariane-3 (rocket) 1984 Aug 4I; 1985 Feb 8I; 1987 Sep 15I; 1988 Mar 11I

Ariane-4 (rocket) 1988 Jun 15I/Dec 10I; 1989 Aug 8I

Ariane-5 (rocket) 1987 Nov 10I

Arizona see also individual governor in the name index (e.g., Mecham, Evan)
energy issues: hydroelectric power 1984 Aug 17H
environmental issues: fossils 1981 Sep 17I; 1985 May 16I; Grand Canyon haze 1989 Aug 29H; water projects 1981 Aug 18F
health care: abortion 1986 Nov 3F; artificial hearts 1985 Sep 29I
immigration and refugees: illegal aliens 1980 Jul 5F
Native Americans: 1981 Apr 18F
politics and government: gubernatorial campaign 1986 Sep 9F; King holiday restored 1989 Sep 22F; presidential campaign 1984 Apr 14F; 1987 Jan 7F; 1988 Feb 18F/Apr 16F

Arizona, University of (Tucson) 1984 Dec 11I; 1985 Mar 8I/Mar 13I; 1987 Jan 1J

Arkansas
education: college desegregation ordered 1983 Mar 24F/Jul 7F; creationism 1981 Mar 19F; 1982 Jan 5F; teacher competency testing 1985 Mar 23F
immigration and refugees: Cuban refugees 1980 Jun 1F/Jun 7F
politics and government: presidential campaign 1980 Feb 16F/May 27F
racial desegregation: 1983 Mar 24F/Jul 7F

Arkansas, University of (Fayetteville) 1980 Jan 1J; 1981 Dec 28J; 1987 Jan 1J; 1989 Jan 2J

Arkansas Gazette 1984 Oct 28F

Arlington National Cemetery (Virginia) 1984 May 28G; 1986 Nov 10G; 1987 Jan 28I

armaments see defense contractors; individual weapon (e.g., MX-missile); specific manufacturer (e.g., Boeing)

Armco Inc. 1985 May 2H/Aug 5H

Armed and Dangerous (film) 1986 Aug 20J

Armed Forces of National Liberation (Puerto Rico) 1982 Dec 31F

Armed Liberation Group of Guadeloupe 1980 Nov 16D

Armed Resistance Unit (anti-imperialist group) 1983 Nov 7F

Armed Revolutionary Nuclei (NAR) (Italy) 1980 Aug 6B

Armenia
demonstrations and protests: 1988 Feb 26B/Feb 27B/Mar 26B
earthquakes: 1988 Dec 15B/Dec 23B/Dec 24B
transcaucasion strife: Azerbaijan clashes 1988 Dec 1B; Nagorno-Karabakh feud 1988 Jun 15B/Jul 12B; 1989 Jan 12B
war crimes: Turkish files on genocide opened 1989 Jan 4B

Armenian National Council 1983 Jul 24A

Armenian Revolutionary Army 1983 Jul 27B; 1985 Mar 12D

Arms and the Man (George Bernard Shaw) (play) 1986 Apr 19J

arms control see individual countries (e.g., Union of Soviet Socialist Republics); specific agreements (e.g., SALT)

Arms Control and Disarmament Agency, U.S. (ACDA) 1983 Jan 12G/Apr 14G; 1987 Apr 17G/Jul 30G

Arms Export Control Act, U.S. 1984 Apr 13G

Army, U.S. see also Green Berets
accidents: helicopter crash 1982 Sep 11G
contract and billing issues: Ford Aerospace 1984 Sep 20G; General Dynamics 1985 Dec 2G
environmental issues: forest fires 1988 Nov 20I; hazardous wastes 1981 Jan 31H; 1983 Dec 9H; 1988 Feb 1H; wetlands controls 1985 Dec 4H
foreign operations: Bolivia drug war 1986 Jul 15D; Czech spy incident 1984 Apr 20B; East German sentry slays U.S. officer 1985 Mar 24B; Grenada invasion 1983 Oct 30G; USSR spy solicitation 1981 Feb 16G; West Germany foils general's assassination 1981 Sep 15G; West German copter crash 1982 Sep 11G
health care issues: AIDS 1985 Oct 18I; 1988 Jun 1I
performance standards: combat readiness 1980 Sep 8G; drug testing 1983 Aug 18G; smoking rules 1986 Jun 11G
personnel issues: Black Americans 1982 Jun 27F; homosexuals 1988 Feb 10G; 1989 May 3G; Medal of Honor warded 1980 Jul 9G; Powell appointment 1988 Dec 1G; recruitment 1984 Feb 2G; 1989 Feb 14G; women 1980 Apr 23G; 1983 Jul 11G
weapons systems: M-1 tank tests 1982 Sep 18G; missile tests 1984 Jun 10G; NATO military exercises 1980 Oct 11G; Pershing II nuclear missiles 1985 Apr 24G; Sergeant York gun cancelled 1985 Aug 27G

Army of God (antiabortion group) 1982 Aug 20F

Around the World in a Day (Prince and the Revolution) (recording) 1985 May 25J/Jun 22J/Jul 27J

arsenic 1981 Jul 28H; 1988 Apr 19H

arthritis 1982 Jul 22I; 1985 Aug 21H

Arthur (film) 1981 Sep 2J/Sep 30J/Dec 2J

Arthur Andersen & Co. 1986 Feb 27H; 1989 Jul 6H

Arthur 2 on the Rocks (film) 1988 Jul 13J

Artie Shaw: Time Is All You've Got (film) 1987 Mar 30J

artificial hearts
ethics issues: federal funding 1988 May 12I/Jul 2I; universities condemn 1984 Nov 27I
implatations: Arizona man 1985 Sep 29I; Burcham, Jack C. 1985 Apr 24I; Chayrez, Bernadette 1986 Feb 9I/Oct 11I; Clark, Barney 1982 Dec 2I/Dec 19I/Dec 27I; 1983 Mar 23I; Creighton, Thomas 1985 Mar 8I/Mar 13I; Haydon, Murray P. 1985 Feb 17I; Lund, Mary 1985 Dec 19I; 1986 Jan 2I; Schroeder, William J. 1984 Nov 25I; 1986 Aug 6I; Stenberg, Leif 1985 Nov 21I

artificial insemination 1984 Aug 1I/Aug 13I; 1987 Mar 10J; see also in vitro fertilization

Artist of the Floating World, An (Kazuro Ishiguro) (book) 1987 Jan 13J

Arts and Letters, American Academy and Institute of see American Academy and Institute of Arts and Letters

Aruba 1985 Jul 20D; 1986 Jan 1D

Aryan Nations World Congress 1986 Jul 14F

Aryan Woodstock 1989 Mar 4F

Asarco Inc. 1980 Nov 10H; 1988 Apr 19H

asbestos
health risks: injury claims 1982 Jan 11H; 1986 Dec 8H; insurer liability 1987 May 29H; merchant seamen lung diseases 1986 Nov 28H; school inspections 1986 Oct 3H

ASEAN see Association of Southeast Asian Nations

Ashland Oil Inc. 1980 Mar 31I; 1988 Jan 2H/Jul 6H/Sep 15H; 1989 Mar 9H/Nov 21H

Ashton Mining Co. 1980 Jan 11E

Asia see also specific country names (e.g., China)
defense and disarmament issues: chemical weapons 1981 Sep 14B; 1982 Mar 22A/Nov 29A/Dec 17A; 1983 May 31A
economy: copyright violations 1989 Apr 25H; growth rate 1983 Apr 15E; news network created 1981 Nov 6J; stock markets 1987 Oct 30A
education: Japanese textbooks protest 1982 Jul 24E; literacy and illiteracy 1980 Dec 4J
foreign relations: Canada 1983 Jan 19D; Great Britain 1985 Apr 14B; PLO 1981 Oct 20A; USSR 1987 May 19B; 1988 Dec 18E
health care: 1989 Sep 24I
international organizations: Commonwealth conference 1980 Sep 8E; Nonaligned Movement anniversary 1985 Apr 25A; UN economic conference 1989 Jul 5E
refugees: 1989 Jun 13A
religion: Roman Catholic cardinals named 1988 May 29J
U.S. relations: 1981 May 2E; 1982 Apr 23E; 1985 Oct 10H/1986 Apr 25G/Aug 6H; 1989 Apr 25H/Jun 26A

Asia (Asia) (recording) 1982 May 5J/Jun 16J/Jul 11J/Aug 18J

Asia (singing group) 1982 May 5J/Jun 16J/Jul 11J/Aug 18J

Asian-Americans 1981 Jun 22F; 1985 Aug 29J; 1989 Jan 17F; see also specific group (e.g., Chinese-Americans)

Asian Development Bank (ADB) 1983 Apr 15E; 1985 Nov 29E; 1986 Mar 11E

Asian Games 1982 Dec 4E; 1986 Oct 5J

Asian Wall Street Journal (newspaper) 1986 Sep 26E

Asia-Pacific News Network 1981 Nov 6J

Asia Watch 1988 Jul 30E/Nov 20E

aspartame (sweetener) 1981 Jul 15I

aspirin 1985 Jan 23I/Dec 10I; 1986 Mar 7F; 1988 Jan 26I/Aug 13I; 1989 Jul 20I

Assam (India)
civil strife: Bodo tribe attacks 1989 Aug 12E; Hindu/Moslem immigrant violence 1980 Apr 19E/Jun 9E/Jul 26E; 1983 Feb 18E/Feb 24E/Feb 25E/Mar 6E/Apr 1E; immigrant rights settled 1985 Aug 15E; road, rail blockade 1982 Jan 1E
politics and government: chief minister sworn 1983 Feb 27E; elections 1985 Dec 16E

Assault, The (film) 1987 Jan 31J/Feb 6J/Mar 30J

assault weapons 1989 Mar 13F/Mar 14F/May 24F

Assemblies of God 1987 May 6J; 1988 Mar 29J/Apr 8J

Associated Press (AP) 1980 Jan 13J; 1985 Jan 8J/Jan 9J/Mar 16C

Association of American Colleges 1985 Feb 10F

Association of American Medical Colleges 1984 Sep 19F

Association of Evangelical Lutheran Churches 1987 Apr 30J

Association of Southeast Asian Nations (ASEAN) 1981 Jun 18E/Jun 20G/1983 Jun 25E/Nov 22E; 1984 Jan 17E/Jul 9E; 1985 Jul 9E; 1986 Jun 23E; 1987 Dec 14E; 1989 Mar 13E

Association of Tennis Professionals (ATP) 1980 Jul 12J

Assurances Generales de France (AGF) 1986 Sep 10B

asteroids 1980 Jan 1I; 1989 Apr 19I

asthma 1983 May 16I; 1986 Jul 8H

astrology 1988 May 9F

Astronomical Society, American see American Astronomical Society

astronomy 1984 Dec 11I; see also specific subjects (e.g., galaxies)

Aswan Dam (Egypt) 1983 Apr 16I

AT (personal computer) 1984 Aug 14I

A-Team (TV show) 1983 Jun 12J; 1984 Oct 21J

Athlete of the Decade 1980 Jan 13J

Atlanta (Georgia)
BNI scandal: 1989 Sep 14B/Dec 14B
business issues: Cable News Network 1980 Jun 1J
crime and law enforcement: antiabortion protests 1988 Oct 8F; child murders 1981 Mar 5F/May 25F/Jun 21F; 1982 Feb 27F; prison siege 1987 Dec 4F
environmental issues: air pollution 1987 Jun 29H
heath care: antiabortion protests 1988 Oct 8F; birth defect study 1984 Aug 16G
immigration and refugees: Cuban refugees 1983 Jul 7F

obituaries: King Sr., Martin Luther 1984 Nov 11F; Woodruff, Robert Winship 1985 Mar 7J

politics and government: Democratic convention (1988) 1987 Feb 10F; 1988 Apr 20F/Jul 18F-19F; mayoral elections 1981 Oct 27F; 1985 Oct 8F; 1989 Oct 3F; presidential library 1986 Oct 1F

Atlanta Braves (baseball team) 1982 Oct 10J/Nov 17J; 1983 Nov 8J

Atlanta Falcons (football team) 1981 Jan 4J; 1988 Apr 24J

Atlanta Journal 500 (auto race) 1986 Nov 2J; 1988 Nov 20J

Atlantic (magazine) 1984 Jun 11F

Atlantic Conveyor (ship) 1982 May 25D

Atlantic Journal-Constitution (newspaper) 1988 Jul 14G

Atlantic Ocean
accidents and disasters: Air-India crash 1985 Jun 23A; Ariane rocket 1982 Sep 10I; Challenger disaster 1986 Apr 19I; Iowa explosion 1989 Apr 19G; Pride of Baltimore sinks 1986 May 14J; Soviet sub sinks 1986 Oct 6I
environmental issues: Hibernia offshore oil field 1988 Jul 18D; oil and gas leases 1989 Sep 15H; sewage sludge dumping 1985 Apr 1H
records and achievements: balloon crossing 1986 Sep 2J
science and technology: meteor impact crater identified 1987 Jun 17I; satellites 1984 Jun 9I/Jul 29I; telephone cables 1984 Feb 6I; Titanic discovered 1985 Sep 1J

Atlantic Recording Corp. 1985 Aug 5J

Atlantic Richfield Co. 1989 Aug 15H

Atlantis (space shuttle) 1985 Oct 7I; 1988 Dec 6I; 1989 May 4I/Oct 18I/Oct 23I

Atlas-Centaur (rocket) 1987 Mar 26I/May 11I

Atlas-E (rocket) 1986 Jan 12I

atmosphere 1982 Mar 6I; 1986 Jan 12I; 1989 Mar 11I/Mar 22H; see also specific aspects (e.g., ozone layer)

atomic and subatomic particles 1980 Jan 31I/Oct 14I; 1983 Jan 26I/Jun 1I; 1984 Jul 3I; 1989 Oct 12I

atomic energy see individual plants (e.g., Chernobyl); specific geographic regions (e.g., China)

atomic particle accelerators 1985 Oct 13I; 1986 Jul 27I; 1987 Jan 30I/Apr 15I/Sep 2I; 1988 Dec 13I

"atomic vets" 1988 May 20G

ATP see Association of Tennis Professionals (ATP)

AT&T see American Telephone and Telegraph Co.

ATU see Amalgamated Transit Union

ATVs see all-terrain vehicles

Auburn University (Alabama) 1984 Jan 2J; 1986 Jan 1J; 1988 Jan 1J/Apr 3J/Apr 24J/Dec 7J; 1989 Jan 2J/Apr 2J

Auca Indians (Brazil) 1987 Sep 30E

auctions see also specific auction houses (e.g., Sotheby)
art: de Kooning painting 1983 May 10J
government securities see Treasury, U.S. Department of the
intellectual property: Clavell novel rights 1986 Jan 11J; Gone with

the Wind sequel rights 1988 Apr 25J
mineral rights: coal leases 1983 May 10H/May 12H/Sep 14H
real estate: low-cost housing mortgages 1987 Apr 24H
statistics: record turnovers reported 1984 Jul 14J
Audi 5000 1986 Dec 23H; 1987 Jan 15H/Jul 29H
Audi of America Inc. 1987 Jan 15H/Jul 29H
August (Judith Rossner) (book) 1983 Aug 14J/Sep 11J/Oct 16J
Augusta National Golf Club (Georgia) 1983 Oct 22F
Au Revoir les Enfants (film) 1987 Sep 9J; 1988 Feb 12J; 1989 Mar 19J
auroras 1985 May 6I
Auschwitz (Nazi death camp) 1989 Jan 25B/Aug 10B/Aug 27B/Sep 19B
austerity measures
Argentina: 1982 Mar 30D; 1984 Sep 25D; 1985 Jun 11D/Jun 14D; 1987 Oct 14D; 1988 Mar 21D
Bolivia: 1985 Oct 2D; 1986 Aug 28D
Brazil: 1983 Feb 18D/Jul 18D/Sep 15D; 1985 Jul 4D
Denmark: 1982 Oct 5B/Oct 16B
Ecuador: 1982 Oct 27D; 1985 Jan 10D; 1987 Mar 25D
El Salvador: 1986 Jan 21D
France: 1983 Mar 25B/May 5B/Jun 8B/Jul 8B
Great Britain: 1980 Nov 29B; 1982 Oct 8B
Greece: 1986 Apr 7B/Sep 6B
Guatemala: 1985 Apr 12D
Hungary: 1987 Jul 20B/Sep 19B
IMF/World Bank: 1981 Oct 2A
Indonesia: 1987 Jan 6E
Ireland: 1987 Mar 31B
Israel: 1983 Oct 10C; 1984 Feb 22C/Sep 4C/Sep 16C/Dec 25G; 1985 Jul 1C; 1989 Jan 1C
Liberia: 1981 Jul 17C
Mexico: 1982 May 15D/Dec 1D; 1985 Nov 21D; 1987 Sep 1D
Netherlands: 1986 Sep 16B; 1988 Sep 20B
Nicaragua: 1989 Jan 30D/May 11D
Nigeria: 1984 May 7C; 1986 Feb 24C; 1989 May 24C/Nov 4C
Norway: 1986 Jun 17B
Panama: 1985 Jul 2E
Peru: 1988 Sep 6D
Philippines: 1984 Oct 13E
Portugal: 1983 Aug 9B
Romania: 1981 Oct 17B
Spain: 1987 Mar 30B
Sudan: 1981 Nov 9C
Trinidad: 1989 Mar 6D
Venezuela: 1989 May 18D
Yugoslavia: 1988 Aug 4B
Australia *see also individual leaders in the name index (e.g.,* Hawke, Robert)
Aborigine policy *see* Aborigines
accidents and disasters: brush fires 1983 Feb 19I; drought 1980 Apr 4E/Apr 24E; 1982 Oct 6E/Dec 1E; 1983 Jun 16I; earthquakes 1989 Dec 28I; monsoon rainfalls 1989 Mar 14I
agriculture: grain exports 1980 Jan 12A/Jun 17E/Jun 24E; grain harvest losses 1986 Jan 1E; meat exports 1983 Aug 12E; 1984 Apr 13E; 1987 Aug 20F; 1988 Jun 24E; U.S. export policy 1986 Apr 18E
arts and culture: Carey wins Booker Prize 1988 Oct 26J; Picasso painting recovered 1986 Aug 19J; rock paintings 1987 Mar 31I; *Taxi Driver* censored 1981 Apr 8J; World Expo 88 1988 Oct 30E
business and industry: automobile industry 1984 May 30E; China iron ore mining 1987 Jun 30E; diamond mining 1980 Jan 11E; 1982 Dec 22E; Japanese auto plant 1981 Jan 20E; mining near Kakadu National Park 1989 Oct 5E; Murdoch denied TV station 1980 Sep 29E; Murdoch purchases media group 1986 Dec 3E; oil yield estimates 1988 Mar 18E; publishing 1987 Mar 13B; tourism 1987 Mar 12E
census data: population 1988 Jan 11E/Jun 6E
crime and law enforcement: arms smuggling 1988 May 31E; Baader-Meinhof member arrested 1981 Feb 28B; bombings 1984 Apr 4E; Chamberlain murder case 1985 Nov 12E; 1986 Feb 7E; 1987 Jun 2E; 1988 Sep 15E; National Safety Council funds theft 1989 Apr 5E; tax avoidance schemes 1982 Aug 25E/Sep 28E
defense and disarmament issues: antinuclear protests 1983 Jul 2I; British A-tests 1984 Jun 5E/Oct 2E; 1986 Jan 10E; chemical weapons conference 1989 Sep 18A; defense spending 1980 Feb 19E; 1987 Mar 19E; 1989 Jul 5E; military staff reorganization 1989 Jul 5E; nuclear-free zone 1985 Aug 6E; nuclear safeguards 1981 Mar 31I; U.S. military cooperation 1980 Sep 9E; 1981 Feb 7G; 1987 Jun 22E; 1988 Nov 22E; white paper 1987 Mar 19E; 1989 Jul 5E
economy: consumer price index 1986 Oct 23E; 1989 Oct 26E; financial system 1981 Nov 17E; 1984 Apr 10E; fringe benefits tax 1986 May 29E; gross domestic product (GDP) 1989 Apr 3E; gross national product (GNP) 1981 Jun 18E; growth rate 1983 Jul 18E; 1986 Mar 20E; 1987 Aug 26B; inflation 1983 Jan 26E; 1987 Jul 14E; Labor Party policy 1981 Aug 25E; prime lending rate 1985 Dec 16E; social security benefits 1985 Mar 21E; stock market fluctuation 1980 Oct 21E; taxes 1982 Jul 19E; 1985 Jun 4E/Jul 4E
education: higher education funding 1988 May 5E/Jun 16E
environmental issues: fossils 1980 Apr 2I; Great Barrier Reef 1980 Jun 10I; 1989 Jan 13E; kangaroos 1984 Sep 5I; 1986 Mar 6I; monsoon rainfalls 1989 Mar 14I; pollution treaty 1986 Nov 25E; tropical rain forests 1984 Aug 7I
espionage and intelligence issues: 1982 Aug 25E
foreign relations: Cambodia 1981 Feb 14E; 1983 Nov 22E; China 1984 Aug 10E; Ethiopia 1985 Jan 13C; Fiji 1987 May 30E; 1988 Feb 9E; France 1983 Jun 9A; Great Britain 1983 Mar 20E/Dec 17E; 1985 Oct 27E; 1986 Feb 17E/Mar 2E; 1987 Mar 13B; 1988 Apr 19E/Aug 17E; Indonesia 1986 Sep 4E; Japan 1984 Apr 13E; 1988 Jun 24E; Libya 1987 May 19E; Malaysia 1986 Jul 6E; New Zealand 1980 Jul 24E; 1982 Nov 10E; 1988 Jun 21E; Pacific regional cooperation 1982 Jun 12E; Papua New Guinea 1985 Nov 10E; South Africa 1984 Mar 2E; 1986 Jun 17E/Aug 5A; USSR 1980 Jan 12A/Jun 17E/Jun 24E; 1981 Mar 4E; 1983 Mar 19E; Vietnam 1983 Nov 22E
government and politics: approval rating 1989 Jun 27E; bill of rights 1988 Jul 11E; budget 1983 Aug 23E; 1986 Aug 19E; 1987 May 13E; 1988 Jul 4E/Aug 23E; cabinet 1982 Apr 19E/Oct 11E; Cocos Islands votes full integration 1984 Apr 6E; constitutional amendments rejected 1988 Sep 3B; Labor Party conference 1986 Jul 7E; Labor Party policies outlined 1981 Aug 25E; Labor Party president named 1986 Jul 13E; Liberal Party/National Party alliance 1987 Apr 28E/Aug 6E; national elections 1980 Oct 15E/Oct 18E; 1983 Mar 5E; 1984 Oct 8E/Dec 1E; 1987 Jul 11E; parliament dissolved 1987 Jun 5E; state elections 1980 Nov 29E; 1981 Sep 19E; 1982 Apr 3E/May 15E/Nov 7E; 1985 Mar 2E/Dec 7E; Victoria Labor government attacks Liberals 1982 Apr 13E
health care: abortion 1980 May 30E; Agent Orange health effects 1980 Jan 3I; AIDS 1984 Nov 15I; 1985 Mar 27E; cold virus treatment 1986 Jan 9I; doctors' strike 1984 Jun 20E; frozen embryos 1983 May 2I; 1984 Apr 10I/Oct 23I; 1985 Feb 22I; life expectancy 1988 May 24I; physical exercise benefit questioned 1980 Jul 5I; public health insurance 1984 Feb 1E; in vitro fertilization 1984 Jun 17I/Aug 13I; 1985 Dec 17I
holidays: Australia Day celebrations 1988 Jan 26E
immigration and refugees: 1980 Jun 19E; 1986 Apr 10E; 1988 Jan 11E/Jun 6E
international organizations *see individual organizations (e.g.,* ANZUS)
labor issues: airline pilots slowdown 1989 Aug 24E/Nov 23E; air traffic controllers job action 1989 Jun 8E; dock workers' strike 1980 Aug 26E; doctors' strike 1984 Jun 20E; employment figures 1985 Jun 6E; metal trades contracts 1981 Dec 7E; New South Wales strikes 1980 Mar 11E; 1989 Jul 25E; Parliament House break-in 1982 Oct 26E; publishing strike 1980 Jun 11E; 35-hour work week 1980 Jul 16E; unemployment rate 1983 Oct 14E; 1984 Jun 8E; 1985 Jul 11E; Victoria walkout 1989 Jul 26E; wage freeze 1982 Dec 23E; wage increases 1980 Jul 14E; 1983 Sep 23E; 1986 Nov 6E; 1987 Mar 10E; 1989 Aug 7E; wage indexation ended 1986 Dec 23E; wage-price accord 1985 Sep 4E
monetary issues: currency 1982 Jul 29E; 1985 Feb 20E; 1986 Jan 23E/Nov 28E; 1988 Jun 20E; 1989 Feb 27E; financial system deregulation 1981 Nov 17E; 1984 Apr 10E; foreign debt 1989 May 31E; inflation 1983 Jan 26E; 1987 Jul 14E; prime lending rate 1985 Dec 16E
obituaries: Burnet, Macfarlane 1985 Aug 31I; Moorehead, Alan 1983 Sep 29J
press and broadcasting: foreign policy articles, book banned 1980 Nov 8E/Dec 2E; Murdoch denied TV station 1980 Sep 29E; Murdoch purchases media group 1986 Dec 3E; publishing strike 1980 Jun 11E; *Spycatcher* publication controversy 1987 Mar 13B
religion: papal visit 1986 Dec 1E; Salvation Army 1986 May 2A; scientology 1983 Nov 2E
rights issues: civil rights legislation 1984 Mar 7E/Aug 2E; homosexuals 1984 Aug 2E; national identity card 1987 Sep 9E/Sep 29E; women 1984 Mar 7E; 1986 May 2A
sports: Boston Marathon 1986 Apr 21J; cricket 1987 Nov 8J; field hockey 1986 Oct 19J; golf 1981 Jun 21J; 1982 Jun 13J; 1983 Jul 31J; 1984 Jun 18J; 1986 Jul 20J; Olympic Games (Moscow) 1980 Mar 18J/Jul 31J; skiing 1989 Aug 12J; tennis 1980 Jul 4J; 1983 Dec 28J; 1986 Dec 28J; 1987 Jul 5J; *see also specific events (e.g.,* America's Cup)
terrorism: 2 Turks slain 1980 Dec 17A; Baader-Meinhof member arrested 1981 Feb 28B; bombings 1984 Apr 4E; Frankfurt bombing 1985 Jun 19B
trade issues: beef exports 1984 Apr 13E; deficits 1982 Jul 12E; 1985 May 10E/Aug 13E; 1987 Aug 18E; 1989 Jun 19E/Aug 16E/Sep 21E/Oct 25E/Nov 23E; grain exports 1980 Jan 12A/Jun 17E/Jun 24E; meat exports 1983 Aug 12E; 1987 Aug 20F; 1988 Jun 24E; protectionism 1987 Oct 22E; steel dumping 1984 Feb 10H; U.S. antitrust accord 1982 May 19A; U.S. export policy 1986 Apr 18E
United Nations policy: 1985 Oct 17A; 1987 Dec 21A
U.S. relations: antinuclear protests 1983 Jul 2I; antitrust accord 1982 May 19A; covert intelligence activities 1982 Aug 25E; meat exports 1983 Aug 12E; 1987 Aug 20F; meetings 1982 Nov 8E; 1983 Jun 14E; 1984 Jul 7G; 1985 Feb 5G; 1986 Apr 18E; 1988 Jun 19G; military cooperation 1980 Sep 9E; 1981 Feb 7G; 1987 Jun 22E; 1988 Nov 22E; pan-Pacific entity proposed 1989 Jun 26A; steel dumping charges 1984 Feb 10H; uranium enrichment 1981 Nov 20I
Australia (yacht) 1980 Sep 25J
Australia, New Zealand, U.S. Treaty Organization (ANZUS) 1982 Jun 22A; 1984 Jul 13A; 1985 Feb 5G; 1987 Jun 22E
Australia II (yacht) 1983 Sep 26J
Australian Cultural Terrorists 1986 Aug 19J
Australian Grand Prix (auto race) 1986 Oct 26J; 1987 Nov 15J; 1988 Nov 13J
Australian Open (tennis tournament)
men's singles: 1980 Jan 2J; 1981 Jan 4J; 1982 Jan 3J/Dec 13J; 1985 Dec 9J; 1987 Jan 25J; 1988 Jan 24J; 1989 Jan 29J
women's singles: 1980 Jan 1J; 1982 Dec 5J; 1985 Dec 8J; 1987 Jan 24J; 1988 Jan 23J; 1989 Jan 28J
Australian Petroleum Exploration Association 1982 May 10E
Austral Plan (Argentina) 1985 Dec 30D; 1986 Mar 25D/Aug 29D
Austria *see also individual leaders in the name index (e.g.,* Kreisky, Bruno)
arts and culture: Habsburg empress buried 1989 Apr 1B; Hollein wins Pritzker 1985 Apr 3J
crime and law enforcement: drug money frozen 1989 Dec 6A; Spain consul kidnapping 1981 Feb 19B/Feb 28B/Jun 19A; wine scandal 1985 Jul 11B/Oct 24B
energy issues: nuclear power 1980 Nov 11B
foreign relations: EC entry application 1989 Jul 17B; Hungary 1989 May 2B/Sep 8B; Libya 1982 Mar 13A; socialist governments meet 1983 Jan 23A; Spain 1981 Feb 19B
government and politics: budget 1988 Sep 29B; coalition government formed 1987 Jan 14B; Kirchschlager elected president 1980 May 18B; national elections 1986 Nov 23B; no confidence vote survived 1985 Feb 1B; provincial autonomy 1980 Jun 15B; Sinowatz becomes chancellor 1983 May 24B
immigration and refugees: East German exodus 1989 Sep 14B
labor issues: job cuts 1986 Sep 2B
obituaries: Bayer, Herbert 1985 Sep 30J; Bergner, Elisabeth 1986 May 12J; Boehm, Karl 1981 Aug 14J; Kokoschka, Oskar 1980 Feb 22J; Lenya, Lotte 1981 Nov 27J; Lorenz, Konrad 1989 Feb 27I; Rahner, Karl 1984 Mar 30J; Schidlof, Peter 1987 Aug 18J; Schneider, Romy 1982 May 29J; von Karajan, Herbert 1989 Jul 16J; Werner, Oskar 1984 Oct 23J
sports: auto racing 1988 Sep 11J; contract bridge 1985 Nov 2J; cycling 1987 Sep 6J; skiing 1986 Mar 23J; 1988 Mar 26J
trade issues: legislation 1985 Jan 2B; wine scandal 1985 Jul 11B/Oct 24B
war crimes: *Anschluss* anniversary 1988 Mar 10B; Hitler anniversary 1989 Apr 20B; Nazi war criminals 1985 Jan 23J/Feb 1B
authors *see individual artists in the name index (e.g.,* Le Carre, John)
Authors League 1984 Dec 3J
Auto da Fe (Elias Canetti) (book) 1981 Oct 15J
automobiles
acceleration: 1986 Aug 15H/Dec 23H/Dec 30H; 1987 Jan 15H/Jul 29H
emissions: 1980 Jul 8H; 1982 Jul 29H/Aug 23H/Nov 23H; 1985 Mar 21B; 1987 Apr 14H; 1988 Feb 17H; 1989 Aug 10H/Aug 15H/Sep 20H/Oct 2H
sales: 1982 May 4H
avalanches 1980 Mar 26I; 1982 Mar 14I; 1985 Nov 13D; 1986 Feb 20I
Avenging Angel (film) 1985 Jan 16J
Avenging Force (film) 1986 Sep 17J
Avianca Airlines 1989 Nov 27D
aviation *see individual airlines (e.g.,* Pan American World Airways)
Aviation Security Act, U.S. 1986 Apr 25C
Avon Books 1986 Jan 11J
AWACS (airborne warning and control system)
Chad: 1983 Aug 18G/Aug 23G

Egypt: 1981 Oct 15C; 1983 Feb 16C/Aug 3C; 1984 Mar 18C/Apr 9G

Europe: 1980 Dec 9G

Pakistan: 1986 Nov 4E

Saudi Arabia

U.S. bases: 1980 Sep 30G

U.S. sales: administration statements 1981 Apr 8G/Apr 21G/Apr 22G/Aug 24G/Sep 11G/Sep 22G/Oct 1G; congressional legislation 1981 Apr 26G/Sep 17G/Oct 14G-15G/Oct 22G/Oct 28G; Israeli response 1981 Apr 22C/Sep 13C/Oct 29C; joint operation proposed 1981 Sep 28C; Saudi statements 1981 Apr 23C

Sudan: 1983 Aug 23G

awards and honors *see specific awards (e.g., Nobel Prize)*

Ayers Rock (Australia) 1983 Nov 11E; 1985 Mar 14E/Oct 26E; 1986 Feb 7E

Azadegan (Born Free) (Iranian group) 1981 Aug 14C

Azerbaijan (USSR) 1988 Mar 4B/Mar 8B/Mar 15B/Mar 27B/Jun 15B/Jul 12B/Dec 1B; 1989 Jan 12B/Aug 14B/Nov 28B

Azores (Portugal) 1983 Dec 13B

AZT (azidothymidine/zidovudine) 1986 Sep 19I; 1987 Jan 16I; 1988 Nov 24I; 1989 Mar 31F/Jul 10I/Aug 3I/Aug 8D/Aug 17I/Sep 18B/Sept 18F/Oct 26F

B

B-1 (aircraft) 1984 Oct 1G

B-2 Stealth (aircraft) 1988 Apr 20G

Baader-Meinhof (West German terrorist group) 1980 Jul 31B; 1981 Feb 28B

Babcock and Wilcox Co. 1980 Mar 4I

Babette's Feast (film) 1988 Mar 4J/Apr 11J

baboons 1984 Oct 26I/Nov 15I

Baby, I Love Your Way/Freebird Medley (Will to Power) (recording) 1988 Nov 26J

"Baby Bells" *see* Bell System

Baby Boom (film) 1987 Oct 21J/Nov 11J

"Baby Doe" rule 1984 Jan 9F/Feb 2F; 1986 Jun 9F

baby food 1987 Nov 13F

Bache Group 1980 Oct 21H

Bache Halsey Stuart Shields Inc. 1980 Apr 1H

Back in Black (AC/DC) (recording) 1980 Dec 3J; 1981 Jan 7J

Back in the Highlife (Steve Winwood) (recording) 1986 Sep 17J

Back to School (film) 1986 Jun 18J/Jul 9J

Back to the Future (film) 1985 Jul 17J/Aug 14J

Back to the Future Part II (film) 1989 Nov 29J/Dec 28J

Back Where You Started (Tina Turner) (recording) 1987 Feb 24J

bacteria

health issues: cheese contamination 1985 Jul 12I; sewage plants 1988 Jul 27H

research: fossils 1980 Apr 2I; gene regulation 1980 Jan 23I; genetic engineering tests 1985 Nov 14I; 1986 Feb 25H/Mar 24I/May 13I; 1987 Apr 24I/Jun 8I/Sep 3H; 1988 Jan 12I; genetic mapping 1987 Feb 16I; patents 1980 Jun 16F

Bad (Michael Jackson) (recording) 1987 Oct 24J/Nov 21J/Dec 26J; 1988 Jan 23J/Feb 20J/Mar 19J/Apr 23J/May 21J

Bad Animals (Heart) (recording) 1987 Jul 22J/Aug 22J/Sep 19J

Bad Boys (film) 1983 Apr 6J

Bad Medicine (Bon Jovi) (recording) 1988 Nov 26J

BAe *see* British Aerospace PLC

BAe 146 (jet airliner) 1985 Jun 1A

Bahais (religious group) 1983 May 22G/May 28C

Bahamas *see also individual leaders in the name index (e.g.,* Pindling, Lynden)

arts and culture: Columbus landing site 1986 Oct 6J

drug trafficking: crime links 1981 Jun 30D; 1982 Nov 13D; 1984 Dec 17D; U.S. rejects sanctions 1988 Apr 15F

foreign relations: Commonwealth summit 1986 Aug 5A

government and politics: general elections 1987 Jun 19D; parliament dissolved 1987 May 12D; Pindling reelected 1982 Jun 10D

immigration and refugees: Cuban attack on patrol boat 1980 May 10D; Haitian aliens 1981 Feb 16D

U.S. relations: military base pact 1984 Apr 5D

Bahia Paraiso (ship) 1989 Jan 28I

Bahrain 1981 Mar 10C; 1982 May 22C; 1983 Jul 19C; 1986 Apr 26C; 1987 Jan 21G

Baikal-Amur Mainline railway 1984 Sep 29B

Baker Plan 1985 Oct 11A/Dec 17D; 1986 Jun29H

Bakuriani (ship) 1984 Nov 6G/Nov 7D

balanced budget amendment 1982 Jul 19F/Aug 4H/Sep 8F/Oct 1F; 1985 Jul 23F/Aug 5F; 1986 Mar 25H/May 19H

balance of payments on current account

statistics: 1980 Jun 19H/Sep 18H; 1982 Dec 16H; 1984 Mar 19H/Jun 18H/Sep 17H/Dec 17H; 1985 Mar 18H/Jun 17H/Sep 16H/Dec 17H; 1986 Mar 18H/Sep 16H/Dec 16H; 1987 Mar 17H/Jun 16H/Sep 15H/Dec 15H; 1988 Mar 15H/Jun 15H/Sep 13H/Dec 13H; 1989 Mar 14H/Jun 13H/Sep 12H

baldness 1987 Mar 16H; 1988 Aug 17H

Balkan economic summit 1989 Mar 15B

ball bearings 1989 May 2H

balloon angioplasty 1989 Mar 9I

balloons 1985 Jul 14I; 1986 Sep 2J; 1987 Dec 17I

Baltic Sea 1981 Sep 8B; 1982 Jan 19B; 1983 Jun 6B; 1986 Nov 14B; 1987 Oct 1B; 1988 Aug 19I

Baltimore Colts (football team) 1984 Mar 29J

Baltimore Orioles (baseball team) 1982 Nov 24J; 1983 Oct 8J/Oct 8J/Oct 16J/Nov 16J; 1989 Nov 7J

Baltimore Stars (football team) 1985 Jul 14J

Bamboo Gang 1986 Dec 17E

Banca Nazionale del Lavoro (BNL) 1989 Aug 17A/Sep 14B/Dec 14B

Banca Privata Italiana 1982 Jul 22B

Banco Ambrosiano scandal 1982 Jul 13B/Jul 19B/Jul 30B/Aug 9B/Nov 26B/Dec 24B; 1983 Feb 18B; 1984 Mar 8B/May 25B; 1987 Feb 26B; 1989 Apr 7B

Banco Central (Spain) 1989 Feb 24B

Banco de Intercambio Regional (Argentina) 1980 Mar 28D/Apr 25D

Banco Espanol de Credito (Banesto) 1989 Feb 24B

Banc One Corp. 1989 Jun 28H

Bandung Conference (1955) 1985 Apr 25A

Bangladesh *see also individual leaders in the name index (e.g.,* Ershad, Hossein Mohammed)

accidents and disasters: cyclones 1988 Nov 29I; ferry sinking 1986 Apr 20E; floods 1987 Sep 4D; 1988 Sep 6I; 1989 Aug 5I; tornados 1989 Apr 26I

assassinations: Ahmed, Manzur 1981 Jun 2E; Rahman, Ziaur 1981 May 30E

civil strife: 8 die in protest march 1988 Jan 24E; coups and coup attempts 1981 Jun 1N/Nov 17E; 1982 Mar 24E; election violence 1988 Feb 10E; martial law protest 1984 Oct 14E

economy: food shortage 1982 Mar 8E

foreign relations: Great Britain 1986 Sep 1B; India 1982 Oct 7E; 1983 Aug 13E; 1984 Jun 10E

government and politics: district elections 1985 May 20E; parliamentary elections 1986 May 21E; 1988 Mar 3E; presidential elections delayed 1986 Sep 13E; Sattar elected president 1981 Nov 15E

international organizations: Commonwealth rejoined 1989 Oct 1A; United Nations 1988 Oct 10A; World Bank aid 1985 May 10E

religion: Islam made state religion 1988 Jun 7E

Bangles (singing group) 1987 Jan 28J/Feb 18J

BankAmerica Corp. 1980 Sep 3D; 1983 Jan 7H; 1984 Nov 15H; 1985 Jul 17H; 1986 Jan 2H/May 12H/Jul 16H/Oct 6H; 1987 Jun 8H

Bankers Trust Co. 1980 May 1H; 1985 May 17H

Bank for International Settlements (BIS) 1984 Jan 25H

Bank of Boston Corp. 1987 Dec 14H

Bank of British Columbia 1985 Jan 10D

Bank of Brunei 1986 Nov 19C

Bank of Canada 1980 Mar 10D; 1984 Mar 15D; 1987 Oct 22D; 1988 Jan 20D; 1989 Feb 16D/May 18D

Bank of Credit & Commerce International Holdings S.A. (BCCI) 1988 Oct 11F

Bank of Crete 1989 Mar 14B

Bank of England 1984 Nov 12B; 1986 Oct 14B; 1987 Mar 9B/Aug 6B/Oct 29B; 1988 Feb 1B/Feb 11B/Mar 17B/May 17B/Jun 22B/Nov 25B

Bank of Greece 1989 Nov 21B

Bank of Israel 1984 Aug 17C/Sep 4C

Bank of Italy 1987 Sep 13B

Bank of Japan 1986 Jan 29E; 1987 Feb 20E; 1989 May 30E

Bank of Korea 1987 Sep 22E/Dec 28E; 1988 Mar 25E

Bank of Mexico 1986 Sep 17D

Bank of New England Corp. 1989 Dec 17H

Bank of New York Co. 1989 Oct 12H

Bank of Spain 1988 Jan 18B

bankruptcies

airlines: Air Florida 1984 Apr 3H/Sep 26H; Braniff International Corp. 1982 May 13H; Eastern Airlines 1989 Mar 9H; Frontier Airlines 1986 Aug 28H

government: Argentina 1980 Apr 25D; 1981 Feb 9D; China 1986 Aug 3E; Detroit 1981 Aug 15H; Japan 1988 Jul 23E

legislation: congressional revisions 1982 Dec 24F; 1983 Apr 27H; 1984 Mar 21H; Supreme Court rulings 1982 Dec 24F; 1984 Feb 22F; 1985 Jan 9H

manufacturers: A.H. Robins Co. 1985 Aug 21H; 1987 Dec 11F; LTV Corp. 1988 May 4H; Manville Corp. 1982 Aug 26H/Aug 27H; 1983 Nov 21H; 1986 Dec 18H; Penn-Dixie Industries Inc. 1980 Apr 7H; Rath Packaging Co. 1983 Nov 1H; Texaco Inc. 1987 Apr 12H; Wedtech Corp. 1986 Dec 15H; Wheeling-Pittsburgh Steel Corp. 1985 Apr 16H; 1986 May 28H; White Motor Corp. 1980 Sep 4H; Wickes Cos. 1982 Apr 24H; Wilson Foods Corp. 1983 Apr 24H

media and the arts: National Public Radio (NPR) 1983 Aug 2F; Oakland (Calif.) Symphony 1986 Sep 12J; PTL (Praise the Lord) ministry 1987 Jun 12H/Oct 8J; United Press International (UPI) 1985 Apr 28H; 1986 Jun 10H

personal issues: applications 1980 Mar 25H

utilities: Public Service Co. (New Hampshire) 1988 Jan 28H

banks and banking *see specific bank (e.g.,* BankAmerica Corp.)

Barajas Airport (Madrid, Spain) 1983 Nov 27D

Barbados 1983 Oct 25G/Nov 8G; 1985 Mar 11D; 1986 May 28D; 1987 Jun 1D

Barbuda *see* Antigua and Barbuda

Barcelona (Spain) 1986 Oct 17J

Barclays Bank PLC 1986 Nov 24B; 1988 Feb 26B

barley 1980 Oct 23B; 1981 Oct 6H; 1986 Apr 9D/Oct 24H

Barnum (musical) 1980 Apr 30J/Jun 8J

Barracks Thief, The (Tobias Wolff) (book) 1985 May 11J

baseball *see also specific league (e.g.,* American League); *individual teams (e.g.,* Oakland Athletics); *players in the name index (e.g.,* Rose, Pete)

awards and honors: Hall of Fame (HOF) 1980 Aug 3J; 1981 Aug 2J; 1982 Aug 1J; 1985 Jan 7J/Mar 6J/Jul 28J; 1986 Jan 8J/Aug 3J; 1987 Jan 14J/Mar 3J; 1988 Jan 12J/Jul31J; 1989 Jan 9J/Feb 28J/Jul 23J

broadcasting: 1988 Dec 14J

executive changes: Giamatti named commissioner 1988 Sep 8J; Kuhn voted out as commissioner 1982 Nov 1J; Ueberroth becomes commissioner 1984 Oct 1J; Vincent named commissioner 1989 Sep 13J

foreign developments: Canada 1984 May 1J; Japan 1988 Mar 18J; USSR 1986 Oct 2J

gambling: Mays, Mantle reinstated 1985 Mar 18J; Rose probe 1988 May 6J; 1989 Jun 25J-26J/Aug 24J

labor and salary issues: contracts 1985 Aug 7J; free agency 1980 May 23J/Nov 13J; 1986 Apr 7J; 1987 Sep 21J; 1988 Jan 22H;

1989 Aug 31J; strikes 1981 Jun 12J/Jun 13H/Jul 31J/Aug 20J

obituaries: Ashford, Emmet 1980 Mar 1J; Giamatti, A(ngelo) Bartlett 1989 Sep 1J; Greenberg, Hank 1986 Sep 4J; Hubbell, Carl Owen 1988 Nov 21J; Maris, Roger 1985 Dec 14J; Martin, Billy 1989 Dec 25J; Paige, Satchel 1982 Jul 8J; Ruffing, Charles "Red" 1986 Feb 17J; Veeck, Bill 1986 Jan 2J

records and achievements: Rose (career hits) 1985 Sep 11J; Ryan (career strikeouts) 1985 Jul 11J

season openings: 1985 Apr 8J

substance abuse: drug suspensions 1986 Feb 28J; drug testing 1985 May 7J/Sep 24J

winners: NCAA title 1987 Jun 7J; World Series 1980 Oct 21J; 1981 Oct 28J; 1982 Oct 20J; 1983 Oct 16J; 1984 Oct 14J; 1985 Oct 27J; 1986 Oct 27J; 1987 Oct 25J; 1988 Oct 22J; 1989 Oct 28J; All-Star Game 1981 Aug 9J; 1983 Jul 6J; 1984 Jul 10J; 1985 Jul 16J; 1986 Jul 15J; 1987 Jul 14J; 1988 Jul 12J; 1989 Jul 11J

Baseball Hall of Fame

Aaron, Henry: 1982 Aug 1J

Barlick, Al: 1989 Feb 28J/Jul 23J

Bench, Johnny: 1989 Jan 9J/Jul 23J

Brock, Lou: 1985 Jan 7J/Jul 28J

Chandler, Happy: 1982 Aug 1J

Dandridge, Ray: 1987 Mar 3J

Doerr, Bobby: 1986 Aug 3J

Foster, Rube: 1981 Aug 2J

Gibson, Bob: 1981 Aug 2J

Hunter, Catfish: 1987 Jan 14J

Jackson, Travis: 1982 Aug 1J

Kaline, Al: 1980 Aug 3J

Lombardi, Ernie: 1986 Aug 3J

McCovey, Willie: 1986 Jan 8J/Aug 3J

Mize, Johnny: 1981 Aug 2J

Robinson, Frank: 1982 Aug 1J

Schoendienst, Red: 1989 Feb 28J/Jul 23J

Slaughter, Enos: 1985 Mar 6J/Jul 28J

Snider, Duke: 1980 Aug 3J

Stargell, Willie: 1988 Jan 12J/Jul 31J

Vaughan, Arky: 1985 Mar 6J/Jul 28J

Wilhelm, Hoyt: 1985 Jan 7J/Jul 28J

Williams, Billy: 1987 Jan 14J

Yastrzemski, Carl: 1989 Jan 9J/Jul 23J

Baseball Writers of America 1980 Nov 18J

Base Realignment and Closure, U.S. Commission on 1989 Jan 5G/Apr 18G

BASF Corp. 1989 Dec 15H

basketball *see also specific teams (e.g.,* Boston Celtics); *individual players in the name index (e.g.,* Abdul-Jabbar, Kareem)

All-Star Game: 1980 Feb 3J; 1982 Jan 31J; 1983 Feb 13J; 1984 Jan 29J; 1985 Feb 10J/Feb 20J; 1986 Feb 9J; 1987 Feb 8J; 1988 Feb 7J; 1989 Feb 8J

awards and honors: Hall of Fame (HOF) 1987 Feb 5J; 1988 Feb 4J; 1989 Feb 10J; Sampson gets Rupp Trophy 1982 Mar 26J

broadcasting: NCAA TV ratings 1983 Apr 10J

collegiate: All-American teams named 1986 Mar 1J; NCAA sanctions upheld 1988 Dec 12F; NCAA scoring mark set 1985 Jan 3J; NCAA TV ratings 1983 Apr 10J; NCAA women's title tournaments OKd 1981 Jan 13J;

Rutgers wins AIAW title 1982 Mar 28J; Sampson gets Rupp Trophy 1982 Mar 26J

European championships: 1987 Jun 14J

NCAA championships: men: 1980 Mar 24J; 1981 Mar 30J; 1982 Mar 20J/Mar 29J; 1983 Apr 4J; 1984 Apr 2J; 1985 Apr 1J; 1986 Mar 31J; 1987 Mar 30J; 1988 Apr 4J; 1989 Apr 3J; women: 1981 Jan 13J; 1983 Apr 2J; 1984 Apr 1J; 1985 Mar 31J; 1986 Mar 30J; 1987 Mar 29J; 1988 Apr 3J; 1989 Apr 2J

obituaries: Maravich, Pete 1988 Jan 5J

Olympics: pros OKd for '92 games 1989 Apr 7J

professional: Afghanistan team defections 1980 Jun 20J; Olympic participation OKd 1989 Apr 7J; USSR/NBA team game 1987 Oct 25J

records and achievements: NCAA scoring mark 1985 Jan 3J

World championships: 1986 Jul 20J/Aug 17J

Basketball Hall of Fame (Springfield, Mass.) 1987 Feb 5J; 1988 Feb 4J; 1989 Feb 10J

Basque region (Spain)
economy and labor: Bilbao nationalists, police clash 1984 Oct 6B; general strike 1984 Feb 24B

floods: 1983 Aug 26I

government and politics: autonomy policy 1982 Jun 30B; 1983 Aug 10B; coalition regional government formed 1987 Feb 23B; parliament regional elections 1980 Mar 9B; taxation powers granted 1980 Dec 30B

terrorism: consul kidnappings 1981 Feb 19B; extraditions 1984 Sep 26B; Spanish/French cooperation 1984 Jun 15B; Torres assassination 1980 Aug 1B; *see also* ETA

Bass Group Inc., Robert M. 1988 Sep 5H

Bastille Day parade (Paris, France) 1986 Jul 14B

Bathers (Pierre Auguste Renoir) (painting) 1985 Oct 27J

bath houses 1984 Apr 9I/Oct 15F/Nov 28F; 1985 Oct 2F

Bath Iron Works Corp. 1985 Oct 7H; 1987 Nov 4H

Batman (film) 1989 Jun 28J/Jul 2J/Jul 26J/Dec 28J

Batman (Prince) (soundtrack) 1989 Jul 29J/Aug 26J

Battelle Memorial Institute 1988 Dec 21H

batteries 1988 Aug 31F

Battle Cry of Freedom: The Civil War Era (James M. McPherson) (book) 1989 Mar 30J

Bayakoa (racehorse) 1989 Nov 4J

Bayern Munich (West German soccer team) 1987 May 27J

BBC *see* British Broadcasting Corp.

BCCI scandal *see* Bank of Credit & Commerce International Holdings S.A.

Beach Boys (singing group) 1983 Apr 7J

Beaches (film) 1989 Jan 25J

Beaches (soundtrack) 1989 May 27J/Jun 24J

Beach of Falesa, The (Robert Louis Stevenson) (book) 1984 Dec 27J

Beagle Channel dispute (Argentina/Chile) 1980 Dec 12A; 1984 Jan 23D/Oct 18D/Nov 29D; 1985 May 2D

Bearing the Cross: Martin Luther King Jr. and the Southern Christian Leadership Conference (David J. Garrow) 1987 Apr 16J

Beastie Boys (singing group) 1987 Feb 18J/Mar 28J/Apr 25J/May 23J

beatification (Roman Catholic Church) 1988 Nov 20J

Beat It (Michael Jackson) (recording) 1984 Jan 11J/Feb 28J

Beatles (singing group) 1985 Feb 24J/Aug 15J

Beatrice Cos. 1980 Jan 6D; 1985 Oct 14H

Beaufort Sea 1980 Aug 23D/Oct 3H; 1985 Dec 30D

Beauty & the Beat (GoGo's) (recording) 1982 Feb 24J/Mar 14J/Mar 17J/May 5J

Bechtel Group Inc. 1982 Jul 25G; 1983 Sep 13H

Bedouins 1981 Jan 12C/Dec 26C

Beecham Group PLC 1989 Apr 12H

Beech-Nut Nutrition Corp. 1987 Nov 13F

beef 1983 Nov 16E; 1984 Apr 7A/Apr 13E/Sep 5I; 1985 Nov 14I; 1986 Dec 16B; 1987 Jul 21H/Aug 20F; 1988 Jun 24E; 1989 Jan 1B

beepers 1983 Mar 2F

beer 1980 Feb 19H; 1985 Dec 17I; 1987 Mar 12B/Aug 19H; 1989 May 31F/Jul 10B; *see also specific companies (e.g., Schlitz)*

Beetlejuice (film) 1988 Mar 30J/Apr 20J/May 18J

Beijing (China)
church developments: Billy Graham sermon 1988 Apr 17E; Catholic church reopened 1985 Dec 24E

defense and disarmament issues: A-weapons testing protested 1985 Dec 22E

economy: currency black market 1980 Mar 1E; food prices 1985 May 10E; 1988 May 15E

human rights: African student protest 1986 Jun 6E; 1987 Jan 8E; dissident receives rights award 1989 Oct 18A; *New York Times* bureau chief expelled 1986 Jul 23E; rural exiles stage sit-in 1985 Apr 27E

pro-democracy movement: 1986 Dec 23E; 1989 Apr 27E/Apr 29E/May 4E/May 15A/May 17E/May 19E/Jun 3E/Jun 30E/Jul 15E/Aug 31A/Oct 28E; *see also* Tiananmen Square

sports: soccer fans riots 1985 May 19E

Tiananmen Square: 1984 Apr 26A; 1987 Jan 1E; 1989 Apr 22E/May 23E/Jun 4E/Oct 1E

Beijing University 1988 May 4E; 1989 May 6E

Being There (film) 1980 Apr 14J/Apr 23J

Beirut Marine barracks bombing (Beirut, 1983) 1983 Oct 23G-24C/Oct 24G/Oct 26C-27C/Oct 27G/Oct 29G-30G/Nov 10C/Nov 23G/Dec 19G; 1984 Jan 16G/Feb 8G

Beirut refugee camp massacre (Sabra/Shatila)
military operation: Christian militia enter 1982 Sep 16C-18C; death count 1982 Sep 27C; Israeli role 1982 Sep 18C/Sep 22C/Sep

24C/Oct 11C/Oct 31C/Nov 17C; 1983 Jun 20C

reaction: PLO urges Arab League sanctions 1982 Sep 21C; Reagan reaction 1982 Sep 18G; UN resolution condemns 1982 Sep 19A; U.S. Jewish reaction 1982 Sep 22C

Beirut University College 1987 Mar 23C

Beitang Church (Beijing, China) 1985 Dec 24E

Belau, Republic of 1981 Jan 1E

Belco Petroleum Corp. 1985 Dec 27D

Belgian Grand Prix (auto race) 1988 Aug 28J; 1989 Aug 27J

Belgium *see also individual leaders in the name index (e.g., Martens, Wilfried)*

accidents and disasters: ferry boat capsizing 1987 Mar 6B/Apr 8B/Jul 24B/Oct 8B; 1989 Jun 22B; Soviet fighter jet crash 1989 Jul 4B

defense and disarmament issues: antinuclear demonstrations 1983 Oct 23B

foreign relations: Argentina 1982 Apr 7D; China 1984 Jun 16E; European Community 1985 Mar 27B; 1989 Oct 3B; Luxembourg 1984 Jan 23B; Persian Gulf minesweeping 1988 Nov 9C; WEU meeting 1984 Jun 12B; Zaire 1989 Jan 14A

government and politics: budget 1988 Aug 15B; Eyskens sworn premier 1981 Apr 6B; general elections 1981 Nov 8B; 1985 Oct 13B; 1987 Dec 13B; regional power increased 1980 Aug 5B; 1989 Jan 9B; spending cuts 1980 Mar 24B

monetary and trade issues: currency 1982 Feb 22B; IMF funding 1983 Jan 18A; steel industry 1984 Jan 23B; 1985 Mar 27B

obituaries: Claude, Albert 1983 May 22I; Leopold III, King 1983 Sep 25J; Simenon, Georges 1989 Sep 4J

press and broadcasting: regulations opposed 1989 Oct 3B

sports: auto racing 1988 Aug 28J; 1989 Aug 27J; Little League 1984 Aug 21J; soccer 1985 May 29B; 1986 Sep 9B; 1987 Sep 9B; 1989 Apr 28B

terrorism: Ahdul slain 1989 Mar 29A; Boeynants kidnapping 1989 Jan 14B/Feb 13B; Jewish diamond district bombed 1981 Oct 20B; Jewish youths attacked 1980 Jul 27B; Lebanese hostages 1988 Dec 29C; 1989 Jun 15C; synagogue gathering attacked 1982 Sep 18B

U.S. relations: 1981 Dec 22H

Believers, The (film) 1987 Jun 17J

Belize (formerly British Honduras) 1981 Mar 11A/Apr 2D/Sep 7D/Sep 21D; 1982 Mar 28D; 1983 Mar 2D; 1984 Jan 20D/Dec 14D; 1986 Oct 15G; 1989 Sep 4D

Bella Donna (Stevie Nicks) (recording) 1981 Sep 9J/Sep 30J

Bell & Beckwith 1983 Sep 6F

Bell System 1982 Jan 8H; 1983 Mar 10H/Mar 25H/Oct 6H/Nov 21H; 1984 Jan 1H/Nov 21H; 1985 May 28H; 1986 Dec 29H; 1987 Sep 10H

Belmont Stakes (horse race)
winners: 1980 Jun 7J; 1981 Jun 6J; 1982 Jun 5J; 1983 Jun 11J; 1984

Jun 9J; 1985 Jun 8J; 1987 Jun 6J; 1988 Jun 11J; 1989 Jun 10J

Beloved (Toni Morrison) (book) 1987 Oct 23J; 1988 Mar 28J/Mar 31J

Bendectin (drug) 1983 Jun 9I

Bendix Corp. 1982 Mar 8H/Aug 30H/Sep 2H/Sep 6H-Sep 7H/Sep 10H/Sep 15H/Sep 17H/Sep 22H/Sep 24H/Dec 22H

Benin 1983 Jan 17C; 1984 Aug 1C; 1989 Dec 8C

Bennington (Vt.) College 1988 Aug 7F

benoxaprofen (drug) 1982 Jul 22I

Benson (TV show) 1985 Sep 12J

Bensonhurst (New York) 1989 Aug 23F/Sep 2F

benzene 1983 Mar 31H/Dec 16H; 1985 Dec 3H; 1987 Jun 24H/Sep 1H; 1988 Jul 20H

Bergen-Belsen (Nazi death camp) 1985 Apr 19G/May 5B

Bering Strait 1987 Aug 7J

Berkeley Barb, The (newspaper) 1980 Jul 3J

Berlin *see* Berlin Wall; West Berlin

Berlin Game (Len Deighton) (book) 1984 Jan 20J/Feb 10J

Berlin Wall 1985 May 21B; 1986 Aug 13B/Nov 24B; 1987 May 6B/Jun 12B/Dec 9B; 1989 Nov 9B

Bermuda 1989 Feb 9D

Berne Convention for the Protection of Literary and Artistic Works 1988 Oct 31H

Berry Gordy's The Last Dragon (film) 1985 Apr 17J

Best Little Whorehouse in Texas (film) 1982 Aug 11J

"best price" rule 1986 Jul 8H

Betamax (recording system) 1988 Jan 11E

Bethlehem Steel Corp. 1984 Jan 24H; 1985 May 2H; 1986 May 26H; 1989 Mar 7H/May 5H

Betrayed (film) 1988 Aug 31J/Sep 21J

Better Be Good to Me (Tina Turner) (recording) 1985 Feb 26J

Bet Twice (racehorse) 1987 Jun 6J

beverages *see specific companies, beverages*

Beverly Hills Cop (film) 1984 Dec 12J; 1985 Jan 16J/Feb 13F/Mar 20J

Beverly Hills Cop (soundtrack) 1985 Mar 30J/Apr 27J/May 25J/Jun 22J

Beverly Hills Cop II (film) 1987 Jun 17J

Beyond the Limit (film) 1983 Oct 12J

B.F. Goodrich Co. 1982 Apr 19H

B-52 (aircraft) 1986 Nov 28G/Dec 5G

Bhopal gas disaster (India) (1984)
chronology: pesticide plant toxic leak 1984 Dec 3E; residents evacuated 1984 Dec 13E; Gandhi visits 1984 Dec 4E; anniversary marked 1985 Dec 2E

liability issues: government suits 1984 Dec 30E; 1985 Apr 8E; 1986 Nov 22E; Union Carbide murder charges filed 1987 Dec 1E; Union Carbide officials arrested 1988 Nov 15E; Union Carbide plant protest bombing 1984 Dec 6B; Union Carbide reports 1985 Mar 20E; 1988 May 10E; U.S court actions 1985 Feb 6A; 1986 May 12E

victim compensation: government payments to heirs 1989 May 9E; government suits 1984 Dec 30E; 1985 Apr 8E; 1986 Nov 22E;

Union Carbide payments 1987 Dec 17E; 1988 Apr 4E; 1989 Feb 14E/Feb 24E; Union Carbide plan rejected 1986 Mar 24E

Bhutan 1988 Oct 10A

Bible, The 1983 Oct 14J; 1989 Feb 6B

Bibliotheque Nationale (French national library) 1987 Nov 22B

bicycle racing *see* cycling; *specific races (e.g., Le Mans)*

bid-rigging 1984 Jan 23H; 1987 Aug 18F; 1989 Nov 23E

Big (film) 1988 Jun 3J/Jun 15J/Jul 13J

"Big Bang" (astronomy) 1980 Jan 20I/Oct 14I; 1985 Jul 14I; 1989 Nov 18I

"Big Bang" (British stock deregulation) 1986 Oct 27B

Big Business (film) 1988 Jun 15J

Big Chill, The (film) 1983 Oct 12J/Nov 2J/Dec 7J

Big Deal (musical) 1986 Apr 10J

Big Easy, The (film) 1987 Sep 9J

Bigger and Deffer (L.L. Cool J) (recording) 1987 Aug 22J

Big River: The Adventures of Huckleberry Finn (musical) 1985 Apr 25J/Jun 2J

Bikini atoll (U.S. territory) 1985 Mar 13I

bilingual education 1985 Sep 26F; 1988 May 5F

Billie Jean (Michael Jackson) (recording) 1983 Apr13J; 1984 Jan 11J

Billionaire Boys Club 1987 Apr 22F; 1988 Jan 25F

Bill of Rights 1987 Jul 29J

Bill & Ted's Excellent Adventure (film) 1989 Feb 22J

Billy Bathgate (E.L. Doctorow) (book) 1989 Mar 31J/Apr 28J

Biloxi Blues (Neil Simon) (play/film) 1985 Mar 28J/Jun 2J; 1988 Apr 20J

binary weapons 1983 Sep 15G/Nov 8G

Bingham family 1986 May 19H

biochemistry 1984 Oct 20I; 1985 Sep 6I; 1986 Mar 4I/Jul 24I/Oct 13I/Oct 22I/Oct 23I; 1987 Nov 28I

Biogen 1980 Jan 16I

Biologics 1986 Apr 3I

biomedical science 1983 May 11I; 1985 Mar 19F/Nov 20F; 1987 Mar 9I; 1988 Feb 11I; *see also* genetic engineering

Bipartisan Budget Appeal 1984 May 3H

birds 1986 May 2I

Birmingham (Alabama) 1981 Mar 1H

Birmingham pub bombings (England) (1974) 1988 Jan 28B

birth certificates 1985 Oct 19J

birth control
Dalkon Shield liability: 1983 Jun 6I; 1984 Feb 29F/Oct 22H/Nov 14H; 1985 Apr 2H/Aug 21H; 1987 May 11F/Dec 11F; 1988 Oct 7F

education: experimental school program 1986 Jul 8F; public service announcements 1985 Aug 1C

family issues: NAS backs teenage use 1986 Dec 9F; parental notification 1983 Jan 10F/Feb 14F/Feb 18F/Jul 8F; teenage pregnancy rate 1985 Mar 12F

foreign developments: Australia 1986 Mar 6I; Great Britain 1985 Oct 17B; Ireland 1985 Feb 20B; US AID funds 1985 Jul 9A

health risks: cancer study 1983 Mar 25I; 1989 Sep 6I; cervical cap approved 1988 May 23I; injury law-

suits 1988 Sep 9F; spermicide risks 1981 Apr 3I
RU 486 controversy: 1986 Dec 18I; 1987 Oct 2I; 1988 Oct 26I/Oct 28I
surveys: 1984 Dec 5F

birth defects 1980 Jan 3I/Apr 3I; 1983 Jun 9I; 1984 Aug 16G; 1988 May 26I/Sep 21I

births and birth rates *see* childbirth

Bir Zeit University (West Bank) 1983 Jan 20C

BIS *see* Bank for International Settlements

bisexuality 1987 May 6J; 1988 Jun 3I

Bitburg (West German military cemetery) 1985 Apr 11G/Apr 16G/Apr 18G/Apr 19G/Apr 20B/Apr 30B/May 5B

Bitter Creek National Wildlife Refuge (California) 1987 Apr 19I

Black, Maroons and White (Mark Rothko) (painting) 1983 Nov 9J

Black Americans *see also individual leaders in the name index (e.g., King Jr., Martin Luther)*
arts and culture: Miss America 1989 Sep 16J; Morrison award issue 1988 Jan 24J; motion pictures 1989 Dec 14J; opera 1985 Jan 3J; Twain letter 1985 Mar 14J; Wright honored 1985 Nov 28J
awards and honors: Morrison bypassed 1988 Jan 24J; Rosa Parks wins Martin Luther King award 1980 Jan 28J
census data: birth certificates 1985 Oct 19J; population 1981 Feb 23F; poverty rates 1985 Jun 3F; 1989 Jul 27F; white perceptions 1989 Jan 12F
crime and law enforcement: Bensonhurst teen slain 1989 Aug 23F/Sep 2F; Brawley case 1988 Feb 29F/Oct 6F; 1989 Apr 27F; Calif drug kingpin funeral 1986 Aug 29F; Dartmouth punishes harassment 1988 Mar 10F; Geter case 1983 Dec 14F; 1984 Mar 26F; imprisonment rates 1985 Jul 28F; jury exclusion 1986 Apr 30F; Ku Klux Klan 1983 Dec 19F; 1984 May 17F; 1987 Feb 12F; mail bombs kill 2 1989 Dec 18F; police brutality 1985 Nov 24F
economy: business ownership 1983 Apr 30J/May 3H; 1984 May 8H; consumer boycotts 1986 May 1F
education: Alabama desegregation suit 1983 Jul 11F; Cincinnati desegregation plan 1984 Feb 16F; college enrollment 1985 May 29F; 1989 Jan 15F; Dartmouth punishes harassment 1988 Mar 10F; Georgia college graduation test 1984 Jun 2F; Harvard course boycott 1982 Aug 27F; high school dropout rate 1989 Sep 14F; Howard bias suit 1983 Jul 22F; increased segregation in 1982 Sep 5F; "Ole Miss" Confederate flag cotroversy 1983 Apr 20J; SAT scores 1982 Oct 4F; 1985 Sep 23F; Spelman College contribution 1988 Nov 4F
employment
affirmative action plans: 1984 Jan 17F; 1986 May 19F; 1987 Feb 25F/Mar 23F
discrimination: Cook County welfare workers 1984 Feb 20F; FBI 1988 Jan 25F; 1989 Jun 30F; federal worker counter-suit 1983 Apr 1F; General Motors 1989 Jan 31F; Honda of Amer-

ica 1988 Mar 23H; *New York Daily News* 1987 Jun 10F
family issues: children's plight studied 1985 Jun 3F
foreign issues: Japan premier 1988 Jul 23E; South Africa 1984 Nov 21G/Dec 3G
housing: Yonkers (New York) controversy 1985 Nov 20F; 1988 Jan 25F/Aug 2F/Sep 10F
medicine and health care: AIDS 1986 Oct 23I; infant mortality rate 1983 Mar 15I; life expectancy 1988 Dec 15F
military issues: racial imbalance 1982 Jun 27F; Robinson promoted 1982 Aug 11G
obituaries: Ailey, Alvin 1989 Dec 1J; Ashford, Emmet 1980 Mar 1J; Baldwin, James 1987 Nov 30J; Bearden, Romare 1988 Mar 12J; Blake, Eubie 1983 Feb 12J; Bowen, Billy 1982 Sep 27J; Bricktop 1984 Jan 31J; Brown, Sterling Allen 1989 Jan 13J; Clark, Mamie 1983 Aug 11J; Fetchit, Stepin 1985 Nov 19J; Gaye, Marvin 1984 Apr 1J; Harris, Patricia Roberts 1985 Mar 23F; Hicks, James L. 1986 Jan 19J; Hill, Abram 1986 Oct 6J; Himes, Chester 1984 Nov 12J; Hurley, Ruby 1980 Aug 9F; King Sr., Martin Luther 1984 Nov 11F; McCree Jr., Wade Hampton 1987 Aug 30J; Mitchell, Clarence M. 1984 Mar 18J; Nixon, E. D. 1987 Feb 25F; Owens, Jesse 1980 Mar 31J; Paige, Satchel 1982 Jul 8J; Pollard, Fritz 1986 May 11J; Redding, J. Saunders 1988 Mar 2F; Rustin, Bayard 1987 Aug 24F; Smith, Muriel 1985 Sep 13J; Smith, Willi 1987 Apr 17J; Van Der Zee, James 1983 May 15J; Ward, Theodore 1983 May 8J; Washington, Chester 1983 Aug 31J; Washington, Harold 1987 Nov 25F; Watson, Barbara 1983 Feb 17F; Wilson, Teddy 1986 Jul 31J
politics and government
congress: Gray elected House budget committee chairman 1985 Jan 4F
Democratic National Committee: Brown elected chairman 1989 Feb 10F
elections: Bussey elected Little Rock mayor 1981 Nov 25F; Chicago city council elections 1985 Dec 30F; 1986 Mar 18F; Cleveland mayoral primaries 1989 Oct 3F; Dinkins elected NYC mayor 1989 Feb 14F/Nov 7F; Goode elected Philadelphia mayor 1983 Nov 8F; Morial reelected New Orleans mayor 1982 Mar 20F; Plaquemines Parish (La.) council 1983 Feb 26F; Sawyer selected acting mayor in Chicago 1987 Dec 2F; Washington elected Chicago mayor 1983 Apr 12F; Wilder elected Virginia governor 1989 Nov 7F
federal appointments: Lucas gets civil rights post 1989 May 9F; Powell named national security adviser 1987 Nov 5G; Powell to head Joint Chiefs 1989 Aug 10G; rights commission chairman controversy 1985 Mar 5F; senior federal positions 1987 Mar 22F

presidential campaign (1984): 1983 Jun 20F
Republican National Committee: 1986 Jun 8F/Jun 26F/Oct 7F/Oct 20F; 1987 Jul 23F
voting issues: city/suburb annexation plan 1987 Jan 21F; congressional redistricting 1984 Nov 13F; eligibility challenges 1986 Oct 7F/Oct 20F; 1987 Jul 23F; fraud 1984 Apr 13F; 1985 Jul 5F/Nov 14F; runoff election laws 1985 Aug 13F
rights issues: anniversary marked 1985 Mar 7F; Lucas gets rights post 1989 May 9F; rights commission chairman controversy 1985 Mar 5F; UN Commission on Human Rights 1987 Mar 11A
riots: Miami 1980 May 17F/May 19F/May 22F/Jun 9F/Jul 15F/Dec 6F; 1982 Dec 28F; 1989 Jan 16F
space program: 1983 Sep 5I; 1987 Jun 5I
sports: baseball 1987 Mar 3J; figure skating 1985 Feb 2J; 1986 Feb 8J/Mar 21J; football 1989 Jan 29J; Frank named NCAA president 1981 Jan 13J; tennis 1985 Jul 13J
welfare and social services: children's plight studied 1985 Jun 3F; poverty rates 1985 Jun 3F; 1989 Jul 27F

Black and Blue (musical) 1989 Jun 4J

Black and White Children in America: Key Facts (Children's Defense Fund) 1985 Jun 3F

Black Economic Agenda, Council for *see* Council for a Black Economic Agenda

black hole (astronomy) 1985 Jun 7I; 1987 Jul 26I

Black Liberation Army 1982 Jan 9F/Jan 20F

black-lung disease 1981 Mar 9F; 1988 Dec 6F

Black Muslims 1980 Jul 23F

Black Panthers 1986 Jun 27F; 1988 Mar 10F

Black Rain (film) 1989 Sep 27J/Oct 25J

Black Sea 1984 May 26B; 1986 Mar 18B/Sep 1B; 1988 Feb 12B

Black September (Palestinian group) 1981 Aug 1C

Black Stallion, The (film) 1980 Apr 23J

Black Widow (film) 1987 Feb 18J

bladder cancer 1980 Mar 6I; 1988 Jun 8H

Blade Runner (film) 1982 Jul 7J

Blair House (Washington, D.C.) 1981 Oct 23J

Blame It on Rio (film) 1984 Mar 7J

Blessings (Belva Plain) (book) 1989 Aug 25J

blimps 1986 Jul 1G

Blind Date (film) 1987 Apr 15J

blizzards *see* snowstorms and blizzards

BL Ltd. (formerly British Leyland) 1980 Dec 31B

blood alcohol tests 1983 Feb 22F

blood banks 1984 Nov 15I; 1986 Jul 9I/Aug 26I/Nov 14I

Blood Banks, American Association of *see* American Association of Blood Banks

blood clots 1980 May 1I; 1986 Mar 10I; 1987 Nov 13I; 1988 Aug 13I; 1989 Mar 9I

blood pressure 1982 Sep 3I; 1984 Nov 11I; 1985 Feb 25H

blood tests
AIDS *see* AIDS
alcohol: 1983 Feb 22F
cancer: 1981 Jan 12I
Down's syndrome: 1989 Nov 22I
radiation: 1986 Nov 23I

blood transfusions 1983 Mar 3I; 1984 Jan 11I; 1987 Mar 19I/Jun 9F; 1989 Oct 5I

Blow Out (film) 1981 Jul 29J

Blue City (film) 1986 May 14J

Blue Cross and Blue Shield Association 1984 Jun 13F

Blue Ribbon Commission on Defense Management 1986 Apr 2G

Blues Brothers, The (film) 1980 Jul 2J

Blue Velvet (film) 1986 Sep 19J; 1987 Jan 4J

B'nai B'rith International 1982 Sep 22C; 1984 Sep 6F

BNL scandal *see* Banca Nazionale del Lavoro

Bobbie Brooks Inc. 1980 Dec 21H

Bob Hope Special (TV show) 1984 Dec 16J

Bob Seger & the Silver Bullet Band (singing group) 1980 Apr 2J/Apr 30J/Jun 4J/Jul 9J; 1981 Sep 30J/Nov 11J; 1986 May 21J/Jun 18J

BOC Challenge (boat race) 1987 May 7J

Bodo tribe (India) 1989 Aug 12E

Body Double (film) 1984 Nov 7J

Body Heat (film) 1981 Sep 30J

Boeing Co.
contract and billing issues: 727 discontinued 1984 Aug 14H; cruise missile 1980 Mar 25G; 1981 Jun 29G; space station 1987 Dec 1I
labor issues: machinists' strike 1989 Oct 4H/Nov 21H
safety and security issues: aging aircraft repairs ordered 1989 May 18H; airplane crashes 1983 Nov 27D; 1985 Aug 12E; 1989 Nov 27D; emergency landings 1983 Jul 29D

Bofors arms scandal 1989 Jul 23E

Boise Cascade Corp. 1986 Aug 25H

Bolero (film) 1984 Sep 12J

Bolivia *see also individual leaders in the name index (e.g., Paz Zamora, Jaime)*
archaeology: 1989 Nov 11I
church developments: churches raided, priests missing 1980 Jul 23D; papal visits 1988 May 7J; rights abuses charged 1980 Sep 10D
civil strife: coups and coup attempts 1980 Jun 9D/Jul 17D/Jul 29D; 1981 Jun 27D/Aug 8D; 1984 Jun 30D/Jul 2E; political repression 1980 Jul 23D; state of seige 1985 Sep 19D; 1986 Aug 28D; 1989 Nov 15D; Zarate Willka arrested 1989 Jun 30D
defense and armed forces: military command replaced 1982 Oct 11D
drug trafficking: 1980 Aug 13G; 1981 Aug 29D; 1986 Jan 11D/Jul 15D/Aug 14D/Nov 15D; 1987 Sep 21D
economy: currency 1987 Jan 1D; foreign investment 1985 Sep 16D; inflation rate 1985 Feb 9D
foreign debt: 1980 Sep 3D; 1984 May 30D/Jun 21D/Sep 14D; 1985 Feb 8D

government and politics: military junta takes power 1982 Jul 19D; Paz Zamora inaugurated president 1989 Aug 6D; president al elections 1980 Jun 29D/Jul 9D; 1985 Jul 15D/Aug 5D; 1989 May 7D; Sanchez de Lozada nominated president 1988 Sep 4D; Siles Zuazo installed president 1982 Oct 10D; Vidoso Calderon as president 1982 Jul 29D/Sep 17D
human rights: 1980 Sep 10D
labor issues: compulsory government service 1980 Aug 1D; general strikes 1982 Sep 18D; 1984 Dec 4D; 1985 Mar 24D/Sep 19D; hunger strikes 1987 Apr 1D; miners' strike 1985 Oct 2D; teachers' strike 1989 Nov 15D
monetary and trade issues: currency 1987 Jan 1D; foreign investment 1985 Sep 16D; IMF loans 1981 Aug 15D; 1986 Jun 20D/Dec 16D; 1987 Jul 16D/Jul 23D
Nazis: 1983 Jan 15D/Jan 25D/Feb 4B
obituaries: Patino, Antenor 1982 Feb 2D
U.S. relations: 1980 Aug 13G; 1983 Aug 11G; 1986 Aug 14D/Nov 15D; 1987 Sep 21D

Bollingen Prize (poetry) 1985 Jan 15J; 1987 Feb 10J

Bolshevik Revolution (1917) 1989 Nov 7B

Bolsheviks 1988 Feb 5B

Bolshoi Ballet 1980 Feb 5J

Bolt (Dick Francis) (book) 1987 Mar 27J

Bombardier Inc. 1986 Aug 18D

bomb detectors 1989 Aug 30H

Bonanno crime group 1987 Aug 26F

B-1 (aircraft) 1981 Jun 30G/Nov 18G; 1982 Jan 20G/Jun 16G; 1983 Sep 15G; 1984 Aug 29G/Sep 4G; 1986 Dec 3G

bone cancer 1983 Sep 21F

bone marrow 1986 Jul 17I

Bone People, The (Keri Hulme) (book) 1985 Oct 31J

Bonfire of the Vanities, The (Tom Wolfe) (book) 1987 Dec 18J; 1988 Jan 29J/Feb 26J/Mar 25J/Apr 29J/May 27J/Jun 24J/Jul 23J

Bon Jovi (singing group) 1986 Oct 22J/Nov 22J/Dec 17J; 1987 Jan 28J/Feb 18J/Mar 28J/Apr 25J/May 23J/Jun 27J; 1988 Oct 29J/Nov 26J/Dec 31J

Bonn, University of (West Germany) 1989 Oct 12I

Booker Prize (literature) 1985 Oct 31J; 1986 Oct 22J; 1987 Oct 29J; 1988 Oct 26J; 1989 Oct 26J

Book Industry Study Group 1984 Apr 11J

Book of Laughter and Forgetting, The (Milan Kundera) (book) 1985 Jan 9J

books *see individual titles (e.g., Cujo); specific authors in the name index (e.g., King, Stephen)*

Bophuthatswana (South African homeland) 1986 Jan 6C

Border, The (film) 1982 Feb 17J

Border Relief Operation, U.N. 1988 May 1E

Born in the U.S.A. (Bruce Springsteen) (recording) 1984 Jul 21J/Aug 25J/Sep 22J/Oct 27J/Nov 24J/Dec 22J; 1985 Jan 26J/Feb 23J/Mar 30J/Apr 27J/May 25J/Jun 22J/Jul 27J/Sep 28J

Born on the Fourth of July (film) 1989 Dec 20J

Bosporus Strait 1985 Apr 27B

Boston (Massachusetts) 1980 Dec 7H; 1982 May 4A; 1985 Sep 3F; 1987 Sep 28F; 1988 Mar 29H/Jun 9I/Oct 12H/Dec 28F; 1989 May 31F

Boston (singing group) 1986 Oct 22J/Nov 22J/Dec 17J; 1987 Jan 28J

Boston Athletic Association 1985 Jul 15J

Boston Bruins (ice hockey team) 1988 May 26J

Boston Celtics (basketball team) 1981 May 14J; 1984 Jun 12J; 1985 May 27J/Jun 3J/Jun 9J; 1986 May 28J/Jun 8J/Jun 19J; 1987 Jun 14J

Boston College (Massachusetts) 1981 Nov 23J; 1984 Dec 1J; 1985 Jan 1J/Dec 11J

Boston Edison Co. 1982 Jan 29I

Boston Globe (newspaper) 1984 Apr 16J; 1988 Oct 23G

Boston Herald American (newspaper) 1982 Sep 7J/Dec 20H

Boston Marathon 1980 Mar 21J/Apr 29J; 1981 Apr 20J; 1982 Apr 19J; 1985 Apr 15J/Jul 15J; 1986 Apr 21J; 1987 Apr 20J; 1988 Apr 18J; 1989 Apr 17J

Boston Pops Orchestra 1980 Jan 10J; 1982 Apr 11J

Boston Red Sox (baseball team) 1980 Dec 6J; 1984 Sep 28J/Oct 15J/Oct 27J/Nov 13J/Nov 18J; 1987 Nov 11J; 1988 Oct 2J/Oct 9J; 1989 Jan 9J

Boston Symphony 1987 Oct 14F

Boston University (Massachusetts) 1984 Nov 27I; 1986 Sep 30H; 1987 Dec 8F; 1989 Jun 13F/Sep 6F

Botswana 1980 Apr 1C/Jul 13C/Jul 18C; 1982 Apr 30C; 1983 Mar 18I; 1985 Jun 14C; 1986 Feb 13C/May 19C; 1988 Sep 19J

Bougainville (Papua New Guinea) 1989 Apr 10E

Boundary Waters Canoe Area (Minnesota/Ontario) 1980 Feb 2I

Bounty, The (film) 1984 May 9J

Bourne Conspiracy, The (Robert Ludlum) (book) 1986 Jul 18J

Bourne Identity, The (Robert Ludlum) (book) 1980 Mar 9J/Apr 6J/May 4J/Jun 8J/Jul 13J/Aug 17J

Bourne Supremacy, The (Robert Ludlum) (book) 1986 Mar 28J/Apr 25J/May 30J/Jun 27J

Bowbelle (ship) 1989 Aug 20B

bowling 1989 Mar 18J

Boys of Summer, The (Don Henley) (recording) 1986 Feb 25J

BP *see* British Petroleum Co.

Bradley Fighting Vehicles 1987 Jan 21G

Bradley University (Peoria, Illinois) 1982 Mar 24J

Brain (Robin Cook) (book) 1981 Mar 8J/Apr 12J

brain cancer 1980 Jul 24H

Brainstorm (film) 1983 Oct 12J

brainwashing 1988 Oct 4D

Braniff International Corp. 1982 Mar 10H/Apr 26H/May 13H; 1989 Nov 6H

Brasilsat-1 (satellite) 1985 Feb 8I

Brave Raj (racehorse) 1986 Nov 1J

Brazil *see also individual leaders in the name index (e.g., Sarney Costa, Jose)*
accidents and disasters: nuclear accidents 1987 Oct 6D/Oct 28D; steamer capsizes 1981 Jan 6D

arts and culture: Niemeyer awarded Pritzker prize 1988 May 24J; Welles documentary found 1986 Aug 27J

church developments: liberation theology criticized by Vatican 1984 Sep 3J; papal visit 1980 Jun 30J

demonstrations and protests: 1984 Jan 25D; 1986 Nov 27D

economy: arms sales 1981 Aug 9D; 1984 Oct 9A; capital controls 1989 Aug 24D; growth plan 1987 Apr 2D; inflation-fighting measures 1987 Feb 5D; 1989 Jan 15D/Jun 14D; inflation rate 1988 Dec 31D; land reform 1980 Feb 5D

energy issues: hydroelectric projects 1982 Nov 5I; 1984 Oct 25D; 1989 Feb 20D; nuclear accidents 1987 Oct 6D/Oct 28D; nuclear power plants 1982 Mar 16D

environmental issues: Amazon rain forests 1989 Feb 4D/Mar 3A

foreign debt: 1980 Mar 5D; 1984 Jan 27D/Jun 21D/Sep 14D; 1985 Feb 8D/Jul 4D; 1986 Sep 6D/Dec 24D; 1987 Jan 21D/Feb 20D/Apr 1D/Apr 13D/Jul 1D/Sep 9D/Sep 25D/Nov 6D/Nov 26D/Dec 10D; 1988 Mar 4D/Nov 2D; 1989 Jan 2D

foreign relations: France 1981 Jan 31A; Italy 1983 Apr 30A; Japan 1989 Mar 3A; Libya 1983 Apr 30A/Jun 8A; Saudi Arabia 1984 Oct 9A; USSR 1981 Jul 15A

government and politics: budget 1980 Dec 17D; Collor de Mello wins presidential elections 1989 Dec 20D; constituent assembly 1987 Feb 1D; 1988 Jul 27D; constitution put into effect 1988 Oct 5D; Neves elected president 1985 Jan 15D; opposition political parties merge 1982 Mar 3D; presidential chief of staff resigns 1981 Aug 6D; Sarney becomes president 1985 Mar 15D/Apr 21D

human rights: 1981 Feb 19D; 1983 Jan 13D; 1988 May 13D; 1989 Feb 7G

labor issues: 1983 Jul 21D; 1985 Jun 3D; 1987 Mar 10D; 1989 Apr 27D

Latin relations: Argentina 1980 May 17D; 1986 Dec 10D; Cuba 1986 Jun 25D; Ecuador 1981 Mar 6D; Mexico 1983 Apr 29D; Nicaragua 1986 Mar 17D; Paraguay 1989 Feb 5D; Peru 1981 Mar 6D

medicine and health care: AIDS 1987 Feb 24D; polio campaign 1980 Apr 16I

monetary and trade issues: arms sales 1981 Aug 9D; 1984 Oct 9A; coffee talks collapse 1989 Oct 3A; currency 1983 Feb 18D; IMF loans 1982 Dec 15D; 1983 Feb 28D/Jul 13D/Jul 18D/Sep 15D/Sep 26D; 1985 Jul 4D; 1987 Nov 6D; manufactured goods exports 1982 Apr 9D; telecommunications satellites 1985 Feb 8I

native rights: 1988 Mar 28D/Jun 1D/May 13D; 1989 Feb 20D

Nazis: 1985 Jun 21A

obituaries: Drummond de Andrade, Carlos 1987 Aug 17J; Freyre, Gilberto 1987 Jul 18D; Mendes, Chico 1988 Dec 22D

sports: auto racing 1985 Apr 7J; 1986 Mar 23J; 1987 Apr 12J; 1988 Jan 31J/Apr 3J; 1989 Mar 26J; May 28J; soccer host nation bid lost 1988 Jul 4J

U.S. relations: 1981 Dec 22H; 1982 Dec 1D; 1983 Sep 30D; 1986 Mar 17D; 1987 Nov 13G; 1988 Feb 29D/Jul 22H; 1989 May 25H/Jun 1A

Brazil (film) 1985 Dec 14J

Brazilian Grand Prix (auto race) 1985 Apr 7J; 1986 Mar 23J; 1987 Apr 12J; 1988 Apr 3J; 1989 Mar 26J

bread 1981 Oct 17B; 1982 Aug 1D; 1983 Nov 12B; 1984 Jan 6C/Jan 22C; 1987 Jul 20B

Breakfast Club, The (film) 1985 Mar 20J

Breakin' (film) 1984 May 9J/Jun 6J

Break In (Dick Francis) (book) 1986 Apr 25J

Break of Dawn (ship) 1987 May 16H

breast cancer
genetic factors: 1980 Mar 29I; 1987 May 21I
mammograms: 1983 Aug 2I
mortality rates: 1985 Feb 8I
risk factors: 1982 Oct 17I; 1983 Mar 25I; 1984 Nov 28I; 1986 Jan 9I; 1987 May 7I; 1989 Aug 3I
treatment: 1981 Jul 1I; 1984 Dec 4I; 1985 Mar 14I; 1988 May 21I

Breast Cancer Society, American *see* American Breast Cancer Society

breast feeding 1984 Dec 19A

breath analyzer tests 1980 Dec 10B

Breathe (singing group) 1988 Nov 26J

Breathing Lessons (Anne Tyler) (book) 1988 Oct 21J; 1989 Jan 27J/Mar 30J

Breathless (film) 1983 Jul 18J

Breeders' Cup Classic (horse race) 1985 Nov 2J; 1986 Nov 1J; 1987 Nov 21J; 1988 Nov 5J; 1989 Nov 4J

Brendan Byrne Arena (East Rutherford, N.J.) 1982 Jan 31J

Bridgeport (Connecticut) 1987 Apr 23J/Oct 24H

bridges
anniversaries: Brooklyn Bridge (New York City) 1983 May 24J; Golden Gate (San Francisco) 1987 May 24F
construction issues: Oklahoma kickbacks 1981 Nov 19F; Rio Grande 1981 Jan 5D
demonstrations and protests: Crow Indian blockade (Montana) 1981 Aug 20F; St. Lawrence Seaway blockade 1984 Dec 9I
foreign developments: El Salvador 1983 May 25D/Sep 3D; Japan 1988 Apr 10E; Lebanon 1981 Jul 16C; Nicaragua 1983 Aug 25D; Turkey 1985 Apr 27B
safety and service issues: in fragile coastal areas 1987 Mar 23H; repair bill 1982 Dec 7H

Brigade Hector Riobe (Haitian exile group) 1983 Jan 2D

Brigham Young University (Provo, Utah) 1985 Jan 3J; 1986 Nov 29J; 1989 Dec 5J

Brighton Beach Memoirs (Neil Simon) (play) 1983 Jun 5J

Brighton bombing (1984) 1984 Oct 12B; 1986 Jun 10B

Bright Shining Lie, A: John Paul Vann and America in Vietnam (Neil Sheehan) (book) 1988 Nov 29J; 1989 Mar 30J

Bring on the Night (Sting) (recording) 1988 Mar 2J

Brink's robbery (1981) (Rockland County, N.Y.) 1981 Oct 20F/Oct 23F; 1982 Jan 9F/Jan 20F/Jan 28F; 1983

Sep 14F/Dec 16F; 1984 Feb 18F/May 3F/Jun 14F/Nov 29F; 1985 May 11F

Bristol-Meyers Co. 1986 Jun 20H

Bristol University (Great Britain) 1988 Apr 29B

British Academy of Film and Television Arts 1980 Aug 18J; 1986 Mar 16J; 1987 Mar 22J; 1988 Mar 20J; 1989 Mar 19J

British Aerospace PLC (BAe) 1985 Jun 1A

British Airtours 1985 Aug 22B

British Airways PLC (BA) 1985 Sep 25B; 1986 Sep 11B

British Broadcasting Corp. (BBC) 1983 Jan 7B; 1985 Aug 7B/Aug 19B; 1987 Feb 1B/Dec 3B

British Coal Corp. 1986 Sep 23B

British Columbia (Canada) 1984 Nov 1D; 1985 Jan 10D; 1986 Feb 20I/May 2D/Oct 8D/Dec 5D; 1987 Jan 5D/Mar 26D/Jun 1D/Jul 11D; 1988 Mar 7D; 1989 May 4D/Nov 23D

British Gas PLC 1988 Mar 1E

British Grand Prix (auto race) 1985 Jul 21J; 1986 Jul 13J; 1987 Jul 12J; 1988 Jul 10J

British Leyland Ltd. *see* BL Ltd.

British Meteorological Office 1989 Feb 3I

British Museum 1983 May 13B

British National Oil Corp. 1983 Mar 30A; 1984 Oct 18A

British Nuclear Fuels Ltd. 1985 Jul 23B

British Olympic Association 1980 Mar 25J

British Open (golf tournament) 1980 Jul 20J; 1981 Jul 19J; 1982 Jul 18J; 1983 Jul 17J; 1984 Jul 22J; 1985 Jul 21J; 1986 Jul 20J; 1987 Jul 19J; 1988 Jul 18J

British Petroleum Co. (BP) 1983 Jul 25B; 1987 Oct 29B

British Rail Corp. 1982 Feb 18B; 1986 Jul 26B; 1988 Jul 14B

British Shipbuilders PLC 1986 May 14B

British Steel Corp. 1980 Jan 2B/Feb 3B/Apr 1B

British Telecommunications PLC 1982 Jul 19B; 1984 Nov 21B

broadcasting *see specific broadcast medium (e.g., radio); individual networks (e.g., American Broadcasting Co.); specific shows (e.g., 60 Minutes)*

Broadcast News (film) 1987 Dec 16J; 1988 Jan 20J

Broadway Album, The (Barbra Streisand) (recording) 1985 Dec 21J; 1986 Jan 29J/Feb 19J; 1987 Feb 24J

Broadway Bound (Neil Simon) (play) 1986 Dec 4J; 1987 Jun 7J

Broadway Danny Rose (film) 1984 Feb 8J

Broken Rainbows (film) 1986 Apr 11J

brokerage firms 1981 Jun 8D; 1982 May 6H/Jul 7H/Oct 20H; 1984 Jun 28H; 1986 Oct 27B/Nov 4H; 1987 Jan 14F/Jul 7H; 1989 Jun 9D; *see also specific companies (e.g., Merrill Lynch)*

Bronx, N.Y., armored car robbery (1982) *see* Sentry Armored Courier Corp.

Bronze Age 1984 Dec 4I

Brookings Institution (Washington, D.C.) 1982 Jun 27F; 1983 Sep 8H; 1985 Jan 23H

Brooklyn Academy of Music (New York City) 1987 Oct 13J

Brooklyn Bridge (New York City) 1983 May 24J

Brotherhood of Locomotive Engineers (BLE) (unaffiliated) 1982 Jul 8H

Brothers in Arms (Dire Straits) 1985 Aug 24J/Sep 28J/Oct 26J/Nov 30J

Browning-Ferris Industries Inc. 1987 Apr 28H

brown lung disease *see* byssinosis

Browns Ferry nuclear power plant 1983 Jan 16H

Brown University (Providence, R.I.) 1984 Oct 11J

Brubaker (film) 1980 Jul 2J

Bruce Hornsby & the Range (singing group) 1986 Dec 17J; 1987 Jan 28J/Feb 18J/Feb 24J/Mar 28J

Bruce Springsteen & the E Street Band (Bruce Springsteen) (recording) 1986 Dec 17J

Bruder Schweigen (Silent Brotherhood) (neo-Nazi group) 1985 Apr 15F/Dec 30F; 1986 Feb 6F

Brunei 1984 Jan 1C/Feb 23C; 1986 Jun 23E/Nov 19C/Dec 24G; 1987 Jan 23G/Sep 20H/Dec 14E; 1989 Sep 11J

Brussels (Belgium) 1989 Jan 9B

bubble chambers 1980 Jan 31I

"bubble" policy 1984 Jun 25H; 1986 Nov 19H

Buchenwald (Nazi death camp) 1985 Apr 13B

buckles 1988 Nov 10H

Buddhist monks 1988 Mar 5E/Sep 24E

budget, U.S. federal
fiscal year 1980: 1980 Jul 8G/Sep 30H; 1981 May 12F
fiscal year 1981: administration actions 1980 Jan 28H/Mar 14H/Mar 31H/Apr 27G; congressional actions 1980 Feb 27H/Jun 12H/Nov 20H
fiscal year 1982: administration actions 1981 Jan 15H/Feb 18H/Mar 10H/Sep 24H/Dec 4F/Dec 7H; 1982 Jul 18H/Oct 26H; CBO deficit estimates 1981 Mar 16H; 1982 Feb 5H; congressional actions 1981 Mar 19H/Apr 2H/Apr 9H; 1982 May 12H/May 27H
fiscal year 1983: administration actions 1982 Feb 6H/Mar 5H/Apr 5H; CBO deficit estimates 1982 Sep 1H; CBO household impact study 1982 Apr 14H; congressional actions 1982 Mar 16F/May 21H/May 28H/Jun 10H/Jun 23H; summit meetings 1982 Apr 28H
fiscal year 1984: administration actions 1981 Oct 28H; 1983 Jan 31H/Oct 1H/Nov 14F; congressional actions 1983 Mar 15F/Mar 23F/May 19H/Jun 23H; Treasury deficit report 1984 Oct 25H
fiscal year 1985: administration actions 1984 Feb 1H/Feb 22H; CBO deficit estimates 1984 Feb 22H; congressional actions 1984 May 18H/Oct 12F/Oct 12H; 1985 Jun 20H/Aug 23G; Treasury deficit report 1985 Jan 25H
fiscal year 1986: administration actions 1984 Nov 14H/Dec 5H; 1985 Feb 4H/Aug 3H/Nov 12H; 1986 Jul 2H/Aug 6H; cities organization calls for spending freeze 1985 Mar 25F; congressional actions 1985 Mar 13H/May 1H/May 10H/May 23H/Jul 24H/Dec 19H/Dec 20H; 1986 Mar 7H/Mar 20H; interest rate drop affecting 1986 Apr 9H; Treasury deficit report 1986 Apr 28H

fiscal year 1987: administration actions 1985 Dec 12H; 1986 Feb 5H/Feb 11H/Aug 19H; 1987 Jul 16H; CBO deficit estimates 1986 Aug 19H; 1987 Jan 2F; congressional actions 1986 Mar 7H/Mar 13H/Mar 15H/Mar 19H/May 2H/Jun 11H/Jun 26H/Sep 30F/Oct 3H; 1987 Apr 24H/Jul 1H; interest rate drop affecting 1986 Apr 9H; state and local losses under Gramm-Rudman 1986 Feb 3H; Treasury deficit report 1987 Jan 27H/Apr 21H

fiscal year 1988: administration actions 1987 Jan 5H/May 14H/Jul 16H/Dec 22H; administration/congressional negotiations 1987 Nov 20H; CBO deficit estimates 1987 Jan 20H; congressional actions 1987 Mar 19H/Apr 1H/Apr 9H/May 7H/Jun 18H/Jun 24H/Dec 22H

fiscal year 1989: administration actions 1988 Feb 18H

Budget Coalition 1981 Feb 27F

Budget Priorities, Center on see Center on Budget Priorities

Buffalo Bills (football team) 1989 Jan 8J

Buffalo Sabres (ice hockey team) 1982 Feb 24J; 1985 Apr 30J

bugging, electronic see wiretapping and electronic surveillance

Built For Speed (Stray Cats) (recording) 1982 Nov 17J/Dec 15J; 1983 Jan 5J/Feb 9J

Bukovina (USSR) 1989 Jun 25B

Bulgaria see also individual leaders in the name index (e.g., Zhivkov, Todor)
accidents and disasters: chemical plant explosion 1986 Nov 1B; pleasure boat sinking 1989 Sep 10B
economy: 1980 Jan 23B
espionage trial: 1982 Dec 22B
ethnic Turks: 1986 Jun 20B; 1989 Feb 22B/May 21B/Jul 16B/Aug 22B/Oct 30B
foreign relations: Balkan conference 1988 Feb 23B; Comecon meeting 1984 Jun 14A; Guyana 1984 Jul 5A; Italy 1982 Dec 22B; Warsaw Pact 1985 Jan 14B
government and politics: Atanasov named premier 1986 Mar 21B; elections 1988 Feb 29B; power-sharing talks 1989 Dec 27B; pro-democracy demonstration 1989 Nov 3B
papal assassination attempt: 1982 Nov 25B/Dec 11B/Dec 18B; 1984 Jun 9B/Oct 26B; 1985 May 27B; 1986 Mar 29B
sports: Olympic Games boycott 1984 May 7J
United Nations policy: 1985 Oct 17A
U.S. relations: 1983 Sep 23G; 1984 Mar 14G

Bull Durham (film) 1988 Jun 15J/Jul 13J

bullfighting 1989 Feb 8J

Bull Run, Second Battle of (1862) 1988 Aug 10H

Bundesbank (West German central bank) 1986 Oct 15B; 1987 Dec 3B; 1988 Jun 21B/Jul 11A

Bunker Ramo Corp. 1981 May 11H

buprenorphine (drug) 1980 Feb 2I

Buran (Soviet space shuttle) 1988 Nov 15I

'Burbs, The (film) 1989 Feb 22J

Burger King Corp. 1982 Oct 29H

Burkina Faso (formerly Upper Volta) 1984 Aug 4C; 1985 Dec 25C; 1986 Jan 17C; 1987 Oct 15C; 1989 Sep 19C; for events before August 1984, see Upper Volta

Burlington (Vermont) 1985 Dec 23G; 1987 Mar 3F

Burma see also individual leaders in the name index (e.g., Ne Win); for events after June 1989, see Myanmar
accidents and disasters: ferry capsizes 1982 Apr 11E
civil strife: anti-insurgency campaigns 1980 Aug 10E; 1988 Sep 30E; demonstrations and protests 1988 Mar 20E
drug trafficking: drug warlord attacked 1982 Feb 23E
economy and labor: food deficit 1982 Mar 8E; strikes 1988 Oct 3E
government and politics: coup 1988 Sep 18E; elections announced 1988 Sep 10E; Maung Maung appointed leader 1988 Aug 19E; name changed to Myanmar 1989 Jun 19E; opposition group formed 1988 Sep 24E; San Yu becomes president 1981 Nov 9E; Sein Lwin chosen party chairman 1988 Jul 26E; Sein Lwin steps down as president 1988 Aug 12E
terrorism: airliner hijacking 1989 Oct 7E; bomb attack on South Koreans 1983 Oct 9E/Oct 10E/Oct 11E/Oct 14E/Nov 4E/Dec 9E; 1984 Jan 11E; train hits land mine 1985 Jul 24E

Burn This (Lanford Wilson) (play) 1987 Oct 14J; 1988 Jun 5J

Burroughs Wellcome Co. 1988 Nov 24I; 1989 Sep 18F/Oct 26F

Burundi 1987 Sep 3C; 1988 Aug 22C

Business (Men at Work) (recording) 1982 Oct 13J/Nov 17J/Dec 15J; 1983 Jan 5J/Feb 9J/Mar 9J

business and industry see specific industry (e.g., automobiles); company name (e.g., Chrysler Corp.); individual executives in the name index (e.g., Iacocca, Lee)

Business Committee for the Arts 1985 Apr 22J

Business International (magazine) 1988 Jun 28A

busing
educational issues: Boston (Mass.) 1985 Sep 3F; Cincinnati (Ohio) 1984 Feb 16F; Los Angeles (Calif.) 1981 Mar 16F; Louisiana 1981 Jan 15F; Norfolk (Va.) 1983 Feb 2F; 1986 Jun 16F/Sep 2F; St. Louis County (Mo.) 1983 Feb 22F
political issues: Carter threatens anti-busing veto 1980 Dec 4F; civil rights commission support 1982 Oct 12F; congressional antibusing legislation 1980 Dec 12F; 1981 Dec 10F; 1982 Feb 4F/Mar 2F/May 6F; state restrictions 1982 Mar 22F/Jun 30F
public opinion poll: 1987 Jan 5F

butachlor (pesticide) 1983 Apr 28I

...But Seriously (Phil Collins) (recording) 1989 Dec 30J

butter 1982 Jun 1H/Nov 21B

Butter Battle Book, The (Dr. Seuss) (book) 1984 Apr 20J/May 11J

buttons 1988 Nov 10H

Byelorussia (USSR) 1986 Mar 7A/Mar 8A

Byron Nuclear Power Station (Rockford, Illinois) 1984 Jan 13H

byssinosis (brown lung disease) 1983 Jun 7H

C

CAB see Civil Aeronautics Board

Cabbage Patch Kids (dolls) 1983 Nov 29J; 1985 Jan 2H

Cable News Network (CNN) 1980 Jun 1J; 1985 Feb 7J

Cable Satellite Public Affairs Network 1986 Jun 2F

cable television
business issues: 1980 Jun 1J; 1983 Oct 12F; 1985 Feb 7J; 1987 Oct 15F; 1989 Aug1F
Emmy Awards: 1988 Aug 28J
programming: free speech protection 1986 Jun 2F; 1987 Nov 1F; Ginsburg nomination 1987 Nov 1F; violence 1989 Aug 1F
rules and regulations: 1980 Jul 22J; 1981 Jul 16J; 1982 Jul 15J; 1983 Apr 21H; 1985 Jul 19F; 1986 Aug 7F; 1987 Dec 11F
sports: 1987 Mar 15J; 1988 Dec 1J

Cabora Bassa hydroelectric plant (Mozambique) 1984 May 2C

Caddyshack (film) 1980 Aug 6J

cadmium 1980 May 17A; 1981 Jul 28H

Cagney and Lacey (TV show) 1984 Oct 21J; 1985 Sep 12J; 1986 Sep 21J; 1987 Sep 20J; 1988 Aug 28J

Cairo Metro (Egypt) 1987 Sep 26C

Calgary Flames (ice hockey team) 1982 Mar 25J; 1986 May 24J; 1989 May 25J

California
accidents and disasters
air crashes: Air Force jet crash 1986 Jul 11G; B-1 bomber crash 1984 Aug 29G; missile explosion 1985 Aug 28I
earthquakes: forecasting 1985 Apr 5I; Fresno County 1983 May 2I; Imperial Valley 1987 Nov 24I; Northern California 1980 Jan 24I; 1984 Apr 24I; San Francisco 1989 Oct 26F; Southern California 1986 Jul 8I; Yosemite National Park 1980 May 25I
fires: 1985 Jul 21I/Aug 28I
storms: 1982 Apr 2I; 1983 Jan 30I/Mar 5I; 1986 Feb 20I
agriculture: Chavez pesticide protest 1988 Aug 21F; fruit tree malathion spraying 1981 Jul 10H; irrigation 1985 Mar 15H/Mar 28H; irrigation controversy 1985 Mar 15H/Mar 28H; Mediterranean fruit fly 1981 Jul 10H/Aug 4H/Aug 26E; 1982 Jun 24I/Sep 21I; watermelon pesticide illness 1986 Feb 14H; water supply contracts 1989 Nov 29H
arts and culture: Getty Trust plans arts center 1983 Sep 20J; Kirov Ballet performs 1986 May 21J; Pasadena Playhouse reopens 1986 Apr 19J
banking: Lincoln Savings scandal 1989 Jan 17F/Oct 13F/Oct 17H/Oct 31H/Dec 4H/Dec 22F; thrift mergers 1982 Oct 26H; 1983 Aug 4H; thrift seizures/rescues 1982 Apr 13H; 1988 Sep 5H
budget and spending programs: 1983 Feb 17H; 1988 Jun 1F
business and economy: AIDS testing for insurance 1985 Sep 26H;

auto manufacturing joint venture 1983 Feb 17H/Dec 22H; building permits 1987 Jun 26H; corporate unitary tax 1986 Sep 5H; economic growth 1986 Jul 10H; gold find 1980 Aug 27H; insurance rate reform 1989 May 4H

crime and law enforcement
bombings: Arab-American committee 1985 Oct 11F; Vincennes captain's wife 1989 Mar 10G
bribery and fraud: Oakland church 1980 Feb 7J; Wells Fargo defrauded 1981 Feb 2H
capital punishment: death sentence upheld 1980 Oct 23F
child abuse: McMartin Pre-School case 1987 Jul 13F
drug trafficking: Oakland kingpin buried 1986 Aug 29F
gun control: 1982 Aug 29F; 1989 Mar 13F/May 24F
kidnappings: 2 boys found 1980 Mar 1F; Hearst companion paroled 1980 Aug 25F
legal issues: Ehrlichman resigns from bar 1980 Jan 19F; "reasonable" attorneys fees upheld 1986 Jun 27F
murder: 5 schoolchildren slain in Stockton 1989 Jan 17F; 21 slain in McDonalds 1984 Jul 4F; Billionaire Boys Club 1987 Apr 22F; 1988 Jan 25F; Liu slaying 1985 Jan 15E/Feb 27E/Apr 9E/Apr 19E1; 1988 Mar 16F; Night Stalker 1985 Aug 25F
prison and parole: Black Panther released 1988 Mar 10F; probation study 1985 Feb 2F; Sirhan denied parole 1985 Jun 25F
educational issues: desegregation plans 1980 May 19F; evolution teaching 1981 Mar 5F; 1985 Dec 13F; 1989 Nov 9F; McMartin Pre-School abuse case 1987 Jul 13F; teachers fired in 1950's reinstated 1982 Nov 1F
energy issues
hydroelectric power: 1984 Aug 17H
nuclear power: A-plants 1980 Apr 23I; 1989 Jun 6H; Diablo Canyon A-plant controversy 1981 Sep 22I/Oct 24I/Nov 19I; 1984 Apr 29H/Aug 2H/Aug 21H/Nov 11I
oil and gas: offshore drilling 1981 Jul 27H; 1983 Jul 28H; 1985 Sep 10H; oil field find 1982 Nov 14I
synthetic fuels project: 1983 Jun 30H
environmental issues
air pollution: anti-smog measures 1989 Sep 14H; auto emissions standard 1989 Oct 2H; clean-air standards 1987 Jun 29H; low-emission gas introduced 1989 Aug 15H; rule and regulations 1989 Mar 17H
food contamination: Chavez pesticide protest 1988 Aug 21F; fruit tree malathion spraying 1981 Jul 10H; watermelon pesticide illness 1986 Feb 14H
oil spills: offshore drilling 1981 Jul 27H; 1983 Jul 28H; 1985 Sep 10H
parks and recreation areas: 1983 May 12H; 1985 Mar 5J
toxic wastes: chemicals 1988 May 31H; hazardous waste dumping 1985 Aug 26H

wildlife protection: condors 1983 Apr 5I; 1987 Apr 19I; 1988 Aug 29H; fruit tree malathion spraying 1981 Jul 10H; irrigation controversy 1985 Mar 15H/Mar 28H; stranded whale 1985 Nov 4J
family issues: divorces 1982 Mar 16J; Madonna/Sean Penn marriage 1985 Aug 16J; McMartin Pre-School abuse case 1987 Jul 13F
foreign issues: Argentine general arrested 1987 Jan 24D; USSR high-technology access 1986 Feb 15G
housing: campground for homeless 1987 Jun 15F; rent control laws 1988 Feb 24F
labor issues: AIDS discrimination suit 1987 Nov 1F; auto workers' contract 1985 Jun 25H; disability leave 1987 Jan 13F; Leary loses radio job 1980 Nov 1J; meat cutters' strike 1985 Dec 29H; workfare bill 1985 Sep 26F
Los Angeles see Los Angeles
lotteries and gambling: 1986 Feb 1J; 1988 Nov 1J
medicine and health care: contaminated cheese 1985 Jul 12I; donated embryo birth 1984 Feb 3I; frozen embryos 1984 Jun 17I/Oct 23I; heart transplants 1984 Oct 26I/Nov 15I; 1986 Jun 10I; pregnancy disability leave 1987 Jan 13F; toxic shock syndrome suit 1982 Dec 24H; watermelon pesticide illness outbreak 1986 Feb 14H
neo-Nazis: 1989 Mar 4F
obituaries: Burton, Phillip 1983 Apr 10F; Christensen, Lew 1984 Oct 9J; Douglas, Helen Gahagan 1980 Jun 28F; Gibson, Phil S. 1984 Apr 28F; Saroyan, William 1981 May 18J; Unruh, Jesse 1987 Aug 4F
politics and government
campaign finance: 1988 Jun 7F
elections: Eastwood elected Carmel mayor 1986 Apr 8F; pro-choice candidate wins Republican primary 1989 Aug 9F
presidential campaigns: 1980 Jun 3F; 1983 Jan 15F; 1984 Jun 5F/Sep 3F; 1988 Jun 7F
Reagan presidential library: 1988 Nov 21F
San Francisco Democratic convention (1984): 1983 Apr 21F; 1984 Apr 23F/Jul 16F/Jul 18F
voting issues: congressional redistricting 1989 Jan 17F
religious issues: papal visit 1987 Sep 10J
San Francisco see San Francisco
science and technology: genetic engineering 1987 Apr 24I/Jun 8I; human growth hormone 1982 Oct 29I; Jet Propulsion lab research 1980 May 6I; 1983 Aug 9I; Livermore lab research 1986 Sep 10I; 1987 Jan 20I; space shuttle 1984 Aug 21I
sports: horse racing 1985 Mar 3J; Breeders' Cup; Little League 1989 Aug 23J; Rose Bowl 1980 Jan 1J; 1982 Jan 1J; 1983 Jan 1J; 1984 Jan 2J; 1985 Jan 1J; 1986 Jan 1J; 1987 Jan 1J; 1988 Jan 1J; 1989 Jan 2J; see also professional teams (e.g., Los Angeles Dodgers)

transportation: coast highway reopened 1984 Apr 11J; vehicle-inspection programs 1980 Dec 11H

California, University of (UC)
Berkeley campus: 1980 Mar 29I/Apr 2I/Oct 9J; 1985 Jan 3I/May 16I; 1986 Apr 3G/May 13I/May 17I; 1989 May 24F
Davis campus: 1982 Dec 11J
Los Angeles campus (UCLA): 1980 Jan 20F/Mar 24J/Apr 3I; 1983 Jan 1J; 1984 Jan 2J; 1985 Mar 29J/Dec 15J; 1986 Jan 1J; 1989 Jan 2J/Mar 21I/Apr 23J
San Diego campus: 1980 Jan 25I; 1985 Feb 25I
San Francisco campus: 1989 Oct 9I

California Angels (baseball team) 1982 Oct 10J; 1984 Sep 17J/Sep 30J; 1985 Aug 4J; 1986 Sep 26J/Oct 15J

California Federal Savings and Loan Association 1982 Oct 26H

California Gold (John Jakes) (book) 1989 Sep 29J/Oct 27J

California Institute of Technology (Pasadena) 1980 Jan 20I; 1981 Oct 9I; 1985 Jan 3I; 1986 Jun 11I; 1987 Sep 21I; 1989 Nov 19I

Cambodia *see also individual leaders in the name index (e.g., Sihanouk, Norodom)*
civil war: chemical weapons use 1980 Aug 7G; 1981 Sep 13G/Nov 10G; death estimates 1980 May 24E; 1981 Jul 8E; famine predicted 1980 Mar 21E; KPNLF offensive 1989 Oct 4E; Thai border clashes 1980 Jun 23E; Vietnamese attack rebel camps 1984 Dec 25E; Vietnamese launch offensive 1984 Apr 15E; Vietnamese overrun KPNLF headquarters 1985 Jan 8E
foreign relations: ASEAN 1981 Jun 18E; 1983 Jun 25E/Nov 22E; 1984 Jul 9E; 1985 Jul 9E; Australia 1983 Jun 14E/Nov 22E; China 1982 Feb 3E; 1988 Jul 1E/Aug 28A; 1989 Jan 16E; Commonwealth 1980 Sep 8E; India 1980 Jul 7E; Thailand 1980 Jul 26E; 1982 Feb 3E; 1984 Apr 17G; 1985 Jan 10E; USSR 1988 Aug 28A
government and politics: Hun Sen named premier 1985 Jan 14E; opposition coalition formed 1982 Jun 22E; Pen Sovan removed as party chief 1981 Dec 5E
human rights: 1984 Feb 10G
peace initiatives: nonaligned nations resolution 1981 Feb 13A; UN resolutions 1980 Oct 22A; 1981 Jul 17A; 1985 Nov 5A; 1986 Oct 21A; 1989 Nov 16E; UN secretary-general visits region 1980 Aug 2A; 1985 Jan 30A; Vienamese talks held 1988 Jul 25E/Nov 8E; 1989 Mar 21E/Jul 30A; Vietnamese exit set 1989 Jan 16E; Vietnamese troop withdrawals 1983 May 2E; 1984 Jun 23E; 1988 May 26E/Jun 30E/Dec 25E; 1989 Apr 5E/Sep 26E
refugee issues: 1000's flee to Thailand 1984 Apr 17G; food distribution ended 1980 Dec 16E; relief efforts 1980 Feb 10E
U.S. relations: 1981 May 2E; 1985 Jul 9G; 1989 Jul 21G
Vietnam conflict: KPNLF headquarters overrun 1985 Jan 8E; offensive launched 1984 Apr 15E; peace talks held 1988 Jul

25E/Nov 8E; 1989 Mar 21E/Jul 30A; rebel camps attacked 1984 Dec 25E; Thailand border issues 1980 Jul 26E; 1982 Feb 3E; 1984 Apr 17G; 1985 Jan 10E; troop exit set 1989 Jan 16E; troops withdraw 1983 May 2E; 1984 Jun 23E; 1988 May 26E/Jun 30E/Dec 25E; 1989 Apr 5E/Sep 26E

Cambodia, U.N. Conference on 1981 Jul 17A

Cambodian-Americans 1989 Apr 25J

Cambridge (Massachusetts) 1985 Dec 23G

Cambridge University (England) 1980 Jan 10I/Oct 14I; 1986 Mar 29J; 1989 Mar 25J

Cameroon 1982 Apr 20C/Nov 6C; 1983 Jan 17C; 1985 Aug 19J; 1986 Aug 21C/Aug 24C

Camorra (Italian crime group) 1983 Jan 26B/Mar 5B

campaign financing
congressional elections: spending totals 1983 May 2F; 1987 May 9F; 1989 Feb 23F
political action committees (PACs): 1983 Apr 28F/Dec 13F; 1984 Apr 27F/Sep 9F; 1985 Mar 18F; 1986 Jan 7F/Jan 23F; 1987 Apr 7F/Apr 29F; 1988 Jul 23F; 1989 Aug 25F
presidential elections: federal matching funds 1984 Jan 3G; 1987 Jan 7F/Jun 4F/Dec 28F; 1988 Jan 4F/Mar 30F; 1989 Aug 25F; spending totals 1989 Aug 25F
reform proposals: 1987 Apr 29F/Jun 18F; 1988 Jun 7F; 1989 Jun 29F
violations: 1987 Jul 2F; 1988 Jan 8F/Apr 12F; 1989 Jan 18F

Campaign for Nuclear Disarmament 1984 Jun 9B

Camp David peace process 1980 Dec 7A/Dec 18C; 1981 Mar 26C; 1982 May 3C/Sep 2C

Campeau Corp. 1988 Jan 25H

Cam Ranh Bay (Vietnam) 1988 Sep 16B

Canada *see also specific provinces (e.g., Ontario); individual leaders in the name index (e.g., Trudeau, Pierre Elliott)*
accidents and disasters: earthquakes 1988 Nov 25I; U.S. cruise missile 1986 Jan 22G
agriculture: Crow's Nest Pass agreement 1982 Feb 13D/Mar 26D; 1983 Feb 1D/Nov 14B; drought assistance 1988 May 31D; farm aid 1986 Sep 10D; farm credit executives fired 1987 Dec 19D; farm income 1989 May 31D; farm prices 1986 Apr 9D; foreclosures 1987 Apr 27D; herbicide curb 1985 Feb 22I
Arctic sovereignty issue: 1985 Sep 10D; 1988 Jan 11C
arts and culture: Genie Awards 1986 Mar 20J; 1988 Mar 22J; 1989 Mar 22J; Munro gets literary award 1987 May 27J; National Gallery opened 1988 May 21D; U.S. classifies films as propaganda 1983 Feb 24J/Sep 8J; 1987 Apr 28F
business and industry: antitrust law ruled unconstitutional 1984 Sep 17D; auto plant closings 1988 Apr 22H; bankruptcies 1983 Jan 17D; brokerage firm merger 1981 Jun 8D; Chrysler loan guarantees 1981 Feb 17D; corporate profits/losses 1980 Jun 12D; 1983

Jun 7D; 1988 Oct 8D; industrial production 1982 Feb 26D; Massey-Ferguson stock guarantee 1981 Feb 7D; oil/gas relief package 1982 May 31D; stock exchanges 1989 Jan 18D; uranium cartel 1981 Jul 7D
census data: population 1982 Apr 3D; 1987 Jan 22D
constitution issues: federal/provincial disputes 1980 Sep 18D; 1981 Jan 12D/Apr 16D/Sep 28D; 1982 Apr 17D; 1983 May 2D; Meech Lake accord 1987 Apr 30D/Jun 3D/Jun 23D/Oct 26D/Dec 7D; 1988 Jun 22D/Dec 19D; 1989 Feb 27D/Nov 10D
crime and law enforcement: "constructive murder" 1987 Dec 9D; death penalty 1987 Jun 30D; hate crimes 1985 Feb 28D; homicide rate 1987 Apr 3D; 1989 Oct 5D; law enforcement study critical 1989 Feb 13D; police anti-subversive activities 1980 Apr 20D; police misconduct charged 1981 Jun 13D/Aug 25D; police uniform rules eased 1989 Oct 13D; prison riots 1982 Jul 25D; taxpayer files stolen 1986 Nov 17D
defense and disarmament issues: 1985 Jun 19D; 1986 Nov 10D; 1987 Feb 5D/Apr 16A/Jun 5D
economy: conferences 1985 Mar 23D; consumer price index 1988 Oct 14D; debtor nation status 1987 Jun 24D; GDP 1989 Mar 1D/Jun 1D; GNP 1980 Aug 29D; 1983 Jun 21D; government program presented 1984 Nov 8D; growth rate 1986 Dec 2D; housing 1989 Jan 14D; income gap for women 1982 Jun 10D; inflation rate 1986 Jan 21D/Aug 22D; poverty 1981 May 11D; 1985 Oct 23D; price/wage hike limits 1982 Aug 26D; provincial incomes gap 1981 Apr 23D; urban cost of living study 1983 Sep 22D; value-added tax 1989 Oct 23D/Dec 19D
education: spelling abilities 1989 Sep 12J
energy issues
electricity: U.S. exports 1987 Jun 18D
nuclear power: A-plants 1988 Jan 20D; uranium cartel 1981 Jul 7D
oil and gas: natural gas prices 1983 Apr 11D; 1985 Oct 31D; natural gas tax 1986 Sep 8D; oil exploration 1983 Jan 20D; oil finds 1980 Jan 3D/Oct 3H; 1985 Dec 30D; oil prices 1981 Jan 1D/Sep 1D; 1985 Jun 24D; oil tax 1981 Mar 2D; 1986 Sep 8D; relief package 1982 May 31D
environmental issues
air pollution: provincial role recommended 1986 Jul 7D; U.S. films called propaganda 1983 Feb 24J/Sep 8J; 1987 Apr 28F
water pollution: acid rain 1980 Jun 23D/Aug 5D; 1981 Oct 8D; 1983 Feb 21I/Aug 23D; 1984 Feb 22H/Mar 21I; 1985 Jul 9I/Sep 20A; 1986 Jan 8D; Great Lakes 1982 Aug 17D; 1983 Oct 16D; 1986 Jul 25D; 1987 Oct 16D; 1989 Oct 11D; herbicide curb 1985 Feb 22I; Niagara River 1983 Feb 15I; 1986 May 14D; shellfish contamination 1989 Nov 23D; wetlands 1989 Nov 19H

espionage and intelligence issues: 1983 May 18D/Jul 1D; 1987 Nov 30D
Expo '86: 1986 Oct 13D
family issues: abortion controversy 1988 Jan 28D/May 18D/Jul 28D; 1989 Mar 9D/Aug 8D/Nov 3D/Nov 16D; divorce 1989 Oct 6D
fishing: French rights dispute 1987 Mar 17D; 1988 Apr 20D/Jun 8D/Sep 12D; mollusk contamination 1987 Dec 11I; 1988 Jan 6I; salmon/herring processing 1989 Nov 6D; seal hunt 1983 Mar 27I; 1984 Mar 8D; 1987 Mar 23D/Dec 30D; shellfish contamination 1989 Nov 23D; tuna scandal 1985 Sep 23D; USSR agreement 1984 May 1A
foreign investments: controls on 1981 Sep 25D; 1984 Dec 7D; by France 1981 Jun 26H; GATT rules 1983 Jul 13A; by U.S. 1984 Oct 12D; in U.S. 1982 May 19D; 1988 Jan 25H; 1989 Jan 20H
foreign relations
Africa: South Africa 1985 Jul 8D
Asia: Japan 1981 May 7E/Jun 4E; 1982 Mar 20A/Aug 11A; 1983 Jun 27A; 1986 Jan 12D
Europe: Commonwealth 1986 Aug 5A; 1988 Feb 2C; France 1987 Mar 17D/May 25D; 1988 Apr 20D/Jun 8D/Sep 12D; Great Britain 1983 Sep 26D; 1984 Sep 24J; NATO 1988 Jun 24B; Poland 1982 Feb 24A; USSR 1980 Jan 12A/Jul 24D/Nov 20A; 1981 May 26D; 1982 Feb 24A; 1983 Nov 1D; 1984 May 1A; 1986 Oct 2D
Latin America: Mexico 1980 May 28D
Middle East: Iran: arms scandal 1986 Dec 12D; hostage crisis 1980 Jan 29A; Iran-Iraq war truce monitors 1988 Aug 15C; Libya 1983 Nov 1D; PLO 1989 Mar 30D; Sinai Desert observers 1986 Mar 16C
government and politics: budget 1982 Jun 28D/Oct 27D; 1986 Sep 18D; 1988 Sep 3D; federal spending criticized 1986 Mar 11D; fishing minister resigns 1985 Sep 23D; foreign policy change set 1981 Jun 22D; Liberal Party leadership convention cancelled 1989 Jun 17D; Liberal Party popularity decline 1982 Aug 4D; Mulroney sworn prime minister 1984 Sep 17D; national elections 1980 Feb 4D; 1984 Aug 15D/Sep 4D; 1988 Nov 10B; New Democratic Party leader resigns 1989 Mar 4D; provincial premiers conferences 1982 Aug 26D; 1985 Aug 22D; 1986 Aug 11D; 1989 Aug 21D; Turner sworn 1984 Jun 30D
immigration and refugees: 1980 Oct 31D; 1986 Nov 24D; 1987 Feb 20D/Jul 12D/Jul 22D; 1988 Dec 28D; 1989 Dec 19D
labor issues
strikes and settlements: airline lockout 1987 Nov 27D; auto worker contracts 1982 Sep 19C; 1984 Oct 29D; auto worker strikes 1982 Nov 5D/Dec 12D; 1983 Nov 5F; 1984 Oct 17D; 1987 Sep 17D; marine engineers' strike 1987 Oct 18D; meat-packing plant strike 1986 Dec 14D; postal worker strike

1981 Jul 14D; 1987 Oct 17D; railroad strike 1987 Aug 28D
unemployment rates: 1982 Jan 8D/Mar 12D/May 7D/Aug 6D/Nov 5D; 1983 Jan 7D/Feb 4D/Mar 11D/Apr 11H/May 3H/Aug 5D/Sep 9D/Oct 7D/Nov 4D; 1984 Jan 6D/Mar 9D/Jun 8D/Sep 7D; 1985 Jan 11D/Apr 4B/Oct 14D; 1987 Jan 9D/Nov 6D; 1988 May 6D/Oct 7D; 1989 Feb 11D/Aug 4D/Dec 8D
unions: Chrysler bailout 1980 Jan 3D; membership 1981 Sep 5D; UAW severs U.S. ties 1985 Mar 30D; 1986 Jun 9D; wage ceiling proposed 1982 Jul 8D
lottery and gambling: 1984 Jan 23J/May 1J
medicine and health care: abortion controversy 1988 Jan 28D/May 18D/Jul 28D; 1989 Mar 9D/Aug 8D/Nov 3D/Nov 16D; AIDS issues 1987 Nov 12D; 1988 Jan 11D/May 25D; 1989 Jan 3D/Aug 3D/Aug 8D; alcoholic beverages 1985 Dec 17I; Canada Health Act 1984 Apr 17D; cystic fibrosis gene found 1989 Aug 24I; physician billing 1983 Dec 12D; 1986 Jun 20D
monetary issues: banking 1980 Mar 10D; 1984 Mar 15D; 1985 Sep 30D; 1987 Oct 22D; 1988 Jan 20D/Apr 2D; 1989 Feb 16D/May 18D; currency 1981 Jul 28H/Aug 3H; 1984 Jun 28H; 1985 Feb 21D; 1986 Feb 11D/Mar 25D; 1987 Feb 2D; 1988 Jan 20D/Apr 15D
native peoples: Dene Indians 1982 Nov 26D; 1987 Jan 15D; 1988 Sep 5D; Inuit (Eskimos) 1982 Jul 8D/Nov 26D; 1987 Jan 15D/Mar 27D/May 26B; 1989 Apr 14D; Metis 1987 Jan 15D/Mar 27D; 1988 Sep 5D; native Canadians 1981 Nov 8D; 1982 Apr 14D; 1983 Mar 16D; 1984 Mar 9D/Jun 21D/Nov 1D; 1987 Jul 11D; 1988 Jul 23D/Oct 20D/Nov 8D/Nov 29D; 1989 Apr 14D/Jul 6D/Jul 10D
Nazis: 1983 Mar 13D; 1987 Mar 12D/Aug 7D; 1989 Jun 26D
obituaries: Acorn, Milton 1986 Aug 20J; Fox, Terry 1981 Jun 28J; Gould, Glenn 1982 Oct 4J; Greene, Lorne 1987 Sep 11J; Hebb, Donald 1985 Aug 20I; Laurence, Margaret 1987 Jan 5J; Levesque, Rene 1987 Nov 1D; Lillie, Beatrice 1989 Jan 20J; McLuhan, Marshall 1980 Dec 31J
press and broadcasting: domestic programming 1986 Nov 18D; newspaper regulation 1981 Aug 18D; 1983 Jul 6D
religious issues: bishops attack economic policies 1983 Jan 1D; ordination of homosexuals 1988 Aug 24J; papal visit 1984 Sep 9J; 1987 Sep 10J
rights issues: 1985 Apr 17D; 1986 Mar 4D; 1988 Sep 22D; 1989 May 24D/Jun 26D
science and technology: astronomers 1986 Jun 11I; chemical weapons 1982 Dec 17A; ice station CESAR 1983 May 21I; impact crater identified 1987 Jun 17I; speed of sound recalculated 1986 Mar 27I; Telesat Canada satellite 1982 Nov 12I
sports
auto racing: 1986 Jun 15J
boxing: 1988 Nov 7J

Calgary Olympics: ceremonies held, records set 1988 Feb 13J/Feb 20C/Feb 27J/Mar 1J; site chosen 1986 Oct 14J

figure skating: 1987 Mar 12J; 1989 Mar 16J

Grey Cup: 1986 Nov 30J; 1987 Nov 29J

ice hockey: 1982 Apr 25J; 1985 May 3J; 1987 Feb 13J/May 3J; 1989 Apr 29J

Moscow Olympics boycott: 1980 Apr 22J/Apr 26J

mountain climbing: 1986 May 20J

Pan American Games: 1983 Aug 28J

Skydome stadium opens: 1989 Jun 3J

substance use: 1989 Jan 11J/Jun 12J

track and field: 1987 Aug 30J

terrorism: Air-India bombing 1985 Jun 23A; engineer kidnapped by pro-Cuban group 1988 Mar 19E; Turkish diplomat 1982 Apr 8A; Turkish embassy 1985 Mar 12D

trade issues

exports: electricity to U.S. 1987 Jun 18D; grain to USSR 1980 Jan 12A/Nov 20A; 1981 May 26D; softwood to U.S. 1986 Jun 10D/Oct 16D/Dec 30D; 1987 Jan 8D; steel dumping 1986 Jun 2D; 1989 Mar 7H; trade surplus 1985 Feb 7D; 1986 Aug 9D; 1989 Aug 17D

imports: autos from Japan 1981 Jun 4E; 1982 Mar 20A/Aug 11A; 1983 Jun 27A; corn from U.S. 1986 Nov 7D; legislation 1983 May 19D; shoe quotas 1985 Nov 20D; U.S. tariffs cut 1989 Nov 30D

pacts and treaties: GATT dairy imports 1989 Sep 19A; GATT investment controls 1983 Jul 13A; Sovt fishing pact 1984 May 1A

U.S./Canada free trade agreement: 1985 Sep 26D/Oct 28D; 1986 Apr 23D; 1987 Sep 23D/Oct 3D/Dec 7D; 1988 Aug 9H/Aug 31D/Sep 19H/Dec 30D

transportation

airlines: Air Canada 1983 Jul 29D; 1986 Apr 27D; 1987 Nov 27D/Dec 18D; deregulation 1988 Jan 1D; deregulation urged 1982 Apr 6D; plane crashes: Air-India 1985 Jun 23A; U.S. troop transport in Gander 1985 Dec 12D; smoking ban 1986 Apr 27D

railroads: safety violations 1986 Feb 16B; tunnels 1989 May 4D

ships: U.S. Arctic water rights 1988 Jan 11C

United Nations policy: 1988 Oct 26A

U.S. relations: CIA brainwashing experiments 1988 Oct 4D; cruise missile tests 1983 Jul 15D; 1984 Mar 6D; 1989 Feb 1D; Gulf of Maine dispute 1984 Oct 12D; North Dakota irrigation project 1983 Nov 21D; SDI research 1985 Sep 8D

welfare and social services: child-care plan 1987 Dec 3D; drug abuse 1987 May 25D; 1989 Jan 11J/Jun 12J; poverty 1981 May 11D; 1985 Oct 23D

Canada Development Corp. 1981 Jun 26H

Canadair Ltd. 1983 Jun 7D; 1986 Aug 18D

Canadian Auto Workers 1986 Jun 9D; 1987 Sep 17D

Canadian First City Financial Corp. 1980 Oct 21H

Canadian Football League
Grey Cup 1986 Nov 30J; 1987 Nov 29J

Canadian Grand Prix (auto race) 1986 Jun 15J

Canadian Lake Carriers Association 1987 Oct 18D

Canadian Life and Health Insurance Association Inc. 1987 Nov 12D

Canadian National Railways 1987 Aug 28D

Canadian Olympic Association 1980 Apr 26J

Canadian Sealers' Association 1984 Mar 8D

Canary Islands 1980 Apr 25B

Canberra (ship) 1982 Jun 19D

cancer see also specific types (e.g., lung cancer)

awards and honors: Bishop/Varmus win Nobel 1989 Oct 9I

chemical hazards: birth-control pills 1989 Sep 6I; DES 1984 Feb 2F; dioxin 1983 Jul 28I; Love Canal 1981 Jun 11H; pesticides 1987 May 20I; 1988 Oct12H; petroleum/chemical plants 1984 Nov 15I

death rates: 1980 Apr 28I; 1985 Feb 12F/Apr 30I; 1986 May 8I/Dec 8I

detection and treatment: blood test for 1981 Jan 12I; experimental drugs 1981 Mar 24I/Apr30I; 1987 May 7I; federal policy guidelines 1984 May 22I; increase in cases 1988 Sep 2I

medical ethics: court-ordered treatment 1983 Sep 21F; euthanasia 1988 Jan 8I; federal policy guidelines 1984 May 22I

prevention: depression 1989 Sep 1I; physical exercise 1989 Nov 3J; workplace regulations 1980 Jan 16H

radiation hazards: Chernobyl 1987 Mar 25I; exposure risks 1981 Aug 20I; 1983 Aug 5G; 1989 Dec 19I; exposure suits 1982 Oct 19F; 1984 Apr 23H/May 25H

research: cancer-suppressing genes 1988 Dec 28I; federal policy guidelines 1988 May 22I; genetic engineering 1988 Apr 21I; immune system activation 1985 Dec 4I; interferon 1981 Mar 24I; interleukin-2 1987 May 7I; Laetrile 1981 Apr 30I; recombinant DNA experiments 1982 Dec 30I

smoking hazards: 1982 Feb 22I

Cancer Society, American see American Cancer Society

canine distemper virus 1988 Aug 19I

Cannes Film Festival (France) 1984 May 23J; 1985 May 20J; 1987 May 19J; 1988 May 23J; 1989 May 23J

Cannonball Run, The (film) 1981 Jul 1J

Can't Slow Down (Lionel Richie) (recording) 1983 Nov 9J/Dec 14J/Dec 14J; 1984 Jan 21J/Feb 18J/Mar 24J/Apr 28J/May 28J/Jun 16J/Jul 21J; 1985 Feb 26J

CAP see Common Agriculture Policy

Cape Times (South African newspaper) 1985 Nov 4C

Cape Verde 1980 Nov 14C; 1982 Dec 8C

Capital Cities Communications Inc. 1985 Mar 18H

capital gains taxes 1988 Aug 16F; 1989 Aug 2H/Sep 14H/Sep 28H/Nov 2H

capital punishment see death penalty

capital spending 1984 Jun 11H/Dec 20H; 1985 Apr 19H/Sep 11H; 1986 Apr 16H; 1988 Dec 28H

Capote (racehorse) 1986 Nov 1J

captan (fungicide) 1985 Jun 18H

carbon dioxide 1981 Jan 13H; 1983 Oct 20H; 1986 Nov 20I; 1989 Nov 7I/Dec 16I

carbon monoxide 1987 Nov 17H

carbon tetrachloride 1987 Jun 24H

Cardinal of the Kremlin, The (Tom Clancy) (book) 1988 Aug 26J/Sep 30J/Oct 21J/Nov 25J/Dec 23J; 1989 Jan 27J/Feb 24J

Cardinals, College of see College of Cardinals

Cargo (Men At Work) (recording) 1983 May 11J/Jun 15J

Caribbean see also specific countries (e.g., Grenada); organizations (e.g., Caricom)

economy: foreign debt 1984 Jan 14D; oil supplies 1981 Apr 10D; 1983 Jul 17D; UNECLA regional report 1987 Dec 22D

foreign relations: Canada 1983 Feb 20D; Mexico 1981 Apr 8D/Apr 10D; 1983 Jul 17D; Venezuela 1981 Apr 8D/Apr 10D; 1983 Jul 17D

Grenada invasion: 1983 Oct 25D; 1985 Feb 7D

hurricanes: 1988 Nov 30I; Allen 1980 Aug 11I; Gilbert 1988 Sep 17I; Hugo 1989 Sep 19D; Joan 1988 Oct 22I

papal visit: 1983 Mar 2D

sports: 1989 Jul 29J

U.S. relations: 1981 Jun 9D/Oct 9D/Dec 4D; 1982 Feb 24D/Apr 8D; 1984 Jan 31G; 1986 Feb 20D

women: 1980 Jul 21D

Caribbean (James A. Michener) (book) 1989 Dec 1J/Dec 22J

Caribbean Championships (track and field) 1989 Jul 29J

Caribbean Community and Common Market (Caricom) 1983 Jul 4D/Oct 30D; 1984 Apr 4D; 1985 Jul 4D; 1988 Jul 4D

Caricom see Caribbean Community and Common Market

Carl Marks Co. Inc. 1982 Mar 2A

Carmelites (Catholic order) 1989 Jan 25B/Sep 19B

Carnegie Corp. 1989 Jun 19F

Carnegie Forum on Education and the Economy 1986 Jul 6F

Carnegie Foundation for the Advancement of Teaching 1983 Sep 14F; 1985 Jan 27F; 1986 Nov 2F; 1988 Mar 15F

Carnegie Hall (New York City) 1986 Dec 15J; 1988 May 11J

Carnegie Institute (Washington, D.C.) 1980 Jan 23I

Carnegie Museum of Natural History (Pittsburgh, Pennsylvania) 1984 Sep 24I

Caron (ship) 1986 Mar 18B

Carroll House (racehorse) 1989 Oct 8J

Cars, The (singing group) 1984 Jul 21J/Aug 25J/Sep 22J

Cartagena Group 1985 Feb 8D/Jul 30D/Dec 17D

Carthage (Tunisia) 1985 Feb 3B

Case of Lucy Bending, The (Lawrence Sanders) (book) 1982 Sep 12J

casinos 1980 Aug 27J/Oct 27J/Dec 12J; 1981 Nov 5B; 1982 Jan 16H; 1985 Mar 18J/Mar 29J/Jun 30J; 1986 Jan 21F

Castillo de Bellver (ship) 1983 Aug 6C

Catalonia (Spain) 1982 Jun 30B

catastrophic illness 1986 Nov 20F; 1987 Feb 15F/Jul 22F/Oct 27F; 1988 Jun 8F/Jul 1F; 1989 Oct 4F/Oct 6F/Nov 22F

Catastrophic Illness Expenses (Health and Human Services) 1986 Nov 20F

Caterpillar Inc. 1986 Jul 4H

Caterpillar Tractor Co. 1983 Apr 23F

Catholic Relief Services 1985 Jan 8C

Catholic University of America (Washington, D.C.) 1980 Nov 16F; 1986 Aug 18J

Cats (musical) 1983 Jun 5J

Cat's Eye (film) 1985 Apr 17J

cattle 1980 Apr 24I/Jun 13D/Jun 13I; 1982 Aug 3I; 1984 Sep 5I; 1986 Mar 28H; 1988 Dec 10B; 1989 Feb 18B; see also specific products (e.g., beef)

Caveat (racehorse) 1983 Jun 11J

Caveman (film) 1981 May 6J

caviar 1980 Mar 15B

CBO see Congressional Budget Office, U.S.

CBS Inc. see also specific television shows (e.g., 60 Minutes)

business issues: video technologies 1980 Jan 31J

Emmy Awards: 1984 Sep 24J

Nielson ratings: 1980 Nov 21J; 1983 Feb 28J; 1984 Apr 17J; 1988 Jan 31J

personnel: employee slayings 1982 Apr 12J/Jun 16J; 1984 May 31F; Paley announces resignation 1982 Sep 9J; Wyman resigns 1986 Sep 10H

programming and sponsorship: baseball contract 1988 Dec 14J; basketball contract 1985 Dec 20J; birth control ads refused 1985 Aug 1C; Bush/Rather shouting match 1988 Jan 25F; FCC rules revision proposed 1983 Aug 4H; Olympic Games broadcast rights 1988 May 24J; 1989 Aug 23J; Soviet screening 1983 Mar 18B; Vietnam documentary 1982 Jan 23G

CBS News (TV show) 1980 Feb 15J/Feb 21C/Jul 1J; 1982 Sep 22F/Sep 29G; 1983 Oct 14J; 1986 Oct 4J

CBS Newsbreak (TV show) 1988 Apr 1J

CBS Records Group 1985 Aug 5J

CBS Reports: The Vanishing Family— Crisis in Black America (TV show) 1987 Mar 4J

CDC see Centers for Disease Control

CDE see Conference on Confidence- and Security-Building Measures and Disarmament in Europe

cedar products 1986 May 22D/Jun 2D

Celebrity (Thomas Thompson) (book) 1982 May 9J/Jun 6J

cell growth 1986 Sep 22I/Oct 13I

cement pipes 1986 Jan 23H

censorship

Canada: 1987 Aug 7D

Chile: 1983 Jun 17D/Aug 26D

Great Britain: 1987 Dec 3B

Indonesia: 1982 Apr 12E

Japan: 1988 Jul 1E; 1989 Oct 3E

Kuwait: 1986 Apr 3C

Nicaragua: 1982 Dec 12D; 1987 Sep 20D

Pakistan: 1983 Mar 27E

Philippines: 1983 May 17E

Poland: 1981 Jul 31B

South Africa: 1986 Dec 11C; 1987 Apr 28C

United States: abortion research 1989 Dec 16F; federal employees 1983 Oct 20H; school classrooms and libraries 1982 Feb 14J; student newspapers 1988 Jan 13F

Uruguay: 1983 Aug 2D

USSR: 1986 Jun 27B

Centerfield (John Fogerty) (book) 1985 Feb 23J/Mar 30J/Apr 27J

Center for Constitutional Rights 1988 Feb 2F

Center for Democratic Policy 1981 Feb 24F

Center for Science in the Public Interest 1985 Nov 14I

Center for Short Lived Phenomena 1986 Nov 26I

Center for Women Policy Studies 1989 Apr 28F

Center on Budget Priorities 1989 Oct 18H

Centers for Disease Control, U.S. (CDC) (Atlanta, Ga.)

AIDS research: 1982 Dec 9I; 1984 Jan 4I/Jan 11I/Apr 21I/Nov 29I; 1985 Aug 29F/Nov 11F; 1986 Jan 9I/Oct 23I/Oct 28F; 1987 Feb 25F/Mar 19I; 1988 May 26F/Jun 3I; 1989 May 13I

chemical hazards research: Agent Orange birth defects 1984 Aug 16G; dioxin 1982 Dec 23I

substance abuse research: cigarette smoking 1987 Sep 11I; cirrhosis of the liver 1984 Nov 23I; hard liquor consumption 1989 Nov 24F; lung cancer 1984 Oct 20I; 1989 Jul 28I

virus/bacteria research: hepatitis B 1984 Dec 13I; laboratory test accuracy 1980 Mar 23I; rubella 1984 Sep 23I; salmonella 1984 Sep 5I; tooth decay 1985 Feb 14F; tuberculosis 1988 Jan 2I

Central African Republic (CAR) 1981 Mar 19C/Mar 20C/Sep 1C; 1983 Aug 18A; 1985 Aug 19J; 1986 Oct 23C; 1987 Jun 12C

Central American peace accord (Guatemala Pact) (1987)

cease-fire: 1987 Oct 27D

compliance measures: El Salvador 1987 Oct 6D/Oct 11D/Nov 12D/Nov 23D; Guatemala 1987 Oct 7D/Oct 28G; Honduras 1987 Dec 4D; Nicaragua 1987 Sep 22D/Sep 26D/Sep 30D/Nov 22D; 1988 Jan 16D

Costa Rican role: Arias Sanchez gets Nobel 1987 Oct 13D; Arias Sanchez sees Castro 1988 Aug 10D; Arias Sanchez visits U.S. 1987 Sep 20D

foreign ministers meet: 1987 Aug 19D

preliminary peace talks: 1984 Nov 8D/Nov 20D; 1985 Feb 14D; 1986 Apr 7D

ratification and support: Central American parliament 1987 Oct 2D; compliance process begins 1987 Nov 5D; Nicaraguan contras

1987 Aug 21D; supervisory committees 1987 Sep 17D; UN resolution backs 1987 Oct 7A signing: 1987 Aug 7D

central banks *see also specific central banks (e.g.,* Bank of England)
capital requirements agreement: 1987 Dec 10A; 1988 Jul 11A
currency interventions: 1985 Feb 27A/Dec 4A; 1987 Oct 28H; 1988 Nov 17A; 1989 May 22A
European Monetary System plan: 1989 Apr 17B
interest rate moves: 1982 Dec 2B; 1986 Mar 7A/Apr 19A; 1987 Dec 3B

Central Council of Jews in Germany 1989 Dec 15B

Central Intelligence Agency, U.S. (CIA) *see also specific agency director in the name index (e.g.,* Casey, William)
appointments and resignations: Casey, William 1980 Dec 11F; 1987 Feb 2G; Gates, Robert 1987 Feb 2G/Mar 3G; Hugel, Max 1981 Jul 14G; Inman, Bobby 1982 Apr 21G; Webster, William 1987 Mar 3G
censorship issues: ABC News fairness violations claimed 1984 Nov 21F; Colby memoir suit 1981 Dec 31G; guerrilla warfare manual 1984 Oct 18G/Oct 22G/Dec 5G; information withholding 1984 Oct 1G; 1985 Apr 16F
covert operations
Afghanistan: 1989 Sep 4G
Africa: Angola 1986 Sep 17G; 1987 Feb 1G; 1989 Nov 27C; Ghana 1985 Nov 25A
Canada: 1988 Oct 4D
Latin America: El Salvador 1984 Mar 21G/Jun 12G/Oct 19D; Nicaragua 1983 May 1G/May 16G/Jun 6D; 1984 Apr 6D/Apr 15G/Apr 18G/Jun 12G/Jun 13G; 1985 Jan 7G; 1986 Oct 7G; 1988 Sep 20G; Nicaraguan contras 1982 Mar 10G; 1984 Apr 21D/May 19G/Sep 18G; 1986 Oct 6G/Oct 7D; 1987 Jan 14G/Jan 17D/Feb 9G/Aug 4G; Panama 1988 Aug 17G
Middle East: Iran 1986 Nov 19G; Iran-Contra 1989 Apr 24F; Iraq 1986 Dec 15G; Lebanon 1983 Nov 1G; 1985 May 12C; Libya 1982 Jan 6G; 1985 Nov 3G
United States: 1981 Mar 17F/Oct 5G/Oct 27F/Dec 4F
USSR: 1981 Nov 26B; 1982 Dec 25B; 1986 Aug 7H; 1987 Mar 27B; 1989 Dec 17G
personnel issues: Chin indictment 1986 Jan 2G; ex-agent pleads guilty 1980 Oct 29G; homosexual employee reinstated 1985 Jan 17F
war crimes: Waldheim WWII papers 1989 Nov 29A

Central Park (New York City) 1988 Mar 25F; 1989 Apr 19F

Century (Fred Mustard Stewart) (book) 1981 Apr 12J

ceramics 1986 Oct 8B; 1987 Oct 14I

CERN *see* European Center for Nuclear Research

Cervantes Prize (literature) 1988 Apr 21J

cervical cancer 1987 Nov 2F

cervical caps 1988 May 23I

CESAR (Canadian ice station) 1983 May 21I

cesium 137 1987 Oct 6D/Oct 28D

Cessna 172 (aircraft) 1987 May 29B/Dec 6D

Cessna 402 (aircraft) 1987 May 28D

CFCs *see* chlorofluorocarbons

CFE *see* Conventional Forces in Europe

C-47 (aircraft) 1987 Mar 9D

CFTC *see* Commodity Futures Trading Commission, U.S.

Chad *see also individual leaders in the name index (e.g.,* Oueddei, Goukouni)
civil war: Aozou strip 1987 Aug 8C/Aug 28C/Sep 6C/Aug 10B; 1988 Oct 3C; cease-fire 1980 Apr 8C; food shortages 1983 Mar 6C; French soldiers killed 1984 Apr 7C; French troop reinforcements 1983 Aug 18A; Libya chemical weapons use 1986 Dec 31C; military operations 1980 Dec 16C; 1983 Jul 30C/Aug 3G/Aug 10C; 1986 Feb 10C; 1987 Jan 9C/Apr 13C/Sep 7C; troop withdrawals 1980 May 16C; 1981 Nov 5C; 1984 Sep 17A/Sep 25C/Nov 10C
government and politics: Libya merger announced 1981 Jan 6C; woman cabinet minister chosen 1982 Oct 22C
peace initiatives: French/African heads of state meet 1983 Oct 3A; French diplomatic efforts 1984 Feb 5C; French-speaking summit 1984 Dec 11C; OAU meetings 1980 Dec 24C; 1982 Feb 11C; peace talks 1984 Jan 13C
refugee issues: Nigeria emigrees to return 1983 Jan 17C
U.S. relations: Egypt military exercises 1983 Aug 10C; Libyan intervention condemned 1983 Aug 10G; military aid 1983 Aug 3C/Aug 4G/Aug23G

Challenger (space shuttle) 1985 Nov 6I; 1986 Apr 19I/Dec 20I

Chaminade University (Honolulu, Hawaii) 1982 Dec 24J

Champion International Corp. 1984 Jul 31H

Chances Are (film) 1989 Mar 29J

Chanel boutique (Paris, France) 1981 Jan 4B

Changes (Danielle Steel) (book) 1983 Oct 16J/Nov 13J

Channel One (TV show) 1989 Mar 5F

Chappaquiddick (Massachusetts) 1980 Jan 15F/Mar 12F

Chapterhouse: Dune (Frank Herbert) (book) 1985 May 24J

Chapter Two (film) 1980 Feb 27J

Chariots of Fire (film) 1981 Sep 26J; 1982 Feb 17J/Mar 10J/Mar 29J

Chariots of Fire (Vangelis) (recording) 1982 Mar 14J/Mar 17J/May 5J

Charles Schwab Corp. 1983 Jan 7H

Charlotte Observer (newspaper) 1981 Apr 13J; 1988 Mar 31J

Charon (moon of Pluto) 1980 Apr 22I

Charter 77 (Czech dissident group) 1980 Jun 1B; 1985 Mar 11B; 1987 Jan 6B; 1988 Jun 17B; 1989 Jun 29B

Chase Manhattan Bank 1980 May 1H/Jul 24H; 1981 Aug 31H; 1985 May 17H/Jul 31C/Sep 4C; 1987 Mar 31H/May 15H

Chase Manhattan Corp. 1989 Oct 12H

Chattanooga (Tennessee) 1980 Jul 22F/Jul 25F

Chaucer: His Life, His Work, His World (Donald R. Howard) (book) 1988 Jan 11J

Chautauqua Institution (Jamestown, N.Y.) 1986 Sep 15A

Cheers (TV show) 1983 Sep 25J; 1984 Sep 24J; 1989 Sep 17J

cheese 1980 Aug 24H; 1982 Jun 1H; 1985 Jul 12I; 1986 Dec 30H

Chelsea (Massachusetts) 1989 Jun 13F/Sep 6F

Chem-Dyne waste dump (Hamilton, Ohio) 1985 Jun 13H

chemical and biological warfare *see also specific types of gas (e.g.,* poison gas)
in Afghanistan: 1980 Aug 7G; 1981 Sep 13G/Sep 14B; 1982 Mar 8A/Mar 22A/Nov 29A/Dec 6A
in Africa: Ethiopia 1980 Aug 7G
disarmament and arms control: Paris conference 1989 Jan 11A; U.S. treaty proposals 1983 Feb 10A; 1984 Apr 4A/Apr 18A; 1989 Jul 18A/Sep 25A; U.S./Soviet data exchange 1989 Sep 26A; Vienna conference 1989 Sep 18A; West German exports curbed 1984 Aug 7B; 1989 Feb 15B
Iraq-Iraq War: 1984 Mar 5C/Mar 30A/Jul 4C; 1988 Mar 21C/Sep 15G/Sep 27G
in Mideast: Libya 1986 Dec 31C; 1988 Dec 21G; 1989 Feb 15B
in Southeast Asia: 1980 Aug 7G; 1981 Sep 13G/Sep 14B/Nov 10G; 1982 Jan 22E/Mar 22A/Nov 29A/Dec 6A/Dec 17A; 1983 May 31A
Soviet policy: 1981 Sep 14B; 1982 Mar 28I; 1984 Jan 10B/Feb 21B; 1987 Oct 3B/Dec 26B; 1989 Jul 18A/Sep 25A
U.S. policy: budget and spending programs 1983 Sep 15G/Nov 8G; Iran-Iraq sanctions 1984 Mar 30A; 1988 Sep 15G/Sep 27G; Libya military options 1988 Dec 21G; plant locations revealed 1986 May 22B; production 1986 May 22B; 1987 Dec 17G; Soviet use disputed 1980 Aug 7G; 1981 Sep 13G/Sep 14B/Nov 10G; 1982 Mar 8A/Mar 22A/Nov 29A; 1983 31a; treaty proposals 1983 Feb 10A; 1984 Apr 4A/Apr 18A; 1989 Jul 18A/Sep 25A
weapons: binary weapons 1983 Sep 15G/Nov 8G; mustard gas 1984 Mar 26A; nerve gas 1984 Mar 26A/Aug 7B; poison gas 1980 Aug 21G; 1984 Mar 26A; 1986 Mar 14C; 1988 Sep 8C/Sep 21C; 1989 Jan 28C/Apr 27B/Jul 7G
in World War II: Japan 1982 Apr 16E; 1988 Sep 18E

Chemical Bank 1983 Aug 3H/Oct 4H; 1985 Apr 22J

Chemical New York Corp. 1989 Oct 12H

Chemical Waste Management Inc. 1986 May 28H

chemistry
awards and honors
Nobel Prize: Berg/Gilbert/Sanger 1980 Oct 14I; Fukui/Hoffman 1981 Oct 19I; Klug 1982 Oct 18I; Taube 1983 Oct 19I; Merrifield 1984 Oct 17I; Hauptman/Karle 1985 Oct 16I; Herschbach/Lee/Polanyi 1986 Oct 15I; Cram/Lehn/Pedersen 1987 Oct 14I; Deisenhofer/Huber/Michel 1988 Oct 19I; Altman/Cech 1989 Oct 12I

obituaries: Brown, Harrison 1986 Dec 8I; Flory, Paul 1985 Sep 9I; Leloir, Luis 1987 Dec 3I; Levi, Primo 1987 Apr 11J; Libby, Willard 1980 Sep 8J; Mulliken, Robert 1986 Oct 31I; Northrop, John 1987 May 27I; Semyonov, Nikolai 1986 Sep 25I; Sokol, Herman 1985 Jun 21I; Urey, Harold 1981 Jan 5I; Wittig, Georg 1987 Aug 26I
research: cold fusion 1989 May 9I/Jul 12I; new state of matter created 1989 Mar 21I

chemotherapy 1983 Sep 21F; 1986 Jul 17I; 1988 Sep 6F

Chernobyl nuclear accident (1986)
A-plant crisis: meltdown 1986 Apr 28B/May 1I/May 11I; contamination 1986 May 7B-8B/May 29B/Jun 5B/Jun 20I; containment 1986 Jun 24I/Nov 15I; death toll 1986 Jul 1B
government response: Gorbachev statement 1986 May 14B; officials punished 1986 Jul 5B/Jul 29B/Aug 14B; 1987 Jul 29B; report issued 1986 Aug 21B
health hazards: 1986 May 15I/Aug 29B/Nov 23I; 1987 Mar 25I; 1988 Jan 22I/Sep 21I; 1989 Nov 8B
international reaction: antinuclear protests 1987 Apr 26I; play opens 1987 Sep 18J
safety measures: Gorbachev proposals 1986 May 14B; IAEA conference 1986 Aug 25I/Aug 29I; IAEA endorses 1987 Jan 16I

Cherokee Indians 1985 Dec 14F

chess 1985 Feb 15J/Sep 2J/Nov 9J; 1986 Oct 9J/Dec 1J; 1987 Mar 31J/Dec 19J; 1988 Feb 22J; 1989 Oct 22J

Chess (musical) 1986 May 14J

Chess Olympiad 1986 Dec 1J

Chevron Corp. 1980 Jan 3D; 1988 Jan 22H

Cheyenne State University (Pennsylvania) 1982 Mar 28J

Chiado district (Lisbon, Portugal) 1988 Aug 25B

Chicago (Illinois) *see also individual leaders in the name index (e.g.,* Washington, Harold)
arts and culture: Barenboim named symphony music director 1989 Jan 30J; flag exhibit 1989 Feb 17J
awards and honors: Stern receives Merit Medal 1985 Mar 23J
business and industry: Playboy Club closed 1986 Jun 30J; Sears restructuring 1988 Oct 31H
census data: population 1984 Apr 7J
crime: aldermen indicted 1986 Nov 21F; diocese head investigated 1981 Sep 10J; Dorfman shot 1983 Jan 20J; Gacy slayings 1980 Mar 13F/Mar 13J; mercy killing of child 1989 Apr 26F; Tylenol poisonings 1982 Oct 6I; Weather Underground leader surrenders 1980 Dec 3F
economy: bond rating lowered 1983 Jul 7H; cost of living comparison 1988 Jun 28A
educational issues: budget deficits 1980 Apr 2F; school decentralization 1989 Sep 5F; school desegregation program 1984 Sep 26F
environmental issues: clean-air standards 1987 Jun 29H; smoking restrictions 1988 Jul 24F
labor issues: firefighters strike 1980 Mar 8H; illegal aliens sanctuary

1985 Dec 23G; job discrimination suit 1989 Jan 10F; teachers strike 1980 Jan 28F/Feb 11F; 1984 Dec 16F/Dec 20F; 1987 Oct 4F
medicine and health care: food poisoning 1985 May 7I; liver transplant 1989 Nov 27I; smoking restrictions 1988 Jul 24F; Tylenol poisonings 1982 Oct 6I
obituaries: Cody, John 1982 Apr 25F; Goodman, Benny 1986 Jun 13J; Gould, Chester 1985 May 11J; Halas, George 1983 Oct 31J; Kroc, Ray 1984 Jan 14J; MacArthur, Roderick 1984 Dec 15J; Pritzker, Abram 1986 Feb 8J; Sykes, Roosevelt 1983 Jul 11J; Waters, Muddy 1983 Apr 30J
politics and government: city council elections 1985 Dec 30F; election fraud probe 1982 Dec 3F; Sawyer selected acting mayor 1987 Dec 2F
religious issues: Bernardin named archbishop 1982 Jul 10J; cardinals named 1983 Feb 2J; diocese head investigated 1981 Sep 10J
sports: Wrigley Field night games 1985 Mar 25J; 1988 Feb 25J
transportation: mass transit 1981 Jun 11J

Chicago (singing group) 1982 Sep 22J; 1985 Jan 26J

Chicago, Art Institute of 1988 May 24J; 1989 Feb 17J

Chicago, University of (Illinois) 1980 Jan 25I/Oct 14I; 1981 Mar 19F/Nov 27I; 1985 Oct 11I; 1989 Nov 11I

Chicago Bears (football team) 1985 Jan 6J; 1986 Jan 5J/Jan 12J/Jan 26J; 1988 Jan 10J/Feb 2J; 1989 Jan 8J

Chicago Board of Trade 1982 Jun 13H/Oct 1H; 1988 Jun 27H; 1989 Aug 2H

Chicago Bulls (basketball team) 1988 Feb 7J/May 25J

Chicago Cubs (baseball team) 1984 Sep 30J/Oct 7J/Oct 17J/Nov 13J/Nov 23J/Mar 25J; 1987 Nov 18J; 1988 Feb 25J/Aug 8J; 1989 Oct 9J/Nov 8J

Chicago Mercantile Exchange 1984 Sep 6H; 1985 Apr 2H; 1989 Aug 2H

Chicago Sun-Times (newspaper) 1984 Apr 12J

Chicago Symphony Orchestra 1989 Jan 30J

Chicago Tribune (newspaper) 1984 Oct 28F

Chicago White Sox (baseball team) 1980 Aug 11J; 1983 Oct 8J/Oct 25J/Nov 23J; 1985 Aug 4J/Nov 25J

chickens 1980 Jan 21H/Mar 8I; 1983 Dec 26H; 1985 May 10E

child abuse 1984 Feb 2F/Oct 9F/Oct 12F; 1987 Jan 24F/Jun 19F/Jul 13F; 1988 Jun 29F/Aug 19F; 1989 Feb 22F/Apr 18F/Nov 20A

childbirth
fetuses and embryos: frozen embryos 1984 Apr 10I; 1985 Feb 22I; 1986 Jun 6I; 1987 Mar 10J; infertile woman with donated embryo 1984 Feb 3I; Tennessee embryo custody suit 1987 Mar 10J; in vitro fertilized quadruplets 1984 Jan 6I
health and safety issues: birth defects 1980 Jan 3I/Apr 3I; 1983 Jun 9I; 1984 Aug 16G; 1988 May 26I/Sep 21I; obstetrics cutback 1989 Oct 11F; premature births 1980 Jan 4I/Jan 25I

infant mortality and infanticide: birth rates 1981 Jun 3B; China girl baby murders 1983 Apr 8E; premature births 1980 Jan 4I/Jan 25I

people: Diana/Charles (son) 1982 Jun 21B; 1984 Sep 15J; Hearst, Patricia (daughter) 1981 May 3F; Hussein, King/Queen Noor (son) 1981 Jun 10C; Sarah/Andrew (daughter) 1988 Aug 8B

pregnancy: 1980 Jan 4I/Jan 25I; 1982 Dec 6F; 1983 May 2I/Jun 9I/Jun 20F/Jul 25I; 1984 Feb 16I; 1987 Jan 13F/Feb 26F

records: Texas woman's 21st child 1980 Jan 12I

surrogacy issues: 1987 Mar 31F; 1988 Feb 3F/Apr 6F/Jun 27F

child-care 1981 May 4F; 1983 Nov 14F; 1984 Oct 12F; 1985 Sep 26F; 1987 Dec 3D; 1988 Aug 16F; 1989 Feb 9F/Mar 15F/May 28H/Nov 9F

child custody 1980 Oct 20F; 1981 Jun 1F; 1984 Apr 25F; 1987 Mar 31F/Oct 29F; 1988 Feb 3F; 1989 Sep 21F/Sep 25F

Childe Holdings 1980 Nov 5C

Child Protection and Obscenity Enforcement Act (1988) 1989 May 16F

children see also international aid organizations (e.g., UNICEF)

adoption see adoption

Black Americans: 1985 Jun 3F

child abuse see child abuse

crime issues: Atlanta child murders 1981 Mar 5F/May 25F/Jun 21F; 1982 Feb 27F; MacDonald murder conviction restored 1982 Mar 31J; McDonald's gunman 1984 Jul 4F; Stockton gunman 1989 Jan 17F; Twilight Zone director acquitted 1987 May 29J

custody issues: 1980 Oct 20F; 1981 Jun 1F; 1984 Apr 25F; 1987 Mar 31F/Oct 29F; 1988 Feb 3F; 1989 Sep 21F/Sep 25F

day-care: 1981 May 4F; 1983 Nov 14F; 1984 Oct 12F; 1985 Sep 26F; 1987 Dec 3D; 1988 Aug 16F; 1989 Feb 9F/Mar 15F/May 28H/Nov 9F

education see education

family issues: single parent families 1985 May 15F; support payments 1984 Aug 16F; 1985 Jul 11F; 1987 Jun 25F; unmarried mothers 1985 Sep 29F

foreign developments: Afghanistan 1983 Jan 27A; Chile 1983 Aug 11D; China 1983 Apr 8E; Colombia 1988 Jul 3D; developing nations 1989 Sep 24I; El Salvador 1985 Feb 3D; Iran 1983 Sep 5A; Iraq 1989 Feb 28C; Kurds 1987 Mar 4C/Jun 20B/Jul 9B; Nicaragua 1982 Dec 11D; 1985 Mar 5D; 1988 Mar 31G/Apr 19D; South Africa 1981 Aug 19C; 1986 Dec 8C; Soviet atrocities 1983 Jan 27A; Turkey 1987 Mar 4C; United Nations 1989 Nov 20A; West Germany 1985 Jun 19B; Zimbabwe 1987 Nov 27C

health and safety issues: Agent Orange 1980 Jan 3I; AIDS 1982 Dec 9I; 1989 Oct 26F; aspirin/Reye's syndrome warning 1985 Jan 23I; birth control information 1985 Oct 17B; five-organ transplant 1988 May 11J; gun owner penalties 1989 Jun 20F; Halloween activities curtailed 1982 Oct 31I; heart transplants 1984 Feb 14I; 1986 Jun 10I; 1987

Oct 16I; INS amnesty rules changed 1987 Oct 8F; labor regulations 1982 Jul 16H; liver transplants 1984 Feb 14I; 1989 Nov 27I; passive smoking risks 1986 Nov 4I; tooth decay 1985 Feb 14F; vaccine injury compensation 1986 Nov 14F

infants see infants

pornography: 1982 Jul 2F; 1989 May 16F

television programming: 1982 May 5J; 1983 Oct 11F/Dec 22F; 1988 Jun 8F/Jul 29H/ Oct 19F/Nov 5F

welfare and social services: 1984 Jan 3F; 1985 May 22F/Jun 3F

Children of a Lesser God (Mark Medoff) (play/film) 1980 Jun 8J; 1986 Oct 3J/Oct 22J; 1987 Mar 30J

Children's Defense Fund 1984 Jan 3F; 1985 Jun 3F; 1987 Feb 2F

Children's Fund, U.N. 1985 Feb 3D; 1988 Dec 20A

Childrens' Hospital (Pittsburgh, Pa.) 1984 Feb 14I; 1988 May 11J

Child's Play (film) 1988 Nov 30J

child support payments 1984 Aug 16F; 1985 Jul 11F; 1987 Jun 25F

Chile see also individual leaders in the name index (e.g., Pinochet Ugarte, Augusto)

accidents and disasters: earthquakes 1985 May 3I; train collision 1986 Feb 17D

church developments: papal visit 1987 Apr 6D

civil strife: antigovernment protests 1980 Aug 27D; 1983 May 11D/May 14D/Jun 14D/Jul 9D/Jul 12D/Jul 29D/Aug 11D/Oct 11D; 1984 Mar 27D/Sep 5D; 1985 Sep 4D/Dec 23D; 1987 Apr 6D; exiles 1983 Jul 21D/Aug 27D; 1987 Mar 31D/Sep 8D; right-wing group arrested 1980 Aug 12D; state of siege 1984 Nov 15D; 1985 Jun 16D

economy: 1981 Dec 20D; 1983 Jan 5B/Mar 23D

energy issues: 1984 Dec 12D

foreign relations: Ecuador 1981 Mar 6D; Israel 1984 Jan 25D; Peru 1981 Mar 6D; United States 1981 Feb 20G; 1985 Jun 18D; 1989 Mar 17I/Jun 16G

government and politics: Aylwin elected president 1989 Dec 14B; constitutional reforms 1989 May 3D/Jul 30D

human rights: Amnesty reports abuses 1980 Sep 8D; bishops defy military subpoena 1989 Feb 15D; Catholics targeted 1985 Aug 24D; deaths squads 1986 Sep 2D; exile returns set 1987 Feb 12D; prison hunger strike 1987 Apr 1D; UN backs U.S. resolution 1986 Mar 14A; UN charges abuses 1983 Dec 9A

labor issues: general strikes 1986 Jul 3D; 1987 Oct 7D; 1989 Apr 18D; miners strike 1981 Apr 22D

monetary and trade issues: foreign debt 1983 Jul 29D; 1984 Jun 21D/Sep 14D; 1985 Feb 8D/Nov 1D; 1987 Feb 26D/Dec 15D; IDB loans 1984 Dec 12D; 1986 Dec 2D; IMF loans 1983 Jan 10D; 1985 Aug 16D; trade surplus, devaluation 1989 Jun 6D; World Bank loans 1985 Jun 18D; 1986 Nov 20D

Nazis: 1984 Jan 25D

obituaries: Frei Montalva, Eduardo 1982 Jan 22B

science and technology: supernova discovered 1987 Feb 24I

China see also individual leaders in the name index (e.g., Deng Xiaoping)

accidents and disasters: earthquakes 1988 Nov 6I; 1989 Oct 18E; flooding 1981 Aug 20E; 1985 Aug 8I

agriculture: food prices 1985 May 10E; 1988 May 15E; food shortages 1981 Apr 24I; grain harvest 1983 Dec 15E

arts and culture: Great Wall find 1983 Feb 26I; historians 1982 Apr 2E; writer's congress 1985 Jan 5E

atomic energy and safeguards: nuclear power plants 1984 Mar 16E; 1985 Sep 24E; 1986 Sep 23I; nuclear testing 1980 Oct 16E/Oct 16I; nuclear waste 1984 Feb 7E; nuclear weapons protest 1985 Dec 22E; U.S. nuclear cooperation pact 1984 Jun 21A; 1985 Nov 21G/Dec 16G

Beijing see Beijing

census data: population 1982 Sep 13E; 1983 Jan 30E/Apr 8E; 1985 Oct 7E; 1988 Feb 15E; 1989 Apr 14E

church developments: archbishop of Canton appointed 1981 Jun 6J; Billy Graham sermon 1988 Apr 17E; Catholic bishop of Shanghai paroled 1985 Jul 3E; Catholic church reopened 1985 Dec 24E; Protestant churches reopened 1982 Jan 10E

crime and law enforcement: abduction ring 1983 Jul 16E; crime rates, other data 1983 Jul 29E; 1984 May 26E; 1985 Nov 16E; hijackers sentenced 1983 Aug 18E; infanticide 1983 Apr 8E

defense and disarmament issues: Geneva disarmament conference 1980 Feb 5A; military leadership shuffled 1980 Feb 14E/Feb 19E; submarine-based ballistic missile 1982 Oct 16E

dissidents: defections 1982 Oct 16E; 1985 Aug 24E; 1986 Apr 30E; Fang addresses students 1988 May 4E; Fang gets rights award 1989 Oct 18A; Gang of Four 1980 Nov 20E/Dec 29E; 1981 Jan 25E; Hu Ping passport revoked 1988 Mar 23E; student/worker protests 1981 Jan 31E/Apr 13E; Xu Wenli arrested 1981 Apr 10E; Yang Jing arrested 1981 Apr 10E

economy and labor

business issues: bankruptcy law 1986 Aug 3E; industrial growth 1987 Feb 20E; privately owned companies 1989 Aug 28E; reforms 1980 Jan 27E; 1984 May 31E/Oct 20E; 1985 Apr 10E; 1987 Jan 29E; 1988 Jul 5E; state controls 1984 Mar 15E; stock market 1986 Sep 26E; trade balance 1983 Feb 6E; 1987 Jul 17E; 1988 Jan 22E; worker idleness 1988 Jun 13E

monetary and fiscal issues: anti-inflationary measures 1988 Sep 30E/Oct 27E; budget cuts announced 1981 Feb 28E; devaluation 1986 Jul 5E; exchange rates 1980 Dec 15E; five-year plan 1986 Apr 12E; 1988 Aug 18E; foreign-currency stores

1980 Mar 1E; gross national product 1983 Apr 29E; 1988 Feb 23E; inflation rate 1988 Jul 19E; 1989 Feb 28E; price controls 1988 Jan 19E/May 15E; readjustment policy 1981 Nov 30E; reforms 1980 Jan 27E; 1984 May 31E/Oct 20E; 1985 Apr 10E; 1987 Jan 29E; 1988 Jul 5E; rural incomes 1987 Feb 20E

education: African student protest 1986 Jun 6E; 1987 Jan 8E; 1988 Dec 27E; 1989 Jan 5E; compulsory work for students 1987 Jul 5E; dual-track education under attack 1981 Dec 19E; graduate students abroad limited 1989 Sep 2E; reforms 1985 May 28E

environmental issues: nuclear waste 1984 Feb 7E; pandas 1985 Jan 12I; 1988 Apr 6I

espionage issues: Chin espionage case 1986 Jan 2G/Feb 7G; Interpol seat taken over 1984 Sep 15E; New York Times journalist expelled 1986 Jul 23E; spy lawyer paroled 1985 May 15E; U.S. joint intelligence-gathering station 1981 Jun 17A

foreign investments: automobiles 1983 May 5H; coal mining 1984 Apr 29A; 1985 Jun 29A; imperial Chinese railway bonds 1983 Aug 18G; 1984 Feb 27A; income tax 1981 Dec 13E; increases in 1986 Jan 30E; International Monetary Fund loan 1986 Dec 12E; land-use rights 1988 Mar 22E; oil drilling 1982 Feb 16E/May 28E; 1983 Aug 6A/Aug 23A; regulations 1983 Sep 26E

foreign relations

Australia: 1984 Aug 10E; 1987 Jun 30E

Belgium: 1984 Jun 16E

Cambodia: 1981 Apr 20E; 1982 Feb 3E; 1988 Jul 1E/Aug 28A; 1989 Jan 16E

Denmark: 1984 Jun 16E

East Germany: 1985 May 16A; 1986 Oct 26E; 1987 Jun 10A

European Community: 1984 Mar 29A; 1987 Jan 16B; 1989 Jun 27A

France: 1980 Oct 17I; 1982 Oct 17A/Dec 27I; 1984 Jun 16E; 1986 Jun 8B

Great Britain: airliner sales 1985 Jun 1A; visits 1985 Jun 19B; 1986 Jun 8B/Oct 18E

Guyana: 1984 Jul 5A

India: 1981 Jun 28E; 1982 May 20E; 1983 Oct 30E; 1987 May 22C; 1988 Dec 23E

Indonesia: 1985 Jul 5E; 1989 Feb 25E

Iran: 1986 Aug 26C

Italy: 1984 Jun 16E; 1985 Apr 7A; 1986 Jun 8B

Japan: 1982 Aug 28E; 1983 Jul 20E; 1984 Mar 16E; 1986 Nov 8E; 1987 May 8E/Jun 27E; 1988 Apr 4E/Aug 25E; 1989 Dec 19E

Laos: 1987 Nov 30E

Macao: 1985 May 23E; 1987 Jan 6E/Mar 26E

Mongolia: 1986 Aug 9A

Netherlands: 1985 Jun 19B

North Korea: 1984 May 4E; 1987 May 21E

Norway: 1984 Jun 16E

Pakistan: 1980 Jan 21E

PLO: 1984 May 7A

Poland: 1986 Sep 30E

Portugal: 1985 May 23E; 1987 Jan 6E/Mar 26E

Southeast Asia: 1981 Feb 1E

South Korea: 1983 May 8E; 1985 Mar 28E

Sweden: 1984 Jun 16E

Taiwan: 1980 Jun 14E; 1981 Sep 30E/Oct 10E; 1986 May 20E; 1987 Oct 14E

USSR: border clashes 1986 Aug 23A; Cambodian conflict talks 1988 Aug 28A; educational and cultural exchanges 1983 Mar 22A; talks on normalizing relations 1980 Jan 19A; 1982 Oct 17A/Nov 19A; 1983 Oct 21A; 1984 Mar 26A; trade agreements 1980 Jun 6A; 1983 Mar 10A; 1984 Feb 10A; 1985 Jul 10A; visits 1982 Mar 7A/Nov 16A; 1984 Dec 29A; 1989 Feb 4A

Vietnam: military actions 1981 May 8E/May 17E; 1984 Apr 6E/Jul 12E; 1987 Oct 5E; 1988 Mar 14E; peace talks 1980 Feb 8E/Mar 6E; talks on Cambodia 1989 Jan 16E; war role admitted 1989 May 16E

West Germany: 1985 Jun 19B; 1986 Jun 8B

government and politics

anniversary: 1984 Oct 1E

appointments and resignations: forestry minister fired 1987 May 29D; Hua Guofeng resignation/dismissals 1980 Sep 7E/Dec 30E; 1981 Feb 6E; 1982 Sep 12E; Hu Yaobang resigns 1987 Jan 16E; leadership shakeups 1982 May 4E/Nov 19E; 1989 Jun 24E; Li Peng named acting premier 1987 Nov 24E; Li Xiannian appointed president 1983 Jun 18E; Wan Li appointed deputy premier 1980 Apr 16E; younger leaders promoted 1984 Sep 7E; 1985 Jun 18E/Sep 16E; Zhao Ziyang appointed deputy premier/premier/general secretary 1980 Apr 16E/Sep 10E; 1987 Jan 16E

organization and structure: bureaucracy reorganization 1982 Mar 8E/May 16E; constitution rewritten 1981 Nov 26E; 1982 Apr 27E/Sep 6E/Dec 6E; leadership shakeups 1982 May 4E/Nov 19E; 1989 Jun 24E; legal reforms passed 1989 Apr 4E; National People's Congress opens 1982 Nov 26E; 1983 Jun 6E; 1987 Mar 25E; 1988 Mar 25E; 1989 Mar 20E; party guidelines issued 1980 Mar 15E; power struggle 1989 May 27E

plots and plotters: Cultural Revolution trials completed 1983 Jun 9E; Kuomintang officials released 1982 Mar 10E; Mao plotters released 1982 Oct 2E; Mao's widow sentence commuted 1983 Jan 25E; party officials executed 1982 Apr 10E; 1983 Jan 17E/Aug 22E

policy issues: ambassadors recalled 1989 Jun 28E; sovereignty claims 1980 Jan 30E

Hong Kong sovereignty issues: 1982 Sep 24A/Nov 20E; 1983 Jul 13A/Oct 6A; 1984 Mar 14E/Aug 1E/Sep 26E/Dec 19A; 1985 May 27E/Dec 22E; 1988 Apr 28E; 1989 Jul 15E/Sep 27E human rights: 1980 Oct 2E; 1981 Dec 9A; 1984 Sep 25A; 1989 Oct 18A

international organizations: Asian Development Bank joined 1985 Nov 29E; 1986 Mar 11E; GATT membership application 1986 Jul 11E; International Atomic Energy Agency joined 1983 Oct 10A; International Monetary Fund loan 1986 Dec 12E; Interpol seat taken over 1984 Sep 15E; UN peace mission approved 1987 Sep 2A

medicine and health care: hepatitis 1988 Mar 21I; Ma Haide receives Lasker 1986 Sep 22I

obituaries: Hu Yaobang 1989 Apr 15E; Wenzhong Pei 1982 Sep 18I; Ye Jianying 1986 Oct 22E

Paracel Islands: 1980 Jan 30E

press and broadcasting: American films 1987 Jul 2E; Hong Kong editor jailed 1983 May 15E; *New York Times* journalist expelled 1986 Jul 23E; *Washington Post* reporter rebuked 1981 Sep 21E

science and technology: high-technology 1980 Jan 24E; 1983 May 25E/Jul 21A; 1984 Feb 11G; 1987 Oct 22G; U.S. sets cooperation 1983 May 11I; 1984 Jan 12A

sports: Asian Games 1986 Oct 5J; Los Angeles Olympics medals 1984 Aug 12J; Moscow Olympics boycott 1980 Feb 1J; Olympic athletes threatened by KKK 1984 Jul 11J

Spratly Islands: 1980 Jan 30E

Tiananmen Square showdown (1989): crackdown protested 1989 Jul 14G; pro-democracy movement 1989 Apr 16E/May 13E/May 27E/Jun 8E-9E/Jun 15E-16E/Jun 21E/Jun 30E/Jul 8E/Jul 11E/Jul 28A/Aug 31A/Dec 11E; secret executions 1989 Aug 30E; U.S. protests crackdown 1989 Jul 14G

Tibet *see* Tibet

U.S.-Beijing trade issues: grain pact 1984 Dec 23E; high-technology 1980 Jan 24E; 1983 May 25E/Jul 21A; 1984 Feb 11G; 1987 Oct 22G; industrial cooperation 1984 Jan 12A; military equipment sales 1980 Jan 24E/May 29G; 1981 Jun 16G; nuclear cooperation pact 1984 Jun 21A; 1985 Nov 21G/Dec 16G; science/technology cooperation 1983 May 11I; 1984 Jan 12A; smuggling 1984 Feb 11G; tax treaty 1984 Mar 21A; textiles 1983 Jan 2E/Jan 13H/Jan 19E/Aug 19A; trade agreements 1980 Sep 17A

U.S.-China visits: Brown 1980 Jan 13E; Bush administration 1989 Dec 9E/Dec 18G; Haig 1981 Jun 16G; Nixon 1989 Oct 28G; Shultz 1983 Jan 30E/Feb 2E; 1987 Mar 5E; U.S. naval port call 1986 Nov 11E; Weinberger 1983 Sep 29E; 1986 Oct 11E; Wu Xueqian 1983 Oct 13G; 1984 Mar 7G; Zhao Ziyang 1984 Jan 12A

U.S. relations: Taiwan policy 1980 Jun 14E; 1981 Jun 10E; 1982 Aug 17A; 1983 Nov 26E; U.S. ambassador named 1985 Jul 22G

china (ceramics) 1986 Oct 8B

China Alive in a Bitter Sea (Fox Butterfield) (book) 1983 Apr 28J

China Aviation Supplies Corp. 1985 Jun 1A

China Beach (TV show) 1989 Sep 17J

China Men (Maxine Hong Kingston) (book) 1981 Apr 30J

China Metalurgical Import and Export Corp. 1987 Jun 30E

China Spring (Chinese dissident magazine) 1988 Mar 23E

Chinese Alliance for Democracy 1988 Mar 23E

Chinese-Americans 1984 Jun 28F/Sep 19F

Chippewa Indians 1989 May 7F

chlordane (insecticide) 1987 Aug 11H

chlorofluorocarbons (CFCs) 1986 Dec 1I; 1987 Sep 16I; 1988 Mar 24H/May 27I/Aug 1H/Sep 26H; 1989 Feb 17I/Mar 2I/May 2I

chloroform 1985 Sep 23H

chocolate 1982 Nov 21B

cholera 1988 Aug 2I

cholesterol 1985 Oct 14I; 1986 Mar 20I/Nov 28I; 1987 Jun 18I/Sep 1I/Oct 5I/Nov 12I; 1989 Jul 7I/Nov 14I

Chorus Line, A (musical) 1983 Sep 29J

Christian Broadcasting Network 1988 Apr 12F

Christian Church (Disciples of Christ) 1984 Nov 30J

Christian Methodist Episcopal Church 1984 Nov 30J

Christic Institute 1988 Jun 23D

Christie Manson & Woods International, Inc. 1980 Dec 12J; 1982 Jul 9J; 1983 May 17J; 1985 Mar 14J/Apr 18J; 1986 Apr 10B; 1987 Mar 30J; 1988 May 3J/Nov 28J; 1989 May 9J

Christine (Stephen King) (book) 1983 Apr 10J/May 15J/Jun 1J/Jun 12J/Jul 10J/Dec 18J

Christmas Island 1983 Feb 26I

Christmas Story, A (film) 1983 Dec 7J

Christ Miracle Healing Center and Church 1982 Nov 23F

Christopher Cross (Christopher Cross) (recording) 1980 Aug 13J/Sep 10J

chromium 1981 Jul 28H

Chrysler Corp.
  business ventures: 1981 May 26H; 1983 Jan 13H/Sep 13H; 1985 Apr 15H/Sep 5D

  Canada operations: 1980 Jan 3D; 1981 Feb 17D; 1982 Nov 5D/Dec 12D; 1987 Sep 17D

  earnings: 1980 Feb 7H/May 7H/Jul 31H; 1981 Jul 22H; 1982 Feb 24H; 1984 Feb 23H/Apr 18H/Jul 19H; 1985 Feb 14H/Apr 25H/Jul 18H; 1987 Apr 27H; 1988 Feb 4H/Apr 27H/Jul 28H

  executive changes: Bieber named to board of directors 1984 Oct 4H; Fraser named to board of directors 1980 May 13H; Iacocca to stay 1983 Dec 8H

  federal loan guarantees: 1980 Jan 7H/Jun 11H; 1983 Jun 15H/Jul 13H

  fuel efficiency standards: 1986 Oct 2H

  labor issues: contracts 1983 Sep 5H; 1985 Oct 23H; 1988 May 4H; 1989 Aug 26H; hiring 1984 Dec 26H; job health and safety violations 1987 Jul 6H; layoffs 1980 Jun 21H; plant closing dispute 1988 Sep 26H; strikes 1983 Nov 5F

Chrysler Corp. Loan Guarantee Board 1980 Apr 10H/May 10H/Jul 15H; 1981 Jan 19H

church and state, separation of 1983 Oct 6F; 1985 Jul 1F; 1987 Jun 19F/Jun 24F/Jun 26F/Nov 9F; 1988 Jun 29F

Church of Christ Congregation 1984 Mar 15J

CIA *see* Central Intelligence Agency, U.S.

Ciba-Geigy Corp. 1983 Dec 13H

Cider House Rules, The (John Irving) (book) 1985 Jun 14J/Jul 19J/Aug 16J

Cigna 1988 Mar 22H

C.I.I.-Honeywell Bull 1980 Apr 15B

Cinchonero People's Liberation Movement (Honduras) 1982 Sep 17D; 1988 Jul 17D

Cincinnati Bengals (football team) 1982 Jan 10J/Jan 24J; 1989 Jan 8J/Jan 22J

Cincinnati Reds (baseball team) 1981 Oct 5J; 1985 Sep 11J; 1988 May 6J/Nov 1J; 1989 Jan 9J/Jun 25J/Jun 26J/Aug 10J/Aug 24J

Cinderella (singing group) 1987 Jan 28J/Feb 18J

cinema *see* motion pictures; *specific film (e.g., Platoon)*

Cinnamon Skin (John D. MacDonald) (book) 1982 Aug 8J

circumcision 1989 Mar 5I

cirrhosis of the liver 1984 Nov 23I

Ciskei (South Africa) 1980 Feb 12C/Dec 17C

CISPES *see* Committee in Solidarity with the People of El Salvador

Citibank *see* Citicorp

Citicorp 1980 Jan 23A/Mar 24F/May 1H; 1982 Mar 4H/Aug 16H; 1985 May 17H; 1986 Feb 4H; 1987 Mar 31H/May 19H; 1988 Jul 19A; 1989 May 11D

cities *see individual mayors in the name index (e.g., Barry, Marion); specific cities (e.g., Washington, D.C.)*

Cities Service Co. 1982 May 28H/May 31H/Jun 6H/Jun 8H/Jun 17H/Aug 6H/Aug 13H/Aug 16H/Aug 25H

Citizens' Committee on the El Salvador Crisis 1981 Dec 15D

Citizens for Tax Justice 1986 Jul 17H

Citizens' Party 1980 Apr 13F

citrus canker 1984 Sep 20H

citrus fruit 1986 Aug 10B/Sep 7B/Oct 27B

City Heat (film) 1984 Dec 12J

City of Angels (musical) 1989 Dec 11J

City University of New York 1987 May 29J

Civic Forum (Czech opposition group) 1989 Nov 21B/Nov 30B

Civil Aeronautics Board, U.S. (CAB) 1980 Jan 12G/May 13H; 1982 Mar 10H/Apr 26H; 1984 Aug 13H/Oct 25H

Civil Rights, U.S. Commission on
  bias and quota issues: "comparable pay" for women rejected 1985 Apr 11F; job bias found pervasive 1982 Nov 23F; job preferences for women 1987 May 15F; Pendleton blasts "new racism" 1985 Mar 5F; quotas renounced 1984 Jan 17F; Reagan record criticized 1982 Sep 12F; 1983 Mar 20F; school busing 1982 Oct 12F; set aside programs 1986 Apr 11F

  budget and spending program: 1982 May 27F

  organization and structure: extended five years 1983 Aug 4F; reconstituted as independent agency

1983 Nov 16F/Nov 30F; staff aide maps new course 1984 Jan 5F

  personnel: appointments 1983 Dec 6F/Dec 16F; dismissals 1981 Nov 16F; 1983 May 25F/Oct 25F

Civil Rights Act (1866) 1989 Jun 22F

Civil Rights Act (1964) 1985 Sep 20F; 1988 Oct 4F; 1989 Jun 5F

Civil Rights Act (1965) 1982 Feb 18F; 1987 Jan 21F

clams 1987 Dec 11I

Clark Air Base (Philippines) 1983 Jun 1E; 1987 Nov 23E; 1988 Oct 17E

Clark Amendment (1976) 1981 Mar 19G

Clean Air Act 1982 Jul 29H/Aug 11H; 1983 May 4H; 1985 Dec 5H; 1988 Oct 4H; 1989 Jun 12H

clean air laws 1981 Jan 22H/May 28H; 1983 Jun 23H; 1984 Jun 25H; 1985 Jun 27H; 1987 Jun 29H/Nov 17H; 1989 Jul 21H/Oct 11H

Clean and Sober (film) 1988 Aug 10J

Clean Water Act 1982 Apr 27F/May 26F; 1984 Jun 26H; 1985 Apr 18H/Jun 13H/Jul 23H; 1986 Oct 16H; 1987 Jan 21H/Feb 4H/Dec 1H; 1988 Jan 28H

Clear and Present Danger (Tom Clancy) (book) 1989 Sep 29J/Oct 27J/Dec 1J/Dec 22J

Clemson University (South Carolina) 1982 Jan 1J/Jan 2J; 1987 Dec 6J

Cleveland (Ohio) 1980 Dec 21H; 1984 Mar 23H; 1985 Oct 2F; 1987 Jun 29H; 1989 Oct 3F

Cleveland Browns (football team) 1986 Jan 4J; 1987 Jan 11J; 1988 Jan 9J/Jan 17J

Cleveland Cavaliers (basketball team) 1982 Nov 3J/Nov 10J

Cleveland Indians (baseball team) 1981 May 15J

Clinch River breeder reactor (Oak Ridge, Tenn.) 1982 Mar 5I/Sep 3F; 1983 Jan 6H/Jun 29H/Oct 26H

clonidine (drug) 1982 Sep 3I

clothing
  health risks: asbestos ban 1986 Jan 23H

  labor issues: home manufacture 1986 Aug 20H; job bias charged 1980 Dec 21H

  price issues: price increases 1988 Apr 20H

  trade issues: import curbs 1983 Jan 2E; 1985 Oct 10H; 1987 Sep 16H; 1988 Sep 9H/Sep 28H/Oct 4H; Japan limits exports 1986 Nov 15E

Clothing and Textile Workers Union, Amalgamated *see* Amalgamated Clothing and Textile Workers Union

Club of London 1987 May 28C

Club of Paris 1987 Jan 21D/Apr 5C/May 28C/Jul 1D/Nov 20D/Dec 8B

clubs 1986 Jun 30J; 1987 May 4F

cluster bombs 1982 Jun 18G/Jul 16G/Sep 29G/Sep 30C

CNN *see* Cable News Network

Coal Exporters Association of the United States 1984 Sep 18H

Coalition for Better Television 1982 Mar 4J

Coalition for Northeastern Governors 1983 Dec 5H

Coal Miner's Daughter (film) 1980 Mar 26J

coal mining
  accidents and disasters: Colorado explosion 1981 Apr 15H; Ken-

tucky explosion 1989 Sep 13H; Utah '84 fire fine 1987 May 11H

  business issues: coal-leasing program 1983 May 10H; joint ventures 1984 Apr 29A; 1985 Jun 29A

  environmental issues: illegal drilling 1983 Apr 1H; water pollution rules 1981 Jan 2H

  strikes and settlements: Great Britain 1981 Feb 18B; 1984 Mar 25B/May 30B/Aug 20B; 1985 Mar 3B; 1986 Sep 23B; Poland 1980 Aug 29B; 1981 Dec 25B; 1988 Sep 3B; 1989 Feb 9B; South Africa 1987 Aug 9C/Aug 30C; United States 1980 Mar 3H; 1981 Mar 23H/Mar 31H/Jun 8H; 1985 Apr 22B; USSR 1989 Jul 26B

coal slurry pipelines 1982 Oct 6G; 1988 Feb 23H

Coast Guard, U.S. 1980 Jul 14D; 1981 Sep 3F; 1984 Nov 17F; 1986 Apr 15C; 1987 Jun 5I; 1988 May 23F

Coast Guard Academy, U.S. 1980 May 21G

Cobra (film) 1986 Jun 18J

Cobra (helicopter) 1984 Apr 26G

Coca-Cola Co. 1982 Mar 19J; 1985 Apr 23J/Jul 10H/Oct 17H; 1986 Apr 9J; 1987 Sep 1H

cocaine
  crack: 1989 Feb 28F/Jul 31F/Aug 30F/Nov 6F

  crime and law enforcement: Congress passes tough penalties 1988 Oct 22F; DEA staff coordinator arrested 1984 Aug 14F; extradited Colombian convicted 1985 Mar 16F; Los Angeles seizure 1989 Sep 29F; military 1984 Mar 22G

  foreign developments: Bahamas 1984 Dec 17D; Bolivia 1981 Aug 29D; 1983 Jan 25D; Colombia 1984 Mar 10D/Nov 23D; 1989 Oct 14D; Great Britain 1986 Nov 27B; Honduras 1984 Nov 1D; Nicaragua 1984 Jul 18G; Peru 1984 Nov 17D

  health risks: deaths 1986 Jul 10F; use 1986 Oct 9F; 1988 Jan 13F; 1989 Jul 31F

  Medellin drug cartel *see* Medellin drug cartel

  people: Barry, Marion 1984 Aug 28F; De Lorean, John 1982 Oct 19J; 1984 Aug 16F; Hoffman, Abbie 1981 Apr 7J; Jordan, Hamilton 1980 May 28F

  sports: 1980 Aug 19J

coca production 1984 Nov 17D; 1986 Jan 11D; 1987 Sep 21D; 1989 Mar 1G

Coca Reduction Organization 1984 Nov 17D

Cocktail (soundtrack) 1988 Oct 29J/Dec 31J

cocoa 1987 May 28C; 1988 Mar 12A; 1989 Sep 18A

Cocom *see* Coordinating Committee for Multilateral Export

coconuts 1985 Nov 18E

Cocoon (film) 1985 Jul 17J; 1986 Mar 24J

Cocoon: The Return (film) 1988 Nov 30J

Cocos Islands (Australia) 1984 Apr 6E

cod 1987 Mar 17D

Coda (Led Zeppelin) (recording) 1982 Dec 15J

Code of Silence (film) 1985 May 15J

Codex (racehorse) 1980 May 17J

coffee 1981 Mar 11I; 1982 Sep 11I; 1984 Oct 1A; 1987 May 28C; 1989 Jul 3A/Oct 3A

coffee machines 1982 Feb 22F

Cogema (French nuclear fuel company) 1980 May 29H

"cohabitation" (French political arrangement) 1986 Aug 13B

coins, gold 1986 Sep 8H/Sep 16B

cold fusion 1989 May 9I/Jul 12I

Coleco Industries Inc. 1983 Nov 29J; 1985 Jan 2H

Collected Short Stories of Eudora Welty, The (Eudora Welty) (book) 1983 Apr 28J

College: The Undergraduate Experience in America (Carnegie Foundation) 1986 Nov 2F

College Entrance Examination Board
ACT: 1986 Sep 22F; 1988 Feb 25F/Sep 19F; 1989 Sep 11F
SAT: 1980 Oct 4F; 1981 Mar 26F; 1982 Sep 21J/Oct 4F; 1984 Sep 1F; 1985 Sep 23F; 1986 Sep 22F; 1988 Feb 25F/Sep 19F; 1989 Feb 3F/Apr 28F/Sep 11F

College Football Association 1981 Aug 22J

College Health Association, American *see* American College Health Association

College of Cardinals (Roman Catholic Church) 1988 May 29J

College of Europe (Bruges, Belgium) 1988 Sep 20B

colleges and universities *see also specific educational institutions (e.g., Harvard)*
careers: degree holder data 1988 Sep 21F; student attitudes 1980 Jan 20F; teaching 1987 Mar 10F
curriculum: home-study 1981 Feb 26J
draft registration: 1983 Jan 21F/Mar 10F; 1986 Jan 22G
enrollment: 1985 May 29F; 1989 Jan 15F
health and safety issues: AIDS 1989 May 22I; student attitudes 1980 Jan 20F
minority issues: apartheid protests 1985 Apr 9G; 1986 Apr 3G; desegregation 1983 Mar 24F/Jul 7F/Jul 11F; 1988 Feb 10F; 1989 May 30F; enrollment 1985 May 29F; 1989 Jan 15F; homosexual groups 1982 Feb 4F; racial bias in testing 1984 Jun 2F; racist incidents 1989 May 22F; student attitudes 1980 Jan 20F; tax-exempt status 1982 Jan 8F
religious issues: campus services 1981 Dec 8F
research: funding 1983 May 20F; 1986 Sep 7I; genetic research rules 1986 Jun 18I; political bias monitoring 1985 Aug 4F
student unrest: apartheid protests 1985 Apr 9G; 1986 Apr 3G; Florida spring break 1986 Mar 28F; South Korea crackdown 1986 Nov 2F; Vietnam War era 1984 Aug 30F
tax issues: 1982 Jan 8F; 1984 Mar 25F
teachers and faculty: student career interest 1987 Mar 10F; unions 1980 Feb 20H
tests and test scores: ACT 1986 Sep 22F; 1988 Feb 25F/Sep 19F; 1989 Sep 11F; racial bias 1984 Jun 2F; SAT 1980 Oct 4F; 1981

Mar 26F; 1982 Sep 21J/Oct 4F; 1984 Sep 1F; 1985 Sep 23F; 1986 Sep 22F; 1988 Feb 25F/Sep 19F; 1989 Feb 3F/Apr 28F/Sep 11F; student skill levels 1985 Feb 10F; 1989 Oct 8F
tuition and student aid: 1983 Aug 3F; 1985 Feb 11F/Jun 2F/Aug 10F; 1986 Aug 3F/Dec 28F; 1987 Nov 4F/Nov 30F; 1988 Aug 7F/Sep 21F/Aug 9F; 1989 Aug 9F

Cologne Declaration (1989) 1989 Jan 26J

Colombia *see also individual leaders in the name index (e.g., Betancur Cuartas, Belisario)*
accidents and disasters: avalanches 1985 Nov 13D; Avianca Airlines crash 1989 Nov 27D/Dec 5D; bull ring bleachers collapse 1980 Jan 21D; earthquakes 1983 Mar 31I; volcanic eruptions 1985 Nov 13D
arts and culture: Garcia Marquez takes refuge 1981 Apr 3D; Garcia Marquez wins Nobel 1982 Oct 21J
civil strife: American killed by guerrillas 1981 Mar 7D; amnesty law 1982 Nov 16D; British woman kidnapped 1980 Jan 5D; Canadian hostage released 1988 Mar 19E; death toll 1987 Aug 7D; government offensives 1980 Aug 26D; peasants march 1988 May 22D; peasants massacred 1988 Jul 3D; truces 1984 May 28D/Aug 30D; *see also* April 19th Movement
crime and law enforcement: Camarena slaying suspect arrested 1985 Apr 30D; kidnapping and adoption ring 1981 Aug 16D; Dominican embassy takeover: 1980 Feb 27D/Mar 2D/Mar 17D/Mar 30D/Apr 6D/Apr 19D/Apr 21D
drug trafficking: amnesty deal rejected 1984 Jul 5D; arrests 1989 Sep 12D; bombings 1989 Dec 6D; cocaine seizures 1984 Mar 10D; government crackdown 1989 Aug 30D; Lehder Rivas captured 1987 Feb 4D; marijuana seizures 1982 Feb 4D; U.S. interdiction 1984 Nov 17F/Nov 23D; U.S. trials 1985 Mar 16F; 1987 Aug 13D/Oct 5F; 1989 Oct 14D; *see also* Medellin drug cartel
foreign debt: 1984 Jun 21D/Sep 14D; 1985 Feb 8D; 1987 Nov 26D; 1988 Dec 30D; 1989 Jun 23D
foreign investment: 1985 Sep 16D
foreign relations: Bolivia 1980 Jul 29D; Central America 1983 Apr 21D/Jul 30D; Venezuela 1987 Aug 9D
government and politics: Barco Vargas elected president 1986 May 25D; Betancur elected president 1982 May 31D; elections 1980 Mar 9D; 1982 Mar 14D; 1986 Mar 9D; Galan assassination 1989 Aug 18D; justice ministry officials quit 1989 Sep 24D; state of siege end ordered 1982 Jun 4D
medicine and health care: malaria vaccine 1988 Mar 10I
Palace of Justice assault: 1985 Nov 7D/Nov 13D
United Nations policy: 1980 Jan 7A; 1988 Oct 26A
U.S. relations: 1982 Mar 3G; 1988 Dec 23D

Colombian Revolutionary Armed Forces 1984 May 28D

Colombo crime group 1986 Jun 13F/Nov 17F

Colony shale oil project 1982 May 2H

Colorado, University of (Boulder) 1989 Oct 12I

Colorado College (Colorado Springs) 1989 Nov 19J

Colored Museum, The (George C. Wolfe) (book) 1986 Nov 2J

"colorization" 1987 May 12J/Jun 19J

Color of Money, The (film) 1986 Oct 17J/Oct 22J/Nov 12J; 1987 Mar 30J

Color Purple, The (Alice Walker) (book/film) 1983 Apr 18J/Apr 28J; 1985 Dec 18J; 1986 Jan 22J/Feb 19J/Mar 19F/Mar 24J

Colors (film) 1988 Apr 20J/May 18J

Colour by Numbers (Culture Club) (recording) 1984 Jan 21J/Feb 18J/Mar 24J/Apr 28J

Colt Industries Inc. 1981 Jul 22H; 1989 Mar 15F

Columbia Cup (boat race) 1982 Jul 31J

Columbia Pictures Inc. 1982 Mar 19J; 1987 Sep 1H/Sep 1H; 1989 Sep 27H

Columbia Presbyterian Medical Center (New York, N.Y.) 1984 Sep 20J

Columbia River 1986 Nov 17H

Columbia University (New York, N.Y.) 1980 Jan 7J; 1981 Feb 20F; 1982 Apr 18F; 1985 Feb 5H/Dec 10F; 1986 Jan 2F; 1987 Oct 14F; 1988 Oct 8J; 1989 Mar 12C; *see also* Pulitzer Prizes

Columbus (manned space laboratory) 1987 Nov 10I

Columbus Circle (New York, N.Y.) 1987 Dec 4H

Comanche Indians 1980 Apr 13F

Comanche Peak nuclear power plant (Texas) 1986 Dec 11H

COMECON *see* Council for Mutual Economic Assistance

Come Pour the Wine (Cynthia Freeman) (book) 1980 Dec 7J; 1981 Jan 11J/Feb 8J; 1987 Dec 7J

comets 1983 Apr 16I/May 11I; 1984 Dec 15I; 1985 Sep 11I; *see also* Halley's Comet

Comex *see* Commodity Exchange Inc.

Comforts of Madness, The (Paul Sayer) (book) 1989 Jan 25J

Coming to America (film) 1988 Jul 13J/Nov 21J

Commando (film) 1985 Oct 23J

Commerce, U.S. Department of *see also specific department heads in the name index (e.g., Baldrige, Malcolm)*
appointments and resignations: Baldrige, Malcolm 1980 Dec 11F/Mosbacher, Robert A. 1988 Dec 6F; Verity Jr., C. William 1987 Aug 10H
budget and spending programs: 1988 Sep 27F; 1989 Aug 10F/Nov 8F
economic boycotts: NCR fined 1987 Aug 25H; Vietnam 1981 May 27G
environmental issues: fishing regulations 1980 Oct 21H; 1986 Jun 30F; 1989 Jun 23H/Sep 5H
fair trade issues: Canada 1986 Oct 16D; 1989 Mar 7H; China 1983 Jul 21A; 1984 Feb 11G; developing nation impact 1988 Sep 27H; Japan 1981 Jul 27H; 1983 Feb 10E; 1986 Jun 30F/Oct 13H; steel imports 1981 Jan 8H; 1982 Jun 11H/Aug 10H/Aug 25A; 1983 Jan 27H; 1984 Feb 10H; 1989 Mar 7H; USSR 1987 Jan 15H
reorganization plans: 1981 Dec 17F; 1982 May 24H

technology issues: high tech export regulations 1984 Jan 18H; NCR fined 1987 Aug 25H; oil-drilling equipment ban lifted 1987 Jan 15H; Soviet gas pipeline violations 1982 Sep 9G/Oct 5G

Commerce Clearing House Inc. 1987 Aug 12F/Nov 19H; 1988 Mar 1H; 1989 Oct 9F

Commercial Space Launch Act Amendments of 1988 1988 Nov 15I

Committee for an Open Convention 1980 Jul 28F

Committee for Social-Defense (KOR) (Polish dissident group) 1981 Sep 28B; 1984 May 12B/Aug 9B

Committee for Solidarity with Arab and Middle Eastern Political Prisoners 1986 Sep 17B

Committee for the Study of the American Electorate (Washington, D.C.) 1985 Jan 8F; 1986 Sep 27F; 1988 Dec 17F

Committee in Solidarity with the People of El Salvador (CISPES) 1987 Feb 20D; 1988 Sep 14F

Committee of Women and Relatives of Prisoners, Disappeared Persons, and Politically Assassinated Persons 1984 Nov 20G

Committee on the Present Danger 1980 May 9G

Committee to Fight Inflation 1980 Jun 21H

Commodity Credit Corp., U.S. (Agriculture Department) 1988 Jun 16H

Commodity Exchange Inc. (Comex) 1989 Aug 24H

Commodity Futures Trading Commission, U.S. (CFTC) 1980 Jan 6H; 1988 Feb 1H; 1989 Aug 29H/Sep 11H

Commodity Research Bureau index 1988 Jun 27H

Common Agriculture Policy (European Community) 1984 Mar 13B/Mar 31B; 1987 Jun 29B

Common Cause 1980 Jul 1F/Aug 28F; 1984 Oct 3F/Dec 18F; 1986 Apr 17F; 1987 Apr 7F; 1989 Oct 13F

common cold 1986 Jan 9I; 1989 Mar 10I

Common Ground: A Turbulent Decade in the Lives of Three American Families (J. Anthony Lukas) (book) 1985 Nov 21J; 1986 Feb 17J/Apr 17J

Commonwealth, The 1980 Sep 8E; 1981 Oct 7A; 1983 Nov 23A; 1986 Jul 13A/Jul 20B/Aug 5A; 1987 Oct 17A; 1988 Feb 2C; 1989 Jul 3E/Oct 1A/Oct 22A

Commonwealth Edison Co. 1984 Jan 13H/Feb 21H

Commonwealth Games 1986 Jul 24J

Communications Act of 1934 1983 Nov 8F

Communications Workers of America (CWA) (AFL-CIO) 1981 Aug 25H; 1982 May 20F; 1986 Jun 26A/Nov 26H; 1989 Aug 6H

Communist Workers Party 1983 Apr 21F; 1985 Jun 7F

Community for Creative Non-Violence 1986 Mar 16F

Community Service Block Grants 1986 Sep 18F

Comoros 1985 Nov 7C; 1989 Nov 26C/Dec 15C

Compagnie de Services Fiduciaries S.A. 1986 Dec 10F

Compagnie Financiere de Paris et des Pays-Bas (Paribas) 1986 Sep 10B

Company of Women, The (Mary Gordon) (book) 1981 Apr 12J

comparable worth 1985 Apr 11F/Jun 17F/Sep 4F; 1987 Mar 18F

Competition, The (film) 1981 Apr 4J

Competitive Equality Banking Act of 1987 1987 Aug 4H

Competitiveness, U.S. Council on 1988 Jun 3H

composers and conductors *see individual artists in the name index (e.g., Bernstein, Leonard)*

Comprehensive Smokeless Tobacco Education Act of 1986 1986 Feb 27F

Comptroller of the Currency, U.S. Office of the (Treasury Department) 1984 Oct 15H

computer chips
business issues: 1982 Dec 22H
fair trade issues: 1981 May 9E; 1983 May 16E; 1986 Jul 31A/Oct 13H; 1987 Mar 27H; 1988 Mar 25A/May 4A
quality issues: 1984 Mar 6G/Sep 10G
research and development: 1983 Sep 14I; 1984 Dec 20I; 1989 Nov 20I

Computer Fraud and Abuse Act 1989 Jul 26I

computers *see also* supercomputers
business issues: 1983 Feb 1B/Mar 27J; 1985 Jan 2H; 1986 Apr 8B/Nov 23E; 1988 Apr 6H/Nov 12H
chips *see* computer chips
colorization: 1987 May 12J/Jun 19J
copyrights and patents: 1981 Mar 3I; 1983 Aug 30H; 1987 Sep 15F; 1988 Mar 17H/Nov 29H; 1989 Apr 25H
crime and piracy issues: bombings 1980 Apr 15B; FBI urges legislation 1983 Oct 18F; file security 1987 Jun 22H; hacker indicted 1988 Dec 22H; viruses 1988 Nov 3H; 1989 Jul 26I; youths penetrate system 1983 Aug 21F
education issues: 1988 Apr 5F
fair trade issues: 1982 Jan 9A; 1983 Dec 2B; 1984 Jul 12A; 1985 Jan 29A; 1986 Oct 20H; 1987 Apr 17H/Aug 25H/Nov 13G; 1988 Feb 29D; 1989 Jul 18H
foreign developments: Australia 1987 Sep 9E; France 1980 Apr 15B; 1982 Jan 27I; Sweden 1983 Dec 2B; West Germany 1983 Dec 2B
games: 1989 Oct 22J
household surveys: 1985 Feb 15J
Iran-Contra arms scandal: 1987 Feb 20G
military issues: 1980 Mar 10G/Jun 6G/Jun 17G
scientific research: 1981 Dec 17I; 1987 Jan 16I
viruses: 1988 Nov 3H; 1989 Jul 26I

computer software *see* computers

Conan the Barbarian (film) 1982 Jun 9J

Conan the Destroyer (film) 1984 Jul 18J

Concealed Enemies (TV show) 1984 Sep 24J

Concordia University (Montreal) 1988 Dec 20I

Concord (Calif.) Naval Weapons Center 1987 Sep 1F

Condition of Teaching, The: A State by State Analysis (Carnegie Foundation study) 1983 Aug 23F condoms 1987 Feb 24D; 1988 Jun 27J

condors 1983 Apr 5I; 1988 Aug 29H

C-130 (aircraft) 1984 Jun 19G

Confederacy of Dunces, A (John Kennedy Toole) (book) 1981 Apr 13J

Confederate flag 1983 Apr 20J; 1987 Jun 7F

Conference for Economic Cooperation 1980 Nov 6A/Nov 6C

Conference of Islamic States 1980 Jan 29A/May 22A/Oct 1A/Oct 9A/Oct 19C

Conference on a Black Agenda for the '80s (Richmond, Va.) 1980 Mar 2F

Conference on Confidence- and Security-Building Measures (CSBM) 1989 Mar 9B

Conference on Confidence- and Security-Building Measures and Disarmament in Europe (CDE) 1984 Jan 17B/Jul 7B; 1986 Aug 19A/Sep 10B/Sep 22A

Conference on Democratization of Communist Countries 1982 Oct 18G

Conference on Security and Cooperation in Europe (CSCE) 1980 Sep 9A/Nov 11A/Dec 19B; 1981 Dec 18B; 1982 Mar 12A; 1983 Sep 7B; 1985 Jan 29B; 1986 Sep 23B/Nov 4B; 1989 Jan 15B

Congo 1984 Jul 30C; 1985 Oct 17A; 1988 Aug 1C; 1989 Sep 19C

Congress, U.S. *see legislative branches* (e.g., Senate); *individual leaders in the name index* (e.g., O'Neill, Thomas)

Congressional Budget Office, U.S. (CBO)
  budget deficits: 1981 Mar 16H; 1982 Feb 5H/Feb 25H/Jul 27H/Jul 28H/Sep 1H; 1983 Aug 19H; 1984 Feb 22H; 1985 Feb 27H; 1986 Feb 26H/Aug 19H; 1987 Jan 2F/Jan 20H; 1989 Jan 4H/Aug 17H
  defense spending: 1983 May 2G
  family incomes: 1982 Feb 27H/Apr 14H; 1983 Aug 25F; 1985 May 22F; 1987 Nov 10H; 1988 Feb 25H
  taxes: 1985 Jun 26H

Congressional Medal of Honor, U.S. 1980 Jul 9G

Congressional Research Service, U.S. 1985 May 22F

Congress Watch 1986 Feb 22F

Connecticut
  economy and labor: Sabbath work law 1985 Jun 26F
  health care: AIDS vaccine 1987 Aug 18I; fetal rights 1982 Jul 7F
  obituaries: Bowles, Chester Bliss 1986 May 25F; Luce, Clare Boothe 1987 Oct 9J
  politics and government: presidential campaigns 1980 Mar 25F; 1984 Mar 27F; 1988 Mar 29F; woman gubernatorial nomination 1986 Sep 9F

Connecticut, University of (Storrs) 1988 Mar 30J

Connecticut General Corp. 1981 Nov 9H

Conn Smythe Trophy *see* Smythe Trophy

Conoco Inc. 1981 May 29H/Jul 12H/Jul 14H/Jul 17H/Jul 20H/Jul 23H/Aug 4H/Aug 5H/Aug 11H

Conquistador Cielo (racehorse) 1982 Jun 5J; 1983 Jan 4J

Conrail (Consolidated Rail Corp.) 1981 May 5H; 1984 Jun 18H; 1986 Aug 22H; 1988 Jan 20H/Oct 9F

Conservation Chemical Co. 1985 Aug 5H

Conservative Political Action Conference 1981 Mar 20F; 1982 Feb 26H; 1985 Mar 2F; 1986 Feb 1F

Consolidated Edison Co. 1983 Aug 13J

Consolidated Rail Corp. *see* Conrail

Consolidation Coal Co. 1980 Mar 3H

Consortium for Superconducting Electronics 1989 May 23I

Constitution (ship) 1986 Aug 14G

Constitution, U.S. *see also specific amendments* (e.g., Fourteenth Amendment)
  amendments: abortion 1981 Dec 16F; 1982 Mar 10F; balanced budget 1982 Jul 19F/Aug 4H/Sep 8F/Oct 1F; 1985 Jul 23F/Aug 5F; 1986 Mar 25H/May 19H; D.C. statehood 1985 Aug 22F; flag desecration 1989 Jun 27F/Jun 29F/Oct 19F; school prayer 1982 May 6F/May 17F; 1984 Mar 15F
  bicentennial celebrations: 1987 May 22F/Jul 16F/Sep 17F
  bill of rights: drug testing 1986 Sep 18F; female conscription 1981 Jun 25F
  ERA *see* Equal Rights Amendment
  judicial branch: Marshall calls "defective" 1987 May 6F; "restraint" debated 1985 Oct 12F/Oct 25F/Nov 15F

constitutional convention 1985 Jul 23F

Constitutional Rights, Center for *see* Center for Constitutional Rights

construction industry *see also specific companies, projects* (e.g.,)
  accidents: 1987 Apr 23J
  budget and spending programs: 1989 Jul 31G
  corruption and ethics issues: 1982 May 18F/Jul 25G; 1984 Oct 1F; 1985 Mar 15F; 1986 Nov 17F; 1987 Aug 18F; 1989 Nov 23E
  foreign developments: Great Britain 1985 Jan 2B; Japan 1987 Nov 20E; 1988 Mar 29G; 1989 Nov 22H/Nov 23E; West Germany 1981 Mar 25B
  housing starts *see* housing starts
  labor issues: 1981 Mar 25B; 1986 Apr 17H; 1987 Feb 17H; 1989 Jan 23H

consumer boycotts 1984 Jan 27B; 1986 May 1F; 1987 Aug 19H; 1988 Aug 21F/Dec 11C

consumer credit
  1984 statistics: 1984 Jan 12H/Apr 23H/May 14H/Jun 14H/Jul 16H/Sep 12H/Oct 12H/Dec 14H
  1985 statistics: 1985 Jan 11H/Feb 14H/Apr 12H/Jun 14H/Aug 15H/Sep 17H/Oct 9H/Nov 13H/Dec 10H
  1986 statistics: 1986 Jan 14H/Feb 11H/Mar 13H/Apr 14H/May 12H/Jun 6H/Aug 7H/Sep 9H/Nov 6H/Dec 5H
  1987 statistics: 1987 Jan 9H/Feb 6H/Mar 9H/Apr 7H/May 7H/Jun 5H/Aug 7H/Sep 4H/Oct 7H/Nov 6H/Dec 7H
  1988 statistics: 1988 Jan 7H/Feb 5H/Mar 7H/Apr 8F/May 6H/Jun 7H/Jul 8H/Aug 5H/Sep 8H/Oct 7H/Nov 7H/Dec 7H
  1989 statistics: 1989 Jan 9H/Feb 7H/Apr 6H/May 5H/Jul 7H/Aug 8H/Sep 8H/Oct 6H/Nov 7H/Dec 7H

Consumer Federation of America 1986 Dec 29H

Consumer Power Co. in Jackson, Mich. 1984 Jul 16H

consumer price index (CPI)
  1980 statistics: 1980 Jan 28F/Feb 22H/Apr 22H/Aug 22H/Oct 24H
  1981 statistics: 1981 Jan 23H/May 22H/Oct 27H
  1982 statistics: 1982 Jan 24H/Apr 23H/Jun 22H/Sep 23H
  1983 statistics: 1983 Jan 21H/Feb 25H/Mar 23H/May 24H/Jun 22H/Jul 22H/Aug 23H/Sep 23H/Oct 26H/Nov 23H/Dec 21H
  1984 statistics: 1984 Feb 24H/Mar 23H/Apr 24H/May 22H/Jun 22H/Jul 24H/Aug 23H/Sep 21H/Oct 24H/Nov 21H/Dec 20H
  1985 statistics: 1985 Jan 23H/Feb 26H/Mar 22H/Apr 23H/May 21H/Jun 20H/Jul 23H/Aug 22H/Sep 24H/Oct 23H/Nov 22H/Dec 20H
  1986 statistics: 1986 Jan 22H/Feb 25 H/Mar 25H/Apr 22H/May 21H/Jun 20H/Jul 23H/Aug 21H/Sep 23H/Oct 23H/Nov 25H/Dec 19H
  1987 statistics: 1987 Jan 21H/Feb 27H/Mar 27H/Apr 24H/May 25H/Jun 23H/Jul 22H/Aug 21H/Sep 23H/Oct 23H/Nov 20H/Dec 18H
  1988 statistics: 1988 Jan 20H/Feb 26H/Mar 23H/Apr 20H/May 20H/Jun 21H/Jul 22H/Aug 23H/Sep 21H/Oct 21H/Nov 22H/Dec 20H
  1989 statistics: 1989 Jan 19H/Feb 22H/Mar 21H/Apr 18H/May 18H/Jun 16H/Jul 19H/Aug 18H/Sep 19H/Oct 19H

Consumer Product Safety Commission, U.S. (CPSC) 1983 Jul 7H/Aug 25H; 1987 Dec 20H

consumer spending
  1983 statistics: 1983 Jul 20H/Sep 20H
  1985 statistics: 1985 Sep 19H/Oct 18H/Dec 23H
  1986 statistics: 1986 Feb 21H/Mar 20H/Apr 18H/Jun 19H/Jul 23H/Aug 20H/Sep 21H/Oct 23H/Nov 20H/Dec 18H
  1987 statistics: 1987 Feb 20H/Mar 19H/Apr 24H/May 25H/Jun 18H/Jul 27H/Aug 24H/Sep 21H/Oct 26H/Nov 26H
  1988 statistics: 1988 Jan 28H/Feb 26H/Mar 24H/Apr 27H/May 27C/Jun 24H/Jul 28H/Aug 26H/Sep 21H/Oct 27H/Nov 30H/Dec 21H
  1989 statistics: 1989 Jan 30H/Mar 1H/Mar 24H/Apr 27H/May 26H/Jun 23H/Jul 28J/Aug 30H/Sep 22H/Oct 27H/Nov 30H/Dec 21H

Contact (Carl Sagan) (book) 1985 Oct 25J/Nov 22J/Dec 20J; 1986 Jan 31J

Contadora Group
  Central American peace initiatives: 1983 May 19A/Jul 17D/Jul 23D/Nov 28D; 1984 Sep 7D/Sep 21D/Sep 22G/Oct 3A/Nov 6D/Nov 8D/Nov 20D; 1985 Feb 14D/Mar 2D/Apr 12D/Sep 12D/Oct 13D/Nov 11D/Dec 7D; 1986 Jan 14D/Apr 7D/May 25D/Jun 7D/Nov 8D; 1987 Jan 19D/Oct 7A

Continental Airlines 1982 Jan 25H; 1983 Sep 30H

Continental Divide (film) 1981 Sep 30J

Continental Illinois Corp. 1982 Jul 21H; 1984 May 17H/Jul 26H/Sep 26H/Dec 1H

Continental Illinois National Bank & Trust Co. (Continental Illinois Corp.) 1982 Jul 21H

continental shelf 1983 Jul 28H; 1987 Apr 27H/Aug 27H

contract bridge 1985 Nov 2J

Control (Janet Jackson) (recording) 1986 Jun 18J/Jul 16J/Aug 13J

Conventional Forces in Europe (CFE) talks 1984 Jan 16G/Mar 16B/Apr 19B; 1987 Jul 27B; 1989 Mar 6B/Jul 13B

Convention on International Trade in Endangered Species 1989 Oct 16C/Oct 30E

Convention on the Rights of the Child 1989 Nov 20A

Conzinc Rio Tinto of Australia Ltd. 1980 Jan 11E

cooking oil 1983 Nov 16E; 1988 Aug 4B; 1989 May 20B

Cook Islands 1985 Aug 6E

Coordinating Committee for Multilateral Export Controls (Cocom) 1988 Apr 4E

Coors Co., Adolph 1987 Aug 19H

Copenhagen (snuff) 1986 Jun 20F

copper 1980 May 17A/Nov 10H; 1981 Mar 12H/Jul 28H; 1983 Apr 16F/Jun 17D; 1984 Jan 26H/Sep 6H; 1985 Dec 3H; 1986 Jun 30H/Jul 28H

Copper-7 (birth control device) 1988 Sep 9F

Coptic Christians 1981 Sep 5C; 1985 Jan 6C

Copyright Act of 1976 1984 Jan 17H

Copyright Office, U.S. (Library of Congress) 1987 Jun 19J

copyrights
  intellectual property: computer chips 1986 Sep 22H; computer programs 1983 Aug 30H; 1988 Mar 17H; film "colorization" 1987 Jun 19J; music 1983 Jul 18J; photocopying 1983 Apr 14F; publishing industry 1982 Jul 13H; VCRs 1981 Oct 19J; 1982 Jun 14H; 1984 Jan 17H
  overseas infringement: 1985 Oct 16H; 1986 Apr 7H; 1988 Apr 29E; 1989 Apr 25H

coral reefs 1984 Aug 16I; 1989 Jan 13E

Corcoran Gallery of Art (Washington, D.C.) 1989 Jun 13J/Dec 18J

Cordillera People's Liberation Army (Philippines) 1986 Sep 13E

Cordis Corp. 1988 Aug 31F

cordless telephones 1985 Feb 15J

corn
  harvests: 1982 Nov 29H; 1983 Aug 1I/Sep 12H; 1984 Jan 13H; 1988 Jul 12H
  herbicides: 1984 Nov 20H; 1985 Feb 22I
  price and production issues: farm prices 1986 Dec 11C; 1988 Jun 27H; payments to farmers 1986 Oct 24H; price-support loan levels 1986 Jan 13H; storage programs 1981 Oct 6H
  Soviet grain embargo: 1980 Jan 12A
  trade issues: 1981 Jul 28G; 1984 Dec 23E; 1986 Nov 7D/Dec 30H

Cornell University (Ithaca, N.Y.) 1981 Oct 19I; 1985 Feb 25I; 1987 May 25J; 1988 May 30J; 1989 Jul 26I

Cornerstone (Styx) (recording) 1980 Jan 2J

coronary bypass surgery 1988 Aug 11I

corporate earnings
  1980 statistics: 1980 Mar 19H

1982 statistics: 1982 Nov 1H/Nov 19H

1983 statistics: 1983 Mar 21H/May 9H/May 15H/Aug 8H/Aug 19H/Nov 3H/Nov 14H/Nov 22H

1984 statistics: 1984 Feb 19H/Mar 20H/May 19H/Aug 4H-6H/Aug 20H/Nov 4H/Nov 10H/Nov 12H/Nov 20H

1985 statistics: 1985 Mar 21H/May 21H

1986 statistics: 1986 Mar 19H/May 20H/Aug 19H/Sep 18H/Nov 19H

1987 statistics: 1987 Mar 18H/May 22H/Aug 7H/Aug 21H/Nov 24H

1988 statistics: 1988 Feb 22H/Mar 23H/May 9H/Jun 23H/Aug 8H/Sept 20H/Nov 7H/Nov 29H

1989 statistics: 1989 Feb 21H/Mar 23H/May 8H/May 25H/Aug 7H/Aug 29H/Nov 6H/Nov 29H

corporate raiding 1985 May 20H; 1987 Jul 3H/Oct 14F

corporate takeovers 1981 Feb 3H/Jul 13H; 1984 Mar 13H; 1985 Dec 6H; 1987 Apr 21H/Jul 3H; 1988 Oct 26H; 1989 Jan 17H; *see also specific companies* (e.g., Nabisco)

Corporation for Public Broadcasting 1981 Feb 26J; 1983 Aug 2F

Corsica 1981 Feb 12B/Dec 1B; 1982 Aug 8B; 1984 Aug 12B/Aug 24B

Corsican National Liberation Front 1981 Jan 30B

Cosa Nostra (crime group) 1980 Jun 30F; 1985 Feb 26F; 1986 Mar 21F/Nov 19F

Cosby Show, The (TV show) 1985 Sep 12J

cosmic background explorer satellite 1989 Nov 18I

Cosmos (soccer team) 1980 Sep 21J; 1985 Jun 22J

Cosmos 1402 (Soviet satellite) 1983 Jan 23I

Cosmos 1443 (Soviet satellite) 1983 Apr 20I

Cosmos 1614 (Soviet spacecraft) 1984 Dec 19I

Cosmos Club (Washington, D.C.) 1984 Sep 18F

Costa Rica *see also individual leaders in the name index* (e.g., Arias Sanchez, Oscar)
  Central American peace accord *see* Central American peace accord
  church developments: papal visit 1983 Mar 2D
  crime and civil disorders: Camarena slaying suspect arrested 1985 Apr 4D; terrorist bombings 1981 Mar 17D
  economy and labor: banana plantations purchased by government 1985 Mar 31D; banana workers strike ends 1980 Jan 17D; IMF loans 1988 Apr 4D
  foreign debt: 1981 Aug 6D/Oct 4D; 1982 Jul 21D; 1983 Sep 9D; 1985 Mar 18G; 1989 Oct 27D
  foreign relations: Cuba 1980 Apr 16D; 1981 May 11D; El Salvador 1980 Jul 11D; 1989 Dec 10D; Honduras 1981 Mar 17D; Nicaragua 1983 Oct 1D
  government and politics: Arias Sanchez elected president 1986 Feb 2D; Monge elected president 1982 Feb 7D
  international organizations: International Monetary Fund 1988 Apr

4D; Organization of American States 1983 May 5D

Nicaraguan conflict: 1983 Oct 12D; 1984 Apr 21D; 1986 Apr 25D/May 16D/Sep 26D; 1988 Feb 5D; 1989 Jul 23D

peace initiatives: Contadora Group talks 1984 Nov 20D; 1985 Feb 14D; 1986 Jan 14D/May 25D/Nov 8D; regional peace talks 1983 Apr 21D/Jul 30D/Oct 5D; 1984 Nov 8D; 1989 Dec 10D; see also Central American peace accord

U.S. relations: Contra supply operations 1986 Dec 25G; 1987 Jan 17D/Mar 16D/May 2G; economic aid 1986 Aug 13G; military advisers 1985 May 6D; military aid 1984 May 10D/Oct 5D; 1984 Nov 1981 Mar 17D

cotton 1982 Dec 9H; 1983 Jan 19E/Mar 22H/Jul 30F

Cotton Bowl (football) 1980 Jan 1J; 1982 Jan 1J; 1983 Jan 1J; 1984 Jan 2J; 1985 Jan 1J; 1986 Jan 1J; 1987 Jan 1J; 1988 Jan 1J; 1989 Jan 2J

Cotton Club, The (film) 1984 Jun 18J/Aug 15J; 1985 Jan 16J

Coumadin (drug) 1986 Mar 19F

Council for a Black Economic Agenda 1985 Jan 15F

Council for Mutual Economic Assistance (COMECON) 1981 Jul 4B; 1983 Oct 20B; 1984 Jun 14A/Nov 31D; 1985 Oct 25B; 1986 Sep 25B/Nov 11A

Council of Economic Advisers, U.S. (CEA) 1981 Aug 30H/Dec 8H; 1982 Feb 10H; 1983 Mar 25H; 1985 Sep 24H; 1988 Feb 19H/Dec 6F; 1989 May 1H

Council of North Atlantic Shipping Associations 1986 Dec 6H

Council on Economic Priorities 1984 Nov 15I

Council on Environmental Quality, U.S. 1980 Feb 19H/Feb 19I/Jul 23H; 1981 Jan 17H

Council on Foreign Relations (New York, N.Y.) 1985 Jul 22G; 1987 Feb 4B

Council on Hemispheric Affairs 1984 Nov 1D

Council on the Environment 1981 Jan 13H

Council on Wage and Price Stability, U.S. 1980 Feb 25H/Dec 16H; 1981 Jan 29H

Counterlife, The (Philip Roth) (book) 1988 Jan 11J

Country (film) 1985 May 6H

coups and coup attempts
Bangladesh: 1981 Jun 1E
Bolivia: 1981 Jun 27D; 1984 Jun 30J
Bophuthatswana (South African homeland): 1988 Feb 10C
Burkina Faso: 1987 Oct 15C
Burma: 1988 Sep 18E
Burundi: 1987 Sep 3C
El Salvador: 1980 May 2D
Ethiopia: 1989 May 20C
Fiji: 1987 May 14E
Gambia: 1981 Jun 30C
Ghana: 1983 Jun 19C
Guatemala: 1983 Aug 7D; 1989 May 9D
Guinea: 1984 Apr 3C; 1985 Jul 4C
Guinea-Bissau: 1980 Nov 14C
Haiti: 1989 Apr 2D
Kenya: 1982 Aug 1C
Lesotho: 1986 Jan 20D

Liberia: 1980 Apr 12C
Maldives: 1988 Nov 3E
Mauritania: 1981 Mar 16C; 1984 Dec 12C
Nigeria: 1983 Dec 31C; 1985 Aug 27C
Panama: 1988 Mar 18D
Paraguay: 1989 Feb 3D
Philippines: 1987 Jan 28E/Apr 18E; 1989 Dec 1E/Dec 7E
Sao Tome and Principe: 1988 Mar 9C
Senegal: 1981 Aug 6C
Sierra Leone: 1987 Mar 23C
Spain: 1981 Feb 23B/Feb 24B
Sudan: 1985 Apr 6C; 1988 Dec 20C
Suriname: 1980 Feb 25D/Aug 13D; 1982 Dec 11D
Syria: 1982 Jan 30C
Thailand: 1981 Apr 3E; 1985 Sep 9E
Transkei (South African homeland): 1987 Dec 30C
Tunisia: 1987 Nov 7C
Turkey: 1980 Sep 12B
Uganda: 1980 May 11C; 1985 Jul 27C
United Arab Emirates: 1987 Jun 17C
Upper Volta: 1980 Nov 25C; 1982 Nov 7C; 1983 Aug 5C
Zambia: 1980 Oct 27C

Courier-Journal (Kentucky newspaper) 1986 Jan 9H

court-martials
Argentina: 1983 Dec 13D
Israel: 1982 Oct 15C
Spain: 1981 Dec 19B; 1982 Feb 19B; 1984 Apr 15B
United States: 1980 Feb 1G; 1983 Dec 1G; 1987 May 15G/Jun 25G/Jul 27G/Aug 24G; 1989 Feb 24G

courts, U.S. see Supreme Court; specific subjects of cases (e.g., abortion); case names (e.g., Roe v. Wade)

Cousins (film) 1989 Feb 22J

Covenant, The (James A. Michener) (book) 1980 Dec 7J; 1981 Jan 11J/Feb 8J/Mar 8J/Apr 12J; 1987 Dec 7J

Coventry (ship) 1982 May 25D

covert aid 1981 Mar 19G; 1984 Nov 27G; 1985 Dec 10G; 1986 Sep 17G; 1989 Jul 21G; see also specific geographic regions (e.g., Nicaragua)

Cozzene (racehorse) 1985 Nov 2J

CPI see consumer price index

CP Rail 1987 Aug 28D; 1989 May 4D

CPSC see Consumer Product Safety Commission, U.S.

crack cocaine 1989 Feb 28F/Jul 31F/Aug 30F/Nov 6F

craters 1987 Jun 17I

Creation (Gore Vidal) (book) 1981 May 10J

creationism 1981 Mar 5F/Mar 19F/Jul 21F; 1982 Jan 5F/Aug 29I/Nov 22I; 1983 Oct 17F; 1985 Jan 10F; 1987 Jun 19F

Credit Agricole III (ship) 1987 May 7J

Credit and Commerce American Investment Inc. 1981 Aug 25H

credit cards 1987 Jul 2F; 1988 Dec 7H

Credit-Suisse 1986 Dec 15B

Cree Indians 1982 Jul 8D; 1988 Nov 29D

Creepshow (film) 1982 Dec 8J

Creepshow 2 (film) 1987 May 20J

cremation 1985 Feb 12I

Creme Fraiche (racehorse) 1985 Jun 8J

Crescent City (Belva Plain) (book) 1984 Oct 19J

cricket (sport) 1986 May 26J; 1987 May 25J/Nov 8J

crime see organized crime; specific crime (e.g. Central Park jogger)

Crimea (USSR) 1987 Jul 28B

crime rates 1983 Sep 11F; 1984 Apr 19F/Sep 8F; 1985 Apr 7F/Jun 9F; 1986 Jul 26F; 1988 Oct 9F; 1989 Apr 9F/Oct 29F

Crimes and Misdemeanors (film) 1989 Nov 13J

Crimes of Passion (Pat Benatar) (recording) 1980 Oct 8J/Dec 3J; 1981 Jan 7J/Feb 11J/Mar 4J

Crimes of the Heart (Beth Henley) (play/film) 1981 Apr 13J/Nov 4J; 1986 Dec 12J

Criminal Justice Reform Act of 1982 1982 Sep 13F

Critical Condition (film) 1987 Jan 21J

Critical Mass (antinuclear group) 1980 Jul 14I; 1982 Aug 18I

Croatia (Yugoslavia) 1986 Feb 15B; 1989 Jan 19B

Crocker National Corp. 1981 Aug 25H; 1985 Jan 2H

"Crocodile" Dundee (film) 1986 Sep 26J/Oct 22J/Nov 12J

"Crocodile" Dundee II (film) 1988 Jun 15J

cross-country running 1981 Jan 13J; 1988 Mar 26J; 1989 Mar 19J

Crossing Delancey (film) 1988 Sep 21J/Oct 19J

Crossings (Danielle Steel) (book) 1982 Oct 17J

Crowds and Power (Elias Canetti) (book) 1981 Oct 15J

Crow Indians 1981 Aug 20F

Crown Trust Co. 1983 Jan 7D

Crow's Nest Pass agreement 1982 Feb 13D/Mar 26D; 1983 Feb 1D/Nov 14B

Crude Oil Windfall Profit Tax Act of 1980 1980 Apr 2H; 1983 May 6H

cruel and unusual punishment 1986 Jun 26F; 1987 Jun 15F; 1989 Jan 14F/Jun 26F

cruise missiles (Soviet)
testing: 1984 Aug 25B
U.S. inspection of: 1989 Jul 8B

cruise missiles (U.S.)
contract issues: Boeing 1980 Mar 25G; Northrop 1987 Dec 20G; stealth technology 1983 Feb 15G
demonstrations and protests: Great Britain 1982 Dec 12B; 1983 Jan 1B/Apr 4B/Nov 16B; Italy 1983 Oct 22B; West Germany 1983 Apr 4B/Oct 22B
deployment
by NATO: Denmark 1984 May 10B; Great Britain 1980 Jun 17B; 1983 Jul 6B/Nov 14B; 1984 Jan 1B; Italy 1983 Nov 16B; Netherlands 1981 Nov 16B; 1985 Nov 1B/Nov 29B; 1986 Feb 28B; Soviet warnings 1982 Nov 29B; 1983 Nov 23A
at sea: 1983 Dec 11G
SALT II violations: 1986 Nov 28G/Dec 5G
testing: 1983 Jul 15D; 1984 Mar 6D; 1986 Jan 22G; 1989 Feb 1D

Cruising (film) 1980 Feb 27J

Crystal River nuclear power plant (Florida) 1980 Feb 26I

CSBM see Conference on Confidence- and Security-Building Measures

CSCE Conference on Security and Co-operation in Europe

Cuba see also individual leaders in the name index (e.g., Castro, Fidel)
accidents and disasters: hurricanes 1985 Nov 22I
Angolan conflict: four-power talks 1988 May 3C/Jun 24C/Jul 13C/Aug 8C/Oct 9C/Nov 15C; peace accord 1988 Nov 18C/Dec 13C/Dec 22C; South African troop skirmishes 1987 Nov 11C; troop withdrawals 1988 Dec 20A; 1989 Jan 10C
arts and culture: poet emigrates 1980 Mar 16D
crime and corruption issues: minister sentenced 1989 Aug 31D; Ochoa Sanchez arrested 1989 Jun 14D; Ochoa Sanchez sentenced to death 1989 Jul 7D
economy: 1985 Jun 4D; 1988 Dec 23D
Ecuadorian embassy seizure: 1981 Feb 21D
foreign debt: 1983 Jan 6D; 1985 Sep 23D
foreign relations: Comecon summit 1984 Jun 14A; El Salvador 1981 Feb 22G; 1982 Mar 8D; Ethiopia 1984 Jan 8C; France 1980 Apr 1D; Great Britain 1986 Jan 31D; 1988 Sep 13B; Morocco 1980 Jul 12A; USSR 1984 Apr 7D
human relations: defections 1987 May 28D; political prisoners 1987 May 29D; 1988 Dec 18D; U.S. charges violations 1984 Feb 10G; 1987 Mar 11A
immigration and refugees: Mariel boatlift 1980 May 1D/Sep 26D; 1983 May 24D; 1984 Jul 12D/Dec 3F/Dec 14D; 1986 Jul 9D; 1987 Nov 20G; 1988 Dec 2F; U.S. emigrees 1981 Jan 18D; 1985 Feb 21F; 1986 Jul 9D; 1987 Nov 20G
international organizations: Comecon summit 1984 Jun 14A; United Nations 1980 Jan 7A/Sep 11A; 1989 Oct 18A
Latin relations: Bahamas 1980 May 10D; Brazil 1986 Jun 25D; Costa Rica 1981 May 11D; El Salvador 1981 Feb 23D; 1989 Dec 25D; Grenada 1983 Oct 26D/Oct 26G/Nov 2D/Nov 4D/Nov 9D; Mexico 1980 Aug 3D; Nicaragua 1983 Nov 25D; 1985 Feb 27D/May 2D/Dec 14G; Uruguay 1985 Oct 17D; Venezuela 1980 Jan 19D
medicine and health care: dengue fever 1981 Jun 30D
obituaries: Dorticos Torrado, Osvaldo 1983 Jun 23D; Lam, Wilfredo 1982 Sep 11J
Peruvian embassy compound occupation: 1980 Apr 6D/Apr 7D/Apr 16D
press and broadcasting: Radio Marti 1982 Jun 27G; 1983 Jun 9G/Sep 29G; 1985 May 20D; U.S. media 1982 Sep 9G; 1989 Jul 21D
science and technology: space program 1980 Sep 18I
sports: high jump record 1989 Jul 29J; Los Angeles Olympics withdrawal 1984 May 23J; Pan American Games 1983 Aug 28J; 1987 Aug 23J

trade embargo: effects 1982 Apr 3G; travel restrictions 1983 May 16G; 1984 Jun 28F
UN Policy: 1980 Jan 7A/Sep 11A; 1989 Oct 18A
U.S. relations: broadcasting 1982 Sep 9G; 1989 Jul 21D; Cuban aid to Salvadoran rebels 1981 Feb 22G; 1982 Mar 8D; Cuban missile crisis conference 1989 Jan 28A; human rights violations charged 1984 Feb 10G; 1987 Mar 11A; Jackson visit 1984 Jun 28A; Roman Catholic bishops visit 1985 Jan 25D; trade embargo impact 1982 Apr 3G; travel curbs 1983 May 16G; 1984 Jun 28F; Vesco residence reported 1984 May 6A

Cuba and His Teddy Bear (Reinaldo Povod) (play) 1986 May 18J

Cubana Airlines 1986 Jul 21D; 1989 Sep 3D

Cuban Adjustment Act of 1966 1984 Feb 12F/Dec 3F

Cuban-Americans 1989 Aug 29F

Cuban-Haitian Task force 1981 Feb 5F

Cuban missile crisis (October 13-28, 1962) 1989 Jan 28A

Cuban refugees 1980 May 21D/May 24F/Jun 1F/Jun 20F/Aug 5F/Aug 29D/Oct 24F/Nov 3F/Nov 19F; 1981 Jan 1F; 1983 Mar 4G/Jul 7F; 1984 Feb 12F; 1987 Nov 29F; Carter, Jimmy 1980 Jun 28A

cucumbers 1989 Apr 27I/Sep 19I

Cujo (Stephen King) (book) 1981 Sep 6J/Oct 4J/Nov 8J/Nov 8J/Dec 6J; 1982 Jan 10J

Cultural Revolution, Chinese (1966-76) 1985 Apr 27E

Culture Club (singing group) 1984 Jan 21J/Feb 18J/Feb 28J/Mar 24J/Apr 28J

curfews
Afghanistan: 1980 May 15E
Bangladesh: 1985 Mar 1E
Chile: 1983 Aug 26D
Colombia: 1989 Aug 30D
El Salvador: 1981 Jan 11D
India: 1984 Nov 1E
Israel: 1988 Jan 24C
Jamaica: 1980 Jul 18D
Nigeria: 1983 Dec 31C; 1987 Mar 13C
Poland: 1981 Dec 22B; 1982 Apr 28B
Sri Lanka: 1987 Jul 29E
Syria: 1980 Mar 5C
Turkey: 1980 Jul 11B
United States: 1984 Aug 9F
Venezuela: 1989 Mar 5D
Zambia: 1980 Oct 27C
Zimbabwe: 1984 Feb 3C/Mar 11C

currency see monetary unit (e.g., dollar, U.S.); organization (e.g., European Monetary System); specific country (e.g., Japan)

Curtiss-Wright Corp. 1981 Jan 28H

Customs Service, U.S. (Treasury Department) 1984 Feb 11G; 1986 Mar 13E; 1987 Jun 26F; 1988 May 23F; 1989 Aug 19G

cyanide 1981 Jul 28H; 1982 Oct 6I/Oct 29I; 1985 Jun 14F; 1986 Jun 20H; 1987 Dec 9F; 1989 Mar 17I

cycling 1985 Jun 23J; 1987 Jul 26J/Sep 6J; 1988 Apr 23J/Aug 1J

cyclone 1988 Nov 29I

Cyclops (Clive Cussler) (book) 1986 Feb 28J

cyclotrons see atomic particle accelerators

Cyprus *see also individual leaders in the name index* (e.g., Denktash, Rauf)
arts and culture: mosaics 1989 Aug 3J
intercommunal talks: Greek Cypriots 1984 Jan 17B; 1985 Mar 1B; 1988 Feb 21B; 1989 Mar 19B; Greek premier visits 1982 Mar 1B; peace talks 1980 Aug 9B; 1985 Jan 20B; 1988 Aug 24B/Nov 23B; Turkish Cypriot state 1983 Nov 15A/Nov 15B; 1984 May 11A; 1985 May 5B/Jun 9B; Turkish premier visits 1986 Jul 4B; Turkish troop withdrawals 1983 May 13A; 1984 Jan 3B; UN mediation efforts 1980 Apr 3B; 1984 Sep 20A; 1985 Jun 12B; 1989 Dec 4B
terrorism: Kuwait Airways hijacking 1988 Apr 8C/Apr 13C; PLO ship bombing 1988 Feb 15C
cystic fibrosis 1989 Aug 24I
Cy Young Award
Carlton, Steve: 1982 Oct 26J
Clemens, Roger: 1986 Nov 13J; 1987 Nov 11J
Davis, Mark: 1989 Nov 14J
Denny, John: 1983 Nov 2J
Fingers, Rollie: 1981 Nov 25J
Gooden, Dwight: 1985 Nov 13J
Hernandez, Willie: 1984 Nov 6J
Hershiser, Orel: 1988 Nov 10J
Hoyt, LaMarr: 1983 Oct 25J
Saberhagen, Bret: 1985 Nov 11J; 1989 Nov 15J
Scott, Mike: 1986 Nov 11J
Sutcliffe, Rick: 1984 Nov 23J
Valenzuela, Fernando: 1981 Nov 11J
Viola, Frank: 1988 Nov 9J
Vuckovich, Pete: 1982 Nov 3J
Czechoslovakia *see also individual leaders in the name index* (e.g., Havel, Vaclav)
arts and culture: Havel released from prison 1989 May 17B; Kafka works to be published 1989 Apr 17J; *Magicians of the Silver Screen* opens 1980 Dec 26J
church developments: Roman Catholic demonstration 1988 Mar 25B
economy: '85 data 1986 Feb 14B; Comecon summit 1984 Jun 14A; food price increases 1982 Jan 30B
environmental issues: Danube River dam project 1989 May 24B
family issues: marriage courses 1981 Sep 27B
foreign relations: East Germany 1989 Oct 3B/Oct 4B/Nov 1B; France 1981 Feb 16B; Hungary 1989 May 24B; Poland 1980 Oct 9B/Nov 5B/Nov 27B; 1982 Apr 5B; USSR 1988 Oct 11B; 1989 Dec 4B
government and politics: Adamec resigns as premier 1989 Dec 7B; Calfa chosen premier 1989 Dec 7B; Central Commmittee mass resignations 1989 Nov 24B; Communist Party congress 1986 Mar 28B; Havel elected president 1989 Dec 29B; Husak resigns as party secretary 1987 Dec 17B; opposition group talks 1989 Nov 21B; premier replaced 1988 Oct 10B
human rights: border shootings 1986 Sep 18B; Charter 77 1980 Jun 1B; 1985 Mar 11B; 1987 Jan 6B; 1988 Jun 17B; 1989 Jun 29B; demonstrations and protests 1988 Mar 25B/Aug 21B; 1989 Jan 15B/Jan 23B/Aug 21B/Oct

28B/Nov 19B; dissidents 1982 Mar 23B; 1986 Sep 2B; 1987 Mar 11B; 1989 May 17B; West German embassy sit-in 1985 Jan 15B
obituaries: London, Artur 1986 Nov 8B
Soviet invasion (1968) 1989 Dec 4B
sports: ice hockey 1985 May 3J; Los Angeles Olympics withdrawal 1984 May 17J; tennis 1980 Dec 7J
U.S. relations: 1984 Mar 14G
Czechoslovakia Invasion (1968) 1989 Dec 4B
Czechoslovak Independent Peace Association 1988 Jun 17B

D

Dachau (Nazi death camp) 1980 Apr 4B
Daddy (Danielle Steel) (book) 1989 Dec 1J/Dec 22J
Daedalus 88 (human-powered aircraft) 1988 Apr 23J
Daewoo Shipyard and Machinery Ltd. 1987 Aug 22E
Dai-Ichi Kangyo Bank Ltd. 1988 Jul 19A
Daily News (New York City newspaper) 1984 Jun 25F
Daily News (Philadelphia newspaper) 1985 Oct 22H
dairy products 1980 Jan 7B; 1981 Mar 31H; 1982 May 5H; 1983 Aug 7A/Nov 19F; 1984 Jun 4H; 1986 Mar 28H/Dec 16B; 1989 Sep 19A; *see also specific products (e.g., milk)*
Dalkon Shield (intrauterine birth control device) 1983 Jun 6I; 1984 Feb 29F/Oct 22H/Nov 14H; 1985 Apr 2H/Aug 21H; 1987 May 11F/Dec 11F; 1988 Oct 7F
Dallas (TV show) 1980 Nov 21J; 1984 Oct 21J/Nov 18J/Dec 16J
Dallas Cowboys (football team) 1980 Aug 1J/Dec 28J; 1981 Jan 4J; 1982 Jan 10J; 1983 Jan 22J; 1986 Jan 4J; 1989 Apr 23J
Dallas-Fort Worth International Airport 1985 Aug 2H
Dallas Morning News (newspaper) 1985 Feb 10F
daminozide (ripener) 1987 Jan 7H; 1989 Feb 1I/Mar 16I
Damnation Alley (TV show) 1983 Jun 12J
Damn the Torpedoes (Tom Petty & the Heartbreakers) (recording) 1980 Mar 5J
dams 1985 Jul 19I; 1986 Nov 17H; 1987 Feb 28E; 1988 Aug 19H; 1989 Feb 20D/May 24B
dance and dancers *see specific dance company* (e.g., American Ballet Company); *individual artists in the name index* (e.g., Nureyev, Rudolf)
Dance Writings (Edwin Denby) (book) 1988 Jan 11J
Dancing Brave (racehorse) 1986 Oct 5J
Dancing in the Dark (Bruce Springsteen) (recording) 1985 Feb 26J
Dancing on the Ceiling (Lionel Richie) (recording) 1986 Sep 17J/Oct 22J/Nov 22J
Dancing Spree (racehorse) 1989 Nov 4J
Danger, The (Dick Francis) (book) 1984 Apr 20J/May 11J
Dangerous Liaisons (film) 1988 Dec 21J
Danube River 1984 May 26B; 1989 May 24B/Sep 10B

Dar al Maal al Islami (DMI) (House of Islamic Funds) 1981 Jun 11J
Dare (Human League) (recording) 1982 Jun 16J
Dark Half, The (Stephen King) (book) 1989 Dec 1J/Dec 22J
Darlington Manufacturing Co. 1980 Dec 14H
Dartmouth College (Hanover, N.H.) 1988 Mar 10F/Mar 28F
Dartmouth Review (college newspaper) 1988 Mar 10F/Mar 28F
databases 1987 Mar 17F
Davis Cup (tennis tournament) 1980 Sep 7J/Dec 7J; 1981 Dec 13J; 1982 Nov 28J; 1983 Dec 28J; 1984 Dec 17J; 1985 Dec 22J; 1986 Dec 28J; 1987 Dec 20J; 1988 Dec 18J; 1989 Dec 17J
Davis Cup Team, U.S. 1980 Sep 7J
Daya Bay nuclear power station (China) 1986 Sep 23I
Day After, The (TV film) 1983 Nov 20J/Nov 23I
daylight savings time 1986 Jul 8F
Day of the Cheetah (Dale Brown) (book) 1989 Jul 28J
Day One (TV show) 1989 Sep 17J
Daytona 24-Hours (auto race) 1985 Feb 3J; 1986 Feb 2J; 1987 Feb 1J; 1988 Jan 31J; 1989 Feb 5J
Daytona 500 (auto race) 1981 Feb 15J; 1985 Feb 17J; 1986 Feb 16J; 1987 Feb 15J; 1988 Feb 14J
DC-6 (aircraft) 1988 Jan 23D
DC-9 (aircraft) 1981 Mar 28E/Mar 31E/Dec 1B
DC-10 (aircraft) 1989 Sep 19C
DDI (dideoxyinosine) (drug) 1989 Oct 21F
DDT (dichlorodiphenyl-trichloro-ethane) 1980 May 17A; 1985 Aug 12H; 1986 May 22H
DEA *see* Drug Enforcement Agency, U.S.
Dead, The (film) 1987 Dec 17J; 1988 Jan 3J
Dead and the Living, The (Sharon Olds) (book) 1985 Jan 14J
Dead Bang (film) 1989 Mar 29J
Dead Poets Society (film) 1989 Jun 2J/Jun 28J
Dead Ringers (film) 1988 Sep 23J; 1989 Mar 22J
Dead Zone, The (film) 1983 Nov 2J
deafness 1988 Mar 13F
Dean's December, The (Saul Bellow) (book) 1982 Mar 7J/Apr 11J
Dean Witter Reynolds Organization Inc. 1981 Feb 20F/Oct 8H
Death and Life of Dith Pran, The (Sydney Schanberg) (article) 1984 Nov 2J
Death of a Princess (film) 1980 May 12J/May 22B
Death on the Rock (TV show) 1988 Apr 28B; 1989 Jan 26B/Mar 19J
death penalty
federal legislation: congressional actions 1984 Feb 22F; 1988 Oct 22F; Federal Espionage Act provision 1984 Apr 3F
foreign issues: Canada 1987 Jun 30D; China 1982 Apr 10E; 1989 Jun 15E; East Germany 1987 Jul 17B; France 1981 Sep 30B; Great Britain 1983 Jul 13B; Philippines 1983 May 16E

rights issues: Amnesty International report 1981 Dec 9A; Christian churches condemn 1984 Dec 8F
Supreme Court rulings *see* Supreme Court
deaths
Abbas, Ferhat: 1985 Dec 24C
Abdullah, Sheik Mohammed: 1982 Sep 8E
Abel, I(orwith) W(ilbur): 1987 Aug 10H
Abell, George: 1983 Oct 7I
Acorn, Milton: 1986 Aug 20J
Adams, Ansel: 1984 Apr 22J
Adams, Harriet: 1982 Mar 27J
Adams, Sherman: 1986 Oct 27F
Adams, Tom: 1985 Mar 11D
Adamson, George: 1989 Aug 20C
Addams, Charles: 1988 Sep 29J
Adler, Luther: 1984 Dec 8J
Ailey, Alvin: 1989 Dec 1J
Albaret, Celeste: 1984 Apr 25J
Albright, Ivan Le Lorraine: 1983 Nov 18J
Alcott, John: 1986 Jul 28J
Aldrich, Robert: 1983 Dec 5J
Algren, Nelson: 1981 May 9J
Alliluyeva, Svetlana: 1986 Apr 16J
Allon, Yigal: 1980 Feb 29C
Alsop Jr., Joseph Wright: 1989 Aug 28F
Alvarez, Luis W.: 1988 Sep 1I
Anaya Sanabria, Herbert Ernesto: 1987 Oct 29D
Anderson, Robert Bernerd: 1989 Aug 14H
Andrade, Carlos Drummond de: 1987 Aug 17J
Andropov, Yuri: 1984 Feb 9B
Andrzejewski, Jerzy: 1983 Apr 20J
Anouilh, Jean: 1987 Oct 3J
Aquino Jr., Benigno: 1983 Aug 21E
Arieti, Silvano: 1981 Aug 7I
Arlen, Harold: 1986 Apr 23J
Armstrong, Herbert: 1986 Jan 15J
Arnaz, Desi: 1986 Dec 2J
Aronson, Boris: 1980 Nov 16J
Asch, Moses: 1986 Oct 19J
Ashby, Hal: 1988 Dec 27J
Ashford, Emmet: 1980 Mar 1J
Ashley, Laura: 1985 Sep 17J
Ashton, Frederick: 1988 Aug 18J
Ashton-Warner, Sylvia: 1984 Apr 28J
Astaire, Fred: 1987 Jun 22J
Astor, Mary: 1987 Sep 24J
Atkinson, Brooks: 1984 Jan 13J
Ayer, A(lfred) J(ules): 1989 Jun 27J
Bader, Douglas: 1982 Sep 5B
Baker, Carlos: 1987 Apr 18J
Baker, Chet (Chesney): 1988 May 14J
Baker, Ella: 1986 Dec 13F
Balanchine, George: 1983 Apr 30J
Baldrige, Malcolm: 1987 Jul 25H
Baldwin, James (Arthur): 1987 Nov 30J
Baldwin, Roger: 1981 Aug 26F
Ball, Lucille Desiree: 1989 Apr 26J
Bane, Frank: 1983 Jan 23F
Bang, Frederik Barry: 1981 Oct 3I
Barber, Samuel: 1981 Jan 23J
Baroni, Geno: 1984 Aug 27F
Barr, Stringfellow: 1982 Feb 3J
Barrett, Emma: 1983 Jan 28J
Barr Jr., Alfred Hamilton: 1981 Aug 15J
Barrow, Errol: 1987 Jun 1D
Barszcz, Edward: 1981 May 24B
Barthelme, Donald: 1989 Jul 23J
Barthes, Roland: 1980 Mar 25J
Barzini, Luigi: 1984 Mar 30J
Basie, Count: 1984 Apr 26J
Bateson, Gregory: 1980 Jul 4I

Bauer, Charita: 1985 Feb 28J
Baxter, Anne: 1985 Dec 12J
Bayer, Herbert: 1985 Sep 30J
Bayne, Beverly: 1982 Aug 29J
Beadle, George Wells: 1989 Jun 9I
Beard, James Andrews: 1985 Jan 23J
Bearden, Romare (Howard): 1988 Mar 12J
Beaton, Cecil: 1980 Jan 18J
Beck, Julian: 1985 Sep 14J
Beckett, Samuel Barclay: 1989 Dec 22J
Belvin, Harry J.W. ("Jimmy"): 1986 Sep 18J
Benchley, Nathaniel: 1981 Dec 14J
Bennett, Gareth: 1987 Dec 7J
Bennett, John: 1980 May 4J
Bennett, Michael: 1987 Jul 2J
Benyahia, Muhammad: 1982 May 3C
Berg, Alan: 1984 Jun 18F
Bergman, Ingrid: 1982 Aug 29J
Bergner, Elisabeth: 1986 May 12J
Berlin, Irving: 1989 Sep 22J
Berlinguer, Enrico: 1984 Jun 12J
Bernbach, William: 1982 Oct 2J
Berrigan, Ted: 1983 Jul 4J
Besse, George: 1986 Nov 17B
Bessie, Alvah: 1985 Jul 21J
Betancourt, Romulo: 1981 Sep 28D
Bettis, Valerie: 1982 Sep 26J
Beuys, Joseph: 1986 Jan 23J
Bhave, Vinoba Acharya: 1982 Nov 15E
Bias, Len: 1986 Jun 19J
Bingham, Jonathan Brewster: 1986 Jul 3F
Bird, Henry: 1980 Jan 30J
Bird, Junius Bouton: 1982 Apr 2I
Bishop, Maurice: 1983 Oct 19D
Bitterman III, Chester Allen: 1981 Mar 7D
Blake, Eubie: 1983 Feb 12J
Blanc, Mel: 1989 Jul 10J
Bloch, Felix: 1983 Sep 10I
Bloomfield, Michael: 1981 Feb 15J
Blunt, Anthony: 1983 Mar 26B
Bobo, Willie: 1983 Sep 15J
Boehm, Karl: 1981 Aug 14J
Bolger, Ray: 1987 Jan 15J
Boll, Heinrich Theodore: 1985 Jul 16J
Borges, Jorge Luis: 1986 Jun 14J
Boult, Adrian: 1983 Feb 23J
Bowen, Billy: 1982 Sep 27J
Bowles, Chester Bliss: 1986 May 25F
Boyd, William: 1983 Feb 19I
Boyle, Tony (William Anthony): 1985 May 31F
Bradford, Robert: 1981 Nov 14B
Bradley, Jenny: 1983 Jun 3J
Bradley, Omar: 1981 Apr 8G
Braine, John: 1986 Oct 28J
Brassai (Gyula Halasz): 1984 Jul 8J
Brattain, Walter Houser: 1987 Oct 13I
Braudel, Fernand: 1985 Nov 28J
Brautigan, Richard: 1984 Oct 25J
Brezhnev, Leonid: 1982 Nov 10B
Bricktop: 1984 Jan 31J
Brisson, Frederick: 1984 Oct 8J
Brooks, Louise: 1985 Aug 8J
Brown, Clarence: 1987 Aug 17J
Brown, Douglas: 1986 Jan 19F
Brown, Harrison ("Scott"): 1986 Dec 8I
Brown, Sterling Allen: 1989 Jan 13J
Bruce, Virginia: 1982 Feb 24J
Bruhn, Erik: 1986 Apr 1J
Bryant, Paul ("Bear"): 1983 Jan 26J
Brynner, Yul: 1985 Oct 10J
Bubbles, John: 1986 May 18J
Bunker, Ellsworth: 1984 Sep 27G

Bunting, Basil: 1985 Apr 17J
Bunuel, Luis: 1983 Jul 30J
Burcham, Jack: 1985 Apr 24I
Burnet, (Frank) Macfarlane: 1985 Aug 31I
Burnham, Forbes: 1985 Aug 6D
Burns, Arthur: 1987 Jun 26H
Burrows, Abe: 1985 May 17J
Burton, Phillip: 1983 Apr 10F
Burton, Richard: 1984 Aug 5J
Butterfield, Lyman Henry: 1982 Apr 25J
Cagney, James: 1986 Mar 30J
Caldwell, Erskine: 1987 Apr 11J
Caldwell, Taylor: 1985 Aug 30J
Calvino, Italo: 1985 Sep 19J
Campbell, Joseph: 1987 Oct 30J
Canaday, John Edwin: 1985 Jul 19J
Capote, Truman: 1984 Aug 25J
Carmichael, Hoagy: 1981 Dec 27J
Carpenter, Karen: 1983 Feb 4J
Carradine, John: 1988 Nov 27J
Carroll, Madeleine: 1987 Oct 2J
Carter III, Billy: 1988 Sep 25J
Carver, Raymond: 1988 Aug 2J
Casey, William: 1987 May 6G
Cassavetes, John: 1989 Feb 3J
Cecil, David: 1986 Jan 1J
Chagall, Marc: 1985 Mar 28J
Chamoun, Camille: 1987 Aug 7C
Champion, Gower: 1980 Aug 25J
Charlotte, Grand Duchess (Luxembourg): 1985 Jul 9B
Chase, Lucia: 1986 Jan 9J
Chayefsky, Paddy: 1981 Aug 1J
Chayrez, Bernadette: 1986 Oct 11I
Cheever, John: 1982 Jun 19J
Chenoweth, Dean: 1982 Jul 31J
Chernenko, Konstantin: 1985 Mar 10B
Choh Hao Li: 1987 Nov 28I
Christensen, Lew: 1984 Oct 9J
Chuikov, Vasily: 1982 Mar 18B
Church, Frank: 1984 Apr 7F
Ciardi, John Anthony: 1986 Mar 30J
Clair, Rene: 1981 Mar 15J
Clark, Barney: 1983 Mar 23I
Clark, Kenneth: 1983 May 21J
Clark, Mamie: 1983 Aug 11J
Claude, Albert: 1983 May 22I
Clurman, Harold: 1980 Sep 9J
Cody, John: 1982 Apr 25F
Cohn, Roy Marcus: 1986 Aug 2F
Cole, Lester: 1985 Aug 15J
Coluche (Michel Colucci): 1986 Jun 19J
Connelly, Marc: 1980 Dec 21J
Conried, Hans: 1982 Jan 5J
Coogan, Jackie: 1984 Mar 1J
Cooke, Terence Cardinal: 1983 Oct 6J
Cooper, Diana: 1986 Jun 16J
Cori, Ferdinand: 1984 Oct 20I
Corn Jr., Ira: 1982 Apr 28J
Corridan, John: 1984 Jul 1J
Cortazar, Julio: 1984 Feb 12J
Cournand, Andre: 1988 Feb 19I
Cowley, Malcolm: 1989 Mar 27J
Crabbe, Buster: 1983 Apr 23J
Crawford, Broderick: 1986 Apr 26J
Crawford, Cheryl: 1986 Oct 7J
Creighton, Thomas: 1985 Mar 8I
Crohn, Burrill: 1983 Jul 29I
Crothers, Scatman: 1986 Nov 22J
Cukor, George: 1983 Jan 24J
Cunningham, Glenn: 1988 Mar 10J
da Costa, Adelino Amaro: 1980 Dec 4B
Dali, Salvador: 1989 Jan 23J
Dangerfield, George: 1986 Dec 27J
Dart, Raymond: 1988 Nov 22I
Dass, Arjun: 1985 Sep 4E
Davis, Bette: 1989 Oct 6J
Davis, Gene: 1985 Apr 6J

Day, Dorothy: 1980 Nov 29F
Dayan, Moshe: 1981 Oct 16C
De Beauvoir, Simone: 1986 Apr 14J
De Broglie, Louis: 1987 Mar 19I
Debus, Kurt Heinrich: 1983 Oct 10I
Debus, Sigurd: 1981 Apr 16B
Defferre, Gaston: 1986 May 7B
DeJouvenel, Bertrand: 1987 Mar 1J
Delamare, Louis: 1981 Sep 4C
Del Monaco, Mario: 1982 Oct 15J
Dempsey, Jack: 1983 May 31J
Denby, Edwin: 1983 Jul 12J
Desmond, Johnny: 1985 Sep 6J
DeVincenzo, Tony: 1983 Nov 18J
Diamond, I.A.L.: 1988 Apr 21J
Dick, Philip: 1982 Mar 2J
Dietz, Howard: 1983 Jul 30J
Dirac, Paul Adrian Maurice: 1984 Oct 20I
Divine: 1988 Mar 7J
Doisy, Adelbert Edward: 1986 Oct 23I
Dorati, Antal: 1988 Nov 13J
Dorfman, Albert: 1982 Jul 27I
Dorfman, Allen: 1983 Jan 20J
Dorticos Torrado, Osvaldo: 1983 Jun 23D
Douglas, Helen Gahagan: 1980 Jun 28F
Douglas, William: 1980 Jan 19F
Drees, Willem: 1988 May 14B
Drew, Richard: 1980 Dec 7I
Dubberstein, Waldo: 1983 Apr 29G
Dubinsky, David: 1982 Sep 17H
Dubos, Rene Jules: 1982 Feb 20I
Dubuffet, Jean: 1985 May 12J
Duk Koo Kim: 1982 Nov 17J
Du Maurier, Daphne: 1989 Apr 19J
Du Pre, Jacqueline: 1987 Oct 19J
Durant, Ariel: 1981 Oct 25J
Durant, Will: 1981 Nov 8J
Durante, Jimmy: 1980 Jan 29J
Eastland, James: 1986 Feb 19F
Edwards, Joan: 1981 Aug 27J
Eitan, Dov: 1988 Nov 30I
Eldridge, Roy: 1989 Feb 26J
Eliade, Mircea: 1986 Apr 22J
Ellin, Stanley: 1986 Jul 31J
Elliot, James ("Jumbo"): 1981 Mar 22J
Ellis, Perry: 1986 May 30J
Ellmann, Richard: 1987 May 13J
Encers, John: 1985 Sep 9I
Erlander, Tage: 1985 Jun 21B
Ervin Jr., Sam: 1985 Apr 23F
Evans, Bill: 1980 Sep 15J
Evans, Gil: 1988 Mar 20J
Evans, Maurice: 1989 Mar 12J
Farrar, Margaret: 1984 Jun 11J
Fassbinder, Rainer Werner: 1982 Jun 10J
Fayad, Alvaro: 1986 Mar 13D
Faylen, Frank: 1985 Aug 2J
Fender, P(ercy) G(eorge) H(enry): 1985 Jun 15J
Fenelon, Fania: 1983 Dec 20J
Fernando, Saman Piyasiri: 1989 Dec 26E
Fetchit, Stepin: 1985 Nov 19J
Feynman, Richard: 1988 Feb 15I
Finley, M(oses) I.: 1986 Jun 23J
Fitzgerald, Robert Stuart: 1985 Jan 16J
Fitzsimmons, Frank: 1981 May 6H
Flory, Paul John: 1985 Sep 9I
Fonda, Henry: 1982 Aug 12J
Fontanne, Lynn: 1983 Jul 30J
Ford II, Henry: 1987 Sep 29H
Foreman, Carl: 1984 Jun 26J
Fortas, Abe: 1982 Apr 5F
Fosse, Bob: 1987 Sep 23J
Foster, Tabatha: 1988 May 11J
Foucault, Michel: 1984 Jun 25J
Fournier, Pierre: 1986 Jan 8J
Fox, Terry: 1981 Jun 28J

Fredericks, Carlton: 1987 Jul 28J
Frei Montalva, Eduardo: 1982 Jan 22B
Freud, Anna: 1982 Oct 9I
Freyre, Gilberto: 1987 Jul 18D
Friedman, Benny: 1982 Nov 23J
Fromm, Erich: 1980 Mar 18J
Fuchs, (Emil) Klaus: 1988 Jan 28I
Fuller, Buckminster: 1983 Jul 1J
Galan, Luis Carlos: 1989 Aug 18D
Gallup, George: 1984 Jul 26F
Gance, Abel: 1981 Nov 11J
Garcia Alvarado, Roberto: 1989 Apr 19D
Garcia Rodriguez, Felix: 1980 Sep 11A
Gardiner, Muriel: 1985 Feb 6J
Garland, William (Red): 1984 Apr 23J
Garner, Peggy Ann: 1984 Oct 16J
Garrido Gil, Rafael: 1986 Oct 25B
Gaye, Marvin: 1984 Apr 1J
Gaynor, Janet: 1984 Sep 14J
Gemayel, Bashir: 1982 Sep 14C
Gemayel, Pierre: 1984 Aug 29C
Genet, Jean: 1986 Apr 15J
Gernreich, Rudi: 1985 Apr 21J
Gershwin, Ira: 1983 Aug 17J
Geschwind, Norman: 1984 Nov 4I
Ghaffar Khan, Abdul: 1988 Jan 20E
Giacometti, Diego: 1985 Jul 15J
Giamatti, A(ngelo) Bartlett: 1989 Sep 1J
Gibson, Phil: 1984 Apr 28F
Ginastera, Alberto: 1983 Jun 25J
Gingold, Hermione: 1987 May 24J
Gleason, Jackie: 1987 Jun 24J
Glubb, John Bagot: 1986 Mar 17B
Godfrey, Arthur: 1983 Mar 16J
Gohlke, Mary: 1986 May 6I
Goldmann, Nahum: 1982 Aug 29C
Gomez, Lefty: 1989 Feb 17J
Gomez Ibarruri, Dolores: 1989 Nov 12B
Gomulka, Wladyslaw: 1982 Sep 1B
Goodman, Benny: 1986 Jun 13J
Goodman, Steve: 1984 Sep 20J
Gordon, Ruth: 1985 Aug 28J
Gould, Chester: 1985 May 11J
Gould, Glenn: 1982 Oct 4J
Grace, Princess (Monaco): 1982 Sep 14J
Graham, Sheila: 1988 Nov 17J
Grant, Cary: 1986 Nov 29J
Graves, Robert (von Ranke): 1985 Dec 7J
Greenberg, Hank: 1986 Sep 4J
Greene, Lorne: 1987 Sep 11J
Griffin, Marvin: 1982 Jun 13F
Griffith, Michael: 1986 Dec 20F
Gromyko, Andrei: 1989 Jul 2B
Grossman, Albert: 1986 Jan 25J
Grosvenor, Melville Bell: 1982 Apr 22J
Gruentzig, Andres: 1985 Oct 27I
Guarnieri, Johnny: 1985 Jan 7J
Guerrero, Manuel: 1985 Mar 30D
Guzman Fernandez, Antonio: 1982 Jul 4D
Hakim, Nadim: 1984 Aug 23C
Halas, George ("Papa Bear"): 1983 Oct 31J
Haley, Bill: 1981 Feb 9J
Halleck, Charles: 1986 Feb 3F
Hallinan, Hazel Hunkins: 1982 May 17F
Hamilton, Margaret: 1985 May 16J
Hammond, Edward: 1986 Nov 3I
Hammond, John: 1987 Jul 10J
Hanley, Edward: 1982 Mar 13H
Hanley, James: 1985 Nov 11J
Hansen, Kenneth: 1981 Aug 27G
Hanson, Howard: 1981 Feb 26J

Harburg, Edgar Y. ("Yip"): 1981 Mar 5J
Hardin, Tim": 1980 Dec 29J
Hardy, Alister: 1985 May 23J
Harnwell, Gaylord: 1982 Apr 18I
Harriman, William Averell: 1986 Jul 26F
Harrington, Michael: 1989 Jul 31J
Harris, Patricia Roberts: 1985 Mar 23F
Hartman, Elizabeth: 1987 Jun 10J
Hayden, Sterling: 1986 May 23J
Hayes, Alfred: 1985 Aug 14J
Hayes, Woody: 1987 Mar 12J
Hayworth, Rita: 1987 May 14J
Hazam, Louis: 1983 Sep 6J
Head, Edith: 1981 Oct 24J
Hebb, Donald Olding: 1985 Aug 20I
Hecht, Harold: 1985 May 25J
Heifetz, Jascha: 1987 Dec 10J
Heinlein, Robert A(nson): 1988 May 8J
Helen, Queen (Romania): 1982 Nov 28B
Heller, Walter W(olfgang): 1987 Jun 15H
Hellman, Lillian: 1984 Jun 30J
Helpmann, Robert (Murray): 1986 Sep 28J
Herbert, Frank: 1986 Feb 11J
Herman, Woody: 1987 Oct 29J
Hess, Rudolf: 1987 Aug 17B
Hicks, James: 1986 Jan 19J
Hill, Abram: 1986 Oct 6J
Hill, Ralph Lee: 1980 Jun 15F
Himes, Chester: 1984 Nov 12J
Hines, Earl (Fatha): 1983 Apr 22J
Hirohito, Emperor (Japan): 1989 Jan 7E
Hitchcock, Alfred: 1980 Apr 29J
Hoareau, Gerard: 1985 Nov 29E
Hofheinz, Roy Mark: 1982 Nov 21F
Holloway, Stanley: 1982 Jan 30J
Hollowood, Bernard: 1981 Mar 28J
Holt, John: 1985 Sep 14J
Hook, Sidney: 1989 Jul 12J
Hopkins, Sam ("Lightnin'"): 1982 Jan 30J
Hornbeck, William: 1983 Oct 11J
Horowitz, Vladimir: 1989 Nov 5J
Hosni, Mohammed Salem: 1982 Mar 14C
Houseman, John: 1988 Oct 30J
Howard, Trevor: 1988 Jan 7J
Hoxha, Enver: 1985 Apr 11B
Hubbard, L. Ron: 1986 Jan 24J
Hubbell, Carl: 1988 Nov 21J
Huberty, James: 1984 Jul 4F
Hudson, Rock: 1985 Oct 2J
Hughes, Francis: 1981 May 12B
Huie, William Bradford: 1986 Nov 22J
Hunter, Alberta: 1984 Oct 17J
Hurley, Ruby: 1980 Aug 9F
Huston, John: 1987 Aug 28J
Hu Yaobang: 1989 Apr 15E
Isherwood, Christopher: 1986 Jan 4J
Iturbi, Jose: 1980 Jun 28J
Jackson, Henry M. ("Scoop"): 1983 Sep 1F
Jackson, Tommy ("Hurricane"): 1982 Feb 14J
Jakobson, Roman: 1982 Jul 18J
James, Harry: 1983 Jul 6J
Jameson, (Margaret) Storm: 1986 Sep 30J
Janson, Horst: 1982 Sep 30J
Jarrell, Tommy: 1985 Jan 28J
Javits, Jacob: 1986 Mar 7F
Jaworski, Leon: 1982 Dec 9F
Jenkins, Gordon: 1984 May 1J
Jessel, George: 1981 May 24J
Jessup, Philip Caryl: 1986 Jan 31A
Joffrey, Robert: 1988 Mar 25J

Jolas, Maria: 1987 Mar 4J
Jonathan, Leabua: 1987 Apr 5C
Jones, Herbert: 1982 May 30D
Jones, Joseph Rudolph ("Philly Joe"): 1985 Aug 30J
Jones, Ralph Waldo Emerson: 1982 Apr 9J
Jones, Thad: 1986 Aug 20J
Jones, William: 1982 Nov 23J
Jorgensen, Christine: 1989 May 3J
Julesberg, Elizabeth: 1985 Feb 19J
Jumbaz, Hisham: 1980 Aug 16C
Kadar, Janos: 1989 Jul 6B
Kahl, Gordon: 1983 Jun 3H
Kahn, Herman: 1983 Jul 7I
Kantorovich, Leonid: 1986 Apr 7J
Kapitsa, Pyotr: 1984 Apr 8I
Kaplan, Henry: 1984 Feb 4I
Karajan, Herbert von: 1989 Jul 16J
Kastler, Alfred: 1984 Jan 7I
Kaufman, Bob: 1986 Jan 12J
Kaufman, Murray ("Murray the K"): 1982 Feb 21J
Kaye, Danny: 1987 Mar 3J
Kaye, Nora: 1987 Mar 3J
Kaye, Sammy: 1987 Jun 2J
Kekkonen, Urho Kaleva: 1986 Aug 31B
Kertesz, Andre: 1985 Sep 27J
Khalid, King (Saudi Arabia): 1982 Jun 13C
Khama, Seretse: 1980 Jul 13C
Khan, Fazlur: 1982 Mar 27I
Khrushchev, Nina: 1984 Aug 8B
Kiesinger, Kurt Georg: 1988 Mar 8B
King Sr., Martin Luther ("Daddy"): 1984 Nov 11F
Kirkwood, James: 1989 Apr 21J
Kirst, Hans Helmut: 1989 Feb 23J
Kishi, Nobosuke: 1987 Aug 7E
Kline, Nathan: 1983 Feb 11I
Kluszewski, Ted: 1988 Mar 29J
Knopf, Alfred A.: 1984 Aug 11J
Koestler, Arthur: 1983 Mar 3J
Kokoschka, Oskar: 1980 Feb 22J
Kondrashin, Kiril: 1981 Mar 7J
Kostelanetz, Andre: 1980 Jan 13J
Kosygin, Alexei: 1980 Dec 18B
Kountche, Seyni: 1987 Nov 10C
Kraft, Joseph: 1986 Jan 10J
Krasner, Lee: 1984 Jun 19J
Kripalani, Jiwatram: 1982 Mar 19E
Krishnamurti, Jiddu: 1986 Feb 17J
Kroc, Ray: 1984 Jan 14J
Kuznets, Simon: 1985 Jul 9J
Kyser, Kay (James King Kern): 1985 Jul 23J
La Follette, Suzanne: 1983 Apr 23J
Laing, R(onald) D(avid): 1989 Aug 23I
Lam, Wilfredo: 1982 Sep 11J
L'Amour, Louis: 1988 Jun 10J
Lanchester, Elsa: 1986 Dec 26J
Landon, Alf(red) M(ossman): 1987 Oct 12F
Lang, Harold: 1985 Jul 26J
Lange, Mark: 1983 Dec 4C
Langer, Suzanne: 1985 Jul 17J
Lansky, Meyer: 1983 Jan 15J
Lara Bonilla, Rodrigo: 1984 May 1D
Larkin, Philip (Arthur): 1985 Dec 2J
Lartigue, Jacques-Henri: 1986 Sep 12J
Lash, Joseph: 1987 Aug 22J
Laszlo, Ernest: 1984 Jan 6J
La Torre, Pio: 1982 Apr 30B
Lattimore, Richmond: 1984 Feb 26J
Laurence, Margaret: 1987 Jan 5J
Lawford, Peter: 1984 Dec 24J
Lawler, Richard: 1982 Jul 24I
Le Duan: 1986 Jul 10E
Lee Sok Kyu: 1987 Aug 22E
Lehninger, Albert Lester: 1986 Mar 4I
Leloir, Luis Federico: 1987 Dec 3I

Lennon, John: 1980 Dec 8J
Lenya, Lotte: 1981 Nov 27J
Leone, Sergio: 1989 Apr 30J
Leopold III, King (Belgium): 1983 Sep 25J
Lerner, Alan Jay: 1986 Jun 14J
LeRoy, Mervyn: 1987 Sep 13J
Levesque, Rene: 1987 Nov 1D
Levi, Julian: 1982 Feb 28J
Levi, Primo: 1987 Apr 11J
Levine, Joseph E(dward): 1987 Jul 31J
Libby, Willard: 1980 Sep 8J
Liberace: 1987 Feb 4J
Liberace, George: 1983 Oct 16J
Lifar, Serge: 1986 Dec 15J
Lillie, Beatrice Gladys: 1989 Jan 20J
Lipmann, Fritz Albert: 1986 Jul 24I
List, Eugene: 1985 Mar 1J
Llewellyn, Richard: 1983 Nov 30J
Lockridge, Richard: 1982 Jun 19J
Loewe, Frederick: 1988 Feb 14J
Loewy, Raymond Fernand: 1986 Jul 14H
Logan, Joshua: 1988 Jul 12J
London, Artur: 1986 Nov 8B
London, George: 1985 Mar 24J
Long, Gillis W.: 1985 Jan 20F
Longowal, Harchand Singh: 1985 Aug 20E
Loos, Anita: 1981 Aug 18J
Lorenz, Konrad Zacharias: 1989 Feb 27I
Loring, Eugene: 1982 Aug 30J
Losey, Joseph: 1984 Jun 22J
Louis, Joe: 1981 Apr 21J
Low, George M.: 1984 Jul 17I
Lowenstein, Allard K.: 1980 Mar 14F
Luce, Clare Boothe: 1987 Oct 9J
Lyle, Sandy: 1988 Apr 10J
MacArthur, Roderick: 1984 Dec 15J
MacBride, Sean: 1988 Jan 15B
MacDonald, Dwight: 1982 Dec 19J
MacDonald, John D.: 1986 Dec 28J
MacDonald, Ross: 1983 Jul 11J
Machel, Samora: 1986 Oct 19C
Mackin, Catherine: 1982 Nov 20J
MacLean, Alistair (Stuart): 1987 Feb 2J
Maclean, Donald: 1983 Mar 6B
MacLeish, Archibald: 1982 Apr 20J
MacMillan, Maurice Harold: 1986 Dec 29B
MacRae, Gordon: 1986 Jan 24J
Madani, Ayatollah Assadollah: 1981 Sep 11C
Magee, Patrick: 1982 Aug 14J
Magnuson, Warren: 1989 May 20F
Mahler, Margaret: 1985 Oct 2I
Malamud, Bernard: 1986 Mar 18J
Maltz, Albert: 1985 Apr 26J
Mamoulian, Rouben (Zachary): 1987 Dec 4J
Mantovani, Annunzio Paolo: 1980 Mar 29J
Mapplethorpe, Robert: 1989 Mar 9J
Maravich, Pete: 1988 Jan 5J
Marchenko, Anatoly: 1986 Dec 8B
Marcos, Ferdinand E.: 1989 Sep 28E
Maris, Roger: 1985 Dec 14J
Markey, Lucille Parker: 1982 Jul 25J
Markham, Beryl: 1986 Aug 3J
Marley, Bob: 1981 May 11J
Martin, Billy: 1989 Dec 25J
Martin, John: 1985 May 19J
Marvin, Lee: 1987 Aug 29J
Masri, Zafir al-: 1986 Mar 2C
Massey, Raymond: 1983 Jul 29J
Massing, Hede: 1981 Mar 8F
Matsushita, Konosuke: 1989 Apr 27E
Mayer, Norman D.: 1982 Dec 8G
Mays, Benjamin E.: 1984 Mar 28J
Maysles, David (Peter): 1987 Jan 3J

McCall, Tom: 1983 Jan 8H
McCarthy, Mary Therese: 1989 Oct 25J
McCloy, John J(ay): 1989 Mar 11G
McCormack, John: 1980 Nov 22F
McCormick, Frank: 1982 Nov 21J
McCree Jr., Wade Hampton: 1987 Aug 30J
McDonnell Jr., James: 1980 Aug 22J
McLuhan, Herbert Marshall: 1980 Dec 31J
McQueen, Steve: 1980 Nov 7J
Meany, George: 1980 Jan 10H
Medawar, Peter (Brian): 1987 Oct 2I
Menard, William Henry: 1986 Feb 9I
Mendes, Chico: 1988 Dec 22D
Mennin, Peter: 1983 Jun 17J
Mercer, Mabel: 1984 Apr 20J
Merman, Ethel: 1984 Feb 15J
Messmer, Otto: 1983 Oct 28J
Michaux, Henri: 1984 Oct 18J
Milgram, Stanley: 1984 Dec 20I
Milland, Ray: 1986 Mar 10J
Miller, Henry: 1980 Jun 7J
Miller, Merle: 1986 Jun 10J
Mills, Irving: 1985 Apr 21J
Minnelli, Vincente: 1986 Jul 25J
Miro, Joan: 1983 Dec 25J
Mitchell, Clarence M.: 1984 Mar 18J
Mitchell, John Newton: 1988 Nov 9F
Mitscherlich, Alexander: 1982 Jun 26I
Molotov, Vyacheslav: 1986 Nov 8B
Monk, Thelonius Sphere: 1982 Feb 17J
Monroe, Marion: 1983 Jun 25J
Moore, Henry: 1986 Aug 31J
Moorehead, Alan: 1983 Sep 29J
Morante, Elsa: 1985 Nov 25J
Morton, Thruston: 1982 Aug 14F
Moses, Robert: 1981 Jul 29F
Muktananda, Swami Paramahansa: 1982 Oct 2E
Mulliken, Robert Sanderson: 1986 Oct 31I
Myrdal, Alva: 1986 Feb 1A
Myrdal, (Karl) Gunnar: 1987 May 17A
Naipaul, Shiva: 1985 Aug 13J
Nathan, Otto: 1987 Jan 27J
Nattino Allende, Santiago: 1985 Mar 30D
Ndlovu, Moven: 1984 Nov 10C
Neagle, Anna: 1986 Jun 3J
Nearing, Scott: 1983 Aug 24J
Neel, Alice: 1984 Oct 13J
Negri, Pola: 1987 Aug 1J
Nelson, Rick: 1985 Dec 31J
Nenni, Pietro: 1980 Jan 1B
Nevelson, Louise: 1988 Apr 17J
Neves, Tancredo de Almeida: 1985 Apr 21D
Newton, Huey Percy: 1989 Aug 22F
Nicholson, Ben: 1982 Feb 6J
Niemoeller, Martin: 1984 Mar 6J
Niven, David: 1983 Jul 29J
Nixon, E(dgar) D(aniel): 1987 Feb 25F
Noguchi, Isamu: 1988 Dec 30J
North, John Ringling: 1985 Jun 4J
Northrop, John H(oward): 1987 May 27I
Nyagumbo, Maurice: 1989 Apr 20C
O'Boyle, Patrick Aloysius Cardinal: 1987 Aug 10J
O'Brien, Pat: 1983 Oct 15J
O'Flaherty, Liam: 1984 Sep 7J
Ohira, Masayoshi: 1980 Jun 12E
O'Keeffe, Georgia: 1986 Mar 6J
Oliver, Sy: 1988 May 27J
Olivier, Laurence Kerr: 1989 Jul 11J
Olszewski, Jerzy: 1981 May 24B
Oppenheimer, Frank: 1985 Feb 3I
Orbison, Roy: 1988 Dec 6J

Orff, Carl: 1982 Mar 29J
Orkin, Ruth: 1985 Jan 16J
Ormandy, Eugene: 1985 Mar 12J
Osborn, Paul: 1988 May 12J
Osborne, John: 1981 May 2F
Ospir, Ivan Maria: 1985 Aug 28D
Owen, Johnny: 1980 Nov 3J
Owens, Jesse: 1980 Mar 31J
Owings, Nathaniel: 1984 Jun 13J
Padover, Saul: 1981 Feb 22J
Page, Geraldine: 1987 Jun 13J
Pahlevi, Mohammed Riza: 1980 Jul 27C
Paige, Satchel: 1982 Jul 8J
Palme, Olof: 1986 Feb 28B
Palmer, Lilli: 1986 Jan 27J
Parada, Jose Manuel: 1985 Mar 30D
Patino, Antenor: 1982 Feb 2D
Paton, Alan: 1988 Apr 12J
Paul, Jean-Claude: 1988 Nov 6C
Paz, Robert: 1989 Dec 16D
Pears, Peter: 1986 Apr 3J
Peckinpah, Sam: 1984 Dec 28J
Peerce, Jan: 1984 Dec 15J
Pepper, Claude Denson: 1989 May 30J
Pereira, Fernando: 1985 Jul 10E
Perkins, Carl Dewey: 1984 Aug 3F
Perkins, Marlin (Richard): 1986 Jun 14J
Perry, Eleanor: 1981 Mar 14J
Petri, Elio: 1982 Nov 19J
Philby, Kim: 1988 May 11B
Phillips, Marjorie Acker: 1985 Jun 19J
Piaget, Jean: 1980 Sep 16I
Pickens, Slim: 1983 Dec 8J
Pignedoli, Sergio: 1980 Jun 15J
Plomley, Roy: 1985 May 28J
Pollard, Fritz: 1986 May 11J
Polya, George: 1985 Sep 7I
Ponselle, Rosa: 1981 May 25J
Porter, Katherine Anne: 1980 Sep 18J
Porter, Robert Rodney: 1985 Sep 6I
Potter, Peter: 1983 Apr 17J
Powell, William: 1984 Mar 5J
Powers, John A. ("Shorty"): 1980 Jan 1I
Preminger, Otto Ludwig: 1986 Apr 23J
Presser, Jackie: 1988 Jul 9H
Preston, Robert: 1987 Mar 21J
Priestley, John Boynton: 1984 Aug 14J
Pritikin, Nathan: 1985 Feb 21I
Pritzker, Abram Nicholas: 1986 Feb 8J
Qoddousi, Hojatolislam Ali: 1981 Sep 5C
Quinlan, Karen Ann: 1985 Jun 11J
Rabi, I(sidor) I(saac): 1988 Jan 11I
Rabia, Hammad Abu: 1981 Jan 12C
Rahman, Ziaur: 1981 May 30E
Rahner, Karl: 1984 Mar 30J
Rainwater, James: 1986 May 31I
Ramachandran, Marudur Gopalan: 1987 Dec 24E
Rambert, Marie: 1982 Jun 12J
Ramsey, Arthur Michael: 1988 Apr 23J
Ramu: 1985 Feb 18I
Rand, Ayn: 1982 Mar 6J
Raphaelson, Samson: 1983 Jul 16J
Raphel, Arnold L.: 1988 Aug 17E
Rappaport, Paul: 1980 Apr 21J
Rauff, Walter Herman: 1984 May 14B
Redding, J. Saunders: 1988 Mar 2F
Redgrave, Michael: 1985 Mar 21J
Reed, Donna: 1986 Jan 14J
Reiser, Pete: 1981 Oct 25J
Remeliik, Haruo I.: 1985 Jun 30E
Renault, Gilbert: 1984 Jul 29J

Renault, Mary: 1983 Dec 13J
Rexroth, Kenneth: 1982 Jun 6J
Rhine, Joseph: 1980 Feb 20I
Rich, Buddy: 1987 Apr 2J
Richardson, Ralph: 1983 Oct 10J
Richter, Charles F(rancis): 1985 Sep 30I
Rickover, Hyman George: 1986 Jul 8G
Ritola, Willie: 1982 Apr 24J
Ritz, Jimmy: 1985 Nov 17J
Robinson, Julia Bowman: 1985 Jul 30I
Robinson, Maurice R.: 1982 Feb 7J
Robinson, Robert E.: 1989 Dec 18F
Robinson, Sugar Ray: 1989 Apr 12J
Robson, Flora: 1984 Jul 7J
Rock, John: 1984 Dec 4I
Rodriguez Gacha, Jose Gonzalo: 1989 Dec 15D
Rodriguez Porth, Jose Antonio: 1989 Jun 9D
Rogers, Carl Ransom: 1987 Feb 4I
Rojas de Negri, Rodrigo: 1986 Jul 3D
Roldos Aguilera, Jaime: 1981 May 24D
Rother, Stanley: 1981 Jul 28D
Rothschild, Alain de: 1982 Oct 17B
Roud, Richard: 1989 Jan 15J
Rowe, James N.: 1989 Apr 21E
Rubinstein, Arthur: 1982 Dec 20J
Rudenko, Lyudmila: 1986 Mar 21J
Ruffing, Charles ("Red"): 1986 Feb 17J
Rustin, Bayard: 1987 Aug 24F
Ryle, Martin: 1984 Oct 14I
Ryskind, Morrie: 1985 Aug 24J
Sa Carneiro, Manuel Lumbrales de: 1980 Dec 4B
Sackler, Arthur: 1987 May 26J
Sakharov, Andrei: 1989 Dec 14B
Salii, Lazarus: 1988 Aug 20E
Salt, Waldo: 1987 Mar 7J
Sands, Robert: 1981 May 5B
Santmyer, Helen Hooven: 1986 Feb 21J
Saragat, Giuseppe: 1988 Jun 11B
Saroyan, William: 1981 May 18J
Sartre, Jean-Paul: 1980 Apr 15J
Savitch, Jessica: 1983 Oct 24J
Schaufelberger, Albert A.: 1983 May 26D
Schidlof, Peter: 1987 Aug 18J
Schiff, Dorothy: 1989 Aug 30J
Schneider, Alan: 1984 May 3J
Schneider, Romy: 1982 May 29J
Scholem, Gershom: 1982 Feb 20J
Scholz, Jackson: 1986 Oct 26J
Schroeder, William J.: 1986 Aug 6I
Scott, Randolph: 1987 Mar 2J
Sebelius, Keith: 1982 Sep 5F
Segovia, Andres: 1987 Jun 2J
Segre, Emilio Gino: 1989 Apr 22I
Seifert, Jaroslav: 1986 Jan 10J
Sellers, Peter: 1980 Jul 24J
Semyonov, Nikolai N.: 1986 Sep 25I
Sert, Josep Lluis: 1983 Mar 15J
Sessions, Roger: 1985 Mar 16J
Shalamov, Varlam: 1982 Jan 30J
Shaw, Irwin: 1984 May 16J
Shearer, Norma: 1983 Jun 12J
Sheldon, Alice: 1987 May 19J
Shinwell, Emanuel: 1986 May 8B
Shockley, William Bradford: 1989 Aug 12I
Sholokhov, Mikhail: 1984 Feb 21J
Short, Robert: 1982 Nov 20J
Shuttleworth, Todd: 1987 Jul 25F
Signoret, Simone: 1985 Sep 30J
Silvers, Phil: 1985 Nov 1J
Simenon, Georges: 1989 Sep 4J
Simpson, Wallis Warfield: 1986 Apr 24J

Sims, John Haley ("Zoot"): 1985 Mar 23J
Sloane, Eric: 1985 Mar 6J
Smith, Kate: 1986 Jun 17J
Smith, Muriel Burrell: 1985 Sep 13J
Smith, Samantha: 1985 Aug 26J
Smith, Walter Wellesley ("Red"): 1982 Jan 15J
Smith, Willi: 1987 Apr 17J
Smyth, Henry DeWolf: 1986 Sep 11I
Snider, Paul: 1980 Sep 15J
Snow, C.P.: 1980 Jul 1J
Soames, Arthur Christopher John Lord: 1987 Sep 16B
Sobhuza II, King (Swaziland): 1982 Aug 21C
Sognnaes, Reidar: 1984 Sep 21I
Sokol, Herman: 1985 Jun 21I
Sokolov, Valentin: 1984 Nov 8J
Sondergaard, Gale: 1985 Aug 14J
Sopwith, Thomas: 1989 Jan 27B
Speer, Albert: 1981 Sep 1B
Speidel, Hans: 1984 Nov 28B
Stankiewicz, Richard: 1983 Mar 27J
Stein, Aaron Marc: 1985 Aug 29J
Stenberg, Leif: 1985 Nov 21I
Steptoe, Patrick (Christopher): 1988 Mar 21I
Sterling, Wallace E.J.: 1985 Jul 1J
Stethem, Robert D.: 1985 Jun 15C
Stevens, Robert T.: 1983 Jan 31F
Stevens, Siaka: 1988 May 29C
Stevenson, Robert: 1986 Apr 30J
Stewart, Ian: 1985 Dec 12J
Stewart, Potter: 1985 Dec 7F
Stitt, Sonny: 1982 Jul 22J
Stone, I(sidore) F(einstein): 1989 Jun 18J
Stone, Irving: 1989 Aug 26J
Strasberg, Lee: 1982 Feb 17J
Strater, Henry: 1987 Dec 22J
Stratten, Dorothy: 1980 Sep 15J
Strauss, Franz Josef: 1988 Oct 3B
Stronge, Norman: 1981 Jan 21B
Sullivan, John L.: 1982 Aug 8G
Surtees, Robert: 1985 Jan 5J
Suslov, Mikhail: 1982 Jan 25B
Susskind, David: 1987 Feb 22J
Swanson, Gloria: 1983 Apr 4J
Sweet, Blanche (Sarah): 1986 Sep 6J
Sykes, Roosevelt: 1983 Jul 11J
Symington, Stuart: 1988 Dec 14F
Szabo, Gabor: 1982 Feb 26J
Szent-Gyorgyi, Albert: 1986 Oct 22I
Tabatabai, Ali Akbar: 1980 Jul 22F
Tailleferre, Germaine: 1983 Nov 7J
Takenaka, Masahisa: 1985 Jan 27E
Taniguchi, Masaharu: 1985 Jun 17J
Tanner, Marion: 1985 Oct 30J
Tarnower, Herman: 1980 Mar 10J
Tarsis, Valery: 1983 Mar 3J
Tati, Jacques: 1982 Nov 5B
Taussig, Helen Brooke: 1986 May 20I
Taylor, Lee: 1980 Nov 13J
Taylor, Maxwell: 1987 Apr 19G
Teale, Edwin Way: 1980 Oct 18J
Terry, Luther Leonidas: 1985 Mar 29I
Thomas, Lowell: 1981 Aug 30J
Thomson, Virgil Garnett: 1989 Sep 30J
Thornton, Willie Mae: 1984 Jul 25J
Tierno, Galvan Enrique: 1986 Jan 20B
Tillstrom, Burr: 1985 Dec 6J
Tinbergen, Nikolaas: 1988 Dec 21I
Tito, Josip Broz: 1980 Apr 4B
Torrijos Herrera, Omar: 1981 Jul 31D
Tosh, Peter: 1987 Sep 11J
Toure, Ahmed: 1984 Mar 27C
Tracy, Honor Lilbush Wingfield: 1989 Jun 13J

Travis, Merle: 1983 Oct 20J
Trifonov, Yuri: 1981 Mar 28J
Troisgros, Jean: 1983 Aug 8J
Truffaut, Francois: 1984 Oct 21J
Tubb, Ernest: 1984 Sep 6J
Tuchman, Barbara: 1989 Feb 6J
Tudor, Antony: 1987 Apr 19J
Turner, Joseph Vernon ("Big Joe"): 1985 Nov 24J
Tworkov, Jack: 1982 Sep 4J
Tynan, Kenneth: 1980 Jul 26J
Ulam, Stanislaw: 1984 May 13I
Unruh, Jesse: 1987 Aug 4F
Urey, Harold: 1981 Jan 5I
Vagnozzi, Egidio: 1980 Dec 26J
Vallee, Rudy: 1986 Jul 3J
Vance, Robert: 1989 Dec 16F
Van Der Zee, James: 1983 May 15J
Van Dyke, Willard: 1986 Jan 23J
Van Niel, Cornelis: 1985 Mar 10I
Veeck, Bill: 1986 Jan 2J
Vidor, King: 1982 Nov 1J
Vinogradov, Ivan: 1983 Mar 20I
Vitale, John: 1982 Jun 5H
Volel, Yves: 1987 Oct 13D
Vreeland, Diana: 1989 Aug 22J
Walker, Joseph: 1985 Aug 1J
Wallace, Lila Bell Acheson: 1984 May 8J
Wallace, Sippie: 1986 Nov 1J
Wallis, Hal: 1986 Oct 5J
Ward, Theodore: 1983 May 8J
Waring, Fred: 1984 Jul 29J
Warren, Robert Penn: 1989 Sep 15J
Washer, Ben: 1982 Sep 5J
Washington, Chester: 1983 Aug 31J
Washington, Harold: 1987 Nov 25F
Waters, Muddy: 1983 Apr 30J
Watson, Barbara: 1983 Feb 17F
Webb, Jack: 1982 Dec 22J
Wechsler, James: 1983 Sep 11J
Weiss, Peter: 1982 May 10J
Weissmuller, Johnny: 1984 Jan 20J
Welles, Orson: 1985 Oct 10J
Wenzhong Pei: 1982 Sep 18I
Werner, Oskar: 1984 Oct 23J
West, Anthony: 1987 Dec 27J
West, Jessamyn: 1984 Feb 25J
West, Mae: 1980 Nov 22J
West, Rebecca: 1983 Mar 15J
Wheeler, Hugh: 1987 Jul 26J
White, Daniel: 1985 Oct 21F
White, Theodore: 1986 May 15J
Whitney, John Hay ("Jock"): 1982 Feb 8J
Wilkins, Roy: 1981 Sep 8F
Williams, Charles ("Cootie"): 1985 Sep 15J
Williams, (George) Emlyn: 1987 Sep 25I
Williams, John Bell: 1983 Mar 26F
Williams, Tennessee: 1983 Feb 25J
Wilson, Dennis: 1983 Dec 28J
Wilson, Meredith: 1984 Jun 15J
Wilson, Teddy: 1986 Jul 31J
Winograd, Garry: 1984 Mar 19J
Winston, Harry: 1986 Dec 12F
Wittig, Georg: 1987 Aug 26I
Wood, Audrey: 1985 Dec 27J
Wood, Natalie: 1981 Nov 29J
Woodruff, Robert Winship: 1985 Mar 7J
Wootton, Barbara: 1988 Jul 11I
Wright, Sewall: 1988 Mar 3I
Wyler, William: 1981 Jul 27J
Wyszynski, Stefan Cardinal: 1981 May 28B
Yadin, Yigael: 1984 Jun 28C
Yanes, Pedro Rene: 1985 Jan 6D
Ye Jianying: 1986 Oct 22E
Yourcenar, Marguerite: 1987 Dec 17J
Zacharias, Jerrold: 1986 Jul 16I

Zia ul-Haq, Muhammad: 1988 Aug 17E
Zimbalist Sr., Efrem: 1985 Feb 22J
Zworykin, Vladimir: 1982 Jul 29I
death squads
    Argentina: 1983 Aug 21D
    Chile: 1986 Sep 2D
    El Salvador: 1983 Jan 15G/Nov 26D/Nov 30G/Dec 25D/Dec 31G; 1984 Mar 3D/Jul 13G/Oct 10G/Nov 1D; 1985 Sep 29D; 1987 Oct 27D; 1988 Oct 26D
    Guatemala: 1984 Nov 1D; 1989 Jun 14D
    Honduras: 1989 Jul 21D
    South Africa: 1989 Nov 19C
Deathtrap (film) 1982 Apr 7J
Death Wish 3 (film) 1985 Nov 20J
Death Wish II (film) 1982 Mar 10J
debt crisis 1986 Jun 29H
debt-for-equity swaps 1988 Feb 18H
debt-for-nature swaps 1989 Feb 4D/Apr 5I/Aug 3C
Declaration of Brussels (1983) 1983 Dec 9A
Declaration of Lima (1985) 1985 Jul 30D
Decline of the American Empire, The (film) 1986 Nov 14J
Decline of Western Civilization, The (film documentary) 1981 Jul 5J
Deenie, Blubber (Judy Blume) (book) 1984 Dec 3J
Deep Six (Clive Cussler) (book) 1984 Jul 20J
Deep Thought (chess computer) 1989 Oct 22J
Deep Throat (film) 1981 Nov 9F
Deere & Co. 1987 Feb 1H
Deering Milliken, Inc. 1980 Dec 14H
defections
    Afghanistan: 1980 Feb 22E/Jun 20J/Sep 15E
    Cuba: 1987 May 28D
    Poland: 1981 Dec 24B; 1982 Oct 22B; 1984 Nov 24B
    Romania: 1981 May 31J; 1989 Nov 29J
    USSR: 1980 Feb 5J; 1981 Apr 11J; 1984 May 28J/Nov 23E; 1985 Sep 12B/Sep 26B
    West Germany: 1985 Aug 23B
Defense, U.S. Department of see also specific department heads in the name index (e.g., Weinberger, Caspar)
    appointments and resignations: Tower, John 1988 Dec 16F; 1989 Feb 23G
    budget and spending programs: 1983 Oct 6G; 1984 Feb 1H/Jul 26G; 1985 Apr 9G; 1988 Aug 11G; 1989 Dec 12G
    contract and billing issues: Boeing 1980 Mar 25G; French/U.S. partnership 1985 Nov 5G; General Dynamics 1983 Feb 21G; General Electric 1985 Mar 28G/Apr 18G; Lockheed 1986 Aug 11G; McDonnell Douglas 1983 Feb 21G; National Semiconductor 1984 Mar 6G; Pratt & Whitney 1984 Feb 21G; Texas Instruments 1984 Sep 10G; top contractors probed 1985 Jun 20G; United Technologies 1983 Feb 21G
    embassy security issues: 1982 Jan 24G; 1985 Nov 21G; 1987 Apr 12G
    environmental issues: toxic waste dumps 1983 Aug 10H
    foreign operations: Australia 1981 Feb 7G; Beirut bombing report 1983 Dec 28G; China 1980 Jan

24E; Costa Rica 1985 May 6D; France 1982 Jul 16B; Grenada 1983 Oct 23G/Oct 25G/Oct 28G; 1984 Jun 21G; Honduras 1983 Jun 9D/Jul 25G; 1984 Jun 24D; Iran hostage rescue report 1980 Aug 23G; Israel 1981 Sep 11G/Sep 13C; Jamaica 1987 Nov 20D; Kenya 1985 Mar 21G; Libya 1981 Aug 20G; Nicaragua 1984 Sep 18G/Dec 16D; Oman 1985 Mar 21G; Persian Gulf 1980 Feb 1G/Oct 11G; 1984 Feb 28C; Saudi Arabia 1981 Nov 2G; Somalia 1985 Mar 21G; Syria 1981 Jul 9A; USSR 1981 Jul 9A/Sep 29G; 1982 Jul 16B/Dec 14G
    media aaccess: 1984 Feb 9F/Aug 23G/Oct 10G; 1985 Sep 19G
    personnel issues: AIDS 1985 Oct 25G; commando units 1984 Jun 8G; dismissal for alleged leaks dropped 1982 May 18G; fatalities 1985 Mar 17G; homosexual ban ease rejected 1989 Oct 21G; Nixon lawsuit 1981 Aug 14F; recruitment goals 1987 Dec 22G; women 1983 Jul 11G
    political campaign issues: 1984 Oct 3F; 1986 Mar 22F
    procurement scandal: 1983 Aug 20G; 1984 Aug 19G; 1985 Jun 17G; 1988 Dec 19G; 1989 Jan 6G
    reorganization: 1986 Apr 2G/Sep 17G
    research and development: university funding 1983 May 20F
    strategic planning and technology: annual report, hi-tech doctrine 1987 Jan 10G; computer warning system flawed 1980 Mar 10G; nuclear forces 1980 Jun 17G; space shuttle 1984 Dec 17G; 1985 Oct 7I; Star Wars 1986 Sep 5G; 1988 Oct 6G; 1989 Jul 13G; stealth fighter unveiled 1980 Aug 20G; strategic planning 1982 Aug 15G; weapons technology study 1984 Feb 28G
    weapons systems: antisatellite missile tests 1985 Sep 20G; chemical weapons 1987 Dec 17G; Maverick missile 1982 Jun 25G/Aug 24G; MX missile 1982 May 19G; stealth fighter unveiled 1980 Aug 20G; technology study 1984 Feb 28G
Defense Advisory Committee on Women in the Services, U.S. 1989 Feb 18G
defense authorization bills 1982 May 14G/Aug 18G; 1983 Jul 26G/Sep 15G/Sep 24G; 1984 Jun 1G/Jun 21G; 1985 Jun 5G/Jun 27G; 1986 Aug 15H; 1987 May 20G/Sep 11G/Oct 2G/Nov 17G; 1988 May 27G/Aug 3G/Sep 29G; 1989 Apr 25G/Jul 27G/Aug 2G/Nov 2G/Nov 15G
Defense Contract Audit Agency, U.S. 1985 May 16G
defense contractors see also specific companies (e.g., General Dynamics)
    contract and billing issues: company listing 1983 Feb 21G; French/U.S. partnership 1985 Nov 5G; reimbursement guidelines 1985 Mar 12G; shortages 1980 Feb 4G
    corruption and ethics issues: audits 1985 May 16G; congressional gifts 1988 Jun 24F; criminal investigations 1985 Jun 20G; fraud scandal 1988 Jun 14G; overcharges 1984 Feb 21G; technology disclosure penalties 1984 Nov 7G

environmental issues: radiation victim suits 1984 Nov 13G; radioactive waste dumping 1981 Jan 31H
Defense Intelligence Agency, U.S. (DIA) 1980 Jul 14I; 1981 Sep 6G; 1987 Mar 27B
Defense Logistics Agency, U.S. (DLA) 1984 Sep 10G
Deficit Reduction Act of 1984 1986 Jun 4H
Def Leppard (singing group)
    Hysteria 1987 Sep 19J/Oct 24J; 1988 Jun 18J/Jul 16J/Aug 27J/Sep 24J
    Open Up and Say...Ahh! 1989 Jan 29J
    Pyromania 1983 Apr 13J/May 11J/Jun 15J/Jul 13J/Aug 17J/Sep 14J/Oct 19J
deforestation 1981 Aug 20E; 1983 Jul 18E; 1987 Apr 11I
Delaware 500 (auto race) 1987 Sep 20J
Delmas trial (1988) 1989 Dec 15C
Deloitte, Haskins & Sells 1989 Jul 6H
De Lorean Motor Co. 1982 Feb 19B/Oct 19B; 1984 Jul 18B; 1986 Dec 17F
Delta (rocket) 1986 May 3I/Sep 5G; 1989 Mar 24I/Aug 27I
Delta Airlines 1985 Aug 2H
Delta Force, The (film) 1986 Feb 19J
Delta Star, The (Joseph Wambaugh) (book) 1983 Apr 10J
Democratic Congressional Campaign Committee 1987 Jul 2F/Oct 20F
Democratic Coordinator (Nicaraguan opposition group) 1988 Jul 10D
Democratic Leadership Council 1986 Feb 18F
Democratic National Committee (DNC) 1981 May 5F/Jun 5F/Jul 2F; 1983 Jan 6F; 1984 Apr 23F; 1985 Feb 1F/Feb 16F; 1986 Feb 18F/Mar 8F/Sep 20F; 1987 Jul 23F; 1989 Feb 10F
Democratic National Convention
    New York City (1980): 1980 Aug 2F/Aug 11F/Aug 12F/Aug 12F/Aug 13F
    San Francisco (1984): 1983 Apr 21F; 1984 Apr 23F/Jul 16F/Jul 18F/Jul 16F/Jul 18F
    Atlanta (1988): 1987 Feb 10F; 1988 Apr 20F/Jul 18F/Jul 19F/Jul 19F
Democratic Party 1982 Jan 15F; 1983 Apr 25F; 1985 May 6F; 1986 May 3F/Oct 7F; 1987 Feb 18F
Democratic Policy, Center for see Center for Democratic Policy
Democratic Revolutionary Alliance (Nicaraguan contra group) 1983 Jul 4D/Sep 8D; 1984 Apr 21D; 1986 May 9D/May 16D
Democratic Revolutionary Front (FDR) (Salvadoran rebel group) 1983 Jan 19D/Jun 9D/Jul 10D/Jul 31D; 1987 Sep 23D/Dec 2D
Democratic Union (Soviet dissident party) 1988 May 7B
Demon Lord of Karanda (David Eddings) (book) 1988 Sep 30J
Dene Indians (Canada) 1982 Nov 26D; 1987 Jan 15D; 1988 Sep 5D
dengue fever 1981 Jun 30D
Denmark see also individual leaders in the name index (e.g., Schluter, Poul)
    arts and culture: Babette's Feast 1988 Mar 4J; Pelle the Conqueror 1988 May 23J/Dec 21J; 1989 Jan 28J/Mar 29J

awards and honors: Jerne wins Nobel Prize 1984 Oct 15I; Pelle the Conqueror 1988 May 23J; 1989 Jan 28J/Mar 29J; Schou wins Albert Lasker Award 1987 Sep 21I
economy: austerity plan 1982 Oct 5B; budget 1986 Aug 15B; 1988 Dec 18B; currency 1982 Feb 22B
foreign aid: 1983 Dec 23A
foreign relations: China 1984 Jun 16E; Iran 1981 Aug 12C; United States 1983 Jun 24G
government and politics: elections 1981 Dec 8B; 1984 Jan 10B; Jorgensen government falls 1981 Nov 12B
Greenland see Greenland
immigration and refugees: 1986 Oct 17B
international organizations: European Community 1986 Feb 27B; 1988 Jun 13B; 1989 Oct 3B; NATO missile deployment 1982 Dec 7B; 1984 May 10B; UN Security Council seat 1985 Oct 17A
obituaries: Bruhn, Erik 1986 Apr 1J
sports: auto racing 1988 Jan 31J; marathons 1988 Apr 17J
Denver Broncos (football team) 1987 Jan 11J/Jan 25J; 1988 Jan 3J/Jan 10J/Jan 17J
Denver Post (newspaper) 1986 Apr 17J
Depository Institutions Deregulation and Monetary Control Act of 1980 1980 Mar 31H
Depository Institutions Deregulation Committee, U.S. 1981 Jun 25H/Sep 22H/Oct 20H; 1982 Mar 22H/Dec 6H
deprenyl (drug) 1989 Aug 4I
depression 1989 Aug 18I/Sep 1I
Deputed Testamony (racehorse) 1983 May 21J
deregulation
    agriculture: 1986 Feb 6H
    airlines: 1980 May 13H
    banks: 1983 Jun 30H; 1986 Feb 6H
    foreign developments: Australia 1984 Apr 10E; Canada 1985 Jun 24D/Oct 31D; 1988 Jan 1D; Great Britain 1985 Jun 5B/Dec 19B; 1986 Oct 26B/Oct 27B; 1988 Nov 7B; New Zealand 1988 May 3E
    railroads: 1980 Oct 14H; 1984 Sep 18H
    telephones: 1980 Apr 7H; 1981 Nov 7H; 1982 Nov 12H
    television: 1981 Jul 16J; 1983 Apr 21H; 1984 Jun 27F
    trucking: 1980 Jun 20H; 1985 Sep 12H
DES (diethylstilbestrol) 1980 Jan 25I/Apr 24I; 1984 Feb 2F/Nov 28I
Desire (U2) (recording) 1988 Nov 26J
Desperately Seeking Susan (film) 1985 Mar 29J/Apr 17J
Destiny (Sally Beauman) (book) 1987 Apr 24J
detergents 1980 May 17A; 1989 Apr 16B
Detroit (Michigan)
    bias issues: affirmative action 1984 Dec 13F; Chin murder 1984 Jun 28F/Sep 19F; 1987 May 1F
    economy: bankruptcy rescue plan 1981 Aug 15H
    energy issues: nuclear power plants 1988 Jan 23H
    labor issues: Labor Day rally 1983 Sep 5H; municipal employees contract 1986 Aug 4H; teachers contract 1987 Sep 19F

obituaries: Ford II, Henry 1987 Sep 29H

politics and government: Carter visit 1980 Jul 8H; GOP convention (1980) 1980 Jul 9F/Jul 14F-15F/Jul 17F; mayoral primary 1985 Sep 10F; presidential campaign 1988 Sep 5F; Reagan urban policy criticized 1982 Jul 13F

religious issues: papal visit 1987 Sep 10J

Detroit Free Press (newspaper) 1984 Oct 28F; 1986 Apr 14F; 1987 Sep 23H/Dec 30H; 1988 Aug 17H; 1989 Mar 20F/Nov 13H

Detroit News (newspaper) 1986 Apr 14F; 1987 Sep 23H/Dec 30H; 1988 Aug 17H; 1989 Mar 20F/Nov 13H

Detroit Pistons (basketball team) 1986 Feb 9J; 1988 Jun 21J; 1989 Jun 8J/Jun 13J

Detroit Tigers (baseball team) 1980 Aug 3J/Dec 6J; 1984 Sep 30J/Oct 5J/Oct 14J/Oct 18J/Nov 6J; 1987 Oct 4J/Oct 12J

Deutsche Presse-Agentur (newspaper) 1981 Sep 2B

developing nations *see also organizations* (e.g.,International Monetary Fund); *specific countries* (e.g., Bangladesh)

aid issues: France 1982 Jan 27I; G-7 1982 Jun 6A; Japan 1989 Jan 24E; OECD 1987 Jun 29A; 1989 Jun 23A

Brandt Commission: 1983 Feb 9A

debt issues: commercial bank lending 1987 Dec 14H; 1988 Feb 26B; 1989 Oct 12H; debt for equity swaps 1988 Feb 18H; OECD 1984 May 18A; statistics 1981 Jan 28A; 1982 Dec 16A; 1988 Jul 20A; U.S. proposals 1986 Jun 29H; 1989 May 24A; U.S. trade deficit policy 1984 May 18A; 1988 Sep 27H

disarmament: 1987 Aug 24A

economy: consumer prices 1988 May 16A; disarmament impact 1987 Aug 24A; growth 1988 Jul 6A

energy issues: 1981 Aug 4A

environmental issues: hazardous wastes 1989 Mar 22A; pollution programs 1983 Feb 15H; tropical forests 1987 Jul 3I

health care: infant formula 1984 Jan 27B; Nestle boycott 1984 Jan 27B; statistics 1989 Sep 24I

information technology: 1982 Jan 27I

religious issues: John Paul II 1988 Feb 19J; liberation theology 1984 Jul 12J/Sep 3J

trade issues: GATT 1984 Nov 30A; Soviet arms sales 1980 Dec 10A; United States 1984 Jan 24H; 1988 Sep 14H

United Nations policy: debt issues addressed 1981 Oct 7A; 1984 Sep 26A; outer space conference 1982 Aug 21I; Syria terror resolution defeated 1987 Dec 1A; UNESCO news study 1983 Dec 25A; UNIDO conference 1980 Feb 9A

Devil's Alternative, The (Frederick Forsyth) (book) 1980 Feb 10J/Mar 9J/Apr 6J/May 4J/Jun 8J

Dev-Yol (Turkish terrorist group) 1980 Jul 19B

Dexedrine (drug) 1988 Apr 15F

DIA *see* Defense Intelligence Agency, U.S.

Diablo Canyon nuclear power plant (California) 1981 Sep 22I/Oct 24I/Nov 19I; 1984 Apr 29H/Aug 2H/Aug 21H/Nov 11I

dialysis 1988 Nov 30F

Diamond Alkali Co. 1983 Jun 2H

diamonds 1980 Jan 11E

Diamond Shamrock Corp. 1980 Oct 17H; 1982 Jul 7H

Diamond-Star Motors Corp. 1989 Aug 26H

Diamond v. Chakrabarty 1980 Jun 16F

Diamond v. Diehr 1981 Mar 3I

diaries

Anne Frank definitive edition: 1986 May 14J

Hitler forgeries: 1983 May 6J; 1984 Mar 21B; 1985 Jul 8B

Reagan Iran-Contra notes: 1987 Apr 8G; 1989 Dec 21F

Soviet cosmonaut: 1983 Aug 16I

Diary of Anne Frank (Anne Frank) (book) 1986 Oct 24F

diazepam (drug) 1985 Sep 4F

diazinon (pesticide) 1986 Oct 7H

dicofol (pesticide) 1985 Aug 12H; 1986 Oct 7H

Die Hard (film) 1988 Jul 15J/Aug 31J/Sep 21J

diesel fuel

pollution standards: 1982 Jan 1H/Nov 23H

prices: 1980 Aug 27B; 1983 Jan 31H; 1987 Jul 20D; 1988 Feb 1B

spills: 1988 Jan 2H; 1989 Jan 28I/Nov 21H

diet 1986 Mar 20I; 1988 Feb 2I; 1989 Mar 2I

dietary fat 1988 Apr 15I/Jul 27I

diethylene glycol 1985 Jul 11B/Oct 24B

diet pills 1982 Oct 5I; 1987 Jul 8F

Different Light (Bangles) (recording) 1987 Jan 28J/Feb 18J

Different Seasons (Stephen King) (book) 1982 Sep 12J

dimethylformamide 1987 Jul 28H

Dingo case (Australia) 1985 Nov 12E; 1986 Feb 7E; 1987 Jun 2E; 1988 Sep 15E

dingos (wild dogs) 1988 Sep 15E

Dinkas (Sudan ethnic group) 1988 Jul 28C

dinosaurs 1980 Jan 1I/Mar 24I; 1985 May 16I; 1986 May 2I

dinoseb (pesticide) 1986 Oct 7H

Dion (Dion DiMucci) (singer) 1989 Jan 18J

dioxin

Agent Orange *see* Agent Orange

foreign health hazard: in France 1983 May 19B; in Italy 1983 Sep 24B; in Switzerland 1983 Jun 4B

U.S. health hazard: EPA site identification 1983 Dec 15H; EPA studies softened 1983 Mar 18H; lawsuits 1982 Aug 25H; 1984 Jan 20H; in Michigan 1983 Mar 31H; in Missouri 1984 Jan 20H; in New Jersey 1983 Jun 2H; research intensifies 1983 Jul 28I; in Times Beach (Missouri) 1982 Dec 23I; 1983 Jan 12H/Feb 22H/Jun 4H; 1985 Apr 10H

diphtheria 1985 Feb 3D

diprotodon (extinct marsupial) 1987 Mar 31I

Direct Action (French terrorist group) 1980 Mar 28B/Apr 15B; 1986 Nov 17B

Dire Straits (singing group) 1985 Aug 24J/Sep 28J/Oct 26J/Nov 30J

Dirk Gently's Holistic Detective Agency (Douglas Adams) (book) 1987 Jul 17J/Aug 21J

Dirty Dancing (film) 1987 Aug 21J/Sep 9J

Dirty Dancing (soundtrack) 1987 Oct 24J/Nov 21J/Dec 26J; 1988 Jan 23J/Feb 20J/Mar 19J/Apr 23J/May 21J/Jun 18J/Jul 16J

Dirty Deeds Done Dirt Cheap (AC/DC) (recording) 1981 May 6J/May 27J/Jul 8J

Dirty Rotten Scoundrels (film) 1988 Dec 28J

"dirty war" (Argentina) 1983 Apr 28D/Aug 21D/Sep 23D; 1985 Dec 21D; 1986 Sep 25D/Dec 23D; 1987 Feb 22D/May 13D/Jun 12D; 1989 Mar 23D

disabled persons

benefit issues: benefit denial cases reopened 1986 Jun 2F; home/job svc funds signed 1988 Aug 19F; Social Security 1983 May 18F/Jun 7F; 1984 Apr 13F/Sep 8F/Sep 19F; 1987 Oct 16F

educational issues: vets benefits 1982 Aug 3F/Sep 29F; vocational rehabilitation program 1983 Sep 13F

family issues: children 1982 Aug 3F; 1988 Aug 19F

health care issues: Agent Orange 1984 Oct 24G; 1989 May 11G; AIDS 1983 May 18F; 1988 Oct 6F; black lung program 1981 Mar 9F; 1988 Dec 6F; catastrophic coverage 1987 Jul 22F/Oct 27F; 1988 Jun 8F/Jul 1F; infants 1983 Apr 14F/Nov 2F/Nov 16F; 1984 Jan 9F/Feb 2F/Oct 9F; 1985 Jul 25J; radiation victims 1988 Apr 25G/May 20G

labor issues: home industrial work 1981 Oct 8H; home/job svc funds signed 1988 Aug 19F; vocational-rehabilitation 1983 Sep 13F

rights issues: anti-bias legislation 1989 Sep 7F

Supreme Court rulings: benefit denial cases reopened 1986 Jun 2F; black-lung disease 1988 Dec 6F; disability rule upheld 1987 Jun 8F; veterans' legal fees 1985 Jun 28G

Disarmament, U.N. Conference on 1987 Aug 24A; 1988 Jul 28G; 1989 Jan 11A

disarmament and arms control *see individual countries* (e.g., Union of Soviet Socialist Republics); *specific agreements* (e.g., SALT)

discotheques 1980 May 28F; 1981 Feb 14B; 1986 Apr 5B/Apr 14C

discount rate 1980 Feb 15H/May 28H/Jul 24H/Jul 25H; 1982 Nov 19H; 1984 Apr 6H/Nov 21H; 1985 May 17H; 1986 Jul 10H/Aug 20H; 1987 Sep 4H; 1988 Aug 9H; 1989 Feb 24H

Discovery II (boat) 1980 Nov 13J

Disease Control, U.S. Centers for *see* Centers for Disease Control, U.S.

diseases *see specific disease* (e.g., cancer)

Disneyland (Marne-la-Vallee, France) 1985 Dec 28J; 1987 Mar 24B

Distant Early Warning Line 1985 Mar 18D

District of Columbia, University of 1982 Mar 20J

DIVAD (antiaircraft gun) *see* Sergeant York

Diver (Jasper Johns) (painting) 1988 May 3J

Diver Down (Van Halen) (recording) 1982 May 5J/Jun 16J

Divine Madness (film) 1980 Oct 1J

diving 1981 Jan 13J

divorce and separation 1985 Mar 5F; 1986 May 6E/Jun 26B; 1987 Jun 8D; 1989 Aug 31B/Oct 6D

D.J. Jazzy Jeff & the Fresh Prince (singing group) 1988 Aug 27J/Sep 24J

Djibouti 1980 Dec 4C; 1981 Mar 21D

DMI *see* Dar al Maal al Islami

DNA (deoxyribonucleic acid) 1980 Apr 3I/Aug 30I/Oct 14I/Oct 14I; 1982 Jan 5I/Dec 30I; 1986 Jun 11I/Sep 29I; 1988 May 13I

DNC *see* Democratic National Committee

DN Galan meet (track and field) 1989 Jul 3J

Doctors (Erich Segal) (book) 1988 Aug 26J

dogs 1986 May 1I; 1988 Sep 15E; *see also* Iditarod

dollar, U.S.

exchange rate: 1980 Mar 17A/Dec 31H; 1981 May 14A/Jun 12H/Aug 3H/Sep 22A/Dec 31H; 1982 Oct 4A; 1983 Dec 30H; 1984 Jun 28H/Sep 10H/Dec 31H; 1985 Mar 21H/Jul 25H; 1986 Apr 23E; 1987 Jan 12B/Jan 21A/Mar 30H/Oct 28H/Nov 5H/Nov 30H; 1988 Dec 30H; 1989 Dec 29H

market intervention: 1983 Jul 29G/Sep 7H; 1985 Feb 27A/Dec 4A; 1987 May 29H; 1988 Mar 4H/Sep 7H; 1989 Sep 23A

Dollmaker, The (film) 1985 May 6H

Dome of the Rock (Jerusalem mosque) 1982 Apr 11C/Apr 12C/Apr 14A/Apr 20A/May 7C; 1983 Apr 7C

Dome Petroleum Ltd. 1980 Aug 23D; 1981 May 29H; 1982 May 19D

Dominica 1980 Jul 21D; 1981 Jun 20D; 1985 Jul 3D; 1987 May 31D

Dominican embassy occupation (1980) (Bogota, Colombia) 1980 Mar 2D/Mar 17D/Mar 30D/Apr 6D/Apr 19D/Apr 21D/Apr 27D

Dominican Republic *see also individual leaders in the name index* (e.g., Balaguer, Joaquin)

Bogata embassy occupation: 1980 Mar 2D/Mar 17D/Mar 30D/Apr 6D/Apr 19D/Apr 21D/Apr 27D

civil strife: 1984 Apr 25D; 1985 Feb 4D; 1988 Mar 8D

ediucation: medical schools 1984 May 11I

foreign debt: 1984 Jun 21D/Sep 14D; 1985 Feb 8D

foreign relations: Haiti 1986 Feb 1D

government and politics: ex-president corruption conviction 1987 Apr 30D; 1988 Nov 27D; Guzman suicide 1982 Jul 4D/Aug 16D

sports: boxing 1982 Mar 21J

Dona Paz (ship) 1987 Dec 20E

Dongui University (South Korea) 1989 Oct 24E

Don't Be Cruel (Bobby Brown) (recording) 1989 Jan 29J/Feb 25J/Mar 25J/Apr 29J/Jun 24J/Jul 29J

Don't Worry, Be Happy (Bobby McFerrin) (recording) 1989 Feb 22J

Doobie Brothers (singing group) 1980 Feb 27J/Oct 8J

dopamine 1980 Jan 10I

Dostoevsky: The Years of Ordeal, 1850-1859 (Joseph Frank) (book) 1985 Jan 14J

Do the Right Thing (film) 1989 Jun 30J

Double Fantasy (John Lennon/Yoko Ono) (recording) 1981 Jan 7J/Feb 11J/Mar 4J; 1982 Feb 24J

double jeopardy 1981 Feb 24F

"double-zero option" 1987 Jun 1B/Jun 12B/Jun 16G

Dow Chemical Co. 1980 Jul 24H; 1983 Mar 31H; 1986 Jan 15D; 1988 Dec 5H

Dow Jones Industrial Average

1981 statistics: 1981 Jan 7H

1982 statistics: 1982 Aug 17H/Aug 18H/Aug 20H/Oct 13H/Oct 25H/Nov 3H/Dec 27H

1984 statistics: 1984 Feb 8H/Aug 3H

1985 statistics: 1985 Jan 29H/Feb 13H/Mar 1H/May 20H/Oct 30H/Oct 30H/Nov 27H/Dec 16H

1986 statistics: 1986 Jan 8H/Jan 31H/Feb 7H/Mar 27H/Apr 21H/Apr 30H/May 29H/Jul 2H/Jul 30H/Sep 4H/Sep 11H

1987 statistics: 1987 Jan 8H/Jan 17H/Jan 22H/Mar 26H/Apr 3H/Apr 23H/Jun 25H/Jul 31H/Aug 25H/Sep 22H/Oct 14H/Oct 16H/Oct 19H/Oct 23H/Nov 6A

1988 statistics: 1988 Feb 4H/Feb 29H/Mar 18H/May 11A/Oct 19H/Oct 21H/Nov 11H

1989 statistics: 1989 May 19H/Aug 24H/Sep 1H/Oct 13H/Oct 16H/Dec 29H

Down and Out in America (film) 1987 Mar 30J

Down and Out in Beverly Hills (film) 1986 Feb 19J/Mar 19F

Down's syndrome 1989 Nov 22I

dowries 1985 Mar 20E; 1988 Nov 24E

Do You Remember Love? (TV show) 1985 Sep 12J

Dr. Feelgood (Motley Crue) (recording) 1989 Oct 28J

Dr. Zhivago (Boris Pasternak) (book) 1987 Feb 12J

draft registration

opposition: demonstrations against 1980 Mar 22F; draft evasion prosecution 1982 Oct 28G/Nov 15G; 1983 Jul 19G; 1984 Feb 3G; 1985 Sep 10G; non-registrants 1980 Sep 4G; 1982 Jul 28G; student financial aid penalties 1983 Jan 21F/Mar 10F; 1986 Jan 22G

political and legislative issues: Carter administration policy 1980 Feb 8G/Mar 6G/Jun 27G/Jul 2G; House votes for 1980 Apr 22G; program ended 1980 Aug 2G; Reagan resumes registration 1982 Jan 7G; student financial aid terms 1983 Jan 21F/Mar 10F; 1986 Jan 22G; task force report downplays 1982 Oct 18G

Supreme Court rulings *see* Supreme Court

Dragnet (film) 1987 Jul 8J

drainage ditches 1988 Feb 23F

Dramatists Guild 1985 Feb 26J

Dreamgirls (musical) 1981 Dec 20J

Dream of the Blue Turtles, The (Sting) (recording) 1985 Aug 24J/Sep 28J

Dream Team, The (film) 1989 Apr 26J

Dressed to Kill (film) 1980 Aug 6J

Drexel Burnham Lambert Inc. 1986 May 12H; 1988 Sep 7H/Dec 21H; 1989 Jan 24H/Mar 29H/Apr 13H/Sep 11H

Dreyfus Fund Inc. 1982 Feb 17H

Drift Net Act of 1987 1989 Jun 23H

drift nets 1989 Jun 23H/Dec 13I

drinking age 1982 Jul 23F; 1984 Jun 7F/Jul 17H; 1987 Jun 23F

drinking water
  conservation: 1980 Dec 1I
  farm worker access: 1987 Feb 6F/Apr 28H
  foreign developments: El Salvador 1980 Feb 19D; Great Britain 1989 Sep 20B
  pollution: 1980 Nov 10H; 1983 Apr 6I/Jun 8H; 1986 Sep 22H; 1987 Dec 15H; 1989 Mar 9H
  safety standards: 1985 May 16H; 1986 Jun 19H; 1987 Jun 24H; 1988 Aug 10H; 1989 Sep 20B

Driving Miss Daisy (Alfred Uhry) (play/film) 1988 Mar 31J; 1989 Dec 13J

drought
  Australia: 1980 Apr 4E/Apr 24E; 1982 Oct 6E/Dec 1E; 1983 Jun 16I
  Canada: 1988 May 31D; 1989 May 31D
  Chad: 1983 Mar 6C
  China: 1981 Apr 24I
  Ethiopia: 1983 Mar 18I; 1985 Jan 13C; 1987 Oct 22C
  India: 1988 Feb 29E
  Italy: 1989 Feb 19B
  Mexico: 1980 Jun 13D/Jun 13I
  OAU fund: 1984 Nov 12C
  southern Africa: 1983 Mar 18I; 1985 Feb 23C
  UN conference: 1985 Mar 11A
  United States: crop levels 1984 Jan 13H; 1988 Jul 12H/Sep 12H; crop prices 1988 Jun 27H; disaster declared 1983 Sep 2I; 1988 Jun 23H; drought relief bill 1988 Jul 28H/Aug 11H; New York-Philadelphia region 1980 Dec 1I; record set 1988 Sep 6I; Southeastern states 1986 Aug 1H

drug czar 1988 Nov 18F; 1989 Jan 12F/Mar 9F

Drug Enforcement Agency, U.S. (DEA) 1982 Jan 21F; 1983 Aug 15F; 1984 Jul 18G/Nov 17F; 1988 Sep 6F/Nov 24F; 1989 Aug 14F

drug tampering 1982 Oct 29I; 1987 Dec 9F

drug tests
  crime and law enforcement: 1988 Jan 21F
  government employment: 1986 Sep 18F; 1988 Nov 14F
  military: 1983 Aug 18G
  sports: baseball 1985 May 7J/Sep 24J; 1986 Feb 28J; NCAA championships 1986 Jan 14J; tennis 1985 Nov 6J; U.S. Olympic Committee 1985 Jan 10J
  statistics: 1989 Jan 11F
  transportation: rail workers 1988 Feb 11F/Oct 9F; 1989 Mar 21F; U.S. department plan 1988 Nov 14F

drug trafficking
  Australia: 1986 Jul 6E
  Bahamas: 1987 Jun 19D; 1988 Apr 15F
  Bolivia: 1980 Aug 13G; 1986 Jul 15D/Nov 15D
  China: 1982 Apr 10E
  Colombia *see* Colombia
  Costa Rica: 1989 Jul 23D

Cuba: 1986 Jan 2G; 1989 Jun 14D

European Community: 1986 Oct 20B

Iran: 1980 Jul 8C

Italy: 1984 Oct 25B; 1985 Nov 9B

Malaysia: 1982 Aug 25E; 1986 Jul 6E

Mexico: 1986 May 22G; 1988 Apr 1F/Apr 15F; 1989 Apr 8D

Nicaragua: 1984 Jul 18G

Panama: 1985 Sep 14D; 1986 Jun 12D; 1987 Jun 26D/Aug 7G/Oct 22D; 1988 Feb 5G/May 7G/May 25D; 1989 Jan 4F/Aug 31D/Dec 20G

Peru: 1984 Nov 17D

Turks and Caicos: 1986 Sep 18F

United Nations: 1988 Dec 20A

United States: Bush plan 1989 Sep 5A; DEA employees 1988 Nov 24F; 1989 Aug 14F; drug courier profile 1983 Mar 23F; FBI director heads probe 1982 Jan 21F; New York 1981 Feb 14F; 1984 Mar 30F; 1989 Jul 7F; organized crime commission report 1986 Mar 3F; Reagan plan 1982 Oct 14F

USSR: 1986 Jan 2G

drunk driving 1980 Dec 10B; 1983 Feb 22F; 1984 Jun 7F/Sep 5F; 1989 Mar 6F/May 31F

Druse Moslems 1982 Jul 20C; 1983 Jul 19C/Aug 2C/Aug 28C/Sep 4C/Sep 7C/Sep 10C/Sep 16C/Sep 19C/Oct 5C; Jumblat, Walid

dry-cleaning solvents 1986 Jan 15D

Drysdale Government Securities, Inc. 1982 May 18H/May 20H/May 21H

Dry White Season, A (film) 1989 Sep 20J

due process 1982 Jun 18F; 1988 Nov 29F

Duke University (Durham, N.C.) 1980 Feb 7I/Feb 20I/May 1I; 1986 Mar 1J/Mar 31J

dumping (trade practice)
  commodities: ball bearings 1989 May 2H; steel 1980 Mar 21A/Mar 27A/Sep 30H; 1982 Aug 10H; 1984 Feb 10H; 1986 Jun 2D; 1989 Mar 7H; telecommunications equipment 1988 Dec 28H; 1989 Nov 20H
  EC report: 1989 May 3B

Dun & Bradstreet Corp.
  business failures: 1983 Jan 21H; 1984 Jan 9H; 1986 Mar 2H

DuPont Awards, Alfred I. (broadcast journalism) 1986 Feb 5J; 1987 Mar 4J; 1988 Jan 28J

Du Pont de Nemours & Co., E.I. 1981 Jul 12H/Jul 14H/Jul 20H/Aug 4H-5H/Aug 11H/Dec 11H; 1986 Mar 19F; 1988 Mar 24H/Oct 15I

Dupont Plaza Hotel (San Juan, Puerto Rico) 1987 Jan 13D/Jan 29D/Jun 22F; 1988 Feb 3F

Duran Duran (singing group) 1984 Dec 22J; 1985 Jan 26J

Dusk & Other Stories (James Salter) (book) 1989 May 13J

Dutch elm disease 1987 Aug 27H/Sep 3H

Dutch Reformed Church 1987 Jun 27C

Dutch Viking (balloon) 1986 Sep 2J

Dynasty (TV show) 1983 Apr 10J; 1984 Oct 21J/Nov 18J/Dec 16J

E

Eagles (singing group) 1980 Jan 2J

Earth (planet) *see also specific features (e.g.,* ozone layer)
  asteroids: 1980 Jan 1I; 1989 Apr 19I
  circumnavigation: by airplane 1986 Dec 14I; by boat 1987 May 7J
  comets: 1983 May 11I
  Cretaceous Era: wildfires 1985 Oct 11I
  magnetic field: 1984 Aug 16I; 1988 Sep 19I
  "mystery" cloud: 1982 Mar 6I

Earth Observation Satellite Co. 1985 Sep 26I

earthquakes
  Armenia: 1988 Dec 15B/Dec 23B/Dec 24B
  Australia: 1989 Dec 28I
  California: Fresno County 1983 May 2I; Imperial Valley 1987 Nov 24I; Los Angeles 1987 Oct 1I/Nov 4I; northern 1980 Jan 24I; 1984 Apr 24I; San Francisco 1986 Mar 31I; San Francisco/Loma Prieta 1989 Oct 17I/Oct 26F/Oct 26I; southern 1986 Jul 8I; Yosemite 1980 May 25I
  Canada/northeastern U.S.: 1988 Nov 25I
  Chile: 1985 May 3I
  China: 1988 Nov 6I; 1989 Oct 18E
  Colombia: 1983 Mar 31I
  Ecuador: 1987 Mar 6D/Mar 11D
  El Salvador: 1986 Oct 10I
  Greece: 1986 Sep 13B/Sep 14B
  India-Nepal border: 1988 Aug 21I
  international data: death toll 1989 Feb 27I; forecasting 1985 Apr 5I; research center 1986 Aug 16I
  Italy: 1980 Nov 23I/Nov 29B/Dec 8I; 1984 May 11I
  Japan: 1983 May 26I
  Mexico: 1980 Oct 24I; 1985 Sep 19D/Sep 20I/Sep 24D/Nov 21D/Dec 18A; 1989 Apr 25I
  North Yemen: 1982 Dec 13I
  Romania/Moldavia: 1986 Aug 31I
  Sicily: 1985 Dec 25I
  Tadzhikistan: 1984 Mar 20I; 1985 Oct 13B; 1989 Jan 23E
  Taiwan: 1986 Nov 15I
  Turkey: 1983 Oct 30I
  Turkmenistan: 1984 Mar 20I
  Uzbekistan: 1984 Mar 20I

East Anglia, University of (Great Britain) 1989 Feb 3I

East Caribbean Central Bank 1983 Oct 30D

Eastern Airlines Inc.
  business issues: antitrust exemption 1984 Aug 13H; bankruptcy filing 1989 Mar 9H; Braniff route takeover 1982 Apr 26H; flight cutbacks sanctioned 1988 Aug 30H; pay-cut-for-stock agreement 1984 Feb 19H; Trump shuttle purchase 1988 Oct 12H; 1989 Mar 31H; Ueberroth investors group purchase 1989 Apr 6H/Apr 12H
  labor issues: layoffs 1989 Dec 28H; pay-cut-for-stock agreement 1984 Feb 19H; strikes 1983 Sep 30H; 1989 Mar 4H/Mar 13H/Nov 23H

Eastern Europe
  economy: EC aid pledge 1989 Nov 18B; growth rate 1980 Jan 18B; trade deficit 1981 Mar 17B
  environmental issues: Chernobyl food contamination 1986 May 7B/May 29B

religious issues: cardinals named 1988 May 29J
  rights issues: Hungarian uprising remembrance urged 1986 Oct 18B; Polish crisis 1980 Dec 5B/Dec 8B; press restrictions 1983 Dec 25A
  Soviet relations: 1989 Apr 25B/Nov 14B
  U.S. relations: 1980 Dec 9G; 1989 Jul 13G/Nov 22F

Eastern Kentucky (Richmond) 1981 Dec 19J

Eastern Orthodox Church 1987 Dec 7A

East Germany *see also individual leaders in the name index (e.g.,* Honecker, Erich)
  Berlin Wall *see* Berlin Wall
  defense and disarmament issues: Warsaw Pact exercises 1981 Mar 26B
  demonstrations and protests: 1982 Nov 21B; 1989 Jan 15B/Jun 7B/Nov 4B/Dec 11B
  economy: food shortages 1982 Nov 21B; growth rate 1980 Jan 18B; national income 1987 Jan 9B; 1989 Jul 21B
  espionage and intelligence issues: spy exchanges 1985 Jun 11A; West German ransom deals 1980 Mar 16B; 1986 Dec 9B; West German spy scandal 1985 Aug 23B
  foreign relations
    Bulgaria: 1984 Sep 9B
    China: 1985 May 16A; 1987 Jun 10A
    Czechoslovakia: 1989 Oct 3B/Nov 1B
    Great Britain: 1985 Apr 9B
    Hungary: 1989 Sep 4B/Sep 10B/Sep 12B/Sep 14B
    Iran: 1980 Apr 23A
    Poland: 1980 Oct 28B/Nov 5B/Nov 21B; 1982 Mar 13B
    USSR: 1984 Jan 17B; 1988 Feb 25B
    West Germany: credits approved 1984 Jul 25B; East Berlin embassy closed 1989 Aug 8B; immigration 1989 Oct 4B/Dec 11B; Prague embassy sit-in 1985 Jan 15B; 1989 Sep 8B; ransom deals 1980 Mar 16B; 1986 Dec 9B; spy scandal 1985 Aug 23B; trade volume 1987 Mar 4B; visitors 1989 Nov 15B
  government and politics: amnesty programs 1987 Dec 13B; 1989 Oct 27B; anniversary 1989 Oct 6B; Gysi elected party chairman 1989 Dec 9B; Honecker removed 1989 Oct 18B; Krenz becomes leader 1989 Oct 18B; leadership resigns 1989 Dec 3B; Modrow named premier 1989 Nov 13B; opposition group formed 1989 Sep 19B; party congress 1986 Apr 21B; 1989 Dec 17B; party membership 1986 Jan 9B
  human rights: Amnesty International assails 1989 Jan 24B; amnesty programs 1987 Dec 13B; 1989 Oct 27B; labor activists arrested 1981 Aug 20B; Prague embassy sit-in 1985 Jan 15B; 1989 Sep 8B
  immigration and refugees: 1989 Sep 4B/Sep 10B/Sep 12B/Sep 14B/Oct 3B-4B/Nov 1B/Dec 11B/Oct 4B/Dec 11B
  obituaries: Fuchs, Klaus 1988 Jan 28I
  religious issues: Christian churches backed 1981 Aug 2B

sports: figure skating 1987 Mar 14J; 1988 Mar 26J; indoor track and field championships 1987 Mar 8J; Olympic Games 1980 Feb 24J; 1984 May 7J; 1987 Dec 21J; 1988 Feb 20C/Oct 2J; shot put 1988 May 22J
  trade issues: Comecon summit 1984 Jun 14A; West German credits/trade 1984 Jul 25B; 1987 Mar 4B
  travel curbs: 1980 Oct 9B; 1982 Feb 12B; 1986 Jun 16B; 1988 Dec 14B; 1989 Nov 15B
  United Nations policy: 1981 Apr 16A; 1987 Sep 15A
  U.S. relations: 1983 Nov 10G; 1984 Jan 22B/Mar 14G; 1985 Mar 24B/Apr 23B; 1989 Oct 4B
  World War II commemorations: Buchenwald liberation 1985 Apr 13B; Elbe River linkup 1985 Apr 25B; outbreak 1989 Sep 1B

Eastman Kodak Co. 1982 Feb 3I; 1985 Sep 13H; 1986 Jan 8H/Feb 11H

East Timor (Indonesia) 1982 Mar 4E/Oct 6G; 1983 Sep 26E; 1985 Jun 25E; 1988 Nov 20E; 1989 Oct 7J

Easy Goer (racehorse) 1989 May 6J/Jun 10J

Easy in the Islands (Bob Shacochis) (book) 1985 Nov 21J

Easy Money (film) 1983 Sep 7J

eavesdropping, electronic *see* wiretapping and electronic surveillance

EBDC *see* ethylene bisdithiocarbamate

EC *see* European Community

Eclipse Awards (horse racing) 1983 Jan 4J; 1984 Feb 3J; 1985 Jan 8J/Feb 8J; 1986 Jan 7J; 1987 Jan 30J; 1988 Jan 27J; 1989 Jan 4J/Jan 28J

Eco-Glasnost (Bulgarian environmental group) 1989 Nov 3B

Economic Cooperation, Conference for *see* Conference for Economic Cooperation

Economic Education, Joint Council on 1988 Dec 28F

economic indicators *see* leading economic indicators

Economic Policy Advisory Board 1981 Feb 10H

Economic Policy Institute 1989 Nov 20I

Economic Priorities, U.S. Council on *see* Council on Economic Priorities, U.S.

economics
  awards and honors
    Nobel Prize: Klein, Lawrence R. 1980 Oct 15H; Tobin, James 1981 Oct 13H; Stigler, George 1982 Oct 20I; Debreu, Gerard 1983 Oct 17I; Stone, Richard 1984 Oct 18J; Modigliani, Franco 1985 Oct 15J; Buchanan, James McGill 1986 Oct 16H; Solow, Robert M. 1987 Oct 21J; Allais, Maurice 1988 Oct 18J; Haavelmo, Trygve 1989 Oct 11A
  educational issues: high school student knowledge 1988 Dec 28F
  obituaries: Kuznets, Simon 1985 Jul 9J; Myrdal, Gunnar 1987 May 17A

Ecuador *see also individual leaders in the name index (e.g.,* Borja Cevallos, Rodrigo)
  accidents and disasters: earthquakes 1987 Mar 6D/Mar 11D; floods 1983 May 8I; landslides 1983 May 8I

church developments: papal visit 1985 Feb 5J

economy and labor: currency 1987 Sep 5E; general strikes 1985 Jan 10D; 1987 Mar 25D; 1989 May 11D; oil exploration 1987 Sep 30E

foreign relations: Bolivia 1980 Jul 29D; Cuba 1981 Feb 21D; Israel 1981 Mar 21G; Lima Group withdrawal 1985 Oct 13D; Nicaragua 1985 Oct 11D; Peru 1981 Jan 28D/Mar 6D

government and politics: Borja Cevallos elected president 1988 May 8D/Aug 10D; constitutional reform referendum 1980 Apr 11D; 1986 Jun 1D; coup attempts 1986 Mar 14D; elections 1984 Jan 28D; 1986 Jun 1D; 1988 Jan 31D; Febres Cordero elected president 1984 May 6D; oil minister resigns 1982 Sep 8D; president held hostage 1987 Jan 16D; revolver fired in national assembly 1980 Sep 30D; state of emergency lifted 1982 Oct 27D

monetary and trade issues: Citibank seizes deposits 1989 May 11D; currency 1983 Mar 18D; debt 1984 May 4D/Jun 21D/Sep 14D; 1985 Feb 8D; 1987 Feb 17D; 1989 Apr 5I; foreign investment 1985 Sep 16D; IMF loans 1983 Jul 26D; 1985 Mar 13D; 1986 Aug 15D

sports: tennis 1986 May 4J

U.S. relations: 1981 Mar 21G; 1983 Aug 11G; 1986 Jan 13G

Eddie Murphy Raw (film) 1987 Dec 23F

Eden Burning (Belva Plain) (book) 1982 Jul 11J/Aug 8J

Edge, The (Dick Francis) (book) 1989 Mar 31J

Edie Brickell & New Bohemians (singing group) 1989 Feb 25J

Edinburgh University (Scotland) 1988 Dec 28I

Edmonton Eskimos (football) 1987 Nov 29J

Edmonton Oilers (ice hockey team) 1982 Jan 20J/Feb 24J/Mar 17J/Mar 25J/Jun 8J; 1983 May 17J; 1984 May 19J; 1985 May 30J; 1987 May 31J; 1988 May 26J

education *see* colleges and universities; *specific institutions* (*e.g.,* Harvard); *geographic regions* (*e.g.,* New York City)

Education, U.S. Department of *see also specific department heads in the name index* (*e.g.,* Bennett, William J.)

appointments: Bell, Terrel 1981 Jan 7F; Bennett, William J. 1985 Jan 10F; Cavazos, Lauro F. 1988 Nov 21F

budget and spending programs: 1983 Oct 20F; 1984 Aug 18F; 1989 Oct 19F

formation: 1980 May 4F

public/private school issues: college desegregation 1983 Jul 7F; high school dropout rate 1989 Sep 14F; parochial school remedial education 1986 Jun 17F

student loan issues: draft registration/aid linkage 1986 Jan 22G; IRS targets deadbeats 1985 Aug 6F

teachers and school staff: AIDS handbook issued 1987 Oct 6F

tests and test scores: college entrance exam scores 1988 Feb 25F

Educational Testing Service (ETS) 1988 Feb 25F/Oct 27F; 1989 Jan 31I/Apr 28F

Education Amendments of 1972 1984 Feb 28F

Education of the Handicapped Act of 1975 1988 Jan 20F

EEOC *see* Equal Employment Opportunity Commission

E.F. Hutton Group Inc. 1985 May 2H; 1987 Dec 3H

E-Ferol Aqueous Solution 1984 May 4I

EFTA *see* European Free Trade Association

Eglin Air Force Base (Florida) 1980 May 24F

Egypt *see also individual leaders in the name index* (*e.g.,* Mubarak, Hosni)

archaeology: fossil primates 1980 Feb 7I

arts and culture: Mahfouz receives death threats 1989 May 3C; Mahfouz wins Nobel Prize 1988 Oct 13J; opera at the Temple of Luxor 1987 May 2J

Camp David peace process *see* Camp David peace process

defense and disarmament issues: Red Sea minesweep 1984 Aug 8A; 1985 Jan 21C; U.S. joint training exercises 1980 Jan 8A; 1983 Aug 10C

economy: Aswan Dam repairs 1983 Apr 16I; food prices 1984 Oct 1C

energy issues: nuclear power plants 1981 Mar 21G/Mar 21I/Jun 7I

foreign relations

Austria: 1981 Aug 29B

Great Britain: 1984 Aug 8A

Iraq: 1982 Apr 9C/Dec 29C

Israel: Arafat reception criticized 1983 Dec 22C; Baker plan welcomed 1989 Dec 7C; economic boycott ended 1980 Feb 5C; high level-contacts resumed 1983 Dec 29C; 1985 Feb 27C; Palestinian autonomy talks 1980 Jan 17C/Feb 1C/Jun 11A/Aug 4C/Sep 3A/Oct 15A; 1981 Sep 23C/Nov 12C; 1982 Mar 21C

Jordan: 1983 Dec 5C

Libya: 1980 Jun 16C; 1984 Nov 17C; 1985 Oct 12C

Oman: 1982 May 8C

Palestinians: 1982 Apr 6C; 1987 Apr 26C

Saudi Arabia: 1982 Oct 5G

USSR: 1981 Sep 15A

government and politics: constitutional reform 1980 May 22C; emergency order suspended 1982 Feb 11C; martial law imposed 1980 Jun 16C; Mubarak becomes president 1981 Oct 7C; parliamentary elections 1987 Apr 10C; Sadat assassinated 1981 Oct 6C

international organizations: Arab League 1987 Nov 8C; 1989 May 23C; IMF 1987 May 15C; Islamic Conference 1984 Jan 19C/Jan 20C/Jan 30C; United Nations 1983 Dec 31A; World Bank 1982 Feb 10C

monetary and trade issues: IMF loans 1987 May 15C; U.S. AWACS plane deal 1980 Feb 25C; 1982 Oct 5G; U.S. debt-relief plan 1986 Dec 24G; World Bank loans 1982 Feb 10C

religious issues: Coptic Christians 1985 Jan 6C

Sinai *see* Sinai

terrorism and unrest: *Achille Lauro* hijacking 1985 Oct 9C/Oct 10C; Beirut embassy bombing 1985 Jul 25C; Copts/Moslems violence 1981 Jun 20C; Egyptair hijacking 1985 Nov 24C; Islamic fundamentalists 1988 Dec 19C; 1989 Apr 26C/May 3C; Vienna synagogue attack 1981 Aug 29B

United Nations policy: Security Council seat 1983 Dec 31A

U.S. relations

defense issues: military exercises 1980 Jan 8A/Nov 28G; 1981 Nov 14G; 1983 Aug 10C; nuclear power plants 1981 Mar 21G/Mar 21I/Jun 7I; Red Sea minesweep 1984 Aug 8A; 1985 Jan 21C

peace initiatives: Baker peace talks plan accepted 1989 Dec 6C; Carter Policy Center conference 1983 Nov 6A; Palestinian autonomy talks 1980 Aug 4C; Shultz visits 1988 Feb 25C; U.S. envoy visits 1985 Aug 18C

trade and aid issues: aid request aired 1985 Jan 8C; Aswan Dam repairs 1983 Apr 16I; AWACS plane deal 1980 Feb 25G; 1981 Oct 15C; 1982 Oct 5G; 1983 Aug 3C; 1984 Apr 9G; debt-relief plan 1986 Dec 24G; tourism 1986 May 29J

Eiffel Tower (Paris, France) 1985 Dec 22B

Eighth Amendment 1987 Jun 15F/Jun 22F

Eighth Commandment, The (Lawrence Sanders) (book) 1986 Jun 27J/Jul 18J

84 Charing Cross Road (film) 1988 Mar 20J

El Al (Israeli airline) 1982 Aug 25C/Sep 2C; 1985 Dec 27A; 1986 May 21B/Oct 24C/Nov 01B

election boycotts

Bangladesh: 1986 Oct 15E; 1988 Mar 3E

Iran: 1984 May 28C

New Caledonia: 1984 Nov 18E

Nicaragua: 1984 Oct 31D

Pakistan: 1985 Feb 25E

Peru: 1985 Apr 13D

Poland: 1984 Jun 9B

Turkey: 1989 Oct 31B

Electoral College 1985 Jan 7F; 1988 Dec 19F; 1989 Jan 4F

Electric Boat (General Dynamics Corp.) 1981 Aug 19G/Oct 22G; 1984 Oct 31G; 1987 May 19G

Electric Horseman, The (film) 1980 Jan 30J

Electricite de France 1980 Feb 26B

electric motors 1989 Nov 30D

Electric Youth (Debbie Gibson) (recording) 1989 Feb 25J/Mar 25J/Apr 29J

Electronic Data Systems Corp. 1985 Oct 15J; 1986 Oct 14H

Electronic Industries Association (Japan) 1989 Jun 12H

Electronic Industries Association (U.S.) 1985 Feb 15J

electronic jamming 1987 Jan 1B; 1988 Nov 30G

electronic surveillance *see* wiretapping and electronic surveillance

electron microscopes 1986 Oct 15I

Elegies (Douglas Dunn) (book) 1986 Jan 28J

---

elephants 1989 May 11I/Jul 18C/Oct 16C/Nov 20C

1100 Bel Air Place (Julio Iglesias) (recording) 1984 Oct 27J

Elf Aquitaine, Societe Nationale 1981 Jun 26H

Elfstedentocht (ice skating race) 1985 Feb 21J

Elgin marbles (sculptures) 1983 May 13B; 1984 Apr 10J

Eli Lilly & Co. 1982 Aug 3I/Aug 4I; 1985 Aug 21H

elm trees 1987 Aug 27H/Sep 3H; 1988 Jan 12I

ELN *see* National Liberation Army (Colombia)

El Nino (climate phenomenon) 1983 Feb 26I

El Pais (Spanish newspaper) 1980 May 9B

El Pavon (Guatemalan prison) 1989 Mar 30D

El Pueblo (Nicaraguan newspaper) 1980 Jan 24D

El Salvador *see also individual leaders in the name index* (*e.g.,* Duarte, Jose Napoleon)

accidents and disasters: CIA plane crash 1984 Oct 19D; earthquakes 1986 Oct 10I; flooding 1982 Sep 20I; military helicopter crash 1984 Oct 23D

Central American peace accord *see* Central American peace accord

church developments: papal address 1982 Feb 28A; papal visits 1983 Mar 2D/Mar 6D

civil strife: blackout 1980 Aug 22D; bridges blown up by rebels 1983 May 25D; Christian Democratic Party headquarters stormed 1980 Feb 12D; Costa Rican embassy occupation 1980 Jul 11D; curfew imposed 1981 Jan 11D; Dutch television crew members killed 1982 Mar 17D; government casualties 1983 Aug 11D; kidnapping ring 1986 Apr 4D; mass kidnapping by rebels 1982 Dec 5D; OAS building occupied 1980 Sep 17D; rebel leadership 1980 Sep 12D; strikes against government 1980 Jun 25D/Aug 15D; university occupation 1980 Mar 17D

defense and armed forces: 1984 Oct 7D/Oct 23D

demonstrations and protests: 1980 Feb 19D; 1983 Sep 27D

economy and labor: banking system 1980 Mar 7D; health workers strike 1985 Jun 2D; land reform 1980 Mar 6D; 1981 Dec 15D; 1982 May 18D/May 20G; 1983 Jul 26D/Sep 27D; 1984 Jan 25G/Jun 28D

foreign relations: Central America 1983 Apr 21D/Jul 30D/Oct 5D; 1987 Oct 2D; 1989 Dec 10D; France 1981 Aug 28A/Sep 2D; Guatemala 1983 Oct 1D; Honduras 1982 Sep 17D; 1983 Oct 1D; 1984 Sep 27D; 1985 Aug 29D; Mexico 1981 Aug 28A/Sep 2D; 1982 Feb 21D; 1985 Aug 28D; Netherlands 1982 Mar 17D; Nicaragua 1983 Nov 25D; 1989 Feb 14D; nonaligned nations 1983 Jan 15D; Spain 1981 Feb 19B/Feb 28B; USSR 1981 Feb 6D/Feb 14B

government and politics

cabinet and ruling parties: coalition government members resign

---

1980 Jan 3D; junta adds civilians 1980 Jan 9D; junta power struggle 1980 Aug 31D; minister of education joins rebels 1980 Jan 8D

constitution: draft version completed 1983 Jun 20D

legislative assembly: elections 1982 Mar 28D/Apr 2D/Jun 4D; 1984 Mar 25D; 1988 Apr 2D/Apr 12D/May 1D; rightist party ends strike 1987 Apr 8D

opposition: coups and coup attempts 1980 May 2D; rebel leadership 1980 Sep 12D

presidency: Cristiani elected president 1989 Mar 19D; Duarte appointed president 1980 Dec 13D; Duarte elected president 1984 May 11D; Magana elected provisional president 1982 Apr 29D; Magana sworn provisional president 1982 May 2D

security forces shake-up: 1983 Nov 26D

human rights: activists honored 1984 Nov 20G; Americas Watch issues report 1988 Aug 4D; Amnesty asks deaths probe 1984 May 21A; Hemispheric Council condemns abuses 1984 Nov 1D; military "death squad" alleged 1988 Oct 26D; rebels free captives 1982 Dec 13D; UN rights resolution 1983 Dec 9A; U.S. certification 1982 Jul 27G/Jul 29G; 1983 Jan 21G/Jul 20G

immigration and refugees: 1980 Jul 5F; 1984 Jan 25G/Sep 26F; 1985 Feb 21F; 1986 May 1F; 1988 Apr 29F

medicine and health care: children vaccinated 1985 Feb 3D; health care workers strike 1985 Jun 2D

military developments

government operations: Honduras joint action 1982 Jul 2D; National University stormed 1980 Jun 25D; rebel raids 1980 Aug 1D/Oct 25D/Dec 28D; 1982 Nov 10D/Nov 19D; 1983 Jun 4D/Jun 10D

rebel operations: 1980 Dec 26D; 1981 Jan 13D/Nov 10D; 1982 Jan 27D/Jan 31D/Jul 5D/Nov 16D; 1983 Jul 8D/Dec 30D; 1984 Feb 8D/Jun 28D; 1985 Oct 10D; 1987 Aug 17D

truces: 1984 Dec 24D; 1985 Feb 3D

peace initiatives

Contadora peace plan: 1984 Nov 8D/Nov 20D; 1985 Feb 14D; 1986 Jan 14D/May 25D

government: amnesty granted rebels 1983 Jul 14D; 1987 Oct 27D/Nov 12D; junta ex-member urges talks 1981 Oct 12D; peace commissions set 1987 Oct 6D

rebels: proposals aired 1981 Jan 14D; 1984 Feb 9D; 1989 Feb 21D; talks agreed 1986 Jun 3D; 1987 Sep 23D; talks called off 1986 Sep 14D; 1987 Oct 29D; truce rejected 1989 Mar 1D

political killings

1980: leftist leaders 1980 Nov 27D; Romero assassination 1980 Mar 24D; 1985 Aug 20D; Romero funeral attack 1980 Mar 30D; statistics 1980 Jun 13D; U.S. churchwomen 1980 Dec 4D/Dec 5D; 1981 May 9D/Jul 12D; 1982 Feb 13D;

1983 Jan 10G/Mar 11D/Mar 16D/Oct 28D/Dec 13G; 1984 May 24D/Jun 18D

1981: Chalatenango Province massacre alleged 1981 Jul 12D; Soyopango slayings 1981 Apr 7D; statistics 1981 Jul 11D/Nov 11D; U.S. agrarian advisers 1981 Jan 3D; 1982 Sep 14D/Oct 1D; 1984 May 22D; 1985 Jul 3D; 1986 Feb 26D

1982: Morazan province massacre 1982 Jan 27D; San Vicente province massacre alleged 1982 Sep 6D

1983: farming cooperative members 1983 Nov 9D; massacre victims found 1983 Oct 7D; statistics 1983 Jul 8D/Dec 25D; U.S. commander Schaufelberger 1983 May 26D/May 27D/May 27G

1984: statistics 1984 Jul 13G

1985: U.S. Marines 1985 Jun 19D/Jun 21D/July 31G

1988: San Francisco massacre 1989 Mar 12D

1989: Attorney General assassinated 1989 Apr 19D; Jesuit priests 1989 Nov 16D/Nov 23D/Nov 26D

terrorism: consul kidnapping in Spain 1981 Feb 19B/Feb 28B; U.S. embassy attack in San Salvador 1980 Sep 16D

United Nations policy: General Assembly 1983 Dec 9A; 1987 Oct 7A

U.S. relations

administration policies and actions

aid issues: military aid, advisers planned 1981 Feb 22G; Nicaraguan dispute 1982 Mar 8D/Mar 12G; Nicaragua rebel aid charged 1984 Aug 8G; policy clarified, solutions backed 1981 Jul 16D; Reagan asks hike 1983 Feb 28G; Reagan stresses support 1983 Feb 22G; U.S. town urges end 1983 Mar 1G

economic reforms: land reform survey 1983 Jul 26D

peace initiatives: leftists asks negotiation role 1981 Jan 14G

personnel: ex-ambassador's wife kidnapped 1983 Jul 8D; Mondale criticism 1983 Jun 19F; Pickering assumes ambassadorship 1983 Sep 6D; Quayle visit 1989 Feb 1G; White loses ambassadorship 1981 Feb 1F

rights issues: abuses targeted 1984 Jan 16G; certification 1982 Jul 27G/Jul 29G; 1983 Jan 21G/Jul 20G; Marine slayers prosecution 1985 Jul 31G

State Department: 1981 Feb 23D/Feb 26D/Jun 9D/Jun 18D; 1982 Oct 27G; 1983 Oct 3G/Dec 31G; 1984 Jan 25G/Apr 12G

congressional policies and actions

aid issues: administration deception charged 1985 Feb 12G; caucus charges misuse 1987 Nov 15G; election aid OKd 1983 Aug 6G; Haig briefs on foreign support 1981 Feb 17G

fact-finding missions: 1982 Feb 11D/Feb 19G; 1983 Jan 15G; 1984 Apr 18D

House of Representatives: 1982 Feb 2G; 1983 Feb 4G; 1984 Feb 7G/Mar 30G/May 10G

legislation: 1982 Feb 10G; 1983 Jul 20G/Nov 12F

Senate: 1982 May 20G/May 26G; 1983 Mar 4G; 1984 Mar 28G/Apr 5G/Oct 10G

demonstrations and protests

against embassy in San Salvador 1980 Sep 16D

against U.S. ambassador 1980 May 12D

against U.S. policy 1981 Mar 24F/May 3F

military advisers and training: 1981 Mar 2G/Mar 22G/Dec 15D; 1982 Jan 9D; 1983 Mar 3G/May 26D/May 27G/Jun 9G/Jun 10D/Jun 13D-14D/Aug 24D; 1984 Mar 21G/Sep 27D

refugee issues: 1980 Jul 5F; 1984 Jan 25G/Sep 26F; 1985 Feb 21F; 1986 May 1F; 1988 Apr 29F

embargos *see also specific embargo (e.g., Soviet grain embargo)*

U.S./Cuba: 1982 Apr 3G; 1986 Aug 22G

U.S./Guatemala: 1983 Jan 7D

U.S./Iran: 1987 Oct 26G; 1988 Mar 7G

U.S./Israel: 1983 May 6G/May 20G

U.S./Nicaragua: 1985 May 1D/May 1G/May 7D/May 10D; 1988 Apr 25G

U.S./South Africa: 1986 Jun 18G

embroidery 1988 Nov 10H

embryos 1984 Jan 6I/Feb 3I/Apr 10I/Jun 17I/Jul 18I/Oct 23I; 1985 Feb 22I; 1986 Jun 6I; 1989 Sep 21F

Emergency Economic Powers Act of 1977 1988 Apr 8G

Emergency Operations, U.N. Office of 1985 Mar 11A

Emergency Veterans Job Training Act (1983) 1983 Aug 15G

Emmy Awards (television) 1980 Sep 7J; 1981 Sep 13J/Sep 13J; 1983 Sep 25J; 1984 Sep 24J; 1985 Sep 12J; 1986 Sep 21J; 1987 Sep 20J; 1988 Aug 28J; 1989 Sep 17J

Emory University (Atlanta, Ga.) 1983 Nov 6A

emotionally disturbed 1988 Jan 20F

Emotional Rescue **(Rolling Stones)** 1980 Aug 13J/Sep 10J

Emotions **(Squier) (recording)** 1982 Sep 22J

Empire State Building (New York City) 1986 Apr 24J

Empire Strikes Back, The **(film)** 1980 May 21J/May 28J/Jul 2J/Aug 6J/Sep 3J/Sep 10J; 1982 Dec 8J

Empty Nest **(TV show)** 1989 Sep 17J

EMS *see* European Monetary System

Encountered Enemy, The: A Vietnam Deception **(TV show)** 1984 Oct 11F

encyclicals, papal 1980 Dec 2A; 1981 Sep 15J; 1986 May 30J; 1987 Mar 25J

endangered species 1984 Aug 6H; 1989 May 11I/Oct 16C/Oct 30E

Endangered Species Act 1982 Jun 8H; 1985 Jan 12I; 1988 Jul 28H/Sep 26H

endrin (pesticide) 1981 Sep 12H

Energia **(Energy) (Soviet rocket)** 1987 May 16I

Energy, U.S. Department of *see also specific department heads in the name index (e.g., Duncan Jr., Charles)*

appointments and resignations: Edwards, James B. 1980 Dec 22F; Herrington, John S. 1985 Jan 10F; Hodel, Donald P. 1982 Nov

5H; Watkins, James D. 1989 Jan 12H

atomic energy and waste: A-research reactors 1987 Mar 28H; A-waste cleanup 1988 Nov 22H; 1989 Jan 4H; A-waste repository 1983 Mar 29H/Dec 27H; 1984 Dec 19H; 1987 Jan 28H; 1988 Mar 10H/Sep 13H; 1989 Nov 28H; A-weapons production 1987 Mar 28H; 1988 Dec 6H; 1989 Jun 30H/Sep 7G/Dec 20G; energy policy plan issued 1981 Jul 17H; nuclear fusion research 1989 Jun 14I; nuclear testing 1986 Sep 30I

budget and spending programs: 1987 Oct 2G; 1988 Sep 29G

government reorganization: abolishment plan 1981 Dec 17F; 1982 May 24H; energy policy plan issued 1981 Jul 17H

health and saftey issues: appliance efficiency standards 1981 Feb 18H; 1987 Mar 17H

oil and gas issues: '79 gas shortage liability 1980 Jul 17H; '80 gas consumption 1980 Mar 20H; coal gasification project 1980 Dec 8H; energy policy plan issued 1981 Jul 17H; Marc Rich subpoena 1983 Sep 21B; oil price control abuses 1984 Jul 13H/Jul 26H

research issues: cold fusion 1989 Jul 12I; Super Collider (atom smashers) 1983 Jul 11I; 1987 Sep 2I; 1988 Nov 10H

energy efficiency standards 1981 Feb 18H; 1987 Mar 17H

Engineers, U.S. Army Corps of 1985 Dec 4H

England *see* Great Britain

English Channel 1982 Aug 28J; 1986 Jan 20B; 1987 Mar 6B/Jul 29B/Nov 27B; 1989 Sep 22B

English Channel tunnel (Eurotunnel) 1980 Mar 19B; 1986 Jan 20B; 1987 Jul 29B/Nov 27B; 1988 Jul 14B

Engraving and Printing, U.S. Bureau of (Treasury Department) 1987 Aug 14J

Eniwetok Atoll (Marshall Islands) 1980 Apr 9E; 1981 May 21A

Enrico Fermi II nuclear power plant (Detroit, Mich.) 1988 Jan 23H

environment *see specific geographic regions (e.g., Canada); organizations (e.g., Greenpeace); related subjects (e.g., endangered species)*

Environment, Council on the *see* Council on the Environment

Environmental Policy Institute 1981 Sep 2I

Environmental Program, U.N. 1986 Dec 1I

Environmental Protection Agency, U.S. (EPA) *see also specific agency head in the name index (e.g., Reilly, William K.)*

acid rain: 1982 Nov 1I; 1985 Jul 26H/Aug 29H/Dec 5H; 1988 Nov 21H

air pollution

guidelines: air particle rules reset 1987 Jun 3H; "bubble policy" set 1984 Jun 25H; 1986 Nov 14H; clean air dispersion plan 1985 Jun 4H; clean air rule delay 1987 Nov 17H; scenic area air rules 1980 Nov 25H

industrial emission standards: city construction ban 1987 Jun 29H; experimental burning 1985 Nov 26H; 1986 May 28H; incinerator

curbs 1989 Nov 30H; oil burning 1985 Nov 8H; oil refinery rules tightened 1984 Apr 17H; polluters listed 1982 Dec 29H; smelter pact 1986 Jul 28H; smokestack rules 1985 Jun 27H

vehicle emission standards: '84 report issued 1986 Apr 22H; '85 report issued 1987 Apr 14H; diesal trucks 1982 Jan 1H/Nov23H/Dec28H; 1984 Oct 10H; emision rule upset by Bork 1987 Jul 28H; fuel efficiency 1985 Jun 26H; GM fuel compromise 1982 Jul 29H; inspection programs 1980 Dec 11H; leaded gas 1982 Aug 23H; 1984 Jul 30H; 1985 Mar 4H; 1986 Dec 2H; 1988 Feb 17H

appointments and resignations: Buford, Anne McGill Gorsuch 1981 Feb 21H; 1983 Mar 9H; Hernandez Jr., John W. 1983 Mar 25H; Lavelle, Rita 1983 Feb 7H; Reilly, William K. 1988 Dec 22F; Ruckelshaus, William 1983 Mar 21H; Thomas, Lee M. 1984 Nov 29H

budget and spending programs: 1982 Oct 22H; 1988 Aug 19F; 1989 Nov 9H

chemical hazards

accidents: West Virgina gas leak 1985 Jan 24H

asbestos: 1985 Aug 6H; 1986 Jan 23H; 1987 Apr 22H/Oct 29H; 1988 Feb 29H; 1989 Jul 6H/Aug 22H

benzene: 1983 Dec 16H; 1988 Jul 20H

chloroform/ethylene oxide labeling: 1985 Sep 23H

cleanup

programs: health record rules issues 1983 Aug 22H; Superfund costs/cleanup 1985 Jan 28H; 1987 Jun 22H; 1989 Dec 19H; toxic dump lists/data 1980 Oct 17H; 1981 Oct 23H; 1983 Aug 3H/Sep 1H; toxic site monitoring/control 1986 Mar 22H; 1987 Jan 16H; voluntary dump cleanup 1982 Feb 1F

sites: Massachusetts/New Hampshire pact 1988 Aug 3H; Michigan dump cleanups set 1982 Nov 18H; New Jersey dump capped 1980 Jan 30H; Tex cleanup set 1987 Jun 22H; Times Beach cleanup 1983 Jan 12H

dioxin: 1983 Mar 31H/Dec 15H; 1984 Jan 20H

fungicides: 1985 Jun 18H; 1989 Dec 4H

herbicides: 1984 Nov 20H; 1986 Oct 7H; 1987 Dec 15H

1,3-butadiene: 1983 Dec 20H; 1985 Oct 2H

PCBs: 1981 May 8H; 1983 May 9H; 1984 Feb 21H

pesticides: 1982 Oct 18I; 1983 Apr 28I/Jul 11H/Sep 30I; 1984 Sep 20H; 1985 Aug 12H; 1986 May 22H/Oct 7H; 1988 Sep 28H/Oct 12H

ripeners: 1987 Jan 7H; 1989 Feb 1I/Mar 16I/Sep 1H

storage issues

dump regulations: 1980 Feb 26H; 1982 Jul 13H/Aug 24H

landfill liquid wastes: 1982 Mar 1F/Mar 17I

storage tanks: 1986 Jul 1H; 1987 Apr 2H

underground water: 1984 Aug 30H

termite-controls: 1987 Aug 11H

wood preservatives: 1984 Jul 11H

corruption and ethics issues

Browning Ferris violations: 1987 Apr 28H

Burford probes: congressional 1982 Dec 16F; 1983 Feb 3F/Feb 7H/Feb 15F/Feb 18F/Mar 3H-4H/Mar 9H/Mar 18/Aug 11H/Sep28H; Justice Department 1983 Feb 16F

Grace indictment/plea: 1987 Jan 28H; 1988 May 31H

Lavelle probes: 1983 Feb 7H/Feb 18F/Feb 23H/Mar 1H/May 18H/May 27H/Jul 22F/Aug 4H/Dec 1H; 1984 Jan 9H; 1985 Apr 19H

Waste Management fined: 1985 Apr 5H

genetic engineering: 1985 Nov 14I; 1986 Jan 30I/Feb 25H/Mar 24I/May 13I; 1987 Aug 27H/Sep 3H/Oct 20I

global warming: 1983 Oct 20H

Love Canal *see* Love Canal

noise pollution: 1980 Dec 24H

ozone protection: 1982 Mar 22I; 1987 Dec 1H; 1988 Aug 1H/Sep 26H

radiation hazards: A-emission standards 1984 Dec 11H; radon gas 1986 Aug 14H; 1987 Aug 4H; 1988 Sep 12H

Superfund *see* Superfund

water pollution

cleanup: clean water enforcement upheld 1980 Dec 2H; Hudson River PCBs 1981 May 8H; ocean dump site ordered moved 1985 Apr 1H

guidelines: "hot spots" listed 1981 Jul 28H; rules tightened 1981 Jan 2H; water quality report issued 1985 Aug 4H

industrial emission standards: chemical rules disputed 1983 Mar 8H; clean water rules disputed 1983 Mar 8H; clean water suit filed 1985 Apr18H; Dow dioxin report issued 1983 Mar 31H; drinking water protection 1980 Nov 10H; 1985 May 16H; 1986 Jun 19H; 1987 Jun 24H/Dec 15H; 1988 Aug 10H; industry rules set 1987 Oct 5H; 1988 Jul 27H; oil refinery rules tightened 1984 Apr 17H

wilderness protection: wetlands 1989 Jan 18H

Environmental Quality, U.S. Council on *see* Council on Environmental Quality, U.S.

Environment and Development, U.N. Commission on 1985 Oct 28A

enzyme-linked immunosorbent assay 1985 Mar 2F

enzymes 1980 Mar 29I

EPA *see* Environmental Protection Agency, U.S.

epidemics *see specific disease (e.g., cholera)*

Episcopal Church 1984 Nov 30J; 1985 Sep 10J/Sep 12J; 1988 Sep 24J; 1989 Feb 11F/Sep 28J/Nov 25E

Epitome (racehorse) 1987 Nov 21J

EPLF *see* Eritrean People's Liberation Front

Equal (artifical sweetener) 1981 Jul 15I

Equal Employment Opportunity Commission (EEOC) 1980 Nov 25H; 1981 Sep 1H; 1983 Oct 18F; 1985 Feb 12F/Jun 17F; 1986 Feb 11F/Jul 23F; 1988 Jan 25F

Equal Rights Amendment (ERA)
advocacy: advocate fined 1980 Nov 7F; hunger strikes 1982 Jun 19F; state rallies 1982 Jun 6F
congressional actions: 1982 Jul 14F; 1983 Nov 15F
party platforms: Democratic Party 1980 Aug 13F; Republican Party 1980 Jul 9F
ratification issues: 1981 Dec 23F; 1982 Jan 25F/Jun 30F
state actions: 1980 Jun 18F; 1982 Feb 10F/Feb 16F/Jun 6F-7F

Equitable Life Assurance Society 1983 Dec 22H

E/R (TV show) 1984 Sep 16J

ERA *see* Equal Rights Amendment

Eritrea (Ethiopia) 1985 Jan 13C; 1987 Oct 22C; 1988 Mar 19C; 1989 Sep 7C

Eritrean People's Liberation Front (EPLF) 1988 Jan 15C/Mar 19C

ESA *see* European Space Agency

Escape (Journey) (recording) 1981 Aug 5J/Sep 9J/Sep 30J/Nov 11J/Dec 9J; 1982 Jan 20J

Escherichia coli (bacterium) 1987 Feb 16I

espionage and intelligence issues *see also specific spy in the name index (e.g., Pollard, Jonathan Jay)*
Bloch spy probe: 1989 Jul 21G/Dec 16G
Chin indictment: 1986 Jan 2G/Feb 7G
CIA budget: 1986 Oct 6G
Daniloff affair: 1986 Aug 30B/Sep 12B/Sep 30A/Oct 22B
Jeffries arrest: 1985 Dec 20G
Miller spy case: 1984 Oct 3G/Nov 13G; 1986 Jun 19G/Jul 14G
Morison arrest: 1984 Oct 1G; 1985 Oct 17G
Moscow embassy scandal: 1987 May 15G/Aug 24G
Nazis post-WWII recruitment: 1985 Jun 28G
New York Times employee expelled from China: 1986 Jul 23E
Pelton sentence: 1986 Dec 16G
Pollard spy case: 1985 Nov 21G/Dec 1C; 1986 Jun 4G; 1987 Mar 4G/May 26C
Soviet UN employee arrested: 1986 Aug 23G
U.S. Army sergeant arrested in West Germany: 1988 Aug 25B
U.S./Australia agreement: 1988 Nov 22E
U.S./Ghana exchange: 1985 Nov 25A
U.S./Soviet diplomatic expulsions: 1986 Oct 22B
U.S./Soviet prisoner exchange: 1986 Feb 11G
Walker spy case: 1985 May 20G/May 22G/May 29G/Jun 3G/Aug 9G/Oct 28G/Nov 12G; 1986 Nov 6G
Whitworth arrest: 1985 Jun 3G; 1986 Aug 28G

Espiritu Santo (New Hebrides) 1980 May 28E/Jun 11E/Aug 31E/Nov 14E

ESPN (cable TV channel) 1987 Mar 15J

est (Erhard Seminar Training) 1984 Dec 14J

Estel-Hoesch AG 1982 Feb 4B

Estimates of School Statistics, 1984-85 (National Education Association) 1985 Apr 9F

Estonia (USSR) 1987 Aug 23B; 1988 Jun 20B/Oct 2B/Nov 16B/Dec 7B; 1989 Jul 27B/Aug 9B/Aug 23B/Dec 24B

E.T.: The ExtraTerrestrial (film) 1982 Jul 7J/Jul 14J/Aug 11J/Sep 15J/Oct 6J/Nov 10J/Dec 8J; 1983 Jan 19J

E.T.: The Extra-Terrestrial Storybook (William Kotzwinkle) (book) 1982 Oct 17J/Nov 14J/Dec 12J

ETA (Euskadi Ta Askatasuna) (Basque terrorist group)
peace initiatives: cease-fire 1989 Mar 18B; talks with government 1984 Aug 23B; 1988 Feb 19B; 1989 Apr 12B
terrorism: assassinations 1982 Nov 4B; 1984 Feb 23B; bombings 1980 Jul 4B; 1982 Aug 8B; 1986 Apr 25B/Oct 25B; 1987 Jun 19B; kidnappings 1981 Feb 28B; leader arrested 1986 Apr 27B

ethanol (grain alcohol) 1987 Jul 14H; 1988 Sep 23H

Ethics in Government Act of 1978 1984 Aug 7F; 1987 Jun 16F; 1988 Apr 8F

Ethiopia *see also individual leaders in the name index (e.g., Haile Mariam, Mengistu).*
accidents and disasters: Leland airplane crash 1989 Aug 7C/Aug 13C
arts and culture: oldest human fossil find 1982 Jun 10E
famine and famine relief: 1983 Mar 18I; 1984 Dec 11C; 1985 Jan 13C/Mar 5C; 1987 Oct 22C; 1988 Jan 15C/Feb 6C; 1989 Oct 21C/Dec 27C
foreign relations: Cuban troop withdrawals 1984 Jan 8C; Somalia 1980 Aug 8C/Aug 27C/Dec 4C; 1982 Jun 1C/Jul 24G; Sudan 1984 Mar 11C
Jews: 1981 Nov 15C; 1985 Jan 3C/Jan 4C
sports: Los Angeles Olympics withdrawal 1984 Jun 1J; marathon 1989 Apr 17J
United Nations policy: Security Council seat 1988 Oct 26A
U.S. relations: 1980 Aug 7G; 1989 May 2F

ethnic jokes 1980 Feb 18F

ethylene bisdithiocarbamate (EBDC) 1989 Dec 4H

ethylene dibromide (pesticide) 1983 Sep 30I/Oct 3H

ethylene oxide 1983 Apr 14H; 1985 Sep 23H

Eureka *see* European Research Agency

Eurobonds 1986 Sep 3B; 1988 Jan 6B/Apr 9B

Europe *see also specific country names (e.g., France)*
accidents and disasters: Chernobyl 1986 Apr 28B; 1987 Apr 26I; weather chill 1985 Jan 10I; 1987 Jan 23B
defense and disarmament issues: antinuclear demonstrations 1983 Oct 22G; CFE talks 1984 Jan 16G/Mar 16B/Apr 19B; 1987 Jul 27B; 1989 Mar 6B/Jul 13B; nuclear-free zones 1982 Dec 8B; 1983 Jun 6B; nuclear fuel reprocessing 1988 May 26E; peace movement 1981 Nov 20B; Reagan arms control speech

1981 Nov 18A/Nov 18B; Reagan statement on limited nuclear war 1981 Oct 16G; US: "no first use" pledge urged 1982 Apr 7G
economy: car sales 1987 Jul 22B; 1988 Jan 18B; cities' cost of living 1988 Jun 28A; currency 1985 Feb 27A; interest rates 1982 Dec 2B; 1987 Dec 3B; stock markets 1985 Jul 10H; 1986 Sep 3B; 1989 Dec 31A; television 1985 Feb 7J; venture capital funds 1988 May 27B; video cassette recorders 1988 Jan 11E
energy and environmental issues: natural gas 1986 Jun 2B; North Sea dumping 1987 Nov 25B; nuclear fuel reprocessing 1988 May 26E; sulfur dioxide emissions 1984 Mar 21I; 1985 Jul 9I; toxic wastes 1988 Aug 1C
foreign relations: Canada 1983 Nov 7A; 1987 Mar 23D; Central America 1984 Sep 28A; Chad 1980 May 16C; China 1984 Feb 7E/Jun 16E; 1986 Jun 8B; Iran 1989 Feb 24A; Japan 1982 Dec 7E; Libya 1986 Apr 24B; Nicaragua 1985 May 7D; 1987 Feb 21D; Sinai peacekeeping force 1981 Dec 3A; South Africa 1984 Jun 14A; 1985 Sep 16C; 1987 Sep 7C; USSR 1982 Jul 1B/Sep 2B; 1986 Jul 13B; West Africa 1988 Aug 1C
immigration and refugees: Poland 1982 Apr 28B; U.S. visas 1989 Jul 13F

INF talks *see* INF talks

labor issues: air traffic controllers 1988 Jul 17B

politics and government: communist party conference 1980 Apr 2B

religion: Roman Catholic Church 1980 Jul 2J/May 29J; 1989 Jan 26J

space program: European Space Agency 1985 Jul 2I; 1987 Nov 10I; 1988 Dec 15I; Spacelab 1983 Nov 28I

sports: golf 1987 Sep 27J; 1989 Sep 24J; Olympic Games in Moscow 1980 Mar 22J

U.S. relations
defense and disarmament issues: allies warned on defense expenditures 1981 Feb 21G; Baker outlines policy 1989 Dec 12G; Carter expects Persian Gulf role 1980 Jan 29C; Carter urges Poland aid 1980 Aug 29G; "no first use" pledge urged 1982 Apr 7G; Reagan on limited nuclear war 1981 Oct 16G; Reagan speech 1981 Nov 18A-18B; Reagan statement on limited nuclear war 1981 Oct 16G; troops 1980 Apr 23G; 1984 Mar 22G/Jun 20G; 1989 Feb 18G
immigration and refugees: 1989 Jul 13F
terrorism issues: airline attack warning 1988 Dec 22H; airline security tightened 1988 Dec 29H; tourism impact 1986 May 29J/Jun 5J
trade issues: interest rate policy 1981 Jul 16H; Nicaraguan trade embargo criticized 1985 May 7D; steel dumping complaints 1980 Mar 21A
visits: 1982 Mar 20A; 1983 Jun 5B/Jun 24G; 1985 Apr 30B

Europe, College of *see* College of Europe

Europe, U.N. Economic Commission for 1981 Mar 17B

European Atomic Energy Community 1981 Mar 31I

European Basketball Championship 1987 Jun 14J

European Center for Nuclear Research (CERN) 1980 Jan 31I; 1983 Jan 26I/Jun 1I; 1984 Jul 3I; 1989 Oct 13I

European Champions Cup (soccer) 1987 May 27J

European Commission (European Community) 1983 May 28A/Jun 30C/Jul 5B/Jul 7B; 1984 Jul 19B/Dec 8B; 1988 Dec 16B

European Commission on Human Rights 1982 Jul 1B

European Community (EC) *see also member nations (e.g., Great Britain)*
agricultural issues: '86 farm budget 1986 Apr 25B; farm pact 1986 Dec 16B; farm subsidy cuts 1987 May 19B; U.S. exports 1986 Jul 2B/Dec 30H; 1987 Jan 29H/Jul 1H; 1989 Jan 5A; wheat exports 1986 Aug 14B; world farm prices 1988 Aug 12B
budget and spending programs: 1984 May 23B; 1985 Nov 27B/Dec 12B; 1986 Apr 25B/Jul 10B
court system *see* European Court of Justice
drug trafficking: 1986 Oct 20B
environmental issues: anti-pollution standards 1989 Jun 9B; car exhaust standards 1985 Mar 21B; chlorofluorocarbons 1989 Mar 2I; ozone treaty 1988 Dec 16I; Rhine River spill 1986 Nov 12B
executive council *see* European Commission
foreign policy: aid issues 1989 Nov 18B; Arab-Israeli conflict 1980 Jun 13A/Jul 31A; famine relief effort 1985 Feb 28A; immigration 1986 Oct 20B; terrorism 1986 Jan 28B/Oct 20B
health and safety issues: Chernobyl disaster 1986 May 7B; 1987 Mar 25I; radiation levels in food 1986 May 29B
internal market issues: anniversary marked 1987 Mar 25B; fishing quotas 1983 Jan 25B; 1985 Dec 23B; television transmission regulation 1989 Oct 3B; unemployment rate 1984 Jul 6B; 1987 Mar 8B/Jun 11B; 1988 Feb 1B/Jul 7B/Nov 10B; value-added tax 1988 Sep 11B
legislative branch *see* European Parliament
membership: 1980 Jun 5B
monetary issues: capital movement 1988 Jun 13B; inflation 1986 Sep 24B; monetary union plan 1989 Apr 17B; *see also* European Monetary System
price fixing: chemical producers fined 1984 Nov 26B; petrochemical concerns fined 1986 Apr 24B
steel import issues: production quotas and subsidies 1983 Jun 30C; 1984 Jan 26B; 1985 Mar 27B; 1987 Dec 22B; U.S. dispute 1982 Jul 24B/Aug 10H/Aug 25A/Oct 21A; 1985 Jan 11A/Nov 1A/Dec 30B; 1986 Sep 7B
summits and meetings: 1981 Nov 27B; 1982 Mar 29B/Dec 4B; 1983 Jun 17B/Dec 6B; 1984 Mar 20B; 1985 Jun 29B/Dec 4B; 1986 Dec

6B; 1987 Jun 29B/Dec 5B; 1988 Feb 13B/Dec 3B/Dec 28B
trade issues: '86 surplus posted 1987 Mar 17B; agricultural exports 1987 Jul 1H; Comecon talks 1986 Sep 25B; European Free Trade Association 1984 Jan 1B; fishing quotas 1983 Jan 25B; 1985 Dec 23B
U.S. policy
agricultural imports/exports: agricultural exports 1986 Jul 2B/Dec 30H; 1987 Jan 29H; 1989 Jan 5A; citrus fruit exports 1986 Aug 10B/Oct 27B; farm subsidies study 1982 Dec 10A; meat war 1988 Dec 10B; 1989 Jan 1B/Feb 18B; pasta war 1986 Aug 10B; wheat exports 1985 Oct 16H
business mergers: '88 takeovers 1989 Jan 17H
manufacturing imports/exports: chemical exports 1984 Jan 13B/Feb 28A; IBM antitrust suit 1984 Aug 2A; Japanese semiconductor pact 1988 Mar 25A/May 4A; plastic exports 1984 Jan 13B; security device sales 1984 Jan 13B/Feb 28A; sporting goods sales 1984 Jan 13B/Feb 28A; steel exports 1982 Jul 24B/Aug 10H/Aug 25A/Oct 21A; 1985 Jan 11A/Nov 1A/Dec 30B; 1986 Sep 7B
raw material imports/exports: Soviet gas pipeline 1982 Jun 22A/Aug 12B
trade barriers report: 1989 May 3B

European Convention (1950) 1988 Nov 29A

European Court of Human Rights 1985 Jul 10B/Dec 9B; 1986 Jul 8B; 1988 Oct 26B/Nov 29A

European Court of Justice 1982 Mar 5B; 1985 May 28B; 1987 Mar 12B

European Cup (soccer) 1985 May 29B

European Football Association, Union of the 1985 Jun 2B

European Free Trade Association (EFTA) 1984 Jan 1B

European Grand Prix 1985 Oct 6J

European Management Forum 1984 Jan 6A

European Monetary System (EMS) 1981 Mar 22B/Oct 4B; 1982 Feb 22B/Jun 12B; 1983 Mar 21B; 1985 Jul 20B; 1986 Apr 6B/Aug 2B; 1987 Jan 12B; 1989 Jun 13B

European Parliament
arms issues: NATO nuclear missile deployment 1983 Nov 16B
budget issues: Fitzgerald speech 1984 Jul 25B; rebate to Britain blocked 1984 Jul 27B; spending plans presented 1980 Jul 9B; 1984 May 23B; 1985 Nov 27B/Dec 12B
elections: Baron Crespo elected president 1989 Jul 25B; Pflimlin elected president 1984 Jul 24B; Plumb elected president 1987 Jan 20B; ruling party suffers setbacks 1984 Jun 17B; 1989 Jun 18B

European Research Agency (Eureka) 1985 Jul 18B/Nov 5B

European Space Agency (ESA) 1985 Jul 2I; 1987 Nov 10I; 1988 Dec 15I; *see also* Ariane rocket

European Strategic Program for Research and Development in Information Technology (Esprit) 1984 Feb 28B

European Track and Field Championships 1986 Aug 31J

European Venture Capital Association 1988 May 27B

euthanasia 1988 Jan 8I; 1989 Apr 26F/May 18F

Evangelical Lutheran Churches, Association of *see* Association of Evangelical Lutheran Churches

Evangelical Lutheran Church in America 1986 Aug 29J; 1987 Apr 30J; 1989 Aug 29J

evaporated milk 1988 Feb 2E

Evening News Association 1985 Aug 29H

Everglades National Park (Florida) 1989 Dec 12H

Every Breath You Take (Police) (recording) 1983 Aug 17J; 1984 Feb 28J

Every Which Way But Loose (film) 1980 Feb 6J

Evil Under the Sun (film) 1982 Mar 10J

Evita (musical) 1980 Jun 8J

evolution, theory of 1981 Mar 5F/Mar 19F/Jul 21F; 1982 Jan 5F/Aug 29I; 1983 Oct 17F; 1984 Apr 14F; 1985 Feb 15F/Dec 13F; 1987 Jun 19F; 1989 Nov 9F

Excalibur (film) 1981 May 6J/May 20J

Excedrin (drug) 1986 Jun 20H; 1987 Dec 9F

exclusionary tender offers 1986 Jul 8H

Executioner's Song, The (Norman Mailer) (book) 1980 Jan 13J/Apr 14J

executions
in Africa: Burkina Faso 1989 Sep 19C; Ghana 1986 Jun 22C
in Asia and Pacific Rim: China 1989 Jul 8E; India 1989 Jan 6E; Indonesia 1986 Oct 9E; Malaysia 1986 Jul 6E
in Europe: Romania - Ceausescu, Nicolae 1989 Dec 25B
in Middle East: Iran 1987 Sep 28C; Lebanon - Higgins, William R. 1989 Jul 31C; Saudi Arabia 1989 Sep 21C
statistics: 1984 Apr 2F; 1988 Dec 19F
in U.S.: Adams Jr., Aubrey 1989 May 4F; Andrade, Richard 1986 Dec 18F; Barfield, Margie Velma 1984 Nov 2F; Bundy, Theodore (Ted) 1989 Jan 24F; Byrne Jr., Edward R. 1988 Jun 14F; Cole, Carroll E. 1985 Dec 6F; Darden, Willie Jasper 1988 Mar 15F; Felde, Wayne Robert 1988 Mar 15F; Funchess, David Livingston 1986 Apr 22F; King, Leon 1989 Mar 22F; Raulerson, James David 1985 Jan 30F; Roach, James Terry 1986 Jan 10F; Smith, John Eldon 1983 Dec 15F; Streetman, Robert 1988 Jan 7F; Taylor Jr., Johnny 1984 Feb 29F; Williams, Robert Wayne 1983 Dec 15F

exercise, physical 1980 May 1I/Jul 5I; 1986 Jan 9I/Mar 6I; 1989 Nov 3J

exhibitions
AIDS: 1989 Nov 16J
art and photography: British art 1985 Nov 9J; Chagall 1987 Sep 2J; contemporary art history 1986 Dec 10J; Impressionist and modern paintings from USSR 1986 May 1J; Israeli archaeological exhibit cancelled 1982 Feb 23J; Mapplethorpe 1989 Jun 13J/Jul 20J/Dec 18J; pre-1930 Soviet art

1981 Jun 3J; U.S. flags 1989 Feb 17J; Wyeth family 1987 Mar 11J

Eximbank *see* Export-Import Bank of the United States

exit polls 1985 Jan 17J

Exocet (missile) 1982 May 4D/May 25D; 1983 Nov 10C; 1987 May 20C

Expo 86 (Vancouver world's fair) 1986 May 2D/Oct 13D

Export Administration Act of 1979 1983 Oct 14H/Dec 2B; 1984 Mar 1H/Mar 30H

Export Enhancement Program 1986 Apr 18E

Export-Import Bank of the United States (Eximbank) 1981 Dec 23G; 1983 Sep 30D; 1989 Jan 8H

extortion
Castellano indicted: 1984 Mar 30F
Colombo crime group: 1986 Nov 17F
Lake Tahoe gambling casino: 1980 Aug 27J
New York construction industry: 1986 Nov 17F; 1987 Aug 18F
North Slope construction boom: 1989 May 23F
Philadelphia police force: 1984 Sep 24F
South Korea: 1989 Jan 31E
Tylenol plot: 1982 Oct 20H
Wedtech scandal: 1987 Jun 3F; 1988 Nov 21F; 1989 Oct 20F
Zaccaro acquittal: 1987 Oct 15F

extremely low frequency signals 1981 Oct 8G

Exxon Corp. 1980 Oct 3H; 1981 Mar 2H/Mar 20I; 1982 May 2H; 1983 Apr 13H/Aug 23A; 1984 Apr 25H; 1986 Jan 27H/Jun 4H/Dec 30C; 1989 Jan 20H/Dec 24H; *see also* Exxon Valdez oil spill

Exxon Valdez oil spill 1989 Mar 24H/Mar 28H/Apr 5H/Apr 7H/May 10H/May 20H/Jul 24H/Jul 28H/Sep 7H/Sep 15H

Eye of the Needle (film) 1981 Jul 24J

Eye of the Tiger (Survivor) (recording) 1982 Jul 11J/Aug 18J

Eyes of the Dragon, The (Stephen King) (book) 1987 Feb 27J/Mar 27J/Apr 24J

Eyes on the Prize (TV show) 1988 Jan 28J

Eyes That See in the Dark (Kenny Rogers) (recording) 1983 Nov 9J

F

FAA *see* Federal Aviation Administration, U.S. (FAA)

Fabulous Baker Boys, The (film) 1989 Oct 25J/Nov 13J

Face Dances (Who) (recording) 1981 Apr 8J/May 6J

facial wrinkles 1988 Jan 22I/Jul 5I

factoring (mathematics) 1988 Oct 11I

Fairchild Industries Inc. 1982 Sep 2H

fairness doctrine 1985 Aug 7F; 1987 Jun 23F/Aug 4F

Fair Warning (Van Halen) (recording) 1981 May 27J

Faith (George Michael) (recording) 1987 Dec 26J; 1988 Jan 23J/Feb 20J/Mar 19J/Apr 23J/May 21J/Jun 18J/Jul 16J; 1989 Feb 22J

Falco (Hans Hoelzel) (singer) 1986 Apr 16J

Falco 3 (Falco) (recording) 1986 Apr 16J

Falcon and the Snowman, The (film) 1985 Feb 13F

Falkland (Malvinas) Islands
Argentina-UK sovereignty dispute *see* Falkland (Malvinas) Islands War
fishing zone dispute: 1986 Oct 29B/Nov 17D/Nov 18B; 1987 Feb 1D; 1989 Jul 12D

Falkland (Malvinas) Islands War (1982)
economic sanctions: European Community imposes curbs 1982 Apr 7D/Apr 14A/May 24A/Aug 3D; Andean Pact boosts trade 1982 Apr 17D; OAS asks sanctions end 1982 Apr 20D/Apr 28D
military operations
March 1982: UK-Argentina dispute heightens 1982 Mar 3A
April 1982: Argentine forces seize control 1982 Apr 1D-2D/Aug 15D; Argentina installs government 1982 Apr 4D-5D/Apr 7D; UK task force puts to sea 1982 Apr 5B; UK political opposition 1982 Apr 5B/Apr 9B/Apr 13B; UK, Argentina declare war zones 1982 Apr 7A/Apr 29D; Galtieri visits 1982 Apr 22D; UK sets air, sea blockade 1982 Apr 28D; British enforce blockade 1982 Apr 30D
May 1982: Stanley airfield bombed 1982 May 1D; *General Belgrano* torpedoed 1982 May 2D; Argentine patrol craft sunk 1982 May 3D; *Sheffield* destroyed 1982 May 4D; Argentina war financing 1982 May 5D; cease-fires 1982 May 6B/May 25A/Jun 2A/Jun 14D; war zone extended 1982 May 7B/May 11D; Argentina drops supplies 1982 May 8D; *Narval* destroyed 1982 May 9B; British attacks near Stanley 1982 May 9B/Jun 12D/Jun 14D; Argentine ship sunk 1982 May 11B; British task force attacked 1982 May 12B; Pebble Island raided 1982 May 14D; Argentine supply ships attacked 1982 May 16D; small-scale bombings 1982 May 20D; *Ardent* sunk 1982 May 21D; British troops land at Port San Carlos 1982 May 21D; Argentine warplanes destroyed 1982 May 22A; air strike against British ships 1982 May 23D/May 24D; British hold Port San Carlos 1982 May 25D; *Coventry* sunk 1982 May 25D; British take Darwin, Goose Green 1982 May 28D-29D; Argentine air attacks end 1982 May 31D; casualties reported 1982 May 30D/Jun 1D/Jun 13D
June 1982: Mount Kent seized 1982 Jun 1D; British claims 1982 Jun 2D; leaflets urge surrender 1982 Jun 3D; Stanley final assault instructions 1982 Jun 3D; Argentine claims 1982 Jun 3D/Jun 13D/Jun 16D; UK consolidates position 1982 Jun 6D; British landing craft attacked 1982 Jun 10D; Argentine troops surrender 1982 Jun 14D/Jun 16D; Thule Island surrenders 1982 Jun 20D
peace initiatives: UK-Argentina hold talks 1982 Mar 1D/Apr 15D/Apr 19B/May 11A/May 20A; non-aligned nations 1982 Mar 6A; UK rejects Argentine plan 1982 Apr

2A; UN resolutions urge talks 1982 Apr 3A/Jun 4A/Nov 4A; U.S. mediation 1982 Apr 14G/Apr 30G/May 1D; Argentina asks OAS role 1982 Apr 20D; UK rejects US plan 1982 Apr 23B; US ends mediation, backs UK 1982 Apr 30D/May 10B/May 10D; UK-Argentina soften stance 1982 May 10B/May 10D; pope urges cease-fire 1982 May 23A; UN cease-fire efforts falter 1982 Jun 2D; Argentine presses claim 1983 Jan 3D; 1989 Sep 25D; UN resolutions urge talks 1983 Nov 16A; 1984 Nov 1A; 1985 Nov 27A; 1986 Nov 25A; British rejects 1984 Jan 4B; UK-Argentina talks break down 1984 Jul 19A; OAS urges talks 1986 Nov 14D
postwar developments
Argentina: POWs repatriated 1982 Jun 19D/Jun 28D/Jul 12B; naval commander relieved 1982 Sep 20D; inquiry 1983 Nov 23D; junta members sentenced 1986 May 16D; government officials pardoned 1989 Mar 23D
Great Britain: British governor returns 1982 Jun 26D; inquiry 1983 Jan 18B; *General Belgrano* sinking coverup charged 1984 Aug 19B
sovereignty issues *see* peace initiatives

Falling in Love (film) 1984 Dec 12J

Family Album (Danielle Steel) (book) 1985 Mar 15J/Apr 19J/May 24J

Family Business (film) 1989 Dec 28J

family income 1980 Jan 22F; 1982 Feb 27H; 1984 Oct 3H; 1985 Aug 27H; 1986 Aug 26H; 1987 Jul 30H; 1988 Feb 25H/Aug 31H/Aug 31H; 1989 May 22F/Oct 18H/Oct 18H

family planning 1980 Jul 30J; 1983 Jul 11E; 1986 Nov 3F; 1987 Jul 30F/Aug 29F; 1988 Jan 29F/Mar 3A

Family Policy Panel 1986 Jan 16F

family size 1982 Nov 19F

Family Support Act (1988) 1988 Oct 13F

Family Ties (TV show) 1986 Sep 21J; 1987 Sep 20J; 1988 Aug 28J

Family Welfare Reform Act 1987 Dec 16F

famine 1980 Mar 21E; 1983 Mar 6C; 1985 Mar 11A; *see also* specific geographical regions (e.g., Ethiopia)

Fanny (Erica Jong) (book) 1980 Sep 14J/Oct 12J; 1987 Oct 12J

Fanny and Alexander (film) 1983 Jun 17J

FAO *see* Food and Agriculture Organization

Farabundo Marti National Liberation Front (FNLM) *see also* Democratic Revolutionary Front
foreign aid: Cuba aid suspected 1989 Dec 25D; Nicaraguan aid alleged 1989 Nov 26D
military offensives: 1987 Mar 31D; 1989 Nov 12D/Nov 15D
peace initiatives: 1988 Oct 31D; 1989 Jan 23D/Sep 15D/Oct 18D/Nov 2D; cease-fires 1985 Dec 24D; 1987 Nov 5D; Duarte rejects peace plan 1989 Jan 25D; U.S. meetings 1983 Aug 30D
terrorism: rebels exchanged for Duarte daughter 1985 Oct 24D

Far Eastern University (Manila, Philippines) 1983 Aug 26E

FarmAid (benefit concert) 1985 Sep 22J

Farm Bureau, American *see* American Farm Bureau

Farm Credit System, U.S. (FCS) 1985 Jul 15H/Nov 4H/Dec 19H/Dec 23H; 1986 Feb 18H/May 6H; 1987 Oct 6H/Dec 19H; 1988 Jan 6F/Jul 5H

Farmers Home Administration, U.S. (FmHA) 1986 Mar 12H/Sep 30H; 1988 Nov 11H/Dec 20H; 1989 Jan 24H

farmland value 1984 May 23H

farm prices
1980 statistics: 1980 Apr 30H/Oct 31H/Nov 20H
1983 statistics: 1983 Feb 28H/Apr 29H/May 31H/Aug 31H/Sep 30H/Oct 31H/Nov 30H/Dec 30H
1984 statistics: 1984 Jan 31H/Feb 29H/Mar 30H/Apr 30H/May 31H/Jun 29H/Jul 31H/Aug 31H/Sep 28H/Oct 31H/Nov 30H/Dec 31H
1985 statistics: 1985 Jan 3H/Feb 28H/Mar 29H/Apr 30H/May 31H/Jul 31H/Aug 30H/Sep 30H/Oct 31H/Nov 29H/Dec 31H
1986 statistics: 1986 Jan 31H/Mar 31H/Apr 30H/May 30H/Jun 30H/Jul 31H/Aug 29H/Sep 30H/Oct 31H/Nov 28H/Dec 31H
1987 statistics: 1987 Jan 30H/Feb 27H/Jul 31H/Aug 31H/Sep 30H/Nov 30H
1988 statistics: 1988 Jan 30H/Feb 29H/Mar 30H/Apr 29H/May 31H/Jun 29H/Jul 29H/Aug 30H/Sep 29H/Oct 31H/Nov 30H/Dec 30H
1989 statistics: 1989 Jan 31H/Mar 30H/Apr 28H/May 31H/Jun 29H/Jul 31H/Aug 31H/Nov 30H

farm workers 1983 Sep 27D; 1985 Sep 1H; 1987 Feb 6F/Apr 28H; 1988 Aug 21F

Farrar, Straus & Giroux 1988 Jan 11J

Fascist Red Army (Colombian terrorist group) 1988 Jul 3D

Fast Car (Tracy Chapman) (recording) 1989 Feb 22J

Faster Than the Speed of Night (Bonnie Tyler) (recording) 1983 Oct 19J

fast-food restaurants 1985 Nov 14I

Fast Times at Ridgemont High (film) 1982 Sep 15J

fast-track negotiations 1986 Apr 23D/May 22D

Fatah Revolutionary Council (FRC) 1989 Nov 12C

Fatal Attraction (film) 1987 Sep 18J/Oct 21J/Nov 11J

Fatal Beauty (film) 1987 Nov 11J

Fatal Vision (Joe McGinniss) (book/TV show) 1984 Nov 18J/Nov 28J; 1987 Aug 21J

fats, saturated 1986 Mar 20I

FBI *see* Federal Bureau of Investigation, U.S.

FCC *see* Federal Communications Commission, U.S.

FDA *see* Food and Drug Administration, U.S.

FDIC *see* Federal Deposit Insurance Corp., U.S.

FDN *see* Nicaraguan Democratic Forces

FDR *see* Democratic Revolutionary Front

Federal Aviation Administration, U.S. (FAA)

accidents: near-collisions 1985 Jun 4H; New Orleans crash damage payments 1985 Aug 25H

appointments: McArtor sworn administrator 1987 Jul 27H

labor issues: air controllers pact 1989 Jan 12H; pilot license rules eased 1989 Aug 31H

safety and security issues: aging plane repairs ordered 1989 May 18H; airline monitoring criticized 1986 May 14H; airplane warning devices 1986 Sep 19H; air traffic control modernization plans 1982 Jan 28I; bomb detection plan set 1989 Aug 30H; Pan Am bomb threat reported 1988 Dec 22H; Pan Am fined $2 million 1986 Aug 22H; security fines imposed 1988 Dec 7H; security tightened abroad 1988 Dec 29H

service issues: flight delays 1984 Dec 4H; flight scheduling 1981 Aug 24H; 1984 Sep 12H

Federal Bureau of Investigation, U.S. (FBI) *see also specific bureau chief (e.g., Webster, William H.)*

appointments: Gates withdraws nomination 1987 Mar 3G; Sessions, William S. 1987 Jul 24F; Webster, William H. 1987 Mar 3G

bias issues: 1988 Jan 25F/Sep 30F; 1989 May 5F/Jun 30F/Sep 21F

corruption and ethics issues: NSC meeting leaks 1983 Nov 24G; Pentagon fraud scandal 1988 Jun 14G

crime and law enforcement: '65 Liuzzo slaying charges dismissed 1983 May 27F; computer legislation urged 1983 Oct 18F; criminal records inaccuracies 1982 Oct 24F; Miami shootout 1986 Apr 11F; New York sting operation 1987 Aug 11F; Selma voting fraud dropped 1985 Jul 5F; statistics 1983 Sep 11F; 1984 Sep 8F; 1986 Jul 26F; 1989 Aug 6F; Tylenol extortion 1982 Oct 20H; Weather Underground fugitive captured 1987 Jan 20F; Wells Fargo robbery arrests 1985 May 30F; white supremacists convicted 1988 Apr 7F

espionage and intelligence issues: Calif engineer arrested 1983 Oct 15G; Honduras coup plot arrests 1984 Nov 1D; Navy ex-officer, son arrested 1985 May 20G; Navy spycase widens 1985 Jun 3G; Nicaraguan contras 1986 Dec 16F/Dec 23F; Northrop engineer arrested 1984 Dec 18G; Soviet UN aide arrested 1986 Aug 23G

privacy issues: break-in authorizations 1980 Nov 6F; 1981 Apr 15F; CISPES break-ins 1987 Feb 20D; Einstein file 1983 Sep 10J; former agents fined 1986 Oct 22F; Latin policy foes surveillance 1988 Feb 2F; Lennon surveillance 1983 Mar 22J; minorities 1981 Oct 14F; nuclear freeze movement 1983 Mar 25G; political probe rules eased 1983 Mar 6F; Reagan campaign staff proobe 1983 Jun 30F; Socialist Workers Party 1986 Aug 25F; Teamsters union informer 1986 Dec 2H

terrorism issues: Los Angeles Olympics security 1984 Apr 15J

Federal Communications Commission, U.S. (FCC)

access fees: AT&T delay confirmed 1983 Dec 1H; AT&T freeze ordered 1984 Mar 28H; long-distance phone rates 1987 Dec 24H; phone access/hookup fees 1984 Mar 21H

business issues: AT&T: 1980 Apr 7H; 1982 Jun 10H; 1983 Dec 1H; 1984 Mar 28H; cable TV operations: 1980 Jul 22J; 1981 Jul 16J; 1982 Jul 15J; 1985 Jul 19F; 1986 Aug 7F; 1987 Dec 11H

deregulation issues: telephone industry 1980 Apr 7H; 1982 Nov 12H; television station 1984 Jun 27F

fairness and equal time doctrines: 1981 Sep 17J; 1983 Nov 8F; 1984 Nov 21F; 1985 Aug 7F; 1987 Aug 4F

licensing rules: license lotteries 1983 Sep 29F; licenses revoked 1987 Aug 12H; television syndication rights 1983 Aug 4H; 1984 Feb 3F

ownership issues: broadcasting stations 1984 Jul 26F; minority policy ruled unconstitutional 1989 Mar 31F; television station 1984 Dec 19H

price issues: long-distance phone rates 1984 Nov 21H; 1986 May 27H/Dec 30H; 1988 May 12H

programming issues: children's TV programming 1983 Dec 22F; indecency curb tightened 1987 Apr 16F/Dec 24F; 1988 Jul 29H; television syndication rights 1983 Aug 4H; 1984 Feb 3F

research: high-definition television 1988 Sep 1H

transmission: broadcast satellite direct service 1982 Jun 23J; satellite dishes 1986 Jan 14H

Federal Deposit Insurance Corp., U.S. (FDIC)

bank bailouts: Continental Illinois Corp. 1984 Sep 26H/Dec 1H; First City Bancorp. 1987 Sep 9H; 1988 Apr 20H; First Pennsylvania Bank 1980 Apr 28H; insolvent thrift seizures 1989 Feb 7H; MCorp 1989 Jun 28H; Penn Square Bank 1983 Jun 17H; 1984 Jun 29H; 1986 Aug 5H; Philadelphia Savings Fund Society 1982 Apr 3H; problem bank list 1983 Sep 29H; record set 1984 Feb 5H; 1988 Dec 29H; statistics 1984 Jan 3H; thrift rescue costs 1989 Oct 4H; Western Savings Bank 1982 Apr 3H

insurance issues: federal limits set 1984 Mar 26H

Federal Election Commission, U.S. (FEC)

congressional campaigns: '81-82 PAC spending 1983 Apr 28F/May 2F; '81-82 party spending 1983 Apr 25F; '82 costs 1983 May 2F; '86 total spending 1987 May 9F; '88 total spending 1989 Feb 23F

corruption and ethics issues: Democrats file suit 1987 Oct 20F; "soft money" challenge denied 1986 Apr 17F

political action committees (PACs) 1980 Aug 28F; 1983 Apr 28F; 1984 Sep 9F; 1985 May 6; 1986 Jan 23F; 1988 Jul 23F

presidential campaigns: '84 spending 1989 Jul 1F; '88 matching funds 1987 Jun 4F/Oct 28F/Dec 28F; 1988 Jan 4F/Mar 30F/Jul 23F/Dec 30F; 1989 Aug 25F

Federal Emergency Management Agency, U.S. 1983 Jun 23I

Federal Energy Regulatory Commission, U.S. 1983 Sep 14H; 1985 Oct 9H

Federal Espionage Act 1984 Apr 3F

federal funds rate 1989 Jul 7H

Federal Home Loan Bank Board, U.S. (FHLBB)

mortgage rates: Dec '84 drop 1985 Jan 7H; variable rates 1980 Apr 3H; 1981 Apr 23H

regulatory issues: deposit brokers 1984 Mar 26H; interstate purchases 1981 Mar 23H; 1982 Aug 16H; investment accounts 1981 May 11H; net worth loan rules 1982 Jan 14H; private borrowing 1982 Jan 14H; stock brokerage business 1982 May 6H; variable rate mortgages 1980 Apr 3H; 1981 Apr 23H

S&L crisis: bank mergers 1982 Jan 18H; 1983 Aug 4H; 1988 Aug 31H; bank seizures 1982 Jun 3H; 1989 Feb 7H; bans bailouts 1981 Sep 7H; 1988 Feb 2H/Mar 18H/Sep 5H; "big 8" accounting firms sued 1989 Jan 26H; deposits 1983 Jan 28H/Mar 2H; losses 1982 Apr 5H/Oct 12H; 1988 Mar 18H/May 11H/Jun 21H/Sep 22H; 1989 Jun 1H; net worth 1982 Jan 28H; sales 1988 Dec 31H; tax breaks 1989 Jan 10H; thrift rescue costs 1988 Jul 7H/Oct 5H; withdrawals 1981 Apr 26H; 1989 Jun 7H

Federal Housing Administration, U.S. (FHA) 1980 Nov 24H; 1981 Sep 14H; 1983 Jul 11H; 1985 Aug 18F; 1986 May 2H/Jun 5H/Sep 30H; 1989 Sep 27F

Federal Insecticide and Rodenticide Act (1986) 1986 Sep 19H

Federal Interagency Fire Center 1985 Jul 11I

Federal Labor Relations Authority 1981 Aug 25H/Oct 22H

federal leasing 1983 Feb 1B

Federal Railroad Administration, U.S. (FRA) 1988 Feb 11F; 1989 Mar 21F

Federal Rehabilitation Act of 1973 1985 Jan 9F

Federal Reserve Bank of New York 1980 Aug 15H; 1983 Sep 7H/Nov 15H; 1988 Mar 4H/Sep 7H

Federal Reserve System, U.S. (Fed) *see also specific board chairmen in the name index (e.g., Volcker, Paul A.)*

appointments and resignations: Angell, Wayne D. 1985 Oct 19H; Greenspan, Alan 1987 Jun 2H; Heller, H. Robert 1986 May 12H; Johnson, Manuel H. 1985 Oct 19H; Seger, Martha 1984 Jul 3F; Volcker, Paul A. 1983 Jun 18H; 1987 Jun 2H

banking issues: brokerage firm purchase approved 1983 Jan 7H; capital requirements 1983 Jun 13H; 1988 Jan 27H; Continental Illinois rescue 1984 May 17H; corporate debt underwriting 1989 Jan 18H; credit controls 1980 May 22H/Jul 3H; foreign bank purchases approved 1981 Aug 25H; international facilities 1980 Nov 19H; merger scrutiny 1982 Jan 27H; "nonbank banks" 1983 Dec 14H; 1986 Jan 22; reserve requirements 1982 Jun 28H; securities underwriting 1988 Jun 13H

business issues: corporate borrowing 1981 Apr 15H; credit controls 1980 May 22H/Jul 3H; junk bond financing in corporate takeovers 1985 Dec 6H

debt issues: commercial banks corporate debt underwriting 1989 Jan 18H; debt for equity swaps 1988 Feb 18H

monetary and fiscal policy: currency intervention 1983 Jul 29G; 1987 May 29H; 1988 Nov 17A; 1989 Feb 27E/May 22A; money supply 1980 Feb 7H; 1982 Oct 5H; 1983 Jun 1H/Jun 10H; 1984 Feb 6H/Nov 9H; 1985 Jul 16H

political issues: administration criticism 1981 Oct 6H; 1984 May 8H; 1988 Feb 19H

statistical data *see specific economic indicator (e.g., consumer credit)*

Federal Savings and Loan Insurance Corp., U.S. (FSLIC)

budget and spending programs: funding shortage 1986 Sep 23H; 1987 Feb 25H/Mar 27H/Aug 4H

S&L crisis: lawsuits 1986 Sep 7H; losses 1988 May 11H; mergers 1982 Jan 18H; 1987 Dec 31H; 1988 May 18H; rescues 1987 Nov 19H; seizures 1982 Apr 13H/Jun 3H

Federal Trade Commission, U.S. (FTC)

budget and spending programs: emergency funds legislation 1980 May 2H; fund shortage shuts 1980 May 1H

business issues: cereal makers 1982 Jan 15H; corporate raiders 1987 Jul 3H

consumer protection: car defects 1983 Nov 17H; children's television programs 1983 Oct 11F; deceptive advertising 1981 Oct 26H; 1982 Mar 18H; 1983 Oct 21F; pain relievers 1983 Jul 13H; telephone rates 1984 May 10H; tobacco 1983 Jul 21I; 1986 Jun 16H/Aug 6H/Oct 24H; used-car rule 1981 Apr 14H; 1982 May 26H/Oct 22H

merger issues: Gulf/Cities Service 1982 Aug 6H; Gulf/Standard Oil 1984 Apr 26H; LTV/Grumman Corp. 1981 Oct 28H; Superior Oil/Mobil 1984 May 15H; Texaco/Getty Oil 1984 Feb 13H

mergers and acquisitions: GM/Toyota venture 1983 Dec 22H

Federated Department Stores Inc. 1988 Jan 25H

F-18 (aircraft) 1982 Nov 9G; 1983 Jan 6G; 1984 Aug 2G

Fences (August Wilson) (play) 1985 May 3J; 1987 Jun 7J

fencing (sport) 1981 Jan 13J

Ferdinand (racehorse) 1986 May 3J/May 17J; 1987 Nov 21J; 1988 Jan 27J

Fermat's last theorem (mathematics) 1988 Jun 3I

Fermi National Accelerator Laboratory (Fermilab) (Chicago) 1985 Oct 13I

Fernald (Ohio) 1989 Jun 30H

Ferris Bueller's Day Off (film) 1986 Jun 18J

fertility rate 1988 May 12D; 1989 Jun 22F

Festival of the Planet's Tribes 1989 Jul 14B

fetal tissue 1987 Jun 30I; 1988 Jun 7I/Apr 15I/Sep 16I; 1989 May 1I/Nov 1I

F-5 (aircraft) 1987 Jun 4G

F-5E (aircraft) 1986 Oct 1G

F-15 (aircraft) 1980 Feb 25G/Jul 8C; 1981 Mar 6C/Aug 11G/Aug 17G; 1983 Aug 23G; 1984 Jan 21G/Feb 24G; 1985 Sep 15C

F-4 (aircraft) 1980 Sep 21C; 1981 Aug 21C; 1986 Aug 15A

F-14 (aircraft) 1981 Aug 19A; 1983 Nov 10C/Dec 14C; 1985 Jul 14G; 1988 Aug 19G; 1989 Jan 4C

FHA *see* Federal Housing Administration

FHLBB *see* Federal Home Loan Bank Board

Fiat S.p.A. 1986 Feb 12A; 1987 Jul 22B; 1988 Jan 18B

Fidelcor Inc. 1987 Aug 2H

Fidelity Savings & Loan Association (San Francisco) 1982 Apr 13H/Jun 3H/Aug 16H

field hockey 1981 Jan 13J; 1986 Oct 19J

Field Medal (mathematics) 1986 Aug 3I

Field of Dreams (film) 1989 Apr 21J/May 31J

Fiesta Bowl (football) 1987 Jan 2J; 1989 Jan 3J

Fifth Amendment 1980 Jun 27F; 1981 May 18F; 1987 Jun 9H/Jun 26H

Fifth Floor, The (film) 1980 Mar 26J

fifth force (physics) 1989 Nov 10I

Fifth Horseman, The (Larry Collins/Dominique Lapierre) (book) 1980 Oct 12J/Dec 7J/Dec 7J; 1987 Oct 12J/Dec 7J

5150 (Van Halen) (recording) 1986 Apr 16J/May 21J/Jun 18J

52nd Street (Billy Joel) (recording) 1980 Feb 27J

52 Pick-Up (film) 1986 Nov 12J

figure skating

compulsory events: figures dropped 1988 Jun 8J

Olympic Games: 1980 Feb 15J-16J/Feb 19J/Feb 21J/Feb 23J

U.S. Championships: 1985 Feb 1J-2J; 1986 Feb 8J; 1987 Feb 7J; 1988 Jan 9J; 1989 Feb 10J

World Championships: 1986 Mar 21J; 1987 Mar 12J/Mar 14J; 1988 Mar 25J/Mar 26J; 1989 Mar 16J/Mar 18J

Fiji

coup and coup attempts: mounted 1987 May 14E; settlement rejected 1987 May 24E; collapses 1987 May 30E

defense and disarmament issues: nuclear-free zone declared 1985 Aug 6E

foreign relations: Australia finds arms cache 1988 May 31E; Australian aid 1988 Feb 9E; Chilean leader visits 1980 Mar 22A; Commonwealth ties severed 1987 Oct 15E; papal visit 1986 Dec 1E

government and politics: elections 1982 Jul 10E; 1987 Apr 12E; president appointed 1987 Dec 5E; raids against dissidents 1988 Jun 6E; republic declared 1987 Oct 6E

filibusters

antiabortion legislation: 1982 Sep 8F/Sep 9F/Sep 15F

antibusing amendment: 1981 Dec 10F

campaign reform bill: 1987 Jun 18F

Meese confirmation: 1985 Feb 23F

Nicaraguan contra aid: 1987 Mar 25G

Senate TV coverage: 1984 Sep 21F

workplace hazards warning: 1988 Mar 29H

Film Institute, American see American Film Institute

Film Recovery Systems Inc. 1985 Jun 14F

films see motion pictures; specific film (e.g., Platoon)

Final Conflict (film) 1981 Apr 1J

Final Countdown, The (film) 1980 Aug 6J

Final Cut (Pink Floyd) (recording) 1983 Apr 13J

Financial Corp. of America 1983 Aug 4H; 1984 Aug 22H; 1988 Mar 18H

Financial General Bankshares (Washington, D.C.) 1981 Aug 25H

Financial Times-Stock Exchange 100 share index 1989 Dec 29B

Fine Arts, U.S. Commission on 1987 Oct 22G

Fine Things (Danielle Steel) (book) 1987 Mar 27J/Apr 24J/May 29J/Jun 26J

Fine Young Cannibals (singing group) 1989 May 27J/Jun 24J/Jul 29J

Finland see also individual leaders in the name index (e.g., Koivisto, Mauno)
budget and spending programs: 1988 Sep 13B
foreign relations: socialist governments meet 1983 Jan 23A; USSR 1987 Jan 7B
government and politics: conservative-led government sworn 1987 Apr 30B; Kekkonen resigns as president 1981 Oct 27B; municipal elections 1980 Oct 20B; parliamentary elections 1987 Mar 16B
medicine and health care: AIDS 1987 Oct 3I; cholesterol study 1987 Nov 12I
obituaries: Kekkonen, Urho Kaleva 1986 Aug 31B; Ritola, Willie 1982 Apr 24J
sports: auto racing 1982 Oct 25J; ice hockey 1980 Feb 24J; Olympic medal taken away 1984 Aug 12J; World Track and Field Championships 1983 Aug 7J
United Nations policy: peacekeeping forces 1985 Jun 7C/Jun 15C; Security Council seat 1988 Oct 26A
U.S. releations: 1983 Jun 24G; 1984 Feb 10H

firearms 1982 Mar 15F/Nov 17G; 1983 Nov 7G; 1986 Apr 10F/May 19F/Jun 19F; 1988 Nov 10F; 1989 May 15F

Firearms Owners Protection Act (1986) 1986 Apr 10F/May 19F

fire extinguishers 1989 May 2I

fires
Australia: brush fires 1983 Feb 19I
Bulgaria: chemical plant 1986 Nov 1B
Canada: Manitoba forest fires 1989 Jul 25D/Jul 25I; Quebec social club 1980 Jan 1D
China: forest fires 1987 May 29D
Cretaceous Era wildfires 1985 Oct 11I
France: forest and brush fires 1986 Aug 7I; Paris Chanel store 1981 Jan 4B
Great Britain: soccer stadium 1985 May 11B; Windscale atomic plant 1988 Jan 1B; York Minster 1984 Jul 9J

Guatemala: Spanish embassy 1980 Jan 31D
Indonesia: Borneo forest fire 1984 Apr 2I; passenger ship 1981 Jan 27E
Ireland: Dublin discotheque 1981 Feb 14B
Italy: Turin movie theater 1983 Feb 13J
Jamaica: Kingston home for women 1980 May 20D
Portugal: Lisbon Chiado district 1988 Aug 25B
Puerto Rico: Dupont Plaza Hotel 1987 Jan 13D/Jan 29D/Jun 22F; 1988 Feb 3F
South Africa: Kinross gold mine 1986 Sep 16C; oil supertanker 1983 Aug 6C
Switzerland: Zurich museum portrait 1985 Jun 13J
United States
Alaska: Dutch luxury liner 1980 Oct 4I; forest fires 1988 Sep 9I
California: Los Angeles Central Library 1986 Apr 29F; Ojai wildfire 1985 Jul 21I; Pryor accident 1980 Jul 25J; Vandenberg Air Force Base 1985 Aug 28I
Florida: Arcadia AIDS family home 1987 Aug 28F
Montana: forest and prairie fires 1984 Sep 1I/Sep 5I
Nevada: MGM Grand Hotel 1980 Nov 21J
New Jersey: Passaic industrial complex 1985 Sep 2F
New York City: Con Ed substation 1983 Aug 13J
Philadelphia: MOVE bombing 1985 May 13F; 1986 Mar 6F
Utah: coal mine 1987 May 11H; Morton Thiokol plant 1987 Dec 29H
Washington: Mount St. Helens eruption 1980 May 18I
West: forest fires 1985 Jul 11I; 1988 Sep 9I/Nov 20I
USSR: nuclear submarine 1986 Oct 4I/Oct 6I; 1989 Apr 7B; Soviet Academy of Sciences library (Leningrad) 1988 Feb 14B
West Germany: Berlin Reichstag fire ruling 1980 Dec 29B; 1981 Apr 22B; Pershing II missile fire 1985 Jan 11B

Firestarter (Stephen King) (book) 1980 Sep 14J/Oct 12J/Dec 7J/Dec 7J; 1981 Jan 11J/Feb 8J; 1987 Oct 12J/Dec 7J

Fire with Fire (film) 1986 May 14J

Firing Line (TV show) 1987 Aug 25F

First Amendment, U.S. (freedom of religion, speech and assembly)
freedom of assembly: public school posting of Ten Commandments 1980 Nov 17F
freedom of religion: abstinence counseling by church groups 1987 Nov 9F; creation science 1987 Jun 19F; job bias 1987 Jun 24F; public school posting of Ten Commancments 1980 Nov 17F
freedom of speech: abstinence counseling by church groups 1987 Nov 9F; broadcasting "fairness doctrine" 1985 Aug 7F; cable TV 1985 Jul 19F; 1986 Jun 2F; 1987 Nov 1F; flag burning 1989 Jun 21F/Jun 27F; PAC spending limits 1985 Mar 18F; pornography 1982 Jul 2F; 1986 Feb 24F; public employee slur of president 1987 Jun 24F; public school book bannings 1982 May 25F; public school post-

ing of Ten Commandments 1980 Nov 17F; public school textbooks 1986 Oct 24F; teacher advocacy of homosexuality 1985 Mar 26F

First Among Equals (Jeffrey Archer) (book) 1984 Aug 24J/Sep 14J/Oct 19J

First Blood (film) 1982 Nov 10J/Dec 8J

First Boston Corp. 1986 May 5H/Oct 14H

First Charter Financial Corp. 1982 Oct 26H; 1983 Aug 4H

First Chicago Corp. 1984 Oct 3H

First City Bancorp 1987 Sep 9H; 1988 Apr 20H

First Federal of America 1982 Oct 26H

First Fidelity Bancorp 1987 Aug 2H

First Interstate Bancorp (Los Angeles) 1986 Jul 14H/Oct 6H

First Monday in October (film) 1981 Sep 4J

First National Bank and Trust Co. (Oklahoma City) 1986 Jul 14H

First National Bank of Boston 1985 Feb 7H

First National Bank of Chicago 1980 May 30H; 1981 Aug 31H; 1983 Feb 25H; 1984 Nov 15H

First Pennsylvania Bank 1980 Apr 28H

fish and fishing industry see also whales and whaling
business issues: Canada salmon/herring processing 1989 Nov 6D
environmental issues: acid rain 1980 Feb 2I/Aug 5D; 1981 Jan 5H; 1986 Mar 14G; Canada seal hunt 1983 Mar 27I; 1984 Mar 8D; 1987 Mar 23D/Dec 30D; endangered species 1984 Aug 6H; oil spills 1988 Jan 2H; sewage sludge dumping 1985 Apr 1H; shrimp fishermen nets 1989 Sep 5H; UN agreement on drift nets 1989 Dec 13I; water quality 1985 Aug 4H
foreign developments: Canada see Canada; China 1985 May 10E; European Community 1983 Jan 25B; 1984 Dec 4B; 1985 Dec 23B; Falkland Islands 1986 Oct 29B/Nov 17D/Nov 18B; 1987 Feb 1D; 1989 Jul 12D; France 1980 Aug 19B/Aug 27B/Sep 5B; Japan 1982 Apr 26G; 1987 Dec 29H; 1988 Mar 14H; 1989 Jun 23H; Poland 1984 Jan 19G; Rhine River 1987 Jan 10B; South Pacific 1986 Oct 22E; USSR 1984 May 1A/Jul 25G
health and safety issues: Canada mollusk contamination 1987 Dec 11I; 1988 Jan 6I; Canada shellfish contamination 1989 Nov 23D; Canada tuna scandal 1985 Sep 23D
Native Americans: 1981 Aug 20F; 1989 May 7F
prices issues: 1984 Apr 13H
territorial waters disputes: Canada/French rights dispute 1987 Mar 17D; 1988 Apr 20D/Jun 8D/Sep 12D; Canada/USSR agreement 1984 May 1A; Falkland Islands 1986 Oct 29B/Nov 17D/Nov 18B; 1987 Feb 1D; 1989 Jul 12D

Fish and Wildlife Service, U.S. (Interior Department) 1984 Aug 6H; 1985 Jan 12I; 1989 Apr 26H/Sep 12H

Fish Called Wanda, A (film) 1988 Jul 15J/Aug 31J/Sep 21J; 1989 Mar 19J/Mar 29J

5,000-meter race (running) 1985 Jul 27J

flag burning 1989 Jun 21F/Jun 27F/Jun 29F/Sep 12F/Oct 12F/Oct 19F

Flamingo Kid, The (film) 1985 Jan 16J

Flanders (Belgium) 1980 Aug 5B; 1989 Jan 9B

Flashdance (film/soundtrack) 1983 May 4J/May 11J/Jun 15J/Jun 15J/Jul 13J/Jul 13J/Aug 17J/Sep 14J

Fleet Financial Corp. 1987 Mar 18H

Fleetwood Mac (singing group) 1982 Jul 11J/Aug 18J/Sep 22J/Oct 13J

Flemish (language) 1981 Dec 17B; 1986 Oct 28B; 1987 Oct 21B

Flesh and Blood (C.K. Williams) (book) 1988 Jan 11J

Fletch (film) 1985 Jun 12J

Fletch Lives (film) 1989 Mar 29J

Flick affair 1984 Oct 25B

Flick Group 1986 Jan 8B

flight attendants 1982 Nov 30H; 1985 Aug 31H; 1986 Oct 7H; 1989 Mar 4H/Mar 13H/Nov 23H

Flight into Egypt, The (John Harbison) (article) 1987 Apr 16J

Flight of the Intruder (Stephen Coonts) (book) 1986 Dec 26J; 1987 Jan 23J

Floating Dragon (Peter Straub) (book) 1983 Mar 13J

flood insurance 1986 Sep 30H; 1987 Mar 23H

floods
Bangladesh: 1987 Sep 4D; 1988 Sep 6I/Oct 10A; 1989 Aug 5I
Bolivia: 1983 Aug 11G
Brazil: 1988 Feb 7I
Canada: 1986 Feb 20I
China: 1981 Aug 20E; 1985 Aug 8I
Ecuador: 1983 May 8I/Aug 11G; 1987 Mar 11D
El Salvador: 1982 Sep 20I
India: 1983 Jun 28I
Italy: 1985 Jul 19I
Peru: 1983 Aug 11G
South Korea: 1984 Oct 1E
Spain: 1983 Aug 26I
Sri Lanka: 1989 Jun 6E
Sudan: 1988 Aug 5I
United States: Alabama 1983 Apr 12I; California 1983 Jan 30I; flood control projects 1985 Nov 13H; Gulf coast 1983 May 23I; Kentucky 1984 May 8I; Louisiana 1983 Apr 12I; Mid-Atlantic region 1983 May 23I; Mississippi 1983 Apr 12I; Oklahoma 1984 May 27I; Tennessee 1983 Apr 12I; 1984 May 8I; Washington State 1980 May 18I; West 1986 Feb 20I; West Virginia 1984 May 8I; Wyoming 1985 Aug 1I

flooring felt 1986 Jan 23H

Florida
accidents and disasters: Hurricane Juan 1985 Oct 26I; Hurricane Kate 1985 Nov 22I
agriculture: citrus crop cold weather damage 1984 Jan 1I; 1981 Jan 18I; 1983 Dec 29I; citrus crop disease 1984 Sep 20H; Mediterranean fruit flies 1981 Aug 4H
arts and culture: human skulls found 1984 Dec 12I
corruption and ethics: Taylor admits lobbying payments 1989 Jul 24F
crime and law enforcement: capital punishment condemned by

churches 1984 Dec 8F; churches condemn capital punishment 1984 Dec 8F; fugitive roundup 1985 Jun 16F; gun laws 1989 Jun 20F; lawyer-client confidentiality 1988 Oct 13F; riots 1980 May 17F/Dec 6F
economy and business: banking 1985 May 21H; insurance laws 1986 Jun 26F
education: college desegregation 1982 Feb 4F; 1983 Mar 24F/Jul 7F; 1988 Feb 10F; high school course retained 1983 May 31F; high school literacy test 1983 May 4F; racial segregation 1983 Mar 24F/Jul 7F; 1988 Feb 10F
environmental issues: hazardous waste sites 1981 Oct 23H; oil and gas exploration 1987 Apr 27H/Aug 27H; parks 1983 Jan 14H; 1989 Dec 12H
executions: Andrade, Richard 1986 Dec 18F; Bundy, Theodore (Ted) 1989 Jan 24F; Darden, Willie Jasper 1988 Mar 15F; Raulerson, James David 1985 Jan 30F
family issues: homosexuals 1982 Feb 4F
foreign issues: Honduran officer sentenced in assassination plot 1986 Jul 23D
immigration and refugees: Cubans 1980 May 21D/May 24F/Oct 24F/Nov 3F; 1987 May 28D; Haitians 1980 Apr 13D/May 7F/Oct 24F/Nov 3F; 1981 Oct 26D; Mariel boatlift (1980) 1980 May 1D/Sep 26D; 1983 May 24D; 1984 Jul 12D/Dec 3F/Dec 14D; 1986 Jul 9D; 1987 Nov 20G; 1988 Dec 2F
lottery: 1988 Sep 7J
medicine and health care: abortion 1989 Oct 10F
obituaries: Pepper, Claude Denson 1989 May 30J
politics and government: Cuban-American elected to Congress 1989 Aug 29F; federal judge impeachment 1988 Aug 3F; 1989 Oct 20F; presidential campaigns 1980 Mar 11F; 1984 Mar 13F; 1988 Jun 18F; presidential primary date moved 1986 Apr 6F; state representative switches to GOP 1989 Feb 21F
religious issues: churches condemn capital punishment 1984 Dec 8F

Florida Southern University (Lakeland) 1982 Mar 20J

Florida State University (Tallahassee) 1980 Jan 1J; 1989 Jan 2J

Flotilla for Peace 1985 Aug 8D

flour 1987 Jul 20B

fluoridation 1985 Feb 14F

fluorocarbon 22 1985 Sep 23H

Fly, The (film) 1986 Aug 20J/Sep 17J

Fly II, The (film) 1989 Feb 22J

Flying Change, The (Henry Taylor) (book) 1986 Apr 17J

Flying Cloud (ship) 1989 Feb 12J

FMC Corp. 1980 Nov 10H; 1983 Jun 8H; 1985 Aug 5H

FmHA see Farmers Home Administration, U.S.

FMLN see Farabundo Marti National Liberation Front

Fog, The (film) 1980 Mar 26J

Folger Shakespeare Library (Washington, D.C.) 1985 Mar 1J; 1987 May 9J; 1989 May 13J

Follies (musical) 1988 Jan 24J

Food, Drug, and Cosmetic Act (1976) 1985 Feb 25H

Food and Agriculture Organization, U.N. (FAO) 1985 Dec 16C; 1986 Oct 23C; 1989 Dec 27C

Food and Drug Administration, U.S. (FDA)
  AIDS issues: 1987 Jan 16I; 1988 Jul 23F/Dec 13I; 1989 Feb 6I/Sep 19I/Oct 21F/Oct 26F
  corruption and ethics: Cordis 1988 Aug 31F; DES use in feed lots 1980 Apr 24I; Eli Lilly 1982 Aug 3I; 1985 Aug 21H
  drug trials and approvals: acyclovir 1982 Mar 30I; 1985 Jan 29I; alpha interferon 1988 Nov 21I; approval policy changed 1988 Oct 19F; AZT 1987 Jan 16I; 1989 Oct 26F; baldness remedy 1987 Mar 16H; diazepam 1985 Sep 4F; dideoxyinosine 1989 Oct 21F; generic drugs testing 1983 Mar 22F; GLQ223 1989 Apr 27I/Sep 19I; hepatitis B vaccine 1981 Nov 16I; 1986 Jul 23I; ibuprofen 1984 May 18H; interleukin-2 1987 May 7I; Laetrile 1980 Jan 3I; lovastatin 1987 Sep 1I; minoxidil 1988 Aug 17H; pentamidine 1989 Feb 6I/Jun 15I; record number of drugs approved 1986 Jan 15F; THA 1987 Jun 21I; timolol 1981 Nov 25I; tissue plasminogen activator 1986 Mar 10I; 1987 Nov 13I
  health and safety issues: Accutane 1988 May 26I; Alar 1989 Mar 16I; benoxaprofen 1982 Jul 22I; Chilean grapes 1989 Aug 16H; generic drugs 1989 Aug 16H; Retin-A 1988 Jul 5I; saccharin 1983 Apr 13I; salmon 1982 Apr 8I; starch-blocker diet pills 1982 Oct 5I; sulfite preservatives 1985 Aug 9H; 1986 Jul 8H; vitamin E 1984 May 4I
  labeling: aspirin 1986 Mar 7F; health claims 1989 Oct 30H
  medical devices: AIDS test 1988 Dec 13I; cervical cap 1988 May 23I; experimental artificial heart 1985 Mar 13I; HTLV-1 virus test 1988 Nov 29I; malfunction notification 1989 Aug 3H; X-ray scanners 1983 Apr 4I

Food for Peace 1983 Aug 6G

food poisoning 1985 May 7I

food prices
  Bolivia: 1984 Dec 4D; 1985 Feb 9D
  China: 1985 May 10E; 1988 May 15E
  Czechoslovakia: 1982 Jan 30B
  Dominican Republic: 1985 Feb 4D
  Egypt: 1984 Oct 1C
  Guatemala: 1985 Aug 29D
  Mexican: 1982 Aug 1D
  Morocco: 1981 Jun 20C
  Poland: 1980 Jul 11B; 1981 Jul 29B/Aug 4B; 1983 Nov 12B; 1988 Feb 1B; 1989 Aug 1B/Aug 11B
  Romania: 1982 Feb 14B
  United States: 1984 Feb 10H/Feb 24H
  Yugoslavia: 1986 Aug 10B
  Zambia: 1986 Dec 11C

Food Research and Action Center 1983 Jan 25F

Food Security Act of 1985 1985 Dec 23H

food shortages *see also* famines
  Chad: 1983 Mar 6C
  China: 1981 Apr 24I

East Germany: 1982 Nov 21B
Poland: 1981 Jul 29B/Aug 4B/Aug 12B/Oct 28B
Romania: 1987 Dec 14B
USSR: 1980 Oct 21B
Vietnam: 1988 May 12E/Jun 25A

food stamp program 1983 Jul 30F; 1985 Oct 8H; 1986 Jan 14F/Oct 2F

foot and mouth disease 1981 Jun 18I

Footloose (film) 1984 Mar 7J

Footloose (soundtrack) 1984 Mar 24J/Apr 28J/May 20J/May 28J/Jun 16J

footwear 1980 Nov 6H; 1984 Jan 23H; 1985 Aug 28H

Forbes (magazine) 1984 Sep 18H; 1985 Oct 15J; 1986 Oct 14H; 1987 May 28J/Sep 20H/Oct 12H; 1988 Oct 10H; 1989 Jul 9H

Ford Aerospace & Communications Corp. 1984 Sep 20G

Ford Foundation 1983 Jul 25J; 1988 Dec 19G; 1989 May 11F

Ford Motor Co.
  business issues: dividend discontinued 1982 Jan 14H; plant closings 1980 Jan 3H
  environmental issues: fuel efficiency 1986 Oct 2H
  foreign operations: Argentina sit-in 1985 Jul 14D; Brazil strike settled 1985 Jun 3D; Western Europe market share 1987 Jul 22B; 1988 Jan 18B
  labor issues: Chrysler parity 1985 Oct 23H; contracts 1982 Feb 13H/Feb 28H; 1984 Oct 14H; 1987 Sep 17H; discrimination case settled 1980 Nov 25H; layoffs 1980 Jan 3H/Jun 21H; plant closings 1980 Jan 3H; work force cuts 1985 Aug 22H
  profits and losses: 1980 Apr 28H/Oct 28H; 1981 Feb 19H; 1982 Feb 18H; 1984 Feb 13H/Apr 26H/Jul 26H; 1985 Feb 13H/Apr 26H/Jul 26H; 1987 Apr 29H/Jul 23H; 1988 Feb 18H/Apr 28H/Jul 27H; 1989 Feb 16H
  safety amd repair issues: recalls 1982 Aug 10H; 1987 Sep 9H

Fore! (Huey Lewis & the News) (recording) 1986 Oct 22J/Nov 22J/Dec 17J

Foreign Affairs (Alison Lurie) (book) 1985 Apr 24J

Foreign Agents Registration Act (1982) 1982 Apr 8G

Foreign Corrupt Practices Act (1977) 1981 May 20H

Foreigner (singing group) 1981 Aug 5J/Sep 9J/Sep 30J/Nov 11J/Dec 9J; 1982 Jan 20J/Feb 24J; 1985 Feb 23J

foreign investment (in U.S.) 1980 Apr 8H; 1982 Jul 9H; 1989 May 30H

Foreign Relations, Council on *see* Council on Foreign Relations

foreign trade *see also organizations* (e.g., European Community); *specific countries* (e.g., Japan)
  1980 statistics: 1980 Feb 28H/Jul 29H/Aug 27H/Sep 26H/Nov 28H/Dec 30H
  1981 statistics: 1981 Feb 27H/Mar 27H/May 28H/Jun 26H/Nov 30G
  1982 statistics: 1982 Feb 26H/Mar 26H/Apr 27H/May 26H/Sep 27H/Nov 26H/Dec 29H
  1983 statistics: 1983 Jan 26H/Mar 29H/Apr 29H/Jun 28H/Aug 29H/Nov 29H
  1984 statistics: 1984 Jan 27H/Feb 29H/Mar 29H/Apr 27H/May

30H/Jun 28H/Jul 27H/Aug 29H/Sep 28H/Oct 31H/Nov 30H/Dec 30H
  1985 statistics: 1985 Jan 30H/Feb 7G/Feb 28H/Apr 30H/May 31H/Jun 28H/Jul 30H/Aug 30H/Sep 27H/Oct 31H/Nov 27H/Dec 31H
  1986 statistics: 1986 Jan 30H/Feb 28H/Mar 27H/Apr 30H/May 30H/Jun 27H/Jul 30H/Aug 29H/Sep 30H/Oct 30H/Nov 26H/Dec 31H
  1987 statistics: 1987 Jan 30H/Feb 27H/Apr 14H/May 14H/Jun 12H/Jul 15H/Aug 16H/Sep 11H/Oct 14H/Nov 12H/Dec 10H
  1988 statistics: 1988 Jan 15H/Feb 12H/Mar 17H/Apr 14H/May 17H/Jun 14H/Jul 15H/Aug 16H/Sep 14H/Oct 13H/Nov 16H/Dec 14H
  1989 statistics: 1989 Feb 17H/Mar 15H/Apr 14H/May 17H/Jun 15H/Jul 18H/Aug 17H/Sep 19H/Oct 19H/Nov 16H/Dec 15H

Forestry Association, American *see* American Forestry Association

Forest Service, U.S. (Agriculture Department) 1984 Sep 5I/Dec 12H; 1987 Aug 14H

Forever Your Girl (Paula Abdul) (recording) 1989 Mar 25J/Aug 26J/Sep 30J/Oct 28J/Dec 25J/Dec 30J

forgeries 1983 May 6J

For Keeps (film) 1988 Jan 20J

formaldehyde 1983 Mar 18H/Aug 25H; 1985 Dec 3H; 1987 Nov 20H

Formula One title (auto racing) 1985 Oct 6J; 1986 Oct 26J; 1987 Nov 1J; 1988 Oct 31J; 1989 Oct 22J

Forsmark nuclear plant (Sweden) 1986 Apr 28B

Fort Apache the Bronx (film) 1981 Apr 1J/Apr 4J

Fort Chaffee (Arkansas) 1980 Jun 1F/Jun 1F/Jun 7F

For the Record: From Wall Street to Washington (Donald Regan) (book) 1988 May 9F

For Those about to Rock (We Salute You) (AC/DC) (recording) 1981 Dec 9J; 1982 Jan 20J

Fort Indiantown Gap (Pennsylvania) 1980 Aug 5F

Fort Lauderdale Strikers (soccer team) 1980 Sep 21J

Fortune (magazine) 1980 May 5H; 1982 May 3H; 1983 Apr 13H; 1984 Apr 30H; 1987 Sep 20H; 1989 Sep 11J

Fort Worth Star Telegram (newspaper) 1985 Apr 24J

48 Hours (film) 1983 Feb 2J

42nd Street (musical) 1981 Jun 7J

For Your Eyes Only (film) 1981 Jul 1J

fossils
  Aegyptopithecus (primate): 1980 Feb 7I
  Archaeopteryx (dinosaur/bird): 1986 May 2I
  dinosaurs: 1980 Mar 24I; 1985 May 16I; 1986 May 2I
  human: 1982 Jun 10E; 1984 Oct 18I/Dec 12I; 1988 Feb 18I
  India hoax claimed: 1989 Apr 20I
  Proconsul africanus (primate): 1984 Aug 22I
  unknown early mammal: 1981 Sep 17I
  Wyoming find: 1984 Sep 24I

Foucault's Pendulum (Umberto Eco) (book) 1989 Dec 1J/Dec 22J

Foundation and Earth (Isaac Asimov) (book) 1986 Oct 31J

Foundation's Edge (Isaac Asimov) (book) 1982 Dec 12J; 1983 Jan 16J

4 (Foreigner) (recording) 1981 Aug 5J/Sep 9J/Sep 30J/Nov 11J/Dec 9J; 1982 Jan 20J/Feb 24J

400-meter freestyle relay (swimming) 1985 Aug 17J

400-meter medley relay (swimming) 1985 Aug 18J

IV (Toto) (recording) 1983 Mar 9J

Fourteenth Amendment, U.S. (life, liberty and property rights) 1982 Jun 18F; 1986 Apr 30F/May 19F; 1987 Jun 22F/Jun 26H

Fourth Amendment, U.S. (search and seizure rules) 1988 Feb 11F

Fourth Deadly Sin, The (Lawrence Sanders) (book) 1985 Aug 16J/Sep 27J

Fourth Protocol, The (Frederick Forsyth) (book/film) 1984 Sep 14J/Oct 19J/Nov 16J/Dec 14J; 1985 Jan 18J; 1987 Sep 9J

Fox Broadcasting Co. 1986 May 6J; 1987 May 15J

Foxfire (TV show) 1988 Aug 28J

FPL *see* Salvadoran Popular Liberation Forces

FP-25 *see* Popular Forces of April 25 (Portugal)

FRA *see* Federal Railroad Administration

France *see also individual leaders in the name index* (e.g., Mitterrand, Francois)
  abortion and birth control: artificial insemination 1984 Aug 1I; RU 486 1986 Dec 18I; 1987 Oct 2I; 1988 Oct 26I/Oct 28I
  accidents and disasters: avalanches 1982 Mar 14I; freighter sinks 1984 Aug 25I; French DC-10 jetliner explodes over Niger 1989 Sep 19C; MiG-23 fighter jet 1989 Jul 4B
  agriculture: farmers protest 1980 Jun 16B; grain sales 1981 Apr 25B
  archaeology: Israeli cave human fossils 1988 Feb 18I
  arts and culture: *Au Revoir les Enfants* 1987 Sep 9J; 1988 Feb 12J; Chagall estate 1988 Feb 1J; cultural conference 1983 Feb 12J; Duras receives Ritz Paris Hemingway Award 1986 Apr 7J; Golden Palm award 1984 May 23J; 1985 May 20J; 1986 May 19J; 1987 May 19J; 1988 May 23J; 1989 May 23J/May 23J; Goncourt Prize 1984 Nov 12J; 1985 Nov 18J; 1987 Nov 16J; *Jean de Florette* 1987 Jun 26J; 1988 Mar 20J; *The Last Metro* 1981 Feb 11J; Malle receives British Academy Award 1989 Mar 19J; national library 1987 Nov 22B; Picasso paintings returned 1987 Jan 20J; Simon awarded Nobel 1985 Oct 17J; Taylor named to arts post 1985 Sep 12J; Yourcenar elected to French Academy 1980 Mar 16J
  awards and honors: Duras receives Hemingway Award 1986 Apr 7J; Golden Palm 1984 May 23J; 1985 May 20J; 1986 May 19J; 1987 May 19J; 1988 May 23J; 1989 May 23J/May 23J; Goncourt Prize 1984 Nov 12J; 1985 Nov 18J; 1987 Nov 16J; Malle receives Brit-

ish Academy Award 1989 Mar 19J; Simon awarded Nobel Prize 1985 Oct 17J; Yourcenar elected to French Academy 1980 Mar 16J
  business and industry: banking 1980 Jan 23A; electronics industry 1982 Jul 28B; Elf Aquitaine transactions 1981 Jun 26H; nationalizations 1981 Jul 8B/Sep 9B/Oct 26B; 1982 Feb 11B; privatization 1986 Jul 23B/Sep 10B; 1987 Sep 24B; steel industry 1981 Dec 22H; 1983 Jun 2A; 1985 Mar 27B; telephone system 1985 Oct 26B; Thompson-Brandt 1982 Nov 19B
  celebrations: D-Day anniversary 1984 Jun 6A; French Revolution anniversary 1989 Jul 14B; military parades 1986 Jul 14B
  corruption and ethics issues: Le Carrefour du Development scandal 1986 Aug 18B
  Corsica *see* Corsica
  crime and law enforcement: death penalty abolished 1981 Sep 30B; hate groups 1981 Jul 3B; kidnapping of industrialist 1980 Jul 9B; legislation approved 1980 Jun 21B; Nantes courtroom hostages 1985 Dec 20B
  defense and disarmament issues: arms sales 1982 Jan 7D; 1984 Aug 27G; 1987 Mar 5B; military exercises with West Germany 1987 Sep 24B; nuclear export limitation pact 1987 Apr 16A; nuclear reactors sales 1980 Feb 27I/Oct 17I; nuclear research 1982 Dec 27I; nuclear tests 1980 Jan 17I; 1981 May 29I; nuclear weapons program 1989 May 28B
  demonstrations and protests: 1980 Mar 19B; 1981 Oct 15B; 1983 May 5B/May 24B; 1986 Dec 4B
  economy: austerity measures 1983 Mar 25B; budget and spending programs 1981 Jun 10B; 1983 Sep 14B/Sep 15B; 1987 Sep 16B; comparisons 1989 Jan 3B; consumer prices 1988 Jan 14B; gross domestic product 1987 Jun 7B; 1988 Feb 15B; 1989 Feb 22B; growth 1988 Jun 28B; inflation-fighting measures 1981 Oct 5B; 1982 Jun 13B; inflation rate 1989 Jan 16B; interest rate 1981 Sep 20B; 1986 Mar 7A/Apr 19A; price controls 1986 Nov 26B; tax rates 1987 Sep 11B; uranium deposits 1980 May 29H
  education: university reforms 1980 Mar 19B; 1983 May 5B/May 24B; 1984 Apr 18B/Aug 29B; 1986 Dec 4B
  energy issues: electricity cuts 1980 Jun 12B; fast-breeder reactors 1980 Feb 26B; nuclear energy increased role 1980 Apr 2B; nuclear fuel sales 1982 Aug 30A/Nov 29I; oil price hikes 1980 Jan 2B; policy proposals 1980 Apr 2B; uranium enrichment process 1980 Sep 10I
  environmental issues: *Rainbow Warrior* incident 1985 Jul 10E/Jul 23E/Aug 26B/Sep 20B/Sep 25B/Nov 4E/Dec 23B; 1986 Jul 7A; 1987 Oct 2B; South Pacific pollution treaty 1986 Nov 25E; toxic waste 1983 May 19B/Jun 4B
  espionage and intelligence issues: 1980 Feb 9B; 1987 Mar 20B
  foreign relations
    Africa: 1983 Oct 3A; 1984 Feb 5C/Dec 11C; Central African Republic 1983 Aug 18A; Chad

1980 May 16C; 1983 Aug 18A/Aug 18C; 1984 Jan 25C/Apr 7C/Sep 17A/Sep 25C/Nov 10C; 1987 Jan 9C/Aug 10B/Sep 7C; Comoros 1989 Dec 15C; Libya 1984 Sep 17A/Sep 25C/Nov 10C; 1987 Sep 7C; 1989 Jan 11A; South Africa 1981 Apr 30A; 1985 Jul 24B; 1987 Feb 20A; Tunisia 1987 Nov 7C

Asia and Pacific Rim: China 1980 Oct 17I; 1982 Oct 17A/Dec 27I; 1984 Jun 16E; 1986 Jun 8B; India 1982 Aug 30A/Nov 29I; Malaysia 1982 Aug 25E; New Hebrides 1980 Jun 11E/Jul 29E; South Pacific pollution treaty 1986 Nov 25E; Vietnam 1986 Oct 11B

Canada: 1982 Nov 8A; 1987 Mar 17D; 1988 Apr 20D/Jun 8D/Sep 12D

Europe: Czechoslovakia 1981 Feb 16B; Great Britain 1980 Feb 18B; Italy 1980 Aug 6B; 1982 Mar 5B; Poland 1981 Dec 23B; Spain 1984 Jun 15B/Sep 26B; West Germany 1984 Aug 1B; 1987 Sep 24B

francophone summits: 1986 Feb 19B; 1987 Sep 4A

Latin America: Argentina 1982 Apr 7D; Brazil 1981 Jan 31A; Costa Rica 1986 Sep 26D; Cuba 1980 Apr 1D; El Salvador 1981 Aug 28A/Sep 2D; Grenada 1983 Oct 25B; Haiti 1986 Feb 7D/Feb 10D; 1987 Jun 23D/Dec 31B; Mexico 1980 May 28D; Nicaragua 1982 Jan 7D; 1984 Apr 12G

Middle East: Iran 1980 Jan 23A; 1981 Jul 29C; 1983 Nov 10C; 1986 Jun 30A; 1987 Jul 17B/Aug 14A; 1988 Jan 13B/Jun 16A; Iraq 1980 Feb 27I; 1981 Jun 17C; 1982 Jan 14A; 1983 Aug 17C/Oct 11C; 1984 Mar 1A/Aug 27G; Israel 1981 Dec 8A; Kuwait 1983 Dec 27C; PLO 1981 Aug 30C; Saudi Arabia 1980 Oct 14A; Sinai peacekeeping force 1982 Jan 13A/Jan 31C

Persian Gulf: 1980 Oct 28B; 1987 Aug 12C/Sep 2A

government and politics: Chirac becomes premier 1986 Mar 20B; communist party 1980 Apr 2B; 1981 Apr 13B/Dec 23B; 1982 Feb 7B/Oct 17A; departmental elections 1982 Mar 14B/Mar 21B; electoral changes 1985 Apr 3B; local elections 1985 Mar 10B/Mar 17B; Mauroy names cabinet 1981 Jun 23B; Mitterrand elected president 1981 May 10B; municipal elections 1983 Mar 13B/Sep 11B; national elections 1980 Nov 30B; 1981 Jun 21B; 1986 Mar 15B/Sep 28B; 1988 Jun 5B/Jun 12B; Rocard reappointed premier 1988 Jun 23B; socialist governments meet 1983 Jan 23A; Socialist Party conference 1985 Oct 13B

Guadeloupe see Guadeloupe

Indochina War: 1986 Oct 11B

international organizations: European Community 1981 Oct 13B; 1984 Jul 19B; 1988 Jun 13B/Sep 11B; European Court of Justice 1982 Mar 5B; European Parliament 1984 Jul 24B; IMF 1983 Jan 18A

labor issues: air traffic controllers 1988 Jul 17B; electric utility workers strikes 1980 Jun 12B; fishermen strike 1980 Aug 19B/Aug 27B/Sep 5B; press strikes 1986 Jul 19B/Dec 18B; purchasing power 1980 Jun 14B; railway strikes 1986 Dec 18B; strikes against government 1980 May 13B; 1987 Jan 11B; unemployment 1984 Apr 11B; 1986 Aug 20B/Oct 17B; unemployment benefits 1982 Nov 22B; union rift 1980 Sep 4B; workweek 1981 Jul 17B; 1982 Jan 13B

language issues: 1986 Sep 10B

Lebanon military developments: air strikes 1983 Nov 17C; ambassador killed 1981 Sep 4C; barracks bombing 1983 Oct 23C/Oct 24C/Oct 26C; cultural center bombing 1984 Jan 1C; embassy bombing 1982 May 24C; hostages 1984 Apr 15C; 1985 Mar 22C/Mar 25C/Mar 31C/Apr 1C; 1986 Mar 5C/Mar 8C/Jun 30A/Dec 24C; 1987 Nov 29A; 1988 May 4C/Dec 29C; military attache killed 1986 Sep 18C; peacekeeping force 1982 Jul 10B; 1983 Feb 4C/Aug 30C/Aug 31B/Sep 7C/Sep 22C/Oct 27A/Dec 24C; 1984 Jan 2B/Mar 25C/Mar 31C; UN peace plan blocked 1981 Apr 16A; UN resolution sponsored 1982 Jun 26A; 1984 Feb 15A/Feb 29A

medicine and health care: AIDS 1984 Apr 21I; 1986 Nov 27B; Pasteur Institute; alcoholism 1980 Dec 10B; suicide rate 1989 Sep 15B

monetary issues: banking 1980 Jan 23A; currency 1981 Aug 3H/Oct 4B; 1982 Jun 12B/Jun 28H/Oct 4A; 1983 Mar 21B; 1984 Sep 10H/Dec 31H; 1986 Apr 6B; 1987 Jan 12B; IMF loans 1983 Jan 18A

New Caledonia see New Caledonia

obituaries: Albaret, Celeste 1984 Apr 25J; Anouilh, Jean 1987 Oct 3J; Barthes, Roland 1980 Mar 25J; Brassai (born Gyula Halasz) 1984 Jul 8J; Braudel, Fernand 1985 Nov 28J; Chagall, Marc 1985 Mar 28J; Clair, Rene 1981 Mar 15J; Coluche (Michel Colucci) 1986 Jun 19J; Dassault, Marcel 1986 Apr 18B; De Beauvoir, Simone 1986 Apr 14J; De Broglie, Prince Louis 1987 Mar 19I; Defferre, Gaston 1986 May 7B; DeJouvenel, Bertrand 1987 Mar 1J; Dubuffet, Jean 1985 May 12J; Foucault, Michel 1984 Jun 25J; Fournier, Pierre 1986 Jan 8J; Gance, Abel 1981 Nov 11J; Genet, Jean 1986 Apr 15J; Jolas, Maria 1987 Mar 4J; Kastler, Alfred 1984 Jan 7I; Lartigue, Jacques-Henri 1986 Sep 12J; Michaux, Henri 1984 Oct 18J; Renault, Gilbert 1984 Jul 29J; Rothschild, Alain de 1982 Oct 17B; Sartre, Jean-Paul 1980 Apr 15J; Signoret, Simone 1985 Sep 30J; Tailleferre, Germaine 1983 Nov 7J; Tati, Jacques 1982 Nov 5B; Troisgros, Jean 1983 Aug 8J; Truffaut, Francois 1984 Oct 21J

Paris see Paris

press and broadcasting: Le Monde editor charged 1980 Nov 7B; press strikes 1986 Jul 19B/Dec 18B; professor convicted on hate crimes 1981 Jul 3B; television network 1985 Dec 22B

religion: Lefebvre defies Vatican 1980 Apr 7J; papal visits 1980 Jun 22B; private schools 1984 Apr 18B/Aug 29B

science and technology: Titanic found 1985 Sep 1J

Soviet relations: Afghanistan invasion 1980 Feb 8A; Andropov disarmament proposal rejected 1982 Dec 21B; credit agreement denied 1982 Jul 16B; export controls 1982 Jan 9A; grain sales 1981 Apr 25B; military exercises protested 1984 Apr 4A; natural gas contract 1982 Jan 23B; natural gas pipeline 1982 Feb 10B/Jul 22B/Aug 26G; 1984 Jan 1B; oil 1986 Nov 20B; spy arrested 1980 Feb 9B; steel plant equipment 1980 Sep 19A; trade limit agreement denied 1982 Nov 13B; trade policy agreement with U.S. 1982 Dec 14A; UN resolution vetoed 1984 Feb 29A; visits 1980 Apr 25A

space and space flights: communications satellites 1985 May 6I; French colonel on Soviet Soyuz 1982 Jun 24I

sports: Albertville chosen for Olympics 1986 Oct 17J; auto racing 1985 Jun 16J/Jul 7J; 1986 Jun 1J/Jul 16J; 1987 Jun 14J/Jul 5J; 1988 Jun 12J/Jul 3J; 1989 Feb 5J/Jun 11J/Jul 9J; boxing 1983 Mar 27J; cycling 1985 Jul 21J; 1986 Jul 27J; 1987 Jul 26J; 1988 Jul 24J; 1989 Jul 23J; Moscow Olympics 1980 May 13J; mountain climbing 1988 Sep 25J; rugby 1987 Jun 20J; tennis 1982 Nov 28J; track and field 1985 Jul 16J; 1989 Jul 10J

terrorism: Basques 1984 Jun 15B/Sep 26B; 1986 Apr 27B; bombings 1982 Aug 21B; Goldenberg's restaurant attack 1982 Aug 9B/Aug 10B; IRA members arrested 1982 Aug 30B; Italian bombing suspect arrested 1980 Aug 6B; Massie slaying 1981 Jul 18B

trade issues: arms sales 1982 Jan 7D; 1984 Aug 27G; 1987 Mar 5B; fishing rights dispute with Canada 1987 Mar 17D; 1988 Apr 20D/Jun 8D/Sep 12D; high technology 1980 Oct 1B; 1982 Jan 27I; nuclear export limitation pact 1987 Apr 16A; nuclear fuel sales 1982 Aug 30A/Nov 29I; nuclear reactors sales 1980 Feb 27I/Oct 17I; trade deficit 1988 Mar 9B; 1989 Feb 26B

transportation: English Channel tunnel (Eurotunnel) 1980 Mar 19B; 1986 Jan 20B; 1987 Jul 29B/Nov 27B; 1988 Jul 14B

United Nations policy: 1981 Apr 30A; 1982 Jun 26A; 1983 Jan 6B; 1984 Feb 15A/Feb 29A; 1985 Sep 30A; 1987 Feb 20A/Sep 2A; 1989 Jan 11A

U.S. relations: 1980 Sep 19A; 1981 Dec 22H; 1982 Jul 16B/Aug 26G/Nov 13B/Dec 14A; 1983 Jun 2A/Oct 25B; 1984 Apr 12G; 1985 Nov 5G; 1989 May 2H/May 28B

war crimes: 1983 Jan 19B; 1989 May 24B

Frankfurt stock market 1988 Apr 30A

franking privileges 1986 May 14F; 1989 Nov 9F

Franklin National Bank 1980 Mar 27H; 1982 Jul 22B

Frantic (film) 1988 Mar 16J

Fraternity of St. Pius X 1988 Jun 30J

FRC see Fatah Revolutionary Council

free agency (sports) 1980 May 23J/Nov 13J/Dec 15J; 1981 Jun 12J/Jul 31J; 1986 Apr 7J; 1987 Sep 21J/Sep 22J; 1988 Jan 22H; 1989 Feb 1J/Aug 31J

Freedom (yacht) 1980 Sep 25J

Freedom and Peace (Polish dissident organization) 1987 Dec 27B

Freedom of Information Act 1980 Mar 3F; 1981 Sep 24G/Oct 15F/Nov 12F; 1982 Jan 25F/May 17F; 1984 Oct 1G; 1985 Nov 26F; 1986 Mar 12F; 1987 Nov 10H; 1988 Feb 2F

Free Fall in Crimson (John D. MacDonald) (book) 1981 May 10J/May 24J/Jul 5J

"freeway murders" 1981 Jan 11F

Freeze Frame (J. Geils Band) (recording) 1982 Jan 20J/Feb 24J/Mar 14J/Mar 17J

French Academy 1980 Mar 16J

French filly All Along (racehorse) 1984 Feb 3J

French fries 1985 Nov 14I

French Grand Prix 1985 Jul 7J; 1986 Jul 16J; 1987 Jul 5J; 1988 Jul 3J; 1989 Jul 9J

French Lieutenant's Woman (film) 1981 Nov 4J/Dec 2J

French Open (tennis tournament)
  men's singles: 1980 Jun 8J; 1981 Jun 7J; 1982 Jun 5J; 1985 Jun 9J; 1986 Jun 8J; 1987 Jun 7J; 1988 Jun 5J; 1989 Jun 11J
  women's singles: 1980 Jun 7J; 1981 Jun 6J; 1982 Jun 6J; 1985 Jun 8J; 1986 Jun 7J; 1987 Jun 6J; 1988 Jun 4J; 1989 Jun 10J

French Revolution (1789) 1989 Jul 14B

Freud Archives, Sigmund 1981 Nov 5I

Friday the 13th (film) 1980 May 28J

Friday the 13th (Part 2) (film) 1981 May 20J

Friday the 13th Part VII—The New Blood (film) 1988 May 18J

Frieda K. (ship) 1984 Sep 19B

Friendship '84 sports festival 1984 Aug 18J

Fright Night (film) 1985 Aug 14J

frogs 1984 Sep 24I

Front for the Liberation of Lebanon from Aliens 1981 Sep 17C; 1983 Feb 5C

Frontier Airlines (People Express) 1986 Aug 28H/Sep 15H

Frontiers (Journey) (recording) 1983 Mar 9J/Apr 13J

Front Line (Italian terrorist group) 1980 Apr 28B

Frostban (bacteria) 1987 Apr 24I/Jun 8I

frost damage 1985 Nov 14I; 1986 May 13I

fruit fly see Mediterranean fruit fly

fruits 1984 Dec 4B; 1985 Aug 9H; 1986 Jul 8H; 1987 Jan 7H; 1989 Jan 5A/Mar 17I/Dec 4H; see also specific types (e.g., apples)

F-16 (aircraft) 1980 Feb 25G; 1981 Jan 10C/Jul 1G/Jul 20G/Aug 11G/Aug 17G/Aug 19E/Sep 15G; 1983 Mar 31G/Apr 13C/May 6G/May 20G; 1986 May 7E; 1987 Jan 21G; 1988 Jan 15B

FSLIC see Federal Savings and Loan Insurance Corp.

FSX (Japanese aircraft) 1989 Mar 21G/May 16G/Jul 31G/Sep 13G

FTC see Federal Trade Commission

F-20 (aircraft) 1986 Nov 17G

fuel efficiency 1985 Jun 26H; 1986 Oct 2H; 1989 May 17H

fuel oil 1983 Mar 18D; 1985 Nov 8H; 1987 Jul 20B

Fugitive Investigation Strike Team (Justice Department) 1984 Nov 20F

Fujisankei Communications Group 1989 Oct 28E

Fujitsu Ltd. 1987 Sep 15F; 1988 Nov 29H

Full Circle (Danielle Steel) (book) 1984 Jun 15J/Jul 20J/Aug 24J

Fullilove v. Klutznick (1980) 1980 Jul 2F

Full Metal Jacket (film) 1987 Jun 26J

Full Moon Fever (Tom Petty) (recording) 1989 Jun 24J/Aug 26J

F/X (film) 1986 Feb 19J

G

Gabon 1980 Nov 9C

Gainers Inc. 1986 Dec 14D

Galapagos (Kurt Vonnegut) (book) 1985 Nov 22J

galaxies 1984 Jul 5I; 1986 Jan 12I; 1987 Jul 26I; 1989 Aug 28I/Nov 17I

Galileo (spacecraft) 1989 Oct 18I/Oct 23I

Gallaudet University (Washington, D.C.) 1988 Mar 13F

Gallup International 1989 Sep 12J

Gambia 1981 Jun 30C/Jul 31C/Aug 6C/Aug 19C

Gambino crime group 1986 Mar 5F; 1987 Mar 13F; 1989 Jan 23F/Jul 7F

gambling 1982 Jan 6F; 1984 Sep 24F; 1985 Jun 30J; 1986 Feb 1J; see also casinos

Game, The (Queen) (recording) 1980 Sep 10J/Oct 8J

gamma ray emissions 1987 Dec 17I

Gandhi (film) 1983 Feb 2J/Mar 9J/May 4J

Gang of Four (China) 1980 Nov 20E/Dec 29E; 1981 Jan 25E

gangs 1981 Aug 7F; 1988 Mar 16F/Dec 16F

Gannett Co. 1981 Jul 24J; 1982 Sep 15J; 1983 Apr 30J; 1984 Jun 25F; 1985 Aug 29H; 1986 May 19H; 1987 Jul 16H

GAO see General Accounting Office, U.S.

Gardens of Stone (film) 1987 May 20J

Garland Publishing 1984 Jun 16J

Garrison Diversion irrigation project 1983 Nov 21D

Garuda Airlines 1981 Mar 28E/Mar 31E

gas exploration 1981 Jul 21H; 1982 May 31D; 1983 Sep 13H; 1984 Aug 8H/Dec 12D; 1986 Nov 24H; 1987 Apr 27H/Aug 27H

gasoline
  consumption: 1981 Apr 23H
  environmental issues: conservation targets 1980 Mar 20H; lead content 1984 Jul 30H; 1985 Mar 4H; 1986 Dec 2H; 1988 Feb 17H; low-emission type introduced 1989 Aug 15H; mileage requirements 1988 Oct 3H; pollution control standards 1982 Dec 28H; refining process improvements 1980 Mar 31I;
  foreign developments: Great Britain 1981 Mar 16B; Israel 1989 Jan 1C; Mexico 1982 Aug 1D; Venezuela 1989 Mar 1D

political campaign issues: 1980 Jun 24F

price and production issues: oil company output 1980 Oct 3H; statistics 1983 Sep 23H; 1985 Jan 15H; taxes: 1982 Dec 7H/Dec 23H; 1983 Jan 31H

gasoline bombs 1982 May 5B

gas pipelines 1984 Dec 12D; 1985 Oct 9H; 1987 Nov 9H; 1989 Jun 3B; Soviet gas pipeline

Gate, The (film) 1987 May 20J

Gate Dancer (racehorse) 1984 May 19J

Gato del Sol (racehorse) 1982 May 1J

Gator Bowl (football) 1981 Dec 28J

GATT *see* General Agreement on Tariffs and Trade

Gay Men's Health Crisis (New York) 1989 Aug 15I

Gay Olympics 1987 Jun 25F

Gaza Strip
civil strife: beatings of protestors 1988 Jan 19C/Jan 24C; deportations of activists 1988 Jan 3C/Jan 13C; fatalities estimated 1988 Oct 18C; firebombs and arson used 1988 Jun 22C; human rights violations charged 1989 Feb 7G; Israel claims cells of PLO faction smashed 1981 May 17C; Israeli crackdown 1987 Dec 25C; 1988 Mar 28C; 1989 Jan 23C; strikes 1981 Dec 1C; 1982 Sep 21C; trials of activists 1987 Dec 27C; unrest 1982 Mar 25C; 1987 Dec 18C; 1988 Jan 10C
Jewish settlements: 1980 Mar 1A/Mar 4G; 1982 Feb 17C; 1984 Apr 11C
Palestinian autonomy: administrative council enlargement 1981 Oct 15C; Egypt election plan 1989 Sep 18C; Israel/Egypt talks 1980 Jan 10C/Jan 17C/Feb 1C/Oct 15A; Palestinian state declaration 1988 Nov 26C; 1989 Nov 15C; PLO/Jordan meeting 1983 Apr 5C; PLO/U.S. meeting 1989 Mar 22C; Shamir election plan 1989 Apr 20C/Apr 27C/Jul 23C

GE *see* General Electric Co.

Genentech Inc. 1980 Oct 14H; 1987 Nov 4I/Nov 13I

General Accounting Office, U.S. (GAO)
budget issues: Gramm-Rudman cuts 1986 Jan 20H/Apr 1H; UNESCO investigation 1984 Mar 26A; year-end report 1985 Dec 25F
crime and law enforcement: federal prison population 1989 Dec 3F; fraud prosecutions 1981 Oct 12F; marijuana cultivation on public lands 1984 Dec 12H
environmental issues: coal-leasing programs 1983 May 10H; hazardous waste 1983 Oct 5H; 1986 Mar 22H; 1987 Jan 16H; oil leases 1985 Jul 26H; Strategic Petroleum Reserve 1982 Mar 19H; toxic chemicals 1984 Jul 9H; wildlife refuges 1989 Sep 12H
farm issues: farm credit 1988 Jun 16H
health issues: Agent Orange medical examinations 1982 Oct 25G; medical research spending 1985 Mar 19F; prescription drug abuse 1982 Nov 14I; women in medical research 1989 Dec 14F
housing issues: FHA deficit 1988 Dec 20H; FHA mortgage programs 1989 Sep 27F

labor issues: government employee pay hikes 1987 Apr 4H
military issues: draft registration 1982 Jul 28G; Honduras military training 1984 Jun 24D; Nicaraguan contra propaganda 1987 Oct 4G; weapons systems 1982 Jun 25G; 1984 May 11G/Sep 18G; 1987 Dec 20G
Nazis: 1982 May 18F/Jun 28G
regulatory issues: government contracts oversight 1985 Mar 27H/Jun 3F; Reagan reelection committee 1986 Mar 22F
savings and loan crisis: audit scores acounting firms 1989 Feb 2H; bailout estimate hiked 1989 May 21H; FSLIC deficit 1987 Feb 25H
South Africa sanctions: 1989 Aug 19G
transportation issues: airline safety monitoring 1986 May 14H; air traffic control 1986 Mar 6H; 1987 May 6H; car defect investigation 1983 Aug 5H; space flight 1980 Feb 16I

General Agreement on Tariffs and Trade (GATT)
agricultural issues: Japan import quotas 1987 Dec 3E; 1988 Feb 2E; Reagan subsidies proposal 1987 Jul 6E; 1988 Nov 17H; U.S.-EC feud 1983 Feb 25B/Aug 7A; 1988 Dec 9A; U.S.-Nicaragua feud 1983 May 11D; 1984 Mar 13A; U.S. sugar quotas 1983 May 11D
computer technology: U.S.-Japan semiconductor agreement 1988 Mar 25A/May 4A
free trade and protectionism: Australia pledges trade barrier elimination 1987 Oct 22E; Canada foreign investment policy review 1983 Jul 13A; debtor nations 1983 May 5A; U.S.-Indian negotiations 1980 Aug 26A; U.S. Omnibus Trade Act 1989 Jun 21A; U.S. policy criticized 1989 Dec 14A
meetings: 1982 Nov 24A; 1984 Nov 30A; 1985 Oct 2B/Nov 28A
membership: China reapplies 1986 Jul 11E; Mexico admitted 1986 Jul 24D; Soviet role rejected 1986 Sep 18A
Uruguay round: agenda agreed 1986 Sep 20A; negotiating guidelines agreed 1989 Apr 8A
world trade statistics: 1980 Sep 16A; 1981 Mar 15A; 1988 Feb 26A/Aug 2A; 1989 Feb 27A/Sep 14A

General Assembly, U.N.
disarmament and arms control: 1988 Jun 26A
presidential elections: 1987 Sep 15A; 1988 Sep 20A; 1989 Sep 21A
Special Committee Against Apartheid: 1985 May 13J

General Belgrano (ship) 1982 May 2D; 1984 Aug 19B

General Dynamics Corp. 1983 Feb 21G; 1985 May 21G/Aug 13G/Nov 12H/Dec 2G; 1986 Feb 7G/Mar 26G; 1987 Mar 10H/Jun 19G

General Electric Co. (GE) 1980 Jun 16F; 1981 Feb 11H; 1985 Mar 28G/Apr 18G/May 13G/Jun 30H/Nov 22F/Dec 11H; 1987 Dec 1I

General Foods Corp. 1982 Jan 15H; 1985 Sep 27H

Generalized System of Preferences (GSP) 1988 Jan 29G

General Mills Inc. 1982 Jan 15H; 1984 May 7H

General Motors Corp. (GMC)
appointments and resignations: Perot ousted 1986 Dec 1H; Smith appointed chairman 1980 Sep 9H
business issues: Fortune 500 ranking 1983 Apr 13H; joint ventures 1981 Aug 12H; 1982 May 24H; 1983 Feb 17H/Dec 22H; 1985 Jun 25H; loans back bond offerings 1986 Oct 14H; plant closings 1986 Nov 6H; 1987 Aug 26H; 1988 Apr 22H; plastic sports car project abandoned 1986 Oct 19H; Saturn plans 1985 Jul 26H; 1986 Oct 30H
foreign operations: Canada 1982 Sep 19C; 1984 Oct 17D/Oct 29D; South Africa 1986 Oct 21C
labor issues: contracts 1982 Mar 21H/Apr 8H; 1983 Aug 23H; 1984 Sep 21H; 1985 Jun 25H/Jul 26H; 1987 Oct 8H; discrimination suit 1983 Oct 18F; 1989 Jan 31F; layoffs 1980 Jun 21H; plant closings 1986 Nov 6H; 1987 Aug 26H; 1988 Apr 22H; strikes 1984 Oct 16H/Oct 17D; wage parity with other companies 1985 Oct 23H
profits and losses: 1980 Apr 22H/Oct 27H; 1981 Feb 2H/Apr 27H/Oct 22H; 1983 Apr 20H; 1984 Feb 7H/Apr 27H/Jul 27H/Oct 23H; 1985 Feb 4H/Apr 23H/Jul 23H; 1987 Jul 23F; 1988 Apr 21H/Jul 21H; 1989 Feb 14H/Feb 16H
safety and repair issues: accident lawsuit settled 1982 Jun 11H; arbitrators for consumer complaints 1983 Nov 17H; brake defects in X-body cars 1983 Aug 3H/Aug 5H; 1987 Apr 14H; emissions of nitrogen oxide 1982 Jul 29H; sudden acceleration 1986 Aug 15H/Dec 30H
sales: incentive program 1986 Aug 28H; United States 1985 Jan 4H; Western Europe 1987 Jul 22B; 1988 Jan 18B

General Public Utilities Corp. (GPU) 1983 Jan 24H/Jun 23H/Sep 13H/Nov 7H/Nov 28H/Nov 30H

General Services Administration, U.S. (GSA) 1985 May 31J; 1986 Dec 5H; 1987 Aug 31J

general strikes
Afghanistan: 1980 Feb 21E
Argentina: 1985 May 23D; 1986 Jan 24D/Mar 25D; 1987 Jan 26D/Dec 9D
Bolivia: 1984 Dec 4D; 1985 Mar 24D/Sep 19D
Brazil: 1983 Jul 21D
Canada: 1987 Jun 1D
Chile: 1986 Jul 3D; 1989 Apr 18D
Dominican Republic: 1987 Aug 11D
Ecuador: 1985 Jan 10D; 1987 Mar 25D/Oct 28D
Gaza Strip: 1981 Dec 1C; 1982 Apr 12C
India: 1982 Jan 19E; 1984 Feb 8E
Israel: 1987 Dec 21C
Morocco: 1981 Jun 20C
Moslem countries: 1982 Apr 14A
Northern Ireland: 1986 Mar 3B
Panama: 1985 Jul 2E; 1986 Mar 19E; 1987 Jul 28D; 1988 Feb 29D
Peru: 1988 Jan 28D
Poland: 1980 Nov 25B; 1981 Feb 6B/Mar 24B/Mar 27B/Mar 30B/Oct 28B; 1982 May 13B
South Africa: 1986 Mar 30C; 1989 Sep 6C

Spain: 1984 Feb 24B; 1988 Dec 14B
Suriname: 1982 Nov 3D
Syria: 1980 Mar 5C
Trinidad: 1989 Mar 6D
Uruguay: 1984 Jan 18D/Jun 27D
Venezuela: 1989 May 18D
West Bank: 1982 Mar 19C/Mar 30C/Apr 12C

General Telephone and Electronics (GT&E) 1980 Apr 7H

generic drugs 1983 Mar 22F; 1984 Sep 24H; 1985 Sep 4F; 1989 Aug 16H

genes *see also* human genome project
alcoholism: 1980 Jun 7I
Alzheimer's disease: 1987 Feb 20I
bacteria regulation: 1980 Jan 23I
bird evolution: 1980 Mar 8I
bone marrow cell transplant: 1980 Apr 3I
breast cancer: 1980 Mar 29I; 1987 May 21I
cancer-suppression: 1988 Dec 28I
Chernobyl victims: 1986 Nov 23I
cystic fibrosis: 1989 Aug 24I
DNA-analysis machine: 1986 Jun 11I
fetal development: 1987 Dec 22I
mapping: 1987 Feb 16I
multiple sclerosis: 1989 Jun 30I
protein synthesis: 1988 May 13I

Genesco Inc. 1980 Nov 6H

Genesis (singing group) 1986 Jul 16J/Aug 13J; 1987 Mar 28J

genetic engineering
blood clot dissolver: 1987 Nov 13I
"engineered" mice sale: 1988 Oct 15I
gene-splice experiment halted: 1984 May 16I
gene-splice risks: 1987 Aug 18I
industry regulation: 1986 Jun 18I
patents: 1980 Jun 16F/Jun 16I; 1987 Apr 16I/Nov 4I/Nov 4I; 1988 Apr 21I/Oct 15I
plant gene-splice breakthru: 1986 Mar 5I
recombinant DNA research: 1986 Sep 29I
vaccines: 1986 Jul 23I

Geneva (Switzerland) 1981 Jul 22B

Geneva Committee (U.N. Conference of the Committee on Disarmament) 1980 Feb 5A; 1983 Feb 10A; 1984 Feb 21B/Apr 4A/Apr 18A; 1985 Feb 5A; 1987 Mar 17B/Jun 9B

Geneva summit (1985) 1985 Nov 14G/Nov 19B

Genie Awards (film) 1986 Mar 20J; 1988 Mar 22J; 1989 Mar 22J

genocide 1982 Feb 23D; 1986 Feb 19A; 1988 Jul 28C/Oct 19G/Nov 4G; 1989 Jan 4B; *see also* Holocaust

Genuine Risk (racehorse) 1980 May 3J/May 17J/Jun 7J

geography 1988 Jul 27F

Geological Survey, U.S. 1983 Oct 30I; 1985 Apr 5I; 1989 Feb 27I

geology 1986 Feb 9I; 1987 Jun 17I

geometry 1988 Dec 20I

Geophysical Union, American *see* American Geophysical Union

George Mason University (Fairfax, Va.) 1985 Nov 24J

George Polk Memorial Awards (journalism) 1983 Feb 25J

Georges Bank (Atlantic fishing area) 1984 Oct 12D

Georgetown University (Washington, D.C.) 1980 Jan 28F; 1982 Mar 29J;

1984 Apr 2J; 1985 Apr 1J/Sep 18J; 1987 Nov 20F; 1989 Feb 23F

Georgia *see also specific cities* (e.g., Atlanta)
accidents and diasters: storms 1982 Apr 2I
agriculture: foreclosure-related suicide 1986 Feb 4H
crime and law enforcement: death sentence overturned by Supreme Court 1980 May 19F; gun laws 1982 Mar 15F; marijuana paraquat spraying 1983 Aug 15F; posthumous pardon of convicted murderer 1986 Mar 11F
ediucation issues: graduation test 1984 Jun 2F; racial segregation 1983 Mar 24F/Jul 7F; 1988 Feb 10F
environmental issues: paraquat spraying against marijuana 1983 Aug 15F
executions: Smith, John Eldon 1983 Dec 15F; Williams, Robert Wayne 1983 Dec 15F
obituaries: Griffin, Marvin 1982 Jun 13F
politics and government: Atlanta Democratic convention (1988) 1987 Feb 10F; 1988 Apr 20F/Jul 18F-19F; Carter to return 1980 Nov 12F; presidential campaigns 1980 Mar 11F; 1984 Mar 13F; presidential primary date changed 1986 Apr 6F
race issues: racial bias 1984 Jun 2F; racial segregation 1983 Mar 24F/Jul 7F; 1988 Feb 10F

Georgia (USSR) 1989 Apr 9B/Apr 27B/Jul 27B

Georgia, University of (Athens) 1981 Jan 3J; 1982 Dec 4J; 1984 Jan 2J; 1985 Mar 31J

Georgia Institute of Technology (Atlanta) 1988 Feb 15I

German Grand Prix (auto race) 1986 Jul 27J; 1989 Jul 30J

German measles (rubella) 1984 Sep 23I

Germany *see* East Germany; West Germany

Gershwin Theater (New York City) 1987 Mar 15J

Gesellschaft fuer Automation 1989 May 10B

Get Nervous (Pat Benatar) (recording) 1982 Nov 17J/Dec 15J; 1983 Jan 5J

Getty Oil Co. 1983 Dec 13H; 1984 Jan 8H/Feb 13H; 1985 Nov 19H; 1987 Feb 12H/Dec 19H

Ghana 1981 Dec 31C; 1982 Jan 2C/Jan 13C/Jan 22E; 1983 Jan 17C/Jun 19C; 1985 Oct 17A/Nov 25A; 1986 Jun 22C/Sep 1B

Ghostbusters (film) 1984 Jul 18J/Aug 15J/Sep 12J

Ghostbusters II (film) 1989 Jun 28J/Jul 2J/Dec 28J

Ghost in the Machine (Police) (recording) 1981 Nov 11J

G.I. Bill 1984 Aug 30F; 1987 Jun 1G

Giacobini-Zinner (comet) 1985 Sep 11I

Gibraltar (British colony) 1982 Apr 5B/Dec 15B; 1983 Apr 11B; 1984 Nov 27B; 1985 Feb 5B; 1988 Mar 6B/Mar 24B/Apr 28B; 1989 Jan 26B

Ginna nuclear power plant, Robert E. *see* Robert E. Ginna nuclear power plant

Ginnie Mae *see* Government National Mortgage Association

Giotto (spacecraft) 1985 Jul 2I
Girls, Girls, Girls (Motley Crue) (recording) 1987 Jun 27J/Jul 22J
Girl You Know It's True (Milli Vanilli) (recording) 1989 Jul 29J/Sep 30J/Oct 28J/Dec 25J/Dec 30J
Giving You the Best That I Got (Anita Baker) (recording) 1988 Dec 31J
"glasnost" 1987 Aug 26G
Glass Houses (Billy Joel) (recording) 1980 Apr 2J/Apr 30J/Jun 4J/Jul 9J/Aug 13J
Glass-Steagall Act (1933) 1987 Jul 7H; 1989 Jan 18H
glassware 1986 Oct 8B
Glengarry Glen Ross (David Mamet) (play) 1984 Mar 25J/Apr 16J
Glitter Dome, The (Joseph Wambaugh) (book) 1981 Aug 9J/Sep 6J
Glitz (Elmore Leonard) (book) 1985 Mar 15J
global warming 1985 Nov 2I; 1986 Nov 20I; 1987 Apr 11I; 1989 Jan 5I/May 12I
Globe Theater (London) 1987 Oct 27J; 1989 Oct 13J
Glory (film) 1989 Dec 14J
gloves 1988 Nov 10H
GLQ223 (tricosanthin) (drug) 1989 Apr 27I/Sep 19I
glutamate-pyruvate transaminase 1980 Mar 29I
GMC *see* General Motors Corp.
G N' R Lies (Guns N' Roses) (recording) 1989 Apr 29J/May 27J
Goddard Institute of Space Studies (Greenbelt, Maryland) (NASA) 1988 Jun 23I
Godel, Escher and Bach: An Eternal Golden Braid (Douglas Hofstadter) (book) 1980 Apr 14J
God Emperor of Dune (Frank Herbert) (book) 1981 May 24J/Jul 5J
God Knows (Joseph Heller) (book) 1984 Oct 19J/Nov 16J
Godplayer (Robin Cook) (book) 1983 Aug 14J
Go For Wand (racehorse) 1989 Nov 4J
GoGo's (singing group) 1982 Feb 24J/Mar 14J/Mar 17J/May 5J
Going In Style (film) 1980 Jan 30J
Golan Heights 1981 Mar 11C/Dec 14C/Dec 17A/Dec 18G/Dec 20C; 1982 Jan 20A/Feb 5A/Feb 17C/Jul 20C; 1984 Jun 28C
gold
- crime and corruption issues: broker fined 1989 Aug 24H; Memphis heist 1983 Nov 26B; NYC heist 1983 Apr 2F/Nov 26B
- exploration and mining: 1980 Aug 27H; 1982 Jan 26F; 1986 Sep 16C; 1987 Aug 9C/Aug 30C
- monetary and trade issues: coins 1982 Feb 12H; 1986 Sep 8H/Sep 16B; gold standard return rejected 1982 Mar 31H; investment returns 1987 Jun 8H
- price and production issues: 1980 Jan 18A; 1982 Jun 21H/Aug 26H; 1985 Mar 19H; 1986 Sep 5H

Goldberg Variations, The (J.S. Bach) (recording) 1983 Feb 23J
Goldenberg's (Paris restaurant) 1982 Aug 9B/Aug 10B
Golden Child, The (film) 1986 Dec 24J; 1987 Jan 21J
Golden Gate Bridge (San Francisco) 1987 May 24F
Golden Girls, The (TV show) 1986 Sep 21J; 1987 Jan 31J/Sep 20J; 1988 Aug 28J
Golden Globe awards (film and television) 1980 Dec 6J; 1987 Jan 31J; 1988 Jan 23J; 1989 Jan 28J
Golden Lion (film award) 1987 Sep 9J
Golden Nugget (casino) 1980 Dec 12J
Golden Palm (Palme d'Or) (film award) 1984 May 23J; 1985 May 20J; 1986 May 19J; 1987 May 19J; 1988 May 23J; 1989 May 23J/May 23J
Golden State Warriors (basketball team) 1982 Nov 10J
Golden Temple (Sikh shrine) (Amritsar, India) 1984 Jun 6E/Jun 7E/Jun 13E/Jun 20E/Jun 25E/Sep 29E/Oct 1E; 1986 Jan 26E/Apr 30E; 1988 May 18E
Goldheart International Ltd. 1983 Apr 2F
golf 1981 Jan 13J; 1983 Oct 22F
Goncourt Prize (literature) 1984 Nov 12J; 1985 Nov 18J; 1986 Nov 17J; 1987 Nov 16J
Gone with the Wind (Margaret Mitchell) (book) 1988 Apr 25J
Gong Show Movie, The (film) 1980 May 28J
Goodbye, Janette (Harold Robbins) (book) 1981 Jul 5J/Aug 9J/Aug 9J
Goodman Theater (Chicago) 1985 Apr 29J
Good Morning, Vietnam (film) 1987 Dec 23J; 1988 Jan 20J/Feb 17J/Mar 16J
Good War, The: An Oral History of World War II (Studs Terkel) (book) 1985 Apr 24J
Goonies, The (film) 1985 Jun 12J
Gorillas in the Mist (film) 1988 Sep 23J/Oct 19J
Gorky Park (Martin Cruz Smith) (book) 1981 May 10J/May 24J/Jul 5J/Aug 9J/Aug 9J/Sep 6J/Oct 4J
Gospels of Henry the Lion, The (illuminated manuscript) 1983 Dec 6J
Gotcha! (film) 1985 May 15J
government *see specific geographic regions* (*e.g.,* Canada); *specific parties* (*e.g.,* Democratic Party); *individual leaders in the name index* (*e.g.,* Carter, Jimmy)
government employees
- benefit issues: charity drive 1983 Sep 15F; state social security exit ban 1986 Jun 19F; student loan repayment 1982 Dec 6H; unemployment benefits 1987 Feb 25F
- corruption and ethics issues: whistleblower legislation 1989 Apr 10F
- foreign developments: Argentina 1985 Dec 30D; Canada 1986 Sep 3D/Oct 6D; 1989 May 24D/Sep 14D; Greece 1980 Nov 6B; Jamaica 1980 Jan 15D; Netherlands 1986 Jan 1B; Nicaragua 1989 Jan 30D; Poland 1982 May 17B; South Korea 1980 Aug 2E; Sweden 1985 May 20B
- health and safety issues: drug testing 1986 Sep 15F/Sep 18F
- job bias and quotas: bias issues 1983 Mar 2F/Apr 1F; 1984 Feb 20F; hiring ceilings 1981 Mar 6H
- politics: Hatch Act revisions 1987 Nov 17F; 1989 Apr 17H; whistleblower legislation 1989 Apr 10F
- privacy issues: privacy in workplace 1987 Mar 31F; secrecy pledge 1987 Aug 11G
- rights issues: censorship 1983 Oct 20H; First Amendment rights 1987 Jun 24F
- strikes and settlements: Philadelphia strike 1986 Jul 22F
- wages, hours and productivity: federal wage laws 1985 Feb 19H; flexible schedules 1982 Mar 26H; overtime time-off 1985 Nov 13F; pay increases 1987 Apr 4H; total employment 1985 Aug 28F

Government Ethics, U.S. Office of 1981 Jul 30G; 1987 Jun 30F; 1988 Jul 27F/Sep 12F
Government National Mortgage Association, U.S. (Ginnie Mae) 1986 May 2H
Governor General's Literary Award (literature) 1987 May 27J
governors 1980 Dec 4F; 1981 Feb 24F/Sep 2H; 1982 Nov 2F/Nov 22H; 1983 Mar 1F/Dec 5H; 1984 Feb 28H; 1986 Aug 23F; 1989 Sep 27F; *individual governors in the name index* (*e.g.,* Cuomo, Mario); *see also* National Governors' Association
Goya (Gian Carlo Menotti) (opera) 1986 Nov 15J
GPU *see* General Public Utilities Corp.
Grace & Co., W.R. 1986 Sep 22H; 1987 Jan 28H; 1988 May 31H
Graceland (Paul Simon) (recording) 1987 Feb 24J/Mar 28J/Apr 25J/May 23J; 1988 Mar 2J
Gramm-Rudman-Hollings Act (1985)
- constitutionality: federal panel rules 1986 Feb 2H; Justice Department brief 1985 Dec 30H; modifications 1986 Jul 30H/Aug 9H/Aug 16H; Supreme Court rules 1986 Jul 7H
- deficit targets: 1985 Dec 12H; 1986 Feb 5H/Feb 26H/Jun 11H/Aug 19H/Oct 21H; 1987 Mar 19H/May 14H/Jul 16H; 1988 Oct 16H; 1989 Jan 9H/Aug 17H/Dec 19H
- spending cuts: 1985 Dec 18G; 1986 Jan 15H/Jan 20H/Feb 5H/Mar 1H/Jul 17H; 1987 Oct 20H; 1989 Oct 16H
- state/local government impact: 1986 Jan 22F/Feb 3H/Feb 24F/Mar17H

Grammy Awards (music) 1980 Feb 27J; 1981 Feb 25J; 1982 Feb 24J; 1983 Feb 23J; 1984 Feb 28J; 1985 Feb 26J; 1986 Feb 25J; 1987 Feb 24J; 1988 Mar 2J; 1989 Feb 22J
Grand Canyon National Park (Arizona) 1987 Aug 19H; 1989 Aug 29H
Grand Challenge Cup (rowing) 1985 Jul 7J; 1986 Jul 6J; 1987 Jul 5J
Grand Colombian Financial Group 1986 Jan 19D; 1987 Jul 30D
Grand Hotel (musical) 1989 Dec 12J
Grand Mosque (Mecca) 1980 Jan 1C/Jan 9C; 1984 Sep 1C; 1987 Jul 31C
Grand National Steeplechase (horse race) 1988 Apr 9J
Grand Slam (tennis) 1988 Sep 10J
grapes 1988 Aug 21F; 1989 Mar 17I
grasshoppers 1985 Jun 29I; 1986 Oct 23C
"Grate American Sleep-Out" (protest event) 1987 Mar 3F
gravity 1980 Mar 8I; 1988 Dec 9I
Grawemeyer Award (music) 1986 Nov 11J; 1987 Sep 29J; 1989 Apr 25J
gray-market goods 1988 May 31H
Great Barrier Reef (Australia) 1980 Jun 10I; 1989 Jan 13E
Great Britain *see also individual leaders in the name index* (*e.g.,* Thatcher, Margaret)
- accidents and disasters: British Airtours crash (Manchester) 1985 Aug 22B; British jetliner crash (Canary Islands) 1980 Apr 25B; British Rail train collision 1986 Jul 26B; ferry sinking 1987 Mar 6B/Apr 8B/Jul 24B/Oct 8B; 1989 Jun 22B; fires 1984 Jul 9J; 1985 May 11B; nuclear power plant accident 1988 Jan 1B; oil spills 1989 Aug 19I; Pan Am flight (Lockerbie) 1988 Dec 21B/Dec 28B; 1989 Nov 1G; weather 1989 Dec 21I
- agriculture: Chernobyl radiation 1986 Jun 20I; farm income 1988 Jan 25B; French import curbs 1980 Feb 18B
- arts and culture: Birtwistle wins Grawemeyer 1987 Sep 29J; Blunt resigns from British Academy 1980 Aug 18J; Booker Prize 1985 Oct 31J; 1986 Oct 22J; 1987 Oct 29J; 1988 Oct 26J; 1989 Oct 26J; *Cats* wins Tony Awards 1983 Jun 5J; *Chariots of Fire* released 1981 Sep 26J; *Chariots of Fire* wins Oscar 1982 Mar 29J; Elgin marbles 1983 May 13B; 1984 Apr 10J; film awards 1980 Aug 18J; 1986 Mar 16J; 1987 Mar 22J; 1988 Mar 20J; 1989 Mar 19J; *A Fish Called Wanda* released 1988 Jul 15J; Golding wins Nobel Prize 1983 Oct 6J; Goya painting to be returned to Spain 1986 Apr 10B; Hughes named poet laureate 1984 Dec 19J; Lawrence enshrined in Poets' Corner 1985 Nov 16J; *The Mission* wins Golden Palm 1986 May 19J; *My Beautiful Laundrette* released 1986 Mar 7J; Olivier Awards 1986 Dec 7J; 1988 Jan 24J; *The Phantom of the Opera* opens 1987 Jul 2J; Redgrave performances cancelled in U.S. 1982 Apr 11J; *Satanic Verses* 1988 Oct 7E/Nov 8J; 1989 Feb 14C/Feb 17C/Feb 24A/Mar 7A/Mar 31J/Apr 28J/May 3C/May 26J; tea drinking 1987 May 2J; Turner painting sold 1984 Jul 5J; Whitbread award 1986 Jan 28J; 1987 Jan 13J; 1988 Jan 19J/Nov 8J; 1989 Jan 25J
- awards and honors: Birtwistle wins Grawemeyer Award 1987 Sep 29J; Booker Prize 1985 Oct 31J; 1986 Oct 22J; 1987 Oct 29J; 1988 Oct 26J; 1989 Oct 26J; Bourdeaux receives Templeton Prize 1984 May 15J; *Cats* wins Tony Awards 1983 Jun 5J; films 1980 Aug 18J; 1986 Mar 16J; 1987 Mar 22J; 1988 Mar 20J; 1989 Mar 19J; Golding wins Nobel 1983 Oct 6J; Hardy receives Templeton Prize 1985 Feb 27J; Hughes named poet laureate 1984 Dec 19J; Klug wins Nobel 1982 Oct 18I; Lawrence enshrined in Poets' Corner 1985 Nov 16J; Milstein receives Nobel 1984 Oct 15I; *The Mission* wins Golden Palm 1986 May 19J; Olivier Awards 1986 Dec 7J; 1988 Jan 24J; Whitbread award 1986 Jan 28J; 1987 Jan 13J; 1988 Jan 19J/Nov 8J; 1989 Jan 25J
- business and industry: banks 1987 Jan 8A; 1988 Feb 26B; business failures 1985 Jan 2B; corporate earnings 1988 Nov 17B; European Court ruling 1986 Jul 8B; financial services bill 1985 Dec 19B; insurance brokers 1982 Sep 8B; pub regulations 1988 Aug 22B; 1989 Jul 10B; securities fraud cases 1986 Sep 23A; stock markets 1983 Jul 27B
- civil strife: racial clashes 1985 Jul 10B; rioting 1981 Jul 10B/Jul 16B; 1985 Sep 10B; soccer violence 1985 Jun 2B; 1989 Apr 15B/Aug 4B
- colonies and dependencies: Anguilla *see* Anguilla; Belize *see* Belize; Bermuda *see* Bermuda; British Honduras *see* Belize; Falkland Islands *see* Falkland (Malvinas) Islands; Gibraltar *see* Gibraltar; Hong Kong *see* Hong Kong; Turks and Caicos *see* Turks and Caicos
- crime and law enforcement: controversial constable reinstated 1986 Aug 22B; death penalty 1983 Jul 13B; Heathrow Airport gold robbery 1983 Nov 26B; prisons 1987 Sep 24B; public order bill 1985 Dec 6B; Security Express robbery 1983 Apr 1B; Yorkshire Ripper 1981 Jan 5B/Apr 29B
- defense and disarmament issues: antinuclear protests 1983 Apr 4B; 1984 Jun 9B; Greenham Common; arms sales 1987 Mar 5B; cruise missile deployment 1980 Jun 17B; 1983 Jul 6B/Nov 14B; 1984 Jan 1B; Gurkha soldiers 1986 Aug 5E; nuclear tests *see* Australia; nuclear weapons exports limits 1987 Apr 16A; nuclear weapons tests 1988 Apr 28B; spending 1981 May 19B; 1982 Dec 14B; training exercises 1986 Feb 13C; Trident missiles 1980 Jul 15B; 1981 Jun 25B
- demonstrations and protests: antigovernment 1980 Nov 29B; antinuclear protests 1983 Apr 4B; 1984 Jun 9B; Stonehenge counterculture festival 1985 Jul 3B
- economy
  - economic indicators: cost of living 1987 Sep 4B; gross domestic product 1987 Jun 22B/Sep 21B; 1988 Mar 18B/May 23B; 1989 Feb 21B/Jun 20B; growth 1985 Jan 10B; 1987 Dec 18B; home appliances 1986 Jan 2B; industrial nation rank 1989 Jan 3B; savings rate 1988 Jan 5B; 1989 Jan 5B; standard of living 1982 Apr 1B; wealth 1987 Sep 4B; 1988 Feb 24J
  - inflation rate 1981 Jun 19B; 1982 Oct 15B; 1986 Jun 13B; 1987 Mar 20B/Nov 13B; 1988 Aug 19B/Sep 15B/Oct 14B/Nov 18B; 1989 Feb 17B/Mar 23B/May 19B/Oct 13B
  - privatizations: British Airways 1986 Sep 11B; British Petroleum Co. 1983 Jul 25B; 1987 Oct 29B; British Telecom 1982 Jul 19B; 1984 Nov 21B; regional water authorities 1986 Jul 3B
  - taxes: 1980 Nov 24B; 1981 Mar 16B; 1986 Sep 24B; 1987 Sep 11B; 1988 Mar 15B/Sep 11B
- education: 1985 May 21B; 1986 Dec 11B; 1987 Nov 28B

environmental issues: Chernobyl radiation 1986 Jun 20I; drinking water 1989 Sep 20B; nuclear power plant accident 1988 Jan 1B; nuclear radiation victim lawsuit 1988 Apr 28B; radioactive waste 1985 Jul 23B; sulfur dioxide emissions 1985 Jul 9I; youth program 1986 Aug 21B

espionage and intelligence issues: anti-Labour government conspiracy probed 1981 Mar 29B; classified document leak 1984 Mar 23B; defector returns to USSR 1984 Sep 18B; foreign minister visits 1986 Jul 13B; trade credits 1988 Oct 20B

family issues: women 1983 May 25B; 1986 Jul 8B; 1989 Sep 4B; youth program 1986 Aug 21B

foreign investment: 1986 Oct 8B; 1988 Apr 8E; 1989 Jan 18H

foreign relations

Afghanistan: 1980 Jan 26A/Feb 28A/Mar 11A

African National Congress: 1986 Feb 3C/Jun 23C

Argentina: 1983 Jun 7A; 1985 Jul 8B

Australia: 1983 Dec 17E

Botswana: 1986 Feb 13C

Brunei: 1984 Jan 1C

Canada: 1982 Jan 18A/Mar 8D/Mar 25A/Apr 17D; 1989 Oct 6D

China: 1985 Jun 1A/Jun 19B; 1986 Jun 8B

Colombia: 1980 Jan 5D

Costa Rica: 1986 Sep 26D

Cuba: 1986 Jan 31D; 1988 Sep 13B

East Germany: 1985 Apr 9B

Egypt: 1984 Aug 8A; 1988 Jan 25C

France: 1980 Feb 18B/Aug 19B

Greece: 1983 May 13B; 1984 Apr 10J

Grenada: 1983 Oct 25B

Guatemala: 1981 Sep 7D; 1986 Aug 19A/Dec 29A

Iran: 1980 May 29B/Jul 25C/Aug 17C; 1987 Jun 4C/Jun 6A; 1989 Mar 7A

Iraq: 1980 Jun 19C

Ireland: 1986 Aug 2B; 1988 May 13B

Israel: 1982 Jun 3C

Lebanon: 1983 Sep 7C/Oct 27A; 1984 Feb 8B; 1985 Mar 14C/Mar 25C/Mar 30C

Libya: 1984 Apr 17A/Apr 22A/Apr 22C/Apr 27A/Apr 30B/Apr 30C; 1985 Feb 5A; 1986 Apr 25C; 1989 Jun 11A

New Hebrides: 1980 Jun 11E/Jul 29E

Persian Gulf: 1987 Aug 12C/Sep 2A

PLO: 1985 Oct 14C

Poland: 1982 Feb 5A

Rhodesia: 1980 Mar 11C

Romania: 1980 Mar 14B

Saudi Arabia: 1980 Jul 28A; 1985 Sep 15C

South Africa: 1981 Apr 30A; 1984 Dec 12C; 1985 Sep 10B/Sep 25B; 1986 Jun 20A/Jul 24J/Jul 29C/Nov 24B; 1987 Feb 20A

Spain: 1986 Apr 22B

Sri Lanka: 1984 Jul 2A

Syria: 1986 May 21B/Oct 24C; 1987 Jul 13B/Dec 1A

USSR: Afghanistan retaliatory measures 1980 Jan 26A; Afghanistan neutrality plan 1980 Feb 28A/Mar 11A; Poland martial law sanctions 1982 Feb 5A; natural gas pipeline 1982 Aug 2B/Sep 9G; British naval attache expelled 1982 Dec 17B; Andropov disarmament proposal rejected 1982 Dec 21B; military exercises protested 1984 Apr 4A; defector returns to USSR 1984 Sep 18B; foreign minister visits 1986 Jul 13B; trade credits 1988 Oct 20B

Vatican: 1982 Jan 16B

West Germany: 1989 Apr 27B

Zimbabwe-Rhodesia: 1980 Jan 18C/Feb 2A

government and politics

budget and spending programs: 1980 Mar 26B; 1982 Mar 9B; 1983 Jul 7B; 1984 Mar 13B; 1988 Mar 15B/Nov 1B

Conservative Party: 1980 Oct 7B; 1989 Oct 10B

corruption issues: Westland PLC controversy 1986 Jan 24B/Feb 12A

elections: local 1980 May 1B; 1981 May 7B; 1984 May 3B; 1986 May 8B; parliamentary by-elections 1980 Mar 13B; 1986 May 8B

Labour Party: conferences 1980 May 31B/Sep 29B; 1981 Jan 24B/Oct 1B; 1986 Oct 3B; 1988 Oct 2B; 1989 Oct 1B; economic program 1982 Nov 23B; leadership 1980 Nov 10B; 1981 Sep 27B; 1982 Oct 27B; 1983 Oct 2B; unilateral nuclear disarmament 1981 Sep 30B

legislation: poll tax 1987 Jul 30B/Dec 4B; 1988 Apr 18B/May 23B

parliament: 1985 Jul 22B/Nov 20B; 1987 May 15B

polls and surveys: party preference 1986 Nov 13B; 1989 Aug 26B/Sep 26B

third parties: Alliance Party 1988 Sep 25B; Green Party 1989 Sep 24B; Liberal Party 1981 Jun 16B/Sep 16B; Social Democratic Party 1981 Mar 2B/Mar 26B/Jun 7B/Jun 16B/Sep 7B/Sep 16B/Oct 9B; 1982 Jul 2B/Sep 23B/Oct 11B

immigration and refugees: 1980 Jul 30B; 1985 May 28B/Jul 10B; 1987 Jun 15C

international organizations

European Community: budget issues 1980 Apr 27B/Apr 28B; 1982 May 18B/May 25B; 1984 Mar 20B/Mar 27B/Jun 26B/Jul 27B; 1985 Nov 27B; 1987 Jun 29B; drinking water standards 1989 Sep 20B; trade issues 1987 Feb 5B; value-added tax 1988 Sep 11B

IMF: 1983 Jan 18A

UNESCO: 1984 Nov 22A; 1985 Oct 8A/Dec 5B

United Nations: 1980 Feb 2A; 1981 Apr 30A; 1984 Dec 9A; 1987 Feb 20A/Sep 2A/Dec 1A; 1989 Jan 11A

labor issues

jobless rate: 1980 1980 Jun 24B/Dec 23B; 1981 1981 Jun 23B; 1982 1982 Jan 26B/Aug

24B; 1983 1983 Sep 2B; 1984 1984 Jun 1B/Aug 2B/Oct 4B; 1985 1985 Jan 31B/Oct 3B; 1986 1986 Jan 31B/Jun 13B/Aug 14B/Dec 18B; 1987 1987 Mar 19B/Jun 18B/Jul 16B/Aug 13B/Sep 17B/Nov 12B/Dec 17B; 1988 1988 Mar 17B/Apr 15B/May 19B/Aug 18B/Sep 15B/Nov 17B/Dec 15B; 1989 1989 Jan 19B/Feb 16B/Dec 14B

job security issues: jobless benefits 1988 Dec 16B; shipyard layoffs 1986 May 14B

strikes and settlements: coal miners strike 1981 Feb 18B; 1984 Mar 25B/May 30B/Aug 20B; 1985 Jan 29B/Mar 3B; coal strike report issued 1983 Jun 23B; ferry service strikes 1982 Aug 3B; seamen strikes 1981 Jan 11B; steelworker strikes 1980 Jan 2B/Feb 3B/Apr 1B; strike statistics 1986 Aug 6B; teacher strikes 1985 Apr 23B; 1986 Mar 3B; 1987 Mar 2B

union issues: conferences 1986 Sep 5B; 1989 Sep 4B; government-miners meet 1986 Sep 23B; miners code of conduct backed 1987 Aug 24B; miners salary increases 1985 Apr 22B; miners union rift 1985 Aug 7B/Dec 6B; regulations proposed 1981 Nov 23B

language issues: 1988 Apr 29B; 1989 Sep 12J

London see London

medicine and health care

abortion and birth control: physicians right to advise minors 1985 Oct 17B; RU486 1987 Oct 2I

AIDS: 1986 Nov 21B; 1988 Jan 28I; 1989 Feb 14B/Sep 18B/Nov 24I

awards: Milstein receives Nobel 1984 Oct 15I

childbirth: reproductive technologies 1984 Jul 18I

National Health Service: 1980 Jan 4B; 1987 Dec 16B; 1989 Jan 31B

radiation hazards: nuclear radiation victim lawsuit 1988 Apr 28B; nuclear weapons tests 1988 Apr 28B

transplant surgery: triple-organ transplant 1986 Dec 17I

mergers and acquisitions: newspapers 1981 Feb 13J; pharmaceuticals 1989 Apr 12H; Sinclair Research sold 1986 Apr 8B; Sotheby takeover 1983 May 4B/Sep 19J; Wedgewood PLC sold 1986 Oct 8B

monetary issues: Bank of England 1984 Nov 12B; 1986 Oct 14B; 1987 May 19B/Aug 6B/Oct 29B; 1988 Feb 1B/Feb 11B/Mar 17B/May 17B/Jun 22B/Nov 25B; currency 1982 Oct 4A; 1984 Jun 28H/Sep 10H/Nov 12B/Dec 31H; 1987 Jan 12B/Nov 9H; Eurobonds 1986 Sep 3B; IMF loans 1983 Jan 18A; interest rates 1980 Nov 24B; 1987 Mar 9B/Apr 28B; 1988 Aug 25B

narcotics and dangerous drugs: Medellin money frozen 1989 Dec 6A

Northern Ireland see Northern Ireland

obituaries: Adamson, George 1989 Aug 20C; Ashley, Laura 1985 Sep

17J; Ashton, Frederick 1988 Aug 18J; Ayer, A(lfred) J(ules) 1989 Jun 27J; Bader, Douglas 1982 Sep 5B; Beaton, Cecil 1980 Jan 18J; Blunt, Anthony 1983 Mar 26B; Boult, Adrian 1983 Feb 23J; Braine, John (Gerard) 1986 Oct 28J; Bunting, Basil 1985 Apr 17J; Burton, Richard 1984 Aug 5J; Carroll, Madeleine 1987 Oct 2J; Cecil, David 1986 Jan 1J; Clark, Kenneth 1983 May 21J; Cooper, Diana 1986 Jun 16J; Du Maurier, Daphne 1989 Apr 19J; Du Pre, Jacqueline 1987 Oct 19J; Evans, Maurice 1989 Mar 12J; Fender, P(ercy) G(eorge) H(enry) 1985 Jun 15J; Finley, Moses 1986 Jun 23J; Glubb, John Bagot 1986 Mar 17B; Graves, Robert 1985 Dec 7J; Hanley, James 1985 Nov 11J; Hardy, Alister 1985 May 23J; Hitchcock, Alfred 1980 Apr 29J; Holloway, Stanley 1982 Jan 30J; Hollowood, Bernard 1981 Mar 28J; Howard, Trevor 1988 Jan 7J; Isherwood, Christopher 1986 Jan 4J; Jameson, Storm 1986 Sep 30J; Laing, R(onald) D(avid) 1989 Aug 23I; Larkin, Philip 1985 Dec 2J; Lawford, Peter 1984 Dec 24J; MacLean, Alistair 1987 Feb 2J; Maclean, Donald 1983 Mar 6B; MacMillan, Harold 1986 Dec 29B; Markham, Beryl 1986 Aug 3J; Medawar, Peter 1987 Oct 2I; Moore, Henry 1986 Aug 31J; Neagle, Anna 1986 Jun 3J; Nicholson, Ben 1982 Feb 6J; Niven, David 1983 Jul 29J; Olivier, Laurence 1989 Jul 11J; Pears, Peter 1986 Apr 3J; Philby, Kim 1988 May 11B; Plomley, Roy 1985 May 28J; Porter, Robert 1985 Sep 6I; Priestley, John 1984 Aug 14J; Rambert, Marie 1982 Jun 12J; Ramsey, Arthur 1988 Apr 23J; Redgrave, Michael 1985 Mar 21J; Renault, Mary 1983 Dec 13J; Richardson, Ralph 1983 Oct 10J; Robson, Flora 1984 Jul 7J; Ryle, Martin 1984 Oct 14I; Sellers, Peter 1980 Jul 24J; Shinwell, Lord (Emanuel) 1986 May 8B; Snow, C.P. 1980 Jul 1J; Soames, Arthur Lord 1987 Sep 16B; Sopwith, Thomas 1989 Jan 27B; Steptoe, Patrick (Christopher) 1988 Mar 21I; Tinbergen, Nikolaas 1988 Dec 21I; Tracy, Honor Lilbush Wingfield 1989 Jun 13J; Tudor, Antony 1987 Apr 19J; Tynan, Kenneth 1980 Jul 26J; West, Rebecca 1983 Mar 15J; Wootton, Barbara 1988 Jul 11I

oil and gas developments: 1981 Oct 19B; 1983 Feb 20A/Mar 30A; 1984 Oct 18A; 1988 Jan 27B/Dec 26B

press and broadcasting 1980 Jul 25C; 1981 Feb 13J; 1986 Oct 7B; 1988 Nov 7B; 1989 Nov 28B/Dec 7B; Death of a Princess controversy 1980 May 12J/May 22B

religion: Bourdeaux receives Templeton Prize 1984 May 15J; Hardy receives Templeton Prize 1985 Feb 27J; Knights of Malta 1988 Apr 8J; papal visit 1982 May 31B/Jun 2B; pope meets archbishop 1980 May 9J

royal family see individual members in the name index (e.g., Elizabeth II)

science and technology: 2 explorers circumvent world 1982 Aug 29I;

cold fusion 1989 Mar 23I/May 9I; global temperature 1989 Feb 3I; "greenhouse" effect 1986 Nov 20I; Klug wins Nobel in chemistry 1982 Oct 18I

Scotland see Scotland

space flights: 1984 Aug 16I; 1987 Nov 10I; 1988 Dec 10I

sports: African organization urges boycott 1984 Jul 1J; auto racing 1986 Jun 1J; 1987 Jun 14J; 1988 Jan 31J/Jun 12J; 1989 Feb 5J; boxing 1980 Sep 27J/Nov 3J; 1983 Mar 19J; 1986 Jul 20J; 1989 Feb 25J; chess 1986 Dec 1J; Commonwealth Games 1986 Jul 24J; contract bridge 1985 Nov 2J; cricket 1986 May 26J; 1987 May 25J/Nov 8J; decathlon 1980 Jul 26J; field hockey 1986 Oct 19J; golf 1987 Jul 28J; 1988 Jun 20J; 1989 Apr 9J; British Open; Hillsborough soccer stampede 1989 Apr 15A/Aug 4B; horse racing 1988 Apr 9J; parachuting 1986 Apr 24J; rowing 1985 Jul 7J; 1986 Jul 6J; 1987 Jul 5J; running 1980 Aug 15J; 1981 Feb 11J/Aug 28J; 1984 Aug 19J; 1985 Jul 16J/Jul 27J; 1986 Mar 23J; 1987 Nov 1J; soccer 1982 May 26J; tennis 1987 Oct 31J; Wimbledon; track and field 1986 Aug 31J; world sports festival 1980 Mar 18J

terrorism: army camp bombings 1980 Feb 7B; Birmingham pub bombings 1988 Jan 28B; British embassy in Iraq attacked 1980 Jun 19C; El Al bombing plot 1986 Oct 24C; Guildford bombings 1989 Jan 16B/Oct 19B; IRA arrests 1985 Jun 25B; Iranian embassy takeover 1980 Apr 30A/May 5B; Israeli ambassador shot 1982 Jun 3C; Libyan embassy gunfire 1984 Apr 17A; London parks bombed 1982 Jul 20B; Marines Music School bombing 1989 Sep 22B; Seychelles opposition leader slain 1980 Nov 29E

trade issues: A-nuclear weapons exports limits 1987 Apr 16A; arms sales 1987 Mar 5B; balance of payments 1986 Mar 7B; 1988 Jan 28B/Mar 25B/Apr 29B/Sep 27B/Nov 25B; 1989 Jun 27B/Aug 24B; current account balance 1987 Jan 28B; 1988 May 27B/Jun 27B; 1989 Mar 1B/Sep 26B

transportation issues: British Airways 1985 Sep 25B; 1986 Sep 11B; bus industry 1986 Oct 26B; English Channel tunnel (Eurotunnel) 1980 Mar 19B; 1986 Jan 20B; 1987 Jul 29B/Nov 27B; 1988 Jul 14B; rail pay hike 1980 Apr 29B; 1982 Feb 18B; rail strikes 1982 Jun 28B/Jul 18B; 1989 Jun 28B

United Nations policy: 1980 Feb 2A; 1981 Apr 30A; 1982 Jan 13A/Jan 31C; 1984 Dec 9A; 1987 Feb 20A/Sep 2A/Dec 1A; 1989 Jan 11A

U.S. relations: antidumping duties 1983 Jun 2A; 1989 May 2H; bank regulations 1987 Jan 8A; extradition refused 1984 Dec 13A; extradition treaty 1985 Jun 24A; 1986 Jul 17G; securities fraud cases 1986 Sep 23A; Strategic Defense Initiative 1985 Dec 6G; 1986 Jun 24B

Wales see Wales

welfare and social services: homelessness 1988 Dec 28B; social welfare system 1981 Aug 5B; 1985 Jun 3B; 1988 Apr 11B/Apr 27B

Great Communicator (racehorse) 1988 Nov 5J

Great Compromise (1787) 1987 Jul 16F

Greatest Hits (Kenny Rogers) (recording) 1980 Dec 3J; 1981 Jan 7J

Greatest Hits on the Radio, Volumes I & II (Donna Summer) (recording) 1980 Jan 2J

Great Lakes 1982 Aug 17D; 1983 Oct 16D; 1986 Jul 25D; 1987 Oct 16D; 1989 Oct 11D

Great Lakes Water Quality Agreement (1978) 1987 Oct 16D

Great Plains Coal Gasification Project 1983 Mar 31H; 1985 Aug 1H

Great Rift (Idaho) 1985 Apr 26H

Great Rift of Cygnus (interstellar gas cloud) 1980 Jan 26I

Great Trek (Afrikaner holiday) 1988 Dec 16C

Great Wall (astronomy) 1989 Nov 17I

Great Wall (China) 1983 Feb 26I

Greece *see also individual leaders in the name index (e.g., Papandreou, Andreas)*
  accidents and disasters: earthquakes 1986 Sep 13B
  arts and culture: Elgin marbles 1983 May 13B; 1984 Apr 10J; Parthenon restoration 1983 Aug 31J; Philip II theater found 1982 Sep 1F
  church developments: Greek Orthodox Church 1987 Apr 3B
  crime and law enforcement: newspaper publisher murdered 1983 Mar 19B
  Cyprus *see* Cyprus
  defense and disarmament issues: 1985 Jan 28A
  demonstrations and protests: 1980 Nov 16B; 1985 Nov 17B; 1986 Apr 7B
  economy: budget issues 1989 Sep 21B; women 1982 Dec 1B
  foreign relations: Albania: 1985 Jan 12B; 1988 Apr 17B; Balkan nations conference: 1988 Feb 23B; Great Britain: 1983 May 13B; 1984 Apr 10J; Iran: 1980 Mar 20A; Iraq: 1984 Jun 24C/Aug 7C; Syria: 1986 Nov 01B; Turkey: 1981 Mar 21B; 1984 Mar 9B; 1987 Mar 28B/Apr 14B; 1988 Jan 31B; USSR: 1984 Jul 13A
  government and politics: cabinet sworn 1982 Jul 5B; Caramanlis elected president 1980 May 5B; elections 1989 Nov 5B; Grivas appointed caretaker premier 1989 Oct 11B; mayoral elections 1982 Oct 25B; Rallis selected premier 1980 May 8B; socialist governments meet 1983 Jan 23A; socialists win parliamentary elections 1981 Oct 18B; Tzannetakis becomes premier 1989 Jul 1B; Zolotas heads coalition government 1989 Nov 21B
  international organizations: European Community 1985 Mar 30B/Nov 18B; 1986 Nov 01B; NATO 1980 Oct 22B
  labor issues: workweek 1980 Nov 6B
  medicine and health care: abortion 1986 Jun 13B; Chernobyl radiation 1987 Mar 25I

oil and gas developments: 1985 Oct 3B; 1987 Mar 28B
  sports: basketball 1987 Jun 14J; human-powered flight 1988 Apr 23J; Olympic torch 1984 Mar 21J
  transportation issues: air traffic delays 1988 Jul 17B
  U.S. relations: 1983 May 20B/Sep 8A; 1984 Aug 20A; 1986 May 29J

Greek-Melkite sect 1980 May 6C

Greek Orthodox Church 1987 Apr 3B; 1989 Aug 3J

Green Bay Packers (football team) 1989 Jan 24J

Green Berets 1981 Mar 22G; 1982 Jan 9D; 1983 Jun 14D/Sep 12G; 1984 Mar 19D/Aug 20D/Sep 27D

Green Desire, A (Anton Myrer) (book) 1982 Apr 11J

Greenham Common air base (Berkshire, Britain) 1980 Jun 17B; 1982 Dec 12B; 1983 Jan 1B/Nov 14B/Nov 16B; 1984 Jan 1B/Apr 4B

greenhouse effect 1986 Nov 20I; 1988 Jun 23I; 1989 May 12I/Nov 7I

Greenland 1982 Feb 23B; 1984 Mar 13A; 1985 Feb 1B; 1987 May 26B

Greenpeace (environmental group) 1983 Jul 18A/Jul 22A
  Rainbow Warrior incident 1985 Jul 10E/Jul 23E/Aug 26B/Sep 20B/Sep 25B/Nov 4E/Dec 23B; 1986 Jul 7A; 1987 Oct 2B

Greens (environmental group)
  European Parliament: 1984 Mar 4B; 1989 Jun 18B
  Great Britain: 1989 Sep 24B
  Sweden: 1988 Sep 18B
  Switzerland: 1987 Oct 18B
  West Germany: 1980 Jan 13B; 1981 Mar 22B; 1983 Feb 20I/Mar 6B; 1984 Mar 4B; 1985 Oct 27B; 1986 Sep 28B/Oct 12B; 1987 Feb 9B/May 3B

Greensboro (North Carolina) 1983 Apr 21F; 1984 Apr 13F; 1987 Jun 7F

Greenwich Savings Bank 1981 Nov 4H

Gremlins (film) 1984 Jul 18J/Aug 15J

Grenada *see also individual leaders in the name index (e.g., Bishop, Maurice)*
  economy: Caricom restrictions ended 1983 Oct 30D
  government and politics: Austin assumes leadership 1983 Oct 20D; Blaize becomes prime minister 1984 Dec 3D; English-speaking federation 1987 May 31D; Gairy returns 1984 Jan 21D; interim government 1983 Oct 29D/Nov 9D/Nov 15D; militia members surrender 1983 Nov 2D
  U.S. relations: economic aid 1983 Nov 4G; Shultz visit 1984 Jan 31G

Grenada Invasion (1983)
  congressional actions: 1983 Oct 27G/Oct 31G/Nov 1G/Nov 8G/Nov 9G; 1984 Jun 21G
  foreign response: Cuba 1983 Nov 2D/Nov 4D/Nov 9D; France 1983 Oct 25B; Great Britain 1983 Oct 25B; North Korea 1983 Nov 4D; OAS 1983 Oct 26D/Nov 16D; UN 1983 Nov 2A; USSR 1983 Oct 25B/Nov 4D
  military operations: contingency plans 1983 Oct 23G; invasion launched 1983 Oct 25G-27G; treaty justification 1983 Oct 26G; casualties 1983 Oct 27G; 1985 Mar 17G; citizens airlifted 1983 Oct 28G; troops withdraw 1983 Oct 30G/Nov 2G/Nov 16G/Dec

15D; 1985 Feb 7D; secret commando units 1984 Jun 8G; female participation 1986 Jan 26G
  news coverage: 1983 Oct 27F/Oct 31F/Dec 15G; 1984 Feb 9F
  U.S. response: Capitol bombed 1983 Nov 7F

Grey Cup (football) 1986 Nov 30J; 1987 Nov 29J

Greyhound Lines Inc. 1983 Nov 3F/Nov 17F/Dec 3F/Dec 19H; 1985 Aug 15H; 1986 Nov 10H/Dec 23H; 1987 Jan 26H/Jul 2H

Greymac Trust Co. 1983 Jan 7D

Greystoke: The Legend of Tarzan, Lord of the Apes (film) 1984 Apr 11J

Grimm & Co. W.T. 1986 Mar 17H

gross national product (GNP)
  1980 statistics: 1980 Jan 18H/Jul 18H/Oct 17H
  1981 statistics: 1981 Apr 20H/Jul 22H/Oct 21H
  1982 statistics: 1982 Jan 20H/Apr 21H/Jul 21H/Oct 20H
  1983 statistics: 1983 Jan 19H/Apr 20H/Jul 21H/Oct 20H
  1984 statistics: 1984 Jan 20H/Apr 19H/Jul 23H/Sept 20H/Oct 19H/Dec 19H
  1985 statistics: 1985 Jan 22H/Apr 18H/Jul 18H/Oct 17H
  1986 statistics: 1986 Jan 22H/Apr 17H/May 20H/Jul 10H/Jul 22H/Aug 19H/Oct 22H/Dec 17H
  1987 statistics: 1987 Jan 22H/Mar 18H/Apr 23H/Jun 17H/Jul 24H/Aug 21H/Oct 23H
  1988 statistics: 1988 Jan 27H/Apr 26H/Jul 27H/Oct 26H/Dec 30H
  1989 statistics: 1989 Jan 29H/Mar 23H/Apr 26H/Jul 27H/Oct 26H

Group of 77 1983 Apr 5A

Group of Eight 1987 Nov 26D; 1988 Nov 29D

Group of Five 1985 Dec 4A; 1986 Jan 9A; 1987 Sep 11B

Group of Seven
  currency issues: 1987 Apr 9A; 1988 Apr 13A/Sep 24A; 1989 Feb 3A/Sep 23A
  economic growth: 1988 Dec 6A
  lending pool: 1987 Dec 29A
  summits: Bonn (West Germany) 1985 May 4A; Chateau Montebello (Canada) 1981 Jul 21A; London (Great Britain) 1984 Jun 7A; Paris (France) 1989 Jul 14A; Tokyo (Japan) 1986 May 6A; Toronto (Canada) 1988 Jun 19A; Venice (Italy) 1987 Jun 8A; Versailles (France) 1982 Jun 5B/Jun 6A; Williamsburg (Virginia) 1983 May 28A/May 30A

Group of Ten 1980 Sep 15A; 1984 Apr 5A; 1985 Jun 21A

Grove City College v. Bell (1984) 1988 Mar 16F/Mar 22F

Grove Press 1985 Mar 4J; 1986 Apr 10J

Growing Up (Russell Baker) 1983 Apr 18J

Grumman Corp. 1981 Jan 24H/Sep 23H/Sep 24H/Oct 28H/Nov 16H

Grundig AG 1982 Nov 19B

GSA *see* General Services Administration, U.S.

GT&E *see* General Telephone and Electronics

GTE Spacenet Corp. 1985 May 6I

Guadeloupe 1980 Nov 16D; 1981 Jan 4B/Jan 30B; 1989 Sep 19D

Guadeloupe Liberation Army 1981 Jan 4B/Jan 30B

Guardian (British newspaper) 1984 Mar 23B

Guatemala *see also individual leaders in the name index (e.g., Rios Montt, Efrain)*
  archaeology: Mayan tomb discovered 1984 May 15I
  Central American peace accord *see* Central American peace accord
  church developments: papal visit 1983 Mar 2D
  civil strife: AID workers killed 1983 Nov 12D; American priest killed 1981 Jul 28D; civil war escalation 1981 Sep 3D; Honduran president's daughter kidnapped 1982 Dec 14D; National Palace bombing 1980 Sep 5D; Red Cross bombing 1989 Dec 27D; repression increased 1981 May 3D; Spanish embassy occupation 1980 Jan 31D/Feb 1A
  coups and coup attempts: air force officers attempt fails 1989 May 9D; army officers attempt fails 1988 May 11D; Garcia overthrown 1982 Mar 23D; Rios Montt overthrown 1983 Aug 7D
  economy: bus fare, food price protests 1985 Aug 29D
  foreign relations: Central America 1983 Apr 21D/Jul 30D/Oct 1D/Oct 5D; 1987 Oct 2D; Cuba 1989 Dec 25D; Great Britain 1981 Mar 11A/Sep 7D; 1986 Aug 19A/Dec 29A; Mexico 1982 Feb 19D; 1984 May 30D; Nicaraguan contras 1984 Sep 8D
  government and politics: amnesty 1983 Aug 13D; 1987 Oct 28G; assembly elections 1984 Jul 2D/Jul 8D; Cerezo Arevalo elected president 1985 Dec 8D; constitution suspended 1982 Mar 24D; elections annulled 1982 Mar 25D; Guevara elected president 1982 Mar 7D; presidential elections 1985 Nov 3D; vice president resigns 1980 Sep 2D
  human rights: 1981 Feb 17D/Oct 15D; 1982 May 24D; 1983 Dec 9A; 1984 Nov 1D; 1987 May 10D; 1988 Aug 4D/Nov 25D; 1989 Mar 30D/Jun 14D
  immigration and refugees: 1982 Feb 19D; 1984 May 30D
  international organizations: Contadora Group 1984 Nov 8D; 1986 Jan 14D/May 25D; IMF 1983 Sep 1D; United Nations 1983 Dec 9A
  peace initiatives: 1987 Oct 7D/Oct 9D/Oct 28G
  U.S. relations: 1983 Jan 7D/May 25G/Jun 12D/Aug 8G/Oct 9D/Nov 12D; 1986 May 1F

Guildford Four 1989 Jan 16B/Oct 19B

Guilty (Barbra Streisand) (recording) 1980 Oct 8J/Dec 3J; 1981 Jan 7J

Guinea 1982 May 10C; 1983 Dec 21I; 1984 Mar 27C/Apr 3C; 1985 Jul 4C

Gulch (racehorse) 1988 Nov 5J

Gulf Canada Ltd. 1982 Apr 30D; 1985 Dec 30D

Gulf Canada Resources Inc. 1983 Jan 20D

Gulf Cooperation Council 1983 Nov 9C; 1984 May 25A; 1988 Jan 9C

Gulf of Maine 1984 Oct 12D

Gulf of Mexico 1982 Aug 15I

Gulf Oil Corp. 1982 Jun 17H/Aug 6H; 1983 Aug 20B; 1984 Mar 5H/Apr 26H

gum disease 1986 Jan 15F

Gun Control Act of 1968 1985 Jul 9F; 1986 Apr 10F/May 19F

Gung Ho! (film) 1986 Mar 19F

Guns N' Roses (singing group) 1988 Jul 16J/Aug 27J/Sep 24J/Dec 31J; 1989 Jan 29J/Feb 25J/Mar 25J/Apr 29J/May 27J

Gurkha National Liberation Front 1988 Aug 6E

Gurkhas 1986 Aug 5E; 1988 Aug 6E

gurus, religious 1983 Oct 6F; 1985 Sep 16J/Nov 14F; 1986 Feb 17J/Jul 22J

Guttmacher Institute, Alan 1985 Mar 12F; 1989 May 2F

Guyana 1980 Apr 8D/Oct 6D/Dec 15D; 1982 Jun 18D/Oct 13D; 1984 Jul 5A/Aug 11D; 1985 Aug 6D/Dec 11D; 1988 Jul 11A

gymnastics 1980 Jul 25J/Jul 31J; 1981 Jan 13J/May 31J; 1985 Jan 8J/Nov 10J; 1989 Nov 29J

Gypsies 1980 Apr 4B; 1986 Feb 15B

Gypsy (musical) 1989 Nov 16J

H

habeas corpus, writs of 1981 Feb 16D; 1983 Oct 5F; 1984 Feb 6F

Habitations of the Word (William Gass) (book) 1986 Feb 17J

Habsburg dynasty 1989 Apr 1B

Haida Indians (Canada) 1987 Jul 11D

Hairspray (film) 1988 Feb 26J

Haiti *see also individual leaders in name index (e.g., Duvalier, Jean-Claude)*
  accidents and disasters: refugee boat capsizes 1981 Oct 26D
  church developments: Aristide expelled from Salesian order 1988 Dec 15D; church congregation attacked 1988 Sep 11D; papal visit 1983 Mar 2D
  crime and law enforcement: battalion commander dies 1988 Nov 6C; secret police head sentenced 1986 Jul 16D
  economy: budget deficit 1989 Nov 28D; foreign debt 1989 Nov 28D
  foreign relations: Bahamas 1981 Feb 16D; Dominican Republic 1986 Feb 1D; France 1987 Dec 31B
  government and politics: Duvalier flees 1986 Feb 7D; presidential elections 1986 Jun 7D; 1987 Nov 2D; constitution approved 1987 Mar 29D; election called off 1987 Nov 29D; national elections 1987 Dec 9D; Manigat wins presidential election 1988 Jan 17D; Manigat sworn 1988 Feb 7D; Celestin chosen premier 1988 Feb 9D; Manigat ousted 1988 Jun 20D; Namphy ousted 1988 Sep 17D; Avril named president 1988 Sep 17D; elections announced 1989 Sep 24D
  human rights: Amnesty charges abuses 1985 Mar 12D; Avril abuses charged 1989 Sep 17D; church congregation attacked 1988 Sep 11D; Duvalier abuses 1986 Feb 26D; opposition arrests 1980 Nov 30D; politicians assassinated 1987 Aug 2D/Oct 13D; post-Duvalier abuses charged 1986

Oct 7D; press members detained 1980 Nov 28D; protesters killed 1987 Jul 29D
immigration and refugees: Belize OKs resettlement 1982 Mar 28D
U.S. relations
aid: 1984 May 14G; 1985 Nov 12D; 1986 Feb 26G; 1987 Nov 29G; 1989 Aug 3G
AIDS: 1983 Mar 3I
refugees: record numbers 1980 Apr 13D; political asylum 1980 May 7F/Jul 2F; Carter clarifies policy 1980 Jun 20F; education for children 1980 Oct 10F; transfer to Puerto Rico 1980 Oct 24F/Nov 3F; expulsion hearings 1981 Jan 30F; government spending 1981 Feb 5F; boat capsizes 1981 Oct 26D; detention camps 1981 Dec 27F; 1982 Jun 29F/Oct 22F; release ordered 1982 Aug 2F; detention policy assailed 1983 Apr 12G; Army officers leave 1989 Jul 22D

Haj, The (Leon Uris) (book) 1984 May 11J/Jun 15J

Haleakala National Park (Hawaii) 1987 Aug 19H

Halley's Comet 1984 Dec 15I; 1985 Jul 2I; 1986 Mar 6I/May 15I

Hall & Oates (singing group) 1983 Jan 5J/Feb 9J

Halloween (holiday) 1982 Oct 31I

Halloween II (film) 1981 Nov 4J

halon gas 1989 May 2I

Hamburg, University of (West Germany) 1986 Oct 21I

Hamburg Savings Bank (Brooklyn, N.Y.) 1985 Dec 31H

Hamersley Iron Ltd. 1987 Jun 30E

Hamilton Tiger-Cats (football) 1986 Nov 30J

Hand, The (film) 1981 May 6J

Handelskreditbank AG 1980 Jul 27B

handguns 1989 Nov 21F

handicapped *see* disabled persons

handkerchiefs 1988 Nov 10H

Handmaid's Tale, The (Margaret Atwood) (book) 1986 Mar 28J

Hands Across America (benefit event) 1986 May 25F/Sep 12F

Hanford Nuclear Reservation (Richland, Wash.) 1986 Oct 8H/Oct 24H/Dec 12H; 1988 Feb 16H/May 15H

hang gliders 1987 Nov 25C

Hangin' Tough (New Kids on the Block) (recording) 1989 Jul 29J/Aug 26J/Sep 30J

Hannah and Her Sisters (film) 1986 Feb 7J/Mar 19F; 1987 Jan 31J/Mar 30J

Hanukkah menorah 1989 Jul 3F

Happy Birthday to Me (film) 1981 May 20J

harbors 1986 Nov 17H; 1988 Aug 19H

Harcourt Brace Jovanovich Inc. 1984 Feb 8J

Hardline According to Terence Trent D'Arby, The (Terence Trent D'Arby) (recording) 1988 May 21J

Harlem Nights (film) 1989 Nov 29J

Harley-Davidson 1983 Apr 1H

"harmonic convergence" 1987 Aug 16J

Harper's (magazine) 1980 Jun 17J/Jul 9J

Harris Trust & Savings Bank of Chicago 1989 Jan 10F

Harrods (London department store) 1983 Dec 17B

Harry S Truman Library (Independence, Mo.) 1983 Mar 7F

Hartford Courant (newspaper) 1984 Oct 28F

Hartford Fire Insurance Co. 1988 Mar 22H

Hartford Whalers (ice hockey team) 1982 Feb 19J

Hart to Hart (TV show) 1983 Jun 12J

Hart Trophy (ice hockey) 1980 Jun 6J; 1988 Jun 8J; 1989 Jun 7J

Harvard-Smithsonian Center for Astrophysics 1986 Jan 12I

Harvard University (Cambridge, Mass.)
appointments: overseer board election 1989 Jun 8F
awards and honors
Lasker Award: Leder 1987 Sep 21I
Nobel Prize: Benacerraf 1980 Oct 10I; Bloembergen 1981 Oct 19I; Gilbert 1980 Oct 14I; Hubel/Wiesel 1981 Oct 9I
endowments, gifts and grants: anniversary celebration 1986 Sep 3F; business ethics program 1987 Mar 30F
minority issues: racial bias course boycott 1982 Aug 27F
people: Estrich named Dukakis campaign manager 1987 Oct 8F
research
arts and culture: Bach preludes found 1984 Dec 19J
medicine and science: Alzheimer's disease 1984 Aug 31I; artificial heart technology 1984 Nov 27I; birth-control pills 1989 Sep 6I; cancer 1986 Jan 9I; 1989 Sep 6I; education reform 1984 Apr 19F; exercise 1986 Jan 9I/Mar 6I; Medicare fee changes 1988 Sep 28F; poverty study 1986 May 21F; recombinant DNA experiments 1982 Dec 30I; saccharin 1980 Mar 6I; sponsorship guidelines 1983 May 20F
sports: ice hockey 1986 Mar 29J; 1989 Apr 1J; rowing 1985 Jul 7J; 1988 Jun 11J

Harvey Milk High School (New York City) 1985 Jun 6F

Hasbro Industries 1984 May 7H

hashish 1988 Jan 13F; 1989 Mar 1G

Hatch Act (1939) 1987 Nov 17F; 1989 Apr 17H

Haunted Mesa, The (Louis L'Amour) (book) 1987 May 29J/Jun 26J

hazardous wastes *see also specific kinds of waste* (e.g., sewage)
cleanup and disposal issues: 1980 Feb 19H; 1983 Jun 8H/Jul 21H/Aug 10H; 1985 Jun 13H; 1988 Feb 26H/May 31H; 1989 Mar 22A
foreign developments: Africa 1988 Aug 1C; Canada 1985 Feb 5D; 1986 Jul 19D/Jul 25D; Europe 1987 Nov 25B
health and safety issues: chemical plant emissions 1985 Mar 26H; ground water supply leaks 1985 Apr 28H; improper disposal 1980 Feb 19H; radioactive waste dumping 1981 Jan 31H; sewer system dumping 1983 May 23H; 1985 Aug 26H; 1988 Jan 28H; violations by dumps 1983 Oct 5H
legal remedies: export control treaty 1989 Mar 22A; indictments 1982 Sep 2H; 1983 May 23H; 1988 Jan

28H; lawsuits 1984 Apr 25H/Jun 8H; regulations 1984 Jul 25H/Nov 8H
Love Canal (Niagara Falls): 1980 Apr 28H/May 21H; 1981 Jun 11H; 1982 Jul 14H; 1987 Nov 26H
Times Beach (Missouri): 1982 Dec 23I; 1983 Jan 12H/Feb 22H/Jun 4H; 1985 Apr 10H

HDTV *see* high-definition television

Head Start 1984 Oct 30F; 1986 Sep 18F; 1989 Nov 9F

Health, Education and Welfare, U.S. Department of (HEW) 1980 May 4F; 1982 Sep 16F

Health and Human Services, U.S. Department of (HHS) *see also individual agency heads in the name index* (e.g., Heckler, Margaret)
appointments and resignations: Bowen, Otis R. 1985 Nov 7F; Heckler, Margaret 1983 Jan 12F; 1985 Jan 12F; Schweiker, Richard 1980 Dec 11F; 1983 Jan 12F; Sullivan, Louis W. 1988 Dec 22F
benefits issue: disability benefits suit 1986 Jun 2F; Medicare reimbursement policy 1988 Nov 1F
budget and spending programs: 1982 Jul 26H; 1983 Oct 20F; 1984 Oct 10F; 1986 Jul 29F; 1988 Nov 18F; 1989 Oct 19F
creation: 1980 May 4F
family issues: abortion 1987 Aug 29F; 1988 Jan 29F; 1989 Dec 16F; birth control 1983 Feb 18F
health care issues: AIDS 1985 Mar 2F; hospital death/discharge rates 1986 Mar 12F; Medicare home dialysis coverage 1988 Nov 30F; Medicare reimbursement policy 1988 Nov 1F; nursing homes 1988 Dec 1F; tobacco 1986 Nov 20H
statistics: death rate 1983 Jan 6I

health care *see also health care professionals* (e.g., physicians); *specific diseases* (e.g., cancer)
costs and fees 1982 Jul 26H; 1983 Jan 21F; 1984 Jun 7F/Oct 10F; 1986 Jul 29F; 1988 Nov 18F
coverage: comprehensive plan proposed 1989 Jan 30F; Massachusetts universal coverage bill 1988 Apr 21F

Health Consequences of Smoking, The: Cardiovascular Disease (surgeon general's report) 1983 Nov 17H

Health Foundation, American *see* American Health Foundation

health insurance 1983 Jun 20F/Aug 3F/Dec 12D; 1984 Feb 1E; 1985 Feb 15F/Jun 3F; 1986 Jun 20D; 1988 Apr 21F; 1989 Jan 30F

health maintenance organizations (HMOs) 1984 Dec 15F; 1986 Aug 20F/Dec 11H; 1988 Dec 15F

"Heard on the Street" (Wall Street Journal column) 1984 May 19H

Heart (Heart) (recording) 1985 Nov 30J/Dec 21J; 1986 Feb 19J/Mar 22J/Apr 16J

Heart (singing group) 1985 Nov 30J/Dec 21J; 1986 Feb 19J/Mar 22J/Apr 16J; 1987 Jul 22J/Sep 19J

Heart Association, American *see* American Heart Association

heart attacks 1985 Dec 10I; 1987 Jun 18I/Sep 1I/Nov 13I; 1988 Jan 26I/Aug 13I; 1989 Mar 9I/Mar 30I/Jul 20I; *see also specific treatments* (e.g., heart transplants)

Heartbeat City (The Cars) (recording) 1984 Jun 16J/Jul 21J/Aug 25J/Sep 22J

Heartbreak Ridge (film) 1986 Dec 24J

Heartburn (Nora Ephron) (book/film) 1983 Jun 1J/Jun 12J/Jul 10J; 1986 Jul 25J/Aug 20J

heart disease 1986 Nov 28I; 1987 Mar 29F/Oct 5I; 1988 Aug 11I; 1989 Nov 3J/Nov 14I

heart transplants 1984 Feb 14I/Feb 21I/Nov 15I; 1985 Nov 20I; 1986 May 6I/Jun 10I/Dec 17I; 1987 Oct 16I; 1989 Dec 3I

heart valves 1985 Nov 13I

Heathrow Airport (London) 1983 Nov 26B

heating gas 1987 Jul 20B

heating oil 1980 Oct 3H; 1989 Dec 24H

Heaven and Hell (John Jakes) (book) 1987 Oct 23J/Nov 20J

Heavens and the Earth, the: A Political History of the Space Age (Walter A. McDougall) (book) 1986 Apr 17J

Heaven's Gate (film) 1980 Nov 19J; 1981 Apr 24J

heavy water 1983 Aug 3D; 1988 May 4I

Hebrew University (Jerusalem) 1982 Dec 12I

Hebron University (West Bank) 1983 Jan 20C

Hehai University (China) 1988 Dec 27E

Heidi Chronicles, The (Wendy Wasserstein) (play) 1989 Mar 9J/Mar 30J/Jun 4J

Heileman Brewing Co., G. 1981 Oct 22H

Heiress (Janet Dailey) (book) 1987 Jun 26J

Heisman Trophy (football)
Allen, Marcus: 1981 Dec 5J
Brown, Tim: 1987 Dec 5J
Flutie, Doug: 1984 Dec 1J
Jackson, Bo: 1985 Dec 7J
Rozier, Mike: 1983 Dec 3J
Sanders, Barry: 1988 Dec 3J
Testaverde, Vinny: 1986 Dec 6J
Walker, Herschel: 1982 Dec 4J
Ware, Andre: 1989 Dec 2J

helicopters 1986 Jul 1G; 1987 May 29J

helium 1980 Jan 20I

Hello Again (film) 1987 Nov 11J

Hell's Angels (motorcycle club) 1980 Aug 18F

Hells Angels Forever (film) 1983 Dec 7J

Helsinki accords 1985 Jul 30A/Dec 3G

Helsinki Conference on European Security and Cooperation (1975) 1985 Jul 30A

Helsinki Final Act (1975) 1986 Nov 4B; 1989 Jan 15B

Helsinki Watch 1984 Dec 17A; 1986 Jun 20B

Hemispheric Affairs, Council on *see* Council on Hemispheric Affairs

hemophiliacs 1980 Aug 30I; 1987 Aug 28F

Henry James: A Life (Leon Edel) (book) 1986 Feb 17J

Henry V (film) 1989 Nov 8J

hepatitis 1981 Nov 16I; 1984 Dec 13I; 1986 Jul 23I/Aug 26I; 1988 Mar 21I/Jun 3I

heptachlor (insecticide) 1987 Aug 11H

Heptavax-B (vaccine) 1981 Nov 16I

Herald of Free Enterprise (ship) 1987 Mar 6B/Apr 8B/Jul 24B/Oct 8B; 1989 Jun 22B

Herald & Weekly Times Ltd. 1986 Dec 3E

Hercules (aircraft) 1989 Nov 27C

Hercules (film) 1983 Sep 7J

Heretics of Dune (Frank Herbert) (book) 1984 Apr 20J/May 11J

Heritage USA (evangelical theme park) 1987 May 26J; 1988 Apr 22H

Hermes (European space shuttle) 1987 Nov 10I

Hero and the Crown, The (Robin McKinley) (book) 1985 Jan 7J

heroin 1980 Feb 2I; 1981 Feb 14F/Feb 15F; 1982 Feb 22F/Aug 25E/Nov 24B; 1983 Mar 18J; 1984 Apr 9F; 1986 Mar 28F/Jul 6E/Aug 29F; 1988 May 16I/Nov 16I

herpes, genital 1982 Mar 30I; 1985 Jan 29I; 1986 Jun 11I; 1989 Jun 28I

herrings 1989 Nov 6D

Hertz Corp. 1984 Nov 25F

He's the D.J., I'm the Rapper (D.J. Jazzy Jeff & the Fresh Prince) (recording) 1988 Aug 27J/Sep 24J

Heublein Inc. 1982 Jul 29H

HEW *see* Health, Education and Welfare, U.S. Department of

Hewlett-Packard Corp. 1983 Mar 27J; 1988 Mar 17H

Hey, Al (Richard Egielski) (book) 1987 Jan 19J

Heysel Stadium (Brussels) 1985 May 29B; 1986 Sep 9B; 1987 Sep 9B; 1989 Apr 28B

HHS *see* Health and Human Services, U.S. Department of

Hibernia oil field (Atlantic Ocean) 1982 Feb 15D; 1988 Jul 18D

Hidden, The (film) 1987 Nov 11J

high-definition television (HDTV) 1988 Sep 1H; 1989 Jan 12I

High Energy Astronomical Observatory 1980 Jan 26I/Mar 20I

Higher Education, American Council on *see* American Council on Higher Education

Higher Education Act of 1965 1986 Jun 3F/Sep 25F

Higher Education Amendment of 1986 1986 Oct 17H

Higher Love (Steve Winwood) (recording) 1987 Feb 24J

high jump 1981 Feb 28J; 1985 Aug 11J; 1987 Jun 30J; 1989 Jul 29J

High Scope Educational Foundation 1984 Aug 11F

highways
budget and spending programs: 1982 Dec 7H; 1985 Mar 13H; 1986 Sep 24H; 1987 Jan 21H/Apr 2H
construction projects: California Route 1 reopened 1984 Apr 11J; Westway project 1981 Mar 14H/Sep 7F
federal aid: 1984 Jun 7F/Jul 17H; 1987 Jun 23F
foreign developments: Afghanistan 1980 Feb 23E; Albania 1985 Jan 12B; Brazil 1989 Mar 3A; Greece 1985 Jan 12B; Japan 1989 Mar 3A; Pakistan 1980 Feb 23E
safety issues: traffic fatalities 1987 Dec 17H; vehicle-inspection programs 1980 Dec 11H

Hi Infidelity (Reo Speedwagon) (recording) 1981 Feb 11J/Mar 4J/Apr 8J/May 6J/May 27J/Jul 8J/Aug 5J

hijackings

Achille Lauro: 1985 Oct 9C/Oct 10C
Air Afrique airliner: 1987 Jul 24B
Air India airliner: 1981 Dec 2C
Burma airliner: 1989 Oct 7E
buses: 1984 May 28C/Jun 1C; 1987 Jul 7E
Chinese plane: 1983 May 8E/Aug 18E
death penalty authorized: 1984 Feb 22F
Egyptian airliner: 1985 Nov 24C
Garuda Airlines: 1981 Mar 28E/Mar 31E
Iraqi Airways airliner: 1986 Dec 25C
Jordanian airliner: 1985 Jun 11C; 1987 Sep 17G; 1989 Mar 14G/Oct 4A
Kuwait Airways airliner: 1988 Apr 5C/Apr 8C/Apr 13C/Apr 20C
Pakistani airliner: 1981 Mar 12E
Pan Am jumbo jet: 1986 Sep 5E
patrol boat: 1981 Aug 14C
Soviet plane: 1988 Dec 2C
Taiwanese cargo plane: 1986 May 20E
Thailand airliner: 1982 Jul 1E
TWA airliner: 1985 Jun 14A/Jun 15C-16C/Jun 26C/Jun 30C/Jul 15B/Oct 17G; 1987 Jan 15A; 1988 Aug 9B; 1989 May 17B
Venezuela airliner: 1980 Dec 5D/Dec 6D

Hill Street Blues (TV show) 1981 Sep 13J; 1983 Sep 25J; 1984 Sep 24J

Himalayas 1983 Jul 18E; 1988 Aug 21I; 1989 Apr 20I

Hiroshima (Japan) 1981 Aug 6I; 1982 Mar 22E; 1985 Aug 6A

Hispanic Americans *see also* Cuban-Americans; Mexican-Americans
census data: population 1981 Feb 23F; 1987 Sep 10F
civil disorders: Lawrence (Mass.) 1984 Aug 9F; Miami (Fla.) 1984 Aug 9F; 1989 Jan 16F
education: college enrollment 1985 May 29F; high school dropout rate 1989 Sep 14F; public schools segregation 1982 Sep 5F; SAT scores 1985 Sep 23F
health care: AIDS 1986 Oct 23I
immigration and refugee issues: reform bill 1983 Oct 4F
labor issues: job bias 1988 Sep 30F; 1989 May 5F/Sep 21F
politics and government: Chicago council elections 1985 Dec 30F; 1986 Mar 18F; Los Angeles council redistricting 1986 Sep 22F; New York primary runoffs 1985 Aug 13F; Reagan record deplored 1983 Jun 24F

history and historiography
intelligence issues: Soviet historian sentenced 1981 Dec 8B; U.S. document theft 1987 Aug 18J; WWII German source revealed 1983 Sep 28A
obituaries: Braudel, Fernand 1985 Nov 28J; Butterfield, Lyman Henry 1982 Apr 25J; Cecil, David 1986 Jan 1J; Clark, Kenneth 1983 May 21J; Dangerfield, George 1986 Dec 27J; Durant, Ariel 1981 Oct 25J; Durant, Will 1981 Nov 8J; Eliade, Mircea 1986 Apr 22J; Finley, M.I. 1986 Jun 23J; Foucault, Michel 1984 Jun 25J; Moorehead, Alan 1983 Sep 29J; Redding, J. Saunders 1988 Mar 2F; Roud, Richard 1989 Jan 15J; Tuchman, Barbara Wertheim 1989 Feb 6J
publications: Anne Frank diary 1986 May 14J

research findings: Columbus landing site 1986 Oct 6J; Taiwan, Peking scholars debate 1982 Apr 2E

Hitachi Ltd. 1983 Jun 27H/Oct 6H/Nov 9H/Dec 21H

Hizballah (Party of God) 1983 Oct 26C; 1984 Oct 4G; 1985 Mar 8C; 1988 May 11C; 1989 Dec 7C

HMOs *see* health maintenance organizations

Hoare Govett PLC 1986 Oct 8B

hockey *see* field hockey; ice hockey

Hoffmann-La Roche Inc. 1983 Jun 4B/Jul 25I; 1988 May 26I

Hold Out (Jackson Browne) (recording) 1980 Aug 13J/Sep 10J

Hold the Dream (Barbara Taylor Bradford) (book) 1985 Jun 14J/Jul 19J

Hollywood Husbands (Jackie Collins) (book) 1986 Oct 31J/Nov 21J/Dec 26J

Hollywood Knights, The (film) 1980 May 28J

Hollywood Wives (Jackie Collins) (book) 1983 Sep 11J/Oct 16J/Nov 13J

Hollywood Women's Political Committee 1986 Sep 6J

Holocaust 1981 Apr 30G; 1985 Feb 28D/May 5B; 1987 Sep 1J; 1989 Dec 15B

Homeless Assistance Act (1988) 1988 Nov 7F

homelessness 1981 Nov 26F; 1984 May 1F/Sep 12F; 1985 Aug 19F; 1986 Jan 21F/Mar 16F/May 25F; 1987 Feb 4F/Mar 3F/Jun 15F/Dec 23F; 1988 Jan 19F/Dec 28B; 1989 Feb 9F

Homestake Mining Co. 1980 Aug 27H; 1982 Jan 26F

homosexuality
AIDS *see* AIDS
demonstrations and protests: 1987 Oct 13F; 1989 Dec 10F
educational issues: 1982 Feb 4F; 1985 Mar 26F/Jun 6F; 1987 Nov 20F
family issues: domestic partnerships 1989 Jul 5F
foreign developments: Australia 1984 Aug 2E; Canada 1985 Jun 19D; 1988 Aug 24J; Ireland 1988 Oct 26B
health issues: bath houses 1984 Apr 9I; hepatitis B 1984 Dec 13I
military issues: 1980 Aug 21G/Nov 24G/Dec 1G; 1984 Aug 17G; 1988 Feb 10G; 1989 May 3G/Oct 21G
obituaries: Genet, Jean 1986 Apr 15J; Isherwood, Christopher 1986 Jan 4J; Rustin, Bayard 1987 Aug 24F
people: Flynn, Errol 1980 Aug 1J; Frank, Barney 1987 May 29F; King, Billie Jean 1981 May 1J
polls and surveys: Kinsey study 1981 Aug 22I
religious issues: 1983 May 13J; 1984 May 10J; 1986 Aug 18J; 1988 May 2J; 1989 Dec 10F
rights issues: 1985 Jan 17F/Jan 19F/Mar 26F; 1986 Mar 11F/Mar 20F; 1987 Nov 20F
sports: 1987 Jun 25F

Honda Motor Co. 1980 Jan 11H; 1986 Mar 17H

Honda of America Manufacturing Inc. 1988 Mar 23H

Honduras *see also individual leaders in name index (e.g., Suazo Cordova, Roberto)*
airplane crashes: cargo plane shot down 1987 Mar 9D; Honduran jetliner 1989 Oct 21D; U.S. helicopters 1984 Jan 11D/Apr 18D
Central American peace accord *see* Central American peace accord
church developments: papal visit 1983 Mar 2D
civil strife: human rights worker killed 1988 Jan 14D; San Pedro Sula siege 1982 Sep 17D/Sep 25D; U.S. soldiers are wounded 1988 Jul 17D
defense and armed forces: commander of armed forces resigns 1984 Mar 31D
foreign relations: Central America 1983 Apr 21D/Jul 30D/Oct 1D/Oct 5D; 1987 Oct 2D; 1989 Feb 14D/Aug 7D; Contadora Group 1984 Nov 8D/Nov 20D; 1985 Feb 14D; 1986 Jan 14D/May 25D; El Salvador 1983 Feb 22G/May 27G/Jun 14D; 1984 Sep 27D
government and politics: Azcona Hoyo elected president 1985 Dec 23D; Callejas claims victory in election 1989 Nov 27D; elections for Constitutional Assembly 1980 Apr 20D; military hands over government 1980 Jul 20D; presidential elections 1985 Nov 25D; Suazo Cordova elected president 1981 Nov 29D
human rights: 1984 Feb 9G; 1988 Jul 29D/Aug 4D; 1989 Jul 21D
Nicaraguan conflict: bishop expelled from Nicaragua 1986 Jul 4D; border opened 1987 Sep 26D; border tensions 1981 May 6D; 1982 Apr 4D; 1983 Mar 23D/Mar 29A/Jun 3D/Oct 1D; 1984 Mar 9D; 1988 Mar 16D; refugee camp raided 1985 Aug 29D; trade debt 1983 Jul 29D
Nicaraguan contras: 1983 Jul 20D; 1985 Jan 9D/Jan 22D/May 15D/Oct 14D; 1988 Apr 19D; 1989 Feb 14D/Aug 7D
press and broadcasting: U.S. journalists killed 1983 Jun 21D
U.S. relations: air bases 1982 Mar 3G; ambassador arrives 1986 Nov 3D; Boland charges violation of law 1983 Apr 13G; Contra aid 1988 Apr 19D; intervention favored if threat from Cuba 1982 Apr 1D; jet fighter sales 1986 Oct 1G; 1987 May 12H/Jun 4G; Kissinger commission visits 1983 Oct 9D; military agreement negotiations 1988 Oct 19D; military aid requests 1983 Jun 9D; military exercises 1983 Jul 20G/Jul 25G; 1984 Mar 19D/Aug 20D; military training 1983 May 27G/Jun 14D; 1984 Jun 24D/Sep 27D; presence said to protect contras 1983 Jul 20D; troops sent to 1988 Mar 24G; troop withdrawals 1988 Mar 23G/Mar 28D; Weinberger visits 1983 Sep 6D

Honey, I Shrunk the Kids (film) 1989 Jun 28J/Jul 26J/Dec 28J

Honeydrippers (singing group) 1984 Nov 24J

Honeymooners, The (TV show) 1985 Jan 26I

Hong Kong (British colony)
economy: stock market 1987 Oct 30A; 1988 Jun 2E; taxi strike 1984 Jan 13E
government and politics: elections favored 1987 Nov 4E; electoral reforms proposed 1988 Feb 10E; legislative elections 1988 Sep 22E; Wilson named governor 1987 Jan 16E
immigration and refugee issues: Vietnamese "boat people" 1989 Jun 13A/Sep 2E/Oct 24A/Dec 12E
press and censorship: China jails editor 1983 May 15E; China dismisses editor 1989 Jul 15E
sovereignty issue: Basic Law draft released 1988 Apr 28E; China status seen 1982 Nov 20E; 1983 Oct 6A; China troop role affirmed 1984 May 25E; Ji visits 1985 Dec 22E; UK administrative role to end 1984 Apr 20A; UK-China accord 1984 Aug 1E/Sep 26E/Dec 19A; 1985 May 27E; UK-China talks 1982 Sep 24A; 1983 Jul 13A; 1984 Mar 14E; 1989 Sep 27E; UK limited citizenship offer 1989 Dec 20E; UK state minister visits 1989 Jul 4E
U.S. relations: 1983 Jan 30E; 1984 Jul 7G; 1988 Jan 29G

Hong Kong Futures Exchange 1988 Jun 2E

Hong Kong Stock Exchange 1988 Jun 2E

Honig v. Doe (1988) 1988 Jan 20F

Honorable Men: My Life in the CIA (William Colby) (book) 1981 Dec 31G

Hooked on Classics (Royal Philharmonic Orchestra) (recording) 1981 Dec 9J; 1982 Jan 20J/Feb 24J/Mar 17J

Hooker Chemical Co. 1980 Apr 28H

Hoover Dam (Colorado) 1984 Aug 17H

Hope and Glory (film) 1987 Oct 16J; 1988 Jan 3J/Jan 23J

Hopi Indians 1981 Apr 18F

Hopscotch (film) 1980 Oct 1J/Dec 3J

Horizon 2000 (space program) 1988 Dec 15I

Hormel & Co., Geo. A. 1986 Feb 8H/Sep 12H

hormones 1988 Dec 10B; 1989 Jan 1B/Feb 18B/Aug 3I

horses 1984 Sep 24I

hospice care 1983 Aug 17F

hospitals
abortion *see* abortion
antitrust issues: 1984 Mar 27F
costs and fees: 1983 Aug 11H/Dec 22H
death/discharge rates: 1986 Mar 12F
disabled care: critically ill patient "dumping" 1985 Dec 14F; handicapped infants 1983 Apr 14F/Nov 2F/Nov 16F; 1984 Jan 9F; 1986 Jun 9F; mentally ill homeless 1988 Jan 19F
foreign developments: Australia 1984 Jun 20E; Canada 1983 Dec 12D; El Salvador 1985 Jun 2D; Great Britain 1989 Jan 31B; Israel 1983 May 22C/May 25C; Israeli occupied territories 1988 Feb 11C
medical personnel: nursing shortage 1988 Dec 12F; surgeon antitrust award 1988 May 16H
Medicare: 1984 Aug 26F/Nov 13F/Dec 12F; 1988 Nov 1F

Hotel (TV show) 1984 Oct 21J

Hotel and Motel Trades Council 1985 Jun 27H

Hotel Employees and Restaurant Employees International Union 1984 Aug 27H

Hotel New Hampshire, The (John Irving) (book) 1981 Oct 4J/Nov 8J/Nov 8J/Dec 6J; 1982 Jan 10J/Feb 7J

"hot line" 1984 Jul 17A

Hot Money (Dick Francis) (book) 1988 Mar 25J/Apr 29J

household income 1986 Aug 5H; 1987 Jun 28H; 1988 Dec 27F

House of Blue Leaves, The (John Guare) (play) 1986 Mar 19J/Jun 1J

House of Islamic Funds 1981 Jun 11J

House of Representatives, U.S.
Administration, Committee on: 1985 May 1F
Aging, Select Committee on: 1984 Dec 6F
Appropriations, Committee on: 1983 Jan 6G/May 17G/Aug 8G/Oct 6G; 1985 Mar 20G; 1987 Mar 25G
Armed Services, Committee on the: 1980 Mar 6G/Mar 11G; 1981 Oct 5G/Oct 6G; 1983 May 3G/Dec 19G; 1985 Jan 4G/May 16G/Oct 6G; 1987 Dec 20G
Arms Control and Foreign Policy Caucus: 1985 Feb 12G
Banking, Finance and Urban Affairs, Committee on: 1983 Apr 12H; 1988 Jul 7H; 1989 Jan 10H/Oct 17H/Oct 31H
Budget, Committee on the: 1981 Apr 9H; 1982 Mar 4G/May 13H; 1983 Jan 5F; 1985 Jan 4F; 1987 Mar 19H/Apr 1H
Children, Youth and Families, Select Committee on: 1986 Feb 9F
Democratic Caucus: 1985 Jan 4G; 1988 Dec 5F
Education and Labor, Committee on: 1985 Sep 14F
Energy and Commerce, Committee on: air pollution 1982 Aug 11F; 1989 Mar 22H/Oct 11H; domestic content bill 1983 May 19H; EPA investigated by 1983 Mar 1H/Mar 9H/Sep 28H; EPA policy assailed 1982 Oct 10F; hazardous waste sites 1985 Apr 28H/Jul 25H; nuclear weapons facilities 1989 Jun 18H; oil companies 1981 Dec 15H; ozone layer 1987 Mar 9I; technology theft 1983 Jun 27H; telecommunications 1982 Mar 25H; tobacco advertising 1986 Jul 18H
Ethics Committee: chairman reveals wife's earnings 1989 Jun 12F; Ferraro inquiry 1984 Aug 7F/Sep 12F/Dec 4F; Frank inquiry 1989 Sep 12F; Gingrich complaint brought to 1989 Apr 11F; sexual misconduct cases 1982 Jul 26F/Dec 14F; 1983 Jul 14F; 1989 Oct 18F; Wright inquiry 1988 Jun 10F/Jul 26F; 1989 Apr 17F
Foreign Affairs, Committee on: Cuba 1983 Jun 9G; El Salvador 1982 Feb 2G/Mar 2D; 1984 Mar 30G; Grenada invasion 1983 Oct 27G; Honduras 1987 Jun 4G; Middle East 1981 Mar 18G; 1986 Dec 8G; Nicaraguan contras 1983 Jun 7G; 1986 May 8G; nuclear freeze resolution 1982 Jun 23G; Philippines 1984 Feb 29G; 1985 Jul 9G; USSR 1981 Mar 18G; 1982 Aug 10G
Government Operations, Committee on: 1988 Sep 30H; 1989 Sep 15F/Oct 27F/Dec 2I/Dec 16F
Hunger, Select Committee on: 1988 Jul 14G

Intelligence, Select Committee on: 1980 Jun 29I; 1982 Sep 22F; 1983 May 16G; 1984 Jun 13G/Dec 5G; 1987 Aug 7F

Interior and Insular Affairs, Committee on: 1981 Jun 23G/Aug 18F; 1983 Feb 1H

Judiciary, Committee on the: 1985 May 8F/Jul 9F; 1987 Feb 20D

Post Office and Civil Service, Committee on the: 1983 Jul 19F

Public Works and Transportation, Committee on: 1983 Aug 10H

Republican Study Committee: 1984 Aug 7F

Science, Space and Technology, Committee on: 1983 Oct 18F; 1984 Feb 7H

Ways and Means Committee: 1981 Jul 14H; 1985 Sep 26H/Nov 23H/Dec 10H/Dec 17H; 1989 May 22F/Aug 9H/Sep 14H

housing see also specific U.S. agencies (e.g., Housing and Urban Development)

homelessness see homelessness

public housing: 1981 Jun 10B; 1985 Nov 20F; 1986 Jun 12H; 1987 Jun 11F; 1988 Apr 11F; 1989 Mar 29F

rentals: '84 budget authorization 1983 Jul 13F; HUD sales blocked 1987 Jul 6F; rent boycotts 1986 Aug 26C; 1989 Apr 24C; rent control 1982 Feb 28F; 1988 Feb 24F; rent increases 1980 Oct 15C; 1988 Feb 1B

sales: 1983 Mar 2H; 1986 Jan 31H; 1989 Oct 31H

starts see housing starts

Housing, U.S. Commission on 1982 Feb 28F

Housing and Urban Development, U.S. Department of (HUD) see also specific department heads in the name index (e.g., Kemp, Jack)

appointments and resignations: Kemp, Jack 1988 Dec 19F; Pierce, Samuel 1980 Dec 22F

budget and spending programs: 1983 Jul 12F; 1988 Apr 11F/Jul 13F/Aug 19F; 1989 Nov 9H

HUD scandal: 1989 Jan 17F/Jun 16F/Dec 22F/Jul 24F

mortgage auctions: 1987 Apr 24H/Jul 6F

social services: homeless 1984 May 1F; illegal aliens 1986 Mar 31F

housing starts

1981 statistics: 1981 Nov 18H

1982 statistics: 1982 May 18H/Jun 16H/Dec 16H

1983 statistics: 1983 Jan 18H/Feb 16H/Mar 16H/Apr 18H/May 17H/Jun 16H/Jul 19H/Sep 19H/Aug 16H/Sep 19H/Oct 19H/Nov 17H/Dec 20H

1984 statistics: 1984 Jan 18H/Feb 16H/Mar 16H/Apr 17H/May 16H/Jun 19H/Jul 18H/Aug 16H/Sep 19H/Oct 17H/Dec 18H

1985 statistics: 1985 Jan 17H/Feb 19H/Apr 16H/May 16H/Jun 18H/Jul 17H/Aug 16H/Sep 18H/Oct 17H/Nov 19H/Dec 17H

1986 statistics: 1986 Jan 17H/Feb 19H/Mar 18H/Jun 17H/Jul 18H/Aug 20H/Sep 17F/Oct 17H/Nov 19H/Dec 16H

1987 statistics: 1987 Jan 21H/Feb 10H/Mar 17H/Apr 16H/May 19H/Jun 16H/Jul 17H/Aug 18H/Sep 17H/Oct 20H/Nov 18H/Dec 16H

1988 statistics: 1988 Jan 20H/Feb 17H/Mar 16H/Apr 19H/May 18H/Jun 17H/Jul 19H/Aug 17F/Sep 21H/Oct 19H/Aug 31E/Nov 17H/Dec 16H

1989 statistics: 1989 Jan 10H/Feb 19H/Mar 19H/Apr 18H/May 16H/Jul 19H/Aug 16H/Sep 19H/Nov 17H/Dec 19H

Houston, University of (Texas) 1980 Jan 1J; 1981 Dec 26J; 1983 Apr 4J; 1984 Apr 2J; 1985 Jan 1J

Houston Astros (baseball team) 1980 Oct 12J; 1981 Sep 26J; 1985 Jul 11J; 1986 Sep 25J/Oct 15J/Nov 11J

Houston Oilers (football team) 1980 Jan 6J/Jan 9J; 1988 Jan 10J

Houston Rockets (basketball team) 1981 May 14J; 1986 Jun 8J

Howard Hughes Medical Institute 1987 Mar 9I

Howard University (Washington, D.C.) 1983 Jul 22F; 1988 Dec 4J; 1989 Mar 7F/Jul 4J

How Can I Fall? (Breathe) (recording) 1988 Nov 26J

Howling, The (film) 1981 May 6J

HTLV see human T-cell leukemia virus

HTLV-1 (virus) 1988 Nov 29I

H20 (Hall & Oates) (recording) 1983 Jan 5J/Feb 9J

H-2 (Japanese rocket) 1984 Jul 13I

Huaorani Indians (Brazil) 1987 Sep 30E

HUD see Housing and Urban Development; Housing and Urban Development, U.S. Department of

Huey Lewis & the News (singing group)
Fore! 1986 Oct 22J/Nov 22J/Dec 17J
Sports 1984 May 20J/May 28J/Jun 16J/Jul 21J/Aug 25J/Sep 22J/Oct 27J

Hughes Aircraft Co. 1984 Aug 22G/Nov 19G; 1985 Sep 16I

Humana Heart Institute (Louisville Ky.) 1984 Nov 25I/Nov 27I

Humana Hospital Audubon (Louisville, Ky.) 1985 Feb 17I/Apr 24I; 1986 Aug 6I

Humana Inc. 1984 Nov 27I

Humana Wellington Hospital (London) 1989 Jun 5I

human genome project 1986 Jun 27I; 1988 Feb 11I/Oct 1I

Human Genome Research, Office for (NIH) 1988 Oct 1I

Human League (singing group) 1982 Jun 16J

human-powered flight 1988 Apr 23J

Human Rights, U.N. Commission on 1980 Feb 5A; 1982 Feb 10A/Feb 18E; 1983 Mar 1A/Sep 5A; 1986 Mar 14A; 1987 Mar 11A/Nov 19E; 1988 Aug 5E; 1989 Feb 6B/Aug 31A/Mar 9B

Human Rights, U.N. Universal Declaration on 1988 Dec 10A

Human Rights Watch 1988 Jul 28C

Human Services Reauthorization Act of 1986 1986 Sep 30F

human T-cell leukemia virus (HTLV) 1983 May 20I

Humphrey (whale) 1985 Nov 4J

100-meter dash (running) 1987 Aug 30J; 1988 Jul 16J

100-meter freestyle (swimming) 1985 Aug 7J

Hungarian uprising (1956) 1986 Oct 18B/Nov 4B

Hungary

arts and culture: Bartok burial 1988 Jul 7J; Wallenberg statue erected 1987 Apr 15B

defense and disarmament issues: border demilitarization proposed 1989 Sep 8B; border fence dismantled 1989 May 2B

economy: austerity plan 1987 Sep 19B; consumer prices 1987 Jul 20B; foreign debt 1988 Nov 29B; private enterprise law 1981 Oct 9B

environmental issues: Danube River dam project 1989 May 24B

foreign relations: Comecon summit 1984 Jun 14A; Israel 1988 May 8C; Romania 1988 Jun 27B/Aug 28B; 1989 Mar 9B/Dec 15B; South Korea 1988 Sep 13A; USSR 1986 Jul 16I; 1989 Apr 25B

government and politics: communist party congress 1980 Mar 28B; 1985 Mar 25B; 1956 uprising anniversary 1986 Oct 18B/Nov 4B; 1989 Oct 23B; communist party conference, Kadar removed 1988 May 22B; Nemeth confirmed as premier 1988 Nov 24B; freedom of assembly approved 1989 Jan 11B; independent parties allowed 1989 Feb 11B; Kadar forced to retire 1989 May 8B; reform within communist party 1989 May 21B; Nagy reburied 1989 Jun 16B; opposition factions talk with government 1989 Jun 13B; reformist named Presidium head 1989 Jun 24B; Nagy posthumously rehabilitated 1989 Jul 6B; noncommunist becomes deputy 1989 Jul 22B; Democratic Forum candidates elected 1989 Aug 5B; communist party renounces Marxism 1989 Oct 7B; constitution changed 1989 Oct 18B; opposition parties legalized 1989 Oct 19B; referendum on presidential election 1989 Oct 31B/Nov 26B; Nemeth resigns from Presidium 1989 Dec 20B; parliamentary elections scheduled 1989 Dec 22B

human rights: demonstrations and protests 1987 Mar 15B; 1988 Jun 27B; dissidents 1986 Jul 21B/Oct 18B

immigration and refugees: East German refugees 1989 Sep 4B/Sep 10B/Sep 12B/Sep 14B

international organizations: IMF membership 1982 May 5A; Warsaw pact summit 1986 Jun 11B

labor issues: workplace party committees abolished 1989 Oct 19B

obituaries: Kadar, Janos 1989 Jul 6B; Szabo, Gabor 1982 Feb 26J

space program: 1980 May 26I

sports: figure skating championships 1988 Mar 25J; Los Angeles Olympics withdrawal 1984 May 17J; Seoul Olympics accepted 1987 Dec 17J

U.S. relations: 1984 Mar 14G; 1989 Oct 19G/Nov 21G

hunger 1982 Oct 6G; 1983 Jul 19F; 1984 Jan 10E; 1985 Feb 26F; 1986 Jan 21F/May 21F; 1988 Sep 15C; see also famine

Hunger, The (film) 1983 May 4J

Hunger Project prize 1988 Sep 15C

hunger strikes

Bolivian workers/students: 1987 Apr 1D

Chilean prisoners: 1987 Apr 1D

Chinese students: 1989 May 13E/May 19E

ERA supporters: 1982 Jun 19F

gypsies in West Germany: 1980 Apr 4B

Haitian Army officers: 1989 Jul 22D

IRA in Northern Ireland: 1981 Apr 23B/Apr 29B/Aug 3G

Iranian dissidents in France: 1988 Jan 13B

Israeli physicians: 1983 Jun 26C

Maze Prison see Maze Prison

Polish dissidents: 1987 Dec 27B

Polish workers: 1981 Aug 4B

South Korean politician: 1983 Jun 2D

Soviet dissident Sakharov: 1981 Dec 10B; 1984 May 2B

U.S. Salvadoran policy protests: 1981 Mar 24F

U.S. war veterans: 1986 Oct 16G

West Bank mayors: 1980 Dec 24C

West German jailed terrorist: 1981 Apr 16B

Hunt for Red October, The (Tom Clancy) (book) 1985 May 24J/Jun 14J/Jul 19J/Aug 16J/Sep 27J

Huntington's chorea 1986 Jan 10F

Hurlyburly (David Rabe) (play) 1984 Jun 21J

hurricanes 1985 May 25I; 1988 Nov 30I
Alicia: 1983 Aug 18I/Aug 22H
Allen: 1980 Aug 11I
Diana: 1984 Sep 13I
Elena: 1985 Sep 2I
Gilbert: 1988 Sep 17I
Gloria: 1985 Sep 27I
Hugo: 1989 Sep 19D/Sep 21I/Sep 22I/Sep 28H
Joan: 1988 Oct 22I/Nov 13D
Juan: 1985 Oct 26I
Kate: 1985 Nov 22I

Husky Oil Co. 1984 Mar 29H

Hustler (magazine) 1983 Nov 8J; 1988 Feb 24F

Hutus (Burundi/Rwanda ethnic group) 1988 Aug 22C

Hyatt Regency Hotel (Kansas City, Mo.) 1981 Jul 17J

Hyde Amendment 1980 Jan 15F

hydroelectric power 1982 Mar 19D/Nov 5I; 1983 Apr 16I/Sep 14H; 1984 May 2C/Jun 28D/Aug 17H/Oct 25D; 1989 Feb 20D/Dec 7D

hydrogen 1980 Jan 20I; 1989 Aug 28I

hydrogen peroxide 1984 Nov 26B

Hydro-Quebec 1987 Jun 18D; 1988 Apr 18D

hyperactivity 1988 Apr 15F

hypodermic needles 1985 Oct 2F; 1987 Feb 24D; 1988 Jan 31I/Jun 9I/Nov 7F; 1989 Mar 8I

Hysteria (Def Leppard) (recording) 1987 Sep 19J/Oct 24J; 1988 Jun 18J/Jul 16J/Aug 27J/Sep 24J/Oct 29J; 1989 Jan 29J

Hyundai Group 1987 Aug 21E

I

IAEA see International Atomic Energy Agency

IATA see International Air Transport Association

IBM see International Business Machines Corp.

IBM Presents Baryshnikov on Broadway (TV show) 1980 Sep 7J

IBP Inc. 1987 Jul 21H/Jul 27H

ibuprofen (drug) 1984 May 18H

ICAO see International Civil Aviation Organization

Icarus Agenda, The (Robert Ludlum) (book) 1988 Mar 25J/Apr 29J/May 27J/Jun 24J/Jul 23J

ICBMs 1980 Sep 18G; 1982 Apr 14G; 1983 Apr 11G/Apr 18G/Apr 19G; 1987 Sep 30B

ICC see Interstate Commerce Commission

ice (illegal drug) 1989 Sep 14F

Ice Age 1987 Mar 31I

ice hockey see also specific teams (e.g., Rangers)
All-Star Game: 1985 Feb 12J; 1988 Feb 9J; 1989 Feb 7J
Canada/Soviet game: 1987 Feb 13J
NCAA championships: 1982 Mar 27J; 1985 Mar 30J; 1986 Mar 29J; 1987 Mar 28J; 1988 Apr 2J; 1989 Apr 1J
Olympic Games (Lake Placid): 1980 Feb 22J/Feb 24J
Stanley Cup: 1980 May 24J; 1981 May 21J; 1982 May 16J; 1983 May 17J; 1984 May 19J; 1985 May 30J; 1986 May 24J; 1987 May 31J; 1988 May 26J; 1989 May 25J
world championships: 1982 Apr 25J; 1985 May 3J; 1987 May 3J; 1989 Apr 29J

Iceland

crime and law enforcement: armed robbery 1984 Feb 18B

economy and labor: whaling 1986 Aug 6I/Nov 9B; 1987 Jun 26E; women strike 1985 Oct 24B

government and politics: budget plan 1988 Nov 1B; coalition government 1980 Feb 8B; 1987 Jul 8B; elections 1987 Apr 25B; Gestsson asked to form government 1980 Jan 16B

health care issues: life expectancy rates 1988 May 24I

U.S. relations: Bush visit 1983 Jun 24G

ice skating see specific form of skating (e.g., figure skating)

IC Industries 1981 Sep 21C

ICO see International Coffee Organization

IDA see International Development Association

Idaho State University (Pocatello) 1981 Dec 19J

IDB see Inter-American Development Bank

Iditarod (dog-sled race) 1985 Mar 20J; 1986 Mar 13J; 1988 Mar 17J; 1989 Mar 15J

If Tomorrow Comes (Sidney Sheldon) (book) 1985 Feb 8J/Mar 15J/Apr 19J/May 24J/Jun 14J

If You Could See What I Hear (film) 1982 May 5J

If You Love This Planet (film) 1983 Feb 24J

IG Bau (West German union) 1981 Mar 25B

illegal aliens

accidents: Arizona 1980 Jul 5F; Texas 1984 Apr 28F

economic issues: employer sanctions 1987 May 26F; federal housing aid 1986 Mar 31F; statistics 1980 Feb 4F; 1986 Feb 20F; worksite raids 1982 May 6F; 1984 Apr 17F

foreign developments: India 1983 Aug 13E; Nigeria 1983 Jan 17C

immigration reform: 1981 Jul 30F; 1982 Dec 18F; 1983 May 18F/Oct 4F; 1984 Jun 20F; 1985 Sep 19F; 1986 Oct 17F

political and legislative issues: amnesty program 1987 May 5F; 1988 May 4F; congressional commission recommendations 1980 Dec 7F; illegal deportations ruling 1987 May 26F; Nicaraguan rules eased 1987 Jul 8F; presidential task force recommendations 1981 May 29G; Salvadorans not exempted 1987 May 14G

sanctuary movement: 1985 Jan 14F/Feb 21F/Dec 23G; 1986 May 1F/Jul 2F

Illinois see also specific cities (e.g., Chicago)

accidents and disasters: tornados 1982 May 29I

economy and business: lottery 1984 Sep 3J; mass transportation 1981 Jun 11H; stock-index futures 1982 Jun 13H

environmental issues: dioxin lawsuit 1982 Aug 25H

family issues: child custody case 1980 Oct 20F

labor issues: teacher strikes 1983 Sep 12F; 1985 Sep 18F; UAW contract 1987 Feb 1H

medicine and health care: abortion clinic abduction 1982 Aug 20F; AIDS 1987 Sep 21F; 1989 Jun 23F; drug paraphernalia ruling 1982 Mar 3F

politics and government: Equal Rights Amendment 1980 Jun 18F/Nov 7F; 1982 Jun 6F/Jun 19F; LaRouche supporters 1986 Apr 9F/Apr 23F; presidential campaigns 1980 Mar 18F; 1984 Mar 20F/Sep 26F; 1988 Mar 15F; Stevenson gubernatorial campaign 1986 Mar 18F/Apr 23F/May 16F

Illinois, University of (Urbana-Champaign) 1982 Dec 29J; 1984 Jan 2J; 1985 Feb 25I

illiteracy 1980 Dec 4J; 1986 Apr 21F

I 'll Take Manhattan (Judith Krantz) (book) 1986 May 30J/Jun 27J/Jul 18J/Aug 29J

ILO see International Labor Organization

I Love Rock "n" Roll (Joan Jett & the Blackhearts) (recording) 1982 Feb 24J/Mar 14J/Mar 17J

ILWU see International Longshoremen's and Warehousemen's Union

Ilyushin-62 (aircraft) 1987 May 9B

Imani Temple 1989 Jul 4J

IMF see International Monetary Fund

Imhausen-Chemie GmbH 1989 May 10B

Immigration Amendments of 1988 1988 Nov 15F

Immigration and Nationalities Act (McCarran-Walter Act) (1952) 1983 Aug 27F

Immigration and Naturalization Service, U.S. (INS)

Cuban refugee issues: 1984 Dec 3F

extraditions and deportations: author deportation dropped 1988 Nov 4F

Haitian refugee issues: 1980 Jul 2F; 1981 Jan 30F; 1989 Jul 22D

illegal aliens: amnesty program 1987 May 5F/Oct 8F; Central Americans 1989 Feb 20F; em-

ployer hiring rules 1987 Jan 20F; employer sanctions 1987 May 26F; Mexicans 1982 May 6F; 1986 Feb 20F; Salvadorans 1984 Jan 25G; work site raids 1982 May 6F; 1984 Apr 17F

immigration and refugees see specific countries (e.g., East Germany); subjects (e.g., refugee camps)

Immigration Reform and Control Act of 1986 1987 May 5F

immune system therapy 1985 Dec 4I

immunization 1984 Dec 19A

I 'm Not Rappaport (Herb Gardner) (play) 1985 Nov 19J; 1986 Jun 1J

Impala Platinum Holdings Ltd. 1986 Jan 6C

impeachment proceedings

Claiborne, Harry E. 1986 Jul 22F/Oct 9F

Hastings, Alcee L. 1987 Mar 17F; 1988 Aug 3F; 1989 Oct 20F

Marcos, Ferdinand E. 1985 Aug 13E

Mecham, Evan 1988 Jan 20F/Feb 5F/Apr 4F

Nixon, Walter L. 1989 May 10F/Nov 3F

Imperial Oil Ltd. (Exxon Corp.) 1989 Jan 20H

Imperial Theatre (New York City) 1981 Dec 20J

Imperiled Generation, An: Saving Urban Schools (Carnegie Foundation) 1988 Mar 15F

import quotas

automobiles: 1980 Jun 12H

beef: 1984 Apr 7A

citrus: 1984 Apr 7A

copper: 1984 Jan 26H/Sep 6H

foreign developments: Australia 1984 Apr 13E; Canada 1985 Nov 20D; China 1983 Jan 19E; European Community 1987 Dec 22E; 1989 May 3B; Japan 1984 Apr 7A/Apr 13E; 1987 Dec 3E; 1988 Feb 2E

shoes: 1984 Jan 23H

steel: 1984 Jul 11H; 1985 Nov 1A; 1989 Jul 25H/Dec 12H

sugar: 1982 May 4H/Jun 5H

textiles: 1983 Jan 19E; 1984 Aug 25H

Impregilo S.p.A. 1985 Apr 27B

INA Corp. 1981 Nov 9H

incest 1980 Jan 15F; 1986 Jun 13B; 1989 Oct 11F/Oct 19F/Oct 21F

incineration 1984 Jun 4B; 1986 May 28H; 1987 Nov 25B/Dec 31H; 1989 Nov 30H

income, per capita 1983 May 1H; 1984 Apr 30H

incomes see specific kinds of income (e.g., family income)

income tax

business issues: bank tax rates 1983 Mar 9H; corporate tax burden 1983 Nov 14H; 1984 Nov 30H; municipal bonds 1986 Mar 19H; windfall profits tax 1989 Apr 3H

foreign developments: Afghanistan 1981 Oct 18E; China 1981 Dec 13E; Finland 1988 Sep 13B; France 1983 Sep 14B; 1987 Sep 16B; Great Britain 1986 Sep 24B; 1988 Mar 15B; Italy 1988 Dec 27B; Japan 1988 Jul 1E; Netherlands 1988 Sep 20B; Norway 1982 Oct 6B; Singapore 1984 Mar 2E; Sweden 1988 Nov 23B

personal income issues: middle class tax burden 1980 Sep 12H; refund withholding 1986 Jun 4H

political campaign issues: 1984 Aug 4F

tax irregularities: 1981 Oct 15J; 1982 May 18J; 1989 Aug 30F

tax reform: indexing 1984 Oct 24H; surcharge proposal to reduce deficit 1982 Feb 22H; tax breaks and shelters 1982 Nov 20H; 1985 Feb 11H; tax code overhaul 1981 Jun 4H; 1983 Jun 29H; 1986 Sep 27H

Incredible Shrinking Woman (film) 1981 Feb 11J

Indecent Obsession, An (Colleen McCullough) (book) 1981 Nov 8J/Dec 6J; 1982 Jan 10J/Feb 7J/Mar 7J/Apr 11J

Independence Bowl (football) 1981 Dec 12J

Independence Hall (Philadelphia) 1987 Sep 17F

Independent, The (British newspaper) 1986 Oct 7B

Independent Bankers Association of America 1981 Apr 23H

Independent Commission on International Development Issues 1983 Feb 9A

Independent Counsel on International Human Rights 1987 Nov 19E

Independent News Service 1984 Apr 12J

Independent Truckers Association 1983 Jan 31H/Feb 10H

India see also individual leaders in the name index (e.g., Gandhi, Indira)

accidents and disasters: Air-India explosion 1985 Jun 23A; Bhopal gas disaster see Bhopal; cyclones 1988 Nov 29I; earthquakes 1988 Aug 21I; flooding 1983 Jun 28I; hurricanes 1982 Jun 4E

arts and culture: Satanic Verses 1988 Oct 7E

census data: population 1988 May 30E

civil strife: Gurkhas 1988 Aug 6E; Hindu caste groups 1985 Apr 23E; Hindu-Moslem violence 1984 May 17E/May 28E; 1987 May 26E; rioting near mosque 1980 Aug 13E; tribal groups/Bengali immigrants in Tripura 1980 Jun 8E; see also Assam; Punjab

crime and law enforcement: Air India jet hijacking 1981 Dec 2C; bandit chief killed 1982 Mar 5E; "bandit king" surrenders 1982 Jun 17E; "bandit queen" surrenders 1983 Feb 14E; police arrested 1982 Aug 17E

defense and disarmament issues: nuclear fuel 1982 Aug 30A/Nov 29I; nuclear reactor parts 1983 Jun 30E; nuclear weapons 1981 Apr 27I; 1988 Mar 20E; surface-to-surface missile 1988 Feb 25E

demonstrations and protests: anti-government strikes 1989 Aug 30E; police 1982 Aug 15E; students 1981 Feb 26E

economy: budget and spending programs 1988 Feb 29E; food shortfall 1982 Mar 8E; gross national product 1987 Feb 24E

energy issues: natural gas production 1983 Mar 1E; nuclear fuel 1982 Aug 30A/Nov 29I

family issues: alimony 1986 May 6E; dowry deaths 1980 Apr 9E;

1983 Jun 5E; 1985 Mar 20E; 1988 Nov 24E

foreign relations

Africa: Maldives 1988 Nov 3E

Asia and Pacific Rim: Bangladesh 1982 Oct 7E; 1983 Aug 13E; 1984 Jun 10E; 1988 Oct 10A; Cambodia 1980 Jul 7E; China 1981 Jun 28E; 1982 May 20E; 1983 Oct 30E; 1987 May 22C; Pakistan 1982 Feb 25E/Nov 1E/Dec 24E; 1986 Dec 21E; 1987 Jan 23E/Feb 19E/Sep 25E; Sri Lanka: peace agreement signed 1987 Jul 29E; peace talks 1985 Aug 17E; visits 1984 Jul 2A

Canada: 1987 Jul 12D; 1989 Dec 19D

Europe: France 1982 Aug 30A/Nov 29I; Great Britain 1986 Sep 1B; USSR 1980 May 28A; 1982 Mar 20E; 1983 Dec 3A; 1986 Nov 28E; 1988 Nov 18E

Middle East: Iran 1982 Jul 7G; Lebanon 1987 Jan 24C/Feb 9C; 1988 Oct 3C; PLO 1980 Apr 9A

government and politics: democracy threat seen 1982 Jan 25E; Indira Gandhi assassinated 1984 Oct 31E; Indira Gandhi sworn prime minister 1980 Jan 14E; Janata Dal party inaugurated 1988 Oct 11E; Maneka Gandhi party members arrested 1982 Sep 25E; opposition resigns in parliament 1981 Sep 16E; parliamentary elections 1980 Jan 6E; 1986 Jun 28E; 1989 Nov 26E; parliament convenes 1984 Jul 23E; Singh government wins confidence vote 1989 Dec 21E; Singh sworn prime minister 1989 Dec 2E; state elections 1980 May 31E; state government of Kerala resigns 1982 Mar 17E; state legislature of Kerala suspended 1981 Oct 21E; Tamil Nadu chief minister dies 1987 Dec 24E

international organizations: Commonwealth summit 1986 Aug 5A; IMF loans 1981 Nov 9A; non-aligned nations 1982 Aug 11A; 1983 Mar 12A; UN Security Council membership 1983 Dec 31A; World Bank loan 1983 Mar 1E

labor issues: dock worker strike 1984 Apr 10E; general strike 1982 Jan 19E; police riots 1982 Aug 15E; strikes banned 1981 Jul 27E

medicine and health care: cholera epidemic 1988 Aug 2I

monetary and trade issues: foreign aid 1986 Jun 16E; IMF loans 1981 Nov 9A; World Bank loan 1983 Mar 1E

obituaries: Abdullah, Sheik Mohammed 1982 Sep 8E; Bhave, Vinoba Acharya 1982 Nov 15E; Gandhi, Indira 1984 Oct 31E; Gandhi, Sanjay 1980 Jun 23E; Khan, Abdul Ghaffar 1988 Jan 20E; Kripalani, Jiwatram Bhagwandas 1982 Mar 19E; Krishnamurti, Jiddu 1986 Feb 17J; Muktananda, Swami Paramahansa 1982 Oct 2E; Ramu (Wolf Boy) 1985 Feb 18I

provences see specific province (e.g., Assam)

religious issues: cooking fat alarm 1983 Nov 16E; papal visit 1986 Feb 1J

space program 1984 Apr 11I; rocket failures 1987 Mar 24I; 1988 Jul

13I; satellite failure 1982 Sep 6I; satellite launch 1980 Jul 18I

sports: cricket 1986 May 26J; 1987 Nov 8J; tennis 1987 Dec 20J

Sri Lanka conflict see under Sri Lanka

United Nations policy: Security Council membership 1983 Dec 31A

U.S. relations: military equipment 1988 Apr 4E; nuclear fuel 1980 Mar 13G/May 16I/Jun 19I/Sep 24F/Sep 24G; nuclear reactor parts 1983 Jun 30E; Pakistan aid 1981 Apr 17G/Jun 16E/Aug 19E; 1986 Nov 4E; supercomputers 1987 Oct 8E; trade disputes 1989 May 25H/Jun 1A; trade negotiations 1980 Aug 26A

Indiana

business issues: corporate takeover regulations 1987 Apr 21H

crime and law enforcement: bid-rigging charges dropped 1984 Jan 23H; racist indicted in Vernon Jordan shooting 1982 Jun 2F

education: 1986 Feb 21F/Jul 16F

energy issues: nuclear power plants 1984 Jan 16H/Jan 23H

environmental issues: hazardous waste sites 1983 Jan 4H

medicine and health care: AIDS 1986 Feb 21F/Jul 16F

obituaries: Halleck, Charles Abraham 1986 Feb 3F; West, Jessamyn 1984 Feb 25J

politics and government: congressional election recount controversy 1985 May 1F; congressional elections 1988 Nov 8F; mayor warns on urban cuts 1981 May 1F; presidential campaigns 1984 May 9F; 1988 May 3F

Indiana Jones and the Last Crusade (film) 1989 May 24J/May 31J/Jun 28J/Jul 2J/Dec 28J

Indiana Jones and the Temple of Doom (film) 1984 Jun 6J/Jul 18J

Indianapolis 500 (auto race) 1981 May 25J; 1982 May 15J/May 30J; 1983 May 29J; 1985 May 26J; 1986 May 31J; 1987 May 24J; 1988 May 29J; 1989 May 28J

Indianapolis Colts (football team) 1988 Jan 9J

Indiana University (Bloomington) 1981 Mar 30J; 1985 Mar 29J; 1986 Mar 1J; 1987 Mar 30J; 1988 Dec 4J

Indian Point nuclear power plant (Buchanan, N.Y.) 1982 Mar 25I; 1983 May 5I/Jun 8H/Aug 26I

"Individuals: A Select History of Contemporary Art, 1945-1986" (art exhibition) 1986 Dec 10J

Indochina War (1945-54) 1986 Oct 11B

Indonesia see also East Timor

accidents and disasters: forest fires 1984 Apr 2I; passenger ship sinks 1981 Jan 27E

crime and law enforcement: ASEAN former secretary sentenced 1986 Jan 9E; executions 1986 Oct 9E; former minister sentenced 1985 May 15E; Garuda Airlines hijacking 1981 Mar 28E/Mar 31E; officer's sentence reduced 1986 May 14E

defense and disarmament issues: atrocities charged 1984 Aug 29E

economy: budget and spending programs 1987 Jan 6E; currency 1986 Sep 12E; economic reforms 1987 Dec 24E; food shortfall 1982 Mar 8E; foreign debt 1984 Mar

12E; oil company debt 1982 Feb 25E

foreign relations: Australia 1980 Dec 2E; 1986 Sep 4E; China 1985 Jul 5E; 1989 Feb 25E; Papua New Guinea 1986 May 28E

government and politics: legislative elections 1982 May 4E; 1987 Apr 23E; press censorship 1982 Apr 12E; riots 1982 Mar 18E; 1984 Sep 12E; Suharto reelected president 1988 Mar 10E

religion: papal visit 1989 Oct 7J

space program: satellites 1984 Aug 16I

U.S. relations: 1982 Nov 8E; 1984 Jul 7G

Indonesia: The Rise of Capital (Richard Robison) (book) 1986 Sep 4E

Industrial Bank of Japan 1988 Jul 17E

industrial capacity utilization 1982 Oct 18H/Nov 17H; 1983 Apr 18H/May 16H; 1988 Aug 16H/Nov 16H/Dec 14H; 1989 Feb 15H/Oct 17H/Nov 15H

industrial production index
1980 statistics: 1980 Nov 14H
1981 statistics: 1981 Apr 15H/Dec 16H
1982 statistics: 1982 Apr 15H/Nov 16H
1983 statistics: 1983 Mar 15H/Apr 15H/May 13H/Jul 15H/Aug 16H/Sep 15H/Oct 14H/Dec 15H
1984 statistics: 1984 Apr 13H/May 15H/Jun 15H/Jul 13H/Aug 15H/Sep 14H/Oct 16H/Nov 15H/Dec 14H
1985 statistics: 1985 jan 15H/Feb 15H/Mar 15H/Jul 18H/Mar 18H/Apr 16H/May 15H/Jun 14H/Aug 15H/Oct 16H/Nov 15H/Dec 13H; 1987 Feb 13H
1986 statistics: 1986 Feb 14H/Mar 14H/Mar 15H/Jun 13H/Jul 15H/Aug 15H/Oct 16H/Nov 14H/Dec 15H
1987 statistics: 1987 Jan 16H/Mar 13H/Apr 15H/May 15H/Jun 16H/Jul 15H/Aug 16H/Sep 15H/Oct 16H/Nov 16H/Dec14H
1989 statistics: 1989 Feb 15H/Mar 16H/Apr 14H/Jun 15H/Jul 14H/Sep 15H/Oct 17H/Nov 14H

inertial confinement fusion 1989 Jun 14I

infant formula 1981 May 20A; 1984 Jan 27B

infant mortality rate 1983 Jan 25F/Mar 15I; 1984 Dec 19A; 1985 May 4F; 1986 Oct 27I; 1987 Feb 2F

infants
crime issues: Dingo case (Australia) 1985 Nov 12E; 1986 Feb 7E; 1987 Jun 2E; 1988 Sep 15E
health and safety issues: AIDS testing 1988 Jan 12I; circumcision benefits 1989 Mar 5I; handicapped care 1983 Apr 14F/Nov 2F/Nov 16F; 1984 Jan 9F; 1986 Jun 9F; heart transplants 1984 Oct 26I; 1985 Nov 20I; vitamin E solution deaths 1984 May 4I
religious issues: baptism 1983 Aug 10J; circumcision benefits 1989 Mar 5I

infertility 1988 May 17I

influenza 1982 Sep 2I

Information Systems (AT&T) 1985 Aug 21H

Infrared Astronomical Satellite 1983 Aug 9I

INF (intermediate nuclear force) talks 1981: Sep 24A

1982: Jan 12A/Feb 9A/Sep 30A
1983: Jan 20B/27B/Jun 24A/Aug 26B/Sep 28A/Oct 14B/Oct 16A/Oct 27A/Nov 14A
1984: Jan 16/Apr 20B
1985: Jan 26A
1987: Mar 12B/Apr 27B/Jun 16G/Aug 26B/Oct 8B

INF (intermediate nuclear force) treaty
Reagan announces tentative treaty 1987 Sep 18B
Bush reassurances to NATO 1987 Oct 3B
U.S./USSR announce last major obstacle removed 1987 Nov 24J
NATO Nuclear Planning Group gives support 1987 Nov 4B
Reagan defends 1987 Dec 3G
Reagan and Gorbachev sign 1987 Dec 8A
allied endorsement of 1987 Dec 8B/Dec 11B
Reagan begins ratification fight 1987 Dec 11G
Senate actions 1988 Jan 25B/Feb 1G/Mar 27G/Mar 30G/May 18G
ABM interpretation issues 1988 Feb 10G
USSR removes missiles 1988 Feb 25B
NATO meeting on 1988 Mar 3B
U.S. destroys missile engines 1988 Sep 8G

In God We Trust (film) 1980 Oct 1J

Inherit the Wind (TV show) 1988 Aug 28J

Inhumane Weapons Convention 1980 Oct 13A; 1981 Apr 10A

Inkatha Freedom Party 1988 Dec 26C; 1989 Aug 8C

Ink Spots (singing group) 1989 Jan 18J

Inland Steel Industries Inc. 1985 May 2H; 1989 Jul 16H

In Memory of a Summer Day (David Del Tredici) (musical composition) 1980 Apr 14J

Innerspace (film) 1987 Jul 8J

Innocent Blood (P.D. James) (book) 1980 Jul 13J

INS *see* Immigration and Naturalization Service

Insat-1 (satellite) 1982 Sep 6I

In Search of Excellence (Thomas J. Peters/Robert H. Waterman) (book) 1983 Aug 14J

In Search of Historic Jesus (film) 1980 Jan 30J

Inside Outside (Herman Wouk) (book) 1985 Apr 19J

insider trading 1980 Mar 18H; 1984 Aug 10H/Aug 30F; 1985 Jun 24H; 1986 Sep 23A/Dec 2H; 1987 Mar 19H/Apr 22H; 1988 Sep 14H/Oct 22F; 1989 Mar 29H

Insider Trading Sanctions Act of 1984 1986 May 5H

In Square Circle (Stevie Wonder) (recording) 1985 Nov 30J

Institute (West Virginia) 1985 May 4H/Aug 11H; 1986 Apr 1H; 1987 Jul 24H

Institute for International Economics (Washington, D.C.) 1987 Jun 24D

Institute of High Energy Physics (Serpukhov, Soviet Union) 1986 Jul 27I

Institute per le Opere di Religione (Vatican bank) 1982 Dec 24B; 1984 Apr 1B

Insurance Association, American *see* American Insurance Association

Integrated Long-Term Strategy, U.S. Commission on 1988 Jan 12G

Integrity in the College Curriculum: A Report to the Academic Community (Association of American Colleges) 1985 Feb 10F

Intel Corp. 1982 Dec 22H; 1986 Sep 22H

Intelligence Oversight Act 1980 Jun 3G

Interagency Task Force on Acid Precipitation 1983 Jun 8H

Inter-American Commission on Human Rights (OAS) 1980 Apr 18D; 1984 Nov 6D

Inter-American Court of Human Rights (OAS) 1988 Jul 29D; 1989 Jul 21D

Inter-American Development Bank (IDB)
member nations: Argentina 1984 Mar 27D; Chile 1984 Dec 12D; 1986 Dec 2D; Nicaragua 1983 Jun 29G/Jul 2A; 1985 Mar 21D; Peru 1987 Jun 3D; 1989 Mar 9D; United States 1983 Jun 29G/Jul 2A
policy issues: capital increase approved 1989 Mar 17D; foreign debt guarantee proposal rejected 1984 Mar 28D; Latin economic gains threatened 1981 Oct 19D
structure and organization: meetings 1984 Mar 26D; 1985 Mar 25D; 1987 Mar 23D; Ortiz Mena elected head of 1980 Nov 1D

Intercambio Ambrosia 1983 Aug 28B

interferon 1980 Jan 16I; 1981 Mar 24I; 1986 Jan 9I; 1988 Nov 21I

Interior, U.S. Department of the *see also specific department heads in the name index (e.g., Watt, James)*
appointments and resignations: Clark, William P. 1983 Oct 13H; Hodel, Donald P. 1985 Jan 10F; Lujan Jr., Manuel 1988 Dec 22F; Watt, James G. 1980 Dec 22F; 1983 Oct 9H
budget and spending programs: 1982 Dec 19F; 1988 Sep 27H; 1989 Oct 7B/Oct 23H
environmental issues: coal leases 1983 Apr 1H/May 10H/Sep 14H; 1984 Jan 9H; coastal areas protection 1987 Mar 23H; ivory ban urged 1989 May 11I; mining halt ordered 1985 Dec 4H; oil and gas exploration and leases 1981 Jul 27H; 1982 Aug 5H/Dec 19F; 1983 Jul 28H; 1986 Nov 24H; 1987 Apr 27H/Aug 27H; 1988 Dec 30H; 1989 Jul 26H/Sep 15H; recreation areas opened to mineral exploration 1981 Dec 18H; water pollution 1985 Mar 15H; wilderness designation removed 1982 Dec 27H
monuments and historic sites: Grand Canyon motorboat use 1981 Dec 18H; White House sleep-in protests prohibited 1984 Jun 29F

interleukin-2 (drug) 1986 Dec 12I; 1987 May 7I

intermediate-range nuclear missiles *see also specific missile (e.g., Pershing II)*
demonstrations and protests: 1981 Oct 10B/Oct 25B
Israeli deployment: 1987 Jul 21C/Jul 23B; 1989 Oct 26C
NATO deployment: West Germany 1980 Jul 15B; 1982 Mar 29B; 1983 Nov 22B; European cost sharing 1981 Apr 7G; linked to arms talks 1982 Nov 30A; 1983 Mar 23B/May 29A; Denmark 1982 Dec 7B; War-

saw Pact response 1983 Apr 7B/Oct 21B; commitment reaffirmed 1983 Jun 2B/Jun 10B; Bush trip to Europe 1983 Jun 24G; Soviet countermeasures 1983 May 28B/Nov 24B/Dec 5A; 1984 Jan 17B; Soviet rejection of "interim solution" 1983 Jun 26A; Soviet withdrawals 1986 Nov 14B; global ban endorsed 1987 Jun 12B
South African deployment: 1989 Oct 26C

Internal Revenue Service, U.S. (IRS) 1980 Nov 10F; 1981 Aug 29H/Sep 3H; 1982 Apr 19F; 1983 May 24F; 1985 Aug 6F; 1987 Nov 10H; 1988 Apr 12F/Apr 22H/Nov 11H

International Air Transport Association (IATA) 1982 Jul 27A; 1984 Dec 30A

International Amateur Athletic Federation (IAAF) 1980 Jul 31J; 1983 Aug 11J

International Association for the Evaluation of Educational Achievement 1988 Mar 2F

International Atomic Energy Agency, U.N. (IAEA) 1982 Sep 24A; 1983 May 6A/Oct 10A; 1985 Feb 21A; 1986 May 11I/Aug 25I/Aug 29I/Sep 26I; 1987 Jan 16I

International Basketball Federation 1989 Apr 7J

International Business Machines Corp. (IBM)
antitrust issues: European Community lawsuit against 1984 Aug 2A; Justice Department case against 1982 Jan 8H/Mar 19H/Aug 13H
appointments and resignations: Opel named CEO 1980 Dec 21H
awards and honors: researchers win Nobel 1986 Oct 15I; 1987 Oct 14I
business issues: competitors to develop standard PC 1988 Sep 13H; home computers 1983 Nov 1H; 1985 Mar 19I; personal computers 1983 Mar 8I; 1984 Aug 14I; 1987 Apr 2I; price reductions 1984 Jun 7H; restructuring plan 1989 Dec 5H; South Africa operations 1986 Oct 21C; toxic waste cleanup settlement 1985 Aug 5H
copyright issues: Fujitsu/IBM software dispute 1987 Sep 15F; 1988 Nov 29H
industrial espionage: executives fired for selling trade secrets 1982 Sep 14H; Hitachi theft suit 1983 Oct 6H/Nov 9H/Dec 21H; Japanese information theft 1982 Jun 22G; 1983 Feb 8H
mergers and acquisitions: Intel stock purchased 1982 Dec 22H
research and development: memory chips 1983 Sep 14I; superconductivity consortium formed 1989 May 23I

International Cancer Congress 1982 Sep 11I

International Center for Development Policy 1986 Nov 29F

International Chess Federation 1985 Feb 15J

International Civil Aviation Organization, U.N. (ICAO) 1983 Dec 13A; 1984 Mar 6A; 1985 Aug 22A; 1988 Dec 2A

International Cocoa Organization 1988 Mar 12A; 1989 Sep 18A

International Coffee Agreement 1989 Jul 3A/Oct 3A

International Coffee Organization (ICO) 1984 Oct 1A; 1989 Jul 3A

International Confederation of Free Trade Unions 1986 Jul 18C

International Congress of Mathematicians 1986 Aug 3I

International Convention on the Prevention and Punishment of the Crime of Genocide 1986 Feb 19A

International Court of Justice (World Court)
Canada/U.S. dispute: 1984 Oct 12D
Iran hostage crisis: 1980 Mar 18A/May 24A
Nicaraguan suit against U.S.: 1984 Apr 8G/Apr 24A/May 10A/Nov 26A; 1985 Jan 18G/Sep 12D/Oct 7G; 1986 Jun 27A/Oct 28A
PLO UN observer mission: 1988 Apr 25A

International Dairy Council 1983 Aug 7A

International Development Association (IDA) 1983 Dec 7G; 1984 Jan 14A/Jan 17A/Apr 13A

International Diamond Corp. 1981 Dec 5H

International Energy Agency (IEA) 1985 Jul 21A

International Environmental and Development Service 1983 Feb 15H

International Federation of Football Associations 1988 Jul 4J

International Harvester Co. 1980 Apr 20H

International Institute for Strategic Studies (London) 1980 Sep 18G; 1981 Sep 23B; 1982 Sep 29B

International Intellectual Property Alliance 1989 Apr 25H

International Labor Organization (ILO) 1980 Feb 11A; 1988 Feb 1H; 1989 Sep 13A

International Longshoremen's and Warehousemen's Union (ILWU) (unaffiliated) 1980 Jan 12G; 1981 Sep 2H; 1982 Apr 20F/Nov 22F; 1986 Dec 6H

International Maritime Organization 1989 Apr 25I

International Mathematical Union 1986 Aug 3I

International Monetary Fund (IMF) *see also* Group of Ten; *specific countries (e.g., Brazil)*
annual reports: 1981 Sep 13A; 1982 Aug 22A; 1984 Sep 12A
debt and loan issues: balance-of-payment loans cut off 1982 Apr 19A; developing countries 1989 Sep 26A; dollar prop-up plan abandoned 1980 Apr 24A; lending procedures changed 1988 Apr 15A; lending resources increase 1982 Dec 9A; 1983 Jan 18A/Feb 11A/Feb 14G; nominal-interest lending pool 1987 Dec 29A; repayment surplus 1988 Feb 3A; Special Drawing Rights calculation changed 1980 Sep 17A; U.S. debt reduction plan 1989 Apr 3A/May 24A
economic forecast: G-7 economic growth projected 1988 Dec 6A; recession prediction 1980 Jun 24A
funding issues: fund contribution quotas increased 1980 Dec 1A; U.S. contribution 1983 Aug 3G
meetings: 1980 Sep 19A/Oct 3A; 1981 Sep 29A/Oct 2A; 1983 Sep 27A/Sep 27G; 1984 Apr 13A/Sep 27A; 1985 Oct 11A; 1986 Sep

24A; 1987 Sep 29A; 1988 Apr 15A/Sep 27A

statistics: consumer prices of developing nations 1988 May 16A; industrial production of developed nations 1988 Apr 4A; international bank lending 1988 Jun 13A; reserve holdings of industrial nations 1988 Mar 7A; trade deficit of industrial nations 1988 May 2A; West Germany tops exporter list 1987 Aug 4A

International Narcotics Matters, U.S. Bureau of (State Department) 1986 Feb 21F

International Physicians for the Prevention of Nuclear War 1985 Oct 11A/Dec 10A

International Press Institute 1983 Jun 28B

International Skating Union 1988 Jun 8J

International Tchaikovsky Music Competition 1986 Jul 3J

International Telecommunications Satellite Organization 1984 Jun 9I

International Tennis Hall of Fame (Newport, R.I.) 1985 Jul 13J

International Theater Institute 1986 Jun 15F

International Thomson Organization Ltd. 1981 Feb 13J

International Tin Agreement 1982 Jun 23A

International Tin Council 1985 Oct 24A

International Trade, U.S. Council on 1982 Jun 5H

International Trade Commission (ITC)
automobiles: 1980 Jun 12H
ball bearings: 1989 May 2H
copper: 1984 Jan 26H
footwear: 1984 Jan 23H/Jun 6H; 1985 Jun 12H/Aug 28H
lumber: 1986 Jun 10D
steel: 1981 Dec 22H; 1983 Mar 24H/Jun 2A; 1984 Jan 24H/Feb 10H/Jul 12F/Jul 11H; 1986 Jun 2D
telecommunications: 1989 Nov 20H

International Trading Group Ltd. 1989 Sep 11H

International Typographical Union 1986 Nov 26H

International Union for Conservation of Nature and Natural Resources 1984 Apr 21I

International Whaling Commission 1981 Jul 25A; 1982 Jul 23A; 1984 Jun 22I; 1985 Apr 3H/Aug 6H; 1986 Jun 9I; 1987 Jun 25A/Jun 26E

International Women's Day 1983 May 25B; 1984 Mar 7E

International Woodworkers of America 1986 Dec 5D

Interpol (International Criminal Police Organization) 1984 Sep 15E

Interstate Commerce Commission, U.S. (ICC) 1980 Sep 15H; 1982 Mar 25H/Sep 13H; 1983 Jan 6H; 1984 Sep 18H; 1986 Jul 24H; 1987 Jul 2H

interstellar matter 1980 Jan 26I

interviews
Adair, Paul (Red) 1983 Jul 31C
Andropov, Yuri V. 1983 Feb 1B
Bakker, Jim 1987 May 26J
Barzani, Massoud 1986 May 22C
Brezhnev, Leonid 1981 Nov 2A
Bush, George 1988 Jan 25F
Carrion Cruz, Luis 1988 Nov 13D
Carter, Jimmy 1980 Apr 13G
Castro, Fidel 1983 Jul 28D; 1985 Feb 3D

Chernenko, Konstantin U. 1984 Sep 1B
Dam, Kenneth W. 1983 Oct 30G
Dhlakama, Afonso 1989 Dec 26C
Ferraro, Geraldine 1984 Aug 25F
Fiallos Navarro, Francisco 1982 Dec 12D
FitzGerald, Garret 1981 Aug 16B
Funderburk, David 1985 May 15B
Gorbachev, Mikhail S. 1985 Aug 26B; 1987 Nov 30G
Haig, Alexander 1982 Feb 5G
Hussein, King 1984 Mar 14C
Jackson, Jesse 1984 Jan 4C
Jumblat, Walid 1983 Aug 13C
Karpov, Viktor P. 1985 Mar 16B
Khan, Abdul Qadir 1987 Mar 1E
Mandela, Nelson 1985 Jan 27C
Meese III, Edwin A. 1985 Oct 14F
Moussavi, Hussein 1983 Apr 13C
Nakasone, Yashiro 1983 Jan 20E
Olszowski, Stefan 1981 Jan 5B
Pahlevi, Riza 1980 Jan 17C
Perez de Cuellar, Javier 1984 Jan 17C
Qaddafi, Muammer el- 1981 Dec 6C
Reagan, Nancy 1981 Nov 13F
Reagan, Ronald 1981 Mar 3G/Oct 16G/Oct 17G; 1982 Mar 17F; 1984 Jul 6F; 1985 Feb 11G/Apr 2H; 1987 Dec 3G; 1988 Dec 22F
Redgrave, Vanessa 1980 Nov 2J
Rehnquist, William H. 1984 Dec 29F
Reischauer, Edwin 1981 May 17G
Rodriguez, Daryl 1989 Apr 27F
Romanenko, Yuri V. 1987 Dec 29I
Ryzhkov, Nikolai 1987 Jan 5I
Sadat, Anwar 1981 Sep 22A
Schmidt, Helmut 1981 Nov 26A
Sharon, Ariel 1982 May 26C
Smith, Richard Craig 1984 May 13G
Stockman, David 1981 Nov 11H
Tambo, Oliver 1985 Nov 4C
Vlascv, Alexander 1987 Jan 6B
Watt, James 1983 Jan 27F
Yamani, Ahmed Zaki 1981 Sep 8A
Zia ul-Haq, Muhammad 1987 Mar 30E

In the Heat of the Night (TV show) 1989 Sep 17J

In the Skin of a Lion (Michael Ondaatje) (book) 1988 Mar 28J

intifada (Palestinian uprising) 1989 Jan 23C/Mar 22C/Sep 4C/Dec 9C

Into the Night (film) 1985 Mar 20J

Into the Woods (musical) 1987 Nov 5J; 1988 Jun 5J

intravenous drug users 1982 Jul 17I; 1985 Oct 2F; 1986 Jun 13I/Oct 23I; 1987 Aug 4I; 1988 Jan 31I; 1989 Feb 17F/Mar 8I

Inuit (Eskimos) 1982 Jul 8D/Nov 26D; 1987 Jan 15D/Mar 27D/May 26B; 1989 Apr 14D

Invincible (ship) 1983 Dec 17E

Invisible Touch (Genesis) (recording) 1986 Jul 16J/Aug 13J; 1987 Mar 28J

in vitro fertilization 1984 Jun 17I/Jul 18I/Oct 23I; 1985 Dec 17I; 1989 Jun 5I/Aug 9I/Dec 2I

INXS (singing group) 1988 Feb 20J/Mar 19J/Apr 23J

IOC *see* Olympic Committee, International

iodine, radioactive 1986 Oct 24H

Iona community (Scotland) 1989 Mar 7J

IOR *see* Istituto per le Opere di Religione

Iowa
blizzards: 1985 Nov 10I

crime and law enforcement: child abuse witness ruling 1988 Jun 29F; farmer kills 3, self 1985 Dec 9F

economy and labor: farmers protest 1985 Feb 27H; UAW auto contract 1987 Feb 1H

politics and government: presidential campaign (1980) 1980 Jan 5F/Jan 11F/Jan 12F/Jan 21F; presidential campaign (1984) 1984 Feb 11F/Feb 20F; presidential campaign (1988) 1987 Mar 19F/Apr 25F/Aug 8F/Aug 23F/Sep 12F/Nov 15F/Dec 30F; 1988 Feb 8F

Iowa (ship) 1989 Apr 19G/Apr 24G

Iowa, University of (Iowa City) 1980 Jun 7I; 1982 Jan 1J; 1986 Jan 1J

IRA *see* Irish Republican Army (IRA)

Iran *see also* individual leaders in the name index (e.g., Khomeini, Ayatollah)
accidents and disasters: defense minister's plane 1981 Sep 29C; Iran Airbus downing by U.S. 1988 Jul 3C/Jul 3G/Jul 11G/Aug 2G/Aug 19G; 1989 Mar 10G/Jul 17G

arts and culture: Rushdie death threats 1989 Feb 14C/Feb 17C/Feb 24A/Mar 7A/Mar 13C/Mar 29A; *see also Satanic Verses*

civil strife: Revolutionary Guards/Azerbaijani clashes 1980 Jan 9C; Sunni/Shiite clashes 1980 Jan 5C

coups and coup attempts: 1980 Jul 10C

defense and disarmament issues: nuclear weapons 1984 Apr 25A/Apr 25G

demonstrations and protests: Afghans 1980 Dec 27A; intellectuals 1981 Feb 16C; opposition group attacked 1980 Jun 12E

economy: food shortfall 1982 Mar 8E; GNP 1983 Dec 18E; rationing 1982 Jan 31E; Teheran cost of living 1988 Jun 28A

executions: Azerbaijani rebels 1980 Jan 12C; drug traffickers 1980 Jul 8C; Ghotbzadeh, Sadegh 1982 Sep 15C; Hashemi, Mehdi 1987 Sep 28C; left-wing counterterrevolutionaries 1981 Jul 6C; new rules for 1981 Sep 18C; statistics 1981 Aug 24C; 1983 Mar 1A

foreign relations: Afghanistan 1980 May 14E; Argentina 1981 Jul 26C; Bahrain 1982 May 22C; China 1987 Oct 22C; East Germany 1980 Apr 23A; France 1983 Aug 17C; 1986 Jun 30A; 1987 Jul 17B/Aug 14A/Nov 29A; 1988 Jan 13B/Jun 16A; Great Britain 1980 Apr 30A/May 5B/Aug 17C; 1987 Jun 4C/Jun 6A; 1989 Mar 7A; India 1989 Jul 7G; Iraq *see* Iran-Iraq War; Israel 1981 Jan 26C; 1982 Oct 25A/Kuwait 1988 Sep 28C; Lebanon 1982 Nov 21C; 1984 Jul 18C/Aug 16C; Hizballah; Islamic Amal/Jihad; Libya 1985 Jun 26C; Nicaragua 1985 Jan 23G; North Korea 1982 Dec 18A; Pakistan 1980 Oct 1A; Panama 1980 Jan 23A; Romania 1980 Apr 23A; Saudi Arabia 1982 Sep 26C; 1984 Jul 24A; 1987 Jul 31C; 1988 Apr 26C; Spain 1984 Jul 24A; Sweden 1986 Oct 4B; Syria 1988 May 26C; 1989 Jan

30C; USSR 1980 Apr 23A/Jun 30C/Oct 5C; 1982 Mar 9A; 1983 May 4B; 1986 Dec 11A; 1989 Jun 20C; West Germany 1984 Jul 22A; 1989 Jul 7G

government and politics: Bani-Sadr elected president 1980 Jan 25C; central bank governor resigns 1981 Jun 7C; commander of Revolutionary Guards resigns 1980 Jun 17E; communist party dissolved 1983 May 4B; defense minister and military leaders killed 1981 Sep 29C; Ghotbzadeh arrested 1980 Nov 7C; Khamenei wins presidential elections 1981 Oct 5C; Khomeini dies 1989 Jun 4C; ministers dismissed 1984 Aug 15C; Montazeri named designated successor to Khomeini 1985 Nov 23C; narcotics prosecutor resigns 1980 Dec 7C; parliamentary elections 1984 May 28C; 1989 Dec 18C; presidential elections scheduled 1981 Jun 24C; Rajai wins presidential election 1981 Jul 24C; revolution anniversary 1982 Feb 12C; social legislation 1981 Sep 3C

hijackings: Kuwaiti airliner 1984 Dec 4C/Dec 9C/Dec 11G; patrol boat near Spain 1981 Aug 14C

human rights: 1981 Sep 3C/Oct 12C; 1983 Mar 1A

international organizations: Arab League 1984 Mar 14C; United Nations 1980 Feb 23A/May 26A; 1981 Sep 26A; 1982 Oct 25A

Kurdish dispute: 1980 Feb 2C/Apr 22C/Oct 14C; 1986 Jan 7C

labor issues: water worker strike 1980 Jul 1C

obituaries: Bahonar, Mohammed Jad 1981 Aug 30C; Beheshti, Ayatollah Mohammed 1981 Jun 28C; Hosni, Mohammed Salem 1982 Mar 14C; Khomeini, Ayatollah Ruhollah 1989 Jun 4C; Qoddousi, Hojatolislam Ali 1981 Sep 5C; Rajai, Mohammed Ali 1981 Aug 30C

press and broadcasting: correspondent released 1987 Feb 4C; critic arrested 1980 Nov 7C; U.S. journalists expelled 1980 Jan 14C/Jul 25C

sports: Olympic Games (Los Angeles) 1983 Aug 1J

terrorist bombings: 1981 Jun 28C/Aug 30C/Aug 31C/Sep 5C; 1982 Oct 2C

trade issues: oil exports 1981 Jan 15C; 1982 Nov 10C; 1984 May 30C; U.S. exports 1982 Apr 22G; 1983 Dec 26E; 1987 Sep 29G

United Nations policy: 1980 Feb 23A/May 26A; 1981 Sep 26A; 1982 Oct 25A

U.S. relations: arms smuggling 1986 Apr 22F; 1989 Jan 4G; CIA operations 1982 Mar 6G; 1986 Nov 19G; conference on U.S. role 1980 Jun 2C/Jun 6C; damages to U.S. companies 1980 Jul 10G; demonstrations in U.S. 1980 Jul 27F; financial claims 1984 Sep 6A; 1986 Dec 29A; Iran called exporter of terrorism 1984 Jan 23C; Iran ex-attache assassinated 1980 Jul 22F; journalists expelled 1980 Jan 14C; secret talks 1986 Nov 6G; Stinger missile evidence found 1987 Oct 8C; suicide attacks feared 1984 Jan 21G; trade 1982 Apr 22G; 1983 Dec 26E;

1987 Sep 29G; U.S. citizen released 1982 Nov 6C; Iran Airbus downing by *Vincennes* 1988 Jul 3C/Jul 3G/Jul 11G/Aug 2G/Aug 19G; 1989 Mar 10G/Jul 17G

Iran Air 1988 Aug 19G/Dec 2A

Iran-contra arms scandal *see also specific players in the name index (e.g., North, Oliver L.)*
administration role: arms smuggling case reassessed 1986 Dec 2F; Casey-Woodward book furor 1987 Sep 27G; CIA involvement 1986 Nov 14G; conservative fundraiser releases audits 1987 Mar 9G; National Security Council computer messages 1987 Feb 20G; political campaign issues 1988 Aug 30F; secret airstrip in Costa Rica 1986 Dec 25G; story broken by Lebanese newspaper 1986 Nov 3C; White House assertions contradicted 1987 Feb 7G; White House response group created 1986 Dec 26F

congressional investigations and independent inquiries: chief counsel for Senate committee named 1987 Jan 22F; congressional hearings begin 1986 Dec 8G/Dec 11F/Dec 16F/Dec 17F; congressmen's conclusions about 1987 Aug 3G; contra aid solicitations 1987 Jan 23G; Hakim files stolen 1986 Dec 13F; immunity granted 1987 Mar 11G; Israel information agreement 1987 Jun 25G; reports 1987 Jan 19G/Jan 29G; Secord to testify voluntarily 1987 Apr 29G; testimony 1987 Feb 18G/May 5G/May 29G/Jun 2G/Jun 3G/Jun 23G/Jul 23G/Jul 29G/Jul 31G/Aug 19G

court procedures and trials: Fernandez charges dropped 1989 Nov 24F; indictments 1988 Jun 20F; 1989 Apr 24F/May 11F; Secord pleads guilty on false statement charge 1989 Nov 8F; trials 1987 Apr 29F; 1988 Jun 24F/Jun 8F/Jun 16F

foreign role: Canada 1986 Dec 12D; Israel 1986 Nov 26C/Dec 10F; USSR 1986 Dec 8B

Tower Commission *see* Tower Commission

Iran hostage crisis
United Nations resolutions: 1980 Jan 13A/Jun 16A
assets freeze: 1980 Jan 23A/Nov 13G/Dec 19C/Dec 27C-28C; 1981 Jan 3A/Jan 16F/Jan 21G
six embassy employees escape: 1980 Jan 29A
hostage families: 1980 Mar 4G
militants hedge on hostage release: 1980 Mar 6C-7C
World Court moves: 1980 Mar 18A/May 24A
hostages visited: 1980 Apr 14A/Dec 25C
rescue mission fails: 1980 Apr 24G-26G/May 1C/May 6C/Jun 5G/Aug 23G
hostages moved: 1980 Apr 26C/Jul 6C; 1981 Jan 3C
foreign reactions: European Community 1980 Mar 20A/Apr 22A; Switzerland 1980 Mar 30A
hostage confessions alleged: 1980 Apr 10C
economic sanctions: EC votes for 1980 May 18B; Great Britain im-

poses 1980 May 29B; USSR vetoes 1980 Jan 13A
ill hostage released: 1980 Jul 11C/Jul 15C
congressional actions: 1980 Jul 30C; 1981 Jan 19G
invasion plan asserted: 1980 Aug 16G
release talks and terms: 1980 Sep 9C/Nov 10C/Oct 22C/Dec 19C/Dec 21C/Dec 27C-28C; 1981 Jan 28C
Iranian parliament role: 1980 Oct 2C/Oct 30C/Nov 2C
militants turn over hostages: 1980 Dec 1C
hostage trials possible: 1980 Dec 31C
proposals for ending: 1981 Jan 3A/Jan 7C
agreements: 1981 Jan 18A-19A/Jan 26C/Feb 18G
hostages freed: 1981 Jan 20C-21J
hostage abuse denied: 1981 Jan 23C
hostages interviewed: 1981 Jan 29C
parade in New York: 1981 Jan 30J
U.S. embassy documents: 1981 Feb 8C/Dec 20G; 1982 Feb 1E
hostages to receive government benefits: 1981 Sep 21G
army intelligence unit: 1983 Aug 23G

Iranian embassy seizure (London, 1980) 1980 Apr 30A/May 5B

Iran-Iraq war (1980-88)
air strikes: Abadan (Iran) 1980 Sep 23C; Ahwaz (Iran) 1985 Mar 4C; Baghdad (Iraq) 1982 Jul 21C; Bandar Khomeini (Iran) 1980 Dec 5C; Baneh (Iran) 1984 Jun 5C; bombing 1983 Nov 27C; Bushehr (Iran) 1985 Mar 4C; Ilam (Iran) 1982 Jul 19C; Iran Airbus downing 1988 Jul 3C/Jul 3G/Jul 11G/Aug 2G/Aug 19G; 1989 Mar 10G/Jul 17G; Khorrambad (Iran) 1982 Jul 19C; Kirkuk (Iraq) 1980 Oct 21C; Larak Island (Iran) 1988 May 14C; military base (Iran) 1981 Apr 4C; Misan (Iraq) 1984 Dec 29C; missile attacks 1982 Dec 20C; 1984 Feb 11C; 1988 Mar 11C/Apr 7C; oil installations (Iran) 1980 Sep 24C; Sirri Island (Iran) 1986 Aug 2C; Teheran (Iran) 1980 Oct 6C; 1986 Dec 13C
casualty counts: 1988 Sep 18C
cease-fires: 1980 Oct 17C; 1982 Jun 10C; 1983 Apr 3C/Jun 8C; 1988 Sep 2C
chemical weapons: 1984 Mar 5C/Mar 7C/Mar 26A/Mar 30A/Jul 4C; 1989 Jan 28C
financing: 1982 Mar 6C
foreign developments: China 1986 Aug 26C; Egypt 1980 Nov 1C; 1981 Mar 31C; 1982 Apr 9C; France 1983 Nov 10C; Israel 1981 Aug 21C; 1982 May 26C; Jordan 1980 Sep 23C/Oct 6C/Oct 8C/Oct 27C; Kuwait 1981 Oct 1C; 1987 Sep 5C; 1988 Mar 30C; Libya 1980 Oct 10C; Morocco 1980 Sep 23C; North Korea 1980 Oct 8A; North Yemen 1980 Sep 23C; Persian Gulf states 1982 May 31C; 1983 Apr 26C; 1986 Mar 12C; 1987 Dec 26C; PLO 1980 Sep 23C; Saudi Arabia 1984 Jun 5C; United States 1980 Sep 23A/Sep 25A; 1982 May 26G; 1984 Aug 27G; 1985 Jul 14G;

1986 Dec 15G; USSR 1980 Sep 23A/Sep 25A
ground war: Abadan 1980 Sep 22C-23C/Sep 27C/Oct 10C; 1981 Sep 20C/Sep 27C; Ahwaz 1980 Sep 27C/Oct 1C; Baneh 1983 Oct 20C; Basra 1982 Jul 22C/Jul 30C; 1984 Feb 23C/Mar 1C; 1985 Mar 19C; 1987 Jan 21C/Jan 29C; 1988 May 25C; central front 1980 Sep 7C; 1982 Sep 30C; 1983 Feb 7C; 1984 Oct 18C; Dizful 1982 Nov 2C/Nov 7C; 1983 Apr 11C; Fao (Faw) 1986 Feb 11C; 1988 Apr 18C; Iran: no territorial ambitions 1982 May 26C; Khorramshahr 1980 Sep 23C/Sep 27C/Oct 1C/Oct 24C; 1982 May 9C/May 24C; Khuzistan 1980 Oct 22C; 1981 Nov 29C; 1982 Apr 30C; 1983 Apr 14C; Kirkuk 1987 Mar 8C; Kurdistan 1983 Jul 23C; 1987 Mar 8C; Marivan 1983 Oct 20C; Mehran 1984 Feb 16C; Misan 1983 Apr 14C; pre-war border dispute 1980 Mar 7C; Qasr-i-Shirin 1980 Sep 13C; shelling of civilians 1983 May 25C/May 26C; 1984 Feb 12C; southern front 1982 Mar 22C/Jul 17C; 1985 Mar 12C; 1986 Dec 25C; 1988 Jun 13C; Sumar 1982 Oct 1C; Susangird 1980 Sep 28C/Nov 14C; 1981 Jan 10C; western border 1981 Dec 9C
human rights: 1983 Sep 5A
international organizations: Arab League 1982 May 20C; 1987 Nov 8C/Nov 12C; Organization of the Islamic Conference 1981 Mar 5A/Mar 12A/Apr 4A; 1987 Jan 26C; Red Cross 1983 May 11C; 1984 Nov 24C; United Nations 1980 Sep 28A/Sep 29A/Oct 22A; 1984 May 25A/Jun 1A; 1988 Mar 5C/Jul 18C/Aug 15C/Aug 20C
peace initiatives: 1980 Sep 25C; 1988 Jul 28C/Aug 26C/Sep 13C/Sep 19C/Dec 16C; Algeria 1982 May 3C; Iraq 1982 Jun 9C; 1983 Apr 16C; Organization of the Islamic Conference 1981 Mar 5A/Mar 12A/Apr 4A; United Nations 1980 Oct 22A; 1981 Jan 16A/Feb 19A; 1988 Jul 18C
political issues: Iranian minister captured 1980 Oct 31C; Iranian war goals 1983 Feb 23C; Iraqi claims 1980 Sep 21C; 1983 Feb 13C; Iraqi morale 1983 Feb 16C; Iraqi threats 1982 Aug 21C; Iraqi war goals 1980 Oct 2C; 1981 Apr 19C
prisoners of war (POWs): 1983 Feb 13C/Sep 5A; 1984 Mar 7C; 1988 Sep 1C; 1989 Dec 25C
shipping war
Iran: antiship missiles set up 1987 Mar 14C; blockade threatened 1983 Jul 24C/Oct 11C; Danish ship seized 1981 Aug 12C; Kuwait oil platform attacked 1987 Oct 22C; naval battles 1983 Apr 13C; naval maneuvers 1987 Aug 7C; oil exports affected by 1987 Oct 7C; oil spills 1983 Mar 29I/Apr 7C/Apr 26C/Sep 21C/Dec 13C; oil supply 1980 Sep 24A/Sep 26C; oil tanker attacks 1984 May 16C; 1985 Aug 18C; 1987 Aug 31C/Oct 16C; Red Sea mining 1984 Jul 31C; Strait of Hormuz passage guarantee 1980 Oct 1C; U.S. presence seen as aggression 1984 Feb 29C; U.S. ship searched 1986 Jan 12C

Iraq: oil tanker attacks 1984 Jun 24C/Aug 7C/Dec 3C; 1987 Jun 20C/Aug 29C; 1988 Jan 12C
statistics: 1987 Oct 2C/Dec 17C
United States: Iranian oil rig bombed 1987 Oct 19C; Iranian vessels attacked 1987 Nov 3C; 1988 Apr 18C; Iranian vessel seized 1987 Sep 21C; Kuwaiti tankers escorted 1987 Aug 12C/Aug 24C; Stingers sold to Saudi Arabia 1984 May 29G

Iraq see also individual leaders in the name index (e.g., Hussein, Saddam)
accidents and disasters: Iraqi Airways jet (Saudi Arabia) 1986 Dec 25C
foreign debt: 1989 Apr 5C
foreign relations: Egypt 1982 Jul 5C/Dec 29C; France 1980 Feb 27I; 1981 Jun 17C; 1982 Jan 14A; 1983 Aug 17C; 1984 Mar 1A; Great Britain 1980 Jun 19C; India 1982 Aug 11A; Iran 1980 Mar 7C/Apr 8C/Sep 20C/Sep 21C; see also Iran-Iraq War; Israel: Osirak nuclear reactor 1981 Jan 10C/Jun 8C-9C/Jun 11C/Jun 15C/Jun 17C/Jun 19A-19C/Jul 16C/Nov 13A; Italy 1989 Sep 14B/Dec 14B; Kuwait 1983 Dec 27C; Lebanon 1981 Dec 15C; PLO 1982 Aug 6C; Saudi Arabia 1980 Nov 20C; Syria 1982 Mar 7C/Apr 8C/Apr 10C/Apr 17C; 1989 May 23C; Turkey 1984 Aug 6C; 1986 Aug 15A; 1987 Mar 4C; USSR 1984 Mar 9A; 1989 Feb 23C; West Germany 1980 Aug 1A
government and politics: elections 1989 Apr 1C; opposition groups form front 1980 Nov 13C
hijackings: Iraqi Airways jet (Saudi Arabia) 1986 Dec 25C
human rights: 1989 Feb 28C
international organizations: non-aligned nations 1982 Aug 11A; Kurds: 1983 Aug 6C; 1984 Jul 29C; 1986 Jan 7C/May 22C/Aug 15A; 1987 Mar 4C; 1988 Mar 21C/Sep 8C/Sep 15G/Sep 21C; 1989 Apr 9C/Oct 12C
oil and gas issues: pipelines 1980 Sep 27C/Nov 20C; 1981 Feb 26C; 1982 Jan 3C/Apr 10C
terrorism: Abu Nidal 1982 Nov 9C; 1984 Jun 8C; British embassy attack 1980 Jun 19C; Iraqi embassy in Beirut bombed 1981 Dec 15C; Vienna synagogue attack 1981 Aug 29B; West Berlin bombing plot 1980 Aug 1A
U.S. relations: 1981 Apr 13G; 1982 Apr 14G; 1984 Nov 8A; 1988 Sep 27G

Iraqi Airways 1986 Dec 25C

IRAS-Araki-Alcock (comet) 1983 May 11I

Ireland
accidents and disasters: Air-India crash 1985 Jun 23A; Dublin discotheque fire 1981 Feb 14B
crime and law enforcement: arms smuggling 1982 Jul 19B; 1983 May 13F; 1984 Sep 29B; extradition of suspects 1988 May 13B/Dec 13B; guerrillas captured 1984 Mar 17B; 1987 Nov 27B; Protestant loyalists arrested 1986 Aug 7B
economy: budget 1982 Mar 26B; 1987 Jan 5B/Mar 31B; currency 1986 Aug 2B; oil drilling 1983 Aug 20B

family issues: abortion and birth control 1983 Sep 7B; 1985 Feb 20B; divorce ban 1986 Jun 26B
foreign relations: Great Britain 1981 Aug 16B/Nov 6B; 1988 May 13B/Dec 13B; see also Anglo-Irish accord
government and politics: FitzGerald becomes prime minister 1981 Jun 30B; 1982 Dec 14B; Haughey becomes prime minister 1982 Mar 9B; 1987 Mar 10B; Haughey government falls 1982 Nov 4B; IRA political wing gets parliament seats 1986 Nov 2B; Labour Party leader resigns 1982 Oct 29B; local elections 1985 Jun 20B; opposition party leader chosen 1987 Mar 21B; parliamentary elections 1981 Jun 11B; 1982 Nov 24B; 1987 Feb 17B
international organizations: European Community 1984 Jul 19B/Jul 25B; 1987 Apr 9B
mergers and acquisitions: Waterford Glass/Wedgewood merger 1986 Oct 8B
sports: cycling 1987 Sep 6J
U.S. relations: 1983 Jun 24G; 1985 Oct 1F

Irian Jaya (Indonesia) 1984 Aug 29E

Irises (Vincent van Gogh) (painting) 1987 Nov 11J

Irish National Liberation Army 1980 Feb 7B; 1982 Aug 30B; 1983 Nov 20B; 1985 Oct 9B/Oct 18B

Irish Republican Army (IRA) see also individual leaders in the name index (e.g., Sands, Robert)
British policy: "Gibraltar 3" expose 1989 Jan 26B
Maze Prison hunger strikes see Maze Prison
Provisional IRA see Provisional Irish Republican Army
Sinn Fein see Sinn Fein
terrorism: 2 UK soldiers slain 1988 Mar 19B; Belfast, London bombings 1981 Oct 10B-11B; Gardiner death plot 1981 Jun 14B; Harrod's blast 1983 Dec 17B; London bombings 1982 Jul 19B; MP slain 1981 Nov 14B; Protestant leader, son slain 1981 Jan 21B/Jun 14B
U.S. policy: extradition treaty 1986 May 31G; gunrunners convicted 1983 May 13F; violence condemned 1983 Mar 17J

Iron and Steel Institute, American see American Iron and Steel Institute

Iron Eagle (film) 1986 Jan 22J

"iron triangles" 1988 Dec 12F

Ironweed (William Kennedy) (book/film) 1984 Apr 16J; 1987 Dec 18J

Irreconcilable Differences (film) 1984 Oct 10J

irrigation 1983 Nov 21D; 1985 Mar 15H/Mar 28H; 1988 Aug 19H

IRS see Internal Revenue Service

Ishikawajima-Harima Heavy Industries Co. 1985 Apr 27B

Ishtar (film) 1987 May 20J

Is It True (racehorse) 1988 Nov 5J

Islam see individual leaders in the name index (e.g., Khomeini, Ayatollah); sects (e.g., Shiite Moslems); specific countries (e.g., Iran)

Islamic Amal 1983 Oct 26C

Islamic College (West Bank) 1983 Jul 26C

Islamic fundamentalists see also specific organizations (e.g., Moslem Brotherhood)
Afghanistan: 1989 Feb 23E
Algeria: 1981 Oct 6C
Egypt: 1981 Oct 9C/Dec 29C; 1982 Mar 6C/Apr 15C; 1984 Sep 30C; 1987 Apr 10C; 1988 Dec 19C; 1989 Apr 26C/May 3C
Iran: 1980 Apr 18C/Jun 17E/Oct 2C/Nov 7C
Jordan: 1985 Dec 27C; 1989 Nov 10C
Malaysia: 1986 Aug 3E
Syria: 1982 Mar 7C
Tunisia: 1987 Oct 2C; 1989 Apr 2C
United States: 1980 Jul 23F

Islamic Jihad (Holy War)
bombings: 1983 Apr 18C/Nov 4C/Dec 12C; 1984 Sep 20C; 1985 Mar 10C/May 18C
hijackings: 1984 Dec 4C
hostages: 1984 Oct 2C; 1985 Mar 14C/Mar 15C/Mar 16C/Mar 25C/Oct 4C; 1987 Mar 23C/Dec 24C; 1988 Oct 1C/Oct 3C
mining of Red Sea: 1984 Jul 31C

Islamic law 1980 May 22C; 1985 Jan 18C; 1987 Sep 28C

Islamic States, Conference of see Conference of Islamic States

Israel see also individual leaders in the name index (e.g., Begin, Menachim)
arts and culture: archaeology 1982 Feb 23J; 1988 Feb 18I
crime and law enforcement: Bedouin parliament member killed 1981 Jan 12C; bus hijackers 1984 Jun 1C; Jewish student's murderers sentenced 1984 May 21C; minister convicted 1982 Apr 23C; minister of religious affairs 1980 Dec 30C
currency: 1980 Feb 24C; 1984 Aug 17C/Sep 16C
defense and disarmament issues: budget 1980 Dec 21C; IDF study 1986 May 21C; intermediate-range ballistic missiles 1987 Jul 21C/Jul 23B; nuclear weapons 1980 Feb 21C/Nov 13A; 1981 May 2C/Jun 24C; 1986 Oct 5C; 1988 Mar 24C; 1989 Oct 26C
economy and business: austerity measures 1983 Oct 10C; 1985 Jul 1C; banking 1985 Jan 6C; 1986 Apr 20C; Bank of Israel; budget 1983 Nov 7C; 1984 Feb 22C; consumer prices 1984 May 15C; El-Al flight curbs 1982 Aug 25C; inflation rate 1980 Jan 15C; 1986 Oct 8C; land expropriations 1980 Mar 12C; optimism about 1986 Oct 8C; Tel Aviv Stock Exchange 1983 Oct 10C/Oct 18C; wage-price freeze 1984 Nov 2C; 1985 Jan 24C
espionage and intelligence issues: nuclear technician convicted 1988 Mar 24C; Pollard case 1985 Nov 21G/Dec 1C; 1986 Jun 4G; 1987 Mar 4G/May 26C
foreign relations
Chile: 1984 Jan 25D
Ecuador: 1981 Mar 21G
Egypt: Baker plan accepted 1989 Dec 7C; Egyptian Arafat reception criticized 1983 Dec 22C; Egyptian commitment to peace 1982 Feb 20C; Egyptian parliament votes to end boycott 1980 Feb 5C; high-level contacts re-

sumed 1983 Dec 29C; 1985 Feb 27C; normalization of relations 1980 Oct 29C; Palestinian autonomy talks 1980 Feb 1C/Jun 11A/Sep 3A; 1981 Feb 22C/Feb 23G/Sep 23C/Nov 12C; 1982 Mar 21C

Ethiopia: 1985 Jan 3C/Jan 4C

France: 1981 Dec 8A; 1982 Mar 3C

Great Britain: 1982 Jun 3C; 1986 May 24C

Iran: 1981 Jul 26C/Aug 21C; 1982 Oct 25A

Iraq: Osirak nuclear reactor 1981 Jan 10C/Jun 8C-9C/Jun 11C/Jun 15C/Jun 17C/Jun 19A/Jun 19C/Jul 16C/Nov 13A

Ivory Coast: 1985 Dec 18C

Lebanon see Lebanon

Liberia: 1983 Aug 28C

Libya: 1986 Feb 4C

Nicaraguan contras: 1984 May 19G/Sep 8D; 1987 Jan 23G/Feb 27C

Poland: 1985 Oct 17A

Saudi Arabia: 1981 Apr 23C/Aug 8C/Aug 11C; 1982 Jan 4C

South Africa: 1987 Mar 18C; 1989 Oct 26C

Syria: 1981 Mar 24C/Apr 5C/May 5A-6A/Jun 1C/Jun 9C; 1985 Dec 15C

Tunisia: 1985 Oct 1C

Turkey: 1980 Dec 2C

USSR: 1982 Jan 17A/Jun 14A; 1985 Dec 25B; 1986 Aug 18A; 1987 Apr 9A/Jul 12C/Jul 23B; 1988 Oct 23C/Dec 2C; 1989 Feb 22C

Zaire: 1982 May 14A

government and politics

cabinet and ministries: Weizman resigns as defense minister 1980 May 25C; Arens becomes defense minister 1983 Feb 11C

celebrations: 1988 Apr 21C

coalition: Peres/Shamir form national unity government 1984 Aug 31C; Shamir OKs 2nd coalition 1988 Dec 19C

elections: Herzog elected president 1983 Mar 22C; Knesset 1981 Jun 30C; 1984 Mar 22C/Jul 23C; 1988 Nov 1C

parliament (Knesset): Begin government survives no confidence vote 1982 Mar 23C/May 19C; elections 1981 Jun 30C; 1984 Mar 22C/Jul 23C; 1988 Nov 1C; Kahane role disputed 1984 Dec 25C; 1987 Jun 8C/Jul 1C

political parties: Labour Party Palestinian plan 1980 Nov 8C; new party formed 1981 Mar 15C

human rights: 1988 Feb 11C

immigration and refugees: Ethiopian Jews 1985 Jan 3C/Jan 4C; statistics 1981 Aug 19C; USSR 1982 Jan 17A; 1985 Dec 25B; 1987 Apr 9A; 1988 Oct 23C

international organizations: Arab League 1982 Sep 9C; European Community 1980 Jun 13A; IAEA 1982 Sep 24A; Red Cross 1983 Dec 13C; United Nations 1980 May 8A/Oct 9A/Nov 13A/Dec 15A; 1982 Apr 28A/Aug 6A/Aug 19A/Oct 25A; 1983 Aug 13A; 1987 Oct 13A/Dec 21A

labor issues: doctors get wage increase 1983 Sep 6C; doctors' strike 1983 May 22C/May 25C/Jun 26C

Nazi war criminals: 1984 Jan 25D; Demjanjuk, John

obituaries: Allon, Yigal 1980 Feb 29C; Dayan, Moshe 1981 Oct 16C; Goldmann, Nahum 1982 Aug 29C; Scholem, Gershom 1982 Feb 20J; Yadin, Yigael 1984 Jun 28C

Palestinian issues: 1980 Dec 1C; 1981 Feb 25C; 1987 Dec 21C; conference in U.S. 1989 Mar 12C; military actions 1980 May 15C/Jun 16C; 1981 Jul 17C; 1985 Oct 1C; 1988 Feb 15C; PLO military chief assassinated 1988 Apr 16C; prisoner exchanges 1983 Nov 24C/Dec 13C; prisoner releases 1985 Jul 24C; recognition of Israel 1982 Jan 22C/Jul 13C; 1988 Nov 15C

religious issues: citizenship 1987 Jul 8C; El-Al flights curbed 1982 Aug 25C; Reform Jewish rabbi ordained 1980 Feb 19C; strife 1986 Jun 24C

security forces: Moslem officer wrongly convicted 1987 May 24C; Palestinian beating deaths 1984 May 28C; 1986 Jun 25C

space program: satellite launching 1988 Sep 19I

terrorism: Antwerp, Belgium attack on Jewish youths 1980 Jul 27B; Arab gunmen from Egypt killed 1989 Dec 5C; army base attacked 1987 Nov 25C; Israeli ambassador in Britain shot 1982 Jun 3C; Jewish extremists arrested 1980 May 14C; London El Al bombing plot 1986 May 21B/Oct 24C; Rome and Vienna airport killings 1985 Dec 27A; 1986 May 21B; tourist bus attacked 1981 Jul 29C; West Berlin restaurant bombing 1982 Jan 15C; : Dome of the Rock killings see Dome of the Rock

United Nations policy: 1980 May 8A/Oct 9A/Nov 13A/Dec 15A; 1982 Apr 28A/Aug 6A/Aug 19A/Oct 25A; 1983 Aug 13A; 1987 Oct 13A/Dec 21A

U.S. relations: aid 1982 Nov 30G/Dec 5C; 1984 Dec 19C; 1985 Jan 30G; ambassador criticizes Reagan administration 1981 Dec 26C; arms smuggling plot 1986 Apr 22F; 1989 Jan 4G; cluster bombs 1982 Sep 29G; conference on peace 1989 Mar 12C; cooperation accord 1981 Nov 30C; 1984 Jan 24A; debt-relief plan 1986 Dec 24G; extradition of terrorist suspect 1981 Dec 13G; F-16 fighter planes 1981 Jul 1G/Jul 20G/Aug 11G; 1983 Apr 13C; Iran-contra arms scandal 1986 Nov 26C/Dec10F; 1987 Jun 25G; 1988 Mar 28F; Kfir fighter planes 1981 Mar 21G; Lavi fighter plane project 1983 Apr 17C/May 2C; military attache to U.S. appointed 1986 Aug 1C; peace proposals 1989 Mar 11C; restraint after terrorist attacks urged 1985 Dec 29G; Saudi Arabia arms sales 1981 Apr 22G/Sep 11G/Sep 22G/Oct 29C; 1986 Mar 11G; Strategic Defense Initiative 1986 May 6C; trade agreement 1985 Mar 4A; U.S. proposals rejected 1982 Sep 2C; visits 1982 Feb 26C; 1985 Aug 18C

Israeli-occupied territories 1980 Jul 29A; 1981 Sep 23C/Nov 12C; 1982 Mar 21C; 1983 Apr 17C; 1988 Jan

25C/Jan 30G/Jun 7C; Gaza Strip; West Bank

Is There No Place on Earth For Me? (Susan Sheehy) (book) 1983 Apr 18J

Istituto per le Opere di Religione (IOR) (Vatican Bank) 1982 Jul 13B/Nov 21A/1984 May 25B; 1985 Mar 15B; 1987 Feb 26B/Jul 17B

Isuzu Motors Ltd. 1981 Aug 12H; 1982 May 24H

It (Stephen King) (book) 1986 Sep 26J/Oct 31J/Nov 21J/Dec 26J; 1987 Jan 23J/Feb 27J

Itaipu Dam (Brazil/Paraguay) 1982 Nov 5I; 1984 Oct 25D

Italian-American Working Group on Organized Crime and Drug Trafficking 1984 Oct 3F

Italian Grand Prix (auto race) 1985 Sep 8J; 1986 Sep 7J; 1987 Sep 6J; 1988 Sep 11J; 1989 Sep 10J

Italmobiliare S.p.A. 1984 Apr 1B

Italy see also individual leaders in the name index (e.g., Andreotti, Giulio)

accidents and disasters: Cubana Airlines jet (Cuba) 1989 Sep 3D; earthquakes 1980 Nov 23I/Nov 29B/Dec 8I; 1984 May 11I; floods 1985 Jul 19I; Heysel stadium soccer riot 1985 May 29B; 1986 Sep 9B; 1987 Sep 9B; 1989 Apr 28B; Mt. Etna volcanic eruption 1983 May 14I; Turin movie theater fire 1983 Feb 13J

arts and culture: da Vinci Last Supper crack detected 1980 Jun 16J; Leaning Tower of Pisa closed for repairs 1989 Dec 15B; playwrights U.S. visa 1983 Aug 27F; 1984 Nov 15G

Banco Ambrosiano scandal: 1982 Jul 13B/Jul 19B/Jul 30B/Aug 9B/Nov 26B/Dec 24B; 1983 Feb 18B; 1984 Mar 8B/May 25B; 1987 Feb 26B; 1989 Apr 7B

banks see Banca Nazionale del Lavoro; Banco Ambrosiano

business and industry: Banca Nazionale del Lavoro (BNL) 1989 Aug 17A/Sep 14B/Dec 14B; Bosporus Strait bridge contract 1985 Apr 27B; Fiat aid for Westland PLC 1986 Feb 12A; Fiat market share 1987 Jul 22B; steel industry 1985 Mar 27B

crime and law enforcement: businessmen and bankers arrested 1980 Mar 4B; Carabinieri official assassinated 1982 Sep 3B; Communist Party leader in Sicily killed 1982 Apr 30B; financier indicted 1982 Jul 22B; Mafia raids 1983 Mar 5B; 1984 Sep 29B/Oct 25B; narcotics smuggling operation 1988 Dec 1B; prison revolt 1980 Dec 29B; publishing group executives arrested 1983 Feb 18B; security company vault robbed 1984 Mar 24B; Seveso chemical plant convictions 1983 Sep 24B; urban guerrillas arrested 1980 Jul 5B; U.S. organized crime cooperation 1984 Oct 3F

currency: 1981 Mar 22B/Aug 3H/Oct 4B; 1982 Jun 12B/Oct 4A; 1985 Jul 20B; 1987 Sep 13B

defense and disarmament issues: antinuclear protests 1982 Apr 17B; 1983 Apr 4B; cruise missile deployment 1983 Nov 16B; nuclear weapons proliferation 1987 Apr 16A

economy: balance of payments 1988 Jan 20B; budget 1982 Jul 31B; 1986 Dec 21B; 1988 Dec 27B; drought 1989 Feb 19B; economic ranking 1989 Jan 3B; gross domestic product 1987 Jul 1B/Dec 19B; tax changes 1988 Dec 27B; wine poisoning 1986 Apr 10B

education: religion in public schools 1987 Oct 10B

environmental issues: algae on coastline 1989 Jul 23I; Venice lagoon cleanup 1988 Sep 12B

family issues: abortion 1981 May 18B

foreign relations: Argentina 1982 Nov 11A; Bulgaria 1982 Dec 11B/Dec 22B; China 1984 Jun 16E; 1985 Apr 7A; 1986 Jun 8B; Libya 1986 Apr 15C; Poland 1981 Apr 13B; Syria 1986 May 21B; Tunisia 1985 Feb 3B; U.S. 1983 Aug 27F; 1984 Oct 3F/Nov 15G; 1989 May 2H; USSR 1982 Jul 24B; 1988 Oct 20B

government and politics: Christian Democrats party conference 1980 Feb 21B; Communist Party 1980 Apr 2B; 1981 Apr 13B; De Mita becomes premier 1988 Apr 13B; elections 1983 Jun 27B; 1987 Jun 15B; Fanfani at G-7 summit 1987 Jun 8A; Fanfani becomes premier 1987 Apr 18B; Goria becomes premier 1987 Jul 29B; Goria resigns as premier 1988 Mar 11B; Goria submits resignation as premier 1988 Feb 10B; officials suspended for Masonic Lodge membership 1981 May 28B; referendum voting 1987 Nov 8B; securities regulatory body president resigns 1982 Aug 11B

international organizations: European Community 1985 Mar 27B; European Court of Justice 1982 Mar 5B; United Nations 1982 Nov 11A; 1985 Mar 11A

labor issues: job action protest 1980 Jan 15B

medicine and health care: abortion 1981 May 18B; Chernobyl radiation effects 1987 Mar 25I

obituaries: Barzini, Luigi 1984 Mar 30J; Berlinguer, Enrico 1984 Jun 12J; Calvino, Italo 1985 Sep 19J; Dalla Chiesa, Carlo Alberto 1982 Sep 3B; Del Monaco, Mario 1982 Oct 15J; La Torre, Pio 1982 Apr 30B; Leone, Sergio 1989 Apr 30J; Levi, Primo 1987 Apr 11J; Morante, Elsa 1985 Nov 25J; Nenni, Pietro 1980 Jan 1B; Petri, Elio 1982 Nov 19J; Pignedoli, Sergio 1980 Jun 15J; Saragat, Giuseppe 1988 Jun 11B

peacekeeping forces: Lebanon 1982 Aug 20G/Aug 27C; 1983 Sep 7C/Oct 27A/Dec 23B/Dec 31C; 1984 Feb 8B/Feb 20C; Sinai Peninsula 1982 Jan 13A/Jan 31C

religion: public schools 1987 Oct 10B; Shroud of Turin 1988 Oct 13J; Vatican agreement signed 1984 Feb 18B

science and technology: Levi-Montalcini receives Nobel Prize 1986 Oct 13I; Rubbia wins Nobel Prize 1984 Oct 17I

sports: auto racing 1985 Jun 16J/Sep 8J; 1986 Sep 7J; 1987 May 3J/Sep 6J; 1988 May 1J/Sep 11J; 1989 Apr 23J/Sep 10J; Heysel soccer riots 1985 May

29B; 1986 Sep 9B; 1987 Sep 9B; 1989 Apr 28B; horse racing 1988 Oct 2J; Olympic Games (Moscow) 1980 May 20J; running 1985 Oct 27J; 1986 Nov 2J; 1987 May 29J; shot put 1987 Aug 12J; skiing 1985 Feb 6J; soccer 1982 Jul 11J; 1989 Dec 9J; tennis 1980 Dec 7J

stock markets: 1981 Jul 8B

terrorism: Achille Lauro hijacking 1985 Oct 9C/Oct 10C; Bologna train station bombing 1980 Aug 2B/Aug 6B; Bolzano bombings 1981 Jul 31B; Moro murder suspects arrested 1980 Mar 12B; Red Brigades 1980 Apr 28B/May 12B/Dec 12B; 1981 Apr 4B/Jul 24B/Dec 17B; 1982 Jan 28B; 1983 Jan 24B; Rome airport massacre 1985 Dec 27A; 1986 May 21B; 1987 Feb 5B; 1988 Feb 12B; statistics 1987 Jan 5B

ITC see International Trade Commission

Ithaca (New York) 1985 Dec 23G

It's All True (film) 1986 Aug 27J

Its Hard (The Who) (recording) 1982 Sep 22J

It's Over, Debbie (euthanasia essay) 1988 Jan 8I

ITT Corp. 1982 May 13H

I've Heard the Mermaids Singing (film) 1988 Mar 22J

ivory 1989 May 11I/Jul 18C/Oct 16C/Oct 30E/Nov 20C

Ivory Coast 1985 Aug 19J/Oct 28C/Dec 18C; 1987 May 28C; 1989 Feb 14C/Oct 18A

I Wanna Dance With Somebody (Whitney Houston) (recording) 1988 Mar 2J

J

J. Geils Band (singing group) 1982 Jan 20J/Feb 24J/Mar 14J/Mar 17J

J. Paul Getty Museum (Malibu, Calif.) 1982 Mar 1J; 1985 Apr 18J

J. Paul Getty Trust 1983 Sep 20J

Jackson Clarion-Ledger (newspaper) 1983 Apr 18J

Jackson Laboratory (Bar Harbor, Maine) 1980 Oct 10I

Jacksons (singing group) 1984 Dec 9J

Jacob Javits Federal Building (New York City) 1985 May 31J

Jaffna University (Sri Lanka) 1989 May 13E

Jagged Edge (film) 1985 Oct 23J/Nov 20J

Jailbird (Kurt Vonnegut) (book) 1980 Jan 13J/Feb 10J

Jamaica

accidents and disasters: fires 1980 May 20D; Hurricane Kate 1985 Nov 22I

business and industry: grain shipments fraud charged 1980 Feb 4D

crime and law enforcement: curfew against armed bands 1980 Jul 18D; reggae singer killed 1987 Sep 11J

foreign debt: 1980 Apr 7D/Apr 15D; 1987 Nov 20D

government and politics: coup plot arrests 1980 Jun 22D; local elections 1986 Jul 29D; Manley wins national elections 1989 Feb 9D; Seaga party wins control of House 1983 Dec 15D; Seaga wins national elections 1980 Oct 30D monetary issues: IMF loans 1980 Jan 15D/Mar 25D/Apr 15D; 1984 Jun 22D; 1987 Jan 15D

obituaries: Marley, Bob 1981 May 11J; Tosh, Peter 1987 Sep 11J

sports: soccer 1988 Aug 13J

U.S. relations: embassy member residence fired on 1980 Jul 4D; grain shipments fraud charged 1980 Feb 4D

Jamaican State Trading Corp. 1980 Feb 4D

James E. Sullivan Memorial Award (athletics) 1987 Feb 23J

Jammu and Kashmir *see* Kashmir

Jane's Defence Weekly (British magazine) 1984 Apr 25A/Apr 25G

Jane's Fighting Ship (British publication) 1984 Oct 1G

Jane's Spaceflight Directory (British publication) 1986 Jun 17I

Janet Jackson's Rhythm Nation 1814 (Janet Jackson) (recording) 1989 Oct 28J/Dec 25J/Dec 30J

Japan *see also individual leaders in the name index (e.g.,* Nakasone, Yasuhiro)

accidents and disasters: earthquakes 1983 May 26I; Japan Airlines crash 1985 Aug 12E; merchant ship/U.S. submarine collision 1981 Apr 20G; Mount Mihara erupts 1986 Nov 21I; nuclear power plant leaks 1981 Mar 8I/May 13E; tidal waves 1983 May 26I; Vietnam boat people/supertanker collision 1989 Mar 8E

arts and culture: Los Angeles museum opens 1986 Dec 10J; Tange wins Pritzger 1987 Mar 18J

automobile industry: 1981 Jul 23E; 1982 Jan 5H; 1983 Jan 26E; 1985 Jan 28E; 1988 Apr 7E

aviation: airline safety talks 1985 May 24A/Jul 30A; Japan Airlines crash 1985 Aug 12E; Japanese airport bombing 1985 Jun 23A; Korean airliner victims remembered 1984 Aug 31E

banks: Bank of Japan 1986 Jan 29E; 1987 Feb 20E; 1989 May 30E; interest rates 1986 Mar 7A/Apr 19A/Oct 31E; international bank lending 1988 Jun 13A; ranking of world's banks 1988 Jul 19A

budget: 1984 Jan 25E; 1986 Dec 30E; 1987 Jul 24E/Nov 23E; 1988 Apr 17E/Jul 1E/Aug 1E; 1989 Jan 19E/Jan 24E/Apr 28E

business and industry: Bosporus Strait bridge contract 1985 Apr 27B; direct investment 1987 May 28E; 1988 May 31E; IBM/Fujitsu Ltd. software dispute 1988 Nov 29H; management praised 1982 Jul 26H; steel industry 1982 Jul 21H; 1987 May 29E; voted most industrially competitive nation 1984 Jan 6A

corruption and ethics issues: IBM/Hitachi lawsuit 1983 Oct 6H; IBM information theft 1982 Jun 22G; 1983 Feb 8H; Lockheed bribery case 1982 Dec 22E; 1983 Oct 12E; Recruit scandal 1989 Feb 13E/Apr 11E/Apr 25E/Apr 27E/May 29E/Jun 2E

crime and law enforcement: crime syndicate leader killed 1985 Jan 27E; security in Tokyo stepped up 1986 Apr 1E

currency: 1980 Mar 2E; 1982 Oct 4A; 1983 Aug 1A/Sep 7H; 1986 Mar 18E/Apr 23E/May 30E/Jul 7H;

1987 Jan 21A/Mar 30H/Apr 9A/Nov 30H/Dec 31H; 1988 Mar 4H/Nov 11H/Dec 30H; 1989 May 22A

defense and disarmament issues: antinuclear movement 1982 Mar 22E/Jun 7G; defense spending 1981 Aug 14E; 1982 Jul 9E/Jul 23E; 1984 Jan 25E; 1985 Sep 18E; 1986 Dec 30E; 1987 Jan 23E/Oct 6A; fighter planes 1987 Oct 2E; missile technology treaty 1987 Apr 16A

economy: billionaires listed 1987 Sep 20H; 1989 Jul 9H; creditor nation status 1986 May 27E; 1987 May 26E; fishing 1989 Dec 13I; five-year development plan 1988 May 23E; GNP 1981 Jun 19E; 1982 Jun 11E; 1986 Jun 24E; 1987 Mar 17E/Jun 16E/Dec 4E; 1988 Mar 17E/Jun 16E; 1989 Mar 17E; growth rate set 1982 Dec 25E; housing starts 1988 Aug 31E; import boosting measures 1989 Dec 28E; inflation rate 1989 Sep 13A; land values 1988 May 20E/Dec 23E; predictions 1982 Jan 17E; ranking in world 1989 Jan 3B; reserve holdings 1988 Mar 7A; standard of living 1988 Jun 3H; stimulus package 1981 Oct 2E; 1982 Oct 8E; 1985 Oct 15E; 1986 Apr 8E/Sep 19E; 1987 Apr 7E/May 29C

energy issues: nuclear power plants 1981 Mar 8I/May 13E; 1988 Mar 21I

environmental issues: whaling 1986 Jun 9I; 1987 Jun 26E

foreign investment

Australia: 1981 Jan 20E

equities; 1988 Apr 8E

United States: banks 1983 Mar 14H; Honda 1980 Jan 11H; 1986 Mar 17H; Mitsubishi 1989 Oct 30H; Nissan 1983 May 9H; 1989 Jul 27H; Sony 1989 Sep 27H; statistics 1988 Apr 5H; 1989 Jan 17H; Toyota 1985 Jun 25H; 1986 Nov 25H

foreign relations

Africa: South Africa 1987 Feb 20A

Asia and Pacific Rim: Australia 1981 Jan 20E; 1984 Apr 13E; 1988 Jun 24E; China 1982 Aug 28E; 1983 Jul 20E; 1984 Mar 16E; 1987 May 8E/Jun 27E; 1988 Apr 4E; 1989 Dec 19E; New Zealand 1984 Jul 2E; North Korea 1988 Sep 13E; Philippines 1982 Jan 18E; 1986 Nov 10E/Nov 13E; South Korea 1980 Nov 28E; 1981 Sep 11E; 1982 Apr 16E/Aug 4E; 1983 Jan 12E; 1984 Sep 8E; Vietnam 1981 Dec 10E

Canada: 1980 Aug 23D; 1981 May 7E/Jun 4E; 1982 Mar 20A/Aug 11A; 1983 Jun 27A

Europe: European Community 1984 Mar 24A/Apr 4A; 1987 Apr 13B; 1988 Jan 18B/Mar 25A; Great Britain 1989 Sep 23A; Italy 1985 Apr 27B; Poland 1982 Feb 23A; Turkey 1985 Apr 27B; USSR 1980 Feb 5J; 1982 Feb 23A/Sep 2B; 1984 Jul 12A; 1985 May 24A/Jul 30A; 1986 Jan 19E; 1987 Mar 20A/Dec 9E; 1988 Dec 18E

Latin America: Brazil 1989 Mar 3A; Mexico 1985 Dec 18A

Middle East: PLO 1981 Oct 14A

government and politics: defense minister Ito resigns 1981 May 16E; governor/state assembly elections 1983 Apr 10E; Kaifu elected premier 1989 Aug 9E; municipal elections 1983 Apr 24E; Nakasone elected premier 1982 Nov 26E; Ohira dies 1980 Jun 12E; Ohira government loses no confidence vote 1980 May 16E; parliamentary by-elections 1987 Mar 8E; 1989 Oct 1E; parliamentary elections 1980 Jun 22E; 1983 Jun 26E/Dec 18E; 1989 Jul 23E; Takeshita elected premier 1987 Nov 6E; Uno elected premier 1989 Jun 2E; woman leads Socialist Party 1986 Sep 6E

immigration and refugees: Bolshoi Ballet defections 1980 Feb 5J; Chinese refugees 1989 Dec 19E

international organizations: GATT 1987 Dec 3E; 1988 Feb 2E/Mar 25A/May 4A; IMF 1983 Jan 18A; United Nations 1987 Feb 20A/Dec 21A

joint ventures: GM/Isuzu 1982 May 24H; GM/Isuzu/Suzuki 1981 Aug 12H; Nissan/Alfa Romeo 1980 Sep 20B; Toyota/GM 1983 Feb 17H; Wheeling-Pittsburgh Steel/Nisshin Steel 1984 Feb 7H

labor issues: jobless rate 1986 Aug 29E; 1987 Mar 2E/Jul 30E/Dec 25E; 1988 Jul 29E; 1989 Aug 1E; union formed 1987 Nov 20E

medicine and health care: AIDS 1987 Mar 24E; average height increase 1980 Apr 6E; life expectancy 1988 May 24I; radiation victims 1987 Dec 18I; tobacco research 1981 Jan 17I; Tonegawa wins Nobel 1987 Oct 12I

mergers: Mitsui Bank/Taiyo Kobe Bank 1989 Aug 29E; National Steel Corp./Nippon Kokan K.K. 1984 Apr 24H

monetary issues: financial markets 1987 May 25E; IMF 1983 Jan 18A; stock markets 1987 Apr 13E; 1988 Dec 28E

obituaries: Kishi, Nobosuke 1987 Aug 7E; Matsushita, Konosuke 1989 Apr 27E; Ohira, Masayoshi 1980 Jun 12E; Takenaka, Masahisa 1985 Jan 27E; Taniguchi, Masaharu 1985 Jun 17J

religious issues: papal visit 1981 Feb 15J

royal family: Akihito 1989 Jan 7E/Aug 4E; Hirohito 1986 Apr 29E; 1988 Sep 19E; 1989 Jan 7E/Feb 24E-25E

science and technology: Fukui wins Nobel 1981 Oct 19I; mathematician retracts Fermat theorem proof 1988 Jun 3I

space program: launch rocket development 1984 Jul 13I; rocket launched 1986 Aug 13I

sports: auto racing 1987 Nov 1J; 1988 Oct 31J; figure skating 1989 Mar 18J; golf 1980 Jun 15J; marathons 1981 Apr 20J; 1987 Apr 20J/May 10J; Olympic Games (Moscow) 1980 Feb 1J; Tokyo Dome inaugurated 1988 Mar 18J

taxes: rates 1987 Sep 11B; reforms 1985 Jan 7E; 1986 Dec 5E; 1988 Jun 14E; sales tax 1989 Apr 1E; on savings 1988 Apr 1E

terrorism: Japanese airport bombing 1985 Jun 23A; rocket attacks 1985 Jan 1E; 1986 Apr 1E

trade issues: current accounts 1989 Feb 3E/Apr 28E; deficits 1980 Mar 15E/Nov 18E; GATT 1987 Dec 3E; 1988 Feb 2E/Mar 25A/May 4A; import duties to be cut 1982 Dec 24E; ivory import ban 1989 Oct 30E; legislation allowing easier access 1983 May 13E; market opening measures 1985 Jul 30E; nontariff barriers to be dismantled 1983 Jan 12E; surpluses 1982 Apr 12E; 1985 Jul 9E; 1986 Jan 17E/Sep 20E; 1987 Dec 10E; 1988 Jan 19E/Apr 11E; 1989 Jan 18E; whaling 1984 Nov 13A; 1985 Mar 5H/Apr 5E/Aug 6H; 1986 Jun 30F; 1988 Feb 10G

transportation: railway tunnel 1988 Mar 13E

U.S. relations

business issues: airline safety talks 1985 May 24A/Jul 30A; antitrust suits 1986 Mar 26H; corporate culture criticized 1988 Jul 17E; financial markets 1984 May 29A; public works projects 1988 Mar 29G; securities fraud investigations 1986 May 27A; space station 1985 May 9I

defense issues: defense spending 1987 Oct 6A; fighter planes 1987 Oct 2E; merchant ship/submarine collision 1981 Apr 20G; nuclear-armed ships 1981 May 17G/May 25E; rocket attack on consulate 1985 Jan 1E; Strategic Defense Initiative 1986 Sep 9E; 1987 Jul 21G; visas denied to antinuclear group 1982 Jun 7G

educational issues: educational systems compared 1987 Jan 3F

political issues: Japanese politician angers U.S. blacks 1988 Jul 23E; lawyers accredited 1987 May 21E; pan-Pacific entity proposed 1989 Jun 26A; Shultz visit 1983 Jan 30E

trade issues: auto domestic content bill 1983 Nov 3H; auto imports/exports 1981 May 1A; 1982 Jul 26H; 1983 May 12H/Jun 30E/Nov 1E; 1984 Jun 19E; 1985 Mar 28E/May 30H; 1986 Feb 13E; 1987 Jan 27E; 1988 Jan 29E; 1989 Jan 10E; ball bearings 1989 May 2H; beef 1984 Apr 7A; California produce fumigation 1981 Aug 26E; cigarettes 1982 Oct 26E; 1986 Oct 3E; citrus fruits 1984 Apr 7A; computer chips 1981 May 9E; 1986 Jul 31A/Oct 13H; 1988 Mar 25A/May 4A; 1989 Jun 12H; congressional pressure for retaliation 1985 Apr 2G; construction industry 1987 Nov 20E; 1989 Nov 22H/Nov 23E; current account surplus 1986 Jun 30E; economic policy coordination 1986 Oct 31E; electronics tariffs 1987 Apr 17H; fishing 1982 Apr 26G; 1987 Dec 29H; 1988 Mar 14H; 1989 Jun 23H; free trade principles adherence urged 1981 Jan 7A; high technology markets 1983 Feb 10E; industrial targeting policy 1983 May 16E; Japan defends policies 1985 Apr 3E; machine tools 1986 Nov 20E; nuclear cooperation pact 1988 Mar 21I/May 26E; rice 1980 Apr 12A; steel dumping 1982 Jul 21H; telecommunications 1988

Dec 28H; 1989 Apr 28G; textile exports 1986 Nov 14E/Nov 15E; Tokyo Round tariff cutting announced 1981 Dec 1E; Toshiba products ban 1987 Jun 30H/Jul 16G; trade concessions 1985 Apr 25A; trade surplus 1984 Oct 6G; 1986 Sep 20E; trade talks 1982 Jan 16A/Feb 25A/Mar 23E/Oct 21G/Dec 3E; 1985 Jan 29A; UAW asks for legislation 1980 Jan 13H; unfair trading partner designation 1989 Jun 1A; U.S. council created 1981 Jul 27H; whaling 1984 Nov 13A; 1985 Mar 5H/Apr 5E/Aug 6H; 1986 Jun 30F; 1988 Feb 10G

World War II: chemical and biological warfare 1982 Apr 16E; 1988 Sep 18E; textbook representation of 1982 Jul 24E/Aug 4E/Aug 26E/Aug 28E; 1988 Jul 1E; 1989 Oct 3E

Japan Airlines 1985 Aug 12E

Japan Automobile Importers Association 1988 Apr 7E

Japan Automobile Manufacturers Association 1981 Jul 23E; 1985 Jan 28E

Japan Economic Council 1982 Jan 17E

Japanese-Americans 1983 Jan 19F/Feb 24F/Jun 16F; 1984 Sep 19F; 1986 Feb 10G/Feb 21F; 1987 Sep 17F; 1988 Apr 20F/Aug 10F; 1989 Nov 8F

Japanese-Canadians 1988 Sep 22D

Japanese Grand Prix (auto race) 1987 Nov 1J; 1988 Oct 31J

Japanese National Oil Co. 1980 Aug 23D

Japan Nuclear Power Co. 1981 May 13E

Jarvik-7 (artificial heart) 1984 Nov 25I; 1985 Feb 17I/Apr 24I/Sep 29I/Nov 21I; 1986 Aug 6I

Jaws 3-D (film) 1983 Aug 10J

Jazz Master Award (music) 1983 May 23J

Jazz Section (Czech dissident group) 1986 Sep 2B; 1987 Mar 11B

Jazz Singer (soundtrack) (Neil Diamond) 1981 Feb 11J/Mar 4J

J .D. Salinger: A Writing Life (Ian Hamilton) (book) 1987 Jan 29J

Jean de Florette (film) 1987 Jun 26J; 1988 Mar 20J

Jefferies Group Inc. 1987 Mar 19H

Jeffersons, The (TV show) 1981 Sep 13J

Jerk, The (film) 1980 Jan 30J

Jerome Robbins's Broadway (musical) 1989 Jun 4J

Jerusalem (Israel)

Begin to shift offices to East Jerusalem 1980 Jun 22C

demonstrations and protests 1981 Nov 22C

Egyptian position on 1980 Feb 1C/Aug 3C/Aug 4C; 1981 May 31C; 1982 Mar 21C

general strikes 1982 Mar 19C; 1987 Dec 21C

Israeli crackdown on protests 1988 Jan 1C

land expropriations 1980 Mar 12C

legislation considered 1980 May 14C

parliament reaffirms as capital 1980 Jul 30C

PLO declaration of independence 1988 Nov 26C

terrorism: bus attacked 1984 Oct 28C/Nov 3C; car bomb discovered 1984 Aug 16C; Dome of the Rock (mosque) 1982 Apr 11C/Apr 12C/Apr 14A/Apr 20A/May 7C; 1983 Apr 7C

United Nations resolutions on 1980 Jun 30A/Jul 29A/Aug 20A

Jerusalem International Book Fair 1987 Apr 9J

Jerusalem Prize (literature) 1985 Jan 9J; 1987 Apr 9J

Jesse Owens Award (track and field) 1988 Dec 3J

Jesuits 1980 May 5J; 1984 Jul 1J; 1989 Nov 16D/Nov 23D

Jet Propulsion Laboratory (Pasadena, Calif.) 1980 May 6I; 1983 Aug 9I

jet stream 1988 Sep 6I

Jewel in the Crown (TV show) 1985 Sep 12J

Jewel of the Nile, The (film) 1986 Jan 22J

jewelry 1983 Apr 2F; 1986 Aug 20H; 1987 Apr 3J/Jun 26F; 1988 Nov 10H

Jewish Defense League 1987 Feb 20F

Jewish settlements (Israeli occupied territories) 1980 Feb 10C; 1981 Jan 26C; 1982 Feb 17C/May 2C/Aug 14G; 1983 Mar 21C/Apr 10C; 1984 Feb 5C; 1985 Jan 10C/Feb 9C/Jul 10C; 1988 Apr 6C

Jewish Theological Seminary of America 1983 Oct 24J

Jews and Judaism

arts and culture: Anne Frank 1986 May 14J; Canetti wins Nobel 1981 Oct 15J; Wiesel wins Nobel 1986 Oct 14A

Catholic/Jewish relations: papal meeting with leaders 1987 Sep 1J; papal meeting with Waldheim critic 1987 Jun 25J; papal visit to synagogue 1986 Apr 13J; papal visit to West Germany criticized 1987 May 4J; Polish convent at Auschwitz 1989 Jan 25B

ecumenical developments: conventions 1985 Jan 26B; women rabbis 1983 Jul 17J/Oct 24J

Ethiopian Jews: 1980 Nov 15C; 1985 Jan 3C/Jan 4C

Nazi war crimes: Artukovic charged by Yugoslav court 1986 Feb 15B; company pays reparations 1986 Jan 8B; reparations funds theft 1988 May 17B; 1989 Dec 15B; Touvier arrested 1989 May 24B

Protestant/Jewish relations: Falwell reverses position 1980 Oct 11J; Southern Baptist Convention 1980 Sep 18J; United Church of Christ 1987 Jun 30J

Soviet emigration: 1980 Jan 11B; 1981 Jan 4B; 1982 Jan 17A; 1987 Apr 9A; 1988 Jan 5B

terrorism: Antwerp bombing 1981 Oct 20B; French president responds to violence 1980 Oct 8B; Istanbul synagogue attack 1986 Sep 6B; Paris machine-gun attacks 1980 Sep 28B; Paris restaurant attack 1982 Aug 9B; Paris synagogue bombing 1980 Oct 3B; Paris travel agency killing 1980 Nov 25B

U.S. issues: PLO meeting 1988 Dec 7C; political campaign issues 1983 Apr 17F; radio talk show host slain 1984 Jun 18F/Oct 18F; 1985 Apr15F; 1987 Nov 17F; Reagan Bitburg visit criticized 1985 Apr 11G

Jews in Germany, Central Council of *see* Central Council of Jews in Germany

Jihad (Holy War) (Egyptian fundamentalist group) 1989 Apr 26C

Jihad Command 1981 Mar 28E

Jimmy Stewart and His Poems (Jimmy Stewart) (book) 1989 Oct 27J

Joan Jett & the Blackhearts (singing group) 1982 Feb 24J/Mar 14J/Mar 17J

job discrimination *see specific areas and subjects of abuse* (e.g., Black Americans)

jobless rate *see* unemployment rate

job training 1982 Jul 1H/Aug 4H/Dec 9E; 1983 Aug 15G/Aug 15H; 1984 Oct 24H; 1985 Sep 26F; 1987 Feb 21F/Apr 2F; 1988 Jan 4B/May 20G/Oct 20F

Job Training Partnership Act 1987 Apr 2F

Joe Egg (play) 1985 Jun 2J

Joe Turner's Come and Gone (August Wilson) (play) 1986 May 2J; 1988 Mar 27J

Joffrey Ballet 1981 Mar 15J

John Brown & Co. Ltd. 1982 Sep 9G

John F. Kennedy Center (Washington, D.C.) 1980 Feb 26J

John Henry (racehorse) 1985 Jan 8J/Feb 8J

John Morrell & Co. 1988 Oct 28H

John Muir and Co. 1981 Aug 17H

John Newberry Medal *see* Newbery Medal (children's literature)

Johns Hopkins University (Baltimore, Md.) 1980 Aug 30I; 1984 Nov 27I; 1985 Aug 13I; 1986 Jul 8F/Jul 22G; 1987 May 25J

Johnson & Johnson 1981 Jul 2H; 1982 Dec 24H; 1983 Mar 4I; 1986 Feb 17F/Jun 2J

Johnson Publishing Co. Inc. 1984 May 8H

Johnson Space Center (Houston, Tex.) 1986 Jan 31F

Joint Chiefs of Staff, U.S. 1984 Feb 9F; 1985 Jul 10G/Oct 1G/Oct 16G; 1987 Jan 10G; 1988 Apr 22G; 1989 Jun 21G/Jul 2G/Aug 10G/Sep 21G

Joint Economic Committee, U.S. Congress 1982 Apr 3G; 1985 Feb 6G; 1986 Mar 17H/Jul 26H/Oct 20H/Dec 28F

Jo Jo Dancer (film) 1986 May 14J

Jones & Laughlin Steel Inc. 1984 Mar 23H

Jordan *see also individual leaders in the name index* (e.g., Hussein, King)

Arab relations: Egypt 1983 Dec 5C; 1984 Sep 25C; Lebanon 1981 Feb 6C; 1983 Aug 16C; PLO 1986 Jul 7C; 1987 Apr 26C; Syria 1980 Nov 26C/Dec 3C/Dec 10C; 1981 Jan 2C/Feb 6C; 1985 Oct 21C; West Bank 1982 Mar 10C/Mar 24A

civil strife: demonstrations and protests 1989 Apr 20C; martial law ended 1989 Dec 19C

economy: water resources 1983 Jun 8C

government and politics: cabinet announced 1989 Dec 6C; national elections 1984 Mar 12C

international organizations: UN-ESCO 1985 Oct 8A; United Nations 1982 Mar 24A

U.S. relations: 1982 Feb 26C/Sep 1A; 1983 Nov 6A; 1985 Nov 12G; 1986 Jan 31G; 1988 Feb 25C

Jordanian airliner hijacking (1985) 1987 Sep 17G; 1989 Mar 14G/Oct 4A

Jose Marti airport (Havana, Cuba) 1989 Sep 3D

Jose Simeon Canas University of Central America 1989 Nov 23D

Joshua Tree, The (U2) (recording) 1987 Apr 25J/May 23J/Jun 27J/Jul 22J/Aug 22J; 1988 Mar 2J

Journey (singing group) 1981 Aug 5J/Sep 9J/Sep 30J/Nov 11J/Dec 9J; 1982 Jan 20J; 1983 Mar 9J/Apr 13J

Joyful Noise: Poems for Two Voices (Paul Fleischman) (poems) 1989 Jan 9J

Joy Luck Club, The (Amy Tan) (book) 1989 Aug 25J

J.P. Stevens & Co. *see* Stevens & Co., J.P.

Jubal Sackett (Louis L'Amour) (book) 1985 Jun 14J/Jul 19J

Judicial Conference of the United States 1980 Aug 2F; 1982 Sep 26F; 1987 Mar 17F

Jumpin' Jack Flash (film) 1986 Oct 22J

June 9 Organization (Armenian terrorist group) 1981 Jul 22B

junk bonds 1985 Dec 6H; 1988 Sep 7H

Jupiter (planet) 1980 May 6I; 1989 Oct 18I/Oct 23I

jury tampering 1988 Jan 22F

Justice, U.S. Department of *see also specific department heads in the name index* (e.g., Meese III, Edwin)

antitrust division and actions: airline exemption 1984 Aug 13H; AT&T 1982 Jan 8H/Jan 21H/Mar 25H/Aug 11H/Aug 24H; 1983 Mar 25H; Baxter denies increased uncertainty 1981 Aug 26H; brewery mergers 1981 Oct 22H; doctors warned on price fixing 1988 Dec 6F; futures markets 1989 Aug 2H; IBM 1982 Jan 8H/Mar 19H; merger guidelines 1982 Jun 14H; 1984 Jun 14H; oil companies 1980 Jul 17H; steel company merger 1984 Feb 15H/Mar 21H; telephone companies 1987 Apr 27H

appointments and resignations: Honegger, Barbara 1983 Aug 22F; Lucas, William 1989 May 9F; Lucas nomination rejected 1989 Aug 1F; Senate committee votes against Reynolds 1985 Jun 27F; Smith, William French 1980 Dec 11F; Thornburgh, Richard L. 1988 Jul 12F/Nov 21F

budget and spending programs 1982 May 2F; 1985 May 8F/Dec 30H; 1988 Sep 27F; 1989 Nov 8F

civil rights: AIDS 1986 Jun 23F; 1988 Oct 6F; fair housing laws 1983 May 19F; housing desegregation plan 1988 Sep 10F; racial hiring quotas 1985 Apr 2F/May 1F; 1986 Mar 28F; school busing 1980 Nov 18F; 1982 Feb 4F/Sep 27F/Nov 12F; school desegregation plan 1982 Dec 10F; school standards for minorities 1985 Sep 20F; severely handicapped infants 1983 Nov 2F

corruption and ethics: Allen gift for Nancy Reagan interview 1981 Dec 1F/Dec 23F; Baxter cleared on conflict of interest 1982 Jun

17H; Billy Carter/Libya investigation 1980 Jul 14F/Jul 24F/Jul 30F/Aug 1F/Aug 4F/Aug 6F/Aug 22G/Sep 17F/Oct2F/Oct29F; 1981 Apr 29F; Carter briefing papers 1984 Feb 29F; CIA director Casey cleared 1982 Apr 8G; Colby breach of security suit 1981 Dec 31G; congressional sexual misconduct 1982 Aug 31F; 1983 Feb 3H/Feb 16F/Aug 11H; Ethics in Government Act 1987 Jun 16F; Ginsburg conflict of interest 1987 Oct 29F/Nov 1F/Nov 7F-8F; 1988 Feb 10F; IBM information theft 1982 Jun 22G; Keating S&L investigation 1989 Oct 13F; North trial document 1989 May 5F; Rich extradition 1983 Sep 22G; Teamsters union 1987 Jun 9H; 1988 Jun 28H; 1989 Mar 13F

crime and law enforcement: *Achille Lauro* hijacking 1988 Jan 17G; arms smuggling 1989 Jan 4G; black activists prosecuted 1985 Nov 14F; CIA operatives investigation 1981 Sep 22G; computer virus indictment 1989 Jul 26I; congressional drug activity 1983 Jul 28F; Cuban refugees 1980 Jun 7F; Kennedy assassination 1980 Jan 4F; Nazi war crimes 1982 Oct 7F; 1983 Mar 15G/Aug 16B; 1987 Apr 27G; neo-Nazi groups 1985 Apr 15F; Noriega charged with drug trafficking 1988 Feb 5G; TWA hijacking 1985 Oct 17G; 1987 Jan 18A

environmental issues: air pollution 1980 Dec 22H; Canadian acid rain films 1983 Feb 24J; foam insulation 1983 Aug 25H; hazardous wastes 1983 Jan 4H/Dec 9H/Dec 13H; 1984 Feb 21H; 1987 Apr 28H; 1989 Jun 6G; office firebombed 1983 Apr 23H; sewage dumping 1988 Mar 22H

foreign issues: Japanese antinuclear group members denied visas 1982 Jun 7G; Nicaraguan contras 1986 Dec 16F; 1987 Jan 9F; PLO UN observer mission 1988 Mar 22G/Aug 29G

health and safety issues: all-terrain vehicles 1987 Dec 20H; prescription drugs 1985 Feb 25H

immigration and refugees: rules for Nicaraguans 1987 Jul 8F; sanctuary movement 1985 Jan 14F

military issues: defense contract fraud 1986 Mar 26G; 1987 May 19G; draft registration evaders 1982 Oct 28G

obituaries: Mitchell, John Newton 1988 Nov 9F

personnel: employees asked about homosexuality 1986 Mar 11F; judicial nominee evaluations 1989 Jun 2F

space flight: *Challenger* disaster settlement 1986 Dec 29I

voting rights: election plans judged by results 1987 Jan 6F; New York City charter revision 1989 Dec 13F; New York State redistricting plans 1982 Jun 22F/Jul 3F; Supreme Court acceptance of cases for review 1984 Mar 23F

Justice Commandos of the Armenian Genocide 1982 May 4A

Justice Statistics, U.S. Bureau of (Justice Department) 1982 Nov 7F; 1984 Apr 8F; 1985 Mar 24F/Apr 7F/Jun 9F/Jul 28F; 1988 Oct 9F

Just One of the Guys (film) 1985 May 15J

K

Kahnawake reserve (Canada) 1988 Jun 1D

Kaiser Permanente Medical Care Program 1986 Dec 11H

Kakadu National Park (Australia) 1989 Oct 5E

Kaleidoscope (Danielle Steel) (book) 1987 Nov 20J/Dec 18J; 1988 Jan 29J/Feb 26J

Kanaks *see* New Caledonia

Kane & Abel (Jeffery Archer) (book) 1980 Aug 17J

kangaroos 1984 Sep 5I; 1986 Mar 6I

Kansas 1980 Apr 1F; 1982 Sep 5F; 1983 Jan 24H/Jan 25F; 1985 Feb 1J/Feb 2J/Jun 28J; 1987 Oct 12F; 1988 Mar 19F; 1989 Nov 6H

Kansas, University of (Lawrence) 1988 Feb 4J/Apr 4J

Kansas City Board of Trade 1982 Feb 24H

Kansas City Royals (baseball team) 1980 Oct 10J/Oct 21J/Nov 18J/Dec 6J; 1984 Sep 30J/Oct 5J; 1985 Oct 16J/Oct 27J/Nov 11J; 1986 Jun 21J; 1989 Jul 11J/Nov 15J

Kaposi's sarcoma 1988 Nov 21I

Karate Kid, The (film) 1984 Jul 18J

Karate Kid Part II, The (film) 1986 Jul 9J

Kashmir (India) 1982 Sep 8E; 1984 Jan 14E/Jul 23E; 1986 Mar 7E/Nov 7E; 1987 Sep 25E

Kate and Allie (TV show) 1984 Dec 16J; 1985 Sep 12J

Kate Vaidan (Reynolds Price) (book) 1987 Jan 12J

Kazakhstan (USSR) 1986 Dec 17B/Dec 25B; 1987 Feb 26B/Mar 12B/Jul 18B; 1988 Sep 14B; 1989 Jun 16B

KC-10 (aircraft) 1984 Jun 5C

KC-135 (aircraft) 1980 Oct 11G

Keeton v. Hustler Magazine Inc. (1983) 1983 Nov 8J

Kellogg Co. 1982 Jan 15H

Kelso (racehorse) 1983 Oct 16J

Kennecott Corp. 1981 Jan 28H/Mar 12H; 1983 Apr 16F; 1986 Jun 30H

Kennedy Center for the Performing Arts (Washington, D.C.) 1982 Dec 18J; 1984 Jun 5J; 1985 Jan 24J; 1986 Aug 8J/Nov 15J

Kennedy Human Rights Award *see* Robert F. Kennedy Human Rights Award

Kennedy International Airport (New York City) 1980 Feb 4B

Kennedy Space Center (Cape Canaveral, Fla.) 1986 Aug 20I

Kenneth Leventhal & Co. 1988 Apr 5H

Kenny (Kenny Rogers) (recording) 1980 Jan 2J

Kentucky 1980 May 27F/Nov 17F/Dec 11H; 1982 Aug 14F; 1983 Mar 24F/Nov 8F; 1984 May 8I/Aug 3F/Sep 24J; 1986 Jan 9H/Apr 6F; 1989 Jun 8F

Kentucky Derby (horse race) 1980 May 3J; 1981 May 2J; 1982 May 1J; 1983 May 7I; 1984 May 5J; 1986 May 3J; 1987 May 2J; 1988 May 7J; 1989 May 6J

Kentucky v. Stincer (1987) 1987 Jun 19F

Kenya *see also individual leaders in the name index* (*e.g.,* Moi, Daniel T. Arap)
environmental issues: conservationist killed 1989 Aug 20C; fossils 1982 Aug 31I; 1984 Aug 22I/Oct 18I; ivory trade 1989 May 11I
foreign relations: Tanzania 1981 Jan 17C; Uganda 1981 Jan 17C; 1987 Dec 14C; Zambia 1981 Jan 17C
government and politics: coup attempt 1982 Aug 2D/Aug 4C; 1985 Sep 18C; one-party state 1982 Jul 9C; parliamentary elections 1983 Sep 26C; 1988 Mar 21C
human rights: 1982 Jul 21C; 1987 Jul 21C; 1988 Sep 21C
obituaries: Markham, Beryl 1986 Aug 3J
papal visit: 1985 Aug 19J
sports: running 1986 Mar 23J; 1987 Nov 1J; 1988 Mar 26J/Apr 18J; 1989 Mar 19J/Jul 3J
U.S. policy: 1980 Apr 21G; 1982 Aug 2D; 1985 Mar 21G
Kerr-McGee Corp. 1981 Dec 11I; 1986 Jan 5H/Aug 22F
Kesterson National Wildlife Refuge (California) 1985 Mar 15H/Mar 28H
Keston College Center for the Study of Religion and Communism 1984 May 15J
Key to Rebecca, The (Ken Follett) (book) 1980 Oct 12J/Dec 7J/Dec 7J; 1981 Jan 11J/Feb 8J/Mar 8J; 1987 Oct 12J/Dec 7J
KEZY (California radio station) 1980 Nov 1J
Kfir (Israeli aircraft) 1981 Mar 21G; 1986 Oct 1G
KGB (Soviet security agency) 1985 Sep 26B; 1986 Aug 30B
Khaibar Brigade (Lebanese terrorist group) 1985 Mar 22C/Mar 31C/Apr 1C
Kharg Island oil terminal (Iran) 1982 Aug 15C/Aug 21C/Aug 30C; 1984 Feb 27C/May 24C/May 30C/Jun 24C/Aug 7C; 1985 Aug 15C/Dec 29C
Khmer People's National Liberation Front (KPNLF) 1985 Jan 8E; 1989 Oct 4E
Khmer Rouge 1980 Aug 4E; 1982 Feb 17E/Jul 11E; 1984 Jan 31E; 1985 Feb 15E; 1988 May 1E; 1989 Aug 30E/Oct 23E; Pol Pot; Samphan, Khieu
Kick (INXS) (recording) 1988 Feb 20J/Mar 19J/Apr 23J
kidnappings
Belgium: former premier Vanden Boeynants 1989 Jan 14B/Feb 13B
Bolivia: President Siles Zuazo 1984 Jun 30D/Jul 2E
Chile: church organization members 1985 Aug 24D; leftist students 1980 Aug 12D
China: kidnapping ring sentencings 1983 Jul 16E
Colombia: Attorney General Hoyos Jimenez 1988 Jan 25D; Beatrice Foods Co. employee 1980 Jan 6D; British rancher 1980 Jan 5D; Canadian engineer 1988 Mar 19E; financier's daughter 1987 Jul 30D; international kidnapping and adoption ring 1981 Aug 16D; judge 1988 Dec 23D
El Salvador: leftist leaders 1980 Nov 27D; President Duarte's daughter 1985 Sep 10D; rightwing kidnapping ring 1986 Apr 4D; soccer spectators 1982 Dec 5D

Ethiopia: foreign relief workers 1983 Jun 9C
France: industrialist Maury-Laribiere 1980 Jul 9B
Guatemala: Honduran president Suazo Cordova's daughter 1982 Dec 14D
Illinois: abortion clinic owner 1982 Aug 20F
Italy: justice magistrate D'Urso 1980 Dec 12B; U.S. Army officer James Dozier 1981 Dec 17B
Lebanon hostages *see* Lebanon
Mexico: U.S. drug agent 1985 Feb 7D
Nicaragua: American volunteer 1988 Mar 9D
Philippines: President Marcos' son-in-law 1982 Jan 3E
Puerto Rico: armored services manager 1980 Nov 21D
Spain: foreign consuls 1981 Feb 19B
United States: bi-athlete Kari Swenson 1984 Jul 16F/Dec 13F; 1985 Jul 12F/Sep 27F; Billionaire Boys Club 1987 Apr 22F; 1988 Jan 25F; religious deprogrammer sentenced 1980 Sep 26J; Synanon members charged 1981 Feb 28F; Tawana Brawley case 1988 Feb 29F/Oct 6F; 1989 Apr27F; Ukiah boys 1980 Mar 1F
kidney transplants 1989 Dec 3I
Kill and Kill Again (film) 1981 May 20J
Killing Fields, The (film) 1984 Nov 2J; 1985 Feb 13F/Mar 25J
Kilroy Was Here (Styx) (recording) 1983 Apr 13J
Kimpo International Airport (Seoul, South Korea) 1986 Sep 14E
King and I, The (musical) 1985 Jun 30J
Kingman Committee (Great Britain) 1988 Apr 29B
Kinross gold mine (South Africa) 1986 Sep 16C
Kinsey Institute 1981 Aug 22I; 1989 Jun 30F
Kiribati 1985 Aug 6E
Kirov Ballet 1986 May 21J; 1988 Aug 6J; 1989 Jan 18J
Kissing a Fool (George Michael) (recording) 1988 Nov 26J
Kiss of the Spider Woman (film) 1985 Jul 26J; 1986 Mar 16J/Mar 24J
Kitty Hawk (ship) 1984 Mar 21A
KLM Royal Dutch Airlines 1989 Sep 29H/Nov 2H
KMBC-TV (Kansas City, Mo. TV station) 1983 Aug 8F/Oct 31F; 1984 Jan 13J; 1985 Jun 28J
Knights of Malta 1988 Apr 8J
Knopf Inc., Alfred A. 1983 Apr 30E
Kodak *see* Eastman Kodak Co.
Koeberg nuclear power station (South Africa) 1982 Dec 19C
Kohlberg Kravis Roberts & Co. 1985 Oct 14H; 1988 Jun 20H/Nov 3H/Nov 30H
Kookaburra III (yacht) 1987 Feb 4J
KOR *see* Committee for Social-Defense
Koran (Moslem holy book) 1984 Jun 18E
Korea *see* North Korea; South Korea
Korean Air Lines bombing (1987) 1989 Apr 25E
Korean Air Lines Flight 007 downing (1983) 1983 Sep 1A
anniversary marked: 1984 Aug 31E

search for wreckage: 1983 Sep 2E
theories about: 1986 Nov 23E
United Nations: 1983 Sep 2A/Sep 12A/Dec 13A; 1984 Mar 6A
United States: allegations called unsupported by experts 1983 Oct 6G; crew found guilty of "willful misconduct" 1989 Aug 2F; Reagan denounces 1983 Sep 5G; reconnaissance plane in area 1983 Sep 4G/Sep 5G; revised version of pilot's remarks 1983 Sep 11G; Shultz claims USSR knew jet was civilian 1983 Sep 1G; Shultz says Soviet explanations unacceptable 1983 Sep 8G
USSR: condemned by UN agency 1984 Mar 6A; general says plane taken for reconaissance plane 1983 Sep 4B; Gromyko charges plane on spy mission 1983 Sep 7B; shootdown admitted 1983 Sep 6B; stops short of admitting shootdown 1983 Sep 2B; UN criticizes 1983 Sep 2A; UN resolution vetoed 1983 Sep 12A
Korean War (1950-53) 1983 Aug 15G; 1985 May 30E/Sep 20E; 1988 Mar 7F
Kosovo (Yugoslavia) 1987 Jun 26B/Oct 25B; 1988 Sep 15B/Nov 19B; 1989 Feb 27B/Mar 29B
Kourou Space Center (French Guiana) 1981 Jun 19I; 1982 Sep 10I; 1984 Mar 4I/Aug 4I; 1985 Feb 8I/Jul 2I; 1986 May 30I; 1987 Sep 15I; 1988 Mar 11I/Jun 15I/Sep 8I/Dec 10I; 1989 Aug 8I
KPMG Peat Marwick 1988 May 27B
KPNLF *see* Khmer People's National Liberation Front
Kramer vs. Kramer (film) 1980 Jan 30J/Feb 27J/Mar 26J/Apr 14J/Apr 23J
Krasnoyarsk radar complex (USSR) 1982 Feb 6B; 1987 Mar 10G/Dec 13G; 1988 Aug 31G; 1989 Oct 23B
Kress & Co., S.H. 1980 Nov 6H
Kristallnacht (1938 German/Austrian pogrom against Jews) 1988 Nov 11B
Krugerrand (South African gold coin) 1986 Sep 8H
Krupp Stahl AG 1982 Feb 4B
krypton-85 gas 1980 Jul 11I
Kuala Lumpur stock exchange 1985 Dec 4E
Ku Klux Klan *see also specific individuals in the name index* (*e.g.,* Duke, David)
Chattanooga racial disorders: 1980 Jul 22F
damage awards against: 1987 Feb 12F/May 20F; 1988 Oct 25F
Decatur attack indictments: 1984 May 17F
demonstrations and protests: 1982 May 15F/Nov 27F; 1987 Jun 7F
Dominica government overthrow plot: 1981 Jun 20D
FBI charged with negligence in trial: 1983 May 27F
Greensboro killings trial: 1983 Apr 21F; 1984 Apr 13F
member convicted of murder: 1983 Dec 19F
Kurdish Workers' Party (PKK) 1987 Jun 20B/Jul 9B
Kurds *see* Iran; Iraq; Turkey
Kurile Islands (USSR) 1981 Sep 10E; 1986 Jan 19E
Kuwait *see also individual leaders in the name index* (*e.g.,* Sabah, Sheik Jabir al-Ahmad al-)

corruption and ethics: Santa Fe insider trading case 1981 Oct 26H; 1984 May 16A
crime and law enforcement: sabotage and subversion convictions 1987 Jun 6C
economy: spending cuts 1982 Apr 29C; stock market collapse 1982 Dec 2C; 1983 Aug 11C
elections: 1985 Feb 20C
foreign investments: 1981 Oct 5H; 1982 Oct 25C
foreign relations: Arab Persian Gulf states 1981 Mar 10C; Iran 1981 Oct 1C; 1987 Sep 5C/Oct 22C; 1988 Mar 30C/Sep 28C; Saudi Arabia 1989 Sep 21C; Syria 1981 May 6C; USSR 1984 Jul 11A/Aug 15A
hijackings: Kuwait Airways airliner (1988) 1988 Apr 5C/Apr 8C/Apr 13C/Apr 20C; Kuwaiti airliner (1982) 1982 Feb 25C; Kuwaiti airliner (1984) 1984 Dec 4C/Dec 9C/Dec 11G
international organizations: World Bank 1980 Aug 2A
oil tanker escorts: 1987 Apr 10C/May 28G/Jun 30G/Jul 22C/Aug 12C/Aug 24C/Oct 21G; 1988 Sep 16C
terrorism: car bombing attacks 1983 Dec 12C/Dec 27C; Mecca bombing 1989 Sep 21C
U.S. relations: 1980 Jan 25G; 1981 Oct 5H/Oct 26H; 1983 Aug 15C
Kuwait Airways 1988 Apr 5C/Apr 8C/Apr 13C/Apr 20C
Kuwait Petroleum Corp. 1981 Oct 5H; 1984 May 16A
Kwangju (South Korea) 1980 May 27E/May 31E
Kyoto University (Japan) 1981 Oct 19I

L

L-1011 Tristar (aircraft) 1985 Aug 2H
La Bamba (film) 1987 Aug 12J
La Bamba (soundtrack) 1987 Sep 19J
Labor, U.S. Department of *see also specific divisions* (*e.g.,* Occupational Safety and Health Administration); *individual leaders in the name index* (*e.g.,* Donovan, Raymond J.)
appointments and resignations: Brock, William E. 1985 Mar 20H; Dole, Elizabeth H. 1988 Dec 24H; Donovan, Raymond J. 1985 Mar 15F; McLaughlin, Ann Dore 1987 Nov 3H
bias issues: discrimination suit 1989 Jan 10F; job bias 1980 Dec 14F; Justice alleges discrimination 1986 Mar 28F
budget and spending programs: 1983 Oct 20F; 1989 Oct 19F
corruption and ethics: Teamsters pension fund 1982 Sep 21H; 1985 Feb 14F; 1987 Nov 10H
Donovan investigation *see the name index for* Donovan, Raymond J.
farm workers: 1987 Apr 28H
health and safety issues: apartment complex collapse 1987 Oct 24H; benzene exposure 1987 Sep 1H; child labor 1982 Jul 16H; disability benefits 1988 Dec 6F; ethylene dibromide exposure 1983 Oct 3H; field work sanitation standards 1987 Feb 6F; formaldehyde 1987 Nov 20H; hazardous chemical ex-

posure 1987 Aug 19H; locks on equipment 1989 Aug 31H; shipyard violations 1987 Nov 4H; Union Carbide chemical leak 1986 Apr 1H; work at home 1981 Oct 8H; 1984 Nov 5H; 1986 Aug 20H; 1988 Nov 10H
statistics: employment changes 1982 Jul 6H; employment cost index 1980 Nov 28H; import prices 1988 Jan 28H; jobless data 1983 Aug 9H; strike activity 1986 Feb 26H; strike-caused idleness 1981 Aug 28H; wage/salary increases 1982 Apr 28H; 1983 Apr 27F; 1984 Jan 27H; 1985 Jan 24H; 1986 Jan 27H; 1987 Jan 27H; *see also specific statistics* (*e.g.,* unemployment rate)
training: job benefits 1983 Aug 15H; 1984 Oct 24H
Labor Day (holiday) 1982 Sep 6J; 1983 Sep 5H
Labor Statistics, U.S. Bureau of (Labor Department) 1983 Jan 21F/Apr 14H; 1985 Feb 7H/Mar 6H/Nov 13F
La Cage aux Folles (musical) 1983 Aug 21J; 1984 Jun 3J
Lacey Act (1985) 1985 Jan 16H
La Costa (California resort) 1982 Jul 9J
lacrosse 1981 Jan 13J; 1987 May 25J; 1988 May 30J
Ladies of Missalonghi, The (Colleen McCullough) (book) 1987 May 29J
Ladies Professional Golf Association Championship 1980 Jun 8J; 1981 Jun 14J; 1982 Jun 13J; 1985 Jun 2J; 1986 Jun 1J; 1987 May 24J; 1988 Aug 28J; 1989 May 21J
Lady Byng Trophy (ice hockey) 1980 Jun 6J
Lady's Secret (racehorse) 1986 Nov 1J; 1987 Jan 30J
Laetrile (drug) 1980 Jan 3I; 1981 Apr 30I
La Francophonie 1987 Sep 4A
Lake Nios (Cameroon) 1986 Aug 21C/Aug 24C
Lake Ontario 1983 Feb 15I
lakes 1980 Feb 2I/Nov 20H; 1985 Aug 29H/Aug 21C/Aug 24C
Lake Superior State College (Sault Ste. Marie, Mich.) 1988 Apr 2J
Lake Tahoe 1980 Aug 27J/Nov 13J
Lake Wobegon Days (Garrison Keillor) (book) 1985 Sep 27J/Oct 25J/Nov 22J/Dec 20J; 1986 Jan 31J/Feb 28J/Mar 28J/Apr 25J/May 30J
L .A. Law (TV show) 1987 Jan 31J/Sep 20J; 1989 Sep 17J
L 'Amant (The Lover) (Marguerite Duras) (book) 1984 Nov 12J; 1986 Apr 7J
Lance (missile) 1981 Aug 10G
Landaluce (racehorse) 1983 Jan 4J
Land Before Time, The (film) 1988 Nov 30J
Land Management, U.S. Bureau of (Interior Department) 1983 Apr 1H
land reform
Afghanistan: 1981 Aug 18E
Brazil: 1985 Oct 10D; 1986 Jul 10D
El Salvador: 1980 Mar 6D; 1982 May 18D/May 20G; 1983 Jun 20D/Jul 26D; 1984 Jun 28D
Philippine: 1987 Mar 3E; 1988 Jan 22E/Jun 10E
San Salvador: 1981 Dec 15D; 1983 Sep 27D/Nov 12F; 1984 Jan 25G
United States: 1984 May 30F

Landsat (satellite) 1983 Mar 8I; 1984 Mar 1I; 1985 Sep 26I
Landscape With Rising Sun (Vincent van Gogh) (painting) 1985 Apr 24J
landslides 1989 Jun 6E
La Nuit Sacree (The Sacred Night) (Tahar Ben Jelloun) (book) 1987 Nov 16J
Laos
chemical weapons: use alleged 1980 Aug 7G; 1981 Sep 13G/Nov 10G; 1982 Jan 22E
foreign relations: China 1987 Nov 30E; Thailand 1988 Feb 17E; Vietnam 1988 Feb 24E
government and politics: elections 1988 Jun 26E; 1989 Mar 26E; president steps down 1986 Oct 31E
sports: Olympic Games withdrawal 1984 May 17J
U.S. relations: herbicide use during Vietnam War revealed 1982 Jan 24G; MIA rescue missions 1981 May 21E; 1983 Jan 31E; 1988 Nov 12E
LAPD *see* Los Angeles Police Department
La Prensa (Nicaraguan newspaper) 1986 Jun 26D; 1987 Sep 20D/Oct 1D; 1989 Sep 2D
La Salle University (Philadelphia, Pa.) 1987 Mar 26J
Lasker Awards, Albert 1983 Nov 16I; 1985 Nov 22I; 1986 Sep 22I; 1987 Sep 21I; 1988 Nov 16I; 1989 Sep 27I
Lassiter (film) 1984 Mar 7J
Lasso (herbicide) 1984 Nov 20H; 1985 Feb 22I
Last Emperor, The (film) 1987 Nov 20J; 1988 Jan 23J/Apr 11J; 1989 Mar 19J
Last Enchantment, The (Mary Stewart) (book) 1980 Jan 13J
Last Metro, The (film) 1981 Feb 11J
Last of the Breed (Louis L'Amour) (book) 1986 Jun 27J/Jul 18J/Aug 29J/Sep 26J
Last Supper, The (Leonardo da Vinci) (painting) 1980 Jun 16J
Last Temptation of Christ (film) 1988 Aug 12J
Last Tycoon (racehorse) 1986 Nov 1J
Las Vegas (Nevada) 1980 Nov 21J; 1982 Nov 13J; 1983 Nov 25J; 1984 Aug 27H/Aug 31J; 1986 Jan 21F/Jul 22F/Nov 22J; 1987 Mar 7J
Las Vegas Grand Prix (auto race) 1982 Oct 25J
Latin America *see also organizations (e.g.,* Organization of American States); *specific countries (e.g.,* Argentina)
accidents and disasters: hurricane damage 1988 Nov 30I
defense and disarmament issues: military arsenals buildup 1982 Jun 4D
economy: 1982 Jan 26D; 1983 Jan 5B; 1987 Dec 22D
foreign debt: 1983 Sep 4D/Sep 9D; 1984 Jan 14D/Jun 21D/Sep 14D; 1985 Feb 8D/Jul 14D/Aug 3D/Dec 17D; 1987 Jan 23D/Nov 26D; 1988 Jul 20A
foreign relations: Central America summit 1983 Jul 30D; Western Europe 1984 Sep 28A
human rights: 1980 Nov 27D; 1984 Feb 10G/Nov 1D/Nov 6D
medicine and health care: malaria vaccine 1988 Mar 10I; report on 1989 Sep 24I; river blindness drug developed 1987 Oct 21I
religious issues: papal visits 1985 Jan 26D/Feb 5J; 1988 May 7J; pope names cardinals 1988 May 29J; priests to be redistributed 1980 Jul 2J
transportation: air traffic rerouted 1980 Jul 14D
U.S. relations: 1981 Mar 3G; 1982 Nov 30D/Dec 1D; 1983 Nov 15H; 1984 Jan 31G; 1985 May 7D; 1988 Nov 29D
Latin America and the Caribbean, U.N. Economic Commission for 1982 Jan 26D; 1983 Jan 5B; 1987 Jan 23D/Dec 22D
L'Attente (Waiting) (Edgar Degas) (painting) 1983 May 18J
Latvia (USSR) 1987 Aug 23B/Nov 18B; 1988 Jun 14B/Jun 21B; 1989 Aug 21B/Aug 23B/Dec 24B/Dec 28B
Launching of Modern American Science, 1846-1876, The (Robert V. Bruce) (book) 1988 Mar 31J
Lavi (Israeli aircraft) 1983 Apr 17C/May 2C
Law of the Sea, U.N. Convention on the 1984 Dec 9A; 1988 Dec 28G
Law of the Sea Conference, U.N. 1980 Aug 29A; 1981 Mar 3A/Aug 5A; 1982 Apr 30A/Jul 8G/Dec 10A
Law of the Sea Treaty, U.N. 1981 Aug 6A; 1982 Jul 8G/Dec 30G
Lawrence (ship) 1984 Feb 28C
Lawrence Livermore National Laboratory (Livermore, Calif.) 1986 Sep 10I; 1987 Jan 20I
Lawyer's Committee for International Human Rights 1984 Feb 9G
layoffs 1980 Jan 3H/Jun 21H; 1986 May 14B/Sep 2B; 1987 Jul 9H; 1988 Jul 5H/Aug 7H
LCA *see* Lutheran Church in America
lead 1981 Jul 28H; 1986 Dec 2H; 1987 Apr 14H; 1988 Feb 11H/Feb 17H/Apr 19H/Aug 10H
leading economic indicators
1980 statistics: 1980 Feb 29H/Mar 31H/May 30H/Jun 30H/Jul 30H
1981 statistics: 1981 Jan 30H/Aug 28H
1982 statistics: 1982 Jan 28H/Mar 1H/Apr 30H/May 28H/Jun 30H/Aug 31H/Sep 30H/Oct 29H/Nov 30H/Dec 30H
1983 statistics: 1983 Jan 28H/Mar 3H/Mar 30H/Apr 29H/May 31H/Jul 29H/Sep 30H/Sep 30H/Nov 30H/Dec 29H/Oct 28H/Nov 30H/Dec 29H
1984 statistics: 1984 Jan 31H/Feb 29H/Mar 29H/Apr 30H/May 31H/Jun 29H/Jul 31H/Aug 29H/Sep 28H/Oct 31H/Dec 28H
1985 statistics: 1985 Mar 1H/Mar 29H/Apr 30H/May 30H/Jun 28H/Jul 31H/Aug 30H/Sep 30H/Oct 31H/Dec 3H/Dec 30H
1986 statistics: 1986 Jan 30H/Mar 4H/Mar 28H/Mar 29H/May 29H/Jul 1H/Aug 1H/Aug 28H/Sep 30H/Oct 31H/Dec 2H/Dec 30H
1987 statistics: 1987 Feb 3H/Mar 3H/Mar 31H/Apr 29H/May 29H/Jun 30H/Jul 30H/Sep 1H/Sep 30H/Oct 30H/Dec 1H/Dec 30H
1988 statistics: 1988 Feb 2H/Mar 1H/Mar 29H/Apr 29H/Jun 1H/Jun 29H/Aug 2H/Aug 30H/Sep 30H/Nov 1H/Dec 1H/Dec 30H
1989 statistics: 1989 Feb 1H/Mar 3H/Mar 29H/Apr 28H/May 31H/Jun 28H/Aug 3H/Sep 1H/Dec 1H
League for Democracy (Burma) 1988 Sep 24E
League of American Theaters and Producers 1989 May 30J
League of Islamic and Arab Peoples 1980 Nov 10A
League of New York Theaters and Producers 1985 Feb 26J
League of United Latin American Citizens 1983 Aug 24F
League of Women Voters 1980 Sep 9F/Sep 25F; 1983 Jan 19F; 1984 Oct 7F
Leaning Tower of Pisa 1989 Dec 15B
Lean on Me (film) 1989 Mar 29J
Leasat 4 (satellite) 1985 Sep 16I
Leaving Home: A Collection of Lake Wobegon Stories (Garrison Keillor) (book) 1987 Oct 23J/Nov 20J/Dec 18J
Lebanese Armed Revolutionary Faction 1982 Aug 21B; 1987 Feb 28B
Lebanon *see also individual leaders in the name index (e.g.,* Gemayel, Amin)
accidents and disasters: Army chief of staff plane crash 1984 Aug 23C
assassinations: French ambassador 1981 Sep 4C; French military attache 1986 Sep 18C; Gemayel (Bashir) headquarters bombing 1982 Sep 14C; Karami helicopter bombed 1987 Jun 1C; Moawad bombing 1989 Nov 22C; PLO official 1982 Sep 27C; Sunni Moslem leader 1989 May 16C
Beirut refugee camp massacre *see* Beirut refugee camp massacre
bombings: church shooting/grenade attack 1982 May 2C; French cultural center 1984 Jan 1C; French embassy 1982 May 24C; Hizballah spiritual leader's home 1985 Mar 8C; Iraqi embassy 1981 Dec 15C; Israeli headquarters compound 1983 Nov 4C; Israeli military headquarters 1982 Nov 11C/Nov 15C; Israeli troop convoy 1985 Mar 10C; Libyan embassy 1984 Jul 12C; Marine barracks (Beirut, 1983) 1983 Oct 23G-24C/Oct 24G/Oct 26C-27C/Oct 27G/Oct 29G-30G/Nov 10C/Nov 23G/Dec 19G; 1984 Jan 16G/Feb 8G; mosque/grand mufti's home 1982 May 6C; oil pipeline 1982 Jan 3C; Paris 1982 Aug 21B; 1986 Sep 17B; PLO command center 1981 Sep 17C; PLO research center 1983 Feb 5C; U.S. embassy (1983) 1982 Jun 24C; 1983 Apr 18C; 1984 Sep 14G/Oct 19C; 1985 Mar 14C/Jul 25C; 1989 Sep 6G
casualties: 1981 Apr 23C; 1982 Sep 1C/Dec 1C
cease-fires: 1981 Apr 8C/Jul 24C; 1982 Jun 11C/Jun 12C/Jul 28C; 1983 Jan 5C/Sep 25C/Dec 27C; 1984 Feb 23C/Mar 13C
environmental issues: water resources 1983 Jun 8C
foreign relations: Austria 1982 Dec 28C; European Community 1982 Jun 29A; France 1984 Feb 29A; Iran 1984 Jul 18C; Libya 1980 Sep 9C; Saudi Arabia 1983 May 17C; USSR 1982 Jul 20A; 1984 Feb 29A; West Germany: terrorist trial 1987 Jan 15A; 1988 Apr 19B/Aug 9B; 1989 May 17B
government and politics: cabinet meeting on government revisions 1984 Sep 19C; Gemayel (Bashir) elected president 1982 Aug 23C; Gemayel (Amin) government to rule by decree 1982 Nov 9C; government abrogates agreement with Israel 1984 Mar 5C; government to assert control over Shouf 1984 Aug 8C; government troop deployments 1984 Nov 26C; Hoss government resigns 1980 Jun 7C; Hrawi elected president 1989 Nov 24C; Karami government resigns 1985 Apr 17C; Moawad elected president 1989 Nov 5C; national unity front formed 1985 Aug 6C; presidential campaign 1982 Jul 23C; Solh asked to form government 1980 Jul 20C; Wazan resigns as premier 1982 Jun 25C
hijackings: Air Afrique airliner 1987 Jul 24B; Jordanian airliner 1985 Jun 11C; 1987 Sep 17G; Kuwaiti airliner 1982 Feb 25C; TWA airliner 1985 Jun 14A/Jun 15C/Jun 16C/Jun 26C/Jun 30C/Jul 15B/Oct 17G; 1987 Jan 15A; 1988 Aug 9B; 1989 May 17B
homeless civilians: 1982 Jun 9A/Jun 17C/Aug 17C/Oct 13C/Dec 10C
hostages: Belgian: 1989 Jun 15C; British: 1985 Mar 14C/Mar 25C/Mar 30C; 1987 Jan 27C/Feb 7C; French: 1984 Apr 15C; 1985 Mar 22C/Mar 25C/Mar 31C/Apr 1C; 1986 Mar 5C/Mar 8C/Jun 30A/Oct 11B/Dec 24C; 1987 Nov 29A; 1988 May 4C/Dec 29C; Indian: 1987 Jan 24C/Feb 9C; 1988 Oct 3C; Jordanian: 1981 Feb 6C; Lebanese mistaken for American: 1985 Mar 15C; Saudi Arabian: 1984 Oct 2C; United States: 1984 Apr 15C/Oct 2C; 1985 Jun 26C/Nov 28C; 1986 Sep 12C/Nov 2C; 1987 Jan 24C/Jan 28G/Feb 9C/Mar 23C/Aug 18C; 1988 Oct 1C; 1989 Aug 3C/Aug 14C; *for individual hostages, see the name index (e.g.,* Anderson, Terry); USSR: 1985 Oct 30C; West German: 1987 Jan 18A/Jan 21C; 1988 Jan 27C/Sep 12C
international organizations: Arab League 1989 May 23C; Red Cross 1982 Jun 17C; 1988 Dec 20C
Israel: Beirut downtown area attacked 1981 Jul 17C; Lebanese Communist Party bases attacked 1989 Dec 26C; Palestinian targets attacked 1980 Apr 9C/Apr 18C/May 15C/Aug 19C/Oct 16C/Dec 3C/Dec 19C; 1981 Apr 9C/Apr 16C/May 28C/Jun 3C/Jul 12C/Jul 16C; 1982 Apr 21C/May 9C/Jun 4C; 1986 Oct 16C; 1988 Jan 2C/Dec 8C; security zone declared success 1985 Dec 13C; Shiite Moslem sheik abducted 1989 Jul 28C; Shiite Moslem village attacked 1988 May 4C; southern Lebanon raid 1980 Apr 14C; Syrian missile deployment 1981 May 5A/May 6A; 1985 Dec 15C; Syrian plane downed 1980 Aug 24C; Syrian targets attacked 1981 Apr 28C; Syria warned 1981 Apr 5C; troops massed on border 1982 May 14C; U.S. arms for hostages deal 1986 Dec 10F
Israeli intervention: Beirut 1982 Jun 10C/Jun 14C/Jun 15C/Jun 18C/Jun 22C/Jun 25C/Jun 26C/Jul 1C/Jul 3C/Jul 7C/Jul 31C/Aug 1C/Aug 4C/Aug 5C/Aug 6C/Aug 9C/Aug 12C/Sep 3C; Bekaa Valley 1982 Jun 9C/Jun 27C/Jul 24C; 1983 May 28C/Aug 2C; 1984 Jan 4C/Aug 16C; 1985 Jan 9C; colonel resigns for reasons of conscience 1982 Jul 25C; conditions for southern Lebanon withdrawal 1984 Oct 17C; cost of intervention 1982 Jul 8C; 1984 Jun 1C; crossing points to south sealed 1983 Dec 31C; Druse forces warned 1983 Sep 5C; general says stay through winter possible 1982 Jun 8C; invasion begins 1982 Jun 6C; Palestinian prisoners held 1982 Jun 22C; Palestinian targets attacked 1982 Jun 7C/Jun 13C/Jul 22C/Jul 30C/Aug 1C; 1983 Nov 20C; 1984 Jun 27C; 1985 Jan 9C; Shiite attacks 1985 Feb 16C; soldiers accused of looting 1982 Sep 28C; Syrian targets attacked 1982 Jun 9C/Jun 22C/Jun 27C/Jul 22C/Jul 24C; Syria warned 1983 Sep 5C; troop-carrying bus ambushed 1982 Oct 3C; troop strength 1982 Jun 23C; troop withdrawal accord 1984 Mar 5C; troop withdrawals 1982 Sep 26C/Oct 10C; 1983 Feb 27C/Jul 20C/Aug 30C/Sep 3C; 1984 Feb 17C; 1985 Jan 14C/Feb 16C/Apr 11C/Apr 21C/Apr 30C/Jun 10C; U.S. asks about cluster bomb use 1982 Jun 18G; U.S. reaction 1982 Jun 7G
Lebanese Army: east Beirut taken over 1982 Oct 15C; extends control in south 1983 Feb 14C; green line dismantled 1984 Jul 28C; militia clashes with 1982 Sep 12C; 1983 Jul 14C-15C/Aug 29C-30C/Aug 31C/Sep 10C/Sep 16C/Sep 24C/Dec 26C; 1984 Jan 13C/Feb 7C/Feb 14C-15C; militia pier seized 1984 Nov 3C; militia positions taken over 1984 Jul 4C; seizes UN troops in south 1985 Jun 7C; sweeps west Beirut 1982 Oct 5C/Oct 14C
militias *see also specific names (e.g.,* Amal)
buffer zone plan 1984 Jan 5C
Christian/Druse accusations 1983 Sep 7C
clashes: Christian/Christian 1980 Feb 17C/Jul 8C/Oct 29C; Christian/Druse 1982 Dec 24C; 1983 Jul 17C/Aug 2C/Sep 4C/Sep 10C; 1984 Dec 6C; 1985 Apr 30C; Christian/Moslem 1981 Apr 19C; 1984 Nov 9C; 1985 Aug 9C; 1989 May 16C; Druse/Druse 1983 Nov 14C; Druse/Shiite 1987 Feb 19C; Druse/Sunni 1984 Mar 23C; Moslem/Moslem 1980 Apr 17C; 1984 Jul 13C; 1987 Feb 23C; Palestinian/Shiite 1985 May 30C; 1986 May 23C; pro/anti-Syrian 1982 May 7C/Dec 15C; 1983 Jan 4C/Jan 9C; Shiite/Shiite 1988 May 25C/May 26C; 1989 Jan 30C
Iran imposes settlement 1989 Jan 30C
Lebanese Forces commander chosen 1984 Oct 9C
Phalangist offer to Syria 1981 Jul 7C
Shiites/Iranians take over Baalbeck 1982 Nov 21C
weapons ban 1982 Sep 1C
obituaries: Chamoun, Camille 1987 Aug 7C; Gemayel, Bashir 1982

Sep 14C; Gemayel, Pierre 1984 Aug 29C; Hakim, Nadim 1984 Aug 23C; Karami, Rashid 1987 Jun 1C; Moawad, Rene 1989 Nov 22C

Palestinians: Arab League evacuation plan 1982 Jul 29C; evacuation 1982 Aug 10C/Aug 21C/Aug 22C/Aug 23C/Aug 27C/Sep 1C/Oct 31C; factional fighting 1983 Jul 24C; full alert 1982 Apr 10C; Iraqi offer to accept guerrillas 1982 Aug 6C; Israeli soldiers captured 1982 Sep 4C; Jordan offer to accept guerrillas 1982 Aug 6C; Shiite militia clashes with 1985 May 19C/May 30C; Sudan offer to accept guerrillas 1982 Jul 26C; Syria agrees to accept guerrillas 1982 Aug 7C; U.S. evacuation plan 1982 Aug 18C/Aug 19C

peace initiatives: Arab League 1989 Apr 26C/Sep 23C/Nov 5C; Israeli-Lebanese 1983 May 16C/May 17C; Syrian-brokered 1985 Dec 28C; U.S.-French peace plan 1981 Apr 16A; U.S. plan 1983 May 6C

peacekeeping forces: France 1983 Feb 4C/Aug 30C/Aug 31B/Sep 7C/Sep 22C/Nov 17C/Dec 24C; 1984 Jan 2B/Feb 8B/Mar 25C/Mar 31C; Great Britain 1984 Feb 8B; Italy 1983 Dec 23B/Dec 31C; 1984 Feb 8B/Feb 20C; joint strategy meeting 1983 Oct 27A; Lebanese government appeals for 1983 Sep 7C

prisoner releases: Israel/PLO exchange 1983 Nov 24C; 1985 May 20C; Israel releases Shiite Moslems 1985 Jul 24C; PLO releases Israelis 1982 Aug 18C

Syria: air strikes 1981 Apr 28C; antiaircraft missiles withdrawn 1986 Jan 4C; Baalbek taken over 1984 Aug 16C; Beirut 1987 Feb 23C; 1988 May 26C; Christian militia clashes with 1980 Feb 17C/Dec 22C; 1981 Apr 2C; 1989 Aug 13C; Christians arrested 1987 Dec 25C; foreign minister visits 1982 Dec 15C; Israeli planes fired on 1981 May 12C/Jun 13C; militia fighting stopped 1984 Jul 13C; missile deployment 1981 May 2C/May 5A/May 6A/Jun 13C; peace settlement imposed on militias 1989 Jan 30C; preparations for Israeli invasion 1982 May 16C; road travel and communications interrupted 1983 May 17C; troop withdrawals 1980 Mar 9C; 1982 Aug 31C; U.S. planes fired on 1983 Nov 10C; U.S. plan for Israeli/Syrian withdrawal rejected 1983 May 13C; U.S. plan for PLO evacuation rejected 1982 Jul 9C

talks and negotiations: Israel/Lebanon 1982 Aug 18C/Dec 28C/Dec 30C; 1983 Jan 13C/Jan 22C; 1984 Oct 31A/Nov 8C/Nov 19C/Dec 20C; 1985 Jan 7C/Jan 8C/Jan 24C; Lebanese parliament 1989 Sep 30C/Oct 22C; national reconciliation talks 1983 Oct 5C/Oct 13C/Oct 23C/Dec 18C; 1984 Mar 13C/Mar 14C/Mar 20C; PLO/U.S. 1982 Jun 17C

trade issues: airport reopened 1983 Aug 16C/Sep 29C

United Nations policy: offices attacked 1980 Dec 23C; peacekeeping forces 1982 Feb 22A; 1983 Jan 18C; 1984 Apr 19A/Oct 12A;

1985 Jun 7C/Jun 15C; PLO guerrilla killing accusations 1981 Jan 2A/Feb 10A; Security Council actions 1982 Jun 6A/Jun 26A/Jul 30A/Aug 1A/Aug 5A/Aug 12A; 1984 Feb 29A/Apr 19A/Sep 6A/Oct 12A; 1985 Mar 11A

U.S. Marines/peacekeeping forces 1982 Sep 10C/Sep 30C; 1983 Feb 2C/Feb 19C/Aug 28C-30C/Aug 29G/Sep 6C/Sep 8C/Sep 12C/Sep 13G/Sep 17C/Sep 19C/Nov 8C/Dec 4C-4G; 1984 Jan 13C/Jan 30C/Feb 8C/Feb 21C/Feb 26C/Jul 30C

U.S. relations: arms for hostages deal 1986 Nov 13G/Dec 8G/Dec 10F; 1987 Feb 26G/Sep 27G; captured U.S. Navy flier Goodman 1983 Dec 4C/Dec 29G/Dec 31C; 1984 Jan 3C-4C/Jan 4G; CIA training of group involved in car bombing 1985 May 12C; congressional actions 1983 Sep 20G/Sep 29G/Nov 2G/Dec 29G; 1984 Jan 10G/Feb 1G; embassy annex security evaluated 1984 Sep 24G; embassy building unfit for use 1983 May 3G; embassy evacuations 1982 Jun 24C; 1984 Oct 19C; 1985 Mar 14C; 1989 Sep 6G; fatalities 1985 Mar 17G; hijacker tried in U.S. 1989 Mar 14G/Oct 4A; New Jersey fires on Syrian positions 1983 Dec 14C; politicians alarmed at combat involvement 1983 Dec 4G; safeguards for Palestinians urged 1982 Oct 6G; UN Security Council resolution vetoed 1984 Sep 6A; 1985 Mar 11A; U.S. embassy annex 1983 May 3G

Le Canard Enchaine (French weekly) 1980 Dec 23B

Le Carrefour du Development (African Crossroads) (French development agency) 1986 Aug 18B

Led Zeppelin (singing group) 1982 Dec 15J

Legacy (James Michener) (book) 1987 Sep 23J

Legacy, The (Howard Fast) (book) 1981 Nov 8J

Legionnaires disease 1980 Jun 9I

legislation, U.S. see specific subjects of bills (e.g., budget)

Le Mans (France) 24 Hours (auto race) 1985 Jun 16J; 1986 Jun 1J; 1987 Jun 14J; 1988 Jun 12J; 1989 Jun 11J

Lemhi Gold (racehorse) 1983 Jan 4J

Le Monde (French newspaper) 1980 Nov 7B

Lend Me a Tenor (musical) 1989 Jun 4J

Lenin Shipyard (Gdansk, Poland) 1980 Aug 14B/Dec 16B; 1982 Oct 12B; 1983 Jan 14B/Mar 9B/Mar 17B; 1987 Jun 12J; 1988 May 10B; 1989 Jul 11B

leprosy 1986 Sep 22I

Les Liaisons Dangereuses (play) 1986 Dec 7J

Les Miserables (musical) 1987 Jun 7J

Les Noces Barbares (Barbaric Wedding) (Yann Queffelec) (book) 1985 Nov 18J

Lesotho 1980 Apr 1C; 1982 Dec 9C; 1986 Jan 20D; 1987 Apr 5C; 1988 Sep 19J

Lesson From Aloes, A (Athol Fugard) (play) 1980 Nov 17J

Less Than One: Selected Essays (Joseph Brodsky) (book) 1987 Jan 12J

Lethal Weapon (film) 1987 Mar 18J/Apr 15J

Lethal Weapon 2 (film) 1989 Jul 26J/Aug 30J/Dec 28J

Let Poland Be Poland (TV show) 1982 Jan 31A

Let's Dance (David Bowie) (recording) 1983 May 11J/Jun 15J

Lettice and Lovage (Peter Shaffer) (play) 1987 Oct 27J

leukemia 1986 Jul 17I/Sep 22H; 1987 Sep 1H; 1988 Jul 20H/Nov 29I

leukopenia (gum disease) 1986 Jan 15F

leveraged buyouts 1985 Oct 14H/Oct 21H; 1988 Oct 26H

Leviathan (film) 1989 Mar 29J

Lewis River 1983 Sep 14H

libel suits 1980 Dec 23B; 1981 Mar 27J; 1982 Jul 9J; 1984 Feb 8J/Mar 20F; 1986 Apr 21F/Jun 25F/Sep 17F; 1988 Mar 7F; see also specific people in the name index (e.g., Westmoreland, William)

Liberal Party (New York) 1980 Sep 6F

liberation theology 1984 Jul 12J/Sep 3J; 1986 Apr 5J

Liberation Tigers of Tamil Eelam (Sri Lankan separatist group) 1987 Aug 5E/Aug 18E/Sep 28E/Oct 25E/Nov 23E; 1989 Jun 28E

Liberia 1980 Apr 12C; 1981 Jul 17C; 1983 Aug 28C; 1984 Jul 26C; 1985 Apr 1C/Jul 18C/Oct 29C/Nov 12C; 1986 Jan 6D; 1987 Mar 4C; 1988 Jul 11A

Libertarian Party 1980 Oct 28F

Liberty (yacht) 1983 Sep 26J

Liberty Bowl (football) 1982 Dec 29J

Liberty University (Lynchburg, Va.) 1988 May 2F

libraries see also Library of Congress
   Bach works discovered 1984 Dec 19J
   book censorship in public schools 1982 Feb 14J/May 25F; 1984 Dec 3J
   Chicago central library architect chosen 1988 Jun 20J
   donation of English Romantic poets collection 1986 Dec 18J
   fires: Los Angeles Central Library 1986 Apr 29F; Soviet Academy of Sciences 1988 Feb 14B
   French national library director appointed 1987 Nov 22B
   New York Public Library president named 1989 Feb 23F
   presidential: Carter library dedicated 1986 Oct 1F; Reagan library construction begun 1988 Nov 21F; Reagan planned library at Stanford abandoned 1987 Apr 23F; Truman Library opens letters to public 1983 Mar 7F

Library of Congress, U.S. 1986 Dec 10J; 1987 Apr 17J/Jul 29J/Aug 18J/Sep 14J/Dec 7F

Librium (drug) 1980 Jul 11I

Libya see also individual leaders in the name index (e.g., Qaddafi, Muammer al-)
   Chad intervention: merger with Chad announced 1981 Jan 6C; military actions 1980 Dec 16C; 1983 Aug 3C/Aug 3G/Aug 10C; 1986 Dec 31C; 1987 Jan 3C/Jan 9C/Apr 13C/Sep 7C; OAU disagreement on 1980 Dec 24C; troop withdrawals 1981 Oct 29C/Nov 5C; 1984

Sep 17A/Sep 25C/Nov 10C; see also Aozou strip
   executions: 1984 Apr 16C; 1987 Feb 20C
   foreign relations: Arab summit meetings 1980 Apr 15C; 1981 Sep 20C; Australia 1987 May 19E; Brazil 1983 Apr 30A/Jun 8A; Canada 1983 Nov 1D; Egypt 1980 Jun 16C; 1983 Feb 16C; 1984 Aug 10C/Nov 17C; 1985 Oct 12C; European Community 1986 Apr 14B; Great Britain 1984 Apr 17A/Apr 22A/Apr 22C/Apr 27A/Apr 30B/Apr 30C; 1986 Apr 25C; Iraq 1985 Jun 26C; Israel 1986 Feb 4C; Italy 1986 Apr 15C; Kurdish rebels 1986 Jan 7C; Lebanon 1980 Sep 9C; 1984 Jul 12C; Malta 1980 Aug 28B; Nicaragua 1981 May 14D; 1983 Apr 30A/Jun 8A; 1985 Jan 23G; OAU 1980 Dec 24C; PLO 1980 Jan 5C; Saudi Arabia 1980 Oct 28C; 1981 Dec 31C; Somalia 1981 Aug 25C; Sudan 1983 Feb 22C; Syria 1980 Sep 2C/Sep 10C/Dec 18C; 1985 Oct 12C; Tunisia 1985 Sep 26C/Oct 12C; 1987 Nov 7C; USSR 1985 Dec 21G; Western Europe 1986 Apr 24B; West Germany 1983 May 8C; 1988 Jan 18B; 1989 Feb 15B/May 10B
   international terrorism: hostages released 1985 Feb 5A; terrorism support cut back 1989 Sep 3C
   labor issues: foreign workers expelled 1985 Oct 12C
   sports: Olympic Games (Los Angeles) withdrawal 1984 Jul 27A
   trade issues: common market 1989 Feb 17C; oil production set aside for African countries 1980 Nov 9C
   United Nations policy: 1989 Jan 11A
   U.S. relations: air strikes 1986 Apr 17G; CIA ex-officials in terrorist training scheme 1982 Jan 6G; Libyan diplomatic mission ordered closed 1981 May 6G; Libyan missile attack on Coast Guard 1986 Apr 15C; naval exercises 1981 Aug 19A/Aug 20G; 1983 Feb 18C/Feb 19C; 1986 Mar 23C/Mar 29G; 1989 Jan 4C; oil companies 1981 Jun 17H; 1982 May 13H/Jul 20H; 1983 Jan 4C; satellite technology 1981 Nov 5G; U.S. firms requested to close operations 1981 Aug 19G

Licence to Kill (film) 1989 Jul 26J

Licensed to Ill (Beastie Boys) (recording) 1987 Feb 18J/Mar 28J/Apr 25J/May 23J

Lidove Noviny (People's News) (Czech dissident newspaper) 1989 Oct 25B

Liechtenstein 1984 Aug 26B

lie detector tests 1985 Nov 21G/Dec 11G/Dec 19F/Dec 20G; 1987 Nov 4F; 1988 Mar 3F

Lie Down With Lions (Ken Follett) (book) 1986 Feb 28J/Mar 28J/Apr 25J

Life and Adventures of Nicholas Nickleby, The (adapted from Charles Dickens) (play) 1982 Jun 6J

Life and Hard Times of Heidi Abromowitz, The (Joan Rivers) (book) 1985 Jan 18J/Feb 8J/Mar 15J

Life and Times of Cotton Mather, The (Kenneth Silverman) (book) 1985 Apr 24J

life expectancy 1981 Feb 8I; 1985 Feb 11F; 1986 Mar 6I; 1987 Jan 19B; 1988 May 24I/Dec 15F

Life Insurance, American Council of see American Council of Life Insurance

Life Its Ownself: The Semi-Tougher Adventures of Billy Clyde Puckett (Dan Jenkins) (book) 1984 Dec 14J

Life's Magic (racehorse) 1985 Nov 2J

Light in the Attic, A (Shel Silverstein) (book) 1985 Jan 13J

Lightning (Dean R. Koontz) (book) 1988 Feb 26J

Like A Prayer (Madonna) (recording) 1989 Apr 29J/May 27J/Jun 24J

Like a Rock (Bob Seger & the Silver Bullet Band) (recording) 1986 May 21J/Jun 18J

Like a Virgin (Madonna) (recording) 1984 Dec 22J; 1985 Jan 26J/Feb 23J

Like Father Like Son (film) 1987 Oct 21J

LILCO see Long Island Lighting Co.

Lili Marleen (film) 1981 Jul 10J

Lilly Poetry Prize see Ruth Lilly Poetry Prize

Lima Group 1985 Oct 13D; 1987 Oct 7A

Lincoln: A Novel (Gore Vidal) (book) 1984 Jul 20J/Aug 24J/Sep 14J

Lincoln: A Photobiography (Russell Friedman) (book) 1988 Jan 11J

Lincoln Center (New York City) 1986 Mar 19J

Lincoln Center Theater Company (New York City) 1985 Apr 29J

Lincoln Savings and Loan Association 1989 Jan 17F/Oct 13F/Oct 17H/Oct 31H/Dec 4H/Dec 22F

Lincoln University (Jefferson City, Mo.) 1981 Jan 13J

line item veto 1985 Jun 20H/Aug 5F

Linkage (racehorse) 1982 May 15J

Lionel Richie (Lionel Richie) (recording) 1982 Nov 17J/Dec 15J; 1983 Jan 5J/Feb 9J/Mar 9J

Lions Club International 1987 Jul 4J

liquor 1985 Dec 17I; 1989 May 31F/Nov 24F

Lisa (personal computer) 1983 Mar 8I

Lisbon (Portugal) 1983 Jul 27B; 1988 Aug 25B

Lisbon Airport (Portugal) 1980 Dec 4B

Listeria monocytogenes (bacterium) 1985 Jul 12I

literacy 1980 Dec 4J; 1986 Apr 21F

literature
   awards and honors see specific awards (e.g., Pulitzer Prizes)
   books see individual titles (e.g., Little Drummer Girl)
   writers see individual artists in the name index (e.g., Le Carre, John)

Lithuania (USSR) 1982 Jan 19B; 1987 Aug 23B; 1989 Jul 27B/Aug 23B/Dec 7B/Dec 20B/Dec 24B/Dec 26B

Little Darlings (film) 1980 Mar 26J/Apr 23J

Little Dorrit (film) 1988 Oct 21J

Little Drummer Girl, The (John le Carre) (book) 1983 Apr 10J/May 15J/Jun 1J/Jun 12J/Jul 10J/Aug 14J

Little Foxes, The (Lillian Hellman) (play) 1981 May 7J

Little League World Series 1980 Aug 30E; 1981 Aug 29J; 1982 Aug 28J; 1984 Aug 21J; 1985 Aug 25J; 1986 Aug 23J; 1988 Aug 27J; 1989 Aug 23J/Aug 26J

Little Mermaid, The (film) 1989 Nov 15J/Nov 29J

Little Shop of Horrors (film) 1986 Dec 24J

Litton Industries Inc. 1981 Jun 29H

Live Aid (benefit concert) 1985 Jul 13J

liver diseases 1984 Nov 23I; 1985 Aug 13I

liver toxins 1987 Jul 28H

liver transplants 1986 Dec 17I; 1989 Nov 27I/Dec 3I

Living Daylights, The (film) 1987 Aug 12J

lizards 1984 Sep 24I

L.L. Cool J (singing group) 1987 Aug 22J

Lloyds Bank PLC 1988 Feb 26B

Lloyd's Maritime Information Services 1987 Dec 17C

Lloyd's of London 1982 Sep 8B; 1983 Feb 1B; 1987 Oct 2C; 1988 Mar 22H

lobbyists 1981 Sep 20F; 1982 Mar 26F; 1983 Sep 21G/Dec 4I; 1984 Mar 18J/Oct 3F/Dec 18F

Loc-Ed After Dark (Tone Loc) (recording) 1989 Apr 29J/May 27J

Lockerbie air crash (1988) 1988 Dec 21B/Dec 28B; 1989 Nov 1G

Lockheed Corp. 1982 Dec 22E; 1983 Oct 12E; 1986 Aug 11G

lockout/tagout rules 1989 Aug 31H

Locomotive Engineers, Brotherhood of *see* Brotherhood of Locomotive Engineers

locusts 1986 Oct 23C; 1988 May 3I

Loma Linda University Medical Center (California) 1982 Aug 26I; 1985 Nov 20I; 1986 Jun 10I; 1987 Oct 16I

Lombard-Wall, Inc. 1982 Aug 12H

London (Great Britain)
　accidents and disasters: boat collision 1989 Aug 20B
　arts and culture: Amnesty International rock concert 1988 Sep 2J; archaeology 1989 Mar 3J/May 14J/Oct 13J; architecture 1987 Dec 1B; Broadway production agreement 1987 Jul 2J; *Chess* opens 1986 May 14J; Elgin marbles 1984 Apr 10J; Elizabethan period theaters uncovered 1989 Mar 3J/May 14J/Oct 13J; Kirov ballet 1988 Aug 6J; Lawrence enshrined in Poets' Corner 1985 Nov 16J; *Lettice and Lovage* opens 1987 Oct 27J; Live Aid concert 1985 Jul 13J; Mandela birthday pop concert 1988 Jun 11J; Olivier theater awards 1986 Dec 7J; 1988 Jan 24J; *Phantom of the Opera* opens 1986 Oct 9J; Royal Ballet 1985 Jun 21J; 1989 Jan 12J; *Serious Money* opens 1987 Mar 21J; Soviet dissident poet arrives 1986 Dec 18B; theater *see also* Olivier awards
　assassinations: Israeli ambassador 1982 Jun 3C; Qaddafi opponent 1980 Apr 11C; Seychelles opposition leader 1985 Nov 29E
　civil strife: racial clashes 1981 Jul 3B; 1985 Jul 10B; riots 1981 Apr 12B
　crime and law enforcement: Heathrow Airport robbery 1983 Nov 26B; Libyan embassy killing 1984 Apr 17A; Queen fired upon 1981 Jun 14B; Security Express robbery 1983 Apr 1B; youth program 1986 Aug 21B
　demonstrations and protests: antinuclear 1980 Oct 26B; 1981 Oct

25B; 1983 Nov 16B; 1984 Jun 9B; economic policies 1981 May 31B; peace-related 1983 May 25B; students 1988 Nov 24B
　economy and business: casinos lose licenses 1981 Nov 5B; London Stock Exchange 1981 Sep 23G/Sep 29H; 1983 Jul 27B; 1984 Jul 19B; 1985 Jan 2B/Jun 5B; 1986 Oct 27B; 1987 Oct 20A; 1988 Feb 11B/Apr 30A/May 11A/Dec 30B; 1989 Oct 16A/Oct 17A
　labor issues: newspapers 1982 Feb 8B/Mar 11B; 1986 Jul 31B
　medicine and health care: in-vitro fertilization 1989 Jun 5I
　press and broadcasting: *Times* and *Sunday Times* 1982 Feb 8B/Mar 11B
　sports: boxing 1980 Sep 27J; rowing 1986 Mar 29J; 1989 Mar 25J; running 1987 May 10J; 1988 Apr 17J
　stock market *see* London Stock Exchange
　terrorism: El Al airliner 1986 May 21B/Oct 24C; Harrods bombing 1983 Dec 17B; IRA bombing 1981 Oct 10B/Oct 11B; Ira hit list 1985 Jun 25B; Iranian embassy seizure 1980 Apr 30A/May 5B; Libyan embassy 1984 Apr 17A/Apr 30B; London park bombings 1982 Jul 20B
　transportation: railways 1988 Jul 14B; traffic jam 1982 Jun 28B

London Marathon 1987 May 10J; 1988 Apr 17J

London Metal Exchange 1985 Oct 24A; 1986 Mar 12B

London Stock Exchange 1981 Sep 23G/Sep 29H; 1983 Jul 27B; 1984 Jul 19B; 1985 Jan 2B/Jun 5B; 1986 Oct 27B; 1987 Oct 20A; 1988 Feb 11B/Apr 30A/May 11A/Dec 30B; 1989 Oct 16A/Oct 17A

London Suppliers Club 1984 Jul 13A

Lonely Passion of Judith Hearne, The (film) 1989 Mar 19J

Lonesome Dove (Larry McMurtry) (book) 1985 Aug 16J; 1986 Apr 17J

Lonesome Gods, The (Louis L'Amour) (book) 1983 Apr 10J/May 15J

Long Distance Voyager (Moody Blues) (recording) 1981 Jul 8J/Aug 5J

Long Island Lighting Co. (LILCO) 1983 Jun 23I/Dec 14H; 1984 Dec 21H; 1985 Feb 21H; 1987 Jan 14H/Jun 11H; 1988 May 27H; 1989 Feb 11H/Feb 28H

Long Island Rail Road 1980 Apr 1H/Apr 2H

long jump 1980 Jul 31J

Long Run, The (Eagles) (recording) 1980 Jan 2J

Looker (film) 1981 Nov 4J

Look Homeward: A Life of Thomas Wolfe (David Herbert Donald) (book) 1988 Mar 31J

Look What the Cat Dragged In (Poison) (recording) 1987 Apr 25J/May 23J

Look Who's Talking (film) 1989 Oct 25J/Nov 29J

Loon Lake (E. L. Doctorow) (book) 1981 Jan 11J

Lord at War (racehorse) 1985 Mar 3J

Lords of Discipline, The (film) 1983 Mar 9J

Los Alamos National Laboratory (New Mexico) 1983 Aug 21F

Los Angeles (California)
　accidents and disasters: Aeromexico airliner/private plane collision 1986 Aug 31F; Central Library fire 1986 Apr 29F; earthquakes 1987 Oct 1I/Nov 4I
　AIDS: 1984 Oct 17I; 1985 Aug 14F
　arts and culture *see also* Emmy Awards; Grammy Awards; fine arts center planned 1983 Sep 20J; Jacksons concert 1984 Dec 9J; Museum of Contemporary Art opens 1986 Dec 10J; Playboy Clubs closed 1986 Jun 30J; *Sarcophagus* opens 1987 Sep 18J
　business and industry: black-owned businesses 1983 May 3H
　census data: population 1984 Apr 7J
　crime and law enforcement: Billionaire Boys Club 1987 Apr 22F; 1988 Jan 25F; cocaine seized 1989 Sep 29F; De Lorean arrested 1982 Oct 19J; "freeway murders" 1981 Jan 11F; gangs 1981 Aug 7F; 1988 Dec 16F; "Night Stalker" 1985 Aug 25F/Sep 27F; Schaeffer slaying 1989 Jul 19F; Stratten slaying 1980 Aug 15/Sep 15J
　demonstrations and protests: Reagan daughter speaks at antinuclear rally 1981 Jul 14F; Taiwan consulate protest 1981 Jul 18F; veterans' sit-in 1981 Jun 9F
　economy: cost of living 1988 Jun 28A
　environmental issues: clean-air standards not met 1987 Jun 29H; sewer dumping fines 1985 Aug 26H
　espionage and intelligence issues: stealth technology 1984 Dec 18G
　family issues: frozen embryo dispute 1984 Oct 23I; 1986 Jun 6I
　foreign issues: Elizabeth II visits 1983 Feb 26G
　immigration and refugees: naturalization ceremony 1981 Jun 22F
　labor issues: female job-bias suit 1982 Nov 22F; teacher strike ended 1989 May 25F
　politics and government: Bradley reelected 1985 Apr 9F; 1989 Apr 11F; city council redistricting plan 1986 Sep 22F; Hispanics 1986 Sep 22F; presidential campaign 1984 Jun 3F
　religious issues: papal visit 1987 Sep 10J
　schools: bilingual education 1988 May 5F; desegregation plan ordered 1980 May 19F; mandatory busing program halted 1981 Mar 16F; teacher strikes 1983 Nov 27F; 1989 May 25F; year-round classes 1986 Feb 24F; 1987 Oct 19F; 1988 Mar 14F
　social services: homeless in "urban campground" 1987 Jun 15F
　sports: football team move 1980 Jan 18J/Mar 1J; running 1985 Jan 19J; *see also* Olympic Games

Los Angeles Ballet 1985 Jan 14J

Los Angeles County Museum of Art 1988 Jan 21J

Los Angeles Dodgers (baseball team) 1981 Sep 26J/Oct 19J/Oct 28J/Nov 11J; 1982 Nov 22J; 1983 Oct 8J; 1985 Oct 16J; 1988 Oct 2J/Oct 12J/Oct 22J/Nov 10J/Nov 15J

Los Angeles Herald-Examiner (newspaper) 1989 Nov 2F

Los Angeles Kings (ice hockey team) 1989 Feb 7J/Jun 7J

Los Angeles Lakers (basketball team) 1980 May 16J/May 29J; 1981 Jun 26J; 1982 Jun 8J; 1983 May 31J; 1984 Apr 5J/Jun 12J; 1985 May 27J/Jun 9J/Nov 23J; 1987 May 18J/Jun 14J; 1988 Jun 21J; 1989 May 22J/Jun 8J/Jun 13J

Los Angeles Memorial Coliseum 1980 Mar 1J; 1981 Jun 22F

Los Angeles Olympic Organizing Committee 1983 Sep 16J; 1984 Dec 19J

Los Angeles Police Department (LAPD) 1984 Apr 15J

Los Angeles Raiders (football team) 1984 Jan 8J/Jan 22J; 1986 Jan 5J; 1989 Jan 24J

Los Angeles Rams (football team) 1980 Jan 6J/Jan 20J; 1986 Jan 4J/Jan 12J

Los Angeles Theater Center 1987 Sep 18J

Los Angeles Times (newspaper) 1984 Apr 16J

Lost Boys, The (film) 1987 Aug 12J

lotteries 1983 Sep 29F; 1984 Jan 23J/Sep 3J; 1988 Sep 7J/Nov 1J

Lou Grant (TV show) 1980 Sep 7J

Louise Bogan: A Portrait (Elizabeth Frank) (book) 1986 Apr 17J

Louisiana *see also individual leaders in the name index* (e.g., Edwards, Edwin); *specific cities* (e.g., New Orleans)
　accidents and disasters: floods 1983 Apr 12I; Hurricane Juan 1985 Oct 26I; oil spill 1984 Jul 30H; sink hole 1980 Nov 20H; train derailment 1982 Sep 28I
　crime and law enforcement: capital punishment 1983 Dec 15F; 1984 Feb 29F; 1988 Mar 15F
　education: creationism 1981 Jul 21F; 1982 Nov 22I; 1983 Oct 17F; 1985 Jan 10F; 1987 Jun 19F; desegregation 1981 Jan 15F; 1989 May 30F
　environmental issues: 1987 Feb 19H
　obituaries: Jones, Ralph Waldo Emerson 1982 Apr 9J
　politics and government: Long announces retirement 1985 Feb 25F; Long's widow wins House seat 1985 Mar 30F; New Orleans GOP convention (1988) 1988 Aug 15F-16F/Aug 18F; parish council elections 1983 Feb 26F; racial reclassification plea denied 1985 Oct 19J
　presidential campaigns: 1980 Apr 5F; 1988 Jun 18F
　sports: Duran fined 1980 Nov 26J

Louisiana State University (LSU) 1983 Jan 1J; 1985 Jan 1J; 1987 Jan 1J; 1989 May 28J

Louisiana Technical University (Ruston) 1982 Mar 28J/Mar 30J; 1983 Apr 2J; 1987 Mar 29J; 1988 Apr 3J

Louisville, University of (Kentucky) 1980 Mar 24J; 1986 Mar 31J; 1987 Sep 29J

Louisville Courier-Journal (newspaper) 1986 May 19H

Louisville Times (newspaper) 1986 May 19H

Louisville Times Co. 1986 Jan 9H

lovastatin (drug) 1987 Sep 1I

Love and War (John Jakes) (book) 1984 Nov 16J/Dec 14J; 1985 Jan 18J

Love Canal (Niagara Falls, N.Y.) 1980 Apr 28H/May 21H; 1981 Jun 11H; 1982 Jul 14H; 1987 Nov 26H

Love in the Time of Cholera (Gabriel Garcia Marquez) (book) 1988 May 27J/Jun 24J

Love Is Never Silent (TV show) 1986 Sep 21J

Love Medicine (Louise Erdrich) (book) 1985 Jan 14J

Low Income Home Energy Assistance Program 1986 Sep 18F

LSD (lysergic acid diethylamide) 1984 Mar 22G

LTV Corp. 1981 Sep 23H/Sep 24H/Oct 28H/Nov 16H; 1984 Mar 21H/Mar 23H; 1985 May 2H; 1986 Mar 15H; 1987 Aug 6H; 1988 May 4H

Lucchese crime family 1988 Aug 26F

Lucky (Jackie Collins) (book) 1985 Sep 27J/Oct 25J

Lulu (Pierre Boulez) (recording) 1981 Feb 25J

lumber 1983 Mar 10A; 1986 Jun 10D/Jul 25H/Aug 25H/Dec 5D/Dec 30D; 1987 Jan 8D/Jul 11D; 1988 Dec 12H

lumpectomy 1984 Dec 4I

lung cancer 1980 Jan 14I; 1981 Jan 17I; 1984 Oct 20I; 1985 Feb 8I/Dec 2F; 1987 Aug 4H; 1989 Jul 28I

lung transplants 1986 May 6I/Dec 17I

Lutheran Church in America (LCA) 1987 Apr 30J

Lutheran Church-Missouri Synod 1987 Apr 30J

Luxembourg 1980 Apr 28B/Jul 31A; 1984 Jan 23B; 1985 Mar 20J/Mar 27B/Jul 9B/Nov 12A; 1986 Mar 23J/Nov 12B; 1989 Apr 18B/Dec 6A

Lyme disease 1989 Dec 22I

Lyons University (France) 1981 Jul 3B

Lyphomed 1989 Oct 12F

M

Mabharata, The (Jean-Claude Carriere) (play) 1987 Oct 13J

Macao 1984 Aug 15E; 1985 May 23E; 1987 Jan 6E/Mar 26E/May 30E/Jul 9E

MacDowell Colony Medal (arts) 1985 Aug 18J; 1986 Aug 17J; 1987 Aug 9J

Machete (pesticide) 1983 Apr 28I

Macheteros (Puerto Rican terrorist group) 1981 Jan 12D

machine tools 1986 Nov 20E

Machinists and Aerospace Workers, International Association of (IAM) (AFL-CIO) 1989 Oct 4H

Macintosh (personal computer) 1984 Jan 24I; 1987 Mar 2H; 1988 Mar 17H

Macy & Co., R.H. 1985 Oct 21H

Madagascar 1985 Oct 17A; 1989 May 6J/Aug 3C

Madison (Wisconsin) 1985 Dec 23G

Mad Love (Linda Ronstadt) (recording) 1980 Mar 5J/Apr 2J

Mad Max Beyond Thunderdome (film) 1985 Jul 17J

Mafia 1980 Sep 2F; 1983 Jan 25B/Mar 5B; 1984 Sep 29B/Oct 18B/Oct 25B; 1985 Sep 6F/Nov 9B; 1986 Feb 10B/Feb 20B/Jun 13F/Nov 19F; 1987 Mar 2F/Mar 13F/Aug 26F/Dec 16B; 1988 Apr 16B

Magellan (spacecraft) 1989 May 4I

Magicians of the Silver Screen (film) 1980 Dec 26J

Magna Carta (British political document) 1984 Sep 25J

Magnum P.I. (TV show) 1983 Apr 10J

mail bombs 1989 Dec 22F

Maine 1980 Feb 10F/Mar 15F/Sep 23I/Oct 10I; 1983 Jul 22A/Oct 1F; 1984 Mar 4F/Mar 5F; 1985 Aug 12F/Aug 26J/Oct 7H; 1986 May 6J; 1987 Jun 1F; 1988 Mar 1F

Maine Yankee nuclear power plant (Wiscassett) 1980 Sep 23I

Maitatsine (Moslem sect) 1984 Mar 4C

Major Fraud Act of 1988 1988 Nov 19F

Major League (film) 1989 Apr 26J

Major League Players Association (baseball) 1987 Sep 21J; 1988 Jan 22H

Major League Umpires Association (baseball) 1984 Oct 5J/Oct 7J

Make It Big (Wham!) (recording) 1985 Feb 23J

Making Love (film) 1982 Feb 17J

Making of the Atomic Bomb, The (Richard Rhodes) (book) 1987 Nov 9J; 1988 Jan 11J/Mar 31J

Malacanang Palace (Manila, Philippines) 1987 Mar 2E

malaria 1988 Mar 10I

malathion 1981 Jul 10H

Malawi 1980 Apr 1C; 1989 May 6J

Malaysia *see also individual leaders in the name index (e.g., Mohamad, Mahathir)*

executions: Australians executed 1986 Jul 6E; French woman's death sentence commuted 1982 Aug 25E

government and politics: Communist Party signs peace agreement 1989 Dec 2E; government crackdown 1987 Oct 29E/Nov 3E; king elected 1984 Feb 9E; 1989 Mar 2E; king's, sultans' power weakened 1983 Sep 5E/Dec 15E; king sworn 1989 Apr 26E; Moslem fundamentalists 1985 Nov 19E; ruling party declared illegal 1988 Feb 4E; state elections 1986 May 6E

press and broadcasting: 1984 Apr 4E; 1986 Sep 26E; 1987 Oct 29E; 1988 Mar 27E

sports: Olympic athletes threatened by KKK 1984 Jul 11J

United Nations policy: 1988 Oct 26A

U.S. relations: Shultz visit 1984 Jul 7G

Maldives 1988 Nov 3E; 1989 Aug 14E

Mali 1983 Jan 17C; 1985 Mar 11C/Dec 25C; 1986 Jan 17C

malpractice 1986 Jun 24F; 1989 Oct 11F

Malta 1980 Aug 28B; 1981 Dec 12B/Dec 19B; 1983 Dec 31A; 1984 Oct 4B/Nov 16B; 1985 Nov 24C; 1987 May 9B/May 12B; 1989 Dec 2A

Maltese Falcon, The (film) 1987 May 12J

mammograms 1983 Aug 2I

Mammoth Hunters, The (Jean M. Auel) (book) 1985 Dec 20J; 1986 Jan 31J/Feb 28J/Mar 28J/Apr 25J/May 30J

Management and Budget, U.S. Office of (OMB) *see also individual leaders in the name index (e.g., Stockman, David)*

appointments: Miller III, James C. 1985 Jul 19H; Stockman, David A. 1980 Dec 11F

budget deficit issues 1985 Aug 8H/Dec 12H; 1986 Jan 15H/Jul 30H/Aug 6H/Oct 23H/Jun 4H;

1987 Jul 16H; 1988 Jan 4H/Oct 16H; 1989 Jan 4H

health care issues: birth control 1983 Jan 10F; Medicare 1988 Nov 28F; video display terminals 1986 Jun 6J

Manassas National Battlefield Park (Virginia) 1988 Aug 10H/Nov 11H

Manchester Airport (Great Britain) 1985 Aug 22B

Man from St. Petersburg, The (Ken Follett) (book) 1982 Jun 6J/Jul 11J/Aug 8J

Maniac (film) 1981 Feb 11J

Manila (racehorse) 1986 Nov 1J

Manitoba (Canada) 1982 Mar 26D; 1983 Oct 6D; 1984 Feb 27D/Mar 20D; 1985 Nov 4D; 1988 Sep 19D; 1989 Jul 25D/Jul 25I/Nov 10D/Dec 7D

Mannequin (film) 1987 Feb 18J

Man of the Year (*Time* magazine) 1987 Dec 26J

Manufacturers Hanover Trust Co. 1985 Jan 14H

Manville Corp. 1982 Aug 26H/Aug 27H; 1983 Nov 21H; 1985 Feb 4F/Aug 2F/Aug 21H; 1986 Dec 18H

Many Faces of AIDS, The: A Gospel Response (U.S. Catholic Conference paper) 1987 Dec 10J

Ma Rainey's Black Bottom (August Wilson) (play) 1984 Oct 11J

Marathon Oil Co. 1980 May 13H; 1981 Oct 30H/Nov 2H/Nov 3H/Nov 19H/Nov 24H/Dec 23H/Dec 24H/Dec 30H; 1982 Feb 17H/Feb 22H/Mar 11H; 1984 Mar 29H/Jul 13H

marathons 1984 Aug 5J; *see also specific race (e.g., Boston Marathon)*

Marble Hill nuclear power plant (Indiana) 1984 Jan 16H/Jan 23H

March for Life (antiabortion rally) 1984 Jan 23F; 1989 Jan 23F

Marchioness (ship) 1989 Aug 20B/Sep 1B

Marco Polo, If You Can (William F. Buckley Jr.) (book) 1982 Feb 7J/Mar 7J

Marc Rich & Co. 1983 Aug 12B/Sep 19H/Sep 21B; 1984 Oct 11H/Dec 17H; 1985 Aug 16B

Margaret Mead and Samoa: The Making and Unmaking of an Anthropological Myth (Derek Freeman) (book) 1983 Jan 31I

Margaret Wade Trophy (basketball) 1982 Mar 30J

Mariel boatlift (1980) 1980 May 1D/Sep 26D; 1983 May 24D; 1984 Jul 12D/Dec 3F/Dec 14D; 1986 Jul 9D; 1987 Nov 20G; 1988 Dec 2F

marijuana

accidents and disasters: Amtrak/Conrail railway collision 1988 Jan 20H

crime and law enforcement: antidrug bill 1988 Oct 12J; cultivation on public lands 1984 Dec 12H; decriminalization recommended 1982 Jul 8I; drug courier profile 1983 Mar 23F; government seizures 1981 Sep 3F; 1982 Feb 4D; long prison sentence upheld 1982 Jan 11F; paraquat spraying 1983 Aug 15F/Sep 14H; U.S. ex-representative sentenced 1982 Nov 10F

foreign developments: Bahamas 1984 Dec 17D; Canada 1981 May 16D

health issues: NAS report 1982 Feb 26I; pot medicinal use 1988 Sep 6F

politics and government: Ginsburg Supreme Court nomination 1987 Nov 7F/Nov 8F

production issues: 1984 Dec 12H; 1989 Mar 1G

statistics: high school seniors 1988 Jan 13F; U.S. troops in Europe 1984 Mar 22G

Marijuana and Health (National Academy of Sciences) 1982 Feb 26I

marine animals 1988 Oct 28H

Marine Corps, U.S.

Beirut Marine barracks bombing *see* Beirut Marine barracks bombing

contract and billing issues: defense contractor liability 1988 Jun 27H

firefighting: 1988 Nov 20I

foreign developments: Costa Rica 1981 Mar 17D; El Salvador 1985 Jun 19D; Grenada 1983 Nov 2G; Moscow embassy 1987 Apr 2G/Apr 7G/May 15G/Jun 12G/Aug 24G; Panama 1988 Apr 8D; 1989 Dec 16D

Lebanon *see* Lebanon

personnel issues: diplomatic outpost guards recalled 1987 Apr 12G; drug tests found faulty 1983 Aug 18G; Gray appointed commandant 1987 Jun 16G; racial imbalance 1982 Jun 27F; Vietnam court-martial 1980 Feb 1G; women's role 1988 Apr 25G

TWA hijacking incident: Stethem slain 1985 Jun 15C; 1988 Aug 9B; 1989 May 17B

Marion Island 1986 Dec 28C

Market Theater (Johannesburg, South Africa) 1987 Sep 16J

Marmottan Museum (Paris) 1985 Oct 27J

marriage

legislation: mandatory AIDS testing 1989 Jun 23F; Swiss laws changed 1985 Dec 22B

people: Benazir Bhutto/Asif Ali Zardari 1987 Dec 18E; Madonna/Sean Penn 1985 Aug 16J; Prince Andrew/Sarah Ferguson 1986 Jul 23G; Prince Charles/Lady Diana Spencer 1981 Jul 29B; Ronald P. Reagan/Doria Palmieri 1980 Nov 24J

statistics: 1981 Oct 18J; 1983 Oct 10F; 1985 Sep 15F; 1987 Jan 13J

Married to the Mob (film) 1988 Aug 31J

Mars (planet) 1983 Apr 16I; 1987 Aug 17I; 1988 Nov 10I/Dec 19I; 1989 Mar 28I/Jul 20I/Aug 22I

Marshall Islands 1980 Apr 9E/Oct 31E; 1981 May 21A; 1985 Mar 13I

Marshall University (Huntington, W. Va.) 1985 Feb 7J

Marshals Service, U.S. (Justice Department) 1985 Jun 16F

marshes 1988 Feb 23F

Martin Beck Theater (New York City) 1987 Nov 5J

Martin Luther King Jr. Nonviolent Peace Prize 1980 Jan 28J

Martin Marietta Corp. 1982 Aug 30H/Sep 2H/Sep 6H/Sep 7H/Sep 10H/Sep 17H/Sep 17H/Sep 22H/Sep 24H/Dec 22H

Mary (mother of Jesus) 1987 Mar 25J

Maryland

crime and law enforcement: Iranian diplomat assassinated 1980 Jul 22F; Mandel convictions overturned 1987 Nov 12F

economy: savings and loan associations 1985 May 14H/May 22H

environmental issues: hazardous waste disposal indictments 1982 Sep 2H

horse racing *see* Preakness Stakes

politics and government: Agnew lawsuit 1981 Apr 27F; 1983 Jan 4F; presidential campaigns 1980 May 13F; 1984 May 8F; primary date moved 1986 Apr 6F; senatorial primaries 1986 Sep 9F; women win senatorial primaries 1986 Sep 9F

religion: sanctuary movement 1985 Dec 23G

Maryland, University of (College Park) 1982 Dec 25J; 1986 Jun 19J

Maryland Savings Share Insurance Corp. 1985 May 22H

*M*A*S*H* (TV show) 1980 Sep 7J; 1983 Feb 28J/Jun 12J

Mask (film) 1985 Apr 17J

Masonic lodge 1981 May 26B/May 28B

Masquerade (film) 1988 Mar 16J

Masquerade (Kit Williams) (book) 1981 Mar 8J/Apr 12J/May 10J

Massachusetts *see also specific cities (e.g., Boston)*

crime and law enforcement: police officers convicted of murder 1983 May 12F; prison drug, gambling operation 1982 Jan 6F

economy: state revenue decrease 1988 Jun 1F

education: Boston University to run Chelsea schools 1989 Jun 13F

energy issues: nuclear power proposal approved 1982 Nov 2I; oil/gas offshore leasing 1983 Jul 28H; 1987 Aug 27H

environmental issues: hazardous waste sites 1988 Aug 3H; oil/gas offshore leasing 1983 Jul 28H; 1987 Aug 27H; sewage dumping charges 1988 Jan 28H

health care issues: AIDS 1987 Jul 8F; artificial skin 1981 Apr 24I; health-insurance plans 1985 Jun 3F; life-sustaining devices 1980 Jan 24F

obituaries: McCormack, John 1980 Nov 22F

politics and government: gubernatorial primary 1982 Sep 14F; Joe Kennedy sets congressional bid 1985 Dec 4F; presidential campaigns 1980 Mar 4F; 1983 Apr 9F; 1984 Mar 13F/Mar 14F

transportation: mass transit 1980 Dec 7H

Massachusetts, University of (Amherst) 1987 Nov 22J; 1988 Feb 17F

Massachusetts General Hospital 1981 Apr 24I

Massachusetts Institute of Technology (MIT) 1980 Apr 22I; 1981 Dec 24I; 1985 Oct 15J; 1986 Sep 10I; 1987 Mar 9F/Sep 21I/Oct 12I/Oct 21J; 1988 May 13I; 1989 May 23I

massage parlors 1985 Oct 2F

Massey Coal Co., A. T. 1985 Dec 20H

Massey-Ferguson Ltd. 1981 Feb 7D

mass transit 1980 Apr 1H/Dec 7H; 1981 Mar 1H/Jun 11H/Jun 13H; 1983 Mar 30H; 1987 Jan 21H/Apr 2H

mastectomy 1984 Dec 4I

Master of the Game (Sidney Sheldon) (book) 1982 Sep 12J/Oct 17J/Nov 14J; 1983 Feb 13J/Mar 13J/Aug 14J

Masters Golf Tournament 1980 Apr 13J; 1981 Apr 12J; 1982 Apr 11J; 1983 Apr 11J/Apr 11J; 1984 Apr 15J; 1985 Apr 14J; 1986 Apr 13J; 1987 Apr 12J; 1988 Apr 10J; 1989 Apr 9J

Matabeleland (Zimbabwe) 1980 Jul 26C; 1983 Mar 12B/Jul 30C; 1984 Feb 3C/Mar 11C; 1987 Nov 27C/Nov 28C

matching funds (presidential elections) 1984 Jan 3G; 1987 Jan 7F/Jun 4F/Dec 28F; 1988 Jan 4F/Mar 30F; 1989 Aug 25F

Mathematical Sciences Research Board (National Academy of Sciences) 1987 Jan 10F

mathematics

awards and honors: Field Medal 1986 Aug 3I

budget and spending programs: 1983 Mar 2F

education issues: college-level program decline 1986 Mar 28F; SAT scores 1980 Oct 4F; 1982 Sep 21J/Oct 4F; 1984 Sep 1F; teacher testing 1985 Mar 23F; teaching reforms sought 1989 Jan 26F; U.S. student weakness 1980 Oct 23F; 1984 Sep 22F; 1987 Jan 10F; 1989 Jan 31I

obituaries: Kantorovich, Leonid V. 1986 Apr 7J; Polya, George 1985 Sep 7I; Robinson, Julia Bowman 1985 Jul 30I; Ulam, Stanislaw Marcin 1984 May 13I; Vinogradov, Ivan M. 1983 Mar 20I

research: 100-digit number factoring 1988 Oct 11I; combinatorial analysis 1988 Dec 20I; Fermat's last theorem proof retracted 1988 Jun 3I; numbers theory conjecture proof 1983 Jul 23I

Matsushita Electric Industrial Co. 1989 Nov 20H

Mattel Inc. 1984 May 7H

matter, fundamental kinds of 1989 Oct 13I

Matter of Honor, A (Jeffrey Archer) (book) 1986 Aug 29J/Sep 26J

Mauna Kea (mountain) 1985 Jan 3I

Mauna Loa (volcano) 1984 Mar 25I

Mauritania 1980 Jan 4C; 1981 Mar 16C/Aug 11C/Oct 21C; 1984 Dec 12C; 1989 Feb 17C/Apr 29C/May 5C/Jul 20C

Mauritius 1982 Jun 11C; 1989 Jul 25C/Oct 7J

mausoleums 1985 Feb 12I

Maverick (missile) 1982 Jun 25G/Aug 24G; 1987 Jun 11G

Max Dugan Returns (film) 1983 Apr 6J

Maximiliano Hernandez Martinez Anticommunist Brigade 1983 Oct 7D

Max Planck Institute for Solid State Research (Stuttgart, West Germany) 1985 Oct 16I

Mayan civilization 1984 May 15I

"Mayflower Madam" 1985 Jul 19J

Maze Prison (Northern Ireland) 1980 Oct 27B/Dec 15B/Dec 18B; 1981 May 5B/May 12B/May 21B/Jun 8B/Jul 10B/Jul 13B/Aug 1B/Aug 2B/Aug 8B/Aug 16B/Aug 20B/Sep 6B/Oct 3B/Oct 6B; 1983 Sep 25B

M. Butterfly (David Henry Hwang) (play) 1988 Mar 20J/Jun 5J

McCarran-Walter Act (1952) 1988 Dec 22F

McCartney II (Paul McCartney) (recording) 1980 Jul 9J

McDonald's Corp. 1982 Oct 29H; 1984 Jul 4F; 1986 Apr 9J/Jul 7H; 1987 Aug 13F

McDonnell Douglas Corp. 1981 Aug 19G; 1982 Nov 9G; 1983 Feb 21G; 1984 Feb 24G/Aug 2G; 1987 Dec 1I; 1989 Aug 27I

MCI Communications Corp. 1980 Jun 13H; 1983 Jan 12F; 1985 May 28H

McMartin Pre-School (Manhattan Beach, Calif.) 1987 Jul 13F

McMoran Oil & Gas Corp. 1984 Oct 12D

MCorp 1989 Jun 28H

Me and My Girl (musical) 1986 Aug 10J; 1987 Jun 7J

measles 1985 Feb 3D

meat *see also specific type* (e.g., beef)
  health and safety issues: hormone-treated cattle 1988 Dec 10B; 1989 Feb 18B; IBP Inc. fined 1987 Jul 21H; John Morrell & Co. fined 1988 Oct 28H; reindeer meat inspections 1986 Sep 19B
  labor issues: 1985 Dec 29H; 1986 Feb 8H/Sep 12H/Dec 14D; 1987 Jul 27H
  price issues: 1982 Jan 30B/Feb 14B; 1985 May 10E
  shortages: 1980 Jun 13B; 1981 Jul 29B; 1982 Nov 21B
  trade issues: Argentina loan 1987 Jan 12D; U.S./Australia agreement 1983 Aug 12E; U.S./EC conflict 1988 Dec 10B; 1989 Feb 18B

Medal of Freedom 1982 Sep 7G; 1984 Mar 26J; 1987 Nov 17G; 1988 Oct 17J; 1989 Jul 6J

Medal of Honor *see* Congressional Medal of Honor

Medellin drug cartel 1987 Nov 21D/Dec 30D; 1988 Jan 25D/Apr 8D/Oct 11F; 1989 Aug 10F/Aug 18D/Sep 6D/Oct 6A/Dec 15D

median age 1985 Apr 19F

Media News Corp. 1982 Jun 2J

Medicaid 1980 Jan 15F/Jun 30F/Sep 17F; 1988 Nov 28F; 1989 Oct 11F/Oct 19F/Oct 21F/Oct 25F

Medical Foundation (Buffalo, N.Y.) 1985 Oct 16I

medical schools 1983 Oct 25D; 1984 Apr 19F/May 11I/Jun 16F/Sep 19F; 1988 Aug 25F/Nov 11F

medical wastes 1988 Aug 9H/Nov 2H

Medicare 1982 Oct 6F; 1983 Aug 17F/Aug 31F; 1984 Aug 26F/Nov 13F/Dec 12F; 1986 Dec 24F; 1987 Jul 22F/Oct 27F; 1988 Jun 8F/Sep 28F/Nov 1F/Nov 15F/Nov 28F/Nov 30F/Dec 15F

Medicare Catastrophic Coverage Act of 1988 1989 Oct 4F/Oct 6F/Nov 22F

Mediterranean fruit fly 1981 Jul 10H/Aug 4H/Aug 26E; 1982 Jun 24I/Sep 21I

Mediterranean Sea 1980 May 17A; 1983 Nov 5C; 1986 Mar 23C

Medora (oil platform) 1988 Dec 26B

Meech Lake Accord 1987 Apr 30D/Jun 3D/Jun 23D/Oct 26D/Dec 7D; 1988 Jun 22D/Dec 19D; 1989 Feb 27D/Nov 10D

Melbourne Age (Australian newspaper) 1980 Dec 2E

Mellon Foundation, Andrew W. 1983 Jul 25J

Memphis State University (Tennessee) 1987 Aug 16J

Men at Work (singing group) 1982 Oct 13J/Nov 17J/Dec 15J; 1983 Jan 5J/Feb 9J/Feb 23J/Mar 9J/May 11J/Jun 15J

Mennonite Church 1981 May 27G

menopause 1989 Aug 3I

Men's International Professional Tennis Council 1983 Jun 8J; 1985 Nov 6J

Mental Health (Quiet Riot) (recording) 1983 Oct 19J

mental hospitals 1981 Mar 4F/May 31B; 1989 Oct 17B

mental illness 1984 Sep 12F; 1988 Jan 19F

mental retardation 1981 Apr 20F; 1982 Jun 18F; 1985 Jul 1F; 1986 Jan 10F; 1987 May 24F; 1988 May 26I; 1989 Jun 26F/Nov 22I

Mercantile Southwest Corp. 1983 Jul 21H

Mercantile Texas Corp. 1983 Jul 21H

Merck & Co. 1987 Oct 21I

mercury 1980 May 17A; 1981 Jul 28H

Mercury (planet) 1989 Aug 22I

mercy-killing *see* euthanasia

mergers and acquisition *see specific subjects* (e.g., steel) *companies* (e.g., LTV Corp.)

Merrell Dow Pharmaceuticals Inc. 1983 Jun 9I

Merrill Lynch & Co. 1987 Apr 29H/Oct 26H/Dec 3H/Dec 14H; 1988 Apr 1H

Mersey River (Great Britain) 1989 Aug 19I

Merwin Dam 1983 Sep 14H

Mesa (Louis L'Amour) (book) 1987 Jul 17J

Mesa Petroleum Co. 1982 May 28H/May 31H/Jun 6H/Jun 8H; 1985 May 20H

metal detectors 1988 Nov 10F

Metal Health (Quiet Riot) (recording) 1983 Nov 9J/Dec 14J

metaproterenol sulfate 1983 May 16I

meteors 1987 Jun 17I

methadone 1988 Nov 16I

methamphetamine 1989 Sep 14F

methane gas 1981 Apr 15H; 1989 Sep 13H

methanol (wood alcohol) 1986 Apr 10B; 1987 Jul 14H; 1988 Sep 23H

methyl isocyanate 1985 Mar 20E/May 4H

Metis (Canadian native group) 1987 Jan 15D/Mar 27D; 1988 Sep 5D

Metromedia Inc. 1983 Aug 8F; 1986 Jul 2J/Oct 14H

Metropolitan Edison Co. 1983 Nov 7H

Metropolitan Museum of Art (New York City) 1982 Feb 23J; 1985 Nov 13J

Metropolitan Opera (New York City) 1980 Jul 24J/Sep 7F/Oct 25J; 1981 Jun 4J; 1983 Sep 15J; 1984 Dec 31J; 1985 Jan 3J/Jun 20J; 1986 Sep 3J; 1988 Mar 16J

Metropolitan Savings Bank 1981 Nov 4H

Mexicana Airlines 1986 Mar 31D

Mexican-Americans 1981 Apr 4F

Mexico *see also individual leaders in the name index* (e.g., De la Madrid, Miguel)
  accidents and disasters: drought 1980 Jun 13D/Jun 13I; gas explosion 1984 Nov 19D; Hurricane Allen 1980 Aug 11I; Mexicana Air-

lines crash 1986 Mar 31D; Mexico City earthquakes 1985 Sep 19D/Sep 20I/Sep 24D/Nov 21D/Dec 18A; 1989 Apr 15I; southern Mexico earthquake 1980 Oct 24I; train derailment 1982 Jul 11D
  arts and culture: Fuentes awarded Cervantes Prize 1988 Apr 21J; Garcia Marquez embassy refuge 1981 Apr 3D
  budget and spending programs: 1988 Apr 17D/Dec 29D
  civil strife: demonstrations and protests 1986 Jan 9D/Jan 22D
  crime and law enforcement: former police head arrested 1989 Jun 13D
  disarmament and arms control: Garcia Robles wins Nobel Prize 1982 Oct 12A; nuclear testing halt called for 1985 Jan 28A
  drug trafficking: trafficker arrested 1989 Apr 8D; U.S. agent slain 1985 Mar 6D; *for details, see* Camarena Salazar, Enrique *in the name index;* U.S. criticizes 1986 Feb 21F
  economy and business: anti-inflation program eased 1988 Dec 12D; Chrysler joint venture 1985 Sep 5D; food prices 1982 Aug 1D; 1986 May 22D; foreign investment 1984 Feb 16D; 1989 May 15D; gasoline prices 1982 Aug 1D; inflation 1982 May 15D; 1983 May 10D; 1986 Jan 13D; 1988 Jun 10D; 1989 Jan 10D; price-control measures 1982 Feb 24D; solidarity pact 1988 Jun 10D; 1989 Dec 3D
  education: university strike 1987 Feb 15D
  energy issues: oil and natural gas 1980 Mar 27D/Nov 19D; 1981 Apr 10D/Jun 2A/Jun 2D; 1983 Jul 17D; 1985 Jul 10D
  environmental issues: smog 1987 Jan 13D
  foreign debt: '81 increase 1981 Dec 24D; '88 decline 1988 Jun 21D; central bank to pay companies' debts 1983 Jul 19D; debt payments postponed 1985 Oct 1D; debt swap 1987 Dec 29D; Latin American meetings 1984 Sep 14D; 1985 Jul 14D; loan guarantees 1983 Sep 30D; loan payments postponed 1982 Aug 20D; new loans 1983 Feb 24D; 1984 Apr 27D; 1987 Mar 20D; reduction agreement 1989 Jul 23D/Sep 13D; rescheduling 1982 Dec 15D; 1983 Mar 18D/Jun 29D/Aug 26D; 1984 Sep 7D; restructuring 1985 Mar 29D; 1989 May 30D
  foreign relations: Brazil 1983 Apr 29D; El Salvador 1981 Aug 28A/Sep 2D; 1985 Aug 28D; Guatemala 1982 Feb 19D; 1984 May 30D; Nicaragua 1981 May 14D/Nov 23D; Panama 1989 May 14D; Venezuela 1981 Apr 8D/Apr 10D; 1983 Jul 17D
  government and politics: de la Madrid elected president 1982 Jul 4D; finance minister resigns 1986 Jun 17D; legislative elections 1988 Jun 6D; midterm elections 1985 Jul 8D; opposition governor sworn 1989 Nov 2D; presidential elections 1988 Jun 6D; PRI loses gubernatorial election 1989 Jul 2D; PRI loses mayoral elections 1983 Jul 3D; PRI presidential candidates list 1987 Aug 13D; Sali-

nas de Gortari named presidential winner 1988 Jul 13D
  immigration and refugees: 1982 Feb 19D/May 6F; 1984 May 30D; 1986 Feb 20F; 1987 May 26F/Jul 2F; 1988 Feb 4F; 1989 May 31D
  labor issues: minimum wage increase 1983 Jun 10D; teachers' strike 1989 May 10D; Volkswagen strike 1987 Aug 26D
  medicine and health care: fetal tissue transplants 1988 Jan 7I
  monetary and trade issues: currency 1982 Aug 5D/Aug 12D/Dec 20D; 1985 Jul 24D; 1987 Nov 18D/Dec 14D; GATT 1986 Jul 24D; IDB loans 1980 Nov 1D; 1984 Mar 26D; IMF loans 1982 Dec 23D; 1986 Jul 22D/Sep 30D/Nov 19D; 1989 Apr 11D; trade surplus 1986 Sep 17D; 1988 Feb 4D
  North-South summit (Cancun) *see* North-South summit (Cancun)
  regional conflicts: foreign ministers meet 1983 Apr 21D/Jul 30D; *see also specific organizations* (e.g., Contadora Group)
  sports: baseball 1985 Aug 25J; boxing 1980 Nov 3J; soccer 1986 May 31J/Jun 29J
  United Nations policy: 1980 Jan 7A
  U.S. relations: 1980 Mar 27D; 1981 Nov 23D; 1982 Mar 6D/Mar 14D/Aug 20G; 1983 Dec 12D; 1985 Apr 23A; 1986 May 22G; 1987 Nov 6D; 1988 Apr 15F

Mexico, National Autonomous University of 1987 Feb 15D

Mexico City (Mexico) 1987 Jan 13D

MGM Grand Hotel (Las Vegas, Nevada) 1980 Nov 21J

MGM/UA 1985 Aug 29J

Miami (Florida)
  crime and law enforcement: drug trafficking/bank links 1980 Jun 5H; Hastings impeachment 1987 May 17F; 1988 Aug 3F; 1989 Oct 20F; Honduran officer arrested 1985 Nov 20D; Merrill Lynch killings 1987 Oct 26H; police brutality 1980 Jul 28F; 1985 Jul 22F; 1989 Jan 23F/Dec 7F; robbers/FBI shootout 1986 Apr 11F; violent crime increase 1981 Aug 12F
  health care: pacemaker defects 1988 Aug 31F
  immigration and refugees: Cuban exile rallies 1980 Apr 7D; Cuban refugees 1980 Apr 7D/Nov 19F; Haitian refugees 1981 Dec 27F; 1982 Oct 22F; Panamanian president in exile 1989 Mar 21D
  politics and government: mayoral election 1985 Nov 5F; school superintendent gets NYC post 1989 Sep 20F
  religion: papal visit 1987 Sep 10J
  riots: Liberty City 1980 May 17F/May 19F/May 22F/Jun 9F/Jul 15F/Dec 6F; Overtown 1982 Dec 28F; 1989 Jan 16F

Miami Dolphins (football team) 1982 Jan 2J; 1983 Jan 23J/Jan 30J; 1984 Dec 20J; 1985 Jan 6J/Jan 20J; 1986 Jan 4J/Jan 12J

Miami Herald (newspaper) 1984 Oct 28F

Miami Vice (soundtrack) 1985 Oct 26J/Nov 30J/Dec 21J; 1986 Jan 29J

Miami Vice (TV show) 1984 Sep 16J

mice 1980 Apr 3I; 1988 Apr 21I/Oct 15I

Michigan *see also specific cities* (e.g., Detroit)
  accidents and disasters: blizzards 1985 Dec 1I
  business and industry: state contract minority/women set asides 1989 Mar 6F; submarine communications system 1981 Oct 8G
  environmental issues: hazardous chemicals 1982 Apr 16I/Nov 18H; 1983 Mar 31H; 1985 Dec 15D; nuclear power plant violations 1986 Sep 10H
  family issues: surrogate motherhood contracts 1988 Jun 27F
  labor issues: auto workers contract 1985 Nov 12H; teacher strikes 1983 Jan 25F/Sep 12F; 1985 Sep 18F
  medicine and health care: DES lawsuits 1984 Feb 2F; surrogate motherhood contracts 1988 Jun 27F
  obituaries: McCree Jr., Wade Hampton 1987 Aug 30J
  people: Miss America pageant 1987 Sep 14J
  politics and government: Detroit GOP convention (1980) 1980 Jul 9F/Jul 14F-15F/Jul 17F; presidential campaign (1980) 1980 Apr 26F/May 20F; presidential campaign (1988) 1986 May 27F; 1987 Apr 25F/Dec 12F; 1988 Jan 30F/Mar 26F; state debt paid off 1985 Nov 8F
  sports: ice hockey 1988 Apr 2J

Michigan, University of (Ann Arbor) 1983 Jan 1J; 1984 Jan 2J; 1985 Dec 12F; 1987 Jan 1J; 1989 Jan 2J/Apr 3J/Aug 24I

Michigan State University (East Lansing) 1986 Mar 1J/Mar 29J; 1987 Mar 28J; 1988 Jan 1J

Micki and Maude (film) 1985 Jan 16J

MicroGeneSys Inc. 1987 Aug 18I

Micronesia, Federated States of 1980 Oct 31E; 1981 May 21A; *see also specific island* (e.g., Palau)

microprocessors 1986 Sep 22H

Microsoft Corp. 1987 Mar 19H; 1988 Mar 17H

microwave radiation 1985 Jul 14I

Middle Core Faction Army (Japanese radical group) 1985 Jan 1E

Middle East *see also specific countries* (e.g., Jordan); *organizations* (e.g., Arab League); *subjects* (e.g., Beirut refugee camp massacre)
  deonstrations and protests: general strike 1982 Apr 14A
  foreign relations: USSR 1981 May 22A; 1982 Jun 14A; 1989 Feb 23C
  health care: river blindness treatment 1987 Oct 21I
  peace process: Egypt 1985 Mar 9G; 1988 Dec 25C; 1989 Oct 6C; European Community 1981 Nov 3A; Iran 1981 Nov 17C; Israel 1980 Nov 13A; 1982 Sep 8C; 1985 Oct 21A; 1987 May 13C; 1989 Jul 5C/Oct 6C; Jordan 1982 Sep 13C/Nov 30C; 1984 Jan 9C/Jan 16C/Mar 1C/Dec 1C; PLO 1982 Nov 9C/Nov 30C; 1983 Feb 22C; 1984 Mar 1C/Nov 29C; Saudi Arabia 1981 Aug 8C/Nov 2C/Nov 17C/Nov 25A; United Nations 1984 Jan 17C; United States 1983 Apr 8C; USSR 1982 Sep 15C
  terrorism: arms smuggling 1981 Sep 22G; 1982 Nov 24B; 1988

May 31E; aviation security rules 1988 Dec 29H

U.S. relations: 1981 Apr 8G/May 7C; 1983 Nov 6A; 1984 Sep 29C; 1985 May 10C/Aug 18C; 1987 Oct 19G

Middle East Airlines 1983 Sep 29C

Middleman and Other Stories, The (Bharati Mukherjee) (book) 1989 Jan 9J

Middle West Governors' Conference 1981 Sep 2H

Midgetman (missile) 1985 Nov 1B

Midland Bank PLC 1981 Aug 25H; 1988 Feb 26B

Midland nuclear power plant (Michigan) 1984 Jul 16H

Midnight (Dean R. Koontz) (book) 1989 Feb 24J/Mar 31J

Midway (ship) 1981 May 25E

Midway Airlines Inc. 1984 Sep 26H

Midwest Leadership Conference 1985 Jun 29F

midwives 1980 Jan 4B; 1989 Oct 11F

Miesque (racehorse) 1987 Nov 21J; 1988 Nov 5J

MI5 (British counterintelligence service) 1987 Mar 13B/Apr 27B/Jul 30B/Aug 13B/Dec 21B

MiG (Soviet aircraft) 1987 Dec 12D

MiG-19 (Soviet aircraft) 1980 May 10D; 1982 Oct 16E; 1986 Apr 30E

MiG-21 (Soviet aircraft) 1980 Aug 24C; 1984 Apr 20B/Apr 26G/Nov 6D/Nov 6G/Nov 7D; 1987 Oct 5E

MiG-23 (Soviet aircraft) 1983 Feb 18C; 1989 Jan 4C/Jul 4B

Miguel de Cervantes Prize (literature) 1985 Apr 23J

mile (running) 1985 Jul 27J; 1989 Ju 10J

Military Academy, U.S. *see* West Point

milk 1983 Mar 18D/Nov 29F; 1985 May 7I; 1988 Feb 2E

Milky Way (galaxy) 1984 Jul 5I; 1985 Jun 7I

Miller Brewing Co. 1980 Feb 19H

Miller Brewing Co. v. Jos. Schlitz Brewing (1980) 1980 Feb 19H

Milli Vanilli (singing group) 1989 Jul 29J/Sep 30J/Oct 28J/Dec 25J/Dec 30J

Milton Bradley Co. 1984 May 7H

Milwaukee Brewers (baseball team) 1980 Dec 6J; 1981 Nov 25J; 1982 Oct 10J/Oct 10J/Oct 20J/Nov 3J/Nov 9J; 1989 Nov 20J

Milwaukee Bucks (basketball team) 1987 Oct 25J

Milwaukee Journal (newspaper) 1984 Oct 28F

Mine Safety and Health Administration (Labor Department) 1987 May 11H

minimum wage
Bolivia: 1985 Mar 24D
France: 1981 Jun 3B
Mexico: 1983 Jun 10D
Peru: 1980 Jan 1D; 1987 Oct 23D
Philippines: 1983 Oct 7E
United States: 1985 Feb 19H; 1986 Aug 20H; 1987 Mar 25F; 1989 Mar 8H/Mar 18H/Apr 12H/May 17G/Jun 13H/Nov 8H/Nov 17H

minivans 1989 Feb 16H

minke whales 1985 Apr 3H

minks 1983 Jul 18A

Minneapolis Star and Tribune (newspaper) 1984 Oct 28F

Minneapolis Star and Tribune Co. 1980 Jun 17J

Minnesota 1980 Feb 2I; 1982 Jan 17I; 1983 Jun 29F; 1984 Mar 20F; 1987 Aug 27F; 1988 Feb 23F/Sep 10J; 1989 Dec 11A

Minnesota, University of (Minneapolis) 1980 Mar 20J/Apr 1J; 1989 Sep 13I

Minnesota Multiphasic Personality Inventory 1989 Sep 13I

Minnesota North Stars (ice hockey team) 1981 May 21J

Minnesota Twins (baseball team) 1985 Aug 4J; 1987 Oct 4J/Oct 12J/Oct 25J; 1988 Nov 9J

Minnesota Vikings (football team) 1988 Jan 9J/Jan 17J/Feb 2J

minorities *see also specific minority (e.g., Black Americans)*
census data: 1989 Jul 17F
crime and law enforcement: jury exclusion 1986 Apr 30F
education: affirmative action 1984 Jun 12F; high schools 1985 Sep 20F; university building occupation 1988 Feb 17F
employment and business: affirmative action 1984 Jun 12F; comparable worth 1987 Mar 18F; federal contracts 1985 Aug 14F; 1986 Mar 28F/Apr 11F; job bias suits 1980 Nov 25H; 1983 Oct 18F; 1988 Jun 29F; 1989 Jan 10F/Jun 5F; radio/television stations 1989 Mar 31F; state contracts 1989 Mar 6F; union claims 1987 Jun 19F
housing: discrimination 1985 Feb 10F; zoning ordinances 1988 Nov 7F
politics and government: Japanese premier's statement 1986 Sep 22E; Reagan administration criticized 1988 Feb 2F
religion: Roman Catholic Church 1985 Sep 15J

minoxidil (drug) 1988 Aug 17H

Minpeco S.A. 1988 Aug 20F/Oct 20H

Minuteman (missile) 1980 Sep 18G; 1981 Dec 31G; 1982 Feb 11G; 1983 May 2G; 1985 Feb 7G/May 23G

Mir (Soviet space station) 1986 Mar 15I/May 6I; 1987 Feb 6I/Feb 8I/Apr 12I/Jul 30I/Dec 29I; 1988 Sep 7I; 1989 Apr 27I

Mirage (Fleetwood Mac) (recording) 1982 Jul 11J/Aug 18J/Sep 22J/Oct 13J

Mirage 2000 (aircraft) 1980 Feb 9B

Miranda v. Arizona (1966) 1981 May 18F

Miranda warning 1984 Jun 12F/Jul 2F; 1985 Mar 4F/Oct 14F; 1986 Jan 14F

miscarriages 1980 Jan 25I; 1988 Jul 28I/Sep 21I

Misery (Stephen King) (book) 1987 Jun 26J/Jul 17J/Aug 21J/Sep 23J

Miskito Indians (Nicaragua) 1982 Feb 23D/Dec 11D; 1983 Dec 1D/Dec 26D; 1985 Jan 9D; 1987 Oct 3D

Miss America (beauty pageant) 1980 Jan 4J; 1984 Jul 23J; 1985 Sep 14J; 1987 Sep 14J; 1988 Sep 10J; 1989 Sep 16J

Miss America Pageant (TV show) 1984 Sep 16J

missile experimental *see* MX missile

missile warning systems 1980 Oct 29G

Missing (film) 1982 Mar 10J; 1984 Feb 8J

Mission, The (film) 1986 May 19J/Oct 31J

Missionary, The (film) 1982 Nov 10J

Mississippi
accidents and disasters: floods 1983 Apr 6I/Apr 12I; Hurricane Elena 1985 Sep 2I
arts and culture: Miss America crowned 1985 Sep 14J; Richard Wright Week declared 1985 Nov 28J
crime and law enforcement: death penalty 1985 Jun 11F; Judge Nixon impeachment 1989 May 10F
economy: boycotts 1982 Jul 2F; tidal lands 1988 Feb 23F
education: school discrimination case 1982 Mar 19F; school improvement 1982 Dec 21F; teacher strikes 1985 Mar 8F/Mar 20F
obituaries: Eastland, James Oliver 1986 Feb 19F; Williams, John Bell 1983 Mar 26F
politics and government: congressional redistricting 1984 Nov 13F; presidential campaigns 1984 Aug 2F; 1988 Jun 18F; primary date moved 1986 Apr 6F

Mississippi, University of (University) 1983 Apr 20J

Mississippi Burning (film) 1988 Dec 9J

Mississippi River 1988 Mar 22H

Mississippi University for Women (Columbus) 1982 Jul 1F

Missouri
accidents and disasters: Hyatt Regency walkway collapse 1981 Jul 17J
arts and culture: Miss America crowned 1989 Sep 16J
crime and law enforcement: Tylenol extortion plot 1982 Oct 20H
education: school desegregation 1980 Mar 3F; 1983 Feb 22F; 1984 Feb 8F; 1988 Feb 10F; teacher strike 1983 Sep 12F
environmental issues: dioxin cleanup 1984 Jan 20H; Times Beach
medicine and health care: abortion 1989 Jan 9F/Jul 3F; infant mortality 1983 Jan 25F
obituaries: Symington, Stuart 1988 Dec 14F; Vitale, John J. 1982 Jun 5H
politics and government: Equal Rights Amendment 1982 Feb 10F; primary date moved 1986 Apr 6F; Republican incumbents reelected 1988 Nov 8F; senatorial, gubernatorial campaigns 1986 Oct 23F

Missouri, University of (Columbia) 1989 Sep 16J

Missouri Pacific Corp. 1980 Jan 8H/Sep 15H; 1982 Sep 13H

Miss Universe (beauty pageant) 1986 Jul 21J; 1988 May 24J

Miss USA (beauty pageant) 1987 Feb 17J; 1988 Mar 1J

Mistaken Identity (Kim Carnes) (book) 1981 Jul 8J

Mistral's Daughter (Judith Krantz) (book) 1983 Jan 16J/Feb 13J/Mar 13J/Nov 13J

Misura (Indian contra group) 1984 Apr 25D; 1985 Apr 22D

MIT *see* Massachusetts Institute of Technology

Mitsubishi Estate Co. 1989 Oct 30H

Mitsubishi Industries 1985 Apr 27B

Mitsubishi Motors Corp. 1985 Apr 15H; 1989 Aug 26H

Mitsui Bank Ltd. 1989 Aug 29E

Mitsui Co. 1982 Jul 21H

mittens 1988 Nov 10H

M-19 *see* April 19 Movement

Mobil Corp.
business issues: price control violations 1984 Jul 26H; ranking among companies 1983 Apr 13H
foreign operations: *Death of a Princess* protested 1980 May 12J; Libya 1982 May 13H/Jul 20H; 1983 Jan 4C; South Africa 1989 Apr 28C

Mobil Grand Prix (track and field meet) 1985 Jul 27J/Aug 4J

Mobro 4,000 (ship) 1987 May 16H

MOCA *see* Museum of Contemporary Art

Modern Problems (film) 1982 Jan 6J

Mohajirs (Pakistan immigrant group) 1988 Oct 2E

Mohawk Indians (Canada) 1988 Jun 1D

Moiseyev Dance Co. 1986 Sep 3J

Moldavia (USSR) 1986 Aug 31I; 1989 Jun 25B

mollusks 1987 Dec 11I; 1988 Jan 6I

Momentary Lapse of Reason, A (Pink Floyd) (recording) 1987 Oct 24J/Nov 21J

Mommie Dearest (film) 1981 Sep 30J

Monaco Grand Prix (auto race) 1988 May 15J; 1989 May 7J

Mona Lisa (film) 1987 Jan 4J/Mar 22J

Monash University (Melbourne, Australia) 1983 May 2I

M-1 (money supply measure) 1980 Aug 15H; 1983 Jun 1H/Jun 10H/Jul 20H; 1985 Jul 16H; 1987 Feb 19H

M-1 (tank) 1982 Sep 18G

Money (magazine) 1988 Feb 24J

money-laundering 1980 Sep 2F; 1986 Sep 18F; 1988 Oct 17F/Nov 24F; 1989 Jun 20F/Aug 31D/Sep 6D

Mongolia 1981 Mar 22I; 1982 Nov 19A; 1984 May 17J/Jun 14A/Aug 23E; 1986 Aug 9A; 1987 Jan 15E/Jan 27A; 1988 Sep 20G

monkeys 1987 Oct 12I; 1989 Dec 8I

monocyte/macrophages 1986 Feb 7I

monoliths 1983 Nov 11E

Monongahela River 1988 Jan 2H/Jul 6H; 1989 Mar 9H/Nov 21H

Monsanto Co. 1983 Apr 28I; 1985 Feb 22I; 1987 Oct 20I/Oct 22H; 1988 Jun 8H

monsoon rains 1983 Jun 28I; 1987 Sep 4D; 1988 Aug 2I; 1989 Mar 14I

Montana
business issues: insurance rate setting 1985 Oct 1F
crime and law enforcement: athlete kidnapping 1984 Jul 16F/Dec 13F; Crow Indian barricades 1981 Aug 20F
environmental issues: coal leases 1983 May 10H/Sep 14H; 1984 Jan 9H; fires 1984 Sep 1I/Sep 5I; pesticides found in birds 1981 Sep 12H; wilderness areas 1988 Nov 3H
politics and government: presidential campaigns 1980 Jun 3F; 1988 Jun 7F; Republican elected 1988 Nov 8F

Montana State University (Bozeman) 1987 Aug 27H; 1988 Jan 12I

Montenegro (Yugoslavia) 1986 Aug 6B; 1987 Jun 26B/Oct 25B; 1989 Jan 11B/Sep 30B

Montgomery Ward & Co. 1985 Aug 2H

Mont Louis (ship) 1984 Aug 25I

Montoneros (Argentine guerrilla group) 1985 Aug 27D

Montreal Canadiens (ice hockey team) 1986 May 24J; 1989 May 25J

Montreal Expos (baseball team) 1981 Oct 19J; 1984 Apr 13J; 1987 Jul 14J; 1989 Aug 15J

Montserrat 1987 May 31D; 1989 Sep 19D

Monty Python's the Meaning of Life (film) 1983 Apr 6J

Moody Blues (singing group) 1981 Jul 8J/Aug 5J

Moody's Investors Service 1983 Mar 10H

Moon 1988 Dec 19I; 1989 Jul 20I

Moonlighting (TV show) 1987 Sep 20J

Moon over Parador (film) 1988 Sep 21J

Moonstruck (film) 1987 Dec 16J; 1988 Jan 20J/Feb 17J/Mar 16J/Apr 11J/Apr 20J

Moon Tiger (Penelope Lively) (book) 1987 Oct 29J

Moral Majority 1987 Nov 3J; 1989 Jun 10F

More Dirty Dancing (soundtrack) 1988 Apr 23J/May 21J

Morgan Guaranty Trust Co. 1980 May 1H; 1985 Jun 18H; 1987 Dec 29D

Morgan Stanley & Co. 1981 Feb 3H; 1987 Apr 13E; 1988 Apr 30A/Jun 27H

Mormon Church 1981 May 5G; 1985 Nov 11J; 1987 Oct 29F; 1989 Jun 30D

Morocco *see also individual leaders in the name index (e.g., Hassan II, King)*
demonstrations and protests: 1981 Jun 20C
foreign relations: Algeria 1988 May 16C; Cuba 1980 Jul 12A; Mauritania 1981 Mar 16C; PLO 1987 Apr 26C
monetary and trade issues: European Community application 1987 Jul 20B; IMF loan 1980 Oct 17A; OAU withdrawal 1984 Nov 12C; regional common market 1989 Feb 17C
papal visit: 1985 Aug 19J
sports: running 1985 Jul 27J; 1987 May 29J; 1989 Aug 20J; soccer 1988 Jul 4J
U.S. relations: 1981 Mar 25G; 1982 Feb 12C/May 27C
Western Sahara *see* Western Sahara

Moro National Liberation Front (Philippine separatist group) 1981 Feb 12E; 1983 Oct 8E

morphine 1986 Nov 27B

Mortgage Bankers Association of America 1982 Jun 1H/Dec 13H; 1983 May 31H; 1985 Jun 22H

mortgage rates 1983 Aug 6H; 1985 Jul 16H/Dec 9H; 1986 Sep 9H/Oct 6H; 1987 Mar 9H/Sep 11H; 1988 Aug 11H

Morton-Norwich Products Inc. 1982 Mar 17H

Morton Thiokol Inc. 1983 Dec 13H; 1986 Feb 19I/May 13I/Jun 9I; 1987 May 6I/May 7I/Dec 29H; 1988 Mar 7I/Aug 22I

mosaics 1989 Aug 3J

Moscow embassy scandal 1987 Apr 2G/Apr 7G/Apr 12G/May 15G/Jun 8G/Jun 12G/Jun 26G/Jul 1G

Moscow on the Hudson (film) 1984 Apr 11J

Moslem Brotherhood 1980 Mar 5C/Aug 16C; 1981 Sep 5C/Nov 29C; 1982 Feb 2C/Apr 8C; 1989 Dec 6C

most-favored-nation (MFN) status *see* Generalized System of Preferences; *specific geographic regions* (e.g., China)

Mother's Day (film) 1980 Oct 1J

Motion Picture Association of America 1983 Nov 8J

motion pictures
actors/directors/producers *see individual artists in the name index* (e.g., Hitchcock, Alfred)
awards and honors *see specific awards* (e.g., Academy Awards)
film companies *see specific company* (e.g., Columbia Pictures)
N.Y. releases: *Accused* 1988 Oct 14J; *Assault* 1987 Feb 6J; *Au Revoir les Infants* 1988 Feb 12J; *Babette's Feast* 1988 Mar 30J; *Beetlejuice* 1988 Jun 3J; *Big* 1988 Jun 3J; *Blue Velvet* 1986 Sep 19J; *Born on the Fourth of July* 1989 Dec 20J; *Brazil* 1985 Dec 14J; *Broadcast News* 1987 Dec 16J; *Broken Rainbows* 1986 Apr 11J; *Bull Durham* 1988 Jun 15J; *Children of a Lesser God* 1986 Oct 3J; *Clean and Sober* 1988 Aug 10J; *Color of Money* 1986 Oct 17J; *Color Purple* 1985 Dec 18J; *Crimes and Misdemeanors* 1989 Nov 13J; *Crimes of the Heart* 1986 Dec 12J; *"Crocodile" Dundee* 1986 Sep 26J; *Dangerous Liaisons* 1988 Dec 21J; *Dead* 1987 Dec 17J; *Dead Poets Society* 1989 Jun 2J; *Dead Ringers* 1988 Sep 23J; *Decline of the American Empire* 1986 Nov 14J; *Decline of Western Civilization* 1981 Jul 5J; *Desperately Seeking Susan* 1985 Mar 29J; *Die Hard* 1988 Jul 15J; *Dirty Dancing* 1987 Aug 21J; *Do the Right Thing* 1989 Jun 30J; *Driving Miss Daisy* 1989 Dec 13J; *Dry White Season* 1989 Sep 20J; *Fabulous Baker Boys* 1989 Nov 13J; *Fanny and Alexander* 1983 Jun 17J; *Fatal Attraction* 1987 Sep 18J; *Field of Dreams* 1989 Apr 21J; *Fish Called Wanda* 1988 Jul 15J; *Full Metal Jacket* 1987 Jun 26J; *Glory* 1989 Dec 14J; *Good Morning, Vietnam* 1987 Dec 23J; *Gorillas in the Mist* 1988 Sep 23J; *Hairspray* 1988 Feb 26J; *Hannah and Her Sisters* 1986 Feb 7J; *Heartburn* 1986 Jul 25J; *Henry V* 1989 Nov 8J; *Hope and Glory* 1987 Oct 16J; *Indiana Jones and the Last Crusade* 1989 May 24J; *Ironweed* 1987 Dec 18J; *Jean de Florette* 1987 Jun 26J; *Kiss of the Spider Woman* 1985 Jul 26J; *Last Emperor* 1987 Nov 20J; *Little Dorrit* 1988 Oct 21J; *Little Mermaid* 1989 Nov 15J; *Mission* 1986 Oct 31J; *Mississippi Burning* 1988 Dec 9J; *Moonstruck* 1987 Dec 16J; *My Beautiful Laundrette* 1986 Mar 7J; *My Left Foot* 1989 Nov 10J; *My Life as a Dog* 1987 May 1J; *Out of Africa* 1985 Dec 18J; *Peggy Sue Got Married* 1986 Oct 8J;

Pelle the Conqueror 1988 Dec 21J; *Platoon* 1986 Dec 19J; *Predator* 1987 Jun 12J; *Prizzi's Honor* 1985 Jun 14J; *Raging Bull* 1980 Nov 14J; *Rain Man* 1988 Dec 16J; *Room With A View* 1986 Mar 7J; *Roxanne* 1987 Jun 19J; *Salvador* 1986 Mar 5J; *Sea of Love* 1989 Sep 15J; *sex, lies and videotape* 1989 Aug 4J; *Sid and Nancy* 1986 Oct 17J; *Stand and Deliver* 1988 Mar 18J; *Thin Blue Line* 1988 Aug 26J; *Three Men and a Baby* 1987 Nov 25J; *Tin Drum* 1980 Apr 11J; *Top Gun* 1986 May 16J; *Trip to Bountiful* 1985 Dec 20J; *Unbearable Lightness of Being* 1988 Feb 5J; *The Untouchables* 1987 Jun 3J; *Wall Street* 1987 Dec 11J; *When Harry Met Sally...* 1989 Jul 12J; *Who Framed Roger Rabbit* 1988 Jun 22J; *Witness* 1985 Feb 8J; *Working Girl* 1988 Dec 21J; *see also individual titles* (e.g., Color Purple)
top-grossing films *see individual titles* (e.g., Empire Strikes Back)

Motley Crue (singing group) 1987 Jun 27J/Jul 22J; 1989 Oct 28J

motorcycle clubs 1980 Aug 18F

motorcycles 1980 Dec 24H

Motorola Corp. 1986 Sep 22H

Motown Industries 1983 May 3H; 1984 May 8H

Motrin (drug) 1984 May 18H

Mountain States Telephone & Telegraph Co. 1981 Feb 21H

Mt. Etna (volcano) (Italy) 1983 May 14I; 1985 Dec 25I

Mt. Everest (Himalayas) 1985 Apr 30J; 1986 May 20J/Sep 25J

Mount Mihara (volcano) (Japan) 1986 Nov 21I

Mt. Rainier (Washington State) 1982 Jul 18J

Mount Rainier National Park (Washington State) 1988 Nov 19H

Mount St. Helens (volcano) (Washington State) 1980 Mar 26I/May 18I

Mt. Wilson Observatory (California) 1980 Aug 7I

mouse (computer) 1983 Mar 8I

MOVE (radical group) 1980 May 8F; 1985 May 13F/Nov 6F; 1986 Mar 6F

Movement of Socialist Renewal (Soviet Union) 1986 Jul 22B

Move Your Shadow: South Africa Black and White (Joseph Lelyveld) (book) 1986 Apr 17J

Movie Channel 1983 Sep 1J

movies *see* motion pictures; *specific film* (e.g., Platoon)

Moving Pictures (Rush) (recording) 1981 Apr 8J/May 27J

Mozambicue *see also individual leaders in the name index* (e.g., Machel, Samora)
civil strife: Machel plane crash 1986 Oct 19C; 1987 Jun 29C; military action against rebels 1980 Jul 10C; prisoner exchanges 1987 Sep 7C; rebel massacres of civilians 1987 Jul 18C/Nov 28C; 1988 Apr 20C; rebels talks 1984 Oct 3C; 1989 Jul 22C/Jul 31C/Dec 26C
drought: 1983 Mar 18I
economy: economic policies 1980 Mar 18C; hydroelectric plant 1984 May 2C; regional development plan 1980 Apr 1C

obituaries: Machel, Samora M. 1986 Oct 19C
papal visit: 1988 Sep 19J
South Africa conflict: 1981 Jan 30C; 1983 May 23C; 1984 Mar 16C/May 2C; 1985 Mar 14C/Sep 16C; 1987 Jul 18C/Aug 6C
U.S. relations: 1981 Mar 13G; 1984 Jun 2G; 1985 Jan 16G

Mozambique National Resistance (Renamo) 1984 Oct 3C; 1987 Nov 28C; 1989 Jul 22C/Jul 31C/Dec 26C

Mr. Mister (singing group) 1986 Feb 19J/Mar 22J

Mr. Mom (film) 1983 Sep 7J

MS. 45 (film) 1981 May 20J

mudslides 1987 Mar 11D; 1988 Feb 7I/Jun 23I

Muhammad Ali Amateur Sports Club 1980 Jan 18J

Multi-Fiber Arrangement 1981 Dec 22A; 1986 Aug 1A/Aug 4E

multiple sclerosis 1989 Jun 30I

Multiple Sclerosis Society 1988 Apr 13F

Muniz Air National Guard base (Puerto Rico) 1981 Jan 12D

Murder of Mary Phagan, The (TV show) 1988 Aug 28J

Murphy Brown (TV show) 1989 Sep 17J

Musee d'Orsay (Paris) 1986 Dec 1J

Museum of Contemporary Art (MOCA) (Los Angeles) 1986 Dec 10J

Museum of Modern Art (New York City) 1988 Feb 10J

music
awards and honors *see specific awards* (e.g., Grammy Awards)
composers and musicians *see individual artists in the name index* (e.g., Streisand, Barbra)
recordings *see individual titles* (e.g., Asia)

musicals *see specific titles* (e.g., Cats)

Musqueam Indians (Canada) 1984 Nov 1D

mussels 1987 Dec 11I

mustard gas 1984 Mar 26A

Mutation (Robin Cook) (book) 1989 Feb 24J

Mutual and Balanced Force Reduction talks 1983 Dec 15A; 1984 Jan 22G; 1985 Jan 30A; 1986 Feb 20B; 1987 Dec 5B

MX missile (missile experimental)
accidents and disasters: plant explosion 1987 Dec 29H
congressional actions: 1981 Jun 23G/Jun 25G/Nov 18G; 1982 Dec 7G/Dec 8G; 1983 May 17G/Jul 26G/Sep 15G; 1984 Jun 1G; 1985 Mar 20G/May 23G
deployment systems: continuous airborne patrol 1982 Jun 22G; Minuteman silos 1982 Feb 11G; 1983 Apr 18G/May 2G; straight-track 1980 May 6G
funding issues: Colorado files suit 1984 Apr 20G; GAO report 1984 May 11G; Mormon Church against 1981 May 5G
military issues: female launch control officers 1985 Feb 7G; testing 1984 Jun 15G; 1985 Aug 23G
Soviet developments: 1982 Nov 26G/Dec 6B/Dec 8A

My American Cousin (film) 1986 Mar 20J

Myanmar (formerly Burma) 1989 Jun 19E/Jul 20E/Sep 13E/Oct 7E/Nov

15E; *for events before June 1989, see* Burma

My Beautiful Laundrette (film) 1986 Mar 7J

My Bodyguard (film) 1980 Sep 3J

My Favorite Year (film) 1982 Nov 10J

My Left Foot (film) 1989 Nov 10J

My Life as a Dog (film) 1987 May 1J; 1988 Jan 23J

My Name is Bill W (TV show) 1989 Sep 17J

My One and Only (musical) 1983 May 1J/Jun 5J

myopia (near-sightedness) 1984 Nov 14I

Mystery of Edwin Drood, The (musical) 1985 Dec 2J; 1986 Jun 1J

N

NAACP *see* National Association for the Advancement of Colored People

Nabisco Brands Inc. 1985 Jun 2H

Nagasaki (Japan) 1981 Aug 6I

Nagorno-Karabakh (USSR) 1988 Mar 27B/Jun 15B/Jul 12B; 1989 Jan 12B/Aug 14B/Nov 28B

Naked Gun, The: From the Files of Police Squad (film) 1988 Dec 28J

NAM *see* Nonaligned Movement

Name of the Rose, The (Umberto Eco) (book/film) 1983 Jul 10J/Aug 14J/Aug 14J/Sep 11J/Oct 16J/Nov 13J/Dec 18J; 1984 Jan 20J/Feb 10J; 1988 Mar 20J

Namibia *see also* South West Africa People's Organization
drought: 1983 Mar 18I
government and politics: Constituent Assembly 1989 Dec 20C; constitutional principles proposed 1981 Oct 26A; Democratic Turnhalle Alliance 1982 Feb 15C; elections 1989 Nov 11C
OAU membership: 1981 Jun 27C
peace agreements: 1988 Aug 8C/Nov 15C/Dec 13C/Dec 22C
peace initiatives and talks: 1980 Oct 24A/Nov 24A; 1981 Jan 14A/Jun 17G; 1982 Jul 13A/Nov 28C/Dec 8C; 1983 Dec 15C; 1984 May 11C; 1985 Nov 27A; 1988 Jan 29C/May 3C/Jun 24C/Jul 13C
South Africa conflict: 1981 May 15C/Jun 1A; 1983 Jan 18C; 1985 Jun 17C/Sep 22C; 1988 Dec 23C; Botha, Pieter
Soviet policy: 1982 Mar 22A
United Nations policy: 1989 Mar 1C
U.S. relations: 1981 May 15C/Jun 27C; 1982 Mar 22A/Nov 23C; 1984 Apr 15C

Namibia, U.N. Transition Assistance Group in 1989 Oct 11C

napalm 1984 Oct 7D; 1986 Dec 31C

NAR *see* Armed Revolutionary Nuclei

Narval (ship) 1982 May 9B

NASA *see* National Aeronautics and Space Administration

NASD *see* National Association of Securities Dealers'

NATCA *see* National Air Traffic Controllers Association

Nation (magazine) 1983 Nov 17F

National Academy of Engineering 1982 Jul 26H

National Academy of Recording Arts and Sciences *see* Grammy Awards

National Academy of Sciences (NAS)
Black Americans: 1989 Jul 27F
budget: 1981 Oct 27I
education: high school graduates 1984 May 23F; mathematics teaching 1989 Jan 26F
environment and pollution: acid rain 1983 Jun 29H; 1986 Mar 14G; global temperatures 1989 Jan 5I
genetics: 1987 Aug 18I; 1988 Feb 11I
medicine and health care: abortion and birth control 1986 Dec 9F; AIDS laboratory 1986 Dec 9F; childbirth 1989 Oct 11F; diet 1988 Apr 15I; 1989 Mar 2I; pesticide residues in food 1987 May 20I; radiation risks 1989 Dec 19I; smoking 1986 Aug 13H/Nov 4I; video display terminals 1983 Jul 11I
narcotics and dangerous drugs: marijuana 1982 Feb 26I/Jul 8I
nuclear weapons plants: 1987 Mar 28H; 1989 Dec 20G
space station: 1987 Jul 6I
technology exports: 1984 Feb 26G

National Acid Precipitation Assessment Program 1987 Sep 17H

National Action Committee on the Status of Women 1984 Aug 15D

National Advisory Committee on Oceans and Atmosphere 1984 Jul 2H/Aug 1H

National Advisory Committee on Semiconductors 1989 Nov 20I

National Aeronautics and Space Administration, U.S. (NASA) *see also individual agency heads in the name index* (e.g., Fletcher, James C.)
accidents and disasters: Atlas-Centaur rocket 1987 May 11I; Challenger 1985 Nov 6I; 1986 Apr 19I/Dec 29I; Delta rocket 1986 May 3I
appointments and resignations: Fletcher, James C. 1986 Mar 1I; Truly, Richard 1989 Apr 12I
budget and spending programs: 1986 Oct 18I/Nov 14I; 1987 Oct 30I; 1988 Aug 19F/Oct 21I; 1989 Nov 9H
exploration and research: greenhouse effect 1988 Jun 23I; ozone concentration 1989 Oct 12I; radiation exposure claims 1981 Aug 20I
interplanetary projects: Mars/Moon probes 1988 Dec 19I; Uranus ring found 1986 Jan 29I; Voyager 2 1981 Aug 28I
manned flights: astronauts trainees named 1987 Jun 5I
satellites and launch vehicles: Landsat satellite 1984 Mar 1I; satellite launches 1984 Jun 9I
shuttle program: '88 crew named 1987 Jan 9I; Challenger 1985 Nov 6I; 1986 Apr 19I/Dec 20I; command structure tightened 1986 Nov 5I; commercial shuttle weighed 1984 Mar 20I; cost overruns defended 1986 Apr 25I; flight schedule slips 1986 Jul 14I; flights cut 1981 Jun 2I; journalist sought for flight 1985 Oct 24I; launch delayed 1989 Dec 18I; launch reset 1988 Jun 28I; launch slated 1986 Oct 3I; management criticized 1987 Jul 23I; new shuttle ordered 1986 Aug 15I; rapid engine wear 1984 Mar 25I; space product sale 1984 May 1I
space station: 1981 Jun 18I; 1982 Jun 24I; 1983 Jul 18I; 1985 May

9I; 1986 May 14I; 1987 Jul 6I/Dec 1I; 1988 Oct 21I; 1989 May 18I Strategic Defense Initiative: 1986 Sep 5G

National Air Traffic Controllers Association (NATCA) 1986 Sep 23H; 1987 Jun 11H; 1989 Jan 12H

National Appliance Energy Conservation Act of 1987 1987 Mar 17H

National Archives (Library of Congress) 1984 Sep 25J; 1986 Dec 1F; 1987 Mar 6F; 1988 Mar 29H/Nov 21F

National Arts Stabilization Fund 1983 Jul 25J

National Assessment of Educational Progress 1986 Apr 12F/Dec 3F; 1988 Feb 25F/Apr 5F/Jun 7F/Sep 22F; 1989 Feb 14F

National Association for the Advancement of Colored People (NAACP) 1980 Jul 4F/Jul 15F; 1981 Jun 29F; 1982 Jul 2F/Jul 28F; 1983 May 20F/May 26F/Jun 11F/Jul 15F; 1985 May 1F/Jun 27F; 1986 Feb 15F; 1988 Sep 10F

National Association of Broadcasters 1983 Apr 18J

National Association of Evangelicals 1983 Mar 8F

National Association of Manufacturers (NAM) 1982 Mar 18F; 1986 May 29H

National Association of Mutual Savings Banks 1982 Mar 3H

National Association of Realtors 1986 Jan 31H

National Association of Recycling Industries 1983 Mar 29H

National Association of Securities Dealers' (NASD) 1984 Nov 16H

National Bank for Cooperatives 1988 Jul 5H

National Basketball Association (NBA)
All-Star Game: 1980 Feb 3J; 1982 Jan 31J; 1983 Feb 13J; 1984 Jan 29J; 1985 Feb 10J/Feb 20J; 1986 Feb 9J; 1987 Feb 8J; 1988 Feb 7J; 1989 Feb 8J
awards and honors: most valuable player (MVP) 1980 May 29J; 1981 May 27J; 1985 Jun 3J; 1986 May 28J; 1987 May 18J; 1988 May 25J; 1989 May 22J; rookie of the year 1988 May 10J
broadcasting: television contracts 1985 Dec 20J
championships: 1980 May 16J; 1981 May 14J; 1982 Jun 8J; 1983 May 31J; 1984 Jun 12J; 1985 May 27J/Jun 9J; 1986 Jun 8J; 1987 Jun 14J; 1988 Jun 21J; 1989 Jun 8J/Jun 13J
college draft: 1986 Jun 17J; 1987 Jun 22J
expansions: 1980 Feb 2J
Olympics: 1989 Apr 7J
records: 1982 Nov 3J; 1984 Apr 5J
Soviet game: 1987 Oct 25J
substance abuse: 1980 Aug 19J

National Bipartisan Commission on Central America 1983 Sep 1G/Oct 9D/Dec 12D; 1984 Jan 11G

National Black American Law Students Association 1982 Aug 27F

National Board for Professional Teaching Standards 1989 Jul 17F

National Book Awards 1987 Nov 9J; 1988 Nov 29J; see American Book Awards, before 1987

National Book Critics Circle Awards 1985 Jan 14J; 1986 Feb 17J; 1987 Jan 12J; 1988 Jan 11J; 1989 Jan 9J

National Broadcasting Co. (NBC)
Emmy Awards: 1981 Sep 13J; 1984 Sep 24J
labor issues: strikes and settlements 1987 Oct 24H
Nielson ratings: prime-time viewership 1986 Apr 22F; television movie tops ratings 1984 Nov 28J
personnel: Brinkley ends career 1981 Sep 18J; CBS correspondent Mudd joins 1980 Jul 1J; Silverman resigns as president/CEO 1981 Jun 30J; "Today" show co-host Pauley to quit 1989 Oct 27J; Wright named CEO 1986 Aug 28H
programming and sponsorship: birth control commercials 1985 Aug 1C; FCC proposes rule revisions 1983 Aug 4H; football TV coverage rights 1981 Aug 22J; Gorbachev interview 1987 Nov 30G; LaRouche lawsuits 1986 Aug 8F/Sep 17F; "New Right" coalition boycott 1982 Mar 4J; Olympics TV coverage rights 1980 Jan 20J/May 6J; 1985 Oct 3J; 1988 May 24J/Dec 1J; Soviet screening 1983 Mar 18B

National Bureau of Economic Research 1980 Jun 3H; 1981 Jul 8H; 1983 Jul 8H

National Bureau of Standards, U.S. (Commerce Department) 1986 Oct 21I; 1987 Jun 22H

National Cancer Institute (National Institutes of Health) 1980 Jan 3I/Mar 6I; 1981 Apr 30I; 1984 Apr 23I; 1985 Feb 7I/Mar 14I/Dec 2F/Dec 4I; 1986 Mar 21I/Dec 8I; 1988 Feb 2I/May 21I

National Center for Education Information 1984 Sep 28F; 1986 Apr 30F

National Center for Health Statistics, U.S. (NIH) 1985 Mar 5F/Sep 29F; 1988 Dec 15F

National Coal Association 1984 Sep 18H

National Coal Board (Great Britain) 1985 Jan 29B/Mar 3B/Apr 22B; 1986 Sep 23B

National Coalition for Haitian Refugees 1989 Sep 17D

National Coalition of Advocates for Students 1985 Jan 28F

National Coastal Barrier Resources System 1987 Mar 23H

National Collegiate Athletic Association (NCAA) 1981 Jan 13J; 1984 Jun 27F; 1986 Jan 14J; 1987 Feb 25J

National Commission for Excellence in Teacher Education 1985 Feb 27F

National Commission on Acquired Immune Deficiency Syndrome (AIDS) 1989 Dec 5F

National Commission on Social Security Reform 1983 Jan 15F

National Commission on Space 1986 May 22I

National Conference of Catholic Bishops 1982 Nov 18A; 1983 Mar 7G/May 3A/Nov 15J/Nov 17J; 1985 Sep 15J; 1986 May 8F/Nov 13J; 1988 Feb 25J; 1989 Nov 6J

National Conference of State Legislatures 1986 Nov 4F; 1989 Aug 7F

National Conference on Soviet Jewry 1980 Jan 11B; 1982 Jan 17A; 1988 Jan 5B

National Congress of American Indians 1983 Jan 27F

National Constructors Association 1987 Feb 17H

National Council of Churches 1980 Nov 6J; 1983 May 13J/Oct 14J; 1986 Jun 21J; 1987 Nov 5J; 1989 Nov 19J

National Council of Community Churches 1984 Nov 30J

National Credit Union Administration 1982 Apr 21H

national debt limit
congressional actions: 1983 Nov 18H; 1984 Jun 29H/Oct 12F; 1985 Nov 1F; 1986 Aug 9H/Aug 16H; 1989 Aug 4H/Nov 7H
presidential actions: Bush abandons bill 1989 Nov 2H; Bush signs increase 1989 Aug 7H; Reagan signs increase 1981 Feb 7H; 1983 Nov 21H; 1984 May 25H; 1985 Sept 10H/1987 May 15H/Jul 30H/Aug 10H/Sep 29H

National Defense (James Fallows) (book) 1983 Apr 28J

National Drug Control Policy, U.S. Office of 1989 Mar 9F

National Education Association (NEA) 1985 Apr 9F/Jul 3F; 1986 Jul 6F; 1987 Dec 3F

National Endowment for the Arts 1983 May 23J; 1985 May 31J/Sep 14F; 1989 Jul 12J/Jul 26J/Sep 29J/Nov 16J

National Endowment for the Humanities 1983 Sep 26J; 1985 Jan 10F

National Enquirer, The (tabloid) 1981 Mar 27J

National Environmental Policy Act (1983) 1983 Sep 13H

National Environmental Protection Act (1970) 1980 Jan 7H

National Eye Institute (HHS) 1984 Nov 14I

National Farmers Union 1982 Oct 18H

National Federation of Republican Women 1989 Oct 8F

National Football League (NFL) see also specific teams (e.g., New York Giants)
awards and honors: most valuable player (MVP) 1984 Dec 20J; 1987 Jan 13J
broadcasting: television rights 1987 Mar 15J
college draft: 1986 Apr 29J; 1987 Apr 28J; 1988 Apr 24J; 1989 Apr 23J
conference championships: 1985 Jan 6J; 1986 Jan 12J; 1987 Jan 11J; 1989 Jan 8J
labor issues: antitrust suit 1984 Nov 17J; 1986 Jul 29J; free agency 1989 Feb 1J; players' strike 1982 Sep 30J
personnel issues: Tagliabue named commissioner 1989 Oct 26J
playoff games: 1986 Jan 4J/Jan 5J; 1988 Jan 9J/Jan 10J

National Football League Players Association (NFLPA) 1987 Sep 22J/Oct 15J

National Forest Service, U.S. 1988 Dec 12H

National Gallery of Art (Washington, D.C.) 1985 Nov 9J; 1986 May 1J

National Gallery of Canada (Ottawa) 1988 May 21D

National Geographic Society 1984 Dec 4I; 1986 Oct 6J; 1988 Jul 27F

National Geological Survey 1987 Nov 24I

National Governors' Association 1981 Aug 11F; 1983 Mar 1F/Aug 1H; 1984 Feb 28F; 1985 Feb 26H; 1986 Feb

24F/Aug 24F; 1987 Feb 21F/Jul 25F; 1989 Jul 30F

National Guard, U.S. 1980 Feb 3F/May 22F; 1988 Aug 17F

National Heart, Lung and Blood Institute, U.S. (NIH) 1987 Oct 5I; 1989 Nov 14I

National Highway Traffic Safety Administration, U.S. (NHTSA) 1983 May 9F/Aug 5H; 1986 Aug 15H/Oct 2H/Dec 30H

National Hockey League (NHL) 1980 May 24J/Jun 6J; 1984 Feb 6J; 1985 Apr 30J; 1987 Feb 13J; see also specific awards (e.g., Stanley Cup)

National Hurricane Center 1988 Nov 30I

national identity cards 1987 Sep 9E/Sep 29E

National Institute for Occupational Safety, U.S. 1986 Jun 6J

National Institute of Allergy and Infectious Diseases, U.S. (NIH) 1989 Jul 10I

National Institute of Child Health and Human Development, U.S. 1989 Oct 17F

National Institute of Justice, U.S. 1984 Nov 25F; 1988 Jan 21F

National Institute of Mental Health, U.S. (HHS) 1984 Oct 19I; 1987 May 24F

National Institute on Drug Abuse of, U.S. (NIH) 1982 Jul 8I; 1986 Jul 10F; 1989 Jul 31F/Oct 9F

National Institutes of Health, U.S. (NIH)
genetic research: 1982 Feb 8I; 1986 Jun 18I; 1988 Jan 12I/Oct 1I
medical research: AIDS 1988 Apr 18I; 1989 May 9F; artificial hearts 1988 May 12I/Jul 2I; clot-dissolving drugs 1986 Mar 10I; fetal tissue 1988 Apr 15I/Sep 16I; fraud investigations 1988 Dec 2I; 1989 Feb 1I/Jun 28I; genital herpes 1986 Jun 11I; obesity 1985 Feb 13F; pain treatment 1986 Jul 21F; Reagan biomedical veto 1985 Nov 20F
smoking/health link: 1984 Feb 16I; 1986 Jan 15F

National Intergroup Inc. 1984 Jan 11F/Apr 24H

National Invitation Tournament (basketball) 1980 Mar 20J; 1981 Mar 25J; 1982 Mar 24J; 1985 Mar 29J; 1987 Mar 26J; 1988 Mar 30J; 1989 Mar 29J

National Labor Relations Board, U.S. (NLRB) 1981 Sep 2H; 1982 Jan 2H; 1983 Oct 20F; 1984 Jan 24H/Apr 19H; 1985 Jun 18H/Oct 28H; 1986 Sep 30H; 1988 Jan 7H

National Lampoon's Christmas Vacation (film) 1989 Dec 28J

National Lampoon's European Vacation (film) 1985 Aug 14J

National Lampoon's Vacation (film) 1983 Aug 10J

National League (baseball) see also All-Star Game
Cy Young Award: 1984 Nov 23J; 1985 Nov 13J; 1986 Nov 11J; 1988 Nov 10J; 1989 Nov 14J
division playoffs: 1984 Sep 30J/Oct 7J; 1986 Sep 17J/Sep 25J; 1987 Oct 4J; 1988 Oct 2J
manager of the year: 1984 Oct 17J
most valuable player (MVP): 1980 Nov 26J; 1981 Nov 17J; 1983 Nov 8J; 1984 Nov 13J; 1985 Nov 18J; 1986 Nov 19J; 1987 Nov 18J; 1988 Nov 15J; 1989 Nov 21J
pennant: 1980 Oct 12J; 1981 Oct 19J; 1982 Oct 10J/Oct 10J; 1983

Oct 8J/Oct 8J; 1985 Oct 16J; 1986 Oct 15J; 1987 Oct 14J; 1988 Oct 12J; 1989 Oct 9J
personnel: Giamatti named baseball commissioner 1988 Sep 8J; Giamatti named league president 1986 Jun 9J; Rose suspension 1988 May 6J
rookie of the year: 1983 Nov 21J; 1984 Nov 19J; 1985 Nov 27J; 1986 Nov 24J; 1987 Nov 4J; 1988 Nov 1J; 1989 Nov 8J

National League of Cities 1981 Mar 2H; 1982 Nov 29F; 1985 Mar 25F; 1986 Mar 10F/Dec 1F

National Liberation Army (ELN) (Colombia) 1980 Jan 5D; 1988 Mar 19E

National Low Income Housing Preservation Committee 1988 Apr 27F

National Oceanic and Atmospheric Administration, U.S. (NOAA) 1983 Mar 8I/Aug 9H; 1988 Mar 14H

National Organization for Women (NOW) 1980 Nov 7F; 1982 Oct 10F; 1983 Sep 30F/Oct 2F/Dec 10D; 1984 Jul 1F; 1985 Apr 10F; 1986 Mar 9F/Jun 9F/Jun 13F; 1987 Jul 8F/Jul 18F

national parks see also specific parks (e.g., Yosemite)
Australia: 1983 Nov 11E/Nov 22E
Canada: 1987 Jul 11D; 1989 May 4D
United States: air quality 1980 Nov 25H; air tour restrictions 1987 Aug 19H; Alaskan land bill 1980 Aug 19H/Dec 2H; wilderness areas 1988 Nov 19H

National Park Service, U.S. 1985 Mar 5J/May 1H; 1989 Aug 29H

National Press Club 1984 Jan 3G; 1987 Jul 8F

National Productivity Advisory Committee 1982 Jan 6H

National Public Radio (NPR) 1983 May 25J/Aug 2F

National Rainbow Coalition 1986 Apr 17F

National Religious Broadcasters 1984 Jan 30F; 1988 Feb 3J

National Research Council (National Academy of Sciences) 1982 Mar 31I/Jul 26H; 1983 Oct 20H; 1984 Feb 26G/Mar 2H/Dec 11H; 1987 Jan 6H/Sep 14I; 1988 Dec 22I; 1989 Apr 11I

National Research Council of Canada 1986 Mar 27I

National Resistance Front (Lebanon) 1985 Mar 10C

National Resources Defense Council 1986 Nov 14A

National Rifle Association (NRA) 1983 May 6F

National Right to Life Committee 1986 Jun 14F

National Safety Council of Australia 1989 Apr 5E

National Savings and Loan League 1982 Feb 15H

National Science Foundation 1980 Jan 20I; 1985 Feb 25I; 1986 Mar 28F/Aug 16I; 1987 Jul 26I

National Security Act (1985) 1985 Apr 16F

National Security Agency, U.S. (NSA) 1984 Oct 6G; 1986 Dec 16G

National Security Council, U.S. (NSC) 1980 Feb 15G; 1982 Jan 12G; 1983 Apr 6G/Nov 24G; 1984 Nov 6D; 1985

Aug 8G/Dec 4G; 1986 Dec 5F; 1987 Nov 5G; 1988 Nov 23G/Dec 28G; see also individual agency heads in the name index (e.g., Powell, Colin L.)

National Security Decision Directive 138 1984 Apr 16G

National Semiconductor Corp. 1984 Mar 6G

National Society of Film Critics 1986 Jan 2J; 1987 Jan 4J; 1988 Jan 3J

National Steel Corp. 1983 Mar 10H/May 4H/Sep 23H; 1984 Apr 24H; 1986 Apr 9H; 1989 May 26H/Jul 16H

National Taxpayers Union 1984 Jul 23F

National Teacher of the Year (award) 1985 Apr 4F

National Theater (Great Britain) 1986 Jun 15F

National Transportation Safety Board, U.S. (NTSB) 1982 Jul 23F; 1988 Jan 20H; 1989 May 20H/Aug 31H

National Tribal Chairmen's Association 1983 Jun 1F; 1985 Jan 11F

National Union for the Total Independence of Angola (UNITA) 1984 Dec 29C; 1985 Mar 14C/Jul 10G/Jul 13C/Nov 11C/Nov 27A; 1987 Nov 25A; 1988 Jan 29C; 1989 Jun 30C/Jul 16C/Nov 20C/Nov 27C/Dec 30C; Savimbi, Jonas

National Union Party 1983 Nov 7F

National Weather Service, U.S. 1983 Sep 20I; 1985 Aug 12F; 1986 May 14F; 1988 Sep 6I; 1989 Feb 26I

National Westminster Bank PLC 1988 Feb 26B

National Wild and Scenic Rivers System 1986 Oct 30H

National Wildlife Federation 1985 Oct 1H; 1989 Aug 10H

National Wildlife Refuge System 1984 Nov 30H

National Women's Political Caucus 1983 Jul 10F; 1985 Jun 30F; 1987 Aug 20F

Native Americans 1982 Dec 8F; 1983 Jan 27F/Jun 1F; 1985 Jan 11F; 1986 May 6J/Nov 10G; 1987 Mar 11A; 1988 Apr 19F/Nov 20J/Dec 12F; 1989 Mar 30J; see also specific group (e.g., Navajo Indians)

Native Canadians 1981 Nov 8D; 1982 Apr 14D; 1983 Mar 16D; 1984 Mar 9D/Jun 21D/Nov 1D; 1987 Jul 11D; 1988 Jul 23D/Oct 20D/Nov 8D/Nov 29D; 1989 Apr 14D/Jul 6D/Jul 10D; see also Inuit

native peoples see Native Americans; specific country (e.g., Canada)

Nativity scenes 1982 Nov 3F; 1989 Jul 3F

NATO see North Atlantic Treaty Organization

Natural, The (film) 1984 Jun 6J

Natural Gas Policy Act of 1978 1985 Jan 1H

naturalization 1981 Jun 22F

Natural Resources Defense Council 1984 Sep 20H; 1989 Jul 8B

Nature Conservancy 1980 Dec 20H; 1989 Apr 5I

nausea 1988 Sep 6F

Nautilus (British rowing team) 1986 Jul 6J

Navajo Indians 1981 Apr 18F/Sep 17I; 1982 Nov 2F; 1985 Apr 16F; 1986 Apr 11J/Nov 4F; 1987 Oct 29F

Naval Academy, U.S. (Annapolis, Md.) 1980 May 21G/May 23G; 1987 Jun 22J

Naval Investigative Service, U.S. 1985 Nov 21G; 1988 Jun 14G

Naval Research Laboratory, U.S. (Washington, D.C.) 1985 Oct 16I

Navistar International Corp. 1986 Apr 10H

Navy, U.S. see also individual leaders in the name index (e.g., Ball III, William L.)
accidents and disasters: Iowa explosion 1989 Apr 19G/Apr 24G; Japanese merchant ship sinking 1981 Apr 20G; Vincennes airbus downing 1988 Jul 3C/Jul 3G/Jul 11G/Aug 2G/Aug 19G; 1989 Mar 10G/Jul 17G
appointments and resignations: Ball III, William L. 1988 Feb 23G; Rickover to be replaced 1981 Nov 13G; Webb Jr., James H. 1988 Feb 22G
combat and equipment issues: fleet readiness report 1980 Sep 30G; missile defects 1984 Aug 15G/Sep 18G; missile testing 1987 Jan 15G; 1989 Dec 4G
contract and billing issues: 1981 Oct 22G; 1983 Jan 6G; 1984 Aug 2G/Aug 22G; 1985 May 21G/Aug 13G; 1986 Feb 7G
drug interdiction: 1984 Nov 17F
espionage and intelligence issues: analyst arrested 1984 Oct 1G
foreign developments: Central America 1983 May 26D/Jul 25G; 1984 Nov 17F; China 1986 Oct 11E/Nov 11E; Japan 1981 Apr 20G; Lebanon 1983 Sep 19C; Libya 1986 Mar 23C; 1989 Jan 4C/Jan 11A; New Zealand 1985 Feb 4B; Persian Gulf 1987 Aug 24C; 1988 Apr 14C/Apr 18C/Apr 22G/Nov 9C; USSR 1986 Mar 18B
personnel issues: drug tests found faulty 1985 Aug 18G; homosexuals 1980 Aug 21G/Nov 24G; 1983 Dec 1G; 1984 Aug 17G; pension law revisions 1989 Nov 2F; women 1980 Jun 28G; 1983 Jul 22G
satellites: 1987 Mar 26I

Nazis and neo-Nazis see also individual Nazis in the name index (e.g., Barbie, Klaus)
Austria: 1985 Feb 1B
Canada: 1983 Mar 13D; 1987 Mar 12D/Aug 7D
Chile: 1984 Jan 25D
France: 1989 May 24B
Gypsy hunger strike: 1980 Apr 4B
Hess burial: 1987 Aug 24B
Israel: 1984 Jan 25D
neo-Nazis: 1980 May 18B; 1981 May 11B; 1983 Apr 21F; 1985 Apr 15F/Sep 28B; 1987 Aug 24B; 1989 Feb 6F/Mar 4F
Romania: 1982 Oct 7F
United States: 1982 May 18F/Oct 7F; 1985 Jun 28G/Sep 27B; 1986 Feb 15B; 1987 Oct 26G
Vatican: 1984 Jan 26G
West Germany: 1980 Apr 4B; 1983 Sep 28A; 1984 Mar 31B; 1985 Sep 27B; 1987 Aug 24B/Oct 26G
Yugoslavia: 1986 Feb 15B

NBC News 1980 Aug 19F; 1987 Dec 1F

NCAA see National Collegiate Athletic Association

NCAA Basketball Championship (TV show) 1983 Apr 10J

NCR Corp. 1987 Aug 25H

NEA see National Education Association; National Endowment for the Arts

near-sightedness (myopia) 1984 Nov 14I

Nebraska 1980 May 13F; 1983 Apr 11G; 1984 May 15F; 1985 Oct 15F; 1988 May 10D

Nebraska (Bruce Springsteen) (recording) 1982 Oct 13J

Nebraska, University of (Lincoln) 1980 Jan 1J; 1982 Jan 1J; 1983 Jan 1J/Dec 3J; 1984 Jan 2J; 1985 Jan 1J; 1987 Jan 1J; 1989 Jan 2J/May 28J

Negotiator, The (Frederick Forsyth) (book) 1989 May 26J/Jun 30J

Negro Leagues (baseball) 1987 Mar 3J

Neighbors (film) 1982 Jan 6J

Nepal 1980 May 2E; 1982 Mar 8E; 1983 Jul 18E; 1986 Feb 17E; 1988 Aug 21I/Oct 10A

Neptune (planet) 1985 Apr 25I; 1989 Aug 24I/Dec 6I

nerve gas 1984 Mar 26A/Aug 7B

Nestle Alimentana S.A. 1984 Jan 27B

Netherlands see also individual leaders in the name index (e.g., Beatrix, Queen)
accidents and disasters: Prinsendam catches fire 1980 Oct 4I
arts and culture: Anne Frank diary edition 1986 May 14J; Assault released in New York 1987 Feb 6J; Assault wins Oscar 1987 Mar 30J
defense and disarmament issues: A-weapons protests 1981 Nov 21B; 1983 Apr 4B; nuclear missile deployment 1986 Feb 28B
environmental issues: dike dedicated 1986 Oct 4B; seal epidemic 1988 Aug 19I
foreign aid: 1983 Dec 23A
foreign relations: China 1985 Jun 19B; El Salvador 1982 Mar 17D; Persian Gulf 1986 Apr 26C; Sinai peacekeeping force 1982 Jan 13A/Jan 31C; Suriname 1988 Jan 25D; West Germany 1980 Dec 29B
government and politics: budget and spending programs 1980 Sep 16B; 1986 Sep 16B; 1988 Sep 20B; immigration rules 1987 Apr 10B; parliamentary elections 1981 May 26B
labor issues: unemployment 1986 Jan 10B; wage freeze 1980 Jan 7B; workweek 1986 Jan 1B
medicine and health care: abortion controversy 1980 Nov 20B
monetary issues: currency 1981 Oct 4B; 1982 Jun 12B; IMF loans 1983 Jan 18A
obituaries: Drees, Willem 1988 May 14B
science and technology: satellite observatory 1983 Aug 9I; van der Meer wins Nobel 1984 Oct 17I
sports: auto racing 1988 Jun 12J; ice skating 1985 Feb 21J; transatlantic balloon crossing 1986 Sep 2J

Netherlands Antilles 1985 Jul 20D; 1986 Jan 1D; 1987 Jun 30H

Neustadt International Prize (literature) 1986 Feb 28J

Neutrality Act (1981) 1981 Jun 20D; 1983 Nov 3F

neutral particle beam 1989 Jul 13G

neutrino particles 1988 Oct 19I

neutron bombs 1980 Jun 26I; 1981 Feb 5G/Aug 10G; 1982 Oct 15B

Nevada
accidents and disasters: nuclear test cave-in 1984 Feb 15H; powerboat racer killed 1980 Nov 13J
crime and law enforcement: casino bombing 1980 Oct 27J; death penalty 1987 Jun 22F; executions 1985 Dec 6F; federal judge incarcerated 1986 May 16F
economy and business: casino revenues 1985 Jun 30J; hydroelectric power 1984 Aug 17H
environmental issues: waste sites 1984 Dec 19H; wilderness area bill 1989 Dec 5H
medicine and health care: infant mortality 1983 Jan 25F; radiation victims 1982 Oct 19F; 1983 Apr 6G; 1984 May 25H
nuclear testing and research: cave-in 1984 Feb 15H; detonations 1982 Aug 5I; 1984 Feb 15H; 1985 Dec 28G; 1986 Dec 13G; 1987 Feb 3G; 1988 Aug 17I; MX missile deployment 1981 May 5G; nuclear fusion 1988 Mar 21I; radiation victims 1982 Oct 19F; 1983 Apr 6G; 1984 May 25H; U.S./USSR cooperation 1985 Jul 29G; 1986 Mar 14G; 1988 Jan 29B/Aug 17I; waste sites 1984 Dec 19H
politics and government: gubernatorial nomination 1986 Sep 9F; presidential campaign (1980) 1980 May 27F; woman wins gubernatorial nomination 1986 Sep 9F

Nevada, University of (Las Vegas) 1985 Jan 3J; 1988 Dec 12F

Nevada Wilderness Area Act (1989) 1989 Dec 5H

Nevado del Ruiz (volcano) (Colombia) 1985 Nov 13D

Never Cry Wolf (film) 1984 Feb 8J

Never Say Never Again (film) 1983 Oct 12J/Nov 2J/Dec 7J

New and Collected Poems (Richard Wilbur) (poetry) 1989 Mar 30J

Newbery Medal (children's literature) 1985 Jan 7J; 1986 Jan 20J; 1987 Jan 19J; 1988 Jan 11J; 1989 Jan 9J

New Brunswick (Canada) 1987 Mar 26D; 1988 Jan 6I; 1989 Sep 17D/Nov 10D

New Caledonia (French territory) 1984 Jul 31E/Nov 18E/Dec 5E; 1985 Jan 7E/Jan 12E/Jan 19A/Apr 25E/May 8E; 1986 Aug 8E; 1987 Sep 13E/Sep 17E; 1988 May 5E/Jun 26E/Aug 20E/Nov 6B; 1989 May 4H

New Choices in America (Democratic National Committee) 1986 Sep 20F

New England Patriots (football team) 1986 Jan 5J/Jan 12J/Jan 26J

New England Power Pool (Nepool) 1987 Jun 18D

New Forum (East German opposition group) 1989 Sep 19B

Newfoundland (Canada) 1980 Jan 3D; 1981 Mar 31D; 1982 Feb 15D; 1984 Jan 26D; 1985 Dec 12D; 1986 Sep 2J/Sep 3D/Oct 6D; 1987 Mar 17D; 1988 Apr 20D/Jun 8D/Jul 18D

New Hampshire 1980 Feb 5F/Feb 26F; 1984 Jan 15F/Feb 28F/Mar 5F; 1986 Oct 27F; 1987 Aug 5H; 1988 Feb 16F/Aug 3H; see also Seabrook nuclear power plant

Newham Seven Defense Committee 1985 Jul 10B

Newhart (TV show) 1984 Dec 16J

New Hebrides 1980 May 28E/Jun 11E/Jul 29E; For events after July 1980 see Vanuatu

New Jersey see also individual leaders in the name index (e.g., Kean, Thomas H.)
accidents and disasters: flooding 1984 May 5I
crime and law enforcement: Brinks robbery arrest 1984 Nov 29F; Lucchese crime family acquittals 1988 Aug 26F; Newark mayor acquitted 1982 Oct 21F; organized crime in pizza industry 1980 Aug 24H; Scarfo convicted 1989 Apr 5F; Schiavone Construction Co. 1982 May 18F
economy and business: casinos 1980 Dec 12J; 1982 Jan 16H; 1985 Mar 29J; corporate taxes 1986 Mar 10H; 1989 Apr 3H
environment and pollution: hazardous wastes 1980 Jan 30H; 1981 Oct 23H; 1983 Jun 2H; 1986 Mar 10H/May 28H; sewage contamination of beaches 1985 Apr 1H
family issues: surrogate motherhood contracts 1988 Feb 3F; see also "Baby M"
foreign issues: Aeroflot landings barred 1983 Sep 17G
labor issues: PATH railroad strike 1980 Sep 1H; teacher minimum salary 1985 Sep 9F; teacher strikes 1983 Sep 12F
mergers and acquisitions: First Fidelity Bancorp/Fidelcor Inc. 1987 Aug 2H
nuclear power plants: 1983 May 6H
obituaries: Quinlan, Karen Ann 1985 Jun 11J
politics and government: congressional reapportionment plan 1983 Jun 22F; Florio elected 1989 Nov 7F; presidential campaign (1980) 1980 Jun 3F; presidential campaign (1984) 1984 Jun 5F/Jul 18F; presidential campaign (1988) 1988 Jun 7F
schools: Jersey City school system takeover 1988 May 24F/Aug 9F; 1989 Oct 5F; "moment of silence" 1987 Dec 1F; sex education 1982 May 25F
sports: soccer 1985 Jun 22J

New Jersey (Bon Jovi) (recording) 1988 Oct 29J/Dec 31J

New Jersey (ship) 1983 Sep 12C/Dec 14C

New Jersey Generals (football team) 1983 Feb 23J; 1985 Jan 25J/Mar 8J

New Kids on the Block (singing group) 1989 Jul 29J/Aug 26J/Sep 30J

New Mexico 1980 Feb 3F/Jun 3F; 1982 Mar 30I/Apr 23F; 1983 Aug 21F; 1984 Jun 5F; 1985 Dec 11I; 1984 Mar 29F; 1988 Mar 10H/Jun 7F/Sep 13H

New Orleans (Louisiana) 1980 Jan 30J; 1982 Mar 20F/Jul 9I; 1983 Jan 16F/Jan 28J/Mar 28F; 1985 Aug 25H/Oct 19F; 1987 Jan 23F; 1988 Aug 15F; 1989 Feb 18F

New Orleans Saints (football team) 1981 Apr 28J

New People's Army (Philippine guerrilla group) 1987 Feb 8E

News Corp. 1988 Aug 7H

News International PLC 1986 Jul 31B

Newspaper Preservation Act of 1970 1989 Nov 13H

New United Motor Manufacturing Inc. 1985 Jun 25H

New York, State University of (Buffalo) 1986 Aug 16I

New York Academy of Medicine 1988 Nov 11F

New York City see also individual leaders in the name index (e.g., Koch, Edward)
accidents and disasters: blackouts 1983 Aug 13J; blizzards 1983 Feb 12I
arts and culture: Carnegie Hall reopens 1986 Dec 15J; Chorus Line sets record 1983 Sep 29J; Eubie Blake birthday celebration 1983 Feb 7J; Gone with the Wind sequel rights auction 1988 Apr 25J; Irving Berlin tribute 1988 May 11J; Joffrey Ballet 1981 Mar 15J; Serra sculpture controversy 1985 May 31J; 1987 Aug 31J; Warhol art auction 1988 May 3J; see also individual companies (e.g., American Ballet Theater); specific performance centers (e.g., Metropolitan Opera)
census data: population 1984 Apr 7J
corruption and ethics issues: Biaggi trial 1987 Mar 16F/Jun 3F/Sep 22F; 1988 Aug 4F; Friedman convicted 1986 Nov 25F; Wedtech scandal 1986 Dec 15H; 1987 Apr 16F/May 11F/Jun 3F/Jul 9F/Dec 22F; 1988 Feb 11F/Aug 4F/Nov 21F; 1989 Aug 8F/Oct 16H/Oct 20F; Zaccaro investigation 1984 Aug 25F; 1987 Oct 15F
crime and law enforcement
assault and battery: CBS anchorman Rather attacked 1986 Oct 4J; police brutality acquittal 1985 Nov 24F
bribery, fraud and extortion: Helmsley trial 1988 Apr 14H; 1989 Aug 30F/Dec 12F; tax fraud convictions 1984 Jun 8H; Tylenol extortion plot 1982 Oct 20H
murder: author Abbott convicted 1982 Jan 21J; Bensonhurst racial slaying 1989 Aug 23F; CBS employees slaying 1982 Apr 12J; 1984 May 31F; Central Park murder 1988 Mar 25F; Donovan witness slain 1982 Aug 25F; Goetz "subway vigilante" shootings 1984 Dec 31F; 1985 Jan 25F/Mar 27F; 1986 Jan 16F/Jul 8F; 1987 Oct 19F; 1989 Jan 13F; Howard Beach racial slayings 1986 Dec 20F; 1987 Jan 13F/Feb 10F/Dec 21F; Lennon slaying 1980 Dec 8J; Lowenstein slaying 1980 Mar 14F; Metropolitan Opera violinist slaying 1980 Jul 24J; Steinberg child abuse case 1989 Jan 30F/Mar 24F
organized crime: Bamboo Gang sentencing 1986 Dec 17E; Bonanno crime family RICO suit 1987 Aug 26F; Castellano indicted 1984 Mar 30F; Castellano killed 1985 Dec 16F; Colombo crime family sentencing 1986 Nov 11F; Cosa Nostra indictments 1980 Jun 30F; 1985 Feb 26F; Gambino crime family convictions 1986 Mar 5F; Gotti arrested 1989 Jan 23F; Gotti trials 1987 Mar 13F; 1988 Jan

22F; Medellin cartel arrest 1989 Aug 10F; Persico/Colombo family convictions 1986 Jun 13F; "Pizza Connection" trial 1987 Mar 2F; Salerno/Genovese family indictments 1986 Mar 21F
prostitution: "Mayflower Madam" 1985 Jul 19J
rape: Central Park jogger attack 1989 Apr 19F; Metropolitan Opera violinist slaying 1980 Jul 24J
robbery: computer break-in 1983 Aug 21F; gold robbery 1983 Apr 2F; Sentry armored car 1982 Dec 12H; 1983 Feb 2F/Feb 18F/Dec 7F; 1985 Mar 7F; Wells Fargo 1983 Nov 26F; 1985 Apr 29F/May 30F
substance abuse: Exxon Valdez captain surrenders 1989 Apr 5H; heroin seized 1982 Feb 22F
terrorism: bombing convictions 1986 Mar 7F; bombings 1982 Dec 31F; Hoffman in minimum-security prison 1981 Jun 2F; Weather Underground 1981 Oct 21F/Oct 22F
demonstrations and protests: 1989 Dec 10F
economy and business: Citicorp assets 1986 Feb 4H; clubs 1988 Jun 20F; Columbus Circle real estate project 1987 Dec 4H; cost of living 1988 Jun 28A; currency 1986 Jul 7H; 1987 Nov 30H; 1988 Nov 9H; 1989 Feb 27F; municipal bonds 1981 Mar 23H; Philippines/Marcos real estate suit 1986 Dec 29E; Playboy Club closed 1986 Jun 30J; Rockefeller Center real estate 1985 Feb 5H/Jul 29H; 1989 Oct 30H
environmental issues: sewage sludge dumping 1985 Apr 1H
espionage issues: Bulgarian trade representative arrested 1983 Sep 23G; CIA ex-agent Wilson arrested 1982 Jun 15G; Soviet UN employee arrested 1986 Aug 23G
film releases see motion pictures
foreign issues: Gorbachev visit 1988 Dec 6G; O'Connor Cuba visit 1988 Jun 5D; Philippines/Marcos lawsuit 1986 Dec 29E; PLO office 1988 Mar 2A/Mar 11G/Aug 29G; Shamir visit 1989 Apr 4C
health care: AIDS: 1985 Sep 9F; 1988 Jan 31I/Nov 7F/Feb 17F; 1989 Jul 8I/Aug 15I; AIDS among IV drug users 1989 Feb 17F
holidays and special events: Brooklyn Bridge centennial 1983 May 24J; St. Patrick's Day parade 1983 Mar 17J; Vietnam veterans parade 1985 May 7G
homosexuality: 1985 Jun 6F; 1986 Mar 20F
immigration and refugees: sanctuary movement 1985 Dec 23G
labor issues: hotel strike 1985 Jun 27H; mass transit strike 1980 Apr 1H/Apr 11H; New York Post agreement 1988 Feb 20H; PATH railroad settlement 1980 Sep 1H; teachers' strike 1983 Sep 18F
marriages: Reagan/Palmieri 1980 Nov 24J
obituaries: Addams, Charles 1988 Sep 29J; Ailey, Alvin 1989 Dec 1J; Baker, Ella 1986 Dec 13F; Balanchine, George 1983 Apr 30J; Berlin, Irving 1989 Sep 22J; Berrigan, Ted 1983 Jul 4J; Bingham, Jonathan Brewster

1986 Jul 3F; Bird, Junius Bouton 1982 Apr 2I; Blake, Eubie 1983 Feb 12J; Brisson, Frederick 1984 Oct 8J; Burrows, Abe 1985 May 17J; Canaday, John Edwin 1985 Jul 19J; Castellano, Paul 1985 Dec 16F; Clurman, Harold 1980 Sep 9J; Cohn, Roy Marcus 1986 Aug 2F; Cooke, Terence Cardinal 1983 Oct 6J; Corridan, John M. 1984 Jul 1J; Crawford, Cheryl 1986 Oct 7J; Farrar, Margaret 1984 Jun 11J; Hicks, James L. 1986 Jan 19J; Hill, Abram 1986 Oct 6J; Hunter, Alberta 1984 Oct 17J; Joffrey, Robert 1988 Mar 25J; Krasner, Lee 1984 Jun 19J; Lerner, Alan Jay 1986 Jun 14J; Mennin, Peter 1983 Jun 17J; Merman, Ethel 1984 Feb 15J; Moses, Robert 1981 Jul 29F; Oliver, Sy 1988 May 27J; Osborn, Paul 1988 May 12J; Peerce, Jan 1984 Dec 15J; Schiff, Dorothy 1989 Aug 30J; Tanner, Marion 1985 Oct 30J; Thomson, Virgil Garnett 1989 Sep 30J; Van Der Zee, James 1983 May 15J; Vreeland, Diana Dalziel 1989 Aug 22J; Warhol, Andy 1987 Feb 21J; Wechsler, James A. 1983 Sep 11J
politics and government: city charter revised 1989 Nov 7F/Dec 13F; city council legality questioned 1981 Nov 17F; city council ruled unconstitutional 1989 Mar 22F; city primaries blocked 1981 Sep 8F; Democratic convention (1980) 1980 Aug 2F/Aug 11F-13F; Dinkins elected mayor 1989 Nov 7F; presidential campaigns 1980 Oct 2F; 1984 Jun 26F/Oct 8F; runoff election law 1985 Aug 13F
press and broadcasting: Murdoch ownership case 1988 Mar 29H; New York Daily News bias case 1987 Jun 10F; New York Post labor agreement 1988 Feb 20H; publishing industry 1985 Mar 4J
religious issues: O'Connor installed archbishop 1984 Mar 19J; Unification Church tax exemption 1982 May 5J
schools: AIDS fears embroil districts 1985 Sep 9F; Fernandez named schools chancellor 1989 Sep 20F; high school for homosexuals 1985 Jun 6F
sports: chess 1988 Feb 22J; 1989 Oct 22J; high jump 1981 Feb 28J; parachuting 1986 Apr 24J; running 1980 Oct 26J; 1981 Feb 27J/Oct 25J; 1982 Oct 24J; 1985 Oct 27J; 1986 Nov 2J; 1987 Nov 1J; 1988 Nov 6J; 1989 Nov 5J; tennis see U.S. Open
stock market see New York Stock Exchange
theater openings see theater
welfare and social services: homeless mentally ill 1988 Jan 19F

New York City Ballet 1983 Mar 16J/Dec 6J; 1989 Sep 13J

New York City Marathon 1980 Oct 26J; 1981 Oct 25J; 1982 Oct 24J; 1985 Oct 27J; 1986 Nov 2J; 1987 Nov 1J; 1988 Nov 6J; 1989 Nov 5J

New York City Opera 1983 Aug 29J; 1988 May 10J

New York City Transit Authority 1986 Sep 30F

New York Coffee, Sugar and Cocoa Exchange 1980 Oct 9H; 1982 Oct 1H

New York Commodity Exchange (Comex) 1980 Jan 21H/Feb 13H; 1981 Dec 28H; 1982 Jun 29H; 1985 Mar 19H; 1986 Sep 5H

New York Cosmos (soccer team) 1982 Sep 19J

New York Daily News (newspaper) 1984 Oct 28F

New Yorker (magazine) 1985 Mar 8J; 1987 Feb 9J

New Yorker Inc. 1985 Mar 8J; 1986 Jan 13J

New York Futures Exchange 1980 Mar 21H/Aug 7H

New York Giants (football team) 1982 Jan 3J; 1986 Jan 5J/Feb 2J; 1987 Jan 11J/Jan 13J/Jan 25J

New York Islanders (ice hockey team) 1980 May 24J; 1981 May 21J; 1982 May 16J; 1983 May 17J; 1984 May 19J

New York Jets (football team) 1983 Jan 23J

New York Knicks (basketball team) 1985 Sep 18J; 1988 May 10J

New York Mercantile Exchange 1986 Feb 20H

New York Mets (baseball team) 1983 Nov 21J; 1984 Nov 19J; 1985 Jul 11J/Aug 25J/Nov 13J; 1986 Sep 17J/Oct 15J/Oct 27J; 1988 May 6J/Oct 2J/Oct 12J

New York Philharmonic 1988 Nov 2J

New York Post (newspaper) 1988 Feb 20H

New York Public Interest Research Group 1987 Jul 29H

New York Public Library 1986 Dec 18J; 1989 Feb 23F

New York Shipping Association 1986 Dec 6H

New York State see also specific cities (e.g., New York City); individual leaders in the name index (e.g., Cuomo, Mario)
crime and law enforcement: Brawley abduction case 1988 Feb 29F/Oct 6F; 1989 Apr 27F; Cohn disbarred 1986 Jun 24F; FBI sting operation 1987 Aug 11F; marijuana seized on Long Island 1981 Sep 3F; prison siege 1983 Jan 11F; Tarnower slaying 1980 Mar 10J; 1981 Feb 24J; tax official bribery plot 1984 Jun 8H
economy and business: insurance reforms 1986 Jun 24F; revenue shortfall 1988 Jun 1F
education: colleges and universities 1989 Feb 3F; SAT-based scholarship ruling 1989 Feb 3F; school desegregation see Yonkers
energy issues: hydroelectric power purchases 1982 Mar 19D; nuclear power plants 1982 Jan 26I; 1987 Aug 5H; see also specific plant (e.g., Indian Point nuclear power plant)
environment and pollution: acid rain 1982 Jul 26D; 1984 Aug 14H; Hudson River PCB cleanup 1981 May 8H; radioactive waste dumping 1981 Jan 31H; salt water dumping 1984 Apr 25H; see also Love Canal
foreign issues: Iran/Pahlevi lawsuit 1983 Jul 1F; Quebec acid rain agreement 1982 Jul 26D; Quebec hydroelectric power purchase 1982 Mar 19D

health care: AIDS 1987 Aug 4I; 1988 Jan 12I; disability benefits lawsuit 1986 Jun 2F; video-display terminals 1988 Jun 14H
horse racing see Belmont Stakes
labor issues: disability benefits lawsuit 1986 Jun 2F; teachers' strike 1983 Sep 18F

New York City see New York City
obituaries: Hanson, Howard 1981 Feb 26J; Javits, Jacob Koppel 1986 Mar 7F; Moses, Robert 1981 Jul 29F
politics and government: Cuomo wins gubernatorial primary 1982 Sep 23F; presidential campaigns 1984 Apr 3F; 1988 Apr 19F; reapportionment plans rejected 1982 Jun 22F
religious issues: abortion debate 1984 Sep 13F; bishops' statement on political candidates 1984 Aug 9F; Unification Church tax exemption 1982 May 5J

New York Stock Exchange 1980 Mar 21H; 1981 Jan 7H; 1982 Aug 26H/Oct 7H/Oct20H; 1983 Nov 21H/Dec 30H; 1984 Aug 3H/Nov 6H; 1985 Jul 10H; 1986 Apr 10H/Sep 11H/Sep 12H/Sep 19H/Dec 19H; 1987 Apr 23H; 1988 Feb 4H/Apr 6H/Jun 1H

New York Times (newspaper) 1983 Feb 25J; 1984 Apr 16J/Oct 28F; 1986 Jul 23E; 1987 Jul 31F

New York University (NYU) 1980 Nov 13F; 1983 Apr 14F; 1988 Feb 10J

New York Yacht Club 1988 Sep 8J

New York Yankees (baseball team) 1980 Aug 11J/Oct 10J/Dec 15J; 1981 Oct 15J/Oct 28J; 1985 Aug 4J/Nov 20J; 1989 Jan 18J

New Zealand see also individual leaders in the name index (e.g., Lange, David)
arts and culture: Hulme wins Booker Prize 1985 Oct 31J
defense and disarmament issues: ANZUS pact 1982 Jun 22A; 1984 Jul 13A; 1985 Feb 5G; nuclear-free zone 1985 Aug 6E; 1987 Jun 4E; nuclear pollution treaty 1986 Nov 25E
demonstrations and protests: 1981 Jul 25E
economy and business: fishing 1989 Dec 13I; oil industry deregulation 1988 May 3E; Petroleum Corp. sale cancelled 1988 Mar 1E
environmental issues: nuclear pollution treaty 1986 Nov 25E
foreign relations: Australia 1982 Nov 10E; 1988 Jun 21E; Fiji 1987 May 30E; Great Britain 1983 Mar 20E; 1986 Feb 17E; Japan 1984 Jul 2E; Pacific islands 1980 Jul 24E; South Africa 1981 Jul 25E
government and politics: elections 1981 Dec 9E; 1984 Jul 14E; Lange to become prime minister 1984 Jul 14E
obituaries: Ashton-Warner, Sylvia 1984 Apr 28J
Rainbow Warrior incident: 1985 Jul 10E/Jul 23E/Aug 26B/Sep 20B/Sep 25B/Nov 4E/Dec 23B; 1986 Jul 7A; 1987 Oct 2B
religious issues: papal visit 1986 Dec 1E; woman named Episcopalian bishop 1989 Nov 25E
sports: rugby 1987 Jun 20J; running 1988 Mar 26J; tennis 1983 Jul 2J; yachting 1988 Jul 25J; 1989 Mar 28J/Sep 19J

U.S. relations: 1982 Nov 8E; 1984 Jul 7G/Jul 13A; 1987 Feb 2G; 1989 Jun 26A

New Zealand (yacht) 1988 Sep 9J

Next (personal computer) 1988 Nov 12H

Next of Kin (film) 1989 Oct 25J

NFL *see* National Football League

NHL *see* National Hockey League

NHTSA *see* National Highway Traffic Safety Administration

Niagara River 1983 Feb 15I; 1986 May 14D

Niagara River Toxic Project 1983 Feb 15I

Nicaragua *see also individual leaders in the name index (e.g., Ortega Saavedra)*
  accidents and disasters: helicopter crash 1982 Dec 11D; Hurricane Joan 1988 Nov 13D
  civil strife: harbor mining 1984 Mar 25A/Apr 12G
  contras *see* Nicaraguan contras
  crime and law enforcement: bombing campaign arrests 1985 Oct 18D; coffee growers' association president killed 1980 Nov 17D
  defense and armed forces: combat alert 1984 Nov 12D; expansion admitted 1982 Mar 9D; military buildup 1984 Mar 9D; militia to be created 1983 Jul 7D
  demonstrations and protests: 1988 Jul 10D/Nov 18D/Dec 7D; 1989 Dec 10D
  economy: 1981 Jul 19D/Sep 9D; 1985 May 10D; 1989 Jun 12D
  foreign debt: 1980 Sep 5D
  foreign relations: France 1982 Jan 7D; Iran 1985 Jan 23G; Libya 1981 May 14D; 1983 Apr 30A/Jun 8A; nonaligned nations 1983 Jan 15D; Soviet-bloc nations 1985 Oct 25B; USSR 1980 Mar 19A; 1981 May 14D; 1982 May 10A; 1984 Mar 25A/Nov 6D/Nov 6G/Nov 7D; 1986 Oct 2J/Oct 3D/Oct 28D; 1987 Mar 2D/Sep 7D; 1989 May 16D
  government and politics: Chamorro chosen opposition presidential candidate 1989 Sep 2D; civil rights to be restored 1980 Jan 3D; contra dialogue ruled out 1987 Oct 29D; contra leader returns 1989 Jun 11D; Council of State members walk out 1980 Nov 12D; critics imprisoned 1981 Oct 29D; elections announced 1984 Jan 14D; elections put off 1980 Aug 24D; elections rescheduled 1984 Feb 21D; electoral law unveiled 1984 Feb 8D; junta members chosen 1980 May 18D; junta resignations 1980 Apr 22D; national dialogue opened 1984 Oct 31D; presidential candidate withdraws 1984 Oct 21D; Sandinista anniversary celebrated 1980 Jul 19D; 1989 Jul 19D; state of siege declared 1982 Mar 15D
  human rights: 1981 May 19D; 1984 Feb 10G; 1989 Nov 9D
  international organizations: World Bank 1984 Sep 28D; 1988 Jul 11A
  Latin relations: Costa Rica 1983 May 5D/Oct 1D; Cuba 1983 Jul 28D/Nov 25D; Ecuador 1985 Oct 11D/Oct 13D; El Salvador 1982 Mar 8D; 1983 Nov 25D; 1984 Jan 12G/Aug 8G; 1989 Nov 26D; Honduras 1981 May 6D; 1982 Apr 4D; 1983 Mar 26D/Jun 3D/Jul 29D/Oct 1D; 1984 Jan 11D; 1985

May 15D; 1986 Dec 7D/Dec 8D; Mexico 1981 May 14D; 1982 Mar 14D
  military operations: cargo plane shootdown 1988 Jan 23D; Denby light plane shootdown 1987 Dec 6D; helicopter shootdown 1984 Jan 11D/Sep 1D; invasion threat seen 1984 Nov 8D; rebel invaders killed 1983 Jan 29D
  Miskito Indians: 1982 Feb 23D/Dec 11D; 1983 Dec 1D/Dec 26D; 1985 Jan 9D; 1987 Oct 3D
  monetary and trade issues: GATT 1983 May 11D; 1984 Mar 13A; IDB loans 1983 Jun 29G/Jul 2A; 1985 Mar 21D; UNCTAD aid 1983 Jul 2A; U.S. embargo 1985 May 1D/May 7D/May 10D; U.S. sugar quota 1983 May 9G/May 11D; 1984 Mar 13A
  peace initiatives: 1983 Apr 21D/Jul 30D/Oct 5D; 1989 Feb 14D/Aug 7D/Dec 10D; amnesty 1983 Dec 1D/Dec 4D; cease-fires 1985 Apr 22D; 1987 Oct 6D; 1988 Mar 23D/Oct 31D; peace talks 1983 Jul 19D; 1987 Dec 4D/Dec 22D; 1988 Jan 28D/Feb 19D/Mar 28D/Apr 30D/Apr 30D/May 28D/Jun 9D/Sep 19D; 1989 Nov 6D/Nov 21D; *see also* Central American peace accord
  press and broadcasting: curbs imposed 1988 May 14D; *El Pueblo* 1980 Jan 24D; *La Prensa* 1986 Jun 26D; 1987 Sep 20D/Oct 1D; Roman Catholic radio station closed 1986 Jan 1D
  religion: Catholic leader deported 1986 Jul 4D; papal visit 1983 Mar 2D/Mar 4D; Roman Catholic pastoral letter 1984 Apr 22D; Roman Catholic radio station closed 1986 Jan 1D; Vatican talks 1984 Sep 12D
  sports: boxing 1982 Jul 31J/Nov 12J
  United Nations policy: Security Council 1982 Mar 19A; 1983 Mar 23D/Mar 29A; UNCTAD aid 1983 Jul 2A
  U.S relations
    covert operations: captured youth recants confession 1982 Mar 12G; charges against Nicaraguan leaders 1984 Jul 18G; classified information leaked 1986 Dec 21G; congressional letter 1984 Mar 20G; covert action plan 1982 Mar 11G; Denby light plane shootdown 1987 Dec 6D; 1988 Jan 13D/Feb 8D; "designs" on neighboring countries charged 1984 Nov 13D; embassy officers accused of spying 1986 May 10D; Hasenfus plane shootdown 1986 Nov 15D; helicopter shot down 1984 Jan 11D/Sep 1D; House vote on combat troops 1985 Jun 27G; military buildup photographs 1982 Mar 9D; military exercises 1983 Jul 20G; Nicaraguan invasion charges 1983 Mar 23G; reconnaissance flights 1984 Apr 26D; secret helicopter unit 1984 Dec 16D
    diplomatic initiatives: diplomats expelled 1983 Jun 6D; 1988 Jul 11D; 1989 May 25D/May 31D; draft agreements 1983 Oct 20D/Oct 20G; Enders visit 1981 Aug 13D; envoy visits 1983 Jun 10D; immigration rules eased 1987 Jul 8F; Nicaraguan ambas-

sador 1982 Dec 12D; 1984 Mar 22G/Apr 18A; talks on reducing tensions 1981 Dec 10D; 1982 Mar 23D/Apr 14D
    trade and aid issues: humanitarian aid 1980 May 19D/Sep 12D; 1981 Jan 23D/Apr 1G; 1983 Nov 18G; 1985 Aug 23G; sugar quota 1983 May 9G/May 11D; 1984 Mar 13A; trade embargo 1985 May 1D/May 7D/May 10D
    World Court suit: 1984 Apr 24A/May 10A/Nov 26A; 1985 Jun 18G/Sep 12D/Oct 7G; 1986 Jun 27A/Oct 28A

Nicaraguan contras *see also individual leaders in the name index (e.g., Calero Portocarrero, Adolfo)*
  criminal activities: gunrunning/drug smuggling 1986 Apr 11D; investigation of 1987 Jan 30F
  foreign aid: Brunei 1986 Dec 24G; Israel 1984 Sep 8D; Taiwan 1984 Sep 8D; West Germany 1986 Jun 10D
  human rights: 1985 Mar 5D; 1987 Feb 25D
  Latin role: Argentina 1984 Sep 8D; Costa Rica *see* Costa Rica; Guatemala 1984 Sep 8D; Honduras *see* Honduras; Venezuela 1984 Sep 8D
  leadership: 1986 Mar 29D; 1987 May 13D; 1988 Jul 18D; 1989 Nov 9D
  military operations: 1983 Mar 23D/Aug 25D/Sep 8D; 1984 Apr 14D; 1985 Aug 8D; 1987 Jul 16D/Dec 20D
  peace initiatives *see* Central American peace accord; Contadora Group; Nicaragua
  U.S. developments
    aid issues: administration campaign for 1986 Mar 12G; congressional actions 1982 Dec 20G; 1984 Oct 22G; 1989 Apr 13G; food deliveries begin 1988 Apr 19D; House actions 1983 Jun 7G/Jul 28G/Oct 20G; 1984 May 24G; 1986 Apr 16G/Apr 30G/May 8G; 1987 Mar 11G/Sep 23G; 1988 Mar 3G/Mar 31G; misuse probe 1986 May 8G; private donors 1984 Sep 8D; Senate actions 1983 Nov 3G; 1984 Mar 28G/Apr 5G; 1985 Jun 6G; 1987 Feb 18G/Mar 18G/Mar 25G; 1988 Mar 31G/Aug 3G/Aug 10G; spending total 1987 Dec 22G; Tambs: administration controls 1987 May 2G
    covert operations: American arrested in Costa Rica flees 1989 Jul 23D; arms-smuggling probe 1986 Dec 23F; Boland charges law violation 1983 Apr 13G; captured peace volunteer released 1988 Mar 9D; demonstrations and protests 1986 Oct 16G; FBI probe 1986 Dec 16F; military presence in Honduras as shield 1983 Jul 20D; military training 1982 Jan 18D; NSC advice 1985 Aug 8G; propaganda financed with federal funds 1987 Oct 4G
    Iran-Contra arms scandal *see* Iran-Contra arms scandal

Nicaraguan Democratic Forces (FDN) (Contra group) 1983 Mar 28D; 1984 Apr 25D; 1986 Dec 23D; 1987 Feb 16D/Mar 4G

Nicaraguan Humanitarian Assistance Office 1985 Aug 30G

Nicaraguan Resistance Movement (Contra group) 1987 May 13D/Nov 19D; 1988 Feb 5D/Jul 18D; 1989 Jun 11D

Nicholas Nickleby (adapted from Charles Dickens) (play) 1981 Oct 4J

Nielsen ratings
  audience-measuring method changed: 1987 Sep 14J
  Olympic Games: 1984 Feb 21J
  Super Bowl: 1985 Jan 20J; 1986 Jan 26J; 1988 Jan 31J
  television movies: 1983 Nov 20J; 1984 Nov 28J
  television networks: 1984 Apr 17J; 1986 Apr 22F; 1989 Apr 18J
  television shows: 1983 Apr 10J/Jun 12J; 1984 Sep 16J/Oct 21J/Dec 28J

Nigeria *see also individual leaders in the name index (e.g., Babangida, Ibrahim)*
  arts and culture: pop music star Fela released from prison 1986 Apr 24C; Soyinka wins Nobel Prize 1986 Oct 16J
  civil strife: Christian/Moslem 1987 Mar 13C; Islamic cults 1981 Jan 12C; Moslem sect 1984 Mar 4C
  coups and coup attempts: Buhari overthrown 1985 Aug 27C; military plot foiled 1985 Dec 20C; Shagari overthrown 1983 Dec 31C
  demonstrations and protests: 1989 May 24C
  economy and business: budget 1984 May 7C
  foreign aid: 1989 Nov 4C
  foreign debt: 1988 Jan 14C
  foreign relations: Great Britain 1986 Sep 1B; 1987 Jun 15C
  government and politics: elections 1983 Aug 6C; 1989 Dec 7C; press and broadcasting curbs 1984 Apr 17C; Supreme Military Council to be formed 1984 Jan 3C
  immigration and refugees: illegal aliens 1983 Jan 17C; 1985 Apr 15C
  international organizations: IMF 1984 May 7C; 1987 Feb 2C; United Nations 1989 Sep 21A
  oil issues: 1980 Aug 8C/Nov 9C; 1981 Aug 26C; 1982 Jan 29C; 1984 Jul 11A/Oct 18A
  sports: football 1989 Dec 5J

nightclubs 1980 Jan 20F

Night & Day (Joe Jackson) (recording) 1982 Nov 17J

Night Hawks (film) 1981 May 6J

Nightline (TV show) 1986 Feb 5J; 1987 May 26J

Nightmare on Elm Street 3, A: Dream Warriors (film) 1987 Mar 18J

Nightmare on Elm Street 4, A: The Dream Master (film) 1988 Aug 31J

'night *Mother* (Marsha Norman) (play) 1983 Apr 1J/Apr 18J

Night of the Fox (Jack Higgins) (book) 1987 Jan 23J/Feb 27J

Night Songs (Cinderella) (recording) 1987 Jan 28J/Feb 18J

"Night Stalker" 1985 Aug 25F/Sep 27F

NIH *see* National Institutes of Health

Nikaia Grand Prix (track meet) (1985) 1985 Jul 16J

Nikkei average 1986 Sep 16E; 1988 Apr 7E/Dec 28E; 1989 Oct 17A

Nimitz (ship) 1983 Feb 18C/Feb 19C; 1985 May 22G

Nine (musical) 1982 Jun 6J

Nineteen Eighty-Four (George Orwell) (book) 1984 Jan 18J

1984 (Van Halen) (recording) 1984 Feb 18J/Mar 24J/Apr 28J/May 20J/May 28J

Nine to Five (film) 1980 Dec 19J; 1981 Jan 7J/Feb 11J/Apr 1J/Apr 4J

Nine Tonight (Bob Seger & the Silver Bullet Band) (recording) 1981 Sep 30J/Nov 11J

90125 (Yes) (recording) 1983 Dec 14J; 1984 Jan 21J

Nippon Kokan K.K. 1984 Apr 24H; 1985 Apr 27B

Nippon Telegraph & Telephone Corp. 1989 May 29E

Nissan Motor Co. 1980 Sep 20B; 1981 Jan 20E/Jan 20E; 1983 May 9H; 1989 Jul 27H

Nisshin Steel Co. 1984 Feb 7H

nitrogen oxide emissions 1984 Aug 14H; 1987 Nov 19H; 1988 Aug 5H/Nov 1I

Nitsuko Ltd. 1989 Nov 20H

Niue 1985 Aug 6E

Nixon v. Fitzgerald (1982) 1982 Jun 24F

Nkomati Accord (1984) 1984 Mar 16C/May 2C; 1985 Mar 14C; 1987 Aug 6C

NLRB *see* National Labor Relations Board

NLT Corp. 1982 Apr 16H

NOAA *see* National Oceanic and Atmospheric Administratio

Nobel Prize
  Allais, Maurice (economics) 1988 Oct 18J
  Altman, Sidney (chemistry) 1989 Oct 12I
  Arias Sanchez, Oscar (peace) 1987 Oct 13D
  Bednorz, J. Georg (physics) 1987 Oct 14I
  Benacerraf, Baruj (physiology or medicine) 1980 Oct 10I
  Berg, Paul (chemistry) 1980 Oct 14I
  Bergstroem, Sune K. (physiology or medicine) 1982 Oct 11I
  Binner, Gerd (physics) 1986 Oct 15I
  Bishop, J. Michael (physiology or medicine) 1989 Oct 9I
  Black, James W. (physiology or medicine) 1988 Oct 17I
  Bloembergen, Nicolaas (physics) 1981 Oct 19I
  Brodsky, Joseph (literature) 1987 Oct 22J
  Brown, Michael S. (physiology or medicine) 1985 Oct 14I
  Buchanan, James McGill (economics) 1986 Oct 16H
  Canetti, Elias (literature) 1981 Oct 15J
  Cech, Thomas (chemistry) 1989 Oct 12I
  Cela, Camilo Jose (literature) 1989 Oct 19J
  Chandrasekhar, Subrahmanyan (physics) 1983 Oct 19I
  Cohen, Stanley (physiology or medicine) 1986 Oct 13I
  Cram, Donald J. (chemistry) 1987 Oct 14I
  Cronin, James W. (physics) 1980 Oct 14I
  Dalai Lama (peace) 1989 Oct 5A
  Dausset, Jean (physiology or medicine) 1980 Oct 10I
  Debreu, Gerard (economics) 1983 Oct 17I

Dehmelt, Hans (physics) 1989 Oct 12I

Deisenhofer, Johann (chemistry) 1988 Oct 19I

Elion, Gertrude B. (physiology or medicine) 1988 Oct 17I

Fitch, Val L. (physics) 1980 Oct 14I

Fowler, William A. (physics) 1983 Oct 19I

Fukui, Kenichi (chemistry) 1981 Oct 19I

Garcia Marquez, Gabriel (literature) 1982 Oct 21J

Garcia Robles, Alfonso (peace) 1982 Oct 12A

Gilbert, Walter (chemistry) 1980 Oct 14I

Golding, William (literature) 1983 Oct 6J

Goldstein, Joseph L. (physiology or medicine) 1985 Oct 14I

Haavelmo, Trygve (economics) 1989 Oct 11A

Hauptman, Herbert A. (chemistry) 1985 Oct 16I

Herschbach, Dudley (chemistry) 1986 Oct 15I

Hitchings, George H. (physiology or medicine) 1988 Oct 17I

Hoffman, Ronald (chemistry) 1981 Oct 19I

Hubel, David H. (physiology or medicine) 1981 Oct 9I

Huber, Robert (chemistry) 1988 Oct 19I

International Physicians for the Prevention of Nuclear War (peace) 1985 Oct 11A/Dec 10A

Jerne, Niels K. (physiology or medicine) 1984 Oct 15I

Karle, Jerome (chemistry) 1985 Oct 16I

Klein, Lawrence R. (economics) 1980 Oct 15H

Klitzing, Klaus von (physics) 1985 Oct 16I

Klug, Aaron (chemistry) 1982 Oct 18I

Koehler, George J. F. (physiology or medicine) 1984 Oct 15I

Lederman, Leon (physics) 1988 Oct 19I

Lee, Yuan T. (chemistry) 1986 Oct 15I

Levi-Montalcini, Rita (physiology or medicine) 1986 Oct 13I

Mahfouz, Naguib (literature) 1988 Oct 13J

McClintock, Barbara (physiology or medicine) 1983 Oct 10I

Merrifield, Robert Bruce (chemistry) 1984 Oct 17I

Michel, Hartmut (chemistry) 1988 Oct 19I

Milosz, Czeslaw (literature) 1980 Oct 9J

Milstein, Cesar (physiology or medicine) 1984 Oct 15I

Modigliani, Franco (economics) 1985 Oct 15J

Mueller, K. Alex (physics) 1987 Oct 14I

Myrdal, Alva (peace) 1982 Oct 12A

Pasternak, Boris (literature) 1989 Dec 10J

Paul, Wolfgang (physics) 1989 Oct 12I

Pedersen, Charles J. (chemistry) 1987 Oct 14I

Perez Esquivel, Adolfo (peace) 1980 Oct 13A

Polanyi, John C. (chemistry) 1986 Oct 15I

Ramsey, Norman F. (physics) 1989 Oct 12I

resignation dispute 1989 Mar 14A/Sep 21J

Rohrer, Heinrich (physics) 1986 Oct 15I

Rubbia, Carlo (physics) 1984 Oct 17I

Ruska, Ernst (physics) 1986 Oct 15I

Samuelsson, Bengt I. (physiology or medicine) 1982 Oct 11I

Sanger, Frederick (chemistry) 1980 Oct 14I

Schawlow, Arthur (physics) 1981 Oct 19I

Schwartz, Melvin (physics) 1988 Oct 19I

Seifert, Jaroslav (literature) 1984 Oct 11J

Siegbahn, Kai M. (physics) 1981 Oct 19I

Simon, Claude (literature) 1985 Oct 17J

Snell, George (physiology or medicine) 1980 Oct 10I

Solow, Robert M. (economics) 1987 Oct 21J

Soyinka, Wole (literature) 1986 Oct 16J

Sperry, Roger W. (physiology or medicine) 1981 Oct 9I

Steinberger, Jack (physics) 1988 Oct 19I

Stigler, George (economics) 1982 Oct 20I

Stone, Richard (economics) 1984 Oct 18J

Taube, Henry (chemistry) 1983 Oct 19I

Tobin, James (economics) 1981 Oct 13H

Tonegawa, Susumu (physiology or medicine) 1987 Oct 12I

Tutu, Desmond (peace) 1984 Oct 16A

U.N. High Commissioner for Refugees (peace) 1981 Oct 14A

U.N. peacekeeping forces (peace) 1988 Sep 29A

van der Meer, Simon (physics) 1984 Oct 17I

Vane, John R. (physiology or medicine) 1982 Oct 11I

Varmus, Harold E. (physiology or medicine) 1989 Oct 9I

Walesa, Lech (peace) 1983 Oct 5A/Dec 10A

Wiesel, Elie (peace) 1986 Oct 14A

Wiesel, Torsten N. (physiology or medicine) 1981 Oct 9I

Wilson, Kenneth G. (physics) 1982 Oct 18J

Noble House (James Clavell) (book) 1981 May 10J/May 24J/Jul 5J/Aug 9J/Aug 9J/Sep 6J/Oct 4J/Nov 8J/Nov 8J/Dec 6J; 1982 Jan 10J/Feb 7J

noise 1980 Dec 24H

No Jacket Required (Phil Collins) (recording) 1985 Mar 30J/Apr 27J/May 25J/Jun 22J/Jul 27J/Aug 24J; 1986 Feb 25J

No Love Lost (Helen Van Slyke) (book) 1980 May 4J/Jun 8J

Nonaligned Movement 1982 Mar 6A/Apr 6C; 1983 Jan 15D/Mar 12A/Sep 28A; 1985 Apr 25A/Sep 9A; 1986 Jun 20A/Sep 7A; 1989 Sep 7A

Norfolk (Virginia) 1983 Feb 2F; 1986 Jun 16F/Sep 2F

Norfolk and Western Railway 1982 Mar 25H

Norfolk Southern Corp. 1986 Aug 22H

Normal Heart, The (Larry Kramer) (play) 1985 Apr 21J

Norma Rae (film) 1980 Apr 14J

Norstar Bancorp. 1987 Mar 18H

North American Soccer League 1980 Dec 5J; 1985 Mar 28J

North and South (John Jakes) (book) 1982 Mar 7J/Apr 11J/May 9J/Jun 6J/Jul 11J

North Atlantic Treaty Organization (NATO) see also specific member countries (e.g., France)

arms control issues: demonstrations and protests 1982 Jun 10A; INF goals endorsed 1986 Dec 5B; limited nuclear war 1981 Oct 20G; SALT II discussed 1985 Jun 7B; U.S./USSR plans 1984 Dec 14A; 1986 Oct 13B

cruise missile deployment see cruise missiles

defense issues: chemical weapons 1984 Jan 10B; 1986 May 22B; conventional forces 1982 Dec 2A; 1985 May 22B; 1986 Dec 12B; 1987 Jul 27B; military exercises 1981 Sep 8B; military spending 1981 May 13B; SDI endorsement 1985 Oct 15G; tactical nuclear weapons 1989 May 29B; warning blast plan 1981 Nov 4G

intelligence issues: spy ring arrests 1988 Aug 25B

intermediate-range nuclear missile deployment see intermediate-range nuclear missiles

obituaries: Speidel, Hans 1984 Nov 28B

organizational issues: Kissinger restructuring proposal 1984 Feb 27G

Soviet bloc issues: Afghanistan invasion 1980 Jan 15A/May 14A/Jun 26B; Polish repression attacked 1982 Jan 11A; Warsaw Pact 1983 Dec 9A; 1984 Jan 10B/Mar 5B; 1986 Sep 10B; 1987 May 29B/Oct 1B; 1988 Dec 8B

North Carolina

accidents and disasters: blizzards 1983 Feb 12I; Hurricane Gloria 1985 Sep 27I; tornadoes 1984 Mar 28H

crime and law enforcement: sniper kills Teamster trucker 1983 Jan 31H

demonstrations and protests: 1982 Jun 6F

education: school desegregation 1983 Mar 24F/Jul 7F

environmental issues: nuclear waste 1986 Sep 11H; wildlife depredation raids 1985 Jan 16H

Equal Rights Amendment: 1982 Jun 6F/Jun 7F

executions: 1984 Nov 2F

obituaries: East, John P. 1986 Jun 29F; Ervin Jr., Sam J. 1985 Apr 23F

politics and government: presidential campaigns 1980 May 6F; 1984 May 8F; Republican incumbents reelected 1988 Nov 8F

North Carolina, University of (Chapel Hill) 1981 Mar 30J/Dec 28J; 1982 Mar 29J; 1987 May 21I/Nov 22J; 1988 Nov 20J; 1989 Nov 19J

North Carolina State University (Raleigh) 1983 Apr 4J; 1986 Jun 17J; 1988 Nov 20J

North Cascades National Park (Washington State) 1988 Nov 19H

North Dakota, University of (Grand Forks) 1982 Mar 27J; 1987 Mar 28J

Northeastern University (Boston, Massachusetts) 1988 Jun 11J

Northern Ireland see also Irish Republican Army; Maze Prison; Provisional Irish Republican Army

Anglo-Irish accord (1985): 1985 Nov 27B/Dec 31B; 1986 Jan 23B/Mar 3B/Jul 12B

arts and culture: pianist wins Tchaikovsky Competition 1986 Jul 3J

business and industry: De Lorean 1982 Feb 19B; 1984 Jul 18B

civil strife: British soldiers killed 1981 May 19B; 1988 Mar 19B/Aug 20B; British troop stationing marked 1989 Aug 14B; Catholic church bombing 1981 Oct 12B; death data 1987 Feb 26B; 1988 Oct 5B; guerrilla extradited from Ireland 1984 Mar 17B; policeman killed 1981 May 6B; Protestant marches 1982 Jul 12B; 1985 Jul 7B/Dec 31B; 1986 Mar 31B/Jul 12B/Aug 7B; rioting 1981 Apr 23B/May 13B; 1984 Aug 15B; Sands death anniversary 1982 May 5B; Ulster security force members arrested 1989 Oct 8B

government and politics: advisory assembly 1981 Jul 2B/Aug 17B; 1982 Apr 5B/Jul 23B/Oct 20B; 1986 Jun 12B; by-elections 1986 Jan 23B; Elizabeth II speaks against violence 1987 Dec 19B; Hurd named state secretary 1984 Sep 10B; local rule plan 1980 Jul 2B; talks on future government system 1980 Jan 7B

human rights: 1988 Nov 29A

labor issues: Catholic job bias 1988 Dec 15B; general strike by unionists 1986 Mar 3B

marches: Republicans 1985 Aug 11B

peace initiatives: women for peace event 1983 May 25B

press and broadcasting: broadcasts banned 1988 Oct 19B; television documentary banned 1985 Aug 7B

security issues: internment without trial 1980 Aug 10B; Republicans 1982 Aug 24B; "shoot to kill" policy 1988 Jan 25B

U.S. relations: 1981 Mar 16A; 1986 Sep 26B

Northern Mining Co. 1980 Jan 11E

North Korea see also individual leaders in the name index (e.g., Kim Il Sung)

bombings: Burma 1983 Oct 9E/Oct 10E/Nov 4E/Dec 9E; KAL airliner 1989 Apr 25E; Seoul airport 1986 Sep 14E

defense and disarmament issues: nuclear weapons 1989 Jul 19E/Oct 24E

demilitarized zone: 1984 Nov 23E; 1986 Aug 19E

foreign debt: 1987 Sep 16E

foreign relations: China 1984 May 4E; Grenada 1983 Nov 4D; Guyana 1984 Jul 5A; Iran 1980 Oct 8A; 1982 Dec 18A; Japan 1988 Sep 13E; 1989 Mar 30E

government and politics: Kim Chong Il promoted 1980 Oct 14E; leftist student world convention 1989 Jul 1E

South Korea relations: relief supplies delivered 1984 Oct 1E; reunification conference called 1982 Feb 10E; ship sunk 1985 Oct 20E; talks 1980 Sep 25E; 1984 Jan 11E/Nov 27E; 1985 Apr 4E; 1986 Jan 20E/Jun 18E; 1988 Dec 28E; 1989 Sep 28E

United Nations policy: 1988 Oct 19A

U.S. relations: 1981 Aug 26E; 1985 Jul 8G; 1988 Oct 31G

Northland Bank of Calgary 1985 Sep 30D

Northrop Corp. 1984 Dec 18G; 1986 Nov 17G; 1987 Dec 20G

North Sea 1980 Mar 27B/Nov 24B; 1983 Mar 14A/Mar 30A; 1986 Jun 2B; 1987 Nov 25B; 1988 Jan 27B/Jul 6B/Dec 26B

North Slope (Alaska) 1989 May 23F

North-South summit (Cancun, Mexico) 1981 Oct 23A/Oct 24A

Northwest Airlines 1982 Nov 30H; 1988 Mar 23H; 1989 Sep 29H/Nov 2H

Northwest Alaskan Pipeline Co. 1982 Apr 30H

Northwestern University (Evanston, Ill.) 1984 Aug 5F; 1987 Jun 17H; 1989 Jun 15I

Northwest Territories (Canada) 1980 Nov 6D; 1982 Apr 14D/Nov 26D; 1987 Jan 15D; 1988 Sep 5D

North Yemen 1980 Sep 23C; 1981 Feb 8C; 1982 Dec 13I

Norton Sound (ship) 1980 Aug 21G

Norway see also individual leaders in the name index (e.g., Brundtland, Gro Harlem)

accidents and disasters: rescue of clipper ship crew 1986 May 14J

defense and disarmament issues: nuclear weapons material lost 1988 May 4I

economy and labor: budget 1982 Oct 6B; 1988 Dec 11B; currency 1982 Oct 4A; Haavelmo wins Nobel 1989 Oct 11A; natural gas agreement 1986 Jun 2B; oil production 1988 Jan 27B; unemployment 1989 Mar 3B

foreign aid: 1983 Dec 23A

foreign relations: Canada 1988 Jun 24B; China 1984 Jun 16E; USSR 1980 Dec 22A; 1989 Apr 7B

government and politics: Syse government sworn 1989 Oct 16B; Willoch government collapses 1986 Apr 30B; Willoch government reelected 1985 Sep 10B; Willoch government takes office 1981 Oct 14B; women cabinet members 1986 May 9B

monetary issues: currency 1982 Oct 4A

science and technology: coffee drinking/cancer link 1982 Sep 11I

sports: boxing 1986 Sep 6J; cross-country 1988 Mar 26J; Lillehammer chosen for Olympics 1988 Sep 15J; marathons 1982 Oct 24J; 1984 Aug 5J; 1985 Oct 27J; 1986 Apr 21J/Nov 2J; 1987 May 10J; 1988 Apr 17J/Nov 6J; 1989 Apr 17J/Nov 5J

trade issues: natural gas agreement 1986 Jun 2B; whaling 1986 Jun 9I/Jul 2B

U.S. relations: 1980 Dec 22A; 1983 Jun 24G

Nothing in Common (film) 1986 Aug 20J/Sep 17J

No Time for Tears (Cynthia Freeman) (book) 1981 Dec 6J

Notre Dame (Julian Schnabel) (painting) 1983 May 20J

Notre Dame, University of (South Bend, Ind.) 1986 Nov 14F; 1988 Jan 1J; 1989 Jan 3J

Nova Scotia (Canada) 1981 Aug 22D; 1983 Aug 29D; 1986 Aug 26D; 1987 Jul 12D/Jul 22D; 1988 Jan 6I

novels see individual titles (e.g., Cujo)

NOW see National Organization for Women

No Way Out (film) 1987 Sep 9J

NPR see National Public Radio

NRA see National Rifle Association

NRC see Nuclear Regulatory Commission

NSC see National Security Council

NTSB see National Transportation Safety Board

nuclear energy see individual plants (e.g., Seabrook); specific geographic region (e.g., Alabama)

nuclear freeze movement 1982 Mar 30G/Mar 31G/Apr 22B/Aug 5G/Oct 28G/Nov 2G/Dec 9G; 1983 Dec 4I

nuclear-free zones 1985 Aug 6E; 1987 Feb 25G/Jun 4E

nuclear fusion 1980 Oct 7H; 1985 Dec 11I; 1988 Mar 21I; 1989 Mar 23I/May 9I/Jun 14I

Nuclear Nonproliferation Treaty (1968) 1987 Sep 21C

Nuclear Planning Group (NATO) 1985 Mar 27B; 1987 May 15B/Nov 4B

Nuclear Power in the Age of Uncertainty (Office of Technology Assessment) 1984 Feb 7H

Nuclear Regulatory Commission, U.S. (NRC)
    congressional report: 1987 Dec 20H
    construction: Clinch River 1982 Mar 5I
    crime and corruption issues: Comanche Peak 1986 Dec 11H; sabotage 1983 Jun 7H/Sep 12G; Three Mile Island 1983 Jun 23H/Sep 13H/Nov 7H
    environmental impact: Three Mile Island nuclear plant 1980 Aug 14I
    health and safety issues: automatic shutdown systems 1983 Apr 11H/Nov 10I; Babcock and Wilcox Co. designs 1980 Mar 4I; cracked pipes 1983 Aug 24I; deadline not met 1980 Jan 2I; Diablo Canyon 1981 Oct 24I; evacuation plans 1980 Jul 24I; 1983 May 5I; federal regulations revision bill 1988 Aug 8H; Georgia Institute of Technology 1988 Feb 15I; Michigan 1986 Sep 10H; Pilgrim Station Unit 1 fines 1982 Jan 29I; reactor vessel cracks 1981 Sep 9H; reported accidents 1981 Jul 26I; safety equipment cost 1987 Aug 4H; safety program criticized 1987 Jan 6H; Salem 1 fines 1983 May 6H; steam generator tubes 1982 Mar 31I; steel reactor components 1983 Jan 22F
    licensing and restarts: Byron 1984 Jan 13H; Clinch River 1983 Jan 6H; Diablo Canyon 1981 Nov 19I; 1984 Aug 2H; environmental considerations 1983 Jun 6H; Indian Point 1983 Jun 8H; inspection shutdowns 1983 Jul 15H; Peach Bottom 1987 Mar 31H; relaxing licensing procedures 1987 Aug 5H; Seabrook 1987 Jun 11H/Oct 29H; Shoreham 1984 Dec 21H; 1985 Feb 21H; 1987 Jun 11H/Oct 29H; shutdown statistics 1982 Feb 6I; Tennessee 1980 Feb 28I; Three Mile Island 1982 Nov 1I; 1985 May 29H/Jun 7H

trade and aid issues: India nuclear fuel sales 1980 May 16I/Jun 19I

Nuclear Research Council (NRC) 1983 Jan 10H

nuclear test ban 1982 Apr 2A/Jul 20G; 1986 Jul 16A

nuclear testing
    Australia: 1984 Jun 5E/Oct 2E; 1985 Dec 5E; 1986 Jan 10E; 1989 Jul 7E
    China: 1980 Oct 16E/Oct 16I; 1985 Dec 22E
    contamination lawsuits: 1982 Aug 4F/Oct 19F/Dec 17F; 1983 Apr 6G/Nov 23F; 1984 May 25H/Nov 13G; 1985 Mar 13I; 1987 Jan 8G; 1988 Apr 28B
    demonstrations: 1983 Oct 22G
    Eniwetok Atoll resettlement: 1980 Apr 9E
    France: 1981 May 29I
    Great Britain: 1984 Jun 5E/Oct 2E; 1985 Dec 5E; 1986 Jan 10E; 1988 Apr 28B; 1989 Jul 7E
    U.S./Soviet joint monitoring: 1986 Nov 14A
    USSR: 1986 Dec 18B; 1987 Jun 9B/Aug 31B

nuclear war 1987 Jan 16I

nuclear waste dumps 1983 Dec 27H; 1984 Dec 19H; 1986 Sep 11H; 1987 Jan 28H; 1989 Nov 28H

Nuclear Waste Policy Act of 1982 1983 Mar 29H

nuclear winter 1984 Dec 11H; 1985 Mar 1H

Nugan Hand Ltd. 1982 Aug 25E

Nuovo Banco Ambrosiano 1982 Aug 9B

nurses 1980 Jan 4B; 1987 Aug 1G/Sep 14J; 1988 Dec 12F; 1989 Sep 5D/Sep 12D/Oct 11F

nursing homes 1986 May 20F; 1988 Dec 1F

Nutcracker, The (ballet) 1983 Dec 6J

NutraSweet (sweetener) 1981 Jul 15I

nutrition 1988 Jun 16H/Jul 27I

NWA Inc. 1989 Sep 29H/Nov 2H

NYNEX Corp. 1989 Aug 6H/Dec 4H

O

Oahe Reservoir (South Dakota) 1988 Feb 23H

Oakland Athletics (baseball team) 1980 Dec 6J; 1981 Oct 15J; 1987 Nov 3J; 1988 Jul 12J/Oct 2J/Oct 9J/Oct 22J/Nov 2J/Nov 16J; 1989 Aug 22J/Oct 8J/Oct 28J

Oakland Invaders (football team) 1985 Jul 14J

Oakland Raiders (football team) 1980 Jan 18J/Mar 1J/Dec 28J; 1981 Jan 11J/Jan 25J; 1982 May 7J; 1988 Feb 2J

Oakland Symphony 1986 Sep 12J

Oakland Tribune (newspaper) 1983 Apr 30J

Oak Ridge atomic complex (Tennessee) 1987 Mar 28H

oats 1986 Apr 9D/Oct 24H

OAU see Organization of African Unity

obesity 1985 Feb 13F

object-oriented programming 1988 Nov 12H

obscenity 1987 Apr 16F/May 4F/Dec 24F; 1988 Jul 29H; 1989 Feb 21F/Jun 23F/Jul 26J

obstetricians 1989 Oct 11F

Obstetricians and Gynecologists, American College of see American College of Obstetricians and Gynecologists

Occidental Chemical Corp. 1985 Nov 26H

Occidental Petroleum Corp. 1980 Apr 28H; 1982 Aug 13H/Aug 16H/Aug 25H; 1983 Aug 6A; 1984 Apr 29A; 1985 Jun 29A; 1988 Jan 21J/Mar 19E

Occupational Safety and Health Administration, U.S. (OSHA)
    criticisms: Congress 1985 May 23H; OTA 1985 Apr 17H
    fines: Bath (Maine) Iron Works Corp. 1987 Nov 4H; Chrysler Corp. 1987 Jul 6H; IBP Inc. 1987 Jul 21H; John Morrell & Co. 1988 Oct 28H; lead-smelting plant 1988 Feb 11H; Union Carbide Corp. 1987 Jul 24H; Uretek Inc. 1987 Jul 28H; USX Corp. 1989 Nov 1H
    health standards: medical records requirement 1982 Jul 12H
    safety standards: asbestos 1984 Apr 9H; 1986 Jun 13H; benzene 1983 Mar 31H; 1985 Dec 3H; brown lung disease 1983 Jun 7H; ethylene dibromide 1983 Oct 3H; ethylene oxide 1983 Apr 14H; formaldehyde 1985 Dec 3H; inspections 1982 Jan 18H; 1986 Jan 7H; substances list overhaul 1989 Jan 13H

ocean dumping 1987 Nov 5H/Dec 29H; 1988 Aug 9H; sewage sludge dumping

Ocean Ranger (oil drilling rig) 1982 Feb 15D

oceans 1989 May 18I/Dec 22I

Ocean Spray Cranberries Inc. 1988 Jan 28H

"October surprise" 1988 Aug 25G/Oct 23G

Octopussy (film) 1983 Jul 6J

OECD see Organization of Economic Cooperation and Development

OECS see Organization of Eastern Caribbean States

Office of Personnel Management, U.S. see Personnel Management, U.S. Office of

Office of Technology Assessment, U.S. (OTA) 1980 Apr 17I; 1982 Oct 24F; 1984 Feb 7H; 1985 Mar 9H/Apr 17H/Sep 24F; 1987 Sep 30G; 1988 Apr 24G/May 17I/Jun 17H; 1989 Jul 17H

Officer and a Gentleman, An (film) 1982 Aug 11J/Sep 15J/Oct 6J/Nov 10J/Dec 8J; 1983 Jan 19J

Official Secrets Act (1982) 1982 Jul 15B

Official Story, The (film) 1986 Mar 24J

Off The Wall (Michael Jackson) (recording) 1980 Mar 5J/Apr 2J/Apr 30J

Ogaden (Ethiopia/Somalia) 1980 Aug 8C

Oglala Sioux Indians 1982 Jan 18G/Jan 26F

Ohbayashi Corp. 1986 Nov 25H

Ohio see also specific cities (e.g., Cleveland)
    accidents and disasters: storms 1982 Apr 2I
    crime and law enforcement: broker sentenced 1983 Sep 6F; Lukens convicted 1989 May 26F
    economy and business: banking 1985 Mar 15H/Mar 19H/Mar 25H; 1989 Jun 28H; GM plant closes 1987 Aug 26H; Honda auto plant 1980 Jan 11H

environmental issues: hazardous waste 1980 Oct 17H; 1985 Apr 5H; 1988 Nov 22H; radiation exposure lawsuit 1989 Jun 30H

labor issues: bias issues 1980 Dec 21H; GM contract rejected 1983 Aug 23H; GM plant closes 1987 Aug 26H; Honda plant organizing drive 1986 Mar 17H; steelworkers 1985 Jul 21H; teacher strikes 1985 Sep 18F; UAW accord at Chrysler Corp. 1983 Nov 5F; UAW contract at General Dynamics 1985 Nov 12H

mergers and acquisitions: Standard Oil/Kennecott Corp. 1981 Mar 12H

obituaries: Hayes, Woody 1987 Mar 12J; Santmyer, Helen Hooven 1986 Feb 21J

politics and government: presidential campaigns 1980 Jun 3F; 1983 Apr 21F; 1984 May 8F; 1988 May 3F

religious issues: Malone elected Catholic group head 1983 Nov 15J

sports: football see Pro Football Hall of Fame; golf 1980 Jun 8J; 1981 Jun 14J; 1982 Jun 13J; 1986 Jul 14J/Aug 11J; 1987 May 24J

Ohio River 1988 Jan 2H/Jan 9H/Jul 6H/Sep 15H; 1989 Mar 9H

Ohio State University (Columbus) 1980 Jan 1J; 1985 Jan 1J; 1987 Jan 1J; 1988 Mar 30J

oil see petroleum

Oil, Chemical and Atomic Workers International Union (OCAW) (AFL-CIO) 1989 Dec 15H

oilseed 1988 May 4A

Okecie Airport (Warsaw) 1987 May 9B

Oklahoma 1980 Jan 20F; 1981 Nov 19F; 1982 Mar 15F/Jun 6F; 1983 Mar 24F/Apr 24H/Jul 7F; 1984 Jul 17F; 1985 Mar 26F/Dec 14F; 1986 Apr 6F/Jul 14H/Aug 22F/Sep 18J; 1988 Feb 10F/Aug 31H; Penn Square Bank

Oklahoma, University of (Norman) 1980 Jan 1J; 1981 Dec 26J; 1985 Jan 1J/Aug 24J; 1986 Jan 1J/Jan 2J; 1987 Jan 1J; 1988 Jan 1J/Apr 4J

Oklahoma State University (Stillwater) 1981 Dec 12J; 1987 Jun 7J; 1988 Dec 3J

Olau Brittania (ship) 1984 Aug 25I

Old Court Savings and Loan Assoc. 1985 May 14H

Old Devils, The (Kingsley Amis) (book) 1986 Oct 22J

Old Dominion University (Virginia) 1985 Mar 31J

Older American Volunteer Programs 1989 Nov 20F

Old Forest and Other Stories, The (Peter Taylor) (book) 1986 Jun 5J

Old Silent, The (Martha Grimes) (book) 1989 Sep 29J

olive oil 1986 Mar 20I

Oliver and Company (film) 1988 Nov 30J

Olivier Awards (drama) 1986 Dec 7J; 1988 Jan 24J

Ollin Yoliztli Prize (literature) 1981 May 12D

Olympia (Washington State) 1985 Dec 23G

Olympic Committee, International (IOC) 1980 Feb 12J/May 27J/Jun 10J; 1982 Oct 13J; 1983 Aug 11J; 1984 Feb 6J/May 18J/May 28J/Jul 1J/Aug 12J; 1986 Oct 14J/Oct 17J; 1988 May

24J/Sep 15J see also individual directors in the name index (e.g., Samaranch, Juan Antonio)

Olympic Committee, U.S. (USOC) 1980 Jan 26J/Feb 12J/Apr 12J; 1985 Jan 10J; 1987 Jun 25F

Olympic committees, national
    Ethiopian: 1984 Jun 1J
    French: 1980 May 13J
    Hellenic: 1984 Mar 21J
    Italian: 1980 May 20J
    Soviet: 1984 Apr 9J/May 7J
    United States see Olympic Committee, U.S. (USOC)

Olympic Games
    Albertville (1992): 1988 May 24J
    Barcelona (1992): 1988 Dec 1J; 1989 Apr 7J
    Calgary (1988): ceremonies held, records set 1988 Feb 13J/Feb 20C/Feb 27J/Mar 1J
    Lake Placid (1980): ceremonies held, medals awarded 1980 Feb 12J/Feb 15J-16J/Feb 19J/Feb 21J-23J
    Lillehammer (1994): 1988 Sep 15J; 1989 Aug 23J
    Los Angeles (1984)
        boycott issues: 1983 Aug 1J; 1984 May 7J/May 8J/May 17J/May 23J/May 28J/May 31J/Jun 1J/Jun 26J/Jul 1J/Jul 27A
        ceremonies: opening 1984 Jul 28J; Reagan greets U.S. team 1984 Aug 13J
        earnings: 1984 Mar 21J/Dec 19J
        medal standings: 1984 Aug 12J
        records and achievements: Benoit wins women's marathon 1984 Aug 5J; Decker/Budd contest 1984 Aug 19J; Lewis wins fourth gold medal 1984 Aug 11J
        security issues: anti-Soviet campaign charged 1984 Apr 9J; measures enforced 1984 Apr 15J/Jul 9J; Soviet attache denied visa 1984 Mar 1J
    Moscow (1980)
        boycott issues: alternative sports festival 1980 Mar 18J; Canada 1980 Apr 22J/Apr 26J; China 1980 Feb 1J; Conference of Islamic States 1980 Jan 29A; Japan 1980 Feb 1J; NBC 1980 Jan 20J/May 6J; Saudi Arabia 1980 Jan 6J; Soviet dissident Sakharov supports 1980 Jan 2B; United States 1980 Jan 18J/Jan 26J; West Germany 1980 Apr 14J; Zaire 1980 Feb 1J
        games held, records set: Jul 19J/22J/Jul 25J/Jul 26J/Jul 31J/Aug 3J
        team participation set, individuals barred: 1980 Feb 12J/Mar 22J/Mar 25J/May 13J/May 20J/May 27J/Jun 10J
    Sarajevo (1984): games held, medals awarded 1984 Feb 6J/Feb 8J/Feb 19J/Feb 21J
    Seoul (1988): attendance 1988 Jan 18J; broadcast rights 1985 Oct 3J; ceremonies held 1988 Sep 17J/Oct 2J; Joyner world record 1988 Jul 16J; North Korea invite 1987 Sep 17J/Dec 21J; site chosen 1984 May 28J; Soviet bloc participation 1987 Dec 21J

Olympic National Park (Washington State) 1988 Nov 19H

Omaha Intermediate Credit Bank 1985 Jul 15H

Omaha World-Herald (newspaper) 1984 Oct 28F

Oman 1980 Apr 21G/Jun 4G; 1981 Mar 10C/Nov 14G; 1982 May 8C/Oct 24C/Dec 5C; 1985 Mar 21G

OMB *see* Management and Budget, U.S. Office of

Omega-7 (terrorist group) 1980 Sep 11A

Omnibus Trade Act (1988) 1989 May 25H/Jun 1A/Jun 21A/Nov 22H

Once Bitten (film) 1985 Nov 20J

Once Upon a Time in America (film) 1984 Jun 6J

One (Richard Bach) (book) 1988 Nov 25J/Dec 23J; 1989 Jan 27J

One of the Living (Tina Turner) (recording) 1986 Feb 25J

One Step Closer (Doobie Brothers) (recording) 1980 Oct 8J

1,3-butadiene 1983 Dec 20H; 1985 Oct 2H

One Tree, The (Stephen R. Donaldson) (book) 1982 May 9J/Jun 6J

On Golden Pond (film) 1981 Dec 4J; 1982 Feb 17J/Mar 10J/Mar 29J/Apr 7J; 1983 Jan 19J

On Human Work (papal encyclical) 1981 Sep 15J

Only When I Laugh (film) 1981 Nov 4J/Dec 2J

Ontario (Canada)
  demonstrations and protests: 1982 Aug 19D
  economy and business: Massey-Ferguson stock issue guarantee 1981 Feb 7D; trust company assets seized 1983 Jan 7D
  education: Catholic school funding 1986 Feb 18D; 1987 Jun 25D
  environmental issues: acid rain 1985 Dec 17D; 1987 Jun 8H; hazardous wastes 1985 Feb 5D/Dec 15D; 1986 Jan 15D/Jul 19D/Jul 25D; hydroelectric power 1989 Dec 7D
  health care: physicians' extra-billing 1986 Jun 20D
  labor issues: grain handler strike 1986 Sep 4D; UAW strikes 1982 Nov 5D
  language rights: 1985 Nov 9D; 1986 Nov 18D
  population shift: 1982 Apr 3D

On Your Toes (musical) 1982 Dec 18J; 1983 Jun 5J

Oosterschelde (Dutch dike) 1986 Oct 4B

OPEC *see* Organization of Petroleum Exporting Countries

Open Convention, Committee for an *see* Committee for an Open Convention

Open Mind (racehorse) 1988 Nov 5J

Open Up and Say...Ahh! (Poison) (recording) 1988 Jun 18J; 1989 Jan 29J

Operation FIST (Fugitive Investigative Strike Team) 1985 Jun 16F

Operation Hat Trick (drug interdiction program) 1984 Nov 17F

Operation Incubator (corruption investigation) 1986 Nov 21F

Operation PUSH Inc. 1987 Jul 4F

Operation Rescue (antiabortion group) 1988 Oct 8F

opium 1989 Mar 1G/Mar 25G

OPM *see* Personnel Management, U.S. Office of (OPM)

Oraflex (drug) 1982 Aug 3I/Aug 4I; 1985 Aug 21H

oral cancer 1986 Jan 15F

oral rehydration therapy 1984 Dec 19A

Orange Bowl (football) 1980 Jan 1J; 1982 Jan 1J; 1983 Jan 1J; 1984 Jan 2J; 1985 Jan 1J; 1986 Jan 1J; 1987 Jan 1J; 1988 Jan 1J; 1989 Jan 2J

Orange Day (Northern Irish Protestant holiday) 1986 Jul 12B

Orange Order (Northern Irish Protestant group) 1982 Jul 12B; 1985 Jul 7B

oranges 1983 Dec 29H

Order, the (neo-Nazi group) 1985 Apr 15F/Dec 30F; 1986 Feb 6F

Ordinary People (film) 1980 Oct 1J/Dec 3J; 1981 Mar 30J

Oregon 1980 May 20F; 1983 Jan 8H/Oct 6F; 1984 May 15F; 1985 Sep 16J/Nov 14F; 1986 Jul 22J/Nov 17H; 1988 May 17F/Dec 12H; 1989 May 2F

Oregon State (Corvalis) 1988 Feb 4J

organic chemicals 1987 Oct 5H

Organization of African Unity (OAU)
  Chad/Libya conflict: 1980 Dec 24C; 1982 Nov 25C; 1984 Jan 13C; 1987 Sep 11C
  organization and structure: anniversary marked 1988 May 24C; foreign debt 1987 Jul 27C
  South African conflict: ANC negotiations plan 1989 Aug 21C; Namibia 1981 Jun 27C; sanctions imposed 1986 Jun 20A; U.S. athletic events boycott 1981 Sep 18J
  Western Sahara conflict: 1981 Jun 26C; 1982 Feb 11C/Feb 22C/Apr 5D/Aug 6D/Oct 30C; 1983 Jun 12C; 1984 Nov 12C; 1988 Aug 30C

Organization of American States (OAS) *see also specific units (e.g.,* Inter-American Court of Human Rights)
  foreign debt: 1983 Sep 4D/Sep 9D
  human rights: 1980 Nov 27D; 1981 Oct 15D
  meetings: 1983 Sep 9D/Oct 26D; 1984 Nov 12D; 1985 Dec 5D; 1986 Nov 14D; 1988 Nov 14D; 1989 May 17D
  membership issues: Canada to join 1989 Oct 27D
  peacekeeping initiatives: Central American peace initiative 1987 Jan 19D/Sep 17D; Costa Rican appeal for peacekeepers 1983 May 5D; Falklands/Malvinas 1982 Apr 20D/Apr 28D; Grenada invasion 1983 Oct 26D/Nov 16D; Nicaragua invites observers 1988 Mar 16D
  terrorism and unrest: El Salvador OAS building seized 1980 Sep 17D
  United States policy: Haig speech 1981 Dec 4D; Noriega attacked 1989 Aug 31D; Reagan speech 1982 Feb 24D; Shultz speech 1982 Nov 17D

Organization of Eastern Caribbean States (OECS) 1983 Oct 23G/Oct 25D/Oct 26G; 1987 May 31D

Organization of Economic Cooperation and Development (OECD)
  aid issues: 1980 Mar 26A/Apr 15A; 1983 Dec 23A; 1987 Jun 29A; 1989 Jun 23A
  capital markets; 1988 Mar 3A/Jun 2A/Jun 22A/May 18A
  Chernobyl disaster: 1988 Jan 22I
  country reports: Australia 1983 Jan 26A/Jul 18E; 1987 Mar 12E; Great Britain 1985 Jan 10B; 1986 Jan 31B/Sep 24B; West Germany: 1984 Jul 30B

debt issues: 1982 Dec 16A; 1984 May 18A; 1988 Jul 20A

economic indicators: growth rate 1982 Jul 6A; 1983 Jul 12A; 1987 Jun 18A/Dec 22A; 1988 Nov 15A/Dec 20A; inflation 1987 Feb 13B; 1988 Nov 15A; steel production 1983 Apr 19A; tax rates 1987 Sep 11B; unemployment 1982 May 11A

education issues: UNESCO reform proposals 1984 Mar 14A

strategy meeting: 1983 May 9A

trade issues: farm subsidies 1987 May 13A; 1988 May 19A; industrially competitive nations 1984 Jan 6A; talks agreement 1985 Apr 12A; U.S. policy criticized 1989 Jun 1A

Organization of Petroleum Exporting Countries (OPEC)
  1980 Feb 22A/May 7A/Jun 10A/Sep 18A/Oct 27G/Nov 9C/Dec 16A
  1981 May 26A/Jun 18A/Aug 21A/Sep 8A/Oct 29A/Dec 11A
  1982 Mar 6A/20A; 1982 Jul 10A/Dec 20A; 1983 Jan 24A/Feb 20A/Mar 14A/Mar 14H/Jul 18A
  1984 Jul 11A/Oct 18A/Oct 31A/Dec 29A
  1985 Jan 30A/Jul 7A/Jul 10D/Jul 21A; 1985 Jul 25D/Sep 17A/Oct 4A/Dec 8A
  1986 Mar 24A/Apr 22A/Aug 4A/Oct 22H/Dec 20A
  1987 Feb 3C/Jun 28A/Aug 17A/Oct 16A/Dec 14A
  1988 May 2A/Jun 11A/Aug 3A/Oct 22A/Nov 28A
  1989 Jan 26A/Feb 21A/Mar 30A/Jun 7A/Sep 27A/Nov 28A

Organization of the Islamic Conference 1981 Mar 5A/Mar 12A/Apr 4A; 1984 Jan 17C/Jan 19C/Jan 20C/Jan 30C; 1987 Jan 26C; 1989 Mar 13C

organ transplants 1986 Jul 15I/Oct 17I; 1988 May 11J; 1989 Jun 15I/Dec 3I; *see also specific transplants (e.g.,* heart transplants)

original intent 1985 Nov 15F

Orion Pictures 1983 Jul 18J

Orphan Drug Act 1985 Aug 11H

Orphans (play) 1986 Dec 7J

Orthodox Church of America 1989 Nov 19J

Oscar and Lucinda (Peter Carey) (book) 1988 Oct 26J

Oscars *see* Academy Awards

Oscar Wilde (Richard Ellmann) (book) 1989 Jan 9J/Mar 30J

OSHA *see* Occupational Safety and Health Administration

Osirak nuclear reactor (Iraq) 1981 Jan 10C/Jun 8C/Jun 9C/Jun 11C/Jun 15C/Jun 17C/Jun 19A/Jun 19C/Jul 16C/Nov 13A

Oslo, University of (Norway) 1989 Oct 11A

Ossining Correctional Facility (New York) 1983 Jan 11F

OTA *see* Office of Technology Assessment, U.S.

Othello (William Shakespeare) (play) 1987 Sep 16J

Ottoman Empire 1989 Jan 4B

OU812 (Van Halen) (recording) 1988 Jun 18J/Jul 16J

Outer Space, U.N. Conference on the Exploration and Peaceful Uses of 1982 Aug 21I

Outland Trophy (football) 1985 Dec 11J; 1986 Nov 29J; 1987 Dec 9J; 1988 Dec 7J; 1989 Dec 5J

Out of Africa (film) 1985 Dec 18J; 1986 Jan 22J/Mar 24J

Outrageous Fortune (film) 1987 Feb 18J

Outsiders, The (film) 1983 Apr 6J

Out the Window (Jasper Johns) (painting) 1986 Nov 10J

ovarian cancer 1983 Mar 25I

Overseas Development Council 1981 Feb 8I

Over the Top (film) 1987 Feb 18J

Owl Moon (Jane Yolen) (book) 1988 Jan 11J

Oxford University (England) 1985 Nov 23J; 1986 Mar 29J; 1987 Mar 14B; 1989 Mar 25J/Aug 2J

oysters 1987 Dec 11I

ozone illness 1980 Feb 12I

ozone layer 1986 Jun 27I/Oct 20I; 1987 Mar 9I/Sep 30I/Dec 1H; 1988 Jan 1I/Mar 14H/Mar 15I/Dec 16I; 1989 Mar 7I/Oct 12I; chlorofluorocarbons

ozone pollution 1987 Nov 17H

P

Pabst Brewing Co. 1981 Aug 4H

PAC *see* Pan-Africanist Congress

pacemakers 1988 Aug 31F

Pacific Islands, U.N. Trust Territory of the 1987 Jul 20E

Pacific Ocean 1983 Aug 10B; 1984 Jan 21G; 1985 Aug 6E; 1987 Dec 8D

Pacific Power and Light Co. 1983 Sep 14H

Packard Electric Division of General Motors Corp. 1983 Aug 23H

Paco's Story (Larry Heinemann) (book) 1987 Nov 9J

PACs *see* political action committees

pain medication 1986 Jul 21F

Painted Desert (Arizona) 1985 May 16I

painting *see also individual artists in the name index (e.g.,* Warhol, Andy)
  appointments and resignations: Varnedoe named to MOMA position 1988 Feb 10J
  archaeology: Mayan wall paintings 1984 May 15I
  auctions: Cassatt, Mary 1983 May 17J; Degas, Edgar 1983 May 18J; de Kooning, Willem 1983 May 10J; Johns, Jasper 1986 Nov 10J; 1988 May 3J; Mantegna, Andrea 1985 Apr 18J; Picasso, Pablo 1988 Nov 28J; 1989 May 9J; Pollock, Jackson 1988 May 2J; Ribera, Jose 1985 Mar 14J; Rothko, Mark 1983 Nov 9J; Schnabel, Julian 1983 May 20J; Turner, J.M.W. 1984 Jul 5J; van Gogh, Vincent 1987 Mar 30J/Nov 11J; Warhol, Andy 1988 May 2J
  awards and honors: Motherwell wins MacDowell Colony Medal 1985 Aug 18J
  donations: Chagall estate donates works to France 1988 Feb 1J; Goya masterwork to be returned to Spain 1986 Apr 10B; Picasso collection returned to France 1987 Jan 20J
  exhibitions: Chagall, Marc 1987 Sep 2J; Impressionist and modern paintings 1986 May 1J
  obituaries: Albright, Ivan Le Lorraine 1983 Nov 18J; Dali, Salvador

1989 Jan 23J; Dubuffet, Jean 1985 May 12J; Kokoschka, Oskar 1980 Feb 22J; Krasner, Lee 1984 Jun 19J; Lam, Wilfredo 1982 Sep 11J; Levi, Julian 1982 Feb 28J; Michaux, Henri 1984 Oct 18J; Miro, Joan 1983 Dec 25J; Neel, Alice 1984 Oct 13J; Nicholson, Ben 1982 Feb 6J; O'Keeffe, Georgia 1986 Mar 6J; Phillips, Marjorie Acker 1985 Jun 19J; Sloane, Eric 1985 Mar 6J; Strater, Henry 1987 Dec 22J; Tworkov, Jack 1982 Sep 4J

thefts: Impressionist paintings 1985 Oct 27J; Picasso painting 1986 Aug 19J

Pakistan *see also individual leaders in the name index (e.g.,* Bhutto, Benazir)
  Afghanistan War *see* Afghanistan War
  civil strife: bombings 1987 Jul 14E; demonstrations and protests 1983 Aug 14E; 1984 Jan 5E; 1987 Jul 5E; ethnic violence 1986 Nov 5E/Dec 15E; 1988 Oct 2E; urban guerrilla group 1982 Jan 17E
  defense and disarmament issues: missile tests 1988 May 24E; nuclear proliferation 1987 Sep 25G; 1988 Jan 15G; 1989 Oct 12G; nuclear weapons 1981 Apr 27I; 1982 Jan 24C; 1987 Mar 1E
  economy: banking 1984 Jun 18E; food shortfall 1982 Mar 8E
  espionage and intelligence issues: Pollard case 1985 Nov 21G
  foreign relations: Great Britain 1986 Sep 1B; USSR 1981 Aug 27E; West Germany 1988 Jan 18B
  government and politics: Ishaq Khan elected president 1988 Dec 12E; Junejo sworn prime minister 1985 Mar 23E; leaders arrested 1981 Feb 25E; opposition party formed 1986 Aug 30E
  hijackings: Pakistani airliner (Damascus, Syria) 1981 Mar 12E/Mar 14E; Pan American Airways (Karachi, Pakistan) 1986 Sep 5E
  Indian relations: border issues 1986 Dec 21E; 1987 Jan 23E/Feb 19E/Sep 25E; cooperation commission 1982 Dec 24E; peace negotiations 1982 Feb 25E/Nov 1E; U.S. aid issues 1980 Jan 16E/Jan 16G; 1981 Jun 16E/Aug 19E; 1986 Nov 4E; 1987 Oct 20G
  international organizations: Commonwealth 1989 Oct 1A; IMF 1980 Nov 25A
  obituaries: Ghaffar Khan, Abdul 1988 Jan 20E
  religion: Ahmedi sect restricted 1984 Apr 27E
  sports: cricket 1987 May 25J
  U.S. relations: humanitarian aid 1980 Jan 12E/Mar 5G; 1981 Apr 21E/Jun 15G/Sep 15G; 1988 Apr 4E; military aid 1980 Feb 3E; nuclear proliferation waiver 1987 Sep 25G; 1988 Jan 15G; 1989 Oct 12G; Shultz visit 1983 Jul 2E

Paks nuclear power plant (Hungary) 1986 Jul 16I

Palapa-B2 (satellite) 1984 Aug 16I

Palau 1980 Oct 31E; 1981 Jan 1E; 1985 Jun 30E/Oct 25E; 1986 Sep 17E/Dec 2E; 1987 Jul 20E/Aug 4E; 1988 Aug 20E/Nov 10E

paleontology 1981 Sep 17I; 1984 Oct 18I; fossils

Pale Rider (film) 1985 Jul 17J

Palestine Liberation Army 1982 Aug 27C

Palestine Liberation Front (PLO faction) 1988 Jan 17G

Palestine National Charter 1989 May 2B

Palestine National Council 1989 Nov 15C

Palestinian Liberation Organization (PLO) see also individual leaders in the name index (e.g., Arafat, Yasir)
Arab League summit: 1988 Jun 7C
Arab nations, PLO meet on A-power: 1981 Jun 19I
European Community: self-determination urged 1980 Jun 13A
independent Palestinian state: 1988 Nov 15C/Nov 26C
Islamic summit: 1981 Jan 29A
United Nations policy: status upgrade defeated 1989 Dec 6A
U.S. relations: Abbas arrest warrant dropped 1988 Jan 17G; Bush administration meeting 1989 Mar 22C; Bush administration proposals 1989 Mar 11C; called terrorist group 1981 Mar 26A; Columbia University conference 1989 Mar 12C; conditions for recognition 1982 Jul 14G; more direct role in peace process sought 1989 Dec 8C; New York City office 1988 Mar 2A/Mar 11G/Mar 22G/Apr 25A/Aug 29C; U.S.-PLO talks reported 1981 Jul 5G; Washington office 1987 Sep 15G

Palestinians 1980 Nov 2J

Palm Bowl (football) 1982 Dec 11J

Palme d'Or see Golden Palm

Pan-Africanist Congress (PAC) 1988 Nov 26C

Panama see also individual leaders in the name index (e.g., Delvalle, Eric Arturo)
accidents and disasters: Torrijos Herrera plane crash 1981 Jul 31D
church developments: papal visit 1983 Mar 2D
Contadora Group see Contadora Group
crime and law enforcement: Diaz Herrera pardoned 1987 Dec 22D
demonstrations and protests: 1987 Jun 11D/Jun 16D
economy and business: foreign debt 1987 Nov 26D; Peoples Temple bank accounts 1980 Feb 28J
foreign relations: El Salvador 1983 Feb 22G; foreign ministers' meeting 1983 Apr 21D/Jul 30D
government and politics: Ardito Barletta resigns as president 1985 Sep 28E; Ardito Barletta sworn as president 1984 Oct 11D; Ardito Barletta wins presidential election 1984 May 16B; de la Espriella becomes president 1982 Jul 31D; de la Espriella resigns presidency 1984 Feb 13D; Noriega critic slain 1985 Sep 14D; presidential elections 1984 May 6D/May 7D; 1989 May 10D; Rodriguez sworn as president 1989 Sep 1D; state of emergency lifted 1987 Jun 30D; Torrijos Herrera killed in plane crash 1981 Jul 31D
human rights: 1988 Apr 23D
international organizations: World Bank 1988 Jul 11A
labor issues: general strikes 1985 Jul 2E; 1986 Mar 19E; 1987 Jul 28D
obituaries: Spadafora, Hugo 1985 Sep 14D; Torrijos Herrera 1981 Jul 31D

sports: boxing 1980 Sep 20J/Nov 25J/Nov 26J; 1982 Jan 16J
U.S. invasion: 1989 Dec 20D/Dec 20G/Dec 22D/Dec 24D/Dec 27G
U.S. relations: aid 1989 Dec 29D; Kissinger fact-finding mission 1983 Oct 9D; Marine killed 1989 Dec 16D; Marine training program 1988 Apr 8D; state of war declared 1989 Dec 15D; Weinberger visit 1983 Sep 6D

Panama Canal 1980 Nov 24A; 1989 Dec 29D

Panama Canal Commission 1983 Feb 3D

Pan American Games 1983 Aug 28J; 1987 Aug 23J

Pan American Health Organization 1985 Feb 3D

Pan American World Airways 1982 Jul 9I; 1985 Mar 27H/Apr 22H/Aug 31H; 1986 Aug 22H/Sep 5E

Pan Am Flight 103 see Lockerbie disaster

Pancontinental Mining Company 1982 Mar 1E

pancreatic cancer 1981 Mar 11I

pandas 1985 Jan 12I; 1988 Apr 6I

Pan-Electric Industries Ltd. 1985 Dec 4E

Panjab University (Chandigarh, India) 1989 Apr 20I

Pan Pacific swimming championships 1985 Aug 17J/Aug 18J

pantyhose 1989 Apr 16B

Pap smear 1987 Nov 2F

Papua New Guinea 1980 Mar 11E/Aug 31E; 1982 Aug 2E; 1984 May 2A/Aug 29E; 1985 Nov 10E/Nov 21E; 1986 May 28E; 1987 Aug 4E; 1988 Jul 4E; 1989 Apr 10E

Papworth Hospital (Cambridge, England) 1986 Dec 17I

Paracel Islands 1980 Jan 30E

parachuting 1986 Apr 24J

Parade (Prince and the Revolution) (recording) 1986 May 21J

parades
China: 1984 Oct 1E; 1989 Oct 1E
France: 1986 Jul 14B
Poland: 1984 May 1B
United States: disarmament 1982 Jun 12G; Iran hostages 1981 Jan 30J; Labor Day 1982 Sep 6J; 1983 Sep 5H; St. Patrick's Day 1983 Mar 17J; Vietnam veterans 1985 May 7G
USSR: 1982 May 1B; 1983 Nov 5B; 1985 May 9B; 1987 Nov 7B

Paradise Theater (Styx) (recording) 1981 Feb 11J/Mar 4J/Apr 8J/May 6J/May 27J/Jul 8J

Paraguay 1980 Sep 17D; 1982 Nov 5I; 1984 Oct 25D; 1985 May 5D; 1987 Apr 3D; 1988 May 7J; 1989 Feb 6D/May 1D; see also individual leaders in the name index (e.g., Stroessner, Alfredo)

Paramount Communications Inc. 1986 Aug 27J; 1988 Nov 21J; 1989 Jul 24H

Parana River 1984 Oct 25D

paraquat 1983 Aug 15F/Sep 14H

parental leave 1988 Oct 7F

Parenthood (film) 1989 Aug 30J/Sep 27J

Parents Music Resource Center 1985 Aug 5J

Paris (France) see also Eiffel Tower
arts and culture: art museum opens 1986 Dec 1J; Creation and Development conference 1983 Feb

12J; Impressionist paintings stolen 1985 Oct 27J; national library director appointed 1987 Nov 22B; see also Paris Opera Ballet
assassinations: Besse, George 1986 Nov 17B; Syrian ex-premier 1980 Jul 21C
bombings: Chanel store 1981 Jan 4B; commercial sites 1986 Feb 5B; courthouse 1981 Jan 30B; government computer facilities 1980 Apr 15B; Lebanese-based group 1986 Sep 17B; synagogue 1980 Oct 3B
demonstrations and protests: disarmament 1981 Oct 15B; 1982 Jun 20B; schools 1980 Mar 19B; 1983 May 5B; 1984 Jun 24B; Turkish immigrants 1980 Mar 3B
Iranian embassy siege: 1987 Aug 14A/Nov 29A
medicine and health care see Pasteur Institute
parades: Bastille Day 1986 Jul 14B
sports: horse racing see Prix de l'Arc de Triomphe; pole vault 1985 Jul 13J
stock market: 1981 May 12B
terrorism: Bakhtiar assassination attempt 1980 Jul 8C; Goldenberg's restaurant attack 1982 Aug 9B/Aug 10B; Jewish/neo-fascist clashes 1980 Oct 12B; Jewish targets attacked 1980 Sep 28B; Jewish woman killed 1980 Nov 25B

Paris, Texas (film) 1984 May 23J

Paris, University of (France) 1980 Apr 5I/Oct 10I

Paris Club 1989 Apr 5C

Paris International Track and Field Meet (1985) 1985 Jul 13J

Paris Opera Ballet 1989 Nov 21J

Paris stock market 1981 May 12B

Paris-to-Dakar car race 1982 Jan 14J

Paris Trout (Pete Dexter) (book) 1988 Nov 29J

Parkinson's disease 1987 Apr 2I/Jun 30I; 1988 Jan 7I; 1989 May 1I/Aug 4I

Parkinson's syndrome 1984 Sep 20J

Parsifal Mosaic, The (Robert Ludlum) (book) 1982 Apr 11J/May 9J/Jun 6J/Jul 11J/Aug 8J

Parthenon (Athens, Greece) 1983 Aug 31J

Partial Accounts: New and Selected Poems (William Meredith) (poetry) 1988 Mar 31J

Parting the Waters: America in the King Years, 1954-63 (Taylor Branch) (book) 1989 Mar 30J

Partners (film) 1982 May 5J

Pasadena Playhouse (Pasadena, Calif.) 1986 Apr 19J

Passage to India, A (film) 1985 Feb 13F/Mar 25J; 1986 Mar 16J

Passamaquoddy Indians 1980 Mar 15F

passive smoking 1984 May 23I; 1986 Dec 16I

passports see visas and passports

pasta 1986 Aug 10B

Pasteur Institute (Paris, France) 1985 Feb 7I/Dec 13B; 1986 Jul 8I

PATCO 1981 Aug 25H/Oct 22H; 1982 Jan 3H

Patent and Trademark Office, U.S. (Commerce Department) 1981 Mar 3I; 1987 Apr 16I; 1988 Oct 21H/Nov 19H

patents

computer programming technology: 1981 Mar 3I
federally financed projects: 1980 Nov 21F
genetic engineering: 1980 Jun 16F/Jun 16I; 1987 Apr 16I/Nov 4I; 1988 Apr 21I/Oct 15I
infringement protection: 1986 Apr 7H
ingredient monopolization: 1980 Jun 27F
Kodak/Polaroid infringement: 1985 Sep 13H; 1986 Jan 8H
pharmaceuticals: 1984 Sep 24H; 1988 Jul 22H
trade issues: 1985 Oct 16H; 1987 Dec 18B; 1988 Jul 22H

PATH railroad 1980 Sep 1H

Patriot Games (Tom Clancy) (book) 1987 Aug 21J/Sep 23J/Oct 23J/Nov 20J/Dec 18J; 1988 Jan 29J

Paul Sacher Foundation 1983 Jun 23J

Paul White Award (broadcast journalism) 1980 Jul 7J

payment-in-kind (PIK) program 1983 Jan 11H/Mar 11H/Jun 13H/Jul 30F/Aug 31H; 1984 Oct 11H

PBB see polybrominated biphenyl

PBS 1980 May 12J; 1984 Sep 24J; 1985 Jun 26J

PCBs (polychlorinated biphenyls) 1980 May 9H; 1981 May 8H/Jul 28H; 1983 Jan 4H/May 9H; 1984 Feb 21H; 1985 Jan 24H/Apr 5H; 1987 Nov 9H

PC jr (personal computer) 1983 Nov 1H; 1984 Jun 7H; 1985 Mar 19I

Peace Corps 1988 Mar 7G

Peace Now (Israeli group) 1980 Jul 1J; 1989 Mar 12C

Peach Bottom nuclear power plant (Delta, Pa.) 1987 Mar 31H

Pebbles (racehorse) 1985 Nov 2J

Pecten Arabian Ltd. 1980 Jul 9C

Pediatrics, American Academy of see American Academy of Pediatrics

Pee-Wee's Big Adventure (film) 1985 Aug 14J

Peggy Sue Got Married (film) 1986 Oct 8J/Oct 22J/Nov 12J

Pelle the Conqueror (film) 1988 May 23J/Dec 21J; 1989 Jan 28J/Mar 29J

PEN (literary organization) 1986 Jan 17J

PEN/Faulkner Award (literature) 1985 May 11J; 1986 Jun 5J; 1987 May 9J; 1988 May 14J; 1989 May 13J

Penn Central Corp. 1981 Jan 22H

Penn-Dixie Industries Inc. 1980 Apr 7H

Penn Square Bank 1982 Jul 5H/Jul 21H; 1983 Jun 17H/Oct 31H; 1984 Apr 12H/Jun 29H/Jul 17F; 1986 Jul 8H/Aug 5H

Pennsylvania
abortion laws: 1986 Jun 11F; 1989 Oct 24F/Nov 18F
crime and law enforcement: antiwar activists' convictions upheld 1985 Nov 22F; mandatory sentencing for firearm use 1986 Jun 19F; organized crime in pizza business 1980 Aug 24H; prison riots 1981 Nov 2F; 1989 Oct 27F
economy and business: Western Savings Bank takeover 1982 Apr 3H
environmental issues: diesel fuel spill penalties 1989 Nov 21H; hazardous waste 1981 Oct 23H
immigration and refugees: refugee camp rioting 1980 Aug 5F

labor issues: autoworker contract ratified 1985 Nov 12H; steelworker strikes 1985 Jul 21H; 1986 Aug 21H; teacher strikes 1983 Sep 12F; USX Corp. fined by OSHA 1989 Nov 1H
nuclear power plants see Three Mile Island
politics and government: presidential campaigns 1980 Apr 22F; 1984 Apr 10F; 1988 Apr 26F; teacher strikes 1985 Sep 18F
school desegregation: 1983 Mar 24F

Pennsylvania, University of (Philadelphia) 1980 Oct 15H; 1986 Jul 6J

Pennsylvania State Correctional Institution (Camp Hill, Pennsylvania) 1989 Oct 27F

Pennsylvania State University (University Park) 1981 Jan 12I; 1983 Jan 2J; 1985 Dec 10J; 1986 Jan 1J; 1987 Jan 2J

Pennzoil Co. 1985 Nov 19H; 1987 Feb 12H/Apr 6H/Apr 12H/Nov 2H/Dec 19H

Penobscot Indians 1980 Mar 15F

pentamidine 1989 Feb 6I/Jun 15I/Oct 12F

Penthouse (magazine) 1981 Aug 6J; 1982 Jul 9J; 1984 Jul 23J

People Express Inc. 1986 Aug 28H/Sep 15H

People for the American Way 1985 Feb 15F

People Like Us (Dominick Dunne) (book) 1988 Jun 24J

"people power" 1987 Mar 29E

Peoples' Army for the Liberation of Kurdistan (ARGK) 1987 Jun 20B

Peoples Front of Estonia 1988 Jun 20B

People's Mujahedeen (Iranian dissidents) 1988 Jan 13B

Peoples Temple 1980 Feb 28J/Apr 8D; 1981 Sep 26F; 1986 Dec 1F

PepsiCo Inc. 1986 Jan 27H

"perestroika" 1988 Sep 30B; 1989 Jan 13B/Apr 22B

Perfect (film) 1985 Jun 12J

Perfect Spy, A (John Le Carre) (book) 1986 May 30J/Jun 27J

perjury
Deaver, Michael K.: 1986 Aug 12F; 1987 Mar 18F/Jul 16F/Dec 16F
Kleindienst, Richard: 1981 Apr 14F
Lavelle, Rita: 1983 Mar 1H/Dec 1H; 1985 Jan 18H
Mecham, Evan: 1988 Jan 8F
Pierce Jr., Samuel R.: 1989 Dec 4F
Secord, Richard V.: 1989 May 11F
Sindona, Michele: 1980 Mar 27H
Swindall, Patrick L.: 1988 Oct 17F; 1989 Jun 20F
Weiss, Solomon: 1982 Nov 27J

Pershing IA (missile) 1987 Apr 27B/Aug 26B/Oct 8B

Pershing II 1982 Jul 22G/Oct 29H/Nov 29B; 1983 Jan 11B/Apr 4B/Jul 27G/Sep 15G/Oct 22B/Nov 14A/Nov 23A; 1984 May 10B; 1985 Jan 11B/Apr 24G; 1988 Sep 8G

Persian Gulf see also Iran-Iraq war; specific countries (e.g., Saudi Arabia)
Canada: 1983 Dec 5E
Egypt: 1981 Jul 27C
Iran: 1980 Oct 1C
oil spills: 1983 Jul 31C/Sep 21C
regional cooperation council: 1981 Mar 10C
regional defense plan: 1982 Jan 26C

Stark attack: 1987 May 17C/May 20C/Jun 19G/Jul 27G; 1989 Mar 27G

United States: amphibious assault force 1980 Feb 12G; capability of defending Gulf asserted 1980 Feb 1G; military deployments 1980 Oct 11G; military installations 1985 Mar 21G; permanent major military command 1981 Apr 24G; presidential campaign issues 1980 Jan 28F; Reagan affirms support for Gulf states 1984 May 21G; Reagan defends policy 1987 Jun 15F; response to Brezhnev proposal 1980 Dec 11A; Sadat offers military facilities 1981 Jul 27C

USSR: 1980 Dec 9A

Vincennes airbus downing: 1988 Jul 3C/Jul 3G/Jul 11G/Aug 2G/Aug 19G; 1989 Mar 10G/Jul 17G

Personal Ensign (racehorse) 1988 Nov 5J

personal income
1982 statistics: 1982 Jan 19H/Feb 19H/Mar 17H/Apr 20H/Jun 18H/Dec 20H
1983 statistics: 1983 Jan 18H/Mar 18H/Apr 19H/May 18H/Jun 20H/Jul 20H/Aug 18H/Sep 20H/Oct 19H/Nov 21H/Dec 20H
1984 statistics: 1984 Jan 19H/Feb 16H/Mar 19H/Apr 18H/May 17H/Jun 19H/Jul 20H/Aug 17H/Sep 19H/Oct 18H/Nov 19H/Dec 18H
1985 statistics: 1985 Jan 18H/Feb 20H/Mar 20H/Apr 17H/May 20H/Jun 19H/Jul 17H/Aug 19H/Sep 19H/Oct 18H/Nov 21H/Dec 23H
1986 statistics: 1986 Jan 23H/Feb 21H/Mar 20H/Apr 18H/May 5H/May 21H/Jun 19H/Jul 23H/Aug 20H/Sep 21H/Oct 23H/Nov 20H/Dec 18H
1987 statistics: 1987 Jan 23H/Apr 24H/May 25H/Jun 18H/Jul 27H/Aug 24H/Sep 21H/Oct 26H
1988 statistics: 1988 Jan 28H/Feb 26H/Mar 24H/Apr 27H/May 27C/Jun 24H/Jul 28H/Aug 26H/Sep 21H/Oct 27H/Nov 30H/Dec 21H
1989 statistics: 1989 Jan 30H/Mar 1H/Mar 24H/Apr 27H/Jul 28J/Aug 30H/Sep 22H/Oct 27H/Nov 30H/Dec 21H

personal spending 1987 Jan 23H

Personal Systems/2 (personal computer) 1988 Sep 13H

Personnel Management, U.S. Office of (OPM) 1983 Sep 15F

Perspective (literary quarterly) 1989 Jun 2J

Peru *see also individual leaders in the name index (e.g., Belaunde Terry, Fernando)*
accidents and disasters: soccer team plane crash 1987 Dec 8D
arts and culture: Vargas Llosa wins Ritz Paris Hemingway Award 1985 Mar 29J
church developments: papal visits 1985 Feb 5J; 1988 May 7J
civil strife: casualties 1983 May 5D; constitutional rights suspended 1982 Jul 12D; general strike 1988 Jan 28D; moment of silence against terrorism 1987 Dec 29D; state of emergency lifted 1983 Sep 19D; terrorist bombings 1982 Aug 20D; universities raided 1987

Feb 18D; *see also* Sendero Luminoso
crime and law enforcement: anti-narcotics workers killed 1984 Nov 17D; army general ordered arrested 1986 Jul 23D; journalist slayings 1983 Jan 29C/Feb 5D; 1985 Mar 27D; 1987 Mar 10D; prisons 1982 Mar 3D; 1986 Jul 23D
Cuban embassy compound occupation: 1980 Apr 6D/Apr 7D/Apr 16D
economy and business: 1980 Jan 1D; 1982 Jul 23D; 1985 Oct 5D; 1988 Sep 6D; inflation 1989 Sep 13A; nationalizations 1985 Dec 27D; 1987 Aug 7D/Sep 29D/Oct 14D
foreign debt: 1983 Jul 26D; 1984 Jun 5D/Jun 21D/Sep 14D; 1985 Feb 8D/Mar 11D; 1986 Feb 2D; 1987 Nov 26D
foreign relations: Bolivia 1980 Jul 29D; Ecuador 1981 Jan 28D/Mar 6D
government and politics: Belaunde Terry elected president 1980 May 18D; Garcia Perez wins presidential election 1985 Jun 1D; municipal elections 1980 Nov 23D; 1986 Nov 9D; presidential elections 1985 Apr 14D; Schwalb resigns as prime minister 1984 Apr 9D; Ulloa Elias resigns as prime minister 1982 Dec 10D; Vargas Llosa declares presidential candidacy 1989 Jul 3D; Villanueva del Campo resigns as prime minister 1989 May 7D
human rights: 1985 Jan 22D; 1987 Feb 9D; 1988 Aug 18D
international organizations: IMF 1986 May 6D/Aug 15D; 1987 Jun 3D; Inter-American Development Bank 1987 Jun 3D; 1989 Mar 9D; United Nations 1981 Dec 15A; 1983 Dec 31A; World Bank 1988 Jul 11A
monetary and trade issues: currency 1988 Sep 6D; 1989 Jan 7D; foreign investment 1985 Sep 16D; IDB loans 1987 Jun 3D; 1989 Mar 9D; IMF loans 1986 May 6D/Aug 15D; 1987 Jun 3D; silver market lawsuit 1980 Feb 15D; 1988 Aug 20F/Oct 20H; World Bank loans 1988 Jul 11A
sports: soccer team plane crash 1987 Dec 8D
United Nations policy: 1981 Dec 15A; 1983 Dec 31A
U.S. relations 1983 Aug 11G

pesticides 1981 Jul 28H; 1983 Dec 9H; 1985 Jun 29I/Sep 11H; 1987 May 20I; 1988 Aug 21F/Sep 28H/Oct 12H/Oct 25H; 1989 Oct 26H; *see also* Bhopal disaster

Peter the Great (TV show) 1986 Sep 21J

Petrobras (Brazilian state oil company) 1987 Mar 10D

petroleum
accidents and disasters: Newfoundland offshore rig sinks 1982 Feb 15D
exploration and drilling
Australia: 1980 Jun 10I; 1982 May 10E
Canada: 1980 Aug 23D; 1982 May 19D/May 31D; 1983 Jan 20D; 1984 Jan 26D
Chile: 1984 Dec 12D
China: 1982 Feb 16E; 1983 Aug 6A/Aug 23A

Ecuador: 1987 Sep 30E
Greece: 1985 Oct 3B
Gulf of Mexico: 1981 Jul 21H
Ireland: 1983 Aug 20B
Libya: 1982 May 13H/Jul 20H
Malta: 1980 Aug 28B
Peru: 1985 Dec 27D
United States: corporate mergers affecting 1984 Mar 8H; environmental impact 1983 Sep 13H; offshore 1984 Aug 8H; 1989 Jul 26H; wilderness areas 1984 Nov 30H
pipelines: Ecuador 1987 Mar 6D; Great Britain 1989 Aug 19I; Iran 1980 Dec 5C; Iraq/Lebanon 1982 Jan 3C; Iraq/Syria 1980 Sep 27C; 1981 Feb 26C; 1982 Apr 10C; Iraq/Turkey 1980 Nov 20C; 1984 Aug 6C; Nigeria 1982 Jan 29C; United States 1982 Aug 1I
spills
Amoco Cadiz fines: 1988 Jan 11H
cleanup: 1980 Jun 16F
environmental liability: 1989 Jul 14H
Exxon Valdez: 1989 Mar 24H/Mar 28H/Apr 5H/Apr 7H/May 10H/May 20H/Jul 24H/Jul 28H/Sep 7H/Sep 15H
foreign developments: Great Britain 1989 Aug 19I; Lithuania 1982 Jan 19B; Persian Gulf 1983 Mar 29I/Apr 26C/Jul 31C/Sep 21C
reporting laws: 1980 Jun 27F; 1989 Aug 4H/Nov 9H
statistics: 1986 Nov 26I
in United States: Delaware 1989 Jun 24H; Monongahela and Ohio Rivers 1988 Jan 2H/Jan 9H/Jul 6H/Sep 15H; 1989 Mar 9H/Nov 21H; Rhode Island 1989 Jun 24H; Texas 1989 Jun 24H; Wyoming 1982 Aug 1I
trade issues: equipment exports 1986 Jun 2D; 1987 Jan 15H

Petroleum Corp. of New Zealand Ltd. 1988 Mar 1E

Peugeot S.A. 1981 May 26H; 1987 Jul 22B; 1988 Jan 18B

Pfizer Inc. 1985 Nov 13I; 1988 Dec 5H

Pforzheimer Foundation 1986 Dec 18J

PGA championship 1980 Sep 10J; 1981 Aug 9J; 1982 Aug 8J; 1983 Aug 7J; 1984 Aug 19J; 1985 Aug 11J; 1986 Aug 11J; 1987 Feb 15J/Aug 9J; 1988 Aug 14J; 1989 Aug 13J

Phantom of the Opera, The (musical) 1986 Oct 9J/Dec 7J; 1987 Jul 2J; 1988 Jun 5J

Phelps Dodge Corp. 1986 Jul 28H

phenols 1981 Jul 28H

Phibro Corp. 1981 Aug 3H

Philadelphia (Pennsylvania) *see also individual leaders in the name index (e.g., Rizzo, Frank)*
accidents and disasters: blizzards 1983 Feb 12I; drought 1980 Dec 1I
arts and culture: Live Aid benefit concert 1985 Jul 13J
Constitution bicentennial: 1987 May 22F/Jul 16F/Sep 17F
crime and law enforcement: antiabortion demonstrators conviction upheld 1989 Mar 2F; MOVE bombing/fire 1980 May 8F; 1985

May 13F/Nov 6F; 1986 Mar 6F; organized crime figures convicted 1988 Nov 19F; 1989 Apr 5F; police officers sentenced 1984 Sep 24F
economy and business: banking 1982 Apr 3H; 1987 Aug 2H
environmental issues: toxic chemicals 1981 Jan 22H
labor issues: city worker strike 1986 Jul 22F; newspaper strike 1985 Oct 22H; newspaper strike averted 1981 Aug 16J
obituaries: Ormandy, Eugene 1985 Mar 12J
politics and government: Kennedy assassination ceremony 1983 Nov 22F; presidential campaign (1984) 1984 Apr 10F/Sep 17F/Oct 11F
religious issues: Catholic nun beatified 1988 Nov 20J
sports: cycling 1985 Jun 23J

Philadelphia 76ers (basketball team) 1980 May 16J; 1981 May 27J; 1982 Jun 8J/Jun 8J; 1983 May 31J/May 31J

Philadelphia Bulletin (newspaper) 1981 Aug 16J; 1982 Jan 29J

Philadelphia Eagles (football team) 1981 Jan 11J/Jan 25J; 1987 Feb 1J; 1989 Jan 29J

Philadelphia Electric Co. 1987 Mar 31H

Philadelphia Flyers (ice hockey team) 1980 May 24J; 1985 May 30J; 1987 May 31J

Philadelphia Inquirer (newspaper) 1983 Feb 25J; 1984 Oct 28F; 1985 Oct 22H

Philadelphia Newspapers Inc. (Knight-Ridder) 1985 Oct 22H

Philadelphia Phillies (baseball team) 1980 Oct 12J/Oct 21J/Nov 26J; 1981 Nov 17J; 1982 Oct 26J; 1983 Oct 8J/Oct 8J/Oct 16J/Nov 2J; 1986 Nov 19J; 1988 Aug 8J

Philadelphia Savings Fund Society 1982 Apr 3H

Philip Morris Inc. 1985 Sep 27H

Philippines *see also individual leaders in the name index (e.g., Aquino Jr., Benigno)*
accidents and disasters: ferry/tanker collision 1987 Dec 20E; Typhoon Ike 1984 Sep 2E; Typhoon Nina 1987 Nov 25E; Typhoon Ruby 1988 Oct 25I
arts and culture: censorship attacked 1983 May 17E
celebrations: Freedom Day 1987 Feb 25E
church developments: bishops call presidential elections fraudulent 1986 Feb 14E; Cardinal Sin accepts Vatican edicts 1987 Mar 6J; papal visits 1981 Feb 15J
civil strife: archbishop Sin urges protest 1984 Oct 2E; arrests in priest murder case 1985 Oct 11E; bombings 1980 Sep 12E/Sep 26E/Oct 19E; communist insurgency 1986 Sep 30E/Nov 27E/Dec 23E; 1987 Feb 8E/Nov 23E; 1988 Dec 15E; government crackdown 1982 Sep 13E; Moro insurgency 1981 Feb 12E; prison attack crushed 1987 Apr 18E; rebellion charges dropped 1986 Sep 1E; union leaders arrested 1982 Aug 13E/Sep 2E; U.S. military adviser killed 1989 Apr 21E; U.S. servicemen killed 1987 Nov 23E
coups and coup attempts: 1986 Nov 7E; 1989 Dec 1E

crime and law enforcement: Benigno S. Aquino III shot 1987 Aug 28E; labor leader Olalia murder 1986 Nov 13E/Dec 2E; Manotoc kidnapping 1982 Feb 9E
defense and disarmament issues: full alert 1985 Sep 21E; nuclear weapons ban legislation 1988 Jun 6E
demonstrations and protests: 1983 Aug 26E/Sep 22E; 1984 Sep 27E; 1985 Oct 21E
economy: aid plan 1989 Jul 5E; economic policy 1983 Oct 7E; food shortfall 1982 Mar 8E
foreign relations: Japan 1982 Jan 18E
government and politics: Aquino assassinated 1983 Aug 21E; campaign use of public funds charged 1984 May 16E; Congress convenes 1987 Jul 27E; constitutional issues 1981 Apr 7E; 1986 Jun 2E/Oct 12E; elections approved by Supreme Court 1985 Dec 19E; Laban party to take part in elections 1984 Feb 26E; local elections 1988 Jan 18E; Marcos dies in Honolulu 1989 Sep 28E; national elections 1987 May 11E; opposition group formed 1988 Aug 27E; opposition groups form coalition 1980 Aug 29E; political party launched 1986 Aug 30E; presidential elections 1986 Feb 14E
human rights: 1982 Sep 14E; 1985 Jun 11E; 1988 Dec 15E
international organizations: IMF 1986 Oct 24E
monetary and trade issues: balance-of-payments gap 1982 Sep 13E; IMF loans 1986 Oct 24E
obituaries: Aquino Jr., Benigno Simeon 1983 Aug 21E; Marcos, Ferdinand E. 1989 Sep 28E; Olalia, Rolando 1986 Nov 13E
U.S. relations 1983 Jun 25E; 1984 Feb 29G; 1985 Jul 9G; 1986 Jun 24E; 1987 Nov 23E; 1988 Oct 17E; 1989 Apr 21E; Subic Bay Naval Base; *see also* Clark Air Base

Philips Data Systems Co. 1980 Apr 15B

Phobos (moon of Mars) 1989 Mar 28I

Phobos 2 (spacecraft) 1989 Mar 28I

Phoenix (Dan Fogelberg) (recording) 1980 Mar 5J

phosphorus 1983 Oct 16D

photosynthesis 1988 Oct 19I

phthalate esters 1981 Jul 28H

physicians
awards and honors: physicians' group wins Nobel 1985 Oct 11A/Dec 10A
crimes: MacDonald murder conviction 1982 Mar 31J; Presley's personal MD 1980 Jan 19J/May 16J; Tarnower slaying 1980 Mar 10J
economic issues: advertising 1980 Jul 22I; antitrust laws 1984 Mar 27F; 1988 Dec 6F; laboratory tests 1980 Mar 23I; malpractice costs 1989 Oct 11F; Medicare payments 1983 Jun 23F; 1984 Nov 13F; 1988 Sep 28F; supply and demand 1980 Apr 17I; 1986 Jun 15F; veterans' hospital salaries 1980 Aug 26F
educational issues: foreign medical school testing 1984 Jun 16F; training 1984 Sep 19F/Dec 6F; 1988 Nov 11F

ethical issues: abortion 1981 Mar 23F; 1988 Jun 27F; AIDS disclosure 1985 Sep 18F; 1987 Mar 19I/Jun 24F/Nov 12F; euthanasia 1984 Apr 12I; 1988 Jan 8I; reproductive technologies 1984 Aug 8I

foreign developments: Australia 1984 Jun 20E; Canada 1983 Dec 12D; 1986 Jun 20D; 1987 Jan 5D; Great Britain 1985 Oct 17B; 1986 Nov 27B; 1989 Jan 31B; Israel 1983 May 22C/May 25C/Jun 26C/Sep 6C

obituaries: Cournand, Andre 1988 Feb 19I; Crohn, Burrill 1983 Jul 29I; Gruentzig, Andres 1985 Oct 27I; Kaplan, Henry 1984 Feb 4I; Taussig, Helen 1986 May 20I; Terry, Luther 1985 Mar 29I

Physicians for Human Rights 1988 Feb 11C

physics

awards and honors

human rights award: 1989 Oct 18A

Nobel Prize: Cronin/Fitch 1980 Oct 14I; Bloembergen/Schawlow/Siegbahn 1981 Oct 19I; Wilson 1982 Oct 18J; Chandrasekhar/Fowler 1983 Oct 19I; Rubbia/van der Meer 1984 Oct 17I; Klitzing 1985 Oct 16I; Binner/Rohrer/Ruska 1986 Oct 15I; Bednorz/Mueller 1987 Oct 14I; Lederman/Schwartz/Steinberger 1988 Oct 19I; Dehmelt/Paul/Ramsey 1989 Oct 12I

obituaries: Alvarez, Luis 1988 Sep 1I; Bloch, Felix 1983 Sep 10I; Brattain, Walter 1987 Oct 13I; De Broglie, Louis 1987 Mar 19I; Dirac, Paul 1984 Oct 20I; Feynman, Richard 1988 Feb 15I; Fuchs, Klaus 1988 Jan 28I; Harnwell, Gaylord 1982 Apr 18I; Kapitsa, Pyotr 1984 Apr 8I; Kastler, Alfred 1984 Jan 7I; Mulliken, Robert 1986 Oct 31I; Oppenheimer, Frank 1985 Feb 3I; Rabi, I(sidor) I(saac) 1988 Jan 11I; Rainwater, James 1986 May 31I; Ryle, Martin 1984 Oct 14I; Sakharov, Andrei 1989 Dec 14B; Segre, Emilio 1989 Apr 22I; Shockley, William 1989 Aug 12I; Smyth, Henry 1986 Sep 11I; Zacharias, Jerrold 1986 Jul 16I

research: antigravitational force 1980 Mar 8I; atomic particle accelerators 1985 Oct 13I; 1986 Jul 27I; 1987 Jan 30I/Apr 15I/Sep 2I; 1988 Dec 13I; quantum jump witnessed 1986 Oct 21I; space shuttle Columbia 1983 Nov 28I; Strategic Defense Initiative 1986 Mar 22G; superconductivity 1987 Feb 16I/Mar 27I/Jul 28H/Oct 14I; 1989 Jan 3I/May 23I; U.S./China cooperation 1983 May 11I; weak force particle 1983 Jan 26I

rights issues: Chinese dissident wins award 1989 Oct 18A; East German charged as spy 1983 Nov 10G; Polish dissident released 1984 Aug 13B

Pictures (Plant) (recording) 1982 Aug 18J

Pilgrim Station nuclear power plant (Plymouth, Mass.) 1982 Jan 29I

Pillars of the Earth, The (Ken Follett) (book) 1989 Sep 29J/Oct 27J

pilot licenses 1989 Aug 31H

pilots *see* airline pilots

pilots, commercial *see* airline pilots

Pine Gap military base (Australia) 1981 Feb 7G

Pink Cadillac (film) 1989 May 31J

Pink Floyd (singing group) 1980 Jan 2J/Mar 5J/Apr 30J/Jun 4J; 1983 Apr 13J; 1987 Oct 24J/Nov 21J

Pink Floyd: The Wall (film) 1982 Oct 6J

Pioneer Bowl (football) 1981 Dec 19J

pipelines *see specific type* (e.g., gas pipelines)

Piper Alpha oil platform (North Sea) 1988 Jul 6B

Pirates of Penzance, The (musical) 1981 Jun 7J

Pisa (Italy) 1989 Dec 15B

Pittsburgh, University of (Pennsylvania) 1983 Jan 1J; 1985 Nov 22I

Pittsburgh Brewing Co. 1981 May 16H

Pittsburgh Penguins (ice hockey team) 1982 Mar 17J; 1988 Jun 8J

Pittsburgh Pirates (baseball team) 1988 Jan 12J

Pittsburgh Press (newspaper) 1987 Apr 16J

Pittsburgh Steelers (football team) 1980 Jan 6J/Jan 20J; 1985 Jan 6J; 1988 Feb 2J/Sep 4J; 1989 Jan 24J

Pittsburgh Symphony 1986 Sep 11J

"Pizza Connection" trial 1987 Mar 2F

pizza industry 1980 Aug 24H

PKK *see* Kurdish Workers' Party

Places in the Heart (film) 1984 Sep 21J/Oct 10J/Nov 7J; 1985 Mar 25J

Plain Dealer (Cleveland newspaper) 1984 Oct 28F

Plains Song (Wright Morris) (book) 1981 Apr 30J

Planes, Trains and Automobiles (film) 1987 Dec 23F

planets 1984 Dec 11I; 1986 Jun 11I

Planned Parenthood Federation of America 1983 Jan 10F/Sep 15F

Plant (singing group) 1982 Aug 18J

plant closings 1985 Nov 21H; 1987 Jun 1F/Jul 9H; 1988 Jul 5H/Jul 13H/Aug 2H

plastics 1981 Jul 28H; 1987 Oct 5H/Nov 5H/Dec 29H; 1988 Oct 28H

platinum 1986 Jan 6C/Sep 2H

Platoon (film) 1986 Dec 19J; 1987 Jan 21J/Jan 31J/Feb 18J/Mar 18J/Mar 30J/Apr 15J

Playboy (magazine) 1980 Aug 15J; 1981 Mar 2J

Playboy Enterprises Inc. 1981 Nov 5B; 1986 Jun 30J

plays *see specific play* (e.g., *Normal Heart*)

Pleasant Colony (racehorse) 1981 May 2J/May 16J/Jun 6J

PLO *see* Palestinian Liberation Organization

plumbing 1988 Aug 10H

Pluto (planet) 1980 Apr 22I

plutonium 1981 Dec 11I; 1984 Apr 23H; 1986 Oct 8H/Dec 12H; 1988 Feb 16H/Mar 21I; 1989 Jul 7E/Oct 6H/Dec 1H/Dec 20G

Plymouth Theater (New York City) 1987 Oct 14J

pneumonia 1980 Jun 9I; 1989 Feb 6I/Jun 15I/Oct 12F

pocket vetoes 1984 Jan 4G/Aug 29F; 1986 Nov 6H; 1987 Jan 14G; 1988 Oct 26F/Nov 3H

poetry

awards and honors

Great Britain: Dunn wins Whitbread award 1986 Jan 28J; Hughes named poet laureate 1984 Dec 19J

Mexico: Borges wins Ollin Yoliztli prize 1981 May 12D

Nobel Prize: Brodsky, Joseph 1987 Oct 22J; Milosz, Czeslaw 1980 Oct 9J; Seifert, Jaroslav 1984 Oct 11J; Soyinka, Wole 1986 Oct 16J

South Africa: Breytenbach wins Rapport Prize 1986 Apr 12J

United States: Nemerov named poet laureate 1988 May 16J; Warren named poet laureate 1986 Feb 26J; Wilbur named poet laureaure 1987 Apr 17J; *see also specific awards* (e.g., Pulitzer Prizes)

grants and gifts: English Romantic poets collection donated 1986 Dec 18J

obituaries: Acorn, Milton 1986 Aug 20J; Berrigan, Ted 1983 Jul 4J; Brautigan, Richard 1984 Oct 25J; Brown, Sterling 1989 Jan 13J; Bunting, Basil 1985 Apr 17J; Carver, Raymond 1988 Aug 2J; Ciardi, John 1986 Mar 30J; de Andrade, Carlos 1987 Aug 17J; Denby, Edwin 1983 Jul 12J; Fitzgerald, Robert 1985 Jan 16J; Graves, Robert 1985 Dec 7J; Hayes, Alfred 1985 Aug 14J; Kaufman, Bob 1986 Jan 12J; Larkin, Philip 1985 Dec 2J; Lattimore, Richmond 1984 Feb 26J; MacLeish, Archibald 1982 Apr 20J; Michaux, Henri 1984 Oct 18J; Rexroth, Kenneth 1982 Jun 6J; Seifert, Jaroslav 1986 Jan 10J; Shalamov, Varlam 1982 Jan 30J; Sokolov, Valentin 1984 Nov 8J; Warren, Robert Penn 1989 Sep 15J

people: Cuban poet emigrates 1980 Mar 16D; South African activist executed 1985 Oct 18C; South African granted asylum 1983 Sep 6F; Soviet dissident arrives in London 1986 Dec 18B; Soviet dissident released from prison 1986 Oct 9B; Soviet poet Yevtushenko leads protest 1989 Mar 5B

scholarship: Shakespeare poem discovered 1985 Nov 23J

P&O European Ferries (formerly Townsend Thoresen) 1989 Jun 22B

Poison (singing group) 1987 Apr 25J/May 23J; 1988 Jun 18J; 1989 Jan 29J

poison gas 1980 Aug 21G; 1984 Mar 26A; 1986 Mar 14C; 1988 Sep 8C/Sep 21C; 1989 Jan 28C/Apr 27B/Jul 7G

Poland *see also individual leaders in the name index* (e.g., Gierek, Edward)

accidents and disasters: Polish airliner (Warsaw) 1980 Mar 14J; 1987 May 9B

arts and culture: Havel play opens in Warsaw 1989 May 25B; intellectuals attacked by press 1982 Jan 12B; intellectuals sign petition 1982 Jan 21B; Milosz wins Nobel Prize 1980 Oct 9J

Auschwitz convent controversy: 1989 Jan 25B/Aug 10B/Aug 27B/Sep 19B

crime and law enforcement: Palestinian leader wounded 1981 Aug 1C; police operations 1981 Mar 19B/Dec 2B; 1982 Feb 17B/May 4B; 1988 May 5B

defections: ambassador to Japan 1981 Dec 24B; banker in U.S. 1982 Oct 22B; travelers in West Germany 1984 Nov 24B

defense and disarmament issues: demobilization 1989 Jan 3B; military units deployment 1981 Oct 26B

demonstrations and protests: amnesty program 1983 Jul 21B; 1984 Jul 21B/Aug 9B/Aug 13B; 1986 Jul 24B; anti-government protests 1981 Dec 17B; 1982 Jan 31B/Apr 18B/Aug 31B; 1983 May 1B; 1989 Feb 25B

dissidents: 1980 Aug 21B; 1981 Jun 5B/Sep 28B; 1982 Sep 3B; 1986 Oct 18B; 1987 Dec 27B

economy and business: currency 1989 Sep 11B; food protests 1981 Aug 10B; national income 1982 Jan 29B; performance 1981 Jul 9B/Sep 17B; personal income 1982 May 17B; prices 1983 Nov 12B; 1987 Nov 14B/Dec 15B; 1988 Feb 1B; 1989 Aug 1B; private curbs lifted 1988 Dec 23B; programs 1980 Nov 19B; 1982 Feb 8B; reforms 1987 Oct 10B; 1988 Feb 1B; 1989 Oct 12B/Dec 30B

environmental issues: acid rain 1985 Jul 9I

espionage and intelligence issues: 1982 Apr 28G

foreign debt: 1981 Feb 5B/Feb 19B/Apr 7B/Apr 27B/Jul 28G/Dec 29A; 1982 Jan 29A/Jul 7B; 1985 Jan 16B; 1987 Dec 8B; 1989 Jun 17B

foreign relations: Austria 1981 Dec 18B; Canada 1982 Feb 24A; European Community 1981 Dec 15B/Dec 23B; 1982 Jan 4B; France 1981 Apr 13B/Dec 23B; Great Britain 1982 Feb 5A; 1988 Nov 2B; Israel 1985 Oct 17A; Italy 1981 Apr 13B; Japan 1982 Feb 23A; NATO 1982 Jan 12B; Switzerland 1982 Sep 9B; West Germany 1982 Jan 6B; 1984 Nov 24B

government and politics: Babiuch removed as premier 1980 Nov 22B; Communist Party Central Committee 1980 Oct 6B/Dec 2B/Dec 4B; 1981 Mar 30B/Apr 30B/Jul 19B/Nov 28B; 1984 Dec 22B; Communist Party Congress 1981 Jul 14B/Jul 20B; 1986 Jul 29B; Communist Party democratization demands 1981 Apr 15B; Communist Party membership 1981 Apr 27B; 1982 Jan 7B; government and party shakeup 1980 Nov 22B; government/opposition talks 1989 Apr 5B; government proposal on unions 1982 Feb 22B; government/striking worker negotiations 1980 Aug 23B/Aug 30B/Aug 31B/Sep 2B; Kania dismissed as party head 1981 Oct 18B; local elections 1984 Jun 9B; Mazowiecki cabinet confirmed 1989 Sep 12B; Messner government resigns 1988 Sep 19B; parliament appeals for strike halt 1981 Oct 31B; parliamentary elections 1985 Oct 14B; parliament delays choosing president 1989 Jul 5B; passport regulations 1981 Apr

26B; Pinkowski dismissed as premier 1981 Feb 9B; Politburo elected 1981 Jul 19B; Rakowski chosen premier 1988 Sep 27B; Rakowski comments on power structure 1980 Sep 14B; referendum on economic and political reforms 1987 Nov 30B; speaker of parliament warning on interference 1980 Dec 13B; World War I observances 1981 Nov 11B; World War II observances 1989 Sep 1B

human rights: 1981 Dec 23B

immigration and refugees: 1982 Apr 28B; 1989 Dec 11B

international organizations: Comecon 1984 Jun 14A; IMF 1984 Dec 14B; 1985 Jan 16B; 1986 May 31B; 1989 Dec 23B/Dec 30B; United Nations 1982 Dec 21A; 1983 Jan 18C; Warsaw Pact 1981 Jan 14B/Mar 26B

labor issues: farmers attempt to form union 1980 Dec 14B; five-day work week 1981 Jan 5B/Jan 31B; funeral of worker 1982 Oct 20B; independent trade unions form federation 1980 Sep 17B; laws on "social ills" 1982 Oct 26B; legislation on worker role in factories 1981 Sep 25B; May Day holiday unrest 1982 May 1B; oil refinery occupation 1981 Dec 24B; organizations banned 1982 Oct 8B; phone service to Gdansk restored 1980 Aug 25B; strikes 1980 Jul 11B/Aug 29B/Sep 19B; 1981 Jan 22B/Mar 10B/Mar 27B/Jul 9B/Jul 29B/Aug 4B/Aug 20B/Oct 28B/Dec 2B/Dec 22B/Dec 25B; 1988 May 5B; 1989 Feb 9B; *see also* Rural Solidarity; Solidarity

martial law: coal mines operating 1981 Dec 30B; death toll 1982 Jan 8B; dissidents charged 1982 Sep 3B; formally lifted 1983 Jul 21B; miner strikes 1981 Dec 22B; petition for end of 1982 Jan 21B; police operations 1982 Feb 17B; restrictions relaxed 1981 Dec 22B; suspended 1982 Dec 21B

monetary issues: currency 1989 Sep 11B

obituaries: Andrzejewski, Jerzy 1983 Apr 20J; Barszcz, Edward 1981 May 24B; Gomulka, Wladyslaw 1982 Sep 1B; Olszewski, Jerzy 1981 May 24B; Wlosik, Bogdan 1982 Oct 20B; Wyszynski, Stefan Cardinal 1981 May 28B

political prisoners and internees: 1982 Apr 18B/Apr 28B/Apr 29B; 1983 Jan 4B; 1985 Nov 9B

Popieluszko murder: 1984 Oct 30B/Nov 3B/Nov 27B; 1985 Feb 7B

press and broadcasting: BBC bureau closed by government 1983 Jan 7B; *Let Poland Be Poland* broadcast 1982 Jan 31A; Roman Catholic mass broadcast 1980 Sep 21J; underground radio station 1982 Apr 12B

Roman Catholic Church: dissidents condemned 1980 Dec 12B; legal status attained 1989 May 17J; martial law criticized 1981 Dec 16B; mass broadcast 1980 Sep 21J; school crucifixes 1984 Apr 6B; Vatican relations established 1989 Jul 17J

Solidarity *see* Solidarity

Soviet bloc relations: Czechoslovakia 1980 Oct 9B/Nov 27B; Eastern Europe 1980 Dec 8B; East Germany 1980 Oct 8B/Oct 28B; 1982 Mar 13B; 1989 Oct 4B; Romania 1980 Oct 21B

Soviet relations: debt repayments deferred 1981 Feb 19B; food shipments 1980 Sep 11B; Gromyko visit 1981 Jul 5B; military exercises 1981 Sep 12B; 1982 Mar 13B; NATO warning to Soviets on interference 1980 Dec 12B; Polish editorial on domestic sovereignty 1989 Oct 24B; Soviet confidence in Poland 1980 Dec 5B; Soviet letter demanding action 1981 Sep 18B/Sep 24B; Soviet press attacks on labor movement 1980 Aug 27B; 1981 Jan 8B; Soviet press attacks on Polish Communist Party 1981 Apr 2B/Apr 25B; Soviet press denies Soviet role in crackdown 1981 Dec 21B; Soviet press supports compromise 1988 Sep 16B; Soviet rallies against Polish "counterrevolution" 1981 Sep 11B; Suslov visit 1981 Apr 23B

sports: Olympic boycott 1984 May 17J

U.S. relations: aid 1981 Jul 28G/Dec 14G; 1988 Feb 3B; 1989 Sep 14B/Oct 19G; ambassador granted asylum 1981 Dec 20B; economic sanctions 1983 Jul 12G; 1984 Jan 19G/Aug 3G/Dec 14B; espionage and intelligence issues 1982 Apr 28G; IMF membership not opposed 1984 Dec 14B; *Let Poland Be Poland* broadcast 1982 Jan 31A; UPI reporter expulsed 1983 Jan 12B; warning on terrorism 1984 Mar 14G

Poland (James A. Michener) (book) 1983 Sep 11J/Oct 16J/Nov 13J/Dec 18J; 1984 Jan 20J/Feb 10J

Polar Express, The (Chris Van Allsburg) (book) 1986 Jan 20J

Polaroid Corp. 1985 Sep 13H; 1986 Jan 8H

Polar Star (Martin Cruz Smith) (book) 1989 Jul 28J/Aug 25J

pole vault 1985 Jul 13J

Police (singing group) 1981 Nov 11J; 1983 Jul 13J/Jul 13J/Aug 17J/Aug 17J/Sep 14J/Oct 19J/Nov 9J; 1984 Feb 18J/Feb 28J

Police Academy (film) 1984 Apr 11J/May 9J

Police Academy 2: Their First Assignment (film) 1985 Apr 17J

Police Academy 4: Citizens on Patrol (film) 1987 Apr 15J

Police Foundation 1983 Apr 5F

polio 1980 Apr 16I; 1985 Feb 3D

Polisario Front 1980 Dec 17A; 1981 Oct 21C; 1982 Feb 22C/Apr 5D/Aug 6D/Oct 30C; 1983 Jun 12C; 1984 Nov 12C; 1988 Aug 30C/Dec 27C; 1989 Jan 4C

political action committees (PACs) 1983 Apr 28F/Dec 13F; 1984 Apr 27F/Sep 9F; 1985 Mar 18F; 1986 Jan 7F/Jan 23F; 1987 Apr 7F/Apr 29F; 1988 Jul 23F; 1989 Aug 25F

Political Studies, Joint Center for 1982 Sep 5F

politics *see specific geographic region* (e.g., Great Britain); *specific parties* (e.g., Republic Party); *individual leaders in the name index* (e.g., Reagan, Ronald)

poll-closing time 1989 Apr 5F

polls and surveys
approval ratings: 1980 Jan 10F; 1981 Jun 20F; 1987 Mar 3F; 1989 Jan 18F/Feb 26F/Jun 27E/Sep 26F

poll tax 1987 Jul 30B/Dec 4B; 1988 Apr 18B/May 23B

pollution *see general areas* (e.g., air pollution); *specific subjects* (e.g., acid rain); *geographic regions* (e.g., Canada)

Poltergeist (film) 1982 Jun 9J/Jul 7J

polybrominated biphenyl (PBB) 1982 Apr 16I

polygraph tests *see lie-detector tests*

polypropylene 1986 Apr 24B

polystyrene 1985 Jul 17I

Pondos (South African ethnic group) 1985 Dec 25C

Poor Little Rich Girl: The Life and Legend of Barbara Hutton (C. David Heymann) (book) 1983 Dec 12J

Popeye (film) 1981 Jan 7J

Popular Forces of April 25 (FP-25) (Portuguese terrorist group) 1987 May 20B

Popular Front of Estonia 1988 Oct 2B

population
Australia: 1988 Jan 11E/Jun 6E
Cambodia: 1980 May 24E
Canada: 1982 Apr 3D; 1987 Jan 22D
China: 1982 Sep 13E; 1983 Jan 30E/Apr 8E; 1988 Feb 15E; 1989 Apr 14E
Chinese: 1985 Oct 7E
India: 1988 May 30E
Soviet Union: 1987 Jan 19B
United Nations conference: 1984 Aug 14A
United States: census undercounting 1980 Sep 25F; elderly 1981 May 23F; farm 1982 Nov 24H; minorities 1981 Feb 23F; Sun Belt 1983 Sep 7H; totals 1980 Dec 31F; 1982 Nov 8F; 1983 Jan 1F; 1984 Dec 28F; 1985 Apr 5F; 1989 Jan 1F
USSR: 1980 Feb 9B; 1986 Oct 1B; 1989 Apr 28B
world population: 1980 Jul 23H; five billionth person 1987 Jul 10J

Population, U.N. Second International Conference on 1984 Aug 14A

Population Activities, U.N. Fund for 1985 Sep 30G; 1987 Jul 10J

Porky's (film) 1982 Apr 7J/May 5J; 1983 Jan 19J

pornography 1986 Feb 24F/Apr 22F/Jul 9F

Pornography, U.S. Commission on (Justice Department) 1986 Jul 9F

porpoises 1980 Oct 21H

Port Authority of New York and New Jersey 1980 Feb 4B

Portland (Oregon) 1988 Jun 9I

Portland Oregonian (newspaper) 1984 Oct 28F

Porto (Portuguese soccer team) 1987 May 27J

Portraits (Cynthia Freeman) (book) 1980 Mar 9J/Apr 6J/May 4J

Portsmouth Uranium Enrichment Complex (Piketon, Ohio) 1988 Nov 22H

Portugal *see also individual leaders in the name index* (e.g., Soares, Mario)
accidents and disasters: Lisbon fire 1988 Aug 25B
crime and law enforcement: Pope threatened 1982 May 12B
economy and business: budget 1988 Nov 27B; GDP 1987 Mar

17B; inflation 1986 Sep 24B; 1987 Mar 17B; reforms blocked 1980 May 21B; unemployment rate 1988 Jan 4B; value-added tax rates 1988 Sep 11B
foreign relations: China 1985 May 23E; 1987 Jan 6E/Mar 26E; Mozambique 1984 May 2C; South Africa 1984 May 2C
government and politics: Balsemao government sworn in 1981 Jan 9B; Balsemao resigns as premier 1981 Aug 11B; constitutional reforms 1982 Aug 12B/Oct 3B; 1989 Jun 1B; Eanes elected president 1980 Dec 7B; interior minister Correia resigns 1982 Feb 13B; municipal elections 1982 Dec 12B; parliamentary elections 1980 Oct 5B; 1985 Oct 6B; 1987 Jul 19B; presidential campaign clashes 1980 Nov 22B; presidential elections 1986 Jan 26B; Soares elected president 1986 Feb 16B; Social Democratic Party conference 1981 Feb 22B; Social Democratic Party withdraws from coalition 1985 Jun 4B; Social Democrats resign from coalition 1985 Jun 13B
international organizations: European Community 1980 Jun 5B; 1984 Dec 4B; 1985 Mar 29B/Mar 30B/Jun 12B; 1986 Jan 1B; IMF 1983 Aug 9B; Western European Union 1988 Nov 14B

Macao *see* Macao

medicine and health care: abortion 1982 Nov 12B

obituaries: da Costa, Adelino Amaro 1980 Dec 4B; Sa Carneiro, Manuel Lumbrales de 1980 Dec 4B

sports: marathons 1987 Apr 20J; 1988 Apr 18J; soccer 1987 May 27J

terrorism: colonel sentenced 1987 May 20B

U.S. relations: 1980 Jun 26B; 1983 Dec 13B

Poseidon (submarine) 1986 May 27G

Posse Comitatus (survivalist group) 1983 Jun 3H

Postal Service, U.S. 1980 Apr 21H; 1984 Dec 24F; 1986 Jan 6H/Aug 20F; 1987 Jul 21H/Aug 14J; 1988 Feb 2H; 1989 Nov 3H

Postman Always Rings Twice, The (film) 1981 Apr 1J

post-traumatic stress disorder 1986 Apr 22F

potassium cyanide 1986 Feb 17F

potatoes 1985 Feb 22I

Potential Effects of Nuclear War on Climate, The (Defense Department) 1985 Mar 1H

poultry *see chickens*

poverty rate 1982 Jul 19H; 1983 Aug 2H; 1984 Aug 2H; 1985 Aug 27H; 1986 Aug 26H/Oct 2F; 1987 Jul 30F; 1988 Aug 31H; 1989 Oct 18H

PPI *see producer price index*

Prague '88 (Czech dissident gathering) 1988 Jun 17B

Pratt & Whitney Aircraft Group 1984 Feb 21G

Pravda (Soviet Communist Party newspaper) 1981 Jan 8B/May 18B; 1982 Jun 4B/Nov 25A; 1986 Jul 5B; 1989 Dec 30B

Prayer for Owen Meany, A (John Irving) (book) 1989 Apr 28J

Preakness Stakes (horse race) 1980 May 17J; 1981 May 16J; 1982 May 15J; 1983 May 21J; 1984 May 19J; 1985 May 18J; 1986 May 17J; 1987 May 16J; 1988 May 21J; 1989 May 20J

Precious Time (Pat Benatar) (recording) 1981 Aug 5J/Sep 9J

Precisionist (racehorse) 1985 Nov 2J

Predator (film) 1987 Jun 12J/Jun 17J

pregnancy 1980 Jan 4I/Jan 25I; 1982 Dec 6F; 1983 May 2I/Jun 9I/Jun 20F/Jul 25I; 1984 Feb 16I; 1987 Jan 13F/Feb 26F

premature births 1980 Jan 4I/Jan 25I

Presbyterians 1982 Jun 29J; 1983 Jun 10J; 1984 Nov 30J; 1985 Jun 11J; 1986 Jun 11J; 1987 Jun 10J/Nov 5J

Presbyterian-University Hospital (Pittsburgh) 1989 Dec 3I

Presidential Commission on AIDS 1987 Sep 9F/Sep 14F/Oct 7F; 1988 Feb 23I/Jun 2F/Jun 12I

Presidential Commission on Strategic Forces 1983 Apr 18G/May 2G

Presidential Task Force on Market Mechanisms 1988 Jan 8H

presidential transitions 1988 Aug 17F

President's Commission for the Study of Ethical Problems in Medicine and Biomedical and Behavioral Research 1983 Mar 21I

President's Commission on Industrial Competitiveness 1985 Feb 13H

President's Commission on Organized Crime 1986 Mar 3F/Mar 6F/Apr 1F

President's Commission on Pension Policy 1980 May 23H

President's Council on Physical Fitness and Sports 1986 Mar 20F

President's Foreign Intelligence Advisory Board 1981 Oct 10G

President's Private Sector Survey on Cost Control 1984 Jan 12H

President's Task Force on Immigration and Refugee Policy 1981 May 29G

President's Task Force on Private Sector Initiatives 1982 Dec 18A

President's Task Force on Regulatory Relief 1987 Jul 14H

Presidio, The (film) 1988 Jun 15J

Presumed Innocent (Scott Turow) (book) 1987 Jul 17J/Aug 21J/Sep 23J/Oct 23J/Nov 20J; 1988 Jan 29J/Feb 26J/Mar 25J

Pretenders (Pretenders) (recording) 1980 Jun 4J

Pretenders (singing group) 1980 Jun 4J

Pretty in Pink (film/soundtrack) 1986 Mar 19F/May 21J

preventive detention 1987 May 26F

price controls and freezes
Argentina: 1987 Oct 14D
Brazil: 1986 Feb 28D/Nov 27D; 1987 Feb 5D/Jun 12D; 1989 Apr 27D
Canada: 1982 Jul 7D; 1984 Nov 8D
China: 1988 Jan 19E/May 15E/Sep 30E
European Community: 1986 Apr 25B
France: 1986 Nov 26B
International Coffee Organization: 1989 Jul 3A
Israel: 1985 Jan 24C
Mexico: 1982 Feb 24D; 1989 Jun 18D/Dec 3D
New Zealand: 1988 May 3E

Nicaragua: 1988 Jun 14D
Peru: 1985 Oct 5D
Poland: 1989 Aug 1B
United States: 1980 Feb 22H/Jun 24F; 1981 Jan 28H; 1984 Jul 26H; 1985 Jan 1H; 1989 Jun 26H
Yugoslavia: 1982 Jul 31B; 1988 Aug 4B

Price Waterhouse & Co. 1989 Jul 6H

Pride of Baltimore (ship) 1986 May 14J

primates 1980 Feb 7I; 1984 Aug 22I/Sep 24I

prime rate (Australia) 1985 Dec 16E

prime rate (Canada) 1985 Jan 10D; 1988 Apr 2D; 1989 Feb 16D

prime rate (U.S.)
1980 statistics: 1980 Mar 7H/Apr 2H/May 1H/May 12H/Jun 12H/Jul 24H/Dec 10H
1981 statistics: 1981 Aug 31H
1983 statistics: 1983 Jan 11H/Feb 25H
1984 statistics: 1984 Apr 5H/May 8H/Jun 25H/Sep 27H/Oct 16H/Oct 26H
1985 statistics: 1985 Jan 14H/May 17H/Jun 18H
1986 statistics: 1986 Aug 26H
1987 statistics: 1987 Mar 31H/May 1H/May 15H/Sep 4H/Oct 7H
1988 statistics: 1988 Feb 2H/May 11A/May 11H/Jul 14H/Aug 11H/Nov 28H
1989 statistics: 1989 Feb 10H/Jun 5H

Prince (singer) 1989 Jul 29J/Aug 26J

Prince and the Revolution (singing group) 1984 Jul 21J/Aug 25J/Sep 22J/Oct 27J/Nov 24J/Dec 22J; 1985 Jan 26J/May 25J/Jun 22J/Jul 27J; 1986 May 31J

Prince Edward Island (Canada) 1983 Mar 27I; 1986 Aug 20J; 1988 Jan 6I

Prince of Tides, The (Pat Conroy) (book) 1986 Nov 21J

Princess Bride, The (film) 1987 Oct 21J

Princess Daisy (Judith Krantz) (book) 1980 Feb 10J/Mar 9J/Apr 6J/May 4J/Jun 8J

Princeton University (New Jersey) 1980 Oct 14I; 1982 Dec 28I; 1985 Feb 25I/Jul 7J; 1988 Oct 8J

Principe *see* Sao Tome and Principe

Prinsendam (ship) 1980 Oct 4I

prisons
foreign developments: Canada 1982 Jul 25D; Chile 1987 Apr 1D; Colombia 1980 Jun 25D; Great Britain 1987 Sep 24B; Guatemala 1989 Mar 30D; Iran 1980 Dec 7C; Italy 1980 Apr 28B/Dec 29B; Peru 1982 Mar 3D; 1986 Jun 18D/Jun 27D; 1987 Feb 9D; *see also* Maze Prison

U.S. policy: construction aid 1981 Aug 17F; drugs/gambling 1982 Jan 6F; incarceration rates by race 1985 Jul 28F; national policy urged 1983 Jan 2F; privacy rights 1984 Jul 3F; refugees 1983 Jul 7F; state jurisdiction 1989 Jan 14F

U.S. riots and unrest: Alabama 1985 Apr 15F; Georgia 1987 Dec 4F; New Mexico 1980 Feb 3F; New York State 1983 Jan 11F; Pennsylvania 1981 Nov 2F; 1989 Oct 27F; Tennessee 1982 Feb 8F; 1985 Jul 2F; West Virginia 1986 Jan 1F

U.S. statistics: 1982 Nov 7F; 1983 Apr 24J; 1984 Apr 8F; 1989 Dec 3F

Prithvi (Indian missile) 1988 Feb 25E

Pritzker Architecture Prize 1983 May 16J; 1985 Apr 3J; 1986 Apr 17J; 1987 Mar 18J; 1988 May 24J; 1989 May 1J

Private Benjamin (film) 1980 Dec 3J

Private Dancer (Tina Turner) (recording) 1984 Aug 25J/Sep 22J/Oct 27J/Nov 24J/Dec 22J; 1985 Mar 30J

Private Lessons (film) 1981 Sep 2J

Private Lives (Noel Coward) (play) 1983 Mar 10J

Prix de l'Arc de Triomphe (horse race) 1986 Oct 5J; 1988 Oct 2J; 1989 Oct 8J

Prized (racehorse) 1989 Nov 4J

Prizzi's Honor (film) 1985 Jun 14J; 1986 Jan 2J/Mar 24J

Pro Bowl (football) 1981 Feb 1J; 1982 Jan 31J; 1983 Feb 6J; 1985 Jan 27J; 1986 Feb 2J; 1987 Feb 1J; 1988 Feb 7J; 1989 Jan 29J

Proconsul africanus (fossil primate) 1984 Aug 22I

Procter & Gamble Co. 1980 Sep 22I; 1982 Mar 17H/Apr 21H

Prodigal Daughter, The (Jeffrey Archer) (book) 1982 Jul 11J/Aug 8J/Sep 12J

producer price index (PPI)
1980 statistics: 1980 Mar 7H/May 9H/Nov 7H
1981 statistics: 1981 Feb 13H
1982 statistics: 1982 Feb 12H/Mar 12H/Apr 9H/Aug 13H
1983 statistics: 1983 Jan 14H/Feb 11H/Apr 15H/May 13H/Jun 15H/Aug 12H/Sep 9H/Oct 14H/Nov 10H/Dec 16H
1984 statistics: 1984 Jan 13H/Feb 10H/Mar 16H/Apr 13H/May 11H/Jun 15H/Jul 13H/Aug 10H/Sep 14H/Oct 12H/Nov 9H/Dec 14H
1985 statistics: 1985 Jan 11H/Feb 15H/Mar 15H/Apr 12H/May 10H/Jun 14H/Jul 12H/Aug 12H/Sep 13H/Oct 11H/Nov 15H/Dec 13H
1986 statistics: 1986 Jan 10H/Feb 14H/Mar 14H/Apr 11H/May 29H/Jun 13H/Jul 11H/Aug 15H/Sep 12H/Oct 10H/Nov 14H/Dec 12H
1987 statistics: 1987 Jan 9H/Feb 13H/Mar 13H/Apr 10H/May 15H/Jun 12H/Jul 12H/Aug 16H/Oct 16H/Nov 13H/Dec 11H/Dec 11H
1988 statistics: 1988 Jan 15H/Feb 12H/Mar 11F/Apr 15H/May 13H/Jun 10H/Jul 15H/Aug 12H/Sep 9H/Oct 14H/Nov 10H/Dec 16H
1989 statistics: 1989 Jan 13H/Feb 10H/Mar 17H/Apr 14H/May 12H/Jun 9H/Jul 14H/Aug 11H/Sep 15H/Oct 13H/Nov 9H

productivity, nonfarm
1983 statistics: 1983 Jul 29H/Oct 27H
1984 statistics: 1984 Jan 30H/Apr 26H/Jul 31H/Oct 29H
1985 statistics: 1985 Jan 29H/Apr 25H/Jul 25H/Oct 28H
1986 statistics: 1986 Jan 29H/Apr 28H/Jul 30H/Aug 27H/Oct 29H
1987 statistics: 1987 Feb 2H/May4H
1988 statistics: 1988 Feb 4H/Apr 4H/Nov 2H/May 2H
1989 statistics: 1989 Feb 6H/May 3H/Aug 3H/Nov 2H

Professional Bowlers Association National Championship 1989 Mar 18J

Pro Football Hall of Fame (Canton, Ohio) 1980 Aug 1J; 1982 Aug 7J; 1985 Jan 22J; 1986 Jan 28J; 1987 Jan 27J/Aug 8J; 1988 Feb 2J/Jul 30J; 1989 Jan 24J

program trading 1988 Feb 4H/Apr 6H/May 10H

Progress 18 (spacecraft) 1983 Oct 20I

Progress of Love, The (Alice Munro) (book) 1987 May 27J

Pro-Life Political Action Committee 1981 Jul 7F

Promise (Sade) (recording) 1986 Jan 29J/Feb 19J/Mar 22J/Apr 16J

Promise (TV show) 1987 Sep 20J

Proof (Dick Francis) (book) 1985 Apr 19J

propanil (herbicide) 1980 Jun 27F

property crime 1989 Aug 6F

property taxes 1982 May 5J; 1985 Mar 22H; 1986 Aug 5H; 1987 Jul 30B/Sep 16F/Dec 4B; 1988 May 9F/Aug 19F

Prophets of Regulation, The (Thomas K. McCraw) (book) 1985 Apr 24J

Proposition 103 (California) 1989 May 4H

prostitution 1985 Jul 19J/Oct 18I; 1987 Mar 24E; 1989 Sep 12F

protein synthesis 1988 May 13I

Protest (Vaclav Havel) (play) 1989 Feb 25B

Protestants 1980 Mar 24F/Nov 15J; 1982 Jan 10E; 1983 May 13J/Jun 8F/Oct 14J; 1984 Mar 6J/Nov 30J; 1989 Dec 15B; see also specific denomination (e.g., Presbyterians)

Proton (Soviet rocket) 1987 Apr 30I; 1988 Feb 18I

Proud Truth (racehorse) 1985 Nov 2J

Providence College (Rhode Island) 1985 Mar 30J

Provisional Irish Republican Army 1981 Aug 21B; 1982 Jul 20B; 1983 Sep 25B; 1984 Sep 29B/Oct 12B/Dec 13A; 1985 Jun 25B; 1986 Jun 10B/Jul 17G; 1987 May 8B/Nov 8B; 1988 Apr 28B/Aug 20B; 1989 Sep 22B; see also Sinn Fein

PS/2 (personal computer) 1988 Sep 13H

Psychiatric Association, American see American Psychiatric Association

psychiatry 1983 Jan 24F/Feb 11I; 1985 Feb 26F/Oct 2I; 1987 Mar 9I/May 26J/Sep 21I; 1989 Aug 23I/Oct 17B/Oct 17I

psychoanalysis 1980 Mar 18J; 1981 Aug 7I/Nov 5I; 1982 Jun 26I/Oct 9I; 1985 Feb 6J

psychological assessment tests 1989 Sep 13I

Psychological Operations in Guerrilla War (CIA manual) 1984 Oct 18G

PTL (Praise the Lord) ministry 1987 Mar 19J/Apr 28J/Jun 12H/Oct 8J; 1988 Apr 22H; 1989 Oct 24F

public choice theory 1986 Oct 16H

Public Citizen (consumer group) 1985 Feb 11H; 1989 Jan 18F/Aug 3H

Public Health Service, U.S. (PHS) 1980 Jan 14I; 1983 Mar 3I/Mar 15I/May 24I; 1985 May 4F; 1986 Jun 12F; 1989 Oct 17F/Dec 16F

public housing 1981 Jun 10B; 1985 Nov 20F; 1986 Jun 12H; 1987 Jun 11F; 1988 Apr 11F; 1989 Mar 29F

Public Service Co. (Indiana) 1984 Jan 16H/Jan 23H

Public Service Co. (New Hampshire) 1984 Apr 18H; 1985 Jan 25H; 1987 Jun 11H/Oct 15H; 1988 Jan 28H

Public Theater (New York City) 1986 May 18J/Nov 2J; 1987 May 28J

Puerto Rico
accidents and disasters: Dupont Plaza Hotel fire 1987 Jan 13D/Jan 29D/Jun 22F; 1988 Feb 3F; Hurricane Hugo 1989 Sep 19D
bombings: aerial navigation stations in Puerto Rico 1980 Jul 14D; buildings in New York 1982 Dec 31F; military jets in Puerto Rico 1981 Jan 12D
crime and law enforcement: ARC Armored Services robbery 1980 Nov 21D; Army instructors attacked 1980 Mar 12D
human rights: Cuban UN resolution 1987 Mar 11A
immigration and refugees: refugee camps 1980 Nov 3F
politics and government: presidential campaigns 1980 Feb 17F; 1988 Mar 20F/Apr 13F; Romero Barcelo wins gubernatorial election 1980 Dec 18D; statehood 1982 Jan 12G; 1989 Nov 14F
sports: boxing 1982 Dec 4J; high jump 1989 Jul 29J

Pulitzer Prizes 1980 Apr 14J; 1981 Apr 13J/Apr 15J; 1982 Apr 12J; 1983 Apr 18J; 1984 Apr 16J; 1985 Apr 24J; 1986 Apr 17J; 1987 Apr 16J; 1988 Mar 31J; 1989 Mar 30J

Punchline (film) 1988 Oct 19J

Punjab (India) see also Golden Temple
central government: appeals for talks 1982 Oct 19E; constitution amended to recognize Sikhism 1984 Mar 31E; direct rule 1983 Oct 6E; 1984 Apr 5E/Aug 23E; 1985 Sep 29E; 1987 May 11E/Nov 9E; 1988 Mar 23E; Gandhi (Indira) announces concessions 1983 Feb 27E; Gandhi (Rajiv) proposals on peace 1989 Mar 3E; Gandhi (Rajiv) signs accord 1985 Jul 24E; "restricted area" declared 1984 Jun 2E; White Paper issued 1984 Jul 10E
civil strife: bus passengers massacred 1986 Nov 30E; 1987 Jul 7E; general strike 1984 Feb 8E; police arrest of militants 1984 Jun 20E; police kill demonstrators 1983 Apr 4E; riots 1981 Sep 21E; Sikh party leader Longowal killed 1985 Aug 20E
elections: 1985 Sep 25E
obituaries: Longowal, Harchand Singh 1985 Aug 20E
world Sikh convention: 1984 Sep 2E

Purdue University (Lafayette, Indiana) 1982 Mar 24J

Purple Rain (film) 1984 Aug 15J/Sep 12J

Purple Rain (Prince and the Revolution) (recording) 1984 Jul 21J/Aug 25J/Sep 22J/Oct 27J/Nov 24J/Dec 22J; 1985 Jan 26J

Purple Rose of Cairo (film) 1986 Mar 16J

Pushkin Museum (Moscow) 1981 Jun 3J; 1987 Sep 2J

Pyotr Vasev (ship) 1986 Sep 1B

Pyromania (Def Leppard) (recording) 1983 Apr 13J/May 11J/Jun 15J/Jul 13J/Jul 13J/Aug 17J/Sep 14J/Oct 19J

Q

Qafzeh cave (Israel) 1988 Feb 18I

Qatar 1981 Mar 10C; 1986 Apr 26C

quahogs 1987 Dec 11I

quantum jump 1986 Oct 21I

quark (subatomic particle) 1984 Jul 3I

quasars 1986 Apr 3I; 1989 Nov 19I

Quebec (Canada) see also individual leaders in the name index (e.g., Bourassa, Robert)
accidents and disasters: blackout 1988 Apr 18D; earthquake 1988 Nov 25I; fire 1980 Jan 1D
business and industry: Bombardier Inc./Canadair Ltd. merger 1986 Aug 18D; Canadair Ltd. losses 1983 Jun 7D; fighter aircraft contract 1986 Oct 31D; U.S. energy sales 1982 Mar 19D; 1987 Jun 18D
census data: population 1982 Apr 3D
constitutional issues: 1981 Oct 2D/Nov 9D; 1982 Dec 6D; Meech Lake agreement
crime and law enforcement: illegal police department operations 1981 Jun 13D; National Assembly massacre 1984 May 8D; prison riot 1982 Jul 25D
economy: Montreal cost of living 1983 Sep 22D; stock exchange 1989 Jan 18D
environmental issues: mollusk contamination 1988 Jan 6I; New York acid rain pact 1982 Jul 26D
federal government relations: 1980 May 2D; 1984 Jul 26D; 1988 Dec 15D
francophone summit: 1987 Sep 4A
health care issues: abortion injunction lifted 1989 Aug 8D; nurses strike 1989 Sep 5D/Sep 12D
labor issues: nurses strike 1989 Sep 5D/Sep 12D; provincial employees strike 1989 Sep 14D; teachers strike settled 1980 Feb 25D
language law: 1982 Sep 8D; 1984 Jul 26D; 1985 Jan 2D; 1986 Dec 22D; 1988 Dec 15D
Meech Lake agreement see Meech Lake agreement
native peoples: 1982 Jul 8D; 1988 Jun 1D
politics and government: Drapeau reelected Montreal mayor 1982 Nov 14D; Levesque death 1987 Nov 1D; Liberal Party confederation plan 1980 Jan 10D; parliamentary elections 1989 Sep 25D; provincial elections 1985 Jun 3D/Dec 2D; provincial minister resigns 1982 Jan 6D
science and technology: combinatorial analysis problem solved 1988 Dec 20I
social service issues: child cash payments 1988 May 12D
sovereignty issue: 1980 Mar 7D/Mar 20D/May 20D; 1982 Jan 6D/Feb 14D; 1985 Jan 19D

Queen (singing group) 1980 Sep 10J/Oct 8J

Queen Elizabeth II (ship) 1982 Jun 6D

Queen of the Damned, The (Anne Rice) (book) 1988 Nov 25J/Dec 23J

Queens University (Ontario) 1981 Sep 5D

Queen Victoria Medical Center (Melbourne, Australia) 1985 Feb 22I

Quiet Riot (singing group) 1983 Oct 19J/Nov 9J/Dec 14J

Quinault Indians 1983 Jun 27H

R

Rabbit Is Rich (John Updike) (book) 1982 Apr 12J

Race Against Time (benefit event) 1986 May 25J

racial bias 1982 Jan 12F/Mar 19F/Aug 27F; 1983 Mar 24F; 1986 Jun 6E; 1987 Sep 16F; 1988 Aug 19F; see also specific minority (e.g., Black Americans)

racial quotas 1983 Apr 13C/May 25F/Oct 25F; 1984 Jan 17F; 1985 Mar 5F/Apr 2F

Racism, U.N. World Conference to Combat 1983 Aug 13A

Racketeer Influenced and Corrupt Organization Act (RICO) 1987 Jun 9H/Aug 26F; 1989 Mar 2F/Jun 26F

radial keratotomy 1984 Nov 14I

radiation 1986 May 29B/Nov 23I; 1987 Dec 18I; 1989 Dec 19I

radio see also specific broadcast (e.g., Voice of America)
business issues: FCC ownership rules 1984 Jul 26F; minority ownership 1989 Mar 31F; National Public Radio woes 1983 May 25J/Aug 2F; RKO General loses license 1987 Aug 12H
foreign issues: France 1981 Jul 3B; 1986 Sep 10B; Great Britain 1981 Sep 23H; 1987 Dec 3B; 1988 Nov 7B; Iran 1980 Oct 12C; Nicaragua 1986 Jan 1D; 1988 May 14D; Nigeria 1984 Apr 17C; Northern Ireland 1988 Oct 19B; Poland 1980 Sep 21J; 1982 Apr 12B; South Africa 1985 Nov 2C; USSR 1983 May 23B
obituaries: Bauer, Charita 1985 Feb 28J; Conried, Hans 1982 Jan 5J; Edwards, Joan 1981 Aug 27J; Fredericks, Carlton 1987 Jul 28J; Godfrey, Arthur 1983 Mar 16J; Greene, Lorne 1987 Sep 11J; Kyser, Kay 1985 Jul 23J; Murray the K 1982 Feb 21J; Plomley, Roy 1985 May 28J; Potter, Peter 1983 Apr 17J; Powers, John (Shorty) 1980 Jan 1I; Tubb, Ernest 1984 Sep 6J; Vallee, Rudy 1986 Jul 3J; Waring, Fred 1984 Jul 29J; Welles, Orson 1985 Oct 10J
people: Berg murder 1984 Jun 18F/Oct 18F; 1985 Apr 15; 1987 Nov 1F; Leary discharge 1980 Nov 1J
politics and government: Cuba broadcasting 1982 Sep 9G; Democratic ad campaign 1986 Apr 27F; live coverage in Senate 1984 Sep 21F; 1986 Feb 27F; Reagan broadcast to Soviet Union 1987 Jan 1B
programming issues: fairness doctrine 1985 Aug 7F; 1987 Jun 23F/Aug 4F; fundamentalist preaching 1980 Feb 25J; obscenity 1987 Apr 16F/Dec 24F
statistics: 1985 Feb 15J

radiocarbon testing 1988 Oct 13J

Radio City Music Hall (New York City) 1985 Feb 1J; 1989 Oct 30H

Radio Free Europe 1988 Nov 30G

Radio Liberty 1988 Nov 30G

Radio Luxembourg 1980 Sep 9C

Radio Marti (radio station) 1982 Jun 27G; 1983 Jun 9G/Sep 29G; 1985 May 20D

Radio Moscow 1987 Jan 1B

Radio-Television News Directors' Association 1980 Jul 7J

radio waves 1980 Mar 21G

radon gas 1986 Aug 14H; 1987 Aug 4H; 1988 Sep 12H/Oct 29H

Rage of Angels (Sidney Sheldon) (book) 1980 Jul 13J/Jul 17J/Sep 14J/Oct 12J; 1987 Oct 12J

Raging Bull (film) 1980 Nov 14J; 1981 Mar 30J

Raiders of the Lost Ark (film) 1981 Jun 12J/Jul 1J/Jul 29J/Sep 2J/Sep 30J/Dec 2J

railroads
  accidents and disasters: Burma 1985 Jul 24E; Chile 1986 Feb 17D; Great Britain 1986 Jul 26B; Louisiana 1982 Sep 28I; Mexico 1982 Jul 11D; Texas 1984 Apr 28F; United States 1988 Jan 20H; USSR 1989 Jun 3B
  bombings: Italy 1980 Aug 2B/Aug 6B; Switzerland 1981 Jul 22B
  business issues: Canadian deregulation 1988 Jan 1D; Polish fares 1988 Feb 1D; U.S. antitrust violations 1981 Oct 20H; U.S. deregulation 1980 Oct 14H; 1983 Jan 6H; 1984 Sep 18H; Yugoslavia fares 1988 Aug 4B
  construction: Albania 1986 Aug 6B; Brazil 1987 May 18D; Canada 1989 May 4D; China 1983 Jul 20E; Japan 1988 Mar 13E/Apr 10E; USSR 1984 Sep 29B
  crime issues: Brazil 1987 May 18D; China 1989 Jun 15E
  English Channel Tunnel *see* English Channel Tunnel
  health and safety issues: Canada 1986 Feb 16B; United States 1982 Aug 25H; U.S. drug testing 1988 Feb 11F/Oct 9F; 1989 Mar 21F
  labor issues: Canada 1987 Aug 28D; France 1986 Dec 18B; Great Britain 1980 Apr 29B; 1982 Feb 18B/Jun 28B/Jul 18B; 1989 Jun 28B; South Africa 1987 Apr 22C; United States 1980 Apr 1H/Apr 2H/Sep 1H; 1981 May 5H; 1982 Jul 8H/Sep 22H; 1985 Jun 22H; 1987 Sep 1F; USSR 1988 Mar 27B
  land rights: Alaska ownership 1985 Jan 5H; Crow's Nest Pass Agreement 1982 Feb 13D/Mar 26D; 1983 Feb 1D/Nov 14B
  mergers and acquisitions: Conrail 1984 Jun 18H; Norfolk and Western/Southern 1982 Mar 25H; Santa Fe/Southern Pacific 1983 Oct 4H; 1986 Jul 24H; Union Pacific/Missouri Pacific 1980 Jan 8H; Union Pacific/Missouri Pacific/Western Pacific 1980 Sep 15H; 1982 Sep 13H

Railway Labor Act 1982 Jul 8H

Rainbow Warrior incident 1985 Jul 10E/Jul 23E/Aug 26B/Sep 20B/Sep 25B/Nov 4E/Dec 23B; 1986 Jul 7A; 1987 Oct 2B

Rainier Bancorp. 1987 Feb 24H

Rain Man (film) 1988 Dec 16J/Dec 28J; 1989 Jan 25J/Jan 28J/Feb 22J/Mar 29J

rains and rainstorms *see also* hurricanes
  Africa: 1985 Feb 23C/Dec 16C
  Atlantic Ocean: 1986 May 14J
  Australia: 1980 Apr 24E; 1983 Jun 16I
  Bangladesh: 1989 Apr 26I/Aug 5I
  Brazil: 1988 Feb 7I/Feb 23D
  Canada: 1982 Feb 15D; 1986 Feb 20I; 1988 Apr 18D
  China: 1985 Aug 8I
  Djibouti: 1981 Mar 21D
  Ecuador: 1983 May 8I
  El Salvador: 1982 Sep 20I
  Great Britain: 1986 Jun 20I
  South Korea: 1984 Oct 1E
  Spain: 1983 Aug 26I
  Sri Lanka: 1989 Jun 6E
  Sudan: 1988 Aug 5I
  United States: Alabama 1983 Apr 12I; California 1983 Jan 30I/Mar 5I; Georgia 1982 Apr 2I; Gulf coast 1983 May 23I; Kentucky 1984 May 8I; Louisiana 1983 Apr 12I; Mid-Atlantic area 1983 May 23I; Mississippi 1983 Apr 6I/Apr 12I; New Jersey 1984 May 5I; Ohio 1982 Apr 2I; Oklahoma 1984 May 27I; Tennessee 1983 Apr 12I; 1984 May 8I; Texas 1982 Apr 2I; Western U.S. 1986 Feb 20I; West Virginia 1984 May 8I; Wyoming 1985 Aug 1I

Raising Hell (Run-D.M.C.) (recording) 1986 Sep 17J

Rajneeshpuram (Oregon commune) 1983 Oct 6F

Rambo: First Blood Part II (film) 1985 Jun 12J/Jul 17J

Rambo III (film) 1988 Jun 15J

Ran (film) 1986 Jan 2J

Rancho Seco nuclear power plant (California) 1989 Jun 6H

Rand Corp. 1984 Jun 7F; 1985 Feb 2F; 1986 Aug 20F

Randolph Caldecott Medal (children's literature) 1985 Jan 7J; 1986 Jan 20J; 1987 Jan 19J; 1989 Jan 9J

Random House Inc. 1983 Aug 2J/Dec 12J; 1985 Aug 28J

Random Winds (Belva Plain) (book) 1980 Jun 8J/Jul 13J/Aug 17J/Sep 14J

Rangers, U.S. Army 1983 Oct 30G

rape 1980 Jan 15F; 1984 Sep 11F; 1985 Mar 24F/Aug 25F; 1986 Jun 13B; 1989 Apr 19F/Jun 21F/Oct 11F/Oct 19F/Oct 21F

Rapid Deployment Force 1980 Nov 28G; 1981 Nov 14G

Rappin' (film) 1985 May 15J

Rapport Prize (literature) 1986 Apr 12J

Rath Packaging Co. 1983 Nov 1H

"Rat Pack" 1988 Mar 13J

rat poison 1986 Mar 21F

Rattle and Hum (U2) (recording) 1988 Dec 31J

Raw and the Cooked, The (Fine Young Cannibals) (recording) 1989 May 27J/Jun 24J/Jul 29J

Raw Deal (film) 1986 Jun 18J

Raymark Industries Inc. 1986 Dec 8H

Ray Miller Inc. 1983 Jan 22F

razor blades 1989 Apr 16B

RCA Corp. 1980 Feb 20I/May 6J; 1982 Mar 4J/Mar 8H; 1985 Aug 5J/Dec 11H

RC-135 (aircraft) 1983 Sep 4B/Sep 4G/Sep 5G

Reading Le Figaro (Mary Cassatt) (painting) 1983 May 17J

"Reaganomics" 1982 Mar 23F; 1986 Apr 22H

Reagan Record, The (Urban Institute) 1984 Aug 15H

real estate 1988 Apr 5H/May 20E/Dec 23E; 1989 May 16F/Dec 17H

Real Thing, The (Tom Stoppard) (play) 1984 Jun 3J

recalls 1980 Sep 22I; 1982 Apr 8I/Jul 29H/Aug 10H; 1983 Dec 12J; 1984 Nov 26H

Reckless (Bryan Adams) (recording) 1985 Jul 27J/Aug 24J

Reckless (film) 1984 Feb 8J

recombinant DNA research 1986 Sep 29I

Recording Arts and Sciences, National Academy of *see* Grammy Awards

Recording Industry Association of America 1985 Aug 5J; 1986 Feb 27H

recordings *see individual titles (e.g., Asia)*

Recruit scandal 1989 Feb 13E/Apr 11E/Apr 25E/Apr 27E/May 29E/Jun 2E

recycling 1983 Mar 29H

Red Army Faction (European terrorist group) 1981 Sep 2B

Red Brigades (Italian terrorist group) 1980 Apr 28B/May 12B/Dec 12B; 1981 Apr 4B/Jul 24B/Dec 17B; 1982 Jan 28B; 1983 Jan 24B

Red Cross, American *see* American Red Cross

Red Cross, International
  Angola: 1985 Mar 14C
  Cambodia: 1980 Aug 4E/Dec 16E
  Cuba: 1983 Nov 2D
  Guatemala: 1989 Dec 27D
  Indonesia: 1982 Mar 4E
  Iran 1980 Jun 14A; 1983 May 11C; 1984 Mar 7C/Nov 24C:
    Iraq: 1983 May 11C
    Israel: 1983 Dec 13C
  Lebanon: 1982 Jun 17C/Aug 18C/Sep 18C; 1988 Dec 20C
  North Korea: 1984 Oct 1E; 1985 Apr 4E/Sep 20E
  South Africa: 1986 Oct 25A
  South Korea: 1984 Oct 1E; 1985 Apr 4E/Sep 20E

Red Dawn (film) 1984 Aug 15J

Red Feet Indians (Brazil) 1987 Sep 30E

Red Flag (Venezuelan terrorist group) 1980 Dec 6D

redistricting 1981 Jun 10F; 1982 Jul 3F; 1983 Jun 22F; 1986 Mar 18F/Sep 22F; 1989 Jan 17F

Redoubt Volcano (Alaska) 1989 Dec 14I

Red Phoenix (Larry Bond) (book) 1989 Jun 30J/Jul 28J/Aug 25J

Reds (film) 1982 Jan 6J/Feb 17J/Mar 29J

Red Square (Moscow) 1983 Nov 5B; 1984 Feb 14B; 1985 May 9B; 1987 Mar 26J/May 29B/Sep 4B/Nov 7B; 1988 Aug 3B

Redstone (Colorado) 1981 Apr 15H

Red Storm Rising (Tom Clancy) (book) 1986 Aug 29J/Sep 26J/Oct 31J/Nov 21J/Dec 26J; 1987 Jan 23J/Feb 27J/Mar 27J/Apr 24J

Reflections of a Public Man (Jim Wright) (book) 1988 Jun 6F

Reflex (Dick Francis) (book) 1981 May 24J

refrigerators 1986 Jan 2B

refugee camps

Gaza Strip (Palestinians): 1988 Jan 24C

Honduras (Nicaraguans): 1983 Dec 1D

Honduras (Salvadorans): 1985 Aug 29D; 1987 Oct 11D

Hong Kong (Vietnamese): 1989 Sep 2E

Hungary (East Germans): 1989 Sep 10B

India: 1989 Aug 12E

Lebanon (Palestinians): 1983 Nov 3C/Nov 16C; 1985 May 19C/May 30C/Jun 17C; 1988 Jan 16C; Sabra and Shatila

Mexico (Guatemalans): 1984 May 30D

Pakistan (Afghans): 1984 Dec 20E

Thailand (Cambodians): 1980 Jan 30E/Feb 24E; 1988 May 1E

Uganda: 1980 Jun 5C

U.S. (Cubans): 1980 Jun 7F/Aug 5F/Aug 29D/Nov 3F

U.S. (Haitians): 1980 Nov 3F; 1982 Jun 29F/Oct 22F

Refugees, U.N. High Commissioner for (UNHCR) 1981 Oct 14A; 1982 Apr 28B/Aug 2D; 1985 Sep 7A/Dec 10A; 1989 Sep 14E

Regional Organization for the Protection of the Marine Environment 1983 Apr 7C

Rehabilitation Act (1973) 1986 Dec 8F

Reichstag fire (1933) 1980 Dec 29B; 1981 Apr 22B

reindeer meat 1986 Sep 19B

Rely tampons 1980 Sep 22I; 1982 Apr 21H

Remains of the Day, The (Kazuo Ishiguro) (book) 1989 Oct 26J

Remo Williams: The Adventure Begins (film) 1985 Oct 23J

Renamo *see* Mozambique National Resistance

Renault 1980 Sep 24H; 1986 Nov 17B; 1987 Jul 22B

Rensselaer Polytechnic Institute (New York) 1985 Mar 30J

rental housing 1983 Jul 13F; 1987 Jul 6F

rent boycotts 1986 Aug 26C; 1989 Apr 24C

rent control 1982 Feb 28F; 1988 Feb 24F

rent increases 1980 Oct 15C; 1988 Feb 1B

Reorganized Church of Jesus Christ Latter Day Saints 1984 Apr 5J

Reo Speedwagon (singing group) 1981 Feb 11J/Mar 4J/Apr 8J/May 6J/May 27J/Jul 8J/Aug 5J

Repeat Offender (Richard Marx) (recording) 1989 Aug 26J/Sep 30J

Repentance (film) 1986 Nov 16J

Republican Mainstream Committee 1986 Apr 26F

Republican National Committee 1982 Nov 6F; 1986 Jun 8F/Jun 26F/Oct 7F/Oct 20F; 1987 Jan 2F/Jan 23F/Jul 23F

Republican National Convention
  Detroit (1980): 1980 Jul 9F/Jul 14F-15F/Jul 17F
  Dalles (1984): 1984 Aug 20F-22F
  New Orleans (1988): 1988 Aug 15F-16F/Aug 18F

Republican Party 1980 Jan 14F; 1981 Jan 5F/Jun 13F; 1982 Mar 14F/Nov 2F; 1983 Apr 25F; 1985 May 6F/Jun

29F; 1986 Apr 26F/Jun 8F; 1987 Feb 18F

Republic Steel Corp. 1984 Mar 21H

research and development 1986 Sep 7I; 1988 Dec 21H

reservoirs 1985 Aug 4H; 1986 Apr 20E; 1988 Feb 23H

Resources Conservation and Recovery Act of 1976 1984 Nov 8H

restaurants *see also* fast-food restaurants
  crimes: 1983 Nov 20F; 1984 Mar 26F; California 1984 Jul 4F; Paris 1982 Aug 9B/Aug 10B; South Africa 1986 Jun 14C; West Berlin 1982 Jan 15C
  health issues: 1985 Aug 9H/Nov 14I; 1988 Jul 24F; 1989 Aug 22H
  hours: 1988 Aug 22B

retail sales: 1983 May 11H/Jun 10H; 1987 May 15B/Dec 28H; 1988 Jan 14H; 1989 Jan 13H/Nov 14H

Retin-A (drug) 1988 Jan 22I/Jul 5I

retirement
  financial issues: savings account 1981 Sep 22H; Social Security 1982 Nov 5H; 1983 Mar 9F; 1988 Nov 15F; women's benefits 1983 Jul 6F; 1984 May 22F/Aug 23H
  government guidelines: federal system 1986 Jun 6F; military system 1985 Feb 5H; 1986 Jul 2G
  legal issues: mandatory 1983 Aug 17F

Retirement Equity Act of 1984 1984 Aug 23H

Retirement Service Center (HUD) 1989 Jul 6F

Return of the Jedi (Joan D. Vinge) (book/film) 1983 Jun 1J/Jun 12J/Jul 10J/Aug 14J/Sep 11J/Jul 6J/Aug 10J/Sep 7J; 1984 Jan 11J

Reunion 1989 May 6J

Revenge of the Nerds (film) 1984 Aug 15J

Revolutionary Cells (West German terrorist group) 1982 Jun 1B

Revolutionary Justice Organization (Lebanese terrorist group) 1986 Oct 11B/Dec 24C

Reye's syndrome 1985 Jan 23I; 1986 Mar 7F

Reynolds Metals Co. 1983 Dec 13H; 1988 Dec 4H

R.H. Macy & Co. *see* Macy & Co., R. H.

Rhine River 1986 Nov 1B/Nov 12B; 1987 Jan 10B/Dec 28B

rhinoviruses 1989 Mar 10I

Rhode Island 1980 Jun 3F; 1982 Nov 3F; 1983 Jan 25F/Sep 12F; 1984 Mar 13F; 1985 Sep 18F; 1988 Nov 8F; 1989 Jun 24H/Sep 15H

Rhyme 'N' Reason (racehorse) 1988 Apr 9J

Rhythm (racehorse) 1989 Nov 4J

rice 1980 Mar 21E/Apr 12A/Jun 27F; 1981 Jul 17C; 1982 Dec 9H; 1983 Apr 28I; 1985 Oct 21E; 1988 May 12E

Richard King Mellon foundation 1980 Dec 20H

Richard Pryor—Here and Now (film) 1983 Nov 2J

Richard Pryor Live on the Sunset Strip (film) 1982 Apr 7J

Rich & Co., Marc *see* Marc Rich & Co.

RICO *see* Racketeer Influenced and Corrupt Organization

Right Stuff, The (Tom Wolfe) (book/film) 1980 May 1J; 1983 Nov 2J rimantadine (drug) 1982 Sep 2I

Risen Star (racehorse) 1988 May 21J/Jun 11J

Rise of Theodore Roosevelt, The (Edmund Morris) (book) 1980 Apr 14J

Risky Business (film) 1983 Aug 10J/Sep 7J

Ritalin (drug) 1988 Apr 15F

Ritz Paris Hemingway Award (literature) 1985 Mar 29J; 1986 Apr 7J; 1987 Apr 6J; 1988 Mar 28J

Rivals (Janet Dailey) (book) 1989 Feb 24J

River, The (Bruce Springsteen) (recording) 1980 Dec 3J

River, The (film) 1985 May 6H

river blindness (onchocerciasis) 1987 Oct 21I

rivers 1986 Oct 30H; 1987 Aug 14H; *see also specific tributary* (e.g., Mississippi River)

Riverside County General Hospital (California) 1983 Dec 26F

Rizzoli Editore S.p.A. 1983 Feb 18B/Aug 28B

R.J. Reynolds Industries Inc. 1982 Jul 29H; 1985 Jun 2H/Sep 27H/Dec 23F

R.J. Reynolds Tobacco Co. 1986 Jun 16H/Aug 6H

RJR Nabisco Inc. 1987 Sep 14H; 1988 Oct 20H/Nov 3H/Nov 30H

RKO General Inc. 1987 Aug 12H

RNA (ribonucleic acid) 1984 Aug 31I; 1988 Nov 16I; 1989 Oct 12I

Road House (film) 1989 May 31J

Road Warrior, The (film) 1982 Sep 15J

robberies and thefts
  Carter papers: 1984 Jun 25F
  foreign incidents: Argentina 1980 Dec 25J; Australia 1989 Apr 5E; Canada 1986 Nov 17D; France 1985 Oct 27J; Great Britain 1983 Apr 1B/Nov 26B; Iceland 1984 Feb 18B; Italy 1984 Mar 24B
  historic documents: 1987 Aug 18J
  IBM secrets theft: 1983 Feb 8H/Dec 21H
  International Diamond theft: 1981 Dec 5H
  NYC gold heist: 1983 Apr 2F
  Sentry Armored Courier robbery: 1982 Dec 12H; 1983 Feb 2F/Feb 18F/Dec 7F; 1985 Mar 7F
  statistics: 1989 Oct 29F
  Wells Fargo Armored Car robbery: 1985 Apr 29F/May 30F

Robert E. Ginna nuclear power plant (Rochester, New York) 1982 Jan 26I

Robert F. Kennedy Human Rights Award 1984 Nov 20G; 1988 Sep 21C; 1989 Oct 18A

Robins Co., A. H. *see* Dalkon Shield

Robocop (film) 1987 Aug 12J

Robot Industries Association 1985 Jun 3H

robots 1985 Jun 3H

Roche Laboratories (Hoffmann-La Roche Inc.) 1988 May 26I

Rock and Roll Hall of Fame 1985 Aug 5J; 1986 Jan 23J; 1989 Jan 18J

Rockefeller Center (New York City) 1985 Feb 5H/Jul 29H; 1989 Oct 30H

Rockefeller Foundation 1983 Jul 25J

Rockefeller Group Inc. 1985 Feb 5H/Jul 29H; 1989 Oct 30H

Rockettes (dance troupe) 1985 Feb 1J

rock paintings 1987 Mar 31I

rocks 1980 Apr 2I

Rock Star (Jackie Collins) (book) 1988 Apr 29J/May 27J

Rockwell International Corp. 1982 Jan 20G; 1984 Sep 4G; 1985 Dec 11G; 1987 Dec 1I; 1989 Mar 6G/Sep 21H/Sep 22H

Rocky Flats nuclear weapons plant (Denver, Colo.) 1984 Apr 23H; 1989 Jun 6G/Sep 21H/Sep 22H/Oct 6H/Dec 1H

Rocky II (film) 1980 Feb 6J

Rocky III (film/soundtrack) 1982 Jun 9J/Jul 7J/Jul 11J; 1983 Jan 19J

Rocky IV (film) 1985 Dec 11J; 1986 Jan 22J

Rocky Mountain Arsenal (Denver, Colo.) 1988 Feb 1H/Dec 19H

rodents 1984 Sep 24I

Roe v. Wade (1973) 1983 Jun 15F; 1986 Jun 11F; 1989 Jan 9F/Apr 19F/Jul 3F

Roe v. Wade (TV show) 1989 Sep 17J

Rogaine (drug) 1988 Aug 17H

Rogers Pass Tunnel (Canada) 1989 May 4D

Rohm & Haas Co. 1980 Jun 27F

Rolling Stones (singing group) 1980 Aug 13J/Sep 10J; 1981 Sep 9J/Sep 30J/Nov 11J/Dec 9J; 1989 Jan 18J/Sep 30J/Oct 28J/Dec 25J

Rollins Environmental Services Inc. 1987 Feb 19H

Roll with It (Steve Winwood) (recording) 1988 Aug 27J/Sep 24J

Romancing the Stone (film) 1984 Apr 11J/May 9J

Romania *see also individual leaders in the name index* (e.g., Ceausescu, Nicolae)
  accidents and disasters: earthquake 1986 Aug 31I; pleasure boat/barge collision 1989 Sep 10B
  economy: consumer prices 1982 Feb 14B; energy crisis 1987 Oct 5B/Nov 15B; foreign debt 1982 Mar 3B
  foreign relations: Balkan nation conference 1988 Feb 23B; Hungary 1988 Jun 27B; 1989 Mar 9B; Iran 1980 Apr 23A; USSR 1980 Mar 14B
  government and politics: Ceausescu executed 1989 Dec 25B; Communist Party conference 1987 Dec 14B; government and party shakeup 1982 May 21B; government overthrown 1989 Dec 15B; Iliescu named interim president 1989 Dec 26B
  human rights: Nadia Comaneci defects 1989 Nov 29J; UN sets probe 1989 Mar 9B
  international organizations: Comecon summit 1984 Jun 14A; IMF 1982 Apr 24B; United Nations 1989 Mar 9B/Oct 18A
  obituaries: Ceausescu, Elena 1989 Dec 25B; Ceausescu, Nicolae 1989 Dec 25B; Helen, Queen 1982 Nov 28B
  sports: Olympics 1980 Jul 31J; 1984 Aug 12J; running 1989 Jul 10J; tennis 1980 Jun 7J
  U.S. relations: 1982 Feb 21G/Feb 27B/Aug 10H/Oct 7F; 1984 Mar 14G; 1985 May 15B/Dec 3G; 1988 Feb 26A; 1989 May 2H

Romantic Comedy (film) 1983 Oct 12J

Rome (Italy) 1980 Dec 12B; 1981 May 13J/Oct 25B; 1982 Oct 9B; 1983 Oct 22B; 1984 Oct 25B; 1985 Feb 3B/May

27B/Sep 25B; 1986 Apr 2B/Apr 13J; 1989 Dec 9J

Rome airport massacre (1985) 1985 Dec 27A; 1986 May 21B; 1987 Feb 5B; 1988 Feb 12B

Ronald Reagan Presidential Foundation 1987 Apr 23F

roofing felt 1986 Jan 23H

Room with a View, A (film) 1986 Mar 7J; 1987 Mar 22J

Rose, The (Bette Midler) (recording) 1980 Jul 9J

Rose Bowl (football) 1980 Jan 1J; 1982 Jan 1J; 1983 Jan 1J; 1984 Jan 2J; 1985 Jan 1J; 1986 Jan 1J; 1987 Jan 1J; 1988 Jan 1J; 1989 Jan 2J

roses 1986 Oct 7J

Rose Theater (London) 1989 Mar 3J/May 14J

Roussel-Uclaf S.A. 1988 Oct 26I/Oct 28I

rowing 1985 Jul 7J; 1986 Jul 6J; 1987 Jul 5J; 1988 Jun 11J; 1989 Mar 25J

Roxanne (film) 1987 Jun 19J; 1988 Jan 3J

Royal Academy (London) 1984 Dec 19J

Royal Ballet (London) 1985 Jun 21J

Royal Court Theater (London) 1987 Mar 21J

Royal Dutch/Shell Group of Companies 1983 Aug 23A; 1989 Aug 19I

Royal Perth Yacht Club of Australia 1988 Sep 8J

Royal Philharmonic Orchestra 1981 Dec 9J; 1982 Jan 20J/Feb 24J/Mar 17J

RU 486 (drug) 1986 Dec 18I; 1987 Oct 2I; 1988 Oct 26I/Oct 28I

rubber 1981 Mar 3I; 1988 Jun 8H

rubella (German measles) 1984 Sep 23I

Rufen (drug) 1984 May 18H

rugby 1980 Jun 20J

Run-D.M.C. (singing group) 1986 Sep 17J

Running Scared (film) 1986 Jul 9J

Rupp Trophy (basketball) 1982 Mar 26J

Rural Solidarity 1981 Feb 1B/Feb 10B/Apr 17B

Rush (singing group) 1981 Apr 8J/May 27J; 1982 Oct 13J

Russia House, The (John le Carre) (book) 1989 Jun 30J/Jul 28J/Aug 25J/Sep 25J

Russian Orthodox Church 1988 Jun 5J

Rustler's Rhapsody (film) 1985 May 15J

Rutgers University (New Brunswick, N.J.) 1982 Mar 28J; 1985 Mar 27F

Ruthless People (film) 1986 Jul 9J

Ruth Lilly Poetry Prize 1986 Jun 6J; 1987 Jul 4J; 1988 Jun 3J; 1989 Jun 2J

Rwanda 1985 Dec 26I; 1986 Aug 21C/Dec 18C; 1988 Aug 22C

Ryder Cup (golf) 1987 Sep 27J; 1989 Sep 24J

S

SA-2 (missile) 1985 Dec 15C

SA-5 (missile) 1985 Dec 21G

SA-7 (missile) 1986 Dec 31C

Sabbath 1985 Jun 26F

Sabra and Shatila refugee camps *see* Beirut refugee camp massacre

Sacahuista (racehorse) 1987 Nov 21J

saccharin (artifical sweetener) 1980 Mar 6I; 1983 Apr 13I

Sacred Congregation for Education (Vatican) 1980 Jan 15J

Sade (singer) 1986 Jan 29J/Feb 19J

Sadler's Wells Royal Ballet 1989 Jan 12J

Safe Drinking Water Act of 1986 1987 Jun 24H

Saga of Baby Divine, The (Bette Midler) (book) 1983 Dec 18J

Saharan Arab Democratic Republic *see* Western Sahara

Sailing (Christopher Cross) (recording) 1981 Feb 25J

Rose, The (Bette Midler) (recording) 1980 Jul 9J

St. Clair Correctional Facility (Odenville, Ala.) 1985 Apr 15F

St. Clair River 1985 Dec 15D; 1986 Jan 15D

St. James Theater (New York City) 1980 Apr 30J

St. John's University (New York, N.Y.) 1986 Mar 1J; 1989 Mar 29J

St. Kitts-Nevis 1983 Sep 18D; 1984 Jun 20D; 1987 May 31D; 1989 Mar 21D

St. Lawrence Island (Alaska) 1988 Feb 11G

St. Lawrence Seaway 1984 Dec 9I

St. Lawrence University (Canton, New York) 1988 Apr 2J

St. Louis Cardinals (baseball team) 1981 Oct 5J; 1982 Oct 10J/Oct 20J/Oct 25J; 1985 Nov 18J/Nov 27J; 1986 Nov 24J; 1987 Oct 4J/Oct 14J/Oct 25J

St. Louis University (Missouri) 1989 Mar 29J

St. Lucia 1987 May 31D

St. Patrick's Cathedral (New York City) 1989 Dec 10F

St. Patrick's Day parade (New York City) 1983 Mar 17J

St. Paul (Minnesota) 1985 Dec 23G

St. Paul's Cathedral (London) 1981 Jul 29B

St.-Pierre and Miquelon 1988 Apr 20D

St. Regis Corp. 1984 Jul 31H

St. Vincent and the Grenadines 1984 Jul 25D; 1987 May 31D

St. Elsewhere (TV show) 1985 Sep 12J; 1986 Sep 21J

St. George and the Dragon (Margaret Hodges) (book) 1985 Jan 7J

Saint-Gobain S.A. 1986 Sep 10B

St. Louis Sun (newspaper) 1989 Sep 25F

St. Petersburg Times (newspaper) 1984 Oct 28F

Salem 1 nuclear power plant (Lower Alloways Creek, N.J.) 1983 May 6H/May 27J

Salesians (Roman Catholic order) 1988 Dec 15D

sales tax 1987 Mar 8E/Apr 23E/May 13E; 1989 Apr 1E

Salk Institute (California) 1982 Oct 29I

Sallie Mae *see* Student Loan Marketing Association, U.S.

salmon 1989 May 7F/Nov 6D

salmonella 1984 Sep 5I; 1985 May 7I

Salomon Brothers Inc. 1980 Feb 22H; 1981 Apr 22H/Aug 3H; 1985 Jul 9H; 1987 Jun 8H/Oct 12H/Dec 4H; 1988 Apr 1H

Salsa (film) 1988 May 18J

SALT I 1980 Sep 14B; 1981 May 19G

SALT II 1980 Mar 14G/Mar 19A; 1981 May 19G; 1982 Apr 9G/May 30G/Nov 26G; 1984 Dec 3G; 1985 May 9B/Jun

7B/Oct 22G; 1986 Jun 30B/Jul 22A/Jul 30A/Nov 11G/Nov 28B/Nov 28G/Dec 5G; 1987 Mar 25G

Salvador (film) 1986 Mar 5J

Salvadoran Popular Liberation Forces (FPL) 1983 May 27D

Salvation Army 1986 May 2A

Salyut 6 (Soviet space station) 1980 Apr 9I/May 26I/Jul 24I/Sep 18I/Nov 27I/Dec 10I; 1981 Mar 10A/Mar 13I/Mar 22I/May 26I/Jun 19I; 1982 Apr 13I

Salyut 7 (Soviet space station) 1982 Apr 13I/May 13I/May 17I/Jun 24I/Jul 2I; 1983 Apr 20I/Oct 20I/Nov 23I; 1984 Apr 11I; 1985 Aug 6I/Sep 17I/Nov 21I; 1986 May 6I; 1987 Feb 6I

Samana Cay (Bahamas) 1986 Oct 6J

Samoa 1983 Jan 31I; Western Samoa

Samuel B. Roberts (ship) 1988 Apr 14C

San Antonio Spurs (basketball team) 1987 Jun 22J

sanctuary movement 1985 Jan 14F/Feb 21F/Dec 23G; 1986 May 1F/Jul 2F

Sandia National Laboratory (New Mexico) 1984 May 16I; 1985 Dec 11I

San Diego Chargers (football team) 1980 Dec 13J; 1982 Jan 2J/Jan 10J

San Diego Padres (baseball team) 1984 Sep 30J/Oct 7J/Oct 14J; 1985 Jul 16J/Aug 25J; 1987 Nov 4J; 1989 Nov 14J

San Diego State University (California) 1987 Dec 6J

San Diego Wild Animal Park 1988 Aug 29H

San Diego Yacht Club 1988 Sep 8J; 1989 Mar 28J/Sep 19J

San Diego Zoo 1983 Apr 5I

Sandoz AG 1987 Dec 28B

Sands of Time, The (Sidney Sheldon) (book) 1988 Nov 25J/Dec 23J; 1989 Jan 27J/Feb 24J

San Francisco (California)
  accidents and disasters: actresses injured in car crash 1982 Sep 5J; earthquakes 1986 Mar 31I; 1989 Oct 17I/Oct 26I
  AIDS/homosexuality issues: 1984 Apr 9I/Oct 15F/Nov 22F/Nov 28F; 1988 Jun 3I
  celebrations: Golden Gate Bridge anniversary 1987 May 24F
  crime and law enforcement: gun-control ordinance 1982 Jul 28F/Aug 29F; Liu slaying 1985 Feb 27E
  economy and business: Bank of America fined 1986 Jan 2H; cost of living 1988 Jun 28A; Crocker National purchased 1981 Aug 25H; Genentech to market TPA 1987 Nov 13I; state tax changes 1980 Mar 8H
  environmental issues: workplace smoking regulations 1983 Jun 3F
  family issues: AIDS/homosexuality 1984 Apr 9I/Oct 15F/Nov 22F/Nov 28F; 1988 Jun 3I; "domestic partnerships" 1982 Jul 5F
  foreign issues: Elizabeth II/Philip visit 1983 Feb 26G
  labor issues: "comparable pay" 1987 Mar 18F; Kaiser strike settled 1986 Dec 11H; workplace smoking regulations 1983 Jun 3F
  medicine and health care: 1984 Apr 9I/Oct 15F/Nov 22F/Nov 28F; 1986 Jan 9I; 1988 Jun 3I
  obituaries: Kaufman, Bob 1986 Jan 12J; White, Dan 1985 Oct 21F

politics and government: Agnos elected mayor 1987 Dec 8F; city planning code 1985 Jul 2F; Democratic convention (1984) 1983 Apr 21F; 1984 Apr 23F/Jul 16F/Jul 18F; Feinstein reelected mayor 1983 Nov 8F; state tax changes 1980 Mar 8H

religious issues: papal visit 1987 Sep 10J; sanctuary movement 1985 Dec 23G

San Francisco, University of (California) 1980 Nov 18J

San Francisco 49ers (football team) 1982 Jan 3J/Jan 10J/Jan 24J; 1984 Jan 8J; 1985 Jan 20J; 1988 Jan 9J; 1989 Jan 8J/Jan 22J

San Francisco Bay National Wildlife Refuge 1988 Oct 28H

San Francisco Examiner (newspaper) 1984 Oct 28F

San Francisco Giants (baseball) 1987 Oct 4J/Oct 14J; 1989 Aug 10J/Aug 15J/Oct 9J/Oct 28J/Nov 21J

San Francisco Giants (football) 1985 Jan 6J

San Jose Pact (1980) 1983 Jul 17D

San Marino Grand Prix (auto race) 1987 May 3J; 1988 May 1J; 1989 Apr 23J

San Quentin Prison (California) 1986 Jun 27F; 1988 Mar 10F

Santa Anita Handicap (horse race) 1985 Mar 3J

Santa Clara University (California) 1989 Dec 3J

Santa Claus: The Movie (film) 1985 Dec 11J

Santa Fe Industries Inc. 1983 Oct 4H/Dec 13H; 1986 Jul 24H

Santa Fe International Corp. 1981 Oct 5H/Oct 26H; 1984 May 16A

Santa Monica Bay (California) 1988 Jan 22H

Sao Tome and Principe 1988 Mar 9C

Sarah, Plain and Tall (Patricia MacLachlan) (book) 1986 Jan 20J

Sara Lee Corp. 1988 Dec 5H

Saratoga (ship) 1985 Oct 10C

Sarcee Indians (Canada) 1989 Jul 10D

Sarcophagus (Vladimir Gubaryev) (play) 1987 Sep 18J

Sarsat (satellite) 1983 Mar 28I

Sarum (Edward Rutherford) (book) 1987 Sep 23J

Sasetru (Argentinian company) 1981 Feb 9D

Saskatchewan (Canada) 1982 Apr 26D; 1988 Apr 4D

SAT *see* Scholastic Aptitude Test

Satanic Verses, The (Salman Rushdie) (book) 1988 Oct 7E/Nov 8J; 1989 Feb 14C/Feb 17C/Feb 24A/Mar 7A/Mar 31J/Apr 28J/May 3C/May 26J

Saving All My Love for You (Whitney Houston) (recording) 1986 Feb 25J

Say Anything (film) 1989 Apr 26J

SBHU Holdings Inc. 1982 Jul 1H

Scanners (film) 1981 Feb 11J

Scarecrow (John Cougar Mellencamp) (recording) 1985 Oct 26J/Nov 30J/Dec 21J; 1986 Jan 29J/Mar 22J

Scarface (film) 1983 Nov 8J; 1984 Jan 11J

Scenic Rivers System 1985 Apr 26H

Schering Corp. 1980 Dec 14F

Schiavone Construction Co. 1982 May 18F

schisms 1988 Jun 30J

schizophrenia 1980 Jan 10I

Sep 15C; United States 1980 Jul 8C/Oct 5C/Oct 11G; 1981 Mar 6C/Nov 2G; 1982 Feb 9G; 1984 May 29G; 1986 Mar 11G/May 7G; 1987 Jan 21G/Oct 8C; *see also* AWACS

business and industry: petrochemical complex 1980 Jul 9C

crime and law enforcement: bombings 1985 May 18C; Khashoggi 1989 Jul 19J; riots 1987 Jul 31C

Death of a Princess controversy 1980 May 12J/May 22B

defense and armed forces 1980 Jan 1C

executions: 1980 Jan 9C; 1989 Sep 21C

family issues: Fassi support payments 1982 Mar 16J

foreign relations: Brazil 1984 Oct 9A; Egypt 1982 Oct 5G; 1988 Jan 9C; Great Britain 1980 Jul 28A; Iran 1984 Jun 5C/Jul 24A; 1988 Apr 26C; Iraq 1980 Nov 20C; 1981 Jul 16C; Israel 1980 May 27C; 1981 Apr 23C/Aug 11C/Nov 1C; 1982 Jan 4C; Jordan 1980 Dec 3C; Lebanon 1981 Jun 30C; 1983 May 17C/Aug 16C/Sep 25C/Oct 5C/Nov 23C/Dec 18C; 1984 Feb 15C/Feb 23C/Oct 2C; Libya 1980 Oct 28C; 1981 Dec 31C; 1984 Sep 1C; Syria 1980 Dec 3C; Uganda 1989 Jan 18C; USSR 1987 Jan 22B

government and politics: King Khalid dies 1982 Jun 13C; Prince Fahd becomes king 1982 Jun 13C

international organizations: Gulf nation cooperation 1981 Mar 10C; IMF 1981 Mar 27A; World Bank 1980 Aug 2A

obituaries: Khalid, King 1982 Jun 13C

oil issues: 1980 Sep 18A; 1981 Apr 19A/May 26A/Jun 24C/Sep 8A; 1983 Jan 24A; 1984 Jul 11A; 1985 Sep 17A; 1987 Feb 3C/Oct 16A

religious issues: pilgrimage to Mecca 1982 Sep 26C; 1987 Jul 31C

sports: Olympic Games (Moscow) boycotted 1980 Jan 6J

U.S. relations 1982 Oct 5G; 1987 Jan 23G; conference on the Middle East 1983 Nov 6A; Iran-Contra arms scandal 1987 Jun 9G; Nicaraguan contras 1984 May 19G

Saudi Basic Industries Corp. 1980 Jul 9C

Savannah River Site nuclear reactor (South Carolina) 1988 Sep 30H; 1989 Sep 7G

Save the Children Fund 1983 Mar 18I

Schlitz Brewing Co., Jos. 1981 Aug 4H/Oct 22H

Scholastic Aptitude Test (SAT) 1980 Oct 4F; 1981 Mar 26F; 1982 Sep 21J/Oct 4F; 1984 Sep 1F; 1985 Sep 23F; 1986 Sep 22F; 1988 Feb 25F/Sep 19F; 1989 Feb 3F/Apr 28F/Sep 11F

school decentralization 1989 Sep 5F

School of American Ballet 1989 Sep 13J

school prayer 1980 Oct 3J; 1981 Nov 16F; 1982 May 6F/May 17F/Sep 8F/Sep 23F; 1983 Mar 8F; 1984 Mar 15F/Jul 26F; 1985 Jun 4F/Sep 10F

schools *see* colleges and universities; *specific institutions (e.g.,* Harvard); *geographic regions (e.g.,* New York City)

school textbooks 1982 Aug 4E/Aug 26E/Aug 28E; 1987 Mar 4F/Mar 27F/Aug 24F/Aug 26F; 1988 Jul 1E; 1989 Oct 3E/Nov 9F

Science, American Association for the Advancement of *see* American Association for the Advancement of Science

Science and Engineering Education for the 1980s (White House) 1980 Oct 23F

Science and Technology Policy, U.S. Office of 1983 Jun 27H; 1986 Jun 30I

Science in the Public Interest, Center for *see* Center for Science in the Public Interest

scientific fraud 1985 May 29F

scientology 1983 Nov 2E

Scotland 1980 May 1B/Jul 20J; 1982 Jul 18J; 1984 Jul 22J; 1986 Jan 28J/Jul 24J; 1988 Apr 10J/Jul 6B/Dec 28I; Lockerbie crash

Scotland Yard (British police agency) 1989 Sep 1B

Screen Actors Guild 1980 Jul 21J/Sep 7J/Oct 23J; 1985 Oct 31J/Nov 5J

Scripps Co.,E.W. 1982 Jun 2J

Scripps-Howard National Spelling Bee 1985 Jun 6J; 1986 May 29J; 1987 May 28J; 1988 Jun 2J; 1989 Jun 1J

Scrooged (film) 1988 Nov 30J

sculpture *see also individual artists in the name index (e.g.,* Nevelson, Louise)

donations: Picasso collection returned to France 1987 Jan 20J; Elgin marbles 1983 May 13B; 1984 Apr 10J

obituaries: Beuys, Joseph 1986 Jan 23J; Dubuffet, Jean 1985 May 12J; Giacometti, Diego 1985 Jul 15J; Lam, Wilfredo 1982 Sep 11J; Moore, Henry 1986 Aug 31J; Nevelson, Louise 1988 Apr 17J; Noguchi, Isamu 1988 Dec 30J; Stankiewicz, Richard 1983 Mar 27J

Tilted Arc controversy 1985 May 31J; 1987 Aug 31J

Vietnam veterans statue 1984 Nov 9G

SDI (strategic defense initiative) *see* Star Wars

Seabrook nuclear power plant (New Hampshire) 1980 May 25F; 1984 Apr 18H; 1985 Jan 25H; 1987 Jun 11H/Oct 15H/Oct 29H; 1988 Jan 28H; 1989 Jun 3H

Seafirst Corp. 1986 Jul 8H

Seagram Co. 1980 Sep 12H; 1981 Jul 12H/Jul 23H/Aug 11H

Sea Grant College Program 1987 Dec 29H

Sea Isle City (ship) 1987 Oct 16C

Sealink 1982 Aug 3B

seals 1983 Mar 27I; 1984 Mar 8D; 1987 Mar 23D/Dec 30D; 1988 Aug 19I

Sea of Love (film) 1989 Sep 15J/Sep 27J/Oct 25J

Search (Jackson Pollock) (painting) 1988 May 2J

Search for Signs of Intelligent Life in the Universe, The (Jane Wagner) (play) 1985 Sep 26J; 1986 Jun 1J

Searle & Co., G. D. 1988 Sep 9F

Sears Roebuck & Co. 1981 Jun 3H/Oct 8H; 1986 Oct 28H; 1988 Oct 31H; 1989 Feb 28H

Sears Tower (Chicago) 1988 Oct 31H

Sears World Trade (Sears Roebuck & Co.) 1986 Oct 28H

Seascape: Folkestone (J.M.W. Turner) (painting) 1984 Jul 5J

Sea Shepherd Conservation Society 1986 Nov 9B

Season in Hell, A (Jack Higgins) (book) 1989 Jan 27J

seat belts 1982 Aug 3H/Nov 18H; 1984 Jul 11H

Seattle Mariners (baseball team) 1984 Nov 20J

Seattle Seahawks (football team) 1980 Dec 13J; 1984 Jan 8J

Seattle Sounders (soccer team) 1982 Sep 19J

Seattle Supersonics (basketball team) 1987 Feb 8J

Seaway Trust Co. 1983 Jan 7D

SEC *see* Securities and Exchange Commission, U.S.

Second International Mathematics Study 1984 Sep 22F

secrecy pledge 1987 Aug 11G

Secret of My Success, The (film) 1987 Apr 15J/May 20J

Secrets (Danielle Steel) (book) 1985 Nov 22J/Dec 20J; 1986 Jan 31J

Secret Service (Treasury Department) 1985 Apr 28F

Section 8 Moderate Rehabilitation Program 1989 Jun 1F

secular humanism 1987 Mar 4F/Mar 27F/Aug 26F

Securities and Exchange Commission, U.S. (SEC)

appointments: Breeden, Richard C. 1989 Oct 6H; Ruder, David S. 1987 Jun 17H

business issues: exclusionary tender offers 1986 Jul 8H; government securities dealers regulation 1986 Oct 28H; NASD stocks changes approved 1984 Nov 16H; "one share, one vote" rule 1988 Jul 7H; options trading 1980 Mar 26H; regulation 1986 Nov 4H; shelf registration process 1983 Nov 10H; S&L stock brokerage services 1982 Jul 7H; volatility of stock prices 1986 Sep 19H

corruption and ethics: Boesky insider trading 1986 Nov 14H/Dec 11H; 1987 Sep 23H; Citicorp foreign-currency dealings 1982 Mar 4H; Drexel Burnham Lambert Inc. 1986 May 12H/Jun 5H; 1988 Sep 7H; 1989 Jan 24H/Apr 13H; Drysdale Government Securities, Inc. 1982 May 20H; First Boston Corp. 1986 May 5H; Hunts silver trading 1980 Apr 1H; insider trading definition proposed 1987 Aug 7H;

Mobil/Marathon buyout 1981 Nov 3H; Morgan Stanley & Co. analyst insider trading 1988 Jun 27H; Santa Fe International Corp. 1981 Oct 26H; 1984 May 16A; *Wall Street Journal* insider trading 1984 May 19H; Washington Public Power Supply System 1983 Nov 29H

mergers, acquisitions and joint ventures: Bendix Corp./RCA Corp. 1982 Mar 8H; takeover laws and regulations changes 1984 Mar 13H; takeovers called good for economy by SEC chairman 1981 Jul 13H

payments issues: ITT 1982 May 13H; Textron Inc. 1980 Jan 31H

reports: 1987 stock market crash 1988 Feb 2H; silver crisis 1982 Oct 20H

Security Council, U.N. 1980 Jan 7A; 1983 Dec 31A; 1985 Oct 17A; 1988 Oct 26A; 1989 Oct 18A

Security Express 1983 Apr 1B

Security Pacific Corp. 1987 Feb 24H

Seems Like Old Times (film) 1981 Jan 7J

See No Evil, Hear No Evil (film) 1989 May 31J

See You in the Morning (film) 1989 Apr 26J

Seibu Railway Group 1987 Sep 20H; 1989 Jul 9H

Seikan train tunnel 1988 Mar 13E

Selacryn (drug) 1985 Feb 25H

Selected Poems (Donald Justice) (book) 1980 Apr 14J

Selected Poems (Galway Kinnell) (book) 1983 Apr 18J

Selective Service System 1980 Apr 22G/Sep 4G; 1986 Jan 22G

self-incrimination 1980 Jun 27F; 1981 May 18F

Sellafield nuclear power plant (Great Britain) 1985 Jul 23B

semiautomatic weapons 1989 Jan 17F/Feb 16F/Mar 13F/Mar 14F

Semiconductor Industry Association 1989 Jun 12H

semiconductors *see* computer chips

Senate, U.S.

Aging, Special Committee on: 1986 May 20F

Appropriations Committee: 1984 Mar 14G; 1986 Jun 6H

Armed Services, Committee on: 1980 Oct 29G; 1981 Jan 28G/Oct 5G/Nov 5G; 1983 Apr 18G; 1984 Feb 2G; 1985 Feb 4G/Apr 4G/Oct 16G; 1986 Feb 5G/Jun 6H; 1989 Feb 2G/Feb 23G

Banking, Housing and Urban Affairs Committee: 1980 Feb 8F/Jun 5H; 1983 Feb 14G/Feb 16H/Jul 14H; 1984 Jul 25H; 1985 Feb 20H; 1987 Apr 22H; 1988 Oct 26H; 1989 Sep 27F

Budget, Committee on the: 1981 Mar 19H/Oct 7F/Oct 30H; 1982 Jul 27H/Jul 28H; 1983 Apr 7G; 1985 Feb 5H/Mar 5G/Mar 13H; 1986 Mar 7H/Mar 19H; 1989 Dec 12G

Campaign Committee: 1982 Dec 2F

Commerce, Science and Transportation, Committee on: 1983 Apr 21H; 1987 Jun 23F

Energy and Natural Resources, Committee on: 1989 Jun 14I

Environment and Public Works, Committee on: 1983 Feb 23H

Ethics, Select Committee on: 1981 Aug 24F; 1989 Jan 17F/Aug 4F/Oct 13F/Dec 22F

Finance, Committee on: 1980 Dec 2H; 1981 Oct 7F; 1982 Jul 2H/Sep 16F; 1985 Apr 2G/Jun 11H/Dec 10H; 1986 Jan 25F/Apr 23D/May 7H; 1987 Jul 21F; 1988 Jul 13H/Aug 9H

Foreign Relations, Committee on: ABM treaty 1987 Sep 21G; Afghanistan chemical weapons use 1982 Mar 8A; Beirut embassy annex bombing 1984 Oct 26G; Cuba radio broadcasts 1982 Sep 9G; El Salvador aid 1982 Feb 2G/Aug 20G/May 26G; INF treaty 1988 Jan 25B/Feb 1G/Mar 30G; Iran-Iraq war 1984 Aug 27G; Iran use of force 1980 Apr 24G; Iraqi poison gas attacks on Kurds 1988 Sep 21C; narcotics and dangerous drugs 1989 Apr 13F; NATO warning blast plans 1981 Nov 4G; Nicaraguan contras 1987 Feb 18G; nominations 1981 Jun 5G; 1984 May 15G; 1989 Jun 20G; Noriega hearings 1988 Feb 8G; nuclear freeze 1982 Jun 9G; 1983 Aug 2G/Sep 20G; Saudi Arabian arms sales 1981 Oct 1G/Oct 15G; Star Wars 1985 Jan 31G; Taiwan status 1983 Nov 15G/Nov 26E; Turkey military aid 1984 Mar 28G

Governmental Affairs, Committee on: 1984 Aug 27H; 1987 Jul 9F; 1988 Sep 30H

Intelligence, Select Committee on: Casey investigation 1981 Jul 29G/Dec 2G; Casey resignation call 1981 Jul 23F; CIA domestic spying 1981 Oct 27F; CIA guerrilla warfare manual 1984 Oct 22G; CIA Nicaragua operations 1984 Apr 11G/Apr 26G; 1985 Jan 7G; covert operations procedures 1987 Aug 7F; 1989 Oct 27G; El Salvador 1984 Oct 10G; Iran-Contra arms scandal 1986 Dec 16F/Dec 19F; 1987 Jan 5G/Jan 19G/Jan 29G/Feb 18G/Apr 8F; Moynihan announces resignation 1984 Apr 15G; Moynihan withdraws resignation 1984 Apr 26G; Nicaraguan contra aid 1983 Sep 22G; Philippines 1985 Nov 1G

Judiciary, Committee on the constitutional amendment on abortion 1981 Dec 16F; 1982 Mar 10F

constitutional convention guidelines 1985 Jul 23F

Freedom of Information Act 1981 Nov 12F

handgun waiting period 1989 Nov 21F

Meese attacked by Justice Department officials 1988 Jul 26F

nomination hearings and recommendations: Bork, Robert H. 1987 Jul 23F/Aug 11F/Sep 15F/Sep 19F/Oct 6F; Civil Rights Commission 1983 Oct 25F; Democratic unit to screen nominations 1986 Dec 22F; Kennedy, Anthony 1987 Nov 14F; Lucas, William C. 1989 Aug 1F; Meese III, Edwin A. 1984 Mar 6F; 1985 Feb 5F; O'Connor, Sandra Day 1981 Sep 16F; Rehnquist, William H. 1986 Aug 1F/Aug 14F; Reynolds, William Bradford 1985 Jun 27F; Sessions III, Jefferson B.

1986 Jun 5F; Siegan, Bernard 1988 Jul 14F

Reagan administration criticized on appointments 1988 Feb 2F

Rules and Administration, Committee on: 1985 Jun 20H; 1987 Apr 29F

Small Business, Select Committee on: 1980 Jan 3H

Western Hemispheric Affairs, U.S. Subcommittee on: 1983 Mar 1G

Sendero Luminoso (Shining Path) 1982 Aug 19D; 1983 Apr 3D/May 5D/May 31D/Jul 2D; 1985 Jan 22D/Apr 13D/Apr 14D; 1986 Jun 18D/Jun 27D; 1987 Feb 9D/Mar 10D

Senegal 1981 Jan 1C/Jul 31C/Aug 6C/Aug 19C/Nov 14C; 1983 Jan 23A; 1988 Feb 28C; 1989 Apr 29C/May 5C

Senegambia 1981 Nov 14C

senility 1980 Apr 19I

Sense of Smell (Jose Ribera) (painting) 1985 Mar 14J

Sentinel Financial Instruments 1984 Jun 8H

Sentinel Government Securities 1984 Jun 8H

Sentry Armored Courier Corp. 1982 Dec 12H; 1983 Feb 2F/Feb 18F/Dec 7F; 1985 Mar 7F

Sequoyah nuclear power plant (Tennessee) 1985 Aug 23H

Serbia (Yugoslavia) 1986 Feb 15B; 1987 Jun 26B/Oct 25B; 1988 Oct 6B/Oct 9B/Oct 17B/Nov 19B; 1989 Feb 27B/May 8B/Nov 29B

Sergeant York (antiaircraft gun) 1985 Aug 27G; 1986 Mar 26G; 1987 Jun 19G

Serious Money (Caryl Churchill) (play) 1987 Mar 21J; 1988 Jan 24J

Serpent and the Rainbow, The (film) 1988 Feb 17J

Service d'Action Civique (French terrorist group) 1981 Jul 18B/Jul 26B

Service Employees International Union 1986 Dec 11H

Servicio Paz y Justicia (Argentine human rights organization) 1980 Oct 13A

Seton Hall University (South Orange, N.J.) 1983 May 21F; 1989 Apr 3J

Seto Ohashi bridge complex (Japan) 1988 Apr 10E

700 Club, The (TV show) 1986 Sep 22F

17 (Chicago) (recording) 1985 Jan 26J

sewage sludge dumping 1985 Apr 1H; 1988 Aug 9H/Oct 19H/Nov 18H

sewer systems 1980 Dec 11H; 1982 May 26F; 1983 May 23H; 1985 Apr 18H/Aug 26H; 1986 Nov 6H; 1988 Jan 28H/Mar 22H/Jul 27H

sex, lies and videotape (film) 1989 May 23J/Aug 4J/Sep 27J

sex bias 1980 Jan 14F; 1982 May 17F/Nov 22F/Nov 23F; 1983 Aug 8F/Aug 11J/Aug 22F/Oct 31F; 1984 Feb 28F/Mar 7E/Jun 26F; 1985 Jun 17F; 1986 Feb 24F/Oct 7H

sex education 1982 May 25F; 1983 Dec 1J; 1985 Jan 13B/Mar 12F; 1986 Jul 8F/Oct 22E; 1989 May 2F

sexual attitudes 1989 Jun 30F

sexual harassment 1986 Jun 19F; 1987 Dec 21G; 1988 Apr 25G; 1989 Feb 18G/Oct 18F

Seychelles 1981 Dec 2C; 1982 Jul 29C/Aug 17C/Nov 27C; 1985 Nov 29E; 1986 Dec 1E; 1987 Dec 6E

Sezai Turkes-Feyzi Akkaya Insaat 1985 Apr 27B

Shakedown (film) 1988 May 18J

shale oil projects 1984 Aug 2H

Sharky's Machine (film) 1982 Jan 6J

"Sharpeville Six" 1988 Mar 17C/Nov 23C

Shatt al-Arab waterway (Iran/Iraq) 1980 Sep 21C/Sep 25C/Oct 10A/Oct 10C; 1988 Aug 26C

Shearson Lehman Brothers Holdings Inc. 1987 Dec 3H

Shearson Lehman Hutton Holdings Inc. 1989 Dec 14H

Shearson Loeb Rhoades Inc. 1981 Apr 21H/Apr 23H

sheep 1986 Jun 20I

Sheffield (England) 1989 Apr 15A/Aug 4B

Sheffield (ship) 1982 May 4D

Shell Canada Ltd. 1982 Apr 30D

shellfish 1989 Nov 23D

Shell International 1982 Jan 29C

Shell Oil Co. 1980 Jul 9C; 1983 Dec 9H; 1984 Jul 13H; 1988 Feb 1H/Dec 19H

Shelter (homeless advocacy group) 1988 Dec 28B

Sheraton Hotel (San Salvador, El Salvador) 1981 Jan 3D

Sherman Antitrust Act (1890) 1985 May 28H; 1989 Aug 1F

She's So Unusual (Cyndi Lauper) (recording) 1984 Jun 16J

Shiite Moslems 1980 Jan 5C; 1982 May 22C; 1983 Dec 27C; 1985 Jul 24C; 1987 Sep 28C; 1988 Dec 1B; 1989 Sep 21C; see also specific groups (e.g., Amal); individual leaders in the name index (e.g., Berri, Nabih)

Shiley Inc. (Pfizer Inc.) 1985 Nov 13I

Shin Bet (Israeli security agency) 1986 Jun 25C; 1987 May 24C

Shining, The (film) 1980 May 23J/May 28J/Jul 2J

Shining Path see Sendero Luminoso

shipbuilding and shipyards 1982 Jan 11H; 1985 Aug 21H/Oct 7H; 1986 May 14B/Jul 8B; 1987 Aug 22E/Nov 4H; see also specific facility (e.g., Lenin Shipyard)

Shirley Valentine (play) 1989 Jun 4J

shoes 1984 Jun 6H; 1985 Jun 12H/Nov 20D/Dec 3H/Dec 17H; 1987 Sep 16H; 1988 Sep 9H/Sep 28H/Oct 4H

Shogun Assassin (film) 1980 Dec 3J

Shooting Rubberbands at the Stars (Edie Brickell & New Bohemians) (recording) 1989 Feb 25J

Shoot to Kill (film) 1988 Feb 17J

Shoreham nuclear power plant (New York) 1983 Jun 5I/Jun 23I/Dec 14H; 1984 Dec 21H; 1985 Feb 21H; 1987 Jan 14H/Jun 11H/Oct 29H; 1988 May 27H; 1989 Feb 28H

Short Circuit (film) 1986 May 14J

short-range nuclear weapons 1983 Oct 27A; 1984 Jan 17B; 1987 Mar 31B; 1988 Feb 6B; 1989 Apr 27B/Apr 30B/May 29B

Short Timers, The (Gustav Hasford) (book) 1987 Jun 26J

shot put 1980 Jun 14J; 1987 Aug 12J; 1988 May 22J

Showtime (cable television channel) 1983 Sep 1J

shrimp 1989 Sep 5H

Shroud of Turin 1988 Oct 13J

Shubert Theater (New York City) 1983 Feb 7J

Sicilian, The (Mario Puzo) (book) 1984 Dec 14J; 1985 Jan 18J/Feb 8J/Mar 15J

Sicily (Italy) 1982 Apr 30B/Sep 3B; 1983 Jan 25B/Mar 5B; 1984 Oct 18B/Oct 25B; 1985 Nov 9B; 1986 Feb 10B/Feb 20B; 1987 Dec 16B; 1988 Apr 16B/Dec 1B; see also Mt. Etna

Sick Children's Hospital (Toronto) 1989 Aug 24I

sickle-cell anemia 1981 Feb 3G

Sid and Nancy (film) 1986 Oct 17J; 1987 Jan 4J

Sidra, Gulf of 1983 Feb 19C; 1986 Mar 23C/Mar 27C/Mar 29G

Siegel Trading Co. 1989 Sep 11H

Sierra Club 1981 Apr 16H; 1983 Sep 13H; 1984 Sep 19H

Sierra Leone 1985 Oct 5C; 1987 Mar 23C; 1988 May 29C/Jul 11A

Sigmor Corp. 1982 Jul 7H

Signals (Rush) (recording) 1982 Oct 13J

Sikhs 1982 Jul 12E/Oct 11E; 1985 May 11E/Sep 4E; 1986 Dec 21E; 1987 Feb 23E; 1988 Aug 10E; 1989 Oct 13D/Dec 19D

silver 1981 Jul 28H; 1987 Jun 8H; 1988 Aug 20F/Oct 20H; 1989 Aug 24H

Simon & Schuster 1989 Jan 26J

Simon & Simon (TV show) 1983 Jun 12J; 1984 Nov 18J

Simple Pleasures (Bobby McFerrin) (recording) 1988 Oct 29J

Simply Irresistible (Robert Palmer) (recording) 1989 Feb 22J

Sinai Peninsula
Egyptian flag raised 1982 Apr 25C
Israeli compensation for settlers 1982 Jun 7C
Israeli/Egyptian talks 1982 Jan 19C/Mar 22C/Apr 15C
Israeli settlement evictions 1982 Mar 2C/Mar 24C/Apr 21C
Israeli withdrawal 1980 Jan 26C; 1982 Jan 19C/Apr 15C/Apr 21C
land route opened across 1980 Oct 29C
peacekeeping force 1981 May 28A/Aug 3C/Oct 19A/Dec 3A; 1982 Jan 13A/Jan 31C/Apr 26C; 1986 Mar 16C
Taba beach resort 1982 Apr 26C; 1988 Sep 29C; 1989 Mar 15C

Sinclair Research Ltd. 1986 Apr 8B

Sindhis (Pakistan ethnic group) 1988 Oct 2E

Singapore see also individual leaders in the name index (e.g., Lee Kuan Yew)
crime and law enforcement: conspiracy arrests 1987 May 21E; former prisoners rearrested 1988 Apr 19D
economy and business: budget 1984 Mar 2E; stock market 1985 Dec 4E
education: 1984 Jan 23E
foreign relations: Nicaraguan contras 1987 Jan 23G
government and politics: Nair resigns as president 1985 Mar 28E; parliament dissolved 1988 Aug 17E; Wee Kim Wee nominated as president 1985 Aug 27E

papal visit: 1986 Dec 1E
sports: Olympic committee receives KKK death threat 1984 Jul 11J
U.S. relations: 1982 Nov 8E; 1984 Jul 7G; 1988 Jan 29G; 1989 May 2H

Singapore International Monetary Exchange 1984 Sep 6H

singers and songwriters see individual artists in the name index (e.g., Lennon, John)

Single European Act (1986) 1987 Apr 9B/May 26B

Sinhalese see Sri Lanka

Sinhalese People's Liberation Front 1989 Jun 20E/Dec 26E

Sinn Fein (Provisional IRA political wing) 1982 Jan 21A; 1984 Mar 14B; 1985 May 15B; 1986 Nov 2B; 1988 Oct 19B

Sioux Indians 1980 Jun 30F; 1982 Jan 18G/Jan 26F

Sire (record company) 1985 Aug 5J

"sistematizarea" (Romanian resettlement program) 1988 Nov 28B

16 (Chicago) (recording) 1982 Sep 22J

Sixteen Candles (film) 1984 May 9J

Sixth Amendment 1988 Jun 29F

60 Minutes (TV show) 1982 Jan 11J; 1983 Jan 16F/Apr 10J; 1984 Sep 16J/Nov 18J

skating see specific type of skating (e.g., figure skating)

Skeleton Crew (Stephen King) (book) 1985 Jul 19J/Aug 16J/Sep 27J

skiing 1980 Dec 27F; 1982 Mar 14I; 1985 Feb 6J; 1989 Feb 2J/Feb 19B; see also World Cup

skin 1984 Aug 15I

skin cancer 1988 Nov 21I

skinheads 1989 Feb 6F

Skydome (Toronto) 1989 Jun 3J

Skywalker (racehorse) 1986 Nov 1J

Slippery When Wet (Bon Jovi) (recording) 1986 Oct 22J/Nov 22J/Dec 17J; 1987 Jan 28J/Feb 18J/Mar 28J/Apr 25J/May 23J/Jun 27J

Sloan Kettering Cancer Center (New York City) 1983 Aug 21F

Slovenia (Yugoslavia) 1989 Feb 16B/Sep 27B/Nov 29B

Small Business Administration 1980 Dec 21F

Smart Women (Judy Blume) (book) 1984 Mar 23J/Apr 20J

Smile (racehorse) 1986 Nov 1J

Smiley's People (John le Carre) (book) 1980 Jan 13J/Feb 10J/Mar 9J/Apr 6J

Smith Barney, Harris Upham & Co. 1982 Jul 1H

SmithKline Beckman Corp. 1985 Feb 25H; 1986 Mar 21F; 1989 Apr 12H

Smithsonian Institution (Washington, D.C.) 1984 Sep 17J

smog 1987 Jan 13D; 1989 Jun 12H/Jul 17H/Sep 14H

smokestacks 1984 Jun 25H; 1985 Jun 27H

Smokey and the Bandit, II (film) 1980 Sep 3J

smoking see tobacco and smoking

Smythe Trophy (ice hockey) 1980 May 24J; 1987 May 31J; 1989 May 25J

snail darter 1984 Aug 6H

SNCF (French rail company) 1986 Dec 18B

Snow Chief (racehorse) 1986 May 17J; 1987 Jan 30J

snowstorms and blizzards 1983 Feb 12I; 1985 Jan 13I/Nov 10I/Dec 1I
snuff 1986 Jan 15F
So (Peter Gabriel) (recording) 1986 Jul 16J/Aug 13J
soccer
accidents and disasters: Great Britain grandstand fire 1985 May 11B; Peru team plane crash 1987 Dec 8D
kidnappings: El Salvador guerrillas kidnap spectators 1982 Dec 5D
NCAA championships: 1980 Nov 18J; 1985 Nov 24J/Dec 15J; 1987 Nov 22J/Dec 6J; 1988 Nov 20J/Dec 4J; 1989 Nov 19J
violence: ban on British teams 1985 Jun 2B; Great Britain 1989 Apr 15A/Aug 4B; Heysel Stadium riot (Belgium) *see* Heysel Stadium
winners: European Champions Cup 1987 May 27J; North American Soccer League 1980 Dec 5J; 1985 Mar 28J
World Cup: 1982 Jul 11J; 1985 May 19E; 1986 May 31J/Jun 29J; 1988 Jul 4J/Aug 13J; 1989 Nov 19J/Dec 9J
Social-Defense, Committee for *see* Committee for Social-Defense
Socialist Workers Party (SWP) 1986 Aug 25F
Social Security System, U.S.
benefits: 1983 May 18F; 1984 Apr 13F/Sep 8F/Oct 2F; 1987 Jun 8F/Oct 16F; 1988 Nov 15F/Dec 3F
funding issues: budget 1985 May 23H; 1988 Oct 28H; reform bill 1983 Mar 9F; solvency problems 1981 Oct 15F; 1982 Apr 1H/Nov 5H; 1983 Jan 15F
labor issues: state and local government employees 1986 Jun 19F
Societe Nationale Elf Aquitaine *see* Elf Aquitaine, Societe Nationale
Society of West End Theater *see* Olivier Awards
sodomy 1987 Oct 13F
softball 1981 Jan 13J; 1988 Aug 1J
"soft money" 1986 Apr 17F
software *see* computers
solar energy 1988 Sep 19I
Solar Maximum Mission Observatory 1980 Feb 14I; 1989 Dec 2I
Solar System Exploration Committee 1983 Apr 16I
solar wind 1984 Aug 16I
Soldiers in Hiding (Richard Wiley) (book) 1987 May 9J
Soldier's Play, A (Charles Fuller) (play) 1984 Sep 14J
Soldier's Story, A (Charles Fuller) (play/film) 1982 Apr 12J; 1984 Sep 14J/Oct 10J/Nov 7J
Solidarity *see also individual leaders in the name index (e.g.,* Walesa, Lech)
amnesty and prisoner releases: 1980 Nov 27B; 1984 May 12B/Aug 9B; 1986 Aug 11B
arrests and trials: 1980 Nov 21B; 1982 Dec 23B; 1985 Jun 14B; 1986 Jan 11B/May 31B
charter: 1980 Nov 10B
demonstrations and protests: 1982 May 3B/Aug 13B/Sep 6B/Nov 27B; 1988 May 1B/Aug 14B
economic and labor issues: economy seen as near collapse 1981 Jun 30B; five-day work week 1981 Jan 9B/Jan 10B/Feb 1B; food and energy costs 1981 Jul 26B; formed by independent trade unions 1980 Sep 24B; free-market economy plan unveiled 1989 Oct 12B
foreign developments: East Germany 1981 Aug 20B; United States 1982 Oct 9G; USSR 1981 Jan 29B/May 18B/Aug 7B/Sep 10B/Sep 14B/Sep 21B/Oct 25B
government and politics: Communist Party attacks on 1981 Feb 3B/Aug 16B/Sep 9B; elections called for 1981 Sep 10B; government asks for mediation help 1988 Aug 26B; government calls illegal 1986 Oct 3B; government sets up officially sanctioned labor unions 1983 Jan 3B; government talks 1980 Oct 31B/Nov 9B; 1981 Mar 25B/Aug 7B/Nov 4B/Nov 18B; 1989 Jan 27B/Feb 6B; legalization of 1980 Oct 24B; 1989 Apr 17B; letter to Soviet-bloc countries 1981 Sep 9B; local election count called inflated 1984 Jun 9B; martial law 1981 Dec 13B; 1983 Jul 21B; Mazowiecki confirmed as premier 1989 Aug 24B; member elected to Politburo 1981 Jul 19B; national referendum on noncommunist government 1981 Dec 12B; opposition in parliament formed by 1989 Jul 4B; parliament approves ban on labor organizations 1982 Oct 8B; parliament approves censorship freedom 1981 Jul 31B; parliamentary caucus votes against joining govt. 1989 Jul 26B; parliamentary elections 1989 Jun 4B; parliamentary election turnout disputed 1985 Oct 14B; parliament passes worker participation legislation 1981 Sep 25B; Politburo warning 1981 Aug 1B; restoration of union demanded 1983 Mar 9B; right to propose legislation sought 1981 Sep 15B; self-management referendum 1981 Sep 8B/Sep 17B; workers' councils proposal 1981 Sep 14B
leadership: chairmanship bids announced 1981 Oct 1B; leaders' meeting 1981 Oct 22B; national congress 1981 Sep 26B/Oct 7B
press and broadcasting: 1982 Apr 12B/Aug 1B; publications moderated 1981 Jun 24B
Roman Catholic Church: activist priest transfer 1984 Mar 15B; John Paul II support for 1982 Jan 1B
strikes and job actions: 1980 Oct 3B/Nov 24B/Nov 25B; 1981 Jan 9B/Jan 10B/Jan 27B/Feb 1B/Feb 6B/Feb 12B/Mar 20B/Mar 24B/Mar 26B/Mar 30B/Aug 12B; 1982 May 13B/Oct 12B; 1988 Aug 26B; 1989 Aug 11B
So Long, and Thanks for All the Fish (Douglas Adams) (book) 1985 Feb 8J
Somalia 1980 Jan 24C/Aug 8C/Aug 21G/Aug 27C/Dec 4C; 1981 Aug 25C/Nov 14G; 1982 Jul 1C/Jul 24G; 1985 Mar 21G; 1987 Jul 2C; 1989 Jul 9C/Jul 14C/Sep 10C
Somali National Movement 1989 Sep 10C
Some Kind of Hero (film) 1982 Apr 7J
Some Kind of Hero (TV show) 1984 Sep 16J
Someone to Watch Over Me (film) 1987 Oct 21J
Something Wicked This Way Comes (film) 1983 May 4J
Somewhere Out There (James Horner/Barry Mann/Cynthia Weil) (recording) 1988 Mar 2J
Song and Dance Man (Karen Ackerman/Stephen Gammell) (book) 1989 Jan 9J
Song & Dance (musical) 1986 Jun 1J
Song of the South (film) 1980 Dec 3J
songs *see specific recording (e.g., Asia)*
Songs from the Big Chair (Tears for Fears) (recording) 1985 Jun 22J/Jul 27J/Aug 24J/Sep 28J/Oct 26J
Sony Corp. 1988 Jan 11E; 1989 Sep 27H
Sophie's Choice (William Styron) (book/film) 1980 May 1J; 1983 Feb 2J/Mar 9J
sorghum 1981 Oct 6H; 1986 Oct 24H/Dec 30H
Sotheby Parke Bernet Group PLC
auctions: 1983 May 18J/May 20J; 1984 Jul 5J; 1985 Apr 24J; 1986 Nov 10J; 1987 Apr 3J/Nov 11J; 1988 May 2J/May 3J; 1989 May 9J
corporate takeover: 1983 May 4B/Sep 19J
sales revenue: 1982 Jul 9J
Souk al-Manakh stock market (Kuwait) 1982 Dec 2C; 1983 Aug 11C
Soul Man (film) 1986 Nov 12J
Soul Stirrers (singing group) 1989 Jan 18J
sound, speed of 1986 Mar 27I
South Africa *see also individual leaders in the name index (e.g.,* Botha, Pieter)
accidents and disasters: drought 1983 Mar 18I; gold mine fire 1986 Sep 16C; mineshaft elevator fall 1980 Mar 27C; supertanker fire 1983 Aug 6C
African National Congress *see* African National Congress
apartheid issues: 1980 Feb 15C/Oct 30D; 1983 May 31C; 1985 Feb 1C; 1986 Mar 4C; 1988 Sep 2C/Dec 11C; 1989 Aug 31C/Sep 27C/Nov 24C
arts and culture: Breytenbach wins Rapport Prize 1986 Apr 12J; Coetzee awarded Jerusalem Prize 1987 Apr 9J; Shakespeare's *Othello* performed 1987 Sep 16J
atomic energy: nuclear weapons 1980 Feb 21C/Jul 14I; 1986 Dec 28C
bombings: 1980 Jun 1C; 1981 Jun 2C; 1982 Dec 19C; 1983 May 20C; 1985 Dec 23C; 1986 Jun 14C
censorship: 1981 Jan 20C; 1985 Nov 2C; 1986 Jun 17C/Dec 11C; 1987 Apr 28C; 1988 Nov 1C
civil strife: Durban riots 1985 Aug 9C; funeral attended by Western diplomats 1985 Dec 3C; Inkatha/ANC fighting 1989 Aug 8C; Inkatha/Congress of South African Trade Unions 1988 Dec 26C; report on causes of 1980 Feb 29C; right-wing white extremists storm rally 1986 May 22C; "sleep-in" protests 1987 Mar 28C; Zulu factions 1988 Feb 15C; Zulu/Pondo 1985 Dec 25C
crime and law enforcement: acquittals of activists 1989 Apr 24C; Afrikaner apartheid foe under ban 1982 Nov 28C; ANC activists sentenced to death 1980 Nov 26C; banning orders expire 1983 Jul 1C; black activists trial 1988 Nov 18C; black police hired 1986 Sep 21C; Delmas trial convictions overturned 1989 Dec 15C; demonstrators arrested 1985 Mar 26C; fugitive government opponents arrested 1984 Dec 12C; "hit squads" 1989 Nov 19C; inquiry in Biko's death 1980 Jun 29C; Moloise execution 1985 Oct 18C; police custody deaths 1982 Feb 5C/Aug 8C/Dec 21C; police/demonstrators clash 1980 Jun 18C/Oct 15C; police fire on schoolchildren rally 1989 Aug 23C; police killings 1985 Mar 21C; 1986 Aug 26C; 1987 Apr 22C; prisoner releases 1987 Nov 5C; 1988 Nov 26C; 1989 Oct 15C; security bills 1986 Jun 20C; squatters deported 1981 Aug 19C; townships raided 1984 Oct 23C; UDF members arrested 1985 Apr 23C; white supremacist group arrests 1982 Dec 11C
defense and armed forces: military spending 1981 Aug 12C; missile program 1989 Oct 26C; pacifist sentenced for refusing conscription 1988 Dec 5C
education: school boycott opposed 1986 Mar 30C; university quotas for nonwhites 1983 Apr 13C
foreign relations: Angola *see* Angola; Australia 1984 Mar 2E; 1986 Jun 17E; European Community 1985 Aug 1A; 1986 Jun 27B; France 1985 Jul 24B; Great Britain 1986 Nov 24B; 1988 Jun 11J; Thatcher, Margaret; Israel 1987 Mar 18C; 1989 Oct 26C; Lesotho 1982 Dec 9C; Mozambique 1981 Jan 30C; 1983 May 23C; 1984 Mar 16C/May 2C; 1985 Mar 14C; 1987 Jul 18C/Aug 6C; Namibia *see* Namibia; Portugal 1984 May 2C; Swaziland 1984 Mar 31C; Zambia 1980 Oct 27C; 1987 Apr 25C; Zimbabwe 1980 Jun 26C; 1981 Apr 18C; 1987 Nov 28C
government and politics: ban on political activities 1988 Feb 24C; community councils 1980 May 10C; de Klerk elected president 1989 Sep 14C; Heunis becomes acting president 1989 Jan 18C; mixed race political role 1982 May 12C/Jul 31C; 1983 May 5C/Nov 2A; multiracial power-sharing recommended 1982 Mar 9C; municipal elections 1988 Oct 27C; parliamentary by-elections 1984 Feb 15C; parliamentary elections 1989 Sep 6C; presidential advisory council 1980 May 8C; republic anniversary marked 1981 Jun 2C; right-wing party launched 1982 Mar 20C; tricameral legislature 1983 Jan 4C; 1984 Aug 28C; triracial President's Council inaugurated 1981 Feb 3C
homelands: 1980 Feb 12C/Dec 17C; 1984 Dec 2J; 1987 Dec 30C; 1988 Feb 10C
international organizations: IMF 1982 Oct 4A; IOC 1984 Jul 1J; Red Cross 1986 Oct 25A; UN 1982 Oct 4A; 1983 Aug 13A; 1986 Jun 20A; 1987 Feb 20A; 1989 Dec 13C
labor issues: international union delegation visits 1986 Jul 18C; miners receive pay raise 1983 Jun 17C; strikers fired 1986 Jan 6C; strikes 1984 Nov 6C; 1986 Jun 16C; 1987 Aug 9C/Aug 30C; 1988 Jun 8C; 1989 Sep 6C; union federation launched 1985 Nov 30C; unregistered black trade union recognized 1980 Nov 5C
monetary issues: currency 1985 Aug 27C
obituaries: Aggett, Neil 1982 Feb 5C; Dipale, Ernest Moabi 1982 Aug 8C; Paton, Alan 1988 Apr 12J
polls: 1985 Aug 25C; 1986 Aug 3C
religion: church-led antiapartheid movement 1988 Mar 13C; Dutch Reformed Church dissidents 1987 Jun 27C; international church organization condemns apartheid 1982 Aug 25C; Vatican condemns apartheid 1989 Feb 10C
sanctions: Canada 1985 Jul 8D; Commonwealth 1985 Oct 22A; 1988 Feb 2C; 1989 Oct 22A; European Community 1985 Sep 10B; 1986 Sep 16B; Great Britain 1985 Sep 25B; 1986 Jun 15B; hailed by "front-line" states 1985 Sep 16C; Nonaligned Movement 1986 Jun 20A; OAU 1986 Jun 20A; polls 1985 Aug 25C; Uited Nations 1981 Apr 30A; 1986 Jun 20A; 1987 Feb 20A; United States 1980 Mar 2F; 1982 Mar 1G; 1985 Jan 13C/Apr 9G/Jun 5G/Jul 11G/Aug 1G; 1986 Jan 10C/Jun 18G/Aug 15G/Oct 2G; 1987 Jun 3H; 1988 Aug 11G; 1989 Aug 19G
science and technology: Pluto's moon 1980 Apr 22I
Seychelles coup attempt: 1981 Dec 2C; 1982 Jul 29C/Nov 27C
sports: boxing 1984 Dec 2J; golf 1980 Jun 8J; rugby 1981 Jul 25E/Sep 19J; running 1980 Aug 15J; 1986 Mar 23J; tennis 1982 Jan 3J/Dec 13J
state of emergency: 1985 Jul 20C/Jul 31C/Aug 18C/Sep 25C; 1986 Jun 12C/Jul 27C/Dec 8C/Dec 11C; 1987 Jun 12C; 1988 Jun 9C
trade issues: foreign debt 1985 Sep 1C
U.S. relations: activist granted asylum 1983 Sep 6F; antiapartheid movement 1980 Mar 24F; 1984 Nov 21G/Dec 3G; 1985 Apr 4F; 1986 Apr 3G; Baker/Botha meeting 1989 May 27G; business divestment 1980 Mar 24F; 1985 Jul 31C; 1986 Oct 21C/Dec 30C; 1989 Apr 28C/Aug 28C; Kirkpatrick secret meeting 1981 Mar 23G; military attache expulsed 1986 May 23G; Nicaraguan Contra aid 1987 Aug 19G; Reagan administration policy 1981 Aug 29G; 1983 Jun 23G; State Department condemns 1985 Aug 28G; steel dumping charges 1984 Feb 10H; trade issues 1981 May 21C
South African Astronomical Observatory 1980 Apr 22I
Southampton, University of (England) 1989 Mar 23I/May 9I
South Asian Association for Regional Cooperation 1985 Dec 7E; 1988 Dec 29E
South Carolina
accidents and disasters: Hurricane Diane 1984 Sep 13I; tornadoes 1984 Mar 28H
atomic energy and safeguards: nuclear weapons fuel plants 1983 Mar 16H; 1987 Mar 28H; 1988 Sep 30H; 1989 Sep 7G
crime and law enforcement: Roach execution 1986 Jan 10F; Texas

asked to retry robber 1983 Nov 20F

labor issues: back pay settlement 1980 Dec 14H

politics and government: presidential campaigns 1980 Mar 8F; 1984 Mar 17F; 1988 Mar 5F/Mar 12F/Jun 18F

South Dakota 1980 Jun 3F/Jun 30F; 1982 Jan 18G/Jan 26F; 1984 Jun 5F/Sep 5I; 1985 Nov 10I/Dec 1I; 1988 Feb 23F/Feb 23H/Mar 19F

Southern African Development Coordination Conf. 1986 Jan 31C

Southern Baptists 1980 Sep 18J; 1981 Jun 9J; 1984 Dec 8F; 1986 Jun 10J; 1987 Jun 16J/Oct 1F; 1988 Jun 14J

Southern California, University of (Los Angeles) 1980 Jan 1J; 1981 Dec 5J; 1983 Apr 2J; 1984 Apr 1J; 1985 Jan 1J; 1986 Mar 30J; 1988 Jan 1J; 1989 Jan 2J

Southern Legislative Conference 1985 Dec 5F

Southern Methodist University (SMU) (Dallas, Texas) 1983 Jan 1J; 1987 Feb 25J

Southern Mississippi, University of (Hattiesburg) 1987 Mar 26J

Southern Pacific Co. 1983 Oct 4H; 1986 Jul 24H

Southern Poverty Law Center 1989 Feb 6F/Nov 5F

Southern Railway 1982 Mar 25H

South Georgia Island (British colony) 1982 Apr 2D/Apr 25D/Apr 25D/Apr 26A/Apr 26B

South Korea see also individual leaders in the name index (e.g., Roh Tae Woo)

bombings: Kimpo International Airport 1986 Sep 14E; Korean airliner bombers sentenced 1989 Apr 25E; Rangoon (Burma) 1983 Oct 9E/Oct 10E/Oct 11E/Nov 4E/Dec 9E

constitutional reform: 1980 Oct 22E; 1987 Aug 31E/Oct 27E

corruption and ethics: general dismissed for corruption 1981 Aug 6E; government officials dismissed 1980 Jun 29E; loan scandal 1982 May 11E/Aug 9E

crime and law enforcement: forced labor camps 1981 Sep 25E; martial law extended 1980 May 18E; policeman massacres villagers 1982 Apr 27E; protests prevented 1987 Mar 3E; students sentenced 1989 Oct 24E

economy: auto production 1988 Aug 2E; DMZ dam construction 1987 Feb 28E; five-year plan 1981 Aug 21E; GNP 1983 Jul 1E; 1987 Dec 28E; 1988 Mar 25E; whaling 1987 Jun 26E

foreign relations: China 1982 Oct 16E; 1983 May 8E/Aug 18E; 1985 Mar 28E/Aug 24E; 1986 Apr 30E; European Community 1987 Dec 18B; Hungary 1988 Sep 13A; Japan 1981 Sep 11E; 1982 Apr 16E/Aug 4E; 1983 Jan 12E; North Korea: spy ship sinking 1985 Oct 20E; papal visit 1984 May 2A/May 6J; 1989 Oct 7J

government and politics: Choi Kyu Hah resigns as president 1980 Aug 16E; Chon Doo Hwan elected president 1980 Aug 27E; general elections 1988 Apr 26D; Roh Tae Woo wins presidential election 1987 Dec 16E; security committee

formed 1980 May 31E; Shin Hyon Hwack resigns as premier 1980 May 20E

government opposition: amnesty 1988 Jun 30E/Dec 21E; protests 1986 Nov 29E; 1987 May 23E/Jun 18E/Aug 22E; 1988 May 23E/Jun 15E; 1989 May 3E

human rights: 1988 Sep 8E

international organizations: United Nations 1988 Oct 19A

Korean airline incident see Korean airline incident

Kwangju uprising see Kwangju

labor issues: independent trade union recognized 1987 Aug 21E; purge of state employees 1980 Aug 2E; strikes 1980 Apr 30E

monetary and trade issues: current account surplus 1987 Sep 22E; 1989 Feb 11E; foreign investment 1985 Oct 14E

North Korea relations: demilitarized zone shooting 1982 Apr 21E; 1984 Nov 23E; 1986 Aug 19E; family reunions allowed 1985 Sep 20E; relief supplies sent by North Korea 1984 Oct 1E; reunification conference called for 1982 Feb 10E; talks 1980 Feb 6E/Sep 25E; 1984 Jan 11E/Nov 27E; 1985 Apr 4E/May 30E/Jul 23E; 1986 Jan 20E/Jun 18E; 1988 Aug 19E/Aug 26E/Nov 17E/Dec 28E; 1989 Mar 2E

obituaries: Duk Koo Kim 1982 Nov 17J

Olympic Games (Seoul) see Olympic Games (Seoul)

sports: Asian Games 1986 Oct 5J; boxing 1982 Nov 13J/Nov 17J; Little League baseball 1985 Aug 25J; Olympic committees receive death threats 1984 Jul 11J

U.S. relations: ambassador nomination approved 1989 Jun 20G; Nicaraguan contra aid 1987 Jan 23G; Pusan information center burning 1982 Aug 11E; Seoul Information Service building occupation 1985 Oct 2E; 1986 Feb 4E; trade issues 1984 Dec 10A; 1986 Aug 4E; 1988 Jan 29G/Dec 28H; 1989 Oct 25E; visits 1983 Jan 30E

Southland Corp. 1984 Jun 8H

South Pacific Forum 1985 Aug 6E; 1986 Aug 8E; 1987 Feb 25G/May 30E

South Sandwich Islands (British colony) 1982 Apr 2D/Jun 20D

South-West Africa People's Organization (SWAPO) 1981 Mar 17C/Sep 14C/Oct 31C; 1982 Mar 16C/Mar 20C; 1984 Mar 11C/Mar 13C/Jun 9C; 1985 Jul 1C; 1988 Nov 17C; 1989 Apr 1D/Sep 12C/Oct 11C/Nov 14C

Southwest Bancshares Inc. 1983 Jul 21H

Southwest Savings Association (Dallas) 1988 May 18H

Southwest Texas State 1982 Dec 11J

South Yemen 1980 Apr 15C/Apr 23C; 1982 Oct 24C; 1984 May 26J; 1986 Jan 23C/Jan 25C; 1987 Dec 12C; 1989 Oct 18A

Soviet Academy of Sciences 1986 Nov 14A/Dec 19B; 1988 Feb 14B; 1989 Jul 8B

Soviet Academy of the Arts 1987 Mar 11J

Soviet-German Nonaggression Treaty (1939) 1989 Aug 23B/Dec 24B

Soviet Institute for Sociological Research 1988 May 26B

Soviet Institute of Space Research 1988 Nov 3I

Soviet Military Power (report) 1983 Mar 9G; 1985 Apr 2G; 1987 Mar 24G; 1988 Apr 29G; 1989 Sep 27G

Soviet National Cup (athletics) 1985 Aug 11J

Soviet Union see Union of Soviet Socialist Republics

Soviet Writers' Union 1989 Jul 4J

Soweto (South Africa) 1980 Oct 15C; 1986 Jun 12C/Jun 16C/Aug 26C/Jun 16C/Aug 26C; 1989 Sep 15C/Oct 15C/Oct 29C/Feb 15C/Oct 29C

soybeans 1981 Jul 15A; 1982 Nov 29H; 1983 Jan 19E; 1984 Jan 13H/Nov 20H; 1985 Feb 22I; 1988 Jun 27H

Soyuz 35 (Soviet spacecraft) 1980 Apr 9I

Soyuz 36 (Soviet spacecraft) 1980 May 26I

Soyuz 37 (Soviet spacecraft) 1980 Jul 23I/Jul 24I

Soyuz 38 (Soviet spacecraft) 1980 Sep 18I

Soyuz 39 (Soviet spacecraft) 1981 Mar 22I

Soyuz-T2 (Soviet spacecraft) 1980 Jun 5I

Soyuz T-3 (Soviet spacecraft) 1980 Nov 27I

Soyuz T-4 (Soviet spacecraft) 1981 Mar 10A/Mar 13I/May 26I

Soyuz T-5 (Soviet spacecraft) 1982 May 13I/Aug 27I

Soyuz T-6 (Soviet spacecraft) 1982 Jun 24I/Jul 2I

Soyuz T-7 (Soviet spacecraft) 1982 Aug 19I/Aug 20I/Dec 10I

Soyuz T-8 (Soviet spacecraft) 1983 Apr 20I

Soyuz T-9 (Soviet spacecraft) 1983 Jun 27I/Nov 23I

Soyuz T-14 (Soviet spacecraft) 1985 Sep 17I

Soyuz T-15 (Soviet spacecraft) 1986 Mar 15I/May 6I/Jul 16I

Soyuz TM5 (Soviet spacecraft) 1988 Sep 7I

Space (James A. Michener) (book) 1982 Oct 17J/Nov 14J/Dec 12J; 1983 Jan 16J/Feb 13J/Mar 13J

Spaceballs (film) 1987 Jul 8J

Spacelab (European spacecraft) 1983 Nov 28I

space manufacturing 1980 Feb 16I

space stations 1987 Feb 12I/Apr 3I/Sep 14I; 1988 Feb 11I; 1989 Apr 11I/Jul 20I/Oct 31H; see also specific craft (e.g., Salyut)

space weapons 1984 Sep 9G; 1985 Jan 28A

Spain see also individual leaders in the name index (e.g., Juan Carlos, King)

accidents and disasters: Colombian airliner crash 1983 Nov 27D; cooking oil deaths 1987 Mar 30B; 1989 May 20B; Spanish embassy fire in Guatemala 1980 Jan 31D

arts and culture: Cela wins Nobel Prize 1989 Oct 19J; Fuentes awarded Cervantes Prize 1988 Apr 21J; Goya masterwork to be returned 1986 Apr 10B; Miles van der Rohe building reconstruction 1986 Jun 2J; oldest known religious shrine found 1981 Nov 27I;

Picasso paintings returned to France 1987 Jan 20J; Sabato receives Miguel de Cervantes Prize 1985 Apr 23J

Basques see Basque region

coup attempt: 1981 Feb 23B; 1982 Feb 19B/Jun 3B; 1983 Apr 6B/Apr 28B

crime and law enforcement: army colonels arrested 1982 Oct 2B; El Pais editor sentenced 1980 May 9B

defense and armed forces: court-martials 1981 Dec 19B; officers receive lenient sentences 1980 May 7B

demonstrations and protests: 1981 Feb 27B/Nov 15B; 1983 Oct 23B; 1984 Jun 3B; 1985 Nov 24B; 1987 Feb 16B

economy and business: bank merger 1989 Feb 24B; fishing 1985 Dec 23B; GDP 1988 Jan 18B; general strike 1988 Dec 14B; inflation 1986 Sep 24B; steel industry 1983 Jul 6B; unemployment 1984 Jun 4B; 1986 Dec 17B; 1988 Jan 13B; value-added tax 1988 Sep 11B

education: 1984 Nov 18B; 1987 Feb 16B

family issues: divorce legislation 1981 Jun 22B

foreign relations: Algeria 1985 Feb 23A; France 1980 Jun 5B/Jun 16B; Great Britain 1988 Oct 17B; Guatemala 1980 Feb 1A; Iran 1984 Jul 24A; Lebanon 1989 May 16C; Western Sahara 1980 Dec 17A

government and politics: Catalonia ruling party chairmanship 1981 Nov 13B; Communist Party leader resigns 1982 Jun 9B; deputy chief of staff dismissed 1981 Feb 25B; general elections scheduled 1986 Apr 21B; regional elections in Andalusia 1982 May 23B; regional elections in Catalonia 1984 Apr 29B; Socialists survive no-confidence vote 1987 Mar 30B; Suarez Gonzalez resigns as premier 1981 Jan 29B

international organizations: European Community 1984 Dec 4B; 1985 Mar 29B/Mar 30B/Jun 12B; 1986 Jan 1B; European Parliament 1989 Jul 25B; NATO 1981 Nov 15B; 1982 May 30A; 1986 Mar 12B; UNESCO 1987 Oct 18A; Western European Union 1988 Nov 14B

obituaries: Bunuel, Luis 1983 Jul 30J; Dali, Salvador 1989 Jan 23J; Gomez Ibarruri, Dolores 1989 Nov 12B; Miro, Joan 1983 Dec 25J; Segovia, Andres 1987 Jun 2J; Sert, Josep Lluis 1983 Mar 15J; Tierno, Galvan Enrique 1986 Jan 20B

press and broadcasting: confidential report published 1981 Mar 18B; El Pais editor sentenced 1980 May 9B

regions: Andalusian vote against home rule 1980 Feb 28B; autonomy policy standardization bill 1982 Jun 30B; Galician referendum on autonomy 1980 Dec 21B; law ruled on by court 1983 Aug 10B

religion: oldest known shrine found 1981 Nov 27I; papal visit 1982 Oct 31B/Nov 9B

royal family: 1986 Jan 30B; 1987 May 2J; see also individual leaders in the name index (e.g., Juan Carlos, King)

sports: Barcelona chosen for Olympics 1986 Oct 17J; bullfighting 1989 Feb 8J; cycling 1988 Jul 24J; golf 1980 Apr 13J; 1983 Apr 11J; 1984 Jul 22J; 1988 Jul 18J; Samaranch elected president of IOC 1980 Jul 16J; tennis 1989 Jun 10J

terrorism: Central Bank hostages freed 1981 May 24B; Iranians arrested 1984 Jul 24A; see also ETA

U.S. relations: 1982 Jul 2G/Dec 15G; 1986 Dec 30H; 1987 Feb 4B/Nov 10B; 1988 Jan 15B/Sep 28B

Spanish embassy occupation (Guatemala, 1980) 1980 Jan 31D/Feb 1A

speaking fees 1988 May 26F/Dec 13F

Special Bulletin (TV show) 1983 Sep 25J

Special Drawing Rights 1980 Apr 24A/Sep 17A

Special Investigations, U.S. Office of (Justice Department) 1984 Oct 17A; 1985 Feb 6G

speed limit 1986 Sep 24H; 1987 Dec 17H

speed skating 1980 Feb 15J/Feb 16J/Feb 19J/Feb 21J/Feb 23J; 1985 Feb 21J

Speed-the-Plow (David Mamet) (play) 1988 May 3J/Jun 5J

spelling bees 1985 Jun 6J; 1989 Sep 12J; Scripps-Howard National Spelling Bee

Spelman College (Atlanta, Ga.) 1988 Nov 4F

Spend a Buck (racehorse) 1986 Jan 7J

sperm banks 1980 Feb 28I

sperm whales 1984 Nov 13A; 1985 Mar 5H

Spies Like Us (film) 1985 Dec 11J

Spike, The (Arnaud de Borchgrave/Robert Moss) (book) 1980 Jul 13J/Aug 17J/Sep 14J

Splash (film) 1984 Apr 11J

Spock's World (Diane Duane) (book) 1988 Sep 30J/Oct 21J

Sport Aid (benefit event) 1986 May 25J

Sport of Nature, A (Nadine Gordimer) (book) 1988 Mar 28J

Sports (Huey Lewis and the News) (recording) 1984 May 20J/May 28J/Jun 16J/Jul 21J/Aug 25J/Sep 22J/Oct 27J

sports utility vehicles 1989 Feb 16H

spotted owl 1988 Dec 12H; 1989 Apr 26H

Spratly Islands 1980 Jan 30E; 1988 Mar 14E

Spring Break (film) 1983 Apr 6J

Spring Moon (Bette Bao Lord) (book) 1982 Jan 10J/Feb 7J/Mar 7J

Spycatcher (Peter Wright) (book) 1987 Apr 27B/Jul 30B/Aug 13B/Dec 21B

Squier (singing group) 1982 Sep 22J

Sri Lanka see also individual leaders in the name index (e.g., Jayewardene, Junius R.)

accidents and disasters: floods 1989 Jun 6E; reservoir bursts 1986 Apr 20E

civil strife: grenade attack on parliament 1987 Aug 18E; Tamil attacks 1984 Nov 20E/Dec 1E;

1985 May 14E; 1987 Apr 21E; Tamil/government clashes 1984 Aug 4E; *see also* Liberation Tigers

foreign aid: 1987 Aug 8E

government and politics: former P.M. Bandaranaike expelled from parliament 1980 Oct 16E; Jayewardene reelected president 1982 Oct 21E; limited autonomy for Tamils 1987 Nov 12E; parliamentary elections 1989 Feb 15E; Premadasa demands Indian withdrawal 1989 Jun 1E; presidential elections 1988 Dec 19E; ruling party chairman assassinated 1987 Dec 23E; Tamil regions to be merged 1988 Sep 10E

hijacking: 1982 Jul 1E

human rights: 1987 Jun 21E; 1989 May 13E/Dec 14E

Indian intervention: 1987 Jun 4E/Jul 29E/Oct 22E; 1988 Feb 6E/Jun 7E; 1989 Jan 1E/May 3E/May 13E/Jun 1E/Jul 28E/Sep 18E

peace initiatives: cease-fires 1985 Jun 18E; 1986 Jan 12E; 1989 Jun 28E; peace agreement 1987 Jul 29E; peace talks 1984 Jan 10E/May 9E; 1985 Aug 17E; 1986 Dec 27E; 1989 May 11E

sports: Olympic committee receives KKK death threat 1984 Jul 11J

state of emergency: 1981 Aug 17E; 1982 Jan 17E/Jul 30E; 1989 Jun 20E

SS (Nazis) 1985 Apr 11G

SS-12 (Soviet missile) 1988 Feb 25B/Aug 1B

SS-18 (Soviet missile) 1987 Sep 30B

SS-20 (Soviet missile) 1983 Jan 11B; 1987 May 19B

SSI *see* Supplemental Security Income

SSN-688 (submarine) 1987 May 19G

Staggers Rail Act of 1980 1980 Oct 14H

Stakeout (film) 1987 Aug 12J/Sep 9J

Stand and Deliver (film) 1988 Mar 18J

Standard Fruit Co. 1980 Jan 17D

Standard Oil Co. of California (Socal) 1984 Mar 5H/Apr 26H

Standard Oil Co. of Ohio 1981 Mar 12H

Standard & Poor's Corp. 1989 Oct 25E

Stand By Me (film) 1986 Sep 17J

Stanford Linear Accelerator (Palo Alto, Calif.) 1987 Apr 15I; 1989 Oct 13I

Stanford University (Palo Alto, Calif.) 1980 Oct 14I; 1981 Oct 19I; 1984 Dec 27J; 1987 Apr 15I/Apr 23F/Jun 7J; 1988 Mar 31F/Dec 6F

Stanley Cup (ice hockey) 1980 May 24J; 1981 May 21J; 1982 May 16J; 1983 May 17J; 1984 May 19J; 1985 May 30J; 1986 May 24J; 1987 May 31J; 1988 May 26J; 1989 May 25J

Star (Danielle Steel) (book) 1989 Mar 31J/Apr 28J/May 26J

Star (Malaysian newspaper) 1988 Mar 27E

starch-blocker diet pills 1982 Oct 5I

starches 1988 Feb 2E

starfish 1989 Jan 13E

Stark (ship) 1987 May 17C/May 20C/Jun 19G/Jul 27G; 1989 Mar 27G

Starlight Express (musical) 1987 Mar 15J

Star of David 1987 Aug 14J

stars 1980 Mar 20I; 1984 Dec 11I; 1986 Jun 11I; 1987 Feb 24I

Stars & Stripes (catamaran) 1988 Sep 9J

Stars & Stripes (yacht) 1987 Feb 4J

Star Trek: The Lost Years (J. M. Dillard) (book) 1989 Oct 27J

Star Trek II: The Wrath of Khan (film) 1982 Jun 9J

Star Trek III: The Search for Spock (film) 1984 Jun 6J

Star Trek IV: The Voyage Home (film) 1986 Dec 24J; 1987 Jan 21J

Star Wars

ABM treaty interpretations: 1987 Jan 31G/Apr 26B/Sep 21G

budget and spending programs: 1986 Dec 29G; 1988 Oct 6G

Bush/Shevardnadze meeting: 1989 Sep 21G

Congress: 1986 Mar 30G

disarmament talks: 1987 Jan 31G/Jul 29B/Jul 31B/Dec 29G; 1988 Jan 22B

foreign developments: Canada 1985 Feb 1D/Sep 8D; Great Britain 1985 Dec 6G; 1986 Jun 24B; Israel 1986 May 6C; Japan 1986 Sep 9E; 1987 Jul 21G; USSR 1985 Mar 16B/Oct 22B; West Germany 1985 Dec 18B

NATO support: 1985 Mar 27B/Oct 15G

opposition: limits urged by ex-administration officials 1986 Aug 17G; poll of physicists 1986 Mar 22G; Roman Catholic bishops 1988 Apr 15J/Jun 25J; scientist resigns 1986 Sep 10I

reports and studies: 1984 Mar 21G; 1985 Sep 24G; 1986 Jul 22G; 1988 Apr 24G

research and testing: 1985 Jun 24I/Dec 28G; 1986 Sep 5G; 1987 Sep 18G; 1989 Mar 24I/Jul 13G

Star Wars (film) 1983 Jan 19J

State, County and Municipal Employees, American Federation of *see* American Federation of State, County and Municipal Employees (AFSCME)

State, U.S. Department of *see also individual agency heads in the name index (e.g., Baker III, James)*

appointments and resignations: ambassador to El Salvador relieved of duties 1981 Feb 1F; appointments blocked 1985 Jul 16F; Kalb resigns as spokesman 1986 Oct 8G

Argentina: 1981 Mar 17D; 1983 Dec 10G

banks: 1981 Jan 16F; 1982 Apr 22G

Bolivia: 1980 Aug 13G

Brazil: 1989 Feb 7G

budget and spending programs: 1987 Dec 22G; 1988 Sep 27F

Chad: 1983 Aug 4G

chemical weapons: Iran-Iraq war 1984 Mar 5C; USSR 1980 Aug 7G/Aug 21G; 1981 Nov 10G; 1982 Mar 22A

Chile: 1981 Feb 20G

China: 1983 Aug 18G

Cuba: 1981 Sep 16G; 1987 Nov 20G

disarmament and arms control: 1981 Sep 2A; 1987 Feb 25G/May 5G/Aug 25A

Egypt: 1980 Feb 25G; 1983 Dec 22G

El Salvador: 1981 Feb 23D/Feb 26D/Jun 9D/Jun 18D; 1982 Oct 27G; 1983 Oct 3G/Dec 13G; 1984 Jan 25G/Nov 1G

environment and pollution: 1980 Jul 23H; 1983 Feb 15H; 1988 Aug 5H

espionage and intelligence issues: Bloch under investigation 1989 Jul 21G

Grenada: 1983 Oct 26G

Guatemala: 1983 Jan 7D

Haiti: 1986 Feb 26G

Honduras: 1986 Oct 1G

human rights annual report: 1983 Feb 8G; 1984 Feb 10G; 1986 Feb 13G; 1988 Feb 10G; 1989 Feb 7G

India: 1980 Mar 13G

International Court of Justice: 1984 Apr 8G; 1985 Oct 7G

Iran: airliner shootdown 1989 Jul 17G; hijackers encouraged by 1984 Dec 11G; hostage crisis 1980 Mar 18A; 1981 Jan 16F/Jan 28C; nuclear materials 1984 Apr 25G; Reagan gives department full control of policy 1986 Nov 25G

Iran-Iraq war: chemical weapons 1984 Mar 5C

Israel: 1982 Jun 7G; 1983 Apr 8C/Apr 17C/May 2C; 1989 Feb 7G

Italy: 1984 Nov 15G

Japan: 1982 Apr 26G

Jordan: 1983 Apr 8C

Korean airliner shootdown: 1983 Sep 11G

Lebanon: 1982 Jun 7G/Sep 28G/Oct 6G; 1984 Sep 24G; 1987 Jan 28G

Libya: 1981 May 6G/Jun 2G/Aug 19G; 1984 Jul 27G; 1985 Dec 21G

Morocco: 1981 Mar 25G

Mozambique: 1981 Mar 13G; 1988 Apr 20C

Nazis: 1984 Jan 26G

Nicaragua: 1981 Apr 1G; 1983 Mar 23G/Oct 20G/Nov 28D; 1984 Sep 22G; 1986 Dec 21G

Nicaraguan contras: 1985 Aug 30G

Northern Ireland: 1981 Dec 21G; 1986 Sep 26B

North Korea: 1988 Oct 31G

obituaries: Watson, Barbara M. 1983 Feb 17F

Panama: 1988 Aug 17G

personnel: AIDS testing 1986 Nov 27F

PLO: 1982 Jul 14G; 1983 Apr 8C/Dec 22G; 1987 Sep 15G

Romania: 1985 Dec 3G

Saudi Arabia: 1980 May 12J

security measures: 1984 Oct 15G

South Africa: 1985 Aug 28G; 1989 Aug 19G

South Pacific: 1987 Feb 25G

travel advisories and bans: El Salvador 1984 Nov 1G; Lebanon 1987 Jan 28G; USSR 1984 Aug 6G; 1987 Jan 29B

TWA airliner hijacking (1985): 1985 Oct 17G

UNESCO: 1983 Dec 28A; 1989 Dec 7A

UN Fund for Population Activities: 1985 Sep 30G

USSR: attitude softening seen 1984 Mar 2G; chemical weapons 1980 Aug 7G/Aug 21G; 1981 Nov 10G; 1982 Mar 22A; disarmament and arms control 1981 Sep 2A; 1984 Jan 29B; 1987 Jul 11B; "hot line" 1984 Jul 17A; Libyan missile sales 1985 Dec 21G; radar complex 1985 Oct 29G; 1988 Jul 20G; travel advisories 1984 Aug 6G; 1987 Jan 29B; visas 1980 Feb 26G; 1981 Apr 2A; 1984 Mar 1J; *see also* Moscow embassy scandal

Vatican: 1984 Jan 26G

Vietnam: 1984 Apr 17G

visas: Cuba 1981 Sep 16G; Italian playwright 1984 Nov 15G; Libya 1984 Jul 27A; Northern Ireland 1981 Dec 21G; USSR 1980 Feb 26G; 1981 Apr 2A; 1984 Mar 1J

Yugoslavia: 1982 Apr 22G

State Colleges and Universities, American Association of *see* American Association of State Colleges and Universities

Stateline (Nevada) 1980 Aug 27J

State of Black America (National Urban League) 1984 Jan 19F; 1985 Jan 16F; 1986 Jan 23F; 1987 Jan 14F

State of the Union address 1980 Jan 23G; 1981 Feb 18H; 1982 Jan 26H; 1984 Jan 25F; 1985 Feb 6F; 1986 Feb 4F; 1987 Jan 27F; 1988 Jan 25F

State Policy Research Inc. 1985 Jun 19F

Statue of Liberty 1986 Jul 3J/Jul 5J

Statue of Liberty-Ellis Island Centennial Commission 1986 Feb 12J

Statue of Liberty-Ellis Island Foundation 1986 Feb 12J

Staying Alive (film) 1983 Aug 10J

Staying Alive (soundtrack) 1983 Aug 17J/Sep 14J

Stealth (aircraft) 1981 Jun 30G; 1985 May 23G

stealth technology 1984 Dec 18G

Steaming (play) 1983 Jun 5J

steel *see also specific companies (e.g.,* U.S. Steel Corp.)

business issues: 1986 Sep 2B; bankruptcy 1980 Apr 7H; 1985 Apr 16H; industry aid package 1980 Sep 30H; mergers 1984 Jan 11B/Feb 15H/Mar 21H/Apr 24H; Spain restructuring 1983 Jul 6B; Weirton Works purchase 1983 Mar 10H; 1984 Jan 11F; West German Krupp/Estel-Hoesch merger 1982 Feb 4B; West German restructuring 1983 Apr 7B

corruption and ethics issues: Mitsui 1982 Jul 21H; Ray Miller Inc. 1983 Jan 22F

labor issues: 1980 Jan 2B; 1985 May 2H

pollution issues: 1980 Sep 30H; 1981 Jan 2H/May 28H; 1983 Dec 16H; 1984 Mar 23H

production: 1982 Dec 31H; 1983 Apr 19A

trade issues: Australia/China 1984 Aug 10E; China/USSR 1983 Mar 10A; France/USSR 1980 Sep 19A; Japan 1987 May 29E; U.S. import levels 1985 Feb 1G/Aug 18H; 1986 Jan 30H; U.S. import restrictions increased 1983 Jul 5H; U.S. quotas 1989 Jul 25H/Dec 12H; U.S./foreign country voluntary restraints 1984 Sep 18H/Dec 10A/Dec 19H; 1989 Nov 22H

U.S. political campaign issues: 1980 Oct 2F

Steel Magnolias (film) 1989 Nov 29J

Steel Wheels (Rolling Stones) (recording) 1989 Aug 26J/Sep 30J/Oct 28J/Dec 25J

Steinlen (racehorse) 1989 Nov 4J

Stephen King's Silver Bullet (film) 1985 Oct 23J

sterilization 1984 Dec 5F

Stern (West German magazine) 1983 May 6J; 1984 Mar 21B

Stevens & Co. J.P. 1983 Oct 20F

stewards and stewardesses *see* flight attendants

stillbirths 1980 Jan 4I; 1985 Jul 12I

Stimulation Technology, Inc. 1981 Jul 2H

Stinger (missile) 1984 May 29G; 1987 Oct 8C; 1989 Jul 5G

Stir Crazy (film) 1981 Jan 7J/Feb 11J/Apr 4J

Stockholm International Peace Research Institute 1981 Jul 4A; 1982 Jun 4D

stock-index arbitrage 1988 May 10H

stock market crash (October, 1987) 1987 Oct 20H/Oct 26H/Oct 30A/Dec 22A/Dec 23H; 1988 Jan 8H/Feb 1H/Feb 2H/Feb 11B/May 16H/Jun 1H/Jun 2E

stock markets 1981 Jul 8B; 1984 Nov 16H; 1985 Aug 27C; 1987 Mar 30H/Oct 30A/Nov 6A; 1988 May 11A/Dec 20H; 1989 Jan 18D/Dec 31A; *see also specific markets (e.g.,* New York Stock Exchange)

Stockton (California) 1989 Jan 17F

Stonehenge (England) 1985 Jul 3B

Stones for Ibarra (Harriet Doerr) (book) 1984 Nov 16J

stone tools 1988 Nov 25I

Stony Brook University Hospital (New York) 1983 Nov 16F

Stories of John Cheever, The (John Cheever) (book) 1981 Apr 30J

Storm Front (Billy Joel) (recording) 1989 Dec 25J/Dec 30J

Strait of Hormuz 1980 Oct 1C/Oct 28B; 1981 Aug 12C; 1984 Feb 28C; 1987 Jul 22C

Strategic Arms Reduction Talks (START) 1982 Jun 29A/Oct 6A; 1983 Feb 2B/Jun 8G/Jul 12A/Oct 4G/Dec 5A/Dec 8A; 1985 Jan 26A; 1988 Sep 23G; 1989 Jun 19B

Strategic Defense Initiative *see* Star Wars

Strategic Forces, U.S. Presidential Commission on 1983 Apr 19G

strategic (long-range) nuclear weapons 1987 May 8A/Jul 31B

Strategic Petroleum Reserve 1980 Oct 27H; 1982 Mar 19H/Apr 22G

strawberries 1985 Nov 14I; 1987 Apr 24I/Jun 8I

Strawberry Fields (Central Park, New York City) 1985 Oct 9J

Stray Cats (singing group) 1982 Nov 17J/Dec 15J; 1983 Jan 5J/Feb 9J

streptokinase (TPA) (drug) 1988 Aug 13I; 1989 Mar 30I

Stringfellow Acid Pits (Riverside, Calif.) 1988 May 31H

Stripes (film) 1981 Jul 1J

strip mining 1981 Jun 15H; 1985 Oct 1H

strokes 1984 Nov 11I

stromatolites 1980 Apr 2I

Strong Medicine (Arthur Hailey) (book) 1984 Nov 16J

student demonstrations

Bolivia: 1987 Apr 1D

Burma: 1988 Mar 20E

China: 1985 Dec 22E; 1986 Jun 6E/Dec 23E; 1987 Jan 1E/Jan 8E/Jul 5E; 1989 Apr 27E/May 4E/May 15A/May 19E

European Community: 1982 Dec 4B

France: 1983 May 5B/May 24B; 1986 Dec 4B/Dec 9B

Greece: 1980 Nov 16B

India: 1981 Feb 26E
Nigeria: 1989 May 24C
Philippines: 1983 Aug 26E; 1984 Oct 2E
South Africa: 1989 Sep 6C
South Korea: 1985 May 26E; 1987 Jun 18E; 1988 May 23E/Jun 15E; 1989 May 3E/Oct 24E
Spain: 1987 Feb 16B
United States: 1989 Mar 7F
Venezuela: 1987 Apr 11D
West Bank: 1980 Nov 18C/Nov 20C; 1982 Apr 8C
Student Loan Marketing Association, U.S. (Sallie Mae) 1983 Aug 3F
Studio 54 (New York City discotheque) 1980 May 28F
Study of Schooling, A (Education Department) 1983 Jul 19F
Styx (singing group) 1980 Jan 2J; 1981 Feb 11J/Mar 4J/Apr 8J/May 6J/May 27J/Jul 8J; 1983 Apr 13J
Subic Bay Naval Base (Philippines) 1983 Jun 1E; 1988 Oct 17E
submarines
accidents and disasters: Soviet mishaps 1983 Aug 10B; 1986 Oct 4I/Oct 6I; 1989 Apr 7B/Jun 26B; U.S./Japanese collision 1981 Apr 20G; U.S./Soviet collision 1984 Mar 21A
arms control: 1986 May 27G/Nov 14B
contract and billing issues: Electric Boat SNN A-sub 1981 Oct 22G; Elf communications systems 1981 Oct 8G; General Dynamics 1984 Oct 31G; 1987 May 19G
defense issues: Canada-US A-sub incident 1987 Jun 5D; Great Britain 1980 Jul 15B; 1982 May 2D; Soviets launch new model 1981 Jan 9G; Soviets off U.S. coast 1984 May 20B; Soviets violate Swedish waters 1981 Oct 28B/Oct 30B/Oct 31B/Nov 6B
subways 1980 Apr 1H; 1982 Jun 28B; 1984 Oct 1F; 1985 Mar 15F; 1987 Sep 26C
"subway vigilante" 1984 Dec 31F; 1985 Jan 25F/Mar 27F; 1986 Jan 15F/Jul 8F; 1987 Apr 27F/Jun 16F/Oct 19F; 1989 Jan 16F
Success Express (racehorse) 1987 Nov 21J
Success Hasn't Spoiled (Rick Springfield) (recording) 1982 Mar 14J/May 5J
Sudan *see also individual leaders in the name index (e.g.,* Nimeiry, Gaffar el-)
accidents and disasters: flooding 1988 Aug 5I; flood relief 1988 Oct 27C; Sudanese airliner shot down 1986 Aug 16C
coups and coup attempts: Jonglei province attempt crushed 1983 May 16C; Mahdi government overthrown 1989 Jun 30C; Nimeiry overthrown 1985 Apr 6C
executions: Taha, Mahmoud Mohammed 1985 Jan 18C
foreign relations: Ethiopia 1984 Mar 11C; Libya 1983 Feb 22C
government and politics: Dahab swears in cabinet 1985 Apr 25C; elections 1986 Apr 12C; government on edge of collapse 1989 Mar 9C; military council hands power to civilians 1986 May 6C; parliaments dissolved 1981 Oct 5C; secession of south being considered 1987 Apr 28C
human rights: 1988 Jul 28C
international organizations: IMF 1986 Apr 2C
U.S. relations: 1981 Aug 13C/Nov 14G; 1983 Aug 23G; 1984 Mar 18C; 1985 Mar 11C
Sudan People's Liberation Army 1986 Aug 16C
Sudden Impact (film) 1984 Jan 11J
sugar 1980 Oct 9H; 1982 May 4H/Jun 5H/Oct 1H; 1983 May 9G/May 11D; 1984 Jan 22C/Mar 13A; 1985 Jun 4D/Nov 18E
sugar beets 1982 Apr 12H
Sugar Bowl (football) 1980 Jan 1J; 1984 Jan 2J; 1985 Jan 1J; 1986 Jan 1J; 1987 Jan 1J; 1988 Jan 1J; 1989 Jan 2J
suicide pills 1984 Oct 11J
suicide rate 1989 Sep 15B
sulfites 1985 Aug 9H; 1986 Jul 8H
sulfur emissions 1983 Feb 21I/Jun 27H/Jun 29H/Dec 5H; 1984 Feb 22D/Feb 28H/Mar 21I/Aug 14H; 1985 Jul 9I/Dec 5H/Dec 17D; 1986 Mar 14G; 1987 Nov 19H; 1988 Nov 21H
sulfuric acid 1982 Mar 6I
Sullivan Award (athletics) 1985 Feb 18J; 1986 Feb 24J
Sullivan Principles 1987 Jun 3H
Summer Rental (film) 1985 Aug 14J
Summing (racehorse) 1981 Jun 6J
Summons to Memphis, A (Peter Taylor) (book) 1987 Apr 6J/Apr 16J
Sumo Indians (Nicaragua) 1982 Dec 11D
Sun 1985 Aug 6I; 1989 Dec 2I
Sunbeam Corp. 1981 Sep 21C
Sun Bowl (football) 1981 Dec 26J
Sun Co. 1980 Sep 12H
Sunday in the Park with George (musical) 1984 May 2J; 1985 Apr 24J
Sunday Silence (racehorse) 1989 May 6J/May 20J/Jun 10J/Nov 4J
Sunday Star (Malaysian newspaper) 1988 Mar 27E
Sunday Times (London newspaper) 1980 Oct 22J; 1982 Feb 8B/Mar 11B
Sunflowers (Vincent Van Gogh) (painting) 1987 Mar 30J
Sunkist Growers Inc. 1981 Feb 20H
Sunkist Invitational (track meet) 1985 Jan 19J
Sunni Moslems 1980 Jan 5C; 1982 May 6C; 1983 Jan 4C; 1984 Mar 23C/Apr 26C; 1985 Apr 17C/Aug 6C/Oct 30C; 1987 Dec 25C; 1989 May 16C
Sunny's Halo (racehorse) 1983 May 7I
Sunrise Savings and Loan Association (Boynton Beach, Fla.) 1986 Sep 7H
Sunshine Mining Co. 1980 Nov 8H; 1982 Jun 12H
Super 301 provision (Omnibus Trade Act) 1989 May 25H/Jun 1A/Jun 21A
Super Bowl (football) 1980 Jan 20J; 1981 Jan 25J; 1982 Jan 24J; 1983 Jan 30J; 1984 Jan 22J; 1985 Jan 20J; 1986 Jan 26J; 1987 Jan 25J; 1988 Jan 3J/Jan 31J; 1989 Jan 22J
"superbubble" (astronomy) 1980 Jan 26I
supercomputers 1985 Feb 25I; 1987 Oct 8E
Superconducting Super Collider 1988 Nov 10H/Dec 13I; 1989 Jun 28H/Sep 29H
superconductivity 1987 Feb 16I/Mar 27I/Jul 28H/Oct 14I; 1989 Jan 3I/May 23I
Super Etendard (French aircraft) 1983 Oct 11C/Nov 10C/Nov 17C
Superfund 1980 Nov 24H; 1982 Dec 20H; 1983 Jan 4H/Dec 13H; 1984 Aug 10H/Oct 2H; 1985 Feb 22H/Mar 26H/Jul 25H/Sep 26H/Dec 10H; 1986 Mar 10H/Apr 1H/Oct 17H; 1988 Feb 1H/Jun 17H; 1989 Jun 15H
Superior Oil Co. 1984 Mar 11H/May 15H
Superman (film) 1980 Feb 6J
Superman II (film) 1981 Jul 1J/Jul 25J/Jul 29J
Superman III (film) 1983 Jul 6J
supermarkets 1985 Dec 29H
supernovas 1987 Feb 24I/Dec 17I
Supplemental Security Income (SSI) Program 1987 Oct 16F; 1988 Nov 15F
supply-side economics 1982 Jan 26H; 1985 Oct 19H; 1986 Apr 22H
Supreme Council for Sports in Africa 1984 Jul 1J
Supreme Court, U.S.
abortion and birth control issues: 1980 Feb 19F/Jun 30F/Sep 17F; 1981 Mar 23F; 1982 May 24F/Nov 30F; 1983 Jun 15F; 1985 Jul 15H; 1986 Jun 11F/Nov 3F; 1987 Nov 9F; 1988 Jun 29F; 1989 Jan 9F/Jul 3F
advertising issues: 1986 Jul 1F
affirmative action: 1980 Jul 2F; 1984 Jun 12F; 1986 May 19F/Jul 2F; 1987 Feb 25F/Mar 23F/Mar 25F; 1989 Jun 12F
alcoholism: 1988 Apr 20G
antiracketeering: 1983 Nov 1F; 1989 Jun 26F
antitrust and merger issues: AT&T Co. breakup 1983 Dec 12H; competitors' challenges of mergers 1986 Dec 9H; doctor/hospital contracts 1984 Mar 27F; football telecasts 1984 Jun 27F; immunity of cities 1985 Mar 27H; lawsuits for financial losses 1989 Apr 18H; manufacturers allowed to drop discount dealers 1988 May 2H; Mobil/Marathon takeover 1982 Feb 22H; newspaper merger 1989 Mar 20F/Nov 13H; state regulation of corporate takeovers 1987 Apr 21H; sugeon/hospital peer-review panel 1988 May 16H; U.S. Steel/Marathon stock purchases 1981 Dec 30H; Zenith lawsuit against Japanese companies 1986 Mar 26H
appointments and resignations: Bork, Robert H. 1987 Jul 1F; Burger, Warren E. 1986 Jun 17F; Ginsburg, Douglas H. 1987 Oct 29F; Kennedy, Anthony 1987 Nov 11F; O'Connor, Sandra Day 1981 Jul 7F; Powell Jr., Lewis F. 1987 Jun 26F; Rehnquist, William H. 1986 Jun 17F; Scalia, Antonin 1986 Jun 17F; Stewart, Potter 1981 Jun 18F; *for confirmation process, see nominees in name index*
arrests and searches: arrests for lack of identification 1983 May 2F; beepers used to track suspects 1983 Mar 2F; drug courier profile 1983 Mar 23F; education 1985 Jan 15F; home arrests without warrant 1980 Apr 15F; police liability for damages 1986 Mar 5F; police liability for illegal search 1987 Jun 25F; police shooting of fleeing suspects 1985 Mar 27F; police use of force 1989 May 15F; search warrants 1983 Jun 8F; 1984 Apr 17F; warrantless arrests 1984 Mar 15F; warrantless searches 1982 Jun 1F; warrant or "probable cause" 1985 Jan 8F
banking and finance issues: arbitration agreements over securities purchases 1989 May 15H; bank affiliates underwriting certain securities 1988 Jun 13H; bank-owned brokerage offices 1984 Jun 28H; 1987 Jan 14F; insider trading 1980 Mar 18H; 1987 Nov 16F; limited-service banks 1986 Jan 22H; regional banking compacts 1985 Jun 10H; securities fraud 1983 Jan 24H
Black Americans: 1986 May 19F; 1987 Jan 21F/Feb 25F/Mar 23F
business issues: bankruptcy code supersedes labor law 1984 Feb 22F; drug paraphernalia 1982 Mar 3F; economic boycott liability 1982 Jul 2F; Exxon overpricing appeal 1986 Jan 27H; federal bankruptcy court system 1982 Dec 24F; government contractor lawsuits over defects 1988 Jun 27H; gray-market goods 1988 May 31H; natural gas prices 1983 Jan 24H; state corporate tax law 1989 Apr 3H; telephone service rates 1986 May 27H; Texaco/Pennzoil court fight 1987 Apr 6H
campaign and election issues: city council plurality voting 1982 Dec 13F; congressional redistricting 1983 Jun 22F; 1984 Nov 13F; 1989 Jan 17F; election procedure changes 1983 Feb 23F; legislative district lines held unconstitutional 1982 Apr 23F; New York City governing body unconstitutional 1989 Mar 22F; PAC spending limits 1985 Mar 18F; political expenditures by nonprofit corporations 1986 Dec 15F; primary election participation of independents 1986 Dec 10F; voting rights 1981 Apr 29F
civil rights: ERA ratification deadline 1982 Jan 25F; private discrimination decision reaffirmed 1989 Jun 15F; public employee slurring of president 1987 Jun 24F; scope broadened 1988 Jan 28F
consumer issues: dairy price challenges 1984 Jun 4H
copyright issues: noncommercial use of home VCRs 1982 Jun 14H; 1984 Jan 17H
death penalty: Alabama law striken down 1980 Jun 20F; in cases of "reckless indifference" 1987 Apr 21F; comparison with other cases not required of states 1984 Jan 23F; execution of Texas murderer indefinitely delayed 1983 Jan 24F; execution stay not lifted 1983 Oct 31F; expedited handling of appeals 1983 Jul 6F; initial sentencing refusal to impose 1984 May 29F; for insane 1986 Jun 26F; juveniles 1988 Jun 29F; mandatory 1987 Jun 22F; for mentally retarded or juveniles 1989 Jun 26F; racial challenge to 1987 Apr 22F; right to lawyer in state appeals 1989 Jun 23F; sentence in Georgia case overturned 1980 May 19F; sentence in Mississippi case overturned 1985 Jun 11F
defendants' rights: armed guards during trial 1986 Mar 26F; child abuse cases 1987 Jan 24F; drunk-driving 1989 Mar 6F; free psychiatric assistance 1985 Feb 26F; immunity grants for grand jury testimony 1983 Jan 11F; ineffective assistance of counsel 1984 May 14F; legal representation for indigent defendants 1988 Nov 29F; Miranda warning 1984 Jun 12F/Jul 2F; 1985 Mar 4F; 1986 Jan 14F; police lawsuits 1983 Jun 13F; presence of lawyer 1986 Mar 10F/Apr 1F
demonstrations and protests: gay rights activists 1987 Oct 13F
disability benefits: black-lung disease 1988 Dec 6F; for mentally disabled 1986 Jun 2F; regulation cutting back on 1987 Jun 8F; veterans' legal fees 1985 Jun 28G
discrimination: against handicapped 1985 Jan 9F; by private clubs 1988 Jun 20F; against those with contagious diseases 1987 Mar 3F
draft registration: 1981 Jun 25F; 1985 Mar 19G; student aid linked to 1983 Jun 29F; 1984 Jul 5F
education issues: books banned from libraries 1982 May 25F; creation science 1987 Jun 19F; denying education to nonresidents 1983 May 2F; dismissal of medical student 1985 Dec 12F; disruptive emotionally disturbed students 1988 Jan 20F; nursing school admission of male 1982 Jul 1F; posting of Ten Commandments 1980 Nov 17F; private schools practicing discrimination 1982 Apr 19F; private schools practicing race discrimination 1983 May 24F; public aid to parochial schools 1985 Jul 1F; racial discrimination in private schools 1988 Apr 25F; religious services on campus property 1981 Dec 8F; school busing 1982 Mar 22F/Jun 30F/Nov 12F; 1986 Jun 16F; school "moment of silence" 1987 Dec 1F; school prayer 1985 Jun 4F; sex bias 1984 Feb 28F; student aid linked to draft registration 1983 Jun 29F; 1984 Jul 5F; student disciplining for speech 1986 Jul 7F; student newspaper censorship 1988 Jan 13F; student searches 1985 Jan 15F; teachers advocating homosexual conduct 1985 Mar 26F; tuition tax credits 1983 Jun 29F; university basketball coach disciplining 1988 Dec 12F
environment and pollution: acid rain 1987 Jun 8H; clean-water violation lawsuits 1987 Dec 1H; environmental impact cases 1980 Jan 7H; hazardous-waste cleanup 1989 Jun 15H; industrial pollution bubble policy 1984 Jun 25H; jury trial for clean-water violations lawsuits 1987 Apr 28F; nuclear power industry 1983 Jun 6H; oil spill reporting 1980 Jun 27F; ozone standards 1982 Mar 22I; strip mining 1981 Jun 15H; toxic waste 1985 Jan 9H; 1986 Mar 10H; water pollution injunctions 1982 Apr 27F; water pollution standards costs 1980 Dec 2H; wetlands 1985 Dec 4H
ethnic bias: 1987 May 18F
evidence: exclusionary rule 1984 Jul 5F; illegally gathered evidence admissible 1984 Jun 11F; oil spill reporting 1980 Jun 27F; police failure to preserve evidence 1988

Nov 29F; police obtaining of evidence 1987 Jan 24F/Mar 9F; refusal to take a blood alcohol test 1983 Feb 22F; self-incrimination 1981 May 18F; 1985 Dec 10F
family issues: child custody 1980 Oct 20F; 1981 Jun 1F; 1984 Apr 25F; child protection from harm by parents 1989 Feb 22F; child sex abuse 1988 Jun 29F; child sexual abuse 1987 Jun 19F; child support payments 1987 Jun 25F
federal powers: criminal sentence appeals if too lenient 1980 Dec 9F; Gramm-Rudman-Hollings budget-balancing law 1986 Jul 7H; interior secretary exceeding of authority 1988 Feb 23H; legislative veto 1983 Jun 23F; local property taken over 1984 Dec 4F; offshore oil and natural gas leases 1984 Jan 11H
federal property rights: 1984 Dec 10F
flag burning: 1989 Jun 21F
handicapped: state liability for discrimination 1985 Jan 9F
health and safety issues: Agent Orange 1987 Nov 16G; asbestos injury suits 1982 Jan 11H; automobile passive restraints 1982 Nov 8H; 1983 Jun 24F; generic drugs 1983 Mar 22F; handicapped infants 1986 Jun 9F; health warnings and liability suits 1987 Jan 12F; nuclear power industry 1982 Nov 1I; 1983 Jan 19F; 1984 Jan 11H; state liability for discrimination 1985 Jan 9F; textile industry worker safety 1981 Jun 17H
housing: rent control law 1988 Feb 24F
immigration and refugees: illegal aliens 1984 Apr 17F; illegal deportations 1987 May 26F; political amnesty 1984 Jun 5F; political asylum 1987 Mar 9F
information: CIA withholding of information 1985 Apr 16F; government agencies retrieval of documents 1980 Mar 3F; IRS data 1987 Nov 10H; raw census data 1982 Feb 24F
job bias: exemption for religious groups 1987 Jun 24F; intentional bias evidence 1983 Apr 4F; overall hiring record not valid as defense 1982 Jun 21F; partnership decisions in law firms 1984 May 22F; racial bias proof required 1989 Jun 5F; state and local employees 1983 Mar 2F
judicial issues: judge's right to overturn convictions 1981 Feb 24F; Justice Department cases 1984 Mar 23F
labor issues: accommodation of employee's religion 1986 Nov 17F; collective bargaining protection for workers 1984 Mar 21F; discrimination in hiring or promotions 1988 Jun 29F; employee drug testing 1988 Oct 9F; 1989 Mar 21F; faculty unions 1980 Feb 20H; labor negotiations interference 1989 Dec 5F; mandatory retirement 1985 Jan 8F/Jun 17F; minimum wage and overtime pay laws 1985 Feb 19H; national security agency lawsuits 1988 Jun 15G; plant closing severance pay 1987 Jun 1F; politically motivated strikes 1982 Jun 24F; pregnancy benefits 1982 Dec 6F; 1983 Jun 20F; 1987 Jan 13F; secondary boycotts 1982 Apr 20F; seniority systems 1984 Jun 12F; strike damage lawsuits 1981 May 4H; unemployment benefits 1987 Feb 25F; union disciplining of members 1987 May 18F; union employees lawsuits of employers 1988 Jun 6H; union fines for returning to work 1985 Jun 27F; union leader penalties 1983 Apr 4F; union's refusal to press discrimination claims 1987 Jun 19F; work on Sabbath 1985 Jun 26F; 1987 Feb 25F; workplace privacy 1987 Mar 31F
land-reform program: 1984 May 30F
libel issues: 1984 Mar 20F; 1986 Apr 21F/Jun 25F; 1988 Feb 24F
mail-fraud law: 1987 Jun 24H
Marcos goods impoundment: 1987 Jun 26F
members: Blackmun death threat 1984 Oct 10F; Blackmun says Court is shifting to right 1984 Sep 18F; Brennan says Court has condoned civil rights violations 1984 Oct 29G; Burger comments on Court workload 1984 Dec 30F; Burger comments on prisons 1983 Jan 2F; Burger reported to have discussed cases with Nixon 1981 Dec 10F; Marshall's comments on Constitution 1987 May 6F; Marshall's criticisms of Reagan 1987 Sep 8F; original intent debate 1985 Oct 12F/Oct 25F/Nov 15F; Rehnquist assails other justices 1981 Apr 27F; Rehnquist criticizes workload 1982 Sep 23F; Rehnquist/Scalia often isolated 1987 Jun 26F; Rehnquist television interview 1984 Dec 29F; Rehnquist warning on federal judiciary funding 1988 Jan 1F; Shakespeare authorship ruling 1987 Sep 25J; Stevens publicly praises Bork qualifications 1987 Jul 17F
mentally retarded: 1981 Apr 20F; 1982 Jun 18F; 1985 Jul 1F
mental patients: 1981 Mar 4F
military issues: damage suits by military personnel 1987 Jun 25G
monetary claims against Iran: 1981 Jul 2F
Native Americans: 1980 Jun 30F; 1983 Jun 27H; 1985 Apr 16F; 1988 Apr 19F
Nazis: 1987 Oct 26G
negligence suits: 1987 May 18G
obituaries: Douglas, William O. 1980 Jan 19F; Fortas, Abe 1982 Apr 5F
obscenity issues: 1981 Nov 9F; 1982 Jul 2F; 1985 Jun 19F; 1986 Feb 24F/Apr 22F; 1987 May 4F; 1989 Feb 21F/Jun 23F
patents: biological organisms 1980 Jun 16F/Jun 16I; computer programs 1981 Mar 3I; monopolization of ingredient of patented process 1980 Jun 27F
presidential powers: civil suits against presidents 1982 Jun 24F; pocket veto 1987 Jan 14G
press and broadcasting: Abscam scandal videotapes 1980 Oct 14F; cable television 1986 Jun 2F; libel issues 1984 Mar 20F; 1986 Apr 21F; political propaganda 1987 Apr 28F; reporter refusing to give information 1981 Jan 19F; student newspaper censorship 1988 Jan 13F; TV broadcast ban refused 1983 Jan 16F
preventive detention: 1984 Jun 4F; 1987 May 26F
privacy issues: aerial surveillance without warrant 1986 May 19F; citizenship data 1982 May 17F; confidentiality between lawyers and clients 1981 Jan 13F; prison inmates 1984 Jul 3F; workplace privacy 1987 Mar 31F
public interest lawyers' legal fees: 1984 Mar 21F
racial bias: damage suits against state and local governments 1989 Jun 22F; grand jury race exclusion 1986 Jan 14F; in job bias suits 1989 Jun 5F; jury selection 1986 Apr 30F; multifamily housing projects 1988 Nov 7F; private schools 1988 Apr 25F; set-aside programs 1989 Jan 23H/Mar 6F
religion: accommodation of employee 1986 Nov 17F; Hanukkah menorah 1989 Jul 3F; Nativity scene 1984 Mar 5F; 1989 Jul 3F; religious group merchandise selling 1981 Jun 22F
sentencing: federal crime code 1988 Jun 13F; federal sentencing rules 1989 Jan 18F; marijuana 40-year prison sentence 1982 Jan 11F; minimum sentences for firearms 1986 Jun 19F
sex bias: 1981 Jun 8F; 1982 May 17F; 1984 Feb 28F; 1987 Mar 25F; 1989 May 1F
sexual harassment: 1986 Jun 19F
sleep-in protests: 1984 Jun 29F
special prosecutor law: 1988 Apr 26F/Jun 29F
sports issues: Gay Olympics 1987 Jun 25F; university basketball coach disciplining 1988 Dec 12F
state and local rights: age bias prohibited 1983 Mar 2F; care for the institutionalized mentally retarded 1981 Apr 20F; cities' antitrust laws immunity 1985 Mar 27H; clubs discrimination forbidden 1988 Jun 20F; clubs required to admit women 1987 May 4F; corporate takeover regulation 1987 Apr 21H; election procedures 1983 Feb 23F; fund-raising groups 1980 Feb 20F; health-insurance plans 1985 Jun 3F; highway funds linked to state drinking age 1987 Jun 23F; jail term for inability to pay fine 1983 May 31F; minimum wage and overtime pay laws 1985 Feb 19H; nuclear power industry 1983 Apr 20I; picketing ban 1988 Jun 27F; public access to beaches 1987 Jun 26H; racial bias damage suits 1989 Jun 22F; raw census data 1982 Feb 24F; religious group merchandise selling 1981 Jun 22F; Social Security System 1986 Jun 19F; state control of lands under tidal water 1988 Feb 23F; taking of private property 1987 Jun 9H; taxation of multinational corporations 1983 Jun 27H; toxic waste cleanup tax 1986 Mar 10H; toxic waste polluters protected by bankruptcy laws 1985 Jan 9H; toxic waste tax 1986 Mar 10H; utilities billing 1989 Jan 11H
tax issues: false tax returns 1984 Jan 17F; state taxation of multinational corporations 1983 Jun 27H; windfall profits tax 1983 May 6H
term begins 1986 Oct 6F
trade issues: Japanese whaling 1986 Jun 30F
trademarks: 1980 Feb 19H
travel restrictions: Cuba 1984 Jun 28F
victim impact statements: 1987 Jun 15F; 1989 Jun 12F
visas to members of communist organizations: 1987 Oct 19F
von Bulow murder conviction: 1984 Oct 1F
women: draft registration 1981 Jun 25F; pension benefits 1983 Jul 6F

Sure Thing, The (film) 1985 Mar 20J
Surface Mining, U.S. Office of (Interior Department) 1985 Oct 1H
Surgeon General's Report on Fitness and Health, The (Public Health Service) 1988 Jul 27I
Suriname 1980 Feb 25D/Aug 13D; 1982 Nov 3D/Dec 9D/Dec 11D; 1986 Oct 25E/Dec 13D/Dec 16D; 1987 Mar 31D/Oct 1D; 1988 Jan 12D/Jan 25D; 1989 Jun 7D/Jul 25D
Suriname Airways 1989 Jun 7D
surrogate mothers 1987 Mar 31F; 1988 Feb 3F/Apr 6F/Jun 27F
surveillance, aerial 1986 May 19F
Survivor (singing group) 1982 Jul 11J/Aug 18J
SU-22 (Soviet aircraft) 1981 Aug 19A
Suzuki Motor Co. 1981 Aug 12H
Swale (racehorse) 1984 May 5J/Jun 9J; 1985 Jan 8J
Swan Lake (ballet) 1988 Aug 6J
SWAPO *see* South-West Africa People's Organization
Swaziland 1980 Apr 1C; 1982 Aug 21C; 1983 Mar 18I; 1984 Mar 31C; 1986 Apr 25C; 1988 Sep 19J
Sweden *see also individual leaders in the name index (e.g.,* Palme, Olof)
arts and culture: Academy of Letters resignations over Rushdie affair 1989 Mar 14A/Sep 21J; *Fanny and Alexander* opens 1983 Jun 17J; *My Life as a Dog* released 1987 May 1J; *My Life as a Dog* wins Golden Globe 1988 Jan 23J
awards and honors: Myrdal wins Nobel Peace Prize 1982 Oct 12A
business and industry: stainless steel companies merge 1984 Jan 11B
Chernobyl accident: 1986 Apr 28B/Sep 19B; 1988 Sep 21I
disarmament and arms control: 1982 Jun 1A/Dec 8B; 1985 Jan 28A
econmomy: GNP 1988 Feb 24B
economy: budget 1989 Jan 10B; GDP 1987 Mar 25B; inflation rate 1987 Jan 22B; tax reform 1988 Nov 23B
foreign aid: 1983 Dec 23A
foreign relations: China 1984 Jun 16E; Mexico 1980 May 28D; USSR 1981 Oct 28B/Oct 30B/Oct 31B/Nov 6B; 1983 Dec 2B; Zimbabwe 1983 Mar 12B
government and politics: Carlson elected premier 1986 Mar 12B; Falldin government collapses 1981 May 4B; general elections 1988 Sep 18B; justice minister resigns 1988 Jun 7B; national elections 1985 Sep 15B; nuclear power referendum 1980 Mar 23B; Palme assassinated 1986 Feb 28B; parliamentary elections 1982 Sep 19B
immigration and refugees: 1986 Oct 4B
labor issues: civil service strike 1985 May 20B; employers association locks out workers 1980 May 1B; harbor worker strike 1980 Jun 10B; public-sector strikes 1986 Oct 30B; wage pact ends strike 1980 May 11B
medicine and health care: breast cancer 1989 Aug 3I
obituaries: Bergman, Ingrid 1982 Aug 29J; Erlander, Tage 1985 Jun 21B; Myrdal, Alva 1986 Feb 1A; Myrdal, Gunnar 1987 May 17A; Palme, Olof 1986 Feb 28B; Stenberg, Leif 1985 Nov 21I; Weiss, Peter 1982 May 10J
science and technology: Bergstroem and Samuelsson win Nobel Prize 1982 Oct 11I; Siegbahn wins Nobel Prize 1981 Oct 19I
sports: golf 1988 Jul 24J; high jump 1987 Jun 30J; ice hockey 1986 Apr 28J; 1987 May 3J; running 1989 Jul 3J; tennis 1983 Dec 28J; 1984 Dec 17J; 1985 Dec 22J; 1986 Jun 8J; 1987 Dec 20J; 1988 May 22J/Dec 18J; Borg, Bjorn; Edberg, Stefan; Wilander, Mats; wrestler disqualified after drug test 1984 Aug 12J
U.S. relations: 1983 Jun 24G; 1989 May 2H
World War II: Wallenberg case 1981 Jan 15A/Oct 31B; 1987 Apr 15B
Swedish Academy of Letters 1989 Mar 14A
Swedish National Defense Research Institute 1980 Jan 17I
Swedish Royal Academy 1989 Sep 21J
sweeteners, artifical 1980 Mar 6I; 1981 Jul 15I; 1983 Apr 13I
swimming 1980 Jul 22J; 1981 Jan 13J; 1982 Apr 18J/Aug 28J; 1983 Apr 23J; 1984 Jan 20J; 1985 Aug 7J/Aug 17J/Aug 18J; 1987 Aug 7J; 1988 Aug 1J
swimming pools 1989 Sep 27C
Swiss Polytechnical Institute 1987 Jan 10B
Switzerland
banking: drug boss funds frozen 1989 Dec 6A; Iran-Contra scandal 1986 Dec 10F/Dec 15B; 1987 Aug 20F; Marcos deposits frozen 1986 Mar 25E; U.S. aided in insider trading case 1984 May 16A
bombings: Geneva train station 1981 Jul 22B
business and industry: Nestle boycott ended 1984 Jan 27B
crime and law enforcement: Khashoggi extradited to U.S. 1989 Jul 19J; Marc Rich & Co. case 1983 Aug 12B/Sep 19H/Sep 21B; 1984 Oct 11H/Dec 17H; 1985 Aug 16B; Polish embassy hostages 1982 Sep 9B
currency: 1982 Oct 4A; 1984 Jun 28H/Dec 27H
economy: cost of living in Zurich 1988 Jun 28A
environment and pollution: dioxin-contaminated soil 1983 Jun 4B; Rhine River chemical spill 1986 Nov 1B/Nov 12B; 1987 Jan 10B/Dec 28B
espionage and intelligence issues: USSR 1980 Feb 18B
foreign relations: France 1984 May 19B; Iran hostage crisis 1980 Mar 30A/Apr 14A

government and politics: federal council nominee rejected 1983 Dec 7B; general elections 1987 Oct 18B; Social Democrats reject withdrawing from coalition 1984 Feb 12B; women 1981 Jun 14B; 1984 Apr 29B; 1985 Dec 22B

hijackings: Air Afrique airliner in Geneva 1987 Jul 24B

initiatives and referendums: army 1989 Nov 26B; foreign workers' rights 1981 Apr 5B; immigration and political asylum 1987 Apr 5B; laboratory animals 1985 Dec 1B; military service alternative rejected 1984 Feb 26B; nuclear power plants 1984 Sep 23B; opening bank records to authorities 1984 May 20B; UN membership 1986 Mar 16B

international organizations: Group of 10 1984 Apr 5A; United Nations 1985 Dec 10A

labor issues: labor costs comparison 1988 Aug 6B

obituaries: Bloch, Felix 1983 Sep 10I; Piaget, Jean 1980 Sep 16I

religion: Roman Catholic Church schism 1988 Jun 30J

science and technology: Rohrer wins Nobel Prize 1986 Oct 15I

sports: figure skating 1986 Mar 21J; skiing 1986 Mar 23J; 1987 Feb 2J; 1988 Mar 24J/Mar 26J; yacht racing 1986 May 9J

Sword and the Sorcerer, The (film) 1982 May 5J/Aug 11J

Sydney Airport (Australia) 1989 Jun 8E

Sydney Morning Herald (Australian newspaper) 1980 Dec 2E

Symphony, RiverRun (Stephen Albert) (musical composition) 1985 Apr 24J

Symphony No. 1 (Ellen Taaffee Zwillich) (musical composition) 1983 Apr 18J

Synanon 1981 Feb 28F

Synchronicity (Police) (recording) 1983 Jul 13J/Aug 17J/Aug 17J/Sep 14J/Oct 19J/Nov 9J; 1984 Feb 18J

synthetic fibers 1987 Oct 5H

synthetic fuels 1983 Mar 31H; 1985 Aug 1H

Syracuse University (New York) 1981 Mar 25J; 1987 Mar 30J; 1988 Jan 1J/May 30J

Syria *see also individual leaders in the name index (e.g., Assad, Hafez al-)*

antigovernment uprisings: 1980 Mar 5C; 1981 Jan 2C; 1982 Feb 2C

bombings: Damascus 1981 Nov 29C

foreign relations: European Community 1987 Jul 13B; Great Britain 1986 Oct 24C; Iraq 1980 Sep 27C; 1982 Apr 8C/Apr 10C/Apr 17C; Jordan 1980 Nov 26C/Dec 3C/Dec 10C; 1981 Jun 2C; 1985 Oct 21C; Hussein, King; Kuwait 1981 May 6C; Libya 1980 Sep 2C/Sep 10C/Dec 18C; 1985 Oct 12C; PLO 1983 May 30C; USSR 1980 Oct 8A; 1981 Jul 9A

Golan Heights *see* Golan Heights

government and politics: Premier Kassem resigns 1987 Oct 31C

hijackings: Pakistani airliner in Damascus 1981 Mar 14E

international organizations: United Nations 1987 Dec 1A; World Bank 1988 Jul 11A

killings: former premier assassinated in Paris 1980 Jul 21C; Muslim

---

Brotherhood leader killed 1980 Aug 16C

Lebanon *see* Lebanon

obituaries: Jumbaz, Hisham 1980 Aug 16C

oil pipelines: 1980 Sep 27C; 1981 Feb 26C; 1982 Apr 10C

terrorism: 1983 Nov 23G; 1986 May 21B/Oct 24C/Nov 01B/Nov 26B/Nov 27C; 1987 Feb 5B/Dec 1A

U.S. relations: 1981 May 20A/Oct 31C; 1982 Feb 26C; 1983 Dec 4C/Dec 25G/Dec 29C/Dec 31C; 1984 Jan 3C/Jan 4C; 1988 Feb 25C

water resources: 1983 Jun 8C

T

tactical nuclear weapons *see* short-range nuclear weapons

Tadzhikistan (USSR) 1984 Mar 20I; 1985 Oct 13B; 1989 Jan 23E

Taiwan *see also individual leaders in the name index (e.g., Chiang Ching-kuo)*

earthquakes: 1986 Nov 15I

economy: foreign-exchange controls 1987 Jul 15E; stock market 1989 Nov 28E

foreign relations: China 1980 Jun 14E; 1981 Sep 30E/Oct 10E; 1984 Oct 1E; 1985 Aug 24E; 1986 Apr 30E/May 20E; 1987 Oct 14E; Nicaraguan contras 1984 Sep 8D; 1987 Jan 23G; South Africa 1980 Oct 13A; South Korea 1985 Mar 28E

government and politics: amnesty 1988 Apr 22E; Chiang Ching-kuo reelected president 1984 Mar 21E; elections 1985 Nov 16E; 1986 Dec 6E; 1989 Dec 2E; Lee Huan appointed premier 1989 May 24E; Lee Teng-hui becomes president 1988 Jan 13E; martial law 1986 Oct 15E; 1987 Jul 14E; Nationalist Party congress 1988 Jul 13E

international organizations: Asian Development Bank 1986 Mar 11E; Interpol 1984 Sep 15E

riots: 1988 May 20E

sports: Little League baseball 1980 Aug 30E; 1981 Aug 29J; 1982 Aug 28J; 1986 Aug 23J; 1988 Aug 27J; 1989 Aug 26J

trade issues: trade surplus 1988 Jan 7E/Feb 8E

U.S. relations: 1981 Jun 17E; 1982 Jan 4E/Jul 8F/Aug 17A/Aug 17E; 1983 Jul 15G/Nov 15G; 1984 Jun 19G; 1988 Jan 29G/Apr 29E/Dec 28H

Taiwan stock exchange 1989 Nov 28E

Taiyo Kobe Bank Ltd. 1989 Aug 29E

Takoma Park (Maryland) 1985 Dec 23G

Talisman, The (Stephen King/Peter Straub) (book) 1984 Nov 16J/Dec 14J; 1985 Jan 18J/Feb 8J

Talk Radio (Eric Bogosian) (play) 1987 May 28J

Talley's Folly (Lanford Wilson) (play) 1980 Apr 14J

Tamil Nadu (India) 1980 May 31E/Oct 26E; 1987 Dec 24E; 1988 Jan 31E; 1989 Jan 21E

Tamils *see* Liberation Tigers; Sri Lanka

Tampa Bay Buccaneers (football team) 1980 Jan 6J; 1986 Jun 21J; 1987 Apr 28J

tampons 1981 Jan 13I; 1982 Dec 24H

tanks 1989 Apr 25B

Tank's Prospect (racehorse) 1985 May 18J

Tanzania 1980 Apr 1C/Oct 26C; 1981 Jan 17C; 1984 Apr 19C/Nov 12C; 1985 Jan 28A/Nov 3C; 1986 Aug 20C; 1987 Oct 31C; 1989 Nov 5J

Taps (film) 1982 Jan 6J

Target (film) 1985 Nov 20J

Tarzan the Ape Man (film) 1981 Jul 29J

Task Force on Food Assistance 1984 Jan 10E

Tasso (racehorse) 1985 Nov 2J

Tatars (Soviet ethnic group) 1987 Jul 28B/Nov 14J

Tattoo You (Rolling Stones) (recording) 1981 Sep 9J/Sep 30J/Nov 11J/Dec 9J

Taubman Co. 1983 Sep 19J

Taxation, U.S. Congress Joint Committee on 1983 Mar 9H; 1984 Nov 30H

Tax Foundation (Washington, D.C.) 1985 Mar 22H

tax havens 1987 Jun 30H

Taxi (TV show) 1980 Sep 7J; 1981 Sep 13J

taxicabs 1988 Jul 24F

Taxi Driver (film) 1981 Apr 2J/Apr 8J

tax indexing 1984 Oct 24H

tax shelters 1982 Jan 20J; 1984 Jun 8H; 1985 Feb 11H

Tchaikovsky Hall (Moscow) 1987 Apr 21J

tea 1987 May 2J

teachers

awards and honors *see* National Teacher of the Year award

career interest: 1987 Mar 10F

foreign issues: Australia 1988 Jan 6E; Bolivia 1989 Nov 15D; Canada 1980 Feb 25D; Great Britain 1985 Apr 23B; 1986 Mar 3B/Dec 11B; 1987 Mar 2B; Mexico 1989 May 10D; Nicaragua 1989 May 25D; South Africa 1986 Mar 30C; South Korea 1980 Aug 2E; Turkey 1982 Feb 26B

job satisfaction: 1986 Apr 30F

labor issues: 1983 Jul 5F; 1984 Feb 14H; 1985 Jul 13F; 1986 Jul 6F; 1989 Jul 21F/Jul 21F; affirmative action plan 1986 May 19F; California 1982 Nov 1F; 1983 Nov 27F; 1989 May 25F; Illinois 1980 Jan 28F/Feb 11F; 1983 Sep 12F; 1984 Dec 16F/Dec 20F; 1985 Sep 18F; 1987 Oct 4F; Michigan 1983 Sep 12F; 1985 Sep 18F; 1987 Sep 19F; Mississippi 1985 Mar 8F/Mar 20F; Missouri 1983 Sep 12F; New Jersey 1983 Sep 18F; New York 1983 Sep 18F; Ohio 1985 Sep 18F; Pennsylvania 1983 Sep 12F; 1985 Sep 18F; Rhode Island 1983 Sep 12F; 1985 Sep 18F; strike statistics 1984 Sep 4F; Washington State 1983 Sep 12F; 1985 Sep 18F

NEA: 1985 Apr 9F/Jul 3F; 1986 Jul 6F; 1987 Dec 3F

salaries: 1983 Oct 11F; 1984 Feb 14H; 1985 Sep 9F; 1987 Mar 15F; 1989 Jul 21F

space program: 1984 Aug 27I; 1985 Jul 19I

---

studies and reports: 1983 Aug 23F/Oct 19F; 1985 Apr 9F; 1986 Jul 6F

Supreme Court rulings: 1985 Jan 15F/Mar 26F

testing of: 1985 Mar 23F; 1986 Mar 10F/May 8F/May 86; 1988 Oct 27F

training: 1984 Sep 28F; 1985 Feb 27F; 1989 Jul 17F

Teachers (film) 1984 Oct 10J

Teachers, American Federation of *see* American Federation of Teachers (AFT)

Teamsters, International Brotherhood of 1981 Apr 14F/Dec 1H; 1982 Jan 15H/Mar 1H/Dec 15H; 1983 Jan 20J/Jan 31H/Feb 10H; 1985 Mar 31H/Jun 12H/Aug 18H/Sep 16H; 1986 Jan 21F/Mar 6F; 1988 Mar 31H/May 19H/Jul 15F/Oct 17F; 1989 May 31H; Justice, Department of; Labor, Department of; Presser, Jackie; Williams, Roy Lee

Tears for Fears (singing group) 1985 Jun 22J/Jul 27J/Aug 24J/Sep 28J/Oct 26J

Technology Assessment, U.S. Office of *see* Office of Technology Assessment, U.S.

teeth 1980 Mar 8I; 1985 Feb 14F

Tel Aviv Stock Exchange 1983 Oct 10C/Oct 18C

telephones 1983 Dec 1H; 1984 Mar 21H/Dec 19H; 1987 Dec 24H; *see also individual companies (e.g., American Telephone and Telegraph)*

Telesat Canada 1982 Nov 12I

telescopes 1985 Jan 3I

television *see* cable television; *specific networks (e.g.,* National Broadcasting System*); individual shows (e.g.,* Cosby Show*)*

Television and Radio Artists, American Federation of *see* American Federation of Television and Radio Artists

Television Arts and Sciences, Academy of *see* Emmy Awards

Television's Vietnam: The Real Story (TV show) 1985 Jun 26J

Temperance Hill (racehorse) 1980 Jun 7J

temperatures 1980 Aug 15I; 1983 Aug 1I/Dec 30I; 1985 Jan 10I/Jan 23I

Tempest (film) 1982 Oct 6J

Temple Mount (Jerusalem mosque) 1982 Apr 12C

Temple of My Familiar, The (Alice Walker) (book) 1989 May 26J/Jun 30J

Templeton Prize 1983 Mar 2J; 1984 May 15J; 1985 Feb 27J; 1986 Feb 26J; 1987 Mar 5J; 1988 Mar 2J; 1989 Mar 7J

Tempo (Indonesian news magazine) 1982 Apr 12E

Temptations, the (singing group) 1989 Jan 18J

10-Year Lunch, The: The Wit and Legend of the Algonquin Round Table (film) 1988 Apr 11J

Tender Mercies (film) 1983 Mar 4J; 1984 Apr 9J

Tennessee

business and economy: American General/NLT Corp. purchase 1982 Apr 16H; GM Saturn project 1986 Oct 30H; Nissan plant in Smyrna opens 1983 May 9H

crime and law enforcement: prison riots 1985 Jul 2F; racial strife 1980 Jul 22F/Jul 25F

---

floods: 1983 Apr 12I; 1984 May 8I

frozen embryo custody case: 1989 Sep 21F

nuclear power plants: 1980 Feb 28I; 1982 Sep 3F; 1983 Jan 6H

politics and government: presidential campaigns 1980 May 6F; 1984 May 1F; presidential primary date moved 1986 Apr 6F; Reagan visits 1982 Mar 15F

religious issues: fundamentalist medical treatment ordered 1983 Sep 21F

World's Fair: 1982 Oct 31J

Tennessee System, University of 1984 Apr 1J; 1986 Jan 1J; 1987 Mar 29J; 1989 Apr 2J

Tennessee-Tombigbee Waterway 1980 Oct 1H

Tennessee Valley Authority (TVA) 1983 Jan 16H; 1984 Jul 16H; 1985 Aug 23H; 1986 Jun 11H

10,000-meter race (running) 1985 Jul 27J

Terminator, The (film) 1984 Nov 7J/Dec 12J

termites 1987 Aug 11H

Terms of Endearment (film) 1983 Nov 23J/Dec 7J; 1984 Jan 11J/Feb 8J/Mar 7J/Apr 9J

territorial waters 1988 Dec 28G

Terror in the Aisles (film) 1984 Nov 7J

Tess (film) 1980 Dec 12J

tetanus 1985 Feb 3D

tetrahydroaminoacridine (THA) (drug) 1987 Jun 21I

Texaco Canada Inc. 1989 Jan 20H

Texaco Inc. 1983 Apr 13H; 1984 Jan 8H/Feb 13H/Jul 13H; 1985 Nov 19H; 1987 Feb 12H/Apr 6H/Apr 12H/Nov 2H/Dec 19H; 1988 Jun 20H; 1989 Jan 20H

Texaco Trophy (cricket) 1986 May 26J; 1987 May 25J

Texas *see also individual leaders in the name index (e.g., Clements, Bill)*

accidents and disasters: Delta Airlines crash (Dallas-Fort Worth) 1985 Aug 2H; frost damage 1983 Dec 29H; Hurricane Alicia 1983 Aug 18I; Hurricane Juan 1985 Oct 26I; storms 1982 Apr 2I

agriculture: citrus crop frost damamge 1983 Dec 29H

arts and culture: Miss America crowned 1987 Feb 17J; 1988 Mar 1J

business and economy: Diamond Shamrock/Sigmor purchase 1982 Jul 7H; First City Bancorp bailout 1988 Apr 20H; MCorp banks purchased 1989 Jun 28H; Mercantile Texas/Southwest Bancshares merger 1983 Jul 21H; savings and loan associations 1987 Nov 19H; 1988 Feb 2H/May 18H/Jul 7H; 1989 Feb 2H; tax increase 1984 Jul 3F; Texaco interference suit 1987 Feb 12H/Nov 2H

crime and law enforcement: Adams conviction overturned 1989 Mar 1F; Adams released from prison 1989 Mar 21F; Autry execution stay 1983 Oct 5F/Oct 31F; execution delayed 1983 Jan 24F; Geter granted retrial 1983 Dec 14F; South Carolina attorney general seeks retrial 1983 Nov 20F

education issues: college bias 1983 Mar 24F; extracurricular activities 1985 Jul 10F; financing ruled unconstitutional 1989 Oct 2F; reform plan 1984 Jul 3F; teacher testing 1986 Mar 10F/May 8F; theory of evolution 1984 Apr 14F

environmental issues: nuclear power plant inspections 1986 Dec 11H; nuclear waste sites 1984 Dec 19H; oil spills 1989 Jun 24H

executions: Brooks Jr., Charles 1982 Dec 7F; King, Leon 1989 Mar 22F

foreign issues: Prince Charles visits 1986 Feb 17F

medicine and health care: brain cancer among petrochemical workers 1980 Jul 24H; "dumping" of critically ill patients 1985 Dec 14F; woman gives birth to 21st child 1980 Jan 12I

obituaries: Corn Jr., Ira G. 1982 Apr 28J; Hopkins, Sam (Lightnin') 1982 Jan 30J; Jaworski, Leon 1982 Dec 9F

politics and government: city council plurality voting 1982 Dec 13F; Dallas GOP convention (1984) 1984 Aug 20F-22F; Dallas Mayor Strauss reelected 1989 May 6F; Gramm wins renomination 1982 May 1F; JFK commemoration ceremony 1983 Nov 22F; presidential campaigns 1980 May 3F; 1984 Aug 2F; 1988 Jan 18F

race issues: college bias 1983 Mar 24F

science and technology: superconducting supercollider 1988 Nov 10H; 1989 Sep 29H

sports: basketball 1980 Feb 2J; football see Cotton Bowl

Texas (James Michener) (book) 1985 Oct 25J/Nov 22J/Dec 20J; 1986 Jan 31J

Texas Air Corp. 1986 Sep 15H; 1988 Oct 12H; 1989 Apr 6H/Apr 12H

Texas A&M University (College Station) 1981 Dec 12J; 1986 Jan 1J; 1987 Jan 1J; 1988 Jan 1J; 1989 May 12G

Texas Eastern Transmission Corp. 1987 Nov 9H

Texasgulf Inc. 1981 Jun 26H

Texas Instruments Corp. 1984 Sep 10G

Texas Oil & Gas Corp. 1985 Oct 30H

Texas Pacific Oil Co. (Seagram Co. Ltd.) 1980 Sep 12H

Texas Rangers (baseball team) 1980 Dec 6J; 1984 Sep 30J; 1989 Aug 22J

Texas System, University of Austin Campus 1982 Jan 1J/Mar 28J; 1984 Jan 2J; 1985 Oct 14I/Nov 22I; 1986 Mar 30J

Texasville (Larry McMurtry) (book) 1987 May 29J

textiles see also Multi-Fiber Arrangement

bankruptcies: 1985 Jan 2B

health and safety issues: 1981 Jun 17H

obituaries: Ashley, Laura 1985 Sep 17J

trade issues: China/European Community 1984 Mar 29A; China/U.S. 1980 Sep 17A; 1983 Jan 2E/Jan 13H/Jan 19E/Feb 2E/Aug 19A; China/USSR 1983 Mar 10A; congressional actions 1985 Oct 10H/Dec 3H; 1986 Aug 6H; 1987 Sep 16H; 1988 Sep 9H/Oct 4H; GATT 1989 Apr 8A; Japan/U.S. 1986 Nov 14E/Nov 15E; Mexico/U.S. 1988 Feb 13D; South Korea/U.S. 1986 Aug 4E; U.S. ad-

ministration actions 1983 Dec 16H; 1984 Aug 25H; 1985 Dec 17H; 1988 Sep 28H; U.S. import volume 1985 Feb 1G

Textron Inc. 1980 Jan 31H

T4 helper cells 1985 Jul 10I

THA see tetrahydroaminoacridine

Thailand see also individual leaders in the name index (e.g., Tinsulanonda, Prem)

arts and culture: Thai chosen Miss Universe 1988 May 24J

Cambodia-Vietnam conflict: 1980 Jun 23E; 1982 Feb 17E; 1984 Mar 25E/Apr 17G; 1985 Jan 10E/May 8E

civil strife: Communists end guerrilla war 1989 Dec 2E

foreign relations: Cambodia 1980 Jul 26E; China 1982 Feb 3E; Laos 1988 Feb 17E

government and politics: coup attempts 1981 Apr 3E; 1985 Sep 9E/Sep 17E; government/military crisis averted 1984 Sep 3E; Kriangsak Chamanand resigns as premier 1980 Feb 19E

hijackings: Burmese students 1989 Oct 7E; Garuda Airlines 1981 Mar 28E/Mar 31E; Sri Lankan hijacker 1982 Jul 1E

immigration and regugees: refugee camps 1988 May 1E; Vietnam "boat people" 1980 Feb 24E/Jan 27E/Apr 20E

religious issues: papal visit 1984 May 2A

U.S. relations: 1980 Jul 5E; 1982 Nov 8E; 1989 May 2H

Vietnam War: POW rescue missions 1983 Feb 28E/Mar 11E

Thames River 1985 Jul 7J; 1986 Mar 29J; 1989 Mar 25J/Aug 20B/Sep 1B

Thames Television 1988 Apr 28B; 1989 Jan 26B

That's What Friends Are For (Burt Bacharach/Carol Bayer Sager) (recording) 1987 Feb 24J

theater

actors/directors/writers see individual artists in the name index (e.g., Mamet, David)

awards and honors see specific awards (e.g., Tony Awards)

openings see individual titles (e.g., Starlight Express)

Theater Communications Group 1985 Mar 13J

Theatrical (racehorse) 1987 Nov 21J

Then Again, Maybe I Won't (Judy Blume) (book) 1984 Dec 3J

Theodore Roosevelt (ship) 1984 Oct 28G

theology 1986 Aug 18J; 1987 Dec 7J; 1989 Jan 26J

thermoluminescence 1988 Feb 18I

Thief (film) 1981 Apr 1J

Thin Blue Line, The (film) 1988 Aug 26J; 1989 Mar 1F/Mar 21F

Things Are Tough All Over (film) 1982 Aug 11J

Thinner (Richard Bachman/Stephen King) (book) 1985 Apr 19J/May 24J

Third Deadly Sin, The (Lawrence Sanders) (book) 1981 Aug 9J/Sep 6J/Oct 4J

Third Force (Northern Irish militant group) 1981 Dec 24B

Third Punic War 1985 Feb 3B

Third Stage (Boston) (recording) 1986 Oct 22J/Nov 22J/Dec 17J; 1987 Jan 28J

thirtysomething (TV show) 1988 Aug 28J; 1989 Jan 28J

This Week (TV show) 1981 Nov 22G

Thomas and Beulah (Rita Dove) (book) 1987 Apr 16J

Thompson-Brandt 1982 Nov 19B

Thomson Organisation Ltd. 1980 Oct 22J

Thorn Birds, The (TV show) 1983 Sep 25J

Thoroughbred Racing Association 1984 Feb 3J

3M Company 1983 Jul 21H

Three Amigos (film) 1986 Dec 24J

Three Men and a Baby (film) 1987 Nov 25J/Dec 23F; 1988 Jan 20J

Three Men on a Horse (play) 1988 Jan 24J

Three Mile Island nuclear power plant (Middletown, Pa.) 1980 Feb 11H/Mar 28F/Jul 11I; 1981 Feb 21F; 1982 Feb 19I; 1983 Jan 24H/Jan 26H/Mar 28H/Nov 7H/Nov 30H; 1984 Nov 7H; 1985 Oct 3H; see also Nuclear Regulatory Commission

Three's Company (TV show) 1983 Apr 10J

Three Servicemen (Frederick Hart) (sculpture) 1984 Nov 9G

3,000 meters (running) 1989 Aug 20J

3,000 meter steeplechase (running) 1989 Jul 3J

Thrift Supervision, U.S. Office of 1989 Dec 4H/Dec 6H

Thriller (Michael Jackson) (recording) 1983 Feb 9J/Mar 9J/Apr 13J/Apr 13J/May 11J/May 11J/Jun 15J/Jun 15J/Jul 13J/Aug 17J/Sep 14J/Oct 19J/Nov 9J/Dec 14J; 1984 Jan 11J/Jan 21J/Feb 18J/Feb 28J/Mar 24J/Apr 28J/May 20J/May 28J

Through a Glass, Darkly (Karleen Koen) (book) 1985 Aug 28J

Throw Momma from the Train (film) 1987 Dec 23F

Thursday's Child (ship) 1989 Feb 12J

Thy Brother's Wife (Andrew M. Greeley) (book) 1982 May 9J

Tiananmen Square (Beijing, China) 1984 Apr 26A; 1987 Jan 1E; 1989 Apr 22E/May 23E/Jun 4E/Oct 1E

Tibet (China) 1985 Sep 1E; 1987 Oct 7E/Oct 7E; 1988 Mar 5E/Jun 15E/Jul 30E; 1989 Jan 2E/Mar 7E/Mar 24E/Oct 5A

tidal waves 1983 May 26I; 1985 May 25I

Tidewater Conference 1982 Mar 14F

Tiffany (singer) 1987 Dec 26J; 1988 Jan 23J/Feb 20J/Mar 19J

Tiffany (Tiffany) (recording) 1987 Dec 26J; 1988 Jan 23J/Feb 20J/Mar 19J

Tightrope (film) 1984 Sep 12J

Tigre (Ethiopia) 1983 Jun 9C; 1985 Jan 13C; 1987 Oct 22C

Tigre Liberation Front 1983 Jun 9C

Tikuna Indians (Brazil) 1988 Mar 28D

Till We Meet Again (Judith Krantz) (book) 1988 Aug 26J/Sep 30J/Oct 21J

Tilted Arc (Richard Serra) (sculpture) 1985 May 31J; 1987 Aug 31J

Time (magazine) 1980 Apr 21F; 1983 Feb 28C/Jun 22J; 1985 Jan 9F; 1986 Dec 27J; 1987 Dec 26J

Time Bandits (film) 1981 Dec 2J

Time Inc. 1983 Feb 28C; 1989 Mar 4H/Jul 24H

Time-Life International 1983 Feb 28C

Times Beach (Missouri) 1982 Dec 23I; 1983 Jan 12H/Feb 22H/Jun 4H; 1985 Apr 10H

Times of Harvey Milk, The (film) 1985 Mar 25J

Times of London (newspaper) 1980 Aug 22B/Aug 29J/Oct 22J; 1981 Feb 13J; 1982 Feb 8B/Mar 11B

timolol (drug) 1981 Nov 25I

tin 1985 Oct 24A; 1986 Mar 12B

Tina Live in Europe (Tina Turner) (recording) 1989 Feb 22J

Tin Drum, The (film) 1980 Apr 11J

Tin Men (film) 1987 Mar 18J

tissue plasminogen activator (TPA) 1986 Mar 10I; 1987 Nov 13I; 1989 Mar 30I

Titan (moon of Saturn) 1983 Apr 16I

Titan (nuclear missile) 1980 Sep 18G/Sep 19G; 1981 Dec 31G

Titan 3-B (rocket) 1987 Feb 11G

Titan 34-D (rocket) 1985 Aug 28I; 1986 Apr 18I; 1987 Oct 26I

Titanic (ship) 1985 Sep 1J; 1986 Jul 13I

TNT see Turner Network Television

tobacco and smoking see also individual agency heads in the name index (e.g., Koop, C. Everett)

advertising: AMA calls for ban 1985 Dec 10F; health warnings 1986 Feb 27F/Apr 17F/Oct 24H; 1987 Jan 12F; legislation banning 1986 Jul 18H

aviation ban: 1986 Apr 27D/Aug 13H; 1987 Jul 13H/Oct 29F; 1988 Mar 23H; 1989 Sep 14H

city restrictions on: Chicago 1988 Jul 24F; New York City 1988 Jan 7F

health and safety issues: 1984 Feb 16I; 1985 Dec 2F; 1986 Jan 15F

liability lawsuits: 1985 Dec 23F; 1988 Jun 13F

military curb on: 1986 Jun 11G

prices: 1987 Jul 20B; 1988 Feb 1B

research and development: 1987 Sep 14H

state age limit on sales: 1986 Nov 20H

statistics: 1985 Dec 2F; 1987 Sep 11I; 1988 Jan 13F; 1989 Jan 5I

trade issues: 1986 Oct 3E

To Be the Best (Barbara Taylor Bradford) (book) 1988 Jul 23J/Aug 26J

Today (TV show) 1982 Jan 6H; 1989 Oct 27J

Togo 1983 Jan 17C; 1985 Aug 19J; 1986 Sep 23C

Tokamak Fusion Test Reactor (Princeton University) 1982 Dec 28I

Tokyo Dome (stadium) 1988 Mar 18J

Tokyo Round (GATT) 1981 Dec 1E

Tokyo Stock Exchange 1986 Sep 16E; 1987 Oct 20A/Dec 16E; 1988 Apr 7E/Dec 28E; 1989 Oct 16A/Oct 17A/Dec 31A

To Live and Die in L.A. (film) 1985 Nov 20J

Tombee: Portrait of a Cotton Planter (Theodore Rosengarten) (book) 1987 Jan 12J

Tommyknockers, The (Stephen King) (book) 1987 Dec 18J; 1988 Jan 29J/Feb 26J

Tom Petty & the Heartbreakers (singing group) 1980 Mar 5J

Tonight Show, The (TV show) 1986 May 6J

Tontons Macoutes (Haitian militia) 1987 Jul 29D

Tony (Antoinette Perry) Awards 1980 Jun 8J; 1981 Jun 7J; 1982 Jun 6J; 1983 Jun 5J; 1984 Jun 3J; 1985 Jun 2J; 1986 Jun 1J; 1987 Jun 7J; 1988 Jun 5J; 1989 Jun 4J

Tony Bin (racehorse) 1988 Oct 2J

Tootsie (film) 1983 Feb 2J/Mar 9J; 1984 Jan 11J

Top Gun (film) 1986 May 16J/Jun 18J

Top Gun (soundtrack) 1986 Jul 16J/Aug 13J/Sep 17J/Oct 22J

Torch Song Trilogy (Harvey Fierstein) (play) 1983 Jun 5J

tornadoes 1982 May 29I; 1983 May 23I; 1984 Mar 28H; 1988 Nov 20I/Nov 28I; 1989 Feb 26I/Apr 26I/Nov 16I

Toronto, University of (Canada) 1989 May 18I

Toronto Argonauts (football team) 1987 Nov 29J; 1989 Jun 3J

Toronto Blue Jays (baseball team) 1981 May 15J; 1985 Oct 16J; 1987 Nov 17J; 1989 Jun 3J/Oct 8J

Toronto Stock Exchange 1980 Feb 27D

Torrejon air base (Spain) 1988 Jan 15B

tortillas 1982 Aug 1D; 1986 May 22D

Toshiba Corp. 1987 Jun 30H/Jul 16G; 1989 Nov 20H

Toshiba Machine Co. (Toshiba Corp.) 1987 Jul 16G; 1988 Mar 22E

To the Citizens of the USSR (manifesto) 1986 Jul 22B

Toto (singing group) 1983 Feb 23J/Mar 9J

Toto IV (Toto) (recording) 1983 Feb 23J

Touche Ross & Co. 1989 Jul 6H

Tough Guys Don't Dance (Norman Mailer) (book) 1984 Sep 14J

Tour de France (bicycle race) 1985 Jul 21J; 1986 Jul 27J; 1987 Jul 26J; 1988 Jul 24J; 1989 Jul 23J

tourism 1980 Jul 4B/Aug 19B; 1981 Jul 29C; 1983 May 16G; 1984 Aug 6G; 1986 May 29J; 1987 Mar 12E; 1989 Sep 3D/Dec 18B

Tower Commission 1987 Feb 26G/Feb 27C/Mar 3F/Mar 4G; 1989 Apr 24F

toxaphene (pesticide) 1982 Oct 18I

toxic-shock syndrome 1980 Jun 6I/Sep 22I; 1981 Jan 13I; 1982 Apr 21H/Dec 24H; 1989 May 20B

Toxic Substances Control Act 1987 Oct 20I

toxic wastes see hazardous wastes

Toyota Championships 1982 Dec 19J

Toyota Motor Corp. 1983 Feb 17H/Dec 22H; 1985 Apr 15H/Jun 25H; 1986 Nov 25H

TPA see streptokinase; tissue plasminogen activator

Tracey Ullman Show, The (TV show) 1989 Sep 17J

Tracy Chapman (Tracy Chapman) (recording) 1988 Aug 27J/Sep 24J

trade see foreign trade; organizations (e.g., OPEC); specific countries (e.g., Japan)

trademarks 1980 Feb 19H; 1983 Mar 22F; 1988 May 31H/Nov 16H

Trade Representative, U.S. 1983 May 13E; 1985 Jan 11A; 1987 Nov 6D;

1988 Feb 29D/Dec 6F; 1989 Jan 31H/Apr 25H/Apr 28G/Nov 22H

trade schools 1988 Feb 9F; 1989 Jun 1F

Trading Places (film) 1983 Jul 6J; 1984 Jan 11J

traffic fatalities 1987 Dec 17H

Trailways Corp. 1987 Jul 2H

Transformation of Virginia, 1740-1790, The (Rhys Isaac) (book) 1983 Apr 18J

Transit Union, Amalgamated *see* Amalgamated Transit Union

Transportation, U.S. Department of *see also individual leaders in the name index (e.g., Dole, Elizabeth)*
  airline rankings 1987 Sep 2F/Nov 10H; 1988 Jan 6H/Apr 5H
  appointments: Burnley IV, James H. 1987 Oct 8H; Dole, Elizabeth 1983 Jan 5H; Lewis Jr., Andrew L. 1980 Dec 11F; Skinner, Samuel K. 1988 Dec 22F
  automobile recalls 1982 Aug 10H; 1986 Dec 23H
  budget and spending programs 1983 Aug 15H; 1988 Sep 28H/Sep 30H
  drug testing 1988 Nov 14F
  private satellite launches 1984 Feb 24H
  seat belt laws 1984 Jul 11H

Transport Workers Union 1980 Apr 2H; 1985 Mar 27H

transsexuality 1989 May 3J

Trans World Airlines (TWA) 1983 Aug 17F; 1985 Jan 8F/Aug 23H; 1986 Apr 2B/Dec 15H

Travel Agents, American Society of *see* American Society of Travel Agents

Traveling Wilburys (singing group) 1989 Jan 29J/Feb 25J/Mar 25J

Traveling Wilburys (Traveling Wilburys) (recording) 1989 Jan 29J/Feb 25J/Mar 25J

Treasure (Clive Cussler) (book) 1988 Mar 25J/Apr 29J

Treasure Houses of Britain (art exhibit) 1985 Nov 9J

Treasury, U.S. Department of the *see also individual agency heads in the name index (e.g., Brady, Nicholas F.)*
  appointments: Baker III, James A. 1985 Jan 8F; Brady, Nicholas F. 1988 Aug 5H; Regan, Donald T. Argentina rescue package 1984 Mar 31G
  auctions 1983 Sep 13H; 1984 Feb 9H; 1985 Aug 8H/Nov 27H; 1986 Feb 6H/May 8H/Aug 7H/Nov 5H; 1987 May 7H/Aug 13H; 1988 May 12H; 1989 Feb 9H/May 11H
  Bank of America fined 1986 Jan 2H
  budget and spending programs 1989 Nov 3H
  budget deficit 1985 Jan 25H; 1986 Apr 28H
  comptroller's office criticized 1983 Oct 31H
  currency market intervention 1983 Jul 29G
  debt strategy 1989 Mar 10H
  federal budget deficit 1984 Oct 25H; 1987 Jan 27H/Apr 21H; 1988 Oct 28H
  household wealth 1986 Aug 21H
  interest rate 1986 Oct 31H
  Netherlands Antilles treaty to be cancelled 1987 Jun 30H
  presidential campaign matching funds 1984 Jan 3G
  Senate tax bill 1986 Jan 25F

tax reform plan 1984 Nov 27H; 1985 Sep 3H

Treaty of Rome 1986 Feb 27B

Triangle Publications Inc. 1988 Aug 7H

Tribune Co. 1985 Mar 25J

tricosanthin (Compound Q/GLQ223) (drug) 1989 Apr 27I/Sep 19I

Trident (missile) 1980 Jul 15B; 1981 Jun 25B; 1984 Aug 15G; 1987 Jan 15G; 1989 Dec 4G

Trinidad and Tobago 1980 Nov 24D; 1981 Nov 10D; 1985 Feb 5J; 1986 Dec 15D; 1989 Mar 6D/Nov 19J

Triple (Ken Follett) (book) 1980 Jan 13J/Feb 10J

triple jump (hop, step, and jump) 1985 Jun 16J

Trip to Bountiful, The (film) 1985 Dec 20J; 1986 Mar 24J

Tripura (India) 1980 Jun 8E/Jun 9E; 1988 Aug 12E

TriStar (aircraft) 1982 Dec 22E

Tri-Star Pictures Inc. 1987 Sep 1H

tritium 1989 Sep 7G

Triumph of Achilles (Louise Gluck) (book) 1986 Feb 17J

Triumph of Politics, The: Why the Reagan Revolution Failed (David A. Stockman) (book) 1986 Apr 22H

tropical forests 1984 Apr 2I/Aug 7I; 1985 Oct 28A; 1987 Jul 3I; 1988 Oct 12D/Dec 22D; 1989 Feb 4D/Mar 3A/Apr 5I

tropical spastic paraparesis 1988 Nov 29I

Tru (Jay Presson Allen) (play) 1989 Dec 14J

Trucking Association, American *see* American Trucking Association

True Blue (Madonna) (recording) 1986 Aug 13J/Sep 17J

True Colors (Cyndi Lauper) (recording) 1986 Nov 22J

True Confession (film) 1981 Nov 4J

True West (Sam Shepard) (play) 1980 Dec 23J

Truly (Lionel Richie) (recording) 1983 Feb 23J

Trusteeship Council, U.N. 1981 May 21A

Tsuruga nuclear power plant (Japan) 1981 Jan 28I/Mar 8I/May 13E

tuberculosis 1986 Jun 13I; 1988 Jan 2I

Tubingen, University of (West Germany) 1980 Feb 5J/Apr 10J

Tufts University (Medford, Mass.) 1981 Dec 24I

Tug of War (Paul McCartney) (recording) 1982 Jun 16J

Tulane University (New Orleans, La.) 1989 Dec 8I

Tulsa, University of (Oklahoma) 1981 Mar 25J

tuna 1980 Oct 21H; 1985 Sep 23D; 1986 Oct 22E

Tunisia 1980 Jan 27C; 1982 Feb 27C; 1985 Feb 3B/Sep 26C/Oct 1C/Oct 12C; 1986 Apr 22C; 1987 Nov 7C; 1988 Apr 16C; 1989 Feb 17C/Apr 2C; Bourguiba, Habib

Tunnel of Love (Bruce Springsteen) (recording) 1987 Nov 21J; 1988 Mar 2J

tunnels
  English Channel Tunnel *see* English Channel Tunnel
  Rogers Pass Tunnel 1989 May 4D
  Seikan train tunnel 1988 Mar 13E

Turkey *see also individual leaders in the name index (e.g., Demirel, Suleyman)*
  accidents and disasters: mudslides 1988 Jun 23I
  Arab terrorist attack on synagogue 1986 Sep 6B
  archaeology: Bronze Age shipwreck 1984 Dec 4I
  Armenian terrorist attacks: Ankara airport 1982 Aug 7B; Australia 1980 Dec 17A; Canada 1982 Apr 8A; 1985 Mar 12D; Portugal 1983 Jul 27B; U.S. 1982 May 4A
  assassinations: Erim, Nihat 1980 Jul 19B
  business and industry: Bosporus bridge contract awarded 1985 Apr 27B
  constitutional reform 1982 Jul 17B/Sep 23B/Nov 7B
  coup 1980 Sep 12B
  earthquakes 1983 Oct 30I
  economic growth 1987 Apr 1B
  foreign relations: Balkan summits 1988 Feb 23B; 1989 Mar 15B; Bulgaria 1989 Feb 22B/Jul 16B/Aug 22B/Oct 30B; Cyprus *see* Cyprus; European Community 1987 Apr 14B; 1989 Dec 18B; Greece 1981 Mar 21B; 1983 May 20B; 1984 Mar 9B; 1987 Mar 28B; 1988 Jan 31B; Iraq 1980 Nov 20C; 1984 Aug 6C; Israel 1980 Dec 2C; U.S. 1980 Mar 29B; 1981 Dec 5G; 1982 May 14B
  government and politics: former premier Ecevit arrested 1982 Apr 10B; former premier Ecevit enters jail 1981 Dec 3B; general elections date set 1983 Apr 29B; 1987 Oct 17B; government files on Armenians to be opened 1989 Jan 4B; government takes over town 1980 Jul 11B; head of central bank replaced 1981 Jan 10B; Ozal elected president 1989 Oct 31B; parliamentary by-elections 1986 Sep 28B; police powers increased 1985 Jun 16B; political activity ban lifted 1983 Apr 24B; political parties dissolved by junta 1981 Oct 17B; Ulusu appointed premier 1980 Sep 21B
  human rights 1982 Mar 16B/Jul 1B; 1985 Jul 23B/Dec 9B; 1989 Jan 3B
  immigration and refugees: Afghanistan 1982 Aug 3A; Turkish immigrants protest in Paris 1980 Mar 3B
  inflation 1988 Jan 6B
  international organizations: IMF 1980 Jun 18A; OECD 1980 Mar 26A/Apr 15A; World Bank 1983 Jun 28B
  John Paul II assassination attempt *see* John Paul II *in the name index*
  Kurds 1980 Sep 22B; 1985 Jan 12E; 1986 Aug 15A; 1987 Mar 4C/Jun 20B/Jul 9B; 1988 Sep 8C/Sep 15G
  labor issues: soldiers take over factory 1980 Feb 14B
  martial law 1980 Feb 20B/Jun 18B; 1982 Feb 26B; 1984 Mar 1B; 1985 Jun 19B/Nov 19B; 1987 Jul 19B
  obituaries: Erim, Nihat 1980 Jul 19B; Gunduz, Orhan 1982 May 4A
  press and broadcasting 1982 Feb 6B; 1983 Jun 28B

Turkmenistan (USSR) 1984 Mar 20I

Turkoman (racehorse) 1987 Jan 30J

Turks and Caicos 1986 Sep 18F; 1988 Mar 3E/Mar 31E

Turner Broadcasting Systems Inc. 1983 Oct 12F; 1985 Feb 7J

Turner Network Television (TNT) 1982 Sep 14J

Turning Points: Preparing American Youth for the 21st Century (Carnegie Foundation) 1989 Jun 19F

turtles 1989 Sep 5H

Tutsis (Burundi/Rwanda ethnic group) 1988 Aug 22C

Tuvalu 1985 Aug 6E

TVA *see* Tennessee Valley Authority

TV Marti 1989 Jul 21D

TWA *see* Trans World Airlines

TWA jet hijacking (1985) 1985 Jun 14A/Jun 15C/Jun 16C/Jun 30C/Jul 15B/Oct 17G; 1987 Jan 15A; 1988 Aug 9B; 1989 May 17B

12 New Etudes for Piano (William Bolcom) (musical composition) 1988 Mar 31J

Twentieth Century Fox Film Corp. 1980 Jan 1J; 1981 Apr 1J; 1987 Jul 2E

Twentieth Century Pleasures: Prose on Poetry (Robert Hass) (book) 1985 Jan 14J

Twilight Ridge (racehorse) 1985 Nov 2J

Twilight Zone: The Movie (film) 1983 Jul 6J; 1987 May 29J

Twins (film) 1988 Dec 28J; 1989 Jan 25J

210 Coca-Cola Bottles (Andy Warhol) (painting) 1988 May 2J

two-mile run 1981 Feb 27J; 1987 May 29J

2,000 meter run (running) 1985 Aug 4J

2010 (film) 1984 Dec 12J

2010: Odyssey Two (Arthur C. Clarke) (book) 1982 Nov 14J/Dec 12J; 1983 Jan 16J/Feb 13J/Mar 13J

Two Weeks in Winter (TV show) 1983 Jan 7B

Two Women (Willem de Kooning) (painting) 1983 May 10J

Tylenol (drug) 1982 Oct 6I/Oct 20H/Oct 29I/Dec 24H; 1986 Feb 17F

Typhoon Ike 1984 Sep 2E

Typhoon Nina 1987 Nov 25E

Typhoon Ruby 1988 Oct 25I

U

UAE *see* United Arab Emirates

UAW *see* United Automobile, Aerospace and Agricultural Implement Workers of America

UBS Switzerland (yacht) 1986 May 9J

UDF *see* United Democratic Front

Uganda
  AIDS: 1986 May 28I
  civil strife: Amin loyalists 1980 Oct 7C/Oct 15C; massacres 1981 Feb 4C/Mar 11C/Mar 15C; 1983 Jun 5C; police civilian roundups 1982 Apr 7C; rebel bombing in Kampala 1981 Apr 10C; rebel peace agreement 1985 Dec 17C; rebels attack army barracks 1982 Feb 23C
  coups: Binaisa overthrown 1980 May 11C; National Resistance Army seizes power 1986 Jan 26C; Obote overthrown 1985 Jul 27C
  foreign relations: Kenya 1987 Dec 14C/Dec 28C; regional cooperation 1981 Jan 17C
  government and politics: Asian community return OKd 1982 Sep 3C;

Museveni assumes presidency 1986 Jan 29C; Obote returns 1980 May 27C; parliamentary elections 1980 Dec 10C/Dec 11C/Dec 13C

Ukraine (USSR) 1983 Dec 31A; 1984 Oct 12A; 1986 Mar 7A/Mar 8A; 1989 Jun 25B/Sep 10B; Chernobyl

Ukrainian Popular Movement for Perestroika (Ruk) 1989 Sep 10B

Ulster Freedom Fighters 1981 Oct 12B; 1984 Mar 14B

Ulysses (James Joyce) (book) 1984 Jun 16J

Unbearable Lightness of Being, The (Milan Kundera) (book/film) 1985 Jan 9J; 1988 Feb 5J

Uncle Buck (film) 1989 Aug 30J

Uncounted Enemy, The: A Vietnam Deception (TV show) 1983 Apr 26J

UNCTAD (Trade and Development, U.N. Conference on) 1983 Apr 5A/Jul 2A/Jul 3A; 1987 Aug 3A; 1988 Sep 2A

underground storage tanks 1987 Apr 2H

Under Satan's Sun (film) 1987 May 19J

Under the Cherry Moon (film) 1986 Jul 9J

Under the Eye of the Clock (Christopher Nolan) (book) 1988 Jan 19J

Undetectable Firearms Act of 1988 1988 Nov 10F

unemployment benefits 1982 Feb 1H; 1983 Mar 24F/Aug 4F/Sep 8H; 1986 Aug 21H; 1987 Feb 25F; 1988 Dec 16B

unemployment rate
  1980 statistics: 1980 Jan 11H/Feb 1H/May 2H/Jun 6H/Jul 3H/Nov 7H
  1981 statistics: 1981 Jun 5H/Jul 2H/Aug 7H/Sep 4H/Oct 2H/Nov 6H/Dec 4H
  1982 statistics: 1982 Jan 8H/Feb 5H/Mar 5H/Apr 2H/May 7H/Jun 4H/Jul 2H/Aug 6H/Sep 3A/Oct 8H/Nov 5H/Dec 3H
  1983 statistics: 1983 Jan 7H/Feb 4H/Mar 4H/Apr 1H/May 6H/Jun 3H/Jul 8H/Aug 5H/Sep 2H/Oct 7H/Nov 4H/Dec 2H
  1984 statistics: 1984 Jan 6H/Feb 3H/Mar 9H/Apr 6H/May 4H/Jun 1H/Jul 6H/Aug 3H/Sep 7H/Oct 5H/Nov 2H/Dec 7H
  1985 statistics: 1985 Jan 9H/Feb 1H/Mar 8H/Apr 5H/May 3H/Jun 7H/Jul 5H/Aug 2H/Sep 6H/Oct 4H/Nov 1H/Dec 6H
  1986 statistics: 1986 Jan 8H/Feb 7H/Mar 4H/Mar 7H/May 2H; Jun 6H/Jul 3H/Aug 1H/Sep 5H/Oct 3H/Nov 7H/Dec 5H
  1987 statistics: 1987 Jan 9H/Feb 6H/Mar 9H/Apr 3H/May 8H/Jun 5H/Jul 2H/Aug 7H/Sep 4H/Oct 2H/Nov 6H
  1988 statistics: 1988 Jan 8H/Feb 5H/Mar 4H/Apr 1H/May 6H/Jun 3H/Jul 8H/Aug 5H/Sep 5H/Oct 5H/Nov 4H/Dec 5H
  1989 statistics: 1989 Jan 6H/Feb 3H/Mar 10H/Apr 7H/May 5H/Jun 2H/Jul 7H/Aug 4H/Oct 6H/Nov 3H/Dec 8H

UNESCO 1980 Oct 25I/Dec 4J; 1982 Dec 3J; 1983 Dec 25A/Dec 28A; 1984 Mar 14A/Mar 26A/Nov 22A/Dec 19A; 1985 Oct 8A/Dec 5B; 1987 Oct 18A; 1989 Dec 7A

UNICEF (International Children's Emergency Fund, U.N.) 1980 Aug 4E; 1984 Dec 19A

Unification Church 1981 Oct 15J; 1982 May 5J/Oct 4J

unified field theory 1980 Mar 8I

UNIFIL see under United Nations

UNIFIL (Lebanon, U.N. Interim Force in) 1981 Feb 10A; 1982 Jun 2J; 1983 Jan 18C

Uniform Code of Military Justice 1983 Nov 18G

UN Interim Forces in Lebanon 1982 Feb 22A

Union Bank of Switzerland 1988 Aug 6B

Union Carbide Corp. 1980 Jul 24H; 1981 Sep 30H; 1984 Dec 6B/Dec 6H; 1985 Jan 24H/May 4H/Aug 11H/Aug 16H/Aug 28H; 1986 Apr 1H; 1987 Jul 24H; see also Bhopal disaster

Union of Concerned Scientists 1984 Mar 21G; 1986 Mar 22G

Union of Soviet Socialist Republics (USSR) see also individual leaders in the name index (e.g., Brezhnev, Leonid I.); republic names (e.g., Armenia)

accidents and disasters
air crashes: Aeroflot in Siberia 1982 Feb 6B; fighter jet 1989 Jul 4B
earthquakes: Armenia 1988 Dec 15B/Dec 23B/Dec 24B; Romania/Moldavia 1986 Aug 31I; Tadzhikistan 1984 Mar 20I; 1985 Oct 13B; 1989 Jan 23E; Turkmenistan 1984 Mar 20I; Uzbekistan 1984 Mar 20I
fires and explosions: Academy of Sciences library blaze 1988 Feb 14B; gas pipeline blast 1989 Jun 3B; naval supply depot blast 1984 Jun 21B; weapons plant blast 1989 Jun 16B
marine collisions: freighter/cruise ship collision 1986 Sep 1B; Lithuania oil spill 1982 Jan 19B; oil tanker hits mine in Nicaragua 1984 Mar 25A; submarines 1983 Aug 10B; 1986 Oct 4I/Oct 6I; 1989 Apr 7B/Jun 26B; submarine/U.S. ship collide 1984 Mar 21A

agriculture: grain harvests 1981 Sep 29B; 1986 Oct 18B; reform plan 1989 Mar 16B

arms control and disarmament: military force ban 1985 Jan 29B; non-aggression accord 1983 Jan 6B; nuclear freeze appeals 1981 Sep 3A; space weapons 1987 Mar 17B; West European poll 1987 Jun 6B; see also specific treaties (e.g., SALT II)

arts and culture
dance: Makarova performs with Bolshoi 1988 Aug 6J; 1989 Jan 18J; Nureyev visits 1987 Nov 14J
film and theater: American theater group performs 1986 Jan 8J; anti-Stalin film popular 1986 Nov 16J
literature: Dr. Zhivago publication set 1987 Feb 12J; Pasternak's son accepts Nobel prize 1989 Dec 10J
music: Brubeck jazz quintet performs 1987 Mar 26J; Feltsman gives concert 1987 Apr 21J; Horowitz performs 1986 Apr 14J; Tchaikovsky piano competition 1986 Jul 3J; Van Cliburn competition 1989 Jun 11J; Vysotsky

satirical songs published 1982 Jan 18B
painting and sculpture: Chagall exhibit 1987 Sep 2J; pre-1930 Soviet art exhibit 1981 Jun 3J; Wyeth art exhibit 1987 Mar 11J

atomic energy and safeguards: nuclear accidents 1985 Feb 21A; nuclear reactors 1980 Apr 8I; 1983 Feb 11B; 1986 Sep 26I; 1989 Jun 16B; nuclear testing 1980 Jan 17I; 1982 Apr 2A; 1985 Apr 17B; 1986 Dec 18B; 1987 Feb 26B/Mar 12B/Jun 9B; see also Chernobyl

budget and spending programs: 1984 Nov 27B; 1988 Oct 27B; 1989 Jan 21B

business and industry: private-sector business activities 1987 May 1B; public bond offering 1988 Jan 6B

census data: death rate 1987 Feb 10B; population 1980 Feb 9B; 1986 Oct 1B; 1987 Jan 19B; 1989 Apr 28B

Chernobyl nuclear accident see Chernobyl nuclear accident

chess 1985 Feb 15J/Sep 2J/Nov 9J; 1986 Oct 9J/Dec 1J; 1987 Mar 31J/Dec 19J; 1988 Feb 22J; 1989 Oct 22J

crime and law enforcement: crime rate 1989 Feb 14B; diamond theft 1982 Mar 5B

defections: Bitov reappears in Soviet Union 1984 Sep 18B; intelligence agent in Great Britain 1985 Sep 12B; Matuzok, Vasily Yakovlevich 1984 Nov 23E; Messerer, Mikhail 1980 Feb 5J; Messerer, Sulamith 1980 Feb 5J; Shostakovich, Maxim 1981 Apr 11J; Yurchenko, Vitaly 1985 Sep 26B; Yurchenko claims kidnapping 1985 Nov 4G

defense and armed forces: arms sales 1980 Dec 10A; 1982 Apr 29G; 1987 Mar 5B; chemical weapons 1980 Aug 7G; 1981 Nov 10G; 1982 Mar 22A/Mar 28I/Nov 29A/Dec 6A; 1983 May 31A; 1984 Jan 10B/Feb 21B; 1987 Oct 3B/Dec 26B; 1989 Apr 27B/Sep 26A; cruise missile test 1984 Aug 25B; ICBM test 1987 Sep 30B; "launch-on-warning" 1982 Nov 29B; military doctrine booklet issued 1981 Nov 20B; military exercises 1981 Sep 8B; 1984 Apr 4A/Apr 7D; military spending 1984 Jan 29B/Jun 13G/Nov 27B; military superiority 1981 Nov 7B; mobile long-range missile development 1983 Aug 18A; modernization call 1982 Mar 10B; nuclear-armed subs increase 1984 May 20B; nuclear-powered attack sub launched 1981 Jan 9G

demonstrations and protests: anti-Stalin 1989 Mar 5B; Azerbaijan 1989 Aug 14B; Baltic republics 1987 Aug 23B; Crimean Tatars 1987 Jul 28B; Kazakhstan 1987 Jul 18B; Latvia 1987 Nov 18B

dissidents see also specific dissidents in the name index (e.g., Sakharov, Andrei D.): Begun freed 1987 Feb 20B; Borisov put in psychiatric hospital 1980 Mar 29B; Brailovsky arrested 1980 Nov 13B; independent political party formed 1988 May 7B; KGB raids 1982 Apr 6B; Lazareva sentenced 1982 Jul 3B; Melyanov freed 1988 Dec 12B; Nudel returns to Moscow 1982 Mar 27B; pardons 1987 Feb 10B; Ratushinskaya re-

leased 1986 Oct 9B/Dec 18B; Roginski sentenced 1981 Dec 8B; Shcharansky freed 1986 Feb 11G; Tolkachev execution 1986 Nov 22B

economy see also perestroika; consumer goods imports 1989 Apr 16B; fishing 1980 Mar 15B; 1984 May 1A; national income 1985 Jan 24B; oil 1982 Jan 19B; 1983 Mar 15B; 1987 Jan 22B/Dec 29B; performance 1980 Jan 25B; 1981 Jan 23B; 1982 Jan 23B/Apr 24B/Dec 25B; 1987 Mar 27B; 1989 Jan 21B; plans 1980 Dec 1B; 1981 Feb 27B; 1988 Sep 21B; reforms 1983 Jul 26B/Aug 2B; 1987 Nov 3B; 1988 Jan 21B; standard of living 1981 Nov 26B; whaling 1983 Jul 18A; 1986 Jun 9I; 1987 May 22B

education: reforms 1984 Jan 4B/Apr 12B; sex education 1985 Jan 13B

emigration: emigres return 1986 Dec 29B; Jews 1980 Jan 11B; 1981 Jan 4B; 1982 Jan 17A; 1987 Apr 9A; 1988 Jan 5B; relatives and spouses in U.S. 1986 Jun 2B; Soviet citizen reunited with American husband 1986 Jan 30F

environmental issues: Greenpeace members 1983 Jul 18A/Jul 22A; nuclear war long-term effects 1983 Nov 1A

espionage and intelligence issues see also KGB
France 1980 Feb 9B
Great Britain 1981 Nov 1B; 1982 Nov 10B; 1985 Sep 12B
Switzerland 1980 Feb 18B
U.S. see also specific spies in the name index (e.g., Walker Jr., John Anthony); Soviet UN employee arrested 1986 Aug 23G

ethnic and nationalist unrest: anniversary of Bolshevik Revolution protests 1989 Nov 7B; Armenia 1988 Mar 26B/Dec 1B; Azerbaijan 1988 Mar 4B/Mar 8B/Mar 15B/Mar 27B/Jun 15B/Jul 12B/Dec 1B; Baltic states 1989 Aug 23B; Georgia 1989 Apr 9B/Apr 27B; Georgians/Abkhazians 1989 Jul 27B; Kazakhstan 1986 Dec 17B/Dec 25B; Moldavia 1989 Jun 25B; nationalist groups meet 1989 Aug 21B; Ordzhonikidze 1981 Nov 24B; Pravda condemns 1989 Apr 11B; Uzbekistan 1989 Jun 12B

foreign policy: Cuban missile crisis conference 1989 Jan 28A; Soviet-German 1939 treaty condemned 1989 Dec 24B

foreign relations
Albania 1982 Nov 29B; 1986 Nov 29B
Angola 1981 Sep 1C/Sep 14C; 1987 Nov 11C; 1988 Jan 29C/Mar 6C/Mar 9A
Argentina 1986 Jan 29A
Australia 1980 Jun 17E/Jun 24E; 1981 Mar 4E; 1983 Mar 19E
Brazil 1981 Jul 15A
Cambodia 1986 Aug 28A
Canada 1981 May 26D; 1982 Feb 24A; 1983 Nov 1D; 1984 May 1A; 1989 Nov 20D
Chad 1981 Mar 13A
China: agreements 1984 Dec 29A; border clashes 1986 Aug 23A; educational and cultural exchanges 1983 Mar 22A; electronic monitoring station 1981 Jun 17A; Soviet threats seen 1982 Nov 19A; talks 1982 Oct

17A; 1983 Oct 21A; 1984 Mar 26A; 1985 Apr 22A; 1988 Aug 28A; trade 1980 Jun 6A; 1982 Mar 7A; 1983 Mar 10A; 1984 Feb 10A/Dec 29A; 1985 Jul 10A
Cuba 1984 Apr 7D; 1985 Jun 4D
Czechoslovakia 1988 Oct 11B
Egypt 1981 Sep 15A
El Salvador 1981 Feb 6D/Feb 14B
Ethiopia 1982 Jul 24G
European Community 1980 Jan 7B/Oct 23B; 1981 Dec 15B; 1982 Jan 4B/Mar 15B; 1987 Jan 16B; 1988 Nov 3B; 1989 Dec 18B
Finland 1987 Jan 7B
France 1980 Sep 19A; 1982 Jan 9A/Jan 23B/Jul 16B/Nov 13B/Dec 14A; 1986 Nov 20B; 1987 May 16B
G-7 1982 Jun 6A
Great Britain 1982 Feb 5A/Dec 3B/Dec 17B; 1988 Oct 20B; Thatcher, Margaret
Greece 1984 Jul 13A
Grenada 1983 Nov 4D
Hungary 1986 Jul 16I; 1989 Apr 25B
India 1980 May 28A; 1982 Mar 20E/Sep 22A; 1983 Dec 3A; 1984 Mar 9E
Iran 1980 Apr 23A/Jun 30C/Oct 5C; 1982 Mar 9A; 1983 May 4B; 1986 Dec 11A; 1989 Jun 20C
Iran-Iraq war 1980 Sep 23A
Iraq 1984 Mar 9A
Israel 1981 May 24C; 1982 Jun 14A; 1985 Jul 15C/Dec 25B; 1986 Aug 18A; 1987 Apr 9A/Jul 12C/Jul 23B/Oct 13A; 1988 Oct 23C/Dec 2C
Italy 1988 Oct 20B
Japan 1981 Sep 10E; 1982 Feb 23A; 1984 Jul 12A; 1985 May 24A/Jul 30A; 1987 Aug 20A/Dec 9E; 1988 Mar 22E
Kuwait 1981 Apr 11A/Aug 15A
Lebanon 1981 Apr 16A; 1984 Feb 29A/Oct 12A; 1985 Oct 30C
Liberia 1985 Jul 18C
Libya 1981 Sep 20C; 1985 Dec 21G
Mongolia 1987 Jan 15E
Mozambique 1987 Jun 29C
Namibia 1982 Mar 22A
NATO 1980 Dec 12B; 1982 Jan 11A; 1983 Jan 6B/Jun 2B; 1984 Jul 12A
Nicaragua 1980 Mar 19A; 1981 May 14D; 1982 May 10A; 1984 Jun 24A/Nov 6D/Nov 6G/Nov 7D; 1986 Oct 3D/Oct 28D; 1987 Sep 7D/Dec 12D
North Korea 1984 May 25A
Norway 1980 Dec 22A
Pakistan 1981 Aug 27E
PLO 1981 Feb 16A/Oct 20A
Poland: anti-Soviet activity 1981 Sep 18B/Sep 22B; compromise supported 1988 Sep 16B; counterrevolution threat in Poland seen 1981 Sep 11B; debt 1981 Feb 19B; food shipments 1980 Sep 11B; Gierek speech quoted in Soviet press 1980 Aug 19B; military exercises 1981 Sep 12B; 1982 Mar 13B; NATO warning to Soviets 1980 Dec 12B; Polish Communist Party criticized 1981 Apr 2B/Apr 25B; Polish workers criticized 1980 Aug 27B; Soviets deny responsibility for crackdown 1981 Dec 21B; talks 1980 Oct 30B/Dec 5B; 1981 Jan 14B/Apr 23B

South Africa 1981 Sep 1C/Sep 14C; 1982 Mar 22A; 1988 Mar 6C/Mar 9A
Sweden 1981 Jan 15A/Oct 28B/Oct 30B/Oct 31B/Nov 6B; 1983 Dec 2B
Syria 1980 Oct 8A; 1981 May 6A/Jul 9A
West Germany 1982 Jan 12B; 1983 Dec 2B; 1985 Jan 22B; 1986 Jul 20B; 1987 May 29B/Sep 4B; 1988 Aug 3B; 1989 Dec 11B; Schmidt, Helmut
Yugoslavia 1988 Oct 11B
Zimbabwe 1981 Feb 21A

government and politics: All-Union Conference of Communist Party 1988 Jun 28B/Jul 1B; anti-Stalin campaign 1988 Apr 17B; Central Committee plenary meeting 1988 Feb 17B; communist leaders concerned over unrest 1981 Jan 8B; Communist Party role defended 1989 Nov 12B; Congress of People's Deputies opens 1989 May 25B; Congress of the Communist Party 1986 Mar 6B; constitutional reform 1988 Dec 1B; Council of Ministers nominations rejected 1989 Jun 27B; former KGB head appointed internal affairs minister 1982 Dec 17B; leadership power struggle 1985 Feb 5B; Lenin criticized by Pravda 1989 Dec 30B; local elections 1987 Jun 21B; manifesto on democratic reforms 1986 Jul 22B; multicandidate parliamentary elections 1989 Mar 26B; parades 1985 May 9B; 1987 Nov 7B; peace forum 1987 Feb 14A; purge victims rehabilitated 1988 Feb 5B; 1989 Jan 31B

human rights 1980 Apr 29B; 1981 Dec 9A; 1989 Feb 6B/Oct 17B; psychiatry 1981 May 31B; 1989 Oct 17I; telephone links 1982 Jul 1B/Sep 2B

international organizations: Comecon 1983 Oct 20B; 1984 Jun 14A/Nov 31D; GATT 1986 Sep 18A; United Nations 1980 Jan 13A/Apr 16A; 1981 Aug 6A; 1982 Aug 6A; 1983 Jan 18C; 1984 Feb 29A/Oct 12A; 1987 Sep 2A/Oct 13A/Oct 15B/Dec 1A; 1989 Nov 3A

labor issues: '62 striking workers massacre confirmed 1989 Jun 2B; auto worker strike 1980 Jun 13B; coal miner strikes 1989 Jul 26B; Kiev strikes 1981 Jul 29B; right to strike approved 1989 Oct 9B; wages and productivity increases 1989 Apr 21B

medicine and health care: abortions 1981 Jun 3B; AIDS 1987 Feb 6B/Aug 25B; alcoholism 1985 May 16B; anthrax epidemic 1980 Mar 20B/Jun 29I; 1982 Jan 14B; drug addiction 1987 Jan 26B; infant mortality 1986 Oct 27I

monetary issues: currency 1988 Dec 11B; foreign debt 1982 Mar 17B; 1989 Jun 9B

Nagorno-Karabakh see Nagorno-Karabakh

obituaries: Andropov, Yuri 1984 Feb 9B; Brezhnev, Leonid 1982 Nov 10B; Chernenko, Konstantin 1985 Mar 10B; Chuikov, Vasily 1982 Mar 18B; Gromyko, Andrei 1989 Jul 2B; Kantorovich, Leonid 1986 Apr 7J; Kapitsa, Pyotr 1984 Apr 8I; Khrushchev, Nina 1984 Aug 8B; Kondrashin, Kiril 1981 Mar 7J;

Kosygin, Alexei 1980 Dec 18B; Malenkov, Georgi 1988 Feb 1B; Marchenko, Anatoly 1986 Dec 8B; Molotov, Vyacheslav 1986 Nov 8B; Philby, Kim 1988 May 11B; Sakharov, Andrei 1989 Dec 14B; Semyonov, Nikolai 1986 Sep 25I; Shalamov, Varlam 1982 Jan 30J; Sholokhov, Mikhail 1984 Feb 21J; Sokolov, Valentin 1984 Nov 8J; Suslov, Mikhail 1982 Jan 25B; Tarsis, Valery 1983 Mar 3J; Trifonov, Yuri 1981 Mar 28J; Vinogradov, Ivan 1983 Mar 20I; Vysotsky, Vladimir 1980 Jul 28B

press and broadcasting: censorship agency to be disbanded 1986 Jun 27B; electronic jamming stopped 1988 Nov 30G; telecast of space walk 1986 May 28I

religion: John Paul II criticized 1982 Dec 29A; Russian Orthodox Church 1000 year anniversary 1988 Jun 5J

republics *see also specific* republics (*e.g.,* Armenia); economic autonomy 1989 Feb 18B/Nov 20B

science and technology: atom smasher 1986 Jul 27I; cholesterol research 1987 Nov 12I

space flight *see also specific craft (e.g., Soyuz);* cosmonaut's diary published 1983 Aug 16I; cosmonauts return after year in space 1988 Dec 21I; customers offered bargains 1987 Jan 5I; director warns of losing lead 1988 Nov 3I; endurance records 1980 Oct 11I; 1982 Nov 14I; 1984 Oct 2I; Halley's comet spacecraft 1984 Dec 15I/Dec 20I; 1986 Mar 6I; interplanetary projects 1989 Aug 22I; "new generation" rocket launched 1987 May 16I; radar satellite launched 1987 Jul 25I; radio contact lost with Mars probe 1989 Mar 28I; reconnaissance satellite falls 1983 Jan 23I; record number of people in space 1984 Feb 8I; research satellite jeopardized by monkey 1987 Oct 12I; rocket launch failure 1987 Apr 30I; 1988 Feb 18I; space shuttle 1984 Jun 8I/Dec 19I; 1988 Nov 15I; telecast of space walk 1986 May 28I; Venus probes 1981 Oct 30I; 1982 Mar 1I/Mar 18I; 1983 Jun 7I; Venus space probe 1984 Dec 21I; Vietnamese cosmonaut 1980 Jul 31I; woman walks in space 1984 Jul 25I

sports: athlete drug use monitoring 1988 Nov 21J; baseball 1986 Oct 2J; basketball 1986 Jul 20J/Aug 17J; 1987 Jun 14J/Oct 25J; figure skating 1986 Mar 21J; 1987 Mar 12J; Friendship '84 sports festival 1984 Aug 18J; gymnastics 1985 Nov 10J; high jump 1985 Aug 11J; ice hockey 1980 Feb 22J; 1982 Apr 25J; 1986 Apr 28J; 1987 Feb 13J/May 3J; 1989 Apr 29J; Olympic Games (Alberta) 1988 Feb 20C; Olympic Games (Lake Placid) 1980 Feb 24J; Olympic Games (Los Angeles) 1983 Sep 16J; 1984 May 7J/May 8J/May 31J; Olympic Games (Moscow) *see* Olympic Games; Olympic Games (Sarajevo) 1984 Feb 19J; Olympic Games (Seoul) 1988 Oct 2J; pole vault 1985 Jul 13J; rowing 1987 Jul 5J; world indoor track and field championships 1987 Mar 8J

terrorism 1981 Oct 18A

trade issues: foreign dependency 1982 Jul 12G; gas pipeline 1981 Nov 20B; 1982 Feb 10B/Jun 22A/Jul 22B/Aug 2B/Aug 26G/Sep 1G/Sep 9G/Oct 5G; 1983 Jul 26B; 1984 Jan 1B

transportation

air travel: Aeroflot flights to U.S. halted 1980 Feb 4B; Aeroflot jet crashes in Siberia 1982 Feb 6B; airspace violation charged 1983 Sep 1B; plane hijakings 1988 Dec 2C; West German pilot lands in Red Square 1987 May 29B/Sep 4B; 1988 Aug 3B

U.S. grain embargo 1980 Jan 6H/Jan 12A/Jan 30F/Jul 24D/Nov 20A

U S. relations *see also individual leaders in the name index* (*e.g.,* Haig, Alexander); Aeroflot flights 1980 Jan 12G/Feb 4B; agreement on accidental confrontations signed 1989 Jun 12G; agreement on preserving future Olympic Games 1984 May 18J; agriculture 1985 Jun 18A; airline safety talks 1985 May 24A/Jul 30A; "Amerika" miniseries broadcast 1986 Jan 22J; anti-Soviet campaign related to Olympics asserted 1984 Apr 9J; Army officer shooting in East Germany 1985 Mar 24B/Apr 23B; athlete drug use monitoring 1988 Nov 21J; chairman of joint chief tours 1989 Jun 21G; chemical weapons treaty 1989 Jul 18A; class action suits against 1982 Mar 2A; coal slurry pipeline 1982 Oct 6G; Defense Secretary Carlucci visits 1988 Aug 4G; delegation inspects military sites 1989 Jul 8B; diplomatic expulsions 1986 Oct 22B; disarmament and arms control 1980 Dec 12A; 1981 Apr 2A/Aug 13A/Sep 2A/Nov 30A; 1982 May 31A; 1984 Jan 29B/Jan 30G/Jun 29B/Jun 29G/Aug 1A/Nov 22A; 1985 Jan 7B/Mar 12A/Mar 16B/May 30B/Jul 16B/Oct 1B/Nov 1B/Nov 14G; 1986 Jun 11B/Jul 30A/Aug 11A/Sep 18A/Nov 12A/Nov 16B/Dec 5B/Dec 8B; 1987 Jan 15B/May 5G/Jul 11B; economic advisers offered 1989 Oct 16G; electronic intelligence-gathering station 1981 Jun 17A; exchange agreements 1986 Aug 5A; exhibition of paintings loaned 1986 May 1J; export restrictions lifted 1989 Jul 18H; false warnings of missile attack 1980 Jun 6G; fishing 1985 Apr 3H; forum on relations 1986 Sep 15A; grain sales 1981 Jun 9A/Aug 5A/Oct 1A; 1983 May 16A/Jul 28A/Aug 25A; 1985 Aug 30A; 1986 Aug 29H/Sep 30G; 1987 Apr 30H/Dec 2G; 1988 Nov 28B; high-technology export controls 1980 Mar 18G; 1982 Jan 9A; homeless advocate given check 1987 Dec 23F; "hot line" 1984 Jul 17A; Iran hostage crisis 1980 Jan 13A; Kiev travel advisory lifted 1987 Jan 29B; Libyan arms sales 1985 Dec 21G; longshoremen stop handing Soviet freight 1980 Jan 12G; Matlock Jr. becomes ambassador 1987 Apr 2G; military comparisons 1981 Sep 6G; 1984 Jun 17G; military spending 1981 Sep 26G/Sep 29G; 1982 Feb 7A; nuclear freeze movement 1983 Mar 25G; nuclear tests 1980 Sep 15I; 1986 Jul 16A/Nov 14A/Dec 19B; 1987 Apr 17G/Aug 31B/Nov 20B; 1988 Jan 29B/Aug 17I/Sep 14B/Dec 15B; oil-drilling equipment 1987 Jan 15H; Olympic attache denied visa 1984 Mar 1J; passenger flights resume 1986 Apr 29A; political campaign issues 1986 Sep 20F; 1988 Aug 16F; prisoner exchange 1986 Sep 30A; radar facility 1985 Oct 29G; 1987 Sep 8G; scientific cooperation 1988 Jan 12I; secret attempt to acquire California banks 1986 Feb 15G; senators pessimistic about relations 1981 Sep 5A; Soviet ambassador appointed 1986 May 20B; Soviet covert visits to Alaska 1988 Feb 11G; Soviet folk ballet troupe visits 1986 Sep 3J; Soviet ICBMs called more accurate 1980 Sep 18G; Soviets welcome MX missile defeat in House 1982 Dec 8A; space cooperation 1988 Nov 10I; space program comparison 1986 Jun 17I; Stalin's daughter returns to U.S. 1986 Apr 16J; Star Wars 1985 Oct 22B; State Department human rights report 1983 Feb 8G; 1984 Feb 10G; 1988 Feb 10G; trade 1980 Feb 20A; 1982 Mar 4A/Nov 16A; 1985 Jan 10A/May 21A; travel advisory for Leningrad 1984 Aug 6G; TV films and tapes screened 1983 Mar 18B; UN resolution cosponsored 1989 Nov 3A; UN staff members reduction 1986 Mar 7A/Mar 8A; U.S. boat and crew released 1984 Sep 19B; U.S. Navy ships incursion 1986 Mar 18B; U.S. nuclear test criticized 1986 Mar 22G; U.S. warships bumped 1988 Feb 12B; Vega spacecraft 1984 Dec 20I; visas denied to Soviet scientists 1980 Feb 26G; warning on anti-satellite missile test 1985 Aug 21B; WWII veterans meet 1985 Apr 25B

women: first woman to walk in space 1984 Jul 25I

Union Pacific Corp. 1980 Jan 8H/Sep 15H; 1982 Sep 13H

UNITA *see* National Union for the Total Independence of

unitary taxation 1985 Nov 8H; 1986 Sep 5H

United Airlines 1985 Apr 22H/May 17H/Jun 15H/Aug 1H; 1986 Oct 7H

United Arab Emirates (UAE) 1981 Mar 10C; 1985 Oct 17A; 1987 Jun 17C/Jun 20C

United Artists (UA) 1980 Nov 19J

United Automobile, Aerospace and Agricultural Implement Workers of America (UAW) (AFL-CIO) *see also individual leaders in the name index* (*e.g.,* Bieber, Owen F.)

contract issues: American Motors 1982 Apr 18H; 1985 Jun 28H; Caterpillar 1983 Apr 23F; 1986 Jul 4H; Chrysler 1983 Sep 5H/Nov 5F; 1985 Oct 23H; 1988 May 4H; Deere 1987 Feb 1H; Diamond-Star Motors 1989 Aug 26H; Ford Motor 1982 Feb 13H/Feb 28H; 1984 Oct 14H; 1987 Sep 17H; General Dynamics 1985 Nov 12H; General Motors 1982 Mar 21H; 1984 Sep 21H; 1985 Jul 26H; 1987 Oct 8H; International Harvester 1980 Apr 20H; New United Motor Manufacturing 1985 Jun 25H

plant and production issues: Chrysler closing 1988 Sep 26H

politics and government: Reagan meeting asked 1980 Dec 20H

trade issues: ITC seeks higher import duties 1980 Jun 12H

union issues: AFL-CIO rejoined 1981 Jul 1H; Canada severs ties 1980 Jan 3D; 1982 Sep 19C/Nov 5D; 1984 Oct 17D/Oct 29D; 1985 Mar 30D; 1986 Jun 9D; Honda drive suspended 1986 Mar 17H; Nissan rejects union 1989 Jul 27H

United Brands Co. 1985 Mar 31D

United Church of Canada 1988 Aug 24J

United Church of Christ 1984 Nov 30J; 1987 Jun 30J

United Democratic Front (UDF) 1985 Apr 23C

United Farm Workers 1988 Aug 21F

United Food and Commercial Workers 1985 Dec 29H; 1986 Feb 8H

United Freedom Front 1987 Jan 18F

United Fruit Co. 1985 Mar 31D

United Kingdom *see* Great Britain

United Klans of America 1987 Feb 12F/May 20F

United Liberation Torchbearers 1985 Jun 20E

United Methodist Church 1984 May 10J/Nov 30J

United Methodist General Conference 1988 May 2J

United Mine Workers of America (UMW) (unaffiliated) 1980 Mar 3H; 1981 Mar 23H/Mar 31H; 1982 Nov 9H/Dec 22H; 1985 Dec 20H; 1989 Jun 20H/Oct 4H

United Nations (U.N.) *see also individual leaders in the name index (e.g.,* Perez de Cuellar, Javier); *specific U.N. agencies* (World Health Organization)

awards and honors

Nobel Peace Prize: High Commissioner for Refugees 1981 Oct 14A; UN peacekeeping forces 1988 Sep 29A

budget and spending programs: 1987 Dec 21A; 1988 Dec 21A

bureaucracy criticized 1985 Sep 30A

children's rights treaty 1989 Nov 20A

conflict resolution role 1984 Sep 18A

crisis response ability 1987 Sep 16A

disarmament and arms control: 1981 Apr 10A; 1982 Jun 12G/Jul 10A/Nov 26A/Dec 13A; 1984 Sep 26A; 1985 Sep 26A; 1987 Aug 24A/Sep 21A; 1988 Jun 26A

drug trafficking and abuse 1988 Dec 20A

failure on declaration of accomplishments and objectives 1985 Oct 24A

famine relief conference 1985 Mar 11A/Mar 11C

financial crisis 1986 Sep 6A

fishing 1989 Dec 13I

food shortfalls 1982 Mar 8E

foreign debt 1982 Mar 17B; 1984 Sep 26A

Human Rights Day 1985 Dec 10G

monority issues: subcommission on prevention of discrimination and protection of minorities 1980 Sep 3A

obituaries: Garcia Rodriguez, Felix 1980 Sep 11A; Myrdal, Gunnar 1987 May 17A

secretary general *see individual leaders in the name index (e.g.,* Waldheim, Kurt)

sessions: opening marked by tensions 1983 Sep 20A

terrorism 1985 Oct 9A; 1987 Dec 1A; hostage taking/abduction 1985 Dec 18A

war crimes: files opened 1987 Nov 6A

United Nations (UN)

women's five-year plan 1980 Jul 30J

United Negro College Fund 1989 May 10F

United Nicaraguan Opposition (UNO) 1986 May 9D; 1987 Feb 16D/May 13D

United Presbyterian Church 1982 Jun 29J

United Press International (UPI) 1983 Jan 2J/Jan 12B; 1985 Apr 28H/May 24H; 1986 Jun 10H

United Rubber Workers 1982 Apr 19H/May 12H

United States Football League (USFL) 1982 May 11J; 1985 Jul 14J; 1986 Jul 29J/Aug 4J

United States v. Mendoza-Lopez (1987) 1987 May 26F

United States v. Ward (1980) 1980 Jun 27F

United Steelworkers of America (USW) 1980 Apr 15H/Nov 8H/Nov 10H; 1981 Dec 11H; 1982 Nov 19H; 1983 Mar 1H/May 30H; 1984 Jan 24H; 1985 May 2H/Jul 21H/Oct 25H; 1986 Jan 16H/Mar 4H/Mar 15H/Apr 9H/May 26H/May 28H/Aug 1H/Aug 21H/Dec 18H; 1987 Jan 17H/Jan 31H/Aug 6H; 1988 Dec 4H; 1989 May 5H/May 26H/Jul 16H

United Technologies Corp. 1982 Sep 7H/Sep 15H/Sep 22H; 1983 Feb 21G; 1986 Feb 12A

United Telegraph Workers 1985 Aug 7H

United Transportation Union (UTU) 1985 Jun 22H

Universal City Studios 1984 Jan 17H

Universal Pictures 1985 Dec 14J

universe 1986 Jan 12I; 1989 Oct 13I/Nov 17I/Nov 18I/Nov 19I

universities *see* colleges and universities

University Boat Race (London) 1986 Mar 29J; 1989 Mar 25J

University Medical Center (Tucson, Ariz.) 1986 Oct 11I

UNO *see* United Nicaraguan Opposition

Unocal Corp. 1985 May 20H

UNRWA (Relief and Works Agency, U.N.) 1982 Aug 17C/Dec 10C; 1985 Mar 25C

Untouchables, The (film) 1987 Jun 3J/Jun 17J/Jul 8J; 1988 Apr 11J

UNTSO (Truce Supervision Organization, U.N.) 1988 Dec 12C

Un Zoo la nuit (Night Zoo) (film) 1988 Mar 22J

UPI *see* United Press International

Upjohn Co. 1987 Mar 16H; 1988 Aug 17H

Upper Volta 1980 Nov 25C; 1982 Nov 7C; 1983 Jan 17C/Aug 5C/Dec 31A; 1984 Aug 4C; *for events after Aug. 1984 see* Burkina Faso

Uppsala University (Sweden) 1981 Oct 19I

Ural Mountains (USSR) 1989 Jun 16B

uranium 1980 May 29H/Sep 10I/Sep 24F/Sep 24G; 1981 Mar 21G/Jul 7D/Nov 20I; 1982 Mar 1E/Nov 29I;

1983 Jun 9A/Nov 22E; 1985 Jun 5H; 1989 Oct 26C

Uranus (planet) 1985 Dec 3I; 1986 Jan 24I/Jan 29I/Jul 4I

Urban Cowboy (film) 1980 Jul 2J/Aug 13J

Urban Cowboy (soundtrack) 1980 Jul 9J

Urban Guerrillas-Mardoqueo Cruz (Salvadoran terrorist group) 1985 Jun 21D

Urban Institute 1984 Aug 15H

Urban League, National 1980 Aug 6F; 1981 Jul 19F; 1982 Aug 1F; 1985 Jul 24F; 1989 Aug 6F

Uretek Inc. 1987 Jul 28H

urinary tract cancer 1980 Mar 6I

Uruguay *see also individual leaders in the name index (e.g.,* Sanguinetti, Julio Maria)
  ambassador escapes Dominican embassy in Colombia 1980 Mar 17D
  amnesty for human rights abuses 1988 May 5D; 1989 Apr 16D
  antigovernment protests 1983 Sep 25D
  constitution rejected by voters 1980 Nov 30D
  foreign debt 1984 Sep 14D
  foreign relations: Cuba 1985 Oct 17D
  general strikes 1984 Jan 18D/Jun 27D
  government and politics: agreement on return to civilian rule 1984 Aug 3D; elections 1982 Nov 29D; Lacalle elected president 1989 Nov 26D; opposition breaks off talks on constitution 1983 Jul 4D; opposition leader arrested 1984 Jun 16D; party elections 1982 Nov 28D; political activity banned 1983 Aug 2D/Nov 12D; presidential elections 1984 Nov 26D
  papal visit 1988 May 7J
  political prisoners 1984 Mar 19D; 1985 Mar 14D
  religion: Uruguayan chosen head of World Council of Churches 1984 Jul 12J
  terrorism: consul kidnapping in Spain 1981 Feb 19B/Feb 28B

U.S. Auto Club 1981 May 25J

U.S. Catholic Conference 1986 May 8F; 1987 Dec 10J

U.S. Conference of Mayors 1980 Jun 10F; 1981 Mar 12F/Jun 17F; 1983 Jun 14I/Jul 19F; 1984 Jun 19F; 1985 Jun 18F; 1986 Jan 21F/Jan 22F; 1987 Jun 13F/Dec 16F

U.S. Figure Skating Championships 1985 Feb 1J/Feb 2J; 1987 Feb 7J; 1988 Jan 9J

U.S. Football League 1984 Feb 29J/Nov 17J; 1985 Jan 15J

U.S. Gold Commission 1982 Mar 31H

U.S. Information Agency (USIA) 1984 Mar 29G/May 15G; 1985 May 26E/Oct 2E; 1986 Feb 4E

U.S. League of Savings and Loan Associations 1982 Mar 3H/Nov 16F

U.S. Memories Inc. 1989 Jun 21I

U.S. Merit System Protection Board 1983 Apr 27F

U.S. Military Academy *see* West Point

U.S. National Outdoor Track and Field Championships 1980 Jun 14J

U.S. Naval Engineering Center (Lakehurst, N.J.) 1986 Jul 1G

U.S. News and World Report, Inc. 1984 Jun 11F

U.S. Open (golf tournament) 1980 Jun 15J; 1981 Jun 21J; 1982 Jun 20J; 1984 Jun 18J; 1985 Jun 16J; 1986 Jun 15J; 1987 Jun 21J; 1988 Jun 20J; 1989 Jun 18J

U.S. Open (tennis tournament)
  ATP dispute settled: 1980 Jul 12J
  men's singles: 1980 Sep 7J; 1981 Sep 13J; 1982 Sep 12J; 1983 Sep 11J; 1984 Sep 9J; 1985 Sep 8J; 1986 Sep 7J; 1987 Sep 14J; 1988 Sep 11J; 1989 Sep 10J
  women's singles: 1980 Sep 6J; 1981 Sep 12J; 1982 Sep 11J; 1983 Sep 10J; 1984 Sep 8J; 1985 Sep 7J; 1986 May 4J/Sep 7J; 1987 Sep 12J; 1988 Sep 10J; 1989 Sep 9J

U.S. Professional Cycling Championship 1985 Jun 23J

U.S. Rabbinical Assembly of Conservative Judaism 1985 Feb 14J

U.S. Short-Course Championships (swimming) 1982 Apr 18J

U.S.-Soviet Trade and Economic Council 1982 Nov 16A

U.S. Steel Corp. 1980 Mar 21A/Mar 27A/Dec 22H; 1981 Nov 19H/Nov 24H/Dec 9H/Dec 23H/Dec 24H/Dec 30H; 1982 Feb 17H/Mar 11H; 1983 Dec 27H; 1984 Feb 10H/Mar 29H; 1985 May 2H/Oct 30H; 1986 Jul 8H; *see* USX Corp.,*for events after July '86*

U.S. Synthetic Fuels Corp. 1980 Jun 26H/Sep 10F; 1982 Dec 5I; 1983 Jun 30H; 1984 Aug 2H; 1986 Apr 18H

U.S. Tennis Association (USTA) 1980 Jul 12J

U.S. Tobacco Co. 1986 Jun 20F

U.S. Trust Co. 1983 Jun 15H

U.S. Women's Open (golf tournament) 1980 Jul 13J; 1981 Jul 26J; 1982 Jul 25J/Jul 25J; 1983 Jul 31J; 1984 Jul 15J; 1985 Jul 14J; 1986 Jul 14J; 1987 Jul 28J; 1988 Jul 24J; 1989 Jul 16J

USA for Africa 1985 May 25J; 1986 Sep 12F

USA/Mobil indoor track and field championships 1981 Feb 27J/Feb 28J

USA Today (newspaper) 1981 Jul 24J; 1982 Sep 15J; 1984 Jun 25F; 1987 Jul 16H

USFL *see* United States Football League

U.S. News & World Report (magazine) 1984 Jun 11F; 1986 Aug 30B

USSR *see* Union of Soviet Socialist Republics

USW *see* United Steelworkers of America

USX Corp. (formerly U.S. Steel) 1986 Jul 8H/Aug 1H/Aug 21H/Oct 6H/Dec 18H; 1987 Jan 17H/Jan 31H; 1989 Nov 1H

Utah, University of (Salt Lake City) 1982 Dec 2I; 1985 Jan 3J; 1989 Mar 23I/May 9I

Utah Jazz (basketball team) 1984 Apr 5J; 1989 Feb 12J

uterine cancer 1983 Mar 25I

Uttar Pradesh (India) 1980 Aug 17E; 1981 Jun 15E; 1982 Oct 3E; 1984 Aug 8E; 1987 May 26E

U2 (singing group) 1987 Apr 25J/May 23J/Jun 27J/Jul 22J; 1988 Mar 2J/Nov 26J/Dec 31J

Uzbekistan (USSR) 1984 Mar 20I; 1989 Jun 12B

V

vaccines 1981 Jun 18I; 1986 Jul 23I/Nov 14F; 1987 Aug 18I; 1988 Mar 10I; 1989 Dec 8I

Valdez Principles 1989 Sep 7H

Valet de Nuit (Night Valet) (Michel Host) (book) 1986 Nov 17J

Valium (drug) 1980 Jul 11I; 1985 Sep 4F; 1987 Feb 9G

Valley Girl (film) 1983 May 4J

Valley of Horses, The (Jean M. Auel) (book) 1982 Sep 12J/Oct 17J/Nov 14J/Dec 12J; 1983 Jan 16J/Feb 13J

value-added tax (VAT) 1988 Sep 11B

Van Biesbroeck 8 (star) 1984 Dec 11I

Van Cliburn International Piano Competition 1985 Jun 2J; 1989 Jun 11J

Vancouver Canucks (ice hockey team) 1982 May 16J

Vangelis (composer) 1982 Mar 14J/Mar 17J/May 5J

Van Halen (singing group)
  best sellers: *Diver Down* 1982 May 5J/Jun 16J; *Fair Warning* 1981 May 27J; *5150* 1986 Apr 16J/May 21J/Jun 18J; *1984* 1984 Feb 18J/Mar 24J/Apr 28J/May 20J/May 28J; *OU812* 1988 Jun 18J/Jul 16J; *Women and Children First* 1980 Apr 30J/Jun 4J

Vanuatu 1980 May 28E/Aug 31E/Nov 14E; 1988 Jul 25E/Dec 21E; 1989 Apr 14E; For events before July, 1980 *see* New Hebrides

VAT *see* value-added tax

Vatican bank *see* Istituto per le Opere di Religione (IOR)

Vatican II 1985 Jan 25A

VCRs *see* video cassette recorders

VDTs *see* video display terminals

Vega (Soviet spacecraft) 1984 Dec 15I/Dec 20I/Dec 21I

Vega (star) 1983 Aug 9I

vegetable oil 1987 Mar 30B

vegetables 1985 Aug 9H; 1986 Jul 8H; 1987 Jan 7H; 1989 Mar 2I/Dec 4H

Veit: The Secret Wars of the CIA, 1981-1987 (Bob Woodward) (book) 1987 Sep 25G

Velsicol Chemical Corp. 1987 Aug 11H

Venera (Soviet spacecraft) 1982 Mar 1I/Mar 18I; 1983 Jun 7I

venereal disease 1986 Sep 22I

Venezuela *see also individual leaders in the name index (e.g.,* Perez, Carlos Andres)
  arts and culture: Miss Universe chosen 1986 Jul 21J
  government and politics: antigovernment protests 1987 Apr 11D; 1989 Mar 1D; corruption scandal 1989 May 1D; curfew lifted 1989 Mar 5D; Lusinchi elected president 1983 Dec 4D; Lusinchi sworn 1984 Feb 2D; municipal elections 1984 May 27D; Perez elected president 1988 Dec 4D
  international organizations: UN council membership 1985 Oct 17A
  labor issues: general strike 1989 May 18D
  Latin relations: Bolivia 1980 Jul 29D; Central American summit 1983 Apr 21D/Jul 30D; Colombia 1987 Aug 9D; Cuba 1980 Jan 19D; Dominican Republic 1987 Apr 30D; El Salvador 1983 Feb 22G; Guyana 1982 Jun 18D/Oct 13D; Mexico 1981 Apr 8D/Apr 10D; 1983 Jul 17D; Nicaraguan contras 1984 Sep 8D; Panama 1987 Dec 22D
  monetary issues: currency 1989 Mar 13D/May 1D
  obituaries: Betancourt, Romulo 1981 Sep 28D
  religious issues: papal visit 1985 Jan 26D
  sports: Pan American Games 1983 Aug 28J
  terrorism: Cuban exile acquitted 1986 Jul 21D; domestic flight hijacked 1980 Dec 5D/Dec 6D
  trade and investment: foreign debt 1984 Jun 21D/Sep 14D; 1985 May 17D; 1986 Feb 26D/Dec 17D; 1987 Sep 18D; 1988 Dec 30D; foreign investment 1985 Sep 16D
  U.S. relations: 1983 Dec 12D; 1984 Jan 31G; 1989 Feb 1G

Venice (Italy) 1988 Sep 12B

Venice Film Festival 1987 Sep 9J

ventriloquists 1986 Jul 2J

venture capital 1988 May 27B

Venus (planet) 1981 Oct 30I; 1982 Mar 1I/Mar 18I; 1983 Apr 16I/Jun 7I; 1984 Dec 21I; 1989 May 4I

Verdict, The (film) 1983 Feb 2J

Verdun (France) 1984 Sep 22B

Vermont 1980 Mar 4F; 1982 May 15F/Sep 2I; 1984 Mar 6F; 1988 Mar 1F/Apr 20F/Nov 8F

Vernon Savings & Loan Association 1987 Jul 2F/Nov 19H

Very Subtle (racehorse) 1987 Nov 21J

veterans 1980 Aug 26F; 1988 May 20G/Nov 18G; see also *specific wars (e.g.,* Vietnam War)

Veterans Administration, U.S. (VA)
  budget and spending programs: 1988 Aug 19F
  health care issues: Agent Orange 1982 Aug 31G/Oct 25G; 1983 Apr 29G; 1984 Oct 24G; AIDS testing 1987 Jun 24F; alcoholism 1988 Apr 20G; disability/pension disputes 1985 Jun 28G; radiation exposure 1983 Apr 6G
  mortgages: 1980 Nov 24H; 1981 Sep 14H; 1983 Jul 11H; 1986 May 2H
  political issues: cabinet-level status 1987 Nov 17G; document destruction fines 1987 Jan 8G

Veterans Affairs, U.S. Department of 1988 Oct 25G/Dec 22F; 1989 Mar 2G/May 11G; *prior to 1988, see* Veterans Administration

Veterans of Foreign Wars 1983 Sep 21G

VHS recording system 1988 Jan 11E

Vicariate of Solidarity (Chilean human rights group) 1989 Feb 15D

Vice Versa (film) 1988 Mar 16J

victim impact statements 1987 Jun 15F; 1989 Jun 12F

Victor (ship) 1987 Dec 20E

Victor Victoria (film) 1982 May 5J

Victory over Japan (Ellen Gilchrist) (book) 1984 Nov 16J

video cassette recorders (VCRs) 1984 Jan 17H; 1985 Feb 15J; 1988 Jan 11E

video display terminals (VDTs) 1983 Jul 11I; 1986 Jun 6J; 1988 Jun 14H

video games 1982 Nov 3J; 1983 Oct 17J; 1985 Feb 15J

Vienna (Austria) 1981 Aug 29B; 1985 Dec 27A; 1989 Apr 1B

Vietnam
  Amerasian children 1982 Oct 7E; 1984 Sep 11G; 1987 Dec 31E; 1988 Jan 20E/Feb 15E
  amnesty program 1988 Feb 11E
  astronaut on *Soyuz* 1980 Jul 23I/Jul 31I
  Cambodian intervention *see* Cambodia
  celebrations: anniversary of end of war 1985 Apr 30E
  crime and law enforcement 1984 Dec 18E; 1985 Jan 3E; 1987 Dec 3E
  economic reforms 1987 Apr 23E
  food shortages 1988 May 12E/Jun 25A
  foreign relations: China 1980 Feb 8E/Mar 6E; 1981 May 8E/May 17E; 1984 Apr 6E/Jul 12E; 1987 Oct 5E; 1988 Mar 14E; 1989 Jan 16E; European Community 1987 Sep 17A; France 1986 Oct 11B; Japan 1981 Dec 10E; Laos 1988 Feb 24E; U.S. 1981 Feb 24G/May 27G/Jun 20G; 1982 Oct 14E; 1984 Sep 11G; USSR 1988 Sep 16B
  government and politics: cabinet reshuffled 1982 Apr 24E; Communist Party Congress 1986 Dec 18E; Do Muoi elected premier 1988 Jun 22E; government shakeup 1987 Feb 17E; national assembly elections 1987 Apr 19E; Politburo members removed 1982 Mar 31E; president and premier removed from office 1987 Jun 18E; Truong Chinh chosen secretary general 1986 Jul 14E; Truong Chinh named chairman of council of state 1981 Jul 4E
  Ho Chi Minh death date corrected 1989 Aug 31E
  international organizations: Comecon 1984 Jun 14A; United Nations 1988 Jun 25A
  obituaries: Le Duan 1986 Jul 10E
  refugees 1980 Feb 24E/Aug 21E; 1981 Aug 13E; 1984 Jun 19A; 1988 Jan 27E/Apr 20E; 1989 Feb 24G/Mar 8E/Mar 13E/Jun 13A/Sep 2E/Sep 14E/Dec 12E
  sports: Olympic Games (Los Angeles) 1984 May 17J

Vietnam: A Television History (TV show) 1985 Jun 26J

Vietnam veterans
  Agent Orange *see* Agent Orange
  commemorations: celebrations honor 1984 Nov 9G; men's war memorial 1982 Nov 13G; 1983 Sep 21G; 1984 Nov 11G; 1986 May 26G; 1987 Oct 22G; parade 1985 May 7G; women's war memorial 1988 Oct 21G/Nov 15G; "unknown soldier" buried 1984 May 28G
  crime and law enforcement: veteran executed 1988 Mar 15F; veteran with PTSD executed 1986 Apr 22F
  health issues: birth defects of children 1984 Aug 16G; combat veterans' problems 1981 Mar 23I; counseling 1981 Jun 16G; 1983 Dec 21G; VA hospital sit-in 1981 Jun 9F
  job training: 1983 Aug 15G
  political issues: national coalition formed 1983 Sep 21G; Native Americans 1986 Nov 10G; woman gets leadership post 1987 Aug 1G

Vietnam Veterans Memorial (Washington, D.C.) 1982 Nov 13G; 1983 Sep

21G; 1984 Nov 11G; 1986 May 26G; 1987 Oct 22G; 1988 Nov 15G

Vietnam Veterans of America 1987 Aug 1G

Vietnam War
Agent Orange see Agent Orange
CBS documentary 1982 Jul 15J; 1983 Apr 26J
CBS/Westmoreland lawsuit see CBS?
Chinese troops in 1989 May 16E
draft avoidance 1988 Aug 17F
Laos 1982 Jan 24G
Marine court-martial recommended 1980 Feb 1G
missing in action: 1982 May 29E; 1984 Jul 17G; 1985 Jul 7G/Dec 4G; 1986 Jan 7E/Apr 18E; 1987 Aug 1E/Nov 25E; 1988 Apr 6E/Nov 12E; 1989 Apr 27G
PBS TV documentaries on 1985 Jun 26J
soldier found guilty of collaboration 1981 Feb 5G

Vietnam Women's Memorial (Washington, D.C.) 1988 Oct 21G/Nov 15G

View to a Kill, A (film) 1985 Jun 12J

Vigilante (film) 1983 Mar 9J

Villanova University (Pennsylvania) 1985 Apr 1J

Vincennes (ship) 1988 Jul 3C/Jul 3G/Jul 11G/Aug 2G/Aug 19G; 1989 Mar 10G/Jul 17G

vinyl chloride 1987 Jun 24H

vinyl floor tiles 1986 Jan 23H

violent crime 1981 Feb 8F/Aug 4F/Aug 12F/Aug 16F/Aug 17F; 1985 Mar 24F/Apr 7F; 1989 Aug 6F

Virginia
accidents and disasters: nuclear power plant pipe ruptures 1986 Dec 9H
colleges and universities 1983 Mar 24F; 1988 Feb 10F
crime and law enforcement: LaRouche organization indictments 1986 Oct 6F; 1987 Feb 17F; marijuana 40-year prison sentence 1982 Jan 11F
environment and pollution: FMC Corp. guilty of obstructing EPA 1980 Nov 10H; National Steel Corp. fined 1983 May 4H
Equal Rights Amendment vote fails 1982 Feb 16F
espionage and intelligence issues: Walker (Arthur J.) arrested 1985 May 29G
labor issues: UMW president sworn in 1982 Dec 22H; UMW strike 1989 Jun 20H
Manassas National Battlefield Park 1988 Aug 10H/Nov 11H
medicine and health care: common cold drug 1986 Jan 9I
politics and government: presidential campaign (1988) 1987 Dec 5F; Wilder elected governor 1989 Nov 7F; Wilder launches campaign for governor 1989 Jan 26F
racial bias 1983 Mar 24F; 1988 Feb 10F
school busing 1983 Feb 2F
sterilization of mental patients 1980 Feb 23F
tenant evictions 1989 Mar 29F
"test-tube baby" clinic 1980 Jan 8I

Virginia, University of (Charlottesville) 1980 Mar 20J; 1982 Mar 26J/Dec 24J; 1989 Dec 3J

Virginia Polytechnic Institute & State University (Blacksburg) 1985 Apr 30J

Virginia Slims Championship (tennis) 1987 Nov 22J

Virgin Islands (U.S.) 1986 Jun 8F; 1988 Apr 2F; 1989 Sep 19D

visas and passports
Australia denies to South Africans 1984 Mar 2E
China revokes students passport 1988 Mar 23E
East German restrictions on travel to Poland 1980 Oct 28B
East German travel to West 1989 Nov 15B
European Community restricts Libyans 1986 Apr 14B
Great Britain requires visas 1986 Sep 1B
Israel tries to prevent emigration by Soviet Jews 1988 Oct 23C
Poland liberalizes regulations 1981 Apr 26B
U.S. bill on Chinese students 1989 Nov 30G
U.S. denies visas to Italian playwrights 1983 Aug 27F
U.S. denies visa to Japanese group 1982 Jun 7G
U.S. increase in 1988 Oct 21F/Nov 15F; 1989 Jun 14D
U.S. invalidates Libyan travel 1981 Dec 10G
U.S. refuses to communist-affiliated visitors 1987 Oct 19F
USSR 1988 Jan 5B
USSR grants visa to Bonner 1985 Oct 28B

Visiting Hours (film) 1982 Jun 9J

VISTA 1989 Nov 20F

vitamin E 1984 May 4I

Voest-Alpine 1986 Sep 2B

Voice of America (radio network) 1982 Jul 19G; 1983 Sep 29G; 1984 Dec 25G; 1985 Nov 9G; 1987 Jan 1B

Voice of the Heart (Barbara Taylor Bradford) (book) 1983 May 15J

Vojvodina (Yugoslavia) 1988 Oct 6B

volcanic lakes 1986 Aug 21C/Aug 24C

volcanoes and volcanic eruptions
Augustine Island (Alaska): 1986 Mar 27I
Mauna Loa (Hawaii): 1984 Mar 25I
Mt. Etna (Sicily): 1983 May 14I; 1985 Dec 25I
Mount Mihara (Japan): 1986 Nov 21I
Mount St. Helens (Washington State): 1980 Mar 26I/May 18I
mystery cloud circling earth: 1982 Mar 6I
Nevado del Ruiz (Colombia): 1985 Nov 13D
Redoubt Volcano (Alaska): 1989 Dec 14I

Volkswagen AG 1985 Jun 3D; 1986 Dec 23H; 1987 Jul 22B/Aug 26D; 1988 Jan 18B

volleyball 1981 Jan 13J

Volume One (Honeydrippers) (recording) 1984 Nov 24J

voluntary export quotas 1981 May 7E; 1983 Jun 30E; 1984 Dec 10A; 1985 Mar 1H/Mar 28E; 1987 Jan 27E

voter registration 1985 Jan 8F

Voting Rights Act (1965) 1981 Jan 6F/Oct 5F; 1982 May 3F/Jun 18F/Jun 23F/Jun 29F; 1983 Feb 23F; 1984 Nov 13F

Vought Corp. 1981 Sep 23H

Voyage, The (Philip Glass) (musical composition) 1988 Mar 16J

Voyager (aircraft) 1986 Dec 14I/Dec 23I

Voyager 1 (spacecraft) 1980 May 6I/Nov 12I

Voyager 2 (spacecraft) 1981 Aug 25I/Aug 26I/Aug 28I; 1985 Dec 3I; 1986 Jan 24I/Jan 29I/Jul 4I; 1989 Aug 24I/Dec 6I

Voyager Petroleums Ltd. 1984 Oct 12D

Voyagers to the West: A Passage in the Peopling of America on the Eve of the Revolution (Bernard Bailyn) (book) 1987 Apr 16J

Vradyn (Greek newspaper) 1983 Mar 19B

VVER-440 (Soviet nuclear reactor) 1986 Jul 16I

VVER 1000 (Soviet nuclear reactor) 1986 Jul 16I

W

Wadsworth Veterans Administration Hospital (Los Angeles) 1981 Jun 9F

Wage and Price Stability, U.S. Council on see Council on Wage and Price Stability, U.S.

wage controls and freezes 1980 Feb 22H/Jun 24F; 1982 Jan 28D/Jul 7D/Dec 23E; 1985 Jan 24C; 1987 Jun 12D/Oct 14D/Nov 15B; 1988 Jun 14D; 1989 Apr 27D/Jun 18D/Dec 3D

Wagmatcook Indians 1981 Aug 22D

Walco National Corp. 1982 Jan 20F

Wales 1980 Nov 3J; 1981 May 7B; 1983 Nov 30J; 1984 Aug 5J; 1985 Jan 2B/Apr 23B; 1986 Mar 3B/Jun 20I; 1987 Mar 2B/Sep 24B/Sep 25I/Dec 4B; 1988 Aug 22B/Nov 6J; 1989 Feb 14B

Walker Cup (golf) 1987 May 28J

Walking Drum, The (Louis L'Amour) (book) 1984 Jun 15J

Wall, The (Pink Floyd) (recording) 1980 Jan 2J/Mar 5J/Apr 2J/Apr 30J/Jun 4J

Wall Street (film) 1987 Dec 11J/Dec 23F; 1988 Apr 11J

Wall Street Journal (newspaper) 1984 Apr 16J/May 19H/Jun 25F/Aug 28H; 1985 Jun 24H/Oct 30H; 1987 Feb 4C/Nov 16F

Wal-Mart Stores Inc. 1984 Sep 18H; 1985 Oct 15J; 1986 Oct 14H

walnuts 1989 Jan 5A

Walt Disney Productions Inc. 1984 Jan 17H; 1985 Feb 1J/Dec 28J; 1987 Mar 24B

Walter E. Heller International Corp. 1983 Mar 14H

Wanderlust (Danielle Steel) (book) 1986 Aug 29J/Sep 26J/Oct 31J

Wanted Dead or Alive (film) 1987 Jan 21J

War and Remembrance (TV show) 1989 Sep 17J

Warhol Foundation for the Visual Arts, Andy 1988 May 3J

Warner Books 1988 Apr 25J

Warner Brothers, Inc. 1981 Jul 25J

Warner Brothers Records, Inc. 1985 Aug 5J

Warner Communications Inc. 1982 Nov 27J; 1989 Mar 4H/Jul 24H

warning labels 1986 Feb 27F/Mar 7F/Apr 17F

War of the End of the World, The (Mario Vargas Llosa) (book) 1985 Mar 29J

War of the Roses, The (film) 1989 Dec 28J

War Powers Act (1973) 1980 Apr 24G; 1983 Mar 15G/Sep 20G/Sep 29G/Oct 27G/Nov 1G/Nov 16G; 1984 Mar 30G; 1987 Oct 21G

Warsaw Pact 1981 Mar 26B; 1982 May 4A; 1983 Jan 6B/Apr 7B/Oct 14B/Oct 21B/Dec 9A; 1984 Jan 10B/Mar 5B/Apr 20B; 1985 Jan 14B; 1987 May 29B; 1988 Feb 6B; 1989 Jul 7B/Oct 26B; see also member nations (e.g., Poland)

Wartime Relocation and Internment of Civilians, U.S. Commission on 1983 Feb 24F

War Without Mercy: Race and Power in the Pacific War (John Dower) (book) 1987 Jan 12J

Washington (state) 1980 Mar 26I; 1981 Nov 9F; 1982 Jan 22I/Jul 18J/Aug 28J; 1983 Jun 15H; 1984 Jan 23H/Dec 19H; 1985 Jun 19F

Washington, D.C. 1980 May 6F; 1984 May 1F; 1985 Aug 22F; 1988 May 3F/Nov 15G; 1989 Aug 3F/Oct 27F; individual leaders in the name index (e.g., Barry, Marion)

Washington, University of (Seattle) 1982 Jan 1J/Dec 25J; 1985 Jan 1J; 1986 Oct 21I; 1987 Jan 20F; 1989 Oct 12I

Washington for Jesus rally (1980) 1980 Apr 29J

Washington Legal Foundation 1984 Aug 7F

Washington Library (Chicago) 1988 Jun 20J

Washington Monument 1982 Dec 8G

Washington Office on Latin America 1984 Feb 9G

Washington Park Wilderness Act of 1988 1988 Nov 16H

Washington Post (newspaper) 1981 Apr 15J/Sep 21E/Oct 23J; 1984 Oct 29F

Washington Project for the Arts (Washington, D.C.) 1989 Jul 20J

Washington Public Power Supply System 1982 Jan 22I; 1983 Jun 15H/Jul 22H/Aug 3H/Aug 9H/Oct 4H/Nov 29H; 1984 Jan 23H

Washington Redskins (football team) 1983 Jan 22J/Jan 30J/Dec 20J; 1984 Jan 8J/Jan 22J; 1987 Jan 11J; 1988 Jan 3J/Jan 10J/Jan 17J/Sep 4J

Washington University (St. Louis, Mo.) 1988 May 16J

Waste Isolation Pilot Plant (WIPP) (New Mexico) 1988 Sep 13H

Waste Management Inc. 1985 Jan 24H/Apr 5H; 1987 Dec 31H

water see drinking water; for pollution issues, see water pollution

Waterford Glass Group 1986 Oct 8B

waterfowl 1989 Nov 19H

Watergate scandal 1983 May 14F; 1987 May 28F

watermelons 1986 Feb 14H

water pollution 1980 Dec 2H; 1981 Jan 2H/Jul 28H; 1982 Apr 27F/Sep 2H; 1984 Apr 17H; 1987 Oct 5H/Oct 16D/Dec 1H; see also specific subjects (e.g., Clean Water Act)

water projects
access issues: 1985 Aug 4H; 1989 Nov 29H
construction programs: 1985 Nov 13H; 1986 Mar 26H/Oct 17H; 1988 Apr 26H; 1989 Sep 29H

wilderness areas: 1985 Nov 26H

waterways 1986 Nov 6H/Nov 17H

Watts Bar nuclear plant (Tennessee) 1985 Aug 23H

Way It Is, The (Bruce Hornsby & the Range) (recording) 1986 Dec 17J; 1987 Jan 28J/Feb 18J/Mar 28J

Wayne State University (Detroit, Michigan) 1987 Mar 27I

wealth 1985 Oct 15J; 1986 Jul 26H/Aug 21H/Oct 14H; 1987 Mar 19H/Sep 20H; 1988 Feb 24J/Oct 10H; 1989 Jul 9H/Sep 11J

Weapons and Hope (Freeman Dyson) (book) 1985 Jan 14J

We Are Still Married: Stories and Letters (Garrison Keillor) (book) 1989 Apr 28J

We Are the World (USA for Africa) (recording) 1985 Jan 28J/Apr 27J/May 25J; 1986 Feb 25J

weather satellites 1984 Jul 29I; 1986 Jan 12I

Weather Underground (terrorist group) 1980 Jul 8F/Nov 6F/Dec 3F; 1981 Apr 15F/Oct 20F/Oct 21F/Oct 22F; 1987 Jan 20F

Wedgewood PLC 1986 Oct 8B

Wedtech Corp. 1986 Dec 15H; 1987 Apr 16F/May 11F/Jun 3F/Jul 9F/Dec 22F; 1988 Feb 11F/Aug 4F/Nov 21F; 1989 Aug 8F/Oct 16H/Oct 20F

Weekend World (British TV show) 1982 Apr 18B

Weekly Mail (South African newspaper) 1988 Nov 1C

Weeping Woman (Pablo Picasso) (painting) 1986 Aug 19J

Weep No More My Lady (Mary Higgins Clark) (book) 1987 Jul 17J/Aug 21J

Weidenfeld Ltd. 1985 Mar 4J

Weirton Steel Corp. 1983 Mar 10H/Sep 23H; 1984 Jan 11F

Welcome to the Real World (Mr. Mister) (recording) 1986 Feb 19J/Mar 22J

welfare
foreign issues: Denmark 1988 Dec 18B
labor issues: racial bias suit filed 1984 Feb 20F
reform proposals: budget cuts 1981 Mar 19F; California workfare bill 1985 Sep 26F; child support payment deductions 1987 Jun 25F; cutbacks proposed 1981 May 4F; 1987 Oct 16F; federal legislation 1987 Apr 2F/Jul 21F/Dec 16F; 1988 Jun 16F/Sep 30F/Oct 13F; Ford Foundation 1989 May 11F; governors 1987 Feb 21F; HEW ex-secretaries 1982 Sep 16F; state experimentation 1986 Dec 12F; state responsibility 1981 Feb 11F

wells 1987 Oct 16J

Wells Fargo Armored Car Services Corp. 1983 Nov 26F; 1985 Apr 29F/May 30F

Wells Fargo Bank 1981 Feb 2H; 1982 Jan 13J; 1984 Jul 18F

Wellwood (ship) 1984 Aug 16I

Wembley Stadium (London) 1980 Sep 27J; 1988 Jun 11J/Sep 2J

Wendy's International, Inc. 1982 Oct 29H

Wen Wei Po (Hong Kong newspaper) 1989 Jul 15E

We're No Angels (film) 1989 Dec 28J

West Bank

American Jewish leaders endorse territorial compromise 1980 Jul 1J
beatings of Palestinian protesters 1988 Jan 19C/Jan 24C
Begin agrees to administrative council enlargement 1981 Oct 15C
Begin says sovereignty will be asserted 1982 May 3C
bombings 1980 Jun 2C
declaration of independence celebrated 1989 Nov 15C
deportations 1980 May 3C/May 11C/May 20A/May 20C/Aug 19C/Oct 14C/Dec 5C/Dec 19A/Dec 24C; 1988 Jan 3C/Jan 13C
economic effects of occupation 1982 Apr 14C
Egypt/Israel talks on Palestinian autonomy 1980 Jan 10C/Jan 17C/Feb 1C/Oct 15A; 1989 Sep 18C
human rights 1989 Feb 7G
independence declared by PLO 1988 Nov 26C
Israeli army officers oppose government policy 1982 May 10C
Israeli crackdowns 1987 Dec 25C; 1988 Jan 1C/Mar 28C; 1989 Jan 23C
Israeli plans for road network 1980 Jun 27C
Israeli raid on Arab village 1989 Apr 13C
Israeli soldiers convicted of harassment 1983 Feb 17C
Israeli soldiers to be court-martialed 1982 Oct 15C
Israeli troops fire on students 1980 Nov 18C
Jewish schools to be built 1980 Mar 23C
Jewish settlements 1980 Feb 10C; 1981 Jan 26C/Feb 25C; 1982 Feb 17C/Sep 5C/Nov 3C; 1983 Mar 21C/Apr 10C; 1984 Feb 5C/Apr 11C/May 23C; 1985 Jan 10C/Feb 9C
Jordan 1982 Mar 10C/Mar 24A; 1988 Jul 31C
killings: campus of Islamic College shootings 1983 Jul 26C; Israeli girl 1988 Apr 6C; Jewish settlers convicted 1985 Jul 10C; mayor of Nablus 1986 Mar 2C; Palestinian attacks on Jewish settlers 1980 May 2C; Palestinians shot by Israeli soldiers 1982 Mar 25C; 1989 Dec 9C
Labor Party partitioning proposal 1980 Apr 24C
local governments dissolved 1982 Mar 18C/Mar 25C/Jun 16C; 1983 Jul 8C
mayors claim PLO cannot be suppressed 1982 Mar 30C
mayors ousted 1982 Mar 26C; 1983 Jul 8C
municipal elections postponed 1981 Mar 26C
obituaries: Masri, Zafir al- 1986 Mar 2C
Palestinian uprising 1987 Dec 18C; 1988 Jun 22C/Oct 18C; 1989 Mar 22C
Reagan peace plan 1982 Sep 1A; 1983 Apr 5C/Apr 10C
schools reopened 1988 May 23C
Shamir plan for elections 1989 Apr 20C/Apr 27C/Jul 23C
strikes 1982 Mar 19C/Mar 30C/Apr 12C/Sep 21C
student demonstrations 1980 Nov 20C
trials of activists 1987 Dec 27C

United Nations 1980 Mar 1A/May 20A/Jun 5A/Dec 19A; 1982 Mar 24A
university faculty members dismissed 1983 Jan 20C
West Berlin (West Germany)
Baker speech 1989 Dec 12G
bombings: Arab social club 1986 Nov 26B; discotheque 1986 Apr 5B/May 21B; Israeli restaurant 1982 Jan 15C; plot to attack congress of Kurdish students 1980 Aug 1A
celebration of city's anniversary 1987 Apr 30B
ceremonies in memory of John F. Kennedy 1983 Nov 22F
coalition government 1989 Mar 10B
East Germany 1986 Jun 16B; 1987 May 6B; 1989 Nov 9B/Nov 15B
Reagan challenges Gorbachev 1987 Jun 12B
Reagan visits 1982 Jun 11B
Reichstag fire 1980 Dec 29B; 1981 Apr 22B
rioting 1980 Dec 15B
Soviet military exercises 1984 Apr 4A
spy exchange 1985 Jun 11A
West Berlin Working Group for Human Rights 1981 Aug 20B
Western 500 (auto race) 1985 Nov 17J
Western European Union (WEU) 1984 Jun 12B/Oct 27B; 1987 Oct 27B; 1988 Nov 14B
Western Pacific Railroad 1980 Sep 15H
Western Railroad 1982 Sep 13H
Western Sahara 1981 Mar 25G/Oct 21C; 1982 Feb 11C/Feb 22c/Apr 5D/Aug 6D/Oct 30C; 1983 Jun 12C; 1984 Nov 12C; 1988 May 16C/Aug 30C; Hassan II, King
Western Samoa 1985 Aug 6E/Dec 27E
Western Savings Bank 1982 Apr 3H
Western Union Corp. 1985 Aug 7H
West German Grand Prix (auto race) 1987 Jul 26J
West Germany see also individual leaders in the name index (e.g., Brandt, Willy)
accidents and disasters: helicopter crash during air show 1982 Sep 11G; nuclear power plant accident 1988 Dec 5I; Pershing II missile fire 1985 Jan 11B
antinuclear protests: 1981 Feb 28B/Oct 10B; 1983 Apr 4B/Aug 6B/Oct 22B/Nov 21B
arts and culture: Boehm wins Pritzker 1986 Apr 17J
assassinations: Karry, Heinz Herbert 1981 May 11B
banking: Bundesbank 1986 Oct 15B; 1987 Dec 3B; 1988 Jun 21B/Jul 11A; commercial lending program 1987 Dec 2B
Berlin see West Berlin
bombings: Frankfurt airport 1985 Jun 19B; Munich Oktoberfest 1980 Sep 26B; Ramstein air base 1981 Aug 31B/Sep 2B; Union Carbide plant 1984 Dec 6B; U.S. military installations and corporate offices 1982 Jun 1B
business and industry: Flick Group pays WWII Jewish victims 1986 Jan 8B; steel-maker merger 1982 Feb 4B; Thompson-Brandt/Grundig purchase 1982 Nov 19B
chemical weapons 1984 Aug 7B; 1989 Feb 15B/Jul 7G

contaminated Austrian wine confiscated 1985 Jul 11B
crime and law enforcement: Adolf Hitler diary forgery 1983 May 6J; 1984 Mar 21B; 1985 Jul 8B; Handelskreditbank AG closed 1980 Jul 27B; Jewish compensation funds theft 1988 May 17B; 1989 Dec 15B; Turkish suspect in papal assassination attempt arrested 1982 Feb 16B
currency 1980 Dec 31H; 1981 Oct 4B; 1982 Jun 12B/Oct 4A; 1983 Mar 21B/Aug 1A; 1984 Sep 10H; 1987 Jan 12B/Nov 30H/Dec 31H; 1988 Mar 4H/Dec 30H; 1989 May 22A
defense and armed forces: budget cuts 1981 Mar 7B; medium-range missile deployment 1982 Mar 29B; 1983 Nov 22B
disarmament and arms control 1987 Aug 26B; double-zero option on nuclear missiles supported 1987 Jun 1B; missile technology export agreement 1987 Apr 16A
discount rate 1987 Jan 22B/Dec 3B
economy: GNP 1983 Jan 10B; 1986 Sep 5B/Dec 4B; 1987 Feb 12B/Sep 1B; 1988 Jan 13B/Jun 1B/Sep 6B; 1989 Jan 11B; net foreign assets 1986 Oct 15B; OECD report 1984 Jul 30B; ranking as economic power 1989 Jun 3B; reserve holdings 1988 Mar 7A; standard of living 1988 Jun 3H
espionage and intelligence issues: counter-intelligence officer defects to East 1985 Aug 23B; NATO espionage ring arrests 1988 Aug 25B
export ranking 1987 Aug 4A; 1988 Aug 2A; 1989 Feb 27A
foreign relations
Albania 1987 Sep 17B
Argentina 1982 Apr 7D
Bulgaria 1984 Sep 9B
China 1985 Jun 19B; 1986 Jun 8B
Czechoslovakia 1985 Jan 15B; 1986 Sep 18B
East Germany 1980 Mar 16B/Apr 30B; 1984 Jul 25B; 1985 Jan 15B; 1986 Dec 9B; 1987 Mar 4B/Aug 12B; 1989 Aug 8B/Sep 8B/Nov 9B/Dec 11B
France 1980 Jul 7B; 1984 Aug 1B; 1987 Sep 24B
Iran 1989 Jan 28C/Jul 7G
Lebanon 1987 Jan 18A/Jan 21C; 1988 Jan 27C/Sep 12C
Libya 1983 May 8C; 1988 Jan 18B; 1989 Feb 15B/May 10B
Mexico 1980 May 28D
Nicaraguan contras 1986 Jun 10D
Pakistan 1988 Jan 18B
Poland 1981 Dec 29A; 1984 Nov 24B
South Africa 1986 Jun 20A; 1987 Feb 20A
Syria 1986 May 21B
U.S. 1983 Jun 2A; 1984 Jul 12A; 1985 Sep 27B/Dec 18B; 1988 Feb 22B; 1989 May 2H
USSR 1981 Nov 20B; 1982 Jan 12B/Oct 5G; 1983 Jan 16B/Dec 2B; 1984 Mar 12B; 1985 Jan 22B; teen makes unauthorized flight 1987 May 29B/Sep 4B; 1988 Aug 3B
government and politics: Brandt resigns as chairman of SDP 1987 Mar 23B; FDP leaves coalition government 1982 Sep 17B; Greens see Greens; Lambsdorff elected FDP leader 1988 Oct 8B; new party formed 1982 Nov 28B; par-

liament president resigns 1988 Nov 11B; parliament speaker resigns 1984 Oct 25B; Vogel to become Social Democratic Party chairman 1987 Jun 14B; Weizsaecker reelected president 1989 May 23B
immigration and refugees: asylum-seekers 1987 Jul 1B
international organizations: European Community 1983 Apr 7B; 1984 Aug 1B; 1985 Jun 12B; United Nations 1984 Dec 9A; 1987 Feb 20A
labor issues: construction union rejects pay agreement 1981 Mar 25B; labor minister favors wage-price freeze 1982 Oct 5B; metalworkers union agreement on workweek 1987 Apr 22B
medicine and health care: Chernobyl disaster health effects 1987 Mar 25I; health care reform package 1988 Nov 25B
Nazis 1984 Mar 31B/Oct 17A; 1985 Sep 28B; 1987 Oct 26G
obituaries: Beuys, Joseph 1986 Jan 23J; Boll, Heinrich Theodore 1985 Jul 16J; Debus, Sigurd 1981 Apr 16B; Fassbinder, Rainer Werner 1982 Jun 10J; Hess, Rudolf 1987 Aug 17B; Karry, Heinz Herbert 1981 May 11B; Kiesinger, Kurt Georg 1988 Mar 8B; Kirst, Hans Helmut 1989 Feb 23J; Mitscherlich, Alexander 1982 Jun 26I; Niemoeller, Martin 1984 Mar 6J; Orff, Carl 1982 Mar 29J; Speidel, Hans 1984 Nov 28B; Strauss, Franz Josef 1988 Oct 3B; Wittig, Georg 1987 Aug 26I
religion: papal visit 1980 Nov 15J; 1987 May 4J; Roman Catholic bishops letter on nuclear arms race 1983 Apr 27B
science and technology: Binner wins Nobel 1986 Oct 15I; Klitzing receives Nobel 1985 Oct 16I; Koehler wins Nobel 1984 Oct 15I; mathematics conjecture proven 1983 Jul 23I; Michel/Huber/Deisenhofer win Nobel 1988 Oct 19I; Paul wins Nobel 1989 Oct 12I; quantum jump witnessed 1986 Oct 21I; Ruska wins Nobel 1986 Oct 15I
space flights: Challenger flight management 1985 Nov 6I; satellite launches 1984 Aug 16I; 1989 Aug 8I
sports: auto racing 1985 Jun 16J; 1986 Jun 1J; 1987 Jun 14J; 1989 Jun 11J; West German Grand Prix; golf 1981 Jul 19J; 1984 Jul 22J; 1985 Apr 14J; Olympic Games (Los Angeles) 1984 Aug 12J; Olympic Games (Moscow) boycott 1980 Apr 14J; running 1982 Apr 19J; soccer 1982 May 26J/Jul 11J; 1986 Jun 29J; 1987 May 27J; tennis 1985 Dec 22J; 1988 Dec 18J; 1989 May 28J/Dec 17J; Becker, Boris; Graf, Steffi
states: Bavarian elections 1982 Oct 10B; 1986 Oct 12B; Hamburg elections 1982 Dec 19B; Hesse coalition government 1985 Oct 27B; 1987 Feb 9B; Hesse municipal elections 1981 Mar 22B; Hesse parliamentary elections 1982 Sep 26B; Lower Saxony parliamentary elections 1982 Mar 21B; North Rhine-Westphalia elections 1980 May 11B; 1985 May 12B

steel industry modernization 1983 Apr 7B
taxes 1987 Feb 24B/Sep 11B
terrorism see also Baader-Meinhof; Lebanese suspect in TWA hijacking arrested 1987 Jan 15A; terrorist Debus dies after hunger strike 1981 Apr 16B; U.S. Army forces commander attacked 1981-Sep 15G
trade surplus 1986 Jan 13B/Jun 4B/Aug 28B; 1987 Apr 29B/Sep 25B; 1988 Feb 22B/Aug 23B
unemployment rate 1983 Jan 5B; 1984 Aug 3B; 1986 Jun 6B/Dec 4B; 1988 Jan 10B/Nov 6B; 1989 May 8B
World War II anniversary marked 1989 Sep 1B
Westinghouse Corp. 1983 Jan 4H
Westland PLC 1986 Jan 9B/Jan 24B/Feb 12A/Jul 24B
Westminster Abbey (London) 1985 Nov 16J; 1986 Jul 23G
Westminster College (Fulton, Mo.) 1988 Oct 18F
Westpac Banking Corp. 1985 Dec 16E
West Point (U.S. Military Academy) 1980 May 21G; 1981 May 27G
West Virginia
Democrats elected 1988 Nov 8F
environment and pollution: FMC Corp. fined in obstruction of EPA 1980 Nov 10H; National Steel Corp. fined over cleanup 1983 May 4H
floods 1984 May 8I
health and safety issues: Union Carbide fined for violations 1987 Jul 24H
infant mortality 1983 Jan 25F
labor issues: coal miner strike 1980 Mar 3H; mineworker strike 1989 Jun 20H; steelworker strike 1985 Jul 21H; UMW president sworn in 1982 Dec 22H; Weirton Steel Works to be purchased by employees 1983 Mar 10H/Sep 23H
presidential campaign (1980) 1980 Jun 3F
presidential campaign (1984) 1984 Jun 5F
presidential campaign (1988) 1988 May 10D
prison riot 1986 Jan 1F
West Virginia University (Morgantown) 1989 Jan 3J
Westway (New York City) 1981 Mar 14H/Sep 7F
Wetherby (film) 1986 Jan 2J
wetlands 1985 Dec 4H; 1988 Feb 23F; 1989 Jan 18H/Nov 19H
WEU see Western European Union
Weyerhaeuser Co. 1986 Jul 25H
whales and whaling 1985 Apr 3H/Nov 4J; 1986 Jun 9I/Jul 2B/Aug 6I/Nov 9B; 1987 May 22B/Jun 25A; Japan
Wham! (singing group) 1985 Feb 23J
What a Fool Believes (Doobie Brothers) (recording) 1980 Feb 27J
"What Is the Proper Way to Display a U.S. Flag?" (art exhibit) 1989 Feb 17J
What's Love Got to Do with It (Tina Turner) (recording) 1985 Feb 26J
What's New (Linda Ronstadt) (recording) 1983 Dec 14J; 1984 Jan 21J
What Works: Research about Learning and Teaching (Education Department) 1986 Mar 4F
wheat

price and production issues: cash payments to farmers 1984 Apr 10H; harvests 1982 Nov 29H; 1983 Jun 13H; 1984 Jan 13H; heat waves 1983 Aug 1I; prices 1988 Jun 27H; price-supports 1986 Jan 13H

trade issues: Algeria 1985 Jun 4H; Argentina 1987 Jan 12D; Australia 1982 Oct 6E; Australia/USSR sales 1980 Jun 17E; Canada 1986 Apr 9D; Crow's Nest Pass agreement; China 1984 Dec 23E; European Community 1986 Aug 14B; European Community/USSR sales 1986 Sep 30G; GATT ruling on U.S./EC dispute 1983 Feb 25B; India 1981 Jul 21E; Nicaragua/USSR agreement 1981 May 14D; unfair trading practices 1985 Oct 16H; USSR 1980 Jan 12A; 1985 Aug 30A; 1986 Aug 1H/Aug 29H; 1987 Apr 30H/Dec 2G; 1989 May 2H

Wheeling-Pittsburgh Steel Corp. 1984 Feb 7H; 1985 Apr 16H/Jul 21H/Oct 25H; 1986 May 28H

When Father Was Away on Business (film) 1985 May 20J

When Harry Met Sally... (film) 1989 Jul 12J/Jul 26J/Aug 30J/Sep 27J

When We Are Married (play) 1986 Dec 7J

While My Pretty One Sleeps (Mary Higgins Clark) (book) 1989 May 26J/Jun 30J/Jul 28J

Whipping Boy, The (Sid Fleischman) (book) 1987 Jan 19J

Whirlpool (James Clavell) (book) 1986 Jan 11J/Nov 21J/Dec 26J; 1987 Jan 23J

Whispers Out of Time (Roger Reynolds) (musical composition) 1989 Mar 30J

Whistleblower bill 1988 Oct 26F

Whistleblower Protection Act (1989) 1989 Apr 10F

Whitbread Book of the Year Award 1986 Jan 28J; 1987 Jan 13J; 1988 Jan 19J/Nov 8J; 1989 Jan 25J

Whitbread round-the-world yacht race 1986 May 9J

white-collar crimes 1989 Jan 18F

White Gold Wielder (Stephen R. Donaldson) (book) 1983 Apr 10J/May 15J/Jun 1J/Jun 12J

Whitehead Institute for Biomedical Research (Cambridge, Mass.) 1987 Dec 22I

White House Conference on Aging 1981 Nov 30F/Dec 3F

White House Staff, U.S. 1980 May 28F; 1981 Oct 29G/Dec 20F; 1985 Jan 8F; 1986 Jan 22F; 1987 Feb 27F/Jul 30G; 1988 May 9F/Jun 14F/Aug 25G/Nov 17F

White Motor Corp. 1980 Sep 4H

White Nights (film) 1985 Dec 11J

White Noise (Don DeLillo) (book) 1985 Nov 21J

Whitesnake (singing group) 1987 Jun 27J/Jul 22J/Aug 22J/Sep 19J/Oct 24J/Nov 21J/Dec 26J; 1988 Jan 23J

Whitesnake (Whitesnake) (recording) 1987 Jun 27J/Jul 22J/Aug 22J/Sep 19J/Oct 24J/Nov 21J/Dec 26J; 1988 Jan 23J

white supremacists 1982 Dec 11C; 1985 Jul 17F; 1986 Jul 14F; 1987 Nov 17F; 1988 Apr 7F; 1989 Feb 6F/Mar 4F

Whitney (Whitney Houston) (recording) 1987 Jun 27J/Jul 22J/Aug 22J/Sep 19J

Whitney Houston (Whitney Houston) (recording) 1985 Sep 28J/Oct 26J; 1986 Feb 19J/Mar 22J/Apr 16J/May 21J/Jun 18J

Who (singing group) 1981 Apr 8J/May 6J; 1982 Sep 22J

Who Censored Roger Rabbit? (Gary K. Wolf) (book) 1988 Jun 22J

Who Framed Roger Rabbit (film) 1988 Jun 22J/Jul 13J; 1989 Mar 29J

Who Killed the Robins Family? (Bill Adler/Thomas Chastain) (book) 1983 Dec 18J; 1984 Jan 20J/Feb 10J/Mar 23J

whooping cough 1985 Feb 3D

whooping cranes 1989 Nov 19H

Who Paid Taxes, 1966-1985 (Brookings Institution study) 1985 Jan 23H

Wickes Cos. 1982 Apr 24H

Wightman Cup (tennis) 1987 Oct 31J

Wildcats (film) 1986 Feb 19J

wilderness areas 1980 Dec 2H; 1982 Feb 21F/Aug 12H/Dec 27H/Dec 30H; 1983 Feb 1H/Apr 12H/May 12H; 1985 Nov 26H; 1988 Nov 19H; 1989 Dec 5H; Reagan, Ronald

Wild Gratitude (Edward Hirsch) (book) 1987 Jan 12J

Wild Heart (Stevie Nicks) (recording) 1983 Jul 13J

wildlife refuges 1980 Aug 19H/Dec 2H; 1984 Nov 30H; 1985 Mar 15H/Mar 28H; 1986 Nov 24H; 1987 Apr 19I/Apr 20H; 1988 Oct 28H; 1989 Sep 12H

Willamette Industries Inc. 1986 Aug 25H

William Morrow & Co. 1986 Jan 11J

Will to Power (singing group) 1988 Nov 26J

"Wilmington 10" 1980 Dec 4F

Wilson Foods Corp. 1983 Apr 24H

Wimbledon (tennis tournament)
men's singles: 1980 Jul 6J; 1981 Jul 4J; 1982 Jul 4J; 1983 Jul 2J; 1984 Jul 8J; 1985 Jul 7J; 1986 Jul 6J; 1987 Jul 5J; 1988 Jul 4J; 1989 Jul 9J
women's singles: 1980 Jul 4J; 1981 Jul 3J; 1982 Jul 3J; 1983 Jul 2J; 1984 Jul 7J; 1985 Jul 6J; 1986 Jul 5J; 1987 Jul 4J; 1988 Jul 2J; 1989 Jul 9J

Winchell Mahoney Time (TV show) 1986 Jul 2J

Windmills of the Gods (Sidney Sheldon) (book) 1987 Feb 27J/Mar 27J/Apr 24J/May 29J/Jun 26J

Window of Opportunity (Newt Gingrich) (book) 1989 Apr 11F

Wind Quintet IV (George Perle) (musical composition) 1986 Apr 17J

Windscale atomic plant (Great Britain) 1988 Jan 1B

Winds of War, The (TV show) 1983 Feb 16J

wine 1982 Mar 5B; 1984 Dec 4B; 1985 Jul 11B/Oct 24B/Dec 17I; 1986 Apr 10B/Dec 30H; 1989 May 31F

Winner in You (Patti La Belle) (recording) 1986 Jun 18J/Jul 16J

Winning Colors (racehorse) 1988 May 7J

Winston 500 (auto race) 1985 May 5J; 1987 May 3J; 1988 May 1J; 1989 May 7J

Winston Cup (NASCAR season title) (auto racing) 1980 Nov 15J; 1985 Nov

17J; 1986 Nov 2J; 1987 Oct 25J; 1988 Nov 20J; 1989 Nov 19J

Winter Tan, A (film) 1989 Mar 22J

wiretapping and electronic surveillance 1980 Jun 21F; 1981 Oct 23J; 1984 Oct 6G; 1985 Sep 16J; 1986 Jul 22J/Dec 5F; 1987 Jun 8G/Jul 1G/Jul 31F/Nov 30D

Wisconsin 1980 Apr 1F; 1981 Sep 19J/Oct 8G; 1983 Jun 11F; 1984 Apr 3F/Apr 7F; 1985 Jul 12H/Sep 26H/Nov 10I; 1988 Apr 5F/Sep 26H; 1989 May 7F

Wisconsin, University of (Madison) 1982 Mar 27J; 1987 May 29J

Wise Guys (film) 1986 May 14J

Wish You Were Here (film) 1988 Jan 3J

witches 1980 Mar 9D

Witches of Eastwick, The (John Updike) (book/film) 1984 Jun 15J; 1987 Jun 17J/Jul 8J

Witness (film) 1985 Feb 8J/Feb 13F/Mar 20J

Witness for Peace 1985 Aug 8D; 1987 Feb 25D; 1988 Mar 9D

Wizard of Oz (Frank L. Baum) (book) 1986 Oct 24F

"Wolf Boy" 1985 Feb 18I

Wolfen (film) 1981 Jul 29J

Woman in Red, The (film) 1984 Sep 12J

Woman in Red, The (Stevie Wonder) (soundtrack) 1984 Nov 24J

Woman Next Door, The (film) 1981 Oct 11J

Woman of the Year (*Time* magazine) 1986 Dec 27J

women *see also specific women in the name index (e.g., Thatcher, Margaret)*
business and industry: managerial positions 1989 Mar 8F; motion picture studio president 1980 Jan 1J; set-aside programs 1986 Apr 11F; 1989 Mar 6F; top-level jobs 1985 Mar 25F
clubs: 1987 Jul 4J
courts and legal system: federal judgeships 1988 Feb 2F
education: black women enrollment 1989 Jan 15F; Columbia Law School dean 1986 Jan 2F; Spellman College president 1988 Nov 4F; University of Wisconsin chancellor 1987 May 29J
family issues: marriage chances 1987 Jan 13J; pension plans 1984 May 22F/Aug 23H
labor and employment 1985 Aug 14F; 1986 Mar 28F/Jul 8B; 1987 May 15F; 1989 Sep 4B
medicine and health care: AIDS 1986 Apr 6I; 1987 Apr 17I; artificial heart recipient 1985 Dec 19I; insurance premiums 1985 Oct 1F; life expectancy 1985 Feb 11F; research representation 1989 Dec 14F
military issues *see also specific branch (e.g., Army)*; Grenada invasion 1986 Jan 26G; U.S. troops in Southern Europe 1989 Feb 18G; veterans' organizations 1987 Aug 1G; Vietnam memorial 1987 Oct 22G; 1988 Oct 21G
politics and government: administration appointments 1989 Oct 8F; election gains 1983 Nov 8F; 1986 Sep 9F; Ferraro vice-presidential candidacy 1984 Jul 12F/Jul 19F; presidency polled 1987 Aug 13F; state legislators 1985 Mar 27F
press and broadcasting: 1980 Jul 7J

religion: Conservative Judaism 1985 Feb 14J; Episcopal Church 1985 Sep 12J; 1988 Sep 24J; 1989 Feb 11F/Sep 28J; Mormons 1984 Apr 5J; Roman Catholic Church 1985 Sep 15J; 1988 Apr 11J/Sep 30J; Salvation Army 1986 May 2A
sex bias *see sex bias*
space flights: 1984 Oct 11I; 1987 Jun 5I
sports: golf 1981 Jul 26J; Iditarod dog-sled race 1986 Mar 13J; Little League baseball 1989 Aug 23J; mountain climbing 1986 May 20J
statistics: 1983 Oct 10F

Women, U.N. Decade for 1980 Jul 30J

Women, U.N. World Conference of 1985 Jul 27A

Women and Children First (Van Halen) (recording) 1980 Mar 30J/Jun 4J

Women Policy Studies, Center for *see Center for Women Policy Studies*

Women Walk Home (Greek-Cypriot group) 1989 Mar 19B

Wonder Years, The (TV show) 1988 Aug 28J; 1989 Jan 28J

Woodrow Wilson International Center for Scholars (Washington, D.C.) 1987 Apr 17J

Woods Hole Oceanographic Institute (Massachusetts) 1986 Jul 13I

workfare 1985 Sep 26F

Working Girl (film) 1988 Dec 21J/Dec 28J; 1989 Jan 25J/Jan 28J

workweek
Australia: 1980 Jul 16E
France: 1981 Jul 17B; 1982 Jan 13B
Greece: 1980 Nov 6B
Israel: 1983 Sep 6C
Netherlands: 1986 Jan 1B
Poland: 1981 Jan 5B/Jan 9B/Jan 10B/Jan 31B/Feb 1B
West Germany: 1987 Apr 22B

World Affairs Council 1981 Oct 15A; 1983 Mar 31G

World Airways Inc. 1986 Sep 3H

World Alliance of Reformed Churches 1982 Aug 25C

World Alpine Skiing Championships 1985 Feb 6J; 1989 Feb 2J

World Anticommunist League 1987 May 21G

World Bank
executive changes: Clausen becomes president 1981 Jul 1A; Conable nominated 1986 Mar 13G; McNamara retires 1981 Jul 1A
lending procedures: capital increase 1988 Feb 22A/Apr 28A; commercial banks 1983 Jan 13A; debt strategy 1988 Dec 18A; 1989 Apr 3A; energy development 1981 Aug 4A; loan/collection comparison 1988 Jul 14A; loan loss provisions 1988 Jul 11A; loan rule changes 1988 Apr 15A
meetings: 1980 Oct 3A; 1981 Oct 2A; 1983 Sep 27A/Sep 27G; 1984 Apr 13A/Sep 27A; 1985 Oct 11A; 1986 Sep 24A; 1987 Sep 29A; 1988 Sep 27A; 1989 Sep 26A
U.S. policy: 1981 Aug 4A; 1984 Jan 17A; 1988 Sep 29G; 1989 Apr 3A

World Championship of Women's Golf 1981 Aug 23J; 1984 Aug 20J/Aug 22J; 1985 Aug 18J

World Championships (basketball) 1986 Jul 20J/Aug 17J

World Championships (figure skating) 1986 Mar 21J; 1987 Mar 12J/Mar 14J; 1988 Mar 25J/Mar 26J; 1989 Mar 16J/Mar 18J

World Championships (gymnastics) 1985 Nov 10J

World Championships (ice hockey) 1982 Apr 25J; 1986 Apr 28J; 1987 May 3J; 1989 Apr 29J

World Championships (track & field) 1983 Aug 7J; 1987 Aug 30J

World Commission on Environment and Development 1987 Apr 27I

World Congress 1986 Oct 15A

World Council of Churches 1981 Jul 4E; 1983 Aug 10J; 1984 Jul 12J; 1986 Jul 27C

World Court *see International Court of Justice*

World Cup (cricket) 1987 Nov 8J

World Cup (field hockey) 1986 Oct 19J

World Cup (rugby) 1987 Jun 20J

World Cup (skiing) 1982 Jan 24J; 1985 Mar 20J; 1987 Feb 2J; 1988 Mar 24J/Mar 26J; 1989 Aug 12J

World Cup (soccer) 1982 Jul 11J; 1985 May 19E; 1986 May 31J/Jun 29J; 1988 Jul 4J/Aug 13J; 1989 Nov 19J/Dec 9J

World Development Report (World Bank) 1980 Aug 17A; 1982 Aug 16A; 1988 Jul 6A

World Economic Outlook (OECD) 1988 Dec 20A

World Expo 88 (Brisbane, Australia) 1988 Oct 30E

World Festival of Youth and Students 1989 Jul 1E

World Food Program, U.N. 1985 Mar 5C; 1989 Oct 21C; United Nations

World Health Organization (WHO) 1981 May 20A; 1985 Feb 3D/Apr 30I; 1986 Jun 6I/Jun 28I/Nov 20I; 1987 Feb 13I; 1988 Jan 28I/Aug 23I; 1989 May 18I/Sep 24I

World Jewish Congress 1985 Jan 26B/Jul 15C; 1989 Nov 29A

World Moslem Congress 1988 Mar 2J

World Professional Road Championship (cycling) 1987 Sep 6J

World Psychiatric Association 1989 Oct 17I

World Refugee Survey 1982 (UN High Commissioner for Refugees) 1982 Aug 2D

World Resources Institute 1987 Apr 11I; 1989 Dec 16I

World's End (T. Coraghessan Boyle) (book) 1988 May 14J

World Series (baseball)
Phillies: 1980 Oct 21J
Dodgers: 1981 Oct 28J
Cardinals: 1982 Oct 20J
Orioles: 1983 Oct 16J
Tigers: 1984 Oct 14J
Royals: 1985 Oct 27J
Mets: 1986 Oct 27J
Twins: 1987 Oct 25J
Dodgers: 1988 Oct 22J
Athletics: 1989 Oct 28J

World's Fair
Brisbane, Australia (1988): 1988 Oct 30E
Chicago, Illinois (1929): 1986 Jun 2J
Knoxville, Tennessee (1982): 1982 May 1I/Oct 31J
Vancouver, Canada (1986): 1986 May 2D/Oct 13D

World's Fair (E.L. Doctorow) (book) 1986 Nov 17J

World Team Cup (tennis) 1988 May 22J; 1989 May 28J

World War I (1914-18) 1984 Sep 22B

World War II (1939-45) *see also specific countries (e.g., Germany); subjects (e.g., Nazis)*

  awards and honors: Congressional Medal 1980 Jul 9G

  ceremonies: Allied linkup in Elbe 1985 Apr 25B; D-Day 1984 Jun 6A; Polish invasion 1989 Sep 1B

  espionage: double agent identified 1984 Jun 3J

  internment camps: Japanese-American 1986 Feb 10G; 1987 Sep 17F

  war crimes: UN files 1987 Nov 6A

Worldwatch Institute 1982 Mar 26I; 1985 Feb 17C

World Wide Military Command and Control System (Wimex) 1980 Mar 10G

World Wilderness Conference 1980 Jun 10I

World Wildlife Fund 1983 Dec 13C; 1988 Apr 6I; 1989 Apr 5I/Aug 3C

W.R. Grace & Co. *see* Grace & Co., W.R.

Wran Committee (Australia) 1988 May 5E/Jun 16E

Wrigley Field (Chicago) 1985 Mar 25J; 1988 Feb 25J/Aug 8J

writers *see individual artists in the name index (e.g., Le Carre, John)*

Writers Guild of America 1981 Jul 11H

W.T. Grimm & Co. *see* Grimm & Co. W.T.

Wyler's Children's Hospital (Chicago) 1989 Nov 27I

Wyoming 1982 Aug 1I

X

Xanadu (film/soundtrack) 1980 Sep 3J/Sep 10J

xenografts (cross-species transplant) 1984 Oct 26I/Nov 15I

X rays 1980 Mar 20I; 1983 Apr 4I; 1985 Dec 28B/Dec 28G; 1986 Sep 10I; 1987 Jan 20I; 1988 Nov 10F/Dec 29H

XT (IBM personal computer) 1983 Mar 8I

Y

Yale Repertory Theater (New Haven, Conn.) 1985 May 3J; 1986 May 2J; 1987 Sep 18J

Yale University (New Haven, Conn.) 1982 Nov 13G; 1984 Dec 19J; 1985 Jan 15J/Mar 14J/Dec 10F; 1987 Feb 10J; 1988 Jun 20J; 1989 Oct 12I

Yankelovich, Skelly and White 1981 Jul 28J

Year in the Life, A (TV show) 1987 Sep 20J; 1988 Aug 28J

Year of Living Dangerously, The (film) 1983 Jan 21J; 1984 Apr 9J

Year of the Dragon (film) 1985 Aug 29J

Yentl (film) 1984 Jan 11J

Yes (singing group) 1983 Dec 14J; 1984 Jan 21J

Yin (Carolyn Kizer) (book) 1985 Apr 24J

Yonkers (New York) 1985 Nov 20F; 1988 Jan 25F/Aug 2F/Sep 10F

Yo Picasso (Pablo Picasso) (painting) 1989 May 9J

"Yorkshire Ripper" 1981 Jan 5B/Apr 29B

Yorktown (ship) 1986 Mar 18B

Yosemite National Park (California) 1980 May 25I; 1985 Mar 5J; 1987 Aug 19H

Young & Rubicam 1989 Oct 30J

Young Sherlock Holmes (film) 1985 Dec 11J

Your Life Is Calling (film) 1986 May 14J

You Should Hear How She Talks about You (Melissa Manchester) (recording) 1983 Feb 23J

Yucca Mountain (Nevada) 1989 Nov 1I/Nov 28H

Yugoslavia *see also individual leaders in the name index (e.g., Milosevic, Slobodan)*

  accidents and disasters: Corsica air crash 1981 Dec 1B

  arts and culture: Golden Palm award 1985 May 20J

  budget and spending programs: 1987 Dec 30B; 1988 Jan 12B

  census data: 1987 Jul 10J

  defense and armed forces: army leaves cancelled 1988 Oct 10B

  economy: foreign debt 1983 Sep 9B; 1987 Jul 3B; inflation rate 1989 Jan 17B/Apr 29B/Oct 2B; prices 1982 Jul 31B; 1986 Aug 10B; 1987 Nov 15B; 1988 Aug 4B; private enterprise 1980 Jun 5B; strikes 1987 Mar 26B; wage freeze 1987 Nov 15B

  foreign relations: Balkan conference 1988 Feb 23B; Hungary 1989 Sep 8B; USSR 1988 Mar 18B/Oct 11B

  government and politics: Central Committee meets 1988 Oct 17B; collective presidency rotated 1981 May 15B; 1985 May 15B; 1986 May 15B; 1988 May 15B; 1989 May 15B; Communist Party congress 1986 Jun 28B; embassies to close 1981 Oct 24B; government shuffled 1984 May 15B; Markovic as premier 1989 Jan 19B; Mikulic as premier 1986 Jan 6B; 1988 Dec 30B; Montenegro president resigns 1989 Jan 11B; one-party rule end urged 1989 Dec 26B; Planinc chosen premier 1982 May 16B; president warns on nationalism 1988 Oct 9B; royal family remains buried 1989 Sep 30B; Slovenian opposition party formed 1989 Feb 16B; Slovenia secession amendment 1989 Sep 27B; Tito surgery 1980 Jan 20B; vice president resigns in finance scandal 1987 Sep 12B

  international organizations: Comecon 1984 Jun 14A

  Kosovo *see* Kosovo

  obituaries: Tito, Josip Broz 1980 Apr 4B

  Serbia *see* Serbia

  sports: Olympics 1984 Feb 8J/Feb 19J

  U.S. relations: 1980 Jun 24B; 1982 Apr 22G; 1985 May 31G; 1986 Feb 15B

Yukon Indians (Canada) 1982 Dec 16D; 1988 Jul 23D/Nov 8D

Z

Zaire *see also individual leaders in the name index (e.g., Mobutu Sese Seko)*

  Angola conflict: 1987 Feb 1G; 1989 Oct 5C

  civil strife: 1985 Jun 21C

  foreign relations: Belgium 1989 Jan 14A; France 1984 Sep 20A; OAU 1982 Oct 8A; Pope 1985 Aug 19J; U.S. 1982 May 13C/May 14A

  government and politics: Mobutu re-elected 1984 Jul 29C

  sports: Olympic boycott 1980 Feb 1J/Oct 7C

  Uganda incursion: 1980 Oct 7C; 1981 Sep 8C

  UN membership: 1989 Oct 18A

Zambesi River 1984 May 2C

Zambia *see individual leaders in the name index (e.g., Kaunda, Kenneth)*

  AIDS: 1987 Oct 4I

  economy: drought 1983 Mar 18I; recovery plan 1987 May 1G; regional unity meetings 1980 Apr 1C; 1981 Jan 17C; World Bank funds 1988 Jul 11A

  foreign relations: East Africa leaders meet 1980 Apr 1C; 1981 Jan 17C; papal visit ends 1989 May 6J; South Africa conflict 1986 May 19C/Aug 5A/Dec 11C; 1987 Apr 25C

Zanzibar 1984 Apr 19C

Zapped (film) 1982 Sep 15J

Zarate Willka Armed Liberation Front (Bolivian terrorist group) 1989 Jun 30D

Zenith Electronics Corp. 1986 Mar 26H

"zero option" 1987 Jun 16G

Zimbabwe *see also individual leaders in the name index (e.g., Mugabe, Robert)*

  civil strife: airline service reestablished 1980 Jan 9C; government/rebel clashes 1981 Feb 13C; rebel strongholds sealed off 1985 Mar 3C; state of emergency extended 1980 Jan 18C

  economy: drought 1983 Mar 18I; foreign debt 1987 Sep 24C; regional development plan 1980 Apr 1C

  foreign relations: South Africa 1986 May 19C/Aug 5A; 1987 Nov 28C; Sweden 1983 Mar 12B; Pope 1988 Sep 19J; U.S. 1983 Dec 19G; 1986 Jul 4C/Sep 2G; USSR 1981 Feb 21A

  government and politics: army deputy commander arrested 1982 Mar 11C; assembly seat quotas abolished 1987 Aug 21C; cabinet minister arrested 1980 Aug 6C; capital city renamed 1982 Apr 18C; government corruption scandal 1989 Apr 14C; government/opposition parties merge 1989 Dec 19C; independence achieved 1980 Apr 17C; national elections 1985 Jul 6C; new parties formed 1981 Apr 12C; 1989 Apr 30C; one-party rule 1984 Aug 12C; 1989 Dec 22C; opposition members expelled 1984 Nov 10C

  international organizations: IMF 1983 Mar 25C; United Nations 1980 Feb 2A/Aug 25A

  obituaries: Ndlovu, Moven 1984 Nov 10C; Nyagumbo, Maurice 1989 Apr 20C

  sports: Olympic committee death threat 1984 Jul 11J

Zimbabwe African People's Union 1984 Mar 11C/Nov 10C/Nov 22C; 1985 Mar 3C; 1987 Apr 17C; 1988 Jan 2C; 1989 Dec 19C

zinc 1980 May 17A

Zionism 1980 Jul 30J; 1982 Aug 29C

Zomax (drug) 1983 Mar 4I

zoning 1985 Jul 1F; 1986 Jan 14H; 1987 Jun 9H; 1988 Nov 7F

Zoya (Danielle Steel) (book) 1988 May 27J/Jun 24J/Jul 23J

Zulus (South African ethnic group) 1985 Aug 9C/Dec 25C; 1988 Feb 15C/Dec 26C; *individual leaders in the name index (e.g., Buthelezi, Mangosuthu)*

ZZ Top (singing group) 1985 Dec 21J

DEC. 1 5 1994